WORDS AND PHRASES
legally defined

THIRD EDITION

under the General Editorship of
David Hay MA, LLM
of the Inner Temple, Barrister

SUPPLEMENT
2006

LexisNexis™
Butterworths

Members of the LexisNexis Group worldwide

United Kingdom	LexisNexis UK, a Division of Reed Elsevier (UK) Ltd, Halsbury House, 35 Chancery Lane, LONDON, WC2A 1EL, and RSH, 1-3 Baxter's Place, eith Walk, EDINBURGH EH1 3AF
Argentina	LexisNexis Argentina, BUENOS AIRES
Australia	LexisNexis Butterworths, CHATSWOOD, New South Wales
Austria	LexisNexis Verlag ARD Orac GmbH & Co KG, VIENNA
BENELUX	LexisNexis Benelux, Amsterdam
Canada	LexisNexis Canada, MARKHAM, Ontario
Chile	LexisNexis Chile Ltda, SANTIAGO
China	LexisNexis China, Beijing and Shanghai
France	LexisNexis SA, PARIS
Germany	LexisNexis Deutschland GmbH, MUNSTER
Hong Kong	LexisNexis Hong Kong, HONG KONG
India	LexisNexis India, NEW DELHI
Italy	Giuffrè Editore, MILAN
Japan	LexisNexis Japan, Tokyo
Malaysia	Malayan Law Journal Sdn Bhd, KUALA LUMPUR
Mexico	LexisNexis Mexico, Mexico
New Zealand	LexisNexis NZ Ltd, WELLINGTON
Poland	Wydawnictwo Prawnicze LexisNexis Sp, WARSAW
Singapore	LexisNexis Singapore, SINGAPORE
South Africa	LexisNexis Butterworths, DURBAN
USA	LexisNexis, DAYTON, Ohio

© Reed Elsevier (UK) Ltd 2006
Published by LexisNexis Butterworths

A CIP Catalogue record for this book is available from the British Library.

ISBN 10: 1 4057 1232 5
ISBN 13: 978 1 4057 1232 3

Typeset by KerryPress Ltd, Luton, Beds
Printed and bound in Great Britain by CPI Bath

Visit LexisNexis UK at www.lexisnexis.co.uk

Preface

This Supplement contains a further selection of definitions from case law and statute.

The law as indicated is, for English sources, that existing at 31 July 2006. For overseas and Scottish cases the law covers judgments published up to 30 June 2006.

This is the twelfth Supplement to the Third Edition to be published and, as in previous years, editorial notes have been revised, particularly references to Halsbury's Laws of England where volumes have been reissued.

The style follows that used in the main volumes, which should be consulted first. Notes of statutory repeals or amendments and any other editorial comments are shown in square brackets.

September 2006

Butterworths
London

The 2005 Supplement is now superseded and may be destroyed.

A

A DANGER TO SOCIETY, OR A PART OF IT

Australia [Section 98(1) of the Sentencing Act 1995 (WA) provides that a superior court may order an offender to be imprisoned indefinitely in certain circumstances. Section 98(2) states that indefinite imprisonment may only be ordered if court is satisfied on the balance of probabilities that when the offender would otherwise be released from custody he or she would be a danger to society, or a part of it, because of: (a) the exceptional seriousness of the offence; (b) the risk that the offender will commit other indictable offences; (c) the character of the offender and in particular (i) any psychological, psychiatric or medical condition affecting the offender; or (ii) the number and seriousness of other offences of which the offender has been convicted; or (d) any other exceptional circumstances.] 'Identifying the meaning of "a danger to society, or a part of it" is not without difficulty. A fundamental premise of the criminal law is that conduct is regarded as criminal for the very reason that its commission harms society, or some part of it. On that basis, any risk that an offender may commit some further indictable offence poses a danger to society, or some part of it; the extent of the "danger" would depend only upon the likelihood of the offender reoffending.

'If, however, s 98 were concerned only with the risk of an offender reoffending, the inclusion of para (a), para (c) and para (d) in subs (2) was unnecessary. Their inclusion suggests that "danger to society, or a part of it" means more than that there is a risk, even a significant risk, that an offender will reoffend.

'It must be noticed that each of the four paragraphs in subs (2) (on which the conclusion that there is a relevant danger must be founded) has a different temporal aspect. Para (a), with its reference to the "exceptional seriousness" of the offence for which the offender is to be sentenced looks to what the offender has already done. Para (b), with its reference to the risk of commission of other offences, looks to the future. Para (c), with its reference to the "character of the offender" requires some assessment of the character of the offender as it is revealed at the time of sentencing. Finally, para (d), with its reference to "any other exceptional circumstances", may permit consideration of a wide variety of matters.

'The breadth of the matters upon which a conclusion of danger to society (or a part of it) may be based suggests that what is required is more than a bare conclusion that it is probable that the offender will commit some indictable offence in the future. That suggestion is reinforced by the use of the word "exceptional" in the phrases "exceptional seriousness of the offence" and "exceptional circumstances". More than the probability of further offending must be shown. Read as a whole, and giving due weight to the repeated reference to "exceptional", the sub-section requires attention to whether, were the offender to be released at the end of the nominal sentence, the offender would engage in conduct, the consequences of the commission of which would properly be called "grave" or "serious" for society as a whole, or for some part of it. Then, and only then, could it be concluded that the offender would be a "danger to society, or a part of it".' *McGarry v R* (2001) 184 ALR 225; 75 ALJR 1682; BC200106510; [2001] HCA 62 at [20]–[23], per Gleeson CJ, Gaudron, McHugh, Gummow and Hayne JJ

Australia 'I do not, with respect, think that there is any difficulty in construing the words "a danger to society, or a part of it". Certainly, all or most criminal conduct is at least an affront to society. But not all criminal conduct necessarily endangers society or a part of it. Some might think that not all crimes of drug use, however harmful to the user, involve a danger to society or a part of it. And whatever view might be held about the reprehensibility of bigamy or the commission of incest by adult siblings, these activities are unlikely to endanger society or any part of it. However, where the part of society involved is especially vulnerable, as in the case of children, different considerations arise. Crimes directed at vulnerable groups, such as children, can more readily be found to be a danger to society or a part of it than other crimes.' *McGarry v R* (2001) 184 ALR 225; 75 ALJR 1682; BC200106510; [2001] HCA 62 at [122], per Callinan J (dissenting)

ABANDON

[The Custody of Children Act 1891 was repealed by the Children Act 1989, Sch 15, as from 14 October 1991 (SI 1991/828).]

ABANDONMENT

Of distress

[For 13 Halsbury's Laws (4th edn) paras 350, 352 see now 13 Halsbury's Laws (4th edn) (Reissue) paras 759, 761.]

Of goods

[For 35 Halsbury's Laws (4th edn) para 1126 see now 35 Halsbury's Laws (4th edn) (Reissue) para 1226.]

Of goods

[As to treasure trove, see now the Coroners Act 1988, s 30.]

Canada '159 The question that the trial judge should have addressed, then, is whether KWG abandoned her property interest in the diary. I believe that she did not, and I would apply this Court's recent unanimous decision in *R. v. Law*, [2002] 1 S.C.R. 227, 2002 SCC 10, to resolve this matter. *Law*, *supra*, clearly provides that where an individual abandons or relinquishes her property, she effectively abandons her privacy interest in it. The logical corollary to this proposition must be that where an individual retains a privacy interest in her property, she cannot be deemed to have abandoned it. While a person can conceivably relinquish her privacy interests in the contents of her property — for example, by reciting every entry in one's diary to the general public — without also giving up the physical good, the law does not seem to allow for the reverse.

'160 In addition, the onus of proving "abandonment" rests with the party alleging it and is a relatively significant burden, which is met only when there is "a giving up, a total desertion, and absolute relinquishment' of private goods by the former owner. It may arise when the owner with the specific intent of desertion and relinquishment casts away or leaves behind his property": R. A. Brown, *The Law of Personal Property* (2nd ed.

1955), at p. 9. According to *Black's Law Dictionary* (6th ed. 1990), "abandonment" is the equivalent of "a virtual, intentional throwing away of property". Reference to these principles indicates that KWG did not abandon the diary ...'. *R v Shearing* [2002] 3 SCR 33 at 94, per L'Heureux-Dubé J

ABATEMENT

Of legacy

[For 17 Halsbury's Laws (4th edn) para 1263 see now 17(2) Halsbury's Laws (4th edn) (Reissue) para 506.]

Of nuisance

[For 34 Halsbury's Laws (4th edn) para 349 see now 34 Halsbury's Laws (4th edn) (Reissue) para 74.]

ABODE

New Zealand 'The provisions of sub-ss (3), (4) and (5) of s 37 [of the Electoral Act 1956] show a legislative intention to equate "place of residence" with "usual place of abode". A place of abode is, we think, a place where a person for the time being, other than for a very brief stay, sleeps and eats and which in general he uses as a base for his daily activities. That a place of abode can be temporary only is clear from sub-s (4). "Usual" in this context we think connotes a degree of regularity and frequency not necessarily continuous in the sense of being uninterrupted, but at least continual in the sense of being repetitive.' *Re Wairarapa Election Petition* [1988] 2 NZLR 74 at 81, per cur

ABOLISH

Australia [As to whether Parliament's intention to 'abolish' an offence included an intention to decree there was no criminal liability for the offence whenever committed; or rather abolish any new criminal liability from accruing after the date of enactment.] 'In my opinion, arguments which rely upon dictionary definitions of the word "abolished" are not decisive ... [I]t would be against common sense and the presumption against retrospective operation to suppose that Parliament intended to abolish the offence in relation to people already tried, convicted and sentenced, or even those who have served their sentences. Nor, in my opinion, does the abolition of the offence extend to the cancellation of an offender's prior criminal record.

For this reason, it is clear that more is involved than conceptual reasoning based on dictionary definitions. The question cannot be determined in absolutes, but rather is to be determined by locating Parliamentary intention on a continuum of possibilities.' *Question of Law Reserved (No 2 of 1996)* (1996) 67 SASR 63 at 67, 70, per Doyle CJ

ABORIGINAL

Australia [Letters Patent issued by the Governor-General authorised the inquiry into certain deaths of 'Aboriginals'.] 'The ordinary meaning of the word "Aboriginal", as used in the community, is a broad one. Ordinary usage would not apply the term to a person believed to have no Aboriginal ancestry, however closely associated with Aboriginals. It would be inconsistent with ordinary usage to describe such a person as an "Aboriginal"; but on the other hand it is not the case that proof of any degree of such ancestry, however slight, would be enough in itself to justify the use of the term. To return to examples given above, which after two centuries of European occupation are by no means fanciful, the discovery that a person had a small trace of Aboriginal descent would not, without more, ordinarily cause those who knew him to describe him as an "Aboriginal"... The weight of authority is against the adoption of a merely genetic notion of the meaning of the word "Aboriginal" and favours the following of ordinary usage. Treating the word "Aboriginal" as including "people of proven 'Aboriginal' descent" was [an] error if [it was meant] to treat as irrelevant social factors such as self-recognition as Aboriginal and recognition by the Aboriginal community.' *State of Queensland v Wyvill* (1989) 90 ALR 611 at 616–617, per Pincus J
[See also *Commonwealth of Australia v Tasmania* (1983) 1 CLR 158 at 274, per Deane J.]

Australia 'In my opinion, in order for someone to be described as an "Aboriginal person" within the meaning of that term in the Aboriginal and Torres Strait Islander Commission Act 1989 (Cth), some degree of Aboriginal descent is essential, although by itself a small degree of such descent is not sufficient. A substantial degree of Aboriginal descent may, by itself, be enough to require a person to be regarded as an "Aboriginal person" ...

'It is I think where a person is either wholly of Aboriginal descent or where the degree of Aboriginal descent is so substantial that the person possesses what would be regarded by the generality of the Australian community as clear physical characteristics associated with Aboriginals that the person would be described in ordinary speech as "Aboriginal". It is racial origin not external physical appearance that governs whether a person is "Aboriginal" for the purposes of the Act ...

'The less the degree of Aboriginal descent, the more important cultural circumstances become in determining whether a person is "Aboriginal". A person with a small degree of Aboriginal descent who genuinely identifies as an Aboriginal and who has Aboriginal communal recognition as such would I think be described in current ordinary usage as an "Aboriginal person" and would be so regarded for the purposes of the Act. But where a person has only a small degree of Aboriginal descent, either genuine self-identification as Aboriginal alone or Aboriginal communal recognition as such by itself may suffice, according to the circumstances.' *Gibbs v Capewell* (1995) 128 ALR 577 at 584–585, per Drummond J

ABORIGINAL TRADITION

Australia '[13] ... The Acts Interpretation Act 1954 (Qld) defines ... "Aboriginal tradition" as "the body of traditions, observances, customs and beliefs of Aboriginal people generally or of a particular community or group of Aboriginal people, and includes any such traditions, observances, customs and beliefs relating to particular persons, areas, objects or relationships.

...

'[47] The definition of "Aboriginal tradition" in the Acts Interpretation Act 1954 (Qld) does not require the establishment of a native title under the common law as described in *Mabo v The State of Queensland [No 2]* (1992) 175 CLR 1 F.C. 92/014 but refers to "the body of traditions, observances, customs and beliefs of Aboriginal people generally or of a particular community or group of Aboriginal people". The ordinary meaning, consistent with dictionary definition of "tradition", is "the handing down of statements, beliefs, legends, customs, etc, from generation to generation, especially by word of mouth or by practice". In *Chapman v Luminis Pty Ltd (No 4)* [2001] FCA 1106, von Doussa J accepted that the word "tradition" in such a context required a degree of antiquity, perhaps more so than the words "observances, customs or beliefs" but that those words nevertheless carry with them the notion that there has been a handing down from generation to generation in accordance with the understanding of Aboriginal lore and practice.' *Stevenson v Yasso* [2006] QCA 40 at [13], [47], per McMurdo P; BC200600746

ABORIGINE

Australia '[13] ... The Acts Interpretation Act 1954 (Qld) defines "Aborigine" as "a person of the Aboriginal race of Australia"...

...

'[38] ... That word should be given its ordinary meaning subject to the assistance given in the Acts Interpretation Act 1954 (Qld) and relevant judicial interpretation. It does not require an ethnological inquiry of a scientific, historical or scholarly character: see *Muramats v Commonwealth Electoral Officer* (WA (1923) 32 CLR 500, Higgins J, 506–507)*; Ofu-Koloi v R* (1956) 96 CLR 172, Dixon CJ, Fullaghar and Taylor JJ, 175. Pertinent considerations are whether the person said to be an Aborigine is of Aboriginal descent, identifies himself or herself as an Aborigine and is recognized in the Aboriginal community as being an Aborigine; see the discussion of this issue by Drummond J in *Gibbs v Capewell* (1995) 54 FCR 503, 507–508 and Merkel J in *Shaw v Wolf* (1998) 83 FCR 113, 118–122, 137.' *Stevenson v Yasso* [2006] QCA 40 at [13], [38], per McMurdo P; BC200600746

ABOUT

Australia 'The relevant *Macquarie Dictionary* definitions of "about" suggest that to ask a question about a subject is to ask a question concerning it, or in regard to it, or connected with it, or concerned with it. The relevant definitions in the *Oxford English Dictionary* (2nd ed) of "about" suggest that to ask a question about a subject is to ask a question touching it, concerning it, in the matter of it, in reference to it, or in regard to it. The word "about" is the "regular proposition employed to define the subject-matter of verbal activity ...".' *R v Le* BC200202750; [2002] NSWCCA 186 at [59], per Heyden JA

ABSCOND

Australia ' "Abscond" is defined in the *Macquarie Dictionary* (3rd ed, 1997) as, "to depart in a sudden and secret manner, especially to avoid legal process." There is, I think, no doubt, and it is not contended otherwise, that the word "abscond" contains the notion of a purpose of avoidance.' *Schnabel v Lui* BC200208087; [2002] NSWSC 1184 at [17], per Hamilton J

ABSENCE

Australia [Section 10(1) of the Extradition Act 1998 (Cth) provides: 'Where a person has been convicted in the person's absence of an offence against the law of an extradition country ... then, for the purposes of this Act, the person is deemed not to have been convicted of that offence but is deemed to be accused of that offence'.] 'Unassisted by reference to the history or context of the relevant provisions or their purpose, one would construe the reference to a conviction in a person's absence in s 10(1) as a reference to a conviction obtained when the person was not present at trial or conviction. Absence simply means not present. On this approach no question would arise as to the reason for the person's non-attendance.

'Such a construction reflects the ordinary use of the language.

'The *New Shorter Oxford English Dictionary* (1993) gives the primary meaning of "absence" as "the state of being away from a place or person". The *Macquarie Dictionary* (1995, 2nd ed) also gives the primary meaning of "absence" as "a state of being away".

'The same meaning was given to s 64 of the Crimes Act 1958 (Vic), which provided a defence to a charge of bigamy where, inter alia, the husband or wife had been "continually absent" for seven years. Hudson J in *R v Darnton* [1960] VR 191 held that the defence was available if the accused had been absent, whether such absence was a result of desertion on his part or not.

'And, in *Gapes v Commercial Bank of Australia Ltd* (1979) 27 ALR 72, Northrop J held that an employee who was physically present at work was not "absent from duty" even though the employee was not performing his duties. His Honour said that "absent from duty" should be "given its ordinary meaning as referring to physical bodily absence from duties".

'In *Ryan v Heiler* (unreported, Supreme Court of New South Wales, Young J, 26 February 1990), Young J was concerned with provisions of the Local Government Act 1990 (NSW) which stipulated that certain absences from council meetings could result in the loss of office by an alderman. "Absence" was construed to mean "not at" rather than "a voluntary or deliberate failure to be present". The assistance of this case is limited because the construction depended on the particular statutory context. His Honour noted that the opposite meaning had been applied in cases dealing with articles of association of companies: *Mack's Claim* [1900] WN (Eng) 114; *McConnell's Claim* [1901] 1 Ch 728; and *Willsmore v Willsmore-Tibbenham Ltd* (1965) 109 Sol Jo 699.' [North J then proceeds to examine *Wiest v DPP* (1988) 23 FCR 472 (which concerns the predecessor of s 10(1), namely, s 4(3) of the Extradition (Foreign States) Act 1966 (Cth)), the common law position, and the history of s 4(3) (at [24]–[82]). He concludes that 'the better construction of s 10(1) is that a conviction in absence means a conviction obtained when the accused was not present for whatever reason'.] *Hellenic Republic v Tzatzimakis* BC200201161; [2002] FCA 340 at [17]–[22], [83], per North J

ABSENCE OF A TEMPORARY NATURE

Australia [Land Tax Act 1958 (Vic) s 13.] '… Like the Tribunal I do not see reason to construe the expression "absence of a temporary nature" in s 13C otherwise than according to the plain, ordinary and natural meaning of the words of the expression and, as the Tribunal said, the ordinary meaning of something which is "temporary" is something that lasts for a time only or which is made to supply a passing need, as opposed to being "permanent". Hence, if one can say of an absence that it is for a time only or to satisfy a passing need, as opposed to being permanent, it is accurate and in my view appropriate to describe the absence as being of a temporary nature; whether short or not.

'That view of the matter finds support in the terms of subsection 13C(3). The express limitation to absences of not greater than two years (or such longer period as the Commissioner may allow) implies that, but for the express limitation, an absence could qualify as a temporary absence though longer than two years.

'No doubt there are limited periods of absence which would be so long that they would not be temporary for the purposes of the section. For example, if an owner absented himself or herself from a principal place of residence with the intention of returning to it in 50 years time, the absence would be for a limited time only but it could not reasonably be regarded as temporary for the purposes of the section. Once, however, one moves away from extreme cases of that kind it is not impossible to suppose that significant periods of absence could be conceived of as "temporary" for the purposes of the section. If an absence of up to two years is within the contemplation of the section, as it plainly is, may not there be cases in which an absence of three years qualifies as "temporary"? Other things being equal, what is the essential difference between two years and three years in the context of this section? And if a period of three years is within the contemplation of the section, what is to say that the section may not

reach to an absence of six years, at least in some cases? After all, a period of that order is no more than the duration of many courses of study and business and professional postings and "short term work assignments or other commitments" were offered in the Second Reading Speech as exemplars of temporary absences to which the exemption was intended to apply.' *Commissioner of State Revenue v Anderson* [2004] VSC 152 at [11], per Nettle J; BC200402772

ABSOLUTE INTEREST

[The Income and Corporation Taxes Act 1970 is largely repealed. The definition has been re-enacted, with minor drafting amendments, by the Income and Corporation Taxes Act 1988, s 701(2).]

ABSTRACT

[For 42 Halsbury's Laws (4th edn) para 147 see now 42 Halsbury's Laws (4th edn) (Reissue) para 141.]

ABSTRACTION

[The Water Resources Act 1963 has been largely repealed, and a definition of 'abstraction' is now contained in s 221(1) of the Water Resources Act 1991, as follows.] 'Abstraction', in relation to water contained in any source of supply, means the doing of anything whereby any of that water is removed from that source of supply, whether temporarily or permanently, including whereby the water is so removed for the purpose of being transferred to another source of supply; and 'abstract' shall be construed accordingly.

ABSURDITY

Canada '[27] If a statute is susceptible of two interpretations, the interpretation that avoids absurdity is to be preferred (*Datacalc Research Corp. v. The Queen*, [2002] T.C.J. No. 99 (QL) (Tax Ct. of Canada) [reported [2002] 2 C.T.C. 2548], at para. 54).

'[28] According to F. Bennion, *Statutory Interpretation*, 4th ed. (London: Butterworths, 2002), the concept of "absurdity" actually encompasses several components. The presumption against an "absurd" interpretation means the avoidance of (1) an unworkable or impractical result, (2) an inconvenient result, (3) an anomalous or illogical result, (4) a futile or pointless result, (5) an artificial result or (6) a disproportionate counter-mischief.' *Wicken (Litigation Guardian of) v Harssar* [2004] OJ No 1935, 240 DLR (4th) 520 (Div Ct), per the Court

ABUSIVE

Australia ' "Abusive" (like "insulting") is a large term. Its subject matter ranges from the trivial to the serious ... The *Macquarie Dictionary* gives as the primary meaning for "abusive" – "Using harsh words or ill treatment" and gives the example of "an abusive author". The second meaning is "characterised by or containing abuse", and the example given is "an abusive satire". The present context is of course the writing or printing of abusive words. There is no reason why it should not be given its ordinary or popular meaning in this context and there is equally no good reason why it should be confined to words towards the upper end of the scale. In common usage it is capable of encompassing fairly trivial and low level, albeit direct, expressions of disapproval.' *Coleman v P* BC200107434; [2001] QCA 539 at [67], per Thomas JA

ACCEPTANCE

[For 4 Halsbury's Laws (4th edn) paras 362–365 see now 4(1) Halsbury's Laws (4th edn) (Reissue) paras 362–365.]

Of offer

[For 9 Halsbury's Laws (4th edn) para 245 see now 9(1) Halsbury's Laws (4th edn) (Reissue) para 650.]

ACCESS

Canada '[11] Section 173(1)(*a*) of the *Code* makes it an offence to wilfully perform an indecent act "in a public place in the presence of one or more persons". In virtue of s. 150, "'public place' includes any place to which the public have access as of right or by invitation, express or implied". Parliament has distinguished legislatively in Part V of the *Criminal Code* – the context that concerns us here – between conduct that is prohibited "in a public place" and conduct that is prohibited if it is "exposed to public view". We should not by judicial interpretation frustrate Parliament's manifest intention by merging these two different foundations of criminal liability.

'[12] Parliament has also created two different offences in ss. 173(1)(*a*) and 173(1)(*b*) of the *Criminal Code*. The former concerns indecent acts committed in a public place in the presence of one or more persons; the latter, indecent acts committed in any place, public or private, with intent to insult or offend any person. Here, the appellant was acquitted under s. 173(1)(*b*). His conviction under s. 173(1)(*a*) can therefore not be supported, as it was to some extent in the Court of Appeal, on grounds that were resolved finally and in the appellant's favour when he was acquitted by the trial judge under s. 173(1)(*b*).

'[13] I agree with the appellant's submission that his living room was not a public place within the meaning of s. 173(1)(*a*). The living room of his private home was not a place "to which the public [had] access as of right or by invitation, express or implied". From both the text and the context, it seems obvious to me that "access", as used here, means "the right or opportunity to reach or use or visit": *The Canadian Oxford Dictionary* (2001), at p. 7. I do not believe it contemplates the ability of those who are neither entitled nor invited to enter a place to see or hear from the outside, through uncovered windows or open doors, what is transpiring within.

'[14] In my respectful view, the trial judge thus erred in concluding that the appellant's living room had been "converted" by him into a public place simply because he could be seen through his living room window and, though he did not know this, was being watched by Mr. and Mrs. S. from the privacy of their own bedroom 90 to 150 feet away.' *R v Clark* [2005] 1 SCR 6 at [11]–[14], 249 DLR (4th) 257 (SCC), per Fish J

Means of access

[The Town and Country Planning Act 1971 was wholly repealed by the Planning (Consequential Provisions) Act 1990, s 3, Sch 1, and the definition of 'means of access' is now contained, in identical terms, in the Town and Country Planning Act 1990, s 336(1).]

To and from highway

'I think ... that, when the statute [see now the definition of "road" in the Road Traffic Act 1988, s 192] speaks of the public having "access" to the road, what is meant is neither (at one extreme) that the public has a positive right of its own to access, nor (at the other extreme) that there exists no physical obstruction, of greater or less impenetrability, against physical access by the public; but that the public actually and legally enjoys access to it. It is, I think, a certain state of use or possession that is pointed to. There must be, as matter of fact, walking or driving by the public on the road, and such walking or driving must be lawfully performed—that is to say, must be permitted or allowed, either expressly or implicitly, by the person or persons to whom the road belongs.' *Harrison v Hill* 1932 JC 13 at 16, per the Lord Justice-General (Clyde)

To computer data

(2) A person secures access to any program or data held in a computer if by causing a computer to perform any function he–
(a) alters or erases the program or data;
(b) copies or moves it to any storage medium other than that in which it is held;
(c) uses it; or
(d) has it output from the computer in which it is held (whether by having it displayed or in any other manner);
and references to access to a program or data (and to an intent to secure such access) shall be read accordingly.

(5) Access of any kind by any person to any program or data held in a computer is unauthorised if—
(a) he is not himself entitled to control access of the kind in question to the program or data; and
(b) he does not have consent to access by him of the kind in question to the program or data from any person who is so entitled.

(Computer Misuse Act 1990, s 17(2), (5))

'Section 17 [of the Computer Misuse Act 1990] is an interpretation section. Subsection (2) defines what is meant by access and securing access to any program or data. It lists four ways in which this may occur or be achieved. Its purpose is clearly to give a specific meaning to the phrase "to secure access". Subsection (5) is to be read with sub-s (2). It deals with the relationship between the widened definition of securing access and the scope of the authority which the relevant person may hold. That is why the subsection refers to "access of any kind" and "access of the kind in question". Authority to view data may not extend to authority to copy or alter that data. The refinement of the concept of access requires a refinement of the concept of authorisation. The authorisation must be authority to secure access of the kind in question. As part of this refinement, the subsection lays down two cumulative requirements of lack of authority. The first is the requirement that the relevant person be

not the person entitled to control the relevant kind of access. The word "control" in this context clearly means authorise and forbid. If the relevant person is so entitled, then it would be unrealistic to treat his access as being unauthorised. The second is that the relevant person does not have the consent to secure the relevant kind of access from a person entitled to control, i e authorise, that access.

'Subsection (5) therefore has a plain meaning subsidiary to the other provisions of the 1990 Act. It simply identifies the two ways in which authority may be acquired—by being oneself the person entitled to authorise and by being a person who has been authorised by a person entitled to authorise. It also makes clear that the authority must relate not simply to the data or program but also to the actual kind of access secured. Similarly, it is plain that it is not using the word "control" in a physical sense of the ability to operate or manipulate the computer and that it is not derogating from the requirement that for access to be authorised it must be authorised to the relevant data or relevant program or part of a program. It does not introduce any concept that authority to access one piece of data should be treated as authority to access other pieces of data "of the same kind" notwithstanding that the relevant person did not in fact have authority to access that piece of data. Section 1 refers to the intent to secure unauthorised access to any program or data. These plain words leave no room for any suggestion that the relevant person may say: "Yes, I know that I was not authorised to access that data but I was authorised to access other data of the same kind."

...

'... The meaning of the statute is clear and unambiguous. But it is right that I should briefly say something about the argument based upon the Law Commission's Working Paper No 110 *Computer Misuse* and report *Computer Misuse* (Law Com No 186) (1989) which (together with the Scottish Law Commission's report *Computer Crime* (Scot Law Com No 106)(1987)) led to the passing of the 1990 Act. The argument was influential in the Divisional Court both in *DPP v Bignell* ([1988] 1 Cr App R 1) and in the present case and was further relied on by the respondent before your Lordships. The respondent quoted passages from the working paper and the report to the effect:

"It should be made clear that 'unauthorised' refers to the obtaining of access to a computer system. Our preliminary view is that it would be undesirable for a hacking offence to extend to an authorised user who is using the computer system for an unauthorised purpose." (Working Paper, para 6.24(iv).)

"… if an employee deliberately seeks to enter part of his employer's system from which he is clearly debarred his conduct is of the same type as the outside hacker, and our proposed offence will apply to him as much as it applies to the outside hacker." (Report, para 3.6.)

"… if the hacking offence is to be aimed at protecting the integrity of the computer (and our view is that it should), then there is no justification for exempting employees who threaten that integrity." (Report, para 3.36.)

'Read as a whole, the report makes it clear that the term "hacking" is used conveniently to refer to all forms of unauthorised access whether by insiders or outsiders and that the problem of misuse by insiders is as serious as that by outsiders (para 3.5). The offence should cover a person who causes the computer to perform a function when he "should know that *that* access is unauthorised" (para 3.33; my emphasis). An employee should only be guilty of an offence if his employer has clearly defined the limits of the employee's authority to access a program or data (para 3.37). Similar passages are to be found in the report of the Scottish Law Commission.

'Whilst the report of the Law Commission supports the correctness of the *decision* in *DPP v Bignell*—the phrase "causing a computer to perform any function" refers to the "manipulation" of a computer (para 3.26)—it does not justify the language used by Astill J followed by Kennedy LJ in the present case. The consideration of the mischief which the 1990 Act was designed to meet confirms and does not contradict the clear meaning of s 1 of the 1990 Act and the equally clear purpose of s 17(2) and (5).' *R v Bow Street Metropolitan Stipendiary Magistrate, ex p Government of the United States of America* [1999] 4 All ER 1 at 7, 9–10, HL, per Lord Hobhouse of Woodborough

ACCESSIBLE

Canada [Student was entitled to attend school in another district if more 'accessible' under Education Act, RSO 1980, c 129, s 40(1)(a).] 'In order to claim the benefit of this important right to education in another school district under s 40(1)(a), a pupil must demonstrate that the school in that district is "more accessible than any secondary school" in the district of residence. The words "more accessible" should be given their plain, ordinary meaning. The Shorter Oxford English Dictionary on Historical Principles (1973), defines "accessible" as: "capable of being entered or reached: get-at-able". Webster's Third New International Dictionary of the English Language (1968), defines "accessible" as: "capable of being reached or easily approached". Broadly speaking, "accessibility" connotes ease of approach. In practice, this must be considered in both the geographical and temporal sense. Realistically, accessibility is a function of distance and travelling time.

'The clause makes it clear that these considerations are not to be viewed in the abstract. The use of the words "more accessible" specifically directs a comparison between the accessibility of schools in both school districts.

'The difference between the terms "reasonably accessible" and "more accessible" is made apparent by the language of Ferguson J. The use of the word "more" instead of the word "reasonably" in s 40(1)(a) indicates a legislative intention to confer on pupils the benefit of a precise and strict test of accessibility. The test is not the reasonableness of the overall arrangements made for education by one or more boards but rather the simple comparison of the accessibility of a school in one district as opposed to a school in another.' *Re Bareham and Board of Education for City of London* (1984) 10 DLR (4th) 406 at 411–412, Ont CA, per Blair JA

ACCESSION

[For 35 Halsbury's Laws (4th edn) para 1138 see now 35 Halsbury's Laws (4th edn) (Reissue) para 1238.]

ACCESSORY

Australia 'The word "accessory" can be either an adjective or a noun. In the Oxford English Dictionary the adjective is defined relevantly to mean: "Coming as an accession; contributing in an additional and hence subordinate degree; additional, extra, adventitious." As a noun its meaning is given as: "An accessory thing; something contributing in a subordinate degree to a general result or effect; an adjunct, accompaniment." In the Macquarie Dictionary, as an adjective its meaning is given as: "contributing to a general effect; subsidiary". As a noun its meaning is given as: "a subordinate part or object; something added or attached for convenience, attractiveness, etc, such as a spotlight, heater, driving mirror, etc, for a vehicle"... As it seems to me, even without a context which may confirm such a conclusion, the word "accessory" whether used as an adjective or a noun does not necessarily connote that the accessory must be joined to something else. An object that is joined to another may well be an accessory although it will not necessarily be so. However, it may still be an accessory even though it is not joined. Adopting as a basis the meaning given in the Macquarie Dictionary, an article will be an accessory if it is a subordinate part or object, added or attached for convenience or effectiveness or other such reason.' *Federal Commissioner of Taxation v Kentucky Fried Chicken Pty Ltd* (1988) 81 ALR 35 at 40–41, per Hope JA

ACCIDENT

[The Road Traffic Act 1972 was repealed by the Road Traffic (Consequential Provisions) Act 1988. See now, as to breath testing after an accident on a road or other public place, the Road Traffic Act 1988, s 6(2).]

[For 25 Halsbury's Laws (4th edn) para 594 see now 25 Halsbury's Laws (4th edn) (2003 Reissue) para 569.]

[Under the Warsaw Convention 1929 art 17 (as set out in Sch 1 to the Carriage by Air Act 1961), the carrier is liable for damage sustained in the event of the death or wounding of a passenger or any other bodily injury suffered by a passenger if the 'accident' which caused the damage so sustained took place on board the aircraft or in the course of the operations of embarking or disembarking. The claimant suffered an indecent assault on an aircraft operated by the defendant airline and, although she sustained no physical injury, she became very distressed, and was later diagnosed as suffering from a clinical depression. On an appeal, the airline contended that the assault was not an 'accident' within the meaning of art 17 since it was not related to the operation of the aircraft or characteristic of air travel.]

'[13] The same word is used in both the English and the French texts and there has been no suggestion that the meaning of that word differs in the two languages ...

'[14] ... Mr Haddon-Cave submitted that the requirement that the accident must be related to air travel could be deduced from (i) the travaux préparatoires, (ii) a purposive approach to interpretation and (iii) a significant body of United States authority. In argument he relied principally on this final factor.

...

'[16] The case on which both parties principally relied was *Air France v Saks* (1985) 470 US 392. The claimant suffered loss of hearing in her left ear as a result of injury which she alleged was caused by the operation of the air pressurisation system as the aircraft lost height before landing. The issue was whether this was an "accident" within the meaning of art 17. The Supreme Court held that it was not. The court drew a distinction between the use of the word "accident" to describe an event *causing* hurt or loss and the use of the same word to describe the *occurrence* of the hurt or loss itself ...

...

'[20] In referring, with approval, to the inclusion in the definition of "accident" of torts committed by fellow passengers, the court said nothing to suggest that those torts had, in some respect, to relate to the operation of the aircraft or to be a characteristic of air travel, although this could be said to have been a feature of cases cited by the court by way of illustration of such accidents ...

...

'[24] The definition of "accident" in *Saks'* case gives that word a natural and sensible meaning in the context in which it appears and has been approved by this court. We propose to apply it in the present case.

'[25] There is nothing in *Saks'* case that justifies the requirement that an "accident" must have some relationship with the operation of the aircraft or carriage by air. Nor do we consider that a purposive approach to interpretation requires that gloss on the word ...

'[26] Liability under art 17 only arises in relation to an accident that occurs on board the aircraft or in the course of embarking or disembarking. Thus the accident will occur at a time when the passenger is in the charge of the carrier. In those circumstances it seems to us to be a logical and reasonable scheme of liability that, whatever the nature of the accident, a passenger should be entitled to be compensated for its consequences where the carrier is not able to discharge the burden imposed by art 20.

'[27] It is not, however, necessary to decide this point, for we agree with Mr Braslavsky that, on the facts of this case, the claimant can satisfy the requirement, if so it be, of demonstrating that the "accident" that occurred related to or was a characteristic of her carriage by air ...

...

'[31] We have no doubt that the accident that befell the claimant exemplified a special risk inherent in air travel and that, whatever the precise test may be, it constituted an "accident" within the meaning of that word in art 17.' *Morris v KLM Royal Dutch Airlines* [2001] EWCA Civ 790 at [13], [14], [16], [20], [24]–[27], [31], [2001] 3 All ER 126 at 130–131, 132, 134, CA, per Lord Phillips of Worth Matravers MR; approved in *Morris v KLM Royal Dutch Airlines, King v Bristow Helicopters Ltd* [2002] UKHL 7, [2002] 2 AC 628, [2002] 2 All ER 565, HL

[On the hearing of preliminary issues, based on a factual matrix agreed only for the purpose of those issues, the court was required to determine, inter alia, whether a culpable act or omission by a carrier resulting in a passenger suffering from a deep vein thrombosis (DVT) on an aircraft which complied with all applicable aviation regulations, on a normal flight which was carried out in accordance with those regulations, and with the carrier's normal procedures and practices, amounted to an 'accident' within the meaning of art 17 of the Warsaw Convention (as set out in Sch 1 to the Carriage by Air Act 1961), which provides that a carrier is liable for damages sustained in the event of the death or wounding of a passenger or any bodily injury suffered by a passenger, if the accident which caused the damage so sustained took place on board the aircraft or in the course of any of the operations of embarking or disembarking. The judge held that for the purposes of art 17 the test was causation by an 'accident', i e an unexpected or unusual event or happening that was external to the passenger, and that the agreed factual matrix did not reveal any such event or happening and accordingly did not disclose a claim under art 17. The claimants appealed, contending that the integral features of carriage on an aircraft pertaining throughout a flight were capable of constituting an 'event'.] '[9] The issue before us depends, essentially, on the meaning of "accident" in art 17 of the Warsaw Convention. The parties start from common ground. In the context of art 17 "accident" refers to the cause of the injury and not to the injury itself. That proposition and the relevant test of an "accident" were accurately identified by the United States Supreme Court in *Air France v Saks* (1985) 470 US 392 at 405:

"We conclude that liability under Article 17 of the Warsaw Convention arises only if a passenger's injury is caused by an unexpected or unusual event or happening that is external to the passenger. This definition should be flex-

ibly applied after assessment of all the circumstances surrounding a passenger's injuries."

The court added (at 406):

"But when the injury indisputably results from the passenger's own internal reaction to the usual, normal, and expected operation of the aircraft, it has not been caused by an accident, and Article 17 of the Warsaw Convention cannot apply."

...

WHAT IS AN "ACCIDENT"?

'[19] I propose to consider this question in the first instance having regard to the natural meaning of the words used in art 17, referring to authority only by way of illustration. I shall consider the effect of my conclusions on the issue under consideration, thereby reaching a provisional view as to the outcome of this appeal. Finally I shall turn to the authorities to see whether they lead me to a result that differs from my provisional view.

'[20] The parties are agreed in taking as their starting point the passage in the opinion of the Supreme Court in *Saks*' case that I have already quoted. In *Morris v KLM Royal Dutch Airlines* [2001] EWCA Civ 790 at [24], [2001] 3 All ER 126 at [24], [2002] QB 100, I remarked that this definition gave the word "accident" a natural and sensible meaning in the context of art 17. In the House of Lords ([2002] 2 All ER 565 at [71]), Lord Hope agreed. I remain of that view.

'[21] Article 17 speaks of the accident causing damage sustained in the event of death or wounding or bodily injury. This is generally treated as requiring that the accident should be the cause of the death, wounding or bodily injury—see, for instance, Shawcross and Beaumont *Air Law* (4th edn reissue) vol 1, para VII (693). It seems to me that the concept of an accident taking place on board an aircraft which causes death, wounding or bodily injury is a simple one. The words naturally suggest an untoward event which impacts on the body in a manner which causes death, wounding or injury. The impact of the event may be physical or it may be an impact on the senses which results in bodily injury, but one would normally expect the untoward event to cause the death or injury directly.

'[22] I do not suggest that these reflections provide an exclusive description of the "accident" in art 17. I note that in *Saks*' case the Supreme Court stated ((1985) 470 US 392 at 406):

"Any injury is the product of a chain of causes, and we require only that the passenger be able to prove that some link in the chain was an unusual or unexpected event external to the passenger."

I have not found it easy, however, to envisage a remote accident in a chain of causation that does not end in a direct cause of the death or injury that is, itself, an accident within art 17. *Shawcross and Beaumont* para VII (694–700) give a wide variety of illustrations of cases where courts have found an accident causing death or injury within art 17 to have been established. Almost all of these constitute untoward events which impacted directly and physically upon the passenger.

'[23] One can break down the definition of an accident into two elements. (1) There must be an event; (2) the event must be unusual, unexpected or untoward. I would indorse the approval by the United States Court of Appeals, Third Circuit, of the following charge to a jury as to the correct legal standard for determining the occurrence of an accident under art 17 (see *Abramson v Japan Airlines Co Ltd* (1984) 739 F 2d 130 at 132):

> "An accident is an event, a physical circumstance, which unexpectedly takes place not according to the usual course of things. If the event on board an airplane is an ordinary, expected, and usual occurrence, then it cannot be termed an accident. To constitute an accident, the occurrence on board the aircraft must be unusual, or unexpected, an unusual or unexpected happening."

AN EVENT

'[24] I turn to consider in a little more detail the first element of an accident. It must be an event. The first meaning of accident that is given by the *Oxford English Dictionary* (2nd edn, 1989), is: "Anything that happens. An occurrence, incident, event." That meaning is however obsolete, in that it has become replaced by the second meaning that the dictionary gives:

> Anything that happens without foresight or expectation; an unusual event, which proceeds from some unknown cause, or is an unusual effect of a known cause; a casualty, a contingency."

The first element of an accident is to be found in all of these.

'[25] A critical issue in this appeal is whether a failure to act, or an omission, can constitute an accident for the purposes of art 17. Often a failure to act results in an accident, or forms part of a series of acts and omissions which together constitute an accident. In such circumstances it may not be easy to distinguish between acts and omissions. I cannot see, however, how inaction itself can ever properly be described as an accident. It is not an event; it is a non-event. Inaction is the antithesis of an accident.

'[26] Mr Thanki drew our attention to a description of the natural meaning of an event given by Lord Mustill, in a quite different context, in *Axa Reinsurance (UK) plc v Field* [1996] 3 All ER 517 at 526, [1996] 1 WLR 1026 at 1035:

> "In ordinary speech, an event is something which happens at a particular time, at a particular place, in a particular way. I believe that this is how the Court of Appeal understood the word. A cause is to my mind something altogether less constricted. It can be a continuing state of affairs; it can be the absence of something happening."

To a degree I consider that this passage can be applied to an accident in the context of art 17. That article postulates that the accident must '[take] place on board the aircraft or in the course of any of the operations of embarking or disembarking". This suggests that the accident will be an ephemeral event. However, the requirement of flexibility and a purposive approach means that one cannot preclude the possibility that an activity that continues for a period, such as circulating contaminated air, could amount to an accident for the purposes of art 17.

DOES THE MATRIX DISCLOSE AN EVENT?

'[27] Mr Cakebread has submitted that it is, or may be, possible to identify two "accidents' in the specimen matrix, as augmented by the further information. The first can, I believe, be fairly described as subjecting the passengers to carriage by air that has the features itemised in the further information. These features have been described by the judge, and by Mr Cakebread, by the generic description "providing cramped seating". The further information also makes allegations about air pressure and the atmosphere and temperature in the cabin. The act of altering the pressurisation, the supply of oxygen or the temperature in the cabin would all, in my opinion, be capable of constituting an "event" that satisfied the first element of an "accident". As I understand it, however, the allegations in respect of those matters are intended to treat them, like cramped seats, as integral features of carriage pertaining throughout the flight rather than the effects of acts of the crew in the course of the flight.

'[28] I do not consider that the existence of these permanent features of the aircraft, or the subjecting of the passengers to carriage in aircraft with these features, is capable of amounting to an event that satisfies the first limb of the definition of an accident which "took place on board the aircraft or in the course of any of the operations of embarking or disembarking". For this reason alone I would hold that the flight itself, albeit that under the matrix it is assumed to have caused the DVT, was not capable of amounting to an "accident" for the purposes of art 17.

'[29] I turn to the failure to warn of the risk of DVT, or to advise on precautions which would avoid or minimise that risk. I cannot see how this failure can be categorised as an accident. It was simply something that did not happen—a non-event. For this reason alone I would hold that the failure to warn of or to advise about the dangers of DVT is not capable of amounting to an accident under art 17.

...

'[37] I am not persuaded that, when considering whether an action has the unusual, unexpected or untoward quality necessary to enable one to qualify it as an accident under the *Saks* test, the questions of whether the actor has knowledge which makes it culpable to perform the action can never be relevant. I am, however, persuaded that it is simply not possible to apply to a state of affairs, or an omission to act, the test that is relevant to deciding whether an event is an accident.

'[38] Looking at the position overall, which is the only realistic way of looking at it, the matrix, as augmented by the further information, discloses nothing which is capable of constituting an "accident" within the meaning of art 17.' *Re Deep Vein Thrombosis and Air Travel Group Litigation* [2003] EWCA Civ 1005 at [9], [19]–[29], [37]–[38], [2004] 1 All ER 445, CA, per Lord Phillips of Worth Matravers MR; affd [2005] UKHL 72, [2006] 1 All ER 786

Australia [In the context of Article 17 of the Convention for the Unification of Certain Rules Relating to International Carriage by Air opened for 1929 signature at Warsaw on 12 October 1929 (the Warsaw Convention) as amended by Protocol done at Montreal on 25 September 1975 (the Montreal Protocol No 4)] 'As was pointed out in *Saks* 470 US 392 at 399 (1985), the Warsaw Convention was drafted in French by continental jurists. And as an international treaty, it would be wrong to read Montreal No 4 as if it reflected some particular cause of action or body of learning that is derived from, say, the common law. It was said

in *Saks* that "the French legal meaning of the term 'accident' differs little from the meaning of the term in Great Britain, Germany, or the United States". Both in French, and in Anglo-American legal discourse (and, we would add, so too in Australian legal discourse) "accident" may be used to refer to the event of a person's injury or to the cause of injury. By contrast, "accidental" is usually used to describe the cause of an injury rather than the event and is often used as an antonym to "intentional".

'In Art 17, "accident" is used to refer to the event rather than the cause of injury. And that event is one which Art 17 requires to be located at a place ("on board the aircraft") or otherwise to be fixed by reference to circumstances of time and place ("in the course of any of the operations of embarking or disembarking").

'Further, in understanding what is meant by "accident", it is necessary to give proper weight to the way in which Art 17 relates three different concepts. Article 17 refers to "damage", to "the death or wounding of a passenger or any other bodily injury suffered by a passenger", and to "the accident which caused the damage so sustained". The damage sustained is treated as being distinct from the accident which caused the damage, and both the accident and the damage are treated as distinct from the death, wounding or other personal injury. What that reveals is that the "accident", in the sense of "an unfortunate event, a disaster, a mishap" is not to be read as being sufficiently described as an adverse physiological consequence which the passenger has suffered. It may be accepted that its happening was not intended. In that sense, what is alleged to have happened may be described as "accidental". But suffering DVT is not an accident. Rather, as the parties to this appeal accepted, "accident" is a reference to something external to the passenger.

'It may also be accepted that an "accident" may happen because of some act or series of acts, or because of some omission or series of omissions; it may happen because of some combination of acts and omissions. If that were not already clear, the reference in Art 25 to damage resulting from "an act or omission of the carrier, his servants or agents" would point in that direction. It by no means follows, however, that asking whether an event was brought about by an act or omission and then classifying the act or omission as "accidental" as distinct from "intentional" is the same as asking whether there has been an "accident" on board an aircraft. In particular, recognising the difficulties in seeking to classify causes of an accident as acts or omissions, or as intended or unintended acts or omissions, does not deny the need, under Art 17, to identify that an accident has occurred on board or in the course of the operations of embarking or disembarking. No other provision of Montreal No 4 suggests any contrary construction of Art 17.

'No doubt as *Saks* indicates, the concept of "accident" is not to be overrefined. It is a concept which invites two questions: first, what happened on board (or during embarking or disembarking) that caused the injury of which complaint is made, and secondly, was what happened unusual or unexpected? And as already pointed out, showing only that while on board or in the course of embarking or disembarking a passenger sustained some adverse physiological change does not identify the occurrence of an accident.

'As the facts in *Husain* demonstrate, the course of events surrounding death or injury to an airline passenger may present difficulties in determining whether there has been an accident. *Husain* concerned the death of a passenger on board an aircraft as a result of exposure to cigarette smoke. A flight attendant had refused requests to move the passenger to a seat further away from those who were smoking on board. The difficulties in determining whether that course of events constituted an accident is sufficiently identified by reference to the competing contentions of the petitioner and the respondents in the Supreme Court of the United States and the contention made by the United States as amicus curiae supporting the respondents (the relatives and legal personal representatives of the deceased passenger). The respondents described the question presented in the proceedings in the Supreme Court as being

> [w]hether the repeated insistence by an airline flight attendant that an asthmatic passenger remain in an assigned seat amidst life-threatening smoke — in direct violation of standard industry practice and the policy of her own airline — is an "unusual" occurrence and thus, under the principles established in [Saks], constitutes an "accident" for purposes of Article 17 of the Warsaw Convention.

'The United States, as amicus curiae, described the question as being "[w]hether an airline's unreasonable refusal to assist a passenger who becomes ill during an international flight, in violation of industry standards and the airline's own policies, constitutes an 'accident' within the meaning of Art 17 of the Warsaw Convention."

'By contrast, Olympic Airways, the petitioner in the United States Supreme Court described the question as being

> [w]hether the court below improperly held that the 'accident' condition precedent to air carrier liability for a passenger's death under Article 17 of the Warsaw Convention can be satisfied when a passenger's pre-existing medical condition is aggravated by exposure to a normal condition in the aircraft cabin, even if the air carrier's negligent omission may have been in the chain of causation?

'These different formulations of the question that arose in *Husain* reveal at least two things. First, unsurprisingly, each sought to emphasise particular aspects of the circumstances surrounding the passenger's death. Secondly, each sought to identify whether something unusual or unexpected had happened on board the aircraft. The United States, as amicus, emphasised the response, or lack of response, to a medical emergency. The respondents emphasised the flight attendant's refusal to move the passenger. The airline sought to say, in effect, that nothing had happened on board that was unusual or unexpected; even if the flight attendant did not react as she should have reacted, there was no accident.

'As already pointed out, neither side in the present appeal sought to challenge the correctness of what was decided in *Husain*. Moreover, questions of the kind considered in *Husain* do not arise in this case because it is central to the appellant's case that nothing happened on board the aircraft which was in any respect out of the ordinary or unusual. Further, what he alleges to be the relevant flight conditions were not said to be unusual or unexpected in any respect. (Indeed, as against CASA, he alleges in his statement of claim that the conditions were "the standard conditions of and procedures relating to passenger travel" on such flights.) And only by the mechanism of describing the absence of warning as a "failure to warn" did the appellant seek to suggest that the absence of warning was in any respect unusual or unexpected on the flights concerned.

'References to "failure" to warn in this context are irrelevant and unhelpful. They are irrelevant because they must proceed from unstated premises about the content or origin of some duty to warn. There is no basis for introducing, for example, concepts of the common law of negligence to the construction or application of an international treaty like Montreal No 4. And unless there is resort to some standard of legal behaviour to determine whether what happened was a "failure", the description of what happened as a failure is, in truth, no more than an assertion that there was no warning.

'The references to failure are unhelpful because they suggest that the only point at which some relevant warning could or should have been given is on board the aircraft. But if some warning was necessary or appropriate, it is not apparent why it should not have been given at a much earlier point of making arrangements to travel by air, rather than on board the aircraft. Further, reference to failure is unhelpful because it diverts attention from what it is that happened on board to what might have, could have, or perhaps should have happened there and why that should be so. If, as earlier indicated, it is appropriate to ask "what happened on board?" the answer in this case is that the appellant alleges that nothing unexpected or unusual happened there.

'The allegations which the appellant makes, if proved, would not establish a cause of action against the carriers.

'That conclusion is consistent with the decisions reached in intermediate courts of appeal in the United States and in England about the application of the Warsaw Convention and subsequent treaties to cases of DVT. In *Re Deep Vein Thrombosis Litigation* [2004] QB 234, the Court of Appeal of England and Wales held that the word "accident" in the Warsaw Convention as modified by the Hague Protocol was to be given a natural and sensible, but flexible and purposive meaning in its context and that for there to be an accident within the meaning of the relevant article, there had to be an event external to the passenger which impacted on the body in a manner which caused death or bodily injury and the event had to be unusual, unexpected or untoward. The Court held that inaction was a non-event which could not properly be described as an accident. Not warning of the risk of DVT and not giving advice on the precautions that would minimise that risk were not events. The conditions in which passengers travelled on flights (with cramped seating and the like) were not capable of amounting to an event that satisfied the first limb of the definition of an accident which "took place on board the aircraft or in the course of any of the operations of embarking or disembarking".' *Povey v Qantas Airways Limited* [2005] HCA 33 at [32]–[44], per Gummow, Hayne and Heydon JJ; BC200504275

Canada 'The Supreme Court of the United States has defined "accident" in Article 17 of the [Warsaw] Convention as "an unexpected or unusual event or happening that is external to the passenger": *Air France v Saks*, 470 US 392 (1985) at 405. This definition has been adopted in Ontario: *Quinn v Canadian Airlines* (1994) 18 OR (3d) 326 (Gen Div), affirmed [1997] OJ No 1832 (QL), application for leave to appeal to SCC dismissed [1997] SCCA No 354 (QL).

'The plaintiff submits that the wrongdoing alleged [exposure of plaintiff to second-hand tobacco smoke] against the defendant is at least in part intentional and deliberate and that accordingly, it simply cannot fall within the meaning of "accident". In my view, this argument is not sustainable.

'The word "accident" in Article 17 is a term of art with a meaning particular to the *Convention*. Reading the *Convention* as a whole, it is apparent that "accident" in Article 17 must be interpreted to embrace intentional acts of wrongdoing. Article 17 is the sole source of liability imposed upon a carrier by the *Convention* for bodily injury to passengers. It follows that if "accident" were interpreted to include only inadvertent or negligent acts by a carrier, it would lead to the extraordinary result that the *Convention* provides a remedy for inadvertence or negligence but fails to provide any remedy for deliberate wrongdoing. It is clear, however, that this is not the case. Article 25, discussed in greater detail below, limits defences or limits on liability for where the carrier is guilty of wilful misconduct, thereby plainly indicating that deliberate wrongdoing is actionable under the *Convention*.

'I turn, accordingly, to the question of whether the facts pleaded bring the case within the definition of "accident" set out above, namely, "an unexpected or unusual event or happening that is external to the passenger".' *Naval-Torres v Northwest Airlines Inc* (1998) 159 DLR (4th) 67 at 75–76, Ont Gen Div, per Sharpe J

New Zealand [Livestock Insurance Policy] 'In the context of an insurance policy it is traditional to commence consideration of whether there had been loss by "accident" by making reference to a definition of Lord McNaughton in *Fenton v J T Thorley & Co Ltd* [1903] AC 443, 448 of "an unlooked-for mishap or an untoward event which is not expected or designed". In *Mount Albert City Council* (supra) Cooke J, as he was then, cautioned that such definitions are helpful but not necessarily exhaustive tests and that it is necessary to come back to the words used to determine whether cover applies to the proved facts. Those cautionary observations are particularly significant in the context of this claim. From the point of view of the plaintiff it might be said that Commodore's death was unlooked-for, untoward, and unexpected. But, in my opinion, any such description cannot be determinative of the claim. It is necessary to go further and consider whether the natural and ordinary meaning of the policy words "from accident", in their context, cover the events relating to Commodore's death. In my opinion, it would be stretching those words beyond their natural and ordinary meaning, and distorting them in their context, to say that Commodore's death was "from accident". His death arose from the processes of nature. There is no evidence to suggest the intervention of factors outside the processes of nature. The stag's death was not "from accident" as that expression would usually be understood.' *Price v New Zealand Insurance Co Ltd* [1996] 3 NZLR 727 at 731, per Chisholm J

Industrial accident

[The Social Security Act 1975 has been repealed. The definition has been re-enacted, with minor drafting amendments in the Social Security Administration Act 1992, s 44(6).]

ACCIDENTAL BODILY HARM

[A fireman suffered post-traumatic stress disorder (PTSD) having attended two particularly horrific fires. The defenders argued that PTSD was not 'bodily injury' and that since he chose to be a fireman, any bodily injury he suffered could not be described as 'accidental'.] 'It makes ... sense to regard PTSD as involving some physical impact on the sufferer ... The pursuer has suffered something which can properly be described as a bodily injury to his person ... An injury suffered by a fireman, while attending a fire, as a result of some fortuitous occurrence during the fire seems to me to be just as much an accidental injury as one sustained in the course of a sport.' *Connelly v New Hampshire Insurance Co* 1997 SCLR 459 at 467–468, per Lord Coulsfield

ACCIDENTAL MEANS

Canada '[24] In discussing what constitutes death by "accidental means", the Court reiterated the principle in *Stats* that the word "accident" is "an ordinary word to be interpreted in the ordinary language of the people" [p. 1164]. The Court continued as follows:

> [19] ... Hence ... we must focus on the ordinary person's understanding of the phrase,

and on "whether in ordinary and popular language the event as it happened would be described as an accident" (para. 26). Only in this way can the reasonable expectations of both the insured and insurer be protected. We must therefore inquire how the phrase "death by accidental means" is used in ordinary language.

[20] As a starting point, we note that the accidental nature of a particular means of death depends, in ordinary parlance, on the consequences that the insured had or did not have in mind. When we speak of an "accidental" means of death, we normally have in mind a situation in which someone's action has had results that this person did not intend or expect. Unintentional or unexpected death is seen as accidental; intentional or expected death as non-accidental.

'[25] The Court referred to other similar authorities and to a number of cases where the general rule that unexpected death is accidental was applied. The Court concluded at para. 23 that "[t]he expectation test can be applied generally to all cases in which death appears to be accidental".

'[26] In my view, it is noteworthy that the entire analysis of the Court relates to the consequences flowing from the *actions* or *conduct* of an insured. Indeed, a good part of the analysis concerns cases where persons engage in risky activities. No reference is made to death resulting from natural causes. The focus of the analysis, as is usually the case, is obviously driven by the factual context of the case, and in that context, it makes eminent sense that "the pivotal question is whether the insured expected to die".

'[27] In my view, the expectation test is not appropriate in a case where death results solely from a natural cause. Such a death is not one "in which death appears to be accidental". If we come back to the examples referred to earlier, a person's unexpected death during his or sleep, caused by aneurysm or other condition with fatal consequences, would not be described as an accident in ordinary and popular language. Nor would such an interpretation accord with the reasonable expectations of the parties.' *Wang v Metropolitan Life Insurance Co* [2004] OJ No 3525, 242 DLR (4th) 598 (CA), per Charron JA

ACCOMMODATE

Canada '[47] When the consultation process suggests amendment of Crown policy, we arrive at the stage of accommodation. Thus the effect of good faith consultation may be to reveal a duty to accommodate. Where a strong *prima facie* case exists for the claim, and the consequences of the government's proposed decision may adversely affect it in a significant way, addressing the Aboriginal concerns may require taking steps to avoid irreparable harm or to minimize the effects of infringement, pending final resolution of the underlying claim. Accommodation is achieved through consultation, as this Court recognized in *R. v. Marshall*, [1999] 3 S.C.R. 533, 179 D.L.R. (4th) 193, at para. 22: "the process of accommodation of the treaty right may best be resolved by consultation and negotiation".

'[48] This process does not give Aboriginal groups a veto over what can be done with land pending final proof of the claim. The Aboriginal "consent" spoken of in *Delgamuukw* is appropriate only in cases of established rights, and then by no means in every case. Rather, what is required is a process of balancing interests, of give and take.

'[49] This flows from the meaning of "accommodate". The terms "accommodate" and "accommodation" have been defined as to "adapt, harmonize, reconcile" ... "an adjustment or adaptation to suit a special or different purpose ... a convenient arrangement; a settlement or compromise": *The Concise Oxford Dictionary of Current English* (9th ed. 1995) at p. 9. The accommodation that may result from pre-proof consultation is just this – seeking compromise in an attempt to harmonize conflicting interests and move further down the path of reconciliation. A commitment to the process does not require a duty to agree. But it does require good faith efforts to understand each other's concerns and move to address them.

'[50] The Court's decisions confirm this vision of accommodation. The Court in *Sparrow* raised the concept of accommodation, stressing the need to balance competing societal interests with Aboriginal and treaty rights. In *R. v. Sioui*, [1990] 1 S.C.R 1025 at p. 1072, 70 D.L.R. (4th) 427, the Court stated that the Crown bears the burden of proving that its occupancy of lands "cannot be accommodated to reasonable exercise of the Hurons' rights". And in *R. v. Côté*, [1996] 3 S.C.R. 139, 138 D.L.R. (4th) 385, at para. 81, the Court spoke of whether restrictions on Aboriginal rights "can be accommodated with the Crown's special fiduciary relationship with First Nations". Balance and compromise are inherent in the notion of reconciliation. Where accommodation is required in making decisions that may adversely affect as yet unproven Aboriginal rights and title claims, the Crown must balance Aboriginal concerns reasonably with the potential impact of the decision on the asserted right or title and with other societal interests.' *Haida Nation v British Columbia (Minister of Forests)* [2004] SCJ No 70, 245 DLR (4th) 33, per McLachlin CJC

ACCOMMODATION

'... "accommodation" in s 58(1) and s 60(1) of the Housing Act 1985 means a place which can fairly be described as accommodation (*Puhlhofer v Hillingdon London Borough Council* [1986] AC 657, [1986] 1 All ER 467) and which it would be reasonable, having regard to the general housing conditions in the local housing authority's district, for the person in question to continue to occupy (s 58(2A) and (2B)). There is no additional requirement that it should be settled or permanent.

'The same is, in my view, true of the "accommodation" which the local housing authority is under a duty to make available to an unintentionally homeless person under s 65(2). I say this fully conscious of the fact that the courts and the Department of the Environment have for some years taken a different view.' *Awua v Brent London Borough Council* [1995] 3 All ER 493 at 499, HL, per Lord Hoffmann

[Under the Housing Act 1996, Pt VII, where a person applies to a local authority for accommodation as a homeless person, the local authority must, if satisfied that the applicant might be homeless and has a priority need, provide accommodation for the applicant pending a final decision.] 'On its true construction the word accommodation in s 188 of the Housing Act 1996 means suitable accommodation. Splitting a family which includes a wife and three children under ten into two hostels some distance apart is not a lawful discharge of the duty under s 188.' *R v Ealing London Borough Council, ex p Surdonja* [1999] 1 All ER 566 at 571, per Scott Baker J

ACCOMMODATION BILL

[For 4 Halsbury's Laws (4th edn) para 383 see now 4(1) Halsbury's Laws (4th edn) (Reissue) para 383.]

ACCOMPANIED

New Zealand [Section 64B(4)(b) of the Immigration Act 1987 requires that an appeal be 'accompanied' by the prescribed fee.] 'It would be difficult to suggest that where the notice of appeal takes the form of a facsimilied communication, and the fee is then despatched by a different method of communication half an hour after the facsimile, and received on the day following the receipt of the facsimile, the appeal is still "accompanied" by the fee, at least within the time limit ... Language is elastic to a certain point but snaps when asked to part company altogether with previously accepted meanings. It could be stretched here to accommodate facsimiles but not, I fear, fees posted but not received within the time limit.' *Wielgus v Removal Review Authority* [1994] 1 NZLR 73 at 79, per Fisher J

ACCOMPANY

New Zealand [Section 234(1) of the Crimes Act 1961 provides that robbery is 'theft accompanied by violence or threats of violence, to any person or property, used to extort the property stolen or to prevent or overcome resistance to its being stolen'.] 'It is implicit in "accompany" that there must be a nexus between the act of stealing, here the act of conversion, and a threat of violence; and further the threat of violence must be used to prevent or overcome resistance to the property's being stolen. Both must be present. "Accompany" does not require that the act of stealing and the threat of violence be contemporaneous. It is sufficient and necessary that they be present together.' *R v Maihi* [1993] 2 NZLR 139 at 141, CA, per cur

ACCOMPLICE

[For 11 Halsbury's Laws (4th edn) para 457 see now 11(2) Halsbury's Laws (4th edn) (Reissue) para 1143.]

ACCORD AND SATISFACTION

[For 9 Halsbury's Laws (4th edn) para 585 see now 9(1) Halsbury's Laws (4th edn) (Reissue) para 1043.]

[For 45 Halsbury's Laws (4th edn) para 1270 see now 45(2) Halsbury's Laws (4th edn) (Reissue) para 386.]

ACCORDANCE

Australia [Regulation 98(1) of the Industrial Relations Regulations (Cth) provides that an application to the Federal Court of Australia must, inter alia, be in 'accordance' with Form 11.] 'Counsel referred to the definition of "accordance"

in the Shorter Oxford Dictionary. He contended that "accordance" in reg 98(1)(a) means "harmony". In my view, the alternative meaning, "conformity", is more appropriate. The notion of a document being in conformity with a form is easier to grasp than the notion of the document and the form being in harmony. Alternatively, disconformity is easier to recognise than disharmony. In my view, "in accordance with" in reg 98(1)(a) means in complete agreement with.' *Re La* (*sub nom Re Federated Furnishing Trade Society of Australasia*) (1993) 41 FCR 151 at 158; 113 ALR 137 at 145, per Gray J

ACCOUNT

Australia '... an "account" [of part of proceedings under the Family Law Act 1975 (Cth)] ... is a narrative, description, retelling, or recital of such proceedings ... There is no account of proceedings merely because some allegations made in the proceedings are reiterated outside the Court. Before there can be an account of proceedings in the relevant sense, a communication must purport to narrate, describe, retell or recite something that has happened in the proceedings, or something about the proceedings.' *Hinchcliffe v Cmr of Police of the Australian Federal Police* BC200107735; [2001] FCA 1747 at [53], per Kenny J

ACCOUNTING DATE

[The Income and Corporation Taxes Act 1970 is largely repealed. The definition has been re-enacted in the Income and Corporation Taxes Act 1988, s 834(1).]

ACCRETION

[For 49 Halsbury's Laws (4th edn) para 294 see now 49(2) Halsbury's Laws (4th edn) (Reissue) para 11.]

ACCRUING DATE

New Zealand 'The expression "accruing due" ... in my judgment means falling due or becoming due. Thus an obligation may be incurred on a certain day and not fall due to be discharged or satisfied until a later day.' *Re Peter Austin Ltd* [1990] 2 NZLR 245 at 252, per Tipping J

ACCUSATION

[Under the Extradition Act 1989 s 11(3)(c) a request for extradition must be refused if the accusation is not made in good faith in the interests of justice. Indian government submitted that 'accusation' related to the state which made the request for extradition, not to those involved in the investigation or prosecution.] '63. Mr Garlick submitted that since "accusation" referred to the request for extradition and the request was being made by the Union of India on behalf of the state of Maharastra and the state was acting through an independent public prosecutor, there was no evidence that any party who could properly be regarded as making the request had acted in bad faith. We do not consider that the ordinary meaning of the word "accusation" is a request, notwithstanding that the nexus between accusation and request may well be obvious. Such a nexus appears from the terms of s 11(3) of the 1989 Act because the subsection refers in turn to the following: (1) "the offence, or each of the offences"; (2) the request, namely "in respect of which the applicant's return is sought"; and (3) "the accusation against him". But the words of the subsection are against the accusation meaning the request because sub-s (3)(c) refers to "good faith in the interests of justice" in relation to the accusation not the request. A request for extradition is not in character an accusation. It is an exercise of sovereign power pursuant to a treaty in respect of an alleged offence. Whether or not it could ever be regarded as an "accusation", for the purposes of an allegation that such an exercise of power was not in good faith, does not arise in this case. But we are satisfied that, even if it could be so regarded, that is not the limit of the meaning of accusation nor the most obvious reflection of what is referred to in the subsection. Accusation is broad enough to encompass the accusation of a witness or witnesses and the offence charged in consequence. By making a request for extradition, reliance is placed upon the evidence of any witness and the offence disclosed thereby. The protection afforded by the subsection would be rendered "sterile", as Mr Nicholls submitted, if the issue of bad faith could be divorced from the underlying facts supporting the request. Certainly Sedley J in *Re Calis* (19 November 1993, unreported) examined the good faith of the complainant to determine the issue under s 11(3). No one appears to have argued to the contrary. Having heard such argument we reject it.' *Re Saifi* [2001] 4 All ER 168 at 190, DC (Eng), per Rose LJ

ACCUSED

[The Extradition Act 1989, s 1(1), allows the extradition to a foreign state with which extradition procedures are available of a person in the United Kingdom who is 'accused' in that state of the commission of an extradition crime.] 'It is common ground that mere suspicion that an individual has committed offences is insufficient to place him in the category of "accused" persons. It is also common ground that it is not enough that he is in the traditional phrase "wanted by the police to help them with their inquiries". Something more is required. What more is needed to make a suspect an "accused" person? There is no statutory definition. Given the divergent systems of law involved, and notably the differences between criminal procedures in the United Kingdom and in civil law jurisdictions, it is not surprising that the legislature has not attempted a definition. For the same reason it would be unwise for the House to attempt to define the word "accused" within the meaning of the 1989 Act. It is, however, possible to state in outline the approach to be adopted. The starting point is that "accused" in s 1 of the 1989 Act is not a term of art. It is a question of fact in each case whether the person passes the threshold test of being an "accused" person. Next there is the reality that one is concerned with the contextual meaning of "accused" in a statute intended to serve the purpose of bringing to justice those accused of serious crimes. There is a transnational interest in the achievement of this aim. Extradition treaties, and extradition statutes, ought, therefore, to be accorded a broad and generous construction so far as the texts permits it in order to facilitate extradition: see *Government of Belgium v Postlethwaite* [1987] 2 All ER 985 at 991–992, [1988] AC 924 at 946–947. That approach has been applied by the Privy Council to the meaning of "accused" in an extradition treaty: see *Rey v Government of Switzerland* [1998] 3 WLR 1 at 7. It follows that it would be wrong to approach the problem of construction solely from the perspective of English criminal procedure, and in particular from the point of view of the formal acts of the laying of an information or the preferring of an indictment. Moreover, it is important to note that in England a prosecution may also be commenced if a custody officer decides that there is sufficient evidence to charge an arrested person and then proceeds to charge him: s 37(7) of the Police and Criminal Evidence Act 1984; and see generally as to the commencement of prosecutions Card, Cross and Jones *Criminal Law* (13th edn, 1995) ch 4. Despite the fact that the prosecuting authorities and the court are not involved at that stage, the charging of an arrested person marks the beginning of a prosecution and the suspect becomes an "accused" person. And that is so even if the police continue to investigate afterwards.

'It is not always easy for an English court to decide when in a civil law jurisdiction a suspect becomes an "accused" person. All one can say with confidence is that a purposive interpretation of "accused" ought to be adopted in order to accommodate the differences between legal systems. In other words, it is necessary for our courts to adopt a cosmopolitan approach to the question whether as a matter of substance rather than form the requirement of there being an "accused" person is satisfied. That such a broad approach to the interpretation of s 1 of the 1989 Act is permissible is reinforced by the provisions of s 20. This provision deals with the reverse position of an extradition of a person "accused" in the United Kingdom and contemplates that "proceedings" against him may not be commenced (begun) for six months after his return. This provides contextual support for a correspondingly broad approach to "accused" in s 1. For my part I am satisfied that the Divisional Court in this case posed the right test by addressing the broad question whether the competent authorities in the foreign jurisdiction had taken a step which can fairly be described as the commencement of a prosecution. But in the light of the diversity of cases which may come before the courts it is right to emphasise that ultimately the question whether a person is "accused" within the meaning of s 1 of the 1989 Act will require an intense focus on the particular facts of each case.' *Re Ismail* [1998] 3 All ER 1007 at 1011–1012, HL, per Lord Steyn

Australia 'As was pointed out in *Narain v Director of Public Prosecutions* (1987) 15 FCR 411 at 421, in the common law, the term "accused" is not a legal term of art. It may be used in legislation with purely domestic concerns so as to encompass terms such as "charge", "indict", "impeach", "arraign", "incriminate", as well as to refer to the laying of an information in a private prosecution: see *Fraser v R (No 2)* (1985) 1 NSWLR 680 at 689–90. But it would not readily be understood as including suspicion by prosecuting authorities but without prosecution: see *Stirland v Director of Public Prosecutions* [1944] AC 315 at 323–4. Much would depend upon the particular statutory or constitutional context. Where what is in issue is a constitutional guarantee then the term may be expected to be used broadly.' *Director of Public Prosecutions (Cth) v Kainhofer* (1995) 132 ALR 483 at 504, per Gummow J

ACQUIESCENCE

Australia 'Strictly used, acquiescence indicates the contemporaneous and informed ("knowing") acceptance or standing by which is treated by equity as "assent" (i.e. consent) to what would otherwise be an infringement of rights ... The word is commonly also used to refer: (i) to a representation by silence of a type which may found an estoppel by conduct (see e.g., *Mitchell v Homfray* [(1881) 8 QBD 587 at 591, 593]); or (ii) to acceptance of a past wrongful act in circumstances which give rise to an active waiver of rights or a release of liability (see, e.g., Brunyate, *Limitations of Actions in Equity* (1932), pp 188–189; Hanbury and Maudsley, *Modern Equity*, 12th edn (1985), pp 621–622); or (iii) to an election to abandon or not enforce rights: see e.g., per Lindley LJ, *Allcard v Skinner* [(1887) 36 Ch D 145 at 186–189]. A plaintiff may, however, lose his right to relief by an "inferior species of acquiescence" ... which does not amount to assent, waiver or election or give rise to an estoppel. In these cases, acquiescence may be used in at least one of three ways. First, it is sometimes used as an indefinite overlapping component of a catch-all phrase also incorporating "laches" or "gross laches" and/or "delay". While such phrases may provide a convenient means of referring to a general area of equity, they tend to obscure principle rather than to assist in its identification. Secondly, acquiescence is used as a true alternative to "laches" to divide the field between inaction in the face of "the assertion of adverse rights" ("acquiescence") and inaction "in prosecuting rights" ("laches") (see, e.g., Smith, *Manual of Equity Jurisprudence*, 14th edn (1889), p 24). Upon analysis, that use of the word "acquiescence" is not helpful since laches ("an old French word for slackness or negligence or not doing": Co. Litt. 380b; *Partridge v Partridge* [[1894] 1 Ch 351 at 360]) comprehends silence or inaction in the face of an unwarranted assertion of adverse rights by another as well as inaction or delay in prosecuting one's own rights. Thirdly, and more commonly, acquiescence is used, in a context where laches is used to indicate either mere delay or delay with knowledge, to refer to conduct by a person, with knowledge of the acts of another person, which encourages that other person reasonably to believe that his acts are accepted (if past) or not opposed (if contemporaneous): see, e.g., *Cashman* [(1897) 7 GLJ at 153]; *Glasson v Fuller* [(1922) SASR 148 at 161–162].' *Orr v Ford* (1989) 167 CLR 316 at 337–338, per Deane J

ACQUIRE

[*Congreve v Inland Revenue Commissioners* was overruled by *Vestey v Inland Revenue Commissioners* (*Nos 1 and 2*) [1979] 3 All ER 976, HL.]

Australia 'Section 50(1) [Trade Practices Act 1947 (Cth)] prohibits a corporation from acquiring, directly or indirectly, any shares in the capital, or any assets, of a body corporate if there ensues the consequence specified in para (a) or (b) of the subsection ... In my opinion when s 50(1) prohibits a corporation from acquiring shares in the capital or assets of a body corporate it is prohibiting the acquisition in the sense of obtaining ownership of any legal or equitable interest in those shares or assets, whether the acquisition is by a person alone or jointly with another person.' *Trade Practices Commission v Australian Iron & Steel Pty Ltd* (1990) 92 ALR 395 at 404–405, per Lockhart J

Australia ' "To acquire", according to its ordinary and natural meaning, connotes in our view to obtain, gain or get something. The first meaning given in the Oxford English Dictionary, 2nd edn (1989), is: "1. To gain, obtain or get as one's own, to gain the ownership of (by one's own exertions or qualities)." The second meaning is: "2. To receive, or get as one's own (without reference to the manner), to come into possession of." The Macquarie Dictionary gives a similar definition. There must be something in existence that can be obtained or gained; but the word is apt to encompass the case where one person creates an asset which at the same time comes into the possession of or is obtained by another person. Some examples are helpful. Where an owner of property grants an option to a person to purchase it, the owner does not own the option before he creates it; it is created by the owner and at the very same time it is acquired by the grantee. Yet, according to the ordinary meaning of the word "acquire", it is clear that the option was acquired by the grantee from the owner of the property: see *Commissioner of Taxes* (*Qld*) *v Camphin* (1937) 57 CLR 127 at 133–134, per Latham CJ, with whose reasons for judgment Rich and McTiernan JJ agreed. Similarly with a lease of property. The owner of property when creating the lease at the same time creates it in favour of the lessee. It is not created by the lessee. It is created by the act of the owner of the property and the lease is obtained by the lessee at the same time. It seems plain to us that the lessee acquires the lease from the owner of the property: see *Camphin*'s case, also per Latham CJ at 133–134.

Other examples of the creation of a fresh set of proprietary rights out of a greater bundle of pre-existing proprietary rights may be found in the judgment of Hill J in *FCT v Cooling* (1990) 22 FCR 42 at 63–64. In such cases, there is an acquisition of those new proprietary rights by the party in whom they are vested.' *Allina Pty Ltd v Federal Commissioner of Taxation* (1991) 99 ALR 295 at 301, per cur

ACQUISITION

Date of acquisition

[The Finance (No 2) Act 1945, s 57(6) is repealed. See now the definition of 'date of sale or purchase' in the Inheritance Tax Act 1984, s 198.]
(1) Subject to the following subsections, the date on which an interest in land is sold or purchased by the appropriate person shall for the purposes of this Chapter [Chapter IV of Part VI] be taken to be the date on which he enters into a contract to sell or purchase it.
(2) If the sale or purchase of any interest by the appropriate person results from the exercise (whether by him or by any other person) of an option granted not more than six months earlier, the date on which the interest is sold or purchased shall be taken to be the date on which the option was granted.
(3) If an interest is acquired from the appropriate person in pursuance of a notice to treat served by an authority possessing powers of compulsory acquisition, the date on which the interest is sold shall, subject to subsection (4) below, be taken to be the date on which compensation for the acquisition is agreed or otherwise determined (variations on appeal being disregarded for this purpose) or, if earlier, the date when the authority enter on the land in pursuance of their powers.
(4) If an interest in land is acquired from the appropriate person—
    (a) in England, Scotland or Wales by virtue of a general vesting declaration within the meaning of the Compulsory Purchase (Vesting Declarations) Act 1981 or, in Scotland, Schedule 24 to the Town and Country Planning (Scotland) Act 1972, or
    (b) in Northern Ireland, by way of a vesting order,
    the date on which it is sold by the appropriate person shall be taken to be the last day of the period specified in the declaration or, in

Northern Ireland, the date on which the vesting order becomes operative.

ACT IN COMPANY

Australia [Section 92D(2) of the Crimes Act 1900 (NSW) provides that a person who, 'acting in company' with another person, engages in sexual intercourse with another person without the consent of that person is guilty of an offence.] 'In *R v Brougham* (1986) 43 SASR 187, the South Australian Supreme Court had to consider a similar question, namely the elements of assault with intent to rob in company, an offence defined by s 158 of the Criminal Law Consolidation Act 1935 (SA)... King CJ, with whom the other members of the court agreed, remarked: "A person commits a robbery, or an assault with intent, in company where that person participates in the robbery or assault together with another or others in the sense that the victim is confronted by the combined force or strength of two or more persons or that the forces of two or more persons are deployed against the victim. It is not necessary that more than one participant actually strike or rob the victim; it is sufficient that the accused and one or more other participants be physically present for the common purpose of robbing, or assaulting with intent, and of physically participating if required." With one reservation, we are of opinion that this test may be applied *mutatis mutandis* to the construction of "acting in company" in s 92D(2). The reservation is that we think it is not essential to show that those persons alleged to have acted in company all had the purpose of "physically participating if required". Even if those with whom the accused is alleged to have acted in company did not all have that purpose, the accused may have acted in company with them in the relevant sense if their intention was to participate in any way, for example by helping to suppress, by threats or their mere presence, thoughts of resistance.' *Kelly v R* (1989) 90 ALR 481 at 483, per cur

ACT OF GOD

[For 9 Halsbury's Laws (4th edn) para 458 see now 9(1) Halsbury's Laws (4th edn) (Reissue) para 907.]

[For 45 Halsbury's Laws (4th edn) para 1251 see now 45(2) Halsbury's Laws (4th edn) (Reissue) para 363.]

ACT ... IN RESPECT OF ANY WILDLFIE

New Zealand '[24] So, it is necessary to consider what is meant by the expression "an act ... in

respect of any wildlife". In the context of the [Wildlife Act 1953], I consider that that expression must mean an act of the kind which is otherwise prohibited by the Act. In essence, that means that it must be an act of the type prohibited by s 63. If an act is not one prohibited by s 63, then no authority is, in general, required for it. If a particular act, performed by a person who was not subject to one of the Acts specified in s 71, did not constitute a breach of s 63, then no authority would be necessary. It would be illogical to interpret s 71 so as to require consent of the two ministers, if that identical act was carried out by a person who was subject to one of those Acts. Conversely, if an act under one of the Acts specified would constitute an offence under s 63, unless lawful authority were obtained, then it would not be in conformity with the scheme and purpose of the Act to hold that lawful authority could not be obtained under s 71, because the act was not an act in respect of wildlife.' *Royal Forest and Bird Protection Society of New Zealand Inc v Minister of Conservation* [2006] NZAR 265 at [24], per MacKenzie J

ACTING IN CONCERT

Australia 'The general principle was clearly stated in *R v Lowery and King (No 2)* [1972] VR 560 at 560 by Smith J who directed the jury in the following terms: "The law says that if two or more persons reach an understanding or arrangement that together they will commit a crime and then, while that understanding or arrangement is still on foot and has not been called off, they are both present at the scene of the crime and one or other of them does, or they do between them, in accordance with their understanding or arrangement, all the things that are necessary to constitute the crime, they are all equally guilty of that crime regardless of what part each played in its commission. In such cases they are said to have been acting in concert in committing the crime". "[E]ven if only one participant performed the acts constituting the crime, each will be guilty as principals in the first degree if the acts were performed in the presence of all and pursuant to a preconceived plan. In this case, the parties are said to be acting in concert." ' *Osland v R* (1998) 159 ALR 170 at 189–190; 73 ALJR 173; BC9806597, per McHugh J

ACTING IN THE ORDINARY COURSE OF THE BUSINESS

[Under s 10 of the Partnership Act 1890 partners may be held vicariously liable where loss was caused to a non-partner by any wrongful act or omission of any partner 'acting in the ordinary course' of his firm's business.] '[13] The second ground on which Mr Al Tajir and Mr Salaam contended that the Amhurst firm was not liable for Mr Amhurst's alleged acts is that these acts were not done by him while acting in the ordinary course of the business of the firm. I say "alleged acts", because Dubai Aluminium's claims against Mr Amhurst and the firm were settled before the trial judge made his findings of fact. Whether Dubai Aluminium's allegations against Mr Amhurst were well founded was never decided.

...

'[16] Mr Sumption QC submitted that whether an act is done in the ordinary course of a firm's business is a question of fact. Here the allegation in the amended points of claim is that the agreements were drafted by Mr Amhurst "in his capacity as a partner" in the Amhurst firm. This, counsel submitted, is an allegation of fact. For the purposes of the Amhurst firm's contribution claim this allegation is assumed to be well founded, pursuant to s 1(4) of the 1978 Act. That is the end of the matter.

'[17] I do not think the issue of vicarious liability is quite so straightforward when, as here, the act in question was not authorised. In order to identify the crucial issue it is necessary first to be clear on what is meant in this context by "acting in the ordinary course of business".

'[18] Partnership is the relationship which subsists between persons carrying on a business in common with a view of profit (s 1 of the 1890 Act). Partnership is rooted in agreement, express or tacit, between the partners. So is the conduct of the partnership business. Clearly, the nature and scope of a business carried on by partners are questions of fact. Similarly, what the ordinary course of the business comprises, in the sense of what is the normal manner in which the business is carried on, is also a question of fact. So also is the scope of a partner's authority.

'[19] Vicarious liability is concerned with the responsibility of the firm to other persons for wrongful acts done by a partner while acting in the ordinary course of the partnership business or with the authority of his co-partners. At first sight this might seem something of a contradiction in terms. Partners do not usually agree with each other to commit wrongful acts. Partners are not normally authorised to engage in wrongful conduct. Indeed, if vicarious liability of a firm for acts done by a partner acting in the ordinary course of the business of the firm were confined to acts authorised in

every particular, the reach of vicarious liability would be short indeed. Especially would this be so with dishonesty and other intentional wrongdoing, as distinct from negligence. Similarly restricted would be the vicarious responsibility of employers for wrongful acts done by employees in the course of their employment. Like considerations apply to vicarious liability for employees.

'[20] Take the present case. The essence of the claim advanced by Dubai Aluminium against Mr Amhurst is that he and Mr Salaam engaged in a criminal conspiracy to defraud Dubai Aluminium. Mr Amhurst drafted the consultancy agreement and other agreements in furtherance of this conspiracy. Needless to say, Mr Amhurst had no authority from his partners to conduct himself in this manner. Nor is there any question of conduct of this nature being part of the ordinary course of the business of the Amhurst firm. Mr Amhurst had authority to draft commercial agreements. He had no authority to draft a commercial agreement for the dishonest purpose of furthering a criminal conspiracy.

'[21] However, this latter fact does not of itself mean that the firm is exempt from liability for his wrongful conduct. Whether an act or omission was done in the ordinary course of a firm's business cannot be decided simply by considering whether the partner was authorised by his co-partners to do the very act he did. The reason for this lies in the legal policy underlying vicarious liability. The underlying legal policy is based on the recognition that carrying on a business enterprise necessarily involves risks to others. It involves the risk that others will be harmed by wrongful acts committed by the agents through whom the business is carried on. When those risks ripen into loss, it is just that the business should be responsible for compensating the person who has been wronged.

'[22] This policy reason dictates that liability for agents should not be strictly confined to acts done with the employer's authority. Negligence can be expected to occur from time to time. Everyone makes mistakes at times. Additionally, it is a fact of life, and therefore to be expected by those who carry on businesses, that sometimes their agents may exceed the bounds of their authority or even defy express instructions. It is fair to allocate risk of losses thus arising to the businesses rather than leave those wronged with the sole remedy, of doubtful value, against the individual employee who committed the wrong. To this end, the law has given the concept of "ordinary course of employment" an extended scope.

'[23] If, then, authority is not the touchstone, what is? Lord Denning MR once said that on this question the cases are baffling (see *Morris v C W Martin & Sons Ltd* [1965] 2 All ER 725 at 730, [1966] 1 QB 716 at 724). Perhaps the best general answer is that the wrongful conduct must be so closely connected with acts the partner or employee was authorised to do that, for the purpose of the liability of the firm or the employer to third parties, the wrongful conduct may fairly and properly be regarded as done by the partner while acting in the ordinary course of the firm's business or the employee's employment. Lord Millett said as much in *Lister v Hesley Hall Ltd* [2001] UKHL 22 at [69], [2001] 2 All ER 769 at [69], [2002] 1 AC 215. So did Lord Steyn (at [15], [28]). McLachlin J said in *Bazley v Curry* (1999) 174 DLR (4th) 45 at 62 (para 37):

> "... the policy purposes underlying the imposition of vicarious liability on employers are served only where the wrong is so connected with the employment that it *can be said* that the employer has introduced the risk of the wrong (and is thereby fairly and usefully charged with its management and minimization)." (My emphasis.)

To the same effect is Professor Atiyah's monograph *Vicarious Liability in the Law of Torts* (1967) p 171: "The master ought to be liable for all those torts which *can fairly be regarded* as reasonably incidental risks to the type of business he carried on." (My emphasis.)

'[24] In these formulations the phrases "may fairly and properly be regarded", "can be said", and "can fairly be regarded" betoken a value judgment by the court. The conclusion is a conclusion of law, based on primary facts, rather than a simple question of fact.

'[25] This "close connection" test focuses attention in the right direction. But it affords no guidance on the type or degree of connection which will normally be regarded as sufficiently close to prompt the legal conclusion that the risk of the wrongful act occurring, and any loss flowing from the wrongful act, should fall on the firm or employer rather than the third party who was wronged. It provides no clear assistance on when, to use Professor Fleming's phraseology, an incident is to be regarded as sufficiently work-related, as distinct from personal (see Fleming *The Law of Torts* (9th edn, 1998) p 427). Again, the well-known dictum of Lord Dunedin in *Plumb v Cobden Flour Mills Co Ltd* [1914] AC 62 at 67, draws a distinction between prohibitions which limit the sphere of

employment and those which only deal with conduct within the sphere of employment. This leaves open how to recognise the one from the other.

'[26] This lack of precision is inevitable, given the infinite range of circumstances where the issue arises. The crucial feature or features, either producing or negativing vicarious liability, vary widely from one case or type of case to the next. Essentially the court makes an evaluative judgment in each case, having regard to all the circumstances and, importantly, having regard also to the assistance provided by previous court decisions. In this field the latter form of assistance is particularly valuable.

...

'[34] ... I turn to consider on which side of the line is the present case. In drafting the consultancy agreements was Mr Amhurst acting solely on his own behalf? Or was he acting, although misguidedly, on behalf of the Amhurst firm? Had the claims against Mr Amhurst and the firm been tried to a conclusion the judge would have made findings of fact on what Mr Amhurst did, how he conducted his relevant business dealings with Mr Salaam and others, whether his conduct was dishonest, and whether he was acting for the firm or solely in his own interests. The court would have looked overall at all the circumstances. The court, and this House, would then have been properly equipped with the appropriate factual material with which to answer these questions. As it is, the only relevant plea in the particulars of claim is the compendious allegation that in doing what he did Mr Amhurst was acting in his capacity as a partner. In so far as this allegation is an allegation of fact, it is assumed to be correct.

'[35] This is a factually meagre basis on which to decide a question of vicarious responsibility for assumed dishonest conduct. But there is no other factual material available. Perforce the House must do its best with this material. Proceeding on this footing, in this context "acting in his capacity as a partner" can only mean that Mr Amhurst was acting for and on behalf of the firm, as distinct from acting solely in his own interests or the interests of others. He was seeking to promote the business of the firm.

'[36] On this assumed factual basis, I consider the firm is liable for Mr Amhurst's dishonest assistance in the fraudulent scheme, the assistance taking the form of drafting the necessary agreements. Drafting agreements of this nature for a proper purpose would be within the ordinary course of the firm's business. Drafting these particular agreements is to be regarded as an act done within the ordinary course of the firm's business even though they were drafted for a dishonest purpose. These acts were so closely connected with the acts Mr Amhurst was authorised to do that for the purpose of the liability of the Amhurst firm they may fairly and properly be regarded as done by him while acting in the ordinary course of the firm's business.

...

'[39] A further point arises here. The additional facts pleaded against Mr Amhurst unwittingly led the Court of Appeal astray. Evans LJ stated ([2001] QB 113 at 133, [2000] 3 WLR 910 at 928) that vicarious liability is not imposed "unless all of the acts or omissions which make the servant personally liable as a tortfeasor took place within the course of his employment". Aldous LJ was of a similar view. I respectfully consider this proposition, as it stands, is ambiguous. The ambiguity would be removed if the proposition were amended to read that vicarious liability is not imposed unless all the acts or omissions which are necessary to make the servant personally liable took place within the course of his employment. That is the present case. That was not the position in *Credit Lyonnais Bank Nederland NV (now known as Generale Bank Nederland NV) v Export Credits Guarantee Dept* [1999] 1 All ER 929, [2000] 1 AC 486, the case relied upon by the Court of Appeal (see [1999] 1 All ER 929 at 935, [2000] 1 AC 486 at 495 per Lord Woolf MR). In the present case, drafting the consultancy agreement and other agreements were acts of assistance by Mr Amhurst and, coupled with dishonesty, they were sufficient in themselves to give rise to equitable liability on his part. That assistance was given by Mr Amhurst while acting in the ordinary course of the firm's business, as discussed above. The firm is liable accordingly. It matters not, for the purpose of establishing vicarious liability, that Mr Amhurst may have done other, additional acts while acting outside the ordinary course of the firm's business.' *Dubai Aluminium Co Ltd v Salaam (Livingstone and others, third parties)* [2002] UKHL 48 at [13], [16]–[26], [34]–[36], [39], [2003] 1 All ER 97, per Lord Nicholls of Birkenhead

ACTION

[Under the new civil procedure, the term 'claim' is used instead of 'action'. For 37 Halsbury's Laws (4th edn) para 17 see now 37 Halsbury's Laws (4th edn) (Reissue) para 15.]

[Under the Employment Protection (Consolidation) Act 1978, s 32(1), an employee has the right not to have action taken against him as an individual by his employer for the purpose of preventing or deterring him from being or seeking to become a member of an independent trade union, or penalising him for so doing. Employers wishing to replace collective bargaining offered pay rises to employees who accepted personal contracts of employment but not to others, claiming that they did not intend derecognition of the union but to get rid of collective bargaining. Employees claimed that their rights under s 23(1) had been infringed by their employers' actions. In the House of Lords it was contended for the employers that although s 153(1) provided that in the 1978 Act, except so far as the context otherwise requires, 'act' and 'action' each includes omission, an omission to confer a benefit on an employee which was conferred on another employee did not amount to 'action ... taken against' that employee for a purpose prohibited by s 23(1).] 'The novel question, raised for the first time before your Lordships, is whether the extended meanings of the word "action" and of the phrase "taking action" provided by s 153(1) are properly to be applied to s 23(1) or whether this is a case where "the context otherwise requires". The crucial phrase to be construed in s 23(1) is "the right not to have action ... taken against him". If this phrase is to be construed as embodying the extended meaning, one must first expand the language so as to include the verb "omit" or the noun "omission" to see how it reads. The attempt to do this grammatically without substantially recasting the phrase and introducing additional words at once exposes the difficulty. If the concept of taking action against some person is to embrace the concept of omitting to act, the omission must be an omission to act in that person's favour. I cannot believe that any competent Parliamentary draftsman, intending that an omission by an employer to take action in favour of an employee should have the same consequences as positive action against him, would fail to spell out the circumstances in which the obligation to take action in favour of the employee was to arise. Otherwise he creates an obvious ambiguity ... To put it no higher, the question whether s 23(1) should be rewritten in some way so as to spell out expressly the meaning of "action" as including omission, or whether the context requires that the definition be not applied, gives rise to a "real and substantial difficulty" in the interpretation of the statute "which classical methods of construction cannot resolve" and thus entitles us to go behind the consolidating 1978 Act to derive whatever assistance we can in resolving the difficulty from the legislative history (see *Farrell v Alexander* [1976] 2 All ER 721 at 726, [1977] AC 59 at 73 per Lord Wilberforce).

'... Thus, prior to the 1978 consolidation, there was no question of applying any definition giving an extended meaning to the word "action" in the context in which we now have to construe it ... [I]f the definition of "action" in s 153(1) of the 1978 Act is applied to s 23(1), not only do we encounter the grammatical difficulty to which I have already referred, but we must also conclude that a consolidation Act has substantially altered the pre-existing law in a way that neither the draftsman nor Parliament can have intended.

'... [I]t remains the golden rule of construction that a statute means exactly what it says and does not mean what it does not say.

'For all these reasons I find it quite impossible to hold that withholding from the applicants in these two appeals the benefits conferred on some of their fellow employees, whatever its purpose may have been, was capable of amounting to a contravention of s 23(1) of the 1978 Act.' *Associated Newspapers Ltd v Wilson, Associated British Ports v Palmer* [1995] 2 All ER 100 at 105–106, 107, 109, HL, per Lord Bridge of Harwich

[The Limitation Act 1980, s 24(1) prevents an 'action' from being brought on any judgment after the expiration of six years from the date on which the judgment became enforceable. A question arose whether bankruptcy proceedings based on a statutory demand for satisfaction of a judgment debt constituted an action on a judgment.] 'It seems to me that bankruptcy proceedings are, first of all, a new proceeding so that it can be properly said that the proceedings are newly brought and are not in any way continuing some previous proceedings pursuant to the judgment or anything of that nature. But while they are not part of the proceedings which led to the judgment — they are not some continuation in any way of those proceedings — they are based on or related to the judgment. The bankruptcy proceedings in the Medway County Court are brought on a judgment obtained in another court. I have stressed that because it is well settled that the limitation period in s 4 [of the Limitation Act 1980] does not apply to a process of execution following a judgment.

...

'... So execution is regulated, inter alia, by Ord 46, r 2, which is supplementary to the action leading to the judgment as contrasted with actions on the judgment, which are the subject of s 24 of the 1980 Act, going beyond normal execution. All that confirms what I took from the reading of the section itself without reference to authorities. From this I deduce that bankruptcy is a new proceeding. It is not a proceeding under the judgment previously obtained.' *Re a debtor*(*No 50A/SD/95*) [1997] 2 All ER 789 at 792, 793, per Judge Paul Baker QC

[Time limit for actions to enforce judgments under the Limitation Act 1980, s 24(1), which states that an 'action' may not be brought on any judgment after the expiration of six years from the date on which the judgment became enforceable. By s 24(2), no arrears of interest in respect of any judgment debt may be recovered after the expiration of six years from the date on which the interest became due.] 'The word "action" is defined by s 38(1) as including "any proceeding in a court of law". The first question is whether s 24(1) bars execution of a judgment after six years, or whether it only bars the bringing of a fresh action on the judgment. If the answer is, as the plaintiffs contend, that it only bars a fresh action, the second question is whether, when a judgment is executed after six years, interest on the judgment is limited under s 24(2) to a period of six years before the date of execution. Tuckey J answered the first question in favour of the plaintiffs, and the second question in favour of the defendant. The Court of Appeal agreed with the judge on the first question but disagreed on the second.

'... I would hold that the first question must be answered in favour of the plaintiffs. "Action" in s 24(1) means a fresh action, and does not include proceedings by way of execution.

...

'With regret, however, I cannot agree with the Court of Appeal on the second question. There would seem to be no reason why the relevant words in s 24(2) "no arrears of interest ... shall be recovered" should not be given their ordinary meaning, so as to bar execution after six years in respect of *all* judgments. It is what the words say. "Recovered" has a broad meaning. It is not confined to recovery by fresh action. But the Court of Appeal has held that the limitation to six years' interest on judgments applies only in a case of actions on judgments, and not to execution of judgments generally. In support of this construction, the Court of Appeal relied strongly on the fact that sub-ss (1) and (2) were part of the same sentence, joined only by a comma, when they were enacted as s 2(4) of the 1939 Act. If the first half of the sentence is confined to actions on judgments, Parliament must have intended that the second half of the sentence should be similarly confined. But in my view this does not follow as a matter of language. "Any judgment" in the first half of the sentence means, quite literally, *any* judgment. There is no warrant for limiting "interest in respect of any judgment debt" in the second half of the sentence to interest in respect of a judgment in an action on a judgment, even if one could think of any good reason why Parliament should so have provided.' *Lowsley v Forbes (t/a L E Design Services)* [1998] 3 All ER 897 at 899, 906, HL, per Lord Lloyd of Berwick

'[2] Put shortly, the issue was this. Section 2(3) of the Fatal Accidents Act 1976 provides: "Not more than one action shall lie for and in respect of the same subject matter of complaint." Did this mean that if a writ was issued in a 1976 Act claim brought on behalf of a deceased's dependants but never served, this automatically precluded the bringing of a new action some years later?

...

'[10] Mr Lawrence originally submitted that it was unlikely that Parliament intended that dependants should be without a remedy in circumstances such as have arisen in this case. He suggested three possible routes by which justice might be done.

'[11] The first involved interpreting the word "action" as meaning "served process" in this context. He said that the fact that the word "action" in other contexts might refer to unserved proceedings was nothing to the point: this statute must be construed by reference to its purpose.

'[12] In my judgment, this route was not open to us. Although the House of Lords has said that if the words of a consolidating statute are clear, one should not go backwards into the legislative history of the words used in it (*Farrell v Alexander* [1976] 2 All ER 721, [1977] AC 59), an action naturally begins when initiating process is issued and a court thereby acquires jurisdiction to make orders against the defendant, notwithstanding that he has not yet been served with process. If there was any lack of clarity there, recourse to the [Fatal Accidents Act 1846] would show that it was inconceivable that Parliament intended the word "action" to have two different meanings in a single short section.

'[13] Mr Lawrence's second route involved withdrawing the concession made in the court below about the meaning of the words "not more than one action shall lie". He now sought to argue, notwithstanding Lord Atkin's dictum, that they should mean that there was only one cause of action, which would merge in any judgment given in any action, and which would be disposed of by any settlement. He conceded that this construction did not wholly deal with all the practical problems that might arise, since it was possible (see *Cooper*

v Williams [1963] 2 All ER 282, [1963] 2 QB 567) for one dependant to be prejudiced by the settlement of (or entry of judgment in) an action brought by another. He suggested, however, that this interpretation did provide a defendant with appropriate protection, in that if a defendant settles a claim, or if a claim goes to judgment, that defendant cannot be troubled by any further proceedings.

'[14] In my judgment, this route was equally illegitimate. If Parliament had wanted to give legislative effect to this concept it would have been easy for it to have found the appropriate language to give effect to its wish. The fact of the matter is that this provision had remained on the statute book for 130 years prior to 1976 without giving rise to any particular difficulty, and it may be that it was only the advent of extended limitation periods for minors, unaccompanied by any similar extension of the period of validity of an unserved writ, that gave rise to the problem that has surfaced in the present case. We must not turn ourselves into legislators if the language used by Parliament simply does not permit it.

'[15] Mr Lawrence's third route was slightly more promising. He suggested that we might be willing to interpret the words of the subsection as meaning that no action should be maintained. If it simply withered away because a protective writ was not served and the defendant had never been troubled with it, it would be a misuse of language to say it had ever been maintained (or had ever "lain" in any real sense of the word). I might have been tempted down that imaginative route of statutory construction to right an obvious injustice to these children if a more orthodox route was not now provided by the 1998 Act.

...

'[19] In my judgment, Mr Treasure was right not to seek to argue that the fortuitous effect of s 2(3) of the 1976 Act in a case where a writ has never been served and a new writ has been issued within the primary limitation period could have any legitimate aim. It was just a procedural quirk, brought about by the chance that Parliament had never considered this particular problem, and because our traditional English methods of interpreting statutes could not right an obvious injustice. He was also right to place no reliance on the words "within a reasonable time" in [the European Convention for the Protection of Human Rights and Fundamental Freedoms 1950] art 6(1) when Parliament permitted children an extended period in which to exercise their right of access to a court. Mr Treasure was also wise to accept, on reflection, that the right to rely on a procedural quirk as a bar to these children's right of access to a court could not possibly amount to a "possession" within the meaning of art 1 of the First Protocol of the convention.

'[20] Since 2 October 2000 we have been under a duty not to act in a way which is incompatible with a convention right (s 6(1) of the [Human Rights Act 1998]), and so far as it is possible to do so, primary legislation must be read and given effect in a way which is compatible with the convention rights (s 3(1)). It is certainly possible to interpret the word "action" as meaning "served process" in order to give effect to the convention rights of these three children. Until the present writ was served in July 1997, no process had been served which asserted a claim to compensation by these children for their mother's death. Section 2(3) of the 1976 Act therefore presents no artificial bar to this claim.' *Cachia v Faluyi* [2001] EWCA Civ 998 at [2], [10]–[15], [19], [2002] 1 All ER 192 at 194–197, CA, per Brooke LJ

See also RIGHT OF ACTION

ACTIONABLE

Canada '[23] *Black's Law Dictionary*, 7th ed. defines "actionable" as: "That for which an action will lie, furnishing legal ground for an action." The requirement that a tort be actionable was described in general terms by Lord Wilberforce in *Chaplin v. Boys*, [1969] 2 All E.R. 1085 (H.L.) at 1102, "The broad principle should surely be that a person should not be permitted to claim in England [the forum] in respect of a matter for which civil liability does not exist, or is excluded, under the law of the place where the wrong was committed." Although that decision, which modified and continued the rule of double actionability, was not followed in *Tolofson*, the principle of actionability remains.' *Castillo v Castillo* [2004] AJ No 802, 244 DLR (4th) 603 (CA), per Wittmann JA

ACTIVELY SEEKING PAID WORK

Australia 'The requirements of s 601(1)(a) [of the Social Security Act 1991 (Cth)] is (*sic*) that the person satisfy the Secretary that he or she is "actively seeking" paid work. In this context the adverb "actively" imports a requirement of active effort as opposed to indolence or procrastination. What the person is required to make an active effort about is the seeking of paid work which is not unsuitable for him or her to undertake – not the seeking of any particular class of such work, nor the seeking of any particular mix of such work.' *Castleman v Secretary, Department of Social Security* (1999) 56 ALD 439; 29 AAR 458; BC9903423; [1999] FCA 836 at [19], per Branson J

ACTUAL BODILY HARM

[Offences against the Person Act 1861, s 47.] '[15] As there are no decisions directly in point, we must address the problem on first principles, noting that, according to Viscount Kilmuir LC in *DPP v Smith* [1960] 3 All ER 161 at 171, [1961] AC 290 at 334, "bodily harm" needs no explanation, and that the phrase "actual bodily harm" consists of "three words of the English language which require no elaboration and in the ordinary course should not receive any [*R v Chan-Fook* [[1994] 2 All ER 552 at 557, [1994] 1 WLR 689 at 694]]". So actual bodily harm means what it says.

'[16] It is necessary to look at definitions because there is nothing to assist us in the decided cases. In ordinary language, "harm" is not limited to "injury", and according to the *Concise Oxford English Dictionary* (11th edn, 2004) p 651 extends to "hurt" or "damage". According to the same dictionary, "bodily", whether used as an adjective or an adverb, is "concern[ed] [with] the body", p 153. "Actual", as defined in the authorities, means that the bodily harm should not be so trivial or trifling as to be effectively without significance.

'[17] Recent authority shows that evidence of external bodily injury, or a break in or bruise to the surface of the skin, is not required. *R v Chan-Fook* [1994] 2 All ER 552 at 558, [1994] 1 WLR 689 at 695 established that actual bodily harm was not limited to "harm to the skin, flesh and bones of the victim". It applies to all parts of the body, including the victim's "organs, his nervous system and his brain". The significant words in that sentence are "all" and "includes". By identifying specific parts of the body, the observations in this judgment were not excluding any others. An assault occasioning actual bodily harm may be committed by words or gestures alone, without the need for any physical contact between the assailant and the body of the victim (see *R v Ireland, R v Burstow* [1997] 4 All ER 225, [1998] AC 147). It follows that physical pain consequent on an assault is not a necessary ingredient of this offence (see *T v DPP* [2003] EWHC 266 (Admin), [2003] All ER (D) (Feb)).

'[18] In my judgment, whether it is alive beneath the surface of the skin or dead tissue above the surface of the skin, the hair is an attribute and part of the human body. It is intrinsic to each individual and to the identity of each individual. Although it is not essential to my decision, I note that an individual's hair is relevant to his or her autonomy. Some regard it as their crowning glory. Admirers may so regard it in the object of their affections. Even if, medically and scientifically speaking, the hair above the surface of the scalp is no more than dead tissue, it remains part of the body and is attached to it. While it is so attached, in my judgment it falls within the meaning of "bodily" in the phrase "actual bodily harm". It is concerned with the body of the individual victim.

'[19] In my judgment, the respondent's actions in cutting off a substantial part of the victim's hair in the course of an assault on her – like putting paint on it or some unpleasant substance which marked or damaged it without causing injury elsewhere – is capable of amounting to an assault which occasions actual bodily harm ... ' *Director of Public Prosecutions v Smith (Michael Ross)* [2006] EWHC 94 (Admin) at [15]–[19], [2006] 2 All ER 16, per Sir Igor Judge P

ACTUAL FRAUD

[A clause in a settlement exempted trustees from liability unless caused by their own 'actual fraud'.] ' "Actual fraud" means what it says. It does not mean "constructive fraud" or "equitable fraud". The word "actual" is deliberately chosen to exclude them.

...

'In my judgment, therefore, cl 15 is apt to exclude liability for breach of trust in the absence of a dishonest intention on the part of the trustee whose conduct is impugned ...

'... The expression "actual fraud" in cl 15 is not used to describe the common law tort of deceit. As the judge appreciated it simply means dishonesty. I accept the formulation put forward by Mr Hill on behalf of the respondents which (as I have slightly modified it) is that it —

> "connotes at the minimum an intention on the part of the trustee to pursue a particular course of action, either knowing that it is contrary to the interests of the beneficiaries or being recklessly indifferent whether it is contrary to their interests or not."

...

'In my judgment cl 15 exempts the trustee from liability for loss or damage to the trust property no matter how indolent, imprudent, lacking in diligence, negligent or wilful he may have been, so long as he has not acted dishonestly.' *Armitage v Nurse* [1997] 2 All ER 705 at 710, 711, CA, per Millett LJ

ACTUAL KNOWLEDGE

New Zealand 'In considering the provisions of ss 18C and 18D of the Companies Act 1955 I have held that the use of the words "actual knowledge of the fraud" eliminated any question of constructive or imputed knowledge or anything other than actual knowledge of the person against whom the lack of authority is being asserted.' *Cricklewood Holdings Ltd v C V Quigley & Sons Nominees Ltd* [1992] 1 NZLR 463 at 478, per Holland J

ACTUAL OCCUPATION

[By s 70(1) of the Land Registration Act 1925 all registered land is deemed to be subject to certain overriding interests, including those of every person in 'actual occupation' of the land.] 'A prospective tenant or purchaser who is allowed, as a matter of indulgence, to go into property in order to plan decorations or measure for furnishings would not, in ordinary parlance, be said to be occupying it, even though he might be there for hours at a time. Of course, in the instant case, there was, no doubt, on the part of the persons involved in moving Mrs Cann's belongings, an intention that they would remain there and would render the premises suitable for her ultimate use as a residential occupier. Like the trial judge, however, I am unable to accept that acts of this preparatory character carried out by courtesy of the vendor prior to completion can constitute "actual occupation" for the purposes of s 70(1)(g).' *Abbey National Building Society v Cann* [1990] 1 All ER 1085 at 1101, HL, per Lord Oliver of Aylmerton

ACTUAL PECUNIARY LOSS

Australia [Trustees Act 1962 (WA) s 20(3). Professional defalcation by solicitor.] 'The word "actual" in the phrase "actual pecuniary loss" in the context of a claim against a solicitors fidelity fund gives added meaning to the words "pecuniary loss" and has a limiting effect on the loss that is recoverable: *Dobcol Pty Ltd v Law Institute of Victoria* [1979] VR 393 at 395, 396; *Ristevski v Kyriacou & Zard Constructions Pty Ltd & Law Institute of Victoria* (unreported; Supreme Court of Victoria; Harper J; 5 August 1997) at 17; *Schofield v Consolidated Interest Fund* (1988) 49 SASR 546 at 554, 555.

'The "actual pecuniary loss" refers only to such pecuniary loss as stems from the value of the money or other property the subject of a defalcation by a solicitor, and does not include other consequential loss suffered as a result of the defalcation: *Dobcol Pty Ltd v Law Institute of Victoria*, (supra). The "actual pecuniary loss" does not refer to the damages suffered by a client as a result of the defalcation by a solicitor.

'The purpose of the Act is to compensate the client for the "actual pecuniary loss" arising from a defalcation, not to settle accounts between the client and the practitioner. The basic measure of a claimant's pecuniary loss is the amount misappropriated by the practitioner. If any payment by the practitioner to the claimant is to be taken into account in determining the "actual pecuniary loss" then the payment must have been made by the practitioner, and accepted by the client, in reduction of the amount misappropriated.

'The value of work done by a solicitor is not to be taken into account in determining the actual pecuniary loss suffered by a client as a result of a defalcation of a solicitor.' *Trustees of the Legal Contribution Trust v Bailey* [2004] WASC 175 at [49], per Le Miere J; BC200405105

ACTUALLY PAID

'The question is whether the words "actually paid" mean that the liability of the reinsurers is limited to the sum in respect of which [the appellant] has discharged its liabilities in respect of the risks which it insured.

...

'Considerations of history, language and commercial background therefore lead me to the conclusion that the word "actually" in the UNL clause is used to emphasise that the loss for which the reinsurer is to be liable is to be net and that the clause does not restrict liability to the amount by which the liability of the reinsured for the loss has been discharged. I think that this is the natural meaning of the clause.' *Charter Reinsurance Co Ltd v Fagan* [1996] 3 All ER 46 at 57, 60, HL, per Lord Hoffmann

ACTUS REUS

New Zealand 'In considering whether the actus reus can be attributed to a defendant, it is important to recognise that this is something which occurs following acts or omissions. It is not the line of conduct which produces the prohibited event, but it is the event itself. It is an occurrence brought about by some activity or inactivity, or by both. The crime therefore (excluding for the moment the possible ingredient of mens rea) is constituted by the event, and not by the discrete acts or omissions which preceded it.' *Kilbride v Lake* [1962] NZLR 590 at 592, per Woodhouse J

ADAPT

[The Road Traffic Act 1972 has been repealed. See now, for the definition of 'goods vehicle', the Road Traffic Act 1988, s 192(1).]

[Section 5(1)(b) of the Firearms Act 1968 makes it an offence for a person to have in his possession, or to purchase or acquire, etc, any weapon designed or 'adapted' for the discharge of any noxious liquid, gas or other thing.] 'We conclude ... that the word "adapted" in s 5(1)(b) ... must mean that the object has been altered so as to make it fit for the use in question.' *R v Formosa* [1991] 1 All ER 131 at 133, CA, per cur

ADAPTATION

[The Copyright Act 1956 has been repealed. The new definition is as below.]

In this Part [Part I: copyright] 'adaptation'—
(a) in relation to a literary or dramatic work, means—
    (i) a translation of the work;
    (ii) a version of a dramatic work in which it is converted into a non-dramatic work or, as the case may be, of a non-dramatic work in which it is converted into a dramatic work;
    (iii) a version of the work in which the story or action is conveyed wholly or mainly by means of pictures in a form suitable for reproduction in a book, or in a newspaper, magazine or similar periodical;
(b) in relation to a musical work, means an arrangement or transcription of the work.

(Copyright, Designs and Patents Act 1988, s 21)

New Zealand [Section 2 (1) of the Copyright Act 1994 provides that:
'adaptation,—
(a) In relation to a literary or dramatic work, includes—
    (i) A translation of the work from one language to another:
    (ii) A version of a dramatic work in which it is converted into a literary work or, as the case may be, of a literary work in which it is converted into a dramatic work:

(iii) A version of the work in which the story or action is conveyed wholly or mainly by means of pictures in a form suitable for reproduction in a book, or in a newspaper, magazine, or similar periodical:

(b) In relation to a literary work that is a computer program, includes a version of the program in which it is converted into or out of a computer language or code or into a different computer language or code, otherwise than incidentally in the course of running the program:

(c) In relation to a musical work, means an arrangement or transcription of the work:']

'[36] Counsel's argument equated the copyright works with the brochures. It was submitted that Benchmark had adapted the brochures for its own purpose. However, this misconceives the nature of the restricted act. It is not directed to using the copyright works or reproductions of them. The act of infringement is the making of an adaptation of the work. Infringement in this way can occur only in respect of literary, dramatic or musical works. It does not apply to artistic works. We must, therefore, concentrate on the written matter in the brochures which might constitute literary works.

...

'[39] Making an adaptation of a work involves producing a different version of the work incorporating the same product of originality of the author but expressing it in a manner which cannot be characterised as copying or reproduction but still presents substantially the same work. Writing a play or film script from a novel, producing object code from a computer program source code, are typical examples. As noted in Laddie (para 3.155) what matters is that the intellectual content of the original work has been taken. Making an adaptation of a work is quite different from making use of a work (or of reproductions of a work). Section 34(2) provides that an adaptation is made when it is recorded, in writing or otherwise. That language makes clear that more is involved than merely taking and using the original work without change.' *Mitre 10 (New Zealand Ltd) v Benchmark Building Supplies Ltd* [2003] 3 NZLR 186

ADAPTOR

Australia 'In my view an adaptor is something which adapts. The *New Shorter Oxford English Dictionary* defines the verb "adapt" as to:

"Fit, adjust, (to); make suitable (to or for) ... Alter or modify to fit for a new use, new conditions, etc ...".

'It also defines "adaptor" as being synonymous with "adapter" which, in turn, it defines as:

"A device allowing connection of pieces of equipment ... unable to be connected directly ... an electrical fitting of this nature, usu. one enabling more than one plug to be connected to the same socket."

'The *Macquarie Dictionary* 2nd ed (1991) relevantly defines "adaptor" as:

"an accessory plug for connecting a piece of apparatus fitted with one type of terminals to a supply point with a different type."

'Although the *Macquarie Dictionary* definition of "adaptor" provides an example of an electrical adaptor, I consider that for present purposes the *New Shorter Oxford English Dictionary* definition is more useful, particularly when read with the definition of the word "to adapt".' *Dick Smith Electronics Pty Ltd v Cmr of Taxation* (1997) 97 ATC 5089 at 5093; 37 ATR 346; BC9706013, per Carr J

ADDRESS

Australia 'In my view, "the address of a person" [referred to in relation to requirements of service of notice of assessment in the Income Tax Regulations (Cth)] means the place at which communications to that person might be received. There is no implication that address be the place where a person resides.' *Sunrise Auto Ltd v Deputy Commissioner of Taxation (Cth)* (1994) 124 ALR 425 at 432, per Spender J

Canada [Company register was required to show the address of every debenture holder.] ' ... a forwarding address is just as good as any other address. Presumably it reflects the wish or business practice of the 32 users not to disclose his or her business or residential address for whatever reason of privacy or convenience led to that decision. There is no juridical reason why that choice should not be respected.' *Hemmerling v IMTC Systems* (1993) 109 DLR (4th) 582 at 583, BC CA, per Gibbs JA

ADEMPTION

[For 25 Halsbury's Laws (4th edn) para 329 see now 25 Halsbury's Laws (4th edn) (2003 Reissue) para 489.]

[For 50 Halsbury's Laws (4th edn) para 342 see now 50 Halsbury's Laws (4th edn) (Reissue) para 393.]

ADEQUACY

Australia [Inheritance (Family and Dependants Provision) Act 1972 (WA) s 6(1).] 'Adequacy of the provision that has been made is not to be decided in a vacuum, or by looking simply to the question whether the applicant has enough upon which to survive or live comfortably. Adequacy or otherwise will depend upon all of the relevant circumstances, which include any promise which the testator made to the applicant, the circumstances in which it was made, and, as here, changes in the arrangements between the parties after it was made. These matters however will never be conclusive. The age, capacities, means, and competing claims, of all of the potential beneficiaries must be taken into account and weighed with all of the other relevant factors.' *Vigolo v Bostin* [2005] HCA 11 at [122], per Callinan and Heydon JJ; BC200500902

ADEQUATE

[Immigration and Asylum Act 1999 s 95.] '[1] This appeal is concerned with a family of asylum seekers with two disabled children who without "adequate" accommodation would be destitute. It raises the questions as to what is "adequate" accommodation for such a family, and who owes the duty to provide it ...

...

'[6] There is furthermore an important point to bear in mind. We are considering the provisions of the 1999 Act and the "adequacy" of accommodation for this family including the disabled children. If we were concerned with a disabled adult asylum seeker we would be concerned, following the language of s 21 of the [National Assistance Act 1948], with whether accommodation "suited" to that disabled adult had been provided. Clearly the words "suited" or "adequate" could mean different things, but it seems scarcely likely that Parliament intended disabled children to receive less favourable treatment at the hands of the state, than a disabled adult would receive at the hands of a local authority. In any event since art 8 of the convention [the European Convention for the Protection of Human Rights and Fundamental Freedoms 1950 (as set out in Sch 1 to the Human Rights Act 1998)] is, it is common ground, engaged in both instances, less favourable treatment for disabled children as compared with disabled adults would be likely to fall foul of art 14. That would lead to it being necessary pursuant to s 3 of the 1998 Act to read both provisions so as not to discriminate.

...

'[51] The adequacy, or "suitability" if that word were preferred ..., of accommodation is relevant in two stages under Pt VI of the 1999 Act. It is relevant to the first stage when a decision is taken as to whether someone with their dependants is destitute. Under s 95 a person is destitute if "he does not have adequate accommodation or any means of obtaining it (whether or not his other essential living needs are met)". A decision that an asylum seeker is destitute triggers the powers under s 95 but where there are children under s 122(3):

> "If it appears to the Secretary of State that adequate accommodation is not being pro-vided for the child, he *must* exercise his pow-ers under section 95 by offering, and if his offer is accepted by providing or arranging for the provision of adequate accommodation for the child as part of the eligible person's household. [emphasis added]"

Thus if a decision is taken that adequate accommodation was not being provided and a decision is thus taken that the asylum seeker with dependants was destitute, the second stage at which adequacy has to be assessed is when considering whether adequate accommodation has been provided pursuant to s 95.

'[52] Adequacy cannot have a different meaning depending on which aspect the court is considering. Although it is only in the context of providing the accommodation once the s 95 powers are being exercised that it is expressly provided by s 96(1) that the accommodation must be "adequate for the needs of the supported person and his dependents (if any)", it must be relevant to the initial decision as to adequacy whether the needs of the asylum seeker and his dependants are being met. But whether the question arises under s 95 in considering whether an asylum seeker is destitute in the first instance, or whether it arises in considering whether accommodation being provided is adequate, the word "adequate" will take its meaning from the context. In the context of different legislation concerned with homeless persons the court has said that "suitability" must be tested by reference to the needs of persons to whom the duty is owed (see *R v Brent London Borough, ex p Omar* (1991) 23 HLR 446). The same must be true of the word "adequate" in the 1999 Act, but the context is important.

'[53] The context for asylum seekers is the provision of accommodation which prevents such people being destitute, and which provides for their essential living needs. Furthermore in considering adequacy or suitability the individual circumstance of each individual, including dependants, must be considered; thus the age of the children and whether any person including the children suffers from a disability will be relevant to the adequacy of accommodation and as to whether the family would be destitute. Lord Hoffmann accepted that s 95(1) prima facie conferred power to accommodate all destitute asylum seekers, including disabled adult asylum seekers, but accepted the argument that regulations made under Pt IV of the 1999 Act made clear that the power was "residual" and could not be exercised if the asylum seeker was entitled to "accommodation under some other provision". See *R (on the application of Westminster City Council) v National Asylum Support Service* [2002] 4 All ER 654 at [38]. It is the fact that Keith J did not appreciate Lord Hoffmann's reasoning which led him wrongly to conclude that adequacy was to be tested without reference to any disability.

'[54] The period during which the accommodation is likely to be occupied is also clearly relevant. Section 95(6)(c) shows that the fact that accommodation is temporary will not be taken into account in considering adequacy. I understand that to mean that its temporary nature cannot be relied on to support the argument of inadequacy. That has to be so to make it consistent with s 97(1)(a) under which in exercising his power to provide accommodation, the Secretary of State must have regard to the fact that "the accommodation is temporary pending determination of the asylum seeker's claim". Adequacy or suitability will vary from case to case; if it takes a very long time for an asylum seeker's claim to be dealt with, that may make accommodation inadequate which was in a shorter time frame adequate.

'[55] In considering whether the Secretary of State is fulfilling a duty to provide adequate accommodation, the position may become different over the passage of time. Just as under homelessness legislation the duty to provide accommodation is a continuing one and thus what may have been suitable at one moment may become unsuitable later (see *R (on the application of Zaher) v Westminster City Council* [2003] EWHC 101 (Admin), [2003] All ER (D) 253 (Jan)), so the same would be true under the 1999 Act.

'[56] In addition just as under the homelessness legislation if a party accepts accommodation as suitable he should not be entitled to challenge its suitability (see *Alghile v Westminster City Council* [2001] EWCA Civ 363, (2001) 33 HLR 57 referred

to in *Zaher*'s case at [28]), so the same principle should apply to the asylum seeker who accepts accommodation as adequate or suitable. But again that does not mean things are set in stone. Circumstances can change and can rekindle the duty (see again *Zaher*'s case at [28] and [29]).

'[57] The distinction between temporary accommodation and permanent accommodation must be borne in mind; but there are also degrees of temporariness and what might be considered adequate or suitable in the short-term may be inadequate or unsuitable in the longer term. One difficulty with the 1999 Act is that although the Act expressly states that the temporary nature of the accommodation is a fact to be taken into account, for some asylum seekers the appeal process may make the length of stay in accommodation quite short whereas for others the delay in the appeal process may make it quite long term. The difficulty for NASS [National Asylum Support Service], and indeed for the court, may be in weighing up to what extent the delay in the process is solely the fault of the system, to be contrasted with the conduct of the asylum seeker who may wish to extend the process as long as possible. However in this case we have heard no argument to the effect that the appeal process has in any way been extended by the action or inaction of the A family and thus the approach of the court must be to the facts as they are ie that the appeal process has in this case taken a very considerable period.

'[58] Adequacy or suitability may also be fact-specific in another way. Accommodation is more difficult to find in London. As has happened in this case, the A family made clear their wish to stay in 50 Clacton Road pending the result of their asylum claim. NASS accepted that they should be entitled to do that albeit being prepared to look for further accommodation which would be more suitable. In the result the children have begun to attend special needs schools and the A family have become keener still to stay in the area. NASS are seeking to find alternative accommodation but only within the relevant area. The argument of Miss Foster for the claimant appears to be that having accepted the constraint of finding accommodation in North London the obligation of NASS can only be fulfilled so as to provide accommodation such that the children can continue to attend their school. In other words the submission appears to be that it is now part of the test of adequacy whether the property fulfils the requirement so far as the children's particular school is concerned. In my view that is not the correct approach. First, accommodation may be adequate in London if that is where NASS has accepted the family should stay, although it would not be adequate in other areas where much more suitable accommodation is available. But *if* the accommodation became such that it was impossible to survive as a family in it, NASS would in my view be entitled to offer accommodation outside London where other schools were available.

'[59] The duty on NASS under which they *must* provide adequate accommodation appears to be absolute. But I suggest that its absolute nature should work in this way. Obviously if asylum seekers are on the streets without any accommodation the duty to provide accommodation is absolute and immediate. The legislature contemplates temporary support until the Secretary of State "is able to determine whether support may be provided under section 95". But when exercising their s 95 powers NASS are in my view entitled to place persons in accommodation which will be adequate in the short-term until they find accommodation adequate for the slightly longer term. That may lead to a family being prepared to accept as adequate the shorter term property for the longer, albeit temporary, term in order to maintain the same schools or doctor etc for the family. Circumstances can of course change so that what was previously accepted as adequate is clearly no longer so, but it would take an extreme change to bring about a duty to provide other accommodation immediately, and that extreme change might be such as to alter the constraints which the family would like to maintain.

'[60] A balancing exercise has to be carried out with the question at the forefront—is the accommodation adequate for the needs of the disabled children in the circumstances which persist at that moment in time? The circumstances of this case, for example, seem to be that the A's wanted to stay in that particular area of London and accepted 50 Clacton Road as adequate while they established their immigration status. It would seem they appreciated that although other accommodation would be sought in the area, the constraints were such that no guarantee of providing better accommodation could be given. If this is right, the questions which would need addressing would be first whether NASS have carried out a proper search for better accommodation, and second whether circumstances have changed so as to render 50 Clacton Road inadequate, that being tested against the accommodation as it was when it was accepted as adequate. That involves a balancing exercise. If no proper search was being carried out that would lead to a finding of a breach of duty. If

circumstances had changed in such a serious way, that may have imposed a duty to find better accommodation come what may, but the constraints may also need further consideration and the balancing exercise will involve considering whether the family should be asked to move from the area or whether it is fair to continue to ask them to accept 50 Clacton Road as acceptable … ' *R (on the application of A) v National Asylum Support Service* [2003] EWCA Civ 1473 at [1], [6], [51]–[60], [2004] 1 All ER 15, CA, per Waller LJ

New Zealand 'An adequate fence—one that as to its nature, condition, and state of repair, is reasonably satisfactory for the purpose it serves or is intended to serve—does not become inadequate by the introduction of a class or type of stock for which the fence was neither built nor intended to serve.' *Grainger v Rossendale Holdings Ltd* [1989] 2 NZLR 389 at 394, CA, per cur

ADJOIN

[On the true construction of Case 2 of Sch 15 to the Rent Act 1977 the word 'adjoining' is used not in the narrow sense of 'contiguous' but in the wider sense of 'neighbouring'.] 'In my judgment the meaning of the word "adjoining" is not restricted to the meaning of "contiguous". Each case must depend on the facts as found by the judge trying the action. It is a question of degree. There may be other ways of approaching the issue, but it may be useful to consider it in this way: namely whether the relevant premises are sufficiently close or related, so that the behaviour or conduct of the tenant of the one affects the access to, or occupation or enjoyment of, that other by its occupiers.' *Cobstone Investments Ltd v Maxim* [1984] 2 All ER 635 at 642–643, CA, per Wood J

Australia 'An examination of the manner in which the word "adjoining" has been construed in decided cases indicates that it may have a range of meanings dependent upon the context in which it occurs. I accept it is permissible to regard it as having a primary meaning of conterminous ie, "connecting with" or "rebutting"; and that it may have a secondary or wider meaning of "near to" or "neighbouring" (*Minister for Works v Antonio* (1966) SASR 54; *New Plymouth Borough Council v Taranki Electric Power Board* [1933] AC 680 at 682; *R v Hedges* (1829) 173 ER 1182; *Cave v Horsell* [1912] 3 KB 533 at 543).' *Solomon v Licensing Court of New South Wales* BC200006367; [2000] NSWSC 974 at [20], per Whealy J

ADMINISTRATION

[For 17 Halsbury's Laws (4th edn) para 703 see now 17(2) Halsbury's Laws (4th edn) (Reissue) para 3.]

ADMISSION

[CCR Ord 9, r 10 provides for striking out a default action where 12 months have expired from the date of service of a default summons and (i) no admission, defence or counterclaim has been delivered and judgment has not been entered against the defendant, or (ii) an admission has been delivered but no judgment has been entered or no notice of acceptance or non-acceptance has been received.] ' "Admission" is defined in Ord 9, r 2(2), but only for the purposes of Ord 9, rr 2, 3 and 6 and, therefore, not r 10 itself, as "the relevant form appended to the summons completed according to the circumstances of the case". "Admission" is further defined for the purposes of the Order, "... unless the context other requires", in much wider terms in Ord 9, r 17 ...

'The difficulty created by these inconsistent definitions is that Ord 9, r 10(ii) takes effect when the plaintiff has falied to enter judgment, not generally but expressly, under Ord 9, r 6(1) in which "admission" is subject to the narrow definition in Ord 9, r 2(2). One consequence is that Ord 9, r 10 may have the effect that "admission" in para (i) may attract the wider meaning while that in para (ii) is limited to the narrow one ... In the language of Ord 9, r 17 the context therefore seems to require that the narrow meaning should be applied when Ord 9, r 10(ii) is under consideration.' *Watkins v Toms* [1998] 2 All ER 534n at 535, 536, CA, per Judge LJ

[CCR Ord 9, r 10(ii) provides for striking out a default action where 12 months have expired from the date of service of a default summons and an admission has been delivered but no judgment has been entered or no notice of acceptance has been received.] 'Both sub-sets of r 10(ii), therefore, are concerned with cases falling within rr 3 and 6, where the word "admission" is defined to mean, in effect, and admission on Form N9.

...

'The effect of this judgment is that Ord 9, r 10 has no application at all in cases in which a defendant to an action for an unliquidated sum does not admit both liability and the whole of the plaintiff's money claim for damages against him. If the defendant makes no admissions as to quantum, ... he must take such alternative steps as

may be available to him under the rules if he wishes of his own motion to bring the proceedings to a premature end before trial.' *Limb v Union Jack Removals Ltd (in liquidation)* [1998] 2 All ER 512 at 522, 527, CA, per Brooke LJ

To benefice

[The Reorganisation Areas Measure 1944 is repealed. A definition of 'admission' is now contained in the Pastoral Measure 1983, s 87(1), as follows.] 'Admission' includes institution and induction, collation, licence and any other process by which a person becomes the incumbent of a benefice or (for the purposes of section 85 [pluralities not to be authorised except under the Measure]) the holder of a cathedral preferment and 'admit' shall be construed accordingly.

ADOLESCENT

Canada [Consideration of possession of child pornography offence of the Criminal Code.] 'The term "adolescent" is defined by *The Shorter Oxford English Dictionary*, 3rd edition (London: Oxford University Press, 1973) at 27, thus:

"A. sb. A person in the age of adolescence.
B. adj. Growing from childhood to maturity 1785."

'and "adolescence" is defined as:

"The process or condition of growing up; the growing age; youth; the period between childhood and maturity, extending from 14 to 25 in males, from 12 to 21 in females."

'As I understand it, the ages given are a reflection of the process of physical maturation. Thus, in males, the broad bones generally do not complete their maturing until the male is about 25. When I use the term "adolescent", however, I mean anyone between fourteen and eighteen.' *R v Sharpe* (1999) 175 DLR (4th) 1 at 13, 14, BCCA, per Southin JA

ADOPT

[The Insolvency Act 1986, s 19(5) refers to contracts of employment 'adopted' by an administrator of a company in carrying out his functions; but an administrator is not to be taken to have adopted a contract of employment by reason of anything done or omitted to be done within 14 days after his appointment.] 'In my judgment, in order to determine Parliament's intention it is necessary to look at the joint effect of adoption followed by the statutory consequences said to flow from it …

'… The word "adopt" is not a term of art but takes its colour from the context in which it is used. In referring to the adoption of children or the adoption by a principal of an agent's unauthorised contract the word has quite different connotations. In s 323(4) of the [Companies Act 1948] the word "adopt" was used to describe the consequence of a liquidator failing to disclaim an unprofitable contract. In that context "adopt" plainly means failure to disclaim, i e leaving in being an existing contractual relationship between the company and the creditor so as to permit the creditor to prove in the liquidation for subsequent breaches. Under the salvage principle, a liquidator who uses leasehold property or goods for the better conduct of a liquidation becomes liable for the rent or contract price: such use by the liquidator has been judicially referred to as "adoption" of the contract by the liquidator: see *Re Anchor Line (Henderson Bros) Ltd* [1936] 2 All ER 941 at 947, 948, 952, [1937] Ch 1 at 8, 9, 15 and *Re S Davis & Co Ltd* [1945] Ch 402 at 406. In those cases adoption does not connote accepting personal liability. Yet in *Re Botibol (decd)*, *Botibol v Botibol* [1947] 1 All ER 26 the word "adoption" was used to describe the acceptance of personal liability by a receiver.

'The meaning of the word "adopt" in ss 19 and 44 of the 1986 Act therefore has to be gathered from the context in which it is used. It is important to bear in mind that the appointment of an administrator or receiver does not terminate the employee's contract of employment with the company. Only if the company (acting by the receiver or administrator) gives notice terminating the employment or, by failing to pay wages as they accrue due, repudiates the contract of employment will the contract with the company terminate. Therefore, so long as wages are paid by the company the employee remains the employee of the company … Therefore, the mere continuation of the employment by the company does not lead inexorably to the conclusion that the contract has been adopted by the administrator or receiver.

'It is common ground that adoption does not mean an assumption of personal liability by the administrator or receiver since there is no question of an administrator accepting personal liability under s 19. Nor in my judgment can it mean "fail to disclaim" as in s 323 of the 1948 Act since, as I have said, the issue is not whether the company is liable on the continued contract but whether the liability on the contract is to have a higher priority. Nor can adoption connote doing such acts as

would be sufficient to make the payments due an expense of the administration, since s 19(4) gives such expenses a different and lower level of priority and in *Nicoll v Cutts* [1985] BCLC 322 it was held that such liability was not an expense of the receivership. In my judgment, as [Counsel] submitted, adoption in ss 19 and 44 can only connote some conduct by the administrator or receiver which amounts to an election to treat the continued contract of employment with the company as giving rise to a separate liability in the administration or receivership.

'If that is the right meaning of "adoption" in ss 19 and 44, the question arises whether adoption of the contract is an all or nothing matter involving the acceptance or rejection of the contract as a whole or whether it is open to an administrator or receiver so to conduct himself as to show that he is only prepared to treat certain liabilities under the contract as liabilities in the administration or receivership. To my mind this is the most difficult question in the case. On the one side it is said that Parliament cannot have intended the administrator or receiver to be able to "cherry-pick", taking the benefits of the contract but rejecting the burdens. On the other, it is said that adoption of a contract is a unilateral act and there is nothing to prevent the adopter from attaching conditions to its adoption.' *Powdrill v Watson* [1995] 2 All ER 65 at 79, 82–83, HL, per Lord Browne-Wilkinson

ADOPTION

[For 24 Halsbury's Laws (4th edn) paras 624–625 see now 5(3) Halsbury's Laws (4th edn) (Reissue) paras 501–707.]

ADULTERATION

[For 18 Halsbury's Laws (4th edn) para 1066 et seq see now 18(2) Halsbury's Laws (4th edn) (Reissue) para 202 et seq.]

ADVENTURE ACTIVITIES

In this section 'facilities for adventure activities' means such facilities, for such sporting, recreational or outdoor activities, as may be prescribed by regulations; but the expression does not include—

(a) facilities which are provided exclusively for persons who have attained the age of 18; or

(b) facilities which do not consist of, or include some element of, instruction or leadership.

(Activity Centres (Young Persons' Safety) Act 1995, s 1(3))

ADVERSE POSSESSION

[For 28 Halsbury's Laws (4th edn) para 768 see now 28 Halsbury's Laws (4th edn) (Reissue) para 977.]

'[68] Where a person in whose favour the period of limitation can run under s 15 of the Limitation Act 1980 is in the possession of land, he is described in para 8(1) of Sch 1 to that Act as being in "adverse possession". This use of the expression "adverse possession" has been followed in the Land Registration Act 2002, which has introduced a new regime for the registration of an adverse possessor of an estate in land or rent charge (see s 97). The details are set out in Sch 6 to that Act. Paragraph 1(1) of the Schedule provides that a person may apply to the registrar to be registered as the proprietor of a registered estate in land if he has been in adverse possession of the estate for a period of ten years ending on the date of the application. The phrase "adverse possession" is defined in para 11 of the Schedule. In brief, a person is in adverse possession for the purposes of the 2002 Act if, but for the disapplication by s 96 of that Act of periods of limitation against a registered proprietor, a period of limitation would run in his favour in relation to the estate under s 15 of the 1980 Act.

'[69] It is plainly of some importance, both now and for the future, to understand what the use of the word "adverse" in the context of s 15 of the 1980 Act was intended to convey. At first sight, it might be thought that the word "adverse" describes the nature of the possession that the squatter needs to demonstrate. It suggests that an element of aggression, hostility or subterfuge is required. But an examination of the context makes it clear that this is not so. It is used as a convenient label only, in recognition simply of the fact that the possession is adverse to the interests of the paper owner or, in the case of registered land, of the registered proprietor. The context is that of a person bringing an action to recover land who has been in possession of land but has been dispossessed or has discontinued his possession (see para 8 of Sch 1 to the 1980 Act). His right of action is treated as accruing as soon as the land is in the possession of some other person in whose favour the limitation period can run. In that sense, and for that purpose, the other person's possession is adverse to his. But the question whether that other person is in fact in possession of the land is a separate question on which the word "adverse" casts no light.

'[70] The general rule, which English law has derived from the Roman law, is that only one person can be in possession at any one time.

Exclusivity is of the essence of possession. The same rule applies in cases where two or more persons are entitled to the enjoyment of property simultaneously. As between themselves they have separate rights, but as against everyone else they are in the position of a single owner. Once possession has begun, as in the case of the owner of land with a paper title who has entered into occupation of it, his possession is presumed to continue. But it can be transferred from one person to another, and it can also be lost when it is given up or discontinued. When that happens, possession can be acquired by someone else. The acquisition of possession requires both an intention to take or occupy the land ("animus") and some act of the body ("corpus") which gives effect to that intention. Occupation of the land alone is not enough, nor is an intention to occupy which is not put into effect by action. Both aspects must be examined, and each is bound up with the other. But acts of the mind can be, and sometimes can only be, demonstrated by acts of the body. In practice, the best evidence of intention is frequently found in the acts which have taken place.

'[71] The question as to the nature of the intention that has to be demonstrated to establish possession was controversial, particularly among jurists in Germany (see, for example, Henry Bond "Possession in the Roman Law" (1890) 6 LQR 259). But it is reasonably clear that the animus which is required is the intent to exercise exclusive control over the thing for oneself (see Bond (1890) 6 LQR 259 at 270). The important point for present purposes is that it is not necessary to show that there was a deliberate intention to exclude the paper owner or the registered proprietor. The word "adverse" in the context of s 15(1) of the 1980 Act does not carry this implication. The only intention which has to be demonstrated is an intention to occupy and use the land as one's own. This is a concept which Rankine The Law of Land-Ownership in Scotland (4th edn, 1909) p 4, captured in his use of the Latin phrase "cum animo rem sibi habendi" (see his reference in footnote 1 to Savigny Das Recht des Besitzes, translated by Perry (1848) (paras 1–11)). It is similar to that which was introduced into the law of Scotland by the Prescription Act 1617, Ch 12 relating to the acquisition of an interest in land by positive prescription. The possession that is required for that purpose is possession "openly, peaceably and without any judicial interruption" on a competing title for the requisite period (see s 1(1)(a) of the Prescription and Limitation (Scotland) Act 1973). So I would hold that, if the evidence shows that the person was using the land in the way one would expect him to use it if he were the true owner, that is enough.

'[72] I agree that the only conclusion that can reasonably be drawn from the evidence is that the Grahams occupied and used the disputed land as their own for 12 years before these actions were brought. The limitation provision in s 15 of the 1980 Act applies. The case has to be treated as one where the registered owner, having been dispossessed, has lost the right to recover the land.

'[73] The question whether this result is incompatible with the Pye's rights under art 1 of the First Protocol to the European Convention for the Protection of Human Rights and Fundamental Freedoms 1950 (as set out in Sch 1 to the Human Rights Act 1998) was answered by the Court of Appeal ([2001] Ch 804, [2001] 2 WLR 1293) in the negative. It was not pursued before your Lordships. This is a civil and not a criminal case (see my observations in *R v Kansal* (*No 2*) [2001] UKHL 62 at [76], [2002] 1 All ER 257 at [76], [2002] 2 AC 69). Nevertheless it was conceded that s 22(4) of the 1998 Act did not apply as this was an appeal against a decision of a court or tribunal which was made before 2 October 2000. The question itself however is not an easy one, as one might have expected the law—in the context of a statutory regime where compensation is not available—to lean in favour of the protection of a registered proprietor against the actions of persons who cannot show a competing title on the register. Fortunately, as my noble and learned friend Lord Bingham of Cornhill has pointed out, a much more rigorous regime has now been enacted in Sch 6 to the 2002 Act. Its effect will be to make it much harder for a squatter who is in possession of registered land to obtain a title to it against the wishes of the proprietor. The unfairness in the old regime which this case has demonstrated lies not in the absence of compensation, although that is an important factor, but in the lack of safeguards against oversight or inadvertence on the part of the registered proprietor.' *J A Pye (Oxford) Ltd v Graham* [2002] UKHL 30 at [68]–[73], [2002] 3 All ER 865, per Lord Hope of Craighead

ADVERTISEMENT

[The Food Act 1984 is largely repealed. The definition of 'advertisement' is re-enacted in the Food Safety Act 1990, s 53(1).]

[The Town and Country Planning Act 1971 has been repealed. The definition of 'advertisement' is re-enacted in the Town and Country Planning Act 1990, s 336(1).]

[The London Cab Act 1968, s 4(5), has been amended by the Cable and Broadcasting Act 1984, s 57(1), Sch 5 para 18, to include advertising by inclusion a cable programme service.]

'Advertisement' includes any means of bringing a matter to the attention of the public and 'advertise' shall be construed accordingly. (Dangerous Dogs Act 1991, s 10(2)).

'In order to constitute an advertisement, it is not necessary for the flags and bunting to be promotional of products or category of products nor that they should indicate the nature of the goods displayed for sale. It is sufficient if they attract or draw attention to the presence of the appellant's premises.' *Taylor v Secretary of State for Scotland* 1997 SCLR 43 at 46, per the Lord Justice-Clerk (Ross)

ADVOCATES OR COUNSELS

Canada 'The second category of child pornography caught by s 163.1(1) [of the *Criminal Code*] is "any written material or visual representation that advocates or counsels sexual activity with a person under the age of eighteen years that would be an offence under this Act".

'This section is more limited than the definition of visual pornography in s 163.1(1)(*a*), which captures sexual "representation[s]" of children. Section 163.1(1)(*b*) is confined to material relating to activity that would be a crime under the *Criminal Code*. Moreover, it is confined to material that "counsels" or "advocates" such crimes. On its face, it appears to be aimed at combating written and visual material that actively promotes the commission of sexual offences with children.

'At stake is not whether the maker or possessor of the material intended to advocate or counsel the crime, but whether the material, viewed objectively, advocates or counsels the crime. "Advocate" is not defined in the *Criminal Code*. "Counsel" is dealt with only in connection with the counseling of an offence: s 22 of the *Criminal Code,* where it is stated to include "procure, solicit or incite". "Counsel" can mean simply to advise; however in criminal law it has been given the stronger meaning of actively inducing: see *R. v Dionne* (1987), 38 CCC (3d) 171 (NBCA.), at p 180, per Ayles J.A. While s 22 refers to a person's actions and s 163.1(1)(*b*) refers to material, it seems reasonable to conclude that in order to meet the requirement of "advocates" or "counsels", the material, viewed objectively, must be seen as "actively inducing" or encouraging the described offences with children. Again, Parliament's purpose of capturing material causing a reasoned risk of harm to children may offer guidance. The mere description of the criminal act is not caught. Rather, the prohibition is against material that, viewed objectively, sends the message that sex with children can and should be pursued.' *R. v. Sharpe* (2001) 194 DLR (4th) 1 at 32–33, SCC, per McLachlin CJC

AERODROME

[The Airports Authority Act 1975 has been repealed.]

AFFAIRS

Australia [Section 28(c)(ii) of the ASC Law of Western Australia refers to an alleged contravention of a law that concerns the management of 'affairs' of a body corporate.] 'Senior counsel for the commission submitted that the term "affairs" is a wide term and covers every aspect of the affairs affecting a corporation. Counsel referred to s 53 of the Corporations Law, which expresses a wide definition of the term "the affairs of a body corporate". Counsel submitted that this definition applied because of the definition in s 60 of the Corporations (WA) Act. However, there are two reasons for thinking that the term "affairs" does not, in s 28 of the ASC Law, have such a wide meaning. The first is that the term appears in the expression "management or affairs". Thus, if the word "affairs" has the meaning given to it by s 53 of the Corporations Law including "(a) the ... business, trading, transactions and dealings ... of the body" and "(c) the internal management and proceedings of the body", the word "management" in s 28(c)(ii) would be unnecessary. The second is that, if a contravention merely "relates to a body corporate", s 28(c)(ii) requires that it "involves fraud or dishonesty".

'I incline to the view that the words "concerns the management or affairs of a body corporate" in s 28 of the ASC Law refer to those matters which arise out of the corporation's business, property and capital and also to those matters which arise out of the internal management of the corporation. If the suspected contravention merely relates to a corporation, that is to say, arises outside the corporation's business, property, capital or management, then the suspected contravention must be of such a nature that it involves fraud or dishonesty. The word "involves" does not denote that fraud or dishonesty must be an element of the offence as charged, merely that the contravention suspected must have involved fraud or dishonesty.'

Australian Securities Commission v Lord (1991) 6 ACSR 350 at 355, per Davies J

Australia [In the context of whether a person is 'capable of managing his or her own affairs' under the (NSW) Protected Estates Act 1983 (PE Act 1983), s 35(1).] '[13] The word "affairs" is one which is capable of a variety of meanings, and can be quite broad: cf *NSW Crime Commission v Murchie* [2000] NSWSC 591; (2000) 49 NSWLR 465 at [21] ff. In the context of the PE Act 1983, the word takes some of its colour from the consequence which might flow from a person being incapable of managing his or her affairs, namely that his or her estate becomes subject to management under this Act.

'[14] Section 4(4) PE Act 1983 says:

> In this Act, a reference to the estate of a person is a reference to the property and affairs of the person ...

'Because of the presence of "and affairs" in this definition, the consequence that it is the estate of a person which becomes subject to management if they are incapable of managing their affairs does not assist much in understanding what counts as a person's "affairs". I note, though, that "property" is a static concept, concerning the things a particular person owns at any one time, while "affairs" has something more of a flavour of activity connected with property. That both the property, and the affairs of a person are expressly stated to become subject to management under the Act when a person is incapable of managing his or her affairs suggests that the "affairs" concerning which the person exhibits incapacity to manage extend to activities connected with property.

...

'[20] In *H v H* (20 March 2000, unreported) Young J considered the rule in *PY v RJS* [1982] 2 NSWLR 700, and gave an ostensive definition of "affairs" at pp 7 and 8:

> However, when looking at that test, the ordinary affairs of mankind do not just mean being able to go to the bank and draw out housekeeping money. Most people's affairs are more complicated than that, and the ordinary affairs of mankind involve at least planning for the future, working out how one will feed oneself and ones family, and how one is going to generate income and look after capital. Accordingly, whilst one does not have to be a person who is capable of managing complex financial affairs, one has to go beyond just managing household bills.

'As necessarily follows from it being an ostensive definition, this passage indicates part of the content of "affairs" when used in the PE Act 1983, without purporting to exhaustively define it.

'[21] In the context of the PE Act 1983, "affairs" are, it seems to me, the various practical dealings that a person needs to engage in, in life, which relate in a significant way to property. These practical dealings are not restricted to ones of investment of money or carrying out transactions like buying, selling, leasing or mortgaging other types of property.' *Re GHI* (*a protected person*) [2005] NSWSC 581 at [13]–[14], [20]–[21], per Campbell J; BC200504621

Canada 'In this regard, the ordinary meaning of "affair" contained in Merriam-Webster's Collegiate Dictionary, 10th ed (1993) at p 18 is "commercial, professional, public or personal business". A similar meaning is to be found in The Shorter Oxford English Dictionary, 3rd ed, vol 1 (Oxford, 1973) at p 32. It follows that "the affairs of the Society", over which the benchers are granted the power to govern and in respect to which convocation is granted the power to make rules, means the professional or public business of the Society. Support for this interpretation is found in the definition of convocation, which is a meeting of benchers held for the purpose of "transacting business of the Society".' *Law Society of Upper Canada v Ontario* (*Attorney-General*) (1995) 121 DLR (4th) 369 at 380, Ont Gen Div, per Borins J

AFFAIRS OF THE BANKRUPT

'Under s 311(1) of the [Insolvency Act 1986] the trustee is under an obligation to take possession of books, papers and other records which relate not only to the bankrupt's estate but also to the bankrupt's affairs.

'Mr Marshall submits that in the present case the two categories of personal correspondence which he is still seeking directions enabling him to sell do, by the definition given to them by Mr Aitken himself in his witness statement, constitute documents relating to Mr Aitken's affairs within the meaning of s 311(1). The relevance of the point is this, that reg 30 of the [Insolvency Regulations 1994], which I have already read, provides that—

"on the authorisation of the official receiver [and in the present case the official receiver has already indicated that he has no objection to the sale of the correspondence

concerned]…[the] trustee [in bankruptcy], may at any time sell, destroy or otherwise dispose of the books, papers and other records of the bankrupt."

So as I understand the argument on this part of the case it is that, since the two categories of correspondence which the trustee now seeks to sell constitute documents relating to Mr Aitken's affairs, and since the trustee in bankruptcy has possession of them, and since the Official Receiver raises no objection to their sale, they can be sold under the terms of reg 30 in just the same way as though they had been part of the bankrupt's estate ab initio.

'I reject that argument. In my judgment the reference to the bankrupt's affairs in s 311(1) of the 1986 Act is a reference to his financial affairs or other affairs which may be relevant to the carrying out of the trustee in bankruptcy's duties under the 1986 Act, or possibly even affairs relevant to the conduct of the official receiver's independent duties under the 1986 Act.

'I reject entirely the proposition that the reference to affairs in s 311 can extend to all affairs concerning the bankrupt's conduct even in relation to his own professional or other activities, except to the extent that that conduct may be relevant to the duties of the trustee in bankruptcy or possibly the Official Receiver under the 1986 Act.

'Moreover, when one comes to look at reg 30 of the 1994 regulations, in my judgment it is clear that that regulation is referring to financial books, papers and other records of the bankrupt or at least books, papers and records of the bankrupt which have been obtained by the trustee in bankruptcy for the purpose of administering the bankrupt's estate in accordance with the trustee's duties under the Act.

'The idea that, although (as in my judgment) Mr Aitken's private, personal letters are not part of his estate as defined by the 1986 Act, none the less, because the trustee in bankruptcy has possession of them, and because they relate to some affairs of Mr Aitken in the widest sense, the trustee has the power against Mr Aitken's wishes to realise those letters by selling them to the media for the benefit of the creditors is in my view repugnant to the true purpose of the 1986 Act.

…

'As I have said, I am only being asked on this application to determine the question raised in relation to personal correspondence. It seems to me that, as I have already said, correspondence properly called "personal correspondence", whatever its subject matter, does not form part of the bankrupt's estate within the definitions in the

1986 Act. While some of it, as I say, may relate to other assets within the bankrupt's estate or to his affairs properly regarded as limited to affairs relevant to the administration of the bankrupt's estate, that does not bring it within the definition of "estate". It does give the trustee a power to see such documents under s 311(1). The trustee has not only seen them, he has them in his possession, but, in my judgment, the application for an order that the two categories of correspondence still in issue comprise documents which the trustee in bankruptcy is entitled to sell for the benefit of the creditors is, for the reasons I have attempted to give, misconceived. In my judgment the trustee in bankruptcy has no right to sell any of those documents.' *Haig v Aitken* [2000] 3 All ER 80 at 88–89, per Rattee J

AFFECT

Canada [The Canadian Human Rights Act provides that nothing in the Act affects any provision of the Indian Act RSC 1970, c I-6.] 'The word "affects" is indeed very wide in scope. I take it to have the meaning of "To act upon or have an effect upon". The opening words of subsection 63(2) of the Canadian Human Rights Act read therefore that nothing in that Act shall have an effect upon … The word "*effet*" in the French version is also general and is equivalent to such words as "*consequence*", "*influence*". Hence: "*La presente loi est sans consequence, sans influence sur*".' *Re Desjarlais* [1989] 3 FCR 605 at 608, FCA, per Desjardins JA

AFFECTED

New Zealand [Guardianship Act 1968, s 17(3).] 'The only qualification for an applicant is that he or she must be "affected" by the order. Someone is "affected" by something which has a material effect on him or her. An affect is a result or consequence.' *B v M* [1997] 3 NZLR 202 at 205, per Ellis J

AFFIRM

Australia 'In a context for limited review of decisions of the [Refugee Review] Tribunal, the use of the term "affirming" is certainly not the most appropriate term to use for disposing of an application which has failed. An order of the Federal Court affirming the decision is open to the construction that that court is affirming that the decision was correctly and lawfully made. However, the term "affirm" is sometimes used in the context

of appellate jurisdiction to indicate that the appeal has failed and that the decision below stands.' *Abebe v Commonwealth* (1999) 162 ALR 1 at 18; 73 ALJR 584; BC9901531, per Gleeson CJ and McHugh J … 'The meaning of the word "affirming" in s 481(1) of the Act [(CTH) Migration Act 1958 No 62] should in any event be taken to be no more than the abstaining from interference with the decision of the Refugee Review Tribunal.' ALR at 75–6, per Callinan J

AFFRAY

[The common law offence of affray was abolished by the Public Order Act 1986. As a statutory offence it is defined as follows.]

(1) A person is guilty of affray if he uses or threatens unlawful violence towards another and his conduct is such as would cause a person of reasonable firmness present at the scene to fear for his personal safety.

(2) Where two or more persons use or threaten the unlawful violence, it is the conduct of them taken together that must be considered for the purposes of subsection (1).

(3) For the purposes of this section a threat cannot be made by the use of words alone.

(4) No person of reasonable firmness need actually be, or be likely to be, present at the scene.

(5) Affray may be committed in private as well as in public places.

(Public Order Act 1986, s 3)

AGAINST

Australia 'In my view the word "against" in the phrase "military operations against the enemy" is used in the sense of "in hostility or active opposition to". This is the common meaning and general usage of the word "against" in such a context. The section [Veteran's Entitlement Act 1986 (Cth), formerly s 36(1)(a)(i); now s 7A(1)(a)(i)] requires service, inter alia, in military operations against the enemy, in the sense of operations in hostility or opposition to the enemy.' *Willcocks v Repatriation Commission* (1992) 111 ALR 639 at 647, per Cooper J

AGE

[The Social Security Act 1975 has been repealed. The definition has been re-enacted in the Social Security Contributions and Benefits Act 1992, s 173.]

AGENT

[For 1 Halsbury's Laws (4th edn) para 701 see now 2(1) Halsbury's Laws (4th edn) (Reissue) para 1.]

General agent

[For 1 Halsbury's Laws (4th edn) para 711 see now 2(1) Halsbury's Laws (4th edn) (Reissue) para 11.]

Of necessity

[For 1 Halsbury's Laws (4th edn) para 724 see now 2(1) Halsbury's Laws (4th edn) (Reissue) para 39.]

Special agent

[For 1 Halsbury's Laws (4th edn) para 711 see now 2(1) Halsbury's Laws (4th edn) (Reissue) para 11.]

AGGRIEVED PERSON

Canada '[12] The expression "person aggrieved" (or its equivalent "aggrieved person") is commonly used in legislation for the purpose of identifying those legally entitled to contest a particular judicial or administrative decision. The quoted expression is generally understood to refer to any person, other than "a mere busybody who is interfering in things which do not concern him", who has a genuine legal grievance because an order or decision has been made that affects his or her interests in a prejudicial manner (see *Attorney-General of the Gambia v. N'Jie*, [1961] 2 All E.R. 504 (P.C.), at 511). It is also generally accepted that the expression, in its ordinary sense, is broad enough to include a party to proceedings, such as Co-op in the case at bar, whose rights are directly and prejudicially affected by an order or decision.' *Co-operators General Insurance Co v New Brunswick* [2004] NBJ No 289, 243 DLR (4th) 371 (CA), per Drapeau CJNB

AGISTMENT

[For 2 Halsbury's Laws (4th edn) para 214 see now 2(1) Halsbury's Laws (4th edn) (Reissue) para 521.]

AGREEMENT

[The Law of Property Act 1925, s 40, has been repealed. See now the Law of Property (Miscellaneous Provisions) Act 1989, s 2.]

AGRICULTURAL HOLDING

[For 1 Halsbury's Laws (4th edn) para 1001 see now 1(2) Halsbury's Laws (4th edn) (Reissue) para 301.]

AGRICULTURAL LAND

[The General Rate Act 1967 and the Rating Act 1971, Part I have been repealed.]

'The expression "agricultural land or pasture" [in the Inheritance Tax Act 1984, s 115(2)] is a composite one. Pasture is undoubtedly bare uncultivated land used for the grazing of animals. The words "agricultural land" when used in association with pasture suggest land of a broadly similar nature, i e undeveloped land in the sense of land, without buildings or other structures, used for agricultural purposes such as the cultivation of crops.' *Starke v IRC* [1994] 1 WLR 888 at 891, per Blackburne J; affd [1996] 1 All ER 622, CA

AGRICULTURAL USE

Canada [A soil composting operation to manufacture potting soil was found to be a permitted 'agricultural use'.] 'As no statutory definition of "agricultural use" is in force, it is my duty to consider how such words in zoning laws have been interpreted in previous decisions in similar cases …

'A decision of a Prince Edward Island court took a broad view of the words "agriculture" and "agricultural". In *Village of West Royalty v PEI Land Use Commission* (1981), 35 Nfld & PEIR 459 (PEISC) at pp 466–467, Mr Justice McQuaid said:

> "While an agricultural operation is, by the regulations, permitted in the zone in which Mr Radanovich proposes to build his greenhouse, the word "agriculture" is not defined by the regulations and we must look elsewhere. The word is thus defined in Funk and Wagnall's *New College Standard Dictionary* and is substantially the same as most dictionary definitions:
>
> > 'The cultivation of the soil; *the raising of food crops*, breeding and raising of livestock, etc.; tillage; farming. The science that treats of the cultivation of the soil [emphasis added].'
>
> 'Webster's *20th Century Dictionary* defined it thus:

'Farming; tillage; *the cultivation of the ground for the purpose of producing vegetables and fruits for the use of man and beast;* or the art of preparing the soil, sowing and planting seeds, dressing the plants and removing the crops. In this sense, the word includes gardening or horticulture and also the raising and feeding of rattle or stock. But in the more common and appropriate sense, the cultivation which intended [is] to raise grain and other feed crops. It is equivalent to husbandry and is the most general occupation of men [emphasis added].'

...

"Among the accepted definitions of "agriculture" is the raising of food crops and the cultivation of the soil for the purpose of producing vegetables and fruits. The operation in question here is the growing of fresh vegetables. While it is true that they are being grown within the confines of a greenhouse that, in my opinion, should not take it out of the category of an agricultural operation. If agriculture, in its broad sense, is permitted within the zone, including the erection of barns and other farm buildings, surely the intent of the regulation is not to prohibit the growing of vegetables in a properly constructed greenhouse."

...

'In my opinion such operations fall within a generous or broad interpretation of the words "preparing the soil" or "cultivation of soil". Spreading the compost material into the long windrows and mixing in additives could be called "tillage".

'In a 1994 zoning case the New Brunswick Court of Appeal indicated a preference for "a generous, as opposed to a narrow interpretation of a quarry's use". *Campbellton (City) v Thompson* (1994) 151 NBR (2d) 1 (NBCA) at p 7.

'The *Campbellton* case strikes me as a strong precedent for the adoption in this case of a generous, as opposed to a narrow interpretation of the words "agricultural use".' *New Brunswick (Minister of Municipalities, Culture and Housing) v B & B Environmental Services Ltd* (1996) 136 DLR (4th) 405, at 407, 408, 409 McLellan J (NBQB)

AGRICULTURE

[The Town and Country Planning Act 1971 and the Water Act 1963 have been repealed. The definition of 'agriculture' is re-enacted in the Town and Country Planning Act 1990, s 336(1); and Water Resources Act 1990, s 221(1) provides that 'agriculture' and 'agricultural' are to have the same meanings as in the Agriculture Act 1947.]

AID

[Under the Race Relations Act 1976 s 33(1), a person who knowingly aids another person to do an act made unlawful by the Act is to be treated as himself doing an unlawful act of the same description.] '[5] The expression "aids" in s 33(1) is a familiar word in everyday use and it bears no technical or special meaning in this context. A person aids another if he helps or assists him. He does so whether his help is substantial and productive or whether it is not, provided the help is not so insignificant as to be negligible. While any gloss on the clear statutory language is better avoided, the subsection points towards a relationship of co-operation or collaboration; it does not matter who instigates or initiates the relationship. It is plain that, depending on the facts, a party who aids another to do an unlawful act may also procure or induce that other to do it. But the expressions "procure" and "induce" are found in ss 30 and 31, not s 33, and are differently enforced; they mean something different from 'aids' and there is no warrant to interpreting "aids" as comprising these other expressions. By s 12 of the Race Relations Act 1968, the predecessor of the 1976 Act, those who deliberately aided, induced or incited another person to do an act made unlawful by Pt I of that Act were to be treated as themselves doing that act, but they could not be subjected to proceedings at the direct suit of the injured party and the 1976 Act adopted a different legislative approach. It is plain that a party who causes another to do an unlawful act does not necessarily aid him to do it. A farmer who starves his sheepdog, with the result that the ravening dog savages a new-born lamb, may reasonably be said to have caused the death of the lamb, but he could not be said to have aided the dog to kill the lamb. In the present appeal no issue arises on the meaning of "knowingly" in this context and it is unnecessary to consider what an aider must know to be liable under s 33(1).' *Anyanwu v South Bank Students' Union* [2001] UKHL/14 at [5], [2001] 2 All ER 353 at 356, HL, per Lord Bingham of Cornhill

AID AND ABET

[For 11 Halsbury's Laws (4th edn) para 42 see now 11(1) Halsbury's Laws (4th edn) (Reissue) para 43.]

Australia 'It is not possible to be an aider through an act which unwittingly provides some assistance to the offender in the commission of the offence and it is not possible to be an aider, whatever the intention, unless support for the commission of the offence is actually provided ... If the word "aids" needs any explanation at all, it might, on occasions be better understood in its effect by the use of words such as "give support to ... help, assist" (see Collins English Dictionary (1979 edn) and the Shorter Oxford English Dictionary)... There must be some deliberate positive involvement, if not active physical involvement, when the offence of aiding occurs.' *R v Beck* [1990] 1 Qd R 30 at 38, per Macrossan CJ

New Zealand 'Where the accused has legal and factual power of control over the activity concerned, and in that sense is more than a passive bystander, non-intervention can amount to "aiding" and "abetting".' *Cooper v Ministry of Transport* [1991] 2 NZLR 693 at 698, per McGechan J

AIR SPACE

Australia 'Since "air space" is a novel juridical concept, it is desirable to characterise it. A transfer of "air space" does not, as its name would suggest, transfer dominion over the space above a building; rather it confers a right on the owner of land to build higher than would normally be permitted if he "acquires" from the owner of another building the rights which the latter would have had if he had utilised them to build the second building as extensively as the relevant codes had permitted. There is, apparently, no statutory basis for this concept, but it arises from a council's power to grant development applications.' *Uniting Church in Australia Property Trust (NSW) v Immer (No 145) Pty Ltd* (1992) 24 NSWLR 510 at 510–511, per Meagher JA

ALIEN—ALIENS

Australia 'As a matter of etymology, "alien", from the Latin *alienus* through old French, means belonging to another person or place. Used as a descriptive word to describe a person's lack of relationship with a country, the word means, as a matter of ordinary language, "nothing more than a citizen or subject of a foreign State" (*Milne v Huber* (1843) 17 Fed Cas 403 at 406 (US)). Thus, an "alien" has been said to be, for the purposes of United States law, "one born out of the United States, who has not since been naturalised under

the constitution and laws" (ibid). That definition should be expanded to include a person who has ceased to be a citizen by an act or process of denaturalisation and restricted to exclude a person who, while born abroad, is a citizen by reason of parentage ... That word is and always has been appropriate to describe the status, vis-a-vis a former colony which has emerged as an independent nation with its own citizenship, of a non-citizen who is a British subject by reason of his citizenship of a different sovereign State.' *Nolan v Minister for Immigration and Ethnic Affairs* (1988) 80 ALR 561 at 563–564, per cur

Australia 'The term "alien" within the meaning of the Constitution is synonymous with the term "non-citizen" within the meaning of the [Migration Act 1958 (Cth) which defines "non-citizen" as covering all persons who are not Australian citizens] (*Nolan v Minister for Immigration and Ethnic Affairs* (1988) 165 CLR 178).' *SZ v Minister for Immigration and Multicultural Affairs* (2000) 101 FCR 342; 62 ALD 64; 173 ALR 353; BC200003413; [2000] FCA 836 at [16], per Branson J

Australia [In the context of naturalisation and citizenship under s 51 xix of the Commonwealth of Australia Constitution] 'In my view it refers to someone who is outside the Australian community and its fundamental loyalties, that is, outside Australian nationality. Applied today and for future application, I would accept that such community and such loyalties are marked off by citizenship of birth and descent, and citizenship by naturalisation. Indeed, so much is accepted by all members of the Court.' *Shaw v Minister for Immigration and Multicultural Affairs* [2003] HCA 72 at [95] per Kirby J; BC200307491

Australia [At argument on appeal is whether in s 51(xix) of the Commonwealth Constitution, the term 'aliens' excludes persons born in Australia (subject to exceptions such as children of foreign diplomats, or of members of visiting armed forces). Section 51(xix) and (xxvii) provides:
51. The Parliament shall ... have power to make laws ... with respect to:
(xix) naturalisation and aliens;

...

(xxvii) immigration and emigration.]

'[4] I have previously stated my view that, subject to a qualification, Parliament, under paras (xix) and (xxvii) of s 51, has the power to determine the legal basis by reference to which Australia deals with matters of nationality and immigration, to create and define the concept of Australian citizenship, to prescribe the conditions on which such citizenship may be acquired and lost, and to link citizenship with the right of abode. In that regard, Brennan, Deane and Dawson JJ said in *Chu Kheng Lim v Minister for Immigration*, that the effect of Australia's emergence as a fully independent sovereign nation with its own distinct citizenship was that alien in s 51(xix) of the Constitution had become synonymous with non-citizen. The qualification is that Parliament cannot, simply by giving its own definition of "alien", expand the power under s 51(xix) to include persons who could not possibly answer the description of "aliens" in the Constitution. Within the class of persons who could answer that description, Parliament can determine to whom it will be applied, and with what consequences. Alienage is a status, and, subject to the qualification just mentioned, Parliament can decide who will be treated as having that status for the purposes of Australian law and, subject to any other relevant constitutional constraints, what that status will entail.

...

'[11] When a word is used to signify a concept, the process involves both inclusion and exclusion. The argument for the plaintiff in this case amounts to the proposition that the meaning of "aliens" in s 51(xix) excludes someone who was born in Australia, regardless of other circumstances and characteristics such as those which apply to the plaintiff. The plaintiff contends that it is an essential characteristic of aliens referred to in s 51(xix) that they were born outside Australia. If that is right, then the power conferred upon the Parliament by s 51(xix) is restricted by that limitation upon the meaning of "aliens". People born in Australia are excluded from the concept, and legislation about such people is not supported by the power to make laws with respect to naturalization and aliens.

'[12] Meaning is always influenced, and sometimes controlled, by context. The context might include time, place, and any other circumstance that could rationally assist understanding of meaning. I referred above to the meaning of "aliens" in s 51(xix). That is a brief description of the immediate context in which "aliens" appears, but the context is much wider than that. It includes the whole of the instrument, its nature and purpose, the time when it was written and came into legal effect, other facts and circumstances, including the state of the law, within the knowledge or contemplation of the framers and legislators who prepared the Constitution or secured its enactment,

and developments, over time, in the national and international context in which the instrument is to be applied ...' Per Gleeson CJ.

...

'[35] In my opinion, a person born in Australia is not, never has been and, without a constitutional amendment, never could be an alien unless that person falls within one of three categories. None of those categories applies to Ms Singh. Over 200 years ago, Sir William Blackstone said that "[t]he children of aliens, born here in England, are, generally speaking, natural-born subjects, and entitled to all the privileges of such." Eight years after the colonies of Australia federated, Griffith CJ, Barton, O'Connor, Isaacs and Higgins JJ made the same comment about a person born in this country in a case where the father was a Chinese alien. Ms Singh is a natural born "subject of the Queen" of Australia for the purpose of s 117 of the Constitution and, unlike an alien, entitled to its protection. If she is a natural born subject of the Queen of Australia, I do not see how anyone could find that she is an alien for the purpose of the Constitution. Furthermore, subject to presently irrelevant exceptions, birth in Australia made her a member of the Australian community and one of "the people of the Commonwealth" to whom the Constitution refers. The Minister has no power to deport Ms Singh. She is not an alien. The Minister has no power to act as if Ms Singh were not a member of the Australian community.

'[36] Section 51(xix) of the Constitution empowers the Parliament of the Commonwealth to make laws with respect to "aliens". By necessary implication or assumption, that grant of power recognises that an alien is a person who can be identified by reference to some criterion or criteria that exists or exist independently of any law of the Parliament or indeed of the Constitution itself. It is a corollary of that implication or assumption that the Parliament of the Commonwealth cannot itself define who is an alien. Thus, s 51(xix) implies or assumes that an alien can be defined — but not by the Parliament.

...

'[38] In the Australian colonies in 1900, the essential meaning — the connotation — of the term "alien" was a person who did not owe permanent allegiance to the Crown. And, subject to three exceptions, in 1900 and now, birth in Australia, irrespective of parentage, gave and still gives rise to an obligation of permanent allegiance to the sovereign of Australia. Even if it is permissible in 2004 to give the constitutional term "aliens" a meaning different from that which it had in 1900

— itself a contestable proposition — the Commonwealth has referred to no circumstance external to the Constitution which demonstrates that the essential meaning of the term in 1900 no longer applies. Indeed, even under a "progressivist" theory of constitutional interpretation, it is hard to conceive of the essential meaning of a constitutional term being entirely displaced and another meaning substituted for it.

'[39] … it is of no relevance in determining the meaning of the constitutional term "aliens" that, under the law of another country, a person, born in this country, may be a citizen of, and owe obligations of allegiance to the sovereign of, the foreign country. Equally irrelevant to determining the meaning of "aliens" in s 51(xix) are concepts of nationality and citizenship. Discussion of those concepts in this constitutional context merely invites error. What was, and is now, central to the meaning of the constitutional term "aliens" is the existence of an obligation of permanent allegiance to our sovereign — once the Queen of the United Kingdom but now, according to the doctrine of this Court, the Queen of Australia. Because the Commonwealth contends that Ms Singh is an alien — and therefore within the operation of s 51(xix) — it must show that upon her birth, she came under no obligation of permanent allegiance to the Queen of Australia. Not only has the Commonwealth failed to show that that is the case, it has not attempted to, nor could it, do so.

…

'[56] When those who framed the Constitution included the term "aliens", they did so against a background of British and colonial history that, for at least six centuries, had regarded an alien as a person who did not owe permanent allegiance to the Crown. The makers of our Constitution enacted s 51(xix) knowing that the principle that a person who did not owe permanent allegiance to the Crown was an alien was an entrenched rule of the common law, a rule as central to the unwritten constitution of the United Kingdom and its colonies as could be found. They also knew that, upon birth in any part of the Crown's dominions, the new born child immediately owed permanent allegiance to the Crown and was entitled to claim a reciprocal duty of protection on the part of the Crown, unless the child fell into one of three categories to which I shall later refer. In 1900, no-one in Australia who knew anything about the subject would think for a moment that a person, born in any part of the Crown's dominions, was an alien unless the child fell into one of the three categories.

'[57] It is a mistake to think that in 1900 an alien was simply a person who was not a British subject. In the then structure of the Empire, a person who was not a British subject was an alien. Nevertheless, "non-British subject" was not the "essential meaning" of the term "alien" in 1900. If it were, the term would have that meaning until amended under s 128 of the Constitution. Most Australians would now be aliens. It is more accurate to say that in 1900 an alien was a person who was not a "subject of the Queen". The essence of the term "alien" was the lack of permanent allegiance to the Crown. While the Crown remained indivisible, a British subject was outside the denotation of the term "alien". However, when the Crown divided, so to speak, the denotation of the term "subject of the Queen" changed. As a result, British subjects no longer owed permanent allegiance to the Queen of Australia and became "aliens" in Australia.

'[58] Against this background, the inevitable conclusion is that in s 51(xix) of the Constitution the term "aliens" means persons who do not owe permanent allegiance to the Queen of Australia. It is only a half-truth to say that an alien is a person who owes permanent or even temporary allegiance to another country. Indeed, in the case of a stateless person, it is not even a half-truth. The meaning of "aliens" in the Constitution does not turn on whether under the law of another country the person in question owes a duty of allegiance to that country. It turns on whether that person owes a duty of permanent allegiance to the Queen of Australia. The history of the concepts of aliens and alienage in England and Australia shows why this is so. To that history, I now turn.

…

'[119] The majority in Nolan accepted the definition of an alien given by Gibbs CJ in Pochi, that is, an alien is "any person who was born outside Australia, whose parents were not Australians, and who has not been naturalized as an Australian." Whether or not the statement of Gibbs CJ in Pochi was an obiter dictum, in Nolan it was the ratio decidendi of the decision. Mason CJ, Wilson, Brennan, Deane, Dawson and Toohey JJ agreed that at federation, the term "aliens" certainly did not extend to British subjects. In a joint judgment their Honours stated:

> The word could not … properly have been used in 1900 to identify the status of a British subject vis-à-vis one of the Australian or other colonies of the British Empire for the reason that those colonies were not, at that time,

independent nations with a distinct citizenship of their own. At that time, no subject of the British Crown was an alien within any part of the British Empire.

'[120] However, their Honours observed that following the creation of separate Australian citizenship by the Nationality and Citizenship Act 1948 (Cth):

> The fact that a person who was born neither in Australia nor of Australian parents and who had not become a citizen of this country was a British subject or a subject of the Queen by reason of his birth in another country could no longer be seen as having the effect, so far as this country is concerned, of precluding his classification as an 'alien'.

'[121] Their Honours referred to developments that "necessarily produced different reference points for the application of the word 'alien'." They identified these developments as the emergence of Australia as an independent nation, the acceptance of the divisibility of the Crown (implicit in the development of the Commonwealth as an association of independent nations) and the creation of a distinct Australian citizenship. They said that the meaning of the word "alien" had not "altered" but that:

> Inevitably, the practical designation of the word altered so that, while its abstract meaning remained constant, it encompassed persons who were not citizens of this country even though they might be British subjects or subjects of the Queen by reason of their citizenship of some other nation. We would add that, to the extent that there would otherwise be inconsistency in the use of the words 'subject of the Queen' in the Constitution, it should be resolved by treating those words as referring, in a modern context, to a subject of the Queen in right of Australia.

'[122] Subsequently, Toohey J in *Cunliffe v The Commonwealth*, after referring to Nolan, said that:

> [A]n alien can generally be defined as a person born out of Australia of parents who were not Australian citizens and who has not been naturalized under Australian law or a person who has ceased to be a citizen by an act or process of denaturalization. Thus the terms "non-citizen" and "alien" are synonymous.

While the terms "alien" and "non-citizen" may be synonymous in some contexts, this does not mean

that a "non-citizen" for the purposes of the Migration Act is an "alien" within the constitutional meaning of the term.

…

'[128] The term "aliens" in s 51(xix) denotes the legal status of alienage. "Naturalization and aliens" in s 51(xix) refers to a process (naturalisation and denaturalisation) and a legal status (alienage). By the late 19th century, international law recognised two well-established rules for acquiring nationality by birth: jus soli and jus *sanguinis*. But those terms provide no more assistance in interpreting s 51(xix) of the Constitution than do the citizenship provisions of the Fourteenth Amendment of the United States Constitution. Both terms are irrelevant. In determining the meaning of the term "aliens" in s 51(xix), the term jus *sanguinis* in particular is no more helpful than the definition of the continental jury would be in determining the meaning of "jury" in s 80 of the Constitution. The terms jus soli and jus *sanguinis* would be relevant only if the term "aliens" had no meaning in the Anglo-Australian world in 1900 or since and Parliament itself could define the term. For the reasons that I have given, Parliament cannot define the constitutional term "aliens".' Per McHugh J.

…

'[163] It is convenient to begin consideration of the plaintiff's contention that, at federation, "aliens" had a fixed legal meaning by reference to Quick and Garran. They commenced their commentary on the term "aliens", when used in s 51(xix), by saying:

> In English law an alien may be variously defined as a person who owes allegiance to a foreign State, who is born out of the jurisdiction of the Queen, or who is not a British subject. The rule of the common law is that every person born out of the British Dominions is an alien, and that every person born within British Dominions is a British subject. This is known as the jus soli or the territorial test of nationality, which is contrasted with the jus *sanguinis* or the parentage test of nationality.

Two aspects of that comment may be noted: the reference to "allegiance" and the contrast between "alien" and "British subject".

'[164] The feudal notion of allegiance has played a significant part in the development of English law respecting aliens. Holdsworth wrote of the appearance in England in the course of the thirteenth century of what were the beginnings of "the modern rules of the common law, which define the persons who are to be accounted as British subjects". As the common law stood before the accession of King James VI of Scotland to the throne of England, "all persons born on English soil, no matter what their parentage, owed allegiance to, and were therefore subjects of the king". As Holdsworth said:

> [I]t is the duty of allegiance, owed by the subject to the crown, which differentiates the subject from the alien. This doctrine has its roots in the feudal idea of a personal duty of fealty to the lord from whom land is held; and, though it has necessarily developed with the development of the position of the king, its origin in this idea has coloured the whole modern law on this topic.

...

'[190] The word "aliens" may have had a fixed legal meaning in the 17th century. (Even then the legislature had altered the rules about alienage in some respects.) By the end of the 19th century the word did not bear the meaning it did at the time of Calvin's Case. There had been numerous legislative interventions in the subject. But there was one feature about the use of the word that was constant: it was that the alien "belonged to another". Often that was expressed by reference to the concept of allegiance and often it was expressed in terms that, by their definitions, assumed that the world could be divided into two groups. Either one was a British subject or one was an "alien". And those groups were defined by reference to the nature of the allegiance they owed. During the 19th century, large numbers of persons emigrated from the British Isles to America and from Europe to the British Isles and America. During the latter half of that century legal thought in Britain and Europe grappled with the consequences of these movements. What may once have been the common law understanding of alienage yielded to these new circumstances. "Aliens", even if it had once had a fixed legal meaning, did not bear such a meaning by the end of the 19th century. But what did remain unaltered was that "aliens" included those who owed allegiance to another sovereign power, or who, having no nationality, owed no allegiance to any sovereign power.' Per Gummow, Hayne and Heydon JJ.

...

'[305] It may also be accepted that the scope of the term "alien" can be affected by changes in the identity of the sovereign and the boundaries of the sovereign's territory. This is to give effect to the reality that allegiance can no longer be owed, and

protection afforded without sovereign power to command the former and to provide the latter. The meaning of the word, however, has not altered. It cannot be modified by Parliament to include persons "who could not possibly answer the description of 'aliens' in the ordinary understanding of the word". As Gibbs CJ observed in *Pochi v Macphee*, in relation to s 12 of the Migration Act 1958 (Cth) ("Migration Act"), as it then was, if the word "alien" did include some persons who were not aliens, it should be given a distributive operation, so as to apply only to those to whom it could validly apply.

'[306] Mr Basten QC who appeared in this appeal for a person given leave to intervene, submitted that the reference to the meaning of "alien" to which I have referred was not made inaccurately or incautiously. The language used reflects established principle in other common law jurisdictions, Great Britain, the United States and Canada. Observations in a Canadian case, *Cunningham v Tomey Homma*, by the Privy Council to the effect that a Provincial enactment denying the franchise to a person of Japanese descent did not necessarily have anything to do with naturalization or alienage are relevant here. The Lord Chancellor said:

> A child of Japanese parentage born in Vancouver City is a natural-born subject of the King, and would be equally excluded from the possession of the franchise.

...

'[315] "Alien" or "non-alien" in any sense in which either term is used calls into question a matter of status. In *Shaw v Minister for Immigration and Multicultural Affairs*, I said and would repeat:

> Courts have long been reluctant to alter the status of a person without a compelling reason to do so.

'[316] This traditional reluctance of courts to interfere with status is itself a factor to be weighed in favour of the plaintiff in resolving ambiguity in the meaning of "alien".

...

'[319] No implication of nationhood or otherwise can validly contradict, or allow the definition by enactment of, an express constitutional term such as "alien". I would reject this submission.

...

'[322] I return to the defendants' principal submission that the constitutional meaning of "alien" includes persons who are born in Australia of non-Australian citizens. I would reject it, in summary, for these reasons. It does not matter that the plaintiff is not a citizen within the meaning of the Citizenship Act. The conclusion that I have reached accords with the view that prevailed at the Federal Convention in 1898. It gives rise to a clear and certain rule. That rule has existed for hundreds of years. It is consistent with the assumptions implicit in s 44 of the Constitution. It is a true reflection of the legal concept of alienage at the time of Federation. It is not inconsistent with any majority holdings of this Court. It falls squarely within the language of Gibbs CJ in *Pochi v Macphee*, and McHugh J in *Re Patterson; Ex parte Taylor*. Because status is involved the Court should not give "alien" any extended meaning. To classify the plaintiff as an alien would be to give the word an extended meaning. No "evolutionary process" or supposed change in the language of the Constitution could, or does require a different outcome. To the extent, if any, that, absent citizenship as conferred or recognized by the Citizenship Act, a person born in Australia as this plaintiff was, is precluded by s 23C of that Act from asserting Australian nationality, the section would be invalid in its operation in relation to her.' *Singh v Commonwealth* [2004] HCA 43 at [4], [11]–[12], [35]–[36], [38]–[39], [56]–[58], [119]–[122], [128], [163]–[164], [190], [305]–[306], [315]–[316], [319], [322], per Callinan J; BC200405816

Alien enemy

[For 49 Halsbury's Laws (4th edn) para 146 see now 49(1) Halsbury's Laws (4th edn) (Reissue) para 632.]

ALIENATION

New Zealand 'In its context in s 60(1) of the Property Law Act the word "alienation" should be given a wide enough meaning to cover a transaction by a debtor, such as a mortgage or charge, whereby he effectively parts with a degree of control over an asset and to that extent puts the asset out of reach of the general body of creditors.' *Re Hale (a bankrupt)* [1989] 2 NZLR 503 at 512, CA, per Richmond J

ALIMONEY

Canada 'My understanding of the words "alimony" and "maintenance" has always been that they are technical and terms of art. "Alimony" strictly refers to an allowance made while the marriage continues to subsist and "maintenance" strictly refers to the allowance made when the marriage is dissolved. Thus an order *nisi* provision for payment of an interim allowance pending the order absolute is "alimony" and a like order after dissolution of the marriage is "maintenance". An allowance ordered to be paid on the grant of a divorce *a mensa et thoro* (less technically known as a judicial separation) is alimony as are payments agreed upon between the parties to a marriage in a written separation agreement.' *The Queen v Burgess* [1982] 1 FCR 849 at 853, Fed Ct TD, per Cattanach J

ALIVE

Canada [Insurance benefits were payable to persons 'alive' sixty days after death of insured.] 'A fiction has developed in the law that in respect of property rights, an unborn child who is subsequently born alive is in the same position as a child living at the time of the death of the benefactor. This fiction has existed for over a century and is so well established that for a statute conferring property rights on children to be interpreted as excluding a child who was *en ventre sa mere* at the time of the death of the father would require specific words of exclusion. In interpreting statutes such as the Insurance Act, RSA 1980, c I-5, I think cognizance must be taken of this fiction. It would be known to legislative draftsmen and the legislation would be passed with this fiction in mind.' *Fitzsimonds v Royal Insurance Co of Canada* (1984) 7 DLR (4th) 406 at 409, Alta CA, per McDermid JA

ALL

New Zealand [Rule 60(1)(a) of the High Court Rules relates to a situation where the sole plaintiff is, or that 'all' the plaintiffs are, resident out of New Zealand.] 'What is required is that the adjective "all" within R 60(1)(a) be interpreted to include "any of" where that is applicable by virtue of the mix of foreign and domestic plaintiffs.' *Schmidt v Bank of New Zealand Ltd* [1991] 2 NZLR 60 at 64, per Jeffries J

All goods that are imported

Canada 'A main item of contention is the meaning of the phrase "all goods that are imported"…

…

'The ordinary meaning to be given to the phrase "all goods that are imported" must consider what might ordinarily be expected of customs legislation. There is no doubt in my mind that any Canadian coming back into Canada and being asked, "Anything to declare?" expects to pay customs duties only on goods acquired outside the country. In addition, those having goods sent from abroad for resale in Canada expect that they might have to pay customs duties on what they bring in. Given this background, the argument made by the Deputy Minister that the phrase "all goods that are imported" should be interpreted as meaning "all goods" is extraordinary, and accordingly, loses weight as against Mr. Flavell's interpretation.

'I find that there is a misinterpretation within the Tribunal's majority decision which undermines its value in determining ordinary meaning. In arriving at its own interpretation of "export", the majority uses Strayer J's quotes from *Old HW-GW Ltd v Canada* (now reported at [1991] 1 CTC 460) that, at page 466:

> … "export" normally involves the transfer of goods from one country to another …
>
> … the most natural meaning in a commercial context for the term "export" or "exportation" is the sending of goods from one country to another, foreign, country". [Emphasis added.]

'From these phrases the majority [at page 204]:

> … adopts the definition of "export", meaning *to send out from one country and into another* or cause to be sent out from one country and into another". [Emphasis mine.]

'The error is that the majority finds from Strayer J.'s words the meaning of "export" to be the downgraded notion of mere mechanical movement from one country to another. The words used by Strayer J. as authority state much more; a "transfer" of goods from one country to another or "a sending" within a commercial context.

'The question is, what would Côté's more properly stated "average person on the street" understand by the words "export" and "import" used in an Act administering the collection of customs. Within my understanding of what generally informed people think, there is no doubt that international trade come to mind with trucks and ships transporting goods to and from Canada and nations around the world. Thus, the words should be interpreted within this clearly commercial context.' *Flavell v Deputy MNR, Customs and Excise* [1997] 1 FC 640 at 663–664, Fed TD, per Campbell J

All other papers and documents in the proceeding

Canada [At issue was whether notes made by a board member were part of the record returnable before the court.] '… "all other papers and documents in the proceeding". In my opinion, the board member's notes are not papers or documents in the proceeding. At common law, not even the evidence formed part of the record …

'What the superior court needs to see are the decision and the reasons in particular, as well as the documents commencing the proceedings before the board. If available, the court wishes to see a transcript of the evidence and the exhibits. A board member's notes are not a reliable record of the evidence and although one might say the handwritten notes are "papers" in the proceeding, in my opinion, considering the factors I have mentioned, I would not interpret the word "papers" to include them. The catch-all clause was intended to require the delivery up of other papers and documents that were *relevant* to the proceeding before the board, not the board member's notes.' *Yorke v Northside-Victoria District School Board* (1992) 90 DLR (4th) 643 at 648–649, NS CA, per Hallett JA

All steps … reasonably practicable to take

New Zealand [Health and Safety in Employment Act 1992, s 2.] 'The requirement to take all reasonably practicable steps is not a counsel of hindsight perfection. It involves, as noted earlier, considerations of "due diligence", "a total absence of fault", of doing what a "reasonable man" would have done under the circumstances, or acting with "all reasonable care".' *Buchanans Foundry Ltd v Department of Labour* [1996] 3 NZLR 112 at 119, per Hansen J

ALL REASONABLE ENDEAVOURS

New Zealand [The Heads of Agreement provided a 'Time Frame for Proceeding' which reads: 'FCE/ECNZ to use all reasonable endeavours to agree a full sale and purchase agreement within three months of the date of this agreement'.] '[114] On the basis that we have found that the HoA is not a binding agreement, the argument that the "Time Frame for Proceeding" clause by itself obligates ECNZ as a matter of law to use all reasonable endeavours to agree a full sale and purchase agreement within three months seems to us quite hopeless. The Judge found that it could not be binding if the HoA was not binding and there has been no cross-appeal on that point. But, even if the clause were part of an otherwise binding HoA, we would have difficulty in seeing that, because of the nature of the "not agreed" items, it could create any legally enforceable obligation to negotiate further. In *Little v Courage Ltd* (1994) 70 P & CR 469 Millett LJ said at p 476:

> "An undertaking to use one's best endeavours to obtain planning permission or an export licence is sufficiently certain and is capable of being enforced: an undertaking to use one's best endeavours to agree, however, is no different from an undertaking to agree, to try to agree, or to negotiate with a view to reaching agreement; all are equally uncertain and incapable of giving rise to an enforceable legal obligation."

'[115] The end in view (the full agreement) is insufficiently precise for the Court to be able to spell out what the parties must do in exercising their reasonable endeavours. Where the objective and the steps needing to be taken to attain it are able to be prescribed by the Court, a best endeavours or reasonable endeavours obligation will be enforceable. That may be possible in relation to some contractual negotiations of relative simplicity and predictability (*Coal Cliff Collieries*). But a negotiation of complex contractual terms is such a variable matter, both in process and in result, and so dependent on the individual positions which each party may reasonably take from time to time during the bargaining, that it is impossible for a Court to define for them what they ought to have done in order to reach agreement. The Court neither knows the result nor is able to say how each offer should have been made, nor whether it should have been accepted. If ECNZ had sat on its hands and absolutely declined to bargain – which was not the case – it would have been necessary, in order to provide a remedy to be able to state what, as a minimum, it was obliged to do as part of the bargaining process. That may have been possible, as can be seen from the presumption for good faith bargaining now to be found in s 32 of the Employment Relations Act 2000 and the code promulgated pursuant to s 35 of that Act, but in fact ECNZ did actively participate in a lengthy bargaining process.

'[116] We take one item at random – the extension of the force majeure clause to the national grid. Did FCE have to agree to it? If so, on what terms? And if FCE was obliged to come to terms on this item, could it seek in return a price adjustment, and by how much? We have no idea

how a Court could resolve these questions – by what standards they would be considered and how value would be attributed to the particular covenant which a party might be seeking. A meaning can, with some trouble, be given to "economic", but the task of assessing the parties' performance during a negotiation of this kind and determining whether a position taken by one side – perhaps influenced by the current position of the other – was or was not consistent with "reasonable endeavours", is beyond the expertise of the Court. In *Coal Cliff Collieries*, notwithstanding Kirby P's view that some contracts to negotiate in good faith may be enforceable, he expressed his conclusion that a Court would be extremely ill-equipped "to fill the remaining blank spaces" which a lengthy negotiation between the parties to a mining contract had failed to remove. He pointed out that the Court could not appeal to objective standards or its own experience. At stake were commercial decisions "involving adjustments which would contemplate binding the parties for years and deciding issues that lie well beyond the expertise of the court". How mining executives, attending to the interests of their corporation and its shareholders, might act in negotiating such a complex transaction was "quite unknowable" (p 27). Those remarks are entirely apposite to the present case.' *Fletcher Challenge Ltd v Electricity Corporation of New Zealand Ltd* [2002] 2 NZLR 433 (CA) at 458–459 per Richardson P, Keith, Blanchard and McGrath JJ

ALLEGIANCE

[For 8 Halsbury's Laws (4th edn) para 862 see now 8(2) Halsbury's Laws (4th edn) (Reissue) para 29.]

ALLODIAL

Australia 'Blackstone contrasted as follows the term "allodial" with the term "fee". "The true meaning of the word fee (feodum) is the same with that of feud or fief, and in its original sense it is taken in contradistinction to allodium; which latter the writers on this subject define to be every man's own land, which he possesseth merely in his own right, without owing any rent or service to any superior. This is property in its highest degree; and the owner thereof hath absolutum et directum dominium, and therefore is said to be seised thereof absolutely in dominico suo, in his own demesne. But feodum, or fee, is that which is held of some superior, on condition of rendering him service; in which superior the ultimate property of the land resides." (Blackstone, *Commentaries on the Laws* *of England*, 17th ed (1830), vol 2, p 104.)' *Wik Peoples v Queensland* (1996) 141 ALR 129 at 227; 71 ALJR 173, per Gummow J

ALLOTMENT

Garden

[For 2 Halsbury's Laws (4th edn) para 1 see now 2(1) Halsbury's Laws (4th edn) (Reissue) para 301.]

Of shares

[For 7 Halsbury's Laws (4th edn) para 366 see now 7(1) Halsbury's Laws (4th edn) (2004 Reissue) para 532.]

ALLOW

Australia [Section 39(3) of the Defence Force Discipline Act 1982 (Cth) provides that a defence member who negligently 'causes' or allows a service ship to be lost is guilty of an offence.] '... the word "allow" refers to permitting or standing by as someone else causes that, effect or consequence.' *Victor v Chief of Naval Staff* (1992) 115 ALR 716 at 723, per cur

Canada [Section 167 of the *Criminal Code* makes it an offence for a person in charge of a theatre to allow an indecent performance.] 'In my view, the court erred in overturning the finding of fact made by the trial judge with respect to *mens rea*. Section 167 requires that the accused "allow" the indecent performance. I agree with the appellant Mara and the respondent that s 167 is a full *mens rea* offence. In my view, the requirement that the accused "allow" an indecent performance implies, at the very least, a requirement of concerted acquiescence or wilful blindness on the part of the accused. Indeed, I would equate "allow" in this context with "knowingly" in the context of *Jorgensen* [*sub nom R. v Hawkins* (1993) 15 OR (3d) 549]. Thus, given that the Court of Appeal's alternative finding is based on a lesser view of *mens rea* than "knowingly", I do not accept their alternative conclusion.' *R v Mara* (1997) 148 DLR (4th) 75 at 93, SCC, per Sopinka J

ALLOWANCE

Australia 'The proper and ordinary meaning of the word in the context of wages, is an agreed amount of money (paid or payable in cash or in kind) by the employer for some purpose directly

related to the provision of services by the employee. The word "allowance" in the context we are concerned with does not merely mean something that is allowed or permitted by the employer. It means an allowance by the employer of a monetary amount (paid in cash or in kind) intended to be related or appropriated directly to a particular feature of the employment of the employee ... and it is not to be understood as merely a permission or allowance by the employer to use the employer's car or a swimming pool built on the premises or the like.' *Terry Shields Pty Ltd v Chief Commissioner of Payroll Tax* (1989) 98 ALR 559 at 567, per Lee CJ

ALLUVION

[For 49 Halsbury's Laws (4th edn) para 294 see now 49(2) Halsbury's Laws (4th edn) (Reissue) para 11.]

ALMOST IDENTICAL

New Zealand [Section 22(2)(b) of the Companies Act 1993] '... almost identical names must be names which are difficult to distinguish or which, on a passing observation would be considered the same.'

'... names where the differences under consideration are geographical, numerical or date markers, ought not to be regarded as "almost identical" unless there are other factors about the names which lead to that conclusion.' *The Paint Factory Ltd v Registrar of Companies* [2000] 3 NZLR 220 at 225, per Williams J

ALMSHOUSE

[The Income and Corporation Taxes Act 1970 has been repealed. See now, as to the exemption of almshouses from income tax, the Income and Corporation Taxes Act 1988, s 505(1)(a).]

ALONE

Australia [Section 24(1)(b) of the Veterans' Entitlement Act 1986 (Cth) stipulates that a veteran is entitled to a special rate of pension if a war-caused injury alone prevents the undertaking of remunerative work.] 'The question whether the veteran by reason of the war-caused condition "alone" has been prevented from continuing to undertake remunerative work can only be answered by reference to all the circumstances in which the war-caused condition exists. The fact that a non war-caused condition is not alone causative of such preventative effect does not prevent it having that effect in combination with the war-caused condition ... Furthermore it is consistent with the application ... of a common sense approach "with an eye to reality".

'[40] As in the case of the present applicant, it is possible that the war-caused condition will be by far and away the more dominant of the causes of the preventative effect where there is also present a non war-caused condition having such effect in combination. The result is that the presence of the latter will deny to a veteran qualification for the special rate of pension.' *Forbes v Repatriation Commission* BC200001248; [2000] FCA 328 at [39], [40], per Nicholson J

ALTERATION

Of picture

[The Copyright Act 1956 has been repealed; see now, as to alteration of an artistic work, The Copyright, Designs and Patents Act 1988, s 84(6).]

AMBIGUITY

[For 50 Halsbury's Laws (4th edn) para 403 see now 50 Halsbury's Laws (4th edn) (Reissue) para 458.]

AMICUS CURIAE

Australia 'According to the Macquarie Dictionary, *amicus curiae* is "a person not a party to the litigation who volunteers or is invited by the court to give advice to the court upon some matter pending before it". In Words and Phrases Legally Defined, there is a reference to the case of *Grice v R* (1957) 11 DLR 699 [Canada] in which Ferguson J said at 702: "*Amicus curiae* ... is one who as a bystander, where a judge is doubtful or mistaken in a matter of law, may inform the court. In its ordinary use the term implies the friendly intervention of counsel to remind the court of some matter of law which has escaped its notice and in regard of which it is in danger of going wrong." My understanding of the matter is that, in general, a court will not entertain submissions from a person as *amicus curiae* unless he or she is a legal practitioner or some other person who has the appropriate qualifications to assist the court ... Order 4, r 7 of the Rules under the Family Law Act [1975 (Cth)] provides that a party to proceedings "... may appear personally or by a legal practitioner". In my view, the effect of this Rule is that the court should not permit persons other than legal practitioners to represent a party to proceedings in the Family Court.' *In the marriage of PW and CA Rogers and Fernandez* (1988) 12 Fam LR 467 at 470, per Gun J

AMOTION

[For 9 Halsbury's Laws (4th edn) para 1266 see now 9(1) Halsbury's Laws (4th edn) (Reissue) para 1069.]

AMOUNT OF THE CLAIM

Australia 'The "amount of the claim" is an expression which has a more or less defined meaning. There are pages and pages of discussion of the phrase in vol 3 of the *American Words and Phrases*, West Publishing Co, Eagan MN, and really the hundreds of cases cited come down to the proposition that the "amount of the claim" means the amount claimed in good faith, so long as that claim is not fictitious or merely colourable: see for instance *Kimel v Missouri State Life Insurance Co* 71 F (2d) 921 at 924 (1934) (US Tenth Circuit Court of Appeals). It may be that one can read those words subject to the claim not being one which is "uncertain, contingent and speculative"; *First English Lutheran Church of Oklahoma City v Evangelical Lutheran Synod of Kansas* decided by the same court 135 F (2d) 702 at 703 (1943), but that is as far as one can go on the American authorities.

'I have looked at cases in this country on the amount of Privy Council appeals and the District Court's jurisdiction so far as amount is concerned, but nothing there seems to deal with this question.' *Jesseron Holdings Pty Ltd v Middle East Trading Consultants Pty Ltd (No 2)* (1994) 13 ACSR 787 at 790; 122 ALR 717 at 721, per Young J

ANALYSIS

[The Food Act 1984 is largely repealed. A definition of 'analysis' is contained in the Food Safety Act 1990, s 53(1), as follows.] 'Analysis' includes microbiological assay and any technique for establishing the composition of food, and 'analyse' shall be construed accordingly.

ANCESTRAL LAND

New Zealand 'Land which was the original home of a Maori tribe—as here the Karikari peninsula was by tradition of the Ngati Kahu the landing place of their first canoe—may still be ancestral land although it has been sold to Europeans. If, even after sale, some special Maori relationship with the land has continued down the generations, that is a factor to be weighed when a zoning change is proposed.' *Environmental Defence Society Inc v Mangonui County Council* [1989] 3 NZLR 257 at 261, CA, per Cooke P

AND

Canada 'No exception can be taken with the promise that the word "and" logically will generally import a conjunctive sense in giving legal effect to written instruments. Moreover, there is no doubt that the judge's rationale for holding the reversion operative, other things being equal, would be compelling if the word "and" bore its normal conjunctive sense.

'However, that general premise is not an inexorable canon of construction to which there can be no exception. Sometimes the word "and" is read as "or", and vice-versa, by force of the context in which they appear. The governing rule must be that both words should be interpreted so as to make sense and give effect to the document being construed. This will at times lead to "and" being construed disjunctively and, conversely, the normal alternative sense of "or" ceding to a conjunctive meaning. (See, for example, *Doe d. Bedford v White* (1827) 4 Bing 276, 130 ER 773, where "and" was construed as "or" and, conversely, *Clergue v H H Vivian and Co* (1909) 41 SCR 607, per Anglin J at p 617, where "or" was interpreted as "and".) In holding use of the word "and" in the reversion proviso left him no alternative but to rule the land reverted to the Crown, the judge must be regarded as falling into the error of not exploring whether the context of its use might import a disjunctive sense to the word.' *Boy Scouts of Canada v Doyle* (1997) 149 DLR (4th) 22 at 58, Nfld CA, per Marshall JA

ANIMAL

[The Road Traffic Act 1972 has been repealed. The definition was re-enacted (with the omission of the word 'any') by the Road Traffic Act 1988, s 170(8).]

[For 2 Halsbury's Laws (4th edn) paras 201, 202, 204 see now 2(1) Halsbury's Laws (4th edn) (Reissue) paras 501–502.]

Domestic

[For 2 Halsbury's Laws (4th edn) paras 201–203, 424–427 see now 2(1) Halsbury's Laws (4th edn) (Reissue) paras 502, 508, 541–545.]

ANIMALS IN QUESTION

[By virtue of s 1 of the Protection of Animals (Amendment) Act 2000, s 2 applies where a prosecutor has brought proceedings under s 1 of the Protection of Animals Act 1911 for cruelty to animals against the owner of the animals to which the offence relates, and the proceedings have not been discontinued or otherwise disposed of. Section 2 of the 2000 Act empowers the court, if it thinks it necessary in the interests of the welfare of 'the animals in question', to authorise the prosecutor to take charge of and care for the animals, sell them, dispose of them otherwise by way of sale, or slaughter them.] '[11] The justices posed for the opinion of the High Court the question whether they "were justified in finding ... that the 'animals in question' were those 'to which the offence relates' namely the seven to which the informations related and as a result dismissing the application".

'[12] Mr Butler for the local authority submitted that the animals in question in s 2(1) of the 2000 Act meant the animals which were the subject of the application, and which might be any animals falling within s 1(2), ie any animal which the respondent kept, or had kept, for commercial purposes. Alternatively, he submitted that the expression "the animals in question" was ambiguous in that it could either bear the meaning for which he contended, or that which the justices found. He sought to refer to extracts from Hansard, when the 2000 Act was passing through Parliament, under the principle of *Pepper* (*Inspector of Taxes*) *v Hart* [1993] 1 All ER 42, [1993] AC 593.

'[13] I concur with the opinion of the justices. I do so for a number of reasons. Firstly, in my opinion, the natural meaning of the expression "the animals in question" in s 2(1) is the animals in question in the proceedings brought by the prosecutor. If the draftsman had intended that the power under s 2 should extend to other animals, I would have expected the section to have been drafted very differently.

'[14] The prosecutor is defined in s 1 of the 2000 Act. If one were to read the words of s 2(1), but incorporating the full definition of the prosecutor, the subsection would read as follows:

> "If, on the application of a person who is mentioned in section 1(3) and who has brought proceedings for an offence under section 1 of the Protection of Animals Act 1911 against the owner of the animals to which the offence relates, and the proceedings have not been discontinued or otherwise disposed of, it appears to the court from evidence given by a

veterinary surgeon that it is necessary in the interests of the welfare of the animals in question, being animals which the owner keeps or has kept for commercial purposes, to do one or more of the things mentioned in subsection (2), the court may make an order authorising him to do so."

So read, there is no room for ambiguity. In other words, in my view the wording of the statute carries with it the clear intention that the animals in question are those which are the subject of the criminal proceedings.

'[15] Secondly, the power given to the court under s 2 of the 2000 Act is an interim power. An order under the section ceases to have effect on the discontinuance or other disposal of the proceedings under s 1 of the 1911 Act: see s 2(4). What was the lacuna intended to be filled by this interim power, and why should the power cease on the termination of the proceedings under s 1 of the 1911 Act? If the section bears the meaning found by the justices, the answers to those questions are readily supplied. The lacuna was that animals which were the subject of cruelty or neglect proceedings might remain in the hands of the owner and continue to suffer while proceedings under the 1911 Act took their course. There would be no need for the power to continue after the conclusion of the proceedings under the 1911 Act for these reasons. If the proceedings resulted in an acquittal of the defendant, there would be no justification for further interference with his custody of his animals. If the proceedings resulted in the conviction of the defendant, then the court would already have its powers under ss 2 and 3 of the 1911 Act to make whatever order was best for the welfare of the animals.

'[16] However, if s 2 was intended to extend the court's intervention powers to protect the welfare of animals which were not themselves the subject of an allegation of cruelty or neglect, but were considered to be at risk of suffering at the hands of a defendant, it is hard to see why such powers should come to an end on the conviction of the defendant. One might think that the conviction of a defendant would be added material for supporting the case that his other animals were at risk. It is true, as Mr Butler points out, that on conviction the court would have powers to disqualify the defendant from holding animals, but those powers would relate to the defendant personally rather than to the animals, and it is not clear why a power to make arrangements or give orders for the safe custody of other animals at risk should automatically be brought to an end on the defendant's conviction,

merely because he would be exposed to the possibility of a disqualification order.

'[17] Thirdly, if there were an ambiguity, it would be permissible to have regard to the long title. In *R v Bates* [1952] 2 All ER 842 at 844, Donovan J said:

"In many cases the long title may supply the key to the meaning. The principle, as I understand it, is that where something is doubtful or ambiguous the long title may be looked to to resolve the doubt or ambiguity, but, in the absence of doubt or ambiguity, the passage under construction must be taken to mean what it says, so that, if its meaning be clear, that meaning is not to be narrowed or restricted by reference to the long title."

'[18] The long title to the 2000 Act suggests, as its language states, that it was to enable provision to be made for the care, disposal or slaughter of animals to which s 1 of the 1911 Act relates, and not to make provisions for the welfare of animals unrelated to such proceedings.

'[19] Mr Butler submitted that the wider construction for which he contends would be subsumed within the words "and for connected purposes", but that is not a persuasive argument. If the purpose of the section was to extend the protective arm of the court not only to animals to which proceedings under the 1911 Act related, but also to any other animals kept by the owner for commercial purposes, that would be a substantial extension rather than merely a connected purpose.

'[20] Lastly, I confess that with considerable hesitation, and wrongly as I now think, I looked at the passages from Hansard on which Mr Butler sought to rely. The 2000 Act resulted from a Private Member's Bill. Mr Butler referred me to the report of the promoter's statement to the House of Commons on the second reading of the Bill. What was said falls far short of satisfying the strict criteria laid down in *Pepper v Hart* for the admission of such material as an aid to construction. In so far as it tends in either direction, it tends, in my view, to support the reading of the justices, for the promoter stated that her aim was to plug what she described as "a very clear gap" in the 1911 Act in that, as matters stood, animals which were the subject of cruelty or neglect proceedings could be left to suffer while the law took its course.' *Cornwall County Council v Baker* [2003] EWHC 374 (Admin) at [11]–[20], [2003] 2 All ER 178, per Toulson J

ANNEX

Canada [An issue arose as to whether a plan of a road was 'annexed' to a grant.] 'Of "annex" the dictionary says: "It implies physical connection or physically joined to, yet physical connection may be dispensed with, and things may be annexed without being in actual contact, when reasonably practicable." That a thing may be annexed without actually being joined is, I think, borne out by the fact that a building performing a satellite function may well be referred to in common usage as an annex although not physically connected to that with which it is so associated.' *British Columbia v Hilyn Holdings Ltd* (1991) 78 DLR (4th) 27 at 32, BC CA, per Taylor JA

ANNUAL PAYMENT

[The Income and Corporation Taxes Act 1970 is now largely repealed. See now, as to Schedule D, the Income and Corporation Taxes Act 1988, s 18. For ss 52, 53 of the Act of 1970 see ss 348, 349 of the Act of 1988.]

ANNUAL PROFITS OR GAINS

[The Income and Corporation Taxes Act 1970 is largely repealed. For Schedule D see now the Income and Corporation Taxes Act 1988, s 18 and for Case VI the Income and Corporation Taxes Act 1988, s 69.]

ANNUITY

[For 39 Halsbury's Laws (4th edn) para 1212 see now 39(2) Halsbury's Laws (4th edn) (Reissue) para 762.]
    [For 23 Halsbury's Laws (4th edn) paras 529, 531 see now 23(1) Halsbury's Laws (4th edn) (Reissue) paras 477, 486.]

Life annuity

[Section 230(6) of the Income and Corporation Taxes Act 1970 has been repealed. The definition was re-enacted (with a minor drafting amendment) in the Income and Corporation Taxes Act 1988, s 657(1).]

Purchased life annuity

[Section 38(6) of the Finance Act 1956 and s 230(6) of the Income and Corporation Taxes Act 1970 have both been repealed. The definition was re-enacted (with a minor drafting amendment) in the Income and Corporation Taxes Act 1988, s 657(1).]

ANONYMOUS WORK

[See generally, as to the copyright position in regard to anonymous or pseudonymous works, the Copyright, Designs and Patents Act 1988, s 57.]

ANOTHER

New Zealand [Section 48 of the Crimes Act 1961 begins 'Every one is justified in using, in the defence of himself or another ... '.] 'This section also involves the question of the legal status of an unborn child. Here the issue is whether an unborn child is within the meaning of the word "another". That word must mean "another person"... an unborn child does not come within the word "another" in the expression "in the defence of himself or another"' *Wilcox v Police* [1994] 1 NZLR 243 at 255–256, per Tipping J

ANY

Any consideration or benefit received by the insider

New Zealand [Section 9(2)(i) of the Securities Amendment Act 1988 refers to 'any consideration received by the insider'.] '... it is clear that in their context those words relate to considerations or benefits received in exchange for or by reason of the giving of a tip ...' *Colonial Mutual Life Assurance Society Ltd v Wilson Neill Ltd* [1994] 2 NZLR 152 at 162, CA, per cur

Any just excuse

New Zealand [Section 13A(1)(b) of the Commissions of Inquiry Act 1908 provides 'Where, in any proceedings before a Commission, a witness, without offering any just excuse, refuses to give evidence when required ...'.] 'The phrase "just excuse" has long been a standard exception in New Zealand legislation concerned with the enforcement of an obligation to give evidence. In addition to s 13A of the Commissions of Inquiry Act 1908 it occurs currently in at least three statutes covering the civil and criminal jurisdiction of the Court:

    ...

    'The words are to be given their ordinary meaning and do not require definition by the Court.' *KPMG Peat Marwick and others v*

Sir Ronald Davison (CA 223/95) [1996] 2 NZLR 278, 319 (CA) at 335, per Henry J

Any person

[The Road Traffic Act 1972 has been repealed. See now the Road Traffic Act 1988, s 157(1)(a).]

'On first reading s 93A(2) [of the Fair Trading Act 1973] does appear positively to confer a right on any person to enforce an undertaking. That wide reading does not in my view bear examination ...

'My reasons for rejecting the very wide prima facie construction are, first, that it would be extraordinary for Parliament to confer a remedy for breach of an undertaking on a far wider basis than the remedy for breach of an order. Secondly, it is not apparent what limit can properly be placed upon "any person" if there is no limitation built into the expression by the latter half of s 93A(2). It could hardly have been Parliament's intention that the whole population of this country should be entitled to bring civil proceedings for failure to fulfil an undertaking. Thirdly, s 93A(2) can be given a sensible meaning if the latter part is allowed to control the expression "any person", so that the subsection means that any person who would be empowered to bring civil proceedings in respect of a contravention of an obligation imposed by the order, will, where the obligation is imposed or assumed by the giving of an undertaking, be empowered to bring civil proceedings in respect of a failure to fulfil such obligation; but that other persons not empowered to bring civil proceedings in breach of an order could not.' *Mid Kent Holdings plc v General Utilities plc* [1996] 3 All ER 132 at 145–146, per Knox J

New Zealand [Land Transfer Act 1952, ss 137 and 146.] '[T]here is a pattern in the use of language in ss 136–148 dealing with caveats, although there is not complete consistency. Having, in ss 136 and 137, given any person claiming a caveatable interest the right to lodge a caveat either in Form M (against the bringing of land under the Act) or Form N (against a dealing) the statute from then onwards generally calls a person who has taken advantage of that right a "caveator": see ss 138, 140, 141, 143, 145, and 147. (In s 144 which deals with the lapsing of a Form M caveat that is not done, but the word "person" is qualified by words describing a caveator ("person by whom or on whose behalf the caveat was lodged"). Section 143(2) speaks of "the caveator or the person on whose behalf the caveat has been lodged". It is difficult to think whom the latter person could

be but this uncertainty does not detract from [the] argument. Section 147, dealing with withdrawal of a caveat, refers both to the caveator and the caveator's attorney or agent.

'Section 146 is the only place in which "person" is not accompanied by a direct reference to the caveator or use of words which can refer only to the caveator. The second time the word "person" appears in this section, referring to someone affected by the caveat, it is not limited to the registered proprietor but extends to anyone who has sustained damage. The section is in both these ways wider in its application than the other caveat sections ... "Any person lodging a caveat" in s 146 is not restricted to the caveator ... If Parliament had intended otherwise, s 146 would surely have referred to a "caveator" like the other sections of which mention has been made. We conclude, then, that both client and solicitor and indeed any other person responsible for lodging a caveat may be liable to pay compensation under s 146.' *Gordon v Treadwell Stacey Smith* [1996] 3 NZLR 281 at 287–288, CA, per cur

Any special property or interest

New Zealand [Crimes Act 1960, s 220.] 'In s 220 the words "the owner, or any person having any special property or interest" encompass persons having a wide range of proprietary and other interests in things capable of being stolen. They are not confined just to owners having general property (see the definition of "property" in s 2 of the Sale of Goods Act 1908) and persons such as pledgees who are conventionally referred to as having a special property: 35 *Halsbury's Laws of England* (4th ed) para 1215; *Chabbra Coporation Pte Ltd v Jag Shakti (Owners) The Jag Shakti* [1986] AC 337, 345. The words must be taken to extend to lawful possession as, for example, in a bailee. They must also extend to the interest of an owner or occupier of land exercising actual control over what is on it as in the cases referred to. Even if that interest is something less than legal ownership no miscarriage of justice can flow from that in this case.' *R v Ellerm* [1997] 1 NZLR 200 at 208, CA, per cur

ANY OTHER SUBSTANCE HARMFUL TO BIRDS

Canada 'The principal objective is to establish the intention of Parliament. The respondent argues that this intention can be established by use of the *ejusdem generis* rule of statutory interpretation, and that application of the rule will result in a narrow interpretation of the words "any other substance" as meaning "any other substance similar to oil?"

'The rule is set out in *National Bank of Greece (Canada) v Katsikonouris*, where, at page 1040 La Forest J says:

"Whatever the particular document one is construing, when one finds a clause that sets out a list of specific words followed by a general term, it will normally be appropriate to limit the general term to the genus of the narrow enumeration that precedes it. [Emphasis added.]"

'La Forest J's use of the term "normally" is instructive. I find it to mean that a general rule of construction is useful unless the intention of Parliament is otherwise clear. I find such to be the case here and therefore, put no weight on the respondent's argument.

'The purpose of the MBC [Migratory Birds Convention] Act is stated in section 4 as follows:

"4. The purpose of this Act is to implement the Convention by protecting migratory birds and nests."

'The Convention referred to in section 4, which was concluded in 1916, is a Schedule to the MBC Act and in the preamble reads:

"His Majesty the King of the United Kingdom of Great Britain and Ireland and of the British dominions beyond the seas, Emperor of India, and the United States of America, being desirous of saving from indiscriminate slaughter and of insuring the preservation of such migratory birds as are either useful to man or are harmless, have resolved to adopt some uniform system of protection which shall effectively accomplish such objects, and to the end of concluding a convention for this purpose have appointed as their respective plenipotentiaries ..."

'Regarding the MBCA Regulations, section 12 of the MBC Act specifies that the Governor in Council may make regulations necessary to carry out the purposes and provisions of the MBC Act and the Convention, including the following:

"12. (1) ...
(*h*) for prohibiting the killing, capturing, injuring, taking or disturbing of migratory birds or the damaging, destroying, removing or disturbing of nests;

(*i*) prescribing protection areas for migratory birds and nests, and for the control and management of those areas;"

'I find on the basis of these provisions that there is a clear intention expressed to provide wide protection to migratory birds, and, therefore, the phrase under consideration should be given a similarly wide interpretation. Therefore, I find that any substance, including oil and oil wastes, is capable of being prohibited if it is "harmful".' *Alberta Wilderness Assn v Cardinal River Coals Ltd* (1999) 3 FC 425 at 470, 471, TD, per Campbell J

ANY PROCEEDS REALIZED FROM ITS DISPOSITION

Canada '... As noted above in respect of s 72(1), read according to its ordinary and grammatical meaning, the phrase "any proceeds realized from its disposition" in s 71 includes proceeds of vessels seized under the *Fisheries Act*. Thus, s 71 merely makes a grant of authority to detain proceeds that is partly superfluous in that only in unusual circumstances could the s 71 power to detain proceeds be practically exercised in respect of proceeds realized pursuant to an authority other than the *Fisheries Act*. Such circumstances could arise if the Federal Court were to make an order pursuant to Federal Court Rule 1007 that proceeds of sale be paid into court and held for the benefit of orders made by other courts. In addition, although there is no authority to dispose of seized property until after the close of proceedings, s 71(1) of the *Fisheries Act* does provide for the detention of the proceeds of "any ... thing seized under this Act". Furthermore, Federal Court Rule 1008 provides that the Federal Court has the power to determine the rights of all claimants to moneys paid into court pursuant to Rule 1007(7). Thus, it is difficult to differentiate, on a principled basis, between a situation where the Crown establishes a claim in the provincial court which is then executed in the Federal Court and the situation in this case where the provincial court purports to order forfeiture of moneys in the hands of a Federal Court. In the result, one is not necessarily driven to infer, as the Court of Appeal concluded, that, taken together, ss 70(3) and 71(1) serve to limit the grant of power to order forfeiture in s 72(1).

'Indeed, had Parliament intended the phrase "any proceeds realized from its disposition" to be limited to proceeds of perishables in ss 71(1) and 72(1), it could have done so expressly, as it did in s 70(3), as well as ss 72(2) and 72(3). Instead, a pattern in the use of the phrase at issue is evident whereby in some sections it is expressly limited to the proceeds of perishables and in other sections it refers more generally to all forms of property seized under the Act and proceeds thereof.

'In addition, it is notable that ss 70(3) and 71(1) are directed at the property of a person at a stage in the proceedings where the person is only accused of an offence. Whereas s 72(1) is directed at the property of a person who has been convicted of an offence. Thus, ss 70(3) and 71(1) are distinct from s 72(1) in that the former address procedural matters and the later is in effect a sentencing provision. In this sense, s 72 stands alone and apart from the immediately preceding sections. This would seem to run against the argument that one must read ss 70(3), 71(1) and 72(1) together in interpreting the phrase "any proceeds realized from its disposition".' *R v Ulybel Enterprises Ltd* [2001] 2 SCR 867 at 890–891, per Iacobucci J

ANY WRONGFUL ACT OR OMISSION

[Under s 10 of the Partnership Act 1890 partners may be held vicariously liable where loss was caused to a non-partner by 'any wrongful act or omission' of any partner acting in the ordinary course of his firm's business.] '[9] The case advanced by Mr Al Tajir and Mr Salaam runs as follows. The claim made by Dubai Aluminium against Mr Amhurst is not that he committed a common law tort such as deceit or negligence. The claim is that he committed the equitable wrong of dishonest participation in a breach of trust or fiduciary duty. Mr Amhurst dishonestly procured or assisted Mr Livingstone in the breach of the fiduciary duties he owed to Dubai Aluminium. Although fault-based, this species of equitable wrong is not a "wrongful act or omission" within the meaning of s 10. Section 10 being inapplicable, the Amhurst firm was not liable for the acts of Mr Amhurst of which Dubai Aluminium complained.

'[10] This argument was rejected by Rix J and the majority of the Court of Appeal. I agree with them. There is nothing in the language of s 10 to suggest that the phrase "any wrongful act or omission" is intended to be confined to common law torts. On the contrary, the reference to incurring a penalty points away from such a narrow interpretation of the phrase. The liability of co-partners for penalties incurred, for instance, for breach of revenue laws was well established when the 1890 Act was passed (see Lindley on Law of Partnership (6th edn, 1893) p 160, and *A-G v Stranyforth* (1721) Bunb 97, 145 ER 608).

'[11] In addition to the language the statutory context points in the same direction. Section 10 applies only to the conduct of a partner acting in the ordinary course of the firm's business or with the authority of his co-partners. It would be remarkable if a firm were liable for fraudulent misrepresentations made by a partner so acting, but not liable for dishonest participation by a partner in conduct directed at the misappropriation of another's property. In both cases the liability of the wrongdoing partner arises from dishonesty. In terms of the firm's liability there can be no rational basis for distinguishing one case from the other. Both fall naturally within the description of a "wrongful act".

'[12] In 1874 Lord Selborne LC's famous statement in *Barnes v Addy* (1874) LR 9 Ch App 244 at 251–252, made plain that a stranger to a trust could be liable in equity for assisting in a breach of trust, even though he received no trust property. On the interpretation of s 10 advanced for Mr Al Tajir and Mr Salaam, a firm could never be vicariously liable for such conduct by one of their partners. I can see nothing to commend this interpretation of the statute.' *Dubai Aluminium Co Ltd v Salaam (Livingstone and others, third parties)* [2002] UKHL 48 at [9]–[12], [2003] 1 All ER 97, per Lord Nicholls of Birkenhead

ANYTHING

Canada 'I begin with the grammatical and ordinary sense of "anything". The *Oxford English Dictionary* (2nd edition 1989), vol 1, defines "anything" as follows: "A combination of ANY and THING, in the widest sense of the latter, with all the varieties of sense belonging to ANY." The dictionary definition suggests a broad interpretation, which would include sexual favours. Such an interpretation is also supported by the immediate context of the provision. "Anything" is referred to three times in s 305(1):

> "305(1) Every one who, without reasonable justification or excuse and with intent to *extort or gain anything*, by threats, accusations, menaces or violence induces or attempts to induce any person, whether or not he is the person threatened, accused or menaced or to whom violence is shown, *to do anything or cause anything to be done*, is guilty of an indictable offence and is liable to imprisonment for fourteen years. [Emphasis added.]"

'In my view, the meaning of "anything" in the immediate context of "to extort or gain anything" and inducing any person "to do anything or cause anything to be done" is clearly in keeping with the wide, unrestricted dictionary definition, and includes sexual favours.

'Mewett and Manning, *supra*, take a differing view. Commenting on *R. v Bird*, they argue at p 833 that:

> Not a great deal of discussion appears in *Bird* on this wide interpretation of "anything", the court being content to say that the word is clear and unambiguous and used in this context is of wide unrestricted application. Yet this is not what is normally meant by "extort or gain". It is true that, in isolation, "anything" can be of the widest meaning, but in the context of "extort or gain", one might have thought that it referred to something of some tangible proprietary or pecuniary nature.

'I respectfully disagree. I do not believe the authors place sufficient weight on the fact that the meaning of "anything" is further qualified by the words "to do anything or cause anything to be done" at the end of the section.' *R v Davis* (1999) 179 DLR (4th) 385 at 402, SCC, per Lamer CJC

APOTHECARY

[For 30 Halsbury's Laws (4th edn) paras 609–610 see now 30 Halsbury's Laws (4th edn) (Reissue) paras 801–802.]

APPARENT

[For 50 Halsbury's Laws (4th edn) para 273 see now 50 Halsbury's Laws (4th edn) (Reissue) para 324.]

APPARATUS

[The pursuer was injured as the result of a fall from a fixed ladder that had a faulty rung. The question was whether the ladder was part of the machinery and 'apparatus' of a mine within the Mines and Quarries Act 1954, s 81(1).] 'To the simple question, is the ladder apparatus used by the respondents for the purpose of carrying on their business in that particular mine, I consider that an affirmative answer ought to be given. In this connection I have to say that I have obtained considerable assistance from a consideration of the case which was not cited to me and arises in another context, of *Inland Revenue v Scottish & Newcastle Breweries Ltd* [1982 SLT 407], and in particular the opinion of the Lord President therein.

That case confirms me in the view that "apparatus" is a word which as a generality extends widely and is not confined to things which are capable of being operated so as to generate some kind of result.' *Brebner v British Coal Corpn* 1988 SLT 736 at 739, per Lord Dervaird

APPEAL

Australia 'It is well established that appeals may generally be divided into three main categories: an appeal strictly so called (sometimes referred to as an appeal stricto sensu); an appeal by way of rehearing; and an appeal de novo. In an appeal in the strict sense the question for consideration is whether the decision subject to appeal was right on the material which the decision-making body below had before it. Fresh evidence cannot be called: *Quilter v Mapleson* (1882) 9 QBD 672 at 676; *Builders Licensing Board v Sperway Constructions (Sydney) Pty Ltd* (1976) 135 CLR 616 at 619… The nature of an appeal by way of rehearing was discussed by Cox J in *Wigg v Architects Board of South Australia* (1984) 36 SASR 111 at 113: "This is a rehearing on the documents, but with a special power to receive further evidence on the appeal. The latter power is necessary, because the question on a rehearing of this kind is whether the order of the court below ought to be affirmed or overturned in the light of the material before the appeal court at the time it hears the appeal." … An appeal [de novo] involves a fresh hearing with the parties being entitled to begin again and adduce new evidence: see *Sweeney v Fitzhardinge* (1906) 4 CLR 716; *Simpson Ltd v Arcipreste* (1989) 53 SASR 9.' *Westend Pallets Pty Ltd v Lally* (1996) 69 IR 1 at 2–3, per the Commission

Australia 'The word "appeal" is defined in s 2 of the Judiciary Act [1903 (Cth)] to include any proceeding to review or call in question the decision of any court or judge. The Full Court correctly held that the stated case procedure under s 350, when invoked in an ordinary case in the exercise of State jurisdiction, involves a proceeding to review or call in question the decision of a primary judge.' *R v Gee* [2003] HCA 12 at [5] per Gleeson CJ; BC200300830

New Zealand [A contract provided for arbitration but under the International Chamber of Commerce Rules of Conciliation and Arbitration 1975, article 24, waived any right of appeal.] 'The jurisdiction to set aside an award for error of law on its face is ultimately an inherent or common law one and is technically classified in New Zealand or English law as review rather than appeal. In substance, however, it gives a limited right of appeal on questions of law. There is no difficulty in concluding that within the meaning of article 24 of the ICC rules this is a form of appeal. It is precisely the kind of derogation from the finality of an award which the framers of the ICC rules would have intended to prevent, so far as that could validly be done under the local law governing the particular arbitration.' *CBI NZ Ltd v Badger Chiyoda* [1989] 2 NZLR 669 at 673–674, CA, per Cooke P

APPLICABLE

[Whether the change from the remission and parole system to the licence system for early release of prisoners was a heavier sentence than that 'applicable' at the time the offence was committed, under the European Convention for the Protection of Human Rights and Fundamental Freedoms 1950 (set out in the Human Rights Act 1998, Sch 1 Pt I art 7(1)). '[18] Article 7(1) prohibits the imposition of a penalty which is heavier than the one that was "applicable" at the time that the offence was committed. No one in the hearings below appears to have focussed on the meaning of the word "applicable". There appears to have been an assumption that this meant "that which would have been applied" and that the sentence that "would have been applied" was one of 12 years' imprisonment. I have already stated my conclusion that the latter assumption may have been unfounded. I now turn to consider the meaning of "applicable" in art 7(1).

[19] This question was recently considered by the Judicial Committee of the Privy Council in *Flynn v HM Advocate* [2004] UKPC D1, 2004 SCCR 281. The issue in that case was whether changes made by Scottish legislation to the release regime applicable in the case of mandatory life sentences infringed art 7(1). My noble and learned friend Lord Carswell, who was a member of the Committee, will in his speech, which I have had the privilege of reading in draft, describe the difference of opinion as to the meaning of "applicable" expressed by members of the Committee.

[20] Had the Committee had cited to them, as we have had cited to us, the decision of the European Court of Human Rights (the Court of Human Rights) in *Coeme v Belgium* [2000] ECHR 32492/96 their task might have been made the easier. Ours certainly is, for at para 145 the court said this in relation to art 7:

"The court must therefore verify that at the time when an accused person performed the act which led to his being prosecuted and convicted there was in force a legal provision which made that act punishable, and that the punishment imposed did not exceed the limits fixed by that provision."

[21] This passage lends strong support to the opinions as to the meaning of "applicable" expressed by my noble and learned friends Lord Rodger and Lord Carswell in *Flynn*'s case. I am persuaded that those opinions correctly state the law. It follows that art 7(1) will only be infringed if a sentence is imposed on a defendant which constitutes a heavier penalty than that which *could* have been imposed on the defendant under the law in force at the time that his offence was committed. I observe, in passing, that if statutory changes are made to the release regime of those serving mandatory life sentences those changes may affect the severity of the sentence that the law requires. That is not this case.' *R* (*on the application of Uttley*) *v Secretary of State for the Home Department* [2004] UKHL 38, [2004] 4 All ER 1 at [18]–[21], per Lord Phillips of Worth Matravers

APPLICATION

[Appeal to Secretary of State under Town and Country Planning Act 1990, s 78 and Planning (Listed Buildings and Conservation Areas) Act 1990, s 20 allowed where local planning authority refuse application for planning permission and listed building consent. Local authority took the view that documents in support of applications were inadequate and applications were therefore invalid.] 'The case turns on the meaning of the word "application" in s 78 of the Planning Act and s 20 of the Listed Buildings Act. In my judgment, and in the context of the statutes, it includes an application which the local planning authority consider to be invalid under the regulations. The words "which the local authority consider to be valid" should not be read into s 78 of the Planning Act and s 20 of the Listed Buildings Act to govern the word "application". A determination of invalidity by the local planning authority does not exclude the right of appeal to the Secretary of State on the question of validity. The applications in this case remained applications for the purpose of triggering the operation of the appeal provisions in the legislation notwithstanding the view of the local planning authority that the applications were invalid.' *R v Secretary of State for the Environment,*

Transport and the Regions, ex p Bath and North East Somerset District Council [1999] 4 All ER 418 at 427, CA, per Pill LJ

APPLIED INDUSTRIALLY

Australia 'The phrase in s 77(5) of the Copyright Act 1968 (Cth) "for determining the circumstances in which a design is, for the purposes of this section to be deemed to be applied industrially" specifies a criterion which may perhaps be described as distinguishing between what in another context the High Court called the fine arts and the useful arts, the latter being more concerned with the field of economic endeavour: see *National Research Development Corpn v Commissioner of Patents* (1959) 102 CLR 252 at 275

'The matter is of ordinary usage, and "industry" may be described as a trade or other particular form or branch of productive labour, and something as "industrialised" when devoted or directed to such an activity. Implicit in this, as French J pointed out in *Kevlacat Pty Ltd v Trailcraft Marine Pty Ltd* (1987) 79 ALR 534 at 546–7 is an element of system'. *Press-Form Pty Ltd v Hendersons Ltd* (1993) 112 ALR 671 at 681, per Gummow J

APPLIED SCIENCE *SEE* SCIENCE

APPLY

Canada '42 The primary factor that supports this conclusion is the very language of s. 48(12)(*j*) [*Labour Relations Act* (Ont.)], which provides that an arbitrator has the power "to interpret and apply human rights and other employment-related statutes, despite any conflict between those statutes and the terms of the collective agreement".

'43 The power to interpret and apply a particular statute would, in my view, ordinarily be understood to include the power to implement and enforce the substantive rights and obligations contained therein. The *Oxford English Dictionary* (2nd ed. 1989), vol. I, at p. 577, states that to "apply" means to "bring (a law, rule, test, principle, etc.) into contact with facts, to bring to bear practically, to put into practical operation". Major J. suggests that my reasons do not respect the intention of the legislature. In my view, the use of the phrase "to interpret and apply human rights and other employment-related statutes" indicates that it was the legislature's intention that an arbitrator would have the power not only to enforce those rights and obligations that are expressly provided for in the

collective agreement, but those that are provided for in human rights and employment-related statutes as well.' *Parry Sound (District) Social Services Administration Board v O.P.S.E.U., Local 324* [2003] 2 SCR 157 at 182–183, per Iacobucci J

APPOINTMENT

[For 24 Halsbury's Laws (4th edn) para 479 see now 5(3) Halsbury's Laws (4th edn) (Reissue) para 80.]

APPREHENSION

[The Extradition Act 1870 has been repealed. See now the Extradition Act 1989, Sch 1, para 5.]

APPRENTICE

[For 16 Halsbury's Laws (4th edn) para 506 see now 16 Halsbury's Laws (4th edn) (2000 Reissue) para 8.]

APPROACH

[A man was charged with breaching a condition of a non-harassment order by approaching the complainer, following her and placing her in a state of fear and alarm. A condition of the order was the accused should not approach the complainer. The Crown's case was that the complainer had seen the accused in the town centre when he had been approximately 100 yards from her and heading in her direction. The accused was looking directly at the complainer, who ran into her solicitor's office where she remained for 15 minutes. On later making her way to the police station, the complainer again saw the accused. While being interviewed by a police officer the complainer saw the accused whom she pointed out to the officer. The accused was looking furtively towards the police office and was later caught on a police surveillance camera on a number of occasions in the course of 17 minutes in the area of the police station. The accused did not give evidence and on being convicted, appealed contending that he had not approached the complainer.] 'We consider that the sheriff was entitled to form the view that the appellant was deliberately lingering about in the area in the hope of seeing the complainer and following her after he had initially spotted her in East High Street. That is supported by the video evidence and by the fact that he did in fact walk past the police station, complete with furtive look, after she had taken refuge there. In the absence of any explanation, therefore, we have come to be of the opinion that the sheriff was entitled to say that the inference could be drawn that this was a deliberate following of the complainer by the appellant. In that situation taking a fairly broad view of the word "approach" we consider that it could be said that the appellant was indeed approaching the complainer by following her about.' *Donaldson v Miller* 2000 SLT 622 at 624, per Lord Sutherland (delivering the opinion of the court)

APPROPRIATE

Canada '48 The word "appropriate" ("*indiqué*") generally confers a very broad latitude and discretion. The Attorney General of Canada refers to the characterization of the expression "appropriate and just in the circumstances", and its French equivalent, in s. 24(1) of the *Charter* by relying upon *Mills v. The Queen*, [1986] 1 S.C.R. 863, at p. 965: "[i]t is difficult to imagine language which could give the court a wider and less fettered discretion."

'49 That, of course, is one of the problems with the Crown's argument. The alleged presence of an "unfettered discretion" with respect to the terms of detention of an NCR accused is precisely the reason why the appellant argues that the whole scheme is unconstitutional as permitting arbitrary infringement of his liberty.

'50 On the hearing of this appeal, the Ontario Review Board and the Nunavut Review Board filed a joint intervention arguing that the "appropriateness" standard urged by the Crown "does not provide guidance, consistency, clarity or fairness. Where a statutory provision affects the liberty of the individual, a clear standard must be established to justify that interference with liberty" (emphasis added). Thus, "[i]t is the position of the [Ontario Review Board] and [Nunavut Review Board] that these [statutory] goals are accomplished by applying to the disposition as a whole, including the conditions, the least onerous and least restrictive standard."

'51 In my view, with respect, the word "appropriate" in the context of s. 672.54 [of the *Criminal Code*] is not at all "unfettered". The word takes its meaning from the context. Conditions must be appropriate, yes, but appropriate having regard to the four enumerated factors (public safety, mental condition of the accused, other needs of the accused, and the reintegration of the accused into society) to fashion a disposition that is "the least onerous and least restrictive to the accused". This

is clear from *Winko, supra*, where, in dealing with the *Charter* challenge under s. 7, McLachlin J. observed, at para. 71, that the scheme "ensures that the NCR accused's liberty will be trammelled no more than is necessary to protect public safety".

'52 This dictum is entirely incompatible with an unfettered "appropriateness" standard. The unnecessary "trammelling" of liberty can often lie in the precise conditions attached to the order and not just in the general mode of detention. The devil, as is so often the case, lies in the details.

'53 *Winko* makes it clear that Part XX.1 of the *Criminal Code* survived the s. 7 *Charter* challenge in that case only because at every step of the process consideration of the liberty interest of the NCR accused was built into the statutory framework. In the following references to *Winko*, it will be noted, there is no distinction drawn between the "disposition", which the Crown concedes must be the "least onerous and least restrictive", keeping in mind the statutory factors, and the "conditions" that form part of the disposition. By way of introduction, McLachlin J. states, at para. 16:

> … Parliament intended to set up an assessment-treatment system that would identify those NCR accused who pose a significant threat to public safety, and treat those accused appropriately while impinging on their liberty rights as minimally as possible, having regard to the particular circumstances of each case. [Emphasis added.]

'54 "[L]iberty rights" obviously extend to more than the bare mode of detention. In this respect, for ease of reference, I refer again to *Winko*, at para. 42:

> … Parliament has signalled that the NCR accused is to be treated with the utmost dignity and afforded the utmost liberty compatible with his or her situation.

'55 Then again, discussing the wording and function of s. 672.54, *Winko* says, at para. 47:

> … the court or Review Board shall make the order that is the least onerous and least restrictive to the accused, consistent with the evidence. [Emphasis added.]

'56 In light of these pronouncements, and the *Charter* challenge to which they were addressed, it seems to me impossible to accept the contention that the word "appropriate" in s. 672.54(*b*) and (*c*) can be read as conferring a discretion unfettered except by the management expertise and medical judgment of the Review Board to fashion such conditions as it thinks fit. In my view, Parliament intended "appropriate" to be understood and applied in the framework of making the "least onerous and least restrictive" order consistent with public safety, the mental condition and other needs of the NCR accused, and the objective of his or her eventual reintegration into society.' *Penetanguishene Mental Health Centre v Ontario* (*Attorney General*) (2003) 237 DLR (4th) 1 at 16–18 (SCC), per Binnie J

APPROPRIATION

Of rights of owner

'The ordinary and natural meaning of "appropriate" is to take oneself, or to treat as one's own, property which belongs to someone else. The primary dictionary meaning is "take possession of, take to oneself, especially without authority", and that is in my opinion the meaning which the word bears in s 1(1) [of the Theft Act 1968]. The act of appropriating property is a one-sided act, done without the consent or authority of the owner.' *R v Gomez* [1993] 1 All ER 1 at 17, HL, per Lord Lowry

APPURTENANCE

[The General Rate Act 1967 has been repealed.]

ARBITRARILY

New Zealand [Section 22 of the New Zealand Bill of Rights Act 1990 provides that 'Everyone has the right not to be arbitrarily arrested or detained'.] ' "Arbitrary" is a somewhat elastic word. Dictionary definitions include "discretionary", "despotic", "capricious". Black's Law Dictionary (5th edn, 1979), includes among its definitions, "without fair, solid and substantial cause; that is, without cause based upon the law", citing *United States v Lotempio* 58 F 2d 358, 359. Chambers English Dictionary (7th edn, 1988), gives as its first definition "not bound by rules".

'Judicial and equivalent authority is also divergent … [Specific reference to this authority then follows.]

'A comprehensive ruling on the meaning of "arbitrary" in s 22 is not now called for. We leave open the possibility that there may be some limited exceptions to the principle that, in general, unlawful detention will be arbitrary detention. We have in mind such cases as detention unlawful yet imperative for the safety of the detainee or other persons, or detention in good faith for reasons falling just short of reasonable and probable grounds

under ss 36, 37 or 38 of the Crimes Act 1961, as envisaged in [*R v Duguay* (1985) 18 DLR (4th) 32, Ont CA; (1989) 56 DLR (4th) 46, SCC].' *R v Goodwin* (*No 2*) [1993] 2 NZLR 390, at 393–394, CA, per cur

ARBITRARY

New Zealand 'Something is arbitrary when it is not in accordance with the law or which is not in accordance with the principles which the law regards as appropriate for a discretion to be operated within.' *Re M* [1992] 1 NZLR 29 at 41, per Gallen J

ARBITRATION

[For 2 Halsbury's Laws (4th edn) paras 501, 507 see now 2(3) Halsbury's Laws (4th edn) (Reissue) paras 1, 8–9.]

ARBITRATOR

[For 2 Halsbury's Laws (4th edn) para 568 see now 2(3) Halsbury's Laws (4th edn) (Reissue) paras 18, 24.]

ARCHITECT

[For 4 Halsbury's Laws (4th edn) para 1301 see now 4(3) Halsbury's Laws (4th edn) (2002 Reissue) para 3.]

ARCHITECTURAL INTEREST

[The Town and Country Planning Act 1971 has been repealed. See now the Planning (Listed Buildings and Conservation Areas) Act 1990, s 1.]

ARGUABLE

Australia '… [M]uch turns on what is meant by "arguable" or "fairly arguable" … [*In General Steel Industries Inc v Commissioner for Railways* (NSW) [(1964) 112 CLR 125 at 129] Barwick CJ said "The test to be applied has been variously expressed; 'so obviously untenable that it cannot possibly succeed'; 'manifestly groundless'; 'so manifestly faulty that it does not admit of argument'; 'discloses a case which the Court is satisfied cannot succeed'; 'under no possibility can there be a good cause of action'; 'be manifest that to allow them' (the pleadings) 'to stand would involve useless expense'. At times the test has been put as high as saying that the case must be so plain and obvious that the court can say at once that the statement of claim, even if proved, cannot succeed; or 'so manifest on the view of the pleadings, merely reading through them, that it is a case that does not admit of reasonable argument'; 'so to speak apparent at a glance'."

'Although various expressions have been employed in this context, all of them may be seen as different ways of saying that a court should not exercise its powers of summary determination of a proceeding except in clear cases ...' *Jackamarra v Krakouer* (1998) 153 ALR 276 at 284–285; [1998] HCA 27 at [32]; BC9801285 at 11–13, per Gummow and Hayne JJ

ARISING

Arising from the same incident or series of incidents

New Zealand 'The expression "incident or series of incidents" serves adequately in the common situation of a number of offences arising out of, say, the one robbery, or a gang rape or some group confrontation but may not be sufficiently sophisticated to cope readily with more complex situations.' *R v O'Brien* [1992] 3 NZLR 464 at 467, per Eichelbaum CJ

Arising out of employment

Canada [Workers' compensation benefits were payable in respect of injury arising out of employment.] 'The words "arising out of employment" refer to the origin of the cause of the injury. There must be some causal connection between the conditions under which the employee worked and the injury which he received (Black's Law Dictionary)...

'However, one cannot interpret the words "arising out of employment" in isolation of the fact that the legislature clearly contemplated that one could suffer an injury arising out of employment which is caused solely by the serious and wilful misconduct of the applicant.' *Gellately v Newfoundland (Workers' Compensation Appeal Tribunal)* (1995) 126 DLR (4th) 530 at 534–535, Nfld CA, per Cameron JA

Arising under

Australia 'It is relevant to notice that several influential decisions contain *dicta* indicating that the concept expressed in the words "a dispute arising under the contract" tends to be regarded as a narrower concept than that expressed, for example, in the words "a dispute arising in connection with" (or "in relation to" or "arising out of") the contract. There are oft-quoted *dicta* in *Heyman v Darwins Ltd* [1942] AC 356 at 383, per Lord Wright, and at 389 and 394 per Lord Porter, which touch the point. I refer also to *Government of Gibraltar v Kenney* [1956] 2 QB 410, in which Sellers J, at 421, said: "The distinction between matters 'arising out of' and 'under' the agreement is referred to in most of the speeches in *Heyman v Darwins Ltd* in the House of Lords and it is quite clear that 'arising out of' is very much wider than 'under' the agreement." ' *Exford Pines Pty Ltd v Vlado's Pty Ltd* [1992] 2 VR 442 at 452, per Tadgell J

Arising under treaty

Australia 'A matter arises under a treaty if, directly or indirectly, the right claimed or the duty asserted owes its existence to the treaty, depends upon the treaty for its enforcement or directly or indirectly draws upon the treaty as the source of the right or duty in controversy.' *Re East; Ex parte Nguyen* (1998) 159 ALR 108 at 132; 73 ALJR 140; BC9806358, per Kirby J

ARMS

Court of Chivalry

[For 35 Halsbury's Laws (4th edn) para 816 see now 35 Halsbury's Laws (4th edn) (Reissue) para 916.]

Officers of arms

[For 35 Halsbury's Laws (4th edn) paras 810–814 see now 35 Halsbury's Laws (4th edn) (Reissue) paras 910–914.]

AROSE

New Zealand [Section 80(5) of the Commerce Act 1986 provides that:

'...

(5) Proceedings under this section may be commenced within 3 years after the matter giving rise to the contravention was discovered or ought reasonably to have been discovered. However, no proceedings under this section may be commenced 10 years or more after the matter giving rise to the contravention.'] '[30] Overall, I draw two conclusions from this survey of the actual words used in s 80(5). First, the word "arose" is capable

of meaning either "occurred" or "was discovered or became discoverable". Secondly, of those two meanings "occurred" is the more likely, particularly in a legal context. That tilts the scales against the meaning advocated by the commission but would not be fatal to it if statutory purposes so required.

...

'[40] I conclude that the word "arose" in s 80(5) means "occurred". The three-year limitation period imposed under that provision was unqualified by questions of discovery or discoverability before it was amended in 2001. It follows that the proceedings are out of time unless saved by some special equitable principle.' *Commerce Commission v Roche Products (New Zealand) Ltd* [2003] 2 NZLR 519 at 527, 529

AROSE OUT OF OR WAS ATTRIBUTABLE TO

Australia [In the context of whether injury 'arose out of or was attributable to defence service' under the (Cth) Veterans' Entitlement Act 1986, s 70(5).] 'The use disjunctively in s 70(5) of the expressions "arose out of" and "attributable" manifest a legislative intention to give "defence-caused" a broad meaning, and certainly one not necessarily to be circumscribed by considerations such as whether the relevant act of the appellant was one that he was obliged to do as a soldier. A causal link alone or a causal connexion is capable of satisfying a test of attributability without any qualifications conveyed by such terms as sole, dominant, direct or proximate.' *Roncevich v Repatriation Commission* [2005] HCA 40 at [27], per McHugh, Gummow, Kirby, Callinan and Heydon JJ; BC200505629

Australia [In the context of whether injury 'arose out of or was attributable to defence service' under the (Cth) Veterans' Entitlement Act 1986, s 70(5).] 'Causal not merely temporal connection: Whatever the provisions for entitlements in workers' compensation or like statutes, or other laws providing repatriation benefits, it follows from the first point that it is essential, certainly so far as the principal claim based on ss 70(1)(b) and 70(5)(a) of the Act is concerned, to focus on the causative relationship postulated between the posited "defence-caused injury" and "any defence service". The need for such a causative relationship is indicated by the phrase "arose out of, or was attributable to". As the primary judge correctly noted, that expression was explained by this Court in *Repatriation Commission v Law* (1981) 147

CLR 635. This Court accepted that the natural meaning of the words pointed to a "causal connexion rather than a temporal one". To this extent, the words were, by 1981 when they were considered in Law, viewed as significantly narrower than the formulae then common in workers' compensation legislation affording an alternative basis for entitlement, namely causal or temporal connection to the posited service.' *Roncevich v Repatriation Commission* [2005] HCA 40 at [55], per Kirby J; BC200505629

ARRANGEMENT

Australia [Section 165(1)(b) of the Bankruptcy Act 1966 (Cth) provides that a trustee of the estate of a bankrupt shall not make an 'arrangement' for giving up a part of his remuneration to the bankrupt or any other person.] 'The term "arrangement" in s 165(1)(b) is a word of wide import. Its ordinary dictionary meaning connotes the act of coming to an agreement or understanding; the term does not refer only to a legally binding agreement, but also encompasses understandings, formal or informal, oral or written, which the parties intend to govern their relationships, even though they may not be intended to have legal force. But as French J said [in *Re Hurt; Ex p Hurt* (1988) 80 ALR 236], it is necessary to read down s 165(1)(b) so as to avoid absurdity. If it was given its literal meaning, it might be wide enough to prevent a trustee who is a partner in a firm of accountants bringing his earnings as trustee into the pool of partnership income, despite the special nature of the interest a partner has in partnership property, including the income he earns which is partnership income. Given the fact that for very many years members of partnerships have commonly been appointed as trustees in bankruptcy and the fact that their trustees' remuneration would commonly be partnership income, that cannot be the legislative intent. Moreover, it is hard to identify any policy of the Bankruptcy Act that would be served by reading s 165(1)(b) as imposing such a restriction on a trustee who is in partnership with others, just as it is difficult to identify any policy in the Act that would be served by reading the subsection as preventing a trustee dealing howsoever he chooses with his remuneration, so long as the dealing was for his own benefit.' *Re Dare; Ex p Dare* (1992) 110 ALR 659 at 662–663, per Drummond J

New Zealand [Section 99(1) of the Income Tax Act 1976 provides: ' "Arrangement" means any contract, agreement, plan, or understanding (whether enforceable or unenforceable) including all steps and transactions by which it is carried into effect'.] '[50] … In short, an arrangement involves a consensus, a meeting of minds between parties involving an expectation on the part of each that the other will act in a particular way. The descending order of the terms "contract, agreement, plan or understanding" suggests that there are descending degrees of enforceability, so that a contract is ordinarily but not necessarily legally enforceable, as is perhaps an agreement, while a plan or understanding may often not be legally enforceable. The essential thread is mutuality as to content. The meeting of minds embodies an expectation as to future conduct. There is consensus as to what is to be done.' *Commissioner of Inland Revenue v BNZ Investments Ltd* [2002] 1 NZLR 450 (CA) at 465–466 per Richardson P, Keith and Tipping JJ.

Arrangement designed to enable the trust to evade

New Zealand [Section 216(c)(v) of the Sale of Liquor Act 1989 refers to an 'arrangement designed to enable the trust to evade'.] 'The word "arrangement" is a word of wide general meaning, and it is not the subject of any special definition. One can infer from this that it was intended to be construed in its ordinary or popular sense …

'The word "designed" clearly connotes purpose. It is not enough that the application should have the effect of evading the prohibitions; it must be intended for that purpose.

'The word "evade" can be used in two senses; one which suggests underhand dealing, and another which means nothing more than the intentional avoidance of something disagreeable … ' *Tararua Foundation v Liquor Licensing Authority* [1995] 2 NZLR 296 at 300–301, CA, per cur

Arrangement or understanding

Australia [Section 45(2)(a) of the Trade Practices Act 1974 (Cth) provides that a corporation shall not make a contract or 'arrangement' or arrive at an 'understanding' if this would be likely to substantially lessen competition.]

'The authorities dealing with s 45(2)(a) of the Act are reviewed in the judgment of Fisher J in *Trade Practices Commission v David Jones (Australia) Pty Ltd* (1986) 64 ALR 67; 13 FCR 446 at 462–4. It appears that "understanding" is to be regarded as a term of wider import than "arrangement". An understanding requires that the minds of the parties to it are "at one that a

proposed transaction proceeds on the basis of the maintenance of a particular state of affairs or the adoption of a particular course of conduct". This passage was from the judgment of Smithers J in *L Grollo & Co Pty Ltd v Nu-Statt Decorating Pty Ltd* (1978) 34 FLR 81 at 89, and was followed by Franki J in *Trade Practices Commission v TNT Management Pty Ltd* (1985) 58 ALR 423; 6 FCR 1 at 25. It appears from the judgment of Fisher J that an arrangement or understanding requires obligations, but does not necessarily require that each party to it accept an obligation to the other or others; it will be sufficient if only one party accepts an obligation to the other or others.

'It is clearly possible for an arrangement or understanding to be constituted when the only communication between the various parties is via a single intermediary. If that intermediary communicates to various persons an intention that each of them should act in a particular way with respect to a particular transaction or situation, and each thereafter acts in that particular way in the hope or belief that the other persons will act similarly, an arrangement or understanding will exist. It is necessary to be careful, however, in distinguishing that situation from one in which the intermediary enters into separate arrangements or understandings with each of the persons. In other words, the terms on which the different persons undertake to act are of crucial importance.

'There is authority to the effect that the mere communication of an intention to act in a particular way does not make the recipient of the information a party to an arrangement or understanding: see *Trade Practices Commission v David Jones (Australia) Pty Ltd* (1986) 13 FCR 446; 64 ALR 67. This proposition accords with common sense; if it were otherwise, every employee of one employer who knew that employees of another employer were intending to stop work would be party to an arrangement or understanding, even if the first-mentioned employees did not intend to stop work themselves. Even if the information of intention to act in a particular way is communicated in the hope or expectations that it will cause the recipient to act in a similar way, it is difficult to see how an arrangement or understanding can result without the recipient communicating in some way an intention to follow the course hoped or expected.' *Australasian Meat Industry Employees Union v Meat and Allied Trades Federation of Australia* (1991) 104 ALR 199 at 210–211, per Gray J

ARREST

[The Road Traffic Act 1972, s 9(1) (as substituted) is repealed. See now the Road Traffic Act 1988, s 6(5).]

[For 11 Halsbury's Laws (4th edn) para 99 see now 11(1) Halsbury's Laws (4th edn) (Reissue) para 693.]

ARRESTED OR DETAINED UNDER ANY ENACTMENT

New Zealand [Section 23(1) of the New Zealand Bill of Rights Act 1990 begins 'Everyone who is arrested or who is detained under any enactment …'.] 'That leads on to the meaning of "detained under any enactment". I take this to refer to the purported exercise of a right of detention conferred by statute. "Detained under any enactment" clearly seems intended to mean something different from arbitrary detention and must be taken to relate to the exercise or purported exercise by officials of statutory powers of detention and perhaps nothing more.' *R v Butcher* [1992] 2 NZLR 257 at 272, CA, per Gault J

New Zealand [Section 23 of the New Zealand Bill of Rights Act 1990 begins 'Everyone who is arrested or who is detained under any enactment …'.] 'I agree with all members of the Court who may take the view that … arrest may be defined as the communication or manifestation by the police of an intention to apprehend and to hold the person concerned in the exercise of authority to do so. Or … so long as the conduct of the arrester, seen to be acting or purporting to act under legal authority, makes it plain that the subject has been deprived of liberty to go where he or she pleases, then there is an arrest within the meaning of s 23(1)… . I have already dwelt on the point that the addition of "under any enactment" after "detained" in s 23(1)(a) is distorted if it is given a narrowing effect, its whole purpose being to underline that there can be no lawful detention by public officers in New Zealand except under an enactment and that any bona fide claim by them to be detaining lawfully must depend on some enactment such as the Crimes Act or the Police Act … the words "or who is detained under any enactment" cannot limit the meaning of the earlier words "who is arrested".' *R v Goodwin* [1993] 2 NZLR 153 at 174, CA, per Cooke P

'No one is arrested within the meaning of s 23 unless he or she is deprived of liberty by the positive act of an official manifesting an intention to exert lawful authority to do so. Detention by the police is not characterised as an arrest unless it is under warrant or where without warrant it is ostensibly justified as being on reasonable of having committed a breach of the peace or an offence punishable by imprisonment (s 315), or under other statutory arrest authority … In the result as I read the judgments in this case all the Judges define "arrest" in terms of the communication or manifestation by the officer of an intention to apprehend and hold the person concerned in the exercise of a purported authority to do so. It follows that if the assumed authority is a power to arrest a deprivation of liberty in those circumstances will constitute an arrest for the purposes of s 23(1)(a) and (b). If the assumed authority is a statutory power to detain it will constitute a detention for those purposes.' *R v Goodwin* [1993] 2 NZLR 153 at 189–190, CA, per Richardson J

'Because of this distinction [in s 23(1)] between arrest and detention, and the limited meaning of detention, arrest is not in my opinion to be given a meaning equivalent to detention. Arrest necessarily involves detention, but the converse is not true. Although both involve a restraint of liberty, the difference between them lies I think in the nature of the authority that is or is purported to be exercised. It is this that determines the meaning of arrest in English law … In the usual course a police officer interrogating a suspect will do so in contemplation of the possibility of arrest, if not with that ultimate intention. Detention or restraint for the purpose of questioning may thus be an arrest … I think the fact of detention or arrest must be marked in some overt way; there must be a clear and deliberate act or statement by the officer whereby he exerts an authority to restrain.' *R v Goodwin* [1993] 2 NZLR 153 at 200, CA, per Hardie Boyes J

ARSON

[For 11 Halsbury's Laws (4th edn) para 1306 see now 11(1) Halsbury's Laws (4th edn) (Reissue) para 594.]

ARTISITC MERIT

Canada 'Section 163.1(6) [of the *Criminal Code*] provides a defence for a representation or written material that constitutes child pornography if it has "artistic merit". Three issues arise regarding the ambit of this defence: (1) the meaning of "artistic merit"; (2) whether artistic works must conform to "community standards" in order to gain the protection of the defence; and (3) the procedure for considering the defence. When construing the defence of artistic merit, we must keep in mind the admonition of Sopinka J. in Butler, *supra*, at p 486: "Artistic expression rests at the heart of freedom of expression values and any doubt in this regard must be resolved in favour of freedom of expression." Simply put, the defence must be construed broadly.

'The first question is what the defence covers. It seems clear the defence must be established objectively, since Parliament cannot have intended a bare assertion of artistic merit to provide a defence. This leaves two possibilities. First, "artistic merit" may refer to the quality of the work in the opinion of objective observers. It is not uncommon in everyday discourse to say of a work of art that, although it is genuinely art, it possesses little or no "artistic merit". If "artistic merit" is used in this sense, then the task of the court would be to determine how good the work of art was. Art students learning their craft, inept artists and artists breaking conventions to establish new idioms might well find their work classified as lacking "artistic merit" and hence lose the benefit of the defence. On the assumption that this was the meaning of "artistic merit", it was argued that the defence is too limited and arbitrary to protect artistic expression adequately.

'The second meaning that can be ascribed to "artistic merit" is "possessing the quality of art", or "artistic character". On this meaning, a person who produces art of any kind is protected, however crude or immature the result of the effort in the eyes of the objective beholder. This interpretation seems more consistent with what Parliament intended. It is hard to conceive of Parliament wishing to make criminality depend on the worth of the accused's art. It would be discriminatory and irrational to permit a good artist to escape criminality, while criminalizing less fashionable, less able or less conventional artists. Such an interpretation would run counter to the need to give the defence a broad and generous meaning. I conclude that "artistic merit" should be interpreted as including any expression that may reasonably be viewed as art. Any objectively established artistic value, however small, suffices to support the defence. Simply put, artists, so long as they are producing art, should not fear prosecution under s 163.1(4).

'What may reasonably be viewed as art is admittedly a difficult question — one that philosophers have pondered through the ages. Although it is generally accepted that "art" includes the production, according to aesthetic principles, of works of the imagination, imitation or design (*New Shorter Oxford English Dictionary on Historical Principles* (1993), vol 1, p 120), the question of whether a particular drawing, film or text is art must be left to the trial judge to determine on the basis of a variety of factors. The subjective intention of the creator will be relevant, although it is unlikely to be conclusive. The form and content of the work may provide evidence as to whether it is art. Its connections with artistic conventions, traditions or styles may also be a factor. The opinion of experts on the subject may be helpful. Other factors, like the mode of production, display and distribution, may shed light on whether the depiction or writing possesses artistic value. It may be, as the case law develops, that the factors to be considered will be refined.' *R. v Sharpe* (2001) 194 DLR (4th) 1 at 34–36, SCC, per McLachlin CJC

ARTISTIC WORK

[The Copyright Act 1956 has been repealed; the new definition is as below.]

In this Part [Part I: Copyright] 'artistic work' means—

(a) a graphic work, photograph, sculpture or collage, irrespective of artistic quality,
(b) a work of architecture being a building or a model for a building, or
(c) a work of artistic craftsmanship.

(Copyright, Designs and Patents Act 1988, s 4)

Canada 'In my view the phrase "artistic work" is used merely as a generic description of the type of works which follow. It is used as a general description of works which find expression in a visual medium as opposed to works of literary, musical or dramatic expression.' *DRG Inc v Datafile Ltd* [1988] 2 FCR 243 at 253, Fed TD, per Reed J

AS OF RIGHT

[In an application for registration of a village green grounded on user 'as of right' within the meaning of s 22 of the Commons Registration Act 1965, the question was raised whether the village's inhabitants had to show that they knew or believed that they had a legalright to use the land for sports and pastimes.] 'The principal issue before your Lordships thus turns on the meaning of the words "as of right" in the definition of a green in s 22(1) of the 1965 Act. The language is plainly derived from judicial pronouncements and earlier legislation on the acquisition of rights by prescription. To put the words in their context, it is therefore necessary to say something about the historical background.

...

'The words "actually enjoyed by the public as of right and without interruption for a full period of 20 years" are clearly an echo of the words "actually enjoyed by any person claiming right thereto without interruption for the full period of 20 years" in s 2 of the [Prescription Act 1832]. Introducing the Bill into the House of Lords (HL Debates), 7 June 1932, col 737, Lord Buckmaster said that the purpose was to assimilate the law on public rights of way to that of private rights of way (84 HL Debates (1931–32), col 637). It therefore seems safe to assume that "as of right" in the 1932 Act was intended to have the same meaning as those words in s 5 of the 1832 Act and the words "claiming right thereto" in s 2 of that Act.

'My Lords, this was the background to the definition of a "town or village green" in s 22(1) of the 1965 Act. At that time, there had been no legislation for customary rights equivalent to the 1832 Act for easements or the 1932 Act for public rights of way. Proof of a custom to use a green for lawful sports and pastimes still required an inference of fact that such a custom had existed in 1189. Judges and juries were generous in making the required inference on the basis of evidence of long user. If there was upwards of 20 years' user, it would be presumed in the absence of evidence to show that it commenced after 1189. But the claim could still be defeated by showing that the custom could not have existed in 1189. Thus in *Bryant v Foot* (1867) LR 2 QB 161 a claim to a custom by which the rector of a parish was entitled to charge 13s for performing a marriage service, although proved to have been in existence since 1808, was rejected on the ground that having regard to inflation it could not possibly have existed in the reign of Richard I. It seems to me clear that class "c" in the definition of a village green must have been based upon the earlier Acts and intended to exclude this kind of defence. The only difference was that it allowed for no rebuttal or exceptions. If the inhabitants of the locality had indulged in lawful sports and pastimes as of right for not less than 20 years, the land was a town or village green. But there is no reason to believe that "as of right" was intended to mean anything different from what those words meant in the 1832 and 1932 Acts.

...

'My Lords, in my opinion the casual and, in its context, perfectly understandable aside of Tomlin J in *Hue v Whiteley* [1929] 1 Ch 440, [1928] All ER Rep 308 has led the courts into imposing upon the time-honoured expression "as of right" a new and additional requirement of subjective belief for which there is no previous authority and which I consider to be contrary to the principles of English prescription. There is in my view an unbroken line of descent from the common law concept of nec vi, nec clam, nec precario to the term 'as of right' in the 1832, 1932 and 1965 Acts. It is perhaps worth observing that when the 1832 Act was passed, the parties to an action were not even competent witnesses and I think that Parke B would have been startled by the proposition that a plaintiff asserting a private right of way on the basis of his user had to prove his subjective state of mind. In the case of public rights, evidence of reputation of the existence of the right was always admissible and formed the subject of a special exception to the hearsay rule. But that is not at all the same thing as evidence of the individual states of mind of people who used the way. In the normal case, of course, outward appearance and inward belief will coincide. A person who believes he has the right to use a footpath will use it in the way in which a person having such a right would use it. But user which is apparently as of right cannot be discounted merely because, as will often be the case, many of the users over a long period were subjectively indifferent as to whether a right existed, or even had private knowledge that it did not. Where Parliament has provided for the creation of rights by 20 years' user, it is almost inevitable that user in the earlier years will have been without any very confident belief in the existence of a legal right. But that does not mean that it must be ignored. Still less can it be ignored in a case like *R v Suffolk CC, ex p Steed* [(1996) 75 P & CR 102] when the users believe in the existence of a right but do not know its precise metes and bounds. In coming to this conclusion, I have been greatly assisted by Mr J G Riddall's article 'A False Trail' (1997) 61 Conv 199.' *R v Oxfordshire County Council, ex p Sunningwell Parish Council* [1999] 3 All ER 385 at 390, 393–394, 395–396, HL, per Lord Hoffmann

AS SOON AS POSSIBLE

New Zealand [Section 23(3) of the New Zealand Bill of Rights Act 1990 provides that 'Everyone who is arrested for an offence and is not released shall be brought as soon as possible before a court or competent tribunal'.] ' ... "as soon as possible" must be interpreted realistically. For example, a reasonable time may be needed for a decision whether or not to charge a person arrested (as by reference of the case to a senior officer) and, if the person is to be charged, for the process of laying the charge and incidental matters. Further, if having been given the information required by s 23(1)(a) and (b) and s 23(4) the person wishes to make a statement or to wait for the arrival of a lawyer, a reasonable time may be allowed for either of these stages. *R v Te Kira* [1993] 3 NZLR 257 at 263, CA, per Cooke P

'From arrest to presentation before the Court the process is to be completed "as soon as possible". The deprivation of liberty before review by a judicial officer is to be as short as possible.' *R v Te Kira* [1993] 3 NZLR 257 at 271, per Richardson J

'The expression "as soon as possible" must be given a meaning that is sensible and practical but that at the same time is not diluted.' *R v Te Kira* [1993] 3 NZLR 257 at 276, per Hardie Boys J

'On the closer scrutiny possible in the context of an actual case giving rise to the relevant facts, the words "as soon as possible" may not be found to preclude reasonable investigatory steps such as those contemplated in England and Canada and by Gibbs CJ in Australia, or to be wholly incompatible with the protection of personal liberty.' *R v Te Kira* [1993] 3 NZLR 257 at 279, per Thomas J

New Zealand [Section 23(3) of the New Zealand Bill of Rights Act 1990 provides that 'Everyone who is arrested for an offence and is not released shall be brought as soon as possible before a court or competent tribunal'.] 'We accept that the expression "as soon as possible" in s 23(3) cannot be absolute, and calls for a reasonable application to time and circumstances. But what is reasonable in a given situation must also be judged in the light of the mandatory language of the subsection, from which it follows that Courts as well as the police can be expected to take whatever steps are necessary to ensure that an arrested person is accorded the rights contemplated by the Act, within the limits of proper administrative and financial constraints.' *R v Greenaway* [1995] 1 NZLR 204 at 207–208, CA, per cur

New Zealand [Section 23(3) New Zealand Bill of Rights Act 1990.] 'The expression "as soon as possible" in s 23(3) is not absolute. It calls for a reasonable application to time and circumstances: see the decision of this Court in *R v Greenaway* [1995] 1 NZLR 204, 207 where the judgment continued that the Courts as well as the police could be expected to take whatever steps are necessary to ensure that an arrested person is accorded the rights contemplated by the Act, within

the limits of proper administrative and financial constraints.' *R v Schriek* [1997] 2 NZLR 139 at 153, CA, per cur

AS SOON AS PRACTICABLE

Australia [Education Services for Overseas Students Act 2000 (Cth) s 20.] 'It is next necessary to determine whether the s 20 notice was sent as soon as practicable after the breach. I have not been referred to, and am not aware of, any authorities directly in point. However, Mr Gibson of Counsel for the applicant referred to a number of decisions of this Court discussing the expression "as soon as reasonably practicable", particularly in the context of s 198(6) of the Act (which deals with the removal of non-citizens). Although s 198(6) includes the word "reasonably" and is in a different context from s 20(2) of the ESOS Act, that discussion still illuminates the problem. A common theme, which I endorse, is that whether something has been done as soon as practicable will depend on the facts of each case considered as a whole (*M38/2002 v Minister for Immigration and Multicultural and Indigenous Affairs* (2003) 199 ALR 290 at [67] and *NATB v Minister for Immigration and Multicultural and Indigenous Affairs* [2003] FCAFC 292 at [51]). The Full Court in NATB also elaborated the concept inherent in the word "practicable" when it said, at [47]–[48];

> The word "practicable" has been defined to mean:
>
> > [c]apable of being put into practice, carried out in action, effected, accomplished or done; feasible. (Oxford English Dictionary online), and:
> >
> > capable of being put into practice, done, or effected, esp with the available means or with reason or prudence: feasible. (The Macquarie Dictionary, 2nd Revised Edition, 1987)

'In *M38*, the Full Court discussed the meaning of the expression "reasonably practicable", and, in particular, the meaning of the word "reasonably" in that expression (at [65]–[69]). Subject to one qualification, we agree with their Honours' observations. The qualification concerns their statement at [66] that "[i]n the context of s 198(6) of the Act, practicability and reasonableness may, on occasion, operate in opposing senses." As the word "feasible" in both of the dictionary definitions suggests, at least some element of reasonableness is inherent in the notion of "practicable" ...

'That observation leads me to conclude that whether something has been done as soon as practicable involves considerations of feasibility and "reasonableness" (notwithstanding the absence of the word "reasonable" from s 20(2) of the ESOS Act).' *Ni v Minister for Immigration and Multicultural and Indigenous Affairs* [2004] FCA 1143 at [29], per Ryan J; BC200405716

Canada [Press release was required to be issued 'as soon as practicable' in respect of material change in securities issuer.] '... The words "as soon as practicable" in s 67 of the *Securities Act* do not mean "as soon as possible". They mean that the press release must be issued and filed with all reasonable dispatch having regard to all the circumstances, including, particularly, the nature and substance of the material change and the proper availability of management personnel to prepare the release and see that it is authorized, issued and filed.' *Pezim v British Columbia (Superintendent of Brokers)* (1992) 96 DLR (4th) 137 at 149, BC CA, per Lambert JA

AS SOON AS REASONABLY PRACTICABLE

[On an appeal where asylum-seekers' claims for support had been refused by the Secretary of State pursuant to the Nationality, Immigration and Asylum Act 2002 s 55, the question of the test to be applied in deciding whether an asylum-seeker had claimed asylum 'as soon as reasonably practicable' had to be determined.] '[37] In the light of the considerations discussed above, we would define the test of whether an asylum-seeker has claimed asylum "as soon as reasonably practicable" as follows:

> "On the premise that the purpose of coming to this country was to claim asylum and having regard both to the practical opportunity for claiming asylum and to the asylum seeker's personal circumstances, could the asylum seeker reasonably have been expected to claim asylum earlier than he or she did?"

R (on the application of Q and others) v Secretary of State for the Home Department [2003] EWCA Civ 364 at [37], [2003] 2 All ER 905, per Lord Phillips of Worth Matravers MR

Australia [Section 198(6) of the Migration Act 1958 (Cth) provides the removal of unlawful citizens 'as soon as reasonably practicable'.] 'The word "practicable" has been defined to mean:

> [c]apable of being put into practice, carried out in action, effected, accomplished or done; feasible. (*Oxford English Dictionary* online)

and:

> capable of being put into practice, done, or effected, esp with the available means or with reason or prudence: feasible. (The *Macquarie Dictionary*, 2nd Revised Edition, 1987)

'In *M38/2002 v Minister for Immigration and Multicultural and Indigenous Affairs* (2003) 199 ALR 290, the Full Court discussed the meaning of the expression "reasonably practicable", and, in particular, the meaning of the word "reasonably" in that expression (at [65]–[69]. Subject to one qualification, we agree with their Honours' observations. The qualification concerns their statement at [66] that "[i]n the context of subs 198(6) of the Act, practicability and reasonableness may, on occasion, operate in opposing senses." As the word "feasible" in both of the dictionary definitions suggests, at least some element of reasonableness is inherent in the notion of "practicable". We find it difficult to accept, for example, that removal would be regarded as practicable, even without the qualifier "reasonably", where no country was willing to admit the unlawful non-citizen.

'Their Honours cited, in support of their statement, *Uebergang v Australian Wheat Board* (1980) 145 CLR 266 at 306, per Stephen and Mason JJ. But Stephen and Mason JJ (at 304–306) were addressing the two words "practicable" (actually "practical", which they accepted had been used in the sense of "practicable") and "reasonable" in the expression "practical and reasonable manner of regulation" used by the *Privy Council in Commonwealth v Bank of New South Wales* (1949) 79 CLR 497 at 641 — a quite different context.

'Contrary to the statement in *M38* at [66], we do not think the word "reasonably" operates in an "opposing sense" to the word "practicable" in subs 198(6); although it is conceivable that it may, in particular circumstances, operate to extend the reasonableness notion, already inherent in the word "practicable", further along what may be described as "the continuum of reasonableness".' *NATB v Minister for Immigration and Multicultural and Indigenous Affairs* [2003] FCAFC 292 at [47]–[50] per Wilcox, Lindgren and Bennett JJ; BC200307783.

ASCERTAIN

See also DESIGNED TO ASCERTAIN

Ascertained goods

[For 41 Halsbury's Laws (4th edn) para 709 see now 41 Halsbury's Laws (4th edn) (Reissue) para 302.]

ASCERTAINED UNDER

Australia [Section 28(1) of IncomeTax Assessment Act 1936 (Cth) provides: 'Where a taxpayer carries on any business, the value, ascertained under this subdivision, of all trading stock on hand at the beginning of the year of income, and all trading stock on hand at the end of that year shall be taken into account in ascertaining whether or not the taxpayer has a taxable income.'] 'The word "under" appears in subs 28(1) and s 29. It is necessary to have regard to the context in order to identify the meaning of the word intended in a particular case. Dictionaries give the relevant definition as "in accordance with" (The *New Shorter Oxford English Dictionary* (1993), 16b; The *Macquarie Dictionary* (1988), 16). Meanings recognised as possibilities in the cases include "in accordance with" (*Gilbert v Western Australia* (1962) 107 CLR 494 at 516), "pursuant to" and "by virtue of" (*R v Clyne; ex parte Harrap* [1941] VLR 200 at 201 per O'Bryan J) and "by" (*R v Tkacz* (2001) 25 WAR 77 at [23]–[26] per Malcolm CJ). The word "under" admits of degrees of precision and exactness on the one hand, and of looseness and inexactness on the other. Since the many provisions of Subdivision B which follow subs 28(1) address the very matter of the manner of ascertainment of value of trading stock, and since s 28 is the general provision requiring the difference between the value of trading stock on hand at the beginning and at the end of a year of income to be taken into account, I think it quite clear that the words "ascertained under" in subs 28(1) mean "ascertained in accordance with". Accordingly, subs 28(1) required the value, ascertained in accordance with the succeeding provisions of Subdivision B, and not otherwise, of all trading stock on hand at the beginning of the year of income, and all trading stock on hand at the end of that year, to be taken into account in ascertaining whether or not the taxpayer had a taxable income.' *Energy Resources of Australia Ltd v FCT* 2003 ATC 4024, [2003] FCA 26 at [37] per Lindgren J; BC200300062

ASSAULT

' "Assault" in the context of this case, that is to say, using the word as a convenient abbreviation for assault and battery, is an act by which the defendant, intentionally or recklessly, applies unlawful force to the complainant. There are circumstances in which force may be applied to another lawfully. Taking a few examples. Firstly, where the victim consents, as in lawful sports, the application of force to another will, generally speaking, not be unlawful. Secondly, where the defendant is acting in self-defence the exercise of any necessary and reasonable force to protect himself from unlawful violence is not unlawful. Thirdly, by virtue of s 3 of the Criminal Law Act 1967, a person may use such force as is reasonable in the circumstances in the prevention of crime or in effecting or assisting in the lawful arrest of an offender or suspected offender or persons unlawfully at large. In each of those cases the defendant will be guilty if the jury are sure that first of all he applied force to the person of another, and secondly that he had the necessary mental element to constitute guilt. The mental element necessary to constitute guilt is the intent to apply unlawful force to the victim. We do not believe that the mental element can be substantiated by simply showing an intent to apply force and no more.' *R v Williams* [1987] 3 All ER 411 at 414, CA, per Lord Lane CJ

[For 11 Halsbury's Laws (4th edn) para 1210 see now 11(1) Halsbury's Laws (4th edn) (Reissue) para 488.]

[For 45 Halsbury's Laws (4th edn) para 1310 see now 45(2) Halsbury's Laws (4th edn) (Reissue) para 427.]

Common assault

[Section 39 of the Criminal Justice Act 1988 provides that common assault and battery are to be summary offences. Section 40 permits a summary offences to which that section applies to be included in an indictment if the charge is founded on the same facts or evidence as a count charging an indictable offence. A defendant was charged with the indictable offence of shoplifting and the summary offence of battery (by spitting at a policeman).] 'Common assault has a different meaning to the man, or even the lawyer, on the street than it might have to the legal pedant ...

'So, we have the narrow meaning, where there is an assault (or putting someone in fear) but no battery (the blow did not strike home), or the everyday meaning, where the word assault encompasses battery. In the courts, assault has

generally become synonymous with battery, that is
to say when the word "assault" was used it normally
meant the intentional use of unlawful force to
another's person without his consent … [Section 39]
emphasises the distinction between common assault
on the one hand and battery on the other hand, and
seemingly distinguishes assault from battery …

'Clearly, the spitting incident was founded on
the same facts or evidence as the count charging
the indictable offence. But the question is whether
the spitting was a summary offence "to which this
section applies". Such offences are listed in
sub-s (3), and the only arguably applicable one is
under "(a) common assault". So we have the
position that s 39 separates the offences of common
assault and battery, and s 40 only applies to common
assault.

'The judge put the position in this way:

"The question there arises whether Parliament
could have intended to have used assault and
battery as separate words in s 39 but in s 40 to
have used assault to embrace battery."

'That is to have used the narrow definition in s 39
and to have used the wider definition in s 40. At
this point angels prepare to dance on needles and
legal pedants sharpen their quill pens.

'If common assault means the same in s 40 as it
clearly means in s 39, then it has the narrow
meaning of the mere apprehension of violence, and
would not embrace battery or the application of
force. If that is right, the appellant succeeds. But
there is no conceivable reason why a blow or a spit
that missed its target could be properly tried on
this indictment, while a blow or spit that connected
could not, as counsel for the appellant concedes.
His point is clear and short. The obvious
presumption is that the words 'common assault'
mean the same in s 39 as they do in s 40, even
though he cannot suggest any reason why in sense
that should be so …

'The judge … gave the word "common assault"
in s 40 the wide meaning, ie he made sense of the
matter, he gave it the meaning which gave it its
most logical force, saying that he was sure that that
was the intention of Parliament.

'In our judgment the judge was right in his
approach. Where the narrow meaning of the phrase
"common assault" makes no sense in its context in
s 40 and cannot possibly reflect any rational policy,
it is entirely permissible as a matter of construction,
in our view, to prefer the wider meaning of the
same phrase, which makes good sense and reflects
a rational policy.' *R v Lynsey* [1995] 3 All ER 654
at 655, 656, 657–658, CA, per Henry LJ

ASSESSABLE

New Zealand 'In the case of a business I think that
ss 9 and 10 of the [Income Tax] Act [1976] and the
prescribed forms envisage a return showing how
the claimed result for the year, whether profit or
loss, is arrived at. In other words, a return of all the
assessable income means a return showing whether
or not the business has assessable income for the
year and how the result is calculated.' *Inland
Revenue Commissioner v Grover* [1987] 2 NZLR
736 at 740, CA, per Cooke P

New Zealand 'Australian authorities clearly
establish that the words "the assessable income"
and "such income" refer to assessable income
generally of the taxpayer and not to the assessable
income of a particular accounting period. In short,
an expenditure may precede or succeed related
income so long as, applying the general tests under
the respective limbs, there is a sufficient nexus
between expenditure and income earning activity.'
Eggers v Inland Revenue Commissioner [1988] 2
NZLR 365 at 374, CA, per cur

ASSESSED

Canada 'The appellant is, in fact, liable to pay the
realty taxes on the property but, on the evidence,
this liability is owed to the landlord, not to the
Township. The liability arises not by virtue of
either the *Municipal Act* or the *Assessment Act*,
RSO 1990, c A.31, but by virtue of the lease.

'The appellant relies upon s 17(1) of the
Assessment Act. It reads as follows:

17(1) Subject to section 18, land shall be
assessed against the owner thereof and against
the tenant to the extent of the assessed value
of the portion of the land occupied by the
tenant.

'Part of the difficulty here is with the use of the
word "assessed" which has at least two meanings,
namely to evaluate and to tax. "The word
'assessment' simply means valuation for property
taxes." J Walker and J Grad, *Ontario Property Tax
Assessment Handbook* (Aurora, Ont: Canada Law
Book, 1993) at p 1.

'At p 12, Walker and Grad say:

An owner-occupied commercial or industrial
property will receive two notices — one indicating the owner's realty portion of the property and the other indicates the business portion. *A tenant of a property will only receive a*

"tenant notice" showing the business assess-ment. The main notice including the realty portion is received by the owner. [Emphasis added.]'

Grey-Bruce Snowmobile Trails Inc v Morris (1997) 151 DLR (4th) 645 at 651, Ont CA, per Austin JA

ASSESSMENT

Australia 'That the process of assessment is one which must produce a definitive liability in a fixed and certain sum, with the corollary that if it does not the process has not been concluded, emerges from numerous statements to that effect by members of the High Court ... In [*FJ Bloemen Pty Ltd v FCT* (1981) 147 CLR 360; 35 ALR 104], Mason and Wilson JJ spoke of the process of ascertainment, that is to say the process of assessment, as involving the rendering certain of the amounts of taxable income and tax payable thereon: see at CLR 372... In *FCT v Prestige Motors Pty Ltd* (1994) 181 CLR 1 123 ALR 306 the joint judgment of Mason CJ, Brennan, Deane, Gaudron and McHugh JJ (at CLR 13) cites *Batagol* as determining that service of the notice of assessment *"fixes* the ascertainment of the amount of the taxable income and the amount of the tax payable by the taxpayer" (emphasis added).' *Federal Commissioner of Taxation v Stokes* (1996) 141 ALR 653 at 663–664, per cur

New Zealand 'To constitute an "assessment" under the section [of a taxing Act] it must be a determination of an amount on which tax is payable and of the amount of that tax. It presupposes that an amount of tax is payable. If there is no taxable income and so no tax payable, the determination is not an assessment even though the Commissioner made income and deduction calculations in arriving at that determination.' *Inland Revenue Commissioner v Lloyds Bank Export Finance Ltd* [1990] 2 NZLR 154 at 157, CA, per cur

New Zealand [Sections 19(1), 21, 23, 25, 26, 27, 29, 32(1) and 33 (111) of the Income Tax Act 1976.] 'An assessment is the quantification by the Commissioner of the statutorily imposed liability of the particular taxpayer to tax for the year in question. The making of an assessment including an amended assessment requires the exercise of judgment on the part of the Commissioner in quantifying that liability on the information then in the Commissioner's possession. It involves the "ascertainment" of the taxable income and of the resulting tax liability just as it does under the

Australian definition of "assessment" which uses the expression ascertainment.

'... to constitute an assessment for income tax purposes the decision of the Commissioner must be definitive as to the liabilty of the taxpayer at the time it is made and final subject only to challenge through the objection process.' *Commissioner of Inland Revenue v Canterbury Frozen Meat Co Ltd* [1994] 2 NZLR 681 at 690, CA, per Richardson J

New Zealand [Income Tax Act 1976] (see *Words and Phrases legally defined* (1995 supplement)) *Golden Bay Cement Co Ltd v Commissioner of Inland Revenue* [1995] 3 NZLR 475 at 483, per Fisher J

ASSET

Australia 'From the viewpoint of the proprietors of a business and subsequent purchasers, goodwill is an asset of the business because it is the valuable right or privilege to use the other assets of the business as a business to produce income.' *Federal Commissioner of Taxation v Murry* (1998) 193 CLR 605 at 615; 155 ALR 67 at 73; 72 ALJR 1065; 98 ATC 4585; BC9802402, per Gaudron, McHugh, Gummow and Hayne JJ

New Zealand [Rule 621(2) of the High Court Rules provides that

'...

(2) Such a party may apply to the Court for an order that the other party or, if the party is a corporation, an officer thereof, do attend before the Court, or any person whom the Court may appoint, and be orally examined as to his income and expenditure, his assets and liabilities, and generally as to his means for satisfying the judgment, or, if judgment has not been obtained, as to such matters as are relevant to the issue of a charging order.'] '[8] The principal purpose of this rule is to enable a plaintiff or judgment creditor to conduct an oral examination of a defendant or judgment debtor as to that party's means for satisfying the judgment which is sought or has been obtained. The rule focuses specifically on the judgment debtor's income, expenditure, assets and liabilities. The words "and generally as to his means for satisfying the judgment" are directed at any other "means" with which the judgment debtor may be able to satisfy the judgment. They signal a broad and non–technical approach to the concept of assets. The word "means" is not, however, wholly unconstrained in its reach.

...

'[19] It may perhaps be helpful, particularly to the Muollos, if we add that in the case of a disputed document R 621(3) involves two straightforward steps. The first is to determine whether the disputed document is relevant to the judgment debtor's means for satisfying the judgment. The expressions "assets" and "means" denote some legally recognised species of property belonging to the judgment debtor and able to be used in whole or in part to satisfy the judgment whether immediately or at some future time: as to that latter aspect see *McCormack v National Australia Bank Ltd* (1992) 106 ALR 647 at p 649. The second step is to determine whether the disputed document is within the judgment debtor's possession or power. A negative answer at either step means that an order to produce cannot be made.' *Hunt v Mullo* [2003] 2 NZLR 322

ASSETS

[The Income and Corporation Taxes Act 1970 is largely repealed. The definition is now to be found in the Income and Corporation Taxes Act 1988, s 779(12).]

[For 2 Halsbury's Laws (4th edn) paras 637–639 see now 7(1) Halsbury's Laws (4th edn) (2004 Reissue) paras 521, 661.]

Canada [Section 56(4)(a) of the Family Law Act authorizes the court to set aside a domestic contract for failure to disclose to the other significant assets or significant debts or other liabilities existing when the domestic contract was made.] 'I have no doubt that the word "assets" when used in the context of this section is intended to include "income" and I so hold.' *Underwood v Underwood* (1994) 113 DLR (4th) 571 at 575, Ont Gen Div, per Brockenshire J

ASSIGNMENT

[For 9 Halsbury's Laws (4th edn) para 336 see now 9(1) Halsbury's Laws (4th edn) (Reissue) para 754 note 3.]

ASSISTANCE

New Zealand [New Zealand Bill of Rights Act 1990, s 24 (g): right to free assistance of an interpreter.] 'Given that the right to an interpreter is grounded in notions of fairness, and given the wording of s 24(g), there seems no justification for limiting the right to assistance to the trial itself, nor for fine distinctions to be drawn between oral and written translations.

'Equally, however, the fact that there is the ability to order written translations does not of itself mean that every accused has the right to have all documents translated at any time. As the Judge noted in *Mosquera* (at 174): "It is up to the trial court to decide on the extent and nature of translation services needed by the defendant".

'The right to the assistance of an interpreter is a flexible one which will depend on the circumstance. This is as illustrated by the statute's use of the somewhat protean term "assistance".' *Alwen Industries Ltd v Collector of Customs* [1996] 3 NZLR 226 at 232, per Robertson J

ASSOCIATED OPERATIONS

[The Income and Corporation Taxes Act 1970 has been repealed. The definition is re-enacted in the Income and Corporation Taxes Act 1988, s 742(1).]

ASSOCIATED WORK

Australia ['Home building work' is defined in s 3(1) of the Home Building Contracts Act 1991 (WA) as including constructing or carrying out any 'associated work' in connection with constructing or re-constructing a dwelling, placing a dwelling on land or altering, improving or repairing a dwelling. 'Associated work' is further defined as including site works, swimming pools, spas, pergolas, carports, garages, sheds, fencing, retaining walls, paving, driveways, landscaping and other like works.] '... where a term such as "associated work" is defined so that it "includes" certain specified forms of work such as swimming pools and carports, the list should not be regarded as exhaustive. One is entitled to give proper weight to the ordinary meaning of the words, that is to say, work "associated" with the construction of a dwelling ...

'According to the *Concise Oxford Dictionary*, the verb to "associate" means to join or to connect as an idea or to combine for a common purpose ... the installation of a floor can be regarded as something that enhances or improves the utility of a house. Looked at in that light, it seems to follow that flooring of a reasonably permanent kind that is measured and made up to fit specific areas in a particular dwelling, such as the flooring in the present case, can properly be regarded as a form of work that is connected to or combined with other work in order to complete the dwelling. I therefore consider that the respondent in the present case was carrying out associated work in connection with the constructing of the subject dwelling.' *Lilley v Lindsay-Smith* BC200102802; [2001] WASCA 168 at [46], [47], per Hasluck J

ASSOCIATION

[In a passing off action by the British Diabetic Association against the Diabetic Society Ltd, it was held inter alia that] '... the crucial issue is whether the single word "society" is sufficiently differentiated from "association"... [T]he two crucial words in this case are very similar in derivation and meaning, and not wholly dissimilar in form. There may be background circumstances in which the small difference between the two words might be sufficient—it is, as the authorities emphasise, a question of fact to be decided in all the circumstances of the particular case—but in the end I have reached the clear conclusion that it is not a sufficient differentiation in this case. For the society to continue to use its existing name would in my judgment be deception, even if unintended, calculated to damage the association's reputation and goodwill.' *British Diabetic Association v Diabetic Society Ltd* [1995] 4 All ER 812 at 831 per Robert Walker J

AT

[The Road Traffic Act 1972 has been repealed. See now the Road Traffic Act 1988, s 9.]

New Zealand 'The proper interpretation of s 198 [of the Crimes Act 1961] requires proof of discharge of a firearm at a person, meaning intending to shoot at that person and not merely recklessly discharging the weapon in a direction which happened to be the direction of the person who was injured.' *R v Pekepo* [1989] 2 NZLR 229 at 232, per Hillyer J

AT AND FROM

[For 25 Halsbury's Laws (4th edn) para 57 see now 25 Halsbury's Laws (4th edn) (2003 Reissue) para 312.]

AT ANY TIME

[Housing Grants, Construction and Regeneration Act 1996, s 108.] '[34]–[35] Mr Ashton submits that it was "an abuse of process" for MJ to start adjudication proceedings so long after it purported on 29 November 2002 to accept a repudiation of the contract by SE. Section 108(1) of the 1996 Act confers the right to refer a dispute arising under the contract for adjudication. Subsection (2) provides that the contract shall "enable a party to give notice *at any time* of his intention to refer a dispute to adjudication" (my emphasis).

'[36] He says that the phrase "at any time" cannot be read literally. Thus, for example, a party cannot refer a dispute to adjudication after the expiry of the relevant limitation period. There is nothing in the 1996 Act, he submits, which indicates what Parliament meant by the words "at any time"...

...

'[38] I cannot accept these submissions. The phrase "at any time" means exactly what it says. It would have been possible to restrict the time within which an adjudication could be commenced, say, to a period by reference to the date when work was completed or the contract terminated. But this was not done. It is clear from Hansard that the question of the time for referring a dispute to adjudication was carefully considered, and that it was decided not to provide any time limit for the reasons given by Lord Lucas. Those reasons were entirely rational.

'[39] There is, therefore, no time limit. There may be circumstances as a result of which a party loses the right to refer a dispute to adjudication: the right may have been waived or the subject of an estoppel. But subject to considerations of this kind, there is nothing to prevent a party from referring a dispute to adjudication at any time, even after the expiry of the relevant limitation period. Similarly, there is nothing to stop a party from issuing court proceedings after the expiry of the relevant limitation period. Just as a party who takes that course in court proceedings runs the risk that, if the limitation defence is pleaded, the claim will fail (and indeed may be struck out), so a party who takes that course in an adjudication runs the risk that, if the limitation defence is taken, the adjudicator will make an award in favour of the respondent.' *Connex South Eastern Ltd v MJ Building Services Group plc* [2005] EWCA Civ 193, [2005] 2 All ER 870 at [34]–[36], [38]–[39], per Dyson LJ

AT ARM'S LENGTH

Australia [Section 160ZH(9)(c) of the Income Tax Assessment Act 1936 (Cth) provides that for the purposes of the application of subs (1), (2) or (3) in determining the cost base, the indexed cost base or the reduced cost base to a taxpayer of an asset, if the consideration paid by the taxpayer is less than the market value of the asset at the time of the acquisition, and the taxpayer and the person from whom the taxpayer acquire the asset were not dealing with each other 'at arm's length', in connection with the acquisition, the taxpayer shall be deemed to have paid an amount equal to the market value of the asset at the time of the acquisition.] 'Whatever the meaning of the expression may be in equity (see *Australian Trade Commission v WA Meat Exports Pty Ltd* (1987) 75 ALR 287 at 291; *Re Hains* (*dec'd*); *Barnsdale v FCT* (1988) 81 ALR 173; 88 ATC 4565 at 4567–8) for the purpose of s 160ZH(9) of the Act the term "at arm's length" means, at least, that the parties to a transaction have acted severally and independently in forming their bargain. Whether parties not at arm's length have dealt with each other at arm's length will be a matter of fact. As Hill J stated in *Trustee for the Estate of the Late A W Furse No 5 Will Trust v FCT* 91 ATC 4007 at 4015, determination of the manner in which parties not at arm's length have dealt with each other requires "an assessment whether in respect of that dealing they dealt with each other as arm's length parties would normally do, so that the outcome of their dealing is a matter of real bargaining".' *Granby Pty Ltd v Federal Commissioner of Taxation* (1995) 129 ALR 503 at 506–507, per Lee J

AT LAW

Australia [Section 44(1) of the District Court Act 1973 (NSW) confers jurisdiction on the District Court in any personal action 'at law' where the amount claimed does not exceed a specified amount.] '… I see no reason for reading the words "at law" in s 44(1) of the District Court Act in a particular sense in which they were sometimes used in the Courts of Westminster immediately before the commencement of the Supreme Court of Judicature Act 1873 (UK). The present claims are founded upon a statute of the Victorian Parliament creating rights enforceable against persons residing in New South Wales, the enforcement of which, if the claims are upheld, will be expressed by a money judgment. They are not claims of an equitable kind, or claims in rem. This seems to me to be quite sufficient for them to be accurately regarded today as personal actions at law.' *Vale v TMH Haulage Pty Ltd* (1993) 31 NSWLR 702 at 707–708, per Priestley JA

AT THE TIME

[The Road Traffic Act 1972 has been repealed; cf now the Road Traffic Act 1988, s 7(3)(a).]

ATROCIOUS

Canada '[23] That being said, I note that in its decision, the Board qualified the treatment suffered by Mr. Suleiman and his family as "deplorable". In *The Canadian Oxford Dictionary*, Toronto: Oxford University Press Canada, 2001, the words "deplorable" and "deplore" have the following meanings:

> **deplorable**: … **1** – exceedingly bad
>
> **deplore**: … **2** – be scandalized by; find exceedingly bad

'[24] On the other hand, in the same dictionary, the words "appalling", "atrocious" and "atrocity" are defined as follows:

> **appalling**: … **1** – shocking, unpleasant; bad
>
> **atrocious**: 1 – very bad or unpleasant … 2 – extremely savage or wicked
>
> **atrocity**: 1 – an extremely wicked or cruel act, esp. one involving physical violence or injury. 2 – extreme wickedness. 3 – something that evokes outrage or disgust

'[25] The Board has saved the reader shocking details of Mr. Suleiman and family's sad story. Be that as it may, it seems to me that if the treatment suffered by Mr. Suleiman and his family, was "deplorable", that is "exceedingly bad", I fail to see then why it would not be "appalling" or "atrocious". Here, the Board accepted that Mr. Suleiman was beaten by the police with canes which, in itself, is certainly a cruel treatment. Luckily, Mr. Suleiman was not killed by the police as was his cousin Mwalim in 2001. Surely, if the treatment suffered by Mr. Suleiman and his family was "deplorable", the Board should state, in the circumstances of the present case, why the acts committed cannot be considered "compelling reasons". The mere fact that such maltreatment "was, lamentably, not unusual for persons running afoul of security forces in Tanzania at the time" does not excuse the gravity of the past persecution which in this case is still fairly recent and has apparently indelibly marked the mental state of Mr. Suleiman. Moreover, the generalized character of the past persecution in Tanzania should not serve as a bar to the application of the "compelling reasons" exception.' *Suleiman v Canada (Minister of Citizenship & Immigration)* [2005] 2 FCR 26 at [23]–[25], [2004] FCJ No 1354 (Fed Ct), per Martineau J

ATTACH

Australia [In the context of attaching a warning statement to a contract.] 'Under its primary meaning, you "attach" one document to another by "fastening, affixing, joining or connecting" (Macquarie Dictionary) the two together. The related meaning offered in the Shorter Oxford English Dictionary is "to tack on; to fasten or join (to) by tacking, tying, sticking etc". As Muir J observed, this would require "some form of physical joinder or incorporation".' *MNM Developments P/L v Gerrard* [2005] QCA 230 at [13], per de Jersey CJ; BC200504347

Canada [Pension plan benefits were not subject to attachment.] '... "attachment" and "set-off" are distinct legal concepts. As I understand it, "attachment" refers to an attachment under legal process ...

'I respectfully agree with the motions judge that the word "attached" in s 65(1) of the *Canada Pension Plan* signifies something that is given to or to be exercised by a third party rather than by the Crown.' *Mintzer v Canada* (1995) 131 DLR (4th) 746 at 756, Fed CA, per Stone JA

ATTACHMENT

Australia 'There is no reason to think that s 118 [of the Bankruptcy Act 1966 (Cth)] uses the word "attachment" in any sense different from that in which it was used in the earlier legislation in England and Australia. If it is not used as a term of art confined to attachments under garnishee orders, there is no reason why it should not be given its widest meaning as an English word with a long history in the law. In the Shorter Oxford English Dictionary (1980), the meaning of the word "attach", in a legal sense, is given as: "To place or take under the control of a court; to arrest or seize by authority of a writ of attachment: (a) a person; (b) property, goods."... In the Macquarie Dictionary, rev edn (1985), the legal meaning of "attach" is given as "to arrest (a person) or distrain (property) in payment of a debt by legal authority". This definition does not confine the requisite legal authority to a court order. It is clear that when the concept of attachment was taken over for the purposes of the Common Law Procedure Act 1854, which instituted the modern garnishee procedure, the word "attachment" had an established meaning in a variety of contexts, referring to a taking, of a person or goods or a debt, by compulsion of legal authority, which was normally that of a court, but was certainly not confined to the ordinary courts of the land. I do not think the association of the word "attachment" with garnishee proceedings in the established courts requires that the word, as used in s 118 of the Bankruptcy Act should be restricted to attachments of that kind. Generally, attachments are by court order, but the legal authority by which an attachment may be given effect may take more than one form. When the word was first used in bankruptcy legislation, the Parliament may well have anticipated that various means of attaching debts might be developed, and have deliberately used a wide word.' *Re Edelsten, Donnelly v Edelsten* (1988) 84 ALR 547 at 559–560, per Burchett J

ATTEMPT

[*Anderton v Ryan* was overruled by a later decision of the House of Lords, *R v Shivpuri*.] 'What turns what would otherwise, from the point of view of the criminal law, be an innocent act into a crime is the intent of the actor to commit an offence. I say "from the point of view of the criminal law" because the law of tort must surely here be quite irrelevant. A puts his hand into B's pocket. Whether or not there is anything in the pocket capable of being stolen, if A intends to steal his act is a criminal attempt; if he does not so intend his act is innocent. A plunges a knife into a bolster in a bed. To avoid the complication of an offence of criminal damage, assume it to be A's bolster. If A believes the bolster to be his enemy B and intends to kill him, his act is an attempt to murder B; if he knows the bolster is only a bolster, his act is innocent.' *R v Shivpuri* [1986] 2 All ER 334 at 344, HL, per Lord Bridge of Harwich

ATTENDANCE

Canada '[9] This appeal depends upon the meaning ascribed to the phrase "enrolled and in attendance as a full-time student" in the definition of "dependent son" in s. 2(1)(b)(*i*) of the Regulations [*Immigration Act*]. Existing jurisprudence on this issue is conflicting. Some cases hold that the Visa Officer is entitled to make a qualitative assessment in order to determine whether there has been full-time attendance at an educational institution as set out in the definition of "dependent son". Other cases hold that the assessment should only be a quantitative one, to be decided based solely on whether the dependent son was physically in full-time attendance at an educational institution. A short review of the prior decisions will illustrate the conflict that has arisen.

'[10] In *Khaira v. Canada (Minister of Citizenship and Immigration)*, [1996] F.C.J. No. 1468 (QL) [reported 35 Imm. L.R. (2d) 257], the Trial Division found that the concept of attendance in the definition of "dependent son" had both quantitative and qualitative elements. The Visa Officer's decision, which held that the student failed to qualify under both the quantitative and qualitative elements of the definition, was confirmed. The student had attended some 77 per cent of his classes and, therefore, was held not to have been a full-time student. The Visa Officer also found that the applicant fell short on the qualitative component in that, while he might very well have been physically in attendance at the classes, his answers to the Visa Officer's questions relating to the contents of the course of study were found to be entirely inadequate. This decision was followed in *Malkana v. Canada (Minister of Citizenship and Immigration)*, [1996] F.C.J. No. 1659 (QL) (T.D.) [reported 37 Imm. L.R. (2d) 288].

'[11] In *Chowdhury v. Canada (Minister of Citizenship and Immigration)*, [1999] F.C.J. No. 514 (QL) (T.D.) [summarized 87 A.C.W.S. (3d) 1014], the Court also appears to have concluded that there is a qualitative aspect contained within the definition of full-time attendance in an educational institution. The Visa Officer concluded that the student had not been in full-time attendance because the student provided no evidence of attendance; could not demonstrate any learning as a result of attendance; and, when he was asked why he had not learned anything, the student had stated that he "did not attend classes well".

'[12] In *Patel v. Canada (Minister of Citizenship and Immigration)*, [1998] F.C.J. No. 1423 (QL) (T.D.) [reported 155 F.T.R. 228], the Trial Division concluded that "if the record states that he or she is enrolled and is in full-time attendance, then that should suffice". The Court added, "Furthermore, given the broad range of academic subjects, in my opinion, it would be inappropriate to allow visa officers to assess the quality of an applicant's academic performance" [paras. 29, 30].

'[13] The learned Motions Judge in the present case followed the decision in *Patel* and specifically disagreed with there being a qualitative element to the "attendance".

'[14] In *Chen v. Canada (Minister of Citizenship and Immigration)*, [2000] F.C.J. No. 1552 (QL) (T.D.) [reported 9 Imm. L.R. (3d) 84], Sharlow J., as she then was, held:

[9] In my view, a visa officer must consider the credibility of an applicant who claims to be enrolled and in attendance as a full-time student. A failure on the part of an applicant to learn the subject matter of a course of studies may be the result of an intellectual failing or difficult personal circumstances. Such factors would not, in my view, support the inference that the applicant is not in attendance as a full-time student. But a failure to learn may also be an indication that the applicant is not being truthful in claiming to be in attendance as a full-time student, and in this regard I accept the suggestion in *Khaira* and *Malkana* that "attendance" necessarily implies both physical and mental presence.

'[15] In *Dhami v. Canada (Minister of Citizenship and Immigration)*, [2001] F.C.J. No. 1160 (QL) (T.D.) [summarized 107 A.C.W.S. (3d) 122], Madam Justice Dawson stated the meaning of "attendance" as follows:

[40] From this jurisprudence I take two principles.

[41] First, where an applicant's credibility is in issue, and the applicant cannot describe the courses taken or the program of study, or cannot demonstrate even a rudimentary knowledge of subjects which the applicant claims to have taken, it is open to a visa officer to conclude that the applicant has failed to establish to the visa officer's satisfaction that the applicant was truly in attendance at the program for which the applicant claims to have been enrolled in.

[42] Second, poor academic performance is by and in itself an insufficient basis upon which to conclude that an applicant was not in attendance as a full-time student. On the plain and ordinary meaning of the words "continuously enrolled and in attendance" there is no requirement for the applicant to demonstrate academic prowess or mastery of the subject matter.

[43] I conclude that because the regulatory definition speaks of both enrolment and attendance, a visa officer is obliged to look beyond the mere fact of registration in a program of study. The reference in the definition to "attendance" is, in my view, for the purpose of testing the reality of a claim to full-time student status. The visa officer must inquire whether an applicant is simply enrolled

on paper or whether an applicant is actually engaged in a *bona fide* manner in a program of study.

[44] When the case law of the Court is reviewed carefully, I find what was argued to be a conflict in the jurisprudence is more apparent than real. In no case has an applicant been required to be a good or a successful student. At the heart of the question certified by Gibson J. was whether a visa officer could look to an applicant's inability to describe what was said to have been taught in courses or evidence of poor physical attendance for the purpose of determining whether the applicant was "in attendance".'

Sandhu v Canada (2002), 211 DLR (4th) 567 at 572–73 (FCA), per Sexton JA

ATTEST

[For 50 Halsbury's Laws (4th edn) para 261 et seq see now 50 Halsbury's Laws (4th edn) (Reissue) para 312 et seq.]

ATTORNEY

[For 44 Halsbury's Laws (4th edn) para 1 see now 44(1) Halsbury's Laws (4th edn) (Reissue) para 1.]

Australia *'Butterworths Australian Legal Dictionary* gives as the primary meaning of "attorney": "a person appointed by another to represent or act in place of that person". *Black's Law Dictionary* is to the same effect: "in the most general sense this term denotes an agent or substitute …". In other words, "attorney" is a synonym for "agent".' *Re NRMA Insurance Ltd* (2000) 33 ACSR 595; BC200000493; [2000] NSWSC 82 at App B para 8, per Santow J

ATTORNMENT

[For 27 Halsbury's Laws (4th edn) para 3 see now 27(1) Halsbury's Laws (4th edn) (Reissue) para 3.]

ATTRIBUTABLE TO *SEE* AROSE OUT OF OR WAS ATTRIBUTABLE TO

AUCTION

[For 2 Halsbury's Laws (4th edn) para 701 see now 2(3) Halsbury's Laws (4th edn) (Reissue) para 201.]

Australia 'Counsel for the plaintiff provided a number of dictionary and text definitions of "auction" which I set out:

a. Oxford English Dictionary: This notes the derivation of auction from the Latin to increase and gives the first meaning as "The action of increasing, growth". The second and more usual meaning attributed is Auction – a public sale in which each bidder offers an increase upon the price offered by the preceding, the article put up being sold to the highest bidder.

b. The Shorter Oxford English Dictionary: Auction – A (usually public) sale in which articles are sold to or reserved for the highest bidder.

'To those can be added some definitions supplied by the defendant, namely,

a. Macquarie Dictionary: Auction – a public sale at which property or goods are sold to the highest bidder.

b. Websters International Dictionary: Auction – a public sale of property or goods to the highest bidder (as by successive increased bids).

c. Shorter Oxford Dictionary: Auction – a public sale in which each bidder offers more than the last previous bid, the article being put up being sold to the highest bidder.

'Halsbury's Laws of England, 4th ed, vol 2, para 901 says that an auction is "a manner of selling or letting property by bids, usually to the highest bidder by public competition" with bids extracted by the auctioneer under the excitement of open competition. There is then a note which states "However, there exist auctions where the lot goes to the highest bidder, but the element of open competition is lacking in that bidders are unaware of rival bids. Postal auctions provide an example. These are conducted in a manner similar to that of selling by tenders."

'I think it fair to say that the predominant idea of an auction as expressed in the foregoing references indicates a public sale where bidders have a chance to re-bid.

'There is an interesting discussion of the difference between a sale by tender and a sale by auction in the judgment of Lord Templeman in *Harvela Ltd v Royal Trust Co of Canada (CI) Ltd* [1986] 1 AC 207 at 230. There his Lordship said:

Where a vendor undertakes to sell to the highest bidder, the vendor may conduct the sale by auction or by fixed bidding. In an auction sale each bidder may adjust his bid by reference to rival bids. In an auction sale the purchaser pays more than any other bidder is prepared to pay to secure the property. The purchaser does not necessarily pay as much as the purchaser was prepared to pay to secure the property ... In a fixed bidding sale, a bidder may not adjust his bid. Each bidder specifies a fixed amount which he hopes will be sufficient, but not more than sufficient, to exceed any other bid. The purchaser in a fixed bidding sales does not necessarily pay as much as the purchaser was prepared to pay to secure the property. But any bidder who specifies less than his best price knowingly takes a risk of being outbid ... Where there are two bidders with ample resources, each determined to secure the property and to prevent the other bidder from acquiring the property, the stronger will prevail in the fixed bidding sale and may pay more than in an auction which is decided not by the strength of the stronger but by the weakness of the weaker of the two bidders. On the other hand an open auction provides the stimulus of perceived bidding and compels each bidder, except the purchaser, to bid up to his maximum. Thus auction sales and fixed bidding sales are liable to affect vendors and purchasers in different ways and to produce different results.

'I consider with respect that this passage expresses the generally held view of the difference between auction and tender.' *Tender Center Pty Ltd v Director-General, Department of Fair Trading* BC200101001; [2001] NSWSC 153 at [8]–[10], per Windeyer J

AUCTIONEER

[For 1 Halsbury's Laws (4th edn) para 713 see now 2(3) Halsbury's Laws (4th edn) (Reissue) para 201.]

AUDIT (TAX)

Australia 'The Commissioner is obviously not confined to the material contained in the returns of income, but may gather information from other sources. To conduct an "audit" of a taxpayer's affairs is one means of gathering such information. What is meant by "audit" in this context? The second and third meanings attributed to the noun "audit" in the Oxford English Dictionary, 1987 re-issue, are apt: "2. official examination of accounts

with verification by reference to witnesses and vouchers; 3. fig. a searching examination or solemn rendering of accounts; esp the Day of Judgment." Plainly the "audit", in either of these senses, of a taxpayer's books and records or of the books and records of third parties but with reference to the affairs of a taxpayer is for one "of the purposes of this Act" (s 263), provided that the audit is related to the ascertainment of the taxable income of, and the amount of tax payable by, the taxpayer.' *Industrial Equity Ltd v Deputy Commissioner of Taxation* (1989) 90 ALR 603 at 608–609, (1990) 170 CLR 649 at 660, per cur

AUNT

Australia [Section 6 of the Adoption of Children Act 1965 (NSW) defines 'relative' as meaning 'a grandparent, uncle or aunt of the child, whether the relationship is of the whole blood or half-blood or by affinity, and notwithstanding that the relationship depends upon the adoption of any person'.] ' "Aunt", according to the common usage of the term in our community, can sometimes include a female person who is one of a child's parents' longest and dearest friends. It can also include a person who is married to an uncle of the child. The question here is whether, within the definition of "relative", "aunt" includes a person who is a sister of the mother's current husband?

'The *Macquarie Dictionary* definition of "aunt" is "the sister of one's father or mother" or the "wife of one's uncle". The first of these definitions covers an aunt by consanguinity, the second an aunt by affinity or, as it is put in the *Shorter Oxford English Dictionary*, an "aunt-in-law".

'The word "affinity" is a relatively ancient word which has been given a definite signification ... The term "aunt by affinity" properly means "wife of an uncle by blood". I do not see any legislative intent to widen the term to include the situation of one's mother's husband's sister.

'Thus, in my view, a sister of one's mother's husband is not, in law, an "aunt".' *Re C and the Adoption of Children Act* (1992) 27 NSWLR 388 at 389–390, per Young J

AUSTRALIAN CONTENT

Australia [The Broadcasting Services Act 1992 (Cth), s 122 gives the Australian Broadcasting Authority power to determine standards for 'the Australian content of programs'.] 'The content of a program for broadcast may be difficult to define in a statute, for it has to do with the communication of sights and sounds that convey ideas and the classification of an idea as "Australian" is a rather elusive concept. But that is not to deny the reality of Australian ideas; they are identifiable by reference to the sights and sounds that depict or evoke a particular connection with Australia, its land, sea and sky, its people, its fauna and its flora. They include our national or regional symbols, our topography and environment, our history and culture, the achievements and failures of our people, our relations with other nations, peoples and cultures and the contemporary issues of particular relevance or interest to Australians ... There is neither historical nor textual foundation for the proposition that the term can be used to classify programs by reference to their provenance.' *Project Blue Sky Inc v Australian Broadcasting Authority* (1998) 153 ALR 490 at 499–500; [1998] HCA 28 at [22], [26]; BC9801389 at 11–12, per Brennan CJ

Australia 'The phrase "the Australian content of programs" in s 122 [of the Broadcasting Services Act 1992 (Cth)] is a flexible expression that includes, inter alia, matter that reflects Australian identity, character and culture. A program will contain Australian content if it shows aspects of life in Australia or the life, work, art, leisure or sporting activities of Australians or if its scenes are or appear to be set in Australia or if it focuses on social, economic or political issues concerning Australia or Australians. Given the history of the concept of Australian content as demonstrated by the provisions of [Television Program Standard] 14, a program must also be taken to contain Australian content if the participants, creators or producers of a program are Australian. Nothing in the notion of the Australian content of programs requires, however, that a standard made pursuant to s 122 must give preference to Australian programs. Nor does the phrase "the Australian content of programs" in s 122 require that such programs should be under Australian creative control.' *Project Blue Sky Inc v Australian Broadcasting Authority* (1998) 153 ALR 490 at 514; 72 ALJR 841; BC9801389, per McHugh, Gummow, Kirby and Hayne JJ

AUTHOR

[The Copyright Act 1956 has been repealed. See now s 9 of the Copyright, Designs and Patents Act 1988.]

[For 9 Halsbury's Laws (4th edn) para 858 et seq see now 9(2) Halsbury's Laws (4th edn) (Reissue) para 110 et seq.]

Joint author

[See now the similar definition in s 10 of the Copyright, Designs and Patents Act 1988.]

Of compilation

Of photograph

Of reprint

[The Copyright Act 1956 has been largely repealed by the Copyright, Designs and Patents Act 1988.]

AUTHORISE

Australia [Where it was submitted that an Act which 'authorised' the Premier to make an agreement did not require him to do so, but merely permitted that course] 'There is not much point in offering, as the Wik did, numerous cases where "authorise" has been held to mean no more than to "sanction, approve, and countenance" or "permit". Just as many cases could be found where the word included the notion that the "authorised" course was required. In the present context, the employment of the term "authorised" was appropriate to the relationship between the Parliament of Queensland and the Executive Government of the State.' *Wik Peoples v Queensland* (1996) 141 ALR 129 at 291; 71 ALJR 173, per Kirby J

Australia [In the context of intellectual property where instructions to an employee to act under the instructions of a third party resulted in acts infringing the copyright in the database of a domain name administrator.] 'The dictionary meanings of the word "authorise" which appears in s 36(1) of the Copyright Act include "give formal approval to; sanction, countenance" — Shorter Oxford English Dictionary, 5th Edition (2002). It was interpreted in that sense in *University of New South Wales v Moorhouse* (1975) 133 CLR 1 at 20–21 (Jacobs J, McTiernan ACJ agreeing) and at 12 (Gibbs J). Authorisation may be inferred. Indeed it may be inferred from indifference of a sufficient degree. In each case it is a question of fact — *Moorhouse* at 21. As Gummow J said of the *Moorhouse* decision in *WEA International Inc v Hanimex Corporation Ltd* (1987) 17 FCR 274 at 286, the construction there adopted:

> ... meant that express or formal permission or active conduct indicating approval was not essential to constitute an authorisation.

'It is necessary that the person said to authorise an infringement has the degree of control and power sufficient to prevent the infringement — *Australian Tape Manufacturers Assn Ltd v The Commonwealth* (1993) 176 CLR 480 at 498. But as Sackville J said in *Nationwide News Pty Ltd v Copyright Agency Ltd* (1996) 65 FCR 399 at 422 (Jenkinson and Burchett JJ agreeing):

> Nonetheless, a person does not authorise an infringement merely because he or she knows that another person might infringe the copyright and takes no step to prevent the infringement.

'In *Australasian Performing Right Assn Ltd v Jain* (1990) 26 FCR 53, musical works were performed publicly in an hotel owned by a company. The company's chief executive officer, who was also a director of it, did not involve himself in the day-to-day operations of the hotel. Bands were selected and performances arranged by an employed manager. No licence to perform copyrighted musical works was obtained from the Australian Performing Rights Assn. In subsequent proceedings the director was held, on appeal, to have authorised the infringement of copyright involved in unlicensed public performances of musical works in which copyright subsisted. The Full Court held that the question of authorisation by the director was one of fact and said at 61:

> The judgment of the members of the High Court in the *Moorhouse* case establishes that one of the meanings of the word "authorise" in the context in which it is here used is "countenance". It may be that not every act which amounts to the countenancing of something is an authorisation. Every case will depend upon its own facts. Matters of degree are involved. But the evidence in the present case reveals, in our opinion, a studied and deliberate course of action in which Mr Jain decided to ignore the appellant's rights and to allow a situation to develop and to continue in which he must have known that it was likely that the appellant's music would be played without any licence from it. It was within his power to control what was occurring be (sic) he did nothing at all. In those circumstances we have reached the conclusion that the appellant established that Mr Jain authorised the infringement of copyright in question contrary to s 36 of the Act.'

Nominet UK v Diverse Internet Pty Ltd [2004] FCA 1244 at [129], per French J; BC200406193

Printing and publishing

[The Copyright Act 1956 has been repealed; see now the Copyright, Designs and Patents Act 1988, s 16(2).]

AUTHORITIES

Canada '[9] The reference materials are not "authorities" in the classic sense. Generally, "authorities" are statutes, jurisprudence and other legal writings that set out or explain laws or legal principles. In oral argument, counsel for AstraZeneca acknowledged that the purpose for introducing the reference materials at this late date was to "shore up" or "nail down" what AstraZeneca asserts is a factual admission made by Dr. Sherman during cross-examination that the tablets will contain a sodium, potassium or aluminum salt. This can only mean that its real value is as evidence to prove a key fact relating to a controversial issue between the parties.' *AstraZeneca Canada Inc v Apotex Inc* [2003] FCJ No 1909, [2004] 2 FCR 364 (CA), per Malone JA

AUTHORITY OF A STATE

Australia '[A body] will be an "authority of a State" if its functions are "impressed with the stamp of government" or if it has been given by the State the power to direct or control the affairs of others on behalf of the State. The role and involvement of the executive, through the Governor in Council or the appropriate minister, is also a relevant factor.' *Stack v Brisbane City Council* (1995) 59 FCR 71 at 78; 131 ALR 333 at 339, per Cooper J

AUTREFOIS CONVICT

'The underlying rationale of autrefois convict, as explained by Blackburn J in *Wemyss v Hopkins* [(1875) LR 10 QB 378] is to prevent duplication of punishment. But if the plea can be supported by a finding of guilt alone, a defendant might escape punishment altogether. Where a defendant is tried before a judge and jury, both have their roles to play and together they constitute the court of trial. If, in any case following trial and conviction by the jury, the judge were to die before passing sentence, there would be no court seised of the case by which sentence could be passed. The defendant, it seems to their Lordships, would in those circumstances have to be rearraigned before another court and if he again pleaded not guilty would have to be retried. But it would be absurd that he should be able to plead the jury's verdict in the first trial as a bar to the second. In the case of autrefois acquit the position is, of course, different, because the jury's verdict of not guilty is a final adjudication and disposal of the case and the judge has no further function to perform.' *Richards v R* [1992] 4 All ER 807 at 813, PC, per Lord Bridge of Harwich

AVAILABLE

[*Rogers v Essex County Council* was reversed by the House of Lords sub nom *R v Rogers*, see below.] 'It is clear that the word "available" qualifies the word "route". The availability of the route cannot be determined by the mere study of a map. That it must be reasonably practicable for a child to walk along it to school does not, to my mind, admit of any argument. Of course, it must be free from obstructions or obstacles which would make its use impracticable. Dangers inherent in a particular route are factors that must be taken into account when considering its availability. A route which involved crossing a river by means of a footbridge would, other things being equal, qualify as an available route. However, if as a result, for example, of recent severe flooding, the bridge became unstable and unsafe to use, that route would cease to be available ... In my judgment a route to be "available" within the meaning of s 39(5) must be a route along which a child accompanied as necessary can walk and walk with reasonable safety to school. It does not fail to qualify as "available" because of dangers which would arise if the child is unaccompanied.' *R v Rogers* [1986] 3 All ER 321 at 326, HL, per Lord Ackner

AVERAGE

[For 43 Halsbury's Laws (4th edn) paras 736, 742 see now 43(2) Halsbury's Laws (4th edn) (Reissue) paras 1791–1793.]

General

[For 25 Halsbury's Laws (4th edn) para 249 see now 25 Halsbury's Laws (4th edn) (2003 Reissue) para 420.]

Particular

[For 25 Halsbury's Laws (4th edn) para 262 see now 25 Halsbury's Laws (4th edn) (2003 Reissue) para 433.]

AVOID

[*Congreve v Inland Revenue Commissioners* was overruled by *Vestey v Inland Revenue Commissioners* (*Nos 1 and 2*) [1979] 3 All ER 976, HL.]

AWARD *SEE* MAKE

B

BAD FAITH

Australia [Decisions of the Refugee Review Tribunal (RRT) made under s 474(1) of the Migration Act 1958 (Cth) are treated as 'final and conclusive'. In this case the RRT affirmed the rejection of a protection visa application under s 474(1). Read in conjunction with *R v Hickman; Ex parte Fox and Clinton* (1945) 70 CLR 598, the power conferred under s 474(1) is broadened such that decisions of the RRT that are made in good faith are treated as beyond review.] 'As with other areas of the law where wrongful intent is in issue, reckless indifference may be the equivalent of intent. But this is not to say that the test is objective. The inquiry is directed to the actual state of mind of the decision-maker. There is no such thing as deemed or constructive bad faith. It is the ultimate decision – in the case of the RRT, affirming the rejection of a protection visa application – which must be shown to have been taken in bad faith. Illogical factual findings or procedural blunders along the way will usually not be sufficient to base a finding of bad faith. Such defects can be equally explicable as the result of obtuseness, overwork, forgetfulness, irritability or other human failings not inconsistent with an honest attempt to discharge the decision-maker's duty.

'Questions of professional ethics arise. An allegation of bad faith, like an allegation of fraud, should not be advanced by an advocate unless there are proper grounds for doing so: *SCAS v Minister for Immigration and Multicultural and Indigenous Affairs* [2002] FCAFC 397 at [19], cf Federal Court Rules O 11 r 1B.

'Bad faith may manifest itself in the form of actual bias. Actual bias in this context is a state of mind so committed to a conclusion already formed as to be incapable of alteration, whatever evidence or argument may be presented. It is something more than a tendency of mind or predisposition: *Minister for Immigration and Multicultural Affairs v Jia* (2001) 205 CLR 507 at [71]–[72]. Apprehended bias, resting as it does on what may be observed objectively, as distinct from the actual state of mind of the decision-maker, is quite different. While it has been suggested that actual bias may occur subconsciously, that would not establish bad faith in the relevant sense for the purposes of s 474(1): *NAAV v Minister for Immigration and Multicultural and Indigenous Affairs* [2002] FCAFC 228 at [4], [113]–[115], [638] and [648].' *Minister for Immigration and Multicultural and Indigenous Affairs v SBAN* BC200207780; [2002] FCAFC 431 at [8]–[10], per Heerey and Kieffel JJ

BAIL

Australia 'The concept of bail evolved to give effect to the presumption of innocence and the right to liberty:

> "When the administration of justice was in its infancy, arrest meant imprisonment without preliminary inquiry till the sheriff held his tourn at least, and, in more serious cases, till the arrival of the justices, which might be delayed for years, and it was therefore a matter of the utmost importance to be able to obtain a provisional release from custody …
>
> "The sheriff was the local representative of the Crown, and in particular he was at the head of all the executive part of the administration of criminal justice. In that capacity he, as I have already shown, arrested and imprisoned suspected persons, and, if he thought proper, admitted them to bail. The discretionary power of the sheriff was ill defined, and led to great abuses, which were dealt with by the Statute of Westminster the First (3 Edw 1, c 12, AD 1275)." [Stephen J F, *A History of the Criminal Law of England*, London, Macmillan & Co, 1883, Vol 1, pp 233–4]

'More recently, bail has been defined as

> "[t]he right to be released from custody granted to a person charged with an offence, on the condition that he or she undertakes to

return to the court at some specified time, and any other conditions that the court may impose." [Nygh P, Butt P (eds), *Butterworths Australian Legal Dictionary*, Sydney, Butterworths, 1997]

'Bail is a mechanism by which the adverse consequences of delay before trial can be minimised. Where appropriate, it is important for accused persons to be released from custody. A grant of bail places the accused in the care of a surety, as distinct from the custody provided by a prison or the police [Donovan B, *The Law of Bail: Practice, Procedure and Principles*, Sydney, Legal Books, 1981].' *R v Collins* BC200200036; [2002] SASC 2 at [10], [11], per Gray J

BAILIWICK

[For 42 Halsbury's Laws (4th edn) para 1111 see now 42 Halsbury's Laws (4th edn) (Reissue) para 1111.]

BAILMENT

[For 2 Halsbury's Laws (4th edn) paras 1501–1502 see now 2 Halsbury's Laws (4th edn) (Reissue) paras 1801–1802.]

BAND *SEE ALSO* INDIAN BAND

Canada '[14] ... An Indian band is a creature of statute, the *Indian Act*. A "band" is defined in the *Indian Act*[1] as:

2. (1) ...
"band" means a body of Indians
(a) for whose use and benefit in common, lands, the legal title to which is vested in Her Majesty, have been set apart before, on or after September 4, 1951,
(b) for whose use and benefit in common, moneys are held by Her Majesty, or
(c) declared by the Governor in Council to be a band for the purposes of this Act;

'[15] The definition of "band" does not constitute an Indian band as a legal entity. Rather, I take it from the definition of "band", and other provisions of the *Indian Act*, that in relation to rights to an Indian reserve, a band is a distinct population of Indians for whose use and benefit, in common, a reserve has been set aside by the Crown. This interpretation was adopted by Macfarlane J.A. in *Oregon Jack Creek Indian Band v. Canadian*

National Railway Co. (1989), 56 D.L.R. (4th) 404 (B.C.C.A.), at pages 409–410:

The members of the band do not constitute a legal entity. The alleged wrong is not to a legal entity (the band) but to the members of the band who are entitled to the use and benefit of the land and the fisheries. For the action to be derivative the band would have to be regarded as a legal entity, like a corporation, and the members of the band would have to be regarded as akin to shareholders. In *Tijani v. Secretary Southern Nigeria*, [1921] 2 A.C. 399 (P.C.), Lord Haldane cautioned against construing aboriginal title in terms which are appropriate only to traditional legal concepts. I think that the same caution must be exercised in considering rights in respect of reserve lands and reserved fisheries.

'[16] However, it does not follow that because an Indian band is not a legal entity, rights accruing to the band are the rights of its members or their descendants in their individual capacities. The definition of "band" uses the term "in common" in relation to the interest that the members of the band have in the reserve. The term "in common" connotes a communal, as opposed to a private, interest in the reserve, by the members of the band. In other words, an individual member of a band has an interest in association with, but not independent of, the interest of the other members of the band.' *Blueberry River Indian Band v Canada* (*Department of Indian Affairs*) (2001) 201 DLR (4th) 35 at 44–45, FCA, per Rothstein JA

BANK—BANKING

[The Bankers' Books Evidence Act 1879, s 9, has been further amended by the Building Societies Act 1986, and the definition is now as follows.] In this Act the expression 'bank' and 'banker' mean—
(a) an institution authorised under the Banking Act 1987 or a municipal bank within the meaning of that Act;
(aa) a building society (within the meaning of the Building Societies Act 1986);
(b) ...;
(c) the National Savings Bank; and
(d) the Post Office, in the exercise of its powers to provide banking services.

(Bankers' Books Evidence Act 1879, s 9(1) (substituted by the Banking Act 1979, s 51(1), Sch 6 Pt I para 1, Pt II para 13; amended by the Trustee Savings Bank 1985, ss 4(3), 7(3), Sch 4, the Building Societies Act 1986, s 120, Sch 18 Pt I para 1, and the Banking Act 1987 s 108(1), Sch 6, para 1))

[For 3 Halsbury's Laws (4th edn) para 38 see now 3(1) Halsbury's Laws (4th edn) (Reissue) para 147.]

BARGAIN

New Zealand [Employment Relations Act 2000, s 32.] '[85] Ms Hornsby argued that the Court should interpret the word "bargain" in s 32(1)(d)(ii) to refer only to specific dealings between one bargaining party and the constituents of another, rather than as part of the definition of bargaining in s 5.

'[86] We do not accept that distinction. Section 5 states that generally the meanings of words apply throughout the 2000 Act unless the context otherwise requires. Section 32(1)(d)(ii) is to be read in the context of Part 5: Good Faith Bargaining for Collective Agreements. The introductory part of the section refers to the duty of good faith on a union and an employer bargaining for a collective agreement and the rest of the section includes frequent references to bargaining. The dictionary definition of "bargain" includes to "negotiate the terms and conditions of a transaction". In that sense "bargain" is a verb and in the context of the 2000 Act means being engaged in the process of bargaining.' *Christchurch City Council v Southern Local Government Officers Union Inc* (2006) 2 NZELR 547 at [85]–[86], per G L Colgan CJ, B S Travis and C M Shaw JJ

BARGAINS FOR ANY REWARD, DIRECTLY OR INDIRECTLY

New Zealand [Section 262 of the Crimes Act 1961 begins 'Every one is liable to imprisonment ... who corruptly takes or bargains for any reward, directly or indirectly ... '.] 'I do not consider that simply to accept an offer of a reward already made comes within the reasonable ambit of the expression "bargains for any reward, directly or indirectly". If someone were to make an unsolicited approach to the owner of stolen property and offer to return it in exchange for a reward then that may well be regarded as bargaining for a reward. Bargaining over the method of exchange rather than the reward itself does not seem to me to come within the intended compass of s 262 which speaks of bargaining *for* any reward.' *Broom v Police* [1994] 1 NZLR 680 at 688, per Tipping J.

BARONET

[For 35 Halsbury's Laws (4th edn) para 863 see now 35 Halsbury's Laws (4th edn) (Reissue) para 963.]

BARRATRY

[For 25 Halsbury's Laws (4th edn) para 165 see now 25 Halsbury's Laws (4th edn) (2003 Reissue) para 342.]

BASE FEE

[For 39 Halsbury's Laws (4th edn) para 449 see now 39(2) Halsbury's Laws (4th edn) (Reissue) para 134.]

BASED ON

Australia 'I am fortified in my view that the phrase "based on" in s 9(1) of the [Racial Discrimination Act 1975 (Cth)] should be construed as encompassing the broader, non-necessarily causative, relationship expressed in the phrase "by reference to" because the words "based on" are taken directly from the definition of "racial discrimination" which appears in Art 1.1 of the Convention, and not from any other anti-discrimination statute.' *Macedonian Teachers' Association of Victoria Inc v Human Rights and Equal Opportunity Commission* (1998) 160 ALR 489 at 509; BC9806928 at 28, per Weinberg J

Canada [Section 3(3) of the British Columbia *Limitations Act*, RSBC 1979, c 236, permits a person to bring an action based on misconduct of sexual nature without time limitation.] '... I am driven to the conclusion that the wording employed by the legislative draftsperson in s 3(3)(*k*) is broad enough to include the negligence action being advanced in this case. As the trial judge noted in her reasons, the phrase "based on" connotes something that serves as a foundation "or starting point and a main or important ingredient". The sexual misconduct here is a main ingredient of the cause of action in negligence, in that no action would lie for negligent hiring or supervision without that component. In this sense, it seems to me this action is fairly described as "based on" the employee's misconduct. We would be taking an unnecessarily narrow and technical view if we were to restrict the section only to causes of action *consisting of* sexual misconduct.' *P (J) v Sinclair* (1997) 148 DLR (4th) 472 at 479, BC CA, per Newbury JA

BATTERED WOMAN SYNDROME

Australia 'Dr Byrne said the [battered woman] syndrome comprised of a "collection of responses, thoughts, feelings and attitudes" which compelled the woman who was the subject of the syndrome meekly to comply with the batterer's wishes without giving any logical thought to her own rights. It entailed a belief on the part of the woman that she could never free herself from the enforced domination of the man, and an induced fear that, if she did not comply with the wishes of the man, it would only serve to worsen her plight. She thus becomes the subject of a "learnt helplessness" which drives her into submission, accompanied by a "learnt hopelessness" that, if she submits, matters will improve.' *Osland v R* (1998) 159 ALR 170 at 234; 73 ALJR 173; BC9806597, per Callinan J

BATTERY

[For 11 Halsbury's Laws (4th edn) para 1210 see now 11(1) Halsbury's Laws (4th edn) (Reissue) para 488.]

BECOMES A BANKRUPT

Australia [Section 120(1) of the Bankruptcy Act 1966 (Cth) provides that a settlement of property in certain circumstances is, if the settlor 'becomes a bankrupt' within two years after the date of settlement, void as against the trustee in the bankruptcy.] '*Florance v Andrew* (1985) 58 ALR 377 is authority of a Full Court of this court [Federal Court of Australia] for the proposition that the reference to the words "becomes a bankrupt" in s 120(1) of the Act in the form which it took at the relevant time (no material change has occurred in the wording of that provision so far as the present point under consideration is concerned) means the date when the sequestration order is made against the debtor's estate or the date when the debtor becomes bankrupt by virtue of the presentation of a debtor's petition; it does not mean the date of commencement of the bankruptcy.' *Corke v Corke* (1994) 121 ALR 320 at 325; 17 Fam LR 698 at 704, per Lockhart J

BED

[For 31 Halsbury's Laws (4th edn) para 12 see now 31 Halsbury's Laws (4th edn) (2003 Reissue) para 16.]

BEFORE TRIAL

New Zealand [The definitions of this phrase appearing in McGechan on Procedure at 3–565 and in Sim's Court Practice at 358 are referred to by Master Gambrill] *Goldsbro v Walker* [1994] 2 NZLR 191 at 194, per Master Gambrill.

BEHEST

Australia [Section 5(1) of the Administrative Decisions (Judicial Review) Act 1977 (Cth) allows a person aggrieved by a decision to which the Act applies to apply for judicial review on the ground, inter alia, that the making of the decision was an improper exercise of the power conferred. Under s 5(2) of the Act, an improper exercise of a power includes an exercise of a personal discretionary power at the direction, or behest, of another person.] 'In the context in which it appears in the Administrative Decisions (Judicial Review) Act, the word "behest" can not simply be a substitution for request. Both words are used against the background of the ordinary administrative law principle that, for a discretion to be valid it must be a real exercise of discretion by the decision-maker, not an acceptance by the decision-maker of a direction by some other person to whom the making of the decision has not been entrusted: cf *R v Anderson; Ex parte Ipec-Air Pty Ltd* (1965) 113 CLR 177 at 189, per Kitto J.' *Telstra Corporation Ltd v Kendall* (1995) 55 FCR 221 at 231–232, per cur

BELIEVE

Australia [Under s 151A(5) of the Workers Compensation Act 1987 (NSW), a person who has elected to claim permanent loss compensation in respect of an injury may revoke the election and commence proceedings in the court for the recovery of damages in respect of the injury if there has been a further deterioration in the person's medical condition that, had it existed at the time of the election, would have entitled the person to additional permanent loss compensation. The election may only be revoked though if at the time of the election, there was "no reasonable cause to believe" that the further deterioration would occur: s 151A(5)(c).] 'The word "believe" must be read in context. Obviously it means something more than having a "suspicion", entertaining a "speculation", or a "fear". The word should not be equated to a firm conviction. That might be a suitable meaning, perhaps, in the sense of a belief in a religious faith.

But that meaning would be liable, in the present context, to deprive para (c) of any real utility as one of the conditions which the applicant for revocation of an election must establish. Belief in that sense, concerning medical prognostications, would rarely if ever be attained. Nonetheless, in the ordinary meaning of the word "believe", it certainly connotes a greater sense of expectation than "think", which Handley JA proposed as a synonym. The word "think" appears but twenty-five words later in s 151A(5)(c) of the Act. Had it been Parliament's purpose to denote no more than "think", it could easily have said so. Instead, it used the word "believe". That is a word that sits higher in the scale of human expectations.

'By inference, Parliament used the word "believe" to indicate recognition of the fact that persons required to make elections of the kind with which s 151A(5) of the Act is concerned will normally have access to medical reports stating prognoses. Of their nature, such reports cannot usually be certain about their predictions. A fear, an apprehension and even a suspicion of the possibility that deterioration in a medical condition would occur will therefore not, without more, establish that there was a reasonable cause to *believe* that such deterioration would happen.' *New South Wales v Taylor* (2001) 178 ALR 32; BC200100871; [2001] HCA 15 at [61]–[62], per Kirby J

BELONGING TO

[Capital allowances under the Finance Act 1971 s 44(1) were granted in respect of machinery and plant if inter alia the machinery or plant "belongs, or has belonged" to the claimant. The question arose whether such capital allowance could be claimed by a taxpayer carrying on the business of finance leasing, ie the purchase of plant and the leasing to end-users of the plant purchased.] 'The equipment in these cases was attached to the land in such a manner that, to all outward appearance, they formed part of the land and were intended so to do. Such fixtures are, in law, owned by the owner of the land. It was suggested in argument that this result did not follow if it could be demonstrated that, as between the owner of the land and the person fixing the chattel to it, there was a common intention that the chattel should not belong to the owner of the land.

'... The terms expressly or implicitly agreed between the fixer of the chattel and the owner of the land cannot affect the determination of the question whether, in law, the chattel has become a

fixture and therefore in law belongs to the owner of the soil (see *Hobson v Gorringe* [1897] 1 Ch 182 at 192–193). The terms of such agreement will regulate the contractual rights to sever the chattel from the land as between the parties to that contract and, where an equitable right is conferred by the contract, as against certain third parties. But such agreement cannot prevent the chattel, once fixed, becoming in law part of the land and as such owned by the owner of the land so long as it remains fixed.'

'... I therefore reach the conclusion that for the purposes of s 44 property belongs to a person if he is, in law or in equity, the absolute owner of it. Such a construction reflects the obvious, prima facie, meaning of the word: what belongs to me is what I own. It produces a coherent and easily applicable formula and, save in relation to fixtures, avoids anomalous results.' *Melluish v BMI (No 3) Ltd* [1995] 4 All ER 453 at 460–461, 464, HL, per Lord Browne-Wilkinson

BENEFICE

[The Reorganisation Areas Measure 1943 has been repealed.]

BENEFICIAL ACTIVITIES

Australia [Section 13(1A) of the Australian Citizenship Act 1948 (Cth) refers to a person engaged in activities outside Australia that are 'beneficial' to the interests of Australia when considering an application for Australian citizenship when the person is not present in Australia.] 'It seems to me that the term "activities beneficial to the interests of Australia" means something in the nature of activities which provide some advantage to Australia , whether commercial or otherwise. The concept necessarily connotes some public interest of Australia , even if of a general or non-specific character, and means more than the private interests, of the respondent. The section requires some objective benefit to Australia.' *Minister for Immigration, Local Government and Ethnic Affairs v Roberts* (1993) 41 FCR 82 at 87, per Einfeld J

BENEFICIAL OWNER

Canada 'As I see it, the expression "beneficial owner" serves to include someone who stands behind the registered owner in situations where the latter functions merely as an intermediary, like a trustee, a legal representative or an agent. The

French corresponding expression "*veritable proprietaire*" (as found in the 1985 revision, RSC, 1985, c F-7) leaves no doubt to that effect.' *Mount Royal Walsh Inc v The Jensen Star* [1990] 1 FCR 199 at 209–210, FCA, per Marceau JA

BENEFICIAL OWNERSHIP

Australia '[24] As the learned Primary Judge pointed out in his careful judgment, the expression "beneficial ownership" appears to have been first used in the Australian income tax context in s 31A of the Income Tax Assessment Act 1922–1934 (Cth), which was concerned with the distinction between public and private companies relevant to provisions which were concerned to ensure that private companies made what were referred to as "sufficient distributions." The successor to s 31A was s 103(2)(b) of the 1936 Act, which treated as a subsidiary of a public company (and thus itself a public company) a company where, inter alia, beneficial ownership of the shares was to be found in the hands of one company or more than one company, and where none of such companies was a public company (cf the later s 103A(4) which replaced s 103(2)(b) and retained the test that the shares be "beneficially owned").

...

'[30] The Court of Appeal in *Wood Preservation Ltd v Prior* [1969] 1 WLR 1077 also considered, this time in the context of a provision which permitted a taxpayer in certain circumstances to take advantage of losses incurred by another taxpayer, the meaning of "beneficial ownership." The case raised the question whether the vendor under a conditional contract for the sale of shares ceased to have the beneficial ownership of the shares. If it did, then the losses were unavailable to the vendor as a deduction. It was held that the vendor on execution of the contract ceased to have the beneficial ownership of the property, even though the purchaser, as a result of the condition, did not itself become the beneficial owner of it. Lord Donovan accepted that a person could cease to be the beneficial owner of property notwithstanding that no other person had become the beneficial owner of it. In the context, "beneficial ownership" involved the ability to appropriate to oneself the benefits of ownership (per Lord Donovan at 1096) or the right to deal with the property as your own (per Harman LJ at 1097).

...

'[31] Later the question of the meaning of "beneficial ownership," again in an income tax context, came to be considered by the House of

Lords in *Ayerst (Inspector of Taxes) v C & K (Construction) Ltd* [1976] AC 167 ('*Ayerst*'). The question was whether a company, which owned 99 out of 100 shares in another company, still beneficially owned the shares in the other company after a winding up order was made against it. It was held that the effect of the winding up order was to divest the company of the beneficial ownership of the shares which it held, and that the company in liquidation could no longer use the shares for its own benefit. In consequence the taxpayer (the subsidiary) was not entitled to use the losses of its parent in liquidation. Lord Diplock, with whom Viscount Dilhorne, Lord Kilbrandon and Lord Edmund-Davies agreed, while recognising the difference between the case of a trustee in bankruptcy on the one hand and the company in liquidation on the other, noted that the company in liquidation, while retaining the legal ownership of its property, was deprived of the possibility of enjoying the fruits of that property or disposing of it for its own benefit. After referring to authorities his Lordship said at 180–181:

...

> My Lords, the expression "beneficial owner" in relation to the proprietary interest of a company in its assets was first used in a taxing statute in 1927...

So when those words were repeated in the Finance Act 1954 not only was there a consistent line of judicial authority that upon going into liquidation a company ceases to be "beneficial owner" of its assets as that expression has been used as a term of legal art since 1874, but also there has been a consistent use in taxing statutes of the expressions "beneficial owner" and "beneficial ownership" in relation to the proprietary interest of a company in its assets which started with the Finance Act 1927, where the context makes it clear that a company upon going into liquidation ceases to be "beneficial owner" of its assets as that expression is used in a taxing statute.'.

'[32] There is a real question as to what *Ayerst* stands for. Certainly, as Lord Diplock demonstrates, the decision in *re Oriental Inland Steam Co; Ex parte Scinde Railway Co* [1873–1874] LR 9 Ch App 557 ('*Re Oriental Inland Steam Co*') is taken by the learned authors of Buckley on the Companies Acts as authority for the proposition that upon a winding up the assets of a company cease to belong beneficially to the company. Perhaps, in saying this, the learned authors were using the expression "beneficial ownership" in the sense which the words would be understood by equity lawyers in the United Kingdom. On the other hand *Ayerst* can be seen as authority for a somewhat narrower proposition, namely that the expression 'beneficial ownership' had come to have a specific meaning in English revenue law which might or might not differ from the ordinary meaning of the expression as understood by equity lawyers.

'[33] As Lord Diplock noted in *Ayerst* the expression "beneficial owner", was first used in revenue statutes in 1927 in the context of provisions relating to relief from capital and transfer stamp duty in cases of reconstruction or amalgamation. Those provisions contained an exception in the case of a company ceasing "'otherwise than in consequence of ... liquidation' to be the beneficial owner of the shares." As his Lordship observed, this provision implied that when a company was in liquidation it ceased to be the beneficial owner of its assets. Put in another way, the 1927 provision through its context gave a particular meaning to the phrase "beneficial ownership." His Lordship was of the view that as later revenue statutes adopted the phrase "beneficial ownership", they did so intending to incorporate the meaning which had been attached to the phrase in 1927. It might be said that the 1927 legislation provided, at least for revenue purposes, a dictionary of the meaning of the phrase, and that later cases had used the phrase and thereby adopted this dictionary definition of it. In other words, while *Ayerst* and the cases which preceded it have been taken, at least by some commentators, as authority for the general law meaning of the phrase "beneficial ownership", the case is not necessarily authority for the general law meaning of the phrase at all.

'[34] The conclusion that *Ayerst* is not authority as to the ordinary legal meaning of the phrase "beneficial owner" proceeds necessarily from the proposition that ordinarily the phrase "beneficial ownership" is used, at least by equity lawyers, only to describe a situation where there is what equity would regard as a trust in the strict sense. Where a trust exists, there will ordinarily be a division of the legal and equitable ownership, so that the legal ownership is in one person, and the equitable ownership is in another. However, it may be accepted that there are some anomalous cases, other than charitable trusts, where at least for a time there is no person entitled in equity but the person with the legal ownership is not to be regarded as the equitable owner of the property. Examples of cases where there is no person regarded in equity as the equitable owner, but where the legal owner does not have beneficial ownership, are the case of the unadministered estate until administration is completed where the executor holds the estate under the obligation to pay the funeral and testamentary expenses: *Commissioner of Stamp Duties (Qld) v Livingston* [1965] AC 694; (1964) 112 CLR 12, *Barns v Barns* [2003] HCA 9 at para50 per Gummow and Hayne JJ; the case of the trustee in bankruptcy who holds the assets vested in him or her subject to an obligation to realise the assets and distribute them pro rata among creditors and to the extent of any surplus to thereafter hold the assets for the bankrupt after payment of the costs of administration; and perhaps certain kinds of discretionary trusts where there is no beneficiary with an interest in the trust property: c f *Gartside v Inland Revenue Commissioners* [1968] AC 553.

...

'[37] *Ayerst* was followed by the Court of Appeal in *J Sainsbury PLC v O'Connor (Inspector of Taxes)* [1991] 1 WLR 963 in the context of group relief from the Corporations Tax. The question was whether the holder of shares (not a company in liquidation) over which there was a put and a call option was the beneficial owner of those shares. It was held that it was. Lloyd LJ noted that the phrase was a term of art and described *Ayerst* as a case where a person or company being the legal owner was deprived of the beneficial ownership of assets by operation of law as a consequence of supervening events. Curiously his Lordship seems to accept that "beneficial ownership" meant no more than "equitable ownership", as indeed was conceded before him. Nourse LJ was not prepared to go so far as to say the phrase was a term of art but said rather that it had a "very well recognised meaning amongst property lawyers." In his Lordship's view the phrase meant "ownership for your own benefit" as opposed to ownership as trustee for another. His Lordship appeared to equate "beneficial ownership" with the holding of an equitable interest in the property.

...

'[47] Professor Good, in his *Principles of Corporate Insolvency Law* (2nd Ed) 1997 at 58, appears to accept that *Re Oriental Inland Steam Co* holds that the company in liquidation holds its assets upon trust, with the consequence that it loses the beneficial ownership of its assets. It is clear that the learned authors use the expression "beneficial ownership" as meaning the right to use or realise the assets for the benefit of the company, and not necessarily in its ordinary meaning.

...

'[56] In our view the fact that the company in liquidation is bound through its liquidator to deal with its assets in accordance with the statutory regime in company law legislation does not mean that the company has ceased to "beneficially own" its assets for the purposes of s 80A(1) of the 1936 Act. It is clear enough that the formula of beneficial ownership was adopted by Parliament to replace the previous formula of "beneficially held", and so as to rectify the difficulty that losses might cease to be available to a company where the person who otherwise was the owner of the shares, was not entered on the register of members so that it could not be said that the person "held" the shares in both the year of income and the year of loss. The substituted requirement of beneficial ownership looked to see not whether the relevant person claiming to hold beneficially was a person whose name had been entered on the register of members but rather who was the real owner of the shares and, in a case where the legal and equitable ownership was divided, who owned the shares in equity. The fact that Parliament saw fit from the time of enactment of the 1936 Act to deal specifically with the case of a bankrupt and to deny to the bankrupt the right to deduct losses which arose in a prior year, even where the assets by statute vested in the trustee in bankruptcy, is not irrelevant either.

...

'[58] The change may, for the purposes of s 80A(1), be in the ownership of the relevant percentage of the share capital or it may involve allotment of new shares with or without changes in rights attaching to shares. The expression "beneficially owned" looks thus merely at equitable ownership. It does not, as counsel for the Commissioner would have it, encompass the case where, as a result of statute, the owner of the shares is subject to the control of another so that it can be said that there is a restraint upon the shareholder as to the disposition of the shares, such that the shareholder cannot dispose of them as it sees fit for its own benefit but no trust in the strict sense is created.

'[59] The present context is quite different from that discussed in the English cases. In our view there is no warrant for giving the phrase "beneficial ownership" some special meaning in the present context.' *Federal Cmr of Taxation v Linter Textiles Australia Ltd (in liq)* [2003] FCAFC 63 per Hill, Goldberg and Conti JJ; BC200301679

Australia [Beneficial ownership of a ship] '[6] It can be seen that subpara 21(4)(b)(ii) of the UK Act enables an action in rem to be brought against a surrogate ship if the relevant person is the beneficial owner of the ship (because they are the beneficial

owner of all the shares in it). Generally, the English Courts have tended to interpret "beneficial owner" broadly, at least in the sense that the section is treated as enabling the Court to inquire into the true ownership of a ship. The legislative antecedent of subs 21(4) of the UK Act, was subs 3(4) of the Administration of Justice Act 1956 (UK) ("the 1956 Act") which provided:

> "In the case of any such claim as is mentioned in para (d) to para (r) of subs (1) of section one of this Act, being a claim arising in connection with a ship, where the person who would be liable on the claim in an action in personam was, when the cause of action arose, the owner or charterer of, or in possession or in control of, the ship, the Admiralty jurisdiction of the High Court ... may ... be invoked by an action in rem against—
> (a) that ship, if at the time when the action is brought it is beneficially owned as respects all the shares therein by that person; or
> (b) any other ship which, at the time when the action is brought, is beneficially owned as aforesaid."

In neither para (a) nor para (b) of subs 3(4) is there express reference to charterers generally or demise charterers specifically (in contrast to subpara 21(4)(b)(i) of the UK Act and para 19(a) of the Act).

'[7] In *Medway Drydock & Engineering Co Ltd v The 'Andrea Ursula' (Owners)* [1973] QB 265, Brandon J had to consider the meaning of the expression "beneficially owned as respects all the shares therein by that person" in para 3(4)(a). His Lordship was not considering whether a surrogate ship was "beneficially owned" but rather whether the wrongdoing or guilty ship was "beneficially owned" by a demise charterer. That this is what his Lordship decided was noted in the ALRC report at p 158 when discussing whether a sufficient nexus would exist between a surrogate ship and the wrongdoing ship if the connection with the former was only as a demise charter. Nothing is said by the ALRC to suggest it disapproved of his Lordship's approach in construing the UK Act when determining ownership of the wrongdoing ship. The issue arose because a ship repairer commenced proceedings against a ship, the "Andrea Ursula", which was chartered under a demise charter to a company which had commissioned the repairs. On the assumption that the demise charterer was liable in personam, was the ship beneficially owned by the charterer? His Lordship noted (at 270) that

that the expression "beneficially owned" (not defined in the 1956 Act (as amended)), was capable of more than one meaning. Brandon J observed that "beneficially owned" could mean owned by someone who, whether the legal owner or not, was in any case the equitable owner. However his Lordship considered that the words were capable of a more practical meaning and said (at 269):

> ... the words [beneficially owned] seem to me to be capable also of a different and more practical meaning related not to title, legal or equitable, but to lawful possession and control with the use and benefit which are derived from them. If that meaning were right, a ship would be beneficially owned by a person who, whether he was the legal or equitable owner or not, lawfully had full possession and control of her, and, by virtue of such possession and control, had all the benefit and use of her which a legal or equitable owner would ordinarily have.

...

'[9] ... Brandon J's conclusion that a demise charterer could be a beneficial owner for the purposes of subs 3(4) of the 1956 Act was criticised by Goff J *in I Congreso del Partido* [1978] QB 500. The facts were comparatively complex. One aspect of the litigation concerned an allegation that a Cuban state enterprise, Mambisa, "beneficially owned" a ship, the "Congreso", which had been arrested by the owners of cargo (sugar) which had not been delivered (as contractually required) by two other ships. Mambisa did not own "Congreso" (it had just been built) in law or in equity (it was legally owned by the Republic of Cuba) but it was to operate and manage the ship. At the time of its arrest, "Congreso" was in the possession of Mambisa. The issue of beneficial ownership arose in relation to the scope of para 3(4)(b) of the 1956 Act, namely, beneficial ownership of the associated ship. Mambisa was the demise charterer of one of the ships (which had carried the sugar) and was in possession of the other ship, which it operated.

'[10] Goff J considered that beneficial ownership (arising from the expression "beneficially owned") included both legal and equitable ownership, but a demise charterer had beneficial use, not beneficial ownership. Goff J's starting point was the natural and ordinary meaning of the words "beneficially owned as respects all the shares therein". His Lordship rejected the suggestion that the words were ambiguous and, accordingly, it was unnecessary to have recourse to the 1952 Arrest Convention. Nonetheless his Lordship did and

expressed the view that the word "owner" in art 3(4) bore its ordinary meaning, namely the person with title to the ship. His Lordship's reconciliation of the 1956 Act with the 1952 Arrest Convention was as follows, at 540–541:

> As I read the Convention, article 3(1), which is expressed to be subject to article 3(4), provides for the arrest of either the particular ship in respect of which the maritime claim arose, or (except in certain specified cases) any other ship which is owned by the person who was, at the time when the maritime claim arose, owner of the particular ship. Furthermore, despite the argument of Mr Alexander for the plaintiffs to the contrary, in this context I read the word "owner" as bearing its ordinary meaning, that is, the person with title to the ship; and I am confirmed in this view by the provision relating to ownership in article 3(2) and by the fact that article 3(4), to which article 3(1) is expressed to be subject, makes special provision for the case of the demise charterer and others. It is to be observed that, if one puts article 3(4) on one side, the draftsman of the Act of 1956 appears to have been seeking to give effect to article 3(1) and (2) of the Convention, subject to the fact that he appears to have been concerned to extend the word "ownership" by the addition of the adjective "beneficial", very possibly to take account of the special English institution of the trust which may form no part of the domestic laws of other signatories to the Convention.
>
> For these reasons, when I place article 3 of the Convention alongside s 3 of the Act, I discern a clear intention on the part of Parliament not to give effect to article 3(4) of the Convention; and I do not think it would be right to impose some special construction on the words of s 3(4) of the Act in an attempt to give effect to one part (though not to others) of article 3(4) of the Convention.

...

In subsequent appeals to both the Court of Appeal [1980] 1 Lloyd's Rep 23 and the House of Lords [1983] 1 AC 244 the case was maintained on behalf of the cargo owners only on the footing that the owner of Congreso was the Republic of Cuba. Issues of sovereign immunity became central to the proceedings. Unlike Brandon J, Goff J was considering the meaning of the expression "beneficially owned" as it might apply to a surrogate or associated ship. His Lordship considered the adjective "beneficially" may have been used to accommodate the construct known to the English law, the trust. One would imagine that his Lordship had in mind that if "beneficial ownership" was, on the facts of the particular case involving a trust, to provide the touchstone of ownership for the purposes of the section, there would be one owner which would not be the legal owner, the trustee.

'[11] I refer to these two authorities in some detail, notwithstanding that in England they have been overtaken by later decisions and legislative changes. I do so because they serve to illustrate two approaches which might be followed in construing legislation giving effect to the 1952 Arrest Convention. The approach of Brandon J is not a narrow one and involves a fairly practical view of the reach of the Convention and legislation intended to give effect to it, bearing in mind the potential application of such legislation to foreign registered ships operated (in the most general sense) by companies or individuals located in countries where the laws which would determine ownership will differ. The Act has been characterised as remedial legislation which should be construed expansively rather than strictly: *Yulianto v The Ship 'Glory Cape'* (1995) 134 ALR 92 at 99. I think it can fairly be said that the thrust of the ALRC report is that rights of arrest and the capacity to bring proceedings in rem should be approached expansively and not narrowly (see particularly the section concerning Australia's national interest at p63–p64), though on the basis that it should not be at odds with the 1952 Arrest Convention and international practices more generally.

'[12] I should note that the difference of approach between Brandon J and Goff J in relation to whether a demise charterer "beneficially owned" the shares in a ship was resolved by the 1981 UK Act, which expressly brought demise charterers of the wrongdoing ship within the purview of the provisions enabling surrogate ship arrest when the demise charterer was also the owner of the surrogate ship. It has been said that by making this amendment, Parliament preferred the view of Goff J: see *The 'Nazym Khikmet'* [1996] 2 Lloyd's Rep 362 at 371.

...

[14] The argument on behalf of the defendants was really that one should take the matters at their face value. Here there had been a change from Armadora to Longan, from Longan to Loquat and that apparently was said to be that. I think that is wrong and that where damages are claimed by cargo-owners and there is a dispute as to the beneficial ownership of the ship, the Court in all cases can and in some cases should look behind the registered owner to determine the true beneficial ownership.

'Slynn J found for the defendants on the evidence. His Lordship did not undertake an analysis of the 1952 Arrest Convention. However his Lordship did point to a legislative intention that because the expression "beneficial ownership" was used, ownership for relevant purposes might arise in the context of a trust. It appears his Lordship thought that a beneficiary under a trust might be viewed as a "beneficial owner". Again, one would imagine that his Lordship had in mind that there would be one owner and the trustee would not be the owner for the purposes of surrogate ship arrest, even if the trustee was the registered owner.

'[15] ... The other situation concerns the arrest of a ship owned by a subsidiary of the company which was the relevant person. Both questions have had to be resolved by interpreting the relevant provisions of the legislation then in force, the Administration of Justice Act 1956 (UK). This Act used the expression "beneficially owned" and similar language is used by its successor, the Supreme Court Act 1981 (UK). It has caused some judicial puzzlement. As Justice Brandon observed, "trusts of ships, express or implied are ... rare". It is unnecessary to cater for them in the proposed legislation. In the event the English courts declined to interpret the expression as a mandate for any general lifting of the corporate veil beyond situations of trusteeship or nominee holdings. Justice Sheen said that he "would not hesitate to lift that veil if the evidence suggested that it obscured from view a mask of fraud rather than the true face of the corporation". But merely because a shipping group chose to operate through a number of one ship companies was, in his view, sufficient reason.

...

'[17] What was intended by the use of the word "owner" in s 19 having regard to the approach of the ALRC, was considered by Sheppard J in *Malaysia Shipyard and Engineering Sdn Bhd v The "Iron Shortland" as the surrogate for the ship "Newcastle Pride"* (1995) 59 FCR 535. Sheppard J reviewed in some detail many of the comparatively recent English authorities including those I have referred to earlier. His Honour concluded that the expression "the owner" in para 19(b) comprehended the beneficial, true or real owner. Sheppard J took into account the ALRC recommendation that there should be no special provision dealing with the corporate veil. His Honour said at 546–547:

It should be said at this point, that there is significant difference between attributing to the legislature on the one hand an intention to embrace within the word "owner" the concept of beneficial ownership, and, on the other, a much more general provision which would have the effect of lifting the corporate veil, making companies who were holding companies responsible for the liabilities of their subsidiaries. The question here is whether a particular company, Capeco Maritime, is the beneficial (ie the real) owner of the vessel. That is the only way in which the plaintiff's case is put. It should be emphasised that counsel for the plaintiff does not seek to advance any proposition based on the fact that Capeco Maritime owns 100 per cent of the shares in each of Newcastle Pride Co and Everbird. Counsel's submission is based on evidence to which I have yet to come that Capeco Maritime was the beneficial owner, not of shares in subsidiary companies, but of the whole 64 shares in each of the ships.

'[18] In determining whether the expression "the owner" in s 19 comprehended a beneficial owner, his Honour said at 547:

I think there are difficulties in taking the simple view that "owner" in the section means only "registered owner". After all, the section does not use those words. Obviously the registered owner will, in the absence of other evidence, be taken to be the beneficial owner. But there seems to me to be no reason of policy why the section should not be construed to mean or to include a beneficial owner. Because the judges who decided *"Shin Kobe Maru"* were dealing with a case directly concerned with the ownership of a vessel and thus with a proprietary, rather than a general, maritime claim, there is a danger in taking too much from the dicta about the meaning of ownership in s 4(2) and applying them to cases under s (3), particularly bearing in mind the terms of both s 17 and s 19. But at least the judgments show that the concept of "owner" and "ownership" in the Act may have a meaning which involves or includes beneficial ownership. There is thus nothing which runs counter to ordinary concepts of admiralty law or jurisdiction which should lead me to reject the plaintiff's submission.

Why should the ability of a plaintiff to take advantage of the remedies provided for in the Act depend on the chance of registration? It is true that most ships will be registered, but some may not be. And if such a plaintiff were able to identify the real or beneficial owner, what in principle should stand in the way of such a plaintiff proceeding against it, even if there is a nominee or trustee between the vessel and the true owner?

'[19] I respectfully agree. What Shepherd J meant by these observations is apparent from their application to the facts. What is revealed, in my opinion, is that his Honour was not using expressions such as "real owner", "true owner" or "beneficial owner" as terms of art to signify a relationship with a precise and fixed legal content ("beneficial ownership" need not always be a concept with fixed legal content: see *Commissioner of Taxation v Linter Textiles Australia Ltd* (*in liquidation*) [2003] FCAFC 63 at [28] and following). In addition, it is comparatively clear from the final sentence in the paragraph set out above that his Honour had in mind that in circumstances involving a trust, the trustee might not be the owner for the purposes of s 19 even if the trustee was the registered owner. Moreover, if the expression "the owner" is not to be taken to be a reference to the registered owner, then the fact that a person or body is the registered owner of a ship, could, in a particular factual setting, be no more than an indicia of ownership of that ship.

'[20] In outline, the facts in *Malaysia Shipyard and Engineering Sdn Bhd v "Iron Shortland"* as *the surrogate for the ship "Newcastle Pride"* (supra) were as follows. Proceedings were commenced (on 24 July 1995) against the "Iron Shortland" by a company which had repaired and equipped another ship, the "Newcastle Pride" (in the period December 1994 to January 1995). The "Iron Shortland" was arrested as a surrogate ship. BHP Transport Pty Ltd ("BHPT") applied to have the ship released from arrest and the warrant set aside. To determine the application, his Honour addressed three questions (identified at 548). The first was whether the company alleged to be the relevant person in the writ, Capeco Maritime NV ("Capeco") was the relevant person in relation to the claim. The second was whether Capeco was the owner or charterer of, or in possession or control of, the "Newcastle Pride" when the cause of action arose. This question arises because of para19(a) of the Act. The third was whether, when the proceedings were commenced, Capeco was the owner of the "Iron Shortland". This question arises because of para 19(b).

...

'[25] In the passage quoted earlier from *The Owners of the Ship "Shin Kobe Maru" v Empire Shipping Co Inc* (1994) 181 CLR 404, the High Court cautioned against construing the Act by reference to prior practices and principles. Moreover the express reference in para 19(a) to "charterer", in contradistinction to "owner", would indicate that the latter does not comprehend the former. However in *McIlwraith McEacharn Ltd v Shell Co of Australia Ltd* (1945) 70 CLR 175, the various members of the High Court concluded that the word "owner" in s 503 of the Merchant Shipping Act 1894 (Imp) could be taken to be include the charterer of the ship in question. In so doing, various references were made in the judgments to taking a broad rather than a narrow and technical approach to what constituted ownership: see Latham CJ at 194, Starke J at 199, Dixon J at 213 and Williams J at 218. Without seeking to overstate its relevance, this authority illustrates that in the realm of Admiralty law, the notion of ownership does not have a fixed content.

'[26] The word "ownership" has neither an historical nor a contemporary universal meaning: see *Bellinz Pty Ltd v Commissioner of Taxation* (1998) 84 FCR 154 at 161 (and, implicitly, the same would be so of a person who commands that relationship over property, an "owner") and that the correlative concept of "property" may be elusive: *Yanner v Eaton* (1999) 201 CLR 351 at 366. As to what might constitute ownership, the Full Court said in *Bellinz Pty Ltd v Commissioner of Taxation* (at 161):

> ... the prima facie meaning of the word ["ownership"], but again subject to context, is the entire dominion of the thing said to be owned: *Union Trustee Co of Australia Ltd v Commissioner of Land Tax* (1915) 20 CLR 526 at 530. Halsbury's Laws of England, 4th ed, (1994) Vol 35, para 1227 and para 1228, cited by the learned primary judge as "a helpful starting point", says:
>
> "**1227. Meaning of "ownership".** Ownership consists of innumerable rights over property, for example the rights of exclusive enjoyment, of destruction, alteration and alienation, and of maintaining and recovering possession of the property from all other persons. Those rights are conceived not as separately existing, but as merged in one general right of ownership.
>
> The ownership of goods differs from the ownership of land in that the common law did not treat land as the subject of absolute

ownership but only of tenure. The common law also did not recognise the possibility of the ownership of goods being split up into lesser successive interests or estates, nor did it contemplate remainders or reversions in chattels.

1228. Division of owner's rights. Ownership is nevertheless divisible to some extent. For example one or more of the collection of rights constituting ownership may be detached. Thus prima facie an owner is entitled to possession or to recover possession of his goods against all the world, a right which a dispossessed owner may exercise by peaceable retaking. He may, however, voluntarily or involuntarily part with possession, for example by the pledging, lending, hiring out, bailment, theft or loss of his goods, in any of which cases he is left with a right of ownership without possession, accompanied or not accompanied, as the case may be, by the right to possess."

... See also the discussion by Finkelstein J in *Wily v St George Partnership Banking Ltd* (1999) 84 FCR 423 at 430–434 and more generally, see J E Penner, *"The 'Bundle of Rights' Picture of Property"* UCLA Law Review vol 43, 1996, p 711–p 820.' *Kent v Vessel 'Maria Luisa'* [2003] FCAFC 93 per Moore J; BC200302365

BENEFICIALLY OWNED

Australia [In the context of the (Cth) Income Tax Assessment Act 1936, s 80A(1).] 'The term "beneficial" is usually employed in trust law as a cognate of "beneficiary". That term identifies those persons for whose benefit the trustee of a private trust (ie not a charitable purpose trust) is bound to administer the trust property. Where A holds Blackacre on a bare trust for B, it may accurately be said that B is the beneficial owner.

'But that use of the word "owner" does not entail enjoyment by B of all the rights which the law as a whole confers in relation to Blackacre. Thus, as Hope JA explained in *DKLR Holding Co (No 2) Pty Ltd v Commissioner of Stamp Duties* [1980] 1 NSWLR 510 at 519–520, although B may be entitled by equitable remedies to be put into possession, B cannot sue A in ejectment. Again, the will or settlement conferring an equitable fee simple may qualify that gift and render it determinable by the conferral upon another of an option to purchase, or by the imposition of a condition subsequent which is certain and does not contravene the policy of the law.

'The authors of a leading Australian text correctly wrote as follows of the effect of a winding-up order:

> Whether the company is insolvent or solvent, the company holds its property beneficially but subject to the statutory scheme of liquidation under which the liquidator is to pay creditors and distribute any surplus among members. Unsecured creditors and contributories have the benefit of the liquidator's administration of the company's estate. Their special interest is to some extent like that of objects of a discretionary trust; they have a right to have a fund of assets protected and properly administered. That interest, although not an interest in specific assets, will be protected against third persons. For example, a holder of an unregistered registrable charge who asks the court to extend the time for registration or a person who seeks rectification of an instrument of charge which could prejudice unsecured creditors will not ordinarily succeed if the company is in liquidation or on the verge of liquidation.

'The critical point is that the change in control of the affairs of the company has no impact upon its beneficial ownership of its assets.

'By analogy with the general law, the circumscribing or suspension by reason of the appointment of the liquidator of the exercise by the usual organs of the company of the incidents of ownership of the assets of the company does not mean that the company itself has ceased to own beneficially its assets within the meaning of s 80A(1). Power to deal with an asset and matters of ownership or title are not interchangeable concepts.

'The 1944 Act used the phrase "beneficially held". In *Dalgety Downs Pastoral Co Pty Ltd v Federal Commissioner of Taxation* (1952) 86 CLR 335, this Court decided that shares registered in the name of X, but as mortgagee from Y, were not "held" by Y within the meaning of s 80(5). Webb, Fullagar and Kitto JJ said that the modification in s 80(5) of "held" by the adverb "beneficially" did not justify acceptance of the displacement of the ordinary meaning of "held" as "registered" when used of shares. Their Honours said of the inclusion of "beneficially":

> This word serves more naturally the purpose of excluding the case of a holding for the

benefit of others than the purpose of so broadening the meaning of the word "held" beyond the particular significance which it normally has in relation to shares as to make it equivalent to "owned" in the most general sense of that word.

'Earlier, in *Avon Downs Pty Ltd v Federal Commissioner of Taxation* (1949) 78 CLR 353 at 364–365, Dixon J had said of the expression, in what was then s 80(6) of the Act, "beneficially held by the trustee of his estate" that it conveyed:

> the idea that the trustee of the estate holds it as part of the estate and not for some person claiming adversely to the beneficiaries. In other words, if the testator was a nominee, his executor is to be in no better position than he is. It seems to me that a transferor of a share who has been paid the consideration for the transfer, holds simply as a passive trustee until the registration of the transfer and the entry of the transferee's name on the register. He could not be said to hold "beneficially."

'The 1964 Act replaced "beneficially held" with "beneficially owned" as the criterion for determining substantial continuity of shareholding and the 1973 Act continued that criterion. Given the outcome in *Dalgety Downs*, the change evidently was made to assist the taxpayer, by allowing the taxpayer to go beyond the face of the share register.' *Commissioner of Taxation v Linter Textiles Australia Ltd* (*In Liquidation*) [2005] HCA 20 at [52]–[57], per Gleeson CJ, Gummow, Hayne, Callinan and Heydon JJ; BC200502292

BENEFIT

Canada 'The classic statement of what comprised a taxable benefit derives from the Supreme Court of Canada case, *R v Savage*. In that case Mr Justice Dickson, as he then was, [quoting from *R v Poynton* [1972] 3 OR 727 at 738] explained in clear and simple terms the principle which distinguishes taxable from non-taxable receipts:

> "If it is a material acquisition which confers an economic benefit on the taxpayer and does not constitute an exemption, e.g., loan or gift, then it is within the all-embracing definition of s 3."

'According to the Supreme Court of Canada, then to be taxable as a "benefit", a receipt must confer an economic benefit. In other words, a receipt must increase the recipient's net worth to be taxable. Conversely, a receipt which does not increase net worth is not a benefit and is not taxable. Compensation for an expense is not taxable, therefore, because the recipient's net worth is not increased thereby.

'Our jurisprudence has long accepted the focus on net gain as the basis for determining whether a receipt is a "benefit" and whether it is therefore taxable.' *Canada v Hoefele* [1996] 1 FC 322 at 330, per Linden JA (FCA)

BENEFITS

New Zealand [Section 27 of the Proceeds of Crime Act 1991.] 'In ordinary usage "benefits" is a wide expression ... The wide and residual meaning of "benefit" had long been recognised in the common law, as in the famous definition of consideration adopted from *Comyn's Digest* in *Currie v Misa* (1875) LR 10 Exch 153, 162: [*quotation follows*].' *R v Pedersen* [1995] 2 NZLR 386 at 390, CA, per Cooke P and Richardson J

' "Benefits" is a word of wide meaning, easily applicable without strain to the payment received by a drug supplier.' *R v Pedersen* [1995] 2 NZLR 386 at 392, CA, per Casey J

BENEVOLENT

[For 5 Halsbury's Laws (4th edn) para 556 see now 5(2) Halsbury's Laws (4th edn) (2001 Reissue) para 58.]

BEQUEST

[For 50 Halsbury's Laws (4th edn) para 469 see now 50 Halsbury's Laws (4th edn) (Reissue) para 523.]

BEST INTERESTS OF JUSTICE

Canada 'The expression "best interests of justice" is the one that has caused difficulty in this case. In another context, the expression has been held to take into consideration both the interests of the accused as well as those of the State; see *R v Bernardo* (1997) 121 CCC (3d) 123 (Ont CA) at p 131.

'In order to determine the proper definition that is applicable, the object of s 530 [of the Criminal Code] must again be considered. Since the rule is the automatic access to a trial in one's official language when an application is made in a timely manner, and a discretionary access when such an application is not timely, the trial judge should therefore consider, foremost, the reasons for the

delay. The first inquiry that comes to mind is directed at the knowledge of the right by the accused. When was he or she made aware of his or her right? Did he or she waive the right and later change his or her mind? Why did he or she change his or her mind? Was it because of difficulties encountered during the proceedings? It is worth mentioning at this point that the right of the accused to be informed of his or her right under s 530(3) is of questionable value because it applies only when the accused is unrepresented. The assumption that counsel is aware of the right and will in fact advise his or her client of that right in all circumstances, absent a duty to do so, is unrealistic, as confirmed by the report of the Commissioner of Official Languages of Canada, *The Equitable Use of English and French Before the Courts in Canada* (1995), at p 105.

'Once the reason for the delay has been examined, the trial judge must consider a number of factors that relate to the conduct of the trial. Among these factors are whether the accused is represented by counsel, the language in which the evidence is available, the language of witnesses, whether a jury has been empanelled, whether witnesses have already testified, whether they are still available, whether proceedings can continue in a different language without the need to start the trial afresh, the fact that there may be co-accuseds (which would indicate the need for separate trials), changes of counsel by the accused, the need for the Crown to change counsel and the language ability of the presiding judge. In fact, a consideration of the requirements of s 530.1(*a*) to (*h*) will provide a good indication of relevant matters.

'I wish to emphasize that mere administrative inconvenience is not a relevant factor. The availability of court stenographers and court reporters, the workload of bilingual prosecutors or judges, the additional financial costs of rescheduling are not to be considered because the existence of language rights requires that the government comply with the provisions of the Act by maintaining a proper institutional infrastructure and providing services in both official languages on an equal basis. As mentioned earlier, in the context of institutional bilingualism, an application for service in the language of the official minority language group must not be treated as though there was one primary official language and a duty to accommodate with regard to the use of the other official language. The governing principle is that of the equality of both official languages.

'The retried accused does not have to justify why he or she is requesting a second trial in his or her official language when he or she failed to do so in the first. The granting of such a request is not an exceptional favour given to the accused by the State; rather, it is the norm. The only relevant factors to consider under s 530(4) are the *additional* difficulties caused by an untimely application.

'Another important consideration with regard to the interpretation of the "best interests of justice" is the complete distinctiveness of language rights and trial fairness. Unfortunately, the distinctions are not always recognized, as can be seen from the reasons of Southin JA of the Court of Appeal:

> "The phrase "the best interests of justice" [encompasses several further principles]...
> 1.   An accused is entitled to make full answer and defence
> 2.   He is entitled to be present at his trial ...
> 3... the jurors ... must be mentally competent and capable of understanding the evidence given before them ... [T]he language of the trial must be a language that the jurors and ... the judge, understand.

...

'Can it be said that an accused who understands both official languages is deprived of his right to make full answer and defence or, to put it another way, that his trial is not fair, if his trial against his wishes is in the other official language, albeit he had an interpreter throughout? If the answer is "yes", it may be argued that the right to make full answer and defence is different for those whose language is English or French from those persons who possess neither language, for instance, many First Nations persons. [(1997), 120 CCC (3d) 16 at paras 63 and 66]"

'The right to full answer and defence is linked with linguistic abilities only in the sense that the accused must be able to understand and must be understood at his trial. But this is already guaranteed by s 14 of the *Charter*, a section providing for the right to an interpreter. The right to a fair trial is universal and cannot be greater for members of official language communities than for persons speaking other languages. Language rights have a totally distinct origin and role. They are meant to protect official language minorities in this country and to insure the equality of status of French and English. This Court has already tried to dissipate this confusion on several occasions. Thus, in *MacDonald v City of Montreal, supra*, Beetz J, at pp 500–501, states that:

> It would constitute an error either to import the requirements of natural justice into ...

language rights ... or vice versa, or to relate one type of right to the other ... Both types of rights are conceptually different ... To link these two types of rights is to risk distorting both rather than reenforcing either.

'I reaffirm this conclusion here in the hope that these rights will no longer be confused. Fairness of the trial is not to be considered at this stage and is certainly not a threshold that, if satisfied, can be used to deny the accused his language rights under s 530.

'While no set infallible method can be provided to ascertain whether it is in the best interests of justice that an application under s 530(4) be accepted, some guidelines can be provided. I have already explained that trial fairness should not be considered; nor should institutional inconvenience. Additional difficulties caused by a late application, as well as the reasons for this delay, are however relevant factors. The basic principle, however, is that, generally, owing to the importance of language rights and the stated intention of Parliament to insure the equality of French and English in Canada, the best interests of justice will be served by accepting the application of the accused to be tried in his official language.' *R v Beaulac* (1999) 173 DLR (4th) 193 at 220, 221, 222, 223, SCC, per Bastarache J

BET

[For 4 Halsbury's Laws (4th edn) para 1 see now 4(1) Halsbury's Laws (4th edn) (2002 Reissue) para 2.]

BEVERAGE

Canada 'The appellants contend that Perrier water is not a "beverage" because that term, when construed in its ordinary and popular sense, excludes water. This is evidenced, they suggest, by the large number of English and American dictionaries that define "beverage" as expressly excluding water. To be sure, the Court was referred to a long list of such definitions, some from dictionaries bearing very unfamiliar names, and indeed many of these definitions are as unambiguous as the appellants suggest. On the other hand, there are dictionary meanings which disagree and indicate that "beverage" does not exclude water. The *Concise Oxford Dictionary* (8th ed), for example, defines "beverage", simply as "a drink". The *Concise Oxford Dictionary*, of course is not an insignificant source for the meanings of English words, especially in Canada. The definitions above suggest that the range of ordinary and acceptable uses of the word "beverage" clearly includes water within its scope.

…

'If a server in a Canadian restaurant asked a customer which "beverage" to bring and the customer responded, "Perrier, please", would the server be surprised that the customer thought that Perrier was a beverage? I think not. Would the server respond to the customer saying, "Perrier is water, and I shall bring it, but do you want a 'beverage' as well?" I think not. In our common speech, most Canadians, in my view, would include water, especially sparkling water, within the meaning of beverage, despite the many dictionary definitions excluding it. Similarly, if a server in French-speaking Canada asked what the customer wished as a "*boisson*", the response "Perrier" would not surprise the server. No one would think that Perrier is not a "*boisson*", despite the advice of the Office de la langue française. Though the word may not always be used to refer to water, therefore, I am of the opinion that it is more natural to interpret "beverage" as including water.' *Perrier Group of Canada Inc v Canada* [1996] 1 FC 586 at 594–595, 597–598, per Linden JA (Fed CA)

BEYOND REASONABLE DOUBT

Australia 'The present case is yet another illustration of the undesirability, in general at all events, of seeking to explain to a jury what is meant by the phrase "beyond reasonable doubt" except by way of contrasting it with the standard of proof in civil proceedings. It is unfortunate that the observations now complained of were made by the learned judge. In a sense it was not wrong to tell the jury that a reasonable doubt was a doubt which they considered reasonable. Had the jury asked his Honour what "reasonable" meant, it would have been correct to reply that a reasonable doubt was a doubt which the jury considered reasonable. In the absence of any request from the jury for elucidation, it is, however, undesirable for a judge to tell the jury that they should first consider whether they have a doubt and then consider whether that doubt is a reasonable one. His Honour did not, however, invite the jury to approach their task in this two stage way. It is, in general at all events, undesirable for a judge even, instead of using the composite phrase "a reasonable doubt" or "beyond reasonable doubt", to distinguish between the doubt and its reasonableness.' *R v Neilan* [1992] 1 VR 57 at 71, per cur

BIAS

Canada 'The test for partiality involves two key concepts: "bias" and "widespread". It is important to understand how each term is used.

'The *New Oxford Dictionary of English* (1998), at p. 169, defines "bias" as "prejudice in favour of or against one thing, person, or group compared with another, especially in a way considered to be unfair". "Bias", in the context of challenges for cause, refers to an attitude that could lead jurors to discharge their function in the case at hand in a prejudicial and unfair manner.

'It is evident from the definition of bias that not every emotional or stereotypical attitude constitutes bias. Prejudice capable of unfairly affecting the outcome of the case is required. Bias is not determined at large, but in the context of the specific case. What must be shown is a bias that could, as a matter of logic and experience, incline a juror to a certain party or conclusion in a manner that is unfair. This is determined without regard to the cleansing effect of trial safeguards and the direction of the trial judge, which become relevant only at the second stage consideration of the behavioural effect of the bias.

'Courts have recognized that "bias" may flow from a number of different attitudes, including: a personal interest in the matter to be tried (*Hubbert*, supra, at p. 295; *Criminal Code*, s 632); prejudice arising from prior exposure to the case, as in the case of pre-trial publicity (*Sherratt*, supra, at p. 536); and prejudice against members of the accused's social or racial group (*Williams*, supra, at para. 14).

'In addition, some have suggested that bias may result from the nature and circumstances of the offence with which the accused is charged: *R. v. L. (R.)* (1996), 3 C.R. (5th) 70 (Ont. Ct. (Gen. Div.)); *R. v. Mattingly* (1994), 28 C.R. (4th) 262 (Ont. Ct. (Gen. Div.)); N. Vidmar, "Generic Prejudice and the Presumption of Guilt in Sex Abuse Trials" (1997), 21 *Law & Hum. Behav.* 5. In *Williams*, supra, at para. 10, this Court referred to Vidmar's suggestion that bias might, in some cases, flow from the nature of the offence. However, the Court has not, prior to this case, directly considered this kind of bias.' *R v Find* [2001] 1 SCR 863 at 882–883, per McLachlin CJ

BILL

[For 34 Halsbury's Laws (4th edn) paras 1222, 1223 see now 34 Halsbury's Laws (4th edn) (Reissue) paras 728, 729.]

BILL OF LADING

[For 43 Halsbury's Laws (4th edn) paras 490, 498 see now 43(2) Halsbury's Laws (4th edn) (Reissue) paras 1532, 1542.]

BILL OF LADING OR ANY SIMILAR DOCUMENT OF TITLE

[At arbitration, the issue arose as to whether s 1(4) of the Carriage of Goods By Sea Act 1971 (derived from art I(b) of the Hague Rules) applied the Rules if the contract of carriage expressly or by implication provided for the issue of a 'bill of lading or any similar document of title'. The question therefore arose whether a straight bill of lading was a 'bill of lading or any similar document of title'.] '[134] The first question is whether a straight bill of lading, but otherwise in the form of any classic bill of lading, is a bill of lading within the meaning of the Hague Rules. If it is, then, it has not been suggested that it should have a different meaning under the 1971 Act, for all that the treatment of the distinction between a bill of lading and a non-negotiable receipt in its s 1(6) may be seen, in retrospect, as a harbinger of the distinction between a bill of lading and a sea waybill to be found in s 1 of the 1992 Act. It is common ground that the point is open. It is open today. It was open and uncertain immediately before the agreement of the Hague Rules.

'[135] In my judgment, a straight bill of lading, for all that it is non-negotiable, should be viewed as a bill of lading within the meaning of the Hague Rules. I say that for the following reasons.

'[136] First, the Hague Rules are predominantly concerned with the content of a contract of carriage in circumstances where such a contract as found in a bill of lading may come to affect a third party into whose hands such a bill is transferred. It seems to me to be plain as a matter of common sense but also on a review of the material cited in this judgment, that in this connection a named consignee under a straight bill of lading, unless he is the same person as the shipper, is as much a third party as a named consignee under a classic bill. Therefore I would view such a named consignee under a straight bill as prima facie within the concern of the Hague Rules.

'[137] Secondly, while it is I suppose true that a straight bill of lading can be used in circumstances where there is no intention of transferring it to the consignee, the authorities considered demonstrate that in practice it is used, just like a classic bill, as a document against which payment is required and

the transfer of which thus marks the intended transfer of property. Therefore, as Professor Tetley says, its nature is that, although it cannot be transferred more than once, for it is not negotiable, it can be transferred by delivery (just like a classic bill) to the named consignee. In these circumstances, the shipper and his bankers and insurers need the same protection as the shipper under a classic bill; and the consignee himself and his insurers in turn need to have rights against the carrier under the contract of carriage. I can see no reason why straight bills of lading have not always been within the 1855 Act. Those needs are in any event recognised under the 1992 Act.

'[138] Thirdly, whatever may be the position as a matter of principle and in the absence of express agreement, the practice appears to be that a straight bill of lading, unlike a mere sea waybill, is written on the form of an otherwise classic bill and requires production of the bill on delivery, and therefore transfer to a consignee to enable him to obtain delivery. (In this respect the position of a straight bill under the Pomerene Act appears to be different, but even so the Harter Act, one of the forerunners of the Hague Rules, would seem to cover straight as well as negotiable bills.)

'[139] Fourthly, suppose the question is asked, in the context of the Hague Rules, in these terms: what of the straight bill? Is this a 'bill of lading' or, being non-negotiable, something else, more akin to a non-negotiable receipt? Then, as it seems to me, the straight bill of lading is in principle, function, and form much closer to a classic negotiable bill, than to a non-negotiable receipt, which, to judge from art VI of the Hague Rules, was viewed as something far more exotic.

'[140] Fifthly, the travaux préparatoires of the Hague Rules, despite lacking unequivocal cogency, to my mind are not only consistent with the view I would prefer, but go far to support it.

'[141] Sixthly, I am unimpressed by the argument derived from the terms of the 1971 and 1992 Acts. They may reflect a developing English view about how to categorise bills of lading and non-negotiable receipts and sea waybills, but, as the learned authors of Benjamin and Carver point out, they are ultimately dealing with different purposes. In any event, I do not see how they can control the meaning of the Hague Rules, which are not only much earlier, but also of international and not merely domestic scope.' *J I MacWilliam Co Inc v Mediterranean Shipping Co SA, The Rafaela S* [2003] EWCA Civ 556 at [134]–[141], [2003] 3 All ER 369, per Rix LJ

[Decision of the Court of Appeal affirmed by the House of Lords: *J I MacWilliam Co Inc v Mediterranean Shipping Co SA, The Rafaela S* [2005] UKHL 11, [2005] 2 All ER 86.]

BILL OF SALE

[For 4 Halsbury's Laws (4th edn) para 601 see now 4(1) Halsbury's Laws (4th edn) (2002 Reissue) para 601.]

BINDER

Australia [Insurance contract; Corporations Act 2001 (Cth) s 716A.] 'The first proposition put forward in this segment of Lumley's submissions was that the Corporations Act 2001 (Cth) contains general provisions relating to responsibility for the conduct of agents and brokers, and also contains specific provisions dealing with the receipt of premiums and other moneys, and with brokers who act under a "binder". That statutory expression "binder" was described by Lumley as a special agreement whereby a broker has authority to make binding decisions on behalf of the insurer in relation to accepting proposals or settling claims.

'The Corporations Act was said to contain in particular a specific provision dealing with cases where a financial services licensee acts under a binder. I was referred to s 916A(1) thereof (presumably that reference was intended to be to s 916E(2) as well), which was described as requiring an agent's authority to be in writing, and for the authority to provide for specific services; subs 916A(1) and 916E(2) respectively reads as follows:

> A financial services licensee may give a person (the authorised representative) a written notice authorising the person, for the purposes of this Chapter, to provide a specified financial service or financial services on behalf of the licensee. (s 916A(1)).

> For all purposes connected with contracts that are risk insurance products, or with claims against the insurer, in respect of which the authorised licensee acts under the binder:
> (a) the authorised licensee is taken to act on behalf of the insurer and not the insured; and
> (b) if the insured in fact relied in good faith on the conduct of the authorised licensee, the authorised licensee is taken to act on behalf of the insurer regardless of the fact that the

authorised licensee did not act within the scope of the binder. (s 916E(2)).

'The definition of "binder" appears in s 716A of the Corporations Act as follows:

> "binder" means an authorisation given to a person by a financial services licensee who is an insurer to do either or both of the following:
> (a) enter into contracts that are risk insurance products on behalf of the insurer; or
> (b) deal with and settle, on behalf of the insurer, claims relating to risk insurance products against the insurer as insurer;

> but does not include an authorisation of a kind referred to in paragraph (a) that is limited to effecting contracts of insurance by way of interim cover unless there is also in existence an authority given by the insurer to the person to enter into, on behalf of the insurer and otherwise than by way of interim cover, contracts of insurance ...'

AON Risk Services Australia Ltd v Lumley General Insurance Ltd [2005] FCA 133 at [141], per Conti J; BC200500548

BLASPHEMY

[For 11 Halsbury's Laws (4th edn) para 1009 see now 11(1) Halsbury's Laws (4th edn) (Reissue) para 348.]

Blasphemous libel

[In this case it was held that the law of blasphemy was confined to protecting only the Christian religion.] 'The offence of blasphemous libel is an offence of strict liability. It is no defence that the defendant did not intend to blaspheme. As it stands, the offence is capable of resulting in unreasonable interferences with freedom of expression ... If the offence is extended to cover attacks on religious doctrines, tenets, commandments or practices of religions other than Christianity, the existence of such an extended law of blasphemy would encourage intolerance, divisiveness and unreasonable interference and interferences with freedom of expression. Fundamentalist Christians, Jews or Muslims could then seek to invoke the offence of blasphemy against each other's religion, doctrines, tenets, commandments or practices, e.g. for denying the divinity of Jesus Christ or for denying that the Messiah has yet to come, or for denying the divine inspiration of the Prophet Muhammed, and so on. An extended law of blasphemy which applied to all religions could be used as a weapon between Protestants and Roman Catholics in Northern Ireland, or by fringe religions, such as the Church of Scientology. The fact that the offence was committed only in cases of scurrilous attacks would mitigate, but not eliminate, the resulting intolerance, divisiveness and unreasonable interference with freedom of expression.' *R v Chief Metropolitan Stipendiary Magistrate, ex p Choudhury* [1991] 1 All ER 306 at 321–322, per cur

BLOCKADE

[For 37 Halsbury's Laws (4th edn) para 1314 see now 36(2) Halsbury's Laws (4th edn) (Reissue) para 814.]

BOARD

'I have no doubt myself that, whether in the seaside or urban context, the concept of "board" has two elements, viz, service and substance—both provided at or about the time of use. By substance I mean the food and drink. By service I mean the preparation and setting out of that food and drink. How much of each is to be provided before "board" can be constituted is a matter of degree but both elements must be present at least in some degree before the concept of board can begin to be established. It would not be "board" to provide a team of waiters and cooks but no food: nor would it be "board" to give the guest unlimited access to a wide range of food and drink but tell him he had to go and collect and prepare it himself.' *Gavin v Lindsay* 1987 SLT 12 at 15, Sh Ct, per Sheriff Kearney

[The bona fide provision by the landlord under a tenancy of a daily 'continental breakfast', consisting of two bread rolls with butter, jam and marmalade, and unlimited tea or coffee with sugar and milk, is more than de minimis and constitutes 'board' for the purposes of s 7(1) of the Rent Act 1977.] 'The relevant definitions of "board" in the Shorter Oxford English Dictionary are: "Food served at the table; daily meals provided according to stipulation; the supply of daily provisions … " With the growing popularity in this country of holidays on the continent, we have grown accustomed to the use of the phrases "full board" and "half board" as corresponding no doubt to the French "pension" and "demi-pension". But, if "half board" relates to breakfast plus one additional

meal, I can see no reason as a matter of language or logic why breakfast by itself should not amount to partial "board", subject always to the implicit requirement that the provision of the meal to the tenant includes the ancillary services involved in preparing it and the provision of crockery and cutlery with which to eat it … A bona fide obligation by a landlord to serve even such a modest daily meal as the continental breakfast with which this case is concerned is hardly likely to appeal to the unscrupulous landlord as a soft option. It will necessarily involve not only the cost of the food and drink provided but also all the housekeeping chores which must be undertaken in shopping for provisions, preparation and service of meals on the premises and clearing and washing up after meals. If a landlord and a tenant genuinely contract on terms which impose such obligations on the landlord, it would, to my mind, be surprising if the legislature had provided for the perpetuation of such a contract in favour of the tenant when the landlord wishes to terminate it.' *Otter v Norman* [1988] 2 All ER 897 at 898, 901, HL

BOARD OR LODGING

Canada [Assistance payments were available for 'board or lodging'.] '… In my opinion the ordinary and plain meaning of the words "board or lodging" is "food and shelter" and "shelter" respectively.' *Our House Ottawa Inc v Ottawa-Carleton (Regional Municipality)* (1992) 92 DLR (4th) 337 at 340, per Craig J (Ont Div Ct)

BOARDING HOUSE

[For 24 Halsbury's Laws (4th edn) para 1210 see now 24 Halsbury's Laws (4th edn) (Reissue) para 1110.]

BOAT

New Zealand '[9] As we have stated, rule 5.7.4B [of the proposed district plan] is that "Commercial boating activity shall not take place on the Kawarau River". Much of the argument focused on the meaning of "boat" (and "boating") and we discuss that shortly. The full phrase used in the rule is "commercial boating activity" and its immediate context is the whole sentence containing that phrase.

'[10] The proposed district plan does not contain definitions of the terms "commercial boating activity" or "boat" in ch 18 – the definition section

– of the proposed district plan. The *New Zealand Oxford Dictionary* defines the constituent terms (relevantly) as follows:

> **Boat** ... **1** a small vessel propelled on water by an engine, oars, or sails. **2** (in general use) a ship of any size ...;
>
> **Boating** –. . . sailing or going in boats as a sport or form of recreation.
>
> **Commercial** – **1** of, engaged in, or concerned with commerce. **2** having profit as a primary aim rather than artistic etc value; philistine.

' "Craft" is defined in the same dictionary as "a boat or vessel". Finally, "vessel" is defined as:

> **Vessel** ... **1** a hollow receptacle esp. for liquid, e g a cask, cup, pot, bottle, or dish. **2** a ship or boat, esp. a large one. **3** a *Anat* a duct or canal etc. holding or conveying blood or other fluid, esp = *blood vessel*. **b** *Bot* A woody duct carrying or containing sap etc. **4** *Bibl* or *joc* a person regarded as the recipient or exponent of a quality (*a weak vessel*).

'[11] Ms Macdonald, for the council, submitted that any "boat" has the following characteristics:

- it is a class of thing that floats;
- it has the ability to travel on or through water; and
- it is used in navigation (its course can be managed or directed).

'As a consequence she submitted to include a bodyboard for surfing – which has those characteristics – within the definition of "boat" is consistent with the plain and ordinary meaning of the word. We consider her argument fails at the first step – Ms Macdonald's definition is too wide because it might include a horse or an elephant, as well as a raft or life jacket, none of which are usually thought of as a boat.

'[12] We conclude that the normal meaning of "boat" does not include "river surfing boards" and by extension, that the normal meaning of "commercial boating activity" does not include "commercial river surfing activity". Further, it appears to us that an individual river surfer is not engaged in "commercial river surfing activity". Most are in the river for thrill-seeking pleasure not for profit. So we are troubled by what "commercial river surfing" could mean, and we return to that issue later.' *Queenstown River Surfing Ltd v Central Otago District Council* [2006] NZRMA 1 at [9]–[12], per Judge Jackson

BODILY FUNCTIONS

[The Social Security Act 1975 has been repealed. See now the Social Security Contributions and Benefits Act 1992, s 64(2).]

Important bodily function

Canada [Claims for personal injuries in motor vehicle accidents were restricted inter alia to specified impairment of an important bodily function.] 'Some bodily functions, however seriously impaired, will not satisfy the legislation. There are bodily functions which obviously are important to everyone. The application of the legislation to them will cause no problems. But there are some bodily functions which are important to some people but not to others. In our view, the legislation was aimed at bodily functions that play a major role in the health and general well-being of the injured plaintiff. The use of the word "important" is intended to differentiate between those bodily functions which are important to the injured person and those which are not. It is only those bodily functions which are important to the particular injured person which can amount to important bodily functions within the meaning of that expression in s 266(1)(b) [of the Insurance Act, RSO 1990, c I.8 [am 1993, c 10, s 23]]. Such an interpretation, in our opinion, is consonant with the obvious intention of the legislature to reduce substantially the number of personal injury claims coming before the courts as a result of motor vehicle accidents.

'If the bodily function is important to the particular injured person, then the bodily function in question is an important one within the meaning of that expression contained in s 266 (1)(b).' *Meyer v Bright* (1993) 110 DLR (4th) 354 at 363, Ont CA

BODILY HARM

Australia 'I consider that the question of whether the injury amounts to "bodily harm" is one of degree, which can only be decided by reference to the facts in each case. In determining this question, it is necessary to focus on the injury and its immediate consequences. The fact that the victim has been left with only a cosmetic disability is irrelevant if the immediate consequences of the injury interfered temporarily with her health. It is relevant also to consider the nature of any treatment received and whether any part of the body was unable to perform its functions fully, either as a result of pain or otherwise and there may well be other relevant matters.' *Wayne v Boldiston* (1992) 85 NTR 8 at 14, per Mildren J

Australia 'There are strong reasons for thinking that the phrase "bodily harm" should receive a wide interpretation and not be restricted to "harm to the skin, flesh and bones of the victim", a narrow meaning which the English Court of Appeal rejected in *R v Chan-Fook* [1994] 1 WLR 689 at 695. In that case it was suggested that a person's body "includes all parts of his body, including his organs, his nervous system and his brain", so that "bodily injury" may "include injury to any of those parts of his body responsible for his mental and other faculties", with the consequence that "bodily harm" is capable of including psychiatric injury although not mere emotions such as fear or distress. The validity of those observations should be recognised in attributing appropriate meaning to "bodily harm" in the definition in s 663A [of the Criminal Code (Qld)].' *West v Morrison* (1996) 89 A Crim R 21 at 23, per Macrossan CJ

BODILY INJURY

[Under the Warsaw Convention 1929 art 17 (as set out in Sch 1 to the Carriage by Air Act 1961), the carrier is liable for damage sustained in the event of the death or wounding of a passenger or any other 'bodily injury' suffered by a passenger if the accident which caused the damage so sustained took place on board the aircraft or in the course of the operations of embarking or disembarking. The claimant suffered an indecent assault on an aircraft operated by the defendant airline and, although she sustained no physical injury, she became very distressed, and was later diagnosed as suffering from a clinical depression. On an appeal, the claimant submitted that 'bodily injury'—'lésion corporelle' in the French text—included mental injury and accordingly was not confined, as the airline contended, to physical injury. The Court of Appeal rejected that submission and the claimant appealed to the House of Lords.] '[3] The expression "bodily injury", or "lésion corporelle", in art 17 means, simply, injury to the passenger's body. The contrast is with absence of injury to a passenger's body. This simple meaning propounds a coherent and workable test. None of the submissions urged upon your Lordships has persuaded me that this phrase should be given a different, more limited meaning. In particular, I see no occasion for limiting art 17 to bodily injuries which are "palpable and conspicuous", whatever those two ambiguous expressions are taken to mean in this context. The

brain is part of the body. Injury to a passenger's brain is an injury to a passenger's body just as much as an injury to any other part of his body. Whether injury to a part of a person's body has occurred is, today as much as in 1929, essentially a question of medical evidence. It may be that, in the less advanced state of medical and scientific knowledge 70 years ago, psychiatric disorders would not have been related to physical impairment of the brain or nervous system. But even if that is so, this cannot be a good reason for now excluding this type of bodily injury, if proved by satisfactory evidence, from the scope of art 17.

'[4] This does not mean that shock, anxiety, fear, distress, grief or other emotional disturbances will as such now fall within art 17. It is all a question of medical evidence. In *Weaver v Delta Airlines* (1999) 56 F Supp 2d 1190 the uncontradicted medical evidence was that extreme stress could cause actual physical brain damage. The judge observed (at 1192) that "fright alone is not compensable, but brain injury from fright is".

. .

'[7] Because I consider it important that the Warsaw Convention (as set out in Sch 1 to the Carriage by Air Act 1961) should have a common construction in all the jurisdictions of the countries that have adopted the convention, I attach crucial importance to the decisions of the United States Supreme Court in *Eastern Airlines Inc v Floyd* (1991) 499 US 530 and *El Al Israel Airlines Ltd v Tsui Yuan Tseng* (1999) 525 US 155, particularly as the United States is such a large participant in carriage by air. But for these decisions, I would have given more weight than does my learned friend to the argument that the word "bodily" and its French counterpart "corporelle" were directed to the distinction between injury to a passenger through loss of baggage or delay on the one hand and injury to his person on the other, rather than to the distinction between bodily injury and mental injury.

'[8] I wish also to say that in my opinion if an injury to the brain of a passenger is found to have occurred, and the other conditions requisite to qualify for compensation under art 17 are present, compensation under the article cannot be refused on the ground that in 1929 this fact would not have been known, with the result that at that time medical opinion would have been that the passenger had suffered only mental injury. Like my noble and learned friend Lord Nicholls of Birkenhead I do not see merit in adding words to the description of injury which are not present in the convention text and I would apply the simple test, does the evidence demonstrate injury to the body, including in that expression the brain, the central nervous system and all the other components of the body?

. .

'[140] The composite expression "bodily injury" involves a combination of two elements. The word "injury" in the context of personal injury involves a condition which departs from the normal, which is not a mere transitory discomfort or inconvenience and which, whilst not permanent or incurable, has, in conjunction with its degree of seriousness, a sufficient duration. It includes a loss of function. A person who is concussed or who is in clinical shock or who is made deaf or blind is properly described as injured. (As to deafness, see, for example, *Daddon*'s case [*Daddon v Air France* (1984) 1 S & B Av R VII/141, Israel SC].) A condition which requires treatment to enable the person to return to the normal is typical of an injury though not essential; many injuries heal over time without intervention. Contracting an illness may amount to an injury depending upon the degree to which the illness departs from the normal. One would not normally describe a person who caught a cold as having suffered an injury but, on the other hand, one would certainly describe someone who contracted a serious disease or condition, say, "AIDS" or hepatitis, as the result of the deliberate or negligent act of another as having suffered an injury.

'[141] The word "bodily" is simpler. It means pertaining to the body. There must be an injury to the body. It is, as it must be, accepted that the brain, the central nervous system and the glands which secrete the hormones which enable the brain and the rest of the central nervous system to operate are all integral parts of the body just as much as are the toes, heart, stomach and liver. They are all susceptible to injury. The mechanisms by which they can be injured vary. An ingested poison might injure the stomach or liver. A lack of oxygen will injure the brain by causing the death of brain cells. An injury to the heart may be caused by a blow or by a traumatic experience or by over-exertion. In every case there is a cause, external to the organ in question, which produces a change in the structure or ability to function of the organ. If the change, either alone or in conjunction with changes in other organs, is properly described as an injury, it is a "bodily" injury. Since the body is a complex organism depending for its functioning and survival upon the interaction of a large number of parts, the injury may be subtle and a matter of inference not direct observation. The medical science of diagnosis exists to enable the appropriate

inferences to be drawn from the observed evidence. Medicinal treatments (as with drugs) are prescribed on the basis that there is a physical condition which can be reversed or alleviated by physical means.

'[142] "Bodily injury" does not import visibility nor palpability nor externality. Its use in art 17 in addition to the use of the words "death" and "wounding" (blessure) and the inclusion of the word "any" confirm this. Take an incident which ruptures a spleen or causes some other internal injury. The doctor infers that the injury has been caused from other signs and symptoms and ultimately confirms it by an invasive (surgery) or non-invasive (ultrascan or X-ray) procedure. An incident may damage someone's optic nerve in a location or manner which cannot be observed; the person may as a result have no sight in that eye; this will be a "bodily injury" even though there is no thing palpable, conspicuous or visible. The use of the word "palpable" in the discussion of the meaning of art 17 typifies the dangers of the use of loose terminology which does not aid clarity but, rather, creates ambiguity. "Palpable" is a term which has a precise meaning—capable of being felt by touch—which is its medical meaning. But it also has a metaphorical usage—readily perceived by the senses or the mind. It will be readily understood that the precise meaning is too restrictive and cannot be justified as a gloss upon the simple phrase "bodily injury". The metaphorical usage likewise cannot be justified and is impractical and unprincipled. Is the judge or arbitrator to say: "Having heard the evidence I am satisfied that the passenger suffered an injury but I cannot say that I readily perceived it?" The obvious attraction of using words such as "palpable" is that they give an illusion of clarity when in truth they enable the user to avoid clarity and simply serve to detract from the clarity of the primary terminology.

'[143] Thus, "bodily injury" simply and unambiguously means a change in some part or parts of the body of the passenger which is sufficiently serious to be described as an injury. It does not include mere emotional upset such as fear, distress, grief or mental anguish (cf argument (8)). A psychiatric illness may often be evidence of a "bodily injury" or the description of a condition which includes "bodily injury". But the passenger must be prepared to prove this, not just prove a psychiatric illness without evidence of its significance for the existence of a "bodily injury". *Morris v KLM Royal Dutch Airlines* [2002] UKHL 7 at [3]–[4], [7]–[8], [140]–[143], [2002] 2 All ER 565 at 568–569, 608–609, HL, per Lord Nicholls of Birkenhead, Lord Mackay of Clashfern and Lord Hobhouse of Woodborough respectively

Australia 'I am of the opinion that the term "bodily injury" was not intended to, and on a proper interpretation of the [Warsaw Convention art 17] does not, include purely psychological injury.' *Kotsambasis v Singapore Airlines Ltd* (1997) 42 NSWLR 110 at 115; 148 ALR 498 at 503; BC9703587 at 13, per Meagher JA

BODY

[For 9 Halsbury's Laws (4th edn) para 1055 see now 9(2) Halsbury's Laws (4th edn) (Reissue) para 857.]

Of persons

[The Income and Corporation Taxes Act 1970 has been largely repealed. The definition is re-enacted in the Income and Corporation Taxes Act 1988, s 832(1).]

Of note

[For 4 Halsbury's Laws (4th edn) para 422 see now 4(1) Halsbury's Laws (4th edn) (2002 Reissue) para 323.]

BODY CORPORATE

Australia 'It is the acquisition by a "corporation" of shares in the capital or assets of a "body corporate" that s 50(1) [Trade Practices Act 1974 (Cth)] prohibits ... The expression "body corporate" is not defined in the Act, so it must be interpreted in accordance with general principles of statutory construction. Plainly the expression "body corporate" has a wider meaning than the statutorily defined word "corporation" because the ordinary meaning of the expression "body corporate" includes a corporation and because the terms of the definition of "corporation" in s 4(1) compel that conclusion. Also s 50 itself draws deliberate distinctions between the expressions "corporation" and "body corporate". "Body corporate" is thus a wider expression than "corporation" for the purposes of s 50.' *Trade Practices Commission v Australian Iron & Steel Pty Ltd* (1990) 92 ALR 395 at 405, per Lockhart J

BOILER PLATE

Canada '[90] A "boiler plate" provision as these words suggest is a standard clause which is

systematically reproduced usually verbatim in a series of instruments having the same object (*Black's Law Dictionary*, 6th ed., at page 175).' *BC Tel v. Seabird Island*, [2003] 1 F.C. 475 at 519 (CA), per Linden JA

BONA FIDE REDUNDANCY

Australia '[20] The respondent submitted that the words "by reason of the bona fide redundancy of the taxpayer" refer to the making of an ETP. However, as a matter of construction, we consider that those words relate to "the dismissal of the taxpayer from any employment". If there were any doubt about the correctness of this view, it is dispelled by reference to the Explanatory Memorandum accompanying the Income Tax Assessment Amendment Bill (No 3) (1984) (Cth) at p 91 where it is said, concerning s 27F:

> This section relates to the second of the "concessional components" in the definition of that term in section 27A(1), for which the taxation treatment is to include only 5 per cent thereof in assessable income. In some respects, where a taxpayer's employment has been prematurely terminated it may seem that, except for the absence of an appropriate scheme, some of the matters referred to in paragraph 27E(1)(b) were in existence in relation to the taxpayer's former employer. However, in section 27F the only test to be satisfied as to the reason for the cessation of the taxpayer's employment is that he or she was dismissed by reason of his or her "bona fide redundancy"

'[21] Clearly the words "by reason of the bona fide redundancy of the taxpayer" refer to "the dismissal of the taxpayer"...

...

'[33] Although para 27A(1)(ja) speaks of "a bona fide redundancy payment" and para 27F(1)(a) speaks of "an eligible termination payment ... made in relation to a taxpayer in consequence of the dismissal of the taxpayer from any employment ... by reason of the bona fide redundancy of the taxpayer", there is no definition of the term "redundancy". The word is often used in the context of industrial relations to describe benefits payable in certain circumstances pursuant to industrial legislation and/or awards ... Paragraph 42 of [Taxation Ruling] 94/12 ... refers to the decision of this Court in *Short v F W Hercus Pty Ltd* (1993) 40 FCR 511. That decision relied heavily upon an earlier South Australian decision, *R v Industrial*

Commission (SA); *Ex parte Adelaide Milk Supply Co-operative Ltd* (1977) 16 SASR 6. In Short, at 520–521, Burchett J said:

> … It can fairly be said that in industrial circles the term redundancy payment has come to mean compensation for losses of various kinds suffered by employees who have given substantial services to an employer and whose services are terminated because, for one reason or another, the employer no longer needs them.

'Mitchell J accepted this statement. Bright J, who dissented on the jurisdictional issue, said (at 26–27):

> The word "redundant" does not occur in the Act. In its industrial sense it is not defined in the Oxford Dictionary. The application which I have already set out attempts the definition for the purpose of the proposed award. A consideration of the cases leads me to think that the question of the redundancy of any employee is linked to the question of the continued utility of the job which he is performing. In other words it does not relate to the personal competence of the employee in the job which he is performing. If I am right in this, then in its widest form the concept of redundancy connotes that an employee becomes redundant whenever (and for whatever reason) his employer no longer desires to have performed the job which that employee was doing. A wide variety of instances are contained in the definition clause in the application but they all seem to fit into this connotation, even the reference to retrenchment of employees for any reason whatsoever.

'It was in connection with this statement of Bright J and the passage quoted by Mitchell J (to each of which he referred at 8–9) that Bray CJ made (at 8) a statement that has since become in part embedded in a number of awards, including the subject award:

> I should begin by saying that I agree with Bright J that the concept of redundancy in the context we are discussing seems to be simply this, that a job becomes redundant when the employer no longer desires to have it performed by anyone. A dismissal for redundancy seems to be dismissal, not on account of any personal act or default of the employee dismissed or any consideration peculiar to him, but because the employer no longer wishes the job the employee has been doing to be done by anyone.

Here the expression containing the words "no longer wishes" was first composed. In its original setting, it is plain that it was not meant to convey the limitation for which the respondent contends. On the contrary, it was meant to capture the full breadth of the concept elaborated by Bright J and referred to in the passage quoted by Mitchell J.

…

'[38] The term must be construed in the context in which it appears. Relevantly, para 27F(1)(a) speaks of " … the dismissal of the taxpayer from any employment … by reason of the bona fide redundancy of the taxpayer". Dismissal is the unilateral act of the employer. The "reason" for a dismissal must be the employer's reason for such dismissal. Paragraph 27F(1)(a) does not contemplate an enquiry by the Commissioner as to the correctness or appropriateness of the employer's decision or the reasons therefore [sic]. Only the bona fides of a relevant transaction may be questioned. The question is not whether the employer used the word "redundant" in such reasons. It is rather whether those reasons indicate that the employee was dismissed by reason of his or her redundancy.

…

[43] The difficulty in this case has been caused by the aphorism which appears in both paras 12 and 42 of [Tax Determination] 94/12 to the effect that the job, not the employee, becomes redundant. However s 27F speaks of the "bona fide redundancy of the taxpayer". We consider that it is more accurate to say that an employee becomes redundant when his or her job (described by reference to the duties attached to it) is no longer to be performed by any employee of the employer, though this may not be the only circumstance where it could be said that the employee becomes redundant. Re-allocation of duties within an organization will often lead the employer to consider whether an employee, previously employed to perform specific functions assigned to a particular "job", will be able to perform any available "job" existing after such re-allocation. Even if the employee's job, defined by reference to its duties, has disappeared, he or she may be able to perform some other available job to the satisfaction of the employer. In that case, no question of redundancy arises. It is only if the employer considers that there is no available job for which the employee is suited, and that he or she must therefore be dismissed, that the question of redundancy arises. If, in good faith, the employer:

> has re-allocated duties;

considers that the employee is not suitable to perform any available job, defined by reference to those re-allocated duties, existing after the re-allocation; and

for that reason, dismisses the employee,

then, for the purposes of s 27F, the employee is dismissed by reason of his or her bona fide redundancy. In the above discussion we have used the word "available" as meaning "vacant", and the word "suitable" as meaning "within the employee's capacity"'. *Dibb v Commissioner of Taxation* [2004] FCAFC 126, per Spender, Dowsett and Allsop JJ; BC200402647

BONA FIDES

Canada 'To be a bona fide occupational qualification and requirement [within s 4(6) of the Code] a limitation, such as a mandatory retirement at a fixed age, must be imposed honestly, in good faith, and in the sincerely held belief that such limitation is imposed in the interests of the adequate performance of the work involved with all reasonable dispatch, safety and economy, and not for ulterior or extraneous reasons aimed at objectives which could defeat the purpose of the Code.' *Ontario Human Rights Commission v Etobicoke* [1982] 1 SCR 202 at 208, SCC, per McIntyre J

BONA VACANTIA

[For 8 Halsbury's Laws (4th edn) para 1503 see now 12(1) Halsbury's Laws (4th edn) (Reissue) para 235.]

[For 17 Halsbury's Laws (4th edn) para 1398 see now 17(2) Halsbury's Laws (4th edn) (Reissue) para 613.]

BOND

[For 4 Halsbury's Laws (4th edn) para 1106 see now 4(1) Halsbury's Laws (4th edn) (2002 Reissue) para 185.]

BOOTY

[For 37 Halsbury's Laws (4th edn) para 1305 see now 36(2) Halsbury's Laws (4th edn) (Reissue) para 805.]

BORDEREAU

Australia [Insurance contract.] 'The meaning of bordereau was said by the applicants to equate with that of a "binder agreement", and in an insurance context, to be defined by s 11(1) of the Insurance Contracts Act 1984 (Cth) as *an authority given by an insurer to an insurance intermediary to enter into, as agent for the insurer, contracts on behalf of the insurer.* I was referred by the applicants to what appears in the joint judgment of the members of the High Court in *Con-Stan Industries of Australia Pty Ltd v Norwich Winterthur Insurance (Australia) Ltd* (1985–1986) 160 CLR 226 at 234–235 (Gibbs CJ, Mason, Wilson, Brennan and Dawson JJ), where the operation of bordereau was explained and illustrated as follows:

> … under the general principles of the law of agency, a broker is the agent of the assured, not the insurer … There will be rare circumstances in which a broker may also be an agent of the insurer, but the courts will not readily infer such a relationship because a broker so placed faces a clear conflict of interest between his duty to the assured on the on hand and to the insurer on the other. An agreement entered into on 1 November 1977 between Norwich and Bedford, known as a Bordereau Agreement, created just such a situation. The agreement authorized Bedford to extend insurance cover in Norwich's name in certain specified categories and within specified monetary limits. Bedford was required to calculate the premiums on the insurance which it accepted on behalf of Norwich and to issue debit notes to the assured. Bedford implicitly had authority to receive payment of the premium from the assured and was required to pay that premium to Norwich, after deducting its commission, within ninety days of the end of the month in which the business was transacted.'

AON Risk Services Australia Ltd v Lumley General Insurance Ltd [2005] FCA 133 at [59], per Conti J; BC200500548

BORNE

Australia 'To "bear" something is to accept or have it as an obligation — e g to bear responsibility, cost or blame: *Macquarie Dictionary*. Something is "borne" which is "carried, sustained or endured": *Oxford English Dictionary*. Thus, in the ordinary meaning of words, a person's expenditure is borne by another when the latter pays the former's bills or provides the funds with which the former pays his bills. Item 126(1)(b) [of (CTH) Sales Tax (Exemptions and Classifications) Act 1992 Sch 1] contemplates that the authority and not the government will actually make the disbursement or payment, and accordingly "borne" does not have the narrow meaning of "paid". To use the example employed in argument — if I give my daughter $2 to buy her lunch, which she does, I bear the expenditure though she pays over the money. I bear the expenditure exclusively, because no one else contributes any part of the $2. If my wife and I pay $1 each, I no longer bear the expenditure exclusively. Nor do I, if my daughter contributes $1 out of her pocket money.' *Totalizator Agency Board v Federal Commissioner of Taxation* (1996) 139 ALR 644 at 660–661, per Sundberg J

BOTTOMRY

[For 43 Halsbury's Laws (4th edn) para 198 see now 43(2) Halsbury's Laws (4th edn) (Reissue) para 1691.]

BOUNDARY

[For 4 Halsbury's Laws (4th edn) para 831 see now 4(1) Halsbury's Laws (4th edn) (2002 Reissue) para 401.]

BREACH OF THE PEACE

[At common law a breach of the peace can occur on private premises even if the only persons likely to be affected by the breach are inside the premises and no member of the public outside the premises is involved: see *McConnell v Chief Constable of Greater Manchester Police* [1990] 1 All ER 423, CA.]

[For 11 Halsbury's Laws (4th edn) para 108 see now 11(1) Halsbury's Laws (4th edn) (Reissue) para 709.]

BREAKDOWN

Canada [Insurance coverage applied to use of replacement vehicle substituted after breakdown of insured vehicle.] '... "Breakdown" connotes some mechanical, electrical or electronic malfunction.' *Clark v Waterloo Insurance Co* (1992) 98 DLR (4th) 689 at 693, per Zalev J (Ont Ct (Gen Div))

BREATH TEST

[The Road Traffic Act 1972 has been repealed. The definition is re-enacted in the Road Traffic Act 1988, s 11(2).]

BRIBERY

[For 1 Halsbury's Laws (4th edn) para 791 see now 1(2) Halsbury's Laws (4th edn) (Reissue) para 107. For 15 Halsbury's Laws (4th edn) para 767 see now 15 Halsbury's Laws (4th edn) (Reissue) para 694.]

BRIDLEWAY

[The Road Traffic Act 1972 has been repealed. The definition, with the omission of the words 'that is to say,' is re-enacted in the Road Traffic Act 1988, s 192(2).]

BRITISH SHIP

[For 43 Halsbury's Laws (4th edn) para 119 see now 43(1) Halsbury's Laws (4th edn) (Reissue) para 103.]

BROADCAST

[The Dramatic and Musical Performers Protection Act 1958 has been repealed. See now the new definition in the Copyright, Designs and Patents Act 1988, s 6.]

BROKER *SEE ALSO* MARKET MAKER

[The Income and Corporation Taxes Act 1970 is largely repealed. The new definition is as below.]

'Broker', in relation to securities, means a member of the Stock Exchange who carries on business in the United Kingdom and is not, at the time the Contract is made, a market maker in securities of the kind concerned. (Income and Corporation Taxes Act 1988, s 737(6))

[For 1 Halsbury's Laws (4th edn) para 712 see now 2(1) Halsbury's Laws (4th edn) (Reissue) para 12.]

[For 41 Halsbury's Laws (4th edn) para 647 see now 41 Halsbury's Laws (4th edn) (Reissue) para 42.]

BROTHEL

New Zealand 'In essence we are asked to decide whether the word "used" appearing in s 147(1) [of the Crimes Act 1961] should be limited in its application to the place where the women engage in acts of intercourse for sexual gratification or whether its application should be extended to include any place where arrangements are made by telephone for that kind of activity to take place elsewhere. If the extended definition is applicable, then an act of prostitution committed at one place (itself a brothel within the narrower definition) would also make into a brothel any other place at which application for that service was made by a male customer or from which the assignment was telephoned to the escort, even though the customer and the woman concerned had never set foot in the second place. Such an extension would not give due weight to the statutory definition of brothel— namely, "any house, room, set of rooms, or place of any kind whatever used for the purposes of prostitution" in the physical sense discussed. That definition does not extend to include any place where arrangements are made for intercourse to be had elsewhere. The statutory definition in its reference to "used for the purposes of prostitution" seems to emphasise that it is of the essence of a brothel for the purposes of s 147(1) that it is the physical place resorted to by persons of both sexes for sexual purposes at which the section is aimed.' *R v Gray* [1984] 2 NZLR 410 at 412, per McMullin J

BROUGHT ABOUT BY

Australia 'While the concept of proximate cause is established in insurance law, at least in causation of loss by an insured peril, the requirement of a proximate cause depends on the words used in the policy and the proper scope to be given to them in the operation of the policy (see generally Davies, 'Proximate Cause in Insurance Law', (1995) 7 ILJ 135 at 135–139). The words 'brought about by' in the fraud and dishonesty exclusion do not have a received interpretation as requiring a proximate cause, and in our view do not require that inquiry into a causal relation between the fraud or dishonesty and the liability be complicated by seeking to distinguish between a proximate cause and some other kind of cause. The words of the policy govern: was the liability brought about by the fraud or dishonesty?' *Switzerland Insurance Australia Ltd v McCann* BC9905358; [1999] NSWCA 310 at [78], per Mason P, Stein and Giles JJA

Australia [An insurance policy included an exclusion clause for liability brought about by a dishonest or fraudulent act or omission of the assured.] 'The language, although redolent of causation, identifies a different kind of connection between the two elements. One of those elements (the liability) is "brought about by" the other (a dishonest or fraudulent act or omission) if the

latter is a component of the former. A liability is brought about by a dishonest or fraudulent act or omission only if the liability is one in which that dishonest or fraudulent act or omission could be a material fact in pleading the claim. It is not brought about by such an act or omission simply because there were dishonest or fraudulent acts or omissions committed at about the time of the events giving rise to liability or because those acts or omissions were committed in the course of some overall relationship between the insured and the claimant. To say that there were "circumstances of dishonesty" attending the relationship between insured and claimant does not identify how or why those circumstances bore upon the nature or extent of the liability giving rise to the loss against which the insured seeks indemnity ...' *McCann v Switzerland Insurance Australia Ltd* (2000) 176 ALR 711; 75 ALJR 325; BC200007594; [2000] HCA 65 at [130], per Hayne J

BUDGET

Australia [Interpretation of clause in retirement village lease] 'The term "budget" is not defined in the 1989 Act. In its ordinary meaning, a budget is an estimate of expected income and expenditure or of operating results for a given period in the future (see The *Macquarie Dictionary*, Second Revision, The Macquarie Library Pty Ltd, Macquarie University, 1987). It might also be described as a periodic, especially annual, estimate of the revenue and expenditure of an organisation (see *Shorter Oxford English Dictionary on Historical Principles*, Fifth Edition, Oxford University Press, Oxford, 2002). Thus, the essence of the concept of the budget is that it is an estimate for the future. The actual expenditure and income may produce a result that is different from the budget because either expenditure or income is underestimated or overestimated.

'In the case of a budget for the Village, the estimate relates only to expenditure, since income by way of contributions levied on Residents is fixed by reference to Outgoings as estimated in the budget ... ' *Brasington v Overton Investments Pty Ltd* [2003] FCA 1523 at [108], [109] per Emmett J; BC200308157

BUILDING

[The Town and Country Planning Act 1971 has been repealed. See now the Town and Country Planning Act 1990, s 336(1).]

BUILDING OPERATION

[The Town and Country Planning Act 1971 has been repealed. The definition is re-enacted in the Town and Country Planning Act 1990, s 336(1). As to s 45(4) of the 1971 Act, see now s 97 of the 1990 Act.]

BURNOUT

Australia [Section 5(B)(2) of the Road Transport (Safety and Traffic Management) Act 1999 (NSW) provides that the driver of a motor vehicle must not 'burnout' a vehicle on a road or related area. Subsection 5(B)(1) provides that the word 'burnout' means, in relation to a motor vehicle other than a motor bike, to 'operate the vehicle in a way that causes the vehicle to undergo sustained loss of traction by 1 or more of the driving wheels'.] '... s 5(b)(2) does not, in my opinion, apply to situations in which a vehicle merely loses traction due to heavy braking or skidding, unaccompanied by any spinning of the driving wheels. As [counsel for the respondent] pointed out, the *Macquarie Dictionary of Slang* defines the word "burnout" as meaning "a car stunt in which the back tyres are made to spin on the spot at very high speed and thus cause as much smoke as possible". It is clear from the Explanatory Memorandum that the legislation creating the offence was directed to conduct of this kind.' *Kempe v Bailey* BC200300952; [2003] ACTSC 13 at [11], per Crispin J

BURSARY

Canada '[31] Having concluded that the SOGD is not an accommodation grant, I must still decide whether it is a "bursary" within the meaning of paragraph 56(1)(*n*) of the [Income Tax] Act. The Judge concluded, in no uncertain terms, that the grant was a bursary.
'[32] At paragraphs 38–42 of his reasons, the Judge turned to the dictionaries for definitions of the words "bursary" and *"bourse"*, which he reproduced:

The *Concise Oxford English Dictionary* – Tenth Edition, Revised, Oxford University Press – defines bursary as:

1. a grant, especially one awarded to a student.

The *New Collegiate Dictionary* – Thomas Allen & Son Limited, Toronto – defines: bursary as:

2. a monetary grant to a needy student.

The *Canadian Oxford Paperback Dictionary* – Oxford University Press – contains the following definition of bursary:

a financial award to a university student made primarily on the basis of financial need or some other criterion in addition to academic merit.

The same dictionary defines "grant" in this manner:

2a: a sum of money given by the state for any of various purposes, e.g. to finance education.

The French version of the paragraph in question uses the term, "bourse d'études" and "bourse", although having other definitions, is also defined by *Larousse – Dictionnaire Général – 1994* – as follows:

3. *Pension accordée par l'État ou par une institution à un élève, à un étudiant ou à un chercheur pour l'aider à poursuivre ses études.*

'[33] To these definitions can be added the following:

Le grand Robert de la langue française: dictionnaire alphabétique et analogique, 2nd ed. Paris: Dictionnaires Le Robert, 1992, at page 132:

1. BOURSE ...

3. Bourse d'études, et, absolt, bourse : pension accordée à un élève, un étudiant, pour subvenir à ses besoins pendant le temps de ses etudes.

The New Oxford Dictionary of English. Oxford: Clarendon Press, 1998, at page 246:

bursary ... **1.** a grant, especially one awarded to someone to enable them to study at university or college.

ITP Nelson Canadian Dictionary of the English Language. Toronto: ITP Nelson, 1997, at page 188:

bursary ... **1.** *a university scholarship based primarily on need.*

Shorter Oxford English Dictionary on Historical Principles, 5th ed. Oxford: Oxford University Press, 2002, at page 311:

bursary ... **3.** An endowment given to a student.

'[34] These definitions of the word "bursary" highlight the fact that bursaries are grants given to students in need of financial help so as to allow them to continue their studies.' *Simser v. Canada* [2006] 1 FCR 253 at [31]–[34], [2004] FCJ No 2075 (Fed CA), per Nadon JA

BUSINESS

[For 47 Halsbury's Laws (4th edn) para 2 see now 47 Halsbury's Laws (4th edn) (Reissue) para 6.]

[The Food Act 1984 is largely repealed. The definition is re-enacted in the Food Safety Act 1990, s 1(3).]

Australia 'The carrying on of a business is any commercial activity undertaken individually or by corporate bodies for fee or reward, usually for profit, not usually of a casual kind, but involving the creation, distribution or supply of goods and/or services: see Macquarie Dictionary and *Lesser v Shire of Wannan* (1897) 23 VLR 446 at 453, per Madden CJ, *Re O'Shea (deceased), National Trustees Executors & Agency Co of Australasia v O'Shea* [1953] VLR 43 and as to business relations see *R v Gallagher* [1986] VR 219... To my mind there is no doubt that the pursuit of professional practice amounts to the conduct of a business.' *Wellington v Norwich Union Life Insurance Society Ltd* [1991] 1 VR 333 at 335, per Nathan J

Australia 'In my opinion, it is more appropriate to consider the provision by the Government of State schools to members of the public, at which school attendance is made compulsory by legislation, save for certain specified exceptions, and the provision of instruction which is free of charge, both historically and traditionally as a service to the community provided by the Government, rather than an activity which, as between the Government and the community, can be characterised as a business, even within the wide definition of business contained in the Act. It may be argued that certain activities conducted by the Government in carrying on schools, for example, the purchase of equipment or the provision of services amounts to the carrying on of a business as between the Crown and the entity with which or with whom it is dealing. But that is not the present case.

'I have been assisted by the various references to the word "business" drawn together by Sheppard J in *State Superannuation Board (NSW) v Federal Commissioner of Taxation* (1988) 82 ALR 63 at 72; 88 ATC 4,382 at 4,389. His Honour sets forth the definition of "business" from the *Shorter Oxford English Dictionary* as including: "trade, commercial transactions or engagement" having earlier referred to the statement by Mason J in *Federal Commissioner of Taxation v Whitfords Beach Pty Ltd* (1982) 150 CLR 355 at 378–379. This passage shows, as Sheppard J readily recognised, that the word "business" has to be read in and take its meaning from its context. I consider that in the context of the Fair Trading Act 1987 (NSW) the word "business" refers to "trade, commercial transactions or engagement".' *Durant v Greiner* (1990) 21 NSWLR 119 at 128, per Rolfe J

Australia [Section 67(4) of the National Health Act 1953 (Cth) defines 'health insurance business' to mean, inter alia, the 'business' of undertaking liability, by way of insurance]. 'In this context the notion of carrying on business should not receive a narrow interpretation, for a wide range of activities could run counter to the policy of the Act. For that purpose it would not matter greatly, and perhaps not at all, whether the business activity in question was conducted as part of some larger business or whether or not it was conducted for a profit'. *Australian Health Insurance Association Ltd v Esso Australia Pty Ltd* (1993) 116 ALR 253 at 261, per Black CJ

Australia [Section 14CD of the Evidence Act 1898 (NSW) gives a wide definition to 'business' to include, among other things, any occupation carried on by a person, for profit or not.] '... it does seem to me that the wide definition of business does indicate that it should not be limited to an activity carried on by the person or company in question in its own right. It seems to me that, by extending "business" to "occupation", the provision leaves open the possibility that a record made by an employee relating to his occupation may be a business record. Whether or not it is a business record, it seems to me, would depend upon whether the document relates in an appropriate way to the occupation, and can correctly be described as a record of the occupation. It must, of course, to be admissible under s 14CE, also be made in the course of the occupation or for the purposes of the occupation.' *Standard Chartered Bank of Australia Ltd v Antico; Bank of New Zealand v Antico* (1993) 35 NSWLR 588 at 590–591, per Hodgson J

Australia ' "Business" is a word which is capable of having a broad meaning. In *Rolls v Miller* (1884) 27 Ch D 71 at 88 in a passage referred to with approval by Williams J in *Tweddle v Commissioner of Taxation* (1942) 180 CLR 1 at 5 Lindley LJ said:

> "The word means almost anything which is an occupation, as distinguished from a pleasure – anything which is an occupation or duty which requires attention as a business."

'However as Mason CJ, Gaudron and McHugh JJ said in *Re Australian Industrial Relations Commission Ex parte Australian Transport Officers Federation* (1990) 171 CLR 216 at 226 "of all words, the word 'business' is notorious for taking its colour and its content from its surroundings …".

'In s 6(2) [of the Contracts Review Act 1980 (NSW)] "business" is used in conjunction with "trade" and "profession" and qualifies "carried on" or "proposed to be carried on". The concept of business thus appears to me to be that encapsulated in the following passage from the judgment of Street CJ, Roper CJ in Eq and Herron J in *Hyde v Sullivan* (1956) SR (NSW) 113 at 119:

> "Speaking generally, the phrase 'to carry on a business' means to conduct some form of commercial enterprise, systematically and regularly, with a view to profit and implicit in this idea are the features of continuity and system."

'It is possible that a business may be carried on by means of a "one-off" transaction without repeated acts of buying and selling if what is done is of sufficient substance and of such a character as to identify it as a trading operation. [*Federal Commissioner of Taxation v Sir Hubert's Island Pty Ltd (in liq)* (1978) 138 CLR 210 at 237–8 per Jacobs J].' *Burrawong Investments Pty Ltd v Lindsay* BC200201218; [2002] QSC 082 at [102]–[105], per Muir J

Australia [In the context of interpreting s 149(1)(d) of the Workplace Relations Act 1996 (Cth).] '[32] … As three members of the Court pointed out in *Re Australian Industrial Relations Commission; Ex parte Australian Transport Officers Federation*, "the word 'business' is notorious for taking its colour and its content from its surroundings: see *Federal Commissioner of Taxation v Whitfords Beach Pty Ltd*. Its meaning depends upon its context." Accordingly, the Court held in the *Transport Officers* case that the expression a "successor or assignee or transmittee of the business" of an entity could, and in that case did, extend to succession between two statutory

authorities, neither of which carried on any commercial undertaking for profit, but both of which discharged governmental functions.

…

'[37] The "business" of an employer may be described in a number of ways. In many contexts it will suffice to describe the kind of activity conducted. A description like "manufacturing", "retailing" or the like may do. In other contexts more detail may be necessary, as, for example, "window frame manufacturing" or "toy retailing". In s 149(1)(d), however, more and different detail is necessary in order to decide whether one employer is the successor to or of the "business" or part of the "business" of another. So much follows inevitably from the need to consider whether the new employer is a successor to a *part* of the former employer's business. But more fundamentally than that, it follows from the fact that s 149(1)(d) focuses upon succession, assignment and transmission to or of a business which is identified as the business *of* an employer. That necessarily directs attention to what it is that the former employer had which is to be described as the "business" of that employer.

…

'[39] The "business" of an employer may be constituted by a number of different assets, both tangible and intangible, that are used in the particular pursuit, whether of profit (if the "business" is a commercial enterprise) or other ends (if the activity is charitable or the "business" of government). In the case of a commercial enterprise, identifying the employer's "business" will usually require identification both of the particular activity that is pursued and of the tangible and intangible assets that are used in that pursuit. The "business" of an employer will be identified as the assets that the employer uses in the pursuit of the particular activity. It is the assets used in that way that can be assigned or transmitted and it is to the assets used in that way that an employer can be a successor.

…

'[43] The conclusion just reached about this example turns upon what is meant by the "business" of the former employer. It understands that word, at least when applied to a commercial venture, as a reference to the combination of the activities pursued in the business and the assets that are used in that business. The conclusion assumes that, either the asset in question (the motor vehicle) is not the sole or principal asset of the business, or that, if it is, it is replaced by another and similar asset which the former employer will use in the same way. That is, the conclusion assumes that the combination of activities and assets which together constitute the former employer's "business" continues largely unaffected by what has happened. There has been no succession because the former employer has not ceased to enjoy any part of its business.' Per Gleeson CJ, Heyne, Callinan and Heydon JJ.

...

'[68] The word "business" in s 149(1)(d) is not defined. Nor is there a universal definition of the phrase "part of the business". However, in s 170LB(3) of the Act (appearing in Pt VIB — "Certified agreements") a definition is provided of the expression "a part of a single business" appearing there. For the purposes of that Part, "a *part* of a single business includes: a geographically distinct part of the single business; or (b) a distinct operational or organisational unit within the single business.

'The adjective "single" affirms that the "business" there mentioned is one that is ultimately integrated into one economic unit. That adjective does not appear in s 149(1)(d) of the Act. Nevertheless, the definition adopted in s 170LB(3) suggests that the Parliament had in mind, for that Part of the Act, a wide and non-exclusive definition. For a provision such as s 149(1)(d), intended to have a much larger ambit of operation, no narrower view would be taken.

...

'[83] In the course of arriving at this conclusion, which was sufficient to decide that appeal, the joint reasons of four members of this Court elaborated the meaning of "business" in a context such as s 149(1)(d):

As was pointed out in Australian Transport Officers Federation, "the word 'business' is notorious for taking its colour and its content from its surroundings". Thus, for example, the expression "the business of government" signifies something quite different from the expression "the business of grazing" which was considered in *Hope v Bathurst City Council*. In the latter case, it was held that the expression "carrying on the business of grazing" meant "grazing activities undertaken as a commercial enterprise in the nature of a going concern, that is, activities engaged in for the purpose of profit on a continuous and repetitive basis".

...

'[92] ... the use of the chameleon-like word "business" must be considered. This is not a technical word of fixed legal connotation. It is not given a particular meaning for the purpose of s 149(1)(d). As R D Nicholson J pointed out in *North Western Health Care Network v Health Services Union of Australia*, the expression "the business" in s 149(1)(d), particularly by reference to the definite article ("the") in the context of succession, assignment and transmission:

requires an asset or property capable of such disposition and not an activity. A succession occurs when there is at law a devolution of property on a person's death. An assignment occurs when there is a transfer of property, particularly personal property. A transmission involves the transfer of a right from one person to another, generally involuntarily, as on death or bankruptcy ... Strictly speaking there cannot be a succession, assignment or transmission of a business or part of a business. For something to occur to that effect it is necessary that it occur in relation to the component parts of the business such as the leasehold or other realty interests; the plant and equipment; or the goodwill. In my view this points to the language in the paragraph being used broadly, not strictly.'

Minister for Employment and Workplace Relations v Gribbles Radiology Pty Ltd [2005] HCA 9, per Kirby J; BC200500900

BUSINESS OF BANKING

Australia 'The essential characteristics of the business of banking are "the collection of money by receiving deposits upon loan, repayable when and as expressly or impliedly agreed upon, and the utilization of the money so collected by lending it again in such sums as are required" [*Commissioners of the State Savings Bank of Victoria v Permewan, Wright & Co Ltd* (1914) 19 CLR 457 at 470–71 per Isaacs J]. It involves the creation of distinct debtor and creditor relationships between the bank and those who deposit money with it and, also, between the bank and those who borrow from it.'
PP Consultants Pty Ltd v Finance Sector Union (2000) 201 CLR 648; 176 ALR 205; BC200006929; [2000] HCA 59 at [17], per Gleeson CJ, Gaudron, McHugh and Gummow JJ

BY

Australia [The court considered whether the Curtin University of Technology was established 'by' the Curtin University of Technology Act 1966 (WA) rather than 'under' it]. 'While in particular contexts [a distinction between "by" and "under"] may be made, there are also contexts where "by" and "under" have the same meaning. For example, both "by" and "under" are commonly used in contexts where the meaning is "pursuant to" or "in accordance with".

'While the word "under" has a primary meaning in the sense of denoting a position beneath or below something which is overhead or above or covered by it, it also has a meaning as an adverb implying covered by or in accordance with some regulative power or principle: *Shorter Oxford English Dictionary* (3rd Ed) Vol II, 2290.

'The word "under" as an adverb also has a meaning in denoting a state or condition including in the sense of denoting inclusion in a group, category or class. Thus the reference to "a member, officer or employee of any … corporation … established under a written law" identifies a corporation as one member of a class of various bodies established under a written law … In this context it matters not that the University was in terms established as a body corporate "by" the Act, as distinct from "under" the Act in the general sense, as it is clear from the definition in the Act that "under" was being used as an equivalent to "by" in the relevant sense. That sense is roughly the equivalent to "in accordance with" or "pursuant to". For example, "by and with" is described in *A Dictionary of Modern Legal Usage* (Oxford 2nd Edn) at 124 as follows:

> "by and with is a classic legal REDUN-DANCY with but one legitimate use: 'For appointments to constitutional offices the phrase by and with the advice of the Senate is a TERM OF ART and should not be changed.' Reed Dickenson Legislative Drafting 75 n 4 (1954)."

'The terms "by law" and "under law" are regarded as synonymous: ibid at 897. The word "under", like "by", is used in the sense of inclusion in a class or category or "in accordance with some regulatory power or principle": *Shorter Oxford English Dictionary* (3rd Ed) Vol II at 2290. Another example is a warrant "under" the King's "own hand": ibid; and see *The Macquarie Dictionary* (3rd Ed) at 229 where the meanings of "under" include "in accordance with" law.' *R v Tkacz* (2001) 25 WAR 77; BC200107679; [2001] WASCA 391 at [23]–[26], per Malcolm CJ

BY REASON OF

Australia 'The expression "by reason of" has been considered in many cases in a variety of contexts …

'In the United States the expression was interpreted as meaning "by virtue of": *United States v William Cramp & Sons Ship & Engine Building Co* 206 US 118 at 127–8.

'Equal opportunity legislation has also used the expression "by reason of" and was considered by the High Court in *Waters v Public Transport Corp* (1991) 103 ALR 513; 173 CLR 349 per Mason CJ and Gaudron J at 359 and interpreted in the sense of "based on". See also *R v Birmingham City Council; Ex parte Equal Opportunities Commission* [1989] AC 1155 per Lord Goff of Chieveley (with whose speech the other members of the House agreed).

…

'In my opinion the phrase "by reason of" in s 5(1) of the [Sex Discrimination Act 1984 (Cth) (SD Act)] should be interpreted as meaning "because of", "due to", "based on" or words of similar import which bring something about or cause it to occur. The phrase implies a relationship of cause and effect between the sex (or characteristic of the kind mentioned in s 5(1)(b) or s 5(1)(c)) of the aggrieved person and the less favourable treatment by the discriminator of that person.

'… Similar legislation in the United Kingdom has received considerable judicial scrutiny and two schools of thought have emerged there. One is that the test requires causation in the sense that there must be a causative link between the defendant's behaviour and detriment to the complainant and does not necessarily involve any consideration of the reason which led the alleged discriminator to treat the complainant less favourably than he treats or would treat a person of a different sex or status. Put another way, one asks the question: would the complainant have received the same treatment from the alleged discriminator *but for* his or her sex (it was thus expressed by Lord Goff of Chieveley in [*James v Eastleigh Borough Council* [1990] 2 AC 751])? This test was adopted by the House of Lords in [*Birmingham City Council v Equal Opportunity Commission* [1989] 1 AC 1155] confirming earlier English authorities and reaffirmed by the House in *Eastleigh Borough Council* by a majority (Lord Bridge of Harwich, Lord Ackner, and Lord Goff of Chieveley; Lord Griffith and Lord Lowry dissenting).

'The other view which appealed to the three members of the Court of Appeal of the United Kingdom in *Eastleigh Borough Council* and to the minority in the House of Lords is what is there referred to as the subjective test, namely, that what is relevant is the defendant's reason for doing an act, not (or perhaps not merely) the causative effects of the act done by the defendant. This view was expressed in the following passage from the speech of Lord Lowry in *Eastleigh Borough Council* at 2 AC 779–80:

> "… the causative construction not only gets rid of unessential and often irrelevant mental ingredients, such as malice, prejudice, desire and motive, but also dispenses with an essential ingredient, namely, the ground on which the discriminator acts. The appellant's construction relieves the complainant of the need to prove anything except that A has done an act which results in less favourable treatment for B by reason of B's sex, which reduces to insignificance the words "on the ground of". The causative test is too wide and is grammatically unsound, because it necessarily disregards the fact that the less favourable treatment is meted out to the victim *on the ground* of the victim's sex."

…

'In my view the Act requires that when an inquiry is being held into alleged discrimination prohibited by s 14(2) on the ground of the sex of an employee, all the relevant circumstances surrounding the alleged discriminatory conduct should be examined. The intention of the defendant is not necessarily irrelevant. The purpose and motive of the defendant may also be relevant.

…

'Ultimately the question must be decided by determining whether there is a relationship of cause and effect between the sex (or characteristic of the kind mentioned in s 5(1)(b) or (c) of the Act) of the aggrieved person and the less favourable treatment of that person, but I do not accept that this inquiry necessarily rejects the motive, intention or purpose of the alleged discriminator.' *Human Rights and Equal Opportunity Commission v Mount Isa Mines Ltd* (1993) 46 FCR 301; 118 ALR 80 at 98–100, 102, 103, per Lockhart J

BY REASON THAT

Australia 'This phrase usually means "because".' *Australian Competition and Consumer Commission v Visy Paper Pty Ltd* (2001) ATPR 41–799; BC200006997; [2000] FCA 164 at [99], per Sackville J

BY VIRTUE OF HIS POSITION AS SUCH

'[11] The statutory provision under challenge is s 548(1) of the Education Act 1996, as amended by the School Standards and Framework Act 1998. The first issue in these proceedings concerns the proper interpretation of this provision. Section 548(1) provides:

> "Corporal punishment given by, or on the authority of, a member of staff to a child—(a) for whom education is provided at any school … cannot be justified in any proceedings on the ground that it was given in pursuance of a right exercisable by the member of staff by virtue of his position as such."

'Corporal punishment means punishment which, justification apart, constitutes battery: s 548(4). Member of staff includes a teacher at the school in control or charge of the child: s 548(6). Child means a person under the age of 18: s 548(7).

'[12] The claimants contend this statutory provision does not apply where parents, having the common law right to discipline their child, expressly delegate this right to a teacher. Then the teacher is exercising an expressly delegated power, not acting as a teacher "as such". This interpretation of s 548 would, it is said, accord proper respect to the deliberate decision of parents in respect of the education and disciplining of their children.

'[13] I consider this interpretation of s 548 is not tenable. It is unnecessary to consider the origins of a teacher's disciplinary powers in relation to school pupils or the extent to which a parent's disciplinary powers are expressly delegable. Suffice to say, the plain purpose of s 548(1) was to prohibit the use of corporal punishment by all teachers in all schools. The claimants' interpretation, if right, would defeat this purpose. The claimants' interpretation would mean the ban on the use of corporal punishment by teachers could be side-stepped by parents expressly giving their consent to the infliction of corporal punishment on their child. Thus the ban would not be mandatory in its operation. It would be optional, at the choice of the parents.

'[14] In my view the phrase "by virtue of his position as such" in s 548(1)(a) is apt to limit the application of s 548(1) to corporal punishment given by a teacher while acting as a teacher, that is, while discharging his functions as a teacher. It excludes cases where, for example, a teacher is himself a parent and is acting in that capacity when punishing a child. Read in context, this phrase is not apt to draw a distinction between cases where the teacher has been expressly authorised by the parents and cases where he has not. In the former case as much as the latter administration of corporal punishment by a teacher derives from a right exercisable by him by virtue of his position as a teacher within the meaning of s 548.' *R (on the application of Williamson) v Secretary of State for Education and Employment* [2005] UKHL 15, [2005] 2 All ER 1 at [11]–[14], per Lord Nicholls of Birkenhead

C

C.I.F.

[For 41 Halsbury's Laws (4th edn) para 612 see now 41 Halsbury's Laws (4th edn) (Reissue) para 13.]

[For 41 Halsbury's Laws (4th edn) para 909 see now 41 Halsbury's Laws (4th edn) (Reissue) para 321.]

CALL

[For 7 Halsbury's Laws (4th edn) para 328 see now 7(1) Halsbury's Laws (4th edn) (2004 Reissue) para 825.]

CALL ON

Australia [Section 11 of the Door to Door Trading Act 1987 (WA) refers to a person who 'calls on' a person for the purpose of negotiating a contract to which the Act applies.] 'The words "call on" in relation to a person normally mean "to visit briefly". They do not ordinarily mean to make a telephone call to a person.' *Ham v Burgess* (1992) 7 WAR 98 at 100, per White J

CALLOUSLY FAIL

Australia [Section 155 of the Criminal Code (NT) provides, inter alia, that it is an offence to 'callously fail' to provide rescue, resuscitation, medical treatment, first aid or succour of any kind to a person when able to do so.] 'To my mind, to "callously fail" involves a deliberate and conscious choice by an informed accused not to provide aid or assistance to the victim; it does not involve an impulsive or an unconscious choice. But, further, I consider that "callous" also requires proof that the accused's failure was such as to offend common standards of respect, decency and kindness in the sense that a reasonable person would regard the accused's failure as callous.' *Re Salmon* (1994) 70 A Crim R 536 at 557, per Kearney J

CANADIAN MARITIME LAW

Canada '1. "Canadian maritime law" as defined in s 2 of the *Federal Court Act* is a comprehensive body of federal law dealing with all claims in respect of maritime and admiralty matters. The scope of Canadian maritime law is not limited by the scope of English admiralty law at the time of its adoption into Canadian law in 1934. Rather, the word "maritime" is to be interpreted within the modern context of commerce and shipping, and the ambit of Canadian maritime law should be considered limited only by the constitutional division of powers in the *Constitution Act, 1867*. The test for determining whether a subject matter under consideration is within maritime law requires a finding that the subject matter is so integrally connected to maritime matters as to be legitimate Canadian maritime law within federal competence: *ITO, supra,* at p 774; *Monk Corp., supra,* at p 795.

'2. Canadian maritime law is uniform throughout Canada, and it is not the law of any province of Canada. All of its principles constitute federal law and not an incidental application of provincial law: *ITO, supra,* at pp 779, 782; *Chartwell, supra,* at p 696.

'3. The substantive content of Canadian maritime law is to be determined by reference to its heritage. It includes, but is not limited to, the body of law administered in England by the High Court on its Admiralty side in 1934, as that body of law has been amended by the Canadian Parliament and as it has developed by judicial precedent to date: *ITO, supra,* at pp 771, 776; *Chartwell, supra,* at pp 695–96.

'4. English admiralty law as incorporated into Canadian law in 1934 was an amalgam of principles deriving in large part from both the common law and the civilian tradition. It was composed of both the specialized rules and principles of admiralty, and the rules and principles adopted from the common law and applied in admiralty cases. Although most of Canadian maritime law with respect to issues of tort, contract, agency and bailment is founded upon the English common law, there are issues specific to maritime law where reference may fruitfully be made to the experience of other countries and specifically, because of the genesis of admiralty jurisdiction, to civilian experience: *ITO, supra*, at p 776; *Chartwell, supra*, at pp 695–97.

'5. The nature of navigation and shipping activities as they are practised in Canada makes a uniform maritime law a practical necessity. Much of maritime law is the product of international conventions, and the legal rights and obligations of those engaged in navigation and shipping should not arbitrarily change according to jurisdiction. The need for legal uniformity is particularly pressing in the area of tortious liability for collisions and other accidents that occur in the course of navigation: *Whitbread, supra*, at pp 1294–95; *Bow Valley Husky, supra*, at pp 1259–60.

'6. In those instances where Parliament has not passed legislation dealing with a maritime matter, the inherited non-statutory principles embodied in Canadian maritime law as developed by Canadian courts remain applicable, and resort should be had to these principles before considering whether to apply provincial law to resolve an issue in a maritime action: *ITO, supra*, at pp 781–82; *Bow Valley Husky, supra*, at p 1260.

'7. Canadian maritime law is not static or frozen. The general principles established by this Court with respect to judicial reform of the law apply to the reform of Canadian maritime law, allowing development in the law where the appropriate criteria are met: *ITO, supra*, at p 74; *Bow Valley Husky, supra*, at pp 1261–68; *Porto Seguro, supra*, at pp 1292–1300.' *Ordon Estate v Grail* [1998] 3 SCR 437 at 489–491, per Iacobucci and Major JJ

CANAL

Australia [An insurance policy under exclusion 3, excluded from insurance cover physical loss, destruction or damage occasioned by flood and referred to, inter alia, escape from a canal'.] 'I do not see in the policy or in exclusion 3 the intention to restrict "canal" to an artificial watercourse used or apt for navigation. There are, no doubt, canals constructed or used essentially for that purpose. The canals in England may have been of this kind, although the canals of Holland may have been designed initially with drainage purposes in mind. But, as the learned judge observed, the term "canal" is applied also to a watercourse used for irrigation, drainage and the passage of stormwater. Once it be accepted that these are ordinary meanings of "canal", I do not see in the present context a reason why the term should be restricted to a navigation canal.' *Provincial Insurance Australia Pty Ltd v*

Consolidated Wood Products Pty Ltd (1991) 25 NSWLR 541 at 562, per Mahoney JA

CANVASSER

[For 15 Halsbury's Laws (4th edn) para 700 see now 15 Halsbury's Laws (4th edn) (Reissue) para 619.]

CAPABLE

Canada [Prohibited weapon included one 'capable' of firing bullets in a defined way.] 'In my view, any uncertainty as to whether the word "capable" means either "immediately capable" or "readily capable" is resolved as soon as the word is interpreted in light of the purpose and goals of the prohibited weapons provisions of the *Code*... The word "capable" as is it defined in the Oxford English Dictionary (2nd edn, 1989) includes an aspect of potential capability for conversion ... Yet, that potential aspect must be given some reasonable restriction. It is the proper role of the court to define the meaning of "capable" as it is used in the definition of "prohibited weapon" in s 84(1). In my view, it should mean capable of conversion to an automatic weapon in a relatively short period of time with relative ease.' *R v Hasselwader* [1993] 2 SCR 398 at 413, 414, 415, 416, per Cory J

CAPITAL

[As to capital see 7(1) Halsbury's Laws (4th edn) (2004 Reissue) para 520.]

Circulating capital

[For 7 Halsbury's Laws (4th edn) para 601 see now 7(1) Halsbury's Laws (4th edn) (2004 Reissue) para 524.]

Issued and unissued capital

[For 7 Halsbury's Laws (4th edn) para 135 see now 7(1) Halsbury's Laws (4th edn) (2004 Reissue) para 521.]

Nominal capital

[For 7 Halsbury's Laws (4th edn) para 135 see now 7(1) Halsbury's Laws (4th edn) (2004 Reissue) para 521.]

Paid up capital

[For 7 Halsbury's Laws (4th edn) para 137 see now 7(1) Halsbury's Laws (4th edn) (2004 Reissue) para 522.]

Reserve capital

[For 7 Halsbury's Laws (4th edn) para 139 see now 7(1) Halsbury's Laws (4th edn) (2004 Reissue) para 526.]

CAPITAL GAIN

Australia 'The term "capital gain" is sometimes used (as it is in this Deed) to refer to the measure of increase in the value of an asset over time. "Capital profit" and "capital gain" appear to have been used synonymously in a number of decisions of this court concerning the operation of the Income Tax Assessment Act: see, e.g., *Blockey v Federal Commissioner of Taxation* [(1923) 31 CLR 503 at 508], per Isaacs J ..., and, most recently, *Federal Commissioner of Taxation v Myer Emporium Ltd* [(1987) 163 CLR 199]. The expression "capital gain", however, has generally been used to connote a gain made in the course of a transaction concerning a capital asset (*Myer Emporium*). Commonly, such a transaction involves the sale or realisation of a capital asset ... However, as is clear from *Californian Copper Syndicate v Harris* [(1904) 5 TC 159 at 167], per Lord Trayner, the transaction may involve the conversion of the asset into a form other than money, as, for example, by the exchange of one asset for another, at least to the extent that the asset is converted into "that which can be turned to pecuniary account": *Tennant v Smith* [(1892) AC 150 at 159]. So employed, the expression "capital gain" is used to mean a realised capital gain, and not a mere increase in the value of the asset. In our opinion a mere increase in the value of an asset does not amount to a capital profit. A profit connotes an actual gain and not mere potential to achieve a gain. Until a gain is realised it is not "earned, derived or received". A capital gain is realised when an item of capital which has increased in value is ventured, either in whole or in part, in a transaction which returns that increase in value.' *Read v Commonwealth of Australia* (1988) 167 CLR 57 at 66, per Mason CJ, Deane and Gaudron JJ

CAPITAL VALUE

New Zealand [Income Tax Act 1976, s 108(1).] ' "Capital value" is not an expression used elsewhere in the Act. It seems likely that it was taken from the Valuation of Land Act 1951 where it is defined in terms of the realisable value if the land (or in this case, the asset) being valued is offered for sale on such reasonable terms as a bone fide seller might be expected to require. This is a market or economic value.' *Poverty Bay Electric Power Board v Commissioner of Inland Revenue* [1999] 2 NZLR 438 at 450, CA, per cur

CAPTAIN

[The Dumping at Sea Act 1974 is repealed. The definition is re-enacted in the Food and Environmental Protection Act 1985, s 24(1).]

CAPTURE

[For 25 Halsbury's Laws (4th edn) paras 157, 161 see now 25 Halsbury's Laws (4th edn) (2003 Reissue) paras 337, 339.]

CARAVAN

In order to qualify for the description "caravan" in section 29 [of the Caravan Sites and Control of Development Act 1960] it is therefore "the structure" that has to possess two qualities. The first part of the section provides that it is necessary for "the structure" to be designed or adapted for human habitation. This, in my view, clearly contemplates the structure as a whole, as a single unit, and not the component parts of it. The second quality which "the structure" has to possess is mobility. The structure has to be capable of being moved by being towed or transported on a single motor vehicle or trailer. "The structure" contemplated by the second part of the section is, in my judgment, precisely the same structure as that contemplated by the first part of the section, not a structure which has been dismantled before loading has taken place. In my view the second limb of the definition can therefore refer only to a whole single structure and not to component parts of it.' *Carter v Secretary of State for the Environment* [1994] 1 WLR 1212 at 1219, CA, per Russell LJ

[As to the erection of a chalet structure on a caravan site see *Wyre Forest District Council v Secretary of State for the Environment* [1990] 1 All ER 780, HL.]

CARE OR CONTROL

[The Children and Young Persons Act 1969, s 70(1) is repealed and the definition of 'care or control' is replaced by that of 'person with care' in the Child Support Act 1991, s 3(3), as follows.] A person is a 'person with care', in relation to any child, if he is a person—

(a) with whom the child has his home;

(b) who usually provides day to day care for the child (whether exclusively or in conjunction with any other person); and

(c) who does not fall within a prescribed category of person.

CARELESS MANNER

Canada [Manslaughter charge alleged use of firearm in a careless manner.] 'In my opinion, the determination of what constitutes "in a careless manner" or "without reasonable precautions for the safety of other persons" is, following *Hundal* [*R v Hundal* (1993) 79 CCC (3d) 97; [1993] 1 SCR 867], to be assessed on an objective standard. I am supported in this view by the plain meaning of the words chosen by Parliament. Neither phrase connotes any subjective knowledge of the standard of care in the circumstances, nor any subjective awareness of the risks arising out of a marked departure from the standard of care.' *R v Gosset* (1993) 105 DLR (4th) 681 at 691, per Lamer CJC (Can SC)

CARGO

[The Dock Workers (Regulation of Employment) Act 1946 has been repealed.]

Deck cargo

[For 43 Halsbury's Laws (4th edn) para 586 see now 43(1) Halsbury's Laws (4th edn) (Reissue) para 682.]

CARRIAGE OF GOODS

[The Road Traffic Act 1972 has been repealed. See now the Road Traffic Act 1988, s 192(1).]

[For 5 Halsbury's Laws (4th edn) paras 328–374 see now 5(1) Halsbury's Laws (4th edn) (2004 Reissue) paras 541–597.]

CARRIER

[For 5 Halsbury's Laws (4th edn) paras 301–327 see now 5(1) Halsbury's Laws (4th edn) (2004 Reissue) paras 501–540.]

CARRY

Australia [Section 15(1) of the Summary Offences Act 1953 (SA) provides that a person who, without lawful excuse, inter alia, 'carries' an offensive weapon is guilty of an offence. Section 15(3) provides that 'carry' includes to have on or about one's person.] 'The word "carries" is, according to its ordinary usage, susceptible of a variety of meanings and that which is apposite depends very much upon the context in which it appears. However, in its normally accepted sense, the word "carry" means to have about the person ready for use or to convey from one place to another or be the bearer of it. So it is that the definition contained in subs (3) of s 15 extends that concept to include the mere fact of having an object on or about one's person, regardless of the purpose for having it or of the bearer's intention in relation to it.

'It is to be noted that a key feature of the word "carry" is that it imports a concept of the object in question being actually on the person or, at the very least, about the person of the carrier.' *Coleman v Zanker* (1992) 58 SASR 7 at 14, per Olsson J

CARRY INTO EFFECT

New Zealand 'The carrying into effect of the Inland Revenue Acts must include their proper implementation or administration. When the Commissioner is properly a party to litigation, whether as a claimant or as a defendant, it seems to me that in the natural and ordinary use of language the conduct of the litigation by him is activity in the carrying into effect or implementation or administration of the Acts.' *Knight v Inland Revenue Commissioner* [1991] 2 NZLR 30 at 35, CA, per Cooke P

CARRY ON BUSINESS

[For 7 Halsbury's Laws (4th edn) para 20 see now 7(1) Halsbury's Laws (4th edn) (2004 Reissue) para 201 note 1.]

Australia 'In our opinion it must be shown that the debtor was carrying on his or her own business. It is not sufficient that the debtor was engaged as an employee in the business of somebody else.' *Turner v Trevorrow* (1994) 126 ALR 263 at 268, per cur

Canada 'The expressions "carry on business", "carrying on business" or "carried on business," while undefined must, when regard is had to the ordinary meaning of the words, refer to the ongoing conduct or carriage of a business". It would seem to follow that where one "carries on" a business in the ordinary sense or by pursuing one or more of the included activities under subsection 248(1) [of the Income Tax Act] over time, one is "carrying on business" under the Act.

'The Trial Judge in his reasons twice refused to confront this definition and in particular the argument that the Department was carrying on business within the defined meaning. The Trial Judge stated:

> "The plaintiff contends that the Department was carrying on an 'undertaking of any kind whatever'. However, the above provision [i.e. the definition of 'business' in s 248(1)] does not define business; rather, it lists a number of examples which are included in the term: *Canadian Marconi Co v The Queen* [1984] CTC 319 (FCA) reversed on other grounds, [1986] 2 SCR 522. [Emphasis added.]"

'The point had indeed been made by this Court in *Canadian Marconi* but only for the purpose of making it clear that beyond the included activities listed in subsection 248(1), the word "business" retains its ordinary meaning.

'Whether one reads the definition of "business" in subsection 248(1) as a definition or as something else, it inescapably brings within the meaning of this word the specific activities which it lists. The result is that profits generated by the carriage of these activities are, for purposes of the Act, business profits and taxable as such. While subsections 8(10) and 122.3(1) do not impose a tax but extend a benefit, it cannot be seriously argued that on that account only, the word business should be construed differently. There is nothing in the language of these subsections which excludes from their application the defined meaning of the word "business".

'Applying this definition, it seems clear that even if it could be said that the Department was not carrying on a business in the ordinary sense, it was at least engaged in an "undertaking of any kind whatever", namely the provision of services under a contract for a fee. As such it was carrying on business under a contract as contemplated by subsections 8(10) and 122.3(1).

'In my view, the Trial Judge ignored the definition set out in subsection 248(1) when he held that business could not be "carried on" within the meaning of subsections 8(10) and 122.3(1) in the absence of a predominant profit motive. The definition in subsection 248(1) reflects no such requirement. Although the word "business" when used in the Act must generally envisage an activity

capable of giving rise to profits, it does not require that this activity be undertaken or carried on for the "predominant" purpose of earning a profit. To incorporate such a requirement into the Act would severely curtail its reach in so far as the taxation of business profits is concerned.' *Timmins v Canada* (1999) 2 FC 563 at 569, 570, 571, CA, per Noël JA

New Zealand [Section 104(b) of the Income Tax Act 1976.] ' "Business" is defined in the Act in s 2 as follows:

> "Business" includes any profession, trade, manufacture or undertaking carried on for pecuniary profit.

'The meaning of the word "business" was extensively explored by Richardson J in *Grieve v Commissioner of Inland Revenue* [1984] 1 NZLR 101 (CA). As I understand it essentially two elements are required: (i) some form of organised commercial activity and (ii) the conduct of that activity for the purpose of making a profit. As to the first, it is not essential that there be a realistic prospect of making a profit when objectively considered. As Richardson J said in *Grieve* at 110:

> "... while the Courts are justified in viewing circumspectly a claim that a taxpayer genuinely intended to carry on a business for pecuniary profit when looked at realistically there seems no real prospect of profit, an actual intention once established is sufficient. The legislation sensibly allows for deductions and allowances to be claimed even where the overall result is a trading loss. It is not for the Courts or the Commissioner to confine the recognition of businesses to those that are always profitable or to do so only so long as they operate at a profit. In my view there is no warrant in the definition of business in its statutory context for reading in a requirement that there must be a reasonable prospect of profit before the gross income derived is assessable under s 88(1)(a) and the deductions sought are allowable under s 111(b) and under the specific deduction provisions requiring the taxpayer concerned to be carrying on a business."

...

'The sole question under this heading is therefore whether the activity which accompanied that purpose was sufficient to amount to a commercial activity for the purposes of a "business". As to the nature of that activity, Richardson J said in *Grieve* at 106:

"In common usage 'business' has and has long had a wide and flexible meaning. In the sense in which it is used in legislation imposing a charge for tax in respect of revenue earning activities *The Oxford English Dictionary* definitions 'a pursuit or occupation demanding time and attention; a serious employment as distinct from a pastime ...; trade; commercial transactions or engagements' and *Webster's Third New International Dictionary* definitions 'a usually commercial or mercantile activity customarily engaged in as a means of livelihood and typically involving some independence of judgment and power of decision ... a commercial or industrial enterprise' reflect the underlying notion. The word has been subject to much judicial discussion in New Zealand and other jurisdictions. Our concern is as to its meaning in the context of the income tax legislation and s 2 provides as it has since 1916 that except where a contrary intention appears 'business' 'includes any profession, trade, manufacture or undertaking carried on for pecuniary profit'. In *G v Commissioner of Inland Revenue* [1961] NZLR 994, 998 McCarthy J considered that notwithstanding the use of the word 'includes' a study of the definition forces the view that it does not add anything to the common meaning of the word and does not catch anything that would not otherwise be caught. In *Harley v Commissioner of Inland Revenue* at 487 North P took the same view. I respectfully agree. While there are obvious shades of difference, and while each of the words 'profession, trade, manufacture or undertaking' has a wide meaning, I cannot readily postulate any activity which they comprehend which is not also included in the general concept of 'business' in ordinary usage.

...

"Underlying each of the words in the definition in s 2 and the term 'business' itself when used in the context of a taxation statute is the fundamental notion of the exercise of an activity in an organised and coherent way and one which is directed to an end result."

...

'As Richardson J said, it must be the exercise of an activity in an organised and coherent way but that too is a wide concept. Two aspects seem to me to refine the meaning: continuity and more than mere preparation.

As to the first, there is an element of continuity involved in carrying on a business but since all courses of conduct must begin somewhere I do not think that there could be any minimum period before a commenced course of conduct would qualify. Richardson J in *Grieve* does say at 110:

"It follows from this analysis that the decision whether or not a taxpayer is in business involves a two-fold inquiry – as to the nature of the activities carried on, and as to the intention of the taxpayer in engaging in those activities. Statements by the taxpayer as to his intentions are of course relevant but actions will often speak louder than words. Amongst the matters which may properly be considered in that inquiry are the nature of the activity, the period over which it is engaged in, the scale of operations and the volume of transactions, the commitment of time, money and effort, the pattern of activity, and the financial results. It may be helpful to consider whether the operations involved are of the same kind and are carried on in the same way as those which are characteristic of ordinary trade in the line of business in which the venture was conducted. However, in the end it is the character and circumstances of the particular venture which are crucial. Businesses do not cease to be businesses because they are carried on idiosyncratically or inefficiently or unprofitably, or because the taxpayer derives personal satisfaction from the venture."

...

Secondly it seems inherent in the statutory provisions that to qualify as the conduct of a business for revenue purposes there must be more than mere preparation. In that respect there could well be some distant analogy with criminal law attempts. The taxpayer must embark on the actual course of conduct which it is hoped would ultimately yield profit if persisted in. I do not think that merely setting up a business structure and purchasing plant or organising the decision-making structures, management and equity structures will suffice. That is not "carrying on a business" but "setting up a business". Nor do I think that activities which are confined to the organisation of relationships between proprietors, or the making of decisions over their future ownership of the business, would normally qualify because they are non-productive of income. As I understand it there must be an operational activity. Other matters may well be preconditions to operational activity but will not suffice in themselves.' *Slater v Commissioner of Inland Revenue* [1996] 1 NZLR 759 at 762, 763, 764 and 765, per Fisher J

CARTRIDGE

Australia [Construction of patent specification.] 'I do not agree that the content of the phrase "self-contained cartridge" or the word "cartridge" is necessarily limited by the notions posited by the respondent. The *Oxford English Dictionary* (2nd Ed 1989) defines the word "cartridge" as: "1(a) the case in which the exact charge of powder for firearms is made up; of paper, parchment, paste board, flannel, serge, metal etc, according to use". The *Chambers Dictionary of Science and Technology* includes the following definition of "cartridge": "a cardboard tube for the carriage of a small quantity of chemical." In Random House Webster's *Unabridged Dictionary* (1999) a meaning of "cartridge" as "any small container for powder, liquid or gas, made for ready insertion into some device or mechanism: an ink cartridge for a pen.

'I agree with the applicants' submissions that in the context of the particular application and of the invention it means something containing a pre-determined amount of powder concentrate to be placed into the hydraulic system for a single use and thereafter to be disposed and replaced.

'I do not accept that either as a matter of ordinary meaning or within the context of the claimed inventions set in the specification, the vessel must have rigid walls to be a cartridge, or somehow fit integrally or snugly into some surrounding fixed framework surrounding the vessel. The biBag here does, in any event, fix to the machine by the outer annulated ring. I do not think that to be a cartridge it needs to be fixed at or by some other part of the vessel.' *Gambro Pty Ltd v Fresenius Medical Care South East Asia Pty Ltd* [2004] FCA 323 at [177]–[179] per Allsop J; BC200401266

CASUAL *SEE* EMPLOYMENT

CASUAL PROFIT

[For 23 Halsbury's Laws (4th edn) para 625 see now 23(1) Halsbury's Laws (4th edn) (Reissue) para 567.]

CATERING PREMISES

[The Food Act 1984 is largely repealed. The definition of 'catering premises' has not been re-enacted, but see now the definition of 'food premises' in the Food Safety Act 1990, s 1(3), as follows.] 'Food premises' means any premises used for the purposes of a food business; 'food business' means any business in the course of which commercial operations with respect to food or food sources are carried out.

CAUSE

Australia [Section 39(3) of the Defence Force Discipline Act 1982 (Cth) provides that a defence member who negligently 'causes' or allows a service ship to be lost is guilty of an offence.] '... the word "cause" refers to an act or actions or antecedent conditions which bring about or produce in a positive sense a certain effect or consequence ...' *Victor v Chief of Naval Staff* (1992) 115 ALR 716 at 723, per cur

CAUSE (LEGAL ACTION)

Cause of action

Australia 'The classic formulation of a "cause of action" is that of Brett J in *Cooke v Gill* (1873) 8 LR CP 107, at 116: "'cause of action' has been held from the earliest time to mean every fact which is material to be proved to entitle the plaintiff to succeed — every fact which the defendant would have a right to traverse." This formulation was adopted by Lord Esher MR in *Read v Brown* (1888) 22 QBD 128, at 131; see also *Trower and Sons Ltd v Ripstein* [1944] AC 254, at 263, per Lord Wright. In *Do Carmo v Ford Excavations Pty Ltd* (1984) 154 CLR 234, at 245, Wilson J said that the "concept of a 'cause of action' would seem to be clear. It is simply the fact or combination of facts which gives rise to a right to sue. In an action for negligence, it consists of the wrongful act or omission and the consequent damage ... Knowledge of the legal implications of the known facts is not an additional fact which forms part of a cause of action. Indeed, a person may be well appraised of all of the facts which need to be proved to establish a cause of action but for want of taking legal advice may not know that those facts give rise to a right to relief." See also *Carter v Egg and Egg Pulp Marketing Board* (Vic) (1942) 66 CLR 557, at 600, per Williams J.' *Torrens Aloha Pty Ltd v Citibank NA* (1997) 72 FCR 581 at 595; (1997) 144 ALR 89 at 101; BC9701370 at 28–29, per Sackville J

Canada [A limitation period for a cause of action arising otherwise than in a province was calculated from the time the cause of action arose.] '... the "cause of action" in a proceeding in tort, as the expression is used therein, must necessarily refer to the damage suffered as well as the act that caused the damage.

...

'... "cause of action" obviously refers to the advent of damage since before such advent, there is no possible action.' *Canada v Maritime Group (Canada) Inc* [1995] 3 FC 124 at 129, Fed CA, per Marceau JA

CAUSE OR PERMIT

[The Road Traffic Act 1972 has been repealed. See now the Road Traffic Act 1988, s 143(1)(b).]

CEASE ... ANYTHING DONE

New Zealand [Section 322(1)(a) of the Resource Management Act 1991.] 'There is some difficulty in the use of the phrase "to cease anything done" since "cease" has an application to continuing activity rather than something which has been done or which has still to be done. I think, however, the meaning of the section is plain and that it is intended to apply to the continuing effects and continuing activities.' *Zdrahal v Wellington City Council* [1995] 1 NZLR 700 at 706, per Greig J

CERTIFICATE

[The Exchange Control Act 1947 has been repealed.]

Australia 'A "certificate", in the ordinary meaning of the term, is "a writing on paper certifying to the truth of something": see the *Macquarie Dictionary*, 2nd ed. In *Costain International Ltd v Attorney-General* (1983) 23 BLR 54, Huggins V-P, in the Hong Kong Court of Appeal, said, at 56, of what is ordinarily conveyed by the term "certificate":

"As I understand it, a certificate is basically a document which speaks to the truth of some existing fact. Often the fact will be that a person other than the certifier has done something, but it may equally be that the certifier himself has done something or has come to some opinion." '

Joam v Minister for Immigration and Multicultural Affairs BC200200501; [2002] FCA 107 at [14], per Drummond J

CERTIORARI

[An order of certiorari was renamed a quashing order by the Civil Procedure Rules 1998,

SI 1998/3132: see CPR 51.1(2)(d). For 11 Halsbury's Laws (4th edn) paras 1521, 1528 see now 1(1) Halsbury's Laws (4th edn) (2001 Reissue) paras 118, 123–128.]

CHAIRMAN

Australia 'A chairman is a person who has control of a meeting. As L W Street J said in *Colorado Construction Pty Ltd v Platus* (1966) 2 NSWR 598 at 600: "It is an indispensable part of any meeting that a chairman should be appointed and should occupy the chair. In the absence of some person (by whatever title he be described) exercising procedural control over a meeting, the meeting is unable to proceed to business. This may perhaps require some qualification if all persons are unanimous. And, in a small meeting, procedural control may pass from person to person according to who for the time being is allowed by the acquiescence of those present to have such control. But there must be some person expressly or by acquiescence permitted by those persons to put motions to the meeting so as to enable the wish or decision of the meeting to be ascertained." It does not seem to me that one can merely say at a meeting, "I am the chairman" unless one also actually behaves at the meeting to show that one exercises procedural control over it. A person exercises procedural control over the meeting by, inter alia, nominating who is to speak, dealing with the order of business (unless that is already set out by a written notice of meeting), putting questions to the meeting, declaring resolutions carried or not carried, in due course asking for any general business, and declaring the meeting closed.' *Kelly v Woltenholme* (1991) 4 ACSR 709 at 712, per Young J

CHALLENGE

[The right to challenge jurors *without* cause (which had already been limited to three such challenges by the Juries Act 1974) was abolished altogether by the Criminal Justice Act 1988, s 118(1). By sub-s (2) of the same section, a Crown Court judge may order that a challenge *for* cause shall be in camera or in chambers.]

[For 11 Halsbury's Laws (4th edn) paras 455–458 see now 11(2) Halsbury's Laws (4th edn) (Reissue) para 984.]

CHAMPERTY

[For 9 Halsbury's Laws (4th edn) para 400 see now 9(1) Halsbury's Laws (4th edn) (Reissue) para 850.]

CHAMPERTY AND MAINTENANCE

Canada 'The threshold issue in this case is whether the arrangements Interclaim has made offend the rules against champerty and maintenance. Champerty is a form of maintenance. *Black's Law Dictionary* defines these terms as follows:

> "Maintenance: An officious intermeddling in a lawsuit by a non-party by maintaining, supporting or assisting either party, with money or otherwise, to prosecute or defend the litigation.
> Champerty: A bargain between a stranger and a party to a lawsuit by which the stranger pursues the party's claim in consideration of receiving part of any judgment proceeds; it is one type of 'maintenance', the more general term which refers to maintaining, supporting or promoting another person's litigation."

'Historically those who offered to assist or assume the pleading of the legal claim of a stranger for reward were barred from doing so by both penal statutes and this common law doctrine. However, the doctrine evolved through the centuries and by the 1840s at least one of England's leading jurists seemed impatient with the rule that had to that point prevented attorneys from assisting those without the means to advance attorney costs and fees in order to allow those without means access to the justice system.

'Lord Abinger, author of the "Assumption of Risk and Fellow Servant Rules" offered this dictum in 1843: "if a man were to see a poor person in the street oppressed and abused, and without the means of obtaining redress, and furnished him with money or employed an attorney to obtain redress for his wrongs, it would require a very strong argument to convince me that that man could be said to be stirring up litigation and strife" (*Findon v Parker* (1843) 152 ER 976 [at 979]).

'The evolution of this law was described by Lord Mustill in *Giles v Thompson*, [1994] 1 AC 142 (HL), at 153–54:

> "My Lords, the crimes of maintenance and champerty are so old that their origins can no longer be traced, but their importance in medieval times is quite clear. The mechanisms of justice lacked the internal strength to resist the oppression of private individuals through suits fomented and sustained by unscrupulous men of power. Champerty was particularly vicious, since the purchase of a share in litigation presented an obvious temptation to the suborning of justices and witnesses and the ex-

ploitation of worthless claims which the defendant lacked the resources and influence to withstand. The fact that such conduct was treated as both criminal and tortious provided a valuable external discipline to which, as the records show, recourse was often required.
> "As the centuries passed, the courts became stronger, their mechanisms more consistent and their participants more self-reliant. Abuses could be more easily detected and forestalled, and litigation more easily determined in accordance with the demands of justice, without recourse to separate proceedings against those who trafficked in litigation."
> …
> "It therefore came as no surprise when Parliament, acting on the recommendation of the Law Commission Report on Proposals for Reform of the Law relating to Maintenance and Champerty (1966) (Law Com. No. 7), abolished the crimes and torts of maintenance and champerty: section 14 of the Criminal Law Act 1967 … section 14(2) of the Act of 1967 … stipulated that the abolition of the civil and criminal liability "shall not affect any rule of [the law of England and Wales] as to the cases in which a contract is to be treated as contrary to public policy or otherwise illegal."

'One of the prerequisites for champerty and maintenance is that there be interference without justification. The doctrine is grounded in public policy and is designed to avoid the "wanton and officious intermeddling in the disputes of others without justification or excuse" (*Giles*).

'In *Martell v. Consett Iron Co*, [1955] 1 Ch 363 (CA), Jenkins LJ referred to this element of maintenance and champerty at pp 399–400 as follows:

> "… the element of impropriety or officious intermeddling being supplied by the fact of interference … coupled with the absence of legal justification for so doing; while, on the other hand, the giving of such aid will not be criminal if it is justifiable in law by reference to one of the specific exceptions … or if the person giving such aid has such an interest in the action as can be held in law sufficient to justify him in giving it." '

Down (Re) (1999), 178 DLR (4th) 294 at 308, 309, 310, BCSC, per Brenner J

CHANNEL

[The Collision Regulations (Ships and Seaplanes on the Water) and Signals of Distress (Ships) Order 1965 has been revoked. See now the Merchant Shipping (Distress Signals and Prevention of Collisions) Regulations 1983, SI 1983/708, Sch 1, r 9.]

[For 43 Halsbury's Laws (4th edn) para 890 see now 43(1) Halsbury's Laws (4th edn) (Reissue) para 809.]

CHARGE

Canada '[34] In my view, when Mervyn leaves his parents' home and goes to a group home, he will leave his parents' charge. The term "charge" is not defined in the *Family Relations Act* either before or after the 1997 amendment. In the *Concise Oxford Dictionary of Current English* (9th ed. 1995), the term "charge" is defined as including: "care, custody, responsible possession". *Black's Law Dictionary* (6th ed. 1990), defines "charge" to include "[a] person or thing committed to the care of another". McEachern C.J.B.C. equated "charge" to "care" and on this basis concluded that when Mervyn left his parents' care for the group home, he would leave their charge. F. L. Woodman, in her article "Financial Obligations of Parents to Adult Disabled Children, Part I" (1997), 17 *Est. Tr. & P. J.* 131, at pp. 140–42, states that "charge" involves an inquiry into whether or not the adult actually lives independently. On this approach, if Mervyn is living in a group home, independent of his parents, he is considered to have withdrawn from their charge. It follows that Mervyn will not fall under the s. 87 definition of "child" when he reaches age 19 and that the *Family Relations Act* could not make his parents responsible for him under s. 88(1).' *Krangle (Guardian ad litem of) v Brisco*, [2002] SCR 205 at 220, per McLachlin CJ

Canada '[19] ...

Section 57 of the [Child and Family Services] Act:

(1) Where the court finds that a child is in need of protection and is satisfied that intervention through a court order is necessary to protect the child in the future, the court shall make one of the following orders, in the child's best interests:

1. That the child be placed with or returned to a parent or another person, subject to the supervision of the society, for a specified period of at least three and not more than twelve months.

2. That the child be made a ward of the society and be placed in its care and custody for a specified period not exceeding twelve months.

3. That the child be made a ward of the Crown, until the wardship is terminated under section 65 or expires under subsection 71(1), and be placed in the care of the society.

4. That the child be made a ward of the society under paragraph 2 for a specified period and then be returned to a parent or another person under paragraph 1, for a period or periods not exceeding an aggregate of twelve months.

(2) In determining which order to make under subsection (1), the court shall ask the parties what efforts the society or another agency or person made to assist the child before intervention under this Part.

(3) The court shall not make an order removing the child from the care of the person who had charge of him or her immediately before intervention under this Part unless the court is satisfied that alternatives that are less disruptive to the child, including non-residential services and the assistance referred to in subsection (2), would be inadequate to protect the child.

(4) Where the court decides that it is necessary to remove the child from the care of the person who had charge of him or her immediately before intervention under this Part, the court shall, before making an order for society or Crown wardship under paragraph 2 or 3 of subsection (1), consider whether it is possible to place the child with a relative, neighbour or other member of the child's community or extended family under paragraph 1 of subsection (1) with the consent of the relative or other person.

...

(9) Where the court finds that a child is in need of protection but is not satisfied that a court order is necessary to protect the child in the future, the court shall order that the child remain with or be returned to the person who had charge of the child immediately before intervention under this Part.

'[20] "Charge", in Black's Law Dictionary, Seventh Edition, states:

... A person or thing entrusted to another's care ...

'[21] "Custody" is defined in Black's Law Dictionary, Seventh Edition, as follows:

The care and control of a thing or person ...

'[22] "Custody" is further defined in the Concise Oxford Dictionary as follows:

Guardianship, care, (parent has custody of child, child is in the custody of father).

'[23] Section 63 of the Child and Family Services Act indicates:

... the Crown has the rights and responsibilities of a parent for the purpose of the child's care, custody and control ...

'[24] In my view, the effect of such an order is to remove the care and control of the child from both parents once a finding has been made that the child is a child in need of protection.' *S (JM) v M (FJ)* (2005) 257 DLR (4th) 158 at [19]–[24], [2005] OJ No 3085 (Ont Sup Ct J), per Meehan J

CHARGE (ACCUSATION)

Australia 'The meaning of the word "charge" was examined by O'Bryan J in *Campagnolo v Attrill* [1982] VR 893. It may be used in the sense of "charged before a Magistrate". In *R v D'Eyncourt* (1888) 21 QBD 109, 119, it was stated that the word in the Act under consideration must be read in its known legal sense, namely, the solemn act of calling before a magistrate an accused person and stating, in his hearing, in order that he may defend himself, what is the accusation against him.' *R v Coroner at Mackay, ex p Butler* [1990] 1 Qd R 451 at 453, per Ryan J

Canada [The right to jury trial was asserted in contempt proceedings on the basis that the accused was 'charged' with an offence.] 'I think the word "charged" bears the sense suggested by the Concise Oxford Dictionary, 6th edn (1974), as "accused". I do not think that the word "charged" imports some technical meaning. A person is charged with an offence whether the proceedings against him are initiated by an indictment, or by a summary procedure initiated by originating notice of motion (as in this case), or by a summary procedure initiated by an oral citation.' *Manitoba (A-G) v Groupe Quebecor Inc* (1987) 45 DLR (4th) 80 at 85, Man CA, per Huband JA

Canada [A person charged with an offence is entitled to trial within a reasonable time.] 'A person is "charged with an offence" within the meaning of s 11 of the *Charter* when an information is sworn alleging an offence against him, or where a direct indictment is laid against him when no information is sworn.' *R v Kalanj* [1989] 1 SCR 1594 at 1607, SCC, per McIntyre J

CHARGES

Australia [A lessee covenanted to pay in addition to the rent all gas and electricity 'charges' and any and all other 'charges' made by any utility or authority against the demised premises.] 'The term "charges" has no precise legal meaning when used in this context. Dictionaries suggest that its ordinary meaning when used in such a context is "a liability to pay money"; it includes "the existence of any pecuniary burden". As such it would prima facie include rates and taxes imposed by a utility or local authority with respect to leased premises.' *Sunskill Investments Pty Ltd v Townsville Office Services Pty Ltd* [1991] 2 Qd R 210 at 220, per Williams J

CHARITABLE INSTITUTION

Australia [In the context of exemption from income tax.] 'In this branch of the law, there are some well-settled principles. First, as already noted, the "charitable" character of an institution is to be determined by reference to the preamble to the Statute of Elizabeth and the four classifications in Lord Macnaghten's speech in *Income Tax Special Purposes Commissioner v Pemsel* [1891] AC 531 ("*Pemsel's Case*"). By reference to the preamble, in *Pemsel's Case*, at 583, Lord Macnaghten classified the following purposes as "charitable" purposes, namely, purposes for: 1) the relief of poverty; 2) the advancement of education; 3) the advancement of religion; and 4) other purposes beneficial to the community, not falling under any of the preceding heads. The present case is primarily concerned with the fourth classification, although Triton also relies on the second classification.

'It is also settled law that whether a particular corporate body is a charitable institution depends on the central or essential object of the institution as determined by reference to its constitution and activities: see, eg, *Salvation Army* at 171–172 per Dixon, Williams and Webb JJ; *Congregational Union of New South Wales v Thistlethwayte* (1952) 87 CLR 375 at 442 per Dixon CJ, McTiernan, Williams and Fullagar JJ; *Stratton v Simpson* (1970)

125 CLR 138 at 150–151 per Windeyer J; and *Crunulla Sutherland Leagues Club Ltd v Federal Commissioner of Taxation* (1990) 23 FCR 82 ("*Crunulla*") at 95–96 per Lockhart J. If the main purpose of such a body is charitable, it does not lose its charitable character simply because some of its incidental or concomitant and ancillary objects are non-charitable. In relation to this process of characterization, Lockhart J said, in *Crunulla* at 96:

> The material facts and circumstances which should be examined to characterise the main purpose of the relevant body include its constitution, its activities, its history and its control. These may alter from time to time and the purpose of establishment may correspondingly change. It is not sufficient to look to the formation of the body and to ascertain what was at the time the purpose of its formation. The statute gives a periodic operation to the words and directs the inquiry to a particular time, namely, the year of income so that consideration must be given not only to the purpose for which the society was established but also the purpose for which it is currently conducted.

'This description of the process is also apposite in this case. The description also indicates that the charitable status of an institution can change over time.

'An institution is not necessarily a charitable institution simply because it has a purpose that is beneficial to the public. In order to qualify as a charitable institution, an institution must have a purpose that is both beneficial to the community and within the spirit and intendment of the preamble to the Statute of Elizabeth. The authorities on this point are clear: see, eg, *ICLR* at 667, 669 per Barwick CJ and *The Royal National Agricultural and Industrial Association v Chester* (1974) 3 ALR 486 at 487 per McTiernan, Menzies and Mason JJ.

'Further, in order to fall within Lord Macnaghten's fourth class, the purpose must be to benefit the public generally, as opposed to individual members of the community, although the fulfilment of the purpose "either directly or indirectly incidentally may benefit such individuals": see *Commissioners of Inland Revenue v Oldham Training and Enterprise Council* (1996) 69 TC 231 ("*Oldham TEC*") at 250–251 per Lightman J. The public may, however, include a section of the public: see *Oldham TEC* at 250; *Commissioners of Inland Revenue v Yorkshire Agricultural Society* [1928] 1 KB 611 ("*Yorkshire*

Agricultural Society") at 622–623 per Lord Hanworth MR, 629–630 per Atkin LJ and 637 per Lawrence LJ; *Crystal Palace Trustees v Minister of Town and Country Planning* [1951] Ch 132 ("*Crystal Palace*") per Danckwerts J; *Commissioners of Inland Revenue v White* (1980) 55 TC 651 ("*White*") and *Royal Australasian College of Surgeons v Federal Commissioner of Taxation* (1943) 68 CLR 436 at 447 per Rich J, 450 per McTiernan, 454 per Williams J; and contrast *Hadaway v Hadaway* [1955] 1 WLR 16 and *New Zealand Society of Accountants v Commissioner of Inland Revenue* (1986) 8 NZTC 5205 at 5208 per Somers J, 5212–5214 per Richardson J, Casey J agreeing with Somers and Richardson JJ.

'In *Royal Australasian College of Surgeons*, the High Court held that the "main or real object of the College [was] the promotion and advancement of surgery", which entitled the College to an exemption pursuant to s 23(e) of the Income Tax Assessment Act 1936–1941 (Cth) and the fact that "some of these subsidiary or ancillary functions and purposes [of the College] may indirectly and incidentally be of benefit to the members of the profession" did not detract from this status: see 447 per Rich J. In *Yorkshire Agricultural Society*, the English Court of Appeal held that the Society, which was formed for the purpose of promoting the general improvement of agriculture, as opposed to a society for the conferral of benefits on its particular members, was charitable within Lord Macnaghten's fourth class in *Pemsel's Case*. Similarly, in *Crystal Palace*, Danckwerts J held, at 858, that the promotion of industry and commerce in general by holding public exhibitions, as opposed to the furtherance of the interests of individuals engaged in trade or industry, was a public purpose of a charitable nature. In *White*, Fox J held that the object of preserving and improving craftsmanship was charitable, though the means required to achieve this end included the provision to craftsmen of particular benefits, including the provision of premises at affordable rent. The fact that individual craftsmen might obtain benefits from the association's activities did not, in this case, operate to deprive the association of charitable status: see *White* at 656, 659–661. Mackenzie J adopted the same reasoning in *Barclay v Treasurer of Queensland* (1995) 95 ATC 4496 ("*Barclay*"). In considering the status of the Queensland Construction Training Fund, his Honour held that the object of fostering and developing the knowledge, skills, training and education of persons employed in the Queensland construction industry was a charitable object, and any benefit to any particular individual in the industry was an incidental object of the Fund: see *Barclay* at 4,500. In *Tasmanian Electronic*, at [56], Heerey J held that, in assisting Tasmanian businesses to adopt electronic commerce, the Tasmanian Electronic Commerce Centre was pursuing a charitable purpose within Lord Macnaghten's fourth category.

'The question whether the purpose is to benefit a section of the public as opposed to individual members of the community does not always admit of a ready answer. In *Dingle v Turner* [1972] AC 601, this consideration led Lord Cross of Chelsea to say, at 624:

> In truth the question whether or not the potential beneficiaries of a trust can fairly be said to constitute a section of the public is a question of degree and cannot be by itself decisive of the question whether the trust is a charity. Much must depend on the purpose of the trust. It may well be that, on the one hand, a trust to promote some purpose, prima facie charitable, will constitute a charity even though the class of potential beneficiaries might fairly be called a private class and that, on the other hand, a trust to promote another purpose, also prima facie charitable, will not constitute a charity even though the class of potential beneficiaries might seem to some people fairly describable as a section of the public.'

Commissioner of Taxation v the Triton Foundation [2005] FCA 1319 at [19]–[24], per Kenny J; BC200506946

CHARITY—GENERAL CHARITABLE PURPOSES

General meaning

[The Charities Act 1960 is largely repealed. The definitions of 'charity' and 'charitable purposes' have been re-enacted in the Charities Act 1993 ss 96(1), 97(1) respectively. The General Rate Act 1967 has been repealed.]

[For 5 Halsbury's Laws (4th edn) para 502 see now 5(2) Halsbury's Laws (4th edn) (2001 Reissue) para 2.]

Exclusively for charitable purposes

New Zealand 'It is therefore clearly established that if a body is established with a main purpose which is clearly charitable but having certain subordinate or incidental purposes which are non-charitable, the latter will not prevent a conclusion that the body was established exclusively for charitable purposes.' *Institution of Professional Engineers New Zealand Inc v Commissioner of Inland Revenue* [1992] 1 NZLR 570 at 573, per Tipping J

Local charity

[The definition of 'local charity' has been re-enacted in the Charities Act 1993, s 96(1).]

Parochial charity

[The definition of 'parochial charity' is now contained in the Charities Act 1993, s 96(1), as follows.]

'Parochial charity' means, in relation to any parish or (in Wales) community, a charity the benefits of which are, or the separate distribution of the benefits of which is, confined to inhabitants of the parish or community, or of a single ancient ecclesiastical parish which included that parish or community or part of it, or of an area consisting of that parish or community with not more than four neighbouring parishes or communities.

CHARTERER

Australia [The Admiralty Act 1988 s 19 (Cth) provides, *inter alia*, that a proceeding on a general maritime claim may be commenced as an action in rem if a relevant person was 'the owner or charterer of, or in possession or control of, the first-mentioned ship'.] 'In substance, the submission [of the appellant] is that the phrase in para (a) of s 19 "the owner or charterer of, or in possession or control of, the first-mentioned ship" creates a genus the indicium of which is possession or control of the ship in question ... In argument the appellant accepted that a salvor or mortgagee in possession, for the purposes of these provisions, might be "in possession or control" to the exclusion of "the owner" or "charterer". It follows that "possession or control" cannot be the common element in a genus comprising "the owner", "charterer" and "in possession or control" ... A further difficulty with the construction urged by the appellant is that s 18 uses both the terms "charterer" and "demise charterer" in respect of the one ship but at different points of time. On a fair reading of s 18, "demise charterer" is used as a narrower term than "charterer".' *Laemthong International Lines Co Ltd v BPS Shipping Ltd* (1997) 149 ALR 675 at 688; BC9706508 at 20–21, per Gaudron, Gummow and Kirby JJ

CHARTERPARTY

[For 43 Halsbury's Laws (4th edn) paras 402–404 see now 43(2) Halsbury's Laws (4th edn) (Reissue) paras 1412–1415.]

CHATTEL—CHATTELS

Australia 'The expression "chattels" ... has its origin in the Norman word for cattle, and from there embraced first "live stock" and then, more generally, articles of property: see *The Oxford English Dictionary* (2nd ed, 1989), where one of the current meanings is given as "any possession or piece of property other than real estate or a freehold".

'According to *Butterworths Australian Legal Dictionary*, property "is either real (that is, an interest or estate in land) or personal (that is, interests in things other than land including chattels and choses in action)." The Dictionary also records that the word "property" is one "which can be used to describe every type of right (that is, a claim recognised by law), interest, or thing which is legally capable of ownership and which has a value". "Ownership" in turn "includes the right to exclude others, the right to alienate and the right to use and enjoy." But "[i]nterests that are less than ownership may also be property." Thus "an incorporeal right such as an easement is a property interest."

...

'*Butterworths Australian Legal Dictionary* (1st ed, 1997) defines the word "chattel" as follows:

"1. Personal property, as distinct from real property.
2. Any property which is not freehold land. The property may be a leasehold (chattel real) or a movable article of property such as household furniture and jewellery (chattel personal) ... As a matter of interpretation or construction, the word 'chattel' in appropriate contexts in deeds, wills, statutes and other instruments can include intangible property (choses in action) as well an tangible property."

'The expressions "chattels real" and "chattels personal" are the subject of para 1203 and para 1204 of volume 35 of *Halsbury's Laws of England* (4th ed re-issue, 1994). The former "are interests concerning or savouring of realty, such as a term of years in land ... which have the quality of immobility which makes them akin to realty, but lack indeterminate duration." They are probably now confined to leaseholds. The latter:

"... are, strictly speaking, things movable, but in modern times the expression is used to denote any kind of property other than real property and chattels real.
"'Personalty' or 'personal property' includes many kinds of property unknown to the common law, such as bills of exchange, bank notes and cheques, land improvement charges, copyrights, patents, shares in joint stock companies, debentures, government annuities and stock in the public funds, goodwill, and the exclusive right of burial in a particular place; but does not include title deeds relating to real estate, heirlooms in the strict sense, fixtures or wild animals, and does not always include growing crops or trees." '

Australian Rice Holdings Pty Ltd v Commissioner of State Revenue (2001) 48 ATR 498; (2002) ATC 4052; BC200107835; [2001] VSC 486 at [16], [17], [32], [33], per Harper J

Australia [The Court of Appeal considered whether goodwill is a chattel within s 63(3) of the Stamps Act 1958 (Vic).] 'If one looks at the cases in which the word "chattels" has been held to include choses in action or other intangible property rights, there has usually been a good reason for considering that the word should be construed as comprehending all that can be characterised as personal property. Sometimes there is an obvious dichotomy between moveables and immovables in the provisions overall, sometimes it is easy to conclude that what was intended was all personal property though excluding (in most cases) chattels real. I have a strong inclination in the present case to believe that this anti-avoidance mechanism, for so it was described, was intended to catch a specific and limited group of potential stamp duty evaders. The conventional contract of sale of land more often than not referred also to "fixtures and fittings" or preferably to a specific list of named movable chattels. The object to be achieved by the section was to prevent an artificial figure being given to the value of the latter, thereby reducing the value of the land for duty purposes. It could, perhaps, be argued that, if shares or other intangibles were sold with real property, there was a similar risk. Marketable securities ordinarily have an easily calculable value (although the same could not necessarily be said of other property which was, from time to time, sold with realty), but transfers of them were already separately charged with duty. No mention was made of any "scam" involving the overvaluing of goodwill, although one may concede that a combination of land and goodwill was not as frequent as the inclusion of specified chattels. If goodwill and the like were to be included, then it is difficult to see why the Treasurer's preference in the first place for "personal property" should not have been repeated in appropriate terms in the legislation as put before Parliament. It was not and at the same time there was an exemption for holders of land used for primary production which excepted those kinds of chattels, which included stock, farm implements and "other chattels", presumably of a similar kind, used by farmers for the purposes of their primary production activities: see s 63(4) of the Act.

'There is no reason why the word "chattels" should be interpreted differently in two subsections not merely of the same Act, not merely of the same section, but of a section inserted by way of amendment at the very same time. I confess to thinking that, if members of Parliament had been asked whether they were referring to different classes of personal property in the one and then in the other subsection, they would have stared at the person responsible for drafting the section with amazement. For the reasons expressed by Callaway JA in *Australian Rice Holdings* I consider that the word has the same meaning in both subsections, and I would here also conclude that it is confined to movable chattels. Although the word "chattels" has apparently, according to some commentators, been given an expanded legal meaning over the last century or so, the legal connotation of the word thereby adopted is not necessarily that which appeals to non-lawyers. That popular meaning is also reflected in dictionary meanings. For example, the first non-obsolete meaning of "chattel" in the Oxford Dictionary (2nd ed) is "a movable possession", although the wider legal meanings are later recognised. Then in the Macquarie Dictionary (revd. 3rd ed) the primary meaning of the word "chattels" is given as "movable articles of property", perhaps a fair reflection of its modern acceptation in this country. In each case, both the context and the related definitions of "movable" show that the concept described in the primary definitions was that of a physical or tangible chattel, capable of being moved from place to place. Having regard to the difficulties inherent in the use of the word "movable" in the law, the meaning here to be given to "chattels" is that of "tangible or physical things".

'It is that popular, straightforward meaning which I think should here be given to the word "chattels", whatever it may mean in other circumstances. I would therefore reject counsel's arguments to the contrary and their attempts to apply the reasoning of Harper J in *Australian Rice Holdings*. With respect, his Honour's conclusions were appropriate neither to that case, nor to the present. Doubtless his reasoning may be applicable in other circumstances where the word "chattels" has to be considered, but, as this Court sought to show in *Australian Rice Holdings*, the particular provisions of s 63(3) should be viewed in their context and as showing that a more limited meaning here should be given to that word. It is unnecessary to repeat here what was said by Callaway JA and me in that case but that reasoning shows why "chattels" should here be read restrictively.' *Commissioner of State Revenue v Uniqema Pty Ltd* [2004] VSCA 82 at [42], per Ormiston JA; BC200402775

Personal

[For 35 Halsbury's Laws (4th edn) para 1104 see now 35 Halsbury's Laws (4th edn) (Reissue) para 1204.]

Real

[For 35 Halsbury's Laws (4th edn) para 1103 see now 35 Halsbury's Laws (4th edn) (Reissue) para 1203.]

[For 39 Halsbury's Laws (4th edn) para 303 see now 39(2) Halsbury's Laws (4th edn) (Reissue) para 3.]

Of person

New Zealand 'The expression *the chattels of a person* is not a term of art with an invariable or even a prima facie legal meaning. In my opinion it would be misleading to assert baldly of chattels that they are the chattels of a person if the truth is that another person holds an equitable charge over them which exhausts their full value. In such a case, the chattels are realistically to a full extent the chattels of a person other than the tenant.' *Metropolitan Life Assurance Co of NZ Ltd v Essere Print Ltd* [1991] 3 NZLR 170 at 172, CA, per Cooke P

CHEESE

[The Food Act 1984 is largely repealed, and the definition is not re-enacted in the Food Safety Act 1990.]

CHEMICAL WEAPONS

Chemical weapons are:

(a) toxic chemicals and their precursors;

(b) munitions and other devices designed to cause death or harm through the toxic properties of toxic chemicals released by them;

(c) equipment designed for use in connection with munitions and devices falling within paragraph (b).

A toxic chemical is a chemical which through its chemical action on life processes can cause death, permanent harm or temporary incapacity to humans or animals; and the origin, method of production and place of production are immaterial.

A precursor is a chemical reactant which takes part at any stage in the production (by whatever method) of a toxic chemical.

(Chemical Weapons Act 1996, s 1(1), (5), (6))

CHEQUE

'It is well established that the normal relation between a banker and his customer is that of debtor and creditor, but it is equally well established that quoad the drawing and payment of the customer's cheques as against money of the customer's in the banker's hands the relation is that of principal and agent. The cheque is an order of the principal's addressed to the agent to pay out of the principal's money in the agent's hands the amount of the cheque to the payee thereof.' *Westminster Bank Ltd v Hilton* (1926) 43 TLR 124 at 126, HL, per Lord Atkinson; dictum applied in *Agip (Africa) Ltd v Jackson*, [1992] 4 All ER 451 at 463, CA, per Fox LJ

[For 4 Halsbury's Laws (4th edn) paras 302–308 see now 4(1) Halsbury's Laws (4th edn) (2002 Reissue) paras 302–308.]

CHILD—CHILDREN

[The Foster Children Act 1980 was repealed by the Children Act 1989, s 108(7), Sch 15.]

[For 24 Halsbury's Laws (4th edn) para 404 see now 5(3) Halsbury's Laws (4th edn) (Reissue) para 3.]

Australia [In an application for guardianship the issue was whether the word 'child' could extend to an intellectually disabled person over the age of 18.] 'The word "child" has two distinctive but dissimilar meanings which the Oxford English Dictionary recognises by grouping its definitions of the word under two major "significations" (there are in fact more than two but the others are not relevant here). Those significations are "I—With reference to state or age" and "II—As correlative to parent". The first grouping corresponds broadly to the term "infant" as understood in the law. The second to the term "offspring" or "issue". In written and spoken communications, the context usually supplies the grouping and one is not particularly troubled by ambiguity. One may use the term "child abuse" or "child education" without any fear of being thought of referring to abuse or education of adults. On the other hand a person making a will leaving his estate to his "children" (naming them) will not be advised by his solicitor that this will not be recognised by the court if the children have become adults before the date of his death ... The general policy of the law, at least until 1983, seems to have been clear that in so far as guardianship, custody and access matters were concerned (and the term "welfare" was used ancillary to those matters), "children" were equated with "infants"... In my view, therefore, so far as the terms "guardianship", "custody", "access" and "welfare" appear in Pt VII of the Family Law Act [1975 (Cth)] in relation to "child" or "children", those terms have always been applied to persons under the age of 18 and no amendment has changed what was clearly that concept from the commencement of the Act.' *Public Guardian v MA* (1990) 14 Fam LR 46 at 53, 57 and 60, per Asche CJ

Australia 'In *Hill v Crook* (1873) LR 6 HL 265 at 282–283, Lord Cairns said that the term "children" in a will, prima facie, meant "legitimate children", but there were two exceptions. His Lordship said:

"But there are two classes of cases in which that prima facie interpretation is departed from. One class of cases is where it is impossible from the circumstances of the parties that any legitimate children could take under the bequest."

'His Lordship went on to say:

"The other class of cases is of this kind. Where there is upon the face of the will itself, and upon a just and proper construction and interpretation of the words used in it, an expression of the intention of the testator to use the term 'children' not merely according to its prima facie meaning of legitimate children, but according to a meaning which will apply to, and which will include, illegitimate children."

'However, it is to be kept in mind that the denotation of the word "children" has altered somewhat over the last century as familial relationships and social attitudes have altered. In *Harris v Ashdown* (1985)

3 NSWLR 193 at 199–200, Kirby P referred to some of the changes which have occurred both in community attitudes and in legislation. At 200, his Honour said:

"… in my view it is no longer safe to approach the construction of words such as 'child' and 'children' from the starting point of Lord Cairns' dictum. Nowadays, it would be much safer to include in the expression 'child', as used in a will, legitimate and exnuptial, adopted and step-children, unless, from the language of the will itself, or from admissible surrounding circumstances, it is shown that a narrower meaning was intended by the testator. Such an approach acknowledges at once the changing nature of personal obligations in today's society and the demise of earlier prejudices against illegitimacy which help to explain the starting point taken by Lord Cairns and, consequently, those who have since followed his dictum. That starting point may well have been appropriate in the social circumstances in which wills were written in 1873. It is scarcely appropriate in modern Australia."

'Notwithstanding his Honour's words, which were not adopted by his colleagues … I consider that, in a will, the word "children" should ordinarily be read as referring to natural children for that is its primary meaning, but that other persons should be included within the term when legislation so requires or when the terms of the will or evidence show that there is reason for doing so.' *Re Estate of Warren* BC200100609; [2001] NSWSC 104 at [3]–[6], per Davies AJ

Australia [Property Law Act 1958 (Vic).]
    '… Meaning of child
'Another issue which arose in the context of the present case is the meaning of the expression "child" where used in s 285(1)(b)(ii) of the Act. Although the word "child" is defined in s 275 of the Act, this definition is only relevant "in relation to domestic partners". Hence, in my opinion, it is necessary to ascertain the intent of the legislature where it used the word child on the first two occasions in s 285(1)(b)(ii). This is not a straightforward task as the word can be used to describe the age of a minor or the familial relationship between a parent and his or her offspring. When used in the former sense it is often used to describe a person not having contractual capacity, that is, less than 18 years of age. However sometimes legislation is framed in the sense of a relationship between persons, rather than their age.

This is the case with a number of provisions in the Family Law Act 1975. In *Dougherty v Dougherty* the High Court of Australia was required to consider the meaning of the word "child" in the context of s 79 of that Act which enabled the Court to make an order requiring a party to a marriage to make a settlement of property "for the benefit of either or both of the parties or a child of the marriage". Mason CJ, Wilson J and Dawson J commented:

It was suggested in argument that s 79 should be construed so as to limit the reference in the section to 'child' to a child under the age of 18 years of age. It was said that the entry into adulthood marks the end of the legal duty of nurture and care resting on the parties to a marriage in respect of the children of the marriage. But clearly, if dependency is to be the test by which the existence of the necessary connection to the marital relationship is to be determined, adulthood is a criterion that is too arbitrary. We do not think that s 79 should be read so as to confine the power to make an order for the benefit of a child to a child who has not attained the age of 18.

'However the context of s 285(1)(b)(ii) of the Act suggests that the word "child", where used on the first two occasions, is used in the sense of the age of a minor, rather than in the sense of a familial relationship. This can be illustrated by an example. Suppose that a woman ("W1") had a relationship with a man ("M1") who had an infant son ("S1") by a previous relationship. Further suppose that this domestic relationship ended and W1 commenced a domestic relationship with another man ("M2") and that S1 was accepted into the household of W1 and M2. In these circumstances, it would make sense for contributions to the welfare of, inter alia, S1 to be taken into account in adjusting the interests of W1 and M2. If the word "child", where used on the first two occasions in s 285(1)(b)(ii) of the Act, was a reference to a familial relationship between a parent and his or her offspring, then such contributions would not be relevant considerations. On the other hand, if the word "child", were used on the first two occasions in s 285(1)(b)(ii) of the Act is a reference to a person who is a minor, then the obvious legislative purpose is given effect to.' *Findlay v Besley* [2003] VSC 247 at [58], per Morris J; BC200303540

Canada [An unborn child was apprehended as being in need of protection.] 'It is my view on examining the Family and Child Service Act that there is nothing to be found in it that assists in expanding the definition of "child" to include an unborn child. The definition of "child" is as follows: "child" means a person under 19 years old.

'There is no definition of "person", but logically a person under 19 must only include children that have been born to be a child "under 19 years", as you do not acquire an age until after birth. The previous Acts authorised the superintendent to apprehend a child only under certain circumstances, such as "children under the age of seventeen ... found begging in the streets, were habitually truant from school; or were dwelling with a thief, drunkard or vagrant". Obviously an unborn child could not come within the class above referred to. Additionally, up until recently it was necessary to bring the child before the court. However, the current Act now enables the department to file a written report to the court within seven days in place of actually physically bringing the child before the court. Although the current Act is considerably more general than its predecessors, nevertheless there is nothing to assist in broadening the definition of "child". The changes in the legislation do not assist in resolving my problem as the definition of "child" has not been changed and there is still nothing in the context of the Act that supports any power in the superintendent to apprehend an unborn child.' *Re Baby R* (1988) 53 DLR (4th) 69 at 77, per Macdonell J (BC SC)

Canada [Consideration of possession of child pornography offence of the Criminal Code.] 'In this judgment, when I myself use the word "child", in contradistinction to when I am quoting someone else's words, I mean those below the age of puberty. At common law, these ages were deemed to be twelve for a girl and fourteen for a boy. As, however, fourteen is the age of consent in Canada and has been, for girls, for over one hundred years (see the *Criminal Code*, SC 1892, c 29, s 269), I define a "child" as anyone under the age of fourteen years.

'I appreciate that in the latter part of this century, fifteen, sixteen and seventeen-year-olds have been considered barely more than children. Our forebears thought no such thing. Boys were sent to sea at thirteen or fourteen and girls could be apprenticed to domestic service, with their consent, at twelve. Boys under eighteen, by lying about their age, fought in the Forces in both wars. The late Mr Justice Harry McKay of this Province joined the army when he was sixteen and went to war. I shall have more to say on this point of adolescents not being children, hereafter.' *R v Sharpe* (1999) 175 DLR (4th) 1 at 13, 14, BCCA, per Southin JA

New Zealand 'The foetus in this case was of about 26 weeks' gestation. It was therefore well past the 20 weeks' gestation period referred to in s 187A(3) of the Crimes Act ... We are of opinion that the ordinary and natural meaning of the word "child" is such as to include the foetus in the present case.' *R v Henderson* [1990] 3 NZLR 174 at 179, CA, per cur

New Zealand [Section 178 of the Crimes Act 1961 is concerned with cases where a woman causes the death of any 'child' of hers.] 'When a child is treated in all respects as a member of the family and has the status of such to all outward appearances, confirmed in all respects by an order of the court, and may be as old as 10 years of age, I think the legislation implicitly contemplates more than just the natural children of an accused.' *R v P* [1991] 2 NZLR 116 at 120, per Heron J

New Zealand [Section 74(b) of the Family Proceedings Act 1980 provides that an application for a maintenance order in respect of a child can be made 'against a parent of parents of the child'.] 'It uses the word child in what can only be the sense of one who is a minor. That is its natural and ordinary meaning in the opening words of the section, and is the only meaning of which the word is capable in para (b); that paragraph cannot apply to one who has attained majority.' *Holley v Andrew* [1992] 3 NZLR 151 at 156, CA, per Hardie Boys J

New Zealand [Section 2 (1) of the Guardianship Act 1968 provides that: 'Child means a person under the age of 20 years'.]

'[63] Having regard to the international obligations which have been assumed by New Zealand under the convention, and the other provisions of New Zealand law which support the interests of unborn children, I hold that the term "child" in s 2(1) of the Act can include an unborn child. Thus, by a different route, I arrive at the same answer as did Judge Inglis in *Re Baby P*. Having concluded that an unborn child may be the subject of jurisdiction under the Act, I agree with the observations of Judge Inglis that it will be a matter of discretion in individual cases whether such jurisdiction should be exercised. This ability to focus on the utility and need for such orders avoids the otherwise impossible task of endeavouring to determine the precise moment in time (for legal purposes) that an unborn child is subject to the Court's jurisdiction: cf *Tremblay v Daigle* [1989] 2 SCR 530 (SCC) at p 533.' *Re an Unborn Child* [2003] 1 NZLR 115 at 133, per Heath J

Illegitimate

[For 1 Halsbury's Laws (4th edn) paras 616–620 see now 5(3) Halsbury's Laws (4th edn) (Reissue) para 125.]

CHILD CONCERNED

[Under the Children Act 1989, s 10, leave to make an application for an order under s 8, including a contact order, must be sought unless the applicant is entitled to apply. By s 10(8) and (9), different considerations apply to the grant of leave depending on whether or not the person applying for leave to make an application is 'the child concerned'. An application was made by a minor for leave to apply for a contact order in respect of her minor half brother who had been adopted by different adoptive parents. It was contended that the applicant was 'the child concerned'] 'I accept that if s 10(8) is read in isolation it could be said that where the applicant for leave is a child the "child concerned" is the child applying for leave. But in my judgment when s 10(8) is construed in its context, and in particular with regard to s 10(1) and (9) and the definitions of s 8 orders in s 8(1), it is clear that this is not the case, and using the words of s 10(1) the "child concerned" is the child with respect to whom the court may make a s 8 order.

'To find out who that child is it is necessary to consider the definition of the relevant s 8 order. When this is done it can be seen that the "child concerned" could be the applicant for leave . . but that often the "child concerned" will not be the applicant for leave.

...

'It follows that an analysis of the definition identifies: (a) the child (or children) with respect to whom a contact order can be made, or who are the subject of the application for a contact order, and the order itself, and thus in my judgment (b) the "child concerned" in s 10(8) and (9).

'In my judgment this conclusion is supported by: (a) the point that s 10(8) and (9) are not in terms that they make alternative provisions where the applicant is or is not a child, and (b) the point that the "child concerned" must identify the same child in both s 10(8) and (9).

'These points indicate that the identification of the "child concerned" is to be made by reference to the s 8 order that the proposed applicant seeks leave to apply for, and not by reference to the identity of the applicant for leave.' *Re S (a minor) (adopted child: contact)* [1999] 1 All ER 648 at 655–656, per Charles J

CHILD OF THE MARRIAGE

Canada '[11] One of the major issues before the motions judge was whether C. is a "child of the marriage" within s. 2(1) of the Divorce Act. The definition is as follows:

"child of the marriage" means a child of two spouses or former spouses who, at the material time,
(a) is under the age of majority and who has not withdrawn from their charge, or
(b) is the age of majority or over and under their charge but unable, by reason of illness, disability or other cause, to withdraw from their charge or to obtain the necessaries of life ...

'[12] The motions judge interpreted paragraph (a) as applying only if the child has taken action to withdraw from the charge of his parents. In his view, an application for Crown wardship by a children's aid society, a parent's consent to Crown wardship or a court order of Crown wardship did not amount to a child's withdrawal from the charge of his parents (at para. 15 of his reasons).

...

'[17] The issue on this appeal is whether the child C., having been made a Crown ward, is still a "child of the marriage". The answer to that question turns on the meaning of paragraph (a) of the definition in s. 2(1) of the Divorce Act, quoted earlier. It provides that a child of the marriage means a child of two spouses or former spouses who, at the material time, "is under the age of majority and who has not withdrawn from their charge". The motions judge concluded that the words "who has not withdrawn from their charge" requires action on the part of the child.

'[18] Prior to 1997, the definition of a child of the marriage made no reference to withdrawal from charge for a child under the age of 16 years. Instead, the right to claim support for a child under 16 years of age rested solely on the criterion of age. The earlier version of the definition read:

"children of the marriage" means each child of a husband and wife who at the material time is
(a) under the age of sixteen years, or
(b) sixteen years of age or over and under their charge but unable, by reason of illness, disability or other cause, to withdraw himself from their charge or to provide himself with the necessaries of life.

'[19] The current definition of "child of the marriage" in both paragraphs (a) and (b) makes reference to a child who has withdrawn from the parents' charge.

'[20] The jurisprudence interpreting withdrawal from the parents' charge for children over 16 years under the prior version of the legislation and over the age of majority in the current legislation emphasizes the child's voluntary withdrawal from the care and support of the parents. Often, this arises in the context where a child attending an educational institution is dependent on the parents for financial support, and a court finds the child still under a parent's charge (see, for example, *Tapson v. Tapson* (1969), 2 R.F.L. 305 (Ont. C.A.), p. 308). In *Tapson*, Laskin J.A. interpreted the phrase "under their charge" broadly to mean "that the parent has assumed the care and maintenance of the child in the parent's premises" (at p. 307). He went on to say (at p. 308):

> An order for maintenance or for interim maintenance based on a child 16 years of age or over being in the charge of a parent assumes, of course, that the child is living with the parent in the parent's care and to that extent, within the parent's responsibility for maintenance.

…

'[22] In interpreting a statute, the words are to be read "in their entire context and in their grammatical and ordinary sense harmoniously with the scheme of the Act, the object of the Act, and the intention of Parliament" (*Rizzo & Rizzo Shoes Ltd.* (*Re*), [1998] 1 S.C.R. 27 at para. 21). While the phrase "has withdrawn from their charge" in paragraph (a) might on first reading suggest some action on the part of the child, in my view, that is not the proper interpretation of the language, when the words are read in context with paragraph (b) and the French version of the definition.

'[23] Both the French and English versions of a federal Act are equally authoritative, and they should be read together so that both versions of the Act are harmonious (Ruth Sullivan, *Statutory Interpretation* (Concord, Ont.: Irwin Law, 1997), p. 91). To read paragraph (a) of the English version as requiring an act by the child is inconsistent with the French version of the Act, which states:

> "enfant à charge" Enfant des deux époux ou ex-époux qui, à l'époque considérée, se trouve dans une des situations suivantes:
> a)   il n'est pas majeur et est à leur charge;

> b)   il est majeur et est à leur charge, sans pouvoir, pour cause notamment de maladie ou d'invalidité, cesser d'être à leur charge ou subvenir à ses propres besoins.

The French version of paragraph (a) of the definition does not suggest that there must be some action on the part of the child; rather, it requires the court to determine whether the child is a minor and still in the charge of a parent.

'[24] One purpose of the definition of a "child of the marriage" is to identify those children for whom support may be ordered under ss. 15 and 17 of the Divorce Act; another is to determine those children for whom a custody or access order may be made pursuant to ss. 16 and 17 of the Act. The French definition of "enfant à charge" makes it clear that the Act is dealing with dependent children – that is, those still under the care of a parent responsible for their maintenance.

'[25] In my view, the words "has not withdrawn from their charge" in paragraph (a) of the English version should be read consistently with the words in paragraph (b) and with the French version of the Act. The issue for a court to determine is whether the child is, at the material time, still under the care and maintenance of a parent and, therefore, dependent on him or her for support.' *S (JM) v M (FJ)* (2005) 257 DLR (4th) 158 at [11]–[12], [17]–[20], [22]–[25], [2005] OJ No 3085 (Ont Sup Ct J), per Meehan J

CHILD PORNOGRAPHY

Australia [Crimes Act 1958 (Vic) s 67A provides: 'Child pornography' means a film, photographic, publication or computer game that describes or depicts a person who is, or looks like, a minor under 16 engaged in sexual activity or depicted in an indecent sexual manner or context.] 'The works constituting pornographic conduct may be of a child who has participated in such conduct or it may be fictional. The fiction may relate to real or imaginary children. The definition catches both visual and written expressions of thought and imagination. Hence child pornography is defined to include computer games. Child pornography is harmful whether it involves real children in its production or whether it is the product of the imagination. Parliament has proceeded on the indisputable assumption that images or writings of the imagination, depicting or describing child pornography would harm children. Material which does not use children in its creation may equally fuel the market for child pornography and the abuse and degradation of children. No argument was, or could be advanced, that the accused's erotic musings could not fall within the ambit of Sub-Division 13 because they were fantasy.' *R v Quick* [2004] VSC 270 at [15], per Redlich J; BC200404938

CHILDREN OF THE DECEASED

New Zealand [Section 3 of the Family Protection Act 1955 provides that:
'...
(1) An application for provision out of the estate of any deceased person may be made under this Act by or on behalf of all or any of the following persons:
    (a) The wife or husband of the deceased:
    (aa) a de facto partner who was living in a de facto relationship with the deceased at the date of his or her death:]
    (b) The children of the deceased:
    (c) The grandchildren of the deceased living at his death:
    (d) The stepchildren of the deceased who were being maintained wholly or partly or were legally entitled to be maintained wholly or partly by the deceased immediately before his death:
    (e) the parents of the deceased, though a parent of the deceased may not make a claim under this Act unless—
        (i) the parent was being maintained wholly or partly or was legally entitled to be maintained wholly or partly by the deceased immediately before his or her death; or
        (ii) the date of the claim, no wife or husband of the deceased, and no de facto partner of the deceased who was living in a de facto relationship with the deceased at the date of his or her death and who the Court can make an order under this Act in favour of, and no child of a marriage or child of a de facto relationship of the deceased, is living.
(2) In considering any application by a grandchild of any deceased person for provision out of the estate of that person, the Court, in considering the moral duty of the deceased at the date of his death, shall have regard to all the circumstances of the case, and shall have regard to any provision made by the deceased, or by the Court in pursuance of this Act, in favour of either or both of the grandchild's parents.']

'[14] More significant than that difficulty is that the expression "children of the deceased" appears in a statute and, to repeat, has to be given a meaning in that context and by reference to the purpose of the statute – and in particular its scheme.
...
'[28] The history of the legislation allows two other relevant conclusions: the initial meaning of "children of the deceased" is biological children so long as, in the language of the day, they were legitimate or had been legitimated by subsequent marriage, plus adopted children; but customary relationships, as with Maori customary marriage and de facto relationships generally, required express statutory inclusion.' *Keelan v Peach* [2003] 1 NZLR 589 at 593, 596, per cur

CHILDREN OF THE MARRIAGE

Australia [Section 79(4)(c) of the Family Law Act 1975 (Cth) refers to the contribution made by a party to the marriage to the welfare of the family constituted by the parties to the marriage and any 'children of the marriage'.] '... s 79(4)(c) does display an intention to place a limit on the children who might be included. If this were not the case the phrase "children of the marriage" would not have been used. In my view, this phrase has achieved the level where it is a term of art; a description with a well-known meaning at law if left otherwise undefined. It refers to any child, provided the child has been treated generally by the parties as though it is their child, that is, a member of their family unit, whether or not one or both of the parties also recognised it as a child of another or others and, in specific respects, treated it as a child of the other or others. It is that definition which I attribute to the term where it appears in s 79 of the Act.' *In the marriage of J E and S J Molen* (1992) 16 Fam LR 203 at 208, per Cohen J

CHIMNEY

[The Clean Air Act 1956 has been repealed. The definition is now contained in the Clean Air Act 1993, s 64(1), as follows.] 'Chimney' includes structures and openings of any kind from or through which smoke, grit, dust or fumes may be emitted, and, in particular, includes flues, and references to a chimney of a building include references to a chimney which serves the whole or part of a building but is structurally separate from the building.

CHOOSE

Australia [Article 87 of a company's articles of association provided that all meetings of the board should be presided over by the chairman if present and in his absence at the time appointed for holding the same or if no chairman had been elected the directors present might 'choose' one of their number as acting chairman to preside at the meeting.] 'The word "choose" in art 87 is a wide one. In quite a different connection in *Judd v McKeon* (1926) 38 CLR 380 at 383 the High Court made it clear that ordinarily the word "choose" is a wide word meaning "no more than to make a selection between different things or alternatives" and it does not necessarily connote any element of a wish that one of those alternatives might come to pass. It seems to me that there may be a choice under art 87 by acquiescence.' *Kelly v Woltenholme* (1991) 4 ACSR 709 at 712–713, per Young J

Canada '[35] Paragraph 15(*c*) of the Regulations [of the *Citizenship Act*] requires that an applicant have an adequate knowledge of one of the four topics mentioned in subparagraphs (i) to (iv), which the judge must choose at random in the questions prepared by the Minister.
    '[36] The *Oxford English Dictionary* (2nd ed.) gives the following definition of:

> *choose*: … To take by preference out of all that are available; to select; to take as that which one prefers …

> *choice*: The act of choosing; preferential determination between things proposed. [Underlining added.]

'[37] It is obvious, from a reading of this paragraph, that this is not what the Judge did in this particular case.
    '[38] Although the wording of paragraph 15(*c*) of the Regulations is not overly clear, it does seem clear that Parliament provided that the Judge should choose one or the other of the four topics, at random.' *Alfonso v Canada* (*Minister of Citizenship and Immigration*) [2003] 2 FC 683 at 694–695 (FCC), per Blais J

CHOSE IN ACTION

[For 6 Halsbury's Laws (4th edn) para 1 see now 6 Halsbury's Laws (4th edn) (2003 Reissue) para 1; for 35 Halsbury's Laws (4th edn) para 1105 see now 35 Halsbury's Laws (4th edn) (Reissue) para 1205.]

Canada '[36] In brief, stock options, like corporate shares, constitute "chattels personal" that fall within the category of legal choses in action, as opposed to choses in possession and, therefore, qualifying as property. A chose in action is an intangible: "a thing incorporeal and only a right; as an annuity, obligation for a debt, a covenant … and generally all causes of suit for any debt or duty, trespass or wrong are to be accounted choses in action." See E.L.G. Tyler and N.E. Palmer, *Crossley Vaines' Personal Property*, 5th ed. (London: Butterworths, 1973) at pp. 11–12, quoting from Blount's *Law Dictionary*, s.v. *Chose in Action.*' *Miller v Miller* (2003) 226 DLR (4th) 71 at 84 (NBCA), per Robertson JA

CHOSE IN POSSESSION

[For 35 Halsbury's Laws (4th edn) para 1105 see now 35 Halsbury's Laws (4th edn) (Reissue) para 1205.]

CHURCHWAY

[For 21 Halsbury's Laws (4th edn) para 6 see now 21 Halsbury's Laws (4th edn) (2004 Reissue) para 6.]
    [For 12 Halsbury's Laws (4th edn) para 437 see now 12(1) Halsbury's Laws (4th edn) (Reissue) para 637.]

CINEMATOGRAPH FILM

[The Copyright Act 1956 and the Dramatic and Musical Performers' Protection Act 1958 have both been repealed. See now FILM.]

New Zealand 'Although a cinematograph film (video) cannot itself be a dramatic work, it can be the medium in which a dramatic work is fixed, ie made.' *Television New Zealand Ltd v Newsmonitor Services Ltd* [1994] 2 NZLR 91 at 100, per Blanchard J

CIRCUMSTANCES … EXCEPTIONAL

New Zealand [Section 80(2) of the Criminal Justice Act 1985 provides that the Court 'shall not impose a minimum period of imprisonment unless it is satisifed that the circumstances of the offence are so exceptional that a minimum period of imprisonment of more than 10 years is justified'.] 'The dictionary meanings of "exceptional" are out of the ordinary course, unusual, uncommon, extraordinary. The Court has to decide first whether the circumstances were exceptional in that they were outside the normal or commonly encountered range in respect of the offence for which the sentence of preventive detention has been imposed. Second, the Court must be satisfied that the exceptionality was of such a character that a minimum period of more than ten years' imprisonment was justified.' *R v Hapi* [1995] 1 NZLR 257 at 260, CA, per cur

CIRCUMVENTION

[The minutes of a company revealed that the aim of certain monetary transactions was the 'circumvention' of the exchange control regulations of a foreign state.] 'They [the defendants] knew that something was concealed. The fact that the concealing was labelled as a "circumvention" does not alter that; it suggests some sort of impropriety ... If the known facts indicate a lack of frankness, the person assisting in effecting the transaction in question must take the risk in the absence of further explanation that it is fraudulent.' *Agip (Africa) Ltd v Jackson* [1992] 4 All ER 451 at 469, CA, per Fox LJ

CITATION

Canada [At issue was the effect of a citation for contempt.] 'Support for this view to equate a citation with notification comes from the definition of "cite" and "citation" in Black's Law Dictionary, 6th ed (St Paul, Minn: West Publishing Co, 1990) at pp 243–4. "Citation" is defined as:

> "A writ issued out of a court of competent jurisdiction, commanding a person therein named to appear on a day named and do something therein mentioned, or *show cause why he should not*." [Emphasis added.]

'While "cite" is defined as:

> "To summon; to command the presence of a person; to notify a person of legal proceedings against him and require his appearance thereto." '

R v K (B) (1995) 129 DLR (4th) 500 at 507, SCC, per Lamer CJC

CIVIL LIST

[For 8 Halsbury's Laws (4th edn) para 1413 see now 12(1) Halsbury's Laws (4th edn) (Reissue) para 207.]

CLAIM

Australia 'The word "claim", when used in an insurance policy, can have different meanings depending on the context: *Transport Industries Insurance Co Ltd v NSW Medical Defence Union Ltd* (1986) 4 ANZ Ins Cas 60–736 (CA(NSW)) at 74,411, per Kirby P; at 74,416 per Glass JA. Nonetheless, the starting point, in a claims made and reported policy, is the dictionary definition (*Macquarie Dictionary*): "1. to demand by or as by virtue of a right; demand as a right or as due. 2. to assert, and demand the recognition of (a right, title, possession, etc); assert one's right to." The cases have generally adopted this meaning as applicable to liability policies. In *Walton v National Employers' Mutual General Insurance Association Ltd* [1973] 2 NSWLR 73 (CA(NSW)) at 82, Bowen JA referred to the "primary sense" of the word "claim" in a liability policy as: "a demand for something as due, an assertion of a right to something. It imports the assertion, demand or challenge of something as a right".' *Drayton v Martin* (1996) 67 FCR 1 at 24; 137 ALR 145 at 164, per Sackville J

CLAIM IN RESPECT OF PERSONAL INJURIES

[The Supreme Court Act 1981, s 33(2) provides for pre-action discovery on the application of a person who appears to the High Court to be likely to be a party to subsequent proceedings in which a 'claim in respect of personal injuries' to a person or in respect of a person's death, is likely to be made.] 'It is plain, in my judgment, that the expression "claim for personal injury" is shorthand for "claim for damages for personal injury". The claim in a statement of claim is that part of the pleading where the relief sought is claimed, be it damages, injunction, specific performance or whatever. A plaintiff does not claim for personal injuries; he claims for damages for personal injury. In the case of a tortious death the plaintiff, personal representative or dependant, claims damages in respect of the death of the deceased.

'... A claim to be indemnified by the insurers under the [Third Party (Rights Against Insurers) Act 1930] is not a claim for damages in respect of personal injuries'. *Burns v Shuttlehurst Ltd* [1999] 2 All ER 27 at 32, CA, per Stuart Smith LJ

CLAIMS WHICH MAY BE MADE

New Zealand [Words in an insurance policy.] 'In my opinion the words "which may be" are no more than an attempt to make in an unnecessarily elegant way the point that no claims may in fact be made during the specified period. I do not think they mean anything more than would have the words "claims made".' *Sinclair Horder O'Malley & Co v National Insurance Co of New Zealand Ltd* [1995] 2 NZLR 257 at 264, CA, per Hardie Boys J

CLASS

[For 50 Halsbury's Laws (4th edn) para 362 see now 50 Halsbury's Laws (4th edn) (Reissue) para 413.]

CLEAR (PERIOD)

[For 45 Halsbury's Laws (4th edn) para 1133 see now 45(2) Halsbury's Laws (4th edn) (Reissue) para 234.]

CLOG

On equity of redemption

[For 32 Halsbury's Laws (4th edn) para 585 see now 32 Halsbury's Laws (4th edn) (Reissue) para 518.]

CLOSE BUSINESS ASSOCIATE

New Zealand [Section 3(2)(a)(i) of the Securities Act 1978.] ' "Close", "business" and "associate" are all relatively imprecise terms. They must be considered in conjunction. None of them is defined in the legislation. The first two are straightforward and require no resort to dictionary definition. Parliament has chosen to use the word "associate" rather than "association", indicating that the focus of the exception is upon a connection of a personal nature between individuals, rather than upon a relationship with a corporate body. The *Oxford English Dictionary* (2nd ed) defines an "associate" as "One who is united to another by community of interest, and shares with him in enterprise, business, or action; a partner, comrade, companion" and also as "One who is frequently in company with another, on terms of social equality and intimacy; an intimate acquaintance, companion, mate". Moreover, the Act is speaking not just of an associate but of a close associate. Closeness too involves nearness or intimacy.

'Although an issuer and a holder of its securities have a relationship through business, the use of the terms "close" and "associate" requires more than this: there must be a degree of intimacy or "business

friendship" in the relationship, though not necessarily a friendship away from business.

'It must be sufficient to overcome any equality which might otherwise be present in the relationship.' *Securities Commission v Kiwi Co-operative Dairies Ltd* [1995] 3 NZLR 26 at 31–32, CA, per cur

CLUB

[For 6 Halsbury's Laws (4th edn) para 201 see now 6 Halsbury's Laws (4th edn) (2003 Reissue) para 101.]

Incorporated club

[For 6 Halsbury's Laws (4th edn) para 206 see now 6 Halsbury's Laws (4th edn) (2003 Reissue) para 106.]

Members' club

[For 6 Halsbury's Laws (4th edn) para 205 see now 6 Halsbury's Laws (4th edn) (2003 Reissue) para 105.]

Proprietary club

[For 6 Halsbury's Laws (4th edn) paras 208–209 see now 6 Halsbury's Laws (4th edn) (2003 Reissue) paras 108–109.]

COASTAL MARINE AREA

New Zealand [Resource Management Act 1991, s 2.] 'It is thus likely that the zone now incorporates land within the coastal marine area, that is to say, the land between high water mark and the line of mean high water springs.' *Freeman v Savage* [1997] 1 NZLR 736 at 742, per Salmon J

CODICIL

[For 50 Halsbury's Laws (4th edn) para 201 see now 50 Halsbury's Laws (4th edn) (Reissue) para 251.]

COERCION

Australia [Section 170NC(1) of the Workplace Relations Act 1996 (Cth) provides that a person must not threaten to take any industrial action with the intention to coerce another person to agree, or not to agree to make an enterprise agreement.] 'The meaning of coercion in the context of s 170NC(1) has been considered in a number of recent cases. In *Cadbury Schweppes Pty Ltd v Australian Liquor Hospitality & Miscellaneous Workers' Union* [2000] FCA 1793 (*Cadbury Schweppes*) at [19] Finkelstein J suggested that coercion in an industrial context usually involves the exertion of illegitimate economic pressure that induces the other party to act.

'In *Finance Sector Union of Australia v Commonwealth Bank of Australia* [2000] FCA 1468 (*Finance Sector Union*) Gyles J at [18]–[38] concluded that for the purposes of s 170NC(1) coercion requires conduct that is:

> compulsive in the sense that the pressure brought to bear, in a practical sense, negates choice; and is
> unlawful, illegitimate or unconscionable.

'More recently, in *National Union of Workers v Qenos* [2001] FCA 178 (*Qenos*) at [128] Weinberg J stated that the analysis of the term "coerce" by Gyles J in *Finance Sector Union* was compelling and correctly stated the reach of s 170NC(1).

'The above cases establish that there must be two elements to prove "intent to coerce" under s 170NC(1). First, it needs to be shown that it was intended that pressure be exerted which, in a practical sense, will negate choice. Second, the exertion of the pressure must involve conduct that is unlawful, illegitimate or unconscionable ...

'The requirement of unlawfulness etc might, in a sense, be said to have been superimposed upon the ordinary meaning of "coercion": cf *Hanley v Automotive, Food, Metals, Engineering, Printing and Kindred Industries Union* (2000) 100 FCR 530 at [11]. However, without such a requirement s 170NC(1) could have an anomalous operation in so far as it might prevent the legitimate exercise of rights by employees or employers. In *Hanley* the Full Court did not really consider this issue. In all the circumstances I consider that it is appropriate to apply the approach taken to s 170NC(1) in *Cadbury Schweppes*, *Finance Sector Union* and *Qenos* unless I am satisfied that that approach is clearly wrong, which I am not.' *Seven Network (Operations) Ltd v Communications, Electrical, Electronic, Energy, Information, Postal, Plumbing and Allied Services Union of Australia (CEPU)* (2001) 109 FCR 378; 184 ALR 65; 106 IR 404; BC200101831; [2001] FCA 456 at [38]–[42], per Merkel J

Australia ' "Coercion" ... carries with it the connotation of force or compulsion or threats of force or compulsion negating choice or freedom to act: see *Hodges v Webb* [1920] 2 Ch 70 at 85–7 per Peterson J. A person may be coerced by another to

do something or refrain from doing something, that is to say the former is constrained or restrained from doing something or made to do something by force or threat of force or other compulsion. Whether or not repetition is involved in the concept of harassment, and it usually will be, it is not in the concept of coercion.' *Australian Competition and Consumer Commission v Maritime Union of Australia* (2001) 187 ALR 487; (2002) ATPR ¶41–849; BC200106710; [2001] FCA 1549 at [61], per Hill J

CODE

Australia [In *Seaegg v R* (1932) 48 CLR 251 Rich, Dixon, Evatt and McTiernan JJ said '[Sections] 72 to 77 of the [Judiciary Act 1903 (Cth)] are headed "Appeal", and contain a code of procedure for an appeal by way of case stated upon a point of law raised at the trial. These special provisions confer a different and narrower right of appeal and different but perhaps wider remedies.'] 'The use in [this passage] of the term "a code of procedure" gives rise to some difficulty. The term "code" may be used in various senses. Used in respect of the Judiciary Act or any provision or group of provisions thereof, it cannot identify a law which restates or replaces the common law, such as the bills of exchange, sale of goods and partnership legislation enacted in the United Kingdom in the second half of the nineteenth century. For at least since the time fairly shortly after its enactment, the Judiciary Act has not been the only law of the Commonwealth made in exercise of its power in s 77(iii) of the Constitution to invest courts of the States with federal jurisdiction. It is not a "code" in the sense of an exercise by the Parliament of the power in s 77(iii) which purports to be exhaustive.

'The term "code" also has been used to point out a particular characteristic with which the section or group of sections is endowed by the relevant statute. An example is the expression a "small self-contained code" used in *Parsons v BNM Laboratories Ltd* [[1964] 1 QB 95 at 119] of s 37 and s 38 of the Finance Act 1960 (UK). In *Seaegg* the phrase "code of procedure" appears to be used in respect of ss 72–7 to "preclude" what otherwise might be the operation of a more generally expressed provision in the same statute.' (footnotes omitted) *R v Gee* (2003) 196 ALR 282; 77 ALJR 812; BC200300830; [2003] HCA 12 at [59]–[60], per McHugh and Gummow JJ

COLLATERAL

Australia 'The prefix "co" imports a sense of "with" or "in addition to", without any necessary concept of primacy or subordination. The Shorter Oxford English Dictionary definition, "[s]ituated or running side by side, parallel", which was quoted with disapproval by counsel for the bank in this court, may well be inapplicable to contractual agreements when interpreted in a spatial sense, but is quite apposite if construed as meaning "related to" or "contributory"... Collateral contracts are so called not because they are subordinate or of lesser importance (although they may well be, depending on the facts of the case), but because they impinge upon and are related to another contract.' *David Securities Pty Ltd v Commonwealth Bank of Australia* (1992) 109 ALR 57 at 64, per Mason CJ, Deane, Toohey, Gaudron and McHugh JJ

COLLIERY

[For 31 Halsbury's Laws (4th edn) para 13 see now 31 Halsbury's Laws (4th edn) (2003 Reissue) para 17.]

COLLISION CLAUSE

[For 25 Halsbury's Laws (4th edn) para 169 see now 25 Halsbury's Laws (4th edn) (2003 Reissue) para 345.]

COLLUSION

Interpleader proceedings

[For 25 Halsbury's Laws (4th edn) para 1019 see now 37(1) Halsbury's Laws (4th edn) (Reissue) para 1436.]

COLOURABLE. *SEE* NOMINAL, TRIVIAL OR COLOURABLE

COMBAT

Australia [For the purposes of disability pension the Administrative Appeals Tribunal interpreted the Veterans' Entitlement Act 1986 (Cth), s 6(1)n as requiring in the applicant some offensive action to 'combat' the enemy compared with mere passive defence.] 'The primary judge favoured the view that the expression "actual combat against the enemy" would include conduct which answered the description of integral participation in an activity directly intended for an encounter with the enemy, whether offensive or defensive in character. We agree with that treatment of the matter.' *Repatriation Commission v Ahrenfeld* (1991) 101 ALR 86 at 93, per cur

COMMAND

[The Collision Regulations, etc Order 1953 has been revoked. See now the Merchant Shipping (Distress Signals and Prevention of Collisions) Regulations 1983, SI 1983/708, Sch 1, r 27(a).]

[For 43 Halsbury's Laws (4th edn) para 884 see now 43(1) Halsbury's Laws (4th edn) (Reissue) para 818 note 9, citing the Collision Regulations 1972 r 3(f).]

COMMANDER

[The Dumping at Sea Act 1974 has been repealed. The definition is now contained in the Food and Environment Protection Act 1985, s 24(1), as follows.] 'Commander', in relation to an aircraft, means the member of the flight crew designated as commander of that aircraft by the operator, or, failing such designation, the person who is for the time being the pilot in command of the aircraft.

COMMENCEMENT

Of arbitration

[Letter by plaintiffs stating that dispute was thereby referred to arbitration; arbitrator appointed six months later; question of limitation depending on when arbitration proceedings were 'commenced'.] 'The issue I have to decide is whether a notice requiring differences to be submitted to arbitration in accordance with an agreement satisfies s 34(3) [of the Limitation Act 1980] because it carries with it by implication a request that the recipient appoint his arbitrator.

'... There is, it seems to me, in this context an important distinction between serving a notice which expressly requires an act to be done and a notice which states something from which that act should follow though it is not referred to. Further, although of course the correct construction of a statutory provision may be affected by its context, if a statutory provision provides for a notice requiring something, it is ordinarily to be expected that the notice must do so expressly.

'... English law has taken the approach that something more must be done than to request that the matter be referred to arbitration. A step must be taken towards getting the arbitration under way, a step towards the appointment of the tribunal.

'... English law has, it seems to me, taken the policy decision that, to stop time running, the notice must take a step further than a requirement to arbitrate.' *Vosnoc Ltd v Transglobal Projects Ltd* [1998] 2 All ER 990 at 999, per Judge Raymond Jack QC

COMMENCEMENT OF THE HEARING

New Zealand [Section 271A of the Resource Management Act 1991.] ' . . it would appear necessary that the words "the commencement of the hearing" be read as relating to the first call of the proceeding for hearing. Any other meaning would result in confusion and difficulty. It is clear that on the first call of the proceeding for hearing it may be disposed of, or the hearing may be adjourned to a later sitting, or the proceeding may be part heard.' *Island Bay Residents' Association (Inc) v Wellington City Council* [2000] 2 NZLR 737 at 745 per Doogue J

'The commencement of the hearing ... is the time and date upon which the proceeding is called in accordance with the first notice of hearing in relation to it.' *Island Bay Residents' Association (Inc) v Wellington City Council* [2000] 2 NZLR 737 at 746 per Doogue J

COMMERCIAL ACTIVITY

Canada [Labour relations board asserted jurisdiction over labour relations of local employees in United States military base in Canada on the basis that this was a commercial activity under s 5 of the State Immunity Act, Can.] '... The section, in combination with the definition of "commercial activity" in s 2, raises two basic questions. First, what is the "nature" of the activity in question—ie, does employment at the base constitute commercial activity? Second, are the proceedings in this case—a union certification application—"related" to that activity? The two questions are, of course, interrelated, and neither can be answered in absolute terms. Certain aspects of employment at the base are commercial, but in other respects the employment relationship is infused with sovereign attributes. Accordingly, the certification proceeding affects both the commercial and sovereign aspects of employment at the base. The issue then becomes whether the effect on the commercial realm is sufficiently strong as to form a "nexus" so that it can truly be said that the proceedings "relate" to commercial activity. In my view, a nexus exists only between the certification proceedings and the *sovereign* attributes of labour relations at the base.

The effect on commercial activity is merely incidental, and cannot trigger the application of s 5 of the State Immunity Act.

'... Whether a contractual relationship exists between employer and employee is wholly irrelevant to the question of whether board proceedings "relate" to employment at the base. The relevant question is whether the connection between conditions of work and the certification proceedings is strong enough to override the competing nexus between these proceedings and management of the base.' *United States of America v Public Service Alliance of Canada, Re Canada Labour Code* (1992) 91 DLR (4th) 449, at 460–461, 469, per La Forest J (Can SC)

Canada '[50] I deal first with the preponderant purpose submissions. I am persuaded that the question of whether any organization is a business for purposes of taxation under the *Assessment Act*, R.S.O. 1990, c. A.31, is not determinative or applicable to the interpretation of the term "commercial activity" under PIPEDA, having regard to the different objectives of the two statutes. However, I am not persuaded that the interpretation submitted by the Association as to the breadth of the words "commercial activity" as defined in PIPEDA is apt.

'[51] The "exchange of consideration" involved in supplying personal information and a prescribed membership fee in exchange for the services and benefits of membership in the Association may constitute consideration under the law of contract. However, consideration in contract does not in itself lead to the finding of commercial activity in the PIPEDA context. In my view, there must be something more than a mere "exchange of consideration", as described by counsel, to be within the definition of "commercial activity".

'[52] Counsel for the Association has in his written submissions referred to a dictionary definition of the words "commerce" and "commercial", in aid of interpreting the meaning of the phrase "commercial activity".

'[53] In that dictionary, the word "commerce" is defined as:

... exchange between men of the products of nature and art; buying and selling together; exchange of merchandise ...

'The word "commercial" is defined as:

... engaged in commerce; trading; of or relating to commerce or trade.

(See Shorter Oxford English Dictionary p. 349 – Appendix B.)

'[54] The same words are defined in the Oxford English Reference Dictionary, Oxford University Press, 2nd ed., 1996, as follows:

"commerce": financial transactions, especially the buying and selling of merchandise, on a large scale;

"commercial": of, engaged in or concerned with commerce; having profit as a primary aim rather than artistic, etc. value.

'The difficulty in dictionary definitions can be readily seen by the absence of the word or notion of profit or gain in the source quoted by counsel for the Association and the presence of the notion of profit or gain in the definition found in the Oxford Reference Dictionary.

'[55] Although the dictionary definitions assist somewhat in interpreting the term "commercial activity" in s. 2(1) of PIPEDA, I rely more heavily on the interpretation from the Privacy Commissioner's Web site noted above wherein it is stated that "collecting membership fees, organizing club activities, compiling a list of members' names and addresses, and mailing out newsletters are not considered commercial activities".' *Rodgers v Calvert* [2004] OJ No 3653, 244 DLR (4th) 479 (SCJ), per MacKenzie J

COMMERCIAL PURPOSES

[Section 4(1) of the State Immunity Act 1978 disapplies state immunity as respects proceedings relating to a contract of employment made between the state and an individual where the contract was made in the United Kingdom or the work is wholly or partly performed there. Section 4(3) provides that the exclusion of sub-s (1) by sub-s (2) does not apply where the work is for an office, agency or establishment maintained by the state in the United Kingdom for 'commercial purposes' unless the individual was habitually resident in that state when the contract was made.] 'As appears from the more recent decision of *Littrell v United States of America (No 2)* [1994] 4 All ER 203 at 211, 212–213, [1995] 1 WLR 82 at 89, 91, the proper approach to the question whether an activity is commercial or in exercise of sovereign authority, involves looking at all the circumstances in relation to the activities and their context and then consider[ing] all the factors together. No one factor is in itself determinative in characterising the activity as sovereign or non-sovereign. It is relevant to look at the nature of the activity, the identity of those who deal with it, and the place where it takes place

in order to resolve this question.' *Arab Republic of Egypt v Gamal-Eldin* [1996] 2 All ER 237 at 247, EAT, per Mummery J

COMMERCIAL RIVER SURFING

New Zealand '[45] What is meant by "commercial river surfing" on the Kawarau River, which is the phrase QRSL used in its application? As described by Mr Ward in his affidavit (quoted earlier) the role of the professionals when in the water is to give advice and training when everyone is in the quieter passages, and to give what assistance they can if a surfer gets into trouble. But a river surfer is, it appears to us, basically on his or her own, particularly when the water gets rough.

'[46] We find that the "commercial" aspects of QRSL's operation on the surface of the Kawarau River are not the river surfing by an individual but the guidance by other, trained surfers. That is quite different to the commercial boating offered by a jetboat operator, where all the passengers are in the same boat. QRSL's in-river activity is "commercial guiding of river surfers", and that is what the commercial river surfing activity on the Kawarau River consists of.

'[47] With the exception of rule 5.7.4B [of the proposed district plan] itself the more specific indications favour an interpretation which includes "river surfing activity" within "boating activity". The principles in Part 2 of the [Resource Management Act 1991] do not assist one way or the other. However, the more important factors in our view are those which flow from the statement of the safety issue, through the objectives and some of the policies to a straightforward reading of rule 5.4.7B which suggests the standard does not apply to river surfing, and certainly not to commercial river surfing activity, on the Kawarau River.' *Queenstown River Surfing Ltd v Central Otago District Council* [2006] NZRMA 1 at [45]–[47], per Judge Jackson

COMMISSION

Australia 'A commission is a sum or percentage allowed to an agent or salesman for his services – *Macquarie Dictionary*. It might also be described as a payment to an agent proportional to an amount involved in a transaction or a percentage of the amount involved in a transaction – see *Shorter Oxford English Dictionary*.' *Brown v Commissioner of Taxation* BC200102688; [2001] FCA 596 at [108], per Emmett J

COMMIT

[The Road Traffic Act 1972 has been repealed. See now the Road Traffic Act 1988, s 4(6).]

COMMON

[For 6 Halsbury's Laws (4th edn) paras 505–507 see now 6 Halsbury's Laws (4th edn) (2003 Reissue) paras 404–406.]

COMMON TERMS AND CONDITIONS OF EMPLOYMENT

[Equal Pay Act 1970, s 1(6).] 'The real question, however, is what is meant by "common terms and conditions of employment" and between whom do such terms and conditions have to be common ... [T]he terms and conditions do not have to be identical, but on a broad basis to be substantially comparable'. *British Coal Corpn v Smith* [1996] 3 All ER 97 at 106, 109, HL, per Lord Slynn of Hadley

COMMONWEALTH

Australia '[23] ... The term "the Commonwealth" is used in various senses particularly in Ch III of the [Commonwealth of Australia] Constitution and the Judiciary Act [1903 (Cth)]. In r 93 [of the High Court Rules], the term "the Commonwealth or a State" is used to identify the body providing the salary to the practitioner whose fee is in question and attention thereby is directed to the party in contract with the practitioner to whom the salary is provided.

...

'[26] It is sufficient for present purposes to indicate that in r 93 the term "the Commonwealth" is not used in any expanded sense which would embrace the AGS [Australian Government Solicitor]. Were the contrary construction to be adopted, a question would arise as to whether the rule altered, impaired or detracted from the operation of s 55P dealing with the charging of fees by the AGS and their recovery by the client of the AGS as costs incurred by the client ...

'[27] A contrary interpretation of r 93 would also raise a question respecting the operation of s 64 of the Judiciary Act. Counsel for the Minister pointed out in his submissions that as an incorporated legal practice the AGS now is not unique in that regard. As is indicated above, r 93 does not apply to a practitioner who is in receipt of a salary from a "private" incorporated legal practice.

If the AGS, a body corporate, fell within the term "the Commonwealth" in r 93, then parties such as the Minister who engage the AGS would be, in respect of recovery of costs, in a different position to private parties who engage another incorporated firm of practitioners. Section 64, which extends to the Minister, gave the Minister in the proceedings in question the same rights, as nearly as possible, as those of the other parties and provided for the award of costs as in a suit between subject and subject.' *Re Minister for Immigration and Multicultural Affairs; Ex parte Goldie; Goldie v Minister for Immigration and Multicultural Affairs* [2004] HCA 27 at [23], [26], [27], per Gummow J; BC200403489

COMMUNICATE

Canada '[44] The Board took the view that "[t]o occur in Canada, a communication must originate from a server located in Canada on which content has been posted" (at p. 459), except perhaps if the content provider has "the intention to communicate it specifically to recipients in Canada" (at p. 460). In my view, with respect, this is too rigid and mechanical a test. An Internet communication that crosses one or more national boundaries "occurs" in more than one country, at a minimum the country of transmission and the country of reception. In *Dow Jones, supra*, the defendant argued that the appropriate law should be that of the jurisdiction where the host server is located, but this was rejected in favour of the law of the State of reception by the High Court of Australia. To the extent the Board held that a communication that does not *originate* in Canada does not occur in Canada, I disagree with its decision.

'[45] At the end of the transmission, the end user has a musical work in his or her possession that was not there before. The work has, necessarily, been communicated, irrespective of its point of origin. If the communication is by virtue of the Internet, there has been a "telecommunication". To hold otherwise would not only fly in the face of the ordinary use of language but would have serious consequences in other areas of law relevant to the Internet, including Canada's ability to deal with criminal and civil liability for objectionable communications entering the country from abroad.

'[46] The word "communicate" is an ordinary English word that means to "impart" or "transmit" (*Shorter Oxford English Dictionary on Historical Principles* (5th ed. 2002), vol. 1, at p. 463). Communication presupposes a sender and a receiver of what is transmitted; see *R. v. Goldman*, [1980] 1

S.C.R. 976 at p. 995, 108 D.L.R. (3d) 17. The "communicator" is the sender, not the recipient.' *Society of Composers, Authors and Music Publishers of Canada v Canadian Association of Internet Providers* [2004] SCJ No 44, 240 DLR (4th) 193, per Binnie J

COMPANY

[For 7 Halsbury's Laws (4th edn) para 1 see now 7(1) Halsbury's Laws (4th edn) (2004 Reissue) para 201.]

Associated company

[The Income and Corporation Taxes Act 1970 has been largely repealed. The definition, with minor drafting amendments, is re-enacted in the Income and Corporation Taxes Act 1988, s 416(1).]

Close company

[Reference should now be made to s 414(1) of the Income and Corporation Taxes Act 1988, in which the definition is re-enacted with the addition of three subsections and other drafting amendments.]

Family company

[The Capital Gains Tax Act 1979 has been repealed. The definition is now contained in the Taxation of Chargeable Gains Act 1992, Sch 6, para 1, as follows.]

'Family company' means in relation to an individual, a company the voting rights in which are—

(i) as to not less than 25 per cent exercisable by the individual, or

(ii) as to more than 50 per cent exercisable by the individual or a member of his family and, as to not less than 5 per cent exercisable by the individual himself.

Subsidiary company

[The extract below should be substituted for that on p 295 of vol 1.]

(1) A company is a 'subsidiary' of another company, its 'holding company', if that other company—

   (a) holds a majority of the voting rights in it, or

   (b) is a member of it and has the right to appoint or remove a majority of its board of directors, or

   (c) is a member of it and controls alone, pursuant to an agreement with other shareholders or members, a majority of the voting rights in it,

or if it is a subsidiary of a company which is itself a subsidiary of that other company.

(2) A company is a 'wholly-owned subsidiary' of another company if it has no members except that other and that other's wholly- owned subsidiaries or persons acting on behalf of that other or its wholly-owned subsidiaries.

(3) In this section 'company' includes any body corporate. (Companies Act 1985, s 736 as substituted by the Companies Act 1989, s 144(1))

Trading company

[The Finance Act 1972, Sch 16, para 11(1), was repealed and re-enacted in the Income and Corporation Taxes Act 1988, Sch 19 para 7, itself repealed by the Finance Act 1989.]

'Trading company' means a company whose business consists wholly or mainly of the carrying on of a trade or trades. (Taxation of Chargeable Gains Act 1992, Sch 6, para 1(2))

COMPEL *SEE* COMPELLING REASONS FOR THE ABSENCE

COMPELLED

New Zealand 'That word has a fairly technical connotation in the law of evidence generally—as meaning "can be mandatorily required".' *R v K* [1995] 2 NZLR 440 at 447, per Hammond J

COMPELLING REASONS

Australia [Migration Act 1958 (Cth) and Migration Regulations 1994 (Cth) cl 820.211(2).] '[4] The Tribunal's statement prepared under s 430(1) of the Act comprises 10 closely typed pages divided into 51 paragraphs. After setting out the background to the review and describing the nature of the evidence and material submitted by the applicant, the Tribunal turned its attention to the waiver provision and said:

> 24. The term "compelling" is not defined in the legislation. According to the Macquarie Dictionary "compel" means "to force or drive, especially to a course of action". The Shorter oxford [sic] Dictionary also defines the word compel as "to bring about by force or moral necessity". The Tribunal has also had regard

to policy guidelines in PAM3 which also refer to the Explanatory Memorandum to the Statutory Rules 1996 No 75 that introduced this provision.

...

'[10] Secondly, counsel for the applicant submitted that the Tribunal misconstrued the term "compelling reasons" in the waiver provision of the criterion. The dictionary definitions, to which the Tribunal referred and which are reproduced in [4] above, are said to involve an impermissibly high standard. This is a silly point. There is no true construction of the expression in question. Reasons for not applying the Sch 3 criteria may appear compelling to one person and not to another. The adjective "compelling" does not introduce an objective standard. The waiver decision will always involve a subjective judgment ...' *McNamara v Minister for Immigration and Multicultural and Indigenous Affairs* [2004] FCA 1096 at [4], [10], per Whitlam J; BC200405413

COMPELLING REASONS FOR THE ABSENCE

Australia [In the context of the criteria applicable to classes of visas: subcl 155.212(3A)(b)(i) of the (Cth) Migration Regulations 1994.] ' "Compel" and "compelling" are words of ordinary meaning and the subclause's expression "compelling reasons for the absence" falls to be construed by reference to well-established principles. In interpreting a statute or delegated legislation the object of the court is to ascertain the legislative intention as "expressed by the words used": *Cooper Brookes (Wollongong) Pty Ltd v Federal Commissioner of Taxation* (1981) 147 CLR 297 at 304. Whilst the construction of a statute is a matter of law, the ordinary or natural meaning of an ordinary English word is generally a question of fact: *Hope v Bathurst City Council* (1980) 144 CLR 1 at 8; *Collector of Customs v Agfa-Gevaert Ltd* (1996) 186 CLR 389 at 396; *Re Minister for Immigration and Multicultural Affairs and Ors; Ex parte Cohen* (2001) 177 ALR 473 at 481. Resort by courts to dictionaries, to assist in the task of establishing the ordinary or natural meaning of an ordinary word has been well recognised over a long period: see the observations of Jordan CJ in *Australian Gas Light Co v Valuer-General* (1940) 40 SR (NSW) 126 at 137, of Mahoney JA in *Provincial Insurance Australia Pty Ltd v Consolidated Wood Products Pty Ltd* (1991) 25 NSWLR 541 at 560/561 and of Mason P in *House of Peace Pty Ltd v Bankstown*

City Council (2000) 48 NSWLR 498 at 504/505. In the final analysis a court must determine the intention of the legislature and the applicability of ordinary words to specific facts by reference to the meaning of the language and purpose of a particular instrument.

'A perusal of commonly used dictionaries indicates that the words "compel" and "compelling" are ordinary English words which have not one, but several connotations. What they have in common is a semantic debt to the Latin pello/pellere — "to force", "to drive", "to stimulate", "to rouse", but it is clear beyond dispute that the idea of "force" common to many of the dictionary entries is not confined to physical or legal force but includes moral force and the "force" of mental stimuli such as from a "compelling argument". The Oxford English Dictionary (2nd ed) Vol III gives four definitions for the verb "compel" ranked from "the usual construction" to "rare":

1. To urge irresistibly, to constrain, oblige, force:
   a. a person to do a thing;
   b. a person to or (into) a course of action, etc.

2.
   a. To take or get by force, to extort;
   b. To constrain (an action); to bring about by force, constraint or moral necessity; to exalt by rightful claim; to command.

3. To force to come, go, or proceed; to drive forcibly, to force

4. To overpower, constrain.

'The same dictionary's entry for "compelling" contains two definitions:

a   That compels: see verb
b   Of a person, his words, writings etc, irresistible; **demanding attention**, respect, etc.'
(emphasis added)

'The entry in the Macquarie Dictionary (3rd ed) for "compelling" states:

(of a person, writer, actor, etc) **demanding attention or interest**.

(emphasis added)

'Webster's Legal Dictionary gives examples of the meanings of "compelling":

that compels: **tending to demand action** or convince

(emphasis added)

'Webster's Third New International Dictionary (unabridged) 1993 contains the following expanded meanings for "compelling":
1. forcing, impelling, driving.
2. **demanding** respect, honour, or **admiration**
3. calling for examination, scrutiny, consideration or thought
4. **demanding** or holding one's **attention**
5. tending to convince or convert by or as if by forcefulness of evidence
(emphasis added)

'The emphasised entries show the sources for the Tribunal's construction of, or gloss upon, "compelling reasons for the absence". The balance, the unemphasised, shows what aspects of the ordinary meaning of "compelling" the Tribunal has omitted from its construction of, or gloss upon, the legislative expression.

'The legislative intention to be discerned in the legislature's use of the word "compelling" in the expression "compelling reasons for the absence" is not an amalgam of every shade of meaning of "compelling" to be found as examples of common usage in dictionaries. A judge must bring to bear to the task of interpreting words of ordinary meaning, his or her understanding of common usage, especially having regard to the purpose, context and language of the relevant delegated legislation.

'The relevant regulations have as their purpose setting out clear criteria for various visas. Clear factual criteria apply for a subclass 155 visa unless the Minister is satisfied there were "compelling reasons for the absence" of more than 5 years. The instruction in para 4.4.40 of MSI 356 is intended to assist in the administration of the subclause, but in its terms it does not purport to construe the delegated legislation which is for the Courts rather than the Executive: *Cakmak v Minister for Immigration and Multicultural and Indigenous Affairs* (2003) 135 FCR 183 at [68].

'The ordinary meaning of the adjective "compelling" is not confined to the meanings used by the Tribunal when it construed the legislative expression. The legislative expression is wide and unqualified. "Compelling" in its wide, ordinary meaning means "forceful". Forceful reasons for an absence may involve physical, legal or moral necessity or may, by reason of their forcefulness, be convincing. There is nothing in the express wording of the relevant subclause which indicates that "compelling", where it occurs, should be read narrowly so as to exclude forceful reasons which

raise moral necessity or which are convincing. Equally, there is nothing in the express wording, or the context, which indicates that "compelling reasons for the absence" must be confined to reasons incorporating an involuntary element, involving circumstances beyond a person's control, involving physical or legal necessity or cognate with the reasons given as examples in MSI 356.

'In *McNamara's* case, Whitlam J had to consider the same waiver provision which was considered in *Bozanich's* case, set out in para 17 above, which contained the expression 'compelling reasons for not applying those criteria'. Whitlam J found:

> Reasons for not applying Sch 3 criteria may appear compelling to one person and not to another. The adjective "compelling" does not introduce an objective standard. The waiver decision will always involve a subjective judgment.

'In *Babicci's* case Moore J considered the expression "compelling circumstances affecting the sponsor or nominator" in reg 1.20J(2):

> Despite subregulation (1), the Minister may approve the sponsorship or nomination of an applicant for a visa if the Minister is satisfied that there are compelling circumstances affecting the sponsor or nominator.

'Moore J decided:

> ... plainly what the regulation had in mind was that the material reveal circumstances such that the Tribunal would be overwhelmingly inclined to exercise the discretion in favour of the applicant and would approve the sponsorship.

'Moore J's decision on the meaning of "compelling" in the subclause he considered is consistent with treating "compelling" as meaning forceful and therefore convincing.

'In both *McNamara* and *Babicci*, the judges treated the Minister, rather than the applicant, as the implied predicate, that is as the person the legislature intended to be "compelled" by the "compelling reasons" or "compelling circumstances" respectively, reflecting the syntax of the waiver provisions under consideration.

'The subclause here is somewhat different syntactically. The expression "compelling reasons for the absence" must, I think refer to the applicant's absence. Whilst the drafting style is one which requires the Minister's satisfaction as to a matter of fact, it seems to me this does not mean the Minster's decision on this aspect involves only a subjective judgment as in McNamara's case. If, as I think is correct, the applicant is the one who must have been "compelled" by the reasons for his absence, the requirement that the Minister be satisfied in respect of them means that the Minister is entitled to make a judgment as to whether the reasons for the absence are forceful, and therefore convincing by reference to some standard of reasonableness such as a reasonable person in the same circumstances as the appellant. Even if I am wrong, and the subclause does not introduce any objective standard, any subjective judgment made by the Minister as to whether the reasons were compelling would still have to be reasonable in the administrative law sense.

'In its reliance on *Bozanich* for the mistaken proposition that "the ordinary meaning of the word 'compelling' incorporates an involuntary element", in its apparent acceptance of *Tumelty* which found the subclause required "circumstances beyond the applicant's control" and in its comparison of the applicant's circumstances with the examples in MSI 356, the Tribunal treated the applicant as the person "compelled" by the reasons for absence. However, in its ratio decidendi it is not clear to me whether the Tribunal was not satisfied the reasons were compelling, because it was not satisfied the reasons "demand or rouse (its) strong attention, interest or admiration or ... tend to demand (its) action", ie. to grant the visa despite the applicant's absence for more than 5 years, or whether it meant it was not satisfied the reasons "demand or rouse (the applicant's), strong attention, interest or admiration or ... tend to demand (the applicant's) action", ie. to remain absent.

'The Tribunal accepted all of the evidence put forward as the "reasons for the absence", namely the psychological dependence of the applicant and his late wife on their only daughter, who grew up, without siblings, with her parents in Australia, during the long depressive illness of the applicant's late wife. Except for a period between 1996 and 1997, when the applicant was finalising his affairs in Italy so he and his late wife could follow their daughter to Australia, he and his late wife had lived with their daughter for over five decades. They had assisted in the care of their grandchildren as they grew up. The Tribunal accepted the psychological dependence arose from the applicant's desire to do the best for his family which the Tribunal described as a "very normal and common human desire."

'Whether the Tribunal treated itself as the person to be "compelled" or the applicant as the person to be "compelled" by such reasons, a conclusion by

the Tribunal that it could not be satisfied the reasons which it had accepted "demand or rouse strong attention, interest or admiration or ... tend to demand action" does not seem reasonable in an administrative law sense.

'The first part of the Tribunal's gloss on the legislative expression, that "compelling reasons for the absence" must "demand or rouse strong attention, interest or admiration" seems strained, awkward and not especially apposite as shown by an examination of the dictionary entries from which it derives. Moreover, it is not possible to be sure what the Tribunal required to satisfy this aspect as it is not possible to identify how the circumstances accepted by the Tribunal as set out in para 43 above could be found, for example, not to "rouse interest".

'The second and alternative part of the Tribunal's construction, namely that "compelling reasons for the absence" must "tend to demand action" is correct and apposite as far as it goes. However, the Tribunal had ascertained "compelling" in its ordinary meaning means "tending to demand action **or to convince**" (emphasis added), but in putting a gloss on the legislative requirement it shortened this ordinary meaning to "tending to demand action'. This seems to me to omit a significant aspect of the ordinary meaning of "compelling".

'The applicant's counsel did not rely on the unreasonableness of the result as a ground of review but rather argued that the Tribunal's construction of the legislative requirement put a gloss upon or derogated from the express words in the subclause. I agree. However, I do not agree that the gloss upon the legislative requirement meant that the Tribunal "required the applicant to demonstrate an involuntary element" as set out in ground (ii)(1). It is not possible to determine what the Tribunal required. It is only possible to say that its gloss on the legislative requirement does not cover all reasons which could come within the legislative expression. Accordingly, it applied a higher test than the express words required, as set out in ground (ii)(2).

'It is necessary at this point to acknowledge the submissions made by the first respondent's counsel. I accept, for the purposes of the decision, that the task of applying the subclause to the particular facts is a task committed to the judgment of the Tribunal. In the absence of matters such as, for example, bad faith or unreasonableness or a characterisation of a fact as a jurisdictional fact, there can be no jurisdictional error arising out of a finding of satisfaction in respect of certain facts, if that state of satisfaction were open on the evidence.

'However, accepting for the purposes of the application that the Tribunal's application of the legislative requirement to a set of facts is a matter committed to it, the antecedent question, is whether the Tribunal's gloss on "compelling reasons for the absence" (if wrong) revealed an error as to a matter of fact (ie. the meaning of ordinary words), which could not give rise to jurisdictional error or an error as to a matter of law.

'Although the Tribunal undertook its decision-making conscientiously and has correctly set out the natural meaning of relevant ordinary words as extracted in para 20 above, it has applied the legislative requirements by a reference to a narrow and not entirely apposite construction of the legislative expression.

'To err in the construction of statutory criteria for the grant of a visa is to err in law: *NAGV and NAGW of 2002 v Minister for Immigration and Multicultural and Indigenous Affairs* [2005] HCA 6. To err in the construction of an expression in delegated legislation, which forms part of the criteria for the grant of a visa, is equally to err in law.

'It is possible that absent the error of construction, the result may have been the opposite of the result complained of, particularly considering the Tribunal's acceptance of certain facts as described in para 43 above. There is authority for the proposition that such a circumstance can give rise to error of law for the purpose of ADJR legislation: *Australian Broadcasting Tribunal v Bond* (1990) 170 CLR 321 at 353 and 384 per Mason CJ.

'As a result of an error in construing the legislative expression, the Tribunal asked itself a wrong question: "Were the reasons for the absence compelling in that they 'demand or rouse strong attention, interest or admiration or … tend to demand action'?" If the Tribunal wished to ask the question posed by the case by reference to the ordinary meaning of "compelling", the correct question was: "Were the reasons for the absence compelling in that they were forceful?" In answering that question, the Tribunal would commit a mistake of law if it put a gloss on "forceful" so as to exclude reasons for the absence which are forceful in that they involve moral necessity, or are convincing by reason of some forcefulness. This distinguishes this case from *Babicci's* case (which is distinguishable on other grounds as well) where Moore J found the mistaken adoption of the meaning of a statutory criterion did not result in the Tribunal misunderstanding the question it had to decide.' *Lorenzo Paduano v Minister for Immigration and Multicultural and Indigenous Affairs and Migration Review Tribunal* [2005] FCA 211 at [31]–[53], per Crennan J; BC200500944

COMPENSABLE INJURY

Australia 'A claimant can only be considered to be a primary, secondary or family victim (s 6) if he/she has crossed the threshold of demonstrating that he/she has been the victim of an "act of violence". It is only after that threshold test has been satisfied that the question of whether the "injury" is a "compensable injury" arises (ss 7 and 8).

'The Dictionary then directs one to s 10 to determine the meaning of "compensable injury". Section 10 is a definition section. It has no substantive effect. It serves the function of indicating that when the phrase "compensable injury" appears in the 1996 [Victims Support & Rehabilitation] Act, it refers to the matters set out in Sch 1: see *Mutual Acceptance Co Ltd v The Federal Commissioner of Taxation* (1944) 69 CLR 389 per Rich J at 398; *Council of the Municipality of Randwick v Rutledge & Ors* (1959) 102 CLR 54 per Menzies J at 62, Windeyer J at 69; *Gibb v The Commissioner of Taxation of the Commonwealth of Australia* (1966) 118 CLR 628 at 635 per Barwick CJ, McTiernan and Taylor JJ and at 640 per Windeyer J; see also *Kelly v R* [2004] HCA 12; (2004) 205 ALR 274 per McHugh J at [84].

'Qualifying the defined term "injury" by the adjective "compensable" does not enlarge the definition of "injury" in the Dictionary. Once a term is given a particular meaning in an Act, prima facie, all references that are derived from or associated with that term should be treated as based on the defined meaning of that term: see Statutory Interpretation in Australia, Pearce and Geddes, Butterworths, 5th Edition, at 6.61. Nothing in the 1996 Act warrants departure from that presumption. Just as the term "injury" should be read wherever it appears in the 1996 Act as referring to "actual bodily harm" and/or "psychological or psychiatric disorder" so, too, "compensable injury" should be read as referring to "compensable actual bodily harm" or "compensable psychological or psychiatric disorder".

' "Injury" is qualified by the adjective "compensable" to ensure that a claimant seeking to recover statutory compensation establishes that he/she has suffered an "injury" (as defined in the Dictionary) but only as set out in Sch 1. This is confirmed by cl 1 of Sch 1 which provides that "[t]he injuries specified in column 1 of the table to this Schedule are compensable injuries for the purposes of this Act."

'The phrase "compensable injury" thus serves the purpose of restricting the category of persons eligible for statutory compensation. Eligibility does not turn merely upon demonstrating that a person has been the victim of an "act of violence" and has suffered some injury. It turns upon both establishing those matters and that the "injury" is "compensable" because it appears in Sch 1. This achieves the legislative purpose of ensuring that "compensation is structured towards those victims suffering the most serious injuries" (Second Reading Speech, New South Wales Legislative Council, Parliamentary Debates (Hansard) 15 May 1996 at p 976).' *Victims Compensation Fund Corporation v GM* [2004] NSWCA 185 at [107], per McColl JA; BC200403610

COMPENSATION

'The word "compensation", when used by lawyers, in connection with the recovery of damages from a wrongdoer, usually means a sum of money designed to repair or make good the loss that the victim has suffered. Of course there is always the proviso: so far as money can do that. Where the wrong is loss of reputation, or pain and suffering and loss of amenity, it cannot in reality be repaired or made good by money. But the law has the fiction that it can.

'In other contexts, compensation can mean something different, such as money paid to a victim on account of his loss, whether or not it be measured so as to repair or make it good …

'In my judgment the word is used in that wider sense in the policy of insurance with which we are concerned.' *Lancashire County Council v Municipal Mutual Insurance Ltd* [1996] 3 All ER 545 at 556, CA, per Staughton LJ

Canada [On a question of compensation for a reinstated employee not exceeding a sum equivalent to remuneration which would have been paid.] ' "Compensation" is defined as follows in Black's Law Dictionary, 5th edn (1979): "Compensation: Indemnification; payment of damages; making amends; making whole; giving an equivalent or substitute of equal value. That which is necessary to restore an injured party to his former position. Remuneration for services rendered, whether in salary, fees, or commissions. Consideration or price of a privilege purchased." It is true that the word does bear the limited meaning of remuneration urged by the applicant, but its primary sense is rather "making amends" or "making whole".' *Canadian Broadcasting Corpn v CUPE* [1987] 3 FCR 515 at 520, FCA, per MacGuigan J

COMPILATIONS

Canada 'Compilations have been known to the Canadian law of copyright for ages, but it is only recently that they have been formally defined in the Act.

'Prior to the 1993 *North American Free Trade Agreement Implementation Act 5* (NAFTA Implementation Act), compilations were only protected in so far as they could be characterized as "literary works".

'In order to implement the North American Free Trade Agreement [North American Free Trade Agreement Between the Government of Canada, the Government of the United Mexican States and the Government of the United States of America, [1994] Can TS No 2] (NAFTA), the Copyright Act was substantially amended. "Artistic work", "dramatic work", "literary work" and "musical work" were from now on to include, respectively, "compilations of artistic works", "any compilation of dramatic works", "compilations of literary works" and "any compilation [of any work of music or musical composition]" (subsection 53(2) of the NAFTA Implementation Act). In the same vein, the definition of "every original literary, dramatic, musical and artistic work" in section 2 was now including "compilations" as "a mode or form of its expression":

2. …

"every original literary, dramatic, musical and artistic work" includes every original production in the literary, scientific or artistic domain, whatever may be the mode or form of its expression, such as compilations, …

Furthermore, a definition of "compilation" was added to section 2 of the *Copyright Act* by subsection 53(3) of the NAFTA Implementation Act. It reads as follows:

2. …

"compilation" means
(*a*) a work resulting from the selection or arrangement of literary, dramatic, musical or artistic works or of parts thereof, or
(*b*) a work resulting from the selection or arrangement of data;

'The 1993 amendments may not be without significance, even though they were down-played by counsel who considered them to be a mere codification of the existing law. Prior to these amendments, "compilations" were seen as "literary works" and courts had therefore to find a way to relate them to literary works. Since the amendments, "compilations" may be related to artistic, dramatic and musical works as well as to literary works, with the result that earlier cases which examined compilations of data as being part of literary works must now be applied with caution: it could be that compilations which did not qualify for copyright protection because they could not be related to literary works, would qualify under the new definition.

'More importantly, the addition of the definition of "compilation" in so far as it relates to "a work resulting from the selection or arrangement of data" appears to me to have decided the battle which was shaping up in Canada between partisans of the "creativity" doctrine — according to which compilations must possess at least some minimal degree of creativity — and the partisans of the "industrious collection" or "sweat of the brow" doctrine — wherein copyright is a reward for the hard work that goes into compiling facts.

'The definition of "compilation" must be interpreted in relation to the context in which it was introduced. Simply put, it was introduced as a result of the signature of the North American Free Trade Agreement and with the specific purpose of implementing it. It is therefore but natural when attempting to interpret the new definition to seek guidance in the very words of the relevant provision of NAFTA which the amendment intends to implement. The applicable provision is Article 1705 which reads as follows:

Article 1705: Copyright

1. Each Party shall protect the works covered by Article 2 of the Berne Convention, including any other works that embody original expression within the meaning of that Convention. In particular:
   (a) all types of computer programs are literary works within the meaning of the Berne Convention and each Party shall protect them as such; and
   (b) compilations of data or other material, whether in machine readable or other form, which by reason of the selection or arrangement of their contents constitute intellectual creations, shall be protected as such.

The protection a Party provides under subparagraph (b) shall not extend to the data or material itself, or prejudice any copyright subsisting in that data or material.

'Clearly, what the parties to the Agreement wanted to protect were compilations of data that "embody original expression within the meaning of [the Berne] Convention" and that constitute "intellectual creations". The use of these last two words is most revealing: compilations of data are to be measured by standards of intellect and creativity. As these standards were already present in Anglo-Canadian jurisprudence — as we shall see later — I can only assume that the Canadian government in signing the Agreement and the Canadian Parliament in adopting the 1993 amendments to the *Copyright Act* expected the Court to follow the "creativity" school of cases rather than the "industrious collection" school.

'Whether compilations of data have been, through the amendments, protected "as such", as is stipulated by Article 1705(1)(b) of NAFTA, remains to be seen. If, at first blush, the fact that "compilations" is also defined as meaning "a work resulting from the selection or arrangement of data" appears to confer on compilations of data a status of their own, equal to that of literary, dramatic, musical or artistic works, yet the definition, when read in context, may not have that effect. Under subsection 5(1) [as amended by SC 1994, c 47, s 57] of the Act, copyright subsists not in a compilation of data *per se*, but in an original work, whether it be literary, dramatic, musical and artistic, with which presumably the type of data can best be related. Furthermore, the definition in section 2 of the words "every original literary, dramatic, musical and artistic work", which are the very words used in subsection 5(1), refers to compilations as being but "the mode or form" of expression of any of these four types of work. Whether, therefore, Canada has fully lived up to its commitments under Article 1705 of NAFTA is an open question which I need not resolve in order to decide this appeal.

'All in all, apart from the possible qualifications one might wish to make with respect to some earlier decisions, I have come to the conclusion that the 1993 amendments did not alter the state of the law of copyright with respect to compilations of data. The amendments simply reinforce in clear terms what the state of the law was, or ought to have been: the selection or arrangement of data only results in a protected compilation if the end result qualifies as an original intellectual creation.' *Tele-Direct (Publications) Inc v American Business Information Inc* [1998] 2 FC 22 at 29–32, FCA, per Déary JA

COMPLAINANT

New Zealand [Under the Summary Proceedings Act 1957, s 185C, the evidence of the complainant in a sexual case at a preliminary hearing is to be given in the form of a written statement, and the complainant is not to be examined or cross-examined on that statement unless certain conditions are met. Here statements made by two girls at depositions hearing were objected to as the girls' mothers (not the girls) had complained to the police.] '[13] The applicant has a straight forward contention that a "complainant" is someone who complains. However, use of such a literal meaning of the word will not achieve the purpose of the provision, namely, to mitigate the ordeal of complainants in giving evidence. This may be illustrated by considering a situation where the mother of some children complains to the police that children have been sexually abused. There is no obvious reason why s 185C should extend to protecting the mother from the stress of giving evidence ...

'[14] Mr Powell, for the police, submitted that the drafters used "complainant" as a substitute for "victim". He submitted that the drafters had a predicament as it would be premature to use the word "victim" in the s 185C provision, for that would prejudge the outcome of the proceedings. Mr Cook submitted that the drafter had the option of using the phrases "alleged victim", or "victims of alleged offences", the latter phrase being used in the Bail Act 2000, s 12(7).

'[15] Mr Powell also observed that the principal focus of the law reform was on rape victims, these being persons who will always feel aggrieved but may or may not complain fearing the future stresses of trial.

'[16] It is plain to me that the term "complainant" was intended to refer to the person involved in the sexual conduct, the alleged victim. To read the word "complainant" any wider would defeat the purpose of the Act. Guided by s 5 of the Interpretation Act the word "complainant" has to be given special meaning to exclude complainants who are not sexual victims. The important consequence of this conclusion, for this case, is that, however it is interpreted, the word "complainant" cannot carry its normal literal meaning of being someone who has complained.' *A v Registrar District Court at Christchurch* [2006] NZAR 195 at [13]–[16], per Fogarty J

COMPLAINT

Australia [Sections 16 and 17 of the Ombudsman (Northern Territory) Act 1978 (NT) refer to the making of 'complaints' to the Ombudsman.] 'I consider that the word "complaint" is used in the sense "to state a grievance or make a formal accusation" (see The Macquarie Dictionary, 3rd Edn, 1997, "complain".)' *Boyce v Owen* (2000) 9 NTLR 177; 156 FLR 321; BC200003627; [2000] NTCA 7 at [18], per Mildren J

COMPLAINT OR PROCEEDING

Australia [Section 152 of the Mining Act 1973 (NSW) provides that where a party to a 'complaint or proceeding' in a warden's court is dissatisfied with that court's decision, he may appeal to the District Court.] 'In a view of the language used, somewhat unsystematically, throughout Pt 9, of "complaints", "applications", "suits", "actions" and "proceedings", and in view of the focus in s 152 upon giving a right of appeal to parties dissatisfied with "decisions" of the warden's court, it seems to me the opening reference in the section to "a complaint or proceeding" is meant to comprehend any kind of matter in regard to which a warden's court may make a decision. So, when a decision is made, and the warden's court had power to make it, an appeal will lie under s 152, no matter what name was given to the proceedings in the court.' *Chief Mining Warden v District Court of New South Wales* (1991) 23 NSWLR 349 at 357, per Priestley JA

COMPLETE SPECIFICATION

Australia [Patents Act 1990 (Cth). Section 40(2)(a) provides: A complete specification must: (a) describe the invention fully, including the best method known to the applicant of performing the invention; ...] '[179] The specification, including the claims, must be read as a whole: *Kimberly-Clark Australia Pty Ltd v Arico Trading International Pty Ltd* (2001) 207 CLR 1 at [14], [16]. In that case the High Court (at [25]) cited the statement in *No-Fume Ltd v Frank Pitchford & Co Ltd* (1935) 52 RPC 231 at 243 that:

(i)t is not necessary that (the patentee) should describe in his specification the manner in which the invention is to be performed, with that wealth of detail with which the specification of the manufacturer of something is usually put before the workman who is engaged to manufacture it.

...

'[197] The Act has a Dictionary in Sch 1. It provides definitions of terms used in the Act "unless the contrary intention appears". One such definition is:

> Complete specification means (other than in section 116) a specification filed in respect of a complete patent application or, if the specification has been amended, the complete specification as amended.

'Section 116 provides that the Commissioner or a court may, in interpreting a complete specification as amended, refer to the specification without amendment.)

'[198] The definition of "complete specification" in its present form with the reference to amendment of the specification was inserted by the Patents Amendment (Innovation Patents) Act 2000 (Cth). As its title suggests, this Act was primarily concerned with the introduction of a system of less formal patents called innovation patents. However, counsel were unable to suggest any connection between innovation patents and the amendment of the definition of "complete specification".

...

'[201] The term "complete specification" is used elsewhere in the Act in a context where it is clear the Act's dictionary meaning, including amendments to the specification, is intended. Examples are s 105 (amendments directed by the court), s 112 (complete specification not to be amended, except by the court, where proceedings pending), s 218 (apportionment of costs where court finds some claims invalid but others not) and s 222(2) (Commissioner to arrange for selling copies of complete specifications). Using the term "complete specification" to mean the specification as amended is therefore a natural usage, and not really an artificial extension of what the term would convey even if the dictionary definition were not present. Therefore we might expect the Act to make it clear where, in a particular context, that meaning is not intended, as indeed it does in a number of instances: see ss 41(1), 42(1)(b), 79B(1)(a), 102(2A).' *Eli Lilly & Co v Pfizer Overseas Pharmaceuticals* [2005] FCA 67 at [179], [197], [198], [201], per Heerey J; BC200500225

COMPLETION

Of contract for sale of land

[For 42 Halsbury's Laws (4th edn) para 191 see now 42 Halsbury's Laws (4th edn) (Reissue) para 262.]

COMPOSITION

[For 3 Halsbury's Laws (4th edn) para 1000 see now 3(2) Halsbury's Laws (4th edn) (2002 Reissue) para 863.]

COMPOSITION OF MATTER

Canada 'The issue is whether claims 1 to 12 amount to an "invention" within the meaning of that term in section 2 of the *Patent Act*. The learned Trial Division Judge found that the oncomouse was new, useful and unobvious. There is no dispute on this appeal with respect to these findings. Because the oncomouse is not "art" or a "process" or a "machine", the controversy is only whether it may be considered to be a "manufacture" or "composition of matter".

'I conclude that the oncomouse is both unobvious and a new and useful "composition of matter". Therefore it is an "invention" within the meaning of that term in section 2 of the *Patent Act*. As I conclude that the oncomouse is a "composition of matter", it is not necessary for me to consider whether it is also a "manufacture".

'In *Chakrabarty, supra,* in dealing with the term "composition of matter" Chief Justice Burger, speaking for the five member majority, stated at page 197:

> ... "composition of matter" has been construed consistent with its common usage to include "all compositions of two or more substances and ... all composite articles, whether they be the results of chemical union, or of mechanical mixture, or whether they be gases, fluids, powders, or solids."

'Burger C.J. noted that the terms "manufacture" and "composition of matter", as modified by the comprehensive "any" in the definition of "invention" in the United States patent statute, were expansive, and "Congress plainly contemplated that the patent laws would be given wide scope". At page 316, the Chief Justice observed that Congress employed broad general language because inventions are often unforeseeable.

> This is especially true in the field of patent law. A rule that unanticipated inventions are without protection would conflict with the core concept of the patent law that anticipation undermines patentability ... Mr. Justice Douglas reminded that the inventions most benefiting mankind are those that "push back the frontiers of chemistry, physics, and the like." ... Congress employed broad general

language in drafting §101 precisely because such inventions are often unforeseeable. [Citations omitted.]

'The majority's approach is clear. The language of patent law is broad and general and is to be given wide scope because inventions are, necessarily, unanticipated and unforeseeable.

'I find this reasoning persuasive. I see no reason why it would not be applicable in interpreting the definition of "invention" in section 2 of the *Patent Act*. Parliament has used the same broad and general language as the United States Congress. The Court must respect Parliament's use of such language and not adopt a narrow approach that would conflict with Parliament's obvious intention.

'In this case, the question is whether the oncomouse is a "composition of matter". What is an "oncomouse" for the purposes of the analysis is to be understood by reference to patent claim 1. It includes both the founder oncomouse, which has had the oncogene introduced at its zygote stage, and subsequent generations of offspring oncomice which will have inherited the oncogene from a parent.

'Using the definition applied in *Chakrabarty*, I am of the view that the oncomouse is a "composition of matter" '.
...

'While what is at issue are living organisms and in particular higher life forms, i.e. non-human mammals, nothing in the term "composition of matter" suggests that living things are excluded from the definition. Indeed, in the Federal Court of Appeal decision in *Pioneer Hi-Bred, supra*, Marceau JA stated at page 12:

> I am prepared to accept that the Canadian patent legislation does not support the assumption that life forms are definitely not patentable.

'At the Supreme Court of Canada in *Pioneer Hi-Bred*, Lamer J., at page 1627 noted that Marceau J.A. was of the opinion that Canadian patent legislation did not expressly exclude living organisms from patentability and did not take exception with this view. In fact, at page 1643, Lamer J. observed that the *Patent Act* contains no provision relating to new forms of life and therefore a new soybean variety in that case would only be patentable if it met the traditional conditions and requirements for a patent. It is apparent that Lamer J. was not excluding life forms from patentability. In *Abitibi, supra*, the Patent Commissioner found that microbial cultures and other lower life forms could constitute inventions for purposes of the

Patent Act. Abitibi was cited before the Supreme Court of Canada in *Pioneer Hi-Bred* and there was no disapproval expressed of that finding. For these reasons, I am satisfied that the *Patent Act* does not exclude living organisms, i.e. non-human mammals, from the definition of "invention".

'That is not to say that the term "composition of matter" has no limits. In both Canada and the United States, natural phenomena, scientific principles and abstract theorems are not patentable. In Canada, subsection 27(8) [as am. by SC 1993, c 15, s 31] of the *Patent Act* excludes scientific principles and abstract theorems from patentability.

> 27(8) No patent shall be granted for any mere scientific principle or abstract theorem.'

Harvard College v Canada (Commissioner of Patents) (2000) 189 DLR (4th) 385 at 399–402, FCA, per Rothstein JA

COMPRISING

Australia [The case concerned patent claims that describe certain 'sensors' and associated equipment as 'comprising' various things.] '… In the context, it is difficult to construe "comprising" as meaning anything other than "consisting of": see *General Clutch Corporation v Sbriggs Pty Ltd* (1997) 38 IPR 359 at 372–6.' *Abbott Laboratories v Corbridge Group Pty Ltd* (2002) AIPC ¶91–824; BC200206154; [2002] FCAFC 314 at [31], per Lee, Emmett and Hely JJ

COMPULSORY ACQUISITION

[For 8 Halsbury's Laws (4th edn) para 1 see now 8(1) Halsbury's Laws (4th edn) (2003 Reissue) para 1.]

COMPULSORY PAYMENT

[For 9 Halsbury's Laws (4th edn) para 642 see now 9(1) Halsbury's Laws (4th edn) (Reissue) para 1104.]

COMPUTER PROGRAM

Australia 'In computer science, the distinction between programs and data in that sense is fundamental. Thus, *Webster's New World Dictionary of Computer Terms* contains the following definitions:

> "Program: a list of instructions written in a programming language, that a computer can

execute so that the machine acts in a predetermined way. Synonymous with software."
"Data: factual information (such as text, numbers, sounds and images) in a form that can be processed by a computer ... "

'Programs cause a computer to perform arithmetic and logical operations or comparisons and to take some additional action based on the comparison or to input or output data in a desired sequence.

'Programs are sometimes called software to distinguish them from hardware, the physical equipment used in the operation of a computer. A distinction can also be drawn between systems programs and processing programs. Systems programs are those that control the operation of the computer. Together, they constitute the operating system for the computer. Processing programs are those whose execution is controlled by the operating system.

'There is a considerable variety of processing programs such as:

- language translators that decode source programs;
- service or utility programs, such as those that "dump" computer memory to external storage for safekeeping;
- application programs, which perform business and scientific functions, such as wordprocessing.

...

' "Computer program" is defined in the [Copyright Act 1968 (CTH) s 10(1)] as "a set of statements or instructions to be used directly or indirectly in a computer in order to bring about a certain result." That requires that a particular result be identified. It is then necessary to identify a set of statements or a set of instructions that are to be used in a computer in order to bring about that result.

...

'... in the current definition, it is necessary to identify precisely the "certain result that the set of statements or instructions" is to be used to bring about.

...

'... The phrase "set of statements or instructions" will still encompass data, so long as those data possess the necessary relationship to the commands in "bringing about a certain result". That is to say, it will suffice if the data and commands are to be used in order to bring about an identified result.'
Australian Video Retailers Assn Ltd v Warner Home Video Pty Ltd (2001) 53 IPR 242; BC200107653; [2001] FCA 1719 at [41]–[44], [70], [79], [82], per Emmett J

CONCERNED WITH THE ADMINISTRATION OF THE SCHEME

[The Pensions Ombudsman had jurisdiction to investigate and determine a complaint of maladministration against an insurance company, an investment management company and the latter's parent company in relation to a pension scheme only if one or other of the companies constituted 'an administrator of the scheme' within the meaning of reg 2(1) of the Personal and Occupational Pension Schemes (Pensions Ombudsman) Regulations 1996. That in turn depended on whether any of the companies was a person 'concerned with the administration of the scheme' within the meaning of reg 1(2) of the 1996 regulations.] '[21] The Pensions Ombudsman appears to have taken the view that a person who undertakes "an act of administration concerned with the Scheme" is a person "concerned with the administration of the scheme". But that view ignores the important distinction between doing an administrative act in connection with a pension scheme and being concerned with its administration. The point was made by the Court of Appeal in Northern Ireland, in *Ewing v Trustees of the Stockham Valve Ltd Staff Retirement Benefits Scheme* [2000] OPLR 257. The question in that case was whether a solicitor to the trustees of a pension scheme, who had written a letter to a beneficiary demanding repayment of benefits said to have been overpaid, was a person concerned with the administration of the scheme. In its judgment, the court said (at 262):

> "The work done by a solicitor may vary considerably from case to case. He may be engaged to perform tasks which are connected with the running of the affairs of his principal. It is, as counsel rightly submitted, a matter of fact and degree, depending on the terms of the solicitor's retainer. Where he is simply instructed to write a letter of claim to a debtor, he is acting as the agent of the principal in carrying out his instructions. We do not consider that it can be said that in these circumstances he is concerned with the administration of the affairs of the principal. Arthur Cox [the solicitors] were in that position. They were merely instructed to seek recovery of certain sums of money from the respondent, and wrote a letter of claim accordingly. In our

view, this cannot be said to have been 'concerned with the administration of the scheme', and the Ombudsman was in error in so holding."

'[22] We have set out the provisions of the Scheme and the policy in some detail in order to show that the administration of the assets of the pensions managed fund and the notional allocation or cancellation of units cannot properly be regarded as "the administration of the scheme". We accept, of course, that those activities, whether carried out by BULA or by BIM, are administrative in nature; and that they are administrative activities which may be described as being carried out in connection with this Scheme. But the relevant question is not whether a person carries out administrative activities in connection with a scheme; the relevant question is whether the person is "concerned with the administration of the scheme". An insurance company which does no more than administer its own assets and calculate, from time to time, the amount which it is liable to pay under a unit-linked policy which it has issued is in much the same position as the trustees' bankers or any other depository. It is no more concerned with the administration of the scheme than others who have contracted to make payments to the trustees or the scheme beneficiaries on request or demand. As we have said, it is significant that the Ombudsman's powers to investigate and determine under Pt X of the [Pension Schemes Act 1993] have not been extended to those concerned only with the financing of, or the provision of benefits under, a scheme.

'[23] It is relevant, in this context, to note that the insurance company was willing to provide administration services in relation to the Scheme, at an additional fee ... We accept that an insurance company which does provide full or partial administrative services may well be a person "concerned with the administration of the scheme"; if not a "manager" of the scheme within s 146(3) of the 1993 Act (see the decision of Dyson J in *Century Life plc v Pensions Ombudsman* [1995] OPLR 351). But that, on the evidence, was not this case.

...

'[25] In our view, the judge was correct to hold that none of the Britannic companies were concerned with the administration of the Scheme; and that, accordingly, the Pensions Ombudsman had no jurisdiction to investigate the complaint in this case.' *R (on the application of Britannic Asset Management Ltd) v Pensions Ombudsman* [2002] EWCA Civ 1405 at [21]–[23], [25], [2002] 4 All ER 860, per Chadwick LJ

CONDITION (STIPULATION)

In lease

[For 27 Halsbury's Laws (4th edn) para 320 see now 27(1) Halsbury's Laws (4th edn) (Reissue) para 108.]

Conditions precedent and subsequent

[For 50 Halsbury's Laws (4th edn) para 317 see now 50 Halsbury's Laws (4th edn) (Reissue) para 368.]

CONDITIONAL TAKE-OVER OFFER

New Zealand [Companies Amendment Act 1963, s 8.] 'The key point of interpretation is whether, when the draftsman of the Act used the expressions "offer" and "take-over offer", the intention was to include conditional contracts; or whether the word "offer" was used in the more precise jurisprudential sense of an offer existing only up to the point of acceptance.

...

'Those terms are used in an extended sense encompassing not only offers in the strict sense but conditional contracts resulting from their acceptance.' *Southfert Co-operative Ltd v Ravensdown Corporation Ltd* [1996] 3 NZLR 196 at 200, 203–204, per Tipping J

CONDUCT (NOUN)

[The Extradition Act 2003, s 65 relates to the conduct of a person where he is alleged to be unlawfully at large after conviction by a court in a category 1 territory of an offence constituted by the conduct, and he has been sentenced for the offence. Section 65(1) provides that:
'(1) This section applies in relation to conduct of a person if—(a) he is alleged to be unlawfully at large after conviction by a court in a category 1 territory of an offence constituted by the conduct, and (b) he has been sentenced for the offence.'

Subsections (2)–(5) provide that 'the conduct' also constitutes an extradition offence in other specified circumstances.] '[28] Turning to s 65(3), we accept that the ordinary meaning of "the conduct" is "all the conduct". But if that is what "the conduct" means, it is impossible to see why Parliament inserted the words "and no part of it occurs in the United Kingdom" in sub-s (2): if all the conduct occurs in the category 1 territory, it is unnecessary to stipulate that none of it occurs in the United Kingdom. The same formulation is found in sub-s (6).

'[29] We think it necessary if possible to arrive at an interpretation of s 65 that does not preclude the extradition of a person who commits a crime in a category 1 territory simply because some of his criminal conduct also occurred in the United Kingdom or in another category 1 territory. If "the conduct of a person" means "all the criminal conduct", then extradition under Pt 1 of the 2003 Act for offences committed partly in one country and partly in another is very difficult and the position illogical. We referred above to a hypothetical drug dealer. Framework offences may be committed in part in more than one category 1 territory, as where some arrangements are made by a person in Belgium and in Germany pursuant to a criminal conspiracy to import drugs into Belgium, and his extradition is sought from the United Kingdom to Belgium. If "the conduct" in sub-s (2) means "all the conduct constituting the offence", it is inapplicable; sub-s (3) is inapplicable, because some of the conduct occurred in Germany; sub-s (4) is not satisfied, because some of the conduct occurred in Belgium; and sub-s (6) is not satisfied, for the same reason.

'[30] However, if "the conduct" in s 65(2)–(6) means "such of the conduct as constitutes a criminal offence (under the law of the category 1 territory)", this highly undesirable conclusion is avoided and a more practical interpretation arrived at. The drug dealer active in Germany and in Belgium carried out acts in Belgium that constituted the offences of drug trafficking (a framework offence) and the illegal importation of drugs into that country. It is irrelevant that as part of the conspiracy he also did acts in Germany (or the United Kingdom). Section 65(2) is satisfied. So is sub-s (3). In this case it is unnecessary to consider sub-s (4)–(5), but the same interpretation applies there and in sub-s (6). The terms of art 4(7) of the Framework Decision, which is permissive in terms, do not require a different conclusion.

'[31] Regrettably, ss 64 and 65 of the 2003 Act have not been drafted with the need to deal with trans-frontier offences taken expressly or clearly into account. We have reached our conclusion because of the need to arrive at a workable interpretation that addresses the nature of framework offences and indeed much crime in the modern world.' *Office of the King's Prosecutor, Brussels v Cando Armas* [2004] EWHC 2019 (Admin), [2005] 2 All ER 181 at [28]–[31], per Stanley Burnton J

The decision was affimed by the House of Lords:

'[16] I would accept the submission of Mr James Lewis QC for the prosecutor that "the conduct" in s 65 means the conduct complained of or relied on in the warrant. Such a reading is consistent with the language and purpose of the Framework Decision, obviates the need for an undesirable inquiry into the niceties of a foreign law and is consistent, so far as that is relevant, with the earlier decision of the House in *Government of Denmark v Nielsen* [1984] 2 All ER 81 at 84, [1984] AC 606 at 614–615. I would accordingly agree with the Deputy Senior District Judge and differ from the Divisional Court in holding that, since some of the conduct complained of or relied on in the warrant occurred in the United Kingdom, the condition in sub-s (2)(a) is not satisfied and sub-s (2) is accordingly inapplicable.

'[17] I cannot, however, accept that sub-s (3) is to be read as requiring that all the conduct complained of should have occurred in the category 1 territory. The subsection does not so provide, and the qualification that no part of the conduct should have occurred in the United Kingdom, expressly stipulated in sub-ss (2)(a), (5)(a) and (6)(a), is not found in (3)(a). It must be inferred that that qualification was not intended. It is enough, under sub-s (3)(a), if some of the conduct complained of or relied on occurred in the category 1 territory. More fundamentally, I cannot accept that, because sub-s (2)(a) is specifically directed to framework list offences, sub-ss (3)–(6) should be understood to exclude such offences. It is only if a case falls within sub-s (2) that the double criminality requirement is dispensed with, as sub-ss (3)(b), (4)(c), (5)(b) and (6)(c) make clear. This reflects the thrust of the Framework Decision. But there is nothing in the section to suggest that sub-ss (3), (4), (5) and (6) cannot apply to framework list offences where the relevant requirement of double criminality is met. No reason of logic or justice was suggested to support such a rule, and it is plain from hypothetical examples suggested in argument that it would lead to results which neither the European Council nor Parliament could ever have intended. I am accordingly of opinion that there is nothing in the language of sub-s (3) which would preclude its application to this case. I would accordingly, for these reasons and those given by my noble and learned friend Lord Hope of Craighead, dismiss the appeal and uphold, for slightly different reasons, the Divisional Court's order that the matter be remitted to the Deputy Senior District Judge to continue the hearing.'

Office of the King's Prosecutor, Brussels v Cando Armas [2005] UKHL 67 at [16]–[17], [2006] 1 All ER 647, per Lord Bingham of Cornhill

'[40] I would construe the word "conduct" in ss 65(2)(a) and 65(3)(a) of the 2003 Act in the light of these authorities. The conduct must occur "in" the category 1 territory if the condition which is set out in these paragraphs to be satisfied. But a purposive meaning must be given to the word "conduct" in this context. It would impose a wholly artificial restriction on the extradition process if it were to be taken as meaning that all the conduct which resulted in the offence must have taken place exclusively within the category 1 territory. Actings elsewhere will be sufficient to constitute conduct in that territory so long as their intended effect was to bring about harm within that territory. It would be immaterial to a request for extradition to Belgium, for example, that the actings which had a harmful effect were all in France or in Germany. The situation would be different, of course, if some part of those actings occurred in the United Kingdom. But that is because of the qualification that s 65(2)(a) has introduced, which prevents cases where some of the conduct occurs in the United Kingdom from being treated as an extradition offence under that subsection. The fact that it was thought necessary to insert this qualification is consistent with the existence of a general rule of the kind that I have described.' *Office of the King's Prosecutor, Brussels v Cando Armas* [2005] UKHL 67 at [40], [2006] 1 All ER 647, per Lord Hope of Craighead

Australia [Section 52 of the Trade Practices Act 1974 (Cth) refers to, inter alia, misleading or deceptive 'conduct'.] '… the making of a statement as to a presently existing state of affairs, if false, may be the engaging in misleading or deceptive conduct, where the statement is embodied as a provision of a contract'. *Accounting Systems 2000 (Developments) Pty Ltd v CCH Australia Ltd* (1993) 42 FCR 470 at 505; 114 ALR 355 at 389, per Lockhart and Gummow JJ

Australia 'In its setting in [the Administrative Decisions (Judicial Review) Act 1979] s 6 the word "conduct" points to action taken, rather than a decision made, for the purpose of making a reviewable decision. In other words, the concept of conduct looks to the way in which the proceedings have been conducted, the conduct of the proceedings, rather than decisions made along the way with a view to the making of a final determination. Thus, conduct is essentially procedural and not substantive in character …

Accordingly, there is a clear distinction between a "decision" and "conduct" engaged in for the purpose of making a decision. A challenge to conduct is an attack upon the proceedings engaged in before the making of the decision. It is not a challenge to decisions made as part of the decision-making process except in the sense that if the decisions are procedural in character they will precede the conduct which is under challenge.' *Minister for Immigration and Multicultural Affairs v Ozmanian* (1996) 141 ALR 32 at 338, per Sackville J

CONDUCT OF DECEASED

Australia [The case concerned whether the conduct of the deceased amounted to provocation under the Crimes Act 1900 (NSW) s 23, thereby founding a case for manslaughter against the accused.] 'In *R v Arden* (1975) VR 449 Menhennitt J, after referring to a number of cases extending back to 1837, said:

> "In light of all those authorities I have concluded that for there to be sufficient to constitute provocation, conduct of some kind, whether it be physical conduct or words, on the part of the person killed must take place in the presence of the accused person. The rationale of this rule appears to me to be as follows. If a person actually sees conduct taking place in respect of a third person and he is provoked thereby, it is understandable that he may be provoked to the extent of taking the other person's life and in circumstances which would reduce murder to manslaughter. Where, however, all that happened is that the accused is told something by a third person there enters immediately the element of belief, and there is nothing tangible upon which the accused can be said to have acted."

'The need for a provocative incident and the requirement that conduct of the deceased occur in the sight and hearing of the Accused hardly leave room for mistake. And if information actually received is not sufficient to amount to conduct constituting provocation, then a fortiori a mistaken belief cannot.

'Nevertheless, it may be accepted that there is a general principle that an honest and reasonable belief in a state of affairs which, if it had existed, would make an Accused's act innocent constitutes a defence to a criminal charge and one which, if there is evidence raising the issue, the Crown must negative pursuant to its obligation to prove a charge beyond reasonable doubt: *Jiminez v R* (1992) 173 CLR 572 at 582 and the cases cited. The requirement that any mistaken belief be held on reasonable grounds applies in the area of self defence: *Zecevic v DPP* (1987) 162 CLR 645 at 661–2.

'However, as the decision of *R v Ianazzone* (1983) 1 VR 649 at 655 and the cases referred to in it make clear, "the honest and reasonable belief doctrine requires belief in a state of facts which, if they existed, would made the defendant's act innocent" and a "belief does not excuse if its truth would have meant, not that no offence was being committed, but that some other and different offence was being committed". Here any mistake as to the deceased's conduct could only assist an accused in obtaining a conviction for manslaughter rather than murder ...

...

'I have no difficulty in accepting the proposition that within s 23 "conduct of the deceased" may include, certainly in circumstances where he is present, conduct for which, in accordance with normal principles of agency, joint enterprise or common purpose, the deceased is responsible. The impact on the person provoked may be just as great and there is nothing in the terms of s 23 to exclude the normal rule that what a person my do personally, he may do by an agent. Actions so done may properly be regarded as "conduct of the deceased"...

...

'In none of the cases in which it has been held that a mistaken belief on the part of an Accused as to the content of the provocative conduct or as to the author of it was relevant has there been any significant consideration as to why, if mistake is to be a relevant factor, it should not be attended with the same limitations as generally in the criminal law. In circumstances where death occurs as a result of provocation, by definition, the provocation occurs before an Accused's loss of control. The Accused is presumably just as able as others to see whence the provocation has come and what it was and while the doctrine of provocation may excuse in some degree his reaction, there is not obviously any reason why he or she should be in any more favoured position than others who have the benefit of the doctrine of reasonable and honest mistake. And insofar as it may be said that the element of lack of self-control is not present in other situations, one might point out that in circumstances of self defence, *Zecevic v R* makes it clear that the requirement of reasonableness is still insisted upon.

...

'... In summary, I doubt whether, as a matter of construction of s 23 mistakes by an Accused can be regarded as "conduct of the deceased". Even if that view be wrong, the principle for which I have cited *R v Ianazzone*, viz that "the honest and reasonable belief doctrine requires belief in a state of facts which, if they existed, would made the defendant's act innocent" and a "belief does not excuse if its truth would have meant, not that no offence was being committed, but that some other and different offence was being committed" precludes regard being had to them. And if that also be wrong, the general principle that mistakes must be both honest and reasonable would limit those to which regard could be had.' *R v Dib* BC200205992; [2002] NSWSC 934 at [39]–[42], [68], [74], [76] per Hulme J

CONDUCTING THE BUSINESS OF A CATERER

New Zealand [Sale of Liquor Act 1989, s 51(1).] *'The New Shorter Oxford English Dictionary* (Clarendon Press, Oxford, 1993) p 353 defines a "caterer" as:

> "a person who caters or provides provisions for a household, club etc, *esp* a person whose trade is to supply, cook, serve etc, food at a social function ... ".

'The Concise Oxford Dictionary (7th ed, 1982) p 145 defines "cater" as to:

> "*vi* purvey food; provide meals *for*; provide amusement, requisites etc; ... hence [caterer] *n*, (esp) one whose trade is to supply food for social events, [catering] *n*, such trade."

'On the evidence, the appellant rarely, if ever, supplies, cooks or serves food itself. Rather, it subcontracts out this part of its "catering" service and the focus of its business is on the sale of liquor. The fact that the appellant might satisfy itself that some third party will supply food for a particular event, or supplies information sheets about the possible provision of food from third party sources is not sufficient to bring its primary business activity as a liquor broker within the definition of the term "caterer".

'The plain meaning of the term "caterer" relates to the supply of food at *receptions, functions or other social gatherings*. The provision of food on such occasions is the primary function of catering for those functions. Section 15(3) does not make the provision of food a discretionary requirement. Rather, it is envisaged by the Act that the provision of liquor on those occasions is in addition to, or complementary to, the provision of food.

...

'I have no hesitation in finding that the essence of catering is the provision of food, and that the clear legislative intent in s 51 of the Sale of Liquor Act 1989 is to provide for the special situation of the caterer who may be required to supply liquor as part of its catering service. It is implicit in s 51 that the endorsed (caterer's) off-licence only authorises the sale of liquor by a caterer while engaging in the provision of food for "receptions, functions, or other social gatherings".' *Bar Systems (New Zealand) Ltd v Wellington District Licensing Agency* [1996] 3 NZLR 100 at 107, per Goddard J

CONFLICT OF LAWS

[For 8 Halsbury's Laws (4th edn) para 401 see now 8(3) Halsbury's Laws (4th edn) (Reissue) para 1.]

CONFRONTED

Australia 'In any event, as a matter of ordinary usage to be "confronted" with something means to be brought face to face with it either physically or, perhaps more commonly, in the mind. If the thing being confronted is an event, usage does not require that the person be present at the event she or he "confronts". This is no less the case when the confronting event is one involving death or serious injury.

'In the present context the point becomes clearer when reference is made to the second paragraph of the definition. This illuminates the definition by giving examples of events that those who drafted it had in mind as falling within it. The second paragraph states that events that qualify as stressors in the setting of service in the Defence Forces include "participation in or observation of casualty clearance". A member of the armed forces taking part in casualty clearance may well have been outside the area of immediate conflict and have neither experienced nor witnessed the events that caused the casualties, yet it is easy to see how such a person could be "confronted with" such events.

'An example taken from earlier conflicts may illustrate the range of situations which, as a matter of ordinary usage and context, the definition can be seen to cover. A sailor in a warship escorting a convoy may come face to face with events involving death in any one (or more) of three ways. He may experience an attack upon his ship, he may witness the loss of another vessel and by attending to casualties in the sickbay he may be confronted with events he has not seen or experienced. There

may of course be an overlap of these stressor events, but that possibility does not deny their separate character.

'The language of the definition provides no warrant to confine the confrontation with an event involving death, of which the definition speaks, to an event involving the death of a family member or other close associate. Indeed, the illumination provided by the second paragraph of the definition would suggest the very opposite, since it is hardly to be supposed that the general reference to casualties and casualty clearance was intended to be qualified in a way which, in the context, would be quite exceptional.' *Woodward v Repatriation Commission* [2003] FCAFC 160 at [123]–[126] per Black CJ, Weinberg and Selway JJ; BC200304136

CONFUSION

[For 35 Halsbury's Laws (4th edn) para 1139 see now 35 Halsbury's Laws (4th edn) (Reissue) para 1239.]

CONNECTED WITH

Australia [Section 78A of the Excise Act 1901 (Cth) and section 164 of the Customs Act 1901 (Cth) refer to rearing of livestock and other operations 'connected with' the rearing of livestock.] 'The words "connected with" are capable of describing a spectrum of relationships ranging from the direct and immediate to the tenuous and remote ... Although the words of the statute are construed according to their ordinary English meaning, that does not mean that their application to a set of facts is simply described as the matching of that set of facts with a factual description. There is necessarily a selection process involved. The range of relationships to which the words apply for the purpose of the Act depends upon a judgment about that purpose.' *Collector of Customs v Pozzolanic Enterprises Pty Ltd* (1993) 115 ALR 1 at 10–11, per cur

CONNOTATION

Australia [Trade Marks Act 1995 (Cth) s 43 provides: An application for the registration of a trade mark in respect of particular goods or services must be rejected if, because of some connotation that the trade mark or a sign contained in the trade mark has, the use of the trade mark in relation to those goods or services would be likely to deceive or cause confusion.] '[25] ... In an opposition to registration, s 43 of the Act requires an opponent to show that: (1) there is a connotation in the proposed trade mark or in a part of it; and (2) because of this connotation, the use of the proposed mark would be likely to deceive or cause confusion. The connotation must be contained within the mark itself: see *TGI Friday's* at 365 per Wilcox, Kiefel and Emmett JJ.

'[26] The word "connotation" is defined in The Oxford English Dictionary (Oxford, 2nd ed, 1989) as meaning:

1.   The signifying in addition; inclusion of something in the meaning of the word besides what it primary denotes; implication.

     ...

     b.   That which is implied in a word in addition to its essential or primary meaning.

'In order for s 43 to apply, the Court must be satisfied that there is a reasonable likelihood of deception or confusion arising because of the connotation within the mark, having regard to the nature of the goods or services to which it is to apply and other relevant considerations: see, eg, the discussion in *Down to Earth* (*Victoria*) *Co-operative Society Ltd v Schmidt* (1998) 41 IPR 632 at 644–5.

...

'[51] Although the word "connotation" was not used in trade marks legislation prior to its appearance in s 43 of the Act, there under the pre-1995 trade marks legislation where registration has been refused on the basis that a mark are in fact numerous instances contained some suggestion of endorsement or approval by a well-known person or entity, or that goods or services to which it was to be applied had been awarded some particular prize or commendation. Such instances include In *re Ferguson and Company's Trade Mark* (1903) 29 VLR 331 ("P&O" in relation to whisky). In this case, Holroyd J observed at 334:

It appears to us that the trade mark is one well calculated to deceive. There is evidence that the Peninsula and Oriental Steamship Company is well known and commonly spoken of by the name "P&O Company", or the "P&O"; and if this trade mark were allowed to be registered there would be upon the register a mark calculated to induce people to believe that the whisky in respect of which it was registered was whisky which was ordered or

used by the P&O Company or purchased and kept by them as part of their stock on ship board.

...

'[53] Plainly enough, however, whether a mark or part of it connotes the sponsorship or approval of a person, entity or institution will depend on all the surrounding circumstances. In each case, it will be a question of fact and degree. In some cases, the implication has been insufficiently direct, as, for example, in *Joseph Bancroft & Sons Co v Registrar of Trade Marks* (1957) 99 CLR 453 ("Joseph Bancroft"). In that case, the High Court reversed the decision of the Registrar of Trade Marks, refusing to register the words "Miss America" as a trade mark in respect of textile products. The Court, which consisted of Williams, Kitto and Taylor JJ, observed at 458–459:

No doubt the words "Miss America", just like the words "Miss Australia", and the corresponding titles in other countries, when used in connexion with female apparel would be capable of suggesting in a vague and indefinable way to likely female purchasers that the goods were suitable in quality to be fashioned for such glamorous beauties, that such vague and indefinable suggestions, emotive as they might be, could hardly be said to refer directly to the character or quality of the goods ... They simply refer to an annual title conferred upon the winner for the year of a beauty competition under this designation and are in essence indistinguishable from the titles conferred upon winners of musical, artistic, sporting and other competitions ... Any reference that the words "Miss America" have to the character or quality of the goods in respect of which registration is sought or indeed to the character or quality of any goods is remote and indirect. Registration could not possibly trespass upon the rights of other traders to use ordinary English words or phrases to inform possible purchasers that the fabrics that they were offering for sale were similar to fabrics that had been worn by "Miss America" or which had in some way received her approval or patronage. Nor would registration of the words as a trade mark be likely to deceive the purchasing public into the belief that "Miss America" had ordered some of the fabrics or had otherwise approved of them. They would at most create the impression that the fabrics were suitable to be worn by a person who desired to be dressed in the same style as such a publicised, attractive, glamorous and popular lady.'

McCorquodale v Masterson [2004] FCA 1247 at [25]–[26], [51], [53], per Kenny J; BC200406282

CONSCIOUS *SEE ALSO* CONSCIOUS, VOLUNTARY AND DELIBERATE ACT

CONSCIOUS, VOLUNTARY AND DELIBERATE ACT

Australia [In the context of the description used by a trial judge in charging juries in murder cases.] '[24] The trial judge gave the jury a two-page note listing the elements of the offence of murder and made use of that document when charging the jury. Item 1(b) of the elements as set out on that document required that there be "a conscious voluntary and deliberate act or acts". His Honour said:

> The second thing that the prosecution has to prove for conviction of murder is that the accused killed the deceased by a conscious voluntary and deliberate act or acts. I will not trouble you further about conscious and voluntary, ladies and gentlemen. That sometimes arises where you have got a person with a mental condition or something like that. I will not trouble you about any of that. I have underlined the word "deliberate" because that is an issue in this case.

'[25] In the above passage a distinction is drawn between, on the one hand, "conscious and voluntary" acts and, on the other hand, "deliberate" acts. By implication, what was in law a "voluntary" act was not the same as a "deliberate" act.

'[26] The word "deliberate" was underlined on the document. His Honour told the jury that that was an issue in the case and he explained the word as follows:

> What does deliberate mean? It means that the fatal stabbing was something which was not intended or foreseen by the accused and could not reasonably have been foreseen by an ordinary person. That is what deliberate means in paragraph 1(b). That the fatal stabbing was not in fact intended or foreseen by the accused and would not reasonably have been foreseen by an ordinary person. So that is what the prosecution has to prove was deliberate.

...

'[28] His Honour's direction continued. His Honour said to the jury:

> Just pause there because there are two steps in this. The first is this. I am proceeding upon the basis that you find that the accused deliberately had the knife out the front. I will say no more about that but it is not enough for murder that he deliberately had the knife out the front. For murder the prosecution has to prove that he deliberately stabbed him in the fatal way and that it was deliberate and it was not an accident. That is to say something which was not in fact intended or foreseen by the accused and would not reasonably have been foreseen by an ordinary person. That is what an accident is and the prosecution has to prove it was not an accident, it was deliberate. That is to say the stabbing was deliberate.

'[29] The standard charge book direction for murder states that this element requires that the act causing death must be "conscious and voluntary", although it expands upon that by stating that "Crime consists of the doing of a deliberate act or acts". The addition of the word "deliberate" to the expression "conscious and voluntary", when describing this element, is sometimes, but not usually, employed by trial judges. At common law it would be by reference to the requirement that the fatal act be "voluntary" that a defence of accident would fall for consideration, when the intended meaning of "accident" was that the fatal act had been an unwilled occurrence. Used in that sense the word "deliberate" could serve a purpose in helping a jury in its assessment and understanding as to whether the fatal act was voluntary, that is unwilled. However, whilst the word "deliberate" might perhaps be usefully employed to emphasise the requirement of intention to perform the very actus reus which caused the death, it might also be applied in addressing a lack of intention to cause the particular result which followed from the act which caused death.

...

'[31] Crockett J in *R v Haywood* [1971] VR 755 at 757–8 and 760 used the expression "a conscious, voluntary and deliberate act" when considering this element of murder, but used it in the context of discussing the mens rea of the accused person at the time when the act causing death happened. In a detailed analysis of the varying uses of the term "voluntary", his Honour acknowledged that the notion of an involuntary act may relate to the actus reus rather than to mens rea. If used in the former sense then, so he held, if the Crown has not established that the act was willed there must be an acquittal; there would be no basis for an unlawful and dangerous act manslaughter verdict.' *R v Peter Schaeffer* [2005] VSCA 306 at [24]–[26], [28]–[29], [31], per Eames JA; BC200510856

CONSEQUENCES

Canada '[27] A direct causation requirement conjures up memories of the famous English tort case of *Re Polemis*, [1921] 3 K.B. 560, where recovery was allowed for damages that were not a foreseeable result of the defendant's negligence but were directly caused by it. When one thinks of direct causation one thinks of something knocking over the first in a row of blocks after which the rest falls down without the assistance of any other act.

'[28] In his text *Handbook of the Law of Torts*, 4th ed. (St. Paul: West Publishing Co., 1971) at pp. 263–64, Dean Prosser defined "consequences" directly caused as "those which follow in sequence from the effect of the defendant's act upon conditions existing and forces already in operation at the time, without the intervention of any external forces which come into active operation later". Here an external force, the gunshots, came "into active operation later". Thus, in Prosser's terms, Chisholm's impairment was not a consequence directly caused by the use or operation of his car.' *Chisholm v Liberty Mutual Group* (2002) 217 DLR (4th) 145 at 154 (Ont CA), per Laskin JA

CONSIDER

Australia 'In my opinion, these various definitions point to a substantial personal involvement on the part of the individual who is required "to consider" the written material. It does not mean that he must read every word of every document. A busy minister of the Crown is entitled to receive assistance from his staff: *Minister for Aboriginal Affairs v Peko-Wallsend Ltd* (1986) 162 CLR 24 at 30 per Gibbs CJ, at 65 per Brennan J. But that entitlement does not, of course, permit him to delegate his decision-making power: see s 31 of the Aboriginal and Torres Strait Islander Heritage Protection Act 1984 (Cth). Nor does it allow him to abrogate his responsibilities. The concept of his considering the representations must involve a balanced mixture of staff assistance and personal involvement.' *Chapman v Minister for Aboriginal and Torres Strait Islander Affairs; Barton v Minister for Aboriginal and Torres Strait Islander Affairs* (1995) 133 ALR 74 at 123–124, per O'Loughlin J

CONSIDERATION

'In my opinion "consideration" cannot be equated with the cash-price element of the offers made ... The cash price is a component, and plainly a very significant component, of the consideration offered. But the expression "consideration" ... is in my view plainly broad enough to include other financial return to the seller under the contract for the disposal of the site. It follows, in my opinion, that the "overage" provisions in the offers (ie the provisions for the payment of a share of development profit by the developer to the seller) are also part of the consideration. Unlike the cash price, however, the overage provision is not a fixed figure but depends on the formula adopted and the profitability of the development as it turns out.' *Stannifer Developments Ltd v Glasgow Development Agency and Scottish Enterprise* 1998 SCLR 870 at 895, per Lord Macfadyen

Australia 'The words "valuable consideration" would seem intended to embrace receipts not in money form, but capable of being valued in money terms. Implicit in them is the notion of a *quid pro quo* or a material "reward, remuneration; a compensation": the Shorter Oxford English Dictionary, 3rd edn (1977). As identified in the judgment of Fisher J in the Federal Court, "valuable consideration" includes "board and lodgings, goods, meals, rent free accommodation or provision of gratuitous services".' *Read v Commonwealth of Australia* (1988) 78 ALR 655 at 659, per Mason CJ, Deane and Gaudron JJ

New Zealand [Goods and Services Tax Act 1985, s 2.] 'The proviso is directed to an "amount agreed to be paid by the authority" in respect of the supply of goods and services and where "the consideration for that supply" is in the nature of a grant or subsidy. It is the character or quality of what is to be paid and of the consideration which is given which is crucial, not its receipt in the hands of the payee. And the extending words "in the nature of" make it clear that even if technically not a grant or subsidy, the consideration will come within the proviso if it is within the nature of a grant or subsidy (cf *Doak v Bedford* [1964] 2 QB 587, 594).

...

'The full charge of each service recipient is met in part by the resident and as to the balance by the department under the rest-home subsidy scheme. Payments to the contractors pursuant to agreements entered into under the scheme in respect of the supply of services to residents are within the meaning of "consideration" in s 2 and come squarely within s 5(6D).' *Director-General of Social Welfare v De Morgan* [1996] 3 NZLR 677 at 683–684, CA, per cur

CONSOLIDATED FUND

[For 34 Halsbury's Laws (4th edn) para 1442 see now 34 Halsbury's Laws (4th edn) (Reissue) para 952.]

CONSPIRACY

[*Lonrho Ltd v Shell Petroleum Co Ltd* was further explained in *Lonrho plc v Fayed* [1991] 3 All ER 303 at 310–312, HL, per Lord Bridge of Harwich.]
   [For 11 Halsbury's Laws (4th edn) para 58 see now 11(1) Halsbury's Laws (4th edn) (Reissue) paras 59–60.]

To defraud

'The question whether particular facts reveal a conspiracy to defraud depends upon, and in particular whether they have agreed to practise, a fraud on somebody. For this purpose it is enough for example that ... the conspirators have dishonestly agreed to bring about a state of affairs which they realise will or may deceive the victim into so acting, or failing to act, that he will suffer economic loss or his economic interests will be put at risk. It is however important in such a case ... to distinguish a conspirator's intention (or immediate purpose) dishonestly to bring about such a state of affairs from his motive (or underlying purpose). The latter may be benign to the extent that he does not wish the victim to suffer harm; but the mere fact that it is benign will not of itself prevent the agreement from constituting a conspiracy to defraud. Of course, if the conspirators were not acting dishonestly, there will have been no conspiracy to defraud; and in any event their benign purpose (if it be such) is a matter which, if they prove to be guilty, can be taken into account at the stage of sentence.' *Wai Yu-tsang v R* [1991] 4 All ER 664 at 671–672, PC, per the Board (Lord Goff of Chieveley)

CONSTITUTIONAL LAW

[For 8 Halsbury's Laws (4th edn) para 801 see now 8(2) Halsbury's Laws (4th edn) (Reissue) para 1.]

CONSUME

[Section 5(1) of the Road Traffic Act 1988 provides that if a person drives a motor vehicle on a road after 'consuming' so much alcohol that the proportion of it in his breath exceeds the prescribed limit he is guilty of an offence.] 'The respondent argued successfully in the court below that the word "consuming" in its most usual sense in the context of alcohol involves imbibing, and possibly eating an alcohol-soaked confection, such as brandy butter, but does not embrace taking alcohol in the form of sniffing it, having it injected, or in the form of a suppository. Thus the man who has been to a wine tasting and has religiously sniffed but then spat out the contents of numerous glasses would not be caught under s 5 because he has not consumed—if this argument is right—any alcohol, whatever amount of alcohol may be in his breath ...
   'For my part, I think that the word "consume" is capable of a whole variety of meanings depending on the context in which it is used. It is not unusual to speak of a house consumed by fire and it would not be strange to speak of a bottle of medical alcohol having been consumed by rubbing its contents onto skin prior to administering an injection. As I say, one can talk of consuming snuff by sniffing. It very much depends on the context.
   'In the present context it is clear that that section was enacted in the context of a parliamentary endeavour to diminish the number of those who drive whilst there is alcohol inside their bodies. I would accept that it is probable that Parliament did not specifically consider the possible modes of entry of alcohol into the body ...
   'Accepting that injecting alcohol into the body is not a usual mode of consumption of significant quantities of alcohol, and that the same may be said of inhalation perhaps, it remains the case that it is possible, without doing violence to the chameleon-like qualities of this word, to construe it widely enough to embrace ingestion in any form.' *DPP v Johnson* [1995] 4 All ER 53 at 55–56, DC, per Schiemann J

CONSUMER

Australia 'The consumer to whom the section [s 52 of the Trade Practices Act 1974 (Cth)] is directed to protect is ... readily recognisable: he is a consumer to whom goods or services are supplied in trade or commerce by a supplier. The "services" which a consumer may have supplied to him are, of course, as diverse as there are trades and businesses in trade and commerce.' *Wright v TNT Australia Pty Ltd* (1988) 80 ALR 221 at 226–228, per Lee J

Canada 'It is common ground that the *Public Utilities Act* provides authority to the Town to collect hydro rates from landlords such as the appellants, as owners, only if the appellants can be taken to be "consumers", as that term is used in the *Public Utilities Act*. That premise was accepted by this court in *Bracebridge Hydro Electric Commission v 796479 Ontario Ltd* (1991), 2 OR (3d) 761 (Ont Ct (Gen Div)); appeal dismissed February 9, 1995, unreported.

'In *Bracebridge*, the issue was whether Bracebridge's policy that required landlords to guarantee payment of tenants' hydro rates was valid as it applied to the subject rented premises, all of which were separately metered. The motions judge held that the landlord was not a "consumer" within the meaning of what is now s 50(4) of the *Act*. Bracebridge appealed. In its brief endorsement dismissing the appeal, the court said:

In the present circumstances where there is individual metering and the tenants are billed individually, we agree with the motions court judge that the owner cannot be considered a "consumer" so as to be required to guarantee the accounts of individual tenants.

'The Town takes comfort from the reference in *Bracebridge* to individual metering and separate billing. Since the appellants' premises are not separately metered, the Town contends that *Bracebridge* does not directly apply to this case. The Town submits that when the apartments are not separately metered, *Bracebridge* suggests that the owner (landlord) would be a consumer.

'In my opinion, if "consumer" is given its plain ordinary meaning, as I think it should be, a landlord-owner is not a consumer. Consumer as referred to in the *Act* is that person who uses, that is consumes, water supplied by a municipal corporation or a public utilities commission. That interpretation of consumer seems to me to accommodate the ordinary meaning of the word "consumer" and it accords with the statutory provisions set out in the *Act* that deal with the obligation to pay for utilities.' *710357 Ontario Ltd v Penetanguishene (Town)* (1998) 164 DLR (4th) 755 at 760–761, Ont CA, per Osborne JA

CONTACT

Australia [Regulation 9(2)(a)(ii) of the Migration Regulations 1989 (Cth) provides that an applicant is disqualified for certain purposes if the applicant has had 'contact' with an overseas near relative during a reasonable period preceding the application.] 'The meaning of the word "contact" is important. In my opinion, it does not refer to physical contact, such as a meeting, but communication in the sense of a social relationship. The *Macquarie Dictionary*, 2nd ed, gives the primary meaning of the word "contact" as "the state of fact of touching", but it goes on to state a sociological meaning as "a condition in which two or more individuals or groups are placed in communication with one another.' *Bagus v Minister for Immigration, Local Government and Ethnic Affairs* (1994) 50 FCR 396 at 402, per Whitlam J

CONTAINER

[The Food Act 1984 is largely repealed. The definition is re-enacted in the Food Safety Act 1990, s 53(1).]

CONTAMINATE

Australia 'The word "contaminate" is defined in the New Shorter Oxford English Dictionary as (among other things) to "[m]ake impure by ... mixture"; and the word "contamination" is there defined as (again, among other things) "[t]he action of making impure ... [s]omething which contaminates". Here, the introduction of pieces of rubber into the woodchips had the result that the two became mixed, to the extent that they could not conveniently be separated. The woodchips were thereafter unmerchantable. It was in these circumstances open to conclude that they were contaminated. It was, accordingly, likewise open to the arbitrator to reject the plaintiff's submission that, in the context of the policy, property only became contaminated upon a change in the physical quality of that property.' *Gunns Forest Products Pty Ltd v North Insurances Pty Ltd and Ors* [2004] VSC 155 at [15], per Harper J; BC200402813

CONTEMPLATED

New Zealand [Section 2(2) of the Crimes Act 1961 provides that 'Where proceedings under this Act are contemplated or taken in respect of any child or young person, the age of that child or young person, for the purposes of those proceedings, shall be that child's or young person's age at the date of the alleged offence or incident in respect of which those proceedings are contemplated or taken.'] 'The word "contemplated" must therefore refer to something more than a state of mind. It must refer

to the initiation of procedures under the Act.'
Police v Edge [1993] 2 NZLR 7 at 13, CA, per
Hardie Boys J

CONTEMPT OF COURT

[For 9 Halsbury's Laws (4th edn) para 2 see now
9(1) Halsbury's Laws (4th edn) (Reissue) para 402.]
   'Contempt of court is an unfortunate term which
conveys to some the concept that the court and the
judges are concerned for their personal dignity. Of
course they are not. Their concern, and that of the
law, is that the authority, impartiality and
independence of the courts shall be upheld, which
is quite different. Accordingly, the principal types
of contempt are (a) conduct which impedes or
prejudices the course of justice and (b) disobedience
of orders made by the court.' *Pickering v Liverpool
Daily Post and Echo* [1990] 1 All ER 334 at
341, CA, per Lord Donaldson of Lymington MR
   'The term "contempt of court" is of ancient
origin having been used in England certainly since
the thirteenth century and probably earlier. The
term has been criticised as inaccurate and
misleading, suggesting in some contexts that it
exists to protect the dignity of the judges. Over 100
years ago Bowen LJ explained in *Re Johnson*
(1888) 20 QBD 68 at 74: "The law has armed the
High Court of Justice with the power and imposed
on it the duty of preventing ... any attempt to
interfere with the administration of justice. It is on
that ground, and not on any exaggerated notion of
the dignity of individuals that insults to judges are
not allowed. It is on the same ground that insults to
witnesses or to jurymen are not allowed." Nearly
70 years ago a similar comment was made by the
Lord President (Clyde) in *Johnson v Grant* 1923 SC
789 at 790. He said: "The phrase 'contempt of
Court' does not in the least describe the true nature
of the class of offence with which we are here
concerned ... The offence consists in interfering
with the administration of the law; in impeding
and perverting the course of justice ... It is not the
dignity of the Court which is offended—a petty
and misleading view of the issues involved—it is
the fundamental supremacy of the law which is
challenged." Approaching 50 years later in *Morris
v Crown Office* [1970] 1 All ER 1079 at 1087
Salmon LJ observed: "The sole purpose of
proceedings for contempt is to give our courts the
power effectively to protect the rights of the public
by ensuring that the administration of justice shall
not be obstructed or prevented ... " Shortly
thereafter Lord Cross of Chelsea in *A-G v Times
Newspapers Ltd* [1973] 3 All ER 54 at 83

commented: "'Contempt of court' means an
interference with the administration of justice and
it is unfortunate that the offence should be continued
to be known by a name which suggests to the
modern mind that its essence is a supposed affront
to the dignity of the court. Nowadays when
sympathy is readily accorded to any one who
defies constituted authority the very name of the
offence predisposes many people in favour of the
alleged offender. Yet the due administration of
justice is something which all citizens, whether on
the left or the right or in the centre, should be
anxious to safeguard." In the same year the Report
of the Committee on Contempt of Court
(Cmnd 5794) (the Phillimore Committee) presented
to Parliament in December 1974 stated in its very
first paragraph: "The law relating to contempt of
court has developed over the centuries as a means
whereby the courts may act to prevent or punish
conduct which tends to obstruct, prejudice or abuse
the administration of justice either in relation to a
particular case or generally." More recently
Lord Diplock in *A-G v Leveller Magazine Ltd*
[1979] 1 All ER 745 at 749 thus summarised the
position: "... although criminal contempt of court
may take a variety of forms they all share a
common characteristic: they involve an interference
with the due administration of justice, either in a
particular case or more generally as a continuing
process. It is justice itself that is flouted by contempt
of court ..." It has accordingly been common
ground throughout this appeal that the aim and
purpose of the law of contempt is to prevent
interference with the due administration of justice.'
A-G v Times Newspapers Ltd [1991] 2 All ER 398
at 406–407, HL, per Lord Ackner

CONTENT

Australia 'The "content" of a "program" is what a
program contains. The [Broadcasting Services
Act 1992 (Cth)] calls that content "matter": it is
what the broadcast audience sees or hears ... The
content of a program for broadcast may be difficult
to define in a statute, for it has to do with the
communication of sights and sounds that convey
ideas ...' *Project Blue Sky Inc v Australian
Broadcasting Authority* (1998) 153 ALR 490 at
499; 72 ALJR 841; BC9801389, per Brennan CJ

CONTINGENT DEBT

Australia [Section 198(2) of the Bankruptcy
Act 1966 (Cth)] disqualifies a creditor from voting
in respect of a 'contingent debt' at a creditors'

meeting.]' 'A question arose in argument as to whether a "contingent debt" within the meaning of s 198(2) was an expression intended to encompass a debt in respect of which there was a doubt if there was any debt at all. This view has its genesis in a passage from a brief judgment of Sir George Mellish LJ in *Ex parte Ruffle; Re Dummelow* (1873) LR 8 Ch App 997 where his Lordship said (at 1001) with respect to s 16(3) of the Bankruptcy Act 1869 (Eng) (the equivalent of s 198(2) of the 1966 Act): "The fair construction of the clause seems to me this: 'a contingent debt' refers to a case where there is a doubt if there will be any debt at all ..." ... It is not entirely clear what Sir George Mellish meant by the words in the passage cited above. In one sense a contingent debt is accurately described in Sir George Mellish's words. A guarantee is an example of a contingent debt; it remains contingent until demand is made by the guarantor upon the debtor, and in that sense it cannot be said with certainty that there will be any debt due by the debtor to the guarantor until demand is made. Until then there is a doubt if there will be any debt at all. In other words it all depends on what Sir George Mellish meant in *Re Ruffle*. But if his Lordship meant that a contingent debt was any debt where there was simply a doubt as to whether a debt would be due in the sense that there may be a dispute about it, then I respectfully disagree with what his Lordship said, at least in the context of bankruptcy law. All debts and liabilities, present or future, certain or contingent to which a bankrupt was subject at the date of bankruptcy are provable in bankruptcy: s 82(1). A contingent debt for purposes of bankruptcy law has a well settled meaning and it certainly does not mean merely any debt which is in dispute.' *Foreshaw v Thompson* (1992) 106 ALR 633 at 643–644, per Lockhart J

CONTINUE TO DO SO

[The Commons Registration Act 1965 s 22 as amended by the Countryside and Rights of Way Act 2000, s 98, enacts in s 22(1A) that land falls within s 22(1A) if it is land on which for not less than twenty years a significant number of the inhabitants of any locality, or of any neighbourhood within a locality, have indulged in lawful sports and pastimes as of right, and either (a) continue to do so, or (b) have ceased to do so for not more than such period as may be prescribed, or determined in accordance with prescribed provisions.] '[91] Two issues arise: (i) Should the recreational use "continue" to the date of the application, the date of registration, or some other date? (ii) Must any

application made after the commencement date of the 2000 Act be considered exclusively in accordance with the amended definition?

'[92] Although the practical effects of these questions are very important, the answers to both seem to me reasonably clear, on the ordinary reading of the statute. (i) The use must "continue" to the date of registration. That is because, in the absence of any other indication, the words "continue to do so" can only be taken as referring to the time when the statute requires the definition to be applied; that is the date when the register is amended under s 13 of the 1965 Act. That is the only formal step referred to in the statute itself. It is also the date at which registration is made conclusive by s 10. In this context, unlike that of the initial registration process, there is no statutory equivalent to the prior step of "provisional registration". The earlier procedures, starting with the application, are the creation of the regulations, and cannot in my view be taken to govern the interpretation of the statute. (ii) The application must be considered under the *amended* Act. This is because, as from the commencement of the 2000 Act, an application can only be made under the Act as so amended. Unless preserved by some specific transitional provision (of which there are none in this statute) or some general provision of the Interpretation Act 1978, the unamended definition is dead, and cannot be resurrected.' *Oxfordshire County Council v Oxford City Council* [2005] EWCA Civ 175 at [91]–[92], [2005] 3 All ER 961, per Carnwath LJ

CONTINUING ASSOCIATION

New Zealand 'The association must be "continuing" — thus, the coming together must not be on a single occasion or event, but must continue over a period of time.' *R v Matau* [1994] 2 NZLR 631 at 637, per Tompkins J

CONTINUOUS SERVICE

Australia 'Given these precedents I am satisfied that "continuous service" for the purpose of this award means the uninterrupted provision of the employee's labour in accordance with the contract of service entered into between the employee and employer.' *Re Restaurant Keepers Award* (1997) 71 IR 286 at 290–291, per Westwood P

CONTRACT

[For 9 Halsbury's Laws (4th edn) paras 201, 210, 206, 422, 212 and 207 see now 9(1) Halsbury's

Laws (4th edn) (Reissue) paras 601, 616, 606, 869, 618 and 607 respectively.]

Contract of insurance

Australia 'In the circumstances of a particular case the determination of whether a contract is properly to be characterised as a contract of insurance may not be easy. Many contracts provide for the payment of money on the happening of contingencies which are not contracts of insurance, for example those which are contracts of suretyship guaranteeing payment, and contracts warranting the quality of performance of a chattel supplied by the warrantor ... It is the requirement of the element of uncertainty which is important in this case. [*Prudential Insurance Co v Commissioner of Inland Revenue* [1904] 2 KB 658 at 662–663.] The element of uncertainty referred to by Channell J concerned the happening of the event upon which the sum insured would become payable. That uncertainty gives rise to uncertainty as to both profit and loss to the insurer which is a distinguishing characteristic of a contract of insurance. Thus, contracts of insurance are said to be aleatory contracts: see *Colinvaux's Law of Insurance*, 6th edn, p 1; MacGillivray and Parkington, *Insurance Law*, 7th edn, p 6.

'A contract of insurance is a contract upon speculation: *Carter v Boehm* (1766) 3 Burr 1905 at 1909; 97 ER 1162 at 1164; *Re Commonwealth Homes and Investment Co Ltd* [1943] SASR 211 at 231. It is a characteristic of a contract of insurance that the amount of the premium is not intended to be equivalent to the present value of the insurer's actual performance: MacGillivray and Parkington, *Insurance Law*, 7th edn, p 3. And conversely the insurer's actual performance, the payment of the sum insured on the happening of the contingency, is not intended to be equivalent to the value of the moneys paid to the insurer by way of premium.

'That a contract of insurance involves an element of speculation is not, of course, a sufficient criterion for distinguishing a contract of insurance from contracts of some other kind. There is an element of speculation in contracts of suretyship and in warranties as to the quality of performance of chattels, but the absence of an element of speculation which carries a risk to the putative insurer that the contract may be worth more or less than the value of the premiums received indicates that the contract is not one of insurance.' *Re Barrett, ex p Young v NM Superannuation Pty Ltd* (1992) 106 ALR 549 at 563–564, per von Doussa J

CONTRIBUTION

[For 16 Halsbury's Laws (4th edn) para 1252 see now 16(2) Halsbury's Laws (4th edn) (Reissue) para 458.]

[Section 1(1) of the Civil Liability (Contribution) Act 1978 provides that any person liable in respect of any damage suffered by another person may recover 'contribution' from any other person in respect of the same damage. By s 6(1) a person is liable in respect of any damage for the purposes of the Act if the person who suffered it is entitled to recover compensation from him in respect of that damage, whatever the legal basis of his liability.] 'The purpose and effect of the 1978 Act was to provide for contribution beyond that of joint tortfeasors for which s 6 of the Law Reform (Married Women and Tortfeasors) Act 1935 had previously provided. The contribution is as to "compensation" recoverable against a person in respect of "any damage suffered by another" (s 1(1)) "whatever the legal basis of his liability, whether tort, breach of contract, breach of trust or otherwise (s 6(1)). It is difficult to imagine a broader formulation of an entitlement to contribution. It clearly spans a variety of causes of action, forms of damage in the sense of loss of some sort, and remedies, the last of which are gathered together under the umbrella of "compensation".' *Friends' Provident Life Office v Hillier Parker May & Rowden (a firm) (Estates and General plc and ors, third parties)* [1995] 4 All ER 260 at 272, CA, per Auld LJ

Insurance

[For 25 Halsbury's Laws (4th edn) paras 538–539 see now 25 Halsbury's Laws (4th edn) (2003 Reissue) paras 496–497.]

CONTRIBUTORY

[For 7 Halsbury's Laws (4th edn) paras 1212–1251 see now 7(3) Halsbury's Laws (4th edn) (1996 Reissue) para 2463 et seq.]

CONTRIBUTORY NEGLIGENCE

Australia 'In our opinion the reasoning of the Court of Appeal in *Daniels* [*v Anderson* (1995) 37 NSWLR 438] is correct. There is no rule that apportionment legislation does not operate in respect of the contributory negligence of a plaintiff where the defendant, in breach of its duty, has failed to protect the plaintiff from damage in respect of the very event which gave rise to the defendant's employment. A plaintiff may be guilty of contributory negligence, therefore, even if the "very purpose" of the duty owed by the defendant is to protect the plaintiff's property. Thus, a plaintiff who carelessly leaves valuables lying about may be guilty of contributory negligence, calling for apportionment of loss, even if the defendant was employed to protect the plaintiff's valuables. A finding of contributory negligence turns on a factual investigation of whether the plaintiff contributed to his or her own loss by failing to take reasonable care of his or her person or property.' *Astley v Austrust Ltd* (1999) 161 ALR 155 at 163; 73 ALJR 403; (1999) Aust Torts Reports ¶81–501; BC9900546, per Gleeson CJ, McHugh, Gummow and Hayne JJ

CONTRIBUTORY SCHEME

New Zealand [Securities Act 1978, s 2(1).] '[The definition of "contributory scheme" in s 2(1) of the Securities Act 1978 was not to exclude the buy-back transaction in the retirement village in this case. Buyers of units invested their money in buying a town house on terms that they would recover all or a large part of their outlay.] [Their Lordships observed concerning:] 'the meaning of "investment of money" in the definition in s 2(1) of "contributory scheme" which is one of the necessary ingredients of the exception to the s 5(1)(b) exemption ... . In the present case ... without any strain of language, buyers of units would say they had invested their money in buying a town house in Culverden Retirement Village on terms they will occupy this with necessary services provided, for so long as they wish and that they will then get back all or a large part of their outlay. The return from their outlay is to be found in the totality of these benefits, not just the financial repayment at the end.

'Their Lordships can see nothing in the context of the definition of contributory scheme to suggest that the undefined words "investment" and "investor" were intended to bear a more restricted meaning excluding this type of transaction from the scope of the definition. Broadly stated, and subject to the somewhat obscure subpara (ii) in s 5(1)(b), the effect of the contributory scheme exception is to take outside the exemption and leave within the scope of the Act interests in land forming part of a joint enterprise involving more than five investors. Their Lordships cannot see any compelling reason for distinguishing between schemes under which the sole return is money and schemes under which the return comes partly as money and partly from the use of land.' *Culverden Retirement Village v Registrar of Companies* [1997] 1 NZLR 257 at 261, PC, per cur

CONTROL

[The Income and Corporation Taxes Act 1970 has been largely repealed. For the definition formerly in s 302(2) see now the re-enactment (with minor drafting amendments) in the Income and Corporation Taxes Act 1988, s 416(2). For that formerly in s 534 see now s 840 of the Act of 1988.]

Australia [Section 221P of the Income Tax Assessment Act 1936 (Cth) provides, inter alia, that a trustee shall be liable to pay an amount which is a deduction made by an employer from salary or wages paid where property has been vested in, or where the 'control' of property has passed to, the trustee.] '... the trustee must, at the very least, have power to realise, by converting into money, all the property in his hands before he can have control of it sufficient for the purposes of s 221P...

'The power to realise the whole of the employer's property is necessary, but not, without more, sufficient to constitute control for the purposes of s 221P. [*Commissioner of Taxation (Cth) v Barnes* (1975) 133 CLR 483 identifies] a further requirement which must be satisfied before the trustee will have sufficient dominion over all of the employer's property to amount to such control: as well as having power to realise the whole of the employer's property in his hands, the trustee must also have an authority to deal with the proceeds of such a realisation that permits him to disburse all of those proceeds (if that be necessary) to pay at least one of the debts of the employer. It is authority in the trustee to pay at least one of the employer's debts from the proceeds of realisation of the entirety of the employer's property (if it should in the circumstances of the particular case, be necessary to turn the whole of the employer's property into cash to do that) that turns actual control by the trustee of the entirety of the employer's property, in the sense of power to prevent others dealing with that property, into "control" within s 221P.' *Australian Securities Commission v Macleod* (1994) 48 FCR 152 at 157–158, per Drummond J

Canada [Under freedom of information legislation, there was a right of access to information under the control of a government institution.] ' ... a principal, in a principal/agent relationship, usually exercises some form of control in the form of dominance or direction over an agent and ... direction over the confidentiality or disclosure of records. However, the definition of "control" also includes the authority to manage, direct, superintend, administer or oversee. An agent would have such power, at least to some degree, with respect to its records and documents including those it maintained or controlled for its principal ... What the dictionary definitions do suggest is that the term "control" is open to a wide variety of meanings depending upon the circumstances in which the word is used.' *Canada Post Corpn v Canada (Minister of Public Works)* [1993] 3 FC 320 at 332–333, per Rothstein J (Fed TD)

Canada [An amalgamated corporation sought to deduct non-capital losses under s 111(1)(a) of the *Income Tax Act*. The question was whether the two corporations were 'controlled' by the same person or groups of persons under s 251(2)(c)(i) of the Act.] 'Though the word "control" is not defined in the *Income Tax Act,* it has been considered many times in the jurisprudence. This jurisprudence has settled that control is based on *de jure* control and not *de facto* control, and that the most important single factor to be considered is the voting rights attaching to shares. In the past, the share register, by itself, has usually been the main basis for determining corporate control, even though the *Income Tax Act* did not adopt that idea expressly. The scope of scrutiny under the *de jure* test has wisely been extended more recently beyond a mere technical reference to the share register ...

...

'... any combination of shareholders that can exert majority control are linked by a "sufficient common connection" for the purposes of the *de jure* test, and therefore, in law, control the corporation. Actual demonstrated control by any such group is not strictly required. Rather, such shareholders need only be in "a position to exercise control".' *Canada v Duha Printers (Western) Ltd* [1996] 3 FC 78 at 109, 115, per Lindern JA (CA)

Canada 'It has been well recognized that, under the *Income Tax Act,* "control" of a corporation normally refers to *de jure* control and not *de facto* control. This Court has repeatedly cited with approval the following test, set out by Jackett P in *Buckerfield's, supra,* at p 507:

Many approaches might conceivably be adopted in applying the word "control" in a statute such as the *Income Tax Act* to a corporation. It might, for example, refer to control by "management", where management and the board of directors are separate, or it might

refer to control by the board of directors ... The word "control" might conceivably refer to *de facto* control by one or more shareholders whether or not they hold a majority of shares. I am of the view, however, that in Section 39 of the *Income Tax Act* [the former section dealing with associated companies], the word "controlled" contemplates the right of control that rests in ownership of such a number of shares as carries with it the right to a majority of the votes in the election of the board of directors [Emphasis added.]

'Cases in which this Court has applied the foregoing test have included, *inter alia, Dworkin Furs, supra,* and *Vina-Rug (Canada) Ltd v Minister of National Revenue* [1968] SCR 193.

'Thus, *de jure* control has emerged as the Canadian standard, with the test for such control generally accepted to be whether the controlling party enjoys, by virtue of its shareholdings, the ability to elect the majority of the board of directors. However, it must be recognized at the outset that this test is really an attempt to ascertain who is in effective control of the affairs and fortunes of the corporation. That is, although the directors generally have, by operation of the corporate law statute governing the corporation, the formal right to direct the management of the corporation, the majority shareholder enjoys the indirect exercise of this control through his or her ability to elect the board of directors. Thus, it is in reality the majority shareholder, not the directors *per se,* who is in effective control of the corporation. This was expressly recognized by Jackett P when setting out the test in *Buckerfield's.* Indeed, the very authority cited for the test was the following dictum of Viscount Simon, LC, in *British American Tobacco Co v Inland Revenue Commissioners* [1943] 1 All E.R. 13, at p 15:

The owners of the majority of the voting power in a company are the persons who are in effective control of its affairs and fortunes. [Emphasis added.]'

Duha Printers (Western) Ltd v Canada [1998] 1 SCR 795 at 815–816, per Iacobucci J

Control the conduct of a proceeding

Australia [Evidence Act 1995 (NSW) s 11.] 'Section 11(1) of the Evidence Act says that the power of a court "to control the conduct of a proceeding" is not affected by the Evidence Act except so far as the Act itself otherwise provides whether expressly or by necessary intendment.

Section 11(2) gives a particular example of what is spoken of in s 11(1). The particular example refers to the powers of the court with respect to abuse of process in a proceeding and says that those powers are not affected.' *Georgeski v Owners Corp Strata Plan No 49833* [2004] NSWSC 945 at [3], per Barrett J; BC200406702

CONTROL, DIRECTION OR INFLUENCE

[Sexual Offences Act 1956, s 31.] 'In our judgment it is clear ... that Parliament in referring to "control, direction or influence" contemplated three different kinds of behaviour in relation to a prostitute's movements. The words, at first blush, suggest progressively wider categories and are plainly to be construed disjunctively. As a matter of construction, although compulsion or persuasion may well be a necessary ingredient of control and, possibly, direction, and although (depending on the circumstances) compulsion or persuasion may be an ingredient of influence, we do not accept that compulsion or persuasion are necessary ingredients of influence.' *A-G's Reference* (*No 2 of 1995*) [1996] 3 All ER 860 at 863, CA, per Rose LJ

CONVERSION

Equitable doctrine

[For 16 Halsbury's Laws (4th edn) para 1372 see now 16(2) Halsbury's Laws (4th edn) (Reissue) para 701.]

Of goods

[For 45 Halsbury's Laws (4th edn) para 1422 see now 45(2) Halsbury's Laws (4th edn) (Reissue) para 548.]

Of securities

[The Capital Gains Tax Act 1979 has been repealed. The definition is re-enacted in the Taxation of Chargeable Gains Act 1992, s 132(3)(a).]

CONVICTED

[A confiscation order may be made under the Criminal Justice Act 1988, s 71 or s 72AA where an offender is convicted of an offence of a relevant description, and by s 72A provision is made for postponed determination up to six months (unless there are exceptional circumstances) beginning with the date of conviction. On a question as to the time

limit the trial judge held that the time ran not from the date of pleading guilty but from the date of sentencing. The appellants claimed that the time had expired and that confiscation orders could not be made.] 'The provisions are contained in a penal statute which provides for a period of imprisonment in default of complying with the order and thus the statute must be construed strictly. In the context it is clear that "conviction" means being found guilty or pleading guilty and does not include the sentence imposed.

...

'Where in s 71(1) and s 72AA(1) the word "convicted" is used in the phrase "where an offender is convicted", it must, we consider, mean the date on which he was either found, or pleaded, guilty. We think this interpretation is borne out by s 72AA(7) and s 72A(11) and by the fact that in the ordinary way it is the duty of the court to determine whether the offender has benefited and, if so, to what extent before sentencing or otherwise dealing with the offender in respect of that offence (see s 71(1A)). Further by s 72(5) the court has to have regard to the amount of any confiscation order before imposing a fine or making a compensation order. Fines and compensation orders are part of the sentencing process. The fact that the court is to leave the orderout of account in determining the appropriate sentence or other manner of dealing with him also supports the conclusion that the Act contemplated the making of the order before sentence was passed.' *R v Shergill* [1999] 2 All ER 485 at 488–489, CA, per Beldam LJ

CONVICTION

'It has been said many times that the word "conviction" is ambiguous and it has sometimes been construed in a statutory context as referring to nothing more than a finding of guilt. But, in the absence of something in the context which suggests that narrower meaning, the authorities in the nineteenth century and earlier all seem to point to the conclusion that the requirement to establish a conviction requires proof not only of the finding of guilt but also of the court's final adjudication by sentence or other order.' *Richards v R* [1992] 4 All ER 807 at 809–810 PC, per Lord Bridge of Harwich

Australia 'The question of what amounts to a conviction admits of no single, comprehensive answer. Indeed, the answer to the question rather depends upon the context in which it is asked. On the one hand, a verdict of guilty by a jury or a plea of guilty upon arraignment has been said to amount to a conviction. On the other hand, it has been said that there can be no conviction until there is a judgment of the court, ordinarily in the form of a sentence, following upon the verdict or plea. Thus Tindal CJ said in *Burgess v Boetefeur* (1844) 7 Man & G 481 at 504; 135 ER 93 at 202: "The word 'conviction' is undoubtedly *verbum aequivocum*. It is sometimes used as meaning the *verdict* of a jury, and at other times, in its more strictly legal sense, for the *sentence* of the court [emphasis added]." The context in which the question arises for present purposes is that of autrefois convict and in that context it would seem clear that a verdict or plea of guilty is insufficient of itself to constitute a conviction.' *Maxwell v R* (1996) 135 ALR 1 at 5, per Dawson, McHugh JJ

CONVINCED

Australia '... to be "convinced" relevantly means no more than to be satisfied by argument or evidence (*New Shorter Oxford English Dictionary*, at 503) or to be persuaded by argument or proof (*Macquarie Dictionary*, revised edition, at p 407).' *Abeysinghe v Minister for Immigration and Multicultural Affairs* BC200202034; [2002] FCA 511 at [14], per Ryan, Carr and Conti JJ

CO–OPERATIVE

[See also 1(2) Halsbury's Laws (4th edn) (Reissue) para 580 note 3.]

COPARCENARY

[For 39 Halsbury's Laws (4th edn) paras 565, 567 see now 39 Halsbury's Laws (4th edn) (Reissue) paras 224–225.]

COPY

[The Copyright Act 1956 has been repealed; see the new definition below.]

(1) The copying of the work is an act restricted by the copyright in every description of copyright work; and references in this Part [Part I: Copyright] to copying and copies shall be construed as follows.

(2) Copying in relation to a literary, dramatic, musical or artistic work means reproducing the work in any material form. This includes storing the work in any medium by electronic means.

(3) In relation to an artistic work copying includes the making of a copy in three dimensions

of a two-dimensional work and the making of a copy in two dimensions of a three-dimensional work.

(4) Copying in relation to a film, television broadcast or cable programme includes making a photograph of the whole or any substantial part of any image forming part of the film, broadcast or cable programme.

(5) Copying in relation to the typographical arrangement of a published edition means making a facsimile copy of the arrangement.

(6) Copying in relation to any description of work includes the making of copies which are transient or are incidental to some other use of the work.

(Copyright, Designs and Patents Act 1988, s 17)

Australia [Under the County Court Act 1958 (Vic), s 80 a judge may make an order prohibiting the publication of a report of certain proceedings, and a copy of such order is to be posted on one of the doors of the court house.] 'At first sight, the question as to what constitutes a copy appears to be decided by reference to the dictionary meaning of the word "copy" as being "an imitation, reproduction or transcript of an original"... In substance, the defence argument had an attractive simplicity to it, namely, that in order to have a copy there must have been an original in writing. This question is not without some difficulty, but I have come to the conclusion that ... in order to have a copy of the judge's order posted it is not necessary that there be an original order made in writing. I so find for the following reasons. The common or ordinary meaning of the word "copy", namely, a reproduction, does not of itself answer the question as to what the document reproduces. It would be otherwise if the word "copy" was taken to mean a facsimile. A document may in my view properly reproduce the terms of an order, even if the order is made orally or if the original order is transmitted in some mechanical form other than conventional writing. The requirement that "copy" meant only a copy of the original would, strictly speaking, lead to the absurd result that if the original signed order of the judge was posted on the door, there would not be compliance with the requirement to post a copy on the door.' *Bailey v Hinch* [1989] VR 78 at 87, per Gobbo J

Australia [The respondents argued that copyright in the motion pictures embodied in certain DVD discs would be infringed by a person who, without licence, rents and plays a DVD disc that embodies those motion pictures. The issue was whether decompression of data and storage in RAM constitutes a 'copy' for the purposes of Copyright Act 1968 (Cth) s 10, which stipulates that 'copy' in relation to a cinematograph film means any article or thing in which the visual images or sounds comprising the cinematograph film (or motion picture) are embodied.] 'I consider that the ephemeral embodiment of tiny fractions of the visual images and sounds that comprise a cinematograph film or motion picture sequentially does not constitute the act of making a copy of the motion picture or cinematograph film … It is clear that neither the whole nor any substantial part of a cinematograph film or motion picture is ever embodied in the RAM of a DVD player or personal computer at any given time. The mere fact that, over a period of time, being the time taken to play the motion picture or cinematograph film, tiny parts are sequentially stored in the RAM of the DVD player or personal computer does not mean that the motion picture or cinematograph film is embodied in such a device. As a result, a consumer, by playing a DVD disc, does not, for the purposes of the Act, make a copy of the whole or a substantial part of the motion picture or cinematograph film embodied in that DVD disc.' *Australian Video Retailers Assn Ltd v Warner Home Video Pty Ltd* BC200107653; [2001] FCA 1719 at [65], per Emmett J

Australia [In the context of the service of a statutory demand under the (Cth) Corporations Act 2001, s 109X(1) and whether service of an original document satisfies the requirement that a copy be served.] 'The construction advanced by Emhill relies on one of the meanings of the word "copy". As the first of multiple meanings of the word, The Macquarie Dictionary states that "copy" means —

> a transcript, reproduction or imitation of an original.

'There is another, different, meaning of the word "copy", which involves no reference to, or distinction from, an original. According to the Oxford English Dictionary, in this usage the word "copy" means —

> one of the various (written or printed) specimens of the same writing or work; an individual example of a manuscript or print.

'Thus, in ordinary usage it is common to speak of (for example) purchasing several copies of a particular book. There is no single original. Rather, the original edition itself consists of some number of copies.' *Emhill Pty Ltd v Bonsoc Pty Ltd* [2005] VSCA 239 at [15]–[16], per Maxwell P; BC200507702

COPYRIGHT

[For 9 Halsbury's Laws (4th edn) para 801 see now 9(2) Halsbury's Laws (4th edn) (Reissue) para 3.]

[The Copyright Act 1956 has been repealed. The new definition is as below.]

Copyright is a property right which subsists in accordance with this Part [Part I: Copyright] in the following descriptions of work—
(a) original literary, dramatic, musical or artistic works,
(b) sound recordings, films, broadcasts or cable programmes, and
(c) the typographical arrangement of published editions.

(Copyright, Designs and Patents Act 1988, s 1)
[See s 2 of the 1988 Act as to rights subsisting in copyright works, and ss 153–156 as to qualification for and extent of copyright protection. See also s 7 of the 1988 Act for provisions relating to cable programmes.]

Period of copyright

[Copyright in a literary, dramatic, musical or artistic work expires (as under the previous Act of 1956) at the end of the period of fifty years from the end of the calendar year in which the author dies. See generally as to the duration of copyright in other works e.g. films, broadcasts etc, ss 12–15 of the Copyright, Designs and Patents Act 1988.]

CORONER

Franchise coroner

[The Coroners Act 1887 was repealed by the Coroners Act 1988. The definition was not re-enacted. For coroner of the Queen's household see now s 29 of, and Schedule 2 to, the Act of 1988.]

CORPORATION

Clearing corporation

United States A 'clearing corporation' is a corporation registered as a 'clearing agency' under the federal securities laws or a corporation:
(a) at least 90 per cent of whose capital stock is held by or for one or more organisations, none of which, other than a national securities exchange or association, holds in excess of 20 per cent of the capital stock of the corporation, and each of which is

(i) subject to supervision or regulation pursuant to the provisions of federal or state banking laws or state insurance laws,

(ii) a broker or dealer or investment company registered under the federal securities laws, or

(iii) a national securities exchange or association registered under the federal securities laws; and

(b) any remaining capital stock of which is held by individuals who have purchased it at or prior to the time of their taking office as directors of the corporation and who have purchased only so much of the capital stock as is necessary to permit them to qualify as directors.

(Uniform Commercial Code 1978, s 8–102(3))

Corporation aggregate

[For 9 Halsbury's Laws (4th edn) para 1204 see now 9(2) Halsbury's Laws (4th edn) (Reissue) para 1005.]

Corporation sole

[For 9 Halsbury's Laws (4th edn) para 1206 see now 9(2) Halsbury's Laws (4th edn) (Reissue) para 1007.]

CORRESPOND

[Backing of Warrants (Republic of Ireland) Act 1965, s 2(2).] 'My Lords, "correspond" is not a term of art: it is an ordinary English word not used in any special sense and must be so applied. In this context it would be unwise to propose a synonym. It would not be right to embark on a search for a legal definition where the legislature thought none was necessary. If one substitutes another word or words for "correspond" one will be inviting magistrates to construe and apply other words: *Brutus v Cozens* [1972] 2 All ER 1297 at 1299, [1973] AC 854 at 861 per Lord Reid. The task of magistrates is simply to apply the word "correspond" and to determine whether the test of correspondence is satisfied on the basis of a perusal of the warrants or, exceptionally, where technical words of expressions are involved, on all the materials before them. Counsel for the appellants invited your Lordships to approach the meaning of the word "correspond" on the basis that it either mandates a test based on the conduct of the accused or by a comparison of the juristic elements of offences specified in the warrant with juristic

elements of putative English offences. While accepting that conduct and juristic elements are relevant matters in an examination of warrants there is no need to make the choice which counsel suggested. The correct approach is much simpler. For my part magistrates should approach the matter in the way indicated by the Divisional Court. May LJ observed (at 10–11):

"The offence specified in the warrant has to 'correspond with any offence under ... [English] law ... which is an indictable offence or is punishable on summary conviction with imprisonment for six months'. The word 'any' shows that the court is not necessarily looking for an English offence which is identical with the offence specified in the warrant nor one whose juristic elements are the same — rather for a sufficiently serious offence which what is specified in the warrant would correspond with in English law if what is specified in the warrant had occurred in England. (Sufficiently serious is defined as an indictable offence or one punishable on summary conviction with imprisonment for six months.) The scheme is, not that the court has to find identical Irish and English offences, but that the offence specified in the warrant is a sufficiently serious Irish offence and that what is specified in the warrant would amount to some sufficiently serious English offence ... The English offence, which may not be an identical offence, is not the offence specified in the warrant but a putative offence with which the offence specified in the warrant has to correspond."

'I would respectfully indorse this reasoning. *Re Gilligan, Re Ellis* [2000] 1 All ER 113 at 122, HL, per Lord Steyn

CORRESPONDING PROVISIONS

New Zealand [The transitional provision of s 227(4) of the Tax Administration Act 1994 reads: '(4) Any express or implied reference in any enactment, instrument, or document (including this Act) to any provision of this Act, or to things done or to be done or failing to be done under or for the purposes of any provision of this Act, shall, if and so far as the nature of the reference permits, be construed as including, in relation to the times, circumstances, or purposes in relation to which the corresponding provision in the repealed enactment has or had effect, a reference to, or to things done or to be done or failing to be done under or for the purposes of, that corresponding provision.']

'In *Winter v Ministry of Transport* [1972] NZLR 539 at p 541, referring to s 20A of the Acts Interpretation Act 1924, Turner J said:

"We read 'corresponding' in s 20A as including a new section dealing with the same subject matter as the old one, in a manner or with a result not so far different from the old as to strain the accepted meaning of the word 'corresponding' as given in the Shorter Oxford English Dictionary – 'answering to in character and function; similar to'. The new s 58A(6) answers to the old one (the second part of the old s 59B(1)) in character and function; it is similar in purpose, prescribes the same thing to be done, and is designed to produce the same result. We hold it to be a 'corresponding section'."

'[28] Clearly the framers of s 227(4) intended an expansive application of s 227(4). It is directed to "any express or implied reference in any enactment …". It is to be construed "if and so far as the nature of the reference permits", as including "in relation to the times, circumstances, or purposes in relation to which the corresponding provision in the repealed enactment has or had effect, a reference … to things … to be done … under or for the purposes of, that corresponding provision".

'[29] The question, then, is whether there is correspondence in that broad sense in relation to the times, circumstances or purposes as regards the continuing operation of s 25. We have no hesitation in holding it to be a corresponding provision to the new s 108. It has the same character and function. It presupposes the amendment of assessments within the time limit. During the four years the amendment function will be exercised as the statute provides. That is intended in each case and s 25 and the new s 108 are intended to produce that result. The altering of assessments during the four-year period is something which is "to be done under or for the purposes of, that corresponding provision.' *Vela Fishing Ltd v Commissioner of Inland Revenue* [2002] 1 NZLR 49 (CA) at 54–55 per cur

CORROBORATION

'Corroboration can only be afforded to or by a witness who is otherwise to be believed. If a witness's testimony falls of its own inanition the question of his needing, or being capable of giving, corroboration does not arise.' *Director of Public*

Prosecutions v Kilbourne [1973] 1 All ER 440 at 452, per Lord Hailsham of St Marylebone LC

[For 11 Halsbury's Laws (4th edn) para 454 see now 11(2) Halsbury's Laws (4th edn) (Reissue) para 1141.]

CORRUPT

Australia 'As Hunt J pointed out in [*Whelan v John Fairfax & Sons Ltd* (1988) 12 NSWLR 148] and elsewhere, the word "corrupt" can have significantly different shades of meaning. This does not make it unusual, but, because it is a word the use of which is apt to give rise to allegations of defamation, it seems to have come in for a high degree of forensic exegesis. Depending upon the context, for example, it can mean that a person takes bribes, or that he abuses power entrusted to him, or that he improperly obtains private benefits from a public position. The range of possible meanings of the word when used in connection with public officials in this State has been substantially expanded by the enactment of the Independent Commission Against Corruption Act 1988 (NSW) which defines "corrupt conduct" in a manner that goes well beyond the ordinary meaning of that expression and is notable for its generality and vagueness.' *Drummoyne Municipal Council v Australian Broadcasting Corpn* (1990) 21 NSWLR 135 at 138, per Gleeson CJ

'I agree with Hunt J that it has at least three substantially distinct meanings [that the plaintiff was open to bribery, was dishonest or was lacking integrity]. I would add also that the word has at least one other common meaning in many contexts; that is a very general and unspecific meaning conveying the idea that the person using the word considers that the person spoken of has a condition of corruptness which would make ordinary, decent members of the community think less of or tend to shun that person.' Ibid at 155, per Priestley JA

CORRUPT PRACTICE

[For 15 Halsbury's Laws (4th edn) para 687 see now 15 Halsbury's Laws (4th edn) (Reissue) para 608.]

CORRUPTLY

Australia 'It follows from *Re Chew* (1992) 173 CLR 626 that, in order for a public officer to "act corruptly", it is not necessary that he or she act in such a way in the performance of his or her duty which was likely to or tended to corrupt, another. It is the exercise of authority for an improper purpose, such as a purpose activated by malice, that constitutes the corrupt action and takes the acting outside of the scope of the officer's authority. This does not necessarily involve doing anything which was likely to or tended to corrupt, another.' *Re Willers* (1995) 81 A Crim R 219 at 225, per Malcolm CJ

Canada [Accused was charged with corruptly accepting a reward, comprising secret commissions.] 'In my view, "corruptly", as used in the section, designates secrecy as the corrupting element of the offence. It is the failure to disclose that makes it impossible for the principal to determine whether to act upon the advice of the agent or accept the actions of the agent. It is the non-disclosure which makes the receipt of the commission or reward corrupt. The word "corruptly", in this context, adds the element of non-disclosure to the *actus reus* of the offence ...

'The word "corruptly" in the context of secret commissions means "secretly" or "without the requisite disclosure". There is no "corrupt bargain" requirement. Thus, it is possible to convict a taker of a reward or benefit despite the innocence of the giver of the reward or benefit. Non-disclosure will be established for the purposes of the section if the Crown demonstrates that adequate and timely disclosure of the source, amount and nature of the benefit has not been made by the agent to the principal.' *R v Kelly* (1992) 92 DLR (4th) 643 at 661, 665, per Cory J (Can SC)

Canada '... The Adjudicator considered that the requirement in paragraph 426(1)(*a*) of the *Criminal Code* that a bribe or advantage be taken "corruptly" was equivalent to the requirement in paragraph 9(1)(*a*) of the [Hong Kong] *Prevention of Bribery Ordinance* that the acceptance of a reward be made "without lawful authority or reasonable excuse". However, I do not believe this is in accordance with established jurisprudence as to the meaning of "corruptly" in paragraph 426(1)(*a*) of the *Criminal Code*. In *R. v Kelly* the majority of the Supreme Court held that in this context "corruptly" means "without disclosure" to the principal. Such disclosure to be a defence must have been effected in an adequate and timely manner, but once made the taking of the reward by an agent cannot be found to have been done "corruptly".' *Li v Canada (Minister of Citizenship and Immigration)* [1997] 1 FC 235 at 253, FCA, per Strayer J

New Zealand [Section 3 of the Secret Commissions Act 1910 begins 'Every person is guilty of an offence who corruptly gives, or agrees or offers to give ... " and s 4 of the same Act begins "Every agent is guilty of an offence who corruptly accepts or obtains ... '.] 'In the context of the section this word would appear to be one designed to describe the mental element which an offender must have when giving or accepting a gift, namely that degree of deliberate criminal intent necessary not only to perform the act itself but also to do it for the purpose of influencing another person or to be influenced to the detriment of a third party's business.' *R v McDonald* [1993] 3 NZLR 354 at 357–358, per Williamson J

New Zealand [Section 262 of the Crimes Act 1961 begins 'Every one is liable to imprisonment for a term not exceeding 3 years who corruptly takes or bargains for any reward ... '.] 'I have found it difficult, indeed impossible, to capture the full connotation of the word "corruptly" in a single synonym or short phrase. The exercise may well be unnecessary and undesirable in any event ...

'While the idea of corruption may not be the same as the idea of dishonesty I take the view that dishonesty is part of the concept of corruption for present purposes. To act corruptly under s 262 I consider the person concerned must (a) have a dishonest purpose and (b) intend to act in a way which can fairly be described as morally wicked or depraved: see The Concise Oxford Dictionary (6th edn, 1976).' *Broom v Police* [1994] 1 NZLR 680 at 687–688, per Tipping J

COST

New Zealand [Section 74(2)(b) of the Income Tax Act 1976.] 'The ordinary meaning of the word as given in *The Shorter Oxford English Dictionary* includes "that which must be given in order to acquire something". The fact that determination of cost may require a valuation exercise does not mean there is no cost.' *Tasman Forestry Ltd v Commissioner of Inland Revenue* [1999] 3 NZLR 129 (CA) at 140 per cur

COST PRICE

New Zealand 'I am in no doubt that "cost price" for the purposes of the calculation of fringe benefit tax means the *effective* cost price, and does not include GST where the person producing the benefit is a registered person and is able to claim a deduction by way of input tax.' *Inland Revenue Commissioner v Atlas Copco (NZ) Ltd* [1991] 2 NZLR 732 at 742, per Sinclair J

COSTS

[For 12 Halsbury's Laws (4th edn) para 1108 see now 12(1) Halsbury's Laws (4th edn) (Reissue) para 807.]

Australia [Section 161 of the Medical Practices Act 1992 (NSW) gives the Medical Tribunal general power to award such 'costs' as the tribunal may determine.] '... the High Court has rejected the notion of litigants recovering costs of attending and instructing. Their costs are to be limited, by the principles in *Cachia v Hanes* (1994) 173 CLR 403 solely to any witnesses' fees to which they are otherwise entitled. This is a stern rule. It is not one apparently required by the breadth of the legislative language (costs). It is one imposed upon that language by judicial presumption upheld by this country's highest court.' *Walton v McBride* (1995) 36 NSWLR 440 at 453, per Kirby P

Of reference to arbitration

[For 2 Halsbury's Laws (4th edn) paras 606–608 see now 2(3) Halsbury's Laws (4th edn) (Reissue) paras 67–70.]

COSTS OF AND INCIDENTAL TO THE PROCEEDINGS

[In connection with charges of VAT and PAYE offences a receiver was appointed to take possession of and manage the defendant's realisable property. The defendant was acquitted and sought an order under the Supreme Court Act 1981, s 51 requiring the respondent, HM Customs and Excise, to pay the costs of the High Court proceedings, including the receiver's remuneration. The application was dismissed and the appellant appealed, contending that the receiver's remuneration constituted costs of and incidental to the High Court proceedings within the meaning of s 51.] 'Section 51(1) of the Supreme Court Act 1981 provides: "Subject to the provisions of this or any other enactment and to rules of court, the costs of and incidental to all proceedings in— ... (b) the High Court ... shall be in the discretion of the court". Section 51(3) gives the court full power to determine by whom and to what extent the costs are to paid. Thence to the rules: Ord 62, r 1(4) defines costs in this way: "References to costs shall be construed as including references to fees, charges, disbursements, expenses and remuneration ..." Those words find an echo in Ord 33, which provides for the proper "remuneration" of the receiver. Mr Joffe submits that "remuneration" must bear the same meaning

and accordingly that s 51(1) is wide enough to include the receiver's remuneration as it is provided for by Ord 30.

'He relies upon the speech of Lord Goff of Chieveley in *Aiden Shipping Co Ltd v Interbulk Ltd, The Vimeira* [1986] 2 All ER 409,[1986] AC 965 to support the wide construction he urges.

...

'As I read the conclusions to Lord Goff's speech, it seems to me that at the heart of his decision on the exercise of the discretionary jurisdiction conferred by the statute lies an evaluation of the interests of justice. Since the unfairness to the appellant is manifest to me, Mr Joffe's argument is attractive.

'Mr Mitchell submits that the regime for dealing with the receiver's costs provided in Ord 30 is distinct and separate—see the special provisions for taxation in Ord 30, r 3(3). He submits that the costs of the receivership are not costs "of and incidental to the proceedings" but are management costs requiring this independent treatment.

'I have not found this an easy point to decide. Eschewing, as I have, any suggestion that the appellant can count himself lucky to have been acquitted, I find it intrinsically unfair that the appellant should be indemnified in the Crown Court but not in the Queen's Bench Division where the proceedings should stand or fall with the criminal proceedings. My first inclination is to accept Mr Joffe's invitation to give a consistent meaning to "remuneration" in Ord 30 and Ord 62 and accordingly in s 51(1).

'On reflection there is another consistency of approach which is more compelling. If the costs of the receivership are to be costs of and incidental to the proceedings, then the costs of the receivership should be costs of the proceedings at all stages of those proceedings and in all events. That produces the difficulty I have. Consistency is impossible if one takes two extremes of its application. Suppose, I asked Mr Mitchell in the course of argument, the ex parte order was made, the receiver moved in immediately and properly incurred expenses in the receivership and was entitled to be remunerated for his efforts. The defendant then applies at the very first moment he has to discharge the order and puts up a compelling case to establish his innocence beyond question. Surely it would wrong, I asked, for him to have suffered loss in such an event. I think he saw the lack of merit in his position. It is, however, Mr Joffe who has problems at the other extreme. Suppose that, as may well often happen, there is long delay between the making of the order and the conclusion of the criminal proceedings with an acquittal which leads to the discharge of the receivership order. Assume, however, that by reason of prudent management by the receiver an ailing business is in fact made profitable to the benefit of the defendant, then why should the defendant not pay for it? Mr Joffe's answer is that could be dealt with by the court's exercise of discretion. I am not happy with that answer. I do not consider that it is proper to engage in an analysis of the cost effectiveness of the receivership and management in order to determine whether the costs of the receivership should be treated as costs of and incidental to the proceedings so as to give the court discretion in the first place.

'The true position, as it now appears to me, is that the investigation of whether or not the defendant has suffered loss by reason of the receivership, is an investigation which should be and ordinarily would be conducted in deciding whether or not damages should be awarded against the plaintiff for breach of the usual undertaking as to damages a plaintiff would normally be required to give. Such an investigation would enable justice to be done …

'I am, with unfeigned reluctance, compelled to conclude that even if the expenses of the receivership are within the definition of costs, they are not costs "of and incidental to the proceedings". They must lie where they fall.' *Re Andrews* [1999] 2 All ER 751 at 759–761, CA, PER Ward lJ

COSTS OF ARREST

Australia [Orders were made that the plaintiff be reimbursed the costs and expenses of arrest and sale of a ship it seized while pursuing claims against the ship's owners. It was reimbursed all expenses except its legal costs in opposing the owners' application for release of the ship.] 'The expression "costs of arrest" is a wide one and is capable of encompassing the maintenance of the arrest against claims for release on the ground that there was no proper basis or jurisdiction for the arrest. If the vessel is released the security provided by the arrest of course comes to an end. Therefore, steps taken in order to keep the security on foot and defend the arrest so that the basic purpose of the arrest can be effected, is a cost of the arrest. It is somewhat artificial to separate out the motive of the arresting party, which is of course to look after its own interests, and then to characterise the incurring of the costs on that basis alone in circumstances where the direct effect of the opposition to release is to ensure that the security remains available to all qualifying claimants.'

Patrick Stevedores No 2 Pty Ltd v Ship MV 'Turakina' (No 3) (1999) 95 FCR 52; BC9907689; [1999] FCA 1615 at [16], per Tamberlin J

COUNTERCLAIM

[For 42 Halsbury's Laws (4th edn) para 407 see now 42 Halsbury's Laws (4th edn) (Reissue) para 407.]

COUNTRY

Australia ' … Hong Kong at the relevant date had a distinct area with identifiable borders. It had its own immigration laws, and was inhabited by a permanent identifiable community, and therefore in my opinion it was appropriate to treat it as a "country" in accordance with the meaning and purpose of that expression as used in [(INT) Convention Relating to the Status of Refugees 1951 art 1A(2)]. In 1965 Hong Kong enjoyed a degree of autonomy in relation to its administration. This lends further support to the submission that it is a "country". In addition, as a matter of everyday usage of language, it is not inappropriate to refer to a person as coming from, belonging to, or returning to Hong Kong. The Territory was not simply a place or area but possessed the foregoing additional elements which it make it appropriate to be treated as a country for Convention purposes.' *Koe v Minister for Immigration and Ethnic Affairs* (1997) 148 ALR 353 at 363; BC9704154 at 15, per Tamberlin J

Australia [The applicant argued that employment at sea was comprehended within the meaning of the words 'service in a foreign country' for the purposes of income tax exemptions under Income Tax Assessment Act 1936 (Cth) s 23AG.] 'We were referred both to the *Oxford English Dictionary* (2nd ed, 1989) and the *Macquarie Dictionary* (3rd ed, 1997) for the meaning of the word "country". The former, gives some fourteen definitions before turning to consider various combinations of words in which the word "country" appears. Many can be said to have no relevance to the particular context. It suffices to say that the first meaning given is "A tract or expanse of land of undefined extent; a region, district". It seems that there was a transition in the meaning of the word to a district with distinct or defined physical characteristics, and that it came to be used for a territory or land of a nation usually, although not necessarily, an independent state. While a perusal of these meanings shows the word is generally used by reference to land, the dictionary does show that, in a technical sense, the word can mean: "A region of the sea or ocean".

'The *Macquarie Dictionary* gives ten meanings before colloquial or adjectival meanings are given. Of these, the first is "a tract of land considered apart from geographical or political limits; region; district". It is instructive to note that no definition given under the word "country" suggests that the high seas might collectively, or for that matter that a particular ocean might individually, be described as a country. Nevertheless, by reference to the same dictionary meaning of "region" which, it will be observed, is included in the definition of "country", it is suggested that the word "country" may be said to mean "a part of the earth's surface (land or sea) of considerable and usually indefinite extent". The suggestion may be said to depend upon the word "region" being a synonym for the word "country", which is surely questionable.

...

'There is, however, some assistance to be gained from s 23AG(3) as originally enacted [which refers to "foreign earnings derived in a foreign country"] in the colour that the subsection gives to the meaning of "country", with which we are concerned. In our opinion, s 23AG(3) does suggest that whatever the word "country" may mean it contemplates some unit, to use a neutral word, capable of imposing a law of income tax – or in other words, a political entity or, perhaps, part of a political entity ...

...

'Ultimately, we think that we should return to the ordinary English use of the word "country" in the context of that being a place where personal service such as employment may be engaged in and where income may be derived. In that context, ordinary usage would not suggest that the high seas, or for that matter some parts of them, were in a composite sense to be regarded as a country, or for that matter a series of countries. Rather the ordinary meaning of the expression "foreign country" in modern usage looks to a political entity, be that a tract of land, a district, or a group of islands. It does not extend to an ocean or region of the sea.

'... The argument advanced on behalf of [the applicant] really sought to suggest that the words "foreign country" be construed as meaning no more than "out of Australia". Had Parliament intended to exempt all personal service income so long as a resident taxpayer served ... outside Australia ... it could have said so in language much more to the point than that which was adopted.' *Chaudhri v Cmr of Taxation* (2001) 47 ATR 126; BC200102220; [2001] FCA 554 at [10], [11], [23], [26], [27], per Hill, Drummond and Goldberg JJ

COUNTY PALATINE

[For 8 Halsbury's Laws (4th edn) para 495 see now 8(2) Halsbury's Laws (4th edn) (Reissue) para 307.]

COUPON

[The Income and Corporation Taxes Act 1970 is largely repealed. The definition is re-enacted in the Income and Corporation Taxes Act 1988, s 45.]

COURSE OF EMPLOYMENT

Australia '*Commonwealth v Oliver* (1962) 107 CLR 353 and the cases which follow it show that an interval or interlude in an overall period or episode of work will ordinarily be seen as being part of the course of employment if the employer, expressly or impliedly, has induced or encouraged the employee to spend the interval or interlude at a particular place or in a particular way. Indeed, the modern cases show that, absent gross misconduct on the part of the employee, an injury occurring during such an interval or interlude will invariably result in a finding that the injury occurred in the course of employment. Accordingly, it should now be accepted that an interval or interlude within an overall period or episode of work occurs within the course of employment if, expressly or impliedly, the employer has induced or encouraged the employee to spend that interval or interlude at a particular place or in a particular way. Furthermore, an injury sustained in such an interval will be within the course of employment if it occurred at that place or while the employee was engaged in that activity unless the employee was guilty of gross misconduct taking him or her outside the course of employment.' *Hatzimanolis v ANI Corpn Ltd* (1992) 106 ALR 611 at 617–618, per Mason CJ, Deane, Dawson and McHugh JJ

Canada 'The words "in course of employment" refer to the time, place and circumstances under which the accident takes place.' *Gellately v Newfoundland (Workers' Compensation Appeal Tribunal)* (1995) 126 DLR (4th) 530 at 534, Nfld CA, per Cameron JA

COURSE OF JUSTICE

Canada [An accused was charged with obstructing the course of justice by statements made during an investigation by the Law Society into allegations of misconduct.] '… "the course of justice" must include the investigatory stage.

'It follows that the phrase "the course of justice", as it appears in s 139(2), is not limited to existing or proposed judicial proceedings. Rather, it must include all those proceedings that fall within the definition of "judicial proceeding" set out in s 118 [of the *Criminal Code*, RSC 1985].' *R v Wijesinha* (1995) 127 DLR (4th) 242 at 252, 255, SCC, per Cory J

New Zealand [Crimes Act 1961, s 116.] 'First, the issue is the meaning of the statutory expression, the course of justice. For the reasons already given we consider that the term should properly be given a broad interpretation. It may be noted that elsewhere in the Crimes Act 1961 (see ss 108 and 110) the term "judicial proceeding" is used. The expression "the course of justice" clearly is broader and we regard the employment of another expression in close adjacent sections as a matter properly to be taken into account … it is necessary to consider the particular function, bearing in mind that the essence of the offence is an agreement to do some act which has a tendency and is intended to pervert the administration of public justice.' *R v Machirus* [1996] 3 NZLR 404 at 412, CA, per cur

COURSE OF SHIP

[The Collision Regulations 1965 have been revoked. See now the Merchant Shipping (Distress Signals and Prevention of Collisions) Regulations 1993, SI 1983/708, Sch 1, r 34 ('manoeuvring as required or authorised by these Rules').]

COURT

Australia [Section 13 of the Appeal Costs Act (1964) (Vic) empowers the court to grant an indemnity certificate where an appeal against the decision of a 'court' on a question of law succeeds. The word 'court' is defined by s 2 of the Act to include '… the Industrial Relations Commission in court session and any board or other body from whose decision there is an appeal to a superior court on a question of law …'] 'The word "court", as defined in s 2 of the Appeal Costs Act, is not confined to a court of law: a "board or other body" of the kind referred to in the definition may very well not be a court of law. Unless, however, the decision which is the subject of the appeal is that of the Industrial Relations Commission in court session or that of a board or other body of the kind

referred to in the definition, I consider that, in order to be the "decision of a court" for the purposes of s 13(1), it must be that of a court recognisable as a court of law: cf *Royal Aquarium and Summer and Winter Garden Society Ltd v Parkinson* [1982] 1 QB 431 at 446–7. In my opinion an award of an arbitrator under the Retail Tenancies Act (1986) Vic is not in that category. For one thing, the structure of Pt 3 of the Retail Tenancies Act recognises an antithesis between an arbitration and a proceeding in a court of law: s 21(4) goes so far as to say that a dispute which is capable of being referred to arbitration under the section is not justiciable in any court. That alone suggests strongly that an award in such an arbitration is not to be equated to the decision of a court.' *Deneys v Delafotis* [1992] 2 VR 701 at 704, per Tadgell J

COURT-MARTIAL

[For 41 Halsbury's Laws (4th edn) para 479 see now 2(2) Halsbury's Laws (4th edn) (Reissue) para 480.]

Air force and army courts-martial

[For 41 Halsbury's Laws (4th edn) para 481 see now 2(2) Halsbury's Laws (4th edn) (Reissue) para 482.]

Naval courts-martial

[For 41 Halsbury's Laws (4th edn) paras 445, 446 see now 2(2) Halsbury's Laws (4th edn) (Reissue) paras 448–449.]

COURT OF JUSTICE

Australia [In the context of whether the Queensland Building Tribunal was a 'court of justice' within the (Qld) Defamation Act 1989, ss 13 and 14.] 'As noted above the Act uses the expression "court of justice" in three different contexts. All of the parties accepted that the expression was used consistently. At common law the three contexts were respectively covered by the defences of absolute privilege, qualified privilege and fair comment. Fair comment was permissible on any matter of public interest, and this included "all political, legal, and ecclesiastical matters". There was no reason for a distinction to be drawn between courts and tribunals in this context. It was otherwise in relation to privilege. The existence of court proceedings was a factor used in the identification of occasions of both absolute and qualified privilege. The defendants submitted that the cases on absolute privilege were relevant in deciding the present matter. By the late nineteenth century it had been settled that no action lay for defamatory statements made in the course of a judicial proceeding before any court of competent jurisdiction; such statements attracted absolute privilege. That was said to have been established in *R v Skinner* [(1772) Lofft. 55, 98 ER 529; cf Cutler v Dixon (1585) 4 Co Rep. 14b, 76 ER 886] over 100 years earlier. In parallel with this a series of cases had established that a fair and accurate report of any proceeding in a court of law was privileged unless the court had prohibited the publication or the subject matter was obscene or blasphemous. However it should be noted that not until 1892 was it unequivocally established that qualified privilege was an available defence in respect of reports of proceedings before magistrates. Until then, the ambit of the defence had been beset by technicalities.

'The nineteenth century was, in short, a period of evolutionary growth of the common law of libel. Cockburn CJ said in 1868:

> Our law of libel has, in many respects, only gradually developed itself into anything like a satisfactory and settled form. The full liberty of public writers to comment on the conduct and motives of public men has only in very recent times been recognized. Comments on government, on ministers and officers of state, on members of both houses of parliament, on judges and other public functionaries, are now made every day, which half a century ago would have been the subject of actions or ex officio informations, and would have brought down fine and imprisonment on publishers and authors. Yet who can doubt that the public are gainers by the change, and that, though injustice may often be done, and though public men may often have to smart under the keen sense of wrong inflicted by hostile criticism, the nation profits by public opinion being thus freely brought to bear on the discharge of public duties? Again, the recognition of the right to publish the proceedings of courts of justice has been of modern growth. Till a comparatively recent time the sanction of the judges was thought necessary even for the publication of the decisions of the courts upon points of law.

'That evolution continued throughout the balance of the century.

'The question whether privilege extended to any body which was not a court in the strict sense seems to have first attracted consideration in depth in the celebrated case of *Dawkins v Lord Rokeby*. Lieutenant-Colonel Dawkins of the First Battalion, the Coldstream Guards, sued Lieutenant-General Lord Rokeby, his brigade commander, for libel. The libel was contained in statements made orally, and substantially repeated in a document handed by the defendant, to a military court of inquiry convened to investigate allegations previously made by the plaintiff against his superior officers. The regulations governing the assembly of such a court provided that its function was to assist the convening officer in arriving at a correct conclusion on any subject; that it had no relevant power to administer an oath nor to compel the attendance of non-military witnesses; and that "a court of inquiry is not to be considered in any light as a judicial body." The defendant had attended and given evidence under military compulsion, but had handed the document to the inquiry on his own initiative. The plaintiff alleged express malice.

'At first instance Blackburn J directed the jury to return a verdict for the defendant on the ground that

> as a matter of law, the action would not lie, if the verbal and written statements were made by the defendant, being a military man, in the course of a military inquiry in relation to the conduct of the plaintiff being a military man, and with reference to the subject of that inquiry, even though the plaintiff should prove that the defendant had acted malá fide and with actual malice and without any reasonable and probable cause, and with a knowledge that the statements so made and handed in by him were false.

'The appeal to the Court of Exchequer Chamber was decided by Kelly CB, Martin, Bramwell, Channell, Piggott and Cleasby BB, and Byles, Keating, Brett and Grove JJ. They unanimously dismissed the appeal. Three grounds were advanced for reaching that decision: first, that a witness at a court of inquiry was protected by absolute privilege to the same extent as if he were a witness in any of the ordinary courts; second, that the entire proceeding before the court of inquiry attracted Crown privilege and could not be produced or read in evidence at any trial at law; and third, that the whole question involved matters of military discipline and military duty alone and was not therefore cognisable in a court of law. In the course of dealing with the first ground, Kelly CB wrote (for all the court):

> The authorities are clear, uniform and conclusive, that no action of libel or slander lies, whether against judges, counsel, witnesses parties, for words written or spoken in the ordinary course of any proceeding before any court or tribunal recognised by law.

'It was said that the principle which pervaded and governed "the numberless decisions" to that effect had been established by cases to which reference was made. In fact, none of the cases referred to mentioned the position of a tribunal. After discussing the plaintiff's argument that a court of inquiry was not a court of justice, the court observed:

> There is, therefore, no sound reason or principle upon which such a witness, called upon to give evidence in such a court, should not be entitled to the same protection and immunity as any other witness in any of the courts of law or equity in Westminster Hall.

'Colonel Dawkins appealed to the House of Lords. In a procedure which seems extraordinary to modern eyes, the House summoned a number of judges. Those recorded in the authorised report as attending the appeal were Kelly CB, Pollock B and Mellor, Brett and Grove JJ, three of whom had sat in the court below. Asked by the House whether the ruling at first instance was right in law, the judges unsurprisingly answered in the affirmative. They said:

> A long series of decisions has settled that no action will lie against a witness for what he says or writes in giving evidence before a Court of Justice ... The authorities, as regards witnesses in the ordinary Courts of Justice, are numerous and uniform. In the present case, it appears in the bill of exceptions that the words and writing complained of were published by the Defendant, a military man, bound to appear and give testimony before a Court of Inquiry. All that he said and wrote had reference to that inquiry; and we can see no reason why public policy should not equally prevent an action being brought against such a witness as against one giving evidence in an ordinary Court of Justice.

'It will be observed that that opinion does not refer to the position of a tribunal and relates existing decisions only to witnesses before "a court of justice". The extension of privilege to witnesses before a court of inquiry is justified only by public policy.

'The House of Lords unanimously dismissed the appeal. Lord Cairns LC gave the leading speech, with which all others participating agreed. After referring in some detail to the reasons given at first instance (particularly the passages quoted above focusing on the position of the parties as military men), he said:

> My Lords, I think it is of great importance that your Lordships should bear in mind these precise expressions which I have now read, because I feel sure that your Lordships would not desire your decision upon the present occasion to go farther than the circumstances of this particular case would warrant. The leading facts which are put in prominence by the learned Judge are these: The statements were made by the Defendant, who was a military man, the inquiry was a military inquiry, the statements were made in relation to the conduct of the Plaintiff as a military man, and were made with reference to the subject of that inquiry.

'Adopting "the expressions of the learned Judges with regard to what I take to be the settled law as to the protection of witnesses in judicial proceedings" he held that

> upon all principles, and certainly upon all considerations of convenience and of public policy, the same protection which is extended to a witness in a judicial proceeding who has been examined on oath ought to be extended, and must be extended, to a military man who is called before a Court of Inquiry of this kind for the purpose of testifying there upon a matter of military discipline connected with the army.

'He did not refer to tribunals, nor did he approve the reference to them in the judgment of Kelly CB in Court of Exchequer Chamber. The judgment of that court was upheld, but with respect, I cannot agree that Kelly CB's opinion was, at least in this respect, affirmed, nor that the decision of the House of Lords established the proposition that absolute privilege applied to evidence given to tribunals which, although not courts of justice, act in a manner similar to that in which courts of justice act. That simply was not part of the ratio decidendi of the decision of the Court of Exchequer Chamber. No dictum to that effect was approved.

'Almost a year later a similar conclusion was reached by a Full Court of the Supreme Court of New South Wales. The reasoning of that court referred only to the military status of the parties. It did not suggest that it was applying some wider doctrine, nor did it refer to the position of tribunals generally.

'To lawyers of the late nineteenth century it must have seemed that *Dawkins v Lord Rokeby* had created a limited and very special extension of what amounted to a privileged occasion. The leading author of the day did not see it as having any application outside the military context in which it was set, an analysis which was unchanged as late as 1906. As will appear, that was subsequently the analysis of a number of judges. So, in my view, it must have seemed to Sir Samuel Griffith in 1889 when he introduced The Defamation Law of Queensland in Parliament. It is legitimate to refer to his second reading speech both as an historical source and as an aid to the interpretation of an ambiguous or obscure provision. That speech makes it clear that ss 11, 13(1)(c) and 14(1)(d) were, subject to an irrelevant exception, intended to reflect the existing law. It provides no foundation for interpreting "court of justice" to refer to anything other than one of the ordinary courts of the judicature.

'When Sir Samuel Griffith made his second reading speech he was, I assume, unaware of the judgment of the English Court of Appeal in *Allbut v General Council of Medical Education and Registration* (1889) 23 QBD 400, delivered only 13 days earlier. There the Court of Appeal held that the publication of the minutes of the defendant containing a statement that the plaintiff's name had been removed from the register of medical practitioners on the ground that he had been guilty of infamous conduct in a professional respect attracted qualified privilege. Characterising the minutes as a report, the court wrote:

> It would be stating the rule to broadly, in our opinion, if it was held, that, to justify the publication of proceedings such as these, the proceedings must be directly judicial, or had in a court of justice. We can find the law nowhere so broadly stated, nor do we think that in these days it would be so laid down. The court must adapt the law to the necessary condition of society, and must from time to time apply, as best it can, what it thinks is the good sense of rules which exist to cases which have not been positively decided to come within them.

'There was no mention of *Dawkins v Lord Rokeby*, even by analogy, which suggests it was not perceived as anything other than a case dealing with the special position of military courts of inquiry.

'The subsequent development of the law relating to absolute privilege provides a case study in the common law method. *Royal Aquarium and Summer and Winter Gardens Society Ltd v Parkinson* [1892] 1 QB 431 was decided in 1892. Relying on *Dawkins v Lord Rokeby*, the defendant submitted he was "entitled to absolute immunity from action in respect of anything said by him while performing his duty as a member of the county council at a meeting for considering applications for licences [for music and dancing]." Not surprisingly, the Court of Appeal unanimously rejected that submission. What is perhaps surprising is that the judges focused on the dictum of Kelly CB in the Court of Exchequer Chamber, rather than the speeches in the House of Lords. It will be recalled that the reference in that dictum to tribunals was not repeated in the judges' advice tendered by Kelly CB to their Lordships, nor in their Lordships' speeches. Lord Esher MR wrote:

> It is true that, in respect of statements made in the course of proceedings before a Court of justice, whether by judge, or counsel, or witnesses, there is an absolute immunity from liability to an action. The ground of that rule is public policy. It is applicable to all kinds of Courts of justice; but the doctrine has been carried further; and it seems that this immunity applies wherever there is an authorized inquiry which, though not before a Court of justice, is before a tribunal which has similar attributes. In the case of *Dawkins v Lord Rokeby* the doctrine was extended to a military Court of inquiry. It was so extended on the ground that the case was one of an authorized inquiry before a tribunal acting judicially, that is to say, in a manner as nearly as possible similar to that in which a Court of justice acts in respect of an inquiry before it. This doctrine has never been extended further than to Courts of justice and tribunals acting in a manner similar to that in which such Courts act.

'The expression "court of justice" seems clearly to refer to the ordinary courts and to be contrasted with tribunals.

'Fry LJ took a different view:

The largest statement of this immunity is that contained in the judgment of the Exchequer Chamber in *Dawkins v Lord Rokeby*, where it is said that "the authorities are clear, uniform, and conclusive that no action of libel or slander lies, whether against judges, counsel, witnesses, or parties, for words written or spoken in the ordinary course of any proceeding before any court or tribunal recognised by law." I accept that proposition with this qualification. I doubt whether the word "tribunal" does not really rather embarrass the matter; because that word has not, like the word "court," an ascertainable meaning in English law. Moreover, the judgment of the Exchequer Chamber appears to me to proceed upon the hypothesis that the word is really equivalent to the word "court," because it proceeds to inquire into the nature of the particular Court there in question, and comes to the conclusion that a military Court of inquiry, "though not a Court of record, nor a Court of law, nor coming within the ordinary definition of a Court of justice, is nevertheless a Court duly and legally constituted and recognised in the articles of war and many Acts of Parliament".

'Lopes LJ expressed a view similar to that of Fry LJ:

This "absolute privilege" has been conceded on the grounds of public policy to insure freedom of speech where it is essential that freedom of speech should exist, and with the knowledge that Courts of justice are presided over by those who from their high character are not likely to abuse the privilege, and who have the power and ought to have the will to check any abuse of it by those who appear before them. It is, however, a privilege which ought not to be extended. It belongs, in my opinion, to Courts recognised by law, and to such Courts only. It was contended that the so confining the absolute privilege was contrary to the decision of *Dawkins v Lord Rokeby*. That contention cannot be supported. The foundation of the decision is that the Court of inquiry in that case was a tribunal constituted, sanctioned, and recognised by law. Kelly CB says: "A Court of inquiry, though not a Court of record, nor a Court of law, nor coming within the ordinary definition of a Court of justice, is nevertheless a Court duly and legally constituted, and recognised in the Articles of War and many Acts of Parliament."

Dawkins v Lord Rokeby, therefore, forms no exception to the general rule which I have stated.

'In those passages both the Master of the Rolls and Lopes LJ used the expression "court of justice" to refer to the traditional courts, not to tribunals.

'Although the Master of the Rolls was in a minority on the question of the extension of privilege to tribunals, it was not long before his view prevailed. The passage quoted above was cited by Collins MR in *Barratt v Kearns* as sufficient to justify a conclusion that a tribunal constituted by a statutory commission issued by a bishop to inquire into the conduct of a vicar attracted absolute privilege. He approached the question by examining the relevant statute and deciding whether the particular tribunal answered Lord Esher's test. Cozens-Hardy LJ reached the same conclusion in reliance on *Dawkins v Lord Rokeby*. By 1918 the matter was regarded as settled. In a case involving the question whether statements made before a local military tribunal constituted under wartime regulations were absolutely privileged, Sankey J said:

A number of cases have been cited, but in my opinion there cannot be any controversy upon the principle of law which is applicable to the present case. That principle I conceive to be this, that where a tribunal is a Court of justice, or a body acting in a manner similar to that in which a Court of justice acts, any statement made by a member thereof is absolutely privileged and no action can be brought thereon.

'He referred to *Dawkins v Lord Rokeby*, but only to the judgment of Kelly CB in the Court of Exchequer Chamber.

'The common law position has continued to be developed gradually in a long series of cases since that time. At least in part the floodgates predictions advanced by Fry LJ in *Royal Aquarium and Summer and Winter Gardens Society v Parkinson* [1892] 1 QB 431 at p 447 have come to pass. It is unnecessary to refer to the cases. They are material to the second question posed above, but not to the question presently under consideration. Today, even administrative tribunals may attract absolute privilege under common law, provided they have a duty to act quasi-judicially. It is in my opinion clear that the application of the defences of privilege to tribunals was an extension of the common law, and that it occurred after 1889. In 1934 Lord Atkin said:

The law as to judicial privilege has in process of time developed. Originally it was intended for the protection of judges sitting in recognized courts of justice established as such. The object no doubt was that judges might exercise their functions free from any danger that they might be called to account for any words spoken as judges. The doctrine has been extended to tribunals exercising functions equivalent to those of an established court of justice. In their Lordships' opinion the law on the subject was accurately stated by Lord Esher in [part of the passage quoted above]

'That extension occurred after 1889.

'The subsequent enthusiasm for Kelly CB's dictum is best explained by the desire of subsequent judges to keep the common law in line with social conditions, particularly the multiplicity of tribunals created by statute. It has sometimes been suggested that the dictum is entitled to particular weight because of the number and identity of the judges who joined in the reasons. Any force which that suggestion might hold is however dispelled when it is realised that in another important respect, the decision has met with disfavour. It will be recalled that the third ground for the decision of the Court of Exchequer Chamber was that the whole question involved matters of military discipline and military duty alone and was not therefore cognisable in a court of law. The correctness of that ground, described by Kelly CB as "another and a higher ground" than the others, has been left open by the House of Lords and rejected by the High Court of Australia.

'In my judgment the expression "court of justice" was understood in 1889 in the context of the law of defamation to mean only a court in the ordinary hierarchy of courts in the judicature. That is the sense in which it is used in the Defamation Act 1889.

'Further support for this view, albeit slight, is to be found in the enactment by the Parliament of specific provisions conferring protection upon tribunals which would, if the defendants' arguments were correct, attract protection under s 11 of the Act. Five provisions in particular are worth noting: the Misconduct Tribunals Act 1997, s 30; the Health Practitioners (Professional Standards) Act 1999, s 387; the Industrial Relations Act 1999, s 337; the Mental Health Act 2000, ss 418 and 477; and, of particular relevance in the present case, ss 19 and 82 of the Queensland Building Tribunal Act 2000. For reasons which are not immediately obvious, all but the last of these Acts adopt the language of the common law by conferring on nominated persons in cases to which they apply "a

defence of absolute privilege" in a proceeding for defamation. There are other acts in which similar language is used without limitation to proceedings for defamation so perhaps the intention was to attract the wider concept of absolute immunity referred to by Gummow J in *Mann v O'Neill*.' *Jackson-Knaggs v Queensland Building Services Authority and Anor* [2004] QSC 289 at [13]–[30], per Fryberg J; BC200405908

COVENANT

[For 27 Halsbury's Laws (4th edn) para 320 see now 27(1) Halsbury's Laws (4th edn) (Reissue) para 107.]

For freedom from incumbrances

[For 42 Halsbury's Laws (4th edn) para 355 see now 42 Halsbury's Laws (4th edn) (Reissue) para 346.]

For further assurance

[For 42 Halsbury's Laws (4th edn) para 356 see now 42 Halsbury's Laws (4th edn) (Reissue) para 347.]

For quiet enjoyment

[For 42 Halsbury's Laws (4th edn) para 354 see now 42 Halsbury's Laws (4th edn) (Reissue) para 345.]

For right to convey

[For 42 Halsbury's Laws (4th edn) para 352 see now 42 Halsbury's Laws (4th edn) (Reissue) para 343.]

COVENANT OR STIPULATION

Australia [Section 261(1) of the Income Tax Assessment Act 1936 (Cth) provides: 'A covenant or stipulation in a mortgage, which has or purports to have the purpose or effect of imposing on the mortgagor the obligation of paying income tax on the interest to be paid under the mortgage … shall be absolutely void.'] 'The word "stipulation" had a technical meaning in Roman law and in the Admiralty Courts, but long ago assumed the more common meaning of anything which forms a material provision of an agreement [Bouvier's Law Dictionary, 1866, Vol 2, p 549]. In *Re Jarvis and Burgess' Contract*, Lowe J used the word to refer generally to a promise [[1932] VLR 1 at 3]. The word "covenant", however, retains the strict legal meaning of a promise under seal, although in general legal parlance it is used to denote any promise, whether contained in a deed or not [*Hayne v Cummings* (1864) 16 CBNS 421 at 426–7; 143 ER 1191 at 1194]. To this extent, the meanings of the two words in s 261(1) overlap. *David Securities Pty Ltd v Commonwealth Bank of Australia* (1992) 109 ALR 57 at 64–65, per Mason CJ, Deane, Toohey, Gaudron and McHugh JJ

CREAM

[The Food Act 1984 is largely repealed. The definition is re-enacted in the Food Protection Act 1990, s 53(1).]

CREDIBILITY

New Zealand 'Convictions may "affect credibility" not only when they are convictions for dishonesty but also where they are convictions which by their nature would bear on the question whether or not the witnesses' evidence would be accepted on the issues to which the witness will be testifying.' *Police v Wilson* [1991] 2 NZLR 492 at 497, per Thorp J

CREDIT

Obtaining of

Australia 'It seems that the word "credit" is not specifically a technical legal term and judges have gone to dictionaries and general sources to provide a meaning: see e.g. Lord Coleridge CJ in *Peters* (1886) 16 QBD 636 at 641 quoting Webster's Dictionary, a "transfer of goods in confidence of future payment". Kitto J refers to this in *Tilley v Official Receiver in Bankruptcy* [(1960) 103 CLR 529 at 535]. Credit is obtained when, with the assent of the creditor and at the behest of the debtor, a debt remains for a time unpaid or, it may be suggested, when goods or services are supplied "in confidence of future payment" being made for them, that is "without insisting on prepayment or upon interchangeable payment" and "relying on the readiness and ability of the (bankrupt) to pay": *Jones* [1898] 1 QB 119 at 125 referred to by Kitto J in *Tilley* at 534. Credit can be obtained when payment otherwise due for goods or services is expressly deferred by consent but there need not be an express arrangement to postpone a payment which would otherwise be due such as would be the case when goods are delivered and the property

in them is passed by delivery: see the majority judgment in *Peters* at 641 and the observations of Kitto J in *Tilley* at 535 where I take his Honour to intend to indicate that credit can be seen to have been given either when liability to pay is postponed or when the discharge of a liability is deferred by consent.' *R v Brown* (1989) 46 A Crim R 28 at 30–31, per Macrossan CJ

CREDIT ADVANCED

Canada 'As a first step, it is necessary to determine whether the relationship between Consumers' Gas and its customers involves any advancement of credit within the meaning of s 347. Although s 347 is not confined to loan-sharking, in general the section arises in transactions which involve an advance of money in some form, whether in a conventional loan, a mortgage, a commercial financing agreement or otherwise. This case presents a more unusual situation, since it is clear that Consumers' Gas does not actually lend any money to its customers.

'In keeping with the thrust of the section in general, "credit advanced" is broadly defined in s 347(2):

> "credit advanced" means the aggregate of the money and the monetary value of any goods, services or benefits actually advanced or to be advanced under an agreement or arrangement minus the aggregate of any required deposit balance and any fee, fine, penalty, commission and other similar charge or expense directly or indirectly incurred under the original or any collateral agreement or arrangement;

Notably, this definition encompasses not only "the money" advanced under an agreement or arrangement, but also "the monetary value of any goods, services or benefits" which may be so advanced. The scope of s 347 therefore is not confined exclusively to loans of money. The respondent submits, however, that the reach of s 347 is limited to cases in which at least some money has been advanced. This argument is based on a grammatical analysis of s 347(2), since "money" is preceded by the definite article "the", whereas the phrase "goods, services or benefits" is modified by the indefinite article "any". Both the motions judge and the Court of Appeal rejected that contention as overly formalistic, and I agree. Section 347 applies to arrangements involving the monetary value of goods, services or benefits even in the absence of an outright advance of money.

'The most plausible interpretation of s 347(2) is that an "advance" of "the monetary value of any goods, services or benefits" means a deferral of payment for such items. A debt is deferred — and credit extended — when an agreement or arrangement permits a debtor to pay later than the time at which payment would otherwise have been due.' *Garland v Consumers' Gas Co* [1998] 3 SCR 112 at 133–134, per Major J

CREDITED

[The Theft Act 1968 s 15A provides that:
'(1) A person is guilty of an offence if by any deception he dishonestly obtains a money transfer for himself or another.
(2) A money transfer occurs when—(a) a debit is made to one account, (b) a credit is made to another, and (c) the credit results from the debit or the debit results from the credit.
(3) References to a credit and to a debit are to a credit of an amount of money and to a debit of an amount of money.']

'[14] However, we agree with the senior district judge that a bank account is not credited, for the purposes of s 15A of the 1968 Act, while the bank with which the account is kept maintains a reservation that precludes the account holder from dealing with the funds in question. "Credited", in this context, means credited unconditionally. If Commerzbank had not apparently confirmed the legitimacy of the transfer of funds to the account of Wolpert Consultants Inc, the entry in its bank account would have been reversed by ABN Amro. Until the reservation was removed, the credit to that account was of no practical effect.' *Re Holmes* [2004] EWHC 2020 (Admin), [2005] 1 All ER 490 at [14], per Stanley Burnton J

CREDITOR

[Meaning of 'creditor' for the purposes of the Insolvency Rules 1986, SI 1986/1925, r 1.17(1) and (3).] 'It was argued by Mr Schaw-Miller for the landlords that in relation to company voluntary arrangements the word "creditor" has to be given what he called its "ordinary meaning"; that is, he said, a person entitled to the benefit of a liability presently due, whether ot not quantified by judgment, where there is a liability to pay damages. That does not, of course, cover rent due in the future under an existing lease because, Mr Schaw-Miller submitted, that is a liability which is both future and contingent. I would prefer for my part to

call it "defeasible" by the determination of the lease rather than "contingent", but nothing much turns on that distinction and I need not pursue it. The liability in question is an existing one but payment is only due in the future.

'I do not accept that a liability to future rent is incapable of inclusion as a matter of law in a company voluntary arrangement. My reasons for that conclusion are both general and specific.

...

'For all those reasons, both general and specific, I prefer the construction of the word "creditor" in r 1.17(1), which includesthose entitled to a right to a future payment under an existing valid instrument such as a lease. The argument to the contrary is based on the proposition that the word "creditor" has a natural or ordinary meaning which is narrow and only includes those with presently enforceable claims. Although that is a possible meaning, I do not accept that it is one which must prevail over other possible meanings notwithstanding the many indications to the contrary from the context and the purpose of the legislation.' *Re Cancol Ltd* [1996] 1 All ER 37 at 41, 46, per Knox J

Australia [Section 122(1) of the Bankruptcy Act 1966 (Cth) renders void, inter alia, a payment made in favour of a 'creditor' having the effect of giving that creditor a preference, priority or advantage over other creditors.] 'It is to be noted that the expressions "creditor" and "creditors" in s 122(1) include not only persons to whom a debt is immediately due and payable at the time of the relevant transaction, but also persons who by reason of a then existing liability of the debtor would be entitled to prove in a hypothetical bankruptcy (or winding up) occurring at that time: see *Re Blackpool Motor Car Co Ltd* [1901] 1 Ch 77; *Burgess v Spooner* (1968) 89 WN (Pt 1) 79; cf in a different context *Re R L Child & Co Pty Ltd* (1986) 5 NSWLR 693.' *Spedley Securities Ltd (in liquidation) v Western United Ltd (in liquidation)* (1992) 7 ACSR 271 at 275, per McLelland J

Any contingent or prospective creditor

New Zealand [Section 219 of the Companies Act 1955 requires applicants for an order for winding up to be the company, a majority of the directors of the company, contributories as defined and their successors in title, the Registrar of Companies, and 'any creditor or creditors (including any contingent or prospective creditors)'.] ['Contingent creditor' was defined by Pennycuick J in *Re William Hockley Ltd* [1962] 2 All ER 111 as follows: 'The expression "contingent creditor" is not defined in the Companies Act, 1948, but must, I think, denotes a person towards whom under an existing obligation, the company may or will become subject to a personal liability on the happening of some future event or at some future date.] 'The matter is one of statutory construction. Free from authority, I should find that the definitions of contingent creditor, and of prospective creditor, could not be exactly the same although in many cases creditors will come within both classes. I should not consider it necessary to add to the qualification of "prospective" the requirement of an "existing obligation" or of certainty of a debt becoming due in the future.

'Little difficulty arises over the definition of contingent creditor. With respect I am content to adopt the definition of Pennycuick J ... I see no necessity to attach any notion of certainty of liability to the definition of "prospective creditor". Clearly the word "prospective" requires the future to be considered. The word can be used in many contexts and I have not found dictionary definitions to be helpful. When the classes of contingent creditor and prospective creditor were added to the general class of creditor I do not accept that the intention was merely to include persons to whom a debt was certainly payable but payment was not due until the future. I am of the opinion and I hold that the addition of prospective creditors was intended to include person in respect of whom there is a real prospect of their becoming creditors.' *Re Austral Group Investment Management Ltd* [1993] 2 NZLR 692 at 695, 698–699, per Holland J

CREDITORS

Australia [Section 477(1)(b) of the Corporations Law provides that the liquidator may, inter alia, pay any class of 'creditors' in full.] 'In my opinion "creditors" in s 477(1)(b) does not include persons not entitled to prove in the winding up. The foreign tax debt, being unenforceable in Australia, is not admissible to proof in the winding up (see *Government of India v Taylor* [1955] AC 491), and the foreign administration debts, being liabilities incurred after the winding up order, are also not admissible to proof in the winding up (see *Re Denton Subdivisions Pty Ltd* (*in liq*) (1968) 89 WN (Pt 1) (NSW) 231).' *Re Oygevault Internation BV* (*in liq*) (1984) 14 ACSR 245 at 248, per McLelland CJ in Eq

CREED

Canada ' "Creed" is not defined by the Ontario *Human Rights Code*. No Ontario Board of Inquiry

has determined whether the definition of "creed" encompasses "political belief". However, an Ontario Board of Inquiry has referred to *Webster's New International Dictionary* where the definition of "creed" includes: "sometimes a summary of principles or a set of opinions professed or adhered to in science or politics, or the like": *Rand v Sealy Eastern Ltd* (1982), 3 CHRR D/938 (Ont Bd Inq) at D/942.

'In *Black's Law Dictionary*, 6th edition, 1990, "creed" is defined as "confession or articles of faith, formal declaration of religious belief, any formula or confession of religious faith, and a system of religious belief". Other definitions are as follows:

Creed 1. a set of principles or opinion, esp. as a philosophy of life (his creed is moderation in everything). 2. a. (often the Creed) = Apostles Creed (see Apostle). b. a brief formal summary of Christian doctrine (cf. Nicene Creed, Athanasian Creed). c. the Creed as part of the Mass. [The Concise Oxford Dictionary of Current English (Eighth Edition) (1990) at p 272]

Creed 1. A formal statement of religious belief; confession of faith. 2. An authoritative statement of certain articles of Christian faith that are considered essential; for example, the Apostles' Creed and the Nicene Creed. 3. Any statement or system of belief, principles, or opinions. [Middle English crede, Old English creda, for Latin credo, "I believe." [The Houghton Mifflin Canadian Dictionary of the English Language (1982) at p 311.]

Creed — any formula or confession of religious faith; a system of religious belief, especially as expressed or expressible in a definite statement; sometimes a summary of principles or set of opinions professed or adhered to in science or politics, or the like: as his hopeful creed. [Webster's New International Dictionary (1977) at p 13]

Creed — 1. A form of words setting forth authoritatively and concisely the general belief of the Christian Church, or those articles of belief which are regarded as essential; a brief summary of Christian doctrine: usually and properly applied to the three statements of belief known as the Apostles', Nicene, and Athanasian Creeds (the Creed, without qualification usually = the Apostles' Creed); b. A repetition of the creed, as an act of devotion; c. More generally: A formula or religious belief; a confession of faith, esp. one held as authoritative and binding upon the members of a communion; 2. An accepted or professed system of religious belief; the faith of a community or an individual, esp. as expressed or capable of expression in a definite formula; b. A system of belief in general; a set of opinions on any subject, e.g. politics or science; c. Belief, faith (in reference to a single fact) rare. [The Oxford English Dictionary (Second Edition) (1989) at p 1141.]

Creed — 1. A brief authoritative formula of religious belief; 2. a set of fundamental beliefs; also: a guiding principle. [Webster's Ninth New Collegiate Dictionary (1991) at p 305.]

Creed — 1. A brief formal summary of Christian doctrine, esp. each of those known as the (Apostles') Creed, the Athanasian Creed, and the Nicene Creed; 2. A repetition of the Creed as a act of devotion, esp. as part of the Mass; 3. A System of Religious belief; 4. A set of opinions or principles on any subject, esp. a political philosophy; 5. Belief or confidence in; an article of faith. [*The New Shorter Oxford English Dictionary on Historical Principles* (1993) at p 545.]

...

'Religious belief is a component of the term "creed" as it appears in human rights and labour legislation: per McRuer CJO in *R. v Ontario Labour Relations Board* (1963) 39 DLR (2d) 593 (HCJ). See also *Morra v Metropolitan Separate School Board* (1981) 3 CHRR D/1034 (Ont Bd Inq).

'It is significant that s 5(1) of the *Code* does not enumerate "religion" as a prohibited ground of discrimination. In my view, although the term creed is capable of including a comprehensive set of principles, its ordinary meaning within s 5(1) requires an element of religious belief.

'Even if it can be said that political opinion may constitute creed, there is no evidence that the applicant's views amount to a creed. I am not prepared to find that the applicant's political views, no doubt shared by others in society, amount to a creed merely because the applicant is from Iraq. On the facts in this case, the applicant's submission that political and religious commitments may be so aligned as to constitute "creed" is not established. Whether a political perspective, such as communism, that is made up of a recognizable cohesive belief *system* or structure may constitute a "creed" is not at issue and is not being determined.

In my opinion, mere political opinion is not within the meaning of "creed" in s 5(1) of the *Code*.' *Jazairi v Ontario (Human Rights Commission)* (1997) 146 DLR (4th) 297 at 306–308, Ont Div Ct, per Corbett J

CRIME

See also OFFENCE

[For 11 Halsbury's Laws (4th edn) para 1 see now 11(1) Halsbury's Laws (4th edn) (Reissue) para 1.]

[The Criminal Law Act 1967, s 3 provides that a person 'may use such force as is reasonable in the circumstances in the prevention of crime'.] '[1] My Lords, the immense, perhaps unprecedented, suffering of many people in many countries during the twentieth century had at least one positive result: that it prompted a strong international determination to prevent and prohibit the waging of aggressive war. This determination found expression in the international legal order, and understandably so, since it is states which wage such wars and states that must suppress them. At issue in these appeals is the extent to which, if at all, this international determination is transposed into the domestic legal order of England and Wales.

'[2] There are 20 appellants before the House. All of them committed acts in February or March 2003 which were, or are alleged to have been, criminal offences, unless there was legal justification for what they did or are said to have done. The issue in each appeal concerns this legal justification, which (depending on the charge in question) differs somewhat from case to case. But the common feature of all the appeals, and the feature which makes the cases important, is that they all raise the question whether the crime of aggression, if established in customary international law, is a crime recognised by or forming part of the domestic criminal law of England and Wales. The appellants acted as they did because they wished to impede, obstruct or disrupt the commission of that crime, or what they believed would be the commission of that crime, by Her Majesty's government or the government of the United States against Iraq in the weeks and days before (as we now know) hostilities began. They accordingly contend, or have contended, that they were legally justified in acting as they did. The House is not asked to rule whether, in preparing to make war against Iraq, the United Kingdom or the United States committed the international law crime of aggression, but it must rule whether, if they may have done, that would justify the appellants' otherwise criminal conduct.

...

'[Argument that] "crime" in s 3 of the 1967 Act covers a crime established in customary international law, such as the crime of aggression

'[26] The main object of the 1967 Act was to amend the law of England and Wales by abolishing the distinction between felonies and misdemeanours as recommended by the Criminal Law Revision Committee. Part I of the 1967 Act, headed "Felony and Misdemeanour", includes s 3 and contains provisions governing matters such as arrest, trial and penalties on conviction. Part II abolished a number of obsolete crimes. Part III abolished tortious liability for maintenance and champerty. The focus of the 1967 Act is entirely domestic, and it would seem to me very highly unlikely that Parliament understood "crime" in s 3 as covering crimes recognised in customary international law but not assimilated into our domestic law by any statute or judicial decision. In construing a domestic statute the ordinary practice is to treat "offence", in the absence of an express provision to the contrary, as referring to an offence committed here against a common law or statutory rule: see *R (on the application of Rottman) v Comr of Police for the Metropolis* [2002] UKHL 20 at [67], [2002] 2 All ER 865 at [67], [2002] 2 AC 692. The same approach must apply to "crime". Nothing in the 1967 Act or in the report on which it was based suggests a contrary intention in this case. I cannot, therefore, accept the appellants' submission on this issue.

'[Argument that] alternatively, "crime" in s 3 means a crime in the domestic law of England and Wales, and the crime of aggression is such

'[27] I approach this proposition assuming the correctness of the conclusions already reached, that "crime" in s 3 means a crime in the domestic law of England and Wales and that a crime recognised as such in customary international law (such as the crime of aggression) may, but need not, become part of the domestic law of England and Wales without the need for any domestic statute or judicial decision.

'[28] The lack of any statutory incorporation is not, however, a neutral factor, for two main reasons. The first is that there now exists no power in the courts to create new criminal offences, as decided by a unanimous House in *Knuller (Publishing, Printing and Promotions) Ltd v DPP* [1972] 2 All ER 898, [1973] AC 435. While old common law offences survive until abolished or superseded by statute, new ones are not created. Statute is now the sole source of new criminal offences. The second reason is that when it is sought to give

domestic effect to crimes established in customary international law, the practice is to legislate. Examples may be found in the Geneva Conventions Act 1957 and the Geneva Conventions (Amendment) Act 1995, dealing with breaches of the Geneva Conventions of 1949 and the Additional Protocols of 1977; the Genocide Act 1969, giving effect to the Convention on the Prevention and Punishment of the Crime of Genocide 1948 (Paris, 9 December 1948; TS 58 (1970); Cmnd 4421); the 1988 Act [Criminal Justice Act 1988], s 134, giving effect to the Convention against Torture and Other Cruel, Inhuman or Degrading Treatment or Punishment 1984 (10 December 1984; UN General Assembly Resolution 39/46, Doc A/39/51; Cmnd 9593); the War Crimes Act 1991, giving jurisdiction to try war crimes committed abroad by foreign nationals; the Merchant Shipping and Maritime Security Act 1997, s 26, giving effect to provisions of the United Nations Convention on the Law of the Sea (Montego Bay, 10 December 1982 to 9 December 1984; Misc 11 (1983); Cmnd 8941) relating to piracy; and ss 51 and 52 of the 2001 Act [International Criminal Court Act 2001], giving effect to the Rome Statute by providing for the trial here of persons accused of genocide, crimes against humanity and war crimes, but not, significantly, the crime of aggression. It would be anomalous if the crime of aggression, excluded (obviously deliberately) from the 2001 Act, were to be treated as a domestic crime, since it would not be subject to the constraints (as to the need for the Attorney General's consent, the mode of trial, the requisite mens rea, the liability of secondary parties and maximum penalties) applicable to the crimes which were included.

'[29] These reasons, taken together, are very strong grounds for rejecting the appellants' contention, since they reflect what has become an important democratic principle in this country: that it is for those representing the people of the country in Parliament, not the executive and not the judges, to decide what conduct should be treated as lying so far outside the bounds of what is acceptable in our society as to attract criminal penalties. One would need very compelling reasons for departing from that principle.

'[30] In the present case, involving the crime of aggression, there are compelling reasons for not departing. A charge of aggression, if laid against an individual in a domestic court, would involve determination of his responsibility as a leader but would presuppose commission of the crime by his own state or a foreign state. Thus resolution of the charge would (unless the issue had been decided by the Security Council or some other third party) call for a decision on the culpability in going to war either of Her Majesty's government or a foreign government, or perhaps both if the states had gone to war as allies. But there are well-established rules that the courts will be very slow to review the exercise of prerogative powers in relation to the conduct of foreign affairs and the deployment of the armed services, and very slow to adjudicate upon rights arising out of transactions entered into between sovereign states on the plane of international law. The first of these rules is vouched by authorities such as *Chandler v DPP* [1962] 3 All ER 142 at 147, 150, [1964] AC 763 at 791, 796, *Council of Civil Service Unions v Minister for the Civil Service* [1984] 3 All ER 935 at 942, [1985] AC 374 at 398, *Lord Advocate's Reference (No 1 of 2000)* 2001 SCCR 296 at 318 (para 60) and *R (on the application of Marchiori) v Environment Agency* [2002] EWCA Civ 3 at [38]–[40], [2002] EuLR 225 at [38]–[40]. The second rule is supported by such authorities as *Buttes Gas and Oil Co v Hammer (Nos 2 & 3)* [1981] 3 All ER 616 at 629, [1982] AC 888 at 932, *Maclaine Watson & Co Ltd v Dept of Trade and Industry* [1989] 3 All ER 523 at 544, [1990] 2 AC 418 at 499, *Westland Helicopters Ltd v Arab Organisation for Industrialisation* [1995] 2 All ER 387 at 397, [1995] QB 282 at 292 and *R (on the application of Campaign for Nuclear Disarmament) v Prime Minister of the United Kingdom* [2002] EWHC 2777 (Admin) at [38], [40], [2003] 3 LRC 335 at [38], [40]. In the *Buttes Gas and Oil* case [1981] 3 All ER 616 at 629–630, [1982] AC 888 at 933, Lord Wilberforce cited with approval the words of Fuller CJ in the United States Supreme Court in *Underhill v Hernandez* (1897) 168 US 250 at 252:

> "Every sovereign State is bound to respect the independence of every other sovereign State, and the courts of one country will not sit in judgment on the acts of the government of another done within its own territory. Redress of grievances by reason of such acts must be obtained through the means open to be availed of by sovereign powers as between themselves."

I do not suggest that these rules admit of no exceptions: cases such as *Oppenheimer v Cattermole* [1975] 1 All ER 538, [1976] AC 249 and *Kuwait Airways Corp v Iraqi Airways Co (No 3)* [2002] UKHL 19, [2002] 3 All ER 209, [2002] 2 AC 883 may fairly be seen as exceptions. Nor, in the present context, is the issue one of justiciability, to which many of these authorities were directed. In considering whether the customary international law crime of aggression has been, or should be, tacitly assimilated into our domestic law, it is none the less very relevant not only that Parliament has, so far, refrained from taking this step but also that it would draw the courts into an area which, in the past, they have entered, if at all, with reluctance and the utmost circumspection.

'[31] The potential and readily foreseeable problems which might arise if it were permissible to impede military preparations or action by the existing government in this country on the ground of their unlawfulness would not end there. For a person so acting could, at least arguably, on facts more significant than those relied on here, be said to "be adherent to the King's enemies in his realm, giving to them aid and comfort in the realm, or elsewhere" within the meaning of the Treason Act 1351, or to commit the common law offence of sedition by exciting disaffection against the government or the constitution. It has never been a defence to such a charge that the Crown or the government had committed itself to an unjust or unlawful cause. It would be strange if the same conduct could be both a crime and a defence. The justification relied on by the appellants would also, if legally available, give rise to applications for disclosure which, if allowed, would be likely to result in the discontinuance of any prosecution. As the House observed in *R v H, R v C* [2004] UKHL 3 at [35], [2004] 1 All ER 1269 at [35], [2004] 2 AC 134: "The trial process is not well served if the defence are permitted to make general and unspecified allegations and then seek far-reaching disclosure in the hope that material may turn up to make them good." I am of the clear opinion that the crime of aggression is not a crime in the domestic law of England and Wales within the meaning of s 3 of the 1967 Act.

...

'[36] For these reasons, which are much the same as those given by the Court of Appeal and followed by the Administrative Court, I would answer the certified questions in [4] and [9] above together, as follows: the crime against peace (or crime of aggression) is not capable of being a "crime" within the meaning of s 3 of the 1967 Act or an "offence" within the meaning of s 68(2) of the [Criminal Justice and Public Order Act 1994]. I would accordingly dismiss all the appeals.' *R v Jones; Ayliffe v Director of Public Prosecutions; Swain v Director of Public Prosecutions* [2006] UKHL 16 at [1]–[2], [26]–[31], [36], [2006] 2 All ER 741, per Lord Bingham of Cornhill

CRIME OF VIOLENCE

[A woman was deceived into entering a bigamous marriage. She sought compensation on the grounds that she would never have had a sexual relationship with the man if she had known he was already married, and that he had committed a crime of violence against her.] 'The reclaimer's original contention to the Board was that she had suffered from the crime of bigamy, but bigamy is plainly not a crime of violence ... The crime committed is simply one of fraud. Since there is nothing in the authorities to require any different view, the Board were, in our opinion, quite entitled to consider the particular circumstances of this case and to come to the conclusion that no crime of violence had been committed.' *Gray v Criminal Injuries Compensation Board* 1999 SCLR 191 at 197–198, per Lord Coulsfield (giving the opinion of the court)

[A woman sought criminal injuries compensation on behalf of her daughter, who had been subjected to three separate incidents of indecent exposure. The Board heard evidence in relation to all three incidents and compensation was refused in respect of all three incidents. The Board refused an award on the basis that indecent exposure was not a crime of violence. The woman sought judicial review of the Board's decision.] 'It is in my view clear from the material before me that the Board was correctly invited to consider the nature of the crimes ... It is also clear that the Board made findings as to what happened on each occasion and then asked itself whether what had happened was a crime of violence. The Board thus, in my view, can be seen to have asked itself the correct question, by adopting the approach approved in *Webb* [*R v Criminal Injuries Compensation Board, ex p Webb* [1987] QB 74, [1986] 2 All ER 478, CA] and in *Gray* [*Gray v Criminal Injuries Compensation Board* 1999 SLT 425, 1999 SCLR 191]. The Board thus, in my opinion, committed no error of law. Nor, in my view, could I hold that the Board's conclusion that the second and third incidents did not constitute crimes of violence was one which the Board could not reasonably reach on the material before it ... I am therefore of opinion that the submission that the Board's decision was unreasonable fails.' *Cameron v Criminal Injuries Compensation Board* 1999 SCLR 992 at 1000, 1001, per Lord Macfadyen

CRIMINAL CAUSE OR MATTER

[By the Supreme Court Act 1981, s 18(1)(a), 'No appeal shall lie to the Court of Appeal ... from any judgment of the High Court in any criminal cause or matter'. Restraint orders made under the Criminal Justice Act 1988 (Designated Countries and Territories) Order 1991 to preserve assets for the satisfaction of an external confiscation order were set aside by the High Court. On appeal by the US Government the respondents contended that the Court of Appeal had no jurisdiction because the judgment was in a 'criminal cause or matter'.] 'It is true of course that the 1991 DCO is concerned with the enforcement of foreign confiscation orders, the order being made as a rule by a foreign criminal court ... It is quite clear in my judgment that orders made under these provisions are civil in character and collateral to the criminal regime.' *United States Government v Montgomery* [1999] 1 All ER 84 at 92, CA, per Stuart-Smith LJ; affirmed [2001] UKHL/3, [2001] 1 All ER 815, HL

CRIMINAL PROCEEDINGS

[The question arose whether extradition proceedings before a magistrate under the Extradition Act 1989 were 'criminal proceedings' for the purposes of the Police and Criminal Evidence Act 1984, ss 69, 72.] 'As previously stated, the magistrate hearing extradition proceedings is hearing evidence to decide whether it discloses proof to the standard necessary to "justify the committal for trial of the prisoner if the crime of which he is accused had been committed in England and Wales" (para 7(1) of Sch 1 to the 1989 Act). When sitting in the ordinary way as examining magistrate on a committal for trial, the proceedings are criminal proceedings to which the 1984 Act applies (see *R v King's Lynn Magistrates' Court, ex p Holland* [1993] 2 All ER 377, [1993] 1 WLR 324 and *R v Oxford City Justices, ex p Berry* [1987] 1 All ER 1224, [1988] QB 507).

'... In our view the proceedings before the committing magistrate are properly classed as criminal, having their birth or origin in acts or conduct punishable under the criminal law. They are not in a separate class of their own.' *R v Governor of Brixton Prison, ex p Levin* [1996] 4 All ER 350 at 356, 358, DC, per Beldam LJ; affd [1997] 3 All ER 289, HL

'I am satisfied that for the purposes of s 19 [of the Legal Aid Act 1988], criminal proceedings means only proceedings before a court of the type identified in that section, which are active in the sense that the court reasonably envisages that a further step in the proceedings will take place, not merely that such a step may be taken dependant on the outcome of proceedings which are taking place elsewhere ...' *R v Bow Street Magistrates' Court, ex p Shayler* [1999] 1 All ER 98 at 101, DC, per Kennedy LJ

CRITERIA

Australia [Migration Act 1958 (Cth) s 31(3) provides that Regulations made under the Act 'may prescribe criteria for a visa or visas of a specified class ...'. Clause 3002 of the Migration Regulations (Cth) states that the application must be validly made within 12 months after 'the relevant day'. The appellant claimed that the time limit imposed by cl 3002 is not a 'criterion' within cl 31(3).] 'The case for a wide meaning of s 31(3) ... is also supported by other factors. Firstly, the ordinary meaning of the word "criteria" supports a wide construction. The *Oxford English Dictionary* Second Edition, Vol IV, p 29 defines "criterion" as meaning "a test, principle, rule, canon or standard, by which anything is judged or estimated". The *Macquarie Dictionary*, revised edition at p 437 defines "criterion" as "a standard of judgment or criticism; an established rule or principle for testing anything". These definitions are sufficiently broad to embrace a time limit for the lodging of a visa application.

'[33] Secondly, there is no reason why a requirement ceases to be a test or standard, or a rule or principle for testing, because it allows for a straightforward answer. The act of judging or weighing, in such an instance, may be brief but it is not eliminated. We therefore share with the primary judge the view that it is not a misuse of language to see a time limitation for visa applications as a matter involving an element of judgment and the application of a standard. For example, the time limit specified in cl 3002 cannot be applied in a particular case without ascertaining the "relevant day", a task that may be far from straightforward.' *Pillay v Minister for Immigration and Multicultural Affairs* BC200000295; [2000] FCA 112 at [32], [33], per Carr, Sackville and Nicholson JJ

CROSS-DEMAND

Australia '... In the context of the [Corporations] Law, a context similar to that in s 41(7) of the Bankruptcy Act 1966 (Cth), a cross-demand will include any claim for damages which exists at the time the application to set aside the statutory demand is made, which is for a monetary amount capable of quantification whether or not it arises out of the same transaction or circumstances as the debt to which the statutory demand relates. There can be no doubt that a claim for damages under the Trade Practices Act or for breach of an implied contractual term will satisfy the description of a cross-demand and thus be an off-setting claim, whether or not it could be relied upon as a defence by way of counter-claim or set-off in proceedings on a bill of exchange on which the person claiming damages is liable.' *John Shearer Ltd v Gehl Co* (1995) 18 ACSR 780 at 786, per cur

CROSS-ELASTICITY OF DEMAND

Australia '[The] authorities made it clear that the test of "significant cross-elasticity of demand between the goods" is a market or economic test in conformity with the meaning given in the Glossary of Terms [prepared by the Comptroller-General of Customs] of "cross-elasticity of demand", and not a mechanical or physical test ... The meaning given to "cross-elasticity of demand" in the "glossary of terms" is consistent with the concept in general economics. It is a concept limited to a change in demand for one product which results from the change in price of another where the two producers compete for sales in the same market. The concept does not extend to different markets in which different products compete.' *Polypacific Pty Ltd v Comptroller-General of Customs* (1993) 123 ALR 392 at 407–408, per Northrop J

CRUEL AND UNUSUAL PUNISHMENT

Canada '[1] Does the mandatory weapons prohibition order under s. 109(1)(c) of the Criminal Code, R.S.C. 1985, c. C-46, when imposed upon conviction of the offence of production of cannabis, violate the appellant's right "not to be subjected to any cruel and unusual treatment or punishment" guaranteed by s. 12 of the Canadian Charter of Rights and Freedoms? If so, is the infringement a reasonable limit prescribed by law as can be demonstrably justified in a free and democratic society under s. 1 of the Charter? These are the constitutional questions raised on this appeal.

'[2] Mr. Wiles entered a plea of guilty on two charges of unlawfully producing cannabis, contrary to s. 7(1) of the Controlled Drugs and Substances Act, S.C. 1996, c. 19 ("CDSA"), the second offence having been committed while he was on release in respect of the first. The marihuana grow operation was discovered on the first occasion when the police responded to a 911 call made accidentally by one of Mr. Wiles' daughters. At this time, the police noted that Mr. Wiles possessed six firearms, all properly stored and licensed. The firearms were left in his possession. At sentencing, the Crown sought the mandatory prohibition orders under s. 109(1)(c) of the Criminal Code in addition to the sentence jointly agreed upon by counsel. Under the terms of s. 109, a 10-year minimum prohibition order is mandatory upon first conviction of any one of certain enumerated drug offences (s. 109(2)). Upon subsequent convictions, the prohibition order is for life (s. 109(3)). Mr. Wiles challenged the constitutionality of s. 109(1)(c), alleging that the imposition of the mandatory weapons prohibition orders constitutes "cruel and unusual punishment" in violation of s. 12 of the Charter. The relevant legislative and Charter provisions are annexed.

'[3] The Crown concedes that a weapons prohibition order constitutes a "treatment or punishment" within the meaning of s. 12 of the Charter. In my view, this concession is well made. Although the purpose of the prohibition order is primarily preventative, in taking away the privilege to possess weapons, it may have some punitive effect on the offender. The question then is whether the loss of this privilege upon conviction of the offence of production is "cruel and unusual".

'[4] This Court has dealt with s. 12 on many occasions and there is no controversy on the test that must be met. Treatment or punishment which is disproportionate or "merely excessive" is not "cruel and unusual": *R. v. Smith*, [1987] 1 S.C.R. 1045 at p. 1072, 34 C.C.C. (3d) 97, 40 D.L.R. (4th) 435. The treatment or punishment must be "so excessive as to outrage standards of decency": *Smith*, at p. 1072; *R. v. Goltz*, [1991] 3 S.C.R. 485 at p. 499, 67 C.C.C. (3d) 481; *R. v. Luxton*, [1990] 2 S.C.R. 711 at p. 724, 58 C.C.C. (3d) 449. The court must be satisfied that "the punishment imposed is grossly disproportionate for the offender, such that Canadians would find the punishment abhorrent or intolerable": *R. v. Morrisey*, [2000] 2 S.C.R. 90, 2000 SCC 39, 148 C.C.C. (3d) 1, 191 D.L.R. (4th) 86, at para. 26 (emphasis in original).

'[5] The court must first determine whether the treatment or punishment is grossly disproportionate for the individual offender having regard to all contextual factors. Relevant factors may include: the gravity of the offence, the personal characteristics of the offender, the particular circumstances of the case, the actual effect of the treatment or punishment on the individual, relevant penological goals and sentencing principles, the existence of valid alternatives to the treatment or punishment imposed, and a comparison of punishments imposed for other crimes in the same

jurisdiction: see *Morrisey*, at paras. 27–28. If the treatment or punishment is grossly disproportionate for the individual offender in light of all relevant contextual factors, the court proceeds to determine whether the infringement can be justified under s. 1 of the Charter. If it is not disproportionate for the individual offender, the court must still consider whether the treatment or punishment is disproportionate having regard to reasonable hypotheticals. In *Goltz*, it was made clear that reasonable hypotheticals cannot be "far-fetched or only marginally imaginable" (p. 515). They cannot be "remote or extreme examples" (p. 515). Rather they should consist of examples that "could commonly arise in day-to-day life" (p. 516).' *R v Wiles* (2005) 260 DLR (4th) 459 at [1]–[5], [2005] SCJ No 53 (SCC), per Charron J

CURATIVE APPARATUS

Australia [Section 26 of the Workers Compensation Act 1958 (Vic) defines medical services to include, amongst others, the provision to the worker of curative appliances or apparatus.] 'A "curative appliance or apparatus" should not be interpreted narrowly. An appliance or apparatus which will improve the condition of an incapacitated person is "curative"... The process of dealing with an incapacitated person may involve a continual war with disease, atrophy of the muscles by lack of use, and even psychological decay by reason of lack of something to do. Any apparatus which helps in this way is a curative apparatus. In *Thomas v Ferguson Transformers Pty Ltd* [[1979] 1 NSWLR 216] the court was concerned with a special hydrotherapy pool. After reviewing the meaning of "apparatus" in several judicial contexts, Hutley JA said, at 220: "... they (judicial remarks) do seem to suggest that an apparatus is a mechanical contrivance or used in connection therewith to achieve a particular purpose, but mere structures such as stairways are not."' *G C Wood & Son (Australia) Pty Ltd v Cullen* [1991] 2 VR 214 at 225, per O'Bryan J

CURRENT

[The Social Security Act 1975 has been repealed. The definition is re-enacted, with minor drafting amendments, in the Social Security Contributions and Benefits Act 1992, s 122(1).]

CURRENT LAND VALUE

Canada 'In construing a lease, our first consideration is the language of the lease itself.

Here that language is clear. In a real estate document, "land" usually means "a right to receive a good title in fee simple". See, e.g., *Ball v Gutschenritter*, [1925] SCR 68, at p 71. "Value" means the "fair market value" of the land or, equivalently, the "exchange value" of the land: what a willing buyer would pay for the land in the open market. See, e.g., *Revenue Properties Co v Victoria University* (1993), 101 DLR. (4th) 172 (Ont Div Ct), at p 180. In British Columbia, the *Property Transfer Tax Act*, RSBC 1996, c 378, s 1, the *Assessment Act*, RSBC 1996, c 20, s 19, and the *Expropriation Act*, RSBC 1996, c 125, s 32, all use substantially the same definition. Nothing in the leases at issue here suggests that either "land" or "value" should be assigned any definition other than the generally accepted one. Thus "current land value" means the price a willing buyer would pay for fee simple title to the land.' *Musqueam Indian Band v Glass* (2000) 192 DLR (4th) 385 at 391–392, SCC, per McLachlin J

CURRENT STATE

[Under s 44 of the Road Traffic Act 1988, s 40A of the 1988 Act, which creates the offence of using a vehicle in a dangerous condition, does not apply to vehicles authorised under the Motor Vehicles (Authorisation of Special Types) General Order 1979. Section 2A(2) of the 1988 Act provides that a person is to be regarded as driving dangerously, for the purposes of ss 1 and 2 of the 1988 Act if it would be obvious to a competent and careful driver that driving the vehicle in its 'current state' would be dangerous. At trial for dangerous driving offences, the defendants submitted, inter alia, that as s 44 of the 1988 Act provided that authorisation of a vehicle under the 1979 order exempted those who used the vehicle on the road from prosecution under s 40A, the exemption should also apply to offences under ss 1 and 2 of the 1988 Act as a matter of public policy.] '[30] ... The offence in s 40A is committed where a vehicle is used when "the condition" of the vehicle is such that it involves a danger of injury to any person. Section 2A(2) differs from s 40A in referring to the "current state" of the vehicle rather than its "condition". The decision in *Wood v Milne* [(1987) Times, 27 March, DC] that "condition" includes inherent or manufactured condition was thus made in respect of different words as well as in the context of latent as well as obvious defects. We are left with the position that the draftsman of the 1991 Act of Parliament [the Road Traffic Act 1991] used the word "condition" for the lesser offence in

s 40A but the different phrase "current state" in s 2A(2) for the more serious offence.

'[31] What is the significance of this difference in the statutory language? The matter is not altogether easy, but we have concluded that the term "current state" in s 2A(2) implies a state different from what might be termed the "original" or "manufactured" state. We are conscious that this was not an argument put to the learned recorder. His careful analysis and conclusion was based on the different submissions made to him on behalf of Mr Marchant and Mr Muntz, submissions which, for the reasons we have given, he was right to reject. In reaching our conclusion as to the construction of s 2A, we have taken account of the following factors.

'[32] First, this case comes before us on the assumption that, apart from the possibility of fitting a guard, there was absolutely no criticism that could be made of the condition of the unit for which either defendant had any responsibility at all. Its condition was as it was when it was new and Mr Muntz bought it from a reputable dealer knowing that it was authorised for use on the public highway.

'[33] Secondly, unlike the submission that was made to the learned recorder, this construction of s 2A does not create a blanket exception from ss 1 and 2 of the 1988 Act, as amended, for those responsible for driving an authorised agricultural motor vehicle on public roads. Liability in respect of dangerous driving in its ordinary sense and in respect of a dangerous condition other than the original inherent manufactured condition of a vehicle remains.' *R v Marchant* [2003] EWCA (Crim) 2099 at [30]–[33], [2004] 1 All ER 1187, per Grigson J

CURTILAGE

Australia '...[R]eference was made to the definition in the *Oxford English Dictionary* of "curtilage": "A small court, yard, or piece of ground attached to a dwelling house, and forming one enclosure with it." It was submitted by counsel for the appellants that the judge erred in adopting that definition for Australian conditions. The meaning of the term has been discussed in *Royal Sydney Golf Club v Commissioner of Taxation (Cth)* (1955) 91 CLR 610 at 626–627 and *Milro Pty Ltd v Associated Securities Ltd* (1970) 92 WN (NSW) 173 at 178–180. It can probably be deduced from those cases that the appropriate test is to ask the question, what land actually or supposedly contributes to the enjoyment of the building for the fulfilment of its purposes? The answer to that question would always be dependent upon the particular facts of the case; what constitutes the curtilage of a building would normally be a question of fact to be determined upon the evidence in the particular case. The relevant evidence may well include the nature of the use of the building, and any visual or physical separation of the building and the land immediately and otherwise surrounding it.' *Grasso v Stanthorpe Shire Council* (1996) 91 LGERA 429 at 435, per Williams J

CUSTODY

Australia [Regulation 38 of the Income Tax Regulations (Cth) provides that the address of a person, as described in any record in the 'custody' of the Commissioner, shall be his address for service.] 'Regulation 38 is part of the scheme providing for service by the Commissioner on persons so as to allow the Commissioner to proceed with his obligations under the Act. It seeks to facilitate the service by providing that certain addresses may be used by the Commissioner. In that context, in my view, "custody" is not restricted to those things which are in the control of the Commissioner, but are the subject of legal ownership or right to possession is in others. It extends to those records which are in the control or guardianship of the Commissioner, regardless of who is the owner of those records.' *Sunrise Auto Ltd v Deputy Commissioner of Taxation (Cth)* (1994) 124 ALR 425 at 436, per Spender J

New Zealand [Fisheries Act 1983, s 80.] 'The question is whether custody pursuant to s 80 should be equated with custody, as distinct from possession, as spoken of by Lord Atkin [in *Government of the Republic of Spain v SS "Arantzazu Mendi", The Arantzazu Mendi* [1939] AC 256, HL]. In this respect note must be taken of the full compass of s 80(1). Not only vessels but other property may be seized thereunder. That other property comprises vehicles, fishing gear, implements, appliances, materials, containers and goods or equipment. In the case of such items of property as these, it is difficult to sever the concepts of custody and of possession; in most such cases having custody will necessarily involve having possession.
    'I therefore consider ... the word "custody" in s 80 should not be regarded as a term of art in the strict admiralty law sense referred to by Lord Atkin. It is, in my judgment, a word of wider import than that: see by analogy *Rural Timber Ltd v Hughes* [1989] 3 NZLR 178, 186 in which the Court of

Appeal said that the word "custody" in s 199 of the Summary Proceedings Act 1957 must be interpreted with reasonable liberality to make the section workable.
    'What then are the incidents of custody for the purposes of s 80 of the Fisheries Act 1983? When property is held in the custody of the Crown under s 80(6) the Crown must generally have a right to the physical possession of the property. How else can the Crown effectively hold the property in its custody? In addition the Crown must have the right to decide where and under what conditions the property is to be held.' *Abel Fisheries Ltd v Stuart* [1997] 2 NZLR 87 at 91, per Tipping J

Legal custody

Australia [Letters Patent issued by the Crown authorised the Royal Commissioner to inquire into deaths of aboriginals whilst in police custody.] 'Elements in the lexical meanings of "custody" include the notion of dominance and control of the liberty of the person, and the state of being guarded and watched to prevent escape. To confine the meaning of "custody" to "that state which follows arrest or similar official act", as the first respondents would have it, is, in our opinion, to pay too close a regard to legal forms rather than the substantive character or quality of police activity.' *Eatts v Dawson* (1990) 93 ALR 497 at 510, per Marling and Gummer JJ

Australia 'One of the definitions of "custody" offered by the Macquarie Dictionary is: "3. imprisonment: *He was taken into custody.*" The Macquarie defines "imprison" as follows: "1. to put into or confine in a prison; detain in custody. 2. to shut up as if in prison; hold in restraint." In my opinion, if a person was shut up by a police officer as if in prison or held in restraint by a police officer, that person would be held in "police custody" for the purposes of the Letters Patent.' Ibid at 521, per Beaumont J

Australia 'However, the question is the meaning of "custody", not in the Queensland legislation, but in s 94 of the Migration Act 1958 (Cth), where the full expression is "entitled to be released from ... custody". It is true that, for some purposes, the word "custody" has been given an extended sense: see *Eatts v Dawson* (1990) 21 FCR 166. But, as an ordinary English word, its appropriate meaning refers to imprisonment, not to release upon terms. In the *Oxford English Dictionary*, 2nd edn, vol IV, it is relevantly defined: "The keeping of the officers of justice (for some presumed offence against the law); confinement, imprisonment, durance." ... my conclusion is that s 94 does not treat release upon parole as custody.' *Gray v Minister for Immigration, Local Government and Ethnic Affairs* (1992) 38 FCR 351 at 353, per Burchett J

New Zealand 'Section 199 of the Summary Proceedings Act requires things seized under s 198 to be retained under the custody of a constable, except while being used in evidence or in the custody of any court. The evidence is that the police allowed Ministry of Transport personnel to have for examination materials that had been seized. As with the case of an expert asked to consider material for similar purposes, we regard the Ministry as holding the materials on behalf of and subject to the direction and control of the police, on which view there was no breach of s 199. "Custody" there must be interpreted reasonably liberally to make the section workable.' *Rural Timber Ltd v Hughes* [1989] 3 NZLR 178 at 186, CA, per cur

Of child

[The definition in s 57(1) of the Matrimonial Causes Act 1973 was repealed by Sch 15 to the Children Act 1989 as from 14 October 1991 (SI 1991/828).]

Canada '[19] ...

Section 57 of the [Child and Family Services] Act:

(1) Where the court finds that a child is in need of protection and is satisfied that intervention through a court order is necessary to protect the child in the future, the court shall make one of the following orders, in the child's best interests:
1. That the child be placed with or returned to a parent or another person, subject to the supervision of the society, for a specified period of at least three and not more than twelve months.
2. That the child be made a ward of the society and be placed in its care and custody for a specified period not exceeding twelve months.
3. That the child be made a ward of the Crown, until the wardship is terminated under section 65 or expires under subsection 71(1), and be placed in the care of the society.
4. That the child be made a ward of the society under paragraph 2 for a specified period and then be returned to a parent or another person under paragraph 1, for a period or periods not exceeding an aggregate of twelve months.

(2) In determining which order to make under subsection (1), the court shall ask the parties what efforts the society or another agency or person made to assist the child before intervention under this Part.

(3) The court shall not make an order removing the child from the care of the person who had charge of him or her immediately before intervention under this Part unless the court is satisfied that alternatives that are less disruptive to the child, including non-residential services and the assistance referred to in subsection (2), would be inadequate to protect the child.

(4) Where the court decides that it is necessary to remove the child from the care of the person who had charge of him or her immediately before intervention under this Part, the court shall, before making an order for society or Crown wardship under paragraph 2 or 3 of subsection (1), consider whether it is possible to place the child with a relative, neighbour or other member of the child's community or extended family under paragraph 1 of subsection (1) with the consent of the relative or other person.

...

(9) Where the court finds that a child is in need of protection but is not satisfied that a court order is necessary to protect the child in the future, the court shall order that the child remain with or be returned to the person who had charge of the child immediately before intervention under this Part.

'[20] "Charge", in Black's Law Dictionary, Seventh Edition, states:

... A person or thing entrusted to another's care ...

'[21] "Custody" is defined in Black's Law Dictionary, Seventh Edition, as follows:

The care and control of a thing or person ...

'[22] "Custody" is further defined in the Concise Oxford Dictionary as follows:

Guardianship, care, (parent has custody of child, child is in the custody of father).

'[23] Section 63 of the Child and Family Services Act indicates:

> ... the Crown has the rights and responsibilities of a parent for the purpose of the child's care, custody and control ...

'[24] In my view, the effect of such an order is to remove the care and control of the child from both parents once a finding has been made that the child is a child in need of protection.' *S (JM) v M (FJ)* (2005) 257 DLR (4th) 158 at [19]–[24], [2005] OJ No 3085 (Ont Sup Ct J), per Meehan J

New Zealand '[7] Section 2 of the Children, Young Persons, and Their Families Act defines "custody" and "guardianship" as follows:

> Custody means the right to possession and care of a child or young person.

> Guardianship has the meaning given to it by s 3 of the Guardianship Act 1968 [since 1 July 2004 this has been altered to read "section 15 of the Care of Children Act 2004"]; and guardian has a corresponding meaning:

'[8] Section 3 of the Guardianship Act 1968 provided:

> Guardianship means the custody of the child ... and the right of control over the upbringing of a child, and includes all rights, powers and duties in respect of the person and upbringing of a child ...

'For comparison, to bring the matter up to date, s 15 of the Care of Children Act 2004 provides:

> **15. Guardianship defined** – For the purposes of this Act, guardianship of a child means having (and therefore a guardian of the child has), in relation to the child,–
>   (a) all duties, powers, rights, and responsibilities that a parent of the child has in relation to the upbringing of the child:
>   (b) every duty, power, right, and responsibility that is vested in the guardian of a child by any enactment:
>   (c) every duty, power, right, and responsibility that, immediately before the commencement, on 1 January 1970, of the Guardianship Act 1968, was vested in a sole guardian of a child by an enactment or rule of law.

...

'[12] By their definitions the bundle of rights known as "custody" falls within the bundle of rights known as "guardianship". Custody is normally an incident of guardianship: the effect of a custody order is to pluck out that smaller bundle of rights and allocate them to the custodian.

'[13] A custodian is not necessarily a guardian. That is the case here, where the Chief Executive is C's custodian, but not one of his guardians.' *Chief Executive of Department of Child, Youth and Family v CM* [2006] NZFLR 289 at [7]–[8], [12]–[13], per Judge J G Adams

Custody or control

Australia [An insurance policy provided for indemnity against damage to property arising from an accident caused by an insured vehicle, but excluded damage done to property in the 'custody or control' of the insured.] '... it may be concluded first, that both custody and control refer not only to legal custody and control but also to actual or de facto custody or control. Secondly, it may be said that the custody or control need not be exclusive of some other person, that is to say, that more than one person may have, at any given point of time, custody or control of the item in question. Thirdly, while control clearly relates to dominion or power over the item ultimately damaged, the exclusion clause will not be attracted where the control is merely in relation to that item but not over it. Nor will the exclusion clause be attracted if the control is of a part only but not the whole of the item.' *Botany Fork v Crane Hire Pty Ltd v New Zealand Insurance Co Ltd* (1993) 44 FCR 27 at 34; 116 ALR 473 at 480, per cur

CUSTOM

[For 12 Halsbury's Laws (4th edn) paras 401, 402 see now 12(1) Halsbury's Laws (4th edn) (Reissue) paras 601, 606.]

CUSTOMS DUTIES

[For 12 Halsbury's Laws (4th edn) para 501 see now 12(2) Halsbury's Laws (4th edn) (Reissue) para1.]

CYCLE

[The Road Traffic Act 1972 has been repealed. See now the Road Traffic Act 1988, s 192(1).]

CY-PRES

Application to charity

[The Charities Act 1960 is largely repealed. See now Part IV of the Charities Act 1993.]

[For 5 Halsbury's Laws (4th edn) para 696 see now 5(2) Halsbury's Laws (4th edn) (2001 Reissue) para 201.]

Application to power of appointment

[For 36 Halsbury's Laws (4th edn) para 874 see now 36(2) Halsbury's Laws (4th edn) (Reissue) para 275.]

D

DAILY

[For 45 Halsbury's Laws (4th edn) para 1113 see now 45(2) Halsbury's Laws (4th edn) (Reissue) para 213.]

Australia [Instrument No 83 of 1995, issued by the Repatriation Medical Authority, sets out a number of factors that could support a hypothesis connecting the applicant's hypertension with his operational service in the Royal Australian Navy, one of which is 'psychoactive substance abuse involving daily consumption of alcohol'] 'Prima facie the word "daily" means "every day"; *London County Council v South Metropolitan Gas Co* [1903] 2 Ch 532 per Joyce J at 537–8. However, as Barry J commented in *Foster v Howard* [1949] VLR 311 at 311, it is an adjective "the precise meaning of which is to be ascertained from the context in which it is used and particularly the substantive which it qualifies". In my opinion, the precision which the term conveys will differ depending on whether it is used prescriptively or descriptively. A doctor's instructions that medicine is to be taken daily may easily be understood as meaning every day. However, we would not generally cavil at the description of a doctor's daily visits to a hospital if he did not generally go on Sundays. We would still regard it as accurate to describe an athlete as training daily even though it turned out that she missed a number of days a year. I do not accept that the phrase, "daily consumption of alcohol" in Instrument 83 could only apply to a veteran who drank every day without exception. Even if that meaning were to be accepted, there would still be the problem of the period over which the "daily" consumption had to be proved. It is neither necessary nor possible to give here a precise meaning to the term. However, for the purposes of formulating a hypothesis to be tested against … Instrument 83, I am satisfied that the qualification, "just about daily", is sufficient for the hypothetical facts to fit the description of daily consumption in … Instrument 83.' *Gorton v Repatriation Commission* BC200101101; [2001] FCA 286 at [27], per Stone J

DAIRY

[The Food Act 1984 is largely repealed. The definition is not re-enacted in the Food Safety Act 1990.]

DAMAGE

[Section 1(1) of the Civil Liability (Contribution) Act 1978 provides that any person liable in respect of any damage suffered by another person may recover contribution from any other person in respect of the same damage. By s 6(1) a person is liable in respect of any damage for the purposes of the Act if the person who suffered it is entitled to recover compensation from him in respect of that damage, whatever the legal basis of his liability.] 'In my judgment, despite the distinction between a claim for restitution and one for damages, each may be a claim for compensation for damage under ss 1(1) and 6(1) of the 1978 Act. The difference between asking for a particular sum of money back or for an equivalent sum of money for the damage suffered because of the withholding of it is immaterial in this statutory context, which is concerned with "compensation" for "damage".' *Friends' Provident Life Office v Hillier Parker May & Rowden (a firm) (Estates and General plc and ors, third parties)* [1995] 4 All ER 260 at 272, CA, per Auld LJ

Australia 'Certain principles may be deduced from the authorities. A clear distinction must be drawn between "injury" and "damage". "Damage" in the rule is to be contrasted with the element necessary to complete a cause of action. Concisely stated, "damage" is used in the rule to encompass the disadvantage or detriment suffered by the plaintiff as a result of the tortious act or omission of the putative defendant. Accordingly it has a much wider meaning than "injury".' *Darrell Lea Chocolate Shops Pty Ltd v Spanish-Polish Shipping Co Inc (The 'Katowice II')* (1990) 25 NSWLR 568 at 576–577, per Carruthers J

Caused by ship

[For 43 Halsbury's Laws (4th edn) para 876 see now 43(1) Halsbury's Laws (4th edn) (Reissue) para 793 et seq.]

Pecuniary damage

[For 12 Halsbury's Laws (4th edn) para 1110 see now 12(1) Halsbury's Laws (4th edn) (Reissue) para 809.]

DAMAGES

[For 12 Halsbury's Laws (4th edn) para 1102 see now 12(1) Halsbury's Laws (4th edn) (Reissue) para 802.]

[Following a failed sterilisation operation, the plaintiff sued the health authority for damages for economic loss in respect of her subsequent conception and the birth of a healthy child.] 'The issue … is whether her action is for damages that "consist of or include damages in respect of personal injuries" within the meaning of s 11(1) of the Limitation Act 1980…

'… In my view, the failure of the attempt to sterilise Mrs Walkin was not of itself a personal injury. It did her no harm; it left her as before … However, it seems to me that the unwanted conception, whether as a result of negligent advice or negligent surgery, was a personal injury in the sense of an "impairment" in the illustrative definition in s 38(1). The resultant physical change in her body resulting from conception was an unwanted condition which she had sought to avoid by undergoing the sterilisation operation …

'The question whether an action is for damages in respect of personal injuries is one of substance, not a matter of pleading … The question is how to determine in any given case the true nature of the claim, by which, in this context, is meant whether it is an action for damages consisting of or including damages in respect of personal injuries … Here the question is … whether the breach of duty, that is the negligence causing the unwanted pregnancy, gave rise to a claim for damages, in this instance, the costs of rearing the child. In my view, it clearly did.' *Walkin v South Manchester Health Authority* [1995] 4 All ER 132 at 134, 139, 141, CA, per Auld LJ

Aggravated damages

[For 12 Halsbury's Laws (4th edn) para 1112 see now 12(1) Halsbury's Laws (4th edn) (Reissue) para 811.]

Liquidated damages

[For 12 Halsbury's Laws (4th edn) para 1109 see now 12(1) Halsbury's Laws (4th edn) (Reissue) para 808.]

Liquidated damages and penalty distinguished

[For 12 Halsbury's Laws (4th edn) para 1116 see now 12(1) Halsbury's Laws (4th edn) (Reissue) para 1065.]

Nominal damages

[For 12 Halsbury's Laws (4th edn) para 1114 see now 12(1) Halsbury's Laws (4th edn) (Reissue) para 813.]

Prospective damages

[For 12 Halsbury's Laws (4th edn) para 1111 see now 12(1) Halsbury's Laws (4th edn) (Reissue) para 810.]

Special damages

[For 12 Halsbury's Laws (4th edn) para 1113 see now 12(1) Halsbury's Laws (4th edn) (Reissue) para 812.]

Statutory damages

[For 12 Halsbury's Laws (4th edn) para 1115 see now 12(1) Halsbury's Laws (4th edn) (Reissue) para 814.]

DANGER

Canada '[51] The "new" definition of "danger", as it currently exists in subsection 122(1) [as am. by S.C. 2000, c. 20, s. 2] of the Code [*Canada Labour Code*], provides as follows:

122. (1) …

"danger" means any existing or potential hazard or condition or any current or future activity that could reasonab ly be expected to cause injury or illness to a person exposed to it before the hazard or condition can be corrected, or the activity altered, whether or not the injury or illness occurs immediately after the exposure to the hazard, condition or activity, and includes any exposure to a hazardous substance that is likely to result in a chronic illness, in disease or in damage to the reproductive system;

'[52] The distinction between the old and new definition of "danger" was explained by the same appeals officer (Mr. Cadieux) [at paragraph 17–19] in the case of *Welbourne and Canadian Pacific Railway Co.*, [2001] C.L.C.A.O.D. No. 9 (QL), as follows.

'[53] The current definition of "danger" sets out to improve the definition of "danger" found in the pre-amended Code, which was believed to be too restrictive to protect the health and safety of employees. Pursuant to the jurisprudence developed around the definition of danger in the pre-amended Code, the danger had to be immediate and present at the time of the safety officer's investigation. The new definition broadens the concept of danger to allow for potential hazards or conditions or future activities to be taken into account. Therefore, the safety officer can look beyond the immediate circumstances that exist at the time of his investigation to determine whether "danger" exists as defined in the Code. However, although the new definition of "danger" allows for a future activity to be taken into consideration, this is not an open-ended expression. The doctrine of reasonable expectation still applies. In order to constitute danger as defined in the Code, it must be reasonable to expect that the prospective hazard, condition or activity will cause injury or illness to a person exposed to it before the hazard or condition can be corrected or the activity modified. Therefore, although the danger can be prospective, the doctrine of reasonable expectation still excludes hypothetical or speculative situations.

'[54] This interpretation of the new definition of "danger" has been adopted and applied by other appeals officers in subsequent cases (*Abood and Air Canada* , [2003] C.L.C.A.O.D. No. 2 (QL); *Canada (Correctional Service) and Schellenberg*, [2002] C.L.C.A.O.D. No. 6 (QL); *International Longshore and Warehouse Union and Pacific Coast Terminals Co.*, [2002] C.L.C.A.O.D. No. 16 (QL); *Bouchard and Canada (Correctional Service)*, [2001] C.L.C.A.O.D. No. 28 (QL)).

'[55] I agree with the above analysis made by Mr. Cadieux in *Welbourne*, *supra*. To paraphrase, the new definition of "danger" in the Code makes it clear that any potential hazard or condition or future activity can constitute a danger. This means that a safety officer can look beyond the immediate circumstances that exist at the time of his investigation to determine whether "danger" exists as defined in the Code.

'[56] Furthermore, it is evident to me that the amended definition still encompasses the concept of reasonable expectation which excludes

speculative situations: the provision specifically provides that the "future activity that could reasonably be expected to cause injury or illness to [the] person exposed" [underlining added]. This requires evidence and obliges the safety officer to perform an objective analysis of a particular situation.

'[57] I agree with the appeals officer that in the absence of specific evidence indicating when grievous bodily harm or death could reasonably occur to a park warden performing law enforcement activity, a safety officer would have to conclude on the absence of danger since he would be faced strictly with a hypothetical or speculative situation.

'[58] However, the new definition also clearly states that a hazard, condition or activity could constitute a danger "whether or not the injury or illness occurs immediately after the exposure to the hazard, condition or activity" [underlining added]. As such, contrary to what was indicated by the appeals officer, I am of the view that it is not necessary that there be a reasonable expectation that the injury or illness will occur immediately upon exposure to the activity in order to constitute danger within the meaning in the Code.

'[59] Nevertheless, in my opinion, the new definition still requires an impending element because the injury or illness has to occur "before the hazard or condition can be corrected, or the activity altered".' *Martin v Canada (Attorney General)* [2004] 1 FCR 625 at 645–647 (FCC), per Tremblay-Lamer J

DANGER TO THE PUBLIC PEACE

Canada '[90] The concept of "public peace" seems very much an old concept from the time that common law offences still existed. Understood in the context of the modern *Criminal Code*, it is difficult to imagine that the public peace could be endangered by something short of harm to persons or property. This Court considered the definition of "peace" or "King's Peace" in the classic case of *Frey v. Fedoruk*, [1950] S.C.R. 517, 97 C.C.C. 1, [1950] 3 D.L.R. 513. In determining whether an officer had falsely imprisoned Frey for a breach of the peace, the majority rejected a definition of "breach of the King's peace" that was given indefinite and overbroad content (at pp. 529–30):

> It appears to me that so understood, the genus is wide enough to include the whole field of the criminal law. As it is put in Pollock and Maitland, History of English Law (1895) Volume 1, page 22:

"all criminal offences have long been said to be committed against the King's peace."

and in Volume 2 of the same work at page 452, it is stated:

"to us a breach of the King's peace may seem to cover every possible crime."

Once the expression "a breach of the King's Peace" is interpreted, as O'Halloran, J.A. undoubtedly does interpret it, not to require as an essential ingredient anything in the nature of "riots, tumults, or actual physical violence" on the part of the offender, it would appear to become wide enough to include any conduct which in the view of the fact finding tribunal is so injurious to the public as to merit punishment. If, on the other hand, O'Halloran, J.A. intended to give to the expression a more limited meaning so that it would include only conduct of a nature likely to lead to a breach of the peace in the narrower sense of which he speaks, the authorities referred to elsewhere in this Judgment seem to me to show that this is not an offence known to the law.

I am of opinion that the proposition implicit in the paragraph quoted above ought not to be accepted.

'[91] The definition I propose of a danger to the public peace is supported in the English authorities. In *R. v. Howell*, [1982] Q.B. 416 (C.A.), at pp. 426–27, Watkins L.J. held for the court that there is no breach of the peace unless an act is done or threatened to be done which (a) actually harms a person or, in his presence, his property; (b) is likely to cause such harm; or (c) puts someone in fear of such harm:

A comprehensive definition of the term "breach of the peace" has very rarely been formulated so far as, with considerable help from counsel, we have been able to discover from cases which go as far back as the 18th century. The older cases are of considerable interest but they are not a sure guide to what the term is understood to mean today, since keeping the peace in this country in the latter half of the 20th century presents formidable problems which bear upon the evolving process of the development of this breach of the common law.

...

We are emboldened to say that there is a breach of the peace whenever harm is actually done or is likely to be done to a person or in his presence to his property or a person is in fear of being so harmed through an assault, an affray, a riot, unlawful assembly or other disturbance.

'I see no principled reason why a similar definition, with the incorporation of recklessness, should not apply to "dangerous to the public peace" under s. 88(1) of the *Code*.' *R v Kerr* [2004] SCJ No 39, 240 DLR (4th) 257, per Lebel J

DANGER TO THE SECURITY OF CANADA

Canada '[80] In order to deny the benefit of s. 53(1) [of the *Immigration Act*] to a person seeking its protection, the Minister must certify that the person constitutes a "danger to the security of Canada". Suresh argues that this phrase is unconstitutionally vague.

...

'[83] We agree with the government and Robertson J.A. that the phrase "danger to the security of Canada" is not unconstitutionally vague. However, we do not interpret the phrase exactly as he or the government suggests. We would not conflate s. 19's reference to membership in a terrorist movement with "danger to the security of Canada". While the two may be related, "danger to the security of Canada", in our view, must mean something more than just "person described in s. 19".

...

'[89] While the phrase "danger to the security of Canada" must be interpreted flexibly, and while courts need not insist on direct proof that the danger targets Canada specifically, the fact remains that to return (*refouler*) a refugee under s. 53(1)(*b*) to torture requires evidence of a serious threat to national security. To suggest that something less than serious threats founded on evidence would suffice to deport a refugee to torture would be to condone unconstitutional application of the *Immigration Act*. Insofar as possible, statutes must be interpreted to conform to the Constitution. This supports the conclusion that while "danger to the security of Canada" must be given a fair, large and liberal interpretation, it nevertheless demands proof of a potentially serious threat.

'[90] These considerations lead us to conclude that a person constitutes a "danger to the security of Canada" if he or she poses a serious threat to the security of Canada, whether direct or indirect, and bearing in mind the fact that the security of one country is often dependent on the security of other nations. The threat must be "serious", in the sense that it must be grounded on objectively reasonable suspicion based on evidence and in the sense that the threatened harm must be substantial rather than negligible.' *Suresh v Canada* (*Minister of Citizenship and Immigration*) [2002] 1 SCR 3 at 47–51, per the Court

DANGEROUS *SEE ALSO* DRIVE—DRIVER; RECKLESS

Act

Australia 'The Court of Criminal Appeal described a "dangerous" act simply as one that is likely to injure another person. This conforms with the dictionary definitions of "dangerous" ("fraught with danger or risk; perilous, hazardous, unsafe": Shorter Oxford English Dictionary) and "danger" ("liability or exposure to harm or injury, risk, peril": Shorter Oxford English Dictionary)... This Court should affirm the English interpretation of "dangerous" as the law in South Australia. It has been applied, in one form or another, by a large majority of the judges of this court who have had to deal with the matter in the 20 years or so since *Holzer* [[1968] VR 481] provided a competitor. The English rule was laid down in *Larkin* [(1942) 29 Cr App R 18 at 23–24] 50 years ago and in 1977 it was affirmed by the House of Lords. It must have been used in countless English trials. In 1980 it was approved by the Privy Council for Jamaica, a common law country. (As to the significance in this court now of the House of Lords and Privy Council decisions, see *Parker v South Australian Housing Trust* (1986) 41 SASR 493, per King CJ at 516–517, and *Cook v Cook* (1986) 162 CLR 376 at 389–390.) It is the law throughout Canada. In Australia it has been endorsed by two, probably three, of the four High Court judges who have said anything about it; the position of the fourth is doubtful. It has been applied in New South Wales without, so far as appears, any hint of dissent. The only exception is Victoria. We are now used to the notion that the common law world contains more than one common law, but I do not think we should in this State depart from what evidently is the only interpretation of the common law rule applied outside Australia, and the interpretation applied by most trial judges in the common law States within Australia, without good reason.' *R v Wilson* (1991) 53 A Crim R 281 at 289, 304, per Cox J

DANGEROUS DOG

[For 2 Halsbury's Laws (4th edn) paras 368–370 see now 2(1) Halsbury's Laws (4th edn) (Reissue) paras 713–714.]

DANGEROUS MACHINERY

[For 20 Halsbury's Laws (4th edn) para 568 see now 20(1) Halsbury's Laws (4th edn) (Reissue) paras 694–695.]

DANGEROUS NATURE

[The Hague Rules art IV r 6 refers to 'Goods of an inflammable, explosive or dangerous nature'; the question arose whether groundnut cargo infested with Khapra beetle was dangerous to other cargo.] 'First, it has been settled law, since *Chandris v Isbrandtsen-Moller Co Inc* [1950] 1 All ER 768, [1951] 1 KB 240; *revsd on issue of interest* [1950] 2 All ER 618, [1951] 2 KB 240, that the word "dangerous" in the expression "goods of ... [a] dangerous nature" must be given a broad meaning. Dangerous goods are not confined to goods of an inflammable or explosive nature, or their like ... Secondly, goods may be dangerous within the meaning of art IV, r 6 if they are dangerous to other goods, even though they are not dangerous to the vessel itself.

'What is the meaning of the word "dangerous" in this context? ... I can see no reason to confine the word "dangerous" to goods which are liable to cause direct physical damage to other goods. It is true that goods which explode or catch fire would normally cause direct physical damage to other cargo in the vicinity. But there is no need to qualify the word "dangerous" by reading in the word "directly" ...' *Effort Shipping Co Ltd v Linden Management SA, The Giannis NK* [1998] 1 All ER 495 at 499–500, HL, per Lord Lloyd of Berwick

DATE UPON WHICH THE TAX BECAME DUE AND PAYABLE

Australia 'At the very least, language is strained by saying that tax becomes "due and payable" on a particular date in circumstances where the Commissioner has issued a document informing the taxpayer that the Commissioner has determined that the taxpayer owes no amount for tax ... Whatever may be the elasticity of the expression "the date upon which the tax became due and payable", it does not, and cannot, accommodate the case where no tax is due and payable.' *Commissioner of Taxation (Cth) v Ryan* (2000) 168 ALR 704; 74 ALJR 471; 43 ATR 694; BC200000085; [2000] HCA 4 at [15], per Gleeson CJ, Gummow and Hayne JJ

DAY

[For 45 Halsbury's Laws (4th edn) para 1113 see now 45(2) Halsbury's Laws (4th edn) (Reissue) para 213.]

DE BONIS NON

[For 17 Halsbury's Laws (4th edn) para 984 see now 17(2) Halsbury's Laws (4th edn) (Reissue) para 201.]

DE NOVO

Canada '[16] In *Kahlon, supra*, the Federal Court of Appeal held that an appeal to the Appeal Board is a hearing de novo in a broad sense. As discussed in Ruth Sullivan, *Statutory Interpretation* (Concord, Ont.: Irwin Law, 1997), at page 41, courts are to use the ordinary meaning of words if there is no reason to reject it in favour of another interpretation. *Black's Law Dictionary*, 6th ed. (St. Paul, Minn.: West Publishing, 1990) at page 721 defines a "hearing de novo" as follows:

> Generally, a new hearing or a hearing for the second time, contemplating an entire trial in same manner in which matter was originally heard and a review of previous hearing. Trying matter anew the same as if it had not been heard before and as if no decision had been previously rendered ... On hearing "de novo" court hears the matter as a court of original and not appellate jurisdiction.

'The *Dictionary of Canadian Law*, 2nd ed., (Dukelow and Nuse, Scarborough, Ont., Carswell, 1995), at page 549, defines "hearing *de novo*" thus:

> "... [I]s ... an altogether fresh or new hearing and not limited to an enquiry to determine if the tribunal acted properly and correctly on the evidence and material before it ..." *New-term Ltd, Re* (1988), 38 M.P.L.R. 17 at 19, 70 Nfld. & P.E.I.R. 216, 215 A.P.R. 216 (Nfld.T.D.), Steele J.'

Kwan v Canada [2002] 2 FC 99 at 115 (TD), per Muldoon J

DEALINGS

Australia [Section 86 of the Bankruptcy Act 1966 (Cth) provides, inter alia, that where there have been mutual credits, mutual debts or other mutual 'dealings' between a person who has become a bankrupt and a person claiming to prove a debt in the bankruptcy, an account shall be taken of what is due from the one party to the other in respect of those mutual dealings.] 'The word "dealings" is used in a non-technical sense in s 86. It has been construed as referring to matters having a commercial or business flavour: if "one man assaults another or injures him through negligence, that gives rise to a claim, but is not a dealing" (per Lord Esher MR, *Eberle's Hotels* ((1887) 18 QBD 459 at 465)). The word is, nonetheless, one of very wide scope which embraces far more than a legally binding contract or "deal". Even if it be correct to construe "dealings" in s 86 as confined to a commercial or business setting, it covers the communings, the negotiations, verbal and by correspondence, and other relations which occur or exist in that setting. Whatever may be the outer limits of the word "dealings" in s 86, it encompasses, as a matter of ordinary language, commercial transactions and the negotiations leading up to them. Where a fraudulent misrepresentation is made in the course of such negotiations, the fraudulent misrepresentation is itself part of the relevant "dealings" (c f *Re Mid-Kent Fruit Factory* ([1896] 1 Ch 567 at 571–572); *Tilley v Bowman Ltd* ([1910] 1 KB 745 at 753)).' *Gye v McIntyre* (1991) 171 CLR 609 at 625, per cur

Australia [Section 86 of the Bankruptcy Act 1966 (Cth) provides for set off where there has been, inter alia, mutual 'dealings' between a bankrupt person and a person claiming to prove a debt in the bankruptcy.] 'The word "dealings" is used in a non-technical sense in s 86. It has been construed as referring to matters having a commercial or business flavour: if "one man assaults another or injures him through negligence, that gives rise to a claim, but is not a dealing" (per Lord Esher MR, *Eberle's Hotels [and Restaurant Co v Jonas* (1887) 18 QBD 459 at 465]). The word is, nonetheless, one of very wide scope which embraces far more than a legally binding contract or "deal". Even if it be correct to construe "dealings" in s 86 as confined to a commercial or business setting, it covers the communings, the negotiations, verbal and by correspondence, and other relations which occur or exist in that setting. Whatever may be the outer limits of the word "dealings" in s 86, it encompasses, as a matter of ordinary language, commercial transactions and the negotiations leading up to them. Where a fraudulent misrepresentation is made in the course of such negotiations, the fraudulent misrepresentation is itself part of the relevant "dealings" (cf *In re Mid-Kent Fruit Factory* [[1896] 1 Ch 567 at 571–572]; *Tilley v Bowman Ltd* [[1910] 1 KB 745 at 753]).' *Gye v McIntyre* (1991) 171 CLR 609 at 625, per cur

Australia [Section 68A of the Companies (Vic) Code states that a person having 'dealings' with a company is entitled to make certain assumptions in relation to those dealings.] 'In the first place the plaintiff denied the operation of the section by contending it could only be relied upon by a party who had had a series of "dealings" with the plaintiff and could not be applied where the parties had entered into only a single transaction. For this purpose it relied on the use of the plural "dealings" as indicating an intention that the section should not apply to a case of a single dealing. It was not suggested why the legislature had restricted this beneficent provision in this way and I cannot see logically it should be so confined. It is not merely a question of reading plural words as including the singular; it is rather a matter of giving a normal English meaning to the word "dealings". Reference was properly made to the Oxford English Dictionary, where in the 2nd edn, vol IV, pp 297–298 the following relevant definition numbered 2 is given: "Intercourse, friendly or business communication, connection. Now usually *pl.*" Examples given in the text of this plural usage commenced as early as 1586 and in my opinion it is a common usage.' *Brick and Pipe Industries Ltd v Occidental Life Nominees Pty Ltd* [1922] 2 VR 279 at 307, per Ormisto J

DEBASE

Australia [As to whether a "techno" dance music adaptation of the chorus of an earlier work "debased" the work under Copyright Act 1968 (Cth) s 55(2)] '1) The term "debase" does not call for substantial sameness or even similarity in style, instruments or performance. They are relevant but not conclusive considerations ... 3) The term "debase" calls for a value judgment based on a significant lowering in integrity, value, esteem or quality of the work. 4) Regardless of which view is taken as to the meaning of "debase", there is, of necessity, a question of degree involved in deciding whether a work is "debased" by an adaptation.' *Schott Musik International Gmbh & Co v Colossal*

Records of Australia Pty Ltd (1996) 141 ALR 433 at 439; 36 IPR 267 at 274, per Tamberlin J

DEBENTURE

[For 7 Halsbury's Laws (4th edn) para 813 see now 7(2) Halsbury's Laws (4th edn) (1996 Reissue) para 1250.]

Stock

[For 7 Halsbury's Laws (4th edn) para 1097 see now 7(2) Halsbury's Laws (4th edn) (1996 Reissue) para 1259.]

DEBT

[The Supreme Court Act 1989, s 35A, provides for the payment of interest in proceedings for the recovery of 'debt'. The question arose whether it covered payment of interest where a claim for judicial review and restitution of sums paid for nursing home care was abandoned after a review panel agreed to reimburse the claimant before the permission stage of judicial review proceedings.] '[80] The claimant can have no claim to interest unless he can show a right to receive it. The only right which he has is if s 35A of the 1981 Act applies, for there is no claim to interest at common law since there is no contract in this case which conveys a right to it. Interest under s 35A is payable only if there is a judgment for damages, or in respect of a debt, or if payment is made before judgment.

'[81] Accordingly, the questions for my determination are: (a) is the sum paid by the defendants properly to be classed as a debt, to which the provisions of s 35A apply even though there has been no judgment? (b) If so, should I exercise the discretion of the court to award interest, knowing as I do that there is no obligation to make such an award, and that the statutory scheme provides for the award of a sum which is called "interest"? (c) If I do think it appropriate to exercise my discretion, at what rate, and in respect of what period is it appropriate to make such an award?

'[82] Resolution of the first of these issues depends upon the proper classification of a claim in restitution in circumstances such as the present. The fact that restitution may be neither properly classed as a claim in debt, or a claim for damages, may be indicated by the fact that the CPR were specifically amended to permit restitution to be brought as an ancillary claim to judicial review where previously it had provided for just "debt or damages". If it had been clear that the latter two words covered "restitution", there would have been no need to add "restitution" specifically to those claims which could be made. Accordingly, the wording of the CPR is either implicitly such as to distinguish restitution from debt or damages, for the purposes of judicial review at any rate or, at best from the claimant's perspective, is unclear.

'[83] In the claimant's submissions, at para 8, Mr Weir claims that the expression "debt or damages" in s 35A has been construed broadly and includes a claim for restitution. He says that it is common ground that interest is payable. That is not the case. The defendants' submissions (para 10(b)) do not accept either proposition.

'[84] Mr Weir relies on *Woolwich Building Society v IRC (No 2)* [1992] 3 All ER 737, [1993] AC 70. That case concerned payments of tax made by a building society to the Revenue under the terms of regulations which it sought to challenge. The regulations being ultra vires, the demand was unlawful. On 31 July 1987 Nolan J held that the regulations were ultra vires and void (a decision subsequently upheld by the House of Lords). The Revenue repaid the building society the moneys with interest from 31 July 1987, but refused to pay any interest in respect of the period up to the date of judgment. The building society claimed repayment of the interest under s 35A of the 1981 Act. The headnote ([1993] AC 70) suggests that once the House had upheld the right of the building society to recover the sums paid, interest was to be paid thereon by s 35A.

'[85] However, it is apparent from the judgment of Ralph Gibson LJ in the Court of Appeal ([1991] 4 All ER 577, [1993] AC 70) that there was there no issue between the parties. It was accepted that interest would be payable as if the sum repaid were a debt within the meaning of s 35A. There is thus no reasoned consideration of the question by any appellate court. Nonetheless, it would be surprising if the point had not been taken if it had been thought there was any substance to it. Thus, although the judgments do not justify the headnote in this respect, the point summarised by that headnote is at least persuasive. The only other citation on which Mr Weir relied – Goff and Jones *The Law of Restitution* (6th edn, 2002) pp 669–670 – provides no independent consideration of the point.

'[86] Does reasoning from first principles compel me to the conclusion indicated by the express addition of "restitution" within the CPR, or to the view expressed in the headnote to the *Woolwich* case [1993] AC 70? If the concession had not been made in the *Woolwich* case, I should in any event have been attracted to the idea that "debt" in s 35A extends so as to cover sums of money subject to an obligation, however arising, to repay them. The sum for which restitution may be ordered (at least in circumstances such as the present) is a liquidated sum. To restrict the scope of "debts" to those arising under a contract would seem to me unduly narrow. The essential characteristic which lies behind Parliament's intention to give a power to award interest in a proper case is that there should be some obligation to pay over the money. Accordingly, I reject the defendants' hesitation over accepting whether s 35A is capable of applying to a sum such as the present, if it is capable of being the subject of a restitutionary claim.' *R (on the application of Kemp) v Denbighshire Local Health Board* [2006] EWHC 181 (Admin) at [80]–[86], [2006] 3 All ER 141, per Langstaff J

Australia [Section 556 of the Companies (NSW) Code refers to a company incurring a 'debt'.] 'The words "incurs" and "debt" are not words of precise and inflexible denotation. Where they appear in s 556 they are to be applied in a practical and commonsense fashion, consistent with the context and with the statutory purposes.

' "Debt" is capable of including a contingent liability. The word was used in that sense in s 291 of the Companies Act 1961 (NSW), which referred to "debts payable on a contingency". That expression did not involve a contradiction in terms. Dictionaries define "debt" as a liability or obligation to pay or render something. Such a liability may be conditional as well as present and absolute ... Once it is accepted that "debt" may include a contingent debt then there is no obstacle to the conclusion that, in the present context, a debt may be taken to have been incurred when a company entered a contract by which it subjected itself to a conditional but unavoidable obligation to pay a sum of money at a future time.' *Hawkins v Bank of China* (1992) 7 ACSR 349 at 357–358, per Gleeson CJ

[See also *Standard Chartered Bank of Australia Ltd v Antico (Nos 1 and 2)* (1995) 38 NSWLR 290 at 314, per Hodgson J]

Australia ' ... [I]n ordinary legal usage, the term "debt", when not expanded (as in [Bankruptcy Act 1966 (Cth) s 82] subs (1) in its primary form) by such phrases as "certain or contingent" and "present or future", identifies an obligation actually incurred, rather than one subjected to a contingency yet to be fulfilled. The absence from the substitute subs (1) [as a result of modifications by Bankruptcy

Rules (Cth) r 84(a) pursuant to Bankruptcy Act 1966 (Cth) s 243] of those words of expansion indicates an intention to use the phrase "all debts and liabilities" in its ordinary legal sense.' *Pyramid Building Society (in liq) v Terry* (1997) 148 ALR 174 at 180; BC9704592 at 11, per Gaudron and Gummow JJ

Australia 'There is authority for the proposition that the term "debt" is used in the Corporations Law in its usual sense which invokes the well recognised distinction between a debt and a liability for unliquidated damages (*Jelin Pty Ltd v Johnson and Anor* (1987) 5 ACLC 463; *Commonwealth Bank of Australia v Butterell* (1994) 14 ACSR 343)... In its usual meaning it does not include a claim for damages for a failure to comply with a covenant in a lease to make good damage caused to the leased premises.' *Molit (No 55) Pty Ltd v Lam Soon Australia Pty Ltd (administrator apptd)* (1996) 68 FCR 319 at 321; (1996) 21 ACSR 157 at 159; (1996) 14 ACLC 1371; BC9603447 at 4–5, per Branson J

Canada [Directors of a corporation were personally liable for debts for wages.] 'The term "debts" cannot be dissociated from the context in which it is used. According to the language used by Parliament, the debts must result from "services performed for the corporation". An amount payable in lieu of notice does not flow from services performed for the corporation, but rather from the damage arising from non-performance of a contractual obligation to give sufficient notice. The wrongful breach of the employment relationship by the employer is the cause and basis for the amounts awarded by the Superior Court as pay in lieu of notice.' *Barrette v Crabtree Estate* [1993] 1 SCR 1027 at 1048–1049, per L'Heureux-Dubé J

DEBT OR DAMAGES

New Zealand 'Equitable interest arising from an implied promise to pay falls fairly within the expression "debt or damages" within s 87(1) of the Judicature Act 1908.' *Hieber v Hieber* [1991] 1 NZLR 315 at 318, CA, per cur

DEBT OR LIQUIDATED DEMAND

Canada 'Professor Dunlop in his text, *Creditor-Debtor Law in Canada*, 2nd ed, criticizes a definition of "debt or liquidated demand" taken from such authorities as *Alm v Tyrone Hotels (Saskatchewan) Ltd et al* (1963) 42 WWR 297 at

301 (Sask QB), which limit "debt" to an express or implied contract. He states (at p 14):

> There are serious difficulties in accepting such a narrow view of debt. The *Burrows* definition would exclude a claim for a statutory penalty or for an equitable debt such as a claim against a trustee for a specific sum of money. It would also exclude those restitutionary causes of action which were not pleaded by use of the common counts. There is no obvious reason in principle or policy why such claims, if quantified, should not be regarded as debts where the context permits such an interpretation. For example, whether a claim for a sum of money is based on contract, restitution or an equitable cause of action should not affect the question whether garnishment before judgment is available. In all cases, the [amount] sued for is liquidated, and this is surely all that the formula "debt or liquidated demand" is seeking to require.

'Later, he defines debt in this manner (at p 16):

> One can say that the most common use of the word "debt" is to describe an obligation to pay a sum certain or a sum readily reducible to a certainty. The obligation may or may not depend on an express or implied contract, depending on the context in which the word is used, but to this writer the essence of the term is that, if there is an obligation to pay a certain or ascertainable sum, the courts should tend not to concern themselves with the precise nature of the cause of action. Claims for unliquidated damages will generally not be describable as debts unless the context suggests or a statute provides otherwise [Footnotes omitted.]

'In *Canadian Imperial Bank of Commerce v Grotsky* (1994) 120 Sask R 305 at 308, 114 DLR (4th) 641, this Court commented favourably on this definition.' *Ross v HVLD Systems (1997) Ltd* (1999) 170 DLR (4th) 600 at 603–604, Sask CA, per Jackson JA

DEBT SECURITY

New Zealand [Securities Act 1978, s 2(1).] 'The right acquired under the buy back provision was not granted in isolation. It cannot be equated with the right of a seller under an ordinary contract for the sale of land. It was a right granted to those who signed the sale and purchase agreement ... the money agreed to be paid back by the appellant to the unit holder under the buy-back provision in due course was by way of repayment of money previously paid to the appellant by the unit holder. It was not repayment in the sense of money repayment of a loan. But it was repayment in the sense of payment back of the same amount, subject to adjustment for charges and inflation.

'... Unit holders are at risk that, having paid the original price to the appellant, the appellant may not be able to honour its repayment commitment. The right granted to the unit holder under the buy-back provision is a debt security. The appellant is the issuer of that security: the buy-back right is granted by the appellant in consideration of the original price paid to the appellant.' *Culverden Retirement Village v Registrar of Companies* [1997] 1 NZLR 257 at pp 260–261, PC, per cur

DECENCY

Australia 'The next matter is whether publication of that evidence is likely to offend against "public decency". The word "decency" is defined by the Shorter Oxford Dictionary as follows: "1. Appropriateness to the circumstances of the occasion; fitness, seemliness, propriety; what is appropriate. 2. Orderly condition of civil or social life. 3. Propriety of demeanour; due regard to what is becoming."

'The Macquarie Dictionary definition is "1. The state or quality of being decent. 2. Conformity to the recognised standards of propriety, good taste, modesty, etc. 3. Something decent or proper".

'Obviously something that is likely to offend against public decency is not necessarily limited to blasphemy, obscenity, profanity or sexual indecency. I think the meaning to be given to the expression is that which would be generally regarded by the public, or a significant section of it, as lacking in propriety or good taste, or unbecoming, or unseemly.' *R v Bara Bara* (1992) 87 NTR 1 at 3, per Mildren J

DECEPTION

Australia 'Deception is the intentional inducing in another of a state of mind which, as the offender knows, does not accord with fact.' *Corporate Affairs Commission v Papoulias* (1990) 20 NSWLR 503 at 506, per Allen J

DECISION. *SEE ALSO* DETERMINATION

Australia [The Administrative Decisions (Judicial Review) Act 1977 (Cth) provides, inter alia, for the judicial review of 'a decision to which this Act applies' (s 5) and 'conduct (engaged in) for the purpose of making a decision to which this Act applies' (s 6). The expression 'decision to which this Act applies' is defined in s 3(1) to mean 'a decision of an administrative character'.] 'A reviewable "decision" is one for which provision is made by or under a statute. That will generally, but not always, entail a decision which is final or operative and determinative, at least in a practical sense, of the issue of fact falling for consideration. A conclusion reached as a step along the way in a course of reasoning leading to an ultimate decision would not ordinarily amount to a reviewable decision, unless the statute provided for the making of a finding or ruling on that point so that the decision, though an intermediate decision, might accurately be described as a decision under an enactment. Another essential quality of a reviewable decision is that it be a substantive determination. The interpretation of "decision" which I favour is not as broad as that preferred by the Federal Court in *Lamb v Moss* [(1983) 76 FLR 296, 49 ALR 533]. My view is more in accord with the tentative opinion expressed earlier by Ellicott J in *Ross v Costigan* [(1982) 59 FLR 184 at 197; 41 ALR 319 at 331] when he said that "it may well be that the word 'decision' means an ultimate or operative determination not a mere expression of opinion or a statement which can of itself have no effect on a person". However, I would not wish for myself to place emphasis on the words "of itself" in this statement. To say that a reviewable decision is an ultimate or operative determination does not mean that antecedent conclusions or findings which contribute to the ultimate or operative decision are beyond reach.' *Australian Broadcasting Tribunal v Bond* (1990) 170 CLR 321 at 337–338, per Mason CJ

Australia [Migration Act 1958 (Cth).] '..."Decision" means result: Whilst it is true that s 430B of the Migration Act refers to the reading of the "outcome of the decision", that provision cannot affect the appellant's case or the meaning, as applicable to his case, of s 478 of the Migration Act. This is because s 430B(1)(b) of that Act makes it clear that the section in which reference is made to "the outcome of the decision" has no application to a person, like the appellant, "who is in immigration detention". The reference to "outcome" in that section cannot therefore distort the meaning of "the decision" throughout the entirety of that Part of the Migration Act. The "decision" is the result of the review undertaken by the Tribunal. Both in its ordinary meaning, and in the differentiations drawn by the Migration Act, the "decision" is thus separate from, and different to, the reasons, findings and reference to material and the "written statement" for which the Migration Act specifically provides. In my respectful opinion, it would involve an artificial and contra-textual interpretation of the Migration Act to adopt a different view.' *WACB v Minister for Immigration and Multicultural and Indigenous Affairs* [2004] HCA 50 at [92], per Kirby J; BC200406533

Canada '... a "decision" is the judicial opinion of the court on the matters in issue and not the procedural judgment or order.' *Johnston (Litigation Guardian of) v Stewart* (1994) 116 DLR (4th) 180 at 185, Ont Gen Div, per Desmarais J

DECISION OF THE JUDGE

[The Administration of Justice Act 1969, s 13(2)(a) provides that where the House of Lords grants leave for an appeal to be brought directly to it no appeal from the 'decision of the judge' to which the 'leapfrog' certificate relates lies to the Court of Appeal. It was contended here that the 'decision of the judge' referred to the order made by the judge that the authority's decision be quashed, and that as the House of Lords had granted leave to appeal from that order, the Court of Appeal had no jurisdiction to entertain the authority's appeal. The authority submitted, inter alia, that to avoid injustice the word 'decision' should be construed as referring to a decision on a particular issue.] '[42] The crucial provision is s 13(2) of the Administration of Justice Act 1969 and in particular the words: "and where leave is granted under this section–(a) no appeal from the decision of the judge to which the certificate relates shall lie to the Court of Appeal ..."

'[43] I am unpersuaded that, in this context, the word "decision" can only mean "judgment or order" in the sense in which those words are used in s 16(1) of the Supreme Court Act 1981.

'[44] It seems unlikely that in 1969 Parliament contemplated the possibility that a certificate under s 12(1) might relate to two issues or grounds in respect of which the House of Lords might grant leave for one but refuse it for the other. We are told that the researches of counsel have failed to unearth a previous example of such a mixed outcome. However, whether as a result of changing practice or increasing complexity, it seems to me that such a situation is likely to recur. For the moment, I shall assume that Collins J granted permission to appeal to the Court of Appeal in respect of both issues. On such an assumption he must have

considered that in respect of each there was a real prospect of success or some other compelling reason justifying the grant of permission. It would seem to me to be surprising if, in such circumstances, a partial grant of leave by the House of Lords were to exclude all possibility of the further pursuit of another ground of appeal which had been considered to have a real prospect of success. To take an example, the House of Lords may grant leave in relation to a ground which plainly involves a matter of general public importance and which calls for an authoritative decision at that level at the earliest opportunity. The second ground may be highly meritorious but case specific and not of general public importance. I would consider it regrettable if the matter could not proceed first by way of the determination of the matter of general public importance in the House of Lords and, thereafter, and if still relevant, by way of the determination of the second ground in the Court of Appeal. I am untroubled by the theoretical possibility that the two appeals might be proceeding in two places at the same time. It would be perfectly possible, for example, for the Court of Appeal to stay the appeal on the second ground pending the resolution of the appeal on the first ground in the House of Lords.

'[45] These considerations dispose me to adopt a broad construction of s 13(2) if that is at all possible. Whilst I accept that the context is not directly in point, I draw some support from the statement of Lord Steyn in *R v Emmett* [1997] 4 All ER 737 at 742, [1998] AC 773 at 781–782, that

> "[t]here is a strong presumption that except by specific provision the legislature will not exclude a right of appeal as of right or with leave where such a right is ordinarily available."

'[46] Mr Giffin QC also seeks to derive further support for this approach from *R (on the application of Zenovics) v Secretary of State for the Home Dept* [2002] EWCA Civ 273, [2002] All ER (D) 77 (Mar). Again, the situation is not wholly analogous, not least because one of the considerations in *Zenovics*'s case was that the narrower construction would have implications relating to the international obligations of the United Kingdom under the Convention Relating to the Status of Refugees (Geneva, 28 July 1951; TS 39 (1953); Cmnd 9171). Nevertheless, it does illustrate a reluctance on the part of the courts to acquiesce in the loss of a right of appeal which would have been the result of a stricter, less purposive construction.

'[47] In my judgment, the conclusion to which Waller LJ has come with, it seems, a measure of reluctance, is not one which is forced upon us by the statutory language. The 1969 Act contains no definition of "decision". Nor does the Act expressly import the words "order or judgment" from ss 3 and 4 of the Appellate Jurisdiction Act 1876. Moreover, I find some significance in the fact that s 15(4) of the 1969 Act uses the words "decision" and "order" differentially. The context is a narrow and exclusionary one (contempt of court) but the language at least justifies the observation that the assimilation of "decision" with "judgment or order" was probably not in the minds of the draftsman or Parliament.' *R (on the application of Jones) v Ceredigion County Council* [2005] EWCA Civ 986 at [42]–[47], [2006] 1 All ER 138, per Maurice Kay LJ

DECISION OR ORDER

Canada 'The issue, in my view, resolves itself into one of statutory construction. It is not clear, however, that similarities in procedure by itself affords a reliable basis for concluding that the findings in issue are "decisions" reviewable under paragraph 18.1(4)(*d*). This Court has been called upon on many occasions to construe the phrase "decision or order ... required by law to be made on a judicial or quasi-judicial basis, made by or in the course of proceedings before a federal board, commission or other tribunal" in section 28 of the Act as it read prior to the 1990 amendments. As has been pointed out in D. J. M. Brown and J. M. Evans, *Judicial Review of Administrative Action in Canada*, loose-leaf ed. (Toronto: Canvasback Publishing, 1998), at paragraph 2:4420, note 376, "initially the Court restricted the term to 'final' decisions or orders, and to those that the tribunal was expressly charged by its enabling legislation to make" but, subsequently, the scope of section 28 was "broadened to include a decision that was fully determinative of the substantive rights of the party, even though it may not be the ultimate decision of the tribunal". Indeed, a recommendation to a Minister of the Crown by an investigative tribunal which by reasonable expectation would lead to a deportation, has been considered reviewable under section 28: *Moumdjian v Canada (Security Intelligence Review Committee)*, [1999] 4 FC 624 (CA).

'I must confess to some difficulty in viewing the findings in issue as "decisions" within the meaning of the section. The decision in *Krever, supra*, [at paragraph 34, page 460] suggests that

the contrary may be true for, as has been seen, the findings of a commissioner under the *Inquiries Act* "are simply findings of fact and statements of opinion" that carry "no legal consequences", are "not enforceable" and "do not bind courts considering the same subject matter". In an earlier case, *Nenn v The Queen*, [1981] 1 SCR 631, at page 636, it was held that the "opinion" required of the Public Service Commission under paragraph 21(*b*) of the *Public Service Employment Act*, RSC 1970, c P-32, was not a "decision or order" that was amenable to judicial review by this Court under section 28. I must, however, acknowledge the force of the argument the other way, that the review of findings like those in issue is available on the ground afforded by paragraph 18.1(4)(*d*) despite their nature as non-binding opinions, because of the serious harm that might be caused to reputation by findings that lack support in the record.' *Morneault v Canada (Attorney General)* (2000) 189 DLR (4th) 96 at 119–120, FCA, per Stone JA

DEDICATION

[For 21 Halsbury's Laws (4th edn) para 62 see now 21 Halsbury's Laws (4th edn) (2004 Reissue) para 108.]

DEED

[For 12 Halsbury's Laws (4th edn) para 1301 see now 13 Halsbury's Laws (4th edn) (Reissue) paras 1, 7.]

An instrument shall not be a deed unless—

(a) it makes it clear on its face that it is intended to be a deed by the person making it or, as the case may be, by the parties to it (whether by describing itself as a deed or expressing itself to be executed or signed as a deed or otherwise); and

(b) it is validly executed as a deed by that person or, as the case may be, one or more of those parties.

An instrument is validly executed as a deed by an individual if, and only if—

(a) it is signed—
 (i) by him in the presence of a witness who attests the signature; or
 (ii) at his direction and in his presence and the presence of two witnesses who each attest the signature; and

(b) it is delivered as a deed by him or a person authorised to do so on his behalf. (Law of Property (Miscellaneous Provisions) Act 1989, s 1(2), (3))

DEED POLL

[For 12 Halsbury's Laws (4th edn) para 1303 see now 13 Halsbury's Laws (4th edn) (Reissue) para 3.]

DEEM

Australia 'In *Muller v Dalgety & Co Ltd* ((1909) 9 CLR 693 at 696), Griffith CJ said that "deemed" is commonly used for the purpose of creating ... a "statutory fiction" ... that is, for the purpose of extending the meaning of some term to a subject matter which it does not properly designate. When used in that sense it becomes very important to consider the purpose for which the statutory fiction is introduced. This passage has been often quoted in Australian courts. It is a recognition that the verb "deem", or derivatives of it, can be used in statutory definitions to extend the denotation of the defined term to things it would not in ordinary parlance denote. This is often a convenient device for reducing the verbiage of an enactment. But that the word can be used in that way and for that purpose does not mean that whenever it is used it has that effect. After all, to deem means simply to judge or reach a conclusion about something. A judge, or a juryman, is a deemster, although, except in the Isle of Man, that name has long been archaic. The words "deem" and "deemed" when used in a statute thus simply state the effect or meaning which some matter or thing has ó the way in which it is to be adjudged. This need not import artificiality or fiction. It may be simply the statement of an indisputable conclusion, as if for example one were to say that on attaining the age of twenty-one years a man is deemed to be of full age and no longer an infant. Hundreds of examples of this usage of the word appear in the statute books. I take two or three only by way of illustration. In England, Lord Brougham's Act, 13 & 14 Vict c 21, s 7, provided that "every Act passed after the 10th June 1850 shall be deemed and taken to be a public Act and shall be judicially taken notice of as such unless the contrary be expressly provided and declared by such Act". No fiction is involved in that. In New South Wales the Real Property Act 1900 (NSW) s 35, states when a grant, certificate of title or instrument affecting land under the provisions of the Act shall be deemed to be registered, and adds that "the person named in any grant, certificate of title, or other instrument so registered as seised of or taking any estate or interest shall be deemed to be the registered proprietor thereof". This provision of the Torrens system is a definition of registered proprietor, not

based in any sense on a fiction.' *Cooper & Dysart Pty Ltd v Sargon* (1991) 4 ACSR 649 at 655–656, per Rowland J

DEEMED

New Zealand 'I accept that, as a matter of construction, the word "deemed" is capable of meaning "rebuttably presumed", that is, presumed until the contrary is proved ... ' *International Bottling Co Ltd v Collector of Customs* [1995] 2 NZLR 579 at 584, per Tompkins J

DEEMED TO BE SERVED

'[15] In the rules [CPR], as originally drafted, r 2.8 was not mentioned at all in r 6.7. As a result of amendments (made by r 4(4) of the Civil Procedure Amendment Rules 2000, SI 2000/221), it is now expressly mentioned in r 6.7 in the following manner, immediately preceding the table:

> "(1) A document which is served in accordance with these rules or any relevant practice direction shall be deemed to be served on the day shown in the following table ...

(Rule 2.8 excludes a Saturday, Sunday, a Bank Holiday, Christmas Day or Good Friday from calculations of periods of 5 days or less) ...'

...

'[43] The court has had the benefit of fuller argument on the point than in *Godwin*'s case [*Godwin v Swindon Borough Council* [2001] EWCA Civ 1478, [2001] 4 All ER 641] and we conclude that, on the natural and ordinary meaning of the language of r 6.7, Saturday and Sunday are not excluded from the calculation of the day of deemed service by first class post. Rule 2.8 does not in terms apply whenever there is a reference in the CPR to the calculation of a period of time of five days or less. It is in restricted terms. It only applies to the calculation of any period of time "for doing any act" which is specified by the CPR, by a practice direction or by a court order. Rule 6.7 does not specify a period of time for doing any act under the CPR. It sets out the methods of calculating the days on which the event of service is deemed to happen as a result of doing acts under other rules involving the use of the various available methods for service of a claim form. Service of a claim form is an act done under rules other than r 6.7.' *Anderton v Clwyd County Council* [2002] EWCA Civ 933 at [15], [43], [2002] 3 All ER 813, per Mummery LJ

DEEMING

New Zealand ' "Deeming" is a statutory technique used to extend the meaning of a word or definition beyond its ordinary or primary meaning, or to make clear something which might otherwise be debatable. Such a provision is not usually an exclusive definition of a category but adds something which would not ordinarily be included.' *Far North District Council v Local Government Commission* [1994] 3 NZLR 78 at 86, per Speight J

DEER

[The Deer Acts 1963 and 1980 have been repealed. The definition of 'deer' is re-enacted in the Deer Act 1991, s 16. Close seasons are prescribed by s 2, Sch 1. As to offences of taking or killing deer see ss 1, 2, 9.]

DEFAMATION

[For 28 Halsbury's Laws (4th edn) para 10 see now 28 Halsbury's Laws (4th edn) (Reissue) para 10.]

[For 28 Halsbury's Laws (4th edn) para 42 see now 28 Halsbury's Laws (4th edn) (Reissue) para 42.]

DEFEASANCE

[For 4 Halsbury's Laws (4th edn) para 704 see now 4(1) Halsbury's Laws (4th edn) (2002 Reissue) para 729.]

DEFECT

Australia [A 'defect' in relation to a statutory demand is defined by s 9 of the Corporations Law to include an irregularity; a misstatement of an amount or total; a misdescription of a debt or other matter; and a misdescription of a person or entity.] 'The definition of "defect" is an inclusive definition, so one must construe the term initially according to its ordinary meaning and then introduce into it, if it is otherwise not included, the deemed statutory connotations. According to its ordinary usage a "defect" means a lack or absence of something necessary or essential for completeness; a shortcoming or deficiency; an imperfection. A defect according to ordinary understanding is not necessarily something which is of a minor nature, it may be either major or minor ... The notion of a "defect" is not to be confined to a misstatement of an amount of a debt to a small or minor

misstatement or to an immaterial or minor misdescription of a debt or a person or entity. Misdescriptions of debts, persons, entities or amounts all fall within the statutory definition of "defect", whether large or small ... ' *Topfelt Pty Ltd v State Bank of New South Wales Ltd* (1993) 47 FCR 226 at 237–238; 120 ALR 155 at 166–167, per Lockhart J

DEFECT OF TITLE

[For 42 Halsbury's Laws (4th edn) para 63 see now 42 Halsbury's Laws (4th edn) (Reissue) para 57.]

DEFENSIVE EQUITY

Australia 'This phrase was used by Deane J in *Commonwealth v Verwayen* (1990) 170 CLR 394 at 435 to denote laches, acquiescence or delay or a mere set-off.' *Giumelli v Giumelli* (1999) 161 ALR 473 at 476; 73 ALJR 547; BC9901018, per Gleeson CJ, McHugh, Gummow and Callinan JJ

DEFICIENCY

[Allocation of Housing and Homelessness (Review Procedures) Regulations 1999, SI 1999/71, reg 8(2).] '[25] ... Regulation 8(2) of the 1999 regulations is an important part of the mechanisms designed to ensure the fairness of the overall procedure, although it seems to have received surprisingly little attention in the numerous reported cases on this legislation. It provides:

> "If the reviewer considers that *there is deficiency or irregularity in the original decision or in the manner in which it was made* but is minded nevertheless to make a decision which is against the interests of the applicant on one or more issues the reviewer shall notify the applicant—(a) that the reviewer is so minded, and the reasons why; and (b) that the applicant, or someone acting on his behalf, may make representations to the reviewer orally or in writing or both orally and in writing." (My emphasis.)

...

'[29] ... The word "deficiency" does not have any particular legal connotation. It simply means "something lacking". There is nothing in the words of the rule to limit it to failings which would give grounds for legal challenge. If that were the intention, one would have expected it to have been stated expressly. Furthermore, since the judgment is that of the reviewing officer, who is unlikely to be a lawyer, it would be surprising if the criterion were one depending solely on legal judgment. On the other hand, the "something lacking" must be of sufficient importance to the fairness of the procedure to justify an extra procedural safeguard. Whether that is so involves an exercise of "evaluative judgment" (see *Runa Begum v Tower Hamlets London BC* [2003] 1 All ER 731 at [114], [2003] 2 AC 430 at [114] per Lord Walker of Gestingthorpe), on which the officer's conclusion will only be challengeable on *Wednesbury* grounds.' *Hall v Wandsworth London Borough Council* [2004] EWCA Civ 1740, [2005] 2 All ER 192 at [25], [29], per Carnwath LJ

DEFRAUD

Australia 'The meaning of the word "defraud" was considered in the speech of Lord Radcliffe in *Welham v Director of Public Prosecutions* [1961] AC 103 at 123–124 ... Those principles find support in *R v Allsop* (1976) 64 Cr App R 29 ... It is not an element of the crime of defrauding that the person obtaining the advantage is not entitled to it. The essence of the crime is the deceit.' *Taylor v R* (1997) 6 Tas R 310 at 336–337; (1997) 93 A Crim R 1; (1997) 137 FLR 250; BC9700447 at 8–9, per Zeeman J

Intent to

Australia [Section 264 of the Criminal Code (Tas) provides that a clerk or servant who, with 'intent to defraud', falsifies his employer's books, documents or accounts, is guilty of fraud as a clerk or servant.] '... for there to be an intent to defraud it is not sufficient merely to induce a course of action by deception. Some prejudice must at least be intended to be caused, to use the expression of Burt CJ, in *Tan v R* [1979] WAR 96 or an intention to deprive another of property or to act to his injury or detriment, to use the expression of Wallace J in the same case, or an intention to deprive another by deceit of some economic advantage or inflict upon him some economic loss, to use the expression of Lord Radcliffe in *Welham v DPP* [1961] AC 103 which was adopted by Burt CJ in *Attorney-General's Reference 1/1981* [1982] WAR 149.' *R v Franklin* [1991] Tas R 54 at 60, per Crawford J

DEL CREDERE AGENT

[For 1 Halsbury's Laws (4th edn) para 713 see now 1(2) Halsbury's Laws (4th edn) (Reissue) para 13.]

DELEGATION

[For 1 Halsbury's Laws (4th edn) para 747 see now 1(2) Halsbury's Laws (4th edn) (Reissue) para 63.]

DELETERIOUS SUBSTANCE

Canada '[60] Subsection 36(3) of the *Fisheries Act*, reproduced again below for ease of reference, prohibits persons from (1) depositing or permitting the deposit of (2) a deleterious substance of any type (3) in water frequented by fish or in any place where the deleterious substance may enter such water:

> 36(3) Subject to subsection (4) [deposits authorized by regulation], *no person shall deposit or permit the deposit of a deleterious substance of any type in water frequented by fish or in any place under any conditions where the deleterious substance* or any other deleterious substance that results from the deposit of the deleterious substance *may enter any such water.* [Emphasis added.]

'[61] In this case, s-s. (4) is not relevant.
'[62] In s. 34(1), "deleterious substance" is defined as:

> (a) any substance that, if added to any water, would degrade or alter or form part of a process of degradation or alteration of the quality of that water so that it is rendered or is likely to be rendered deleterious to fish or fish habitat or to the use by man of fish that frequent that water.

'[63] On an ordinary and plain reading of para. (a), a substance is deleterious if, when added to any water, it would alter the quality of the water such that it is likely to render the water deleterious to fish, fish habitat or to the use by man of fish that frequent the water. There is no stipulation in para. (a) that the substance must be proven to be deleterious to the receiving water. There is no reference to the receiving water in para. (a). On the contrary, the language makes it clear that the substance is deleterious if, when added to any water, it degrades or alters the quality of the water to which it has been added. The "any water" referred to in para. (a) is not the receiving water. Rather, it is any water to which the impugned substance is added, after which it can be determined whether the quality of that water is rendered deleterious to fish, fish habitat or the use by man of fish that frequent that water.' *R v Kingston (City)* [2004] OJ No 1940, 240 DLR (4th) 734 (CA), per Gillese JA

DELIBERATE

See also CONSCIOUS, VOLUNTARY AND
DELIBERATE ACT

Canada '[92] It is our view that such an error is
disclosed in paragraph 77, where the Judge said,
"at least one other potential inference may be
drawn: that the dedication was deliberate arising
out of confusion or miscommunication". The
conclusion that the dedication arose out of confusion
or miscommunication is antithetical to the
conclusion that the dedication was deliberate.
Indeed, it is axiomatic that a step taken on account
of confusion or miscommunication cannot be
deliberate. According to *The Oxford English
Dictionary* (2nd ed.), an act is deliberate if it is
"[w]ell weighed or considered; carefully thought
out; formed, carried out, etc. with careful
consideration and full intention; done of set purpose;
studied; not hasty or rash." While it may be that the
dedication documents were deliberately sent, this
does not mean that there was a deliberate act or
intention to include the 768 patent in the list of
patents to be dedicated.' *Parke-Davis Division v
Canada (Minister of Health)* [2003] 2 FC 549–550
(FCA), per the Court

DELIBERATELY ABSENTED HIMSELF
FROM HIS TRIAL

[Under the Extradition Act 2003, s 83(1), at an
extradition hearing, if the judge is required to
proceed under s 83 he must decide whether the
person whose extradition is sought was convicted
in his presence. Under s 83(3), if the judge decides
that question in the negative he must decide whether
the person 'deliberately absented himself from his
trial'.] '[48] I reach the following conclusions: (a)
In s 85(3) Parliament has adopted the expression
"deliberately absented himself from his trial".
Consideration must be given to the concept of
deliberate absence and to the concept of a trial.
The respondent has deliberately absented himself
from Albania but there is no evidence that he knew
of the existence of a trial or of any proceedings
which might lead to a trial. (b) The word "trial"
was adopted by Parliament in the context of the
presence of art 6 [of the European Convention for
the Protection of Human Rights and Fundamental
Freedoms 1950 (as set out in Sch 1 to the Human
Rights Act 1998)] with its use of the word "hearing"
and its reference to a right to a hearing and a right
to be informed of the nature and cause of the
accusation. Article 6 confers the right to a fair trial

and the word "trial" would not have been used by
Parliament in s 85(3) if a wider view of absence
had been intended. (c) The subsection must be
construed in a context in which capital importance
is attached to the appearance of a defendant at his
trial. The focus is on a specific event at which the
respondent could expect to be present. Other factors,
as well as the need to facilitate extradition, are at
work. (d) Parliament could have used an expression
such as "deliberately absenting himself from legal
process" which could, on appropriate findings of
fact, include leaving a jurisdiction to avoid arrest
but Parliament has not done so and the sub-section
cannot be construed as if it had. The expression
"his trial" contemplates a specific event and not
the entire legal process. (e) In the result, I am
unable to construe the words of s 85(3) as covering
the present circumstances. While the absence from
the jurisdiction of Albania is established, it is not
established that the respondent left that jurisdiction,
or remained in the United Kingdom, with the
intention expressed in the subsection.' *Government
of the Republic of Albania v Bleta* [2005] EWHC
475 (Admin), [2005] 3 All ER 351 at [48], per
Pill LJ

DELIVERY

Of goods

[For 41 Halsbury's Laws (4th edn) para 747 see
now 41 Halsbury's Laws (4th edn) (Reissue)
para 163.]

[For 41 Halsbury's Laws (4th edn) paras 757–
789 see now 41 Halsbury's Laws (4th edn) (Reissue)
paras 163–195.]

DEMANDS DELIVERY

[Section 3(1) of Carriage of Goods by Sea Act 1992
provides that where s 2(1) operates in relation to
any document to which the Act applies and the
person in whom rights are vested by virtue of that
subsection takes or 'demands delivery' from the
carrier of any of the goods to which the document
relates (para (a)); makes a claim under the contract
of carriage against the carrier in respect of any of
those goods (para (b)); or is a person who, at the
time before those rights were vested in him, took
or 'demanded delivery' from the carrier of any of
those goods (para (c)), that person becomes subject
to the same liabilities under that contract as if he
had been a party to it. Section 2(1) transfers to, and
vests in, the lawful holder of the bill of lading all
rights of suit under the contract of carriage as if it

had been a party to that contract. The House of Lords had to determine what constituted a 'demand' for 'delivery' for the purposes of s 3(1) and whether the sellers had made such a demand.] '[32] In giving effect to this intention, s 3 of the 1992 Act postulates first that the holder in question must be a person in whom the contractual rights of suit have been vested by s 2(1). The language of s 2(1) adopts and is identical to the corresponding words in the 1855 Act [Bills of Lading Act 1855], "shall have transferred [to] and vested in him all rights of suit". Section 3(1)(a) and (b) relate to a person who, being a person who has those rights, chooses to exercise them either (a) by taking or demanding delivery of the goods or (b) by making a claim under the contract of carriage contained in or evidenced by the bill of lading. Both involve an enforcement by the endorsee of the contractual rights against the carrier transferred to him by s 2(1). Under (a) it is by enjoying or demanding the performance of the carrier's contractual delivery obligation. Under (b) it is by claiming a remedy for some breach by the carrier of the contract of carriage. Each of (a) and (b) involves a choice by the endorsee to take a positive step in relation to the contract of carriage and the rights against the carrier transferred to him by s 2(1). It has the character of an election to avail himself of those contractual rights against the carrier. There are however difficulties which neither the drafting nor the report [Law Commission and Scottish Law Commission: *Rights of suit in respect of carriage of goods by sea* (Law Com No 196, Scot Law Com No 130, March 1991)] faces up to. Whilst taking delivery is a clear enough concept—it involves a voluntary transfer of possession from one person to another—making a "demand" or "claim" does not have such a specific character and, what is more, may be tentative or capable of being resiled from, a point commented upon by Millett LJ in the Court of Appeal ([1998] 4 All ER 821 at 836, [1999] QB 863 at 884). Delivery brings an end to the actual bailment of the goods and is (save in special circumstances) the final act of contractual performance on the part of the carrier. Claims or demands may on the other hand be made at any stage (although usually only made after the end of the voyage) and there may at the time still be performance obligations of the carrier yet to be performed.

'[33] To "make a claim" may be anything from expressing a view in the course of a meeting or letter as to the liability of the carrier to issuing a writ or arresting the vessel. A "demand" might be an invitation or request, or, perhaps, even implied

from making arrangements; or it might be a more formal express communication, such as would have sufficed to support an action in detinue. From the context in the 1992 Act and the purpose underlying s 3(1), it is clear that s 3 must be understood in a way which reflects the potentially important consequences of the choice or election which the bill of lading holder is making. The liabilities, particularly when alleged dangerous goods are involved, may be disproportionate to the value of the goods; the liabilities may not be covered by insurance; the endorsee may not be fully aware of what the liabilities are. I would therefore read the phrase "demands delivery" as referring to a formal demand made to the carrier or his agent asserting the contractual right as the endorsee of the bill of lading to have the carrier deliver the goods to him. And I would read the phrase "makes a claim under the contract of carriage" as referring to a formal claim against the carrier asserting a legal liability of the carrier under the contract of carriage to the holder of the bill of lading.

'[34] But this is not the end of this problem. The use of the word "demand" is problematic as is the phrase "or at least attempting to enforce rights" in para 3.18 of the report. (It seems that those who wrote para 3.18 had in mind such exceptional situations as where the cargo is destroyed while the vessel is waiting to discharge at the discharge port and after a demurrage liability recoverable under the bill of lading has arisen—an intriguing and, if I may be forgiven for saying so, a relatively unilluminating example.) If the carrier accedes to the demand and gives delivery as demanded, the demand is subsumed in the taking of delivery. If the carrier rejects the demand, a new scenario arises: is the endorsee going to make a claim against the carrier for refusing to comply with the demand? If the endorsee chooses to let the matter drop and not to make a claim, what significance of the demand remains? What principle of mutuality requires that the endorsee shall nevertheless be made subject to the liabilities of a contracting party? What if the endorsee chooses to endorse over the bill of lading to another to whom the carrier is willing to and does deliver the goods? The task of the judge, arbitrator or legal adviser attempting to construe s 3(1) is not an easy one and it is necessary to try and extract from it some self-consistent structure.

'[35] So far I have been concentrating on paras (a) and (b). Paragraph (c) presents further problems. It raises the relatively common situation where the vessel and its cargo arrive at the destination before the bills of lading have completed their journey down the chain of banks and buyers. The intended receiver has not yet acquired any rights under s 2(1). He is not entitled to demand delivery of the goods from the carrier. He may or may not be the owner of the goods but he quite probably will not at that time have the right to the possession of the goods; an earlier holder of the bill of lading may be a pledgee of the goods. This situation is dealt with commercially by delivering the goods against a letter of indemnity provided by the receiver (or his bank) which will include an undertaking by the receiver to surrender the bill of lading to the carrier as soon as it is acquired and will include any other stipulations and terms which the situation calls for. It may well at that time, either expressly or by implication, give rise to a *Brandt* type of contract on the terms of the bill of lading. But again the question arises: what is the character and the role of the demand referred to in para (c)? Ex hypothesi, the intended receiver had no right to make the demand and the carrier had no obligation to accede to it unless there was some other contract between the receiver and the carrier, e g a charterparty, which gave rise to that right and obligation in which case ss 2 and 3 have no application to that transaction. Paragraph (c) clearly involves an anticipation that the s 2(1) rights will be transferred to the receiver. The parenthesis which follows emphasises this "by virtue of having the rights vested in him". This shows that it is a necessary condition of the receiver's becoming liable under s 3(1) that the rights are vested in him by the operation of s 2(1). The inclusion of the word "demanded" remains problematical. A rightly rejected demand for delivery by one who is not entitled to delivery is an act devoid of legal significance. What is significant is if the carrier decides (voluntarily) to accede to the demand and deliver the goods to the receiver notwithstanding the non-arrival of the bill of lading. Paragraph (c) does not include the making of a claim. The draftsman has accepted the irrelevance of a claim made by one who has no contractual standing to make it. Unless facts occur which give a relevance to the inclusion of the word "demanded" in para (c), in my view the scheme of ss 2 and 3 requires that any such demand be treated as irrelevant for the purposes of s 3(1) and that the 1992 Act be construed accordingly. A "demand" made without any basis for making it or insisting upon compliance is not in reality a demand at all. It is not a request made "as of right", which is the primary dictionary meaning of "demand". It is not accompanied by any threat of legal sanction. It is a request which can voluntarily be acceded to or refused as the person to whom it is made may choose. Accordingly it will be unlikely in the extreme that para (c) will ever apply save where there has been an actual delivery of the cargo.' *Borealis AB v Stargas Ltd, The Berge Sisar* [2001] UKHL/17 at [32]–[35], [2001] 2 All ER 193 at 209–211, HL, per Lord Hobhouse of Woodborough

DEMISE

[For 27 Halsbury's Laws (4th edn) para 107 see now 27(1) Halsbury's Laws (4th edn) (Reissue) para 106.]

DEMISED PREMISES

'[44] Section 106(b) of the Property Law Act provides:

> (b) That he will, at all times during the continuance of the said lease, keep, and at the termination thereof yield up, the demised premises in good and tenantable repair, having regard to their condition at the commencement of the said lease, accidents and damage from fire, flood, lightning, storm, tempest, earthquake, and fair wear and tear (all without neglect or default of the lessee) excepted:
> Provided that this covenant shall not be implied in any lease of a dwellinghouse.

'[45] The first issue is whether the term "demised premises" in s 106(b) includes land. The term is not defined in the Property Law Act. The words of s 106(b) itself suggest that it is directed to the repair of buildings and structures on land rather than the land itself. But I see no reason to construe the covenant narrowly so as to exclude land.

...

'[48] The context in which the words are used in s 106(b) does not require that "demised premises" be confined to buildings in cases where land is also part of the property leased. Although the section is plainly directed principally to the repairs of structures on land, it makes perfect sense if the words "demised premises" are given their accepted meaning. The application of this section can be modified if necessary by other means as I will now discuss.

...

'[51] BP's position is that the express repair clauses have deliberately limited the lessee's repair obligation to buildings and other structures on the land. Mr Lange pointed out that the repair clauses make specific reference to the land, in the case of the leases of 36–54 and 58–90 Brigham Street by referring to "the demised premises", the words of s 106(b) exactly. This, he says, demonstrates an intention that s 106(b) is not to be implied.' *BP Oil New Zealand Ltd v Ports of Auckland Ltd* [2004] 2 NZLR 208 at 222, 223

DEMOCRATIC INSTITUTIONS

Canada '[34] In applying subparagraph 19(1)(*f*)(i) of the *Immigration Act*, the visa officer must examine firstly, the status of the organization, i.e., is it a democratic institution – *institution démocratique* within the meaning of the subparagraph, and secondly the conduct of the non-citizen, i.e., whether the non-citizen has engaged in acts of espionage or subversion against that democratic institution. The conduct of the non-citizen for the purpose of the subparagraph is only relevant if a determination has been made that the organization has the required status.

'[35] In our view, the application Judge erred when he held that the expression "democratic government, institutions or processes" (or "*institutions démocratiques*" as used in the French text) was restricted to institutions and processes involving "political governance". The expression also encompasses institutions and processes which although non-governmental, are part and parcel of the democratic fabric of Canada and there is no basis for limiting the purpose of paragraph 19(1)(*f*) in the manner suggested by the application Judge.

'[36] Both the case law and the plain dictionary meaning of the relevant terms support the view that the expression in issue as it is understood in Canada is capable of a wide meaning. For instance, in *Lavigne v. Ontario Public Service Employees Union*, [1991] 2 S.C.R. 211, the Supreme Court recognized that a union is a democratic institution different from government [at pages 326 and 330-331]:

I would also add that some of the concerns which might normally be raised by a compelled association are tempered when that association is, as in this case, established in accordance with democratic principles. Professor Norman Cantor, "Forced Payments to Service Institutions and Constitutional Interests in Ideological Non-Association" (1983), 36 Rutgers L. Rev. 3, is clear in his view that government should be able to confer on democratic institutions powers to receive payments for services and to contribute to causes serving their ends even though these may be objected to by dissenters.

...

The essential question is whether democracy in the workplace has been kept within its proper or constitutionally permissible sphere. The experience of the United States is helpful in considering this difficult issue. The courts in that country have attempted to make a clear distinction between an individual's relationship with government and his or her relationship with other democratic institutions, such as professional associations and unions.

...

With respect to democratic institutions other than the government, and to unions in particular, the United States Supreme Court has attempted to draw the line between those actions designed "to promote the cause which justified bringing the group together" ... and those actions which fall outside that sphere.

'[37] We can conclude from *Lavigne* that there are democratic institutions in Canada other than the government, such as, but not limited to, professional associations and unions.

...

'[42] The *Blackwell Encyclopaedia of Political Science*, Oxford (U.K.): Blackwell Publishers, 1991, at pages 167 and 168 also acknowledges that democratic processes and democratic institutions are not always related to government:

Modern Democratic regimes are distinguished by the existence, legality and legitimacy of a variety of autonomous organizations and associations that are relatively independent in relation to the government and to one and another. This characteristic is often referred to as PLURALISM.

'[43] In the *Oxford Companion to Politics of the World*, New York: Oxford University Press, 1993, at page 223, in contemporary circumstances, marked by a high degree of social, economic, and political differentiation, the author concluded that: A system of institutions to promote discussion, debate, and competition among divergent views, a system encompassing the formation of movements, pressure group, and/or political parties with leaderships to help press their cases appears both necessary and desirable.

...

'[45] It follows that both the words "institution" and "process" when qualified by the word "democratic" are capable of a meaning which transcends government.

'[46] In Canada, a democratic institution is not limited to a political institution, it includes organized groups who seek through democratic means to influence government policies and decisions.

...

'[50] Accordingly, a democratic institution for the purpose of subparagraph 19(1)(f)(i) of the Immigration Act consists of a structured group of individuals established in accordance with democratic principles with preset goals and objectives who are engaged in lawful activities in Canada of a political, religious, social or economic nature.' *Qu v Canada* [2002] 3 FC 3 at 15–20 (CA), per Richard J

DEMURRAGE

[For 43 Halsbury's Laws (4th edn) para 469 see now 43(2) Halsbury's Laws (4th edn) (Reissue) para 1508.]

DENIZEN

Canada [Appellant claimed de facto citizenship as 'denizen'.] 'It was contended that there was even a common-law basis for such a category in the "denizens" distinguished by Blackstone from "aliens" and "natives": Blackstone, Commentaries on the Laws of England, [abridgement] 3rd edn by W C Sprague, 1895, at page 65, defines a denizen as "an alien born, but who has obtained *ex donatione regis* letters patent to make him an English subject: a high and incommunicable branch of the royal prerogative". However, even though naturalization is recognized by Blackstone as a separate process under the control of Parliament, it is clear that a denizen, like a naturalized person, is more properly to be analogized to a present-day citizen rather than to a non-citizen immigrant. Both denizens and naturalized persons were incapable of being members of the Privy Council or of Parliament, or of holding any office of trust or any grant of lands from the Crown. Both were so created by a formal act, the former by a high and incommunicable branch of the royal prerogative, the latter by an Act of Parliament.' *Canepa v Canada (Minister of Employment and Immigration)* [1992] 3 FC 270 at 275–276, FCA, per MacGuigan JA

DENTAL SURGEON

[For 30 Halsbury's Laws (4th edn) para 199 see now 30 Halsbury's Laws (4th edn) (Reissue) para 301.]

DEPARTMENT

Australia [Section 5 and item 74 in the First Schedule to the Sales Tax (Exemptions and Classifications) Act 1935 (Cth) has the effect that sales tax is not payable on the sole value of goods for official use, and not for sale, by a 'department' of the Government of a State.] 'In my opinion the term "department", in the context of item 74 and especially in light of the distinction drawn there between departments and authorities, means a part of the Public Service of the Commonwealth or a State organised for the carrying out of particular governmental functions and for which a Minister of the Crown is responsible. A department in that sense does not have an identity in law separate from the persons who from time to time constitute it.' *Government Insurance Office of New South Wales v Commissioner of Taxation* (1992) 35 FCR 247 at 251, per Heerey J

Canada ' ... In my view the definition of "department" is sufficiently wide to include independent boards, commissions, agencies and foundations. Section 3(d) of the Freedom of Information Act is as follows:

> (d) "minister" means a member of the Executive Council and, in the case of a board, commission, foundation, agency, association or other body of persons not reporting directly to a minister in respect of its day-to-day operations, means the chief executive officer;

'This definition implies that it is not necessary for an independent commission to be reporting directly to a Minister in order to be subject to the Freedom of Information Act.' *McLaughlin v Halifax-Dartmouth Bridge Commission* (1993) 108 DLR (4th) 506 at 516, NS CA, per Roscoe JA

DEPENDENT

Australia [Section 6(1) of the Family Provision Act 1982 (NSW) provides that an eligible person, who may apply for provision out of the estate of a deceased person, is, inter alia, a person wholly or partly 'dependent' on the deceased person.] 'The word "dependent" is an ordinary English word, and whether a person is or has been wholly or partly dependent upon another is a question of fact. No doubt one of the commonest forms of dependence is a financial one, in the sense that the dependence flows from the fact that accommodation, food, clothing and other necessities or amenities of life are provided by the person who owns or is otherwise entitled to the accommodation and pays for the other things. But I do not think that the word, as used in the statute or otherwise, has this very limited meaning. In ordinary parlance, young children are properly and commonly said to be dependent on their mother as well as their father, regardless of where the money comes from. A contrary view, that young children are not dependent on their mother if she has no independent means, seems to me to be a misuse of language. This accords with what Samuels JA said in *Ball v Newey* (1988) 13 NSWLR 489 at 491, that "'Dependent' in the ordinary sense of the word, means the condition of depending on something or on someone for what is needed". If the correct view were that the context of the statute requires a limitation of the word to "financial or material" matters as McLelland J said in *Re Fulop Deceased* [(1987) 8 NSWLR 679] or to "other forms of dependence analogous to but distinct from financial dependence" as Samuels JA suggested in *Ball v Newey* (at 491), then surely a mother's services to a young child satisfy the test. The child could not survive without the provision of those services; he or she needs them. To suggest that, in a money sense, they are valueless, is simply wrong. If the provision of accommodation by a father for a young child, that is, having the child live in a house which he owns and lives in, can make the child partly dependent upon the father, as it undoubtedly can, I am unable to see why the provision by a mother to her children, living with her, of the services essential for their well-being does not make them partly dependent upon her. In my opinion it does. The same considerations apply to a step-child or his or her step-mother, when the child lives with the step-mother and is looked after by her.' *Petrohilos v Hunter* (1991) 25 NSWLR 343 at 346–347, per Hope A-JA

Dependent child

Australia '*Secretary, Dpt of Social Security v Field* (1989) 25 FCR 425 is, I think, clear authority for the following … 'A child is a dependent child of an adult only if the adult has the legal right to have, and to make decisions concerning, the daily care and control of the child. Care and control in fact, without the legal right, is irrelevant (*Re Juren* (1993) 30 ALD 613 is a good example of the way in which that proposition may apply in practice).' *Elliott v Secretary, Dpt of Social Security* (1995) 134 ALR 439 at 444, per Lehane J

Australia 'In my view, the definition of dependent child [in reg 1.03 of the Migration Regulations (Cth)] recognises that, in the case of a child over 18, the qualifying relationship will not exist routinely but will require a real state of dependency in the particular circumstances. The fact that the

definition is drawn in that way also seems to reflect an intention on the part of the legislature to require a child over 18 to have the need to rely upon a parent or parents rather than simply having chosen, for a time, not to exercise the independence which that person may enjoy … I have reached the view that the Tribunal erred in assessing financial dependence only by reference to the respondent's immediate situation imposed by the restriction upon her working whilst in Australia. I consider that the proper approach at law required consideration to be given to the respondent's capacity to support herself in her country of origin, or the country from which she came into Australia, having regard to her physical and mental wellbeing, her skills and training, her resources, her background, and her general personal circumstances, and to her capacity to continue to do so. The focus upon her situation whilst in Australia in my view is too narrow a focus for responding to the question which the definition dictates. In my view, the definition of "dependent child" does not contemplate that the existence of the state of financial dependency should be inquired into only in relation to the respondent's situation in Australia, dictated by criteria for eligibility for a visa or by the visa conditions which preclude the visa applicant from working whilst in Australia.' *Minister for Immigration and Multicultural Affairs v Pires* (1998) 160 ALR 97 at 103–104; BC9806872 at 9–10, per Mansfield J

DEPENDENT RELATIVE REVOCATION

[For 50 Halsbury's Laws (4th edn) para 298 see now 50 Halsbury's Laws (4th edn) (Reissue) para 348.]

DEPICT

Australia 'According to the Oxford Dictionary, the word "depict" means represent in drawing or colours or portray in words. It is the latter meaning which was relied upon by the Commonwealth in this case.

'According to The New Shorter Oxford Dictionary on Historical Principles Vol 1 at 637, "depict" is given the following meanings:

1. Portray or represent (as if) in colours or in drawing, painting or sculpture …
2. Portray or represent in words; describe graphically.

'In the same work "depiction" means:

the action of depicting; painted representations; graphic description.

'The word "describe" means "Portray in words" or "give a detailed or graphic account of [someone or something]. The word "description" means, among other things: "detailed account of a person ... a verbal portrait" and "a verbal representation of portraiture".

'In September 1999, Guidelines for the Classification of Publications (the "Guidelines") were published following their approval by Commonwealth, State and Territory Censorship Ministers in accordance with s 12(3) of the Classification (Publications, Films and Computer Games) Act 1995 (Cth) to take effect from 1 September 1999. The definition of "depiction" in the Guidelines is:

> Representation through image. Realistic depictions include photographs or illustrations which are close to real life; stylised depictions include cartoons and other unrealistic illustrations and images.

' "Description" is defined as:

> Representation through text. Generally descriptions of classifiable elements may contain more detail than depictions.

'According to Roget's Thesaurus of English Word and Phrases (Twelfth Impression, 1978) p 808, "depict" is a verb which means "represent" or "describe". In the same work at p 344, "representation" is a synonym for "depiction" or "portrayal". According to Roget's New Millenium Thesaurus First Edition 2005 at p 344, "depict" is a synonym of "describe" the meanings of which include delineate, draw, picture and represent. The word "represent" is defined at p 326 as a synonym for "imitate", "depict", "picture" or "portray". It follows that a written description of a person and the behaviour of that person is a depiction or portrayal of that person whether in terms of appearance or behaviour. For these reasons, ground 2 has not been made out to that extent.

'In my opinion, the learned Judge did not define the meaning of the words "depict" and "person" too broadly. The meaning adopted was consistent with the generally accepted usage of those words. I will deal separately with the issue whether the words were defined in such a way that contravened ss 7 and 24 of the Constitution.' *Holland v the Queen* [2005] WASCA 140 at [24]–[31], per Malcolm CJ; BC200505554

Australia '[169] "Depict" is not defined in the Act. The meanings given in the "Macquarie Dictionary" (2nd revised ed) are:

1. to represent by or as by painting; portray; delineate
2. to represent in words; describe.

'[170] "The New Shorter Oxford English Dictionary" defines "depict" as:
1. portray or represent (as if) in colours or in drawing, painting or sculpture.
2. portray or represent in words; describe graphically.

'[171] The "Australian Concise Oxford Dictionary" gives a similar definition.

'[172] The explanatory memorandum accompanying the Bill is of some assistance. Paragraphs 63 and 64 read:

> 63. New subsection 233BAB(2) confirms that the regulations must not specify an item as constituting a tier 2 good unless the importation or exportation of the item is already prohibited (conditionally or absolutely) by regulation. Thus, this new section does not establish a new class of prohibited goods, rather it creates new penalties relating to the unlawful importation or exportation of existing classes of prohibited goods.

> 64. New subsection 233BAB(3) defines child pornography for the purposes of the offence. It provides that for the purposes of new subsection 233BAB(1) an item is taken to be an item of child pornography if it is a document or other goods that depicts a person who is, or appears to be, under the age of 16 years, who is involved in a sexual pose or sexual activity, and that depiction is likely to cause offence to a reasonable adult. Section 4 defines 'document' as including books.

...

'[181] Notwithstanding that expressed view — which is only an aid to construction — the terms of reg 4A(1A) itself at that time necessarily draw a distinction between "depict in pictorial form" and "depict". If they are both construed to mean pictorial material, the words "in pictorial form" are wholly redundant. In my view, in that context, "depict" must mean represent in writing

...

'[189] It is plain that the evil to which s 233BAB of the Customs Act was directed is the importation of child pornography, whether in the form of literature or photographs. The underlying purposes were both to shield the community from injury and protect children from exploitation. It would be inconsistent with the legislative purpose, and create an unnecessary anomaly, were the section to be construed to allow proscription of pictorial publications of serious child pornography as tier 2 goods but not allow such proscription of descriptive texts of serious child pornography. The terms "describe" or "depict" are not defined in the Customs Act. The ordinary meaning of the word "depict" includes "describe". There is no textual constraint in the Act which would require the word "depict" to be construed in a restricted sense to exclude "describe".' *Holland v the Queen* [2005] WASCA 140 at [169]–[172], [181], [189], per Roberts-Smith JA; BC200505554

DEPICTED

Canada 'Section 163.1(1)(*a*)(i) [of the *Criminal Code*] brings within the definition of child pornography a visual representation of a person "who is or is depicted as being under the age of eighteen years and is engaged in or is depicted as engaged in explicit sexual activity" (emphasis added). Does "depicted" mean: (a) intended by the maker to depict; (b) perceived by the possessor as depicting; or (c) seen as being depicted by a reasonable observer?

'The first and second interpretations are inconsistent with Parliament's objective of preventing harm to children through sexual abuse. The danger associated with the representation does not depend on what was in the mind of the maker or the possessor, but in the capacity of the representation to be used for purposes like seduction. It is the meaning which is conveyed by the material which is critical, not necessarily the meaning that the author intended to convey. Moreover, it would be virtually impossible to prove what was in the mind of the producer or possessor. On the second alternative, the same material could be child pornography in the possession of one person and innocent material in the hands of another. Yet the statute makes it an offence for anyone to possess such material, not just those who see it as depicting children. The only workable approach is to read "depicted" in the sense of what would be conveyed to a reasonable observer. The test must be objective, based on the depiction rather than what was in the mind of the author or possessor. The question is this: would a reasonable observer perceive the person in the representation as being under 18 and engaged in explicit sexual activity?' *R. v Sharpe* (2001) 194 DLR (4th) 1 at 29, SCC, per McLachlin CJC

DEPLORABLE

Canada '[23] That being said, I note that in its decision, the Board qualified the treatment suffered by Mr. Suleiman and his family as "deplorable". In *The Canadian Oxford Dictionary*, Toronto: Oxford University Press Canada, 2001, the words "deplorable" and "deplore" have the following meanings:

> **deplorable**: ... **1** – exceedingly bad

> **deplore**: ... **2** – be scandalized by; find exceedingly bad

'[24] On the other hand, in the same dictionary, the words "appalling", "atrocious" and "atrocity" are defined as follows:

> **appalling**: ... **1** – shocking, unpleasant; bad

> **atrocious**: 1 – very bad or unpleasant ... 2 – extremely savage or wicked

> **atrocity**: 1 – an extremely wicked or cruel act, esp. one involving physical violence or injury. 2 – extreme wickedness. 3 – something that evokes outrage or disgust

'[25] The Board has saved the reader shocking details of Mr. Suleiman and family's sad story. Be that as it may, it seems to me that if the treatment suffered by Mr. Suleiman and his family, was "deplorable", that is "exceedingly bad", I fail to see then why it would not be "appalling" or "atrocious". Here, the Board accepted that Mr. Suleiman was beaten by the police with canes which, in itself, is certainly a cruel treatment. Luckily, Mr. Suleiman was not killed by the police as was his cousin Mwalim in 2001. Surely, if the treatment suffered by Mr. Suleiman and his family was "deplorable", the Board should state, in the circumstances of the present case, why the acts committed cannot be considered "compelling reasons". The mere fact that such maltreatment "was, lamentably, not unusual for persons running afoul of security forces in Tanzania at the time" does not excuse the gravity of the past persecution which in this case is still fairly recent and has apparently indelibly marked the mental state of Mr. Suleiman. Moreover, the generalized character of the past persecution in Tanzania should not serve as a bar to the application of the "compelling reasons" exception.' *Suleiman v Canada* (*Minister of Citizenship & Immigration*) [2005] 2 FCR 26 at [23]–[25], [2004] FCJ No 1354 (Fed Ct), per Martineau J

DEPOSIT

Australia [Land and Business (Sale and Conveyancing) Act 1994 (SA) s 6:

6(1) A contract for the sale of land or a business that provides for the payment of part of the purchase price of the land or business (except a deposit) before the date of settlement is void.

(2) Money paid under a contract that is void under subsection (1) may be recovered by action in any court of competent jurisdiction.

(3) In this section —

'deposit' means an amount paid by a purchaser in a lump sum, or in not more than three instalments, towards the purchase price of land or a business before the date of settlement.]

'Much of the argument in this case turned on what constituted a "deposit" for the purposes of s 6 and in particular whether the payment of $50,000 on 4 April 2002 formed part of the deposit. I was referred to a number of cases including *Howe v Smith* (1884) 27 ChD 89 at 101; *Mehmet v Benson* (1963) 81 WN (NSW) 188 at 191; *Coates v Sarich* [1964] WAR 2 at 6 and 15; *Brien v Dwyer* (1978) 141 CLR 378 at 386, 398, 401 and 406. There is no doubt that at common law the word, when undefined, usually means something in the nature of an earnest given by a purchaser to bind the bargain as security for its performance. However, that is not necessarily its meaning in this case.

'For the purpose of s 6 the word is defined as meaning "an amount paid by a purchaser in a lump sum, or in not more than three instalments, towards the purchase price ... before the date of settlement". It does not matter whether the contract concerned treats it as an earnest or as a non-refundable sum in the event of default. It does not matter to whom the payment is made, whether to a stakeholder, a trustee or beneficially to the purchaser. To qualify as a deposit for the purpose of s 6 it need only be paid by the purchaser towards the purchase price. Provided that it is an amount also paid before settlement in one, two or three instalments, it will qualify as a deposit for the purpose of s 6. In most cases, it will be able to be inferred from the terms of the contract that the deposit is treated as an earnest or that, as in this case, it is non-refundable in the event of default by the purchaser. However, it is not necessary that that qualification apply to the payments which may constitute a deposit for the purpose of s 6.' *Ethnic Earth Pty Ltd v Quoin Technology Pty Ltd (in liq)* [2004] SASC 257 at [43], Bleby J; BC200405432

Canada 'As I see it, a deposit is a contract by which a customer lends money to a bank. The terms of the loan may vary as agreed upon by the banker and the customer. In the absence of such expressly agreed upon terms, the common law dictates that what is intended is a loan that is repayable on demand ... It includes all monies received by an institution in the usual course of business, that it is obligated to repay either on demand or in accordance with the provisions of any receipt of payment instrument issued by it in exchange for the money received.' *Saskatchewan Co-operative Credit Society Ltd v Canada (Minister of Finance)* [1990] 2 FCR 115 at 124–125, FCTD, per Collier J; affd 77 DLR (4th) 186, FCA

Of chattel

[For 2 Halsbury's Laws (4th edn) para 1506 see now 2 Halsbury's Laws (4th edn) (Reissue) para 1806.]

DEPOSITOR

[The Banking Act 1987, s 58(1) provides for compensation payments to 'depositors' where an institution becomes insolvent and certain conditions apply.] 'It is, in my view, clear that no one can be a "depositor" unless he is entitled or deemed to be entitled to a "deposit" within the statutory definition. Under s 5(3) sums paid by someone who falls within the classes excluded by paras (a) to (e) of s 5(3) are not deposits within the meaning of the Act. Therefore, apart from the modifications introduced by s 60(9), in the case of a sum paid to the institution by a trustee, its status as a "deposit" under s 5(3) depends upon the personal characteristics of the payer (the trustee) not the beneficiary. Thus, if A (who is a close relative of a director of the institution) pays a sum to an institution as bare trustee for B (who is not a close relative) under s 5(3)(e) the sum is not a deposit, since it was "paid by" A, a close relative, and sums so paid are excluded from the definition of "deposit". The characteristics of B, the beneficiary, are irrelevant for the purposes of s 5(3).

'When Parliament determined that compensation should be payable to certain beneficiaries under trusts, this necessarily required a modification of the definition of "deposit" so as to determine whether or not a debt owed by an institution is a "deposit" by reference to the characteristics of the beneficiary, B. This variation was effected by s 60(9)(a) and (b) under which the status of the sum as a "deposit" is made to depend on the characteristics of the beneficiary, not those of the trustee. Thus, in the example given above, for the purposes of ss 60 and 61 of the Act, a sum which would have been excluded by s 5(3)(e) from being a "deposit" falls to be treated as a deposit since it was paid by A, as trustee, for B who, not being a close relative, was not an excluded person under s 5(3)(e).

'It follows that the provisions of s 61(3) which say that the nominee "shall be treated as entitled to the deposit" do not, as the courts below consider, lead to the conclusion that he is a 'depositor'. A claimant who is a beneficiary under a bare trust also has to show that, within the definition in s 5(3) as amended by s 60(9), the sum falls to be treated as a "deposit": unless it is a deposit he will not be the depositor.

'Once the importance of the definition of "deposit" is apparent, the analogy between the rights to compensation of a beneficiary under a bare trust and the right of an assignee to such compensation becomes very strained. A (a close relative) pays a sum to the institution as trustee for B (not a close relative): B is entitled to compensation since the sum is to be treated as a deposit (s 60(9)(a)). Compare the case where A (a close relative) assigns an existing deposit to B (not a close relative). B is not entitled to compensation: the sum is not a "deposit" since its status falls to be determined according to the characteristics of A at the date of payment under s 5(3), there being nothing to modify that definition for the purposes of Pt II of the Act. Therefore the rights of an assignee to compensation would not be the same as a beneficiary under a bare trust.

'Take another case. A (not a close relative) pays the sum to the institution as trustee for B (a close relative). The sum is not a "deposit" (s 60(9)(b)): therefore no compensation is payable. Contrast the case where A, instead of declaring himself trustee, assigns the debt to B (a close relative). If assignees are to be treated as 'depositors', B would be entitled to compensation since there is nothing to link the definition of "deposit" to the status of the assignee as opposed to that of the person who made the original payment. One would therefore have the remarkable result that close relatives who obtained assignments of debts would be entitled to compensation where, if they had made the original deposit themselves or were beneficiaries under a bare trust, they would have been expressly excluded.

'For these reasons, in my judgment s 60 provides no clear guidance as to the meaning of the word "depositor".

'In the courts below it was thought that the draftsman of the Act had probably overlooked the position of assignees. However, s 60(9)(c) deals specifically with one type of assignment, viz deposits evidenced by transferable certificates of deposit or other transferable instruments (CDs). Therefore the rights of assignees of at least one kind were in the mind of the draftsman.

'It is interesting to see how Parliament dealt with the definition of "deposit" in the context of CDs. The subject matter of a CD is to be included in the definition of "deposit" 'if it had been paid by the person who is entitled to it at the time when the institution in question becomes insolvent. There are two points to be noted. First, the assignee is to be deemed to have made the initial payment, ie he is deemed to be the deposit maker. This strongly suggests that Parliament was, throughout, considering a depositor to be the original payer and therefore had to deem an assignee to have paid the deposit. Second, unlike the personal characteristics of beneficiaries under a trust which are ascertained at the date of the original payment, it is the personal characteristics of the assignee at the date of insolvency which determines the status of the CD. As one would expect in the case of compensation for assignees, the entitlement to compensation is not made to depend on the personal characteristics of the original depositor.

'However, the most significant feature of s 60(9)(c) is that it deals only with one type of assignment, viz assignments of sums deposited under CDs. If 'depositor' includes all assignees, this would lead to extraordinary results. If A (not a close relative) makes a CD deposit and then transfers it to B (a close relative), B is not entitled to compensation since the sum is not a deposit by virtue of s 60(9)(c). If, on the other hand, A were to make an ordinary deposit (not a CD) and then assign it to X (a close relative), X is entitled to compensation since there is nothing to exclude the debt from the definition of deposit. I find it impossible to accept that Parliament, having been to such lengths to exclude from compensation a close relative who was either the original depositor, or a beneficiary under a trust, or the holder of a CD, intended an assignee who is a close relative at the date of insolvency to receive compensation. For these reasons I can find nothing in the provisions of s 61 which clearly indicate that an assignee is to be treated as a depositor and indications in s 60 that he is not to be so treated.' *Deposit Protection Board v Dalia* [1994] 2 All ER 577 at 585–587, HL, per Lord Browne-Wilkinson (also reported in [1994] 2 AC 367 at 398–400)

DEPRIVE

Canada [A father was charged with child abduction under s 283(1) of the *Criminal Code*, which makes it an offence for a parent to take a child, not subject to custody order, with intent to deprive the other parent of possession of that child.] 'Indeed, to "deprive" a person of something means, among other things, to keep that person from that which he or she would otherwise have: *Oxford English Dictionary, supra,* vol IV, at p 490. Similarly, the French verb *"priver"* means *"empecher (qqn) de jouir d'un bien, d'un avantage présent ou futur; enlever à (qqn) ce qu'il a ou lui refuser ce qu'il espère, ce qu'il attend": Le Grand Robert, supra,* t. VII, at p 779. This suggests that the accused would have the requisite intent if he or she intended to keep the other parent from having a possession to which he or she would otherwise be entitled.' *R v Dawson* [1996] 3 SCR 783 at 796, (1996) 141 DLR (4th) 251, per L'Heureux-Dubé J

DEPRIVE OF POSSESSION

Canada 'In order to interpret the intent requirement in s 281 [of the Criminal Code, RSC 1985 c C-46] a brief discussion of the meaning of the phrase "deprive ... of the possession" is a prerequisite. I agree with the appellant that, given the fact that children are not inanimate objects, this wording must be interpreted to encompass the idea that parents have the right to the care and control of their children.

'It is clear that "possession" is not limited to circumstances in which the parent or guardian is actually in physical control of the child at the time of the taking.

'Moreover, in order for there to be deprivation of possession, there need not be any withholding of the child. Indeed, where withholding is made a necessary element of deprivation, the deprivation arises as a result of "detention" rather than by "taking, or enticing".' *R v Chartrand* (1994) 116 DLR (4th) 207 at 224–225, SCC, per L'Heureux-Dubé J

DERELICT

[For 43 Halsbury's Laws (4th edn) para 1008 see now 43(1) Halsbury's Laws (4th edn) (Reissue) para 1031.]

DERIVED

New Zealand [Section 65(2)(a) of the Income Tax Act 1976.] 'The question of what income can be treated as "derived" during an accounting year is, unlike the question of deductions, a matter governed by normal accounting principles.' *Commissioner of Inland Revenue v Mitsubishi Motors New Zealand Ltd* [1995] 3 NZLR 513 at 520, PC, per cur

New Zealand [Section 38(2) of the Income Tax Act 1976 provides 'Subject to this Act, income tax shall be payable by every person on all income derived by him during the year for which the tax is payable'.] 'The expression "derived" is not defined. It means flowing, springing, or emanating from and is synonymous with the English tax expression "arising from or accruing" (*Commissioner of Inland Revenue v Farmers' Trading Co Ltd* [1982] 1 NZLR 449, 457).' *Egmont Co-operative Dairies Ltd (In Liquidation) v Commissioner of Inland Revenue* [1996] 2 NZLR 419 at 426, CA, per cur

DEROGATION FROM GRANT

[For 12 Halsbury's Laws (4th edn) para 1354 see now 13 Halsbury's Laws (4th edn) (Reissue) para 57.]

DESCENDANT

[For 50 Halsbury's Laws (4th edn) para 521 see now 50 Halsbury's Laws (4th edn) (Reissue) para 575.]

DESCRIPTION *SEE* DEPICT; SALE OF GOODS

DESIGN

[For 48 Halsbury's Laws (4th edn) para 371 see now 35 Halsbury's Laws (4th edn) (Reissue) paras 776–777.]

In this Act 'design' means features of shape, configuration, pattern or ornament applied to an article by any industrial process, being features which in the finished article appeal to and are judged by the eye, but does not include—
(a) a method or principle of construction, or
(b) features of shape or configuration of an article which—
   (i) are dictated solely by the function which the article has to perform, or
   (ii) are dependent upon the appearance of another article of which the article is intended by the author of the design to form an integral part.

(Registered Designs Act 1949 as amended by the Copyright, Designs and Patents Act 1988: see Sch 4 to the latter Act)

Australia [In the context of a clause in an insurance policy which covered design and consulting/advisory services] 'In order to determine the context to be given to the expression "design", in the context of an insurance policy of the kind here involved, both Pioneer and QBE made reference to standard dictionary definitions, as well as to the decision in *Vosten v Commonwealth* (1989) 1 Qd R 693.

'The dictionary definitions drawn to attention, relevantly defined "design" in the following inclusive ways:

   (a) *The Shorter Oxford English Dictionary*:
        a plan or scheme conceived in the mind;
        a project;
        a plan or purpose of attack upon a person or thing;
        a preliminary sketch, a plan or pattern from which a picture, building, machine, etc, may be made;
        the action or art of planning and creating in accordance with appropriate functional or aesthetic criteria.
   (b) *The Macquarie Dictionary*:
        to prepare the preliminary sketch or the plans for a work to be executed;
        to plan or fashion artistically or skilfully;
        to intend for a definite purpose;
        to form or conceive in the mind; contrive; plan;
        an outline, sketch or plan, as of a work of art, an edifice or a machine to be executed or constructed;
        the combination of details or features of a picture, building, etc;
        a plan; a project; a scheme.'

...

'Ryan J, in delivering judgment in the Full Court, observed (at 708):

"However, I do not consider that the design in the sense of the clause in the policy should be confined to matters set out on the plans submitted to the government department. The design of the product and the construction of the product itself are distinct matters. The design is an idea or conception; it is, as his Honour stated, quoting from the *Oxford English Dictionary* 'a plan or a scheme conceived in the mind of something to be done, the preliminary conception of an idea that is to be carried into effect by action.' When a decision

was made on the site to fit a particular method of anchorage that involved two things: a decision on the design of the method of anchorage and the execution of that decision by fitting that anchorage. If the design decision was not defective but its execution was it could not be said that the injury arose out of the defective design of the product. On the other hand if the design itself was defective and the injury arose from that defect the insurer could rely upon the clause to exempt itself from liability." '

Pioneer v QBE Insurance Ltd BC200200846; [2002] NSWSC 137 at [15]–[16], [18], per Wood CJ at CL

DESIGNATED BY DESCRIPTION

New Zealand [Contracts (Privity) Act 1982, s 4.] '... the question is whether "X's nominee" or "the lessor's nominee" is a person designated by description. In my judgment a person so "described" is a person designated by description for the purposes of s 4. Conceptually there can be no doubt whether a person claiming to qualify does in fact answer to the description. X or the lessor has the power to nominate only one person to take the benefit of the contract. That person, once nominated, is identifiable with certainty. The fact that until nominated the person could be anyone at all does not, in my view, alter the fact that the nominee is designated as the person intended to benefit from the contract and such designation is by description. The identity of the person is described with precision in the contract.

'The criterion which the third party promisee must fulfil is specified exactly in the contract. What is the difference between the following descriptions: "X's nominee", "the winner of the next Olympic marathon" and "Y's first grandchild"? Each allows the intended beneficiary to be positively identified if and when the event takes place. The fact that the person may not exist at the date of the contract is not a problem. Nor is the fact that there may never be a nomination. In that event liability will remain with the person holding the power of nomination.' *Rattrays Wholesale Ltd v Meridyth-Young & A'Court Ltd* [1977] 2 NZLR 363 at 382–383, per Tipping J

DESIGNED

See also DESIGNED TO ASCERTAIN

Canada [An insurance policy excluded vehicles 'designed' for travel on public roads, and the exclusion was alleged to apply to a snowmobile.] 'The policy intends to make a distinction between a "land motor vehicle designed for travel on public roads" and a "land motor vehicle designed for recreational use off public roads". I conclude then that the words "designed for" as used in the policy are not to be read as meaning "capable of".

'The Oxford English Dictionary states the meaning of "designed" as follows: "b. planned, purposed, intended". Black's Law Dictionary gives its meaning as follows: "contrived or taken to be employed for a particular purpose. Fit, adapted, prepared, suitable, appropriate, intended, adapted or designated". The Random House Dictionary states its meaning as: "made or done intentionally; intended, planned". These definitions of the word "designed" suggest the word has two general meanings: (1) intended or purposed for a particular purpose and (2) fit or suitable …

'In my view, to ensure as the policy surely intends that the two phrases have distinct meanings, the word "designed" must be given the number (1) meaning set out above, that is to say, "intended for a particular purpose". When used in that sense one must conclude that a snowmobile is designed for use off public roads and, in particular, for use on snow-covered areas off public roads. In that sense of the word "designed", a snowmobile is not designed for travel on public roads, roads that are usually bare of snow.' *Martin v Redshaw* (1990) 65 DLR (4th) 476 at 478–479, Ont HCJ, per O'Leary J

New Zealand 'It can be mentioned here that the word "designed" in the expression "a vehicle designed for amusement purposes" is by definition to be read as referring to the construction of the vehicle and not to its use or intended use.' *Police v Sinclair* [1991] 3 NZLR 569 at 571, per Tipping J

DESIGNED TO ASCERTAIN

Australia [The Road Safety (Alcohol & Drugs) Act 1970 (Tas) s 2 provides that a breath analysing instrument 'means any apparatus that is designed for ascertaining, by analysis of a person's breath, the concentration of alcohol present in his blood'.] 'The word "design" has a wide range of meanings, which might be interpreted according to its legal context (*Edwards Hot Water Systems v S W Hart & Co Pty Ltd* (1983) 49 ALR 605; *Shacklady v Atkins & Anor* (1994) 126 ALR 707) and the fact that the design is dictated solely by function does not preclude it from being a "design" within the framework legislation such as patent legislation

(*Ogden Industries Pty Ltd & Ors v Kis (Australia) Pty Ltd* (1981) 45 ALR 129) …

'The word "design" has been given a variety of meanings in areas of construction (*Independent Authority v EMI Electronics Ltd* (1980) 14 BLR 1) and intellectual property (*Dalgety Austlake Operations Ltd v F F Sealy Nominees Pty Ltd* (1986) 10 FCR 403) and in general terms can be said to be a process intended to achieve a result. *Oxford*, (3 Ed) includes the meanings "to indicate", "to purpose intend have in view", "delineate", while *Webster* (1971 Ed) adds "plan", "a project", "the object of a plan or purpose; the end in view; the adaptation of means to a preconceived end". The Alcotest 7110 apparatus was constructed to achieve an object and was an adaptation of means in accordance with scientific principle. Variation of the calculations produced a result different from that which could have been achieved if the machine had been programmed to accept a different assumption of scientific principle, but that variation, based on assumption, was permitted by the "designer"…

'The word "ascertain" likewise has a range of meaning, ranging from "to make subjectively certain", to "make objective certain". Oxford, (3 Ed) includes the meanings "to assure, inform, appraise, to decide, fix limit". Webster includes "to make certain, to make sure or find out by trial or examination, to establish; to determine with certainty".

'… The apparatus proclaimed fulfilled the purpose for which it was employed by a methodology for which it was "designed".' *Horton v White* (2002) 37 MVR 347; BC200204900; [2002] TASSC 57 at [24]–[27] per Slicer J

DESIRABLE

[Prospective claimants in proceedings against the prospective defendant companies for unlawful conspiracy to manipulate markets and/or anti-competitive behaviour sought pre-action disclosure under s 33(2) of the Supreme Court Act 1981, which applies to persons who are likely to be party to subsequent proceedings, and CPR 31.16. One question was whether pre-action disclosure was within any of the three reasons set out in CPR 31.16(3)(d), which are that it is 'desirable' in order to dispose fairly of the anticipated proceedings; assist the dispute to be resolved within proceedings; or save costs.] '[79] This is a difficult test to interpret, for it is framed both in terms of a jurisdictional threshold ("only where") and in terms of the exercise of a discretionary judgment ("desirable").

'[80] Three considerations are mentioned in CPR 31.16(3)(d): disposing fairly of the anticipated proceedings; assisting the dispute to be resolved without proceedings; and saving costs. The first of this trio obviously contemplates the disposal of proceedings once they have been commenced—in that context the phrase "dispose fairly" is a familiar one (see e g RSC Ord 24, r 8); the second as clearly contemplates the possibility of avoiding the initiation of litigation altogether; the third is neutral between both of these possibilities.

'[81] It is plain not only that the test of "desirable" is one that easily merges into an exercise of discretion, but that the test of "dispose fairly" does so too. In the circumstances, it seems to me that it is necessary not to confuse the jurisdictional and the discretionary aspects of the sub-rule as a whole. In the *Bermuda International* case Waller LJ contemplated (at [26]) that CPR 31.16(3)(d) may involve a two-stage process. I think that is correct. In my judgment, for jurisdictional purposes the court is only permitted to consider the granting of pre-action disclosure where there is a real prospect in principle of such an order being fair to the parties if litigation is commenced, or of assisting the parties to avoid litigation, or of saving costs in any event. If there is such a real prospect, then the court should go on to consider the question of discretion, which has to be considered on all the facts and not merely in principle but in detail.

'[82] Of course, since the questions of principle and of detail can merge into one another, it is not easy to keep the two stages of the process separate. Nor is it perhaps vital to do so, provided however that the court is aware of the need for both stages to be carried out. The danger, however, is that a court may be misled by the ease with which the jurisdictional threshold can be passed into thinking that it has thereby decided the question of discretion, when in truth it has not. This is a real danger because first, in very many if not most cases it will be possible to make a case for achieving one or other of the three purposes, and secondly, each of the three possibilities is in itself inherently desirable.

'[83] The point can be illustrated in a number of ways. For instance, suppose the jurisdictional test is met by the prospect that costs will be saved. That may well happen whenever there are reasonable hopes either that litigation can be avoided or that pre-action disclosure will assist in avoiding the need for pleadings to be amended after disclosure in the ordinary way. That alternative will occur in a very large number of cases. However, the crossing of the jurisdictional threshold on that basis tells you practically nothing about the broader and more particular discretionary aspects of the individual case or the ultimate exercise of discretion. For that, you need to know much more: if the case is a personal injury claim and the request is for medical records, it is easy to conclude that pre-action disclosure ought to be made; but if the action is a speculative commercial action and the disclosure sought is broad, a fortiori if it is ill-defined, it might be much harder.

'[84] In the present case, I think with respect that Deputy Judge Brindle fell into this error. Thus he dealt with CPR 31.16(3)(d) in a single paragraph in which he decided that disclosure relating to the China deal and generally was desirable and should be made. He said that his reasoning or much of it was already dealt with under the heading of the "likelihood of proceedings". There, however, he had in turn applied the wrong test; and even though in doing so he had considered666 matters which properly belonged to the question of discretion, by dealing with them for the different purpose of asking himself whether proceedings were likely, he was led into thinking that having decided that proceedings were likely, therefore pre-action disclosure should be made. That is demonstrated by his very next paragraph (headed "Discretion") where he simply says that "It is clear from what I have said above that an order should be made …"

'[85] In effect, Deputy Judge Brindle never stood back, having dealt with the jurisdictional thresholds, and asked himself whether this was a case where his discretion should be exercised in favour of disclosure. It cannot be right to think that, wherever proceedings are likely between the parties to such an application and there is a real prospect of one of the purposes under CPR 31.16(3)(d) being met, an order for disclosure should be made of documents which would in due course fall within standard disclosure. Otherwise an order for pre-action disclosure should be made in almost every dispute of any seriousness, irrespective of its context and detail. Whereas outside obvious examples such as medical records or their equivalent (as indicated by pre-action protocols) in certain other kinds of disputes, by and large the concept of disclosure being ordered at other than the normal time is presented as something differing from the normal, at any rate where the parties at the pre-action stage have been acting reasonably.

'[86] It is to be observed that because of the way in which he proceeded, Deputy Judge Brindle decided the question of discretion even before considering the breadth of the discovery requested or the allegation of oppression.' *Black v Sumitomo*

Corp [2001] EWCA Civ 1819 at [79]–[86], [2003] 3 All ER 643, per Rix LJ

DESTITUTE

Canada '[16] The term "destitute" has long been a term of art in our law. When our Legislature enacted that word in 1955 (R.S.A., c. 188) [s. 3(1)], it clearly meant to use its accepted legal sense. Legislatures and precedent fix the concept; trial judges apply it to a multitude of factual circumstances. As a result, the old language shapes a mere concept, which modern courts adapt to modern circumstances.

'[17] The *Maintenance Order Act* and its antique terminology follow closely the wording of parts of the old English poor laws, notably the *Poor Relief Act, 1601* (U.K.), 43 Eliz. 1, c. 2: see the citations in *A.-G. v. Merthyr Tydfil U.*, [1900] 1 Ch. 516 (C.A.). The concept of "destitute" has been shaped by what courts have considered sufficient reasons for lack of income and therefore, a basis for a claim for support:

1. Refusal to work for fear of coercion or violence, or union discipline or expulsion: *Lewisham U. v. Nice*, [1924] 1 K.B. 618 (Div. Ct.); *cf. A.-G. v. Merthyr Tydfil U.*
2. The job would ruin the person's chances for future employment: *Lewisham U. v. Nice.*
3. Present illness, even if caused by previous voluntary drunkenness: *St. Saviour's U. v. Burbridge*, [1900] 2 Q.B. 695 (Div. Ct.).
4. The only work available required extraneous activities, such as abstinence from alcohol, attending religious services, etc.: *Poplar Guardians v. Martin*, [1905] 1 K.B. 728 (Div. Ct.).
5. Private charitable support for the poor dependent: *State v. Waller*, 136 P. 213, 90 Kans. 829, 49 L.R.A. (ns) 588 (1913) (C.A.); *State v. Sayre*, 222 N.W. 20, 206 Iowa 1334 (1928) (C.A.); *State v. Weldin*, 189 A. 586 (1937) (Del. C.A.); *State v. Greer*, 144 N.W.2d 322, 259 Iowa 367 (1966).
6. An independent life and part-time college course auditing, but illness: *Stern v. Stern*, 473 A. 2d 56, 58 Md. App. 280 (1984) (C.A.).

'[18] Mr. B. contends that his daughter lacks funds because she freely chooses to get a university degree, and not to work full time. But the case law surrounding the word suggests that the courts should approach this with a longer-term view.

'[19] A child confined to light work by an accident or illness could reasonably quit his or her job and stay off work for two months to have an operation, and so fit herself for regular employment. One without English language skills could work only part time for a few months in order to take English lessons and earn more. One prevented by law to work in Canada could surely spend a few months getting landed immigrant status, or a work permit, to be able to take legal employment. A judge might hold that such persons had acted reasonably, and not forfeited the right to support.

'[20] Whether the child was "able to maintain himself or herself" depends whether his or her choice was reasonable in the circumstances, and whether he or she was "able to work". That is a question of fact and of degree, for the trial court.' *PT v RB* [2004] AJ No 803, 242 DLR (4th) 30 (CA), per Paperny JA

DESTRUCTION

Of tree

[As to tree preservation orders see now the Town and Country Planning Act 1990, s 198.]

Of will

[For 50 Halsbury's Laws (4th edn) para 291 see now 50 Halsbury's Laws (4th edn) (Reissue) para 341.]

DETAINS

New Zealand [Crimes Act 1961, s 210.] 'As Richardson P states, the word "detains" has a number of meanings. The President quotes the definition contained in *The Shorter Oxford Dictionary*; "to keep in confinement or custody; to keep back, withhold; to keep, retain, to hold, hold down; to keep from proceeding; to keep waiting; to stop". The *Oxford English Dictionary* expands this definition. The second meaning ascribed to the word "detain" (after the first meaning given of keeping in confinement or under restraint) is "to keep back, withhold; especially to keep back what is due or claimed".

'To our mind, the word "detains", in its natural and ordinary sense, connotes the notion of keeping or holding back something. That something may already be in the other person's physical possession, but it is detained in being kept or held back. It does not seem a strained use of the English language to suggest that an intending abductor who already has physical possession of a child can detain that child in the sense of keeping or withholding the child from the person who is at that time entitled to the lawful possession of the child.

'Moreover, many words have different shades of meaning and we cannot see why it is necessary to prefer one recognised meaning or another. Why cannot the words be used in both senses? Thus, for the purposes of s 210, the abductor may "detain" a child by keeping the child in confinement or custody or by keeping or withholding the child from the parent entitled to the custody of the child. In both cases the child is literally detained.' *R v Tauiliili* [1997] 1 NZLR 525 at 534, CA, per Gault, Thomas and Blanchard JJ

DETENTION

Canada [The question was of the right to counsel in the event of 'detention'.]

'1. In its use of the word "detention", s 10 of the Charter [of Rights and Freedoms] is directed to a restraint of liberty other than arrest in which a person may reasonably require the assistance of counsel but might be prevented or impeded from retaining and instructing counsel without delay but for the constitutional guarantee.

'2. In addition to the case of deprivation of liberty by physical constraint, there is a detention within s 10 of the Charter, when a police officer or other agent of the state assumes control over the movement of a person by a demand or direction which may have significant legal consequence and which prevents or impedes access to counsel.

'3. The necessary element of compulsion or coercion to constitute a detention may arise from criminal liability for refusal to comply with a demand or direction, or from a reasonable belief that one does not have a choice as to whether or not to comply.

'4. Section 10 of the Charter applies to a great variety of detentions of varying duration and is not confined to those of such duration as to make the effective use of *habeas corpus* possible.' *R v Thomsen* [1988] 1 SCR 640 at 649, SCC, per Le Dain J

DETERMINATION

Australia [Section 60 (1) of the Safety, Rehabilitation and Compensation Act 1988 (Cth) (the 'SRC Act') provides: 'determination means a determination, decision, or requirement made under s 8, s 14, s 15, s 16, s 17, s 18, s 19, s 20, s 21, s 21A, s 22, s 24, s 25, s 27, s 29, s 30, s 31, s 34, s 36, s 37 or s 39, under para 114B(5)(a) or under Division 3 of PtX'.]

'[37] The definition of "determination" in the SRC Act thus becomes an inclusive definition of substantial breadth. In general it refers to whole sections and not subsections, even though the sections referred to do contain subsections. Moreover, it refers to several sections, such as s 14, s 15, s 18, s 20, s 21, s 21A and s 36, which do not use the language of "determination" but give work to do to the other concepts of "decision" and "requirement" embraced by the s 60(1) definition of "determination".

...

'[40] The way in which s 37(7) must operate also suggests that a "determination" is required. The inclusion of the words "without reasonable excuse" introduces a distinctive requirement for some deliberative human action. An assessment needs to be made at some point — by a person — as to a refusal or failure to undertake a rehabilitation program, and to the reasonableness or unreasonableness of that refusal or failure. Such a process requires that the person at least consider the circumstances surrounding the employee's failure or refusal to undertake a rehabilitation program and to evaluate what is reasonable in the circumstances. This intellectual process involves matters of judgment and degree. The suspension of rights under s 37(7) can only occur by force of law once some such assessment has been made. The process cannot be conducted in a manner analogous to the mechanistic operations of a sorting machine. The process that is required would seem unequivocally to fall, at least, within the s 3(3)(g) AAT Act definition of "decision" as "doing or refusing to do any other act or thing" and hence within the definition of "determination" under the SRC Act.

...

'[49] It was accepted in *Buck*, and in the subsequent cases that, as a practical matter, some person or body must make a decision as to the application of s 37(7) in any specific case (c f *Trajkovski* at 464). This cannot be controversial. The question is whether it is correct to conclude that what are said to be the self-executing aspects of s 37(7) deprive the processes required for the application of s 37(7) of any relevant decision-like character. Framed in terms of the definition of "determination" in s60(1), which includes the definition of "decision" in s 3(3) of the AAT Act, the question is whether or not those processes constitute, at least, "doing or refusing to do any act or thing".

'[50] The correct approach to the interpretation of the word "decision" in the AAT Act was discussed by Lockhart J, with whom Sheppard J agreed, in *Director-General of Social Services v Hales* (1983) 47 ALR 281 ("*Hales*"). *Hales* followed the decisions in *Director-General of Social Services v Hangan* (1982) 45 ALR 23 and *Re Matteo and Director General of Social Services* (1981) 4 ALD 398, and was followed in *Secretary, Department of Social Security v Alvaro* (1994) 50 FCR 213.

'[51] In *Hales*, Lockhart J held (at 305–306):

"One cannot look to the definition in s 3(3) [of the AAT Act] to determine definitively the meaning of the word 'decision'. It must take its colour and content from the enactment which is the source of the decision itself. No narrow or pedantic approach is called for in determining whether a decision falls within the scope of review of the Administrative Appeals Tribunal. The multiplicity of statutes which continue to grow and to confer jurisdiction on the Administrative Appeals Tribunal, and the manifold and diverse circumstances which attract the power of the decision maker, all call for a liberal approach to the definition of the word 'decision' ... It is necessary to examine the Act which confers jurisdiction on the Administrative Appeals Tribunal and the administrative framework in which it operates to determine whether there is a 'decision' susceptible to review under the Administrative Appeals Tribunal Act. A pronouncement which alters rights or imposes liabilities is readily classified as a 'decision', but the word has a wider scope. It may include a declaration or statement which has a real practical effect although not altering rights or imposing liabilities: *Duncan v Defence Force Retirement and Death Benefits Authority and Commonwealth of Australia* (1980) 30 ALR 165 at 169–170."

...

'[64] The broad definition of "determination" in s 60(1) and its application to specific sections is consistent with an intention to give a wide measure of merits review within the field – limited as it is – marked out by the definition. Within that field there would seem to be no occasion to take a narrow view, since to do so would be inconsistent with the beneficial object of legislation for the compensation of employees (see DC Pearce and RS Geddes, *Statutory Interpretation in Australia*, 5th ed Butterworths, Australia, 2001 at 9.2–9.3)'

Australian Postal Corp v Forgie [2003] FCAFC 223 per Black CJ, Merkel and Stone JJ; BC200305847

DETERMINING

New Zealand ' ... the word "determining" indicates a process, a continuing action, rather than the conclusion of the process which is the "determination".' *R v S* [1993] 2 NZLR 142 at 149, CA, per cur

DETRIMENT

New Zealand 'I am reluctantly forced to the view that the language used necessarily implies ... loss or damage to the position of the other. It cannot be interpreted on the basis that a failure to grant a right or hypothetical benefit can constitute a detriment.' *Brewer v R* [1994] 2 NZLR 229 at 235, per Robertson J

DEVASTAVIT

[For 17 Halsbury's Laws (4th edn) para 1542 see now 17(2) Halsbury's Laws (4th edn) (Reissue) para 792.]

DEVELOPMENT

Of property

[The Town and Country Planning Act 1971 has been repealed. The definition is re-enacted, with minor drafting amendments, in the Town and Country Planning Act 1990, s 55. For Schedule 8 to the 1971 Act see now Schedule 3 to the 1990 Act.]

Town planning

[The Town and Country Planning Act 1971 has been repealed. See now the Town and Country Planning Act 1990, s 75(2).]

DEVELOPMENT PLAN

[The Town and Country Planning Act 1971 has been repealed. The definition is now contained in the Town and Country Planning Act 1990, ss 27, 54, as follows.]

(1) Subject to subsection (4), for the purposes of this Act and any other enactment relating to town and country planning, the Land Compensation Act 1961 and the Highways

Act 1980, the development plan for any district outside Greater London and the metropolitan counties (whether the whole or part of the area of a local planning authority) shall be taken as consisting of—

(a) the provisions of the structure plan for the time being in force for that area or the relevant part of that area, together with the Secretary of State's notice of approval of the plan;

(b) any alterations to that plan, together with the Secretary of State's notices of approval of them;

(c) any provisions of a local plan for the time being applicable to the district, together with a copy of the authority's resolution of adoption or, as the case may be, the Secretary of State's notice of approval of the local plan; and

(d) any alterations to that local plan, together with a copy of the authority's resolutions of adoption or, as the case may be, the Secretary of State's notices of approval of them.

(2) References in subsection (1) to the provisions of any plan, notices of approval, alterations and resolutions of adoption shall, in relation to a district forming part of the area to which they are applicable, be respectively construed as references to so much of those provisions, notices, alterations and resolutions as is applicable to the district.

(3) References in subsection (1) to notices of approval shall, in relation to any plan or alteration made by the Secretary of State under section 51, be construed as references to notices of the making of the plan or alteration.

(4) This section has effect subject to Part III of Schedule 2 (old development plans).

(5) Any reference in the Land Compensation Act 1961 to an area defined in the current development plan as an area of comprehensive development shall be construed as a reference to an action area for which a local plan is in force.

(Town and Country Planning Act 1990, s 54)

For the purposes of this Act and any other enactment relating to town and country planning, the Land Compensation Act 1961 and the Highways Act 1980, the development plan for any district in Greater London or a metropolitan county (whether the whole or part of the area of a local planning authority) shall be taken as consisting of—

(a) the provisions of the unitary development plan for the time being in force for that area or the relevant part of it, together with a copy of the local planning authority's resolution of adoption or the Secretary of State's notice of approval or, where part of the plan has been adopted and the remainder approved, copies of the resolution and the notice; and

(b) any alteration to that plan, together with a copy of the authority's resolution of adoption, or the Secretary of State's notice of approval, of the alteration or, where part of the alteration has been adopted and the remainder approved, copies of the resolution and the notice.

(Town and Country Planning Act 1990, s 27)

DEVIATION

Of ship

[For 25 Halsbury's Laws (4th edn) para 143 see now 25 Halsbury's Laws (4th edn) (2003 Reissue) para 322.]

[For 43 Halsbury's Laws (4th edn) para 431 see now 43(2) Halsbury's Laws (4th edn) (Reissue) para 1467.]

DEVOLVE—DEVOLUTION

[For 17 Halsbury's Laws (4th edn) para 1073 see now 17(2) Halsbury's Laws (4th edn) (Reissue) para 337.]

[For 17 Halsbury's Laws (4th edn) paras 1071–1115 see now 17(2) Halsbury's Laws (4th edn) (Reissue) paras 335–373.]

Australia [Marshall J accepted (at [15]) the following contentions made by the respondents.]

'10. Devolution is the involuntary passing of property from one person to another by operation of law, for example upon death, bankruptcy or insolvency (*Butterworths Australian Legal Dictionary*, Butterworths, Sydney, 1997, p 356).

'11. The word devolution refers, in its common usage, to the passing of property to a successor in a deceased estate. To devolve means to pass property from a person dying to a person living. Devolution is marked by the absence of voluntariness (Mason J in *O'Brien v Komesaroff* (1982) 41 ALR 255 at 261).' *Wheaton (t/as Marketing Advisory Services) v Football Tasmania Ltd* BC200106588; [2001] FCA 1518 at [14], per Marshall J

DIGNITY

Canada [The right to personal dignity is protected under s 4 of the *Quebec Charter of Human Rights and Freedoms*.] 'In the *Petit Robert 1,* at p 541, the expression *"dignité"* is defined as follows: [TRANSLATION] "1 Respect merited by someone. *Dignity of man compared with other beings.* See Grandeur, noblesse. *Principle of the dignity of the human person:* which holds that a human being must be treated as an end in himself or herself. *'All of the dignity of man lies in thought'* (PASC.). 'The *only dignity of man: the tenacious revolt against his condition'* (CAMUS). 2 Self-respect. See Amour-propre, fierté, honneur. *To have dignity. To lack dignity. 'His haughty dignity that … kept him honest and solitary'* (LOTI)". It is in these two senses, which could be characterized as internal and external that we must understand "dignity" within the meaning of the *Charter,* which itself makes no distinction.

'Having regard to the manner in which the concept of personal "dignity" has been defined, and to the principles of large and liberal construction that apply to legislation concerning human rights and freedoms, I believe that s 4 of the *Charter* addresses interferences with the fundamental attributes of a human being which violate the respect to which every person is entitled simply because he or she is a human being and the respect that a person owes to himself or herself.

'Moreover in my opinion, because of the underlying concept of respect, the right to personal dignity, unlike the concept of inviolability, does not require that there be permanent consequences in order for interference with that right to be found. Thus, even a temporary interference with a fundamental attribute of a human being would violate s 4 of the *Charter…* ' *Quebec (Public Curator) v Syndicat National des Employés de l'hôpital St-Ferdinand* [1996] 3 SCR 211 at 254, 256, per L'Heureux-Dubé J

DILIGENCE

Canada 'Upon reflection, it seems arguable to me that the term "diligence" is synonymous with the term "care". That is, diligence is simply the degree of attention or care expected of a person in a given situation. At least, that is the way the term is employed in *City Equitable.* If attention to one's obligations is the essence of diligence, then that aspect of the standard neither adds to nor detracts from the statutory statement in subsection 227.1(3) of the *Income Tax Act.* Others, however, have taken a different approach by contending not only that diligence is an independent element of the statutory standard but also that that requirement, unlike the statutory requirements for skill and care, is more onerous than at common law: see Welling, *supra,* at pages 333–334; see also the Ontario case of *Kerr v Law Profession Indemnity Co* (1994) 22 CCLI (2d) 28 (Ont Gen Div), which deals with the Ontario *Business Corporations Act* [RSO 1990, c B.16].' *Soper v Canada* [1998] 1 FC 124 at 151, FCA, per Robertson JA

DIRECT CAUSE

Australia [Identifying causation under an insurance contract.] '[15] Plainly enough, the meaning of the phrase "directly caused" is ultimately a question of construction of the policy. The ordinary rules of contractual interpretation apply to the construction of a policy of insurance, although a liberal interpretation in favour of the insured should be adopted in so far as the ordinary and natural meaning of the words used by the insurers permits this to be done: *Australian Casualty Co Ltd v Federico* [1986] 160 CLR 513 at 520–521, per Gibbs J.

…

'[32] Ultimately, the court's decision is clearly assisted by the fact that a close examination of the whole of the policy throws up a variety of descriptions of causal connections, as the plaintiff usefully pointed out in their own written submissions:

> The policy contains a broad spectrum of descriptions of causal connections. The weakest of these is the phrase "directly or indirectly caused by or contributed to by or arising from" under cl 2 of the section headed "General exclusions." The strongest of these is "caused solely as a result of" in cl 6(1)(a)(iii) in the section headed "Electronic Equipment Section".

'Between these two descriptions are a variety of descriptions of causal connections: "caused by" (see, for example, cl 3.5(c) in the "Property Section"), "occasioned by or in consequence of", "arising out of" (see, for example, cl 3.7 of the "Property Section"), "direct result" (see, for example, cl 4.7 of the "Property Section"), "resulting from" (see, for example, cl 2.1 of the "Business Interruption Section", "in consequence of" (cl 3.1 of the "Business Interruption Section"), "caused by or arising out of" (see, for example, cl 2.3 of the "Broadform Liability Section"); "arising directly or indirectly out of or in the course of" (cl 3.1(a) of the "Broadform Liability Section"), "due to" (see, for example, cl 3.3 of the "Broadform Liability Section"), "caused by or naturally resulting from" (cl 5.3(c) of the Electronic Equipment Section"), "occurring by reason of" (cl 6.1 of the "Electronic Equipment Section"), "consequent upon" (cl 2.1 of the "Theft Section"), "attributed to" (cl 3.3 of the "Money Section"), "arising out of or resulting from" (cl 3.4 of the "Money Section"), "directly or indirectly caused by or arising from" (cl 3.14 of the "Broadform Liability Section"), "caused directly or indirectly by" (cl 3.25 of the "Broadform Liability Section"), "directly or indirectly caused to or contributed to by" (cl 7 of the "General Exclusions").

...

'[35] The plaintiff has taken the court to a number of authorities where courts have dealt in general terms with issues of causation and in particular have interpreted the words "proximate cause" as appropriate to mean "direct cause", and have held that there are in particular contexts, no difference in meaning between the word "direct" and the word "proximate". Those authorities, for example, include *City Centre Cold Store v Preservatrice Skandia Insurance Ltd* (1985) 3 NSWLR 739, where at 742 Clarke J observed that the approach which the trial judge took accorded with the statement of Lord Porter in *Boiler Inspection and Insurance Co of Canada v Sherwin-Williams Co of Canada Ltd* [1951] AC 319 at 333:

> Whatever meaning the word "direct" may have in qualifying the word "result", it does not imply that there can be no step between the cause and the consequence. It is unnecessary to multiply examples.

'Likewise in *State Government Insurance Commission v Sinfein Pty Ltd* (1996) 15 WAR 434, Ipp J observed at 452:

> Senior counsel for the appellant accepted (correctly, in my view,) that "directly" did not mean "immediately" (ie coming in time immediately after the driving of the vehicle.).
> [proceeding to cite the above passage from Lord Porter's speech]

'[36] Notwithstanding those authorities to which the court was taken in such detail and notwithstanding acceptance of the notion that in determining the issue of causation for the purpose of the law of tort, causation is to be determined in accordance with common-sense notions *March v Stramare*, to my mind, the proper approach to the question which is separated out here is simply one of construction of the particular policy before the court.' *Lasermax Engineering Pty Ltd v QBE Insurance (Aust) Ltd* [2004] NSWSC 483 at [15], [32], [35]–[36], per Einstein J; BC200403607

Canada '[30] The motions judge and the Financial Services Commission have essentially adopted the same test of direct causation by relying on a definition of "direct cause" in *Black's Law Dictionary*: "The active, efficient cause that sets in motion a train of events which brings about a result without the intervention of any force started and working actively from a new and independent source". See, for example, *Petrosoniak v. Security National Insurance Co.*, *supra*. Applying this definition the motions judge correctly concluded that "there was not an unbroken chain of events". Instead "the shooting constituted an intervening act, independent of the vehicle's use or operation which clearly broke the chain of causation", thus disentitling Chisholm to accident benefits.' *Chisholm v Liberty Mutual Group* (2002) 217 DLR (4th) 145 at 155 (Ont CA), per Laskin JA

DIRECTLY AFFECTED

Canada '[1] This is a judicial review of a decision of the Ontario Civilian Commission on Police Services ("the Commission") in which the Commission refused to deal with a complaint of police misconduct based on its determination that the complainant, Roger Rolfe, was not a person "directly affected" by the conduct at issue.

'[2] The sole issue in this proceeding is the proper interpretation of the words "directly affected" as used in sections 57(1) and 59(5) of the Police Services Act, R.S.O. 1990, c. P.15 ("the Act"). The relevant sections state:

> 56(1) Any member of the public may make a complaint under this Part about the policies of or services provided by a police force or about the conduct of a police officer.
>
> 57(1) A complaint may be made by a member of the public only if the complainant was directly affected by the policy, service or conduct that is the subject of the complaint.
>
> 59(5) The chief of police shall not deal with any complaint made by a member of the public if he or she decides that the complainant was not directly affected by the policy, service or conduct that is the subject of the complaint.

...

'[12] There is no case law interpreting the words "directly affected" in the context of the Police Services Act. However, the Alberta Court of Appeal dealt with a similar issue in *Canadian Union of Public Employees, Local 30 v. Alberta (Public Health and Advisory Board)*, [1996] A.J. No. 48 (C.A.), a case to which both counsel in this proceeding made reference. In the Alberta case, the Edmonton Board of Health made a decision approving the development of a waste management facility. The applicant union ("C.U.P.E.") had made submissions objecting to the proposal when it was in the planning stages. When the decision approving the facility was released, C.U.P.E. filed an appeal with the Public Health and Advisory Board. The applicable legislation provided a right of appeal to "a person who is directly affected by a decision of a local board". The Alberta Court of Appeal upheld the tribunal and lower court decisions that C.U.P.E. was not "directly affected" and therefore had no right of appeal.

'[13] In considering the appropriate interpretation of the words "directly affected", the Alberta Court of Appeal (at para. 18) relied on a common law interpretation enunciated by Lord Hobhouse in *Re Endowed Schools Act*, [1898] A.C. 477 (P.C.) at 483 as follows:

> That term points to a personal and individual interest as distinct from the general interest which appertains to the whole community.

'[14] The Alberta Court of Appeal then reasoned that the words "directly affected" must mean more than "affected" and held, at para. 19:

> In our view, the inclusion of the word "directly" signals a legislative intent to further circumscribe a right of appeal. When considered in the context of the regulatory scheme, it is apparent that the right of appeal is confined to persons having a personal rather than a community interest in the matter.

'[15] Although different legislation was involved in the Alberta case, the words used are virtually identical to the words in our statute ("directly affected"), and the context in which they are used is also very similar (a right of appeal to a tribunal in respect of an issue of public interest). Further, the reasoning of the court is logical and persuasive. In my view, the interpretation of "directly affected" adopted by the Albert Court of Appeal in the C.U.P.E. case is appropriate to apply to those same words as used in our Police Services Act.

'[16] The respondent argues that Mr. Rolfe does not fit within the definition because he was not the person injured by the police conduct. Rather, the police conduct was directed towards the woman in the store and Mr. Rolfe was a mere witness to it.

'[17] In my opinion, that it is a far too restrictive definition, and not one that is required by the plain meaning of the words used. Indeed, it is the most restrictive interpretation of the words "directly affected" one could possibly apply. Such an approach is not consistent with the broad public purpose of the legislation and the fact that it is meant to protect the most vulnerable in society against the most powerful agents of the state. If the respondent's interpretation is correct, only actual victims would have a right of complaint. The orphaned children of a person killed by police would not have a complaint; the parents of a teenager the police failed to protect would not have a complaint; a wife who saw her husband shot in front of her would not have a complaint. That is an overly narrow reading of the statute.

'[18] On the other hand, the legislation should not be interpreted so broadly that a right of complaint is vested in anybody who is unhappy with the police. There must be some direct link between the person filing the complaint and the police conduct which is the subject of the complaint, something that distinguishes the complainant's interest from that of any other member of the community.' *Corp of the Canadian Civil Liberties Assn v Ontario (Civilian Comm. on Police Services)* (2005) 260 DLR (4th) 754 at [1]–[2], [12]–[18], [2005] OJ No 3875 (Ont Sup Ct J), per Molloy J (Lane J concurring)

DIRECTLY ATTRIBUTABLE

Canada 'Ms Poole for the Ministry did cite two Canadian authorities for the proposition that the phrase "directly attributable to" means "wholly" or "entirely attributable to": see *Haley v Canadian Northern Railway Co* [1920] 1 WWR 460 (Sask KB), and *Butler v Grand Trunk Pacific Railway Co* [1940] 2 WWR 532, [1940] 3 DLR 544 (Alta CA). In the latter case, Harvey CJA said for the Court:

> Can it be said that it is "directly attributable" to something if it is only partly so? It seems to me that question must be answered in the negative and that perhaps leads to the dictionary meaning of "directly" for "wholly directly attributable" is of course the same thing as "wholly attributable". [At 542.]

'The *Oxford English Dictionary on Historical Principles* (1993) gives two [meanings] for the word "directly" that are relevant in this context, namely (1) "completely, absolutely; exactly" and (2) "without an intermediary; by a direct process". The two cases cited by the Ministry obviously adopted the first meaning, without indicating why the second is not equally apposite. I am not persuaded a more modern reader would understand "directly" to mean "solely", or that something cannot have more than one "direct" cause. If, as was stated by the Supreme Court of Canada in *Dell Holdings, supra*, the *Expropriation Act* is to be construed in a broad and liberal way, the approach adopted in the older railway cases seems overly narrow. Even accepting the meaning adopted by those cases, it is arguable that once the Ministry decides to insist on concrete barriers between the Highway and Deloume Road, the necessity to relocate *will* be "directly attributable to" the Ministry's works.' *Bayview Builders Supply (1972) Ltd v British Columbia (Ministry of Transportation & Highways)* (1999) 170 DLR (4th) 751 at 762–763, BC CA, per Newbury JA

DIRECTLY IN CONNECTION WITH

New Zealand 'One example given by counsel was the painting of a vessel. That service would be directly in connection with the vessel, but services rendered to the passengers and crew of a vessel would not be rendered directly in connection with the vessel.' *Wilson & Horton Ltd v Commissioner of Inland Revenue* [1994] 3 NZLR 232 at 236, per Hillyer J

DIRECTORY

Australia [Section 64(3) of the Trade Practices Act 1974 (Cth) prohibits demands for payment for entries in a directory relating to a person or his business unless the making of the entry has been authorised.] 'Black's Law Dictionary adopted the following meaning of directory: "Book containing names, addresses, and occupations of inhabitants of city. Also any list or compilation, usually in book or pamphlet form, of persons, firms or corporations forming some class separate and distinct from others, e.g., telephone directory, hotel directory, etc". The word "directory" used in s 64 seems to me to bear some such meaning or connotation as that ascribed by Black.' *Kennan v Monahan* [1991] 1 Qd R 401 at 404, per McPherson J

Australia 'In *Pearse v Morrice* [(1834) 2 Ad & E 84 at 96; 111 ER 32 at 37], Taunton J said "a clause is directory where the provisions contain mere matter of direction and nothing more". In *R v Loxdale* [(1758) 1 Burr 445 at 447; 97 ER 394 at 395], Lord Mansfield CJ said "[t]here is a known distinction between circumstances which are of the essence of a thing required to be done by an Act of Parliament, and clauses merely directory". As a result, if the statutory condition is regarded as directory, an act done in breach of it does not result in invalidity ... In our opinion, the Court of Appeal of New South Wales was correct in *Tasker v Fullwood* [[1978] 1 NSWLR 20 at 23–24] in criticising the continued use of the "elusive distinction between directory and mandatory requirements" and the division of directory acts into those which have substantially complied with a statutory command and those which have not. They are classifications that have outlived their usefulness because they deflect attention from the real issue which is whether an act done in breach of the legislative provision is invalid.' *Project Blue Sky Inc v Australian Broadcasting Authority* (1998) 153 ALR 490 at 516; [1998] HCA 28 at [92]; BC9801389 at 36–37, per McHugh, Gummow, Kirby and Hayne JA

DISABILITY

[The Disability Discrimination Act 1995, s 1(1) contains the following definition.]

Subject to the provisions of Schedule 1, a person has a disability for the purposes of this Act if he has a physical or mental impairment which has a substantial and long-term adverse effect on his ability to carry out normal day-to-day activities.

Australia [Section 4 (1) of the Disability Discrimination Act 1992 (Cth) provides:
'disability', in relation to a person, means:
(a) total or partial loss of the person's bodily or mental functions; or
(b) total or partial loss of a part of the body; or
(c) the presence in the body of organisms causing disease or illness; or
(d) the presence in the body of organisms capable of causing disease or illness; or
(e) the malfunction, malformation or disfigurement of a part of the person's body; or
(f) a disorder or malfunction that results in the person learning differently from a person without the disorder or malfunction; or

(g) a disorder, illness or disease that affects a person's thought processes, perception of reality, emotions or judgment or that results in disturbed behaviour;

... and includes a disability that:

(h) presently exists; or

(i) previously existed but no longer exists; or

(j) may exist in the future; or

(k) is imputed to a person.]

'[4] The definition of "disability" lists a series of physical conditions. The problem in the case arises partly because para (g) begins by reference to physical conditions and then adds a reference to a consequence ("disturbed behaviour") of a condition. It is necessary to relate para (g), with its added reference to resulting behaviour, to the provisions of s 5 as to what amounts to discrimination.

...

'[11] It may be accepted, as following from paras (f) and (g) of the definition of disability, that the term "disability" includes functional disorders, such as an incapacity, or a diminished capacity, to control behaviour. And it may also be accepted, as the appellant insists, that the disturbed behaviour of the pupil that resulted from his disorder was an aspect of his disability.' *Purvis v New South Wales (Department of Education and Training);* [2003] HCA 62 per Gleeson CJ; BC200306678

Australia [Section 4 (1), Disability Discrimination Act 1992 (Cth).] 'In our view, the Federal Court's characterisation of disability as merely referring to the underlying condition does not accord with the proper construction of s 4(1) of the Act. Disability is defined broadly in s 4(1), the legislative intent being to capture the full range and nature of disabilities. As defined, it includes the functional limitations that result from the underlying condition. This interpretation gives the definition an operation consistent with the ordinary meaning of disability, viz, a "lack of ... physical or mental ability". The Act's definition draws upon existing definitions in Commonwealth and State legislation, as well as the meaning of disability in the international community. The paragraphs of the definition that arguably apply to Mr Hoggan's behavioural problems are (a), (e) and (g).

'Paragraph (a) states that disability means the "total or partial loss of the person's bodily or mental functions". The focus of this paragraph is on loss of functions rather than the cause of any such loss. The ordinary meaning of the phrase "mental functions" would include the manner in which the mind functions through processes of

thought and capacities to learn and control behaviour. Dictionaries define the term "mental" to include "performed by or existing in the mind" or "relating to the intellect" [*The Macquarie Dictionary*, 3rd ed (1997) at 1345–1346] and "done by the mind" [*The Australian Oxford Dictionary*, (1999) at 846]. They define "function" to mean "to perform a function; act; serve; operate ... to carry out normal work, activity, or processes." [*The Macquarie Dictionary*, 3rd ed (1997) at 859].

...

'Paragraph (e) states that disability means "the malfunction ... of a part of the person's body". This paragraph also focuses on functional ability, rather than underlying cause. "Malfunction" is defined in dictionaries to mean "a failure to function in a normal or satisfactory manner" [*The Australian Oxford Dictionary*, (1999) at 816] or "failure to function properly" [The Macquarie Dictionary, 3rd ed (1997) at 1304].

...

'Paragraph (g) declares that disability means "a disorder, illness or disease that affects a person's thought processes, perception of reality, emotions or judgment or that results in disturbed behaviour".

...

'The disabilities referred to in para (g) are confined by the adjectival phrases introduced by the word "that". The words that follow describe the type of disorder, illness or disease encompassed by the Act. The adjectival clauses cannot be definitive of the "disorder, illness or disease"; otherwise the Act would not protect persons who had a condition that did not manifest itself in disturbed behaviour because of the stage of the condition or because it was being effectively treated.

'The interpretation given to the words "disorder, illness or disease" by the Full Court, however, is too narrow. The Macquarie Dictionary defines "disorder" to mean "a derangement of physical or mental health or functions" [*The Macquarie Dictionary*, 3rd ed (1997) at 617]. Thus, Mr Hoggan's behaviour is part of his disability because it includes his incapacity to adapt his behaviour to a standard consistent with the safety of other pupils, teachers and aides. His disability is not confined to his brain damage.

'International organisations also recognise that the term "disability" includes functional difficulties. When the Act was drafted, the most widely accepted classification scheme covering all disability types, both internationally and domestically, was that of the World Health Organisation's International Classification of Impairments, Disabilities, and Handicaps: A Manual of Classification Relating to the Consequences of Disease ("the ICIDH"). It recognised that a disability may include functional difficulties. The Act's definition of "disability" incorporates the key terminology of the ICIDH. The ICIDH provides a conceptual framework for "disability" that describes three dimensions — impairment, disability and handicap.

'Impairment is defined as "any loss or abnormality of psychological, physiological, or anatomical structure or function". It includes the existence or occurrence of an anomaly, defect or loss in a limb, organ, tissue or other structure of the body, or a defect in a functional system or mechanism of the body, including the systems of mental function.

'Disability is defined as "any restriction or lack (resulting from an impairment) of ability to perform an activity in the manner or within the range considered normal for a human being". It is concerned with compound or integrated activities expected of the person or of the body as a whole, such as those represented by tasks, skills and behaviour.

'Handicap is defined as "a disadvantage for a given individual, resulting from an impairment or a disability, that limits or prevents the fulfilment of a role that is normal (depending on age, sex, and social and cultural factors) for that individual". Handicap focuses, therefore, on the person as a social being and reflects the interaction with, and adaptation to, the person's surroundings.

'The definition of disability in the Act encompasses both the concept of "impairment" and "disability". The Draft Position Paper in relation to the Act refers to the ICIDH and states:

'This approach to definition has been valuable in focussing attention on the fact that for many people with disabilities, restrictions on their ability to participate equally in different aspects of life are not the inevitable, medical consequence of a particular impairment. Rather, in many cases restrictions on equality for people with disabilities result from features of the social or physical environment — features which can be altered, and which in some cases the law can help to change.

'This statement and the overall structure of the Act show that the Act was aimed at removing the handicaps faced by persons with disabilities that arise from their interaction with their social environment.

'To construe "disability" as including functional difficulties gives effect to the purposes of the Act. Such a construction accords with the Act's beneficial and remedial nature. In this case, the damage to Mr Hoggan's brain is a "hidden" impairment — it is not externally apparent unless and until it results in a disability. It is his inability to control his behaviour, rather than the underlying disorder, that inhibits his ability to function in the same way as a non-disabled person in areas covered by the Act, and gives rise to the potential for adverse treatment. To interpret the definition of "disability" as referring only to the underlying disorder undermines the utility of the discrimination prohibition in the case of hidden impairment.' *Purvis v New South Wales (Department of Education and Training);* [2003] HCA 62 at [67]–[80] per McHugh and Kirby JJ; BC200306678

Australia [Workers' Compensation and Rehabilitation Act 1981 (WA) ss 5(1), 5(4).] '[42] The essential question raised by this appeal is whether a review officer applied correctly the definition of "disability" in s 5 of the Workers' Compensation and Rehabilitation Act 1981 ("the Act"), in holding that the respondent worker's depressive illness was "a continuation of, and "mere" recurrence of "a pre-existing illness caused by excluded factors, and was not, therefore, compensable under the Act.

...

In Section 5 of the Act "disability" and "disease" are defined as follows:

"disability" means –
(a) a personal injury by accident arising out of or in the course of the employment, or whilst the worker is acting under the employer's instructions;
(b) a disabling disease to which Part III Division 3 applies;
(c) a disease contracted by a worker in the course of his employment at or away from his place of employment and to which the employment was a contributing factor and contributed to a significant degree;
(d) the recurrence, aggravation or acceleration of any pre-existing disease where the employment was a contributing factor to that recurrence, aggravation, or acceleration and contributed to a significant degree; or
(e) a disabling loss of function to which Part III Division 4 applies,
(f) but does not include a disease caused by stress if the stress wholly or predominantly arises from a matter

mentioned in subsection (4) unless the matter is mentioned in paragraph (a) or (b) of that subsection and is unreasonable and harsh on the part of the employer;

...

"disease" includes any physical or mental ailment, disorder, defect, or morbid condition whether of sudden or gradual development

Section 5(4) provides as follows:

For purposes of the definition of "disability", the matters are as follows –
(a) The worker's dismissal, retrenchment, demotion, discipline, transfer or redeployment;
(b) the worker's not being promoted, reclassified, transferred or granted leave of absence or any other benefit in relation to the employment; and
(c) the worker's expectation of —
    (i) a matter; or
    (ii) a decision by the employer in relation to a matter,
    referred to in paragraph (a) or (b).

Section 5(5) provides as follows:

In determining whether the employment contributed, or contributed to a significant degree, to the contraction, recurrence, aggravation or acceleration of a disease for purposes of the definitions of "disability" and "relevant employment", the following shall be taken into account –

(a) the duration of the employment;
(b) the nature of, and particular tasks involved in, the employment;
(c) the likelihood of the contraction, recurrence, aggravation or acceleration of the disease occurring despite the employment;
(d) the existence of any hereditary factors in relation to the contraction, recurrence, aggravation or acceleration of the disease;
(e) matters affecting the worker's health generally; and
(f) activities of the worker not related to the employment.

'[63] In my opinion, the question should be answered in the affirmative. That is because the Act allows a recurrence (etc) of a pre-existing disease to be a disability, where the employment contributed significantly to that recurrence. And it does so, without placing any restriction on the kind of pre-existing disease which might recur, or be aggravated or accelerated by the subsequent employment.

'[64] If a pre-existing disease was caused by stress, but was not excluded by s 5(4), then it would be a disability. The "recurrence, aggravation, or acceleration" limb of the definition would then be unnecessary: the worker would already be disabled.

'[65] Thus, in my view, the Act does not prevent a disability arising where a pre-existing disease — albeit caused by matters which are excluded — recurs or is aggravated or accelerated by matters which are not.' *FAI General Insurance Co Ltd (De-Registered) v Goulding* [2004] WASCA 167 at [42], [63]–[65], per Templeman J; BC200405078

Canada 'Subsection 3(1) of the *Canadian Human Rights Act*, RSC 1985, c H-6, as amended, the appropriate text, proceeds as follows:

3.(1) For all purposes of this Act, race, national or ethnic origin, colour, religion, age, sex, marital status, family status, disability and conviction for which a pardon has been granted are prohibited grounds of discrimination.

'Section 25 of that Act runs thus:

25...
"disability" means any previous or existing mental or physical disability and includes disfigurement and previous or existing dependence on alcohol or a drug.

'The expression "mental or physical disability" is not further defined in that Act nor in the *Interpretation Act*, RSC 1985, c I-21.

'This Court is satisfied that the definition of "disability" was intended by Parliament to include SDD, dyslexia and dysgraphia, just as Parliament must have intended to include, say, the dumbness which is caused by congenital deafness. This Court interprets that statutory expression in a large, liberal, purposive manner to comprehend such a learning disability even although it might not obviously be "physical" or "mental" in their restrictive senses.' *Arnold v Canada (Human Rights Commission)* [1997] 1 FC 582 at 598, Fed TD, per Muldoon J

Canada '[114] The first ground of appeal illustrates the importance of formulating the correct "comparator" in any s. 15 analysis. As McIntyre J. said in *Andrews v. Law Society of British Columbia*, [1989] 1 S.C.R. 143, 56 D.L.R. (4th) 1, equality "is a comparative concept, the condition of which may only be attained or discerned by comparison with the condition of others in the social and political setting in which the question arises". (At 164.) In challenging the Chambers judge's rejection of the comparators of persons disabled by child sexual abuse and persons disabled by child abuse of other kinds, Mr. Berry on behalf of the plaintiffs explained in oral argument that he uses the word "disability" (which of course is one of the grounds enumerated in s. 15(1)) or "disabled" to refer to "any injury" suffered, presumably at any time, by a person. Any injury, he said, is "disabling".

'[115] This is not the usual meaning of the term. *The Canadian Oxford Dictionary* (1998) defines "disability", for example, as a "physical or mental handicap" or "incapacity created or recognized by the law", and "disabled" as "having reduced physical or mental abilities, esp. through injury or disease". *The Concise Oxford Dictionary* (8th ed., 1990) also defines "disabled" to include "a lack of some asset, quality or attribute that prevents one's doing something", while *Black's Law Dictionary* (7th ed., 1999) includes in the definition of "disable" the "depriving of (someone or something) of the ability to function". Similarly, *Merriam-Webster's Dictionary of Law* (1996) defines "disability" to mean an inability to pursue an occupation because of a physical or mental impairment, and "disable" to mean "to make incapable or ineffective".

'[116] These dictionary definitions are consistent with the definition of "disabled" in the Canada Pension Plan scheme at issue in Granovsky, which required that an applicant for a disability pension suffer from a severe condition that made him or her "incapable regularly of pursuing any substantially gainful occupation". (Granovsky, para. 10.) The Supreme Court of Canada seemed to accept the same definition in its discussion of the word "disability" as it appears in s. 15(1) of the Charter (*Granovsky*, para. 26), although the Court also affirmed at para. 27 the statement of Sopinka J. in *Eaton v. Brant County Board of Education*, [1997] 1 S.C.R. 241, 142 D.L.R. (4th) 385, that disability "means vastly different things depending upon the individual and the context". Elsewhere in *Granovsky*, Binnie J. stated that "The concept of disability must ... accommodate a multiplicity of impairments, both physical and mental, overlaid on a range of functional limitations, real or perceived, interwoven with recognition that in many important aspects of life the so-called 'disabled' individual may not be impaired or limited in any way at all". (Para. 29; my emphasis.)' *Arishenkoff*

v British Columbia [2004] BCJ No 1101, 241 DLR (4th) 385 (CA), per Newbury JA

DISABLED PERSON

[The Disability Discrimination Act 1995, s 1(2) contains the following definition.]

In this Act, 'disabled person' means a person who has a disability.

DISBURSEMENTS

By solicitor

[For 44 Halsbury's Laws (4th edn) para 164 see now 44(1) Halsbury's Laws (4th edn) (Reissue) para 191.]

DISCHARGE

Australia 'The Full Court held that "discharge" and "satisfaction", when used in s 160M(3) [of the Income Tax Assessment Act 1936 (Cth)], were not to "be construed as extending to the performance of obligations under an agreement giving rise to the rights in accordance with the terms of the agreement" and were words which "must be confined to cases where the rights are satisfied or discharged otherwise than by performance of the obligations which give rise to the rights by the other party to the contract" [(1996) 68 FCR 122 at 139, per Lockhart J]. There is no basis for confining "discharge" or "satisfaction" in this way. First, as a matter of ordinary language, "discharge" can be used in the sense of "[t]he act of clearing off a pecuniary liability; payment" or "[f]ulfilment, performance, execution (of an obligation, duty, function, etc)". Secondly, it is common for lawyers to speak of a contractual obligation being discharged by performance ... Thirdly, when the sub-section speaks, as it does, of the "discharge" of a debt it is plainly using the word "discharge" in a way that at least includes payment of the debt according to the terms of the obligation incurred by the debtor.' *Federal Commissioner of Taxation v Orica Ltd* (1998) 154 ALR 1 at 29–30; [1998] HCA 33 at [93]–[96]; BC9801652 at 41–42, per Gaudron, McHugh, Kirby and Hayne JJ

New Zealand [The word "discharge" is defined in s 2(1) of the Resource Management Act 1991.] 'In the ordinary and natural use of language, a person discharges something when he causes it to be discharged.

'... because of its context the word discharge is to be construed as extending to cause to discharge'. *McKnight v NZ Biogas Industries Ltd* [1994] 2 NZLR 664 at 670, per cur

DISCIPLINARY ACTION

Australia [Section 4(1) of the Commonwealth Employees Rehabilitation and Compensation Act 1988 (Cth) provides that the term injury does not include any disease or injury suffered by an employee due to reasonable 'disciplinary action' taken against the employee.] 'In the context of the definition of "injury" in s 4(1) of the Act, the phrase "disciplinary action" means no more than reasonable action lawfully taken against an employee in the nature of or to promote discipline. The relevant discipline is constituted by the body of duties and such rules of conduct or behaviour as are applicable to and enforceable against the employee by virtue of his or her employment by the Commonwealth. The disciplinary action referred to in the definition is action which has been taken against the employee prior to the injury being suffered by the employee as a result of such action. What is clear to my mind is that it is the disciplinary action itself and not the steps anterior to the decision to take such action which is covered by the definition.' *Commission for Safety and Rehabilitation of Commonwealth Employees v Chenhall* (1992) 109 ALR 361 at 369, per Cooper J

DISCIPLINE

Australia [Workers Compensation and Rehabilitation Act 1981 (WA).] 'The word "discipline" is to be given its ordinary meaning. It must be interpreted in context. The context in which it appears is as follows. The effect of s 18 of the Act read in conjunction with the definition of "disability" in s 5, is that a worker who in the course of his employment contracts a disease caused by stress is entitled to compensation. The proviso to the definition of disability limits the instances in which a worker who contracts a disease caused by stress will be entitled to compensation. Thus a worker is not entitled to compensation where the disease was caused by stress that arose wholly or predominantly from the matters set out in para 5(4)(a), unless there has been conduct that is unreasonable and harsh on the part of the employer. The matters set out therein include the worker's dismissal, retrenchment, demotion, discipline, transfer or redeployment.

'That is the context within which the word discipline is to be defined. It should therefore be given its ordinary meaning in an employment context. It is not helpful to attempt to define the outer boundaries of what is included within "discipline". However, it clearly includes the issue of a written warning such as the written warning of 17 April 2000 given by the appellant to the respondent.

'Whether the discipline of the worker is unreasonable and harsh only falls to be determined if the disease contracted by the worker was caused by stress that wholly or predominantly arose from the discipline of the worker. In this case, the review officer found that the respondent's stress predominantly arose from discipline, being the issue of the formal warning notice to him on 17 April 2000. Accordingly, it was that discipline that the review officer had to determine to be unreasonable and harsh in order for the respondent to be entitled to compensation.' *Housing Industry Assn Ltd v Murten* [2004] WASCA 139 at [21], per Le Miere J; BC200403939

Canada '[28] To recall, the disputed section [of the Alberta *Labour Relations Code*] reads as follows:

> 142(2) If an arbitrator, arbitration board or other body determines that an employee has been discharged or otherwise disciplined by an employer for cause and the collective agreement does not contain a specific penalty for the infraction that is the subject-matter of the arbitration, the arbitrator, arbitration board or other body may substitute some other penalty for the discharge or discipline that to the arbitrator, arbitration board or other body seems just and reasonable in all the circumstances.

'[29] I agree with the chambers judge's finding (at para. 52) that s. 142(2) reasonably supports two differing interpretations. The first such approach views the term "discharged" as informed by the word "disciplined", thereby requiring "discharged" to be interpreted as discharged solely for disciplinary reasons. However, this was not the interpretative route taken by the arbitration board. The board adopted the comments of Arbitrator Moreau in *Re Alberta and A.U.P.E. (Van Steenoven)*, [1998] A.G.A.A. No. 43 (QL) [summarized 52 C.L.A.S. 367], wherein the predecessor provision to s. 142(2) was found to permit review of both culpable and non-culpable dismissals. In his reasons, Arbitrator Moreau relied upon the inclusion of both "discharge" and "discipline" in the phrase "may substitute some other penalty for the discharge or discipline that to the arbitrator, arbitration board or other body seems just and reasonable in all the circumstances" as support for his interpretation [para. 27].

'[30] A broad interpretation of the verb "discipline" is also supported by the *Oxford English Dictionary* (2nd ed. 1989), vol. IV, at p. 735, which defines "discipline" using terms such as "to instruct, educate, train … to bring under control", concepts not habitually associated with punishment *per se*. Similarly, the inclusion of broad language enabling the board to substitute "some other penalty" that in the view of the arbitrator "seems just and reasonable in all the circumstances" suggests a broad and inclusive reading of the provision. As s. 142(2) equally invites either interpretation, there was ample reason for the arbitration board to conclude that the provision applied to both culpable and non-culpable dismissals.' *Alberta Union of Provincial Employees v Lethbridge Community College* [2004] SCJ No 24, 238 DLR (4th) 385, per Iacobucci J

DISCLAIMER

[For 3 Halsbury's Laws (4th edn) paras 701–718 see now 3(2) Halsbury's Laws (4th edn) (2002 Reissue) paras 472–489.]

Australia 'Lord Chelmsford's definition in *Ralston v Smith* [11 HLC 223 at 254] was, and it is as good a one as could be given, "the renunciation of some previous claim actually or apparently made, or supposed to be made".' *Minerals Separation Ltd v Petter's Sulphide Ore Treatment Ltd* (1990) 8 CLR 779 at 793, per Griffith CJ

DISCLOSE

[Under section 5(2)(d) of the Data Protection Act 1984 it is an offence for a registered data user to 'disclose' personal data to any person who is not described in the entry in the register of data users relating to the user.] 'The same principles apply to disclosure as they do to use. Although there is a particular reference to the meaning of "disclosing" in s 1(9) of the Act, … disclosure as such is not defined in the Act, and the word "disclose", like the word "use", should where it appears in the Act be given its natural and ordinary meaning. Subject to exceptional circumstances, information which is recorded in computer-readable form cannot be disclosed unless it has first been retrieved from the database and changed into a form in which it can be communicated to that person …

'I add in parenthesis that a question may arise whether the unauthorised transfer of data from the database of one computer to the database of another within the United Kingdom (cf s 5(2)(e)) could of itself amount to disclosure of data contrary to s 5(2)(d) of the Act. No such question arises for decision in the present case. I however incline to the view that such a transfer would not of itself amount to disclosure of data "to any person who is not described in the entry" contrary to s 5(2)(d), although it may readily be inferred that the person effecting the transfer was inevitably thereby disclosing the data to another person or persons who, as he well knew, would retrieve the information from the second database and so have the information disclosed to him. On this basis, I cannot see that this exceptional case detracts from the approach to the construction of the Act which I favour.' *R v Brown* [1996] 1 All ER 545 at 549–550, HL, per Lord Goff of Chieveley

DISCLOSURE

[Section 71 of the Social Security Administration Act 1992 provides that the Secretary of State is entitled to recover a payment which has been made in consequence of a misrepresentation or failure to disclose any material fact, whether fraudulent or otherwise.] '[18] I find the statement by Hely J in *Condon*'s case [*Condon v Comr of Taxation* [2000] FCA 1291, Aust Fed Ct] persuasive. The word "disclosure" requires something to be revealed or made apparent. That can only happen if the fact as stated is unknown to the recipient. The distinction between disclosure and stating a fact is that in the former there is revelation and in the latter there may not be. Revelation does not depend upon whether or not the discloser realises that the information was known or unknown to the recipient. Thus a person who makes a statement may believe that it amounts to a disclosure or may believe that it is only a statement of fact, which does not depend upon his belief but upon the knowledge of the recipient.'

…

'[38] I agree that the word "disclose" implies revelation of that which was previously unknown to the recipient. That is the ordinary meaning of the word, and it is supported by the cases to which Aldous LJ has referred. Furthermore, although s 71 of the Social Security Administration Act 1992 does not say so in terms, it is implicit in my view that the disclosure must be to the person responsible for the decision, and, accordingly, that it is his or her knowledge accordingly which must be considered.' *Hinchy v Secretary of State for Work and Pensions* [2003] EWCA Civ 138 at [18], [38], [2003] 2 All ER 289, per Aldous LJ and Carnwath LJ

[The Civil Procedure Rules 1998 (CPR) 31.22(2) gives the power to make an order restricting or prohibiting the use of a document which had been disclosed. In CPR Pt 31, 'disclosure' is defined as meaning that a party discloses a document by stating that the document existed or had existed. An order under CPR 31.22(2) was made that further use of documents should be permanently prohibited, but the party against whom the order was made applied for an order permitting it to use the documents in other proceedings. That party appealed against both orders. In the first appeal, it argued that as the documents had been produced voluntarily and had been referred to in the report of an expert witness instructed by the opposing party, they were not documents which had been 'disclosed', so that the court had not possessed the power to restrict their use under CPR 31.22(2) and they were available for use in all proceedings. In the second appeal, it sought to use the documents under conditions of confidence in the second proceedings.] '[1] There are before the court two appeals against orders of Pumfrey J which had the effect of preventing SmithKline Beecham plc (SB) from using certain documents in their case against Apotex which is currently before the judge ...

...

'[28] Mr Turner accepted that CPR 31.22 was a complete code. The first 25 words were a substitute for the implied undertaking that applied pre-CPR. CPR 31.22(1)(a), (b) and (c) contained exceptions which also applied pre-CPR. CPR 31.22(2) enabled the court to make a restriction or prohibition order in respect of a document "which has been disclosed ...". Such documents are those produced pursuant to the obligation of disclosure under such rules as CPR 31.5 and 31.6. There was a difference between a document which had been disclosed and one which a party had a right to inspect. CPR 31.14 gave a right to inspect documents. At the date of the application the rule included a right to inspect documents referred to in experts' reports. That difference between documents disclosed and those which could be inspected perpetuated the difference which existed under the RSC between documents produced on discovery which were subject to the implied undertaking and those which had to be produced or were produced voluntarily and those which were not. It followed that documents which were produced voluntarily or in experts' reports were not documents "which have been disclosed"

and therefore the court did not have power to restrict their use under CPR 31.22(2).

'[29] I agree with Mr Turner that CPR Pt 31 is a complete code, but I reject his submission that that code perpetuated in all respects the distinction between documents disclosed in a list of documents and those that might be disclosed in another way. The obligation to disclose and the ability to inspect are dealt with separately as is the ability to use a document after disclosure. CPR 31.3 is concerned with disclosed documents but reserves an ability to refuse inspection. CPR 31.14 adds to CPR 31.3. In any case the wide definition in CPR 31.2 must be determinative. That states that: "A party discloses a document by stating that the document exists or has existed." No distinction is sought to be drawn between documents obtained from third parties and no limitation is placed on the way that the statement is made. In my view a reference by a party to a document in a witness statement is a statement that the document exists. I therefore reject Mr Turner's submission. It follows that the judge was right to consider the application by Generics as an application under CPR 31.22(2). He was also right to conclude that the *Lilly Icos* case [*Lilly Icos LLC v Pfizer Ltd (No 2)* [2002] EWCA Civ 02, [2002] 1 All ER 842, [2002] 1 WLR 2253] gave guidance as to the considerations he should have in mind.

...

'[43] The interests of justice are paramount. In the present case, the interests of the owners of the documents can be protected by an order under CPR 31.22. The interests of SB favours modification of the order made in the Generics proceedings to allow the documents to be deployed in the Apotex proceedings. There is a real argument that they would be discoverable under CPR 31.17 and refusal of use could reflect adversely on the administration of justice. In those circumstances I conclude that the documents should be released from the CPR 31.22(2) order for use in the Apotex proceedings with an order protecting the interests of the owners of the documents in the way that the judge did in the BASF proceedings.' *SmithKline Beecham plc v Generics (UK) Ltd; BASF AG v SmithKline Beecham plc* [2003] EWCA Civ 1109 at [1], [28]–[29], [43], [2003] 4 All ER 1302, CA, per Aldous LJ

DISCONTINUANCE

Canada [Notice requirement for police officers as public servants was specified in the event of a 'discontinuance of a function'.] 'Therefore, a "discontinuance of a function" will occur when that set of activities which form an office is no longer carried out as a result of a decision of an employer acting in good faith. For example, if a particular set of activities is merely handed over in its entirety to another person, or, if the activity or duty is simply given a new and different title so as to fit another job description then there would be no "discontinuance of a function". On the other hand, if the activities that form part of the set or bundle are divided among other people such as occurred in *Mudarth*, there would be a "discontinuance of a function". Similarly, if the responsibilities are decentralized, as happened in *Coulombe*, there would also be a "discontinuance of a function"'. *Flieger v New Brunswick* [1993] 2 SCR 651 at 664, per Cory J

DISCOVER

[For 23 Halsbury's Laws (4th edn) para 1577 see now 23(1) Halsbury's Laws (4th edn) (Reissue) para 1732.]

DISCRETION

Australia ' "Discretion" is a notion that "signifies a number of different legal concepts". In general terms, it refers to a decision-making process in which "no one [consideration] and no combination of [considerations] is necessarily determinative of the result." Rather, the decision-maker is allowed some latitude as to the choice of the decision to be made. The latitude may be considerable as, for example, where the relevant considerations are confined only by the subject-matter and object of the legislation which confers the discretion. On the other hand, it may be quite narrow where, for example, the decision-maker is required to make a particular decision if he or she forms a particular opinion or value judgment.' (footnotes omitted) *Coal and Allied Operations Pty Ltd v Australian Industrial Relations Commission* (2000) 174 ALR 585; (2000) 74 ALJR 1348; BC200005034; [2000] HCA 47 at [19], per Gleeson CJ, Gaudron and Hayne JJ

DISCRIMINATION

[The Sex Discrimination Act 1975, s 1(a), as applied by s 2, defines sex discrimination by a person as treating a man less favourably on the ground of his sex than he treats or would treat a woman. By s 5(3), a comparison of the cases of persons of different sex or marital status must be

such that the relevant circumstances in the one case are the same, or not materially different, in the other. An action was brought by a homosexual barman claiming unlawful discrimination contrary to s 1(1)(a) after he was dismissed following complaints made by a female fellow employee. The industrial tribunal decided, on a preliminary issue, that the applicant's claim of discrimination on grounds of his sexual orientation was not within its jurisdiction under the provisions of the 1975 Act. The applicant appealed to the Employment Appeal Tribunal, which upheld the decision of the industrial tribunal. The applicant appealed to the Court of Appeal.] 'The industrial tribunal and the Appeal Tribunal were, therefore, correct to conclude that there is a difference between discrimination on the ground of sex and discrimination on the ground of sexual orientation and that a person's sexual orientation is not an aspect of his or her sex.

...

'The right question framed in terms of s 1(1)(a) is whether the applicant, *a man*, had been *less favourably treated than* his employers treated or would have treated *a woman*. By focusing on the applicant's homosexuality, the drift of the argument pushes one almost ineluctably—as I myself was carried along—to ask the wrong question: was he discriminated against because he was a man (sex) or because he was a homosexual (sexual orientation)? In concentrating on that, one falls into the error that one does not make the comparison which the statute requires namely between his position as *a man*, and the comparative position of *a woman*. The fault in the argument is that it precludes consideration of a vital question, namely whether or not discrimination against him based upon his homosexuality may not also be discrimination against him as a man ... I have come to the conclusion that the task imposed on the tribunal by s 1(1)(a) read with s 5(3) is to ascertain: (a) what, as a matter of fact, was the treatment received by the employee; (b) was he treated less favourably than the woman with whom he falls to be compared; and (c) would he have been so treated but for his sex?' *Smith v Gardner Merchant Ltd* [1998] 3 All ER 852 at 863, 864, CA, per Ward LJ

[The Disability Discrimination Act 1995, s 5 includes the following definition.]

For the purposes of this Part, an employer discriminates against a disabled person if—
    (a) for a reason which relates to the disabled person's disability, he treats him less favourably than he treats or would treat

others to whom that reason does not or would not apply; and

(b) he cannot show that the treatment in question is justified.

Australia 'A distinction is often drawn between two forms of discrimination, namely "direct" or "disparate treatment" discrimination and "indirect" or "adverse impact" discrimination. Broadly speaking, direct discrimination occurs where one person is treated in a different manner (in a less favourable sense) from the manner in which another is or would be treated in comparable circumstances on the ground of some unacceptable consideration (such as sex or race). On the other hand indirect discrimination occurs where one person appears to be treated just as another is or would be treated but the impact of such "equal" treatment is that the former is in fact treated less favourably than the latter.' *Waters v Public Transport Corpn* (1991) 103 ALR 513 at 545, per Dawson and Toohey JJ

Australia ' "[D]iscrimination", as a matter of ordinary English, has quite distinct shades of meaning. Some of these lack the critical if not pejorative connotation the term has in human rights legislation. Thus, "discrimination" may identify the ability to observe accurately and make fine distinctions with acuity, good judgment or taste, as well as the making of unjust or prejudicial distinctions. In Australia, discrimination is also a constitutional concept ... In *Street v Queensland Bar Association* [(1989) 168 CLR 461 at 570–571] ... Gaudron J said: "Although in its primary sense 'discrimination' refers to the process of differentiating between persons or things possessing different properties, in legal usage it signifies the process by which different treatment is accorded to persons or things by reference to considerations which are irrelevant to the object to be attained. The primary sense of the word is 'discrimination between'; the legal sense is 'discrimination against'." Further, in *Castlemaine Tooheys Ltd v South Australia* [(1990) 169 CLR 436 at 478] ... , Gaudron and McHugh JJ said: "A law is discriminatory if it operates by reference to a distinction which some overriding law decrees to be irrelevant or by reference to a distinction which is in fact irrelevant to the object to be attained; a law is discriminatory if, although it operates by reference to a relevant distinction, the different treatment thereby assigned is not appropriate and adapted to the difference or differences which support that distinction. A law is also discriminatory if, although there is a relevant difference, it proceeds as though there is no such difference, or, in other words, if it treats equally things that are unequal — unless, perhaps, there is no practical basis for differentiation." ' *IW v City of Perth* (1997) 146 ALR 696 at 721–722; BC9703257 at 38–39, per Gummow J

Australia 'In its ordinary signification discrimination means differential treatment, or put another way, the failure to treat all persons equally where there is no reasonable distinction to justify different treatment. The discrimination may be positive, such as by conferring a benefit, or negative, for example by imposing a restriction.' *Telstra Corp Ltd v Hurstville City Council* BC200201288; [2002] FCA 385 at [39], per Sundberg and Finkelstein JJ

DISEASE OF THE MIND

New Zealand 'If the primary cause of the state of abnormality was internal to the accused — e.g. psychosis, arteriosclerosis, epilepsy, psychological inability to cope with the ordinary stresses of life, or hyperglycaemia due to the failure to take insulin — the condition will be classified as a disease of the mind.' *Police v Bannin* [1991] 2 NZLR 237 at 242, per Fisher J

DISFIGUREMENT

Canada 'According to its ordinary English meaning "disfigurement" means the marring of the figure or appearance of something: see Shorter Oxford English Dictionary, 3rd ed, vol 1, at p 566. (The meaning of "figure" in this context is the appearance of something as seen by others — ibid at p 749.) Jowitt's Dictionary of English Law, 2nd ed, vol 1, at p 625, defines "disfigurement" as an external injury which detracts from personal appearance.

'Section 266(1)(a) [of the Insurance Act (RSO 1990, c I.8)] speaks of the injured person sustaining disfigurement. It does not speak of the disfigurement of any particular part of the injured person's body. It follows that in order for a disfigurement to come within s 266(1)(a), while the injury will be to one or more specific parts of the body, it must have the effect of marring or detracting from the appearance of the individual as a person.' *Meyer v Bright* (1993) 110 DLR (4th) 354 at 366–367, Ont CA

DISGRACEFUL CONDUCT IN A PROFESSIONAL RESPECT

New Zealand [Medical Practitioners Act 1968, s 58(1).] 'In *Doughty v General Dental Council*

[1987] 3 All ER 843 at p 847, the Privy Council adopted the following passage from the judgment of Scrutton LJ in *R v General Council of Medical Education and Registration of the United Kingdom* [1930] 1 KB 562 at p 569:

> "It is a great pity that the word 'infamous' is used to describe the conduct of a medical practitioner who advertises. As in the case of the Bar so in the medical profession advertising is serious misconduct in a professional respect and that is all that is meant by the phrase 'infamous conduct'; *it means no more than serious misconduct judged according to the rules written or unwritten governing the profession.*" (Emphasis added.)

'In our view the same test should be applied in judging disgraceful conduct. In *Doughty* the Privy Council pointed out that Lord Jenkins' observation in *Felix* was in the context of a case in which dishonesty was very much the issue.

'In considering whether conduct falls within that category, regard should be had to the three levels of misconduct referred to in the [Medical Practitioners] Act, namely disgraceful conduct in a professional respect, s 58(1)(b); professional misconduct, s 43(2); and unbecoming conduct, s 42B(2). Obviously, for conduct to be disgraceful, it must be considered significantly more culpable than professional misconduct, that is, conduct that would reasonably be regarded by a practitioner's colleagues as constituting unprofessional conduct, or as it was put in *Pillai v Messiter (No 2)* (1989) 16 NSWLR 197, 200, a deliberate departure from accepted standards or such serious negligence as, although not deliberate, to portray indifference and an abuse of the privileges which accompany registration as a medical practitioner.

'The standard of proof is not the criminal standard. The preliminary proceedings committee is required to prove the charge to the civil onus, that is, proof on the balance of probabilities. But the authorities have recognised that the degree of satisfaction for which the civil standard of proof calls, will vary according to the gravity of the fact to be proved: *Ongley v Medical Council of New Zealand* (1984) 4 NZLR 369, 375–376. The charges against the appellant were grave. The elements of the charge must therefore be proved to a standard commensurate with that gravity.' *Brake v Preliminary Proceedings Committee of the Medical Council of New Zealand* [1997] 1 NZLR 71 at 77, per cur

DISHONEST

Canada 'Webster's Third New International Dictionary (Springfield, MA: Merriam-Webster Inc, 1986), defines "dishonest" as "characterized by a lack of truth, honesty, probity, or trustworthiness".' *63398 Alberta Ltd v Saskatchewan Government Insurance* (1995) 131 DLR (4th) 561 at 569, Sask CA, per Jackson JA

DISHONESTY

Australia [Section 81(1) of the (Vic) Crimes Act 1958 provides that 'A person who by any deception dishonestly obtains property belonging to another, with the intention of permanently depriving the other of it, is guilty of an indictable offence'.] '... In England, courts have adopted the view that the word "dishonestly" in comparable legislation has a residual meaning, and that the meaning is to be determined by the jury expressing the moral standards of the ordinary person. In *R v Feely* ([1973] (Q)B 530 at 537–8), Lawton LJ said —

> Jurors, when deciding whether an appropriation was dishonest can be reasonably expected to, and should, apply the current standards of ordinary decent people. In their own lives they have to decide what is and what is not dishonest. We can see no reason why, when in a jury box, they should need the help of a judge to tell them what amounts to dishonesty.

'Then in *R v Ghosh* ([1982] (Q)B 1053, especially at 1064 per Lord Lane CJ), the Court of Appeal added to the test for dishonesty by requiring that the accused must also realise that the conduct was "by the ordinary standards of reasonable and honest people" dishonest.

'Victorian courts have not accepted this approach in the context of ss 81(1) and 82(1) of the Crimes Act. In *R v Salvo* ([1980] VR 401), the accused was charged with obtaining property by deception. He relied on the defence of bona fide claim of legal right. Three members of the Full Court considered the meaning of the word "dishonestly" in this context. Fullagar and Murphy JJ (McInerney J dissenting) held that the test in Feely was not a correct statement of the meaning to be given to the word "dishonestly" in s 81. Their Honours held that the word was not used, in the context of s 81(1), in its ordinary sense but in a special and technical sense, and that a claim of legal right negated the existence of "dishonesty" for the purposes of an offence under s 81. Murphy J said. —

If the jury gained the impression from the judge's charge that in deciding what was in the accused's mind they should simply rely on the fact that he "did make the false representations that the cheque would be met", then in my view, in the circumstances of the case, they would have been acting under a misapprehension. For the deception was admitted. The accused admitted that he performed it for the purpose of obtaining possession of the car and he succeeded in his purpose.

The question always remained, was the obtaining by deception done dishonestly, and, up to this point in his charge, the learned trial judge had not given the jury any express assistance as to what they should consider in arriving at an answer to that question. Up to this point, the jury could have been misled inferentially into thinking that they should have regard only to the fact that the accused admitted making the false representation to enable them to decide whether they were satisfied that he acted dishonestly.

But his Honour continued: "It is not to the point for you to say — each of you to yourself — 'Would I have acted in that way? Would I, if I had done that, have regarded myself as acting dishonestly?' That is not the point. The point is that you must determine are you satisfied beyond reasonable doubt that the accused man knew that he was acting dishonestly in doing what he did? And that is the crux of this case"...

'The reasoning in *Salvo* was applied in *R v Brow* [1981] VR and in *R v Bonollo* [1981] VR 633. In *Peters v R* (1998) 192 CLR 493, the High Court considered the element of dishonesty in the trial of an accused charged with conspiracy to defraud. Gaudron and Toohey JJ distinguished the Victorian cases just mentioned, saying that they should be confined in their application to offences against statutory provisions in which the word "dishonest" was held to have been used in a special sense. Professor Williams has argued that the approach of cases such as *Peters* has significantly undermined the standing of the Victorian decisions based on *Salvo* and that these authorities are open to further review. But in *McLeod v R* (2003) 214 CLR 230; 197 ALR 333, the High Court considered a charge under s 173 of the Crimes Act 1900 (NSW) that a director of a body corporate fraudulently took or applied property of the body corporate for his own use or benefit. All members of the Court mentioned the line of authorities commencing with *Salvo* without any suggestion that the Victorian authorities

are wrongly decided.' *R v Masoko Tado* [2004] VSCA 177 at [23], per Charles JA; BC200406516

DISMISS

[For 16 Halsbury's Laws (4th edn) para 616 see now 16 Halsbury's Laws (4th edn) (2000 Reissue) para 477.]

DISMISSAL

Australia ' ... we find no difficulty in accepting the ordinary meaning of "dismissal" suggested by Brereton J in *Ex parte Wurth; Re Tully* (1954) 55 SR (NSW) 47 as being "the termination of services by the employer without the employee's consent"; we would add that where an employee does not freely consent to the termination, understood in a broad sense, then the circumstances may still amount to a dismissal by the employer as a constructive dismissal ...' *Smith v Director-General of School Education* (1993) 31 NSWLR 349 at 366, per cur

New Zealand 'In *Auckland Shop Employees Union v Woolworths (NZ) Ltd* [1985] 2 NZLR 372, this court held that, in the context of the Industrial Relations Act, the word "dismissal" included cases where, in substance, the employer had dismissed a worker although, in form, the worker had resigned ... In the context of an Act aimed at good industrial relations, it was right to assume that Parliament had intended the word "dismissal" to cover cases where the employer had effectively dismissed the worker, although technically the worker had resigned. I do not think that the court is justified in taking a similar approach in a situation where there was a fixed contract in which the worker agreed to work for a stated period and where there was no evidence of an express or implied promise of renewal.' *Actors Industrial Union of Workers v Auckland Theatre Trust Inc* [1989] 2 NZLR 154 at 162, CA, per Barker J

DISMISSED

New Zealand [Rule 28 of the Court of Appeal Rules includes the phrase 'Where an action is dismissed or a judgment of nonsuit is pronounced or an application is refused ... '.] 'I am of the view that a proceeding is not "dismissed" when a defendant succeeds and judgment is entered in his or her favour. [There follow at pp 477–478 the Judge's five specific reasons for his view.] *Nimmo v Westpac Banking Corpn* [1994] 1 NZLR 472 at 477, per Thomas J

DISORDERLY HOUSE

[For 11 Halsbury's Laws (4th edn) para 1057 see now 11(1) Halsbury's Laws (4th edn) (Reissue) para 379.]

'The offence is keeping a disorderly house. That is a house having the characteristic of disorderliness, as that expression has been defined in the cases. It seems to me that a house does not acquire the legal character of disorderliness because disorder occurs there on one occasion any more than a house becomes a gaming house because cards are played there once or a house becomes a brothel because it is used for purposes of prostitution by more than one woman on a single occasion. Moreover, it appears to me that the mischief at which the common law offence is aimed is the mischief of keeping a house to which members of the public resort for purposes of the disorderly recreation, if one can so describe it, which is available there, whether it takes the form of indecency or illicit pugilism or cock fighting or whatever. The essence of the mischief is the continuity which exists where the use of premises for a given unlawful purpose becomes notorious.'
Moores v Director of Public Prosecutions [1991] 4 All ER 521 at 525, per Bingham LJ

DISPENSING

Canada '[22] The appellants submit that the trial judge erred by failing to define the controlled act of dispensing eye glasses in terms of risk of harm; by finding that dispensing is part of prescribing; by finding that dispensing eye glasses to a person of visual maturity presents a risk of harm; and by failing to define the controlled act of dispensing within the spirit and intent of the *RHPA* [*Regulated Health Professions Act*].
...
'[28] Here the trial judge heard expert evidence as to the meaning of dispensing. He defined the term in a manner consistent with that evidence, dictionary definitions and the definition of dispensing as it appeared in predecessor legislation.
'[29] For example, the defence expert optician agreed that dispensing an optical prescription for eye glasses would include: "selection, designing, measuring, manufacturing, verification, fitting/delivery".
'[30] Dictionary definitions of dispensing include:

The Concise Oxford Dictionary of Current English (1998),

dispense ...make up and give out (medicine etc.) according to a doctor's prescription.

The Dictionary of Canadian Law, 2d ed.,

Ophthalmic Dispensing. (i) Supplying, preparing and dispensing ophthalmic appliances; (ii) interpreting prescriptions of legally qualified medical practitioners and optometrists; and (iii) the fitting, adjusting and adapting of ophthalmic appliances to the human face and eyes in accordance with the prescriptions of legally qualified medical practitioners and optometrists.

'[31] "Ophthalmic dispensing" was formerly defined in s 1 of the *Ophthalmic Dispensers Act*, R.S.O. 1990, c. O.43 as the:
(a) supplying, preparing, and dispensing ophthalmic appliances;
(b) interpreting prescriptions of legally qualified medical practitioners and optometrists, and
(c) the fitting, adjusting and adapting of ophthalmic appliances to the human face and eyes in accordance with the prescriptions of legally qualified medical practitioners and optometrists ...

'[32] I see no error in the definition of dispensing adopted by the trial judge. However, I add that I do not view the words chosen by him as exclusive or all encompassing. Further, I wish to clarify that I do not equate the term "preparation" with "fabrication". Rather, I view its meaning as "all actions necessary to be performed prior to adaptation and delivery".' *King Optical Group Inc v College of Opticians of Ontario* (2001) 207 DLR (4th) 72 at 79–81, Ont CA, per Simmons JA

DISPOSAL OR CESSATION OF ... BUSINESS

New Zealand [Section 43(2) of the Accident Compensation Act 1982 uses the phrase "Every employer who, on the disposal or cessation of his business".] 'On the ordinary and natural reading of the words they are directed only to those cases where only the business or each and every business of the employer is disposed of or otherwise ceases.' *NZ Forest Products Ltd v Accident Compensation Corporation* [1994] 3 NZLR 150 at 155, CA, per cur

DISPOSE—DISPOSAL

Australia [By section 160M(6) of the Income Tax Assessment Act 1936 (Cth) a 'disposal' of an asset that did not exist before the disposal but is created by the disposal shall be deemed to be disposal without consideration nor costs or expenditure.] 'The notion of "disposal" is critical to the operation of Pt IIIA but, curiously, the term is not defined in the Act. The word "disposal" in relation to an asset is of wide import and includes the act or process of transferring something to or providing something for another. It is a very comprehensive term. The word "disposal" according to its ordinary meaning presupposes that there is some proprietary right vested in the disposer at the time of the disposal. Ordinarily the creation of an asset must precede its disposal and would not generally comprehend property which was created by the act of disposal. One talks of disposing of something that one has.' *Hepples v Federal Commissioner of Taxation* (1990) 21 ATR 42 at 50–51, per Lockhart J

Canada [An insurance policy covered a substitute vehicle where the original vehicle was 'disposed' of or sold.] 'The definition of "dispose" in the definition section s 29 [of the Interpretation Act]: "dispose" means to transfer by any method and includes assign, give, sell, grant, charge, convey, bequeath, devise, lease, divest, release and agree to do any of those things. Counsel for the appellant's first argument on the meaning of "disposed of" was that sub-s 2(1), the application section, of the Interpretation Act permitted definitions in the Interpretation Act not to be applied where a contrary intention appears in the Interpretation Act or in the enactment itself.

'In my opinion, the Interpretation Act definitions ought to be applied unless it is clear from the context that they cannot be sensibly applied. That is what is meant by a contrary intention appearing in the Act. It is not a sufficient ground for ignoring the defined term in the Interpretation Act that there are alternative meanings which could give a sensible construction. If there is no reason for not applying the definition in the Interpretation Act then it must be applied. In my opinion there is no reason for not applying the definition of "dispose" in this case.' *Sealey v Crystal* (1987) 39 DLR (4th) 151 at 153–154, BC CA, per Lambert JA

Canada 'In selecting the words "disposed of" in s 30 of the [Environmental Protection Act (RSO 1990, c E.19)], it is my view that the legislature intended that these words have a meaning distinct from the other activities notwithstanding the broad dictionary meaning. The meaning of the phrase which is most consistent with the general scheme and objective of the Act is "final disposal of waste at the site". It is this latter activity that would generate the greater environmental concerns and therefore should attract closer scrutiny.' *Banks v Northumberland* (*County*) (1994) 114 DLR (4th) 360 at 366, Ont CA, per Griffiths JA

DISPOSITION

' "Disposition" must involve some transfer of an interest in property, in the technical sense of the word "property", as contrasted with mere possession.' *Worcester Works Finance Ltd v Cooden Engineering Co Ltd* [1971] 3 All ER 708 at 714, CA, per Megaw LJ

[Matrimonial Causes Act 1973, s 37. Husband and wife had claimed the right to buy the property of which they were joint secure tenants but parties separated and wife gave notice terminating joint tenancy. Husband was served with possession notice but claimed avoidance of the disposition by his wife under s 37.] 'The service of a notice ending the joint tenancy is not a disposition of property. That is the only act performed by the wife on which Mr Bater can rely. I do not see how its nature can change simply because it ends not merely the secure tenancy but also the right to buy which depended on the secure tenancy. The House of Lords has held that the serving of the notice to end a periodic tenancy is not a dispositive act. It does no more than remove one of the requirements needed for the existence of the right to buy, namely the continuation of the secure tenancy. The termination of the right to buy comes about because of the effect of the statutory provisions creating the right to buy and not because of any act or disposition by Mrs Bater.' *Bater v Bater* [1999] 4 All ER 944 at 950, CA, per Roch LJ

[The defendant charity exchanged contracts for the sale of premises to the second defendant, who subsequently assigned the benefit of the contract to the claimant in consideration of a payment. Subsequently, the charity contended that its contract with the second defendant was void on the ground of its own non-compliance with certain requirements of the Charities Act 1993. In response, the claimant sought to rely on s 37(4) of the 1993 Act, a provision which operated in favour of a person who in good faith acquired an interest in land held by a charity for money or money's worth, but was applicable only in relation to a 'disposition' of such land. On an application by the claimant for a summary order for specific performance, the master rejected his contention that a contract for sale constituted a 'disposition' for the purposes of s 37(4). He therefore dismissed that application, and the claimant appealed.] '[6] Subsection (4) of Section 37 provides as follows:

"Where—(a) any land held by or in trust for a charity is sold, leased or otherwise disposed of by a disposition to which subsection (1) or (2) of section 36 above applies, but (b) sub-section (2) above has not been complied with in relation to the disposition, then in favour of a person who (whether under the disposition or afterwards) in good faith acquires an interest in the land for money or money's worth, the disposition shall be valid whether or not—(i) the disposition has been sanctioned by an order of the court or of the Commissioners, or (ii) the Charity trustees have power under the trusts of the Charity to effect the disposition and have complied with the provisions of that section so far as applicable to it".

It will be seen that the question of the applicability of sub-s (4) depends on, for present purposes, two questions. First, whether by virtue of the contract the property was "sold, leased or otherwise disposed of by a disposition to which subsection (1) or (2) of s 36 above applies"; and, secondly, whether the second defendant "under the disposition" acquired an interest in the land "in good faith". To put the matter another way, (i) was the contract a "disposition" for the purposes of s 37(4) and (ii) did the second defendant act in "good faith"?
...
'[15] In my judgment, it is signal that s 37 does in sub-s (1) expressly describe separately, on the one hand, "a contract for the sale, or for a lease or other disposition" (the words "any other" not being deployed before "disposition") and, on the other hand, an instrument "effecting a disposition". There is, therefore, a distinction drawn in s 37 itself between a contract for a disposition and an effected disposition. The presence of this distinction is also apparent from s 37(5) which refers, on the one hand, to "any contract for the sale, or for a lease or other disposition, of land which will, *as a result of the disposition*, be held by or in trust for a charity" and, on the other hand, to an "instrument effecting a disposition of such land".
'[16] This distinction is yet further apparent in s 37(2) which talks of land being "sold leased or otherwise disposed of by a disposition". In my judgment, this addition of the words "by a disposition" to the very same words which also appear in s 36(1) make it clear that the subject

matter of s 37(2) is, therefore, not a contract for a disposition, but rather only a disposition which has been actually effected. This is confirmed by the later words in s 37(2) which refers to "the disposition" and require the insertion of the prescribed certificate in "the instrument by which the disposition is effected".
'[17] Accordingly, in my judgment, the expression "sold, leased or otherwise disposed of by a disposition" which also appears in s 37(4) has the same consequence, given the addition of the words "by a disposition", namely that this sub-section applies only to an effected disposition and does not apply to a transaction which is merely a contract to make a disposition. This is confirmed, in my judgment, by the fact that sub-s (4) applies only where "subsection (2) has not been complied with"... ' *Bayoumi v Women's Total Abstinence Educational Union Ltd* [2003] EWHC 212 (Ch) at [6], [15]–[17], [2003] 1 All ER 864, per Simon Berry QC (reversed in part [2003] EWCA Civ 1548, CA (see below))
'[26] It is important, in the context of the present appeal, to note that the legislature has had well in mind, when enacting ss 36 and 37 of the 1993 Act, the distinction between a contract (or agreement) for the sale or other disposition of charity land and the transfer, conveyance or other instrument by which the sale or other disposition is effected. The distinction is emphasised in s 37(1). It is recognised, also, in s 36(3)—the requirements of which must be complied with "before entering into an agreement for the sale or (as the case may be) for a lease or other disposition" of charity land; in s 36(5)—"Where the proposed disposition is the granting of a lease ... before entering into an agreement for the lease"; and in s 37(2)—which requires the charity trustees to include the certificate for which that subsection provides "in the instrument by which the disposition is effected". But, having regard to the decision in *Milner*'s case [*Milner v Staffordshire Congregational Union (Inc)* [1956] 1 All ER 494, [1956] Ch 275], it is less clear whether the prohibition in s 36(1) of the Act—"no land ... shall be sold, leased or otherwise disposed of"—is intended to extend to the making of a contract for the sale of charity land. It is to that point that I now turn.
...
'[43] Although, as I would hold, s 36(1) of the 1993 Act does not, itself, have the effect of making void an agreement for the sale of charity land into which charity trustees have entered without first complying with the requirements of s 36(3) of the Act, it is plain that (absent an order of the court or

of the commissioners) a transfer made in purported performance of such an agreement will be void; unless saved by s 37(4). It follows that, in a case such as the present, where the purchaser becomes aware, before completion of the contract by transfer or conveyance, of the failure by the charity trustees to comply with the requirements of s 36(3), he cannot compel performance of the contract. Section 37(4) of the 1993 Act does not assist him in such a case. That section can have no application to an uncompleted contract for the sale of charity land. No "disposition" is capable of being made valid by the operation of that section unless it is a "disposition" within para (a)—that is to say, a "disposition" to which sub-ss (1) or (2) of s 36 applies. An uncompleted contract for the sale of charity land is not, itself, a "disposition" of that land for the purposes of s 36(1) or (2) of the Act.' *Bayoumi v Women's Total Abstinence Educational Union Ltd* [2003] EWCA Civ 1548 at [26], [43], [2004] 3 All ER 110, CA, per Chadwick LJ

Australia ' "Disposition" is a term that has given rise to much litigation, particularly in reference to definitions in revenue legislation where it has meanings extended to include such things as releases of rights, creation of new rights, and the moving of property from the sole ownership of A to the co-ownership of A and B, and the exercise of general powers of appointment. The saga culminating in *FCT v St Helens Farm (ACT) Pty Ltd* (1981) 146 CLR 336; 34 ALR 23 is a striking example.

' "Disposition" is not a word with a technical legal meaning, although it frequently is used in legal instruments; speaking generally, it covers all forms of alienation: *FCT v Wade* (1951) 84 CLR 105 at 110; [1951] ALR 962. "Alienation" indicates a transaction whereby property is transferred to another person otherwise than by involuntary operation of law: see *Re Gaskell and Walters' Contract* [1906] 2 Ch 1 at 10'. *Australian Trade Commission v Film Funding and Management Pty Ltd* (1989) 87 ALR 49 at 67, per Gummow J

Australia [Section 368(1) of the Companies (NSW) Code provided relevantly: (1) Any disposition of property of the company ... made after the commencement of the winding up by the Court is ... void.] 'The words "dispose" or "disposition" may have very wide meanings depending on the context: see, e.g., *Henty House Pty Ltd (In Vol Liq) v Federal Commissioner of Taxation* (1953) 88 CLR 141 at 152 and *McGain v Federal Commissioner of Taxation* (1966) 116 CLR 172. Even presenting one's own bankruptcy petition

may amount to a disposition, *Re Cotgrave, Mynors v Cotgrave* [1903] 2 Ch 705 and *In Marriage of Bassola, Official Trustee in Bankruptcy (Intervener)* (1985) 10 Fam LR 413. The concept associated with the use of such word involves the presence of both a disponor and a disponee. In a situation where a person ceases to own property because he forfeits it, it is hard to see how there is a disponee. It would not seem to me that such transaction would be affected by s 368 of the Code because it does not involve a disposition within the meaning of that section.' *Mosaic Oil NL v Angari Pty Ltd [No 2]* (1990) 20 NSWLR 280 at 284–285, per Young J

DISPOSITION OF THE COMPLAINANT IN SEXUAL MATTERS

Australia [Section 36BA of the Evidence Act 1906 (WA) states: 'In proceedings for a sexual offence, evidence relating to the disposition of the complainant in sexual matters shall not be adduced or elicited by or on behalf of a defendant.'] 'In discussing evidence concerning the character of an accused in a criminal trial, the New Zealand Law Commission has pointed out that:

> "On the one hand, the law distinguishes between evidence of general reputation and evidence of individual opinion and, in the case of the defendant in criminal proceedings, has historically recognised only the former. On the other hand, it is not always clear what is meant by reputation. On occasion, it appears to be used interchangeably with *character*. It may be important therefore to distinguish between character as *public estimation* – which is perhaps more correctly referred to as reputation – and character as *disposition* – which is something more intrinsic to the individual in question." (original emphasis)

'[58] The concept of disposition referred to in this passage obviously refers to a person's tendencies or propensities as things intrinsic to the individual in question which exist independently of other persons' opinions of those features. They are part of the character of the person so that given a relevant set of conditions or circumstances the person concerned has a tendency or propensity to act in a particular way. In contrast, the general opinion that others have of those features may constitute part of the person's reputation. Thus, a person who anonymously donates large sums of money to charity may have a reputation for being miserly, but in truth that person's disposition is charitable.

'[59] As we pointed out earlier, an important object of the 1985 amendments [to the Evidence Act 1906 (WA)] was to ensure that in trials for sexual offences a person's sexual reputation or disposition would not be used as a basis for reasoning that the complainant was the kind of person who would have consented to the conduct in question. That being so, it seems proper to construe "disposition" in s 36BA as referring to any characteristics of the complainant which suggests that he or she is the "kind of person" who would have engaged in the conduct in question. Thus, evidence relates to the "sexual disposition" of the complainant for the purpose of s 36BA only when it tends to prove that he or she is that "kind of person". A contrast is therefore to be drawn between statements and conduct which reveal the intrinsic character of the complainant and those which, although relevant to the particular occasion, do not. It is statements and conduct falling within the former category to which s 36BA is directed. It may not always be easy to draw the distinction between statements and conduct which reveal the intrinsic character of the complainant and those which, although relevant to the particular occasion, do not. But generally, the more direct and confined the relationship between the statement or conduct and the particular occasion, the less likely it is to reveal intrinsic character.

'[60] Absent an admission, a person's disposition, like a person's feelings, intentions or wishes, can only be proved indirectly. In most cases, a person's disposition can only be proved by:

(a) the person in question expressly or impliedly declaring that he or she has a certain disposition, or

(b) drawing inferences as to a person's disposition from the past conduct of the person, or

(c) drawing an inference from a person's reputation.' (footnotes omitted)

Bull v R (2000) 171 ALR 613; BC200002276; [2000] HCA 24 at [57]–[60], per McHugh, Gummow and Hayne JJ

DISPUTE

[Arbitration agreement to refer 'any dispute' to arbitration. Omission in Arbitration Act 1996, s 9 of ground for refusing a stay formerly in Arbitration Act 1975, s 1(1), ie that 'there is not in fact any dispute between the parties with regard to the matter agreed to be referred'.] 'In my view, ... there is a dispute once money is claimed unless

and until the defendants admit that the sum is due and payable ... In my judgment if a party has refused to pay a sum which is claimed or has denied that it is owing then in the ordinary use of the English language there is a dispute between the parties.

...

'The important distinction between s 9 of the 1996 Act and s 1(1) of the 1975 Act is the omission of the words "that there is not in fact any dispute between the parties with regard to the matter agreed to be referred". Accordingly the court no longer has to consider whether there is *in fact* any dispute between the parties but only whether there is a dispute within the arbitration clause of the agreement, and the cases which turn on that distinction are now irrelevant.' *Halki Shipping Corpn v Sopex Oils Ltd* [1998] 2 All ER 23 at 56, CA, per Swinton Thomas LJ

DISSOLUTION

Australia '... [I]n relation to nomenclature there is no real difference between "dissolution", "termination" or the "ending" of a partnership. Butterworths Australian Legal Dictionary defines "dissolution" as "ending or breakup of a partnership" and goes on to say "A dissolution may be followed by a winding up of the partnership where both the firm and the assets are realised and distributed". Lindley and Banks On Partnership (17th ed) at 10–20 refers to a partnership surviving as a partnership at will following a dissolution. This is an indication that it is permissible to refer to the dissolution of a partnership even where what follows is a partnership at will on similar terms.' *Leisure Investments Pty Ltd v Bilioara Pty Ltd* BC200007168; [2000] NTSC 94 at [80], per Thomas J

DISTINCTIVE

[The test of distinctiveness is no longer applied.]

[For 48 Halsbury's Laws (4th edn) para 34 see now 48 Halsbury's Laws (4th edn) (2000 Reissue) para 58.]

Canada [Aboriginal rights are protected under s 35 of the *Canadian Charter of Rights and Freedoms*.] 'The standard which a practice, custom or tradition must meet in order to be recognized as an aboriginal right is not that it be distinct to the aboriginal culture in question; the aboriginal claimants must simply demonstrate that the practice, custom or tradition is distinctive. A tradition or custom that is distinct is one that is unique — "different in kind or quality; unlike" (*Concise Oxford Dictionary*). A culture with a distinct tradition must claim that in having such a tradition it is different from other cultures; a claim of distinctness is, by its very nature, a claim relative to other cultures or traditions. By contrast, a culture that claims that a practice, custom or tradition is distinctive — "distinguishing, characteristic" — makes a claim that is not relative; the claim is rather one about the culture's own practices, customs or traditions considered apart from the practices, customs or traditions of any other culture. It is a claim that this tradition or custom makes the culture what it is, not that the practice, custom or tradition is different from the practices, customs or traditions of another culture. The person or community claiming the existence of an aboriginal right protected by s 35(1) need only show that the particular practice, custom or tradition which it is claiming to be an aboriginal right is distinctive, not that it is distinct.' *R v Van der Peet* [1996] 2 SCR 507 at 560–561, per Lamer CJ

DISTRESS

[For 13 Halsbury's Laws (4th edn) para 201 see now 13 Halsbury's Laws (4th edn) (Reissue) para 601.]

DISTRIBUTION

By company

New Zealand '[44] The term "distribution" is defined by s 2(1) of the Act as follows:
2. Interpretation — (1) Distribution, in relation to a distribution by a company to a shareholder, means –
    (a) The direct or indirect transfer of money or property, other than the company's own shares, to or for the benefit of the shareholder; or
    (b) The incurring of a debt to or for the benefit of the shareholder –
in relation to shares held by that shareholder, and whether by means of a purchase of property, the redemption or other acquisition of shares, a distribution of indebtedness, or by some other means.

'[45] Section 52(3) of the Act provides:
    (3) If, after a distribution is authorised and before it is made, the board ceases to be satisfied on reasonable grounds that the

company will, immediately after the distribution is made, satisfy the solvency test, any distribution made by the company is deemed not to have been authorised.

...
'[48] The "distribution" provisions of the Act have their origin in comprehensive work undertaken by the Law Commission on company law reform in New Zealand: see "Company Law" (NZLC PP5, 1987), "Company Law: Reform and Restatement" (NZLC R9, June 1989) and "Company Law Reform: Transition and Revision" (NZLC R16, September 1990). The regime for distributions created by the Act was intended to be a radical departure from the old law on capital maintenance ...

'[56] Viewed in that context, the definition of the term "distribution" ought not to be construed in a narrow manner. Reform of the capital maintenance doctrine would be undermined if the definition was interpreted narrowly. Yet, interpretation of the definition must also accord with the underlying purposes of the distribution provisions read in light of the Act as a whole: s 5 of the Interpretation Act 1999. The main purpose of enacting the legislative change was to strengthen the capital maintenance doctrine to avoid prejudice to creditors and higher ranking shareholders ...

...
'[72] The starting point for analysis is the definition of distribution in s 2(1) of the Act. A company seeking relief against a director under s 56(4) of the Act must be able to point to a benefit gained by a shareholder, in its capacity as a shareholder, arising out of either the transfer of an asset (or the transfers of assets) from the company or the incurring of a liability (or liabilities) by the company on behalf of the shareholder ...

...
'[86] In my view the definition of "distribution" ought to be given a wide meaning to facilitate the purposes of the distribution provisions of the Act: namely, protection of the interests of creditors and higher ranking shareholders once insolvency intervenes.' *Re DML Resources Ltd* (*In Liquidation*) [2004] 3 NZLR 490

Of estate

New Zealand 'When Parliament [in the Law Reform (Testamentary Provisions) Act 1949] referred to a "distribution of any part of the estate" it must at least have meant to include actual transfers of assets to beneficiaries, whether all or part of a bequest to a legatee or part of an expected residue to a residuary beneficiary. A legacy which becomes vested in the legatee by the assent of the executor, although not paid or transferred to the legatee, is also, in my judgment, relevantly distributed for it is as much the legatee's property as that actually paid or conveyed to him.' *Jurkovich v Fortune* [1988] 2 NZLR 442 at 446, CA, per Somers J

DISTURBANCE

Canada [See section 175(1)(a) of the Criminal Code, RSC 1985, c C–46.] 'The word "disturbance" is capable of many meanings. The task is to choose the meaning which best accords with the intention of Parliament. The following arguments support the conclusion that "disturbance" in s 175(1)(a) involves more than mere mental or emotional annoyance or disruption ... First, the noun "disturbance" may have a different connotation than the verb "to disturb". Not everything that disturbs people results in a disturbance (e.g., smoking). A definition which posits identity between "disturb" and "disturbance" is contrary to ordinary usage, the most fundamental principle of statutory construction. This is not to say that one cannot speak of a purely emotional disturbance, but rather that "disturbance" has a secondary meaning which "disturb" does not possess; a meaning which suggests interference with an ordinary and customary conduct or use ... The disturbance contemplated by s 175(1)(a) is something more than mere emotional upset. There must be an externally manifested disturbance of the public peace, in the sense of interference with the ordinary and customary use of the premises by the public. There may be direct evidence of such an effect or interference, or it may be inferred from the evidence of a police officer as to the conduct of a person or persons under s 175(2). The disturbance may consist of the impugned act itself, as in the case of a fight interfering with the peaceful use of a bar room or it may flow as a consequence of the impugned act, as where shouting and swearing produce a scuffle. As the cases illustrate, the interference with the ordinary and customary conduct in or near the public place may consist in something as small as being distracted from one's work. But it must be present and it must be externally manifested. In accordance with the principle of legality, the disturbance must be one which may reasonably have been foreseen in the

particular circumstances of time and place.' *R v Lohnes* [1992] 1 SCR 167 at 178, 181–182, SCC, per McLachlin J

Of franchise

'Both at common law and under statute the right to establish and conduct a market authorises the market to be established in a defined place or within a defined area, in the present case the City of Birmingham. In addition to the area within which the market may be established, the market owner is given further protection over a wider area, that is to say over an area having a radius of 6 miles. The purpose of this wider protection is to protect the market owner from competition for customers who would normally use his market. The source of the 6 miles distance appears to be in the writings of Bracton. Bracton treated 6 miles as being one-third of the Roman "dieta", a day's journey (Bract (1640 edn) bk IV ch 46 fo 235*a*-*b*). A man going to market should have one third of a day to get to market, one third to attend the market and another third to return home (see Pease "Some Early Cases on Disturbance of Market" (1916) 32 LQR 199 at 203). If the rival market was within 6 miles, it would attract customers who might otherwise come to the authorised market. If the authorised market was given a wider protection than 6 miles, users of markets would have to spend too long getting to the nearest market. Hence the limit of 6 miles. The whole basis of that rule, unbelievably archaic as it is, is therefore linked to the distance from an actual market, the customers of that market and their ability to get to it.' *Birmingham City Council v Anvil Favis* [1989] 1 All ER 147 at 149, per Browne-Wilkinson V-C

DIVERT

[For 21 Halsbury's Laws (4th edn) para 143 see now 21 Halsbury's Laws (4th edn) (2004 Reissue) paras 781–783.]

DIVIDEND

'The word "dividends" originally referred to the dividing up of something, usually a profit, among several people so that each had a fraction or share of the whole. The rebate allowed by co-operative societies to members who made purchases at the society's shop was called a "dividend". I believe that the payment out of a share of a football pool to a successful forecaster of the results of matches is called a "dividend". Both these uses refer to sharing out of something. In ordinary language today among people having some understanding of business a "dividend" refers to a payment out of a part of the profits for a period in respect of a share in a company. The dividend may be a fixed amount on a preference share or a fluctuating amount on an equity share. It is distinguished in the Taxes Acts generally by being accompanied, under the "imputed corporation tax" system operative in the United Kingdom, by a "tax credit". The distinction in both ordinary understanding and in taxation legislation is between "dividends" on the one hand and "interest" on the other, the latter being paid less basic rate tax in contradistinction to the tax credit attributed to a dividend.' *Esso Petroleum Co Ltd v Ministry of Defence* [1990] 1 All ER 163 at 165, per Harman J

[For 7 Halsbury's Laws (4th edn) para 596 see now 7(1) Halsbury's Laws (4th edn) (2004 Reissue) para 905.]

DIVORCE

[For 13 Halsbury's Laws (4th edn) paras 501 et seq see now 29(3) Halsbury's Laws (4th edn) (Reissue) paras 401 et seq.]

DIVULGE

Australia [Section 8XB(1)(b) cf the Taxation Administration Act 1953 (Cth) states, inter alia, that a person shall not 'divulge' or communicate to another person any taxation information relating to a third person.] 'It is part of the ordinary meaning of the word "divulge" as used in s 8XB that the act of divulging involves the exposure of information. The mere delivery of a document containing statements prepared by the Australian Taxation Office in code form would not constitute the divulging of information. The disclosure of statements in code would not be a divulging of information unless further disclosure of the meaning of the code was made by an officer of the Australian Taxation Office in breach of a taxation law.' *R v Lovell* (1991) 52 A Crim R 340 at 347, per Lee J

DO WORK

Australia [In the context of the (Cth) Veterans' Entitlements Act 1986 s 37(1) and the (Cth) Veterans' Entitlements (Income Support Supplement – Permanent Capacity for Work) Determination 1999.] 'In our view, the expression to "do work" in cl 5(2)(b), when read in context, requires the decision-maker to focus upon the applicant, and

not some hypothetical person. Consideration must be given to whether a person of the applicant's background, suffering from his or her condition, is, solely by reason of the impairment, permanently unable to do remunerative work of the type that he or she would otherwise be fitted to undertake. In answering that question, it must be determined whether the applicant can undertake such work for more than eight hours per week. In other words, the test looks at the individual applicant, treats "work" as remunerative activity, and assesses the applicant's ability to carry out that activity by reference to that person's qualifications, background and skills.

'The test that we consider appropriate does not go as far as that seemingly applied by the primary judge. His Honour's analysis would treat an applicant as relevantly incapacitated in circumstances where that person could not readily find alternative employment. That goes too far. It imposes an unwarranted gloss upon the language used by the legislature. The correct test, in our view, does not focus upon employability, but rather the capacity to perform remunerative work of a kind for which the person is otherwise suited.' *Repatriation Commission v Hill* [2005] FCAFC 7 at [57], per Wilcox, French and Weinberg JJ

DOCK

[For 36 Halsbury's Laws (4th edn) para 401 see now 36(1) Halsbury's Laws (4th edn) (Reissue) para 604.]

[The Capital Allowances Act 1968 has been repealed. The definition is re-enacted in the Capital Allowances Act 1990, s 18(9).]

DOCK WORKER

[The Dock Workers (Regulation of Employment) Act 1946 has been repealed.]

DOCUMENT

'The word "document" in normal usage is most frequently used in relation to written, typed or printed paper documents ... However, terminological emphasis in description in such cases on the means or surface for recording information does not deprive such alternative stores of information from qualifying as a "document"... It seems to us that the essential essence of a document is that it is something containing recorded information of some sort. It does not matter if, to be meaningful, the information requires to be processed in some way such as translation, decoding or electronic retrieval.' *Rollo v HM Advocate* 1996 SCCR 874 at 877, per Lord Milligan

New Zealand 'I agree ... that "document" includes a tape-recording of oral evidence given before a tribunal such as the Commission.' *Standen v Licensing Control Commission* [1990] 2 NZLR 722 at 725, per Greig J

New Zealand [Section 263 of the Crimes Act 1961 provides that:

...

"Document" means–
  (a) Any paper, parchment, or other material used for writing or printing, marked with matter capable of being read; or
  (b) Any photograph, or any photographic negative, plate, slide, film, or microfilm, or any photostatic negative; or
  (c) Any disc, tape, wire, sound track, card, or other material or device in or on which information, sounds, or other data are recorded, stored, or embodied so as to be capable, with or without the aid of some other equipment, of being reproduced therefrom; or
  (d) Any material by means of which information is supplied, whether directly or by means of any equipment, to any device used for recording or storing or processing information; or
  (e) Any material derived, whether directly or by means of any equipment, from information recorded or stored or processed by any device used for recording or storing or processing information:

...

  (2) For the purposes aforesaid–
    (a) It is immaterial in what language a document is expressed or in what country or place it is expressed to have effect:
    (b) A crossing on any cheque, draft on a banker, post office money order, postal note, postal order, coupon, or other document of which the crossing is authorised or recognised by law shall be deemed to be a material part of it.]

'[31] Putting to one side any relevant implications of the enactment of s 263, we have no difficulty accepting that the computer program and computer disk in question are each a "document" for the purposes of s 229A. Essentially, a document is a thing which provides evidence or information or serves as a record. The fact that developments in technology may improve the way in which evidence or information is provided or a record is kept does not change the fundamental purpose of that technology, nor a conceptual appreciation of that function. Legislation must be interpreted with that in mind.

'[32] It is unarguable that a piece of papyrus containing information, a page of parchment with the same information, a copper plate or a tablet of clay, are all documents. Nor would they be otherwise if the method of notation were English, Morse code, or binary symbols. In every case there is a document because there is a material record of information. This feature, rather than the medium, is definitive.

'It is sufficient for us to observe that the program and disk in issue constitute material things which record and provide information and that as such they are readily comprehended by the term "document".' *R v Misic* [2001] 3 NZLR 1 (CA) at 8–9 per cur

DOCUMENT OF THE COURT

Australia [Section 5 of the Freedom of Information Act 1982 (Cth) provides, inter alia, that the Act does not apply to any access to a 'document of the court' unless the document relates to administrative matters.] 'It is not necessary for the purposes of this appeal to define the outer limits of the field covered by the expression "a document of the court" in s 5. It is sufficient to say that a transcript of ex tempore reasons for judgment produced by a court reporting service at the request of a judge, not for general publication but for the confidential use of the judge to enable him or her to prepare published reasons for decision, is a document of a court within the meaning of s 5. Such a document is produced to enable a member of a court to perform one of his or her essential judicial functions, namely the publication of reasons for judgment. A document of that character is so closely connected with the court for which it is produced as to fall easily within the description of "a document of the court" as that expression is used in s 5. It is quite different in character from a document produced by a member of the public for his or her own purposes from shorthand notes taken during the hearing.' *Loughnan* (*Principal Register, Family Court of Australia*) *v Altman* (1992) 111 ALR 445 at 451, per cur

DOCUMENT OR PROCEEDING

Australia 'Secondly, the definition of "document" in the dictionary [Corporations Law s 9] was much wider than the earlier statutory definition. It provided that it includes:

"(a) any paper or other material on which there is writing or printing or on which there are marks, figures, symbols or perforations having a meaning for persons qualified to interpret them …".

The expressions "document" and "proceeding" are of such a width as to include a deed of company arrangement. Clearly it is, of course, a "paper … on which there is writing or printing" and it may well be that it is properly characterised as a "proceeding" (but again we need not stay to consider that matter).' *MYT Engineering Pty Ltd v Mulcon Pty Ltd* (1999) 30 ACSR 705 at 714; 17 ACLC 86; BC9902256, per Gleeson CJ, Gaudron, Gummow and Hayne JJ

DOMESTIC FURNACE

'Domestic furnace' means any furnace which is (a) designed solely or mainly for domestic purposes, and (b) used for heating a boiler with a maximum heating capacity of less than 16.12 kilowatts. (Clean Air Act 1993, s 64(1))

DOMESTIC VIOLENCE

Australia '[60] The phrase used by the regulations is "domestic violence". The word "violence" is not defined, other than to include a threat of violence. Domestic violence is "suffered", "committed" and "perpetrated". It must be of a kind, to be "relevant domestic violence" (reg 1.23(2)(b)) to cause the relevant fear or apprehension there referred to. It is of the kind dealt with by the Courts in the applications referred to in reg 1.23(1)(c) to (f) and by the police reports referred to in reg 1.24(1)(a)(ii). "Violence" is an ordinary English word. The phrase "domestic violence" refers to the social context of its occurrence. This is reflected in the spousal and familial relationship found in the regulations. The phrase is not a term of art It describes something: "violence" occurring in the domestic context. "Violence" has the following meanings in accepted dictionaries:

(a) *Oxford English Dictionary* (2nd Ed)
Violence: 1. a. The exercise of physical force so as to inflict injury on, or cause damage to, persons or property; action or conduct characterized by this; treatment or usage tending to cause bodily injury or forcibly interfering with personal freedom.

(b) *The Macquarie Dictionary* (3rd Ed)
Violence: noun 1. rough force in action: the violence of the wind. 2. rough injurious action or treatment: to die by violence. 3. any or unjust or unwarranted exertion of force or power, as against rights, laws, etc; injury; wrong; outrage. 4. a violent act or proceeding. 5. rough or immoderate vehemence, as of feeling or language; fury; intensity; severity. 6. a distortion of meaning or fact.

(c) *New Oxford Dictionary of English*
Violence noun [mass noun] behaviour involving physical force intended to hurt, damage, or kill someone or something.

'[61] In some contexts in ordinary usage, the notion of "violent" as intense, passionate or furious is expanded into areas of feeling, emotions and mental state. People do speak of emotional violence or verbal violence to express a meaning as to the furiousness, passion or venom of someone's behaviour. That is not, however, to say that someone who belittles, criticises, rejects, insults, humiliates or hurts the feelings of another, or who raises his or her voice to another, is committing an act of violence. It is the plainest use of language, we think, that to "commit" or "perpetrate" violence or the threat of violence involves the act, or threat of, application of physical force. It goes without saying that the application of force (especially the threat of it) may be exhibited by, and in the context of, a myriad of factual circumstances. The person disposed to commit the acts of violence may have to do little by way of word or deed to strike fear into someone as to their safety. Also, it goes without saying, that violence by spouse against spouse or other family member may well be accompanied by belittling, expressions of contempt and other conduct likely or intended to bring about coercion, humiliation, surrender or abasement.

'[62] However, belittling, lowering self esteem, "emotional violence" or "psychological violence" and such behaviour as surrogates or synonyms for violence is, we think, to broaden the scope of the regulations beyond their words. There must be "violence", or the "threat of violence", involving the application, or threat of application, of force such that the alleged victim is caused to fear for, or be apprehensive about, his or her well-being or personal safety.

...

'[64] As we have said, "violence" is an ordinary word and "domestic violence" is an ordinary concept.

...

'[67] Belittlement and expressed contempt may have their place in the creation of a climate of fear. But we reject the extension of "violence" to encompass "emotional" and "psychological" violence as the subject of these regulations, in the absence of the application, or threat of application, of physical force.

...

'[69] Even if one approaches the appeal on the conceded basis of the width of the word "violence" and the phrase "domestic violence", there must still be violence committed or perpetrated by the spouse of the alleged victim.' *Cakmak v Minister for Immigration and Multicultural and Indigenous Affairs* (2003) 31 Fam LR 29; [2003] FCAFC 257 per Gyles, Conti and Allsop JJ; BC200307047

DOMICILE

[For 8 Halsbury's Laws (4th edn) para 421 see now 8(3) Halsbury's Laws (4th edn) (Reissue) para 35.]

Of origin and of choice distinguished

[For 8 Halsbury's Laws (4th edn) para 425 see now 8(3) Halsbury's Laws (4th edn) (Reissue) para 39.]

DOMINANT

Australia 'Much turns upon the identification, among various purposes, of that which is "dominant" [under the Income Tax Assessment Act 1936 (Cth) Pt IVA]. In its ordinary meaning, dominant indicates that purpose which was the ruling, prevailing, or most influential purpose.' *Commissioner of Taxation v Spotless Services Ltd* (1996) 186 CLR 404 at 416; (1996) 141 ALR 92 at 98; (1996) 71 ALJR 81; 96 ATC 5201; BC9605762 at 8, per Brennan CJ, Dawson, Toohey, Gaudron, Gummow and Kirby JJ

New Zealand [Commerce Act 1986, s 3(8).] 'Although adopting language differing to come extent, the Judges in *Telecom v Commerce Commission* case held that the word dominant is to have its normal meaning of "prevailing", "commanding", "governing" or the like. The statute requires a position in a market in which that degree of influence can be exercised over the production, acquisition, supply or price of goods or services in that market. That is to be determined by reference to the stated matter and, because they are not exhaustive, such other relevant matters as may be found in the particular case. It is a broad factual assessment in the nature of a jury question.

'The decision in *Telecom v Commerce Commission* has been criticised as setting too high a level of market power so as to limit the value of the section as an effective regulator or abusive anti-competitive conduct. In this respect it must be noted that the Commerce Act was amended in 1994 without any change being made to s 3(8) or s 36 ... Further, the decision of this Court did not, in our view, shift the concept of dominant position away from that from which it had been derived— art 86 of The Treaty of Rome. The judgment of Richardson J, which on the meaning of dominance, was agreed with by the majority of the other members of the Court, compares (p 443) the non-exhaustive factors to be regarded under s 3(8) in determining the existence of a dominant position with the attributes of an undertaking in a dominant position formulated in the decision of Commission of the European Community in *Re Continental Can Co Inc* [1972] CMLR D11, D27. There is to be borne in mind the distinction between the concept (dominant position in a market) and the test for its existence (market share, vertical and horizontal constraints—which economists assess as elements of market power).

'The *Telecom* case really decided no more than "dominant" means dominant; that in testing for dominant position s 3(8) prescribes non-exhaustive matters to be considered; that potential competition may impose constraints and that the evidence of economists (so long as it is empirically based) will be helpful ... There is no indication in the judgments that a dominant position is one of absolute control or monopoly. The very tests in s 3(8)(a), (b), and (c) contemplate less than that.

'Much has been read into the passage of Richardson J's judgment commenting on the earlier decision of the Commerce Commission in *Proposal by Broadcast Communications Ltd* [1990] NZAR 443, 448 which had said:

"... the dominance test is not an absolute test based on an ability to act independently. Indeed, no person, not even a monopolist, acts without regard to competitors, suppliers or customers. Rather, the concept of dominance is based on the degree of control a person has over the market involving his or her goods or service. Dominance exists when a person is in a position of economic strength such that it can behave to a large extent independently of that person's competitors. A person in a dominant position will be able to effect an appreciable change in the price and or other aspects of supply of his goods and services and to maintain this change for an appreciable length of time without suffering a serious adverse impact on profitability."

'Richardson J said of this at p 442:

"There could be no criticism of the first three sentences. There is, however, a concern that 'large' and 'appreciable' used as synonyms for 'dominant' set too low a standard. They are ambiguous expressions and as the High Court noted in criticising the commission's resort to 'appreciable' that word can mean perceptible, discernible, noticeable; and it can also mean considerable, large, or fairly large, perhaps a different shade of meaning, material."

'The ambiguity or elasticity of the terms "large" and "appreciable" is plain. Large, like "high" in the expression "high market power", will mean what the user intends it to mean. We understand Richardson J not to be rejecting the language as wrong but to be criticising it as unhelpful because to some it could convey meanings inappropriate to reflect dominant position. It is not a rejection of the view that dominance reflects the ability to act to a large extend independently across every possible interpretation of "to a large extent". Indeed, in the next paragraph Richardson J said:

"And s 3(8) requires that the influence which the person concerned is in a position to exercise is so high or great or large as to be characterised as a 'dominant influence'.".'

Port Nelson Ltd v Commerce Commission [1996] 3 NZLR 554 at 573–575, CA, per cur

DOMINANT POSITION

New Zealand 'Words can have overtones not quite caught by any paraphrase, and "dominant" is one of them. But so far as any paraphrase can be helpful I think that words such as "a prevailing, commanding, ascendant, governing, primary, principal or leading influence" convey much the same idea.' *Telecom Corpn of New Zealand Ltd v Commerce Commission* [1992] 3 NZLR 429 at 434, CA, per Cooke P

DOMINANT POSITION IN A MARKET

New Zealand [Section 47 of the Commerce Act 1986.] 'For our purposes, no elaborate discussion of the meaning of "dominant position" is required and we are happy to adopt the recent formulation reached by McGechan J in *Commerce Commission v Port Nelson Ltd* (1995) 5 NZBLC 103, 762 after an exhaustive review of the authorities and, in particular, of the Court of Appeal's judgment in *AMPS-A* [*Telecom Corporation of New Zealand Ltd v Commerce Commission* (1991) 4 TCLR 473]. We quote a key passage from McGechan J at 103, 787:

"'Dominance' includes a qualitative assessment of market power. It involves more than 'high' market power; more than mere ability to behave 'largely' independently of competitors; and more than power to effect 'appreciable' changes in terms of trading. It involves a high degree of market *control*." '

Power New Zealand Ltd v Mercury Energy Ltd [1996] 1 NZLR 686 at 710 per Barker J and Dr M Brunt

DOMINATE

Australia [Section 50 of the Trade Practices Act 1974 (Cth) prohibits a corporation from acquiring shares in the capital of a corporate body if the result would put the corporation in a position to 'dominate' a market for goods.] 'An enterprise will be in a position to dominate a market when there is a probability that the other enterprise or enterprises in the market will act in a way calculated not to affect adversely the dominant concern's short term interests. Dominance, unlike control, is not primarily concerned with the formal relationship between entities but rather with their conduct towards each other within a particular market environment. If the size or strength of a particular entity is such that, in practice, other entities are unable or unwilling actively to compete with it in a particular market, that entity is dominant in that market. The dominant position relates to a position of economic strength enjoyed by an undertaking which enables it to prevent effective competition being maintained in the relevant market by affording it the power to behave to an appreciable extent independently of its competitors, its customers and ultimately of the consumers. Such a position does not preclude some competition but enables the undertaking which profits by it, if not to determine, at least to have an appreciable influence on, the conditions under which the competition will develop and, in any case, to act largely in disregard of it so long as such conduct does not operate to its detriment.' *Trade Practices Commission v Arnotts* (1990) 93 ALR 657 at 668, per Beaumont J

Australia [Section 50 of the Trade Practices Act 1974 (Cth) prohibits a corporation from acquiring directly or indirectly any shares in the capital or any assets of a body corporate which would put the corporation in a position to dominate a market for goods or services.] 'The word "dominance" is not defined in the Act. Its natural and ordinary meaning is "having a commanding influence on": see *Trade Practices Commission v Ansett Transport Industries (Operations) Pty Ltd* (1978) 32 FLR 305 at 325. A dominant firm has a high degree of "market power", a term defined in *Queensland Wire Industries Pty Ltd v Broken Hill Pty Co Ltd* [(1989) 167 CLR 177, 83 ALR 577].' *Arnotts Ltd v Trade Practices Commission* (1990) 97 ALR 555 at 579, per cur

DONATIO MORTIS CAUSA

[For 17 Halsbury's Laws (4th edn) para 1076 see now 17(2) Halsbury's Laws (4th edn) (Reissue) para 340.]

'The conditions which are essential to a valid donatio mortis causa were concisely stated by Farwell J in *Re Craven's Estate, Lloyds Bank Ltd v Cockburn* [1937] 3 All ER 33 at 37–40. Those conditions, which must be "exactly complied with" in any case, are as follows. (1) There must be a clear intention to give, but only if the donor dies, whereas if the donor does not die then the gift is not to take effect and the donor is to have back the subject matter of the gift. The gift must, therefore, be conditional in that sense, either expressly or by inference. (2) The gift must be made in contemplation of death, by which is meant not the possibility of death at some time or other, but death within the near future, which may be called death for some reason believed to be impending. If the gift is made in contemplation of death, it may be readily inferred from the circumstances that it was on condition that it was to be held only in the event of death: see *Re Lillingston (decd), Pembery v Pembery* [1952] 2 All ER 184 at 187. (3) The donor must effectively part with dominion over the subject matter of the gift. Mere words of gift are not enough. There must be some clear act taken towards a transfer of the property.' *Sen v Headley* [1990] 1 All ER 898 at 902, per Mummery J

'First, the gift must be made in contemplation, although not necessarily in expectation, of impending death. Secondly, the gift must be made upon the condition that it is to be absolute and perfected only on the donor's death, being revocable until that event occurs and ineffective if it does not. Thirdly, there must be a delivery of the subject matter of the gift, or the essential indicia of title thereto, which amounts to a parting with dominion and not mere physical possession over the subject matter of the gift.' *Sen v Headley* [1991] 2 All ER 636 at 639, CA per Nourse LJ

[For 20 Halsbury's Laws (4th edn) paras 66–67 see now 20(1) Halsbury's Laws (4th edn) (Reissue) para 71 et seq.]

DONE BY A SHIP

New Zealand [Section 4 of the Admiralty Act 1973.] 'It seems possible to extract from the decisions four core requirements for a damage maritime lien. First, some physical part of the ship or its gear must play an essential part in the chain of events which leads to the damage. The "ship" must be the "instrument" by which the damage is done (per Lord Diplock in *The Escherscheim* at p 8; see further *Currie v M'Knight* at pp 101, 108). Damage caused by human activity on a ship unaccompanied by the use of some part of the ship or its gear is therefore insufficient. Thus in *Hamilton v SS "Monterey"* [1940] NZLR 31 (SC) it was fatal to categorisation as damage by ship that the passenger claimant had been assaulted by the ship's night steward without the involvement of any part of the ship's gear in its operation.

'Secondly, the part played by the ship or its gear must be a significant and active one. It is trite to say that accidents in or on ships could not occur but for the existence of the ship. The ship is one of the conditions which makes the accident possible. In that theoretical sense the ship forms an essential part of the chain of causation. However, the mere fact that the injury could not have occurred without the environment provided by the ship is not enough. The part played by the ship or its gear must go beyond the provision of a passive environment which made it possible for the accident to occur (*SS "Monterey"*, and see further *Mulvey v The Barge "Neosho"* (1919) 47 DLR 437 (injury to seaman tripping on ropes negligently left on a barge deck held not to be damage "done" by the barge but merely "on" the barge)).

'Thirdly, human conduct must also play an essential part. It is the human contribution to the accident which gives rise to the liability, not the association of the ship with the damage per se. Ironically, damage caused by the state of the ship alone does not amount to "damage done by a ship" for present purposes. Contrary to the anthropomorphism much beloved by Admiralty lawyers, the damage must in fact be "done by a human". Accidents resulting from the condition of the ship, without more, do not qualify (*The Vera Cruz*; *The "Queen Eleanor"*; *The Zeta* and *Union Steamship Co*).

'Fourthly, it seems that the only form of human conduct which qualifies is the crew's active operation of the ship or its gear. The precise scope of the active operation is open to argument. On the one hand it has been suggested that the lien is limited to damage which is "the direct result or natural consequence of something done by those engaged in the *navigation* of the ship" (emphasis added) (*The Escherscheim* at p 926). But the breadth which would have to be given to the word "navigation" in this context seems to rob it of much of its utility. Hoisting equipment by crane (*The Minerva*), moving hatch covers by winch (*Union Steamship Co*), and abandoning salvaged vessels (*The Minerva*) do not amount to "navigation" in any usual sense of that word. No doubt for that reason the activity has more recently been described as "management or navigation" (per Dixon J in *The "Regis"* at p 700 and Clark J in *The Rama* at p 293). Unfortunately in this context "management" is an even more opaque expression. Evidently it does not extend to negligently leaving the vessel in a dangerous condition which is later encountered by the plaintiff.

'(For illustrations see *The Barge "Neosho"*; *The Vera Cruz*; *The "Queen Eleanor"*; *The Zeta* and *Union Steamship Co*. As Dixon J said in *The "Regis"* (ibid) the decided cases "show that when the injury arises from some defect in the condition of the ship considered as premises or as a structure upon which the person injured is standing, walking or moving, the ship is treated as no more than a potential danger of a passive kind, a danger to the user, whose use is the active cause of the injury. But where the injury is the result of the management or navigation of the ship as a moving object or of the working of the gear or of some other operation, then the damage is to be regarded as done by the ship as an active agent or as the 'noxious instrument'.")

'What does seem probable is that the activity must be an operational one in the sense that the ship or its gear is actively used for its designed operational purpose. Neither the purposes of the lien nor precedent requires one to go further. Accordingly it seems doubtful whether a lien would follow if an enraged crew member used a hatch cover for the extraneous purpose of hitting a passenger. Plainly in such a case no "navigation" is involved, no matter how strained the meaning given to that word. Nor is there any operation of the ship as a ship or the hatch cover as a hatch cover. What is required, it is suggested, is the use of the ship or its gear within the purposes for which it was designed or installed. To that tenuous extent at least, some link is retained with the original navigational purposes of the lien.' *Fournier v The ship "Margaret Z"* [1999] 3 NZLR 111 at 124–125 per Fisher J

DOWNLOAD

'At the heart of these applications lies a difference of view as to the meaning of the word "download". It is a word of relatively recent origin. The applicant contends its meaning is that contained in the *Concise Oxford Dictionary* (9th edn) "transfer from one storage device or system to another". The Serious Fraud Office … considers that downloading includes not only the imaging process … ie transferring information from the computer to another storage device, but also the next stage of writing the image to compact disk. Only when this exercise has been carried out is the information secure. If this is not done there is a risk, albeit a small one, that the information will be lost or tampered with …

'In our judgment the correct meaning of download is that described in the *Concise Oxford Dictionary*.' *R v City of London Magistrates' Court, ex p Green* [1997] 3 All ER 551 at 554, DC, per Scott Baker J

DRAINAGE

[The Land Drainage Act 1976, although not s 116(1), is largely repealed. A similar definition of 'drainage' was to be found in the Land Drainage Act 1991, s 72(1); but this has now been substituted as follows (by the Environment Act 1995, s 100(2)).]
'Drainage' includes—
(a) defence against water (including sea water);
(b) irrigation, other than spry irrigation;
(c) warping; and
(d) the carrying on, for any purpose, of any other practice which involves management of the level of water in a watercourse.

DRAMATIC WORK

[The Copyright Act 1956 has been repealed. See below.]

In this Part [Part I: Copyright] 'dramatic work' includes a work of dance or mime. (Copyright, Designs and Patents Act 1988, s 3(1))

New Zealand 'The protection which copyright gives creates a monopoly and "there must be certainty in the subject-matter of such monopoly in order to avoid injustice to the rest of the world": see *Tate v Fullbrook* [1908] 1 KB 821 per Farwell LJ at 832–833. The subject matter of the copyright claimed for the "dramatic format" of "Opportunity Knocks" is conspicuously lacking in certainty. Moreover, it seems to their Lordships that a dramatic work must have sufficient unity to be capable of performance and that the features claimed as constituting the "format" of a television show, being unrelated to each other except as accessories to be used in the presentation of some other dramatic or musical performance, lack that essential characteristic.' *Green v Broadcasting Co of New Zealand* [1989] 2 All ER 1056 at 1058, PC, per cur

New Zealand 'It seems, then, that a scenario or script can be a dramatic work and that copyright protection extends beyond the scenario or script, a distinction being drawn between the dramatic work itself, on the one hand, and the material on which it is fixed, on the other.' *Television New Zealand Ltd v Newsmonitor Services Ltd* [1994] 2 NZLR 91 at 100, per Blanchard J

DRAWBACK

[For 12 Halsbury's Laws (4th edn) para 553 see now 12(2) Halsbury's Laws (4th edn) (Reissue) para 1103.]

DRAWING

[The Copyright Act 1956 has been repealed. The Copyright, Patents and Designs Act 1988 does not define 'drawing', but 'graphic work' includes drawing (s 4(1)).]

DREDGING

[The Capital Allowances Act 1968 has been repealed. The statutory definition in s 67(10) is re-enacted in similar terms in the Capital Allowances Act 1990 s 125(3).]

DRIVE—DRIVER

[The Road Traffic Act 1972 has been repealed. The statutory definition in s 196(1) is re-enacted, with drafting amendments, in the Road Traffic Act 1988, s 192(1).

For ss 6, 8 of the former Act see now ss 5, 6 of the Act of 1988; for s 25 see now s 170 of the Act of 1988.]

Careless driving

[Section 3 of the Road Traffic Act 1960 has been repealed. See now the definition of 'Careless, and inconsiderate driving,' in s 3 of the Road Traffic Act 1988 (as substituted by s 2 of the Road Traffic Act 1991) as follows.]
'If a person drives a mechanically propelled vehicle on a road or other public place without due care and attention, or without reasonable consideration for other persons using the road or place he is guilty of an offence.'

Dangerous driving

[Section 2A of the Road Traffic Act 1988 (as substituted by the Road Traffic Act 1991, s 1, as from a date to be appointed) sets out what is meant by dangerous driving.]
(1) For the purposes of sections 1 and 2 above ['causing death by dangerous driving' and 'dangerous driving'] a person is to be regarded as driving dangerously if (and, subject to subsection (2) below, only if)—
  (a) the way he drives falls far below what would be expected of a competent and careful driver, and
  (b) it would be obvious to a competent and careful driver that driving in that way could be dangerous.
(2) A person is also to be regarded as driving dangerously for the purposes of sections 1 and 2 above if it would be obvious to a competent and careful driver that driving the vehicle in its current state would be dangerous.
(3) In subsections (1) and (2) above 'dangerous' refers to danger either by injury to any person or of serious damage to property; and in determining for the purpose of these subsections what would be expected of, or obvious to, a competent and careful driver in a particular case, regard shall be had not only to the circumstances of which he could be expected to be aware but also to any circumstances shown to have been within the knowledge of the accused.
(4) In determining for the purposes of subsection (2) above the state of a vehicle, regard may be had to anything attached to or carried on or in it and to the manner in which

it is attached or carried. (Road Traffic Act 1988, s 2A as substituted by s 1 of the Road Traffic Act 1991).

Reckless driving

'One may perhaps pause for a moment to consider what factors in the driving may tend to aggravate the offence [of reckless driving], and what factors tend to mitigate it. The following, amongst others, may be regarded as aggravating features: first of all, the consumption of alcohol or drugs, and that may range from a couple of drinks to what was described by the court in *R v Wheatley (John)* (1982) 4 Cr App R(S) 371, as a "motorised pub crawl". Second, the driver who races: competitive driving against another vehicle on the public highway; grossly excessive speed; showing off. Third, the driver who disregards warnings from his passengers, a feature which occurs quite frequently in this type of offence. Fourth, prolonged, persistent and deliberate course of very bad driving, ... a person who over a lengthy stretch of road ignores traffic signals, jumps red lights, passing other vehicles on the wrong side, driving with excessive speed, driving on the pavement and so on. Next, other offences committed at the same time and related offences, that is to say driving without ever having had any licence, driving whilst disqualified, driving whilst a learner driver without a supervising driver and so on. Next, previous convictions for motoring offences, particularly offences which involve bad driving or offences involving the consumption of excessive alcohol before driving. In other words the man who demonstrates that he is determined to continue driving badly despite past experience. Next, where several people have been killed as a result of the particular incident of reckless driving. Then, behaviour at the time of the offence, for example, failure to stop, or, even more reprehensible, the driver who tries to throw off the victim from the bonnet of the car by swerving in order that he may escape. Finally causing death in the course of reckless driving carried out in an attempt to avoid detection or apprehension ... On the other hand the mitigating features may be numbered as follows amongst others. First of all the piece of reckless driving which might be described in the vernacular as a "one off", a momentary reckless error of judgment; briefly dozing off at the wheel (see *R v Beeby* (1983) 5 Cr App R(S) 56) ... sometimes failing to notice a pedestrian on a crossing. Next, a good driving record will serve the defendant in good stead. Good character generally will also serve him in

good stead. A plea of guilty will always be taken into account by the sentencing court in favour of the defendant. Sometimes the effect on the defendant, if he is genuinely remorseful, if he is genuinely shocked. That is sometimes coupled with the final matter which we wish to mention as being a possible mitigating factor, namely where the victim was either a close relative of the defendant or a close friend and the consequent emotional shock was likely to be great.' *R v Boswell* [1984] 3 All ER 353 at 356–357, CA, per Lord Lane CJ

[Under s 1 of the Road Traffic Act 1991, which came into force in July 1992, there were substituted for ss 1, 2 of the Road Traffic Act 1988, as from a date to be appointed, new ss 1, 2 and 2A, under which the offence of reckless driving will cease to exist and be replaced by that of dangerous driving.]

DRIVING

Australia [The Transport Accident (Amendment) Act 1988 (Vic) amended the definition of 'transport accident' to refer to the 'driving' of a motor car.] 'In our opinion, when Parliament made its amendments in 1988 and substituted for the concept of use the more limited and concise concept of driving, it intended to use the word "driving" in its ordinary sense. In its ordinary sense driving does not include being in charge of a motor car although it may have that meaning in a particular context or through a definition. The cases decided under this Act on what amounted to the use of a motor car show that concept to have a wide ranging operation going far beyond the concept of driving. We consider that, by these amendments, Parliament was seeking to limit traffic accident to an incident with the necessary connection with a particular activity. That activity is narrower than, and more concise and easily recognisable than, the use of a motor car. To treat a person in charge of a motor car as driving it would be inconsistent with that intention of Parliament. It would widen the activity of driving beyond its normal meaning. It would introduce a rather vague basis for compensation if an incident which was directly caused by or which directly arose out of a person being in charge of a motor car amounted to a transport accident.

'We consider that in s 4(1)(c)(ii) of the Transport Accident (Amendment) Act 1988 the word "driving" is used in its ordinary sense.' *Transport Accident Commission v Treloar* [1992] 1 VR 447 at 449–450, per McGarvie and Gobbo JJ

DRUG

[The Food Act 1984 is largely repealed. By the Food Safety Act 1990, s 1(2), 'food' does not include controlled drugs within the meaning of the Misuse of Drugs Act 1971.]

DUE TO

[Section 10(1) of the Crown Lands Resumption Ordinance (Hong Kong) provides that the amount of compensation payable on the resumption of land is to be determined on the basis of the loss or damage suffered by the claimant 'due to' the resumption of the land specified in the claim.] 'First, it goes without saying that a prerequisite to an award of compensation is that there must be a causal connection between the resumption or acquisition and the loss in question ... [A]s a matter of general principle, to qualify for compensation the loss must not be too remote. That is the second condition.

'Fairness requires that claims for compensation should satisfy a further, third condition in all cases. The law expects those who claim recompense to behave reasonably. If a reasonable person in the position of the claimant would have taken steps to eliminate or reduce the loss, and the claimant failed to do so, he cannot fairly expect to be compensated for the loss or the unreasonable part of it. Likewise if a reasonable person in the position of the claimant would not have incurred, or would not incur, the expenditure being claimed, fairness does not require that the authority should be responsible for such expenditure. Expressed in other words, losses or expenditure incurred unreasonably cannot sensibly be said to be caused by, or be the consequence of, or be due to the resumption ...

'To qualify for compensation a loss suffered post-resumption must satisfy the three conditions of being causally connected, not too remote, and not a loss which a reasonable person would have avoided. A loss sustained post-scheme and pre-resumption will not fail for lack of causal connection by reason only that the loss arose before resumption, provided it arose in anticipation of resumption and because of the threat which resumption presented. In the terms of the Resumption Ordinance, a pre-resumption loss which satisfies these criteria is as much "due to" the resumption of the land as a post-resumption loss.' *Director of Buildings and Lands v Shun Fung Ironworks Ltd* [1995] 1 All ER 846 at 853, 863 PC, per Lord Nicholls

DUMPING

[The Dumping at Sea Act 1974 has been repealed. The Food and Environment Protection Act 1985 makes provision as to the deposit of substances or articles at sea in similar terms to the definition of 'dumping' (see s 5(a)).]

DUPLICATING PROCESS

[The Copyright Act 1956 has been repealed. The definition is not re-enacted in the Copyright, Designs and Patents Act 1988.]

DURESS

See also **NECESSITY**

[For 9 Halsbury's Laws (4th edn) para 297 see now 9(1) Halsbury's Laws (4th edn) (Reissue) para 710.]

[For 18 Halsbury's Laws (4th edn) para 332 see now 31 Halsbury's Laws (4th edn) (2003 Reissue) para 841.]

[The case of *Lynch v Director of Public Prosecutions for Northern Ireland* [1975] 1 All ER 913 was overruled by *R v Howe* [1987] 1 All ER 771, HL, in which it was held that the defence of duress is not available to a person charged with murder whether as principal in the first degree (the actual killer) or as principal in the second degree (the aider and abettor). An extract from the latter case is given below.] 'There is, of course, an obvious distinction between duress and necessity as potential defences: duress arises from the wrongful threats or violence of another human being and necessity arises from any other objective dangers threatening the accused. This, however, is, in my view, a distinction without a relevant difference, since on this view duress is only that species of the genus of necessity which is caused by wrongful threats. I cannot see that there is any way in which a person of ordinary fortitude can be excused from the one type of pressure on his will rather than the other.' *R v Howe* [1987] 1 All ER 771 at 777, HL, per Lord Hailsham of St Marylebone LC

'The reason why duress has for so long been stated not to be available as a defence to a murder charge is that the law regards the sanctity of human life and the protection thereof as of paramount importance. Does that reason apply to attempted murder as well as to murder? ... An intent to kill must be proved in the case of attempted murder but not necessarily in the case of murder. Is there logic in affording the defence to one who intends to kill but fails and denying it to one who mistakenly kills intending only to injure? If I may give two examples. (1a) A stabs B in the chest intending to kill him and leaves him for dead. By good luck B is found whilst still alive and rushed to hospital where surgical skill saves his life. (1b) C stabs D intending only to injure him and inflicts a near identical wound. Unfortunately D is not found until it is too late to save his life. I see no justification of logic or morality for affording a defence of duress to A who intended to kill when it is denied to C who did not so intend. (2a) E plants in a passenger aircraft a bomb timed to go off in mid-flight. Owing to bungling it explodes while the aircraft is still on the ground with the result that some 200 passengers suffer physical and mental injuries of which many are permanently disabling, but no one is killed. (2b) F plants a bomb in a light aircraft intending to disable the pilot before it takes off but in fact it goes off in mid-air killing the pilot who is the sole occupant of the airplane. It would in my view be both offensive to common sense and decency that E if he established duress should be acquitted and walk free without a stain on his character notwithstanding the appalling results which he has achieved, whereas F who never intended to kill should, if convicted in the absence of the defence, be sentenced to life imprisonment as a murderer.' *R v Gotts* [1992] 1 All ER 833 at 840, HL, per Lord Jauncey of Tullichettle

[Duress therefore not a defence in either cases of murder or attempted murder.]

DURING

Australia [Regulation 9(2)(a)(ii) of the Migration Regulations 1989 (Cth) provides that an applicant is disqualified for certain purposes if the applicant has had contact with an overseas near relative 'during' a reasonable period preceding the application.] '... the word "during" has two ordinary meanings, namely "throughout the continuance of" and "in the course of": *Macquarie Dictionary* ... I think that the natural meaning in the context of the word "during" is that of "throughout the continuance of". As Gummow J indicated in admittedly obiter observations [in *Hunt v Minister for Immigration and Ethnic Affairs* (1993) 41 FCR 380], the language of reg 9(2)(a)(ii) is apt to focus on the "current state of the social and emotional ties" between the overseas near relative and the relevant applicant. Regulation 131A(1)(d) is, after all, designed to deal with "compassionate grounds" for the grant of an entry permit. It would be extraordinary if an applicant's "contact" under reg 9

were not assessed up to and at the time of the application being lodged.' *Bagus v Minister for Immigration, Local Government and Ethnic Affairs* (1994) 50 FCR 396 at 402–403, per Whitlam J

DUTIES OF OFFICE

Australia [Section 87 of the Criminal Code (Qld) creates the offence of procuring for the holder of a public office a benefit on account of any act or omission in the discharge of the 'duties of the office'.] 'Whilst it is possible to point to particular statutory functions which may be regarded as imposing a duty upon the Minister, these by no means exhaust the whole of his executive or administrative responsibilities. Conferred upon him by his office were many other functions of a general as well as a particular kind. It is hardly likely that s 87 was aimed against the corrupt performance by public officials of the responsibilities of their office only where a specific statutory duty could be identified and not otherwise. There is, moreover, nothing in the section which requires it to be construed in that way. In the context of s 87 the phrase "duties of his office" may be read, as it ought to be, in the sense of "functions of his office"... An act of a public official, or at all events a Minister, can constitute an act "in the discharge of the duties of his office" when he performs a function which it is his to perform, whether or not it can be said that he is legally obliged to perform that function in a particular way or at all ... The section is concerned with the violation or attempted violation of official duty rather than with the actual performance of official duty. Official corruption necessarily involves impropriety and it is not to be supposed that s 87 is limited to those cases where the act or omission in question would, apart from the corrupt influence, be proper.' *Re Herscu* (1991) 56 A Crim R 270 at 273–275, per Mason CJ, Dawson, Toohey and Gaudron JJ

DUTY

New Zealand [Section 105(5)(b) of the Child Support Act 1991 speaks of a 'duty to maintain the child'.] 'The Act is intended to operate in a family or domestic context and we see no occasion to depart from the ordinary meaning of duty, defined in *The Concise Oxford Dictionary* (6th ed, 1976) as "Moral or legal obligation, what one is bound or ought to do".' *Lyon v Wilcox* [1994] 3 NZLR 422 at 431, CA, per cur

Discharge of

Australia 'In ordinary speech, "the discharge of the duties" of the holder of a public office connotes far more than performance of duties which the holder of the office is legally bound to perform: rather the term connotes the performance of the functions of that office. The functions of an office consist in the things done or omitted which are done or omitted in an official capacity. The phrase "being charged with the performance of any duty" thus means no more than being responsible for performing the functions of the public office. That phrase distinguishes the holder of a merely honorific public office from the holder of a public office responsible for the performance of official functions ... When the office is such that the holder wields influence or is in a position to wield influence in matters of a particular kind, the wielding of influence in a matter of that kind is a discharge of the duties of the office. Such a wielding of influence is something done in an official capacity.' *Herscu v R* (1991) 103 ALR 1 at 9, per Brennan J

Duty to act judicially

New Zealand [Defamation Act 1992, s 14(1)(b).] '... the requirement of recognition by law is, we think, inherent in the expression, "a tribunal or authority that has a duty to act judicially". The wording, legislative history and relevant policy considerations all lead to that conclusion.' *Gray v M* [1998] 2 NZLR 161 at 164, CA, per cur

DWELLING

'[2] This appeal concerns the words, "a dwelling-house ... let as a separate dwelling" in s 1 of the Housing Act 1988. A single room, as part of a house, may be a dwelling house ... The key issue is whether the room which [the appellant] occupied ... could in law qualify as a "dwelling" only if cooking facilities were there available. Unless constrained to the contrary by authority, I would impose no such restrictive interpretation. Such a restrictive interpretation would both be unwarranted by the statutory language and an inappropriate gloss on provisions designed to give some protection to tenants in modest rented accommodation under assured tenancies.

'[3] "Dwelling" is not a term of art, but a familiar word in the English language, which in my judgment in this context denotes a place where one lives, regarding and treating it as home. Such a place does not cease to be a "dwelling" merely because one takes all or some of one's meals out; or brings take-away food in to the exclusion of home cooking; or at times prepares some food for consumption on heating devices falling short of a full cooking facility.

'[4] Decisions on the infinite factual variety of cases are for judges of trial and their decisions on the facts of individual cases should neither be treated nor cited as propositions of law. I would not myself, for example, regard a bed, any more than cooking facilities, as an essential prerequisite of a "dwelling": every case is for the judge of trial, but I would have no difficulty with a conclusion that one could live in a room, which is regarded and treated as home, although taking one's sleep, without the luxury of a bed, in an armchair, or in blankets on the floor.' *Uratemp Ventures Ltd v Collins* [2001] UKHL 43 at [2]–[4], [2002] 1 All ER 46 at 48, HL, per Lord Irvine of Lairg LC

'[30] The words "dwell" and "dwelling" are not terms of art with a specialised legal meaning. They are ordinary English words, even if they are perhaps no longer in common use. They mean the same as "inhabit" and "habitation" or more precisely "abide" and "abode", and refer to the place where one lives and makes one's home. They suggest a greater degree of settled occupation than "reside" and "residence", connoting the place where the occupier habitually sleeps and usually eats, but the idea that he must also cook his meals there is found only in the law reports. It finds no support in English literature. According to the Book of Common Prayer, "the fir trees are a dwelling for the stork" (Psalm 104, v 17); while W S Gilbert condemned the billiard sharp "to dwell in a dungeon cell" (where it will be remembered he plays with a twisted cue on a cloth untrue with elliptical billiard balls) (see The Mikado, Act II). It is hardly necessary to observe that Victorian prison cells did not possess cooking facilities. Of course, the word "dwell" may owe its presence to the exigencies of the rhyme, but it does not strike the listener as incongruous. If faintly humorous, it is because the occupation of a prison cell is involuntary, not because of the absence of cooking facilities. As I shall show hereafter, Gilbert, who had qualified at the Bar, had got his law right. An earlier and greater poet wrote of Lucifer being hurled "to bottomless perdition, there to dwell in adamantine chains and penal fire' (see Milton *Paradise Lost*, I.47).

'[31] In both ordinary and literary usage, residential accommodation is "a dwelling" if it is the occupier's home (or one of his homes). It is the place where he lives and to which he returns and which forms the centre of his existence. Just what use he makes of it when living there, however, depends on his mode of life. No doubt he will sleep there and usually eat there; he will often prepare at least some of his meals there. But his home is not the less his home because he does not cook there but prefers to eat out or bring in ready-cooked meals. It has never been a legislative requirement that cooking facilities must be available for a premises to qualify as a dwelling. Nor is it at all evident what policy considerations dictate that a tenant who prepares his meals at home should enjoy security of tenure while a tenant who brings in all his meals ready-cooked should not ...

...

'[58] In my opinion the position is relatively straightforward. The first step is to identify the subject matter of the tenancy agreement. If this is a house or part of a house of which the tenant has exclusive possession with no element of sharing, the only question is whether, at the date when the proceedings were brought, it was the tenant's home. If so, it was his dwelling. (He must also occupy it as his only or principal home, but that is a separate requirement.) If the tenancy agreement grants, in addition, the right to the shared use of other rooms, the question is whether the room or rooms of which he has exclusive possession are his dwelling place or only part of it. This depends on the nature and extent of the right and the character of the other rooms. The right to occupy a living room in common with and at the same time as the landlord is such an invasion of his privacy that Parliament cannot be taken to have intended that the tenant should enjoy security of tenure. For this purpose a kitchen is a living room, at least if it is possible to occupy it and not merely cook and wash up in it; so that a right to occupy a kitchen (as distinct from a right to make some limited use of its facilities) in common with the landlord will take the tenancy out of the Acts. The presence or absence of cooking facilities in the part of the premises of which the tenant has exclusive occupation is not relevant.'
Uratemp Ventures Ltd v Collins [2001] UKHL 43 at [30]–[31], [58], [2002] 1 All ER 46 at 53–54, 62–63, HL, per Lord Millett

[The claimant was a married man with eleven children, eight of whom were dependent on him. He owned two three-bedroomed houses in which he and his family lived which were on the same street but separated by two other properties. He claimed income-based jobseeker's allowance, entitlement to which was subject to a requirement that a claimant's capital did not exceed the prescribed amount. The effect of reg 108(2) of and para 1 of Sch 8 to the Jobseeker's Allowance Regulations 1996 was that 'the dwelling occupied as the home' was to be disregarded in the calculation of a claimant's capital.] '[1] This is the question which arises in this appeal: is there one dwelling or two dwellings occupied as the home where a claimant for jobseeker's allowance normally occupies as his home two houses separated from each other by other houses in the street, each house being overcrowded if the claimant and his large family were removed from both houses into only one of them? On 23 May 2002 the Social Security Commissioner, Mr EAL Bano, so construed the Jobseeker's Allowance Regulations 1996, SI 1996/207 as to lead him to the conclusion that there could be only one dwelling in those circumstances (Social Security Decision CJSA 4620 2000) but he gave the Secretary of State permission to appeal to us.

...

'[20] As the commissioners have pointed out, there is a sad lack of coherence in the drafting of this wide range of social welfare legislation. One might have hoped for some uniformity in the definition of the essential building blocks, like a claimant's home, which affect the allowing or disallowing of a social security-type benefit. Because of the non-application of the definition of "dwelling" contained in s 84(1) of the [Social Security Act 1986] and s 137(1) of the [Social Security Contributions and Benefits Act 1992], not even the 1981 [Supplementary Benefit (Resources) Regulations 1981, SI 1981/1527] and 1996 regulations are wholly and exactly comparable.

'[21] Given these differences, be they large or small, I find it impossible to derive from another set of provisions any support for any convincing argument, one way or the other, as to the meaning of the regulations we have to construe. I can only look for clues as to the true meaning of "dwelling occupied as the home" from within the 1996 regulations themselves.

'[22] The first clue is within para 1 of Sch 8 itself in the words "notwithstanding regulation 88". Under reg 88 the capital and income of the claimant's partner or polygamous "wife", which by virtue of s 13(2) of the [Jobseekers Act 1995] are to be treated as his, are to be aggregated with his. Without the qualification "notwithstanding regulation 88", it seems likely or highly arguable that any separate home of the partner/"wife" would also be disregarded. Certainly one can be sure at least that the legislature had in mind the possibility that there would be two dwellings competing for being or both claiming to be disregarded.

'[23] The provisions of Sch 2 to the 1996 regulations confirm that the legislature was alive to the possibility of there being two dwellings available for consideration. Paragraph 3(6) of Sch 2 shows that the draftsman had in mind the possibility that a person was liable to make payments in respect of two dwellings and treated him to be occupying both dwellings as his home in the circumstances prescribed, viz, in cases of domestic violence, university residence, and moving house.

'[24] I find it difficult, however, to draw any satisfactory conclusion from these fact-specific examples in para 3 of Sch 2 or from the cases of the partner/polygamous "wife" in reg 88. None of this seems to me to throw light on the crucial question whether separate buildings can constitute a single dwelling occupied as the claimant's home. As Mr Kolinsky submits, simply to conclude that two separate buildings cannot be a single dwelling begs the question.

'[25] Given that the draftsman had the possibility of two dwellings in mind, what did he intend to include in or exclude from the meaning of "dwelling".

'[26] If one approaches construction of the words literally, one notes that the word "dwelling" has been chosen, not, for example, "dwelling-house" nor "residential accommodation". "Dwelling" is defined by the Oxford English Dictionary as "place of residence; a dwelling-place, habitation, house". "Dwelling-place" is "A place of abode", whereas "Dwelling-house" is "A house occupied as a place of residence, as distinguished from a house of business, warehouse, office, etc." Because the single word is expanded into a phrase "dwelling occupied as the home" I am given the impression that the legislature intended to convey the function to be served by the concept of a dwelling rather than to connote its constituent elements, the bricks and mortar of the dwelling. The function is a place serving as home for the claimant. That place is not necessarily confined to a single building. For me this emphasis is reinforced by the inclusion within "dwelling" of "any garage, garden and outbuildings normally occupied by the claimant as his home including any premises not so occupied …" (see reg 1 of the 1996 regulations). A barn converted for residential accommodation is part of the dwelling constituted by the farmhouse and that converted barn. I appreciate that not too much can be derived from that analogy because they both lie within the same curtilage, but it gives the flavour.

'[27] A test for determining where home is can conveniently be expressed in the way Mr Commissioner Bano directed the tribunal to approach the question (Social Security Decision CJSA 4620 2000 at para 14), viz, by asking whether—

"the claimant's arrangements were such that one house was, in effect, used as an annex of the other, or to put it another way, whether this was a single home on a split site. Occasional use of the second house by the claimant or his dependent children will not assist him, because the tribunal must be satisfied that the second house was 'normally' occupied by the claimant as his home."

'[28] If one needs to look further, one should look to see where common sense, fairness and justice take one. Taking the latter consideration first, the facts of this case provide a proper background for the question. Here is a man who organised his domestic life at a time when he was in good and apparently stable employment. He bought the property two doors away to house his growing family. Then he fell upon hard times. If in 1992 he had sold number 11A and bought a single five/six-bedroom property, that property would have to be disregarded. It surely cannot be fair that he should suffer when the purpose of having two properties is exactly the same as having only one.

'[29] Simple justice seems to me to dictate that a man in the applicant's position should not be discriminated against adversely to the owner of a single but large property for his family.

'[30] Common sense dictates that the court can construe the words in a way which does not make them unworkable or impractical. Assume, as the tribunal subsequently found, the claimant truly does use both houses as his home, how is a decision-maker to determine which of the two is to be disregarded? Can the claimant elect? Is it the property of greater or of lesser value? Is it the first he acquired or the last? Has some (but goodness knows what) attempt have to be made to ascertain which is the more significant home? Those questions seem to me impossible of answer and militate against the Secretary of State's submissions. One cannot have a scheme which is incapable of easy, sensible and certain application.

'[31] On the other hand, the claimant's construction does allow common sense to prevail. In requiring both properties to be occupied as the home at the same point in time, it is perfectly easy to distinguish those two properties seen as a unit from the second home which a hypothetical claimant may have in the country as a weekend retreat. Allowing only one of those homes to be disregarded is entirely just and fair as between the public purse and the claimant for this benefit.

'[32] If one applies this functional test as opposed to a structural test, a decision-maker can with common sense determine what the claimant is using as his home. It is the place where he lives, where he eats, sleeps, bathes, relaxes, enjoys with his family. Such a test avoids the absurdities that two semi-detached houses would not be a single dwelling, however used, so long as they remain detached. Not even going out of the back door of one, through the communal garden and in the back door of the other could make it one dwelling. But knock a hole through the party wall and then there is structural integration and presumably two dwellings have been converted into one. The subtleties of such distinctions produce an absurdity that has to be avoided by a more realistic interpretation.

'[33] I would test this by applying a purposive construction. The purpose of these provisions is surely to provide benefits for those in need. A liberal, as opposed to a strict, construction demands that they be construed in favour of a claimant to relieve hardship rather than in favour of the Secretary of State to protect the public purse out of which the benefits are to be paid. If the Secretary of State who laid the regulations before Parliament could not do so in a way which made his position clear, then the regulations are to be construed against him.

'[34] I am not impressed with Mr Maurici's argument that Parliament must have intended first that the 1996 regulations should have the same meaning as the 1987 income support regulations [the Income Support (General) Regulations 1987, SI 1987/1967], and, secondly, that Social Security Decision CIS 81/91 has received Parliamentary approval. My rejection of that submission owes as much to the absence of an equivalent to s 84(1) of the 1986 Act in the 1995 Act, and hence to a small difference between the two provisions, as to complete cynicism about the adequacy of parliamentary scrutiny of subordinate legislation of this kind.

'[35] I do not find it necessary to consider the unfairness and discriminatory effect of the regulations as a discrete human rights point. I am satisfied that domestic principles of construction lead to the conclusion that Mr Commissioner Bano was correct.' *Miah v Secretary of State for Work and Pensions* [2003] EWCA Civ 1111 at [1], [20]–[35], [2003] 4 All ER 702, CA, per Ward LJ

DWELLING HOUSE

'In some statutory contexts and often in ordinary everyday language the word "dwellinghouse" is indeed used to describe a house in which people are actually living as a private residence. Actual residential occupancy is not, however, a necessary characteristic of a dwelling house. As a matter of ordinary language "dwellinghouse" is capable of including not only a house which is dwelt in but also a house which is constructed or adapted for dwelling in although it may at the relevant time be vacant or even not fit and ready for occupation. For example, a family may be forced out of their dwelling house by fire, flood or other natural disaster. The house may remain empty for a long period while building works are carried out on it. I do not think it would be a misuse of the English language to say of such a house that it was at all times, even when empty, a dwelling house.' *Re 1–4 White Row Cottages Bewerley* [1991] 4 All ER 50 at 53, per Mummery J

E

EARNINGS

[The Social Security Act 1975 has been repealed. The definition is re-enacted in the Social Security Contributions and Benefits Act 1992, s 3(1).]

EASEMENT

Australia 'I accept the definition of easement as submitted by Mr Lee for the second defendant which is set out in the Butterworths Australian Legal Dictionary (1997 First Edition) at p 401, which defines easement as:

"A right enjoyed by a person with regard to the land of another person, the exercise of which interferes with the normal rights of the owner or occupier of the land." '

City Developments Pty Ltd v Registrar General of the Northern Territory (2000) 135 NTR 1; 156 FLR 1; BC200002941; [2000] NTSC 33 at [34], per Thomas J

Canada In *Re Ellenborough Park; Re Davies; Powell v Maddison* [1956] 1 Ch 131 at 163, [1955] 3 All ER 667 at 673, the English Court of Appeal accepted the following as essential requirements for a valid easement:
(1) there must be a dominant and a servient tenement;
(2) the easement must accommodate the dominant tenement;
(3) the dominant and servient owners must be different persons; and
(4) the easement must be capable of forming the subject matter of a grant.

Shelf Holdings Ltd v Husky Oil Operations Ltd (1987) 38 DLR (4th) 441 at 447, Alta QB, per Andrekson J

ECONOMIC EVIDENCE

Australia [Rule 149A of the District Court Rules 1968 (Qld) relevantly requires a defendant in an action for damages for personal injury in a District Court to make pre-trial disclosure of expert and 'economic evidence' in his possession to the plaintiff.] 'The only sensible construction I can place upon "economic evidence" is that it is not limited to expert evidence, and that it connotes evidence of the kind that will assist in the computation of damages. It requires the disclosure of evidence that will allow the calculation of special damages, or of components that may be quantified with reasonable particularity. Lay evidence of physical movements does not have that character. The rule does not apply to evidence that is merely relevant to something else that leads by chain reaction to relevance on the issue of economic loss.' *Martin v Kennedy* [1992] 2 Qd R 109 at 112, per cur

EDITION

[For 37 Halsbury's Laws (4th edn) para 1002 see now 36(2) Halsbury's Laws (4th edn) (Reissue) para 402.]

EDITOR

[For 37 Halsbury's Laws (4th edn) para 1058 see now 36(2) Halsbury's Laws (4th edn) (Reissue) para 452.]

EDUCATION

General meaning

[The Income and Corporation Taxes Act 1970 has been repealed. See now the Income and Corporation Taxes Act 1988, s 259(5)(a).]

EFFECTED BY THE INSURED

Canada [An insurer was not liable for the replacement cost of damaged property until replacement had been effected by the insured.] 'The words "effected by the insured" appear on their face to be broad enough to include the case where an insured effects replacement by imposing contractual terms on a third party. It would be unreasonable to interpret the clause as meaning that in order to recover replacement costs an insured must do the work of repair or replacement itself.

'In my view, the phrase "effected by the insured" is sufficiently broad that it can be satisfied by the insureds' interpretation, namely, effected either directly, or indirectly by the insureds through the agency or agencies of others.' *Brkich & Brkich Enterprises Ltd v American Home Assurance Co* (1995) 127 DLR (4th) 115 at 131, 132, BCCA, per Finch JA

EFFECTIVE CONTROL

Australia ' "Effective control" in the context of the statute [Crimes (Confiscation of Profits) Act 1988 (WA)] means de facto control. The expression contemplates control that is practically effective, in the sense that the person concerned has in fact the capacity to control the possession, use, or disposition of the property. This is, in my opinion, the meaning of "effective control" unadorned or unencumbered by the definition in s 3(1) in terms of s 52A of the Act.' *Connell v Lavender* (1991) 5 ACSR 33 at 46–47, per Malcolm CJ

EFFECTS

In will: generally

[For 50 Halsbury's Laws (4th edn) para 473 see now 50 Halsbury's Laws (4th edn) (Reissue) para 527.]

EGGSHELL TENANCY

'[3] This case concerns what is commonly referred to as an "eggshell tenancy" because the demise is of the internal skin of the part of the building occupied by the tenant. No load-bearing parts of the building are included in the demise. Counsel confirmed that this was not an uncommon type of business lease.' *Pumperninks of Piccadilly Ltd v Land Securities plc* [2002] EWCA Civ 621 at [3], [2002] 3 All ER 609 at 612, CA, per Charles J

EJUSDEM GENERIS

[For 12 Halsbury's Laws (4th edn) para 1526 see now 13 Halsbury's Laws (4th edn) (Reissue) para 233.]

ELDEST

[For 50 Halsbury's Laws (4th edn) para 517 see now 50 Halsbury's Laws (4th edn) (Reissue) para 571.]

ELECTION

[For 16 Halsbury's Laws (4th edn) para 1392 see now 16(2) Halsbury's Laws (4th edn) (Reissue) para 724.]

Australia 'In submissions, the term "election" was used as a synonym for "option" as it appears in cl 2 [of the Order made by the Governor in Council under the BLF (De-recognition) Act 1985 (Vic): Victoria Government Gazette, No S39, 13 October 1987]. The true nature of "election" is the confrontation of the person electing with two mutually exclusive courses of action between which a choice must be made, for example, to terminate or keep a contract on foot. In its setting in cl 2 of the Order, "option" is best understood as identifying a power, but not a duty, which is thereby conferred upon the Custodian.' *Victoria v Sutton* (1998) 156 ALR 579 at 590; 72 ALJR 1386; BC9804343, per Gaudron, Gummow and Hayne JJ

ELUDE

Canada 'The relevant meaning of "elude" in the Shorter Oxford English Dictionary, 3rd edn (1973), is "to evade compliance with or fulfilment of," or simply "to evade". "Evade", in turn, is defined as "to escape by artifice from". The respondent referred us to the definition in the Consolidated Webster Encyclopedia Dictionary: "to evade, to avoid by artifices, stratagem, wiles, deceit or dexterity. To remain unseen, undiscovered, or unexplained". Again, the respondent referred to the definition of "evasion" in Black's Law Dictionary, 5th edn (1979): "An act of eluding, dodging, or avoiding, or avoidance by artifice ... A subtle endeavouring to set aside truth or to escape the punishment of the law". It seems to me, therefore, that "elude" has the connotation either of artifice or surreptitiousness, or of the intention to repudiate the obligation or escape the effect of the law in a general way.' *Rios v Canada (Minister of Employment and Immigration)* [1990] 3 FCR 632 at 636, FCA, per MacGuigan JA

EMBARRASSMENT

'The court's power to direct amendment of a notice [of payment into court under RSC Ord 22, r 1(5)]

only arises if it appears to the court that the plaintiff is embarrassed by the payment. The expression "embarrassed" is not defined in the rules. In this context the underlying concept is that a plaintiff is embarrassed if he is placed in a difficulty which he ought not fairly to have to face. ... I am not to be taken as indicating that in every case where there are two plaintiffs joined together with separate causes of action there will be embarrassment if a payment is not apportioned between them. There may well be cases where this is not so. One example is of alternative claims'. *Walker v Turpin* [1993] 4 All ER 865 at 872, 874, CA, per Sir Donald Nicholls V-C

EMBODIED

Australia 'This word, as is made clear by *The New Shorter Oxford English Dictionary*, 1993, generally refers to the giving of "a material or discernible form to (an abstract principle, concept, etc.)". The precise sense conveyed by it, as a matter of English idiom, appears in the lines W S Gilbert put into the mouth of the Lord Chancellor in *Iolanthe*:

"The Law is the true embodiment
Of everything that's excellent.
It has no kind of fault or flaw,
And I, my Lords, embody the Law."

The Lord Chancellor is claiming that the law contains and reflects all excellence, and that he himself holds (and therefore will pronounce) the law ... The word "embodied" may well have been taken, by the draftsman of s 10 [of the Copyright Act 1968 (Cth)], from a usage in copyright law that closely paralleled that of Gilbert's Lord Chancellor ... ' *Sega Enterprises Ltd v Galaxy Electronics Pty Ltd* (1996) 139 ALR 518 at 521–522, per Burchett J

EMBRACERY

[For 11 Halsbury's Laws (4th edn) para 953 see now 11(1) Halsbury's Laws (4th edn) (Reissue) para 313.]

EMBRYO

[A question arose whether human embryos created by the cell nuclear replacement technique were not embryos within the meaning of s 1(1) of the Human Fertilisation and Embryology Act 1990, and were therefore not subject to regulation under that Act.] '[1] The first stage of reproduction of a human being involves the creation of an embryo. An embryo is a live organism containing a full set

of 46 chromosomes that has the potential to develop into a foetus and subsequently into a person. In 1990 the only way in which an embryo had ever been created was by the fertilisation of the female egg by the male sperm. Such fertilisation takes place naturally as a result of sexual union between man and woman. Scientists have, however, developed other methods of fertilising a female egg with a male sperm so as to produce an embryo and can, in particular, achieve this outside the body (in vitro).

'[2] In 1984 a committee of inquiry, chaired by Dame Mary Warnock, published a *Report of the Committee of Inquiry into Human Fertilisation and Embryology* (Cmnd 9314) (the Warnock report) which dealt, in particular, with the ethical problems raised by scientific intervention in these processes. The report made a large number of recommendations which included, in particular, that the creation of embryos outside the body, and the use of these, should be regulated by a statutory licensing authority. The government published a White Paper that proposed the implementation of the Warnock recommendations and, in accordance with this, introduced the Human Fertilisation and Embryology Act 1990.

'[3] The 1990 Act contains a definition of an embryo, and a number of provisions, which reflect the fact that it was drafted at a time when the only known way of producing an embryo was by fertilisation.

...

'[5] Since the introduction of the 1990 Act, scientists have developed a method of creating an embryo that does not involve fertilisation. It bears a close resemblance to the nucleus substitution that the Warnock report had identified as a possibility and has the same potential for producing a clone. The difference is that it involves introducing a nucleus taken from an adult human into an egg that has not been fertilised. This method of creating an embryo is known as cell nuclear replacement or CNR. I have described the organism produced by CNR as an embryo because it is now common ground that the nature of that organism so resembles that of an embryo produced by fertilisation that it is appropriate to describe it by the same term. Certainly, it is generally so described by scientists.

...

'[14] The relevant provisions of the 1990 Act are the following:

"1. *Meaning of 'embryo', 'gamete' and associated expressions.*—(1) In this Act, except where otherwise stated—(a) embryo means a live human embryo where fertilisation is complete, and (b) references to an embryo include an egg in the process of fertilisation and, for this purpose, fertilisation is not complete until the appearance of a two cell zygote.

"(2) This Act, so far as it governs bringing about the creation of an embryo, applies only to bringing about the creation of an embryo outside the human body ...

...

'[19] The definition of an embryo in s 1(1) of the 1990 Act is manifestly designed to identify the stage at which the process of fertilisation produces, or should be deemed to produce, a live human embryo. References to fertilisation can have no application to an embryo produced by CNR. Arguably, the term "two cell zygote" is not appropriate to describe the embryo produced at the stage at which the single cell organism produced by CNR divides into two cells.

'[20] On behalf of the Secretary of State, Mr Parker QC has submitted that it is permissible and appropriate to imply words into the definition of an embryo in s 1(1) in order to embrace an embryo produced by CNR. This he would achieve by implying a phrase into the subsection, so that it defines embryo as "a live human embryo where [*if it is produced by fertilisation*] fertilisation is complete". Mr Parker accepts that this construction involves "straining" the natural meaning of the words of the subsection, but submits that a purposive approach to construction requires such an approach.
...

'[35] There is one difference between an embryo produced by CNR and one produced by fertilisation. The former, if it is permitted to develop, will grow into a clone of the donor of the implanted nucleus ...
...

'[42] For the reasons that I have given, I consider that a regulatory regime that excludes from its ambit embryos created by CNR is contrary to the intention of Parliament in introducing the 1990 Act. The prospect of such a regime is both startling and alarming. These considerations provide the most cogent reason to reach an interpretation of the 1990 Act which embraces embryos produced by CNR, subject to consideration of any countervailing considerations, or incoherence.
...

'[49] My conclusion is that there are most compelling reasons for giving s 1 of the 1990 Act the strained construction for which Mr Parker contends, and very little that weighs against this. I

would reverse the decision reached by the judge and hold that an organism created by cell nuclear replacement falls within the definition of "embryo" in s 1(1) of that Act.' *R (on the application of Quintavalle) v Secretary of State for Health* [2002] EWCA Civ 29 at [1]–[3], [5], [14], 19]–[20], [35], [42], [49], [2002] 2 All ER 625 at 627, 630–631, 634, 636–637, CA, per Lord Phillips of Worth Matravers MR

[Decision of the Court of Appeal affirmed: *R (on the application of Quintavalle) v Secretary of State for Health* [2003] UKHL 13, [2003] 2 All ER 113.]

EMERGENCY

[The Radioactive Substances Act 1960 has been repealed. The definition is re-enacted in the Radioactive Substances Act 1993, s 31(11).]

EMERGENCY WORKS

'Emergency works' means works whose execution at the time when they are executed is required in order to put an end to, or to prevent the occurrence of, circumstances then existing or imminent (or while the person responsible for the works believes on reasonable grounds to be existing or imminent) which are likely to cause danger to persons or property. (New Roads and Street Works Act 1991, s 52(1))

EMPLOYEE

Australia 'The word "employee" in its ordinary meaning, in my view, includes an employee engaged on a casual basis. A casual during the course of employment is just as much an employee of the employer as a full-time or part-time weekly employee or a permanent employee, the only difference being that the engagement is on a different basis.' *Richens v Tresilian* (1993) 32 NSWLR 301 at 312, per Hungerford J

EMPLOYER

Canada [A trustee in bankruptcy was allegedly liable as employer for pension contributions after continuing the business operation.] ' ... these plans in question have not been wound up; in fact the trustee had made fresh contributions to these plans. Then too there is the recognition that these workers re-engaged by the trustee are members of the plans. It may not have intended that it come within the definition of "employer" as set out above but it seems that the trustee fits that definition in relation to what it has done—notwithstanding its disclaimer in its re-engagement agreement with the workers. It has dealt with these workers who are members of the plan and it has paid these workers for their services now being rendered to the trustee. In addition as part of the package the trustee has made payments into the plan fund for the benefit of the members of these plans. It seems to me that the trustee has become (albeit it appears inadvertently) an employer within the meaning of the legislation.' *Re St Mary's Paper Inc* (1993) 107 DLR (4th) 715 at 718–719, per Farley J (Ont Gen Div)

EMPLOYERS' ASSOCIATION

[The Trade Union and Labour Relations Act 1974 has been repealed. The definition is re-enacted with modifications in the Trade Union and Labour Relations (Consolidation) Act 1992, as follows.] An 'employers' association' is an organisation (whether temporary or permanent)—
(a) which consists wholly or mainly of employers or individual owners of undertakings of one or more descriptions and whose principal purposes include the regulation of relations between employers of that description or those descriptions and workers or trade unions; or
(b) which consists wholly or mainly of—
  (i) constituent or affiliated organisations which fulfil those conditions or themselves consist wholly or mainly of constituent or affiliated organisations which fulfil the conditions specified in paragraph (a) (or themselves consist wholly or mainly of constituent or affiliated organisations which fulfil those conditions), or
  (ii) representatives of such constituent or affiliated organisations,

and whose principal purposes include the regulation of relations between employers and workers or between employers and trade unions, or the regulation of relations between its constituent or affiliated organisations. (Trade Union and Labour Relations (Consolidation) Act 1992 s 122(1))

Statutory references to employers' associations include combinations of employers and employers' associations. (ibid s 122(2))

A 'federated employers' association' is an employers' association which consists wholly or mainly of constituent or affiliated organisations, or representatives of such organisations, as described in paragraph (b) above. (ibid s 135(1))

See 47 Halsbury's Laws (4th edn) (Reissue) para 1201.

EMPLOYMENT

Canada '... the assumption of the Deputy Tax Court Judge that the word "employment" in paragraph 3(2)(*c*) necessarily means employment under a contract of service is overly restrictive, and does not accord with the overall purpose and intent of the *Unemployment Insurance Act*. I note that the definition of "employment" in subsection 2(1) of the Act is not restricted to contracts of service, but rather broadly states that it is "the act of employing or the state of being employed." In my view, the Act, as reflected in sections 3 and 4 [as am by SC 1990, c 40, s 3], is designed to create an unemployment insurance regime in which some employment in the nature of contracts of service is *excluded* from insurable employment, and other employment is *included* in insurable employment even though it is not under contracts of service. The Act, in other words, is designed to create an unemployment insurance regime which recognizes that the line between contracts *of* service and contracts *for* service is very often blurred. As stated by Beetz J in *Martin Service Station Ltd. v Minister of National Revenue*, and quoted with approval by MacGuigan JA in *Can. (A.G.) v Skyline Cabs (1982) Ltd*, "Whether they be self-employed or employed under a contract of service, taxi drivers and bus drivers for instance are exposed to the risk of being deprived of work. This risk is, in my opinion, an insurable one." ' *Canada v Schnurer Estate* [1997] 2 FC 545 at 558, FCA, per Isaac CJ

Canada 'On the language of s 34 [of the *Residential Tenancy Act*] the issue is whether Mr. Fraser had "employment" as a caretaker (s 34(1)) or was employed as a caretaker (s 1 "caretaker's premises").

'The words "employer" and "employee" are commonly used to refer to the persons formerly referred to as master and servant. That terminology is used to describe situations of contracts of service. I think it is safe to conclude that the words "employer" and "employee", included in s 34(3) through the definition of "employment premises", refer to a situation of a contract of service, that is, in the old language, master and servant. The Parks Board has deposed that Mr. Fraser is not an employee. It follows that his arrangement with the Parks Board does not fit within s 34(3).

'Notwithstanding Mr. MacInnis's able argument, I am not satisfied, however, that the words "employment" and "employed", found in s 34(1)

and the s 1 definition of "caretaker's premises" are restricted to the narrow master and servant, contract of service situation.

'I observe, firstly, that the Act does not have as its primary purpose the regulation of master and servant situations or contracts of service, as do the *Employment Standards Act*, RSBC 1996, c 113, and the *Labour Relations Code*, RSBC 1996, c 244. Nor is it a licensing statute requiring protection of the public, such as the *Real Estate Act*, RSBC 1996, c 397. A requirement in that Act that a salesperson be employed by an agent has been held to refer to a traditional master and servant relationship: *Gene Drennan Ltd v Bohun* (1997), 29 BCLR (3d) 179 *sub nom. F W C. The Land Co. (Receiver-Manager of) v Bohun* (C.A.).

'I consider that the words "employment" and "employed" used in s 34(1) are susceptible of meanings both large and narrow. Largely read, "employment" may refer to work, or an activity in which a person receives valuable consideration, and "employed" may mean occupied or engaged: *The Dictionary of Canadian Law*, 2nd ed. (Scarborough: Carswell, 1995). More narrowly read, "employment" may refer to the position of a person in the service of another or performance of services under a contract of service, and "employed" may mean performing the duties of an office or employment: *The Dictionary of Canadian Law*. Other dictionaries provide a similar range of meanings.

'It may be thought that the references in s 34(3) to "employer" and "employee", captured in the definition of "employment premises", suggest that the words "employment" and "employed" in s 34(1), coming as they do from the same root word "employ", refer to the same sort of relationship. While reference to the common roots of these several words provides a useful starting point in assessing the true meaning of s 34(1), it is not, however, conclusive and the same word even may be used in different senses in the same statute: *Sommers v The Queen*, [1959] SCR 678 at 685. The approach is summarized by Elmer Driedger in *Construction of Statutes* (2nd ed., 1983) at p 87, cited with approval in *Rizzo & Rizzo Shoes Ltd. (Re)*, [1998] 1 SCR 27 at para. 21, 154 DLR (4th) 193:

> Today there is only one principle or approach, namely, the words of an Act are to be read in their entire context and in their grammatical and ordinary sense harmoniously with the scheme of the Act, the object of the Act, and the intention of Parliament.

'In s 34(1) the focus is upon a tenancy that lasts as long as the employment and in which there is no inherent connection between the services provided and the actual premises. In contrast, the premises discussed in s 34(1) are inextricably tied to the services provided: the term "caretaker's premises" requires that the residence be situated in the premises receiving the caretaker's services. I consider that the focus in s 34(1) is upon the caretaking function whether or not the context is technically a contract of service.' *Fraser v Vancouver Board of Parks & Recreation* (2001) 198 DLR (4th) 569 at 574–575, BCCA, per Saunders JA

Casual employment

Australia 'A characteristic of engagement on a casual basis is, in my opinion, that the employer can elect to offer employment on a particular day or days and when offered, the employee can elect to work. Another characteristic is that there is no certainty about the period over which employment of this type will be offered. It is the informality, uncertainty and irregularity of the engagement that gives it the characteristic of being casual.' *Reed v Blue Line Cruises Ltd* (1996) 73 IR 420 at 425, per Moore J

Australia '... it is not inconsistent with a casual employment relationship for employees to be engaged on a regular basis pursuant to a roster ... it is not necessarily the case ... that casual employment will always be informal, uncertain or irregular.' *Community and Public Sector Union v Victoria* BC200000013; [2000] FCA 14 at [12], per Marshall J

South Africa 'Employment cannot be casual when the employee cannot cease work without giving notice and the employer cannot dismiss him without notice.' *Pretoria City Council v Minister of Labour* 1945 TPD 245, per Solomon J

EMPLOYMENT HISTORY

Canada '25 In my view, there is no reason to limit the scope of the expression "employment history" to particular aspects of employment or to modify its usual meaning. Parliament referred broadly to "employment history" and did not qualify that expression. There is no evidence of an intent to limit its meaning. Further, the wording of s. 3(*b*) [*Privacy Act*] suggests that it has a broad scope. Indeed, the provision does not state that personal information includes "employment history" itself. Rather, it stipulates that it includes "information relating to ... employment history" (emphasis added). *Black's Law Dictionary* (6th ed. 1990) defines the word "relate" at p. 1288 as "to bring into association with or connection with". The wording of the French version of s. 3(*b*) is equally general: "*Les renseignements, quels que soient leur forme et leur support, concernant un individu identifiable, ... relatifs à ... ses antécédents professionnels ...*" (emphasis added). The *Dictionnaire de droit québécois et canadien* (2nd ed. 2001) defines "*relatif*" at p. 477 as "*[q]ui concerne, qui se rapporte à*". Considering the wording of the provision, it would seem that the personal information referred to is that relating to employment history. In the absence of clear legislative intent to the contrary, the ordinary meaning of the legislative provision must prevail. The ordinary meaning of "employment history" includes not only the list of positions previously held, places of employment, tasks performed and so on, but also, for example, any personal evaluations an employee might have received during his career. Such a broad definition is also consistent with the meaning generally given to that expression in the workplace.' *Canada (Information Commissioner) v Canada (Commissioner of the Royal Canadian Mounted Police)* [2003] 1 SCR 66 at 82–83, per Gonthier J

ENACTMENT

[For 44 Halsbury's Laws (4th edn) para 803 see now 44(1) Halsbury's Laws (4th edn) (Reissue) para 1232.]

New Zealand 'The argument is that in the paragraphs mentioned, and in various other places in the Acts Interpretation Act [1924], "enactment" means only an Act or any provision of an Act but does not correspondingly apply to regulations. We can see no sensible reason why that restricted interpretation should be adopted in relation to para (h) or para (g) [of s 20].' *Black v Fulcher* [1988] 1 NZLR 417 at 419, CA, per cur

ENCROACHMENT

Australia 'It is clear from those decisions that "encroachment" was used to describe occupation or usurpation not merely by cross-boundary occupation or usurpation but also that which was free-standing. In the *Earl of Lisburne's* case [(1866) LR 1 CP 259] the term was seen as potentially applicable to land which was divided from the leased land by a small river. In other cases a road had intervened. And, was pointed out in *Kingsmill*

v Millard (1855) 11 Exch 313 at 318, the term has been applied to the occupation of land "at a distance" beyond the boundary of the leased land.

'There is, I think, nothing in the purpose or the policy of the [Encroachment of Buildings Act 1992 (NSW)] which would require the exclusion from the ordinary meaning of "encroachment" of a free-standing encroachment and limit the meaning of the term merely to cross-boundary encroachment.' *Googoorewon Pty Ltd v Amatek Ltd* (1991) 25 NSWLR 330 at 333, per Mahoney JA

ENCUMBER

Canada '... in my view, the motions judge erred in holding that the term "encumber" in s 21 of the *Family Law Act* [RSO 1990, c F3] applied to either the guarantee or the acknowledgment. If the motions judge is correct then taken to its logical conclusion no spouse could enter into any unsecured financial transaction without violating s 21 of the *Family Law Act* unless he or she had the consent of the other spouse. Even as simple a transaction as purchasing goods on credit could eventually lead to summary judgments against the spouse and ultimately execution against his or her interest in the matrimonial home. The Supreme Court of Canada in *Maroukis v Maroukis*, [1984] 2 SCR 137, 12 DLR (4th) 321, has held that the term "encumber" in s 42 of the predecessor legislation does not apply to an execution taken by creditors of one of the parties to the marriage. It would be an odd result if the term could nevertheless be applied to an even more remote transaction such as the obtaining of a commercial loan or, as in this case, the giving of a personal guarantee by one spouse for the debts of his or her company.

'There is no doubt that, as pointed out by the motions judge, the matrimonial home occupies a special place in family property relations. That is not, however, sufficient reason to give the term "encumber" such an unusual meaning that would seriously interfere with normal commercial transactions. It should also be borne in mind that s. 64 of the Act provides that "[f]or all purposes of the law of Ontario, a married person has a legal personality that is independent, separate and distinct from that of his or her spouse". It would seem inconsistent with this fundamental principle that by virtue of s 21 a man or woman would nevertheless require the consent of his or her spouse before entering into any kind of commercial transaction that could result in the creation of an unsecured debt.

'In my view, the term "encumber" in s 21 must be given its ordinary meaning as a burden on property, a claim, lien or liability attached to property.' *Bank of Montreal v Bray* (1997) 153 DLR (4th) 490 at 506–507, Ont CA, per Rosenberg JA

END

Of engagement

[For 43 Halsbury's Laws (4th edn) para 229 et seq see now 43(2) Halsbury's Laws (4th edn) (Reissue) para 1701 et seq.]

ENDANGER

Canada '41 The requirements of an aggravated assault include those of the assault itself plus, as mentioned, certain listed consequences:

> 268. (1) Every one commits an aggravated assault who wounds, maims, disfigures or endangers the life of the complainant. [*Criminal Code*]

The prosecution must establish all of the elements of an assault *plus* the aggravating circumstance.
'42 In *R. v. Leclerc* (1991), 67 C.C.C. (3d) 563 (Ont. C.A.), Lacourcière J.A. wrote for the court, at pp. 567–68:

> The case-law interpreting the sections quoted [ss. 265 and 268] makes it clear that the essential intent required for an assault, as defined, remains the same for all forms of assault, including aggravated assault. Parliament intended that the severity of the punishment should increase to reflect the more serious consequences of the assault. [Emphasis added.]

'43 In *Godin, supra*, Cory J. stated, at p. 485, "[t]he section pertains to an assault that has the consequences of wounding, maiming or disfiguring" (emphasis added) or (to complete the list) endangering life. "Endanger" means to "[p]ut in danger ... put in peril ... [i]ncur the risk": *New Shorter Oxford English Dictionary on Historical Principles* (1993), vol. 1, at p. 816. As to the focus on consequences, see generally *R. v. Brodie* (1995), 60 B.C.A.C. 153, at para. 4; *R. v. Dewey* (1999), 132 C.C.C. (3d) 348 (Alta. C.A.), at para. 9; and *R. v. Ross*, [1998] O.J. No. 3427 (QL) (Gen. Div.), at para. 23. See also *R. v. Vang* (1999), 132 C.C.C. (3d) 32 (Ont. C.A.), at para. 12.' *R v Williams* [2003] 2 SCR 134 at 148–149, per Binnie J

ENFORCEMENT

Australia 'There is no doubt that as a matter of ordinary English usage the "enforcement" of a charge refers to compelling the observance of the rights asserted. Thus mere passive receipt of property the subject of the claimed right would not amount to what ordinary usage would describe as an "enforcement" of that right by the person having the benefit of the right ... [Section 267 of the Corporations Law] applies only where the chargee purports to take a step in the enforcement of the charge; it does not apply to all charges of a particular kind ... it emphasises that it is the characterisation of the chargee's conduct which is critical.' *400 Lonsdale Nominees Pty Ltd v Southern Cross Airlines Ltd (in liq)* (1993) 10 ACSR 739 at 746, per Hayne J

ENGAGE IN ANY BUSINESS

New Zealand [Section 112(2)(a) of the Income Tax Act 1976.] ' "Business" is defined in the Act in s 2 as follows:

> "Business" includes any profession, trade, manufacture or undertaking carried on for pecuniary profit.

'The meaning of the word "business" was extensively explored by Richardson J in *Grieve v Commissioner of Inland Revenue* [1984] 1 NZLR 101 (CA). As I understand it essentially two elements are required: (i) some form of organised commercial activity and (ii) the conduct of that activity for the purpose of making a profit. As to the first, it is not essential that there be a realistic prospect of making a profit when objectively considered. As Richardson J said in *Grieve* at 110:

> "... while the Courts are justified in viewing circumspectly a claim that a taxpayer genuinely intended to carry on a business for pecuniary profit when looked at realistically there seems no real prospect of profit, an actual intention once established is sufficient. The legislation sensibly allows for deductions and allowances to be claimed even where the overall result is a trading loss. It is not for the Courts or the Commissioner to confine the recognition of businesses to those that are always profitable or to do so only so long as they operate at a profit. In my view there is no warrant in the definition of business in its statutory context for reading in a requirement that there must be a reasonable prospect of

profit before the gross income derived is assessable under s 88(1)(a) and the deductions sought are allowable under s 111(b) and under the specific deduction provisions requiring the taxpayer concerned to be carrying on a business."

...

'The sole question under this heading is therefore whether the activity which accompanied that purpose was sufficient to amount to a commercial activity for the purposes of a "business". As to the nature of that activity, Richardson J said in *Grieve* at 106:

"In common usage 'business' has and has long had a wide and flexible meaning. In the sense in which it is used in legislation imposing a charge for tax in respect of revenue earning activities *The Oxford English Dictionary* definitions 'a pursuit or occupation demanding time and attention; a serious employment as distinct from a pastime ...; trade; commercial transactions or engagements' and *Webster's Third New International Dictionary* definitions 'a usually commercial or mercantile activity customarily engaged in as a means of livelihood and typically involving some independence of judgment and power of decision ... a commercial or industrial enterprise' reflect the underlying notion. The word has been subject to much judicial discussion in New Zealand and other jurisdictions. Our concern is as to its meaning in the context of the income tax legislation and s 2 provides as it has since 1916 that except where a contrary intention appears 'business' 'includes any profession, trade, manufacture or undertaking carried on for pecuniary profit'. In *G v Commissioner of Inland Revenue* [1961] NZLR 994, 998 McCarthy J considered that notwithstanding the use of the word 'includes' a study of the definition forces the view that it does not add anything to the common meaning of the word and does not catch anything that would not otherwise be caught. In *Harley v Commissioner of Inland Revenue* at 487 North P took the same view. I respectfully agree. While there are obvious shades of difference, and while each of the words 'profession, trade, manufacture or undertaking' has a wide meaning, I cannot readily postulate any activity which they comprehend which is not also included in the general concept of 'business' in ordinary usage.

"... Underlying each of the words in the definition in s 2 and the term 'business' itself when used in the context of a taxation statute is the fundamental notion of the exercise of an activity in an organised and coherent way and one which is directed to an end result."

...

'As Richardson J said, it must be the exercise of an activity in an organised and coherent way but that too is a wide concept. Two aspects seem to me to refine the meaning: continuity and more than mere preparation.

'As to the first, there is an element of continuity involved in carrying on a business but since all courses of conduct must begin somewhere I do not think that there could be any minimum period before a commenced course of conduct would qualify. Richardson J in *Grieve* does say at 110:

"It follows from this analysis that the decision whether or not a taxpayer is in business involves a two-fold inquiry – as to the nature of the activities carried on, and as to the intention of the taxpayer in engaging in those activities. Statements by the taxpayer as to his intentions are of course relevant but actions will often speak louder than words. Amongst the matters which may properly be considered in that inquiry are the nature of the activity, the period over which it is engaged in, the scale of operations and the volume of transactions, the commitment of time, money and effort, the pattern of activity, and the financial results. It may be helpful to consider whether the operations involved are of the same kind and are carried on in the same way as those which are characteristic of ordinary trade in the line of business in which the venture was conducted. However, in the end it is the character and circumstances of the particular venture which are crucial. Businesses do not cease to be businesses because they are carried on idiosyncratically or inefficiently or unprofitably, or because the taxpayer derives personal satisfaction from the venture."

...

'Secondly it seems inherent in the statutory provisions that to qualify as the conduct of a business for revenue purposes there must be more than mere preparation. In that respect there could well be some distant analogy with criminal law attempts. The taxpayer must embark on the actual course of conduct which it is hoped would ultimately yield profit if persisted in. I do not think that merely setting up a business structure and purchasing plant or organising the decision-making structures, management and equity structures will suffice. That is not "carrying on a business" but "setting up a business". Nor do I think that activities which are confined to the organisation of relationships between proprietors, or the making of decisions over their future ownership of the business, would normally qualify because they are non-productive of income. As I understand it there must be an operational activity. Other matters may well be preconditions to operational activity but will not suffice in themselves.' *Slater v Commissioner of Inland Revenue* [1996] 1 NZLR 759 at 762, 763, 764 and 765, per Fisher J

ENGAGED IN

[The Interception of Communications Act 1985 s 1 provides that a person who intentionally intercepts a communication by means of a public telecommunications system commits an offence. Section 9 excludes evidence (inter alia) tending to suggest that an offence has been committed by any person engaged in the running of a public telecommunication system (s 9(1)(a), (2)(c). A recording of a telephone conversation of the defendant made by a telephone engineer for his own private purpose was admitted in evidence; the defendant contended that it should have been excluded as tending to show that an offence under s 1 had been committed.] '[8] The words "engaged in" which appear in both s 9(2)(b)—"engaged in the business of the Post Office"—and in s 9(2)(c)— "engaged in the running of a public telecommunication system"—are capable of two meanings. On one view, the words are used simply to indicate the person's office, status or position within the relevant organisation. On this view, it would be enough to show that the person was an employee or other agent of that organisation when he carried out the intercept. The other view is that the words are used to indicate that at the time the person was embarked upon a particular activity. On this view, it would be necessary to examine what he was doing at the time and to determine whether or not it was within the scope of his duties or his instructions. The admissibility of the intercept would depend not on whether he was employed by the organisation but on whether he was acting within the scope of his employment or on his instructions at the time of the interception.

'[9] It is plain that the second of these two alternatives would require more detailed investigation than the first to determine whether the intercept was inadmissible under s 9(1) of the 1985 Act or was admissible. Indeed, it is hard to see how an investigation into the person's activities at the time of the intercept could be conducted without entering into what was described by Steyn LJ in *R v Effik* (1992) 95 Cr App R 427 at 432 as the "forbidden territory". Section 9(1)(a) provides that no evidence shall be adduced and no question asked in cross-examination which tends to suggest that an offence under s 1 of the 1985 Act has been committed by the person who carried out the intercept or whether a warrant has been or is to be issued to him. The underlying purpose, as Lord Mustill said in *R v Preston* [1993] 3 All ER 638 at 667, [1994] 2 AC 130 at 167, is to protect information as to the authorisation and carrying out of official intercepts. But the prohibition extends to unauthorised as well as to authorised activity. It reflects the public interest that the circumstances in which the activities of those involved in serious crime came to the knowledge of the police should not be capable of being explored at a trial.

'[10] Questions as to the scope of the person's duties, the extent of his authority and the instructions which he had been given would be hard to avoid if the decision as to admissibility were to depend on evidence as to whether he was acting within the scope of his employment at the time when the interception was carried out. They would be almost certainly crucial to the issue of admissibility if the intercept was carried out, as it was in this case, at the person's place of work using his employer's equipment within normal working hours. They indicate the difficulties which the prohibition in s 9(1) would create in the conduct of such an investigation. These difficulties suggest quite strongly that the first alternative meaning of the phrase is the one which it bears in the present context.'

. . .

'[31] There is a reference to the purpose for which the interception has been made in s 1(3)(a) already referred to. If the call had been intercepted for a purpose connected with the provision of a public telecommunication service, it would have not come within s 1 and no offence under that section would have been committed. The question in the present case under s 9 only arises because the intercept was for an alien purpose. Section 9(2) is concerned with defining the three categories of persons to whom s 9(1) refers. It already presupposes that they have (or may have) committed an offence under s 1, ie that, where a public telecommunications employee is concerned, his purpose was not connected with the services which his employers provided. It is in this context that s 9(2)(b) and (c) have to be construed. The effect of the Court of Appeal's interpretation would be to confine these paragraphs to authorised acts of the employee done in the interests of his employer. This focus upon the act or conduct of the person both detracts from the force of s 1(3)(a) and conflicts with the drafting of s 9(2) which is concerned with categorising the person. The words "engaged in" denote the person's employment at the relevant time not whether he was acting within his authority.' *R v Sargent* [2001] UKHL 54 at [8]–[10], [31], [2002] 1 All ER 161 at 164–165, 172–173, HL, per Lord Hope of Craighead and Lord Hobhouse of Woodborough respectively

ENJOIN

Canada 'At issue on the enjoinment motion was the right of the *Sheena M* interests to avoid facing actions on another front, specifically in the BC Supreme Court, until their limitation action had been dealt with. The motion was purely under paragraph 581(1)(*c*) of the *Canada Shipping Act*, which grants this Court jurisdiction to prevent the continuation of a proceeding before any court "other than the Admiralty Court". This section does not grant and indeed does not need to grant to the Federal Court, as the Admiralty Court, the procedural power to stay proceedings in its own Court, but rather it grants the Federal Court the ability to enjoin other courts from proceeding with their actions in certain circumstances. The test for such an enjoinment is that of appropriateness as set out in the preamble to subsection 581(1) of the *Canada Shipping Act*. In contrast, the present motion is for a stay under section 50 of the *Federal Court Act*.

'To complete this line of reasoning, there is a difference between enjoining and staying. The former, is defined in the revised 4th edition of *Black's Law Dictionary* in terms of an injunctive direction to perform or to abstain from some act. The *New Shorter Oxford English Dictionary on Historical Principles* reflects this injunctive aspect of the verb "enjoin":

Prohibit, forbid; *esp.* (*Law*) prohibit or re-strain by an injunction.

'In contrast a stay, or a stay of proceedings as it is correctly called, is an order by which a court suspends its own proceedings, either temporarily, until something is done, or permanently, where it is improper to proceed: see for example *Osborn's Concise Law Dictionary*, Sweet & Maxwell, 5th edition. That a stay is a procedure internal to the

Court issuing the order is clear from the dissertation on the nature of a stay set out in the 4th edition (1982) of *Halsbury's Laws of England*, Volume 37, at page 325, which includes the following:

A stay of proceedings arises under an order of the court which puts the stop or "stay" on the further conduct of the proceedings in that court at the stage which they have then reached, so that the parties are precluded thereafter from taking any further step in the proceedings. [Emphasis added.]

'The test for a stay, in the interests of justice, is generally acknowledged to be the three-part test set out in *RJR—MacDonald Inc v Canada (Attorney General)*, [1994] 1 SCR 311, being the three-part *American Cyanamid* test [*American Cyanamid Co v Ethicon Ltd*, [1975] AC 396 (HL)] although in this instance the appropriate test for a stay of proceedings is a two-part test set out in *Mon-Oil Ltd v Canada* (1989), 26 CPR (3d) 379 (FCTD), a point that I shall touch on again in due course. The test for a stay is very different concept and test from that of an enjoinment of a proceeding in another court under the *Canada Shipping Act*.' *Canadian Pacific Railway Co v Sheena M (The)* [2000] 4 FC 159 at 172–173, FCTD, per Hargrave Proth

ENROLLED

Australia [Migration Act 1958 (Cth) s 137J and Education Services for Overseas Students Act 2000 (Cth) s 20.] '… The ordinary meaning of "enrolled" in this context connotes a relationship between student and education provider in relation to a particular course. The student does not cease to be "enrolled" merely because the particular series of lectures might have concluded. Usually an education provider will not be able to certify that academic result was satisfactory or otherwise, thereby discharging its own obligations, until the completion of some examination or other assessment. Of necessity, this will normally take place after lectures have concluded.' *Rajbhandari v Minister for Immigration and Multicultural and Indigenous Affairs* [2004] FCA 1130 at [10], per Heerey J; BC200405650

ENTAIL

To be entailed upon it

[A testator bequeathed a collection of works of art to his heir of entail, on condition that 'at his death he makes over to the College of Edinburgh to be entailed upon it [the collection] which I bequeath for the purpose of laying a foundation for a Gallery for the encouragement of the fine Arts'. Dispute arose as to whether or not a trust had been created.] 'We agree that the words "to be entailed upon it" … should be construed as disclosing an intention that the collection should be settled, that is, held in trust.' *University of Edinburgh v The Torrie Trustees* 1997 SLT 1009 at 1013–1014, per Lord Justice Clerk Ross (delivering the opinion of the court)

ENTAILED INTEREST

[For 39 Halsbury's Laws (4th edn) paras 418–421 see now 39(2) Halsbury's Laws (4th edn) (Reissue) paras 117–120.]

ENTIRE CONTRACT

[For 4 Halsbury's Laws (4th edn) para 1145 see now 4(1) Halsbury's Laws (4th edn) (2002 Reissue) para 8.]

ENTITLED

[For 35 Halsbury's Laws (4th edn) para 1111 see now 35 Halsbury's Laws (4th edn) (Reissue) para 1211.]

[Insolvency Act 1986, s 435(10)(b).] '[31] Subsection (10) provides:

> "For the purposes of this section a person is to be taken as having control of a company if–(a) the directors of the company or of another company which has control of it (or any of them) are accustomed to act in accordance with his directions or instructions, or (b) he is entitled to exercise, or control the exercise of, one third or more of the voting power at any general meeting of the company or of another company which has control of it; and where two or more persons together satisfy either of the above conditions, they are to be taken as having control of the company."

…

'[58] The phrase I have to construe in s 435(10)(b) is a typically compressed piece of draftsmanship. The verb "entitled" governs both the exercise of voting power and the control of voting power. In looking at control of voting power, the word "entitled" must, in my judgment, mean "entitled as between the registered shareholder and the controller of the voting power". Why, then, should the word "entitled" in its application to the

exercise of voting power be construed as meaning "as between the registered shareholder and the company"? There is a further slight clue to the meaning of s 435. Unlike s 736 and s 736A of the 1985 Act [Companies Act 1985], which refer to "voting rights", s 435 refers to "voting power". The word "rights" naturally directs attention to legal rights, especially since s 736A(2) goes on to explain that voting rights means "rights conferred on shareholders in respect of their shares". The word "power", by contrast, gives me some encouragement to look to the economic reality of the case. A registered shareholder who holds his shares on a bare trust under which he is required to cast his vote in accordance with the directions of the beneficial owner might be said to have voting rights, but I do not consider that in any real sense he can be said to have voting power. The Court of Appeal, in two cases I have mentioned (*Bibby*'s [*IRC v J Bibby & Sons Ltd* [1944] 1 All ER 548] and *IRC v Silverts Ltd* [1951] 1 All ER 703, [1951] Ch 521), were clearly impressed by the appeal to the common sense and economic reality of the case of a bare trustee. I do not consider that the wording of s 435 compels me to take a different view. In addition Holdings was a corporate shareholder. If I ask whose voice would be heard if, after the declaration of trust, Holdings were to cast the votes attached to the shares registered in its name at a general meeting of the company, the only answer, in my judgment, is Kozo's.

'[59] I hold, therefore, that following the execution of the declaration of trust Holdings is not to be regarded, for the purposes of s 435(10)(b) of the 1986 Act, as being entitled to exercise the voting power of those shares. Since such a person is bound to act in accordance with the directions of the beneficial owner, he does not control their voting power either. Thus Holdings was not associated with the company when the debenture was executed.' *Re Kilnoore Ltd (in liquidation); Unidare plc v Cohen* [2005] EWHC 1410 (Ch) at [31], [58]–[59], [2005] 3 All ER 730, per Lewison J

To practise

Australia [Section 49(1) of the Judiciary Act 1903 (Cth) provides than any person 'entitled' to practise as a barrister or solicitor or both in any state shall have the like right to practise in any federal court.] 'Its sense is to be derived from the ordinary meaning of the word "entitle" which is "to give a rightful claim to anything": Shorter Oxford English Dictionary. In that ordinary sense it attaches only to a practitioner who has satisfied all conditions necessary to establish the rightful claim to practise. And most telling in the immediate context of these proceedings is the fact that the second reading speech which introduced the 1966 amendments proceeded upon the express assumption that the entitlement to practise would be conditioned upon the holding of a current practising certificate.' *Little v Registrar of High Court of Australia* (1991) 101 ALR 244 at 255, per cur

ENTITLEMENT

Canada [A wife sought to garnish her husband's pension benefits to enforce her entitlement to support payments under their separation agreement.] 'The word "entitlement" is defined in the New Shorter Oxford Dictionary, 1993, at p 830 as: "(c) something to which a person is entitled, esp. a state benefit".

'In Black's Law Dictionary, 6th ed, at p 532, "entitlement" is defined as: "Right to benefits, income or property which may not be abridged without due process".

'In my view, keeping in mind the judicial trend of endeavouring to ensure fairness between both parties to a matrimonial dispute, the word "entitlements" in the phrase "subject to entitlements arising under a separation agreement" in s 64 of the Act [*Pension Benefits Standards Act*] should be interpreted to include a claim for maintenance under a separation agreement …

…

'I interpret s 64 to mean that, in this case, the entitlement of the appellant to receive a benefit under his Telecommunication Workers' Pension Plan is subject to the claim of the respondent to receive maintenance under the Separation Agreement. To enforce that claim, the attachment proceedings taken in this case under the *Family Maintenance Enforcement Act* and the *Family Relations Act* were not invalid.' *Vellow v Vellow* (1996) 134 DLR (4th) 657 at 664, 665, per Hinds JA (BCCA)

ENTRAPMENT

'[1] [E]very court has an inherent power and duty to prevent abuse of its process. This is a fundamental principle of the rule of law. By recourse to this principle courts ensure that executive agents of the state do not misuse the coercive, law enforcement functions of the courts and thereby opress citizens of the state. Entrapment, with which these two appeals are concerned, is an instance where such

misuse may occur. It is simply not acceptable that the state through its agents should lure its citizens into committing acts forbidden by the law and then seek to prosecute them for so doing. That would be entrapment.

…

'[36] Entrapment occurs when an agent of the state—usually a law enforcement officer or a controlled informer—causes someone to commit an offence in order that he should be prosecuted.' *R v Looseley* [2001] UKHL 53 at [1], [36], [2001] 4 All ER 897 at 899–900, 907, HL, per Lord Nicholls of Birkenhead and Lord Hoffmann respectively

ENTRUST

Canada 'The word "entrusted" has been common to policies of insurance for a long time but has rarely been subjected to judicial scrutiny. Only one Canadian case has been cited by the two parties — each finding comfort in the decision.

'The House of Lords considered a similar case which arose in 1922. In *Lake v Simmons* [1927] AC 487, [1927] All ER Rep 49 (HL), Viscount Haldane explained the difficulty in interpreting the scope of the policy exception. He said [at p 499]:

> "[T]he first of the questions is partly, at least, one of mixed fact and law, the interpretation to be placed on the application of the word 'entrusted' in the exceptions. 'Entrusted' is not necessarily a term of law. It may have different implications in different contexts. In its most general significance all it imports is a handing over the possession for some purpose which may not imply the conferring of any proprietary right at all. I hand my umbrella to a servant to enable me to be free of it while I am taking off my coat. In a very general sense I entrust him with the umbrella. But there is no easily definable bailment in such an instance. What I have really done is to divest myself of the embarrassing circumstances of holding it. Entrusting may, of course, introduce a bailment, conferring some definite, but restricted, proprietary right. It is a question, then, of a contract entered into, and whether there is such a contract depends on more than a bare parting with possession."

…

'Although not dealing with an insurance problem, the meaning of "entrusted" was considered by a Canadian Court as early as 1900. In *Moshier v Keenan* (1900) 31 OR 658 (Ch) Boyd, C was required to determine the meaning of "entrusted" in an agency case. He said [at p 660]:

> "It [entrusted] imports that confidence has been reposed in the agent by principal — the owner of the goods — and that the possession of the goods at the particular time and in the particular way they are in the hands of the agent is intended and contemplated by the owner. If the possession has been obtained in violation of instructions or by means of a breach of faith — that is not all 'entrusted' possession within the provisions of the Act."

'The decision on which both parties have relied is *Hinks v Canadian Home Assurance Co* (1985) 12 CCLI 93 (Alta QB). There, Mr Justice Sulatycky dealt with the interpretation of a similar insurance policy clause which excepted coverage for loss resulting from the dishonesty of a person to whom the insured property is entrusted.

'He followed *Lake v Simmons* in preferring the interpretation of "entrusted" that meant more than bare physical delivery.

'So it was held that "entrusted" in the contract between the plaintiff and defendant "entails a delivery or parting with possession coupled with real consent on the part of the insured, for a mutually understood purpose, on the condition that the recipient return or account for the property in given circumstances."

'In *Lake v Simmons*, Viscount Sumner said [at p 508]: "In my opinion, the natural meaning of 'entrusted' invokes that the assured should be (by) some real and conscious volition have imposed on the person to whom he delivers the goods some speciesof fiduciary duty.".' *Harris v Boreal Insurance Inc* (1996) 139 DLR (4th) 187 at 189, 190, 191, per Miller J (NBQB)

ENVIRONMENT

New Zealand [Section 322(1)(a) of the Resource Managemnt Act 1991 provides for the service of an abatement notice on any person doing anything likely to have an adverse affect on the environment.] 'The environment in this sense is more than the physical surroundings, the objects and substances which are in the vicinity. With its emphasis on people and communities, which must be the people in the communities, the resource management legislation intends that the environment includes the people, and must give them in this particular context predominant significance. Environment, in its definition in the Act, includes people and the social, economic, aesthetic and cultural conditions which affect people.

...

'It is not, I think, possible, nor is it proper, to attempt to define the scope of the environment beyond what must necessarily be deduced from the proper interpretation of the Act and its parts and sections. It certainly is not necessary to define the environment widely so as to include the whole of Wellington or the whole of Karori. It may be too narrow in all cases to say that the environment is your neighbour and no other.' *Zdrahal v Wellington City Council* [1995] 1 NZLR 700at 708–709, per Greig J

EQUIPMENT

[The Road Traffic Act 1972 has been repealed. See now the Road Traffic Act 1988, s 190(2).]

[A labourer flagger employed by the appellant council was injured when a flagstone he was manhandling broke because of a defect in its manufacture. The Employers' Liability (Defective Equipment) Act 1969, s 1(1) provides for the employer to be liable in defined circumstances where an employee is injured in the course of his employment in consequence of a defect in equipment provided by his employer.] 'I have no hesitation in concluding that the word "equipment" in s 1(1)(a) [of the Employers' Liability (Defective Equipment) Act 1969] is habile to cover the flagstone in this appeal. In the first place, the requirement of the subsection is that the equipment is provided "for the purposes of the employer's business" and not merely for the use of the employee. Thus a piece of defective equipment which causes injury to a workman would fall within the ambit of the subsection even although the workman was neither required to use nor had in fact used it. Whatever the meaning of "equipment" this would go further than the circumstances in *Davie v New Merton Board Mills Ltd* [1959] 1 All ER 346, [1959] AC 604, where the defective tool had been provided to the employee for the purposes of his job. In this case the flagstone had undoubtedly been provided by the appellants for the purpose of their business of repairing and relaying the pavement. In the second place, there can be no logical reason why Parliament having recognised the difficulties facing workmen, as demonstrated by *Davie v New Merton Board Mills Ltd*, should have removed those difficulties in part rather than in whole. ... In my view, the only reasonable conclusion is that Parliament intended the 1969 Act to provide a remedy in the situations where an employer had provided for the purpose of his business an article which was defective and caused injury to a workman but where he was for the reasons set out in *Davie v New Merton Board Mills Ltd* not in breach of a common law duty of care owed to that workman.' *Knowles v Liverpool City Council* [1993] 4 All ER 321 at 326–327, HL, per Lord Jauncey of Tullichettle

EQUITY

[For 16 Halsbury's Laws (4th edn) paras 1204–1205 see now 35 Halsbury's Laws (4th edn) (Reissue) paras 654–655.]

Australia 'The phrase "an equity" can be used in the narrow sense of referring to an immediate right to positive equitable relief. Used in that sense, the phrase does not encompass the entitlement of a promise under a promissory estoppel. The phrase "an equity" can ... be used in a broader and less precise sense to refer to any entitlement or obligation ("the equities") of which a court of equity will take cognisance. In that sense, the phrase can be used to refer to a "defensive equity" such as "laches, acquiescence or delay" or a mere set-off or to an interest or entitlement which does not of itself found equitable relief. It is in that broader and less precise sense that it is permissible to speak of the operation of estoppel in equity as giving rise to "an equity". This use of the phrase "an equity" in relation to the operation of promissory estoppel can be illustrated by reference to cases in the Supreme Court of New South Wales where, until 1972 when a Judicature Act system was first introduced, old phraseology was preserved and the distinction between "an equity" which of itself founded a claim for relief and "an equity" which did not remained of critical importance in some circumstances.' *Commonwealth of Australia v Verwayen* (1990) 170 CLR 394 at 434–435, per Deanne J

Equitable charge

[For 32 Halsbury's Laws (4th edn) para 406 see now 32 Halsbury's Laws (4th edn) (Reissue) para 306.]

Equitable interest

[For 39 Halsbury's Laws (4th edn) para 347 see now 39(2) Halsbury's Laws (4th edn) (Reissue) para 46.]

Australia 'As has been often observed, the Courts have not laid down a clear dividing line between an equitable interest in property and what is described as "a mere equity". The difficulties of categorisation were recognised well before the decision in *Phillips v Phillips* (1861) 4 De GF & J 208; (1861) 45 ER 1164 and have not been resolved despite much erudite judicial and academic discussion since then: see e g *Double Bay Newspapers Pty Ltd v A W Holdings Pty Ltd* (1996) 42 NSWLR 409 at 423E; Megarry and Wade, *The Law of Real Property* (2000) 6th ed, para 5–013; *Snell's Equity* (2000) 30th ed, para 2–05; (1955) 71 LQR 480; Meagher, Gummow and Lehane, *Equity Doctrines and Remedies* (1992) 3rd ed, para 427ff.

'Equitable, or proprietary, interests and "mere equities" alike depend for their very existence upon the fundamental concept that equity acts *in personam* and that the rights which it recognises and enforces are not rights *in rem* but rights *in personam*. So, for example, the beneficiary of a bare trust of land is said to have an equitable interest in the land because an equity court, acting upon the conscience of the trustee, will compel the trustee to deal with the land in a certain way for the benefit of the cestui que trust. Likewise, the purchaser of land under an uncompleted contract for sale is said to have an equitable interest in the property, but only because it is tacitly assumed that a court of equity will grant specific performance of the contract. In examples such as these, the equitable interest is commensurate with the availability and extent of the corresponding right *in personam*: see e g *Glenn v Federal Cmr of Land Tax* (1915) 20 CLR 490 at 503–4 per Isaacs J; *Central Trust and Safe Deposit Co v Snider* [1916] 1 AC 266 at 272; *Brown v Heffer* (1967) 116 CLR 344 at 349; *DKLR Holding Co (No 2) Pty Ltd v Cmr of Stamp Duties* [1980] 1 NSWLR 510 at 518ff.

'It follows that if the equity court would not enforce the right *in personam* – where, for example, it has been lost by acquiescence, laches, delay or some other circumstance affording a defence – then the equitable interest might either never have existed in the first place or might have ceased to exist: see *Central Trust and Safe Deposit Co* at 272.

'A right enforceable *in personam* in equity confers an equitable, or proprietary, interest only when there is a nexus of sufficient propinquity between the right and the specific property to which the right relates. What is a nexus of sufficient propinquity is the conundrum. It has been recognised that "there is some circuity involved in finding the starting point for the existence of ... an equitable interest, the problem being to isolate as the initiating factor the proprietary interest or the right to enforce the interest … This problem is almost a jurisprudential mystery": per Kearney J in *Burns Philp Trustee Co Ltd v Viney* [1981] 2 NSLWR 216 at 223.

'Many definitions of an equitable interest have been attempted and found wanting. For example, in *National Provincial Bank Ltd v Ainsworth* [1965] AC 1175, at 1248, Lord Wilberforce identified such an interest as being one which was "definable, identifiable by third parties, capable in its nature of assumption by third parties and [having] some degree of permanence or stability". That definition has been much criticised: see Meagher, Gummow and Lehane, *Equity Doctrines and Remedies* (1992) 3rd ed, para 428. There is probably no point in attempting any universal definition. As Kearney J said in *Burns Philp Trustee Co Ltd v Viney* at 223–4:

"… there is an obvious difficulty in endeavouring both to analyse and to formulate any general principle in this area of the law. The administration of equity has always paid regard to the infinite variety of interests and has refrained from formulating or adhering to fixed universal and exhaustive criteria with which to deal with such varying situations. The approach traditionally adopted by equity has been to retain flexibility so as to accommodate the multitudinous instances in which fundamental equitable rules fall to be applied."

'Like an "equitable interest", a "mere equity" is a slippery creature. It can be cornered and illuminated by example but not captured and confined by definition. For present purposes, the most illuminating example is found in [*Latec Investments Ltd v Hotel Terrigal Pty Ltd (in liq)* (1965) 113 CLR 265]. There, a mortgagee fraudulently exercised a power of sale, so that as against the mortgagee and the collusive purchaser the mortgagor had a right in equity to set aside the conveyance. However, the rights of a third party had intervened in the meantime so that the competition was between the mortgagor, claiming an equitable interest in the land which was prior to that of the third party, and the third party who claimed a subsequent equitable interest acquired for value without notice of what it said was the mortgagor's "mere equity".

'There was disagreement between Kitto and Taylor JJ as to whether the mortgagor had a prior equitable interest in the property. Kitto J was of the view, on the authority of *Phillips v Phillips*, that the mortgagor had to make good its right in equity

to have the fraudulent conveyance set aside before the mortgagor could be said to have an equitable interest in the land, namely, its equity of redemption. As between the mortgagor and the third party, the competition was, according to his Honour, between a "preliminary equity" – that is, a claim to set aside the conveyance for fraud – and an admitted subsequent equitable interest. His Honour was of the opinion that *Phillips v Phillips* compelled the conclusion that the "preliminary equity" was a "mere equity" which could not compete with the subsequent equitable interest acquired for value without notice: at 277–9.

'On the other hand, Taylor J was of the view that the mortgagor had never been deprived of its equitable interest in the property by the voidable fraudulent conveyance. On the authority of cases decided both before and after *Phillips v Phillips*, his Honour concluded that the owner of an equitable interest in property who is induced by fraud to transfer it continues to retain that equitable interest: it does not cease upon the transfer and then come into existence again when the transfer is set aside: at 281–4.

'However, Taylor J concluded that the true principle enunciated in *Phillips v Phillips* was simply that where the person entitled to a prior equitable interest requires the assistance of a court of equity to remove an impediment to his or her title as a preliminary to asserting it, the court will not interfere if a third person has acquired an equitable interest in the property for value without notice before the prior equitable interest holder comes to the court for assistance: at 286.

'The approach of Menzies J was to attempt to reconcile the two apparently conflicting streams of authority relied upon by Kitto and Taylor JJ. His Honour would recognise that an equitable right could be a "mere equity" in the sense adopted by Kitto J for the purpose of a priority contest with an equitable interest and yet could be an "equitable interest" for the purpose of transmission by devise or assignment: at 290–1. In the result, therefore, Menzies J agreed with the position taken by Kitto J.

'*Latec Investments* has been judicially considered on very many occasions and I will not contribute yet another exegesis. My own view, which reflects the approach taken by Menzies J, is that *Phillips v Phillips* can be explained as a policy decision rather than a decision resting on distinctions in the qualities of various equitable rights. The policy is simply this: where the holder of a prior equitable interest needs the assistance of the equity court to perfect his or her title to it, that equitable interest will be defeated if, before the title is perfected, a third party takes an equitable interest for value without notice.

'Perfecting the title to an equitable interest does not mean resolving a dispute as to its existence in the first place, as where, for example, parties disagree as to whether a document has created an equitable charge and a declaration is sought from the equity court. Perfecting the title means seeking an equitable remedy without which a previously existing equitable interest would be lost.' *Mills v Ruthol Pty Ltd* BC200201632; [2002] NSWSC 294 at [121]–[132], per Palmer J

Equity of redemption

[For 32 Halsbury's Laws (4th edn) para 407 see now 32 Halsbury's Laws (4th edn) (Reissue) para 307.]

ERECTION

[The Town and Country Planning Act 1971 has been repealed. The definition is re-enacted in the Town and Country Planning Act 1990 s 336(1).]

ERRONEOUS ADVICE

Canada [A member of the public service who is given 'erroneous advice' respecting the counting of a period of service for pension purposes is, under certain circumstances, entitled to a remedy under the *Public Service Superannuation Act*.] '... The trial judge agreed with the Minister and held that "erroneous advice" contemplates a positive misstatement, and that no such misstatement was made to the appellant ...

...

'With respect, this was an error of law. The phrase "erroneous advice" should not be so narrowly construed, especially in remedial legislation such as this. It seems to me that where one party is advising another, the failure to divulge material information may be just as misleading as a positive misstatement. Missing information can be just as harmful as mistaken information. Both types of advice are equally erroneous. This is especially the case where, as here, the information in question is of a specialized nature, which is easily available to the advisor but not easily obtainable by the party being advised. In such a context, the duty of an advisor is to advise competently, accurately, and fully.' *Spinks v Canada* (1996) 134 DLR (4th) 223 at 229–230, per Linden JA (FCA)

ESCAPE

[For 11 Halsbury's Laws (4th edn) para 967 see now 11(1) Halsbury's Laws (4th edn) (Reissue) para 325.]

Rule in Rylands v Fletcher

[For 32 Halsbury's Laws (4th edn) paras 341, 342 see now 34 Halsbury's Laws (4th edn) (Reissue) paras 42–43.]

ESCHEAT

[For 39 Halsbury's Laws (4th edn) para 597 see now 39(2) Halsbury's Laws (4th edn) (Reissue) para 254.]

ESCROW

[For 12 Halsbury's Laws (4th edn) para 1332 see now 13 Halsbury's Laws (4th edn) (Reissue) para 36.]

Australia 'A deed delivered in escrow is delivered conditionally, to take effect or become operative when a specified event occurs or some condition is fulfilled. It binds the maker of the deed, who cannot subsequently resile, and once the condition is fulfilled the deed becomes binding absolutely: see *Butterworths Australian Legal Dictionary* (1997) p 429, citing *Monarch Petroleum NL v Citco Australia Petroleum Ltd* [1986] WAR 310; *Hooker Industrial Developments Pty Ltd v Trustees of the Christian Bros* [1997] 2 NSWLR 109; *Alan Estates Ltd v WG Stores Ltd* [1982] Ch 511. The statement that a deed is held in escrow expresses a legal conclusion.' *Vickery v JJP Custodians Pty Ltd* (2002) 11 BPR 20,333; BC200205296; [2002] NSWSC 782 at [10], per Austin J

ESTABLISHMENT

[An appeal to cancel the registration of care homes under the Care Standards Act 2000, s 3 of which provides for the circumstances in which an 'establishment' is a care home.] '[4] On appeal to the Care Standards Tribunal, Futures referred to s 3 of the 2000 Act which reads as follows:

"**3.** (1) For the purposes of this Act, an establishment is a care home if it provides accommodation, together with nursing or personal care, for any of the following persons.

(2) They are–(a) persons who are or have been ill; (b) persons who have or have

had a mental disorder; (c) persons who are disabled or infirm; (d) persons who are or have been dependent on alcohol or drugs.

(3) But an establishment is not a care home if it is–(a) a hospital; (b) an independent clinic; or (c) a children's home, or if it is of a description excepted by regulations."

'[5] Futures contended that the 11 homes no longer functioned as care homes as defined in s 3 as they provided supported living. That contention was based upon the reorganisation that had taken place within the Alternative Group. The freehold of the houses had been transferred to Housing with Futures providing care. Housing had then granted an assured tenancy to each of the residents. Put shortly, Features contended that because the accommodation element was provided by means of an assured tenancy the establishment ceased to be a care home as defined by s 3.

'[6] The hearing before the tribunal lasted 11 days and involved many issues ranging from submissions on onus of proof to human rights and investigation of the tenancies. The tribunal concluded:

"108. We have reached the unanimous decision that the 11 homes are establishments providing accommodation together with nursing or personal care for persons with a mental disorder (s 3(1) Care Standards Act 2000)… "

…

'[15] The appellants did not rely upon the division of responsibility between Housing and Futures. They argued their case upon the basis that Housing and Futures with their houses were an 'establishment'. They submitted that once a tenancy was granted, the relationship between them and the tenants changed. The tenants occupied their homes as of right not under licences. It followed that the tenants were being provided with care in their own homes. That being so, neither Housing nor Futures were providing accommodation within the meaning of that word in s 3 of the 2000 Act …

'[16] The appellants submitted that Housing and Futures did not supply accommodation. They were a domiciliary care agency supplying care to them in their own homes.

'[17] The judge rejected that submission. He put forward ([2004] All ER (D) 116 (Nov) at [30]) this working definition of the word establishment as used in s 3 of the 2000 Act: ' "a place, including a building, in which organised activities are

conducted" and "the conduct of organised activities in a place, including a building."' He went on as follows:

"[31] The 'establishment' or 'it' must provide accommodation together with 'nursing or personal care'. As far as accommodation is concerned, it is provided by a room and facilities within a building which the owner permits the resident to occupy and make use of. As far as nursing or personal care is concerned, they have to be provided by a person or persons. Accommodation and care must be provided 'together', but they need not be provided by the same company or individual. Although 'person' is referred to in the singular in s 11(1), the Interpretation Act 1978 permits that singular to include the plural. Thus, as the tribunal held, there was nothing to prevent an establishment from being carried on by two companies, Alternative Housing and Alternative Futures together. Both could carry it on, and if they did so, both required to be registered. In fact, as the facts found by the tribunal and the terms of the tenancy agreements show, both accommodation and services were to be provided, and were provided, by Alternative Housing."

'[18] Mr Berkley submitted the judge's view was contrary to the meaning of s 3. Neither Housing nor Futures were providing accommodation for the purposes of s 3 of the 2000 Act. Their buildings were occupied by the appellants, not as residential institutions, but comprised separate dwellings. The intention of the legislature expressed in the 2000 Act and in the regulations under the 2000 Act (the Care Homes Regulations 2001, SI 2001/3965) was to offer a range of different models for living and imposed different schemes of regulation upon residential care homes, domiciliary care agencies and other agencies and establishments.

'[19] Mr Roger McCarthy QC for the commission supported the conclusion of the judge. He drew attention to the consequences of the appellants' submissions, namely that it would be impossible for a person to be a tenant in a care home whether or not the lessor and care provider were the same person. It followed that an establishment could move away from being a registered care home by granting assured tenancies, even though the residents' needs and circumstances were unchanged and there was no actual difference in the way that the care was provided.

'[20] Mr McCarthy submitted, rightly in my view, that the word establishment did not have a technical meaning and therefore should be given its ordinary meaning. However that word must be construed in the context of s 3(1) and as part of it. As such an "establishment" must include a building to be a home, but can include a controller or organiser formed as a partnership, a company or companies. The word is wide enough to encompass Housing and Futures and their houses.' *R (on the application of Moore) v Care Standards Tribunal* [2005] EWCA Civ 627 at [4]–[6], [15]–[20], [2005] 3 All ER 428, per Sir William Aldous

ESTATE

[For 39 Halsbury's Laws (4th edn) para 302 see now 39(2) Halsbury's Laws (4th edn) (Reissue) para 2.]

Australia '[105] The starting point of the analysis in *Schaefer v Schuhmann* [1972] AC 572 at 585 was the assumption that, whilst the legislation contained no definition of the "estate" out of which the court is empowered to make provision, the term "estate" could not mean "the gross estate passing to the executor" but must be given a confined meaning, to identify only "the net estate" which is "available to answer the dispositions made by the will". It may be significant that s 1(1) of the Inheritance (Family Provision) Act 1938 (UK) (since repealed by the Inheritance (Provision for Family and Dependants) Act 1975 (UK)) spoke of provision "out of the testator's net estate" and in s 5(1) "net estate" was said to mean:

> "all the property of which a testator had power to dispose by his will (otherwise than by virtue of a special power of appointment) less the amount of his funeral, testamentary and administration expenses, debts and liabilities and estate duty payable out of his estate on his death".

But the NSW Act at issue in *Schaefer* did not contain these provisions. Nor does the Inheritance Act.

'[106] However that may be, there is no reason to confine the South Australian statutory expression "estate" in this way. The detailed provisions in the legislation respecting the nature and extent of the orders which may be made and the effect given to such orders, as explained in the subsequent decisions in Easterbrook and Schultz, suggest the contrary.

...

'[170] It was also suggested in argument that because s 10 of the Act provides that any provision made by the court is to operate and take effect as if

it were a will or a codicil executed immediately before death, it should be inferred that the Act was intended to operate as if the testator had, in effect, resolved, and was entitled to resolve, to renounce his contractual obligations at the moment before death. To that I would give the answer that the majority of their Lordships did in *Schaefer* in respect of the similar provision under consideration there, that the presence of such a section is instead, a contrary indication. Of it, their Lordships said at 585:

> "The Act contains no definition of the 'estate' out of which the court is empowered by s 3(1) to make provision for members of the family. It is, however, clear that it cannot mean the gross estate passing to the executor but must be confined to the net estate available to answer the dispositions made by the will. Again if one reads the section without having in mind the particular problem created by dispositions made in pursuance of previous contracts the language suggests that what the court is given power to do is to make such provision for members of the testator's family as the testator ought to have made, and could have made, but failed to make. The view that the court is not being given power to do something which the testator could not effectually have done himself receives strong support from s 4(1) which says that a provision made under the Act is to operate and take effect as if it had been made by a codicil executed by the testator immediately before his death. That being the apparent meaning of the Act their Lordships pass to consider what are the rights of a person on whom a testator has agreed for valuable consideration under a bona fide contract to confer a benefit by will.".' *Barns v Barns* [2003] HCA 9 per Gummow and Hayne JJ; BC200300694

ESTATE OR INTEREST

New Zealand 'The reference in s 101(6) of the Property Law Act to "an estate or interest which has priority over the mortgage" must at least include an estate or interest as defined in s 2 of the Land Transfer Act, that is to say a mortgage under that Act, and does not, in the present case at least, add to what is set out in s 105 of the Land Transfer Act [1952].' *Bank of New Zealand v Development Finance Corpn of New Zealand* [1988] 1 NZLR 495 at 503, CA, per cur

ESTIMATE

Australia 'The concept of "estimate" does not involve arbitrarily seizing upon any figure. What is involved is the formation of a judgment or opinion based upon reason. That judgment or opinion must necessarily be made bona fide but it need not be exact, for the process of estimation involves a process of approximation.' *Australia and New Zealand Banking Group Ltd v Federal Commissioner of Taxation* (1994) 119 ALR 727 at 741, per Hill J

ESTOPPEL *SEE ALSO* RES JUDICATA

[For 16 Halsbury's Laws (4th edn) para 1501 see now 16(2) Halsbury's Laws (4th edn) (Reissue) para 951.]

By agency

[For 1 Halsbury's Laws (4th edn) para 725 see now 1(2) Halsbury's Laws (4th edn) (Reissue) para 29.]

By approbation

[For 16 Halsbury's Laws (4th edn) para 1507 see now 16(2) Halsbury's Laws (4th edn) (Reissue) para 962.]

By deed

[For 16 Halsbury's Laws (4th edn) para 1504 see now 16(2) Halsbury's Laws (4th edn) (Reissue) para 954.]

Feeding the estoppel

[For 16 Halsbury's Laws (4th edn) para 1505 see now 16(2) Halsbury's Laws (4th edn) (Reissue) para 1033.]

By record

[For 16 Halsbury's Laws (4th edn) para 1503 see now 16(2) Halsbury's Laws (4th edn) (Reissue) para 953.]

Promissory

[For 16 Halsbury's Laws (4th edn) para 1514 see now 16(2) Halsbury's Laws (4th edn) (Reissue) para 958.]

Cause of action estoppel

'Cause of action estoppel arises where the cause of action in the latter proceedings is identical to that in the earlier proceedings, the latter having been between the same parties or their privies and having involved the same subject matter. In such a case the bar is absolute in relation to all points decided unless fraud or collusion is alleged, such as to justify setting aside the earlier judgment. The discovery of new factual matter which could not have been found out by reasonable diligence for use in the earlier proceedings does not, according to the law of England, permit the latter to be reopened. The rule in Scotland, which recognises the doctrine of res noviter veniens ad notitiam is different: see *Phosphate Sewage Co Ltd v Molleson* (1879) 4 App Cas 801 at 814, per Earl Cairns LC. There is no authority there, however, for the view that a change in the law can constitute res noviter. The principles upon which cause of action estoppel is based are expressed in the maxims nemo debet bis vexari pro una et eadem causa and interest rei publicae ut finis sit litium. Cause of action estoppel extends also to points which might have been but were not raised and decided in the earlier proceedings for the purpose of establishing or negativing the existence of a cause of action.' *Arnold v National Westminster Bank plc* [1991] 3 All ER 41 at 46, HL, per Lord Keith of Kinkel

Issue estoppel

[The following extract should be substituted for that given in Main Volume 2, p 181 for *Mills v Cooper*.] 'This doctrine, so far as it affects civil proceedings, may be stated thus: a party to civil proceedings is not entitled to make, as against the other party, an assertion, whether of fact or of the legal consequences of facts, the correctness of which is an essential element in his cause of action or defence, if the same assertion was an essential element in his previous cause of action or defence in previous civil proceedings between the same parties or their predecessors in title and was found by a court of competent jurisdiction in such previous civil proceedings to be incorrect, unless further material which is relevant to the correctness or incorrectness of the assertion and could not by reasonable diligence have been adduced by that party in the previous proceedings has since become available to him.' *Mills v Cooper* [1967] 2 All ER 100 at 104, per Diplock LJ

'In order to create an estoppel of that kind [issue estoppel], three requirements have to be satisfied. The first requirement is that the judgment in the earlier action relied on as creating an estoppel must be (a) of a court of competent jurisdiction, (b) final and conclusive and (c) on the merits. The second requirement is that the parties (or privies) in the earlier action relied on as creating an estoppel and those in the later action in which that estoppel is raised as a bar must be the same. The third requirement is that the issue in the later action in which the estoppel is raised as a bar must be the same issue as that decided by the judgment in the earlier action.' *DSV Silo-und Verwaltungsgesellschaft MBH v Sennar (owners), The Sennar* [1985] 2 All ER 104 at 110, HL, per Lord Brandon

[An extract from the speech of Lord Diplock in the above case appears in Main Volume 2. In the case citation the name of the vessel was incorrectly printed as '*The Sennan*'.]

Per rem judicatam

'The particular type of estoppel relied on by the husband is estoppel per rem judicatam. This is a generic term which in modern law includes two species. The first species, which I will call "cause of action estoppel", is that which prevents a party to an action from asserting or denying, as against the other party, the existence of a particular cause of action, the non-existence or existence of which has been determined by a court of competent jurisdiction in previous litigation between the same parties. If the cause of action was determined to exist, i.e., judgment was given on it, it is said to be merged in the judgment, or, for those who prefer Latin, transit in rem judicatam. If it was determined not to exist, the unsuccessful plaintiff can no longer assert that it does; he is estopped per rem judicatam. This is simply an application of the rule of public policy expressed in the Latin maxim, "nemo debet bis vexari pro una et eadem causa". In this application of the maxim, causa bears its literal Latin meaning. The second species, which I will call "issue estoppel", is an extension of the same rule of public policy. There are many causes of action which can only be established by proving that two or more different conditions are fulfilled. Such causes of action involve as many separate issues between the parties as there are conditions to be fulfilled by the plaintiff in order to establish his cause of action; and there may be cases where the fulfilment of an identical condition is a requirement common to two or more different causes of action. If in litigation on one such cause of action any of such separate issues whether a particular condition has been fulfilled is determined

by a court of litigation, neither party can, in subsequent litigation between them on any cause of action which depends on the fulfilment of the identical condition, assert that the condition was fulfilled if the court has in the first litigation determined that it was not, or deny that it was fulfilled if the court in the first litigation determined that it was.' *Thoday v Thoday* [1964] 1 All ER 341 at 352, CA, per Diplock LJ

[Applied in *Thrasyvoulou v Secretary of State for the Environment* [1990] 1 All ER 65 at 75–76, HL, per Lord Bridge of Harwich.]

ESTOVERS

[For 16 Halsbury's Laws (4th edn) para 579 see now 6 Halsbury's Laws (4th edn) (2003 Reissue) para 474.]

EVERY ALIENATION OF PROPERTY

New Zealand [Section 60(1) of the Property Law Act 1952 refers to 'every alienation of property with intent to defraud creditors'.] 'I can see no justification for reading those words so as necessarily to exclude transactions to which a foreign person is a party …

'… the expression "every alienation of property" must bear its literal and natural meaning.' *Springfield Acres Ltd (In Liquidation) v Abacus (Hong Kong) Ltd* [1994] 3 NZLR 502 at 508–509, per Henry J

EVERY PARTY

Canada [A collecting bank claimed to be a party to a cheque paid in due course.] 'The words "every other party thereto or named therein" are broad enough to describe a collecting bank. Those words suggest that the section applies to two classes of parties, those named in the cheque such as the drawer and those not named in the cheque such as the collecting bank.

'… if the effect of s 48(4) [of the *Bills of Exchange Act*, RSC 1985, c B-4] was to extend the protection from proceedings beyond the drawee to other parties such as the collecting bank, then the words "party thereto" have meaning and the concluding phrase would operate to allow an action to proceed against a party, in the absence of notice by the drawer, if that party had previously commenced proceedings to protect its own rights.' *Enoch Band of the Stony Plain Indian Reserve No 135 v Morin* (1995) 128 DLR (4th) 754 at 763, 764, Alta QB, per Costigan J

EVERYONE

New Zealand [Section 11 of the New Zealand Bill of Rights Act 1990 states that 'Everyone has the right to refuse to undergo any medical treatment'.] '"Everyone" in respect of s 11 must mean "every person who is competent to consent".' *Re S* [1992] 1 NZLR 363 at 374, per Barker J

New Zealand [New Zealand Bill of Rights Act 1990, s 11.] '... it is sufficient for present purposes to say that s 11 of the New Zealand Bill of Rights Act 1990 provides that ... "Everyone has the right to refuse to undergo any medical treatment" and that this is in accord with the position at common law. "Everyone" in this context means everyone who is competent to do so, and if persons are incompetent then in certain cases consent can be given on behalf of that person by the Court.' *Re G* [1997] 2 NZLR 201 at 210, per Fraser J

EVICTION

[For 27 Halsbury's Laws (4th edn) para 326 see now 27(1) Halsbury's Laws (4th edn) (Reissue) para 238.]

EVIDENCE

Refreshing memory

'In our judgment ... it should be open to the judge, in the exercise of his discretion and in the interests of justice, to permit a witness who has begun to give evidence to refresh his memory from a statement made near to the time of events in question, even though it does not come within the definition of contemporaneous, provided he is satisfied (1) that the witness indicates that he cannot now recall the details of events because of the lapse of time since they took place, (2) that he made a statement much nearer the time of the events and that the contents of the statement represented his recollection at the time he made it, (3) that he had not read the statement before coming into the witness box and (4) that he wished to have an opportunity to read the statement before he continued to give evidence. We do not think that it matters whether the witness withdraws from the witness box and reads his statement, as he would do if he had had the opportunity before entering the witness box, or whether he reads it in the witness box. What is important is that, if the former course is adopted, no communication must be had with the witness, other than to see that he can read the statement in peace. Moreover, if either

course is adopted, the statement must be removed from him when he comes to give his evidence and he should not be permitted to refer to it again, unlike a contemporaneous statement which may be used to refresh memory while giving evidence.' *R v Da Silva* [1990] 1 All ER 29 at 33, CA, per cur

EXAMINATION

Australia [Section 353A(2) of the Crimes Act 1900 (NSW) provides that a medical practitioner may make an 'examination' of a person who is in custody where there are reasonable grounds for believing that an examination of the person will afford evidence of the commission of a crime or an offence.] 'Considering merely the words of s 353A when enacted in 1924, my opinion would be that an examination of the person of someone in custody as permitted by subs (2) would permit an external examination involving an examination by eye and by touch. The words of subs (2) do not suggest to me an intention to make lawful the taking of some part of the body itself from within the body of the person in lawful custody. None of the subsequent amendments to the section, in my opinion, enlarges the authorisation made by subs (2) when enacted in 1924.

'My impression of the meaning of the words is influenced both by my understanding of what an examination, as understood in ordinary language, would have meant in 1924 and by recognition that the section plainly, as noted by the Court of Criminal Appeal in *Re Hass* [1972] 1 NSWLR 589, made lawful *some* actions by a legally qualified medical practitioner acting at the request of an appropriate police officer which would not have been lawful in absence of the section. The extent of the actions thus converted from being unlawful to lawful was limited by subs (2) in a number of ways ...

'None of these conditions suggests to me that the statutory authority to commit what in technical terms would be, but for the statutory authority, an assault upon the person in custody, went to the extent of authorising the taking from within the body of person in custody part of the body, namely blood.' *Fernando v Commissioner of Police* (1995) 78 A Crim R 84 at 68–69, per Priestley JA

EXCEPTIONAL

[The Crime (Sentences) Act 1997, s 2 provides for a life sentence to be imposed where a person is convicted of a second serious offence, unless the court is of the opinion that there are 'exceptional circumstances' which justify its not doing so.] 'We must construe "exceptional" as an ordinary, familiar English adjective, and not as a term of art. It describes a circumstance which is such as to form an exception, which is out of the ordinary course, or unusual, or special, or uncommon. To be exceptional, a circumstance need not be unique, or unprecedented, or very rare; but it cannot be one that is regularly, or routinely, or normally encountered.' (*R v Kelly* [1999] 2 All ER 13 at 20, CA, per Lord Bingham of Cornhill CJ

Australia [Circumstances in which accounting period for taxation purposes can be changed.] '[62] Wilcox J [in *Nikac v Minister for Immigration and Ethnic Affairs* (1988) 20 FCR 65 ("Nikac") at 81] said that "the term 'exceptional circumstances' postulates a criterion which is both vague and subjective"; that although his Honour thought the circumstances "not exceptional", it was "impossible to categorise a different view as being devoid of plausible justification"; and that "[l]ike beauty, 'exceptional circumstances' lies in the eye of the beholder" (all at 81). This passage was referred to with approval by a Full Court in *Hicks v Aboriginal and Torres Strait Islander Commission* (2001) 110 FCR 582 at 586–587.

...

'[76] In my opinion, however, the word "exceptional" is not used in the Taxation Rulings or the Statement of Reasons merely with the literal and neutral dictionary meaning of "pertaining to an exception", as the Commissioner's submission suggests. The significance of the use of the word "exceptional" must be assessed in the context in which it is used. IT 2360 used the word "rare" (para 10) (see [20] above) and IT 2497 uses the expression "the most exceptional circumstances" (para 4) (see [21] above). This last expression shows that the word "exceptional" was being used in a qualitative sense which admits of degrees of exceptionality. I suggest that the expression "most exceptional" bears a meaning akin to "very rare".

'[77] In the Statement of Reasons Mr Thaler referred to both Taxation Rulings. In my opinion, when he used the word "exceptional" in the Statement of Reasons, he was using it in the sense similar to that of "rare". A particular illustration is his statement that IT 2497 "clearly precluded entities such as these from being granted SAPs except in cases where exceptional circumstances existed". The category of taxpayers, "large investment or property (unit) trusts" is being addressed. Mr Thaler notes that this particular category of taxpayer has already been determined by IT 2497 not to be allowed to adopt an SAP unless the circumstances of a particular trust make it "exceptional". An

exception to the firm determination that has previously been made in respect of such a class of taxpayers can be properly described as a "rare" case.' *MLC Investments Ltd v Cmr of Taxation* [2003] FCA 1487 per Lindgren J; BC200307716

EXCEPTIONAL CIRCUMSTANCES

Australia 'The Administrative Appeals Tribunal has considered the meaning of "exceptional circumstances" in *Re O'May and Australian Fisheries Management Authority* (1999) 57 ALD 181 and in *Re Glendon Lane Pty Ltd and Australian Fisheries Management Authority* (1995) 36 ALD 376. It was also considered in *Re Secretary, Department of Family and Community Services and Selke* (1993) 31 ALD 770; 18 AAR 457 and *Re Secretary, Department of Family and Community Services and Tran* (1991) 23 ALD 449; 13 AAR 346. In summary, I am satisfied "exceptional circumstances"; means to "form an exception; unusual instance; extraordinary".' *Re Graham and Australian Fisheries Management Authority* 71 ALD 700, [2002] AATA 862 at [29] per J Handley (Senior Member) and C Ermert (Member)

Australia 'The test which I am compelled to apply in considering whether to grant bail is a stringent one. For many offences bail is presumed unless there is some argument against it. For more serious offences it is necessary for the Court to be satisfied that there is an acceptable risk. For even more serious offences, including trafficking in drugs in a commercial quantity and murder and treason, it is necessary that the Court be satisfied that "exceptional circumstances" exist. Thus, by reason of the law, I have a duty to adopt a high hurdle in considering bail in this case.

'It has been said that exceptional circumstances should not be defined; but, rather, one should examine the facts and see if those facts show circumstances which are exceptional ...' *Re Application for Bail by Barbaro* [2004] VSC 404 at [7], per Morris J; BC200407237

New Zealand [Section 17(2)(c) of the Legal Aid Act 1969.] '... the term "exceptional circumstances" when used in a statute is never free from difficulty. As a matter of general approach, it is usually construed as meaning something like "quite out of the ordinary".' *Awa v Independent News Auckland Ltd* [1996] 2 NZLR 184 at 186 per Hammond J

EXCESS OF JURISDICTION

Australia 'The expressions "excess of jurisdiction" and "want of jurisdiction" are well understood.

The expressions are not terms of art. Speaking generally, it can be said that there is a "want of jurisdiction" when a court or tribunal does an act which is beyond its general power or authority and that there is an "excess of jurisdiction when it does an act, the doing of which is within its general authority or power, but which was done in breach of the conditions which authorise the doing of acts of that class or nature": *Public Service Association Case* (above) per McHugh J at 164 and the cases there cited.' *Tsimpinos v Allianz (Aust) Workers' Compensation (SA) Pty Ltd* (2004) 88 SASR 311, (2004) 233 LSJS 300, [2004] SASC 124 at [28], per Debelle J; BC200402488

EXCESSIVE DEMANDS

Canada *Issue 1: May a finding of 'excessive demands' be based exclusively on the predicted additional cost of the health services that an applicant for permanent residence in Canada, if admitted, might reasonably be expected to require?*

'[15] In *Yogeswaran, supra*, McKeown J. seems only to have considered the cost of the special education required by a visa applicant's dependent son in reaching his conclusion that the son's admission would impose "more than normal" and, therefore, excessive demands on social services. While this Court affirmed *Yogeswaran, supra*, it did not expressly address this point. Accordingly, I do not regard it as determinative of the issue raised by counsel in this appeal.

'[16] More recently, in *Pervez v. Canada (Minister of Citizenship and Immigration)*, 2001 FCT 1420 [summarized 110 A.C.W.S. (3d) 892], Simpson J. stated (*supra*, at para. 14):

[14] The applicant also argues that the Medical Officer's report was unreasonable because it considered only the cost element of the excessive demand. However, given the high costs of dialysis and transplant surgery, it is my view that the report was sufficient when it addressed only cost. I should add that, had the Medical Officer addressed the availability of transplant and dialysis services, I am confident that his conclusion about excessive demand would not have changed.

'[17] In her reasons, Simpson J. did not refer to the cases decided in the Trial Division that counsel for Ms. Deol says establish that cost alone cannot constitute excessive demands and should be followed in this case. Before examining these decisions, I should note that s. 22 of the *Immigration Regulations, 1978*, SOR/78–172, purports to prescribe a non-exhaustive list of factors to be considered by medical officers in determining whether a person is medically inadmissible. These factors include limitations on the supply of the health services likely to be required by an applicant for a permanent residence visa, but not, explicitly, their cost.

'[18] However, it was held in *Ismaili v. Canada (Minister of Citizenship and Immigration)* (1995), 100 F.T.R. 139, that the Minister has no statutory power to enact regulations dealing with medical inadmissibility on the ground of excessive demands, but only on the ground of public health and safety. Thus, there is no statutory definition of "excessive demands". The correctness of *Ismaili, supra*, is not challenged in this appeal. Accordingly, it is important to treat with care "excessive demands" cases decided before *Ismaili, supra*, which relied on s. 22, including *Jim v. Canada (Solicitor General)* (1993), 69 F.T.R. 252.

'[19] Of the cases decided after *Ismaili, supra*, counsel for Ms. Deol relies particularly on *Poon v. Canada (Minister of Citizenship and Immigration)* (2000), 198 F.T.R. 56 at para. 21, where Pelletier J. (as he then was) said:

Cost alone cannot be the determining factor. If it were, one would expect the statute and the regulations to refer to excessive cost instead of excessive demand.

This view of the applicable law has been followed recently in *Manto v. Canada (Minister of Citizenship and Immigration)*, 2001 FCT 572 at paras. 28–29 [reported 205 F.T.R. 165].

'[20] However, on closer examination these cases do not seem to me to decide that a person who requires an expensive but low demand service is not for that reason medically inadmissible. Rather, they are authority for the more limited proposition that, since both cost and availability are relevant to determining the existence of excessive demands, the record must indicate that evidence relating to both factors was considered by the medical officer. Other cases relied on in this manner by counsel for Ms. Deol also seem to me to make this point: *Fei v. Canada (Minister of Citizenship and Immigration)*, [1998] 1 F.C. 274, and *Shan v. Canada (Minister of Citizenship and Immigration)* (1998), 153 F.T.R. 238.

'[21] *Pervez, supra*, may be difficult to reconcile with these cases in that Simpson J. specifically stated that it was unnecessary for the medical report to go beyond the question of cost. However, she was also prepared to conclude that, on the facts before her, a consideration of availability would not have changed the decision.

'[22] In my opinion, cost alone can constitute "excessive demands" under subpara. 19(1)(*a*)(ii). In *Poon* (*supra*, at para. 21), Pelletier J. agreed that, even though not mentioned in the Act or the Regulations, cost is a relevant consideration. The "excessive demands" limb of medical inadmissibility expresses a legislative concern to protect from unusually high demands the public resources devoted to health care.

'[23] In addition, I would note that the statutory phrase is "excessive demands", not "excessive demand". The singular, "excessive demand", might well have been regarded as the correlative of "inadequate supply". However, it requires no linguistic stretch to interpret the plural, "excessive demands", as including both the cost and the availability of health services that a visa applicant is likely to require if admitted to Canada.' *Deol v Canada* (*Minister of Citizenship & Immigration*) (2002) 215 DLR (4th) 675 at 684–686 (FCA), per Evans JA

EXCHANGE OF CONTRACTS

'In my opinion, the authorities show that even if the expression "exchange of contracts" is not a term of art, it is a well-recognised concept understood both by lawyers and laymen which has the following features.

(1) Each party draws up or is given a document which incorporates all the terms which they have agreed, and which is intended to record their proposed contract. The terms that have been agreed may have been agreed either orally or in writing or partly orally or partly in writing.

(2) The documents are referred to as "contracts" or "parts of contract", although they need not be so entitled. They are intended to take effect as formal documents of title and must be capable on their face of being fairly described as contracts having that effect.

(3) Each party signs his part in the expectation that the other party has also executed or will execute a corresponding part incorporating the same terms.

(4) At the time of execution neither party is bound by the terms of the document which he has executed, it being their mutual intention that neither will be bound until the executed parts are exchanged.

(5) The act of exchange is a formal delivery by each party of its part into the actual or constructive possession of the other with the intention that the parties will become actually bound when exchange occurs, but not before.

(6) The manner of exchange may be agreed and determined by the parties. The traditional method was by mutual exchange across the table, both parties or their solicitors being present. It also commonly takes place by post, especially where the parties or their solicitors are at a distance. In such a case exchange is sequential and does not take place until the second document to be dispatched has been received or posted (see *Eccles v Bryant & Pollock* [1947] 2 All ER 865 at 866, [1948] Ch 93 at 97–98 per Lord Greene MR). Exchange can also take place by telephone, in which case it will be simultaneous (see *Domb v Isoz* [1980] 1 All ER 942 at 949, [1980] Ch 548 at 558 per Buckley LJ).' *Commission for the New Towns v Cooper* (*GB*) *Ltd* [1995] 2 All ER 929 at 950–951, CA, per Stuart-Smith LJ

EXCLUSIONARY PROVISION

Australia '[6] S 4D of the Act defines an "exclusionary provision". It includes a provision of a contract, arrangement or understanding made, or proposed, between persons, any two or more of whom are competitive with each other, which has the purpose of preventing, restricting or limiting the supply of goods or services to, or the acquisition of goods or services from, particular persons or classes of persons, by all or any of the parties.

'[7] The word "provision" is used here and elsewhere in Pt IV in a comprehensive rather than any technical sense reflecting its usage in contract law. It invites attention to the content of what has been, or is to be, agreed, arranged or understood, rather than any particular form of expression of that content adopted, or to be adopted, by the parties. This is emphasised by the statement in s 4(1) that "in relation to an understanding" provision means "any matter forming part of the understanding".

...

'[9] The definition of exclusionary provision in s 4D encompasses more than that identified above but it is not necessary to consider those wider applications. What is important is that the definition of exclusionary provisions extends to provisions which deal with the supply or the acquisition of goods or services. Accordingly, s 45(2) prohibited corporations who are competitors from making a contract, or arrangement, or arriving at an understanding, which had the purpose or effect of restricting or limiting the supply, or the acquisition, of goods or services, to or from particular persons. By contrast, the form of exclusive dealing said to be relevant in this appeal (that described in s 47(4)) does not deal with conditions which restrict both supply and acquisition. It deals with the acquisition of goods or services on the condition that the person from whom the goods or services are acquired will not supply goods or services to particular persons (as distinct from acquire goods or services from them).

...

'[32] The answer to the inquiry just described is not dictated by the particular drafting adopted by parties. There may be no written record of an agreement, let alone of any arrangement made by, or understanding reached between, the parties. Where there is no written record, there could be no resort to drafting. Further, and no less importantly, it is necessary to recognise that "contract, arrangement or understanding" encompasses such a wide range of consensual arrangements that the word "provision" and cognate expressions cannot be understood as confined to what might appear as a single clause of a written agreement. "Provision", when it is used in s 45(6), directs attention to the content of the agreement, arrangement or understanding rather than the manner of its expression. *Visy Paper Pty Ltd v Australian Competition and Consumer Commission* [2003] HCA 59 per Gleeson CJ, McHugh, Gummow and Hayne JJ; BC200305828

EXCLUSIVELY

Australia 'The word "exclusively" connotes a degree of absoluteness. It is an adverb meaning "in an exclusive sense or manner; solely". Exclusive means "excluding all but what is specified", generally see the Shorter Oxford English Dictionary. The Macquarie Dictionary is even more emphatic; thus "not admitting of something else"; "incompatible"; "limited to the object or objects designated"; "shutting out all other activities".' *Federal Commissioner of Taxation v Manchester Unity IOOF* (1993) 113 ALR 113 at 126, per Northrop J

EXECUTION

Australia 'The word "execution" is generally understood as signifying the enforcement of or giving effect to a judgment or orders of a court ...'

Osborne Computer Corp Pty Ltd v Airroad Distribution Pty Ltd (1995) 37 NSWLR 382 at 387, per Rolfe J

EXECUTOR

[For 17 Halsbury's Laws (4th edn) para 702 see now 17(2) Halsbury's Laws (4th edn) (Reissue) para 2.]

EXISTING STATE OF THE LAW

Australia 'The phrase "the existing state of the law" embraces the then understanding of the common law. In this way there is discerned the state of affairs for the remedy or establishment of which the statute was designed.' *Wik Peoples v Queensland* (1996) 141 ALR 129 at 222; 71 ALJR 173, per Gummow J

EXPECT

Australia 'The meaning of the word "expect" should not lead to difficulty. It is to be understood according to its usage in ordinary parlance, namely, "to regard as likely to happen" or "to expect to find" or "to expect that it will turn out that": see Macquarie Dictionary, Shorter Oxford English Dictionary and Fowler's Modern English Usage, 2nd edn and *Commonwealth of Australia v Friedrich* (1991) 5 ACSR 115 at 126–7. Thus what s 556 [of the Companies (SA) Code] requires to be provide is whether a reasonable and prudent director of the company has reasonable grounds for regarding it as likely to happen that the company will not be able to pay its debts as and when they fall due.' *Carrier Air Conditioning Pty Ltd v Kurda* (1993) 11 ACSR 247 at 250, per Debelle J

EXPECTATION

Australia 'The distinction between "expectation" loss and "reliance" loss for the purposes of the law of contract is well recognised. However, it is a distinction that is apt to mislead if transposed into other contexts. Contrary to what might be thought, the term "expectation" loss does not indicate that damages are payable simply for thwarted expectations. Rather, damages are payable for the loss involved in non-performance of the contract. Even if a contract is not susceptible of specific performance, the other party is legally entitled to expect its performance. Hence the expression "expectation loss"!

'The matter may be put another way. Non-performance is, in effect, the loss of a contractual promise which, itself, is a valuable right. That loss must be compensated by an award of damages in the sum that represents the value of that right.' *Marks v GIO Australia Holdings Ltd* (1998) 158 ALR 333 at 338–339; 73 ALJR 12; BC9805922, per Gaudron J

EXPEDIENT

Canada 'In his oral submissions, counsel for the Crown submitted that "not to be expedient" could be equated with unfettered discretion. That is clearly not the case. If that had been the intent of the Legislature it could have, in s 8(1) [of the *Public Tender Act*], merely said "if the government funded body inviting the tender does not wish to award the contract to the preferred bidder" rather than "if it appears to the government funded body inviting the tender not to be expedient to award the contract to the preferred bidder." The Shorter Oxford English Dictionary defines "expedient" as "advantageous; fit, proper, or suitable to the circumstances of the case: Useful, politic, as opp. to just or right." I do not accept that the Legislature intended to use the word in the depreciative sense.I am satisfied that the meaning as used in the *Public Tender Act* is "whatever is suitable and appropriate in reason for the accomplishment of a specified object". (See Black's Law Dictionary.)' *Health Care Developers Inc v Newfoundland* (1996) 136 DLR (4th) 609 at 635, per Cameron JA (Nfld CA)

New Zealand [Criminal Justice Act 1985, s 75(2).] ' "Expedient" is frequently used in statutes … While there may be shades of meaning of the word, depending on the context, reference to standard dictionaries brings out its basic meaning … Clearly, "expedient" as used in the section sets a lower threshold than "necessary", a conclusion reinforced by the consideration that the legislature often employs the alternative standards of "necessary or expedient". . .' *R v Leitch* [1998] 1 NZLR 420 at 428–429, CA, per cur

EXPENDED FOR REPAIR

Canada [A fire insurer was liable only for the amount expended for repair.] 'Turning to the phrase "expended for repair", it is similarly not clear to me that these words should have the interpretation contended for by the insurer. In most cases of substantial property loss, an insured will be unable initially to bear the cost of replacement. The insured may borrow the money, or make other financial arrangements to pay those replacement costs. If, as suggested in *Machson, supra*, the rebuilding were financed through a mortgage loan, where the bank pays the builder, and the insured incurs a debt secured by a mortgage to the bank, one would think an insured entitled to recover under the language of this policy.' *Brkich & Brkich Enterprises Ltd v American Home Assurance Co* (1995) 127 DLR (4th) 115 at 132, BCCA, per Finch JA

EXPENDITURE

Canada '[10] As the Tribunal pointed out, the word "expenditures" is not defined in the Act. *Black's Law Dictionary*, 5th ed. defines the noun "expenditure" as:

> Spending or payment of money; the act of expending, disbursing, or laying out of money; payment.

'[11] It defines the verb "expend" as:

> To pay out, lay out, consume, use up; normally implying receiving something in return.

'[12] It defines the noun "expense" as:

> That which is expended, laid out or consumed. An outlay; charge; cost; price. The expenditure of money, time, labor, resources, and thought.

'[13] I am satisfied these definitions, with "expenditure" including the "spending of money" and "expend" including "consuming" and "using up", are broad enough to include the Board's internal operating costs of the Board's third party unit.

'[14] In the definitions of these words in the *Random House Dictionary of the English Language* (2nd ed. 1987), "consumption" is included in the definition of the word "expenditure" and "to use up" is included in the definition of the word "expend":

> Expenditure: 1. The act of expending; disbursement; consumption. 2. that which is expended; expense
> Expend: 1. to use up. 2. To pay out; disburse; spend
> Expense: 1. Cost or charge. 2. A cause or occasion of spending. 3. The act of expending; expenditure.'

Fowler v Nova Scotia (Workers' Compensation Board) [2004] NSJ No 271, 242 DLR (4th) 588 (CA), per Hamilton JA

EXPENSES

Australia 'The word "expenses" in the context of ss 90 and 91 [of the Australian Securities Commission Act 1989 (Cth)] bears its ordinary and natural meaning as being confined to moneys expended by a person or an obligation incurred by the person. It does not include sums which the person claims a right to charge against others for his own services: *Parr v Australasian Asiatic Trading & Engineering Co Pty Ltd* [1958] VR 198 at 200–1; *Attorney-General (NSW) v Hunter* [1983] 1 NSWLR 366 at 378–80.' *Westpac Banking Corp v Australian Securities Commission* (1997) 143 ALR 35 at 45, per Cooper J

EXPENSES OF THE WINDING UP

[The question arose whether tax liabilities arising during provisional liquidation were 'expenses of the winding up' for the purposes of the Insolvency Act 1986, s 156.] 'In *Re Mesco Properties Ltd* [1980] 1 All ER 117, [1980] 1 WLR 96 a company in compulsory winding up sold several properties at a profit and thus became liable for tax on the gains. The Court of Appeal held that since the tax was a consequence of the realisation of the company's assets in the winding up it was "a charge or expense incurred in the winding up of the company" for the purpose of the predecessor of s 156 of the Act. The same result should in my view apply whenever the tax liability is a consequence of the proper performance by the liquidator of his duties, for example where the liquidator continues the trading of the company in order to be able to sell its business in due course as a going concern.

'Is the position different where the tax liability is incurred as the result of the proper performance by a provisional liquidator of his duties? That turns on whether the provisional liquidator can be said to have been acting "in the winding up of the company", to use the words of s 156. I see no reason of principle against such a conclusion, given that once a winding-up order has been made the winding up is deemed to have commenced on the presentation of the petition (ie before the appointment of the provisional liquidator). More concretely, in the present case, the purpose of carrying on the business of the company was to preserve its goodwill, thus making possible in due course the sale of its business as a going concern as part of the liquidation.

'Indeed, it appears to be implicit in the insolvency legislation that all acts of the provisional liquidator in performance of his functions are expenses of the winding up. Rules 4.218(1)(f) and 4.30(3) treat all the remuneration of a provisional liquidator (without differentiation) expressly as an expense of the liquidation. And r 4.30(3) makes the same assumption for expenses 'incurred by' the provisional liquidator, even if—by apparent drafting oversight—such expenses are not mentioned in r 4.218(1).

'I therefore conclude that the court has power under s 156 to make an order for payment of these tax liabilities out of the assets and to determine their place in the order of priority.' *Re Grey Marlin Ltd* [1999] 4 All ER 429 at 433, per David Donaldson QC

EXPERIENCED

Australia '… In that case, the AAT [in *Re Slattery and Repatriation Commission* (1998) 52 ALD 90] said at 108:

> "The word 'witnessed' suggests that the person was present at the event involving real or present (ie actual) or threatened death. The word 'experienced' suggests that the person observed or encountered such an event and the word 'confronted' that he or she was faced with such an event."

To limit the definition of the word "experienced" in this way was plainly at odds with its ordinary and natural meaning.' *Woodward v Repatriation Commission* [2003] FCAFC 160 at [58], [59] per Black CJ, Weinberg and Selway JJ; BC200304136

EXPERIENCING A SEVERE STRESSOR

Australia '[39] The term "experiencing a severe stressor" is defined in cl 8 of the SoP [Statement of Principles] for PTSD [Post Traumatic Stress Disorder]. Cl 8 of the SoP defines that expression in the following terms:

> "'experiencing a severe stressor' means the person experienced, witnessed, or was confronted with an event or events that involved actual or threat of death or serious injury, or a threat to the person's, another person's, physical integrity.
> In the setting of service in the Defence Forces, or other service where the Veterans' Entitlement Act applies, events that qualify as stressors include:
> (i) threat of serious injury or death; or
> (ii) engagement with the enemy; or

(iii) witnessing casualties or participation in or observation of casualty clearance, atrocities or abusive violence."

'[40] The definition of "experiencing a severe stressor" in cl 8 of the SoP for Alcohol Dependence or Alcohol Abuse is in essentially the same terms, although it contains the qualification that the event or events might evoke intense "fear, helplessness or horror".

...

'[112] ... As a matter of ordinary English usage it may be easier to read the definition of "experiencing a severe stressor" as being entirely subjective than it is the definition of "stressful event" considered by North J.

...

'[122] The definition of "experiencing a severe stressor" has three elements that relate to a person's encounter with an event involving death – the person must have "experienced, witnessed or [have been] confronted with an event that involved death ...". Plainly enough, although the elements may overlap in any particular situation, the definition will be satisfied if any one of them is present. As a matter of ordinary language, the field that the definition is intended to cover is bounded by the three different elements. It follows that for the purposes of the definition a person may be "confronted with" an event that he or she has neither experienced nor witnessed.

'[123] In any event, as a matter of ordinary usage to be "confronted" with something means to be brought face to face with it either physically or, perhaps more commonly, in the mind. If the thing being confronted is an event, usage does not require that the person be present at the event she or he "confronts". This is no less the case when the confronting event is one involving death or serious injury.

...

'[137] In *Stoddart v Repatriation Commission* (2003) 197 ALR 283 ("Stoddart"), Mansfield J held that the AAT had erred in requiring that a "threat" be one that, judged objectively and remote from the circumstances and state of knowledge of the person experiencing it, has a real or actual prospect of resulting in death or serious injury. His Honour considered that by doing so the Tribunal had thereby imported into the concept of "threat" in the applicable SoPs more than was demanded by their wording and their purpose: see at [41].

'[138] Mansfield J observed:

"[47] It is not apparent to me why the SoPs should distinguish between events which ac-

tually involved the threat of death or serious injury leading to ALD [alcohol liver damage] or PTSD and events which were perceived (and for the sake of considering the contention, I assume reasonably perceived) as involving the threat of death or serious injury leading to ALD or PTSD. The respondent contends, and the tribunal accepted, that in the former case the conditions are consistent with an hypothesis of being war-caused, but in the latter case they should be seen beyond reasonable doubt as not consistent with an hypothesis of being war-caused. In this matter, if the applicant is believed about the occasions he referred to, his operational service was in an area where his vessel might come under attack (but did not) and battle stations were signalled and he feared for his personal integrity and suffered ALD and PTSD as a result.

...

"[50] In my judgment, the meaning of the word 'threat' as used in the definition of 'experiencing a severe stressor' does not require the construction or meaning contended for by the respondent and accepted by the tribunal. The adjectival clause 'that involved actual or threat of death or serious injury' explains the nature of the event or events which must be experienced. It contemplates an objective and assessable state of affairs. I do not think it provides for idiosyncratic and personal perceptions of events which, judged objectively, do not in fact fall within the adjectival clause. But it does not follow that the 'threat' there referred to must involve events which judged objectively and with full information involve an actual threat of death or serious injury ... That construction would appear to go beyond the purpose of SoPs. It would involve the Repatriation Medical Authority in the two SoPs being interpreted as saying (for example) that on medical-scientific evidence PTSD cannot be related to operational service where events actually experienced, and which a person with the knowledge and in the circumstances of a particular claimant could reasonably lead to that person perceiving a threat of death or serious injury or to physical integrity, did not, judged objectively and with full knowledge of all the circumstances, in fact amount to such a threat. Such an interpretation would lead to excluding from the scope of the word 'threat' a range of circumstances, some of which are referred to above, which common sense indicates are matters not directly within medical-scientific evidence. That is, if a threat of serious injury or death is perceived by a claimant from actual events experienced in circumstances where, judged objectively with the knowledge and in the circumstances of the claimant, it was reasonable to perceive the threat, I do not understand it to be a medical-scientific opinion that no reasonable hypothesis can be raised connecting the condition resulting from those events with them. The definition of 'sound medical-scientific evidence' in s 5AB(2) also indicates that the Repatriation Medical Authority would not intend to impose a prescriptive exclusion of the kind which would result from the interpretation of the SoPs which the tribunal adopted."

'[139] Mansfield J concluded that the AAT erred in law in its understanding of the expression "experiencing a severe stressor" in each of the relevant SoPs by requiring there to be an actual threat, judged objectively and with full knowledge of all the circumstances.. In his Honour's opinion, the definition extended to a person experiencing or being confronted with an event involving threat of death or serious injury (etc), if the event said to constitute the threat, judged objectively from the point of view of a reasonable person in the position of the applicant experiencing it, was capable of conveying, and did convey, the risk of death or serious injury. In other words, "experiencing" should be construed as having at least this partially subjective connotation.

'[140] It would be open to the AAT to conclude the situation involving Mr Woodward was similar, in relevant respects, to that considered by Mansfield J in Stoddart. It would be open to the AAT to find that the material pointed to Mr Woodward believing that he was in danger whilst he was on patrol and that such a belief was reasonable. It would also be open to conclude that the material pointed to Mr Woodward perceiving a threat of serious injury or death from actual events, experienced in circumstances in which it was reasonable to perceive a threat. It would be open to conclude that there were one or more "events" which precipitated the perception and that the events were real in the sense that they had an objective existence. If the reasoning of Mansfield J is accepted, the material before the AAT was capable of satisfying the requirements of the definition of "experiencing a severe stressor" in the SoP in relation to the incident on patrol.

'[141] We consider that the reasoning of Mansfield J in Stoddart is persuasive and that it

should be followed. In doing so, however, we express no opinion about a situation in which the perception of a threat, although real in the mind of an individual, is not objectively reasonable.' *Woodward v Repatriation Commission* [2003] FCAFC 160 per Black CJ, Weinberg and Selway JJ; BC200304136

EXPIRATION OF AN ACT

New Zealand [Section 22 of the Acts Interpretation Act 1924 begins 'The expiration of an Act shall not affect … '.] 'To interpret the word "expiration" in the section as excluding the revocation of an Act by repeal is altogether too narrow and stilted.' *Ewart v England* [1993] 3 NZLR 489 at 492, per Thomas J

EXPLICIT SEXUAL ACTIVITY

Canada 'Section 163.1(1)(*a*)(i) [of the *Criminal Code*] catches visual representations of "explicit sexual activity". Sexual activity spans a large spectrum, ranging from the flirtatious glance at one end, through touching of body parts incidentally related to sex, like hair, lips and breasts, to sexual intercourse and touching of the genitals and the anal region. The question is where on this spectrum Parliament intended to place the boundary between material that may be lawfully possessed and material that may not be lawfully possessed. A number of indications suggest that Parliament intended to draw the line at the extreme end of the spectrum concerned with depictions of intimate sexual activity represented in a graphic and unambiguous manner.

'The first indication is Parliament's use of the word "explicit" to describe the activity depicted. Parliament could have simply referred to "sexual activity". Instead, it chose "explicit sexual activity". "Explicit" must be given meaning. According to the *Canadian Oxford Dictionary* (1998), "explicit" in the context of sexual acts means "describing or representing nudity or intimate sexual activity". Similarly, "explicit" according to the *New Oxford Dictionary of English* (1998) means "describing or representing sexual activity in a graphic fashion". This suggests that the law catches only depictions of sexual intercourse and other non-trivial sexual acts.

'This restricted meaning is supported by the fact that in creating other offences, like sexual assault, Parliament uses the word "sexual" without any modifiers. To constitute sexual assault, the sexual aspect of the contact must be clear. The addition of the modifier "explicit" in s 163.1 suggests that this at least is required.

'A restrained interpretation of "explicit sexual activity" is also supported by reading s 163.1(1)(a)(i) and s 163.1(1)(a)(ii) together. They are designed to cover two types of depiction: (i) the depiction of explicit sexual *activity*; and (ii) the *static depiction* of the sexual organs or anal regions of children. Subparagraph (ii) clearly indicates that Parliament's concern was with visual representations near the extreme end of the spectrum. While it is possible in the abstract to argue that Parliament intended a much broader sweep for subpara (i) than for (ii), it seems more likely that Parliament was seeking to catch in subpara (i) the activity-related counterpart to subpara (ii).

'Finally, Parliament's goal of preventing harm to children related to child pornography supports a restrained interpretation of "explicit sexual activity". The evidence suggests that harm to children produced by child pornography arises from depictions of explicit sexual acts with children at the extreme end of the spectrum. The literature on harm focuses mainly on depictions of sexual activity involving nudity and portrayal of the sexual organs and anal region. It is reasonable to conclude that this sort of material was uppermost in Parliament's mind when it adopted this law.

'I conclude that "explicit sexual activity" refers to acts which viewed objectively fall at the extreme end of the spectrum of sexual activity — acts involving nudity or intimate sexual activity, represented in a graphic and unambiguous fashion, with persons under or depicted as under 18 years of age.' *R. v Sharpe* (2001) 194 DLR (4th) 1 at 29–31, SCC, per McLachlin CJC

EXPORT

Australia 'The ordinary meaning of "export" is to send commodities from one country to another using the verb "send" as indicating that which occasioned or brought about the carriage of the commodity from one country to another: see *Canton Railroad Co v Rogan* 340 US 511 (1951) at 515.' *Australian Trade Commission v Goodman Fielder Industries Ltd* (1992) 36 FCR 517 at 563, per cur

Canada '[5] The dictionary meaning of the term "export" is "to take away or carry off" or "to send out [commodities] from one country to another" (*The Shorter Oxford English Dictionary on Historical Principles*, 3rd ed., 1990). Certainly diesel fuel purchased in Canada but consumed in the United States by commercial trucks transporting

goods from Canada to the United States would fit within the dictionary definition of the term "export". However, for taxation purposes, the Supreme Court of Canada has provided the authoritative interpretation of the term in the taxation context that is binding on this Court and must be applied. Interestingly, the interpretation appears to derive from an opinion given to the President of the United States, Chester A. Arthur, by the Solicitor General and Acting Attorney General of the United States, Samuel F. Phillips, in 1883. The words used in the Phillips opinion were adopted verbatim by the Supreme Court of the United States in *Swan and Finch Company v. United States*, 190 U.S. 143 (1903). At pages 144 and 145, Mr. Justice Brewer stated:

> Whatever primary meaning may be indicated by its derivation, the word "export" as used in the Constitution and laws of the United States, generally means the transportation of goods from this to a foreign country. "As the legal notion of emigrating is a going abroad with an intention of not returning, so that of exportation is a severance of goods from the mass of things belonging to this country with an intention of uniting them to the mass of things belonging to some foreign country or other." 17 Op. Attys. Gen. 583. [Emphasis added.]

'[6] In *Swan and Finch*, it was found that rapeseed oil used and consumed in vessels bound for foreign ports was not "exportation" and was, therefore, not entitled to the drawback of duties paid on the rapeseed oil when it was originally imported.

'[7] The words used by the Supreme Court of the United States in *Swan and Finch* were adopted almost verbatim by the Supreme Court of Canada in *The King v. Carling Export Brewing and Malting Co. Ltd.*, [1930] S.C.R. 361, at pages 371–372:

> Generally speaking, export, no doubt, involves the idea of a severance of goods from the mass of things belonging to this country with the intention of uniting them with the mass of things belonging to some foreign country. It also involves the idea of transporting the thing exported beyond the boundaries of this country with the intention of effecting that. [Underlining added.]

The case involved the purported export of beer from Canada to the United States between 1924 and 1927. If the beer was exported, it would be exempt from sales tax and gallonage tax. This was the time of "Prohibition" in the United States. Duff J. stated at page 372:

> As I shall point out, there are difficulties in reconciling with the ordinary notion of export, as commonly understood in commerce, and as contemplated by this statute, the kind of operation in which the respondents were engaged.

At page 374, he elaborated as follows:

> The Crown argues that as the export alleged in this case involves, as already indicated, a deliberate violation of the United States laws to the extent pointed out, it cannot be treated as "export" within the meaning of the statute. I think there is a great deal to be said in favour of the view that "export" in the sense of the statute may be limited in such a way as to exclude export so entirely beyond the ordinary course of commerce. The considerations in favour of this view are so numerous and so obvious that they need not be dwelt upon.

The Supreme Court decision in *Carling Export Brewing* was reversed by the Privy Council, [1931] 2 D.L.R. 545, but not on this point.

'[8] The *Swan and Finch* and *Carling Export Brewing* cases indicate that the dictionary definition of "export", in its broadest sense, may not be apt in determining questions of taxation with regard to goods sent out of the country. We are not concerned with illegality as in *Carling Export Brewing*. However, the circumstances here are, in some respects, similar to the facts in *Swan and Finch*. Having regard to the Supreme Court's interpretation of the term "export", the question is whether the diesel fuel in question in this case was severed from the mass of things belonging to Canada with the intention of uniting it with the mass of things belonging to the United States.

'[9] It must first be noted that the Supreme Court's words must be read having regard to context and cannot be read literally. The term "belonging to" does not mean state ownership by Canada or the United States. The rapeseed oil in *Swan and Finch* and the beer in *Carling Export Brewing* did not belong to the governments of the United States or Canada in the ownership sense. The terms "severance" and "uniting" also do not mean the physical parting or joining of goods.

'[10] Having regard to context, I think what is contemplated is the removal of goods from one country with the intention that they be destined to, and remain to be used or sold in another country

without being returned to the country of origin. This view is supported by the words of the United States Supreme Court in *Swan and Finch, supra,* at page 145.

> Another country or State as the intended destination of the goods is essential to the idea of exportation.'

Penner International Inc v Canada [2003] 2 FC 581 at 589–591 (FCA), per Rothstein JA

EXPORTER

Australia [In determining the identity of an "exporter" for the purpose of s 269TAB(1) of the Customs Act 1901 (Cth).] 'Although "exporter" is not defined in the Act, its meaning has been judicially considered. In *Henty v Bainbridge-Hawker* (1963) 36 ALJR 354, Owen J of the High Court of Australia [found that] "... For the purposes of this case it is sufficient to say that if, in the case of an f.o.b. contract with an overseas buyer the seller places the goods sold on board a ship bound for foreign parts and engages with the shipowner to carry them to the overseas buyer and the goods are carried overseas, the seller has, in my opinion, exported the goods within the meaning of the Customs Act." ... In *Australian Trade Commission v Goodman Fielder Industries Ltd* (1992) 36 FCR at 517 a Full Court of this court considered the meaning of the word "export" in the context of the Export Market Development Grants Act 1974 (Cth). At 523 the court said: "The ordinary meaning of "export" is to send commodities from one country to another using the verb "send" as indicating that which occasioned or brought about the carriage of the commodity from one country to another." There is, perhaps, some ambiguity in the words "that which occasioned or brought about the carriage". In one sense, an order from an importer can be said to occasion or bring about the despatch, and therefore the carriage, of goods from one country to another. However, for the reason indicated, this sense is not relevant to s 269TAB(1)(a) of the Customs Act.' *Companhia Votorantium de Celluse e Papel v Anti-Dumping Authority* (1996) 141 ALR 297 at 307, 308, per Wilcox, RD Nicholson JJ

EXPRESS PROVISION TO THE CONTRARY

Australia 'The phrase, in [Contracts Act 1984 (Cth)] s 8(2), "but for an express provision to the contrary" identifies that part of the logical universe (the normal common law rules of private international law as understood in Australia and which identify the proper law) which remains after allowance for the operation of the objective test to select the law of a State or a Territory. The words "express provision" in that phrase embrace those provisions of the contract from which, or by recourse to which, it would be determined that the parties to the contract had selected or chosen a proper law which was not the law of a State or a Territory ... We conclude that the phrase "but for an express provision to the contrary" in s 8(2) is not to be read as identifying only what in the texts and judgments often is called an express choice of law clause, of which the first sentence of cl 19 [of the insurance policy] is an example.' *Akai Pty Ltd v The People's Insurance Co Ltd* (1996) 188 CLR 418 at 436, 439; (1996) 141 ALR 374 at 386–387, 389; (1996) 71 ALJR 156; BC9606281 at 18, 21, per Toohey, Gaudron and Gummow JJ

EXPROPRIATION PROCEEDINGS

Canada 'The Board reasoned that the word "proceedings" must refer to "the administrative law process involving a claimant's claim for compensation, beginning with the filing of the Form A Application to Determine Compensation". Thus the expropriating authority's actions or omissions before Bayview filed its final Form A were held not to fall within the scope of "proceedings under this *Act*".

'The Board found support for this interpretation in both the *Supreme Court Act*, SBC 1989, c 40, and the *Supreme Court Rules*, where "proceeding" is defined to include "an action, suit, cause, matter, appeal or originating application". The tribunal read these definitions as "limiting the term 'proceeding' to a matter before the court, and not extending to incidents that occurred prior to the issuance of the originating court documents". Thus while expressing sympathy with Bayview "about the way this whole series of events has unfolded", the Board did not consider itself at liberty to consider any period pre-dating the filing of the *final* Form A that was before it.

'It will be recalled that Bayview had filed a Form A first in November 1991. Later amendments were required when the Ministry's plans for the intersection of the Trans Canada Highway and Deloume Road changed, and later again when 16 square metres of Bayview's property were expropriated, contrary to the Ministry's revised plans. As Mr McDaniel points out, the date of filing of the original Form A was not referred to by the Board in its consideration of s 46. Ms Poole submits that the original Form A was not *before* the Board and that therefore it was correct not to consider it; but while the formal document may not have been included in the record, the fact of the Ministry's original plans beginning back in 1989, the changes in those plans prior to the date of formal expropriation, and the fact of Bayview's original and amended claims, were certainly in the record before the Board. Thus even if the word "proceedings" is limited to formal steps in the expropriation process as the Board suggested, the Board in my view erred in restricting itself to considering the period commencing with the filing only of the *final* Form A.

'Mr McDaniel submits, moreover, that the expropriation "proceedings" may be regarded as extending back even further — to February 1990, when the Ministry informed Bayview that it intended to acquire some of its property, or May 1990, when construction of the highway alterations began. (Bayview's award for business losses was calculated from that month.) He cites the decision of the Supreme Court of Canada in *Dell Holdings, supra*, which, among other things, confirmed that a statute such as the *Expropriation Act* is a remedial statute and "must be given a broad and liberal interpretation consistent with its purpose. Substance, not form, is the governing factor" (para 21). *Dell Holdings* involved a different question than that at issue here, namely, whether damages for disturbance may be awarded where an expropriation has occurred; but in the course of his judgment, Cory J for the majority observed:

> The courts have long determined that the actual act of expropriation of any property is part of a continuing process. In [*City of Montreal v Daniel J McAnulty Realty Co* [1923] SCR 273] at p 283, Duff J noted that the term "expropriation" is not used in the restrictive sense of signifying merely the transfer of title but in the sense of the *process of taking the property* for the purpose for which it is required. Thus whether the events that affected the value of the expropriated land were part of the expropriation process, or, in other words, a step in the acquisition of the lands, is a significant factor for consideration in many expropriation cases. [Para 37.]

'From this, Mr McDaniel argues that "proceedings" should include "*the process* that commences with the decision by the expropriating authority to acquire the Claimant's land to undertake the construction of works associated with the acquisition".

'*The Dictionary of Canadian Law* (2nd ed, 1995) defines (or describes) "proceeding" very broadly indeed — "one of those words of very wide import that must be interpreted according to that context in which it is used". The context in this case is that of a remedial statute — a context quite different from court rules of procedure.'

Bayview Builders Supply (1972) Ltd v British Columbia (Ministry of Transportation & Highways) (1999) 170 DLR (4th) 751 at 766–767, BC CA, per Newbury JA

EXTERNAL APPEARANCE

Australia [A body corporate by-law prohibited each proprietor of a unit in a residential building from doing anything to vary the 'external appearance' of his lot without prior consent of the body corporate council.] 'The concept of appearance necessarily connotes the existence of an observer who has the capacity to see the appearance. Otherwise the term is devoid of practical content. In the context of the by-laws and in the factual context in which they exist, the expression "external appearance" must mean the appearance which the lot presents to a person outside it who might reasonably be able to view it; and this must take in any limitations as to possible viewing locations. The purpose behind the by-law is obviously to preserve the view of the lot for the pleasure of the owners of other lots and for ensuring that the appearance of the building remains of the same quality in the eyes of other persons who might reasonably be expected to look at it for various reasons. In all of these cases, it is predicated that such views are limited to those which can reasonably be taken. The concept does not extend to a theoretical appearance as it might be seen, by a person placed in a position which is not practically possible or likely.' *Re Saunders* [1993] 2 Qd R 335 at 338, per Derrington J

EXTINGUISHMENT

Australia [The essential issue raised in these proceedings is whether, and to what extent, the traditional owners of parts north-east Arnhem Land can exclude fishermen and others from the claim area and from certain sites. In one of the two proceedings that were issued, the relevant applicants sought a determination of native title rights under the Native Title Act 1993 (Cth) (the NTA).] '[123] It can be seen that the "recognition" of native title in a particular case and at a particular point in time was necessarily a limited and transitory recognition. Not only could the native title rights evolve over time in accordance with Aboriginal tradition, they were subject to extinguishment. They could also be lost if the holders of the native title ceased to maintain their traditional connection with the land.

...

'[257] The question then is whether Parliament has used the word "extinguishment" in s 47A NTA in a general sense where it might include "non-recognition" or in its more precise sense where it would not. It seems to me most unlikely that the Commonwealth Parliament would have intended that all "non-recognition" be disregarded. "Non-recognition" is not limited to inconsistency with common law rights. It includes non-recognition on the basis that the rights claimed, or the traditions on which they are based, are ones that the common law would not recognise for reasons of judicial policy.

...

'[261] In my view the word "extinguishment" in s 47A(2) NTA means extinguishment by an act of sovereign will (usually legislation or an act done pursuant to legislation) of a right capable of recognition by the common law as at the date of settlement. That would seem to be the sense in which the word was understood by Olney J in *Yorta Yorta Aboriginal Community v Victoria* [1998] FCA 1606 at [133]. In my view his Honour's understanding was correct.

'[262] The same result seems to me to flow from the requirement in s 47(2)(b) of the NTA that the extinguishment arise from the "creation" of a right ...' *Gumana v Northern Territory* [2005] FCA 50 at [123], [257], [261]–[262], per Selway J; BC200500180

EXTORT OR GAIN

New Zealand [Section 238(1)(a) of the Crimes Act 1961.] 'There is no cause to read the words other than disjunctively or to give the word "extort" anything other than its ordinary meaning. The primary meaning of "extort" in *The Oxford English Dictionary* (2nd ed) is "To wrest or wring (something) from a person". Certainly it carries an overtone of illegitimate action, but the expression itself is very broad. The word originates from the Latin torquere (to twist) and in its general sense connotes the obtaining of something by means of force or intimidation ...

'Again the primary meaning of "gain" used as a verb is to obtain or secure. On an ordinary use of language, to get anything that one does not presently have, is to gain that thing. To recover what is owed or what has been wrongfully taken is to gain what is received.' *R v Cargill* [1995] 3 NZLR 263 at 269, CA, per cur

EXTRADITION

[For 18 Halsbury's Laws (4th edn) para 201 see now 17(2) Halsbury's Laws (4th edn) (Reissue) para 1101.]

EXTRAORDINARY TRAFFIC

[For 21 Halsbury's Laws (4th edn) para 241 et seq see now 21 Halsbury's Laws (4th edn) (2004 Reissue) paras 313–315.]

EXTRADITION CRIME

[The Extradition Act 1870, Sch 1, contains a list of extradition crimes and continues to apply despite the repeal of the 1870 Act by the Extradition Act 1989 where a relevant Order in Council is in force.] 'It must be borne in mind that the list is intended to cover conduct that falls within any of the generic descriptions of crime in the list. The issue does not turn on the ability to match a course of conduct with a listed offence ... It turns on whether an offence of broad scope, in the sense that there can be a criminal conspiracy to commit a whole range of specific offences, is intended to be covered, though not named, by a specific entry in a varied list.

'I have considered the history of the list and am not able to conclude that where the description of the listed offence was what Lord Lowry in [*US Government v Bowe* [1990] 1 AC 500, [1989] 3 All ER 315, PC] described as specific, for example embezzlement and larceny, the offence of a conspiracy to commit the offence can be included in the list by implication.' *R v Secretary of State for the Home Department, ex p Gilmore* [1998] 1 All ER 264 at 269, CA, per Pill LJ

'In general, a state only exercises criminal jurisdiction over offences which occur within its geographical boundaries. If a person who is alleged to have committed a crime in Spain is found in the United Kingdom, Spain can apply to the United Kingdom to extradite him to Spain. The power to extradite from the United Kingdom for an "extradition crime" is now contained in the Extradition Act 1989. That Act defines what constitutes an "extradition crime". For the purposes of the present case, the most important requirement

is that the conduct complained of must constitute a crime under the law both of Spain and of the United Kingdom. This is known as the double criminality rule.

'... Since torture outside the United Kingdom was not a crime under UK law until 29 September 1988, the principle of double criminality which requires an Act to be a crime under both the law of Spain and of the United Kingdom cannot be satisfied in relation to conduct before that date if the principle of double criminality requires the conduct to be criminal under United Kingdom law *at the date it was committed*. If, on the other hand, the double criminality rule only requires the conduct to be criminal under UK law *at the date of extradition* the rule was satisfied in relation to all torture alleged against Senator Pinochet whether it took place before or after 1988. The Spanish courts have held that they have jurisdiction over all the crimes alleged.

'In these circumstances, the first question that has to be answered is whether or not the definition of an "extradition crime" in the 1989 Act requires the conduct to be criminal under UK law at the date of commission or only at the date of extradition.

...

'My Lords, if the words of s 2 are construed in isolation there is room for two possible views. I agree with Lord Bingham CJ and Lord Lloyd that, if read in isolation, the words "if it occurred ... would constitute" read more easily as a reference to a hypothetical event happening now, i e at the request date, than to a past hypothetical event, i e at the conduct date. But in my judgment the right construction is not clear. The word "it" in the phrase "if it occurred" is a reference back to the actual conduct of the individual abroad which, by definition, is a past event. The question then would be "would that past event (including the date of its occurrence) constitute an offence under the law of the United Kingdom". The answer to that question would depend upon the United Kingdom law at that date.

'But of course it is not correct to construe these words in isolation and your Lordships had the advantage of submissions which strongly indicate that the relevant date is the conduct date ...

'... The scheme of the 1870 Act was to define "extradition crime" as meaning – "a crime which, if committed in England ... would be one of the crimes described in the first schedule to this Act": s 26. Schedule 1 to the 1870 Act contains a list of crimes and is headed: "The following list of crimes is to be construed according to the law existing in England ... *at the date of the alleged crime*, whether by common law or by statute made before or after the passing of this Act ..." It is therefore quite clear from the words I have emphasised that under the 1870 Act the double criminality rule required the conduct to be criminal under English law at the conduct date not at the request date. Paragraph 20 of Sch 1 to the 1989 Act provides—

"... 'extradition crime', in relation to any foreign state, is to be construed by reference to the Order in Council under section 2 of the Extradition Act 1870 applying to that state as it had effect immediately before the coming into force of this Act and to any amendments thereafter made to that Order ..."

Therefore in this class of case regulated by Sch 1 to the 1989 Act the same position applies as it formerly did under the 1870 Act, ie the conduct has to be a crime under English law at the conduct date. It would be extraordinary if the same Act required criminality under English law to be shown at one date for one form of extradition and at another date for another. But the case is stronger than that. We were taken through a trawl of the travaux préparatoires relating to the Extradition Convention and the departmental papers leading to the 1989 Act. They were singularly silent as to the relevant date. But they did disclose that there was no discussion as to changing the date on which the criminality under English law was to be demonstrated. It seems to me impossible that the legislature can have intended to change that date from the one which had applied for over a hundred years under the 1870 Act (ie the conduct date) by a side wind and without investigation.' *R v Bow Street Metropolitan Stipendiary Magistate, ex p Pinochet Ugarte (No 3)* [1999] 2 All ER 97 at 100–101, 105–107, HL, per Lord Browne-Wilkinson

EXTRAORDINARY EXPENSES FOR EXTRACURRICULAR ACTIVITIES

Canada 'The Applicant seeks contribution from the Respondent for the cost of the children's hockey, being approximately $1,400 annually, and for the cost of the proposed swimming lessons for the children, being $228 annually. The first issue to decide is whether these expenses fall within the category of "extraordinary expenses for extracurricular activities" contemplated under section 7(1)(f) of the [Child Support] *Guidelines*.

'In arriving at the amounts stipulated in the Tables to the *Guidelines*, Parliament theoretically took into account all types of expenses that Canadian parents as a collectivity incur on behalf of their children. The Table amount represents an average amount which a parent at that income level will spend on his or her child or children. It does not necessarily equal what a particular parent who has that income actually spends on his or her child or children. The child support payment itself is considered a global sum available to cover a portion of whatever expenses the custodial parent incurs in order to meet the needs of a child or children. Those applying the *Guidelines* cannot make any assumptions regarding what portion of a Table amount represents expenses relating to extracurricular activities, aside from assuming that some portion does.

'The word "extraordinary" in section 7(1)(f) does not refer to the fact that the expense may be incurred infrequently by that parent or by parents in general. Nor does it refer to the unusualness of the expense in the jurisdiction where the matter is being considered. In other words, the fact that a small number of Canadian children may pursue a particular extracurricular pursuit has no bearing on the analysis of whether the expense incurred by a parent for a child in regard to such a pursuit should be considered "extraordinary".

'The real focus of the analysis must be the extent to which the expense or expenses for an extracurricular activity or activities would be inordinately burdensome for the custodial parent to pay, taking into account his or her income (as defined in the *Guidelines*). It is in this sense that the word "extraordinary" is being used.

'There are at least two ways in which the term "extraordinary" may be interpreted within the context of section 7(1)(f). The expenses for one particular extracurricular activity for one particular child may be considered extraordinary because of its amount in relation to the income from all sources of the parent who is paying the expense. As well, the totality of expenses for extracurricular activities for one child or for all of the children for whom a parent is paying such expenses may be considered extraordinary in relation to the income from all sources of that parent.' *Camirand v Beaulne* (1998) 160 DLR (4th) 749 at 755–756, Ont Gen Div, per Aitken J

F

FACILITIES

[Under the National Health Service Act 1977, s 3, the Secretary of State has a duty (devolved to health boards) to provide throughout England and Wales, to such extent as he considers necessary to meet all reasonable requirements, hospital accommodation and other facilities and services, including '(e) such facilities for the prevention of illness, the care of persons suffering from illness and the after-care of persons who have suffered from illness as he considers are appropriate as part of the health service'.] '[19] The main issue to be determined on this appeal is whether the word "facilities" in s 3(1)(e) of the 1977 Act can be interpreted as including not only the accommodation, plant and other means by which services are provided or by which they more readily achieve their purpose, but also as including the human beings who actually provide the services referred to in that subsection.

...

'[41] I agree that the judge adopted too restrictive an approach to the meaning of the word "facilities" where it appears in s 3(1)(e). As the case law suggests–and Mr Drabble added *R v Secretary of State ex p Kirklees BC* (1971) Times, 24 January, where Taylor J proceeded on the basis that the provision of the services of a housing steward was the provision of a "facility" for the occupants of the relevant housing–its meaning will be derived from the context in which the word is used. It means "that which facilitates". Sometimes the word refers to tools, or accommodation, or plant, which facilitate the provision of a service. Sometimes it refers to an entire service provision, like a laundry service, or the provision of a day centre, which facilitates the prevention of illness, or the care of persons suffering from illness, or the after-care of persons who have suffered from illness. If a local health board wishes to provide a non-nursing day centre, or a hydro-therapy pool, for s 3(1)(e) purposes, because it thinks it appropriate to provide these facilities as part of the health service, it would be absurd, as Mr Drabble argued (with the full support of counsel for the department), if it

was limited to providing the accommodation and the "plant", and somebody else had to provide the personnel to run the facility.

'[42] Of course it is true, as the judge observed, that in other parts of the 1977 Act, the meaning of the word "facilities" is more narrowly focused, but that is only what one would expect when the draftsman uses a chameleon-like word like "facilities" which takes its colour from its context. Mr Herberg, for his part, was constrained to accept that the word "facilities" might embrace "services" as well in other statutory contexts, but he continued to maintain his clients' stance robustly, notwithstanding the icy winds that assailed his submissions from other bodies with immense knowledge of how the health service works in practice.

'[43] What this case is concerned to identify is the extent of the health service functions under s 3(1)(e) that may be appropriately and lawfully provided by a local health board. The modern legislation which Mr Herberg showed us was not concerned with such basic definitions. It enabled a whole host of sensible ways in which a local health board exercising health service functions can now co-operate with a local social services authority exercising allied functions in providing an optimum service for the public. This co-operation may be achieved through partnership arrangements, through payments of money, or through the preparation and implementation of joint strategies, but at the end of the day the question remains: what is a local health board lawfully obliged to provide under s 3(1)(e) of the 1977 Act if it considers it appropriate as part of the health service? The answer to that question can only be found in the language of the 1977 Act, and in my judgment it is lawfully able to provide funding for services like the Riverside project, if it considers it appropriate as part of the health service.'
R (on the application of Keating) v Cardiff Local Health Board (Secretary of State for Health, intervening) [2005] EWCA Civ 847 at [19], [41]–[43], [2005] 3 All ER 1000, per Brooke LJ

FACILITIES AND INFORMATION

Australia [Section 25(1) of the Evidence Act 1910 (Tas) entitles the defendant's medical practitioner to examine the injured person and, at the same time, imposes on the injured person, and all other parties (if any) to the proceedings, an obligation to give the defendant's medical practitioner, 'all such facilities and information as may be necessary to enable him to ascertain fully the nature and extent of the injury'.] '... the facilities and information referred to in s 25 are something different from, and/or additional to, the medical examination ... The facilities and information that have to be given are not those which are necessary to enable the practitioner to examine the plaintiff, but those necessary to enable him to ascertain fully the nature and extent of the injury in respect of which there is a claim for damages.

'In the context of s 25(1), "facilities" are something that has to be given by one person to another in order to make something else easier. The obligation imposed on the plaintiff by the first limb of subs (1), is to submit to an examination by the defendant's medical practitioner. The obligation imposed by the second limb is to do or say something that will make something else easier to achieve. Facilities is a word of wide import. The subsection imposes an obligation on the plaintiff to facilitate the full ascertainment by the defendant's medical practitioner of the nature and extent of the injury in respect of which the proceedings have been taken. The only other possible matter in respect of which the subsection could impose a duty on the plaintiff to facilitate, is the medical examination. However, in my view, the concluding words of subs (1) are not linked to the examination. A failure to facilitate an examination, eg, by failing to undress or move limbs as directed by the defendant's medical practitioner, or even to undergo radiological examination, would constitute a failure to "submit" to an examination as enacted by subs (2).' *Papson v Woolworths (Vic) Pty Ltd (No 2)* BC200005270; [2000] TASSC 124 at [25], [30], per Underwood J

FACT

'[A] "fact" in a criminal trial is something that is established to the satisfaction of the jury by competent and sufficient evidence adduced, and in relation to a person indicted in that trial. A "fact" of that character has no existence outside the context of the trial; and the facts established at a trial against one accused may well differ from the facts established against a co-accused in the same proceedings; they commonly do.' *Howitt v HM Advocate* 2000 SLT 449 at 453, per Lord McCluskey (delivering the opinion of the court)

FACTOR

[For 1 Halsbury's Laws (4th edn) para 712 see now 1(2) Halsbury's Laws (4th edn) (Reissue) para 12.]

FAIL

[The Road Traffic Act 1972 has been repealed. The definition is re-enacted in the Road Traffic Act 1988, s 11(2).]

Australia [An offence arises pursuant to s 67(2) of the Road Traffic Act 1974 (WA) where a person fails to comply with the requirement of providing a sample of his breath for analysis.] 'The word "fails" is to be interpreted in those subsections [ss 67A(1) and 67(2)] as meaning "does not". As a consequence, if no sample of breath for preliminary testing or analysis results there is a requisite failure. There is no proper basis in law ... to imply any element of wilfulness in construction of the word.' *Adair v Gough* (1990) 10 MVR 558 at 560ñ561, per Nicholson J

New Zealand [Section 10(3)(b) of the Criminal Justice Act 1985 begins 'Refuses or fails to apply for legal aid ...'.] 'The word "fails" must necessarily be understood in its objective sense of "does not succeed".' *Parkhill v Ministry of Transport* [1992] 1 NZLR 555 at 559, CA, per cur

FAIR

Canada 'The relevant meaning of "fair" in such Oxford Dictionary is:

1. A regular gathering of buyers and sellers at a time and place ordained by charter, statute or custom. Now *esp* (a part of) such a gathering devoted entirely to amusements (also *fun-fair*). ME. *b.* an exhibition, esp. one designed to publicize a particular product or the products of one industry, country, etc.

The said Webster's dictionary gives the following:

1. orig, a gathering of people held at regular intervals for barter and sale of goods 2. a festival or carnival where there is entertainment and things are sold, often for

charity; bazaar [Americanism] 3. a) an event consisting of a usually competitive exhibition of livestock, household and manufactured products, etc plus amusement facilities and educational displays.

The Oxford American Dictionary (1980), gives the following:

1. a periodical gathering for the sale of goods, often with shows and entertainments. 2. an exhibition of commercial or industrial goods. 3. an exhibition of agricultural produce, farm animals, etc.

These dictionary meanings suggest that fairs include the sale or display of goods or livestock. Such activities do not occur at an outdoor music festival or concert. On the other hand, the dictionary meanings suggest that fairs include shows and entertainments. An outdoor music festival or concert is a show or entertainment.' *Mosport Park Ltd v Clarington (Municipality)* (1994) 116 DLR (4th) 763, Ont Div Ct, per Southey J

FAIR COMMENT

[For 28 Halsbury's Laws (4th edn) paras 131, 132 see now 28 Halsbury's Laws (4th edn) (Reissue) paras 135–136.]

'The civil law of libel is primarily concerned to provide redress for those who are the subject of false and defamatory factual publications. Thus in the simplest case A will be entitled to relief against B if B publishes a defamatory factual statement concerning A which B cannot show to be true. The law is not primarily concerned to provide redress for those who are the subject of disparaging expressions of opinion, and freedom of opinion is (subject to necessary restrictions) a basic democratic right. It is, however, plain that certain statements which might on their face appear to be expressions of opinion (as where, for example, a person is described as untrustworthy, unprincipled, lascivious or cruel) contain within themselves defamatory suggestions of a factual nature. Thus the law has developed the rule ... the comment may only be defended as fair if it is comment on facts (meaning true facts) stated or sufficiently indicated. Failing that, the comment itself must be justified.' *Brent Walker Group plc v Time Out Ltd* [1991] 2 All ER 753 at 760, CA, per Bingham LJ

Rolled-up plea

[For 28 Halsbury's Laws (4th edn) para 188 see now 28 Halsbury's Laws (4th edn) (Reissue) para 192.]

FAIR DEALING

Canada '[144] Necessarily, fairness depends upon the context and facts of each particular case, and for that reason, "fair" is not defined in the Act. In the case of *Hubbard v. Vosper*, [1972] 2 Q.B. 84 (C.A.) at 94, Lord Denning recognized that "[i]t is impossible to define what is 'fair dealing.' It must be a question of degree ... [I]t must be a matter of impression." In *Cie Générale des Établissements Michelin-Michelin & Cie v. C.A.W.-Canada* (1996), 71 C.P.R. (3d) 348 ("*Michelin*") at 384, the Trial Division of this Court accepted that the overall use of the copyright must be fair and the copyright must be treated in a good faith manner. Like Lord Denning, the Court admitted that it was "a question of impression" (at 384). The Ontario Court (General Division) *in Allen v. Toronto Star Newspapers Ltd.* (1997), 78 C.P.R. (3d) 115 at 123, 152 D.L.R. (4th) 518, viewed the test as "essentially purposive".

'[145] Despite these remarks, an assessment of fairness is not simply a subjective exercise, and there are a number of identifiable factors that might influence one's conclusion. A list of these factors has not been compiled by a Canadian court, nor is one contained in the Act. As our Act does not describe any specific factors to consider, it is incumbent upon this Court to do so as best it can.

'[146] In *Hubbard v. Vosper, supra*, Lord Denning described (at 94) some of the factors that may be relevant to a determination of the fairness of dealing for the purposes of criticism and review. He analyzed the number and extent of quotations, the purpose of the dealing, whether the use was for a rival purpose, and the proportions of the extracts compared to independent comments. Some of these factors have been subsequently accepted and explained by the Court of Appeal in England in cases such as *Pro Sieben Media AG v. Carlton UK Television Ltd.*, [1999] F.S.R. 610 ("*Pro Sieben*"), and *Hyde Park Residence Ltd. v. Yelland*, [2000] E.W.J. 514 (QL) [reported [2000] 3 W.L.R. 215]. However, these considerations, which are related to fair dealing in the context of criticism or review or reporting current events, do not neatly apply in every situation. Nevertheless, they may provide guidance for this Court to explore the factors relevant to fair dealing under Canadian law.

'[147] 17 U.S.C. § 107, which outlines the doctrine of fair use in the United States, directs American courts to consider a non-exhaustive list of factors, including the purpose and character of the use, the nature of the copyrighted work, the amount and substantiality of the portion used in relation to the copyrighted work as a whole and the effect of the use upon the potential market for or value of the copyrighted work.

'[148] I realize the differences in the American legislation as compared to our own Act. Generally, American law is more favourable to copyright users than is Canadian law. In particular, 17 U.S.C. § 107 leaves open the types of purposes that may constitute fair use, unlike our Act, which specifies allowable purposes (see *Hager, supra*, at 309; *Michelin, supra*, at 379; and Vaver, *Copyright Law, supra*, at 190). However, this fact alone does not mean that we cannot "find some assistance in examining the experience in the United States", as Estey J. suggested, and consider these factors in an analysis of fair dealing (see *Compo, supra*, at 367). Importantly, the distinction between Canadian and American law regarding allowable purposes has limited bearing on a discussion of the factors that influence whether dealing is fair.

'[149] I am further comforted by the fact that Professor Vaver has described (in *Copyright Law, supra*, at 191) many similar factors and implied that they may be applicable to Canadian law:

> Several factors have been used to determine whether a dealing is fair: the purpose and character of the dealing; the nature of the source work; what and how much has been dealt with; the effect of the dealing on the potential market for or value of the source work; whether the source work was available within a reasonable time at an ordinary commercial price; and any reasonable guidelines accepted by joint owner and user interests.

'[150] Assessing these observations in combination with the American and British factors, I have compiled a list of factors that should influence the fairness of the Law Society's dealings with the Publishers' works on behalf of patrons of the Great Library. Importantly, the elements of fairness are malleable and must be tailored to each unique circumstance. None of the factors are conclusive or binding, and additional considerations may well apply uniquely in the Canadian context. However, the following factors are usually among the non-exhaustive list of considerations: (1) the purpose of the dealing; (2) the nature of the dealing; (3) the amount of the dealing; (4) alternatives to the dealing; (5) the nature of the work in question; and (6) the effect of the dealing on that work.' *CCH Canadian Ltd. v Law Society of Upper Canada* (2002) DLR (4th) 385 at 447 (FCA), per Lindeen, J.A.

New Zealand '... fair dealing for the purposes of research or private study does not encompass an activity in which the material concerned is simply appropriated and passed on to others for the commercial profit of the appropriator.' *Television New Zealand Ltd v Newsmonitor Services Ltd* [1994] 2 NZLR 91 at 106, per Blanchard J

FAIR MARKET VALUE

Australia [In the context of share market valuation.] '[52] There are a number of contractual, statutory and accounting standards contexts in which the administration of justice must determine the "fair value" of property. The meaning of that formulation will vary with the context. In some contexts the formulation refers to what is just or equitable in all the circumstances. In such a case the scope of the relevant considerations which may be taken into account by the requisite decision-maker, whether an arbitrator or a judge, is wide. (See, e g with respect to oppression suits in corporations law: *Scottish Co-operative Wholesale Society Ltd v Meyer* [1959] AC 324 at 369; *Re Bird Precision Bellows Ltd* [1986] 1 Ch 658 at 669; *Coombs v Dynasty Pty Ltd* (1994) 14 ACSR 60 at 102; *United Rural Enterprises Pty Ltd v Lopmand Pty Ltd* [2003] NSWSC 910; (2003) 47 ACSR 514 at [36]; *Re An Arbitration Fletcher Humphreys & Co Ltd v Middleton* [1944] NZLR 502 esp at 507–508. In another statutory context see, e g *Holt v Cox* (1994) 15 ACSR 313 esp at 334 and 336–337; *E S Gordon Pty Ltd v Idameneo (No 123) Pty Ltd* (1994) 15 ACSR 536 esp at 539–541; c f *Capricorn Diamonds Investments Pty Ltd v Catto* [2002] VSC 105; (2002) 5 VR 61 pp 71–77.) Where the relevant test is "fair value", a market value is often not decisive. (See, e g *Gambotto v WCP Ltd* [1995] HCA 12; (1995) 182 CLR 432 at 457–458.)

'[53] A number of authorities suggest a distinction between a "market value" test and a "fair value" or "fair market value" test. (See, e g *Fletcher Humphries & Co Ltd v Middleton* supra at 507; *Holt v Cox* supra at 334; c f *Cattanach v Water Conservation and Irrigation Commission* [1963] NSWR 304 at 308–309.) The overall context will be determinative.

...

'[55] A test of a "market value", whether in a statutory or contractual context, usually invokes the test long established and frequently applied in *Spencer v The Commonwealth of Australia* (1907) 5 CLR 418 esp at 432 and 440–441 of a willing but not anxious purchaser and vendor, bargaining with each other. This approach was most recently expressed in a joint judgment of three judges of the High Court in *Marks v GIO Australia Holdings Ltd* [1998] HCA 69; (1998) 196 CLR 494 at 514:

> ... The value ... is to be identified according to what price freely contracting, fully informed parties would have offered and accepted for it.

'[56] It is convenient to refer to the Spencer's case formulation as the exchange value test (*Spencer* supra at 431.5 per Griffith CJ, as did Gleeson CJ *in Boland v Yates Property Corporation Pty Ltd* [1999] HCA 64; (1999) 74 ALJR 209 at [79].)

'[57] Where the focus of the valuation process is on a "market value", even in a context, as so often occurs, where there is no or little trading history in the relevant property, the approach will usually be quite different to that which arises where a "fair value" is required to be determined. The range of relevant circumstances to be taken into account is not as wide and regard is not had to the particular history of the commercial or personal relationships between the prospective vendor and purchaser of the property to be valued.

'[58] Where, as here, the formulation is "fair market value", the valuation test requires a similarly limited focus on the range of circumstances relevant to a process of determining exchange value. A "fair market value" may diverge from a "market value" for numerous reasons, e g where property is thinly traded, or the parcel is small, or there exist market distortions.

...

'[60] Nevertheless, the word "fair" has, in my opinion, work to do. In a contractual context, this additional word suggests that the valuation should proceed on the assumption, which may be contrary to the facts of a particular contractual relationship, that there is no impediment to the process of bargaining, whether in terms of availability of information or restraints arising from the characteristics of a particular vendor or purchaser or otherwise. Issues will arise, however, when determining what aspects of the particular relationship are of a character which inhere in the item of property itself, as distinct from those which should be treated as excluded by the concept of a "fair market value".

'[61] It is not possible to set out in abstract terms how a fair market value should be computed. It is necessary to focus on the particular issues which arise in order to determine what the formulation requires in a particular case." *MMAL Rentals P/L v Bruning* [2004] NSWCA 451

at [52]–[53], [55]–[58], [60]–[61], per Spigelman CJ; BC200408896

FAIRLY ARGUABLE

Australia 'We do not think it useful to fasten upon one verbal formula in preference to all others as a description of the necessary degree of satisfaction. What must be shown is that it is clear that the appeal will fail and in that sense is not "arguable" or not "fairly arguable".' *Jackamarra v Krakouer* (1998) 153 ALR 276 at 285; 72 ALJR 819; BC9801285, per Gummow and Hayne JJ

FAIRLY BASED ON THE MATTER DESCRIBED IN THE SPECIFICATION

Australia [Patents Act 1990 (Cth) s 40(3) provides in part: (1) A provisional specification must describe the invention. (2) A complete specification must: (a) describe the invention fully, including the best method known to the applicant of performing the invention; and (b) where it relates to an application for a standard patent — end with a claim or claims defining the invention ...(3) The claim or claims must be clear and succinct and fairly based on the matter described in the specification. (4) The claim or claims must relate to one invention only.] '[27] This appeal turns upon the phrase in s 40(3) "fairly based on the matter described in the specification". This subsection is concerned purely with the relationship between the body and claims of the one specification. However, the criterion of fair basing appears elsewhere in patent law, in particular to establish a sufficient connection with an earlier disclosure to support that earlier date as the priority date for a claim or claims. The Patents Regulations 1991 (Cth) use the phrase "the claim is fairly based on matter disclosed" in provisional applications, applications under the Patent Cooperation Treaty and divisional applications.

...

'[50] To some extent, various of the judgments below assume that the relevant test under s 40(3) requires a comparison between the claims and the "inventive step", or a comparison between the claims and the "merit" of the invention, or a comparison between the claims and the "technical contribution to the art" made by the patent.

'[51] There are some key features of the legislation which suggest that these assumptions are wrong.

'[52] *The imprecision of "inventive merit"*. This Court has recently warned against use of the expression "inventive merit". It was employed in the 19th century to express ideas now relevant to what is novel and to what is an inventive step (ss 18(1)(b)(i) and (ii) of the Act). "The phrase invites error through imprecision of legal analysis."

[53] *The language of s 40(3)*. Further, conceptions like "inventive step", "merit" and "technical contribution to the art" find no support in the statutory language of s 40(3). Section 40(1) speaks of a provisional specification describing "the invention" and s 40(2)(a) speaks of a complete specification describing "the invention fully". Section 40(2)(b) speaks of the claims "defining the invention". Section 40(4) speaks of the claims relating "to one invention only". Although s 40(3) does not use the word "invention", this context suggests, and the parties agreed, that the requirement in s 40(3) that the claims be fairly based on the matter described in the specification is a requirement that they be fairly based on the matter in it that discusses the "invention" (an expression which includes the "alleged invention"). In s 40(1), "invention" means "the embodiment which is described, and around which the claims are drawn". It has the same meaning in s 40(2). So far as s 40(3) implicitly refers to an invention, it must bear the same meaning there. It does not mean the "inventive step taken by the inventor" or the "advance in the art made by the inventor". Nor does it refer to inventive "merit" or to any "technical contribution to the art".

'[54] Even if s 40(3) did not impliedly refer to an invention, the language points to a comparison between the claims and what is described in the specification only, and again it does not call for any inquiry into an "inventive step", or inventive "merit" or a "technical contribution to the art".

. . .

'[68] *Erroneous principles*. The comparison which s 40(3) calls for is not analogous to that between a claim and an alleged anticipation or infringement. It is wrong to employ "an over meticulous verbal analysis". It is wrong to seek to isolate in the body of the specification "essential integers" or "essential features" of an alleged invention and to ask whether they correspond with the essential integers of the claim in question.

'[69] *"Real and reasonably clear disclosure"*. Section 40(3) requires, in Fullagar J's words, "a real and reasonably clear disclosure." But those words, when used in connection with s 40(3), do not limit disclosures to preferred embodiments.

The circumstance that something is a requirement for the best method of performing an invention does not make it necessarily a re-

quirement for all claims; likewise, the circumstance that material is part of the description of the invention does not mean that it must be included as an integer of each claim. Rather, the question is whether there is a real and reasonably clear disclosure in the body of the specification of what is then claimed, so that the alleged invention as claimed is broadly, that is to say in a general sense, described in the body of the specification.'

Fullagar J's phrase serves the function of compelling attention to the construction of the specification as a whole, putting aside particular parts which, although in isolation they might appear to point against the "real" disclosure, are in truth only loose or stray remarks.

. . .

'[89] Doric submitted that the expression "fairly based" is a composite expression, not calling for any separate inquiry into "fairness" and "basis". The expression required that the claim must fairly reflect what the specification teaches or describes to the addressee. It required a "qualitative" comparison between the claim and the matter described (ie the matter describing the invention fully pursuant to s 40(2)(a)). The matter to be described is "[t]he embodiment ... around which the claims are drawn." The claim should not be "wider than warranted by the disclosure made in the body of the specification." This "qualitative" comparison was, it was repeatedly said, a "matter of substance". These contentions were said to be supported by the history of fair basing before it became expressed as a statutory test in the 1949 UK Act and the 1952 Act: but it must be said that no part of the identified history suggested any particular solution to the present problem.

'[90] The essential difficulty with these arguments is that they never made it plain what quality was being sought or used as the basis of comparison. They tended towards circularity: it is not helpful to say that in making a qualitative comparison for the purposes of fair basing, the relevant quality is fairness. They contended that the quality was "fairness" in the sense of what was "reasonable" or "warranted" or "commensurate", but these expressions take the inquiry no further. The arguments asserted that the measure of fairness or reasonableness was that the claim must not travel beyond the disclosure, but this begs the question of what the disclosure was. Nor were the arguments advanced by the insistence that the matter was one of substance, not form.

'[91] Doric contended that if its arguments were rejected and the consistory clause on which the Patentee relied was sufficient to provide a fair basis, s 40(3) could be satisfied in every case by an assertion of the kind it contained. That is not so. Section 40(3) would only be satisfied if the specification read as a whole corresponded with the consistory clause; it cannot be satisfied by mere assertion in a consistory clause.

...

'[93] Further, there are examples of cases in which courts have refused to construe the specification as disclosing an invention limited to the preferred embodiment because of statements that it is not so limited, and have treated the consistory clause as disclosing the invention. Indeed, the employment of consistory clauses "co-extensive with or equivalent to the widest claim" was said by Blanco White in 1955, after the precursors to s 40(3) of the Act had come onto the statute book, to be usual. This was referred to without disapproval by Dixon CJ, Kitto and Windeyer JJ, who also said that in a modern specification, after a statement of the objects of the invention, "one might expect to find a general description of what the inventor asserts his invention consists of, commonly called a 'consistory clause'. This, however, is not an essential part of the body of a specification."

...

'[101] Doric's reliance on the decision of the Full Federal Court in *Atlantis Corporation Pty Ltd v Schindler* also was misplaced. The invention in that case was said in its title to relate to the provision of adequate drainage by artificial means with particular application to landscape gardening. The consistory clause described a particular apparatus but went on immediately to state that the invention taught a method of providing drainage utilising that apparatus. Claim 1 claimed the apparatus but with no limitation to its use for the purpose of drainage. Claim 1 was held to be unambiguous, not to be construed with such a limitation respecting drainage (as the primary judge McLelland CJ in Eq had construed it) and so to be not fairly based.

'[102] Although Doric did not explicitly request this Court to change settled principles in Australia respecting fair basing, it advanced arguments which could only be accepted if the law were changed. Thus its reliance on *Biogen Inc v Medeva plc* was an implicit invitation to adopt for s 40(3) the United Kingdom construction of a different provision.' *Lockwood Security Products Pty Ltd v Doric Products Pty Ltd* [2004] HCA 58 at [27], [50]–[54], [68]–[69], [89]–[91], [93], [101]–[102], per Gleeson CJ, McHugh, Gummow, Hayne and Heydon JJ; BC200407622

FAIRWAY

[The Collision Regulations and Distress Signals Order 1977 has been revoked. See now the Merchant Shipping (Distress Signals and Prevention of Collisions) Regulations 1983, SI 1983/708, Sch 1, r 9.]

FALSE

New Zealand [Following an earlier unreported decision of which Hillyer J approved the judge said:] 'His Honour held that the word "false" in s 151 was intended to mean more than merely erroneous and must involve an element of knowledge or intention to defraud so as to be deceitful in that sense.' *Collector of Customs v Thorn EMI Lighting (NZ) Ltd* [1988] 1 NZLR 705 at 708, per Hillyer J

FALSE IMPRISONMENT

[For 45 Halsbury's Laws (4th edn) para 1325 see now 45(2) Halsbury's Laws (4th edn) (Reissue) para 442.]

'For false imprisonment it is not necessary that the plaintiff should be aware of the fact of the imprisonment (see per Atkin LJ in *Meering v Grahame-White Aviation Co Ltd* (1920) 122 LT 44 at 53ñ54); although the damages might be diminished if the plaintiff was unconscious of the imprisonment. Atkin LJ continued (at 54): "If a man can be imprisoned by having the key turned upon him without his knowledge, so he can be imprisoned if, instead of a lock and key or bolts and bars, he is prevented from, in fact, exercising his liberty by guards and warders or policemen. They serve the same purpose. Therefore it appears to me to be a question of fact. It is true that in all cases of imprisonment so far as the law of civil liability is concerned that 'stone walls do not a prison make,' in the sense that they are not the only form of imprisonment, but any restraint within defined bounds which is a restraint in fact may be an imprisonment". It is clear that the policy of the law is jealously to protect personal liberty. Thus, it appears that, if a man is without justification confined in a room, it would be no defence to show that, if he had not been locked in, he would not in fact have had occasion to leave the room during the period of time over which he was so confined, although, again, that would be relevant to damages. The wrong done is the infringement of the right to the ability to leave and go elsewhere. Further, it would appear to follow that, if a man should be under some restraint not to leave a particular place for a period of time, for example because he does not have the means to leave, or because he has contracted to stay there to guard the place, or because, as a soldier or policeman, he has been ordered to remain there, he could, nevertheless, claim damages for false imprisonment if, without justification, he should be imprisoned within that place. The immediate and wholly unrestricted freedom and ability to go somewhere else are not, therefore, a precondition for asserting a claim in false imprisonment.' *Weldon v Home Office* [1990] 3 All ER 672 at 677, CA, per Ralph Gibson LJ

[A prisoner who had been segregated under prison rules for disciplinary offences claimed damages for 'false imprisonment'.] 'False imprisonment is the wrongful deprivation of a person of his liberty: P is wrongfully detained by D in a particular place (or places). Thus if P is *lawfully* detained by D in a particular place, ex hypothesi the detention cannot constitute wrongful imprisonment by D. But that is precisely what occurs when a person is committed to prison. When a person is committed to prison, the prison authorities may lawfully detain him in any place authorised by statute, viz today, in any prison. Likewise, it is for the prison authorities to decide whereabouts within a prison an inmate shall be confined. A prisoner's loss of freedom to go where he will is total. In this way it is inherent in lawful committal to prison that, in law, the prisoner has no right of action arising from the fact of his being detained by the prison authorities in any prison or in any particular place within a prison.' *R v Deputy Governor of Parkhurst Prison, ex p Hague* [1990] 3 All ER 687 at 709, CA, per Nicholls LJ

FALSE IN A MATERIAL PARTICULAR

Australia 'The expression "false in a material particular" appears in many statutes, both in this country and overseas. It has been discussed in *R v Lord Kylsant* [1932] 1 KB 442; *Murphy v Griffiths* [1967] 1 WLR 333; *R v Mallett* [1978] 1 WLR 820; *R v M* [1980] 2 NSWLR 195; *R v Brott* [1988] VR 1. In the last mentioned case, Brooking J pointed out that the concept is well understood. As his Honour said at 11: "An assertion that a document is false is to be taken as an assertion that it is false in a material particular". The term "material" requires no more and no less than that the false particular must be of moment or of significance, not merely trivial or inconsequential.

'Section 20(1) [of the Migration Act 1958 (Cth) referring to information on a passenger card] does not apply to statements that are merely false or misleading; there is the added requirement that the statement must be false or misleading in a material particular. In the context of s 20(1), a statement will be false or misleading in a material particular if it is relevant to the purpose for which it is made: see *Jovcevski v Minister for Immigration, Local Government and Ethnic Affairs* (Federal Court, Lockhart J, 12 October 1989, unreported). A statement will be relevant to that purpose if it may—not only if it must or if it will—be taken into account in making a decision under the Act as to the grant of the visa or entry permit in respect of which the statement is made.' *Minister for Immigration, Local Government and Ethnic Affairs v Dela Cruz* (1992) 110 ALR 367 at 371, per cur

FALSIFY

Australia [Section 560(1) of the Companies (Qld) Code provides that an officer of a company who 'falsifies' any books relating to the affairs of the company is guilty of an offence.] 'In my opinion, "falsifies" in s 560(1) simply means "make false" and does not require an alteration to a previously existing document: *R v Webber* (1988) 15 NSWLR 49.' *Dempster v National Companies and Securities Commission* (1993) 10 ACSR 297 at 355, per Malcolm CJ

FAMILY

[The Family Income Supplements Act 1970 has been repealed. The definition is now contained in the Social Security Contributions and Benefits Act 1992, s 137(1), as follows.] 'Family' means—
  (a) a married or unmarried couple;
  (b) married or unmarried couple and a member of the same household for whom one of them is or both are responsible and who is a child or a person of a prescribed description;
  (c) except in prescribed circumstances, a person who is not a member of a married or unmarried couple and a member of the same household for whom that person is responsible and who is a child or a person of a prescribed description.

[The Capital Gains Tax Act 1979 has been repealed. The definition is re-enacted, with minor drafting amendments, in the Taxation of Chargeable Gains Act 1992, Sch 6 para 1(2).]

'Family' in, relation to [a child in need], includes any person who has parental responsibility for the child and any other person with whom he has been living. (Children Act 1989, s 17(10))

[The Rent Act 1977, Sch 1 para 2(1), allows the 'surviving spouse' of a statutory tenant to succeed to the tenancy on the death of the original tenant. Where a homosexual couple had lived together for a long period, the surviving partner claimed to be entitled to succeed to the statutory tenancy as 'a person who was living with the original tenant as his or her wife or husband' as permitted by Sch 1 para 1(2), or alternatively to succeed to an assured tenancy as a 'member of the original tenant's family' within Sch 1 para 3(1).] 'Is it fatal to a claim to be a member of the family of the original tenant that the appellant cannot show that he was living with Mr Thompson as his husband or wife, the nearest family relationship he asserts? In my view it is not. If a person does not succeed on the first he may still succeed on the second category. Here the partner fails because the first category requires partners of different sexes. That he cannot satisfy. If he satisfies the definition of family he may still qualify.

'I turn then to the second question which I, at any rate, have found a difficult one — difficult largely because of preconceptions of a family as being a married couple and, if they have children, their children; difficult also because of the result in some of the earlier cases when applying the law to the facts. It is, however, obvious that the word "family" is used in a number of different senses, some wider, some narrower. "Do you have any family?" usually means "do you have children?" "We're having a family gathering" may include often distant relatives and even very close friends. The "family of nations", "the Christian family" are very wide. This is no new phenomenon. Roman law, as I understand it, included in the familia all members of the social unit though other rights might be limited to spouses or heirs.

'It is not an answer to the problem to assume (as I accept may be correct) that if in 1920 people had been asked whether one person was a member of another same-sex person's family, the answer would have been "no". That is not the right question. The first question is what were the characteristics of a family in the 1920 Act [Increase of Rent and Mortgage Interest (Restrictions) Act 1920], and the second whether two same-sex partners can satisfy those characteristics so as today to fall within the word "family". An alternative question is whether the word "family" in the 1920 Act has to be updated so as to be capable of including persons who today would be regarded as being of each other's family, whatever might have been said in

1920 (see Lord Steyn in *R v Ireland, R v Burstow* [1997] 4 All ER 225 at 232, [1998] AC 147 at 158, Bennion *Statutory Interpretation* (3rd edn, 1997) p 686 and 44(1) *Halsbury's Laws* (4th edn) (1995 reissue) para 1473).

'If "family" could only mean a legal relationship (of blood or by legal ceremony of marriage or by legal adoption) then the appellant must obviously fail. Over the years, however, the courts have held that this is not so.

'In the first place, it has been said that the ordinary meaning of the word is to be taken; "family" where it is used in the Rent Acts is not a term of art (per Lord Diplock in *Carega Properties SA (formerly Joram Developments Ltd) v Sharratt* [1979] 2 All ER 1084 at 1086, [1979] 1 WLR 928 at 931, though the meaning for Viscount Dilhorne ([1979] 2 All ER 1084 at 1087, [1979] 1 WLR 928 at 932) is a question of law and "family" is not the same as "household".

'In the second place, it has been accepted that de facto relationships can be recognised as constituting a family …

'In the application of this "ordinary meaning", "de facto" approach there are not surprisingly decisions on both sides of the line …

…

'The issue is in my view open for your Lordships to decide.

'Given, on the basis of these earlier decisions that the word is to be applied flexibly, and does not cover only legally binding relationships, it is necessary to ask what are its characteristics in this legislation and, to answer that question, to ask further what was Parliament's purpose. It seems to me that the intention in 1920 was that not just the legal wife but also the other members of the family unit occupying the property on the death of the tenant with him should qualify for the succession. The former did not need to prove a qualifying period; as a member of the tenant's family a two-year residence had to be shown. If more than one person qualified, then, if no agreement could be reached between them, the court decided who should succeed.

'The hallmarks of the relationship were essentially that there should be a degree of mutual inter-dependence, of the sharing of lives, of caring and love, of commitment and support. In respect of legal relationships these are presumed, though evidently they are not always present, as the family law and criminal courts know only too well. In de facto relationships these are capable, if proved, of creating membership of the tenant's family. If, as I consider, this was the purpose of the legislation, the question is then who in 1994 or today (I draw no distinction between them) are capable in law of being members of the tenant's family. It is not who would have been so considered in 1920. In considering this question it is necessary to have regard to changes in attitude. The point cannot have been better put than it was by Bingham MR in *R v Ministry of Defence, ex p Smith* [1996] 1 All ER 257 at 261–263,[1996] QB 517 at 552–554 when, although dealing with the validity of an administrative decision rather than the meaning of a few words in a statute, said, after referring to changes of attitude in society towards same-sex relationships:

> "I regard the progressive development and refinement of public and professional opinion at home and abroad, here very briefly described, as an important feature of this case. A belief which represented unquestioned orthodoxy in Year X may have become questionable by Year Y, and unsustainable by Year Z. Public and professional opinion are a continuum." (See [1996] 1 All ER 257 at 263, [1996] QB 517 at 554.)

If "meaning" is substituted for "opinion" the words are no less appropriate. In *Barclays Bank plc v O'Brien* [1993] 4 All ER 417 at 431, [1994] 1 AC 180 at 198 Lord Browne-Wilkinson (with whom other members of the House agreed) said that in relation to the equity arising from undue influence in a loan transaction:

> "But in my judgment the same principles are applicable to all other cases where there is an emotional relationship between cohabitees. The "tenderness" shown by the law to married women is not based on the marriage ceremony but reflects the underlying risk of one cohabitee exploiting the emotional involvement and trust of the other. Now that unmarried cohabitation, whether heterosexual or homosexual, is widespread in our society, the law should recognise this."

'In particular, if the 1988 amendment had not been made ("as his or her wife or husband") I would have no hesitation in holding today when, it appears, one-third of younger people live together unmarried, that where there is a stable, loving and caring relationship which is not intended to be merely temporary and where the couple live together broadly as they would if they were married, that each can be a member of the other's family for the purpose of the 1977 Act.

'If, as I think, in the light of all the authorities this is the proper interpretation of the 1920 Act I hold that as a matter of law a same-sex partner of a deceased tenant can establish the necessary familial link. They are capable of being, in Russell LJ's words in *Ross v Collins*, "a broadly recognisable de facto familial nexus"(see [1964] 1 All ER 861 at 866,[1964] 1 WLR 425 at 432). It is then a question of fact as to whether he or she does establish the necessary link.

'It is accordingly not necessary to consider the alternative question as to whether by 1999 the meaning of the word in the 1920 Act needs to be updated. I prefer to say that it is not the meaning which has changed but that those who are capable of falling within the words have changed.

...

'It seems to be suggested that the result which I have so far indicated would be cataclysmic. In relation to this Act it is plainly not so. The onus on one person claiming that he or she was a member of the same-sex original tenant's family will involve that person establishing rather than merely asserting the necessary indicia of the relationship. A transient superficial relationship will not do even if it is intimate. Mere cohabitation by friends as a matter of convenience will not do. There is, in any event, a minimum residence qualification; the succession is limited to that of the original tenant. Far from being cataclysmic it is, as both the county court judge and the Court of Appeal appear to recognise, and as I consider, in accordance with contemporary notions of social justice. In other statutes, in other contexts, the same meaning may or may not be the right one. If a narrower meaning is required, so be it. It seems also to be suggested that such a result in this statute undermines the traditional (whether religious or social) concept of marriage and the family. It does nothing of the sort. It merely recognises that, for the purposes of this Act, two people of the same sex can be regarded as having established membership of a family, one of the most significant of human relationships which both gives benefits and imposes obligations.

'It is plain on the findings of the county court judge that in this case, on the view of the law which I have accepted, on the facts the appellant succeeds as a member of Mr Thompson's family living with him at his death.' *Fitzpatrick v Sterling Housing Association Ltd* [1999] 4 All ER 705 at 710–711, 714–715, 716–717, HL, per Lord Slynn of Hadleigh

'The question calling for decision in the present case is a question of statutory interpretation. It is whether a same-sex partner is capable of being a member of the other partner's family for the purposes of the Rent Act legislation. I am in no doubt that this question should be answered affirmatively. A man and woman living together in a stable and permanent sexual relationship are capable of being members of a family for this purpose. Once this is accepted, there can be no rational or other basis on which the like conclusion can be withheld from a similarly stable and permanent sexual relationship between two men or between two women. Where a relationship of this character exists, it cannot make sense to say that, although a heterosexual partnership can give rise to membership of a family for Rent Act purposes, a homosexual partnership cannot. Where sexual partners are involved, whether heterosexual or homosexual, there is scope for the intimate mutual love and affection and long-term commitment that typically characterise the relationship of husband and wife. This love and affection and commitment can exist in same-sex relationships as in heterosexual relationships. In sexual terms a homosexual relationship is different from a heterosexual relationship, but I am unable to see that the difference is material for present purposes. As already emphasised, the concept underlying membership of a family for present purposes is the sharing of lives together in a single family unit living in one house.

...

'I must also mention the "ordinary person" test enunciated by Cohen LJ in *Brock v Wollams* [1949] 1 All ER 715 at 718, [1949] 2 KB 388 at 395. He suggested that the trial judge should ask himself this question: would an ordinary person, addressing his mind to the question whether the defendant was a member of the family, have answered "yes" or "no"? This oft-quoted test has tended to bedevil this area of the law. It may be useful as a reminder that family is not a term of art. But the test gives uncertain guidance when, as here, the members of the Court of Appeal and also your Lordships are divided on how the question should be answered. Contrary to what seems implicit in this form of question, the expression "family" does not have a single, readily recognisable meaning. As I have emphasised, the meaning of family depends upon the context in which it is being used. The suggested question does not assist in identifying the essential ingredients of the concept of family in the present context.

'In the course of a well-reasoned and attractively presented argument, Mr Chapman submitted that homosexual relationships have always existed and that at the inception of the Rent Act regime in the 1920s a homosexual partner would not have been regarded as a member of the tenant's family. In those days homosexual acts between men constituted a criminal offence. This remained so until they were decriminalised by the Sexual Offences Act 1967.

'This submission raises the question whether the word "family" as used in the Rent Acts may change its meaning as ways of life and social attitudes change. Can the expression family legitimately be interpreted in 1999 as having a different and wider meaning than when it was first enacted in 1920? The principles applicable were stated cogently by Lord Wilberforce in *Royal College of Nursing of the UK v Dept of Health and Social Security* [1981] 1 All ER 545 at 564–565, [1981] AC 800 at 822. A statute must necessarily be interpreted having regard to the state of affairs existing when it was enacted. It is a fair presumption that Parliament's intention was directed at that state of affairs. When circumstances change, a court has to consider whether they fall within the parliamentary intention. They may do so if there can be detected a clear purpose in the legislation which can only be fulfilled if an extension is made. How liberally these principles may be applied must depend upon the nature of the enactment, and the strictness or otherwise of the words in which it was expressed.

'In the present case Parliament used an ordinary word of flexible meaning and left it undefined. The underlying legislative purpose was to provide a secure home for those who share their lives together with the original tenant in the manner which characterises a family unit. This purpose would be at risk of being stultified if the courts could not have regard to changes in the way people live together and changes in the perception of relationships. This approach is supported by the fact that successive Rent Acts have used the same undefined expression despite the far-reaching changes in ways of life and social attitudes meanwhile. It would be unattractive, to the extent of being unacceptable, to interpret the word "family" in the 1977 Act without regard to these changes.

...

'In one respect of crucial importance there has been a change in social attitudes over the last half-century. I am not referring to the change in attitude toward sexual relationships between a man and woman outside marriage or toward homosexual relationships. There has been a widespread change in attitude toward such relationships, although differing and deeply felt views are held on these matters. These differing views are to be recognised and respected. The crucial change to which I am referring is related but different. It is that the morality of a lawful relationship is not now regarded as relevant when the court is deciding whether an individual qualifies for protection under the Rent Acts. Parliament itself made this clear in 1988, when amending the Rent Acts in the 1988 Act. Paragraph 2(3) of Sch 1 envisages that more than one person may be living with the tenant as a surviving spouse under the extended definition. In so enacting the law, Parliament was not expressing a view, either way, on the morality of such relationships. But by this provision Parliament made plain that, for purposes of Rent Act protection, what matters is the factual position. The same must be true of homosexual relationships.

'It is for this reason that I do not accept the argument that the inclusion of a tenant's homosexual partner within the ranks of persons eligible to qualify as members of his family is a step which should be left to Parliament. It really goes without saying that in cases such as this the courts must always proceed with particular caution and sensitivity. That is not to say the courts can never proceed at all …

'In this regard, at the risk of repetition, it is necessary to stress the limited nature of the decision in this case. The courts have already decided that the undefined expression "family" is to be given a wide meaning in the context of the Rent Acts. The courts have already decided that family includes relationships other than those based on consanguinity or affinity. To include same-sex partners is to do no more than apply to them the same rationale as that underlying the inclusion of different sex partners. The decision goes no further than this. The decision leaves untouched questions such as whether persons of the same sex should be able to marry, and whether a stable homosexual relationship is within the scope of the right to respect for family life in art 8 of the Convention for the Protection of Human Rights and Fundamental Freedoms (Rome, 4 November 1950; TS 71 (1953); Cmd 8969).' *Fitzpatrick v Sterling Housing Association Ltd* [1999] 4 All ER 705 at 720, 721–723, HL, per Lord Nicholls of Birkenhead

Australia [Whether family is family within or sub-group of 'native title group' for purposes of (Cth) Native Title Act 1993 s 61(1).] 'The word "family" as applied to people can be used in a variety of senses. The *Oxford English Dictionary* (2nd ed), for example, includes the following amongst possible meanings of "family":

"3.a. The group of persons consisting of the parents and their children, whether actually living together or not; in wider sense, the unity formed by those who are nearly connected by blood or affinity.

4.a. Those descended or claiming descent from a common ancestor: a house, kindred, lineage."

Alternatively the term as used in the application may have its own dictionary or conventional meaning. There is no evidence to suggest this is the case, but the additional description of the claim group "and other related people etc" suggests this might be so.

'The additional description merely compounds the fatal flaw in the formula used. While it purports to be an inclusive formula, it is an ambiguous one in several respects. The first ambiguity inheres in the word "related" and this is because of the varying possible meanings of family. The second and more important ambiguity is whether the formula is intended to be definitive of the group, i e a related person is a member. Or is it permissive, i e it includes such related persons who wish to participate in the claim.

…

'The description used is incapable, without elaboration, of conveying meaning to the Court, or to individuals who may be contemplating applying to be joined: *Ford v NSW Minister for Land & Water Conservation* [2000] FCA 1913.' *Colbung v Western Australia* [2003] FCA 774 at [38]–[41] per Finn J; BC200304122

FAMILY ARRANGEMENT

[For 18 Halsbury's Laws (4th edn) para 304 see now 42 Halsbury's Laws (4th edn) (Reissue) paras 1002, 1004.]

FAMILY MEMBER

New Zealand [Domestic Violence Act 1995, s 2.] 'My conclusion is that for the purpose of establishing family relationships under the Domestic Violence Act, a live-in same-sex relationship is equated to legal marriage. Putting it another way, if one woman lives together with another woman in a relationship in the nature of marriage, her partner is the "family member" of her brother for jurisdictional purposes under the Act.' *P v M* [1998] 3 NZLR 246 at 252 per Fisher J

FARMING

Australia ' "Farming" is defined in vol 12 of the Second Edition of the *Oxford English Dictionary*, inter alia, to be "business of cultivating land, raising stock, etc, agriculture husbandry". In *Lowe (Inspector of Taxes) v J W Ashmore Ltd* [1971] Ch 545 at 553 Megarry J stated that: "It [farming] must at least include the raising of beasts, the cultivation of land and the growing of crops … " The case of *Camden Park Estate Pty Ltd v Commissioner of Land Tax (NSW)* (1983) 84 ATC 4,334 can be distinguished factually. In that case the storage of milk at an intermediary location in order to cool it down did not in substance add anything whereas the processing and pasterisation of the milk did … The Tribunal is satisfied that the processing of livestock does not fall within the definition. Processing, by its very nature, is part of the secondary stage of production and cannot be classified as primary production.' *Inghams Enterprises Pty Ltd v Commissioner of State Taxation* (1996) 16 SR (WA) 88 at 92, per the Tribunal

FASHION HOUSE

Australia 'The expression "fashion house" is a basic English expression: see the *New Shorter Oxford Dictionary* 1993, where the definition of "house" includes "[a] place of business; a business establishment, a firm; spec. a printing or publishing firm, *a couture or fashion establishment*" (emphasis added). Under the definition of "fashion", the dictionary refers to the usage of the expression "fashion" in the context of "fashion house", and refers to "a business establishment displaying and selling high-quality clothes". The *Macquarie Dictionary*, 2nd ed 1995, defines the expression "fashion house" as an expression in its own right to mean "a firm which designs and manufactures fashionable clothing primarily for the very rich". The expression is frequently used in relation to prestigious enterprises.' *Gianni Versace SpA v Monte* BC200200707; [2002] FCA 190 at [159], per Tamberlin J

FAST FOOD

Australia 'The expression "fast food" is well established in the English language, both here and overseas. It is to be found, for instance, in Sch 1 of the Retail Leases Act 1994 (NSW), and is used in combination with the word "outlets" by Hill J in *Pepsi Seven-Up Bottlers Perth Pty Ltd v*

Commissioner of Taxation (1995) 62 FCR 289 to describe types of establishment that include those belonging to the Pizza Hut chain and hamburger stores. In The Oxford English Dictionary, 2d Ed (1989), Vol V, it is stated to have originated in the United States, and is defined, according to the well known method of that dictionary, with examples of the usage from which the meaning has been derived, as follows:

> ***Fast food.*** Orig. US. Also fast-food, fastfood. [f. FAST a. + FOOD sb.] a. Used attributively with reference to catering outlets where foods are kept hot and ready to serve, or partially prepared so that they can be served quickly. 1951 Fountain & Fast Food Service Oct. 39/1 The partners have become old hands at spotting the type of conventioneer that will patronize their fast food service. 1960 Fast Food July 17/2 Fast food type restaurants do the lion's share of business for breakfast and noon meals eaten out. 1968 N.Y. Times 23 June III. 2/3 Another star performer in the fast-food field has been A-G Foods, which … operates a string of quick-service restaurants. 1975 New Yorker 14 Apr. 80/1 Supermarkets and fast-food shops are gaining great ground. 1978 Tucson Mag. Dec. 6/3 Nothing but a glorified, garlic-flavoured fastfood operation with the poorest example of Italian cuisine. 1984 Verbatim X. III. 20/2 Fastfood eateries often dispense plastic "silverware".
> b. The type of food served in these restaurants; convenience food which can be prepared quickly at home. 1954 (title) Fountain and fast food. 1960 Fast Food Feb. 48/1 Delicate scallops are really fast food … because they come ready to cook. 1977 Times 6 June 2/5 "Fast food" requires no preparation by the customer. Traditional "fast food outlets" like fish-and-chip shops are being superseded by Chinese, Indian, Kebab and fried chicken houses. 1980 Guardian 24 May 19/8 Fastfoods have managed to get rid of their junk tag and cash in on new attitudes to leisure. 1985 Times 11 Nov. 3 /4 (heading) £1,000 for a British fast food.

'Similarly although less comprehensively, in the Macquarie Dictionary, revised 3d Ed (2001), the expression is defined:

> ***fast food*** noun food for sale, as chicken, chips, hamburgers, etc, which can be provided without delay.

'It would, of course, be wrong simply to apply a dictionary definition in a mechanical way, which failed to draw from the whole clause all that is actually expressed by the language defined when used as it is used in cl 19.1(a). As I put it in *Gantry Acquisition Corp. v Parker -; Parsley Petroleum Australia Pty Ltd* (1994) 51 FCR 554 at 569:

> [N]o word [and the same applies to an expression such as "fast food"] has a meaning which remains rigidly fixed, however it is used. A word is not a locked box with static contents; it is more like a living cell, changing as it responds to the environment, which is its context.

'But nothing in the context or use here can move the meaning away from the essential ideas of quick service and of the style of food and establishment associated with that quick service. Both Sea King Seafood and Oporto exhibit these characteristics. In the words of one of the quotations selected by the Oxford Dictionary, both are "quick-service restaurants", and they serve the type of food to be found in such restaurants — fish and chips, or chicken or hamburgers with chips. Another of the Oxford Dictionary's illustrative quotations refers, as the traditional paradigm of "fast food outlets", to "fish-and-chip shops" and goes on to mention "fried chicken houses", while the Macquarie Dictionary takes "chicken, chips, hamburgers, etc which can be provided without delay" for its exemplification of "fast food".' *Owners Corp Strata Plan v Charbel CJ Pty Ltd* [2004] NSWSC 1286 at [18]–[19], per Burchett AJ; BC200503617

FAVOURABLE

Canada [Increased costs were available where judgment obtained was more favourable than settlement offer.] 'The shorter Oxford English Dictionary defines "favourable" as including that which facilitates one's purposes or wishes, and that which concedes what is desired. As mentioned earlier, my view is that the concept of favourability requires only comparability between the offer and the judgment, not equivalence, and not correspondence.' *Hunger Project v Council on Mind Abuse (COMA) Inc* (1995) 121 DLR (4th) 734, Ont Gen Div, per J Macdonald J

FEDERAL BOARD

Canada ' "Federal board, commission or other tribunal" is defined in s 2(1) of the Federal Court Act:

> "federal board, commission or other tribunal" means any body or any person or persons having, exercising or purporting to exercise jurisdiction or powers conferred by or under an Act of Parliament or by or under an order made pursuant to a prerogative of the Crown
> ...

'When the Governor in Council acts pursuant to a statute, it is a federal board.' *Saskatchewan Wheat Pool v Canada (A-G)* (1993) 107 DLR (4th) 190 at 192, per Rothstein J (Fed TD)

FEDERAL JURISDICTION

Australia '[I]t has been accepted that the exercise by this Court or any other federal court of jurisdiction with respect to any of the matters of the description in s 75 and s 76 of the Constitution is the exercise of federal jurisdiction within the meaning of s 79.' *Northern Territory v GPAO* (1999) 161 ALR 318 at 327; 24 Fam LR 253; 73 ALJR 470; BC9900714, per Gleeson CJ and Gummow J

FEE

Canada '... In the Concise Oxford Dictionary (8th ed), "fee" is defined as

> 1. a payment made to a professional person or to a professional or public body in exchange for advice or services. 2. money paid as part of a special transaction, for a privilege, admission to a society, etc. (enrolment fee).

' "Charge" is said to be "a price asked for goods or services" or "a financial liability or commitment".

'Counsel for the respondent stated that only *R. v Churchill*, *supra*, has held that legislation which authorized a "fee" also permits the levying of a tax. The term "tax" is, of course, one with a profoundly legal history. In *Lawson v Interior Tree Fruit & Vegetable Committee*, *supra*, at p 363, the Supreme Court of Canada defined the components of a tax as, (1) enforceable by law, (2) imposed by authority of a legislature, (3) imposed by a public body, and (4) for a public purpose. *R. v Churchill*, *supra*, was a case where the levy imposed by a provincial statute on mobile homes, while it was said to be a "fee", was treated by McIntyre J throughout as a tax. The operative provision in the British Columbia statute was:

> 2. Subject to section 4, every person who is in charge of, or operates, a mobile home park shall, on or before the fifteenth day of each

month, pay a fee to the collector in whose jurisdiction the mobile home park is situated, in an amount to be determined by multiplying the number of mobile homes of each class designated in the schedule located in a mobile home park during the preceding month or any part thereof by the rate set out in the Table of Fees in the Schedule. [*Mobile Home Park Fee Act*, SBC 1971, c 35.]

'The issue in *Churchill* was not, as here, whether a fee as distinct from a tax was authorized, but whether what was accepted as a tax imposed by the provincial legislature was *ultra vires* as an indirect tax which s. 92(2) of the *British North America Act, 1867*, would not allow. It is a case where what was said to be a fee was in reality a tax and readily accepted without analysis as such. It is quite distinct from this case on the issue of "fee" or "tax" because (1) the statute required or provided nothing to the payor in return, and (2) the levy came within the *Lawson* criteria for a tax.

'In *The Law of Municipal Corporations, supra*, Ian Rogers wrote at p 737 that there is a distinction between the authority for a municipality to impose a tax and its authority to collect a fee such as a licensing fee. He agreed, however, that sometimes the terms fee, charge and tax are used interchangeably. *R. v Churchill* is an example where the term "fee" was used merely as a synonym for a tax and no distinction was required …

…

'The types of cases where a distinction between "fee" or "charge" and "tax" become important were those where an institution or corporation had been granted a statutory exemption from "taxation" and a municipality attempted to levy a charge against it, or those where a charge was made for a service under a provincially authorized scheme and the "fee" was upheld as a fee for service used toward the cost of the overall service-provider and not invalid as an indirect tax *ultra vires* of the province.' *Ontario Private Campground Assn v Harvey (Township)* (1997) 146 DLR (4th) 347 at 361–362, Ont Gen Div, per Howden J

FEE FARM RENT

[For 39 Halsbury's Laws (4th edn) para 1206 see now 39(2) Halsbury's Laws (4th edn) (Reissue) para 756.]

FENCE

[For 4 Halsbury's Laws (4th edn) para 877 see now 4(1) Halsbury's Laws (4th edn) (2002 Reissue) para 917.]

FILING

[Under the relevant statutory provisions and rules of court, the claimant had a certain number of days in which to file an appeal notice to bring a statutory appeal in the county court. CPR 2.3(1) provides that 'filing' a document means delivering it, by post or otherwise, to the court office.] '[9] At this point it is necessary to refer to the definition of "filing" in CPR 2.3(1). That sub-rule provides as follows: "'filing', in relation to a document, means delivering it, by post or otherwise, to the court office …"

…

'[41] I can now state my own conclusions. I turn to the first issue. In my judgment, this is a *Swainston* case [*Swainston v Hetton Victory Club Ltd* [1983] 1 All ER 1179] rather than an *Aadan* case[*Aadan v Brent London BC* (2000) 32 HLR 848], in that mere delivery of an appeal notice to the appropriate court office is sufficient to constitute the "filing" of the notice within the terms of the definition of that word in CPR 2.3(1), without any additional requirement that there should be someone at the court office to receive it, and/or to authenticate it.

…

'[45] In my judgment the instant case is stronger than *Swainston*'s case, in that whilst, as Browne-Wilkinson J noted ([1983] 1 All ER 1179 at 1182), the concept of presentation requires "some form of collaboration by the person to whom the presentation is being made", the concept of delivery to an office does not. If presentation to a court or tribunal is a unilateral act, in the sense in which Browne-Wilkinson J used that word, then in my judgment, a fortiori delivery to an office is.'

'[55] Counsel, for whose excellent submissions I am grateful, agree that the essential task of the court is to construe the definition of "filing" in CPR 2.3(1). The words are: "'filing', in relation to a document, means delivering it, by post or otherwise, to the court office …"

'[56] The current rule can be contrasted with the old Ord 2, r 4 of the County Court Rules, which referred to "filing it [the document] in the court office by delivering it to the proper officer for entry by him in the records of the court". So one notes that under that old rule we were told where the document was being filed (in the court office); how (by delivery to a person, the court officer); and even why (for entry by him in the record). The current rule is considerably simpler.

'[57] I look first to the opening words: "'filing', in relation to a document, means delivering it". To file a document the party has to do something, namely deliver it. It is his act, no one else's. Next, I take the words "by post or otherwise". This indicates to me that the method of delivery by post is an acceptable form of delivery. The postman delivers the post, usually, one hopes, before the court office is open. It involves no further act by anyone, unless perhaps to pick it up later out of the letterbox or off the floor and carry it to a more convenient place. So too with the document pushed by a party through the same letterbox. The final words, "to the court office", show that delivery is to a place, not to a person, suggesting again that there is no reciprocal act of acceptance required.

'[58] Taking all of that together, delivery seems to me to involve a unilateral, not a transactional, act. The ordinary meaning of the words, therefore, "posting through the letterbox", as was done here, would be sufficient.

'[59] I see the force of Mr Bhose's argument that this construction may lead to uncertainty. If no one is in the office to verify whether the document arrived before or after midnight, there is a potential difficulty. Under 5PD, paras 5.1 and 5.2 the court is required to record on the document the date on which it was filed and enter that date and other information on the court records. It will be apparent, however, to the court staff that a document of the kind we have been dealing with here will have been personally delivered by hand, not by the postman. It may, therefore, be necessary for enquiry to be made by the court office of the filing party to ascertain when delivery was effected. That is a nuisance, but it does enable the date of delivery to be ascertained and the uncertainty dissolved. I hope, in any event, that this does not happen often.'
Van Aken v Camden London Borough Council [2002] EWCA Civ 1724 at [9], [41], [45], [55]–[59], [2003] 1 All ER 552, per Jonathan Parker and Ward LJJ

FILM

In this Part [Part I: Copyright] 'film' means a recording on any medium from which a moving image may by any means be produced. (Copyright, Designs and Patents Act 1988, s 6)

FINAL ORDER

Australia 'The inclusion of the expression "final order" in s 40(1)(g) of the Bankruptcy Act 1966 (Cth) gives the section a wider application than earlier provisions that operated only by reference to a "final judgment". The section also acknowledges that a final order can be made in

either an action or a proceeding; so even if there is reason for holding that a judgment in an action will only be "final" for the purposes of s 40(1)(g) if this requirement is satisfied, there is, in my opinion, no justification for holding that an order in a proceeding will be final only if the proceeding possesses a common but not invariable characteristic of an action, viz, that it is a proceeding in which it would have been open to the defendant debtor to have raised a counter-claim or set-off. There is no justification for finding, by reference to cases decided on the bankruptcy statutes when they did not permit a bankruptcy notice to issue in respect of a final order in a proceeding, but only in respect of a final judgment in an action, limitations on the phrase "final order in a proceeding" which was introduced into the Acts to widen their operation. The only limitations on whether an order is a final one are those to be gathered from the words of the section ...' *Re Gibbs; ex p Triscott* (1995) 133 ALR 718 at 729, per Drummond J

FINANCE (VERB)

Canada [An employee was disentitled to unemployment insurance benefits if he was, inter alia, 'financing' a labour dispute.] 'The term "financing" has to have an air of reality to it. It ought to be read as requiring active and voluntary involvement by the claimant and as implying a meaningful connection between the payment and the dispute. An individual, generally speaking, pays dues to insure membership in good standing in his or her local, to insure continued service from local executives, and to insure strike payments to him or her if the local decides to engage in a lawful strike.' *Hills v Canada (A-G)* [1988] 1 SCR 513 at 559, SCC, per L'Heureux-Dube J

FINANCIAL ASSISTANCE

New Zealand 'In practical terms, there is no relevant distinction between money and money's worth. To regard the section [s 62 of the Companies Act 1955] as dealing with the one and not the other would be to treat it as if it read "monetary" assistance, rather than "financial" assistance. The latter is a word of much less precise meaning, indicative of value rather than of a particular form in which value may be given. Indeed it is clear from the words of the section itself that it extends beyond purely monetary assistance. Further, we see no difference in principle between a purchase and a sale. If there is no reason for the company in the pursuit of its own commercial interests to sell an asset, and if the only reason is to enable the purchaser to use the asset to buy shares in the company, we think there is the provision of financial assistance and therefore contravention of s 62.' *Catley v Herbert* [1988] 1 NZLR 606 at 615, CA, per cur

FIND OUT

Australia [Under s 17(1) of the Sentencing Act 1995 (NT) the court, in determining the amount of a fine and the way in which it is to be paid, is required to take into account the financial circumstances of the offender and the burden its payment will impose. However, s 17(2) states that a court is not prevented from fining an offender only because it has been unable to 'find out' the matters referred to in s 17(1).] 'The use of the words "unable to find out" import that there is a duty on the court. Amongst other things the Oxford English Dictionary defines "find out" as (a) to discover by attention, scrutiny, study etc; (b) to come upon by searching or enquiry. All of that brings about the notion of activity by the court to ascertain the required information, not mere reception of information if any is offered.' *Nelson v Meredith* BC200100222; [2001] NTSC 4 at [10], per Martin CJ

FIRE

[For 25 Halsbury's Laws (4th edn) para 618 see now 25 Halsbury's Laws (4th edn) (2003 Reissue) paras 591–594.]

Loss by

[For 25 Halsbury's Laws (4th edn) para 155 see now 25 Halsbury's Laws (4th edn) (2003 Reissue) para 334.]

FIREARM

Antique firearm

'I have … reached the conclusion that in defining "an antique firearm" it is necessary, first, to look at its age, and without sufficient age a gun, no matter what its history and interest, cannot be considered to be "an antique firearm". I consider age to be an essential prerequisite in this matter. I am, however, not prepared to put a definite time-scale on this although I would be surprised if, without very strong other factors, a twentieth-century gun came within this definition. As Everleigh J pointed out in *Richards v Curwen* [[1977] 3 All ER 426] the age at which something is entitled to the adjective "antique" must vary depending on the "article". Once a gun has been shown to be of sufficient age, other factors can be considered in deciding whether it can truly be regarded as "an antique firearm". Among these factors are its historical or other interest, its design and status and also its value.' *Walkingshaw v Wallace* 1990 SCCR 203 at 209, Sh Ct, per Sheriff Dixon

Meaning of 'lethal'

[*Moore v Gooderham* was approved in *R v Thorpe* [1987] 2 All ER 108, CA.]

FIREPLACE

[The Clean Air Act 1956 has been repealed. The definition is re-enacted in the Clean Air Act 1993, s 64(1).]

FIRM

Australia 'The word "firm", in its ordinary meaning, covers a wide variety of organisations including corporations. This is confirmed by an examination of relevant dictionaries. For example, in the *New Shorter Oxford English Dictionary* (1993) the third meaning attributed to the word is as follows:

> "A partnership or company for carrying on a business; a group of people working together, orig. (derog.) to further their own interests; (a criminal) organisation or gang; a group of hospital doctors and their assistants."

'*Butterworths Australian Legal Dictionary* (1997) contains a number of definitions. The first refers to an unincorporated body of persons associated together for the purpose of carrying on business. The second definition is as follows:

> "An undertaking providing legal services to the public for reward comprising a sole practitioner or partners or a solicitor corporation, employed solicitors and other staff, and other assets including work in progress, good will and liabilities. The sole practitioner or partners carry on professional practice under a business or firm name. For some purposes, a "firm of solicitors" includes solicitors who share remuneration as solicitors, whether or not on the same basis for each of them …"

'The third meaning given is that of the collective name for persons who have entered into partnership with one another.' *Re Kidd* BC200204368; [2002] VSC 300 at [7]–[9], per Smith J

FIRST

[The claimants claimed title to certain land by adverse possession. The defendant disputed the claim on the ground that even if the claimants proved all the adverse possession they asserted, the intervention of the Crown's ownership during that period meant that the relevant limitation period had not expired. The Limitation Act 1980, Sch 1 para 12 provides that notwithstanding the statutory time limit for actions to recover land in s 15(1), where in the case of any action brought by a person other than the Crown the right of action first accrued to the Crown through whom the person in question claims, the action may be brought at any time before the expiration of (a) the period during which the action could have been brought by the Crown or (b) 12 years from the date on which the right of action accrued to some person other than the Crown, whichever period first expires. The defendant contended that the word 'first' in the phrase 'first accrued to the Crown' in para 12 meant 'earlier' or 'previously' rather than 'originally' and that para 12 so interpreted provided it with a complete answer to the claim.] '[18] The difference between these rival submissions turns on the sense of the word "first" in the phrase "first accrued to the Crown" in para 12. Mr Jefferies submitted that it means "earlier" or "previously" rather than "originally". If that is right, then even if the right of action to recover the disputed land *originally* accrued to the GLC, it "first accrued to the Crown" within the true sense of the word "first" as used in para 12. So interpreted, para 12 defeats the claim.

'[19] Mr Reynolds's submission was that "first" in that phrase does not mean "earlier" or "previously". It means "first" in the sense of "originally", and he pointed to the use of the same word in s 15(1), where he said it obviously means "originally", not "earlier" or "previously". As Pt II of Sch 1 modifies s 15, it would, he said, be odd if para 12 was using the word in a different sense. If this interpretation of para 12 is correct, Mr Reynolds's further submission was that, subject to one qualification, para 12 has no application to this case. That is because the claimants' case is that their adverse possession dates from November 1985, when the right of action "first" accrued to the GLC. If, however, they did not commence any

adverse possession prior to the Crown's acquisition of the title on 1 April 1986, but only did so afterwards, Mr Reynolds conceded that this *would* be a para 12 case (since the right of action would then have "first accrued to the Crown"). In that event, he accepted that the claimants could not succeed, because TfL would be entitled to the extended limitation period conferred by para 12.

'[20] So does "first" in para 12 mean "originally" or does it mean "earlier" or "previously"? For reasons submitted by Mr Reynolds, an interpretation in harmony with s 15(1) points to the former meaning and my initial instinct was that that was likely to be the better interpretation. If so, however, it produces odd consequences.

'[21] First, para 10 shows that the Crown enjoys a 30-year limitation period from the date when the cause of action originally accrued. Second, the *Tomlin* case [*Secretary of State for Foreign and Commonwealth Affairs v Tomlin* (1990) Times, 4 December, CA] shows that it will enjoy that period even if it claims as a successor in title to one who originally had the right of action. Third, the primary intention of para 12 is to prescribe the limitation period applicable to a person claiming *through* the Crown. It is agreed that "some person other than the Crown" in para 12(b) refers to that person; and the basic scheme of para 12 appears to be to give that person a limitation period of (a) 30 years from when the cause of action *originally* accrued (see my first and second points), or (b) 12 years from when he (or the first non-Crown owner through whom he claims) acquired the title from the Crown, whichever period expires first.

'[22] Mr Reynolds would not, I think, disagree with most of that. But he would say that that analysis of para 12 only applies to cases in which the cause of action *originally* accrued to the Crown, because that is the sense of the word *first*. If the Crown is merely a successor to the owner to whom the right of action so accrued, para 12 has no application. The consequence is that, although para 10 and the *Tomlin* case show that, as such a successor, the Crown has 30 years from the *original* accrual of that right of action in which to sue, a successor to the Crown who purportedly acquires title more than 12 years after the original accrual of the right of action will acquire no right of action at all. According to Mr Reynolds, the Crown has a full title to the relevant land immediately before the purported transfer to the Crown's successor: but at the very moment of such transfer the title is extinguished by s 17. The successor in title will only have a right of action if that right is one that *originally* accrued to the Crown.

'[23] In my judgment, Mr Reynolds's interpretation of para 12 does not identify the correct sense of Pt II of Sch 1 read as a whole. The period during which the Crown could have brought an action is 30 years from the date when the right of action originally accrued, whether that right accrued to the Crown or to a predecessor. Paragraph 12 gives the Crown's successor in title the benefit of that same period or the alternative para 12(b) one, whichever expires first. That shows that the feature of paramount importance in the scheme of para 12 is that the claimant to possession is someone claiming through the Crown, which itself had a right of action. Whether or not the right of action *originally* accrued to the Crown or to someone else appears to be of no importance since, whether it did or not, the longer 30-year period anyway runs from the date of that original accrual. Mr Reynolds's submission that the Crown's successor will only enjoy the benefit of the extended para 12 period if the right of action originally accrued to the Crown rather than to its predecessor appears, therefore, to be a subtlety lacking a rational basis. The argument of course has the support of the narrower, and perhaps more natural, meaning of the word "first" in the relevant phrase. But in my judgment it is not possible to derive from Pt II as a whole, and para 12 in particular, any logical reason for interpreting "first" in that narrow way. Nor does it have to be so construed: in an appropriate context it can undoubtedly mean "earlier" or "previously", for example a condition that a particular course of action cannot be followed without "first" serving a notice.

'[24] Moreover, if Mr Reynolds is right in his suggested interpretation, what is the limitation period prescribed by the 1980 Act which bars TfL's claim? As I understand it, it is said to be the basic 12-year one prescribed by s 15(1), even though during the Crown's tenure that period was superseded by the 30-year period. That being so, the argument must be that, once the Crown's tenure has expired (after the 12-year period), that basic period was retrospectively re-activated so as to provide an immediate bar to the bringing of a claim by TfL. I accept that this is conceptually possible but I cannot discern in Pt II an indication that it forms part of the legislative intention. If it had been, I regard it as likely that Pt II would have spelt it out in terms approximately as follows:

"12A. For the avoidance of doubt, and notwithstanding anything in paragraphs 10 and 12, where in the case of any action brought by a person other than the Crown ... the right of

action originally accrued to a person other than the Crown but subsequently accrued to the Crown ... through whom the person in question claims, the action may not be brought by that person after the expiration of twelve years from the date on which the right of action originally accrued."

'[25] Part II does not spell that out and I consider that that is because that was not the intention. The omission to spell it out creates, if Mr Reynolds is right, a lacuna in the legislation. How can the claimants in the present case assert, or the court hold, that the freeholder's title became extinguished in November 1997, after 12 years' adverse possession, when para 10 shows that the title had not become so extinguished by then? If in fact it only became extinguished at midnight on 2/3 July 2000–after something over 14 years of adverse possession–then under which provision in the 1980 Act is that said to be the prescribed limitation period? In my judgment, the answer to these questions is that para 12 provides a complete code for claims brought by persons claiming through the Crown, whether the right of action accrued originally to the Crown, or only so accrued earlier, and I so hold. I agree with, and accept, Mr Jefferies's submission that the true sense of the word "first" in para 12 is that of "earlier" or "previously".' *Hill v Transport for London* [2005] EWHC 856 (Ch) at [18]–[25], [2005] 3 All ER 677, per Rimer J

FIRST RIGHT OF REFUSAL *SEE* PREFERRED SUPPLIER

FISHERY

Canada [Indian treaty rights included liberty for the band to carry on their fisheries as formerly.] '... "fishery" may be used to denote not only the right to catch fish but also the place where the right can be exercised.' *R v Little* (1995) 131 DLR (4th) 220 at 236, BCCA, per cur

FISHING

Australia '... the notices to produce in the present case are simply not fishing at all, in the sense in which that term is used metaphorically in the law relating to discovery, interrogatories, subpoenas, notices to produce and other forms of compulsive interlocutory process, that is to say where:

"... a person who has no evidence that fish of a particular kind are in a pool desires to be at liberty to drag it for the purpose of finding whether there are any there or not." (*Associated Dominions Assurance Society Pty Ltd v John Fairfax & Son Pty Ltd* (1952) 72 WN(NSW) 250 at 254 per Owen J)

'In the present case it can be safely assumed that the documents sought by the notices to produce in fact exist, they being standard financial documents which the law and proper accounting practice would require companies of any substance to generate. Likewise, as already mentioned, there can be no doubt that these documents contain information relevant to the issues which arise on a security for costs application. The only uncertainty is whether that information would help or hinder the security application. But unpredictability of response has never been a bar to the pursuit of relevant evidence, as many a hapless cross-examiner who received an unexpected answer will attest.' *Bailey v Beagle Management Pty Ltd* (2001) 105 FCR 136; BC200100211; [2001] FCA 60 at [25], [26], per Heerey, Branson and Merkel JJ

FIXED CAPITAL

[For 7 Halsbury's Laws (4th edn) para 600 see now 7(1) Halsbury's Laws (4th edn) (2004 Reissue) para 524.]

FIXED PLANT AND MACHINERY

New Zealand 'Fixed machinery as the phrase is used in the debenture in my judgment connotes plant which is attached to premises in some way. Similarly, fixed plant is that which is attached to premises in the sense that it is not readily transportable or freely moveable. Both are to be contrasted with freely moveable items which may nevertheless be retained by the company for use in its ordinary business. Such a construction also gives the word "fixed" its ordinary meaning of "placed or attached firmly".' *National Bank of New Zealand Ltd v Commissioner of Inland Revenue* [1992] 1 NZLR 250 at 255–256, per Henry J

FIXTURES

[For 27 Halsbury's Laws (4th edn) para 142 see now 27(1) Halsbury's Laws (4th edn) (Reissue) para 143.]

FLAGRANT INCOMPETENCE

Australia [In the context of conduct by counsel at trial] 'I would therefore, with respect, adopt the

principle stated by Gleeson CJ, [in *R v Birk* (1990) 19 NSWLR 677)] using the term "flagrant incompetence" in the sense that the conduct of counsel was so far outside the standard of competency to be reasonably expected of counsel, as to have caused or plainly likely to have caused a miscarriage of justice.' *Ella v The Queen* (1991) 103 FLR 8 per Asche CJ cited in *McKenzie v Edmondson* (1996) 15 WAR 391 at 402, per Scott J

FLOATING CHARGE

[For 7 Halsbury's Laws (4th edn) para 824 see now 7(2) Halsbury's Laws (4th edn) (1996 Reissue) para 1260.]

FLOOD

Australia 'The word "flood" is also one which, in Australia, conjures up different visual messages than it probably does in England or Europe where water run-off is typically more common, more confined and better controlled. In this comparatively flat and arid country, mention of "flood", undefined, will usually produce images of vast tracts of country under water and farmers awaiting rescue on the roofs of their houses. Doubtless this is why the insurer provided specific definitions of "flood" in each of the present policies: see, generally, D St L Kelly & M Ball, *Principles of Insurance Law in Australia and New Zealand*, 1991, pp 358 ff.' *Provincial Insurance Australia Pty Ltd v Consolidated Wood Products Pty Ltd* (1992) 25 NSWLR 541 at 552, per Kirby P

Canada [A claim was made under an insurance policy for damage to a ferry terminal by the battering of waves.] 'In my opinion the exclusionary clause excludes liability for loss or damage caused, directly or indirectly, by flood, and then the clause goes on to give a meaning to the word "flood". It says: "'Flood' means waves, tides, tidal waves …" and then the word "and" appears used in its conjunctive sense and, in my opinion, the use of the word "and" at that place in the exclusionary clause is of significance, because what follows thereafter appears as follows: "… and the rising of, the breaking out or the overflow of, any body of water … ". It appears to me that in interpreting this clause the learned trial judge lost sight of the words following "tidal waves" in the clause. He attached no meaning to the words "and the rising of, the breaking out or the overflow of, any body of water". Properly construed, in my opinion, what the draftsman of the clause has done is to provide that flood is to be interpreted as covering both cause and effect. Thus, the flood may be caused by waves, tides, tidal waves, and if, for example, as in this case, waves result in the rising of, the breaking out, or the overflow of a body of water that would amount to a flood within the meaning of that term as defined in the exclusionary clause.' *British Columbia Ferry Corpn v Commonwealth Insurance Co* (1987) 40 DLR (4th) 766 at 768, BC CA, per Hinkson JA

FLOOR AREA

Australia [Section 3(1) of the Retail Tenancies Act 1986 (Vic) provides that the definition of 'retail premises' does not include 'premises that have a floor area that exceeds 1000 square metres …'.] 'Floor areas are those surfaces of a durable and cleansable nature covered overhead and used to provide the retail services for which the premises are dedicated. It follows from this analysis that the open parking areas, despite fitting some of the criteria, and despite being specifically assigned, to a particular accommodation unit, do not fall within the ambit of floor area.' *Robert v Besford* [1991] 1 VR 606 at 609, per Nathan J

FOLDCOURSE

[For 6 Halsbury's Laws (4th edn) para 575 see now 6 Halsbury's Laws (4th edn) (2003 Reissue) para 470.]

FOOTPATH

[The Road Traffic Act 1972 has been repealed. The definition, with the mention of the words 'in relation to England and Wales', was re-enacted in the Road Traffic Act 1988, s 192(1).]

FOR AND TO

New Zealand [Sections 8(1)(e) and 11(2)(e) of the Goods and Services Tax Act 1985.] 'Reference to any standard dictionary brings home the wide variety of senses in which the preposition "for" may be employed. *The Oxford English Dictionary* (2nd ed) identifies 11 separate categories of meaning and many distinct usages within particular categories. The discussion in the text extends over nine columns in the dictionary. Again the *Tasman Dictionary,* which as its name suggests is directed to Australian English and New Zealand English, lists 33 meanings of the word. The particular

meaning intended necessarily hinges on the context in which the word is used and how it is used in that context.

'In the context of s 11(2)(e), services supplied "for" a person not resident in New Zealand may indicate several possible senses in which "for" may be intended. It may refer simply to the person to whom the services were supplied. It may be used in a representative sense, on behalf of or on account of a foreign client. In that meaning it contemplates that the person placing the order is acting on behalf of a third party. It may be used in the sense of purpose, for the purposes of the foreign client. It may connote benefit, for the benefit of the foreign client or in favour of foreign client. Such a rubbery word has various shades of meaning. Frequently, too, it is deliberately employed to convey emphasis, as in the Gettysburg address, government of the people, by the people, for the people.

'Section 11(2)(e) employs the composite expression "for and to a person"…

'While it is important to seek to give adequate meaning to all the words actually employed in the legislation, it is not realistic to expect that busy drafters or legislators will always ensure that each provision is tautly and precisely drawn without any surplusage. Also it is not uncommon for legislative drafting to convey emphasis through a combination of words. Some apparent repetition by the use of different or added words may be explicable for those reasons …

'I am inclined to think that the framers of s 11(2)(e) employed both expressions to convey emphasis and perhaps to bring out the intent that the contract must be genuine and so the services must be supplied under that contract to and for the other contracting party.' *Wilson & Horton Ltd v Commissioner of Inland Revenue* [1996] 1 NZLR 26 at 32–33, CA, per Richardson J

'I have come to the conclusion that the words "for" and "to" are used as a composite phrase, meaning no more than that the supply of the goods and services is pursuant to a contract with, and in that sense is both for and to, an overseas resident.' *Wilson & Horton Ltd v Commissioner of Inland Revenue* [1996] 1 NZLR 26 at 36, CA, per McKay J

FOR THE BENEFIT OF EMPLOYEES

New Zealand 'The shares must be held "for the benefit" of employees. "For" in that context means with the object and purpose of benefiting employees and the "benefit" to employees must be discernible and real. As in the case of the exercise of trustees' powers to make advances for a person's benefit, it must confer an advantage which can be enjoyed by employees. It must be of value to employees. An arrangement does not qualify as being "for the benefit of employees" unless employees actually stand to benefit.' *NZI Bank Ltd v Euro-National Corpn Ltd* [1992] 3 NZLR 528 at 544, CA, per Richardson J

FOR THE PURPOSES OF A JUDICIAL PROCEEDING

New Zealand '… a situation in which a work is required to be reproduced so that legal advisers can properly advise a client whether or not it is appropriate to commence legal proceedings threatened against the client.' *Television New Zealand Ltd v Newsmonitor Services Ltd* [1994] 2 NZLR 91 at 109, per Blanchard J

FOR THE PURPOSES OF RESEARCH OR PRIVATE STUDY

New Zealand 'The defendants, by means of the *Oxford Dictionary,* defined research as the searching into a matter or subject or the investigation or close study of it. That definition seems appropriate. "Research" and "study" are obviously connected with one another. Research involves the study of things, including written materials or those captured in electronic form … It is, I think, significant that the word "private" qualifies only the word "study". "Private study" connotes a form of study which is personal to the person undertaking it. Although I am inclined to think that a corporation can engage in private study, as when its personnel endeavour to place themselves in a position to be better able to perform their functions in or related to the corporation, "research" is even more clearly something of which a business organisation is capable.' *Television New Zealand Ltd v Newsmonitor Services Ltd* [1994] 2 NZLR 91 at 106, per Blanchard J

FOR THE PURPOSES OF THE MEDIATION

New Zealand [The Employment Relations Act 2000, s 148 provides for confidentiality in relation to mediation.] '[11] The phrase in subs (1) "… created or made for the purposes of the mediation and any information that, for the purposes of the mediation, is disclosed orally in the course of the mediation" is at the heart of the case. The meaning of the phrase is not entirely clear on its

face. It may mean for the purpose or purposes for which the mediation has been arranged or conducted as opposed to other extraneous or earlier purposes. The "purpose" may, potentially, be as narrow as the resolution of the particular issue brought to the mediation by the party instigating it, or as broad as the state of health of the employment relationship as a whole at the date of mediation. The phrase may mean created for the purposes of mediation as opposed to created at an earlier time for other purposes.

…

'[42] The scheme of the Employment Relations Act 2000 and, in particular, Part 9 (Personal grievances, disputes, and enforcement) and Part 10 (Institutions), assists in determining the meaning of the phrase "for the purposes of the mediation". As has already been noted, that is at the heart of the question for decision. The first object in s 101, addressing Part 9, is the recognition that, "in resolving employment relationship problems", access to information and mediation services is more important than rigid formulaic procedures.

'[43] The first object set out in s 143 in relation to the institutions established under the Act (including the Mediation Service) should support successful employment relationships and the good faith obligations that underpin them. The second object is to "recognise that employment relationships are more likely to be successful if problems in those relationships are resolved promptly by the parties themselves;".

'[44] The question for decision is affected by a number of other relevant sections of the Employment Relations Act including ss 143(a)–(da), 144(2) (particularly (d)), 147, 149, 150, 152, 153, and 159. We accept Mr Corkill's submission for the plaintiff that from these sections a number of conclusions about "the purposes of the mediation" can be drawn. Where there is an employment relationship problem, mediation is to be the first port of call. The legislation places emphasis on the parties themselves resolving employment problems but assistance is also provided by mediators. Mediators are not also adjudicators unless the parties specifically request them to so act. Fast and effective resolution of employment relationship problems is promoted using a variety of communication tools with flexibility being emphasised. Section 144 emphasises the provision of information, the assisting of the smooth conduct of employment relationships, and the resolving, promptly and effectively, of employment relationship problems.

…

'[48] We conclude that the parliamentary reference (during the enactment process) to the *Crummer* case [*Crummer v Benchmark Building Supplies Ltd* [2000] 2 ERNZ 22], and its intention to alter what had been found or confirmed by *Crummer*, related to the conclusion that, under the 1991 Act, confidentiality and inadmissibility had to be agreed upon by the parties on a case-by-case basis in mediation. Parliament's intention in 2000 was that such conditions should attach automatically to all mediations and that there should be a form of blanket privilege on all mediations irrespective of whether or not the parties had agreed to this in advance.

'[49] We do not consider that Parliament can be said to have gone further and, in particular, to have altered well-established and well-known common law principles relating to "without prejudice" communications and the admissibility of them in subsequent proceedings. To alter the common law would have required a clearly expressed intention to do so. Rather, we find it was the legislature's intention to enshrine in the Act the relevant principles stated in *Crummer*, perhaps for the guidance of people who are not lawyers (of whom many are involved in mediations) and therefore perhaps unfamiliar with such evidential concepts. The common law of confidentiality and admissibility of "without prejudice" statements is reflected in s 148(1).

...

'[56] We hold that the phrase "for the purposes of the mediation" reflects the common law requirement that such communications must be genuinely for the purpose of settling litigation or potential litigation and the protections (including inadmissibility) are lost where such communications are for other purposes.' *Jesudhass v Just Hotel Ltd* (2006) 3 NZELR 106 at [11], [42]–[44], [48]–[49], [56], per G L Colgan CJ

FOR THE TIME BEING

[Agriculture and Horticulture Act 1964 s 11(3).]
'[12] When the United Kingdom joined the European Economic Community on 1 January 1973 there were already in existence Community regulations governing the grading of certain types of horticultural produce. So this country's law on this topic had to be brought into line with the existing Community rules. Further, criminal sanctions had to be provided in respect of contraventions of Community grading rules because, as already noted, Community law requires that contravention of Community grading rules must

attract criminal sanctions similar to those attaching to contraventions of domestic grading regulations. The 1964 Act therefore had to be amended.

'[13] The amendment was made by s 4(1) and Part C of Schedule 4 to the 1972 Act [the European Communities Act 1972]. It consisted of adding a new subsection, sub-s (3), to s 11 of the 1964 Act. The structure of the new subsection was as follows. First, produce of a description for the time being subject to Community grading rules was, automatically and without further ado, removed from the scope of the regulation-making power in s 11(1) of the 1964 Act. Thenceforward such produce would not be "regulated produce" as defined in s 12 of the 1964 Act. Second, a new regulation-making power was created by which provision could be made to apply the 1964 Act, with or without modification, to such produce "as if" it were regulated produce. The new sub-s (3) of s 11 provided:

> "Regulations under subsection (1) above shall not apply to produce of any description for the time being subject to Community grading rules; but in relation to any such produce the Ministers may by regulations ...(b) provide for the application, subject to any modifications specified in the regulations, of all or any of the following provisions of this Part of this Act as if the produce were regulated produce and as if the standards of quality established by those rules were prescribed grades."

'[14] Community grading rules were defined as "any directly applicable Community provisions establishing standards of quality for fresh horticultural produce": see para 4(1)(c) of Part C of Schedule 4 to the 1972 Act.

'[15] I have mentioned that the need for this amendment arose from the fact that directly applicable Community grading rules were already in existence. The new regulation-making power was plainly apt to apply to produce which was subject to existing Community rules. That is not disputed. But was it apt to apply to Community grading rules made subsequently, that is, after the 1972 Act came into force? This is the issue in the present proceedings, because the Community grading rules said to have been contravened in the ASDA store on 1 November 2000 were all made after 1972.

'[16] With all respect to those who have considered otherwise, to my mind it is abundantly plain that the scope of the new regulation-making power was not confined to produce falling within Community grading rules existing in 1972.

'[17] Let me take this in stages. The first stage is to note that the scope of the new regulation-making power was co-extensive with the types of produce excluded from the definition of "regulated produce". The scope of the new regulation-making power marched hand-in-hand with the scope of the disapplication provision in the opening words of the new sub-s (3). This is clear as a matter of both language and context. This is clear as a matter of language, because the new power applied to "such produce" which is a reference back to the produce mentioned in the opening words ("produce of any description"). This is as one would expect. One would expect to find that, sub-s (3) having excluded certain produce from the scope of s 11(1), the new power would enable the ministers to make alternative provision regarding the self-same horticultural produce. One would expect to find that the new regulation-making power would fill the gap created by the exclusionary provision. So language and context were in harmony.

'[18] The second step is to note the language used to define the scope of these two matching provisions. The new sub-s 11(3) of the 1964 Act excluded from the scope of regulated produce "produce of any description *for the time being* subject to Community grading rules" (my emphasis). The ambulatory words I have emphasised can only have been intended to indicate that this exclusionary provision was not confined to produce which was subject to Community grading rules at the time this provision in the 1972 Act came into force. Rather, the applicability of the exclusionary provision was to depend upon the content of Community grading rules at any given time in the future. The phrase "for the time being" envisages, and is intended to encompass, a changing state of affairs. This, again, is what one would expect, in relation to both the disapplication provision and the new regulation-making power. One would expect to find that the new power would extend to produce which, for the time being, was subject to Community grading rules.' *Department for Environment, Food and Rural Affairs v ASDA Stores Ltd* [2003] UKHL 71 at [12]–[18], [2004] 1 All ER 268, HL, per Lord Nicholls of Birkenhead

FORAGE

Australia [The definition of 'traditional Aboriginal owners' in s 3(1) of the Aboriginal Land Rights (Northern Territory) Act 1976 (Cth) requires that they are 'a local descent group of Aboriginals who ... are entitled by Aboriginal tradition to forage

as of right over that land'.] 'On the face of things, in its primary meanings, the word "forage" seems inapt to activities upon under-sea land, at least when that land is more than a few metres from the shore line. But if the expression "forage ... over that land" is to have application to submerged land, it must be understood as extending at least to fishing in and taking the resources of the sea. The assertion of entitlement to forage over the area the subject of the claim ... seems contrary to any narrow understanding of the subject of the present claim as being only the seabed, as distinct from the superjacent waters.' *Risk v Northern Territory of Australia* BC200202743; [2002] HCA 23 at [32], per Gleeson CJ

Australia [The definition of 'traditional Aboriginal owners' in s 3(1) of the Aboriginal Land Rights (Northern Territory) Act 1976 (Cth) requires that they be a that they are 'a local descent group of Aboriginals who ... are entitled by Aboriginal tradition to forage as of right over that land'.] 'The term "forage" includes "the act of searching for provisions of any kind" [*Macquarie Dictionary*, 3rd ed (1998) at 825]. In that sense, it is wide enough to include fishing in the seas below the low water mark and the recovery of clams, oysters and other edibles attached to or on the sea-bed. But the more natural meaning of the term "forage" is the search for food on land above the low water mark. The historic and primary meaning of the term was and still is "food for horses and cattle" [*Shorter Oxford English Dictionary*, vol 1, 3rd ed (rev) (1975) at 784; *Macquarie Dictionary*, 3rd ed (1998) at 825]. Although in s 3 "forage" obviously has a wider meaning than obtaining food for horses and cattle, it requires a strained construction of the term to regard it as including fishing or the recovery of edibles on or attached to the sea-bed.' *Risk v Northern Territory of Australia* BC200202743; [2002] HCA 23 at [62], per McHugh J

FORCE

Canada 'Section 265 of the *Criminal Code* describes the general elements that underlie all of the assault offences, including assault, assault causing bodily harm, aggravated assault, sexual assault and aggravated sexual assault. The essence of all forms of assault, as laid out in s 265, is the intentional, non-consensual application of force, or the threat thereof. "Force" can include any touching, no matter the degree of strength or power applied, and therefore is not only those physical acts designed to maim or cause injury.' *R v Cuerrier* [1998] 2 SCR 371 at 385, per L'Heureux-Dubé J

New Zealand [Section 48 of the Crimes Act 1961 provides 'Every one is justified in using, in the defence of himself or another, such force as, in the circumstances as he believes them to be, it is reasonable to use'.] 'In my judgment the word "force" in s 48 means force which, but for its justification, would amount to an assault. It is the same force as is encompassed in the definition of assault, ie physical force or the threat of same.' *Wilcox v Police* [1994] 1 NZLR 243 at 255, per Tipping J

FORCIBLE ENTRY

Australia 'The meaning of "entry" in the statute of 1381 [5 Rich II, c 7] and in its statutory successors is well established. The "entry" of which they speak is an entry by which the offender takes possession of the premises or which the offender makes with the intention of taking possession: see Blackstone's Commentaries, Bk IV, Ch 11, pp 147–148; Hawkins, Pleas of the Crown, 8th edn (1824), Bk I, Ch 28, ss 20 and 21, p 500; *R v Child* (1846) 2 Cox CC 102. The meaning of "entry" in the statute accords with its primary legal meaning. The Oxford English Dictionary (Murray, 1897) defines the legal meaning of "enter" thus: "To make entry (into lands) as a formal assertion of ownership; to take possession", and defines "to enter on" in corresponding terms. The Macquarie Dictionary contains a similar definition for "entry": "the act of taking possession of lands or tenements by entering or setting foot on them". Legal dictionaries agree that the primary legal meaning of "entry" is not a mere going or coming onto land. Thus Jowitt's Dictionary of English Law, 2nd edn (1977), defines "entry" to mean "the act of going on land, or doing something equivalent, with the intention of asserting a right in the land".' *Prideaux v Director of Public Prosecutions* (*Vic*) (1981) 61 ALJR 600 at 601, per cur

FOREIGN COUNTRY

Australia [The applicant argued that employment at sea was comprehended within the meaning of the words 'service in a foreign country' for the purposes of income tax exemptions under Income Tax Assessment Act 1936 (Cth).] '... [T]he ordinary meaning of the expression "foreign country" in modern usage looks to a political entity, be that a tract of land, a district, or a group of islands. It does not extend to an ocean or region of the sea.

'... The argument advanced on behalf of [the applicant] really sought to suggest that the words "foreign country" be construed as meaning no more than "out of Australia". Had Parliament intended to exempt all personal service income so long as a resident taxpayer served ... outside Australia ... it could have said so in language much more to the point than that which was adopted.' *Chaudhri v Cmr of Taxation* (2001) 47 ATR 126; BC200102220; [2001] FCA 554 at [26], [27], per Hill, Drummond and Goldberg JJ

FOREIGN POWER

Australia [Section 44(i) of the Commonwealth Constitution states that any person who is a 'citizen of a foreign power' 'shall be incapable of being chosen' as a Senator or a Member of the House of Representatives, or of sitting as a Senator or Member.] 'The point of immediate significance is that the circumstance that the same monarch exercises regal functions under the constitutional arrangements in the United Kingdom and Australia does not deny the proposition that the United Kingdom is a foreign power within the meaning of s 44(i) of the Constitution. Australia and the United Kingdom have their own laws as to nationality so that their citizens owe different allegiances. The United Kingdom has a distinct legal personality and its exercises of sovereignty, for example in entering military alliances, participating in armed conflicts and acceding to treaties such as the Treaty of Rome, themselves have no legal consequences for this country. Nor, as we have sought to demonstrate ... does the United Kingdom exercise any function with respect to the governmental structures of the Commonwealth or the States.' (footnotes omitted) *Sue v Hill* (1999) 163 ALR 648; 73 ALJR 1016; BC903377; [1999] HCA 30 at [96], per Gleeson CJ, Gummow and Hayne JJ

FORESEEABILITY

See **PRACTICABLE** [in the context of employers' obligations to provide and maintain a working environment: (WA) Occupational Safety and Health Act 1994 s 191(1)(a)]

FORESTRY LAND

[The Capital Allowances Act 1968 was repealed and the definition re-enacted in the Capital Allowances Act 1990, s 133(1); but that definition ceased to have effect on 6 April 1993 (s 133(2)).]

FORFEIT

New Zealand [Section 107B(2) of the Fisheries Act 1983.] ' "Forfeit" has its ordinary meaning, namely that the property in question is "given up" or "surrendered" to the Crown.' *Equal Enterprise Ltd v Attorney-General* [1995] 3 NZLR 293 at 297, CA, per cur

FORFEITURE

Australia 'The word forfeiture and its derivatives has meant an immediate loss of all interest in property as well as a loss of the right of possession. The concept of forfeiture does not evolve out of any administrative decision to which the provisions of the Judicial Review Act might attach; on the contrary it arises by force of statute upon the happening of certain prior events.' *Whim Creek Consolidated NL v Colgan* (1991) 103 ALR 204 at 210–211, per O'Loughlin J

Canada 'The appellant argues that the Court of Appeal erred by finding that continued physical detention of seized property is a precondition to an order of forfeiture under s 72(1) [of the *Fisheries Act*]. The only clear and express precondition to such an order is the conviction of the accused. Otherwise, the words in s 72(1) are equivocal on this point. A continued physical detention precondition might make sense were the word "seized" to be read only in the present tense. However, the word "seized" can also be read in the past tense and so may also refer to things formerly seized under the Act. Furthermore, the legal definition of "forfeiture" is "a divestiture of specific property without compensation": see *Black's Law Dictionary* (6th ed. 1990), at p. 650. It may be that after a bare divestiture of the property rights of the owner, without more, the title to property would necessarily vest in the party holding possession, i.e. the Crown, where the property was detained under its authority up until forfeiture.' *R v Ulybel Enterprises Ltd* [2001] 2 SCR 867 at 891, per Iacobucci J

FORTHWITH

Australia [The Family Court ordered the wife to pay a certain amount of money to the husband 'forthwith'. The next day the husband brought an application to enforce that order.] 'The word means "as soon as practicable" rather than "within a reasonable time".' *Re the Marriage of Rubie* (1991) 15 Fam LR 47 at 49, per Nygh J

Canada '[10] The relevant text of s. 254(2) [Criminal Code] reads:

> (2) Where a peace officer reasonably suspects that a person who is operating ... or who

has the care or control of a motor vehicle ... has alcohol in the person's body, the peace officer may, by demand made to that person, require the person to provide *forthwith* such a sample of breath as in the opinion of the peace officer is necessary to enable a proper analysis of the breath to be made by means of an approved screening device ...

'[11] As we shall presently see, the police made *two* ASD demands, one at the roadside and the other at the police station – more than an hour after the respondent had been arrested for failing to comply with the demand made at roadside. Plainly, this second demand, made at the station, was not a lawful demand under s. 254(2) of the *Code*.

'[12] What we are left with, then, is the respondent's *refusal* to provide a breath sample forthwith pursuant to the only lawful demand made upon him pursuant to s. 254(2). That is the factual obstacle to the Crown's appeal.

'[13] We are left as well with the ASD breath sample provided by the respondent at the police station, approximately 1 hour and 20 minutes after his arrest for refusing to provide a sample at roadside. "Forthwith" means "immediately" or "without delay": *Canadian Oxford Dictionary* (2nd ed. 2004), at p. 585. Without doing violence to the meaning of the word, "forthwith" cannot be stretched to bring within s. 254(2) of the *Criminal Code* the long-delayed "compliance" that occurred in this case. This semantic obstacle to the Crown's position, like the factual one, is in my view insurmountable.' *R v Woods* (2005) 254 DLR (4th) 385 at [10]–[13], [2005] SCJ No 42 (SCC), per Fish J

FORTUITOUS

Canada ['Peril of the seas', for insurance purposes, includes two elements, the first of which is that the cause of the loss be 'fortuitous'.] 'The requirement that the cause of the loss be "fortuitous" excludes the natural and inevitable action of wind and waves, ordinary wear and tear, inherent defects and intentionally caused losses. Events which are not fortuitous, as defined in the cases, are reflected in the exclusions found in s 56 of the Act [Insurance (Marine) Act 1979] and the definition in the Act of "perils of the seas". In general, the word "fortuitous", as interpreted by the cases, carries the connotation that the cause of the loss not have been intentional or inevitable.' *CCR Fishing Ltd v British Reserve Insurance Co* (1990) 69 DLR (4th) 112 at 115, SCC, per McLachlin J

FOSTER CHILD

[The Foster Children Act 1980 was repealed by the Children Act 1989, s 108(7), Sch 15. See now, as to private arrangements for fostering children ss 66–70 of the Act of 1989.]

FRAUD

[For 16 Halsbury's Laws (4th edn) para 1219 see now 16(2) Halsbury's Laws (4th edn) (Reissue) para 413.]

Australia [In the following extract, Kay J was quoting from observations he made in *Slatinsek v Slatinsek*, unreported.] 'The Oxford English Dictionary defines "fraud" as: "the quality of being deceitful, criminal deception, the using of false representations to obtain an unjust advantage, or to injure the rights or interest of another, an act or instance of deception, a dishonest trick, a fraudulent contrivance; a spurious or deceptive thing". The Macquarie Dictionary says that fraud is: "Deceit, trickery, sharp practice or breach of confidence by which it is sought to gain some unfair or dishonest advantage". At common law fraud consists of: "a false statement of fact which is made by one party to a transaction to the other knowingly, or without belief in its truth or recklessly without caring whether it be true or false, with the intent that it should be acted upon by the other party and which was in fact so acted upon": *Derry v Peek* (1889) 14 App Cas 337 at 374. Where a court has been made the involuntary instrument of depriving others of their just rights by intention, or deception, it will if possible set aside the transaction against the innocent party: *Brooke v Lord Mostyn* (1864) 33 Beav 457 at 462. The Courts of Equity have developed broader principles of fraud than those in common law so that suppression or non-disclosure of material facts would also enable the courts to intervene and set aside agreements breached as a result of such conduct: see *In the Marriage of Green and Kwiatek* (1982) 8 Fam LR 419; [1982] FLC 91–259; *Robinson v Robinson* [1982] 2 All ER 699. In my view however, whatever view one takes of fraud, there must be some element of deceit before the court can act ... That can either be deceit by one party of the other or in certain circumstances deceit by either or both parties of the court.' *In the marriage of MC and EA Cameron* (1988) 12 Fam LR 265 at 277, per Kay J

Australia [Section 121 of the Bankruptcy Act 1966 (Cth) provides, *inter alia*, that 'a disposition of property ... with intent to defraud creditors ... is ...

void.] 'It is notoriously difficult to provide an exhaustive statement as to what is involved in the concepts of "fraud" and "intent to defraud". "Fraud" involves the notion of detrimentally affecting or risking the property of others, their rights or interests in property, or an opportunity or advantage which the law accords them with respect to property. Conversely, it is not fraud to detrimentally affect or risk something in or in relation to which others have no right or interest or in respect of which the law accords them no opportunity or advantage. And there is no intent to defraud if the person in question believes that others have no right or interest in or in relation to the property concerned and that the law accords them no opportunity or advantage with respect to that property.' *Cannane v J Cannane Pty Ltd (in liq)* (1998) 153 ALR 163 at 172; (1998) 27 ACSR 603 at 612; [1998] HCA 26 at [30]; BC9801073 at 12, per Gaudron J

Australia 'In *Butterworth's Australian Legal Dictionary* "fraud" is defined as "an intentional dishonest act or omission done with the purpose of deceiving". In its everyday usage, and frequently when used in the context of the criminal law, "fraudulently" simply means dishonestly; it does not necessarily carry the connotation of the intentional deprivation of someone's property rights ... Used in that context, the term "fraudulent" does not imply any adverse effect on property rights; it really means no more than dishonestly or with moral opprobrium.' *R v Cushion* (1997) 150 ALR 45 at 52–53; BC9705917 at 52–53, per Williams J

Canada 'From its inception, the concept of criminal fraud has had two constituent elements. Stephen, *A History of the Criminal Law of England* (1883) vol 2, described them in this way at pp 121–22:

> ... there is little danger in saying that whenever the words "fraud" or "intent to defraud" or "fraudulently" occur in the definition of a crime, two elements at least are essential to the commission of the crime; namely, first, deceit or an intention to deceive or in some cases secrecy; and, secondly, either actual injury or possible injury or an intent to expose some person either to actual injury or to a risk of possible injury by means of that deceit or secrecy.

'This was the approach adopted in *In re London and Globe Finance Corp* [1903] 1 Ch 728, Buckley J described the act of fraud as follows, at pp 732–33:

> To defraud is to deprive by deceit: it is by deceit to induce a man to act to his injury.

More tersely it may be put, that to deceive is by falsehood to induce a state of mind; to defraud is by deceit to induce a course of action.

'A broader definition of fraud was given in *Scott v Metropolitan Police Commissioner* [1975] AC 819 (HL). There, the definition of fraud which was adopted did not include deceit as an essential element. Rather, dishonesty and deprivation were held to be basic to the concept.

'In *R. v Olan* [1978] 2 SCR 1175, 41 CCC (2d) 145, 86 DLR (3d) 212, the reasoning in *Scott* was adopted and it was held that the two elements of fraud are dishonesty and deprivation. It was put in these words (at p 1182):

Courts, for good reason, have been loath to attempt anything in the nature of an exhaustive definition of "defraud", but one may safely say, upon the authorities, that two elements are essential, "dishonesty" and "deprivation". To succeed, the Crown must establish dishonest deprivation.

'As well the requirement of deprivation was widened so that the risk of deprivation alone is sufficient. Thus, the defrauded party need not show actual harm or loss resulted from the actions of the accused (at p 1182):

The element of deprivation is satisfied on proof of detriment, prejudice or risk of prejudice to the economic interests of the victim. It is not essential that there be actual economic loss as the outcome of the fraud.

'The *Olan* approach was endorsed in *R. v Théroux* [1993] 2 SCR 5, 79 CCC (3d) 449, 100 DLR (4th) 624. There the importance of defining the offence of fraud in light of the underlying objective of promoting honesty in commercial dealings was emphasized. McLachlin J described the requisite elements of criminal fraud in these words, at pp 25–26:

To establish the *actus reus* of fraud, the Crown must establish beyond a reasonable doubt that the accused practised deceit, lied, or committed some other fraudulent act ... [I]t will be necessary to show that the impugned act is one which a reasonable person would see as dishonest. Deprivation or the risk of deprivation must then be shown to have occurred as a matter of fact. To establish the *mens rea* of fraud the Crown must prove that the accused knowingly undertook the acts which constitute the falsehood, deceit or other

fraudulent means, and that the accused was aware that deprivation could result from such conduct.

'It was held that mere negligent misrepresentation would not amount to a fraudulent act. However, "deliberately practised fraudulent acts which, in the knowledge of the accused, actually put the property of others at risk" should be subject to criminal sanction.

'Next it must be determined whether non-disclosure can constitute fraud. Traditionally, courts were of the view that fraud does not include non-disclosure (*R v Brasso Datsun (Calgary) Ltd* (1977) 39 CRNS 1 (Alta SCTD)). However, *Olan, supra*, and *Théroux, supra*, have endorsed a wider interpretation of fraud which can include non-disclosure in circumstances where it would be viewed by the reasonable person as dishonest. This view was upheld in *R v Zlatic* [1993] 2 SCR 29, 79 CCC (3d) 466, 100 DLR (4th) 642. At p 44 McLachlin J, speaking for the majority, held that if the means to the alleged fraud can be characterized objectively as dishonest they are fraudulent. This, it was observed, can include the non-disclosure of important facts.

'In summary, it can be seen that the essential elements of fraud are dishonesty, which can include non-disclosure of important facts, and deprivation or risk of deprivation.' *R v Cuerrier* (1998) 162 DLR (4th) 513 at 556–558, SCC, per Cory J

FRAUDULENT BREACH OF TRUST

[The question arose whether for the purposes of s 281(3) of the Insolvency Act 1986, dishonesty was an essential ingredient of fraudulent breach of trust.] '[42] ... I ask myself whether there is anything in the policy of the 1986 Act which suggests that in s 281(3) of the Act Parliament was intending to give the words "fraudulent breach of trust" a different meaning from that which they had for the purposes of ss 26 and 28 of the 1914 Act and their predecessor sections. In my judgment this question must be answered in the negative.

'[43] The main changes in legislative approach and social views as to the relevant conduct in respect of the law of bankruptcy which occurred between 1914 and 1986 were the abandonment of a retributive approach and the giving of a new emphasis to rehabilitation. This explains why there is no direct equivalent of s 26 of the 1914 Act in the 1986 Act. Discharge from bankruptcy as the result of the exercise of discretion by the court has now in most cases been replaced by automatic discharge after the lapse of the prescribed time. However s 281 still provides, as had s 28 of the 1914 Act, exceptions to the scope of the release from debts consequential upon discharge. One would expect, however, that the effect of the new climate would be to limit the scope of the exceptions rather than to enlarge them.

...

'[50] I see no reason for regarding "fraudulent breach of trust" in s 281(3) of the 1986 Act as meaning anything different from what the same expression meant in s 28 of the 1914 Act. Dishonesty therefore remains an essential ingredient.

...

'[68] Nevertheless I am not persuaded that the Ombudsman's decision gives rise to an issue estoppel which establishes that Mr Woodland was not only guilty of breaches of trust but that these breaches were fraudulent. I do not think that the issue which the Ombudsman had to consider was the same as that which has to be considered in relation to s 281(3). It does not appear to me that "wilful default" is precisely the same as "fraudulent breach of trust" so that a finding of the first necessarily involves a finding of the second as well.' *Woodland-Ferrari v UCL Group Retirement Benefits Scheme* [2002] EWHC 1354 (Ch) at [42]–[43], [50], [68], [2002] 3 All ER 670 at 681, 683, 687, per Ferris J

FREE

Australia ["Free" goods or services.] 'The word "free" is rich and diverse in meaning, and "there is no dictionary meaning of the word 'free' which can be applied in all cases": *Adelaide Co of Jehovah's Witnesses Inc v Commonwealth* (1943) 67 CLR 116 at 127 per Latham CJ. Of the many definitions of the word which will be found in any dictionary, the following ones are pertinent to offers of "free" goods or services in commercial advertising: The Macquarie Dictionary, 2nd Revised ed, definition (26): "provided without, or not subject to, a charge or payment". The New Shorter Oxford English Dictionary, 1993, definition (13): "Given or provided without charge or payment, gratuitous".' *Nationwide News Pty Ltd v Australian Competition and Consumer Commission* (1996) 142 ALR 212 at 221, per Lindgren J

Australia [At issue, was whether the phrase "free shares" was misleading.] 'In essence the word "free", as here used, is a word of straightforward meaning. It conveys, of course, a secondary meaning

of a word with far greater import. Most of its primary meanings connote an absence of restriction, whether of an intellectual, moral, legal, physical or any other practical kind. In the *Oxford English Dictionary* the present use appears only as the thirty-second meaning of the adjective and its relationship to the other, more significant, meanings is explained by the authors stating that it is "in full, free of cost, charge, or the like". Consequently the definition then stated is relatively simple: "given or provided without payment, costless, gratuitous".' *Heydon v NRMA Ltd* (2000) 36 ACSR 462; (2001) 19 ACLC 1; BC200007998; [2000] NSWCA 374 at [687], per Ormiston AJA

Freely and voluntarily

Australia [Section 13(2)(c) of the Wills, Probate and Administration Act 1898 (NSW) requires that a testator knew of and approved of a gift and that the gift was 'given or made freely and voluntarily by the testator'.]

'The *Macquarie Dictionary* defines "freely" as, "in a free manner". The adjective "free" cannot have its meaning dealt with so shortly – the *Macquarie Dictionary* records 31 different shades of meaning. Those shades of meaning which could bear upon s 13(2)(c) are:

"5. Exempt from external authority, interference, restriction, etc, as a person, the will, thought, choice, action etc; independent, unfettered.

6. At liberty, permitted, or able at will (to do something): free to choose ...

12. Exempt or released from something specified that controls, restrains, burdens, etc (fol. by from or of): free from matrimonial ties, free of taxes.

13. Having immunity or being safe (usu. fol. by from): free from criticism ...

25. Given without consideration of a return, as a gift".

'The *Macquarie Dictionary* lists seven shades of meaning of "voluntary" when used as an adjective. Those which could bear upon s 13(2)(c) are:

"1. Done, made, brought about, undertaking, etc of one's own accord or by free choice: a voluntary contribution.

2. Acting of one's own will or choice: a voluntary substitute.

3. Pertaining to or depending on voluntary action or contribution.

4. Law (a) acting or done without compulsion or obligation. (b) done by intention or not by

accident: voluntary manslaughter. (c) made or done without valuable consideration: a voluntary conveyance or settlement."

'The notion of acting "freely and voluntarily" occurs in many areas of the law outside probate. Concerning the admissibility of a confession in a criminal trial, the High Court in *R v Lee* (1950) 82 CLR 133 at 144 said:

> "(1) That such a statement may not be admitted in evidence unless it is shown to have been voluntarily made in the sense that it has been made in the exercise of free choice and not because the will of the accused has been overborne or his statement made as the result of duress, intimidation, persistent importunity or sustained or undue insistence or pressure, and
> (2) That such a statement is not voluntary if it is preceded by an inducement, such as a threat or promise, held out by a person in authority, unless the inducement is shown to have been removed.

'These two "rules" ... seem to be not really two independent and coordinate rules. There seems to be really one rule, the rule that a statement must be voluntary in order to be admissible. Any one of a variety of elements, including a threat or promise by a person in authority, will suffice to deprive it of a voluntary character.

'Also concerning confessions in criminal cases, Brennan J said, in *Cleland v R* (1982) 151 CLR 1, at 18:

> "The conduct of police before and during an interrogation fashions the circumstances in which confessions are made and it is necessary to refer to those circumstances in determining whether a confession is voluntary. The principle, focussing upon the will of the person confessing, must be applied according to the age, background and psychological condition of each confessionalist and the circumstances in which the confession is made. Voluntariness is not an issue to be determined by reference to some hypothetical standard: it requires a careful assessment of the effect of the actual circumstances of the case upon the will of the particular accused."

'A plea of guilty, in a criminal case, is one which is required to be made freely and voluntarily. In *Meissner v R* (1994) 184 CLR 132 at 143, Brennan, Toohey and McHugh JJ said:

> "A plea made as a result of intimidation has not been made freely and voluntarily, and the court that acts on the plea has been misled and its proceedings have been rendered abortive, whether or not it ever becomes aware of the impropriety. For similar reasons, improper conduct of any kind that has the tendency to interfere with the accused person's right to make a free and voluntary decision to plead not guilty to a charge must be regarded as having a tendency to pervert the course of justice ...
> "It will often be difficult to determine whether conduct that falls short of intimidation but which has the tendency to induce an accused to plead guilty is improper conduct that interferes with the accused's free choice to plead guilty or not guilty. Argument or advice that merely seeks to persuade the accused to plead guilty is not improper conduct for this purpose, no matter how strongly the argument or advice is put. Reasoned argument or advice does not involve the use of improper means and does not have the tendency to prevent the accused from making a free and voluntary choice concerning his or her plea to the charge. As long as the argument or advice does not constitute harassment or other improper pressure and leaves the accused free to make the choice, no interference with the administration of justice occurs.
> "Conduct is likely to have the tendency to interfere with a person's free choice to plead not guilty, however, when the conduct consists of a promise or benefit that is offered in consideration of the accused pleading guilty. The difficulty in such cases is to draw the line between offers of assistance that improperly impact on the accused's freedom of choice and offers of assistance that are legitimate inducements. In most cases, that difficulty can be resolved by determining whether, in all the circumstances of the case, the offer could reasonably be regarded as intended to protect or advance the legitimate interests of the accused having regard to the threat to those interests that arises from the institution of the criminal prosecution. Thus, to offer to pay an accused person's legal expenses if he or she pleads guilty is not improper conduct for this purpose if the advantages in pleading guilty can reasonably be regarded as outweighing the consequences to the accused that might flow from a conviction after a plea of not guilty and the offer is made only for that

reason. On the other had, to pay the accused's legal expenses in consideration of the accused changing his or her plea to a plea of guilty when the payment is made for the purpose of protecting the interests of the payer or some other person is an interference with the course of justice. Such an offer has the tendency to interfere with the accused's freedom of choice and seeks to serve an interest other than those interests of the accused that are threatened by the prosecution."

'It has been recognised, in some other legal contexts, that lack of information, or misinformation, can result in a decision not being made "freely and voluntarily". In *Soterious v Police* [2000] SASC 256 (unreported, 4 September 2000) Duggan J said, at [33]:

"In my view, the plea which was entered in these circumstances could not be regarded as being made freely and voluntarily with sufficient knowledge by the appellant to make an informed decision. The appellant is a young woman who had not been in trouble with the law before this incident. She did not commit the offence with which she was charged and it is clear that when she consulted the solicitor her instructions were to that effect. For reasons which appealed to the solicitor and which he did not wish to communicate to the appellant, he did not accept her version as being truthful. I am confident in finding that the solicitor did not intend to pressure the appellant in an improper manner into changing her instructions and that he considered that he was acting in her best interests. However, I have no doubt that she considered herself to be under pressure. I bear in mind that in *Meissner's* case it was held that pressure emanating from a legal adviser does not necessarily vitiate the plea. However the appellant was not only under pressure, but there were significant gaps in the advice which she was given. It was in these circumstances that she admitted to an offence which she did not commit."

'In *Karam v ANZ Banking Group Ltd* [2001] NSWSC 709 Santow J said, in a case concerning the avoidance of a guarantee (at [387]):

"The same Solicitor's Certificate adds as a further question, "Are you signing the acknowledgment freely and voluntarily?" with again each of the signatories needing to answer that question in the affirmative. On the

view of matters the Bank contends for, each of the signatories were signing the acknowledgment freely and voluntarily, though under the pressure, not illegitimate, of needing the further accommodation that the Bank would only provide if they did sign it. On the other hand, they could not be said to have signed the acknowledgment freely and voluntarily if they did not understand and could not be properly advised of its true effect. They were moreover, as Mr Marsden's letter attests, faced with the threat of terminating all bank accommodation of which the earlier cheque dishonour was a clear signal, with its inevitable consequence of the business collapsing and enforcement, whether by the Bank or the Karams at the Bank's behest. The overall effect was to take away any rights they might otherwise have had to prevent the Bank from using the mortgage over their personal homes to secure personal guarantees; and for the guarantees in turn to be treated as covering all of the Company's indebtedness. They lost any capacity to negotiate. *To sign an acknowledgment "freely and voluntarily" presupposes amongst other things that one is not precluded from an understanding of the rights that one is giving away.* Denial of the security documents to the independent adviser beyond any doubt meant that his advice could not provide such an understanding. This is quite apart from the pressure to which they were subjected and the Bank's lack of candour." (emphasis added)

...

'Of course, given the vastly different contexts in which the judicial statements which I have just been quoting about when an act is free and voluntary have been made, one cannot expect to transfer those statements directly into the context of s 13 of the Wills, Probate and Administration Act. They serve, though, to remind one that the notion of acting "freely and voluntary" is one which has a relationship implicit in it. One acts "freely and voluntarily" when one acts free from circumstances constraining one's actions. The sort of circumstances which the cases I have quoted recognise as being ones which can, sometimes, result in action not being free and voluntary included duress, intimidation, persistent importunity, sustained or undue insistence or pressure, harassment, force, threats, fear, fraud, being induced by a threat or promise or some offered advantage, undue influence, and being deprived of relevant information or advice. However, as the discussion and the quoted extract from *Meissner* shows, the mere fact that an action occurs in a context where the actor is subject to one or more of these types of constraints, an action is not always sufficient, in itself, to lead to the conclusion that the actor has not acted freely and voluntary. One legal context in which one enquires whether an action is done "freely and voluntarily" might require the absence of a different range of constraining conditions to a different legal context in which one enquires whether an action is done "freely and voluntarily". Or one such legal context might call for those factors to be weighted differently to the way they are weighted in a different legal context. Further, as the quoted extract from *Cleland* shows, whether an action is in fact not free and voluntary depends on the interaction of the constraining circumstances with the particular actor.

'As well, a person could fail to act "freely and voluntarily" for reasons which were to do with their own mental capacity or condition, rather than because of some constraining external circumstances. A particular student leaving school might have free choice whether to become a labourer or a factory worker, but not have a free choice whether to become a labourer or a nuclear physicist.

'The equitable jurisdiction to set aside catching bargains:

> "... applies whenever one party to a trans-action is at a special disadvantage in dealing with the other party because illness, igno-rance, inexperience, impaired faculties, finan-cial need or other circumstances affect his ability to conserve his own interests, and the other party unconscientiously takes advantage of the opportunity thus placed in his hands." (Per Kitto J, *Blomley v Ryan* (1956) 99 CLR 362 at 415.)

'It is a small step to say that part of the rationale for equity interfering in such cases is that the victim of the catching bargain is not in a position to act freely and voluntarily. Kitto J's list of factors which brings into play the jurisdiction to relieve against catching bargains, includes both external and internal constraints on freedom of action.

'The notion of "acting freely" is well recognised in probate law. One of the preconditions for admission of a will to probate is "that the will propounded is the last will of a free and capable testator" (eg per Isaacs J, *Bailey v Bailey* (1924) 34 CLR 558 at 570). A testator's inability to perform the mental tasks necessary for will-making, or insane delusion, relevant to the subject matter of

the will, prevents probate being granted because the testator cannot make a free choice about how to leave his property.'

'Turning now to s 13, there is a distinction between the two limbs of s 13(2)(c) which arises as a matter of the meaning of the language used. The test that the testator "knew and approved" of the gift requires there to be two identified states of the testator's mind – that he or she knew of the gift, and that he or she approved of the gift. The test "that the gift was given or made freely and voluntarily" looks at a categorisation of the testator's action. Whether an act is one done freely and voluntarily depends to some extent, but only to some extent, on the state of the testator's mind. As well, whether an action is committed freely and voluntarily looks to whether there are constraining external circumstances on the testator which prevent his or her action from being free and voluntary.

'It is the context in which the "acting freely and voluntarily" expression is used which conveys what sort of constraints on action, whether external or internal, are the relevant ones. We need to know what sorts of constraints on action are the relevant ones, to decide whether a testator acted "freely and voluntarily" within the meaning of s 13(2)(c).

...

'Section 34 of the Interpretation Act 1987 (NSW) enables an explanatory note relating to the Bill for the Act to be taken into account to determine the meaning of a provision, if the provision is ambiguous or obscure. The term "freely and voluntarily", in s 13(2)(c), is one which has considerable potential for ambiguity. It is therefore appropriate, given the terms of the explanatory note, to look to the terms of the Law Reform Commission Report to seek to elucidate the meaning of "freely and voluntarily" in s 13(2)(c).

...

'By reference to the Law Reform Commission report one can conclude that, in enacting this test, Parliament is not to have been taken to have expected testators to be making decisions about what gifts to include in a Will in circumstances devoid of any of the impulses to action coming from affection, gratitude or a sense of moral obligation. Motives such as these underlie many wills, and there is no impropriety in them. The type of freedom and voluntariness which Parliament intended is that identified by the Law Reform Commission, namely freedom and voluntariness of a kind which results in there being no impropriety in the making of the Will.

'I should add that in s 13(2)(c) the expression "voluntarily" is not used in its usual legal sense of "without consideration". This emerges from the consideration of the Law Reform Commission's reasoning which led to the inclusion of the "freely and voluntary" test in s 13(2)(c). It also emerges from realising that it would often be pointless to construe "voluntary" as meaning "without consideration". In the situation where a testator included a particular provision in the will because he had received consideration for doing so, if s 13(2)(c) were to make void that disposition, equity would, in many cases, then step in to impose a constructive trust, to require that the person who had given the consideration should receive from the estate the property he or she had been promised. The jurisdiction to impose a constructive trust where someone promises, for valuable consideration, to leave property by will in a particular fashion (other than as a pecuniary legacy), but does not, is well established: *Synge v Synge* (1894) 1 QB 466 at 470; *Horton v Jones* (1935) 53 CLR 475 at 484, 489; *Birmingham v Renfrew* (1937) 57 CLR 666 at 683; *Schaefer v Schuhmann* [1972] AC 572; *Jacobs on Trusts*, 6th ed, [266]–[272].' *Tonkiss v Graham* BC200206010; [2002] NSWSC 891 at [67]–[73], [77]–[79], [82]–[84], [86], [94]–[95], per Campbell J

FREE ON BOARD

[For 41 Halsbury's Laws (4th edn) para 612 see now 41 Halsbury's Laws (4th edn) (Reissue) para 13.]

FREEDOM OF EXPRESSION

New Zealand ' "Freedom of expression" does not mean freedom to copy the form in which authors have expressed themselves and without consent having been given.' *Television New Zealand Ltd v Newsmonitor Services Ltd* [1994] 2 NZLR 91 at 95, per Blanchard J

FREEDOM OF THE PRESS

'The need for a free press is axiomatic, but the press cannot be allowed to charge about like a wild unbridled horse.' *A-G v News Group Newspapers Ltd* [1988] 2 All ER 906 at 921, per Watkins LJ

FREIGHT

[For 43 Halsbury's Laws (4th edn) para 443 et seq see now 43(2) Halsbury's Laws (4th edn) (Reissue) para 1753 et seq.]

Contract of affreightment

[For 43 Halsbury's Laws (4th edn) para 401 see now 43(2) Halsbury's Laws (4th edn) (Reissue) para 1410.]

Dead freight

[For 43 Halsbury's Laws (4th edn) para 591 see now 43(2) Halsbury's Laws (4th edn) (Reissue) para 1646.]

FRESH CAUSE OF ACTION

New Zealand 'In essence, "cause of action" means the act on the part of the defendant which gives the plaintiff the cause of complaint (*Smith v Wilkins and Davies Construction Co Ltd* [1958] NZLR 958, 961). The test of whether an amended pleading raises a "fresh" cause of action for the purposes of the rules as to amendment is well settled. [*McCarthy J in Smith* (*supra*) *at 961 is then quoted, and Court of Appeal and Australian authority cited.*]

' It is then a matter of comparing the allegations in the new pleadings with what has previously been alleged, recognising that questions of degree are involved.' *Chilcott v Goss* [1995] 1 NZLR 263 at 273, CA, per cur

FRESH IN THE MEMORY OF

Australia 'The word "fresh", in its context in s 66 [of the Evidence Act 1995 (NSW)], means "recent" or "immediate". It may also carry with it a connotation that describes the quality of the memory (as being "not deteriorated or changed by lapse of time" [The Oxford English Dictionary, 2nd ed (1989), "fresh" sense 7a]) but the core of the meaning intended, is to describe the temporal relationship between "the occurrence of the asserted fact" and the time of making the representation. Although questions of fact and degree may arise, the temporal relationship required will very likely be measured in hours or days, not, as was the case here, in years.' *Graham v R* (1998) 157 ALR 404 at 405; 72 ALJR 1491; 102 A Crim R 438; BC9804990, per Gaudron, Gummow and Hayne JJ

FRIENDLY SOCIETY

[For 19 Halsbury's Laws (4th edn) para 10 see now 19(1) Halsbury's Laws (4th edn) (Reissue) para 103.]

FROM THE WILD

Australia '... it may be useful to consider the necessary connotation of the words "from the wild". It seems to me that the relevant dichotomy is with a state of domestication, rather than a state wherein the animal in question has been placed under control or restraint by a human agency (cf *Reeve v Wardle; Ex parte Reeve* [1960] Qd R 143). It seems to me that a creature is still "in the wild" if it is within its natural environment or habitat and that it has not necessarily been removed from that environment or habitat because it has been trapped or confined by the action of man. Plainly enough, questions of fact and degree will always be involved in considering this issue, but it cannot be automatically assumed that, because a creature has been captured or even reduced into possession, it has been removed from the wild so that its further abduction can no longer be regarded as a taking of it from the wild. A simple illustration will suffice. Flathead fish live and breed on or near the bottom. If hooked by an angler's line, a flathead is clearly "in the wild" in the relevant sense, at least until it is brought into the boat and deposited in the fish bin. In my opinion, a sea creature will normally be regarded as being "in the wild" until it is removed from the sea to a boat or to a land environment where it will be unable to survive without the provision of an artificial marine habitat.' *Lloyd v Snooks* BC9907337; [1999] TASSC 117 at [13], per Wright J

FRONTAGE

New Zealand '[58] With respect, I do not accept the view that "frontage" in the condition meant contiguous frontage to a side of a house to a street uninterrupted by any other building in between. If this is what was determined in English, I, with respect, do not follow it. I am attracted to the view of Hammond J in *Bailey*, that the condition was meant to preclude the erection of a building which had the right-of-way as its only frontage. This is reinforced by the use of the word "wholly" in the condition. I also prefer the view of Elias J in *Rental Space* that "frontage" as used in the condition applies to access to a public street. It is a legal and not a practical concept.

'[60] There are other pointers to the meaning of "frontage". That word is used in s 125 of the Public Works Act 1928 which, presumably, the drafters of the condition had in mind. Clearly, in that section it means a legal boundary between the section and an existing street. There is no limitation in the section to a minimum conjoint legal boundary, nor is there a reference to practical vehicular access. Further "frontage" in its usual dictionary meaning is "land abutting on street ...". It has other dictionary meanings but this is the common meaning which, in my view, is consistent with both its use in s 125 of the Public Works Act 1928, and in the condition. Finally, reference to "wholly" means that the condition only applies if the only legal boundary of the section which abuts a street is through the right-of-way. "Frontage" clearly applies to a conjoint legal boundary between the section and the street, and does not apply to the building as such.' *Wright v Tan* [2002] 3 NZLR 703 at 716–717, per Paterson J.

FRUSTRATION

[For 9 Halsbury's Laws (4th edn) para 950 see now 9(1) Halsbury's Laws (4th edn) (Reissue) para 897.]

FUGITIVE

[The Fugitive Offenders Act 1967 has been repealed. See now the Fugitive Offenders Act 1989, s 1, where the term 'fugitive' is not used.]

FUGITIVE CRIMINAL

[The Extradition Act 1870 has been repealed. The definitions are re-enacted in the Fugitive Offenders Act 1989, Sch 1 para 20.]

[For 18 Halsbury's Laws (4th edn) para 210 et seq see now 17(2) Halsbury's Laws (4th edn) (Reissue) para 1194 et seq.]

FULL AND SATISFACTORY EXPLANATION FOR THE DELAY IN MAKING THE CLAIM

Australia [Section 40(2), Motor Accidents Act 1988 (NSW).] 'The concept of a "full and satisfactory explanation" is, to some extent, explained by s 40(2), which deals with the two elements as follows. A full explanation is said to be a full account of the conduct, including the actions, knowledge and belief of the claimant, from the date of the accident until the date of providing the explanation. The word "full" takes its meaning from the context. It refers to the conduct bearing upon the delay, and the state of mind of the claimant. The subsection goes on to provide that an explanation is not a satisfactory explanation unless a reasonable person in the position of the claimant would have been justified in experiencing the same delay.

'Pt 5 is replete with legislative declarations of its objects. This is not an exercise in apologetics. Rather, it gives practical content to terms such as "reasonable", "justification" and "satisfactory". What would constitute justifiable delay on the part of a reasonable person in making a claim is to be considered in the light of the legislative purposes explained in the Act. That matter is taken further by a specific provision (in s 43A(3)) that evidence as to delay in the onset of symptoms of physical injury may form part of an explanation.' *Russo v Aiello* [2003] HCA 53 at [4], [5] per Gleeson CJ; BC200305655

FULL DESCRIPTION

Australia [The Customs Act 1901 (Cth) s 269F requires "a full description of the goods" in respect of which a Tariff Concession Order is sought.] '... the appropriate test of a "full description" was enunciated by Deputy President McMahon in *Re SMS Autoparts Pty Ltd and Chief Executive Officer of Customs* (1996) 41 ALD 615 at 619 when he said that: "A full description must be an objective description and must be such as to enable those who import, or who supervise importation, to identify the goods by an informed inspection".' *Re Cameco Downunder Pty Ltd and Chief Executive Officer of Customs* (1996) 44 ALD 129 at 135, per the Full Tribunal

FUMES

[The Clean Air Act 1956 has been repealed. The definition is re-enacted in the Clean Air Act 1993, s 64(1).]

FUNCTION

Canada [Notice requirement for police officers as public servants was specified in the event of a 'discontinuance of a function'.] 'A "function" must be the office that is to say the bundle of responsibilities, duties and activities that are carried out by a particular employee or group of employees.

'It is this definition of "function", in the sense of "office" which best comports with the environment of the work place. The very word "employment" indicates the existence of an employee and an employer. A term such as "function" or "office" must have a meaning for both these parties. For example, a person may have the "office" of plant superintendent. A person functioning as a plant superintendent carries out a regime or set of activities and duties that forms the office of plant superintendent. Both the employer and the employee understand what is required in order to perform or to carry out that particular office. Similarly the "office" of secretary or punch press operator carries with it a particular set of activities and duties. A particular bundle of skills is required to perform the duties and activities required by each of these offices. Once again, both the employer and the employee will know exactly what is required to perform the activities of the particular office.' *Flieger v New Brunswick* [1993] 2 SCR 651 at 663–664, per Cory J

FURNITURE

[For 27 Halsbury's Laws (4th edn) paras 622–623 see now 27(1) Halsbury's Laws (4th edn) (Reissue) para 718.]

G

GAIN

[For 7 Halsbury's Laws (4th edn) para 20 see now 7(1) Halsbury's Laws (4th edn) (2004 Reissue) para 201 note 1.]

GALE

[For 31 Halsbury's Laws (4th edn) para 848 see now 31 Halsbury's Laws (4th edn) (2003 Reissue) para 611.]

GAMBLING LOSS

'A gambling loss, whenever paid, is a completed voluntary gift from the loser to the winner.' *Lipkin Gorman (a firm) v Karpnale Ltd* [1991] 2 AC 548 at 562, [1992] 4 All ER 512 at 519, HL, per Lord Templeman

GAME (ANIMALS OR BIRDS)

[Land was appointed to the Forestry Commission for a term of 999 years subject to the reservation of sporting rights to the estate owner. The reservation was expressed to be in respect of 'all game, woodcocks snipe and other wild fowl hares rabbits and fish.' The question arose as to whether the word 'game' covered deer.] 'The phrase ... was "all game woodcocks snipe and other wild fowl hares rabbits and fish". To my mind, there is a plain implication in the first eight words of *noscitur a sociis*: the phrase "other wild fowl" ... gives one a feeling that in the collocation of words the draftsman was speaking about feathered creatures ... The word "game" has a real and adequate meaning and, knowing it by its neighbours, which is all the Latin words mean, the phrase "woodcocks snipe and other wild fowl" points to birds which are habitually shot for sport and eaten, and the word "game" is coloured by that collocation, so that it means, in my view, feathered game, not anything else. In my view, trying as best I can to bear in mind all the multitude of influences that come to one's thought, I have myself really no doubt at all that "game" in this reservation means

only feathered game and not terrestrial game and does not include deer.' *Inglewood Investment Co Ltd v Forestry Commission* [1988] 1 All ER 783 at 789–790, per Harman J

[For 2 Halsbury's Laws (4th edn) para 211 see now 2(1) Halsbury's Laws (4th edn) (Reissue) para 517.]

GAMING

[For 4 Halsbury's Laws (4th edn) para 2 see now 4(1) Halsbury's Laws (4th edn) (2002 Reissue) para 3.]

GAVELKIND

[For 139 Halsbury's Laws (4th edn) para 322 see now 39(2) Halsbury's Laws (4th edn) (Reissue) para 14.]

GENDER

'[23] The words "sex" and "gender" are sometimes used interchangeably, but today more frequently denote a difference. Mrs Cox submitted that gender was broader than sex. Her suggested definition was that "gender" related to culturally and socially specific expectations of behaviour and attitude, mapped on to men and women by society. It included self-definition, that is to say, what a person recognised himself to be. See also Sir Brian Neill in *S-T (formerly J) v J* [1998] 1 All ER 431 at 476, [1998] Fam 103 at 153). It would seem from the definition proposed by Mrs Cox, with which we would not disagree, that it would be impossible to identify gender at the moment of the birth of a child.' *Bellinger v Bellinger* [2001] EWCA Civ 1140 at [23], [2002] 1 All ER 311 at 317–318, CA, per Dame Elizabeth Butler-Sloss P and Robert Walker LJ

GENERAL WARRANT

Australia 'The term "general warrant" strictly refers to a warrant issued in times past under the prerogative power, commonly in sedition cases, and which purported to authorise the arrest of unnamed persons (and the seizure of all their papers). Such warrants were held to be unlawful as lacking statutory authority in the old case of *Entick v Carrington*: see Jowitt's *Dictionary of English Law*, 2nd ed, p 856 and *Inland Revenue Commissioners v Rossminster Ltd* [1980] AC 952 at 1008–9. However, the term is now sometimes used to describe a warrant issued under statutory authority that is so vague in its operation as to permit an unlimited search and seizure; cf *Arno v Forsyth* (1986) 65 ALR 125 at 130, 139–40 and *Inland Revenue Commissioners v Rossminster Ltd* at 1005–6.' *Harts Australia Ltd v Commissioner, Australian Federal Police* (1996) 141 ALR 493 at 498–499, per Drummond J

GENERATING STATION

[The Electricity (Supply) Act 1919 has been repealed. The Electricity Act 1989, s 64(1), defines the term as follows.] 'Generating station', in relation to a generating station wholly or mainly driven by water, includes all structures and works for holding or channelling water for a purpose directly related to the generation of electricity by that station.

GENUINE

Australia [The Industrial Relations Act 1979 (Vic) enabled associations to be recognised as such with respect to certain trades. Section 55(3) stated that an application must be granted if it appeared that the applicant was a 'genuine' association.] 'I should state first that in my view (a view which as I understood them was conceded by counsel to be correct) the question whether an association is "genuine" within the meaning of s 55(3) involves both a subjective and objective test. It is not "genuine" if the applicant has an improper motive, but on the other hand, it is not necessarily "genuine" merely because the applicant has a sincere belief in the justice of its cause and an honest wish to obtain recognition.

'In some cases the absence of any "track record" of which the commission speaks may throw light on the question whether the application is genuine; it might tend to show that the applicants have no genuine interest in an industrial sense in the establishment of a board or in relation to other industrial matters. It might tend to show that the application was not genuine in the sense that the applicants must have some ulterior or improper motive in making the application, or that it was a

sham.' *Sonnemann v Industrial Relations Commission of Victoria* [1992] 1 VR 531 at 538, per Southwell J

GENUINE DISPUTE

Australia 'One statement which has been approved on a number of occasions is that of the Chief Judge in Equity in *Eyota Pty Ltd v Hanave Pty Ltd* (1994) 12 ACLC 669 at 671: "It is, however, necessary to consider the meaning of the expression 'genuine dispute', where it occurs in [Corporations Law] s 459H. In my opinion that expression connotes a plausible contention requiring investigation, and raises much the same sort of considerations as the 'serious question to be tried' criterion which arises on an application for an interlocutory injunction or for the extension or removal of a caveat ..." ' *Seventeenth Febtor Ltd v National Australia Bank Ltd* (1997) 23 ACSR 585 at 587; BC9701921 at 4, per Sundberg J

GETS POSSESSION

New Zealand [Crimes Act 1961, s 210 (Abduction of child under 16).] 'First, following the standard rule of statutory construction, the phrase "gets possession" in subs (3) must be interpreted in the context of the section as a whole. Unless the context suggests otherwise, the word "possession" in the phrase "gets possession" and in the phrase "right to the possession of the child" in subs (3) should be given the same meaning. The possession referred to must then relate back to the word "possession" in the substantive provision contained in subs (1). The pertinent words in that section are "with intent to deprive any parent ... having lawful care or charge of any child ... of the possession of the child". The possession which the alleged abductor gets, and in respect of which good faith is needed, is possession contrary to that of which the abductor intends to deprive the other person. It is the possession resulting from the act of taking or enticing away or detaining. When this occurs, the state of mind of the abductor is material, both as to the intention to deprive the other person of possession and the good faith claimed to accompany the act ... . It is at the time the child is detained with an intent to deprive the parent having lawful custody of the possession of the child that the right to possession must be claimed.

...

'The word "gets" has an over-abundance of meanings. The definition takes up ten pages of the *Oxford English Dictionary* which provides a wide variety of meanings. We doubt that reference to the dictionary meaning is therefore of much assistance, particularly as the word should be interpreted as part of the phrase "gets possession" and in the context in which it is used. A number of meanings given, however, confirm that the word "gets" properly can be used where a person may already have the article in his or her possession. Thus, while the first meaning given is "to obtain, procure", a later meaning is "to obtain, come to have ...". Again, we do not consider that it is strained to say that a person can get possession in the sense of obtaining or coming to have possession of a child already in his or her physical possession when the child is kept or withheld from another person who is entitled to possession.

...

'It is virtually impossible to suggest that at the time Parliament anticipated exempting persons from the crime of kidnapping, whether by unlawfully carrying off or detaining the victim, who happened to already have possession of the person "kidnapped". The phrase "gets possession" can then only be sensibly interpreted to refer to the time when the victim is carried off or detained.' *R v Tauiliili* [1997] 1 NZLR 525 at 533–536, CA, per Gault, Thomas and Blanchard JJ

GIFT

Class gift

[For 50 Halsbury's Laws (4th edn) para 362 see now 50 Halsbury's Laws (4th edn) (Reissue) para 413.]

Inter vivos

[For 20 Halsbury's Laws (4th edn) para 1 see now 20(1) Halsbury's Laws (4th edn) (Reissue) para 1.]

GIPSY—GYPSY *SEE ALSO* TRAVELLER

'One of the difficulties in the present case, in my view, is that the word "gipsy" has itself more than one meaning. The classic dictionary meaning can be found as the primary meaning given in the Oxford English Dictionary (1933): "A member of a wandering race (by themselves called *Romany*), of Hindu origin, which first appeared in England about the beginning of the 16th c. and was then believed to have come from Egypt". Hence the word "gipsy", also spelt as "gypsy"... Alongside this meaning, the word "gipsy" also has a more colloquial, looser meaning. This is expressed in the

Longman Dictionary of Contemporary English (1984), where two meanings are attributed to "gipsy". The first meaning is along the lines I have already quoted. The second is "a person who habitually wanders or who has the habits of someone who does not stay for long in one place"; in short, a nomad. I can anticipate here by noting that if the word "gipsy" is used in this second, colloquial sense it is not definitive of a racial group within the 1976 [Race Relations] Act. To discriminate against such a group would not be on racial grounds, namely on the ground of ethnic origins. As the judge [in the court below] observed, there are many people who travel around the country in caravans, vans, converted buses, trailers, lorries and motor vehicles, leading a peripatetic or nomadic way of life. They include didicois, mumpers, peace people, new age travellers, hippies, tinkers, hawkers, self-styled "anarchists", and others, as well as Romany gipsies. They may all be loosely referred to as "gipsies", but as a group they do not have the characteristics requisite of a racial group within the Act.' *Commission for Racial Equality v Dutton* [1989] 1 All ER 306 at 309, CA, per Nicholls LJ

Canada '[4] In response to the argument of the defence, the Crown sought to amend the information to read "Roma a.k.a. gypsies". The trial judge refused. The Crown then asked the trial judge to take judicial notice of the dictionary definitions of Roma. Again, the trial judge declined. Finally, the Crown asked the trial judge to reopen the trial to permit the Crown to call evidence that gypsies are the same as Roma. The trial judge refused this application as well and as a result he dismissed the charges.

'[5] The Crown appealed, challenging each of the three rulings referred to in the previous paragraph. Ewaschuk J. dismissed the appeal. The Crown's application for leave to appeal to this court challenges the same three rulings that were considered by the summary conviction appeal court.

'[6] As to judicial notice, at trial the Crown asked that the court take judicial notice of the dictionary definitions of Roma (singular – Rom) in order to establish that Roma are gypsies or are known as gypsies. In support of its application, the Crown referred to five dictionaries. Although the language in each is not exactly the same, all of the dictionaries referred to Rom as a gypsy. In some instances, the definitions were limited to a man or boy gypsy.

'[7] There are two bases on which a court may take judicial notice of a fact. The one that is relevant to this case covers facts which are capable of immediate and accurate demonstration by resorting to readily accessible sources of indisputable accuracy: Sidney W. Lederman and Alan W. Bryant, *Sopinka's The Law of Evidence in Canada*, 2nd ed. (Toronto: Butterworths Canada Ltd., 1999) at para. 19.13.

'[8] Given that the Crown asked nothing more than that the trial judge take judicial notice of definitions found in standard dictionaries and given that those definitions were relatively consistent, the trial judge should probably have acceded to the Crown's request and taken notice of those definitions. However, the trial judge's error, if there was one, is not dispositive of the application before this court.

'[9] In dismissing the summary conviction appeal, Ewaschuk J. found that there was no evidence that the respondents had targeted Roma. He reasoned that even if one accepted that Roma are a subset of gypsies (as the dictionary definitions would have shown), that would not have been sufficient to found convictions; rather, it would be necessary to show that the words Roma and gypsies are interchangeable (according to the dictionaries they are not). Only then would it be established that the hatred targeted at gypsies was targeted at Roma. Put another way, Ewaschuk J. concluded that even if the trial judge had taken judicial notice of the fact that gypsies include Roma, the result of the trial would have been the same. That conclusion turned on an assessment of the evidence.

'[10] It was suggested in argument before us that the reason that the Crown specified Roma rather than gypsies as the identifiable group in the information was in order to be sensitive to the Roma people. The term gypsy in its broadest sense is often used to refer to people who lead a nomadic life, and for many Roma, the term gypsy conjures up unflattering or stereotypical images. For example, one dictionary definition of a gypsy is "a cunning rogue": *Oxford English Dictionary* 2nd ed. We understand the Crown's concern for sensitivity; however, what seems to be common ground is that not all people who are referred to as gypsies are in fact Roma.' *R v Krymoski* (2003) 227 DLR (4th) 504 at 506–507 (Ont CA), per the Court

Canada '[22] A court may accept without the requirement of proof facts that are either "(1) so notorious or generally accepted as not to be the subject of debate among reasonable persons; or (2) capable of immediate and accurate demonstration by resort to readily accessible sources of indisputable accuracy": *R. v. Find*, [2001] 1 S.C.R. 863, 2001 SCC 32, 154 C.C.C. (3d) 97, 199 D.L.R. (4th) 193, at para. 48. The dictionary meaning of words may fall within the latter category: see J. Sopinka, S.N. Lederman and A.W. Bryant, *The Law of Evidence in Canada* (2nd ed. 1999), at paras. 19.13 and 19.22.

'[23] The Crown presented the trial judge with five dictionaries demonstrating a relationship between "Roma" and "gypsy". For example, the New Oxford Dictionary of English (1998) contained the following definitions:

> gypsy (also gipsy) > noun (pl. –ies) a member of a travelling people with dark skin and hair, speaking a language, (Romany) related to Hindi, and traditionally living by seasonal work, itinerant trade, and fortune-telling. Gypsies are now found mostly in Europe, parts of North Africa, and North America, but are believed to have originated in the Indian subcontinent.

> Rom > noun (pl. Roma/...) a gypsy, especially a man. – origin mid 19th cent.: abbreviation of ROMANY.

> Romany > noun (pl. –ies) 1 (mass noun) the language of the gypsies, which is an Indo-European language related to Hindi. It is spoken by a dispersed group of about 1 million people, and has many dialects. 2 A gypsy.

'[24] The dictionary definitions presented to the trial judge hence showed that "gypsy" can refer to an ethnic group properly known as "Roma", "Rom", or "Romany". I see no reason why the trial judge should not have taken judicial notice of that fact and then considered it, together with the rest of the evidence, to determine whether there was proof beyond a reasonable doubt that the respondents did in fact intend to target Roma.' *R v Krymoski* (2005) 249 DLR (4th) 28 at [22]–[24], [2005] SCJ No 8 (SCC), per Charron J

GIVE

Australia [Migration Act 1958 (Cth) s 430D.] '... At the relevant time, the word "give" used in s 430D(2), the applicable provision in this case, was not defined. Accordingly, it is the ordinary meaning of the word, understood in its context, that must be considered. The context is that the RRT must give the applicant a copy of the written statement. In that setting, to give a document ordinarily requires its physical delivery, not some act of constructive delivery of possession which, at general law, may suffice to transfer property in a chattel. It will not be enough to communicate to the applicant orally that the document has arrived, or to communicate the gist of the document, or even to read the document to the applicant. What is required is that the written statement be physically given to the applicant. Only once this has occurred can it be said that s 478(1)(b) is enlivened and time begins to run. The appellant's evidence that the written statement was not "given" until requested by him from Ms Alamar "some" weeks after he was told of the adverse decision by the RRT has not been controverted by the Minister who had the burden of establishing the objection to competency.

'Although the word "give" in s 430D(2) was not defined, it was defined for the purposes of s 430B(6) (and s 368B(6)). Section 430B(6) dealt with the third method of notification described earlier in these reasons. It provided that, if the applicant was not present at the handing down of the decision, then a copy of the written statement was to be given to the applicant within 14 days by one of the methods specified in s 441A. Section 441A was provided for by Sch 3, Item 12 of the 1998 Act. However, Item 12 may have been ineffective because the amendment was misdescribed. The amendment sought to insert s 441A "[a]t the end of Div 7 of Part 6". No such Division existed. Presumably the Parliament intended to insert s 441A at the end of Div 7 of Pt 7, which is concerned with the RRT.' *WACB v Minister for Immigration and Multicultural and Indigenous Affairs* [2004] HCA 50 at [37], per Gleeson CJ, McHugh, Gummow and Heydon JJ; BC200406533

GIVE EFFECT TO

Australia [Section 45(2), Trade Practices Act 1974 (Cth)] '[15] S 45(2) stated, among other prohibitions, that a corporation shall not make a contract, arrangement or understanding containing an exclusionary provision (s 45(2)(a)(i)). Nor shall a corporation "give effect to" an exclusionary provision (s 45(2)(b)(i)). Here and in s 45(6), the expression "give effect to" included the doing of "an act or thing in pursuance of or in accordance with" a provision of a contract, arrangement or understanding, and the enforcement or purported enforcement thereof (s 4(1)).

...

'[33] That conclusion is reinforced when due account is paid to the use of the expression "the giving effect to which". That is an expression of wide meaning and its use requires consideration of the various kinds of conduct which it encompasses. As has been indicated above, s 4(1) of the Act requires that "give effect to", in relation to a provision of a contract, arrangement or

understanding, "includes do an act or thing in pursuance of or in accordance with or enforce or purport to enforce". Necessarily, then, the relevant inquiry is about what may be done under the contract, arrangement or understanding, not how it is drafted. That is, the inquiry must focus upon the content of the stipulations which the parties have made or agreed. Thus, upon analysis, the one verbal composite may contain stipulations each of which is a "provision" in the statutory sense, and with different statutory characteristics. Do the stipulations which cause a contravention of s 45(2) meet the criterion in s 45(6)?' *Visy Paper Pty Ltd v Australian Competition and Consumer Commission* [2003] HCA 59 per Gleeson CJ, McHugh, Gummow and Hayne JJ; BC200305828

GOOD AND SUFFICIENT CAUSE

'Under [the Prosecution of Offences Act 1985] s 22(3)(a) the court must be satisfied that there is a good and sufficient cause for extending or further extending the period of custody specified in the [Prosecution of Offences (Custody Time Limits) Regulations 1987]. The seriousness of the offence with which the defendant is charged cannot of itself be good and sufficient cause within the section (see *R v Governor of Winchester Prison, ex p Roddie* [1991] 2 All ER 931 at 934, [1991] 1 WLR 303 at 306); nor can the need to protect the public (see *R v Central Criminal Court, ex p Abu-Warech* [1997] 1 All ER 159 at 164, [1998] 1 WLR 1083 at 1088 per Auld LJ). If conditions of that kind are not satisfied, the defendant is entitled to bail and the question of extending custody time limits will not arise. Nor, as again Lloyd LJ held in *Ex p Roddie* [1991] 2 All ER 931 at 934, [1991] 1 WLR 303 at 306, can it be a good cause that the extension is only for a short period. As Auld LJ said in *Ex p Abu-Warech* [1997] 1 All ER 159 at 164, [1998] 1 WLR 1083 at 1088:

"To amount to 'good ... cause' there must be some good reason for the sought postponement of the trial carrying with it the need to extend the custody time limit."

'While it is possible to rule that some matters, such as those we have just mentioned, are incapable in law of amounting to good and sufficient cause for granting an extension, there is an almost infinite variety of matters which may, depending on the facts of a particular case, be capable of amounting to good and sufficient cause. It is neither possible nor desirable to attempt to define what may or may not amount to good and sufficient cause in any given case, and it would be facile to propose any test which would be applicable in all cases.' *R v Crown Court at Manchester, ex p McDonald* [1999] 1 All ER 805 at 810, DC, per Lord Bingham of Cornhill CJ

GOOD BEHAVIOUR

Canada [Judicial office continued during good behaviour.] '... one could fail to meet the requirement of good behaviour without wilful misconduct, even under the Act of Settlement, 1701. It appears to me that such an interpretation is fully appropriate today in relation to s 99(1) of the Constitution Act, 1867, at least to the extent that a permanent disability could give rise to a breach of good behaviour or, as the Inquiry Committee suggested, "non-behaviour". It is most consistent with meeting the purpose of judicial independence which is not only that the public should be served by decisions rendered without fear or favour but also that it should simply be served. I respectfully adopt the language of the Inquiry Committee: "We are of the view that it is important for continued public confidence in the administration of justice that a person who holds the office of judge not be permanently incapable of fulfilling the office of judge". (Decision, at pp 37–8) At the same time it adequately protects judges from improper threats to their security of tenure.' *Gratton v Canada (Judicial Council)* (1994) 115 DLR (4th) 81 at 100, Fed TD, per Strayer J

GOOD CAUSE

Australia [It is a defence to a prosecution for refusal to, inter alia, submit to an alcotest or breath analysis when there is, in the circumstances of the case, 'good cause' for refusal: Road Traffic Act 1961 (SA) s 47(e).] 'A perusal of the decided cases on this issue reveals that the court has, as I have indicated, accepted that appropriate evidence which establishes the existence of a genuine belief, based on reasonable grounds, that blowing will be injurious to health or that events subsequent to relevant driving which could render a breath analysis suspect as to its accuracy, may well amount to good cause. On the other hand, there is little, if anything, in the way of published authority which bears on conduct based on genuinely held religious beliefs, non-observance of which may give rise to deleterious spiritual, rather than physical, consequences.

'Bearing in mind the nature of the multi-cultural society in which we now live, I would not be

prepared to reject out of hand the possibility that serious spiritual distress likely to be caused to a defendant by being compelled to blow contrary to the tenets of that person's religious beliefs may be capable of constituting good cause. A perceived probability, for example, according to a genuinely held belief, that a person might be condemned to eternal damnation by particular conduct, is not a matter to be lightly dismissed, if a reasonable basis for such a belief (eg the specific teachings of a religious sect as actually known to a defendant) was demonstrated.' *Re Chaousis* (1995) 76 A Crim R 257 at 259–260, per Olsson J

GOOD CHARACTER

Australia 'It should also be observed that the term "good character" is not precise in its denotation. In one sense, it refers to the mental and moral qualities which an individual has. In another sense, it refers to the individual's reputation or repute: see *Oxford English Dictionary*, meanings 11, 12 and 13; *The Macquarie Dictionary* meanings 1, 2, 3, 4 and 5. Necessarily, when decisions are made in Australia under the Act in relation to persons who are overseas, greater attention tends to be given to objective facts and to reputation or repute rather than to a detailed analysis of the person's inherent qualities. I do not suggest that, in the context, "good character" refers to reputation and repute as such. It does not. But criminal convictions or the absence of them and character references are likely to be an important source of primary information. If there is a criminal conviction, the decision-maker will have regard to the nature of the crime to determine whether or not it reflected adversely upon the character of the applicant.' *Irving v Minister for Immigration, Local Government and Ethnic Affairs* (1996) 139 ALR 84 at 87–88, per Davies J

GOOD FAITH

[Meaning of 'good faith' in relation to protected disclosure under Employment Rights Act 1996, ss 43C(1), 43G(1)(a).] '[41] Shorn of context, the words "in good faith" have a core meaning of honesty. Introduce context, and it calls for further elaboration. Thus in the context of a claim or representation, the sole issue as to honesty may just turn on its truth. But even where the content of the statement is true or reasonably believed by its maker to be true, an issue of honesty may still creep in according to whether it is made with sincerity of intention for which the Act provides protection or for an ulterior and, say, malicious, purpose. The term is to be found in many statutory and common law contexts, and because they are necessarily conditioned by their context, it is dangerous to apply judicial attempts at definition in one context to that of another. This is so even in closely related legislation such as the Sex Discrimination Act 1975, the Race Relations Act 1976 and the Disability Discrimination Act 1995, in which s 4(2) of the 1975 Act, s 2(2) of the 1976 Act and s 55(4) of the 1995 Act prevent as being discriminatory for the relevant purpose treatment prompted by an allegation that is "false and not made in good faith". In such a formulation which is concerned with the stark difference between truth or falsity, not, as here "reasonable belief in [its substantial truth]", the notion of "good faith" is the only vehicle for considering the honesty or dishonesty of the allegation. For those reasons, I do not consider that it is helpful to turn in this context to some of the more distant examples of the use of the expression that have been cited to us ...

'[42] I should, however, say something about one other example, *Central Estates (Belgravia) Ltd v Woolgar* [1971] 3 All ER 647, [1972] 1 QB 48 which concerned the meaning of "in good faith" in the Leasehold Reform Act 1967 on the issue whether motivation is relevant to whether something is done or said in good faith, Lord Denning MR's words in that context are a frequent point of reference ([1971] 3 All ER 647 at 649, [1972] 1 QB 48 at 55): "... under this Act a claim is made 'in good faith' when it is made honestly and with no ulterior motive." However, the issue in that case was whether claims by two tenants under the 1967 Act to acquire the freehold and an extended lease of their respective properties were made in good faith so as to enable them to defeat their respective landlords' claims for re-entry and forfeiture for breach of covenant under their leases. The issue was, therefore, the good faith of a claim, which does not necessarily involve consideration of the truth of any statement of fact in making it, and where motive, or honesty of motive was all. It is thus understandable that Megaw LJ in that context equated "in good faith" with "honestly", saying ([1971] 3 All ER 647 at 651, [1972] 1 QB 48 at 57):

"The words 'in good faith', in my opinion, mean 'honestly'. A claim is not made honestly if it is made with the intention of committing a criminal offence, or of facilitating the future commission of a criminal offence.

It does not make it any the less a dishonest claim because the intended criminal offence is itself not what is called an offence involving dishonesty."

'[43] Whereas in Mrs Street's case, the issue is the good faith of a disclosure containing a statement of fact—an allegation. If it falls within s 43C it involves no separately identified issue as to its truth or reasonable belief in its truth or other indicia of honesty. If it falls within s 43G there is required, in addition to good faith, reasonable belief in its truth, no motive of personal gain, on the contrary a good reason for not disclosing to the employer, and reasonableness. In short, these provisions may require employment tribunals on occasion to distinguish between good faith and honesty in a way not called for in the Central Estates case, notwithstanding Lord Denning MR's seemingly conjunctive rather than disjunctive use of the words "honestly and with no ulterior motive".

'[44] I say "may" require such a distinction because where a statement is made without reasonable belief in its truth, that fact would be highly relevant as to whether it was made in good faith (see, for example, *Darnton v University of Surrey* [2003] IRLR 133 at 136, [2003] ICR 615 at 623 (para 24) per Judge Serota QC), as indeed it would also be highly relevant as to its reasonableness. Mr Donovan accepted—indeed he prayed in aid—that degree of overlap between good faith, reasonable belief in substantial truthfulness and reasonableness in all the circumstances. But it does not necessarily follow that, where a statement is made in that belief, it necessarily follows that it is made in good faith or reasonably. Where, as in a statutory provision like s 43G(1), the parliamentary draftsman has included the notion of good faith among a set of cumulative conditions of the qualification in question, it is plain that he contemplated that the notion of good faith should be capable of adding, according to the circumstances, something to that of reasonable belief in truth, as Mummery LJ appears to have accepted in his analysis of these provisions in *ALM Medical Services Ltd v Bladon* [2002] IRLR 807 at [4](iii), [2002] ICR 1444 at [4](iii) (see [10], above). It is noteworthy too that in s 43G, and also in s 43F, good faith is the first of the cumulative conditions stipulated.

...

[48] Turning more closely to the construction and effect of the cumulative conditions of protection set out in s 43G, even if one defines "in good faith" as requiring simply "honesty of intention", that still requires more than a reasonable belief in the

truth of the allegations made. The draftsman must be taken to have intended some additional, even if partially overlapping, requirement with that of reasonable belief in the truth of the disclosure, when continuing in s 43G(1)(a) the requirement of good faith in the earlier provisions of Pt IVA of the 1996 Act.' *Street v Derbyshire Unemployed Workers' Centre* [2004] EWCA Civ 964, [2004] 4 All ER 839 at [41]–[44], [48], per Auld LJ

Australia '... each of the three formulations mentioned by Fisher J [in *Barton v Official Receiver* (1986) 161 CLR 75] is concerned with the actual state of mind of the person who took under the disposition. Negligence, stupidity, or blindness to what others might be well able to see are not equivalent to lack of good faith.' *Official Trustee in Bankruptcy v Mitchell* (1992) 16 Fam LR 87 at 95, per cur

Australia [Section 149(6) of the Environmental Planning and Assessment Act 1979 (NSW) provides that a council shall not incur any liability for any advice provided in 'good faith' pursuant to an earlier subsection relating to including advice on relevant matters affecting the land of which it may be aware.] '... in a particular statutory context, a criterion of "good faith" may go beyond personal honesty and the absence of malice, and may require some other quality of the state of mind or knowledge of the relevant actor ...

'The statutory concept of "good faith" with which the legislation in this case is concerned calls for more than honest ineptitude. There must be a real attempt by the authority to answer the request for information at least by recourse to the materials available to the authority.' *Mid Density Developments Pty Ltd v Rockdale Municipal Council* (1993) 44 FCR 290 at 299–300; 116 ALR 460 at 468–469, per cur

Australia [Decisions of the Refugee Review Tribunal (RRT) made under s 474(1) of the Migration Act 1958 (Cth) are treated as 'final and conclusive'. In this case the RRT affirmed the rejection of a protection visa application under s 474(1). Read in conjunction with *R v Hickman; Ex parte Fox and Clinton* (1945) 70 CLR 598, the power conferred under s 474(1) is broadened such that decisions of the RRT that are made in good faith are treated as beyond review.] 'In *R v Murray; Ex parte Proctor* (1949) 77 CLR 387 at 400, Dixon J expressed the good faith requirement in terms of an "honest attempt to deal with a subject matter confided to the tribunal and to act in pursuance of the power of the tribunal in relation

to something that might reasonably be regarded as falling within its province". In like vein, a "person honestly acting in the supposed course of the duties or authorities arising from [an] enactment" would enjoy the protection of provisions of the enactment limiting or qualifying rights of action in respect of decisions made under it: *Little v Commonwealth* (1947) 75 CLR 94 at 108 (Dixon J).

' "Good faith" is a "protean term" which appears in a variety of statutory and common law contexts: *Secretary, Department of Education, Employment, Training and Youth Affairs v Prince* (1997) 152 ALR 127 at 130 per Finn J. It has also been applied both broadly and narrowly in administrative law, particularly in England. Courts have not traditionally limited it to a requirement of "honesty" in decision-making. In *Westminster Corp v London and North Western Railway Co* [1905] AC 426, Lord Macnaghten said, at 430:

> "It is well settled that a public body invested with statutory powers ... must take care not to exceed or abuse its powers. It must keep within the limits of the authority committed to it. It must act in good faith. And it must act reasonably. The last proposition is involved in the second, if not in the first."

'The learned authors of the Eighth edition of Wade and Forsyth's *Administrative Law*, Clarendon Press, 1994 have remarked that courts continually accuse public authorities of bad faith merely because they have acted unreasonably or on improper grounds (at 413–14):

> "Again and again it is laid down that powers must be exercised reasonably and in good faith. But in this context 'in good faith' means merely 'for legitimate reasons'. Contrary to the natural sense of the words, they impute no moral obliquity."

'See also *Webb v Minister of Housing and Local Government* [1965] 1 WLR 755 at 784 and *Roberts v Hopwood* [1925] AC 578 at 603. In its ordinary meaning the term "good faith" imports the idea of honesty. Wade and Forsyth observe that "bad faith" should be restricted to cases of actual dishonesty: *Cannock Chase DC v Kelly* [1978] 1 WLR 1 and *Western Fish Products Ltd v Penwith DC* [1981] 2 All ER 204 at 215.

'De Smith, Woolf and Jowell in the Fifth Edition of their text, *Judicial Review of Administrative Action*, Sweet & Maxwell, 1995 equate bad faith with dishonesty, malice and self interest (at 553):

"These motives, which have the effect of distorting or unfairly biasing the decision-maker's approach to the subject of the decision, cause the decision to be taken in bad faith or for an improper purpose (the term "improper" here bearing a connotation of moral impropriety). Some of the decisions based on bad faith will also violate the ground of illegality, as the offending motive may take the decision outside the "four corners" of the authorised power. Irrespective of whether this be so, any ingredient of bad faith may in itself cause a decision to be invalid."

'For a brief statement of a like view of bad faith see also Craig, *Administrative Law*, 4th ed, Sweet & Maxwell, 1999 at 546 and Supperstone & Goudie, *Judicial Review*, 2nd ed, Butterworths, 1997 at 6.11–6.13.

[French J then examines a number of recent cases brought under the Migration Act 1958 (Cth), namely, SAAG v Minister for Immigration and Multicultural and Indigenous Affairs [2002] FCA 547; SBAN v Minister for Immigration and Multicultural and Indigenous Affairs [2002] FCA 591; SBAP v Refugee Review Tribunal [2002] FCA 590; NAAG v Minister for Immigration and Multicultural and Indigenous Affairs [2002] FCA 713; NACL v Refugee Review Tribunal [2002] FCA 643; NAAP v Minister for Immigration and Multicultural and Indigenous Affairs [2002] FCA 805; SBAU v Minister for Immigration and Multicultural and Indigenous Affairs [2002] FCA 1076; NADR v Minister for Immigration and Multicultural and Indigenous Affairs [2002] FCAFC 293; SBBS v Minister for Immigration and Multicultural and Indigenous Affairs [2002] FCAFC 361.]

'The authorities referred to above and the propositions set out by the Full Court in *SBBS* make it clear that absence of good faith, for the purposes of the *Hickman* provisos, is not limited to cases of dishonesty or malice or personal interest. It may be found in a reckless or capricious approach to the exercise of the power in question. Consistently with the language of Dixon J in *Hickman* and *Proctor* and in *Little*, the term "good faith" is not to be considered in isolation from the process to which it is applied. An authority exercising a statutory power is required to act in good faith in the sense that the authority is required to make an honest attempt to exercise the power entrusted to it. An honest attempt to exercise the power is not demonstrated merely by the absence of dishonesty or malice or personal interest. And with respect to the contrary view expressed by Heerey J in *SBAP*

it seems to me on the authorities that bad faith is not necessarily the obverse of good faith. Good faith requires more than the absence of bad faith. It requires a conscientious approach to the exercise of power.

'Neither unreasonableness nor irrationality nor error of law or fact nor failure of procedural fairness is sufficient of itself to establish want of good faith. But a substantial departure from minimal standards of decision-making may be such as to indicate that a decision-maker has failed to adopt a conscientious approach to the task before it. It may be indicative of dishonesty or malice or actual bias or recklessness or capriciousness in the exercise of the power. The concept of "good faith" is evaluative. The threshold for finding its absence is high. It may in practice vary according to the nature and subject matter of the power being exercised as well as according to the circumstances of the particular case. In this sense it may be analogous to the variable standard imposed by the requirements of procedural fairness.

'In assessing the requirements of good faith for the Refugee Review Tribunal, it is necessary to bear in mind that its decisions may have the most profound consequences for those affected by them. They may quite literally be life or death decisions or significantly affect the liberty of the individual whether within Australia or outside. On the other hand, it is also necessary to bear in mind that the legislature has set up the Refugee Review Tribunal as a high volume administrative decision-making mechanism which is required by the [Migration Act] to carry out its functions economically, informally and quickly as well as fairly and justly (s 420). The question whether there has been a want of good faith in the given case will depend upon an assessment of all the relevant circumstances of that case.

...

'Breach of natural justice may, according to the circumstances, evidence want of good faith. Where there is shown to be actual bias on the part of the Tribunal which prevents it from carrying out its function at review there is a case for finding want of good faith in the exercise of its powers notwithstanding that the bias may be the result of opinions honestly held. And it may be that in some cases want of fairness on the part of the Tribunal will be so serious as to evidence a reckless or capricious approach to the conduct of the review which would negative good faith.' *Applicant WAFV of 2002 v Refugee Review Tribunal* BC200300027; [2003] FCA 16 at [39]–[41], [52]–[54], [59], per French J

Australia '[49] His Honour [Primary Judge] held that the section required an objective finding on the evidence whether the conduct which would otherwise be unlawful pursuant to s 18C was said or done reasonably and in good faith in the circumstances referred to in paras (a), (b) or (c) of that section. He referred to the judgment of Kirby J in *Cannane v J Cannane Pty Ltd (In Liquidation)* (1998) 192 CLR 557 at 596 where Kirby J observed, with respect to the terms "good faith" and "acted in good faith", that there are two divergent meanings given to them according to their statutory context:

> The first is a broad or subjective view which requires inquiry into the actual state of mind of the person concerned, irrespective of the causes which produce it. The second involves the objective construction of the words by the introduction of such concepts as an absence of reasonable caution and diligence. The particular interpretation apt to the use of the words in a given legislative context will depend on the decision-maker's elucidation of the purpose of the legislature.

...

'[83] The requirement in s 18D that the protected conduct be done in "good faith" raises the definitional question — what is meant by "good faith" in this context? Associated with that is the question whether good faith is to be assessed subjectively or objectively, or by some combination of subjective and objective factors and whether, and to what extent, it overlaps the requirement of reasonableness.

'[84] The term "good faith" has been described as "protean" in character with "long standing usage in a variety of statutory and ... common law contexts" — *Secretary, Department of Education, Employment, Training and Youth Affairs v Prince* (1997) 152 ALR 127 at 130 (Finn J). A search of Commonwealth statutes discloses 154 Acts in which the term is used. Its applications are diverse and reflected in a variety of constructions according to its particular applications. Since 1999 it has defined a central duty of company directors and other officers of corporations who must act in good faith in the best interests of their corporations and for proper purposes (s 181 Corporations Act 2001 (Cth)) — recently discussed in *Australian Securities and Investments Commission v Adler* (No 3) (2002) 30 ACLC 576 at [735] (Santow J). It is a requirement of governments and other parties negotiating with respect to future acts affecting native title — s 31 Native Title Act 1994 (Cth) — considered in *Strickland v Minister for Lands for*

Western Australia (1998) 85 FCR 303; *Walley v Western Australia* (1999) 87 FCR 565 and *Brownley v Western Australia (No 1)* (1999) 95 FCR 152. It is a condition of the protection of antecedent transactions from avoidance by a trustee in bankruptcy — s 123 Bankruptcy Act 1966 (Cth). In industrial law it supports the validation of things done by a collective body that would otherwise be invalid — s 225 Workplace Relations Act 1996 (Cth).

'[85] The valid exercise of statutory powers is conditional upon their exercise in good faith. That is so notwithstanding their protection by the most robust of privative clauses — *R v Hickman; Ex parte Fox and Clinton* (1945) 70 CLR 598. The content of good faith in that context has been the subject of considerable attention in this Court in connection with the scope of s 474 of the Migration Act 1958 (Cth), a privative clause framed in very wide terms. It is not necessary here to revisit the review of the authorities undertaken in *WAFV v Refugee Review Tribunal* (2003) 125 FCR 351. But for the reasons there expressed, absence of good faith which will amount to jurisdictional error, vitiating the exercise of a statutory power, is not limited to cases of dishonesty or malice or personal interest. It may be found in a reckless or capricious approach to the decision-maker's task. The exercise of a power in good faith requires an honest and conscientious approach. The latter aspect accords with the requirement of fidelity to the obligation cast upon the decision-maker.

'[86] The duty to act in good faith defines, at equity, the content of various classes of obligation which are described as fiduciary — Finn, *Fiduciary Duties*, Law Book Co, (1976) at 78–81. There is authority for the existence in Australia of an implied duty at common law to act in good faith in the performance of contracts, albeit it has been much debated — see e g Renard *Constructions (ME) Pty Ltd v Minister for Public Works* (1992) 26 NSWLR 234; *Alcatel Australia Ltd v Scarcelli* (1998) 44 NSWLR 349; *Hughes Aircraft Systems International v Air Services Australia* (1997) 76 FCR 151 and *Burger King Corp v Hungry Jacks Pty Ltd* [2001] NSWCA 187 and various commentaries in Mason, *Contract, Good Faith and Equitable Standards in Fair Dealing* (2000) 116 LQR 66; Carlin, *The Rise and Rise (And Fall?) of Implied Duties of Good Faith in Contractual Performance in Australia* (2002) 25 NSW Law Journal 99; Peden, *The Meaning of Contractual "Good Faith"*; (2002) 22 Australian Bar Review

225; Carter and Peden, *Good Faith in Australian Contract Law* (2003) 19 Journal of Contract Law 155.

'[87] These are examples of the range of circumstances in which the words "good faith" are to be applied. They are not exhaustive of those circumstances. For each example there is a body of judicial decisions construing and applying the words. The particular construction will be adapted to the particular statute or rule of law in which the words are used. In some cases there will be a statutory definition which will confine their meaning. For example, in Sale of Goods legislation there is a provision that a thing is deemed to be done in "good faith" within the meaning of the Act when it is done "honestly whether it be done negligently or not".

'[88] The variety of particular applications of "good faith" does not deny the conclusion that the words have a core meaning which is of general application manifested in different ways according to the environment in which they must be applied. Its content is found in the ordinary English meaning of the words. That, in accordance with established principle, is the starting point of all statutory construction.

'[89] It has been implied in some commentary that the search for meaning is fruitless. Professor Roy Goode said of English jurists, " … we do not know quite what [good faith] means" — EA Farnsworth, *"Good Faith in Contract Performance"*, Beatson and Friedmann (eds) *Good Faith and Fault in Contract Law*, Clarendon Press Oxford (1995) at 157 n 13. Nevertheless the occurrence of the words in a multiplicity of statutes suggests they bear meaning to those who draft the laws and to at least some of the legislators who vote for them. And it is not unreasonable to expect that those bound by them have a sense of their meaning which can be derived from their ordinary usage.

'[90] The ordinary English meaning of the word "faith" as defined in the *Shorter Oxford English Dictionary* includes the following:

1. The duty of fulfilling one's trust; fealty; the obligation of a promise or engagement.

2. The quality of fulfilling one's trust, fidelity, loyalty.

The term "good faith" is noted against the second meaning as reflecting fidelity and loyalty and is contrasted with bad faith meaning faithlessness or having an intent to deceive. In *Black's Law Dictionary*, 7th Edition, West Group (1999) at 701, "good faith" is defined thus:

A state of mind consisting in (1) honesty in belief or purpose, (2) faithfulness to one's duty or obligation, (3) observance of reasonable commercial standards of fair dealing in a given trade or business, or (4) absence of intent to defraud or to seek unconscionable advantage. — Also termed bona fides.

'[91] Honesty is an element embedded in the ordinary meaning of good faith. It is the antithesis of bad faith. The idea of fidelity or loyalty goes beyond honesty. It is a relational concept. It involves adherence to a commitment or an obligation or a principle. Because it is relational it is ambulatory and because it is ambulatory so too is the concept of "good faith" as a whole. In a less direct sense so too is honesty. In the context of an implied term of good faith in the performance of a contract, Sir Anthony Mason used the words "mainly in the sense of loyalty to the promise itself and as excluding bad faith behaviour" — AF Mason op cit at 69. These elements are not contingent upon context. They emerge from the ordinary meaning of the words although, like "fairness" in administrative justice, they take their content from the particular circumstances in which it is sought to apply them.

'[92] In the *United States Second Restatement of Contracts* para 205, it was said:

The phrase "good faith" is used in a variety of contexts and its meaning varies somewhat with the context. Good faith performance or enforcement of a contract emphasizes faithfulness to an agreed common purpose and consistency with the justified expectations of the other party; it excludes a variety of types of conduct characterized as involving "bad faith" because they violate community standards of decency, fairness or reasonableness.

'[93] In a statutory setting a requirement to act in good faith, absent any contrary intention express or implied, will require honest action and fidelity to whatever norm, or rule or obligation the statute prescribes as attracting the requirement of good faith observance. That fidelity may extend beyond compliance with the black letter of the law absent the good faith requirement. In ordinary parlance it may require adherence to the "spirit" of the law. This may attract the kind of penumbral judgments by courts of which Professor Stone wrote. That is not necessarily a matter for concern in the case of civil proscriptions. They are evaluative judgments which the courts are authorised and required by the legislature to make. A good faith provision offers a warning that game playing at the margins of a statutory proscription or obligation may attract a finding of liability. There is nothing in principle to prevent the legislature protecting a rule by attaching an uncertain risk of liability to conduct in the shadow of the rule.

...

'[96] It follows from the preceding discussion that good faith may be tested both subjectively and objectively. Want of subjective good faith, i e seeking consciously to further an ulterior purpose of racial vilification may be sufficient to forfeit the protection of s 18D. But good faith requires more than subjective honesty and legitimate purposes. It requires, under the aegis of fidelity or loyalty to the relevant principles in the Act, a conscientious approach to the task of honouring the values asserted by the Act. This may be assessed objectively.

'[97] Constructional choices between subjective and objective approaches to good faith have been considered in a number of different statutory contexts. *Cannane v J Cannane Pty Ltd*, was a case arising under s 121 of the Bankruptcy Act 1966 (Cth) involving a disposition with intent to defraud creditors, not being for valuable consideration, in favour of a person who acted in good faith. Kirby J in a part of his dissenting judgment which did not conflict with the majority judgments, said (at 596):

> The words "good faith" and "acted in good faith" appear in many statutes in virtually all countries of the common law. It would be erroneous to suggest that a single meaning could be adopted, indifferent to the particular statutory context. It has been remarked that, putting it broadly, the words "good faith", or their Latin equivalents, have received "two divergent meanings" ... The first is a broad or subjective view which requires inquiry into the actual state of mind of the person concerned, irrespective of the causes which produce it. The second involves the objective construction of the words by the introduction of such concepts as an absence of reasonable caution and diligence. The particular interpretation apt to the use of the words in a given legislative context will depend on the decision-maker's elucidation of the purpose of the legislature.

...

'[101] Generally speaking the absence of subjective good faith, e g dishonesty or the knowing pursuit of an improper purpose, should be sufficient to establish want of good faith for most purposes. But it may not be necessary where objective good faith, in the sense of a conscientious approach to

the relevant obligation, is required. In my opinion, having regard to the public mischief to which s 18C is directed, both subjective and objective good faith is required by s 18D in the doing of the free speech and expression activities protected by that section.

...

'[103] It may be that there will be an overlap between the assessment of reasonableness and of good faith. This does not necessarily mean that they overlap conceptually. It just means that there may be common factual elements underpinning them in a particular case. In *Burger King Corp v Hungry Jacks Pty Ltd*, the New South Wales Court of Appeal, in dealing with the implied obligation of good faith in the performance of contracts, said (at [169]–[170]):

> ... it is worth noting that the Australian cases make no distinction of substance between the implied term of reasonableness and that of good faith. As Priestley JA said in [*Renard Constructions (NE) Pty Ltd v Minister for Public Works* (1992) 26 NSWLR 234 at 263] "the kind of reasonableness I have been discussing seems to me to have much in common with the notions of good faith". Priestley JA commented further at 265 that "... in ordinary English usage there has been constant association between the words fair and reasonable. Similarly there is a close association of ideas between the terms unreasonableness, lack of good faith and unconscionability".

Peden op cit at 242 criticised this approach:

> ... as more courts are incorporating good faith obligations into contracts, the meaning of "good faith" must be given a much more precise meaning than "fairness", "justice", or even "reasonableness".

Beyond the practical interaction which will occur because they involve consideration of common facts, it is not necessary here to search for any conceptual overlap between reasonableness and good faith nor to be too concerned if on the constructional approaches so far adopted such an overlap exists.' *Bropho v Human Rights and Equal Opportunity Commission* [2004] FCAFC 16 per French J; BC200400209

Australia 'The words "good faith" as used in s 18D involve more than the absence of bad faith, dishonesty, fraud or malice. Having regard to the context provided by the Act, the requirement to act in good faith imposes a duty on a person who does an act because of race, an act reasonably likely to inflict the harm referred to in s 18C, to show that before so acting that person considered the likelihood of the occurrence of that harm and the degree of harm reasonably likely to result. In short the risk of harm from the act of publication must be shown to have been balanced by other considerations. The words "in good faith" as used in s 18D import a requirement that the person doing the act exercise prudence, caution and diligence, which, in the context of the Act would mean due care to avoid or minimize consequences identified by s 18C. (See: *Mid Density Developments Pty Ltd v Rockdale Municipal Council* (1993) 44 FCR 290 per Gummow, Hill, Drummond JJ at 298).' *Bropho v Human Rights and Equal Opportunity Commission* [2004] FCAFC 16 at [144] per Lee J; BC200400209

Australia [Local Government Act 1993 (NSW) s 733(1)(b) provides: (1) A council does not incur any liability in respect of: ... (b) anything done or omitted to be done in good faith by the council in so far as it relates to the likelihood of land being flooded or the nature or extent of any such flooding.] '[32] A statutory standard of "good faith" is protean and always takes its colour from its context. The most significant feature of s 733 in this regard is that the section protects a governmental body from legal liability for losses incurred by others.

...

'[37] More significant, for present purposes, is the "good faith" standard in s 733. The issue often arises whether this formulation imports a subjective or objective standard. (See e g *Cannane v J Cannane Pty Ltd* (*in liq*) (1998) 192 CLR 557 at 596). The principle that an exemption provision should be construed strictly leads to the conclusion that a test of good faith in such a provision is not concerned only with the state of mind of the accused. A public authority seeking to take advantage of an exemption provision should, in the absence of a contrary indication, be required to satisfy an objective test of good faith. This is because such a test imports reasonable conduct on its part, including tests of prudence, caution, conscientiousness and, in some cases, of diligence. (See Cannane supra; *Bropho v Human Rights and Equal Opportunity Commission* (2004) 204 ALR 761 at [96]–[102], [144].

'[38] Accordingly, it has been held that the "good faith" standard in s 733 does not involve a test of honesty so that just "honest ineptitude" is not enough. (See *Mid Density Developments Pty Ltd v Rockdale Municipal Council* (1993) 44 FCR 290 at 299–300; *Douglas v Water Administration*

Ministerial Corporation (NSWCA (unreported 12 September 1995).) I prefer to base this conclusion on the principle of statutory interpretation I have mentioned, rather than on the concept advanced in *Mid Density Developments* at 299, that s 733 is concerned to strike a balance between the interests of a public authority and private interests in property or reliance on the conduct of a public authority.

'[39] It will often be the case that the identification of the precise act of a defendant which causes a nuisance is not controversial and does not require rigorous analysis. Where, however, as in the present case, a council seeks to rely on the exemption from liability in s 733 of the Act, it is necessary to give careful attention to the acts said to have been done or omitted, in order to determine whether those acts have been "in good faith". *Bankstown City Council v Alamdo Holdings Pty Ltd* [2004] NSWCA 325 at [32], [37]–[39], per Spigelman CJ (Giles and Ipp JJA agreeing); BC200406123

GOOD MARKETABLE TITLE

[Agreement by bank to make secured advance to customer to purchase land. Undertaking by customer's solicitor to bank in standard form to apply sums received from bank or client solely for acquiring a 'good marketable title' to the land.] 'The bank submits that this means "a freehold title free from incumbrances"; and that such a title is better than "a good title" since it must be both "good" (in the sense of being without blemish) and "marketable" (in the sense of relating to property which is readily saleable). Both propositions are quite untenable. They are the product of a growing unfamiliarity with the language which was once the common currency of conveyancers of unregistered land. They confuse the subject matter of the sale (what has the vendor agreed to sell?) with the vendor's duty to prove his title to the subject matter of the sale (has the vendor sufficiently deduced title to what he has agreed to sell?).

'These are two quite separate questions.

...

'The obligation of a vendor is to deduce sufficient title to the property which he has contracted to sell. The expression "good marketable title" describes the quality of the evidence which the purchaser is bound to accept as sufficient to discharge this obligation. It says nothing about the nature or extent of the property contracted to be sold to which title must be deduced. The expression is a compendious one which describes the title and not the property. It is used in contradistinction to "a good holding title", by which is meant a title which a willing purchaser might reasonably be advised to accept, but which the court would not force on a reluctant purchaser.' *Barclays Bank plc v Weeks Legg & Dean (a firm)* [1998] 3 All ER 213 at 221, 222, CA, per Millett LJ

GOODS

[The Road Traffic Act 1972 has been repealed. See now the Road Traffic Act 1988, s 192(1).]

'In both the Sale of Goods Act 1979, s 61, and the Supply of Goods and Services Act 1982, s 18, the definition of "goods" includes "all personal chattels other than things in action and money". Clearly, a disk is within this definition. Equally clearly, a program, of itself, is not.

'If a disk carrying a program is transferred, by way of sale or hire, and the program is in some way defective, so that it will not instruct or enable the computer to achieve the intended purpose, is this a defect in the disk? Put more precisely, would the seller or hirer of the disk be in breach of the terms as to quality and fitness for purpose implied by s 14 of the 1979 Act and s 9 of the 1982 Act? ...

'Suppose I buy an instruction manual on the maintenance and repair of a particular make of car. The instructions are wrong in an important respect. Anybody who follows them is likely to cause serious damage to the engine of his car. In my view, the instructions are an integral part of the manual. The manual including the instructions, whether in a book or a video cassette, would in my opinion be "goods" within the meaning of the 1979 Act, and the defective instructions would result in a breach of the implied terms in s 14.

'If this is correct, I can see no logical reason why it should not also be correct in relation to a computer disk onto which a program designed and intended to instruct or enable a computer to achieve particular functions has been encoded. If the disk is sold or hired by the computer manufacturer, but the program is defective, in my opinion there would prima facie be a breach of the terms as to quality and fitness for purpose implied by the 1979 Act or the 1982 Act.' *St Albans City and District Council v International Computers Ltd* [1996] 4 All ER 481 at 493, CA, per Sir Iain Glidewell

[Clause II(9) in a lease granted in 1924 provided that 'no goods shall at any time be or remain placed outside the said premises which or of any nature which the Lessor shall have forbidden to be or to remain so placed'. As a consequence of alterations, it became possible to park a motor car on covered areas which had formerly been open basement areas, and for many years the occupiers had parked one or more motor cars on the skylights. The lessor gave formal notice in reliance on cl II(9), that it was forbidden with immediate effect to place any motor vehicles, motor cycles or other goods outside of the premises demised to it pursuant to the lease. The question arose whether motor cars were 'goods' within the meaning of the clause.] '[15] It is common ground, as the dictionary definition makes clear, that "goods" can be widely understood to mean "property or possessions", or more narrowly "saleable commodities, merchandise, wares" or, as Mr Walker puts it, "tangible moveable property viewed as an item or items of commerce". There is clear authority that a motor car was goods for the purposes of the Factors Act 1889 (see *Stadium Finance Ltd v Robbins* [1962] 2 All ER 633, [1962] 2 QB 664). There Ormerod LJ ([1962] 2 All ER 633 at 636, [1962] 2 QB 664 at 670) said: "The word 'goods' in the section does not appear to have anything other than the ordinary meaning ... I cannot see why ... [a motor car] does not come within the definition 'goods'." Danckwerts LJ ([1962] 2 All ER 633 at 639, [1962] 2 QB 664 at 676) agreed with that judgment and said: "In my view, the word 'goods' must include all chattels of which physical possession is possible, notwithstanding that they are not easily moveable ..." The case was, of course, one concerned with the meaning of the word in the statute but the reference to the ordinary meaning of the word is at least persuasive even if it is not conclusive.

'[16] The issue for us is whether a motor car is excluded from the wide range of property or possessions ordinarily encompassed within the meaning of "goods". That task of interpretation has to be carried out against the background knowledge which would reasonably be available to the contracting parties in the situation in which they were at the time of the execution of this lease (see *Earl of Lonsdale v A-G*, [1982] 3 All ER 579, [1982] 1 WLR 887). Because the basement areas were open in 1924, parking motor cars was not likely to have been in the immediate contemplation of the parties. Motor cars were, however, familiar on the streets of London in 1924 and the user clause at cl II(8) contains a prohibition against the premises being used for the business of "Dealer in Motors or Hirer Out or keeper of Motors". This was a 999-year lease so it must have been within the contemplation of the parties that the premises might be altered perhaps in a way to make a motor business feasible and allow the display of motor cars in the way in which they are presently parked.

We do not consider that the physical state of the property at the time of the lease takes the vexed question of interpretation much further.

'[17] In our view the crucial question is whether or not the words taken in the whole context of the clause are limited by the preceding words which place a restriction on any placard, advertisement or announcement "relating to goods actually dealt in by and in the ordinary course of the business or occupation of the occupant or occupants of the said premises". We conclude the words are not so restricted.' *Spring House (Freehold) Ltd v Mount Cook Land Ltd* [2001] EWCA Civ 1833 at [15]–[16], [2002] 2 All ER 822 at 828–829, CA, per Ward and Rix LJJ

In marine insurance policy

[For 25 Halsbury's Laws (4th edn) para 113 see now 25 Halsbury's Laws (4th edn) (2003 Reissue) para 295.]

GOODS VEHICLE

[The Road Traffic Act 1972 has been repealed. For s 196 thereof see now the Road Traffic Act 1988, s 192(1).]

Articulated goods vehicle

[See now the Road Traffic Act 1988, s 108(1).]

Heavy goods vehicle

[See now s 120 of the Road Traffic Act 1988 (prospectively repealed and re-enacted by the Road Traffic (Driver Licensing and Information Systems Act 1989)).]

Small goods vehicle

[See now the Road Traffic Act 1988, s 108(1).]

GOODWILL

[For 35 Halsbury's Laws (4th edn) paras 1106–1109 see now 35 Halsbury's Laws (4th edn) (Reissue) paras 1206–1210.]

Australia 'For legal purposes, goodwill is the attractive force that brings in custom and adds to the value of the business. It may be site, personality, service, price or habit that obtains custom. But with the possible exception of a licence to conduct a business exclusive of all competition, a licence that authorises the conduct of a business is not a source of goodwill. A taxi licence therefore is simply an item of property whose value is not dependent on the present existence of a business. It is not and does not contain any element of goodwill.' *Federal Commissioner of Taxation v Murry* (1998) 193 CLR 605 at 630; 155 ALR 67 at 85; 72 ALJR 1065; 98 ATC 4585; BC9802402, per Gaudron, McHugh, Gummow and Hayne JJ

Australia 'Whilst it is in existence, a partnership has goodwill. Goodwill "is a composite thing referable in part to its locality, in part to the way in which (the business) is conducted and the personality of those who conduct it, and in part the likelihood of competition, many (clients) being no doubt actuated by mixed motives in conferring their custom": *Federal Commissioner of Taxation v Williamson* (1943) 67 CLR 561. Goodwill is the attractive force which brings in custom: *Inland Revenue Commissioners v Müller & Co's Margarine Ltd* [1901] AC 217, 224.

'With a solicitor's practice, part of the goodwill is represented by the name of the firm and its reputation, part of the goodwill is represented by the clients who consistently resort to the firm for advice and part of the goodwill is brought about from other factors. Traditionally, when one is valuing the goodwill of a solicitor's practice as one once had to do for death duty purposes if a partner should die during the course of the partnership, the valuation was usually about 18 months purchase of the gross annual takings or of profits of the partnership. As Rost and Collins *Land Valuation and Compensation in Australia* (Commonwealth Institute of Valuers Sydney, 1971) put it at pp 510–11:

"In the case of practising solicitors and accountants, factors to be taken into account include the proportions of gross fees of a recurring and a non-recurring nature; also the number of clients and the type of clientele. Practices with a limited number of clients, even though earning substantial fees, would, other things being equal, have a lower value than those having a wider spread of clients yielding an equivalent amount in fees."

'However, a purchaser buying the goodwill is really buying the super profit, that is, the profit over and above a reasonable return from the investment of capital, brought about by the likelihood that old clients will return to the firm and the reputation of the continuing partners to attract work over and above the likelihood of the hypothetical average solicitor's ability to attract work.

...

'The goodwill of a solicitor's partnership is the super profit, that is, the profit that can be earned over and above the reasonable return from the investment of the capital by virtue of the special distinguishing features of the practice which makes people resort to that practice rather than go somewhere else.' *Ryan v Rouen* BC200002876; [2000] NSWSC 468 at [15]–[17], [23], per Young J

GOVERNMENT

[For 8 Halsbury's Laws (4th edn) para 804 see now 8(2) Halsbury's Laws (4th edn) (Reissue) para 354.]

[Bank account of company wholly owned by Sierra Leone government; purported change of mandate for signatories after coup. Question of validity depending on construction of 'the Government of Sierra Leone'.] 'Accordingly, the factors to be taken into account in deciding whether a government exists as the government of a state are: (a) whether it is the constitutional government of the state; (b) the degree, nature and stability of administrative control, if any, that it of itself exercises over the territory of the state; (c) whether Her Majesty's government has any dealings with it and if so what is the nature of those dealings; and (d) in marginal cases, the extent of international recognition that it has as the government of the state.' *Republic of Somalia v Woodhouse Drake & Carey (Suisse) SA, The Mary* [1993] 1 All ER 371 at 384 per Hobhouse J, applied in *Sierra Leone Telecommunications Co Ltd v Barclays Bank plc* [1998] 2 All ER 821

Australia ' "Government" is a word which can be used in various senses. It can be used to describe the concept of control or direction exercised over the actions of people in a community. It can also be used to describe an entity which exercises such control or direction.' *Brisbane City Council v Albietz* BC200102407; [2001] QSC 160 at [8], per Wilson J

GOVERNOR

Of dependent territory

[For 6 Halsbury's Laws (4th edn) para 1033 see now 6 Halsbury's Laws (4th edn) (2003 Reissue) para 826.]

GRANT

Canada '[18] The next step is to consider the terms of s. 196 [Immigration and Refugee Protection Act]. The Minister and majority of the Federal Court of Appeal conclude that the use of the term "granted" indicates an actively ordered, as opposed to an automatic stay. This is supported by the Concise Oxford English Dictionary's definition of the term "grant" which defines it as: "give (a right, property, etc.) formally or legally to … legal conveyance or formal conferment" (p. 620). This definition supports a deliberate act. The English version of s. 196 suggests that it applies only to stays actively granted. This said, it is possible to argue, for instance, that statutes can "grant" a right of appeal and that consequently the English version of s. 196 is not as clear as the Minister contends.' *Medovarski v Canada (MCI)* [2005] 2 SCR 539 at [18], [2005] SCJ No 31 (SCC), per McLachlin CJC

GRANT OR SUBSIDY

New Zealand [Section 78(2) of the Goods and Services Tax Act 1985 provides that:
'…
(2) Where an alteration in the law is made and a supplier [has, at any time] entered into any agreement or contract in respect of the supply of goods and services with a recipient, unless express provision for the exclusion of any such alteration in the law is contained in the agreement or contract, or [where] the alteration in the law has been taken into account, every such agreement or contract shall be deemed to be modified as follows:
(a) Where the alteration in the law renders that supply liable to be charged with tax or increases the amount of any tax charged or chargeable in relation to that supply, the supplier may add to the agreed price in the said agreement or contract the amount of that tax or the increase of that tax; or
(b) Where the alteration in the law renders that supply exempt from tax or reduces the amount of tax charged or chargeable in relation to that supply, the supplier or the recipient may deduct from the agreed price in the said agreement or contract the amount of that tax or the reduction of that tax:
Provided that this subsection shall not apply where that contract or agreement is entered into after the expiry of the period of 3 months that commences with the coming into force of the alteration in the law:

Provided further that this subsection shall not apply to require a public authority to alter any amount agreed to be paid by the authority in respect of any supply of goods and services where the consideration for that supply is in the nature of a grant or subsidy.']

'[14] Their Lordships think that the policy behind the proviso was to leave the level of grants or subsidies, whether paid directly to the beneficiaries or by way of contracts with service providers, to government decision. It therefore looks at the question of whether the payment is a grant or subsidy from the government's point of view. It is a matter for the government to decide whether an increase in GST requires the level of subsidy to be correspondingly increased. No automatic contractual provision is necessary or desirable. In the case of the rest home subsidy scheme it was taken into account in the next adjustment of the fee-for-service rate. In another case the government might consider that the level of subsidy did not need to be changed.

'[15] Their Lordships therefore think that the Court of Appeal in *De Morgan's* case was right in saying that the question was whether, from the point of view of the department, the character or quality of the payment was in the nature of a grant or subsidy and not whether it was for the benefit of the service provider rather than the recipient of the service. If that is the question, there can be no doubt about the answer ...' *Kena Kena Properties Ltd v Attorney-General* [2002] 2 NZLR 597 at 601 per cur (PC)

GRAPHIC WORK

'Graphic work' includes (a) any painting, drawing, diagram, map, chart or plan and (b) any engraving, etching, lithograph, woodcut or similar work. (Copyright, Designs and Patents Act 1988, s 4)

GRATUITY

New Zealand [Finance Act (No 2) 1941, s 6.] 'The question is whether the expression "gratuity" as used in the context of s 6 is apt to cover a payment or provision made and received as of right. In ordinary usage "gratuity" means payment without a claim of right. In *The Oxford English Dictionary* the relevant meanings are: "2. A gift or present (usually of money) often in return for favours or services, the amount depending on the inclination of the giver ... . 3. Spec a. A bounty given to soldiers on re-enlistment, retirement, or discharge." The dictionary refers to the meaning "Payment;

wages" as obsolete. Australian and New Zealand dictionaries reinforce the conclusion that that is the standard meaning of the word in New Zealand. *The Tasman Dictionary* and *The Macquarie Dictionary* both define "gratuity" as "1. a gift usu. of money, over and above payment due for service; tip. 2. that which is given without claim or demand. 3. a bounty given to soldiers". The *Heinemann, New Zealand Dictionary* definition is "something given freely, especially a gift of money, such as a tip or a payment to an employee on retirement."

...

'There may be circumstances in which the context requires a different meaning to be accorded ... The context may show that the standard meaning was not intended ... But this is not a case where "gratuity" may take colour from its association in the section with other expressions. In s 6 "gratuity" stands alone as the subject. The short question then is whether there is any other justification derived from the statutory context for reading the word as extending beyond its ordinary meaning of a voluntary payment.

'In our view there is nothing in the scheme and language of s 6 to justify extending the meaning. On the contrary, on its face, subs (2) is directed to the circumstance where, on the retirement of an employee, he or she is not entitled to a retirement payment or retirement leave. Where there is no preceding contractual entitlement, the local authority "may pay to him by way of gratuity" an amount not exceeding an amount calculated in terms of the subsection.' *Wellington Regional Council v Edwards* [1997] 2 NZLR 129 at 136–137, CA, per cur

GREEN

[For 6 Halsbury's Laws (4th edn) para 525 see now 6 Halsbury's Laws (4th edn) (2003 Reissue) para 425.]

[For 34 Halsbury's Laws (4th edn) para 507 see now 34 Halsbury's Laws (4th edn) (Reissue) para 293.]

GRIEVE

'Where an employer who is either not a farmer or is liable to be absent from the farm employs another to manage or run his farm, that person can properly be described as a farm manager ... On the other hand, a grieve ... reports to and receives instructions from the employer "or his representative" who, for example, might be a farm manager. The grieve is thus in a subordinate position to his employer or his representative. The grieve is not qualified to run the farm but acts on the instructions of one who has the necessary knowledge. His function is to act as overseer or head foreman and supervise the work done by other workers on the farm.' *Teviot Scientific Publications Ltd v McLeod* 1995 SCCR 188 at 192, per Lord Allanbridge

GRIEVOUS BODILY HARM

[The defendant, who was HIV positive, had unprotected consensual sexual intercourse with the two complainants on several occasions in the course of long-term relationships with them. Both complainants contracted HIV. The defendant was charged with inflicting grievous bodily harm on the complainants contrary to s 20 of the Offences against the Person Act 1861. It was not alleged that the defendant had deliberately set out to infect the complainants. Instead, the prosecution alleged that he had been reckless as to whether they might become infected.] '[29] In *R v Ireland* [*R v Ireland, R v Burstow* [1997] 4 All ER 225], much argument also centred around the difference between the concept of inflicting grievous bodily harm in s 20 and causing it in s 18. Lord Steyn recognised that the two words, "inflict" and "cause", are not synonymous. In relation to *R v Clarence* [(1889) 22 QBD 23], he acknowledged that the possibility of inflicting or causing psychiatric injury would not then have been in contemplation, whereas nowadays it is. In his view the infliction of psychiatric injury without violence could fall within the ambit of s 20. Lord Steyn ([1997] 4 All ER 225 at 235, [1998] AC 147 at 160) described *R v Clarence* as a "troublesome authority", and in the specific context of the meaning of "inflict" in s 20 said expressly that *R v Clarence* "no longer assists". Lord Hope of Craighead similarly examined the consequences of the use of the word "inflict" in s 20 and "cause" in s 18. He concluded that for practical purposes, and in the context of a criminal act, the words might be regarded as interchangeable, provided it was understood that "inflict" implies that the consequence to the victim involved something detrimental or adverse.

'[30] Such differences as may be discerned in the language used by Lord Steyn and Lord Hope respectively do not obscure the fact that this decision confirmed that even when no physical violence has been applied, directly or indirectly to the victim's body, an offence under s 20 may be committed. Putting it another way, if the remaining ingredients of s 20 are established, the charge is not answered simply because the grievous bodily harm suffered

by the victim did not result from direct or indirect physical violence. Whether the consequences suffered by the victim are physical injuries or psychiatric injuries, or a combination of the two, the ingredients of the offence prescribed by s 20 are identical. If psychiatric injury can be inflicted without direct or indirect violence, or an assault, for the purposes of s 20 physical injury may be similarly inflicted. It is no longer possible to discern the critical difference identified by the majority in *R v Clarence*, and encapsulated by Stephen J in his judgment, between an "immediate and necessary connection" between the relevant blow and the consequent injury, and the "uncertain and delayed" effect of the act which led to the eventual development of infection. The erosion process is now complete.

'[31] In our judgment, the reasoning which led the majority in *R v Clarence* to decide that the conviction under s 20 should be quashed has no continuing application. If that case were decided today, the conviction under s 20 would be upheld. Clarence knew, but his wife did not know, and he knew that she did not know that he was suffering from gonorrhoea. Nevertheless he had sexual intercourse with her, not intending deliberately to infect her, but reckless whether she might become infected, and thus suffer grievous bodily harm. Accordingly we agree with Judge Philpot's first ruling, that notwithstanding the decision in *R v Clarence*, it was open to the jury to convict the appellant of the offences alleged in the indictment.

...

'[58] We repeat that the Crown did not allege, and we therefore are not considering the deliberate infection, or spreading of HIV with intent to cause grievous bodily harm. In such circumstances, the application of what we may describe as the principle in *R v Brown (Anthony Joseph)* [1993] 2 All ER 75, [1994] 1 AC 212 means that the agreement of the participants would provide no defence to a charge under s 18 of the 1861 Act.

'[59] The effect of this judgment in relation to s 20 is to remove some of the outdated restrictions against the successful prosecution of those who, knowing that they are suffering HIV or some other serious sexual disease, recklessly transmit it through consensual sexual intercourse, and inflict grievous bodily harm on a person from whom the risk is concealed and who is not consenting to it. In this context, *R v Clarence* (1889) 22 QBD 23, [1886–90] All ER Rep 133 has no continuing relevance. Moreover, to the extent that *R v Clarence* suggested that consensual sexual intercourse of itself was to be regarded as consent to the risk of consequent disease, again, it is no longer authoritative. If , however, the victim consents to the risk, this continues to provide a defence under s 20. Although the two are inevitably linked, the ultimate question is not knowledge, but consent. We shall confine ourselves to reflecting that unless you are prepared to take whatever risk of sexually transmitted infection there may be, it is unlikely that you would consent to a risk of major consequent illness if you were ignorant of it. That said, in every case where these issues arise, the question whether the defendant was or was not reckless, and whether the victim did or did not consent to the risk of a sexually transmitted disease, is one of fact, and case specific.' *R v Dica* [2004] EWCA Crim 1103 at [30]–[31], [58]–[59], [2004] 3 All ER 593, CA, per Judge LJ

Australia 'In the end, I think the better conclusion is that any injury which, if not life endangering or likely so to be, is nevertheless one which either permanently impairs the efficient functioning of the body or permanently impairs its prior condition of physical soundness falls within the definition of "grievous bodily harm".' *R v Tranby* [1992] 1 Qld R 432 at 437, per Macrossan CJ

Canada '[41] For the guidance of the judge who will preside at the appellant's new trial, I nonetheless believe it helpful to add that "grievous bodily harm", within the meaning of ss. 34 and 35 of the *Criminal Code*, is not limited to harm or injury that is permanent or life-threatening. In ordinary usage, "grievous" bodily harm means harm or injury that is "very severe or serious": see *The Canadian Oxford Dictionary* (2nd ed. 2004), at p. 664. These terms respect the statutory context in which that expression was adopted by Parliament in the relevant provisions of the *Code*.' *R v Paice* [2005] 1 SCR 339 at [41], [2005] SCJ No 21 (SCC), per Fish J

GROUND

Australia [(WA) Criminal Property Confiscation Act 2000.] '... The word "ground" or "grounds" is not defined in the Confiscation Act. To some extent, it appears to be used interchangeably with the word "basis". Thus, for example, "grounds" is used in s 43(8) ("Reasonable grounds for suspecting" property is crime-used or crime-derived); the expression "ground" for making the order is used in s 44(a) or "grounds" on which the order may be made in s 44(b); two or more "grounds" for making a freezing order (s 48(3)); whereas s 48(4) refers to a freezing order made

under s 43(1) "on the basis" that another order has been, or is likely to be made and " ... on the basis of advice given to the court ..."; and s 48(7) speaks of a freezing order made " ... on the basis that the property was suspected of being crime-used or crime-derived ... ".

'As there is no statutory definition of the word "ground" in the Confiscation Act, it must be given its ordinary dictionary meaning. The "Macquarie Dictionary" (2nd Revised Ed) defines "ground" as "the foundation or basis on which a theory or action rests; motive; reason ... " The word is also to be construed in the context of the particular provision in which it appears and the statute as a whole and having regard to the purpose and objects of the legislation. The preamble states the purpose of the Act is " ... to provide for the confiscation in certain circumstances of property acquired as a result of criminal activity and property used for criminal activity ... "' *Re Smith; Ex parte; Director of Public Prosecutions for Western Australia (No 1)* [2004] WASC 145 at [80], per Roberts-Smith J; BC200403971

GROUND RENT

New Zealand [Lease.] '[53] In pure theory, a ground rent is simply what it says it is, a rent for the ground. Buildings or improvements on the land and the use to which the land is put by the lessee are disregarded so that a rent is assessed for the bare land. A hypothetical exercise is undertaken pursuant to which the land is valued at its highest and best use. Very commonly, because of the difficulty identifying comparable rentals, the rent is arrived at as a percentage of the resulting valuation by applying an appropriate rate of interest.

'[54] In determining the highest and best use of the land regard is had to any encumbrances affecting the land, the location of the site, the infrastructure, zoning restrictions, the availability of services and utilities, and such other factors as may affect the site. It is as if the valuer for the willing but not eager lessee (or prudent lessee) stood on the opposite side of the road from the subject land and envisaged it devoid of buildings and improvements while everything around it and relating to it remained intact.' *S & M Property Holdings Ltd v Waterloo Investments Ltd* [1999] 3 NZLR 189 (CA) at 200 per Thomas and Blanchard JJ

(1) The "ground rent"

'[69] It is instructive to begin with the commonly accepted meaning of "ground rent". The meaning ascribed to the concept in case law, judicial dictionaries and enactments of Parliament is wholly consistent with the exclusion of buildings from the calculation of the ground rent.

'[70] In *Bartlett v Salmon* (1855) 6 De GM & G 33 at p 41, the Lord Chancellor, Lord Cranworth, stated: "The term ground rent is well understood and has a definite meaning: it *is the sum paid by the owner or builder of houses for the use of land to build on*, and is therefore much under what it lets for when it has been built on" (emphasis added). This definition is adopted in 27(1) *Halsbury's Laws of England* (4th ed) para 212 at p 202, ft 1. See also Hill & Redman's *Law of Landlord and Tenant* (18th ed) para E82. To the same effect is the definition of ground rent in *Stroud's Judicial Dictionary of Words and Phrases* (5th ed, 1986) vol 2 at p 1128: "By the expression 'ground rent', if unexplained, is to be understood a rent less than the rack-rent of the premises; its proper meaning is *the rent at which land is let for the purpose of improvement by building*" (emphasis added). The same meaning has often been adopted when the expression has been used in statutes. For example, cl 1 of the Second Schedule to the Public Bodies Leases Act 1969 refers to the "valuation of the fair annual ground rent of the said land, *without the buildings or improvements so to be valued*" (emphasis added). (See also cl 11.) Similarly in s 24 of the Landlord and Tenant (War Damage) Act 1939, (UK), a "ground lease" is: "a lease at a rent ... which does not substantially exceed the rent which a tenant might reasonably have been expected, at the commencement of the term created by the lease, to pay for the land comprised in the lease, *excluding any buildings*, for a term equal to the term created by the lease" (emphasis added). While these references may not be conclusive as to the meaning of the phrase "ground rent" in the context of a particular lease, they ineluctably point to a commonly accepted meaning which has remained durable for over a century.' *S & M Property Holdings Ltd v Waterloo Investments Ltd* [1999] 3 NZLR 189 (CA) at 203 per Thomas and Blanchard JJ

'Ground rental is what is paid for the use of land for building purposes. Rental of land for building purposes has been the generally-understood meaning of ground rental for well over 100 years.

'[94] In *Bartlett v Salmon* (1855) 6 De GM & G 33, Lord Cranworth LC said at p 41:

> "The term ground rent is well understood and has a definite meaning: it is the sum paid by the owner or builder of houses for the use of land to build on, and is therefore much under what it lets for when it has been built on."

'[95] This meaning is confirmed in 27(1) *Halsbury's Laws of England* (4th ed) para 212 at p 202. To the same effect are the definitions in *Stroud's Judicial Dictionary of Words and Phrases* (5th ed, 1986) vol 2 at p 1128 "rent at which land is let for the purpose of improvement by building" and in *Words and Phrases legally defined* (3rd ed, 1989) vol 3 at pp 28–29 in reference to the term ground lease "rent ... for the land comprised in the lease, excluding any buildings ...".' *S & M Property Holdings Ltd v Waterloo Investments Ltd* [1999] 3 NZLR 189 (CA) at 209 per Tipping J

GROUP OF COMPANIES

New Zealand 'It is my conclusion that the phrase "a group of companies" in s 191(3) [of the Income Tax Act 1976] should be interpreted by applying the definition of "companies" in s 2. It therefore means a group of companies, whether incorporated in New Zealand or elsewhere. I do not find any sufficient reason for qualifying that literal meaning further by restricting it to a group of companies incorporated in New Zealand or elsewhere who are New Zealand taxpayers.' *Alcan New Zealand Ltd v Commissioner of Inland Revenue* [1993] 3 NZLR 495 at 506, per Tompkins J

GUARANTEE

[For 20 Halsbury's Laws (4th edn) para 101 see now 20(1) Halsbury's Laws (4th edn) (Reissue) para 101.]

Australia [Section 230 of the Companies (Vic) Code provides that a company shall not give a 'guarantee' or provide security in connection with a loan made to a director or related company.] 'It was argued that in order to effect the purpose of s 230 the word "guarantee" should be given a meaning which includes the obligation of indemnity on which the respondents sue. In our opinion there are two reasons for rejecting that submission. First when used in a statute the word "guarantee" more readily conveys the concept of an obligation to answer for the debt, default or miscarriage of another. The second is that it is a wholesome and established approach to legislation to treat Parliament, which can alter any rights present or future by an expression of intention, as not intending to alter the rights which would otherwise exist, to a greater extent than is shown by the words it uses or by a consideration of the statute as a whole, to have been its clear intention. There is weight in the argument that within the area with which s 230 deals an indemnity is socially and commercially as undesirable as a guarantee. There is, however, nothing in the context which indicates that Parliament used the word "guarantee", with a meaning which extends beyond its usual and conventional meaning.' *Brick and Pipe Industries Ltd v Occidental Life Nominees Pty Ltd* [1992] 2 VR 279 at 370; (1991) 6 ACSR 464 at 486, per cur

GUARDIAN

[For 24 Halsbury's Laws (4th edn) para 527 see now 5(3) Halsbury's Laws (4th edn) (Reissue) paras 143–149.]

Australia [In the context of (SA) Criminal Law Consolidation Act 1935.] '[18] As I have said, there is no definition of "guardian" in the CLCA, nor was there a definition of the word in the earlier and equivalent sections.

'[19] There is not a great deal in the context of the section which provides an indication of the meaning of the word. The reference to a schoolmaster, a schoolmistress or teacher suggests that the section is directed at close relationships involving influence, care, control and vulnerability. In the ordinary case, the relationship of parent and child, including an adoptive parent and child, is the prime example of a relationship exhibiting those features.

'[20] Subject to one matter which I will mention, in 1885 when s 11 was introduced, "guardian" had a clear meaning at common law. In the first edition of Halsbury's Laws of England Vol 17 the guardianship of the person and estate of an infant is discussed in Pt 7. The learned authors state (I omit footnote references):

> The disabilities of an infant and his legal incapacity to manage his own affairs render it necessary that for the protection of his interests and the management of his property he should have a guardian of his person and property, to whom he stands in the relation of ward. A person may be the guardian of an infant either (1) in socage; (2) by nature in the case of an heir-apparent; (3) by custom; (4) for nurture; (5) naturally, or by parental right; (6) by parental appointment, or (7) by appointment by a court of competent jurisdiction.

'[21] Guardianship in socage and by custom are not relevant in this case. Guardianship by nature and for nurture are described in the following terms:

> Guardianship by nature, in its original and strict sense, is that of a father over his infant heir-apparent of either sex. It lasts until the infant attains full age, but is exercisable only over the person of the infant.

...

> A father, and after his death a mother, has the guardianship for nurture of an infant child up to the age of fourteen.

...

'[23] Guardianship by parental appointment is described (relevantly) as follows:

> Both a father and mother have power, if under age by deed, and if of full age by deed or will, to appoint persons to act as guardians of an infant child, in the case of a father, after his death, and, in the case of a mother, after the death of herself and the father, if the child is then an infant and unmarried. Where the appointment is made by deed, it is of a testamentary nature, and is revocable by a subsequent will making a different appointment; but it is not admissible to probate. The intended guardian may attest the deed. No special words are necessary in making the appointment, but it is not sufficient to appoint a person guardian of the estate of the child.

...

'[25] The relevant definition for the purposes of this case is guardianship by parental right which is described in the following terms:

> A father, and after his death a mother, has by parental right the guardianship of the person of an infant child up to the age of twenty-one, as his natural guardian in the wider sense of the term.'

R v R, WD [2005] SASC 191 at [18]–[21], [23], [25], per Besanko J; BC200503542

GUARDIAN AD LITEM

[For 24 Halsbury's Laws (4th edn) para 765 see now 5(3) Halsbury's Laws (4th edn) (Reissue) paras 327, 332.]

GUARDIANSHIP *SEE* CUSTODY

GUILT

Australia [Section 475 of the Crimes Act 1900 (ACT) provides that, where a person has been convicted of a crime and "any doubt or question arises as to his or her guilt", a judge of the Supreme Court of the Australian Capital Territory could direct a magistrate to examine all persons likely to give material information on the matter.] 'Even when the primary facts are admitted, the "guilt" of an accused person depends on the law that has to be applied to those facts. Without applying the law to the facts as found or admitted, "guilt" in a legal sense is a meaningless concept. Whether the accused is guilty of murder or, alternatively, manslaughter, rape or, alternatively, indecent assault, burglary or, alternatively, housebreaking depends on the law that has to be applied to the primary facts. In some cases, the "guilt" of the prisoner may even depend on the assessment of a jury as to whether the conduct of the prisoner was reasonable in the circumstances. If the prisoner pleads self-defence to a charge of murder, for example, whether that person is guilty or not guilty of murder or guilty or not guilty of manslaughter depends on the assessment the jury makes of the reasonable grounds for the prisoner's alleged response. In some cases, "guilt" may be found only after the jury determines the nature of the office or employment of the prisoner or the nature of his or her relationship with other persons. Whether a person is guilty of fraudulent misappropriation, for example, may depend on whether the relationship between the prisoner and another person is that of trustee and beneficiary or debtor and creditor. Whether a person is guilty of embezzlement will depend on a finding that at the relevant time the prisoner was a clerk or servant of the person whose money has been taken. In other cases, "guilt" may depend on the acts, intentions or mental states of persons other than the accused. Rape and indecent assault depend on the victim's absence of consent. Larceny, embezzlement and misappropriation depend on whether the owner of the property consented to the taking by the accused. Larceny by finding depends on whether the "owner" of the property has or has not abandoned possession of it.

'In all these cases, it is fanciful to speak of "guilt" as being an entity that is independent of the jury's verdict. It is the conviction recording the jury's verdict that establishes the "guilt" of the prisoner. Like Bishop Berkeley who "maintained that material objects only exist through being perceived", the lawyer maintains that "guilt" exists in a criminal law context only when it is perceived as the concomitant of a conviction. To assert otherwise is to deny the presumption of innocence, a presumption that operates until the entry of a conviction rebuts it.

…

'It is true, as the [respondent] pointed out, that the term "guilt" is often used to mean "state of guilt". But used in that sense, "guilt" usually refers to culpable or morally reprehensible conduct that is deserving of punishment, penalty or social condemnation. It is not necessarily synonymous with the legal quality of the acts, omissions and state of mind that together constitute a particular criminal offence. In support of his argument that s 475 was not concerned with a finding of "guilt", the [respondent] pointed out that lawyers and others refer to "consciousness of guilt" and "admission of guilt", concepts that exist independently of any finding of guilt by a judge, magistrate or jury. But these examples of "guilt" are not really helpful. They refer to the state of mind of the accused. Such states of mind constitute evidence that a jury can use to infer that the accused is guilty of the offence with which he or she is charged. Sometimes those states of mind refer to the actus reus of the offence. Sometimes they refer to the mens rea of the offence. Sometimes, particularly in the case of simple criminal offences, they refer to both the actus reus and the mens rea of the offence. But the conduct recognised or admitted by those states of mind is not always or necessarily synonymous with the legal quality of the acts and omissions that constitute the elements of any particular criminal offence. A person may believe that he or she is "guilty" of a breach of the law when in fact no law has been breached. In the context of s 475, it was the legal quality of the acts and omissions of the prisoner that identified the "guilt" of the prisoner, not the prisoner's or other persons' beliefs as to his or her guilt.' (Footnote omitted.) *Eastman v Director of Public Prosecutions (ACT)* (2003) 198 ALR 1; BC200302601; [2003] HCA 28 at [10]–[11], [19], per McHugh J

GYPSY

See GIPSY

H

HABEAS CORPUS

Ad deliberandum

[For 11 Halsbury's Laws (4th edn) para 511 see now 1(1) Halsbury's Laws (4th edn) (2001 Reissue) para 250.]

Ad respondendum

[For 11 Halsbury's Laws (4th edn) para 1510 see now 1(1) Halsbury's Laws (4th edn) (2001 Reissue) para 250.]

Ad subjiciendum

[For 11 Halsbury's Laws (4th edn) para 1452 see now 1(1) Halsbury's Laws (4th edn) (2001 Reissue) para 207.]

Ad testificandum

[For 11 Halsbury's Laws (4th edn) para 1509 see now 1(1) Halsbury's Laws (4th edn) (2001 Reissue) para 250.]

HABITUALLY RESIDENT

'A person may cease to be habitually resident in country A in a single day if he or she leaves it with a settled intention not to return to it but to take up long-term residence in country B instead. Such a person cannot, however, become habitually resident in country B in a single day. An appreciable period of time and a settled intention will be necessary to enable him or her to become so.' *C v S* [1990] 2 All ER 961 at 965, HL, per Lord Brandon of Oakwood

[Entitlement to income support only if 'habitually resident' in the United Kingdom, by the Income Support (General) Regulations 1987, reg 21(3), Sch 7, para 17.] 'Left to myself and guided only by the ordinary English meaning of words, I would say that a person is not habitually resident here on the day when she arrives, even if she takes up residence voluntarily and for settled purposes. "Habitually", to my mind, describes

residence which has already achieved a degree of continuity.' *Nessa v Chief Adjudication Officer* [1998] 2 All ER 728 at 731, CA, per Sir Christopher Staughton

'In addition to the ordinary meaning of the word "habitual" and the judicial and legislative background to its use it is permissible to take account of the purpose for which and the context in which it is used, namely to impose a restriction on entitlement to income support reasonably capable of being applied. It does not seem to me that physical presence in the United Kingdom together with a settled intention to remain but without the lapse of any appreciable period of time since arrival is best calculated to introduce the restriction intended. The additional requirement for the lapse of an appreciable period of time since arrival adds to the fact of physical presence a further fact more easily ascertainable than and confirmatory of a settled intention to remain.

'... What is an appreciable period will depend on the facts of each individual case for all that is required is what is necessary to give to the fact of residence the quality of being habitual in accordance with the normal meaning of that word.' *Nessa v Chief Adjudication Officer* supra at 742–743, per Morritt LJ

[Income Support (General) Regulations 1987, reg 21(3), Sch 7 para 17; appeal in the case above.] 'The tribunal thus decided that the appellant was "habitually resident" as on the date of arrival; she had to prove no more than, and she did prove that, she came voluntarily and for settled purposes ...

'It is said that "ordinarily resident" and "habitually resident" have the same meaning. It follows that for habitual, as for ordinary residence, voluntary residence with a settled purpose is enough. If this is right, it is perfectly possible for habitual residence to be acquired on the first day.

'The counter-argument is that voluntariness and settled purpose are not enough. In order to be "habitual," residence must both be established and have continued for a period sufficient for it to be said as a matter of ordinary language that the individual has the habit of residing in the United Kingdom. The case relied on here is *C v S* (*minor:*

abduction: illegitimate child) [1990] 2 All ER 449, sub nom *Re J* (*a minor*) (*abduction: custody rights*) [1990] 2 AC 562. The question there, however, was whether the child had ceased to be habitually resident in Western Australia when his mother took him away with the settled intention of living in England. Thus the issue was not whether he had acquired an habitual residence in England.

...

... In the present case, the question whether any or an appreciable period of time is needed to establish "habitual residence" is the key issue.

'There is an overlap between the meaning of "ordinary" and "habitual" residence and one is sometimes defined in terms of the other ...

'I am not satisfied, but it is unnecessary to decide, that they are always synonymous. Each may take a shade of meaning from the context and the object and purpose of the legislation. But there is a common core of meaning which makes it relevant to consider what has been said in cases dealing with both ordinary and habitual residence.

...

'With the guidance of these cases it seems to me plain that as a matter of ordinary language a person is not habitually resident in any country unless he has taken up residence and lived there for a period. There may be cases where for the purposes of making particular legislation effective (as for founding jurisdiction), it is necessary that a person should be habitually or ordinarily resident in some state at any one time. In other words, there cannot be a gap. Whether that is so does not have to be decided here. It seems to me, however, that whilst of course realising that some people seeking to come here may need immediate financial assistance, it is not necessary to the working of this particular legislation that the ordinary meanings of the word should be set aside in order that there is no gap between habitual residence in one state and habitual residence in another state.

'If Parliament had intended that a person seeking to enter the United Kingdom or such a person declaring his intention to settle here is to have income support on arrival, it could have said so. It seems to me impossible to accept the argument at one time advanced that a person who has never been here before who says on landing, "I intend to settle in the United Kingdom" and who is fully believed is automatically a person who is habitually resident here. Nor is it enough to say, "I am going to live at X or with Y." He must show residence in fact for a period which shows that the residence has become "habitual" and, as I see it, will or is likely to continue to be habitual.

'I do not consider that when he spoke of residence for an appreciable period, Lord Brandon [in *C v S* [1990] 2 All ER 961 at 965, [1990] 2 AC 562 at 578–579] meant more than this. It is a question of fact to be decided on the date when the determination has to be made on the circumstances of each case whether and when that habitual residence had been established. Bringing possessions, doing everything necessary to establish residence before coming, having a right of abode, seeking to bring family, "durable ties" with the country of residence or intended residence, and many other factors have to be taken into account.

'The requisite period is not a fixed period. It may be longer where there are doubts. It may be short (as the House accepted in *Re S* (*a minor*) (*custody: habitual residence*) [1997] 4 All ER 251 at 257, [1998] AC 750 at 763 in my speech; and *Re AF* (*a minor*) (*child abduction*)[1992] 1 FCR 269 at 277 where Butler-Sloss LJ said "a month can be ... an appreciable period of time").

'There may indeed be special cases where the person concerned is not coming here for the first time, but is resuming an habitual residence previously had ... On such facts the adjudication officer may or of course may not be satisfied that the previous habitual residence has been resumed. This position is quite different from that of someone coming to the United Kingdom for the first time.

'In my opinion, the tribunal was wrong in law in considering only the voluntariness of her presence and her intention to reside. The commissioner and the majority in the Court of Appeal were right in law to say that the facts must be investigated to see whether there was a residence which could be accepted as "habitual".' *Nessa v Chief Adjudication Officer* [1999] 4 All ER 677 at 680–682, HL, per Lord Slynn of Hadley

HACKING *SEE* ACCESS–To computer data

HANSARD INTERVIEW

'[12] So far as we are aware, a Hansard interview is unique to investigations carried out by the Revenue ...

...

'[16] Before considering the application or otherwise of Code C, it is appropriate to refer briefly to the nature of a Hansard interview, set in its historical context. It is a somewhat curious expression. At the time of the interview in this case on 8 March 1995 the interview was conducted in accordance with the practice set out in a reply to a parliamentary question given by the Chancellor of the Exchequer (Mr John Major) on 18 October 1990 (see 177 HC Official Report (6th series) written answers col 882). In the communication subsequently prepared by the SCO [Special Compliance Office] the Chancellor was stated to have given "the following answer regarding tax fraud":

"The practice of the Board of Inland Revenue in cases of tax fraud is as follows: 1. The Board may accept a money settlement instead of instituting criminal proceedings in respect of fraud alleged to have been committed by a taxpayer. 2. They can give no undertaking that they will accept a money settlement and refrain from instituting criminal proceedings even if the case is one in which the taxpayer had made a full confession and has given full facilities for investigation of the facts. They reserve to themselves full discretion in all cases as to the course they pursue. 3. But in considering whether to accept a money settlement or to institute criminal proceedings, it is their practice to be influenced by the fact that the taxpayer has made a full confession and has given full facilities for investigation into his affairs and from examination of such books, papers, documents or information as the Board may consider necessary. The above statement of practice should be regarded as replacing the one given by the then Chancellor of the Exchequer on 5 October 1944." '

R v Gill [2003] EWCA Crim 2256 at [12], [16], [2003] 4 All ER 681, CA, per Clarke LJ

HARASSMENT *SEE ALSO*
UNDUE HARASSMENT

[Section 1(3) of the Protection from Eviction Act 1977 makes it an offence to do certain acts with intent to cause residential occupiers of premises to give up occupation.] 'The 1977 Act is a consolidating Act which re-enacts, inter alia, Pt III of the 1965 [Rent] Act, which is headed "Protection against Harassment and Eviction without due process of Law". The 1965 Act created the criminal offence of harassment as a response to the Report of the Committee on Housing in Greater London (Cmnd 2605 (1965)), more familiarly known as the Milner Holland Report. That report revealed a shocking variety of abuses to which landlords were subjecting their tenants in order to obtain vacant possession of rent-restricted properties. Discussing these abuses the report said (pp 162–163, 176):

"We began our inquiry into this part of the field by attempting a classification of the different forms of malpractice under separate heads, categorizing them all under the general head of 'abuses'. This gave rise to two difficulties. First, it was not easy to draw a line between those acts which were plainly illegal, either as breaches of the criminal or civil law, and those which, while we regarded them as wholly reprehensible abuses, might possibly involve no actual illegality; indeed, many cases reported to us were of such complexity that the dividing line between what was illegal and what was just lawful became so shadowy as to be impossible to determine ... We have given much thought to the question how far the existing criminal or civil law gives effective protection to tenants who are subjected to abuses of the kinds we have found to exist. Few of them are breaches of the criminal code; rather more may perhaps be sufficient to support a claim in a civil court for an injunction or damages; many are manifestations of unconscionable and anti-social behaviour which cannot be brought squarely within the purview either of crime or civil wrong". The report abounds in examples of unconscionable harassment designed to make life intolerable for occupiers and thus to drive them out of the premises and cited a New York police statute as an example of a statute that made criminal this type of abuse, which at present fell short of a civil or criminal wrong. When s 30(2) of the 1965 Act was enacted it closely followed the form of the New York police statute. The social evil is so clearly set out in the report that I am quite satisfied that Parliament deliberately chose the language of s 30(2) of the 1965 Act to make any action likely to interfere with the peace or comfort of the occupier a criminal offence if it was performed with the evil intention of forcing the occupier to give up occupation of the premises, "intention" in this context meaning with the purpose or motive of causing the occupier to give up occupation of the premises.' *R v Burke* [1990] 2 All ER 385 at 389, HL, per Lord Griffiths

Australia 'The *Macquarie Dictionary* gives several meanings,

"1. To trouble by repeated attacks, incursions, etcetera, as in war or hostilities; harry; raid.

2. To disturb persistently; torment, as with troubles, cares, etcetera."

'It points out that the word derives from an old French word meaning "to set a dog on".

'It seems to me that if there is persistent disturbance of a person, by conduct, that can be sufficient to amount to harassment.' *Nguyen v Scheiff* BC200201118; [2002] NSWSC 151 at [65]–[66], per Campbell J

HARBOUR

Canada '... a person does not harbour a dog, within the ordinary meaning of "harbour", unless he or she exercises some degree of care or control over the dog.' *Purcell v Taylor* (1994) 120 DLR (4th) 161, Ont Gen Div, per Borins J

HARDSHIP

Australia 'Any condition which presses with particular asperity upon a person may be described as a hardship. The sense is conveyed by the definition in the Oxford English Dictionary, 2nd edn, which includes "hardness of fate or circumstance".' *Re Kabalan* (1993) 113 ALR 330 at 332, per Gummow J

Australia [Section 44(4)(a) of the Family Law Act 1975 (Cth) refers to 'hardship' as a criterion, inter alia, for granting leave to institute proceedings in certain circumstances.] 'Hardship is caused by the inability of a person to pursue a claim which in the circumstances of the case appears on the prima facie evidence to be substantive and not merely trifling: see *In the marriage of Whitford* (1979) 4 Fam LR 754 at 760, per cur.' *In the Marriage of P and A Neocleous* (1993) 16 Fam LR 557 at 561, per Fogarty and Nygh JJ

Australia [Property Act 1958 (Vic) s 282(2).] 'A two-stage approach is to be adopted by the Court dealing with an application for leave under s 282(2). It should first weigh up the respective hardship to the parties and then consider whether to grant leave in the exercise of its discretion: *Harris v Harris; Moore v Clarke*.

In *Harris v Harris*, Gillard J considered the meaning of the word "hardship" in s 282(2) stating:

> In my opinion the word "hardship" is a well understood word and nothing is gained by substituting other English words for it. The subsection requires the court to consider the relative hardships depending on the outcome of the application.

'His Honour went on to adopt the words of Fogarty and Nygh JJ in In *The Marriage of Neocleous* (1993) 16 Fam LR 557 at 561 where they said:

> Hardship is caused by the inability of a person to pursue a claim which in the circumstances

of the case appears on the prima facie evidence to be substantive and not merely trifling.'
Joyce v Delany & La Patrice Holdings Pty Ltd [2004] VSC 338 at [7], per Williams J; BC200406024

HARMFUL EVENT

[Article 5(3) of the Brussels Convention on Jurisdiction and the Enforcement of Judgments in Civil and Commercial Matters 1968 (as set out in Sch 1 to the Civil Jurisdiction and Judgments Act 1982) provides that a person domiciled in a contracting state can, in another contracting state, be sued in matters relating to tort, delict or quasi-delict, in the courts for the place where the 'harmful event' had occurred. The claimant suffered injuries in a road accident in France, sued and recovered damages in France and was given the right to return to the tribunal to seek a further award in the event of a subsequent deterioration in his condition ('*en cas d'aggravation*'). He did bring further proceedings before the tribunal but abandoned them and sued in England, claiming that the deterioration in his medical condition on the ground that the 'harmful event' occurred in England. An application to strike out the claim for want of jurisdiction was refused and an appeal was brought against that order.] '[15] It is common ground that the term "harmful event" is an autonomous convention concept, not to be determined by reference to national law. As we think is already apparent, Mr Henderson's case, in summary, is as follows. Self-evidently, the accident occurred in France, and the original action, which concluded in 1983, was properly brought in France. However, *aggravation* is a fresh cause of action under French law. Mr Henderson has been domiciled and has lived in England throughout the period from 1983 to date. Therefore, the deterioration in his condition which founds the basis for his cause of action *en cas d'aggravation* occurred exclusively in England. Accordingly, the "harmful event" identified by art 5(3) has occurred exclusively in England, and the English courts have jurisdiction to entertain his claim.

'[16] This is the reasoning which persuaded the Senior Master that the English courts had jurisdiction ...

...

'[19] We are unable to accept the Senior Master's conclusions for a number of reasons. First and foremost, we are satisfied that for the purposes of art 5(3) of the convention the "harmful event" in this case was the original "tort, delict or quasi-delict", which occurred in France on 8 July 1978. The *aggravation*, in our judgment, is not a fresh wrong done to the claimant: it is a worsening of his condition deriving directly from the original wrong. The fact that in French law it constitutes a fresh cause of action is, in our judgment, at best procedural. We see nothing in this process which requires the court to equate the *aggravation* with a new and different "harmful event" for the purposes of art 5(3).

...

'[30] ... In our view, the harmful event in this case was M Jaouen's negligence in causing the accident and injury to Mr Henderson. That act had no extra-territorial effect. It gave Mr Henderson no cause of action in England. He could not choose where to sue in 1981: his only cause of action was in France.

'[31] We do not think that the deterioration in Mr Henderson's condition can properly be described as a fresh "harmful event". It is a most unfortunate consequence which flows directly from the original tort, delict or quasi-delict and is recognised as such by the French court, which provides a fresh cause of action to cater for it.

...

'[44] Whilst we cannot but have sympathy for Mr Henderson, whose life has been blighted by his injuries sustained in the accident, we think there is some force in the submission made by the appellants that the definition of "harmful event" for which Mr Brooke argues could result in forum shopping at will simply by a claimant moving to live in a different jurisdiction. Were a choice of jurisdictions genuinely open to Mr Henderson, he would plainly be well advised to choose that which was likely to give him the greater award. The fact that he would get more in England than in France cannot otherwise, however, be a good reason for conferring jurisdiction on England.' *Henderson v Jaouen* [2002] EWCA Civ 75 at [15]–[16], [19], [30]–[31], [44], [2002] 2 All ER 705 at 710, 711, 712–713, 715, CA, per Wall J

HARSH AND OPPRESSIVE

New Zealand [Employment Contracts Act 1991, s 57(1)(b).] 'With Hardie Boys J, we see no need to give the words "harsh and oppressive" anything other than their natural collective meaning. In contexts relating to the impact of particular terms on a party or parties to a contract any difference in meaning they may bear must be slight indeed. In dictionary definitions there is considerable overlap.

Both connote considerably more than imbalance; rather, the sense of unreasonably or unjustifiably onerous to the degree suggested by the dictionary meanings such as severe, cruel, burdensome, merciless.' *Steelink Contracting Services Ltd v Manu* [1999] 1 NZLR 722 at 727, CA, per cur

HAS FAILED TO USE OR HAS PALPABLY MISUSED HIS OR HER ADVANTAGE

Australia 'More recently, it has become common to cite the well-known passage in Lord Sumner's speech in *SS Hontestroom v SS Sagaporack* [1927] AC 37 at 47. But that speech did not, in my respectful opinion, add anything of substance to what had been said 30 years earlier in *Coghlan*. Nor for that matter to what had been said by Griffith CJ in *McLaughlin*. All that was added was the somewhat unfortunate reference (as it seems to me) to the consideration of whether "it can be shown that [the trial judge] has failed to use or has palpably misused his advantage" [1927] AC 37 at 47. These words carry the flavour of judicial misconduct which is rarely shown, or even suggested. How one distinguishes an alleged judicial "misuse" of advantage which is "palpable" from one which exists but is not "palpable" has never been clear to me. Nor is it clear why misuse must be "palpable" but the failure to use the advantage given to the judge need not be "palpable". Lord Sumner's formula is, in my respectful opinion, flawed. It may lead appellate courts to an assumption about the burden of demonstrating error that is unduly onerous: warranted neither by the statutory formulae applicable to such cases nor by the notion of "appeal" itself.' *State Rail Authority of New South Wales v Earthline Constructions Pty Ltd (in liq)* (1999) 160 ALR 588 at 611; 73 ALJR 306; BC9900187, per Kirby J

HASTEN DEATH

New Zealand [Section 164 of the Crimes Act 1961 provides that 'Every one who by any act or omission causes the death of another person kills that person, although the effect of the bodily injury caused to that person was merely to hasten his death while labouring under some disorder or disease arising from some other cause'.] 'There is a significant difference between hastening the death of a living person who may nevertheless be terminally ill and discontinuing a life-support system which is artificially prolonging manifestations of "life".' *Auckland Area Health Board v A-G* [1993] 1 NZLR 235 at 255, per Thomas J

HEALTH

Australia [The complainant suffered permanent cosmetic disfigurement when the appellant bit his left ear. The question was whether this constituted permanent injury to health.] 'As the learned judge pointed out to the jury, the word "health" is not defined in the Criminal Code. Resort to the dictionaries confirms that a cosmetic disability with no consequence upon the functioning of the body does not involve impairment of "health" as that word is ordinarily understood. The definitions of "health" in the dictionaries focus on the *functioning* of the body ... The Macquarie Dictionary's (1981) principal definition is: "soundness of body; freedom from disease or ailment; the general condition of the body or mind with reference to soundness and vigour"... One concludes, therefore, that the concept of "health", as ordinarily understood, covers the functioning of the body, and in relation to that, freedom from disease or ailment, and that it does not extend to the presence within or on the body of organs or parts which perform no function, the absence of which causes no disease or ailment ... It does not mean physically entire or intact, regardless of significance to functioning.' *R v Tranby* (1991) 52 A Crim R 228 at 237–238, per de Jersey J

HEALTH SERVICE

Australia [The court considered whether a religious practice called a 'Purification Rundown' was correctly considered a 'health service' according to the definition provided by s 4 of the Community and Health Services Complaints Act 1993 (ACT).] 'In my opinion, the definition of the term "health service" is not limited to services that are of direct benefit to a person's health. It would extend to the provision of pathology tests or other services of an exploratory or diagnostic nature. However ... the benefits or ostensible benefits must relate specifically to the treatment and care of physical or mental illness or injury or to services such as carried out in order to prevent illness. Furthermore, they must ultimately be directed, or purportedly directed, toward achieving such health benefits by virtue of the intrinsic therapeutic value of the service itself or of those further services that might be provided as a consequence of the diagnosis made or information ascertained. Hence, the question of whether a procedure constitutes a health service requires a judgment as to whether the dominant purpose or purported purpose is to cause or facilitate some benefit to a person's health by

means of the service itself rather than by the invocation of divine intervention or by means of spiritual development.' *Hanna v Cmr Community and Health Services Complaints (ACT)* (2002) 171 FLR 185; BC200206546; [2002] ACTSC 111 at [26], per Crispin ACJ

HEIRLOOMS

[For 39 Halsbury's Laws (4th edn) paras 390, 391 see now 39(2) Halsbury's Laws (4th edn) (Reissue) paras 89–90.]

HENRY VIII POWER

'[13] It will at once be apparent that the [Weights and Measures Act 1963] contained provisions, set out in ss 8(2) and 10(10), which conferred power on a subordinate body (the Board of Trade) to amend the statute itself. Such a power, of course, ordinarily belongs to the sovereign legislature, the Queen in Parliament, which passes, amends and repeals primary legislation. But by force of its very sovereignty, Parliament may delegate the power of amendment or repeal. A provision by which it does so is known as a "Henry VIII" clause, as it has been said "in disrespectful commemoration of that monarch's tendency to absolution". I doubt whether this is a just memorial to his late Majesty, who reigned 100 years before the civil war and longer, yet before the establishment of Parliamentary legislative supremacy in our constitutional law. But the label is old and convenient. In the last century constitutional lawyers and others expressed a wary suspicion of the use of Henry VIII clauses, because they transfer legislative power to the executive branch of government. As I shall show, it is central to the argument advanced by Mr Shrimpton in this case that the lawful use of such power is subject to very stringent limitations, which have been exceeded ... ' *Thoburn v Sunderland City Council* [2002] EWHC 195 Admin at [13], [2002] 4 All ER 156, per Laws LJ

HEREDITAMENT

[For 27 Halsbury's Laws (4th edn) para 131 see now 27(1) Halsbury's Laws (4th edn) (Reissue) para 132.]

New Zealand [Acts Interpretation Act 1924, s 4.] 'An easement, such as the access easement in the present case, is an incorporeal hereditament, which is a right in respect of land and therefore an interest in land, but it is not land in the tangible sense nor an estate in land in the common law sense. Nevertheless, it is contemplated as land by the Acts Interpretation Act 1924 since the generic "hereditaments" must encompass both those which are corporeal and those which are incorporeal. It is the case that Chitty J in *Re Danson (Deceased)* (1895) 11 TLR 455 is reported to have held that the reference to "hereditaments" in the definition of "land" in the Interpretation Act 1889 (UK) was confined to corporeal hereditaments. But in *Re Clutterbuck* [1901] 2 Ch 285, 289 Bryne J suggested that the *Times Law Report* must have been erroneous, thereby making plain his view that the statutory definition comprehended both corporeal and incorporeal hereditaments. There was nothing in the definition to suggest that the term should be given an amputated meaning and, as Bryne J pointed out, it was unnecessary for the purpose of Chitty J's judgment for such a meaning to be selected. In the Law of Property Act 1925 (UK) the definition of "land" includes incorporeal hereditaments which is consistent with conventional jurisprudence. The New Zealand Land Transfer Act 1952 similarly provides that in the Act and in all instruments purporting to be made and executed under that Act, unless the context otherwise requires, "land" includes hereditaments corporeal and incorporeal, of every kind of description and easements.

'These references demonstrate that at least for certain legislative purposes an incorporeal hereditament, such as an easement, may be treated for certain purposes the same as terrestrial land.' *Auckland City Council v Man O'War Station Ltd* [1996] 3 NZLR 460 at 465, per Anderson J

[For 39 Halsbury's Laws (4th edn) paras 375, 380 see now 39(2) Halsbury's Laws (4th edn) (Reissue) paras 74, 79.]

Corporeal hereditament

[For 39 Halsbury's Laws (4th edn) para 381 see now 39(2) Halsbury's Laws (4th edn) (Reissue) para 80.]

Incorporeal hereditament

[For 39 Halsbury's Laws (4th edn) para 382 see now 39(2) Halsbury's Laws (4th edn) (Reissue) para 81.]

Real and personal hereditaments

[For 39 Halsbury's Laws (4th edn) para 383 see now 39(2) Halsbury's Laws (4th edn) (Reissue) para 82.]

HIGH-CLASS SHOP

[Sub-tenants of a shopping centre advertised a closing-down sale. The landlords sought to enforce a clause of the sub-lease requiring the sub-tenants to keep the shop open as a high-class shop for carrying on business for the sale of footwear, hosiery, and handbags of all descriptions. The sub-tenants argued that the clause lacked precision, gave rise to wholly subjective tests and was unenforceable by specific implement.] 'No difficulty is, in my view, presented by the expression "high-class shop"; it is a familiar commercial expression readily capable of objective assessment.' *Co-operative Wholesale Society Ltd v Saxone Ltd* 1997 SCLR 835 at 838, per Lord Hamilton

HIGH SEAS

[For 49 Halsbury's Laws (4th edn) para 284 see now 49(2) Halsbury's Laws (4th edn) (Reissue) para 1.]

HIGHWAY

[For 21 Halsbury's Laws (4th edn) paras 1–8 see now 21 Halsbury's Laws (4th edn) (2004 Reissue) paras 1–8.]

HINDER

Australia [Section 45D(1)(b) of the Trade Practices Act 1974 (Cth) prohibits, inter alia, engaging in conduct that 'hinders' or prevents supply of goods or services.] 'Further, it cannot be, and indeed was not, suggested in argument that the notion "direct" is inherent in either of the words "hinder" or "prevent". "Hinder" has been construed in England "in the general sense of *in any way* affecting to an appreciable extent the ease of the usual way of supplying the article" (emphasis added): *Tennants (Lancashire) Ltd v CS Wilson and Co Ltd* [1917] AC 495 at 513–514], per Lord Dunedin; *Peter Dixon and Sons Ltd v Henderson, Craig & Co* [[1919] 2 KB 778 at 786]. What was there said in relation to hindrance of supply would apply with equal force to hindrance of acquisition. The comments of Gibbs J relating to the words "prevent or hinder" in *R v Bell, ex p Lees* [(1980) 146 CLR 141 at 147–148], must be seen in the context of that case. As his Honour observed, a broad construction would have effected a very drastic interference with ordinary civil rights. There is no similar reason for rejecting a broad interpretation of those words in this case. As has been said, such an interpretation is entirely consonant with the purpose of the section.' *Devenish v Jewel Food Stores Pty Ltd* (1991) 172 CLR 32 at 45–46, per Mason CJ

HOLIDAY

[For 45 Halsbury's Laws (4th edn) para 1119 see now 45(2) Halsbury's Laws (4th edn) (Reissue) para 219.]

HOLIDAYS, ON PAY, ...

New Zealand [Holidays Act 1981, s 7A(1).] 'The crucial question is the meaning of the expression "holidays, on pay" in s 7A in the statutory context. The words "on pay" are not defined. The ordinary and natural meaning of "pay" in that context is the remuneration received for a working day. It is payment for labour or service. It is an earned benefit in the sense that the holiday and so the pay accrues because the recipient has been working under an employment contract. That is reflected in the definition of "paid holidays" in *The New Shorter Oxford English Dictionary*: "an agreed holiday period for which wages are paid as normal".

'The scheme of the section itself also provides some guidance as to the meaning of the words. First, it is directed to "Every employment contract" and to the provision "in relation to every worker bound by it" for the grant of public holidays. In that respect it is directed to all employees affected, rather than focussing on the work that the particular worker would have done or might have done on a particular day. Second, it provides globally in respect of not less than 11 "holidays on pay". That theme carries through the next group of words referring to holidays "where they fall on days that would otherwise be working days for the worker". Those features all point to the use of the same calculation basis to arrive at the pay for each holiday and to the pay being that received for a working day's work.

'Elsewhere in the statute somewhat different terminology is used. The calculation of pay for annual holidays is based on a worker's "average weekly earnings", a defined term which through the further defined term "gross earnings" means "the total amount of remuneration payable to him by his employer or by way of salary, wages, allowances or commission" (s 3). Again, "ordinary pay" means "the remuneration for the worker's normal weekly number of hours worked calculated at the ordinary time rate of pay" (s 4). The expression is used in s 16(4) which requires that holiday pay be at a rate not less than the worker's current rate of ordinary pay. "Ordinary pay" would often be a lower figure than "average weekly earnings", for example where a worker has seen substantial amounts of overtime during the year in question. Special sick and bereavement leave under s 30A uses the formula of "pay at the ordinary time rate of pay for the normal number of hours that that worker normally works on that day."

'Of particular significance in this regard are the provisions of s 25 for payment for public holidays to persons employed in a factory (extended to employment in an "undertaking" under s 30). The expression used in s 25 for the calculation required is "wages for an ordinary working day"...

'Sections 7A and 24 are both directed to pay for public holidays. They are not mutually exclusive. Section 7A applies to all employment under employment contracts including employment in factories ... The entitlement under the employment contract provided for in terms of s 7A is to holidays on pay ... There is no room in the statutory scheme for a mismatch, for arriving at different base figures under the two provisions. And, as earlier indicated, pay for a working day is what underlies the expression "on pay" in the context of s 7A ...

'While the interpretation task would have been facilitated by use of the same set of words in both s 7A and s 25, we consider there is no distinction of substance in the meaning of the two expressions in their statutory context and in the scheme of the Act as a whole. In each case the pay for the statutory holiday is that for an ordinary working day. Nor does it seem that the meaning of "ordinary pay" as defined in s 4 can be any different ... [T]he workers are entitled to observe public holidays without loss of what they habitually receive for ordinary working days. Any lesser remuneration is something less than "pay" using that word in its ordinary sense.' *Ports of Auckland Ltd v New Zealand Waterfront Workers Union Inc* [1996] 3 NZLR 268 at 271–273, CA, per cur

HOMEWORKER

[The Wages Councils Act 1979 has been repealed. See now the Wages Act 1986, s 26(1), where the definition is as follows.]

'Homeworker' means an individual who—
    (a) contracts with a person, for the purposes of that person's business, for the execution of work to be done in a place not under the control or management of the person with whom he contracts, and

(b) does not normally make use of the services of more than two individuals in the carrying out of contracts for the execution of work in relation to which statutory minimum remuneration is provided by any order under section 14 [of the Wages Act 1986]

New Zealand [The Employment Contracts Act 1991, s 2.] 'The appellants [professional homecare workers] come within the definition of homeworkers in the ordinary and natural meaning of the words used by the legislature. But is there anything in the purposes of the legislation which might limit that meaning? Are there any policy reasons ... which might lead to a different result?
...
'... homecare workers are in a vulnerable position of the kind contemplated by those responsible for promoting the extended definition in 1987 if they are ineligible to receive the protections accorded to employees under the Employment Contracts Act and allied statutes. Although their position is quite different from outworkers engaged in piecework they are similarly vulnerable and susceptible of manipulation if allowed to be treated as independent contractors ... They are very much, therefore, the type of worker who needs the protection of the Act by being deemed an employee notwithstanding a contractual description of "independent contractor".
...
'The intention of the extended definition is to deem to be an employee anyone who has been engaged in the course of some other person's trade or business to do non-tradesman's work in a dwelling (not necessarily their own). An engagement, employment or contract is within the definition if it is expressly or impliedly a term that the place where the work will be done is to be a dwelling house.

'Such an interpretation will include people like the appellants, but would not extend to those like artists, journalists or designers who choose to work from home, but in respect of whose place of work the other party to the engagement is indifferent and in respect of whom no term can be implied about where work is to be done.

'The interpretation will extend to a traditional outworker in respect of whom the place of work is to be, on a proper interpretation of the contract, a dwelling house, but not necessarily to a traditional outworker in respect of whom no term is express or to be implied as to the use of a dwelling house

as a workplace.' *Cashman v Central Regional Health Authority* [1997] 1 NZLR 7 at 11, 13–14, CA, per cur

HOMICIDE

[For 11 Halsbury's Laws (4th edn) para 1151 see now 11(1) Halsbury's Laws (4th edn) (Reissue) para 425.]

HONEST BELIEF

[A trust deed provided by cl 15(1)(a)(iv) that no trustee would be liable by reason of 'any other matter or thing other than wilful fraud or dishonesty on the part of the Trustee whom it is sought to make liable'.] 'With respect, however, I find myself unable to agree with the third proposition, if stated without qualification. At least in the case of a solicitor-trustee, a qualification must in my opinion be necessary to take account of the case where the trustee's so-called "honest belief", though actually held, is so unreasonable that, by any objective standard, no reasonable solicitor-trustee could have thought that what he did or agreed to do was for the benefit of the beneficiaries. I limit this proposition to the case of a solicitor-trustee, first, because on the facts before us we are concerned only with solicitor-trustees and, secondly, because I accept that the test of honesty may vary from case to case, depending on, among other things, the role and calling of the trustee: compare *Twinsectra Ltd v Yardley* [1999] Lloyd's Rep 438 at 464 per Potter LJ. In that case (at 465), the court regarded the standard of honesty applicable in the case of the defendant solicitor, Mr Leach, as being "that to be expected of a reasonably prudent and honest solicitor".

'The word "honest" at first sight points exclusively to a state of mind. But, as the *Twinsectra Ltd* case illustrates, its scope cannot be so limited. A person may in some cases act dishonestly, according to the ordinary use of language, even though he genuinely believes that his action is morally justified. The penniless thief, for example, who picks the pocket of the multi-millionaire is dishonest even though he genuinely considers the theft is morally justified as a fair redistribution of wealth and that he is not therefore being dishonest.
...
'For all these reasons the judge in my judgment erred in his approach to the construction of the effect of cl 15(1)(a)(iv) of the Bacchus trust deed. That clause in my judgment would not exempt the

trustees from liability for breaches of trust, even if committed in the genuine belief that the course taken by them was in the interests of the beneficiaries, if such belief was so unreasonable that no reasonable solicitor-trustee could have held that belief.' *Walker v Stones* [2000] 4 All ER 412 at 443–444, 446, CA, per Sir Christopher Slade

HOSPITAL

[The Road Traffic Act 1972 has been repealed. The definition was re-enacted in the Road Traffic Act 1988, s 11.

See also s 161(1) of the Act of 1988.]

HOSPITIUM

[For 24 Halsbury's Laws (4th edn) para 1228 see now 24 Halsbury's Laws (4th edn) (Reissue) para 1127

HOSTILITIES

[For 25 Halsbury's Laws (4th edn) para 158 see now 25 Halsbury's Laws (4th edn) (2003 Reissue) para 336.]

HOTCHPOT

[For 42 Halsbury's Laws (4th edn) para 929 see now 42 Halsbury's Laws (4th edn) (Reissue) para 924.]

HOTEL

[For 24 Halsbury's Laws (4th edn) paras 1205, 1207 see now 24 Halsbury's Laws (4th edn) (Reissue) paras 1105, 1107.]

HOUR

[For 45 Halsbury's Laws (4th edn) para 1143 see now 45(2) Halsbury's Laws (4th edn) (Reissue) para 214 .]

Australia 'Experience in this profession shows that the word "hour" is sometimes interpreted differently by solicitors and clients, and by different solicitors amongst themselves. Some solicitors appear to take the view that an hour means the time that a solicitor of reasonable competence of the grade specified (ie partner, senior associate, ordinary solicitor), would have spent on the problem, not the time that the actual solicitor did spend on the problem. Another view is that a time

should be allowed for mind-switching purposes, so that if a solicitor makes a telephone call for one minute, the solicitor requires another five minutes to get his or her mind back on to the job that he or she was doing before the phone call was made, so the client is charged for six minutes. Another view is taken that if the solicitor does not know the answer to the problem (even though a reasonable bystander would have thought that a solicitor of reasonable competence would have known), the client is to be charged for the reading and research that it takes the solicitor to get himself or herself up to scratch. I would think that unless it is spelt out, where there is an informal agreement between solicitor and client that the client will be charged at an hourly rate, ordinarily that means that the client will be charged only for the time actually spent on the client's matter and not including time that was necessary for the solicitor to spend on self-education.' *Bartex Fabrics Pty Ltd v Phillips Fox* (1994) 13 ACSR 667 at 678–679, per Young J

HOUSE

[The Leasehold Reform Act 1967, s 1(1) confers the right on a tenant of a leasehold house, occupying the house as his residence, to acquire the freehold or an extended lease in certain circumstances. Section 2(1) defines 'house' as including any building designed or adapted for living in and reasonably so called, notwithstanding that the building is not structurally detached, or was or is not solely designed or adapted for living in, or is divided horizontally into flats or maisonettes.] 'In construing these provisions, it is in my view important to distinguish between s 1(1), by which the right of acquisition is conferred and s 2(1), by which the building to be acquired is identified. The functions of the two provisions being quite different, I would have thought it clear, authority apart, that the requirement that the tenant should occupy the house as his residence ought not to have any influence on the identification of the house …

'In my view the correct approach to the construction of ss 1(1) and 2(1) is as follows. The first requirement of s 1(1) is that there should be a leasehold house held by the tenant. In order to find out whether that requirement is satisfied you go straight to s 2(1), which invites you to identify a building held by the tenant and designed or adapted for living in; it need not be structurally detached, nor solely designed or adapted for living in. If and when you have identified such a building you must consider whether it is reasonable to call it a house. If it is, then you go back to the other requirements of s 1(1) and consider next whether the tenant is occupying the building as his residence. You do not consider that question unless and until the requirements of s 2(1) are satisfied.' *Duke of Westminster v Birrane* [1995] 3 All ER 416 at 420–421, CA, per Nourse LJ

[The Leasehold Reform Act gives a tenant of a leasehold 'house' who occupies the 'house' or part of it as his residence the right to acquire on fair terms the freehold of the 'house'. By virtue of s 2(1), 'house' includes any building designed or adapted for living in and reasonably so called, notwithstanding that the building was not structurally detached. Where a building is divided vertically, sub-s (1)(b) provides that the building as a whole is not a 'house'. Section 2(2) provides that references to a house do not apply to a house which is not structurally detached and of which a 'material part' lies above or below a part of the structure not comprised in the house.] '[12] In the Court of Appeal ([2001] EWCA Civ 761, [2001] 3 EGLR 47, [2002] QB 364) Robert Walker LJ was of the view that the whole of the built structure, or building, comprising 76 Harley Street and 27 Weymouth Mews can reasonably be called a "house". I have some sympathy with this view. The fact that for some years 27 Weymouth Mews was occupied and used as a separate residential unit has only a limited bearing on the question whether the whole of this single structure can reasonably be called a "house". 76 Harley Street is itself divided into several separate residential units. Despite this the whole of 76 Harley Street can reasonably be called a "house", as the 1967 Act itself envisages: see s 2(1), and the observations of Dillon LJ in *Malpas v St Ermin's Property Ltd* [1992] 1 EGLR 109 at 110.

'[13] Where I part company with the Court of Appeal is that, even if the whole structure can reasonably be called a "house", I do not think that is the end of the matter. The scope of the opening words of s 2(1) ("'house' includes any building designed or adapted for living in and reasonably so called") is cut down, when the circumstances require, by s 2(1)(b) ("where a building is divided vertically the building as a whole is not a 'house'"). That is this case. The structure comprising 76 Harley Street and 27 Weymouth Mews is divided vertically at the point where the eastern end of the extended ground floor and basement of 76 Harley Street meets 27 Weymouth Mews. The division is vertical (from top to bottom), even though part of the basement of 76 Harley Street lies under 27 Weymouth Mews.

'[14] Accordingly there can be no question of Mr Malekshad being entitled to enfranchise 27 Weymouth Mews as well as 76 Harley Street. Each of these two units comprises a house for the purposes of the 1967 Act. Of these two houses, Mr Malekshad was, it seems, occupying the third floor flat in 76 Harley Street as his residence. His claim to enfranchise 27 Weymouth Mews must fail.

'[15] Thus far I have applied the provisions of s 2(1) to the particular facts of this case. The next step is to apply s 2(2), given that at the point of division between 76 Harley Street and 27 Weymouth Mews part of the basement of 76 Harley Street lies below 27 Weymouth Mews. The basement of 76 Harley Street extends back to a wall which divides the front part of the basement from the rear part of the basement under 27 Weymouth Mews.

'[16] In applying s 2(2) Judge Ryland ([2000] EGCS 37) was bound to follow the test enunciated by the Court of Appeal in the *Duke of Westminster*'s case [*Duke of Westminster v Birrane*] [1995] 3 All ER 416 at 422–423, [1995] QB 262 at 270–271. If that test is put aside in favour of the approach outlined above, the application of s 2(2) is straightforward and admits of no doubt: the portion of 76 Harley Street underlying 27 Weymouth Mews is not a material part of 76 Harley Street. It does not have the effect that 76 Harley Street as a whole underlies 27 Weymouth Mews to a substantial or important extent. In terms of figures, it represents an insubstantial part, just over 2%, of the overall floor area of 76 Harley Street and about 7% of the overall basement area of 76 Harley Street.

'[17] Accordingly, s 2(2) does not operate to exclude 76 Harley Street from the scope of the enfranchisement provisions in the 1967 Act ... ' *Malekshad v Howard De Walden Estates Ltd* [2002] UKHL 49 at [12]–[17], [2003] 1 All ER 193, per Lord Nicholls of Birkenhead

Australia [The primary restrictions in a covenant registered in 1927 were that only a 'house' designed to meet certain limitations as to height and roof design should be built and when built should be 'used as a private residence only'.] 'While it may well be that a structure—such as one containing two semi-detached cottages (*Munns v Watson* [[1937] VLR 178]) or a duplex block of flats (see, e.g., *Yorkshire Fire and Life Insurance Co v Clayton* (1881) LR 8 QBD 421 at 424–425 per Jessel MR) may qualify as "a house", and that such a structure, if occupied and used only for its intended purposes, may properly be described as being used "for the purposes of residence", or "for residential purposes", it seems to me that, when, as here, one finds a reference to "*the* house" and to "*a* private residence", one must conclude that what the draftsman had in mind was "a house" in the sense of a structure of a permanent character structurally severed from other such structures, under its own separate roof, adapted for, and used as, the place of residence of a single family or family group: see, e.g., *Kimber v Admans* [1900] 1 Ch 412; *Rogers v Hosegood* [1920] 2 Ch 388; *Ilford Park Estates Ltd v Jacobs* [1903] 2 Ch 522; *Ex parte High Standard Constructions Ltd; Cobbold v Abraham* [1933] VLR 385; *Re Naish and the Conveyancing Act* [(1960) 77 WN(NSW) 892]. If this be so, then, for the purposes of the restrictions, the proposed structure must be regarded—as it has been described—as five (town) houses; and thus, as infringing the restrictions.' *Post Investments Pty Ltd v Wilson* (1990) 26 NSWLR 598 at 640–641, per Powell J

Australia '... on the basis of ordinary English understanding and usage, the expression "house" particularly in the context of clothing and fashion, would include a fashion house or haute couture business.

'The expression "fashion house" is a basic English expression: see the *New Shorter Oxford Dictionary* 1993, where the definition of "house" includes "[a] place of business; a business establishment, a firm; spec. a printing or publishing firm, *a couture or fashion establishment*" (emphasis added).' *Gianni Versace SpA v Monte* BC200200707; [2002] FCA 190 at [158], [159], per Tamberlin J

HOUSEHOLD

Australia 'There was an extensive discussion of the meaning of "household" in *Kingsland v MacIndoe* [1989] VR 273 and it seems clear that the word in its ordinary sense is as set out in the Oxford dictionary:

> "The holding or maintaining of a house or family; house keeping; domestic economy ... the inmates of a house collectively; an organised family, including servants or attendants, dwelling in a house; a domestic establishment".'

Lawrence v Public Trustee BC200102208; [2001] NSWSC 375 at [7], per Macready M

Canada [Insurance benefits were available for members of the 'household' of the insured.] 'I consider the use of the word "member" to be significant. The legislature could have used such words as "tenant", "resident" or "occupant" but it chose the word "member". To my mind to be a "member" of a household implies a constituent, an integral part or a component of a whole, thus supporting the trial judge's concept of a bond or affinity as an essential element of what constitutes a member of a household ... .

'The word "household" in the statute implies a "householder" which in turn implies some form of relationship between the "member" and the "householder". This relationship imposes on the "member" a certain deference to the "householder", compliance with a degree of propriety and responsibility and an active sense of participation in "household" functions and to defer to the wishes of the "householder" in this regard.' *Gray v Insurance Corpn of British Columbia* (1987) 46 DLR (4th) 269 at 273–274, BC CA, per Carrothers JA

New Zealand [Section 30(2) of the Rating Powers Act 1988.] 'The essential connotation of the term is familial domesticity.

'In my judgment the institutional provision of board with or without medical care and irrespective of the attentiveness of the providers of board, does not come within the ambit of the term "household" as such term is commonly understood in New Zealand society. The ordinary New Zealander would not regard as a "household" an institution which provides board as a commercial activity or as a community facility or service, such as a hotel, hospital or rest-home. That persons may reside in an institution, even on a long-term basis, participating to a substantial degree in the organisation of the institution, submitting to the rules of it and recognising someone as the head of it, may frequently be features of, but are not necessarily definitive elements of, a "household". If they were a prison could be called a "household" as an acceptable description in ordinary use. Plainly any such use would be simply wry.

...

'Institutions of a commercial or public nature whose services or functions include the provision of accommodation, or board and accommodation, such as boarding-houses, rest-homes, hospital, boarding-schools and prisons, do not, in common usage and therefore as used in s 30(2) of the Act, come within the scope of the term "household".' *Hopper Nominees Ltd v Rodney District Council* [1996] 1 NZLR 239 at 242 and 243, per Anderson J

HOUSEHOLD ITEM

New Zealand [Section 4(1)(a)(i) of the Shop Trading Hours Act Repeal Act 1990 provides that the trading restrictions on Good Friday and Easter Sunday (provided for in s 3(1) of the Act) do not apply to a shop if it is a shop where:

'(i)   The goods for sale include nothing that is not food, drink, a household item, a personal item, an automotive fuel, an automotive lubricant, an automotive part, or an automotive accessory of a kind that people may reasonably need to be able to buy at any time …']

'[30] In *Department of Labour v Cavanagh* [1996] DCR 657, Judge Callander at p 662 held that the term "household item" included anything properly used for domestic purposes in or about a home, being an article of domestic use or ornament. He considered that the expression would also include items in the immediate vicinity of the house, provided they are used for domestic purposes by the householders. … These suggested definitions seem a sensible starting point.' *Woolworths (New Zealand) Ltd v Attorney-General* [2001] 3 NZLR 123 at 130 per Glazebrook J

HUMILIATE. *SEE* OFFEND, INSULT, HUMILIATE OR INTIMIDATE

HYPOTHECATION

[For 43 Halsbury's Laws (4th edn) para 635 see now 43(2) Halsbury's Laws (4th edn) (Reissue) para 1691.]

Australia 'An example of what has been accepted as a letter of hypothecation was the document relied upon in *Lloyds Bank Ltd v Bank of America National Trust and Savings Association* [1938] 2 KB 147. At 157 there is set out the terms of a letter sent by a trader to its bank for the purpose of obtaining finance. It was agreed that all bills or documents against which advances might be made should be held by the bank as a continuing security for the payment on demand of the bills so purchased or discounted and for all advances which were made by the bank. This was in fact described as a letter of hypothecation and was accepted by the court as a general agreement of hypothecation.' *Askrigg Pty Ltd v Student Guild of Curtiss University of Technology* (1989) 1 ACSR 40 at 46, per Cohen J

I

IDENTICAL

Canada '[15] The crucial question, therefore, is whether claim 21 of the reissued patent is "identical" to claim 14 of the patent within the meaning of subsection 47(2) [of the *Patent Act*]. If it is, the cause of action pleaded in the counterclaim is not affected by the surrender of the patent. If, on the other hand, the claims are not identical, that cause of action could no longer be pursued in the courts. The Motions Judge turned to a dictionary source for assistance in construing the word "identical" in subsection 47(2). Thus *The Canadian Oxford Dictionary* (Oxford University Press: Toronto, 1998), defines that word as meaning things that are "exactly the same in every detail". At the same time, the Motions Judge found American jurisprudence touching the meaning of "identical" in the corresponding provisions of United States patent legislation to be of no assistance.

…

'[20] I shall turn next to consider the American jurisprudence. The construction of the word "identical" in the United States statute has attracted the attention of the courts of that country for more than three decades. Reference to some of the decided cases is illustrative. Thus in *Austin v. Marco Dental Products, Inc.*, 560 F.2d 966 (9th Cir. 1977), at page 973, the Court did not speak in terms of a literally exact requirement in order for claims to be "identical" but only that the claims be "substantially identical". Subsequently, in *Seattle Box Co., Inc. v. Industrial Crating & Packing, Inc.*, 731 F.2d 818 (Fed. Cir. 1984), the meaning of the word "identical" was again addressed. In referring to the requirements of section 252, the Court stated at page 827:

> Congress, in this statute, has explicitly limited claim continuity to claims in the reissued patent *identical* to claims in the original patent. The statute does not allow the claims of the original patent some other form of survival. The original claims are dead. The statute permits, however, the claims of the reissue patent to reach back to the date the original patent issued, *but only if* those claims are identical with claims in the original patent. With respect to new or amended claims, an infringer's liability commences only from the date the reissue patent is issued.

The Court went on to state, at page 827, that while it was not asked to decide exactly what "identical" meant in section 252, it was clear "that 'identical' means, *at most*, 'without substantive change' ".

'[21] In *Kaufman Co., Inc. v. Lantech, Inc.*, 807 F.2d 970 (Fed. Cir. 1986), the Court agreed with the test enunciated in *Seattle Box, supra*. In *Slimfold Mfg. Co., Inc. v. Kinkead Industries, Inc.*, 810 F.2d 1113 (Fed. Cir. 1987), the Court was of a similar view. After referring to earlier cases, it concluded at pages 1115–1116:

> In essence, courts have held that it is the scope of the claim that must be identical, not that the identical words must be used. In *Seattle Box Co. v. Industrial Crating & Packing, Inc.*, 731 F.2d 818, 221 USPQ 568 (Fed. Cir. 1984), the court held it unnecessary to define "identical" as applied to that case, but expressed the view that it means "at most, without substantive change". *Id.* at 827–28, 221 USPQ at 575 (emphasis in original). In *Kaufman Co. v. Lantech Inc.*, 807 F.2d 970, 977 (Fed. Cir. 1986) this court discussed section 252 as applied to reexamination and held that "'identical' within the meaning of s. 252 first paragraph, means 'without substantive change' ".

'In *Laitram Corp. v. NEC Corp.*, 952 F.2d 1357 (Fed. Cir. 1991), the Court expressed a substantially similar view, at page 1361: "'Identical' does not mean verbatim". The Court then went on to adopt the "no substantive change in scope" test of *Kaufman* and *Slimfold, supra*. To the same effect is *Bloom Engineering Co., Inc. v. North American Mfg. Co., Inc.*, 129 F.3d 1247 (Fed. Cir. 1997), at page 1250.

'[22] It seems to me that the approach taken by the American courts to the construction of the word "identical" is to be preferred to a strict literal interpretation of that word in subsection 47(2) of the Act. The focus should be on whether the scope of the reissue claim has been changed over that of the original claim because of use of different language in the reissue claim. If the language of claim 21 did not work a substantive change on the scope of claim 14, the former claim must be viewed as "identical" to the latter claim even though the language of the one is not in all respects the same as the other.' *Stamicarbon BV v Urea Casale SA* [2002] 3 FC 347 at 359 and 363–365 (CA), per Stone JA

IDIOT

[The Curators Act 1585 (Scotland), which allows a petition to be presented to the Court of Session for the appointment of a future-in-law to a natural fool, an 'idiot' or a furious person was held to be still in force. The question was as to the adaptation of its language to modern times.] 'I was referred to the definition of "idiot" in The Oxford English Dictionary and in particular the second meaning of that word: "A person so deficient in mental or intellectual faculty as to be incapable of ordinary acts of reasoning or rational conduct. Applied to one permanently so afflicted, as distinguished from one who is temporarily insane, or "out of his wits", and who either has lucid intervals, or may be expected to recover his reason". My attention was also directed to the Mental Health (Scotland) Act 1984, section 1(2) where "mental disorder" is defined and it was suggested that the distinction between an "idiot" and a "furious" person may be the same as that between mental handicap and mental illness ... That language or at least the last part of it is as apt today ... for the definition for present purposes of the insane or, as it is sometimes put, the incapax. The phraseology used today as the test for the appointment of a curator bonis or tutor-dative is that the incapax is in such a mental condition as to be incapable of managing his or her affairs or of giving directions for the management thereof. If, as I have held, the Act of 1585 is still in force, I see no reason why the words of the Act should not be read and interpreted in the modern phraseology which is their equivalent. To do so would not in my view do any undue violence to the words of the 1585 Act as those words have come to be understood over the centuries.' *Britton v Johnstone (Curator Bonis)* 1992 SCLR 947 at 1991–1992, per Lord Abernethy

ILLEGAL

Canada 'I will not repeat the historical foundations for the doctrine of illegality, which have been ably summarized by my colleague, Bastarache J. I simply note that the meaning of the term "illegal" within the context of the doctrine of illegality does not always mean "unlawful" in the traditional sense of being "contrary to, prohibited, or unauthorized by law" (*Black's Law Dictionary* (6th ed, 1990)). The need to exercise caution in the use of the term "illegal" in this area was underlined by C Boyle and D R Percy, eds, in *Contracts: Cases and Commentaries* (5th ed 1994), at p 721:

'A word of warning is necessary with respect to terminology. It will be evident already that the expressions "illegal" and "contrary to public policy" are used somewhat loosely and interchangeably. The approach of the British Columbia Law Reform Commission may be helpful. After recognizing that the word "illegal" is not always entirely appropriate, the Commission stated in its *Report on Illegal Transactions* (1983), at 2:

The term "illegal" is used as a convenient shorthand expression, signifying that the transaction so designated is one which a court will decline to enforce on the ground that it infringes some public policy, or the terms or object of an enactment. [Emphasis added.]

'The fact that the court determines that a contract is void or unenforceable for public policy reasons under the doctrine of illegality does not render either the contract itself or the subject of the contract unlawful. As noted by G H Treitel in *The Law of Contract* (9th ed 1995), at p 399: "Such contracts are often called 'illegal'. It is sometimes said that they are only 'void' or 'unenforceable'; but these statements only emphasise that no specific legal wrong is involved. So long as this point is borne in mind, no harm is done by using the traditional terminology in which these contracts are 'illegal'." (Emphasis added.)' *Continental Bank Leasing Corp v Canada* [1998] 2 SCR 298 at 355, per McLachlin J

ILLEGITIMATE

[Section 14 of the Family Law Reform Act 1969 has been repealed. For further reform of the law, so as to remove, so far as possible, the legal disadvantages of illegitimacy, see now the Family Law Reform Act 1987.]

IMMEDIATE

[Section 4(1) of the Public Order Act 1986 makes it an offence to use towards another person such threatening, abusive etc words or behaviour with intent to cause such person to believe that 'immediate' unlawful violence will be used against him.] 'It seems to us that the word "immediate" does not mean "instantaneous", that a relatively short time interval may elapse between the act which is threatening, abusive or insulting and the unlawful violence. "Immediate" connotes proximity in time and proximity in causation, that it is likely that violence will result within a relatively short period of time and without any other intervening occurrence.' *R v Horseferry Road Metropolitan Stipendiary Magistrate, ex p Siadatan* [1991] 1 All ER 324 at 329, per cur

Canada '[57] I now turn to the issue of the immediacy of the serious danger. Before concluding that the serious danger was "immediate", the Board first determined the meaning of the word as it appears in section 87.4 [of the *Canada Labour Code*]. The Board's reasoning is primarily found in paragraph 288 of the decision, which I have already reproduced. I agree with the applicant and PIPSC that the Board appears, at least at first glance, to have eliminated the temporal element which might have been thought to attach to the word "immediate". The Board supported its view of the meaning of the word by having recourse to the French version of the statute, where "immediate" is translated as *"imminent"*. In consulting *Le Nouveau Petit Robert: Dictionnaire alphabétique et analogique de la langue française* on the word *"imminent"*, the Board concluded that that dictionary specifically defined *"danger imminent"* as *"danger menaçant"*, which suggests less temporality. However, as is obvious from a reading of the *Le Nouveau Petit Robert*, the first and foremost definition of the word *"imminent"* is the following: *"qui va se produire dans très peu de temps"*. Moreover, the antonyms offered by that dictionary are *"éloigné"* and *"lointain"*. The definition and the antonyms clearly convey a sense that the word *"imminent"* has a temporal dimension.

'[58] The Board also purported to support its interpretation of the word "immediate" by citing various synonyms provided for that word in *Roget's Thesaurus*, namely "in a short time, soon, at once, awhile, anon, by and by, briefly, presently ... straightaway, quickly, speedily, promptly, presto, slapdash, directly". These synonyms, in my view, give support to the view that the word "immediate" does have a temporal dimension.

'[59] The word *"imminent"* used in the French version and the word "immediate" in the English version can be easily reconciled. Both words must mean, in the context of the subsection, that the serious danger must occur soon or within a short time. However, as to what constitutes a short time or soon in a given case must be determined on the facts of that case.' *Chalk River Technicians and Technologists v Atomic Energy of Canada Ltd* [2003] 3 FC 313 at 340–341 (FCC), per Nadon J

IMMEDIATE RIGHT, DUTY OR LIABILITY

Australia 'To be a "matter" there must be "some immediate right, duty or liability to be established by the determination of the Court" which the party invoking jurisdiction propounds ... It is also true that the "matters" referred to in s 75 [of the Commonwealth Constitution] are not the proceedings but the subjects of the controversy which are amenable to judicial determination in the proceedings. However, the party asserting jurisdiction must be able to demonstrate the existence of a legal right or duty which is apt to judicial determination; not mere "abstract questions of law without the right or duty of any body or person being involved".' *Re East; Ex parte Nguyen* (1998) 159 ALR 108 at 132–3; 73 ALJR 140; BC9806358, per Kirby J

IMMEDIATE SUPERVISION

Australia [Clause 19(b) of the Brisbane City Council Salaried Staff Award 1992 states that the 'ordinary hours of duty of officers having other officers or employees under their immediate supervision or working in close association with employees, whether in the employ of the Brisbane City Council or otherwise employed, whose ordinary hours of duty exceed 36¼ per week shall be the same as the ordinary hours of duty of such officers, workers or employees.'] 'According to the *Macquarie Dictionary*, 3rd ed, the ordinary meanings of the word "immediate" include: "without intervening medium or agent; direct: an immediate cause". The word "supervision" has the meaning "the act or function of supervising; oversight; superintendence" while "supervise" has the meaning: "to oversee (a process, work, workers, etc) during execution or performance; superintend; have the oversight and direction of".

'The word "immediate" in the phrase here in question in cl 19(b) can, I think, be accepted as serving to identify officers within cl 19(b) as officers who exercise supervisory functions over others directly, without their being any intermediary in the chain of supervision between such officers and those they supervise.

'So far as ordinary English usage is concerned, to say that one officer has another under his supervision conveys something different from saying that one officer is responsible to higher authority for another officer. One officer can be responsible to higher authority for another or for the way that other performs his or her duties without necessarily having involvement in the kind of oversight of the performance by the subordinate of his or her duties that is conveyed by the expression "supervision".

'As the ordinary meaning of "supervise" suggests, "supervise" or "supervision" connotes a temporal connection between the activity of supervision and the carrying out of work by those supervised. The ordinary meaning of the words "immediate supervision" suggests a relationship involving a temporal nexus between the activity of supervisory oversight and the work activities of those supervised. The context in which the phrase is found in cl 19(b) supports this interpretation. That cl 19(b) operates by fastening on the ordinary hours of duty that supervised employees must work and making that the ordinary hours of duty which their salaried supervisors must themselves work suggests that the concept of "immediate supervision" in cl 19(b) involves oversight by the supervisor of the work of those supervised throughout the whole of the period the latter are required to work. Moreover, cl 19(b) confers exactly the same benefit on the Council in relation to salaried staff who, though not performing any supervisory duties, work in close association with Council or external employees whose own ordinary hours of duty exceed the general 36¼ hour per week standard for salaried staff. So far as this class of salaried staff is concerned, non-supervisory salaried staff must work the same increased ordinary hours of duty as non-salaried employees where they are, in fact, working in close physical proximity during the period the other employees are performing their own work, provided that work "is of direct interest to the [salaried] officer in the performance at that time of the officer's duties". Such salaried staff can only be required to work the same ordinary hours of duty that the other employees must work if they have to work in both close physical and temporal proximity to the other employees.

'For the reasons given, I think that before an officer can be said to have the "immediate supervision" of others within cl 19(b), there must be some temporal link between the period the supervisor is required to be on duty and the period those he is said to supervise are required to be on duty, even if it is not necessary that there be an exact overlap between the two periods of duty.' *Brisbane City Council v Australian Municipal Administrative Clerical & Services Union* BC200300464; [2003] FCA 106 at [13]–[16], per Drummond J

IMMEDIATELY AFTER

New Zealand [Section 31 of the District Courts Act 1947 provides that "A duplicate of the notice of motion [to appeal] shall be served on all parties directly affected by the appeal either before or immediately after the notice of motion is lodged in the High Court ...".] 'The thrust of the authorities is that the service requirement of "immediately" after the notice of appeal is lodged is regarded as jurisdictional and very little lee way is permitted.' *McNicholl v McNicholl* [1996] 1 NZLR 611 at 613, per Barker J

IMMINENT

'In my judgment, where a prosecution is virtually certain to be commenced and particularly where it is to be commenced in the near future, it is proper to describe such proceedings as imminent.' *A-G v News Group Newspapers Ltd* [1988] 2 All ER 906 at 921, per Watkins LJ

IMPERIAL STANDARD

[For 50 Halsbury's Laws (4th edn) paras 59–62 see now 50 Halsbury's Laws (4th edn) (Reissue) paras 26–51.]

IMPLIED TERM

[For 9 Halsbury's Laws (4th edn) paras 351–362 see now 9(1) Halsbury's Laws (4th edn) (Reissue) paras 778–789.]

IMPORT

Australia [It was contended that 'importation' of prohibited substances within the meaning of the Customs Act 1901 (Cth), s 233B terminates at the landing of goods at a port.] 'A section addressed simply to the act of landing would not only fail to exhaust in a proper and understandable way the relevant Federal head of power. It would also fail to achieve the plain objective of preventing importation by attacking those within Australia who become concerned in arranging the act of importation and in moving the goods, once imported, into the community where they do their mischief. Legal authority, both of the High Court of Australia and of this court supports that construction of the word "importation". In *Forbes v Traders Finance Ltd* (1970) 126 CLR 429 Barwick CJ said (at 432): "'[I]mportation' extends on both sides of the actual act of importing into the country. The importation does not cease at the moment of an import. But the relevant use of a vehicle must be proximate to the act of importing. Whether it is so or not is a question of degree for decision in the particular case." ' *R v Courtney-Smith (No 2)* (1990) 48 A Crim R 49 at 63, per cur

New Zealand ' "To import" involves active conduct; and the bringing of goods into the country or causing them to be brought into the country does not cease as the aircraft or vessel enters New Zealand territorial limits. Importing into New Zealand for the purposes of s 6(1)(a) [of the Misuse of Drugs Act 1975] is a process. It does not begin and end at a split second of time. The element of importing exists from the time the goods enter New Zealand until they reach their immediate destination.' *R v Hancox* [1989] 3 NZLR 60 at 62, CA, per cur

IMPORTER

[For 'Customs and Excise Management Act 1929' substitute 'Customs and Excise Management Act 1979'. The Food Act 1984 is largely repealed. In the Food Safety Act 1990, s 53(1), 'importer' is not defined, but 'exportation', 'importation', 'export' and 'import' are expressed to have the same meanings as in the Customs and Excise Management Act 1979.]

Australia 'The ordinary meaning of "import" is 'to bring in from a foreign country merchandise or commodities for sale, use, processing or re-export': *Macquarie Dictionary*, 3rd edition. As Senior Counsel for [the Respondent] acknowledges, in the ordinary meaning of the word an "importer" is someone who brings the goods into Australia. This meaning does not require that the importer be the owner at law of the goods, or even that the goods will be owned in Australia at all.' *Granite Arms Pty Ltd v Chief Executive Officer of Customs* BC200302505; [2003] FCA 506 at [42], per Spender J

IMPOSSIBLE OR IMPRACTICABLE ... TO FORMULATE HIS CLAIM

New Zealand [High Court Rules, R 299.] '[T]his means an inability to plead in accordance with the

requirement of the rules. The focus is on pleading, not on proof. Further and more general discovery can be sought once the pleadings have been completed. Precommencement discovery is limited to what is required to enable the intended claim to be properly pleaded. As Somers J pointed out, there is some, but not much, difference between the words "impossible or impracticable". The fact that both are used shows that something less than impossibility will suffice: see Wylie J in *British Markitex Ltd v Johnston* (1987) 2 PRNZ 535 at p 540.' *Hetherington Ltd v Carpenter* [1997] 1 NZLR 699 at 705, CA, per cur

IMPROPER

Australia 'The *Macquarie Concise Dictionary* gives the word "improper" the following meanings:

"1. not proper; not strictly belonging, applicable or right; *an improper use for a thing*.

2. not in accordance with propriety of behaviour, manners, etc: *improper conduct*.

3. unsuitable or inappropriate, as for the purpose or occasion: *improper tools*.

4. abnormal or irregular."'

'The *New Shorter Oxford English Dictionary* includes in its treatment of the word "improper" the meaning "unbecoming, unseemly, indecorous". In our view the word "improper" appearing as part of the expression "improper conduct" in reg 18(1)(d) of the Australian Federal Police (Discipline) Regulations 1979 (Cth) is used in the second sense of the *Macquarie Concise Dictionary* definition set out above. That is, we conclude that reg 18(1)(d) is directed at conduct which may be regarded as lacking propriety or as unbecoming or unseemly in the circumstances. We do not regard the regulation as seeking to embrace in addition conduct which is merely technically irregular.' *O'Connell v Palmer* (1994) 53 FCR 429 at 434, per cur

Australia [Directors were charged with making 'improper' use of their positions.] '... that case [*Re Chew* (1992) 173 CLR 626] has rightly been taken to approve an objective test of impropriety ... Impropriety does not depend on an alleged offender's consciousness of impropriety. Impropriety consists in a breach of the standards of conduct that would be expected of a person in the position of the alleged offender by reasonable persons with knowledge of the duties, powers and authority of the position and the circumstances of the case. When impropriety is said to consist in an abuse of power, the state of mind of the alleged offender is important ... the alleged offender's knowledge or means of knowledge of the circumstances in which the power is exercised and his purpose or intention in exercising the power are important factors in determining the question whether the power has been abused. But impropriety is not restricted to abuse of power. It may consist in the doing of an act which a director or officer knows or ought to know that he has no authority to do.' *Re Byrnes* (1995) 81 A Crim R 138 at 147–148, per Brennan, Deane, Toohey and Gaudron JJ

IMPROPER PURPOSE

Australia [Production of documents for liquidators.] 'It is accepted that an applicant cannot "fish" for a case. Before he or she may be permitted to examine a confidential affidavit there must be material before the Court "from which it appears that the applicant has an arguable case, to which the material is relevant, before the discretion should be exercised in favour of that applicant" and that once that arguable case appears, the discretion will normally be exercised so as to grant the application: *Re Excel Finance Corporation Ltd (Receiver and Manager Appointed); Worthley v England* (1994) 52 FCR 69 at 94. This test was approved in *Re Southern Equities Corporation* at 422. In *Worthley*, in applying the test, the Court said at 94:

> In the present case the commencement by the Trustee and debenture holders of proceedings against Mr Worthley raised, without more, the possibility that Mr England had sought the examination summons against Mr Worthley for an improper purpose. The material filed in support of the application in which Mr England stated its purpose was clearly relevant to the issue of that purpose. In our view his Honour was in error in refusing inspection in a case where so to do would cause prejudice to Mr Worthley in the proceedings, and that error was an error of principle which justifies the Court granting leave to appeal against what is otherwise a matter of practice and procedure.

'In *Southern Equities Corporation*, Lander J, with whom the other members of the Court agreed, said that there must be some evidence before the Court from which it may be inferred that the examinee had an arguable case and that the content of the affidavit is relevant to that arguable case. He went on to say, at 422:

The authorities are clear that there is no right, on the part of an examinee, to access to the material lodged in support of the application for the examination summons. It is clear enough that while the court has a discretion to allow an examinee to inspect an affidavit supporting the application, which discretion should be exercised in favour of the examinee where the justice of the case so requires, there must be some evidence before the court from which it may be inferred that the examinee has an arguable case and that the affidavit material is relevant to that arguable case ...

'In *Re Moage Ltd (In Liq)* Mansfield J expressed his view about what is meant by an arguable case. He said at 67:

> In my view it involves no more than that the court requires to be satisfied to an appropriate level of satisfaction that the applicant is not pursuing the application without good cause or without good reason, and in particular is not doing so purely in the hope that, by procuring the release of the affidavit, some evidentiary foundation for the allegation will be made out. In other words, if the applicant is merely "fishing" for a case, then no reason for exercising the discretion in its favour will exist; if it presents material from which it is shown that it has passed the threshold beyond fishing, and has an arguable case based on that material, then the discretion may be exercised in its favour. Refinements of degrees of arguability is, in my view, unnecessary.'

Re Normans Wines Ltd; Harvey v Burfield (2004) 88 SASR 541, (2004) 207 ALR 644, (2004) 49 ACSR 628, [2004] SASC 171 at [59], per Mulligan J; BC200403417

IMPROPER, UNREASONABLE OR NEGLIGENT

[Section 51 of the Supreme Court Act 1981, as substituted by the Courts and Legal Services Act 1990, s 4(1), relates to costs in the civil division of the Court of Appeal, the High Court and county courts. Section 51(7) defines "wasted costs" as, inter alia, any costs incurred by a party as a result of any "improper, unreasonable or negligent" act or omission on the part of any legal or other representative or any employee of such a representative.] 'A number of different submissions were made on the correct construction of these crucial words in the new s 51(7) of the Supreme Court Act 1981. In our view the meaning of these expressions is not open to serious doubt.

' "Improper" means what it has been understood to mean in this context for at least half a century. The adjective covers, but is not confined to, conduct which would ordinarily be held to justify disbarment, striking off, suspension from practice or other serious professional penalty. It covers any significant breach of a substantial duty imposed by a relevant code of professional conduct. But it is not in our judgment limited to that. Conduct which would be regarded as improper according to the consensus of professional (including judicial) opinion can be fairly stigmatised as such whether or not it violates the letter of a professional code.

' "Unreasonable" also means what it has been understood to mean in this context for at least half a century. The expression aptly describes conduct which is vexatious, designed to harass the other side rather than advance the resolution of the case, and it makes no difference that the conduct is the product of excessive zeal and not improper motive. But conduct cannot be described as unreasonable simply because it leads in the event to an unsuccessful result or because other more cautious legal representatives would have acted differently. The acid test is whether the conduct permits of a reasonable explanation. If so, the course adopted may be regarded as optimistic and as reflecting on a practitioner's judgment, but it is not unreasonable.

'The term "negligent" was the most controversial of the three. It was argued that the 1990 Act, in this context as in others, used "negligent" as a term of art involving the well-known ingredients of duty, breach, causation and damage. Therefore, it was said, conduct cannot be regarded as negligent unless it involves an actionable breach of the legal representative's duty to his own client, to whom alone a duty is owed. We reject this approach. (1) As already noted, the predecessor of the present Ord 62, r 11 made reference to "reasonable competence". That expression does not invoke technical concepts of the law of negligence. It seems to us inconceivable that by changing the language Parliament intended to make it harder, rather than easier, for courts to make orders. (2) Since the applicant's right to a wasted costs order against a legal representative depends on showing that the latter is in breach of his duty to the court it makes no sense to superimpose a requirement under this head (but not in the case of impropriety or unreasonableness) that he is also in breach of his duty to his client.

'We cannot regard this as, in practical terms, a very live issue, since it requires some ingenuity to postulate a situation in which a legal representative causes the other side to incur unnecessary costs without at the same time running up unnecessary costs for his own side and so breaching the ordinary duty owed by a legal representative to his client. But for whatever importance it may have, we are clear that "negligent" should be understood in an untechnical way to denote failure to act with the competence reasonably to be expected of ordinary members of the profession.

'In adopting an untechnical approach to the meaning of negligence in this context, we would however wish firmly to discountenance any suggestion that an applicant for a wasted costs order under this head need prove anything less than he would have to prove in an action for negligence—

> "advice, acts or omissions in the course of their professional work which no member of the profession who was reasonably well-informed and competent would have given or done or omitted to do ... [an error of judgment] such as no reasonably well informed and competent member of that profession could have made". (See *Saif Ali v Sydney Mitchell & Co* [1978] 3 All ER 1033 at 1041, 1043, [1980] AC 198 at 218, 220 per Lord Diplock.)

'We were invited to give the three adjectives (improper, unreasonable and negligent) specific, self-contained meanings, so as to avoid overlap between the three. We do not read these very familiar expressions in that way. Conduct which is unreasonable may also be improper, and conduct which is negligent will very frequently be (if it is not by definition) unreasonable. We do not think any sharp differentiation between these expressions is useful or necessary or intended.' *Ridehalgh v Horsefield* [1994] 3 All ER 848 at 861–862 CA, per Sir Thomas Bingham MR

IMPROVEMENT

[The Leasehold Reform Act 1967 gives a qualifying tenant a statutory right to buy the freehold of the house of which he is the leaseholder. Section 9(1A) of the Act provides that, in the case of houses over a certain rateable value, the price is to be the amount which, at the time when the tenant gave notice of his desire to purchase, the freehold of the house and premises might be expected to realise on the open market. Section 9(1A)(d) requires that the price be diminished by the extent to which the value of the house and premises had been increased by 'any improvement' carried out by the tenant or his predecessors in title at their own expense. The

appellant was the tenant of a large house. It had originally been one dwelling for family occupation, but had been converted into five flats in 1947. While the 1947 works had originally increased the value of the house, the converted state made it worth less in the 1980s than it would have been in its original state. In 1987 the tenant's predecessor converted the house into two dwellings. In 1991 the tenant made further alterations. By 1997, when he gave notice of his desire to buy the freehold, the house was again arranged for single family occupation, more or less as it had originally been constructed. In subsequent proceedings, the Lands Tribunal held that both the conversion and the reconversion were improvements, but that the reconversion works did not entitle the tenant to pay a diminished price because their effect was to reverse the conversion works carried out and return the house to its original configuration. That decision was upheld by the Court of Appeal. On the tenant's appeal to the House of Lords, their Lordships considered the correct approach to s 9(1A)(d).]
'[17] In my opinion the language of s 9(1A)(d) is clear. A diminution in the open market value is to be allowed only by the extent to which that value has been increased by "any improvement" which has been carried out by the tenant or a predecessor at their own expense. For the tenant to secure a reduction, he must therefore, first, identify improvements which he or his predecessors have carried out at their own expense, and secondly, satisfy the tribunal that but for those improvements the house and premises would have been worth less.

'[18] The first of these two conditions requires consideration of any changes which have been made to the premises during the term of the lease, or the period which s 3(3) deems to have been the term of the lease. "Improvement" is a word of ancient lineage in the law of landlord and tenant and land law generally: see, for example, s 25 of the Settled Land Act 1882. In general terms it means additions or alterations to the house and premises which are not mere repairs or renewals: see Hague on Leasehold Enfranchisement (3rd edn, 1999) pp 198–199 (para 9–30). It is important to bear in mind that an improvement is a physical and not an economic concept. It refers to the works themselves and not to the effect, if any, which they have upon the value of the premises. It is the second condition which deals with the effect on value. So the Lands Tribunal was in my opinion quite right to say that the 1947 conversion and the subsequent reconversion were both improvements, even though the 1947 improvements had been

stripped out before the valuation date and, even if they had remained intact, would have reduced rather than increased the value of the house and premises.

'[19] The issue in this appeal turns upon what I have called the second condition. What does it mean to say that the value of the house and premises has been increased by the improvement? In my opinion, it signifies a simple causal relationship: but for the improvement, the house and premises would have been worth less. The comparison is between the value of the house as it stands and what its value would have been if the improvement had not been made.

'[20] The hypothetical house envisaged by this comparison is in my opinion one which has all the features of the real house, including its history, save for one: that the improvement in question had not been made. By that test, the 1947 improvements made no difference to the value of the house at the valuation date, because they had ceased to exist. On the other hand, if the reconversion had not taken place, the 1947 improvements would still have existed and the house would have been worth less. To the extent that it was worth more, the tenant was entitled to a reduction in the open market value.

...

'[24] Similarly, I see no justification for taking the approach of the Lands Tribunal and aggregating the net effect of all improvements made during the course of the lease, so as to compare the house as it stands at the valuation date with the house as it was let in 1843 or 1921 or 1947. If that was what Parliament had meant, it would have said that the price was to be diminished by the extent to which its value had been increased by "all the improvements" carried out by the tenant or his predecessors at their own expense and not "any improvement" so carried out. The words "any improvement" mean that each improvement relied upon by the tenant must be separately considered in comparison with what the house would otherwise have been worth. If it has added nothing to the value, it is disregarded; it does not play a ghostly role in the calculation of the value added by a later improvement by assuming its absence as part of the hypothetical unimproved property.' *Shalson v Keepers and Governors of the Free Grammar School of John Lyon* [2003] UKHL 32 at [17]–[20], [24], [2003] 3 All ER 975, per Lord Hoffmann

IMPUGN

Australia [Section 14(1) of the Criminal Code (NT) states that a 'person cannot be found guilty of an offence unless the conduct impugned would have constituted an offence under the law in force when it occurred'. Subsection 14(2) states that if 'the law in force when the conduct impugned occurred differs from that in force at the time of the finding of guilt, the offender cannot be punished to any greater extent than was authorized by the former law or to any greater extent than is authorized by the latter law.'] 'This in our view begs the question as to what is meant by "the conduct impugned" and whether or not that includes conduct which justifies or excuses an accused from criminal responsibility. One view is that conduct is only "impugned" if that conduct results in criminal responsibility. Where a person is not criminally responsible because he acted in self defence, the conduct was not impugned at all. Therefore, where the law relating to self defence changes so that conduct is impugned under the former definition, but not impugned under the latter, s 14 applies so that the accused must be acquitted. This would give the word "impugn" a meaning "to find fault with" (see definition 2 in the *Shorter Oxford Dictionary*). Alternatively "impugn" might mean simply "to call into question" (see definition 1 of the *Shorter Oxford* and also the *Macquarie Dictionary*). The conduct which is impugned in this sense would include the conduct relied upon by the accused as amounting to self-defence, because the whole of the accused's conduct must be called into question in order to decide whether he is guilty or not. Under s 14, it is the same conduct which is considered in each case, and the question is whether that conduct would have constituted an offence under the law at the time of its occurrence and also at the time he is proceeded against. Which ever way you look at it, the result is the same.' *Nguyen v R* BC200302420; [2003] NTCCA 4 at [9], per Martin CJ, Mildren and Riley JJ

IN AND FOR VICTORIA

Australia 'The Constitution Act 1975 (Vic) [s 16] provides that the Parliament of Victoria 'shall have power to make laws in and for Victoria in all cases whatsoever'. It further provides that: 'A Court shall be held in and for Victoria and its dependencies which shall be styled "The Supreme Court of the State of Victoria" ...' [s 75].

'Other State Constitutions use expressions other than "in and for" the State in describing the power of the State legislature. "[F]or the peace, welfare, and good government" of the State [for example, Constitution Act 1902 (NSW) s 5], or "for the

peace, order, and good Government"[for example, Constitution Act 1889 (WA), s 2] of the State are expressions in some State Constitutions. But just as a power to make laws for the peace, welfare, and good government (or peace, order, and good government) of a State is a plenary power [*Union Steamship Co of Australia Pty Ltd v King* (1988) 166 CLR 1 at 9 per Mason CJ, Wilson, Brennan, Deane, Dawson, Toohey and Gaudron JJ; *Durham Holdings Pty Ltd v New South Wales* (2001) 75 ALJR 501 at 503 [9] per Gaudron, McHugh, Gummow and Hayne JJ; 177 ALR 436 at 439] so, too, is the power of the Victorian Parliament to make laws "in and for Victoria". Neither the words "peace, welfare [or order], and good government" nor the words "in and for" the State are to be read as words of limitation [*Union Steamship* (1988) 166 CLR 1 at 10 per Mason CJ, Wilson, Brennan, Deane, Dawson, Toohey and Gaudron JJ]. Nor is there any reason to give the words "in and for Victoria" some narrower meaning when used in s 75 of the Constitution Act 1975 in relation to the Supreme Court.

'It has been said, however, that it is in the words "peace, order and good government" or, in this case "in and for Victoria", that some territorial limitation on the power of a State parliament is to be found [*R v Foster; Ex parte Eastern and Australian Steamship Co Ltd* (1959) 103 CLR 256 at 307. See also *Broken Hill South Ltd v Cmr of Taxation* (NSW) (1937) 56 CLR 337 at 375 per Dixon J; *Union Steamship* (1988) 166 CLR 1 at 12–13 per Mason CJ, Wilson, Brennan, Deane, Dawson, Toohey and Gaudron JJ; *Johnson v Cmr of Stamp Duties* [1956] AC 331; *Thompson v Cmr of Stamp Duties* [1969] 1 AC 320 at 335–6; Australia Act 1986 (Cth), s 2(1)]. Or, perhaps, territorial limitations on the parliaments of the States are to be found by reference to the federal structure of which each State is a part [*State Authorities Superannuation Board v Cmr of State Taxation* (WA) (1996) 189 CLR 253 at 271 per Brennan CJ, Dawson, Toohey and Gaudron JJ. See also *Port MacDonnell Professional Fishermen's Assn Inc v South Australia* (1989) 168 CLR 340 at 369–73].

'It is clear that legislation of a State parliament "should be held valid if there is any real connexion – even a remote or general connexion – between the subject matter of the legislation and the State"[*Pearce v Florenca* (1976) 135 CLR 507 at 518 per Gibbs J.]. This proposition has now twice been adopted in unanimous judgments of the Court [*Union Steamship* (1988) 166 CLR 1 at 14; *Port MacDonnell* (1989) 168 CLR 340 at 372] and should be regarded as settled. That is not to say, however, that there may not remain some questions first, about what is meant in a particular case by "real connexion" and, secondly, about the resolution of conflict if two States make inconsistent laws [*Port MacDonnell* (1989) 168 CLR 340 at 374; *State Authorities Superannuation Board* (1996) 189 CLR 253 at 285–6 per McHugh and Gummow JJ].' *Mobil Oil Australia Pty Ltd v Victoria* (2002) 189 ALR 161; 76 ALJR 926; BC200203432; [2002] HCA 27 at [45]–[48], per Gaudron, Gummow and Hayne JJ

IN CHARGE OF

[Section 5 of the Road Traffic Act 1972 has been repealed. See now s 4 of the Act of 1988 (prospectively amended by s 4 of the Road Traffic Act 1991).

A person will be 'in charge' if he is voluntarily in de facto control of the vehicle as if, in all the circumstances, he may be expected imminently to assume control: *DPP v Watkins* [1989] 1 All ER 1126.]

IN COMPANY

Australia [Section 61J(1) of the Crimes Act 1900 (NSW) provides that any person who has sexual intercourse with another person without the consent of the other person and in circumstances of aggravation and who knows that the other person does not consent to the sexual intercourse is liable to imprisonment for 20 years. Subsection (2) defined 'circumstances of aggravation' as circumstances in which 'the alleged offender is in the company of another person or persons ...'.] 'Before fixing upon a construction of the section, it is convenient to consider the second argument, which depends upon the way in which the cases have defined the phrase "in company". Most of the cases are concerned with robbery in company, rather than sexual assault. You would expect the same meaning in the context of both offences, although there are obvious differences between the offence of robbery and the offence of sexual assault. The common purpose in robbery is the taking of property for division between participants. Sexual offences involve individual gratification. The common purpose is in achieving, or facilitating, that objective. [Kirby J then examines the caselaw.]

...

'What emerges from these cases? A number of propositions can be stated:

- First, the statutory definition (s 61J(2)(c) [of the Crimes Act 1900 (NSW)]) requires that the offender be "in the company of another person or persons".
- Secondly, the accused and such person, or persons, must share a common purpose (either to rob, or as here, sexually assault).
- Thirdly, the cases appear to assume that each participant is physically present.
- Fourthly, participation in the common purpose without being physically present (for example, as a look-out or as an accessory before the fact) is not enough.
- Fifthly, the perspective of the victim (being confronted by the combined force or strength or two or more persons) is relevant, although not determinative. If two or more persons are present, and share the same purpose, they will be "in company", even if the victim was unaware of the other person.

'The physical presence of another is, therefore, required for the crime to be committed in company. However, two questions remain. First, what is meant by physical presence? Secondly, in respect of which aspect of the crime identified by s 61J is physical presence required? That is the construction question identified earlier. Is it penetration, as the appellant asserts, or would it be enough that the events giving rise to the accused's knowledge of the absence of consent took place in company?

'For the purposes of this appeal, I believe it is really only necessary to answer the first question, that is: what is meant by physical presence, and whether, in the context of this case, the separation of 50 metres was capable of satisfying that requirement?

'Physical presence is an elastic concept. The concept is best explained by example. Assume the robbery of a large warehouse, with a number of persons involved. The robbers scatter in search of valuables. They may, at any point, be separated by 50 metres and yet, throughout, will remain "in company". Assume that one robber demanded the Bankcard of the owner, and his PIN number. He then separated from his companions, went to the bank one kilometre away, and used the card to withdraw cash, before returning to the warehouse. Is the theft of that money part of the crime committed in company? The Bankcard and the PIN number were, no doubt, obtained with the aid of the coercion exerted by the group.

'Take another illustration, closer to the facts in this appeal. Assume a sexual assault in a large house, involving a number of individuals. If, for reasons of privacy, the victim were taken to an adjacent bedroom, and the door closed, the offence would plainly still be one committed in company. And the result, I suggest, would be no different if the bedroom were upstairs, so that some distance separated the offender at the time of penetration, and other members of the group.

'However, there must be limits. The point must be reached where the separation between the offender and the group is such that the offence can no longer be characterised as being in the presence of a group. How are those limits determined? I believe the learned trial Judge accurately identified the test. The test is the coercive effect of the group. There must be such proximity as would enable the inference that the coercive effect of the group operated, either to embolden or reassure the offender in committing the crime, or to intimidate the victim into submission.' *R v Button; R v Griffen* (2002) 54 NSWLR 455; 129 A Crim R 342; BC200202229; [2002] NSWCCA 159 at [103], [120]–[125], per Kirby J

IN CONCERT

Australia 'The phrase "in concert" has been construed as involving knowing conduct, the result of communication between the parties and not simultaneous actions occurring spontaneously. It has been said to involve contemporaneity and a community of purpose which requires a consensual element.' *Australasian Meat Industry Employees Union v Meat and Allied Trades Federation of Australia* (1991) 104 ALR 199 at 215, per French J

Australia [Section 45D(1) of the Trade Practices Act 1974 (Cth) provides, inter alia, that a person shall not, 'in concert' with a second person, engage in conduct hindering or preventing goods or services supply to a third or fourth person.] 'The notion of engaging in conduct "in concert" with another involves knowing conduct which is the result of communication between the parties and not simply simultaneous actions occurring spontaneously. It also involves contemporaneity and community of purpose. The requirement of contemporaneity does not mean that the acts constituting the relevant conduct must coincide precisely with the notion of concert: *Tillmanns Butcheries Pty Ltd v Australasian Meat Industry Employees' Union* (1979) 27 ALR 367 at 373; *Australasian Meat Industry Employees' Union v Mudginberri Station Pty Ltd* (1985) 61 ALR 417 at 424; *Epitoma Pty Ltd v Australasian Meat Industry Employees' Union (No 2)* (1984) 54 ALR 730 at 734; *Flower Davies Wemco Pty Ltd v Australian Builders Labourers' Federated Union*

of Workers (WA Branch) (1986) 20 IR 88 at 96… Conduct involving direction and response may, according to the circumstances of the case, be conduct in concert on the part of the person directing and the person acting upon that direction.' *J-Corp Pty Ltd v Australian Builders Labourers Federated Union of Workers—Western Australian Branch* (1992) 111 ALR 502 at 535–536, per French J

IN CONNECTION WITH

Australia [Section 3(1) of the Crimes (Confiscation of Profits) Act 1985 (NSW) defines 'tainted property' as follows: '"tainted property" means property that — (a) was used in, or in connection with, the commission of a serious offence; or (b) was derived or realised, directly or indirectly, by any person, as a result of the commission of a serious offence.'] 'The section refers to "use *in* the commission of an offence" and such a use would comprehend "use of the property" as an integral part of the crime, and that plainly relates to the time period over which the offence is committed. The words "in connection with" are equally related to that same time period, but they have a connection with the crime which is not so direct as in the case of "property used in the commission of the crime". The purpose of the composite expression "in, or in connection with" is to bring in, as "tainted property" all property which *at the time of the committing* of the offence is used in, or in connection with, the crime … The words "in, or in connection with, the commission of a serious offence" relate to the use of the property under consideration temporally to the period over which the happenings and events constituting the commission of the crime occurred. That period will not be restricted to the actual moments in which the crime, in law, was committed and it will be a question of fact in every case whether the user of the property had the necessary contemporaneous association with "the commission of the crime".' *R v Milienou* (1991) 53 A Crim R 271 at 274–275, per Lee CJ

Australia [Section 233 of the Companies (Qld) Code states that it is unlawful for a company to give a prescribed benefit to a person 'in connection with' the retirement of a person from a prescribed office of the company.] 'Contemporaneity may support an inference of connection, but it is not enough that the payment was made at about the time of retirement.

'The phrase "in connection with" is one of wide import, as I had occasion to observe in a different context in *Our Town FM Pty Ltd v Australian*

Broadcasting Tribunal (1987) 16 FCR 465 at 479–80; 77 ALR 577 at 591–592:

' "The words 'in connection with' ... do not necessarily require a causal relationship between the two things: see *Commissioner for Superannuation v Miller* (1985) FCR 153 at 154, 160, 163; 63 ALR 237 at 238, 244, 247. They may be used to describe a relationship with a contemplated future event: see *Koppen v Commissioner for Community Relations* (1986) 11 FCR 360 at 364; 67 ALR 215; *Johnson v Johnson* [1952] P 47 at 50–1. In the latter case the United Kingdom Court of Appeal applied a decision of the British Columbia Court of Appeal, *Re Nanaimo Community Hotel Ltd* [1945] 3 DLR 225, in which the question was whether a particular court, which was given 'jurisdiction to hear and determine all questions that may arise in connection with any assessment made under this Act', had jurisdiction to deal with a matter which preceded the issue of an assessment. The trial judge held that it did, that the phrase 'in connection with' covered matters leading up to, or which might lead up to an assessment. He said ...: 'One of the very generally accepted meanings of "connection" is "relation between things one of which is bound up with or involved in another"; or, again "having to do with". The words include matters occurring prior to as well as subsequent to or consequent upon so long as they are related to the principal thing. The phrase "having to do with" perhaps gives as good a suggestion of the meaning as could be had.' This statement was upheld on appeal." ' *Claremont Petroleum NL v Cummings* (1992) 110 ALR 239 at 280, per Wilcox J

Canada '[35] Firstly, I turn to the words "in direct connexion with". The *Oxford Compact Thesaurus*, 2001, 2nd ed., Oxford University Press, at page 161, provides the following meaning for the words "in connection with":

> **in connection with: regarding**, concerning, with reference to, with regard to, with respect to, respecting, relating to, in relation to, on, ... connected with, on the subject of, in the matter of, apropos, re, ... in re.

'[36] The French text of paragraph 1(a) of Article 2 of the Convention uses the words "*en relation directe avec*". *Le Nouveau Petit Robert: dictionnaire alphabétique et analogique de la langue française*, 1996, revised and expanded by Josette Rey-Debove et Alain Rey, at page 1915, defines, *inter alia*, the word "*relation*" as follows:

> *II. Lien, rapport. A. 1... . rapport; connexion, corrélation ... 2. Caractère de deux ou plusieurs choses entre lesquelles existe un lien. = rapport; liaison. Établir une relation entre deux phénomènes. Mettre deux événements en relation. Ce que je dis n'a pas de relation avec ce qui précède.*

This meaning is in line with that given to the words "in connection with" in the *Oxford Compact Thesaurus*, which, amongst other things, associates these words with the words "relating to" or "in relation to".' *Isen v Simms* [2005] 4 FCR 563 at [35]–[36], [2005] FCJ No 756, 2005 FCA 161 (Fed CA), per Nadon JA

New Zealand [R 5.4 of the New Zealand Law Society Solicitors' Nominee Company Rules 1988.] ' "In connection with" may signify no more than a relationship between one thing and another. The expression does not necessarily require that it be a causal relationship: *Our Town FM Pty Ltd v Australian Broadcasting Tribunal* (1987) 16 FCR 465, 479 per Wilcox J. But, as Davies J warned in *Hatfield v Health Insurance Commission* (1987) 15 FCR 487, at 491:

> "Expressions such as 'relating to', 'in relation to', in connection with' and 'in respect of' are commonly found in legislation but invariably raise problems of statutory interpretation. They are terms which fluctuate in operation from statute to statute ... . The terms may have a very wide operation but they do not usually carry the widest possible ambit, for they are subject to the context in which they are used, to the words with which they are associated, and to the object or purpose of the statutory provision in which they appear."

Strachan v Marriott [1995] 3 NZLR 272 at 279–280, CA, per Hardie Boys J

IN COURSE OF DELIVERY

[The Food Act 1984 is largely repealed.]

IN EVIDENCE

Australia [Section 63A(1) of the Telecommunications (Interception) Act 1979 (Cth) provides that in certain circumstances, a person may give 'in evidence' information obtained by intercepting a communication.] 'The first [submission] was that the tendering of the tapes did not constitute the giving in evidence of information and, accordingly, did not fall within the ambit of s 63A(1)... There is no substance in the first of these submissions. The evidence in a proceeding is not necessarily confined to sworn oral testimony given in court by a witness. It includes any documents received in evidence. It includes also any tape recordings received in evidence of relevant conversations. As Mason CJ, Brennan and Deane JJ said in their joint judgment in *Butera v Director of Public Prosecutions for the State of Victoria* (1987) 164 CLR 180 at 184:

> "... Of course, a conversation can be proved by the oral testimony of anyone who heard it but that is not the only means by which a conversation might be proved. The courts have now accepted tape recordings as evidence of the conversations or other sounds recorded on the tape."

'The tapes, in the present proceedings, recorded what the appellant said. The tendering of the tapes was giving in evidence that information, information obtained by the interception performed by Mr Beaver. It may be asked rhetorically: "But who gave the evidence? Surely the Crown Prosecutor did not himself give evidence by tendering the tapes?" The answer is that the wrong question has been posed. Section 63A does not speak of a person giving evidence. What it speaks of is a person giving "*in* evidence". The Crown Prosecutor did not, in ordinary language, give evidence of the information contained in the tapes. What he did, by tendering the tapes in evidence, was to give "*in* evidence" that information.' *R v Edelsten* (1990) 21 NSWLR 542 at 550, per cur

IN EXCESS OF JURISDICTION OR WITHOUT JURISDICTION

New Zealand 'The proper exercise of judicial responsibility requires that the Judge act with integrity and competence. A cushion of immunity provides appropriate protection against error. Absolute immunity would undermine judicial responsibility and give no weight at all to the public policy goals of tort and public law liability. As the word "excess" indicates it is a matter of degree. In extreme circumstances the Judge's conduct may so egregiously overstep the mark as to take the resulting decision beyond any colour of authority. While purporting to act in a judicial capacity a Judge who acts in bad faith or is grossly careless or indifferent to the performance of responsibilities can properly be characterised as acting without jurisdiction or in excess of

jurisdiction.' *Harvey v Derrick* [1995] 1 NZLR 314 at 326, CA, per Richardson J

IN GOOD FAITH

Australia [Section 122(2) of the Bankruptcy Act 1966 (Cth) refers to a payee 'in good faith'.]

'I respectfully agree with the observation of Wootten J in *Re Chisum Services Pty Ltd* (1982) 7 ACLR 641 that for the purpose of s 122(2), "good faith is a subjective condition, requiring that the payee act with propriety and honesty". In my opinion, subject to the operation of s 122(4)(c), a creditor is a "payee ... in good faith" within the meaning of s 122(2)(a) if at the time of the payment to him he neither believed nor suspected that the payment was such as to give him a preference over other creditors of an insolvent debtor: cf *Re Chisum Services*, loc cit.' *Spedley Securities Ltd (in liquidation) v Western United Ltd (in liquidation)* (1992) 7 ACSR 271 at 278, per McLelland J

IN LIEU OF

Canada '[82] The chambers judge concluded that this was clearly a case where Mr. Forsen had elected to take action in "addition to or in lieu of" coverage under workers' compensation legislation.

'[83] Section 9 of the *Workers Compensation Act*, R.S.B.C. 1996, c. 492, provides:

> 9(1) Where by the law of the country or place in which the injury or occupational disease occurs the worker or the worker's dependants are entitled to compensation in respect of it, they must elect whether they will claim compensation under the law of that country or place or under this Part, and to give notice of the election. If the election is not made and notice given, it must be presumed that they have elected not to claim compensation under this Part; but if there is in existence an agreement entered into, or arrangement made, under section 8.1, any right of election is subject to the terms of that agreement or arrangement.
>
> (2) Notice of the election must be given to the Board within 3 months after the occurrence of the injury or disablement from occupational disease, or, if it results in death, within 3 months after the death, or within any longer period that either before or after the expiration of the 3 months the Board allows.

'[84] The parties agreed that Mr. Forsen did not elect to claim compensation under the *Workers Compensation Act*. In order to avoid a statutory time limitation under that Act, Mr. Forsen was required to make a claim for benefits by October 1, 1998. It is agreed that he did not do that. He filed his action in Washington on September 21, 1999. Thus, says Co-Operators, at the time he filed his claim in Washington, Mr. Forsen was out of time under the *Workers Compensation Act* and therefore had no choice but to file in Washington. Co-Operators argued that this lack of choice at the time of filing the Washington State action is significant.

'[85] Co-Operators submitted that the language of the exclusion clause is unambiguous, the action must be taken "in lieu of" a claim under workers' compensation legislation. "In lieu of" is defined by *Black's Law Dictionary* as "instead of or in place of". Thus, counsel for Co-Operators submitted that two possible courses of conduct or options must be available to a person so that they may select between the two courses of conduct or options. When Mr. Forsen filed the Washington State action, the time for filing a claim under the *Workers Compensation Act* had long passed. If the workers' compensation claim was no longer available to him, it follows that the Washington State action could not be "in lieu of" it.

'[86] The argument is meretricious. Nothing in the wording of the clause in issue dictates that a choice must be available at the time of filing the action. On the contrary, the wording of s. 9 expressly deems an election to have been made where no notice of election is provided: "If the election is not made and notice given, it must be presumed that they have elected not to claim compensation under this Part; ..." (Emphasis added.)

'[87] I would dismiss the cross-appeal. *Marjak Services Ltd v Insurance Corp of British Columbia* [2004] BCJ No 1838, 244 DLR (4th) 700 (CA), per Ryan JA

IN OBEDIENCE TO

New Zealand [Section 39 of the Police Act 1958 provides immunity from prosecution to a memeber of the police doing anything "in obedience to" any process issued out of any Court, or by any Judge, District Court Judge, or Justice.] 'I regard these words as being equally applicable to the execution of a warrant whether expressed in mandatory or in authorising terms. In the latter case the warrant does not expressly require that it be executed, but if a police officer does execute it then he is acting

in obedience to it by doing so and by keeping within its authority. The obvious purpose of the section is against confining the word "obedience" to its narrow meaning of obedience to a command. The protection will not apply, however, if the officer goes beyond the warrant and conducts a search which he knows is beyond the purpose for which the warrant was issued. He cannot then claim to be acting in obedience to the warrant.' *Simpson v Attorney-General [Baigent's Case]* [1994] 3 NZLR 667 at 716, CA, per McKay J

IN PUBLIC

Australia [Section 31(1)(a)(iii) of the Copyright Act 1968 (Cth) provides that copyright in relation to a work, is the exclusive right to, inter alia, perform the work 'in public'.] 'The phrase in s 31(1)(a)(iii) of the 1968 Act is "to perform the work *in public*" not before "members of the public" or "a public audience" or "the general public". Running through the authorities I have discussed is the notion that for the purposes of this performing right a performance will be "in public" if it is not "in private", and the perception of an antithesis between performances which are in public and those which are "domestic" or "private" in character. In determining whether a performance answers the latter description, the nature of the audience is important. In coming together to form the audience for the performance were the persons concerned bound together by a domestic or private tie or by an aspect of their public life? Their "public life" would include their presence at their place of employment for the supply of a performance to assist the commercial purposes of their employer.

'Looked at in that way, the reasoning in the authorities supports the proposition in [Wei, *The Law of Copyright in Singapore*, 1989] that if a performance occurs as an adjunct to a commercial activity the performance is likely to be regarded as public, indeed, in the learned author's view "almost certainly so".' *Australasian Performing Right Association Ltd v Commonwealth Bank of Australia* (1992) 111 ALR 671 at 685, per Gummow J

IN RELATION TO

Australia 'It may be accepted that there will always be a question of degree involved where the issue is the relationship between two subject matters. The words "in relation to" are wide words which do no more, at least without reference to context, than signify the need for there to be some relationship or connection between two subject matters: see *Smith v Federal Commissioner of Taxation* (1987) 164 CLR 513 at 533 per Toohey J and *PMT Partners Pty Ltd (in liq) v Australian National Parks and Wildlife Service* (1995) 184 CLR 301 at 328 per Toohey and Gummow JJ. But the phrase is both "vague and indefinite": see per Taylor J in *Tooheys Ltd v Cmr of Stamp Duties (NSW)* (1961) 105 CLR 602 at 620. Like the phrase "in respect of", the phrase "in relation to" will not, at least normally, apply to any connection or relationship no matter how remote: see *Technical Products Pty Ltd v State Government Insurance Office (Qld)* (1989) 167 CLR 45 at 51 per Dawson J. The extent of the relationship required will depend upon the context in which the words are used.

'As Beaumont and Lehane JJ said in *Joye v Beach Petroleum NL* (1996) 67 FCR 275 at 285 in discussing a number of the cases dealing with "relates to":

"… it will depend upon context whether it is necessary that the relationship be direct or substantial, or whether an indirect or less than substantial connection will suffice." '

'… What is required is that there be a connection, which, while direct or indirect, close or even distant, can fairly be described as one which relates to the particular subject matter under consideration which here is (to paraphrase it) international trade.' *Australian Competition and Consumer Commission v Maritime Union of Australia* (2001) 187 ALR 487; (2002) ATPR ¶41–849; BC200106710; [2001] FCA 1549 at [68], [69], [74] per Hill J

IN RESPECT OF

[By virtue of the Policyholders Protection Act 1975, where an insurance company becomes insolvent the Financial Services Compensation Scheme (the Scheme) is obliged to indemnify the policyholder in respect of compulsory insurance for any damages and costs for which it is found liable to an employee. By the terms of the policy in the instant case, a claimant's costs were to be allowed where they were 'in connection' with the claim to which the indemnity applied and defence costs were similarly indemnified if they were 'in relation to' the claim. A dispute arose as to whether the Scheme was liable to pay the policyholders' costs for defending the claim against its employee. Section 6(4) of the Act requires the Scheme to secure that a sum equal to the full amount of any liability of a company in liquidation towards any policyholder under the terms of any policy to which s 6 section applies is

paid to the policyholder as soon as reasonably practicable after the beginning of the liquidation. Inter alia s 6(5) states that the indemnity does not apply otherwise than 'in respect of' a liability of the policyholder which is a liability subject to compulsory insurance. The judge at first instance had found that the Scheme was liable to pay the policyholders' costs of defending the claim and the Scheme appealed arguing that s 6(5) was to be narrowly construed so that it only related to established liabilities in respect of which the policy holder was obliged to have compulsorily insured.]

'[3] Once Independent became insolvent there has never been any dispute that by virtue of s 6(4) and (5) of the 1975 Act the Scheme was obliged to indemnify Geologistics for: (1) any damages for which Geologistics had been found liable to pay to the employee; (2) any costs which Geologistics had been found liable to pay the employee. The dispute related to whether the Scheme was obliged to pay the costs which Geologistics were as at the time of Independent's liquidation bound to pay their solicitors Davies Arnold Cooper (DAC) for defending the claim.

…

'[17] I do not get much assistance from the authorities. They simply demonstrate that the proper construction of the words will depend on their context.

'[18] I come back therefore to the wording of s 6(4) and (5) of the 1975 Act. If the narrow construction advocated by Sir Sydney were adopted in relation to s 6(5), that construction would have the following consequences: first there would be covered the damages for which Geologistics have been found liable in this case because those are damages for breach of an employer's duty to an employee, and the liability has been established; second unless the costs which Geologistics have been ordered to pay their employee whether in relation to the unsuccessful defence of the claim or the unsuccessful appeal are something in relation to which Geologistics were required "compulsorily" to carry insurance, those costs would be irrecoverable; third if the employee had in some interlocutory proceeding recovered an order for costs, but had then abandoned their action conceding there was no liability, those costs would not be recoverable (even in this instance if there was a requirement to compulsorily insure against the same); fourth costs of defending this claim against the claimant although recoverable under the terms of the policy if Independent had remained solvent, would not be recoverable unless there was a requirement to compulsorily insure against the same; fifth costs of defending any claim successfully, incurred with the approval of Independent and recoverable under the policy if Independent remained solvent, would be irrecoverable.

...

'[23] In any event it seems to me that the narrow construction placed on s 6(5) of the 1975 Act by Sir Sydney is inconsistent with there being the two subsections. If s 6(4) and (5) were intended to provide an indemnity against only that which was required to be the subject of compulsory insurance, s 6(4) could have so provided without the need for s 6(5). That alone supports the view that the words "otherwise than in respect of a liability of the policyholder which is a liability subject to compulsory insurance", must be intended to produce the result that what the policyholder can recover under s 6(4) goes beyond the liability which must be compulsorily insured. What is contemplated is therefore that under a policy which is required to be taken out, the policyholder will be entitled to recover against the insurance company some indemnity beyond that for which statute compels insurance, but by virtue of s 6(5) that right to indemnity must still be "in respect of ... the ... liability subject to compulsory insurance".

...

'[28] The points made do not in my view face up to the interpretation of the language of s 6(5). In s 6(5) the words are descriptive of the type of insurance. "In respect of" has to mean "in connection with", and that is the reason why a claimant's costs are recoverable. Once the narrow construction is rejected, and "in connection with" becomes the route to the claimant's costs being recovered, I do not see how defence costs "in connection with" or "in relation to" fall into some different or irrecoverable category. Certainly the object or purpose of the statute relied on does not require a strained construction to be placed on s 6(5) to achieve that result.

'[29] What then it may be said is s 6(5) concerned with? The answer is clear. Many policies as indeed the very policy with which this appeal is concerned, cover matters for which insurance is not compulsory. One could have claims falling both under a section relating to compulsory insurance and a section of the policy concerned with non-compulsory insurance. Clearly the Scheme was not intended by s 6(4) to cover matters which were not the subject of compulsory insurance nor any costs incurred in respect of the same. Section 6(5) is intended to make that position clear and no more.' *R (on the application of*

Geologistics Ltd) v Financial Services Compensation Scheme [2003] EWCA Civ 1905 at [3], [17]–[18], [23], [28]–[29], [2004] 3 All ER 39, CA, per Waller LJ

Australia 'Of the words "in respect of", Brennan, Deane and Gaudron JJ said, admittedly in another context, in *Technical Products Pty Ltd v State Government Insurance (Qld)* (1989) 167 CLR 45 at 47; 85 ALR 173 at 175 : "The words "in respect of" have a very wide meaning. Indeed, they have a chameleon-like quality in that they commonly reflect the context in which they appear. The nexus between legal liability and motor vehicle which their use introduces in s 3(1) is a broad one which is not susceptible of precise definition. That nexus will not, however, exist unless there be some discernible and rational link between the basis of legal liability and the particular motor vehicle." ' *Fraser v Deputy Commissioner of Taxation* (1996) 138 ALR 689 at 700, per Beaumont J

Canada 'The phrase "in respect of" was considered by this court in *Nowegijick v Canada* (1983) 144 DLR (3d) 193 at 200, [1983] 1 SCR 29, [1983] CTC 20:

> The words "in respect of" are, in my opinion, words of the widest possible scope. They *import such meanings as "in relation to"*, "with reference to" or "in connection with". The phrase "in respect of" is probably the widest of any expression intended to convey some connection between two related subject-matters.

'(Emphasis added.) In my view, these comments are equally applicable to the phrase "relating to". The Pocket Oxford Dictionary, 7th edn (1984) defines the word "relation" as follows:

> ... what one person or thing has to do with another, way in which one stands or is related to another, kind of connection or correspondence or contrast or feeling that prevails between persons or things ...

'So, both the connecting phrases of s 241(3) suggest that a wide rather than narrow view should be taken when considering whether a proposed disclosure is in respect of proceedings relating to the administration or enforcement of the Income Tax Act.' *Slattery (Trustee of) v Slattery* (1993) 106 DLR (4th) 212 at 226, per Iacobucci J (Can SC)

Canada '[26] The appellant's submission turns on whether these proceedings are undertaken "in respect of a cause of action". The words "in respect of" have been held by this Court to be words of the broadest scope that convey some link between two subject matters. See *Nowegijick v. The Queen*, [1983] 1 S.C.R. 29, at p. 39, *per* Dickson J. (as he then was):

> The words "in respect of" are, in my opinion, words of the widest possible scope. They import such meanings as "in relation to", "with reference to" or "in connection with". The phrase "in respect of" is probably the widest of any expression intended to convey some connection between two related subject matters.'

Markevich v Canada (2003) 223 DLR (4th) 17 at 31 (SCC), per Major J

IN RESPECT OF *SEE ALSO* IN RELATION TO

IN RESPECT OF THE EMPLOYMENT

Australia ['Fringe benefit' is defined in s 136(1) of the Fringe Benefits Tax Assessment Act 1986 (Cth) to include 'a benefit provided ... to the employee or to an associate of the employee ... by ... the employer ... in respect of the employment of the employee ...'] 'While the width of the definition of "fringe benefit" was designed to capture benefits that, in truth, were other than remuneration, the stated purpose [to "ensure that all forms of remuneration paid to employees bear a fair measure of tax"] suggests that asking whether the benefit is a product or incident of the employment will be helpful. If it is not then the benefit is likely to be extraneous to the employment and will not bear [fringe benefits tax], notwithstanding that the employment might have been a causal factor in the provision of the benefit. In particular, the fact that a benefit is provided to a director because it was authorised by that director will not, of itself, be sufficient to characterise the benefit as one which is "in respect of" the employment. Without more, it is not a product or incident of that office.

'[29] To put the matter another way, although the process of characterising the benefit provided in a particular case can involve questions of fact and degree, it is not sufficient for the purposes of the Act merely to inquire whether there is some causal connection between the benefit and the employment: see *Commissioner of Taxation v Rowe* (1995) 60 FCR 99 at 114 and 123. Although Brennan, Deane and Gaudron JJ observed in [*Technical Products Pty Ltd v State Government*

Insurance Office (Qld) (1989) 167 CLR 45; 85 ALR 173; 8 MVR 385; 63 ALJR 392] (at 47), that the requisite connection will not exist unless there is "some discernible and rational link" between the two subject matters which the statute requires to be linked, as was pointed out by Dawson J (at 51), the connection must be "material".' *J & G Knowles & Associates Pty Ltd v Federal Commissioner of Taxation* (2000) ATC 4151; 44 ATR 22; BC200000725; [2000] FCA 196 at [28], [29], per Heerey, Merkel and Finkelstein JJ

IN THE COURSE OF A BUSINESS

[Defendant, who had been a fisherman for 20 years, sold a fishing boat which he had used for his business and bought another. He contended that this was not a sale of goods 'in the course of a business' and thus did not give rise to an implied term that the vessel was of merchantable quality under the Sale of Goods Act 1979, s 14(2).] 'In approaching the construction of the words "in the course of a business", it is of course the task of the court to construe s 14(2) as it appears in the 1979 Act. In that respect, not only does s 14(2) embody a deliberate change in the wording of its equivalent in the 1893 Act, but it is to be construed as part of an overall code embodied in the 1979 Act which is different and more extensive in nature from the codification contained in its predecessor.

...

'It seems to me clear that, free of any constraints imposed by the decisions to which we have been referred, this court, making use of the tools of construction now available to it, should construe the words of s 14(2) of the SOGA 1979 at their wide face value. In my view, it is not necessary to do more than to turn to the statutory change of wording in s 14(2) as between the 1893 Act and s 3 of the Supply of Goods (Implied Terms) Act 1973 (which s 14(2) of SOGA 1979 simply re-enacted), to see that it was the intention of SOG(IT)A 1973 to widen the protection afforded to a purchaser by s 14(2) from a situation where the seller was a *dealer* in the type of goods sold, to one where he simply made a sale "in the course of a business"; the requirement for regularity of dealing, or indeed any dealing, in the goods was removed. Given the removal of that requirement there is, on the face of it, no reason or warrant (at any rate in a civil rather than a criminal context) to re-introduce some implied qualification, difficult to define, in order to narrow what appears to be the wide scope and apparent purpose of the words, which is to distinguish between a sale made in the course of a seller's business and a purely private sale of goods outside the confines of the business (if any) carried on by the seller.' *Stevenson v Rogers* [1999] 1 All ER 613 at 623, CA, per Potter LJ (holding that the sale was a sale in the course of a business)

IN THE COURSE OF HIS EMPLOYMENT

[By the Race Relations Act 1976, s 32(1), anything done by a person 'in the course of his employment' is to be treated for the purposes of the Act as done by his employer as well as by him. The plaintiff was ill-treated by fellow employees.] 'When an industrial tribunal is considering whether, for the purposes of s 32(1) any conduct complained of does or does not amount to a "thing done by a person in the course of his employment", is the tribunal bound to answer that by reference to: (a) the words "course of employment" in the sense in which they are employed in everyday speech; or (b) the principles laid down by case law for the establishment of vicarious liability by an employer for the torts committed by an employee during the course of his employment?
...
'It would be particularly wrong to allow racial harassment on the scale that was suffered by the complainant in this case at the hands of his workmates — treatment that was wounding both emotionally and physically — to slip through the net of employer responsibility by applying to it a common law principle evolved in another area of the law to deal with vicarious responsibility for wrongdoing of a wholly different kind. To do so would seriously undermine the statutory scheme of the Discrimination Acts and flout the purposes which they were passed to achieve.
'The tribunals are free, and are indeed bound, to interpret the ordinary and readily understandable words "in the course of employment" in the sense in which every layman would understand them ... The application of the phrase will be a question of fact for each industrial tribunal to resolve, in the light of the circumstances presented to it, with a mind unclouded by any parallels sought to be drawn from the law of vicarious liability in tort.' *Jones v Tower Boot Co Ltd* [1997] 2 All ER 406 at 413, 416, CA, per Waite LJ

IN THE NATURE OF A COMMERCIAL VENTURE

[Council Directive (EEC) 77/197 (the directive) is designed to safeguard the rights of employees on the transfer of undertakings and art 1 of the directive states that it applies to 'the transfer of an undertaking, business or part of a business to another employer as a result of a legal transfer or merger'. In the Transfer of Undertakings (Protection of Employment) Regulations 1981 (TUPE), by which the United Kingdom attempted to give effect to the directive, 'undertaking' is defined in reg 2(1) as including 'any trade or business' but not to include 'any undertaking or part of an undertaking which is not in the nature of a commercial venture'. A local authority transferred its refuse collection service to a company and the claimants claimed that by defining 'undertaking' in TUPE as not including an undertaking which was not in the nature of a commercial venture, the United Kingdom had erroneously excluded the transfer of the refuse service from protection.] '[30] The distinction that Mr Underhill makes between the refuse disposal service before transfer and the same undertaking after transfer is that before transfer it was not operated for profit whereas after transfer it is so operated. It is not possible to see any reason in principle why employees should not have the protection of TUPE when their employers, who do not operate for profit the undertaking in which they are employed, transfer that undertaking to employers who intend to operate it for profit. The truth is, of course, that the wording of TUPE was designed to do no more and no less than give effect to the acquired rights directive. The aquired rights directive draws no such distinction.
'[31] Our conclusion is that where (i) the undertaking after transfer is a commercial venture and (ii) the undertaking before transfer had all the characteristics that it had after transfer, save that it was not operated for profit, the undertaking before transfer will normally be capable of being described as "in the nature of" a commercial venture. We are satisfied that that is so in the present case. The elastic phrase "in the nature of" bridges the gap between before and after and enables the provisions of TUPE, prior to amendment in 1993, to be read in a manner which accords with the acquired rights directive.' *Alderson v Secretary of State for Trade and Industry* [2003] EWCA Civ 1767 at [30]–[31], [2004] 1 All ER 1148, CA, per Lord Phillips of Worth Matravers MR

IN THE ORDINARY COURSE OF BUSINESS

New Zealand [Section 266 of the Companies Act 1955.] 'The phrase "in the ordinary course of business" in the context of s 266(2)(b) was considered briefly by Hansen J in *Builders*

Hardware Co Ltd v Steel (High Court, Christchurch, M 386/94, 15 March 1995). The learned Judge accepted the dictum of Somers J in the Court of Appeal in *Julius Harper Ltd v F W Hagedorn & Sons Ltd* [1991] 1 NZLR 530; the Court of Appeal had adopted the view of Rich J in the High Court of Australia in *Downs Distributing Co Pty Ltd v Associated Blue Star Stores Pty Ltd (In Liquidation)* (1948) 76 CLR 463, 477:

> "... it does suppose that according to the ordinary and common flow of transactions in affairs of business there is a course, an ordinary course. It means that the transaction must fall into place as part of the undistinguished common flow of business done, that it should form part of the ordinary course of business as carried on, calling for no remark and arising out of no special or particular situation."

'The Court of Appeal in *Hagedorn* had to determine the meaning of the phrase in a debenture given by a company—"ordinary course of its business"—meaning the business of the company under consideration. Nevertheless, the Court adopted Rich J's interpretation of the phrase "ordinary course of business".

'I consider that the tests imposed in the Australian cases, as adopted by the Court of Appeal, of the phrase "ordinary course of business" impute an objective view of the course of business rather than a subjective one such as the way in which particular parties carry on their business. As was pointed out by Kennedy J in the Supreme Court of Western Australia in *Katoa Pty Ltd (In Liquidation) v Dartnall* (1983) 74 FLR 202, 205:

> "The dividing line between transactions which are and those which are not in the ordinary course of business is not always easy to define in a particular case." '

James Hardie Building Products Ltd v Meltzer [1996] 2 NZLR 506 at 510, per Barker J

IN THE PRESENCE OF

[For 50 Halsbury's Laws (4th edn) para 261 see now 50 Halsbury's Laws (4th edn) (Reissue) para 310.]

IN TRADE

New Zealand [Section 9 of the Fair Trading Act 1986] ' "Trade" is defined [in the Fair Trading Act 1986] to include any activity of commerce

relating to the supply of goods. There is authority the promotional activities of a trade association or organisation fall within that description: e g *Glorie v W A Chip & Pulp Co Pty Ltd* (1981) ATPR 40–259; *Kosky v Outstanding Doors* (High Court, Auckland, HC 246/94, 6 June 1995, Fisher J).' *Pharmaceutical Management Agency Ltd v Research Medicines Industry Association New Zealand Inc* [1996] 1 NZLR 472 at 475, per McGechan J

IN TRADE OR COMMERCE

Australia [Section 52, Trade Practices Act 1974 (Cth).] '[27] The preliminary question was initially argued before a single Judge of this Court who answered it in the affirmative. On appeal to the High Court that decision was reversed. The relevant reasoning appears at 602–604 (per Mason CJ, Deane, Dawson & Gaudron JJ):

> "It is well established that the words 'trade' and 'commerce', when used in the context of s 51(i) of the Constitution, are not terms of art but are terms of common knowledge of the widest import. The same may be said of those words as used in s 52(1) of the Act. Indeed, in the light of the provisions of s 6(2) of the Act which give an extended operation to s 52 and which clearly use the words 'trade' and 'commerce' in the sense which the words bear in s 51(i) of the Constitution, it would be difficult to maintain that those words were used in s 52 with some different meaning. The real problem involved in the construction of s 52 of the Act does not, however, spring from the use of the words 'trade or commerce'. It arises from the requirement that the conduct to which the section refers be 'in' trade or commerce. Plainly enough, what is encompassed in the plenary grant of legislative power 'with respect to ... Trade and commerce' in s 51(i) of the Constitution is not of assistance on the question of the effect of the word 'in' as part of the requirement that the conduct proscribed by s 52(1) of the Act be 'in trade or commerce'.

> "The phrase 'in trade or commerce' in s 52 has a restrictive operation. It qualifies the prohibition against engaging in conduct of the specified kind. As a matter of language, a prohibition against engaging in conduct 'in trade or commerce' can be construed as encompassing conduct in the course of the myriad of activities which are not, of their

nature, of a trading or commercial character but which are undertaken in the course of, or as incidental to, the carrying on of an overall trading or commercial business. If the words 'in trade or commerce' in s 52 are construed in that sense, the provisions of the section would extend, for example, to a case where the misleading or deceptive conduct was a failure by a driver to give the correct handsignal when driving a truck in the course of a corporation's haulage business. It would also extend to a case, such as the present, where the alleged misleading or deceptive conduct consisted of the giving of inaccurate information by one employee to another in the course of carrying on the building activities of a commercial builder. Alternatively, the reference to conduct 'in trade or commerce' in s 52 can be construed as referring only to conduct which is itself an aspect or element of activities or transactions which, of their nature, bear a trading or commercial character. So construed, to borrow and adapt words used by Dixon J in a different context in *Bank of NSW v The Commonwealth* [(1948) 76 CLR 1 at 381], the words 'in trade or commerce' refer to 'the central conception' of trade or commerce and not to the 'immense field of activities' in which corporations may engage in the course of, or for the purposes of, carrying on some overall trading or commercial business.

"As a matter of mere language, the arguments favouring and militating against these alternative constructions of s 52 are fairly evenly balanced. The scope of the prohibition ... is ... governed not only by 'the terms in which it is created' but by 'the context in which it is found' ... . In that regard, it is of particular significance that the words 'trade' and 'commerce' have 'about them a chameleon-like hue, readily adapting themselves to their surroundings'... S 52(2) precludes limiting the scope of s 52(1) by implication drawn from the contents of other provisions of Pt V. Nonetheless, when the section is read in the context provided by other features of the Act, which is 'An Act relating to certain Trade Practices', the narrower (ie the second) of the alternative constructions of the requirement 'in trade or commerce' is the preferable one. Indeed, in the context of Pt V of the Act with its heading 'Consumer Protection', it is plain that s 52 was not intended to extend to all conduct, regardless of its nature, in which

a corporation might engage in the course of, or for the purposes of, its overall trading or commercial business. Put differently, the section was not intended to impose, by a sidewind, an overlay of Commonwealth law upon every field of legislative control into which a corporation might stray for the purposes of, or in connection with, carrying on its trading or commercial activities. What the section is concerned with is the conduct of a corporation towards persons, be they consumers or not, with whom it (or those whose interests it represents or is seeking to promote) has or may have dealings in the course of those activities or transactions which, of their nature, bear a trading or commercial character. Such conduct includes, of course, promotional activities in relation to, or for the purposes of, the supply of goods or services to actual or potential consumers, be they identified persons or merely an unidentifiable section of the public. In some areas, the dividing line between what is and what is not conduct 'in trade or commerce' may be less clear and may require the identification of what imports a trading or commercial character to an activity which is not, without more, of that character. The point can be illustrated by reference to the examples mentioned above. The driving of a truck for the delivery of goods to a consumer and the construction of a building for another pursuant to a building contract are, no doubt, trade or commerce in so far as the relationship between supplier and actual or potential customer or between builder and building owner is concerned. That being so, to drive a truck with a competitor's name upon it in order to mislead the customer or to conceal a defect in a building for the purpose of deceiving the building owner may well constitute misleading or deceptive conduct 'in trade or commerce' for the purposes of s 52. On the other hand, the mere driving of a truck or construction of a building is not, without more, trade or commerce and to engage in conduct in the course of those activities which is divorced from any relevant actual or potential trading or commercial relationship or dealing will not, of itself, constitute conduct 'in trade or commerce' for the purposes of that section. That being so, the giving of a misleading handsignal by the driver of one of its trucks is not, in the relevant sense, conduct by a corporation 'in trade or commerce'. Nor, without more, is a misleading statement by one of a building company's own employees to another employee in the course of their ordinary activities. The position might well be different if the misleading statement was made in the course of, or for the purposes of, some trading or commercial dealing between the corporation and the particular employee."

'[28] The following propositions emerge from the above extract:

● The phrase "in trade or commerce" has a restrictive operation, in the sense that it narrows the operation of s 52.
● The phrase is capable of both a wider and a narrower interpretation.
● The wider interpretation would include "… the myriad of activities which are not, of their nature, of a trading or commercial character but which are undertaken in the course of, or as incidental to, the carrying on of an overall trading or commercial business."
● Such an approach would impose an overlay of Commonwealth law upon any area in which a corporation might act in carrying on its trading or commercial activities.
● The second, and narrower construction is that s 52 applies only to conduct "… which is itself an aspect or element of activities or transactions which, of their nature, bear a trading or commercial character."
● The narrower construction is correct.
● The section is concerned with the conduct of a corporation towards persons with whom it has, or may have dealings in the course of its trading activities or transactions which dealings, of their nature, bear a trading or commercial character.
● The dividing line between conduct which is in trade or commerce and conduct which is not may be unclear, in which case it may be necessary to identify the features which import a trading or commercial character to an activity which would not, without more, have that character.
● The mere driving of a truck or construction of a building is not, without more, in trade or commerce.
● To engage in conduct which is divorced from any relevant actual or potential trading or commercial relationship or dealing will not, of itself, constitute conduct "in trade or commerce" for the purposes of the section.

…

'[33] Brennan J disposed of the matter upon the basis that the injured party was not misled or likely to be misled in his capacity as a consumer. However his Honour also said something about the alternative basis for limiting the operation of s 52 preferred by the majority and by Toohey J. At 606 Brennan J said:

"Although I agree with the majority that the phrase 'in trade or commerce' qualifies the operation of s 52, I am respectfully unable to agree that that phrase restricts the operation of s 52 to conduct which is in itself of a trading or commercial character. The question whether conduct is engaged in 'in trade or commerce' cannot be answered by reference to the conduct divorced from the circumstances in which it is engaged in; it can be answered only by reference to the surrounding circumstances. Those are the circumstances 'in' which the conduct is engaged in. There is no scalpel of principle which can dissect the conduct out of the activity or transaction 'in' which it is embedded. Therefore, in my opinion, if misleading or deceptive conduct occurs in the course of carrying on an activity or carrying out a transaction of a trading or commercial character, the test imported by the phrase 'in trade or commerce' is satisfied.

"The activity in which the defendant corporation was engaging in this case — building construction for reward — was its business and was clearly a trading activity. It is therefore unnecessary to consider the different meanings which may be attributed to the terms 'trade' and 'commerce' in differing contexts. The conduct on which the plaintiff relies was engaged in in the course of and as an integral part of the defendant corporation's trade.

"There is only one argument of substance which might be thought to justify a reading down of the general language of s 52 by restricting the meaning of the phrase 'in trade or commerce', namely, that s 52 can hardly have been intended to apply across the broad canvas of activities which reach out to the periphery of trade or commerce."

'[34] His Honour then went on to explain that his preferred approach, limiting the protection offered by s 52 to consumers, avoided the need to adopt a narrow construction of the expression "in trade or commerce", which approach his Honour obviously considered to be unsatisfactory.

'[35] The approach taken by McHugh J was similar in most respects to that adopted by Brennan J. His Honour first held that the s 52 protection should be limited to consumers. Having set out reasons for this conclusion his Honour then observed (at 619) that it appeared to be "almost paradoxical" to take a broad view as to the operation of s 52 (by rejecting the notion that it was limited to consumer protection) and, at the same time, to construe narrowly the expression "in trade or commerce". In particular, his Honour observed at 619–620:

"If the general words of the section require that it be read as going beyond the protection of consumers, then I can see no reason for confining those words to misleading or deceptive conduct of a trading or commercial character or to conduct in the course of activities which are of the essence of trade or commerce. Rather the general nature of the words would require them to be read as including any misleading or deceptive conduct which occurs in the course of trade or commerce. It would seem most unlikely that the Parliament, ex hypothesi, having gone beyond consumer protection, would intend those general words to proscribe only some kinds of misleading or deceptive conduct occurring in the course of trade or commerce.

"Moreover, to interpret the words 'in trade or commerce' by reference to the trading or commercial character of the conduct rather than by reference to its relationship with the course of trade or commerce must result in a reduction of protection for consumers, the very persons whose interests Pt V was intended to protect."

'[36] In summary, in both the reasons of the majority and those of Toohey J, the focus is upon the conduct which is said to be misleading or deceptive and the circumstances in which it occurred. It is not a question of assessing the degree of "proximity" between the relevant conduct and the overall business undertaking of the relevant corporation. That is not to say that the nature of such undertaking may not be relevant to the question of whether or not the conduct in question occurred "in trade or commerce". See for example *Tobacco Institute of Australia Ltd v Australian Federation of Consumer Organisations Inc* (1992) 38 FCR 1. I will discuss that decision at a later stage.' *Hearn v O'Rourke* [2003] FCAFC 78 per Dowsett J; BC200302019

IN TRANSIT

Australia 'The ordinary meaning of "transit" essentially connotes that goods are in motion between two points, but the period of transit may continue during intervals or periods when they may be loaded or unloaded and temporarily housed provided that this is reasonably referable to the furtherance of the carriage of goods to the final destination. The notion of "in transit" accepts that the movement of the goods may be interrupted by circumstances associated with the requirements of their transportation.' *NEC Australia Pty Ltd v Gamit Pty Ltd* (1993) 42 FCR 410 at 417–418, per Lockhart J

New Zealand '... there is no universal answer to the question what is meant by transit. It is a matter of construing the words used in the particular contract, and applying them to the facts.' *Kelly v National Insurance Co of New Zealand Ltd* [1995] 1 NZLR 641 at 646, CA, per cur

IN WHICH THE BUSINESS OF A CATERER WAS CONDUCTED

New Zealand [Sale of Liquor Act 1989, s 36(5).] '[F]or s 36(5) to apply, the premises concerned must be the operational headquarters of a "caterer's" business and must therefore be the premises from which food for "receptions, functions, or other social gatherings" is provided, complemented by the provision of liquor, if that is required.' *Bar Systems (New Zealand) Ltd v Wellington District Licensing Agency* [1996] 3 NZLR 100 at 107, per Goddard J

INABILITY

Australia 'The meaning of the term "inability" in the phrase "inability to obtain appropriate clinical management" was considered by a Full Court of this Court in *Brew v Repatriation Commission* (1999) 94 FCR 80. At first instance, Sundberg J said ((1999) 56 ALD 403):

"[10] It was submitted that the Tribunal had misconstrued factor (e). The meaning of 'inability' is that given by the *Macquarie Dictionary* (2nd ed 1991) — 'lack of ability; lack of power, capacity, means'. See also the *New Shorter Oxford English Dictionary* (1993) — 'The condition of being unable; lack of ability, power or means'. The tribunal was in my view correct in saying that a person who chooses not to seek medical treatment is not for that reason unable to obtain it. The word 'inability' is directed to an objective barrier to obtaining treatment, such as the absence of medical officers, and not to a lack of willingness to obtain treatment. It was also argued that the applicant was unable to obtain medical treatment because she did not during her service know she had varicose veins. If this would otherwise be an 'inability' for the purposes of factor (e), it is ruled out by cl 2 of the SoP, because her lack of awareness is not a factor that is related to her service."

On appeal, it was argued that Sundberg J had erred in focusing on the "objective barriers" to obtaining appropriate clinical management. The majority of the Full Court in the judgment of Merkel J agreed with by Mansfield J, said (at 87 paras[23]–[28]):

"[23] The primary contention of the appellant was that the AAT and Sundberg J had misconstrued cl1(e) by focusing entirely upon 'objective barriers' to obtaining appropriate clinical treatment and thereby failing to have regard to 'subjective barriers' to obtaining treatment. It was contended that in a particular case, but more specifically in the present case, the subjective barriers believed by the appellant to exist were capable of constituting or resulting in an 'inability' to obtain appropriate clinical management for her varicose veins.

"[24] Counsel for the respondent did not dispute that subjective factors may, in an appropriate case, constitute or result in an inability to obtain appropriate clinical management but submitted that, as the arbiter of fact, it was plainly open to the AAT to conclude from the material before it that the matters relied upon by the appellant did not fall within cl1(e).

"[25] It is well established that the Court is here concerned with beneficial legislation intended to confer significant benefits on veterans with the consequence that a beneficial, rather than a strict or narrow, approach should be taken to the construction of the legislation. In the present context that means that whether 'inability' is established in a particular case is to be approached as a matter of practical reality rather than by a theoretical approach to that issue.

"[26] In my view Sundberg J was quite correct in treating the meaning of 'inability' in cl (1)(e) as 'lack of ability; lack of power, capacity, means' (The *Macquarie Dictionary*)

or 'the condition of being unable; lack of ability, power or means' (The *New Shorter Oxford Dictionary*). The dictionary definitions embrace what may fairly be described as objective barriers such as lack of power, capacity or means or a subjective barrier such as the 'condition of being unable'. Whether the objective or subjective barrier to obtaining treatment is made out in a particular case depends upon the facts of that case".' *Brown v Repatriation Commission* [2003] FCA 1130 at [11], [12] per Cooper J; BC200306102

Canada [Social assistance was available for person in need because of inability to find regular employment.] 'The ordinary meaning of inability is "the condition of being unable; lack of ability, power or means": The New Shorter Oxford English Dictionary (1993), vol 1, p 1331.

'In the context of this regulatory scheme, it seems to me that a person in need by reason of inability to obtain regular employment is a person who is unable to find a regular job for a reason beyond that person's control. At least the expression "inability to obtain regular employment" connotes something more than being unavailable for work or being unemployed no matter what the reason.' *Kerr v Social Services of Metropolitan Toronto* (*General Manager*) (1995) 121 DLR (4th) 250 at 260–261, Ont CA

INAPPROPRIATE

Canada 'The appellant points to the *Canadian Oxford Dictionary* (1998) definition of "inappropriate", at p 712, as being "not appropriate" or "unsuitable". As noted above, in *Dergousoff, supra*, Cameron JA also used the term "unsuitable" to describe the meaning of the word "inappropriate". Abella JA also recognized at p 490 that the ordinary or plain meaning of "the word inappropriate appears, on the surface, to be wide in its discretionary reach". I agree that the ordinary meaning of this word is "unsuitable". This view is further reinforced by reference to the French text of s 4 of the [Child Support] Guidelines which reads: "*si le tribunal est d'avis que ce montant n'est pas indiqué*" (emphasis added). The English equivalents of the term "*indiqué*" given in *Le Robert & Collins Super Senior* (1995) are "advisable", "suitable", and "appropriate". I find no ambiguity in the language of s 4 of the Guidelines.

'Nor do I think that the plain language of s 4 leads to an absurd result. Turning to the broader context, the word "inappropriate" is also found in s 3(2)(b) of the Guidelines, which deals with children over the age of majority. Abella JA acknowledges, at p 491 of her reasons, that for the purposes of s 3(2)(b) "inappropriate" means that "a more flexible needs and means analysis can be undertaken". This statement would seem to indicate that she agrees that trial judges have the discretion to both increase and reduce Guideline figures under s 3(2)(b). Yet despite the similarity between the wording of ss 3(2)(b) and 4, Abella JA finds that the word "inappropriate" means "inadequate" for the purposes of s 4 and therefore authorizes only increases from the Table amounts in cases where the paying parent has an income of more than $150,000 per annum. With respect, such an interpretation is inconsistent with the established principle that where the same word is used on multiple occasions in a statute, one is to give the same meaning to that word throughout the statute: see *R v Zeolkowski* [1989] 1 SCR 1378, at p 1387; *Thomson v Canada* (*Deputy Minister of Agriculture*) [1992] 1 SCR 385, at p 400; *Driedger on the Construction of Statutes* (3rd edition 1994), at p 163.

...

'Based on the wording of s 1 and the legislative history, a fair description of the purpose of the Guidelines is to establish fair levels of support for children from both parents upon marriage breakdown, in a predictable and consistent manner. They are designed to ensure, as I said in a different context in *Chartier, supra*, at para 32, "that a divorce will affect the children as little as possible", or as the Minister said, to put children first. Indeed, s 4(b)(ii) itself emphasizes the centrality of the actual situation of the children by expressly requiring that the "condition, means, needs and other circumstances of the children" be considered in the assessment of an appropriate amount of support payable in respect of income over $150,000. In my opinion, it is not at all clear from the statute or the words of the Minister that any single element of this general legislative purpose is to be given more weight than any other, and certainly not more weight than the actual circumstances in which the children find themselves. While Abella JA is correct to point out that predictability, consistency and efficiency are among the Guidelines' objectives, these are not the only considerations. I thus respectfully disagree with the Court of Appeal's suggestion that these legislative objectives dictate that child support awards can never be reduced under s 4.

'A proper construction of s 4 requires that the objectives of predictability, consistency and efficiency on the one hand, be balanced with those of fairness, flexibility and recognition of the actual "condition, means, needs and other circumstances of the children" on the other. Furthermore, this balancing must take into account the ordinary meaning of the word "inappropriate", as well as its use elsewhere in the statute. In my opinion, the plain language of s 4 is consistent with such an interpretation. Accordingly, the word "inappropriate" in this section must be broadly defined to mean "unsuitable" rather than merely "inadequate". Courts thus have the discretion to both increase and reduce the amount of child support prescribed by the strict application of the Guidelines in cases where the paying parent has an annual income exceeding $150,000. I would note that the respondent did not take issue with this interpretation in either her written or oral submissions.' *Francis v Baker* [1999] 3 SCR 250 at 267, 268, 269, 270, per Bastarache J

INCAPACITY

[For 24 Halsbury's Laws (4th edn) paras 492–493 see now 5(3) Halsbury's Laws (4th edn) (Reissue) paras 4–5.]

Australia 'The word "incapacity" is defined by s 3(1) of the [Work Health Act 1986 (NT)] to mean "an inability or limited ability to undertake paid work because of an injury". The right to receive weekly compensation under the Act depends upon there being, inter alia, incapacity (see s 53) which in broad terms, is productive of financial loss to the worker (see s 64 and s 65). However, neither the above definition of incapacity nor the other provisions of the Act require or compel a conclusion that all incapacity ceases once a worker is able to return to employment which is as well paid as that which he would have earned but for the injury. A person might have the capacity to work in several fields of employment. Supposing, as a result of an injury, he loses the ability to work in all of those fields except one, and he obtains employment in the one field left open to him with the result that there is no financial loss, it could not be said that the worker no longer had a limited ability to undertake paid work because of his injury. The receipt, post injury, of the same or higher wages than that received pre-injury has long been rejected as sufficient to deny the existence of partial incapacity for work: see *Thompson v Armstrong and Royse Pty Ltd* (1950) 81 CLR 585; *Arnotts*

Snack Products Pty Ltd v Yacob (1985) 155 CLR 171; 57 ALR 229; *Watkins Ltd v Renata* (1985) 8 FCR 65 especially at 68–9; 61 ALR 153 especially at 156–7.' *Foresight Pty Ltd v Maddick* (1991) 79 NTR 17 at 19, per Mildren J

INCHMAREE CLAUSE

[For 25 Halsbury's Laws (4th edn) para 168 see now 25 Halsbury's Laws (4th edn) (2003 Reissue) para 344.]

INCHOATE

Australia [Gray J, in a discussion of inchoate offences, noted the following.] ' "The term 'inchoate' is not one in general use. It stems from the Latin 'inchoare' which means to start work on and it therefore can be defined as only partly formed or just begun … [T]he common thread amongst these crimes is that they are committed even though the substantive offence that was intended is not completed and no harm is caused.": Bronitt and McSherry, Principles of Criminal Law, LBC Information Services, Sydney, 2001, p 431.' *R v Haines* (2001) 80 SASR 363; (2001) 216 LSJS 122; BC200106583; [2001] SASC 347 at note 9, per Gray J

Canada '[65] The criminalization of counselling the commission of an offence creates a form of secondary liability. Where the counselled offence is committed, the act of counselling constitutes participation; where the counselled offence is not committed, the crime is said to be inchoate. *Black's Law Dictionary* (8th ed. 2004) defines an inchoate crime as "[a] step toward the commission of another crime, the step in itself being serious enough to merit punishment". The rationale for imposing criminal liability for participation and inchoate offences is the same as that for primary liability. As noted by my colleague Fish J., the Law Reform Commission of Canada, as it was then called, provided a useful summary of the rationale in its Working Paper 45, *Secondary Liability: Participation in Crime and Inchoate Offences* (1985). I repeat it here for convenience:

> Primary liability attaches to the commission of acts which are outlawed as being harmful, as infringing important human interests and as violating basic social values. Secondary liability attaches on the same ground to their attempted commission, to counselling their commission and to assisting their commission.

This is clear with participation. If the primary act (for example, killing) is harmful, then doing it becomes objectionable. But if doing it is objectionable, it is also objectionable to get another person to do it, or help him do it. For while killing is objectionable because it causes actual harm (namely, death), so too inducing and assisting killing are objectionable because of the potential harm: they increase the likelihood of death occurring.

The same arguments hold for inchoate crimes. Again, if the primary act (for example, killing), is harmful, society will want people not to do it. Equally, it will not want them even to try to do it, or to counsel or incite others to do it. For while the act itself causes actual harm, attempting to do it, or counselling, inciting or procuring someone else to do it, are sources of potential harm – they increase the likelihood of that particular harm's occurrence. Accordingly, society is justified in taking certain measures in respect of them: outlawing them with sanctions, and authorizing intervention to prevent the harm from materializing. [Emphasis added; pp. 5–6.]'

R v Hamilton [2005] 2 SCR 432 at [65], [2005] SCJ No 48 (SCC), per Charron J

INCIDENTAL TO

[Under the Supreme Court Act 1981, s 51, the costs 'of and incidental to' the proceedings are in the discretion of the court.] '[11] In my judgment, save in exceptional cases, costs incurred by a defendant at the stage of a pre-action protocol, in dealing with and responding to issues which are subsequently dropped from the action when the proceedings are commenced, cannot be costs "incidental to" those proceedings. If, say, the original pre-action protocol claim letter included claims 1, 2, 3, 4, and 5, but the subsequent particulars of claim in the court proceedings were limited to claims 1, 2 and 5, it is very difficult to see how, in ordinary circumstances, the costs incurred in refuting original claims 3 and 4, which were not included within or formed any part of those subsequent proceedings, were costs incurred "incidental to" such proceedings.

…

'[16] Accordingly, I consider that, as a matter of principle, unless the circumstances are exceptional and thereby give rise to some sort of unreasonable conduct, costs incurred by a defendant at the pre-action protocol stage in successfully persuading a claimant to abandon a claim (either in whole or in part) are not costs incidental to any subsequent proceedings if, in those subsequent proceedings, such claims do not feature at all. Accordingly, such costs are not recoverable under s 51 of the 1981 Act. Mr Stewart, quite properly, does not suggest that there has been unreasonable conduct and does not suggest that this is in any way an exceptional case. Accordingly, I conclude as a matter of general principle that the costs thrown away, which are the subject matter of this application, are not recoverable under s 51.' *McGlinn v Waltham Contractors Ltd* [2005] EWHC 1419 (TCC) at [11], [16], [2005] 3 All ER 1126, per Judge Peter Coulson QC

INCITE *SEE* PROMOTE, INCITE OR INSTRUCT

INCLUDE

Canada '... "Include" as defined in the *Black's Law Dictionary* is a "[t]erm [which] may, according to context, express an enlargement and have the meaning of *and* or *in addition,* or merely specify a particular thing already included within general words theretofore used." "Including" within a statute is interpreted as a word of enlargement or of illustrative application as well as a word of limitation." ...' *Allen v Grenier* (1997) 145 DLR (4th) 286 at 293, per Mazza J (Ont Gen Div)

INCLUDES

Australia 'The use of the statutory formula "means ... and includes ..." to provide an expanded definition is not uncommon. The use may be such that the "and includes" shows that the "means" is not exclusive, in the discussion in Burrows, *Statute Law in New Zealand,* 2nd ed, 243–4.' *Howes v Dobson Developments Pty Ltd* BC200101611; [2001] NSWCA 96 at [148], per Giles JA

Australia 'The word "includes" has been given an exhaustive meaning where the context in which it appears indicates an intention to confine a general word by providing a limited list of words. Indeed, even though the primary meaning of "include" is expansive, where the words that follow would ordinarily fall within the meaning of the general word, the fact that they are expressed will often indicate an exhaustive or exclusive use of "includes". (See e g *YZ Finance Co v Cummings* (1964) 109 CLR 395 at 398–9, 401–2, 403; *Dilworth v Cmr of Stamps* [1899] AC 99 at 105–106. A number of authorities have recently

been discussed by Malcolm CJ in *R v Tkacz* [2001] WASCA 391 esp at [45]–[56]. See also Pearce and Geddes, *Statutory Interpretation in Australia* (5th ed) at 6.56–6.60.)

...

'... each of the lists contained in (c), (d) and (e) [of the Victims Support and Rehabilitation Act 1996 (NSW) Sch 1] is, in my present opinion, intended to provide an exhaustive list. In this context the word "include" in each of these paragraphs of cl 5 must be understood in the sense of "means and includes". I can see no statutory purpose to be served by a partial list of possible psychological and physical symptoms, let alone of possible disabilities. It would be the only such list in the Act.' *Victims Compensation Fund v Brown* (2002) 54 NSWLR 668; 129 A Crim R 538; BC200203034; [2002] NSWCA 155 at [30], [34] per Spigelman CJ

INCOME

Australia 'Income is not a technical concept. As used in the [Income Tax Assessment Act 1966 (Cth)] the word is to be construed in accordance with the ordinary usages of mankind: *Scott v Commissioner of Taxation* (*NSW*) (1935) 35 SR (NSW) 215.

'Perhaps the most usual usage of the word "income" in ordinary speech is to describe that which comes in as a reward for services. Amounts such as salary, wages, commission, tips and the like, are universally regarded as income and it is immaterial whether they are paid under or pursuant to a contract of service or services on the one hand, or gratuitously on the other. So, too, for income tax purposes, it would be immaterial whether an amount which is a reward for services is paid to the taxpayer in advance of the services being performed (eg, a signing-on fee) or after the services have been performed, or whether the payment is made by the person for whom the services are performed or by some other person. It will also be generally immaterial whether the amount paid is paid periodically or in a lump sum. What will matter is the character of the payment as a reward for services or, as it was put by Fullager J in *Hayes v FCT* (1956) 96 CLR 47 at 57–8, whether the receipt is a "product" of the taxpayer's services.' *Reuter v Federal Commissioner of Taxation* (1993) 111 ALR 716 at 730, per Hill J

Australia 'That expression "income according to ordinary concepts" has of course frequently appeared in reported authorities on income taxation in Australia. One instance is the dictum of Jordan CJ in *Scott v Federal Commissioner of Taxation* (1935) 35 SR (NSW) 215 at 219, cited by counsel for SGL in the present proceedings, as follows:

> The word "income" is not a term of art, and what forms of receipts are comprehended within it, and what principles are to be applied to ascertain how much of those receipts ought to be treated as income, must be determined in accordance with the ordinary concepts and usages of mankind, except in so far as the statute states or indicates an intention that receipts which are not income in ordinary parlance are to be treated as income, or that special rules are to be applied for arriving at the taxable amount of such receipts."

McNeil v Cmr of Taxation [2004] FCA 420 at [43] per Conti J; BC200401849

Australia [In the context of the sale of shares and trusts.] 'Turning to the ordinary meaning of the term "income", it appears to me that the income tax cases are of considerable assistance, and, in particular, [*Federal Commissioner of Taxation v Myer Emporium Ltd* (1987) 163 CLR 199] is of relevance. By way of background, I would note that the lack of definition of the term "income" in the Income Tax Assessment Act 1936 (Cth), s 25, meant that it was necessary for the courts to determine, for the purposes of that Act, what should in accordance with ordinary concepts and usages, be treated as income. Further, in determining what was income for that purpose, the distinction between income and capital gains which is a feature of trust law, was imported into the income tax cases: Laws of Australia 31.1 [13] and [17]. One would therefore expect the income tax cases to be dealing with income in its "ordinary" sense, in the absence of any special statutory provision to the contrary.

'In *Myer Emporium*, it is plain, in my view, that the Court considered that the receipts there in question were both income pursuant to s 25 of the Income Tax Assessment Act 1936 — that is, in its ordinary sense — and also in the special sense of profit arising from the carrying on of a profit-making undertaking pursuant to the particular provisions in s 26(a). It is not necessary, I think, to canvass the facts of *Myer Emporium* in detail, save to note that the receipt arose as a single, very large sum which resulted from one isolated transaction. At 209–210, Mason ACJ, Wilson, Brennan, Deane and Dawson JJ said the following:

> Because a business is carried on with a view to profit, a gain made in the ordinary course

of carrying on the business is invested with the profit-making purpose, thereby stamping the profit with the character of income. But a gain made otherwise than in the ordinary course of carrying on the business which nevertheless arises from a transaction entered into by the taxpayer with the intention or purpose of making a profit or gain may well constitute income. Whether it does depends very much on the circumstances of the case. Generally speaking, however, it may be said that if the circumstances are such as to give rise to the inference that the taxpayer's intention or purpose in entering into the transaction was to make a profit or gain, the profit or gain will be income, notwithstanding that the transaction was extraordinary judged by reference to the ordinary course of the taxpayer's business. Nor does the fact that a profit or gain is made as the result of an isolated venture or a "one-off" transaction preclude it from being properly characterized as income: *Federal Commission of Taxation v Whitfords Beach Pty Ltd* (1982) 150 CLR 355 at pp 366–367, 376.

'That the concept of income for trust purposes and for the purposes of s 25 of the Income Tax Assessment Act 1936 would be relevantly the same, appears from the discussion at 215, where their Honours observed:

> The periodicity, regularity and recurrence of a receipt has been considered to be a hallmark of its character as income in accordance with the ordinary concepts and usages of mankind. Likewise, the need to distinguish capital and income for trust purposes and other purposes has focused attention on the difference between the right to receive future income and the receipt of that income, a difference which has given rise to the analogical difference between the fruit and the tree: see *Shepherd v Federal Commissioner of Taxation* (1965) 113 CLR 385 at p 396.
>
> …
>
> For present purposes it is sufficient for us to say, without necessarily agreeing with these criticisms, that, valuable though these considerations may be in categorizing receipts as income or capital in conventional situations, their significance is diminished when the receipt in question is generated in the course of carrying on a business, especially if it should transpire that the receipt is generated as a profit component of a profit-making

scheme. If the profit be made in the course of carrying on a business that in itself is a fact of telling significance. It does not detract from its significance that the particular transaction is unusual or extraordinary, judged by reference to the transactions in which the taxpayer usually engages, if it be entered into in the course of carrying on the taxpayer's business. And, if it appears that there is a specific profit-making scheme, it is pointless to say that it is unusual or extraordinary in the sense discussed.

'The important distinction is, as their Honours noted at 213 in particular, between profits derived in a business operation or in carrying out a profit-making scheme, which are income, as distinct from proceeds of a "mere" realisation or change of investment. Their Honours said in respect of that distinction that:

> The proposition that a mere realization or change of investment is not income requires some elaboration. First, the emphasis is on the adjective "mere": *Whitfords Beach* (1982) 150 CLR at p 383. Secondly, profits made on a realization or change of investments may constitute income if the investments were initially acquired as part of a business with the intention or purpose that they be realized subsequently in order to capture the profit arising from their expected increase in value: see the discussion of Gibbs J in *London Australia* (1977) 138 CLR at pp 116–188. It is one thing if the decision to sell an asset is taken after its acquisition, there having been no intention or purpose at the time of acquisition of acquiring for the purpose of profit-making by sale. Then, if the asset be not a revenue asset on other grounds, the profit made is capital because it proceeds from mere realization. But it is quite another thing if the decision to sell is taken by way of implementation of an intention or purpose, existing at the time of acquisition, of profit-making by sale, at least in the context of carrying on a business or carrying out a business operation or commercial transaction.'

Orr v Wendt and Ors [2005] WASCA 199 at [37]–[40], per Wheeler JA; BC200508859

INCOME YEAR

New Zealand [Accident Rehabilitation and Compensation Insurance Act 1992, s 41(2) importing the definition of s 2 of the Income Tax Act 1976.] 'The legislature has seen fit in s 41(2) to require the appellant to divide the earnings of the respondent in his most recent income year other than his earnings as an employee by the number of weeks in that income year. The number of weeks in that income year were 52 and not 41. There is nothing in s 41(2) which enables any other interpretation ... Neither the long title nor the previous legislation allow an interpretation of s 41(2) which is contrary to the plain meaning. Nor, given the plain meaning of s 41(2), is a purposive approach attempting to enlarge the definition of "income year" in the Income Tax Act 1976 open to this Court.' *Accident Rehabilitation and Compensation Insurance Corporation v Tarr* [1996] 3 NZLR 715 at 720, per cur

INCUMBRANCE

[Meaning of 'incumbrance' for the purposes of the Landlord and Tenant Act 1987s 12(4).] 'The 1987 Act does not define "incumbrance". The authorities yield no conclusive answer to the question whether a lease is an incumbrance or not ... The answer is in my view that the meaning to be given to the expression depends on the context, as is confirmed by the legal dictionaries.

...

'In the present context I regard it as critical (1) that Pt I of the Act is triggered when the immediate landlord of qualifying tenants proposes to (or does) part with the reversion to the tenants' leases; (2) that the object of this Part of the Act is to give qualifying tenants an overriding right to buy the reversion on appropriate terms if they wish; (3) that where the reversion passes from immediate landlord A to new landlord B to purchaser C the Act enables the tenants to pursue their claim not only against A and B but also C; and (4) that the situation described in (3) would appear to fall aptly within s 16.

'These considerations lead me to conclude that where a new immediate landlord grants a lease which has the effect of transferring the reversion of the tenants' leases from himself to another immediate landlord, the former must be regarded as no longer holding the estate or interest that had been the subject matter of the original disposal. The estate or interest relevant for present purposes must be the reversion, and the intermediate landlord (B in my example above) no longer has it. The type of concurrent lease which Frogmore granted to Atherton is, as explained in 27(1) *Halsbury's Laws* (4th edn reissue) para 81, correctly characterised as a lease of the reversion (sometimes referred to as a "reversionary" lease). The grant of a lease which has that effect is not in my view an incumbrance within s 12(4); it is an event which triggers the operation of s 16 (although not, on facts such as the present, a relevant disposal).

'It does not follow from this that no lease can ever be an incumbrance within the meaning of s 12(4). When a new landlord acquires his interest, a flat may be vacant in the block and the landlord may let it. That in no way affects the reversion to the leases of the other tenants. But it could affect the appropriate purchase consideration. I would regard such a lease as an incumbrance within s 12(4).' *Belvedere Court Management Ltd v Frogmore Developments Ltd* [1996] 1 All ER 312 at 326, 327–328, CA, per Sir Thomas Bingham MR

INCUR

Australia 'The words "incurs" and "debt" are not words of precise and inflexible denotation ... the word "incurs" takes its meaning from its context and is apt to describe, in an appropriate case, the undertaking of an engagement to pay a sum of money at a future time, even if the engagement is conditional and the amount involved uncertain.' *Hawkins v Bank of Chicago* (1992) 7 ACSR 349 at 357–358, per Gleeson J

INCURRED

Canada 'The appellant relies on a line of cases that restrict the word "incurred" to the narrow meaning that an expense is not incurred until there is a legal liability to pay for it. The respondent relies on a competing line of cases that give the word "incurred" a wider purposive meaning. These cases say that expenses are incurred if their reasonable necessity and the amount of the expenditure are determined with certainty within the time period, even if a legal obligation to pay has not yet been incured.

'The clearest way to address the authorities is first to review them briefly in chronological order.

'In *Hasson v Hamel* (1977) 16 OR (2d) 517, 526, 78 DLR (3d) 573, Zalev Co Ct J held that domestic services performed by the insured's daughter were not "incurred" within the meaning of a similar provision because dictionary definitions of the word "incurred" demonstrated that expenses were not incurred unless there is some legal liability to pay for them and the insured did not contract with her daughter to pay for the services, nor did her undertaking to pay for them create any legal liability.

'In *Stokes v State Farm Mutual Insurance Co* (1982), Ont County Ct, referred to in Newcombe, *The Standard Automobile Policy Annotated* (Butterworths, 1986), the insured had completed some dental procedures but more work remained to be done. The nature and cost of the remaining work was known. The court held the insurer liable because the work was necessitated and its cost known within the four years. The insurer would not have been liable if the nature or cost of the work was unascertained within the four years.

'In *MacDonald v Travelers Indemnity Co of Canada* [1987] ILR ¶1–2220 p 8575, 42 DLR (4th) 204 (Ont HCJ), the court interpreted a Michigan statute which required a determination of the point in time at which expenses were "incurred" for a terribly disabled young woman. Although the precise issue in this case was not there addressed, Osler J at p 8602 adopted a wide meaning of the word "incurred":

> I have not been referred to any case or to any other authority in which the word "incur" has been specifically defined or dealt with. The ordinary meaning of the word is given in the *Shorter Oxford Dictionary* as "to run into; to render oneself liable to". In the context of the Michigan statute, it does not seem to me that the word implied a strict necessity to be legally obligated to make payments before expenses can be said to have been incurred.

'Osler J supported this interpretation with a purposive analysis of the statute and noted that a narrower interpretation would penalize a destitute insured and reward an insured with greater financial means [p 8602]:

> 'Suppose, for example, Lynne MacDonald had not had the support of her family and had been destitute. She could never have made payments with respect to her care or rehabilitation and thus made herself entitled to be reimbursed. It seems to me that if a reasonable necessity for the item claimed is established and the cost of obtaining such a service or product is shown, the expense may be said to have been incurred and the obligation to pay within thirty days must then be assumed by the defendant.

'This purposive interpretation, that an insured has "incurred" or "run into" an expense for an item when its reasonable necessity is demonstrated and its cost is known, will be revisited below.

'In *Virginia Farm Bureau Mutual Insurance Co v Hodges*, 385 SE 2d 612 (1989) at 614, the

Supreme Court of Virginia overturned a trial judgment requiring the insurer to pay for medical treatment diagnosed as necessary within the specified year but required to be performed after the expiry of the year. Whiting J, for the court, held at p 614 that anticipated medical expenses are not "incurred" within one year from the date of the accident unless the insured within that period has paid the expense or has contracted for it:

> During the first year after her accident, Hodges did not pay Dr Brobst nor was she contractually obligated to pay him. She could have decided to go to another doctor or not have the surgery at all. Therefore, she did not "incur" the expense of Dr Brobst's suggested surgical procedure within the meaning of the policy.
>
> ...
>
> In our opinion, the language unambiguously requires that Hodges pay or be legally obligated to pay these medical expenses within the one-year period in order for them to have been "incurred" within the terms of the policy.

'In *Placken v Canadian Surety Co* (1990) 47 CCLI 268 (Ont Dist Ct), Kurisko DCJ, the insured had his right leg amputated after a motorcycle accident and the court held the insurer liable for future expenses for the repair and replacement of the prosthesis, which would continue throughout his life, to the policy limit. The prosthesis expenses were incurred at the time of the amputation because the plaintiff at that time became liable to, or subject to, those expenses for the rest of his life and it was not necessary that the prosthesis expenses be ascertained, actually incurred or paid within the four-year period. The court relied upon a number of cases on the meaning of "incurred" including *R v Allan* (1979) 45 CCC (2d) 524 (Ont CA), 529–30 where Lacourciere JA relied on dictionary definitions such as "to render oneself liable to", "to bring upon oneself", to be "subject to" as meanings of the word "incurred".

'In *MacLeod v Lumberman Mutual Casualty Co* (1993) 15 CCLI (2d) 59, the Nova Scotia Supreme Court held that in deciding whether medical expenses required to be performed by a specialist in Sault Ste Marie had been "incurred" within four years from the date of the accident, there was a gray area between possible speculation or optional future expenses on the one hand and, on the other hand, expenses so certainly required that they are incurred even though their execution is deferred. Goodfellow J at pp 70–71 held that the Sault Ste

Marie expenses were incurred because of the certainty of their requirement at the material time:

> ... the evidence establishes that sufficient degree of certainty of treatment, determined and required prior to the limitation date so as to have been "incurred" within four years from the date of the accident but the execution of the treatment and its continuation was merely deferred post the limitation period. Any other conclusion would ignore the purpose of Sched B benefits and produce, in my view, an unrealistic result.

'The court, in holding that expenses for medical procedures performed in Georgia after the expiry of four years were not "incurred" within the period, found that there was "by a wide margin, no balance of probability that the degree of certainty of such treatment was determined or required prior to the limitation date".

'To sum up the "incurred" cases, there are no Ontario appellate decisions on point. The trial judgments range from the narrow interpretations in *Hasson* and *Virginia State Farm* through the gray area described in *MacLeod v Lumberman* to the liberal interpretation that favours the insured in *Stokes, MacDonald,* and *Placken.*' Smith *(Committee of) v Wawanesa Mutual Insurance Co* (1998) 168 DLR (4th) 750 at 754–757, Ont Div Ct, per Campbell J

INDECENT

New Zealand ['Indecent' is defined in section 2 of the Indecent Publications Act 1963.] 'It should be noted that the definition is inclusive not exclusive. By using the word "includes" Parliament has clearly left open the view that the word "indecent" may be apt to cover ground not expressly stated in the definition. However it is now clear beyond argument, at least in this Court, that for material to be indecent for the purposes of the Act under any criterion it must have the capacity for causing injury to the public good.' *Society for the Promotion of Community Standards Inc v Waverley International (1988) Ltd* [1993] 2 NZLR 709 at 717, per Tipping and Jaine JJ

INDECENT AND OBSCENE

Australia 'Just as the words do not have the same denotation in ordinary parlance, neither do they at common law. What is obscene will also be indecent but it does not follow that what is indecent is necessarily obscene. The line between what is indecent and what is obscene may on occasions be difficult to draw but, as in ordinary usage, the common law recognises that the word "obscene" is a stronger epithet than "indecent". It denotes a higher degree of offensiveness.' *Phillips v Police* (1994) 75 A Crim R 480 at 488, per Debelle J

INDECENT ASSAULT

'An indecent assault is an assault committed in circumstances of aggravation. It seems to us that at least it must be proved that the accused intentionally assaulted the victim with knowledge of the indecent circumstances or being reckless as to the existence of them.' *R v Court* [1987] 1 All ER 120 at 124, CA, per Ralph Gibson LJ

INDEMNITY

[For 20 Halsbury's Laws (4th edn) para 305 see now 20(1) Halsbury's Laws (4th edn) (Reissue) para 109.]

INDENTURE

[For 12 Halsbury's Laws (4th edn) para 1303 see now 13 Halsbury's Laws (4th edn) (Reissue) para 3.]

INDIAN

Canada '[70] Guided by the proper principles of constitutional interpretation when dealing with a claim to an aboriginal right, what is the meaning of the word "Indian" in sec. 13 of the *NRTA [National Resources Transfer Agreement]*?

'[71] In *R. v. Grumbo* (1998), 168 Sask.R. 78, the Court of Appeal of Saskatchewan dealt with the identical issue to the one before us, namely, whether the Métis accused in that case was an Indian within the meaning of sec. 12 of the Saskatchewan *NRTA*. In a previous decision of the Saskatchewan Court of Appeal, *R. v. Laprise* (1978), 6 W.W.R. 85, it had been decided that sec. 12 did not include the Métis. The court in *Grumbo* by a majority concluded that *Laprise* had been decided *per incuriam* because it based its decision on the definition of Indian in the *Indian Act* of the day. Sherstobitoff J.A., for the majority, explained (at para. 24):

> "[24] It seems also apparent that if the court had realized that it was interpreting a part of the Constitution when it interpreted s 12 of the *Natural Resources Transfer Agreement*, it would not have incorporated by reference, as

it has done, as a definition of the word Indian in that section, the definition of that word found in an ordinary statute, the *Indian Act* (Canada). The result of this incorporation by reference would be that Parliament is empowered to amend the Constitution by simply amending the definition of the word Indian in the Indian Act from time to time as it has done. This cannot be right. The Constitution cannot be amended by a simple Act of Parliament.

> "See as well *R. v. Sutherland, Wilson et al. and Canada (Attorney General)*, [1980] 2 S.C.R. 451."

'[72] He went on to conclude (at paras. 35–36):

> "[35] No evidence or argument was presented relating to this fundamental issue of whether the legislation confirming the *Natural Resources Transfer Agreement* was passed in the context of whether, constitutionally speaking, Métis were Indians so that the Métis had the same rights thereunder as Indians, or in the context of the Métis being a separate people from the Indians with their own distinct aboriginal rights. The issue before the court cannot be properly decided without evidence respecting that context. Both the Crown and Mr. Grumbo should have an opportunity to present evidence and argument in respect of it. There must be an order for a new trial in respect of this issue.

> "[36] There is another reason for a new trial. While the judgment in the Queen's Bench was based on the facts established by the evidence and affected only Mr. Grumbo, both counsel, as well as the Métis people and the general public have treated it as having definitively settled the question of whether Métis are Indians for the purposes of the *Natural Resources Transfer Agreement*. On the appeal, counsel for both parties made it clear that they wished this court to definitively settle the question. As noted above, there is not a sufficient foundation of evidence to do so. That evidence can only be made available through a new trial."

'[73] It was therefore an error of law to accept that the definition of "Indian" as used in the *NRTA* was the same as that contained in the *Indian Act* as amended from time to time. But this does not necessarily mean that the word "Indian" in the *NRTA* was not understood and intended to be consistent with the meaning of the word "Indian" as it was in the *Indian Act* at the time the *NRTA* was enacted. This is an important distinction. This conclusion is entirely consistent with the expert evidence of Mr. Gallow, whose opinion was accepted and applied by the trial judge. There is no logical or legal reason why the same meaning cannot be attributed to the word "Indian" in the *NRTA* as that word was then used and understood in the *Indian Act*. I entirely agree that the meaning of a word in a constitutional document cannot be altered simply by amendments to an ordinary statute (see *Grumbo*), but this is not to say that a word in a constitutional document cannot be interpreted the same as in an ordinary contemporary statute, if the court is satisfied that is in fact what the words were intended to mean. In such circumstances, of course, the meaning of the word ("Indian" in our case) will not change with amendments to the ordinary statute.

'[74] It is entirely a question of contextual purposive interpretation, aided by the historical record available to the court.

'[75] The appellant and intervenor argue that there is a distinction between the meaning of the word "Indian" in the *NRTA* and in the *Indian Act*, and that Wright J. erred when he concluded that the intention of the drafters of the *NRTA* was to define the term "Indian" consistently with the 1927 *Indian Act*. As counsel for the intervenor put it, the Métis want to be "Indian" under the *NRTA*, but for no other purpose.

'[76] The intervenor also argues that examination of the terms of the *NRTA*, together with the historical testimony presented at trial, supports the conclusion that for the Métis and Indians respectively scrip and treaty rights were accepted in 1870 on the understanding that their rights to hunt, trap and fish would not be affected. The honour of the sovereign mandates that these solemn undertakings be respected unless expressly taken away. It must be presumed therefore, the intervenor argues, that the *NRTA* was intended to confirm and protect the existing right to hunt.

'[77] The province relies on the findings and conclusions of the trial judge and the Queen's Bench judge on appeal with respect to the purpose and meaning of sec. 13. It is submitted that acceptance of the appellant's interpretation of sec. 13 would have the effect of creating a new Métis hunting right which had not been in existence at any time before the *NRTA*. This is contrary to the historical evidence and would be impossible to administer given that there is "no objective way to determine who is and who is not Métis." Furthermore, the *NRTA* by its very terms makes it clear that the use of the word "Indian" does not include "Métis." Paragraphs 11 and 12 of the *NRTA*, along with sec. 13, are grouped together under a single heading "Indian Reserves." Only Indians under the *Indian Act* (but not Métis) live on "Indian reserves".' *R v Blais* (2001) 198 DLR (4th) 220 at 242–244, Man CA, per Scott CJM

Canada '27 The common usage of the term "Indian" in 1930 also argues against a view of this term as encompassing the Métis. Both the terms "Indian" and "half-breed" were used in the mid-19th century. Swail Prov. Ct. J. cites a North American census prepared by the Hudson's Bay Company in 1856–57 (pp. 146–47). The census records 147,000 "Indians", and breaks this down into various groups, including "The Plain Tribes", "The Esquimaux", "Indians settled in Canada", and so forth. A separate line indicates the number of "Whites and half-breeds in Hudson's Bay Territory", which is estimated at 11,000, for a total of 158,000 "souls". This document illustrates that the "Whites and half-breeds" were viewed as an identifiable group, separate and distinct from the Indians.

'28 The Red River Métis distinguished themselves from the Indians. For example, the successive Lists of Rights prepared by Métis leaders at the time of the creation of the Province of Manitoba excluded "the Indians" from voting. This provision could not plausibly have been intended to disenfranchise the Métis, who were the authors of the Lists and the majority of the population. The Third and Fourth Lists of Rights emphasized the importance of concluding treaties "between Canada and the different Indian tribes of the Province", with the "cooperation of the Local Legislature" (Morton, *supra*, at pp. 246 and 249). The Local Legislature was, at that time, a Métis-dominated body, underscoring the Métis' own view of themselves and the Indians as fundamentally distinct.

'29 There might not have been absolute consistency in the use of the terms "Indian" and "half-breed", and there appears to have been some mobility between the two groups. However, as evidenced by the historical documents statement cited above, the prevailing trend was to identify two distinct groups and to differentiate between their respective entitlements. Dr. Ens indicated in his report: "By 1850 'Half-Breed' was the most frequently used term among English-speaking residents of the North West to refer to all persons of mixed ancestry. It was a term that clearly differentiated between Indian and Metis populations" (respondent's record, at p. 176). At trial, the appellant's expert, Dr. Shore, could not cite any source in which the Canadian government used the term "Indian" to refer to all Aboriginal peoples, including the Métis.

'30 This interpretation is supported by the location of para. 13 in the *NRTA* itself. Quite apart from formal rules of statutory construction, common sense dictates that the content of a provision will in some way be related to its heading. Paragraph 13 falls under the heading "Indian Reserves". Indian reserves were set aside for the use and benefit of Status Indians, not for the Métis. The placement of para. 13 in the part of the *NRTA* entitled "Indian Reserves", along with two other provisions that clearly do not apply to the Métis, supports the view that the term "Indian" as used throughout this part was not seen as including the Métis. This placement weighs against the argument that we should construe the term "Indians" more broadly than otherwise suggested by the historical context of the *NRTA* and the common usage of the term at the time of the *NRTA*'s enactment.

'31 We find no basis in the record for overturning the lower courts' findings that, as a general matter, the terms "Indian" and "half-breed" were used to refer to separate and distinguishable groups of people in Manitoba from the mid-19th century through the period in which the *NRTA* was negotiated and enacted.' *R v Blais* (2003) 230 DLR (4th) 22 at 33–34 (SCC), per the Court

INDICTMENT

[For 11 Halsbury's Laws (4th edn) para 193 see now 11(2) Halsbury's Laws (4th edn) (Reissue) para 913.]

Australia 'Strictly speaking, an indictment was a document making a formal accusation of crime on the basis of evidence found credible by a grand jury. A presentment was a document of the same character that was based, not upon evidence presented to the grand jury, but upon the grand jury's personal knowledge of the facts ... When the Crimes Act 1956 (Vic) speaks of a presentment, it is referring to the procedure now described in other States and in the Judiciary Act as a proceeding by way of indictment, and that the reason for this different terminology was to distinguish this procedure from that of indictment by means of the grand jury which is a procedure unknown in other States. This view is, I believe, supported by the following passage from the joint judgment of Dixon and Evatt JJ in *R v Federal Court of Bankruptcy; Ex parte Lowenstein* (1938) 59 CLR 556 at 582, where their Honours said: "But, even if this means of avoidance be allowable, what is meant by an indictment? In English law it is a Bill of accusation preferred before a grand jury and found true by the oaths of at least 12 men whereupon it is to be prosecuted at the suit of the King. But in Australia the word has inevitably been used in a wider sense. Since 9 Geo IV c 83, the means of putting a prisoner upon his trial before a petit jury has been by an accusation under the hand of a law officer or prosecutor for the King. Grand juries have been little used. The accusation at different times and in different States has been variously called an information, an indictment and a presentment." ' *R v Nicola* (1987) 79 ALR 469 at 474–476, per Nicholson J

INDORSEMENT

[For 4 Halsbury's Laws (4th edn) para 308 see now 4(1) Halsbury's Laws (4th edn) (2002 Reissue) para 308.]

INDUCE

Australia '... The Oxford English Dictionary (2nd Ed) defines "induce" in the relevant sense as:

> to lead (a person) by persuasion or some influence or motive ... to **do** something (original emphasis).

'In that sense, inducing is different from holding out an inducement to a person which may or may not have an operative effect on his or her mind.' *Hawker De Havilland Aerospace Pty Ltd (ACN 103 165 466) v Automotive, Food, Metals, Engineering, Printing and Kindred Industries Union* [2005] FCA 804 at [25], per Ryan J; BC200504053

INDUCEMENT

Australia '... [T]he fact that the Department told him what he already knew cannot amount to an inducement. "Inducement" is a word defined in the New Shorter Oxford Dictionary as (among other definitions) "lead, persuade, influence (a person)". Another definition is to be found in Butterworths Australian Legal Dictionary under the sub-heading "Criminal Law". The following appears: "A persuasion of temporal or worldly as opposed to moral or religious character aimed at producing some willing action on the part of an accused by a person with authority."

'But a statement of the obvious cannot be persuasive or influential. In this context, the observations of Brennan J in *Collins v R* (1980) 31 ALR 257 at 309 are pertinent.

'His Honour there said:

"Of course, the motive to confess, like the motive for many human actions, may be mixed and if there be a congeries of motives it is necessary to determine whether the confession would not have been made but for pressure placed upon the confessionalist or some fear of prejudice or hope of advantage induced by a person in authority, or whether the making of a confession is really to be accounted for by motives of the confessionalist which are not referable to such pressure, fear or hope. This is a question of fact and of degree to be resolved according to the particular circumstances of the case."

'Here Mr Dempsey's motives for making the confession of 5 August 1999 were not referable to pressure, fear or hope emanating from anything the Department said. The source of any pressure, fear or hope existed quite independently of any statement, however emphatically made, to Mr Dempsey by the Department. Accordingly, in my opinion, the argument based upon the proposition that Mr Dempsey was induced by departmental statements cannot be accepted.' *R v Dempsey* BC200007430; [2000] VSC 521 at [17]–[20], per Harper J

New Zealand [Section 20 of the Evidence Act 1908] 'It is desirable to return to s 20. The word "inducement" is coupled with the words "promise or threat". The composite phrase is "a promise or threat or any other inducement". Promises and threats are apt to incline suspects to accept guilt when they are not guilty. That is the rationale for being careful about admitting confessions which have resulted from promises and threats. The same rationale must apply to 'other inducement'. In broad terms therefore an inducement may be anything which might logically incline a suspect falsely to admit guilt. *R v Potae* [2000] 3 NZLR 375 at 380, CA, per cur

INDUSTRIAL ACTION OR OTHER ACTION

Australia 'The conjunction of the words "other action" with the words "industrial action" [in s 170NC(1)(a) of the Workplace Relations Act 1996 (Cth)] is strongly suggestive of an intent on the part of the legislature to limit the scope of what might otherwise be an extraordinarily wide definition of the conduct caught by the section.

'The words "or other action" in the composite expression "industrial action or other action" should be read in accordance with the maxim noscitur a sociis. A word or phrase in an enactment must always be construed in the light of the surrounding text. In *Attorney-General v Prince Ernest Augustus of Hanover* [1957] AC 436, Viscount Simonds said, at 461:

"... Words, and particularly general words, cannot be read in isolation; their colour and their content are derived from their context."

'The expression "industrial action" is defined in s 4 of the Workplace Relations Act 1996 (Cth). It describes conduct of various types on the part of employers and employees, and organisations registered under the Act, and is limited to matters relating to the performance of work. Significantly, there is no mention of conduct by third parties within that definition. Section 4 also describes action which is not "industrial action", but it too only relates to employers and employees. The expression "other action" in s 170NC(1)(a) can be given a sensible interpretation if one reads it as including conduct of a kind taken by an employer, or employee, or an organisation registered under the Act, which related to the performance of work but is not included within the definition of "industrial action". Picketing is one example of such conduct.

'Given that s 170NC is penal in character (albeit a contravention does not create an offence: s 170NF) the expression "other action" should not be accorded any undue width. Penal provisions are construed strictly, although this is now a canon of construction of less significance than was formerly the case: *Beckwith v The Queen* (1976) 135 CLR 569 at 576.' *National Tertiary Education Industry Union v Commonwealth* BC200201567; [2002] FCA 441 at [93]–[96], per Weinberg J

INDUSTRIAL BUILDING OR STRUCTURE

[The Capital Allowances Act 1968 has been repealed. The definition is re-enacted in the Capital Allowances Act 1990, s 18.]

[The Town and Country Planning Act 1971 has been repealed. A definition of 'industrial building' is given in the Town and Country Planning General Development Order 1988, SI 1988/1813, Sch 2 Part 8 para E, as follows.] 'Industrial building' means a building used for the carrying out of an industrial process and includes a building used for the carrying out of such a process on land as a dock, harbour or quay for the purposes of an industrial undertaking but does not include a building or land in or adjacent to and occupied together with a mine.

INDUSTRIAL DISPUTE

Australia 'To my mind it is clear that the amendment of the definition [in the Industrial Relations Act 1979 (Vic)] of "industrial dispute" in 1983 to include "a dispute arising from the dismissal ... from his employment of an employee" was intended to extend the definition to a dispute between an employer and an employee whose employment had been determined. It places no strain upon the language of the definition to construe the reference to "a dispute arising between an employer and one or more of his employés" as including a dismissed employee when identifying the disputants in a dispute arising from a dismissal. Clearly, the definition was always intended to embrace a dispute between an employer and one of his employees and, at least after the wording of the definition was expanded to cover specifically a dispute from a dismissal, it can scarcely have been intended to exclude a dispute between the employer and the very person dismissed. To construe the definition in such a way would, I think, be unduly narrow and pedantic and contrary to the evident intention of the legislature.' *Downey v Trans Waste Pty Ltd* (1991) 172 CLR 167 at 178–179, per Dawson J

Australia 'The Industrial Relations Act 1988 (Cth) (the Act), in s 4(1), relevantly defines "industrial dispute" to mean:

"(a) an industrial dispute (including a threatened, impending or probable industrial dispute):
  (i) extending beyond the limits of any one State; and
  (ii) that is about matters pertaining to the relationship between employers and employees; or
(b) a situation that is likely to give rise to an industrial dispute of the kind referred to in paragraph (a)."

'... The effect of para (b) of the present definition of "industrial dispute" is that an industrial dispute may be constituted by "a situation that is likely to give rise to" a dispute, but it an actual, threatened, impending or probable dispute, "about matters pertaining to the relationship between employers and employees". When regard is had to the language of that paragraph, the definition appears to be quite wide enough to encompass a dispute with a company that is not an employer but, like Shell Australia, is in a position, because of the relevant corporate structure and because of its powers and rights with respect to a superannuation fund, directly

to affect the relationship between an employer and its employees with respect to their superannuation entitlements.' *Re Amalgamated Metal Workers Union of Australia; Ex p the Shell Company of Australia Ltd* (1992) 174 CLR 345 at 345–5; 108 ALR 229 at 234–235, per Mason CJ, Deane, Toohey and Gaudron JJ

INEXPEDIENT

New Zealand [Section 32 of the Charitable Trusts Act 1957 provides that:

'(1) Subject to the provisions of subsection (3) of this section, in any case where any property or income is given or held upon trust, or is to be applied, for any charitable purpose, and it is impossible or impracticable or inexpedient to carry out that purpose, or the amount available is inadequate to carry out that purpose, or that purpose has been effected already, or that purpose is illegal or useless or uncertain, then (whether or not there is any general charitable intention) the property and income or any part or residue thereof or the proceeds of sale thereof shall be disposed of for some other charitable purpose, or a combination of such purposes, in the manner and subject to the provisions hereafter contained in this Part of this Act.

(2) Subject to the provisions of subsection (3) of this section, in any case where any property or income is given or held upon trust, or is to be applied, for any charitable purpose, and the property or the income which has accrued or will accrue is more than is necessary for the purpose, then (whether or not there is any general charitable intention) any excess property or income or proceeds of sale may be disposed of for some other charitable purpose, or a combination of such purposes, in the manner and subject to the provisions hereafter contained in this Part of this Act.

(3) This section shall not operate to cause any property or income to be disposed of as provided in subsection (1) or subsection (2) of this section—
  (a) If in accordance with any rule of law the intended gift thereof would otherwise lapse or fail and the property or income would not be applicable for any other charitable purpose:
  (b) In so far as the property or income can be disposed of under Part 4 of this Act'].

'[14] The general connotation of the word "inexpedient" in its present context is of the original charitable purpose or purposes having become unsuitable, inadvisable or inapt. Parliament's wish to expand the concepts of impossibility and impracticability should not be inhibited by too narrow an interpretation of the word "inexpedient". Clearly Parliament wished to give the Courts power to approve a scheme of variation in circumstances beyond those where the original purpose could no longer be carried out. The concept of inexpediency introduced a value judgment rather than simply an assessment of feasibility. It may remain possible and practicable to carry out the original purpose but it may have become inexpedient to do so … It may be worth repeating here that the question is not whether the scheme carries out the purposes of the trust better. Rather it is whether it is now inexpedient to carry them out.' *Re McElroy Trust* [2003] 2 NZLR 289 at 293, per cur

INFLUENCE/INDUCED

'This part of the case depends on the words "which would influence the judgment of a prudent insurer in fixing the premium, or determining whether he will take the risk" (ss 18(2) and 20(2) of the [Marine Insurance Act 1906]).

'The main thrust of the argument for Pan Atlantic is that this expression calls for the disclosure only of such circumstances as would, if disclosed to the hypothetical prudent underwriter, have caused him to decline the risk or charge an increased premium. I am unable to accept this argument.

'In the first place I cannot find the suggested meaning in the words of the Act. This is a short point of interpretation, and does not yield to long discussion. For my part I entirely accept that part of the argument for Pan Atlantic which fastens on the word "would" and contrasts it with words such as "might". I agree that this word looks to a consequence which, within the area of uncertainty created by the civil standard of proof, is definite rather than speculative. But this is only part of the inquiry. The next step is to decide what kind of effect the disclosure would have. This is defined by the expression "influence the judgment of the prudent underwriter". The legislature might here have said "*decisively* influence"; or *conclusively* influence; or "determine the decision"; or all sorts of similar expressions, in which case Pan Atlantic's argument would be right. But the legislature has not done this, and has instead left the word "influence" unadorned. It therefore bears its ordinary meaning, which is not, as it seems to me, the one for which Pan Atlantic contends. "Influence the judgment" is not the same as "change the

mind". Furthermore, if the argument is pursued via a purely verbal analysis, it should be observed that the expression used is "influence the judgment of a prudent insurer or [the underwriter] in … determining *whether* he will take the risk". To my mind, this expression clearly denotes an effect on the thought processes of the insurer in weighing up the risk, quite different from words which might have been used but were not, such as "influencing the insurer *to take* the risk".

'My Lords, this conclusion accords with what I regard as the practicalities. Looking at the matter through the eyes of a court, called upon to rule after the event on whether an undisclosed circumstance was material, the proposition that "influence" means "decisively influence" takes as its point of reference a hypothetical underwriter personifying the generality of those who know their job and perform it carefully, without exceptional timidity or boldness; it assumes that this underwriter has had before him all the material which was before the actual underwriter; it also assumes that after weighing up the conflicting factors which enter into a decision of this kind the hypothetical underwriter has decided that the balance comes down in favour of writing the risk on the terms on which it was actually written; and then on these assumptions requires a firm conclusion on whether or not the undisclosed facts would (not might) have tipped the balance the other way and caused him to reach a different decision. Even looking at the matter after the event, this exercise presents great difficulties, for the reasons given by Parker LJ in the *CTI* case [1984] 1 Lloyd's Rep 476 at 510–511 in the passage quoted above. But the point is that it is not the court after the event, but the prospective assured and his broker before the event, at whom the test is aimed; it is they who have to decide, before the underwriter has agreed to write the risk, what material they must disclose. I am bound to say that in all but the most obvious cases the "decisive influence" test faces them with an almost impossible task. How can they tell whether the proper disclosure would turn the scale? By contrast, if all that they have to consider is whether the materials are such that a prudent underwriter would take them into account, the test is perfectly workable.

Furthermore, the argument for Pan Atlantic demands an assumption that the prudent underwriter would have written the risk at the premium actually agreed on the basis of the disclosure which was actually made. Yet this assumption is impossible if the actual underwriter, through laziness, incompetence or a simple error of judgment has made a bargain which no prudent underwriter would have made, full disclosure or no full disclosure. This absurdity does not arise if the duty of disclosure embraces all materials which would enter into the making of the hypothetical decision, since this does not require the bargain actually made to be taken as the starting point …

'Accordingly, treating the matter simply as one of statutory interpretation I would feel little hesitation in rejecting the test of decisive influence …

'I turn to the second question which concerns the need, or otherwise, for a causal connection between the misrepresentation or non-disclosure and the making of the contract of insurance. According to ss 17, 18(1) and 20(1) [of the Marine Insurance Act 1906] if good faith is not observed, proper disclosure is not made or material facts are misrepresented, the other party, or in the case of ss 18 and 20 the insurer, "may avoid the contract". There is no mention of a connection between the wrongful dealing and the writing of the risk. But for this feature I doubt whether it would nowadays occur to anyone that it would be possible for the underwriter to escape liability even if the matter complained of had no effect on his processes of thought. Take the case of misrepresentation. In the general law it is beyond doubt that even a fraudulent misrepresentation must be shown to have induced the contract before the promisor has a right to avoid, although the task of proof may be made more easy by a presumption of inducement. The case of innocent misrepresentation should surely be a fortiori, and yet it is urged that so long as the representation is material no inducement need be shown. True, the inequalities of knowledge between assured and underwriter have led to the creation of a special duty to make accurate disclosure of sufficient facts to restore the balance and remedy the injustice of holding the underwriter to a speculation which he had been unable fairly to assess; but this consideration cannot in logic or justice require courts to go further and declare the contract to be vitiated when the underwriter, having paid no attention to the matters not properly stated and disclosed, has suffered no injustice thereby. How then does it happen that the 1906 Act seems to contemplate that once a material misrepresentation or non-disclosure is established the underwriter has an invariable right to avoid? …

'My Lords, in my judgment little or nothing can be gleaned from twentieth century cases to indicate a solution to the problem of causation. Before stating my own opinion on this problem there are two more points to be made.

'First, one suggested explanation for the absence from s 20 of any requirement that the misrepresentation shall have induced the contract is that any such requirement had been swept away 30 years before in *Ionides v Pender* (1874) LR 9 QB 531. Consistently with the views already expressed I am unable to accept this, and I should add that even if the effect of *Ionides v Pender* had been to make the influence on the hypothetical underwriter the benchmark of materiality I am unable to see why this should not have left behind such requirements of actual causation as had previously formed part of the common law. However, as I have said, although *Ionides v Pender* was an important case it did not in my opinion have the effect contended for.

'Secondly, it has been suggested that the absence from the 1906 Act of any reference to causation stems from a disciplinary element in the law of marine insurance. The concept is that persons seeking insurance and their brokers cannot be relied upon to perform their duties spontaneously; that the criterion of whether or not the misrepresentation or non-disclosure induced the contract would make it too easy for the assured to say that the breach of duty made no difference; and that accordingly the law prescribes voidability as an automatic consequence of a breach by way of sanction for the enforcement of full and accurate disclosure. For my part, although I think it possible to detect traces of this doctrine in the earlier writings I can see nothing to support it in later sources; and I would unhesitatingly reject any suggestion that it should now be made part of the law. The existing rules, coupled with a presumption of inducement, are already stern enough, and to enable an underwriter to escape liability when he has suffered no harm would be positively unjust, and contrary to the spirit of mutual good faith recognised by s 17, the more so since non-disclosure will in a substantial proportion of cases be the result of an innocent mistake.

'For these reasons I conclude that there is to be implied in the 1906 Act a qualification that a material misrepresentation will not entitle the underwriter to avoid the policy unless the misrepresentation induced the making of the contract, using "induced" in the sense in which it is used in the general law of contract. This proposition is concerned only with *material* misrepresentations. On the view which I have formed of the present facts the effect of an immaterial misrepresentation does not arise and I say nothing about it …

'Before embarking on this long analysis I suggested that the questions in issue were short. I propose the following short answers. (1) A circumstance may be material even though a full and accurate disclosure of it would not in itself have had a decisive effect on the prudent underwriter's decision whether to accept the risk and if so at what premium. But, (2) if the misrepresentation or non-disclosure of a material fact did not in fact induce the making of the contract (in the sense in which that expression is used in the general law of misrepresentation) the underwriter is not entitled to rely on it as a ground for avoiding the contract.' *Pan Atlantic Insurance Co Ltd v Pine Top Insurance Co Ltd* [1994] 3 All ER 581 at 600–601, 610, 616–618, HL, per Lord Mustill

INDUSTRIAL DISPUTE

Australia 'It has long been recognised that an industrial dispute may be generated by a written demand. Disputes of that kind are commonly called "paper disputes". They have sometimes been described with a touch of irony; sometimes in terms suggesting that they are not quite the real thing. However, the Constitution, in s 51(xxxv), speaks of "industrial disputes", not "industrial disturbances". Leaving aside questions that may arise with respect to the parties to a dispute, its subject matter and interstateness, all that is necessary to constitute an industrial dispute is disagreement as to the terms or conditions that should, in fact, apply as between employer and employee.' *Re State Public Services Federation; Ex p A-G (WA)* (1993) 178 CLR 249 at 266–267; 113 ALR 385 at 387–388, per Mason CJ, Deane and Gaudron JJ

INFORMATION

Australia [The applicant sought access under the Freedom of Information Act 1982 (Cth) to documents obtained by the Department of Immigration and Multicultural Affairs. Access to the documents was denied under s 503A of the Migration Act 1958 (Cth) on the basis that the documents did not contain 'information' pursuant to this section, namely the name of the agency which provided the information on which the applicant's visa was rejected and why the agency requested confidentiality of the information] 'By approaching the section with regard to the ordinary and natural meaning of the expression "information", it is my view that the name of the agency and the terms of the request for confidentiality can be said to be "information". As the Full Court pointed out in *Win v Minister for Immigration and Multicultural Affairs* (2001) 105 FCR 212 at 217–18, the expression "information" is a broad expression and can include, according to the Oxford English Dictionary (2nd ed, 1989), "[k]nowledge communicated concerning some particular fact, subject or event; that of which one is apprised or told". The name of the agency giving the information and the terms of the request, if disclosed, would clearly communicate knowledge about facts.' *Kwok v Minister for Immigration and Multicultural Affairs* BC200106288; [2001] FCA 1444 at [20] per Tamberlin J

Australia 'A helpful discussion of what might constitute "information" for present purposes is found in the judgment of the Full Court in *Win v Minister for Immigration & Multicultural Affairs* (2001) 105 FCR 212. That judgment concerned a "dob-in" letter received by the Tribunal. Their Honours said at 217:

> ... it may not strictly be necessary to consider the meaning of the word "information" as used in s 424(1) of the Migration Act. Nonetheless, we should record our view that the construction advanced by the appellant is too narrow.

The *Macquarie Dictionary* includes these definitions of the word "information":

> "1. Knowledge communicated or received concerning some fact or circumstance; news. 2. Knowledge in various subjects, however acquired".

The *Oxford English Dictionary* (2nd ed, 1989) includes among its definitions of "information":

> "3.a. Knowledge communicated concerning some particular fact, subject or event; that of which one is apprised or told".

As these definitions show, "information" is capable of different shades of meaning, depending on the context.' *HAJ v Minister for Immigration and Multicultural and Indigenous Affairs* [2003] FCAFC 186 at [31] per Moore J; BC200304551

INFRINGEMENT

Of copyright

[The Copyright Act 1956 has been repealed. See now, as to the meaning of infringement of copyright, the Copyright, Designs and Patents Act 1988, s 27.]

INHERENT JURISDICTION

Australia 'S[ection] 21 of the Family Law Act 1975 (Cth) provides that a court "to be known as the [Family Court] is created" by that statute. Original jurisdiction is conferred on the Family Court by s 31 and appellate jurisdiction by s 93A(1). Jurisdiction is also conferred by other statutes, including the Child Support Act 1988 (Cth) (s 101, s 102, s 105), the Bankruptcy Act 1966 (Cth) (s 35A), and the Trade Practices Act 1974 (Cth) (s 86B).

'[25] The Family Court is thus not a common law court as were the three common law courts at Westminster. Accordingly, it is "unable to draw upon the well of undefined powers" which were available to those courts as part of their "inherent jurisdiction". The Family Court is a statutory court, being a federal court created by the Parliament within the meaning of s 71 of the Constitution. A court exercising jurisdiction or powers conferred by statute "has powers expressly or by implication conferred by the legislation which governs it" and "[t]his is a matter of statutory construction"; it also has "in addition such powers as are incidental and necessary to the exercise of the jurisdiction or the powers so conferred". It would be inaccurate to use the term "inherent jurisdiction" here and the term should be avoided as an identification of the incidental and necessary power of a statutory court.

'[26] In [*R v Forbes; Ex parte Bevan* (1972) 127 CLR 1 sub nom *Re Forbes and Commonwealth Industrial Court; Ex parte Bevan* [1972–73] ALR 1046; (1972) 46 ALJR 401], Menzies J, with whose judgment Barwick CJ, Walsh and Stephen JJ agreed, distinguished in the manner identified above "inherent jurisdiction" or "inherent power" and jurisdiction or power derived by implication from statutory provisions conferring a particular jurisdiction. The distinction between these sources of power is not always made explicit but is fundamental.' *DJL v Central Authority* (2000) 170 ALR 659; 74 ALJR 706; 26 Fam LR 1; (2000) FLC 93–015; BC200001746; [2000] HCA 17 at [24]–[26], per Gleeson CJ, Gaudron, McHugh, Gummow and Hayne JJ

INHERENT REQUIREMENT

Australia [Inherent requirement of a particular employment.] '[115] In *X v The Commonwealth* [(1999) 200 CLR 177] (at 187–188), McHugh J paraphrased the "inherent requirements" of a particular employment, for the purposes of s 15(4) of the DD Act, as the "essential element" thereof,

and as relating to "much more than the physical ability to carry out the physical tasks encompassed by the particular employment", and also to obligations of fidelity and good faith on the part of the employee, and to an implied warranty of an employee to exercise reasonable care and skill in carrying out the employment.

...

'[117] In the joint reasons for judgment of Gummow and Hayne JJ, with which Gleeson CJ and Callinan J agreed, the following appears at 208:

> "The reference to 'inherent' requirements invites attention to what are the characteristics or essential requirements of the employment as opposed to those requirements that might be described as peripheral. Further, the reference to 'inherent' requirements would deal with at least some, and probably all, cases in which a discriminatory employer seeks to contrive the result that the disabled are excluded from a job. But the requirements that are to be considered are the requirements of the particular employment, not the requirements of employment of some identified type or some different employment to meet the needs of a disabled employee or applicant for work".'

Daghlian v Australian Postal Corp [2003] FCA 759 per Conti J; BC200303964

INHERENT REQUIREMENTS

Australia 'In the report of the International Labour Organisation's Commission of Inquiry into the observance of the Discrimination Convention by the Federal Republic of Germany, "inherent" was interpreted to mean "existing in something as a permanent attribute or quality; forming an element, especially an essential element, of something; intrinsic, essential". The term "inherent" in [the Industrial Relations Act 1988 (Cth)] s 170DF(2) should be given the same meaning. Importantly, for the purposes of this case, that which is essential to the performance of a particular position must be regarded as an inherent requirement of that position.' *Qantas Airways Ltd v Christie* (1998) 152 ALR 365 at 383; (1998) 79 IR 120; [1998] HCA 18 at [74]; BC9800685 at 25, per McHugh J

INHERENT REQUIREMENTS OF PARTICULAR EMPLOYMENT

Australia [Section 15(4) of the Disability Discrimination Act 1992 (Cth) provides that discrimination by an employer against a person on the ground of the person's disability is not unlawful if the person, because of his or her disability 'would be unable to carry out the inherent requirements of the particular employment'.] 'Whether something is an "inherent requirement" of a particular employment for the purposes of the Act depends on whether it was an "essential element" of the particular employment. However, the inherent requirements of employment embrace much more than the physical ability to carry out the physical tasks encompassed by the particular employment. Thus, implied in every contract of employment are obligations of fidelity and good faith on the part of the employee with the result that an employee breaches those requirements or obligations when he or she discloses confidential information or reveals secret processes. Furthermore, it is an implied warranty of every contract of employment that the employee possesses and will exercise reasonable care and skill in carrying out the employment. These obligations and warranties are inherent requirements of every employment. If for any reason – mental, physical or emotional – the employee is unable to carry them out, an otherwise unlawful discrimination may be protected by the provisions of s 15(4).

'[32] Similarly, carrying out the employment without endangering the safety of other employees is an inherent requirement of any employment. It is not merely "so obvious that it goes without saying" – which is one of the tests for implying a term in a contract to give effect to the supposed intention of the parties. The term is one which, subject to agreement to the contrary, the law implies in every contract of employment. It is but a particular application of the implied warranty that the employee is able to and will exercise reasonable care and skill in carrying out his or her duties.

'[33] It would be extremely artificial to draw a distinction between a physical capability to perform a task and the safety factors relevant to that task in determining the inherent requirements of any particular employment. That is because employment is not a mere physical activity in which the employee participates as an automaton. It takes place in a social, legal and economic context. Unstated, but legitimate, employment requirements may stem from this context. It is therefore always permissible to have regard to this context when determining the inherent requirements of a particular employment.' (footnotes omitted) *X v Commonwealth* (1999) 167 ALR 529; 74 ALJR 176; (2000) EOC ¶93–054; BC9907850; [1999] HCA 63 at [31]–[33], per McHugh J

INHERENT VICE

[For 25 Halsbury's Laws (4th edn) para 177 see now 25 Halsbury's Laws (4th edn) (2003 Reissue) para 354.]

INITIATION OF PROCEEDINGS

Canada 'The information that formally launched the criminal proceedings against Robert Wood was sworn by the police and not by Lauren Kennedy or her parents. The issue of whether the initiation of proceedings includes conduct falling short of swearing the formal information amounts to initiation of criminal charges was reviewed at length by the House of Lords in *Martin v Watson* [1995] 3 All ER 559. In that case, there was an acrimonious history between the parties who were neighbours. The defendant complained to the police that the plaintiff had exposed himself to her. The police laid an information, the plaintiff was arrested, but the charge was dismissed when the prosecution offered no evidence. The plaintiff sued for malicious prosecution and succeeded at trial, but the Court of Appeal set aside the judgment on the ground that it could not be said that the defendant had "set the law in motion" merely by providing false information to the police. After a detailed review of the English and Commonwealth authorities, the House of Lords restored the trial judgment, holding at 567–568:

> Where an individual falsely and maliciously gives a police officer information indicating that some person is guilty of a criminal offence and states that he is willing to give evidence in court of the matters in question, it is properly to be inferred that he desires and intends that the person he names should be prosecuted. Where the circumstances are such that the facts relating to the alleged offence can be within the knowledge only of the complainant, as was the position here, then it becomes virtually impossible for the police officer to exercise any independent discretion or judgment, and if a prosecution instituted by the police officer the proper view of the matter is that the prosecution has been procured by the complainant.

'Counsel for the defendants conceded that there was authority for the proposition that providing false information to the police which led them to lay charges could amount to initiation of proceedings, and I can see no reason not to adopt the test as laid down by the House of Lords.' *Wood v Kennedy* (1998) 165 DLR (4th) 542 at 560, Ont Gen Div, per Sharpe J

INJUNCTION

[For 24 Halsbury's Laws (4th edn) para 901 see now 24 Halsbury's Laws (4th edn) (Reissue) para 801.]

Mandatory

[For 25 Halsbury's Laws (4th edn) para 902 see now 24 Halsbury's Laws (4th edn) (Reissue) para 802.]

Perpetual

[For 25 Halsbury's Laws (4th edn) para 903 see now 24 Halsbury's Laws (4th edn) (Reissue) para 803.]

Mareva injunction

[A Mareva injunction covering assets abroad should provide that it does not affect the rights of third parties except to the extent that the order is enforced by the courts of states in which the defendant's assets are located: *Babanaft International Co SA v Bassatne* [1989] 1 All ER 433, HL.]

INJURIOUS, OR LIKELY TO CAUSE INJURY, TO HEALTH

[The local council claimed that residential premises containing a steep staircase were 'prejudicial to health' and thus a statutory nuisance within the meaning of the Environmental Protection Act 1990, s 79, sub-s (1) of which provides that statutory nuisances include any premises in such a state as to be prejudicial to health or a nuisance. Section 79(7) defines the expression 'prejudicial to health' as meaning 'injurious, or likely to cause injury, to health' but the Act does not define 'injury' or 'health'.] 'By a combination of s 79(1) and 79(7) of the Environmental Protection Act 1990 the issue in this case is whether because of the manner of construction or arrangement of its staircase 14 Bannerman Road is "in such a state as to be injurious, or likely to cause injury, to health". Although the judge did not regard the reading as the most obvious available, he was persuaded that this statutory formula could as a matter of language alone extend to a case where the state of the premises was likely to cause physical injury ... I do not agree. It is very unnatural to describe a

physical accident as causing injury to health. First, such incidents as a broken ankle or sprained wrist are in ordinary usage not described as interfering with the victim's health, as opposed to afflicting or injuring his body. Second, once the concept of injury is introduced into the definition, the specific limitation to injury to health underlines the fact that "injury" here is not used in its normal sense of bodily injury.

'There are at least two pointers in the bare wording of the present legislation that support that view. First, s 79(1)(f) of the 1990 Act, which has been linked to the present s 79(1)(a) since at least s 91 of the Public Health Act 1875, and which concerns any animal kept in such a place or manner as to be prejudicial to health or a nuisance, is difficult to reconcile with the argument that "prejudicial to health" as used generally in s 79(1) can extend to physical injury. If the purpose of s 79(1)(a) indeed extended to physical injury caused by an animal, it would be surprising that it limited that protection to injuries resulting from the "place or manner" in which the animals were kept. And it is especially odd to single out for prohibition cases where the "place" of the keeping threatens physical injury: since if an animal is dangerous it is dangerous wheresoever it may be. A further pointer in this direction is to be found in s 81 of the Public Health Act 1936, which gives local authorities powers to make "Byelaws for the prevention of certain nuisances", including, by s 81(b), byelaws preventing the keeping of animals so as to be "prejudicial to health". It strains belief to think that this latter expression, defined generally for the purposes of both the 1936 Act and the 1990 Act, can in this context extend to danger of physical injury.

'Second, the contrast between prejudice to health and physical danger is underlined in the emergency provisions under the Building Act 1984, where separate regimes are supplied in respect of s 79 statutory nuisances on the one hand (s 76 of the 1984 Act) and, on the other hand, "dangerous" buildings (s 77 of the 1984 Act). The latter expression, seen as referring to a different case from the s 79 statutory nuisance, is the obvious and natural way of referring to danger of physical injury: which "injury to health" is not.

'However, whatever may be thought of the verbal infelicities forced on the 1990 Act by the appellant's case, as the judge said everything falls into place once one looks at the history of the legislation, as expounded by Mummery LJ in his judgment. It is quite clear, as the judge indeed concluded, that the provisions of s 79(1) come without significant amendment from nineteenth century statutory provisions directed at premises that create a risk of disease or illness. The provisions with which we are concerned are first found in general public health legislation of a recognisably modern type, in almost identical terms to the 1990 Act formulation, in s 91 of the 1875 Act. Reading through that Act, and referring to its predecessors, it cries out from the page that the target of the legislators was disease and not physical injury. And that was clearly understood or assumed at the time the legislation was passed. One of the predecessor statutes, consolidated in the 1875 Act, was the Nuisances Removal Act 1855, s 8 of which addressed "... Premises in such a State as to be a Nuisance or injurious to Health". In *Great Western Rly Co v Bishop* (1872) LR 7 QB 550, where the issue was whether water running from a railway bridge on to highway users below constituted such a nuisance, Mr Lopes QC (at 551) pointed to the origins of the legislation and concluded that the Act was a sanitary Act, and so a "nuisance" under it must affect health. Cockburn CJ agreed with him (at 552). True it is that the actual issue in the case was whether the inconvenience, as opposed to physical injury, suffered by the passers-by could be a nuisance; but that point was seen as concluded by the status of the legislation as, in nineteenth century terms, a sanitary provision. That perception was expressed in the 1875 Act by the nuisance provisions in s 91 being included in Pt III, "Sanitary provisions"; and by the implementation of that Act being in the hands of the sanitary authorities that had been created by the Public Health Act 1872. Changing the language, but not the concept, into twentieth century form, the successor provisions of 1990 are about disease or ill-health, and not about physical danger.' R v Bristol City Council, ex p Everett [1999] 2 All ER 193 at 203–204, CA, per Buxton LJ

INJURY

Australia 'Nor do we accept that the extension by s 4K [of the Trade Practices Act 1974 (Cth)] of loss or damage to "injury" leads to any different conclusion. It may be that "injury" in s 4K is intended to refer to injury to the person but we do not need to decide if that is so. Even if "injury" is to be given some wider meaning than personal injury, we do not accept that a person suffers injury simply because a hoped for advantage does not materialise. The central inquiry is what consequence has the contravention of the Act had on the party in question. That requires comparison between the position in fact of the party which alleges loss and the position that would have obtained had there been no contravention.' *Marks v GIO Australia Holdings Ltd* (1998) 158 ALR 333 at 348; 73 ALJR 12; BC9805922, per McHugh, Hayne and Callinan JJ

To person

Australia [Section 5 of the Accident Compensation Act 1985 (Vic) defines 'injury' to mean any physical or mental injury including (a) industrial deafness; (b) a disease contracted by a worker in the course of the worker's employment whether at or away from the place of employment and to which the employment was a contributing factor; and (c) the recurrence, aggravation, acceleration, exacerbation or deterioration of any pre-existing injury or disease where the worker's employment was a contributing factor to that recurrence, aggravation, acceleration, exacerbation or deterioration. The question before the court was whether the rupture of an artery and consequent cerebral haemorrhage suffered by the respondent was a physical injury.] '"Injury" means in its normal usage — harm or damage, and it must be "physical" to fall within the definition with which we are concerned. Unless there is binding authority to the contrary, there is no reason that I can see why the rupture of an artery should not be considered to be physical harm. It clearly is so ... It has always been accepted in Victoria that any ascertainable lesion or dramatic physiological change causing incapacity and occurring during a protected period is an "injury" within the meaning of the Workers Compensation Act (Vic).' *Accident Compensation Commission v McIntosh* [1991] 2 VR 253 at 256–257, per Murphy J

Australia [Safety, Rehabilitation and Compensation Act 1988 (Cth) s 4(1).] 'The task is one of statutory construction. This is a beneficial statute. Nevertheless, conformably with that, it is necessary to construe the words used by the Parliament.

'The so-called proviso in the definition does not exclude causes. It provides that if a disease or injury which would otherwise fall within the definition ("any such") is one which answers a description (relevantly here: "suffered as a result of ... the failure to obtain a promotion"), the disease or injury is not an "injury" as defined. The words are satisfied here. There was no debate that the factual findings made by the Tribunal amount to a conclusion that the disease or injury suffered was as a result of the failure to obtain the promotions.

'In order to succeed, the appellant must assert, as she does, that operative causes are not excluded and that given the provision's purpose some modifier should be read into the words to restrict the effect of the exclusion to circumstances where there were no other employment related causes. We do not agree. The operation of the provision had the evident purpose of removing from the field of compensation a disease, injury or aggravation which was a result of something. We see no evident purpose to remove from the field of compensation a disease, injury or aggravation which was only a result of that thing. The words do not readily admit that construction. The cases on multiple causes in tort or general law do not assist that enquiry.

'It will in any case be for the Tribunal to examine the facts, assess the reasons for the disease, injury or aggravation and come to conclusions in respect thereof. Whether in any given case, those findings allow a conclusion that the condition was suffered as a result of one or more of the matters referred to in the proviso, may be a factual question, or perhaps a legal question. Here, however, the findings were clear. The failure to obtain the promotions materially contributed to the condition and there is no issue but that the condition was suffered as a result of the failure to obtain the promotion.

'To the extent that Drummond J in *Comcare v Mooi* (1996) 69 FCR 439 at 448 took a different view as to the operation of the definition, we respectfully disagree. To the extent that his Honour did, it was clearly obiter.

...

'As to the way the primary judge approached the matter, we are of the view that as a matter of construction of the definition the distinction drawn by the Tribunal was not necessarily inappropriate. The events which surround a promotion process may, conceivably, be such as to cause serious injury, mental or physical. Injury as a result thereof could be quite distinct from any injury suffered as a result of a failure to obtain a promotion. However, equally, distress at or with the process of assessing the candidates for promotion may, as a matter of fact, be suffered as a result of failure to obtain the promotion. It is possible to envisage circumstances where someone who would have had no, or limited, criticism of the events surrounding a promotion process had he or she achieved the promotion, becomes aggrieved by those processes to the extent of suffering psychological harm following a failure to obtain the promotion. In such circumstances, there may be factual issues, including medical issues, as to what was the role of the events in the procedure and of the failure to obtain the promotion.

However, we do not think that it can be concluded, as a matter of construction of the definition, that events concerned with the process of evaluation of the promotion application are necessarily bound up with the decision as to the promotion and any failure to obtain the promotion.' *Hart v Comcare* [2005] FCAFC 16 at [20], per Branson, Conti and Allsop JJ; BC200501180

Australia [Evidence of injury is required to establish that a sexual assault victim is a victim of an act of violence. 'Injury' is defined in the Dictionary section of the Victims Support and Rehabilitation Act 1996 (NSW).]

'[46] "Injury" is defined in the Dictionary as follows:

"Injury" means:
(a) actual physical bodily harm,
(b) psychological or psychiatric disorder,

...

but does not include injury arising from loss or damage to property.

...

'[104] Identifying a person who is prima facie eligible for statutory compensation depends first upon determining whether or not that person has been a victim of an "act of violence" within the meaning of s 5. Relevantly that requires the claimant for compensation to demonstrate that the offence to which he or she has been subjected "resulted in injury or death" (s 5(1)(c)). This requirement is reflected in Pt 4, dealing with compensation awarded by the Court, which requires the aggrieved person to establish that he/she has "sustained injury" by reason of the offence.

'[105] Proof of "injury" turns upon demonstrating the victim suffered either actual bodily harm or psychological or psychiatric disorder.' *Victims Compensation Fund Corporation v GM* [2004] NSWCA 185 at [46], [104]–[105], per McColl JA; BC200403610

Australia [In the context of the (NSW) Motor Accidents Act 1988.] 'In *Leo N Dunn & Sons Pty Ltd v McPhillamy* [2000] NSWCA 343, the plaintiff pleaded that he suffered back injury through sitting over a period in a twisted seat in the shuddering cabin of a prime mover. It was held that he did not make a "claim" as defined in s 40(1) of the Motor Accidents Act 1988 ("the MAA"), which referred to a claim to damages "in respect of the death of or injury to a person caused by the fault of the owner or driver of a motor vehicle in the use or operation of the vehicle", and that the claim as pleaded was "one relating to something different, namely an injury arising out of the nature and conditions of employment" (at [18]).

'This did not directly turn on the meaning of "injury", the definition of which in the MAA at the relevant time was materially the same as that in the MACA. *Leo N Dunn & Sons Pty Ltd v McPhillamy* involved a time limit for commencing proceedings, which did not apply to the commencement of proceedings in respect of a claim within the meaning of the MAA (s 151D(4)). It was submitted that the trial judge had wrongly imported the concept of a motor accident as defined in the MAA. Mason P said (at [16]–[18]—

[16] I have no difficulty with the submission that what happened here does fall within the concept of a "claim" as that definition stands alone in s 40(1). That definition does not pick up provisions relating to a motor accident or require that the claim arise out of a motor accident or even a series of motor accidents, at least in the sense of motor accidents as events occurring at a particular point of time.

[17] However, I have concluded that his Honour was correct in his broad reasoning. In my view, one should start with examining the purpose of s 151D(4) as it appears on the face of that section. I have indicated what I think it to be. It is not looking just at picking up the definition of the word "claim" as found in s (1) [sic: s 40(1)] of the Motor Accidents Act, even though that definition serves the function of defining that word for the purpose of the whole of Part 5 thereof. The word "claim", when found in s 40, appears in a context and with a purpose, namely that of regulating due notice to insurers and the timely and efficient prosecution of proceedings in courts. That Part seems to me to be directed and only to be directed at the type of accident that occurs at a fixed point of time.

[18] I am not suggesting that there cannot be more than one accident giving rise to perhaps a single injury and an overlapping set of obligations with respect to traffic reports, proceedings and the like. Nevertheless, I would accept the submission of counsel for the opponent that the claim as propounded in the draft statement of claim is one relating to something different, namely an injury arising out of the nature and conditions of employment.

'Meagher JA said succinctly (at [22]) that "the word claim when used in Pt 5 of the Motor Accidents Act means claim arising out of a motor accident, notwithstanding the more limited definition in s 40(1)". Heydon JA agreed with his brethren. The distinction was between an accident causing injury and nature and conditions of work causing injury.

'In *Emad Trolley Pty Ltd v Shigar* [2003] NSWCA 231 the plaintiff, who was injured when he fell from a trolley truck while collecting shopping trolleys, pleaded that he suffered his injury due to an unsafe system of work. It was held that, despite the pleading, his was a claim within the similar definition of a claim in the MACA. With reference to *Leo N Dunn & Sons Pty Ltd v McPhillamy*, Hodgson JA observed (at [6]) that it would have been different if it had been "in respect of an injury caused progressively over a period of time, even if caused by the fault of the owner of a motor vehicle, and even if a result of and caused by the driving of that vehicle ...". However, his Honour went on —

Chapter 4 of the MAC Act is plainly directed at regulating claims arising out of motor accidents, and has no application where an alleged injury is caused, not by a motor accident, but progressively over a period of time: see s 67. Accordingly, ss 70 and 108 have no application where there is no motor accident, even though there may be an injury and a claim as defined by the MAC Act.

'Accordingly, his Honour's observation did not turn on the meaning of "injury".

'These cases were applied in *Owen v State of New South Wales* [2004] NSWCA 165. The plaintiff's painful back was aggravated by a bumpy ride on an unpadded bench in a prison van. A defence was raised that his claim in that respect fell within the MAA and must fail because steps required prior to bringing proceedings in respect of a claim had not been taken. Campbell AJA, with whom Beazley and Ipp JJA agreed, said that it was not necessary to decide whether the plaintiff's injury was an injury as defined in the MAA (at [47]), but that for the injury to be caught by Pt 5 of the MAA (which required the steps) it must be "caused by a motor accident which occurred at a fixed point of time" (at [58]). A fixed point of time was distinguished from a fixed instant of time, with recognition that a motor accident can occur over some seconds or longer, but it was said that for a motor accident to be caught by Pt 5 it must be "sufficiently circumscribed in time to allow it to be identified as such and to set in train the reporting and other provisions of the Part" (at [62]). Again, the distinction was between injury occurring at a particular time (caused by an accident) and injury not so occurring.

'The appellant accepted that the provisions of the MACA "as they related to motor accident claims" had no application where an injury was caused progressively over a period of time. The submissions on appeal were directed to whether the appellant's back injury was an injury within the meaning of the MACA, and the appellant submitted that, on the balance of probabilities, he had sustained disc lesions or herniations on 18 January 2001 which constituted the requisite injury.

'Section 122(1) does not refer to a claim or to a motor accident, although s 122(2) does say that Ch 5 "does not apply to or in respect of a motor accident occurring before the commencement of this Act". By extension from the above cases, however, Ch 5 of the MACA dealing with damages is concerned with injury from "the type of accident that occurs at a fixed point of time" (*Leo N Dunn & Sons Pty Ltd v McPhillamy* at [17]). While it may come down to whether there was a frank injury, the phrase hallowed by usage in contrast with injury from the nature and conditions of work, the task is one of identifying the injury and determining whether it was an injury occurring at a particular time as distinct from one arising out of the nature and conditions of work. If it was, it is then of course necessary to address the other elements in the definition of injury in the MACA.' *Khaya v Container Terminals Australia Ltd* [2005] NSWCA 433 at [9]–[15], per Giles JA; BC200510757

Canada [Two-year limitation period applied in respect of injury to person or property.] '... "injury to property" in s 3(1)(*a*) [of Limitation Act, RSBC 1979, c236] should be construed to refer to a circumstance where property has received direct damage from or by "an extrinsic act" or, putting it another way, from or by "an identifiable external event". In my view the phrase "injury to person" in s 3(1)(*a*) should be construed in the same manner.' *Zubrugg v Bowie* (1992) 91 DLR (4th) 599 at 605, BC CA, per Hinds JA

New Zealand 'Looking at the Act [Accident Compensation Act 1972] as a whole ... it is designed to provide compensation for those who suffer injury (or death). The injury (or death) is qualified by the term "by accident" which seems to me to preclude the test from being an inquiry into whether or not the person who caused the injury was an intentional wrongdoer, reckless wrongdoer, negligent wrongdoer or merely the innocent cause of injury. That is the description of the actor and not a description of what the victim suffered. Indeed, an accident may happen without the intervention of a second party but result from something done solely by the injured person. The legislation must be construed from the point of view of the person who suffers the injury and in the light of the wide language used.' *G v Auckland Hospital Board* [1976] 1 NZLR 638 at 641, per Henry J

New Zealand 'Once there is a personal injury by accident within the scope of the Act [Accident Compensation Act 1982], all the emotional or psychological effects fall within the statutory words "The physical and mental consequences of any such injury or of the accident". Those words are not limited to mental consequences identifiable by some particular medical or psychiatric description, nor to what is often called shock or trauma. Parliament cannot have intended fine distinctions in this area.' *Green v Matheson* [1989] 3 NZLR 564 at 572, CA, per cur

INLAND WATERS

[The Water Resources Act 1963 has been repealed. A definition of 'inland waters' is now contained in the Water Resources Act 1991, s 221(1), as follows.] 'Inland waters' means the whole or any part of—

   (a) any river, stream or other watercourse (within the meaning of Chapter II of Part II of this Act), whether natural or artificial and whether tidal or not;

   (b) any lake or pond, whether natural or artificial, or any reservoir or dock, in so far as the lake, pond, reservoir or dock does not fall within paragraph (a) of this definition; and

   (c) so much of any channel, creek, bay, estuary or arm of the sea as does not fall within paragraph (a) or (b) of this definition.

INN KEEPER

[For 24 Halsbury's Laws (4th edn) para 1206 see now 24 Halsbury's Laws (4th edn) (Reissue) paras 1105–1106.]

INNOCENT ... OF ANY FRAUDULENT CONDUCT OR INTENT TO DECEIVE

New Zealand [Professional Indemnity Insurance Policy.] 'There is an element of surplusage in the clause if "innocent" is given its ordinary meaning. We think, however, that it would distort the apparent purpose of the provision if "innocent" were to be given the gloss suggested by counsel ... Upon an ordinary use of the language an insured which has not acted dishonestly would be taken to have acted innocently ... We have real difficulty in seeing where the line could be drawn between innocent but unconscionable behaviour and that which was innocent simpliciter. We are not persuaded that the natural meaning of the words in a clause proffered by an insurer should be strained in this manner to enable avoidance of the policy where an insured is found to have acted without fraud or deceit. It is more appropriate, we think, to accept that the clause has an element of surplusage or to read it as meaning "innocent *and so* free of any fraudulent conduct or intent to deceive." The provision as a whole is clearly directed to the subjective intention or state of mind of the insured, not to the effect of their conduct.' *Switzerland Insurance (Australia) Ltd v Gooch* [1996] 3 NZLR 525 at 531, per cur

INNUENDO

[For 28 Halsbury's Laws (4th edn) paras 44, 46 see now 28 Halsbury's Laws (4th edn) (Reissue) paras 39, 47.]

INPUT TAX

[The Value Added Tax Act 1983 has been repealed. The definition is now contained in the Value Added Tax Act 1994, s 24(1) as follows.] Subject to the following provisions of this section, 'input tax', in relation to a taxable person, means the following tax, that is to say—

    (a) VAT on the supply to him of any goods or services;

    (b) VAT on the acquisition by him from another member State of any goods; and

    (c) VAT paid or payable by him on the importation of any goods from a place outside the member States,

being (in each case) goods or services used or to be used for the purpose of any business carried on or to be carried on by him.

[*See also* OUTPUT TAX.]

INSANE

Australia [Section 393(1) of the Crimes Act 1958 (Vic) provides, inter alia, that if any person indicted or presented for any indictable offence is 'insane' and is upon arraignment so found by a jury lawfully empanelled for that purpose so that such person cannot be tried upon such indictment or presentment, the court may order such person to be kept in strict custody until the Governor's pleasure be known.] '... it has long been recognised that, in a context such as s 393, the word "insane" does not mean "insane in the colloquial sense" (*R v Presser* [1958] VR 45 at 48) or "insane within the M'Naughten Rules" (*Ngatayi v R* (1980) 147 CLR 1 at 7) ... In England, the courts have always applied Alderson B's interpretation in *R v Pritchard* (1836) 7 Car & P 303; 173 ER 135 of s 2 of the Criminal Lunatics Act, namely, that "the question is, whether the prisoner has sufficient understanding to comprehend the nature of this trial, so as to make a proper defence to the charge". In the context of s 393, the word signifies inability, by reason of some physical or mental condition, to follow proceedings of the trial and to make a defence in those proceedings: *Ngatayi* at 9. Thus, it has been said that the test needs to be applied "in a reasonable and commonsense fashion": *Presser* at 48; *Ngatayi* at 8. The test looks to the capacity of the accused to understand the proceedings and, in some cases, complete understanding may require intelligence of quite a high order: *Ngatayi* at 8. But it does not mean that the accused is required to have sufficient capacity to make an able defence: *Presser* at 48; *Ngatayi* at 8.' *Kesavarajah v R* (1994) 181 CLR 230 at 244–245, per Mason CJ, Toohey and Gaudron JJ

INSOLVENCY

'All legal systems have to deal with the situation which arises where a debtor is unable to pay his debts. Under English law, where the debtor is a corporate body, its assets are sold, the proceeds distributed among its creditors, and then the debtor ceases to exist, ie it is dissolved. The law is more merciful to an individual. His property is sold and the proceeds distributed among his creditors. Thereafter, in due course, he is discharged from bankruptcy and is permitted to resume normal life, freed from the burden of his past debts. This simple scheme has to be buttressed by statutory provisions concerned to prevent abuse by debtors and to achieve a fair distribution of a debtor's property among his creditors. In some circumstances it would not be reasonable that a disposition of property made by an individual before his bankruptcy, or by a company before being wound up, should be allowed to stand. This may be because of the purpose for which the disposition was made, or because of the time at which it was made. One instance is where a debtor, anticipating insolvency, seeks to discharge one of his debts in priority to the others. For example a company may pay off its bank overdraft ahead of its other liabilities because the directors have given personal guarantees to the bank. The directors are anxious to relieve themselves of their personal liability, so they decide to use what money is available in repaying the bank and to leave those who have supplied goods to the company to whistle for their money. Another instance is when an individual, anxious about the consequences of his insolvency, gives away his property shortly before he becomes bankrupt. For example he transfers his share of his house to his wife. Fairness to his creditors demands that he should not be able to deplete his assets in this way in a deliberate attempt to put them beyond the reach of his creditors. Successive statutes, principally the Bankruptcy Acts and the Companies Acts, contained provisions regulating this subject matter. They were something of a hotchpot. The provisions are to be found now in the Insolvency Act 1986. They comprise a coherent, modernised and expanded code.' *Re Paramount Airways Ltd* [1992] 3 All ER 1 at 3–4, CA, per Sir Donald Nicholls V-C

INSTITUTION

[The Charities Act 1960 has been repealed. The definition is now reproduced in the Charities Act 1993, s 97(1).]

Australia [A foundation applied for a certificate of exemption from liability to pay tax on debits made to accounts held with banks and non-bank financial institutions pursuant to s 11(1) of the Debits Tax Administration Act 1982 (Cth) on the ground that it was a 'religious institution' under s 3 of that Act.] 'The context in which the expression "religious institution" appears includes the juxtaposed term "public benevolent institution" which tends to suggest that the word "institution" is to be given a meaning greater than a structure controlled and operated by family members and friends.' *Pamas Foundation (Inc) v Deputy Commissioner of Taxation* (1992) 35 FCR 117 at 125; 106 ALR 229 at 237–238, per Beaumont and Lee JJ

Canada '[40] In the *Dictionary of Politics*, 7th ed., Lawrenceville, Virginia: Brunswick Publishing Corp., 1992, by Walter John Raymond, the word "institution" is defined as follows:

> **Institution.** The delivery system for the implementation of an idea, a will, or a certain

desired end, consisting of people who are behaving and interacting according to preset patterns (e.g., discipline and loyalty), and who perform their designated functions according to preset goals and objectives.

'[41] According to Le Grand Robert de la Langue Française, 1985, the current meaning of the word "institution" is as follows:

> [TRANSLATION] **Institution** … . Court. That which is instituted (body politic, group, foundation, legal or social regime) … human, national, international, political, religious institutions
>
> …
>
> An institution can take the form of a legal entity of public (e.g.: State, Parliament) or private (e.g.: association) law, a non-personalized group, a foundation or a legal regime …
>
> …
>
> Collective. Educ. The *Institution:* a group of organized structures that perpetuate themselves in each area of social activity. *The legal, litterary, artistic … institutions of a society.*'

Qu v Canada [2002] 3 FC 3 at 17–18 (CA), per Richard J

INSTRUCT *SEE* PROMOTE, INCITE OR INSTRUCT

INSULT. *SEE* OFFEND, INSULT, HUMILIATE OR INTIMIDATE

INSULTING WORDS

Australia 'Considerable reliance was placed upon the primary definition of "insult" given in the *Macquarie Dictionary* namely, "to treat insolently with or contemptuous rudeness; affront". [The intervener] submitted that if "insult" is confined to contemptuous rudeness, the term has only a relatively narrow application, so that such conduct could properly be prohibited without imposing an unacceptable burden upon free political speech. However I do not think the term "insult" can be properly confined to the first part of the Macquarie definition, and note that it also includes "affront" which is not a meaning that aids the submission. It is interesting to note that the example of usage given in the same entry is: "The crowd piled up at the windows and added insult to injury by laughing at them." Laughter of course can be a very hurtful insult, and cartoons with emphatic captions are a well-established form of political comment.

'In *Thurley v Hayes* (1920) 27 CLR 548 at 550 Rich J delivering the judgment of the court stated:

"'Insulting' is a very large term, and in a statement of this kind is generally understood to be a word not cramped within narrow limits. In the *Oxford Dictionary* under the word 'insult', we find it means in a transitive sense 'to assail with offensively dishonouring or contemptuous speech or action; to treat with scornful abuse or offensive disrespect; to offer indignity to; to affront, outrage'. We find in the same dictionary: 'Hence "insulted," treated with contemptuous abuse, outrage'. There is, therefore, in this case no warrant for saying that the words complained of and found to have been used were not legally capable of being regarded as insulting words."

'The words there in question were "You are sponging on the government and you waste public money and I will report you", spoken to a returned soldier. Similarly, in the Victorian case of *Annett v Brickell* [1940] VLR 312 the expression "insulting words" was held to be not limited to words disparaging a person's moral character. They were held to include scornful abuse of a person or the offering of any personal indignity or affront. Similarly, in the United Kingdom under analogous legislation it has been considered that the word should be given its ordinary or popular meaning, and it is interpreted neither more widely nor more narrowly than such a meaning requires.

'In Queensland, in *Voigt v Loveridge; Ex parte Loveridge* [1938] St R Qd 303, the Full Court upheld a conviction under s 7A(1)(c) [of the Vagrants, Gaming and Other Offences Act 1931 (Qld)] of a political candidate for distributing circulars alleging that his opponent had offered himself as a Free Labourer (scab) in 1911 "when unionists were fighting for their existence", and that his opponent had "worked for the 'boss' to crush his fellow unionists in Mackay district". It continued, "trade unionists, please remember this: you know what its effect is and you know it is an action which cannot be forgotten or forgiven". The court held the magistrate entitled to find the circular insulting. The word "insulting" plainly cannot be successfully insulated from a political and governmental context.

'I do not think that the term can be properly limited to the narrow meaning suggested by [the intervener]. A person who printed or distributed a statement that a member of parliament lacked integrity or had been selfish and lazy, or had let down his electorate and deserved to be sacked could not in my view defeat a charge brought under s 7A(1) [of the Vagrants, Gaming and Other Offences Act 1931 (Qld)] even if the words were true. As earlier mentioned there is no available defence of truth or any other defence that could be made such as those that would be available in a charge of defamation. At least a significant minority of political cartoons might likewise offend the prohibition both of abusive and insulting words, and might in any event satisfy counsel's preferred connotation of "contemptuously rude".' *Coleman v P* BC200107434; [2001] QCA 539 at [52]–[55], per Thomas JA

INSURABLE INTEREST

[For 25 Halsbury's Laws (4th edn) para 190 see now 25 Halsbury's Laws (4th edn) (2003 Reissue) para 366.]

INSURANCE

[For 25 Halsbury's Laws (4th edn) para 2 see now 25 Halsbury's Laws (4th edn) (2003 Reissue) para 2.]

Contingency

[For 25 Halsbury's Laws (4th edn) para 791 see now 25 Halsbury's Laws (4th edn) (2003 Reissue) para 780.]

Double

[For 25 Halsbury's Laws (4th edn) para 534 see now 25 Halsbury's Laws (4th edn) (2003 Reissue) para 495.]

Industrial assurance

[For 25 Halsbury's Laws (4th edn) para 550 see now 25 Halsbury's Laws (4th edn) (2003 Reissue) para 528.]

Australia 'When the term "insurance" is used in the Constitution it cannot, in my view, be taken to be so restricted as to exclude from its scope transactions that have all the characteristics of insurance except the suggested need for the premium to be proportionate to the risk. That would involve a limitation on the scope of the power that could not have been intended because it would exclude from possible legislative regulation transactions having every outward appearance of insurance and serving, from the viewpoint of the policyholder, every function of insurance and involving the creation of rights indistinguishable from those created by a policy of insurance in respect of which the premiums were, in fact, proportioned to the risk'. *Australian Health Insurance Association Ltd v Esso Australia Pty Ltd* (1993) 116 ALR 253 at 260, per Black CJ

INSURANCE BUSINESS

[The question arose whether reinsurance business is 'insurance business' within the meaning of the Insurance Companies Act 1982.] 'Section 1 of the Act speaks of "insurance business" which it then divides into "long term business" and "general business". Insurance business is defined by section 95 of the Act so as to include the matters therein specifically referred to. That form of definition does not preclude the ordinary meaning of words which, as to one of the meanings of the word "insurance"given in the Oxford English Dictionary is as follows:

"A contract by which the one party (usually a company or corporation) undertakes, in consideration of a payment (called a premium) proportioned to the nature of the risk contemplated, to secure the other against pecuniary loss, by payment of a sum of money in the event of destruction of or damage to property (as by disaster at sea, fire or other accident), or of the death or disablement of a person."

'I do not see the mention of destruction of or damage to property nor that parenthetical reference to premium as at the heart of an up-to-date meaning of the word, but the notion of a securing against pecuniary loss in consideration of a payment proportioned to the risk contemplated is, and, as such, I do not see the ordinary meaning of the word insurance to exclude but rather to include reinsurance.

'If, then, the ordinary meaning of words permits or requires reinsurance to be regarded as "insurance", is there anything in the Act of 1982 to suggest otherwise? ... [A]s I see it, [the references in ss 3(2), 9(3), 32(1)(b), 32(3), 37(2)(d), 63(1) of the Act to "reinsurance"] either make sense, in some cases, only if the word "insurance" as used in the Act includes reinsurance or, at lowest, are, in other cases, not inconsistent with "insurance" having that meaning. The Act itself, in other words, points irresistibly in the same direction as the ordinary meaning of words ... I conclude that for the purposes of the Act of 1982 reinsurance business is included within the broader term "insurance business".' *Re NRG Victory Reinsurance Ltd* [1995] 1 WLR 239 at 241–242, per Lindsay J

Long term business

'If insurance business includes reinsurance business [see *Re NRG Victory Reinsurance Ltd* supra] then reinsurance business has to be capable of being examined to see whether it falls into long term business within the classes specified in Schedule 1 to the [Insurance Companies Act 1982] or "general business" of the classes specified in Part I of Schedule 2 to that Act — see section 1(1). However, there is in neither Schedule any specific reference to reinsurance. It must follow that the terms of Schedule 1 and of Schedule 2 Part I are themselves sufficient to effect any necessary division of reinsurance notwithstanding that they do not in terms refer to reinsurance. As no other machinery for a division is provided and as the machinery provided has to suffice, the inevitable conclusion, in my view, is that the Act contemplates that reinsurance of insurance which is insurance within the classes of business in Schedule 1 is long term reinsurance and is long term business, with a corresponding conclusion as to reinsurance of insurance which is insurance of the general business classes of Schedule 2 Part I. Long term reinsurance is thus long term business.' *Re NRG Victory Reinsurance Ltd* [1995] 1 WLR 239 at 242, per Lindsay J

INTENT TO DEFRAUD

New Zealand 'An intent to defraud [under s 229A of the Crimes Act 1981] does not necessarily require an intent to inflict a pecuniary or economic injury or have to result in loss of that nature. It may apply for example where a document is brought into existence to deceive a person responsible for the discharge of a public duty into doing something he would not have done but for the deceit, or not doing something which but for the deceit, he would have carried out. As pointed out in *Weiham v Director of Public Prosecutions* [1961] AC 103 deceit in this form may result in an advantage to the deceiver without any corresponding loss to the deceived. Examples given in the same case were of a drug addict forging a doctor's prescription so as to enable him to obtain drugs from a chemist, although intending to pay the chemist the full price; or a character reference forged for purposes of a job application. See also *Scott v Metropolitan Police Commissioner* [1975] AC 819, and *Wai*

Yu-tsang v R [1992] 1 AC 269.' *R v Firth* [1998] 1 NZLR 513 at 519, CA, per cur

INTEREST

New Zealand [Who may object under the Public Works Act 1981, s 23 to the proposed acquisition of land for public works.] '[4] Section 23(3) of the PWA prescribes who may object and it is restricted to:

> (3) Every person having an estate or interest in the land intended to be taken ...

...

'[9] I hold that the effect of s 23(3) of the PWA is that only one class of persons may lodge an objection under s 23 of the PWA: persons with any estate or interest in the land. From its context in the phrase "estate or interest" I hold that "interest" means "proprietary interest" rather than "concern".' *Bird v Nelson City Council* [2006] NZRMA 39 at [4], [9], per Judge Jackson

INTEREST (RETURN ON CAPITAL)

[For 32 Halsbury's Laws (4th edn) para 106 see now 32 Halsbury's Laws (4th edn) (Reissue) para 106.]

Australia [Section 9(1) of the Taxation (Interest on Overpayment) Act 1983 (Cth) provides for 'interest' to be paid on certain refunds of tax overpayments.] 'The word "interest" is a term in ordinary English usage. In the context of the payment of money it means "compensation for injury 'damages" ' or "money paid for the use of money lent (the principal) or for forbearance of a debt, according to a fixed ratio" (The Oxford English Dictionary, 2nd edn, 1980, vol VII, p 1099), or "a charge for the use of credit or borrowed money; such a charge expressed as a percentage per time unit of the sum borrowed or used": Collins English Dictionary (Australian Edition), 1982, p 761. At law the different senses of the ordinary usage of the word have been reflected in the concepts of "interest proper" (being interest due under a contract, statute or due for any reason in law) and "interest by way of damages" (being interest for deprivation of the use of money or delay in its payment): *Riches v Westminster Bank Ltd* [1947] AC 390 at 400. A useful definition of "interest" in its common usage and at law and in equity is that given by Rand J in *Re Farm Security Act 1944 of the Province of Saskatchewan* [1947] SCR 394 at 411:

"Interest is, in general terms the return or consideration or compensation for the use or retention by one person of a sum of money, belonging to, in a colloquial sense, or owed to, another ... But the definition ... assumes that interest is referable to a principal in money or an obligation to pay money".

'The term "interest" is used in s 9(1) of the Act in its widest sense and includes both the concept of a return on the money represented by the overpaid tax or compensation for the loss of its use for such period as it has been held by the revenue. The terms "simple interest" and "compound interest" do not alter the essential character of interest. Rather, the adjective denotes the method of calculation and thus the type of interest. Simple interest is the interest paid on the principal lent or the obligation to pay money. Compound interest is the interest eventually paid on a principal periodically increased by the addition of each fresh amount of interest as it becomes due and remains unpaid. The type of interest contemplated by s 9(1) of the Act is determined by the method of calculation specified in s 10. *Consolidated Fertilizers Ltd v Deputy Commissioner of Taxation* (1992) 107 ALR 456 at 461–462, per Cooper J

New Zealand [Insolvency Act 1967, s 75(4). Counsel had argued that 'interest' in subs (4) need not be read as requiring an existing interest and could encompass ... a divested or determined interest.] 'A divested interest is no longer an interest ... "any interest" in subs (4) refers only to an interest recognised by law.' *Auckland City Council v Glucina* [1997] 2 NZLR 1 at 5, per cur

INTEREST IN LAND

New Zealand 'The view that I have reached is that a right to work mines and carry away the minerals won is an incorporeal hereditament (because it is a right over land in the possession of another). If of indeterminate duration it is a freehold interest; if of fixed duration a chattel interest. In either case it is an interest in land.' *Tainui Maori Trust Board v A-G* [1989] 2 NZLR 513 at 523, CA, per Cooke P

New Zealand 'When considering whether a right of first refusal creates an interest in land, it is convenient to analyse the general point in four stages. Stage one is where all that exists is a bare right of pre-emption. Stage two is reached when a triggering event occurs requiring an offer to be made to the person with the right of pre-emption. Stage three relates to the time after an offer has been made pursuant to the right of pre-emption and stage four, for completeness, relates to the stage, if reached, when a contract results from the acceptance of such offer.

'At stage one the position is clear. A bare right of pre-emption, before there is any suggestion of an event triggering the right, does not create any interest in land: see *Mackay v Wilson* (1947) 47 SR (NSW) 315, *Re Rutherford* [1977] 1 NZLR 504, *Pritchard v Briggs* [1980] 1 All ER 294, *Anderson v Te Wharau Investments Ltd* (1990) ANZ ConvR 156 and *Gainford v Stinson* (1993) 2 NZ ConvC 191,768 (CA).

'At the other end of the spectrum it is perfectly plain that once a contract exists between the parties for the sale and purchase of land an interest in land is created in the purchaser. The fact that the contract may still be conditional will not of itself necessarily prevent an interest in land from arising: see *Bevin v Smith* [1994] 3 NZLR 648; and *McDonald v Isaac Construction Co Ltd* [1995] 3 NZLR 612, 619.

'Working backwards we come to stage three. This is where, pursuant to the right of pre-emption, the vendor has actually made an offer to the holder of the right, which offer is normally open for acceptance for a stipulated period of time. The offer will be couched on the basis of the terms which the vendor is prepared to offer elsewhere. This situation cannot be materially distinguished from an option in the conventional sense and thus creates an interest in land: see *Morland v Hales* (1910) 30 NZLR 201 (CA) and *Bevin v Smith* (supra) at p 665.

'It is at stage two where the difficulties arise. At this stage an event has occurred which requires the vendor to make an offer to the person holding the right of pre-emption but no such offer has been made. The distinction between stage two and stage one is that at stage one no triggering event has occurred. That is why at that stage it is clear no interest in land can arise because the vendor has decided to sell but, in breach of the right, has failed or refused to make the necessary offer to the holder of the right. It is at this point that the holder of the right will usually be most vulnerable. Clearly an injunction may be appropriate but a caveat may well be better because of its effect as notice to others interested in buying.

'When analysing the point at stage two, it should not matter whether the right of pre-emption is couched as a negative covenant or as a positive one, i e not to sell without first offering as opposed to offering before looking elsewhere. In substance the effect is the same. Once the triggering event has occurred, the holder of the right is entitled to

receive an offer.' *Motor Works Ltd v Westminster Auto Services Ltd* [1997] 1 NZLR 762 at 765, per Tipping J

INTERESTS OF JUSTICE

Australia 'The interests of justice in a particular criminal case are to ensure that a person who is accused of a crime is convicted if guilty and acquitted if innocent after he has had a fair trial. The interests of justice also extend to the public interest in the due administration of justice.' *Re Mickelberg* (1992) 59 A Crim R 288 at 302–303, per Malcolm CJ

INTERIM

Canada 'In my view, the impugned order ought to be set aside on the ground that it does not grant the interim protection provided for in Article 9 of the *Commercial Arbitration Code*. I agree with the plaintiff's submission that interim protection is "interim" in that it is something done pending final determination of the issues on the merits. It is protection, not payment. Here, the Prothonotary awarded costs to be collected now, without any determination whatsoever on the merits. There is no opportunity to alter this award. There is nothing "interim" about the award, and it is not "protective" in nature"it is payment.' *Frontier International Shipping Corp v Tauros (The)* [2000] 2 FC 445 at 448, FCTD, per Pinard J

INTERPLEADER

[For 25 Halsbury's Laws (4th edn) para 1001 see now 37(1) Halsbury's Laws (4th edn) (Reissue) para 1419.]

INTERPRETER

New Zealand [New Zealand Bill of Rights Act 1990, s 24(g).] 'The phrase "assistance of an interpreter" is broad and inclusive: nothing on the face of the provision limits it application to contemporaneous oral interpretation. I accept that "interpreters" are commonly understood as those persons who orally translate the spoken language of others in their presence, but I do not consider that the meaning is necessarily restricted in this way—particularly in the present context where it is the "assistance" of an interpreter which is referred to.

'If the purpose of the right is to ensure an accused person understands and participates meaningfully in the proceeding, then to restrict interpretative assistance to the spoken word (when much of significance in legal proceedings appears in written form) would rob the right of true force.' *Alwen Industries Ltd v Collector of Customs* [1996] 3 NZLR 226 at 230, per Robertson J

INTIMIDATE. *SEE* OFFEND, INSULT, HUMILIATE OR INTIMIDATE

INTIMIDATES

[The Criminal Justice and Public Order Act 1994, s 51(1) provides that a person commits an offence if (a) he does an act which 'intimidates, and is intended to intimidate', another person ('the victim'), (b) he does the act knowing or believing that the victim is assisting in the investigation of an offence or is a witness or potential witness or a juror or potential juror in proceedings for an offence, and (c) he does it intending thereby to cause the investigation or the course of justice to be obstructed, perverted or interfered with.] '[16] "Intimidation" and "to intimidate" are ordinary English words with a normally understood primary meaning of putting someone in fear. Fear is part of the Latin derivation. As with most words, there are shades of possible meaning, such that to attempt a definition which is intended to be comprehensive is unnecessary and undesirable. An intention by the defendant to intimidate is not alone enough, for that is the other limb of the relevant part of the statutory offence. Accordingly we consider that the appellant was entitled to be acquitted if "an act which intimidates ... another person" is limited to circumstances where in consequence the victim is intimidated in the sense that he is put in fear. '[17] We accept, however, that the *Oxford English Dictionary*'s modern usage of "to intimidate" as including "to force to or deter from some action by threats or violence" is capable of embracing a shade of meaning whereby the intimidator does not in fact succeed in putting the victim in fear. For this meaning, some element of threat or violence is necessary. '[18] In our judgment, a person does an act which intimidates another person within s 51(1)(a), if he puts the victim in fear. He also does so if he seeks to deter the victim from some relevant action by threat or violence. A threat unaccompanied by violence may be sufficient, and the threat need not necessarily be a threat of violence. The act must be intended to intimidate. The person doing the act has to know or believe that the victim is assisting

in the investigation of an offence or is a witness or potential witness or juror or potential juror in proceedings for an offence. He has to do the act intending thereby to cause the investigation or the course of justice to be obstructed, perverted or interfered with. If the other ingredients are established, this intention is presumed unless the contrary is proved (sub-s (7)). The intimidation does not necessarily have to be successful in the sense that the victim does not have actually to be deterred or put in fear. But it will obviously be material evidence if the victim was not in fact deterred or put in fear. A person may intimidate another person without the victim being intimidated. This apparent contradiction arises from different shades of meaning of the active and passive use of the verb. An act may amount to intimidation and thus intimidate, even though the victim is sufficiently steadfast not to be intimidated.' *R v Patrascu* [2004] EWCA Crim 2417, [2004] 4 All ER 1066 at [16]–[18], per May LJ

INTOXICATING LIQUOR

[In the definition of 'intoxicating liquor' in the Licensing Act 1964, s 201(1), the following paragraph is substituted for para (a) by the Licensing (Low Alcohol Drinks) Act 1990, s 1.]
> '(a) any liquor which is of a strength not exceeding 0.5 per cent at the time of the sale or other conduct in question; ...'

INTOXICATION

Australia [Hulme J found that there was a duty owed by the second defendant to the plaintiff to take reasonable care in and about the serving of alcohol.] '... [I]t is one thing to say that a duty existed. It is another to define or describe its (minimum) content. Having regard to the subject matter, I think this must be done by reference to the term "intoxicated" despite the difficulties arising from the lack of precision in that term. Thus there is common acceptance that there are degrees of intoxication – see *Words and Phrases (Judicially Defined in Canadian Courts)* and *Judicial and Statutory Definitions of Words and Phrases* collected by the staff of the American National Reporter System and the cases cited in those publications. The word is used by some to describe any altered state arising from the use of alcohol even if the manifestations of that state are but an increase in willingness to laugh, increase in the volume of speaking or some greater excitability, but it is difficult to see that any duty should be defined by that sort of test. And even the definition in the *Oxford* (2nd ed, on compact disk) raises as many questions as it answers:

"The action of rendering stupid, insensible, or disordered in intellect with a drug or alcoholic liquor; the making drunk or inebriated … The action or power of exhilarating or highly exciting the mind; elation or excitement beyond the bounds of sobriety"

'The definition of Fair J in *R v Ormsby* (1945) NZLR 109 that under the New Zealand Motor Vehicles Act a person is in a state of intoxication "when as a result of his consumption of intoxicating liquor, his physical or mental faculties, or his judgment, are appreciably and materially impaired in the conduct of the ordinary affairs or acts of daily life" is more useful but there is some scope for differences in view as to what was intended to be encompassed by the phrase "appreciably and materially". Does "appreciably" refer to manifestations apparent to an observer?

'For the purposes of my use of the term "intoxicated" in this part of my reasons I would define it as a state wherein there is, due to the effects of alcohol or drugs, a loss of self-control or judgment which is more than of minor degree. Experience suggests that once a state answering that description is reached, the person affected has a significantly increased risk both of going on to become even more intoxicated and of suffering injury. By the time the effect of loss of self-control or judgment can be described as "moderate", that stage of significantly increased risk has arrived.' *Cole v Lawrence* (2001) 33 MVR 159; BC200100562; [2001] NSWSC 92 at [56]–[58], per Hulme J

INTRODUCED

[The pursuers were a firm of estate agents who were employed by the defender in connection with the sale of heritable property. The contract provided that, even after the period during which the pursuers were sole selling agents had expired, they would still be entitled to receive payment if the sale took place to a purchaser who was 'introduced to [the defender] during that period or with whom [the pursuers] had negotiations about the property during that period'. After the contract had expired, the defender sold the property to a company the principals of which had been sent information about the property by the pursuers.] 'In the present case the purchasers were not introduced to the defender by the pursuers. They may have been made aware of the fact that the property was for sale by the pursuers but the pursuers did not put them in touch with the defender.' *Christie Owen & Davis plc v Alan King* 1998 SCLR 149 (Notes) at 152, per Sheriff Principal Maguire

[Estate agents were employed to sell heritable property. The contract with the owner provided that, even after the period during which the estate agents were sole selling agents had expired, they would still be entitled to receive payment if the property were sold to a purchaser who was 'introduced to [the owner] during that period or with whom [the estate agents] had negotiations about the property during that period' (clause 5(b)). The estate agents subsequently sued the owner.] 'It is in our view sufficient to being a potential purchaser within the ambit of clause 5(b) of this contract if it is established that he was introduced to the property or brought into a relationship with it through the actings of the agent. We do not consider that any personal introduction to the defender [ie the owner] is required. This construction is consistent with the various authorities to which reference was made and is also supported by the commercial realities. We observe in this connection that there was evidence that potential purchasers who have been sent sale details by the agents do from time to time contact the seller directly; a situation can accordingly be envisaged where an unscrupulous seller having been contacted directly by a potential purchaser might immediately terminate the contract with the agents and then complete the sale. The commercial purpose of a clause of this type is to take account of such a temptation and the consequent need for vigilance on the part of the agents. We consider further that the inference that the agents introduced the purchaser to the defender's property can legitimately be drawn from the primary facts in this case. In so deciding, we are influenced by the discreet nature of the marketing of the property and by the absence of evidence of any other factor which could have generated an approach by the ultimate purchaser. Although no direct evidence was led as to the causal connection, it is significant in our view that there was no competing explanation for the purchasers' interest or for the fact that Mr Douglas [the purchaser], according to the defender's own evidence, asked when he telephoned him if the property was "still" on the market.' *Christie Owen & Davis plc v Alan King* 1998 SCLR 786 (Updates).

INVALID CARRIAGE

[See also the Road Traffic Act 1988, s 185(1).]

INVENTION

Australia 'The term "invention" may give rise to difficulty because both in ordinary parlance and in patent legislation it is used in various senses. In *British United Shoe Machinery Co Ltd v A Fussell & Sons Ltd*, Fletcher-Moulton LJ observed that the word "invention" is used in at least three distinct senses. His Lordship continued:

> "First of all we say that to support a Patent there must be 'invention.' There it means an inventive act. Then we talk about a person getting a monopoly for an 'invention.' There it means a thing which is new and that has required an inventive act to produce it. There is also an intermediate sense in which it is used, that is to say, you sometimes speak of a patentee's 'invention' meaning the particular inventive act which this inventor has performed. When you talk about the patentee's 'invention', in such a connection you do not mean that which is claimed in any one or another of the Claims. You are speaking generally as if you were giving a history of the subject, and saying, – 'So-and-so's invention was that for the first time he applied electricity for such and such a purpose.' It is quite possible that he has never claimed the universal use of it for such and such a purpose; he may have claimed something much narrower. Yet if he was the first to do it you may without inaccuracy say that it was his 'invention', meaning his particular inventive act."

'... In the fourth edition [of Blanco White, *Patents for Inventions*, 3rd ed, 1962], the learned author referred to the adoption by the statutory definition of "invention" of the body of law attached to s 6 of the Statute of Monopolies and observed that the word "invention" was not always used in that sense; he identified the judgment of Fletcher-Moulton LJ in *British United Shoe* and said that, in speaking of a person's invention, four possible meanings are involved. He went on:

> "They are: 1. The embodiment which is described, and around which the claims are drawn. This is the sense used in the Act: cf the phrase of s 32, 'the invention so far as claimed in any claim.' 2. The subject-matter of a claim – especially that of the broadest claim. 3. The inventive step taken by the inventor. 4. The advance in the art made by the inventor; as (to take Lord Justice Moulton's example) 'he applied electricity for the first time to such-and-such a purpose.' This is likely to be

broader and more fundamental than would correspond with any claim."

'It is the first meaning which, with respect, McTiernan J correctly adopted [in *AMP Incorporated v Utilux Pty Ltd* (1971) 45 ALJR 123] in construing s 40(1) of the [Patents Act 1952 (Cth)], and the same is true of s 40(2) of the [Patents Act 1990 (Cth)].' *Kimberley-Clark Australia Pty Ltd v Arico Trading International Pty Ltd* (2001) 177 ALR 460; 50 IPR 513; BC200100261; [2001] HCA 8 at [20]–[21], per Gleeson CJ, McHugh, Gummow, Hayne and Callinan JJ

INVENTIVE MERIT

Australia 'The expressions "inventive merit" and "appreciable merit" appear to have come into use during the development in the last century of modern patent law. The notion of "merit" was used by the courts and by commentators, including Fletcher Moulton [*The Present Law and Practice Relating to Letters Patent for Inventions*, (1913) at 19], to express what under the Act is conveyed by the principles concerning novelty and, more frequently, inventive step. By the beginning of this century, it had no distinct and independent doctrinal meaning: it was used sometimes in reference to subject-matter, sometimes in reference to novelty. The phrase invites error through imprecision of legal analysis.' *Advanced Building Systems Pty Ltd v Ramset Fasteners (Aust) Pty Ltd* (1998) 152 ALR 604 at 612; [1998] HCA 19 at [26]; BC9800864 at 13, per Brennan CJ, Gaudron, McHugh and Gummow JJ

INVESTMENT

Australia 'Investment is usually understood as it is defined in *Butterworths Australian Legal Dictionary*:

> "Investment: conversion of money or circulating capital and some species of property from which an income or profit is expected. It is spending which adds to the stock of capital, traditionally regarded as spending on capital goods such as machinery, factory buildings, information, technology and infrastructure. It also includes the purchase of securities and other financial instruments."

Re Fraser; Ex Parte Public Trustee BC200000408; [2000] WASC 36 at [16], per McKechnie J

INVESTMENT OF MONEY

New Zealand [Securities Act 1978, ss 2(1) and 5(1)(b). Their Lordships made an observation concerning the meaning of "investment of money":] 'As the Courts below recognised, one of the everyday meanings of investment is the laying out of money in the acquisition of property in the hope of return. The return may come in the form of capital or income or both. It may be in cash, or it may be in kind such as the provision of services. There may be no prospect of capital growth, as with the purchase at par of short-dated government stock. There may be no prospect of any lump sum return at all, as happens with an annuity. The purchaser of an annuity would readily say that he has invested his money in buying an annuity.

'Likewise in the present case, Their Lordships consider that, without any strain of language, buyers of units would say they have invested their money in buying a town house in Culverden Retirement Village on terms that they will occupy this, with necessary services provided, for so long as they wish and that they then get back all or a large part of their outlay. The return from their outlay is to be found in the totality of these benefits, not just the financial payment at the end.' *Culverden Retirement Village v Registrar of Companies* [1997] 1 NZLR 257 at 261, PC, per cur

INVESTMENT TRUST

[For 23 Halsbury's Laws (4th edn) para 1185 see now 23(1) Halsbury's Laws (4th edn) (Reissue) para 1444.]

INVIOLABILITY

Canada 'Section 1 of the *Charter* guarantees the right to personal "inviolability"... The statutory amendment enacted in 1982 (see *An Act to amend the Charter of Human Rights and Freedoms*, SQ 1982, c.61, in force at the time this cause of action arose) which, *inter alia,* deleted the adjective "*physique*", in the French version, which had previously qualified the expression "*intégrité*" (inviolability), clearly indicates that s 1 refers inclusively to physical, psychological, moral and social inviolability. The question is rather one of determining what the concept of "inviolability" must be understood to mean.

'The *Petit Robert 1* (1989) defines the word "*intégrité*" as follows, at p 1016: [TRANSLATION] "1 (1530). Condition of a thing that has remained intact. See Intégralité, plénitude, totalité. *The*

integrity of a whole, of an entire thing. Integrity of a work. "The integrity of the organism is essential to the manifestations of consciousness" (CARREL). *The integrity of the territory.* REM. *Integrity* is more qualitative than *integrality,* which is generally reserved for that which is measurable". Having regard to this definition, the Superior Court made the following comments in *Viau v Syndicat canadien de la fonction publique* [1991] RRA 740, at p 745:

> "[TRANSLATION] When applying this concept to persons, we find that it is a threshold of moral damages below which there is no interference with personal inviolability. This threshold will be exceeded when the interference has left the victim less complete or less intact than he or she previously was. This diminished condition must also be of some lasting, if not permanent nature. [Emphasis added.]"

'This approach to the interpretation of the concept of inviolability set out in s 1 of the *Charter* appears to me to be appropriate. The common meaning of the word "inviolability" suggests that the interference with that right must leave some marks, some sequelae which, while not necessarily physical or permanent, exceed a certain threshold. The interference must affect the victim's physical, psychological or emotional equilibrium in something more than a fleeting manner.' *Quebec (Public Curator) v Syndicat National des Employés de l'hôpital St-Ferdinand* [1996] 3 SCR 211 at 252–253, per L'Heureux-Dubé J

INVOLUNTARY

Canada ' "Involuntary" means "not voluntary; done or happening without exercise or co-operation of the will; not done willingly or by choice; independent of volition, unintentional". See *The Oxford English Dictionary*, Vol. XII (Oxford: Clarendon Press, 1970). Antonyms include "voluntary" and "wilful". The corresponding expression in the French legislative text is "involontaire". Its meaning mirrors that of "involuntary". Antonyms of "involontaire" include "volontaire", "intentionnel" and "voulu". See P. Robert, *Le Grand Robert de la Langue Française*, 2nd edition (Montreal: Les dictionnaires Robert Canada, 1987). By defining in such terms the type of loss for which a mortgagee is not answerable, the legislature has mandated courts to focus on whether the mortgagor's loss was the object of the mortgagee's exercise and execution of his statutory power of sale.' *Bérubé v Lévesque* (1999) 180 DLR (4th) 694 at 701, NBCA, per Drapeau JA

INVOLVEMENT

New Zealand [Under s 18(2) of the Crimes Act 1991, the court has discretion to refuse relief against forfeiture of property if the applicant was 'involved in the commission of the offence'.] 'We agree that something less than participation as a party may amount to an involvement. If the legislature had intended that only party status gave rise to the Court's right to refuse relief it would surely have said so ... We understand the legislature to be saying that a material association with the offending is enough. It may take the form of assistance of a kind which would make the applicant a party to the crime. Or it may simply be a failure to prevent property in which the applicant has an interest being used for criminal purposes which are known to the applicant in circumstances in which the applicant should have taken practical preventative steps. Mere knowledge of the criminal use of the property does not amount to involvement, even when the applicant benefits from the use, as in *R v Matamua* (Court of Appeal, Wellington, CA 569/95, 10 July 1996) where the applicant was never in a position to control the drug dealing and had no active involvement in it, but knew that money being paid to her was "dirty money". The Court said that to be involved required more than mere suspicion or awareness of an offence and "more than mere reluctance through fear to give early assistance to police investigations." ' *Lyall v Solicitor-General* [1977] 2 NZLR 641 at 649, CA, per cur

INVOLVES

Australia '... Although it is difficult to conceive of an offence as involving an intent to steal unless the intent to steal is an element of the offence, it has been held in another context that the word "involves" is not necessarily to be equated to an element of an offence. In *Australian Securities Commission v Lord* [(1991) 33 FCR 144 at p 149] Davies J held that it was not necessary to establish that fraud or dishonesty was an element of an offence the subject of investigation for the purposes of the expression "involves fraud or dishonesty" in s 28 of the Australian Securities Commission Law. It was enough that it was suspected that there was associated fraud or dishonesty. The word "involved" also has an established meaning in the area of revenue law concerned with the problem of whether

a decision the subject of appeal is one that involves a question of law. In as much as those lines of authority ascribe a meaning to "involved" that is equivalent or close to "associated with", as opposed to "part of", they may be thought of as some support for the idea that a s 76(1)(b) [Crimes Act 1958 (Vic)] offence is one that involves an intent to steal if committed in conjunction with an offence of stealing.

'But I do not think that is the case. The words of a statutory provision take their meaning from their context, and in the context of s 102A of the Justices Act I do not think that there can be any doubt that "involves" was used in the sense of "an element of the offence". The section referred to an offence that "involves the stealing of property and the amount or value of the property *the subject-matter* of the offence" (my emphasis). Regardless of the circumstances, the only form of burglary of which it could be said that it had the stealing of property as its "subject matter" was burglary of which the intent to steal was an element of the offence.' *Director of Public Prosecutions v Verigos* [2004] VSC 97 at [26], per Nettle J; BC200402119

IS SUFFERING

[Under the Children Act 1989, s 31(2) a court may only make a care order or supervision order if it is satisfied that the child concerned 'is suffering, or is likely to suffer', significant harm, which is attributable to the care being given to the child, or likely to be given if the order were not made, or to the child's being beyond parental control.] 'The trial judge heard argument that the requirements in s 31(2)(a) and (b) were not satisfied in the present case. She said:

> "... I am satisfied that [M] is suffering significant harm within the meaning of s 31(2)(a) in that he has suffered ill-treatment by being permanently deprived of the love and care of his mother when she was murdered in his presence, and in the presence of his half-brothers and sisters in October 1991. I am also satisfied that under s 31(2)(b) the significant harm is attributable to the care given to the child by the father not being what it would be reasonable to expect a parent to give to him, in that the father deprived the child, by his actions, of the care of a loving mother ... The relevant date for the words "is suffering" in s 31(2)(a) I find relates to the period immediately before the process of protecting

the child is first put into motion, that is when the father deprived the child for all time of his mother."

'In my opinion the opening words of s 31 link the making of an order by the court very closely with the application to the court by a local authority or authorised person ... There is nothing in s 31(2) which in my opinion requires that the conditions to be satisfied are disassociated from the time of the making of the application by the local authority. I would conclude that the natural construction of the conditions in s 31(2) is that where, at the time the application is to be disposed of, there are in place arrangements for the protection of the child by the local authority on an interim basis which protection has been continuously in place for some time, the relevant date with respect to which the court must be satisfied is the date at which the local authority initiated the procedure for protection under the Act from which these arrangements followed. If after a local authority had initiated protective arrangements the need for these had terminated, because the child's welfare had been satisfactorily provided for otherwise, in any subsequent proceedings it would not be possible to found jurisdiction on the situation at the time of initiation of those arrangements. It is permissible only to look back from the date of disposal to the date of initiation of protection as a result of which local authority arrangements had been continuously in place thereafter to the date of disposal ...

... [It] is now permissible under the second branch of s 32(2)(a) to look to the future even if no harm has already occurred in the past. This is an important difference from the previous legislation ... It is also clear that while Parliament added the new provisions looking to the future without any necessary connection with harm already suffered, it wished to retain the first branch in respect of harm which the child is suffering.' *Re M (A Minor) (Care Order: Threshold Conditions)* [1994] 2 AC 424 at 430–431, 433–434, 437, HL, per Lord Mackay of Clashfern LC

ISSUE

Australia 'The term "issue" is defined as follows:
- "Give or send out authoritatively or officially; publish, emit, put into circulation" – the *New Shorter Oxford English Dictionary*;
- "To put out; deliver for use; to send out, discharge" – the *Macquarie Dictionary*;
- "The act of delivery; emission; sending" – *Butterworths Australian Legal Dictionary*.

'[19] The word "issue" involves the idea of something passing from one person to another, sending forth or delivering. Thus, a document which is at all times retained by a person in his own sole control cannot be said to have been issued by him. He might execute or create the document and then decide not to give it to anybody. In such a case, he would not have issued the document – *Koon Wing Lau v Calwell* (1949) 80 CLR 533 at 568 per Latham CJ. More specifically, a certificate is not "issued" to a person until it is delivered to him, which means that it must pass from the possession of the authorities either into his manual custody or under his control or into his legal possession so as to be at his command – per Dixon J at 574.' *Prudential-Bache Securities (Aust) Ltd v Warner* BC9905004; [1999] FCA 1143 at [18], [19], per Emmett J

IWI

New Zealand [Maori Fisheries Act 1989, Sch 1A, para 2.] 'Williams' *Maori Dictionary* (7th ed, revised 1985) defines *iwi* as "Nation, people". At the present day the expression is commonly used to refer to a tribe, and we have no doubt that it was used in that sense in the resolutions adopted at the annual general meeting of the Maori Fisheries Commission in 1992 set out in Sch 1A of the Maori Fisheries Act 1989 as inserted in 1992. A point not to be lost sight of is that, as the definition in Williams suggests, the reference is to *the people* of the tribe. The leaders or representatives are not the *iwi*.

' "Iwi" refers, as we have said, to the people of tribes; and this must include those entitled to be members although their specific tribal affiliation may not have been and cannot be established.' *Te Runanga o Muriwhenua and others v Te Runanganui o Te Upoko o Te Ika Association Inc and others (CA 155/95)* [1996] 3 NZLR 10 at 18, per cur

New Zealand [Section 6 of the Maori Fisheries Act 1989.] 'The waka/iwi/hapu/whanau paradigm has been said to be at the centre of Maori society. There is not universal agreement as to the structure of this paradigm but it is generally accepted that each Maori traces his or her genealogy from a waka (canoe), then to an iwi (tribe), then to a hapu (sub-tribe), and then to a whanau (an extended family). It is not accepted by all historians that the term "iwi" in this paradigm means tribe and some give it the meaning of people with a common ancestry.' *Te Waka Hi Ika o Te Arawa v Treaty of*

Waitangi Fisheries Commission [2000] 1 NZLR 285 (HC & CA) at 301 per Paterson J

'The evidence of the experts makes it clear that "iwi" has several meanings, some of which may not have been given prominence at particular times. The meaning concentrated on by the opponents of the commission's scheme was the word "people". It was suggested that "iwi" did not mean "tribe" at the time of the Treaty and was used at that time as meaning "people". This being so, it was submitted that the word could not have meant "tribe" when it was used in the resolutions and must mean "people", namely all Maori people. There was evidence which establishes that "iwi" was sometimes synonymous with "tribe" at the time of the Treaty. While "hapu" may have been the more common Maori word for "tribe" at that time, the use of the word "iwi" for "tribe" was not unknown. There was a dictionary published by the Church Missionary Society in 1820 which gave "tribe" as one of the meanings of "iwi". However, it was further submitted that even if it is accepted that "iwi" may have meant "tribe" in 1840, this was not the primary meaning of the word at that time and may not be the primary meaning of the word at this time. One of the most authoritative Maori dictionaries, Williams *A Dictionary of the Maori Language*, did not give "tribe" as a meaning of "iwi" in its fifth edition published in 1917, although it had given "tribe" as the meaning of "iwi" in its earlier editions the first of which was published in 1844...

'While great emphasis was placed on the meaning of the word "iwi" at the time of the Treaty, it is the meaning of "iwi" used in the statute in the modern context that is important. Even most of the witnesses who did not accept that "iwi" meant "tribe" in 1840, agreed that it has been used to mean "tribe" in more recent times. There was ample evidence before me, notwithstanding what appears in the latest edition of Williams *A Dictionary of the Maori Language* published in 1971, to this effect. The *Reed Dictionary of Modern Maori* (2nd ed, 1995) gives the meaning of "iwi" as "tribe, bone, race, people, nation, strength". Ngata's *English-Maori Dictionary* (1994) gives the meaning of "tribe" as either "iwi" or "waka". Witnesses called on behalf of the UMAs conceded that "iwi" is used to refer to a single tribal group which traces its descent from an eponymous ancestor. Some witnesses, particularly those supporting the commission including well-known Maori language experts, took the view that the primary meaning of "iwi" is "tribe". I conclude from the evidence given on both sides of the

debate that the word "iwi" can have several meanings, one of which is "people" and one of which is "tribe". This latter meaning is an important, if not a primary meaning. I also note that the word without a modifier may be either singular or plural.' *Te Waka Hi Ika o Te Arawa v Treaty of Waitangi Fisheries Commission* [2000] 1 NZLR 285 (HC & CA) at 326–327 per Paterson J

'... "iwi" means traditional Maori tribes in the sense that a tribe includes all persons who are entitled to be a member of it because of kin links and genealogy.' *Te Waka Hi Ika o Te Arawa v Treaty of Waitangi Fisheries Commission* [2000] 1 NZLR 285 (HC & CA) at 329 per Paterson J

New Zealand [Schedule 1A to the Maori Fisheries Act 1989 provides:

"Resolutions Adopted At Hui-A-Tau On 25 July 1992
ALLOCATION
AUTHORITY

1. That the hui endorse the decision made by the Commission to seek legislative authority to further secure the Commission's intention to allocate its assets to iwi.

METHOD

2. That MFC examine the alternative methods to allocate, consult with iwi, and have prepared discussion material to enable agreement to be reached on the optimum method for allocation.

LEGAL RIGHTS: 50%

3. That MFC ensure that no allocation of the 10% be made before the position of the pursuit of the legal rights of iwi to secure the complete 50% is secure.

EVENT OF DELAY

4. That the hui agree that, in the event of significant delay to the implementation of the allocation strategy, the MFC hold a further tender of MFC/AFL quota for the 1992/93 fishing year only.

AOTEAROA FISHERIES LIMITED (AFL)

5. That MFC allocate the assets of AFL as part of the allocation strategy.

AFL CASH & OTHER ASSETS

6. That MFC allocate the assets of AFL cash, and other assets on the same basis as the quota is allocated.

MAORI FISHERY NEGOTIATORS (MFN) BUDGET (6)

7. That this hui supports the continued funding of the MFN up to $350,000 for the next year on terms to be agreed by the MFC/MFN.

MANDATE

8. That this hui affirms the fact that the negotiators represent all the interests of all iwi in the negotiations with and litigation against the Crown.

MAORI FISHERIES COMMISSION FUTURE

9. That the future of the MFC be subject to further consideration by MFC/iwi and a position paper be circulated to iwi by October 1992.

MAORI CONGRESS BUDGET

10. That the Congress and the negotiators meet with the Commission to discuss the servicing and financial requirements of the negotiating process.']

'[17] The arguments have ranged widely, both in the lower Courts and before the Board, but Their Lordships consider that the point is a very short one. The commission, as a statutory body, has no power to distribute its assets except in accordance with the terms of the Act. Section 19(2) of the 1992 Act makes it clear that the commission's only power to dispose of quota or its shares in Aotearoa is that conferred by s 9(2)(l) of the 1989 Act as amended. That paragraph provides only for a distribution under a scheme which gives effect to the resolutions of the hui. Those resolutions plainly provide for distribution to iwi. The concurrent findings of Paterson J and the Court of Appeal, which were scarcely challenged in argument, were that in using the term "iwi" the resolutions intended to refer to traditional tribes. As Thomas J said in his dissenting judgment "there is not the slightest doubt that those representatives of iwi gathered at the hui-a-tau on 25 July 1992 intended the pre-settlement assets to be distributed to iwi and that they meant iwi in the sense of traditional tribes.

'[18] This reasoning leads in Their Lordships' opinion to the inescapable conclusion that Paterson J and the majority in the Court of Appeal were right.' *Te Waka Hi Ika o Te Arawa v Treaty of Waitangi Fisheries Commission* [2002] 2 NZLR 17 (PC) at 27 per cur

J

JETSOM

[For 1 Halsbury's Laws (4th edn) para 350 see now 1(1) Halsbury's Laws (4th edn) (2001 Reissue) para 350 note 4.]

JETTISON

[For 25 Halsbury's Laws (4th edn) para 163 see now 25 Halsbury's Laws (4th edn) (2003 Reissue) para 341.]

JOB

Australia ['Job' contrasted with 'position'.] 'A person's job is therefore primarily concerned with the tasks that he or she is required to perform. No doubt the term "job" is often used to signify a paid position of employment. But in the context of determining the requirements of a job, it seems more natural to regard the term as referring to particular work or tasks that the person must perform. A person's position, on the other hand, is primarily concerned with the level or rank from which he or she performs those tasks. Position concerns rank and status. What is required of a person's position, however, will usually require an examination of the tasks performed from that position. That is because the capacity to perform those tasks is an inherent requirement of the particular position.' *Qantas Airways Ltd v Christie* (1998) 152 ALR 365 at 382–383; (1998) 79 IR 120; [1998] HCA 18 at [72]; BC9800685 at 25, per McHugh J

JOINTURE

[For 36 Halsbury's Laws (4th edn) para 847 see now 36 Halsbury's Laws (4th edn) (Reissue) para 248.]

JUDGMENT

[For 26 Halsbury's Laws (4th edn) para 501 see now 26 Halsbury's Laws (4th edn) (Reissue) para 501 .]

[Under the Limitation Act 1980, s 10(3) if the person in question is held liable by 'a judgment' given in civil proceedings or by an award in arbitration, the relevant date for limitation is the date on which the judgment was given or the date of the award. The issue arose whether for the purposes of s 10 the judgment included a judgment on liability only, in which case the claimant's action was statute-barred, or whether a judgment on quantum was required in order to start time running.] '[1] Section 10 of the Limitation Act 1980 provides that a claim for contribution under the Civil Liability (Contribution) Act 1978 shall have a limitation period of two years from the date on which a person seeking contribution is "held liable ... by a judgment".

'[2] The issue on this appeal is whether for these purposes the judgment spoken of by the statute includes a judgment on liability only, for damages to be assessed, or whether a judgment on quantum as well as liability is required to start time running.

...

'[9] As stated above, the issue on this appeal is whether, for the purposes of s 10(3)(a), Aer Lingus was "held liable ... by [the] judgment" given on 9 May 2001 for damages to be assessed, or only by the judgment for £490,000 given on 3 October 2003.

...

'[32] With this mainly historical background, I return to the language of s 10 itself. It is common ground that there is no express reference to the ascertainment of quantum in the language "held liable ... by a judgment ... or ... award"; and that an award, like a judgment, can be limited to a pure declaration or finding of liability without any ascertainment of quantum. It is also common ground that "that damage" is not a reference to damages, but to the victim's original loss or injury. In these circumstances, attention has been concentrated on the subscript to sub-s (3) and on sub-s (4), for both those passages do contain references to damages.

'[33] As for the subscript to sub-s (3), Mr Harvey and Mr Heathcote Williams (for the respondents) both accept that it is unnecessary on their construction of the section, since time will begin to run as soon as liability is established, whether or not quantum has also been ascertained. In their submission, therefore, the subscript is merely a piece of cautious draftsmanship, to make clear, even if unnecessarily so, that any change in the level of damages will not delay the relevant date.

'[34] In my judgment, however, this is not a cogent explanation, although it was accepted by Simon J. If the ascertainment of damages is not a necessary condition for the accrual of the right to recover contribution, then it is confusing, rather than clarifying, to stress that a change in the level of quantum on appeal will not delay the accrual of the right or the running of time. On the contrary, the reference to a judgment or award varying the amount of damages is suggestive of the underlying assumption that the judgment or award already referred to earlier in the subsection is a judgment or award which ascertains damages. It seems to me, therefore, that on balance the subscript supports the case made by Mr Pooles on behalf of Aer Lingus, although perhaps not strongly so.

'[35] It seems to me that this pointer is underlined, but more strongly, by s 10(4). Where there is no judgment or award, but the victim's claim is dealt with simply by agreement, the relevant date is the earliest date on which "the amount to be paid ... is agreed", and that is so whether liability is admitted or not. If, however, the ascertainment of quantum is irrelevant, it is difficult to understand why, where settlement proceeds by agreement in the absence of judgment, the statute does not focus on the earliest date on which liability is agreed, where it is, even before the settlement sum is arrived at. It is true that a settlement sum may be agreed without any admission of liability; but equally a settlement sum may be agreed for the very reason that liability is admitted. Indeed, that not infrequently happens: a tortfeasor admits liability, for that is not in dispute, but it may take time to work out the quantum for a settlement. The respondents submit that in such a case, a judgment for damages to be assessed is normally consented to, as in these proceedings: and that the statute looks to the formality of such a judgment, rather than to the relative informality of the mere agreement. However, there need be nothing informal about an admission of liability–on the contrary; and in any event, s 10(4) is intended to operate equally whether liability is admitted or not: in other words the subsection expressly contemplates the case where liability is admitted, and even so, the admission of liability is ignored for providing the relevant date. Section 10(4) therefore suggests

that the critical matter is the ascertainment by agreement of the settlement sum. Parity would therefore suggest that, where the matter is dealt with by judgment or award, the critical matter is again the ascertainment of the quantum of liability. The judge accepted that s 10(4) is anomalous, but he regarded the statute as being otherwise too clear to permit any regard being paid to this anomaly. In my judgment, however, the language he relied on ("held liable") is not determinative.

'[36] What happens where there is agreement on a settlement sum followed by a consent judgment for payment of that sum, as must often occur? Or a judgment for damages to be assessed followed by agreement on a settlement sum? Are such cases governed by sub-s (3) or sub-s (4)? They cannot be governed by both: there can in logic be only one "relevant date", and this is emphasised by the words which introduce sub-s (4)–"If, in any case not within subsection (3) above ..." If sub-s (3) requires only a judgment for damages to be assessed, then it must follow that, given such a judgment, sub-s (4) never comes into play, for the case will already fall within sub-s (3). If, however, sub-s (3) requires a judgment for damages, then an agreement within sub-s (4) could both follow a mere judgment for damages to be assessed and anticipate a consent judgment for the payment of the agreed sum: but it would be the agreement which comes first at a time when there is no judgment within sub-s (3), and it would then seem that the relevant date is fixed by sub-s (4). Do such considerations throw any light on the issue under appeal? I think they do, for sub-s (4) appears to highlight the importance of the date of agreement of the settlement sum, but this would be undermined by allowing an earlier judgment for damages to be assessed to be determinative of the relevant date.

...

'[39] I bear in mind that the words "held liable ... by a judgment" are in themselves a powerful reason for thinking that a judgment on liability in the absence of a determination of quantum is sufficient for the application of sub-s (3), a fortiori since, if the appellants' submission is correct, the subsection could easily have said "is held liable and quantum is determined ... by a judgment". Nevertheless, for the reasons I have sought to set out above, I think that the language of the section is at least consistent with and marginally favours Aer Lingus's submissions.

...

'[43] For all these reasons, in respectful disagreement with the judge, who preferred the arguments of the respondents, I would hold that the judgment or award referred to in s 10(3) of the 1980 Act as setting the relevant date for the running of time against a tortfeasor who seeks contribution under the 1978 Act is a judgment or award which ascertains the quantum, and not merely the existence, of the tortfeasor's liability. I would therefore allow Aer Lingus's appeal.' *Aer Lingus plc v Gildacroft Ltd* [2006] EWCA Civ 4 at [1]–[2], [9], [32]–[36], [39], [43], [2006] 2 All ER 290, per Rix LJ

Australia [Order 10, r 7(b) of the Federal Court Rules 1979 (Cth) provides that where a party fails to comply with an order of the court directing that party to take a step in the proceeding, any other party may move the court on notice for 'judgment' or an order against him if the party in default is a respondent.] 'The expression "judgment" in this rule does not have the meaning given to that term by s 4 of the Federal Court of Australia Act 1976 (Cth) because it is used in the rule to distinguish judicial determinations in the form of judgments from orders, ie, other judicial determinations. The term "judgment" in its technical sense means a decision that concludes an action while an order is any other judicial determination:' *Onslow v Commissioners of Inland Revenue* (1890) 25 QBD 465 at 466; *Opie v Opie* (1951) 84 CLR 362 at 372.' *Australian Securities Commission v Macleod* (1994) 54 FCR 309 at 311–312, per Drummond J

Australia [After citing *Halsbury's Laws of England,* 4th ed (1976) vol 26, para 501] 'Lord Selborne LC in *Re Faithfull; Ex parte Moore* (1885) 14 QBD 627 at 632 (Court of Appeal) said although the words "judgment" and "order" have sometimes been used: "… to constitute an order a final judgment, nothing more is necessary than that there should be a litis contestatio and a final adjudication between the parties." I note with respect that the High Court in *Driclad Pty Ltd v Federal Commissioner of Taxation* [(1968) 121 CLR 45] referred to the word "judgment" often being used as a convenient abbreviation for "reasons for judgment". I conclude from the foregoing that the use of each of the words "judgment", "decree" or "order" has been flexible, and that to refer to the dicta in the reported cases may not be of great assistance.' *In the Marriage of Moore* (1996) 20 Fam LR 495 at 499; 125 FLR 420 at 424, per Butler J

Australia [Direction to Registrar by judge under (Cth) Federal Court Rules 1979 O 46 r 7A.] 'The word "judgment" as used in O 52 r 10 may be taken to refer to an "operative judicial act". (See: *Driclad Pty Ltd v Commissioner of Taxation* (1968)

121 CLR 45 per Barwick CJ, Kitto J at 64). A judgment as defined in s 4 of the Act has the same meaning as "judgments, decrees, orders and sentences" used in s 73 of the Constitution, namely, a formal order made by a court which disposes of, or deals with, the proceeding then before it. (See: *Moller v Roy* (1975) 132 CLR 622 per Mason J at 639). S 73 is confined to decisions made in the exercise of judicial power (See: *Mobil Oil Australia Pty Ltd v Victoria* (2002) 76 ALJR 926 per Gaudron, Gummow, Hayne JJ at [63]; *Consolidated Press Ltd v Australian Journalists' Association* (1947) 73 CLR 549; *Director of Public Prosecutions (SA) v B* (1998) 194 CLR 566 per Gaudron, Gummow, Hayne JJ at [9]–[10]).

'As Barwick CJ said in *Minister for Works for the Government of Western Australia v Civil and Civic Pty Ltd* (1967) 116 CLR 273 at 277:

> "It is of the essence of a judgment within the meaning of the Constitution that it is binding upon parties and definitive of legal rights. It is not enough that the judge or Court exercises a jurisdiction of the Supreme Court in a matter judicial in its substance. The judge or Court must authorizedly give a binding judgment which determines or settles rights."

'The extent to which a judgment defines legal rights may be, of course, a question of construction of the terms of the judgment. (See: *Australian Telecommunications Commission v Colpitts* (1986) 12 FCR 395 per Toohey J at 400–402). Whether a bare determination by a Judge not to accede to a request for recusal made by a party to a proceeding can be said to define a right and, thereby, constitute a judgment is an issue for which there is opposing authority. (See: *Brooks v Upjohn Co* (1998) 85 FCR 469, 472–476; *Barton v Walker* [1979] 2 NSWLR 740, 749; *The Queen v Watson; Ex parte Armstrong* (1976) 136 CLR 248, 266). It is to be noted that in Brooks formal orders were made on a notice of motion filed by the party seeking the recusal.' *Bizuneh v Minister for Immigration and Multicultural and Indigenous Affairs* [2003] FCAFC 42 at [3]–[5] per Lee, Whitlam and Jacobson JJ; BC200300845

Declaratory

[For 1 Halsbury's Laws (4th edn) para 185 see now 1(1) Halsbury's Laws (4th edn) (2001 Reissue) paras 120, 151.]

JUDICIAL AUTHORITY

New Zealand 'Some of the broader definitions of "judicial" include "Having the function of judgment;

invested with authority to judge causes" (*Shorter Oxford English Dictionary*), and "judge-like, impartial" (*Chambers English Dictionary*). The narrower definitions emphasise the relationship with a Court of justice and derivation of power from the law. Although I am of the view that the word is more often used in relation to a Judge of a Court of justice (to paraphrase *Chambers*), it is possible that the wider meaning is also understood from the word. It is not unambiguous.

'It is used together with and modifies the word "authority". Authority again is capable of being read as including an arbitrator if it is read as a person or body holding power. (*Chambers English Dictionary*). It can have a more restrictive meaning, only including power derived from an enactment, or in some other way from the state. I do not think it can be said that either meaning is clearly what was intended, but it seems the more natural of the two in this context is that implying a power derived from the state. Reading the two words together does not, to my mind, give more certainty. The more natural and ordinary reading of judicial authority would seem to be a person or body having power to judge a matter before it, which power is derived from the state.' *Arbitrators' Institute of New Zealand Inc v Legal Services Board* [1995] 2 NZLR 202 at 204, per Heron J

JUDICIALLY

Australia [Role of Refugee Review Tribunal.] 'In carrying out that assessment, involving as it does a determination of great importance to an applicant, the Tribunal must act "judicially" and according to law. In so acting the Tribunal does not exercise judicial power, but by reason of the importance of its task, the Tribunal must observe the "practical requirements of fairness" appropriate for the exercise of judicial power. As Sedley J stated in *R v Higher Education Funding Council, ex parte Institute of Dental Surgery* [1994] 1 WLR 242 at 258:

> In the modern state the decisions of administrative bodies can have a more immediate and profound impact on people's lives than the decisions of courts, and public law has since *Ridge v Baldwin* [1964] AC 40 been alive to that fact. While the judicial character of a function may elevate the practical requirements of fairness above what they would otherwise be, for example by requiring contentious evidence to be given and tested orally, what makes it "judicial" in this sense is

principally the nature of the issue it has to determine, not the formal status of the deciding body.

'While the expression "acting judicially" is not now often used when referring to administrative decision making, it usefully comprehends concepts relevant to this appeal. (See: *Australian Broadcasting Tribunal v Bond* (1990) 170 CLR 321 per Deane J at 365).

'Failure of the Tribunal to act "judicially" will necessarily stamp the review procedure as one which did not accord an applicant practical fairness or justice. To act "judicially" and according to law the Tribunal must carry out its decision-making function rationally and reasonably and not arbitrarily. (See: Bond per Deane J at 366–367). That is to say, the Tribunal cannot determine the matter by a "tossing a coin" or by making a "snap decision" or by acting on instinct, a "hunch" or a "gut-feeling".' *WAIJ v Minister for Immigration and Multicultural and Indigenous Affairs* [2004] FCAFC 74 at [19]–[21] per Lee and Moore JJ; BC200401353

JURISDICTION

Australia 'The "jurisdiction" of a court is its *authority* to take cognisance of, and to decide, proceedings brought before it; its jurisdiction delimits its area of competence and authority. The concept is one of authority or capacity; and the essence of an inquiry into "jurisdiction" in this sense is as to its limits — whether a court has power to hear and determine the particular case: see *Commonwealth v Kreglinger & Fernau Ltd* (1926) 37 CLR 393 at 408 per Isaacs J.' *Braun v R* (1997) 112 NTR 31 at 39, per Kearney and Thomas JJ

Australia 'This is a "generic term" [*Baxter v Commissioners of Taxation (NSW)* (1907) 4 CLR 1087 at 1142] generally signifying authority to adjudicate. It is used in various senses. The jurisdiction of a court to hear and determine a personal action and to grant relief may depend upon no more than effective service of that court's process upon the defendant within the territorial bounds of its competence or pursuant to the exercise of a "long-arm" jurisdiction; or it may depend also upon the proceeding being with respect to a particular subject-matter [*Flaherty v Girgis* (1987) 162 CLR 574 at 598; *John Pfeiffer Pty Ltd v Rogerson* (2000) 172 ALR 625; 74 ALJR 1109; BC200003351; [2000] HCA 36 [13]–[14]]. *Australian Securities and Investments Commission* *v Edensor Nominees Pty Ltd* (2001) 177 ALR 329; 37 ACSR 1; [2001] HCA 1; BC200100154 at [2], per Gleeson CJ, Gaudron and Gummow JJ

New Zealand 'As Lord Bridge of Harwich noted in [*Re McC (A Minor)* [1985] AC 528] at 536 "jurisdiction" is a term used with many different shades of meaning. It has long been accepted in English law that, for what would now be called administrative law purposes (as in proceedings for judicial review, certiorari or prohibition), the term bears a meaning narrower than it does in the context of actions seeking to make Judges of Courts of limited jurisdiction personally liable in tort: see for example *Pease v Chaytor* (1863) 3 B & S 620, 639–644 per Blackburn J. The distinction stems from recognition, on the one hand, that some effective remedy is required for acts of limited Courts which prove to be contrary to law and, on the other hand, that it is unduly harsh to mulct a judicial officer in damages for making a mistake in a matter which he or she is bound to determine.' *Harvey v Derrick* [1995] 1 NZLR 314 at 317, CA, per Cooke P.

'It is plain, then, that as used in s 193, the word "jurisdiction" must embrace a wider area of activity than the mere lawful exercise of the Court's powers. The error will be beyond "jurisdiction" for present purposes only if in some way it is so extraordinary that it falls outside the implied penumbra of protected error which supplements the lawful exercise of the Court's powers.' *Harvey v Derrick* [1995] 1 NZLR 314 at 336, CA, per Fisher J

JURISDICTIONAL FACT

Australia 'The term "jurisdictional fact" (which may be a complex of elements) is often used to identify that criterion, satisfaction of which enlivens the power of the decision-maker to exercise a discretion. Used here, it identifies a criterion, satisfaction of which mandates a particular outcome.' *Corporation of the City of Enfield v Development Assessment Commission* (2000) 169 ALR 400; 74 ALJR 490; BC200000174; [2000] HCA 5 at [28], per Gleeson CJ, Gummow, Kirby and Hayne JJ

JURY

[For 26 Halsbury's Laws (4th edn) paras 601, 602 see now 26 Halsbury's Laws (4th edn) (Reissue) paras 401–402.]

[By the Criminal Justice Act 1988, s 118(1), the right of peremptory challenge *without* cause was

abolished: *see* CHALLENGE. By sub-s (2) of that section, a Crown Court judge may order that the hearing of a challenge *for* cause shall be in camera or in chambers.

By s 119 of the Act of 1988, persons aged between sixty-five and seventy are to be eligible as jurors, although persons over sixty-five may be excused jury service as of right.

Other provisions of the Act of 1988 are: discretionary deferral of jury service (s 120); continuation of trials for murder on death or discharge of juror (s 121); and the position where an accused pleads autrefois acquit or autrefois convict (decision by judge alone) (s 122).]

JUST AND REASONABLE

Australia [Section 52 of the Land and Environment Court Act 1979 (NSW provides that where a judge, inter alia, convicts any person of an offence punishable in the summary jurisdiction of the court, the judge may include in the conviction an order for costs, such costs as to the judge seem 'just and reasonable'.] 'The requirement that such an order must be both just and reasonable entails both that there will be a fair hearing on the merits of the application for the order, and that the terms of the order finally made will be in themselves reasonable.' *Caltex Refining Co Pty Ltd v Maritime Services Board of New South Wales* (1995) 36 NSWLR 552 at 564, per Sully J

JUST CAUSE

Canada ' "Just cause" is undefined under the [Unemployment Insurance] Act. Its meaning is one of law. In *Tanguay v Unemployment Ins Comm*, a group of employees had left their jobs so as to make room for younger ones. The Board of Referees accepted the reason given as amounting to "just cause" but the Umpire rejected it. Pratte JA, for the Court, confirmed stating the following:

> ... it seems clear that the board decided as it did because it was of the view that the applicants had acted reasonably in leaving their employment. This indicates a complete misunderstanding of the words "just cause" in s. 41(1). In the context in which they are used these words are not synonymous with "reason" or "motive". An employee who has won a lottery or inherited a fortune may have an excellent reason for leaving his employment: he does not thereby have just cause within the meaning of s. 41(1). This subsection is an

important provision in an Act which creates a system of insurance against unemployment, and its language must be interpreted in accordance with the duty that ordinarily applies to any insured, not to deliberately cause the risk to occur. To be more precise, I would say that an employee who has voluntarily left his employment and has not found another has deliberately placed himself in a situation which enables him to compel third parties to pay him unemployment insurance benefits. He is only justified in acting in this way if, at the time he left, circumstances existed which excused him from thus taking the risk of causing others to bear the burden of his unemployment.

'Pratte JA cited with approval the following statement of Donaldson LJ of the English Court of Appeal in *Crewe v Social Security Comr*:

> It is of the essence of insurance that the assured shall not deliberately create or increase the risk.

'In the case at bar, the applicant voluntarily increased the risk of losing his employment. He sought employment in the area of trucking while his driving licence was clouded with the likelihood of a suspension. Can he, in those circumstances, expect to share the unemployment insurance fund causing others to bear the burden of his unemployment? I do not think so. Under the basic principles of insurance, the applicant placed himself from the beginning in a situation of high risk in terms of losing his employment without "just cause".

...

'... Admittedly, the applicant in the case at bar had no other reasonable alternative but to leave his employment. But the reason for his leaving was the loss of his driving licence for which he was responsible, having been found guilty of a drinking and driving offence. This was not a "just cause".' *Smith v Canada (Attorney General)* [1998] 1 FC 529 at 537–538, FCA, per Desjardins JA

JUST EXCUSE [FOR NOT GIVING EVIDENCE]

New Zealand [Commissions of Inquiry Act 1908, s 13A.] '[I]n the present case the statutory "sufficient cause" and "just excuse" exceptions provide ample scope for all the circumstances to be taken into account. Inherent in these two expressions, which are synonymous in this context,

is the concept of weighing all the consequences of the refusal to give evidence: the adverse consequences to the inquiry if the questions are not answered, and the adverse consequences to the witness if he is compelled to answer.

'In his ruling of 27 September 1995 the Commissioner expressed a different view. He ruled that the exceptions do not extend beyond the scope of the privileges and immunities preserved by s 6 of the Commissions of Inquiry Act 1908. A witness who does not enjoy the common law privilege against answering a question therefore lacks sufficient cause within s 9 or just excuse within s 13A. Their Lordships agree with the Court of Appeal that on this the Commissioner misdirected himself. The width and elasticity of the relieving exceptions are not to be confined and restricted in this way.' *Brannigan v Sir Ronald Davison* [1997] 1 NZLR 140 at 147–148, PC, per cur

JUSTICE

Australia [Section 352 of the Crimes Act 1900 (NSW) requires the officer arresting a person without warrant to take that person before a justice to be dealt with according to law.] '"Justice" is defined by s 4(1) of the Crimes Act as meaning a justice of the peace, but s 352 clearly contemplates that the justice before whom the person must be brought is one who is acting in a capacity to be able to deal with him according to law. It does not include any police officer authorised to grant bail pursuant to s 17 of the Bail Act 1978 (NSW): *Burns* (unreported, Court of Criminal Appeal, NSW, 19 August 1988), pp 7–8; *Zorad* (1990) 19 NSWLR 91 at 98–99; 47 A Crim R 211 at 218.

'In *Burns* at p 7, Street CJ (with whom the other members of the Court agreed) expressed the view that the word "justice" in s 352 should be interpreted as referring to

> "... a magistrate. That is to say, a judicial officer vested with the powers and charged with the responsibilities that are conferred and imposed upon a judicial officer".

'That statement was, of course, made in the context of an issue as to whether the word "justice" included a police officer authorised to grant bail, so that the description which the Chief Justice gave was intended merely to exclude such a police officer. In my view it would not exclude a justice of the peace who was exercising the judicial powers given to him as a judicial officer by, for example, the Justices Act 1902 (NSW) or the Bail Act.' *Re Ainsworth* (1992) 57 A Crim R 174 at 181, per Hunt J

JUSTIFICATION

[For 28 Halsbury's Laws (4th edn) para 81 see now 28 Halsbury's Laws (4th edn) (Reissue) para 82.]

JUSTLY ENTITLED TO BE HEARD

Australia [Section 222(1) of the Workplace Relations Act 1996 (Cth) permits the court to allow to appear before it persons whom the court considers to be justly entitled to be heard.] '... [T]here must be a standard according to which it can be determined when a person should or should not be allowed to appear. That standard is that the person is "justly entitled to be heard". To satisfy this requirement a person must show that he or she has a sufficient interest in the inquiry. What will constitute a sufficient interest will vary from case to case and will often depend upon the nature of the alleged irregularities. It is therefore inappropriate, if not impossible, to define the outer limits of what would constitute a sufficient interest.' *Re an inquiry relating to elections for officers in the United Firefighters' Union of Australia (Vic Branch)* (2000) 102 IR 247; BC200006529; [2000] FCA 1493 at [3], per Finkelstein J

K

KEEPING

Australia 'In ordinary use of language I would understand keeping as discharging some responsibility in respect of operations at an establishment. Such keeping may be only part of the overall operations, for example the keeping of a green at a golf or bowling club, or it may be essentially the whole operation such as keeping a lighthouse or keeping a brothel.' *Re Rahme* (1993) 70 A Crim R 357 at 362, per Grove J

KEPT

Australia 'There is no reason, in my view, to attribute … a restrictive meaning to the word "kept". In its ordinary meaning it includes the narrow meaning given to it by Perry J [in *Residues Treatment and Trading Co Ltd v Southern Resources Ltd* (1989) 52 SASR 54 at 77; 15 ACLR 416 at 420] but it includes the well understood wider meanings of "keep" of which "kept" is the past participle, namely "to have in stock", "to have charge or custody of": *The Macquarie* Dictionary, 2nd rev; or "to guard, defend, protect, preserve, save", "to take care of, to look after": *Shorter English Oxford Dictionary.*' *Duke Group Ltd* (*in liq*) *v Pilmer* (1994) 15 ACSR 255 at 272, per Mullighan J

Australia [Subsection 1305(1) of the Corporations Act 2001 (Cth) states that '[a] book kept by a body corporate under a requirement of this Act is admissible in evidence in any proceeding and is prima facie evidence of any matter stated or recorded in the book.' Subsection 1305(2) states that '[a] document purporting to be a book kept by a body corporate is, unless the contrary is proved, taken to be a book kept as mentioned in subs (1)'. Section 1305 of the Corporations Law (the predecessor of the Corporations Act) was essentially in the same terms.] 'In a number of cases concerning evidentiary provisions as to records kept by companies, the word "kept" has been given a narrow interpretation. In *Residues Treatment and Trading Co Ltd v Southern Resources Ltd* (1989)

52 SASR 54, Perry J was concerned with the Companies (South Australia) Code, s 550 … It was argued that a company's annual report, which it had a statutory obligation to create, was a "book kept by a corporation pursuant to a requirement of this Code". His Honour said, at 77:

> "In my opinion, given its context, the word 'kept' in s 550(1) does not simply mean a document which is retained by a corporation. It seems to me that it is an essential part of the quality of a document which is said to come within the scope of s 550, that it should be in the nature of a document or record which is in some way maintained by the corporation in a systematic or periodic fashion.
>
> "It is true, as Mr Bathurst QC put in the course of his argument, that a company would normally keep a copy of its Annual Report and make it available, from time to time, for inspection by people who had a legitimate reason to see it.
>
> "But that consideration is not sufficient to lead me to the view that the Annual Report should be regarded as within the scope of the relevant words of s 550, as it does not seem to me to answer to description of a book 'kept' by the corporation in the relevant sense of that word."

'The first of the paragraphs I have just quoted was cited with approval by Drummond J in *The Tubby Trout Pty Ltd v Sailbay Pty Ltd* (1993) 42 FCR 595 at 600. His Honour had to rule as to the admissibility of a letter received by a corporate respondent in that case from the credit manager of a company that was providing supplies to a restaurant, confirming that it was opening a separate account for the restaurant, and that that respondent would be responsible for that account until a separate licence was granted for the restaurant by a licensing authority. It was argued that the company was obliged by the Corporations Law to keep that letter as a written financial record that correctly recorded and explained its transactions and financial position.

Drummond J did not reject the submission that the relevant company was obliged to retain the letter pursuant to a provision of the Corporations Law, but held that the letter did not fall within the scope of s 1305 because it was not a document or record that the corporation was required to maintain in a systematic or periodic fashion.

'A similar approach was taken by Olsson J, with whom Mohr and Nyland JJ agreed, in *Sheahan v Northern Australian Land and Agency Co Ltd* (unreported, Supreme Court of South Australia, Full Court, 6 May 1994). At first instance, Perry J had refused to allow two purported contracts of sale to be tendered pursuant to s 1305. After setting out s 1305 and the definition of "books", Olsson J said, at para 50:

> "What is manifestly in contemplation is that class of document which is brought into existence, by or on behalf of a company, and maintained in its custody by virtue of an express obligation to do so imposed by the Corporations Law itself."

'However it is not clear from the judgment whether the appellants in that case identified any statutory provision as the source of an obligation to retain the purported contracts, or argued that "kept" included "retained". His Honour's comments, insofar as they related to the scope of the word "kept", may well have been obiter.

'It seems that a wide interpretation of the word "kept" was adopted for the first time in *Duke Group Ltd v Pilmer* (1994) 63 SASR 364. In that case, Mullighan J declined to follow *Residues Treatment and Trading Co Ltd v Southern Resources Ltd* (supra), and held that the annual report of a company constituted a book "kept" by the company under a requirement of the Companies Code. He did so on the basis that the Code, s 274(1), obliged the company to furnish a member of the company, in specified circumstances, with copies of the last of its annual accounts, directors' reports, and auditor's reports. He reasoned that, since a company could not provide such documents without retaining them, there was an implied requirement to keep them, and that that requirement fell within the scope of s 1305. It seems no such argument was advanced in *Residues Treatment*. As to the reasoning for not following *Residues Treatment*, his Honour said the following at 273:

> "With respect, I disagree. There is no reason, in my view, to attribute such a restrictive meaning to the word 'kept'. In its ordinary meaning it includes the narrow meaning given

to it by Perry J but it includes the well understood wider meanings of 'keep' of which 'kept' is the past participle, namely 'to have in stock', 'to have the charge or custody of': *Macquarie Dictionary* 2nd rev; or 'to guard, defend, protect, preserve, save', 'to take care of, to look after': *Shorter English Oxford Dictionary*."

'In *R v Connell* (1996) 14 ACLC 32 at 35, White J (of the Supreme Court of Western Australia) followed Perry J in *Residues Treatment* and Drummond J in *Tubby Trout*, rejecting the interpretation favoured by Mullighan J in *Duke Group*. His comments were obiter, since he concluded that the documents in question were kept by the relevant company on either construction of the word "kept". He had held that s 1305(2) not only deemed a document to which it applied to be a book and to have been kept by a body corporate, but also deemed its keeping to have been under a requirement of the Corporations Law or a previous law corresponding to a provision of the Corporations Law. He said that the narrow construction of "kept" went "a long way towards overcoming any difficulty which might otherwise be thought to exist as a result of the construction of s 1305(2) which I prefer and to avoiding what Mr Connell has called an 'absurd result'." Mr Connell had argued that a wide interpretation of s 1305(2) would lead to the "absurd result that any piece of paper in the possession of a body corporate, whatever its nature, would … be prima facie evidence of its truth". His Honour had rejected that submission, on the basis that s 1305(2) dealt only with a document that purported to be a book kept by a body corporate. Having reached that conclusion, it is difficult to understand what difficulty a wide interpretation of "kept" could create.

'A very compelling reason for adopting a wide interpretation was advanced by Finkelstein J in *Valoutin v Furst* (1998) 154 ALR 119. After referring to the competing views expressed in *Residues Treatment* and *Duke Group*, his Honour said (at 128–9):

> "In deciding which of these decisions is to be preferred it must be remembered that since the last century the narrow traditional common law view of the admissibility of business records has been the subject of statutory modification to facilitate the admission of those records in almost every common law jurisdiction. This is because the common law rules were recognised as an inhibition to the proper administration of justice in both the

civil and criminal courts. Thus there is no warrant for giving a provision such as s 1305 a narrow construction especially when the admissibility of a document under the section is only on a prima facie basis and will often give way to other conflicting evidence. In my view there is no reason why the word 'kept' should be given the restrictive meaning preferred by Perry J. I agree with Mullighan J that the word should be given its ordinary meaning which includes 'to maintain' and 'to retain'."

'In *Caratti v R* (2000) 22 WAR 527 at 546, Malcolm CJ, with whom Kennedy and Anderson JJ agreed, cited those comments with approval. However what Malcolm CJ said was obiter, since he concluded that the relevant documents were admissible on either construction of the word "kept".

'The fact that s 1305 and its predecessors involve a departure from the common law is one factor weighing in favour of a narrow interpretation of "kept". It could also be argued that Parliament intended "kept" in s 1305 to be understood in the same way as "keep" in s 286(1), which imposes the obligation to keep written financial records that correctly record and explain a company's transactions, financial position, and financial performance, and would enable true and fair financial statements to be prepared and audited. However I think that those factors are outweighed by the requirement of the Acts Interpretation Act 1901 (Cth), s 15AA, to prefer a construction that would promote the purpose or object underlying the Act to one that would not. Like Malcolm CJ, I agree with the views expressed by Finkelstein J in *Valoutin*. Further, the wide approach gives the word "kept" its ordinary meaning, as Mullighan J pointed out in *Duke Group*. For these reasons, I consider that s 1305 applies to all books retained in the custody of a corporation under a requirement of the Corporations Act 2001 (Cth) or the Corporations Law and not just to books that are the subject of a requirement that they be maintained in a systematic fashion.' *R v Turner (No 17)* BC200201966; [2002] TASSC 18 at [8]–[16], per Blow J

KNACKER'S YARD

[The Food Act 1984, is largely repealed. The definition is re-enacted in the Food Safety Act 1990, s 53(1).]

KNEW

[The Second Council Directive (EEC) 84/5 on compulsory motor insurance, art 1(4) makes provision regarding unidentified and uninsured vehicles, but exempts the Motor Insurers Bureau from liability in respect of an injured passenger who voluntarily entered the vehicle which caused the damage or injury, if it can be proved that he knew it was uninsured. '[12] … Thus, member states may exclude compensation for damage or injury caused by the driver of an uninsured vehicle if the person who suffered damage or injury "voluntarily" entered the vehicle and "knew" it was uninsured. It should be noted that, unlike the corresponding exception in the MIB agreement ("knew or ought to have known"), the exception permitted by the directive uses the word "knew" without any adornment. It is this difference in language which gives rise to the issues arising on this appeal.

'[13] What is meant by "knew" in the context of the directive? The interpretation of the directive is a matter governed by community law. If the meaning of "knew" in art 1 is doubtful, and it is necessary to resolve the doubt in order to decide this appeal, then a reference to the Court of Justice of the European Communities must be made. Rightly so, because it is important that the provisions of this directive are applied uniformly throughout the community. So I turn to consider what "knew" means in the directive and whether there is any relevant ambiguity.

'[14] The context is an exception to a general rule. The Court of Justice has stressed repeatedly that exceptions are to be construed strictly. Here, a strict and narrow interpretation of what constitutes knowledge for the purpose of art 1 is reinforced by the subject matter. The subject matter is compensation for damage to property or personal injuries caused by vehicles. The general rule is that victims of accidents should have the benefit of protection up to specified minimum amounts, whether or not the vehicle which caused the damage was insured. The exception, therefore, permits a member state, contrary to the general rule, to make no provision for compensation for a person who has suffered personal injury or damage to property. Proportionality requires that a high degree of personal fault must exist before it would be right for an injured passenger to be deprived of compensation. A narrow approach is further supported by the other prescribed limitation on the permissible ambit of any exclusion: the person claiming compensation must have entered the vehicle voluntarily. The need for the passenger to have entered the vehicle voluntarily serves to confirm that the exception is aimed at persons who were consciously colluding in the use of an uninsured vehicle. And it can be noted that the directive emphasises the exceptional nature of the exclusion of compensation by placing the burden of proving knowledge on the party who seeks to invoke the exception, namely, the institution responsible for paying compensation.

'[15] This, then, is the context in which "knew" is used in this directive. In this context, knowledge by a passenger that a driver is uninsured means primarily possession of information by the passenger from which the passenger drew the conclusion that the driver was uninsured. Most obviously and simply, this occurs where the driver told the passenger that he had no insurance cover. Clearly, information from which a passenger drew the conclusion that the driver was uninsured may be obtained in many other ways. Another instance would be when the passenger was aware, from his family or other connections with the driver, that the driver had not passed his driving test ("if he'd taken the test, I would have known"). Knowledge of this character is often labelled actual knowledge, thereby distinguishing other types of case where a person, although lacking actual knowledge, is nevertheless treated by the law as having knowledge of the relevant information.

'[16] There is one category of case which is so close to actual knowledge that the law generally treats a person as having knowledge. It is the type of case where, as applied to the present context, a passenger had information from which he drew the conclusion that the driver might well not be insured but deliberately refrained from asking questions lest his suspicions should be confirmed. He wanted not to know ("I will not ask, because I would rather not know"). The law generally treats this state of mind as having the like consequences as would follow if the person, in my example the passenger, had acted honestly rather than disingenuously. He is treated as though he had received the information which he deliberately sought to avoid. In the context of the directive that makes good sense. Such a passenger as much colludes in the use of an uninsured vehicle as a passenger who actually knows that the vehicle is uninsured. The principle of equal treatment requires that these two persons shall be treated alike. The directive is to be construed accordingly.

'[17] Thus far I see no difficulty. I consider that it is acte clair that these two categories of case fall within the scope of the exception permitted by the directive. Conversely, I am in no doubt that "knew" in the directive does not include what can be described broadly as carelessness or "negligence". Typically this would cover the case where a passenger gave no thought to the question of insurance, even though an ordinary prudent passenger, in his position and with his knowledge, would have made inquiries. He "ought" to have made inquiries, judged by the standard of the ordinary prudent passenger. A passenger who was careless in this way cannot be treated as though he knew of the absence of insurance. As Lord Denning MR said in *Cia Maritima San Basilio SA v Oceanus Mutual Underwriting Association (Bermuda) Ltd, The Eurysthene* [1976] 3 All ER 243 at 251, [1977] QB 49 at 68, negligence in not knowing the truth is not equivalent to knowledge of it. A passenger who was careless in not knowing did not collude in the use of an uninsured vehicle, and he is not to be treated as though he did. To decide otherwise would be to give a wide, rather than a narrow, interpretation to the exception permitted by the directive. This also seems to me to be acte clair.' *White v White* [2001] UKHL/9 at [12]–[17], [2001] 2 All ER 43 at 47–49, HL, per Lord Nicholls of Birkenhead

KNEW OR HAD REASON TO BELIEVE

[The liability of insurers to satisfy judgments against uninsured drivers is excluded under the Road Traffic Act 1988, s 151(4) in the case of a person who 'knew or had reason to believe that the vehicle had been stolen or unlawfully taken'.] '[9] Section 151 of the Road Traffic Act 1988 requires insurers to satisfy judgments obtained against drivers arising out of their use of a motor vehicle where the judgment relates to a liability which is required to be covered by a policy of insurance under s 145 of the 1988 Act. Section 145 of the 1988 Act requires the driver of a motor vehicle to be covered by a policy of insurance for any liability which may be incurred by the driver in respect of the death of, or bodily injury to, any person, or any damage to property, caused by, or arising out of, the use of the vehicle on a road or other public place. It follows that Iain's liability for Andrew's injuries was a liability which was required to be covered by a policy of insurance.

'[10] Subject to an important exception, s 151 applies when the vehicle is being driven by uninsured drivers as well as insured ones. Insured drivers are covered by s 151(2)(a), which requires insurers to satisfy judgments where the liability is "a liability covered by the terms of the policy ... and the judgment is obtained against any person who is insured by the policy ..." And uninsured drivers are covered by s 151(2)(b), which requires insurers to satisfy judgments where the liability is "a liability, other than an excluded liability, which would be so covered if the policy insured all persons ... and the judgment is obtained against any person other than the one who is insured by the policy ..." It is common ground that Iain's liability to Andrew was not covered by the terms of the policy, and that Iain was not insured by the policy, because he had not attained the age of 25, he did not hold a driving licence, and he had not been authorised by MEL to drive the van. So if the insurers are required to satisfy any judgment obtained by Andrew against Iain, it will have to be a judgment which satisfies the conditions of s 151(2)(b). It is common ground that Iain's liability to Andrew would have been a liability to which s 151(2)(b) related if that liability had not been "an excluded liability". That is the important exception to the generality of s 151. The critical question is whether Iain's liability to Andrew was an excluded liability.

'[11] The manifest purpose of the exception is to relieve insurers from their duty to satisfy judgments obtained against uninsured drivers by their passengers if the passenger knew or had reason to believe that the vehicle had been stolen or unlawfully taken. Thus, s 151(4) provides, so far as is material, as follows:

"In subsection (2)(b) above 'excluded liability' means a liability in respect of the death of, or bodily injury to, or damage to the property of any person who, at the time of the use which gave rise to the liability, was allowing himself to be carried in or upon the vehicle and knew or had reason to believe that the vehicle had been stolen or unlawfully taken, not being a person who–(a) did not know and had no reason to believe that the vehicle had been stolen or unlawfully taken until after the commencement of his journey, and (b) could not reasonably have been expected to have alighted from the vehicle."

It is accepted, of course, that Andrew was allowing himself to be carried in the van at the relevant time. And it is not suggested that he only became aware of the facts relating to Iain's lack of authority to drive the van after the journey to the garage had started. So the critical question is whether Andrew "knew or had reason to believe that the [van] had been stolen or unlawfully taken". The insurers accept that the burden of proof on that issue rests with them. It is therefore for them to prove, on the balance of probabilities, that Andrew knew or had reason to believe that that was the case.

...

'[16] In my judgment, the word "knew" in s 151(4) does not mean something other than actual knowledge or such knowledge as the law regards as equivalent to it. But there is an alternative to proof that the injured passenger *knew* that the vehicle had been stolen or unlawfully taken. Insurers will avoid liability if they prove that the injured passenger had *reason to believe* that the vehicle had been stolen or unlawfully taken. Whereas the words "knew or ought to have known" in the MIB agreement were intended to be co-extensive with the word "knew" in the directive [Second Motor Insurance Directive (Council Directive (EEC) 84/5 (on the approximation of the laws of the member states relating to insurance against civil liability in respect of the use of motor vehicles) (OJ 1984 L8 p 17)], s 151 does not fall to be construed in the light of the directive, so that the words "knew or had reason to believe" in s 151(4) need not be co-extensive with the word "knew" in the directive. To be fair, Mr Braslavsky did not contend for that.

'[17] So if the words "had reason to believe" in s 151(4) have to be construed independently of the word "knew", what do they mean? Mr Braslavsky accepted–in my opinion, rightly–that insurers do not have to prove that the injured passenger actually believed that the vehicle had been stolen or unlawfully taken. What has to be proved is that the injured passenger had the information–or what Mr Adrian Palmer QC for the insurers called "the building blocks"–which would have afforded him good reasons for believing that the vehicle had been stolen or unlawfully taken had he applied his mind to the topic. Shutting one's eyes to the obvious is therefore enough, provided that it would indeed have been obvious to the injured passenger if he had thought about it.' *McMinn v McMinn* [2006] EWHC 827 (QB) at [9]–[11], [16]–[17], [2006] 3 All ER 87, per Keith J

KNEW OR OUGHT TO HAVE KNOWN

[Clause 6(1)(e)(ii) of (Motor Insurers' Bureau (Compensation of Victims of Uninsured Drivers) Agreement) 21 December 1998 absolves the MIB from liability where an injured passenger 'knew or ought to have known' that the vehicle was uninsured, as permitted by the Second Council Directive (EEC) 84/5 on compulsory motor insurance, art 1(4).] '[20] Against this background I turn to the interpretation of the phrase "knew or ought to have known" in cl 6(1)(e) of the 1988 MIB agreement. This question of interpretation is governed by English law. "Ought" imports a standard by reference to which conduct is measured.

Such is the prevalence of negligence in English law that the phrase immediately prompts the thought that the standard imported by "ought" is the standard of the reasonable person. In cases of professional negligence the standard is that of the reasonably competent and careful professional in the relevant discipline. But this is not necessarily the standard. The meaning of the phrase depends upon its context. Here the context is the directive. The MIB agreement was entered into with the specific intention of giving effect to the directive.

'[21] Had the MIB agreement been embodied in legislation, whether primary or secondary, the English court would have been under an obligation to interpret its provisions, as far as possible, in a way which gives effect to the directive (see *Marleasing SA v La Comercial Internacional de Alimentación SA* Case C-106/89 [1990] ECR I-4135). As Lord Oliver of Aylmerton observed in *Litster v Forth Dry Dock and Engineering Co Ltd* [1989] 1 All ER 1134 at 1140, [1990] 1 AC 546 at 559, a purposive construction will be applied to legislation even though, perhaps, it may involve some departure from the strict and literal application of the words which the legislature has elected to use.

'[22] The present case does not involve legislation. Despite the contrary argument submitted to your Lordships, I do not see how the *Marleasing* principle, as such, can apply to the interpretation of the MIB agreement. Article 5 of the EC Treaty obliges member states to take all appropriate measures to ensure fulfilment of their obligations arising out of the treaty. The rationale of the *Marleasing* case is that the duty of member states under art 5 is binding on all the authorities of member states, including the courts. The courts must apply national law accordingly, whenever the law was enacted or made. But it is one matter to apply this principle to national law. Whatever form it may take, law is made by authorities of the state. It is quite another matter to apply this principle to contracts made between citizens. The *Marleasing* principle cannot be stretched to the length of requiring contracts to be interpreted in a manner that would impose on one or other of the parties obligations which, the *Marleasing* case apart, the contract did not impose. This is so even in the case of a contract where one of the parties is an emanation of government, here, the Secretary of State. The citizen's obligations are those to which he agreed, as construed in accordance with normal principles of interpretation.

'[23] So the *Marleasing* principle must be put on one side. Even so, I consider that the application

of conventional principles of interpretation of documents arrives at the same result. The purpose for which the MIB agreement was made furnishes a compelling context. The exception spelled out in cl 6(1)(e)(ii) of the MIB agreement was intended by the parties to carry through the provisions of the directive. The phrase "knew or ought to have known" in the MIB agreement was intended to be co-extensive with the exception permitted by art 1 of the directive. It was intended to bear the same meaning as "knew" in the directive. It should be construed accordingly. It is to be interpreted restrictively. "Ought to have known" is apt to include knowledge which an honest person who enters the vehicle voluntarily would have. It includes the case of a passenger who deliberately refrains from asking questions. It is not apt to include mere carelessness or negligence. A mere failure to act with reasonable prudence is not enough. Hence it does not embrace the present case. Brian White's claim is not excepted from the MIB agreement. On this I respectfully differ from the view of the Court of Appeal (sub nom *Mighell v Reading, Evans v Motor Insurers' Bureau, White v White* [1999] 1 CMLR 1251).' *White v White* [2001] UKHL/9 at [20]–[23], [2001] 2 All ER 43 at 49–50, HL, per Lord Nicholls of Birkenhead

KNIFE

Folding pocketknife

[Under the Carrying of Knives etc (Scotland) Act 1993, s 1 it is an offence to carry any article which has a blade or is sharply pointed. A folding pocketknife with a cutting edge which does not exceed 3 inches is exempted.] 'In our opinion a knife which has a blade which can be fixed in the open position by a locking device is not a folding pocketknife within the meaning of section 1(3)... It is not enough that the knife can be placed in the pocket, or that the blade can be folded to enable it to be placed there. It must be a folding pocketknife. It cannot be described as a knife of that kind if it has a device which is designed, until it has been overcome, to prevent the blade from being folded ... The description which it would be natural to give to a knife of that kind is that it is a lock knife or a locking knife, to distinguish it from a knife whose blade is always and immediately foldable.' *Stewart v Friel* 1995 SCCR 492 at 495, per the Lord Justice-General (Hope)

KNIGHT

[For 35 Halsbury's Laws (4th edn) paras 867–869 see now 35 Halsbury's Laws (4th edn) (Reissue) paras 967–969.]

KNOCK FOR KNOCK

[For 25 Halsbury's Laws (4th edn) para 753 see now 25 Halsbury's Laws (4th edn) (2003 Reissue) para 726.]

KNOWINGLY

[The defendant was stopped at Heathrow Airport on arrival from Amsterdam. He was in possession of two video cassettes which bore the labels of two ordinary films on general release, but which actually contained material whose importation was prohibited, namely indecent photographs of boys under 16. In his defence, he claimed that he had not known that the cassettes had contained indecent photographs of children, and had instead believed them to contain two other films which he thought were prohibited, but were not in fact prohibited. Such a belief, if accepted by the jury as a reasonable possibility, would have required the defendant's acquittal, and the judge directed the jury accordingly. He was convicted and appealed.] '[53] In the present case it is not in dispute that the goods carried by the appellant were prohibited goods. Once the jury had rejected (as they did) the "*Taaffe* defence" [*R v Taaffe* [1984] 1 All ER 747, HL] advanced on behalf of the appellant that he believed he was carrying two prohibited video films but that, in reality, those films were not prohibited, the only issue for the jury to decide was whether the defendant knew that the goods which he was carrying were subject to a prohibition. The judge on a number of occasions correctly directed the jury that this was the issue which they had to decide. He also correctly told the jury that the prosecution had to satisfy them that the defendant "by his behaviour, and the situation which you will find as a matter of fact, that he knew he was bringing in prohibited photographs".
...
'[56] ... The offence created by s 170(2)(b) of the 1979 Act is the offence of being "knowingly concerned in any fraudulent evasion ... of any prohibition ... with respect to the goods". The essence of the offence is being knowingly concerned in the evasion of a prohibition. The jury were fully entitled to find that the behaviour of the appellant satisfied them that he was knowingly concerned in

the evasion of a prohibition. His behaviour in buying genuine video films of "Spartacus" and "The Godfather Part 2" in the airport shop at Amsterdam Airport and obtaining receipts for them, leaving the genuine video films in the lavatory at Heathrow, and then producing the receipts which appeared to relate to the two video films containing indecent material, pointed quite clearly to the conclusion that he knew that he was involved in the evasion of a prohibition against importation.

'[57] In many cases a person who, at the request of another and, it may be, in return for a payment, brings into the United Kingdom an article, knowing that he is taking part in the fraudulent evasion of a prohibition against importation, will not know the precise nature of the article which he is carrying. In such a case the task for the prosecution in proving an offence would be virtually impossible if, in addition to having to prove that the article was a prohibited one and that the defendant knew that he was involved in the evasion of a prohibition, it also had to prove that he knew the precise nature of the article. In my opinion the application of the principle stated in *R v Hussain* [[1969] 2 All ER 1117, CA] gives rise to no injustice in a case such as the present one, as it is open to the defendant to seek to rely on the "*Taaffe* defence" if his case is that he believed that he was carrying an article which in reality and contrary to his belief was not prohibited.' *R v Forbes* [2001] UKHL 40 at [53], [56], [57], [2001] 4 All ER 97, HL [22] [56]

Canada [The accused was charged with knowingly selling obscene material without lawful justification or excuse, where the materials had film board approval.] 'It is a general rule of statutory construction that when the term "knowingly" is used in a criminal statute, it applies to all elements of the *actus reus*.' *R v Jorgensen* [1995] 4 SCR 55 at 93, SCC, per Sopinka J

KNOWINGLY AND VOLUNTARILY

Australia [In the context of disclosure of documents under Evidence Act 1995 (NSW) s 122(2).] 'The meaning of the words "knowingly and voluntarily" was touched upon by Rolfe J in *Ampolex v Perpetual Trustee Co (Canberra) Pty Ltd* (1996) 40 NSWLR 12 at 22, where his Honour said:

I assume that the word "voluntarily" is intended to mean something other than "under compulsion of law" which appears in paragraph (c). I think the distinction is that the disclosure was made voluntarily, in the sense

that it was not made by way of mistake, it being possible that a disclosure may be made "knowingly" yet by way of mistake, and accordingly, perhaps not voluntarily.'
Australian Securities and Investments Commission v Rich [2004] NSWSC 934 at [3], per Austin J; BC200406700

KNOWLEDGE

Constructive knowledge

'What types of knowledge are relevant for the purposes of constructive trusteeship? Mr Price [counsel for the plaintiff] submits that knowledge can comprise any one of five different mental states which he described as follows: (i) actual knowledge; (ii) wilfully shutting one's eyes to the obvious; (iii) wilfully and recklessly failing to make such inquiries as an honest and reasonable man would make; (iv) knowledge of circumstances which would indicate the facts to an honest and reasonable man; (v) knowledge of circumstances which would put an honest and reasonable man on inquiry. More accurately, apart from actual knowledge they are formulations of the circumstances which may lead the court to impute knowledge of the facts to the alleged constructive trustee even though he lacked actual knowledge of those facts. Thus the court will treat a person as having constructive knowledge of the facts if he wilfully shuts his eyes to the relevant facts which would be obvious if he opened his eyes, such constructive knowledge being usually termed (though by a metaphor of historical inaccuracy) "Nelsonian knowledge". Similarly the court may treat a person as having constructive knowledge of the facts (type (iv) knowledge) if he has actual knowledge of circumstances which would indicate the facts to an honest and reasonable man.' *Baden v Societe Generale pour Faranises le Developpment du Commerce et de l'Industrie en France SA* [1992] 4 All ER 161 at 235, per Peter Gibson J

[See also *Lipkin Gorman v Karpnale Ltd* [1992] 4 All ER 409 at 416, CA, per May LJ; on appeal [1992] 4 All ER 512, HL]

KNOWS OR REASONABLY SUSPECTS

Australia [Section 189(1) of the Migration Act 1958 (Cth) provides that if an officer 'knows or reasonably suspects' that a person is an unlawful non-citizen then the officer must detain that person. Section 196 provides that an unlawful non-citizen detained under s 189 must be kept in immigration detention until he or she is removed from Australia, deported or granted a visa.] 'The definitions of the words "suspect" and "suspicion" in the *Macquarie Dictionary* make it plain that a suspicion may be formed "with insufficient proof or with no proof", or "on little or no evidence", or "on slight evidence or without evidence". By itself, the word "suspects" would be capable of being construed to include the formation of an imagined belief, having no basis at all in fact, or even conjecture. Plainly, to empower an arrest on the basis of an irrational suspicion would offend the principle of the importance of individual liberty underlying the common law. It would also allow the possibility of arbitrary arrest, with the consequence that Australia would be in breach of its international obligations pursuant to art 9 of the International Covenant on Civil and Political Rights. To avoid these consequences, the word "reasonably" has been placed before the word "suspects" in s 189(1). The adverb makes it clear that, in order to justify arrest and detention, the suspicion that a person is an unlawful non-citizen must be justifiable upon objective examination of relevant material. Given that deprivation of liberty is at stake such material will include that which is discoverable by efforts of search and inquiry that are reasonable in the circumstances.

'The phrase "reasonably suspects" is used as an alternative to "knows". Before an officer could know that a person is an unlawful non-citizen, the officer would have to have reached a level of satisfaction of that fact approaching certainty. If, as in the present case, the person concerned were not an unlawful non-citizen, because he or she was the holder of a visa entitling him or her to be in Australia, it would be impossible for the officer to know the contrary. The context of the phrase "reasonably suspects" suggests that something substantially less than certainty is required. Reasonable suspicion, therefore, lies somewhere on a spectrum between certainty and irrationality. The need to ensure that arrest is not arbitrary suggests that the requirement for a reasonable suspicion should be placed on that spectrum not too close to irrationality.

'It is trite to say that what is reasonable in a particular case depends upon the circumstances of that case. It is worth remembering, however, that all of the circumstances must be considered. If, as in the present case, an officer is aware of conflicting facts, the reasonableness of any suspicion formed by that officer must be judged in the light of the facts available to him or her at the particular time. It may be that the existence of a particular fact would ground a reasonable suspicion in the mind of the officer if it were the only fact known to him or her. If, at the time of forming the suspicion, the officer is aware of conflicting facts, it may not be reasonable simply to discard those facts and to form a suspicion on the basis of the single fact capable of supporting such a suspicion. That is, the officer is not empowered to act on a suspicion reasonably formed that a person may be an unlawful non-citizen. The officer is to detain a person whom the officer reasonably suspects is an unlawful non-citizen. That, of course, is consonant with the serious act the officer is empowered to carry out. Section 196 operates upon a person detained under s 189 who is an unlawful non-citizen, not upon a person reasonably suspected of being an unlawful non-citizen. The scheme contemplated under the Migration Act 1958 (Cth) is indefinite detention pending removal or deportation under administrative fiat. It is not detention for the purpose of curial review or determination of status. These provisions confirm that the appropriate construction of s 189 is that an officer in forming a reasonable suspicion is obliged to make due inquiry to obtain material likely to be relevant to the formation of that suspicion.

'One further consideration should be mentioned. A suspicion that is not grounded in fact to the point of becoming reasonable does not become reasonable because of a perceived need to act quickly. In the present case, the fact that Mr Cain knew that the appellant was about to be dismissed from his employment by Fluor Daniel Pty Ltd ..., and that he would be at the premises of that company at a particular time, did not bear upon the reasonableness of the suspicion. It created precisely the situation in which the need for a suspicion to be grounded in fact to the point of being reasonable became even more acute than normal, so that precipitate action, based on a misapprehension, might be avoided. The fact that the appellant was employed at a significant level with a national employer suggested that the appellant held a visa permitting him to obtain such employment.' *Goldie v Commonwealth* (2002) 188 ALR 708; BC200201595; [2002] FCA 433 at [4]–[7], per Gray and Lee JJ

L

LACHES

[For 16 Halsbury's Laws (4th edn) paras 1476–1477 see now 16(2) Halsbury's Laws (4th edn) (Reissue) para 910.]

LAMMAS LANDS

[For 6 Halsbury's Laws (4th edn) para 517 see now 6 Halsbury's Laws (4th edn) (2003 Reissue) para 417.]

LAND

[The Capital Gains Tax Act 1979 has been repealed. The definition in re-enacted in the Taxation of Chargeable Gains Act 1992, s 288(1).]

[For 39 Halsbury's Laws (4th edn) paras 377, 378 see now 39(2) Halsbury's Laws (4th edn) (Reissue) paras 76–77.]

New Zealand [Acts Interpretation Act 1924, s 4; Reserves Act 1977, s 2(1).] 'The Reserves Act 1997 does not define the term "land". Section 4 of the Acts Interpretation Act 1924 provides that in every Act, if not inconsistent with the context thereof and unless there are words to exclude or restrict such meaning:

> "Land" includes messuages, tenements, hereditaments, houses, and buildings unless there are words to exclude houses and buildings, or to restrict the meaning to tenements of some particular tenure.

'An easement, such as the access easement in the present case, is an incorporeal hereditament, which is a right in respect of land and therefore an interest in land, but it is not land in the tangible sense nor an estate in land in the common law sense. Nevertheless, it is contemplated as land by the Acts Interpretation Act 1924 since the generic "hereditaments" must encompass both those which are corporeal and those which are incorporeal. It is the case that Chitty J in *Re Danson* (*Deceased*) (1895) 11 TLR 455 is reported to have held that the reference to "hereditaments" in the definition of "land" in the Interpretation Act 1889 (UK) was confined to corporeal hereditaments. But in *Re Clutterbuck* [1901] 2 Ch 285, 289 Bryne J suggested that the *Times Law Report* must have been erroneous, thereby making plain his view that the statutory definition comprehended both corporeal and incorporeal hereditaments. There was nothing in the definition to suggest that the term should be given an amputated meaning and, as Bryne J pointed out, it was unnecessary for the purpose of Chitty J's judgment for such a meaning to be selected. In the Law of Property Act 1925 (UK) the definition of "land" includes incorporeal hereditaments which is consistent with conventional jurisprudence. The New Zealand Land Transfer Act 1952 similarly provides that in the Act and in all instruments purporting to be made and executed under that Act, unless the context otherwise requires, "land" includes hereditaments corporeal and incorporeal, of every kind of description and easements.

'These references demonstrate that at least for certain legislative purposes an incorporeal hereditament, such as an easement, may be treated for certain purposes the same as terrestrial land.

'... It is necessary to bear in mind, in the present case that the term "land" may have a special legislative meaning. Thus, although generally speaking land cannot be appurtenant to land—*Lister v Pickford* per Romilly MR (1864) 34 LJ Ch 582, 584—in terms of which principle an easement could not be land, nevertheless the Acts Interpretation Act 1924 and the Land Transfer Act 1952, for example, envisage that for certain legislative purposes an easement can be land.' *Auckland City Council v Man O'War Station Ltd* [1996] 3 NZLR 460 at 465, per Anderson J

A piece of land

New Zealand [Section 129B(1)(a) of the Property Law Act 1952 provides that 'A piece of land is landlocked if there is no reasonable access to it'.] 'The ordinary meaning of the words used suggests that land is to be regarded as landlocked if it does not in a practical sense have reasonable access.

The section confers a discretion to be exercised after consideration of all relevant factors, and it would seem contrary to the remedial purpose of the legislation to adopt an artificially limited view as to what is a piece of land ... There must be "a piece of land" which is a distinct and separate whole in the sense that the contours or character of the terrain are such that it should be so regarded.' *Cleveland v Roberts* [1993] 2 NZLR 17 at 23, CA, per cur

In lease

[For 27 Halsbury's Laws (4th edn) para 129 see now 27(1) Halsbury's Laws (4th edn) (Reissue) para 130.]

In mining law

[For 31 Halsbury's Laws (4th edn) para 15 see now 31 Halsbury's Laws (4th edn) (2003 Reissue) para 19.]

LAND DISTURBANCE

Australia [Clause 5.3 of an agreement between the plaintiffs and defendants provided that during the construction of a pipeline the defendants would implement measures outlined in a Cultural Heritage Plan including the employment of an Aboriginal Archaeological Consultant and two Aboriginal Monitors selected by the Archaeological Consultant 'at all stages of construction involving land disturbance (clearing, grading and trenching)'] 'the word "disturbance" in this sort of agreement in both the Australian and American cases tends to be very widely construed, and includes indirect action as well as direct physical injury.

'[9] ... Although the word "disturbance" is usually construed very widely, and there have been a few cases involving disturbing fisheries, in which it is said that things like fouling the water disturb the fishery (see, for instance, *Fitzgerald v Firbanks* [1897] 2 Ch 103), there are also decisions to the effect that one must be sensible in construing the term. If one construes the term too widely, one gets far beyond what the parties must have intended. That is illustrated by a case in quite a completely different connection, that is whether standing to take communion in an Anglican church is disturbing public worship (*Skoke-Graham v R* (1985) 16 DLR (4th) 321, 331).

'[10] What is to be disturbed is "land". As pointed out last week, "land" could mean "soil" or "surface" or "general topography". Even if it has

the connotations of "soil", one must look further as there are a number of decisions as to whether "soil" means the surface, or whether it means the whole of the land. Perhaps the most instructive is *Micklethwait v Winter* (1851) 6 Ex 644; 155 ER 701; and see *Wakefield v Duke of Buccleuch* (1866) LR 4 Eq 613 at 625.' *Carriage v Duke Australia Operations Pty Ltd* BC200001303; [2000] NSWSC 239 at [8]–[10], per Young J

LAND DRAINAGE

[The Water Resources Act 1963 has been repealed. A similar definition of 'drainage' is given in the Water Resources Act 1991, s 113(1), as follows.] 'Drainage' includes defence against water (including sea water), irrigation other than spray irrigation, and warping.

LAND OF ANY OTHER DESCRIPTION

[Subject to certain immaterial exceptions, the Road Traffic Act 1988 s 34(1)(a) provides that a person commits an offence if, without lawful authority, he drives a motor vehicle onto or upon 'any common land, moorland or land of any other description not being land forming part of a road'. Section 192 of the 1988 Act defines road as any highway and 'any other road to which the public has access'. At trial of an action for a declaration of a prescriptive right of way over a track crossing a village green, the judge accepted the defendants' contention that the track did not form part of a road for the purposes of s 34(1)(a). He nevertheless gave judgment for the claimants, holding that the village green did not constitute 'land of any other description' since that phrase was to be construed ejusdem generis with the preceeding words, 'common land' and 'moorland'.] '[15] Mr Chapman submits that the language of s 34(1)(a) is unambiguous, first because the introductory words "any common land, moorland" themselves give rise to no genus—there being no real common feature between common land and moorland (at least until the latter came to be recognised as such in the [Countryside and Rights of Way Act 2000])—and secondly because the insertion of the words "of any other description" (previously, "land of whatsoever description") demonstrates Parliament's intention to exclude the ejusdem generis rule of construction: see the House of Lords decision in *Larsen v Sylvester & Co* [1908] AC 295, [1908–10] All ER Rep 247. He might too have pointed to the sharply contrasting words at the end of s 34(4): "any other *like* emergency" (my emphasis).

'[16] Mr Harrison's contrary submission rests essentially upon there being express reference in s 34(1)(a) to "common land" and "moorland". Why, he asks forensically, refer to these specific types of land at all unless it is to limit the scope of the general words. The difficulty with this argument, however, is that it would arise in every case where the application or otherwise of the ejusdem generis principle falls for consideration, and cannot therefore be decisive in bringing the principle into play.

'[17] For my part, I accept Mr Chapman's submission that s 34(1)(a) is unambiguous although I recognise that the use of the word "whatsoever" in residuary words is not of itself necessarily sufficient in every case to disapply the principle: see Bennion on Statutory Interpretation (3rd edn, 1997) in particular sections 382 and 385 (pp 961 and 963). That conclusion notwithstanding, I think it right still to consider both the other arguments with regard to the application of s 34(1)(a) on the facts of this case since, as Mr Harrison points out, the somewhat striking consequence of so construing the section is that prescriptive rights to vehicular access can never be acquired save over "land forming part of a road" ie over a public highway or over a road to which the public already has de facto access (as to which see below); there will accordingly be those, say, using a neighbour's private drive to access their own houses who, contrary to their long-held belief, have never gained the prescriptive right of way they thought they enjoyed.
...

'[23] I turn therefore to the question arising under the second limb of s 34(1)(a), whether the track across The Pinn is "land forming part of a road", "road" for this purpose being defined by s 192 to mean "any highway and any other land to which the public has access". Has the public access to the track? Assuming, as I do, that the inhabitants of Bonnington who are entitled to use The Pinn as their village green are sufficient to constitute "the public", the answer to this question is clearly Yes in the sense that the public can and probably do walk over the track during their use of the green. Is that, however, sufficient for this purpose, or, as Mr Chapman submits, for the definition to be satisfied must the public have access to the track in the sense of using it as a road? In my judgment Mr Chapman is right on this argument too. Perhaps the most helpful authorities on the point are *DPP v Vivier* [1991] 4 All ER 18 and *DPP v Coulman* [1993] RTR 230. Although neither of them address the narrow question arising, to my mind they lend general support to the view that it is only if walkers use the road qua road that this use is regarded as relevant access: see, for example, the discussion of Harrison v Hill 1932 JC 13 in the court's judgment in *DPP v Vivier* [1991] 4 All ER 18 at 21.

'[24] There was some suggestion during the course of argument that unless the track were to be regarded as "land forming part of a road" those driving along it would not be subject to the breathalyser law—the particular context in which *DPP v Vivier* and *DPP v Coulman* were decided. That, however, is not so: the breathalyser law applies to those driving "on a road or other public place". As, indeed, was stated in *DPP v Vivier* (at 20), it was there "unclear, and immaterial, whether the respondent was driving upon one of the roads or at some other place within the caravan park". Even assuming, therefore, that the track is not within the s 192 definition of "road", it is undoubtedly a "public place".

'[25] It follows from all this that I for my part accept Mr Chapman's submission that the relevant use of this track down the years has at all times contravened s 34(1)(a).' *Massey v Boulden* [2002] EWCA Civ 1634, [2003] 2 All ER 87, per Simon Brown LJ

LAND ... VALUE

Canada 'Unless the parties specify otherwise, the meanings of "land" and of "value" are well established in law. When land is sold, "land" refers to "a right to receive a good title in fee simple" unless the agreement states otherwise (*Ball v Gutschenritter*, [1925] SCR 68, at p 71). "Land" is not given a special meaning in the Musqueam leases; in particular, it is *not* defined as a 99-year leasehold interest in the property under the lease.

' "Value" in real estate law generally means the fair market value of the land, which is based on what a seller and buyer, "each knowledgeable and willing," would pay for it on the open market. See *Revenue Properties Co v Victoria University* (1993), 101 DLR (4th) 172 (Ont Div Ct), at p 180; *Re Farlinger Developments Ltd. and Borough of East York* (1975), 61 DLR (3d) 193 (Ont CA), at p 205, and *Sun Life Assurance Co. of Canada v City of Montreal*, [1950] SCR 220, [1950] 2 DLR 785.' *Musqueam Indian Band v Glass* (2000) 192 DLR (4th) 385 at 401, SCC, per Gonthier J

LANDLOCKED

New Zealand [Section 129B(1)(a) of the Property Law Act 1952 provides that 'A piece of land is landlocked if there is no reasonable access to it'.] 'The ordinary meaning of the words used suggests that land is to be regarded as landlocked if it does not in a practical sense have reasonable access. The section confers a discretion to be exercised after consideration of all relevant factors, and it would seem contrary to the remedial purpose of the legislation to adopt an artificially limited view as to what is a piece of land … There must be "a piece of land" which is a distinct and separate whole in the sense that the contours or character of the terrain are such that it should be so regarded.' *Cleveland v Roberts* [1993] 2 NZLR 17 at 23, CA, per cur

LANGUAGE OF THE ACCUSED

Canada 'The expression "language of the accused" was not addressed at trial or in the Court of Appeal because it posed no problem to the parties. Admittedly, French was the maternal language of the accused and that fact was accepted as justification for invoking s 530(4) [of the Criminal Code]. The Attorney General of Canada explained that the definition of the language of the accused has been a contentious issue for many years. In *R v Yancey* (1899) 2 CCC 320 (Que QB (Crown Side)) at p 323 the "habitual" language of the accused was adopted. This solution was accepted in *Piperno v The Queen* [1953] 2 SCR 292 at p 296, 107 CCC 241, and more recently in *Saraga v The Queen* Que Sup Ct, No. 500-01-01624L-876, November 18, 1988 [summarized 6 WCB (2d) 201]. Other courts have adopted the maternal language, or first language learned and still spoken: see *R v Brown*, Que Sup Ct, No 700-01-3172-840, March 28, 1985, RJPQ 85–215; *R v Lorentz-Aflalo*, Que Sup Ct, No 500-01-006114-877, October 8, 1987. In those cases, the court considered the language of education, the language used at home, the language used for social contacts and the language of the community to which the accused identifies. In *Saraga, supra*, Martin J accepted the language of the preferred form of communication.

'A simple approach, such as maternal language or language used in the home, is inappropriate *inter alia* because it does not provide a solution for many situations encountered in a multicultural society and does not respond to the fact that language is not a static characteristic. Some persons insist that they have two maternal languages. Some persons have a maternal language that is neither French nor English, and use in the home either the maternal language, or the maternal language and French, or English, or both English and French.

Their language at work may be English or French. Their language in social contacts may not be the same as their language of work. Language of use can change when a person changes employment, marries or divorces, or makes new friends. Many other situations of this nature could be described. This is not necessary.

'The solution to the problem, in my view, is to look at the purpose of s 530. It is, as mentioned earlier, to provide equal access to the courts to accused persons speaking one of the official languages of Canada in order to assist official language minorities in preserving their cultural identity: *Ford, supra*, at p. 749. The language of the accused is very personal in nature; it is an important part of his or her cultural identity. The accused must therefore be afforded the right to make a choice between the two official languages based on his or her subjective ties with the language itself. The principles upon which the language right is founded, the fact that the basic right is absolute, the requirement of equality with regard to the provision of services in both official languages of Canada and the substantive nature of the right all point to the freedom of Canadians to freely assert which official language is their own language. I note that s 530(2) will apply to individuals who do not speak either of the two official languages. An accused's own language, for the purposes of s 530(1) and (4), is either official language to which that person has a sufficient connection. It does not have to be the dominant language. If the accused has sufficient knowledge of an official *language to instruct counsel*, he or she will be able to assert that that language is his or her language, regardless of his or her ability to speak the other official language. The Crown may challenge the assertion made, but it will have the onus of showing that the assertion is unfounded. The court, in such a case, will not inquire into specific criteria to determine a dominant cultural identity, nor into the personal language preferences of the accused. It will only satisfy itself that the accused is able to instruct counsel and follow the proceedings in the chosen language.

'The assertion of language is a prerequisite to an application under s 530(1) or s 530(4). Once entitlement is established and an application is made under s 530(4), the judge will be required to determine whether the best interests of justice will be served by granting the application.' *R v Beaulac* (1999) 173 DLR (4th) 193 at 218, 219, 220, SCC, per Bastarache J

LANGUAGE USED

New Zealand [New Zealand Bill of Rights Act 1990, s 24(g).] 'The phrase "language used" is broad enough to encompass both spoken and written language—not just, as counsel for the respondent argued, the extracts from the documentary exhibits which are read out or articulated in Court.' *Allwen Industries Ltd v Collector of Customs* [1996] 3 NZLR 226 at 230, per Robertson J

LAPSE

[For 50 Halsbury's Laws (4th edn) para 347 see now 50 Halsbury's Laws (4th edn) (Reissue) para 398.]

Australia ' "Lapse" is an event that marks the end of the period during which a caveat, in the words of s 74H [of the Real property Act 1900 (NSW)], "remains in force" in such a way as to provide protection to the caveator by way of notice of the estate or interest asserted. Lapse entails termination of the command addressed to the Registrar-General by s 74H that he not take certain defined actions which he would otherwise be able and required to take in relation to the relevant title but which appear to him to be prohibited by the caveat. A caveat that has lapsed is no longer of any efficacy to achieve the legal results that caveats produce. It has no continuing existence (*Wilson v McIntosh* [1894] AC 129) and is to all intents and purposes dead. And this is so whether or not the recording in relation to it remains on the title in unqualified form.' *St Abanoub Properties Pty Ltd v Registrar-General* BC200203813; [2002] NSWSC 615 at [15], per Barrett J

LARGE-SCALE

[The definition in the Harbours Act 1964, s 57, has been repealed by the Transport and Works Act 1992, s 68(1), Sch 4.]

LAST KNOWN ADDRESS

Australia [Regulation 16.01(1)(c) of the Bankruptcy Regulations 1996 (Cth) provides that, unless the contrary intention appears, where a document is required or permitted to be served on a person, the document may be left at the last known address of the person.] 'In my view, on the language of reg 16.01(1)(c), the reference to "last-known address of the person" is to that address which has been made known by the applicant as at the time closest to the date in question.' *Drake t/as TH Drake &*

Associates v Stanton BC9907684; [1999] FCA 1635 at [8], per Tamberlin J

LAW MERCHANT

[For 12 Halsbury's Laws (4th edn) para 460 see now 12(1) Halsbury's Laws (4th edn) (Reissue) para 662.]

LAWFUL

Australia 'The word "lawful" can mean, simply, permitted, i.e. something which can be done without an infraction of the law, for example a lawful trade. Or it can mean something which is supported by the law, for example lawful authority. Or again it may connote a quality of being legally enforceable, for example a lawful demand which can be enforced by action [*Crafter v Kelly* [1941] SASR 237 at 243]. In many cases it is easier to see what the word does not mean than to define with precision what it does.' *Taikato v R* (1995) 139 ALR 386 at 412, per Kirby J

Australia 'The meaning of "lawful" depends on its context, as Napier J pointed out in *Crafter v Kelly* [[1941] SASR 237 at 243]. As a result, a "lawful purpose" may mean a purpose not forbidden by law or not unlawful under the statute that enacts the term [*Bear v Lynch* (1909) 8 CLR 592 at 600, 603, 606]; or it can mean a purpose that is supported by a positive rule of law [*Crafter v Kelly* [1941] SASR 237 at 243–5].' *Taikato v R* (1995) 139 ALR 386 at 390, per Brennan CJ, Toohey, McHugh and Gummow JJ

LAWFUL ADMISSION

Canada 'The first issue is what meaning is to be given to the term "lawful admission". I do not agree that an immigrant who obtained leave to enter Canada by fraud or deception can be said to have been "lawfully" admitted. By qualifying the word "admission" with the term "lawful", Parliament clearly intended "lawful admission" to mean something more than having a port-of-entry inspector rubber stamp the ship's manifest or an individual's passport with the words "landed immigrant". Lawful admission requires compliance with *all* of the requirements of the Act in force at the time the immigrant entered Canada. *Canada (Minister of Citizenship and Immigration) v Nemsila* [1997] 1 FC 260 at 266, Fed TD, per Jerome ACJ

LAWFUL AUTHORITY

[Section 19 of the Firearms Act 1968 makes it an offence for a person, 'without lawful authority or reasonable excuse (the proof whereof lies on him)' to have with him in a public place a loaded shotgun or air weapon, or any other firearm (whether loaded or not) together with ammunition suitable for use in that firearm.] 'The first issue is whether a certificate for a firearm and ammunition is in itself lawful authority for the holder of the certificate to have the firearm and ammunition for it in a public place ...

'It is plain from the structure and wording of the relevant provisions of the 1968 Act that such a certificate is not itself lawful authority for the purpose [of having the firearm and ammunition in a public place]. The holding of a certificate is the primary requirement under ss 1 and 2 of the Act to save the possessor of a firearm or shotgun, wherever he has it, from committing an offence under those sections. Section 19 is one of a group of sections, starting with s 16, imposing additional restrictions on the holders of firearms or shotguns, for the purpose, as the group heading accurately describes it, of "Prevention of Crime and preservation of public safety". Just as ss 1 and 2 say nothing about possession or holding of a firearm or shotgun "in a public place", so s 19 says nothing about a firearm or shotgun certificate. Moreover, s 19 also applies to (loaded) air weapons, for which no certificate is required unless it is declared a weapon by rules made by the Secretary of State to be specially dangerous (see s 1(3)(b) of the 1968 Act). The two sets of provisions are quite independent of each other ... Accordingly, in our judgment, a holder in a public place of a shotgun or any other firearm in the respective circumstances specified in s 19 may be without lawful authority and in breach of the section for that reason, whether or not he holds a valid firearm or shotgun certificate.' *R v Jones* [1995] 3 All ER 139 at 141–142, CA, per Auld J

New Zealand '[5] The Wildlife Act 1953 relates to the protection and control of wild animals and birds. It applies to wildlife, which means "any animal that is living in a wild state". The term "animal" is defined to include "any terrestrial or freshwater invertebrate declared to be an animal under section 7B of this Act". Section 7B declares the terrestrial and freshwater invertebrates specified in the Seventh Schedule to be animals. The Seventh Schedule includes all species of *Powelliphanta*. So it is clear that *Powelliphanta Augustus*, whether it be a separate species or not, is "wildlife". That means that the interesting question posed by A P

Herbert, in one of his misleading cases, *Cowfat v Wheedle* (A P Herbert, *Uncommon Law*), namely whether snails are ferae naturae (wild animals), does not arise here.

'[6] Section 3 of the Act provides that all wildlife is declared to be subject to the Act and, with a number of separate categories of exceptions, to be absolutely protected throughout New Zealand. *Powelliphanta* does not fall within one of the exceptions, so that it is declared to be subject to the Act and to be absolutely protected throughout New Zealand. The extent of that protection, as set out in the Act, is contained in s 63(1) ...

...

'[26] ... Section 63 provides that the various actions concerned are prohibited "without lawful authority". Solid Energy submits that it has lawful authority, by virtue of the mining licence, and the conditions which deal with the protection of wildlife, the reinstatement of overburden, and such matters. There are essentially two questions which need to be addressed in relation to that issue:
(a) Whether the mining licence itself constitutes "lawful authority" for the purposes of s 63, so that no consent under s 71 is required; and
(b) Whether the conditions in the mining licence which deal with the protection of wildlife constitute a consent of the relevant ministers under s 71.

'[27] As to the first question, I do not consider that the licence itself constitutes lawful authority for a breach of s 63. As I have already noted, an obligation by a licence holder to comply with other statutes in carrying out activities under the licence is commonplace. I do not consider that the present circumstances constitute an exception. The licence itself recognises that activities under the licence may have an effect on wildlife, and contains specific conditions directed towards minimising those effects. But I do not consider that the licence is to be construed as a code, replacing the provisions of the Wildlife Act and any other relevant legislation, so far as the protection of wildlife, flora and the environment are concerned. The imposition of conditions with specific requirements to act in certain ways is more consistent, in my view, with those conditions being additional to other statutory obligations than in place of them.

'[28] As to the second question, Mr Rennie submits that no form of consent is required, and submits that the licence, when viewed in the light of the conditions which address the protection of wildlife, may properly be regarded as a consent. I do not consider that the licence or its conditions constitute consent for the purposes of s 71. The licence is issued under delegated authority from the Minister of Energy. There is no evidence that the Minister of Conservation participated in the issue of the licence. That is fatal to the submission. However, I prefer not to base my decision only on that absence of evidence. I consider that, even if officials with delegated authority from the Minister of Conservation had participated in the issue of the licence, or in the formulation of the conditions, the licence or its conditions would not constitute consent under s 71. If they were so regarded, they would necessarily constitute consent to any action otherwise in breach of the Act, so long as the conditions of the licence were met. I do not consider that the licence is properly to be construed as having that effect. The licence in this case was issued in 1990. *Powelliphanta Augustus* was apparently not discovered until about 1996. To hold that the conditions of the licence constituted consent under s 71 would mean that any act of hunting or killing the snails in the course of the mining activity had the consent of the relevant ministers, even although their existence was unknown. I do not consider that the requirement for consent in s 71 should be read down in that way.

'[29] For these reasons, I consider that neither the Coal Mines Act, nor the coal mining licence, constitute lawful authority for any act otherwise in breach of s 63 of the Act in respect of *Powelliphanta*; nor do the terms of the licence constitute consent pursuant to s 71 to any act otherwise in breach of s 63.' *Royal Forest and Bird Protection Society of New Zealand Inc v Minister of Conservation* [2006] NZAR 265 at [5]–[6], [26]–[29], per MacKenzie J

LAWFUL CUSTODY

Canada '[54] I note that the section 1(1) [Education Act] definition of "guardian" uses the expression "lawful custody" as distinct from merely "custody". I have performed a search of Ontario legislation on the e-Laws database and found that the word "custody" occurs 1343 times in 231 statutes and regulations. Sometimes it means merely physical care or control of a person or possession of a thing and sometimes it connotes care or control under some lawful authority. Often it is used in the criminal law sense of imprisonment. In family law statutes and regulations and many other instances, it is used in the family law sense of some or all of the bundle of rights and obligations mentioned in paragraph [21] above, but sometimes in those provisions it appears in the phrase "lawful custody".

I also did a search for the occurrences in Ontario statutes and regulations of the expression "lawful custody". The search showed 148 "hits", which for a two word search means 74 occurrences of the two words, in 24 statutes and regulations. There are 11 occurrences in the Education Act.

'[55] I then did a database search for cases in which "lawful custody" appeared. The only non criminal case I found that actually interprets the meaning of the expression was *Re K.M.*, [2000] O.J. No. 5810 (O.C.J., Kukurin J.). Part of the Quicklaw headnote of the case, which accurately summarizes the judge's conclusion, is as follows:

> Statutes – Interpretation – Words and phrases – "Lawful custody" in clause 3(2)(c), in clause (c) of the definition of "parent" in subsection 37(1) and in clause 137(1)(c) of Child and Family Services Act includes not only custody granted by court order or written agreement but also other situations not contrary to law, such as informal surrender of parental rights to trusted friends who then exercise de facto custody.

...

'[58] In the end, then, Kukurin J. concluded that the adoption applicants acquired the status of "parents" for purposes of the adoption provisions of the Child and Family Services Act by virtue of a declaration in writing by the child's mother purporting to give custody of the child to them. This was sufficient to clothe the applicants with "lawful custody". I would not go so far as to say that any custodial parent can just "transfer custody", in the sense of all custodial rights. Custody can be conferred only by birth, court order or one of the agreements authorized by law to confer custody: see paragraphs [22] and [23] above. However, I do agree that a custodial parent can transfer some of the incidents of custody, such as physical care and control, actual residence and daily discipline authority. It is done every day, without court order or agreement in writing. There are probably other incidents of custody that a parent could transfer as well.

'[59] A child can live in the "lawful custody" of a person who does not have authority to exercise all the incidents of "custody". That seems to me to be the basis of the decision in *Re K.M.* It seems to refer to the transfer of day to day residence, care and control, which are enough to make the situation one of the child living in the "lawful custody" of the foster parents.

Conclusions on "guardian" and "lawful custody" for attendance rights

'[60] The situation in *Re K.M.* is similar to the case before me. Here the parents have authorized the residence of the child in the care and control of her aunt, for purposes much less important and less stringently regulated than an adoption. It seems to me the situation in this case would fall within the ordinary meaning of the words "lawful custody". Anyone would say that the aunt's physical custody of Valerie was lawful. Anyone would say that Valerie's residence with the aunt was lawful, that her being subject to her aunt's house rules and discipline regime was lawful. If you asked anyone whether the aunt has lawful custody of Valerie, the answer would be yes, because Valerie lives with her aunt with the express written permission of her parents, and that amounts to lawful custody. There is nothing in the attendance rights provisions themselves or the surrounding provisions in the Education Act that prevents the words "person who has lawful custody of a child" from having this plain and ordinary meaning.' *Chou v Chou* (2005) 253 DLR (4th) 548 at [54]–[55], [58]–[60], [2005] OJ No 1374 (Ont Sup Ct J), per Perkins J

LAWFULLY PRESENT

'[5] My Lords, is a person temporarily admitted to the United Kingdom under the written authority of an immigration officer pursuant to para 21 of Sch 2 to the Immigration Act 1971 "lawfully present in the United Kingdom" within the meaning of para 4 of the Schedule to the Social Security (Immigration and Asylum) Consequential Amendments Regulations 2000, SI 2000/636? That is the single question raised on this appeal …

…

'[17] The Secretary of State's main argument is that the phrase "lawfully present" in para 4 of the Schedule to the 2000 regulations has to be read as a whole and that lawful presence for this purpose is a status gained only by having lawfully entered the United Kingdom with leave to enter (and having subsequently remained within the terms of that leave). Not having been granted leave to enter, the appellant accordingly lacks the required immigration status and is not to be regarded as lawfully present. The Secretary of State's fallback argument is that, even if one takes the words "lawfully present" separately, the appellant was not to be regarded as "present": s 11(1) deems him not to have entered the United Kingdom and, not having entered, he must be deemed not to be present either.

…

'[26] To my mind the only way the respondent could succeed in these proceedings would be to make good his core argument, that the word "lawfully" in this context means more than merely not unlawfully; rather it should be understood to connote the requirement for some positive legal underpinning. Mr Giffin QC illustrates the argument by reference to *Taikato v R* [1997] 1 LRC 433, a decision of the High Court of Australia on very different facts. The question there was whether an individual carrying a formaldehyde spray possessed it "for a lawful purpose", and it was held that she did not do so even though her purpose (self-defence) was one not prohibited by law. Brennan CJ (at 440) said:

> "'Lawful purpose' in [the relevant legislation] should be read as a purpose that is authorised, as opposed to not forbidden, by law because that meaning best gives effect to the object of the section. The meaning of 'lawful' depends on its context, as Napier J pointed out in *Crafter v Kelly* [1941] SASR 237 at 243. As a result, a 'lawful purpose' may mean a purpose not forbidden by law or not unlawful under the statute that enacts the term … or it can mean a purpose that is supported by a positive rule of law …
>
> As a general rule, interpreting 'lawful purpose' in a legislative provision to mean a purpose that is not forbidden, rather than positively authorised, by law is the interpretation that best gives effect to the legislative purpose of the enactment. This is because statutes are interpreted in accordance with the presumption that Parliament does not take away existing rights unless it does so expressly or by necessary implication … Nevertheless, the purpose, context or subject matter of a legislative provision may indicate that Parliament has used the term 'lawful purpose' to mean a purpose that is positively authorised by law."

'[27] So too here, submits the respondent: para 4 of the Schedule to the 2000 regulations confers an entitlement to certain state benefits (or, more accurately, displaces a prima facie disqualification from receiving such benefits) upon persons who are nationals of a relevant state and who are "lawfully present" in the United Kingdom. Unless, submits Mr Giffin, the applicant's presence in the United Kingdom has been positively authorised by a specific grant of leave to enter, rather merely than by temporary admission, his disqualification from the benefits should not be found displaced.

'[28] I would reject this argument. There is to my mind no possible reason why para 4 should be construed as requiring more by way of positive legal authorisation for someone's presence in the United Kingdom than that they are at large here pursuant to the express written authority of an immigration officer provided for by statute. (Much of the argument before the House assumed that if a temporarily admitted applicant were "lawfully present" in the United Kingdom for para 4 purposes, so too would be any asylum seeker even were he in fact detained under Sch 2 to the 1971 Act: he too would be legally irremovable unless and until his asylum claim were rejected. It now occurs to me that that assumption may be ill-founded: certainly Mr Giffin's *Taikato*-based argument would have greater force in that type of case. For present purposes, however, it is unnecessary to decide the point.)' *Szoma v Secretary of State for the Department of Work and Pensions* [2005] UKHL 64 at [5], [17], [26]–[28], [2006] 1 All ER 1, per Lord Brown of Eaton-under-Heywood

LAY DAYS

[For 43 Halsbury's Laws (4th edn) para 466 see now 43(2) Halsbury's Laws (4th edn) (Reissue) para 1503.]

LAYOFF

Canada 'The labour agreement in the case at bar does not define "layoff". We must therefore look at the cases to see how courts and labour arbitrators have defined it. They suggest that "layoff" is used in the law of labour relations to describe an interruption of the employee's work short of termination. A "layoff", as the term is used in the cases, does not terminate the employer-employee relationship. Rather, it temporarily discharges the employee. The hope or expectation of future work remains. But for the time being, there is no work for the employee. Such an employee, it is said, is laid off.

'Reference to a few of the cases illustrate this use of the term. In *Air-Care Ltd v United Steel Workers of America* [1976] 1 SCR 2, at p 6, Dickson J (as he then was) adopted the following definition of layoff:

> "Lay-Off" is not defined in the Quebec *Labour Code*, RSQ 1964, c 141. However, the *Shorter Oxford English Dictionary* defines "lay-off" as follows: "Lay-off, a period during which a workman is temporarily discharged" and *Nouveau Larousse Universel*, Tome 2 "Mise à pied": "retrait temporaire d'emploi".

'The controlling idea of a layoff as a disruption (as opposed to termination) of the employment relationship is echoed by Vancise JA in *University Hospital v Service Employees International Union, Local 333 UH* (1986) 46 Sask R 19. Stating that a layoff occurs when the employee-employer relationship is "seriously disrupted", Vancise JA noted at p 28 that *Black's Law Dictionary* (5th ed 1979) defines layoff as "[a] termination of employment at the will of employer. Such may be temporary (*e.g.* caused by seasonal or adverse economic conditions) or permanent".

'While in common parlance the term "layoff" is sometimes used synonymously with termination of the employment relationship, its function in the lexicon of the law is to define a cessation of employment where there is the possibility or expectation of a return to work. The expectation may or may not materialize. But because of this expectation, the employer-employee relationship is said to be suspended rather than terminated.

'The suspension of the employer-employee relationship contemplated by the term "layoff" arises as a result of the employer's removing work from the employee. As stated in *Re Benson & Hedges (Canada) Ltd and Bakery, Confectionery and Tobacco Workers International Union, Local 325* (1979) 22 LAC (2d) 361, at p 366:

> Arbitrators have generally understood the term "lay off" as describing the situation where the services of an employee have been temporarily or indefinitely suspended owing to a lack of available work in the plant ...

'It follows that for there to be a layoff, there must be a cessation of work. If the employee continues to work substantially the same number of hours, his or her grievance is not, whatever else it may be, a layoff. As the Arbitration Board stated in *Re Benson & Hedges, supra*, at p 370, "there is ... a general arbitral consensus that lay-off refers to cessation of work by an employee and that if it is to bear any other meaning it should be clearly spelled out by appropriate adjectival words or phrases [in the collective agreement]".' *Canada Safeway Ltd v RWDSU, Local 454* [1998] 1 SCR 1079 at 1111–1113, per Cory and McLachlin JJ

LEASE

[For 27 Halsbury's Laws (4th edn) para 51 see now 27(1) Halsbury's Laws (4th edn) (Reissue) para 50.]

[The Capital Allowances Act 1968 has been repealed. The definition is re-enacted in the Capital Allowances Act 1990, s 161(2).]

Agreement for lease

[For 27 Halsbury's Laws (4th edn) paras 53, 57 see now 27(1) Halsbury's Laws (4th edn) (Reissue) para 52.]

Lease of land

New Zealand [Municipal Corporations Act 1954, s 305(2).] 'The latter was seen as empowering a council to "grant leases of land at such rental for such term and on such conditions as it thinks fit" to non-profit making bodies, the principal object of which was to carry on stated purposes including recreation. The reference to "land" is to be read in terms of s 4 of the Acts Interpretation Act 1924 so as to include "buildings". The section invoking s 5(j) of the Acts Interpretation Act 1924, is to be read as applying to this lease to clubs.' *Upper Hutt City Council v Upper Hutt District Cricket Club* [1996] 3 NZLR 87 at 93, per McGechan J

Mining lease

[For 31 Halsbury's Laws (4th edn) para 222 see now 31 Halsbury's Laws (4th edn) (2003 Reissue) para 292.]

LEGAL ADVISER

[The claimant, a prisoner remanded in custody pending sentencing, applied for judicial review of the decision of the defendant to refuse access to his lawyer, an avvocato, on the basis that he was not a legal adviser within r 2 of the Prison Rules 1999. Rule 2(1) provides that, where the context so admits, the expression 'legal adviser' means, in relation to a prisoner, his counsel or solicitor, and includes a clerk acting on behalf of his solicitor, and r 38(1) provides that the legal adviser of a prisoner in any legal proceedings, civil or criminal, to which the prisoner is a party is to be afforded reasonable facilities for interviewing him in connection with those proceedings.] '[7] The claimant contends that Mr Di Stefano is a legal adviser within the meaning of the 1999 rules and that, accordingly, pursuant to r 38(1) of the rules, Mr Di Stefano must be permitted to visit him in prison.

...

'[16] By a claim form issued on 17 September (which was six days ago) the claimant challenged the governor's decision refusing access to Mr Di Stefano on the following grounds:

"The decision is unlawful as it breaches art 6(3)(b) and (c) of the convention [the European Convention for the Protection of Human Rights and Fundamental Freedoms 1950 (as set out in Sch 1 to the Human Rights Act 1998], ie the defendant, by refusing the claimant access to his chosen legal representative, is restricting his need for adequate time and facilities to prepare for his sentence (part of trial process) to be heard on 2 October 2002—and his appeal against conviction."

...

'[24] It is common ground that Mr Di Stefano is not a member of the English legal profession. He is neither a solicitor nor a barrister. The claimant's evidence shows, and the defendant's evidence does not contradict, that Mr Di Stefano is an avvocato who is qualified to practise, and does practise, at the Italian Bar.

'[25] Article 59 of the EC Treaty (now art 49 EC) provides:

"Within the framework of the provisions set out below, restrictions on freedom to provide services within the Community shall be progressively abolished during the transitional period in respect of nationals of Member States who are established in a State of the Community other than that of the person for whom the services are intended."

'[26] As a result of the Treaty of Amsterdam (Amsterdam, 2 October 1997) (OJ C340 10.11.97 p 1), the numbering of that article has since May 1999 been changed to art 49 EC.

'[27] On 22 March 1977, the Council of the European Communities adopted Council Directive (EEC) 77/249 (OJ 1977 L078 p 17) (the directive). The purpose of the directive is to facilitate the effective exercise by lawyers of freedom to provide services in accordance with art 59 of the EC Treaty (now art 49 EC). Article 1 of the directive defines "lawyer". That definition includes an Italian avvocato. Article 2 of the directive requires each member state to recognise any such person as a lawyer ...

'[28] The directive has been implemented in this country by the European Communities (Services of Lawyers) Order 1978, SI 1978/1910. Article 2 of the 1978 order defines "EEC lawyer" as—

"a person entitled to pursue his professional activities under the designation, in Belgium of an avocat—advocaat, in Denmark of an advokat, in Germany of a Rechtsanwalt, in

France of an avocat, in the Hellenic Republic of a dikegoros, in the Republic of Ireland of a barrister or solicitor, in Italy of an avvocato, in Luxembourg of an avocat-avoué, or in the Netherlands of an advocaat ..."

'[29] Article 5 of the 1978 order provides:

"No enactment or rule of law or practice shall prevent an EEC lawyer from providing any service in relation to any proceedings, whether civil or criminal, before any court, tribunal or public authority (including appearing before and addressing the court, tribunal or public authority) by reason only that he is not an advocate, barrister or solicitor; provided that throughout he is instructed with, and acts in conjunction with, an advocate, barrister or solicitor who is entitled to practise before the court, tribunal or public authority concerned and who could properly provide the service in question."

...

'[33] Section 27 of the Courts and Legal Services Act 1990 identifies the persons who have a right of audience before the English courts. Section 28 of the 1990 Act identifies the persons who have a right to conduct litigation before English courts.

'[34] In his second supplemental skeleton argument delivered on Friday afternoon, Mr Johnson conceded that art 5 of the 1978 order impacts upon ss 27 and 28 of the 1990 Act. In my view this concession is correct. An Italian avvocato who conforms with the requirements of the 1978 order is entitled to exercise either (a) a right of audience before the English courts, or (b) a right to conduct litigation before the English courts.

'[35] At this point it is necessary to turn to art 6 of the convention, upon which the claimant relies in his claim form. Article 6 provides:

"1. In the determination of his civil rights and obligations or of any criminal charge against him, everyone is entitled to a fair and public hearing within a reasonable time by an independent and impartial tribunal established by law ...

2. Everyone charged with a criminal offence shall be presumed innocent until proved guilty according to law.

3. Everyone charged with a criminal offence has the following minimum rights: (a) to be informed promptly, in a language which he understands and in detail, of the nature and cause of the accusation against him; (b) to

have adequate time and facilities for the preparation of his defence; (c) to defend himself in person or through legal assistance of his own choosing ..."

'[36] The claimant is currently in the midst of the trial process. He has been found guilty of manslaughter by the jury. The trial judge has not yet addressed the question of sentence. The claimant continues to enjoy the rights set out in art 6 of the convention. He is entitled to have adequate time and facilities for the preparation of his plea in mitigation in accordance with art 6(3)(b). In relation to sentence he is entitled to defend himself through legal assistance of his own choosing in accordance with art 6(3)(c).

'[37] In the course of his opening submissions Mr Johnson said that it was an oddity that the claimant should dismiss the solicitors and counsel who represented him at trial, and then instruct an Italian advocate as his principal legal adviser rather than fresh English solicitors and counsel.

'[38] On this point I agree with the observation of Mr Newman: it is no business either of the court or of the defendant whom the claimant wishes to instruct to represent him in criminal proceedings. Of course the claimant cannot engage an excessive number of lawyers, or change his legal team with undue frequency. Subject to that, however, the claimant is entitled to instruct anyone who has rights of audience under s 27 of the 1990 Act, or anyone who has rights to conduct litigation under s 28 of that Act. Accordingly, the claimant is entitled if he wishes to instruct an Italian lawyer who has rights under those provisions to represent him in ongoing criminal proceedings.

'[39] Let me now turn to r 2 of the 1999 rules. Section 3(1) of the Human Rights Act 1998 requires this court so far as possible to read and give effect to the 1999 rules in a way which is compatible with convention rights. Accordingly, I shall construe r 2 of the 1999 rules in a manner which conforms with art 6(3)(b) and (c) of the convention.

'[40] The term "legal adviser" in r 2 must embrace any lawyer who (a) is chosen by the prisoner, and (b) is entitled to represent the prisoner in criminal proceedings to which the prisoner is a defendant. On the evidence before the court, Mr Di Stefano is an Italian avvocato who falls within the definition of "EEC lawyer" in the 1978 order. He has been chosen by the claimant to represent him in ongoing criminal proceedings. It therefore follows that Mr Di Stefano falls within the term "his counsel or solicitor" in r 2 of the 1999 rules.' *R (on the application of Van Hoogstraten) v Governor of*

Belmarsh Prison [2002] EWHC 1965 (Admin) at [7], [16], [24]–[29], [33]–[40], [2003] 2 All ER 309, per Jackson J

LEGALLY ENTITLED

Canada 'The parties both made submissions with respect to the interpretation of another exception to section 107 of the *Customs Act* contained in section 108.

> 108. (1) An officer may communicate or al-low to be <u>communicated information obtained</u> under this Act or the *Customs Tariff,* or allow inspection of or access to any book, record, writing or other document obtained by or on behalf of the Minister for the purposes of this Act or the *Customs Tariff* to or by
>
> …
>
> (c) any person otherwise legally entitled thereto [Underlining added.]"

'Mr Kubrick argued that the applicant was "legally entitled" to the information on the DAS [Detailed Adjustment Statement] by virtue of the duty of procedural fairness which requires the respondent to give to the applicant the information that it needs to enable it to exercise its statutory rights of re-determination and review of the section 55 assessment.

'Ms Turley, on the other hand, pointed out that the words "any person otherwise legally entitled thereto" also appear in the *Income Tax Act*, and have been given a narrow interpretation by the courts. Therefore, she argued, it was reasonable to presume that Parliament intended them to have the same meaning in the *Customs Act* that has been ascribed to them by the courts for the purposes of the *Income Tax Act* where there is a similar concern about maintaining the confidentiality of information that individuals are statutorily obliged to provide to the government.

'The leading case on the interpretation of the words "legally entitled" in the *Income Tax Act* is *Glover v Glover et al* (1980) 29 OR (2d) 392 (CA); affd by *sub nom Glover v Minister National Revenue* [1981] 2 SCR 561. In this case, it was held that neither a wife who had been granted custody of her children, nor a judge of the Supreme Court of Ontario, was "legally entitled" to information in the possession of Revenue Canada that would have enabled them to locate a husband who had absconded with the parties' children in contravention of a custody order.

'The Ontario Court of Appeal stated in Glover that, when considered in the context of the other provisions of the *Income Tax Act*, the "legally entitled" exception should be construed narrowly as referring only to the provisions in certain statutes, such as the *Statistics Act* [SC 1970-71-72, c 15] and the *Canada Pension Plan* [RSC 1970, c C-5], that authorize government departments to obtain the information needed for the administration of the statutory schemes for which they are responsible.

'However, it should also be noted that the basis of the claim for disclosure made in *Glover* was different from that made by the applicant in this case. Moreover, the *Income Tax Act* also included a provision specifically prohibiting Revenue Canada from disclosing for the purpose of civil litigation information provided to it by taxpayers.

'Nonetheless, I conclude that the exception in paragraph 108(1)(c) of the *Customs Act* should be narrowly construed, as it was in *Glover* by virtue of the similarities between the wording of the exceptions to the prohibition against disclosure in the *Income Tax Act* and the *Customs Act*, and the importance of the principle that government must keep confidential information in its possession that it could legally have required the individual to provide.

'Accordingly, any right that the applicant may have under the duty of fairness to obtain the DAS and related worksheets from the respondent does not make the applicant "legally entitled" to the information for the purpose of paragraph 108(1)(c). This phrase should be limited in the same manner as the analogous provision in the *Income Tax Act,* so that it applies only to the statutory powers conferred by those federal statutes that authorize particular departments or officials to obtain information for administrative purposes.' *Johns Manville Int'l, Inc v Deputy MNR* (1999) 3 FC 95 at 117, 118, 119, TD, per Evans J

LEGACY

[For 17 Halsbury's Laws (4th edn) paras 1228–1230 see now 17(2) Halsbury's Laws (4th edn) (Reissue) paras 472–474.]

Demonstrative legacy

[For 17 Halsbury's Laws (4th edn) para 1230 see now 17(2) Halsbury's Laws (4th edn) (Reissue) para 474.]

Specific legacy

[For 17 Halsbury's Laws (4th edn) paras 1228–1230 see now 17(2) Halsbury's Laws (4th edn) (Reissue) paras 472–474.]

LEGAL REPRESENTATION

New Zealand [Section 10(1) of the Criminal Justice Act 1985 provides that a full-time custodial sentence cannot be imposed on an offender who has not been 'legally represented'.] 'The omission in sub-s (1) of the words "in the court" must be treated as recognition that there may be representation, extending beyond mere advice or assistance, out of court. Legal representation is not limited to appearances by counsel or a solicitor in court.' *Parkhill v Ministry of Transport* [1992] 1 NZLR 555 at 559, CA, per cur

LEGATEE

[The Capital Gains Tax Act 1979 has been repealed. The definition is re-enacted in the Taxation of Chargeable Gains Act 1992, s 64(2), (3).]

LEGITIMATE

[For reform of the law so as to remove, so far as possible, the legal disadvantages of illegitimacy, see now the Family Law Reform Act 1987.]

LEGITIMATE EXPECTATIONS

Australia 'Judicial review may protect "legitimate expectations", in the sense of interests which do not amount to legal rights, powers or privileges. That was the sense in which the term was first used, as Dawson J pointed out in *Haoucher v Minister for Immigration and Ethnic Affairs* ((1990) 169 CLR 648 at 658–659). When used in that sense, a "legitimate expectation" falls within the category of those interests which, being liable to adverse affection by an exercise of the relevant power, import observance of the principles of natural justice as a condition of its valid exercise. But the protection of a "legitimate expectation" in the sense of an interest not legally enforceable is a consequence of the availability of a remedy to give effect to the statute; the protection of a "legitimate expectation" is not an independent foundation of a jurisdiction to grant a remedy. If the jurisdiction to grant a judicial review remedy is thought to arise from the existence of a legitimate expectation rather than an implied statutory condition, what is the criterion of legitimacy? Legitimacy has been attributed to expectations which originate in specified ways, such as representations, practices and assurances: see *Council of Civil Service Unions v Minister for the Civil Service* ([1985] AC 374 at 401); *Attorney-General (NSW) v Quin* ((1990) 170

CLR 1 at 20). But the list of ways in which a "legitimate" expectation may arise is not exhaustive and the characteristic of legitimacy remains undefined. No doctrine of administrative estoppel has emerged ... The term "legitimate expectation" is sometimes used in a different sense, describing an expectation by a person that procedural fairness will be extended to him before a power is exercised: see, for example, the decision in *Macrae v Attorney-General (NSW)* ((1987) 9 NSWLR 268).' *Annetts v McCann* (1990) 170 CLR 596 at 605, per Brennan J

LESION

Australia 'The word "lesion", for example, in its ordinary use, connotes primarily an injury, in the sense of a sudden impairment of the function of affected tissue or a morbid change in the functioning of the body. But medical and forensic dictionaries indicate that the word is sometimes used in modern medical parlance to include changes in organs and tissues through a disease process.' (footnotes omitted) *Kennedy Cleaning Services Pty Ltd v Petkoska* (2000) 200 CLR 286; (2000) 174 ALR 626; BC200005035; [2000] HCA 45 at [8], per Gleeson CJ and Kirby J

LET

New Zealand [Physical Welfare and Recreation Act 1937, s 12(2).] 'I do not regard the word "let" within s 12(2) as carrying some implied restriction to periodic or other short term tenancies. The word can carry the latter sense; vide s 143 of the Municipal Corporations Act 1954, read in the context of ss 152 and 153. However, that sense is not inflexible. It seems unlikely that Parliament would have intended to introduce such an uncertainty, in absence of further definition or provision into the statutory powers concerned. Moreover, the "letting" involved would not necessarily always be short term. Circumstances could well dictate otherwise, particularly if a local authority was seeking to shed any close municipal involvement. I read "let" in its wider sense of "lease". Further, in the absence of any express restrictions as to duration of term, restrictions which very easily could have been imposed. I see no call to limit duration.' *Upper Hutt City Council v Upper Hutt District Cricket Club* [1996] 3 NZLR 87 at 97–98, per McGechan J

LETTER OF CREDIT

[For 3 Halsbury's Laws (4th edn) para 131 see now 3(1) Halsbury's Laws (4th edn) (Reissue) para 252.]

LIABLE TO SERVE

[Part 2 of the Sexual Offences Act 2003 sets out notification periods, specified in the context of terms of imprisonment, during which certain information has to be notified by a sex offender to the police. Section 131 applies the notification provisions to young offenders and s 131(a) provides that Part 2 of the Act applies to a period of detention which a person is 'liable to serve' under a detention and training order or a secure training order as it applies to an 'equivalent sentence of imprisonment'.] '[17] … In our view, for practical purposes the period of detention which a person "is liable to serve" under a detention and training order is fixed at the date of sentence. Without a further order of the court, the period may not be extended. The notification provisions are, as we have already explained, directly linked with the sentence of the court. The statutory provisions are not susceptible to judicial alteration. By definition, those made subject to a detention and training order are young offenders who have not been sentenced to detention in a young offender institution. Bearing that in mind we can see no particular reason why the double discount (as it was described) should lead to the wide construction of s 131(a) for which the Crown contends. If Mr Branston were right, it would have been perfectly straightforward for the statutory provision under s 131(a) to have referred simply to "a detention and training order" or "the term of a detention and training order" or "a sentence of detention and training" rather than the "period of detention which a person is liable to serve". Under the detention and training order therefore the offender is not liable to serve a sentence of detention and training: he is liable to serve a period of detention and training. By contrast with s 131(f)–(j), the detention and training order is one of a group of provisions included in s 131(a)–(e) which focused specifically on the "period" of detention, or training, or keeping in secure accommodation.

'[18] We must now consider s 131(f)-(j). Section 131(f) refers to a "sentence of detention" in a young offender institution, para (g) to "sentence under a custodial order", para (h) a "sentence of detention" under ss 90 or 91 of the Powers of Criminal Courts (Sentencing) Act 2000, para (i) to "a sentence of custody for life" and finally, para (j) to "a sentence of detention, or custody for life". These paragraphs produce equivalents between various "sentences" of detention and the equivalent "sentence" of imprisonment. The distinction between the "sentence" of detention and the "period" of detention must be deliberate. This is consistent with the express distinction already identified between the respective periods of detention and training, and of supervision, and the term of the order which is one of the marked characteristics of the detention and training order.

'[19] In our judgment, for the purposes of s 131(a) the period of detention which the offender is "liable to serve" is and should be treated not as a reference to the entire term of the detention and training order, but to what it says it is, the period of detention and training itself … ' R v Slocombe [2005] EWCA Crim 2297 at [17]–[19], [2006] 1 All ER 670, per Sir Igor Judge P

LIABILITY—LIABLE

[For 43 Halsbury's Laws (4th edn) para 964 et seq see now 43(1) Halsbury's Laws (4th edn) (Reissue) para 880 et seq.]

LIBEL

[For 28 Halsbury's Laws (4th edn) para 11 see now 28 Halsbury's Laws (4th edn) (Reissue) para 11.]

LIBERTY

Canada '… I have difficulty understanding how the refusal of a discretionary exemption from a lawful deportation order, as applied to a non-refugee who has no legal right to be in the country, must be seen as involving a deprivation of liberty. Unless "liberty" is taken to include the freedom to be anywhere one wishes, regardless of the law, how can it be "deprived" by the lawful execution of a removal order?

'Counsel for the respondent has invoked pronouncements of the Supreme Court in cases having little to do with immigration in order to assert a broader interpretation for "liberty" and "security of the person". He cited Wilson J in R. v Morgentaler to the effect that liberty interests include a general guarantee of "personal autonomy over important decisions intimately affecting … private lives". Suffice it to say that the four judges who concurred in the result declined to consider the application of "liberty" in this context and based their decision on "security of the person". It was clear that their conclusion that section 7 [of the Canadian Charter of Rights and Freedoms] was engaged was directly related to the very intrusive character of abortion availability and the fact that criminal sanctions were potentially involved. Two judges found no violation of section 7. Counsel cited to us another invocation of "personal autonomy" as an aspect of "liberty", in the case of *B (R.) v Children's Aid Society of Metropolitan Toronto* in which four judges of the Supreme Court considered that the protection of "liberty" in section 7 gave parents the right to refuse medical treatment for their children. It may be noted that four other judges declined to give "liberty" that scope and one judge considered it unnecessary to decide the matter as he found no violation of section 7 requirements of fundamental justice.

'On the basis of the jurisprudence to date, then, I am unable to conclude that "liberty" includes the right of personal choice for permanent residents to stay in this country where, as the Supreme Court said in *Chiarelli*:

> They have all deliberately violated an essential condition under which they were permitted to remain in Canada.'

Williams v Canada (Minister of Citizenship and Immigration) [1997] 2 FC 646 at 666–667, FCA, per Strayer J

LICENCE

[For 27 Halsbury's Laws (4th edn) paras 8, 9, 12 see now 27(1) Halsbury's Laws (4th edn) (Reissue) paras 9, 14.]

New Zealand 'A licence is simply an authority or permission to do what is otherwise wrongful or illegal, and in ordinary usage it extends to the document certifying or recording that the appropriate permission has been given by the competent authority.' *Edwards v O'Connor* [1991] 2 NZLR 542 at 550, CA, per cur

LICENSED PREMISES

[For 26 Halsbury's Laws (4th edn) para 382 see now 26 Halsbury's Laws (4th edn) (Reissue) para 28.]

New Zealand [Sale of Liquor Act 1989, s 2.] 'If the holder of an endorsed (caterer's) off-licence sells liquor at premises at which it is catering for a "reception, function or other social gathering" pursuant to that licence, those premises are licensed premises within the meaning of s 2 of the Act. "Licensed premises" are therefore wherever the holder of the licence is selling liquor as part of its catering activity.' *Bar Systems (New Zealand) Ltd v Wellington District Licensing Agency* [1996] 3 NZLR 100 at 109, per Goddard J

LIEN

[For 28 Halsbury's Laws (4th edn) paras 502, 503 see now 28 Halsbury's Laws (4th edn) (Reissue) paras 702–703.]

Australia 'The word "lien" is a word of far from certain content that is used in the law in a number of different contexts. This is illustrated by the entries "Lien" and "Equitable lien" in *Butterworths Australian Legal Dictionary* (1997) edited by the Hon Dr Peter E Nygh and Peter Butt. Among the contexts in which the word is used are contexts of bailment, corporations, insurance, legal practitioners and real property (as listed in the general entry "Lien") and also the context of liens created and enforced in equity as noted in the entry "Equitable lien". Liens in these various contexts may be created by contract, by statute, by operation of general law or by order of an equity court. In some contexts, particularly that of an artificer's lien, the lien does undoubtedly confer only possessory rights and confers no power of sale: *Mulliner v Florence* (1878) 3 QBD 484 at 489; *Bolwell Fibreglass Pty Ltd v Foley* [1984] VR 97 at 117. However, in other contexts a lien does confer not only a right of possession but rights of action to recover moneys, as in the case of legal practitioners' liens over the fruits of litigation: *Ex parte Patience; Makinson v The Minister* (1940) 40 SR (NSW) 96 at 100; *Worrell v Power* (1993) 46 FCR 214 at 222–4; *Akki Pty Ltd v Martin Hall Pty Ltd* (1994) 35 NSWLR 470 at 473–4.' *Ell (t/as GNP Printing) v Cisera* BC200106725; [2001] NSWSC 784 at [8], per Hamilton J

Equitable lien

[For 28 Halsbury's Laws (4th edn) para 551 see now 28 Halsbury's Laws (4th edn) (Reissue) para 754.]

Innkeeper's

[For 24 Halsbury's Laws (4th edn) paras 1245–1246 see now 24 Halsbury's Laws (4th edn) (Reissue) paras 1144–1146.]

Maritime lien

[For 43 Halsbury's Laws (4th edn) para 1131 see now 43(2) Halsbury's Laws (4th edn) (Reissue) para 1901.]

Solicitor's lien

[For 44 Halsbury's Laws (4th edn) para 226 see now 44(1) Halsbury's Laws (4th edn) (Reissue) para 254.]

LIFE INTEREST

[For 39 Halsbury's Laws (4th edn) paras 459, 460 see now 39(2) Halsbury's Laws (4th edn) (Reissue) paras 144–145.]

LIKE

Canada [Exception to recorder of mining claims applied to specified reserves, parks 'or other like reservations'.] '… The word "like" indicates that the reservation should be similar to or comparable with one or more of those expressly mentioned in that it possesses the common characteristic of those reservations. This common characteristic is that the lands are required by the Government of Canada for a broadly stated public purpose. Only a reservation of that kind may fall within the description "other like reservations", in my opinion.' *Halferdahl v Canada* (*Mining Recorder, Whitehorse Mining District*) [1992] 1 FC 813 at 824, FCA, per Stone JA

LIKELY

[Prospective claimants in proceedings against the prospective defendant companies for unlawful conspiracy to manipulate markets and/or anti-competitive behaviour sought pre-action disclosure under s 33(2) of the Supreme Court Act 1981, which applies to persons who are 'likely' to be party to subsequent proceedings and CPR 31.16.] '[70] The application has to be made by "a person … likely to be a party to subsequent proceedings" against "a person … likely to be a party to the proceedings" (s 33(2) of the 1981 Act) and those requirements are reflected (in reverse order) in CPR 31.16(3)(a) and (b). There is no longer any statutory requirement that "a claim … is likely to be made".

'[71] Of course, in one sense it might be said that a person is hardly likely to be a party to subsequent proceedings whether as a claimant or otherwise unless some form of proceedings is itself likely to be issued. Two questions, however, arise. One is whether the statute requires that it be likely that proceedings are issued, or only that the persons concerned are likely to be parties *if* subsequent proceedings are issued. The other is whether "likely" means "more probably than not" or "may well". As to the first question, in my judgment the amended statute means no more than that the persons concerned are likely to be parties in proceedings if those proceedings are issued. That was what Lord Woolf had in mind when he wrote of the

requirement that "there is a likelihood that the respondent would indeed be a defendant if proceedings were initiated" (*Access to Justice* p 127 (para 50) (see [46], above)). The omission of any language which expressly requires that the initiation of proceedings itself be likely, which could have been included in the amended section, appears to me to reflect the difficulties which the earlier authorities had explored in the sort of circumstances found in *Dunning v Board of Governors of the United Liverpool Hospitals* [1973] 2 All ER 454, [1973] 1 WLR 586. What the current language of the section appears to me to emphasise, as does the rule of court, is that the parties concerned in an application are parties who would be likely to be involved if proceedings ensued. The concern is that pre-action disclosure would be sought against a stranger to any possible proceedings, or by a party who would himself be unlikely to be involved. If the statute and rule are understood in this sense, then all difficulties, which might arise where the issue of proceedings might depend crucially on the nature of the disclosure sought and where it is impossible at the time of making the application to say whether the disclosure would critically support or undermine the prospective claim, disappear.

'[72] As to the second question, it is not uncommon for "likely" to mean something less than probable in its strict sense. It seems to me that if I am wrong about the first question, then it is plain that "likely" must be given its more extended and open meaning (see Lord Denning MR in *Dunning*'s case), because otherwise one of the fundamental purposes of the statute will have been undermined. If, however, I am right about the first question, the second question is of less moment. Even so, however, I am inclined to answer it by saying that "likely" here means no more than "may well". Where the future has to be predicted, but on an application which is not merely pre-trial but pre-action, a high test requiring proof on the balance of probability will be both undesirable and unnecessary: undesirable, because it does not respond to the nature and timing of the application; and unnecessary, because the court has all the power it needs in the overall exercise of its discretion to balance the possible uncertainties of the situation against the specificity or otherwise of the disclosure requested. Clearly, the narrower the disclosure requested and the more determinative it may be of the dispute in issue between the parties to the application, the easier it is for the court to find the request well founded; and vice versa.'

Black v Sumitomo Corp [2001] EWCA Civ 1819 at [70]–[72], [2003] 3 All ER 643, per Rix LJ

[In the course of proceedings brought by them against the defendant, the claimants applied, under CPR 31.17, for an order for disclosure against a non-party. Such an order could only be made where, inter alia, the documents sought were 'likely to support the case of the applicant or adversely affect the case of one of the other parties to the proceedings' (CPR 31.17(3)(a)). The power to grant discovery against non-parties derived from s 34(2) of the Supreme Court Act 1981, which also used the word 'likely' in relation to the conditions for the exercise of the power. That word could also be found in CPR 31.16(3)(a) and (b), two of the threshold conditions for the exercise of the jurisdiction to order pre-action disclosure–a jurisdiction derived from s 33(2) of the 1981 Act, which had again used the word 'likely'. On the claimants' application, the judge granted a declaration that the requirements of CPR 31.17(3)(a) had been satisfied in relation to the classes of document which formed the subject matter of the application. On appeal, the meaning of the word 'likely' was considered.] '[4] It is against that background that the claimants made the applications for disclosure of documents with which we are now concerned. They are made, respectively, under CPR 31.12 and CPR 31.17. It is convenient to set out the relevant provisions in those rules:

"31.12 (1) The court may make an order for specific disclosure or specific inspection.

"(2) An order for specific disclosure is an order that a party must do one or more of the following things—(a) disclose documents or classes of documents specified in the order ...

"31.17 (1) This rule applies where an application is made to the court under any Act for disclosure by a person who is not a party to the proceedings.

"(2) The application must be supported by evidence.

"(3) The court may make an order under this rule only where—(a) the documents of which disclosure is sought are likely to support the case of the applicant or adversely affect the case of one of the other parties to the proceedings; and (b) disclosure is necessary in order to dispose fairly of the claim or to save costs.

"(4) An order under this rule must—(a) specify the documents or the classes of documents which the respondent must disclose ..."

Each of those rules must be read in conjunction with CPR 31.8, which provides:

"(1) A party's duty to disclose documents is limited to documents which are or have been in his control.

"(2) For this purpose a party has or has had a document in his control if—(a) it is or was in his physical possession; (b) he has or has had a right to possession of it; or (c) he has or has had a right to inspect or take copies of it."

And it must be kept in mind that disclosure is not sought as an end in itself. The object of disclosure (at least in this case) is to enable the claimants to inspect the documents disclosed. In that context, the provisions of CPR 31.3(1) are relevant:

"A party to whom a document has been disclosed has a right to inspect that document except where—(a) the document is no longer in the control of the party who disclosed it; (b) the party disclosing the document has a right or a duty to withhold inspection of it ..."

...

'[16] The grounds upon which Mr Hollander QC, on behalf of the Treasury, submitted that the judge had been wrong to reach the conclusion that the threshold condition in sub-para (a) of CPR 31.17(3) was satisfied—as developed in argument in this court—may, we think, fairly be considered under two main heads. First, that the judge failed to direct himself correctly in relation to the requirement that the only documents which a person who is not party to the proceedings can be ordered to disclose are documents "likely to support the case of the applicant or adversely affect the case of one of the other parties to the proceedings" in that (i) he failed to give to the word "likely" the meaning "more probable than not" which (it is said) that word should bear in that context and (ii) he failed to appreciate that the test "likely to support ... or adversely affect" had to be applied to each individual document or (if the documents were to be described as a class) to each document in the class. Second, that the judge failed to recognise that the effect of CPR 31.17(2) is to require the applicant to adduce evidence of the matters on which he relies to establish that the threshold condition in CPR 31.17(3)(a) is met. In the present case, it is said, the claimants made no attempt to adduce evidence of the matters on which they relied.

...

The test which the threshold condition requires

'[20] We turn, therefore, to consider the criticism that the judge failed to apply the correct test when reaching the conclusion that the claimants had satisfied the threshold condition in sub-para (a) of CPR 31.17(3) in relation to the scheduled material. As we have indicated, there are two limbs to that criticism. The first is that the judge failed to give to the word "likely" the meaning "more probable than not".

'[21] The meaning of the word "likely" in a statutory or regulatory context has been considered by the courts on a number of occasions; in particular, in the context of the requirement, in s 8(1)(b) of the Insolvency Act 1986, that an administration order may only be made if the court considers that the making of an order "would be likely to achieve" one or more of the statutory purposes set out in s 8(3) of that Act. In *Re Consumer and Industrial Press Ltd* [1988] BCLC 177 at 178, Peter Gibson J held that the evidence must go beyond establishing a mere possibility that a statutory purpose would be achieved: it must enable the court to hold "that the purpose in question will more probably than not be achieved". In *Re Harris Simons Construction Ltd* [1989] BCLC 202, [1989] 1 WLR 368, Hoffmann J took a different view. He pointed out ([1989] BCLC 202 at 203–204, [1989] 1 WLR 368 at 370) that, on a scale of probability of 0 (impossibility) to 1 (absolute certainty) the test of "more probable than not" required a factor greater than 0.5—which he thought too high. Two of the reasons which he gave are of general application:

> "First, 'likely' connotes probability but the particular degree of probability intended must be gathered from qualifying words (very likely, quite likely, more likely than not) or context. It cannot be a misuse of language to say something is likely without intending to suggest that the probability of its happening exceeds 0.5, as in 'I think that the favourite, Golden Spurs at 5–1 is likely to win the Derby' ... Fourth, as Peter Gibson J said, s 8(1) only sets out the conditions to be satisfied before the court has jurisdiction. It still retains a discretion as to whether or not to make the order. It is therefore not unlikely that the legislature intended to set a modest threshold of probability to found jurisdiction and to rely on the court's discretion not to make orders in cases in which, weighing all the circumstances, it seemed inappropriate to do so."

He preferred, in the context of s 8(1)(b) of the 1986 Act, a test of "real prospect". His view was followed by Vinelott J in *Re Primlaks (UK) Ltd* [1989] BCLC 734, and was adopted, in preference to his own earlier view, by Peter Gibson J in *Re SCL Building Services Ltd* [1990] BCLC 98.

'[22] Decisions on the meaning of the word "likely" in the context of s 8(1)(b) of the 1986 Act are not, of course, determinative of the meaning to be given to that word in the context of CPR 31.17(3)(a). In particular it is pertinent to have in mind that a "real prospect" test is adopted, expressly, in CPR 24.2 (grounds for summary judgment) and in CPR 52.3 (permission to appeal); and it may be supposed, at least prima facie, that, if the rule-making body had intended the test under CPR 31.17(3)(a) to be a "real prospect" test, it would have said so. But the decisions on s 8(1)(b) of the 1986 Act to which we have referred illustrate the point—which may, perhaps, need no authority—that "likely" does not carry any necessary connotation of "more probable than not". It is a word which takes its meaning from context. And, where the context is a jurisdictional threshold to the exercise of a discretionary power, there may be good reason to suppose that the legislature—or the rule-making body, as the case may be—intended a modest threshold of probability.

'[23] The context in which the meaning of "likely" in CPR 31.17(3)(a) has to be determined includes (i) the statutory power to which CPR 31.17 was intended to give effect, (ii) the corresponding provisions in CPR 31.16 (disclosure before proceedings start) and the statutory power to which that rule was intended to give effect and (iii) the circumstances in which the new rules as to disclosure, contained in CPR Pt 31, were introduced. It is necessary, therefore, to examine those provisions.

'[24] Section 33(2) of the Supreme Court Act 1981 empowers the court to order pre-action disclosure; s 34(2) of the 1981 Act empowers the court to order disclosure against a non-party. The two sections—as amended by the Civil Procedure (Modification of Enactments) Order 1998, SI 1998/2940—are in these terms, so far as material:

> "33... (2) On the application, in accordance with rules of court, of a person who appears to the High Court to be *likely* to be party to subsequent proceedings in that court ... the High Court shall, in such circumstances as may be specified in the rules, have power to order a person who appears to the court to be *likely* to be a party to the proceedings and to

be *likely* to have or to have had in his possession, custody or power any documents which are relevant to an issue arising or likely to arise out of that claim—(a) to disclose whether those documents are in his possession, custody or power; and (b) to produce such of those documents as are in his possession, custody or power to the applicant ...

"34... (2) On the application, in accordance with rules of court, of a party to any proceedings ..., the High Court shall, in such circumstances as may be specified in the rules, have power to order a person who is not a party to the proceedings and who appears to the court to be *likely* to have in his possession, custody or power any documents which are relevant to an issue arising out of the said claim—(a) to disclose whether those documents are in his possession, custody or power; and (b) to produce such of those documents, as are in his possession, custody or power to the applicant ..." (Our emphasis.)

It can be seen that the structure of the two sections is very similar. They are derived, respectively, from ss 31 and 32 of the Administration of Justice Act 1970. They must be regarded as complementary provisions extending the powers of the court in relation to disclosure.

'[25] Each of ss 33(2) and 34(2) of the 1981 Act provides that the power which it confers shall be exercisable "in such circumstances as may be specified in the rules". The relevant rules are, now, respectively CPR 31.16 and CPR 31.17. We have already set out the provisions of CPR 31.17, so far as material. The corresponding provisions in CPR 31.16 are:

"(1) This rule applies where an application is made to the court under any Act for disclosure before proceedings have started.

"(2) The application must be supported by evidence.

"(3) The court may make an order under this rule only where—(a) the respondent is *likely* to be a party to subsequent proceedings; (b) the applicant is also *likely* to be a party to those proceedings; (c) if proceedings had started, the respondent's duty by way of standard disclosure, set out in rule 31.6, would extend to the documents or classes of documents of which the applicant seeks disclosure; and (d) disclosure before proceedings have started is desirable in

order to—(i) dispose fairly of the anticipated proceedings, (ii) assist the dispute to be resolved without proceedings; or (iii) save costs

"(4) An order under this rule must—(a) specify the documents or the classes of documents which the respondent must disclose ..." (Our emphasis.)

'[26] Again, it can be seen that the structure of CPR 31.16 and CPR 31.17 is very similar; indeed, paras (2), (4) and (5) are identical and para (1) differs only in identifying the different circumstances in which each rule is to apply. In each case para (3) imposes threshold conditions. The threshold conditions in CPR 31.16(3)(a) and (b) require that the applicant and the person against whom the order for disclosure is sought are likely to be parties to subsequent proceedings. There is, of course, no corresponding provision in CPR 31.17(3)—for the obvious reason that CPR 31.17 applies to a case where there are existing proceedings to which892 the person against whom disclosure is sought is not—and is not likely to be—a party. The threshold conditions in CPR 31.16(3)(d)(i) and (iii) are reproduced in CPR 31.17(3)(b).

'[27] CPR 31.16(3)(c) requires that, if proceedings had started, the respondent's duty by way of standard disclosure, set out in CPR 31.6, would extend to the documents or classes of documents of which the applicant seeks disclosure. Standard disclosure requires a party to disclose only (a) the documents on which he relies, (b) the documents which (i) adversely affect his own case, (ii) adversely affect another party's case or (iii) support another party's case, and (c) the documents which he is required to disclose by a relevant practice direction. It is to be noted that the rule-making body has not adopted the wider test of "relevance" which is found in s 33(2) of the 1981 Act. There can be no doubt that that reflects a deliberate intention to curtail the process of discovery; to get away from the traditional approach based on "telling the story" or "leading to a train of inquiry" as exemplified by the decision in *Cie Financiere et Commerciale du Pacifique v Peruvian Guano Co* (1882) 11 QBD 55—see Access to Justice: Final Report to the Lord Chancellor on the Civil Justice System of England and Wales (July 1996) ch 12 at paras 37–40 (pp 124–125) and the note in the *White Book* (*Civil Procedure* (*Spring 2002*)) para 31.6.3. The statutory power to order disclosure (in accordance with rules of court) where a prospective party is likely to have had in his possession custody or power any documents which are relevant to an issue has been curtailed by the new rules so as to be exercisable only in respect of documents which fall within the first two categories identified by Lord Woolf MR at para 38 of Access to Justice: Final Report.

'[28] CPR 31.17(3)(a) reflects a similar approach. The rule-making body has eschewed the wider test of relevance which is found in s 34(2) of the 1981 Act. It has confined the documents of which disclosure may be ordered to those within categories (a) and (b) of CPR 31.6; but with modifications which take account of the twin premises (i) that the applicant does not have (and may never have seen) the documents of which he seeks disclosure and (ii) that the person against whom an order for disclosure is sought is a stranger to the dispute. So, "documents on which he relies" in CPR 31.6(a) and "documents which adversely affect another party's case" in CPR 31.6(b)(ii) have become "documents ... likely to support the case of the applicant" and "documents ... likely to adversely affect the case of one of the other parties to the proceedings" in CPR 31.17(3)(a). The statutory power to order disclosure where a person who is not a party is likely to have had in his possession, custody or power any documents which are relevant to an issue has been curtailed by CPR 31.17(3)(a) in much the same way as the corresponding statutory power to order pre-action disclosure has been curtailed by CPR 31.16(3)(c). But there is a difference in language in two respects. First, CPR 31.17(3)(a) does not provide, in terms, for disclosure of "documents which adversely affect his own case" or of "documents which support another party's case"; that is to say, there is no mention in CPR 31.17(3)(a) of the categories identified in CPR 31.6(b)(i) and (iii). An obvious explanation for that apparent omission is that the rule-making body thought it unnecessary to provide for the possibility that a party would pursue an application, supported with evidence, for disclosure of documents which would adversely affect his own case or which would support the case of his opponent. The difference in language does not reflect any difference in substance.

'[29] Second, the threshold condition in CPR 31.17(3)(a) is lowered by the qualification "likely to". It is not necessary that the documents of which disclosure is ordered will support the applicant's own case or that they will adversely affect the case of another party; it is enough that they are likely to do so. The explanation for that difference is also obvious; the rule-making body appreciated that an applicant cannot be expected to specify which documents under the control of another—which he may never have seen—will support his case or adversely affect that of another party, or to know whether he will wish to rely upon them. It further appreciated that the person against whom disclosure is sought—being a stranger to the dispute—cannot be expected to decide for himself which of the documents under his control do support the applicant's case or adversely affect the case of one of the other parties to an action in which he is not a party. Nor can the court be expected to decide whether documents which it has not seen will support the applicant's case or adversely affect that of another party. The test has to be one of probability. The question, of course, is what degree of probability does the test require.

'[30] The judge found assistance in the judgment of Rix LJ in *Black v Sumitomo Corp* [2001] EWCA Civ 1819, [2002] 1 WLR 1562. The question in that case was whether pre-action disclosure should be ordered pursuant to s 33(2) of the 1981 Act and CPR 31.16. Rix LJ (with whose judgment Ward and May LJJ agreed) identified two questions: (i) whether s 33(2) of the 1981 Act required that it be likely that proceedings are issued, or only that the persons concerned are likely to be parties if subsequent proceedings are issued; and (ii) whether "likely" means "more probable than not" or "may well". He held (at [71]), in answer to the first of those questions, that the requirement was no more than that the persons concerned were likely to be parties in proceedings if those proceedings are issued. He went on to say (at [72]):

"As to the second question, it is not uncommon for 'likely' to mean something less than probable in its strict sense. It seems to me that if I am wrong about the first question, then it is plain that "likely" must be given its more extended and open meaning (see Lord Denning MR in [*Dunning v Board of Governors of the United Liverpool Hospitals* [1973] 2 All ER 454, [1973] 1 WLR 586]), because otherwise one of the fundamental purposes of the statute will have been undermined. If, however, I am right about the first question, the second question is of less moment. Even so, however, I am inclined to answer it by saying that 'likely' here means no more than 'may well'. Where the future has to be predicted, but on an application which is not merely pre-trial but pre-action, a high test requiring proof on the balance of probability will be both undesirable and unnecessary: undesirable, because it does not respond to the nature and timing of the application; and unnecessary, because the court has all the power it needs in the overall exercise of its discretion to balance the possible uncertainties of the situation against the specificity or otherwise of the disclosure requested. Clearly, the narrower the disclosure requested and the more determinative it may be of the dispute in issue between the parties to the application, the easier it is for the court to find the request well founded, and vice versa."

He observed (at [73]) that, apart from the two questions of principle which he had identified, the word "likely" itself presented no difficulties: "Temptations to gloss the statutory language should be resisted. The jurisdictional threshold is not, I think, intended to be a high one."

'[31] Mr Hollander submits that the judge was wrong to place reliance on those observations. It is said that there is no real parallel between the provisions relating to pre-action discovery which were under consideration in *Black v Sumitomo* and the provisions relating to discovery against third parties which fall for consideration in the present case. We reject that submission. It seems to us that there is a close parallel between rr 16 and 17 in CPR Pt 31; as there is between the statutory provisions to which those rules are respectively intended to give effect. In particular, it is plain that the word "likely" has a common root in the provisions of ss 31 and 32 of the Administration of Justice Act 1970; that that word is used in the same sense wherever it appears in ss 33(2) and 34(2) of the 1981 Act; and that that word is used in the same sense in CPR 31.16(3)(a) and (b). It would be remarkable if the rule-making body had intended the same word to be understood in a different sense in CPR 31.17(3)(a).

'[32] In those circumstances, unless there were reasons which compelled a different conclusion, we would think it right to reject the submission that the word "likely", in the context of the threshold condition in CPR 31.17(3)(a), means "more probable that not"; and to hold that the word has, in that context, the meaning "may well" which this court thought it should bear in CPR 31.16(3)(a) and (b). We are not persuaded that there are reasons which compel a different conclusion. Indeed, it seems to us that the reasons which led this court to reach the conclusion which it did in *Black v Sumitomo* have equal force in the context of CPR 31.17(3)(a). As Rix LJ pointed out, a high test requiring proof on the balance of probability would be both undesirable and unnecessary; for the reasons which he gave.

'[33] In rejecting the submission that the test which the threshold condition in CPR 31.17(3)(a) requires is "more probable than not", we should not be taken to accept that the hurdle posed by that condition is, necessarily, as low as that which has to be surmounted when applying the "real prospect" test under other provisions in the CPR. In the context of CPR 24.2, or CPR 52.3, "real prospect" has been held to mean "realistic, as opposed to fanciful" (see *Swain v Hillman* [2001] 1 All ER 91 at 92 and *Tanfern Ltd v Cameron-MacDonald* [2000] 2 All ER 801 at 807, [2000] 1 WLR 1311 at 1316). We have already pointed out that, if the rule-making body had intended the test under CPR 31.17(3)(a) to be a "real prospect" test, it may be supposed that it would have said so. We think that the word "likely", when used in the CPR, connotes a rather higher threshold of probability than merely "more than fanciful". But a prospect may be more than fanciful without reaching the threshold of "more probable than not". We share the view expressed by Rix LJ in *Black v Sumitomo* that, properly understood, the word "likely" presents no difficulties; and that the temptation to gloss the statutory (or regulatory) language should be resisted. We should add, also, that it follows from our conclusion that, in the context of CPR 31.17(3)(a), "likely" does not mean "more probable than not" that it is no bar to an order for disclosure that the court is of the view that the document to be disclosed is as likely—or more likely—to support the case of one of the other parties to the proceedings as it is to support the case of the applicant. It is enough that the court is satisfied that the document is likely to support the case of the applicant. The fact that the court (without sight of the document) may think that, if it turns out not to support the case of the applicant, then it is likely that the document will support the case of one of the other parties is irrelevant.' *Three Rivers District Council v Bank of England (No 4)* [2002] EWCA Civ 1182 at [4], [16], [20]–[33], [2002] 4 All ER 881, per Chadwick LJ

[The Human Rights Act 1998 s 12(3) provides that no relief affecting the exercise of the Convention right to freedom of expression is to be granted so as to restrain publication before trial unless the court is satisfied that the applicant is 'likely' to establish that publication should not be allowed. This provision fell to be construed in an application for an interim injunction restraining publication by the press of confidential information.]
'[12] Although it is unusual in this court to state one's conclusions so early in the judgment, I propose to do so here because they necessarily

dictate whether the confidentiality in much of the material before us needs to be preserved pending trial and what therefore can be said at this stage in an open court judgment. These then, stated in the most summary form, are my conclusions. (i) The judge below was correct in his approach to s 12(3): the test is not that of the balance of probabilities but rather that of a real prospect of success, convincingly established. (ii) The judge below was entitled, on the material before him and the findings he made, to form the judgment that he was satisfied that Cream has a real prospect of success at trial (and, the s 12(3) threshold having thus been crossed, was entitled then in all the circumstances of the case to exercise his discretion in favour of an order involving prior restraint). (iii) The appeal therefore fails and should be dismissed. (iv) Were the threshold test to be that for which the appellants contend (more likely than not), then the judge could not properly have been satisfied on the findings he made that Cream's prospects of success at trial were good enough to justify the grant of interlocutory relief. On that basis, therefore, I would have allowed the appeal.

...

'[54] There is no inconsistency between *A v B* guideline (xii) and what, for example, Lord Steyn said in *Reynolds v Times Newspapers Ltd* [1999] 4 All ER 609 at 628, [2001] 2 AC 127 at 207 as to the right to freedom of expression being a constitutional right and that "[b]y categorising this basic and fundamental right as a constitutional right, its higher normative force is emphasised". It is one thing to say, as indeed I myself said in *Al-Fagih v HH Saudi Research & Marketing (UK) Ltd* [2001] EWCA Civ 1634, [2002] EMLR 215, in a passage repeated with approval by this court in *Loutchansky v Times Newspapers Ltd (No 2)* [2001] EWCA Civ 1805 at [22], [2002] 1 All ER 652 at [22], [2002] QB 783, that the media's right to freedom of expression, particularly in the field of political discussion "is of a higher order" than "the right of an individual to his good reputation"; it is, however, another thing to rank it higher than competing basic rights. See too in this regard what Sedley LJ said in *Douglas v Hello! Ltd* [2001] 2 All ER 289 at 323, [2001] QB 967 at 1004 (para 135), set out in [17], above.

'[55] Section 3 of the 1998 Act legislation (including therefore s 12(3)) is to "be read and given effect in a way which is compatible with the Convention rights". This in my judgment requires that s 12(3) will in all cases be able to be applied compatibly with and as between competing human rights. It seems to me essentially this argument

which Mr Tugendhat was advancing in *Douglas'* case as described in Keene LJ's judgment there ([2001] 2 All ER 289 at 326, [2001] QB 967 at 1007–1008 (para 149)) (see [15], above).

'[56] There is an important distinction between the *American Cyanamid* approach and that now required by s 12(3) even if the threshold test created by the latter is, as I would hold, that of a real prospect of success convincingly established. The distinction is that under *American Cyanamid* the court is concerned only to find a serious issue to be tried, not to resolve either conflicts of fact or difficult questions of law so as to gauge the merits of the claim. I accordingly have some difficulty with Sir Andrew Morritt V-C's views expressed in *Imutran Ltd v Uncaged Campaigns Ltd* [2001] 2 All ER 385 (see [19], above). It seems to me that there will indeed be a number of claims for injunctive relief which now will fail when earlier they would have succeeded: they will fail because the court is required by s 12(3) actually to consider their merits (so as to reach a judgment as to the prospects of their eventual success) and cannot grant relief unless satisfied on cogent evidence that the claim does indeed have a real prospect of succeeding at trial notwithstanding the defendant's ex hypothesi conflicting right to freedom of expression. To construe s 12(3) as I would propose is by no means to rid it of all force and effect. Nor is the comparative imprecision of the test of real prospect of success fatal to its adoption: see the final paragraph of Hoffmann J's judgment in the *Harris Simons Construction* case set out in [39], above.

'[57] What Mr Straw said in Committee on 2 July 1998 (see [41], above) is, I would suggest, consistent equally with both contended-for constructions. On either side's approach courts in future will not "grant an interim injunction simply to preserve the status quo ante" and the new test will be "much higher ... than that there should simply be a prima facie case to get the matter into court".

'[58] Although, as I have already indicated (see [25], above), it seems to me that the more obvious meaning of the words in s 12(3) is "more likely than not to establish" (rather than "has a real prospect of establishing"), the latter meaning is undoubtedly an available one on the language used, the synonym for the word "likely" being, as Professor Smith suggested (see [34], above), "not unlikely".

'[59] Recognising, as of course I do, the importance of the right to freedom of expression— "the lifeblood of democracy" as Lord Steyn described it in *R v Secretary of State for the Home Dept, ex p Simms* [1999] 3 All ER 400 at 408, [2000] 2 AC 115 at 126—an importance, indeed, to which s 12(4) of the 1998 Act itself requires us to have "particular regard", and accepting too, as I do, that the higher threshold test for which the appellants contend represents the more natural meaning of the words used, it is tempting to construe sub-s (3) in this way. I have concluded, however, that it would be wrong to do so given the impact that such a construction would have on competing convention rights as I have sought to explain in [51], [52], above. In short, I have come to accept the argument which Mr Tugendhat appears unsuccessfully to have advanced, first in *Douglas'* case and later, notwithstanding the assistance he then had from Sir Andrew Morritt V-C's judgment in the *Imutran* case, in *Theakston's* case.

'[60] Although the reasoned rejection of that argument by both Keene and Sedley LJJ in *Douglas'* case (see respectively [16], [17], above) for the most part seems compelling, the one feature of the case which I would respectfully suggest neither judgment directly addresses is the different situation arising at the interlocutory stage from that which will exist at trial. Of course it is possible at the interlocutory stage for the court to look ahead and reach a judgment as to the prospects of success at trial and clearly, in determining those prospects, the court will have regard to the possible risks and consequences of interfering with the respective rights which each party is seeking to vindicate. That does not, however, take account of the possibility that in certain cases, although the claimant at the interlocutory stage looks more likely eventually to lose than to win, there may be compelling reasons why nevertheless his ultimate chance of victory, odds against though it be, should be preserved rather than pre-empted at the interlocutory stage.

'[61] That is the possibility I have sought to illustrate above and, of course, on the appellants' contended-for construction, the court is forbidden to have regard to it. It is this which has convinced me that s 12(3) must after all be construed to provide the lower threshold test. That is not, of course, to say that, whenever the test is satisfied, the court will grant interlocutory relief. On the contrary, the lower threshold test merely gives the court a discretion in a greater number of cases. Often the court will not think it right to exercise that discretion in favour of prior restraint unless it is indeed satisfied that the claim will more probably than not succeed at trial. As, moreover, is stated in the judgment in *A v B (a company)* [2002] 2 All ER

545 at [12] (see [23], above): "In many situations the balance [between conflicting rights] may not point clearly in either direction [in which event] interim relief should be refused." There is, of course, no inconsistency between this paragraph and the test of real prospect of success. How could there be, given, as already indicated, this court's adoption of that lower test in [11](iii) of the same judgment. I reject Miss Sharp's submission to the contrary.'

How likely is 'likely'?

'[69] It seems to me, as it does to Simon Brown LJ, that the natural meaning of the word "likely" in the immediate context of s 12(3) of the Human Rights Act 1998 is "more probable than not". As Ouseley J said in *Theakston v MGN Ltd* [2002] EWHC 137 (QB), [2002] EMLR 398, it is not easy to envisage, as a matter of ordinary English, an injunction which is likely to be granted but which more probably than not will be refused. It seems to me no easier as a matter of logic to say that it is likely that an injunction will be granted but more likely that it will not be.

'[70] To say this is not to cast doubt on the many instances in which, in other contexts, the statutory purpose has been held to require one of the milder meanings of "likely" also to be found in the dictionary. A good example—and I cite it for a reason to which I shall be coming—is the decision of this court in *Black v Sumitomo Corp* [2001] EWCA Civ 1819, [2002] 1 WLR 1562, a case on pre-action disclosure by a person likely to be a party to eventual proceedings, where Rix LJ said (at [72]):

"As to the second question, it is not uncommon for 'likely' to mean something less than probable in its strict sense. It seems to me that if I am wrong about the first question, then it is plain that 'likely' must be given its more extended and open meaning (see Lord Denning MR in (*Dunning v Board of Governors of the United Liverpool Hospitals* [1973] 2 All ER 454, [1973] 1 WLR 586)), because otherwise one of the fundamental purposes of the statute will have been undermined. If, however, I am right about the first question, the second question is of less moment. Even so, however, I am inclined to answer it by saying that 'likely' here means no more than 'may well'. Where the future has to be predicted, but on an application which is not merely pre-trial but pre-action, a high test requiring proof on the balance of probability will be both undesirable and unnecessary:

undesirable, because it does not respond to the nature and timing of the application; and unnecessary, because the court has all the power it needs in the overall exercise of its discretion to balance the possible uncertainties of the situation against the specificity or otherwise of the disclosure requested."

'[71] When therefore in *Douglas v Hello! Ltd* [2001] 2 All ER 289 at 322–323, [2001] QB 967 at 1004 (para 134), I paraphrased s 12(3) as requiring a probability of success at trial, it was in the "strict sense" described by Rix LJ that I was using the word. The other two members of the court, Brooke and Keene LJJ, used the statutory word "likely" without expanding it. Our decision did not depend on the precise register of the word. Having now heard full argument on the present appeal, I am satisfied for the reason I have given that in s 12(3) the word in its immediate context does mean probable in its strict sense.

'[72] But the overarching question which emerged late in the argument before us, and which I now think is crucial, is whether the process of construction stops there, or whether s 3 of the 1998 Act itself requires us to read the word "likely" down from the meaning conferred by its immediate context in order to make s 12(3) compliant with the European Convention for the Protection of Human Rights and Fundamental Freedoms 1950 (as set out in Sch 1 to the 1998 Act). There is no reason whatever to suppose that Parliament, in mandating us so far as possible to read all legislation and give it effect compatibly with the convention rights, did not mean to include the 1998 Act itself in that obligation.

'[73] Suppose, first of all, a case where it is manifest that if an interim injunction is not granted the claimant may be seriously and irreparably harmed, while if it is granted the defendant will suffer little if at all. Where s 12 does not apply—that is, in all but freedom of expression cases—the fact that the legal or factual basis of the claim at the interlocutory stage appears weak is a factor, but by no means a conclusive one, in the court's decision as to how best to hold the situation until trial. The same is true of a case where the most the judge can find is that the chances of final success are even, as in my reading of [40] of his open judgment, Lloyd J found in the present case. That, it seems to me, is as it should be: not only is a modest risk of a catastrophic event something against which the court ought to be able temporarily to guard a claimant; every lawyer knows that by the time of trial the claimant's prospects of success may have grown, sometimes through the disclosure of the

defendant's own documents, to a very strong probability. It takes a great deal, in my judgment, to justify a rule which denies such a claimant the possibility of the temporary protection of the law without which success at trial will be hollow.

'[74] The case of *Venables v News Group Newspapers Ltd* [2001] 1 All ER 908, [2001] Fam 430 furnishes a disturbing illustration. Dame Elizabeth Butler-Sloss P was able to grant the appropriate injunctions without regard to s 12(3) because her decision was final, not interlocutory. But suppose that an emergency application had had to be made for a temporary restraint on the publication of the claimants' identities and whereabouts pending trial, and that the evidence of a threat to their lives and safety consequent on publication had not been strong, so that one could not say that they were probably going to succeed at trial. Despite the gravity of the possible consequences of publication and the inconsequentiality of a moratorium until trial, the President's hands would have been tied by s 12(3). Her eventual decision in the claimants' favour would have been entirely abortive.

'[75] To the interpretation of statutes by close reading, which has historically been the first principle of judicial construction, s 3 has now added a second and more radical principle which seeks to give effect to a new Parliamentary intent: that the meaning to be ascribed to its words, whenever they were enacted, is so far as possible to be a meaning which respects convention rights. One has only to look at a dictionary to see that the word "likely" in s 12(3) is capable of bearing what Rix LJ calls a more extended and open meaning than literal probability. But is it capable of bearing it in the context of s 12(3), or does such an extension go beyond what is legally and linguistically possible? And if it is permissible, is it requisite?

'[76] I am satisfied that "likely" in s 12(3) is quite capable of bearing its milder meaning. While the logical difficulty remains of something being likely but its opposite being more likely, the practical usage of the word to convey something which is reasonably or realistically possible has ample judicial support in other contexts; and the full present context is larger than s 12(3) or s 12 itself, for it includes s 3.' *Cream Holdings Ltd v Banerjee* [2003] EWCA Civ 103 at [12], [54]–[61], [69]–[76], [2003] 2 All ER 318, per Simon Brown and Sedley LJJ

Australia [Section 29 of the Criminal Law Consolidation Act 1935 (SA) refers to an act that was 'likely' to endanger the life of another.] 'The word "likely" in this sort of context conveys the notion of a substantial or real chance, not a mere possibility (cf *Boughey v R* (1986) 161 CLR 10), but it must be a likelihood of danger to someone's life, not just to his physical well being. The offences created by subsections (2) and (3) of s 29 do not require proof of an intention to cause grievous bodily harm or mere harm respectively—reckless indifference will do—, but it must also be proved that the defendant knew that his act or omission was likely to cause such harm. Again, realisation of the risk of harm, without more, would not be enough.' *R v Teremoana* (1990) 54 SASR 30 at 40, per Cox J

Australia [Section 20(2B) of the Aboriginal Land Rights (Northern Territory) Act 1976 (Cth) imposed restrictions on repeat land claims unless certain factors existed and it was 'likely' that the applicants would be found to be the traditional Aboriginal owners of the subject land.] 'If a meaning is given to the word "likely" so that it refers "to a real or not remote chance or possibility, regardless of whether it is less or more than 50%" (*Tillmanns Butcheries Pty Ltd v Australasian Meat Industry Employees' Union* (1979) 27 ALR 367 at 380), that construction will be an appropriate beneficial construction, it will also be a construction that would better promote the purpose or object underlying the Act: s 15AA of the Acts Interpretation Act 1901 (Cth). Moreover, it will accord with the minister's second reading speech in the sense that the minister explained that "the criteria to be applied by a Commissioner" when considering repeat land claims "are aimed at ensuring that claimants are not disadvantaged ..."; the repeat claims that were to be summarily rejected were, according to the minister, those that had "little or no chance of success".' *Jungarrayi v Olney* (1992) 105 ALR 527 at 538, per cur

Australia [Under s 237(a) of the Native Title Act 1993 (Cth), acts that are not likely to interfere directly with the carrying on of the community or social activities of the persons who are the holders of native title in relation to land or waters, attract an expedited procedure under the Act.] 'The term "likely" in this context is not directed to a judgment on the balance of probabilities as to interference or major disturbance. Such a judgment would potentially permit, without benefit of any negotiation, quite significant risks (of that interference or major disturbance) to be incurred. To put it crudely and quantitatively, on that construction a forty nine per cent chance of interference or major disturbance flowing from the act proposed would keep it within the realm of the expedited procedure. Consistently with the objects of the [Native Title Act 1993 (Cth)], the word "likely" requires a risk assessment by the Tribunal that will exclude from the expedited procedure any proposed act which would involve a real chance or risk of interference or major disturbance of the kind contemplated by s 237. Such an approach to the construction of the word "likely" is familiar in Australia although it depends upon the particular statutory context in which the word is used – see *Tillmanns Butcheries Pty Ltd v Australian Meat Industry Employees' Union* (1979) 27 ALR 367 at 375 (Bowen CJ) and 380–381 (Deane J); *Jungarrayi v Olney* (1992) 105 ALR 527 at 537–8. *Smith* (*on behalf of the Gnaala Karla Booja People*) *v WA* BC200100042; [2001] FCA 19 at [23], per French J

Australia [Under the Supreme Court Rules 1970 (NSW) Pt 55 r 10(b) the Supreme Court may issue a warrant for the arrest of a contemnor and his or her detention in custody until he or she is brought before the Court to answer the contempt charge where 'it appears that the contemnor is likely to abscond or otherwise withdraw himself from the jurisdiction'.] '... difficulty arises from the use of that slippery word "likely". I describe the word as "slippery" because there is no doubt that the meaning to be attributed to it differs widely in different contexts: see the definition of "Likely" in *Butterworths Australian Legal Dictionary* (1997); and see *Tillmanns Butcheries Pty Ltd v Australian Meat Industry Employees' Union* (1979) 42 FLR 331 at 339–40 per Bowen CJ; and *Boughey v R* (1986) 161 CLR 10 at 20 per Mason, Wilson and Deane JJ. In some contexts it means "probable" as opposed to "possible": *Australian Telecommunications Commission v Krieg Enterprises Pty Ltd* (1976) 14 SASR 303 at 311–12 per Bray CJ. In other contexts it means only "having a substantial, real, and not remote chance of causing the result.": *R v Teremoana* (1990) 54 SASR 30 at 40 per Cox J. Where it is to be found in the spectrum between these extremes varies according to the statutory context.

'In the present context it seems to me that "likely" should be construed as requiring the establishment of a probability on the balance of probabilities. I come to this conclusion because the rule is draconian in effect, permitting the arrest and deprivation of liberty of a person at an early stage of contempt proceedings and before the alleged contemnor has in any way defaulted in appearing to answer the charge, much less been found guilty of contempt. In those circumstances it seems to me that the rule should be construed as justifying arrest only where a case is made out on the probabilities that the person will absent himself or herself as outlined in the balance of the rule.' *Schnabel v Lui* BC200208087; [2002] NSWSC 1184 at [15]–[16], per Hamilton J

Canada [A landed immigrant who was a member of or likely to participate in activities of a terrorist organization is liable for deportation.] 'I accept the submissions of the applicant that the ordinary meaning of the English word "likely" is "probable" or "more probable than not". I accept as well the submissions of the Attorney General for the respondents that the French text of paragraph 19(1)(*g*), which cannnot be ignored in interpretation of the provision, includes the phrase "*ou qu'elles appartiennent à une organisation susceptible de commettre de tels actes ou qu'elles sont susceptibles de prendre part aux activités illégales d'une telle organisation*" (underlining added) for the English "or are members of or are likely to participate in the unlawful activities of an organization that is likely to engage in such acts of violence". The French text uses "*susceptible*" for "likely" and it is noteworthy that the report of SIRC in its conclusion about the PFLP states that it is found to be a "terrorist organization likely (*susceptible*) to engage in acts of violence". In *Petit Robert I: Dictionnaire alphabétique et analogique de la langue française* (Paris, 1987) "*susceptible*" is defined as "*capable*" or "*sujet à*". In *Harrap's Standard French and English Dictionary* (London, 1987), "*susceptible*" is translated as "capable of, admitting of, liable to", and in some phrases as "likely to".

'In my opinion paragraph 19(1)(*g*) is to be interpreted so that "likely", "*susceptible*", with reference to the organization referred to, means "capable of" and not simply "probable"...' *Al Yamani v Canada (Solicitor General)* [1996] 1 FC 174 at 213–214, per MacKay J (FC TD)

Canada 'In assessing the *risk* of future harm (which is called the *threat* of future harm in s 2), there is room for a variable assessment depending on the nature of the threatened harm which is in contemplation. A threat of harm through neglect of the child's hygiene might well have to be much more probable in order to meet the balance of probability test than a threat of serious permanent injury through physical or sexual abuse. Generally speaking, a risk sufficient to meet the test might well be described as a risk that constitutes "a real possibility".

'I have received a good deal of stimulation on this subject from the decision of the House of Lords in *Re H* [1996] AC 563. In that case five law lords reached considerable agreement with each other on some of the issues of proof under the English legislation but split 3–2 on one point about the balance of probability and split 3–2 in the result. I would be disinclined to adopt any particular approach that was presented in that case because the English legislation is markedly different in some important respects from our legislation. However, I wish to say that I would adopt the views expressed by all five law lords that the word "likely" has a primary meaning of "more probable than not", but a recognized secondary meaning of "a real possibility", and that the secondary meaning captures the intent of Parliament in the use of the word "likely" in relation to the possibility of a child suffering harm in the future.' *S(B) v British Columbia (Director of Child, Family & Community Services)* (1998) 160 DLR (4th) 264 at 277, BC CA, per Lambert JA

New Zealand [As to the meaning of "likely" and in particular the degree of probability it contemplates:] '[B]earing in mind the purpose of the provision the appropriate level is that above mere possibility but not so high as more likely than not and is best expressed as a real and substantial risk that the stated consequences will happen. That is the construction adopted in a different context in *Colonial Mutual Life Assurance Society Ltd v Wilson Neill Ltd* [1994] 2 NZLR 152, 161 and one well-known in the criminal law: *R v Harney* [1987] 2 NZLR 576, 581.' *Port Nelson Ltd v Commerce Commission* [1996] 3 NZLR 554 at 562–563, CA, per cur

LIKELY TO RESULT

New Zealand 'With respect we think that is not the appropriate approach to provisions of s 61(6) and (7) [of the Commerce Act 1986]. In each instance the expression "likely to result" is preceded by the expression "will in all the circumstances result". A finding in compliance with the last-mentioned rubric requires the Court to reach the point of probability. The alternative of "likely to result" envisages something less.' *Rugby Union Players' Association Inc v Commerce Commission (No 2)* [1997] 3 NZLR 301 at 319, per Smellie J

LIMITATION OF ACTIONS

[For 28 Halsbury's Laws (4th edn) para 601 see now 28 Halsbury's Laws (4th edn) (Reissue) para 801.]

LIQUIDATED DAMAGES

Canada 'Liquidated damages is a pre-estimate of damages, agreed upon in advance by the parties to a contract, as to what damages will be paid in the event of a breach of that contract.' *Pick O'Sea Fisheries Ltd v National Utility Service (Canada) Ltd* (1995) 130 DLR (4th) 472 at 480, NSCA, per Flinn JA

LIQUIDATED DEMAND

Canada [Default judgment was available for a liquidated demand.] ' "Liquidated demand" is not defined in the rules. The present English rule, with respect to entering judgment in default of defence (Order 19, Rule 2), is similar to our Rule in that it refers to the case where the plaintiff's claim "is for a liquidated demand only". The words "liquidated demand", as they are used in that English rule, are defined in *Precedents of Pleadings*, Bullen & Leake, 12th ed (1975) at p 153, as follows:

"A liquidated demand is a debt or other liquidated sum. It must be a specific sum of money due and payable, and its amount must be already ascertained or capable of being ascertained as a mere matter of arithmetic. Otherwise even though it be specified, or quantified, or named as a definite figure that requires investigation beyond mere calculation, it is not a 'liquidated demand' but constitutes 'damages'."

'Similarly, these words are defined in *The Supreme Court Practice* (1988), vol 1 at p 35, as follows:

"A liquidated demand is in the nature of a debt, i.e., a specific sum of money due and payable under or by virtue of a contract. Its amount must either be already ascertained or capable of being ascertained as a mere matter of arithmetic. If the ascertainment of a sum of money, even though it be specified or named as a definite figure, requires investigation beyond mere calculation, then the sum is not a 'debt or liquidated demand', but constitutes 'damages'."

'In Odgers, *Principles of Pleadings and Practice*, supra, at p 46 the author says the following:

"When the amount to which the plaintiff is entitled can be ascertained by calculation, or fixed by any scale of charges or other positive data, it is said to be 'liquidated' or made clear ... But when the amount to be recovered

depends upon the circumstances of the case and is fixed by opinion or by assessment or by what might be judged reasonable, the claim is generally unliquidated ... But if the claim is in its nature a claim for damages at large, it is not in law treated as a 'liquidated demand' even if the plaintiff puts a figure on the damages which he is claiming." '

Pick O'Sea Fisheries Ltd v National Utility Service (Canada) Ltd (1995) 130 DLR (4th) 472 at 480–481, NSCA, per Flinn JA

LIQUIDATOR

[For 7 Halsbury's Laws (4th edn) para 1552 see now 7(3) Halsbury's Laws (4th edn) (1996 Reissue) para 2315.]

LITERARY WORK

[For 9 Halsbury's Laws (4th edn) para 835 see now 9(2) Halsbury's Laws (4th edn) (Reissue) para 66.]

LITIGANT IN PERSON

'A company is a persona ficta. As has been said of a company, "it does not have a soul to be damned or a body to be kicked". It is a consequence of the artificial nature of a company as a legal person that inevitably actions by it and decisions for it have to be taken by natural persons. The law of agency is at the root of company law (see Gower's *Principles of Modern Company Law* (5th edn, 1992) pp 139, 164). The acts of the authorised agent, acting within the scope of his authority, are under the ordinary principles of agency the acts of the company. When a company authorises a director to act and appear for it in court proceedings, and the court allows the director to act and appear, the company acts and appears by the director. The company is the litigant.

'The crucial question is whether it can be said of the company so acting and appearing that it is a litigant in person for the purposes of the [Litigants in Person (Costs and Expenses) Act 1975]... I would unhesitatingly answer the question in the negative. I do so for the following reasons.

'(i) A litigant in person in ordinary parlance is a party to litigation who represents himself by appearing in court himself. If someone other than himself represents him, then notwithstanding that that other person is his agent, that party is not a litigant in person ... The company appears by a representative, its director, and hence it is not a litigant in person.

'(ii) It has repeatedly and authoritatively been stated that a company cannot appear in person ... Against that background, it is to my mind highly improbable that without any indication that Parliament intended the term "litigant in person" to apply to a company, the 1975 Act applied to a company represented by a director.' *Jonathan Alexander Ltd v Proctor* [1996] 2 All ER 334 at 340–341, CA, per Peter Gibson LJ

[The Official Receiver obtained company directors' disqualification orders in the High Court against three individuals, together with an order for costs against each of them. He submitted a bill of costs which included work done by himself in part of the proceedings, and he sought to have those costs taxed as a litigant in person under the Litigants in Person (Costs and Expenses) Act 1975, s 1(1) and RSC Ord 62, r 18. It was necessary to determine whether the Official Solicitor was a litigant in person.] 'As the holder of a statutory office, each Official Receiver is empowered to bring proceedings, including disqualification proceedings, in his or her own name, and each is accorded by law a right of audience before the court to which he or she is attached. Does this make an Official Receiver who exercises the right a litigant in person? There are only two possible bases for the answer: either a litigant in person is anyone who conducts proceedings in his or her own name without representation, or there is a hitherto unnoticed third category between the represented and the unrepresented litigant, namely the litigant ex officio. The latter is not entirely fanciful. An Official Receiver litigates not in his or her personal name but as "The Official Receiver" — the definite article being appropriate since in each case one such officer alone is ordinarily empowered to act — and there is an intelligible sense in which it can be said that it is the office and not the individual occupying it which possesses the right to litigate and to conduct proceedings. The possibility of an office, as distinct from its holder, being a party to litigation derives some support, in the present state of the law, from the decision of the House of Lords in *M v Home Office* [1993] 3 All ER 537 at 566,[1994] 1 AC 377 at 424:

> "I do not believe there is any impediment to a court making such a finding [of contempt], when it is appropriate to do so, not against the Crown directly, but against a government department or a minister of the Crown in his official capacity." (See per Lord Woolf.)

Their Lordships' House accordingly substituted "the Secretary of State for Home Affairs" as the person against whom the contempt finding was to be made, in preference to the Crown (impleaded as the Home Office pursuant to the list published under s 17 of the Crown Proceedings Act 1947) or Kenneth Baker (the Home Secretary) himself. But it would be a further and unwarranted step to devise for procedural purposes a corresponding and novel category of official litigants. The legal and physical fact in a case such as the present is that the Official Receiver is empowered by law to act without representation in certain civil proceedings. When he or she does so, the description "litigant in person" is apposite. Although Ord 5, r 6 includes among litigants in person, those acting in a representative capacity, Mr Crow claims no such capacity for the Official Receiver. If the Official Receiver does not represent the Crown or the public, he or she acts as an individual, albeit with statutory authority. It would follow, no doubt, that any order for costs made against the Official Solicitor would be made against him or her in a personal capacity; but the department will always, without doubt, ensure that they are indemnified out of public funds, just as any costs which they recover go back into public funds.' *Re Minotaur Data Systems Ltd, Official Receiver v Brunt* [1999] 3 All ER 122 at 128, CA, per Aldous LJ

[Civil Procedure Rules r 48.6.] '[23] In the course of his reply, Mr Way accepted that the appellant is a litigant in person within the meaning of [CPR] r 48.6. But Mr Speaight QC maintained as his primary submission that he is not. In short, he contends that a party cannot be a litigant in person if, as was this appellant, he is represented at the final hearing. There is no definition of a "litigant in person" in the Litigants in Person (Costs and Expenses) Act 1975, or in the CPR. In *Jonathan Alexander Ltd v Proctor* [1996] 2 All ER 334 at 338, [1996] 1 WLR 518 at 523 Hirst LJ referred to "the ordinary meaning, as I understand it, of the description 'litigant in person', viz an unrepresented individual". Peter Gibson LJ said ([1996] 2 All ER 334 at 341, [1996] 1 WLR 518 at 525):

> "A litigant in person in ordinary parlance is a party to litigation who represents himself by appearing in court himself. If someone other than himself represents him, then notwithstanding that that other person is his agent, that party is not a litigant in person."

That was a case where a company brought a claim and was represented at the trial by one of its directors. It did not instruct solicitors or counsel at any stage of the proceedings.

'[24] But the court did not have in mind an arrangement of the kind entered into in the present case, where the litigant employs a professional person, who is not a lawyer, to conduct litigation on his behalf and to instruct counsel to conduct an appeal. It is common ground that Tenon does not have the right to conduct litigation within the meaning of the [Courts and Legal Services Act 1990]. That right may only be exercised in one of the cases mentioned in s 28(2)(a)–(d). Of these, the most important are: (i) persons who have been granted the right by an appropriate authorised body (s 28(2)(a)) and thereby become legal representatives within the meaning of CPR 2.3(1), and (ii) litigants in person (see s 28(2)(d)). We shall refer to the former as "authorised litigators". Section 28(2)(b) and (c) have no application in the present case. It follows that, if the appellant is not a litigant in person, nobody had the right to conduct this litigation within the meaning of the 1990 Act.

'[25] In our judgment, the observations made by this court in *Jonathan Alexander Ltd v Proctor* do not support the proposition that a person is not a litigant in person if he or she is represented by counsel through the agency of the Licensed Access Scheme. Even before the 1990 Act, a litigant might have been acting in person for only part of the proceedings: for example, a litigant might have commenced the proceedings on his own, but later instructed solicitor and counsel. Such a person would properly have been regarded as a 'litigant in person', if and so long as he acted on his own behalf. At the time of the *Jonathan Alexander Ltd v Proctor* decision, the general position was that a person could either appear in court in person or be represented, having instructed solicitors or solicitors and counsel (i e by a legal representative). It is easy to see why, against that background, it was considered that, if a person was represented in court, he was not acting in person. Under the more prescriptive scheme of the 1990 Act, however, there is no reason why a party should not be a litigant in person for the purpose of conducting litigation (under s 28(1)(d)), even if rights of audience on his behalf (under s 27) are exercised by an authorised advocate.

'[26] The introduction of the Licensed Access Scheme, therefore, has meant that the *Jonathan Alexander Ltd v Proctor* approach will no longer suffice as an all-embracing definition of a litigant in person. In our view, where a member of the Chartered Institute of Taxation instructs a barrister under the Licensed Access Scheme, the presence of the barrister does not prevent the party on whose behalf the barrister has been instructed from being a litigant in person. After the BarDIRECT committee informed the Chartered Institute of Taxation on 1 August 2001 that members of that body were now permitted to instruct a barrister on an appeal to the High Court and Court of Appeal, it issued Guidance Notes. We have already noted (see [18], above) how these notes made it clear that "any litigation will have to be conducted on the basis that the litigant is a litigant in person" (para 8). In all the circumstances we agree with the Bar Council's statement that, unless a member of the Chartered Institute of Taxation is also a solicitor, any litigation must be commenced on the basis that the litigant is a litigant in person.' *Agassi v Robinson (Inspector of Taxes) (Bar Council and another intervening)* [2005] EWCA Civ 1507 at [23]–[26], [2006] 1 All ER 900, per Dyson LJ

LIVE TOGETHER

[The Social Security Act 1975 has been repealed. See now the Social Security Contributions and Benefits Act 1992, s 122(3), under which regulations may be made as to the circumstances in which persons are to be treated as 'residing or not residing together'; and the Social Security Benefit (Persons Residing Together) Regulations 1977, SI 1977/956 (as amended by SI 1983/186 and SI 1984/1303).]

LIVESTOCK

[The Town and Country Planning Act 1971 has been repealed. See now the Town and Country Planning Act 1990, s 336(1).]

LIVING APART

New Zealand [Social Security Act 1964, s 63(a).] 'The parties to a marriage are not "living apart" unless they not only are physically separated, but at least one side regards the marriage tie as dead.' *Director-General of Social Welfare v W* [1997] 2 NZLR 104 at 108–109, per McGechan J

LIVING TOGETHER

Australia 'I consider that that phrase connotes a continuing period of residing together, and that the requirement of "living together" is not fulfilled by occasional and short periods during which the parties are physically located in the same premises.' *Mao v Peddley* BC200102595; [2001] NSWSC 254 at [84], per McLaughlin M

LOAN

[The Building Societies Act 1962 has been repealed. Cf now the Building Societies Act 1986, s 7.]

LOCK–OUT

[For 47 Halsbury's Laws (4th edn) para 568 see now 47 Halsbury's Laws (4th edn) (Reissue) para 1403.]

Australia [Section 170ML(3) of the Workplace Relations Act 1996 (Cth) provides that an employer is entitled, for the purpose of supporting or advancing claims made by the employer in respect of a proposed workplace agreement, or responding to industrial action by any employees, to lock out from their employment all or any of those employees. If the employer does so, the lock out is a 'protected action'. Section 170ML(4) states that the 'reference in subs (3) to the employer locking out employees from their employment is a reference to the employer preventing employees from performing work under their contracts of employment without terminating those contracts.'] 'I do not accept the Union's submission that in order for a lock out to come within the provisions of subs (3) and subs (4) of s 170ML it must constitute a total shutdown of an employer's business. Those provisions are not expressed in terms that employees are to be locked out from the whole of their employment in order for the provisions to be satisfied. In particular s 170ML(4) refers to an employer preventing employees "from performing work". It does not say that a lock out is a reference to an employer preventing employees from performing *any* work under their contracts of employment. This view is consistent with the observations of Marshall J in [*Lennie v Hawkes & Butterworth* (unreported, Industrial Relations Court (NT), Marshall J, 472/96, 4 October 1996)] at 22:

> "Whilst s 170PG(4) of the Act [the predecessor of s 170ML(3)] does not require either the complete cessation of work or the physical exclusion of employees from the workplace, it demands a clear and unambiguous act by reference to which employees can know that they are locked out as a matter of fact."

This approach to the construction of the expression "lock out" in s 170ML(3) and (4) is consistent with the policy which lies behind the concept of "protected action" in s 170ML. The purpose of giving action or conduct the protection of "protected action" is to enable the bargaining party to engage in activities to further their industrial ends. In the case of a union or group of employees they are entitled to undertake any activity which comes within the scope of "industrial action" as defined in the Act which covers a considerable number of actions and activities … An employer has a lesser armoury. It can only deny its employees the opportunity to work. It would be a curious result in an industrial relations context if a union or employees could undertake the range of industrial action in the varying degrees of intensity which the definition of "industrial action" allows, yet the employer had to undertake an all-or-nothing approach – either full-time work or no work at all. There is nothing in the provisions of Div 8 of Pt VIB of the Act which leads to, or requires, the conclusion that the lock out allowed by s 170ML(3) must be total. In the same way as the industrial action available to employees allows employees to place bans or limitations on the performance of particular aspects of their work, the imposition of a lock out allows an employer to limit or restrict the amount of work it will allow its employees to undertake.' *Construction, Forestry, Mining and Energy Union v Master Builders' Assn of Victoria (No 2)* (2000) 171 ALR 140; BC200001177; [2000] FCA 169 at [30], per Goldberg J

LODGING HOUSE

[For 24 Halsbury's Laws (4th edn) para 1210 see now 24 Halsbury's Laws (4th edn) (Reissue) para 1110.]

LOSS *SEE ALSO* RISK

Of ship

[For 43 Halsbury's Laws (4th edn) para 964 et seq see now 43(2) Halsbury's Laws (4th edn) (Reissue) para 880 et seq.]

LOSS OF EARNINGS

Australia [The Criminal Injuries (Compensation) Act 1970 (WA) authorises an assessment for 'injury or loss', loss being defined as '… any loss … caused by or directly arising from injury, namely loss of earnings … '.] '… I consider that the reference in the definition of "loss" to "loss of earnings" includes a reference to loss of earning capacity. Such position follows from the understanding of the nature of the damage to be covered (subject to the other limitations in the legislation providing for compensation) in all States as accepted by the Full Court of this State and is consistent with the position in at least South Australia and the Australian Capital Territory as disclosed at relevant periods by reported decisions.' *Re A* (1994) 73 A Crim R 56 at 70, per Nicholson J

LOST MODERN GRANT

'I come ... to the contention that the plaintiff succeeds on the basis of lost modern grant. That doctrine arises from the inadequacies of common law prescription. At common law, acquisition of a prescriptive right depended upon the claimant establishing (amongst other things) the requisite period of user. Thus, common law prescription was based upon a presumed grant. The grant would be presumed only where the appropriate user had continued from time immemorial. That was fixed as the year 1189; that date originated in a medieval statute. It was usually impossible to satisfy that test. Accordingly, the courts held that if user "as of right" for 20 years or more was established, continued user since 1189 would be presumed. That was satisfactory as far as it went, but there were gaps. In particular the presumption of immemorial user could be rebutted by showing that, at some time since 1189, the right did not exist. For example, an easement of light could not be claimed in respect of a house built after 1189. It was because of the unsatisfactory nature of common law prescription that the doctrine of lost modern grant was introduced. It was judge made. The doctrine presumed from long usage that an easement

had, in fact, been granted since 1189 but the grant had got lost. The form which the doctrine took was, initially, that juries were told that from user during living memory, or even during 20 years, they could presume a lost grant. After a time the jury were recommended to make that finding and finally they were directed to do so. Nobody believed that there ever was a grant.

'But it was a convenient and workable fiction. The doctrine was ultimately approved by the House of Lords in *Dalton v Henry Angus & Co* (1881) 6 App Cas 740, [1881–5] All ER Rep 1.' *Simmons v Dobson* [1991] 4 All ER 25 at 27, CA, per Fox LJ

LUGGAGE

[For 5 Halsbury's Laws (4th edn) paras 390–392 see now 5(1) Halsbury's Laws (4th edn) (2004 Reissue) paras 613–615.]

LUMP SUM

New Zealand [Income Tax Act 1976 (rep), s 68(2).] 'The manner of payment in a lump sum is a payment made only once and is not apt to describe the payment of the objector's one year's salary entitlement by annual instalments. The payment in question was not "any payment made in a lump sum" ... a lump sum is either a single payment containing a number of components or, less frequently, one to which a number of payees may be entitled.' *Commissioner of Inland Revenue v Lupton* [1997] 2 NZLR 759 at 764–765, per Williams J

M

MACHINERY

New Zealand [Section 6 of the Rating Powers Act 1988 and para 16 of Part II of the First Schedule to the Rating Powers Act 1988.] ' "Machinery" is defined in the *Oxford English Dictionary* (2nd ed) as "machines, or the constituent parts of a machine, taken collectively; the mechanism or 'works' of a machine or machines" and in *Webster's Third New International Dictionary* (1966) as "machines as a functioning unit ... the constituent parts of a machine or instrument". In other words a length of hydraulic tubing in itself may not be a machine but once it forms an integral part of a diesel engine, it can properly be regarded as "machinery". I accept Telecom's point that whether or not one might regard wire cables and optic fibres as machines in themselves, they can properly be regarded as "machinery" if they are constituent parts of some larger entity which is a machine.

...

'Meanings change. So long as it remained consistent with statutory context and intent I would have no difficulty in opting for a modern and expansive definition of "machine" in preference to the more traditional and narrow definition found in the *Oxford*. Equally, however, it would be illusory to think that the answer could be found by simply taking one of the modern definitions and applying it literally to a telecommunications network. In operation a network has a form of input a transmitting and an output. It could be described as a device that assists in the performance of a human task. But the *American Heritage* definition as a "device ... that ... assists in the performance of a human task" would in its literal terms include a pencil. The *Encyclopaedia Britannica* definition "an input, an output and a transforming or modifying and transmitting device" could in its literal terms be taken to include the entire national railway system as would the *Webster* definition. There must be very few contexts in which pencils and national railway systems would be regarded as "machines". Everything must turn upon the context.'

Telecom Auckland Ltd v Auckland City Council [1995] 3 NZLR 489 at 502 and 503, per Fisher J

MADE AVAILABLE

Canada 'The Minister argues that the learned Tax Court Judge erred in concluding the term "made available" found within paragraph 6(1)(*e*) of the [Income Tax] Act. Specifically, it is argued that the right to impose a standby charge is not dependent on whether a taxpayer has unrestricted or exclusive use of an employer's automobile. In support thereof, reliance is placed on two earlier decisions of the Tax Court which held that "exclusive use" of an employer's automobile is not required to trigger paragraph 6(1)(*e*).

'I agree with the Minister that the term "made available" cannot bear the restricted or narrow interpretation adopted by the learned Tax Court Judge.

'It is one thing for a court to define a statutory phrase in terms of what it does not mean and quite another to articulate its precise scope. For purposes of deciding this appeal, however, it is unnecessary to pursue the latter task. At the same time, much can be gleaned by reference to both the English and French versions of paragraph 6(1)(*e*). The English version speaks of an automobile being "made available" to an employee and of an employee reimbursing an employer for "the use of" an automobile. The language chosen by the legislative draftsperson is undeniably broad. The same holds true with respect to the French version of paragraph 6(1)(*e*). But, in my opinion, that version offers greater insight into the circumstances that trigger the right of the Minister to impose a standby charge. It reads:

'**6.**(1) Doivent être inclus dans le calcul du revenu d'un contribuable tiré, pour une année d'imposition, d'une charge ou d'un emploi, ceux des éléments appropriés suivants:

...

(*e*) lorsque son employeur ou une personne liée à son employeur a mis dans l'année une automobile à sa disposition (ou à la disposition d'une personne qui lui est liée), l'excédent, si excédent il y a,

(i) de la somme qui représente les frais raisonnables pour droit d'usage de l'automobile pendant le nombre total de jours dans l'année durant lesquels elle a ainsi été disponible, sur

(ii) le total de toutes les sommes dont chacune représente une somme (autre qu'une dépense liée au fonctionnement de l'automobile) payée dans l'année à l'employeur ou à la personne liée à l'employeur par le contribuable ou par la personne qui lui est liée pour l'usage de l'automobile; [Emphasis mine.]

'What the French and English versions share in common is the use of broad language to describe the criterion which brings paragraph 6(1)(*e*) into play. At the same time, the French version appears more precise, referring to an automobile which is at the "disposal" of an employee (*à sa disposition*) and to an employee's "right to use" an employer's automobile (*pour droit d'usage de l'automobile*). In short, an automobile is made available to an employee if it is at his or her disposal and there is a concomitant right of usage. Indeed, actual usage by an employee, for either personal or business purposes, is not expressly required. A mere right of usage is sufficient, of which more will be said below. Within this context, it is clear to me that the broad and unqualified language found in both linguistic versions of paragraph 6(1)(*e*) reinforces the Minister's argument that unrestricted use of an automobile is not a condition precedent to the application of that provision. Further support for this understanding is found in the legislative history of that provision.' *Canada v Adams* [1998] 3 FC 365 at 372, 373–374, FCA, per Robertson JA

MADE UNDER

Australia [Section 60(1) of the Safety, Rehabilitation and Compensation Act 1988 (Cth) provides: 'determination means a determination, decision, or requirement *made under* s 8, s 14, s 15, s 16, s 17, s 18, s 19, s 20, s 21, s 21A, s 22, s 24, s 25, s 27, s 29, s 30, s 31, s 34, s 36, s 37 or s 39, under para 114B(5)(a) or under Division 3 of Pt X'.] 'The question that now remains is whether such a decision has been "made under" s 37(7) so as to satisfy the "made under" element of the

definition in s 60(1). In *Hutchins v Commission of Taxation* (1996) 65 FCR 269 in the context of interpreting the phrase "made under an enactment" in s 3(1) of the ADJR Act, Black CJ said (at 271):

"It is clear that there may be a decision 'under an enactment' within the meaning of that expression in the ADJR Act notwithstanding that the enactment concerned does not expressly require or authorise the decision in question but does so impliedly."

'Similarly in *Electricity Supply Association of Australia Ltd v Australian Competition and Consumer Commission* (2001) 113 FCR 230, Finn J held (at 250–251):

"The second quality required of a 'reviewable decision' is that it be a decision 'made under' an enactment ... This test requires there to be a 'sufficient connection' between the text of the statute in question and the decision sought to be reviewed ... This 'sufficient connection' requirement itself effects a balance between the policy, on the one hand, of allowing effective redress to persons aggrieved by administrative decision making processes (so enhancing those processes), and that, on the other hand, of protecting the efficient administration of government from impairment by an extended conception of a reviewable decision".'

Australian Postal Corp v Forgie [2003] FCAFC 223 at [60], [61] per Black CJ, Merkel and Stone JJ; BC200305847

MADE ... UNDER AN ENACTMENT

Australia [The issue in the present appeal is whether the decision to exclude the respondent was a decision to which the Judicial Review Act applied. By virtue of s 4 of the Judicial Review Act, the answer depends upon whether it was 'a decision of an administrative character made ... under an enactment'.] '[59] The defining expression "a decision of an administrative character made ... under an enactment" has given rise to a considerable body of case law under the ADJR Act, some of it indeterminate in outcome. The focus has been upon three elements of the statutory expression. The first is "a decision"; the second, "of an administrative character"; and the third, "made ... under an enactment".

'[60] The cases, particularly in the Federal Court, have tended to see these as discrete elements. But there are dangers in looking at the definition as other than a whole. The interrelation between them appears from the following passage in the joint judgment of Toohey and Gaudron JJ in *Australian Broadcasting Tribunal v Bond* respecting the ADJR Act:

> It does not follow that, because s 5 is not confined to acts involving the exercise of or a refusal to exercise a substantive power, the acts which constitute a decision reviewable under s 5 of [the ADJR Act] are at large. They are confined by the requirement in s 3(1) that they be made "under an enactment". A decision under an enactment is one required by, or authorized by, an enactment. The decision may be expressly or impliedly required or authorized. If an enactment requires that a particular finding be made as a condition precedent to the exercise of or refusal to exercise a substantive power, a finding to that effect is readily characterized as a decision "under an enactment". However, it is otherwise with respect to findings which are not themselves required by an enactment but merely bear upon some issue for determination or some issue relevant to the exercise of a discretion. Findings of that nature are not themselves "decisions under an enactment"; they are merely findings on the way to a decision under an enactment.

...

'[64] This appeal involves particular consideration of the third element; that presented by the requirement that the decision be "made ... under an enactment". Here again, as with the earlier two elements just discussed, there is involved a question of characterisation of the particular outcome which founds an application for review under the statute. Questions of characterisation provide paradigm examples of the application of the precept that matters of statutory construction should be determined with regard to the subject, scope and purpose of the particular legislation, here the *Review Act*.

'[65] In considering the present case, some care is needed lest an answer is given at odds with the subject, scope and purpose of the *Review Act*. In a leading Australian text, the following passage is in point:

> Many of the difficulties stem from the fact that no statute could possibly spell out the detail of every single decision or step in the decision-making process, which it requires of its administrators. Some statutes are admit-

tedly more detailed than others, whilst some do little more than stipulate the administrator's end goals and a few methods. But, whether the statute be detailed or broad brush, they all need to contain a provision which states in substance and in very broad terms that a Minister, bureaucrat or other agency has the power (or even the duty) to administer this Act, and to do all things necessary in that regard. The recent trend is to treat decisions which can find no other statutory source of authority than such a clause as not being made under an enactment for ADJR purposes, although there has been scant attempt to identify why that approach should be adopted as a matter of principle.

...

'[69] Notions of immediacy and proximity have given rise to much difficulty elsewhere in the law, particularly with questions of attribution of legal responsibility for tortious acts and omissions. Moreover, there is evident from the reasoning of Jerrard JA in the present case uncertainty whether the suggested criterion applies only where there are arguably competing statutory sources of power. The circumstance that a decision could not have been made but for the concurrence of a range of circumstances of fact and law does not deny that in the necessary sense it was "made under" a particular enactment. The search for "immediate" and "proximate" relationships between a statute and a decision deflects attention from the interpretation of the *Review Act* and the *ADJR Act* in the light of their subject, scope and purpose.

...

'[77] In *NEAT [NEAT Domestic Trading Pty Ltd v AWB Ltd* [(2003) 77 ALJR 1263; 198 ALR 179] the written approval of AWB (International) Ltd ("AWB") was a statutory condition which had to be satisfied before the authority established by the *Wheat Marketing Act 1989* (Cth) might give its consent to the bulk export of wheat. It was held in the joint judgment in *NEAT* that the circumstance that the production of the written approval by AWB was given statutory significance did not provide the basis for an implication of the conferral by the statute of authority upon *AWB* to give approval and to express its decision in writing; that power derived from the incorporation of *AWB* under the applicable companies legislation, s 124 of the Corporations Law of Victoria. The determination to give written approval was not a decision under an enactment for the purposes of the *ADJR Act*; rather, the provision of the approval was a condition precedent to consideration by the authority as to whether it would give its consent to export.

'[78] There is a line of authority in the Federal Court, beginning with the judgment of Lockhart and Morling JJ in *Chittick v Ackland* and including the judgments of Kiefel J and Lehane J in *Australian National University v Lewins*, which assists in fixing the proper construction of the phrase "decision of an administrative character made … under an enactment". As noted earlier in these reasons, the presence in the definition in the *ADJR Act* of the words "(whether in the exercise of a discretion or not …)" indicates that the decision be either required or authorised by the enactment. Mayer shows that this requirement or authority may appear sufficiently as a matter of necessary implication. However, whilst this requirement or authority is a necessary condition for the operation of the definition, it is not, by itself, sufficient.

'[79] The decision so required or authorised must be "of an administrative character". This element of the definition casts some light on the force to be given by the phrase "*under* an enactment". What is it, in the course of administration, that flows from or arises out of the decision taken so as to give that significance which has merited the legislative conferral of a right of judicial review upon those aggrieved?

'[80] The answer in general terms is the affecting of legal rights and obligations. Do legal rights or duties owe in an immediate sense their existence to the decision, or depend upon the presence of the decision for their enforcement? To adapt what was said by Lehane J in Lewins, does the decision in question derive from the enactment the capacity to affect legal rights and obligations? Are legal rights and obligations affected not under the general law but by virtue of the statute?

'[81] If the decision derives its capacity to bind from contract or some other private law source, then the decision is not "made under" the enactment in question. Thus, in *Lewins*, a decision not to promote to Reader a member of the staff of the Australian National University was not "made under" the *Australian National University Act* 1991 (Cth) ("the ANU Act"). Lehane J explained:

> In this case, the relevant statutory power (in s 6(2)(k) of the ANU Act) is simply one 'to employ staff'. Obviously that, taken together with the general power to contract, empowers the University to enter into contracts of employment, to make consensual variations of employment contracts and to enter into new

contracts with existing employees. But I cannot see how it is possible to construe a mere power to employ staff as enabling the University unilaterally to vary its contracts with its employees or to impose on them, without their consent, conditions which legally bind them — except, of course, to the extent that contracts of employment may themselves empower the University to make determinations which will be binding on the employees concerned.

'[82] For these reasons, a statutory grant of a bare capacity to contract does not suffice to endow subsequent contracts with the character of having been made under that enactment. A legislative grant of capacity to contract to a statutory body will not, without more, be sufficient to empower that body unilaterally to affect the rights or liabilities of any other party. The power to affect the other party's rights and obligations will be derived not from the enactment but from such agreement as has been made between the parties. A decision to enter into a contract would have no legal effect without the consent of the other party; the agreement between the parties is the origin of the rights and liabilities as between the parties.

…

'[89] The determination of whether a decision is "made … under an enactment" involves two criteria: first, the decision must be expressly or impliedly required or authorised by the enactment; and, secondly, the decision must itself confer, alter or otherwise affect legal rights or obligations, and in that sense the decision must derive from the enactment. A decision will only be "made … under an enactment" if both these criteria are met. It should be emphasised that this construction of the statutory definition does not require the relevant decision to affect or alter existing rights or obligations, and it will be sufficient that the enactment requires or authorises decisions from which new rights or obligations arise. Similarly, it is not necessary that the relevantly affected legal rights owe their existence to the enactment in question. Affection of rights or obligations derived from the general law or statute will suffice.

'[90] The character of the *ADJR Act* as a law of the Commonwealth which confers federal jurisdiction to hear and determine applications for review supports the construction of the critical phrase "decision … made … under an enactment" in these reasons. Reference has been made earlier in these reasons under the heading "The definition" to the importance in construing this phrase of the expression in s 76(ii) of the Constitution "arising

under any laws made by the Parliament". There must be a "matter" so arising. The meaning of the constitutional term "matter" requires some immediate right, duty or liability to be established by the court dealing with an application for review under the ADJR Act. A recent example of the practical operation of the constitutional requirements of a "matter" is provided by *Re McBain;Ex parte Australian Catholic Bishops Conference.* As a State law, the Review Act does not have the constitutional underpinning which controls the interpretation of the ADJR Act. However, as noted at the beginning of these reasons, s 16(1) of the *Review Act* explicitly links the text and structure of that statute to the ADJR Act.' Per Gummow, Callinan and Heydon JJ
…

'[146] … Nonetheless, the words "under an enactment", appearing in the ADJR Act and in the Review Act, remain to be interpreted. In *Australian National University v Burns* Bowen CJ and Lockhart J, writing of the same phrase in the ADJR Act, observed:

> The difficulty in the present case does not lie in the definition of the expression "under an enactment" … [T]he word "under", in the context of the [ADJR Act], connotes "in pursuance of" or "under the authority of" … The difficulty lies in the application of the expression to particular circumstances. The present case poses the problem in an acute form.
> …
> In one sense every decision of the [university] Council may be said to be made "under" the University Act namely, in the sense of in pursuance of or under its authority … If the Council makes statutes with respect to the "manner of appointment and dismissal" of professors … those statutes arguably may also constitute a source of the Council's authority to engage and dismiss professors; but as no such by-laws have yet been made we need not pause to consider that provision further on this point.

'[147] Although "in one sense" every "decision" of the governing body of a statutory authority such as the University (and every decision made "under" such decisions) might be seen as being made "under" the University Act, this has not been the approach that courts have taken, virtually from the start of the operation of the *ADJR Act*, and hence of the Review Act. The reason is simple. And it is grounded in the language of each statute.

'[148] If it had been the purpose of the two Acts to cast the net of their application so widely, there would have been no reason to include in the definition of a "decision to which this Act applies" the phrase "under an enactment". It would have been sufficient simply to require "a decision" and that it was one "of an administrative character" and perhaps one made by an identified authority or officer of the polity concerned. Instead, the precondition was added, applicable to every case that enlivened the reforming legislation. The "decision" in question had to be one "made … under an enactment". Plainly, therefore, the phrase was intended to impose an additional requirement. It is one that, to the extent of its language and purpose, cuts back the availability of the new law to provide simplified judicial review. Accordingly, although "in one sense" every decision made by or under the governing body of the University might be said to be made "under" the University Act, this was not the sense in which the phrase is used either in the *ADJR Act* or in the *Review Act*. The respondent did not argue otherwise.

'[149] … The appreciation in the courts that this was so has led to successive attempts, principally in the Federal Court, which long enjoyed exclusive jurisdiction under the *ADJR Act*, to explain the meaning of the requirement that the administrative decision in question was one "made … under an enactment". The Federal Court has sought to do so by using alternative words, or description of appropriate approaches. The attempted explanations include the following:

(1) The core functions test: This was the view that the phrase was intended to refer to a decision in pursuance of a "core function" of the public official or authority concerned. It represented an approach expounded at first instance in *Burns* by Ellicott J, whose part as one of the federal law officers instrumental in designing and piloting the *ADJR Act* into law made his opinion one of special significance. It was this approach that led Ellicott J in Burns to his conclusion that *the ADJR Act* applied in that case which concerned the termination by a university council of a professor's appointment. Such an action was found to lie "at the very heart of its existence and [was] essential to the fulfilment of the basic function for which the University was set up by Parliament". There are resonances of this approach in the earlier opinion of Kitto J in this Court in *Board of Fire Commissioners (NSW) v Ardouin*. There, in construing a statutory provision exempting a statutory authority from liability, Kitto J asked whether the negligence on which the plaintiff

sued "would have been the very thing, or an integral part of or step in the very thing, which the provisions of the Act other than [the exemption] ... gave power in the circumstances to do". In his reasoning in the Court of Appeal in this case, Jerrard JA came close to a similar exposition. He described the decision made affecting the respondent as one "as to a central or core function of the University". However, on appeal in *Burns*, that approach was criticised as incorrectly focussed. The Full Court in *Burns* found that it was impossible to distinguish between decisions affecting professors and decisions relating to other employees including "registrars, librarians, groundsmen or security officers". By hypothesis, the latter decisions were thought not to have been made "under an enactment" by reason only of the general powers under the statute belonging to the university council. Therefore, some other and different connection was required. The orders of Ellicott J were set aside.

(2) The proximate source test: In place of the test suggested by Ellicott J, the Full Court in *Burns* propounded no principle better than that the outcome of the statutory criterion depends on "the circumstances of each case". However, whilst this approach was undoubtedly correct, it scarcely gave much guidance. It was in this context (and perhaps reflecting developments happening at the same time in the law of tort) that judges began to suggest that whether a "decision" was made "under an enactment" depended upon whether the propounded enactment was the "immediate" or "proximate" source of the power deployed in the given case. This was the way in which a number of decisions were reasoned in the Federal Court including *Australian Film Commission v Mabey; Australian Capital Territory Health Authority v Berkeley Cleaning Group Pty Ltd*; and *James Richardson Corporation Pty Ltd v Federal Airports Corporation*. In such cases, the Federal Court was at pains to draw a distinction between the enactment which afforded the capacity for the public decision-maker to make the "decision" in question and the subordinate source (usually a contract made under general powers) which was the proximate foundation or justification of the "decision". Where such a distinction could be made, the impugned decision was held not to have been made "under" the enactment but "under" the more

proximate source of power. However, the difficulty with the supposed distinction between "proximate" and "remote" sources of "decisions" is obvious. Essentially, the distinction is self-fulfilling. Debates over "remote" and "proximate" sources are unhelpful because the words are descriptive of the outcome. They are not prescriptive of the way in which that outcome is to be reached.

(3) The "authorised or required" test: A realisation that this was so led, in turn, to renewed attempts to find a discrimen that would mark out an applicable statutory conferral of power from that which was inapplicable when applying the test required by the statute. This resulted in the suggestion in *General Newspapers Pty Ltd v Telstra Corporation* that it was necessary to ask whether the impugned decision amounted to an "ultimate or operative determination which an enactment authorises or requires, and thereby gives it statutory effect" or otherwise. This new test came as something of a surprise because the facts in General Newspapers were substantially indistinguishable from those in James Richardson, decided shortly before by reference to the concept of "proximate" and "remote" decisions. Moreover, as particular members of the Federal Court were quick to point out, if the Federal Parliament, in the *ADJR Act*, had meant to confine judicial review to "decisions" expressly identified for that purpose in the legislation, it would have proceeded in the *ADJR Act* in the manner that it had adopted in the *AAT Act*; yet it did not. In *Chapmans Ltd v Australian Stock Exchange Ltd*, Lockhart and Hill JJ remarked with telling effect:

> The question of characterisation must be determined as one of substance and it would seem not to be determinative that the statute did not spell out precisely the power to make the decision.

This view conformed to the opinion that had been stated by the Full Court in *Burns*, at the beginning of this series of cases, that "[t]he [*ADJR*] *Act* should not be confined to cases where the particular power is precisely stated". Notwithstanding these conflicting signals, the Federal Court continued to favour an approach restricting the ambit of the phrase "made ... under an enactment". It became generally disinclined to characterise a decision in that way if the only source of the legislative power relied upon was stated in general terms in the enactment and if a different, more specific source could be identified, usually a contract, to explain and justify the "decision" made.

(4) The rights and duties test: Now, on the proposal of the University in the present appeal, a majority of this Court has endorsed a new and different test altogether. It requires consideration of whether, in the given case, the enactment "under" which the applicant for review says that the impugned "decision" was made, was one affecting the applicant's "legal rights and obligations". The test as thus stated is "do legal rights or duties owe in an immediate sense their existence to the decision or depend upon the presence of the decision for their enforcement?" I shall turn shortly to criticise this test. However, let me at once state what, in my view, is the correct test:

(5) The need for statutory authority test: According to the correct test, the question whether a decision challenged in the *Review Act* proceedings was "made ... under an enactment" is answered by first determining whether the lawful source of the power to make the "decision" lies in the enactment propounded and, secondly, deciding whether an individual would, apart from that source, have the power outside of the enactment (either under the common law or by some other statute) to make the "decision" concerned. If the answer to that question is in the affirmative, the "decision" was not made "under" the propounded enactment. If it is in the negative, the source of power in the statute is established as governing the case. The "decision" is therefore made "under" the statute or it is made without power.

...

'[152] No view could be taken of the phrase "made ... under an enactment" that is inconsistent with the clear parliamentary purpose that "persons aggrieved" by an administrative decision are entitled by law to enliven the *Review Act* if they can show no more than that their "interests" are "adversely affected by the decision". To provide such a wide definition of "person aggrieved" and then, by a judicial gloss, to narrow severely the parliamentary purpose in so providing (by obliging demonstrations of the "affecting of legal rights and obligations" as a precondition to relief) is unacceptable as a simple matter of statutory construction. The text is not then internally harmonious and consistent as it should be assumed the Parliament intended. Judges must not impose interpretations on parliamentary

law that contradict express provisions of such law or deny, or frustrate, its application. There is no textual foundation for glossing the Review Act in this way. To the contrary, there are clear textual provisions that forbid it.

'[153] Reducing the review ambit: From the start of the operation of the *ADJR Act*, as relevantly followed in the Review Act, courts have tried, in the ways that I have summarised, to reduce the apprehended over-reach of judicial review. The phrase "made ... under an enactment" is but one of the statutory provisions invoked for this purpose. Others have sometimes proved fruitful in confining the ambit of the legislation. These include determinations that the person concerned is not "a person aggrieved"; rejection of the claim that the determination is a "decision"; and suggestions that any "decision" is not "of an administrative character" because it does not involve the governmental action for which the Review Act and its federal predecessor were designed. None of these controls was available to, or was ultimately relied upon by, the University in this appeal. In elaborating the phrase "made ... under an enactment", courts should not strain themselves to adopt artificial interpretations in order to confine the text. The text itself provides for its own restrictions. Unnecessary restraints, without the clearest foundation in the statute, should not be introduced by judges to undermine beneficial legislation of this kind.' *Griffith University v Tang* [2005] HCA 7 at [59]–[60], [54]–[65], [69], [77]–[82], [89]–[90], [146]–[149], [152]–[153], per Kirby J; BC200500644

MAGISTRATE

[For 29 Halsbury's Laws (4th edn) para 201 see now 29(2) Halsbury's Laws (4th edn) (Reissue) para 501.]

MAIN BUSINESS

Australia [Cl 845.215 of Sch 2 to the Migration Regulations 1994 (Cth) provides: 'The total value of the net assets owned by the applicant, or by the applicant and the applicant's spouse together, in the *main business or main businesses* in Australia: a) is; and b) has been throughout the period of 12 months immediately preceding the making of the application; at least AUD100,000'.] 'A crucial issue to be determined on this application is the meaning of the expressions "main business" and "main businesses" in the context of cl 845.215. As is mentioned above, no statutory definition of "business" is available to assist the determination of this issue. The dictionary definitions of "business" are so numerous and so diverse that they provide little assistance for present purposes. I note, however, a few of the apparently more relevant definitions to be found in the *Oxford English Dictionary*, 2nd edn, and the *Macquarie Dictionary, 2nd* edn, respectively.

'The *Oxford English Dictionary*, 2nd edn, includes the following definitions of "business" amongst many others:

"12.a. A person's official or professional duties as a whole; stated occupation, profession or trade.

...

13.a. In general sense: action which occupies time, demands attention and labour; esp. serious occupation, work, as opposed to pleasure or recreation.

...

14.a. (With pl.) A pursuit or occupation demanding time and attention; a serious employment as distinguished from a pastime. b. spec. A particular occupation; a trade or profession.

...

23. A commercial enterprise regarded as a 'going concern'; a commercial establishment with all its 'trade', liabilities etc".

'The *Macquarie Dictionary*, 2nd edn, includes the following definitions of "business":

"1. one's occupation, profession or trade.

2. Econ. the purchase and sale of goods in an attempt to make a profit.

3. Comm. a person, partnership, or corporation engaged in this; an established or going enterprise or concern: to be in business

...

6. that with which one is principally and seriously concerned."

'In *Re Australian Industrial Relations Commission; ex parte Australian Transport Officers Federation* (1990) 171 CLR 216 Mason CJ, Gaudron and McHugh JJ observed at 226:

"[o]f all words, the word 'business' is notorious for taking its colour and its content from its surroundings ..." (citation omitted)

'In the present case the most relevant aspect of the surroundings of the word "business" is the definition of "main business" contained in r 1.11 (see [5] above). To understand the nature of a business that can be a "main business" it is necessary to give consideration to the definitions contained in s 134(10) of the Act and r 1.03 respectively of "ownership interest" and "qualifying business" (see [6] and [7] above). Each of these expressions is used in r 1.11.

'It is convenient to consider first the definition of "qualifying business". This is because a "main business" in relation to an application for a visa must be a "qualifying business" (see r 1.11(1)(d)). It is significant, in my view, that a "qualifying business" is defined to mean an "enterprise" of a particular kind (see [7] above). Each of the *Oxford English Dictionary* and the *Macquarie Dictionary* confirms that "enterprise" is a word of general meaning which is broadly synonymous with "undertaking". Had it been intended that an "enterprise" within the meaning of r 1.03 was to be limited to the commercial activities of a single legal entity, whether a natural person, a partnership or a company, one would have expected the regulation to say so.

'The inference to be drawn from the use in the definition of "qualifying business" of the word "enterprise" is strengthened by the use in the s 134(10) definition of "ownership interest" of the indefinite article in respect of the words "company" and "partnership" (see [6] above). It seems plainly to be intended that an "ownership interest" in relation to a business can derive from, for example, a shareholding in a company that carries on the business together with another entity. Were it not so intended, para (a) of the s 134(10) definition would presumably read:

"a shareholder in the company that carried on the business."

'I conclude that it is not a necessary characteristic of a "main business" for the purpose of the criterion specified by cl 845.215 that the business be carried on by a single entity. I do not understand the respondent to have contended that, as a matter off construction of cl 845.215, a "main business" may not extend beyond the commercial activity of a single entity. Rather, as I understood the case of the respondent, it was argued that, by completing form 1138 in the way in which he did (see [12] above), the applicant limited his claim to be entitled to the business visa to a claim based on his interest in Holdmark. To this extent the respondent supported the approach adopted by the Tribunal.'
Nassif v Minister for Immigration and Multicultural

and Indigenous Affairs [2003] FCA 481 at [28]–[35] per Branson J; BC200302446

MAIN TRANSMISSION LINES

[The Electricity (Supply) Act 1919 has been repealed. See now the definition of 'electric line' in the Electricity Act 1989, s 64(1).]

'Electric line' means any line which is used for carrying electricity for any purpose and includes, unless the context otherwise requires—

(a) any support for any such line, that is to say, any structure, pole or other thing in, by or from which any such line is or may be supported, carried or suspended;

(b) any apparatus connected to any such line for the purpose of carrying electricity; and

(c) any wire, cable, tube, pipe or other similar thing (including its casing or coating) which surrounds or supports, or is surrounded or supported by, or is installed in close proximity to, or is supported, carried or suspended in association with, any such line.

MAINTAIN

'My Lords, s 41 of the Highways Act 1980 requires a highway authority for a highway maintainable at the public expense "to maintain the highway". By s 329(1) of the Act "'maintenance' includes repair, and 'maintain' and 'maintainable' are to be construed accordingly".

'On 14 November 1991 at 7.10 in the morning, Mr Goodes was driving his car on a highway maintainable by East Sussex County Council. The car skidded on ice on the road and crashed into the bridge. Mr Goodes was gravely injured. He has claimed damages from the highway authority for breach of their duty to "maintain the highway". In view of what the authority's officers knew of the forecast weather conditions at that time of the morning, they should have taken steps in sufficient time to put down salt or grit and thus to prevent the ice forming. Whether the gritting lorry which had been scheduled to cover the road could and should have arrived earlier in time to prevent ice forming has been contested at the trial and before the Court of Appeal ([1999] RTR 210). The issue before your Lordships has, however, been whether the duty to "maintain" includes a duty to keep the road safe by preventing ice from forming. It has not been contended that there is a liability at common law in negligence.

'As a matter of ordinary language "maintain" is wide enough to include the taking of preventive steps and to include steps to keep the road safe for ordinary use by motor cars. Gritting is a perfectly normal practice and no suggestion is made that extraordinary or novel steps should have been taken. If this Act stood alone, there would be much force in the conclusion of the majority in the Court of Appeal that there could be liability in some circumstances for a failure to maintain by keeping the road safe subject to the local authority establishing a defence under s 58(1) of the Act that the authority—

"had taken such care as in all the circumstances was reasonably required to secure that the part of the highway to which the action relates was not dangerous for traffic."

'The 1980 Act cannot, however, be seen in isolation. Section 41 has its antecedents in earlier legislation and in the obligations of the inhabitants of the parish responsible for keeping a highway in repair. My noble and learned friend Lord Hoffmann, whose speech I have had the advantage of reading in draft, has analysed the extent of the duty both by statute and at common law. I agree with his conclusion that the earlier obligation to maintain or repair a highway would not have included preventing the formation of ice or danger created by snow and that "maintain" in s 41(1) and "maintenance" in s 329(1) must be read in the same way.' *Goodes v East Sussex County Council* [2000] 3 All ER 603 at 604–605, HL, per Lord Slynn of Hadleigh

Australia [Section 36 of the Prisons Act 1952 (NSW) makes it an offence to knowingly harbour, 'maintain' or employ an escaped prisoner.] 'The very word "maintain" itself, in my view, denotes at least some degree of regularity in the giving of such assistance: cf *Kallin v Kallin* [1944] SASR 73 at 75 …

'Applying … the interpretation of the verb "maintain" which I have accepted — that the maintenance must be of such a nature that objectively it assists the escapee to continue to exist without being taken back into custody — means that the mere provision of a Kentucky Fried Chicken meal does not *necessarily* amount to maintenance. There is a very good argument available that, because there was no degree at all of regularity involved, it did not amount to maintenance.' *Re Blinkhorn* (1994) 32 NSWLR 706 at 709, 711; 71 A Crim R 472 at 475, 477, per Hunt CJ at CL

Canada [Section 3 of the Patented Medicines (Notice of Compliance) Regulations, SOR/93–133, provides that the Minister "shall ... maintain a register".] 'The applicants cited two definitions for the word "maintain". They are:

> To keep up, preserve, cause to continue in being ... to guard from loss or derogation. [*Compact Edition of the Oxford English Dictionary*, 1971, page 1698].

> To keep in an existing state ... [*Merriam-Webster's Collegiate Dictionary*, 10th Ed, page 702]

'To the above definitions I would add from the *New Shorter Oxford English Dictionary on Historical Principles*, L. Brown, ed (Oxford: Clarendon Press, 1993) "to keep vigorous, effective, or unimpaired;". The respondent replies that "maintain" must refer to a continuous obligation. Additionally, the respondent Minister looks to the French version of subsection 3(1) which states:

> 3.(1) *Le 30ᵉ jour suivant la date d'entrée en vigueur du présent règlement, le ministre ouvre un registre de tout renseignement soumis aux termes de l'article 4 et le tient à jour.*

...

'I must also acknowledge that the English and French versions of the Regulations are equally authoritative and one should look carefully at both in interpreting the meaning of any term. (See the *Official Languages Act*, RSC 1985 (4th Supp), c 31, s 13 and *Thomson v Canada* (*Deputy Minister of Agriculture*) [1992] 1 SCR 385.) The phrase "*tient à jour*" necessarily implies an on-going function, i.e. updating. In the context of these Regulations the term "maintain" can support the same interpretation. Thus, the duty imposed on the Minister by subsection 3(1) is to maintain, in an up-to-date state, the Register.' *Merck Frosst Canada Inc v Canada* (*Minister of National Health and Welfare*) [1997] 3 FC 752 at 765–766, Fed TD, per Nadon J

MAINTENANCE

New Zealand '[17] ... An agreement under s 21 of the Property (Relationships) Act 1976 cannot be varied under s 182(2) even if payments made pursuant to it could be characterised as maintenance for the purposes of the Family Proceedings Act.

...

'[27] The Family Proceedings Act also defines "maintenance agreement" as, relevantly:

> A written agreement made between a husband and wife, and providing for the payment by either party of a periodical sum of money or lump sum of money or both towards the maintenance of the other party.

...

'[34] Maintenance agreements survive remarriage. However, s 182(2) of the Family Proceedings Act allows the Family Court to vary or cancel a maintenance agreement following dissolution. It provides:

> (2) Where an order under Part 4 of this Act, or a final decree under Part 2 or Part 4 of the Matrimonial Proceedings Act 1963, has been made and the parties have entered into an agreement for the payment of maintenance, a Family Court may at any time, on the application of either party or of the personal representative of the party liable for the payments under the agreement, cancel or vary the agreement or remit any arrears due under the agreement.

'[35] In the exercise of its discretion under s 182(2), the Court may have regard to the parties' circumstances and change of circumstances since the date of the agreement, and anything else that the Court thinks relevant: s 182(3). Relevant considerations plainly include the grounds on which spousal maintenance may be ordered under the Family Proceedings Act. For present purposes there are two relevant factors. First, liability to maintain a spouse following dissolution is limited to the extent that maintenance is necessary to meet the reasonable needs of the other party where that other party cannot practicably meet the whole or any part of those needs for any one or more of a number of specified reasons, such as children or the division of responsibilities within the marriage. Where a marriage is dissolved, each spouse is required to assume responsibility, within a period of time that is reasonable in all the circumstances, for meeting his or her own needs. Secondly, in determining the amount payable by one party to a marriage for the maintenance of the other, including maintenance after dissolution, the Court must have regard to the means of each party, including means derived from any division of property under the Property (Relationships) Act.' *Bellamy v Townshend* [2004] 2 NZLR 692

MAINTENANCE (OF AN INFANT)

[For 48 Halsbury's Laws (4th edn) para 900 see now 48 Halsbury's Laws (4th edn) (2000 Reissue) para 944.]

MAKE

'An award [in arbitration proceedings], whilst it is no doubt the final culmination of a continuing process, is not in itself a continuing process. It is simply a written instrument and I can see no context for departing from what I apprehend to be the ordinary, common and natural construction of the word "made". A document is made when and where it is perfected. An award is perfected when it is signed, at any rate in the absence of something in the arbitration agreement or the rules under which the arbitration is conducted requiring some further formality before the award becomes effective.' *Hiscox v Outhwaite (No 1)* [1991] 3 All ER 641 at 646, HL, per Lord Oliver

[The Town and Country Planning Act 1971 has been repealed. See now the Town and Country Planning Act 1990, s 115.]

MAKE AN AGREEMENT IN WRITING

Australia [Legal Practitioner's Act (SA) ss 42(6), 42(7).] '[13] There is a long line of authority supporting the Master's conclusion. That authority, in relation to the English and interstate counterparts of s 42(6), establishes that for a legal practitioner and a client to make an agreement in writing, the parties must show, by writing, their accession to the written terms. Usually accession to the agreement will be indicated by a signature, but that may not be the only means by which such accession can be indicated.

...

'[18] A similar view has been taken in Australia. In *Jovetic v Stoddart & Co* (1992) 7 WAR 208 at 218, Seaman J held that the solicitor and the client must both join by writing in some document or documents which constitute the agreement. In that case, as the solicitor had not signed or indicated by any other means in writing his accession to the agreement, it did not have effect under the Western Australian counterpart of s 42(6). In *Re Walsh Halligan Douglas' Bill of Costs* [1990] 1 Qd R 288, Dowsett J, in circumstances which are factually analogous to those of the present case, was not prepared to find that there was an agreement in writing since there was no document evidencing the acceptance by the client of the terms of the proposed agreement.

'[19] The traditional way by which an agreement in writing to be bound was indicated was the placing of a signature on the document containing the terms of the agreement. However, in my opinion, that need not be the only way. A signature is not critical. What is important is that the acceptance of the terms be in writing. In my opinion, that could be achieved by the sending of an email, or some other form of written communication which did not include a signature. However, a signature is, as I say, the conventional way by which a party indicates his or her accession in writing to an agreement.

...

'[21] In *Heppingstone v Stewart*, Griffith CJ said:

> it cannot be disputed that a written offer, containing all the terms of a proposed contract, may be accepted verbally, and if it is accepted verbally then there is a complete contract satisfying the Statute of Frauds.

'In the same case, Barton J said:

> It is plain that the document in question was not until acceptance a binding agreement. It was only an offer to make one. But the acceptance of the offer, even if merely verbal, converted it into a binding contract of which every term was in writing.

'[22] In *O'Young v Walter Reid & Co* at 508, Dixon J said:

> it could not be said that a contract existed but was unenforceable for want of sufficient writing. For the only contract offered by the intending guarantors would be in writing, and it would be immaterial that the creditors simple assent or acceptance was not also expressed in writing.

'In the same case, at 513 Evatt J said:

> A memorandum may be sufficient to satisfy sec 4 of the Statute of Frauds although it is signed by the party to be charged, before the agreement is concluded by verbal acceptance. When the signed offer is accepted by parol, such writing is not merely a memorandum or note of the agreement, it is "the agreement" itself "in writing and signed by the party to be charged therewith."

'In each of *Heppingstone v Stewart* and *O'Young v Walter Reid & Co*, the High Court applied a passage from the judgment of Willes J in *Reuss v Picksley* (1866) LR 1 Exch 342 at 351:

The only question is, whether it is sufficient to satisfy the statute that the party charged should sign what he proposes as an agreement, and that the other party should afterwards assent without writing to the proposal? As to this it is clear, both on reasoning and authority, that the proposal so signed and assented to, does become a memorandum or note of an agreement within the 4th section of the statute.

...

'[24] In my opinion the approach of the High Court in the two cases concerning the counterparts of the Statute of Frauds is not determinative of the issue which arises in this case.

'[25] One starts with the language used in s 42(6). It provides that the practitioner "may make an agreement in writing with a client" with respect to costs. Section 42(6) is an empowering provision. It authorises the *doing* of something. It authorises an agreement of a particular kind to be made in a particular way. Section 42(6) does not merely authorise the practitioner to make an agreement with the client concerning costs. Nor does s 42(6) authorise the making of an agreement the terms of which are in writing. Section 42(6) speaks not only to what the practitioner may produce with the client (viz., an agreement) but also to the manner in which that agreement may be produced (viz., in writing). Thus s 42(6) is to be understood as though it read "the practitioner may make, in writing, an agreement with the client". In this way effect is given to all words in s 42(6), and in particular to the requirements for the *making* of the agreement which it contains.

'[26] Where two parties agree orally that the terms of their agreement are those contained in a specified document, they do not, in my opinion, *make* an agreement in writing. Rather, they make an oral agreement with a term of that oral agreement being that the written terms contained in the specified document form part of their agreement. One can say, sensibly, that they have an agreement in writing but not that they have *made* an agreement in writing. The position is the same, in my opinion, when one party makes a proposal in writing which is accepted orally by the other.

'[27] The distinction is between the manner of the making of the agreement on the one hand, and the effect of that which has been made, on the other. In my opinion, the passages from *Heppingstone v Stewart* and *O'Young v Walter Reid & Co*, to which I have referred above, are directed to the latter circumstance only. One can say, as did Evatt J in *O'Young v Walter Reid & Co*

that when a signed offer is accepted orally, the writing constitutes a written agreement, but that falls short of a conclusion that the parties have *made* an agreement in writing. That which the parties have agreed upon may be in writing without the parties having made an agreement in writing.' *McNamara Business & Property Law v Kasmeridis* [2004] SASC 336 at [13], [18]–[19], [21]–[22], [24]–[27], per White J; BC200407129

MAKES A CLAIM

[The Carriage of Goods by Sea Act 1992, s 3(1)(b) refers to a person who 'makes a claim under the contract of carriage'.] '[33] To "make a claim" may be anything from expressing a view in the course of a meeting or letter as to the liability of the carrier to issuing a writ or arresting the vessel. A "demand" might be an invitation or request, or, perhaps, even implied from making arrangements; or it might be a more formal express communication, such as would have sufficed to support an action in detinue. From the context in the 1992 Act and the purpose underlying s 3(1), it is clear that s 3 must be understood in a way which reflects the potentially important consequences of the choice or election which the bill of lading holder is making. The liabilities, particularly when alleged dangerous goods are involved, may be disproportionate to the value of the goods; the liabilities may not be covered by insurance; the endorsee may not be fully aware of what the liabilities are. I would therefore read the phrase "demands delivery" as referring to a formal demand made to the carrier or his agent asserting the contractual right as the endorsee of the bill of lading to have the carrier deliver the goods to him. And I would read the phrase "makes a claim under the contract of carriage" as referring to a formal claim against the carrier asserting a legal liability of the carrier under the contract of carriage to the holder of the bill of lading.' *Borealis AB v Stargas Ltd, The Berge Sisar* [2001] UKHL/17 at [33], [2001] 2 All ER 193 at 209–210, HL, per Lord Hobhouse of Woodborough

MALICE

[For 28 Halsbury's Laws (4th edn) para 145 see now 28 Halsbury's Laws (4th edn) (Reissue) para 149.]

Australia [The principal issue raised by this appeal is whether the author and distributor of certain defamatory matter before and during an election, were entitled to defend claims for damages made against them by the respondent on the basis of qualified privilege. The respondent pleaded that the defence of qualified privilege was not available, the publication in each case allegedly being made with actual malice.] 'An occasion of qualified privilege must not be used for a purpose or motive foreign to the duty or interest that protects the making of the statement. A purpose or motive that is foreign to the occasion and actuates the making of the statement is called express malice. The term "express malice" is used in contrast to presumed or implied malice that at common law arises on proof of a false and defamatory statement. Proof of express malice destroys qualified privilege. Accordingly, for the purpose of that privilege, express malice ("malice") is any improper motive or purpose that induces the defendant to use the occasion of qualified privilege to defame the plaintiff. In *Browne v Dunn* (1893) 6 R 67 at 72, Lord Herschell LC said that malice "means making use of the occasion for some indirect purpose". Early in the history of the law of qualified privilege – which did not come into the common law until the end of the eighteenth century – Lord Campbell CJ said that malice was "any indirect motive, other than a sense of duty" [*Dickson v Earl of Wilton* (1859) 1 F & F 419 at 427]. Similarly, in an action for slander of title, Parke B [in *Brook v Rawl* (1849) 19 LJ Ex 114 at 115] said that "acting maliciously means acting from a bad motive". "If the occasion is privileged", said Brett LJ [in *Clark v Molyneux* (1877) 3 QBD 237 at 246], "it is so for some reason, and the defendant is only entitled to the protection of the privilege if he uses the occasion for that reason." In *Horrocks v Lowe* [[1975] AC 135 at 149] – the leading English case on malice – Lord Diplock said:

> "So, the motive with which the defendant on a privileged occasion made a statement defamatory of the plaintiff becomes crucial. The protection might, however, be illusory if the onus lay on him to prove that he was actuated solely by a sense of the relevant duty or a desire to protect the relevant interest. So he is entitled to be protected by the privilege unless some other dominant and improper motive on his part is proved. "Express malice" is the term of art descriptive of such a motive."

'Improper motive in making the defamatory publication must not be confused with the defendant's ill-will, knowledge of falsity, recklessness, lack of belief in the defamatory statement, bias, prejudice or any other motive than

duty or interest for making the publication. If one of these matters is proved, it usually provides a premise for inferring that the defendant was actuated by an improper motive in making the publication. Indeed, proof that the defendant knew that a defamatory statement made on an occasion of qualified privilege was untrue is ordinarily conclusive evidence that the publication was actuated by an improper motive. But, leaving aside the special case of knowledge of falsity, mere proof of the defendant's ill-will, prejudice, bias, recklessness, lack of belief in truth or improper motive is not sufficient to establish malice. The evidence or the publication must also show some ground for concluding that the ill-will, lack of belief in the truth of the publication, recklessness, bias, prejudice or other motive existed on the privileged occasion and actuated the publication. Even knowledge or a belief that the defamatory statement was false will not destroy the privilege, if the defendant was under a legal duty to make the communication. In such cases, the truth of the defamation is not a matter that concerns the defendant, and provides no ground for inferring that the publication was actuated by an improper motive. Thus, a police officer who is bound to report statements concerning other officers to a superior will not lose the protection of the privilege even though he or she knows or believes that the statement is false and defamatory unless the officer falsified the information. Conversely, even if the defendant believes that the defamatory statement is true, malice will be established by proof that the publication was actuated by a motive foreign to the privileged occasion. That is because qualified privilege is, and can only be, destroyed by the existence of an improper motive that actuates the publication.

'If the defendant knew the statement was untrue when he or she made it, it is almost invariably conclusive evidence of malice. That is because a defendant who knowingly publishes false and defamatory material almost certainly has some improper motive for doing so, despite the inability of the plaintiff to identify the motive. In *Barbaro v Amalgamated Television Services Pty Ltd* [(1985) 1 NSWLR 30 at 51], Hunt J said that "[i]n some of the older authorities, an absence of honest belief on the part of the defendant is treated merely as some evidence of an indirect motive which alone is said to constitute express malice, but the better view, in my opinion, is to treat the two as different kinds of malice". His Honour cited no authority for this novel proposition. Some years later, in *Hanrahan v Ainsworth* [(1990) 22 NSWLR 73 at

102–3], Clarke JA said that, since *Horrocks*, "it has been accepted that if it is proved that a person has made a defamatory statement without an honest belief in its truth or for a dominant improper purpose … malice will be made out".

'The knowledge and experience of Justice Hunt in defamation matters is well recognised. But with great respect to his Honour and Clarke JA, they erred in asserting that lack of honest belief defeated a defence of qualified privilege. There is no basis in principle or authority for treating knowledge of falsity or lack of honest belief as a separate head of, or equivalent to, malice. In the law of qualified privilege, the common law has always regarded malice as the publishing of defamatory material with an improper motive. Knowledge of falsity is "almost conclusive evidence" that the defendant had some improper motive in publishing the material and that it actuated the publication. That judges have treated knowledge of falsity as almost conclusive evidence of malice is no ground, however, for treating it as a separate head of, or equivalent to, malice. In some circumstances, lack of honest belief in what has been published may also give rise to the inference that the matter was published for a motive or purpose that is foreign to the occasion of qualified privilege. Nothing in Lord Diplock's speech in *Horrocks* supports treating the defendant's knowledge or lack of belief as a separate head of, or equivalent to, malice. Indeed, Lord Diplock expressly said [at 149–50] that, if it is proved that the defendant did not believe that what he or she published was true, it was "generally conclusive evidence" of improper motive.

'As we have said, malice means a motive for, or a purpose of, defaming the plaintiff that is inconsistent with the duty or interest that protects the occasion of the publication. It is the motive or purpose for which the occasion is used that is ultimately decisive, not the defendant's belief in the truth of the matter. As Cotton LJ said in *Clark v Molyneux* [(1877) 3 QBD 237 at 249–50]:

> "The question is not whether the defendant has done that which other men as men of the world would not have done, or whether the defendant acted in the belief that the statements he made were true, but whether he acted as he did from a desire to discharge his duty."

'The conceptual difficulties with using lack of honest belief as equivalent to malice have increased since Rules of Court have required plaintiffs to plead the meanings on which they rely even when those meanings are the natural and ordinary meanings of the publication. When the author of a written or oral statement gives evidence, that person is invariably asked whether he or she intended to convey each of the pleaded meanings. If the author denies intending any of those meanings and the tribunal of fact finds that the publication had that meaning, the author is then said to have no honest belief in the defamatory meaning and, relying on *Barbaro*, that the privilege is destroyed …

'In *Austin v Mirror Newspapers Ltd* [(1985) 3 NSWLR 354], the Judicial Committee had to consider a similar problem in considering the issue of reasonableness under the statutory defence of qualified privilege given by s 22 of the Defamation Act 1974 (NSW). The Judicial Committee held, correctly in our opinion, that an author may have an honest belief in what he or she writes even though the author does not intend the writing to have one of the defamatory meanings found by the jury. Lord Griffiths, giving the Advice of the Committee, said [at 362]:

> "Although the answer to the interrogatory is evidence that can be used in an attempt to defeat a defence of comment it does not follow that it will necessarily defeat the defence of statutory qualified privilege. *Words are often capable of more than one meaning, and because the jury may attach to them a defamatory meaning which the writer did not intend, it does not follow that the writer did not honestly believe in the truth of what he wrote and reasonably intended a different meaning to be given to his language.* In this case Mr Casey gave evidence and said that he did honestly believe in the truth of what he wrote. The trial judge believed him and the answer to the interrogatory is a wholly insufficient basis to undermine the opinion of the trial judge which the Court of Appeal were free to accept." (Emphasis added)

'These remarks of Lord Griffiths apply where the issue is the malice of the defendant. The defence of qualified privilege would be dramatically curtailed if defendants had to intend and believe in the truth of every meaning that a judge or jury later gave to the publication. The privilege is not curtailed if lack of belief in a particular meaning is merely some evidence from which it may be inferred in some circumstances that the defendant was actuated by an improper motive. Nor is it curtailed if one applies the doctrinally sound view of Cotton LJ [*Clark v Molyneux* (1877) 3 QBD 237 at 249–50] that the question is not "whether the defendant acted in the belief that the statements he made were true, but whether he acted as he did from a desire to discharge his duty [or interest]".

'In our opinion, neither lack of honest belief nor knowledge of falsity ipso facto destroys a defence of qualified privilege. But knowledge of falsity is "almost conclusive evidence" of improper motive, except where the defendant is under a legal duty to publish the defamation.

'In exceptional cases, the sheer recklessness of the defendant in making the defamatory statement, may justify a finding of malice. In other cases, recklessness in combination with other factors may persuade the court that the publication was actuated by malice. In the law of qualified privilege, as in other areas of the law, the defendant's recklessness may be so gross as to constitute wilful blindness, which the law will treat as equivalent to knowledge. "When a person deliberately refrains from making inquiries because he prefers not to have the result, when he wilfully shuts his eyes for fear that he may learn the truth", said this Court in *R v Crabbe* [(1985) 156 CLR 464 at 470], "he may for some purposes be treated as having the knowledge which he deliberately abstained from acquiring." In less extreme cases, recklessness, when present with other factors, may be cogent evidence that the defendant used the occasion for some improper motive. This is particularly so when the recklessness is associated with unreasoning prejudice on the part of the defendant. In *Royal Aquarium and Summer and Winter Garden Society v Parkinson* [[1892] 1 QB 431 at 444], Lord Esher MR said:

> "If a person charged with the duty of dealing with other people's rights and interests has allowed his mind to fall into such a state of unreasoning prejudice in regard to the subject-matter that he was reckless whether what he stated was true or false, there would be evidence upon which a jury might say that he abused the occasion."

'Fifteen years earlier, as Brett LJ, Lord Esher MR had said [*Clark v Molyneux* (1877) 3 QBD 237 at 247]:

> "[I]f it be proved that out of anger, or for some other wrong motive, the defendant has stated as true that which he does not know to be true, and he has stated it whether it is true or not, recklessly, by reason of his anger or other motive, the jury may infer that he used the occasion, not for the reason which justi-fies it, but for the gratification of his anger or other indirect motive."

'In Lord Diplock's speech in *Horrocks*, there are passages that standing alone suggest mere recklessness or indifference to truth and falsity is sufficient to constitute malice. But we do not think that Lord Diplock was intending to change the law, as it was laid down by Lord Esher MR in the above quotations. In fact, in *Horrocks* Lord Diplock referred to Lord Esher MR's judgments in these cases as correctly stating the law. Furthermore, Lord Diplock introduced his discussion of "recklessness" by saying that, if the defendant "publishes untrue defamatory matter recklessly, without considering or caring whether it be true or not, he is in this, *as in other branches of the law*, treated as if he knew it to be false" (emphasis added). This statement makes it clear that Lord Diplock was using the term "reckless" in the sense of "wilful blindness", as explained by this Court in *Crabbe*.

'Further, mere lack of belief in the truth of the communication is not to be treated as if it was equivalent to knowledge of the falsity of the communication and therefore as almost conclusive proof of malice. The cases contain many statements to the effect that the privilege will be lost if the defendant did not honestly believe in the truth of a defamatory statement made on a privileged occasion. If those statements mean no more than that qualified privilege is lost when the defendant knows or believes the defamatory statement is false, they are in accord with settled principle and authority. But if they mean that the defendant loses the privilege unless he or she has a positive belief in the truth of the publication, it is not easy to reconcile them with basic principle. They are not reconcilable, for example, with the principle that recklessness as to the truth or falsity of a publication, short of wilful blindness, will not destroy an occasion of qualified privilege unless it appears that the recklessness is accompanied by some other state of mind. A person who is reckless as to whether the statement is true or false has no positive belief in the truth of the statement. Yet as the above statements of Lord Esher MR in Royal *Aquarium* and *Clark* show, recklessness, short of wilful blindness, is not enough to destroy the privilege. It must be accompanied by some other state of mind. Where that is so, the recklessness is evidence that the publication was actuated by the accompanying state of mind, be it anger, hatred, bias or unreasoning prejudice. As Jordan CJ pointed out in *Mowlds v Fergusson* [(1939) 40 SR (NSW) 311 at 323]:

"All that the *Royal Aquarium Case* decides is that if a defendant is proved to be affected by a particular prejudice and is proved to have made a defamatory statement on a privileged occasion, not to serve the legitimate purposes of the occasion but to indulge this prejudice, express malice is made out. In such a case, proof of the prejudice may serve both to explain how the defamatory statement came to be made, and also to justify the inference that it was made for the purpose of indulging the prejudice."

'The proposition that the defendant must have a positive belief in the defamatory imputation is also difficult to apply to the case of a true innuendo. In many – perhaps the great majority of – such cases, an innocent statement is transformed into a defamatory statement by reason of external circumstances known to a recipient or recipients of the innocent statement but unknown to the publisher. If lack of belief in the truth of the defamatory statement defeated the privilege, the publisher would not be protected even though he or she honestly believed in the truth of the innocent statement.

'The proposition that the defendant must have a positive belief in the defamatory imputation is also inconsistent with the proposition that malice is not proved merely because a person does not intend and therefore does not believe in a defamatory meaning found by the judge or jury. As *Austin* [(1985) 3 NSWLR 354 at 362] shows, a person may have an honest belief in what he or she publishes although he or she has no belief in the truth of a defamatory imputation that that person has published. Where malice is the issue, the case for holding that mere lack of belief is not equivalent to knowledge of falsity or malice is overwhelming. That is because the ultimate issue is always whether the publication was made for a purpose foreign to the duty or interest that protects the occasion of the publication, not whether the defendant believed the matter to be true.

'Moreover, there are many statements in the cases that indicate that it is only knowledge or belief in the falsity of the defamatory statement that will ordinarily be treated as conclusive evidence of an improper motive. In *Jenoure v Delmege* [[1891] AC 73 at 79], Lord Macnaghten, giving the Advice of the Judicial Committee, said:

"The privilege would be worth very little if a person making a communication on a privileged occasion were to be required, in the first place, and as a condition of immunity, to prove affirmatively that he honestly believed the statement to be true. In such a case bona fides is always to be presumed."

'This statement was made in the context of a decision that the trial judge had wrongly placed the onus on the defendant to prove that he believed the truth of the communication. But it also emphasises that the onus is on the plaintiff to show that the publication was actuated by an improper motive.

'In *White v Mellin* [[1895] AC 154 at 160] – an action for injurious falsehood – Lord Herschell LC, after referring to a statement by Lopes LJ that it was actionable to publish, maliciously and without lawful occasion, a false statement disparaging the goods of another, said that it would be necessary to show that the statement was intended to injure the plaintiff and was not published bona fide or was published with knowledge of its falsity. In *Shapiro v La Morta* [(1923) 40 TLR 39 at 41] – another case of injurious falsehood – Lush J said that the publication of a statement which to the defendant's "knowledge is false and calculated to injure is malicious". In the same case on appeal, Atkin LJ said that "a statement made by a man who knows that it is likely to injure and knows that it is false is made maliciously". In *Godfrey v Henderson* [(1944) 44 SR (NSW) 447 at 452], Jordan CJ referred to the way that the plaintiff in that case might prove malice and said:

"He might be able to establish that the defendant, in reflecting on the accuracy of his circular, was in fact animated by some particular illegitimate purpose ... or, without being able to put his finger on any improper purpose, *he might be able to show that the defamatory statement was, in whole or part, false to the defendant's knowledge.* If he could prove the latter, it would be open to a jury to find that the statement must have been made for some improper purpose." (Emphasis added)

'In drafting his Defamation Code, Sir Samuel Griffith also took the view that to establish malice – lack of good faith under the Code – the plaintiff must show a belief in the untruth of the defamatory material.

'In *Horrocks*, Lord Diplock spoke of both a positive belief and a lack of honest belief by the defendant in the truth of the defamation. But it is clear that he was referring to the defendant's knowledge of the falsity of the defamatory material or recklessness in publishing that amounted to wilful blindness. In a key passage that is frequently overlooked, Lord Diplock said (footnotes omitted):

"So the judge was left with no other material on which to found an inference of malice except the contents of the speech itself, the circumstances in which it was made and, of course, the defendant's own evidence in the witness box. Where such is the case the test of malice is very simple. It was laid down by Lord Esher himself, as Brett LJ, in *Clark v Molyneux*. It is: has it been proved that the defendant did not honestly believe that what he said was true, *that is, was he either aware that it was not true or indifferent to its truth or falsity?* In *Royal Aquarium and Summer and Winter Garden Society Ltd v Parkinson* Lord Esher MR applied the self-same test." (Emphasis added)

'Thus, when Lord Diplock applied the law of malice to the facts in *Horrocks* and defined honest belief, he made it clear that the plaintiff had to prove that the defendant was aware of the falsity of the publication or so wilfully blind to it that knowledge of its falsity was imputed to him.

'An earlier passage in Lord Diplock's speech [*Horrocks v Lowe* [1975] AC 135 at 149–50] also shows that by lack of honest belief, he meant knowledge of falsity:

> "If it be proved that he *did not believe that what he published was true* this is generally conclusive evidence of express malice, for no sense of duty or desire to protect his own legitimate interests can justify a man in *telling deliberate and injurious falsehoods* about another, save in the exceptional case where a person may be under a duty to pass on, without endorsing, defamatory reports made by some other person." (Emphasis added)

'Statements in the cases to the effect that the defendant will lose the protection of the privilege unless he or she had an honest belief in the truth of what that person published must be understood in the light of two matters. First, honesty of purpose is presumed in favour of the defendant. It is for the plaintiff to prove that the defendant did not use the occasion honestly or, more accurately, for a proper purpose. Second, in many – perhaps most – cases, a defendant who has no belief in the truth of what he or she publishes will know or believe that it is untrue. It is understandable therefore that judges will often say that qualified privilege is destroyed when the defendant has no honest belief in the truth of the matter but really mean that it is destroyed when the defendant knew that the matter was false. Indeed, as the quotation that we have just set out shows, Lord Diplock does that very

thing in *Horrocks* [[1975] AC 135 at 149–150]. Lack of honest belief in the law of qualified privilege does not mean lack of belief; it means a belief that the matter is untrue.

'Because honesty is presumed, the plaintiff has the onus of negativing it. That is to say, the plaintiff must prove that the defendant acted dishonestly by not using the occasion for its proper purpose. Unless that is kept in mind, there is a danger that reference to the honesty of a defendant will reverse the onus of proof. If the tribunal of fact rejects the defendant's evidence that he or she positively believed in the truth of what he or she published, it does not logically follow that the plaintiff has proved that the defendant did not believe in the truth of the publication or had an improper motive. Rejection of the defendant's evidence, combined with other evidence, may lead to the conclusion that the defendant had no belief in the truth of the publication or knew that it was false. But mere rejection of the defendant's evidence does not logically and automatically lead to any conclusion as to what his or her state of mind was. "[B]y destroying that evidence you do not prove its opposite." [*Hobbs v Tinling* [1929] 2 KB 1 at 21 per Scrutton LJ]

'When the plaintiff proves that the defendant knew the defamatory matter was false or was reckless to the point of wilful blindness, it will constitute almost conclusive proof that the publication was actuated by malice. A deliberate defamatory falsehood "could not have been for a purpose warranted by any privilege; and hence it is unnecessary to determine what the exact purpose was in order to ascertain whether the privilege has been lost for the particular defamatory statement which has been proved to be wilfully false" [*Mowlds v Fergusson* (1939) 40 SR (NSW) 311 at 329 per Jordan CJ, Davidson and Halse Rogers JJ agreeing]. When the plaintiff can only prove that the defendant lacked a belief in the truth of the defamatory material, however, it will be no more than evidence that may give rise with other evidence to an inference that the publication was actuated by malice.

'In some cases, proof of lack of belief will not even be evidence from which an inference of malice can be drawn. Thus, the circumstances of the case may be such that the defendant is entitled to communicate defamatory matter even though he or she has no belief in its truth. In *Clark* [(1877) 3 QBD 237 at 244], Bramwell LJ said "a person may honestly make on a particular occasion a defamatory statement without believing it to be true; because the statement may be of such a character that on that occasion it may be proper to communicate it to a particular person who ought to be informed of it". This passage was approved by Lindley LJ in *Stuart v Bell* [[1891] 2 QB 341 at 351] where the Court of Appeal held that the defendant had a social or moral, but not legal, duty to report to the plaintiff's employer that the plaintiff was suspected of stealing.

'In a case like the present, persons handing out how-to-vote cards may honestly believe that they are informing the electorate of their candidate's views and may not themselves have thought about whether much or any of the content of the how-to-vote card is true. Such persons will not lose the protection of the occasion because they had no positive belief in the truth of any defamatory matter in the how-to-vote card. It is proper for them to communicate their candidate's views to voters, and they do not lose their protection because, although acting for the purpose of the privileged occasion, they had no positive belief in the truth of the defamatory matter.

'If the common law did hold that lack of belief or lack of honest belief in the truth of the defamatory matter was equivalent to knowledge of falsity or malice, it would have to be developed in respect of electoral communications to accord with the freedom of communication in respect of political matters that the Constitution protects ...

...

'Carelessness of expression or carelessness in making a defamatory statement never provides a ground for inferring malice [*Clark v Molyneux* (1877) 3 QBD 237 at 244 per Bramwell LJ; *Moore v Canadian Pacific Steamship Co* [1945] 1 All ER 128 at 133 per Lynskey J]. The law of qualified privilege requires the defendant to use the occasion honestly in the sense of using it for a proper purpose; but it imposes no requirement that the defendant use the occasion carefully. Even irrationality, stupidity or refusal to face facts concerning the plaintiff is not conclusive proof of malice [*Clark v Molyneux* (1877) 3 QBD 237 at 249 per Cotton LJ; *Horrocks v Lowe* [1975] AC 135 at 150 per Lord Diplock] although in "an extreme" case it may be evidence of it [*Turner v Metro-Goldwyn-Mayer Pictures Ltd* [1950] 1 All ER 449 at 463 per Lord Porter]. And mere failure to make inquiries [*Clark v Molyneux* (1877) 3 QBD 237 at 249 per Brett LJ] or apologise [*Horrocks v Lowe* at 152 per Lord Diplock] or correct the untruth when discovered [*Howe and McColough v Lees* (1910) 11 CLR 361 at 372 per Griffith CJ, Barton J agreeing] is not evidence of malice.

'Finally, in considering whether the plaintiff has proved malice, it is necessary that the plaintiff not only prove that an improper motive existed but that it was the dominant reason for the publication. In *Godfrey* [(1944) 44 SR (NSW) 447 at 454], Jordan CJ said:

"It is of the utmost importance in the case of statements made on occasions of qualified privilege, that the privilege which the law casts around such statements should not be nullified by a readiness to treat as evidence of express malice destroying the privilege anything which does not definitely, and as a matter of commonsense, point to the actual existence of some express malice which was really operative in the making of the statement; and substantial evidence is required, not surmise or a mere scintilla: *Oldfield v Keogh* [(1941) 41 SR (NSW) 206 at 214]. Any other approach to the subject would in substance destroy the doctrine of qualified privilege altogether." '

Roberts v Bass (2002) 194 ALR 161; (2003) Aust Torts Reports ¶81–683; BC200207519; [2002] HCA 57 at [75]–[101], [103]–[104], per Gaudron, McHugh and Gummow JJ

Australia [In the context of involuntary manslaughter.] '[25] ... Sir James Fitzjames Stephen summarised the state of the common law in 1877 by saying that malice aforethought covered any one or more of the following states of mind: intent to kill or cause grievous bodily harm; knowledge that the act causing death will probably cause death or grievous bodily harm although such knowledge is accompanied by indifference whether death or grievous bodily harm is caused; an intent to commit any felony whatever; or an intent to oppose by force an officer executing a duty of arrest or custody.

...

'[31] In Pt 1 of the Crimes Act there are a number of interpretation provisions, including s 5 which defines the word "maliciously". That section is as follows:

Maliciously: Every act done of malice, whether against an individual or any corporate body or number of individuals, or done without malice but with indifference to human life or suffering, or with intent to injure some person or persons, or corporate body, in property or otherwise, and in any such case without lawful cause or excuse, or done recklessly or wantonly, shall be taken to have been done maliciously, within the meaning of this Act, and of every indictment and charge where malice is by law an ingredient in the crime. *The Queen v Lavender* [2005] HCA 37 at [25], [31], per Kirby J; BC200505502

Actual malice

Canada [Defendant in libel action was entitled to plead in mitigation the absence of actual malice and gross negligence.] "'Actual malice", [is] a term which relates to the actual state or condition of the mind of the person who did the act. It implies some personal hatred or ill will or wanton intention to injure and denotes a condition which is directly imputable to the publisher concerned. The same considerations apply to the words "without gross negligence".' *Allan v Bushnell TV Co Ltd* (1969) 4 DLR (3d) 212 at 221, Ont CA, per Schroeder JA

MALICE AFORETHOUGHT

[For 11 Halsbury's Laws (4th edn) para 1157 see now 11(1) Halsbury's Laws (4th edn) (Reissue) para 431.]

MALICIOUS PROSECUTION

[For 45 Halsbury's Laws (4th edn) para 1340 see now 45(2) Halsbury's Laws (4th edn) (Reissue) para 458.]

MANAGEMENT

Of ship

[For 43 Halsbury's Laws (4th edn) para 779 see now 43(2) Halsbury's Laws (4th edn) (Reissue) para 1835.]

MANDAMUS

[An order of mandamus was renamed a mandatory order by the Civil Procedure Rules 1998, SI 1998/3132: see CPR 51.1(2)(b). See now 1(1) Halsbury's Laws (4th edn) (2001 Reissue) para 133 et seq.]

MANDATE

[For 2 Halsbury's Laws (4th edn) para 1520 see now 2 Halsbury's Laws (4th edn) (Reissue) para 1820.]

MANDATORY

Australia 'Traditionally, the courts have distinguished between acts done in breach of an essential preliminary to the exercise of a statutory power or authority and acts done in breach of a procedural condition for the exercise of a statutory power or authority. Cases falling within the first category are regarded as going to the jurisdiction of the person or body exercising the power or authority. Compliance with the condition is regarded as mandatory, and failure to comply with the condition will result in the invalidity of an act done in breach of the condition. Cases falling within the second category are traditionally classified as directory rather than mandatory.' *Project Blue Sky Inc v Australian Broadcasting Authority* (1998) 153 ALR 490 at 515–516; [1998] HCA 28 at [92]; BC9801389 at 36–37

MANSION HOUSE

Principal mansion house

[For 42 Halsbury's Laws (4th edn) para 585 et seq see now 42 Halsbury's Laws (4th edn) (Reissue) paras 789, 791.]

MANSLAUGHTER

[For 11 Halsbury's Laws (4th edn) para 1161 see now 11(1) Halsbury's Laws (4th edn) (Reissue) para 436.]

MANUFACTORY

[For 8 Halsbury's Laws (4th edn) para 131 see now 8(1) Halsbury's Laws (4th edn) (2003 Reissue) para 10.]

MANUFACTURED

New Zealand 'The observation by Darling J in *McNicol v Pinch* [1906] 2 KB 352 at 361 that the essence of making or manufacturing is that what is made shall be a different thing from that out of which it is made, has been adopted in subsequent cases.' *International Bottling Co Ltd v Collector of Customs* [1995] 2 NZLR 579 at 583, per Tompkins J

MANUFACTURING

Canada [Business assessment was levied against respondent as being a manufacturer.] 'Apparently then, the activity of restoring and retreading a tire cannot be distinguished from the activities involved in manufacturing a new tire. It would appear to follow that if the activity of producing an automotive part from entirely new components constitutes manufacturing, the activity of making the same product out of partly old and partly new components also constitutes manufacturing.' *Cantire Products Ltd v Ontario (Regional Assessment Commissioner Region No 15)* (1993) 106 DLR (4th) 755 at 756, per curiam (Ont Div Ct)

MARITIME AND ADMIRALTY

Canada '... In my view, the third party claim is integrally connected to the Court's admiralty and maritime jurisdiction. That jurisdiction, as McIntyre J. pointed out in *ITO, supra*, is not "frozen by *The Admiralty Act, 1934*" and that the words "maritime" and "admiralty" should be interpreted "within the modern context of commerce and shipping". This view was echoed by Iacobucci J in *Monk, supra*, where he stated, at pages 800–801:

> Finally, I would say that the claims of Monk are maritime in character and are not in any way an encroachment of what is in "pith and substance" a matter falling within s 92 of the *Constitution Act, 1867*. The claims here advanced do not in my view have as their foundation or source sale of goods elements of the telex arrangement between Monk and Island therefore are not within the provincial scope of property and civil rights or within any other heading of s 92.
> *I should also like to add that the approach I have taken in this matter corresponds with McIntyre J.'s urging that the terms "maritime" and "admiralty" should be interpreted within the modern context of commerce and shipping and should not be static or frozen. Such terms should rather be capable of adjusting to evolving circumstances unencumbered by rigid doctrinal categorization and historical straitjackets.* [Emphasis added.]'

Pakistan National Shipping Corp v Canada [1997] 3 FC 601 at 625–626, FCA, per Stone JA

MARITIME PERILS

Australia '... the definition of "maritime perils" strongly indicates that the Act is also concerned with voyages across the open sea.

'Most of the enumerated perils in the definition of "maritime perils" are not perils that are likely to be encountered by boats that never leave the safety of the rivers of a country. Boats on rivers are not likely to be seized by pirates, captured by the vessels of other nations, detained by the rulers of other countries or sunk by enemy vessels. In *Hamilton, Fraser & Co v Pandorf & Co* [(1887) 12 App Cas 518], Lord Bramwell and Lord Macnaghten, respectively, thought that the definition given by Lopes LJ sitting in the Queen's Bench Division of "dangers or accidents of the sea" — which they equated with "perils of the sea" — was "very good" and could not "be summed-up better". Lopes LJ said [in *Pandorf v Hamilton* (1885) 16 QBD 629] at 635: "it is sea damage occurring at sea and nobody's fault." Similarly, Professor Sutton has written that "the definition ... of maritime perils as 'perils consequent on, or incidental to, the navigation of the sea ...' etc implies that the vessel must either be on a sea voyage or at least be waterborne on the sea". For that reason, he expressed the view that "pleasure craft (or commercial craft for that matter) used exclusively on lakes and rivers would appear to come within the provisions of the Insurance Contracts Act 1984 and not the Marine Insurance Act 1909.' *Gibbs v Mercantile Mutual Insurance (Aust) Ltd* (2003) 199 ALR 497, [2003] HCA 39 at [44], [45] per McHugh J; BC200304263

Australia 'The first of the phrases used in explanation of the general expression "the perils consequent on, or incidental to, the navigation of the sea" found in the definition of "maritime perils" in s 9(2) of the Marine Insurance Act is "perils of the seas". Over the years, much attention has been given to what is meant by "perils of the seas". The discussion of that expression, in cases decided after the passing of the UK Act and the Marine Insurance Act, has necessarily given close attention to r 7 of the rules for construction of the policy found in the Second Schedule to the Marine Insurance Act. In this case the operation of that rule may be put to one side.

'In earlier decisions considering what are "perils of the seas", much attention was given to distinguishing between the fortuitous or unexpected and the inevitability of a ship's decay. The former kinds of event might be caused by perils of the seas; the inevitable decay of the ship was not. Often, the discussion of such issues embraced distinctions between proximate and other causes. Sometimes, the discussion in the cases reflected the way in which the claim was pleaded. So, for example, in *Phillips v Barber* [(1821) 5 B & Ald 161 [106 ER 1151]], the court considered whether damage to a ship lying in a graving dock in the harbour of St John, New Brunswick, when blown on its side, was a loss by the perils of the seas or a loss "by other perils and misfortunes".

'Attention to particular provisions of policies, especially to the common provision concerning perils of the seas, should not distract attention from the more general questions that are presented by the expression "maritime perils". It is an expression that includes more than "perils of the seas". Perils of the seas are but one species of that genus. Reference to the cases about what are perils of the seas is important, but only to the extent that those cases reveal the nature of the perils embraced by the words "maritime perils".

'The emphasis given in early cases to identification of the proximate cause of the loss caused some uncertainty in cases where the vessel's master or crew were negligent. By the early 19th century, the better view was that underwriters were answerable for perils insured against, however the operation of those perils may have been affected by the measures taken by the vessel's master or crew. So, the insured recovered under policies of marine insurance in cases where vessels were burnt through the negligence of the master or crew, where a vessel was stranded in a river because the cargo was loaded carelessly, and where the vessel was blown over in consequence of the master's discharging ballast. The negligence of the master or crew did not preclude recovery. What mattered was whether an insured risk had occurred. That did not turn on where the event occurred but on what happened and why. Was what happened a peril consequent on, or incidental to, the navigation of the sea — a fortuitous or unexpected event consequent on, or incidental to, the operation of the vessel?' *Gibbs v Mercantile Mutual Insurance (Aust) Ltd* (2003) 199 ALR 497, [2003] HCA 39 at [187]–[190] per Hayne and Callinan JJ; BC200304263

MARGINAL

Australia '… in the *Oxford English Dictionary* (2nd ed), "marginal" is relevantly defined as meaning "of minor importance, small, having little effect". At the present day, it appears to us to carry also the ordinary meaning of "small and insignificant or unimportant".' *Shumilov v Minister for Immigration and Multicultural Affairs* BC200200149; [2002] FCA 36 at [11], per Branson, Mansfield and Katz JJ

MARKET

See also DISTURBANCE

[For 29 Halsbury's Laws (4th edn) para 601 see now 29(2) Halsbury's Laws (4th edn) (Reissue) para 1001.]

Australia [By section 46 of the Trade Practices Act 1974 (Cth) a corporation that is in a position to control a 'market' shall not take advantage of the power to eliminate competition.] 'The Act does not otherwise seek to define what is meant by the word "market". That is not surprising since the word is not susceptible of precise comprehensive definition when used as an abstract noun in an economic context. The most that can be said is that "market" should, in the context of the Act, be understood in the sense of an area of potential close competition in particular goods and/or services and their substitutes … The economy is not divided into an identifiable number of discrete markets into one or other of which all trading activities can be neatly fitted. One overall market may overlap other markets and contain more narrowly defined markets which may, in their turn, overlap, the one with one or more others. The outer limits (including geographic confines) of a particular market are likely to be blurred; their definition will commonly involve assessment of the relative weight to be given to competing considerations in relation to questions such as the extent of product substitutability and the significance of competition between traders at different stages of distribution. While actual competition must exist and be assessed in the context of a market, a market can exist if there be the potential for close competition even though none in fact exists. A market will continue to exist even though dealings in it be temporarily dormant or suspended. Indeed, for the purposes of the Act, a market may exist for particular existing goods at a particular level if there exists a demand for (and the potential for competition between traders in) such goods at that level, notwithstanding that there is no supplier of, nor trade in, those goods at a given time—because, for example, one party is unwilling to enter any transaction at the price or on the conditions set by the other.' *Queensland Wire Industries Pty Ltd v Broken Hill Proprietary Co Ltd* (1989) 83 ALR 577 at 588, per Deane J

Australia 'The concept of "market" has long involved elements of both activity and location. The ordinary meanings set out in the Shorter Oxford English Dictionary include "the meeting together of people for the purchase and sale of provisions or livestock, publicly exposed at a fixed time and place" and "the action or business of buying and selling". At common law it was a "franchise right of having a concourse of buyers and sellers to dispose of commodities in respect of which the franchise was given": *Downshire (Marquis) v O'Brien* (1887) 19 LR Ir 380 at 389.

'In competition law it has a descriptive and a purposive role. It involves fact finding together with evaluative and purposive selection. In any given application it describes a range of economic activities defined by reference to particular economic functions (eg manufacturing, wholesale or retail sales), the class or classes of products, be they goods or services, which are the subject of those activities and the geographic area within which those activities occur. In its statutory setting the market designation imposes on the activities which it encompasses limits set by the law for the protection of competition. It involves a choice of the relevant range of activity by reference to economic and commercial realities and the policy of the statute. To the extent that it must serve statutory policy, the identification will be evaluative and purposive as well as descriptive.' *Singapore Airlines Ltd v Taprobane Tours WA Pty Ltd* (1991) 104 ALR 633 at 648–649, per French J

Australia 'In s 4E of the [Trade Practices Act 1974 (Cth)] the term "market" is defined to mean "a market in Australia". The definition goes on to say "and when used in relation to any … services, includes a market for those … services and other … services that are substitutable for, or otherwise competitive with the first mentioned … services". The part of the definition dealing with substitutability is concerned with the outer limits of any given market, not the central concept of a market, something which the Act does not attempt to define. It was put on behalf of [the appellant], and I accept, that, at least in the context of s 46, a market is a place or circumstance in which actual or potential exchanges can occur between buyers and sellers of economic goods or services, that is to say, goods or services which are relatively scarce, have utility and are transferable. To similar effect, Bannock, Baxter and Davis in their *Dictionary of Economics* (Penguin, 1998, at 262) define "market" as:

> "A collection of homogeneous transactions. A market is created whenever potential sellers of a good or service are brought into contact with potential buyers and a means of exchange is available."

'Both the foregoing definitions speak of sellers and buyers in the plural. Of course, a market can exist even if there is only one seller (or buyer). This is because the concept is as much concerned with potentialities as present actualities. Barriers to entry may be formidable, for example in pre-privatisation Australia where telephone services were provided by a statutorily entrenched monopolist. But this could change, as in fact it did. In such a case the good or service is something external to the monopolist. The possibility always exists, however theoretical, for the good or service to be provided by new entrants to the market. But the position is different when the good or service is incapable of separation from the identity of the supplier. To take another example, there might be said to be an Australian novelists' market in which novelists compete to sell their novels to publishers. But one would not say there was a separate Tim Winton novels market or a separate Richard Flanagan novels market.' *Monroe Topple & Associates Pty Ltd v Institute of Chartered Accountants in Australia* (2002) ATPR ¶41–879; BC200203308; [2002] FCAFC 197 at [81]–[82], per Heerey J

MARKET MAKER

'Market maker', in relation to securities of a particular kind, means a person who—

(a) holds himself out at all normal times in compliance with the rules of the Stock Exchange as willing to buy and sell securities of that kind at a price specified by him; and

(b) is recognised as doing so by the Council of the Stock Exchange. (Income and Corporation Taxes Act 1988, s 737(6))

MARKET OVERT

[The rule of law relating to the sale of goods in market overt was abolished by the Sale of Goods (Amendment) Act 1994.]

MARKET POWER

Australia [Section 50(1) of the Trade Practices Act 1974 (Cth) prohibits a corporation from acquiring any shares of a body corporate which would substantially strengthen its power to control or dominate that market.] 'Market power can be defined as the ability of a firm to raise prices above the supply cost without rivals taking away customers in due time, supply cost being the minimum cost an efficient firm would incur in producing the product …' *Queensland Wire Industries Pty Ltd v Broken Hill Pty Co Ltd* (1989) 167 CLR 177 at 188, 83 ALR 577 at 583, per Mason CJ and Wilson J

'The term "market power" is ordinarily taken to be a reference to the power to raise price by restricting output in a sustainable manner ... But market power has aspects other than influence upon the market price. It may be manifested by practices directed at excluding competition such as exclusive dealing, tying arrangements, predatory pricing or refusal to deal ... The ability to engage persistently in these practices may be as indicative of market power as the ability to influence prices.' *Queensland Wire Industries Pty Ltd v Broken Hill Pty Co Ltd* (1989) 167 CLR 177 at 200, 83 ALR 577 at 591, per Dawson J

MARKET VALUE

[The Capital Allowances Act 1968 has been repealed. See now the definition in the Taxation of Chargeable Gains Act 1992, s 272(1), as follows.] 'Market value' in relation to any assets means the price which those assets might reasonably be expected to fetch on a sale in the open market.

MARRIAGE

[For 22 Halsbury's Laws (4th edn) paras 905, 907 see now 29(3) Halsbury's Laws (4th edn) (Reissue) paras 33, 35.]

Canada 'I find that under the common law of Canada applicable to Ontario a valid marriage can take place only between a man and a woman and that persons of the same sex do not have the capacity to marry one another ... That principal purpose of marriage cannot, as a general rule, be achieved in a homosexual union because of the biological limitations of such a union. It is this reality that is recognized in the limitation of marriage to persons of opposite sex ... Unions of persons of the same sex are not "marriage", because of the definition of marriage.' *Layland v Ontario (Minister of Consumer and Commercial Relations)* (1993) 107 DLR (4th) 214 at 218–219, 222–223, per Southey J (Ont Div Ct)

Canada '[53] The authority to define "marriage" is found under the head of power set out in s. 91(26) of the *Constitution Act, 1867* and is, therefore, under federal jurisdiction. Specifically, this head of power authorizes the Parliament of Canada to make laws for "Marriage and Divorce". [*Constitution Act, 1867* (U.K.), 30 & 31 Vict., c. 3, s. 91(26) (see also R.S.C. 1985, App. II, No. 5)]. To date, the only statutory pronouncement that can be said to amount to a definition of "marriage" in the exercise of this head of federal power is found

in the recent *Modernization of Benefits and Obligations Act (MBOA).* [S.C. 2000, c. 12].

'[54] The *MBOA* amended 68 federal statutes to include same-sex spouses in the definition of "common-law partners". This statute was the federal Parliament's response to the Supreme Court of Canada decision of *M. v. H,.* [1999] 2 S C.R. 3, 171 D.L.R. (4th) 577 that found s. 29 of the *Family Law Act* of Ontario to be discriminatory because it excluded same-sex partners from spousal support obligations and benefits. The *MBOA* grants unmarried different and same-sex "common-law partners" almost all the same rights and obligations as married spouses in federal law.

'[55] The only specific provisions of the *MBOA* that are relevant to the within applications are found in the interpretation clause. That clause provides that:

1.1 For greater certainty, the amendments made by this Act do not affect the meaning of the word "marriage", that is, the lawful union of one man and one woman to the exclusion of all others.

'[56] The actual legal definition of "marriage" is said to have its roots in the common law and the statutory marriage laws of England. It is generally understood that at common law the definition that is routinely referred to is found in the statement of Lord Penzance in the 1866 English case of *Hyde v. Hyde and Woodmansee.* That definitional statement is said to be "the voluntary union for life of one man and one woman, to the exclusion of all others". And, because it will be a continuous point of reference throughout these reasons, the entire statement of Lord Penzance is as follows [(1866), L.R. 1 P. & D. 130 at 133]:

I conceive that marriage, as understood in Christendom, may for this purpose be defined as the voluntary union for life of one man and one woman, to the exclusion of all others.

Layland v. Ontario
'[57] In 1993 this Divisional Court had occasion to consider the issue of marriage and it was generally within the same context as the within applications. The case is *Layland v. Ontario (Minister of Consumer and Commercial Relations)* [(1993), 14 O.R. (3d) 658 at 663, 104 D.L.R. (4th) 214 (Div. Ct.)] and is one in which the majority of the court, and relying on English authority including *Hyde v. Hyde,* found that:

... under the common law of Canada applicable to Ontario a valid marriage can take place only between a man and a woman, and that persons of the same sex do not have the capacity to marry one another.

'[58] However, to complete the judicial pronouncement, Greer J. offered a dissenting opinion and held that [at p. 668]:

... restricting marriages to heterosexual couples infringes and violates the applicants' s. 15(1) Charter rights and that such violation cannot be justified under s. 1 of the Charter. I also agree ... that there is no common law prohibition against same-sex marriages in Canada.'

Halpern v Canada (Attorney General) (2002) 215 DLR (4th) 223 at 304–306 (Ont Div Ct), per LaForme J

Canada '[1] The definition of marriage in Canada, for all of the nation's 136 years, has been based on the classic formulation of Lord Penzance in *Hyde v. Hyde and Woodmansee* (1866), L.R. 1 p. & D. 130 at 133: "I conceive that marriage, as understood in Christendom, may for this purpose be defined as the voluntary union for life of one man and one woman, to the exclusion of all others." The central question in this appeal is whether the exclusion of same-sex couples from this common law definition of marriage breaches ss. 2(*a*) or 15(1) of the *Canadian Charter of Rights and Freedoms* ("the *Charter*") in a manner that is not justified in a free and democratic society under s. 1 of the *Charter*.

...

'[46] In our view, "marriage" does not have a constitutionally fixed meaning. Rather, like the term "banking" in s. 91(15) and the phrase "criminal law" in s. 91(27), the term "marriage" as used in s. 91(26) of the *Constitution Act, 1867* has the constitutional flexibility necessary to meet changing realities of Canadian society without the need for recourse to constitutional amendment procedures.

...

'[108] ... [I]t is our view that the dignity of persons in same-sex relationships is violated by the exclusion of same-sex couples from the institution of marriage. Accordingly, we conclude that the common-law definition of marriage as "the voluntary union for life of one man and one woman to the exclusion of all others" violates s. 15(1) of the *Charter*.

...

'[155] In summary, we have concluded the following:

(1) the existing common law definition of marriage is "the voluntary union for life of one man and one woman to the exclusion of all others";

(2) the courts have jurisdiction to alter the common law definition of marriage; resort to constitutional amendment procedures is not required;

(3) the existing common law definition of marriage does not infringe MCCT's freedom of religion rights under s. 2(*a*) of the *Charter* or its equality rights on the basis of religion under s. 15(1) of the *Charter*;

(4) the existing common law definition of marriage violates the Couples' equality rights on the basis of sexual orientation under s. 15(1) of the *Charter*; and

(5) the violation of the Couples' equality rights under s. 15(1) of the *Charter* cannot be justified in a free and democratic society under s. 1 of the *Charter*.

'[156] To remedy the infringement of these constitutional rights, we:

(1) declare the existing common law definition of marriage to be invalid to the extent that it refers to "one man and one woman";

(2) reformulate the common law definition of marriage as "the voluntary union for life of two persons to the exclusion of all others";

(3) order the declaration of invalidity in (1) and the reformulated definition in (2) to have immediate effect; ...'

Halpern v Canada (Attorney General) (2003) 225 DLR (4th) 529 at 537, 547, 562 and 572–573 (Ont CA), per the Court

New Zealand 'But in my view before there can be a "marriage partnership" for the purposes of the Matrimonial Property Act there must also be a subsisting legal marriage. "Marriage" is given no more than an inclusive definition in s 2(1) but there is nothing there to rebut the normal assumption that in a legal context "marriage" means legal marriage in the absence of express indications to the contrary.' *Cossey v Bach* [1992] 3 NZLR 612 at 620, per Fisher J

MARSHALLING

[For 16 Halsbury's Laws (4th edn) para 1426 see now 16(2) Halsbury's Laws (4th edn) (Reissue) para 758.]

MASTER AND SERVANT

Canada 'In *The Law of Master and Servant*, 5th ed (London: Sir Isaac Pitman and Sons Ltd, 1967)

Judge F.R. Batt commented at page 1, that the relationship between a master and servant is so fundamental that it eludes precise definition. He described a "servant" as "one who is under an obligation to render services and obey the orders of a person or body of persons, especially in return for wages and salary." He goes on at page 1 to state that a "master" is "one having direction or control over the actions of others".

'At page 5, Judge Batt discusses the relationship between a master and servant:

> Whether any relation is that of master and servant is entirely a question of fact … the law is not concerned with the terminology used by the parties but only with the nature of the relation which the parties intended, or, in the absence of clearly expressed intention, must be deemed to have intended to create …

'In *Vicarious Liability in the Law of Torts* (London: Butterworths, 1967), P.S. Atiyah discusses the master and servant relationship at 47 and 48. He states:

> … what the courts now look for is not so much the power to direct *how* the work shall be done, but the power to control the servant in relation to the incidental features of his employment – what has been termed the "when" and the "where" of the work.
>
> …
>
> Insofar as control is still an important test it is the "ultimate" control that matters, the power of the employer to tell the servant what he is to do, when he is to do it and where he is to do it. [Emphasis in original.]

'For vicarious liability to exist, the employer must have effective control over the employee: see *Montreal v Montreal Locomotive Works Ltd*, [1947] 1 DLR 161 (PC) at 169. The British Columbia Court of Appeal affirmed the need to find this element of control in *A (C) v C (J.W.)* (1998), 60 BCLR (3d) 92 at 121, 166 DLR (4th) 475.' *P (NI) v B (R)* (2000) 193 DLR (4th) 752 at 757, BCSC, per Bouck J

MASTER OF OR ANY SEAMAN EMPLOYED IN … A SHIP

[The Merchant Shipping Act 1995, s 58 creates an offence, applying to the master of or any seaman employed in a ship, of doing of an act which causes death or serious injury to any person.] '[40] While s 58 states that it applies to "the master of,

or any seaman employed in", a United Kingdom ship, reg 4 of the Merchant Shipping Act 1970 (Unregistered Ships) Regulations 1991, SI 1991/1366, provides that s 58 applies to a "masters and seamen employed in" an unregistered ship. Mr Persey submitted that the section only applies to a master who is *employed* as such. Not without some hesitation we have concluded that he is correct. Part III deals largely with the terms under which masters and crew serve. Some sections in Pt III expressly apply to a master employed as such. We have concluded that the same must be true of s 58. Were this not so, the owner/master of a yacht registered in the United Kingdom who causes serious damage to its engines or navigational equipment when under the influence of drink will be guilty of a criminal offence punishable, on indictment, with up to two years' imprisonment. We find it hard to believe that Parliament intended to make it a criminal offence to damage one's own property.' *R v Goodwin* [2005] EWCA Crim 3184 at [40], [2006] 2 All ER 519, per Lord Phillips of Worth Matravers CJ

MATERIAL

[For 31 Halsbury's Laws (4th edn) para 1075 see now 31 Halsbury's Laws (4th edn) (2003 Reissue) para 774.]

MATERIAL CONSIDERATION

[The Town and Country Planning Act 1990, s 70(2) provides that a planning authority is required to have regard to 'material considerations' when dealing with an application for planning permission.] 'Sir Thomas Bingham MR, in the course of his judgment in this case, said that "material" in sub-s (2) meant "relevant", and in my opinion he was correct in this. It is for the courts, if the matter is brought before them, to decide what is a relevant consideration. If the decision-maker wrongly takes the view that some consideration is not relevant, and therefore has no regard to it, his decision cannot stand and he must be required to think again. But it is entirely for the decision-maker to attribute to the relevant considerations such weight as he thinks fit, and the courts will not interfere unless he has acted unreasonably in the *Wednesbury* sense (see *Associated Provincial Picture Houses Ltd v Wednesbury Corp* [1947] 2 All ER 680, [1948] 1 KB 223)…

'An offered planning obligation which has nothing to do with the proposed development, apart from the fact that it is offered by the developer, will plainly not be a material consideration and could be regarded only as an attempt to buy planning permission. If it has some connection with the proposed development which is not de minimis, then regard must be had to it. But the extent, if any, to which it should affect the decision is a matter entirely within the discretion of the decision-maker and in exercising that discretion he is entitled to have regard to his established policy.' *Tesco Stores Ltd v Secretary of State for the Environment* [1995] 2 All ER 636 at 642, 647, HL, per Lord Keith of Kinkel

'... I shall, if I may, look at the question from a slightly different perspective. The law has always made a clear distinction between the question of whether something is a material consideration and the weight which it should be given. The former is a question of law and the latter is a question of planning judgment, which is entirely a matter for the planning authority. Provided that the planning authority has regard to all material considerations, it is at liberty (provided that it does not lapse into *Wednesbury* irrationality) to give them whatever weight the planning authority thinks fit or no weight at all. The fact that the law regards something as a material consideration therefore involves no view about the part, if any, which it should play in the decision-making process.

'This distinction between whether something is a material consideration and the weight which it should be given is only one aspect of a fundamental principle of British planning law, namely that the courts are concerned only with the legality of the decision-making process and not with the merits of the decision. If there is one principle of planning law more firmly settled than any other, it is that matters of planning judgment are within the exclusive province of the local planning authority or the Secretary of State.' *Tesco Stores Ltd v Secretary of State for the Environment* supra at 657 per Lord Hoffmann

MATERIAL LOSS OR DAMAGE

[An aircraft of the defendant airline crashed at a site near to where the claimants lived. They issued proceedings to recover damages for psychiatric injury allegedly caused by seeing or hearing the crash and the events following it. The claimants relied on s 76(2) of the Civil Aviation Act 1982, which provides, inter alia, that where 'material loss or damage' was caused to any person on land by an aircraft while in flight, taking off or landing, damages in respect of the 'loss or damage' were recoverable without proof of negligence or intention

'as if the loss or damage had been caused by the wilful act, neglect or default of the owner of the aircraft'.]

ISSUE 1: THE CONSTRUCTION OF SECTION 76(2) OF THE 1982 ACT

'[14] If one is looking at the words "loss or damage" in [the Civil Aviation Act 1982] s 76(2), as interpreted by s 105 of the 1982 Act, it is my view that the words are wide enough to include psychiatric injury. First, psychiatric injury was a recognised form of personal injury in 1982. Secondly, the parties have not been able to find any statutes where "personal injury" is defined as excluding mental impairment. Thirdly, it is difficult to see why Parliament should have intended to exclude psychiatric injury from recoverable loss in a 1982 statute.

'[15] In *Morris v KLM* [2002] 2 All ER 565 at [17] Lord Steyn drew a distinction between the restrictive words "bodily injury" and the wider usage "personal injury":

"In this context it is reasonable to expect that if it had been intended to cover mental injury or illness, it would have been provided for expressly. In the absence of such an express reference it is reasonable to interpret 'bodily injury' and 'lésion corporelle' as words of restriction, i e as referring to non-fatal injury which is physical rather than mental: contrast the *wide term* "personal injury" in the Guatemala Protocol which never came into force ..." (My emphasis.)

The context that Lord Steyn was referring to was, (1) the fact that mental injury was not the subject of compensation in many of the contracting states at the time of the Warsaw Convention, and (2) the large number of circumstances implicit in air travel which might give rise to claims by passengers for mental injury: from in-flight turbulence to delayed gate departure due to mechanical problems with aircraft. So far as the second point is concerned, the circumstances giving rise to a claim under s 76(2) are, fortunately, uncommon. I was told that this is the first case in which it has been necessary to decide the present point.

'[16] Mr Pugh (counsel for the defendant) submits that the determination of this issue depends on the proper construction of the word "material". He submits that, in its 1920 context, the word means "physical or bodily" damage or loss to625 the exclusion of mental or physical damage or loss. He accepts that, looking at the matter in 1982, the word "material" would not be used to mean "physical" damage; but he submits that, once the word acquired that meaning, it was preserved in succeeding statutes, subject to one qualification. The qualification is that, if the 1982 Act and its legislative predecessors were "always speaking" statutes, then the 1982 Act should be construed in the light of contemporary circumstances.

'[17] Mr Shepherd (counsel for the claimants) relied on another meaning of the word "material", as meaning "legally significant" or "relevant".

'[18] Looking at the terms of ss 76 and 105 of the 1982 Act as a whole, it is my view that the statutory tort in s 76(2) is drawn in sufficiently wide terms to permit the recovery of psychiatric or mental loss or damage. The word "material" would have been an inapt choice of word to use if the intention had been to limit recovery to physical or bodily loss or damage.

'[19] The proper interpretation of the 1920 Act is more problematic. There was no definition of "damage or loss" until 1936. "Material" in its context might mean "legally significant" or "relevant"; but, if this were so, it would be necessary to identify the contrast that is being drawn. If no contrast is being drawn then it seems to me that Mr Pugh is correct in his submission that the word "material" would be superfluous. It may be that the draftsman was seeking to exclude disturbance and inconvenience damage from s 76(2). However, if that was the intention then it was clumsily executed since, as Mr Pugh submitted, s 76(1) and (2) of the 1982 Act are dealing with discrete issues. Section 76(1) is dealing with a limitation on a common law right to sue in nuisance and trespass, whereas s 76(2) is dealing with a self-standing statutory tort.

'[20] Despite this uncertainty, I am prepared to assume for the purposes of the defendant's argument that they are right in their submission that the "material damage or loss" in the 1920 Act meant physical or bodily damage or loss. The issue then is whether that meaning remained fixed in all subsequent enactments so as to provide the key to the proper construction of the 1982 Act.

CONCLUSION ON ISSUE 1

'[33] I have therefore concluded that the "loss or damage" referred to in s 76(2) of the 1982 Act is not limited to "physical loss or damage" and (subject to my conclusions on issue 3) includes psychiatric injury.

ISSUE 2: THE MEANING OF 'PERSONAL INJURY' IN SECTION 105 OF THE 1982 ACT

'[34] This matter is largely covered by my conclusions on issue 1, since I have (implicitly) rejected the defendant's submission that "personal injury" in s 105 of the 1982 Act is to be treated as

"bodily injury". But in any event, the defendant very properly accepted that, in the light of the majority opinion in *Morris v KLM*, a person can recover on the basis of a bodily injury if that person can establish that the mental injury is evidence of structural change to the brain or central nervous system.

ISSUE 3: WHETHER THE LOSS AND DAMAGE RECOVERABLE UNDER SECTION 76(2) IS LIMITED TO DAMAGES RECOVERABLE AT COMMON LAW?

'[35] The defendant submits: (1) that, if personal injury in s 76(2) of the 1982 Act covers psychiatric injury, the words "*as if* the loss and damage had been caused by the wilful act, neglect, or default of the owner of the aircraft" (my emphasis) limits the categories of people who can recover damages in respect of such injuries; (2) that, if negligence were proved, the law would restrict the categories of persons who can recover damages in respect of psychiatric injury, see for example *White v Chief Constable of the South Yorkshire Police* [1999] 1 All ER 1 at 41, 43, [1999] 2 AC 455 at 502, 504–505; (3) on this approach, the claimants can only recover damages for psychiatric injury if they are primary victims or secondary victims with sufficient proximity and ties of love and affection.

'[36] The claimants submit that: (1) this approach places too much emphasis on the word "neglect" and ignores the other words in the phrase, in particular "wilful act"; (2) there is no reason to restrict the right to recover damages for this statutory tort on the basis of rules relating to the recovery of damages for negligence; and (3) by referring to "wilful act" the 1982 Act treats the defendant's act as if it were the deliberate infliction of injury, see *Wilkinson v Downton* [1897] 2 QB 57, [1895–9] All ER Rep 267.

'[37] I accept the defendant's submissions on this issue. Where there is damage to land and an action for trespass the claimant would have to show an intentional or wilful act of trespass. Where there is injury to a person, there might be an action in negligence; and the claimant would have to show carelessness. In my view, the effect of s 76(2) is that the claimant is absolved from having to show either a deliberate act or carelessness. In this context, "wilful act" means a deliberate act and not "intentional wrongdoing". On this basis I can see no reason why the normal rules as to foreseeability and remoteness should not apply.

'[38] I am reinforced in this conclusion by three further points. First, as the defendant points out, if the claimants' construction were correct, then there would be potentially two different approaches to the recoverability of damages (one arising from a "wilful act", and the other from "neglect or default") without any statutory indication as to which approach applies in any particular case. This is an inherently unlikely legislative intention. Secondly, the conclusion I have reached is more easy to reconcile with the reference to contributory negligence. Thirdly, if claimants can always proceed on the basis that there has been an intentional wrongdoing as if there had been a deliberate assault, then they could recover damages for injury to feelings, see McGregor on Damages (16th edn, 1997) para 1844. This too seems an inherently unlikely legislative intention.

'[39] It follows that I find that the answer to issue 3 is that loss or damage is only recoverable under s 76(2) if such loss or damage would be recoverable at common law.' *Glen v Korean Airlines Co Ltd* [2003] EWHC 643 (QB) at [14]–[20], [33]–[39], [2003] 3 All ER 621, per Simon J

MATERIAL PART

[The Leasehold Reform Act 1967, s 1(1) confers the right on a tenant of a leasehold house, occupying the house as his residence, to acquire the freehold or an extended lease in certain circumstances. Section 2(2) excludes from the definition of 'house' a house which is not structurally detached and of which a material part lies above or below a part of the structure not comprised in the house.] 'Although the question is one of fact and degree on which the view of the judge at first instance is of prime importance, the test he is to apply is a matter of law on which it may be necessary, as it is here, for an appellate court to express a view …

'Stephenson LJ [in *Parsons v Viscount Gage* [1973] 3 All ER 23, [1973] 1 WLR 435] assumed that in s 2(2) "material" did not, as it sometimes does, simply point the contrast with "trivial" or "insignificant". As a matter of language I agree with him. In ordinary legal parlance "material", used adjectivally, is not found in a vacuum. It imports a reference to something else. The thing to which it is applied must be material to some inquiry or for some purpose. It must be of sufficient substance or significance to have an effect of some kind. So Parliament must have intended that the part of the house, in order to be material, would be of sufficient substance or significance to have an effect of some kind. What might that effect be? Bearing in mind the primary purpose of s 2(2), I think it must be prejudice to the enjoyment of the house or another part of the structure caused by enfranchisement, in particular by reason of the

inability of one freehold owner to enforce positive obligations against successors in title of the other.

'I would therefore hold that if the part of the house which lies above or below a part of the structure not comprised in it is of sufficient substance or significance to make it likely that enfranchisement will prejudice the enjoyment of the house or another part of the structure, whether by reason of the inability of one freehold owner to enforce positive obligations against successors in title of the other or otherwise, then it is a material part of the house within s 2(2). In practice it may be found that that test will exclude from the operation of the Act houses of which little more than a trivial or insignificant part lies above or below a part of the structure not comprised in it. But that is not a reason for rejecting the only test that Parliament can reasonably be supposed to have intended.' *Duke of Westminster v Birrane* [1995] 3 All ER 416 at 422–423, CA, per Nourse LJ

[The Leasehold Reform Act gives a tenant of a leasehold house who occupies the house or part of it as his residence the right to acquire on fair terms the freehold of the house. By virtue of s 2(1), 'house' includes any building designed or adapted for living in and reasonably so called, notwithstanding that the building was not structurally detached. Where a building is divided vertically, sub-s (1)(b) provides that the building as a whole is not a 'house'. Section 2(2) provides that references to a house do not apply to a house which is not structurally detached and of which a 'material part' lies above or below a part of the structure not comprised in the house.] '[2] This appeal raises the question of the proper interpretation of the phrase "material part" in s 2(2) of the Leasehold Reform Act 1967. The context is that the 1967 Act confers a right of enfranchisement on the tenants of some, but not all, residential units. Houses may be enfranchised, flats may not. So the statute has to draw a demarcation line between houses and flats. Typically a flat comprises one floor, or part of one floor, of a building. So s 2(1)(a) of the 1967 Act excludes from the concept of a "house" the flats or other units resulting from the horizontal (side to side) division of a building. Typically also a house may be structurally attached to other property, as with a semi-detached house or a terraced house. So s 2(1)(b) provides that where a building is divided vertically (from top to bottom), the building as a whole is not a "house" though any of the units into which it is divided may be.

'[3] So far so good. But divisions of a building, either as originally constructed or later adapted, are frequently not wholly along straight lines. A building may be divided from top to bottom, but the dividing line may have a "kink" or a "dog-leg" in it. The division may be along what has been described as a broken vertical line, partly vertical and partly horizontal. Then one unit will, in part, lie over or under the other. Clearly, it would be absurd if every such deviation from a straight vertical line, however trivial or unimportant, were to take a unit outside the scope of s 2(1)(b).

'[4] Section 2(2) provides how the concept of a "house" is to be applied in such "mixed" cases. The effect of this subsection is that if a material part of a (structurally attached) "house", ascertained in accordance with s 2(1), lies above or below a part of the structure not comprised in the house, then the enfranchisement provisions are inapplicable to that house. In this context "material part" must mean material part of the house, namely, of the unit identified as a house by application of s 2(1). This unit is to be excluded from enfranchisement by s 2(2) if, but only if, a material part of it lies above or below a part of the structure to which it is attached.

'[5] The criterion by which materiality is to be judged for this purpose must depend upon the purpose which s 2(2) is intended to serve. On this there has been some difference of judicial emphasis. I think the better view is that the purpose of the section is simply to avoid the absurdity mentioned above. The subsection is concerned to ensure that the right of enfranchisement is not lost by reason of the fact that a trivial or unimportant part of the house overhangs or underlies another part of the structure to which it is attached. The subsection achieves this result by excluding from the scope of the 1967 Act cases where a material part of the house lies above or below a part of the structure to which it is attached.

'[6] This suggests that in this context materiality calls for a broad assessment of the relative importance or unimportance of the part as a feature of the house. Does this part have the effect that the house as a whole overhangs or underlies the structure to which it is attached to a substantial, or important, extent? If, judged by this standard, the underlying or overhanging part of the house is immaterial, then the landlord's interests, if any, in the adjoining property are protected by s 2(5), not by exclusion of the whole house from enfranchisement.

'[7] In *Parsons v Trustees of Henry Smith's Charity* [1973] 3 All ER 23 at 30, [1973] 1 WLR 845 at 854, Stephenson LJ said that material "must mean material to the tenant or to his enjoyment of the house". This formulation seems to link materiality to the use made of the part by the tenant. I do not think this can be correct. Whether a part is material cannot vary according to the use made of the part by the particular tenant or, indeed, according to the potential use of the part. A very small area is often capable of valuable use. But this ought not to make "material" a part of the house which otherwise would not be such. It ought not to exclude the house from enfranchisement. Section 2(1)(b) uses the physical state of the building as the criterion ("divided vertically"). Section 2(2) is concerned to ease the rigour of the "vertical division" criterion.

'[8] When *Parsons'* case reached your Lordships' House Lord Wilberforce left open the exact meaning of this phrase in this context (see *Parsons v Viscount Gage (trustees of Henry Smith's Charity)* [1974] 1 All ER 1162 at 1165, [1974] 1 WLR 435 at 439–440). He did note that whether a part is material is an issue which must be largely factual and one of common sense. This suggests a simple, non-technical approach. The question I have posed conforms with this approach.

'[9] It follows from what I have said that on this question of interpretation I respectfully differ from the view expressed by Nourse LJ in *Duke of Westminster v Birrane* [1995] 3 All ER 416 at 422–423, [1995] QB 262 at 270–271. He identified the primary purpose of s 2(2) as follows:

"The primary purpose of s 2(2) must have been to exclude from the operation of the Act houses in respect of which the inability of one freehold owner to enforce positive obligations against successors in title of the other would be likely to prejudice the enjoyment of the house or another part of the structure." (See [1995] 3 All ER 416 at 422, [1995] QB 262 at 269.)

'[10] He then stated the test to be applied when deciding whether a part is material:

"... if the part of the house which lies above or below a part of the structure not comprised in it is of sufficient substance or significance to make it likely that enfranchisement will prejudice the enjoyment of the house or another part of the structure, whether by reason of the inability of one freehold owner to enforce positive obligations against successors in title of the other or otherwise, then it is a material part of the house within s 2(2)." (See [1995] 3 All ER 416 at 423, [1995] QB 262 at 271.)

'[11] I recognise that difficulties of enforcement of positive obligations against successors in title, and other difficulties of this nature, may well have led, or contributed, to the policy decision to exclude flats from the scope of the 1967 Act. But I am not persuaded that s 2(2) is aimed directly at these difficulties. Rather, s 2(2) is aimed more generally at elucidating, and giving effect to, the broad distinction drawn by the 1967 Act between houses, which may be enfranchised, and flats, which cannot. If, having given effect to this distinction, the unit in question is not excluded from enfranchisement by s 2(2), and there are potential difficulties arising from the fact that an (immaterial) part of the house underlies or overhangs structurally attached property of the landlord, the provisions of s 2(5) are apt to produce an adequate, balanced solution. Therein lies the landlord's protection against the risk of possible prejudice in the respects identified by Nourse LJ. The test enunciated in the *Duke of Westminster*'s case, on the other hand, would go far to emasculate what must have been the intended operation of s 2(5).' *Malekshad v Howard De Walden Estates Ltd* [2002] UKHL 49 at [2]–[11], [2003] 1 All ER 193, per Lord Nicholls of Birkenhead

MATERIAL RISK

Australia 'The law should recognize that a doctor has a duty to warn a patent of a material risk inherent in the proposed treatment; a risk is material if, in the circumstances of the particular case, a reasonable person in the patient's position, if warned of the risk, would be likely to attach significance to it or if the medical practitioner is or should reasonably be aware that the particular patient, if warned of the risk, would be likely to attach significance to it. This duty is subject to the therapeutic privilege.' *Rogers v Whitaker* (1992) 175 CLR 479 at 490, per Mason CJ, Brennan, Dawson, Toohey and McHugh JJ

MATRIMONIAL HOME

[For 22 Halsbury's Laws (4th edn) paras 1046 et seq see now 29(3) Halsbury's Laws (4th edn) (Reissue) paras 277 et seq.]

MATTER (LEGAL PROCEEDING)

Australia 'A "matter" [in the Commonwealth Constitution s 76(i) and the Judiciary Act 1903 (Cth) s 30(a)] must be distinguished from the action or judicial proceeding which is commenced in order to obtain a determination of a controversy between the parties. The "matter" is not the proceeding but the subject of the controversy which is amenable to judicial determination in the proceeding. Such a controversy has particular characteristics ... It is a long-standing doctrine that a "matter" may consist of a controversy between a person who has a sufficient interest in the subject and who asserts that a purported law is invalid and the polity whose law it purports to be.' *Croome v Tasmania* (1997) 142 ALR 397 at 400; (1997) 91 A Crim R 238; BC9700297 at 3–4, per Brennan CJ, Dawson and Toohey JJ

Australia 'To be a "matter" there must be "some immediate right, duty or liability to be established by the determination of the Court" which the party invoking jurisdiction propounds ... [T]he "matters" referred to in s 75 [of the Commonwealth Constitution] are not the proceedings but the subjects of the controversy which are amenable to judicial determination in the proceedings. However, the party asserting jurisdiction must be able to demonstrate the existence of a legal right or duty which is apt to judicial determination; not mere "abstract questions of law without the right or duty of any body or person being involved". The full rigour of these words has undoubtedly been affected by the judicial extension, in the course of this century, of the beneficial remedy of declaration. They may need reconsideration one day.' *Re East; Ex parte Nguyen* (1998) 159 ALR 108 at 132–3; 73 ALJR 140; BC9806358, per Kirby J

Australia 'The term "matter" has meaning only in the context of a legal proceeding ... A "matter" cannot exist in the abstract. If there is no legal remedy for a "wrong", there can be no "matter". A legally enforceable remedy is as essential to the existence of a "matter" as the right, duty or liability which gives rise to the remedy. Without the right to bring a curial proceeding, there can be no "matter". If a person breaches a legal duty which is unenforceable in a court of justice, there can be no "matter".' *Abebe v Commonwealth* (1999) 162 ALR 1 at 11–12; 73 ALJR 584; BC9901531, per Gleeson CJ and McHugh J

MATTER (SUBSTANCE)

Canada '43 "Composition of matter" (*composition de matières*) is an open-ended expression. Statutory subject matter must be framed broadly because by definition the *Patent Act* must contemplate the unforeseeable. The definition is not expressly confined to inanimate matter, and the appellant

Commissioner agrees that composition of organic and certain living matter can be patented. In the case of the oncomouse, the modified genetic material is a physical substance and therefore "matter". The fertilized mouse egg is a form of biological "matter". The combination of these two forms of matter by the process described in the disclosure is thus, as pointed out by Rothstein J.A. ([2000] 4 F.C. 528, at para. 120), a "composition of matter".

'44 What, then, is the justification under the *Patent Act* for drawing a line between certain compositions of living matter (*lower* life forms) and other compositions of living matter (*higher* life forms)?

'45 My colleague, Bastarache J., quotes from the *Oxford English Dictionary* (2nd ed. 1989), vol. IX, at p. 480, the entry that "matter" is a "[p]hysical or corporeal substance in general ..., contradistinguished from immaterial or incorporeal substance (spirit, soul, mind), and from qualities, actions, or conditions", but this, of course, depends on context. "Matter" is a most chameleon-like word. The expression "grey *matter*" refers in everyday use to "intelligence" — which is about as incorporeal as "spirit" or "mind". Indeed, the same Oxford editors define "grey matter" as "intelligence, brains" (*New Shorter Oxford English Dictionary* (1993), vol. 1, at p. 1143). The *primary* definition of matter, according to the *Oxford English Dictionary*, is "[t]he substance, or the substances collectively, out of which a physical object is made or of which it consists; constituent material" (p. 479). The definition of "*matière*" in *Le Grand Robert de la langue française* (2nd ed. 2001), vol. 4, quoted by my colleague, is to the same effect ... ' *Harvard College v Canada* (*Commissioner of Patents*) [2002] 4 SCR 45 at 76–77, per Binnie J

MATTERS IN DIFFERENCE

[For 2 Halsbury's Laws (4th edn) para 610 see now 2(3) Halsbury's Laws (4th edn) (Reissue) para 9.]

MATRIMONIAL PROPERTY.
SEE PROPERTY

MAXIMUM LENGTH

Australia [Section 321I(1) of The Crimes Act 1958 (Vic) refers to a penalty of imprisonment for a term the 'maximum length' of which is not prescribed by law.]

'When the phrase "maximum length" is used in such a context, it seems to import a length which is known when the discretion is to be exercised, not a length which is unknown and will remain unknown until the natural life expires. The better view of s 321I(1) is that "maximum length" referred to in para (b) describes a term of imprisonment fixed or calculable in years, months or days; it does not describe a term of indeterminate duration such as the term of a prisoner's natural life.' *Dimozantos v R* (1992) 174 CLR 504 at 507 109 ALR 115 at 117, per cur

MAY

See also MUST

Australia 'It is true that [the Offenders Community Corrections Act 1963 (WA), s 40D] subs (2a) states that the court "may" order that the prisoner in question is not to be eligible for parole. The power thus reposed in the court is conditioned upon a determination by the court that it considers that the making of the order "is appropriate". But it does not follow that, if the court has concluded that such an order is appropriate, the court then has a discretion in the matter. The point may be illustrated by reference to the following passage from the judgment of Windeyer J in *Finance Facilities Pty Ltd v Federal Commissioner of Taxation* [(1971) 127 CLR 106]. His Honour said of the question of whether a permitted power must be exercised if the stipulated conditions be fulfilled: "This does not depend on the abstract meaning of the word 'may' but [on] whether the particular context of words and circumstance make it not only an empowering word but indicate circumstances in which the power is to be exercised — so that in those events the 'may' becomes a 'must' ...".' *Mitchell v R* (1996) 184 CLR 333 at 345; (1996) 134 ALR 449 at 457; (1996) 70 ALJR 313; (1996) 85 A Crim R 304; BC9600434 at 11, per Dawson, Toohey, Gaudron, McHugh and Gummow JJ

Canada '14 The Crown submits that an offender who meets the criteria in s. 753(1)(*a*) or (*b*) must be declared a dangerous offender and must be given an indeterminate sentence, without regard to whether the offender might also meet the criteria for a long-term offender designation. There are two branches to this argument: first, that under s. 753(1), courts have no discretion to decline to declare an offender a dangerous offender once the statutory criteria have been satisfied; and second, that s. 753(5)(*a*) of the *Criminal Code* prevents a sentencing judge from considering the long-term offender provisions on a dangerous offender application until after the court has already found that an offender is not a dangerous offender. We consider each aspect of the argument in turn.

(1) The Sentencing Judge's Discretion

'15 Section 753(1) provides that "[t]he court may, on application made under this Part following the filing of an assessment report under subsection 752.1(2), find the offender to be a dangerous offender" if it is satisfied that the statutory criteria set out in paras. (*a*) or (*b*) are met. The Crown submits that the word "may" in s. 753(1) does not create a true discretion, but rather grants a power that is contingent only upon proof of the statutory conditions. On this view, the word "may" in the phrase "[t]he court may ... find the offender to be a dangerous offender" should be treated as imperative; a sentencing judge who finds that the dangerous offender criteria are met must make a dangerous offender designation. For the following reasons, it is our opinion that this submission must fail.

'16 The language of s. 753(1) indicates that a sentencing judge retains a discretion whether to declare an offender dangerous who meets the criteria for that designation. As mentioned above, s. 753(1) provides that the court may find an offender to be a dangerous offender if it is satisfied that the statutory criteria set out in paras. (*a*) or (*b*) are met. On its face, the word "may" denotes a discretion, while the word "shall" is commonly used to denote an obligation: see for example *R. v. Potvin*, [1989] 1 S.C.R. 525, at p. 549. Indeed, s. 11 of the *Interpretation Act*, R.S.C. 1985, c. I-21, requires "shall" to be construed as imperative and "may" to be construed as permissive. If Parliament had intended that an offender must be designated dangerous if each of the statutory criteria have been satisfied, one would have expected Parliament to have used the word "shall" rather than "may".

'17 That said, cases do exist in which courts have found that the power conferred by "may" is coupled with a duty once all the conditions for the exercise of the power have been met: R. Sullivan, *Sullivan and Driedger on the Construction of Statutes* (4th ed. 2002), at p. 58. See for example, *Brown v. Metropolitan Authority* (1996), 150 N.S.R. (2d) 43, in which the Nova Scotia Court of Appeal ruled that Sackville's Metropolitan Authority was obliged to pay the claimant pursuant to s. 8(1) of the *Community of Sackville Landfill Compensation Act*, S.N.S. 1993, c. 71, despite the fact that the section provided that the Authority may pay an amount to a person who is a resident, or an owner or occupier of real or personal property in the

municipality on account of damages arising out of the operation of the landfill. But as Sullivan observes, at pp. 59–60:

> In a case like *Brown*, it is wrong to say that "may" means "shall" or "may" is imperative. As Cotton L.J. wrote in *Nichols v. Baker*,
>
>> I think that great misconception is caused by saying that in some cases "may" means "must". It can never mean "must", so long as the English language retains its meaning; but it gives a power, and then it may be a question in what cases, where a Judge has a power given him by the word "may", it becomes his duty to exercise it. (*In re Baker*; *Nichols v. Baker* (1890), 44 Ch. D. 262, at 270.)
>
> *The duty, if it arises, is inferred from the purpose and scheme of the Act or from other contextual factors.* [Emphasis added.]

'18 In this case, there is no indication of a duty to find an offender dangerous once the statutory criteria have been met.' *R v Johnson* (2003) 230 DLR (4th) 296 at 308–309 (SCC), per Iacobucci and Arbour JJ

New Zealand 'Where the word "may" was used in a statute there was a prima facie presumption that its meaning was permissive. The real question, however, was that of ascertaining the intention of the legislature, and the "context or circumstance" of that word's use might lead to mandatory construction (see p 84 line 9, p 84 line 14, p 84 line 35).' *Far North District Council v Local Government Commission* [1994] 3 NZLR 78 at 84, per Speight J (above passage cited from headnote holding 3 at 79).

New Zealand [Securities Amendment Act 1988, s 5(1)(f)(iii).] 'The *Collins English Dictionary* (3rd ed, 1991) relevantly describes "may" as "an auxiliary ... to indicate possibility: *the rope may break*". The role of the word in s 5(1)(f)(iii) is thus to indicate uncertainty: there is a possibility that the grantee will "have the power to acquire" the shares but equally there is the possibility that power will never accrue.' *Mercury Energy Ltd v Utilicorp NZ Ltd* [1997] 1 NZLR 492 at 501, per Fisher J

Mandatory

Australia 'The authorities on when the word "may" can be considered mandatory rather than facultative were outlined by a Full Court of this court in *Commissioner for Superannuation v Hastings*

(1986) 70 ALR 625 where Woodward, Keely and Wilcox JJ said at 629: "The leading Australian authorities dealing with the circumstances under which the word 'may', when used in a statute, should be interpreted as imposing an obligation are *Ward v Williams* (1955) 92 CLR 496 and *Finance Facilities Pty Ltd v FCT* (1971) 127 CLR 106. In the former case Dixon CJ, Webb, Fullager, Kitto and Taylor JJ said (at 505) that 'it is necessary to bear steadily in mind that it is the real intention of the legislature that must be ascertained and that in ascertaining it you begin with the prima facie' presumption that permissive or faculative expressions operate according to their ordinary natural meaning".' *Australian Telecommunications Commission v Bartley* (1988) 84 ALR 261 at 265–266, per Einfeld J

Permissive

[For 44 Halsbury's Laws (4th edn) para 932 see now 44(1) Halsbury's Laws (4th edn) (Reissue) para 1238.]

MAY AGREE

New Zealand [Crown offering to sell back to original owner land that had been compulsorily acquired; original owner agreeing to repurchase but price was not agreed; Crown seeking to withdraw the offer; was the offer binding?; meaning of "may agree" in the Public Works Act 1981, s 40(2A).] 'It seems to me that the words "may agree" can properly be interpreted as being jurisdictional. I think they must import that if there is a dispute as to price, the matter can be referred to the Land Valuation Tribunal.

...

'As I see it, s 40(2A) is there for the protection of the former owner, and it should not be read down to a preemptive power in the hands of the Crown.' *Deane v Attorney-General* [1997] 2 NZLR 180 at 194, per Hammond J

MAY AT ANY TIME [HAVE THE POWER TO ACQUIRE OR DISPOSE OF THE VOTING SECURITY]

New Zealand [Securities Amendment Act 1988, s 5(1)(f)(iii).] 'The phrase "may at any time" is not to be equated with the word "will". Section 5(1)(d) ("Has the power to acquire") in combination with s 5(4)(f) ("Is exercisable ... in the future") already caters for the case in which it is known that the power to acquire will arise in the future. The significant element introduced by s 5(1)(f)(iii) is that in place of certainty it becomes sufficient if by virtue of the agreement the power "may at any time" accrue.' *Mercury Energy Ltd v Utilicorp NZ Ltd* [1997] 1 NZLR 492 at 501, per Fisher J

MEAN HIGH WATER SPRINGS

New Zealand ['Under the Town and Country Planning Act 1977 which was the Act in force at the time the district plan became operative, 'mean high water mark' was an important jurisdictional boundary for planning purposes. Under the Resource Management Act 1991 similar importance has been attributed to the line of 'mean high water springs'. The two lines are not necessarily coincidental. Mean high water mark is calculated by reference to the high tide mark of all tides, whereas] 'mean high water springs is calculated by reference to the line of the high spring tides.' *Freeman v Savage* [1997] 1 NZLR 736 at 739, per Salmon J

MEANS

Australia [Order 43, r 31 of the Rules of the Supreme Court of the Australian Capital Territory provides for oral examination of a judgment debtor as to any 'means' of satisfying the judgment.]

'The term "means" refers to the pecuniary resources which may be available for satisfaction of the judgment debt: see e g *Watkins v Ross* (1893) 68 LT 423 in which Lindley LJ said at 424: "The object of this rule is plain enough; it is to make a judgment debtor tell what assets he has got to satisfy the judgment". At 425, Kay LJ commented to like effect. In *Watkins v Ross*, their Lordships therefore refused to order that a debtor be examined as to the circumstances relating to a debenture bond, the validity of which was the subject of legal proceedings. Their Lordships considered that such an examination went "beyond the limit of the rule": per Lord Esher MR at 424.

'We would not read the term "means" as limited to pecuniary resources presently, in the sense of instantly or currently, available. Order 43, r 31 uses no such description. The term "means" of its very nature denotes not only existing property or assets but also resources or sources whereby assets or property may become available for satisfaction of the judgment debt. But nevertheless, the rule allows only an examination as to the property and means which the judgment debtor has to satisfy the judgment.

'Order 43, r 31 does not, as does s 81 of the Bankruptcy Act 1966 (Cth), allow for a general, wide ranging inquiry into the financial transactions of the debtor. The purpose of the examination is to ascertain from what sources the debtor may satisfy the judgment debt. The term "means" does not denote other possible methods by which the judgment creditor may obtain satisfaction of the debt. It is the means of the debtor which are the subject of the examination.' *McCormack v National Australia Bank Ltd* (1992) 106 ALR 647 at 649, per cur

MEANS AND INCLUDES

Australia [General statutory interpretation of composite expression.] 'Generally, when a definition is framed "exclusively" in the sense that the defined term is said to "mean" a particular form of words, then that is the only meaning that can be assigned and there is little or no room for elaboration or development. This task is then to determine the meaning of the definition

'In contrast, where the definition uses the expression "includes", then it is generally open to use other appropriate definitions to supplement the defined term by reference to them.

'The use of the composite expression "means and includes" is considered by Pearce and Geddes, *"Statutory Interpretation in Australia"* 5th ed 2001, at [6.56]. They suggest that the correct approach to the understanding and effect of this composite expression is that the expression "means" is used where the definition is intended to be exhaustive, while the expression "includes" is used where it is intended to enlarge the meaning of the term defined. In [6.60], they strongly counsel against the use of the expression "means and includes", because it is based on terms which, to some extent, are incompatible with one another in the sense that one limits and the other extends.' *Visa International Service Assn v Reserve Bank of Australia* [2003] FCA 977 at [284]–[286] per Tamberlin J; BC200305436

MEASURE

[For 34 Halsbury's Laws (4th edn) para 1226 see now 34 Halsbury's Laws (4th edn) (Reissue) para 731.]

MEASURE (LEGISLATIVE)

[For 44 Halsbury's Laws (4th edn) para 802 see now 44(1) Halsbury's Laws (4th edn) (Reissue) para 1205.]

MEDIATION

Australia 'The word "mediation" is defined as "action in mediating between parties, as to effect an agreement or reconciliation": *The Macquarie Dictionary* 2nd ed at p 1105. The word "mediate" means "to bring about (an agreement ...) between parties by acting as mediator" and "to settle (disputes, etc) by mediation; reconcile" and "to act between parties to effect an agreement, compromise or reconciliation": *The Macquarie Dictionary* at p 1105.

'The objectives of mediation as provided for in this Court are made patent by the content of [Federal Court Rules (Cth)] O 72 r 7 [which outlines how a mediation conference must be conducted]. What is required, is that there be "a structured process" involving the mediator in assisting the parties. That is done "by encouraging and facilitating discussion between the parties". The object of that is that they should "communicate effectively with each other about the dispute". There is the possibility that they might reach agreement and consent to an order. Those objectives are important curial objectives in the court process.

...

'It is not the case that mediation can only be ordered where respondents admit the whole or part of the case against them or that it should not be held even where an applicant has a reasonable prospect of success. The point of mediation, as the nature of the word implies, is that there is give and take on both sides and that neither party enters a mediation session with any prescriptions. All parties ordered or directed to attend a mediation pursuant to the rules of the Court in this Registry are advised:

> "the mediator will encourage free and frank discussion about the matters in dispute. The parties are the negotiators. They negotiate with each other in an endeavour to resolve their differences. The mediator may facilitate the process by suggesting options and possible solutions to resolve the whole or part of the differences between the parties." '

Australian Competition and Consumer Commission v Lux Pty Ltd BC200102543; [2001] FCA 600 at [25], [26], [28], per Nicholson J

Australia 'The word "mediation" is defined as "action in mediating between parties, as to effect an agreement or reconciliation": *Macquarie Dictionary* 2nd ed at p 1105. The word "mediate" means "to bring about (an agreement ...) between parties by acting as mediator" and "to settle (disputes, etc) by mediation; reconcile" and "to act between parties to effect an agreement, compromise or reconciliation": *Macquarie Dictionary* at p 1105.

'The objectives of mediation as provided for in this Court are made patent by the content of Federal Court Rules O 72 r 7. What is required, is that there be "a structured process" involving the mediator in assisting the parties. That is done "by encouraging and facilitating discussion between the parties". The object of that is that they should "communicate effectively with each other about the dispute". There is the possibility that they might reach agreement and consent to an order. Those objectives are important curial objectives in the court process.

'It has been recognised by Lehane J in *Kilthistle No 6 Pty Ltd (rec and mgr apptd) v Austwide Homes Pty Ltd* (Lehane J, 10 December 1997, unreported) that ordinarily mediation is a consensual procedure and that there can be little doubt it is most likely to achieve results if all parties are willing participants. However, as acknowledged by his Honour, the amendment of the Federal Court Act to empower the Court to refer a proceeding to mediation even if all parties do not agree and consequential amendment of the rules to take account of that provision, reflect a view that mediation may be productive even if a party is initially a reluctant participant.

'It is not the case that mediation can only be ordered where respondents admit the whole or part of the case against them or that it should not be held even where an applicant has a reasonable prospect of success. The point of mediation, as the nature of the word implies, is that there is give and take on both sides and that neither party enters a mediation session with any prescriptions. All parties ordered or directed to attend a mediation pursuant to the rules of the Court in this Registry are advised:

> "the mediator will encourage free and frank discussion about the matters in dispute. The parties are the negotiators. They negotiate with each other in an endeavour to resolve their differences. The mediator may facilitate the process by suggesting options and possible solutions to resolve the whole or part of the differences between the parties." '

Australian Competition and Consumer Commission v Lux Pty Ltd BC200102543; [2001] FCA 600 at [25]–[28], per Nicholoson J

MEDICAL MISADVENTURE

New Zealand [It was necessary to consider whether a cardio-vascular incident could have been the result of medical misadventure defined in s 2 of the Accident Rehabilitation and Compensation Insurance Act 1992 as 'personal injury resulting from medical error or medical mishap'.] ' "Medical mishap" arises out of "adverse consequence of treatment by [or at the direction of] a registered health professional, properly given, if —" ...

'As Matthew was being transported to Kingseat Hospital for the purposes of an assessment and prospectively treatment his situation does not fall within the meaning of medical mishap ... ' *Innes v Wong* [1996] 3 NZLR 238 at 244, per Cartwright J

New Zealand [Accident Compensation Act 1982, s 2.] 'The expression "medical misadventure" is merely one species of "personal injury by accident". The latter phrase involves two elements – the injury as well as the accidental means by which it was brought about. "Medical misadventure" is merely declaratory of that which had always been implicit in the concept of "personal injury by accident". In its natural and ordinary sense it extends to "any adverse consequences to a patient's health caused by wrong medical treatment ..."

'The conclusion that there must be an injury before there could be a "medical misadventure" also follows from the nature of cover under the Act. Of the various provisions in s 26(1) of the Act, the relevant statutory purpose is contained in para (c): "To make provision for the compensation of persons who suffer personal injury by accident ...". Until there has been an injury there is nothing to compensate. Deficient medical advice does not in itself harm anybody. It is only when the advice is acted upon to the patient's detriment that it could be said that there has been a "personal injury by accident" which in turn may be susceptible to compensation.

'I accept ... that deficient advice per so does not amount to "medical misadventure". The deficient advice must lead to some adverse physical or mental consequence, and thus provide the "injury" element of a "personal injury by accident". On the other hand, it is sufficient if the physical or mental consequence is an adverse one seen from the patient's point of view ..." *Doyle v Accident Compensation Corporation* [1997] 3 NZLR 161 at 165–166, per Fisher J

MEDICAL PRACTITIONER

[The Social Security Act 1975 has been repealed. The definition is re-enacted in similar terms in the Social Security Administration Act 1992, s 191(1).]

(1) In any enactment passed before 1 January 1979 the expression 'legally qualified medical practitioner', or 'duly qualified medical practitioner', or any expression importing a person recognised by law as a medical practitioner or member of the medical profession, shall, unless the contrary intention appears, be construed to mean a fully registered person.

(2) In any enactment passed before 1 January 1979 references (however expressed) to a person registered under the Medical Acts or as a medical practitioner shall, unless the contrary intention appears, be construed as references to a fully registered person. (Medical Act 1983, Sch 1 para 11)

'Fully registered person' means a person for the time being registered under section 3, 19 or 27 [of the Medical Act 1983; primary United Kingdom or primary EC qualifications; recognised overseas qualifications; visiting overseas specialists] as a fully registered medical practitioner, or under section 18 above as a visiting EEC practitioner, and—

(a) so far as mentioned in subsection (3) of section 15 or 21 [of the Medical Act 1983: provisional registration], but not further, includes a person for the time being provisionally registered;

(b) in relation to such employment and such things as are mentioned in paragraphs (a), (b) and (c) of subsection (7) of section 22 [of the Medical Act 1983: employment during currency of limited registration of persons by virtue of overseas qualifications], but not in relation to other matters, includes a person for the time being registered under that section with limited registration;

and "fully registered" shall be construed accordingly. (Medical Act 1983, s 55)

[For 30 Halsbury's Laws (4th edn) paras 3–4 see now 30 Halsbury's Laws (4th edn) (Reissue) paras 3–4.]

MEDICAL TREATMENT

[The Social Security Act 1975 has been repealed. The definition is re-enacted in the Social Security Administration Act 1992, s 191(1).]

MEET TOGETHER

Australia [The articles of association of a company required that resolutions of that company be made by a quorum of directors 'meet[ing] together'.] 'I agree with the view expressed by Santow J in *Wagner v International Health Promotions* (1994) 15 ACSR 419 at 421–2 that the words "meet together" when ordinarily used in respect of a meeting of directors connote a meeting of minds made possible either by physical proximity or by technology.

'In my view, provided that each participating director is able to be aware of the contributions to the meeting made by each other director and to contribute himself or herself to the meeting without significant impediment, it is not of importance that the meeting together of the directors is achieved with the assistance of the telecommunications industry. I conclude that directors can, generally speaking, meet together by video links or by using telephone conference connections. A meeting of two directors only can by analogy of reasoning, in my view, generally speaking, be held using an ordinary telephone connection.' *Re Ferguson* (1995) 58 FCR 106 at 111–112; sub nom *Re GIGA Investments Pty Ltd* (*in admin*) 17 ACSR 472 at 477, per Branson J

MEETING

General

[For 7 Halsbury's Laws (4th edn) para 685 see now 7(1) Halsbury's Laws (4th edn) (2004 Reissue) para 1130 et seq.]

Canada [A municipality held an in camera 'workshop'.] 'Black's Law Dictionary, 5th edn (1979), at p 886 reflects common parlance when it defines "meeting" as: "... an assembling of a number of persons for the purpose of discussing and acting upon some matter or matters in which they have a common interest ...". In the context of a statutory committee, "meeting" should be interpreted as any gathering to which all members of the committee are invited to discuss matters within their jurisdiction. And that is precisely what was being done on that occasion. No matter how the meeting might be disguised by the use of terms such as "workshop", or the failure to make a formal report, the committee members were meeting to discuss matters within their jurisdiction. What the committee was trying to do was to have a meeting in camera, something expressly forbidden under [a] by-law.' *Southam Inc v Hamilton-Wentworth (Regional Municipality) Economic Development Committee* (1988) 54 DLR (4th) 131 at 135, Ont CA, per Grange JA

Of company

'The fact that a meeting cannot pass a valid resolution in certain circumstances does not necessarily mean that there has been no meeting at all. Thus in many cases (including the present) the articles of a company provide that, in the event of there being no quorum present at a meeting, the meeting shall be adjourned for a fixed period. In such a case it is clear that the inquorate meeting was a meeting notwithstanding the fact that it could conduct no business.' *Byng v London Life Association Ltd* [1989] 1 All ER 560 at 565, CA, per Browne-Wilkinson VC

MEMBER

Australia [Section 45 of the Companies (Acquisition of Shares) (SA) Code provides that the court may make orders on the application, inter alia, of a 'member' of the company where a person has acquired shares in the company in contravention of s 11.] 'In my opinion, the court is bound to construe s 45 and to give it a definite meaning as to the categories of members given statutory standing. That meaning must be as consistent as possible with the Takeover Code's policy and with the avoidance of the evils which the Code was designed to remedy. The Code's policy can be discerned from s 59 which give guidance to the Commission as to the factors it should take into account in exercising its powers under ss 57 and 58. The Commission must "take into account the desirability of ensuring that the acquisition of shares in companies takes place in an efficient, competitive and informed market" and some specific guidelines are added. I think that s 45 should be construed in such a way that a "member" of company has standing if he, she or it was a member of the company at the time of the contravening transaction and also at the time of the application of the court, except in the case of the limited class of members "from whom the shares were acquired", such members being in a special category for the obvious reason that they have a direct interest in the quality of the information given in a Notice designed to tempt them to part with their shares in a takeover situation ... What about the necessity to be a member at the time of the alleged contravention? By way of contrast with s 45, s 47(1) expressly

confers standing to seek relief under that section both upon persons who hold shares at the time of the application and upon persons who held shares at the time of service of the impugned Pt A statement. Section 45 is silent on the point ... It is sufficiently clear that the language of s 45 and the purposes of the Code gathered from its provisions as a whole and from s 59 in particular, combine to point on substantial balance to a construction which requires membership by the applicant both at the time of the contravention and at the time of the application to the court. *Niord Pty Ltd v Adelaide Petroleum NL* (1990) 54 SASR 87 at 96–98, per White J

Of company

[For 7 Halsbury's Laws (4th edn) para 338 see now 7(1) Halsbury's Laws (4th edn) (2004 Reissue) para 750.]

In his character of a member

[The Insolvency Act 1986, s 74(2)(f) provides that a sum due to any member of the company (in his character of a member) by way of dividends, profits or otherwise is not deemed to be a debt of the company.] 'There is no doubt that the words "in his character of a member" limit the scope of what is a sum due to any member. A sum due to that member in some other capacity, for example as a director, would not come within the section. In considering what is comprehended by the reference to the member's character of a member, it is natural to look to the bundle of rights and obligations which make up a share, the holding of which is the essential characteristic of a member. Those rights and obligations are conferred or imposed on members by or under the articles and the memorandum which bind the company and its members inter se (s 14 of the [Companies Act 1985]), as well as any rights or obligations conferred or imposed by statute (e g a right to a return of capital pursuant to a reduction of capital confirmed by the court: s 138(2) of the 1985 Act). Sums due under rights obtained by a member under a separate contract with the company or as a result of a wrong done to him by the company would not appear to be sums due to the member in his character of a member.'

...

'We doubt if it is right to describe a member claiming damages for misrepresentation or breach of a contractual warranty when induced to subscribe for shares as being entitled to the damages in his character of a member, as his claim does not arise from a right which is part of the bundle of rights and obligations which make up his shares, though we acknowledge it has a relation to what the judge called the corporate nexus. But in our judgment, when a member claims damages for misrepresentation inducing him to purchase shares in the market, the damages are not due to him in his character of a member.' *Soden v British and Commonwealth Holdings plc (in administration)* [1996] 3 All ER 951 at 957, 963, CA, per Peter Gibson LJ

MEMBER OF A MISSION

[By s 16(1)(a) of the State Immunity Act 1978, the exception to immunity in s 4 does not apply to proceedings concerning the employment of 'members of a mission' within the meaning of the Vienna Convention on Diplomatic Relations (set out in Sch 1 to the Diplomatic Privileges Act 1964).] '[I]t is not disputed ... that as a secretary [the appellant] was a member of the embassy's administrative and technical staff, being employed in the embassy's administrative and technical service. But it is submitted for her that she was not a member of the mission because the ordinary meaning of "mission" is a body of persons sent to a foreign country to serve their home government, and Mrs Ahmed was not sent from Saudi Arabia but was a locally recruited British citizen, employed in a clerical capacity and without any diplomatic status. However, Mr Hoyle recognises from the convention itself, if nowhere else, that the members of the mission cannot be limited to those who enter the United Kingdom by reason of being sent from the state in question: they include those who are already in the United Kingdom and whose appointments are notified to the Foreign and Commonwealth Office (art 39). Mrs Ahmed's appointment was not so notified. More particularly, he said that the term "members of a mission" means those who are actually or notionally sent from abroad by the state.

'The industrial tribunal were unanimous in rejecting the argument based on membership of a mission, and in my judgment they were plainly right to do so. In my opinion the only question on this point is whether Mrs Ahmed is a member of a mission within the meaning of art 1, that question being relevant to whether Saudi Arabia is immune as respects proceedings relating to her contract of employment ... There is nothing in s 16(1)(a) of the 1978 Act nor in art 1 of the convention that links membership of a mission with the tests laid down, for example, in art 39 as to the persons who are entitled to enjoy privileges and immunities and as to the time when that enjoyment commences ...

'In my judgment, whether or not the appointment of a member of the mission is notified to the Foreign and Commonwealth Office, a person who falls within the definition of "members of a mission" is a member of the mission for the purposes of s 16(1)(a). To my mind it is clear that by being a member of the embassy staff employed in the administrative and technical service of the embassy, she was a member of the mission.' *Ahmed v Government of the Kingdom of Saudi Arabia* [1996] 2 All ER 248 at 251–252, CA, per Peter Gibson LJ

MEMBERSHIP (OF A TRADE ORGANISATION)

[Person offered a pupillage by a set of chambers was unable to take up pupillage because of ill-health and asked for postponement for one year, which was refused. He brought a claim for disability discrimination before an employment tribunal, relying on s 13 of the Disability Discrimination Act 1995 which makes it unlawful for a trade organisation to discriminate against a disabled person in the terms on which it was prepared to admit him to 'membership' of the organisation, or by refusing to accept, or deliberately not accepting, his application for 'membership'. The definition of 'trade organisation' includes an organisation whose members carry on a particular profession. On a challenge by the chambers to its jurisdiction, the tribunal held that the complainant could pursue his claim because his application for pupillage was an application for 'membership' of a trade organisation for the purposes of s 13 of the 1995 Act. That decision was reversed by the Employment Appeal Tribunal, which held that a person applying to a set of chambers for pupillage was not applying to become a member of those chambers.] '[2] The issue on this appeal is whether a pupil barrister has "membership" of a trade organisation. It is not in dispute on this appeal that the barristers' chambers where the pupil is doing his pupillage with a pupil master who is a member of those chambers is a trade organisation within s 13(4) of the 1995 Act.

...

'[7] On the issue of membership, the ET referred to the definitions in the *Shorter Oxford English Dictionary* of "member" and "membership". It said that there were various definitions of "member" but that the only one relevant for its purposes was: "Each individual belonging to a society or assembly ... one who takes part in anything." It referred to "membership" being defined as: "The condition or status of being a member of a society etc." It looked at what it called "the components of a set of chambers' and referred to five categories: (1) barristers who are the members of chambers as defined in the chambers' constitution, (2) the senior and deputy clerk who have under that constitution the status of members, (3) barristers who are not members of the chambers under the constitution but practise from the chambers as "door tenants' or "squatters', (4) pupils, (5) staff. Of pupils, the ET said:

> "Then we have the pupils, who spend a fixed term of one year in chambers. During the first six months they are not allowed to undertake any court work, although they do assist the other members of chambers in connection with research and general preparation. They receive a modest regular payment during their pupillage and in the second six months they are able to undertake court work, and when they do so they go to court as representatives of the chambers."

'[8] The ET asked itself which of those categories were members of the trade organisation under s 13. It considered that a purposive construction should be applied and the ordinary dictionary meaning of the term used rather than the specified definition in the chambers' constitution. It accepted that pupils could not be members of the chambers under their constitution nor under Bar Council regulations, but it said that that did not mean that pupils could not qualify for protection under s 13 and it said that it was persuaded that "the pupils are at least members of the chambers in the sense that they have the statutory protection accorded to such persons". It referred to the fact that the Sex Discrimination Act 1975 and the Race Relations Act 1976 have sections which are the equivalent of s 13 and that in 1990 by amending legislation a new s 35A was introduced into the 1975 Act and a new s 26A was introduced into the 1976 Act to deal with discrimination by barristers against applicants for pupillage or tenancy. It noted that the 1995 Act contained no provision equivalent to s 35A and s 26A, but that it is to be amended from October 2004 to contain such a provision. However, the EAT thought it purposeless to speculate on the reasons for such omission in the 1995 Act and for the intended inclusion later this year. It looked at the chambers' constitution and drew a distinction between a trainee, which is what a pupil is, and a tenant in the chambers ...

...

'[15] The issue before us is one of statutory construction. The terms "member" and "membership" are not defined and accordingly they must be given their ordinary meaning in the context in which they are used. That does not mean that one out of a number of dictionary meanings should be adopted as the ET did, particularly when the dictionary meanings it selected were those for membership of a society or assembly. The context of "member" and "membership" which is relevant is that of being a member or membership of a trade organisation, and by s 13(4) the definition includes an organisation whose members carry on a particular profession or trade. That in itself is sufficient to invalidate Mr O'Dempsey's impossibly wide definitions of all who, he says, fall within the concept of membership of a trade organisation. If he is right on his test of not being a mere visitor to the organisation or having a relationship other than that of a member of the public with the organisation or his ground 5 definition, included within the membership of a trade organisation would be persons who in ordinary parlance would never be called members of it, for example the cleaning lady engaged to dust and clean the premises, or the junior clerk in a set of barristers' chambers, or the mini-pupil still at school or university, wanting to see what life was like at the Bar and obtaining some work experience. None of them carries on the profession of a barrister.

'[16] Mr O'Dempsey's invocation of a purposive approach in social legislation such as the discrimination legislation so as to give an inclusive meaning to "membership" and "member" is one that I view with caution. The 1995 Act is not like the Act referred to in *Jones'* case [*Jones v Secretary of State for Social Services*] by Lord Diplock in his dissenting speech. There, as Lord Diplock pointed out ([1972] 1 All ER 145 at 181, [1972] AC 944 at 1005), the social purpose of injury benefit was to provide the claimant with an income for a period not exceeding six months from the date of the accident while he was incapable of work. The benefit would fail in its social purpose unless it was allowed quickly, and Parliament, Lord Diplock said, must have contemplated a simple and speedy procedure in the majority of cases. In the discrimination legislation, Parliament has not proscribed all discrimination but has made unlawful discrimination in certain fields only and in those fields by the statutory language it has limited the circumstances where discrimination is unlawful. Of course it is right to give the statutory language determining those circumstances as broad a construction as the language can reasonably bear, but it would be wrong to give the ordinary and readily understandable words in s 13 some artificially extended meaning, and in my judgment that is what Mr O''Dempsey is asking us to do.

'[17] However, I would also reject Mr Napier's submission that assistance on the meaning of "membership" in s 13, applying as it does to trade organisations and not making specific references to the Bar, can be obtained from the meaning given in s 35A of the 1975 Act and s 26A of the 1976 Act to terms other than "member" or "membership" in a section confined to the Bar.

...

'[23] I conclude that as a matter of ordinary language a pupil in a set of barristers' chambers is not a member of that set and that Mr Horton in applying for pupillage with the chambers was not applying for membership of the chambers. We have not been referred to the position in respect of other trade organisations. I do not doubt that there could be situations analogous to that of pupillage at the Bar, to which the same approach should apply.' *Horton v Higham* [2004] EWCA Civ 941 at [2], [7]–[8], [15]–[17], [23], [2004] 3 All ER 852, CA, per Peter Gibson LJ

MEMORANDUM OF ASSOCIATION

[For 7 Halsbury's Laws (4th edn) para 197 see now 7(1) Halsbury's Laws (4th edn) (2004 Reissue) para 285.]

MENS REA

[For 11 Halsbury's Laws (4th edn) para 4 see now 11(1) Halsbury's Laws (4th edn) (Reissue) para 10.]

MENTAL DISORDER

[For 30 Halsbury's Laws (4th edn) paras 1001, 1003 see now 30 Halsbury's Laws (4th edn) (Reissue) paras 1202, 1203.]

MENTALLY SUBNORMAL

New Zealand [Section 138 of the Crimes Act 1961 provides:

'138. Sexual intercourse with severely subnormal woman or girl—
(1) Every one is liable to imprisonment for a term not exceeding 7 years who has or attempts to have sexual intercourse with a woman or girl who is severely subnormal, if he knows or has good reason to believe that she is severely subnormal.
(2) For the purposes of this section, a woman or girl is severely subnormal if she is mentally subnormal, within the meaning of the Mental Health Act 1969, to the extent that she is incapable of living an independent life or of guarding herself against serious exploitation or common physical dangers.'

The Mental Health Act 1969 defines mentally subnormal as 'suffering from subnormality of intelligence as a result of arrested or incomplete development of mind'.]

'[7] As it happens the Mental Health Act 1969 has been repealed and replaced by the Mental Health (Compulsory Assessment and Treatment) Act 1992, which came into force on 1 November 1992. It is plain however that the definition remains for the purposes of the Crimes Act and prescribes when a person is mentally subnormal: that is "suffering from subnormality of intelligence as a result of arrested or incomplete development of mind". Important of course, is the additional requirement prescribed by subs (2) of s 138 of the Crimes Act, namely that the person must be incapable of living an independent life or of guarding herself against serious exploitation or common physical dangers.' *R v Richardson* [2001] 3 NZLR 620 (CA) at 621 per cur

MERCANTILE AGENT

[For 1 Halsbury's Laws (4th edn) para 712 see now 1(2) Halsbury's Laws (4th edn) (Reissue) para 12.]

MERE EQUITY

Australia 'As has been often observed, the Courts have not laid down a clear dividing line between an equitable interest in property and what is described as "a mere equity". The difficulties of categorisation were recognised well before the decision in *Phillips v Phillips* (1861) 4 De GF & J 208; (1861) 45 ER 1164 and have not been resolved despite much erudite judicial and academic discussion since then: see e g *Double Bay Newspapers Pty Ltd v A W Holdings Pty Ltd* (1996) 42 NSWLR 409 at 423E; Megarry and Wade, *The Law of Real Property* (2000) 6th ed, para 5–013; *Snell's Equity* (2000) 30th ed, para 2–05; (1955) 71 LQR 480; Meagher, Gummow and Lehane, *Equity Doctrines and Remedies* (1992) 3rd ed, para 427ff.

'Equitable, or proprietary, interests and "mere equities" alike depend for their very existence upon the fundamental concept that equity acts *in personam* and that the rights which it recognises and enforces are not rights *in rem* but rights *in personam*. So, for example, the beneficiary of a bare trust of land is said to have an equitable interest in the land because an equity court, acting upon the conscience of the trustee, will compel the trustee to deal with the land in a certain way for the benefit of the cestui que trust. Likewise, the purchaser of land under an uncompleted contract for sale is said to have an equitable interest in the property, but only because it is tacitly assumed that a court of equity will grant specific performance of the contract. In examples such as these, the equitable interest is commensurate with the availability and extent of the corresponding right *in personam*: see e g *Glenn v Federal Cmr of Land Tax* (1915) 20 CLR 490 at 503–4 per Isaacs J; *Central Trust and Safe Deposit Co v Snider* [1916] 1 AC 266 at 272; *Brown v Heffer* (1967) 116 CLR 344 at 349; *DKLR Holding Co (No 2) Pty Ltd v Cmr of Stamp Duties* [1980] 1 NSWLR 510 at 518ff.

'It follows that if the equity court would not enforce the right *in personam* – where, for example, it has been lost by acquiescence, laches, delay or some other circumstance affording a defence – then the equitable interest might either never have existed in the first place or might have ceased to exist: see *Central Trust and Safe Deposit Co* at 272.

'A right enforceable *in personam* in equity confers an equitable, or proprietary, interest only when there is a nexus of sufficient propinquity between the right and the specific property to which the right relates. What is a nexus of sufficient propinquity is the conundrum. It has been recognised that "there is some circuity involved in finding the starting point for the existence of … an equitable interest, the problem being to isolate as the initiating factor the proprietary interest or the right to enforce the interest … This problem is almost a jurisprudential mystery": per Kearney J in *Burns Philp Trustee Co Ltd v Viney* [1981] 2 NSLWR 216 at 223.

'Many definitions of an equitable interest have been attempted and found wanting. For example, in *National Provincial Bank Ltd v Ainsworth* [1965] AC 1175, at 1248, Lord Wilberforce identified such an interest as being one which was "definable, identifiable by third parties, capable in its nature of assumption by third parties and [having] some degree of permanence or stability". That definition has been much criticised: see Meagher, Gummow

and Lehane, *Equity Doctrines and Remedies* (1992) 3rd ed, para 428. There is probably no point in attempting any universal definition. As Kearney J said in *Burns Philp Trustee Co Ltd v Viney* at 223–4:

"… there is an obvious difficulty in endeavouring both to analyse and to formulate any general principle in this area of the law. The administration of equity has always paid regard to the infinite variety of interests and has refrained from formulating or adhering to fixed universal and exhaustive criteria with which to deal with such varying situations. The approach traditionally adopted by equity has been to retain flexibility so as to accommodate the multitudinous instances in which fundamental equitable rules fall to be applied."

'Like an "equitable interest", a "mere equity" is a slippery creature. It can be cornered and illuminated by example but not captured and confined by definition. For present purposes, the most illuminating example is found in [*Latec Investments Ltd v Hotel Terrigal Pty Ltd (in liq)* (1965) 113 CLR 265]. There, a mortgagee fraudulently exercised a power of sale, so that as against the mortgagee and the collusive purchaser the mortgagor had a right in equity to set aside the conveyance. However, the rights of a third party had intervened in the meantime so that the competition was between the mortgagor, claiming an equitable interest in the land which was prior to that of the third party, and the third party who claimed a subsequent equitable interest acquired for value without notice of what it said was the mortgagor's "mere equity".

'There was disagreement between Kitto and Taylor JJ as to whether the mortgagor had a prior equitable interest in the property. Kitto J was of the view, on the authority of *Phillips v Phillips*, that the mortgagor had to make good its right in equity to have the fraudulent conveyance set aside before the mortgagor could be said to have an equitable interest in the land, namely, its equity of redemption. As between the mortgagor and the third party, the competition was, according to his Honour, between a "preliminary equity" – that is, a claim to set aside the conveyance for fraud – and an admitted subsequent equitable interest. His Honour was of the opinion that *Phillips v Phillips* compelled the conclusion that the "preliminary equity" was a "mere equity" which could not compete with the subsequent equitable interest acquired for value without notice: at 277–9.

'On the other hand, Taylor J was of the view that the mortgagor had never been deprived of its equitable interest in the property by the voidable fraudulent conveyance. On the authority of cases decided both before and after *Phillips v Phillips*, his Honour concluded that the owner of an equitable interest in property who is induced by fraud to transfer it continues to retain that equitable interest: it does not cease upon the transfer and then come into existence again when the transfer is set aside: at 281–4.

'However, Taylor J concluded that the true principle enunciated in *Phillips v Phillips* was simply that where the person entitled to a prior equitable interest requires the assistance of a court of equity to remove an impediment to his or her title as a preliminary to asserting it, the court will not interfere if a third person has acquired an equitable interest in the property for value without notice before the prior equitable interest holder comes to the court for assistance: at 286.

'The approach of Menzies J was to attempt to reconcile the two apparently conflicting streams of authority relied upon by Kitto and Taylor JJ. His Honour would recognise that an equitable right could be a "mere equity" in the sense adopted by Kitto J for the purpose of a priority contest with an equitable interest and yet could be an "equitable interest" for the purpose of transmission by devise or assignment: at 290–1. In the result, therefore, Menzies J agreed with the position taken by Kitto J.

'*Latec Investments* has been judicially considered on very many occasions and I will not contribute yet another exegesis. My own view, which reflects the approach taken by Menzies J, is that *Phillips v Phillips* can be explained as a policy decision rather than a decision resting on distinctions in the qualities of various equitable rights. The policy is simply this: where the holder of a prior equitable interest needs the assistance of the equity court to perfect his or her title to it, that equitable interest will be defeated if, before the title is perfected, a third party takes an equitable interest for value without notice.

'Perfecting the title to an equitable interest does not mean resolving a dispute as to its existence in the first place, as where, for example, parties disagree as to whether a document has created an equitable charge and a declaration is sought from the equity court. Perfecting the title means seeking an equitable remedy without which a previously existing equitable interest would be lost.' *Mills v Ruthol Pty Ltd* BC200201632; [2002] NSWSC 294 at [121]–[132], per Palmer J

MERGER

[For 39 Halsbury's Laws (4th edn) paras 598, 599 see now 39(2) Halsbury's Laws (4th edn) (Reissue) paras 255–256.]

MESNE PROFITS

[For 27 Halsbury's Laws (4th edn) para 255 see now 27(1) Halsbury's Laws (4th edn) (Reissue) para 258.]

MIDNIGHT

New Zealand 'In ordinary usage, I think, midnight means the end of the day.' *Secretary for Justice v New Zealand Public Service Association Inc* [1990] 2 NZLR 36 at 42, CA, per Cooke P

MILK

[The Food Act 1984 is largely repealed.]
'Milk' includes cream and skimmed or separated milk. (Food Safety Act 1990, s 53(1))

MINE

[The Mines and Quarries Act 1954, s 180 has been further amended by the Management and Administration of Safety and Health in Mines Regulations 1993, SI 1993/1897. The definition is now as follows.] 'Mine' means an excavation or system of excavations, including all such excavations to which a common system of ventilation is provided, made for the purpose of, or in connection with, the getting, wholly or substantially by means involving the employment of persons below ground, of minerals (whether in their natural state or in solution or suspension) or products of minerals.

[For 31 Halsbury's Laws (4th edn) para 1 see now 31 Halsbury's Laws (4th edn) (2003 Reissue) para 5.]

Open mine

[For 31 Halsbury's Laws (4th edn) para 3 see now 31 Halsbury's Laws (4th edn) (2003 Reissue) para 7.]

MINERAL DEPOSITS

[The Capital Allowances Act 1968 has been repealed. The definition is now contained in the Capital Allowances Act 1990, s 161(2), as follows.] 'Mineral deposits' includes any natural deposits capable of being lifted or extracted from the earth and, for this purpose, geothermal energy, whether in the form of aquifers, hot dry rocks or otherwise, shall be treated as a natural deposit.

MINERALS

[For 31 Halsbury's Laws (4th edn) para 8 see now 31 Halsbury's Laws (4th edn) (2003 Reissue) para 12.]

MINING OPERATIONS

Australia 'Pursuant to the definition of "mining operations" now inserted in s 164(7) [of the Customs Act 1901 (Cth)], "mining operations" means, inter alia, the mining for minerals or the beneficiation of minerals as an integral part of operations for the recovery of minerals and that meaning extends to the production of common salt by evaporation.' *Dampier Salt (Operations) Pty Ltd v Collector of Customs* (1995) 133 ALR 502 at 509, per Lee J

MISAPPROPRIATION

Australia 'The word "misappropriates" in [the Crimes Act 1914 (Cth)] s 71(1) does not refer to the way in which the property is used but to its wrongful appropriation. That is not to deny that use can, in appropriate circumstances, constitute an appropriation. Cf *Wilson v Woodrow* (1987) 26 A Crim R 387, a case on s 73(4) of the Crimes Act 1958. But if, for example, I use my own stationery to perpetrate a deception, that is not a fraudulent misappropriation of the stationery. Accordingly, if the accused believed that the money order forms belonged to them, they could not be convicted of the offences with which they were charged even if they subsequently used the forms for a fraudulent purpose.' *Lawrence* (1996) 86 A Crim R 412 at 420, per Calloway JA

MISAPPROPRIATION OR DEFALCATION WHILE ACTING IN A FIDUCIARY CAPACITY

Canada 'Thus, there appear to be two approaches which have been taken to the interpretation of the words "misappropriation or defalcation while acting in a fiduciary capacity". On the one hand, the approach reflected in *Ironwood Investments Joint Venture v Leggett* and in *Jerrard v Peacock* views the words in the context of those with which they are associated in the paragraph and attributes to

them some element of dishonesty, wrongdoing, or misconduct. On the other hand, decisions such as that of the British Columbia Court of Appeal in *Smith v Henderson* suggest a broader interpretation which eschews the need for dishonesty, wrongdoing or misconduct and is prepared to extend the exception to all cases in which a fiduciary is in breach of any fiduciary obligation.

'In my view, the former approach is the correct one, having regard to the purposes of bankruptcy legislation and to the language used in section 178, and keeping in mind as well that not all breaches of obligation by a fiduciary are breaches of a *fiduciary* obligation. They may simply be inadvertence, negligence or incompetence.

'The courts have resisted a rigid approach to the determination of what constitutes a fiduciary relationship, as previously noted, emphasizing that it is "the nature of the relationship and not the category of actors involved" which is important for purposes of that exercise. In this same spirit, it seems to me, the courts should avoid attempting to sweep into concepts such as "misappropriation" or "defalcation"—which in their ordinary meanings connote some element of wrongdoing, improper conduct, or improper accounting—any and all failures by the fiduciary to comply with the obligations attending upon that capacity. When it comes to the application of insolvency legislation, the results of not resisting that temptation can be far reaching and inconsistent with the purposes of such legislation.

'The *Shorter Oxford Dictionary* defines the words "misappropriate", "defalcate", and "defalcation" as follows:

Misappropriate
To appropriate to wrong uses; chiefly, to apply dishonestly to one's own use. So, misappropriation.

Defalcate
To cut or lop off (a portion from the whole); to retrench, deduct; to curtail, reduce; to commit defalcations; to misappropriate property in one's charge.

Defalcation
To reduce by deductions; to lop off; to abate; defection; shortcoming; failure; a fraudulent deficiency in money matters; also, the amount misappropriated.

'*Black's Law Dictionary*, 6th ed, defines "misappropriation" as "the unauthorized, improper, or unlawful use of funds or other property for purpose other than that for which intended".

'In *Smith v Henderson*, Legg JA cited the definition of "defalcation" from *Black's Law Dictionary*, 5th ed, in the following fashion (*supra*, p 158):

> "Defalcation: The act of a defaulter ... failure to meet an obligation ..."

'Respectfully, this citation omits important aspects of the full definition, and takes the phrase "failure to meet an obligation" out of context. The full definition in the 5th edition of *Black's Law Dictionary* reads as follows:

> Defalcation
> The act of a defaulter; act of embezzling; failure to meet an obligation; misappropriation of trust funds or money held in any fiduciary capacity; failure to properly account for such funds. Commonly spoken of officers of corporations or public officials.

'Looked at in its entirety, then, the *Black's* definition demonstrates that the reference to a failure to meet an obligation must be read in the context of the references to "embezzling", to "misappropriation of trust funds" and to a "failure to properly account". Moreover, an examination of the American authorities on which the inclusion by *Black's* of "failure to meet an obligation" within the concept of defalcation for purposes of bankruptcy legislation, confirms that they can be explained in these terms, notwithstanding that they may appear on the surface to stand for the proposition that an innocent default in duty on the part of a fiduciary will suffice to create a debt that survives bankruptcy.' *Simone v Daly* (1999) 170 DLR (4th) 215 at 230–231, 231–233, Ont CA, per Blair J (ad hoc)

MISBEHAVIOUR

Australia [In the context of summary dismissal under a written contract of employment.] '[446] The concept of "misbehaviour" used in the contract is not a concept that appears to have been the subject of judicial consideration in respect of the right of summary dismissal.

'[447] However "misbehaviour" is analogous to "misconduct" at common law. In *North v Television Corporation Ltd* (1976) 11 ALR 599 at 608–9 Smithers and Evatt JJ of the Australian Industrial Court held:

> It is of assistance to consider the expression "misconduct" by reference to subject matter to which it is related and the context in which it appears. The subject matter is the termina-

tion by one party against the will of another of a continuing contract of employment on the ground of breach of one of the terms of the contract. And the context is such as to indicate that certain breaches of a non-serious nature, some of which would be within the connotation of misconduct, are not regarded as grounds for termination. In such a situation it is reasonable to interpret the expression "misconduct" as referring to *conduct so seriously in breach of the contract that by standards of fairness and justice the employer should not be bound to continue the employment*.

(Emphasis added)

'[This passage was cited with approval by the Full Industrial Court in *Brackenridge v Toyota Motor Corporation Australia Ltd* (1996) 142 ALR 99 at 107, Wilcox CJ in *Gooley v Westpac Banking Corp* (1995) 129 ALR 628 and Young J in *Galipienzo v Solution 6 Holdings Ltd* (1998) 28 ACSR 139. Also see Einfeld J in *Sheldrick v WT Partnership (Aust) Pty Ltd* (1998) 89 IR 206.]

'[448] Revisiting the common law situation is of utility, remembering always that the Court is of course presently dealing with a question of contract construction:

- It is trite law to state that, since the early nineteenth century, a defined spectrum of classes of conduct have developed within the common law of employment which justify the summary dismissal of an employee. Such behaviours include:
  - "Misconduct", being a general term encompassing (without restriction) insolence (*Vardy v Cuthbert* (1872) 3 AJR 25), abusive language (*Farley v Lums* (1917) 19 WALR 117), drunkenness (*Meyrick v Stirling Bros Ltd* (1899) 1 WALR 51), physical assault (*Brackenridge v Toyota Motor Corp Australia Ltd* (1996) 142 ALR 99) and sexual impropriety (*Orr v University of Tasmania* (1957) 100 CLR 526).
  - "Disobedience", being the wilful disregard of instructions lawfully and reasonably made: *Turner v Mason* (1845) 14 M & W 112; *Adami v Maison de Luxe Ltd* (1924) 35 CLR 143.
  - "Incompetence", being the failure by an employee to afford an employer of the degree of skill expressly or impliedly warranted: *Harmer v Cornelius* (1858) 5 CB (NS) 236.

- Notwithstanding the plethora of authorities bearing upon the question of the circumstances in which a summary dismissal will be justified, there are no rules of law which dictate either, first, the precise nature of the manifold behaviours that potentially give rise to a right of summary dismissal or, second, the degree of such conduct required before that right is enlivened. That is to say, as put by Lord James of Hereford, speaking for the Privy Council on appeal from the New Zealand Court of Appeal in *Clouston & Co Ltd v Corry* [1906] AC 122 at 129, the resolution of this question is a matter of fact alone in that "[t]here is no fixed rule of law defining the degree of misconduct which will justify dismissal." Alternatively expressed by Starke and Evatt JJ in *Blyth Chemicals Ltd v Bushnell* (1933) 49 CLR 66 at 73, "[t]he degree of misconduct that will justify dismissal is usually a question of fact."

- Since the progressive repeal of the cognate Masters and Servants Acts in the late nineteenth century, the common law has posited the employment relationship as, at least in form, merely a species of commercial exchange governed by general principles of contract law. Consistency with this conception demands that the question of whether conduct justifying summary dismissal has occurred be determined by reference to the ordinary principles regarding the repudiation of contracts. In an early exposition of such an approach, Blackburn J in *Bettini v Gye* (1876) 1 QBD 183 at 188 posited as concerning whether the breach in question was of a term:

  > going to the root of the matter, so that a failure to perform it would render the performance of the rest of the contract by the plaintiff a thing different from what the defendant has stipulated for ...

'[449] To my mind both in terms of determining at common law whether or not the conduct of an employee is to be regarded as repudiatory or not such as to justify summary dismissal, as well as in terms of endeavouring to assess whether or not misbehaviour or breach of duty as used in cl 5.1(a) which here requires construction and application, the following considerations remain of particular significance:

- Emphasis on the whole of the relationship: As noted above, the most important consequence of the modern shift towards the application of general principles of contract law to the

summary dismissal context is that the conduct of the employee must be viewed in the context of the employment relationship as a whole. Rather than merely quantify the 'seriousness' or otherwise of the misconduct, the question must be considered in light of the employee's length of service, their demonstrated ability and their standards of prior conduct. Thus in *Sheldrick v WT Partnership (Aust) Pty Ltd & Ors* (1998) 89 IR 206 (FCA), an engineer employed by the respondent broke into a colleagues office by removing a pane of glass and inspected confidential memoranda in the course of an ongoing dispute as to management structures. While Einfeld J was of no compunction (at 235) in deeming such behaviour "thoughtless, immature and unwise", it was "certainly not grounds for the summary dismissal of a dedicated, loyal and longstanding employee who had proved his commitment to his employer by relocating to Asia from Australia with his entire family and agreeing to remain there for a significant period."

- Approach when misconduct isolated: There are authorities suggesting that the "contract of employment cannot be brought to an end by a single act of misconduct unless such single act of misconduct is of such aggravated character that it strikes the employment contract down immediately, completely and permanently": *Elcom v Electrical Trades Union of Australia, New South Wales Branch* (1983) 5 IR 267 (NSW Industrial Commission) at 270, per Macken J. My own view is that no such rule of thumb exists. I note however that in *Jupiter General Insurance Co Ltd v Ardeshir Bomanji Shroff* [1937] 3 All ER 67, and in consideration of the fact that "the immediate dismissal of an employee was seen as a strong measure", Lord Maugham stated (at 73–4) that:

  > it can be in exceptional circumstances only that an employer is acting properly in summarily dismissing an employee on his committing a single act of negligence.

- Motives of the employee relevant: Commensurate with the position that it will ordinarily be necessary to demonstrate that the employee has intended to repudiate his or her obligations under the contract of employment, the motives laying behind the conduct in question will be of relevance. Thus in *Blyth Chemicals*, it was stated by Dixon and McTiernan JJ (at 82) that "the effect to be given to all the acts combined, which have been established against the respondent, must in the end be governed by an estimate of his honesty and motives." (See also *Boston Deep Sea Fishing and Ice Co v Ansell* (1888) 39 Ch D 339 at 358, per Cotton LJ. Specifically, it will ordinarily be fatal for an employee to have acted contrary to the interests of the employer for his or her own personal pecuniary gain, given that such actions are inherently repugnant to the former remaining in a relationship of personal service with the latter.

'[450] Dixon and McTiernan JJ in *Blyth* at 81 spoke of:

conduct which in respect of important matters is incompatible with the fulfilment of an employee's duty, or involves an opposition, or conflict between his interest and his duty to his employer, or impedes the faithful performance of his obligations, or is destructive of the necessary confidence between employer and employee

'as being a ground of dismissal and at p 83 held that:

In the view we take of the circumstances of the case, the motives and intentions of the respondent [employee] become all-important; for the significance and sufficiency as a justification of the other items of misconduct relied upon appear to us to depend upon the truth of his explanation or the bona fides of his acts. Further, the effect to be given to all the acts combined, which have been established against the respondent, must in the end be governed by an estimate of his honesty and motives.

'[451] Significantly, the High Court held in that case that the burden of justifying the basis for a summary dismissal rests with the employer.

'[452] In the result "misbehaviour" in terms of cl 5.1(a) means substantial wrongful conduct such as to constitute an act of repudiation of the employment contract, being conduct inconsistent with the fulfilment of the employee's obligations to the employer. In that regard, Mr Randall's intentions in conducting himself in relation to the matters that are the subject of the dispute are important in determining the existence or otherwise of "misbehaviour".

...

'[471] The word "misbehaviour" should be read as one would read the expression "misconduct" as

referring to conduct so seriously in breach of the contract that by standards of fairness and justice the employer should not be bound to continue the employment.' *Randall v Aristocrat Leisure Ltd* [2004] NSWSC 411 at [446]–[452], [471], per Einstein J; BC200406880

MISCARRIAGE

[For 20 Halsbury's Laws (4th edn) para 119 see now 20(1) Halsbury's Laws (4th edn) (Reissue) para 140.]

MISCONDUCT (MEDICAL PRACTITIONER)

Australia 'The words used in the statutory test ("misconduct in a professional respect") plainly go beyond that negligence which would found a claim against a medical practitioner for damages: *Re Anderson* [(1967) 85 WN (NSW) at 575]. On the other hand gross negligence might amount to relevant misconduct particularly if accompanied by indifference to, or lack of concern for, the welfare of the patient: cf *Re Anderson* [at 575]. Departures from elementary and generally accepted standards, of which a medical practitioner could scarcely be heard to say that he or she was ignorant could amount to such professional misconduct: ibid. But the statutory test is not met by mere professional incompetence or by deficiencies in the practice of the profession. Something more is required. It includes a deliberate departure from accepted standards or such serious negligence as, although not deliberate, to portray indifference and an abuse of the privileges which accompany registration as a medical practitioner: cf *Allinson* [(1894) 1 QB 750] (at 760–761).' *Pillai v Messiter (No 2)* (1989) 16 NSWLR 197 at 200, per Kirby J

MISFEASANCE

[For 7 Halsbury's Laws (4th edn) para 1692 see now 7(3) Halsbury's Laws (4th edn) (1996 Reissue) para 2452.]

MISREPRESENTATION

[For 31 Halsbury's Laws (4th edn) paras 1044, 1045 see now 31 Halsbury's Laws (4th edn) (2003 Reissue) paras 742–743.]

Fraudulent misrepresentation

[For 31 Halsbury's Laws (4th edn) paras 1058, 1059 see now 31 Halsbury's Laws (4th edn) (2003 Reissue) paras 756–757.]

Innocent misrepresentation

[For 31 Halsbury's Laws (4th edn) para 1064 see now 31 Halsbury's Laws (4th edn) (2003 Reissue) para 763.]

MISSILE

Australia 'According to the *Shorter English Oxford Dictionary* (3rd ed), a "missile" is an object "capable of being thrown, adapted to be discharged from the hand or from a machine or engine … applied to weapons that discharge arrows, bullets, etc". The meaning is expressed in a similar way in the *Macquarie Dictionary* (2nd rev) — "an object or weapon that can be thrown, hurled or shot, as a stone, a bullet, a lance, or an arrow … capable of being thrown, hurled, or shot, as from the hand, or gun, etc"… I do not think the dictionary definitions exclude a liquid from being a missile. It is capable of being thrown and from the hand … If an object is capable of being thrown, it comes within the ordinary English meaning of "missile".' *Field and South Australia v Gent* (1996) 87 A Crim R 225 at 229, per Mullighan J

MISLEADING OR DECEPTIVE

New Zealand [Section 9 of the Fair Trading Act 1986 provides that 'No person shall, in trade, engage in conduct that is misleading or deceptive …'.] 'An omission to provide information may be misleading or deceptive conduct.

…

'Silence may constitute misleading or deceptive conduct, but whether it does is to be objectively assessed in all the circumstances: *Gregory v Rangitikei District Council* [1995] 2 NZLR 208; *Mills v United Building Society* [1988] 2 NZLR 392; *Smythe v Bayley's Real Estate Ltd* (1993) 5 TCLR 454; *Lam v Austinel Investments Australia Pty Ltd* (1989) ATPR 40–990; *Rhône-Poulenc Agrochimie SA v UIM Chemical Services Pty Ltd* (1986) 12 FCR 477. Conduct not misleading or deceptive may become so by an omission to inform arising out of altered circumstances: *Gregory v Rangitikei District Council*. Conduct may be misleading or deceptive within the meaning of s 9 of the Fair Trading Act 1986 by an omission to provide information even if no obligation to provide such information exists as a matter of general law, outside the standards of conduct required by the Fair Trading Act. The question whether conduct is misleading or deceptive is substantially a question of fact and degree: *Goldsbro v Walker* [1993] 1

NZLR 394 at p 401 per Richardson J. Whether conduct is to be so characterised does not turn on any intention to mislead or deceive: *Hornsby Building Information Centre Pty Ltd v Sydney Building Information Centre Ltd* (1978) 140 CLR 216 at p 233 per Murphy J. It is to be objectively assessed: *Mills v United Building Society* at p 413. It is necessary, however, that the conduct is deceptive or misleading or is "likely" to mislead or deceive, a point emphasised by McGechan J in *Gregory.*' *Des Forges v Wright* [1996] 2 NZLR 758 at 764 per Elias J

MISTAKE

[For 32 Halsbury's Laws (4th edn) paras 3, 4 see now 32 Halsbury's Laws (4th edn) (Reissue) paras 3–4.]

MODEL

New Zealand [Defined in s 2 of the Copyright Act 1976.] 'While initially hesitant I now see the force of the conclusion that a true prototype garment can be regarded as a model. The medium in which the model is made can hardly be decisive. Models are often made of wood or clay or plasticine but there seems no reason in logic why for the purposes of the fashion industry, a model should not be made of some other material, i e the material with which the finished product is to be made. I therefore accept that a prototype garment is capable of being a model with the definition.' *Bonz Group (Pty) Ltd v Cooke* [1994] 3 NZLR 216 at 221, per Tipping J

MODIFY

New Zealand [The Law Practitioners Act 1982, s 118(3) allows the court on appeal from the New Zealand Law Practitioners Disciplinary Tribunal to 'confirm, reverse, or modify the order or decision appealed against'.] 'General dictionary meanings suggest that the word "modify" in respect of a penalty generally carries a connotation of reduction in severity. Thus:

Funk & Wagnall's New Standard Dictionary (1924):

> "**1.** To make somewhat different; change more or less in character, properties, form, or application; limit or restrict; vary; as, to modify the details of a plan; local causes modify climate; adverbs modify verbs. **2.** To make more moderate or less sweeping; reduce in degree or extent; qualify; as, to modify a punishment."

Webster's New International Dictionary (1938):

"**1.** To limit; also, to mitigate; assuage. Obs.
2. To reduce in extent or degree; to moderate; qualify; lower; as, to modify heat, pain, punishment. 'He modifies his first severe decree'. Dryden.
3. To differentiate into, or diversify by, different forms, as light, sound, passion; – now merged in sense **4.**
4. To change somewhat the form or qualities of; to alter somewhat; as, to modify the terms of a contract."

New Standard Oxford English Dictionary (1993):

"**2.** Limit, restrain; appease, assuage.
3. Make partial or minor changes to; alter without radical transformation. Orig esp qualify or moderate (a statement etc), alter so as to improve."

'In *Souter v Souter* [1921] NZLR 716 where the words used in a codicil to a will were "to modify and alter my said will", Cooper J held that:

"One of the primary meanings of the word 'modify' is, no doubt, 'to limit' or 'restrict', but it also means 'to vary' and there is authority that it may even mean 'to extend' or 'enlarge' [referring to *Stevens v General Steam Navigation Co* [1903] 1 KB 890 which related to the word 'modification' used in respect of an Act re-enacting a repealed Act]."

'Notwithstanding that the general tenor of dictionary definitions favours as a primary meaning of "modify" to assuage or reduce in severity, there are two matters arising from the context of the Act which persuade us that the word "modify" in s 118(3) allows the Court to impose on appeal a more severe penalty than has been imposed by the tribunal:
'(1) It is illogical to suggest that the Court on appeal can only reduce the severity of an order of the tribunal as to penalty when a right to appeal is given to the complainant as well as to the practitioner;
'(2) Section 119(2) as to publication in the *Gazette* of the result of a disciplinary proceeding provides specifically for situations "Where an appeal against any such order [of the tribunal] results in the name of a practitioner being ordered to be struck off or restored to the roll". This plainly contemplates that the most severe penalty against a practitioner may be imposed as well as remitted on appeal.'

Wellington District Law Society v Cummins [1998] 3 NZLR 363 at 366–367, per cur

MOLESTATION

Australia 'The Oxford English Dictionary 2nd ed, vol IX (1991) refers to "molestation" as "the action of molesting, or the condition of being molested; annoyance; hostile or vexatious interference; vexation; distress". "Molest" is given a number of meanings including "to cause trouble, grief, or vexation"; "to interfere with or meddle with (a person) injuriously or with hostile intent". Interestingly, none of the meanings refer to sexual assault. Similarly, the Macquarie Dictionary (1981 1st ed) defines "molest" to mean "to interfere with annoyingly, injuriously or with hostile intent" but the 2nd edition (1990) and the 3rd edition (1997) give as its prime meaning "to assault sexually", and as its second meaning "to interfere with annoyingly or injuriously". Butterworths Australian Legal Dictionary (eds Dr P E Nygh and P Butt) (1997) also refer to two meanings:

"to act with the intent to annoy, and to annoy with ordinary and reasonable feeling: *In the Marriage of Moio* [1984] FLC 91–575 … In relation to a child, to abuse sexually."

'In *R v Cook* (1983) 37 RFL (2d) 93 (Ontario Provincial Court) Naismith Prov J said of the expression "sexual molestation" appearing in s 47 of the Child Welfare Act (Ontario):

"There has been much said about the fact that there is no definition of sexual molestation in the Act. And we were referred to some definitions. Oxford defines molestation as annoyance, hostile or vexatious interference. Webster defines it as a cause or state of harassment. Counsel has shown me a definition of molest which begins: 'molest is a wide ranging word which I should be reluctant to define or paraphrase …' I don't think I want to go any further with definitions. Obviously there are a number of definitions of 'molestation'; and of 'condition' and of 'sexual', but unfortunately none in the Act to help us as to just exactly what the legal test is … it is not clear as to precisely what a 'condition of sexual molestation' is."

'I think what these references show is that the word "molestation" had, at the time … at least two principle meanings, one of which was to assault sexually.' *JSV (by their Litigation Guardian SRV) v*

Christian Outreach Centre (2000) 156 FLR 174; BC200003108; [2000] NTSC 36 at [7], [8], per Midren J

MONEY

General meaning

[For 32 Halsbury's Laws (4th edn) paras 102, 102 see now 32 Halsbury's Laws (4th edn) (Reissue) paras 101–102.]

Australia 'The question is whether … credit by term deposit with the respondent is properly described as "money" within the meaning of the Companies (WA) Code s 401(3). I am inclined to think that money placed on term deposit would remain "money" within the meaning of the section. The term "money" itself is commonly regarded as being one which does not bear a single precise meaning in the eyes of the law. The meaning of the term depends on the context in which it is used. And so, since the House of Lords decision in *Perrin v Morgan* [1943] AC 399, in the context of testamentary instruments one finds the term taking on a number of possible meanings to include, as in that case, all the testator's personal property and sometimes, even all real and personal property. The term has been held, because of the context, to include sums standing to the credit of a bank account: *Re Collings, Jones v Collings* [1933] Ch 920.' *Lean as liquidator of Trison Australian Pty Ltd (in liq) v Commissioners of the Rural & Industries Bank Ltd* (1991) 5 ACSR 455 at 459, per Murray J

In will

[For 50 Halsbury's Laws (4th edn) para 478 see now 50 Halsbury's Laws (4th edn) (Reissue) para 532.]

MONOPOLY

[For 47 Halsbury's Laws (4th edn) paras 68, 71 see now 47 Halsbury's Laws (4th edn) (Reissue) paras 102, 105.]

MONTH

[For 45 Halsbury's Laws (4th edn) paras 1107–1111 see now 45(2) Halsbury's Laws (4th edn) (Reissue) paras 207–211 .]

Calendar month

[For 45 Halsbury's Laws (4th edn) paras 1107–1111 see now 45(2) Halsbury's Laws (4th edn) (Reissue) paras 207–211.]

MOORED

In good safety

[For 25 Halsbury's Laws (4th edn) para 137 see now 25 Halsbury's Laws (4th edn) (2003 Reissue) para 316.]

MORAL DUTY

Australia [Inheritance (Family and Dependants Provision) Act 1972 (WA) s 6.] '[18] Of all the cases that have come to this Court under the testator's family maintenance legislation of the various States, I have been able to find only three in which there is no reference in any of the judgments to concepts of moral claims or moral obligations. There may be others but, in any event, they are rare. Sometimes, reference has been made to "natural claims". In *Coates v National Trustees Executors and Agency Co Ltd*, Dixon CJ, having referred to the decision of the Privy Council in *Bosch*, spoke of an adult son's "natural claims upon [his mother's] testamentary bounty" which "were much strengthened by his co-operation and support in the conduct of her business and of her affairs." The context makes it plain that what Dixon CJ described as "natural claims" were the same as what Salmond J had in mind in referring to a testator's "moral duty".

'[19] The same approach has been taken by the Supreme Court of Canada to corresponding legislation. In 1994, in *Tataryn v Tataryn*, McLachlin J, responding to an argument that the "moral duty" approach was inappropriate because of its uncertainty, said:

> If the phrase "adequate, just and equitable" is viewed in light of current societal norms, much of the uncertainty disappears. Furthermore, two sorts of norms are available and both must be addressed. The first are the obligations which the law would impose on a person during his or her life were the question of provision for the claimant to arise. These might be described as legal obligations. The second type of norms are found in society's reasonable expectations of what a judicious person would do in the circumstances, by

reference to contemporary community standards. These might be called moral obligations, following the language traditionally used by the courts.

...

'[24] Reference has been made earlier to various elements of the legislative scheme to which, in the past, judges have related ideas of moral claims and moral duty: the matter of "proper" provision; the making, by court order, of "fit" provision; the determination as to where the burden of an order should fall; and the question of character or conduct disentitling an applicant to provision. The same ideas have also been significant as a restraint upon unwarranted judicial intervention ...'

...

'[68] In his judgments in *Goodman v Windeyer* and in *Hughes*, Murphy J expressed dissatisfaction with this focus upon notions of "moral duty" and "moral claim". His Honour stressed that the entitlement to make a claim was to be found in the terms of the statute. The applicant was not to be put additionally to the proof of a "moral claim". Nor did the existence of a "moral claim" remedy the absence in a particular case of an ability to make a claim under the legislation ...

...

'[73] "Moral duty" may often have been used as a convenient shorthand expression intended to do no more than invite attention to the questions presented by the relevant legislation. Its use, however, has led to reference being made to the "moral claims" of those who seek further provision and that is an expression which is liable to being misunderstood just as its progenitor "moral duty" may mislead. It is therefore better to forgo any convenience that these shorthand expressions may offer in favour of adherence to the relevant statutory language. In *Permanent Trustee Co Ltd v Fraser*, Kirby P and Sheller JA correctly indicated that what was said in the joint judgment in *Singer* should henceforth provide an appropriate guide to the construction and operation of the family provision legislation.' *Vigolo v Bostin* [2005] HCA 11 at [18]–[19], [24], per Gleeson CJ, [68], [73], per Gummow and Heydon JJ; BC200500902

MORE APPROPRIATE TO THE CASE IN QUESTION

[Under s 1(1) of the Damages Act 1996, the court was required, when determining the rate to be expected from the investment of a sum awarded as damages for future pecuniary loss in an action for personal injury, to take into account such rate of return as might from time to time be prescribed by the Lord Chancellor. Section 1(2) provided that sub-s (1) did not prevent the court taking a different rate of return into account if any party to the proceedings showed that it was 'more appropriate to the case in question'. Pursuant to s 1(1), the Lord Chancellor prescribed a single discount rate of 2.5%.] '[33] We are told that this is the first time that this court has had to consider the 1996 Act, and that guidance is needed as to the meaning of "more appropriate in the case in question" in s 1(2). The phrase "more appropriate", if considered in isolation, is open-textured. It prompts the question: by what criteria is the court to judge whether a different rate of return is more appropriate in the case in question? But the phrase must be interpreted in its proper context, which is that Lord Irvine LC has prescribed a rate pursuant to s 1(1) and has given very detailed reasons explaining what factors he took into account in arriving at the rate that he has prescribed. I would hold that in deciding whether a different rate is more appropriate in the case in question, the court must have regard to those reasons. If the case in question falls into a category that Lord Irvine did not take into account and/or there are special features of the case which (a) are material to the choice of rate of return and (b) are shown from an examination of Lord Irvine's reasons not to have been taken into account, then a different rate of return may be "more appropriate".

...

'[35] If s 1(2) is interpreted in this way, it is likely that it will be in comparatively few cases that s 1(2) will be successfully invoked, at any rate as long as the 2·5% rate and Lord Irvine's reasons for it continue to apply. The construction that I have given to s 1(2) seems to me to accord with and promote the policy considerations to which I have already referred. A generous and open-ended interpretation of s 1(2) would undermine the policy that was clearly articulated by Lord Irvine in his reasons, and by the courts before that.' *Warriner v Warriner* [2002] EWCA Civ 81 at [33], [35], [2003] 3 All ER 447, per Dyson LJ

MORE OR LESS

[Certificate of title.] New Zealand '... there are prior authorities in this Court holding that the words "more or less" in a title (as in this case) prevent the statement of area in the title from prevailing over an actual survey" [authorities then cited].' *Melville-Smith v Attorney-General* [1996] 1 NZLR 596 at 603, per Hammond J

MORTGAGE

[For 32 Halsbury's Laws (4th edn) paras 401, 402 see now 32 Halsbury's Laws (4th edn) (Reissue) paras 301–302.]

Equitable mortgage

[For 32 Halsbury's Laws (4th edn) para 405 see now 32 Halsbury's Laws (4th edn) (Reissue) para 305.]

Legal mortgage

[For 32 Halsbury's Laws (4th edn) para 404 see now 32 Halsbury's Laws (4th edn) (Reissue) para 304.]

Puisne mortgage

[For 32 Halsbury's Laws (4th edn) para 544 see now 32 Halsbury's Laws (4th edn) (Reissue) para 318 note 4.]

MOTOR VEHICLE

Australia [Motor Accidents Compensation Act 1999 (NSW) s 3 provides: Motor vehicle means a motor vehicle or trailer within the meaning of the Road Transport (General) Act 1999.] '[12] The Road Transport (General) Act 1999 contains the following definitions:

> Motor vehicle means: a vehicle which is built to be propelled by a motor that forms part of the vehicle.
>
> Vehicle means:
> (a) any description of vehicle on wheels (including a light rail vehicle) but not including any other vehicle used on a railway or tramway or,
> (b) any other vehicle prescribed by the regulations

'[13] The Road Transport (General) Act 1999 is one of a number of interrelated acts. The same definition of motor vehicle as is incorporated by reference in the Motor Accidents Compensation Act appears, either expressly or by reference, in a number of cognate New South Wales statutes, referred to in s 5 of the Road Transport (General) Act 1999 as the "road transport legislation": the Road Transport (General) Act s 3; the Road Transport (Vehicle Registration) Act 1997 s 4; the Road Transport (Driver Licensing) 1998 Act s 4 and the dictionary; the Road Transport (Heavy

Vehicles Registration Charges) Act 1995 s 3; the Road Transport (Safety And Traffic Management) Act 1999 s 4 and the dictionary.

'[14] In the scheme for compensation for road accidents in existence immediately before the Motor Accidents Compensation Act 1999 the words "motor vehicle" had been defined in identical terms (see the Motor Accidents Act 1988 s 3 and Traffic Act 1909 s 2).

'[15] This amended definition was inserted into the Traffic Act 1909 by the Traffic Legislation Amendment Act 1997 which inserted the same definition in a wide variety of acts including the Driving Instructors Act 1992, the Industrial Relations Act 1986, the Motor Vehicle Sports (Public Safety) Act 1988, the Road Obstructions (Special Provisions) Act 1979, the Stamp Duties Act 1920, the Supreme Court Act 1970 and the Tow Truck Act 1989.

…

'[19] Within the Motor Accidents Compensation Act itself the word "motor vehicle", as defined, is found in a number of operative provisions, in addition to its use in the definition of claim, which word relevantly appears in s 108. These instances include the definition of motor accidents, s 3; the definition of the owner of motor vehicle which is registered, s 4; the definition of the use of an uninsured motor vehicle on a road, s 8; the statutory third party policy for the owner of a motor vehicle, s 10 (see also ss 11–13, 15, 18 and 19).

'[20] Of particular significance is the use of the words motor vehicle in the definition in s 3 of "motor accident". This concept is central to the scheme under the Act with respect to uninsured or unidentified motor vehicles in 2.4, motor accidents injury in Ch 3; motor accident claims in Ch 4; and the scheme for award of damages in Ch 5.

'[21] There is an element of circularity in the statutory definition; a "motor vehicle" is a "vehicle" of a particular character: However, the word "vehicle" is defined in terms of itself, relevantly, as a "vehicle on wheels". Where a word is defined, in part, in terms of itself then, subject to the context, the Act uses the word as appearing in the definition in its natural and ordinary meaning.

'[22] In my opinion, the natural and ordinary meaning of the word "vehicle" conveys the idea of conveyance or carriage and, perhaps, of movement within or upon the object. A device which does no more than push is not, in my opinion, a vehicle unless, perhaps, the person operating it also travels in some way on the object. I do not find it necessary to decide that particular issue.

'[23] The primary meaning in the Macquarie Dictionary is: "any receptacle, or means of transport, in which something is carried or conveyed or travels" (see also *Fawcett v BHP By-Products Pty Ltd* (1960) 104 CLR 80 at 918 per Windeyer J).

...

'[26] It is not sufficient, in my opinion, that a piece of equipment on wheels provides propulsion to an object.' *Murad v Pacific Services Pty Ltd* [2004] NSWCA 251 at [12]–[15], [19]–[23], [26], per Spigelman CJ; BC200404751

MURDER

[For 11 Halsbury's Laws (4th edn) para 1152 see now 11(1) Halsbury's Laws (4th edn) (Reissue) para 426.]

MUSICAL WORK

Canada ' ... the definition of the words "every original literary, dramatic, musical and artistic work" makes it plainly obvious that musical work is not meant to refer to or to include "composition with or without words" as the legislator opposes the two notions in that definition. It makes sense for Parliament to do that as section 5, in which the definition of "every original work" is used, broadly protects copyright in every original work. In the case of music, it is appropriate that it extends also to every original composition, not only to music work as narrowly defined in section 2 to mean every combination of melody and harmony printed, reduced to writing or graphically produced.' *CTV Television Network Ltd v Canada (Copyright Board)* [1993] 2 FCR 115 at 130, FCA, per Letourneau JA

MUST

Australia [Section 34(2) of the Road Traffic Act 1961 (SA) provides that the mass of a vehicle with or without its load and the mass carried on an axle or axles of a vehicle 'must' be determined in accordance with the regulations.] 'It seems to me that "must be determined" imposes an obligation which cannot be regarded as directory only. I have looked both in the dictionary and in Maxwell. The appropriate meaning of "must" in the Shorter Oxford English Dictionary is: "expressing necessity: Am (is, are) obliged or required to; have (has) to; it is necessary that (I, you, he, it, etc) should". "In ordinary usage, 'may' is permissive and 'must' is imperative" (Maxwell on Interpretation of Statutes, 12th edn (1969), p 324) ... If the wish of Parliament

had been to make the subsection directory it could easily have done so by using the word "may" instead of the word "must".' *Kosovich v Mancini* (1982) 31 SASR 272 at 275–276, per Millhouse J

MUTINY

Australia [Section 92(5) of the Corrective Services Act 1988 (Qld) penalises with 14 years' imprisonment a prisoner who while taking part in a riot or 'mutiny' escapes or attempts to escape ...] 'Perhaps the best modern definition of "mutiny" is that given by the Courts-Martial Appeal Court in *R v Grant* [1957] 2 All ER 694. It was said in that case at 696 that "there is no doubt now that mutiny is an offence which deals with collective insubordination, collective defiance or disregard of authority or refusal to obey authority". In my view it is the element of challenge to authority which distinguishes a "mutiny" from a "riot". That is confirmed by a consideration of a number of dictionary definitions of the term which stress revolt against constituted authority as an essential element of "mutiny". There is also a valuable discussion of the offence of "mutiny" in Winthrop, *Military Law and Precedents*, 2nd edn at 578 ff. That learned author stresses that intention to overthrow lawful authority is an essential element of the crime. The examples he gives, which include some from English naval and military history, clearly support the conclusion. The intent may, of course, be inferred from the acts done by way of subverting superior authority. In my view intent to subvert authority is also an essential element of the offence of mutiny created by s 92. Given the difference in character between a "mutiny" and a "riot" there is no problem in concluding that two or more persons may "mutiny" whilst for purposes of s 92 there have to be at least three prisoners to constitute an unlawful "assembly" or "riot".' *R v Aston (No 3)* [1991] 1 Qd R 443 at 448, per Williams J

MUTUAL

Australia [Section 86 of the Bankruptcy Act 1966 (Cth) provides for set off 'where there have been mutual credits, mutual debts or other mutual dealings between a person who has become a bankrupt and a person claiming to prove a debt in bankruptcy ...'] 'In the context of s 86, the word "mutual" conveys the notion of reciprocity rather than that of correspondence. It does not mean "identical" or "the same". So understood, there are three aspects of the section's requirement of mutuality. The first is that the credits, the debts, or the claims arising from other dealings be between the same persons. The second is that the benefit or burden of them lie in the same interests. In determining whether credits, debts or claims arising from other dealings are between the same persons and in the same interests, it is the equitable or beneficial interests of the parties which must be considered: see eg *Hiley* [*v Peoples Prudential Assurance Co Ltd* (1938) 60 CLR 468 at 497]. The third requirement of mutuality is that the credits, debts, or claims arising from other dealings must be commensurable for the purposes of set-off under the section. That means that they must ultimately sound in money.' *Gye v McIntyre* (1991) 171 CLR 609 at 623, per cur

N

NAME

[For 30 Halsbury's Laws (4th edn) paras 796–800 see now 35 Halsbury's Laws (4th edn) (Reissue) paras 12725–1275.]

NATIONAL DEBT

[For 32 Halsbury's Laws (4th edn) paras 218–220 see now 32 Halsbury's Laws (4th edn) (Reissue) paras 166–168.]

NATIONAL ORIGIN

Australia 'National origin may in some cases be resolved by a person's place of birth. In other cases it may be necessary to have regard to the national origin of a parent or each parent or other ancestors either in conjunction with the person's place of birth or disregarding that factor. If by reference to matters of national origin one can expose a racially-discriminatory law, then the Convention will have served its purpose. However, no Convention purpose is in any manner frustrated by drawing a distinction between national origin and nationality, the latter being a purely legal status (and a transient one at that)... In our opinion, there would have to be very cogent reasons advanced why we should diverge from what we perceive to be a growing body of English and Australian authority and international learning in the field. That body of learning distinguishes between, on the one hand, "national origin" as an indicator of race and, on the other hand, nationality or citizenship as being a sometimes transient legal status.' *Macabenta v Minister for Immigration and Multicultural Affairs* (1998) 159 ALR 465 at 474, 475; 52 ALD 8, per Carr, Sundberg and North JJ

NATIONAL SECURITY

Australia 'It was submitted by counsel for Mr Irving that the term "national security" in reg 177(d) [of the Migration Regulations 1989 (Cth)] refers to external security rather than to internal security. "National security" is not, however, limited to external matters. It looks to matters affecting the country in general rather than individual persons.' *Irving v Minister for Immigration, Local Government and Ethnic Affairs* (1996) 139 ALR 84 at 89, per Davies and R D Nicholson JJ

NATIONALITY

[See now 4(2) Halsbury's Laws (4th edn) (Reissue) para 1 et seq.]

NATIVE TITLE RIGHTS

Australia [Right to live on the land and to erect structures.] '[122] Paragraph 3(b) of the determination [of the learned judge] identified the following right:

> (b) the right to live on the land, to camp, erect shelters and other structures, and to travel over and visit any part of the land and waters.

...

'[129] The underlying issue in relation to this right is the scope of inconsistency between the historic pastoral leaseholders' rights and the applicants' native title rights and interests. The content of the reservations is incidental. They do not define the limits of native title rights and interests in relation to the land. They may however be taken into account in determining the scope of the pastoral leaseholder's rights in assessing the extent of their inconsistency with the asserted native title rights and interests — *Ward HC* at [417]. Despite some emphasis on reservations in its written submission the Northern Territory's core argument was that a right to live permanently on the land or to erect permanent structures on it was inconsistent with the rights of pastoralists to use the land as conferred by their pastoral leases.

'[130] The question of permanency in living arrangements on the land including the erection of permanent structures was not expressly considered by the Full Court or the High Court in the *Ward* litigation. However in *Daniel v State of Western*

Australia (*No 2*) [2003] FCA 1425, Nicholson J identified but did not resolve what he regarded as a potential inconsistency between a pastoral leaseholder's rights and a right to live permanently at a place on the land. His Honour accepted that a native title right to "remain" on the land could be exercised consistently with the pastoral leaseholder's rights. In the event he construed the right to "live" on the land as a right to "live temporarily on the areas as part of camping and for that purpose to build shelters". So construed there was no inconsistency with pastoral leasehold rights. In *Neowarra*, Sundberg J considered a propounded native title right to live, build structures and establish and maintain communities anywhere on a pastoral lease. He found this to be inconsistent with the general right to conduct pastoral activities on the whole of the land and with many of the particular rights conferred on pastoral leaseholders — [502]. As for "camping", on the other hand, his Honour said (at [504]):

> This activity is encompassed in the notion of access to land for traditional purposes. Setting up a temporary camp as opposed to permanent settlements is not inconsistent with the rights of the pastoralist, though in the event of a conflict of activities, the rights of the pastoralist will prevail.

'In *Attorney-General* (*NT*) *v Ward* (2003) 134 FCR 16 (Ward FC 2), the Full Court, on remittal from the High Court, determined by consent native title rights and interests held by the applicants by way of non-exclusive rights to occupy, use and enjoy land and waters in accordance with their traditional laws and customs including as an incident of that entitlement:

> (b) the right to live on the land, to camp, to erect shelters and to move about the land.

'[131] The pastoral leases which have affected the claim area in the present case are historical grants. The relevant extinguishment of native title rights and interests derives only from inconsistency with the rights historically conferred by those leases. No question of prospective activity under a subsisting pastoral lease arises. Consistently with what was said by Nicholson J in *Daniel* (*No 2*) and Sundberg J in *Neowarra*, the right to "live" on the land can be interpreted as a right to live permanently on the land without any conflict with pastoral leaseholders' rights. That right does not necessarily involve permanent settlement at a particular place. The issue therefore reduces to the question whether a native title right of permanent settlement is inconsistent with a pastoral leaseholder's rights.

There is no logical reason why it must be so. Just as the right to live permanently on the land does not necessarily give rise to inconsistency with the pastoral leaseholder's rights, neither does the right to erect a permanent structure. The existence of such a structure does not preclude a pastoralist's right to require its removal in the event that it conflicts with a proposed exercise by the pastoralist of a right under the lease. It is not inevitable that such a conflict will arise.

'[132] The inconsistency posited by the Northern Territory in respect of the grant of historical pastoral leases long expired, is based on a theoretical conflict which would not inevitably have occurred. No inconsistency of rights giving rise to extinguishment of the native title right to live on the land and to erect permanent structures thereon is demonstrated. The concept of "permanency" referred to here is, in any event, a relative one.

'[133] The right defined in para 3(b) to live on the land, to camp, to erect shelters and other structures, and to travel over and visit any part of the land and waters, should stand.' *Northern Territory of Australia v Alyawarr, Kaytetye, Warumungu, Wakaya Native Title Claim Group* [2005] FCAFC 135 at [122], [129]–[133], per Wilconx, French and Weinberg JJ; BC200505385

Australia [Teaching physical and spiritual attributes on the land.] 'Paragraph 3(c) of the determination [of the learned judge] defined the following right:

> the right to engage in cultural activities on the land, to conduct ceremonies and hold meetings, to teach the physical and spiritual attributes of places and areas of importance on or in the land and waters and to participate in cultural practices relating to birth and death, including burial rights;

'The Northern Territory submitted that the right asserted in para (c) to teach the physical and spiritual attributes of places and areas of importance on or in the land or waters is akin to a right to maintain and protect cultural knowledge. This was a right rejected by the High Court in *Ward HC* as a right in relation to land or waters. It relates to information not land.

'The right to teach the physical and spiritual attributes of places and areas of importance, if specified as a right to teach on the land, requires access to and use of the land for that purpose. So defined, it is a right in relation to the land. In order to avoid ambiguity para 3(c) should be reworded. A reformulation to limit the rights by confining their exercise to activities on the land was proposed by the applicants and not opposed by the Northern Territory. The proposed reformulated para 3(c) is in the following terms:

the right to do the following activities on the land:
(i) engage in cultural activities;
(ii) conduct ceremonies;
(iii) hold meetings;
(iv) teach the physical and spiritual attributes of places and areas of importance on or in the land and waters; and
(v) participate in cultural practices relating to birth and death, including burial rights.

'The right so reformulated should be substituted for that in para 3(c) of the determination.' *Northern Territory of Australia v Alyawarr, Kaytetye, Warumungu, Wakaya Native Title Claim Group* [2005] FCAFC 135 at [134]–[135], per Wilcox, French and Weinberg JJ; BC200505385

Australia [Right to protect sites of importance.] 'Paragraph 3(d) of the determination [of the learned judge] defined a right of access to the land and to protect sites on the land in the following terms:

the right to have access to, maintain and protect places and areas of importance on or in the land and waters, including rock art, engraving sites and stone arrangements.

'The Northern Territory submitted that the right to protect sites under traditional laws and customs necessarily involves the assertion of a right to control access and to exclude others from the land. The native title rights and interests recognised could not include elements allowing for the exclusion of others. The historical grant of pastoral leases in the area had extinguished the right to exclude and control access to the land so removing the very substance of the right to protect sites.

'The applicants submitted that the word "protect" does not, in ordinary usage, imply the exercise of control over the matter or thing being protected. The right could include protecting places from environmental damage or degradation and seeking to prevent unwitting damage or disturbance by animals or people. None of these activities, it was said, would necessarily involve any control over access to the land by others.

'The learned trial judge said (at [322]):

I do not regard the use of the word "protect" as inappropriate. It contemplates conduct in relation to places and areas of importance which may fall well short of controlling access to those places in a way which is incon-

sistent with previously granted rights, and the exercise of the right to be recognised is subject to the prevailing activities under the exercise of other rights: s 44H of the NT Act. It is a right which I consider exists independently of the Northern Territory Aboriginal Sacred Sites Act (NT).

'One answer to the Northern Territory objection is that the rights determined in para 3 are expressly stated in para 4 to be not exclusive of the rights and interests of others in relation to the land (other than the land covered by the townsite of Hatches Creek). In *Ward FC 2*, the Full Court considered a submission by the Commonwealth that the word "protect" would give native title holders an entitlement to exclude others from the land. The Court there said (at [25]):

We do not agree. The notion of protection of significant Aboriginal sites is well understood. It may involve physical activities on the site to prevent its destruction, but it also extends to control of ceremonial activities. Particularly having regard to the existence of subclause (e), we do not think the words would be read as implying a general control of access.

'Notwithstanding the decision of the Full Court in *Ward FC 2*, counsel for the Northern Territory pressed for a formulation of para 3(d) which would make clear the limitation on the scope of the right to protect. However, the determination read as a whole does not allow ambiguity of the kind propounded in connection with the word "protect". His Honour has not been shown to have erred in this matter. The right as formulated in para 3(d) of the determination should stand.' *Northern Territory of Australia v Alyawarr, Kaytetye, Warumungu, Wakaya Native Title Claim Group* [2005] FCAFC 135 at [136]–[140], per Wilcox, French and Weinberg JJ; BC200505385

Australia [Right to make decisions about access to and use and enjoyment of the land.] 'The native title rights stated in paras (e) and (f) of the determination [of the learned judge] can be dealt with together. They are in the following terms:

(e) the right to make decisions about access to the land and waters by people other than those exercising a right conferred by or arising under a law of the Northern Territory or the Commonwealth in relation to the use of the land and waters;
(f) the right to make decisions about the use and enjoyment of the land and waters

and the subsistence and other traditional resources thereof, by people other than those exercising a right conferred by or arising under a law of the Northern Territory or the Commonwealth in relation to the use of the land and waters.

'The applicants accepted at trial that the right to exclude all others from the claim area had been extinguished by the grant of pastoral leases that conferred rights inconsistent with a native title right to control access to the land. In the joint judgment in *Ward HC*, dealing with the extinguishing effect of the grant of pastoral leases by the State of Western Australia, their Honours said (at [192]):

> These were acts involving the grant of rights and interests inconsistent with so much of the native title rights and interests as stipulated for control of access to the land the subject of the grants. The pastoral leases were acts attributable to the State which denied to the native title holders the continuation of a traditional right to say who could or who could not come onto the land in question. That consequence flowed apart from the provisions of the State Validation Act. It followed that to that extent the grants of pastoral leases extinguished native title rights and interests within the meaning of par (b)(i) of s 12M(1).

'And at [194]:

> The right to control access apart, many other native title rights to use the land the subject of the pastoral leases probably continued unaffected.

'The learned trial judge said (at [270]):

> It is obvious that rights under pastoral leases and statutory rights of entry for explicit purposes meant that native title holders would not have been able to prevent persons from entering the land in the exercise of those rights. On the other hand, the rights granted to the pastoral lessees were not rights granted to all persons, and pastoral lessees were obliged to exercise their rights for the purpose of the lease. The preserved rights are those to a pastoral lessee permitting access by the lessee or persons to whom the lessee permitted to enter, and reserved or (sic) statutory rights for reserved purposes such as stock routes. I do not consider that it is inconsistent with such rights that the native title right to control access to the land should survive to exclude persons who might wish to enter the land to

do things unrelated to the pastoral lease or without some other reserved or statutory rights.

'His Honour said further (at [271]):

> … the inconsistency arises because the pastoral lease authorised the entry of a definable group of persons under it. It did not authorise the entry of all or any persons under it. The lessee could exclude uninvited persons, subject to the reservation in favour of Aboriginal persons. That right would run in tandem with the right in the native title holders to control access: s 44H of the NT Act. Once the lease came to an end, the Aboriginal native title holders would have whatever rights survived to control access to the claim area. Their right would have been extinguished to the extent that it was exclusive for the reason already given, and to the extent that it might otherwise have been exercisable in relation to the previous pastoral lessee and the lessee's authorised entrants. But it does not follow, in my view, that the right of a definable group of persons under the lease to access the claim area is inconsistent with (and so extinguishes) the non-exclusive native title right to control access to the claim area in respect of persons outside that definable group of persons.

'His Honour gave examples of persons who were seeking to enter the land to film a sacred site or to set up a fishing camp at a water hole where camping or taking fish was prohibited or regulated by the traditional laws and customs of the native title holders. His Honour also held (at [272]) that it was consistent with the reservation in the historical leases that the native title holders, in accordance with their traditional practices could continue to control entry to their country by other Aboriginal people to the extent that that right was not in conflict with rights under the pastoral leases. At [274] his Honour said:

> I have reached the view that the native title rights to control access to the claim area and to make decisions about its use are not so inconsistent with rights under the pastoral leases as to lead to their total extinguishment.

'His Honour also considered the effect of the current lease CLP 1117 in favour of the Corporation. He concluded, however, that the applicants' native title rights and interests had not been further extinguished by CLP 1117 beyond the extinguishment effected by previous pastoral leases. This conclusion was the subject of a separate challenge under appeal ground 47.

'In the course of the hearing the Court raised the possibility that paras 3(e) and (f) could be replaced by a native title right defined in terms of para 5(e) in the decision of the Full Court in *Ward FC 2*. That provided for:

> 5(e) The right to make decisions about the use and enjoyment of the NT determination area by Aboriginal people who are governed by the traditional laws and customs acknowledged and observed by the native title holders.

'This, however, was not supported by the Northern Territory which pointed out that it had taken a neutral position on that aspect of the determination in *Ward FC 2* albeit the inclusion of the right in 5(e) had been opposed by the Commonwealth and Western Australia.

'The grant of historical pastoral leases had a partially extinguishing effect upon native title rights and interests in the determination area insofar as they comprised rights to exclude other persons from entering upon the land. The question is whether that partial extinguishment left in place a qualified right to exclude persons other than the relevant pastoral lessees and their invitees or other statutory entrants. The Northern Territory contended that the native title rights and interests set out in the determination must be native title rights and interests that existed at sovereignty. It was not open to determine, post-extinguishment, a qualified residual right which did not exist at sovereignty.

'In *Neowarra*, the applicants sought the right to make decisions about use and enjoyment of the claim area expressed as a qualified right to make access decisions in relation to persons other than persons holding a pastoral lease or exercising a statutory right in relation to the use of the land and waters. Sundberg J said (at [475]):

> The amendment does not avoid the difficulties. It confuses the separate processes required by the legislation. First there must be a determination of each native title right and interest. Then there must be a comparison between that right and interest and other interests that exist in the claim area. Each right or interest now propounded by the applicants for comparative purposes must be a native title right or interest. No native title right approximating to the reformulation is established by the evidence ... It is not surprising that the evidence does not establish the amended right. The subject matter of the qualification (a pastoral leaseholder and a person exercising a statutory right) did not then exist.

'His Honour went on to identify a further difficulty with the amendment by reference to the decision of the High Court in *Yarmirr* (at [98]). In that case the applicants sought to express wide-ranging native title rights in the sea as subject to public rights to navigate and fish and the right of innocent passage. Gleeson CJ, Gaudron, Gummow and Hayne JJ in their joint judgment said the two sets of rights were fundamentally inconsistent and could not stand together. It was not sufficient to attempt to reconcile them by providing that exercise of the native title rights and interests was to be subject to the other public and international rights. Sundberg J in *Neowarra* said (at [475]):

> That applies to the attempt to reconcile the fundamentally inconsistent native title right to make decisions about the use and enjoyment of the land and waters and the rights granted by a pastoral lease.

'His Honour applied the same reasoning to reject a proposed right to control the access of others to the claim area — [477].

'There are dicta in the joint judgment of Gleeson CJ, Gaudron, Gummow and Hayne JJ in *Ward HC* which militate against the applicants' contentions. Reference has already been made to what their Honours said in paras [192] and [194] of the joint judgment. Moreover their Honours said at [62] that without a right, as against the whole world, to possess the land "it may greatly be doubted that there is any right to control access to the land or make binding decisions about the use to which it is put". Having regard to what was said in the High Court it seems that the right to control access cannot be sustained where there is no right to exclusive occupation against the whole world. The underlying rationale for that conclusion is that particular native title rights and interests cannot survive partial extinguishment in a qualified form different from the particular native title right or interest that existed at sovereignty. The rights set out in paras 3(e) and (f) of the determination do not resemble the holistic right of exclusion which went with exclusive possession and occupation at the time of sovereignty. In this respect the appeal should be allowed and paras 3(e) and 3(f) deleted from the determination save as to the area of the Hatches Creek townsite where prior extinguishment can be disregarded because of the application of s 47B of the NT Act.

'The applicants proposed as an alternative to paras 3(e) and 3(f), a para (fa) in the following terms:

… As an incident of their rights in relation to the use and enjoyment of the land and waters, a right to take appropriate steps according to law to prevent or mitigate any activity or presence of persons on the land which —
(a) is without or in excess of lawful authority; and
(b) interferes with or impairs the use and enjoyment of the land in accordance with rights and interests identified above.

'The difficulty with that alternative is that it imports a right of exclusion which is inconsistent with the reasoning upon which paras (e) and (f) are wanting. Moreover it is very difficult to interpret and apply para (fa) to support a right to exclude a person from the land in the circumstances defined in that paragraph.

'Although para 5(e) of the determination in *Ward FC 2* had the sanction of the Full Court in that case, it is not without difficulty. There is a risk that it may be seen as creating a criterion for exclusion based in part upon Aboriginality. In any event it does not appear in this case that there are persons other than the native title holders who are bound by their traditional laws and customs. The position would be different were the native title holders a subset of a wider society incorporating other groups bound by the same traditional laws and customs. An example of such a case is *De Rose v State of South Australia* [2002] FCA 1342 where the native title holders were found to be a subset of a society comprising the Western Desert Bloc. To the extent that the native title holders could collectively exclude particular members from particular areas, such as women from law grounds, that is a matter best left to the intramural workings of the traditional laws and customs. It is not a matter requiring determination as a distinct native title right.' *Northern Territory of Australia v Alyawarr, Kaytetye, Warumungu, Wakaya Native Title Claim Group* [2005] FCAFC 135 at [141]–[151], per Wilcox, French and Weinberg JJ; BC200505385

Australia [Right to trade.] 'Paragraph 3(g) of the determination defined the following right:

the right to share, exchange or trade subsistence and other traditional resources obtained on or from the land and waters;

'The Northern Territory contended that the right to trade is not a right or interest in relation to land or waters notwithstanding that the asserted objects of the trade are resources of the land and waters. The same, it was said, is true of the right to share or

exchange resources. The applicants however responded that the right is a right to trade in the produce of the land and therefore has a relationship to the land. The Northern Territory argued that in *Yarmirr* at first instance Olney J held that a claimed right to trade was not a right or interest in relation to land or waters notwithstanding that its asserted objects were the resources of the claim area.

'The right to trade is a right relating to the use of the resources of the land. It defines a purpose for which those resources can be taken and applied. It is difficult to see on what basis it would not be a right in relation to the land.

'Olney J in *Yarmirr* at first instance referred to evidence of exchange of goods. The evidence was that of Mary Yarmirr. It related to trade by way of exchange, between indigenous groups of items including spearheads, stone axes, bailer shells, cabbage palm baskets and turtle shells. His Honour said (at 587):

Whilst there can be no doubt that the trade here described related to objects which can properly be categorised as resources of the waters and land, the trading was constituted by the exchange of goods. The so-called "right to trade" was not a right or interest in relation to the waters or land. Nor were any of the traded goods "subsistence resources" derived from either the land or the sea.

'Olney J's observation does not involve the proposition that trade in the resources of the land can never be a "right" in relation to the land. There the evidence was of an activity. It did not amount to evidence of the exercise of a right. Indeed his Honour referred to it in his judgment as a "so-called right to trade". Further evidence to which Olney J referred fell short of establishing an asserted historic trade between the forbears of the Croker Island applicants and the Macassans. There was no evidence that, since European contact, members of the Croker Island community had engaged in trade by way of sale or exchange in the resources of the waters of the claimed area. Nor was there evidence to suggest that trade in the resources of the claimed area form part of the traditional customs of their ancestors. Although cited by the Northern Territory in relation to the right to trade in this case, *Yarmirr* cannot be taken as authority for the proposition that there cannot be a right to trade in the resources of the land as a right in relation to the land.

'The Northern Territory argued that the right to trade in the resources of the land necessarily implies a native title right to exclusive possession thereof. It was submitted that his Honour's reference to

Yanner and the absence of any right to own flora and fauna implied a view that the evidence was consistent with a native title right to take flora and fauna but not to own it. In any event the evidence was said not to support any right to "trade" in the resources of the land as that term is generally understood. The evidence was limited to:

(a) evidence of sharing and exchanging (using the term "swapping") ochre, spears, boomerangs, feathers and hair belts for personal use;

(b) evidence of sharing and exchanging goods in a ceremonial context, referred to as "tyenkerr", which witnesses described as "[l]ike a thank you" or "to pay him off";

(c) evidence of the collection of beans to make beads sold to a shop for purchase by tourists.

'The Northern Territory argued that that evidence made no reference at all to any commercial or profit motives or any level of organised business operation.

'In his reasons for judgment the learned trial judge found that the use or exercise of the right to use and enjoy the resources of the claim area was well supported. Evidence had also been given by the applicants that they had asserted the right to use the natural resources of the claim area including water, trees, bush medicines, soakages, sacred sites and other things including ochre from various places in the claim area. His Honour said (at [160]):

In my judgment, it is also consistent with the evidence to which I have referred that the applicants, under their traditional laws and customs, have the right to share, exchange or trade subsistence and other traditional resources obtained from or on the land and waters constituting the claim area.

'The evidence relied upon by his Honour in this respect was not exposed in any detail beyond his earlier reference to the evidence of the applicants that they had asserted the right to use the natural resources of the claim area. In the circumstances, it is difficult to see how this evidence was capable of supporting a finding of a native title right to trade in the resources of the area. There appears to have been no evidentiary support for this aspect of the determination. Paragraph 3(g) should therefore be varied to read:

the right to share or exchange subsistence and other traditional resources obtained on or from the land and waters."

Northern Territory of Australia v Alyawarr, Kaytetye, Warumungu, Wakaya Native Title Claim Group [2005] FCAFC 135 at [152]–[157], per Wilcox, French and Weinberg JJ; BC200505385

Australia [Right to control disclosure of spiritual beliefs and practices.] 'Paragraph 3(h) of the determination related to the protection of traditional knowledge:

the right to control the disclosure (otherwise than in accordance with traditional laws and customs) of spiritual beliefs or practices, or of the paraphernalia associated with them (including songs, narratives, ceremonies, rituals and sacred objects) which relate to any part of or place on the land or waters;

'The Northern Territory contended before the learned trial judge that the propounded right was not one which meets the requirement of s 223(1)(b) namely that it be in relation to the claim area. It was argued before his Honour that the spiritual beliefs upon which the claimed right is based may be about the claimed area and its surrounding areas but did not have the quality necessary to fall within the definition of native title rights and interests.

'His Honour considered that the right is one which has a connection with the claim area so as to come within the definition in s 223(1). The critical question which he identified was whether the claim group by the traditional laws and customs which give rise to the particular native title rights and interests has a connection with the claimed area. He said (at [324]):

The expression of the claimed right is more refined, or more specifically directed to meeting the requirement of s 223(1)(b), than those considered by the High Court in Ward at 31–32, [58]–[60] or by O'Loughlin J in De Rose at [51]. The evidence discloses that certain of the spiritual beliefs or practices of the claim group are "site specific", and the activities conducted pursuant to them relate to particular locations in the claim area. As expressed, the proposed right firstly relates only to the spiritual beliefs which concern particular locations in the claim area. And secondly, it seeks to "control" the disclosure of those beliefs and the material objects and other "paraphernalia" associated with them. It is not directed to controlling the use of some intellectual property, but to controlling its acquisition. I am confident there is a right to control the acquisition of such information in accordance with traditional laws and customs of the claim group. By the "site specific" nature of those particular spiritual beliefs, in my view the claim group has a connection with the claim area. As expressed, I do not consider the right is "something approaching an incorporeal right akin to a new species of intellectual property" (c f the majority in *Ward* at 31 [59]). 'In *Ward FC 1* the Full Court majority said of the claimed right to protect and prevent the misuse of cultural knowledge (at [666]):

> Although the relationship of Aboriginal people to their land has a religious or spiritual dimension, we do not think that a right to maintain, protect and prevent the misuse of cultural knowledge is a right in relation to land of the kind that can be the subject of a determination of native title.

'In the High Court in *Ward HC* the majority joint judgment held that the Full Court had not erred in their rejection of the proposed right. Their Honours identified the imprecision of the term "cultural knowledge" as the first difficulty facing that submission (at [58]). They also characterised the claimed right as "something approaching an incorporeal right akin to a new species of intellectual property to be recognised by the common law under para (c) of s 223(1)". — (at [59]). The essential point was the requirement of 'connection' in para (b) of the definition in s 223(1) of native title and native title rights and interests. They said (at [60]):

> The scope of the right for which recognition by the common law is sought here goes beyond the content of the definition in s 223(1).

'The Northern Territory submitted that the term "spiritual beliefs and practices" suffered from the same imprecision as the term "cultural knowledge" considered by the High Court in Ward HC. Moreover it is not a right "in relation to land". The fact that the spiritual beliefs and practices are about areas of land or waters within the claim area does not change their fundamental nature of the right asserted.

'In *Neowarra* the applicants sought to formulate this class of native title right to avoid the difficulties exposed in Ward HC. They expressed it thus:

> To prevent the disclosure otherwise than in accordance with traditional laws and customs [of] tenets of spiritual beliefs and practices (including songs, narratives, rituals and ceremonies) which relate to areas of land or waters, or places on the land or waters.

'However, as Sundberg J observed (at [487]):

The reformulation does not avoid "the fatal difficulty" to which the joint judgment referred at [60]. It will still involve the "restraint of visual or auditory reproductions of what was found [on the land] or took place there".

'The propounded right, notwithstanding its formulation in the present case in para 3(h) of the determination, is not a right in relation to land.

'The applicants proposed a further reformulation at the hearing of the appeal thus:

> (h) the right to such control of access to places on the land and waters as will prevent the disclosure (otherwise than in accordance with traditional laws and customs) of spiritual beliefs or practices, or of the paraphernalia associated with them (including songs, narratives, ceremonies, rituals and sacred objects) which relate to any part of or place on the land or waters.

'This reformulation runs into the difficulty facing paras (e) and (f) in purporting to confer a right to exclude persons from entry onto the land under certain circumstances.

'For the preceding reasons para 3(h) should be deleted from the determination.' *Northern Territory of Australia v Alyawarr, Kaytetye, Warumungu, Wakaya Native Title Claim Group* [2005] FCAFC 135 at [158]–[164], per Wilcox, French and Weinberg JJ; BC200505385

Australia [Right to determine membership of the landholding group.] 'Paragraph 3(i) of the determination [of the learned judge] identified a further right in the following terms:

> the right to determine and regulate the membership of and recruitment to a landholding group.

'Notwithstanding the inclusion of this right in the determination, the applicants accepted that it is more appropriately recognised as part of their laws and customs rather than as a right or interest in relation to the claim area. It does not appear to be a native title right or interest in relation to the land or waters. In any event it is subsumed by the provisions of para 2 of the determination in relation to the identification of the native title holders. Paragraph 3(i) should therefore be deleted from the determination. *Northern Territory of Australia v Alyawarr, Kaytetye, Warumungu, Wakaya Native Title Claim Group* [2005] FCAFC 135 at [165], per Wilcox, French and Weinberg JJ; BC200505385

Australia [Right to be acknowledged as the Aboriginal owners of the land.] 'The applicants sought, in their cross appeal, the insertion of an additional right 3(j) defined thus:

the right as against the whole world, including other Aboriginal groups or persons, to assert and be acknowledged as the Aboriginal owners of the land and waters in accordance with traditional laws and customs.

'It is said that the omission of this right from the determination was an oversight. The applicants referred to [67] in his Honour's judgment in which he referred to the proposed para 3(j). His Honour discussed at [324] the native title rights set out in para 3(h) which he found to have "a connection with the claim area so as to come within the definition in s 223(1) of the NT Act". For the reasons expressed earlier in relation to the appeal against the inclusion of para 3(h) in the determination that paragraph could not stand.

'His Honour then proceeded to make a finding in favour of the inclusion of the proposed para 3(j) for reasons which were substantially the same as his reasons for including 3(h). He said (at [325]):

The right claimed in (j) is, in my judgment, for the same reasons a native title right possessed under the traditional laws and customs of the claim group by reason of which the claim group has a connection with the claim area. Olney J in *Hayes* at 148 made a similar determination.

'As his Honour pointed out, Olney J in *Hayes v Northern Territory* (1999) 97 FCR 32 made a determination which included a similar right expressed thus:

3(b) The right to be acknowledged as the traditional Aboriginal owners of the land and waters of their respective estates within the determination area.

'There is no doubt that the omission of the proposed para 3(j) from the determination was an oversight on the part of his Honour. However, the question remains whether it is a native title right that can properly be the subject of a determination under the NT Act.

'The meaning of the proposed right to be acknowledged is elusive. The questions posed by the Northern Territory are fundamental. How would the right be infringed? How could it be enforced? Native title which is recognised by the common law, albeit not as a common law tenure "... may be protected by such legal or equitable remedies as are appropriate to the particular rights and interests established by the evidence, whether proprietary or personal and usufructuary in nature and whether possessed by a community, a group or an individual" — *Mabo* (*No 2*) at 61 (Brennan J). Although that passage did not mandate enforceability as a condition of common law recognition, there is a real question whether common law recognition has any role to play in relation to a right or interest which is incapable of enforcement. This is not to adopt the tendency deprecated by the Privy Council in *Amodu Tijani v Secretary, Southern Nigeria* [1921] 2 AC 399 at 403 of rendering native title "conceptually in terms which are appropriate only to systems which have grown up under English law" — *Mabo* (*No 2*) at 84 (Deane and Gaudron JJ). But symbolic statements which are empty of content have no place in a determination of rights. They promise much and deliver little but disappointment. Paragraph 3(j) is incapable of precise definition and incapable of enforcement. It should not be included in the determination. Paragraph 8(e)(vi) of the determination, which refers to it, should also be deleted.' *Northern Territory of Australia v Alyawarr, Kaytetye, Warumungu, Wakaya Native Title Claim Group* [2005] FCAFC 135 at [166]–[168], per Wilcox, French and Weinberg JJ; BC200505385

NATURAL

Australia '... "natural" means that which has been formed or constituted by nature in contradistinction to that which is artificially made or constructed: see *Macquarie Dictionary* and *Oxford English Dictionary*. As the *Oxford English Dictionary* notes, when qualifying land, "natural" means that which is not cultivated.' *City of Mitcham v Mol Pty Ltd* BC200302734; [2003] SASC 166 at [24], per Debelle J

NATURAL JUSTICE

Australia [Administrative Law Act 1978 (Vic).] '[47] The phrase "natural justice" has a particular meaning in modern administrative law. At its least, it consists of two common law rules requiring that fair procedure is followed in the decision making process affecting rights or interests of an individual. The two rules are —

(i) The hearing rule (audi alteram partem) which requires the decision-maker to give an opportunity to the person adversely affected by the decision to be heard in respect to matters relevant to the decision.

(ii) The rule that the decision-maker shall not be a judge in his own cause namely that the decision-maker is free from bias.

'[48] The rules are concerned with the decision making process and not the merits of the decision itself. See *Chief Constable of North Wales Police v Evans*. The better view appears to be that there is no third rule that the decision maker must act fairly. In *Footscray Football Club Ltd v Commissioner of Payroll Tax*, Lush J said:

> I find myself unable to accept the proposition that a duty formulated merely as a duty to act fairly is a duty to comply with the rules of natural justice. In one sense it can be said that any person exercising public power is under a duty to act fairly.
>
> The rules of natural justice are usually crystallised into two categories; the first rule, as sometimes formulated, was in the form that no person shall act as judge in his own cause, and perhaps may be formulated in the form that the deciding body must be free of bias; and the second rule stated the requirement that the person whose rights may be affected is entitled to be heard. Within each of those rights there may again be a requirement of fair acting.

'[49] Barwick CJ in *Salemi v MacKellar (No 2)* made it clear that the duty to act fairly flowed from the obligation to accord natural justice. His Honour said:

> It is in this connexion that the concept of fairness is relevant: that is, once it is concluded that the power of decision or action is dependent on the observance of natural justice, fairness in the particular circumstances will determine what must needs be done to satisfy natural justice. The fairness is what is required of a repository of power when on the proper construction of the statute that power is qualified by the need to accord natural justice. But the basic question is whether the statutory power is so qualified. Whether it is to be so qualified is a matter for the Parliament. It is for the courts to decide in point of construction what the Parliament has relevantly enacted, both expressly and implicitly. The courts by construction of the statute educe and make express the qualification of the granted power inherent in the statute. Having decided that the statute makes the exercise of the power contingent on the observance of natural justice, the courts then decide what is required in the particular circumstances to satisfy the statute so construed. But it is fundamental that what the courts do

in qualifying the powers is no more than to construe the statute. Failure to meet the qualification of the power, that is to accord natural justice in the manner in which the courts decide is required in the circumstances, results in an invalidity of the decision or act, because neither is authorized by the statute as construed by the courts.

'[50] More recently Deane J has identified what he described as another requirement of natural justice and that is that decisions must be based upon logically probative and relevant material. See *Australian Broadcasting Tribunal v Bond*. However, the High Court has not come that far as yet.

...

'[55] It is well established that the application of the rules of natural justice and their content depends upon a proper construction of the statutory provisions relating to the decision making process.' *Lewenberg v Victoria Legal Aid* [2005] VSC 28 at [47]–[50], [55], per Gillard J; BC200500462

NECESSARIES

Of infant

[For 24 Halsbury's Laws (4th edn) paras 416–417 see now 5(3) Halsbury's Laws (4th edn) (Reissue) paras 18–21.]

[For 41 Halsbury's Laws (4th edn) para 642 see now 41 Halsbury's Laws (4th edn) (Reissue) para 37.]

Canada '[66] Counsel for the appellant suggested that this claim fell under paragraph 22(2)(*m*) of the *Federal Court Act*:

> 22.(2) Without limiting the generality of subsection (1), it is hereby declared for greater certainty that the Trial Division has jurisdiction with respect to any one or more of the following:
>
> ...
>
> (*m*) any claim in respect of goods, materials or services wherever supplied to a ship for the operation or maintenance of the ship, including, without restricting the generality of the foregoing, claims in respect of stevedoring and lighterage.

'[67] This argument has no merit. A fishing licence, and even more so a quota attributed to a fishing licence, cannot be equated with "goods, materials or services ... supplied to a ship". This Court, in *Joys v. M.N.R.*, [1996] 1 F.C. 149 (C.A.), has held that fishing licences are not "goods" (at page 162), that they are not an integral part of the vessel (at pages 164 and 173) and that they are not, properly speaking, issued to a vessel, but to a person in respect of a vessel (at page 165).

'[68] It is also very doubtful that the concept of "necessaries" in maritime law could be invoked in the present case. Counsel for the appellant has not referred the Court to any authority for the proposition that a fishing licence could form part of the "necessaries" provided to a ship. Necessaries, in my view, do not extend to fishing licences issued by the Minister with respect to a ship. As noted by William Tetley, in *Maritime Liens and Claims*, 2nd ed., (Montréal: International Shipping Publications, Blais, 1998) (at p age 551):

> Necessaries may be defined as supplies, repairs and equipment (and in some jurisdictions other goods and services) ordered on the credit of the ship and which are generally beneficial to the ship, so that it may carry out the common venture.

(For a list of goods or services to which the concept of "necessaries" has been extended, and which does not include fishing licences, see Nigel Meeson, *Admiralty Jurisdiction and Practice*, 2nd ed., London: LLP Professional Publications, 2000, at 2–163.) Fishing licences are not issued on the credit of a ship and the Minister of Fisheries and Oceans can hardly be compared with a claimant for necessaries or a creditor.' *Radil Bros Fishing Co v Canada* (*Department of Fisheries and Oceans, Regional Director General*) (2001) 207 DLR (4th) 82 at 103, FCA, per Décary JA

NECESSARIES OF LIFE

Canada 'Generally speaking, the criminal law imposes liability for acts, some conduct that is prohibited. But there are certain situations where an omission to act may lead to criminal liability. But that can only arise if there is a legal duty, not merely a moral duty, to act.

'Section 215 of the *Criminal Code* imposes a specific legal duty to act, that being, to provide necessaries of life in certain categories of relationships. Specifically, s. 215(1)(b) requires every person to provide necessaries of life to their spouse. It also makes it a criminal offence to fail, without lawful excuse, to provide necessaries of life where the failure to do so endangers the life of their spouse. Thus Parliament clearly intended to make the omission to provide necessaries of life, in certain circumstances, a crime.

'I think it is agreed that the term "necessaries of life" encompasses more than just food, clothing and shelter. It includes anything necessary to preserve life, such as medical aid or intervention to prevent serious harm or risk of death.' *R v Kirby* [2004] NWTJ No 57, 245 DLR (4th) 564 (SC) at 566–67, per Vertes J

New Zealand '... the provision of artificial respiration may be regarded as a necessary of life where it is required to prevent, cure or alleviate a disease that endangers the health or life of the patient. If, however, the patient is surviving only by virtue of the mechanical means which induces heartbeat and breathing and is beyond recovery, I do not consider that the provision of a ventilator can properly be construed as a necessary of life.' *Auckland Area Health Board v A-G* [1993] 1 NZLR 235 at 249–250, per Thomas J

New Zealand [Section 151 of the Crimes Act 1961 provides that: '(1) Every one who has charge of any other person unable, by reason of detention, age, sickness, insanity, or any other cause, to withdraw himself from such charge, and unable to provide himself with the necessaries of life, is (whether such charge is undertaken by him under any contract or is imposed upon him by law or by reason of his unlawful act or otherwise howsoever) under a legal duty to supply that person with the necessaries of life, and is criminally responsible for omitting without lawful excuse to perform such duty if the death of that person is caused, or if his life is endangered or his health permanently injured, by such omission.'] '[23] So a parent's common law duty is undoubted. But it does not follow, it seems to us, that when in s 151 Stephen framed a duty to provide the necessaries of life – and more specifically in s 152 a duty upon a parent, or upon a person in place of a parent, to provide them for a child under 16 years in that person's actual custody – he was setting down in statutory form the parent's common law duty to take reasonable steps to protect his or her child from the type of harm which we have just been discussing. The expression "necessaries of life" (or "necessaries" in s 152, which in context bears the same meaning) has long been well understood as encompassing goods and services food, clothing, housing, medical care) necessary to sustain life. Apart from the dictum in *Popen* to which the Judge referred, it has never, so far as the diligence of counsel and our own researches have discovered, been understood to include the taking of an action other than providing goods and services for the purpose of sustenance, albeit in relation to goods and services it is a flexible expression capable of adjusting to changing times and circumstances. It is noticeable that Stephen himself, in giving in his *History* at pp 10 – 11 an illustration of the duties of parents or guardians, refers only to their duty to provide food, warmth and clothing etc for children. We note too that Simister and Brookbanks at para 3.2.1 plainly do not regard a failure to effect an easy rescue of a child as the omission to supply a necessary.

'[24] In other contexts, such as bankruptcy and infants' contracts, necessaries may include anything suitable or appropriate for the person in the particular circumstances or social situation, not merely those things which the person must absolutely have to sustain life, but again in those contexts we do not find the expression used save in relation to a commodity or service able to be acquired by or made available for the use of the person in question. It might of course be the case that the employment of a personal security service could be a necessary for a celebrity, even a very young celebrity, but such a purchasable service is not comparable with the ordinary function performable by parents in protecting their child from harm. In our view, and with respect to the contrary obiter opinion of the Court in *Popen*, it would be a distortion of plain words, totally inappropriate in interpreting a statute imposing criminal liability, to describe that parental function as one of the necessaries of life.' *R v Lunt* [2004] 1 NZLR 498

NECESSARILY INCURRED

[Child Support (Maintenance Assessments and Special Cases) Regulations 1992, SI 1992/1815, Sch 3 para 4(1): 'Subject to the following provisions of this paragraph the housing costs referred to in this Schedule shall be included as housing costs only where—(a) they are necessarily incurred for the purpose of purchasing, renting or otherwise securing possession of the home for the parent and his family, or for the purpose of carrying out repairs and improvements to that home …'.] '[1] This appeal concerns the approach to "housing costs" for the purpose of determining exempt income when making a maintenance assessment under the Child Support Act 1991…

'[2] As part of the overall process of making a maintenance assessment under the 1991 Act, it is necessary to calculate the "assessable income" of each parent. This is his or her net income minus his "exempt income, calculated or estimated in accordance with regulations" (Sch 1, para 5)…

'[3] These calculations are performed in accordance with the 1991 Act itself and the Child

Support (Maintenance Assessments and Special Cases) Regulations 1992, SI 1992/1815. In what appears to be the jargon of those who work daily with these regulations, I will refer to them as the MASC Regulations 1992.

…

'[30] An appeal lies to this court from a decision of a child support commissioner only "on a question of law" (see s 25(1) of the 1991 Act). The focus of the present appeal is upon the application of the words "are necessarily incurred for the purpose of purchasing … or otherwise securing possession of the home for the parent" where they appear in para 4(1)(a) of Sch 3 to the MASC Regulations 1992, and in particular on the word "necessarily". The word "necessarily" is an ordinary English word, not a technical legal term. It is accordingly important first to establish the task of, and permissible discretion in, this court on an appeal of this kind. There is clear guidance from the House of Lords.

…

'[37] In my view "necessarily" where it appears in para 4(1)(a) of Sch 3 is a linguistically irreducible word. We should be very careful not to replace it with a synonym in this case nor to paraphrase para 4, and I eschew any attempt to do so.

'[38] It is also a word which accommodates a range of meanings, although it is far less protean or wide than the word "substantial" which Lord Mustill was considering [in *South Yorkshire Transport Ltd v Monopolies and Mergers Commission* [1993] 1 All ER 289 at 294–295, [1993] 1 WLR 23 at 29, HL].

'[39] In my view it is possible and permissible to say where on the spectrum of exigency the word "necessarily" is placed, and to say what it does not mean. It does not mean merely reasonably, or sensibly or justifiably. It is higher on the spectrum than that. Nor does it mean "reasonably necessarily". The maker of the regulation has not qualified the word necessarily, so if there is a different shade of meaning, or a different band on the spectrum, between "reasonably necessarily" and "necessarily" simpliciter, it is the latter meaning and the latter band which the regulation requires. But nor does the word "necessarily" convey an absolute meaning, such as absolutely essentially or inescapably. The context is, as Mr Castle accepts, too subjective for that; and I agree with the submission of Ms Demetriou that the regulation cannot sensibly require that minute scrutiny is given not only to all possible mortgage options at the time of commencement, but to continuing possible remortgage options. Further, "necessarily incurred" in para 4(1)(a) qualifies both the purpose of purchasing, renting or otherwise securing possession of the home; and also "the purpose of carrying out repairs and improvements to that home". There is a definition of "repairs and improvements" in para 2, quoted in [10], above. In relation to repairs it means "major repairs necessary to maintain the fabric of the home". In relation to improvements it means any of the measures listed in sub-paras (a) to (k) "undertaken with a view to improving its fitness for occupation". The measures themselves include at (k) "other improvements which the child support officer considers reasonable in the circumstances". So it is clear that although all repairs and improvements must, because of para 4(1)(a), be "necessarily incurred", consideration of repairs and improvements requires the application of a range of judgments by the decision-maker. The breadth and elasticity of para 2 (which employs words like "major", "maintain[ing] the fabric of the home", "improving its fitness for occupation" and "reasonable in the circumstances") would be otiose if "necessarily incurred" was given too restrictive or absolute a meaning in para 4(1)(a).

'[40] So "necessarily" must be given its proper force, but not a strained force. I agree with paras 39 and 40 of the decision of Mr Commissioner Jacobs (quoted in [22], above) where he said that para 4(1)(a) set a "high threshold" but also that "it must be interpreted and applied sensibly, with appropriate regard to the realities of property acquisition and of the mortgage market". In my view Mr Castle was right to accept the appropriateness of that comment.

'[41] I also agree with the sense of the observations of Mr Commissioner Jacobs when he said (at para 52) (quoted more fully in [24], above:

"In practice the focus is likely to be on the sequence of events that led to the mortgage arrangement … and the reasons the parent gives for making that decision. A parent will need a more persuasive reason to explain some decisions than others."

'[42] Beyond what I have stated in [37]–[41], above, I do not believe it possible to "sharpen" the test where it appears in para 4(1)(a) of Sch 3 to the MASC Regulations 1992.'

…

'[52] I agree that this appeal should be dismissed for the reasons given by Holman J. I add a few words of my own because the word "necessarily" which lies at the heart of the appeal has given rise to difficulty. The appeal turns on the meaning of this word where it is used to describe housing costs

that are "necessarily incurred for the purpose of purchasing, renting or otherwise securing possession of the home for the parent …" (see para 4(1)(a) of Sch 3 to the Child Support (Maintenance Assessments and Special Cases) Regulations 1992, SI 1992/1815).

'[53] "Necessary" is a somewhat protean word whose meaning depends on the context in which it is used. In some contexts, it means "indispensable" or "essential". Thus, for example, s 2(1) of the Law of Property (Miscellaneous Provisions) Act 1989 provides that a contract for the sale of an interest in land "can only be made in writing". To say that it is "necessary" for such a contract to be in writing is to use the word in its strongest sense. It is indispensable that such a contract be in writing. There is no contract unless it is in writing.

'[54] In *R v Shayler* [2002] UKHL 11 at [23], [2002] 2 All ER 477 at [23], [2003] 1 AC 247 Lord Bingham of Cornhill said of the word "necessary" where it appears in the phrase "necessary in a democratic society" in art 10(2) of the European Convention for the Protection of Human Rights and Fundamental Freedoms 1950 (as set out in Sch 1 to the Human Rights Act 1998):

"It is plain from the language of art 10(2), and the European Court has repeatedly held, that any national restriction on freedom of expression can be consistent with art 10(2) only if it is prescribed by law, is directed to one or more of the objectives specified in the article and is shown by the state concerned to be necessary in a democratic society. 'Necessary' has been strongly interpreted: it is not synonymous with 'indispensable', neither has it the flexibility of such expressions as 'admissible', 'ordinary', 'useful', 'reasonable' or 'desirable' (see *Handyside v UK* (1976) 1 EHRR 737 at 754 (para 48))."

'[55] In some contexts, the word "necessary" has a weaker meaning. But it will usually bear the connotation of some degree of compulsion or exigency. The context will determine where on the spectrum of compulsion or exigency the word "necessary" is placed (I adopt the words of Holman J at [39], above).

'[56] It could be argued in the present context (costs incurred in securing possession by means of a mortgage) that, to the extent that costs are incurred in excess of the minimum necessary to secure possession of the house, they are not necessarily incurred; or putting it another way, that costs are "necessarily incurred" only if they are unavoidably or indispensably incurred. But

Mr Castle does not so contend, and he is right not to do so. Such an approach is unrealistic and would in any event be difficult to apply in practice. It would mean that it had to be established that the parent had incurred the lowest possible mortgage costs. But, in the real world, many considerations are taken into account by a would-be mortgagor when choosing a mortgage. The level of the interest rate is obviously an important consideration. But mortgage A may offer a rate of interest of 6% which is fixed for five years, and mortgage B may offer a variable interest rate of 5%. Which of these two offers the cheaper costs? Is the position affected if mortgage A includes a penalty for early redemption, whereas mortgage B does not do so? And what if the level of redemption penalty differs as between the two mortgages? There are many different types of mortgages available. It may be quite impossible to say whether the costs incurred in relation to any particular mortgage are the cheapest possible mortgage costs. This is the practical reason why, in the present context, it cannot have been intended that the necessity test requires the making of detailed comparisons of mortgage costs of this kind.

'[57] But, in my view, this is not the only reason why the necessity test is not limited to an objective assessment of the question whether the costs incurred are the cheapest possible costs. It may be very important to a mortgagor to have the security of a fixed-rate mortgage and/or to know that he can redeem his mortgage without penalty. It may be of importance to him that the mortgagee is a front rank building society, rather than a relatively unknown secondary bank. From his point of view, it may be necessary to obtain a mortgage from a well-known building society and on terms that enable him, so far as possible, to plan his affairs with some certainty. In my judgment, it would be most surprising if these entirely normal considerations were required to be left out of account when determining whether the mortgage costs were necessarily incurred.

'[58] I do not consider that, in the context of para 4(1) of Sch 3 to the MASC Regulations 1992, the phrase "necessarily incurred" requires such considerations to be ignored. In my judgment, in deciding whether costs are necessarily incurred, account can also be taken of the absent parent's circumstances. That is not to introduce a test of reasonableness. But it recognises that it may not be possible to say whether a person has necessarily incurred costs without having regard to his or her circumstances. These will, of course, include whether the person could have secured the possession of his house by incurring lower costs, i e whether lower costs were actually available to him or her as an option. But they may also include whether, having regard to those circumstances, he or she considered it to be possible to incur lower costs. To give another example: the absent parent may have a rational fear that he will be made redundant within the next ten years, and that he will then find it very difficult to find employment. He may be a somewhat cautious person, and want to pay off his mortgage as soon as possible, so as to allay his concern that he may be saddled with a mortgage after he has stopped earning. From his point of view, it is necessary to pay off the mortgage as soon as possible. In my judgment, this is a consideration to which a tribunal may have regard when deciding the question.' *Pabari v Secretary of State for Work and Pensions* [2004] EWCA Civ 1480, [2005] 1 All ER 287 at [1]–[3], [30], [37]–[42], per Holman J, [52]–[58], per Dyson LJ

NECESSARY

[Under the Contempt of Court Act 1981, s 4(2) publication of any report of legal proceedings held in public may be postponed by an order of the court where it appears 'necessary' for avoiding a substantial risk of prejudice.] 'As for the second of my three questions ("appears to be necessary for avoiding" the described risk), again there is some learning on the same word in a different part of the same Act: see *Re an inquiry under the Companies Securities (Insider Dealing) Act 1985* [1988] 1 All ER 203, [1988] AC 660 (HL) which suggests that the word "necessary" in s 10 has a meaning somewhere between "indispensable" on the one hand and "useful" or "convenient" on the other. Again, there could be argument that within the same Act one should expect the same word to have the same meaning, but in the context of s 4(2) and given the respect habitually accorded by the legislature and the courts to the freedom of the press to report public events, I cannot see "necessary" as here intended to mean no more than, say, merely "convenient": see eg *R v Clerkenwell Magistrates' Court, ex p Telegraph plc* [1993] 2 All ER 183 at 187, [1993] QB 462 at 469 and *R v Horsham Justices, ex p Farquharson* [1982] 2 All ER 269 at 287–288, [1982] QB 762 at 795. More important in this area is the consideration that the necessity is not general or abstract but is specifically related to the avoidance of the described risk. [Counsel] argues on behalf of the press that the purpose of the "necessity" provision is threefold: firstly, to ensure that an order is made only if it is needed in the practical sense that the prejudice cannot be avoided save by an order; secondly, and again looking to practicalities, to be sure that an order, if made, would be likely to cause the prejudice to be avoided and, thirdly, that the order, if made, is to be no wider in its ambit than is needed to avoid the predicated risk. I confess to being attracted by this submission (which requires the judicial discretion I shall describe below to be the last stage in a three-stage approach) but I shall have to examine later whether I am free to adopt it. 'I am attracted because the section does not simply say, as it could so easily have done, that the court may make a postponement order where an order is necessary by reason of a substantial risk of that prejudice but only where it appears necessary for avoiding that prejudice. I see [Counsel's] submission as giving full weight to the words "for avoiding".' *MGN Pension Trustees Ltd v Bank of America National Trust and Savings Association* [1995] 2 All ER 355 at 361–362, per Lindsay J

Australia ' "Necessary" is a word which has the same connotations as words such as "needs" and "need".' *Re Action Food Barns (WA) Pty Ltd* (1996) 17 SR (WA) 317 at 344, per Judge Greaves

Australia 'The term "necessary" in such a setting as this is to be understood in the sense given it by Pollock CB in *The Attorney-General v Walker* [(1849) 3 Ex 242 at 255–256; 154 ER 833 at 838–839], namely as identifying a power to make orders which are reasonably required or legally ancillary to the accomplishment of the specific remedies for enforcement provided in Div 4 of Pt 3 of the District Court Act [1973 (NSW)]. In this setting, the term "necessary" does not have the meaning of "essential"; rather it is to be "subjected to the touchstone of reasonableness".' *Pelechowski v Registrar* (1999) 162 ALR 336 at 348; 73 ALJR 697; BC9902072, per Gaudron, Gummow and Callinan JJ

Canada '[86] The 1988 amendments to the *Copyright Act* specify that participants in a telecommunication who only provide "the means of telecommunication necessary" are deemed not to be communicators. The section as presently worded provides as follows:

2.4(1) For the purposes of communication to the public by telecommunication,

...

(b) a person whose only act in respect of the communication of a work or other subject-matter to the public consists of providing the means of

telecommunication necessary for another person to so communicate the work or other subject-matter does not communicate that work or other subject-matter to the public; [Emphasis added.]

'[87] Parliament did not say that the intermediaries are engaged in communication of copyright content *but* enjoy an immunity. Instead, s. 2.4(1)(b) says that such intermediaries are deemed, for purposes of the *Copyright Act*, not to communicate the work to the public at all. Whether or not intermediaries are parties to the communication for legal purposes other than copyright is an issue that will have to be decided when it arises.

...

'[91] The words of s. 2.4(1)(b) must be read in their ordinary and grammatical sense in the proper context. "Necessary" is a word whose meaning varies somewhat with the context. The word, according to *Black's Law Dictionary*,

may mean something which in the accomplishment of a given object cannot be dispensed with, or it may mean something reasonably useful and proper, and of greater or lesser benefit or convenience, and its force and meaning must be determined with relation to the particular object sought. [Emphasis added.] (*Black's Law Dictionary* (6th ed. 1990), at p. 1029)

'In context, the word "necessary" in s. 2.4(1)(b) is satisfied if the means are reasonably useful and proper to achieve the benefits of enhanced economy and efficiency.' *Society of Composers, Authors and Music Publishers of Canada v Canadian Association of Internet Providers* [2004] SCJ No 44, 240 DLR (4th) 193, per Binnie J

NECESSARY ... FOR THE PURPOSE OF PRESERVING THE POSITION

New Zealand [Judicature Amendment Act 1972, s 8.] 'Section 8 confers discretion on the Court to make interim orders in an application for review where the Court is of "the opinion it is necessary to do so for the purpose of preserving the position of the applicant" (s 8(1)). Where the Crown is the respondent the Court may, by interim order, "Declare that the Crown ought not to take any further action that is or would be consequential on the exercise of the statutory power" (s 8(2)(a)).

'In *Carlton & United Breweries Ltd v Minister of Customs* [1986] 1 NZLR 423, this Court emphasised the width of the discretion and the undesirability of trammelling it by formulations not found in the section itself.

...

'*Carlton & United Breweries Ltd v Minister of Customs* concerned the imposition of anti-dumping duties under Part VA of the Customs Act 1966. In assessing the viability of the action it was relevant that the legislative scheme indicated a limited role for the Court ... Just as the nature and apparent strength of the applicant's case are to be weighed, so too is the need to protect the applicant's position. Necessity to protect a position requires that there be a legal and factual position to protect.' *New Zealand Maori Council v Attorney*-General [1996] 3 NZLR 140 at 150–151, CA, per cur

NECESSITY

'English law does, in extreme circumstances, recognise a defence of necessity. Most commonly this defence arises as duress, that is pressure on the accused's will from the wrongful threats or violence of another. Equally however it can arise from other objective dangers threatening the accused or others. Arising thus it is conveniently called "duress of circumstances".' *R v Martin* [1989] 1 All ER 652 at 653, CA, per cur

Agency of

[For 1 Halsbury's Laws (4th edn) para 724 see now 1(2) Halsbury's Laws (4th edn) (Reissue) para 28.]

NEED

New Zealand [Section 4(1)(a)(i) of the Shop Trading Hours Act Repeal Act 1990 provides that the trading restrictions on Good Friday and Easter Sunday (provided for in s 3(1) of the Act) do not apply to a shop if it is a shop where:
'(i) The goods for sale include nothing that is not food, drink, a household item, a personal item, an automotive fuel, an automotive lubricant, an automotive part, or an automotive accessory of a kind that people may reasonably need to be able to buy at any time ...']

'[35] ... In the case already referred to (*Department of Labour v Cavanagh*) Judge Callander considered at p 662 that the term "need" should be given its ordinary and more extensive meaning of "want" or "requirement" as against a meaning of "basic necessity" or "essential". I would agree with this analysis. However, at p 663 Judge Callander went on to say that any need must be reasonable. This means, said Judge Callander, that the Court must

examine the needs subjectively to determine whether they are "moderate, sensible or rational wants or requirements or whether, on the other hand, on an objective analysis, they may be considered excessive, exorbitant, inordinate, unnecessary or extravagant.

'[36] In addition Judge Callander drew attention to the requirement that they must be items that people may need to be able to buy at any time. He thus suggested that an appropriate question may be whether the purchase of the item may reasonably be put off until another day not given special protection by Parliament. Again this seems to me to be the correct analysis.

'[37] For food and drink, household cleaning items, items for personal ablutions and essential items of household maintenance there would seem little argument that there could be a reasonable need to purchase these items at any time. Indeed, in respect of many of the items, assuming that the householder did not have supplies of those items to hand, supplies would even come within the more imperative definition of the term "need". Given, however, the wider definition of need accepted I see no reason to restrict the range of goods available in these categories to exclude what some may regard as luxury goods.

'[38] There may, however, be some questions over items which would be or could be seen as occasional purchases (for example the purchase of patio furniture) rather than more everyday items on the basis that it would be difficult to see why the purchase of occasional items could not reasonably be put off until another day not given special protection by Parliament. However, even this is subject to the caveat that this only applies if it would not create hardship if a person was deprived of the use of those items for a day.

'[39] ... given Waiheke is a holiday destination where people may have brought limited supplies with them, where they may have limited storage and limited transport facilities, the ability to shop every day for items in those categories could be seen as a necessity.' *Woolworths (New Zealand) Ltd v Attorney-General* [2001] 3 NZLR 123 at 131–132 per Glazebrook J

NEGLECT

Australia [The accused sought a certificate for costs in respect of adjourned days of the trial resulting from illness of a juror. For the certificate to issue it is necessary, inter alia, that the order for a new trial be not attributable to the act, neglect or default of the accused.] '"Neglect", as with the word "default", is passive in its quality. It is to be interpreted in the context of s 18 of the [Appeal Costs Fund Act 1964 (Vic)] as something which results in a trial being discontinued and a new trial being ordered. I am of the view that, within that context, the appropriate and proper meaning to be given to the word "neglect" is to fail to perform a duty or obligation or to omit or to fail, through carelessness or negligence, to do something. The omission to do something, however, in this context, in my view, should be an omission to do something which the accused or his legal practitioner is able to do.' *R v Grimwade* (1990) 51 A Crim R 470 at 476, per McDonald J

NEGLIGENCE

[For 34 Halsbury's Laws (4th edn) para 1 see now 33 Halsbury's Laws (4th edn) (Reissue) para 601.]

Contributory negligenc e

[For 34 Halsbury's Laws (4th edn) para 68 see now 33 Halsbury's Laws (4th edn) (Reissue) para 675.]

Criminal

[For 11 Halsbury's Laws (4th edn) para 1171 see now 11(1) Halsbury's Laws (4th edn) (Reissue) para 445.]

NEGOTIATE

Due negotiation

United States A negotiable document of title is 'duly negotiated' when it is negotiated in the manner stated in this section [by indorsement and delivery or, if the indorsement is in blank, by delivery alone] to a holder who purchases it in good faith without notice of any defense against or claim to it on the part of any person and for value, unless it is established that the negotiation is not in the regular course of business or financing and involves receiving the document in settlement or payment of a money obligation. (Uniform Commercial Code 1978, s 7ñ501(4))

NEGOTIATIONS

New Zealand [Sections 9 and 12(2) of the Employment Contracts Act 1991.] 'Negotiations are as I have said a process of mutual discussion and bargaining, involving putting forward and debating proposal and counter-proposal, persisting,

conceding, persuading, threatening, all with the objective of reaching what will probably be a compromise that the parties are able to accept and live with.' *Capital Coast Health Ltd v New Zealand Medical Laboratory Workers Union Inc* [1996] 1 NZLR 7 at 19, CA, per Hardie Boys J

NERVOUS

Mental shock and nervous shock

Australia 'As Wooten J observed in *Fraser* [1975] 2 NSWLR 521 at 525–6 the terms "mental shock and nervous shock" are not words of narrow technical meaning and have long been used interchangeably in the law of tort to include any mental or psychological disturbance ... The phrase should be construed as including the full range of psychiatric illnesses whether or not they would, in the absence of the phrase in the definition of "injury", have been taken to be included within "bodily harm".' *West v Morisson* (1996) 89 A Crim R 21 at 23, per Macrossan CJ

Nervous shock

'Her [the plaintiff's] claim is ... one for what have in the authorities and the literature been called damages for nervous shock. Judges have in recent years become increasingly restive at the use of this misleading and inaccurate expression, and I shall use the general expression "psychiatric damage", intending to comprehend within it all relevant forms of mental illness, neurosis and personality change.' *Attia v British Gas plc* [1987] 3 All ER 455 at 462, CA, per Bingham LJ

'To my mind the expression "nervous shock", as used in the decided cases, connotes a reaction to an immediate and horrifying impact. I have no doubt that the kinds of psychiatric illness to which nervous shock may give rise could equally be brought about by an accumulation of more gradual assaults upon the nervous system, but the law as it stands does not appear to me to provide for the latter category.' *Jones v Wright* [1991] 3 All ER 88 at 123, CA, per Nolan LJ

' "Shock", in the context of this cause of action [for damages for nervous shock] involves the sudden appreciation by sight or sound of a horrifying event, which violently agitates the mind. It has yet to include psychiatric illness caused by the accumulation over a period of time of more gradual assaults on the nervous system.' *Alcock v Chief Constable of South Yorkshire Police* [1991] 4 All ER 907 at 918, HL, per Lord Ackner

NEW OR NEWLY DISCOVERED FACT

[The Criminal Justice Act 1988, s 133(1) provides that, when a person has been convicted of a criminal offence and when subsequently his conviction has been reversed on the ground that a 'new or newly discovered fact' shows beyond reasonable doubt that there has been a miscarriage of justice, the Secretary of State must pay compensation for the miscarriage of justice to the person who has suffered punishment as a result of such conviction or, if he is dead, to his personal representatives, unless the non-disclosure of the unknown fact was wholly or partly attributable to the person convicted.]

'[46] The first reason given in the decision letters for the refusal of compensation is that the new evidence about Pollitt's possession of a gun does not amount to a "new or newly discovered fact" but is simply new evidence of a matter that was in issue at the trial. Mr Starmer submits that that is wrong. New evidence can be a new or newly discovered fact even if it does relate to an issue at trial. For example, at trial there may be an issue as to identification. Later evidence (e g in the form of a confession and/or DNA evidence) may show that the true offender was someone else and that the identification of the defendant at trial was erroneous. It would be absurd if the subsequent evidence could not amount to a new or newly discovered fact because the identity of the offender was in issue at the trial.

'[47] Mr Sales seeks to meet this challenge in two ways. He submits first that the decision letters were right to draw the distinction they did between evidence and fact; and secondly, that even if the matters relied on amount to a "fact", they are not a "new" or "newly discovered" fact within the meaning of s 133.
...

'[50] It seems to us that those authorities [*R v Secretary of State for the Home Dept, ex p Priestley* [1994] COD 505, and *R v Secretary of State for the Home Dept, ex p Garner* (1999) 11 Admin LR 595] do not get Mr Sales very far. We would certainly accept the distinction drawn in them between evidence and fact. Evidence that 'x' is the case does not make 'x' a fact: for example, the evidence may not be not credible (as posited in *Ex p Priestley*) or it may in any event not result in relevant findings of fact (as happened in *Ex p Garner*). We do not read the decision letters in this case, however, as being based on that simple distinction between evidence and fact. The reasoning appears to be that, because Pollitt's possession of a gun was in issue at the trial, new evidence relating to that issue cannot meet the

statutory condition as to a "new or newly discovered fact". If that is the reasoning, then in our judgment it is erroneous. Where new evidence results in a finding of fact and the fact so found can properly be described as a new or newly discovered fact, then the relevant statutory condition can be met even if the evidence and the resulting finding of fact relate to a matter that was in issue at trial. Mr Starmer's example, where later evidence shows that the offence was committed by someone other than the original defendant, is a good one.

'[51] In any event the evidence/fact distinction does not meet the real point in this case. The fact relied on here is the fact that at trial the prosecution was in possession of undisclosed material showing that the police had received information about Pollitt's possession of a gun before they interviewed Murphy and Brannan. That is plainly a fact and not merely a matter of evidence: it was agreed at the 2002 appeal. It is capable in principle of being a new or newly discovered fact. That Pollitt's possession of a gun was an issue at trial does not affect the point.

'[52] We therefore reject the first of Mr Sales's submissions on this issue. His second submission, however, has more substance to it. What he says is that the undisclosed material relied on by the Court of Appeal in 2002 was not "new or newly discovered" within the meaning of s 133 since it was in the possession of the applicants before the hearing of the first appeal in 1993; and it is from the conclusion of the first appeal, rather than from the date of the trial, that time runs for the purpose of determining whether a fact is "new or newly discovered".
...

'[56] It follows from the above, submits Mr Sales, that the reference to a "new or newly discovered fact" in s 133(1) of the 1988 Act must be to a fact that is new or newly discovered since the date of the final decision, i e since the conclusion of any appeal brought within the ordinary time limit (or, if no appeal has been brought, since the expiry of the time limit for bringing one).

'[57] The way Mr Sales puts this second submission does not reflect the actual reasoning in the decision letters, which focus in this respect on the information available to the defence at trial (and do not thereby provide a sufficient answer to a case based on the undisclosed material). In our judgment, however, the submission is well founded.

'[58] We accept that s 133, read in the light of art 14(6) of the ICCPR [International Covenant on Civil and Political Rights], is concerned only with facts that emerge after the ordinary appellate process has been exhausted. The disclosure of a fact between trial and the determination of an appeal brought within the normal time limit cannot engage the operation of the section. In this case the undisclosed material was disclosed to Murphy and Brannan before the hearing of the first appeal in 1993. If it had resulted in the quashing of their convictions on that appeal, it could not have given rise to an entitlement to compensation under s 133; and although the same material played a part in the quashing of the convictions on the second appeal in 2002, it was still incapable of meeting the statutory conditions for compensation. Since it was already known at the time of the first appeal, at no time did it amount to a "new or newly discovered fact".

'[59] That position is not affected by the way in which the undisclosed material was dealt with on the 1993 appeal, ie on the basis of a "realistic concession" that the ground of appeal relating to non-disclosure of that material must fall with the court's rejection of the evidence it had heard. Indeed, the position would remain the same even if the concession should not have been made or accepted. As Lord Steyn put it in *Mullen's* case [*R (on the application of Mullen) v Secretary of State for the Home Dept*] [2004] 3 All ER 65 at [45]:

"If there is no new or newly discovered fact, but simply, for example, a recognition that an earlier dismissal of an appeal was wrong, the case falls outside art 14(6). That is so, however palpable the error in the first appellate decision may have been …'

'[60] Accordingly, although Mr Sales's second submission is not the way in which the decision letters were reasoned, the point made is in our judgment a good one and provides a sufficient basis for the refusal of statutory compensation … '
R (on the application of Murphy) v Secretary of State for the Home Department [2005] EWHC 140 (Admin), [2005] 2 All ER 763 at [46]–[47], [50]–[52], [58]–[60], per Richards J

NEWSPAPER

Australia 'In *Attorney-General v Bradbury* (1851) 7 Ex 97 … Martin B gave (at p 103) a definition of the word "newspaper" in its ordinary sense. He said: "The ordinary understanding of the word 'newspaper' is, a publication containing a narrative of recent events and occurrences published regularly at short intervals from time to time". That definition seems to me as satisfactory as it was 120 years ago

…' *Downland Publications Ltd v Deputy Commissioner of Taxation* (1982) 64 FLR 216 at 223, per Starke J

Australia 'The meaning of "newspaper" which has received approval in the High Court as at 1971–72 is that adopted by Gibbs J in the *Rotary Offset Press* case (1971) 45 ALJR at 522C: "The ordinary understanding of the word 'newspaper' is a publication containing a narrative of recent events and occurrences, published regularly at short intervals from time to time". That definition does not, in terms, refer to the advertising material which may appear in such a publication, and the significance, for the purposes of determining whether a publication is a "newspaper", of the advertising content of it may require ongoing consideration.' *John Fairfax & Sons v Deputy Commissioner of Taxation (NSW)* (1988) 91 ALR 111 at 122, per Mahoney JA

NEWSREEL

[There are no longer special special provisions relating to newsreels following the repeal of the Films Act 1960 by the Films Act 1985.]

NEXT FRIEND

[For 24 Halsbury's Laws (4th edn) para 895 et seq see now 5(3) Halsbury's Laws (4th edn) (Reissue) para 327; for 30 Halsbury's Laws (4th edn) paras 1017–1019 see now 30 Halsbury's Laws (4th edn) (Reissue) paras 1423–1425.]

NEXT OF KIN

[For 50 Halsbury's Laws (4th edn) paras 526, 527 see now 50 Halsbury's Laws (4th edn) (Reissue) paras 580–581.]

NO REASONABLE CAUSE TO BELIEVE

Australia 'It is true that the notion of "reasonable cause", although often used in legal instruments, is an awkward expression. A cause is a cause is a cause. Beliefs about causes may be reasonable, but causes are neither reasonable nor unreasonable. They are facts even if, as current legal doctrine insists, they often involve value judgments [*March v Stramare (E & M H) Pty Ltd* (1991) 171 CLR 506]… "no reasonable cause to believe" means "no cause for reasonably believing".' *New South*

Wales v Taylor (2001) 178 ALR 32; BC200100871; [2001] HCA 15 at [15], per Gleeson CJ, McHugh and Hayne JJ

NOMINAL, TRIVIAL OR COLOURABLE

Australia [It was common ground that consideration was not 'real and substantial' for the purposes of the Bankruptcy Act 1966 s 120 (Cth) if it was nominal, trivial or colourable.] 'The first two adjectives in the phrase "nominal or trivial or colourable" are directed to the quantum of the consideration. The first to consideration which is of only token value. The second to that which is not a mere token but is very small in relation to the value of the property for which it is exchanged. "Colourable" on the other hand goes to the genuineness of the consideration. Colourable consideration is that which is "pretended, feigned, counterfeit, collusory": *Oxford English Dictionary*.' *Wansley* (*trustee of the bankrupt estate of Edwards*) *v Edwards* (1996) 68 FCR 555 at 559–560; (1996) 148 ALR 420 at 425; BC9604145 at 8–9, per Olney, Whitlam and Sundberg JJ

NON EST FACTUM

[For 12 Halsbury's Laws (4th edn) para 1365 see now 13 Halsbury's Laws (4th edn) (Reissue) para 68.]

NON-ARM'S LENGTH TRANSACTION

Australia [Section 94 of the Sales Tax Assessment Act 1992 (Cth) applies to a taxpayer if '(a) the taxpayer (or an associate) has been party to a non-arm's length transaction; and (b) if the transaction had instead been an arm's length transaction, it would have been the case (or could reasonably be expected to have been the case) that: (i) the liability of the taxpayer to tax on the non-arm's length transaction, or any other transaction, would have been increased; or (ii) the entitlement of the taxpayer to a credit in connection with the non-arm's length transaction, or any other transaction, would have been reduced.] 'The section begins by postulating "a non-arm's length transaction". This expression is not only inelegant; it masks an ambiguity. Does it refer to a transaction between parties who are not at arm's length? Or does it refer to a transaction which is not conducted at arm's length, whether or not the parties themselves would be described as at arm's length from each other? The case law shows that similar, if not identical, expressions have been construed in

each of these ways, and that the difference between the two constructions has been emphasised. One approach is exemplified by *Australian Trade Commission v WA Meat Exports Pty Ltd* (1987) 75 ALR 287, where a Full Court (Beaumont, Wilcox and Burchett JJ) was concerned with the meaning of the expression "any person determined by the Board to be a person not at arm's length with the claimant or the association", an expression appearing in s 4(8) of the Export Market Development Grants Act 1974 (Cth). Having drawn attention to the fact that the phrase "not at arm's length" is often found in revenue statutes, the joint judgment of the Court (at 291) took the "ordinary meaning of the phrase" to be that explained in *Osborn's Concise Law Dictionary*, 6th ed, 32: "the relationship which exists between parties who are strangers to each other, and who bear no special duty, obligation, or relation to each other, e g vendor and the purchaser". The Court commented: "[T]he context of s 4 is consistent with the disqualification of expenditure by one party in favour of another where one of them has the ability to exert personal influence or control over the other." ...

'[11] But in *Granby Pty Ltd v F C of T* (1995) 95 ATC 4240, where the expression "dealing with each other at arm's length" in s 160ZH of the Income Tax Assessment Act 1936 (Cth) was in question, Lee J said (at 4243):

> "The expression 'dealing with each other at arm's length' involves an analysis of the manner in which the parties to a transaction conducted themselves in forming that transaction. What is asked is whether the parties behaved in the manner in which parties at arm's length would be expected to behave in conducting their affairs. Of course, it is relevant to that enquiry to determine the nature of the relationship between the parties, for if the parties are not parties at arm's length the inference may be drawn that they did not deal with each other at arm's length."

...

'[13] ... I think the better view of s 94 is that it does not refer to the relationship between the parties to a transaction, but to the manner of their dealing, although any relationship will obviously be important for the inferences it may raise.' *Pontifex Jewellers* (*Wholesale*) *Pty Ltd v Commissioner of Taxation* BC9908502; [1999] FCA 1822 at [10], [11], [13], per Burchett J

NON-RESIDENT

[The Capital Gains Tax Act 1979 has been repealed. The definition is re-enacted in the Taxation of Chargeable Gains Act 1992, s 14(4).]

NORMAL RESIDENCE

[Whether the occupation of interim accommodation pending a decision of an application for assistance could be 'normal residence' for the purposes of the Housing Act 1996 s 199(1)(a).] '[18] It is clear that words like "ordinary residence" and "normal residence" may take their precise meaning from the context of the legislation in which they appear but it seems to me that the prima facie meaning of normal residence is a place where at the relevant time the person in fact resides. That therefore is the question to be asked and it is not appropriate to consider whether in a general or abstract sense such a place would be considered an ordinary or normal residence. So long as that place where he eats and sleeps is voluntarily accepted by him, the reason why he is there rather than somewhere else does not prevent that place from being his normal residence. He may not like it, he may prefer some other place, but that place is for the relevant time the place where he normally resides. If a person, having no other accommodation, takes his few belongings and moves into a barn for a period to work on a farm that is where during that period he is normally resident, however much he might prefer some more permanent or better accommodation. In a sense it is "shelter" but it is also where he resides. Where he is given interim accommodation by a local housing authority even more clearly is that the place where for the time being he is normally resident. The fact that it is provided subject to statutory duty does not, contrary to the appellant authority's argument, prevent it from being such.
...
'[22] In *Eastleigh BC v Betts* [1983] 2 All ER 1111 at 1120, [1983] 2 AC 613 at 628 Lord Brightman stressed that "the real exercise will be to decide whether the normal residence has been such as to establish a subsisting local connection". In my opinion the occupation of interim accommodation can be taken into account in deciding whether such a local connection exists.' *Mohamed v Hammersmith and Fulham London Borough Council* [2001] UKHL 57 at [18], [22], [2002] 1 All ER 176 at 182–183, HL, per Lord Slynn of Hadley

NOT LESS THAN

[Under terms of a lease, tenants were required to give 'not less than nine months written notice' 'prior to' the effective date of termination of the lease. The tenants gave notice on 31 October 1995 that they wished to terminate the lease on 31 July 1996. There was dispute over whether the notice was timeous.] ['I agree ... both the first day and the last day fall to be excluded in computing the period of uninterrupted time that must elapse between the giving of notice and the expiry of the period for notice stipulated.' *Esson Properties Ltd v Dresser UK Ltd* 1997 SLT 949 at 952, per Lord Penrose

NOTARY

[For 34 Halsbury's Laws (4th edn) para 201 see now 33 Halsbury's Laws (4th edn) (Reissue) para 701.]

NOTICE

' "Notice" is often used in a sense or in contexts where the facts do not support the inference of knowledge. A man may have actual notice of a fact and yet not know it. He may have been supplied ... with a document and so have actual notice of its content, but he may not in fact have read it; or he may have read it some time ago and have forgotten its content.' *Eagle Trust plc v SBC Securities Ltd* [1992] 4 All ER 488 at 497–498, per Vinelott J

Of intended prosecution

[For 40 Halsbury's Laws (4th edn) para 532 see now 40(2) Halsbury's Laws (4th edn) (Reissue) para 728.]

NOTIFIED OF THE DECISION

Australia [Migration Act 1958 (Cth) s 478(1)(b).] '... The appellant submitted that for the Minister, as statutory guardian, the interests of the minor were paramount and took precedence over the Minister's statutory obligations under the Act as the opposing litigant in the Federal Court and this Court. This submission is ill-founded. Any role the Minister may have as guardian is not altogether clear given the language of the relevant sections of the Guardianship Act. However, any such role is irrelevant to the question of construction raised by this appeal. The question is how to construe the phrase "notified of the decision" in s 478(1)(b) of the Act. Any obligation of the Minister under a different enactment can have no effect on that construction. In any event, although s 6A(1) of the Guardianship Act provides that a non-citizen child shall not leave Australia except with the consent in writing of the Minister, s 6A(4) qualifies this, stating:

> This section shall not affect the operation of any other law regulating the departure of persons from Australia.

'At [42], per Gleeson CJ, McHugh, Gummow and Heydon JJ; BC200406533.

'[84] The appellant disputed the conclusions of the Federal Court that being "notified of the decision" meant no more than being notified of the result of the Tribunal's hearing. To construct this argument, the appellant relied on four steps.

'[85] First, he said that the word "notified" connoted something more than mere provision of information. From the meaning of the word and from its context in s 478 of the Migration Act, it implied a formal or official notification for a particular purpose. That purpose was to set in train proceedings of considerable importance to persons, such as himself, claiming refugee status. It engaged the jurisdiction of the Federal Court, a court established under Ch III of the Constitution. Moreover, as s 478(1) of the Migration Act indicated, the notification of the decision was to be such as to permit an "application" to the Federal Court to be made as specified under the Rules of that Court. Those Rules contemplate appropriate particularity in the identification of the grounds of an application for judicial review. In the context, therefore, the requirement to "notify" the appellant of the "decision" had to be one that involved a notification apt for its purpose, namely the initiation with appropriate specificity of an application to the Federal Court.

'[86] Secondly, the appellant argued that s 478 had to be read as an integral part of the "code" provided by the Migration Act for the delivery of "decisions" of the Tribunal. That "code" included s 430(1) of the Act, which contemplated the provision of a "written statement" that would afford precisely the material upon which a person (such as the appellant) in immigration detention could effectively initiate judicial review of the kind envisaged by ss 476 and 477 of the Migration Act. The obligation to provide copy of that "statement" to a potential applicant for judicial review, within a brief time, indicated the intended interaction of notification of the "decision" and provision of the "statement". In the case of a person (such as the appellant) in immigration detention, the "code"

required the Tribunal to give an applicant (and the Secretary) a copy of the "statement" within fourteen days after the "decision" concerned was made. Where this was not done, the appellant submitted, time would not run because the provision of the statement as well as a notification of the "decision" was part of the inter-related scheme of the Migration Act.

'[87] Thirdly, the appellant pointed out that the amendments to the Migration Act, enacted in 1998, drew an express distinction between the provision of "the outcome of the decision" and "being notified of a decision". By inference, after 1998, "being notified of a decision" meant more than mere notification of the "outcome of the decision". It followed, according to the appellant, that the notification by Mr Wallis of the result of the appellant's application to the Tribunal was not enough to notify the appellant of the decision. Nor did Ms Alamar's oral elaboration immediately thereafter amount to such a notification.

'[88] Fourthly, the appellant emphasised the need to construe the Migration Act with its purpose in mind, namely to facilitate effective engagement of the Federal Court by an application under s 476 or s 477 of that Act. In the case of illiterate unaccompanied minors (but also in many other cases) it was of the nature of the "applications" for which the Parliament has provided that they were of great importance to the persons affected and to the fulfilment of Australia's national protection obligations under the Refugees Convention. In such circumstances, the words "notified of the decision" should be construed to amount to a real and effective notification — one that would fulfil the purpose of engaging the jurisdiction of the Federal Court. It was not sufficient, in the case of a blind applicant, to provide such a person silently with a document typed in the ordinary way in the English language. Similarly, in the case of an illiterate minor, it was not sufficient to "notify ... the decision" by telling him of its "outcome". It was essential to provide him with the statement envisaged by s 430(1) and indeed a translation of that statement or its main part into the language that could be read to (and understood by) him, as constituting the essential "reasons" and "findings" of the Tribunal. Nothing less was sufficient to render the statutory right to judicial review a substantive reality. Because it was common ground that no such translation had been provided, the appellant had not been "notified of the decision". The time limit in s 478 of the Migration Act was not engaged. The Federal Court had jurisdiction to hear the application.

...

'[90] *Critical notification of a "decision":* The essential problem for the appellant's construction is that the time limit fixed by the Migration Act for applications for judicial review to the Federal Court is expressed by reference to being "notified" of the "decision". That is how s 478(1)(b) is worded. When regard is had to s 430 of the Migration Act, it is clear from its language that it draws a sharp distinction between the "decision on a review" and the "reasons for the decision", "findings on any material questions of fact" and reference "to the evidence or any other material". The "written statement", to which s 430 of the Migration Act refers, is also differentiated from the "decision of the Tribunal". In such a context, the reference to being "notified of the decision" must be taken to be a reference to notification of the result of the Tribunal's review. Separate provision is made for the "written statement". That separate provision is also reflected in the sections that were added to the Migration Act in 1998.

...

'[99] When the requirements of s 478(1)(b) of the Migration Act are read against the background of the foregoing considerations, it is clear that the appellant was "notified" of the "decision" of the Tribunal on 16 March 2001. The duty of the Tribunal to give an applicant a copy of the statement under s 430(1) of the Migration Act was a separate and distinct obligation. Originally, it was integrated with notification but that integration was deliberately repealed. In the appellant's case, the time when that statement was provided was therefore distinct from the time of being "notified" of the "decision".

'[100] However desirable it might be to afford to persons in the position of the appellant a notification, in a language in which they are fluent, of the "decision", the substance of the s 430(1) "statement" and a warning about the strict time limit for commencing proceedings in the Federal Court, the Migration Act makes no provision in that respect. It would not be a valid performance of this Court's duty of interpretation of s 478(1)(b) for it to import a precondition of the supply of the "statement" (still less a translation of the whole or some unspecified part thereof) into the clear language of that paragraph.

'[101] *Conclusion: the decision was "notified":* By the clear language of s 478(1)(b) of the Migration Act and the equally clear purpose of the Parliament, the time for the lodgment of the application for judicial review in the Federal Court began to run from the moment the appellant was notified of the "decision". Whatever problem might arise where an applicant had no ability at all to understand the limited information to be contained in such notification, it does not arise in this case. The notification was given orally. The appellant was told that he had lost. That much was not contested. That much was translated into the appellant's language. His awareness of it is confirmed by his immediate emotional response which was common ground. He broke down and sobbed. The primary judge and the Full Court were correct as a matter of law to decide as they did. They were doing no more than the Constitution requires. They were giving effect to the language and purpose of a valid enactment of the Federal Parliament according to its terms. That is also the duty of this Court.' *WACB v Minister for Immigration and Multicultural and Indigenous Affairs* [2004] HCA 50 at [83]–[88], [90], [99]–[101], per Kirby J; BC200406533

NOTORIETY

[For 12 Halsbury's Laws (4th edn) para 1365 see now 12(1) Halsbury's Laws (4th edn) (Reissue) para 657.]

NOTWITHSTANDING

Canada '[61] I do not find this argument persuasive. While I agree that "notwithstanding" in subsections 9(2) and 11(1) [of the *Canadian Human Rights Act*] indicates an exception to an earlier provision, in my view it does nothing more than create that exception. In *Engineered Buildings Ltd. and City of Calgary, Re* (1966), 57 D.L.R. (2d) 322, at page 325 the Alberta Supreme Court, Appellate Division held that "notwithstanding anything in this Act" means "that where the facts come within that subsection no other part of the Act applies". Similarly, in *Mitchell (Re)* (1996), 25 B.C.L.R. (3d) 249, at paragraph 17 the British Columbia Supreme Court concluded that "a provision beginning with 'notwithstanding X' creates an exception to X".

'[62] To construe "notwithstanding" as including the additional meaning of "to the contrary" would require that the word notwithstanding was being used to resolve an inconsistency or conflict between the relevant provisions. But in the provisions referred to by the applicants, no such inconsistencies or conflicts exist. Therefore, the use of "notwithstanding" in these instances signals only an exception to an earlier provision. Subsection 11(1) states it is a discriminatory practice to maintain different wages for male and female employees performing work of equal value. Subsection 11(4) simply creates an exception where certain facts exist, namely, if the difference in wages is based on a factor prescribed by the EWG 1986. Similarly, subsection 9(1) provides that it is a discriminatory practice for an employee organization to exclude, expel, or suspend an individual from membership in the organization on a prohibited ground of discrimination. Subsection 9(2) creates an exception where the individual has reached normal retirement age.

'[63] Accordingly, I reject the applicants' submission that the phrase "notwithstanding any collective agreement" should be read to mean "notwithstanding any collective agreement to the contrary".

'[64] The applicants also take the position that the Tribunal's interpretation of section 10 does not give effect to the plain meaning of the word "notwithstanding", which is "in spite of" or "without prevention by". They argue that "notwithstanding any collective agreement", therefore, means that the contents of collective agreements are of no relevance and should be ignored in the inquiry into the existence of common personnel and wage policies.

'[65] According to the *New Shorter Oxford English Dictionary on Historial Principles*, 1993 ed., "notwithstanding" means "In spite of, without regard to or prevention by". The courts, in a number of instances, have accepted that the plain meaning of "notwithstanding" is "in spite of". (See, for example: *Money v. Alberta* (*Registrar of Motor Vehicles*) (1995), 170 A.R. 321 (Q.B.); *Mattabi Mines Ltd. v. Mine Assessor* (1990), 72 O.R. (2d) 88 (C.A.); *Engineered Buildings Ltd. and City of Calgary, Re* (1966), 57 D.L.R. (2d) 322 (Alta. s C. (A.D.).)

'[66] While I accept that the plain meaning of "notwithstanding" is "in spite of", the plain meaning of the word notwithstanding on its own is insufficient to give meaning to its use here. Regard must be had to its contextual use within the provision itself and with respect to the statute to which it applies. The phrase within which the word notwithstanding appears states: "employees of an establishment include, notwithstanding any collective agreement applicable to any employees of the establishment". The "notwithstanding" phrase within the context of section 10 as a whole, simply adds additional information about the "employees of an establishment". The additional information provided is that, even if, the employees are subject to a collective agreement, they are still in the establishment if they are subject to a common

personnel and wage policy … ' *Canada* (*Human Rights Commission*) *v Canadian Airlines International Ltd* [2001] 1 FC 158 at 182–183, TD, per Hansen J

NOVATION

[For 9 Halsbury's Laws (4th edn) para 580 see now 9(1) Halsbury's Laws (4th edn) (Reissue) para 1036.]

[For 44 Halsbury's Laws (4th edn) para 496 see now 44(1) Halsbury's Laws (4th edn) (Reissue) para 896.]

NOVUS ACTUS INTERVENIENS

'In cases of homicide, it is rarely necessary to give the jury any direction on causation as such. Of course, a necessary ingredient of the crimes of murder and manslaughter is that the accused has by his act caused the victim's death. But how the victim came by his death is usually not in dispute. What is in dispute is more likely to be some other matter: for example, the identity of the person who committed the act which indisputably caused the victim's death; or whether the accused had the necessary intent; or whether the accused acted in self-defence, or was provoked. Even where it is necessary to direct the jury's minds to the question of causation, it is usually enough to direct them simply that in law the accused's act need not be the sole cause, or even the main cause, of the victim's death, it being enough that his act contributed significantly to that result. It is right to observe in passing, however, that even this simple direction is a direction of law relating to causation, on the basis of which the jury are bound to act in concluding whether the prosecution has established, as a matter of fact, that the accused's act did in this sense cause the victim's death. Occasionally, however, a specific issue of causation may arise. One such case is where, although an act of the accused constitutes a *causa sine qua non* of (or necessary condition for) the death of the victim, nevertheless the intervention of a third party may be regarded as the sole cause of the victim's death, thereby relieving the accused of criminal responsibility. Such intervention, if it has such an effect, has often been described by lawyers as a *novus actus interveniens*. We are aware that this time-honoured Latin term has been the subject of criticism. We are also aware that attempts have been made to translate it into English; though no simple translation has proved satisfactory, really because the Latin term has become a term of art which conveys to lawyers the crucial feature that there has not merely been an intervening act of another person, but that that act was so independent of the act of the accused that it should be regarded in law as the cause of the victim's death, to the exclusion of the act of the accused. At the risk of scholarly criticism, we shall for the purposes of this judgment continue to use the Latin term.' *R v Pagett* (1983) 76 Cr App R 279 at 288, CA, per Robert Goff LJ

NUISANCE

[For 34 Halsbury's Laws (4th edn) paras 301–309 see now 34 Halsbury's Laws (4th edn) (Reissue) paras 1–10.]

Private nuisance

[For 34 Halsbury's Laws (4th edn) para 307 see now 37 Halsbury's Laws (4th edn) (Reissue) para 7.]

Statutory nuisance

[For 38 Halsbury's Laws (4th edn) para 403 see now 38 Halsbury's Laws (4th edn) (Reissue) para 604.]
   [For 34 Halsbury's Laws (4th edn) para 304 see now 33 Halsbury's Laws (4th edn) (Reissue) para 4.]

Nuisance to highway

[For 21 Halsbury's Laws (4th edn) para 419 see now 21 Halsbury's Laws (4th edn) (2004 Reissue) para 322.]

Public nuisance

[For 34 Halsbury's Laws (4th edn) para 305 see now 37 Halsbury's Laws (4th edn) (Reissue) para 5.]
   'If it is correct, in general, that a public nuisance cannot arise out of the lawful use of a highway, …

it is not, in my judgment, because there is no unlawful act. It is because a consideration of the neighbourhood in the vicinity of the highway will lead to the conclusion that the noise or fumes, are not an actionable wrong in all the circumstances of the case. In other words, those who live close by public highways must accept the inevitable disturbance for the greater good of the public. Certainly this principle applies in private nuisance (see *Sturges v Bridgman* [(1879) 11 Ch D 852 at 856] and I can see no reason for a different approach in public nuisance, at least of the kind alleged in this case [passage of heavy goods vehicles]. Also many types of road which might otherwise give rise to noise nuisance will have been constructed pursuant to statutory powers after all relevant planning procedures have been complied with and compensation paid where appropriate. Actions in nuisance, if successful, would make a nonsense of the whole scheme. The private right must usually yield to the greater public interest.' *Gillingham Borough Council v Medway (Chatham) Dock Co Ltd* [1992] 3 All ER 923 at 932, per Buckley J

NURSERY GROUNDS

[For 1 Halsbury's Laws (4th edn) para 1002 see now 1(2) Halsbury's Laws (4th edn) (Reissue) para 302.]

NURSING HOME

[The Registered Homes Act 1984 has been amended by the National Health Service and Community Care Act 1990, s 66(1), Sch 9, para 27, to substitute in sub-s (3) for 'hospital', 'health service hospital, within the meaning of the National Health Service Act 1977'.]

O

OATH

Australia 'An oath, … is an appeal to a Supreme Being in whose existence the person taking the oath believes so as to bind his conscience but the form of taking the oath is not essential to the oath. That seems to be the position at common law. It would also appear to be the position under the Evidence Act [1906 (WA)] for s 97, providing as it does that every witness, with certain exceptions, shall give evidence on oath, declares that each oath shall be binding which is administered and taken in a form and manner that the person taking it declares to be binding on his conscience.' *R v Sossi* (1985) 17 A Crim R 405 at 408, per cur

OBJECTION

Australia 'The word "objection" [the Income Tax Assessment Act 1936, s 186] probably means no more than the entire writing which has been lodged with the Commissioner signifying the "objection" of the taxpayer and the grounds of that objection. But if this be not the case, the "objection" referred to in the section must be then confined to the statement by the taxpayer to the effect that he objects to the assessment of his taxable income and tax payable as notified to him. It is not a document confined to a particular claim as to taxable income or deduction as the Commissioner would suggest.' *Lighthouse Philatelics Pty Ltd v Federal Commissioner of Taxation* (1991) 103 ALR 156 at 164, per cur

OBJECTIONABLE

New Zealand [Section 3 of the Films, Videos and Publications Classification Act 1993 provides that:
'(1) For the purposes of this Act, a publication is objectionable if it describes, depicts, expresses, or otherwise deals with matters such as sex, horror, crime, cruelty, or violence in such a manner that the availability of the publication is likely to be injurious to the public good.

(2) A publication shall be deemed to be objectionable for the purposes of this Act if the publication promotes or supports, or tends to promote or support,—
(a) The exploitation of children, or young persons, or both, for sexual purposes; or
(b) The use of violence or coercion to compel any person to participate in, or submit to, sexual conduct; or
(c) Sexual conduct with or upon the body of a dead person; or
(d) The use of urine or excrement in association with degrading or dehumanising conduct or sexual conduct; or
(e) Bestiality; or
(f) Acts of torture or the infliction of extreme violence or extreme cruelty.

(3) In determining, for the purposes of this Act, whether or not any publication (other than a publication to which subsection (2) of this section applies) is objectionable or should be given a classification other than objectionable, particular weight shall be given to the extent and degree to which, and the manner in which, the publication—
(a) Describes, depicts, or otherwise deals with—
(i) Acts of torture, the infliction of serious physical harm, or acts of significant cruelty:
(ii) Sexual violence or sexual coercion, or violence or coercion in association with sexual conduct:
(iii) Other sexual or physical conduct of a degrading or dehumanising or demeaning nature:
(iv) Sexual conduct with or by children, or young persons, or both:
(v) Physical conduct in which sexual satisfaction is derived from inflicting or suffering cruelty or pain:
(b) Exploits the nudity of children, or young persons, or both:
(c) Degrades or dehumanises or demeans any person:

(d) Promotes or encourages criminal acts or acts of terrorism:

(e) Represents (whether directly or by implication) that members of any particular class of the public are inherently inferior to other members of the public by reason of any characteristic of members of that class, being a characteristic that is a prohibited ground of discrimination specified in section 21(1) of the Human Rights Act 1993.

(4) In determining, for the purposes of this Act, whether or not any publication (other than a publication to which subsection (2) of this section applies) is objectionable or should be given a classification other than objectionable, the following matters shall also be considered:

(a) The dominant effect of the publication as a whole:

(b) The impact of the medium in which the publication is presented:

(c) The character of the publication, including any merit, value, or importance that the publication has in relation to literary, artistic, social, cultural, educational, scientific, or other matters:

(d) The persons, classes of persons, or age groups of the persons to whom the publication is intended or is likely to be made available:

(e) The purpose for which the publication is intended to be used:

(f) Any other relevant circumstances relating to the intended or likely use of the publication'].

[Section 23 of the Films, Videos and Publications classification Act 1993 provides that:

'...

(2) After examining a publication, and having taken into account the matters referred to in section 3 of this Act, the Classification Office shall classify the publication as—

(a) Unrestricted; or

(b) Objectionable; or

(c) Objectionable except in any one or more of the following circumstances:

(f) the availability of the publication is restricted to persons who have attained a specified age:

(fi) the availability of the publication is restricted to specified persons or classes of persons:

(fii) the publication is used for one or more specified purposes.

(3) Without limiting the power of the Classification Office to classify a publication as a restricted publication, a publication that would otherwise be classified as objectionable may be classified as a restricted publication in order that the publication may be made available to particular persons or classes of persons for educational, professional, scientific, literary, artistic, or technical purposes'].

'[31] The High Court ruled that classification of the book and particular photographs as objectionable under the deeming provisions of s 3(2)(a) precluded any alternative classification under s 23, while noting that the board had nevertheless considered restriction to Mr Moonen alone. Then, as to the photographs classified as objectionable under s 3(3), the Full Court concluded that s 3(4) factors referred only to existing publications and, similarly, publications which were merely planned or proposed were outside s 23.

'[32] ... We agree. In *Moonen 1*, the Court para [39] (para [16] above) concluded, for the reasons it gave, that s 23(3) provided the sole exception to the otherwise mandatory requirement that a publication deemed objectionable under s 3(2) be classified as objectionable and allowed for availability on the very limited basis envisaged by that section (s 23(3)). And, of course, photographs found objectionable under s 3(3) could also, if satisfying the statutory criteria under s 23(3), be classified for restricted availability under the section.' *Moonen v Film and Literature Board of Review* [2002] 2 NZLR 754 at 764–765, per cur

OBJECTS ... WHOLLY OR MAINLY OF A POLITICAL NATURE

[The Broadcasting Act 1990, s 92(2)(a) prohibits the broadcasting of any advertisement inserted by or on behalf of any body whose 'objects are wholly or mainly of a political nature'.] 'The definition of "body" [in s 202 as a body of persons whether incorporated or not, and including a partnership] helps in reaching a conclusion as to what the section is referring to as being "objects". They are not necessarily the technical objects of an incorporated body. None the less where the body has formally set out its objects as has Amnesty International (British Section), I would expect the authority to decide, at any rate in the first instance, whether the body's objects fall within the subsection by doing no more than examine the statement of its objects. Where, however, there is doubt as to whether the formal statement reflects the true position or it is not possible to determine the position by merely looking at the objects the authority is quite entitled to examine any other material which is available. If there are no formal objects then obviously it is necessary to look at what other material there is available in order to determine what its objects are. In doing so the authority has to decide the purpose for which the body exists, recognising that a body may exist for more than one purpose.

'Where there is more than one object and some are political and others are not then it may be essential to go beyond the mere formal statement of the objects in order to decide whether the objects are mainly political. It needs to be remembered that if the body is not considered at least of a mainly political nature it is not subject to the prohibition.' *R v Radio Authority, ex p Bull* [1997] 2 All ER 561 at 569–570, CA, per Lord Woolf MR

OBLIGATION

[For 12 Halsbury's Laws (4th edn) para 1387 see now 13 Halsbury's Laws (4th edn) (Reissue) para 90.]

OBLIGEE–OBLIGOR

[For 12 Halsbury's Laws (4th edn) para 1385 see now 13 Halsbury's Laws (4th edn) (Reissue) para 88.]

OBLITERATION

[For 50 Halsbury's Laws (4th edn) para 273 see now 50 Halsbury's Laws (4th edn) (Reissue) para 345.]

OBSCENE AND INDECENT

Australia 'Just as the words do not have the same denotation in ordinary parlance, neither do they at common law. What is obscene will also be indecent but it does not follow that what is indecent is necessarily obscene. The line between what is indecent and what is obscene may on occasions be difficult to draw but, as in ordinary usage, the common law recognises that the word "obscene" is a stronger epithet than "indecent". It denotes a higher degree of offensiveness.' *Phillips v Police* (1994) 75 A Crim R 480 at 488, per Debelle J

OBSOLETE

Canada [Respondents sought cancellation of easement as obsolete.] 'No technical meaning is to be given to the word "obsolete" in this provision. It is an ordinary English word which is defined in the Shorter Oxford Dictionary, 3rd edn, thus: "1. That is no longer practised or used; discarded; out of date. 2. Worn out; effaced through wearing down, atrophy or degeneration".' *Collinson v La Plante* (1992) 98 DLR (4th) 459 at 467, BC CA, per Southin JA

OBSTACLE

Canada '*Issue 1*:Did the Agency provide adequate reasons for its finding that section 13-D of the tariff constitutes an obstacle to the mobility of passengers with disabilities?'

'In the words of the tariff, did the Agency's reasons provide sufficient indication of the reasoning process by which it determined that it is an obstacle to the mobility of a disabled passenger to require that an attendant, travelling on the same ticket as the passenger, be capable of assisting the passenger in getting on and off the train?

'The Agency determined that the tariff was an obstacle in its November 1994 decision. The decision under appeal treats this earlier finding as a given. The only portion of the 1994 decision dealing with the reasons for the Agency's determination is reproduced in paragraph 6 above. It is worth noting that the tariff was not a subject of the original complaint filed by Mr. Lemonde. Its provisions seem to have come before the Agency only as a result of VIA's reference to it in its submission responding to the complaint.

'In my view, the conclusion that the tariff was an obstacle is not supported by sufficient indication of the reasoning process engaged in by the Agency. The reasons provide no intimation of what constitutes an obstacle to the mobility of a disabled passenger nor are they sufficiently clear.

'The *Concise Oxford Dictionary of Current English* defines "obstacle" as a "thing that obstructs progress". Not only has the Agency failed to articulate any definition but it also does not appear to have engaged in any reasoned consideration of the tariff provisions. How does the requirement that an attendant be capable of assisting the disabled person with whom they are travelling to board and deboard a train constitute an obstacle to the mobility of the disabled person? This is a question which the Agency did not answer and hence it erred in law.' *VIA Rail Canada Inc v Canada (National*

Transportation Agency) (2000) 193 DLR (4th) 357 at 365, FCA, per Sexton JA

Canada 'Issue 1: Did the Agency provide adequate reasons for its finding that section 13-D of the tariff constitutes an obstacle to the mobility of passengers with disabilities?

'[26] In the words of the tariff, did the Agency's reasons provide sufficient indication of the reasoning process by which it determined that it is an obstacle to the mobility of a disabled passenger to require that an attendant, travelling on the same ticket as the passenger, be capable of assisting the passenger in getting on and off the train?

...

'[29] The *Concise Oxford Dictionary of Current English* defines "obstacle" as a "thing that obstructs progress". Not only has the Agency failed to articulate any definition but it also does not appear to have engaged in any reasoned consideration of the tariff provisions. How does the requirement that an attendant be capable of assisting the disabled person with whom they are travelling to board and deboard a train constitute an obstacle to the mobility of the disabled person? This is a question which the Agency did not answer and hence it erred in law.' *VIA Rail Canada Inc v National Transportation Agency* [2001] 2 FC 25 at 36–37, CA, per Sexton JA

OBSTRUCT

Canada '[14] The Village submits that the Triathlon Festival, as it occurred in 2002 and was expected to occur in 2003, obstructed "part of a highway or other public place" and created a nuisance thereon, in contravention of s. 532(2). Mr. Sullivan notes that the *Shorter Oxford English Dictionary* defines "obstruct" to mean:

1. To block, close up, or fill ... with obstacles or impediments; to render impassable or difficult of passage. 2. To interrupt or render difficult the passage or progress of; to impede, hinder, or retard ... 3. To stand in the way of, or persistently oppose the progress or course of ... to impede, retard, withstand, stop

'He argues that the 2002 Triathlon Festival as described in the affidavit evidence rendered passage "difficult or impassable" and clearly hindered or retarded normal traffic. The case authorities cited by the appellant are rather aged (see *e.g.*, *R. v. Plummer* (1870), 30 U.C.Q.B. 41, *Horner v. Cadman* (1886), 55 L.J.C.C. 110, and *The Queen v. Watson and Kenway* (1895), 6 C.C.C. 331 (N.S. Co. Ct.)), but generally support the principle that even a temporary or impermanent hindering of

traffic constitutes an "obstruction" of the highway.' *Harrison Hot Springs* (*Village*) *v Kamenka* (*cob World Endurance Sport*) [2004] BCJ No 1251, 243 DLR (4th) 141 (CA), per Newbury JA

OBVIOUS

Australia '... in the present case, the invention claimed is a new combination of three integers. [The appellant] does not suggest any of those integers in itself is inventive. The issue is whether the *combination of the three integers* ... constitutes an inventive step or whether such a combination of integers would have been obvious to the non-inventive skilled worker in the field of pharmaceutical formulation. It must be emphasised that the prior existence of publications revealing the three integers, as separate items, does not of itself make the alleged invention obvious. It is the selection of the integers – out of, perhaps, many possibilities – which must be shown to be obvious: see *Minnesota Mining* at 293.

'However, it is important to note exactly what is meant by "obvious" in this context. The law does not require that it be apparent, at the outset, to the non-inventive skilled worker, that a particular combination of integers will succeed in obtaining the desired result. It is enough that it be apparent to such a worker that it would be worthwhile to try each of the integers that was ultimately successfully used. The point was made in a classic statement of Buckley LJ in *Beecham Group Ltd's* (*Amoxycillin*) *Application* [1980] RPC 261. At 290–1, his Lordship said (omitting citations):

"It is clearly established that, for a particular step or process to be obvious for the purpose of either section, *it is not necessary to establish that its success is clearly predictable ... It will suffice if it is shown that it would appear to anyone skilled in the art but lacking in inventive capacity that to try the step or process would be worthwhile* ... Worthwhile to what end? It must, in my opinion, be shown to be worth trying in order to solve some recognised problem or meet some recognised need. The uninventive expert ... should not be supposed to be attempting to discover something new, that is, to be striving for inventiveness. Having been shown what was disclosed by the prior art, he must be supposed to be attempting to solve some problem or fulfil some need which has not been resolved or satisfied by the prior art but which appears to his uninventive mind to be possibly capable of solution or satisfaction by taking the step or doing the thing under consideration. This, it seems to me, must involve the uninventive but skilled man having a particular problem or need in mind. If on carrying out his test he finds that the new step has the sort of consequence he had hoped but in an unexpectedly high degree, this would or might not mean that the new step was inventive or other than obvious; it might merely mean that a new obvious step has solved the problem or met the need unexpectedly well. The question would, I think, be one of degree. If, on the other hand, the new step produces some unexpected result productive of an improvement or benefit of an unexpected kind it may well be held to be inventive, the association of the new step with its result not having been obvious." [Emphasis added]'

Aktiebolaget Hassle v Alphapharm Pty Ltd (2000) AIPC 91–636; BC200005958; [2000] FCA 1303 at [35]–[36], per Wilcox, Merkel and Emmett JJ

OCCASION

'That, however, does not resolve the present problem, which is whether on a single occasion the court may both activate a sentence and impose a new sentence so as together to exceed the maximum sentence of two years provided by the statute. Speaking for myself, and in the light of the submissions made by [the amicus curiae], I am in no doubt that the "occasion" for the purposes of s 14(1) [of the Contempt of Court Act 1981] is the occasion on which the order of committal is made, whether or not it relates to one application or more than one application, and, furthermore, that the relevant occasion is that on which the contemnor actually leaves the court to go to prison. The effect of the section, in my view, is that whether a previously suspended sentence is activated or not a contemnor must not, on any single occasion, leave court subject to a new sentence of more than two years' imprisonment for contempt. By "new" I mean a sentence which the contemnor was not actually serving before. If a contemnor had been sentenced to an immediate term of 12 months, and on a later occasion was brought from prison to answer a further charge of contempt for which he was sentenced to a consecutive term of 18 months, there would be no breach of the section.' *Villiers v Villiers* [1994] 2 All ER 149 at 154, CA, per Sir Thomas Bingham MR

OCCASIONED BY A MOTOR VEHICLE

Canada [Shorter limitation period applied in respect of damage occasioned by a motor vehicle.] 'Although snow and ice accumulated on the steps of a bus, the fact that the bus was a motor vehicle is only incidental to the circumstances of the case.' *Renaud v OC Transpo* (1992) 91 DLR (4th) 755 at 759, per Chadwick J (Ont Ct (Gen Div))

OCCUPANCY

[For 35 Halsbury's Laws (4th edn) para 1136 see now 35 Halsbury's Laws (4th edn) (Reissue) para 1236.]

OCCUPANT

Canada [Which of two insurers was liable to a plaintiff, who was injured when clearing snow from his car, depended on whether the plaintiff was an 'occupant' or a 'pedestrian'.] 'The word "occupant" is defined by reference to various physical activities or processes. An "occupant" is a person who is driving an automobile, being carried in or upon an automobile, entering or getting onto an automobile or alighting from an automobile. The plain meaning of the words used, it seems to me, suggests an intention to draw the line between an occupant and a non-occupant at the point that an individual, who is not driving, can no longer be said to be either entering or getting onto an automobile or, alternatively, alighting from an automobile. To apply, it seems to me, a zone of connection test to determine an issue of occupancy in the face of such a definition would have the effect of extending the definition of "occupant" beyond that which seems plainly to have been intended. It would confer occupancy status on a person who had completed the process of either entering or getting onto the automobile or the process of alighting from the automobile, but nevertheless was within a zone defined by factors which would appear to me inconsistent with the definition. Those factors focus largely upon the intention or purpose of the person concerned and upon other considerations related not to the actual activity of the individual at the time of the accident, but rather to his or her previous and proposed activity in order to determine the degree of connection of the person at the time of injury to the vehicle.' *Kyriazis v Royal Insurance Co of Canada* (1991) 82 DLR (4th) 691 at 703, Ont Gen Div, per Abbey J

OCCUPANT/PEDESTRIAN

Canada [Plaintiff driver was outside vehicle to clean windows.] 'We agree with the trial judge that on the facts of this case the plaintiff does not come within the definition of "occupant" in the policies involved. It is not necessary to agree or disagree with the comment of the trial judge on p 29 of his reasons [p 705 DLR] to the effect that it is "unlikely, that the legislature, by the use of the word 'pedestrian' intended to isolate and exclude from the operation of s 236 altogether a category of persons considered to be neither occupants nor pedestrians", since in our view on the agreed facts the plaintiff is a pedestrian within the clear meaning of that word.' *Kyriatis v Royal Insurance Co of Canada* (1993) 107 DLR (4th) 288, Ont CA, per curiam

OCCUPATION (OF PROPERTY)

Australia ' "Occupied" [in regard to land] ... contemplates a physical presence and control. Occupation, one might say, requires some form of user but is more than mere user. All buildings which are "occupied" are used for some purpose or purposes.' *Gosford RSL Club Co-operative Ltd v Commissioner of Land Tax (NSW)* (1981) 11 ATR 805 at 810, per Lee J

OCCUPATIONAL PENSION SCHEME

'Occupational pension scheme' means any scheme or arrangement which is comprised in one or more instruments or agreements and which has, or is capable of having, effect in relation to one or more descriptions or categories of employments so as to provide benefits, in the form of pensions or otherwise, payable on termination of service, or on death or retirement, to or in respect of earners with qualifying service in an employment of any such description or category. (Pension Schemes Act 1993 s 1)

OCCUPIED ... FOR A PUBLIC PURPOSE

[Licensing Act 1964, s 15(1)(a).] '[9] I return therefore to the substantive appeal. The question is whether, after it acquired ownership on 15 November 2002, the Newcastle City Council was occupying the premises for a public purpose. The justices did not try to answer this question because they thought that whether the council had gone into occupation or not, the making of the compulsory purchase order created a "special removal situation", presumably on the ground that the council was "about to" occupy the premises for a public purpose. Lightman J said ([2004] All ER (D) 272 (Mar) at [27]) that this was wrong: there had to be "practical certainty and imminence of outcome" and this did not exist when the compulsory purchase order was made. The order had still to be confirmed; this would involve a public inquiry and the outcome was uncertain. He rejected an alternative argument that the council had actually occupied the premises on the ground that it was not considered by the justices and that there was no up-to-date evidence of the "physical presence or degree of control" necessary to establish occupation: para [29]).

'[10] In the Court of Appeal, Jacob LJ (who gave the principal judgment) agreed with Lightman J on both points. On the second point, he said (at [26]) that "occupied ... for [a] public purpose" does not include "mere public ownership of a vacant property".

'[11] As Lightman J correctly observed, there appears to have been no evidence before the justices about exactly what happened when the sale by Ultimate to the council was completed. However, in the absence of evidence to the contrary I think that one should assume that it was an ordinary sale with vacant possession. The premises had been closed for business for the previous four months. The council would in law have obtained possession by virtue of being given the land certificate and the keys or other indicia or means of control. If squatters had entered, it would have been the council and not Ultimate who would have been entitled to bring an action for trespass. But, as the judge also said, one cannot assume that the council actually entered upon the premises or did anything to exercise control.

'[12] In *Madrassa Anjuman Islamia of Kholwad v Johannesburg Municipal Council* [1922] 1 AC 500 at 504 Viscount Cave said that "occupy" was a word of uncertain meaning, the precise meaning of which in any particular statute or document "must depend on the purpose for which, and the context in which, it is used". One must start, therefore, by inquiring into the purpose of the provisions for special removal. The grounds upon which a licensee may apply for a special removal are now set out in para (a) and (b) of s 15(1), but the language remains substantially unchanged since (at the latest) the Alehouses Act 1828. The common element in the statutory grounds is that something outside the control of the licensee has happened (or shortly will happen) to the licensed premises which makes (or will make) it impossible for him to carry on business. As Jacob LJ put it, "some force majeure either of God or man" (see [2004] 3 All ER 493 at [21]). Thus the purpose which one derives from the context of the other grounds for special removal suggests that the section is more concerned with whether the "occupation" for public purposes is such as immediately or shortly to exclude the licensee than with whether it is immediately beneficial to the occupier. One may contrast occupation for the purposes of rating, where, in addition to legal possession, "use and enjoyment" of the hereditament is required: see *Hampstead BC v Associated Cinema Properties Ltd* [1944] 1 All ER 436, [1944] KB 412. By contrast, I consider that a public authority which obtains legal possession of licensed premises with a view to putting them to some future public use is in immediate occupation of those premises for the purposes of s 15. The possession of the authority is sufficient to exclude the licensee, who would be committing a trespass if he attempted to re-enter and carry on his business. I agree with Jacob LJ that "mere public ownership" of a vacant property is not sufficient but I think that possession is. But once one treats the council as having gone into occupation when they took possession, then it is clear that their occupation must have been for a public purpose, namely for the implementation of the statutory scheme.' *R* (*on the application of Bushell*) *v Newcastle upon Tyne Licensing Justices* [2006] UKHL 7 at [9]–[12], [2006] 2 All ER 161, per Lord Hoffmann

OCCUPIER

[Under the Fire Precautions Act 1971 the occupier of premises used without a fire certificate for specified purposes is guilty of an offence. The respondent was the owner of a guest house. He was charged with a breach of the 1971 Act in that while he was on holiday the premises were used for purposes requiring a fire certificate. At first instance it was held that he was not the occupier at the relevant time and he was acquitted. *On appeal*] ' ... it is perfectly plain that somebody who is away temporarily on holiday remains the occupier of premises, if he is in fact the owner occupier before he leaves and has every intention of remaining the owner occupier when he returns.' *McClory v MacKinnon* 1996 SCCR 367 at 370, per Lord Sutherland

OF

Australia [Section 77A(2) (c) of the Bankruptcy Act 1966 (Cth) permits the investigator to require a person to produce specified books that are books 'of' an associated entity of the bankrupt.] 'Books may be those "of" an associated entity, within the meaning of s 77A if the associated entity claims under a trust for which the relevant books are "trust documents" within the general law ... The term "of" in s 77A(2)(c) is apt to embrace a connection or association falling short of absolute ownership.' *Re Simersall; Blackwell v Bray* (1992) 108 ALR 375 at 382, per Gummow J

Australia [Section 23(3)(c) of the Industrial Relations Act 1979 (WA) states that the Western Australian Industrial Relations Commission shall not make an order empowering a representative of an organization to enter any part of the premises of an employer.] ' "Of" is a preposition meaning in context, "belonging or possession, connection, or association" [*Macquarie Dictionary*].

'The premises of the employer are those premises which have a connection or association with the employer.' *Molina v Zaknich* [2001] BC200106701; WASCA 337 at [39], [40] per McKechnie J.

OFFENCE

See also CRIME

[Under the Criminal Justice and Public Order Act 1994, s 68(1) a person commits the offence of aggravated trespass if he trespasses on land and in relation to any 'lawful activity' which persons were engaging in did anything which was intended to have the effect of obstructing or disrupting that activity. Under s 68(2) activity is lawful for the purposes of s 68 if the person or persons 'may engage on the activity on the land on that occasion without committing an offence or trespassing on the land'.] '[26] ... In construing a domestic statute the ordinary practice is to treat "offence", in the absence of an express provision to the contrary, as referring to an offence committed here against a common law or statutory rule: see *R* (*on the application of Rottman*) *v Comr of Police for the Metropolis* [2002] UKHL 20 at [67], [2002] 2 All ER 865 at [67], [2002] 2 AC 692...

...

'[33] The 1994 Act is a long and detailed statute, addressing a large number of criminal justice matters, particularly in England and Wales but also in Scotland and Northern Ireland. Although some provisions of the 1994 Act have a wider reach (s 160 extends the powers of constables to United Kingdom waters), s 68 is directed to land within one or other of the three domestic jurisdictions. There is no suggestion that those whose activities the Marchwood appellants and the appellant Swain sought to obstruct or disrupt were themselves trespassers. So the only question is whether "offence" in s 68(2) should be understood to cover an offence under customary international law.

'[34] The answer to that question must be negative, for very much the same reasons as are given in [26] above. "Offence" is not defined in the 1994 Act. It must be understood as meaning an offence under the domestic criminal law of the relevant United Kingdom jurisdiction.

...

'[36] For these reasons, which are much the same as those given by the Court of Appeal and followed by the Administrative Court, I would answer the certified questions in [4] and [9] above together, as follows: the crime against peace (or crime of aggression) is not capable of being a "crime" within the meaning of s 3 of the [Criminal Law Act 1967] or an "offence" within the meaning of s 68(2) of the 1994 Act. I would accordingly dismiss all the appeals.' *R v Jones; Ayliffe v Director of Public Prosecutions; Swain v Director of Public Prosecutions* [2006] UKHL 16 at [26], [33]–[34], [36], [2006] 2 All ER 741, per Lord Bingham of Cornhill

Australia 'There is nothing novel in the idea that an offence is constituted by the combination of acts and attendant circumstances which expose a person to a specified penalty by way of punishment. Thus, for example, robbery and armed robbery are distinct offences under the criminal laws of the States and Territories, as are assault, assault occasioning actual bodily harm and assault occasioning grievous bodily harm. Moreover, as Brennan J pointed out in *Kingswell*, "[a] criminal offence can be identified only in terms of its factual ingredients, or elements, and the criminal penalty which the combination of elements attracts." His Honour added "[i]f a particular combination of elements attracting a particular penalty is one offence, a different combination of elements attracting a different penalty is another offence."

...

'The word "offence" in that section is clearly capable of bearing a meaning of the kind ascribed to it by Brennan J in *Kingswell*. It does no violence to the language of s 80 [of the Commonwealth Constitution 1901] to construe "offence" as an act or omission which exposes a person to a specified penalty by way of punishment and, also, as any combination of factual elements which directly

pertain to an act or omission which exposes a person to a distinct penalty by way of punishment. And in my view it cannot be given any narrower meaning consistent with the settled approach to the construction of constitutional guarantees.' (footnotes omitted) *Cheng v R* (2000) 175 ALR 338; 74 ALJR 1482; BC200005825; [2000] HCA 53 at [90], [94], per Gaudron J

Canada [Section 11 of the Charter of Rights and Freedoms provided rights for persons charged with an offence.] 'Accordingly, the term "offence" in s 11 applies to the breach of a law of the sort which could result in the accused being deprived of life, liberty or security of the person through criminal or penal proceedings.' *Re Petroleum Products Act* (1986) 33 DLR (4th) 680 at 708–709, PEI CA, per Mitchell J

Motoring offence

[For 40 Halsbury's Laws (4th edn) para 479 see now 40(2) Halsbury's Laws (4th edn) (Reissue) para 680.]

Political offence

[For 18 Halsbury's Laws (4th edn) para 259 see now 17(2) Halsbury's Laws (4th edn) (Reissue) para 1174.]

OFFEND, INSULT, HUMILIATE OR INTIMIDATE

Australia 'The words "offend, insult, humiliate or intimidate" are open textured. They are sometimes used in ordinary parlance to describe a level of response to another person's conduct which is relatively minor. Their definitions in the *Shorter Oxford English Dictionary* include:

offend — to vex, annoy, displease, anger, now esp to excite personal annoyance, resentment, or disgust (in anyone) (Now the chief sense).

insult — to assail with scornful abuse or offensive disrespect; to offer indignity to; to affront, outrage ...

humiliate — to make low or humble in position, condition or feeling, to humble ... to subject to humiliation; to mortify.

intimidate — to render timid, inspire with fear; to overawe, cow, now esp to force to or deter from some action by threats or violence.'

Bropho v Human Rights and Equal Opportunity Commission [2004] FCAFC 16 at [67] per French J; BC200400209.

OFFENSIVE INSTRUMENT

Australia 'The noun "instrument", in this context, means a thing with or through which something is being done, or effected. The adjective "offensive" means something that is adopted or used for the purpose of attack. The question whether an object or article is an offensive instrument raises for consideration the nature of the object, the uses of which it is capable, and the intention of the person who is using it on the occasion in question. An object which in its nature and in its ordinary use is not offensive may become an offensive instrument by reason of the use to which a person puts it, and the intent which accompanies such use.' *Re Hamilton* (1993) 66 A Crim R 575 at 577, per Gleeson CJ

OFFENSIVE MATERIAL

Australia [Schedule 5 cl 2(3) to the Local Government Act 1989 (Vic) provides that a returning officer at a local government election must refuse to register a sample how-to-vote card which the officer is satisfied contains 'offensive material'.] 'It is plain that the nature of the clause contemplates that the returning officer has to make a judgment as to whether it is capable of giving offence and not proceed upon a factual finding that it has in fact offended anyone ... The evidence is that it had before it dictionary meanings. Those dictionary meanings included a general meaning which comprehended what I have just covered, namely, that offensive material is material capable of giving offence or which is aggressive or shocking.' *Patrick v Cobain* [1993] 1 VR 290 at 293, per Gobbo J

OFFENSIVE OR OBJECTIONABLE

New Zealand 'Offensiveness or objectionability cannot be measured by a machine or by some standard with arithmetical gradations. It is a matter of perception and the interpretation of that perception in the mind.' *Zdrahal v Wellington City Council* [1995] 1 NZLR 700 at 708, per Greig J

OFFER

[For 9 Halsbury's Laws (4th edn) para 227 see now 9(1) Halsbury's Laws (4th edn) (Reissue) para 632.]

Of shares to public

[For 7 Halsbury's Laws (4th edn) paras 190, 293 see now 7(1) Halsbury's Laws (4th edn) (2004 Reissue) paras 579, 678.]

New Zealand [Companies Amendment Act 1963, First Schedule, Part A, para 1.] '[T]he terms ["offer" and "take-over offer"] are used in an extended sense encompassing not only offers in the strict sense but conditional contracts resulting from their acceptance.' *Southfert Co-operative Ltd v Ravensdown Corporation Ltd* [1996] 3 NZLR 196 at 200, 203–204, per Tipping J

OFFICE

Public office

[For 1 Halsbury's Laws (4th edn) para 9 see now 1(1) Halsbury's Laws (4th edn) (2001 Reissue) para 9.]

OFFICER

Of company

Australia [Section 173 of the Crimes Act 1900 (NSW) provides that whosoever being a director, 'officer' or member of any body corporate or public company fraudulently takes or applies for his own use or benefit any property of such body corporate or company shall be liable for penal servitude for ten years.] 'The word "officer" is not one of fixed or precise denotation. Its meaning and signification vary according to the context. Views as to the appropriateness of its application in a given case may change over time and may be influenced by changes in fashions of speech, including the use of what might once have been thought rather grandiloquent job descriptions ... To be an officer it is neither necessary nor sufficient that a person be an employee of the company in question ... The proposition that the word "officer" in s 173 of the Crimes Act does not have a meaning in accordance with the definition in s 5(1) of the Companies (New South Wales) Code, but has its ordinary meaning, is one of law: *Hope v Bathurst City Council* (1980) 144 CLR 1 at 7. The jury should have been directed that it has its ordinary meaning. That meaning, however, is not one with which many people would be familiar and the concept of an officer of a public company calls for explanation. In the present case the jury should have been instructed that, although the issue was ultimately one of fact for them to determine, they should approach it as follows. To establish that the appellant was an officer, the Crown would need to show that the appellant held an office by virtue of which he participated in the management or administration of the affairs of the company. In this context the word "office" refers to a specific position which usually (although not necessarily) carries a title and which has identifiable functions and responsibilities. The position must be part of the managerial or administrative structure of the company, and the person who occupies it must be one who takes part in the management or administration of the company. That part need not necessarily be powerful or dominant, but it would need to go beyond performing duties of a kind that might be performed by a clerk or a messenger or a stenographer or a person of similar rank. The fact that a person is called an "executive" does not necessarily mean that the person is in truth an officer, any more than the fact that a person is not so described means that the person is not an officer. Nevertheless, in distinguishing between employees who are officers and those who are not, the distinction between employees who are regarded by a company as executives and those who are not will in many cases give useful practical guidance in applying the test stated above.' *R v Scott* (1990) 49 A Crim R 96 at 101–103, per Gleeson CJ

OFFICIAL RECEIVER

[For 3 Halsbury's Laws (4th edn) para 483 see now 3(2) Halsbury's Laws (4th edn) (2002 Reissue) paras 31–35.]

ON BEHALF OF

[A firm of solicitors signed a letter of obligation in a conveyancing transaction without qualification but the obligations therein were undertaken 'on behalf of our above named clients'.] 'The expression "on behalf of" signifies more than the fact that the defenders were the agents for the sellers ... In my view, it meant that what was undertaken was undertaken by the defenders as the agents of the sellers, and hence that it was the sellers' undertaking which was given. It may be that the phrase "on behalf of" has no strict legal meaning. This may well mean that it can bear different meanings according to the context in which it is used. However, it does not follow that it is incapable of having a certain legal effect in the particular context in which it is found.' *Digby Brown & Co v Lyall* 1995 SLT 932 at 933–934, OH, per Lord Cullen

Australia [A document was signed 'For and on Behalf of ... [Banque National De Paris]' with execution in the form of a 'Banker's signature' accompanied by an official stamp of BNP.] 'Authority suggests that the meaning of the phrase "on behalf of" has no "strict legal meaning" and that context "will always determine" its meaning in any particular circumstance of usage. In *R v Toohey: Ex parte Attorney-General* (*Northern Territory*) (1980) 145 CLR 374 at 386 the joint judgment of the Court illustrated the point as follows:

"The phrase 'on behalf of' is, as Latham CJ observed in *R v Portus; Ex parte Federated Clerks Union of Australia* (1949) 79 CLR 428 at 435, 'not an expression which has a strict legal meaning', it bears no single and constant significance. Instead it may be used in conjunction with a wide range of relationships, all however in some way concerned with the standing of one person as auxiliary to or representative of another person or thing.

"In what is perhaps its least specific use, 'on behalf of' may be applied to someone who does no more than express support for persons or for a cause, as with one who speaks on behalf of the poor or on behalf of tolerance. It may be used when speaking of an agency relationship, but also of some quite ephemeral relationships, such as that which exists between a party to litigation and the witness he calls, a witness "on behalf of" the defence. Again, it may, as the Northern Territory here contends, be used where the relationship is that of trustee and cestui que trust. It was of such a use that Lord Cairns LC spoke when he said, in *Gillespie v City of Glasgow Bank* (1879) 4 App Cas 632 at 640, that the phrase could describe a relationship of trustee and cestui que trust 'if the circumstances of the case are consistent with that interpretation'. Context will always determine to which of the many possible relationships the phrase 'on behalf of' is in a particular case being applied; 'the context and subject matter' (per Dixon J in the *Federated Clerks' Case* (1949) 79 CLR, at 438) will be determinative."

'In *R v Portus; Ex parte Federated Clerks Union of Australia* (1949) 79 CLR 428 the court was concerned with the use of the words "on behalf of" in a sense wider than that denoting the relationship of principal and agent. Dixon J expressed that wider sense of the phrase as follows:

> "… It means for the purposes of, as an instrument of, or for the benefit and in the interest of …" (at 438)

'In my view, there is no warrant in giving the phrase anything other than its ordinary meaning of conveying that the signatory, Dhiri, beside the words "Bankers signature" is the signatory as agent for, or the instrument of, BNP in executing the document: that BNP has executed the document by its agent, or instrument.' *Pacific Carriers Ltd v Banque Nationale de Paris* BC200106929; [2001] NSWSC 900 at [285]–[287], per Hunter J

ON DEMAND

New Zealand 'The true distinction is therefore that if the obligation to repay is expressed as "on demand" simpliciter there is no requirement to make demand and time starts to run from the date the moneys were advanced. This is because the law has treated the words "on demand" as adding nothing to the implied promise immediately to repay. In a sense the words "on demand" simply reinforce and declare what the law takes to be implicit anyway. If, however, the parties have either expressly or by necessary implication demonstrated an intention that a demand is required in order to create a liability to repay, time does not start to run until the making of the demand. In the case of a loan on demand simpliciter the demand is not part of the cause of action . The position is otherwise if the demand is intended to be part of the cause of action.' *DFC New Zealand Ltd v McKenzie* [1993] 2 NZLR 576 at 583, per Tipping J

ON OR ABOUT HIS PERSON

Canada 'Section 98(1) allows an officer to conduct a search if the officer suspects that the traveller has contraband "secreted on or about his person". In this case, once the officers from Interdiction and Intelligence had performed the strip search they could have no suspicion that the appellant had drugs secreted "on or about" his person. In my view, the plain meaning of "on or about his person" would not include "inside" his person.' *R v Monney* (1997) 153 DLR (4th) 617 at 649, Ont CA, per Rosenberg JA

ON THE FAITH OF THE RECEIPT

Australia 'It was accepted by the parties to the appeal [in *David Securities Pty Ltd v Commonwealth Bank of Australia* (1992) 175 CLR 353, 385–6] that the words on the faith of the receipt (which are italicised in the original reasons for judgment of the High Court) refer to the act or process of receiving the money. To my mind, what is meant by this passage in the reasons of their Honours is that the defendant must have acted to its detriment on the faith of (meaning in reliance on) its having received the money. The phrase was considered by the New South Wales Court of Appeal in *State Bank of New South Wales Ltd v Swiss Bank Corp* (1995) 39 NSWLR 350 …

'The Court of Appeal affirmed the decision of the trial judge giving judgment for Swiss Bank and holding that the defence of change of position was not available to State Bank. In considering that question, the Court placed a slight gloss on the critical phrase in *David Securities* saying in effect that on the faith of the receipt meant in good faith, which must, the Court said, (39 NSWLR 350, 355):

> "… be linked to the payee acting *on the faith of the receipt* (repeating the emphasis in *David Securities Pty Ltd* (at 385). This is inherent in the passage where the italicised words appear. The court held that the critical moment for the payee is when payment is made, for it is then the unjust enrichment occurs. The critical moment for the payee is the moment of change of position but that, in order to be relevant, must be on the faith of the receipt.
>
> "'It seems to us that knowledge derived otherwise than from the payer cannot be relevant in deciding whether a change of position by the payee occurred on the faith of the receipt …".'

Port of Brisbane Corp v ANZ Securities Ltd BC200202254; [2002] QCA 158 at [13]–[14], per McPherson JA

ON THE GROUND THAT

[The Criminal Justice Act 1988, s 133(1) provides that, when a person has been convicted of a criminal offence and when subsequently his conviction has been reversed 'on the ground that' a new or newly discovered fact shows beyond reasonable doubt that there has been a miscarriage of justice, the Secretary of State must pay compensation for the miscarriage of justice to the person who has suffered punishment as a result of such conviction or, if he is dead, to his personal representatives, unless the non-disclosure of the unknown fact was wholly or partly attributable to the person convicted.]

'[61] Another of the reasons given in the decision letters was that, even if the undisclosed material did amount to a new or newly discovered fact, the conviction was not quashed "on the ground that" that the new or newly discovered fact showed that there had been a miscarriage of justice. It was not the undisclosed material, but the combined effect of all the evidence considered by the Court of Appeal, which resulted in the convictions being quashed. (This issue is therefore concerned only with the words "on the ground that", not with the separate question whether there has been shown to be a "miscarriage of justice".)

'[62] Mr Starmer takes issue with the Secretary of State's reasoning. He submits that the undisclosed material was the principal reason for the decision to quash the convictions. The other evidence was of limited materiality, especially given that much of it could not have been called at the trial. That is sufficient to meet the statutory test. Alternatively, the test is satisfied if the new or newly disclosed fact was at least a *contributory* factor in the decision to quash, which it plainly was.

'[63] Mr Sales submits that the words "on the ground that" in s 133(1), picking up the same wording in art 14(6) of the ICCPR [International Covenant on Civil and Political Rights], mean that the new or newly discovered fact must be *the* reason, in the sense of being the sole or principal reason, for the decision. It is the new or newly discovered fact, and not other matters, that must show beyond reasonable doubt that there has been a miscarriage of justice. The focus is on the effect of the particular matter that constitutes the new or newly discovered fact. This poses an insuperable obstacle for the claimants. It is clear from the judgment of the Court of Appeal in 2002 that the convictions were quashed on the basis of the totality of the evidence now available. The undisclosed material formed only a part and in no sense can the decision to quash convictions be said to have been taken "on the ground that" such material showed beyond reasonable doubt that there had been a miscarriage. The acid test of that is what happened in 1993, when the material was disclosed in advance of the appeal but the appeal was unsuccessful.

'[64] We accept Mr Sales's submissions on this issue. In our judgment it is not sufficient that the new or newly discovered fact makes some contribution to the quashing of the conviction. It must be the principal, if not the only, reason for the quashing of the conviction. Only then could it be said that the new or newly discovered fact showed beyond reasonable doubt that there had been a miscarriage of justice.' *R (on the application of Murphy) v Secretary of State for the Home Department* [2005] EWHC 140 (Admin), [2005] 2 All ER 763 at [61]–[64], per Richards J

ON THE RESERVE

Canada [Indian band council was entitled to pass by-laws affecting hunting and fishing 'on the reserve'.] 'The appellants submit that the ordinary meaning of the word "on" embraces the concept of being adjacent to a thing. In fact, the *Concise Oxford Dictionary* (9th ed 1995), defines the term as "supported by or attached to or covering or enclosing". In my opinion, however, while the expression "on" can, in some situations, mean "adjacent to" or "near", that is not its primary meaning. Its principal usage denotes a situation where one object or thing is over or supported by another, not beside or contiguous with it. In *Webster's Third New International Dictionary* (1986) the word "on" is defined as "1: in or into the position of being in contact with the upper surface of something or of being supported from beneath by the upper surface". Thus the word "on" used in the connection of "on the reserve", in its ordinary and natural meaning, signifies "within the reserve", not "adjacent to the reserve".

...

'... I conclude that the phrase "on the reserve" in the context of s 81(1)(*o*) should receive its ordinary and common sense meaning and be interpreted as "within the reserve" or "inside the reserve" or "located upon or within the boundaries of the reserve".' *R v Lewis* [1996] SCR 921 at 955, 959, (1996) 133 DLR (4th) 700 at 725, 728, SCC, per Iacobucci J

OPEN COUNTRY

[For 34 Halsbury's Laws (4th edn) para 470 see now 34 Halsbury's Laws (4th edn) (Reissue) para 250.]

OPEN COURT

New Zealand [At the end of the case, the Judge was taken ill before he could give judgment, and later died. Before he died, he conveyed to the Registrar his decision by telephone. The Registrar repeated it phrase by phrase to the parties and counsel, who were present in the Judge's chambers during the call. Through the Registrar the Judge then inquired of each counsel whether there were any further matters requiring attention. Counsel made limited inquiries through the Registrar who then gave the Judge's answers to counsel and parties. An application was then made seeking orders that: judgment was not nullified by reason of its not being pronounced in open court pursuant to R 540 of the High Court Rules.] 'Despite dicta in some of the cases which seem to suggest that "open Court" means something other than open Court, I am not persuaded that those refinements should be applied to the straightforward words in R 540 of the High Court Rules ... today the average intelligent New Zealander would take the view that only a lawyer would argue that what occurred ... could be described as taking place "in open Court" ... My conclusion to this point therefore is that judgment was not given pursuant to [R 540] (because it was not pronounced by the Judge in open Court).' *Bell-Booth v Bell-Booth* [1998] 1 NZLR 375 at 381, per Smellie J

OPEN LAND

[The Town and Country Planning Act 1971 has been repealed. See now the Town and Country Planning Act 1990, s 215.]

OPEN-MARKET PRICE

[The definition in the Capital Allowances Act 1968 is now spent. See MARKET VALUE.]

OPEN SPACE

[The Town and Country Planning Act 1971 has been repealed; the definition is re-enacted in the Town and Country Planning Act 1990, s 336(1). The Housing Act 1985, s 581(4) has been repealed.]

OPEN TO THE PUBLIC

Canada 'The issue in this appeal is whether a restaurant is an "enclosed public place, including any public transit vehicle or any building or part of a building that is open to the public" within the meaning of s 142 of *The Urban Municipality Act, 1984*, SS 1983–84, c U-11.

'The City of Saskatoon passed a by-law regulating smoking in restaurants. Thirty-five restaurateurs sued to have the by-law set aside or declared to be void and of no force and effect. The parties applied to the Queen's Bench under Queen's Bench Rule 188 for an order determining certain points of law, one of which was that stated in the preceding paragraph. The application was supported

by an agreed statement of facts, of which we need be concerned with only the following paragraph:

6. Restaurants are privately owned business establishments to which members of the public are customarily invited and admitted and in which food or drink is served and sold to members of the public.

'The judge found that restaurants were public places within the meaning of the Act.

'The full text of s 142 of the Act is as follows:

142. A council may, by bylaw, prohibit, control and regulate the lighting, carrying or smoking of any lighted cigar, cigarette, pipe or other smoking device in any enclosed public place, including any public transit vehicle or any building or part of a building that is open to the public.

'Neither the Act nor any other provincial legislation defines public place for the purposes of s 142.

'The appellants argued that since restaurateurs, although they invite the general public into their premises, reserve the right to refuse entry to anyone they choose, (subject only to human rights legislation), restaurants are not public places within the meaning of s 142. They argued that only places to which the public has a right of access are public places within the meaning of s 142. They cited a number of authorities dealing with the term "public place" in other statutes such as the *Criminal Code*, RSC 1985, c C-46.

'We cannot agree with their argument. The term "public place" as used in s 142 is modified by the words which follow: "including ... any building or part of a building that is open to the public". The words "open to the public", in their plain and ordinary meaning, include places to which "members of the public are customarily invited and admitted" as described in para 6 of the agreed statement of facts. The reservation of the right to deny access to anyone, or to remove anyone, does not alter the fact of the general invitation of the public. In sum, a place to which the public is invited is clearly "open to the public". If the legislators had intended to restrict the scope of s 142 to places to which the public had a right of access, as opposed to a revocable invitation to enter, they would have said so.

'Furthermore, this interpretation conforms with the obvious purpose of s 142: to permit a municipality to protect public health by regulating smoking in places where the public gathers, and to thereby protect the public from the deleterious effects of second-hand smoke. To confine the municipality's power to legislate to places to which the public has a right of access would render the legislation almost meaningless.' *Albertos Restaurant v Saskatoon (City)* (2000) 194 DLR (4th) 343 at 344–345, Sask CA, per Sherstobitoff JA

OPERATION

Australia [Section 4(3)(m) of the Admiralty Act 1988 (Cth) provides that: 'A reference in this Act to a general maritime claim is a reference to: ... (m) a claim in respect of goods, materials or services (including stevedoring and lighterage services) supplied or to be supplied to a ship for its operation or maintenance ...'] 'I am of the view that the term "operation" should not be confined in its interpretation to matters relating to the mere movement or propulsion of the ship from one port to another. In *The "River Rima"* in the Court of Appeal [1987] 2 Lloyd's Rep 106 at 113, Nourse LJ said in relation to the supply of the containers under consideration that he was "also prepared to accept that it is possible to concede of a state of affairs in which they would have been goods supplied to a ship for the operation". He did not consider that such a state of affairs had been disclosed on the evidence. In the circumstances of the case he found that the containers had been provided to the shippers rather than to the ship. In the House of Lords, Lord Brandon was prepared to assume without deciding that "the use of a container ... on board a ship designed to carry containers ... is a use for the operation of such a ship within the meaning of para (m)": [1988] 1 WLR 758 at 762–3. I can see no valid reason for excluding from the concept of "operation of a ship" considerations relating to any special characteristics of the ship, such as its being a freighter or tanker or to any special use or voyage upon which it may be engaged, at least when these latter factors were reasonably within the contemplation of the supplier or the services and the operator of the ship.' *Port of Geelong Authority v The Ship 'Boss Reefer'* (1992) 109 ALR 505 at 518–519, per Foster J

OPERATION OF THE SHIP

Canada '[39] I now turn to the words "the operation of the ship" and *"avec l'exploitation [du navire]"*. The *Compact Oxford English Dictionary of Current English*, 2nd ed., 2002, Oxford University Press, edited by Catherine Soanes, at pages 602–603 defines "operation" as follows:

1. *the slide bars ensure smooth operation*: functioning, working, running, performance, action. 2. **the operation of the factory: management, running, governing, administration, supervision.** 3. *a heart bypass operation*: surgical operation. 4. *a military operation*: action, activity, exercise, undertaking, enterprise, manoeuvre, campaign. 5. *Their mining operations*: business, enterprise, company, firm; *informal* outfit. [Emphasis added.]

...

'[42] I conclude that the words "occurring ... in direct connexion with the operation of the ship", found in paragraph 1(a) of Article 2 of the Convention, are broad enough to encompass the appellants' claims. Firstly, I am satisfied that the injuries suffered by Mr. Simms occurred as a result of the operation of the respondent's boat. In my view, the "operation of the ship" necessarily includes all activities arising from the running of the ship in a general sense, such as the launching of the boat into water, its navigation and its removal from water. Hence, claims for personal injury will not be limited to those which arise by reason of injuries caused by the vessel itself, such as collisions between two or more ships, the striking of a dock or other object by a ship, etc.' *Isen v Simms* [2005] 4 FCR 563 at [39], [42], [2005] FCJ No 756, 2005 FCA 161 (Fed CA), per Nadon JA

OPERATIONAL INCONSISTENCY

Australia 'The Defence Regulations [(Cth)] do not operate to prevent entry or activity on the perimeter area, except if a defence operation or practice has been authorised by a chief of staff pursuant to reg 51(1). It would seem clear that, were authority to be granted pursuant to the Mining Act [1978 (WA)] to enter upon or conduct mining activities on land in the perimeter area at a time or times specified in an authorisation under reg 51(1) for the conduct of a defence operation or practice, there would be direct inconsistency between that authorisation and the authority granted under the Mining Act. That inconsistency would result from the inconsistent operation in the particular circumstances of the Mining Act and the Defence Regulations – "operational inconsistency", as it is called: *Victoria v The Commonwealth ("The Kakariki")* (1937) 58 CLR 618; *Re Tracey; Ex parte Ryan* (1989) 166 CLR 518 at 599–600 per Gaudron J.' *Commonweath v Western Australia* (1999) 160 ALR 638 at 653; 73 ALJR 345; BC9900217, per Gleeson CJ and Gaudron J

OPPRESSION

'Section 76(2) of the 1984 Act [Police and Criminal Evidence Act 1984] distinguishes between two different ways in which a confession may be rendered inadmissible: first, where it has been obtained by oppression (para (a)); second, where it has been made in consequence of anything said or done which was likely in the circumstances to render unreliable any confession which might be made by the defendant in consequence thereof (para (b)). Paragraph (b) is wider than the old formulation, namely that the confession must be shown to be voluntary in the sense that it was not obtained by fear of prejudice or hope of advantage, excited or held out by a person in authority. It is wide enough to cover some of the circumstances which under the earlier rule were embraced by what seems to us to be the artificially wide definition of oppression approved in *R v Prager* [1972] 1 All ER 1114. This in turn leads us to believe that "oppression" in s 76(2)(a) should be given its ordinary dictionary meaning. The Oxford English Dictionary as its third definition of the word runs as follows: "Exercise of authority or power in a burdensome, harsh, or wrongful manner; unjust or cruel treatment of subjects, inferiors, etc.; the imposition of unreasonable or unjust burdens". One of the quotations given under that paragraph runs as follows: "There is not a word in our language which expresses more detestable wickedness than *oppression*". We find it hard to envisage any circumstances in which such oppression would not entail some impropriety on the part of the interrogator.' *R v Fulling* [1987] 2 All ER 65 at 69, CA, per Lord Lane CJ

[For 11 Halsbury's Laws (4th edn) para 930 see now 11(1) Halsbury's Laws (4th edn) (Reissue) para 211.]

OPPRESSIVE

New Zealand [Credit Contracts Act 1981, s 9.] 'I begin by noting that the Act clearly provides ... that such [credit contracts] may be "re-opened" if such were "oppressive", which "means oppressive, harsh, unjustly burdensome, unconscionable, on [sic] in contravention of reasonable standards of commercial practice."

'As to the meaning of those expressions, some of the existing authorities are canvassed in *Gault on Commercial Law* vol 2, paras 10.02–10.09, and more fully in Pol, "Credit Contracts: The Factors going to Oppression" (1989) 6 Auckland Univ Law Review 139. In general, the New Zealand case law to date appears to establish the following general propositions. Subject to the particular problems created by the summary judgment procedure and the rules relating thereto, the onus is on the party asserting oppression. The cases evidence real caution against upsetting commercial bargains. The cases also evidence a disinclination on the part of our Courts to proceed on anything other than a case-by-case basis.

'That said, some useful sub-principles have evolved. First, the mere fact that the contract is disadvantageous is insufficient to make it oppressive (*Italia Holdings (Properties) Ltd v Lonsdale Holdings (Auckland) Ltd* [1984] 2 NZLR 1). Second, the oppression must be that of the lender (*Burbery Mortgage Finance & Savings Ltd (In Receivership) v Haira* (High Court, Rotorua, CP 93/89, 21 April 1994, Barker J). Third, the exercise of rights (without more) does not amount to oppression; such may however become unreasonable in light of collateral undertakings (see *Manion* (supra); *Shotter v Westpac Banking Corporation* [1988] 2 NZLR 316). But, an action can be oppressive, notwithstanding that it is contractually permitted (*Robinson v United Building Society* (High Court, Dunedin, CP 35/87, 7 May 1987, Tompkins J) and see the note thereon in [1988] NZLJ 416). Fourth, in alleged cases of unreasonable standards of commercial practice there should be led evidence of the reasonable market practice sought to be relied on. See, for instance, *Cambridge Clothing Co Ltd v Simpson* [1988] 2 NZLR 340; *Didsbury v Zion Farms Ltd* (High Court, Auckland, CP 2501/88, 22 February 1989, Wallace J) at pp 19, 20; *Robinson v United Building Society* (supra).

'Whether it can be said that any unifying principle has emerged in New Zealand law is problematical.

...

'[T]o my mind "oppression" is primarily an economic concept. Given that superior bargaining power on the market risks is not per se objectionable—and that is how commercial life really is—what Courts should be looking for, is an inequality of exchange arising where there is superior bargaining power but coupled with the likes of ignorance, harsh contract clauses or such like matters. In that sense, then, "oppression" is a market corrective, but to be utilised only in a relatively narrow range of cases.' *Prudential Building and Investment Society of Canturbury v Hankins* [1997] 1 NZLR 114 at 123–125, per Hammond J

OPTIMUM UTILIZATION

Australia [Section 5B of the Fisheries Act 1952 (Cth) provides that, in administering the Act, the minister shall have regard to the objectives of, inter alia, achieving the 'optimum utilization' of the living resources of the Australian fishing zone.] '... the phrase "optimum utilization" is not limited to avoidance, by proper conservation and management measures, of the danger of over-exploitation of living resources of the Australian Fishing Zone ... In my view, "optimum utilization" is a phrase broad enough to include economic exploitation for the benefit of the littoral state, namely Australia, by, for example, the raising of revenue from a resources tax. Certainly, in my view, there may be "optimum utilization" by having regard to the economic interests and prosperity of those, taken as a whole, who exploit the fishery when adopting a regime for the reduction in the number of units.' *Bienke v Minister for Primary Industries and Energy* (1994) 125 ALR 151 at 171, per Gummow J

OPTION

'An option in gross for the purchase of land is a conditional contract for such purchase by the grantee of the option from the grantor, which the grantee is entitled to convert into a concluded contract of purchase, and to have carried to completion by the grantor, on giving the prescribed notice and otherwise complying with the conditions on which the option is made exercisable in any particular case.' *Griffith v Pelton* [1957] 3 All ER 75 at 83, CA, per Jenkins LJ

'The granting of [an] option imposes no obligation upon the purchaser and an obligation upon the vendor which is contingent upon the exercise of the option. When the option is exercised, vendor and purchaser come under obligations to perform as if they had concluded an ordinary contract of sale. And the analogy of an irrevocable offer is ... a useful way of describing the position of the purchaser between the grant and exercise of the option.' *Spiro v Glencrown Properties Ltd* [1991] 1 All ER 600 at 604, per Hoffman J

Australia 'In submissions, the term "election" was used as a synonym for "option" as it appears in cl 2 [of the Order made by the Governor in Council under the BLF (De-recognition) Act 1985 (Vic): Victoria Government Gazette, No S39, 13 October 1987]. The true nature of "election" is the confrontation of the person electing with two mutually exclusive courses of action between which

a choice must be made, for example, to terminate or keep a contract on foot. In its setting in cl 2 of the Order, "option" is best understood as identifying a power, but not a duty, which is thereby conferred upon the Custodian.' *Victoria v Sutton* (1998) 156 ALR 579 at 590; 72 ALJR 1386; BC9804343, per Gaudron, Gummow and Hayne JJ

OR

Australia ' "Or" quite commonly and grammatically can have a conjunctive sense: *Minister for Immigration & Ethnic Affairs v Baker* (1997) 73 FCR 187 at 195. Thus the phrase, "I need a computer for use at home or in the office", conveys that the computer should be suitable for both uses.' *Abbott Laboratories v Corbridge Group Pty Ltd* (2002) AIPC ¶91–824; BC200206154; [2002] FCAFC 314 at [39], per Lee, Emmett and Hely JJ

Australia [At issue on appeal was whether the magistrate had the power to sentence the appellant to a term of imprisonment in addition to imposing a fine pursuant to section 49(3)(b) of the Road and Safety Act 1986 (Vic).] '[4] Section 49(3) of the Act reads, so far as relevant:

> (3) A person who is guilty of an offence under para ... (f) ... of subs (1) ... is liable
>   (a) ...
>   (b) in the case of a subsequent offence, to a fine of not more than 25 penalty units or to imprisonment for a term of not more than 3 months.

...

'[8] In *Re The Licensing Ordinance* Blackburn J pointed out that there are two categories of circumstances in which courts have been prepared to read the word "or" in a statute as meaning "and" and vice versa. The first is where the court is persuaded that the legislature has made a mistake in the Act and the wrong conjunction has been used. The second is by reading the words in context, as where a list of items joined by "and" is governed by words showing that the list is a list of alternatives. Neither of these circumstances is present here. There is no reason to suppose that the word "or" in s 49(3)(b) is to be read as meaning "and".

'[9] This view is strengthened by a comparison with s 64 of the Act, which reads, so far as relevant:

> 64. Dangerous driving

    (1) A person must not drive a motor vehicle at a speed or in a manner which is dangerous to the public, having regard to all the circumstances of the case.

    (2) A person who contravenes subs (1) is guilty of an offence and is liable to a fine of not more than 240 penalty units or to imprisonment for a term of not more than 2 years or both and …

'Thus s 64(2), in contrast to s 49(b), expressly provides for a penalty of a fine or imprisonment or both.

'[10] Hodges J said in *Craig Williamson Pty Ltd v Barrowcliff*:

> I think it is a fundamental rule of construction that any document should be construed as far as possible so as to give the same meaning to the same words wherever those words occur in that document, and that that applies especially to an Act of Parliament, and with especial force to words contained in the same section of an Act. There ought to be very strong reasons present before the Court holds that words in one part of a section have a different meaning from the same words appearing in another part of the same section.

'Mason J said in *Registrar of Titles (WA) v Franzon*:

> It is a sound rule of construction to give the same meaning to the same words appearing in different parts of a statute unless there is reason to do otherwise.'

Dunlop v Anstee [2004] VSC 139 at [4], [8]–[10], per Balmford J; BC200402724

ORDER

New Zealand 'In ordinary language "order" is a command or direction although as Bridge J observed in *R v Recorder of Oxford, ex p Brasenose College* [1969] 3 All ER 428, 431, while a linguistic purist would say that its most accurate connotation was to require taking an affirmative course of action, it is equally clear that the word may have a much wider meaning covering in effect all decisions of court.' *Walls v Calvert & Co* [1994] 1 NZLR 424 at 427, CA, per cur

[*NB: The Court of Appeal here endorses the broad definition of 'order' given in 1969 by Bridge J in the case referred to above.*]

Interlocutory

[For 26 Halsbury's Laws (4th edn) para 506 see now 26 Halsbury's Laws (4th edn) (Reissue) para 506.]

ORDER AS TO COSTS

Australia 'The power conferred by s 117(2) of the Family Law Act 1975 (Cth) ("the Act") is a power to "make such order as to costs and security for costs, whether by way of interlocutory order or otherwise, as the court considers just". That power is not simply a power to make an order for costs. Were it so, it would only authorise orders to indemnify for "costs actually incurred in the conduct of litigation" [*Cachia v Hanes* (1994) 179 CLR 403 at 410]. However, a power to make an "order as to costs" is a broader power. And when regard is had to the consideration that s 117(2) expressly authorises interlocutory orders, that subsection must, in my view, be construed as authorising orders requiring a party to proceedings under the Act to provide another party with funds to conduct those proceedings … One other matter should be noted with respect to s 117(2), namely that its terms are, if anything, wider than the bare power "to award costs" considered in *Knight v FP Special Assets Ltd* (1992) 174 CLR 178. Accordingly, it follows that the subsection authorises orders against persons who are not parties to proceedings in the exceptional circumstances in which that course is appropriate. At least that is so if the order is one which indemnifies for costs actually incurred, an order of that kind being properly described as an "order as to costs".' *Re JJT; Ex parte Victoria Legal Aid* (1998) 155 ALR 251 at 253; 23 Fam LR 1 at 3; 72 ALJR 1141; BC9802630, per Gaudron J

ORDER IN COUNCIL

[For 44 Halsbury's Laws (4th edn) para 982 see now 44(1) Halsbury's Laws (4th edn) (Reissue) para 1500.]

ORDER OF COUNCIL

[For 44 Halsbury's Laws (4th edn) para 982 see now 44(1) Halsbury's Laws (4th edn) (Reissue) para 1500.]

ORDINARILY

Canada [A deduction was available for expenses where a taxpayer was 'ordinarily' required to carry on duties away from his employer's place of business.] 'Considering first the meaning of "ordinarily", the jurisprudence indicates that this term describes activities which are normal, or of regular occurrence; in other words, activities which are not rare or abnormal or minimal. The Federal Court of Appeal in interpreting the word "ordinarily" ... has said that it means "in most cases" or as a general rule. While the trend in the jurisprudence appears to be away from a purely quantitative test of time spent away from the employer's place of business as determinative, it must still be of some relevance in ascertaining whether such duties to be performed away are so trivial or insignificant as not to detract from the employer's place of business as the essential focus of the employer's work.' *Verrier v Canada* [1989] 2 FCR 71 at 75, Fed TD, per Stroyer J

ORDINARY COURSE OF BUSINESS

New Zealand 'The essence of the concept of the ordinary course of business seems to me to be not the ordinary or extraordinary character of the particular transaction but whether or not that transaction was entered into bona fide in the company's interests and genuinely as part of the continued operation of the company's business.' *Julius Harper Ltd v F W Hagedorn & Sons* [1989] 2 NZLR 471 at 493, per Tipping J

ORDINARY PLACE OF RESIDENCE

Canada [Relocation costs were payable to employees.] 'In my view the phrase "ordinary place of residence" involves essentially a question of fact as to where one is found at the time of appointment. If one is induced to move to the city where the relevant board office is situated and is compensated therefore by the payment of relocation expenses, then that becomes his ordinary place of residence and he ceases to receive travel and living expenses because he has accepted relocation costs.' *Petryshyn v Canada* [1993] 3 FCR 640 at 662, per Strayer J (Fed TD)

ORDINARY TIME EARNINGS

Australia [In relation to casual employees under the Clerical Employees Award (State) (Qld). The expression 'ordinary time earnings' is defined, in cl 3.5(3)(d), to mean 'the actual ordinary rate of pay the employee receives for ordinary hours of work', to include 'casual rates received for ordinary hours of work', and to exclude 'overtime'.] 'For a full-time or part-time employee it represents the amount calculated by the base rate that such an employee receives for the hours of work for which the employee is engaged. A casual employee, on the other hand, receiving "casual rates", is in a different category. By definition, a casual employee is not employed by reference to a given weekly interval of hours, whether full-time or part-time. On the contrary, a casual employee, as the Award itself makes clear, is "an employee who is engaged by the hour and who may terminate employment or be discharged at any moment without notice"

'It follows that the "ordinary hours of work" of an employee paid casual rates are not fixed by reference to the hours of the week. For a casual employee the "ordinary hours of work" are the hours that the casual employee actually works. This construction is compatible, in my view, with the reference in the definition of "ordinary time earnings" in cl 3.5(3)(d) of the Award to the inclusion in "ordinary time earnings" of "casual rates received for ordinary hours of work". The words of that paragraph show the imperfections of the text. But such difficulties can be overcome by approaching the meaning of cl 3.5 of the Award with the purposes of the Award provisions, and the related provisions of the Administration Act, kept firmly in mind. Approached in that way the "notional earnings base" of a casual employee, established by reference to "ordinary time earnings" (as defined in cl 3.5(3)(d) of the Award) is all time earnings for all hours actually worked. No other construction does justice to the fundamental difference between the time obligations of full-time and part-time employees and the completely different time arrangements for casual employees.' *Australian Communication Exchange Ltd v DCT* [2003] HCA 55 at [76], [77] per Kirby J; BC200305681

ORGAN

Canada [Bank claimed immunity as organ of foreign state.] 'The word "organ" is a very broad one. The Oxford English Dictionary defines it as "a means of action or operation, an instrument, a 'tool'; a person, a body of persons, or thing by which some purpose is carried out or some function performed".

'The use of the broad word "organ" in the Act, which was promulgated to codify the application of the doctrine in Canada, indicates the intention of Parliament to protect individuals and institutions who act at the request of a foreign state in situations where that state would enjoy sovereign immunity.'

Walker (*Litigation Guardian of*) *v Bank of New York Inc* (1994) 111 DLR (4th) 186 at 190–191, Ont CA, per McKinlay JA

ORIGINAL

Canada '[53] It is widely accepted that an "original" work must be independently produced and not copied. In attempts to further explain this cornerstone of copyright law, different judges and commentators have described the word "original" with a host of words and phrases mentioned above, including various combinations of the terms "labour", "judgment", "skill", "work", "industry", "effort", "taste" or "discretion" (see for example *Ladbroke Football, supra*, and *Slumber-Magic, supra*). To me, these are all possible ingredients in the recipe for originality, which may be altered to suit the flavour of the work at issue. Each term may help to determine whether a work is, in fact, original, but it is a mistake to treat any of these words as if they were statutory requirements. These are not, in themselves, prerequisites to copyright protection, but rather evidence of the sole prerequisite, originality. To determine whether or not the materials in issue are "original" works, a principled and reasoned approach based upon evidence is required, not reliance on a particular word or phrase that merely seeks to explain the concept of originality.

'[54] Moreover, I am not convinced that a substantial difference exists between an interpretation of originality that requires intellectual effort, whether described as skill, judgment and/or labour or creativity, and an interpretation that merely requires independent production. As discussed above, any skill, judgment and/or labour must be directed at an exercise other than mere copying for the result to be an original work (see *Interlego, supra*, at 262–3; *Tele-Direct, supra*, at para. 29). Clearly, therefore, the crucial requirement for a finding of originality is that the work be more than a mere copy. The vast majority of works that are not mere copies will normally require the investment of some intellectual effort, whatever that may be labelled. Works that are entirely devoid of such effort are, almost inevitably, simply copies of existing material.

'[55] I acknowledge that it is more difficult to apply the standard of originality to some types of works, such as compilations, than to traditional forms of expression, such as novels, sculptures or plays. The further one gets away from traditional literary works, the less obvious it becomes that a work has not been copied. Compilations of data, for instance, typically do not display an author's uniquely identifiable flare, nor "exhibit, on their face, *indicia* of the author's personal style or manner of expression" (*Hager, supra*, at 308). This makes it difficult to establish whether compilations are original or are merely copies. In addition, some compilations may be comprised of elements that are copied from other works or parts of works in which copyright may or may not otherwise subsist. Because the selection and arrangement of the underlying elements, not the elements themselves, must be original, a compiler must demonstrate something more than merely copying those elements into a new work before the Act will award copyright protection. However, Anglo-Canadian copyright law does not require "creativity" to establish that such a work is not a mere copy.

'[56] Even where "creativity" has been employed as a label for the intangible effort required to distinguish an original work from a mere copy, courts have emphasized that the standard is extremely low. British, Canadian and American jurisprudence has firmly established that copyright law is unlike patent law in that novelty or non-obviousness are not required, and that courts must not subjectively judge the quality or merit of an author's work (see *Fox, supra*, at 112–14). In *Apple Computer, supra* (F.C.A.), Hugessen J.A. stated that the sole distinguishing characteristic of literary work is that it be print or writing. In *Ladbroke, supra*, the court noted that aesthetic quality or virtue is not required for copyright protection. In *University of London Press, supra*, it was said that copyright could subsist "irrespective of the question whether the quality or style is high" (*supra*, at 608). The House of Lords held in *Walter v. Lane*, [1900] A.C. 539 at 549, that copyright could subsist in a book whether it was "wise or foolish, accurate or inaccurate, of literary merit or of no merit whatever", and (at 558) that a work "devoid of the faintest spark of literary or other merit" may have a copyright, "worthless and insignificant as it would be". American law also warns against judges constituting themselves judges of worth (see U.S. House Report No. 1476 (1976), 94th Cong., 2d Sess. 51; and *Bleistein v. Donaldson Lithographing Co.*, 188 U.S. 239 (1903) (*per* Justice Holmes at 251)).

'[57] To ignore this basic axiom is to intrude on the domain of critics and become appraisers of merit instead of arbiters of originality. It is not necessary for a copyright work to evince qualities of novelty, ingenuity, innovation, genius, merit, virtue, beauty, brilliance, imagination, creative spark and other such attributes, for copyright law is not necessarily concerned with them. Of course, most, if not all "creative" and "imaginative" works would be original, but not all original works must be "creative" or "imaginative"; those attributes, though praiseworthy, are not mandatory characteristics of every original work.' *CCH Canadian Ltd v Law Society of Upper Canada* (2002) DLR (4th) 385 at 418–420 (FCA), per Linden JA

ORPHAN RELATIVE

Australia [In the context of inter-country adoption and an application for a Child (Migrant) visa enabling the adopted child to enter and remain in Australia in order to be cared for by her Australian citizen adoptive parents. Migration Act 1958 (Cth).] '[11] The expression "orphan relative" is defined in reg 1.14. Regulation 1.14 provides:

> An applicant for a visa is an orphan relative of another person who is an Australian citizen, an Australian permanent resident or an eligible New Zealand citizen if:
> (a) the applicant:
>   (i) has not turned 18; and
>   (ii) does not have a spouse; and
>   (iii) is a relative of that other person; and
> (b) the applicant cannot be cared for by either parent because each of them is either dead, permanently incapacitated or of unknown whereabouts; and
> (c) there is no compelling reason to believe that the grant of a visa would not be in the best interests of the applicant.

...

'[26] As counsel for the applicant acknowledged, the adopted child in this case cannot satisfy cl 117.211(a) because she cannot satisfy the definition of "orphan relative" in reg 1.14. As already noted, it was her contention that the adopted child satisfies cl 117.211(b) since she was not an orphan relative "only because" the sponsoring Australian relative had adopted her. The submission was that the adopted child could not satisfy the definition of "orphan relative" in reg 1.14 "only because", following her adoption, she could not satisfy para (b) of this definition since her adoptive parents, who were within the definition of "parent" in reg 1.03, were not dead, permanently incapacitated or of unknown whereabouts.

'[27] I reject this submission. It is not correct to say that the adopted child is not an orphan relative "only because" she has been adopted. If the applicant and his wife had not adopted her, then she would have no relevant relationship with them.

When cl 117.211(b) is read with cl 117.211(a), the meaning of cl 117.211(b) is patent. Clause 117.211(b) applies where the visa applicant would be "an orphan relative of an Australian relative of the applicant" if he or she had not been adopted by that Australian relative. The adopted child would not have been an "orphan relative" of either the adoptive parent but for her adoption, because, but for her adoption, she would not be "a relative" of either of them and could not satisfy reg 1.14(a)(iii).

'[28] As the respondent's counsel submitted, the Explanatory Statement, which accompanied the Migration Amendment Regulations 2002 (No 2) (Cth) that introduced subcl 117.211(b), confirms that this subclause was intended to prevent "an orphan relative" from *losing* this status upon his or her adoption by a sponsoring Australian relative: see Acts Interpretation Act 1901 (Cth), ss 15AB and 46...

'[29] The Explanatory Statement confirms that para (b) of cl 117.211 provides for the situation where an adoption *prevents* a person satisfying the definition of "orphan relative" and not for the circumstance where an adoption *enables* a person to satisfy the definition of "relative" but not "orphan relative".' *EC v Minister for Immigration and Multicultural and Indigenous Affairs* [2004] FCA 978 at [11], [26]–[28], per Kenny J; BC200404794

OTHER CAUSE

Canada [Parent had continuing obligation to support child who was unable to withdraw from parents' charge for 'other causes'.] 'I conclude, accordingly, that inability to obtain employment in a depressed economy is one of the "other cause(s)" within the contemplation of s 2 of the Divorce Act.' *Baker v Baker* (1994) 109 DLR (4th) 548 at 556, per Berger J (Alta QB)

OTHER NEEDS

Canada '... The export of logs was placed on the Export Control List "to ensure that there is an adequate supply and distribution of [logs] in Canada for defence *or other needs*" (emphasis added). The respondent's argument is that "other needs" allows control of export in order to accord with provincial policies of restricting export to ensure a supply within the province, or to limit export for environmental purposes, or for reasons of international trade. Reference is made to the decision in *Teal Cedar Products (1977) Ltd v Canada*, [1989] 2 FC 158 (CA).

'I do not think the *Teal Cedar* case assists the respondent. It was an order in council that was challenged in that case, not the exercise of a delegated decision-making authority. More importantly, the argument being made was that unless the timber in question was being added to the list to satisfy a need related to a national emergency, or some need similar thereto, the order in council would not be valid. The Court held that "other needs" could refer to need other than defence. While this is clearly so, phrases such as "for ... other needs", when used as those words are used in paragraph 3(*e*), must be interpreted in accordance with the *ejusdem generis* rule of construction. The words "other needs" must at least have a national or federal character and there must be a "need". I have difficulty accepting that the existence of a provincial policy, *simpliciter*, falls within the wording "defence or other needs".' *K F Evans Ltd v Canada* (*Minister of Foreign Affairs*) [1997] 1 FC 405 at 425, Fed TD, per Reed J

OTHER PROCEEDINGS ... OR OTHER LEGAL PROCESS

[Section 252(2) of the Bankruptcy Act 1986 provides that an interim order in respect of a debtor may be made having the effect that while it is in force no bankruptcy petition relating to the debtor may be presented or proceeded with, and 'no other proceedings, and no execution or other legal process' may be commenced or continued against the debtor or his property except with the leave of the court.] 'In my judgment, when one finds in s 252(2)(b) the words "other proceedings" used as an alternative to a bankruptcy petition expressly mentioned in the subsection and the words "other legal process" used as an alternative to "execution", the ordinary meaning of "proceedings" and "legal process" adopted by Millett J in *Re Olympia and York Canary Wharf Ltd* [1993] BCLC 453, namely as embracing all steps in legal proceedings from the initiation of proceedings to enforcement of judgment—but not "non-judicial steps" which do not require the assistance of the court—is confirmed. For both a bankruptcy petition and execution are clearly legal (in the sense of judicial) proceedings ...

'I appreciate that Millett J was considering the meaning of the words in s 11(3) of the 1986 Act and not s 252(2), which I am concerned to construe. However, one would expect the same words to be used with the same meaning in two sections of the same Act ...

'Section 11(3)(d) contains an express reference to the levying of distress inconsistent with its inclusion in the words "other proceedings" or "other legal process". It is therefore clear, in my judgment, that in s 11(3)(d) Parliament did not intend the words "proceedings" or "legal process" to include the levying of distress. It would, in my judgment, require a clear contextual indication of a different intention to s 252(2) to justify construing the same words as including the levying of distress. In my judgment, there is no such indication ...

'Since, as I have already indicated, I see no sensible reason for construing the words of s 252(2) as excluding one self-help remedy, namely distress, but including another, namely peaceable re-entry, it follows that, in my judgment, a peaceable re-entry such as that in the present case does not require the leave of the court under s 252 of the 1986 Act.' *Re a debtor* (*No 13A/IO/95*) [1996] 1 All ER 691 at 703, per Rattee J

OTHER RECORDS

[In the Bankers' Books Evidence Act 1879 s 9(2), it is provided that expressions in that Act relating to 'bankers' books' include ledgers, day books, cash books, account books and other records used in the ordinary business of the bank, whether those records are in written form or are kept on microfilm, magnetic tape or any other form of mechanical or electronic data retrieval mechanism.'] 'It is plain that none of the classes of documents in the order made by Mr Registrar Rawson include copies of entries in ledgers, day books, cash books, account books, and I am therefore concerned only with the meaning of the words "other records used in the ordinary business of the bank" in its context in s 9(2) of the 1879 Act. If the matter were free from authority, I should be inclined to the view that these words should be construed restrictively. It seems to me clear that the purpose of the statute is to provide a convenient mode of proof for documents inherently probative of particular facts, and for this purpose one can refer to ss 3, 4 and 5 of the 1879 Act. However, the matter is not free from authority.

...

'In *Williams v Williams, Tucker v Williams* [1987] 3 All ER 257, [1988] QB 161 Sir John Donaldson MR was confronted with the problem of a request for paid cheques and credit slips relating to specified accounts with a named bank. In his judgment, with which Parker LJ and Sir George Waller agreed, having reviewed the history of the 1879 Act and its amendment, he said this, after dealing with the bank in question's policy in relation to the retention of cheques and paying-in slips:

"In this situation counsel appearing for [the applicant] has to submit, and does submit, that the bundles of cheques and paying-in slips constitute bankers' books within the modern definition and that adding each cheque or paying-in slip to the bundle constitutes making an entry in those books. Whilst I would be prepared to accept that the cheques constitute part of the bank's records used in the ordinary business of the bank ... I am quite unable to accept that adding an individual cheque or paying-in slip can be regarded as making an 'entry' in those records. Putting the matter in another way, 'other records' in the new definition has, I think, to be construed ejusdem generis with 'ledgers, day books, cash books [and] account books' and unsorted bundles of cheques and paying-in slips are not 'other records' within the meaning of the Act.' (See [1987] 3 All ER 257 at 261, [1988] QB 161 at 168.)

'I take this case as clear authority that the words "other records" have to be construed to cover records of the same kind as ledgers, day books, cash books and account books, which are, as is well known, the means by which a bank records day-to-day financial transactions. The words are not, it seems to me, apt to cover records kept by the bank of conversations between employees of the bank, however senior, and customers. The records in the present case are essentially the records of meetings, and it seems to me that those sort of notes of meetings cannot be properly regarded as entries in books kept by the bank for the purpose of its ordinary business within the definition of s 9(2) of the 1879 Act.' *Re Howglen Ltd* [2001] 1 All ER 376 at 380, 381–382, per Pumphrey J

OTHER THAN THOSE OF OR IN CONNECTION WITH A PRIVATE DWELLINGHOUSE

[The claimant contended that a restrictive covenant on plots of land on an estate not to use the premises 'for any purpose other than those of or in connection with a private dwellinghouse' was not a restriction to a single dwelling house since the phrase 'other than those of or in connection with a private dwellinghouse' meant 'other than for residential purposes'.] '[14] The claimant's construction of the first sentence of para (2) (the first covenant) essentially involves reading the words "other than those of or in connection with a private

dwellinghouse" as meaning "other than for residential purposes". The defendant's reading of the first covenant means that the plot as a whole cannot be used other than for or in connection with a single private dwelling house. As with any issue of construction, other than where the answer seems plain, the fact that one can reformulate a particular interpretation so as to make it clear can always enable the opponent of that interpretation to contend that, if that was the meaning intended, it would have been only too easy to express it in that way. As both Mr Vivian Chapman, who appears for the claimant, and Mr Kim Lewison QC, who appears for the defendant, sensibly accept, such an argument rarely takes a dispute as to construction further. The very reason that the question of interpretation is before the court is normally because the provision has not been as clearly drafted as it might have been.

'[15] I have reached the conclusion that the defendant's interpretation of the first covenant is to be preferred. First, as a matter of ordinary language, the indefinite article "a" tends to carry with it the concept of singularity as opposed to plurality. Restriction to use as "a private dwellinghouse" appears to me, at least in the absence of contextual or factual contra-indications, to mean restriction to a single dwelling house. The fact that the first covenant is not a restriction to "a private dwellinghouse" but to "[purposes] of or in connection with a private dwellinghouse" does not appear to me to call that conclusion into question in the present case. What the draftsman had in mind is the various uses to which one might put the land and buildings, and provided that the various purposes could fairly be said to be "those of or in connection with" a private dwellinghouse, they would be within the covenant. However, the use of those anterior words does not, to my mind, cast doubt on the simple fact that "a private dwellinghouse" tends to denote singularity. Given that it is "the premises", i e the plot as a unit, which is not to be used other than for purposes "of or in connection with a dwellinghouse", it seems to me that the natural meaning of the words is that there can be only "a" dwelling house, i e one dwelling house, on the premises, i e the plot.

'[16] Secondly, it seems to me that that conclusion is reinforced by the closing words of the first covenant, namely 'or for professional purpose(s)'. As Mr Chapman accepted in argument, a simple way of formulating the construction preferred by the claimant so far as the first covenant is concerned is that it limits the use of the plot to that of residential purpose or purposes. The fact that the draftsman self-evidently had in mind the concept of a particular type of purpose (or purposes), appears to me rather to reinforce the contention that he used the concept of "a private dwellinghouse" to emphasise the singularity (as well as the use) of the permitted building. Thus, there is the contrast between that expression and the permitted types of use, namely 'those of or in connection with' such a dwelling house, and professional purpose(s).

…

'[30] Obviously, when construing an expression in a document, one must be very careful of relying on authority. Indeed, there are cases which suggest that, in such a case, it is almost impermissible to refer to authorities as to the meaning of other documents, even when they involve interpreting the same expression. However, it does appear to me that it is not illegitimate to bear in mind the desirability of certainty and consistency in relation to the court's approach to the prima facie meaning of fairly common expressions in conveyances, leases, and, indeed, other types of document. It is desirable, where possible, for people to know with a reasonable certainty what their rights may be: uncertainty breeds costs, worry, and litigation. Where, as in *Dobbs'* case [*Dobbs v Linford* [1952] 2 All ER 827, [1953] 1 QB 48], the Court of Appeal has taken a pretty clear view as to the natural meaning of an expression such as "a private dwellinghouse", it seems to me that, while accepting that the same expression can obviously have a different meaning because of its textual or factual context, as the decision in *Downie*'s case indicates, the court should be slow to depart from that meaning without some reason. I am reinforced in that view in this case, because both Romer LJ and Evershed MR referred to authority as assisting them in construing a covenant whose central words were identical to those in the present case (see[1952] 2 All ER 827 at 830, 831, [1953] 1 QB 48 at 53, 54).

'[31] Mr Lewison very properly drew attention to s 61 of the [Law of Property Act 1925] which provides that, in all deeds, unless the context otherwise requires, the singular includes the plural (and vice versa). As explained by Russell J in *Re A Solicitors' Arbitration* [1962] 1 All ER 772 at 774, [1962] 1 WLR 353 at 356, that statutory provision "is designed to shorten the drafting of deeds and nothing more". However, that obviously does not mean that the provision can effectively be ignored. None the less, as exemplified by that very case, such a statutory provision "which is designed to save verbosity cannot properly be relied on" to

alter the meaning of a provision, if the court is satisfied that the provision was not intended to have the extended meaning which would result from applying s 61 (see [1962] 1 All ER 772 at 774, [1962] 1 WLR 353 at 357). It is fair to say that it is not as obvious to me that s 61 should not be applied in the present case as it appears to have been to Russell J in relation to the provision before him. However, it seems to me that the factors which have persuaded me that "a private dwellinghouse" is to be given its natural meaning, ie to be limited to singular, should lead to the conclusion that "the context otherwise requires". Apart from the natural reading of "a private dwellinghouse", and the contrast with "for professional purpose [or purposes]", it is to be noted that the application of s 61 in *Dobbs'* case would have produced a different result from that which obtained.' *Crest Nicholson Residential (South) Ltd v McAllister* [2002] EWHC 2443 (Ch) at [14]–[16], [30]–[31], [2003] 1 All ER 46, per Neuberger J

OUGHT TO HAVE KNOWN

Australia '*Boughey v The Queen* (1986) 161 CLR 10 establishes that, when the prosecution relies on the "ought to have known" limb of s 157(1)(c) [Criminal Code (Tas)], the Crown must prove beyond a reasonable doubt that the accused, and not some hypothetical person, ought to have known, if he or she had thought about it, that there was "a 'real and not remote' chance" [at 21 per Mason, Wilson and Deane JJ] that the unlawful act would bring about the death of the deceased [at 28–29 per Mason, Wilson and Deane JJ]. That is to say, on the proven facts, the jury must be satisfied beyond reasonable doubt that this accused with his or her knowledge ought to have known that there was a real chance that the unlawful act would bring about the death of the deceased. In *Boughey*, Mason, Wilson and Deane JJ, who gave the leading judgment, said that "the content of the knowledge laid at the door of an accused is [not] to be assessed by reference to the notional knowledge and capacity of some hypothetical person" … nothing in that case requires the conclusion that a prosecution under the "ought to have known" limb of s 157(1)(c) must fail unless the Crown proves the state of the accused's knowledge or "expertise" by direct evidence … their Honours said that the starting point in the inquiry whether the accused ought to have known that his unlawful act was likely to cause death "must be the knowledge, the intelligence and, where relevant, the expertise which the particular accused actually possessed." [at 28–29] Nothing in that passage or in the decision itself gives any support for the notion that the Crown cannot prove the accused's knowledge inferentially or that the prosecution must fail unless the Crown directly proves the knowledge and expertise of the accused concerning the relevant circumstances.' *Simpson v R* (1998) 155 ALR 571 at 573; 72 ALJR 1199; BC9803287, per Gaudron and McHugh JJ

OUGHT TO KNOW

New Zealand [Companies Act 1955 s 18C.] 'The proviso to s 18C(1) prevents a party relying on the section if "that person knows or by reason of his position ought to know" of the lack of authority. The proviso has not been the subject of any detailed examination in the cases in this jurisdiction so far. Several points of interpretation presented themselves. The first was the meaning to be given to the phrase "position with or relationship to". I held this phrase was not limited to an inside relationship with the company, but did require an ongoing relationship (*Story v Advance Bank Australia Ltd* (1993) 10 ACSR 699, 710 (NSW CA)). The next point was the meaning of the words "ought to know" which I held differed from the common law concept of being "put upon inquiry" and required something more (*Brick and Pipe Industries Ltd v Occidental Life Nominees Pty Ltd* [1992] a VR 279, 359). The question then became what is the relationship between these two phrases. The wording of the proviso conveys that what the person ought to know is determined by his or her position with, or relationship to, the company. Therefore information acquired is only relevant if it forms part of the relationship between the person and company (which is to be defined having regard to its particular characteristics).' *Equiticorp Industries Group Ltd* (*In Statutory Management*) *v The Crown* (*Judgment no 47: Summary*) [1996] 3 NZLR 586 at 612–613, per Smellie J

OUT OF

[The Social Security Act 1975 has been repealed. See now the Social Security Contributions and Benefits Act 1992, s 94.]

OUTGOINGS

[For 42 Halsbury's Laws (4th edn) para 131 see now 42 Halsbury's Laws (4th edn) (Reissue) para 125.]

OUTLET (IN THE BOTTOM THEREOF)

Australia [Construction of patent specification.] 'There is no hole or aperture in the biBag at the bottom. Rather, a tube inside the vessel, with a filter at its end at the bottom of the vessel draws fluid from the bottom of the vessel and takes it to the intermediate annulated ring at the top of the vessel. There are three rings. The middle ring has a hole which acts as the ingress of water. The intermediate ring has a hole to which the tube delivers fluid from the bottom of the vessel. The outer ring is used in affixing the biBag to the machine …

'An outlet is defined in the *Macquarie Dictionary* as "an opening or passage by which anything is let out, a vent or exit". The *New Shorter Oxford* (1993) defines outlet as "an opening by which something escapes or is released; a means of issue or exit".

…

'[156] In this way, there is an outlet at the bottom of the vessel into the third fluid conducting means. The commencement of the passage by which the concentrate is let out of or exits the vessel is at the filter. The ingress or openings into the filter is or are how the concentrate escapes or is released from the vessel into the third fluid conducting means.

…

'[158] Examining the matter functionally, the fluid concentrate leaves the powder column and the vessel at the point it passes through the filter into the third fluid conducting means at the bottom of the vessel. In this sense, though the vessel is not cut or pierced at the bottom, nevertheless there is an outlet at the bottom.

'[159] The tube could exit the skin of the vessel from the bottom. No functional advantage is obtained by running it inside the bag up to the standard annulated fixture. The essence of the invention is as I have earlier described it. One essential integer is the use of powder in a vessel and dissolution of it by water on-line. In claim 4 the concentrate solution is conducted from the bottom of the vessel, where there is an outlet. Looking at the claim purposively (*Populin v HB Nominees* at 41–2) and recognising that the essential matter to which the words of claim 4 are directed is to conduct the concentrate solution from the bottom of the vessel into the third fluid conducting means out of the vessel and to the mixing point, it can be seen that how much tubing that constitutes part of the third fluid conducting means that is within the boundaries of the skin of the vessel is functionally immaterial, just as the precise location of the break in the skin of the vessel through which the fluid passes into the intermediate ring and continues along the third fluid conducting means is functionally immaterial. What is taught by the claims, read in the light of the specification, is that the outlet of the vessel is where the concentrate enters the third fluid conducting means (and thereby leaves, exits or is let out of the vessel) and as such is at the bottom of the vessel. That occurs in types 2 and 3.' *Gambro Pty Ltd v Fresenius Medical Care South East Asia Pty Ltd* [2004] FCA 323 per Allsop J; BC200401266

OUTPUT TAX

Subject to the following provisions of this section, 'output tax', in relation to a taxable person, means VAT on supplies which he makes or on the acquisition by him from another member State of goods (including VAT which is also to be counted as input tax by virtue of subsection (1)(b) above). (Value Added Tax Act 1994, s 24(2))

[*See also* INPUT TAX.]

OUTRAGE

[For outraging public decency see 11(1) (Reissue) Halsbury's Laws (4th Edn) para 372; and *R v Rowley* [1991] 4 All ER 649, CA.]

OVEN

[The Clean Air Act 1956 has been repealed, and the definition is not re-enacted in the Clean Air Act 1993.]

OVERAGE

'In my opinion "consideration" cannot be equated with the cash-price element of the offers made … The cash price is a component, and plainly a very significant component, of the consideration offered. But the expression "consideration" … is in my view plainly broad enough to include other financial return to the seller under the contract for the disposal of the site. It follows, in my opinion, that the "overage" provisions in the offers (ie the provisions for the payment of a share of development profit by the developer to the seller) are also part of the consideration. Unlike the cash price, however, the overage provision is not a fixed figure but depends on the formula adopted and the profitability of the development as it turns out.' *Stannifer Developments Ltd v Glasgow Development Agency and Scottish Enterprise* 1998 SCLR 870 at 895, per Lord Macfadyen

OVERPAYMENT

Australia [Section 26 of the Sales Tax Assessment (No 1) 1930 (Cth) refers to tax being 'overpaid' by a person.] 'In the view I take of it, "overpayment" is not confined to a situation where some tax is payable but more than that sum has been paid, but can encompass the situation where no tax is payable, with the consequence that the entirety of that which has been paid is an overpayment.' *Precision Pools Pty Ltd v Federal Commissioner of Taxation* (1992) 109 ALR 679 at 688, per Spender J

OVERTIME

[The Factories Act 1961, s 89(10), has been repealed.]

[The respondent's retirement pension was related to his 'remuneration' as defined in Pt C of the Local Government Pension Scheme Regulations 1995. He had worked overtime. His contract of employment had set out an agreed rate for overtime, but had not provided that either the authority or the pensioner could insist upon any overtime working. Regulation C2(2)(a) provided that 'remuneration', as defined in para (1), did not include payments for 'non-contractual overtime'. On a complaint by the pensioner to the Pensions Ombudsman, the latter found that the pensioner had not been contractually bound to work overtime, but held that his overtime payments did not constitute payment for 'non-contractual overtime' within the meaning of para (2)(a) since the contract had provided for a rate of pay if overtime were worked. The Ombudsman therefore concluded that any overtime was contractual, that accordingly payments for such overtime fell within the general definition of 'remuneration' in para (1) and that they were therefore to be taken into account for the purposes of calculating the pensioner's retirement benefits. The local authority appealed to the High Court.] '[5] This case is concerned with the meaning of exception (a)—what does "non-contractual overtime" mean? Were Mr Skingle's overtime earnings "payments for non-contractual overtime"?

'[6] I proceed initially on the same premise as did the Ombudsman, namely that Mr Skingle's contract of employment provided for a basic salary for a basic working week (of 36 hours). The contract also set forth an agreed rate for overtime. But it did not provide that either the authority or

Mr Skingle could insist upon any overtime working. There was no compulsory overtime.

…

'[8] So the Ombudsman's reasoning ran: the contract provided for the rate of pay if overtime was worked. Hence any overtime was contractual. It was not outside the contract.

'[9] The borough say that is wrong: "non-contractual overtime" means overtime not called for by the contract—non-compulsory, that is voluntary, overtime is what is meant. The mere provision in the contract of employment for a rate of pay if optional overtime is worked does not make the overtime "contractual". Despite Mr Randall's attractively-presented argument, I have concluded that the borough are right. Here are my reasons.

'[10] Focus first on the word "overtime". This indicates time spent working beyond the basic hours provided by the contract. But it does not mean time spent working at some other employment—it is work on the job that is being referred to. Now if payment for all work on the job (normal hours plus all overtime, voluntary or not) counts as the "remuneration", the exclusion is meaningless. That cannot be right. Some payment for work on the job is clearly to be excluded—and that can only be payment for work done on the job which is not required by the contract—namely voluntary overtime.

'[11] Mr Randall felt the force of this, as did the Ombudsman. The latter could not find any meaning to "non-contractual overtime" ("it is not clear to me what payments for overtime could fall within [the definition]"). Mr Randall suggested ex gratia payments for voluntary additional hours not recognised officially as overtime. That is too loose a concept—an ex gratia payment is just a gift and would not fall within the basic definition of remuneration at all. Remuneration is "payments … in respect of employment".

'[12] I am confirmed in this view by a second order argument. This is based on exclusion (c)—payment for loss of holidays. If an employee works for part of his holiday entitlement and gets paid, he is in effect doing much the same thing as overtime during a working week. It hardly seems rational that voluntary overtime should be included, but similar voluntary work during holidays excluded. Originally it was Mr Randall who prayed this provision in his aid. He said: "look, payment for work done in lost holiday time is excluded specifically, the same could have been done for voluntary overtime but it was not." When the provision was turned against him he suggested

instead that it was aimed at something altogether different—payments for lost holidays that were never taken at all, as for instance may happen when an employee leaves without having taken his full holiday entitlement. But the provision is not so limited—it covers both payments in lieu of holidays and payments for working during holidays.

'[13] Mr Randall raised several other points which I should mention briefly. He submitted that the provision, being an exception, should be construed narrowly. Whilst this is a principle of interpretation of European legislation, I am not aware that it is a principle for the construction of our domestic legislation. Besides, even if one applies the principle one must give the exception some sensible meaning. As I have said, none can be found if "non-contractual overtime" covers both compulsory and voluntary overtime.

'[14] Next he submitted that the alternative argument did violence to the actual language, that it amounted to substitution of the word "compulsory" for the word "contractual". That at first appealed to me, but on reflection I think it appealed because of the way Mr Randall put it. If one reads "contractual" as "called for by the contract" there is no such violence.

'[15] Mr Randall also submitted that the borough's construction made no sense in the real workplace. There, he said, many workers in practice do overtime and are happy to do so. It makes no difference whether they are required to do so or not. Many workers indeed do overtime not just for more money but because they want to see their jobs done properly. From his evidence Mr Skingle, as a good public servant, fell in that class. Why in practice should one sort of overtime be included, but another not? The answer is that is what the exception does—it differentiates between contractual and non-contractual overtime.' *Newham London Borough Council v Skingle* [2002] EWHC 1013 (Ch) at [4]–[6], [8]–[15], [2002] 3 All ER 287 at 289–291, per Jacob J

[Reversed, *Newham London Borough Council v Skingle* [2003] EWCA Civ 280, [2003] 2 All ER 761, but not on the definition of overtime.]

OWNER

See also OWNERSHIP

[For 35 Halsbury's Laws (4th edn) paras 1127–1128 see now 35 Halsbury's Laws (4th edn) (Reissue) paras 1227–1228.]

[Environmental Protection Act 1990, s 80(2)(b).] 'The principal thrust of Mr Williams' submission in support of this appeal is that a whole series of statutes regulating statutory nuisances from 1848 up until the present time have defined "owner" in the same way, namely:

"... the Person for the Time being receiving the Rack Rent of the Lands or Premises in connexion with which the said Word is used, whether on his own Account or as Agent or Trustee for any other Person ..."

Such a definition is to be found, purely by way of example, in s 2 of the Public Health Act 1848, and (with slight but immaterial variations) in the Nuisances Removal and Diseases Prevention Act 1855, in s 4 of the Public Health Act 1875, in the Public Health Act 1936, the Public Health Act 1961, the Control of Pollution Act 1974, the Local Government (Miscellaneous Provisions) Act 1976 and the Clean Air Act 1993. Furthermore, that definition has also been used in other regulatory acts concerning fire precautions, highways and housing.

'That being so, Mr Williams submits that as "owner" in s 80(2) of the 1990 Act is not defined, and as the definition in s 81A(9) of "owner" is expressly, by that subsection, limited to that subsection and does not extend to the use of the word "owner" elsewhere in the Act, it follows that there is a potential ambiguity and, indeed, potentially a different meaning where the word "owner" appears in s 80(2).

'As a matter of history, over the last 150 years, "owner" has, in this legislation, acquired a technical meaning where statutory nuisances are being dealt with and the word "owner" in s 80(2) should be given that same well-established, historically-based meaning ...

'Mr Williams submits that, in the light of ... authority, the approach of this court to the word "owner" in s 80(2) should be similarly historically based. He stresses that the long title to the Act indicates a restatement of the law defining statutory nuisances. He submits that the principal purpose of Pt III of the Act is to ensure that statutory nuisances are promptly abated or prevented. To this end, the enforcing authority or private individual, who also has powers under the Act, should be able readily to identify a person connected with the premises who can speedily be served with a notice. By targeting the person receiving the rack rent, or the person entitled to receive the rack rent, the enforcing authority or private individual is able to identify persons sufficiently closely connected to the premises to be held responsible for their condition. Mr Williams submits that in restricting, in s 81A(9),

the definition of "owner", Parliament was concerned to ensure that that definition was not to apply to the word "owner" when used in the Act, other than in s 81A(9). He does not shrink from the submission that the consequence is that "owner" means more than one thing in the same Act.

'He submits that no injustice is done to a managing agent served with such a notice, first, because enforcement proceedings can be taken only against a true managing agent: see, for example, *Bottomley v Harrison* [1952] 1 All ER 368 and *Midland Bank Ltd v Conway BC* [1965] 2 All ER 978. Furthermore, the managing agent has the right of appeal against the notice contained in the regulations to which we have referred. Thirdly, although failure to comply with an abatement notice is a criminal offence, there is a defence for a managing agent of reasonable excuse provided by s 80(4), to which I have already referred. Finally, a managing agent can recover expenses incurred by making deductions from rent collected on behalf of the landlord.

'So far as s 81A(9)'s definition is concerned, Mr Williams submits that s 81A is concerned with the imposition of a land charge and it would not make sense in relation to a land charge to speak of an agent as being the owner because the agent does not have the legal title which a land charge would affect. That, submits Mr Williams, provides a perfectly good reason why a different definition is provided in s 81A(9).

...

'In my judgment, Mr Williams's submissions are correct. I pay full regard to the penal nature of the statute, creating, as it does, a criminal offence, or more accurately, one should say, restating a criminal offence. But, as I have already indicated, the regulations provide, for example, a means of challenge where the wrong person has been served with an abatement notice and there is also a defence, which I have indicated, in relation to reasonable excuse.

'It seems, to my mind, that the reference in s 81A(9) to "this section" immediately poses a question mark or ambiguity as to the meaning of "owner", where it appears undefined in s 80(2). That being so, a judge is entitled to resolve that ambiguity by recourse to the overwhelming legislative history to which I have referred, a legislative history which, it is to be noted, not only precedes this Act by 150 years but also succeeds it in the terms of s 64 of the Clean Air Act 1993. That being so, the answer to the question posed by the case stated, as to whether the Crown Court was correct in concluding that the respondent was not the owner of the premises within the meaning of s 80(2)(b), is No.' *Camden London Borough Council v Gunby* [1999] 4 All ER 602 at 605–606, 607, 608, CA, per Rose LJ

Australia [Section 19(3) of the Circuit Layouts Act 1989 (Cth) provides that infringement occurs, inter alia, where the alleged infringer knows or ought reasonably to know that he or she is not licensed by the 'owner' of the relevant eligible layout right.] 'The words "the owner" can, however, be at least as readily understood not as a specific designation of a particular person in that sense (the specific designation construction) but as a non-specific reference to a possessor of the attributes which constitute ownership of the relevant right … the non-specific construction is the preferable one.' *Nintendo Co Ltd v Centronics Systems Pty Ltd* (1994) 121 ALR 577 at 586, per Mason CJ, Brennan, Deane, Toohey, Gaudron and McHugh JJ

Australia [Section 19 of the Admiralty Act 1988 (Cth) provides that a proceeding on a general maritime claim concerning a ship may be commenced as an action in rem against some other ship if a relevant person in relation to the claim was, inter alia, the 'owner' of the first-mentioned ship and that person is, when the proceeding is commenced, the 'owner' of the second-mentioned ship.] 'I think there are difficulties in taking the simple view that "owner" in the section means only "registered owner". After all, the section does not use those words. Obviously the registered owner will, in the absence of other evidence, be taken to be the beneficial owner. But there seems to me to be no reason of policy why the section should not be construed to mean or to include a beneficial owner.' *Malaysia Shipyard v 'Iron Shortland' as surrogate for the ship 'Newcastle Pride'* (1995) 131 ALR 738 at 749, per Sheppard J

Canada '[8] Section 181(b) of the *Highway Traffic Act, supra* states that a person who is driving a motor vehicle and is in possession of it with the consent of the owner is deemed to be the agent or servant of the owner and to be driving the motor vehicle in the course of his employment. The effect of this provision is to make the owner of the vehicle vicariously liable for any loss or damage sustained as a result of the driver's negligence.

'[9] The term "owner" is defined in s 1(m.1) of the *Highway Traffic Act, supra* as:

> (m.1) "owner" includes any person renting a motor vehicle or having the exclusive use of it under a lease or otherwise for a period of more than 30 days.

'[10] It is common ground that Solis had exclusive possession of the Escort from April 14, 1998 until after the collision in question. Accordingly, he was an "owner" for purposes of the Act. However, the definition of "owner" in the Act is not exhaustive.

'[11] In *Hayduk v. Pidoborozny*, [1972] S.C.R. 879 the Supreme Court of Canada determined that the registered owner of a vehicle may also be treated as an owner within the meaning of the Act. The majority in *Bois v. McDonald* (1975), 60 D.L.R. (3d) 184 (Alta. s C.A.D.) interpreted *Hayduk v. Pidoborozny* to mean that the registered owner should *prima facie* be considered an owner unless and until it is established that they are not an owner at common law or do not fall within the extended definition of "owner" contained in the Act. In the present case, it was Solis who was the registered owner of the vehicle.

'[12] The Defendant Ford Credit suggests that it was not the owner of the vehicle as Solis had not breached the lease. Therefore, it was not entitled to possession of the Escort and had no "dominion" over the vehicle. In making this submission it relied on the following comments of Ford J. in *Charlebois v. Wells,* [1947] 3 D.L.R. 919 at p. 921 (Alta. s C.T.D.):

> In order to apply *The Vehicles and Highway Traffic Act* of Alberta to the question of liability arising from an accident in which a motor vehicle is involved, ownership must be determined according to the use of the word "owner" in our Act. Bearing in mind the object of the Act, it is also my opinion that the usual criteria of ownership must exist; and among these dominion over the car is very important. One who has the right to authorize its use, including what is implied in or that follows from such authority, would, I think, be the owner, but this is not an attempt at a definition of the term.

'[13] The Ontario Supreme Court (Appellate Division) in *Wynne v. Dalby* (1913), 16 D.L.R. 710 at 714 referred to the word "owner" as an elastic term. Its meaning in a statutory enactment depends on the object the enactment is intended to serve. The issue before the court in *Wynne v. Dalby* was essentially the same as the issue with which I am confronted. The specific question posed in that case was whether the conditional seller of a motor vehicle was an owner for purposes of s 19 of the Ontario *Motor Vehicle Act* (statutes of 1912, ch 48), which provided:

19. The owner of a motor vehicle shall be responsible for any violation of this Act or of any regulation prescribed by the Lieutenant-Governor in Council.

'[14] In concluding that a conditional seller was not an "owner" for purposes of that section, Meredith C.J.O., who delivered the judgment of the court, stated at pp. 715–716:

> The purpose of sec. 19 was, I think, to avoid any question being raised as to whether a servant of the owner, who was driving a motor vehicle when the violation of the Act or regulation took place, was acting within the scope of his employment, and to render the person having the dominion over the vehicle, and in that sense the owner of it, answerable for any violation in the commission of which the vehicle was the instrument, by whosoever it might be driven; and I do not think that it can have been intended to fix the very serious responsibility which the section imposes upon one who, like the respondent, at the time the accident happened, had neither the possession of nor the dominion over the vehicle, although he may have been technically the owner of it in the sense in which the owner of the legal estate in land is the owner of the land.

'[15] *Wynne v. Dalby, supra* was referred to by Laskin J. in his minority judgment in *Hayduk v. Pidoborozny, supra*. He indicated that it was this case which underlay the "dominion" test upon which the Alberta Appellate Division had proceeded. Laskin J. suggested that while it might be appropriate to apply this test in litigation between two parties claiming ownership to a vehicle, it should not be applied in situations where the registered owner is attempting to escape vicarious liability by proof that the legal or beneficial interest in the vehicle rested with someone else. Ritchie J., on behalf of the majority in *Hayduk v. Pidoborozny, supra* also cautioned at pp. 886–887 that:

> The respondents cited and relied upon a number of decisions of the Court of Appeal of Ontario in this regard and I think it sufficient to say that these cases were decided under *The Highway Traffic Act of Ontario* and in my opinion are of no assistance in interpreting the *Alberta Vehicles and Highway Traffic Act, supra.*

'[16] The Supreme Court of Canada again dealt with the issue of ownership in *Honan (Next Friend of) v. Doman Estate*, [1975] 2 s C.R. 866. Doman,

the original owner of the vehicle in that case, fearing that the car might be seized under execution of an alimony judgment obtained by his wife, persuaded the defendant Gerhold to register the vehicle in his name. Doman executed a transfer of the vehicle to Gerhold but retained sole control of the car. Gerhold obtained insurance coverage for the car and renewed the registration in his own name on several occasions. The court held that while Doman retained exclusive possession of the vehicle, the actions of the defendant in applying for and renewing the registration and insurance was consistent with his ownership of the vehicle.

'[17] Given these two Supreme Court of Canada decisions it is apparent that dominion and control is no longer the sole test for ownership under the *Highway Traffic Act, supra* in terms of vicarious liability. Where the registered owner has some earmarks of title, that person may also be regarded as an owner of the vehicle (*McEwan v. Iles* (1981), 128 D.L.R. (3d) 447 at 452–453, cited with approval in *Theriault (Litigation Guardian of) v. Aubin* (1991), 121 N.B.R. (2d) 235 (N.B.C.A.)).' *Alas v Solis* (2001) 203 DLR (4th) 409 at 412–413, Alta QB, per Nash J

Canada '2 In each appeal only one issue was raised. Where there is a long-term lease of an automobile with an option to buy the vehicle at the end for a significant price, is the lessor or its assignee an "owner" under s. 181 of the *Highway Traffic Act*, R.S.A. 2000, c. H-8? That section makes the owner vicariously liable for the driver's fault.

'3 Counsel for Ford Credit argued that it was not an "owner" because it had no real dominion or control, citing *Wynne v. Dalby* (1913) 30 O.L.R. 67, 16 D.L.R. 710 (C.A.).

'4 In our view, there are two crucial points. First, Alberta's statute permits more than one "owner" at the same time, for purposes of this section: *Hayduk v. Pidoborozny* [1972] S.C.R. 879, 886, 29 D.L.R. (3d) 8.

'5 Second, the statute does not really define an "owner". Section 1 (m.1) merely says that

> "'owner' includes any person renting a motor vehicle …"

That extends the meaning of the word "owner", but does not confine it. It does not say that the word in question "means" a lessee, just that it "includes" a lessee. Such a non-exclusive definition clause in an Act is presumed not to remove common or dictionary meanings of the term. See Burrows, *Interpretation of Documents* 106–07 (2d ed. 1946); *Re Parsons*, [1943] Ch. 12, 15, [1942] 2 All E.R.

496, 497F (C.A.); Côté, *Interpretation of Legislation in Canada*, 62 (3d ed. 2000); *Canadian Pacific Ltd. v. Canada (Attorney General)*, [1986] 1 S.C.R. 678, 687–9, 66 N.R. 321; *Nova v. Amoco Canada Petroleum Co.*, [1981] 2 S.C.R. 437, 460–61, 38 N.R. 381. Plainly and admittedly Ford Credit was the owner (or an owner) at common law.' *Ford Credit Canada Ltd. v Solis* (2003) 226 DLR (4th) 744 at 746 (Alta CA), per the Court

OWNER–OCCUPIER

[The Town and Country Planning Act 1971 has been repealed. See now the Town and Country Planning Act 1990, s 168.]
(1) Subject to the following provisions of this section, in this Chapter [Chapter II of Part VI] 'owner-occupier', in relation to a hereditament, means—
    (a) a person who occupies the whole or a substantial part of the hereditament in right of an owner's interest in it, and has so occupied that hereditament or that part of it during the whole of the period of six months ending with the date of service; or
    (b) if the whole or a substantial part of the hereditament was unoccupied for a period of not more than 12 months ending with that date, a person who so occupied the hereditament or, as the case may be, that part of it during the whole of a period of six months ending immediately before the period when it was not occupied.
(2) Subject to the following provisions of this section, in this Chapter [Chapter II of Part VI] 'owner-occupier', in relation to an agricultural unit, means a person who—
    (a) occupies the whole of that unit and has occupied it during the whole of the period of six months ending with the date of service; or
    (b) occupied the whole of that unit during the whole of a period of six months ending not more than 12 months before the date of service,
and, at all times material for the purposes of paragraph (a) or, as the case may be, paragraph (b) has been entitled to an owner's interest in the whole or part of that unit.
[Subsection (3) defines 'resident owner-occupier', and sub-s (4) defines 'owner's interest' and 'date of service'.]

OWNERSHIP

See also BENEFICIAL OWNERSHIP

Australia [Beneficial ownership of a ship.] '[61] The word "owner" cannot be given any general description. But ordinarily the incidents of ownership of a chattel include the right to make physical use of the chattel, the right to the income from it, the power of management, and the right of alienation: Lawson & Rudden (supra) at p 8. In the *Malaysia Shipyard and Engineering Sdn Bhd v The "Iron Shortland" as the surrogate for the ship "Newcastle Pride"* (1995) 59 FCR 535 (at 544) Sheppard J quoted from the decision of the Singapore Court of Appeal in *The "Ohm Mariana" The ex "Peony"; Pacific Navigation Co Pty Ltd v Owners "Ohm Mariana" ex "Peony"* [1993] 2 SLR 698 that the term "owner" means any person who is vested with such ownership as to have the right to sell, dispose of or alienate the ship, and that a beneficial owner of the ship comes within that term. See also to similar effect *"The Permina 3001"* [1979] 2 Lloyd's Rep 327, 329.

'[62] The notion of "ownership" carries a connotation of dominance, ultimate control and of ultimate title against the whole world: cf O W Holmes The Common Law 1882 at 242–246; *Blackstone's Commentaries*, 18th ed 1829, Vol 2, at 389; and Holdsworth, A History of English Law, 1925 vol VII at 449.

'[63] In *Jeffries v Great Western Railway Co* (1856) 5 E & B 802, at 805, Lord Campbell CJ said:

> "I am of opinion that the law is that a person possessed of goods as his property has a good title as against every stranger, and that one who takes them from him, having no title in himself, is a wrongdoer, and cannot defend himself by shewing that there was title in some third person; for against a wrongdoer possession is a title."

'[64] That approach was applied by the Court of Appeal in *"The Winkfield"* [1902] P 42 at 55 by Collins MR. These statements accord with the primary definition of "owner" in The *Oxford English Dictionary* as: ... "(a) ... One who owns or holds something as his own; a proprietor; one who has the rightful claim or title to a thing (although he may not be in possession) ..."

'[65] A helpful description of "ownership" is formulated by Jordan CJ in *Gatward v Alley* (1940) 40 SR (NSW) 174 at 178, where his Honour said in relation to a question as to ownership of a car:

> "A good title to property, in the sense of such ownership as the law allows, consists in having the legal right to exercise with respect to it

all such rights, as against all such persons, as by law are capable of being exercised with respect to property of the class in question. A person who has possession of property but not ownership has, as a general rule, the same legal rights as the owner, save to the extent to which those rights are qualified as against the owner …"

'[66] Ownership, whether legal or equitable, therefore involves something greater than beneficial interest. Equitable ownership of property is commensurate with the right to relief in a Court of Equity: *The Trustees Executors & Agency Co Ltd v The Acting Federal Commissioner of Taxation* (1917) 23 CLR 576 at 583; Meagher, Heydon and Leeming, Meagher, Gummow & Lehane's *Equity Doctrines & Remedies* 4th ed 2002 at [4–120]. If a person has contractual rights in relation to a ship which, if performed will result in the person becoming the owner of the ship, then the person will be regarded as the equitable owner of the ship provided that specific performance of the contract would be decreed: *KLDE Pty Ltd v Commissioner of Stamp Duties (Qld)* (1984) 155 CLR 288, 296–297. Thus entitlement to a vesting order or

equivalent relief would be necessary before AFE could be regarded as the equitable owner of the ship as at the relevant date: *Stern v McArthur* (1988) 165 CLR 489, 523–524; *Chan v Cresdon Pty Ltd* (1989) 168 CLR 242, 252–253. But that does not mean that AFE does not have an interest in the trust property, including the ship, which equity would protect regardless of whether AFE could be called the equitable owner.

…

'[72] … But "owner" in s 19(b) of the Act is concerned with title to, or proprietorship of the ship at a particular point in time. Such capabilities as AFE had in relation to the ship at the relevant date lack the directness and immediacy necessary to confer on AFE title to or ownership of the ship as at that date. The existence of a power in AFE to cause Everdene to terminate the trust does not have any impact prior to the exercise of the power upon Everdene's ownership of the ship. It simply means that ownership existing at a point in time could be displaced thereafter by unilateral action.' *Kent v Vessel 'Maria Luisa'* [2003] FCAFC 93 per Tamberlin and Hely JJ; BC200302365

P

PAID

[Payments of interest made by a property investment company were claimed to be 'charges on income' paid by the company within the meaning of s 338 of the Income and Corporation Taxes Act 1988 and therefore allowable deductions in computing its profits or losses. The question arose whether interest was 'paid' within the meaning of s 338, where the company paid the interest out of money which it had been lent by the lender for the specific purpose of enabling it to pay, ie a circular transaction.]
'[14] Section 338(1) of the 1988 Act provides, in short, that charges on income shall be allowed as deductions against profits in computing the corporation tax of a company. "Charges on income" are defined in s 338(2) as "payments of any description mentioned in subsection (3) below". So far as relevant, sub-s (3) provides that "the payments referred to in subsection (2)(a) above are — (a) any yearly interest". Prima facie, payment of interest in s 338 has its normal legal meaning, and connotes simply satisfaction of the obligation to pay. In the present case, WIL's obligation to pay the accrued interest to the trustees was discharged by satisfaction. Thus, if the Revenue are to succeed, "payment" in s 338 must bear some other meaning. Ultimately, applying in full the purposive *Ramsay* approach [*W T Ramsay Ltd v IRC* [1981] 1 All ER 865, [1982] AC 300, HL] to interpretation, I can find no justification for giving "payment" in s 338 some other meaning. Moreover, I am unable to see what that other meaning could be.

'[15] I must elaborate a little. In the ordinary case the source from which a debtor obtains the money he uses in paying his debt is immaterial for the purpose of s 338 of the 1988 Act. It matters not whether the debtor used cash-in-hand, sold assets to raise the money, or borrowed money for the purpose. Does it make a difference when the payment is made with money borrowed for the purpose from the very person to whom the arrears of interest are owed? In principle, I think not. Leaving aside sham transactions, a debt may be discharged and replaced with another even when the only persons involved are the debtor and the

creditor. Once that is accepted, as I think it must be, I do not see it can matter that there was no business purpose other than gaining a tax advantage. A genuine discharge of a genuine debt cannot cease to qualify as a payment for the purpose of s 338 by reason only that it was made solely to secure a tax advantage. There is nothing in the language or context of s 338 to suggest that the purpose for which a payment of interest is made is material.'

...

'[78] Section 338(1) of the Income and Corporation Taxes Act 1988 provides that there shall be allowed as deductions for the relevant accounting period "any charges on income paid by the company in the accounting period, so far as paid out of the company's profits brought into charge to corporation tax". Subsection (2)(a) of that section provides that "charges on income" means for the purposes of corporation tax "payments" of any description mentioned in sub-s (3). Subsection (3)(a) states that the payments referred to in sub-s (2) include "any yearly interest". Those are the provisions on which WIL's claim to an allowable deduction in the end depends. There is no question in this case of the taxpayer company having to demonstrate that it has sustained a "loss" or achieved a "gain" in circumstances where the result of the transaction was to leave it in no different position from that which it was in before. Had that been the question, the issue, as in *W T Ramsay Ltd v IRC, Eilbeck (Inspector of Taxes) v Rawling* [1981] 1 All ER 865, [1982] AC 300, would have been whether at the end of the day there was a real loss or a real gain. But those are not the concepts which are used in the statutory provisions that are in issue in this case. They do not depend upon an assessment of the result of the transaction. They depend upon the taxpayer being able to demonstrate that a charge on income has been "paid" by the company.

'[79] The Special Commissioners ([1997] STC (SCD) 69) found as a fact that the loans which were made by the scheme to WIL were real loans. It is clear that, but for the loans, WIL could not have afforded to pay the interest which it owed to the scheme. Nevertheless the fact is that the loans were made and the interest was paid. WIL's claim is therefore based upon transactions which have been found by the commissioners to be genuine. There was no step that falls to be ignored because it was artificial. It cannot be said that there was no business or commercial reason for the interest to be paid. The payment reduced the amount of WIL's accrued liability to pay interest. It was received as interest in the hands of the payee. WIL's obligation to pay interest to that extent was discharged. Nothing was inserted into the transaction to make it appear to be different from what it was. It was a payment of yearly interest which was paid out of the company's profits for the relevant accounting period.

'[80] The question that has to be addressed in these circumstances relates, as Lord Steyn said in *IRC v McGuckian* [1997] 3 All ER 817 at 826, [1997] 1 WLR 991 at 1001, to the fiscal effectiveness of the transaction entered into by the taxpayer. The answer to the question is to be found in the words used by the statute. A course of action that was designed to defeat the intention of Parliament would fall to be treated as tax avoidance and dealt with accordingly. But one must discover first what the statute means. The ordinary principles of statutory construction must then be applied to the words used by Parliament which describe the effect of the transaction for tax purposes.

'[81] On this approach the case does not seem to me, in the end, to give rise to any real difficulty. The words 'paid" and "payment" are to be construed according to their ordinary meaning. The question whether a payment has been made is a question of fact. That question has been answered by the findings made by the commissioners. The evidence established to their satisfaction that a loan was in fact made by the scheme to WIL and that WIL used that loan to pay interest to the scheme. The interest was a charge on income because it was a payment of a description mentioned in s 338(3) of the 1988 Act. That point having been established, the rule in s 338(1) determines the fiscal effectiveness of the transaction for the purposes of WIL's liability to corporation tax.' *MacNiven (Inspector of Taxes) v Westmoreland Investments Ltd* [2001] UKHL/6 at [14]–[15], [78]–[81], [2001] 1 All ER 865 at 870–871, HL, per Lord Nicholls of Birkenhead and at 888–889, per Lord Hope of Craighead

PALPABLE OR OVER-RIDING ERROR

Canada 'Surely what is meant by the descriptive adjectives "palpable" and "manifest" must be that

the error can be identified and can be shown to be an error. The importance of identifying the error is stressed in *Beaudoin-Daigneault v Richard* [1984] 1 SCR 2 at p 9. Surely, also, what is meant by the adjective "over-riding" must be that the error is one which either must have altered the result or which may well have altered the result.' *Van Mol (Guardian ad Litem of) v Ashmore* (1999) 168 DLR (4th) 637 at 645, BC CA, per Lambert JA

PANNAGE

[For 6 Halsbury's Laws (4th edn) para 515 see now 6 Halsbury's Laws (4th edn) (2003 Reissue) para 415.]

PARCEL

Canada '[23] The Terminal City Club contends that *East* is distinguishable because it dealt with strata lots under the *Condominium Act*, R.S.B.C. 1979, c. 61, not air space parcels, and thus did not address ss. 138 and 139 of the *Land Title Act*, R.S.B.C. 1996, c. 250. Those sections of the *Land Title Act* provide:

> 138. In this Part:
>
> …
>
> *"air space parcel"* means a volumetric parcel, whether or not occupied in whole or in part by a building or other structure, shown as such in an air space plan;
> *"air space plan"* means a plan that
> (a) is described in the title to it as an air space plan,
> (b) shows on it one or more air space parcels consisting of or including air space, and
> (c) complies with the requirements of section 144;
>
> …
>
> 139. Air space constitutes land and lies in grant.

'[24] The Assessor contends that as an air space parcel is land as provided by s. 139 of the *Land Title Act*, an air space parcel is within the definition of "parcel" in the *Assessment Act* because land is real property. The Assessor says it then follows from the reasoning of East that these strata lots are both on parcel LMS3324 and, because they are of an air space parcel that in turn is located above another air space parcel, on air space parcel LMS3323.

'[25] In response, Terminal City Club Tower contends that the term "parcel" must be read as connoting the ground (seeking to use, for the moment a word other than land for the piece of earth involved in the discussion) that is the base for the various air space parcels above it. On this reading the parcel is the ground located on Hastings Street. There are 225 strata lots on that parcel. Therefore, says Terminal City Club Tower, the 60 units do not comprise 85 per cent of the strata lots on the parcel (s. 1(a)(iii)(B)). The Terminal City Club observes that the *Condominium Act*, R.S.B.C. 1979, c. 61, in effect when East was decided, deemed each strata lot to be a separate parcel of land, but that Esson C.J.B.C. rejected an approach that would have relied upon that provision, looking instead to the underlying real property.

'[26] I am not satisfied that the provisions of the Land Title Act definitively resolve the issue, as the Assessor contends, even considering the principle that "presumes a harmony, coherence, and consistency between statutes dealing with the same subject matter": *R. v. Ulybel Enterprises Ltd.*, [2001] 2 S.C.R. 867, 2001 SCC 56, 203 D.L.R. (4th) 513, at para. 52. We are concerned here with a Regulation passed under the Assessment Act and a provision that uses different words than are employed by the *Land Title Act*. One must ask whether the section of the Regulation in which the term "parcel" is used supports the Assessor's submission. In my view the answer is no. I consider that the meaning intended for the word "parcel" may be discerned from its use with the word "on" in the phrase "on a parcel", and that as in East, it connotes a physical relationship between the strata lot and the land. Air space is, as determined by s. 138 of the *Land Title Act*, volumetric. I do not read the common meaning of the word "on" as implying a position within a volume, as must be the case if the Assessor is correct that these strata lots are "on" LMS3324. Rather, in dealing with the physical positioning of one thing to another, the word "on" most naturally refers to a relationship of adjacency, involving surface nearness or surface touching. While one may say that these strata lots are "in" an air space parcel, I would not say that in plain and ordinary English, they are "on" the air space parcel of which they are a part, and to so say is to strain the word's plain meaning.' *Terminal City Club Tower v. British Columbia (Assessor of Area No 9 – Vancouver)* [2004] BCJ No 1895, 243 DLR (4th) 529 (CA), per Sanderson JA

PARENT

[The definition in s 114(1) of the Education Act 1944 was repealed by Sch 15 of the Children Act 1989 as from 14 October 1991 (SI 1991/828).]

[The definition in the Mines and Quarries Act 1954, s 182(1) has been amended by the Children Act 1989, s 108(5), Sch 13, para 13. The definition is now as follows.] 'Parent' means a parent of a young person or any person who is not a parent of his but who has parental responsibility for him (within the meaning of the Children Act 1989).

[The definition in the Factories Act 1961, s 176(1) has been amended by the Children Act 1989, s 108(5), Sch 13, para 15. The definition is now as follows.] 'Parent' means a parent of a child or young person or any person who is not a parent of his but who has parental responsibility for him (within the meaning of the Children Act 1989), and includes any person having direct benefit from the young person's wages.

Australia [Section 4 of the Immigration (Guardianship of Children) Act 1946 (Cth) defines non-citizen children and refers to a 'parent' of the non-citizen child.] 'I conclude that the word "parent" in s 4 of the Immigration (Guardianship of Children) Act, as it stood in 1991, did not include a person who had adopted a child in another country, where that adoption order was not recognised in Australia. I consider that this view of the proper construction of the Act can be discerned, particularly, from the legislative history.' *Re Application of Mr and Mrs K* (1995) 128 ALR 562 at 568, per Brownie J

PARKING METER

New Zealand [Traffic Regulations 1976, Reg 123.] '[17] It is obvious that in terms of Reg 123 controlling authorities are bound to provide and maintain appropriate parking signs indicating restrictions and their extent of the type set out in Schedule 4 of the Regulations. Equally obviously if parking is controlled by parking meters no signs are required pursuant to the Regulations. It is likely to be the case that that Regulation was enacted at that time when the newer form of pay and display machines had not been in general operation. But in interpreting the Regulation if the words are plain, clear and unambiguous and incapable of bearing another meaning – unless absurdity arises – interpretation rules are not required.

'[18] Naturally, if statutory words are capable of bearing different meanings, or interpretations, an approach concentrating on the purpose of the statutory provision is preferred (e g see *R v Karpavicius* [2004] 1 NZLR 157 (PC). But here the words "parking meter" are clear. The only issue is whether the machine before the District Court falls within such description.

'[19] Counsel for the respondents argued that, a "meter" carried with it the implication that it measured time. As the pay and display machine, to be contrasted with an individual parking meter, did not do so it could not be categorised as a parking meter. It did not have an "internal clock" which wound down. But meters are things or instruments for recording a quantity of a substance, or for the measuring of something. For example, a barometer measures air pressure, a thermometer measures temperature. Of course some types of meters are in the nature of clocks such as a taxi meter which in one respect fixes fees as against time elapsed, but more usually against distance travelled.

'[20] Dictionary definitions sometimes are helpful in determining whether an object falls within the statutory words, although in the end the instrument requires a purposive interpretation. The Concise Oxford Dictionary defines parking meter as.

> a coin-operated meter receiving fees for parking vehicle in the street and indicating time allowed.

'[21] New Webster's Dictionary (1990 ed) says that a meter "measures". The American Heritage Dictionary of English Language (4th ed) provides a definition of a parking meter as follows:

> a coin-operated device that registers the amount of time purchased for the parking of a motor vehicle, at the expiration of which the driver is liable for a fine.

'[22] A pay and display machine for issuing parking receipt tickets registers for the benefit of the motorist the time within which he or she may legally park in the designated spaces, such time measured or fixed as against the amount of money paid into the machine. On that basis it the machine would appear to be a "parking meter". The term is not defined in the regulations although in the Council Bylaws a "multiple parking meter" includes a pay and display parking meter. Of course, this Bylaw definition cannot determine the meaning to be applied to the Regulation.

'[23] The Judge considered that the apparent intention of Reg 123(1) was to ensure the public was aware of the area that was the subject of parking restrictions and that signs were not necessary in the case of individual parking meters because such was adjacent to a parking space and it would be immediately apparent that it was such space that was subject to a restriction. She therefore concluded that pay and display machines were not parking meters because they did not govern individual parking spaces but rather a number of individual marked spaces which were bounded at each end by yellow no parking lines. But that is saying no more than that to be a "parking meter" the machine has to govern only an individual space. It is not the space that is governed that determines whether the machine is a meter, but the inherent nature of the machine. A pay and display machine has to be adjacent to or beside, at least one parking space so that it may apparently govern at least that space.

...

'[26] The plain and ordinary meaning of "parking meter", supported by dictionary definitions, encompasses the type of machine which measures the permitted time that a motorist may park as against moneys inserted with the issue of a receipt simply evidence of the forward projection of the allowable time. It regulates the length of time a vehicle may be parked, and is activated by the insertion of money by a road user. In my view such a machine comes squarely within the meaning of "parking meter" in the Regulations.

'[27] I conclude therefore in terms of the first question asked in para 6.1 pay and display machines in issue in this case constituted a "parking meter" under the Regulations ... ' *Wellington City Council v McBride* [2006] DCR 452 at [17]–[23], [26]–[27], per Gendall J

PARLIAMENT

[For 34 Halsbury's Laws (4th edn) paras 1001, 1029, 1030, 1035 see now 34 Halsbury's Laws (4th edn) (Reissue) paras 501, 527, 528, 533.]

PART

Canada '[199] By definition, a part is something less than a whole. *The Shorter Oxford English Dictionary* (3rd ed.) defines "part" as:

> 1. That which with another or others makes up a whole; a certain amount, but not all, of any thing or number of things; a portion, division, section, element, constituent, piece.

'Therefore, one attribute of a work which may be inferred from the [*Copyright Act*] Act's reference to parts of a work is that a work, at least generally, implies something that is whole or complete.' *CCH Canadian Ltd v Law Society of Upper Canada* (2002), 212 DLR (4th) 385 at 462 (FCA), per Rothstein JA

Of premises

'I agree with counsel for the defendant that if after an assignment or underletting of the whole of the premises one asked the question "Has there been an assignment or underletting of any part of the premises?" the answer plainly would be Yes. The answer would be Yes because what had been assigned or underlet would be every part of the premises and this covenant against assignment or underletting of any part of the premises in my view plainly embraces the assignment or underletting of every part.' *Field v Barkworth* [1986] 1 All ER 362 at 364, per Nicholls J

PARTICULAR CIRCUMSTANCES

Australia [Section 37(2) of the Misuse of Drugs Act 1990 (NT) provides that a sentence for an offence under the Act shall require the person to serve a term of actual imprisonment, unless having regard to the 'particular circumstances' of the offence or the offender, the court is of the opinion that such a penalty should not be imposed.] 'The Act refers to "particular" rather than special, which is somewhat unusual.

'The Australian Concise Oxford Dictionary includes as meanings of "particular": "relating to one as distinguished from others, special; one considered apart from others, individual; worth notice, special more than ordinary".

'The Macquarie Dictionary includes the following meanings: "pertaining to some one person, thing, group, class, occasion, etc, rather than to others or all; special, not general; being a definite one, individual, or single, or considered separately; distinguished or different from others or from the ordinary; noteworthy; marked; unusual; exceptional or especial".

'It seems to me that "particular circumstances" when referred to in s 37(2) of the Act means circumstances sufficiently noteworthy or out of the ordinary, relative to the prescribed conduct constituting the offence, or of the offender, to warrant a non-custodial sentence.' *Maynard v O'Brien* (1991) 78 NTR 16 at 22, per Angel J

Australia [Section 37(2) of the Misuse of Drugs Act 1990 (NT) provides that the court shall have regard to the 'particular circumstances' of the offence or the offender in considering whether a term of actual imprisonment should be imposed.] 'In the end I consider that the preferable interpretation to be given to s 37(2) is, as Angel J concluded in *Maynard v O'Brien* [(1991) 78 NTR 16], that the circumstances must be "sufficiently noteworthy *or* out of the ordinary, relative to the proscribed conduct constituting the offence, or of the offender, to warrant a non-custodial sentence", but, like Kearney J, I do not consider that the circumstances need to be so noteworthy or out of the ordinary as to convey the meaning that only in rare cases will there be found circumstances that fall within that class.' *Duthie v Smith* (1992) 83 NTR 21 at 30, per Mildren J

PARTICULAR SOCIAL GROUP

[Women from Pakistan had been forced by their husbands to leave their homes and feared that they would be unprotected by the state and be at risk of prosecution for sexual immorality if forced to return to Pakistan. They sought asylum claiming that they had a well-founded fear of persecution for reasons of 'membership of a particular social group' within the meaning of the Convention and Protocol relating to the Status of Refugees, art 1A(2).]

'The travaux préparatoires for the Geneva Convention shed little light on the meaning of "particular social group". It appears to have been added to the draft at the suggestion of the Swedish delegate, who said that ' "experience had shown that certain refugees had been persecuted because they belonged to particular social groups". It seems to me, however, that the general intention is clear enough. The preamble to the convention begins with the words:

> "*Considering* that the Charter of the United Nations and the Universal Declaration of Human Rights approved on 10 December 1948 by the General Assembly have affirmed the principle that human beings shall enjoy fundamental rights and freedoms without discrimination ..."

In my opinion, the concept of discrimination in matters affecting fundamental rights and freedoms is central to an understanding of the convention. It is concerned not with all cases of persecution, even if they involve denials of human rights, but with persecution which is based on discrimination. And in the context of a human rights instrument, discrimination means making distinctions which principles of fundamental human rights regard as inconsistent with the right of every human being to equal treatment and respect. The obvious examples, based on the experience of the persecutions in Europe which would have been in the minds of the delegates in 1951, were race, religion, nationality and political opinion. But the inclusion of "particular social group" recognised that there might be different criteria for discrimination, in pari materiae with discrimination on the other grounds, which would be equally offensive to principles of human rights. It is plausibly suggested that the delegates may have had in mind persecutions in Communist countries of people who were stigmatised as members of the bourgeoisie. But the concept of a social group is a general one and its meaning cannot be confined to those social groups which the framers of the convention may have had in mind. In choosing to use the general term "particular social group" rather than an enumeration of specific social groups, the framers of the convention were in my opinion intending to include whatever groups might be regarded as coming within the anti-discriminatory objectives of the convention.

'The notion that the convention is concerned with discrimination on grounds inconsistent with principles of human rights is reflected in the influential decision of the US Board of Immigration Appeals in *Re Acosta* (1985) 19 I & N 211 where it was said that a social group for the purposes of the convention was one distinguished by—

> "an immutable characteristic … [a characteristic] that either is beyond the power of an individual to change or that is so fundamental to his identity or conscience that it ought not to be required to be changed."

This was true of the other four grounds enumerated in the convention. It is because they are either immutable or part of an individual's fundamental right to choose for himself that discrimination on such grounds is contrary to principles of human rights.

'It follows that I cannot accept that the term "particular social group" implies an additional element of cohesiveness, co-operation or interdependence. The fact that members of a group may or may not have some form of organisation or interdependence seems to me irrelevant to the question of whether it would be contrary to principles of human rights to discriminate against its members. Among the other four categories, "race" and "nationality" do not imply any idea of

co-operation; "religion" and "political opinion" might, although it could be minimal. In the context of the convention it seems to me a contingent rather than essential characteristic of a social group. In the opinion of Judge Beezer for the US Court of Appeals in *Sanchez-Trujillo v Immigration and Naturalization Service* (1986) 801 F 2d 1571 at 1576 it was said that ' "*particular social* group" implies a collection of people closely affiliated with each other, who are actuated by some common impulse or interest'. This remark has been taken up in some (but not all) other US cases. It has however been rejected by the Supreme Court of Canada in *A-G of Canada v Ward* (*UN High Comr for Refugees et al intervening*) (1993) 103 DLR (4th) 1 and the High Court of Australia in *A v Minister for Immigration and Ethnic Affairs* (1997) 2 BHRC 143. I would reject it also. I agree with La Forest J in *Ward*'s case (1993) 103 DLR (4th) 1 at 34 when he said that "social group" could include individuals fearing persecution on "such bases as gender, linguistic background and sexual orientation". None of these implies any form of interdependence or co-operation.

'To what social group, if any, did the appellants belong? To identify a social group, one must first identify the society of which it forms a part. In this case, the society is plainly that of Pakistan. Within that society, it seems to me that women form a social group of the kind contemplated by the convention. Discrimination against women in matters of fundamental human rights on the ground that they are women is plainly in pari materiae with discrimination on grounds of race. It offends against their rights as human beings to equal treatment and respect. It may seem strange that sex (or gender) was not specifically enumerated in the convention when it is mentioned in art 2 of the Universal Declaration of Human Rights (Paris, 10 December 1948; UN TS 2 (1949); Cmd 7662). But the convention was originally limited to persons who had become refugees as a result of events occurring before 1 January 1951. One can only suppose that the delegates could not think of cases before that date in which women had been persecuted because they were women. But the time limit was removed by the 1967 New York Protocol and the concept of a social group is in my view perfectly adequate to accommodate women as a group in a society that discriminates on grounds of sex, that is to say, that perceives women as not being entitled to the same fundamental rights as men. As we have seen, La Forest J in *Ward*'s case had no difficulty in saying that persecution on grounds of gender would be persecution on account of membership of a social group. I therefore think that women in Pakistan are a social group.' *R v Immigration Appeal Tribunal, ex p Shah* [1999] 2 All ER 545 at 562–564, HL, per Lord Hoffmann

[The appellant asylum-seeker was an Albanian citizen. He claimed that his family had become involved in a dispute in Albania about ownership of land; that the dispute had led to a member of his family killing a member of the other family; that he feared that he would be killed by the other family in revenge; and that he had left Albania as a result. The Secretary of State rejected the claim to asylum, concluding, inter alia, that it did not amount to a well-founded fear of persecution for reason of the asylum-seeker's membership of 'a particular social group' as required by art 1A of the Convention and Protocol relating to the Status of Refugees 1951. The issue arose on appeal.] '[16] Before turning to the submissions of counsel on this issue, I should briefly refer to the meaning of the term "particular social group" and to its main non-contentious and contentious elements. In doing so, I recognise that it is an imprecise and fact-sensitive term which, depending on the circumstances, can also involve difficult questions of judgment. I also acknowledge the number of recent and highly authoritative judicial analyses of the term in this and other common law countries and do not intend what follows to be another attempt at a comprehensive analysis of the topic.

'[17] To put counsel's respective submissions in context, I suggest that membership of a particular social group exhibits the following uncontroversial and sometimes over-lapping features: (1) some common characteristic, either innate or one of which, by reason of conviction or belief, its members, cannot readily accept change; (2) some shared or internal defining characteristic giving particularity, though not necessarily cohesiveness, to the group, a particularity which, in some circumstances can usefully be expressed as setting it apart from the rest of society; (3) subject to possible qualification that I discuss below, a characteristic other than a shared fear of persecution; and (4) subject to possible qualification in non-state persecution cases, a perception by *society* of the particularity of the social group.

'[18] Though guidance can be derived from the particular groups identified in art 1A(2) and the application of the ejusdem generis rule, there is potential for a broad range of collectivities. Whether there is a particular social group of which a claimant is a member is essentially a mixed question of fact, policy and judgment in the context of the society in which it is claimed to exist. Persons with common innate characteristics, such as persons of the same gender or family, do not necessarily constitute a particular social group. And particular social groups can be very large or very small and, depending on the circumstances, can consist of a clan or a family. See for example *Re Acosta,* (1985) 19 I & N Dec 211; *Re GJ* [1998] INLR 387; *A-G of Canada v Ward* [1993] 2 SCR 689; *Applicant A v Minister for Immigration and Ethnic Affairs* (1997) 190 CLR 225; *Minister for Immigration and Multicultural Affairs v Sarrazola* (1999) 166 ALR 641; *R v Immigration Appeal Tribunal, ex p Shah (UN High Comr for Refugees intervening), Islam v Secretary of State for the Home Dept (UN High Comr for Refugees intervening)* [1999] 2 All ER 545, [1999] 2 AC 629; *Chen Shi Hai v Minister for Immigration and Multicultural Affairs* (2000) 201 CLR 293; *Refugee Appeal No 71427/99* [2000] INLR 608; and *R v Secretary of State for the Home Dept, ex p Montoya* (27 April 2001, unreported), IAT decision 00TH0016.

'[19] Those familiar with the issue and the authorities may wonder why, in the light of the House of Lords' treatment of the matter in *Shah*'s case, I have qualified the notion of "setting apart from society" and have made no mention of discrimination or stigmatisation as defining characteristics of a particular social group. I acknowledge that the protection provided by the refugee test as a whole is undoubtedly inspired by anti-discrimination notions; see, for example *Refugee Appeal No 71427/99* [2000] INLR 608 and *Shah*'s case. But I have held back on them for the moment because they have been live issues in this appeal and because I believe it is open to question whether, in a non-state persecution case as here, it is a *necessary* defining characteristic of a particular social group. There is a particular difficulty where the persecution is by somebody other than the state. In such a case, if setting apart, discrimination or stigmatisation is an essential element, who is doing the setting apart, discriminating or stigmatising? Not necessarily society. It may just be those doing the persecuting. The state comes into it if it fails to protect, as some of their Lordships observed in *Shah*'s case, but that failure, though a product or symptom of discrimination, goes to a different part of the refugee test. In short can a claimant, in a non-state persecution case, establish that he is a member of a particular social group simply by proving that someone—anyone—has marked out his group, in this case a family, for special attention, say, a quarrelsome and violent neighbour or a gang leader in pursuit of some private spite or vengeance?

...

'[22] Miss Grey submitted that there was no evidential basis for recognising Mr Skenderaj's family as a "group apart" or stigmatised in any way or discriminated against. She said that the family was not, on the facts of this case, recognised as a distinct group by society and to the extent that it was so regarded by the family with whom it was feuding, it was essentially a private matter, as in *Pedro v Immigration Appeal Tribunal* [2000] Imm AR 489. And the state's non-intervention, to the extent that it resulted either from incapacity, unwillingness or ignorance of the matter did not provide the discrimination, because it did not intervene generally in such feuds. She added that unless every land-owning family in Albania were to constitute a particular social group, which is not Mr Skenderaj's case, only the start of a feud can mark a family group out. Such an approach would impermissibly rely on the act or acts of persecution to define the group. Accordingly, she submitted, neither Mr Skenderaj's family nor the male members of it formed a particular social group within the convention.

'[23] Now that I have identified the area of dispute on this issue, I return to R v Immigration Appeal Tribunal, ex p Shah (UN High Comr for Refugees intervening), Islam v Secretary of State for the Home Dept (UN High Comr for Refugees intervening) [1999] 2 All ER 545, [1999] 2 AC 629. There was clear discrimination of Pakistani women in that case, but I doubt whether that factor was necessary to the House of Lords' determination that they or some of them constituted a particular social group. The main reason for the resort to anti-discriminatory principles was to dismiss the notion that cohesiveness was a necessary element of such a group. Given the approach of the United States Board of Immigration and Appeals in Re Acosta (1985) 19 I & N Dec 211 and of the reasoning of La Forest J in the Supreme Court of Canada in A-G of Canada v Ward [1993] 2 SCR 689 on which their Lordships drew heavily in Shah's case, it may be that, on this part of the refugee test at least, discrimination was not an essential. Thus, as Lords Steyn and Hoffmann mentioned ([1999] 2 All ER 545 at 556–557, 563, [1999] 2 AC 629 at 644, 651–2 respectively), in Acosta's case, the Board said that a particular social group was one distinguished by an immutable characteristic; and in A-G of Canada v Ward [1993] 2 SCR 689, La Forest J said simply, and by reference, to the whole refugee concept, that it

could include individuals fearing persecution on "such bases as gender, linguistic background and sexual orientation".

...

'[29] As I have already indicated there is powerful authority that kinship or family membership may, depending on the circumstances, qualify as membership of a particular social group. Lord Steyn indicated as much in *Shah*'s case [1999] 2 All ER 545 at 556, [1999] 2 AC 629 at 644, drawing on what he described as "the seminal reasoning" of the United States Board of Immigration Appeals in *Re Acosta* (1985) 19 I & N Dec 211:

> "Relying on an ejusdem generis interpretation the Board interpreted the words 'persecution on account of membership in a particular social group' to mean persecution 'that is directed toward an individual who is a member of a group of persons all of whom share a common immutable characteristic'. The Board went on to say that the shared characteristic might be an innate one 'such as sex, color or kinship ties'".

See also *R v Immigration Appeal Tribunal, ex p de Melo* [1997] Imm AR 43 at 49 per Laws J; *Quijano v Secretary of State for the Home Dept* [1997] Imm AR 227 at 229, 230 (per Thorpe LJ), 233 (per Morritt LJ) and 234 (per Roch LJ); and *Minister for Immigration and Multicultural Affairs v Sarrazola* (1999) 166 ALR 641.

'[30] In my view, on the evidence accepted by the adjudicator and not challenged before the tribunal, Mr Skenderaj has not made out his claim that he was a member of a particular social group so as to engage the other elements of the test of a refugee in art 1A(2). I say that, not for the reason principally relied on by Miss Grey that there was no setting apart or stigmatisation of, or discrimination against, the family outside the persecution alleged. For the reasons I have given, I do not regard that as a necessary part of the definition of a particular social group, particularly in a non-state persecution case. I say it because, as Miss Grey also submitted, the Skenderaj family was not regarded as a distinct group by Albanian society any more than, no doubt, most other families in the country. To rely on the attitude of the family with whom it was feuding, as a marking out of the Skenderaj family so as to make it a particular social group for this purpose would be artificial. The threat was, as in *Pedro v Immigration Appeal Tribunal* [2000] Imm AR 489 (which concerned the rape of a woman in Angola by a soldier) a private matter, just as would be a long-standing and violent feud between neighbours or threats of violence from criminals for some actual or perceived slight or with some motive of dishonest gain. It would be absurd to regard the first limb of the refugee test as engaged every time a family is on the receiving end of threatening conduct of that sort.' *Skenderaj v Secretary of State for the Home Department* [2002] EWCA Civ 567 at [16]–[19], [22]–[23], [29]–[30], [2002] 4 All ER 555, per Auld LJ

Australia [The applicant applied for refugee status on the basis that he had a well-founded fear of being persecuted for reasons of membership of a 'particular social group' within the meaning of both the 1951 Convention Relating to the Status of Refugees and the 1967 Protocol Relating to the Status of Refugees.] 'In my opinion for a person to be a member of a "particular social group" within the meaning of the Convention and Protocol what is required is that he or she belongs to or is identified with a recognisable or cognisable group within a society that shares some interest or experience in common. I do not think it wise, necessary or desirable to further define the expression.' *Morato v Minister for Immigration, Local Government and Ethnic Affairs* (1992) 111 ALR 417 at 432, per Lockhart J

[See also *Jahazi v Minister for Immigration and Ethnic Affairs* (1995) 133 ALR 437 at 443, per French J

Australia [The Convention Relating to the Status of Refugees Art 1A(2) defined a refugee as, *inter alia*, 'any person who ... owing to a well-founded fear of being persecuted for reasons of ... membership of a particular social group ... is outside the country of his nationality and is unable or ... unwilling to avail himself of the protection of that country.'] '[N]umerous individuals with similar characteristics or aspirations in my view do not comprise a particular social group of which they are members. I agree with the statement in *Ram* [(1995) 57 FCR 565 at 569; 130 ALR 314]: "There must be a common unifying element binding the members together before there is a social group of that kind. When a member of a social group is being persecuted for reasons of membership of the group, he is being attacked, not for himself alone or for what he owns or has done, but by virtue of his being one of those jointly condemned in the eyes of their persecutors, so that it is a fitting use of language to say that it is 'for reasons of his membership of that group'." ' *'Applicant A' v*

Minister for Immigration and Ethnic Affairs (1997) 142 ALR 331 at 375–376; BC9700274 at 63, per Gummow J

Australia [Article 1A(2) of the Convention relating to the Status of Refugees (Geneva, 28 July 1951; Aust TS 1954 No 5; 189 UNTS 150) art 1A(2) (as amended by the Protocol relating to the Status of Refugees (New York, 31 January 1967; Aust TS 1973 No 37; 606 UNTS 267)) provides that the term 'refugee' shall apply to any person who 'owing to well-founded fear of being persecuted for reasons of race, religion, nationality, membership of a particular social group or political opinion, is outside the country of his nationality and is unable or, owing to such fear, is unwilling to avail himself of the protection of that country; or who, not having a nationality and being outside the country of his former habitual residence, is unable or, owing to such fear, is unwilling to return to it.' The respondent claimed that she was a victim of serious and prolonged domestic violence on the part of her husband and members of his family and that the police in Pakistan refused to enforce the law against such violence or otherwise offer her protection.] 'In my view, it would be open to the Tribunal, on the material before it, to conclude that women in Pakistan are a particular social group.

'The size of the group does not necessarily stand in the way of such a conclusion. There are instances where the victims of persecution in a country have been a majority. It is power, not number, that creates the conditions in which persecution may occur. In some circumstances, the large size of a group might make implausible a suggestion that such a group is a target of persecution, and might suggest that a narrower definition is necessary. But I see nothing inherently implausible in the suggestion that women in a particular country may constitute a persecuted group, especially having regard to some of the information placed before the Tribunal on behalf of Ms Khawar. And cohesiveness may assist to define a group; but it is not an essential attribute of a group. Some particular social groups are notoriously lacking in cohesiveness.

'In *Applicant A v Minister for Immigration and Ethnic Affairs* (1997) 190 CLR 225 at 263, McHugh J explained why the persecutory conduct itself cannot define the particular social group in question for the purposes of art 1A(2), but went on to add that the actions of the persecutors may serve to identify or even cause the creation of such a group [at 264]. He held that couples in China who want to have more than one child, contrary to the one child policy, were not a particular social group, as there was no social attribute or characteristic which linked them independently of the alleged persecutory conduct.

'Women in any society are a distinct and recognisable group; and their distinctive attributes and characteristics exist independently of the manner in which they are treated, either by males or by governments. Neither the conduct of those who perpetrate domestic violence, or of those who withhold the protection of the law from victims of domestic violence, identifies women as a group. Women would still constitute a social group if such violence were to disappear entirely. The alleged persecution does not define the group.' (footnotes omitted) *Minister for Immigration and Multicultural Affairs v Khawar* (2002) 187 ALR 574; BC200201536; [2002] HCA 14 at [32]–[35], per Gleeson CJ

Australia [The Shtjefni family were from Albania where Mr Shtjefni had been forced to pay ransom money to prevent his children being kidnapped and to secure the release of his daughter when she had been kidnapped. The Refugee Review Tribunal had found that Mr Shtjefni's daughter was a refugee under art 1A(2) of the Convention relating to the Status of Refugees (Geneva, 28 July 1951; Aust TS 1954 No 5; 189 UNTS 150) art 1A(2) (as amended by the Protocol relating to the Status of Refugees (New York, 31 January 1967; Aust TS 1973 No 37; 606 UNTS 267)). She had based her claim on the basis of a fear of persecution for reasons of her membership of a 'particular social group'. The 'particular social group' of which Leonia claimed to be a member was her immediate family. The Minister for Immigration and Multicultural Affairs appealed the decision.] 'The tribunal held that a family can be a "particular social group" for the purposes of the Refugees Convention. It referred to a number of decisions in the Federal Court where this proposition has been accepted. For example, in *Sarrazola v Minister for Immigration and Multicultural Affairs* [1999] FCA 101 at [36] Hely J said: "A family is cognisable as a group in society such that its members share something which unites them and sets them apart from the general community". In *Giraldo v Minister for Immigration and Multicultural Affairs* [2001] FCA 113 at [42], Sackville J said: "A particular family or extended family is capable of constituting a particular social group for the purposes of the Convention." In *Minister for Immigration and Multicultural Affairs v Sarrazola (No 4)* [2001] FCA 263 at [31], Merkel J, with whom Sundberg and Heerey JJ agreed, said: "[I]t is entirely consistent with the Convention that a person's freedom from persecution on the basis that he or she is a member of a particular social group, namely, a family, can be one of the fundamental rights and freedoms assured to refugees."

' ... the view that a family can be a "particular social group" has been accepted by some justices of the High Court. For example, in *Applicant A v Minister for Immigration and Multicultural Affairs* (1997) 190 CLR 225 at 241 Dawson J said: "I can see no reason to confine a particular social group to small groups or to large ones; a family or a group of many millions may each be a particular social group". It is also a view that has been accepted by courts in other countries. Both Canada and the United States have adopted the Refugees Convention as local law. The following are examples of United States cases that have ruled on the issue. In *Sanchez-Trujillo v Immigration and Naturalization Service* 801 F 2d 1571, 1576 (9th Cir 1986) the Ninth Circuit Court of Appeals said that: "a prototypical example of a 'particular social group' would consist of the immediate members of a certain family, the family being a focus of fundamental affiliational concerns and common interests for most people." In *Gebremichael v Immigration and Naturalization Service* 10 F 3d 28, 36 (1st Cir 1993) the First Circuit Court of Appeals said: "There can, in fact, be no plainer example of a social group based on common, identifiable and immutable characteristics than that of the nuclear family." More recently in *Castillo v Immigration and Naturalisation Service* 242 F 3d 1169 (9th Cir 2001), the Ninth Circuit Court of Appeals, after a review of many authorities, said (at 1176) that: "Consistent with decisions from our circuit, our sister circuits and the [Board of Immigration Appeals], we hold that a family group may qualify as a particular social group within the meaning of [the relevant US Act]."

'As to the position in Canada, see for example *Al-Busaidy v Canada (Minister of Employment and Immigration)* 31 ACWS (3d) 457 ACWSJ LEXIS 29598, p 5 (1992) ("[T]he [Immigration Appeal Board] has committed reviewable error in not giving due effect to the applicant's uncontradicted evidence with respect to his membership in a particular social group, namely, his own immediate family."); *Montoya v Canada* 48 ACWS (3d) 391, para 5 (1994) ("[T]he Applicant's immediate family can be considered a particular social group."); *Vyramuthu v Canada* 53 ACWS (3d) 385, para 7 (1995) ("[J]urisprudence establishes that a family may constituted (sic) a particular social group ..."); *Campos v Minister of Citizenship and Immigration* 1997 Fed Ct Trial

LEXIS 695, p 5 ("The [Convention Refugee Determination Division of the Immigration and Refugee Board] determined that the applicants' family was capable of constituting a particular social group ..."). In *Castellanos v Solicitor General of Canada* [1995] 2 FC 190, the Federal Court of Canada said (at 204):

"When considering such associations or social groups, one cannot imagine a closer-knit or easier to confirm unit than the family. This is especially true with respect to immediate family, being a person's sons, daughters, parents and any other blood relative they permanently reside with. There can be absolutely no doubt that the family unit forms a social group which is protected against persecution by the Act."

...

'While the Minister accepts that it was open to the tribunal to find that a family is a "particular social group", the Minister says that the tribunal's finding in relation to this particular family was in error because the tribunal did not apply the correct test to arrive at its decision. The Minister says that the relevant test is that laid down in *Minister for Immigration and Multicultural Affairs v Zamora* (1998) 85 FCR 458. In *Zamora* the Full Court said (at 464) that a particular social group must have the following features:

"First, there must be some characteristic other than persecution or the fear of persecution that unites the collection of individuals; persecution or fear of it cannot be a defining feature of the group. Second, that characteristic must set the group apart, as a social group, from the rest of the community. Third, there must be recognition within the society that the collection of individuals is a group that is set apart from the rest of the community."

...

'The Minister says that [the tribunal's] findings are not sufficient to meet the requirements of the third limb of the criteria stated in *Zamora*. In particular, the Minister says that before the tribunal could find that a family constitutes a "particular social group", the particular family must be publicly recognised as a group, and it is not sufficient that families generally are recognised as a separate group within the relevant community.

'There are two answers to this argument. The first is that the Minister's "construction" of the third requirement in *Zamora* is not correct. A proper reading of the third requirement does not

suggest that it is necessary for a particular collection of individuals to be regarded by the community as a separate group, such as a family group, before it will qualify as a "particular social group". There are many examples of potentially relevant social groups. They include groups defined by kinship, ethnicity, territory, age, sex, language, place of residence, class, occupation, recreation, business, education, and so on. What is important is that the relevant group be recognised as separate from the general community. Then there will be a "particular social group" for the purposes of the Refugees Convention. That is all that is required to meet the third limb of the *Zamora* "test". It would be too limiting to impose a further requirement that a particular social group must also be defined by reference to the identity of its particular members.

'The second reason for rejecting the Minister's contention is that it is contrary to authority. In *Sarrazola* (*No 4*), the Full Court considered the three factors mentioned in *Zamora*. Merkel J, with whom Heerey and Sundberg JJ agreed, said in relation to the second and third factors (at para 36 and para 37):

"In order to determine the existence of the second and third factors in *Zamora* the RRT was required to address whether the characteristics of the family configuration raised by the material and evidence before it (see *Minister for Immigration and Multicultural Affairs v Singh* (2000) 98 FCR 469 at 482) set the group apart as a social group from the rest of the community, and whether the group was recognised by the relevant section of Columbian society as a group that is so set apart. The characteristics that usually unite a family as a collection of individuals and that which will set it apart from the rest of the community will be familial links of the kind described by Wilcox J in *C*. The determination of which of those links apply in a particular case will identify, and thereby define, the relevant group as the particular social group for the purposes of Art 1(2A).

"Importantly, in addressing the third factor in *Zamora* the question is whether the family unit considered to be a social group is publicly recognised as being set apart as such. It is not whether the particular family (ie the members of the family however configured) is well known as such." '

Minister for Immigration and Multicultural Affairs v Shtjefni (2001) BC200105564; [2001] FCA 1323 at [6]–[8], [10], [11], [13], [14], per Finkelstein J

Canada [Persecution, in relation to refugee claimant, included the membership in a particular social group.] 'The meaning assigned to "particular social group" in the Act should take into account the general underlying themes of the defence of human rights and anti-discrimination that form the basis for the international refuge protection initiative. The tests proposed in *Mayers*, *Cheung* and *Matter of Acosta*, supra, provide a good working rule to achieve this result. They identify three possible categories:

(1) groups defined by innate or unchangeable characteristic;

(2) groups whose members voluntarily associate for reasons so fundamental to their human dignity that they should not be forced to forsake the association; and

(3) groups associated by a former voluntary status, unalterable due to its historical permanence.

'The first category would embrace individuals fearing persecution on such bases as gender, linguistic background and sexual orientation, while the second would encompass, for example, human rights activists. The third branch is included more because of historical intentions, although it is also relevant to the anti-discrimination influences, in that one's past is an immutable part of the person.' *Canada (A-G) v Ward* [1993] 2 SCR 689 at 739, per La Forest J

PARTIES

Canada 'It appears to me that the plain meaning of section 11 of the contract is that either party to the contract may elect to have a matter in dispute that is covered by the contract referred to arbitration. In this case, since the respondents had initiated proceedings in the courts, the appellants were presented with a choice between electing binding arbitration or acquiescing in the respondents' decision to resort to the courts.

'To suggest otherwise is to render the clause surplusage. As the appellant points out, the parties to a dispute can always refer the matter to arbitration if they can agree between themselves to do so. The respondents, on the other hand, submit that the court would have to read "may" as "shall" to obtain the result sought by the appellant. However, this interpretation would remove all choice. The parties would be restricted to one

avenue of dispute resolution that might not in every case be to the advantage of either.

'In my view, the correct interpretation of the clause is that "parties" means "either party". Thus either party may refer a dispute to binding arbitration and arbitration then becomes mandatory. Failing such an election by one of the parties, the matters in dispute can be resolved in the courts.' *Canadian National Railway v Lovat Tunnel Equipment* (1999) 174 DLR (4th) 385 at 388, Ont CA, per Finlayson JA

PARTIES ... AFFECTED

New Zealand [Rule 235 of the High Court Rules provides an interlocutory application must be 'served on all other parties intended to be affected thereby'.] 'A person certainly can be described as "affected" by an application for leave to issue against him. He is put at potential risk. The application is one to change his status from immune to vulnerable. If that application is not something which "affects" him, a very special meaning is being given to the word.' *Colonial Mutual Life Assurance Society Ltd v Wilson Neill Ltd* [1993] 2 NZLR 617 at 626, per McGechan J

PARTITION

[For 39 Halsbury's Laws (4th edn) para 552 see now 39(2) Halsbury's Laws (4th edn) (Reissue) para 215.]

PARTNER

New Zealand [Domestic Violence Act 1995, s 2.] ' "Partner" is there defined to include not only participants in legal marriage (first of the three limbs of the definition of "partner") but also "Any other person (whether the same or the opposite gender) with whom the person lives or has lived in a relationship in the nature of marriage ..." (second limb of the second definition of "partner"). The express inclusion of the words "whether the same or the opposite gender" makes it clear that same-sex partnerships are included. The combination of those words with the requirement that "the person lives or has lived in a relationship in the nature of marriage" presupposes that there can be same-sex relationships which are "in the nature of marriage". The concluding words of the second limb of the definition of partner reinforce that conclusion. They make it immaterial that these persons "are not, or were not, or are not or were not able to be, legally married to each other".' *P v M* [1998] 3 NZLR 246 at 251–252, per Fisher J

PARTNERSHIP

[For 35 Halsbury's Laws (4th edn) para 2 see now 35 Halsbury's Laws (4th edn) (Reissue) para 2.]

PARTS, PERTINENTS AND OTHERS

[In a dispute over a commercial lease of unfurnished office premises, a landlord sought to recover the cost of installing new carpets and vinyl floor coverings. There was no specific reference to carpeting and other floor coverings in the lease, but the landlord relied on the phrase 'parts, pertinents and others therein or thereon'.] 'The expression "parts, pertinents and others" is comprehensive in its application to the heritage, but it cannot support a claim for damages quantified by reference to the cost to the landlord of introducing moveables such as carpeting to the premises. If as wide as counsel for the pursuer suggested, the clause would apply alike to all soft furnishings, and to furniture of every description.' *Lowe v Quayle Munro Ltd* 1997 SLT 1168 at 1172, per Lord Penrose

PARTY

Australia ' "Party" is defined in s 170VA to mean "in relation to an AWA or ancillary document ... the employer or employee." In my view, that definition, in conjunction with the extension effected by s 170VB of the concept of an AWA to include a "proposed AWA" has the effect that a person who is proposed to be an employer or employee in relation to a proposed AWA is a party for the purposes of s 170VV(3). This is consistent with my observations in *Maritime Union of Australia v Burnie Port Corp Pty Ltd* (2000) 101 IR 435, where, referring to the judgment of a Full Court of this Court in *Schanka v Employment National (Administration) Pty Ltd* (2000) 170 ALR 42 ("Schanka"), I said, at 27;

> "That case dealt, in part, with a claim in respect of an applicant who had been a party to negotiations for an AWA which had not resulted in his entering into a completed agreement. However, the application of the principle recognised in Schanka means that it is not necessary that a contract (or AWA) be concluded for the question of duress on which s 170WG is predicated to arise. Nor will the

standing of applicants raising that question depend upon their being parties to the AWA in question."

'It was also argued on behalf of the respondents that, even if Canturi and Napoli had been comprehended as "parties" to a proposed AWA by force of the extended definition in s 170VB(1), in order to have standing to prosecute these applications, they had to answer the description of "parties" at the date of instituting the applications, ie 22 December 1999. Because no relevant AWA, or proposed AWA, was then in existence, or under negotiation, so the argument went, neither applicant was a "party" at that date. I reject that contention. In my view, the time at which an applicant must be a "party" to an actual or proposed AWA is the time of the alleged application of duress which is said to contravene s 170WG(1).' *Canturi v Sita Coaches Pty Ltd* 116 FCR 276, [2002] FCA 349 at [34], [35] per Ryan J; BC200201159

PARTY WALL

[For 4 Halsbury's Laws (4th edn) para 889 see now 4(1) Halsbury's Laws (4th edn) (2002 Reissue) para 962.]

PASSENGER

[By s 28 of the Town Police Clauses Act 1847, every person who in any 'street', to the annoyance of 'passengers', committed certain offences, e.g. indecent exposure, became liable to a penalty. The meaning of 'street' for the purposes of the section was extended to include places of public resort and recreation grounds by the Public Health Acts Amendment Act 1907.] 'The Oxford English Dictionary shows that in 1847 when the Act was passed "passenger" had a meaning, now unusual except in the expression "foot-passenger", of "A passer by or through ... A traveller (usually on foot), a wayfarer". Before the meaning of "street" was enlarged in 1907 this dictionary definition of "passenger" was not hard to apply: it clearly covered anyone using the street for ordinary purposes of passage or travel. The dictionary definition cannot be so aptly applied to a place of public resort such as a public lavatory, but on a commonsense reading it seems to me that when applied in this context "passenger" must mean anyone resorting in the ordinary way to the place of public resort for one of the purposes for which people normally resort to it.' *Cheeseman v Director of Public Prosecutions* [1991] 3 All ER 54 at 63, per Bingham LJ

PASSING OFF

'The essence of the action for passing off is a deceit practised on the public and it can be no answer, in a case where it is demonstrable that the public has been or will be deceived, that they would not have been if they had been more careful, more literate or more perspicacious. Customers have to be taken as they are found.' *Reckitt & Colman Products Ltd v Borden Inc* [1990] 1 All ER 873 at 888, HL, per Lord Oliver of Aylmerton

PASTORAL PURPOSES

Australia 'The ordinary meaning of the phrase "for the purpose of pasture" is the feeding of cattle or other livestock upon the land in question [*Westropp v Elligott* (1884) 9 App Cas 815 at 819–20]. The phrase "for pastoral purposes" would include the feeding of cattle or other livestock upon the land but it may well be broader, and encompass activities pursued in the occupation of cattle or other livestock farming.' *Wik Peoples v Queensland* (1996) 141 ALR 129 at 245; 71 ALJR 173, per Gummow J

PASTURE

[For 6 Halsbury's Laws (4th edn) paras 547–575 see now 6 Halsbury's Laws (4th edn) (2003 Reissue) paras 452–464.]

PATENT

[For 35 Halsbury's Laws (4th edn) para 303 see now 35 Halsbury's Laws (4th edn) (Reissue) para 303.]

PAWN

[For 36 Halsbury's Laws (4th edn) paras 101, 103 see now 36 Halsbury's Laws (4th edn) (Reissue) paras 101, 103.]

PAWN, PAWNED GOODS OR PLEDGE

Australia '[16] Both "pawn" and "pledge" are words having a long-established legal meaning. That is hardly surprising when the ancient origins of such transactions are recalled. For centuries, pawn or pledge (the terms are used interchangeably) has been recognised as one class of bailment of goods. It was treated as such in Roman law. This understanding of pawn or pledge was established very early in the common law and was reflected in the writings of the great commentators. It underpinned the way in which legislation regulating the activities of pawnbrokers was framed in Great Britain, in the Australian colonies and later in the Australian States.

'[17] Commentators and the courts have long recognised that pawn or pledge is "a bailment of personal property, as a security for some debt or engagement". They have identified such a transaction as distinct and different from mortgage where "the whole legal title passes conditionally to the mortgagee". This distinction was sometimes expressed in terms of the difference between the "special property" of the pledgee and the "general property" which remained in the pledgor. The "special property" of the pledgee was described as the right to detain the goods for the pledgee's security and "is in truth no property at all". That "special property" depends upon delivery of possession, whereas in the case of a mortgage of personal property the right of property passes by the conveyance and possession is not essential to create or support the title.

'[18] It has also long been recognised that pawn and pledge must also be distinguished from lien. "One who has a lien has only a right of detaining the res until the money owing is paid: a lien disappears if possession is lost, and there is no right of sale". A lien is merely a personal right and cannot be taken in execution; a pledge creates an interest in the pledgee that can be seized in execution.

'[19] Time has not dulled these distinctions. They are distinctions that underpinned the nineteenth century decisions referred to in the reasons of the Court of Appeal. But they are distinctions which still are to be observed. In his third edition of Commercial Law, published in 2004, Professor Sir Roy Goode wrote:

A pledge ... involves the transfer of possession of the security, actual or constructive, to the creditor. *But the delivery of possession does not necessarily signify the existence of a pledge; it may equally be referable to an intention to create an equitable mortgage or charge.* The capacity in which the creditor holds possession depends on the agreement of the parties. Is he intended merely to have possession, with a right of sale in the event of the debtor's default, or is he to be a security owner (mortgagee) or chargee? *It seems clear that the three types of security are mutually exclusive and that it is not possible, for example, for the creditor to be both a pledgee and a mortgagee of the same asset at the same time.* (emphasis added)

...

'[25] ... "Pawn" and "pledge" refer to a bailment of personal property as security for a debt. That is a transaction which is distinct from a chattel mortgage and the distinction is not to be elided by treating one kind of transaction as being subsumed in the other.' *Palgo Holdings Pty Ltd v Gowans* [2005] HCA 28 at [16]–[19], [25], per McHugh, Gummow, Hayne and Heydon JJ; BC200503300

Australia '[78] A pawn or pledge is a bailment of personal property as a security for a debt or other promise. In Roman law, pledge (pignus) was one of three contracts (deposit, loan for use, and pledge) classified by Justinian as involving mutuum under "obligations contracted re". Each of these contracts was "real", in the sense that, for their formation, there was needed, in addition to the agreement of the parties, the handing over by one party to the other of the thing that was the object of the contract. The main duty that arose under the contract was that of the recipient to return the thing, in the case of pawn or pledge, if and when the debt was repaid.

'[79] A feature of the obligation of the pawnee or pledgee in Roman law was that, because it did not become the owner, it had to return the identical thing received when the conditions were fulfilled. However, even in ancient times, the overlap between the case of fiducia (where the recipient became an owner) and that of pignus (where it did not) led to uncertainty, having regard to the development of special actions. As Professor Jolowicz explained:

> from the point of view of the layman both pignus and fiducia cum creditore are ways of raising money on security, and both depositum and fiducia cum amico are ways of getting someone to look after property.

'[80] The flexibility of various forms of pignus according to Roman law is noted by many writers. This flexibility also came to be reflected in the common law of England. Thus Coke in his Institutes sometimes treated goods delivered to a bailee as a "gage", as alternative to goods delivered as a "pledge".

'[81] Possession as the essential feature: The essential feature of pawn or pledge in Roman law, and later in civil law in the states of modern Europe and also in the common law, was that "possession is necessary to complete the title by pledge". Thus, Sir William Jones defined a pledge to be "a bailment of goods by a debtor to his

creditor, to be kept till the debt is discharged". Holt CJ defined a pledge thus: "[W]hen goods or chattels are delivered to another as a pawn, to be a security to him for money borrowed of him by the bailor; and this is called in Latin vadium, and in English a pawn or a pledge." As Story put it in his Commentaries on the Law of Bailments, in Roman law a pawn or pledge "is properly called pignus". Transfer of possession of the borrower's property was the essence of it.

'[82] Pawn and chattel mortgage: While the essential feature of a "pawn" is the transfer of possession, it may be conceded that on the existing authorities a distinction is drawn between a chattel mortgage (where title passes to the creditor) and a pawn. At common law, if a security is a chattel mortgage it cannot also be a pawn. However, the common law meaning of "pawn" and any rigid distinction between a pawn and a chattel mortgage cannot be determinative of the issue in this case, which concerns the construction of an Act of the New South Wales Parliament. The joint reasons assume that the common law definitions of "pawn" or "pledge", as expressed in the cited cases and commentaries, are determinative of the statutory construction question. As explained above, this is an error. The statute must be interpreted so as to give effect to the purpose of the legislature as expressed in the natural and ordinary meaning of the terms used in the particular context; and not by uncritical importation of a technical legal meaning, disjoined from the context.

...

'[95] ... According to The Macquarie Dictionary133. "pawn", as a verb, has as its primary meaning "to deposit as security; as for money borrowed: to pawn a watch".' *Palgo Holdings Pty Ltd v Gowans* [2005] HCA 28 at [78]–[82], [95], per Kirby J; BC200503300

PAWNBROKER

[For 36 Halsbury's Laws (4th edn) para 101 see now 36 Halsbury's Laws (4th edn) (Reissue) para 101.]

PAWNED GOODS *SEE* **PAWN, PAWNED GOODS OR PLEDGE**

PAY

Australia [In the context of a liquidated damages dispute under Building and Construction Industry Security of Payment Act 1999 (NSW).] 'The Oxford

English Dictionary defines the verb "pay" to mean: "To give (a person) what is due in discharge of a debt, or as a return for services done, or goods received, or in compensation for injury done; to remunerate, recompense." In turn, "payment" is defined as "[t]he action, or an act, of paying." From this it can readily be concluded that the touchstone of the ordinary and natural meaning of the expressions "to pay" and "receives payment" in the present context is the act of a debtor transferring by way of satisfaction whatever is owed by him or her to a creditor. It therefore follows that the defendant's payment to the plaintiff of the judgment debt arising from the summary judgment of 18 October 2002 falls within this definition on the basis that it is not concerned with any restrictions on the right of the payee to apply the funds paid, but merely the act of payment in itself.

'However, particularly with respect to a remedial statute such as this Act, the "importance of interpreting legislation with the general purpose of the statute in mind rather than by simply relying on the literal meaning approach to statutory construction" requires emphasis: *Cole v Director-General of Department of Youth and Community Services and Anor* (1986) 7 NSWLR 541, per McHugh JA. In the specific instance of the Act this general purpose could hardly be less unambiguous, expressed in s 3(1) to be:

> to ensure that any person who undertakes to carry out construction work (or who undertakes to supply related goods and services) under a construction contract is entitled to receive, and is able to recover, progress payments in relation to the carrying out of that work and the supplying of those goods and services.

'From this statement it is critical for present purposes to observe the emphasis on the creation of rights to the recovery of progress payments, in addition to rights vesting a mere entitlement to receive such payments.

'The case law is replete with statements emphasising that the mischief to which the Act is directed, is the delay in contractors and subcontractors receiving milestone payments for work performed in an industry that, as expressed by Smart J in *Abignano Ltd v Electricity Commission of New South Wales* (1986) 3 BCL 290 at 297, has long been "notorious" for its extremely tight profit margins. Thus in *Multiplex Constructions Pty Ltd v Luikens* [2003] NSWSC 1140 at [96], Palmer J characterised the payment claim, payment schedule and adjudication mechanism as being one in which

the respondent is obliged to "pay now, argue later", with the presumed need of claimants for security of cash flow taking precedence in the interim to any full and final determination of the rights of the parties (s 3(4)). Equally in *Brodyn Pty Ltd t/as Time Cost and Quality (ACN 001 998 830) v Philip Davenport & Ors* [2003] NSWSC 1019 at [14] at [14], Einstein J observed that "[w]hat the legislature has effectively achieved is a fast track interim progress payment adjudication vehicle", going onto conclude (at [18]) that "the legislation was aimed at permitting contractors and subcontractors to obtain a prompt interim progress payment on account, pending final determination of all disputes."

'It is with this general purpose in mind that the right to suspend construction work provided by ss 15 and 27 of the Act must be read. Specifically, it is evident that the right of suspension is intended to allow contractors, while shielded from liability by virtue of s 27(3), to cease incurring additional expenses and liabilities during periods in which their cash flow has been interrupted by a failure on the part of the principal to pay progress payment claims made in accordance with the Act or the relevant contract. Indeed, this right of suspension pending payment takes on a special importance given that s 12 of the Act has abrogated the effect of "pay when paid" provisions in applicable construction contracts, placing head contractors at additional risk when facing a recalcitrant principal.

'Accordingly to apply the above-discussed ordinary meaning of "pay" and "payment" to circumstances wherein a claimant has been provided with a conditional payment the benefit of which the claimant is deprived pending the outcome of an appeal is contrary to:

(a) the purpose of the Act generally in its emphasis on the maintenance of cash flow regardless of the final rights and obligations of the parties to a construction contract;

(b) the purpose of the payment claim, payment schedule and adjudication mechanism specifically, being to ensure that monies owed as progress payments are actually recoverable; and

(c) the purpose of the right of suspension provided by ss 15 and 27, potentially depriving a claimant of both rights to the benefit of progress payments and to avoid the incurring of additional expenses and liabilities pending payment of the same.

'Indeed the imperative of giving effect to the purpose of the statutory right of suspension when construing the Act was recently reinforced by the

Court of Appeal in *Brodyn Pty Ltd t/as Time Cost and Quality v Davenport & Anor* [2004] NSWCA 394. In the context of a discussion concerning the availability of judicial review of the decisions of adjudicators, Hodgson JA (with whom Mason P and Giles JA agreed) said (at [51]) that:

> the scheme of the Act appears strongly against the availability of judicial review on the basis of non-jurisdictional error of law. The Act discloses a legislative intention to give an entitlement to progress payments, and to provide a mechanism to ensure that disputes concerning the amount of such payments are resolved with the minimum of delay. The payments themselves are only payments on account of a liability that will be finally determined otherwise: ss 3(4), 32. The procedure contemplates a minimum of opportunity for court involvement: ss 3(3), 25(4). The remedy provided by s 27 can only work if a claimant can be confident of the protection given by s 27(3): if the claimant faced the prospect that an adjudicator's determination could be set aside on any ground involving doubtful questions of law, as well as of fact, the risks involved in acting under s 27 would be prohibitive, and s 27 could operate as a trap.

'By parity of reasoning, the remedy provided by s 27 of the Act is capable of achieving its full intended function only if the payment which terminates the claimant's right of suspension can be applied to defray expenses and liabilities incurred in carrying out the work to which the progress payment relates. To this end it bears repeating, as emphasised by Hodgson JA above, that progress payments made pursuant to the Act are interim payments; rather than operating as a discharge of a finally determined liability, their sole purpose is to ensure that contractors have sufficient cash on hand to continue work pursuant to the applicable contract. As this purpose was instrumental in the decision of the Court of Appeal in *Brodyn* to effectively deny the judicial review of adjudicators' determinations, so it must be in respect of the issue under consideration here.

'Relevantly, s 33 of the Interpretation Act 1987 (NSW) compels the court, when construing a statutory provision, to prefer a construction "that would promote the purpose or object underlying the Act" over "a construction that would not promote that purpose or object." It has been held that this provision and its equivalents in other jurisdictions go further than merely declaring the purposive approach to statutory construction; rather,

it permits the court to, first, identify whether a particular provision admits more than one possible meaning and, second, to prefer that alternative meaning if it is more consistent with the purpose of the enactment under consideration. As stated by Dawson J in *Mills v Meeking* (1990) 169 CLR 214 at 235 in the context of his Honour's discussion of the operation of s 35 of the Interpretation of Legislation Act 1984 (Vic):

> the literal rule of construction, whatever the qualifications with which it is expressed, must give way to a statutory injunction to prefer a construction which would promote the purpose of an Act to one which would not, especially where that purpose is set out in the Act. Section 35 of the Interpretation of Legislation Act must, I think, mean that the purposes stated in Pt 5 of the Road Safety Act are to be taken into account in construing the provisions of that Part, not only where those provisions on their face offer more than one construction, but also in determining whether more than one construction is open. The requirement that a court look to the purpose or object of the Act is thus more than an instruction to adopt the traditional mischief or purpose rule in preference to the literal rule of construction. The mischief or purpose rule required an ambiguity or inconsistency before a court could have regard to purpose: *Miller v The Commonwealth* (1904) 1 CLR 668, at p 674; *Wacal Developments Pty Ltd v Realty Developments Pty Ltd* (1978) 140 CLR 503, at p 513. The approach required by s 35 needs no ambiguity or inconsistency; it allows a court to consider the purposes of an Act in determining whether there is more than one possible construction. Reference to the purposes may reveal that the draftsman has inadvertently overlooked something which he would have dealt with had his attention been drawn to it and if it is possible as a matter of construction to repair the defect, then this must be done. However, if the literal meaning of a provision is to be modified by reference to the purposes of the Act, the modification must be precisely identifiable as that which is necessary to effectuate those purposes and it must be consistent with the wording otherwise adopted by the draftsman. Section 35 requires a court to construe an Act, not to rewrite it, in the light of its purposes.

'Thus an analysis of both the general and specific purposes of the Act permits the court to identify an alternative construction to the ordinary meaning of "pay" and "payment." That is that a claimant will not have "received payment" pursuant to s 27(2), and that a respondent will still have failed "to pay" pursuant to s 15(1)(b), in circumstances where the claimant is unable to obtain the benefit of that payment due to conditions, such as the provision of a secured bank guarantee, placed on its receipt. The adoption of such a construction does not constitute a "re-writing" of ss 15 and 27 as proscribed by the dictum of Dawson J above, but is rather a departure from the ordinary meaning of "payment" in circumstances where the context and purpose of its use demands such a modification.' *Beckhaus Civil Pty Ltd v Brewarrina Shire Council (No 2)* [2004] NSWSC 1160 at [74], per Macready M; BC200408473

PAYABLE

Australia [Sections 68 and 69 of the Defence Force Retirement and Death Benefits Act 1973 (Cth) allows a contributing member to extend the period of his service if he had previous employment upon the termination of which a transfer value became 'payable'.] 'It was contended by the appellant that the possibility of his making that election was sufficient for the benefit under the New Zealand scheme to qualify as a benefit by way of a lump sum *payable* to or in respect of him. That contention involves treating "payable" in s 68(1) as equivalent to "which is payable or could become payable". We can find no warrant in the legislation for giving it that extended meaning. "Payable" is an ordinary English word signifying that something is presently capable of being paid. If an amount is not capable of being paid unless and until a specified election shall have been made, or some other event shall have happened, it is not "payable" in accordance with that ordinary meaning. This view conforms with that expressed by Gummow J, in *Edelsten v Health Insurance Commission* (1988) 90 ALR 595 at 599.' *Glass v Defence Force Retirement and Death Benefits Authority* (1992) 38 FCR 534 at 537, per cur

Australia 'For money to be "payable", in a context where that word is used in distinction to "due" or "owing", there must generally be an immediate obligation to pay (*Macquarie Dictionary*). In the expression "due and payable", "payable" means required to be immediately or presently paid (*Peacock v Commonwealth Trading Bank of Australia* [1979] 2 NSWLR 412 at 416; *Deputy Cmr of Taxation v Peacock* [1980] 2 NSWLR 130

at 134, 138, 141; *Clyne v Deputy Cmr of Taxation* (1981) 150 CLR 1 at 15).' *Helou v Mulligan Pty Ltd* BC200302156; [2003] NSWCA 92 at [26], per Mason P

New Zealand [Section 15 of the Accident Rehabilitation and Compensation Insurance Act 1992.] 'It is not apparent that there is a temporal limitation on the use of the word "payable"… *The Shorter Oxford English Dictionary* definition of "payable" is not confined to "yet to be paid"… The definition also includes "able to be paid". *Schlaadt v Accident Rehabilitation and Compensation Insurance Corporation* [2000] 2 NZLR 318 at 322 per John Hansen J

PAYBACK

Australia [A judge took into account 'payback' in sentencing an Aboriginal person pleading guilty to manslaughter.] 'Payback is not vendetta. There must be clear evidence of the difference. As I understand it, payback, in certain cases which must be carefully delineated and clearly understood, can be a healing process; vendetta never. It would be a serious and impermissible abrogation of the court's duty to reduce a sentence on any person of whatever race or creed because of assurances that friends or relatives of the victim were preparing their own vengeance for the assailant. If payback is no more than this it is nothing to the sentencing process. If, however, it transcends vengeance and can be shown to be of positive benefit to the peace and welfare of a particular community it may be taken into account; though even then I do not believe the court could countenance any really serious bodily harm. But, as Mildren J has pointed out, the action contemplated may not in fact come within the prohibitions of the criminal law. In some cases the payback is purely symbolic. In one such case before me, payback consisted of merely touching the assailant on the thigh with a blunt-nosed spear, the families concerned having previously come to certain financial arrangements. The formal ceremony, however, was an important and necessary part in the reconciliation of the families, because only through that ceremony could certain relatives be relieved of what, to them, was otherwise a solemn and sacred obligation to avenge the wrong inflicted on the victim.' *R v Minor* (1992) 79 NTR 1 at 2, per Asche CJ

PAYMENT

[Under the Civil Liability (Contribution) Act 1978, s 1(1), any person liable in respect of any damage suffered by another person may recover contribution from any other person liable in respect of the same damage (whether jointly with him or otherwise). Sub-s (2) provides that a person is entitled to recover contribution notwithstanding that he has ceased to be liable in respect of the damage in question since the time when the damage occurred, provided that he was so liable immediately before he made or was ordered or agreed to make the payment in respect of which the contribution is sought; and under s 1(4) a person who has made or agreed to make any payment in settlement or compromise of any claim made against him in respect of any damage is entitled to recover contribution. The Limitation Act 1980, s 10 specifies a limitation period, where a person becomes entitled to a right to recover contribution under the 1978 Act, s 1, of two years from the date on which the right accrued, and under s 10(4) of the 1980 Act, where the person in question makes or agrees to make any payment to one or more persons in compensation for the damage, the relevant date is the earliest date on which the amount to be paid by him is agreed between him and the person to whom the payment is to be made.] '[9] ... Mr Chapman submitted that the right to recover contribution arises only where the person seeking contribution has made, or been ordered or agreed to make, payment of a monetary sum to the person who has suffered the damage. Where, or in so far as, the person seeking compensation has made reparation in some other way, specifically by carrying out works at his own expense, he has no entitlement under the 1978 Act to recover contribution from any other person liable in respect of the same damage. Mr Chapman relied on the use of the word "payment" in sub-ss (2) and (4) of s 1 of that Act.

'[10] In further support of the above proposition, Mr Chapman submitted that the right to recover contribution arises only in the circumstances mentioned in sub-ss (3) and (4) of s 10 of the 1980 Act. Otherwise, there could be a right to contribution which would not be the subject of accrual under s 10(1) and there would be no limitation period. It could not have been the intention of the legislature, he submitted, that there should be circumstances in which there was no limitation period.

'[11] There is no question of sub-s (3) of s 10 of the 1980 Act applying. I am concerned here only with sub-s (4). Mr Chapman submitted that apart from the comparatively small monetary sum, the settlement agreement was not an agreement to make payment by way of compensation to the employer. It was an agreement to carry out, or cause to be carried out, work at no cost to the employer. Moreover, though it was true that payment was agreed to be made between the claimants and the contractors who carried out the remedial works, no amount to be paid by the claimants was agreed between the claimants and any person to whom payment was to be made in compensation for the damage. Mr Chapman submitted, and I accept, that the expression at the end of sub-s (4) "the person ... to whom the payment is to be made" must refer to a person receiving the payment by way of compensation for the damage.

...

'[15] Mr Chapman's submissions were cogent, but I reject them. They lead to a conclusion as to the intention of Parliament which in my judgment is not borne out by the legislation as a whole. That intention could readily have been stated expressly if it had existed, and I can see no reason for it. The primary provision giving rise to the right to claim contribution is s 1(1) of the 1978 Act. There is no suggestion there of any limit or restriction on the right of a person to claim contribution from another person liable in respect of the same damage. Subsections (2)–(4) of s 1 are designed not to restrict the right, but to remove restrictions or defences that might otherwise be raised. Section 10 of the 1980 Act, albeit that it arises out of an enactment of the 1978 Act, is directed to time limitation and not to narrowing the nature of the right to contribution.

'[16] The word "payment" in ordinary parlance is capable of including a payment in kind, as that well-known expression exemplifies. One talks, for example, of paying a debt to society by the performance of community service. In my judgment, the word "payment" in these statutory provisions includes a payment in kind, at any rate where the payment in kind is capable of valuation in monetary terms. In such a case the "amount to be paid by him" in s 10(4) of the 1980 Act refers not to the amount of the work, but to its value. That construction, in my judgment, best gives effect to what appears to me to be the intention of Parliament.' *Baker & Davies plc v Leslie Wilks Associates (a firm)* [2005] EWHC 1179 (TCC) at [9]–[11], [15]–[16], [2005] 3 All ER 603, per Judge Richard Havery QC

Canada [Entitlement to welfare assistance depended on income, which included all 'payments' received by claimant. Appellant had borrowed funds to pay mortgage, and board held that borrowings constituted income.] '... In ordinary parlance, the debtor receives the proceeds of a loan and "payments" are paid to the creditor or mortgagee. In ordinary parlance, when one refers to a mortgage or a loan agreement, a person does not speak of "payments" being made to a debtor or a mortgagor.' *Rubino v Metropolitan Toronto* (*Dept of Social Services*) (1992) 98 DLR (4th) 424 at 430, per O'Driscoll J (Ont Div Ct)

PECUNIARY

New Zealand 'The word simply means pertaining to or of money.' *Presbyterian Church of New Zealand Beneficiary Fund v Commissioner of Inland Revenue* [1994] 3 NZLR 363 at 376, per Heron J

Pecuniary advantage

'[I]t seems to me clear that the purpose of the November order was to deprive a person ... of the pecuniary advantage obtained by them as a result of Mr Barnette's crime, within s 71(1)(b) [of the Criminal Justice Act 1988 (Designated Countries and Territories) Order 1991]. I see no reason to give a restricted meaning to the wide words 'pecuniary advantage'. It is repugnant to common sense to suggest that someone who has retained valuable shares for 11 years (now 14) in defiance of a court order, who has meanwhile been drawing dividends on them and whose value may be expected to have increased over that time, has not obtained a pecuniary advantage from the crime.' *United States Government v Montgomery* [1999] 1 All ER 84 at 96, CA, per Stuart-Smith LJ

New Zealand 'We have not been referred to any case which specifically discusses the point but we think it is implicit in the term "advantage" that if a defendant were legally entitled to receive the money in question, he has not obtained a pecuniary advantage [under s 229A of the Crimes Act 1961] to which he was not entitled. In *Ruka v Department of Social Welfare* [1997] 1 NZLR 154 at 163 this Court recorded, seemingly without argument on the point, that that was the position in regard to the Social Welfare benefit there in issue.' *R v Firth* [1998] 1 NZLR 513 at 516, CA, per cur

PEERAGE

[For 35 Halsbury's Laws (4th edn) paras 802–805 see now 35 Halsbury's Laws (4th edn) (Reissue) paras 902–905.]

PENALTY OR FORFEITURE

New Zealand ' "Penalty" would appear to be a broad term covering all possible forms of imposed

disadvantage. In a legal context, "forfeiture" would appear to be more specific in its emphasis upon loss of some existing property or other advantage.' *Re Network Agencies International Ltd* [1992] 3 NZLR 325 at 328, per Fisher J

PENDENT JURISDICTION

Australia 'As explained in *Philip Morris Inc v Adam P Brown Male Fashions Pty Ltd* ((1981) 148 CLR 457 at 515) the expression "pendent jurisdiction" is one that originated in United States Constitutional jurisprudence, where there arose a question, which has also arisen in Australia, of the content of Federal judicial power. It frequently happens that a dispute about a question arising under a Federal law will form part of a wider controversy between parties. There may then arise a problem as to the extent of the jurisdiction of a federal court to resolve the entire controversy. In so far as the Federal Court's jurisdiction to resolve the controversy extends beyond the Federal question it is called "pendent". The expression "pendent jurisdiction", it must be emphasised, is a description of a conclusion, not a reason for reaching that conclusion.' *National Parks and Wildlife Service v Stables Perisher Pty Ltd* (1990) 20 NSWLR 573 at 579, per Gleeson CJ

PENDING

Australia 'The [CTH] Child Support (Assessment) Act carries no definition as to when an application can be said to be "pending in a court having jurisdiction under this Act". The term "pending" is defined in the *Macquarie Dictionary* as "remaining undecided, awaiting decision". In *Dunn v Bevan; Brodie v Bevan* [1922] 1 Ch 276 Sargant J quoted *Oswald on Contempt of Court*, 2nd ed, p 62: "Proceedings are pending immediately the writ is issued, and as long as any proceedings can be taken", agreed with that statement, and cited in support *Metzler v Gounod* 30 LT 264 and *Dallas v Ledger* 4 Times LR 432.

'Once instituted therefore, until dealt with, any application may properly be described as "pending".' *McGuiness v Cowie* (2002) 29 Fam LR 441; BC200205707; [2002] FamCA 461 at [34]–[35], per Kay J.

PERAMBULATION

[For 12 Halsbury's Laws (4th edn) para 440 see now 12(1) Halsbury's Laws (4th edn) (Reissue) para 640.]

PEREMPTORY

[For 45 Halsbury's Laws (4th edn) para 1149 see now 45(2) Halsbury's Laws (4th edn) (Reissue) para 252.]

PERFECTED *SEE* MAKE

PERFORMANCE

Canada [Copyright fees were payable on basis of performance of musical works.] 'The appellant first submits that it does not perform musical works because it does not, as required by the definition of "performance" in section 2 of the Act, broadcast an acoustic representation of a melody or harmony. Under the Act, performance means "any acoustic representation of a work or any visual representation of any dramatic action in a work, including a representation made by means of any mechanical instrument or by radio communication". What it transmits, appellant says, are electrical signals to individual subscribers' premises. Such signals are electro-magnetic waves which are completely distinct from acoustic or sound waves and cannot be heard at any time during their distribution to subscribers' premises. While the acoustic or sound waves are generated by compression of air or some other medium, electro-magnetic waves are generated by a change in an electric or magnetic field. In the words of the appellant, a cable system is simply a medium for the transmission of electrical signals to the subscribers' premises and their transmission of non-broadcast services by cable television systems to individual subscribers' premises is through a closed circuit network as opposed to being propagated through space by radio waves.

'I do not think this whole case ought to depend on whether it is this kind or that kind of waves which are transmitted to the subscribers. The definition of 'performance' in section 2 speaks of any acoustic representation. It does not speak of acoustic waves as opposed to electro-magnetic waves or vice-versa. When a subscriber turns on the television set and listens to the music broadcasted or transmitted by the appellant, it is an acoustic representation of a melody that he or she gets: it is the very performance of a musical work as contemplated by the Act.' *Canadian Cable Television Association v Canada (Copyright Board)* [1993] 2 FCR 138 at 150–151, FCA, per Letourneau JA

PERILS OF THE SEAS

[For 25 Halsbury's Laws (4th edn) para 153 see now 25 Halsbury's Laws (4th edn) (2003 Reissue) para 332.]

[For 43 Halsbury's Laws (4th edn) para 454 see now 43(2) Halsbury's Laws (4th edn) (Reissue) para 1490.]

Australia '[P]erils of the sea should not be treated as having some esoteric meaning. Nor can its meaning be identified in a single all embracing definition capable of unvarying application to all circumstances. There is no single criterion which, standing alone, will identify whether what happened is or is not properly to be called a peril of the sea ... In *Gamlen* [(1980) 147 CLR 142 at 166] Mason and Wilson JJ said that "sea and weather conditions which may reasonably be foreseen and guarded against may constitute a peril of the sea" ... To that extent we agree with what was said by Mason and Wilson JJ in *Gamlen*. Such an approach, even if it is different from the American and Canadian approach, better reflects the history of the rules, their international origins and is the better construction of the rules as a whole.' *Great China Metal Industries Co Ltd v Malaysian International Shipping Corp Berhad* (1998) 158 ALR 1 at 12, 14; BC9805441, per Gaudron, Gummow and Hayne JJ

Canada ['Peril of the sea', for insurance purposes, includes two elements, the second of which is that the loss be 'of the sea'.] 'The ... requirement, that the loss be "of the sea", excludes losses which would not have occurred in an accident on land: ... The sinking of a ship as a result of the ingress of sea water due to a fortuitous act has without exception been considered to be an accident which is "of the sea"... The test is not whether the defect which started the causal chain that led to the loss is one that could occur exclusively at sea, but rather whether the accident itself—in this case the sinking of the ship—is one which could only occur at sea. Many sinkings result from causes which could occur on land—for example, the piercing of the hull of the ship with a rock could occur on land. No one would suggest that coverage under insurance for "perils of the sea" would not lie where a ship founders and sinks at sea for that reason.' *CCR Fishing Ltd v British Reserve Insurance Co* (1990) 69 DLR (4th) 112 at 116, SCC, per McLachlin J

PERISH

New Zealand [Section 9 of the Sale of Goods Act 1908 provides that 'Where there is an agreement to sell specific goods, and subsequently the goods, without any fault on the part of the seller or buyer, perish before the risk passes to the buyer, the agreement is thereby avoided'.] 'There has been some disagreement in the cases as to the meaning of this term. In *Horn v Minister of Food* [1948] 2 All ER 1036, the contract involved the sale and purchase of potatoes. They were found to have become rotten to the point that they could not be used. The Judge nevertheless held that the goods could still appropriately be described as potatoes and accordingly had not perished. The decision was however complicated by the fact that the Court also held that the risks of deterioration were in the particular circumstances, with the buyer.

'By contrast in *Rendell v Turnbull & Co* (1908) 27 NZLR 1067, Cooper J was dealing with an action where potatoes were to all outward appearances in good condition, but in fact had deteriorated to the point where they were unsuitable for consumption. The potatoes had been described as "table potatoes" and the Judge accepted that that meant potatoes which were fit to eat. The Judge considered that because of their condition they had ceased to be table potatoes and had perished for the purposes of the Sale of Goods Act. Although it is suggested that this case arrived at a decision in conflict with that in *Horn v Minister of Food* (supra), that is not necessarily so because of the significance which was given to the descriptive term "table".

'In *Benjamin's Sale of Goods* (5th ed, 1997) para 6–029, pp 298–299, the word "perished" as used in the section is defined in terms that the goods have been so altered in nature by damage or deterioration that they have become for business purposes something other than that which is described in the contract of sale.

'In *Asfar & Co v Blundell* [1896] 1 QB 123, a cargo of dates had been underwater for two days and when brought up were described by the Court as being simply a "mass of pulpy matter impregnated with sewage and in a state of fermentation". Lord Esher MR said at pp 127–128:

"... that test is whether, as a matter of business, the nature of the thing has been altered ... it becomes for business purposes something else, so that it is not dealt with by business people as the thing which it originally was, ... has become a total loss."

'The Court accepted that all that was necessary was destruction of the merchantable character of the goods.

'These cases indicate that a significant factor is the intended use, the purpose to which the parties contemplate the goods will be put. In such cases although the substantial nature of the goods may not have changed, nevertheless they may still be regarded as having perished for the purposes of the section.

'In *Barr v Gibson* (1838) 3 M & W 390, a ship had gone aground in a storm and was left by the crew. Baron Parke giving the judgment of the Court indicated that the vessel still had the form and structure of a ship and was a ship, although incapable of being used as such. By contrast in *Nickoll & Knight v Ashton, Edridge & Co* [1901] 2 KB 126, a cargo had to be shipped by a named steamship. The particular steamship was at the time stranded upon a rock in the Baltic and the Court held that the ship, for the purpose of being a cargo carrying ship, had at the time perished. It is significant as appears from the dissenting judgment of Vaughan Williams LJ, that the ship concerned had not been destroyed and after its removal from the rock, would have been available to perform the contract. The impossibility which arose was a question of time since the mishap which occurred prevented the ship from being available at the time contemplated. Nevertheless the majority considered that for the purposes of the contract the ship was to be seen as having perished, using that term.

'The view is expressed in *Benjamin*, that *Barr v Gibson* (supra) would no longer be followed. Again the question of purpose is of importance. As in the case of the potatoes, the present tendency of the law would seem to be against determination on the basis of nomenclature, rather a recognition of the situation as contemplated by the contracting parties.' *Oldfield Asphalts Ltd v Grovedale Coolstores (1994) Ltd* [1998] 3 NZLR 479 at 486–487, per Gallen J

'In context and bearing in mind those principles which the Courts have formulated in interpreting both s 9 and in applying the doctrine of frustration generally, the term "perish" must be interpreted as meaning not that the goods concerned should have been physically destroyed, but that the nature of the goods should have been so affected by the supervening incident that they have ceased to have those qualities which led to the parties entering into the contract for their disposition. The question then in each case as to whether or not the subject-matter of the contract can be said to have perished, will be one of degree.' *Oldfield Asphalts Ltd v Grovedale Coolstores (1994) Ltd* [1998] 3 NZLR 479 at 491, per Gallen J

PERJURY

[For 11 Halsbury's Laws (4th edn) para 938 et seq see now 11(1) Halsbury's Laws (4th edn) (Reissue) para 299 et seq.]

PERMANENT INCAPACITATION

Australia [Regulation 127(1) of the Migration Regulations 1989 (Cth) refers to an applicant for an entry permit being a special need relative as the result of a death or 'permanent incapacitation'.] 'It was common ground that a permanent incapacitation which brings the applicant within the defined meaning of "special need relative" may be an incapacitation either of the Australian citizen (or permanent resident usually resident here) to whom the relationship relates or of another person. If that be so, the "incapacitation" contemplated by reg 127 includes an inability to feed and clothe oneself unaided, and may extend to include other inability to maintain oneself unaided. So interpreted, the word might be understood accurately to describe the condition of a normal infant in this country until he was well advanced in adolescence. (On the other hand it might be said that so to understand the word is to ignore usage and context.) The context in which the word occurs, where it is given, like death, a causal operation by the phrase "as the result of", might suggest that it is intended to describe not a condition, but an occurrence: "being rendered incapable", as the Oxford English Dictionary, 2nd edn, has it. But an occurrence cannot have the quality of permanence. A condition can. And the same dictionary has also for the word, "the fact of being incapacitated".

'None of the several normal disabilities of infancy which may attract the description which the word "incapacitation" expresses can, in my opinion, be described as "permanent". In the context which reg 127 supplies, the word "permanent" in my opinion means likely to continue indefinitely, that is for a substantial but undetermined period. The incapacitation of a normal infant, such as that postulated in this case, is likely, on the contrary, to continue for a substantial period of time the duration of which can be, and is habitually, prophesied confidently by reference to common experience. If the applicant's child's condition may be said to be an incapacitation, as to which it is unnecessary to express a conclusion, the incapacitation cannot in my opinion be called permanent.' *Chen v Minister for Immigration, Local Government and Ethnic Affairs* (1992) 110 ALR 192 at 194, per Jenkinson J

PERMANENT SERIOUS IMPAIRMENT

Australia [Accident Compensation Act 1985 (Vic) s 134AB.] '[20] Subsection (38) of s 134AB is altogether novel. So far as presently relevant, it makes elaborate provision for what must be shown in order to establish that impairment or loss of a body function is "serious" within the meaning of the phrase "permanent serious impairment" in para (a) of the definition of serious injury in subs (37). It does this by reference only to the consequences to the plaintiff of the relevant impairment or loss, para (b) serving to confine attention exclusively to pain and suffering (which by definition includes loss of enjoyment of life) and loss of earning capacity. Paragraph (b) — which in fact deals with the first three paragraphs of the definition of serious injury — reads thus —

> (b) the terms "serious" and "severe" are to be satisfied by reference to the consequences to the worker of any impairment or loss of a body function, disfigurement or mental or behavioural disturbance or disorder, as the case may be, with respect to—
> > (i) pain and suffering; or
> > (ii) loss of earning capacity—
> when judged by comparison with other cases in the range of possible impairments or losses of a body function [or] disfigurements or mental or behavioural disturbances or disorders, respectively.

'Paragraph (c), dealing with paragraphs (a) and (b) only of the definition of serious injury, reads:

> (a) an impairment or loss of a body function or a disfigurement shall not be held to be serious for the purposes of subsection (16) unless the pain and suffering consequence or the loss of earning capacity consequence is, when judged by comparison with other cases in the range of possible impairments or losses of a body function, or disfigurements, as the case may be, fairly described as being more than significant or marked, and as being at least very considerable.

'In weighing the consequences of an impairment or loss of a body function, any psychological or psychiatric consequences of the physical injury are to be excluded from consideration. Paragraph (d) of subs (38) (which is not directly relevant here) deals with mental or behavioural disturbance; it provides that such is not "severe" unless the relevant consequences are "more than serious to the extent of being severe". Thus, all three paras (b), (c) and

(d) build on the definition of serious injury in subs (37) and in conjunction with that definition they constitute the so-called narrative test of which the Minister spoke in the Second Reading Speech. That test was the central point of the argument on the four appeals before us.

...

'[32] Having now dealt, however briefly, with the consequences (being consequences as to pain and suffering and economic loss) by which alone an impairment stands to be adjudged serious or not for the purpose of the expression "permanent serious impairment or loss of a body function" in para (a) of the definition of serious injury in s 134AB(37), we return to the word permanent; for the proper construction of the phrase "permanent serious impairment" was much debated before us, the argument suggesting that there was some ambiguity lurking there. Now, there can be no doubt but that, if a relevant impairment of a body function is to answer the statutory definition, the impairment must be "serious" in the sense dictated by paras (b) and (c) of subs (38) — that is, the consequences of the impairment (and more particularly the consequences as to economic loss or pain and suffering) must be such as can be "fairly described as being more than significant or marked, and as being at least very considerable" (which we shall refer to as the "very considerable" test). But given that that is so, is it the *impairment* (as Mr Maxwell tended to suggest) or (as Mr Gorton submitted) the *serious impairment* which must answer to the description "permanent" if the statutory definition is to be satisfied? Indeed Mr Gorton submitted that in the result the consequences, which were already required to meet the "very considerable" test, had to be permanent as well. That followed, he said, from the order in which the adjectives now appeared in the definition in para (a) of subs (37).

'[33] In some ways the debate seemed rather hypothetical. In practical terms, one can scarcely proceed to consider the consequences to the plaintiff of either the injury or the impairment before one has identified precisely the nature and extent of the injury relied upon and of the consequent impairment of a body function said to have been produced. A necessary part of that task of identification will be to determine how far, if at all, the alleged impairment is permanent, in the sense of likely to last for the foreseeable future. Only then, it seems to us, can one proceed to the inquiry about the consequences for the plaintiff: are the consequences such that they satisfy the "very considerable " test set forth in paras (b) and (c)? Thus, in order the questions must be: first, what is the injury and

what is the impairment said to be produced in consequence; secondly, is the impairment permanent, ie, likely to last for the foreseeable future; and thirdly, are the consequences for the plaintiff such as to satisfy the "very considerable" test? If the answer to the second or third of these is no, the injury is not a serious injury as defined by para (a) of subs (37). If the answer to both is yes, it is a serious injury, but then one has identified an impairment which is both permanent and serious (as defined) and the fact that the impairment is permanent will obviously have been a consideration when weighing the consequences; after all, they are the consequences *of that impairment*. It is hardly likely, if the impairment of the body function will probably last for the foreseeable future, that the consequences *upon which the plaintiff relies* to satisfy the "very considerable" test will be otherwise.

'[34] Having given the matter much thought, we think it enough to say this: that the impairment of a body function will answer the description "permanent serious impairment" if it is an impairment which, with consequences (as to economic loss or pain and suffering or both) that meet the "very considerable" test, is permanent, in the sense of likely to last for the foreseeable future. That sufficiently couples both adjectives — permanent and serious (as defined) — and beyond that it seems unnecessary to go. Certainly nothing in these four appeals raised any problem in that regard.' *Barwon Spinners Pty Ltd v Podolak* [2005] VSCA 33 at [20], [32]–[34], per Ormiston, Chernov and Phillips JJA; BC200500543

PERMANENTLY INCAPACITATED FOR WORK

Australia [In the context of the (Cth) Veterans' Entitlements Act 1986 s 37(1) and the (Cth) Veterans' Entitlements (Income Support Supplement – Permanent Capacity for Work) Determination 1999.] 'In adopting what was in substance a test of "employability", we consider that his Honour fell into error. A test of that nature may be appropriate in the context of whether an employee who has been injured in the course of his or her employment is relevantly incapacitated, and entitled by reason of that fact to compensation. An invalidity service pension is genealogically different. It is analogous to a social security entitlement. There is no need for any link to be shown between the incapacity that the veteran now suffers, and any service that has been rendered. There is nothing to suggest that s 37(1) of the VE Act contains an implication that, in considering whether a person is "permanently incapacitated for work" regard must be had to the availability of the type of work for which that person is suited.' *Repatriation Commission v Hill* [2005] FCAFC 7 at [61], per Wilcox, French and Weinberg JJ; BC200500302

PERMIT

Canada 'The application of the following statutory conditions in the *Insurance Act,* RSO 1990, c.I.8, s 234 as amended, is at issue.

"5. The insured shall not drive or operate or permit another person to drive or operate the automobile unless the insured or other person is authorized by law to drive or operate it."

'The issue of the father's "permitting" his son to drive when he was "not authorized" is not so simple. It seems to be "settled law" that the word "knowingly" cannot be implied before the word "permit". *Cecconi v State Farm Automobile Insurance Co* [1991] OJ No 1059 (6 pp) (QL) (Ont Ct (Gen Div)) [reported at 6 CCLI (2d) 138]. In order for the father not to have permitted the son to drive while not authorized he would be required to "take all reasonable and prudent precautions to see that the Statutory Condition is not contravened" (*Cecconi* supra, per Scott J at p 2).' *Henckel v State Farm Mutual Automobile Insurance* (1997) 145 DLR (4th) 765 at 766–767, per McWilliam J (Ont Gen Div)

PERSECUTION

'The parties are agreed that the issues in this appeal all relate to the proper construction of art 1A(2) of the Geneva Convention relating to the Status of Refugees (Geneva, 28 July 1951; TS 39 (1954); Cmnd 9171) (the convention). The problem to which these issues are directed arises from the fact that the appellant's claim to refugee status is based upon the alleged insufficiency of state protection against persecution by non-state agents. It is not part of his case that he has a well-founded fear of persecution by the state itself or by organs or agents of the state. His claim is based on his fear of violence by skinheads, who are not agents of the state, and on the alleged failure of the state through its police service to provide him with protection against their activities. He also based his claim on discrimination in the field of employment, the right to marry and education, but the tribunal concluded that any abuse of his rights in respect of these matters did not amount to persecution. The Court

of Appeal held that the tribunal were fully entitled to reach that conclusion, and there has been no appeal against that part of its decision to this House. Your Lordships are concerned only with the allegation of failure by the state to protect the appellant against the activities of non-state agents.

'Article 1A(2) of the convention, as amended by the 1967 Protocol (New York, 31 January 1967; TS 15 (1969); Cmnd 3906), provides that the term "refugee" shall apply to any person who—

"owing to a well-founded fear of being persecuted for reasons of race, religion, nationality, membership of a particular social group or political opinion, is outside the country of his nationality and is unable or, owing to such fear, is unwilling to avail himself of the protection of that country; or who, not having a nationality and being outside the country of his former habitual residence as a result of such events, is unable or, owing to such fear, is unwilling to return to it º"'

'The following issues arise in the determination of the question raised by the problem that the parties have identified in regard to the allegation of persecution by non-state agents. (1) Does the word "persecution" denote merely sufficiently severe ill-treatment, or does it denote sufficiently severe ill-treatment against which the state fails to afford protection? (2) Is a person "unwilling to avail himself of the protection" of the country of his nationality where he is unwilling to do so because of his fear of persecution by non-state agents despite the state's protection against those agents' activities, or must his fear be a fear of being persecuted there for availing himself of the state's protection? (3) What is the test for determining whether there is sufficient protection against persecution in the person's country of origin—is it sufficient, to meet the standard required by the convention, that there is in that country a system of criminal law which makes violent attacks by the persecutors punishable and a reasonable willingness to enforce that law on the part of the law enforcement agencies? Or must the protection by the state be such that it cannot be said that the person has a well-founded fear?

'These three issues raise questions about the structure of art 1A(2) and about the meaning of words and phrases used in various parts of that article. The point is commonly made in regard to the convention that it is not right to construe its language with the same precision as one would if it had been an Act of Parliament. The convention is an international instrument. So, as my noble and learned friend Lord Lloyd of Berwick has observed, its choice of wording must be taken to have been the product of the inevitable process of negotiation and compromise: *Adan v Secretary of State for the Home Dept* [1998] 2 All ER 453 at 458, [1999] 1 AC 293 at 305. And the general rule is that international treaties should, so far as possible, be construed uniformly by the national courts of all states. This point also suggests that the best guide to the meaning of the words used in the convention is likely to be found by giving them a broad meaning in the light of the purposes which the convention was designed to serve. It will be necessary to examine the wording of the article. But it may be helpful as a starting point to identify the relevant purpose or purposes.

'It seems to me that the convention purpose which is of paramount importance for a solution of the problems raised by the present case is that which is to be found in the principle of surrogacy. The general purpose of the convention is to enable the person who no longer has the benefit of protection against persecution for a convention reason in his own country to turn for protection to the international community ... This purpose has a direct bearing on the meaning that is to be given to the word "persecution" for the purposes of the convention. As Professor James C Hathaway *The Law of Refugee Status* (1991) p 112 has explained:

> "persecution is most appropriately defined as the sustained or systemic failure of state protection in relation to one of the core entitlements which has been recognised by the international community."

At p 135 he refers to the protection which the convention provides as "surrogate or substitute protection", which is activated only upon the failure of protection by the home state. On this view the failure of state protection is central to the whole system. It also has a direct bearing on the test that is to be applied in order to answer the question whether the protection against persecution which is available in the country of his nationality is sufficiently lacking to enable the person to obtain protection internationally as a refugee. If the principle of surrogacy is applied, the criterion must be whether the alleged lack of protection is such as to indicate that the home state is unable or unwilling to discharge *its* duty to establish and operate a system for the protection against persecution of its own nationals.

...

'Fortunately the situation in Slovakia is not such as to give rise to the problems which may arise in other jurisdictions where there is no effective state authority or the state authority is unable to provide protection. The present case is relatively straightforward. The institutions of government are effective and operating in the Republic of Slovakia. The state provides protection to its nationals by respecting the rule of law and it enforces its authority through the provision of a police force. But, as the tribunal said in para 59 of its judgment, there is racial violence against the Roma perpetrated by skinheads. The police do not conduct proper investigation in all cases and there have been cases where their investigation has been very slow. But there was also evidence that the police have intervened to provide protection when they have been asked to do so and that stiff sentences are imposed at times for crimes that are racially motivated. The tribunal's conclusion was that the violent attacks on Roma are isolated and random attacks by thugs.

...

'I agree with the view of the majority [in the Court of Appeal]. For my part, I would regard the analysis of the article which was provided by Lord Lloyd in *Adan v Secretary of State for the Home Dept* [1998] 2 All ER 453, [1999] 1 AC 293 as being both helpful and instructive. It is an important reminder that there are indeed two tests that require to be satisfied. A person may satisfy the fear test because he has a well-founded fear of being persecuted, but yet may not be a "refugee" within the meaning of the article because he is unable to satisfy the protection test. But it seems to me that the two tests are nevertheless linked to each other by the concepts which are to be found by looking to the purposes of the convention. The surrogacy principle which underlies the issue of state protection is at the root of the whole matter. There is no inconsistency between the separation of the definition into two different tests and the fact that each test is founded upon the same principle. I consider that it has a part to play in the application of both tests to the evidence.

'I would hold therefore that, in the context of an allegation of persecution by non-state agents, the word "persecution" implies a failure by the state to make protection available against the ill-treatment or violence which the person suffers at the hands of his persecutors. In a case where the allegation is of persecution by the state or its own agents the problem does not, of course, arise. There is a clear case for surrogate protection by the international community. But in the case of an allegation of persecution by non-state agents the failure of the state to provide the protection is nevertheless an essential element. It provides the bridge between persecution by the state and persecution by non-state agents which is necessary in the interests of the consistency of the whole scheme.

...

'To sum up therefore on this issue, I consider that the obligation to afford refugee status arises only if the person's own state is unable or unwilling to discharge its own duty to protect its own nationals. I think that it follows that, in order to satisfy the fear test in a non-state agent case, the applicant for refugee status must show that the persecution which he fears consists of acts of violence or ill-treatment against which the state is unable or unwilling to provide protection. The applicant may have a well-founded fear of threats to his life due to famine or civil war or of isolated acts of violence or ill-treatment for a convention reason which may be perpetrated against him. But the risk, however severe, and the fear, however well-founded, do not entitle him to the status of a refugee. The convention has a more limited objective, the limits of which are identified by the list of convention reasons and by the principle of surrogacy.

'The tribunal said in para 53 of its judgment that in its view it was the failure of the state to provide protection that converts the discriminatory acts into persecution. On that approach, having considered the evidence, it decided that the appellant fell below the threshold which it believed was required for international protection in a case where the fear was of discriminatory acts and where it was alleged that there was not a sufficiency of protection from non-state agents. In para 60 the tribunal stated: "It is our view that his fear is not that of persecution." For the reasons which I have given I consider that the tribunal approached the matter in the right way, by examining the question as to the sufficiency of state protection at the first stage when they were considering whether the appellant's fear was of "persecution" within the meaning of the convention. In the view of the conclusion which the tribunal reached as to this part of the definition in art 1A(2), it was unnecessary for it to consider whether the second part of the definition was satisfied. But it is obvious that, as the appellant had failed to show that he had a well-founded fear of being "persecuted" for the purposes of the first part, he would be bound to fail the requirements of the second part also. The words "such fear" in that part assume that the fear which he has is a fear of being "persecuted".

'Where the allegation is of persecution by non-state agents, the sufficiency of state protection is relevant to a consideration whether each of the two tests—the "fear" test and the "protection" test—is satisfied. The proper starting point, once the tribunal is satisfied that the applicant has a genuine and well-founded fear of serious violence or ill-treatment for a convention reason, is to consider whether what he fears is "persecution" within the meaning of the convention. At that stage the question whether the state is able and willing to afford protection is put directly in issue by a holistic approach to the definition which is based on the principle of surrogacy. I consider that the Tribunal was entitled to hold, on the evidence, that in the appellant's case the requirements of the definition were not satisfied. I would refuse the appeal.' *Horvath v Secretary of State for the Home Department* [2000] 3 All ER 577 at 579–581, 585, HL, per Lord Hope of Craighead

Australia 'Persecution involves the infliction of harm, but it implies something more: an element of an attitude on the part of those who persecute which leads to the infliction of harm, or an element of motivation (however twisted) for the infliction of harm. People are persecuted for something perceived about them or attributed to them by their persecutors. Not every isolated act of harm to a person is an act of persecution.' *Ram v Minister for Immigration and Ethnic Affairs* (1995) 130 ALR 314 at 317, per Burchett J

Australia 'In ordinary usage, the primary meaning of "persecution" is [The *Oxford English Dictionary*, 2nd ed (1989), vol 11 at 592] "The action of persecuting or pursuing with enmity and malignity; esp the infliction of death, torture, or penalties for adherence to a religious belief or an opinion as such, with a view to the repression or extirpation of it; the fact of being persecuted; an instance of this". Accordingly, I agree with the ... formulation by Burchett J in giving the judgment of the Full Federal Court in *Ram v Minister for Immigration* [(1995) 57 FCR 565 at 568; 130 ALR 314 at 317] ... ".' '*Applicant A' v Minister for Immigration and Ethnic Affairs* (1997) 142 ALR 331 at 375; BC9700274 at 62, per Gummow J

Australia [The term 'refugee' is defined in the Convention relating to the Status of Refugees (Geneva, 28 July 1951; Aust TS 1954 No 5; 189 UNTS 150) art 1A(2) (as amended by the Protocol relating to the Status of Refugees (New York, 31 January 1967; Aust TS 1973 No 37; 606 UNTS 267)), as a person who has a well-founded fear of being persecuted for reasons of race, religion, nationality, membership of a particular social group or political opinion.] 'Where discriminatory conduct is motivated by "enmity" or "malignity" towards people of a particular race, religion, nationality, political opinion or people of a particular social group, that will usually facilitate its identification as persecution for a Convention reason. But that does not mean that, in the absence of "enmity" or "malignity", that conduct does not amount to persecution for a Convention reason. It is enough that the reason for the persecution is found in one or more of the five attributes listed in the Convention.' *Chen Shi Hai v Minister for Immigration and Multicultural Affairs* BC200001745; [2000] HCA 19 at [33], per Gleeson CJ, Gaudron, Gummow and Hayne JJ

Australia [Under art 1A(2) of the Convention relating to the Status of Refugees (Geneva, 28 July 1951; Aust TS 1954 No 5; 189 UNTS 150) (as amended by the Protocol relating to the Status of Refugees (New York, 31 January 1967; Aust TS 1973 No 37; 606 UNTS 267)) Australia has protection requirements in respect of a person who 'owing to a well-founded fear of being persecuted for reasons of race, religion, nationality, membership of a particular social group or political opinion, is outside the country of his nationality and is unable or, owing to such fear, is unwilling to avail himself of the protection of that country ...'] 'The object and purpose of international refugee law, which presently has the Convention at its heart, has been described by Professor Hathaway in *The Law of Refugee Status* [(1999) Butterworths], at p 124 as follows:

> "... refugee law is designed to interpose the protection of the international community only in situations where there is no reasonable expectation that adequate national protection of core human rights will be forthcoming. Refugee law is therefore 'substitute protection' in the sense that it is a response to disenfranchisement from the usual benefits of nationality.' As Guy Goodwin-Gill puts it, '... the degree of protection normally to be expected of the government is either lacking or denied.'"

'[19] It is in the light of the object and purpose of the Convention, which are fairly summarised in the above paragraph, that the ordinary meaning of the words in art 1A(2) of the Convention is to be determined. That light suggests that art 1A(2) is concerned with persecution in the sense discussed by Mr Atle Grahl-Madsen in *The Status of Refugees in International Law* A W Sijthoff-Leyden, 1966, Vol I at p 189:

> "... The label 'persecution' may, as a rule, only be attached to acts or circumstances for which the government (or, in appropriate cases, the ruling party) is responsible, that is to say: acts committed by the government (or the party) or organs at its disposal, or behaviour tolerated by the government in such a way as to leave the victims virtually unprotected by the agencies of the State."

'[20] The above approach to the interpretation of the word "persecuted" in art 1A(2) of the Convention is supported by Australian jurisprudence. Brennan CJ stated in [*Applicant A v Minister for Immigration and Ethnic Affairs* (1997) 190 CLR 225; 142 ALR 331; 71 ALJR 381] at 233:

> "The feared 'persecution' of which art 1A(2) speaks exhibits certain qualities. The first of these qualities relates to the source of the persecution. A person ordinarily looks to 'the country of his nationality' for protection of his fundamental rights and freedoms but, if 'a well-founded fear of being persecuted' makes a person 'unwilling to avail himself of the protection of [the country of his nationality]', that fear must be a fear of persecution by the country of the putative refugee's nationality or persecution which that country is unable or unwilling to prevent."

Although the Chief Justice was in dissent in *Applicant A*, there is nothing in the majority judgments which suggests disagreement with the above para (see also *Islam v Secretary of State for The Home Department* [1999] 2 WLR 1015, considered in *Khawar v Minister for Immigration and Multicultural Affairs* (1999) 168 ALR 190; BC9907235; [1999] FCA 1529).

'[21] It is thus strictly speaking incorrect to speak of a person who has a well-founded fear of being persecuted within the meaning of art 1A(2) of the Convention nonetheless having available to him or her the protection of the country of his or her nationality. A person who has available to him or her the protection of his or her country of nationality may have a well-founded fear of being harmed in a discriminatory way (see per McHugh J in *Applicant A* at 258) but that feared harm will not amount to persecution within the meaning of art 1A(2) of the Convention. Persecution in the Convention sense involves discriminatory harm which the putative refugee's country of nationality is not willing or not able to prevent to the degree that is normally to be expected of a country sensibly concerned with the human rights of its citizens.'

Hellman v Minister for Immigration and Multicultural Affairs BC200002559; [2000] FCA 645 at [18]–[21], per Branson J

Australia [Article 1A(2) of the Convention relating to the Status of Refugees (Geneva, 28 July 1951; Aust TS 1954 No 5; 189 UNTS 150) art 1A(2) (as amended by the Protocol relating to the Status of Refugees (New York, 31 January 1967; Aust TS 1973 No 37; 606 UNTS 267)) provides that the term 'refugee' shall apply to any person who 'owing to well-founded fear of being persecuted for reasons of race, religion, nationality, membership of a particular social group or political opinion, is outside the country of his nationality and is unable or, owing to such fear, is unwilling to avail himself of the protection of that country; or who, not having a nationality and being outside the country of his former habitual residence, is unable or, owing to such fear, is unwilling to return to it.'] 'Article 1A(2) does not refer to any particular kind of persecutor. It refers to persecution, which is conduct of a certain character. I do not see why persecution may not be a term aptly used to describe the combined effect of conduct of two or more agents; or why conduct may not, in certain circumstances, include inaction.

'Whether failure to act amounts to conduct often depends upon whether there is a duty to act. Sometimes, for example, silence, where there is an obligation to speak, might bear a positive as well as a negative aspect. In some circumstances, silence in the face of an accusation can amount to an admission. Or failure to contradict what somebody else says might, in some circumstances, involve a representation that what is said is true. It depends upon the circumstances; and a relevant circumstance might be what would ordinarily be expected, or whether the person who remains silent has a legal or moral duty to speak. Similarly, the legal quality of inaction in the face of violence displayed by one person towards another might depend upon whether there is a duty to intervene. If X sees A assaulting B, then there may be no duty upon X to intervene, and the mere failure to do so might not amount to conduct of any description. But if A and B are schoolchildren, and X is a teacher responsible for their supervision, the failure to intervene will take on a different complexion.

'If there is a persecutor of a person or a group of people, who is a "non-state agent of persecution", then the failure of the state to intervene to protect the victim may be relevant to whether the victim's fear of continuing persecution is well-founded. That would be so whether the failure resulted from a state policy of tolerance or condonation of the

persecution, or whether it resulted from inability to do anything about it. But that does not exhaust the possible relevance of state inaction.

'The references in the authorities to state agents of persecution and non-state agents of persecution should not be understood as constructing a strict dichotomy. Persecution may also result from the combined effect of the conduct of private individuals and the state or its agents; and a relevant form of state conduct may be tolerance or condonation of the inflicting of serious harm in circumstances where the state has a duty to provide protection against such harm. As was noted earlier, this is not a case in which it is necessary to deal with mere inability to provide protection; this is a case of alleged tolerance and condonation. In *Ex parte Shah* [1999] 2 AC 629, Lord Hoffmann, in giving the example of the Jewish shopkeeper set upon with impunity by business rivals in Nazi Germany, referred to the failure of the authorities to provide protection, based upon race, as an "element in the persecution" [at 654]. The same expression was used by Lord Hope of Craighead in [*Horvath v Secretary of State for the Home Department* [2001] 1 AC 489 at 497–8].

'Where persecution consists of two elements, the criminal conduct of private citizens, and the toleration or condonation of such conduct by the state or agents of the state, resulting in the withholding of protection which the victims are entitled to expect, then the requirement that the persecution be by reason of one of the Convention grounds may be satisfied by the motivation of either the criminals or the state.' (footnotes omitted) *Minister for Immigration and Multicultural Affairs v Khawar* (2002) 187 ALR 574; BC200201536; [2002] HCA 14 at [27]–[31], per Gleeson CJ

PERSON

[For 7 Halsbury's Laws (4th edn) para 80 see now 7(1) Halsbury's Laws (4th edn) (2004 Reissue) para 284.]

[Under the Housing Act 1985, s 65 a local authority has a duty to an unintentionally homeless person with a priority need to secure that accommodation becomes available for his occupation, and by s 75 accommodation is to be regarded as available for a person's occupation only if it is available for occupation both by him and by any other person who might reasonably be expected to reside with him. A local authority offered a one-bedroomed flat to an applicant for accommodation and her husband, knowing that the applicant was eight months pregnant. The applicant refused the offer and the council treated her refusal as unreasonable. She applied by way of judicial review to quash the decision and succeeded at first instance. The council appealed.] 'The first and main question at issue in this appeal is, when an applicant (or an applicant's wife or partner) is pregnant, is the unborn child she is carrying a "person who might reasonably be expected to reside" with the applicant? Even more succinctly, the question narrows down so that it becomes, "Is the unborn child a person within that phrase?" Sir Louis Blom-Cooper, sitting as a deputy judge of the High Court, decided as a matter of law that the answer to that question is Yes ...

'We have to interpret this section according to the normal rules of construction, first seeking the ordinary and natural meaning and secondly, interpreting it within the context of the statute. In my judgment this is a case in which it is proper to interpret the relevant phrase within the context of Pt III of the 1985 Act, that part which deals with housing the homeless. Within that context I can find nothing ... which disturbs or in any way undermines the interpretation of the word "person" in s 65 as having its normal and natural meaning ... For my part I have no doubt that in this section it must be given its proper and ordinary meaning—a person who is alive at the time that the offer is made.' *R v Newham London Borough Council, ex p Dada* [1995] 2 All ER 522 at 525, 528, 529, CA, per Glidewell LJ

[Companies which operated supermarkets were prosecuted for offences contrary to s 169A of the Licensing Act 1964. That provision, which had been inserted into the 1964 Act by the Licensing (Young Persons) Act 2000, made it an offence for a 'person' in licensed premises to sell intoxicating liquor to a person under 18. In contrast, only the licensee and his employees had been capable of committing the equivalent offence under the predecessor provision to s 169A. In both cases the sales had taken place on licensed premises, the licensees being named employees of the companies, and had been carried out by employees of the companies. It had to be determined whether the companies came within the meaning of 'person' in s 169A.] '[6] It was clear that the offences under s 169 could only be committed by the licensee or *his* employees. There was clear authority to that effect in *Brandish v Poole* [1968] 2 All ER 31, [1968] 1 WLR 544, *Boucher v DPP* (1996) 160 JP 650 and *Russell v DPP* (1996) 161 JP 185.

'[7] It was also common knowledge that in practice licences are customarily granted to named employees of off-licence and supermarket companies, not as a result of any desire on the part of the companies to avoid the responsibilities of a licensee, but because justices insist on those responsibilities being vested in named individuals. Although the business is that of the ultimate employer the licence relates to specific premises and is issued locally to one or more named employees. Experienced counsel in this case know of no example of a licence of this kind having been granted to a corporate body ...

'[8] By s 1 of the 2000 Act it is provided:

"For section 169 of the Licensing Act 1964 ... there shall be substituted the following sections—

"**169A**. *Sale of intoxicating liquor to a person under 18.*—(1) A person shall be guilty of an offence if, in licensed premises, he sells intoxicating liquor to a person under eighteen ...

'[9] This gives rise to the question at the heart of these appeals. Is Marks & Spencer or Somerfield Stores "[a] person" for the purposes of s 169A? On behalf of the appellant prosecuting authorities, it is submitted by Mr Butler and Mr Knapp that the answer is clear: "a person" means "any person", whether natural or corporate, whether employer or employee, and whether or not he, she or it is the licensee. Where the consequences would otherwise be unfair, a person charged by reason of the act or default of some other person may avail himself of the due diligence defence referred to in sub-s (3).

'[10] It is suggested that that conclusion flows from the language of the new provision, assisted, if necessary, by s 5 of the Interpretation Act 1978 which provides that in any Act, unless the contrary intention appears, words and expressions listed in Sch 1 are to be construed in accordance with that schedule. Schedule 1 defines a "person" as including a body of persons corporate or unincorporated.

'[11] Mr Haggan QC, on behalf of Marks & Spencer, and Mr Light on behalf of Somerfield, submit that the new statutory provision lacks clarity. They say it is ambiguous. If construed as the appellant suggests it would lead to absurd results. They refer to s 160(1) whereby it is an offence for a "person" to sell or expose for sale any intoxicating liquor without holding a justices' licence. They submit that a "person" in s 160 cannot refer to persons in the position of Marks & Spencer and Somerfield because, if it did, they would commit the offence under s 160 every time intoxicating liquor is sold in their shops. It would be absurd if a "person" were given different meanings in s 160 and the new s 169A. Indeed they make a similar point by reference to s 3, the basic licensing provision, which refers to a "fit and proper" person, but in a context which has always been understood to be limited to natural persons.

'[12] In my judgment these submissions of Mr Haggan QC and Mr Light are correct. It is essential to read s 169A in the context into which it has been inserted. That context certainly includes s 160 and for that matter s 3. Given that context, the results which would follow from differential meanings being accorded to "a person" in ss 160 and 169A can properly be described as absurd.

'[13] It can also be said that when considered in that context s 169A is inherently ambiguous because "[a] person [who] sells" may refer to one or more of the contractual seller (in the sense of the person with title to the goods), the licensee or the sales assistant or check-out operator.

'[14] On this basis I consider that the threshold delineated in *Pepper (Inspector of Taxes) v Hart* [1993] 1 All ER 42, [1993] AC 593 has been crossed and it is appropriate for us to consider what was said in Parliament during the passage of the Bill in 1999 and 2000…

…

'[16] It is abundantly clear from the many extracts from *Hansard* to which we have been referred, that the Bill had "a narrow remit". That quotation is from the debate on 12 May 2000 (see 349 HC Official Report (6th series) col 1141). The "narrow remit" was to end the distinction which the 1964 Act had been found to draw between employees of a licensee and employees of a proprietor, whether incorporated or not, who was not the licensee.

'[17] The passages to which we have been referred show unequivocally that the target was previously omitted employees, without, of course, removing responsibility from the licensee. There is nothing to support the proposition that the proprietor/employer, who is not a licence-holder, was within the contemplation of the promoter of the Bill or indeed his Parliamentary colleagues. Availing myself of this material I conclude that the purpose of s 169A was the limited one contended for by Mr Haggan and Mr Light, and that the provision can and should be construed so as to give effect to that purpose.

…

'[22] The striking thing about the present case is that the new provision has been slotted into the traditional regime of the licensing legislation which has for centuries concentrated its control on the licence-holder and those under his direction. The amendment provides a limited extension to that structure. However, Parliament has yet to put the legislation on a footing which truly reflects modern patterns of retailing. Rightly or wrongly, and the policy arguments are not all one way, the proprietor, whether incorporated or not, is beyond the reach of the statutory offences.

…

'[24] For my part I would dismiss both appeals. In so doing I would answer the questions possessed by the stated cases as follows. In the Marks & Spencer case the question is: "Does '[a] person]' in s 169A(1) of the 1964 Act include the owner of the business or employer where that person is not the licence holder and/or the actual individual involved in the sale?" The answer is "No".' *Haringey London Borough Council v Marks & Spencer plc, Liverpool City Council v Somerfield Stores plc* [2004] EWHC 1141 (Admin) at [6]–[14], [16]–[17], [22], [24], [2004] 3 All ER 868, CA, per Maurice Kay LJ

Australia [As to whether a child in utero who is injured and is subsequently born, lives independently and then dies is a "person" under the Crimes Act 1900 (NSW) s 52A.] ' "Person" is undefined in the Crimes Act save to extend its meaning to societies, companies and corporations. As observed by the learned trial judge the common law has long recognised that where an unborn child receives injuries, is born alive but dies of those antenatal injuries, the perpetrator may suffer criminal liability for homicide: *R v Senior* (1832) 1 Mood CC 346; 168 ER 1798; *R v West* (1848) 2 Cox CC 500. In New South Wales the definition of murder in s 18 of the Crimes Act refers to "intent to kill or inflict grievous bodily harm on some person" and there is no reason to hold that the common law principle as to liability would not continue to apply … An offender may be convicted of the murder or manslaughter of a "person" being an unborn infant at the time of the felonious act causing death and it can be noted that one arraigned for those crimes may by express provision (s 52A(5)) be convicted of an offence under s 52A.' *R v F* (1996) 40 NSWLR 245 at 247, per Grove J

Australia '[T]he word "person" in s 6(3) and s 75B(1) [of the Trade Practices Act 1974 (Cth)] does not extend to the Commonwealth body politic … It is extremely unlikely that the Commonwealth Parliament intended that s 75B(1) should apply to activities of the State engaged in solely for traditional governmental purposes, particularly when it limited the Act's application to the Commonwealth to its business activities. And there is no basis for thinking that the word "person" bears different meanings in s 6(3) and s 75B(1). Given these considerations and given, also, that the word "person" in s 6(3) and s 75B(1) does not extend to the Commonwealth, it is to be concluded that the Act evinces an intention that, contrary to s 22(1)(a) of the Acts Interpretation Act [(Cth)], a State is not a "person" for the purpose of those sections.' *Bass v Permanent Trustee Co Ltd* (1999) 161 ALR 399 at 409; 73 ALJR 522; BC9901019, per Gleeson CJ, Gaudron, McHugh, Gummow, Hayne, Callinan JJ

Australia 'Section 22(1) of the Acts Interpretation Act 1901 (Cth) provides that:

> In any Act, unless the contrary intention appears:
> (a) expressions used to denote persons generally (such as "person", "party", "someone", "anyone", "no-one", "one", "another" and "whoever"), include a body politic or corporate as well as an individual;
> (aa) individual means a natural person.

'Reliance was placed by the appellant upon the primary meaning of the word "person" in the New Shorter Oxford English Dictionary Vol II at p 193, which relevantly defines a "person" as an individual human being and, specifically, a human being as opposed to a thing or an animal. It was submitted by the appellant that the meaning of the term did not extend to a fictitious or imaginary person, but only to an actual human being.

'In my opinion, it is a notorious fact of which judicial notice could be taken that the word "person", as it is commonly used in every day speech and language, extends to both real and fictitious persons. As the New Shorter Oxford Dictionary itself makes clear, the word "person" includes a person who plays a part in a drama or a character in a play or story. It is clear that the word extends to real, imaginary and fictitious persons.

'The appellant pointed out that the same dictionary also indicated that in a legal context, the term "person" meant:

> An individual (also natural person) or a group of individuals as a corporation (also artificial person), regarded as having rights and duties recognised by the law.

'The appellant submitted that the meaning of a "person" as a character in a story was not actually in general use. It was contended that a character in a story is usually called just that.

'Reference was also made to Osborne's Concise Law Dictionary 17th Ed (1983) at p 197 which contains the following definition of "person":

> The object of rights and duties that is, capable of having rights and of being liable to duties. Persons are of two kinds, natural and artificial. A natural person is a human being; an artificial person is a collection or succession of natural persons forming a corporation. "Individual" denotes a human being.

'This definition is a legal definition. It is apparent that there are many senses in which the word "person" can be used. The point which the appellant was seeking to make was that, while he acknowledged that characters exist in literature, including fiction, in those instances they were not real people and they had no rights or duties at law. With respect, that is not to the point by reason of the references in s 233BAB to a document or other goods that "depicts a person" with the characteristics stipulated in a way that is likely to cause offence to a reasonable adult. In my view it makes no difference whether the person depicted is real, imaginary or fictitious. It was submitted, however, that if the word "person" was not limited to a real person, the legislation would contravene ss 7 and 24 of the Constitution because material such as that in Street Boy Dreams and the material in the magazine Koinos could not be disseminated which, in turn, would constitute suppression of political discussion. It was further submitted that the language in s 233BAB(3) and (4) the phrase:

> That depicts a person:
> (i) who appears to be under 16 years of age; and
> (ii) who is involved in a sexual pose or in sexual activity …

must refer to a real being and that the provision does not extend to fictional characters.

'The argument was that the relevant law was directed at prohibiting the importation of child pornography so as to protect children from abuse in the making of pornography, whereas in the case of fictional children, there was no interest to protect. It was, for example, to prevent taking photographs of real children who were being abused. Significantly, the appellant in his written submissions also contended that it was:

> (b) to protect real people from having to read or view unsolicited material that they would find offensive; and
> (c) to maintain public policy.

'It was contended that, so far as the protection of real people was concerned, in fiction or in literary articles, there was no real person who was being abused. There was no actual child there. Further, as the appellant put it in his submission, inasmuch as the magazine Koinos and the novel Street Boy Dreams comprise written material, there was no real person, apart from the author, involved in the writing and publication of the work.' *Holland v the Queen* [2005] WASCA 140 at [15]–[23], per Malcolm CJ, Roberts-Smith and McLure JJA; BC200505554

PERSON AGGRIEVED.

See also AGGRIEVED PERSON

'The question of who is "a person aggrieved" for the purpose of giving a right to make an application to a court or other judicial or quasi-judicial body has been the subject of a great many reported decisions of the courts going back from the present day to the nineteenth century. However, the majority of the decisions are at first instance and not binding on this court. They draw arbitrary and unsatisfactory distinctions between different statutes and situations and lead to needless highly technical arguments as to locus standi. In these circumstances it is, I hope, useful if I set out certain general propositions which I would expect to apply where the expression "a person aggrieved" is used in relation to a right of appeal in the absence of a clear contrary intention in a particular statutory context. (a) A body corporate, including a local authority, is just as capable of being a person aggrieved as an individual. (b) Any person who has a decision decided against him (particularly in adversarial proceedings) will be a person aggrieved for the purposes of appealing against that decision unless the decision amounts to an acquittal of a purely criminal offence. In the latter case the statutory context will be all important. (c) The fact that the decision against which the person wishes to appeal reverses a decision which was originally taken by that person and does not otherwise adversely affect that person does not prevent that person being a person aggrieved. On the contrary it indicates that he is a person aggrieved who is entitled to exercise the right of appeal in order to have the original decision restored.' *Cook v Southend Borough Council* [1990] 1 All ER 243 at 246, CA, per Woolf LJ

Australia 'I adopt the following statement from the judgment of Olney J in *Salter v NCSC* [1989] WAR 296 at 301: "Although the term 'a person aggrieved' is frequently used in statutes it is one which has defied concise definition. No universal test has been devised to provide an instant test as to the meaning of these words. Whenever they are used their meaning will be conditioned by the context in which they appear. With respect, it seems to me that the most helpful dictum to be derived from a consideration of the authorities is that of Burt CJ in *Turner v Corporate Affairs Commission* (SC (WA), 26 May 1987, unreported) at 3: 'A person is aggrieved, I think, when you can see that he will suffer or may well suffer financial loss by the fact of the Company being struck off. I do not think that you should attempt to construe that expression in any technical way. It is simply a question of looking at the facts and asking whether the person who is making the application has a genuine interest in maintaining it'." ' *Colarc Pty Ltd v Donarc Pty Ltd, Colarc Pty Ltd v Arcus Holdings Pty Ltd* (1991) 4 ACSR 155 at 157, per Walsh J

Australia 'Standing under the Administrative Decisions (Judicial Review) Act 1977 (Cth) to challenge a decision (s 5) or conduct (s 6) is conferred upon a person "who is aggrieved" by the decision or conduct ... In my opinion, not only must there be the existence of a special interest in a decision, but also a person must show that the decision sought to be challenged will in some way expose that interest in peril.' *Queensland Newsagents Federation Ltd v Trade Practices Commission* (1993) 46 FCR 38 at 42, per Spender J

Australia 'The meaning of "a person aggrieved" is not encased in any technical rules; much depends upon the nature of the particular decision and the extent to which the interest of the applicant rises above that of an ordinary member of the public.

'The applicant's interest must not be remote, indirect or fanciful. The interest must be above that of an ordinary member of the public and must not be that of a mere intermeddler or busybody. The Administrative Decisions (Judicial Review) Act 1977 (Cth) has selected in ss 5 and 6 as its criterion for standing the expression "a person aggrieved". The word "interest" is not used in ss 3 and 5. The term a "person aggrieved" is not a restrictive one; it is of very wide import.' *Right to Life Association (NSW) Inc v Secretary, Department of Human Services and Health* (1995) 128 ALR 238 at 251–252, per Lockhart J

Australia [Section 202(1) of the Copyright Act 1968 (Cth) provides, inter alia, that where a person, by means of circulars, advertisements etc threatens a person with an action or proceeding in respect of an infringement of copyright, a 'person aggrieved' may bring an action against the first mentioned person and may recover damages sustained.] '[The term] is plainly intended to include any person adversely affected by the threat or threats. The supplier to the recipient of a threatening letter of the goods the subject of the threat, who loses sales or potential sales, as a result of the letter, falls within the concept of a "person aggrieved".' *Cowan v Avel Pty Ltd* (1995) 58 FCR 157 at 164, per Wilcox J

Australia [Section 601AH of the Corporations Act 2001 (Cth) provides, inter alia, that the Court may make an order that the Australian Securities and Investments Commission reinstate the registration of a company if an application for reinstatement is made to the Court by a person aggrieved by the deregistration and the Court is satisfied that it is just that the company's registration be reinstated.] 'The mere fact that a person is a shareholder or a director of a deregistered company is insufficient to establish that that person is a person aggrieved within s 601AH; see e g *Re Waterbury Nominees Pty Ltd* (1986) 11 ACLR 348. As Olney J said in *Re Waldcourt Investment Co Pty Ltd* (1986) 11 ACLR 7 at 12:

> "I do not think that either a shareholder or a director as such must necessarily be aggrieved by the cancellation of the registration of a company. An applicant must, in my opinion, show that his interests have been or are likely to be prejudicially affected by the cancellation of registration."

'That prejudice might be shown by the shareholder showing that he or she was also a creditor of the company or that there might well be a surplus of assets if the company were reinstated and certain events occurred.

'The *Peter Conyers case* at 1850–1 makes it clear that if the company was insolvent and in liquidation before deregistration then, at least ordinarily, a shareholder and a director are not aggrieved by the deregistration. This is because the shareholder has no asset of any value and the director's office was displaced by the liquidator.' *Casali v Crisp* BC200106002, [2001] NSWSC 860 at [27], [28], per Young CJ in Eq

Australia 'The meaning of the term "person aggrieved" in s 39 was considered recently by Heerey J in *Supaproducts Pty Ltd v Alesevic & Ano* [2003] FCA 1145. His Honour in that case adopted the interpretation applied to corresponding provisions of the Trade Marks Act 1995 (Cth) in *The Ritz Hotel Ltd v Charles of the Ritz Ltd* (1988) 12 IPR 417 at 454. In that case McLelland J held at 454 that:

> ... the expression would embrace any person having a real interest in having the register rectified ... and thus would include any person who would be, or in respect of whom there is a reasonable possibility of his being, appreciably disadvantaged in a legal or practical sense by the register remaining unrectified ...

'As Heerey J observed at [14], the approach taken by McLelland J was followed by Full Courts of this Court but also in the context of trade marks in *Kraft Foods Inc v Gaines Pet Foods Corporation* (1996) 65 FCR 104 at 112–113 and *Campomar Sociedad Limitada v Nike International Ltd* (1998) 85 FCR 331 at 363, 381.

'Heerey J also held, following McLelland J in *Ritz Hotel* at 455, that the jurisdiction of the Court was to be established as at the time the proceedings were commenced, although should the facts change between then and the hearing a question of discretion could arise.

'In *Powell v Birmingham Vinegar Brewery Co Ltd* [1894] AC 8, Lord Watson said at 12:

> "In my opinion, any trader is, in the sense of the statute, 'aggrieved' whenever the registration of a particular trade mark operates in restraint of what would otherwise have been his legal rights. It is implied, of course, that the person aggrieved must manufacture or deal in the same class of goods to which the registered mark applies, and that there shall be a reasonable possibility of his finding occasion to use it. But the fact that the trader deals in the same class of goods and could use it, is prima facie sufficient evidence of his being aggrieved ...".'

MacPhee v Peters Foods Australia Pty Ltd (in liq) [2003] FCA 1528 at [68]–[71] per Hill J; BC200308125.

PERSON CHARGED WITH AN OFFENCE

[By the Criminal Law Act 1977 s 38(3), a warrant issued in England, Wales or Scotland 'for the arrest of a person charged with an offence' can be executed in Northern Ireland by any member of the RUC. A person arrested in Scotland falsely gave the particulars of another man, who was then arrested in Northern Ireland and on release sued for wrongful arrest.] '[21] I turn next to the question of the construction of s 38(3). There can be no doubt that the warrant was "a warrant issued in Scotland". Indeed, as I have already said, the warrant was validly issued, even although it was directed against a person who was in fact not the person who had earlier appeared before the sheriff and whom the sheriff intended should be returned for sentence. The problem then arises regarding the following phrase "for the arrest of a person charged with an offence". On the view which the Court of Appeal took, these words require that the person named in the warrant is a person who has actually been charged with an offence. But that is not the only possible construction. It is also possible that they are simply describing the kind of warrant with which the subsection is concerned, namely a warrant to arrest, as distinct from a warrant to search, or any other kind of warrant. On this approach the words are not detailing the substance of the warrant so as to require that the person arrested has in fact been charged with an offence.

'[22] In my view counsel for the defendants was correct in submitting that the latter construction is to be preferred. As he pointed out, if the plaintiff had been in Scotland and the warrant had been executed in Scotland the arrest in conformity with the warrant would have been lawful. That position should still be the same when by virtue of the legislation the power is given to execute it in Northern Ireland. Section 38(3) simply gives the power to execute the warrant within another jurisdiction. If the execution is lawful in the one country, then it should be lawful in the other. The purpose of the section is to enable warrants granted in one of the stated jurisdictions to be readily enforceable in another within the United Kingdom. Endorsation of the warrant is expressly declared in sub-s (4) not to be required. The phrase "for the arrest of a person charged with an offence" appears in all of the first three subsections, covering the three jurisdictions in which the warrants in question may be executed. In each case it seems to me that the words have no greater significance than to denote that the warrants are, to use the language of the sidenote, "warrants of arrest". The construction adopted by the Court of Appeal would have more weight if the subsection had read "may be executed against that person". But those last three words do not appear in the legislation and there is no obvious reason for construing the subsection as if they were there.

'[23] Even if the construction which I prefer was incorrect and the critical phrase should be understood as requiring that the warrant should in its substance be for the arrest of a person who has been charged with an offence, the situation here was that the plaintiff had been, albeit mistakenly, charged with an offence. It was against the plaintiff by name that the indictment had been issued. The plaintiff can thus qualify as a person "charged with an offence" for the purposes of the subsection. While I prefer to base my decision on the construction of the critical phrase, this alternative approach also seems to me to be acceptable. But I do not consider that the Court of Appeal was correct in requiring that the warrant could only be executed against the plaintiff if he had in fact been the person who actually appeared before the sheriff and whom the sheriff intended to be arrested. That construction involves a questioning of what appeared clearly, even although mistakenly, on the face of the warrant. Where there is no reason to question what appears on the face of the warrant, the constable enforcing it has no obligation to do so: indeed on the contrary he has the duty to enforce it. And if in executing it he complies with the terms of the instruction embodied in the warrant he should not be regarded as having acted unlawfully.' *McGrath v Chief Constable of the Royal Ulster Constabulary* [2001] UKHL 39 at [21]–[23], [2001] 4 All ER 334 at 342–343, HL, per Lord Clyde

PERSON DEALING WITH A COMPANY

[The Companies Act 1985 s 35A provides:
'(1) In favour of a person dealing with a company in good faith, the power of the board of directors to bind the company, or authorise others to do so, shall be deemed to be free of any limitation under the company's constitution.
(2) For this purpose—(a) a person "deals with" a company if he is a party to any transaction or other act to which the company is a party ...']

'[14] The judge accepted the argument put forward on behalf of Mr Phipps and Mr Paul that each shareholder who received bonus shares was a person dealing with the company and that the issue and allotment of bonus shares constituted a "transaction or other act to which the company is a party". The judge indicated that Mr Reid, Mr Spickernell and Mr Bryson and their shareholder companies did not know that the issue and allotment of the bonus shares were beyond the power of the directors for the purposes of s 35A(2)(b). He expressed his strong inclination to conclude that the directors acted in good faith for the purposes of s 35A(2)(c). If wrong on the applicability of s 35A, the judge would have concluded that the effect of the two defects would not have rendered any bonus shares invalid, but would only have rendered the paying up of some of the shares invalid. That conclusion, expressed tentatively in the judge's first judgment, was expressed as a final decision in the judge's further judgment.

...

'[34] For s 35A(1) to validate the bonus issue it was necessary to find that the shareholders receiving the shares were persons dealing with the company in good faith and that the reasons why the bonus issue would otherwise have been invalid were limitations under the company's constitution on the power of the board of directors to bind the company. The judge held that a shareholder of a company receiving shares (whether or not bonus shares) from the company is "a person dealing with the company" within the scope of s 35A(1). He considered that as a matter of ordinary language, such a shareholder would be within the ambit of those words, and he said that, in the absence of a powerful reason to the contrary, it is inappropriate to treat naturally wide words in a statute as subject to an implied limitation. The judge also referred to the decision of this court in *Smith v Henniker-Major & Co* [2002] EWCA Civ 762, [2002] 2 BCLC 655, [2003] Ch 182 and found that the reasoning of each member of this court appeared, if anything, to support his conclusion. He also found that s 322A of the 1985 Act indirectly supported his conclusions. That section sets out circumstances in which s 35A cannot be relied on. Those circumstances are limited to transactions between a company and a director of it or of its holding company or a person connected with the directors or a company with whom such a director is associated. Finally the judge expressed the view that the present case plainly fell within the policy behind s 35A as expressed by Carnwath LJ in *Smith v Henniker-Major & Co* ([2002] 2 BCLC 655 at [108], [2003] Ch 182):

> "The general policy seems to be that, if a document is put forward as a decision of the board by someone appearing to act on behalf of the company, in circumstances where there is no reason to doubt its authenticity, a person dealing with the company in good faith should be able to take it at face value ..."

'[35] I have to say that my immediate reaction to the question whether a shareholder receiving bonus shares is "a person dealing with the company" is

not the same as that of the judge. Having regard to the nature of a bonus issue (see paras [17] and [18] above) and the fact that it is an internal arrangement with no diminution or increase in the assets or liabilities of the company, with no change in the proportionate shareholdings and with no action required from any shareholders (see *Whittome v Whittome (No 1)* 1994 SLT 114 at 124 per Lord Osborne), I do not think that the shareholder is a person dealing with the company as a matter of ordinary language. The section contemplates a bilateral transaction between the company and the person dealing with the company or an act to which both are parties such as will bind the company only if the section applies and it will not apply if the person deals with the company other than in good faith. It would be very surprising if a bonus issue made by a single resolution applicable to all shareholders were to be rendered by the section binding in part but void in part depending on the circumstances of the individual shareholders. Nor do I agree with the judge that it matters not whether the shareholder receives a bonus issue or pays for his new shares. If a shareholder receives shares otherwise than by way of a bonus issue (for example, by a rights issue requiring payment of new consideration), then he would have to deal with the company, and the question would be whether a shareholder is within the intended reach of the section.' *EIC Services Ltd v Phipps* [2004] EWCA Civ 1069, [2005] 1 All ER 338 at [14], [34]–[35], per Peter Gibson LJ

PERSON IN AUTHORITY

Australia [Section 410 of the Crimes Act 1900 (NSW) provides that no confession, admission or statement shall be received in evidence against an accused person if it has been induced by, inter alia, any threat or promise held out to him by some 'person in authority'.] 'I would accordingly hold that a person in authority includes any person concerned in the arrest, detention or examination of the accused, or who has an interest in respect of the offence, or who otherwise is seen by the accused by virtue of his position, as capable of influencing the course of the prosecution, or the manner in which he is treated in respect of it.' *Re Dixon* (1992) 62 A Crim R 465 at 483, per Wood J

Canada ' "Person in authority" typically refers to those persons formally engaged in the arrest, detention, examination or prosecution of the accused: see *AB, supra*, at p 26. However, it may take on a broader meaning. Canadian courts first considered the meaning of "person in authority" in *R v Todd* (1901) 4 CCC 514 (Man KB). In that case, the accused made a statement to two men he believed to be fellow prisoners, but who were in fact acting as agents of the police. It was held, at pp 526–27, that:

> A person in authority means, generally speaking, anyone who has authority or control over the accused or over the proceedings or the prosecution against him ... [T]he authority that the accused knows such persons to possess may well be supposed in the majority of instances both to animate his hopes of favour on the one hand and on the other to inspire him with awe, and so in some degree to overcome the powers of his mind ... [Emphasis added.]

'Thus, from its earliest inception in Canadian law, the question as to who should be considered as a person in authority depended on the extent to which the accused believed the person could influence or control the proceedings against him or her. The question is therefore approached from the viewpoint of the accused. See also *R v Roadhouse* (1933), 61 CCC 191 (BCCA) at p 192.

'The subjective approach to the person in authority requirement has been adopted in this Court. See *Rothman*, *supra*, at p 663. The approach adopted by McIntyre JA (as he then was) in *R v Berger* (1975) 27 CCC (2d) 357 (BCCA), at pp 385–86 is, in my view, a clear statement of the law:

> The law is settled that a person in authority is a person concerned with the prosecution who, in the opinion of the accused, can influence the course of the prosecution. The test to be applied in deciding whether statements made to persons connected in such a way with the prosecution are voluntary is subjective. In other words what did the accused think? Whom did he think he was talking to? ... Was he under the impression that the failure to speak to this person, because of his power to influence the prosecution, would result in prejudice or did he think that a statement would draw some benefit or reward? If his mind was free of such impressions the person receiving this statement would not be considered a person in authority and the statement would be admissible.'

R v Hodgson [1998] 2 SCR 449 at 471–472, per Cory J

PERSONAL *SEE* **PERSONAL CARE**

PERSONAL AFFAIRS

Australia 'The "personal affairs" of a person within the meaning of ss 41(1) and 12(2) of the Freedom of Information Act 1982 (Cth) connotes information which concerns or affects the person as an individual whether it is known to other persons or not. For example, a document may contain statements about a person's private life in the sense of his personal life which is widely known in various sections of the community. Something may be notorious, but its notoriety does not deprive it of the character of information relating to the person's "personal affairs". Such a document would therefore prima facie answer the description of one which relates to the "personal affairs" of a person within s 41(1). Whether any disclosure of the information would be an "unreasonable disclosure" within s 41(1) is a different question ... I agree with the Full Court in *Dyrenfurth* [(1988) 80 ALR 533] that it would be inappropriate to attempt to define the meaning of "personal affairs" in some definitive way. It would be unwise to substitute for the word "personal" some other word such as the word "private" because one generally accepted meaning of the word "private" is confidential or not widely known. In my opinion a person's affairs may be personal to him notwithstanding that they are not secret to him. In conclusion on this point I observe that in s 3, which states the object of the FOI Act, reference is made (in s 3(1)(b)) to the "private" affairs of persons. I do not regard that circumstance as confining the meaning of "personal affairs" in s 41(1) to affairs that are private in the sense of secret to the person.' *Colakovski v Australian Telecommunications Corpn* (1991) 100 ALR 111 at 118–119, per Lockhart J

PERSONAL CARE

Australia 'Some of the primary meanings of "personal" include:

> (a) Of or pertaining to concerning of affecting the individual person or self; individual; private; one's own.
>
> (b) Of or pertaining to one's person body or figure; bodily.

'Accordingly, personal care connotes care taken in connection with such matters. It could be provided by:

> (a) The person concerned.

(b) An employed valet or lady in waiting,

(c) A mother for her sick child or

(d) A daughter for her elderly incapacitated mother.'

Devonshire v Hyde BC200200245; [2002] NSWSC 30 at [22], [23], per Macready M

Australia 'Apart from the exclusionary matters in s 5(2) there is no definition of "close personal relationship". Little help is obtained from the reading speeches as to the meaning of "close personal relationship". It is apparent from the terms of the separate definition of a de facto relationship that a close personal relationship does not necessarily involve the concept of living together as a couple. Instead s 5(1)(b) refers to persons "who are living together, one or each of whom provides the other with domestic support and personal care". It is notable that both domestic support and personal care must be provided. One of them alone would not be sufficient. The "close personal relationship" has to be between two adult persons who are "living together". Given that they may be members of the same family, such as a grandparent and grandchild and the different definition for a "de facto relationship" concepts relating to a "couple" are not relevant. Instead the definition calls for two different links. The first is that the parties are "living together". The second is that "one or each of whom provides the other with domestic support and personal care."

'So far as the first requirement is concerned since one is not concerned with concepts applicable to couples the requirement would be met if the parties shared accommodation together. For example, a boarder in an elderly widow's home would qualify. It may not be necessary for there to be a sharing of food or eating arrangements together.

'The second requirement is cumulative. There must be both domestic support and personal care.

'It is the provision of "personal care" which provides the clue to the meaning of the composite expression "domestic support and personal care". Some of the primary meanings of "personal" include:

(a) Of or pertaining to concerning or affecting the individual person or self; individual; private; one's own.

(b) Of or pertaining to one's person body or figure; bodily.

'Accordingly, personal care connotes care taken in connection with such matters. It could be provided by:

(a) The person concerned.

(b) An employed valet or lady in waiting.

(c) A mother for her sick child or.

(d) A daughter for her elderly incapacitated mother.'

Blyth v Spencer; Spencer v Neville [2005] NSWSC 653 at [14]–[18], per Macready AJ; BC200504866

PERSONAL EFFECTS

Australia 'I treat the expression "personal effect" in the will as equivalent to "personal effects" and as meaning, therefore, physical chattels having some personal connection with the testator and not money or any entitlement to money ... The expression "personal effects" will of course take colour from its context.' *State Trust Corpn of Victoria v Taylor* [1993] 1 VR 282 at 286, per Tadgell J

PERSONAL EQUITY

Australia '... I am of the view that the expressions "personal equity" and "right in personam" encompass only known legal causes of action or equitable causes of action, albeit that the relevant conduct which may be relied upon to establish "a personal equity" or "right in personam" extends to include conduct not only of the registered proprietor [of an estate or interest in land recorded in the Land Titles Register] but also of those for whose conduct he is responsible, which conduct might antedate or postdate the registration of the dealing which it is sought to have removed from the Register.' *Grgic v Australian and New Zealand Banking Group Ltd* (1994) 33 NSWLR 202 at 222–223, per Powell JA

PERSONAL INFORMATION

Canada [Personal information was exempt from disclosure under freedom of information legislation.] 'Given this qualification, we are all of the opinion that the information sought is not within the intendment of the definition of "personal information". The plain language of s 24(1)(k) indicates that the bare name of an individual is not personal information. Furthermore, the plain language of s 24(2)(e) indicates that details of a licence or permit are excluded from the operation of s 24(1). "Details of a licence or permit" does not contemplate release of a core of personal data that one provides in confidence. One must take a practical approach when confronted with an issue of interpretation of this Act. It has endeavoured to provide a workable balance between the interests of public access and protection of legitimate personal privacy interests. One should look at the reasons for the exemption from the disclosure requirements in determining whether the agency head has properly invoked a particular exemption.' *General Motors Acceptance Corpn of Canada Ltd v Saskatchewan Government* Insurance (1993) 109 DLR (4th) 129 at 136, Sask CA, per Tallis JA

PERSONAL INJURY

[A child born as a result of an act of incestuous sexual intercourse suffered from severe mental handicap and various physical abnormalities. An application for compensation was made on her behalf to the Criminal Injuries Compensation Board. The Board refused to grant compensation on the view that congenital deficiencies could not properly be regarded as 'injuries'. The child's curator bonis sought judicial review of the Board's decision.] 'It appears to me that the concept of injury, in the context of a situation in which compensation for it must be assessed, presupposes a pre-injury state which is capable of assessment and comparison with the post-injury state. It is obvious from the circumstances of this case that the child concerned never had, nor could have, any existence save in a defective state. Accordingly, in my opinion, it is inevitable that her plight, grievous though it may be, cannot be seen as "personal injury" within the meaning of paragraph 5 of the Revised 1969 Scheme [of the Criminal Injuries Compensation Board].' *P's Curator Bonis v Criminal Injuries Compensation Board* 1997 SCLR 69 at 97, per Lord Osborne

Australia [Section 3 of the Magistrates' Court Act 1971 (Vic) provides for a jurisdictional limit of $5,000 where damages include damages in respect of 'personal injury'.] 'In the absence of express authority, I have come to the conclusion that the expression "personal injury" does not extend beyond physical injury and mental illness to include emotional hurt. I am encouraged to this view by the fact that the law has rejected grief or sorrow as a form of injury which can be relied on to mount a claim in negligence: *Mount Isa Mines Ltd v Pusey* (1970) 125 CLR 383 at 394 and *Jaensch v Coffey* (1984) 155 CLR 549 at 587. It is true that damages are awarded for pain and suffering in the typical personal injury case. They are awarded, however, where pain and suffering flow from and are connected with physical or mental injury and may therefore be said to be damages "in respect of personal injury". To interpret the legislation in this way would enable it to encompass the typical

personal injury case and also the "nervous shock" cases. It would address the object of the legislation to give litigants in typical personal injury, cases the opportunity of seeking jury trial where the claim exceeds $5,000.' *Graham v Robinson* [1992] 1 VR 279 at 281, per Smith J

New Zealand 'The "personal injury" referred to [in the Accident Compensation Act 1982] must mean a physical injury of some kind. If the claimant has suffered a personal physical injury by accident then quite clearly by virtue of the provisions of s 2(1) any mental or physical consequences that flow from that injury or from that accident will be compensatable, but where as here there has been no physical injury to the respondent, even by the merest physical touch, he cannot be said to have suffered personal injury by accident so as to allow his mental illness to be compensatable. In other words, the mental consequences must be parasitic on a contemporaneous or earlier physical injury to the claimant.' *Accident Compensation Corpn v F* [1991] 1 NZLR 234 at 240, per Holland J

New Zealand 'On the plain language of the definition, without reference to any authority, it is I think implicit that external action or event is not an essential qualification for personal injury by accident. Furthermore, it is equally implicit in my view that disease or other similar bodily or mental damage if not expressly excluded could fall within the definition of personal injury by accident.' *Mitchell v Accident Compensation Corpn* [1991] 2 NZLR 743 at 747, per Greig J

PERSONAL ITEM

New Zealand [Section 4(1)(a)(i) of the Shop Trading Hours Act Repeal Act 1990 provides that the trading restrictions on Good Friday and Easter Sunday (provided for in s 3(1) of the Act) do not apply to a shop if it is a shop where:

'(i) The goods for sale include nothing that is not food, drink, a household item, a personal item, an automotive fuel, an automotive lubricant, an automotive part, or an automotive accessory of a kind that people may reasonably need to be able to buy at any time …']

'[30] In *Department of Labour v Cavanagh* [1996] DCR 657 … [Judge Callander] considered "personal items" meant anything intended to provide for a particular individual's needs rather than that of a group, being an article of individual use or ornament. These suggested definitions seem a sensible starting point.' *Woolworths (New Zealand) Ltd v Attorney-General* [2001] 3 NZLR 123 at 130 per Glazebrook J

PERSONAL NEEDS

Canada [Assistance was payable for 'personal needs' and applicants sought payments in respect of counselling.] 'The more difficult interpretation of s 12(3)(*b*) relates to the meaning of the words "personal needs". The Director interprets those words to mean grooming supplies, toiletries, tobacco and other such amenities. The applicants submit that those words should be interpreted to include counselling and vocational rehabilitation; and that counselling and vocational rehabilitation services are provided by the applicants ... The words "personal needs" should not be read as including counselling, because counselling is expressly provided for in a separate section.' *Our House Ottawa Inc v Ottawa-Carleton (Regional Municipality)* (1992) 92 DLR (4th) 337 at 340, 346, per Craig J (Ont Div Ct)

PERSONAL PENSION SCHEME

'Personal pension scheme' means any scheme or arrangement which is comprised in one or more instruments or agreements and which has, or is capable of having, effect so as to provide benefits, in the form of pensions or otherwise, payable on death or retirement to or in respect of employed earners who have made arrangements with the trustees or managers of the scheme for them to become members of it (Pension Schemes Act 1993 s 1)

PERSONAL PROPERTY

[For 35 Halsbury's Laws (4th edn) paras 1101, 1104 see now 35 Halsbury's Laws (4th edn) (Reissue) paras 1201, 1204.]

Canada 'I say that wages paid to and received by an employee of a band as compensation for his or her services cannot fall under the scope of application of subsection 90(1) [of the *Indian Act*] simply because, in my opinion, neither money as such nor the receipt of money as wages were meant to be included in the term "personal property" ("*biens meubles*", in the French version) as used by Parliament in formulating this deeming provision.
    'The terms "personal property" in common law and its correspondent "*biens meubles*" in French

Quebec law, even if they can both be understood as extending to all things other than real estate or "*biens immeubles*" subject to personal ownership, may be less inclusive according to the context in which they are used. On a mere reading of subsection 90(1) in both its versions, it appears clear to me that the two terms were not used by Parliament in their all-inclusive sense. On enacting paragraph 90(1)(*a*), Parliament could obviously not have in mind a notion of personal property that included money *per se*. Theoretically, we may speak of moneys being acquired with moneys, if we think of foreign moneys. However, nothing within the *Indian Act* would appear to contemplate such speculative monetary transactions leading me to conclude that transactions of such a type could have been in any one's mind when the text was adopted. *Canada v Kakfwi* [2000] 2 FC 241 at 253, FCA, per Marceau JA

PERSONAL REPRESENTATIVE

[For 17 Halsbury's Laws (4th edn) para 704 see now 17(2) Halsbury's Laws (4th edn) (Reissue) para 4.]

PERVERSE

Australia [The plaintiff alleged a tribunal had used a perverse process of reasoning.] '... [T]he authorities use the word "perverse" in different senses. It is sometimes used to describe a finding which is against the overwhelming weight of the evidence: see, for example, *Azzopardi*, at 156, per Glass JA. It is also used in the sense of acting without *any* probative evidence to support a material finding of fact: *Minister for Immigration and Ethnic Affairs v Teo* (1995) 57 FCR 194, at 199, per curiam. The authorities suggest that the latter is capable of constituting an error of law, but the former, of itself, is not: *Australian Broadcasting Tribunal v Bond* (1990) 170 CLR 231, at 359, per Mason CJ.' *Dibeek Holdings Pty Ltd v Notaras* BC200005161; [2000] FCA 1212 at [52], per Miles, Sackville and Katz JJ

Canada '[2] Lurking within the issues so framed are other questions:
1. Is a perverse verdict in a civil case an error of law?
2. Is a verdict which is "inordinately" high or low an error of law?

'[3] To put it another way, is there any real conceptual difference between that which is "perverse" and that which is "inordinate", or are the two words merely different ways of saying the same thing? To put it yet another way, is attributing different legal outcomes to whichever of the two labels one chooses, specious? Another question is whether, in this context, "perverse" and "unreasonable" are synonymous. I note that *The Shorter Oxford English Dictionary* (1973), in its definition of "perverse", says:

> c. spec. Of a verdict: against the weight of evidence or the direction of the judge on a point of law.

and gives, as the first date for that use, 1854. In *Allcock v. Hall*, infra para. 104, that great judge, Lindley L.J., speaks of a verdict as "unreasonable and almost perverse", from which one can infer that the two words are not synonymous.' *Johnson v Laing* [2004] BCJ No 1313, 242 DLR (4th) 48 (CA), per Southin JA

PHOTOGRAPH

[Images stored on computer in digital form which enabled it to display and print out indecent pictures of children; also available on internet.] 'Was the disk storing the first appellant's archive ... an "indecent photograph" within s 1(1)(c) of the [Protection of Children Act 1978]? It cannot be said that the disk itself was a photograph within the dictionary definition, because that requires—"a picture or other image obtained by the chemical action of light or other radiation on specially sensitised material such as film or glass".

...

'If not a "photograph", is the computer disk nevertheless "a copy of an indecent photograph" within s 7(2)? It contains data, not visible to the eye, which can be converted by appropriate technical means into a screen image and into a print which exactly reproduces the original photograph from which it was derived. It is a form of copy which makes the original photograph, or a copy of it, available for viewing by a person who has access to the disk. There is nothing in the Act which makes it necessary that the copy should itself be a photograph within the dictionary or the statutory definition, and if there was, it would make the inclusion of the reference to a copy unnecessary. So we conclude that there is no restriction on the nature of a copy, and that the data represents the original photograph, in another form.

...

'There remains the basic question whether the 1978 Act should properly be interpreted so as to include a form of technology which, we are

prepared to assume, was either not anticipated or was in its infancy when the Act was passed. In this context, both parties rely on s 7(5), which includes "any form of video recording" within the statutory definition ... It is difficult to read the inclusion of s 7(5) as restricting the scope of the general definitions in ss 1 and 7(2), and these definitions are wide enough, in our judgment, to include later as well as contemporary forms of copies of photographs.' *R v Fellows* [1997] 2 All ER 548 at 556–557, CA, per Evans LJ

PHYSICAL ACCESS

New Zealand [Section 129B(1)(c) of the Property Law Act 1952] 'In our view the word "physical" was used to place the emphasis upon access in fact. A property owner normally has both a legal right of access and the physical means to exploit it. In exceptional cases there can be one without the other. Paper roads can be physically impassable. Routes which are physically passable are not always supported by strict legal rights. In our view the phrase "physical access" was used in s 129B(1)(c) to make it clear that in this context the factual situation may be decisive.' *Kingfish Lodge (1993) Ltd v Archer* [2000] 3 NZLR 364 at 371–372, CA, per cur

PHYSICAL IMPEDIMENTS

Canada [Development permit could be issued for undersized property in situation of specified impediments.] 'The issue resolves itself into the meaning of the words "buildings or other physical impediments". These words are not terms of art having a fixed legal meaning. Nor are they ambiguous. The plain meaning of the word "physical" is "material as opposed to moral and spiritual", and the plain meaning of the word "impediments" is "hindrances, obstructions or obstacles". Therefore, the plain meaning of the two words together is material hindrances, obstructions or obstacles. The material hindrances, obstructions or obstacles must be like buildings. I accept the submission on behalf of the applicants that "physical impediments" are something in the nature of a sheer cliff, a body of water or a city street. I reject as unreasonable and wrong the submission on behalf of the respondents that "physical impediments" include ownership of abutting lots by different persons. Ownership or title of land might be impediments, but not physical impediments like buildings.' *Mountain Ash Court*

Property Owners Association v Dartmouth (*City*) (1993) 109 DLR (4th) 738 at 744–745, per Nathanson J (NS SC)

PHYSICAL ILLNESS

Canada '[77] The insurance policy does not contain a medical definition of "physical illness". Indeed, Metropolitan Life chose not to define the term at all. Thus, as with the word "accident", the term "physical illness" must be given its ordinary and popular meaning. What matters is the ordinary person's understanding of the term. To suggest that the ordinary person would think that any time a woman becomes pregnant she has a physical illness because she has a cluster of emboli and open uterine veins, which in .00007 per cent or fewer live births combine to produce a fatal amniotic fluid embolism is, respectfully, nonsensical. None of the usual *indicia* that ordinary people think of when they think of a physical illness are present no symptoms, no outward manifestations of illness, no progressively worsening condition.

'[78] To establish a sensible working definition of "physical illness" – a definition that accords with insureds' reasonable expectations – I again turn to Justice Cardozo. Exclusions for" physical illness", "disease" or "bodily infirmity" are typical in accidental death benefit policies and they essentially mean the same thing. In interpreting these terms, most American courts apply the reasons of Cardozo J. in *Silverstein v. Metropolitan Life*, 254 N.Y. 81 (N.Y. 1930). In that case, Cardozo J. held at 84, that the meaning of the term in common parlance should govern, and he distinguished between a "disease" or "infirmity" and a "predisposing tendency":

> In a strict or literal sense, any departure from an ideal or perfect norm of health is a disease or an infirmity. Something more, however, must be shown to exclude the effects of accident from the coverage of a policy. The disease or the infirmity must be so considerable or significant that it would be characterized as disease or infirmity in the common speech of men ... A policy of insurance is not accepted with the thought that its coverage is to be restricted to an Apollo or a Hercules.
> A distinction, then, is to be drawn between a morbid or abnormal condition of such quality or degree that in its natural and probable development it may be expected to be a source of mischief, in which event it may fairly be described as a disease or an infirmity, and a

condition abnormal or unsound when tested by a standard of perfection, yet so remote in its potential mischief that common speech would call it not disease or infirmity, but at most a predisposing tendency. [Citations omitted.]

'See also J.A. Bryant Jr., "What Conditions Constitute 'Disease' Within Terms of Life, Accident, Disability or Hospitalization Insurance Policy", 461 A.L.R. 3d 822; *Katskee v. Blue Cross/Blue Shield of Nebraska*, 515 N.W.2d 645 (Neb. 1994).

'[79] Cardozo J.'s common sense distinction shows that amniotic fluid embolus or embolism is not a physical illness. It is not an abnormal condition of such quality or degree that in its *natural and probable development* may be expected to be a source of mischief. Amniotic fluid emboli and open maternal uterine veins do not "naturally and probably" produce a fatal embolism. The opposite is the case. Their existence in pregnant women is a condition *so remote in its potential mischief* that common speech would call it not a physical illness, but at most a predisposing tendency. It could hardly be otherwise when at most .00007 per cent of pregnant women die from it.' *Wang v. Metropolitan Life Insurance Co* [2004] OJ No 3525, 242 DLR (4th) 598 (CA), per Charron JA

PICKETING

[The Trade Union and Labour Relations Act 1974 has been repealed. The definition is re-enacted in the Trade Union and Labour Relations (Consolidation) Act 1992, s 220. See also 47 Halsbury's Laws (4th edn) (Reissue) paras 1441–1444.]

PIRACY

[For 18 Halsbury's Laws (4th edn) para 1536 see now 18(2) Halsbury's Laws (4th edn) (Reissue) para 732.]
  [For 25 Halsbury's Laws (4th edn) para 162 see now 25 Halsbury's Laws (4th edn) (2003 Reissue) para 340.]

PISCARY

[For 6 Halsbury's Laws (4th edn) para 581 see now 6 Halsbury's Laws (4th edn) (2003 Reissue) para 476.]

PIT

[For 31 Halsbury's Laws (4th edn) para 14 see now 31 Halsbury's Laws (4th edn) (2003 Reissue) para 18.]

PLACE OF PUBLIC ENTERTAINMENT

Australia [The Local Government Act 1993 (Cth) provides that an approval is required in order to use a building 'as a place of public entertainment'. A 'place of public entertainment' is defined in the Act to include, inter alia, premises that are the subject of a liquor licence and 'used or intended to be used for the purpose of providing entertainment'.] '… not every hotel which provides some form of music or other amusement for its patrons will be being used for the purpose of providing entertainment. A single violin or guitar, providing background music in a dining room, would not comfortably be described as a use of the premises for the purpose of providing entertainment. Rather, the activity will be an accompaniment to the dining and thus incidental to the use as an hotel. However, if the activity has a character of its own, so that it is proper to describe it as a "use for the purpose of providing entertainment", then the premises will be being used both as an hotel and also for the purpose of "a place of public entertainment" and must be approved to be used for that purpose.' *Director of Public Prosecutions v La Forest* [2001] NSWSC 828; BC200105795 at [13], McClennan J

PLACE OF WORK

[The Factories Act 1961, s 29(1) provides that every place of work has to be made and kept safe for anyone working there. When leaving the cab of a forklift truck an employee injured his hand on its defective door. The employers argued that the cab was 'plant' rather than a 'place of work'.] 'There does not appear to me to be anything that suggests that "plant" and "place" are to be regarded as mutually exclusive for the purposes of s 29(1). The only qualification to "place" that is provided in the section is that the person has to work there … it appears from the cases to which I was referred that a rung of a ladder or the cab of a fire engine are both to be regarded as places within the meaning of the section … I cannot see any reason why the cab of a forklift truck is not a place also.' *Gunion v Roche Products Ltd* 1995 SLT 38 at 39, OH, per Lord Morton of Shuna

PLACED

[Clause II(9) in a lease provided that 'no goods shall at any time be or remain placed outside the said premises which or of any nature which the Lessor shall have forbidden to be or to remain so placed'. The question arose whether it was apt to

say that a motor car was 'placed' outside the said premises.] '[10] The judge dealt with this as follows:

"'Placed' is a general word which may be apt to describe vehicles which would be parked. I accept, of course, that if one were using a phrase specifically directed to the parking of vehicles, one would be unlikely to use the word 'placed' and 'park' would be the apt word. But if one needs a generic word to cover both vehicles and other things, 'placing' is as apt a description of leaving them in a position on the ground as any and is the most general word available."

'[11] (1) We agree with the judge. As the *Oxford English Dictionary* observes, "place" is "often a mere synonym of *put*" (our emphasis). In ordinary discourse when asking, "Where shall I park?", the answer may well be, "Put your car over there". When Mr Walker submits that placing has a connotation of arranging goods for a purpose, Mr David Hodge QC for the appellant, observes that the task of parking these three cars in the quite tight space available involves exactly that skilful arrangement. (2) In our judgment "place" is such a colourless, general word that it throws no light on the shades of meaning to be given to "goods".' *Spring House (Freehold) Ltd v Mount Cook Land Ltd* [2001] EWCA Civ 1833 at [10]–[11], [2002] 2 All ER 822 at 826–827, CA, per Ward and Rix LJJ

PLANT

Australia [Whether a cutting is a 'plant' under the (NSW) Drugs, Poisons and Controlled Substances Act 1981.] 'The word "plants", as used in the definition of "commercial quantity" in s 70 of, and in Sch 11 to, the Drugs, Poisons and Controlled Substances Act 1981, as in force between 1st October and 7th December 2000, is an ordinary English word. The expert botanical evidence led, both by the prosecution and the defence, was inadmissible. The jury should not have been left to decide the meaning of "plants" for themselves in the light of that evidence, but nor should they have been left at large to determine whether the cuttings were plants. It was for the judge to tell them the meaning of the word in its statutory context, to the extent that that meaning was relevant to the issues at the trial. They could not be told simply that "plants" was an ordinary English word, because it has a wide range of meanings and the fate of an accused person should not depend on whether a particular jury thinks that a pruning lying on the ground is a plant or that something more is required.

'In my opinion, a cutting becomes a plant, for present purposes, when it develops a root. That is a meaning that fits the context and conduces to a practical system of criminal justice. It does not depend on the intention of the accused or anyone else. The root need not be a root system, nor need it be viable. Once a cutting becomes a plant, it continues to be a plant even if it dies. There is no reason to think that Parliament intended proof of the number of plants to depend on expert evidence, whether as to the viability of a root system, the viability of a substrate, the capacity of a putative plant to photosynthesize, whether fungi or algae are plants or other similar matters.' *R v Kevin Francis-Wright* [2005] VSCA 79 at [2]–[3], per Callaway JA; BC200502052

PLEADING

[For 36 Halsbury's Laws (4th edn) para 1 see now 36 Halsbury's Laws (4th edn) (Reissue) para 1.]

PLEDGE *SEE* PAWN, PAWNED GOODS OR PLEDGE

POINT OF LAW

Australia [Pursuant to the Criminal Code (Qld), s 669A(2), the Attorney-General may refer any point of law to the court for its consideration and opinion if the defendant has been acquitted of the charge.] 'While from some of the authorities referred to earlier I would accept that the phrases "point of law" or "question of law" can, in some contexts, have a wide and somewhat technical meaning, I am not persuaded that the wide and special meaning represents the sense in which the phrase is used in s 669A(2)... I think that s 669B requires the court to express an opinion on a point of law said to be contained in a reference or at least requires the court in expressing its opinion to answer the question said to be raised, only if the point is of the character to which it can be assumed the subsection intends to refer. It is concerned with a point involving principle capable of some general application as opposed to rulings which are dependent upon the manner in which an assessment is made of particular factual situations which are not readily capable of wider application to other situations.' *Re Lewis* (1990) 48 A Crim R 218 at 223, per Macrossan CJ

POISON

[For 30 Halsbury's Laws (4th edn) para 782 see now 30 Halsbury's Laws (4th edn) (Reissue) para 1051 et seq.]

POLICIES

New Zealand [Sections 59 and 62 of the Resource Management Act 1991.] ' "Policy" and "policies" must bear their natural and ordinary meaning in the context of the Act. As an appropriate definition Mr Salmon cited what is described in *The Oxford English Dictionary* (2nd ed), as "the chief living sense":

> "**5.** A course of action adopted and pursued by a government, party, ruler, statesman, etc; any course of action adopted as advantageous or expedient."

'The definition "a course of action" is also given by other dictionaries, such as *Chambers*. It may readily be accepted as appropriate in the present context. The word "policy" is very old. One of the examples given in *The Oxford Dictionary,* dating from 1599, is "Eche one ... did, in the begynnynge of the months of Januarye ... presente somme gyfte unto his frende ... a pollicye gretly to be regarded". A familiar modern usage in this country is "New Zealand's anti-nuclear policy". Often, as in the Resource Management Act, the word has governmental or administrative connotations. The name of our "police" comes from the same source.

'It is obvious that in ordinary present-day speech a policy may be either flexible or inflexible, either broad or narrow. Honesty is said to be the best policy. Most people would prefer to take some discretion in implementing it, but if applied remorselessly it would not cease to be a policy. Counsel for the defendants are on unsound ground in suggesting that in everyday New Zealand speech or in parliamentary drafting or in etymology, policy cannot include something highly specific. We can find nothing in the Resource Management Act adequate to remove the challenged provisions from the permissible scope of "policies". In our opinion they all fall within the term and are intra vires the regional council.' *Auckland Regional Council v North Shore City Council* [1995] 3 NZLR 18 at 23, CA, per cur

POLICY OF INSURANCE

[For 24 Halsbury's Laws (4th edn) para 215 see now 25 Halsbury's Laws (4th edn) (2003 Reissue)

para 83; for 25 Halsbury's Laws (4th edn) para 405 see now 25 Halsbury's Laws (4th edn) (2003 Reissue) para 798.]

POLITICAL

[The Extradition Act 1870 has been repealed. See now the Extradition Act 1989, Sch 1, para 1(2).]

[The regulatory authority for commercial radio in the United Kingdom is required by s 92 of the Broadcasting Act 1990 to ensure that advertisements broadcast on commercial radio do not include advertisements 'inserted by or on behalf of any body whose objects are wholly or mainly of a political nature' or any 'advertisement which is directed towards any political end'.] 'Clearly the word "political" is wider than "party political". I take "objects of a political nature" and "political ends" to be synonymous … In its ordinary sense, and distinguishing it, as one must, from "party political", the word "political" means pertaining to policy or government. The word "political" is familiar to the courts in other contexts. Claims are made to "political asylum", but in that context the word is effectively defined by reference to the definition of a "refugee" in art 1 of the Convention relating to the Status of Refugees (Geneva, 28 July 1951; TS 39 (1954); Cmd 9171). The word is also known in the field of extradition. Extradition will not lie if the person whose extradition has been requested has been convicted or accused of "an offence of a political character": see the Extradition Act 1989, s 6(1)(a), which replaced the Extradition Act 1870, s 3(1). It has also been considered in relation to the law of charities, notably by the House of Lords in *Bowman v Secular Society Ltd* [1917] AC 406, [1916–17] All ER Rep 1 and *National Anti-Vivisection Society v IRC* [1947] 2 All ER 217, [1948] AC 31 and by Slade J in *McGovern v A-G* [1981] 3 All ER 493 at 508–509, [1982] Ch 321 at 340… The significance of the judgment [in *McGovern*'s case], for present purposes, lies in the clear unquestioned assumption, running through the whole of [Slade J's] reasoning, that political objects are those which seek to effect a change in the law or a change in governmental policy or the promotion of a political party, and it is on this that Mr Pannick, in my view rightly, relies.' *R v Radio Authority, ex p Bull* [1995] 4 All ER 481 at 496–497, DC, per McCullough J; affd [1997] 2 All ER 561, CA

POLITICAL DISCUSSION

New Zealand [Her Honour stated, 'I am of the view that it is for the "common convenience and

welfare" of New Zealand society that the common law defence of qualified privilege should apply claims for damages for defamation arising out of political discussion' and continued:] ' "Political discussion" is discussion which bears upon the function of electors in a representative democracy by developing and encouraging views upon government.' *Lange v Atkinson and Australian Consolidated Press NZ Ltd* [1997] 2 NZLR 22 at 46, per Elias J

POLITICAL OPINION

Australia 'In a political context, an assertion of fact can be perceived by those in authority (or by others whom those in authority cannot control) as just as dangerous, perhaps more so, than an expression of opinion (in the strict sense) and thus warranting the persecution of those who state such facts … I agree with counsel for the applicant that the Tribunal erred in relying on a supposed dichotomy between "political opinion" and "personal knowledge"… Asylum seekers are more likely to come from troubled countries where political violence is rife than from peaceful and stable societies. Accusations of involvement in violence and other criminal conduct is likely to form part of political discourse. It would be a surprising intention to impute to the drafters of the Convention that only people who were persecuted because their "opinion" consisted of views on abstract questions of legislative policy or political philosophy would be within its protection.' *Ranwalage v Minister for Immigration and Multicultural Affairs* (1998) 159 ALR 349 at 352–353; 53 ALD 58; BC9806217, per Heerey J

POP MUSIC

'Pop music' includes rock music and other kinds of modern popular music which are characterised by a strong rhythmic element and a reliance on electronic amplification for their performance (whether or not, in the case of any particular piece of rock or other such music, the music in question enjoys a current popularity as measured by the number of recordings sold): Broadcasting Act 1990 s 85(6).

PORT

[For 25 Halsbury's Laws (4th edn) para 135 see now 25 Halsbury's Laws (4th edn) (2003 Reissue) para 314.]

[For 36 Halsbury's Laws (4th edn) para 401 see now 36(1) Halsbury's Laws (4th edn) (Reissue) para 603.]

Dockyard port

[For 36 Halsbury's Laws (4th edn) para 401 see now 36(1) Halsbury's Laws (4th edn) (Reissue) para 606.]

PORTION

[For 42 Halsbury's Laws (4th edn) para 725 see now 42 Halsbury's Laws (4th edn) (Reissue) para 727.]

PORTRAYAL *SEE* DEPICT

POSITION

Australia [In the context of whether an employee's position became redundant following the reorganization of the company. Workplace Relations Act 1996 (Cth).] '[32] Clauses 55.2 and 55.5 [of the employment agreement] provided for the cases where an employee became "redundant and [was] transferred to a lower paid job" (cl 55.2) and where an employee accepted "an offer to transfer to another location" (cl 55.5). Both these cases assumed that the employee, or the "position", had become redundant but that the employee's employment continued. No clear distinction was drawn between the *employee* being redundant and the *position* being redundant. Thus, cl 55.2 spoke of "[s]hould an *employee* become redundant" and then said that the employee should "retain the hourly rate applicable to the redundant *position*" (emphasis added).
...
'[52] ... "Position" was not used in the Agreement as a legal term of art. It was used in a colloquial sense. In the collocation of words found in cl 55.1.1 (when understood against the background of the various considerations earlier mentioned) "position" refers to a position in a business — a business to or of which another employer may be successor, transmittee or assignee (whether immediate or not). If, for example, there had been some change in the terms and conditions offered by the new employer from those offered by Amcor, or there had been some change in the tasks to be undertaken by the employee, there may have been some question about whether the "position" continued. Issues of that kind do not arise in the present matter.

'[53] This conclusion about the meaning of "position" is reinforced by a number of other considerations. First, there is the treatment, in cl 55.1.1, of retrenchment as a further necessary element for it to be engaged, and there are those other provisions of cl 55 which are engaged only if the employee concerned is no longer employed in the business. These provisions suggest that a "position" is to be identified in relation to a business rather than identified by reference to employment by a particular employer.

'[54] Secondly, reading the provisions as focusing upon a position in a business is consistent with the approach to redundancy taken by the Commission in the *Termination, Change and Redundancy Case*. There, as already noted, the emphasis was upon a "job" becoming redundant rather than a worker becoming redundant. As the Commission pointed out, the definition of "redundancy" which it adopted from the *Adelaide Milk Supply Co-operative Case* recognised that "redundancy situations may not necessarily involve dismissals" and emphasised that the job or work had disappeared through no fault on the part of the employee. To find that a position is redundant whenever an employer leaves an industry (regardless of whether another employer continues to operate the business concerned) would give insufficient emphasis to the need to identify whether a "job" had become redundant.

'[55] No doubt, as the Union submitted, the clause now in question is different from the model clauses which the Commission adopted in its supplementary decision in the *Termination, Change and Redundancy Case*. It follows that what is said in the decisions in that case is not determinative of the present issue. Nonetheless, the clause now in question is informed by considerations similar to those which the Commission sought to reflect in the drafting it adopted. So much follows from the emphasis given, in cl 55.1.1, to the concept of "position".' Per Gummow, Hayne and Heydon JJ.
...
'[81] What is the meaning of "position" in this context? Is it, as Amcor urged, a disembodied notion of the work or "job", disjoined from the particular employer or any specific employer? Or is it the position held by the employee with the employer concerned? Amcor's submissions before this Court urged the disjuncture, under the Agreement, between the work and the specific employer providing the work. I agree with the other members of this Court that the Agreement, viewed as a whole, presumes such a disjuncture. However, it must be acknowledged that there are a

number of textual considerations (pointed out by the Federal Court) that appear to indicate a contrary conclusion.

...

'[112] ... this statutory provision ... makes very difficult, if not impossible, the construction of cl 55.1.1 that confines the meaning of "a position", as there provided, solely to "a position" with the original employer, namely the Company (Amcor). Because of the statutory provision for transmission of employer liabilities under a certified agreement, it must be possible to read "a position", in cl 55.1.1 of the Agreement, as relating not only to a position with Amcor but also to a position with a successor, transmittee or assignee of Amcor.

'[113] Once this outcome is acknowledged (as the Act requires), the restriction of "a position" to "a position with Amcor" evaporates. It is not to the point that the present case is not, or may not be, an instance of such transmission under the Act. The mere possibility of such an application of the Act to the Agreement refutes the purist or literal interpretation of cl 55.1.1 urged for by the Union.' *Amcor Ltd v Construction, Forestry, Mining and Energy Union* [2005] HCA 10 at [32], [52]–[55], [81], [112]–[113], per Kirby J; BC200500901

Australia [Construction of the (NSW) Workplace Relations Act 1996, s 170CH(3): 'an order requiring the employer to reinstate the employee by ... reappointing the employee to the position in which the employee was employed immediately before the termination'.] ' "Position", when used in s 170CH(3)(a), refers to the place in the employer's commercial structure which the employee occupied before termination. It refers not only to the pay and other benefits which an employee may earn in a position, but also to the work which the person filling that position does. It follows that an employer, ordered to reinstate an employee by reappointing the employee to the position in which the employee was employed immediately before the termination, not only must recommence paying or providing the financial or other benefits attached to the position, but also must put the employee back to the performance of those duties which the employee was fulfilling before termination.

'There are two principal reasons to reach this conclusion. First, s 170CH(3) provides for two different kinds of order for reinstatement. It distinguishes between, on the one hand, orders requiring an employer to reinstate an employee by reappointing the employee to the position in which the employee was employed immediately before termination, and, on the other, reinstatement by appointing the employee "to another position on terms and conditions no less favourable than those on which the employee was employed immediately before the termination". This distinction between reinstatement by reappointing to the former position and reinstatement by appointing to another position reveals that the concept of "position" is insufficiently described by reference only to the pay or other benefits which an employee is to receive from the employer. Yet in essence the respondent's contention was that the appellant was reinstated to his former position because he was paid the same pay and benefits, and that it did not matter whether he was given any work to do. Secondly, both the drawing of that distinction and the Act's reference to "position" rather than "employment" or "contract of employment" reveal that more is required by an order of the kind now in question than recreation of the contractual nexus that existed between the parties before the termination of employment or recreation of that nexus to the extent of giving the employee the benefits available under the terms and conditions which previously existed. Rather, reinstatement by reappointing to a former position requires the recreation of the circumstances of employment that preceded the termination. The contractual nexus between the parties must be re-established. The terms and conditions of that contract must be the same. The employer must provide work to be done by the employee of the same kind and volume as was being done before termination. In cases where that last element cannot be achieved (as, for example, where the work formerly done is no longer required) the form of reinstatement for which s 170CH(3)(a) provides would not be appropriate and the question would become whether the alternative form of reinstatement (by appointing to another position) should be made.' *Blackadder v Ramsey Butchering Services Pty Ltd* [2005] HCA 22 at [43]–[44], per Hayne J; BC200502369

POSITION OF AUTHORITY

Canada [It is an offence under s 153(1) of the *Criminal Code* to touch a young person for a sexual purpose while in a position of trust or authority towards the young person.] 'The courts have had little to say on a theoretical level about the scope of these expressions, which are nowhere defined in the *Criminal Code*. Proulx JA wrote the following about the "position of authority" concept in *Léon, supra,* at p 483:

"[TRANSLATION] In its primary meaning, the notion of authority stems from the adult's role in relation to the young person, but it will be agreed that in the context of this statutory provision, to be in a "position of authority" does not necessarily entail just the exercise of a legal right over the young person, but also unlawful power to command which the adult may acquire in the circumstances."

'For his part, Blair J made the following comment in *P.S., supra*:

"… [a position of authority] invokes notions of power and the ability to hold in one's hands the future or destiny of the person who is the object of the exercise of the authority … "

…

'In the absence of statutory definitions, the process of interpretation must begin with a consideration of the ordinary meaning of the words used by Parliament. *Le Grande Robert de la langue française* (2nd ed 1986) defines the French word "*autorité*" as a [TRANSLATION] "[r]ight to command, power (recognized or unrecognized) to enforce obedience", which is, at least in substance, quite similar to the definition proposed by Proulx JA. It adds that another meaning of "*autorité*" is [TRANSLATION] "[s]uperiority of merit or seductiveness that compels unconstrained obedience, respect, trust". *The Oxford English Dictionary* (2nd ed 1989) suggests similar definitions for the English word "authority": "[p]ower or right to enforce obedience" and "[p]ower to influence the conduct and actions of others". I am in complete agreement with Proulx JA that the meaning of the term must not be restricted to cases in which the relationship of authority stems from a role of the accused but must extend to any relationship in which the accused actually exercises such a power. As can be seen from these definitions, the ordinary meaning of the word "authority" or "*autorité*" does not permit so restrictive an interpretation.' *R v Audet* [1996] 2 SCR 171 at 193–194, per La Forest J

POSITION WITH OR RELATIONSHIP TO

New Zealand [Companies Act 1955 s 18C.] 'The proviso to s 18C(1) prevents a party relying on the section if "that person knows or by reason of his position ought to know" of the lack of authority. The proviso has not been the subject of any detailed examination in the cases in this jurisdiction so far. Several points of interpretation presented themselves. The first was the meaning to be given to the phrase "position with or relationship to". I held this phrase was not limited to an inside

relationship with the company, but did require an ongoing relationship (*Story v Advance Bank Australia Ltd* (1993) 10 ACSR 699, 710 (NSW CA)). The next point was the meaning of the words "ought to know" which I held differed from the common law concept of being "put upon inquiry" and required something more (*Brick and Pipe Industries Ltd v Occidental Life Nominees Pty Ltd* [1992] 2 VR 279, 359). The question then became what is the relationship between these two phrases. The wording of the proviso conveys that what the person ought to know is determined by his or her position with, or relationship to, the company. Therefore information acquired is only relevant if it forms part of the relationship between the person and company (which is to be defined having regard to its particular characteristics).' *Equiticorp Industries Group Ltd* (*In Statutory Management*) *v The Crown* (*Judgment no 47: Summary*) [1996] 3 NZLR 586 at 612–613, per Smellie J

POSSESS

'[1] My Lords, can a person who has his hand inside a zipped-up jacket, forcing the material out so as to give the impression that he has a gun, be held to have in his possession an imitation firearm within the meaning of s 17(2) of the Firearms Act 1968? That is the short question raised by this appeal. Judge Badley, sitting in the Crown Court at Preston, ruled that he could and the Court of Appeal (Criminal Division) (Kennedy LJ, Curtis and Forbes JJ) ([2003] EWCA Crim 3751, [2004] 2 All ER 549, [2004] 1 Cr App R 487) upheld that decision. The appellant, who pleaded guilty on the basis of the judge's ruling, challenges its correctness.

…

'[8] In my respectful opinion, the conclusion reached by the lower courts is insupportable. One cannot possess something which is not separate and distinct from oneself. An unsevered hand or finger is part of oneself. Therefore, one cannot possess it. Resort to metaphor is impermissible because metaphor is a literary device which draftsmen of criminal statutes do not employ. What is possessed must under the definition be a thing. A person's hand or fingers are not a thing. If they were regarded as property for purposes of s 143 of the [Powers of Criminal Courts (Sentencing) Act 2000] the court could, theoretically, make an order depriving the offender of his rights to them and they could be taken into the possession of the police. *R v Morris* [(1984) 79 Cr App R 104], cited by the Court of Appeal, does not assist on this point, since the defendant in that case had with him, with intent to commit robbery, a separate object, namely two metal pipes bound together, which had the appearance of a double-barrelled shotgun. The criticisms of the Court of Appeal's decision made by Richardson (Criminal Law Week issue 45, 15 December 2003, para 6 and Comment) and Professor Spencer ("Is that a gun in your pocket or are you purposively constructive?" [2004] CLJ 543) are in my opinion unanswerable.

...

'[10] Rules of statutory construction have a valuable role when the meaning of a statutory provision is doubtful, but none where, as here, the meaning is plain. Purposive construction cannot be relied on to create an offence which Parliament has not created. Nor should the House adopt an untenable construction of the subsection simply because courts in other jurisdictions are shown to have adopted such a construction of rather similar provisions.' *R v Bentham* [2005] UKHL 18, [2005] 2 All ER 65 at [1], [8], [10], per Lord Bingham of Cornhill

POSSESSION

[For 35 Halsbury's Laws (4th edn) paras 1111–1114 see now 35 Halsbury's Laws (4th edn) (Reissue) paras 1211–1214.]

[Whether a tenant had parted with possession of premises to a company contrary to terms of lease.] '[17] The central questions are the extent and meaning of the covenants in cl 4.18.1 of the lease not to "part with possession" of part of the premises, not to "share possession" of the whole or any part of the premises, and not to "part with possession" of the whole of the premises without consent.

'[18] The judge held that Mr Akici could not have broken the covenant against parting with possession by his arrangement with the company, unless the arrangement had "wholly oust[ed] him from legal possession" of the premises and that "nothing short of a complete exclusion of [Mr Akici] from the legal possession for all purposes amounts to a parting of possession". In this connection, he was purporting to apply the reasoning in a number of cases, culminating with, and considered and applied by, the decision of the Privy Council in *Lam Kee Ying Sdn Bhd v Lam Shes Tong* [1974] 3 All ER 137 at 142–143, [1975] AC 247 at 255–256. As was stated by the Privy Council in that case ([1974] 3 All ER 137 at 143, [1975] AC 247 at 256):

"A covenant which forbids a parting with possession is not broken by a lessee who in law retains the possession even though he allows another to use and occupy the premises."

'[19] However, in so far as cl 4.18 precluded sharing possession, the judge held that "possession" was not to be given the strict legal meaning which it was given in the covenant against parting with possession, and that it should be construed as referring to sharing occupation. In that connection, he was following the decision of Sir Douglas Frank QC sitting as a deputy judge of the High Court, in *Tulapam Properties Ltd v De Almeida* [1981] 2 EGLR 55.

...

'[23] The difference between possession and occupation is rather technical, and, even to those experienced in property law, often rather elusive and hard to grasp. None the less, it is very well established, and is particularly important, and indeed well known, in the field of landlord and tenant law, especially in relation to the question of whether an agreement creates a tenancy or a licence, and in relation to alienation covenants such as cl 4.18.

'[24] While interpretation of a word or phrase in a document must ultimately depend upon the documentary and factual circumstances in which it was agreed, it is desirable that the courts are as consistent as they properly can be when construing standard phrases in standard contexts. In that connection, a covenant against parting with possession is included in many, quite possibly most, modern commercial leases. Further the courts have consistently given the strict meaning to such covenants as was adopted in unreserved terms by the Privy Council in the *Lam Kee Ying* case, and in the five cases therein referred to ([1974] 3 All ER 137 at 142–143, [1975] AC 247 at 255–256).

'[25] Accordingly, while one cannot lay down any immutable rule as to how a particular word or expression is to be construed in every document or lease, I consider that any court must be very cautious before construing the word "possession" as extending to occupation which does not amount to possession, especially in a familiarly expressed covenant against parting with possession in a detailed professionally drafted commercial lease, such as that in the present case.

'[26] In these circumstances, I consider that it would require a very strong and clear case before a covenant against parting with possession should be construed in any way other than that adopted by the Privy Council in the *Lam Kee Ying* case, particularly in the light of the consistent approach taken in the earlier authorities cited therein. In agreement with Judge Dean, therefore, I would hold that the covenant against parting with possession of the whole or part of the premises in the present case should be given its normal, and technically legally correct, meaning, unless there is any good reason to construe it in some other way.

'[27] I turn to the covenant against sharing possession. On the face of it, one would expect the word "possession" to have the same meaning each time it appears in cl 4.18, particularly in light of the fact that it is a word which is familiar, especially in the context of leases, to lawyers. The only reason for not giving the word "possession" its normal technical meaning in a covenant against sharing possession appears to be that identified by Sir Douglas Frank, namely that possession is, as it were, unitary and cannot be shared.

'[28] I do not accept that possession cannot be shared. It seems to me that, as a matter of principle, it would have been open to Mr Akici to share possession of the premises in this case with the company, or indeed with Mr Gultekin. I accept that, as stated by Sir Douglas Frank, possession in those circumstances would be joint, and, in a sense, therefore unitary. However, it seems to me that, as a matter of ordinary language, a lessee who lets another person into possession of the demised premises, so that they are both in possession, can properly be said to "share" possession with that other person. Joint owners can be said to enjoy "shared" ownership. Indeed, I note that both s 34 of the Law of Property Act 1925 and s 36 of the Settled Land Act 1925, which are concerned with joint ownership of land, refer to the land being owned in "undivided *shares*" (my emphasis).

'[29] In consequence, I do not agree with Sir Douglas Frank that to give the word "possession" its usual meaning in the context of the phrase "sharing possession" deprives the covenant of any legal effect. It has a real effect, namely to prevent the conversion of a tenancy to a single lessee into what, in practical terms, will amount to a joint tenancy.

'[30] It may be said that this conclusion will result in a covenant against sharing possession having relatively little value. The answer to that point may be said to be same as that given in the *Lam Kee Ying* case [1974] 3 All ER 137 at 143, [1975] AC 247 at 256, namely that "the words of the covenant must be strictly construed, since if the covenant is broken a forfeiture may result". That approach may well be a little less powerful than it was 30 years ago, on the basis that such canons of construction are now given rather less weight.

None the less, the modern approach, namely that such covenants should be given what is, in their documentary, factual and commercial context, their natural and commercially sensible meaning, indicates, in my judgment, the same result. Further, I do not think one should lean in favour of giving a wide meaning to an absolute covenant (i e one which is not subject to a proviso that consent cannot be unreasonably withheld).' *Akici v LR Butlin Ltd* [2005] EWCA Civ 1296 at [17]–[19], [23]–[30], [2006] 2 All ER 872 at, per Neuberger LJ

Australia [Section 33 of the Australian Securities Commission Act 1989 (Cth) provides that the Commission may require production of specified books in a person's 'possession'.] 'The sense in which "possession" is used in a statute requires a consideration of statutory policy. By s 33 and its associated provisions in Div 3 of Pt 3 of the ASC Law, wide investigative powers are conferred upon the commission. They must, like all such investigative powers be limited by its legitimate statutory functions: *SA Brewing Holdings Ltd v Baxt* (1989) 89 ALR 105 at 116.

'It is, however, a minimum requirement of the statutory policy that the investigative power be effective. A limitation of the word "possession" in s 33 to actual physical custody would leave open to persons connected with the corporation whose affairs are under investigation, the possibility of avoidance of the section by the simple artifice of placing sensitive documents in the hands of some third party. Once it is posited that the policy of the statute is not to leave open that possibility then the application of the definition of possession in s 86 of the Corporations Law follows, it being consistent with a minimum requirement for effective exercise of the power under s 33. And if that be right, there can be no basis for saying that the word "possession" as used in s 33, has some different meaning in relation to documents in the hands of a party's lawyer who is required by the client to raise and maintain a claim of legal professional privilege. Whatever the effect of s 69 of the ASC Law, it does not, in my opinion, support a construction of "possession" that shifts according to whether a person holding documents for the recipient of a notice relating to such documents, is or is not a lawyer and is or is not asserting legal professional privilege.' *Australian Securities Commission v Dalleagles Pty Ltd* (1992) 108 ALR 305 at 313–314, per French J

Australia [Section 3(1) of the Misuse of Drugs Act 1981 (WA) provides that 'to possess includes to control or have dominion over, and to have the order or disposition of, and inflections or derivatives of the verb "to possess" have correlative meanings.'] 'For possession to be established there needs to be proof of an intent to possess or to exercise control over the drugs in question. Proof of knowledge will normally be sufficient to show an intention to control. Ultimately, possession is a question of fact and intention to control is to be inferred from the circumstances: *Davis v The Queen*, above, at 276 per Malcolm CJ; and *R v Cumming* (1995) 86 A Crim R 156 at 163.' *Atholwood v R* BC200001354; [2000] WASCA 76 at [55], per Malcolm CJ

Of land

[For 39 Halsbury's Laws (4th edn) para 487 see now 39(2) Halsbury's Laws (4th edn) (Reissue) para 167.]

POSSESS/DISPOSSESS

[Possession of land by a person in whose favour the period of limitation can run under the Limitation Act 1980, s 15.] '[36] Many of the difficulties with these sections which I will have to consider are due to a conscious or subconscious feeling that in order for a squatter to gain title by lapse of time he has to act adversely to the paper title owner. It is said that he has to "oust" the true owner in order to dispossess him; that he has to intend to exclude the whole world including the true owner; that the squatter's use of the land has to be inconsistent with any present or future use by the true owner. In my judgment much confusion and complication would be avoided if reference to adverse possession were to be avoided so far as possible and effect given to the clear words of the Acts. The question is simply whether the defendant squatter has dispossessed the paper owner by going into ordinary possession of the land for the requisite period without the consent of the owner.

'[37] It is clearly established that the taking or continuation of possession by a squatter with the actual consent of the paper title owner does not constitute dispossession or possession by the squatter for the purposes of the Act. Beyond that, as Slade J said, the words possess and dispossess are to be given their ordinary meaning.

'[38] It is sometimes said that ouster by the squatter is necessary to constitute dispossession (see for example *Rains v Buxton* (1880) 14 Ch D 537 at 539 per Fry J). The word "ouster" is derived from the old law of adverse possession and has overtones of confrontational, knowing removal of the true owner from possession. Such an approach

is quite incorrect. There will be a "dispossession" of the paper owner in any case where (there being no discontinuance of possession by the paper owner) a squatter assumes possession in the ordinary sense of the word. Except in the case of joint possessors, possession is single and exclusive. Therefore if the squatter is in possession, the paper owner cannot be. If the paper owner was at one stage in possession of the land but the squatter's subsequent occupation of it in law constitutes possession, the squatter must have "dispossessed" the true owner for the purposes of para 1 of Sch 1 (see *Treloar v Nute* [1977] 1 All ER 230 at 234, [1976] 1 WLR 1295 at 1300; and Professor Dockray "Adverse Possession and Intention" [1982] Conv 256). Therefore in the present case the relevant question can be narrowed down to asking whether the Grahams were in possession of the disputed land, without the consent of Pye, before 30 April 1986. If they were, they will have "dispossessed" Pye within the meaning of para 1 of Sch 1 to the 1980 Act.

'[39] What then constitutes "possession" in the ordinary sense of the word?

POSSESSION

'[40] In *Powell v McFarlane* (1977) 38 P&CR 452 at 470 Slade J said:

> "(1) In the absence of evidence to the contrary, the owner of land with the paper title is deemed to be in possession of the land, as being the person with the prime facie right to possession. The law will thus, without reluctance, ascribe possession either to the paper owner or to persons who can establish a title as claiming through the paper owner. (2) If the law is to attribute possession of land to a person who can establish no paper title to possession, he must be shown to have both factual possession and the requisite intention to possess ('animus possidendi')."

Counsel for both parties criticised this definition as being unhelpful since it used the word being defined—possession—in the definition itself. This is true: but Slade J was only adopting a definition used by Roman law and by all judges and writers in the past. To be pedantic, the problem could be avoided by saying there are two elements necessary for legal possession: (1) a sufficient degree of physical custody and control ("factual possession"); (2) an intention to exercise such custody and control on one's own behalf and for one's own benefit ("intention to possess"). What is crucial is to understand that, without the requisite intention, in law there can be no possession. Remarks made by Clarke LJ in *Lambeth London BC v Blackburn*

[2001] EWCA Civ 912 at [18], (2001) 82 P&CR 494 ("it is not perhaps immediately obvious why the authorities have required a trespasser to establish an intention to possess as well as actual possession in order to prove the relevant adverse possession") provided the starting point for a submission by Mr Lewison QC for the Grahams that there was no need, in order to show possession in law, to show separately an intention to possess. I do not think that Clarke LJ was under any misapprehension. But in any event there has always, both in Roman law and in common law, been a requirement to show an intention to possess in addition to objective acts of physical possession. Such intention may be, and frequently is, deduced from the physical acts themselves. But there is no doubt in my judgment that there are two separate elements in legal possession. So far as English law is concerned, intention as a separate element is obviously necessary. Suppose a case where A is found to be in occupation of a locked house. He may be there as a squatter, as an overnight trespasser, or as a friend looking after the house of the paper owner during his absence on holiday. The acts done by A in any given period do not tell you whether there is legal possession. If A is there as a squatter he intends to stay as long as he can for his own benefit: his intention is an intention to possess. But if he only intends to trespass for the night or has expressly agreed to look after the house for his friend he does not have possession. It is not the nature of the acts which A does, but the intention with which he does them which determines whether or not he is in possession.

FACTUAL POSSESSION

'[41] In *Powell*'s case (1977) 38 P&CR 452 at 470–471 Slade J said:

"(3) Factual possession signifies an appropriate degree of physical control. It must be a single and [exclusive] possession, though there can be a single possession exercised by or on behalf of several persons jointly. Thus an owner of land and a person intruding on that land without his consent cannot both be in possession of the land at the same time. The question what acts constitute a sufficient degree of exclusive physical control must depend on the circumstances, in particular the nature of the land and the manner in which land of that nature is commonly used or enjoyed ... Everything must depend on the particular circumstances, but broadly, I think what must be shown as constituting factual possession is that the alleged possessor has

been dealing with the land in question as an occupying owner might have been expected to deal with it and that no-one else has done so."

I agree with this statement of the law which is all that is necessary in the present case. The Grahams were in occupation of the land which was within their exclusive physical control. The paper owner, Pye, was physically excluded from the land by the hedges and the lack of any key to the road gate. The Grahams farmed it in conjunction with Manor Farm and in exactly the same way. They were plainly in factual possession before 30 April 1986.'

INTENTION TO POSSESS

'[42] There are cases in which judges have apparently treated it as being necessary that the squatter should have an intention to own the land in order to be in possession. In *Littledale v Liverpool College* [1900] 1 Ch 19 at 24 Lindley MR referred to the plaintiff relying on "acts of ownership" (see also *George Wimpey & Co Ltd v Sohn* [1966] 1 All ER 232 at 240, [1967] Ch 487 at 510). Even Slade J in *Powell v McFarlane* (1977) 38 P&CR 452 at 476, 478, referred to the necessary intention as being an intention to "own". In *Buckinghamshire CC v Moran* (1988) 56 P&CR 372 at 378–379 the trial judge (Hoffmann J) had pointed out that what is required is "not an intention to own or even an intention to acquire ownership but an intention to possess". The Court of Appeal in that case ([1989] 2 All ER 225 at 238, [1990] Ch 623 at 643) adopted this proposition which in my judgment is manifestly correct. Once it is accepted that in the Limitation Acts, the word "possession" has its ordinary meaning (being the same as in the law of trespass or conversion) it is clear that, at any given moment, the only relevant question is whether the person in factual possession also has an intention to possess: if a stranger enters onto land occupied by a squatter, the entry is a trespass against the possession of the squatter whether or not the squatter has any long-term intention to acquire a title.

'[43] A similar manifestation of the same heresy is the statement by Lindley MR in *Littledale v Liverpool College* [1900] 1 Ch 19 at 23 that the paper owners—

"could not be dispossessed unless the plaintiffs obtained possession themselves; and possession by the plaintiffs involves an animus possidendi—i.e., occupation with the intention of excluding the owner as well as other people."

This requirement of an intention to exclude the owner as well as everybody else has been repeated in subsequent cases. In *Powell v McFarlane* (1977) 38 P&CR 452 at 471–472 Slade J found difficulty in understanding what was meant by this dictum since a squatter will normally know that until the full time has run, the paper owner can recover the land from him. Slade J reformulated the requirement (to my mind correctly) as requiring an—

> "intention, in one's own name and on one's own behalf, to exclude the world at large, including the owner with the paper title if he be not himself the possessor, so far as is reasonably practicable and so far as the processes of the law will allow." '

J A Pye (Oxford) Ltd v Graham [2002] UKHL 30 at [36]–[43], [2002] 3 All ER 865 at 876–877, per Lord Browne-Wilkinson

POST OBIT

[For 12 Halsbury's Laws (4th edn) para 1393 see now 13 Halsbury's Laws (4th edn) (Reissue) para 96.]

POUNDBREACH

[For 2 Halsbury's Laws (4th edn) para 438 see now 2(1) Halsbury's Laws (4th edn) (Reissue) para 633; for 11 Halsbury's Laws (4th edn) para 972 see now 11(1) Halsbury's Laws (4th edn) (Reissue) para 330; and for 13 Halsbury's Laws (4th edn) para 363 see now 13 Halsbury's Laws (4th edn) (Reissue) para 771.]

POWER

[For 36 Halsbury's Laws (4th edn) paras 801–806 see now 36(2) Halsbury's Laws (4th edn) (Reissue) paras 201–206.]

New Zealand [Securities Amendment Act 1988, s 5 (2).] '[I]n this context "power" is concerned with the ability to do something, that the ability to bring about the effect required must lie within one's own hands and not those of another, and that a notion of domination or command is involved. None of these facilities necessarily exists at the time that a right of first refusal is conferred but of course s 5(1)(f)(iii) does not demand the existence of the power from the beginning. Nor is it necessary to postulate that the power will necessarily ever arise in the future. It is sufficient if at the time of the agreement one can say that the grantee "may at any time" have such power. And of course the possibility that the power may arise only in the

future, and be exercisable only on the fulfilment of conditions, is expressly provided for in s 5(4)(f) and (g).' *Mercury Energy Ltd v Utilicorp NZ Ltd* [1997] 1 NZLR 492 at 501, per Fisher J

New Zealand [The plaintiff claimed discovery pursuant to R 293 of the High Court Rules of the defendant's medical records held by third parties on the basis that they were within his power.] 'I am satisfied, having considered the provisions of the Privacy Act 1993, that the plaintiff has an enforceable right of access to the documents relating to him held by the parties named in the defendants' application and that those documents are therefore within his power, as that word is understood for the purpose of the law relating to discovery.' *Johansen v American International Underwriters (New Zealand) Ltd* [1997] 3 NZLR 765 at 768, CA, per cur

PRACTICABLE

[The Clean Air Act 1956 has been repealed. The definition is re-enacted in the Clean Air Act 1993, s 64(1).]

Australia [In the context of (WA) Occupational Safety and Health Act 1994 s 19(1)(a): An employer shall, so far as is practicable, provide and maintain a working environment in which his employees are not exposed to hazards and in particular, but without limiting the generality of the foregoing, an employer shall: (a) provide and maintain workplaces, plant, and systems of work such that, so far as is practicable, his employees are not exposed to hazards.] '[28] The question of what is "practicable" in any given context may differ from one situation to another and may well differ over the course of time by reason of an increasing state of knowledge that employers have about the risk of injury or harm to health occurring and the means available of removing or mitigating that risk, as well as the availability, suitability and cost of the means of removing or mitigating the risk being more advantageous to an employer from a practical and commercial point of view. Indeed, concerning what is practicable from time to time, it might be said that, what was said by Mason, Wilson and Dawson JJ in *Bankstown Foundry Pty Ltd v Braistina* (1986) 160 CLR 301 at 308–309, in respect of what reasonable care requires under the general law — namely, that what it requires "will vary with the advent of new methods and machines and with changing ideas of justice and increasing concern with safety in the community" — applies with equal force.

'[29] As what may be practicable to avoid or minimise hazard may change from time to time, this perhaps suggests that at any point in time it may be appropriate to ask whether any particular form of hazard is or was foreseeable. Depending on whether or not it is, a particular form of hazard avoidance or minimisation might be available, cost effective and so on, that is to say "practicable" in terms of s 3 of the Act.

'[30] In this regard it is interesting to note that in their joint judgment in *Chugg* (supra), Dawson, Toohey and Gaudron JJ (with whom Brennan J and Deane J in separate judgments generally agreed) reflected on the relevance of foreseeability in this type of statutory context. In that case, the High Court, in the course of deciding that the prosecution, and not the defendant, bore the onus of showing whether measures to mitigate exposure to harm were "practicable", considered the terms of the duty imposed by s 21 of the Occupational Health and Safety Act 1985 (Vic) and the definition of "practicable" in s 4 of that Act. These sections respectively were similar in content to s 19 and s 3 of the Act in this State. Section 21 of the Victorian Act relevantly provided that:

(1) An employer shall provide and maintain so far as is practicable for employees a working environment that is safe and without risks to health.

(2) Without in any way limiting the generality of subsection (1), an employer contravenes that subsection if the employer fails —

(a) to provide and maintain plant and systems of work that are so far as is practicable safe and without risks to health.

'Under s 4 of the Victorian Act, the term "practicable" was relevantly defined to mean:

practicable having regard to —
(a) the severity of the hazard or risk in question;
(b) the state of knowledge about the hazard or risk and any ways of removing or mitigating that hazard or risk;
(c) the availability and suitability of ways to remove or mitigate that hazard or risk; and
(d) the cost of removing or mitigating that hazard or risk.

'[31] Without finally needing to determine the question, their Honours noted, at 265:

It is clear from the definition of "practicable" in s 4 of the Act that the issue of practicability requires some consideration of the question of foreseeability.

'[32] In *R v Australian Char Pty Ltd* [1999] 3 VR 834; (1995) 79 A Crim R 427, the Victorian Court of Criminal Appeal (Phillips CJ, Smith and Ashley JJ) also addressed the question of foreseeability in the context of s 21 of the Victorian Act. A worker was injured when he placed his hand between a conveyor belt and a drum. A prosecution alleging breach of s 21 on two counts went before a jury. The trial judge charged the jury on the meaning of "practicable" by telling them it required an objective test and by referring to dicta of *Harper J from Holmes v R E Spence & Co Pty Ltd* (1992) 5 VIR 119 at 123–124. He also directed the jury that an employer is bound to have regard to the risk that its employees would act inadvertently or without reasonable care for their own safety.

'[33] The dicta of Harper J from *Holmes* (supra) that the trial judge quoted to the jury was that:

The act does not require employers to ensure that accidents never happen. It requires them to take such steps as are practicable to provide and maintain a safe working environment. The courts will assist the attainment of this end by looking at the facts of each case as practical people would look at them, not with the benefit of hindsight, nor with the wisdom of Solomon, but nevertheless remembering that one of the chief responsibilities of all employers is the safety of those who work for them. Remembering also that, in the main, such a responsibility can only be discharged by taking an active, imaginative and flexible approach to potential dangers in the knowledge that human frailty is an ever present reality. This, indeed, is an element which often turns what would otherwise be a positive result into a negative one, so that, for example, the minor but less obvious traps may present a greater danger than the major and more obvious ones ... One must then weigh the chances of spontaneous stupidity, or a fall, or the like, against the practicability of guarding the machine so as to maintain its function while preventing the human factor from resulting in injury. If the danger is slight and the installation of a guard would be impossibly expensive, or render the machine unduly difficult to operate, then it maybe that the installation of that guard is properly to be regarded as impracticable. Each case must be decided on its own facts.

'[34] In *Australian Char* (supra), the Court of Criminal Appeal held there was no misdirection by the trial judge in putting the issue of practicability to the jury in these terms. In particular the Court considered, at 846, the exposition of the law of Harper J to have been "full and accurate". The Court there added:

> The necessity for an objective approach was implicit in the judgment of Harper J ... He was careful to warn against the dangers of use of hindsight. When he referred to "the knowledge that human frailty is an ever present reality" of which an employer's responsibility under the Act must take account, he was no doubt referring to an aspect of practicability derived from principles pertaining to common law actions in negligence for damages. When he referred to "the chances of spontaneous stupidity, or a fall, or the like" he was doubtless adverting to the types of matters which may bear upon foreseeability of risk of injury and hence may bear, inter alia, upon "the severity of the hazard or risk in question".

'[35] The Court, at 847, then went on to observe:

> It is one thing to say that s 21 imports concepts applicable to the tort of negligence — a proposition implicit in the joint judgment of Dawson, Toohey and Gaudron JJ in *Chugg v Pacific Dunlop Ltd* (1990) 170 CLR 249 at 265. But it is another matter to conclude that s 21 requires the occurrence of an accident to an employee against which to consider an employer's acts or omissions. The obligation cast upon the prosecution is that it identify, with sufficient particularity, the breach of s 21(1) upon which it relies. In that context the prosecution carries the onus of proof in relation to practicability: *Chugg* at 249. Nothing in that obligation requires that an accident involving injury to an employee has occurred. It is consistent with this analysis that s 21 "confers neither a civil cause of action nor a defence to a civil action: s 28": *Chugg* at 260
> ...

'It follows from what we have said that proof of an offence against ss 21 and 47 is not dependent upon there having been an accident and injury to an employee. So, considerations apposite to the common law tort of negligence are not, in the context of an alleged breach of s 21, necessarily confined by a requirement of foreseeability of injury to a particular employee, that employee having in fact suffered injury. That does not mean, however, in the event that an accident has occurred and injury has been sustained, that the prosecution is precluded from conducting its case on a narrow basis. That was here the situation. The prosecution sought to establish breach of s 21 simply by reference to the circumstances in which injury was sustained by Evans. It was not obliged to take such a course in principle; but that is the forensic choice it made. Even limited by that context, however, the passage cited from Holmes did no more than set a proper framework for the jury's inquiry.

'[36] It is also worthy of note, though not a passage the trial Judge quoted to the jury in *Australian Char*, that in Holmes (above), at 126, in relation to the argument that the employee's actions were not reasonably foreseeable by the employer, Harper J added:

> The question in cases such as the present is not whether the detail of what happened was foreseeable, but whether accidents of some class or other might conceivably happen, and whether there is a practicable means of avoiding injury as a result.

'[37] The approach taken by the Victorian Court of Criminal Appeal in *Australian Char* (supra) has been endorsed and applied in this State in a number of cases. Most recently, in *Tenix Defence Pty Ltd v MacCarron* [2003] WASCA 165 at [47], EM Heenan J rejected a submission that the approach taken in *Australian Char* should not be adopted in this State by reason of differences between s 21 of the Victorian Act and s 19 of the Act in this State. While accepting that the terms of the two provisions were not identical, EM Heenan J was satisfied, at least in relation to the circumstances of the case then before him, that the differences were not material and that the judgment in Australian Char "contains an accurate description of the principles which apply in the case of a complaint alleging an offence against s 19". With his Honour I respectfully agree.

'[38] ... His Honour also accepted that the Magistrate was not unappreciative of the fact that "practicable" means reasonably practicable, having regard to the factors mentioned in the definition of that term in s 3, including the degree of the risk of the potential injury or harm occurring and the means of removing or mitigating that risk and the availability, suitability and cost of the means referred to for avoiding it.

'[39] It is plain the authorities require the "balancing exercise", as EM Heenan J called it, to be conducted by reference to the facts of each case. Consequently, in *MacCarron v Coles Supermarkets Australia Pty Ltd* [2001] WASCA 61; (2001) 23 WAR 355, where a 13-year-old boy employed to collect shopping trolleys from around a shopping centre and return them to the Coles and Kmart stores at the centre was struck by an elastic strap which had been used to keep a number of shopping trolleys together whilst he was returning the trolleys to the Woolworths store at the centre and died from injuries, the majority was not satisfied the s 19 duty had been breached on the knowledge available. Murray J, at 389, with whom Wallwork J agreed on this question, said:

> The evidence of those persons who were associated with the operation of Rosalie's Trolleys was effectively that they had no knowledge of any danger associated with the use of elastic straps …
>
> The question of practicability, in my opinion, had to be related back to the identified hazard that in some undefined way the employee might be struck by an elastic strap in such a way as to cause the kind of injury and the death which in fact ensued. Certainly it was reasonably practicable to take simple steps to obviate the risk if it was known, or reasonably foreseeable. Another means of securing the trolleys was in fact available at the time and other similar perfectly safe means might be readily imagined. The severity of the potential injury or harm of the kind which in fact occurred was, of course, very great, but the degree of risk of it occurring at the time was entirely unknown … At the time the accident happened, it was, I think, on the evidence before the learned magistrate, an entirely surprising event.

'[40] By contrast, Kennedy J, at 372, dissented in relation to this view, and would have found that the evidence before the Magistrate was capable of supporting a verdict of guilty. His Honour there stated that:

> In the present case, the third respondent's work practices might be held to have been deficient. The evidence was that parts of the area over which the trolleys had to be moved sloped. There might be held to be a risk that

trolleys would break loose unless tied together. There were, however, no instructions given to the boys to use ropes to tie the trolleys together, it being left up to them to obtain ropes if they wished to do so. A practical system of work might have involved the compulsory use of ropes. Andrew had obtained for himself an occy strap to secure the trolleys. His use of the occy strap caused his death. Whether there was a work environment in which Andrew was exposed to the risk of being struck by an occy strap and whether the failure to maintain a safe work environment caused Andrew's death is for the magistrate to determine.

'[41] In *Tenix* (supra), EM Heenan J noted, at [44], that when one speaks of foreseeability in the context of s 19 of the Act, whether objective foreseeability of a reasonable employer or the subjective foreseeability of a particular employer:

> … it is not necessary to show that the precise sequence of events which led to the death was foreseen or foreseeable. This is not the test for foreseeability because it is sufficient in the circumstances to ask whether a consequence of the same general character as that which followed was reasonably foreseeable as one not unlikely to follow from the use of electric arc welding apparatus in a confined space and in hot working conditions — see *Chapman v Hearse* (1961) 106 CLR 112 at 120.

'[42] Again, having regard to what the Victorian Court of Criminal Appeal said in *Australian Char* (supra) at 487, and also to what was said by Harper J in Holmes (supra) at 126, the question of whether the statutory duty in s 19(1)(a) of the Act has been breached in any given case is not governed by whether a particular injury, in the present case death, of an employee was foreseeable by the particular means by which it occurred, but rather whether an accident of some class, including the class by which injury, or, as in this case, death, might follow, might conceivably happen, and whether there is a practicable means of avoiding the injury, or, in the present case, death.' *Western Power Corporation v Shepherd* [2004] WASCA 233 at [28]–[42], per Barker J; BC200406840

PRACTICE

Australia [(ACT) Supreme Court 1933 s 23).] 'The identification of "practice" relevant to s 23(3) raises two issues. The first is the meaning of the word "practice". The second is the point in time by reference to which its content is to be determined.

'The ordinary meaning of the word "practice" in its application to the law is defined in the Second Edition of the Oxford English Dictionary (1989) as "the method of procedure used in the law-courts". This refers back to a definition in Tomlins Law Dictionary of 1809 of "Practice of the Courts" as:

> ... the form and manner of conducting and carrying on suits or prosecutions at Law or in Equity, civil or criminal ... ; according to the principals of Law and the rules laid down by the several courts.

'The definition applicable to the law fits within the wider concept of "practice" as:

> A habitual way or mode of acting; a habit, custom; (with pl.) something done constantly ...'

Byrnes v Barry [2004] ACTCA 24 at [66], per French J; BC200408139

PRACTITIONER OR FIRM OF PRACTITIONERS

Australia [Order 71 r 93 of the High Court Rules provides that 'a practitioner or firm of practitioners' 'are those persons whose names are entered in the Register of Practitioners kept at the Registry of the Court under s 55C of the Judiciary Act [1903 (Cth)]'.] 'Subject to what may be wider rights conferred on them by s 55Q(1)(b) ..., AGS [Australian Government Solicitor] lawyers who practise in the High Court would be expected to appear in that Register (ss 55C, 55D and 55I). The AGS itself, as a corporate entity, is not such a person and is not a "practitioner or firm of practitioners" within the meaning of r 93.' *Re Minister for Immigration and Multicultural Affairs; Ex parte Goldie ; Goldie v Minister for Immigration and Multicultural Affairs* [2004] HCA 27 at [22], per Gummow J; BC200403489

PREAMBLE

[For 44 Halsbury's Laws (4th edn) para 814 see now 44(1) Halsbury's Laws (4th edn) (Reissue) para 1265.]

PRECEPT

Canada '189 I accept that Mr. Amselem has met the threshold test of bringing his claim within the protected zone of religious freedom. (For present purposes, as I conclude the appeal should be dismissed, it is unnecessary to dwell on the alleged insufficiencies of the evidence of the other appellants.) Mr. Amselem clearly respects the succah ritual as a religious precept, by which I understand him to mean a divine command (*Shorter Oxford English Dictionary* (5th ed. 2002), vol. 2, at p. 2316). There is no doubt expressed by any of the parties that in general terms the precept exists as an article of the Jewish faith. We are not dealing here with a religion of one phenomenon, or a non-traditional claim such as the smoking of peyote as part of a claimed religious experience (*Employment Division, Department of Human Resources of Oregon v. Smith*, 494 U.S. 872 (1990)). Those types of issues will have to be addressed when they arise.' *Syndicat Northcrest v Amselem* [2004] SCJ No 46, [2004] 2 SCR 551, per Binnie J

PRECINCTS

Australia [Section 33(1) of the Queensland Heritage Act 1992 (Qld) prohibits development in a registered place unless it is approved by the council. Section 33(2) provides that approval is not required 'in relation to a church or the precincts of a church' in certain circumstances.] 'The most difficult question is the identification of the area in the neighbourhood of the church that is affected by the exemption's reference to "precincts". It may mean the ground immediately surrounding the church, or the district in which the church is situated or some intermediate meaning, and the section does not identify which is intended. But it might comfortably be said that the general context and purpose of the legislation would exclude a connotation extending to the district or general locality of the church. Conversely, it is certainly not confined to the lots on which the church is built according to their real property subdivisions ...

['[Footnote 2:] It appears to be inconsequential that "precincts" is used rather than "precinct". Although the *Oxford English Dictionary* provides an alternative meaning for the word, especially in the plural, that is, "often applied more vaguely to the region lying immediately around a place, without distinct reference to any enclosure; the environs", the breadth of that meaning and its vagueness make it unfit to apply to a provision of this nature.']

...

'[16] ... the construction of this expression should not be technical or pedantic but should accord with the purpose for which the exemption is provided. One meaning given by both the *Macquarie* and *Oxford English Dictionaries* is the ground immediately surrounding a religious house or place of worship, and in that context, "immediately" means directly or without anything intervening; but the dictionary definition does not expressly require the ground to be vacant. Another meaning is "the environs", which is more general and vague, meaning no more than surroundings. These definitions refer in one direction to proximity to the church, but do not refer in the other direction to the outer limits of a precinct, presumably because, apart from the need for immediacy, they are variable depending on the circumstances.

'[17] None of this is very enlightening in the present problem but another meaning given by the *Oxford English Dictionary* provides some assistance. It is, "The space enclosed by the walls on other boundaries of a particular place or building, or by an imaginary line drawn round it." This is etymologically consistent, for the word is derived from *praecinctum*, meaning enclosure, and ultimately from *cingere*, to gird. This injects a flavour of enclosure supporting the view that where that occurs, the wall of a neighbouring building that does not have any ecclesiastical use will form part of the boundary enclosing the precincts, so that the building itself is outside them. This also suggests that the reference to "ground immediately surrounding a religious house" refers to empty ground that is enclosed by alien buildings or at least by some imaginary boundaries.

...

'[19] ... it is unlikely that in referring to [precincts] in the context of this exemption, the legislature intended that the concept should encompass an area outside that currently used by the church for its liturgical practices or ancillary uses, such as housing for the clergy or other supporting persons.

...

'[23] If the expression draws colour from its purpose, then it might be construed as meaning the ground and buildings thereon connected with the church, which are in some way, even perhaps indirectly, used, at least, for purposes associated with the church's function as a place of public worship.

'[24] This approach is not uncomfortable with the reverse position where a church is surrounded in every direction by a large area of vacant and unused land. The precincts of the church would not necessarily extend to the wall of first building to be found or to the borders of land owned by others.

Although precise identification of the imaginary boundaries might be difficult, they would normally be limited to an area associated with the church as a place of worship. Beyond that, land not used for that purpose would be outside the church's precincts, even though it be owned by the church.' *Queensland Heritage Council v Roman Catholic Archdiocese of Brisbane* BC9907787; [1999] QSC 353 at [9], n 2, [16], [19], [23], [24], per Derrington J

PREFERRED SUPPLIER

Australia 'The expression "preferred supplier" has been used extensively in the course of dealings between the Nationwide entities and Franklins during the period from 1994 to 1998. The contention of Nationwide Holdings is that the use of the expression is inconsistent with the notion that there was a series of one-off contracts for a supply of specific quantities of commodities at specific prices as agreed by the parties on a weekly basis. The expression "preferred supplier" is said to have been used in the sense of conferring not merely a de facto status of preferred supplier, that is, being a supplier who is preferred in practice, but rather as giving rise to the conferral or grant of a legally enforceable contractual right of first refusal.

'The expression "preferred supplier" denotes, in normal usage, a commercial course of conduct. In contrast, the expression "right of first refusal" or "first right of refusal" is framed to the law and usually confers a legally enforceable right. However, as is evident from the authorities discussed below, the latter expression does not have a fixed and definite meaning.

'In *Mackay v Wilson* (1947) 47 SR(NSW) 315 at 325, Street J said in relation to a right of first refusal:

> But an agreement to give "the first refusal" or "a right of pre-emption" confers no immediate right upon the prospective purchaser. It imposes a negative obligation on the possible vendor requiring him to refrain from selling the land to any other person without giving to the holder of the right of first refusal the opportunity of purchasing in preference to any other buyer. It is not an offer and in itself it imposes no obligation on the owner of the land to sell the same. He may do so or not as he wishes. But if he does decide to sell, then the holder of the right of first refusal has the right to receive the first offer, which he also may accept or not as he wishes. The right is

merely contractual and no equitable interest in the land is created by the agreement.

'The High Court considered the expression in *Woodroffe v Box* (1954) 92 CLR 245 at 257, where Fullagar and Kitto JJ said:

> The term "first refusal" is not a technical term. It is a colloquial term, and indeed a somewhat inept term, because what the potential offeree wants is an opportunity of accepting an offer rather than an opportunity of refusing an offer. It may, and does, occur in various phrases, such as "give the first refusal", "have the first refusal", "give the right of first refusal", "have the right of first refusal", etc.
>
> It seems clear that a mere promise to give the first refusal should be taken prima facie as conferring no more than a pre-emptive right. If I promise to give you the first refusal of my property, I am making prima facie only a negative promise: I am saying; "I will not sell my property unless and until I have offered it to you and you have refused it."

'The meaning of the expression "first right of refusal" was considered by Madgwick J in *White Property Developments Ltd v Richmond Growth Pty Ltd* (unreported, Federal Court of Australia, Madgwick J, 28 January 1998), where his Honour said:

> The obligation not to sell the land "unless and until" (to adopt the language of *Woodroffe v Box*) it had been offered to White Property, could not be satisfied unless White Property had been given the chance, and had failed, to accept an offer on the terms (or on terms more favourable to White Property than those) upon which the property would actually be sold by Richmond Growth. That is, if an offer rejected by White Property was not accepted by anyone else, and Richmond Growth was forced to lessen its demands, White Property was entitled to have the opportunity to accept the lesser offer before any one else did. If White Property rejected an offer but Richmond Growth was then able to obtain better terms elsewhere, White Property was not entitled to be re-offered the property on the more onerous terms.

'It is evident that the content of a "right of first refusal" is by no means fixed, specific or certain and in order to ascertain its meaning in any particular case one needs to pay careful regard to the surrounding facts and circumstances and the conduct of the parties. But we are not here dealing with a right of first refusal. The expression used in the present case is that of the status of "preferred supplier", which is more in the nature of describing a de facto trading relationship. The expression "status of preferred supplier" connotes a sense of commercial practice rather than contractual commitment. It is a long way from providing a platform on which to construct any type of "right of first refusal".

'There are a number of alternative formulations of the concepts of "preferred supplier" and "right of first refusal". Two of these formulations are discussed below.

'According to the first formulation, the supplier has the right of first refusal to supply the needs of the retailer. If the parties cannot agree on quality, volume, price and terms, the retailer can then buy from other persons at the same price and on the same terms as it wanted from the supplier. If the retailer varies the terms favourably to the third party, i e other potential suppliers, the retailer must give the supplier the opportunity to sell on such equally favourable terms as its offer to the third party. It is only if the supplier still refuses, that the retailer can purchase from the third party on those terms. The retailer is otherwise bound not to purchase from anyone else.

'According to the second formulation, if the retailer decides to buy any fresh fruit and vegetable produce, it must give the supplier the first chance of supplying it as a matter of commercial practice. If the supplier refuses, the retailer may then go to the market at large even if it is on more favourable terms. There is no obligation on the retailer to offer the more favourable terms to the supplier before purchasing from the third party supplier.

'These two formulations clearly illustrate the very significant differences that can exist as to the meaning of the concept of "right of first refusal" and even more so as to the concept of "preferred supplier". The vague and indeterminate nature of the expression "preferred supplier" makes it unlikely that there was any point reached in communications between Nationwide Holdings and Franklins, or evidenced by their subsequent conduct, whereby there arose any binding obligation or right in either party

'In this case, Nationwide Holdings submits that it was entitled to compel Franklins to make an offer to it to supply all or any part of its needs for fruit and vegetables before approaching anyone else. The evidence makes reference to the concept of having "earned" the status of a preferred supplier, which is really indicative of satisfactory commercial performance. There is no reference in the evidence, however, to a contract preventing Franklins from approaching any other supplier without providing a prior opportunity for Nationwide Holdings to supply it with produce, such that Nationwide Holdings could enforce a restriction on Franklins from approaching any other supplier.

'The tentative evidence relied on by Franklins in relation to the meaning of the expression "preferred supplier" is set out in the affidavit of Mr Cassone at [34], which reads as follows:

> In addition, I may have said words to Mr Prestia the effect of which were "[w]e want you with us for the long-term. Keep supplying the quality." At that time, Nationwide Australia was a "preferred supplier" in respect of certain varieties of fruit and vegetables for the Big Fresh stores. The term "preferred supplier" in the fruit and vegetable industry refers to an informal way of designating a particular category of suppliers that retailers intend to use on a regular basis. The "preferred supplier" is generally the first supplier the buyer approaches when purchasing produce. Provided that the quality of the produce supplied is of a standard acceptable to the buyer, that the quantity required by the buyer can be provided by the supplier, that the price of the produce is competitive, and that the services provided by the supplier are reliable, the buyer will purchase produce from the "preferred supplier". I was pleased with the quality of Nationwide Australia's produce and service at this stage. I was also of the view that, so long as Nationwide Australia continued to supply quality produce, Franklins would probably continue to place its business with the company. However, Franklins did not bind itself to Nationwide Australia for the long-term by agreeing to a formal arrangement.

'It should be noted that Mr Cassone's statements fall far short of suggesting a "right of first refusal". Instead, Mr Cassone's statements refer to an informal industry practice of designating a particular category of suppliers who have demonstrated satisfactory performance.' *Nationwide Produce (Holdings) Pty Ltd (in liquidation) v Linknarf Limited (in liquidation)* [2005] FCAFC 129 at [56]–[68], per Tamberlin, Conti and Jacobson JJ; BC200505043

Australia 'In *Beecham Group Ltd v Bristol Laboratories Pty Ltd* (1967–8) 118 CLR 618 the High Court, in respect of the matters to be considered in an application for an interlocutory injunction, said at 622:

> The first is whether the plaintiff has made out a prima facie case, in the sense that if the evidence remains as it is there is a probability that at the trial of the action the plaintiff will be held entitled to relief.

'The notion of probability in this setting was explored by Mahoney JA (with whom Glass and Samuels JA agreed) in *Shercliff v Engadine Acceptance Corp Pty Ltd* (1978) 1 NSWLR 729 at 737.

' "Probability" may mean "more likely than not". In that sense the use of the expression prima facie sometimes describes the sufficiency of evidence required to shift the burden of disproof to the other party.

'However "probability" may also denote a lesser standard of satisfaction. In *Koufos v C . Czarnikow Ltd* [1969] 1 AC 350 Lord Reid, in considering remoteness of damage and the principles of *Hadley v Baxendale* (1854) 9 Exch 341, used the words "not unlikely" as denoting a degree of probability considerably less than an even chance but nevertheless not very unusual and easily foreseeable (at 383).

'I have referred to this case simply to show that "probability" does not always mean "more likely than not" but may, both in the common and technical use, embrace a notion of sense of persuasion somewhat less than an even balance.

'Mahoney JA also thought so because in *Shercliff v Engadine Acceptance Corp Pty Ltd* he said at 736:

> In my opinion the "probability" to which the High Court was referring, was a probability in the sense to which Lord Reid referred and I think that the degree of probability or likelihood of success is simply that which the Court thinks sufficient, in the particular case, to warrant preservation of the status quo.'

Shaw v Attorney General for the State of Western Australia and Anor [2005] WASC 149 at [57]–[61], per McKechnie J; BC200504712

PRELIMINARY HEARING

New Zealand [Summary Proceedings Act 1957, s 158.] 'When the provisions of Part V are considered in context, it is clear in my view, that Part V is a code which deals with the summonsing of, the conduct of and the disposition of a preliminary hearing in those cases where the charge is laid indictably. It contemplates that a proceeding commences with the information and that the defendant is either then summonsed or brought on a warrant to the Court to answer that information. As part of that process there is a deposition hearing and if the police are not in a position to proceed with the taking of depositions at the time the defendant is brought before the Court, there is power to adjourn given by s 152.' *Robinson v North Shore District Court* [1997] 1 NZLR 64 at 68, per Paterson J

PREMISE

Australia 'In our view, the relevant definition of a "premise" is "a basis stated or assumed from which a conclusion is drawn" – see the *Macquarie Dictionary* 2nd ed 1992 at p 1341.' *Aala v Minister for Immigration and Multicultural Affairs* BC200203343; [2002] FCAFC 204 at [47], per Gray, Carr and Goldberg JJ

PREMISES

[The Food Act 1984 is largely repealed. The definition is now contained in the Food Safety Act 1990, s 1(3), as follows.] 'Premises' includes any place, any vehicle, stall or moveable structure and, for such purposes as may be specified in an order made by the Ministers, any slip or aircraft of a description so specified.

[Clause II(9) in a lease granted in 1924 provided that 'no goods shall at any time be or remain placed outside the said premises which or of any nature which the Lessor shall have forbidden to be or to remain so placed'. As a consequence of alterations, it became possible to park a motor car on covered areas which had formerly been open basement areas, and for many years the occupiers had parked one or more motor cars on the skylights. The lessor gave formal notice in reliance on cl II(9), that it was forbidden with immediate effect to place any motor vehicles, motor cycles or other goods outside of the premises demised to it pursuant to the lease. The question arose on appeal whether the words 'outside the said premises' meant outside the building even though within the demise, thereby incorporating the area where the vehicles were parked, as the trial judge had held.] '[28] Whilst not referring to *Alice in Wonderland*, both counsel seem to be agreed that in the same lease, indeed in the same clause of the lease, the word "premises" may bear one meaning at one time and another at another time. In our judgment it is clear that

"premises" is a chameleon-like word which takes its meaning from its context. Since it can mean almost anything the task of the court is to give the word the meaning which it most naturally bears in its context and as reasonably understood by the commercial men who entered into the agreement.

...

'[52] ... [W]here do we find the meaning of this phrase? In the context of the lease as a whole the words tend almost invariably to mean the whole of the demised premises. In the context of the preceding parts of sub-cl (9) their natural reference to the building is displaced by the lack of consistency and there is much uncertainty as to that meaning. We are driven reluctantly to conclude that the uncertainty pervades the meaning of the clause we have to construe. We are left in real doubt as to what was intended. It follows that the expression is ambiguous and, very much as the last resort, we are driven to construe the clause against the grantor. "Outside the said premises" means outside the boundaries of the premises the subject of the demise.' *Spring House (Freehold) Ltd v Mount Cook Land Ltd* [2001] EWCA Civ 1833 at [28], [52], [2002] 2 All ER 822 at 831, 836, CA, per Ward and Rix LJJ

[The appellant tenant had an 'eggshell tenancy' of a ground floor shop in a building. The tenant applied for the grant of a new tenancy under Pt II of the Landlord and Tenant Act 1954. The landlord opposed the application on the ground set out in s 30(1)(f), namely that it intended to demolish the "premises" comprised in the holding.] '[3] This case concerns what is commonly referred to as an "eggshell tenancy" because the demise is of the internal skin of the part of the building occupied by the tenant. No load-bearing parts of the building are included in the demise. Counsel confirmed that this was not an uncommon type of business lease. However they did not refer us to any reported case under the 1954 Act relating to such a lease.

...

'[24] It follows that in this case the landlord has to show that he intends to demolish or reconstruct the premises comprised in the property comprised in the tenancy that is occupied by the tenant. This is not necessarily the same as the "demised premises" because: (i) "property" is a word which, as its definition in s 205 of the Law of Property Act 1925 shows, is capable of a wider meaning than the extent of the "demised premises" and thus the eggshell, and (ii) "occupied" is also a word with a breadth of meaning. The definition of "property" in s 205 of the 1925 Act is that it "includes any thing in action, and any interest in real or personal property". Naturally that definition does not apply but in my judgment it reflects the natural breadth of meaning of the word and provides a pointer to the extent of its meaning when used to describe the subject matter of a tenancy. Leading counsel for the tenant pointed out that normally a person does not "occupy" a right or an easement; I agree. Further it seems to me that this is reflected and catered for by s 32(3) which recognises the possibility of there being "rights enjoyed ... with the holding" and that they need to be included in the new tenancy which s 32(1) requires to be a new tenancy of the holding.

...

'[63] The tenant argues that the judge was wrong to hold that works intended by the landlord were within s 30(1)(f) because in the context of works of demolition (and reconstruction) the word "premises" in s 30(1)(f) applies only to parts of a built structure which perform some structural function.

'[64] In support of this argument the tenant accepts that it means giving "premises" a narrower meaning than it has in s 23 where the tenant accepts it includes open land (see *Coppen v Bruce-Smith* (1999) 77 P & CR 239 at 245). It follows that the tenant accepts that the possible breadth of meaning of the word "premises" in s 30(1)(f) is wide enough to include open land but points out that (i) it is difficult to see how open land could be demolished or reconstructed, and (ii) the second part of s 30(1)(f) (which refers to substantial work of construction on the holding) could apply to open land and from those points argues that there is nothing odd in a result that both parts of s 30(1)(f) should not apply to the subject matter of all tenancies covered by the 1954 Act and thus that the first part should apply to some tenancies and not to others. On the assumption, but without deciding, that open land cannot be demolished I agree. But this does not mean that the dividing line between what is included and excluded from the first part of s 30(1)(f) should be drawn where the tenant asserts, when as the tenant correctly accepts the word "premises" can include open land and thus to my mind can also include an eggshell within a building.

'[65] Further in my judgment the ordinary meaning of the words demolish and reconstruct is wide enough to apply to an eggshell. In other words, in my judgment in this case the eggshell (and thus in this case the outside skin of the enclosed shop that is occupied by the tenant and includes the floor, the ceiling, the plaster and tiling and the shop front) is capable of being demolished

and reconstructed. In my judgment strong support for this view is found in *City Offices (Regent Street) Ltd v Europa Acceptance Group plc* [1990] 1 EGLR 63 (in particular at 65). I accept that that case was concerned with the construction of the lease in question so that the court was giving meaning to the phrase "redevelopment or reconstruction of the demised premises" as used in the lease itself and thus in circumstances in which the parties to the lease plainly intended it to apply to the eggshell demised. The *City Offices* case would therefore be a closer analogy with cl 5 of the lease in this case (see [11], above) albeit that that clause does not refer to works on, or to, the demised premises. None the less in my judgment the *City Offices* case provides clear support for the view that as a matter of language an eggshell with no structural element can, as found in that case, be reconstructed and thus, in my view, demolished.

'[66] To support the argument that in the context of s 30(1)(f) of the 1954 Act "premises" applies only to parts of a built structure which perform some structural function leading counsel for the tenant referred us to a number of authorities, these included the two cases referred to in the *City Offices* case ...

'[67] As I have already mentioned, none of these cases deal with an eggshell tenancy and thus one where a part of a building is demised but the demise excludes the load-bearing structure of the building and includes nothing which performs a structural function in relation to the building. When that is taken into account, in my judgment none of the passages in those cases are authority for the proposition advanced on behalf of the tenant that in s 30(1)(f) "premises" refers only to parts of a built structure which perform some structural function.

...

'[69] Here any load-bearing parts of the building and its enclosing walls are excluded from the demised premises but they include the floor, ceiling and roller-blind. In my judgment having regard to the language of s 30(1)(f) and the purpose of the 1954 Act the works intended by the landlord (leaving aside the work relating to the roller-blind which involves demolition or reconstruction— see the *Bewlay* case [*Bewlay (Tobacconists) Ltd v British Bata Shoe Co Ltd* [1958] 3 All ER 652]) are works which involve demolition of the premises comprising the holding, or a substantial part of those premises, because, either: (i) as found by the judge they involve the demolition of the eggshell that was demised, or (ii) they involve the demolition of that eggshell together with the rights of support which render the eggshell demised capable of occupation and use by a tenant. For the purposes of deciding this appeal it does not matter which.' *Pumperninks of Piccadilly Ltd v Land Securities plc* [2002] EWCA Civ 621 at [3], [24], [63]–[67], [69], [2002] 3 All ER 609 at 612, 618, 631–632, CA, per Charles J

[Under s 146(2)(a) of the Water Industry Act 1991, an undertaker is entitled to charge for the connection to a water supply of 'premises' which had never at any previous time been connected to a supply of water provided for domestic purposes by a water undertaker. Subsection (2)(b) contained a similar provision in respect of connection to a public sewer. The question arose whether in regard to two buildings converted into 109 flats, the original buidings or the separate flats were to be regarded as the 'premises'. The Court of Appeal considered the purpose and scope of s 146(2).] '[36] … In my judgment, the interpretation of s 146(2) has to be considered not only by reference to the word "premises" but also by reference to the use there of the word "connection". "Premises" is an ordinary word whose precise meaning is to be derived from its context. It is to be noted that neither "premises" nor "connection" or "connected" are defined in the definition section of this Act, s 219. "Premises", it seems to me, will usually include buildings but may not be limited to buildings and might in some circumstances refer to a place with few or no buildings on it. Premises may in its context also consist of a part of a larger building. A garden centre or a builder's merchant may have premises which include one or more buildings but the premises may extend to the larger site used for the keeping of plants or bricks and sand. A garden centre might conceivably have premises with no buildings on it at all. The premises of a farming business might consist of a group of farm buildings but it would be a somewhat strange context perhaps, though not impossible, which included 100 acres of fields as part of the farm premises. The premises of a large corporation might in context consist of the entirety of a large office block. The premises of a small firm or company might consist of one or two rooms on an upper floor of a much larger building. In the general context of the supply of water and sewerage services premises are likely to include buildings or parts of buildings to which the water is supplied and from which the sewage is taken away. There are a number of references to premises in various other sections of this statute. Those include, but are not perhaps limited to, ss 41, 45, 52 and 64. These show that in this statute

the expression "premises" is used in various contexts with various contextual shades of meaning.

'[37] In my judgment, as I have said, the relevant meaning of s 146(2)(a) and (b) is to be derived not only from the use of the word "premises" but from its use in the context of the word "connection". The full relevant expression is—

"a charge for the connection to a water supply of premises which have never at any previous time … been connected to a supply of water provided for domestic purposes by a water undertaker …"

I think that the heading of s 146 may be misleading. At first blush, it appears to refer to the making of a physical connection so that the charge would be a charge for doing so. But the undertaker does not have to go to s 146(2) to be able to charge the costs of the physical connection. Section 45(6) provides the power to make such charge for water and ss 106 and 107 do so also for sewerage. Section 146(2) is concerned, I think, with the connection to the water and sewerage systems of premises which have not previously been so connected and must include new premises which are likely to place an additional burden on the system as a whole. If the premises are in this sense new premises, there is I think no need to establish positively that there will be a volumetric additional burden. It may be taken that in the round there will be. The section applies to a new housing development on what was formerly an unoccupied site. It would probably not apply to a modest alteration to an existing house which did not constitute the building of new premises. Where existing buildings are converted, it will be a question of fact and degree whether the result is or includes the construction and connection of premises which have never previously been connected, or whether the conversion retains the identity of premises which existed and were connected before the conversion took place …

'[38] On the facts of the present case the 109 flats were new premises which had never previously been connected and the claimants were entitled to make a charge for each of them under s 146(2). Although the expression "infrastructure charge" does not appear in the statute, I am satisfied that the charge to which s 146(2) refers is in the nature of a contribution to the capital and maintenance cost of providing services, subject to the additional demand which the connection of premises not previously connected must in general generate. I reach this conclusion without reference to Hansard or to condition C of the claimants' conditions of appointment. Mr Watson did not persuade me that condition C was properly available as an aid to construing s 146(2) but it is not necessary for me to decide.' *Thames Water Utilities Ltd v Hampstead Homes (London) Ltd* [2002] EWCA Civ 1487 at [36]–[38], [2003] 3 All ER 1304, CA, per May LJ

Australia [Section 23(3)(c) of the Industrial Relations Act 1979 (WA) states that the Western Australian Industrial Relations Commission shall not make an order empowering a representative of an organization to enter any part of the premises of an employer.] 'The word "premises" is an example of a word which started out with one meaning and has now gained a second meaning. It is important to trace its history because that history explains why the word "premises" does not bear a precise meaning, but is a word which bears different meanings according to context.

'The origin of the word is Latin, entering the English language probably through the Law French. The Latin *prae missa*, means a proposition set out before. It is used in logic to refer to the parts of a syllogism being previously stated. Sometimes in that use it is spelt "premisses".

'The word "premises" was adopted for use in conveyancing deeds to save constant reference to parcels of land within deeds, conveniently referring to "the premises" as meaning land originally described in detail at the commencement of the deed.

'Because of its pervasive use in conveyancing deeds, over the centuries the word "premises" has come to apply to real property of one sort or another. A history of the evolution of the word is conveniently set out by Lord Goddard CJ in *Gardiner v Sevenoaks Rural District Council* [1950] 2 All ER 84 at 85; see also *Beacon Life & Fire Assurance Co v Gibb* (1862) 1 Moore NS 73, per Lord Chelmsford at 97; 15 ER 630 at 639. Because of the nature of its evolution, the word "premises" is a noun, capable of varying meanings, depending on the context in which it is used. It generally denotes a connection with real property, but not always.

'In *Turner v York Motors Pty Ltd* (1951) 85 CLR 55, the High Court considered, amongst other things, the use of the expression "prescribed premises" within the meaning of s 8 of the Landlord and Tenant Amendment Act 1948–1949 (NSW). It was also concerned with whether the tenancy was a tenancy at will or from month to month. Williams J dissented on this latter question. Both he and

Dixon J considered that "prescribed premises" as defined did not include bare land. At 75 Dixon J said:

"The word 'premises' is no doubt a vague one but in legislation of this sort there are great advantages in a test of its application which is objective and consists in a readily ascertainable physical fact."

'Williams J at 83 said:

"The word 'premises' is used in a popular sense and in this sense has a wide meaning. It is wide enough to include bare land. Its true meaning in any particular statute must be ascertained from the context in which it appears and from an examination of the scope and purpose of the statute as a whole."

'Even though he was in dissent on the main issues in the case, I adopt this statement of Williams J as correctly stating the proper approach to the meaning of the word.

'In *Andrews v Andrews & Meers* [1908] 2 KB 567, Kennedy LJ in a correction to the judgment of Buckley LJ, which Buckley LJ accepted, said:

"I do not quite accept my brother Buckley's view about 'premises' being necessarily confined to land. There are cases which indicate that 'premises' may have a wider meaning."

'There are many cases which show that the word "premises" as used in statute may be given different meanings according to the purpose of the statute. Sometimes the question whether a particular place is "premises" is a legal question but usually it is a question of mixed law and fact. In construing the Industrial Relations Act, it is not helpful to refer generally to the cases because they are merely examples of different meanings to be ascribed to the word "premises" in different contexts. They do not provide a prescriptive meaning in the Industrial Relations Act but merely confirm that the meaning may vary from statute to statute. Some assistance can be gained from *FCT v Reynolds* (1987) 77 ALR 543 per Wilcox J at 558:

"At first sight it may appear incongruous to regard as a single set of premises to substantial areas of land, upon which different industrial activities are carried on, and their linking corridor 51 kms in length. But I see no reason why the term 'premises' in the relevant definition should be read so as to exclude such a result. The term 'premises' is capable of application to vacant land. There is no implication in the definition that all parts of the premises be held subject to the same instrument of title, or even the same tenure, and there is no limitation as to size. Where a particular person holds a parcel of contiguous land, regardless of title or tenure, for the purpose of conducting a single integrated activity, it is not inappropriate to describe the whole of that land as a single set of premises. As was submitted on behalf of the respondents, even if the conveyor itself is used neither for mining operation nor for the treatment of mining products the whole area actually occupied by the respondents constitutes the premises within which they conduct an integrated business activity consisting of those disparate parts".

'This illustrates the breadth that the word "premises" may connote in particular circumstances. By analogy this breadth may include multiple tenants or occupants of the same premises.' *Molina v Zaknich* [2001] BC200106701; WASCA 337 at [40]–[50] per McKechnie J

PREMIUM

Insurance

[For 25 Halsbury's Laws (4th edn) para 458 see now 25 Halsbury's Laws (4th edn) (2003 Reissue) para 129.]

Rent

[For 27 Halsbury's Laws (4th edn) para 759 see now 27(1) Halsbury's Laws (4th edn) (Reissue) para 782.]

Australia 'The word is not defined in the [Commercial Tenancy (Retail Shops) Agreement Act 1985 (WA)], but in ordinary parlance means, in the context of landlord and tenant, any money in addition to the rent, paid by the tenant as an incentive for the grant of a new lease or renewal of the existing lease.' *O F Gamble Pty Ltd v Whitemore Pty Ltd* (1990) 2 WAR 327 at 330–331, per Com Anderson QC

PREPARATION

[The Food Act 1984 is largely repealed. The definition is now contained in the Food Safety Act 1990, s 53(1), as follows.] 'Preparation', in relation to food, includes manufacture and any form of processing or treatment, and 'preparation

for sale' includes packaging, and 'prepare for sale, shall be construed accordingly.

Australia [Schedule 3 to the Customs Tariff Act 1987 (Cth) contains a heading 3808 specifying that herbicides put up in forms or packings for retail sale or as 'preparations' are subject to customs duty.] 'In essence the test expounded in *Re Bayer Australia Ltd and Collector of Customs* (*NSW*) (1985) 7 ALN N84 is that the product cannot be a preparation of an intermediate nature not presented in the form ready to be marketed. The learned primary judge accepted this definition and held that: "A preparation is a presentation of a substance which is ready to be used for a particular application or purpose". In our respectful opinion this is the correct interpretation of the word "preparation" in heading 3808.' *Collector of Customs v Chemark Services Pty Ltd* (1993) 42 FCR 585 at 593; 114 ALR 531 at 539, per cur

PRESCRIBED FORM OF IDENTIFICATION

Canada 'The real issue is precisely the one identified by the trial judge in her reasons: "What is an issue in the matter before this court is whether it was acceptable I.D." That issue falls to be determined on the interpretation to be given to the words "prescribed form of identification" in s 3(3) of the Act.

'By O Reg 613/94, the Ontario government has defined the contents of "prescribed form of identification". Section 1 of the regulation states that "[t]he following forms of identification are prescribed for the purposes of subsection 3(3) of the Act." Five forms of identification are then listed – an Ontario driver's licence with a photograph of the person to whom the licence is issued, a Canadian passport, a Canadian citizenship card including photograph, a Canadian Armed Forces card, and a photo card issued by the Liquor Licence Board of Ontario.

'In my view, subject to a minor qualification I will make at the conclusion of these reasons, these five items constitute an exhaustive list of the forms of identification that a vendor of tobacco products may examine when deciding whether a prospective customer is entitled to buy a package of cigarettes. I reach this conclusion for several reasons.

'First, the dictionary definition of the word "prescribed" suggests exclusivity and compulsion. In her judgment, the trial judge stated:

""Prescribed" not being defined in the *Interpretation Act*, I then verified the definitions in

the dictionary. The dictionary definitions of "prescribed" are as follows:
1. "To set down as a direction or rule to be followed; to lay down the rules of the law." – Canadian Law Dictionary.
2. "To lay down as a guide, direction, or rule of action." – Webster's Collegiate Dictionary.
3. "To lay down or impose authoritatively." – Oxford English Dictionary."

'This is a fair selection of dictionary definitions. Having set them out in her reasons, the trial judge did not state explicitly how she interpreted these definitions. In my view, the words "rule to be followed", "rule of action" and "impose authoritatively" suggest something that is mandatory. In the context of s 3(3) of the Act that means that a vendor must insist that a customer produce one of the five statutory forms of identification.' *R v Seaway Gas & Fuel Ltd* (2000) 183 DLR (4th) 412 at 419, 420, Ont CA, per MacPherson JA

PRESENCE OR HEARING OF THE DEFENDANT

Australia 'Given the modern purpose of committal proceedings, the words "in the presence or hearing of the defendant" should not be treated as having only a formal significance. When regard is had to the purpose of committal proceedings and the context of the Justices Act [1928 (NT)], particularly s 110, those words are to be construed as meaning that the defendant is able to understand what "facts and circumstances" are being alleged against him or her. The text of s 106 and s 110 and the nature of the proceedings indicate that it is insufficient that the evidence is given in the physical presence or hearing of the defendant. Rather it is necessary "that the defendant, by reason of his presence, should be able to understand the proceedings and decide what witnesses he wishes to call, whether or not to give evidence and, if so, upon what matters relevant to the case against him." [*Kunnath v The State* [1993] 1 WLR 1315 at 1319; [1993] 4 All ER 30 at 35].' *Ebatarinja v Deland SM* (1998) 157 ALR 385 at 391; 72 ALJR 1499; BC9804989, per Gaudron, McHugh, Gummow, Hayne and Callinan JJ

PRESENTED

'[31] Until a simpler regime is introduced, the following guidance may be helpful. (1)

Section 111(2) of the Employment Rights Act 1996 speaks of "presenting" a complaint to a tribunal. It is now well established that a complaint is "presented" when it arrives at the Central Office of Employment Tribunals or an Office of the Tribunals (the Office). (2) If a complainant or his/her agent proves that it was impossible to present a complaint in this way before the end of the time prescribed by s 111(2)(a)—for example because the Office was found to be locked at a weekend and it did not have a letter box—then it will be possible to argue that it was not reasonably practicable for the complaint to be presented within the prescribed period. (3) If a complainant chooses to present a complaint by sending it by post, presentation will be assumed to have been effected, unless the contrary is proved, at the time when the letter would be delivered in the ordinary course of post (see, by analogy, s 7 of the Interpretation Act 1978). (4) If the letter is sent by first class post, it is now legitimate to adapt the approach contained in CPR 6.7 and conclude that in the ordinary course of post it will be delivered on the second day after it was posted (excluding Sundays, Bank Holidays, Christmas Day and Good Friday, being days when post is not normally delivered). (5) If the letter does not arrive at the time when it would be expected to arrive in the ordinary course of post, but is unexpectedly delayed, a tribunal may conclude that it was not reasonably practicable for the complaint to be presented within the prescribed period. (6) If a form is date-stamped on a Monday by a tribunal office so as to be outside a three-month period which ends on the Saturday or Sunday, it will be open to a tribunal to find as a fact that it was posted by first class post not later than the Thursday and arrived on the Saturday, alternatively to extend time as a matter of discretion if satisfied that the letter was posted by first class post not later than the Thursday. (7) This regime does not allow for any unusual subjective expectation, whether based on inside knowledge of the postal system or on lay experience of what happens in practice, to the effect that a letter posted by first class post may arrive earlier than the second day (excluding Sundays etc: see (4), above) after it is posted. The "normal and expected" result of posting a letter must be objectively, not subjectively, assessed and it is that the letter will arrive at its destination in the ordinary course of post. As the present case shows, a complainant knows that he/she is taking a risk if the complaint is posted by first class post on the day before the guillotine falls, and it would be absurd to hold that it was not reasonably practicable for it to be presented in time if it arrives in the ordinary course of post on the second day after it was posted. Nothing unexpected will have occurred. The post will have taken its usual course.

'[32] For the avoidance of doubt, the strict litigation rule in *Godwin*'s case [*Godwin v Swindon Borough Council* [2001] EWCA Civ 1478, [2001] 4 All ER 641] does not apply in employment tribunal cases. If in such a case a complainant takes a chance and the letter containing the complaint happens to arrive at the Office on the day after it was posted and therefore within the permitted three-month period, it will have been presented in time.' *Sealy v Consignia plc* [2002] EWCA Civ 878 at [32], [2002] 3 All ER 801 at 811–812, per Hart J

PRESENTATION

Australia 'The word "presentation" has numerous nuances of meaning. It may mean, for example, "the action of presenting or introducing ..." or it may mean that "... style or manner in which something is presented, described or explained" (The *New Shorter Oxford English Dictionary*, Fourth Ed, 1993). In its former sense, it includes the act of offering, delivering or giving and is frequently used in that sense in the bankruptcy jurisdiction (e.g. *Purden Pty Ltd v Registrar in Bankruptcy* (1982) 43 ALR 512)... It is, however, a word whose meaning will depend upon its context (*Bartlett v Holmes* (1853) 13 CB 630, 138 ER 1347, per Jervis CJ).' *Re Bullivant's Natural Health Products Pty Ltd and Health and Family Services* (1996) 43 ALD 305 at 316, per Dep Pres S A Forgie and Mem Smithurst

PRESERVE

[Section 277(8) of the Town and County Planning Act 1971 (repealed; see now the Planning (Listed Buildings and Conservation Areas) Act 1990, s 72) provided that where any area was for the time being designated as a conservation area, special attention should be paid to the desirability of 'preserving' or enhancing its character or appearance.] 'Neither "preserving" nor "enhancing" is used in any meaning other than its ordinary English meaning. The court is not here concerned with enhancement, but the ordinary meaning of "preserve" as a transitive verb is "to keep safe from harm or injury; to keep in safety, save, take care of, guard": Oxford English Dictionary, 2nd edn (1989). In my judgment character or appearance can be said to be preserved where they are not harmed.

Cases may be envisaged where development would itself make a positive contribution to preservation of character or appearance. A work of reinstatement might be such ... The statutorily desirable object of preserving the character or appearance of an area is achieved either by a positive contribution to preservation or by development which leaves character or appearance unharmed, that is to say preserved.' *South Lakeland District Council v Secretary of State for the Environment* [1992] 1 All ER 45 at 49, CA, per Mann LJ

PREVENTIVE

Canada '60 In my view, nothing inherent in the Commission's public interest jurisdiction, as it was considered by this Court in *Asbestos*, *supra*, prevents the Commission from considering general deterrence in making an order. To the contrary, it is reasonable to view general deterrence as an appropriate, and perhaps necessary, consideration in making orders that are both protective and preventative. Ryan J.A. recognized this in her dissent: "The notion of general deterrence is neither punitive nor remedial. A penalty that is meant to generally deter is a penalty designed to discourage or hinder like behaviour in others" (para. 125).

61 The *Oxford English Dictionary* (2nd ed. 1989), vol. XII, defines "preventive" as "[t]hat anticipates in order to ward against; precautionary; that keeps from coming or taking place; that acts as a hindrance or obstacle". A penalty that is meant to deter generally is a penalty that is designed to keep an occurrence from happening; it discourages similar wrongdoing in others. In a word, a general deterrent is preventative.' *Re Cartaway Resources Corp* [2004] SCJ No 22, [2004] 1 SCR 672, per LeBel J

PRICE

Australia 'The question, which arises under this section, is whether the delivery charge was part of the price for the goods. There is an inclusive definition of "price" in s 4 of the [Trade Practices Act 1974 (Cth) (TPA)]. "Price" includes a charge of any description.

'In *Australian Competition and Consumer Commission v Nationwide News Pty Ltd* (1996) ATPR ¶41–519 at 42,493–42,494, Heerey J construed the word "price" in s 53(e) narrowly. His Honour said that "price" means the money consideration for the goods. His Honour observed that the word "price" is well understood in sale of goods of legislation and he gave it the same meaning in s 53(e) of the TPA.

'Although his Honour did not refer in the judgment to the definition in s 4 of the TPA, it seems to me that his Honour was applying that definition of "price" to the word appearing in s 53(e). It follows that even though the definition of "price" in s 4 of the TPA includes a charge of any description, on the approach taken by his Honour, the charge must be part of the money consideration for the purchase of the goods. I respectfully adopt this approach to the construction of the word "price" in s 53(e) of the TPA.' *Australian Competition and Consumer Commission v Dell Computer Pty Ltd* (2002) ASAL ¶55–082; (2002) ATPR ¶41–878; BC200203645; [2002] FCA 847 at [35]–[37], per Jacobson J

PRICE LIST

Australia 'In ordinary parlance, a "price-list" is a list of articles for sale, with a statement of the prices sought for them; of course, such prices may not be those at which purchasers agree to buy. The word "catalogue" has a wider meaning. The Oxford English Dictionary definition includes as a presently obsolete or archaic meaning "a list, register, or complete enumeration"; it goes on: "Now usually distinguished from a mere list or enumeration, by systematic or methodical arrangement, alphabetical or other order, and often by the addition of brief particulars, descriptive, or aiding identification, indicative of locality, position, date, price, or the like".

'A price list is thus a species of catalogue. But, as a list of articles for sale, a price list ordinarily will be directed at activities in trade or commerce, treating that term as embracing commercial dealings with new and used articles. Not all catalogues will have this character, as a matter of ordinary usage.' *Federal Commissioner of Taxation v Thomson Australian Holdings Pty Ltd* (1989) 87 ALR 682 at 692, per Gummow J

PRIMA FACIE

Australia 'The phrase can have various shades of meaning in particular statutory contexts but the ordinary meaning of the phrase "prima facie" is: "At first sight; on the face of it; as appears at first sight without investigation" [Oxford English Dictionary, 2nd ed (1989), vol XII at 470–471].' *North Ganalanja Aboriginal Corp (on behalf of the Waanyi People) v Queensland* (1996) 185 CLR

595 at 615–616; 135 ALR 225 at 235; BC9600680 at 14, per Brennan CJ, Dawson, Toohey, Gaudron and Gummow JJ

PRIMA FACIE GROUNDS

Australia '... The ordinary meaning of the words prima facie is "at first sight; on the face of it; as appears at first sight without investigation": *North Ganalanja Aboriginal Corp v Queensland* (1996) 185 CLR 595 at 615–16; *Macquarie Dictionary*. In the present context, the phrase "prima facie grounds" means, in my opinion, that there is a legal basis for the claim and that there is some evidence referred to in the affidavit in support of the application which, if accepted, would be capable of sustaining the proceedings: c f *North Ganalanga* (supra) at 639; *May v O'Sullivan* (1955) 92 CLR 654 at 658.

'... An arguable case is not merely one which is capable of being argued, but one which has some prospect of success: *Dempster v National Companies and Securities Commission* (1993) 9 WAR 215 at 261. If prima facie grounds exist, then they will be "arguable".' *Hunter v Cmr of Police* BC200300042; [2003] WASC 10 at [18], [19], per Pullin J

PRIMARILY DEPENDENT

Australia [Section 4 of the Motor Accidents (Compensation) Act (NT) provides 'dependent child', in relation to a person, means a child of the person, or a child in relation to whom the person stands or stood in loco parentis, who is not the spouse of another person and who

   (a) has not attained the age of 16 years; or

   (b) having attained that age but not having attained the age of 21 years, is a full-time student or is physically or mentally handicapped,

   and is primarily dependent on the person for financial support.']

'[8] There is no ambiguity in the wording of the definition. When regard is had to the scheme of the Act in its entirety, it is readily apparent that the Legislature intended to compensate only those in specified categories who were "primarily dependent" on the deceased for financial support. The applicant must establish both that the child had not attained the age of 16 years and that, at the time of the death of the deceased, the child was primarily dependent on the deceased for financial support.

...

'[46] The ordinary and natural meaning of the word "primarily" is usually equated with the word "principally". The Oxford English Dictionary (2nd Edition) defines "primarily" in the following terms:

1. In the first order in time or temporal sequence; at first, in the first instance, firstly; originally
2. With reference to other than temporal order: in the first place, first of all, pre-eminently, chiefly, principally; essentially.

'[47] The Macquarie Dictionary defines primarily as meaning "in the first place; chiefly; principally".

'[48] Superficially there is some attraction in the submission of the respondent that the word "primarily" requires a comparison between sources of financial support and a conclusion as to which single source is the primary or principal source. By way of analogy, ordinarily it might be thought that if a person is wholly dependent upon another person for financial support, that fact would exclude partial or complete dependence upon a third person. However, in the context of workers compensation legislation, numerous authorities including *Aafjes v Kearney* have held that a dependant may be wholly dependent upon more than one person. Perhaps the answer is found in the remarks of Mason J in *Aafjes v Kearney* [212]:

> The dominating consideration here and in the United Kingdom is a strong disinclination, founded on common sense, to attribute to the Legislature an intention to deprive an applicant of a claim based on total dependency for support where a legal obligation to provide that support exists which has not been abandoned, merely because the applicant is in receipt of benefits from others, whether proceeding from charity or some other motive.

...

'[51] In the context of the scheme introduced by the Act, in my opinion the Legislature did not contemplate a strict comparison and limitation to a single source of financial support as contended by the respondent. It is not difficult to envisage a circumstance where the principal source of financial support comes jointly from two parents, but other minor financial support is also provided by a third person. In such circumstances it might reasonably be said that the child is primarily dependent upon both parents for financial support. If the respondent's contention is correct, if a child relied upon both parents equally but a court found one parent's contribution to the financial support was greater than the other, albeit by a very small

amount, upon the death of the parent whose contribution was the lesser, the child would be deprived of the benefits under the Act. Such an interpretation does not sit well with the scheme of the Act and the remedial nature of it." *Malbunka v Territory Insurance Office Board* [2004] NTSC 30 at [8], [46]–[48], [51], per Martin CJ; BC200403755

PRINCIPAL PLACE OF RESIDENCE

Australia [In the context of succession.] '[36] ... The ordinary meaning of "residence", according to dictionary definitions, includes "the place of a person's home or habitation; the place where he abides" or "to have one's usual dwelling-place or abode; the circumstance of having one's permanent or usual abode in or at a certain place."

'[37] Courts have been required to consider the concept of "residence" in various different contexts. The connotation of some "permanence" or "settled purpose" seems to be inherent in the concept of residence. However, the precise meaning of expressions such as "residence" and "principal residence" must depend heavily on the context in which they are used.

'[38] [Counsel for the Halls submitted that] I would be assisted by a consideration of cases on the meaning of "principal place of residence" or "principal residence" in the context of taxation and other revenue legislation. Various factors are considered in that context, including: whether it is the place the person actually resides; how often the person is present at the premises and spends the night there; whether the premises are used as a business; what connection they have with any other place of residence; where the person "eats and sleeps and has a settled abode"; continuity of living arrangements; use of electricity and services; the presence of furniture. In stamp duty cases at least, it appears that the intention of the relevant person is a relevant, although not a dominant, factor in deciding the factual question as to whether or not a place can be described as a person's principal place of residence. In determining the issue, the Court "has to make a common sense assessment taking into account a number of varying and even conflicting circumstances."

'[39] Factors that may be relevant in the interpretation of revenue legislation may be less relevant in the context of interpretation of a will. Obviously, death often occurs at times when a person is seriously ill or incapacitated. At such a time, they may be in hospital or some other form of care. They may have been absent from their principal place of residence and in such care for a short or long time prior to their death. They may have lost full mental capacity at some time prior to their death. It would be undesirable if a testator's otherwise clearly expressed testamentary intention could be thwarted by the mere fact of hospitalisation or relocation from their customary abode prior to death.

'[40] There have been a few first instance decisions that have considered what is meant by expressions such as "my principal place of residence at the date of my death".

'[41] In *Re Rowell* (1982) 31 SASR 361, the testatrix made a will in 1974, by which she made a gift of "my principal place of abode at the time of my death." In 1976 she was admitted as a patient to a psychiatric hospital, suffering from personality disorder and neurotic depression. In January 1977 her affairs came under the control of the Public Trustee, who administered them until her death. She remained in the hospital continuously until her death in 1979. At the time of her death, she owned one house which she had apparently never actually moved into. The house remained unoccupied throughout her period of hospitalisation.

'[42] Wells J held that the house fell within the description "my principal place of abode." His Honour concluded that the testatrix had intended the house to be her abode, but said that her mental illness was "a trick of fate" which prevented her from ever actually going into occupation of the house. He said he would be loath to hold that her 3-year presence in the hospital, and her receipt of sustenance and treatment there, had the effect of making the hospital her abode.

> Furthermore, I am of the opinion that the testatrix's inability, and consequent failure, to enter into occupation of her intended home makes no difference to the operation of the disputed passage in the will. Where a person has established a place of abode, mere physical absence from it does not, in his or her contemplation of it, change its status. It would require the sort of choice or decision referred to above to effect such a change.

...

'[44] In *Re Baulkhorn*, Derrington J considered a gift expressed in terms of "my principal place of residence." The testatrix made her last will in April 1992 and a codicil to that will in September 1992. At the time of execution of her will and codicil, the testatrix owned the Silver Bridle property. She had lived at that property for some years prior to execution of her will, but moved out of it in July 1992 to live in a hostel in Ashmore. As in the present case, the testatrix's agreement with the hostel involved the provision of a room and the supply of meals and access to personal support and care, social activities and security. She sold the Silver Bridle property at the end of 1992. In January 1993, she bought some vacant land at Chisholm Rd and then entered into a contract to have a residence built on the land. On 11 March 1993 she had a serious stroke and was taken from the hostel to a nursing home, where she lapsed into a coma and died on 17 March 1993. The house was constructed to "lock up" stage at the date of her death. She never occupied the Chisholm Rd property. The Chisholm Rd property was the only real property owned by the testatrix at the time of her death.

'[45] Derrington J concluded that the Chisholm Rd property was not the testatrix's principal place of residence, because it was never actually her place of residence and only represented a place of "intended future residence". Had it been her principal place of residence, his Honour's reasoning seems to be that it would not have lost that character merely by reason of her residence at the hostel or the nursing home.

'[46] Derrington J considered the issue again in the case of *Re Willis*. The testatrix devised "the house property in which I shall be residing at the time of my decease." At the time of her death she owned a house property in which she had last resided 13 years before. During the intervening period she lived only in a psychiatric hospital and nursing homes. The house was left vacant throughout that period and her personal belongings were left there. For most of the 13 years she lacked the capacity to have any intention whether to reside in the house or not. Immediately prior to her death she was incapable of residing in the property or of having the intention to do so.

'[47] His Honour held that a will should not be construed in a strictly technical or legalistic sense, but with sensitivity to the factual context of ordinary life and circumstances, and according proper influence to special personal circumstances of the testator having a bearing on the meaning of an expression used in the will. Accordingly, the will should be construed as referring to the "house which I shall keep and maintain as my residence though I cannot physically be there."

'[48] Derrington J arrived at that conclusion notwithstanding that for 13 years prior to her death it would have been practically impossible for the testatrix to physically return to the property, initially for medical reasons and later for psychiatric reasons. His Honour noted the evidence that, until her mental incompetence overtook her, the testatrix intended to reside in the property whenever she could and so intended the relevant devise to apply to it. I agree in particular with the following observations:

> It is a matter of general experience that some people suffer total incapacity in institutions away from their normal home for a long period immediately prior to death and the concept of their residence must be sufficiently flexible to accommodate this.
>
> In such cases, an expression in a will referring to a house in which the testator is residing at the time of death clearly could not be construed as applying only to a house in which there was continuing active daily occupation as a residence. A person of ordinary understanding and knowledge of the factual context would understand that, used in such circumstances in a will, a testator meant the words to carry more than the narrow meaning of the house in which he was or would be in physical occupation.
>
> … It follows that the concept connoted by the word 'residing' should if possible be given such breadth as to accommodate what would seem from all the available material to coincide with the wishes and intent of the testatrix. It is not insignificant that if this is not done the gift would fail because of circumstances outside the control of the testatrix which did not exist at the time when she had her last testamentary capacity.

'[49] I do not disagree with the statements of principle or conclusions expressed in those cases. Obviously each case will depend on its own facts.' *State Trustees Ltd v Hall* [2004] VSC 328 at [36]–[42], [44]–[49], per Hollingworth J; BC200406348

PRINCIPLES OF THE TREATY OF WAITANGI

New Zealand 'Both the [Treaty of Waitangi Act 1975] and the [State-Owned Enterprises Act 1986] refer to the "principles" of the Treaty. In their Lordships' opinion the "principles" are the underlying mutual obligations and responsibilities which the Treaty places on the parties. They reflect the intent of the Treaty as a whole and include, but are not confined to, the express terms of the Treaty. (Bearing in mind the period of time which has elapsed since the date of the Treaty and the very different circumstances to which it now applies, it is not surprising that the Acts do not refer to the terms of the Treaty.) With the passage of time, the "principles" which underlie the Treaty have become much more important than its precise terms.

'Foremost among those "principles" are the obligations which the Crown undertook of protecting and preserving Maori property, including the Maori language as part of taonga, in return for being recognised as the legitimate government of the whole nation by Maori.' *New Zealand Maori Council v A-G* [1994] 1 NZLR 513 at 517, [1994] 1 All ER 623 at 629, PC, per cur

PRIVATE *SEE* PERSONAL AFFAIRS

PRIVATE DWELLING

[The Clean Air Act 1956 has been repealed. The definition is now contained in the Clean Air Act 1993, s 64(4), as follows.] In this Act, except so far as the context otherwise requires, 'private dwelling' means any building or part of a building used or intended to be used as such, and a building or part of a building is not to be taken for the purposes of this Act to be used or intended to be used otherwise than as a private dwelling by reason that a person who resides or is to reside in it is or is to be required or permitted to reside in it in consequence of his employment or of holding an office.

PRIVATE PURPOSES

New Zealand [Need to quote s 15(4) of the Copyright Act 1976.] 'I do not think that it can have been intended that the references to "private purposes" was to allow a taping of broadcasts in order to exploit all or part of their content commercially. It is immaterial that end users, namely customers, may themselves not have intended to use the transcripts for anything other than internal reference. In other words, I equate "private" not only with non-public, but also with an absence of commercial exploitation involving, directly or indirectly, a disposition of the work.' *Television New Zealand Ltd v Newsmonitor Services Ltd* [1994] 2 NZLR 91 at 104, per Blanchard J

PRIVIES

Canada '… I start with the observation that there is a dearth of authority upon the question of who are "privies".

'In the leading text on the subject we read:

A judicial decision *inter partes* operates as an estoppel, in favour of, and against, parties and privies only, not third person or strangers.

...

'Conversely, two persons distinct in name, but substantially identical in title and interest, constitute in law one and the same party for the purposes of estoppel by *res judicata*, as for all others.

...

' "Persons", for the purposes of the rules now under discussion, means an artificial, as well as a natural, person. It therefore comprises corporations, whether aggregate, or sole, such as the Crown, which can take advantage of, and is bound by, any estoppel *per rem judicatam*, as much as any of the Queen's subjects.

'Counsel for Nu-Pharm relied on the *Black's Law Dictionary*, the definition of "privy" which reads as follows:

A person who is in privity with another. One who is a partaker or has any part or interest in any action, matter, or thing. In connection with the doctrine of res judicata, one who, after the commencement of the action, has acquired an interest in the subject matter affected by the judgment through or under one of the parties, as by inheritance, succession, purchase or assignment. *Rhyne v Miami-Dade Water and Sewer Authority*, Fla.App., 402 So.2d 54, 55. *See* Insider; Privies; Privity.

'As an adjective, the word has practically the same meaning as "private".

'In my opinion, the present day notion of "privies" in the third prong of the *res judicata* doctrine goes beyond the examples given in Black's dictionary.

'In *Carl Zeiss Stiftung v Raymer & Keeler Ltd (No 2)*, Lord Guest wrote as follows:

The next requirement is that the judgment should have been between the same parties or their privies ... "Privies" have been described as those who are "privy to (the party) in estate or interest" (Spencer Bower on Res Judicata, p 130). Before a person can be privy to a party there must be community or privity of interest between them ... It was argued for the respondents, although without clear authority in this country, that "privy" covers a person who is in control of proceedings. Reference was made to the American Restatement of the Law (Judgments) (1942), s 84, where it is said that

a person who is not a party but who controls an action is bound by the judgment as if he were a party if he has a proprietary or financial interest in the judgment as a privy ... We were referred to a number of American cases dealing with privies. I am not prepared in this country to extend the doctrine to the extent which it apparently has reached in that country.

'In *Roberge v Bolduc*, Madam Justice L'Heureux-Dubé wrote as follows:

This is not to say that the parties must be physically identical in both cases. It is the juridical identity of the parties that is required for the presumption of *res judicata* to apply, as Mignault, op cit, contends, at p 110:

[Translation] And by identity of person must be understood *legal* identity, not *physical* identity. (Emphasis in original.) Nadeau and Ducharme, op. cit., at No. 573, p 472, emphasize this distinction:

[Translation] For *res judicata* there must be legal identity of the parties, not mere physical identity. The one may exist without the other. There is legal identity whenever one person represents another or is represented by him (References omitted.)

...

'The examples of representation by one party of another are too numerous to list or discuss here. Aubry and Rau, op. cit., at pp 335–56, review them in detail and even such review is not necessarily exhaustive. Representation may depend on the facts of the particular case and the interest of the parties involved. Suffice it to say that, for the identity of parties in so far as it relates to *res judicata*, juridical identity is all that is required.' *Hoffman-La Roche Ltd v Canada (Minister of National Health and Welfare)* [1997] 2 FC 681 at 687–689, Fed TD, per Richard J

PRIVILEGE

Absolute privilege

[For 28 Halsbury's Laws (4th edn) paras 95, 97 see now 28 Halsbury's Laws (4th edn) (Reissue) paras 95, 96.]

Qualified privilege

[For 31 Halsbury's Laws (4th edn) para 108 see now 28 Halsbury's Laws (4th edn) (Reissue) para 109.]

PRIVITY

[For 16 Halsbury's Laws (4th edn) para 1543 see now 16(2) Halsbury's Laws (4th edn) (Reissue) para 999.]

PRIZE

Admiralty

[For 37 Halsbury's Laws (4th edn) paras 1301–1303 see now 36(2) Halsbury's Laws (4th edn) (Reissue) paras 801–803.]

PRIZE COMPETITION

New Zealand 'The definitions "game of chance" and "prize competition" are mutually exclusive. In other words something which is a prize competition is by definition not a game of chance.' *Department of Internal Affairs v Machirus* [1992] 1 NZLR 503 at 505–507, per Tipping J

PROBABLE

Australia [Section 8 of the Criminal Code (Qld) provides that where two or more persons form a common intention to prosecute an unlawful purpose and in the prosecution an offence is committed of such a nature that its commission was a 'probable' consequence, each of them is deemed to have committed the offence.] 'The overall effect of the passages emphasised [from *Re Brennan* (1936) 55 CLR 253 at 260–261] is that it is sufficient to satisfy s 8 if a consequence was a real or substantial possibility; indeed, the second passage appears to assert that probability can be proved by linking cause and effect.' *Re Hind* (1995) 80 A Crim R 105 at 116, per Fitzgerald J

PROBABLE CONSEQUENCE

Australia [In the context of the (Qld) Criminal Code 1989, s 8.] 'In *Johns v R* (1980) 143 CLR 108, Stephen J discussed the genesis of the notion of "probability" as a basis under the common law for sheeting home criminal responsibility for the acts of the principal offender to an accessory. His Honour said:

> That the notion of "probability" as a suggested criterion of an accessory's liability for what I have called "the other crime" finds its place in the literature is perhaps due to Sir Michael Foster's use of the term. In his Crown Cases, 3rd ed (1809), in treating of

accessories before the fact, he says, at p 370: "So where the principal goeth beyond the terms of the solicitation, if in the event the felony committed was a probable consequence of what was ordered or advised, the person giving such orders or advice will be an accessary (sic) to the felony" (emphasis added). However it is clear from the illustrations which the learned author then gives that he cannot intend "probable" in any such sense as the applicant would use it; that is, as meaning "more probable than not", almost as a question of percentage calculation. The second illustration given by Foster aptly demonstrates this, it is as follows: "A adviseth B to rob C, he doth rob him, and in so doing, either upon resistance made, or to conceal the fact, or upon any other motive operating at the time of the robbery, killeth him. A is accessary (sic) to this murder." The same point may be made of other illustrations which Foster gives. In *Reg v Radalyski* ((1899) 24 VLR 687) counsel for the appellant, an accessory before the fact to abortion, sought to rely on the passage from Foster for the proposition that, for his conviction of murder to stand, the death of the woman during an attempted abortion had to be shown to be a probable consequence. When this was put, Williams J pertinently observed, in the course of argument ((1899) 24 VLR at p 691), that the "extension of the instances given (that is to say, Foster's examples) is against you": Street CJ made a similar observation when the present matter was before the Court of Criminal Appeal.

'Sir James Stephen, when he came to write his Digest of the Criminal Law, cited (8th ed (1947), p 21) the above passage from Foster J in support of his own statement of an accessory's criminal responsibility. He used the phrase "likely to be caused" rather than "probable consequence" but repeated verbatim Foster's illustration which I have set out above. The meaning of "probable" for which the applicant must contend, that of something which is more probable to happen than not to happen, seems to be no more intended by Stephen's use of "likely" than by Foster's use of "probable".

'In *Brennan v R* (1936) 55 CLR 253, Dixon and Evatt JJ also noted that the use of the word "probable" in s 8 of the Criminal Code, seems to have been derived from Sir Michael Foster's use of the term in the common law in relation to criminal responsibility for acts done in the prosecution of a common criminal purpose.

'These considerations confirm my opinion that, for the purposes of s 8 of the Criminal Code, the reference to "a probable consequence" is to a consequence which is a "substantial risk" or "real chance" or "real possibility" of occurring in the prosecution of the common unlawful purpose.' *R v Deemal-Hall, Darkan and McIvor* [2005] QCA 206 at [59]–[61], per Keane JA; BC200503990

PROCEEDING

Australia [The Jurisdiction of Courts (Cross-vesting) Act 1987 (Vic), s 5, confers power on the court to transfer the 'proceeding' to certain interstate or federal courts for determination.] 'The meaning depends on the context in which the word is used. In some cases it is equivalent to "an action" whereas in others it may mean a step in an action. Sometimes it may include a counter claim ... The word "proceeding" is capable of such a variety of meaning that dictionary definitions as to its ordinary or natural meaning are not of much use. They tend to highlight the number of meanings which the word can bear. Any assistance as to its meaning has to be derived from the statutory context and the objects of the legislation in question. If there are several causes of action, there is power to transfer one of those causes of action. A separate cause of action is a proceeding. Issues cannot be instituted in a court ... [The Act cannot] be construed as authorising the transfer of issues, such as the issue of liability.' *Blake v Norris* (1990) 20 NSWLR 300 at 306–308, per Smart J

Australia [Section 3(1) of the Supreme Court Act 1986 (Vic) defines 'proceeding' as meaning any matter in the court other than a criminal proceeding.] 'It appears to me to be clear that the word "proceeding", as defining in s 3 of the Supreme Court Act 1986, is used as a generic expression to embrace what was formerly comprehended individually and respectively by the expressions "action", "cause" and "matter". The expression "matter in the court" in the definition of "proceeding" in s 3 refers on that assumption to a proceeding in the sense of a vehicle by which the jurisdiction of the court is invoked and not to the subject matter of a justiciable dispute.' *Braeside Bearings Pty Ltd v H J Brignell & Associates (Boronia)* [1996] 1 VR 17 at 20, per Tadgell JA

PROCEEDING BY WAY OF APPEAL

Australia [Section 7(3) of the Jurisdiction of Courts (Cross-vesting) Act 1987 (NSW) refers to a proceeding by way of an appeal'.] 'The better view is that the drafter has used this elliptical phrase to extend the meaning of "appeal" somewhat. Proceedings are thus included which, though not an "appeal" strictly so-called, can properly be viewed as being in the nature of an appeal or for the purpose of an appeal or "by way of" an appeal. The word "appeal" can, in a particular context, be given a wide meaning. For example, it was held in the Full Court of the Supreme Court of this State that an application for an order in the nature of prohibition to correct an error made in the Court of Petty Sessions was an "appeal" for the purposes of s 6(1) of the Suitors' Fund Act 1951: see *Ex parte Parsons; re Suitors' Fund Act* (1952) 69 WN (NSW) 380; see also, *Builders Licensing Board v Pride Constructions Pty Ltd* [1979] NSWLR 607 at 618 and *Onions v Government Insurance Office of New South Wales* (1956) 73 WN (NSW) 279 at 283. These decisions simply underline the importance of giving effect in every case to the apparent purpose of the statute and avoiding an overly narrow construction of the language which would defeat the achievement of that purpose.' *NEC Information Systems Australia Pty Ltd v Lockhart* (1991) 22 NSWLR 518 at 522, per Kirby P

New Zealand 'It is not disputed that reference to "proceedings" can include an arbitration, and although one normally associates the word "proceedings" with a Court, I think it is not unnatural to refer to arbitration proceedings.' *Arbitrators' Institute of New Zealand Inc v Legal Services Board* [1995] 2 NZLR 202 at 203, per Heron J

New Zealand [Section 14(1) of the Defamation Act 1992.] 'In my view where a matter which is of a statutorily recognised character is brought before the Court, it is a "proceeding" within s 14 whether or not the Court ultimately rules that it lacks jurisdiction in the circumstances of the particular case.' *Rawlinson v Oliver* [1995] 3 NZLR 62 at 68, CA, per Richardson J

PROCEEDINGS

Canada '[24] Interpreted in their grammatical and ordinary sense, these words clearly encompass the statutory collection procedures in the *ITA* [*Income Tax Act*]. Although the word "proceeding" is often used in the context of an action in court, its definition is more expansive. The Manitoba Court of Appeal stated in *Royce v. MacDonald (Municipality)* (1909), 12 W.L.R. 347, at p. 350, that the "word 'proceeding' has a very wide meaning, and includes steps or measures which are not in any way connected with actions or suits". In *Black's Law Dictionary* (6th ed. 1990), at p. 1204, the definition of "proceeding" includes, *inter alia*, "an act necessary to be done in order to obtain a given end; a prescribed mode of action for carrying into effect a legal right".

...'

Markevich v Canada (2003) 223 DLR (4th) 17 at 30 (SCC), per Major J

Canada '[73] The purpose of s. 11(*c*) is to protect a person charged with an offence against self-incrimination. This protection should not depend solely on the terminology associated with the procedure established by Parliament.

'[74] In the instant case, Parliament decided that an appeal from a decision of the Minister must be made by way of an action in the Federal Court (s. 135 of the *CA*). However, this choice of procedure does not alter the actual relationship between the parties.

'[75] The *Petit Robert* (1990) defines the word "*poursuite*" as follows: [TRANSLATION] "legal action taken against someone who has violated a law ..." (p. 1501). In the case at bar, the customs officer, a representative of the state, served a notice of ascertained forfeiture on the appellant. There can therefore be no doubt that the service of the notice of ascertained forfeiture by the customs officer, who had reasonable grounds to believe that a provision of the *CA* had been contravened, constituted a "*poursuite*" against the appellant.

'[76] From that moment, the appellant was required to follow the path set out by Parliament for contesting the proceeding against him. To this end, he asked the Minister to review the officer's decision (ss. 129 and 131 of the *CA*) and he subsequently appealed the Minister's decision to the Federal Court. Thus, although the appellant is designated a "plaintiff", it is not he who actually initiated the "*poursuite*". On the contrary, he is simply defending himself in a proceeding against him that was initiated by the respondent.

'[77] In the English version of s. 11(*c*) of the *Charter*, the term "*poursuite*" is rendered as "proceedings". The *Oxford English Dictionary* (2nd ed. 1989) defines "proceeding" as follows, at p. 545: "The instituting or carrying on of an action at law; a legal action or process; any act done by authority of a court of law; any step taken in a cause by either party" (emphasis added). It should be added that, in ss. 13 and 14 of the *Charter*, the word "proceedings" is rendered as "*procédures*" in

the French version. In s. 24(2) of the *Charter*, "proceedings" is rendered as "*instance*".

'[78] This shows that the word "proceedings" has a much broader meaning than "*poursuite*" (see, for example, *Markevich v. Canada*, [2003] 1 S.C.R. 94, 2003 SCC 9, at paras. 23–37), and it applies regardless of whether the individual seeking the protection of s. 11(*c*) of the *Charter* is a "plaintiff" or a "defendant".' *Martineau v Canada (Minister of National Revenue)* [2004] SCJ No 58, [2004] 3 SCR 737, 247 DLR (4th) 577, per Fish J

PROCEEDINGS ... IN RESPECT OF ANY CAUSE OF ACTION

Canada '[33] The words at issue in section 32 [of the *Crown Liability and Proceedings Act*] are "proceedings by or against the Crown in respect of any cause of action". I have no difficulty rejecting the appellant's opening argument that the word "proceedings" is to be interpreted without regard to the words "in respect of any cause of action". The word "proceedings" must be read together with the words that modify it.

'[34] Nonetheless, I am not satisfied "proceedings ... in respect of any cause of action" necessarily only refer to court proceedings.

'[35] The term "proceedings" is one of broad scope. While in a legal context, the term "proceedings" will usually relate to a court action or steps taken under a court order, it may also include "any legal action or process" (*Shorter Oxford Dictionary*, Vol. II 3rd ed. Oxford: Clarendon Press, 1990). A requirement to pay under section 224 [as am. by S. C. 1994, c. 21, s 101] is analogous to a garnishing order issued by a court. Failure to honour a requirement to pay may result in an assessment under the *Income Tax Act*. Seizure and sale of chattels under subsection 225(1) is a provision closely parallel to a writ of execution issued by a court. Parliament has empowered the Minister to take enforceable collection action without the necessity of first obtaining a judgment in Court. These procedures are legal processes.

'[36] The words "in respect of" are words of the widest scope connecting two related subject matters. In *Slattery (Trustee Of) v. Slattery*, [1993] 3 S.C.R. 430, Iacobucci J., for the majority, refers to the words "in respect of" as they were previously considered by the Supreme Court in *Nowegijick v. The Queen*, [1983] 1 S.C.R. 29. He states at page 445:

The phrase "in respect of" was considered by this Court in *Nowegijick v. The Queen*, [1983] 1 S.C.R. 29, at p. 39:

> The words "in respect of" are, in my opinion, words of the widest possible scope. *They import such meanings as "in relation to"*, "with reference to" or "in connection with". The phrase "in respect of" is probably the widest of any expression intended to convey some connection between two related subject matters. [Emphasis in original.]

'Thus, the words "proceedings ... in respect of any cause of action" simply mean that the proceedings contemplated have some connection to a cause of action.' *Markevich v Canada* [2001] 3 FC 449 at 464–465, TD, per Rothstein JA

PROCESS

Australia [Commonwealth Constitution s 51(xxiv).]
'[2] His Honour concludes that the word "process" in s 51(xxiv) should be confined to proceedings which are directly connected with the determination of legal rights or the enforcement of the law. The alternative contention is that the relevant phrase "service and execution ... of the civil and criminal process ... of the States" extends to encompass compulsory attendance for the purpose of giving evidence in the course of a criminal investigation by a statutory authority.

...

'[4] Mason P collects the relevant references in the two basic authorities: *Amman v Wegener* (1972) 129 CLR 415 and *Alliance Petroleum Australia NL v Australian Gaslight Co Ltd* (1983) 34 SASR 215. The emphasis given therein to the close connection between a committal proceeding and a criminal prosecution and to the close analogy between an arbitration proceeding and civil action in the courts, reflects the facts in issue in those cases. In neither case was the Court concerned to determine the limits of the word "process".
'[5] I add one additional reference. Gibbs J said in *Amman* at 438:

> A summons issued by a justice for the purpose of securing the attendance of a witness at a committal proceeding is not only 'process' within the ordinary meaning of that expression, but is part of the criminal process of a State within par (xxiv), whether or not it can properly be described as the process of a court.

'[6] The significance of this passage is in his Honour's use of the phrase "not only" and what is said thereafter. Gibbs J emphasised that a summons to attend a committal proceeding is "part of the criminal process of a State". However, his Honour also indicated that a summons "for the purpose of securing the attendance of a witness at a committal proceeding" is also "process", within the ordinary meaning of that expression. This confirms that the word "process" should not be given a narrow meaning.
'[7] The New South Wales Crime Commission, with its special statutory powers of criminal investigation, stands in a long tradition in Australia of statutory authority for royal commissions of inquiry, which were frequently invoked for purposes of determining whether criminal offences had occurred. (See, e g *McGuinness v Attorney-General of Victoria* (1940) 63 CLR 73 at 99; William Harrison Moore "Executive Commissions of Inquiry" (1913) 13 Columbia Law Rev 500 esp at 508.)
'[8] The words "criminal process" are capable, in their natural and ordinary meaning, of extending to encompass compulsory powers to force attendance to give evidence in a criminal investigation by such a statutory authority. The context which suggests that the words should be read down is the reference to "service and execution". However, the force of that context in narrowing the interpretation is considerably attenuated by the fact, established by *Amman*, that the words "of the courts" do not qualify the words "civil or criminal process". These words are at large, albeit in the immediate context of "service and execution". No authority has been cited to the Court which would suggest that these words, in such a context, should be confined to the determination of legal disputes or the enforcement of laws.
'[9] Section 51(xxiv) should be given a broad and purposive construction. Its purpose extends, in my opinion, to the authorisation of federal laws designed, relevantly, to facilitate and ensure the efficacy of the enforcement of the criminal laws of the states, so as to ensure that in this respect Australia is, in substance, borderless.

...

'[12] This object of a borderless operation of the legal system is not well served if the s 51(xxiv) power is confined to the determination of legal disputes or the enforcement of the law. It is best served if the power extends to ensuring the efficacy of criminal investigations by a statutory authority. It is not desirable to speculate further about the limits of the word "process".' *Dalton v NSW Crime Commission* [2004] NSWCA 454 at [2], [4]–[9], [12], per Spigelman CJ; BC200408735

PROCESSING

[On appeal by publishers, the Court of Appeal considered, inter alia, (1) whether the publishers' entitlement to disclose that the claimant was a drug addict and was receiving treatment for drug addiction carried with it the entitlement to publish such details as had been provided in relation to that treatment; (2) whether the act of publishing the newspapers containing the articles constituted 'processing' as defined by s 1 of the Data Protection Act 1998, namely obtaining, recording or holding the information or data or carrying out any operation or set of operations on it, including its use; and (3) if so, whether the publications fell within s 32 of the Act, which provided, in relation to journalistic material, an exemption from the provisions imposing substantive obligations on the data controller if he reasonably believed that publication would be in the public interest and that compliance with the provisions was incompatible with journalism. The judge had held that s 32 applied only to pre-publication processing, and that accordingly the publishers had not been entitled to rely on the exemption.] '[75] The new case advanced by the appellants renders important some of the definitions in ss 1(1) and 2 of the [Data Protection Act 1998]. These are:

"'data' means information which—(a) is being processed by means of equipment operating automatically in response to instructions given for that purpose, (b) is recorded with the intention that it should be processed by means of such equipment, (c) is recorded as part of a relevant filing system or with the intention that it should form part of a relevant filing system, or °

"'personal data' means data which relate to a living individual who can be identified—(a) from those data, or (b) from those data and other information which is in the possession of, or is likely to come into the possession of, the data controller, and includes any expression of opinion about the individual and any indication of the intentions of the data controller or any other person in respect of the individual;

"'processing', in relation to information or data, means obtaining, recording or holding

the information or data or carrying out any operation or set of operations on the information or data, including—(a) organisation, adaptation or alteration of the information or data, (b) retrieval, consultation or use of the information or data, (c) disclosure of the information or data by transmission, dissemination or otherwise making available, or (d) alignment, combination, blocking, erasure or destruction of the information or data …

"'using' or 'disclosing', in relation to personal data, includes using or disclosing the information contained in the data …

"2. In this Act 'sensitive personal data' means personal data consisting of information as to—(a) the racial or ethnic origin of the data subject, (b) his political opinions, (c) his religious beliefs or other beliefs of a similar nature, (d) whether he is a member of a trade union (within the meaning of the Trade Union and Labour Relations (Consolidation) Act 1992), (e) his physical or mental health or condition, (f) his sexual life, (g) the commission or alleged commission by him of any offence, or (h) any proceedings for any offence committed or alleged to have been committed by him, the disposal of such proceedings or the sentence of any court in such proceedings."

…

'[101] The definition of "processing" in the directive [EP and Council Directive (EC) 95/46 (on the protection of individuals with regard to the processing of personal data and the free movement of such data) (OJ L281/31 p 50)] and the Act alike is very wide. "Use of the information or data" and "disclosure of information or data by transmission, dissemination or otherwise making available" are phrases, given their natural meaning, which embrace the publication of hard copies of documents on which the data has been printed. Is such a meaning consistent with an interpretation which gives effect, in a sensible manner, to the objects of the Act?

'[102] While the Act extends to certain manual filing systems, it is otherwise concerned with the automated processing of personal information. Almost all of the provisions of the Act relate to activities prior to the moment when that information is transferred to hard copies. It would conflict with the overall nature and object of the directive and the Act to seek to apply their provisions to the acts of those who distribute and make available to the public the product of prior data processing in which they have not been concerned. Extending "processing" to embrace such activities need not, however, have that result.

'[103] The directive and the Act define processing as "any operation or set of operations". At one end of the process "obtaining the information" is included, and at the other end "using the information". While neither activity in itself may sensibly amount to processing, if that activity is carried on by, or at the instigation of, a "data controller", as defined, and is linked to automated processing of the data, we can see no reason why the entire set of operations should not fall within the scope of the legislation. On the contrary, we consider that there are good reasons why it should.

'[104] While an individual may reasonably find it objectionable that another should record and hold personal data about himself, the greater invasion of privacy, damage and distress is likely to be caused when that information is made public. Article 23 of the directive provides:

"1. Member States shall provide that any person who has suffered damage as a result of an unlawful processing operation or of any act incompatible with the national provisions adopted pursuant to this directive is entitled to receive compensation from the controller for the damage suffered.

"2. The controller may be exempted from this liability, in whole or in part, if he proves that he is not responsible for the event giving rise to the damage."

If publication were not treated as part of a "processing operation" this provision would be deprived of much of its force.

'[105] Section 13 of the Act gives effect to art 23. It provides:

"(1) An individual who suffers damage by reason of any contravention by a data controller of any of the requirements of this Act is entitled to compensation from the data controller for that damage.

"(2) An individual who suffers distress by reason of any contravention by a data controller of any of the requirements of this Act is entitled to compensation from the data controller for that distress if—(a) the individual also suffers damage by reason of the contravention, or (b) the contravention relates to the processing of personal data for the special purposes.

"(3) In proceedings brought against a person by virtue of this section it is a defence to prove that he had taken such care as in all the circumstances was reasonably required to comply with the requirement concerned."

Once again, if these provisions are to be effective, publication must be treated as part of the operations covered by the requirements of the Act.

'[106] Accordingly we conclude that, where the data controller is responsible for the publication of hard copies that reproduce data that has previously been processed by means of equipment operating automatically, the publication forms part of the processing and falls within the scope of the Act.' *Campbell v Mirror Group Newspapers Ltd* [2002] EWCA Civ 1373 at [75], [101]–[105], [2003] 1 All ER 224, per Lord Phillips of Worth Matravers MR

PROCESSOR

Exclusive

United States   The term 'exclusive processor' means any securities information processor or self regulatory organisation which, directly or indirectly, engages on an exclusive basis on behalf of any national securities exchange or registered securities association which engages on an exclusive basis on its own behalf in collecting, processing, or preparing for distribution or publication any information with respect to (i) transactions or quotations on or effected or made by means of any facility of such exchange or (ii) quotations distributed or published by means of any electronic system operated or controlled by such association. (Securities Exchange Act of 1934, s 3(a)(22)(B))

PROCURE

Australia   [Section 354(2) of the Criminal Code (Qld) states that a 'person kidnaps another person if the person unlawfully and forcibly takes or detains the other person with intent to gain anything from any person or to procure anything to be done or omitted to be done by any person.'] 'The term "procure" is found on a number of occasions throughout the Code, but it does not appear to have any uniform legal meaning. It is first found in s 7, the provision defining who is a principal offender. Any person who "procures" any other person to commit an offence may be charged with actually committing it. To my mind the term "procure" in s 354 is used in the same way, and with the same meaning. I will return to that meaning in a moment.

'Section 217 of the Code creates the offence of procuring a person to engage in carnal knowledge. For purposes of that section the term "procure" is defined as meaning "knowingly entice or recruit for the purposes of sexual exploitation". That definition cannot strictly apply to the use of the term in s 354 but, in my view, it is significant to observe that the words "entice or recruit" fundamentally involve the notion of bringing about or causing the particular result – for s 217 that result being sexual exploitation.

'Section 417 of the Code is headed "Procuring Execution of Deed by Threats", but neither the term "procure" nor one of its derivatives is used in the section itself. Relevantly the section is in the following terms:

> "Any person who, with intent to defraud, and by means of any unlawful violence to, or restraint of, the person of another, or by means of any threat of violence or restraint to be used to the person of another, ... compels or induces any person ... to execute ... any valuable security ... is guilty of a crime".

'The critical words there are "compels or induces" and again those words connote some causal connection between the conduct directed towards the person and the act in question of that person. It is those words which justify the use of the term "procuring" in the description of the offence.

'A consideration of ss 217 and 417 strongly suggests that procuring means bringing about or causing the relevant result.

'The *New Shorter Oxford English Dictionary* gives a number of meanings for "procure"; relevantly it gives the following definitions: "bring about ... cause to be done ... prevail on or persuade ... try to induce."

'There is not a lot of authority on the meaning of the term "procure" in the criminal law. It was specifically considered by the Court of Appeal in *Attorney-General's Reference (No 1 of 1975)* [1975] QB 773. The facts of the case are not relevant for present purposes. Lord Widgery CJ (with whom Bristow and May JJ agreed) said at 779–80:

> "To procure means to produce by endeavour. You procure a thing by setting out to see that it happens and taking the appropriate steps to produce that happening. We think that there are plenty of instances in which a person may be said to procure the commission of a crime

by another even though there is no sort of conspiracy between the two ... .

> "You cannot procure an offence unless there is a causal link between what you do and the commission of the offence ... .

> "Giving the words their ordinary meaning in English, and asking oneself whether in those circumstances the offence has been procured, we are in no doubt that the answer is that it has. It has been procured because, unknown to the driver and without his collaboration, he has been put in a position in which in fact he has committed an offence which he never would have committed otherwise".

'That reasoning was applied by the Court of Criminal Appeal (Shaw LJ, Cusack and Slynn JJ) in *Broadfoot* (1976) 64 CrAppR 71. Relevantly the court said at 74:

> "His first complaint is that the learned judge told the jury that the word 'procure' was really equivalent to the word 'recruit'. Let it be said at an early stage that the word 'procure' in the statute is not a term of art. It is a word in common usage and word which a jury is well able to understand. Each case in which it is alleged that there has been a procurement or attempted procurement must be related to the facts of the particular case. It is essential for a jury to make up their minds, when they have heard the evidence and decided what to accept, whether what they do accept does amount to 'procuring'.

> "Counsel has quoted to the Court several decisions dealing with the interpretation of the word 'procure' in cases involving quite different facts. The Court does not find those references, though no doubt attention has properly been drawn to them, particularly helpful in this case. Nor indeed do the dictionary definitions of the word have much bearing upon what is to be decided.

> "Perhaps a useful guide is to be found in *Attorney-General's Reference (No 1 of 1975)* ...

> "There is another expression which can be used as guidance in determining what should be decided on particular facts. During the course of argument in this Court, Shaw LJ suggested that 'procuring' could perhaps be regarded as bringing about a course of conduct which the girl in question would not have embarked upon spontaneously of her own volition.

"It is essential … that the interpretation of the word is a matter of commonsense for the jury concerned, and this court can see nothing wrong in the judge having suggested to the jury the word 'recruited' as being a useful expression to consider in deciding what they thought on this particular issue".

'It is interesting to note that the term "recruited" referred to in *Broadfoot* is the word used in s 217 of the Code. I also mention that the reasoning of Lord Widgery was cited with approval by Bowen CJ, Lockhardt and Beaumont JJ in *Yorke v Lucas* (1983) 49 ALR 672 at 681.

'Those cases to my mind indicate the relevant considerations here. In the context of this case it would be open to a jury to conclude that an intent to bring about, cause, or facilitate an assault by A on J was a sufficient intent to constitute the offence defined in s 354.

'As used in ss 7, 217 and 417 of the Code, and in cases such as *Attorney-General's Reference* and *Broadfoot*, the term procure is used in the context of procuring a person to do something. In that context it may often be relevant, at least from an evidentiary perspective, that the person would not have done the act "spontaneously of her own volition" to use the language quoted above from *Broadfoot*…

'However it seems that such a qualification is not universal. In *Gough v Rees* (1929) 46 TLR 103 the proprietor of a bus was charged with counselling and procuring the conductor, his employee, to commit the offence of allowing more than a specified number of passengers to be on board the bus. Lord Hewart CJ, with the concurrence of Swift and Branson JJ, said (105):

"… it is said that a man cannot counsel or procure unless he knows and intends what is to be done … In form that statement is correct. But it is clear that the appellant knew what would happen unless he took precautions. He took no precautions and was rightly held responsible for the consequences. That which he did and that which he omitted to do seem to me as much a counselling and procuring as if he had called the conductor and instructed him to overload to his utmost capacity and best opportunity".

'That strongly suggests initial unwillingness of the person to do the act intended to be procured is not always an essential element of procuring.

'Sections 354 speaks not of procuring a person to do something, but of procuring an act to be done by someone. If the essence of the offence is the doing of an act, ensuring that an act is done, it is difficult to see why whether or not the person procured to do the act was initially willing to do it was a relevant consideration. *Yorke v Davis* was a case concerned with contravention of a provision of the Trade Practices Act 1974 (Cth). Section 75B of the Act included in the phrase "a person involved in a contravention" any person who "aided, abetted, counselled or procured the contravention". There, as with s 354, the procurement was of an act. As already noted the court considered Lord Widgery's formulation of the test for procurement was apposite.

'Some assistance can be gleaned from the discussion of Pennycuick J in *Re Royal Victoria Pavilion Ramsgate* [1961] Ch 581. There on the sale of a number of properties, mainly theatres, the vendor covenanted with the purchaser to "procure that until … [a certain date] … the premises known as … shall not (a) be open to the public between … [certain dates] … except for entertainment by living actors … and … any entertainment by means of cinematography … shall be deemed to be specifically precluded". Subsequently the plaintiff purchased the subject premises from the vendor and the question for the court was whether he was bound by the covenant given by the vendor to the purchaser of the other properties. At 587 the following was said:

"The word "procure" is defined in the *Oxford English Dictionary* … as meaning; "obtain by care or effort", and can be more simply paraphrased as "see to it". The obligation undertaken by … is to see to it that a certain state of affairs prevails during the specified term".

'Again that was a case of procuring an act, namely the continuance of certain state of affairs, and the context demonstrates, as acknowledged in *Broadfoot*, that the word is not a term of art and its meaning is to be derived from its usage on a particular occasion.' *R v Faagutu* BC200300586; [2003] QCA 70 at [28]–[42], per Williams JA

PRODUCTION

New Zealand [The approach adopted by Lockhart J in *Federal Commissioner of Taxation v Jax Tyres Pty Ltd* (1984) 58 ALR 138 at 142 was agreed with by Justice Tompkins.] *International Bottling Co Ltd v Collector of Customs* [1995] 2 NZLR 579 at 583, per Tompkins J

PROFESSED

'The exemption conferred on the trustees by cl 15 of the Bacchus trust deed would be available, according to its terms, only if they had acted "in the professed execution of the trusts and powers hereof". If a trustee knows that he is acting beyond his powers, it is submitted, he cannot be said to be so acting. Both Mr Stones and Mr Osborne, it is submitted, must have known that they were acting outside their powers and therefore in breach of trust; accordingly neither of them is in a position to invoke cl 15 and each of them must be liable.

...

'The suggested construction of cl 15 would thus confine its operation to unconscious or accidental, as opposed to conscious, breaches of trust. It would afford no protection in regard to a "judicious breach of trust" ... In my judgment, on the ordinary use of language, this construction attaches too narrow a meaning to the phrase "in the professed execution of the trusts and powers hereof". The Shorter Oxford English Dictionary (1993 edn) includes among other definitions of the word "professed" the meaning "alleged, ostensible". I agree with the judge that cl 15, on its true construction, must apply so as to exonerate the trustees, save to the extent excluded by the clause, in particular dishonesty, for anything done by them in the purported execution of the trusts and powers of the Bacchus trust deed—that is to say even though in fact not done in the exercise of such trusts or powers.' *Walker v Stones* [2000] 4 All ER 412 at 440, CA, per Sir Christopher Slade

PROFESSIONAL ACTIVITY

Australia [Contrasting "profession" and "professional activity" in the Fair Trading Act 1987 (NSW) s 4.] 'However, I consider the words "professional activity" may well point to a wider range of those who provide services to the public in an analogous way to traditional professionals. They may, depending on how they are organised and conduct themselves, include, for example, taxation consultants, brokers, teachers and conceivably, if at a particular level, mediators ... The term "professional activity" refers at least to particular activity which a member of a profession would characteristically carry out in that capacity and which is in fact so carried out by that member as such a professional.' *Prestia v Aknar* (1996) 40 NSWLR 165 at 186, per Santow J

PROFESSIONAL SERVICES

Canada 'While it is appropriate to classify as medical practice that which is carried out by a physician in furtherance of a patient's care, there must always be some direct involvement by the defendant doctor. In other words, there must be no question that the plaintiff was the defendant doctor's patient. There must be some doctor/patient relationship for it to be said that the doctor is providing medical professional services even if the extent of the connection as we have seen need not be overwhelming. The nature and basis of the plaintiff's claim must have its roots in the care (broadly defined) provided to the patient by his or her defendant physician.

...

'... While undoubtedly the referral by a doctor to have the mammogram done constitutes the practice of medicine, as does the review of the x-ray itself, and the performance of the mammogram if personally performed or directly supervised by the attending physician, general supervision of an employee in circumstances where no true doctor/patient relationship exists cannot be characterized in my opinion as a provision of a medical professional service within the meaning of s 61 of *The Medical Act.*' *Narynski v Dow Corning Canada Inc* (1997) 147 DLR (4th) 208 at 214 215, Man CA, per Scott CJM

PROFIT À PRENDRE

[For 31 Halsbury's Laws (4th edn) para 19 see now 31 Halsbury's Laws (4th edn) (2003 Reissue) para 23.]

PROFITS AND GAINS

New Zealand [Section 65(2)(a) of the Income Tax Act 1976.] 'Income tax is levied upon "assessable income", which by s 65(2)(a) of the Income Tax Act 1976 includes "all profits or gains derived from any business". The term "profits or gains" is not defined. Prima facie, therefore, it bears its ordinary meaning as it would be understood by a businessman or accountant. As Dixon J said in *Commissioner of Taxes (South Australia) v Executor Trustee and Agency Co of South Australia Ltd* (1938) 63 CLR 108, 152:

"Income profits and gains are conceptions of the world of affairs and particularly of business ... in nearly every department of enterprise and employment the course of affairs and the practice of business have developed methods of estimating or computing in terms of money the result over an interval of time produced by the operations of business, by the work of the individual, or by the use of capital. The practice of these methods of computation and the general recognition of the principles upon which they proceed are responsible in a great measure for the conceptions of income, profit and gain and, therefore, may be said to enter into the determination or definition of the subject which the legislature has undertaken to tax."

Commissioner of Inland Revenue v Mitsubishi Motors New Zealand Ltd [1995] 3 NZLR 513 at 515, PC, per cur

PROHIBITED ACTIVITY

New Zealand [When it is permissible for a planning authority to use the 'prohibited activity' status provided for in the Resource Management Act 1991, s 77B(7).] '[9] It is inevitable that, in the course of this judgment, significant extracts from the ruling under appeal will be cited. It is therefore convenient to set out in full paras [12]–[15] of the judgment since these contain the Environment Court's reasoning on the point:

[12] The *Concise Oxford* defines "prohibit" as ... formally forbid by law, rule etc ... and that seems an entirely appropriate way of regarding the term in this context. In the abstract, "prohibiting" an activity is a legitimate planning tool, but one to be used sparingly and in a precisely targeted way. Section 77B(7) provides that if an activity is so classified, "... no application may be made for that activity and a resource consent must not be granted for it". It is, therefore, a distinct exception to the permissive, effects based, philosophy of the Act as a whole. It is not, we think, legitimate to use the "prohibited" status as a de facto, but more complex, version of a non-complying status. In other words, it is not legitimate to say that the term "prohibited" does not really mean "forbidden", but rather that while the activity could not be undertaken as the Plan stands, a Plan Change to permit it is, if not tacitly invited, certainly something that would be entertained ...

[13] We think that the correct approach to a "prohibited" status is that offered by Mr Serjeant, a consultant planner for MIA; viz that it should be used only when the activity in question should not be contemplated in the relevant place, under any circumstances. That would be the first of the two "extreme exam-

ples" given in the decision in *Re an Application by Amoco Minerals NZ Ltd* (1982) 8 NZTPA 449:

To give two extreme examples there could be cases where social and/or environmental factors are so important that no mining should occur on certain land notwithstanding the importance of the mineral resources there; or in another case, the importance of the mineral resources in a particular place in national terms might outweigh very substantial local environmental damage.

That approach both fits the meaning of "prohibited", and requires a precise targeting of the status at areas of land for which, or circumstances in which, the activity in question should never be contemplated.

...

'[19] Five points were then advanced in support: (1) it was wrong to place weight on the dictionary definition; (2) the RMA contains no restrictions on when prohibited activity status can be used; (3) the Court's ruling is inconsistent with the purposes of the RMA; (4) the Court's ruling is inconsistent with the scheme of the RMA; (5) the Court's ruling undermines the intent of s 61(1A) of the Crown Minerals Act 1991.

'[20] The first point was really the flip side of the other four. In the appellants' submission the predominant factor must be the legislation, and it is to that rather than dictionary meanings that one should turn in order to determine the meaning and intent of concepts such as "prohibited activity". To deal with this aspect immediately, I do not consider anything turns on the Court's reference to the dictionary. Of itself it is nothing unusual. Further, the Court merely uses it to confirm that the statutory definition of "prohibited" matches the ordinary meaning of the word. What is in issue are the implications of the definition on the issue of when "prohibited activity" status should be used.'

Coromandel Watchdog of Hauraki Inc v Ministry of Economic Development [2005] NZRMA 497 at [9], [19]–[20], per Simon France J

PROHIBITED NAME

[Section 216 of the Insolvency Act 1986 provides that it is an offence, for, inter alia, directors, to act, without the leave of the court, in relation to a company known by a 'prohibited name', and under s 216(2) a company name is a 'prohibited name' if

it is a 'name which is so similar' to the name by which the liquidated company was known 'as to suggest an association with that company'.]
'[11] The essential question for the district judge was whether the name of Air Equipment was a "prohibited name" within s 216(2)(b). That turns on whether the name of Air Equipment was so similar to the name of Air Component as to suggest an association with Air Component.

'[12] In his careful judgment the district judge concluded that the name of Air Equipment was a prohibited name. He observed that the word "Air" was in the name of both companies; in an industry dealing with the sale of air compressors the words "equipment" and "component" could be used interchangeably; the two companies were operating in a very similar, if not the same, market from the West Midlands region; and there was continuity of Mr Ricketts' interest in the two companies.
...
'[14] The approach of the judge to the interpretation of s 216(2) was criticised on the ground that it did not take account of the particular purpose for which the provisions were enacted or the severity of the criminal sanctions imposed for contravention of the section.

'[15] It is common ground that the sections were enacted to curb the "phoenix syndrome", a vivid expression coined to cover those cases in which the privileges of limited liability are exploited by those—

> "who set up companies with vestigial capital; immediately run up debts, often taking deposits from consumers for goods and services which are never delivered; transfer the assets of the first company at an undervalue to a second company; allow the first company to cease trading, with its creditors confined to that company's inadequate assets; and then begin the process all over again with the second (or third or fourth) company." (See Davies *Introduction to Company Law* pp 99–100.)

'[16] This is not a "phoenix syndrome" case: there was no transfer of assets by Air Component to Air Equipment at an undervalue; there was no evidence that the companies were used to run up debts and to avoid their payment either on the part of Air Component or Air Equipment; there was no evidence that creditors of Air Equipment or anyone else had been misled by the similarity of the names of the two companies or the fact that Mr Ricketts was a director of both of them.

'[17] In those circumstances it was contended that, if a purposive approach had been adopted to the construction of s 216(2), the judge would not have concluded that the name of Air Equipment was a prohibited name, especially in the context of the harsh consequences of criminal sanctions for offences of strict liability committed in contravention of the restrictions (see *R v Cole* [1998] 2 BCLC 234).

'[18] I appreciate the relevance of a purposive interpretation, but the legal position is that, if the name of Air Equipment is a prohibited name within the natural and ordinary meaning of the language of s 216(2), this case is caught by the restrictions, even if this is not a "phoenix syndrome" case and even if the sanctions of criminal liability seem to be harsh. In *Thorne v Silverleaf* [1994] 1 BCLC 637 at 642–643 Peter Gibson LJ said:

> "But it is clear that the sections as enacted apply to a wider set of circumstances than the case of a person attempting to exploit the goodwill of a previous insolvent company. However, in the absence of an application under s 216(3) for leave, the court is left with no discretion on the application of the sections, and so long as the statutory provisions remain unaltered a creditor of a company is entitled to take advantage of them, if they can be shown to be applicable."

...
'[24] I agree with Mummery LJ's judgment and conclusion on this appeal but, because of the surprisingly long reach of this legislation and the obvious importance of the point at issue, I wish to add a short judgment of my own. In doing so I gratefully adopt Mummery LJ's exposition of the relevant facts and law, repeating none of this save for the all-important provision around which this appeal must necessarily turn, s 216(2) of the Insolvency Act 1986:

> "... a name is a prohibited name ... if—(a) it is a name by which the liquidating company was known ... or (b) it is a name which is so similar to [the name by which the liquidating company was known] as to suggest an association with that company."

'[25] The issue in these proceedings is whether Air Equipment Co Ltd is a prohibited name. The name of the liquidating company here was The Air Component Co Ltd. The critical question therefore arising is whether Air Equipment Co Ltd is "a name so similar to [The Air Component Co Ltd] as to suggest an association with that company".

'[26] In holding that Air Equipment Co Ltd *is* a prohibited name, the district judge below said that—

> "within the industry dealing with the sale of air compressors the words "equipment" and "component" might be interchangeable … It is a matter of commonsense interpretation that these two words could be used interchangeably."

He furthermore repeatedly emphasised that "the statute requires the one name only to "suggest" an association". "That", he observed, "is a very low threshold."

'[27] For my part I have some difficulty with each limb of that approach. As to the words "equipment" and "component", they do not seem to me interchangeable. Rather I find it unsurprising that the two names were not in fact the names of successor companies but rather the names of related companies within the same group. Mummery LJ has for convenience from time to time in his judgment adopted the expression "successor company" to refer to Air Equipment Co Ltd, the longer lasting of the two companies in question here. As he makes plain, however, it was itself already in existence before The Air Component Co Ltd went into liquidation, the appellant simultaneously having been a director of both.

'[28] At one point in the argument I wondered whether s 216(2)(b) applied in the case of companies within the same group of companies as opposed to the case of a phoenix company as that concept is ordinarily understood: the use of a new successor company, often trading under the same or similar name, using the old company's assets, often acquired at an undervalue, and exploiting its goodwill and business opportunities. It became plain, however, that the provision is no less applicable in the case of group companies than phoenix companies. Indeed, certain of the exceptions provided for by the rules (see [10] of Mummery LJ's judgment, above) necessarily imply it.

'[29] It is accordingly not necessary to conclude that the words "equipment" and "component" are, as the district judge thought, "interchangeable". It is sufficient if the respective names of these companies considered in the context of all the circumstances in which they were actually used or likely to be used (see [22] of Mummery LJ's judgment, above), suggested an association, suggested in other words that they were part of the same group.

'[30] I turn to the other aspect of the district judge's judgment about which I am uneasy, his view that the legislative requirement that an association be merely "suggested" indicates "a very low threshold". In construing this provision it is important to bear in mind the draconian consequences, both criminal and civil, which can all too easily flow from finding a company's name to be a prohibited name. As stated in s 271 of *Bennion on Statutory Interpretation* (4th edn) p 705, the court should strive to avoid adopting a construction which penalises someone where the legislator's intention to do so is doubtful, or penalises him in a way which is not made clear. With this well-established principle of construction in mind, I would construe the phrase "as to suggest" in s 216(2)(b) rather more stringently than indicated by the judgment below. To my mind the similarity between the two names must be such as to give rise to a probability that members of the public, comparing the names in the relevant context, will associate the two companies with each other, whether as successor companies or, as here, as part of the same group.

'[31] Even, however, adopting this somewhat stricter approach to the construction and application of this provision, I for my part would conclude, in common with the judge below and with Mummery LJ, that there was indeed an association between these two companies. I too, therefore, would dismiss this appeal.' *Ad Valorem Factors Ltd v Ricketts* [2003] EWCA Civ 1706 at [11]–[12], [14]–[18], [24]–[31], [2004] 1 All ER 894, CA, per Mummery and Simon Brown LJJ

PROHIBITION

[An order of prohibition was renamed a prohibiting order by the Civil Procedure Rules 1998, SI 1998/3132: see CPR 51.1(2)(c). For 1 Halsbury's Laws (4th edn) paras 128–129 see now 1(1) Halsbury's Laws (4th edn) (2001Reissue) paras 118, 123–125, 129–132.]

PROMOTE—PROMOTION

Australia [Fair Trading Act 1987 (WA).] '[10] … The learned Stipendiary Magistrate referred to two sets of dictionary definitions, those in the Oxford English Dictionary and the Macquarie Dictionary. He was of the view that the Oxford English Dictionary's definition of "promotion" in terms of "to further anything" was, at least at first glance, wide enough to catch the board master activity in the prosecution's case.

'[11] However, he also noted the Macquarie definitions included, apart from a furtherance part, "activity designed to increase public awareness of, and hence the sale of, a product". He went on to consider authority on the understanding of "promoter" in corporate law, which he appears to have concluded offered some support for the view that the terms I have quoted in the Fair Trading Act meant "encouragement" of the scheme "in the sense of drawing in participants".

...

'[13] I consider that the learned Stipendiary Magistrate's construction of "promotion" and its related terms was too narrow, however. The authorities on corporate law understandings, discussed briefly in Ford HAJ, et al, *Ford's Principles of Corporations Law*, 11th ed (2003), [5,270], indicate that taking an active and substantial part in the organisation of the venture, including a non-corporate one, is sufficient for these purposes.

'[14] Here there is reason to take an even wider view. It is that s 24(4) refers to "promotes or takes part in the promotion of" a scheme. The original complaints are framed in terms of the latter phrase. The additional words "takes part in the promotion" seem to me to suggest that more is intended to be caught than the corporate law concept of being a promoter.

'[15] It thus seems to me that the statutory context does not appear to require the restriction of the promotion or take part in the promotion idea to advertising or similar activity. This is because of the broader meanings the dictionary sources use, the approach adopted to "promoter" in corporate law, and the apparent purpose of s 24(4) which was stressed by the appellant. That purpose appears to be to stamp out pyramid trading schemes. Reaching them before advertising has begun or participants have been recruited would seem to me to be part of this.

...

'[17] The line should fall short of those more ministerial or advisory acts which in ordinary language would not be called "promotion" or "taking part in promotion". Various examples were discussed in argument. One was the simple anonymous recording of details and mailing of details to participants without any meaningful role in the design or origination of the recording system or the mail-out or any responsibility for a meaningful part of scheme activity that might be represented by such recording system of mail-out. Another was introducing persons to the scheme so they could advise on the scheme's lawfulness.

...

'[19] I should add that my analysis of the meaning of "promoter" or "take part in promotion" in s 24(4) has had to be conducted without the benefit of any relevant authorities on this provision or its counterparts elsewhere in this country or overseas, or extrinsic material on the provision of the sort the Interpretation Act 1984 (WA) s 19 allows. I am not aware of any such material and counsel for the appellant informed me that their research had not turned up any." *Hawkins v Price* [2004] WASCA 95 at [10]–[11], [13]–[15], [17], [19], per Simmonds J; BC200402726

PROMOTE, INCITE OR INSTRUCT

Australia [The National Classification Code provided for classification of publications that 'promote, incite or instruct' in matters of crime or violence.] 'The phrase, "promote, incite or instruct" is a collocation of overlapping meanings. According to the *Shorter Oxford English Dictionary*, to promote is to further the growth, development, progress or establishment of (anything); to further advance, encourage. To incite, is to urge or spur on; to stir up, instigate, stimulate. To instruct, is relevantly to furnish with knowledge or information; to teach or educate ... Reflecting the theme of promotion or incitement the provision of information on matters of crime will constitute instruction if it appears from the content and context of the article, objectively assessed, as purposive, the relevant purpose being to encourage and equip people with the information to commit crimes.' *Brown v Members of the Classification Review Board of the Office of Film and Literature Classification* (1998) 154 ALR 67 at 81; BC9801120, per French J

PROMOTER

[For 7 Halsbury's Laws (4th edn) para 37 see now 7(1) Halsbury's Laws (4th edn) (2004 Reissue) para 244.]

PRO–MUTUUM

[For 2 Halsbury's Laws (4th edn) para 1536 see now 2 Halsbury's Laws (4th edn) (Reissue) para 1836.]

PRONOUNCE

Australia [In the context of Family Law Rules 1984 (Cth) O 38 r 18.] 'In my view, the word "pronounce" is not used in the sense of uttering or speaking, but in the sense of defining the reasons for judgment by the provision of a judgment, order or decree. This may be either by the spoken word or by the written word. I am confirmed in this view by the clear principle that emerges from the striking facts of [*In the Marriage of Blamey* (1994) 18 Fam LR 481], and the authorities therein referred to, namely that a judge is entitled to change his or her reasons for judgment and to amend his or her orders provided such change is carried out before the formal orders issue from the court.' *In the Marriage of Moore* (1996) 20 Fam LR 495 at 500; 125 FLR 420 at 424, 425 per Butler J

PROPER NAVIGATION

Australia 'It seems to me as a matter of common English usage that the proper navigation of a passenger vessel necessarily includes whether she is carrying a safe or unsafe number of passengers from a stability point of view.' *R v Warner* (1991) 25 NSWLR 382 at 396, per Carruthers J

PROPER WORKING ORDER

[Covenants implied by s 11(1)(b) of the Landlord and Tenant Act 1985. Under that provision, a lessor was obliged, inter alia, to keep in 'proper working order' the installations in the dwelling house for the supply of water, gas and electricity.] '[15] ... There is an obvious distinction between the duty to keep "in repair" and the duty to keep "in proper working order". We are concerned with the latter duty. An installation cannot be said to be in proper working order if, by reason of a defect in construction or design, it is incapable of working properly.

'[16] Accordingly we have no difficulty in resolving the first issue. At the commencement of the tenancy the installations for the supply of water, gas and electricity must be so designed and constructed as to be capable of performing their functions. The assumed facts of this case demonstrate, however, that the question of whether installations for the supply of water, gas or electricity are capable of performing their function can raise a difficult question as to how this is to be judged. This brings us to the second issue.

...

'[27] Our conclusion is that, in so far as installations for the supply of water, gas and electricity are concerned an installation will be in proper working order if it is able to function under those conditions of supply that it is reasonable to anticipate will prevail. While the test as formulated may appear to involve uncertainty, we suspect that if the evidence relevant to the test is considered, it may be easier to apply in practice.' *O'Connor v Old Etonian Housing Association Ltd* [2002] EWCA Civ 150 at [15]–[16], [27], [2002] 2 All ER 1915 at 1020, 1023, CA, per Lord Phillips of Worth Matravers MR

PROPERLY

[In a dispute over a commercial lease of unfurnished office premises, a landlord sought to recover various costs which in terms of the lease had to be 'properly incurred'.] 'When one seeks content for the term "properly" in relation to the right of a landlord to recover expenditure from a tenant, it must take account of the context. The landlord, on this hypothesis, has a right to incur expenditure without consent of the tenant, or reference of the proposals to the tenant, and to demand payment of a proportion of that expenditure. The expenditure would not be properly incurred if it were incurred unreasonably, having regard to the respective interests of the landlord and tenant.' *Lowe v Quayle Munro Ltd* 1997 SLT 1168 at 1172, per Lord Penrose

PROPERTY

[For 44 Halsbury's Laws (4th edn) para 657 see now 44(1) Halsbury's Laws (4th edn) (Reissue) para 1032.]
'I agree that the liberty or freedom to trade, enjoyed by everyone, is not a form of "property" within the meaning of s 22 [of the Finance Act 1963]. This liberty, or freedom, is a "right" if that word is given a very wide meaning, as when we speak of a person's "rights" in a free society. But in s 22 the words used are "assets" and "property". "Property" is not a term of art, but takes its meaning from its context and from its collocation in the document or Act of Parliament in which it is found and from the mischief with which that Act or document is intended to deal: see Lord Porter in *Nokes v Doncaster Amalgamated Collieries Ltd* [1940] 3 All ER 549 at 574, [1940] AC 1014 at 1051. The context in the instant case is a taxing Act which is concerned with assets and with disposals and acquisitions, gains and losses. I can see no reason to doubt that in s 22 "property" bears the meaning of that which is capable of being owned, in the normal legal sense, and that it does not bear the extended meaning that would be needed if it were to include a person's freedom to

trade.' *Kirby (Inspector of Taxes) v Thorn EMI plc* [1988] 2 All ER 947 at 953, CA, per Nicholls LJ

'Treating the matter purely as a matter of construction, I am quite unable to accept that the word "property" when it is used in the definition of property [in the Insolvency Act 1986, s 436] is intended to describe anything other than an existing item. In other words, I do not accept that it is susceptible of referring to something which has no present existence but may possibly come into existence on some uncertain event in the future. There seems to me a very clear distinction between two situations. The first is where there is a contingent interest in property, for example the right to receive £50,000 under a legacy on attaining the age of "x" years when one is "x" minus "y" years old. That is an interest which is contingent and future but, if there is a trust fund—which I assume in my example there is—there is existing property in respect of which there is a contingent interest. That seems to me to be quite different from the second situation, the possibility of achieving an interest in something which presently does not exist but may exist in the future.

...

'Accordingly, I have come to the conclusion that the hope that Mrs Campbell had of being awarded an award [by the Criminal Injuries Compensation Board], which in fact fructified two years later, was not at the date when she became bankrupt part of her property in such a way as to vest in the trustee in bankruptcy when she became bankrupt.' *Re Campbell (a bankrupt)* [1996] 2 All ER 537 at 540, 544, per Knox J

[The question arose whether a waste management licence under the Environmental Pollution Act 1990 could be discalimed as onerous property under the Insolvency Act 1986, s 178, which depended on whether the licence was 'property' within s 436 of the 1986 Act.] 'It is contended on behalf of the agency that a waste management licence is not "property" because it is expressly and correctly described as a licence. It appears to me that merely because something is or can be categorised as a "licence" does not mean that it is incapable of constituting "property". It would be a triumph, not merely of form, but of bare linguistics if the legal characterisation of a right under one statute were to be determined by the nomenclature which the legislature chose to use in another statute concerned with a wholly different area of law.

'In the context of a case involving the acquisition of interests in land enforeceable against third parties, Lord Wilberforce said in *National Provincial*

Bank Ltd v Ainsworth [1965] 2 All ER 472 at 494, [1965] AC 1175 at 1247–1248:

> "Before a right or an interest can be admitted into the category of property, or of a right affecting property, it must be definable, identifiable by third parties, capable in its nature of assumption by third parties, and have some degree of permanence or stability."

'It seems to me that a waste management licence even satisfies that rather strict test.

'Furthermore, the fact that the legislation creating waste management licences provides for their transfer (in s 40) and that there is in fact a market in such licences, provide support for the contention that a waste management licence is "property" within the wide definition of s 436 of the 1986 Act.

...

'In all the circumstances, I am of the view that a waste management licence granted pursuant to s 35 of the 1990 Act constitutes "property" within the definition of that word in s 436 of the 1986 Act, and hence ... such a licence may be disclaimed by the liquidator of the company that holds it pursuant to s 178 of the 1986 Act.' *Re Mineral Resources Ltd* [1999] 1 All ER 746 at 753, 755, per Neuberger J

[Insolvency Act 1986, ss 178, 436.] '1. These appeals raise two questions:(1) is a waste management licence granted under the Environmental Protection Act 1990 "property" within the meaning of that word as defined in s 436 of the Insolvency Act 1986? And if so, (2) if it is onerous, is the liquidator or trustee in bankruptcy of the holder of the waste management licence entitled to disclaim it pursuant to s 178 of the 1986 Act? In *Re Mineral Resources Ltd, Environment Agency v Stout* [1999] 1 All ER 746 Neuberger J answered the first question in the affirmative and the second in the negative ...

...

'23. It is apparent that unless the object sought to be disclaimed is property within s 436 it cannot be "onerous property" within the scope of s 178(3). It was common ground that if a waste management licence is property then it falls within para (b) of the definition of onerous property. Thus the first issue is whether a waste management licence comes within the definition in s 436 of the 1986 Act. Neuberger J held that it did. If it does then, prima facie, s 178 would apply so as to enable the liquidator to disclaim it. The Agency claims that s 178 does not apply to a waste management licence on the grounds that the application of the section to such an item of property would be inconsistent with the overriding purpose of the 1990 Act in general and the provisions of s 35(11) in particular. This is the second issue. Neuberger J decided that the application of s 178 was excluded.

...

'26. The word "property" is not a term of art but takes its meaning from its context: *Nokes v Doncaster Amalgamated Collieries Ltd* [1940] 3 All ER 549 at 574, [1940] AC 1014 at 1051 and *Kirby (Inspector of Taxes) v Thorn EMI plc* [1988] 2 All ER 947 at 953, [1988] 1 WLR 445 at 452... Thus in successive statutes dealing with bankruptcy and insolvency the definition of "property" has been progressively extended (*Morris v Morgan* [1998] CA Transcript 524); though, however wide the definition, it is subject to the implied exclusion of rights of the bankrupt with reference to his body, mind or character: *Heath v Tang, Stevens v Peacock* [1993] 4 All ER 694, [1993] 1 WLR 1421. It is apparent from the terms of s 436 that the definition is to some extent circular but is not exhaustive. Further, as Browne-Wilkinson V-C observed in *Bristol Airport plc v Powdrill* [1990] 2 All ER 493 at 501, [1990] Ch 744 at 759, it is hard to think of a wider definition of "property".

...

'33. It appears to me that [the] cases indicate the salient features which are likely to be found if there is to be conferred on an exemption from some wider statutory prohibition the status of property. First, there must be a statutory framework conferring an entitlement on one who satisfies certain conditions even though there is some element of discretion exercisable within that framework (*A-G of Hong Kong v Nai-Keung* [[1987] 1 WLR 1339, PC], *Re Rae* [[1995] BCC 102] and *Commonwealth of Australia v WMC Resources Ltd* [(1998) 152 ALR 1]). This condition is satisfied by the provisions of ss 35(2), 36(3) and 43 of the 1990 Act. Second, the exemption must be transferable (*National Provincial Bank Ltd v Ainsworth* [[1965] 2 All ER 472, [1965] AC 1175, HL], *A-G of Hong Kong v Nai-Keung*, *Commonwealth of Australia v WMC Resources Ltd* and *De Rothschild's* case [*De Rothschild v Bell (a bankrupt)* [1999] 2 All ER 722, [1999] 2 WLR 1237, CA]). This is satisfied by the terms of s 40(1). The requirement that the transferor and transferee should join in the application demonstrates the transferability of the waste management licence even though it takes the form of a surrender and regrant by the agency. Third, the exemption or licence will have value (*A-G of Hong Kong v Nai-Keung, Re Rae* and *Commonwealth of Australia v WMC Resources Ltd*). In *Re Mineral Resources Ltd, Environment Agency v Stout* [1999] 1 All ER 756 at 753 Neuberger J commented that there is a market in waste management licences. There was no evidence to that effect in these cases and the agency did not agree that there was any market. However it was common ground that money does change hands as between transferor and transferee. Further the very substantial fees the agency is entitled to charge and in fact receives is a good indication of the substantial value a waste management licence possesses for the owners or occupants of the land to which it relates.

'34. In my view a waste management licence comes within the definition of "property" contained in s 436. It is in my view "property" properly so called. In the alternative I consider that it is an "interest ... incidental to property", namely the land to which it relates.' *Re Celtic Extraction Ltd* [1999] 4 All ER 684 at 685–686, 691–692, 694, CA, per Morritt LJ

[Where a contractual tenancy of residential property on a long lease comes to an end by effluxion of time, a sole residing tenant is entitled to a continuation tenancy under the Landlord and Tenant Act 1954, Pt I, notwithstanding that the contractual tenancy had originally been granted to two or more tenants jointly. The question arose whether such a right was 'property' for the purposes of the Insolvency Act 1986, s 283.] 'First, and crucially, the issue under s 238 is whether the interest or right is, in juristic terms, "property". If the right is, in its legal nature, property, it only falls outside the bankrupt's estate by some specific exclusion. That in practical terms the "property" when held by a bankrupt may be of no value to the creditors is nothing to the point. The issue is of the general nature of the right created by Pt I of the 1954 Act, and not of its value in particular circumstances. I regard the continuation tenancy as having clear incidents of a property nature, in particular because it retains from the contractual tenancy the character of assignability: see the concluding parts of paras (a) and (b) of s 3(2) of the 1954 Act.

'Second, even if the criterion stated in the first point is not correct, and one does have to consider the value of the right in the hands of a bankrupt, it is far from being so clear that a continuation tenancy would never have value in the hands of a trustee in bankruptcy so as to disqualify the right from being ever a component of the bankrupt's estate.

...

'I therefore conclude, differing from the judge, that a continuation tenancy is part of the bankrupt's estate under s 283 of the 1986 Act.' *De Rothschild v Bell* [1999] 2 All ER 722 at 734–735, 736, CA, per Buxton LJ

'Clearly, any documents having any value, whether they are letters, or whatever they are, are prima facie property within the definition of property in s 436 of the [Insolvency Act 1986], and therefore part of the bankrupt's estate within the definition in s 283. However, there are some clearly established exceptions from the width of the definition of estate, and not only those expressed by the statute itself in s 283, but others which have been established as exceptions by the common law ...

...

'What is clear in my judgment from the authorities ... is that the courts recognise that, consistently with the purpose of the 1986 Act, even valuable assets of a peculiarly personal nature, especially, for instance, rights of action for damages to body, mind or reputation, are not included in the wide definition of property for the purposes of the definition of a bankrupt's estate in the 1986 Act.

'In my judgment it is inconceivable that Parliament really envisaged, by passing the 1986 Act, that the effect of bankruptcy should be that a bankrupt's personal correspondence should be available for publication to the world at large by sale at the behest of the trustee in bankruptcy. In my opinion, the concept of such a gross invasion of privacy is repugnant. I do not believe that Parliament intended it any more than it intended creditors to have the benefit of a bankrupt's right to damages for injury to his person or character. In my judgment, on its proper construction, in the context of its apparent legislative purpose, the effect of the 1986 Act is that a bankrupt's estate does not include the bankrupt's personal correspondence which, like a right of action for damages for libel, is of a nature peculiarly personal to him and his life as a human being. This is so, in my judgment, even in the case of a famous bankrupt whose correspondence as a result may be worth a considerable sum to the media. As I have said, it is accepted by the terms of the trustee's own application in this case that the documents in respect of which the trustee seeks directions enabling him to sell them are all "personal correspondence", and I quote from the application.

'I reach this conclusion apart from the provisions of art 8 of the European Convention on Human Rights, but I am confirmed in that conclusion by the fact that it seems to me at least strongly arguable that the construction of the 1986 Act contended for by the trustee in bankruptcy would indeed constitute an infringement of art 8.

'I recognise of course that personal correspondence may include letters relating to other property of the bankrupt that is included in his estate which it may be necessary for the trustee to have possession of in order properly to administer that estate. That situation is covered in my judgement by s 311(1) of the 1986 Act which I have already read, and which entitles the trustee in bankruptcy to possession of documents relating to the bankrupt's estate, even though such documents are not themselves comprised in the estate. Indeed, the very terms of s 311(1) to my mind contemplate the possibility that there may be documents belonging to the bankrupt which are not part of his estate and therefore for which express provision has to be made by s 311(1).' *Haig v Aitken* [2000] 3 All ER 80 at 86, 87–88, per Rattee J

[The State Immunity Act 1978, s 13(2)(b) provides that the property of a state is not to be subject to any process for the enforcement of a judgment or arbitration award, or in an action in rem, for its arrest, detention or sale, while s 13(4) states that this privilege does not apply in respect of property which is for the time being in use or intended for use for commercial purposes. Section 14(4) provides that property of a state's central bank or monetary authority is not to be regarded for the purposes of s 13(4) as in use or intended for use for commercial purposes.] '[44] The word "property" in s 13(4) clearly refers to "the property of a State", which is the phrase used in s 13(2)(b). So s 13(2)(b) and (4) set out the rules on immunity from enforcement with respect only to the property of a state. It is noteworthy that even if a state can be sued because one of the exceptions set out in the earlier sections of the 1978 Act applies, still it may not be possible to enforce a judgment obtained against it on that state's property in the jurisdiction, unless the state's property falls within the scope of s 13(4).

'[45] There is no definition of "property" in the 1978 Act. However, in the *Alcom* case [*Alcom Ltd v Republic of Colombia (Barclays Bank plc, garnishees)* [1984] 2 All ER 6, [1984] AC 580, HL], Lord Diplock stated that the expression "property" in s 13(2)(b) and (3) "is broad enough to include, as being the property of a banker's customer, the debt owed to him by the banker which is represented by the total amount of any balance standing to the customer's credit on current account". In *AIC Ltd v Federal Govt of Nigeria*, Stanley Burnton J stated (albeit obiter) that the word "property" in s 14(4) included a chose in action constituted by the debts owed by the Bank of England to the Central Bank of Nigeria that had accounts with the Bank. In my view the word "property" must have the same meaning and scope in both ss 13 and 14 of the Act. Moreover, I think it clear from Lord Diplock's statement in the *Alcom* case, which I have quoted above, that the word should be given a broad scope. So, in my view, "property" will include all real and personal property and will embrace any right or interest, legal, equitable, or contractual in assets that might be held by a state or any "emanation of the State" or central bank or other monetary authority that comes within ss 13 and 14 of the 1978 Act.' *AIG Capital Partners Inc v Republic of Kazakhstan* (*National Bank of Kazakhstan intervening*) [2005] EWHC 2239 (Comm) at [44]–[45], [2006] 1 All ER 284, per Aikens J

Australia 'Interests in a permit under the Petroleum (Submerged Lands) Act 1967 (Cth) may be recorded in a register of titles kept by the Designated Authority which also records the approval of transfers: ss 76 and 78. The fact that permits can be transferred and dealt with for valuable consideration and that such dealings are recorded in a register of titles is, in my view, a clear legislative indication that the permittee enjoys a stable interest which is capable of constituting a valuable asset. It is incorporeal but it is nonetheless property: see *Commonwealth v Tasmania* (1983) 158 CLR 1 at 287 per Deane J. I have reached the conclusion that the rights granted under a permit are stable and permanent enough for them properly to be regarded as property. Regulatory machinery is not antithetical to the concept of property and I do not regard the limitations on assignment of permits as inconsistent with a proprietary right. I regard the statutory limitations on permittees as no more than an acceptable level of regulation of the exploitation of an important natural resource which, at the same time, confers on the permit holder a sufficiently stable title.' *Western Mining Corpn Ltd v Commonwealth of Australia* (1994) 50 FCR 305 at 335, per Ryan J

Australia 'The word "property" is often used to refer to something that belongs to another. But in the [Fauna Conservation Act 1974 (Qld)], as elsewhere in the law, "property" does not refer to a thing; it is a description of a legal relationship with a thing. It refers to a degree of power that is recognised in law as power permissibly exercised over the thing. The concept of "property" may be elusive. Usually it is treated as a "bundle of rights".

But even this may have its limits as an analytical tool or accurate description, and it may be, as Professor Gray has said: that "the ultimate fact about property is that it does not really exist: it is mere illusion". Considering whether, or to what extent, there can be property in knowledge or information or property in human tissue may illustrate some of the difficulties in deciding what is meant by "property" in a subject matter. So too, identifying the apparent circularity of reasoning from the availability of specific performance in protection of property rights in a chattel to the conclusion that the rights protected are proprietary may illustrate some of the limits to the use of "property" as an analytical tool. No doubt the examples could be multiplied.

'[18] Nevertheless, as Professor Gray also says, "An extensive frame of reference is created by the notion that 'property' consists primarily in control over access. Much of our false thinking about property stems from the residual perception that 'property' is itself a thing or resource rather than a legally endorsed concentration of power over things and resources."

'[19] "Property" is a term that can be, and is, applied to many different kinds of relationship with a subject matter. It is not "a monolithic notion of standard content and invariable intensity". That is why, in the context of a testator's will, "property" has been said to be "the most comprehensive of all the terms which can be used, inasmuch as it is indicative and descriptive of every possible interest which the party can have".' (footnotes omitted) *Yanner v Eaton* (1999) 166 ALR 258; 73 ALJR 1518; BC9906413; [1999] HCA 53 at [17]–[19], per Gleeson CJ, Gaudron, Kirby and Hayne JJ

Australia [At issue on appeal was whether interest in a trust fund is property and therefore an asset within the meaning of the *Social Security Act 1991* (Cth).] '[22] ... The meaning of the word "property" is ... to be derived from the context of the Act and its purpose: *Project Blue Sky Inc v Australian Broadcasting Authority* (1998) 194 CLR 355 at 368 and 381. Its evident purpose is to provide financial assistance to persons whose means are limited. Even before the amendments of 2000 it could be seen that the Act was concerned to ensure that persons who had assets and income beyond a certain level should not be recipients of benefits and that they should utilise the means available to them.

...

'[24] Even on a wider view of property a discretionary trust would not qualify. It could in no sense be said to be the property of a person who is not yet identified as a beneficiary of it. For the purposes of the Social Security Act however some beneficiaries of discretionary trusts in reality, if not in law, have access to the trust assets because they are in a position to control the trust. The amendments of 2000 recognise and deal with such a situation. They and the Explanatory Memorandum tend to confirm, in my view, that it is assets which are in truth available to a person which are relevant for the purposes of the Act.' Per Keifel J.

...

'[31] Some assistance may be gained from the decision of the Privy Council in *Commissioner of Stamp Duties (Queensland) v Livingston* [1965] AC 694. In that case, the Privy Council dismissed an appeal from the High Court of Australia, and held that a person who is entitled to a deceased's estate has no proprietary interest therein while the executor or administrator is administering that estate. Their Lordships' advice distinguished between a "property right" in any of the items making up the assets of the estate, and a right to ensure that "the assets are properly dealt with and the rights that they hope will accrue to them in the future are safeguarded". This latter right was characterised as a "chose in action" as distinct from "a beneficial interest" in property. The holder of the proprietary interest was said to be the executor. The beneficiary could make the executor act to protect his interest. However, he could not protect his interest from interference by a third party without invoking the assistance of the executor. The Privy Council held that this meant that he did not hold a proprietary interest.

'[32] I note, of course, that the decision of the Privy Council has been the subject of strong criticism. See, for example, D C Jackson *Principles of Property Law*, Sydney, The Law Book Co Ltd, 1967, at pp 40–41. I am also mindful of the fact that when the matter was before the High Court (*Livingston v Commissioner of Stamp Duties* (Q) (1960) 107 CLR 411), Dixon CJ, with whom Windeyer J agreed, dissented.' *Secretary, Department of Family and Community Services v Geeves* [2004] FCAFC 166 at [22], [24], per Keifel J, [31]–[32], per Weinberg J; BC200403803

Canada [Wife claimed share in value of husband's university degree'] 'I am satisfied that one of the inherent qualities of "property" is that it may be transferred, bought, sold, exchanged, gifted, inherited, or hypothecated; a university degree is not "property" and therefore is not matrimonial property within the meaning of the Matrimonial Property Act. In the division of matrimonial property, it should be given no value.' *Storey-Bishoff v Storey-Bishoff* (1993) 108 DLR (4th) 452 at 457, per Gagne J (Sask UFC)

Canada '[21] Section 2 of the *Bankruptcy and Insolvency Act* provides that "property" includes "every description of property, whether real or personal, legal or equitable ... and includes ... every description of ... interest ..., present or future, vested or contingent, in, arising out of or incident to property". Having regard to that wording, it is difficult to imagine how Parliament could have cast a wider net. In *Bristol Airport Plc v. Powdrill*, [1990] Ch. 744, the broad wording of the definition of "property" found in the English statute led Sir [Nicolas] Browne-Wilkinson V.-C. to observe, at p. 759D, that it was "hard to think of a wider definition of property". The equally broad wording of s. 2 of the *Bankruptcy and Insolvency Act* evinces a clear legislative intention to catch every conceivable type of property right and interest. See *Chetty v. Burlingham Associates Inc.* (1995), 31 C.B.R. (3d) 161 (Sask. C.A.), leave refused (1995), 34 C.B.R. (3d) 73 (S.C.C.). After all, one of the goals of the statute is to ensure the equitable distribution of a bankrupt's assets among the creditors in bankruptcy. See *Husky Oil Operations Ltd. v. Minister of National Revenue*, [1995] 3 S.C.R. 453, per Gonthier J., for the majority, at para. 7 and *Western Tire & Auto Supply Ltd. v. Fundy Supplies Ltd.* (1971), 3 N.B.R. (2d) 723 (C.A.), per Hughes J.A., as he then was, at p. 727.

'[22] The Supreme Court of Canada has given a broad interpretation to the word "property". In *Marzetti v. Marzetti*, [1994] 2 S.C.R. 765, it held that a taxpayer's "right" to an income tax refund constituted "property" even though that "right" was not legally enforceable. English courts have adopted the same interpretative approach. Thus, in *Re Rae*, [1995] B.C.C. 102 the court held that the entitlement of a licence holder to be considered for a new licence constituted "property" under the English bankruptcy statute. The same conclusion was reached in *Dear v. Reeves*, [2001] 3 W.L.R. 662 regarding a grantee's right of first refusal under a deed. See, as well, Houlden & Morawetz, *The 2002 Annotated Bankruptcy & Insolvency Act*, (Toronto: Carswell, 2002), at pp. 269–344 and *Halsbury's Laws of England*, vol. 3(2), 4th ed. (London: Butterworths, 2002 reissue): "Bankruptcy and Individual Insolvency", at 227–28, para. 400. Under s. 2 of the *Bankruptcy and Insolvency Act*, an interest arising out of or incident to property need not be vested to constitute "property"; a contingent interest is sufficient.'

PricewaterhouseCoopers Inc v Manulife Financial (2003) 225 DLR (4ᵗʰ) 340 at 350–351 (NBCA), per Drapeau JA

New Zealand [Corporations (Investigation and Management) Act 1989, s 54; as to whether 'property' as used in that section included money:] 'Giving the provision a "fair, large and liberal construction and interpretation" as required by s 5(j) of the Acts Interpretation Act 1924, however, I held it was inconceivable that Parliament intended to cover all forms of property "save that most commonly used in commerce and most likely to be involved" in cases under s 54, namely, money (*MacMillan Builders Ltd v Morningside Industries Ltd* [1986] 2 NZLR 12). Furthermore, on settlement the Crown received and assignment of bank deposits from A14 which are *choses in action* and unquestionably property.' *Equiticorp Industries Group Ltd (In Statutory Management) v The Crown (Judgment no 47: Summary)* [1996] 3 NZLR 586 at 610–611, per Smellie J

New Zealand 'The Court is asked to decide whether a spouse's earning capacity is "property" within the meaning of s 2 of the Matrimonial Property Act 1976. The consequence would be that any enhancement of that capacity during the marriage would be matrimonial property and would at the end of the marriage be subject to assessment and division, generally equal division … While the concept of property is a fluid one, including for instance intangible property and in matrimonial property law non-assignable or non-transferable interests, a basic distinction still remains between rights in respect of the person and rights in respect of things. Property law, while of an extensive and never finally determined scope, is limited to the latter It does not extend, for example, to entirely personal characteristics which are part of an individual's overall make up. Relevant provisions of the Act confirm that limit.

'The Court in carrying out its role of interpreting legislation must of course read it in context, and the relevant social and economic context has changed, in some ways dramatically, in the last 20 years. But it is not within the proper interpretative role of the Court by reference to that context to give a radically different meaning to the word "property" in the way proposed. While the Court is not confined to the words of the Act, it is confined by them. Accordingly earning capacity is not property and an enhancement of that capacity is not matrimonial property.' *Z v Z (No 2)* [1997] 2 NZLR 258 at 264, CA, per cur

See also MATRIMONIAL PROPERTY

PROPERTY OF A STATE'S CENTRAL BANK OR OTHER MONETARY AUTHORITY

[The State Immunity Act 1978, s 14(1) details the entities which are entitled to the immunities and privileges conferred by Part I of the Act, but excludes 'any entity (hereafter referred to as a "separate entity") which is distinct from the executive organs of the government of the State and capable of suing or being sued', except in the circumstances set out in s 14(2). Section s 13(4) states that the privilege of the property of a state against enforcement does not apply in respect of property which is for the time being in use or intended for use for commercial purposes, while s 14(4) provides that 'property of a state's central bank or monetary authority' is not to be regarded for the purposes of s 13(4) as in use or intended for use for commercial purposes.] '[50] In my view the scheme of the Act in relation to the immunity of a central bank (or other monetary authority) from suit and the immunity of its property from the enforcement processes of United Kingdom courts has the following pattern. First, if the central bank (etc) is a department of the government of the state, but is not a "separate entity" as defined by s 14(1), then the central bank is immune from the adjudicative process unless it falls within one of the exceptions in the Act, including the "commercial transaction" exception set out in s 3. That is the effect of s 14(1).

'[51] Secondly, any process for the enforcement of a judgment or arbitration award may only be issued as against a state's property if, "for the time being [it] is in use or intended for use for commercial purposes". That is the effect of ss 13(2)(b) and 13(4). As I have already stated, in my view what constitutes "property" must be given a broad interpretation and "property" must mean the same in ss 13(2)(b), 13(4) and 14(4). Of course, whether a particular enforcement provision can be used against a state's property by the United Kingdom court will depend on three matters: (a) proof that the state concerned does have an interest in the particular asset; (b) proof that the state's property comes within the exception expressed in s 13(4); and (c) the nature of the property to be the subject of enforcement and the scope of the particular enforcement process under English law.

'[52] Thirdly, because s 14(1) defines what is covered by the words "a State", it must mean that the property of any department of the government of the state will constitute "State property", for the purposes of ss 13(2)(b) and (4), unless the department or other emanation of the state is a "separate entity" as defined in s 14(1). This must follow from the wording of the opening sentence of s 14(1).

'[53] Therefore, if s 14(4) did not exist, then because central banks and other monetary authorities are not excluded from the scope of s 14(1), a central bank (etc) that is a department of the government of a state and is not a "separate entity", (as defined), and its property could be the subject of an enforcement process in respect of a judgment obtained against the relevant state. But to be so the property of the central bank (etc) would have to fall within the scope of s 13(4).

'[54] Fourthly, as to the immunity of "separate entities", which is dealt with in s 14(2), the same rules as to immunity of a state apply, (for both the adjudicative and enforcement jurisdictions), if the two pre-conditions set out are fulfilled. If s 14(4) did not exist, then it seems to me that s 14(2) would be applicable to a central bank (etc) that fell within the definition of a "separate entity" as set out in s 14(1). This means that, but for the existence of s 14(4), the property of a central bank that is a "separate entity" could be the subject of the enforcement jurisdiction of United Kingdom courts in respect of a judgment against the central bank (etc), provided the property came within the scope of s 13(4) – ie that the relevant property is in use or intended for use for commercial purposes at the relevant time.

'[55] Fifthly, if a "separate entity" (which is not a central bank etc), is entitled to immunity, but it submits to the jurisdiction of the United Kingdom courts, then its property can be the subject of process to enforce a judgment against it. If the exclusion of central banks (etc) from the scope of s 14(3) was not present, then that subsection would have dealt with the situation when a central bank (etc) was indeed a "separate entity" as defined in s 14(1) and the central bank (etc) had submitted to the jurisdiction in circumstances when it could have asserted immunity. In that case, there could be enforcement of a judgment obtained against a central bank (etc) as against "the property" of the central bank (etc) that is a "separate entity", but only if that property of the central bank (etc) as a "separate entity" was in use or intended for use for commercial purposes: s 13(4).

'[56] But, sixthly, s 14(4) does exist and effect must be given to its wording. It is specifically directed to the question of enforcement processes against "Property of a State's central bank or other monetary authority". In my view it is clear that Parliament intended that the position of a central bank or other monetary authority should be dealt

with distinctly from either any other department of the government of a state, or any "separate entity" as defined in s 14(1). As I have attempted to show, it would have been possible to deal with the position of central banks (etc) using s 14(1), (2) and (3) without the need for a separate subsection. But s 14(4) was specifically introduced as an amendment. To my mind that makes it clear that Parliament intended this separate subsection to have a different effect from the preceding subsections of s 14 so far as they concern the ability to use enforcement processes against states and "emanations of the State".

'[57] In my view the wording of s 14(4) is clear and imperative; hence the wording "The property of a State's central bank ... shall not be regarded ..." The words are, in their natural meaning, not capable of qualification. When they are set in their context, as I have tried to do, it is clear that they should not be qualified. This has the following consequences:

(1) All "property" of a state's central bank or other monetary authority is covered by s 14(4). The only question is whether the central bank (etc) has one of the types of interests in the property concerned, as I have described the interests above, so that the assets concerned can be described as the "property" of the central bank concerned.

(2) It does not matter whether the central bank is a department of the state or a separate entity. In all cases the central bank's property "shall not be" regarded as in use or intended for use for commercial purposes "for the purposes of [s 13(4)]".

(3) Given the wording of s 14(4), then the property of a state's central bank (or other monetary authority) must enjoy complete immunity from the enforcement process in the United Kingdom courts.

(4) If the central bank (etc) has an interest in the property concerned, but the state of the central bank has another interest in the same property, then in my view the effect of s 14(4) is that the relevant property is immune from enforcement in respect of a judgment against that state, whether the property concerned is in use or intended for use for commercial purposes or not.

'[58] One can only speculate on why a separate subsection was introduced by amendment to deal with the position of property of central banks and other monetary authorities with regard to the enforcement process in United Kingdom courts. But one can note, first, that generally speaking, when a central bank or a state's monetary authority is performing its key functions of acting as guardian and regulator of the state's monetary system, it will be exercising governmental or sovereign authority; it will not be acting for commercial purposes. Secondly, it is likely that the most obvious "property" of a central bank, a state's reserves, will be held and used for governmental, or sovereign purposes and not for commercial purposes. It may be that it was recognised by the draftsmen of the Act that it would be difficult, if not impossible, to determine whether a particular asset of a central bank or monetary authority was, at a relevant time, being used or intended for use for sovereign purposes or for commercial purposes. The assets of a state's central bank (or monetary authority) would be an obvious target for the enforcement process in relation to judgments against the state or its central bank (etc). This might lead to unwelcome and perhaps embarrassing litigation in United Kingdom courts. Therefore this possibility was pre-empted by the all-embracing and imperative immunity granted by s 14(4).

'[59] Contrary to the submissions of Mr Salter, the wording of s 14(4) will work in relation to "property" of the central bank whether the central bank is a department of a state or a separate entity. Take first the case where the central bank is a department of the state. If the central bank handles "property", then it will do so as a part of the state. But, as a department of state, it might have the capacity to sue and be sued and it could have the right to enter contracts. That capacity will all depend on the law of the particular state concerned. If the central bank has no interest in the relevant property, then s 14(4) does not apply. But if it is established that the central bank has "property" in the asset in the sense I have described above, then this asset is immune from any enforcement process, whether the judgment is against the state as such, or it is the central bank that has been sued.

'[60] In the case of a central bank that is a separate entity from a department of the state, there can be no problem (in English law at least) about it having "property" in assets. Thus in the present case it is clear that the NBK has "property" of some form in the London assets; viz a contractual right to the payment of debts in the case of the cash accounts held by AAMGS, and a beneficial interest in the securities held by AAMGS. At the same time the state could also have an interest in the same property; it may be some kind of beneficial interest, as it is agreed to be in this case. But in all cases, whatever the nature of the "property" right

of the central bank, the assets concerned are immune from the enforcement process.

'[61] Therefore I conclude that the words "Property of a State's central bank or other monetary authority" in s 14(4), when construed using common law principles of construction, mean any asset in which the central bank has some kind of "property" interest as I have described, which asset is allocated to or held in the name of a central bank, irrespective of the capacity in which the central bank holds it, or the purpose for which the property is held.' *AIG Capital Partners Inc v Republic of Kazakhstan (National Bank of Kazakhstan intervening)* [2005] EWHC 2239 (Comm) at [50]–[61], [2006] 1 All ER 284, per Aikens J

PROPHYLAXIS

Canada '88 ... Dictionaries tend to include prophylaxis as an aspect of treatment:

> *Oxford English Dictionary* (2nd ed. 1989), vol. XII, at p. 644

> > *Med.* The preventive treatment of disease ...

> *Black's Medical Dictionary* (39th ed. 1999), at p. 446

> > Treatment or action adopted with the view of warding off disease.

In *Butterworths Medical Dictionary* (2nd ed. 1978), at p. 1385, the following definitions (amongst others) are given:

> *Clinical prophylaxis.* The prevention of the development of signs and symptoms of the disease without necessarily eradicating the causal factor, e.g. in malaria, by schizonticidal drugs.

> *Drug prophylaxis.* The administration of drugs as protection against infection, in particular malarial infection.
> *Gametocidal prophylaxis.* The administration of drugs in order to kill malarial gametocytes in individuals.

See also *Dorland's Illustrated Medical Dictionary* (27th ed. 1988), at p. 1365.

'89 If "prophylactic" treatment of malaria may post-date the initial infection, it would seem appropriate that prophylaxis can also include "prevention of the development of signs and symptoms of the disease [AIDS] without necessarily eradicating the causal factor [HIV]".' *Apotex Inc v Wellcome Foundation Ltd* [2002] 4 SCR 153 at 195, per Binnie J

PROPOSAL

Merger or takeover proposal

New Zealand 'The statute enacts a concept of "proposal". It is something which is put forward. It need not be a concluded enforceable contract. It may not yet be fully detailed, and it may still be in the balance or worse. However, it is something sufficiently formulated and determined to be put up for clearance and ultimately implemented. It is not something still a vague and unsettled notion. It is not something which is still merely under discussion, undecided. It has moved on past the discussion stage to a stage of formulation and acceptance.' *Commerce Commission v Fletcher Challenge Ltd* [1989] 2 NZLR 554 at 608, per McGechan J

PROPOSES

[By s 5 of the Landlord and Tenant Act 1987, where a landlord 'proposes' to make a relevant disposal affecting premises he must serve a notice on qualifying tenants affording them the right of first refusal.] 'It is in our view clear that the expression "proposes" describes a state of mind somewhere between mere consideration of a possible course of action at one extreme and a fixed and irrevocable determination to pursue that course of action at the other ... A "proposal" under the 1987 Act means that a project must have moved out of "the zone of contemplation ... into the valley of decision" (see *Cunliffe v Goodman* [1950] 1 All ER 720 at 725, [1950] 2 KB 237 at 254 per Asquith LJ).

'... It is necessarily implicit in the legislation that a proposal is none the less such because the tenants may assert their right to buy. Furthermore, it flies in the face of common sense to suggest that a party does not propose to do that which he binds himself to do by contract. The fact that a third party may succeed in defeating or frustrating his proposal does not mean that he ceases to propose, only that he may be unsuccessful in implementing his proposal.' *Mainwaring v Trustees of Henry Smith's Charity* [1996] 2 All ER 220 at 233–234, CA, per Sir Thomas Bingham MR

PROPRIETARY RIGHT

Australia 'Registration in the council's register confers an exclusive entitlement to the floor space. The transferee of the transferable floor space has a right recognised by the council to have a development application considered by the council taking into account the existence of the transferable floor space. This is a valuable right not possessed by an applicant for development approval without transferable floor space. The reality is that commerce regards transferable floor space as a proprietary right. The courts should do likewise.' *Halwood Corpn Ltd v Chief Commissioner of Stamp Duties* (1992) 33 NSWLR 395 at 403, per Loveday J

PROPRIETOR

[The appellant company was the parent company of a number of wholly-owned subsidiary companies. One of those subsidiaries owned a public house, and others provided that public house with employees. The environmental health department of the respondent local authority found breaches under reg 4(2) of the Food Safety (General Food Hygiene) Regulations 1995, and prosecuted the company under reg 4(1) which provides that a proprietor of a food business has to ensure that the handling and offering for sale or supply of food are carried out in a hygienic way. The company was convicted in the magistrates' court and appealed to the Crown Court. As a preliminary issue, the company submitted that it was not a 'proprietor' as defined by s 53 of the Food Safety Act 1990, since it was not 'the person by whom that business is carried on'. It argued that a wholly-owned subsidiary was a different legal entity in law to its parent and that it carried out none of the activities within the definition of food business in reg 2 of the 1995 regulations in that it did not carry out any handling or offering for sale or supply of food.] '[33] Proprietor for the purposes of s 53 is therefore a term of art. The proprietor does not have to be the owner of the business, although it may be. It does not have to be involved in its day-to-day running. Provided it can be said that on the evidence it is the person by whom the business is carried on, it is the proprietor. Such a person may of course be an individual or a limited company.

'[34] It follows that on the basis of such a definition, there may be more than one proprietor. It will all depend upon the facts of the particular case.

'[35] Moreover, it seems to me that Mr MacDonald is right in his approach to these provisions. It is not necessary for the proprietor to carry out any, let alone all, of the functions which appear in the definition of "food business' in reg 2. Once it is established that the business in question is a food business, the only remaining issue is whether the defendant is the proprietor, having regard to the statutory definition in s 53. If on the evidence the court is sure it is and is sure (as here) of a breach of reg 4, the case is made out.

'[36] The issue therefore comes to this. Was the Crown Court, on the evidence adduced before it, entitled to be sure that the appellants were carrying on that business? If it was, the appeal fails. If not, it succeeds.

'[37] In deciding whether the evidence disclosed that the appellants were carrying on a business, the court was in my view entitled to make a realistic assessment of the actual role of the appellants in the group. It was entitled to bear in mind that there may be much involved in carrying on a food business which falls outside the purely physical processes listed in reg 2. That is what the Crown Court did. It carried out a careful analysis of the evidence before it. It placed considerable weight on what was said in the appellants' annual report. It was entitled to. It came to the conclusion that the appellants did much more than act simply as a shareholder. The company took an independent and active role in the management of the company. In short, it seems to me that given the court's findings of fact, it was entitled to come to the views expressed in paras 7(b) and 7(c) of the case.'
Greene King plc v Harlow District Council [2003] EWHC 2852 (Admin) at [33]–[37], [2004] 2 All ER 102, per Goldring J

PROSECUTION

[For 45 Halsbury's Laws (4th edn) para 1342 see now 45(2) Halsbury's Laws (4th edn) (Reissue) para 460.]

PROTECTION

Australia [Article 1A(2) of the Convention relating to the Status of Refugees (Geneva, 28 July 1951; Aust TS 1954 No 5; 189 UNTS 150) art 1A(2) (as amended by the Protocol relating to the Status of Refugees (New York, 31 January 1967; Aust TS 1973 No 37; 606 UNTS 267)) provides that the term 'refugee' shall apply to any person who 'owing to well-founded fear of being persecuted for reasons of race, religion, nationality, membership of a particular social group or political opinion, is outside the country of his nationality and is unable or, owing to such fear, is unwilling to avail himself of the protection of that country; or who, not having a nationality and being outside the country of his former habitual residence, is unable or, owing to such fear, is unwilling to return to it.']

'There is a broader sense, and a narrower sense, in which the term "protection" is used in the present context.

'An example of the broader sense is to be found in the following passage in the judgment of Brennan CJ in *Applicant A v Minister for Immigration and Ethnic Affairs* (1997) 190 CLR 225 at 233:

"The feared 'persecution' of which art 1A(2) speaks exhibits certain qualities. The first of these qualities relates to the source of the persecution. A person ordinarily looks to 'the country of his nationality' for protection of his fundamental rights and freedoms but, if 'a well-founded fear of being persecuted' makes a person 'unwilling to avail himself of the protection of [the country of his nationality]', that fear must be a fear of persecution by the country of the putative refugee's nationality or persecution which that country is unable or unwilling to prevent."

'The relationship between persecution as the inflicting of serious harm in violation of fundamental rights and freedoms, and the responsibility of a country of nationality, or state, as the primary protector of fundamental rights and freedoms, has been taken up in the interpretation of the Convention. It is reflected in what was said by Lord Hope of Craighead in *Horvath v Secretary of State for the Home Department* [2001] 1 AC 489 at 497–8:

"I would hold therefore that, in the context of an allegation of persecution by non-state agents, the word 'persecution' implies a failure by the state to make protection available against the ill-treatment or violence which the person suffers at the hands of his persecutors. In a case where the allegation is of persecution by the state or its own agents the problem does not, of course, arise. There is a clear case for surrogate protection by the international community. But in the case of an allegation of persecution by non-state agents the failure of the state to provide the protection is nevertheless an essential element. It provides the bridge between persecution by the state and persecution by non-state agents which is necessary in the interests of the consistency of the whole scheme."

'His Lordship went on to quote Dawson J in *Applicant A* [at 248], who said that it was a well-accepted fact that international refugee law was meant to serve as a substitute for national protection where such protection was not provided due to discrimination against persons on grounds of their civil or political status.

'The narrower sense in which "protection" is used is that of diplomatic or consular protection extended abroad by a country to its nationals. As Professor Kälin has demonstrated [in Kälin, "Non-State Agents of Persecution and the Inability of the State to Protect", (2001) 15 *Georgetown Immigration Law Journal* 415 at 426], the history of the Convention and textual considerations suggest that, in art 1A(2), in the expression "the protection of that country", the word "protection" is used in this sense. The historical background to the Convention includes the 1946 Constitution of the International Refugee Organisation, which referred to external protection and viewed a refugee as a person having no consul or diplomatic mission to whom to turn. The drafting history appears to support Professor Kälin's view. And the inability or unwillingness of the refugee referred to in art 1A(2) to avail himself of the protection of his country, by hypothesis, occurs when he is outside his country. It does not follow, however, that the broader sense of protection is irrelevant to art 1A(2).

'It is accepted in Australia, and it is widely accepted in other jurisdictions, that the serious harm involved in persecution may be inflicted by persons who are not agents of the government of the country of nationality referred to in art 1A(2). However, the paradigm case of persecution contemplated by the Convention is persecution by the state itself. Article 1A(2) was primarily, even if not exclusively, aimed at persecution by a state or its agents on one of the grounds to which it refers. Bearing that in mind, there is a paradox in the reference to a refugee's inability or unwillingness to avail himself of the protection of his persecutor. But accepting that, at that point of the Article, the reference is to protection in the narrower sense, an inability or unwillingness to seek diplomatic protection abroad may be explained by a failure of internal protection in the wider sense, or may be related to a possibility that seeking such protection could result in return to the place of persecution. During the 1950s, people fled to Australia from communist persecution in Hungary. They did not, upon arrival, ask the way to the Hungarian Embassy.

'The opening portion of art 1A(2) postulates that a putative refugee is outside the country of his nationality owing to a fear of persecution. That contemplates a fear of persecution within the country of his nationality. It is "such fear" that makes the person unwilling to avail himself of the protection of his country. It is not a fear of being persecuted by the country's diplomats that causes the unwillingness; although the possibility that if he puts himself in their hands he may be returned to his own country may be a consideration.

'When a national of another country applies, under the Act, for a "protection visa", claiming that Australia "has protection obligations" under the Convention, and contends that his or her case falls within art 1A(2), unwillingness to seek the diplomatic protection of the country of nationality may be self-evident. But on the questions whether persecution is a threat, (which usually involves consideration of what has occurred in the past as a basis for looking at the future), and whether such persecution is by reason of one of the Convention grounds, and whether fear of persecution is well-founded, the obligation of a state to protect the fundamental rights and freedoms of those who are entitled to its protection may be of significance.' (footnotes omitted) *Minister for Immigration and Multicultural Affairs v Khawar* (2002) 187 ALR 574; BC200201536; [2002] HCA 14 at [17]–[24], per Gleeson CJ

PROTECTIVE MEASURE/ PROVISIONAL MEASURE

[Article 12 of Council Regulation (EC) 1347/2000 (the Brussels II regulation) on the jurisdiction and the recognition and enforcement in matrimonial matters provides that in 'urgent cases' the provisions of the regulation are not to prevent courts of a member state from taking 'such provisional, including protective measures' in respect of persons or assets in that state as may be available under the law of that state even if, under the regulation, another court has jurisdiction as to the substance of the matter.] '[32] However it is necessary to look beyond the facts of the present case to consider more generally the application of arts 11 and 12 to financial claims ancillary to the proceedings for divorce, judicial separation or nullity. Plainly the Brussels II Regulation has no direct application to such claims. In modern times the real issues litigated as a consequence of the breakdown of relationships are usually money and children. In modern times the utility of the power to order maintenance pending suit has much diminished and the right to apply for it is much less often exercised. For those with little means there is the safety net of benefit entitlement. The affluent generally have capital reserves or the ability to borrow. The procedures for the preparation of the substantive financial claims have been streamlined, partly in an attempt to avoid the unnecessary expense of a contested hearing to determine the level of temporary provision only to be followed by a contested hearing to settle the long-term future. In these cases with an international dimension the temptation on the parties first to manoeuvre and then to fight to establish the jurisdiction which one believes will be more generous and the other believes will be less generous need to be firmly kerbed. It does not require great insight to see that a judgment on pending suit provision is likely to impact upon the outcome of the substantive application, even if it does not pre-empt the operation of the alternative jurisdiction. It is manifest, in my judgment, that an application for maintenance pending suit cannot be categorised as a protective measure. The *de Cavel* [*de Cavel v de Cavel* Case 143/78 [1979] ECR 1055, ECJ] and *Reichert* [*Reichert v Dresdner Bank AG (No 2)* Case C-261/90 [1992] ECR I-2149, ECJ] cases make that plain and the principles there stated should equally be applied to art 12 of the Brussels II Regulation.

'[33] I am also myself of the opinion that an application for maintenance pending suit cannot even be categorised as a provisional measure. Over-payments or payments obtained by material non-disclosure are at best given some indirect reflection in a later quantification of substantive orders. Furthermore if the duty to quantify the substantive order is to be discharged in the court of another member state the payee may well escape even that reflection.

'[34] If this last point be finely balanced then the balance should in my judgment be settled by a strict construction of art 12 for policy reasons. First we must espouse the regulation and apply it wholeheartedly. We must not take or be seen to take opportunities for usurping the function of the judge in the other member state. Once another jurisdiction is demonstrated to be apparently first seised, this jurisdiction must defer, by holding itself in waiting in case that apparent priority should be disproved or declined. Second one of the primary objectives of the convention is to simplify jurisdictional rules and to eliminate expensive and superfluous litigation. A divorcing couple that has to litigate the consequences of the marital breakdown is not blessed. The couple that first litigates where to litigate might be said to be cursed. In reality it is a curse restricted to the rich. Only they can afford such folly ... All this might perhaps be prevented for the future were this appeal to contribute to the adoption of a narrow construction of art 12 here and in other member states pending a possible future ruling of the Court of Justice of the European Communities.' *Wermuth v Wermuth* [2002] EWCA Civ 50 at [32]–[34], [2003] 4 All ER 531, CA, per Thorpe LJ

PROTEST

[For 43 Halsbury's Laws (4th edn) para 193 see now 43(1) Halsbury's Laws (4th edn) (Reissue) para 469.]

PROVIDED FOR

Australia 'In my opinion, the phrase "provided for" means that the service must be provided for the purpose of causing or facilitating such a benefit. Confirmation of that meaning may be found in the presence of the alternative phrase "or purportedly for" which in this context clearly means that the service must be professedly or ostensibly provided for such a purpose.' *Hanna v Cmr Community and Health Services Complaints (ACT)* (2002) 171 FLR 185; BC200206546; [2002] ACTSC 111 at [26], per Crispin ACJ

PROVIDING FOR

Australia [In the context of providing for fixing of retail petrol prices; (Cth) Trade Practices Act 1974 s 45A.] 'We were not referred to any authority on the term "providing for" in s 45A. In this context the term, coming from the Latin *providere*, to see before, suggests arranging for or stipulating beforehand (Macquarie) or to make preparation for, get ready (Shorter Oxford). What is it that is to happen in the future as a result of these arrangements or preparations? It must be price fixing, that is to say competitors agreeing on prices they will charge consumers for good or services.

'Examples of "providing for" price fixing in this sense would be an arrangement that prices would increase by a particular formula, or an agreement that if one competitor increases prices the others will follow. In short, "providing for" must be a means to the end of price fixing.' *Apco Service Stations Pty Ltd v Australian Competition and Consumer Commission* [2005] FCAFC 161 at [49]–[50], per Heerey, Hely and Gyles JJ; BC200505938

PROVISION. *SEE* EXCLUSIONARY PROVISION

PROVISION THAT HAS THE PURPOSE

New Zealand [Commerce Act 1986, s 2(5)(a).] 'First, it is the "provision" that must be shown to have the purpose. Secondly, the inquiry as to the purpose of the provision must be undertaken having regard to the deeming provision in s 2(5)(a) which reads:

(a) A provision of a contract, arrangement, or understanding, or a covenant shall be deemed to have had, or to have, a particular purpose if—

  (i) The provision was or is included in the contract, arrangement or understanding, or the covenant was or is required to be given, for that purpose or purposes that included or include that purpose; and

  (ii) That purpose was or is a substantial purpose:

'That deems a provision to have the purpose if it was required to be included (by the person or persons so requiring) for that purpose. This indicates plainly that not all parties need be shown to share the purpose. In any event, in a case which is concerned with contracts and intended contracts it is unproductive to point to the purpose of only one party. Once the contract is concluded the parties must be taken to share the purposes of its provisions.' *Port Nelson Ltd v Commerce Commission* [1996] 3 NZLR 554 at 563, CA, per cur

PROXIMATE CAUSE

[For 25 Halsbury's Laws (4th edn) para 180 see now 25 Halsbury's Laws (4th edn) (2003 Reissue) para 356.]

PROXY

Australia 'The question is whether, for the purpose of the [Corporations Act 2001 (Cth) s 250A(1)], voting by attorney is encompassed within the provisions dealing with voting by proxy.

'In *Totally & Permanently Incapacitated Veterans' Association v Gadd* (1998) 28 ACSR 549 at 557 Young J drew attention to *Monmouthshire Canal Navigation Co v Kendall* (1821) 4 B & Ald 453 at 458 (106 ER 1003 at 1005) where counsel said that the word "proxy" is an abbreviation of the word "procuracy." The word is not recognised in Dr Samuel Johnson's "A Dictionary of the English Language" W Strahan, London, 1755. The *Oxford English Dictionary*'s second, and now obsolete, meaning is a document empowering a person to act as the representative of another; a proxy, a letter of attorney. In *In re English, Scottish and Australian*

Chartered Bank [1893] 3 Ch 385 at 409 Lindley LJ described the word "proxy" as meaning some agent properly appointed. In my view the word "proxy" in the Corporations Act is sufficiently broad to include an attorney.' *New South Wales Henry George Foundation Ltd v Booth* BC200201438; (2002) 41 ACSR 288; [2002] NSWSC 245 at [20]–[21], per Gzell J

New Zealand 'A "proxy", which is a contraction of "procuracy", is defined in *The New Shorter Oxford Dictionary* (1993) as:

"1. The agency of a person who acts by appointment instead of another; the action of a substitute or deputy. Chiefly in by *proxy*, by the agency of another, by or through a substitute, not in person. 2. A document empowering a person to represent and act for another; a letter of attorney. Now only *spec*, a document authorizing a person to vote on behalf of another, a vote cast by proxy. 3. A person appointed or authorized to represent and act for another; an attorney, a substitute, a representative."

'In *Cousins v International Brick Co Ltd* [1931] 2 Ch 90 at 100 Lord Hanworth MR defined a proxy in relation to a company as:

' "A person representative of the shareholder who may be described as his agent to carry out a course which the shareholder himself has decided upon".'

Maori Development Corporation Ltd v Power Beat International Ltd [1995] 2 NZLR 568 at 575, per Blanchard J

PSYCHOPATHIC DISORDER

[For 30 Halsbury's Laws (4th edn) para 1002 see now 30 Halsbury's Laws (4th edn) (Reissue) para 1003.]

PUBLIC

Australia 'The phrase in s 31(1)(a)(iii) of the 1968 Act [Copyright Act 1968 (Cth)] is "to perform the work in public" not before "members of the public" or "a public audience" or "the general public". Running through the authorities I have discussed is the notion that for the purposes of this performing right a performance will be "in public" if it is not "in private", and the perception of an antithesis between performances which are in public and those which are "domestic" or "private" in character.

In determining whether a performance answers the latter description, the nature of the audience is important. In coming together to form the audience for the performance were the persons concerned bound together by a domestic or private tie or by an aspect of their public life? Their "public life" would include their presence at their place of employment for the supply of a performance to assist the commercial purposes of their employer.' *Australasian Performing Right Association Ltd v Commonwealth Bank of Australia* (1992) 40 FCR 59 at 74, per Gummow J

Canada '[244] The ordinary meaning of the word "public" appears to be the community or people as an aggregate, or at least a particular section, group or portion of a community, and certainly is more than a single person. *Black's Law Dictionary* (6th ed.) provides the following definition:

> n. The whole body politic, or the aggregate of the citizens of a state, nation, or municipality. The inhabitants of a state, county, or community. In one sense, everybody, and accordingly the body of the people at large; the community at large, without reference to the geographical limits of any corporation like a city, town, or county; the people. In another sense the word does not mean all the people, nor most of the people, nor very many of the people of a place, but so many of them as contradistinguishes them from a few. Accordingly, it has been defined or employed as meaning the inhabitants of a particular place; all the inhabitants of a particular place; the people of the neighbourhood. Also, a part of the inhabitants of a community.

Having regard only to the broad definition of the word "public", one might conclude that the term "to the public" would suggest that a communication must be aimed or targeted at more than one person. '[245] On the other hand, Australian jurisprudence suggests that in some circumstances, a single person might be the public for purposes of the Australian *Copyright Act*: see *Telstra v Australasian Performing Rights Association, supra,* at pp. 156–7.' *CCH Canadian Ltd v Law Society of Upper Canada* (2002) DLR (4th) 385 at 475 (FCA), per Rothstein JA

PUBLIC AUTHORITY

[For 1 Halsbury's Laws (4th edn) para 6 see now 1(1) Halsbury's Laws (4th edn) (2001 Reissue) para 6.]

[A Parochial Church Council (PCC) submitted, inter alia, that it was not a 'public authority' within the meaning of s 6(1) of the Human Rights Act 1998 and that accordingly it was not subject to that provision, which made it unlawful for such a body to act in a way that was incompatible with convention rights. Under s 6(3), 'public authority' includes 'any person certain of whose functions are functions of a public nature'.]'[6] The expression "public authority" is not defined in the Human Rights Act, nor is it a recognised term of art in English law, that is, an expression with a specific recognised meaning. The word "public" is a term of uncertain import, used with many different shades of meaning: public policy, public rights of way, public property, public authority (in the Public Authorities Protection Act 1893), public nuisance, public house, public school, public company. So in the present case the statutory context is all important. As to that, the broad purpose sought to be achieved by s 6(1) is not in doubt. The purpose is that those bodies for whose acts the state is answerable before the European Court of Human Rights shall in future be subject to a domestic law obligation not to act incompatibly with convention rights. If they act in breach of this legal obligation victims may henceforth obtain redress from the courts of this country. In future victims should not need to travel to Strasbourg.

'[7] Conformably with this purpose, the phrase "a public authority" in s 6(1) is essentially a reference to a body whose nature is governmental in a broad sense of that expression. It is in respect of organisations of this nature that the government is answerable under the convention. Hence, under the Human Rights Act a body of this nature is required to act compatibly with convention rights in everything it does. The most obvious examples are government departments, local authorities, the police and the armed forces. Behind the instinctive classification of these organisations as bodies whose nature is governmental lie factors such as the possession of special powers, democratic accountability, public funding in whole or in part, an obligation to act only in the public interest, and a statutory constitution: see the valuable article by Professor Dawn Oliver "The Frontiers of the State: Public Authorities and Public Functions under the Human Rights Act" [2000] PL 476.

'[8] A further, general point should be noted. One consequence of being a "core" public authority, namely, an authority falling within s 6 without reference to s 6(3), is that the body in question does not itself enjoy convention rights. It is difficult to see how a core public authority could ever claim to be a victim of an infringement of convention rights. A core public authority seems inherently incapable of satisfying the convention description of a victim: "any person, *non-governmental organisation* or group of individuals" (see art 34; my emphasis). Only victims of an unlawful act may bring proceedings under s 7 of the Human Rights Act, and the convention description of a victim has been incorporated into the Act, by s 7(7). This feature, that a core public authority is incapable of having convention rights of its own, is a matter to be borne in mind when considering whether or not a particular body is a core public authority. In itself this feature throws some light on how the expression "public authority" should be understood and applied. It must always be relevant to consider whether Parliament can have intended that the body in question should have no convention rights.

'[9] In a modern developed state governmental functions extend far beyond maintenance of law and order and defence of the realm. Further, the manner in which wide-ranging governmental functions are discharged varies considerably. In the interests of efficiency and economy, and for other reasons, functions of a governmental nature are frequently discharged by non-governmental bodies. Sometimes this will be a consequence of privatisation, sometimes not. One obvious example is the running of prisons by commercial organisations. Another is the discharge of regulatory functions by organisations in the private sector, for instance, the Law Society. Section 6(3)(b) gathers this type of case into the embrace of s 6 by including within the phrase "public authority" any person whose functions include "functions of a public nature". This extension of the expression "public authority" does not apply to a person if the nature of the act in question is "private".

'[10] Again, the statute does not amplify what the expression "public" and its counterpart "private" mean in this context. But, here also, given the statutory context already mentioned and the repetition of the description "public", essentially the contrast being drawn is between functions of a governmental nature and functions, or acts, which are not of that nature. I stress, however, that this is no more than a useful guide. The phrase used in the Act is public function, not governmental function.

'[11] Unlike a core public authority, a "hybrid" public authority, exercising both public functions and non-public functions, is not absolutely disabled from having convention rights. A hybrid public authority is not a public authority in respect of an act of a private nature. Here again, as with s 6(1), this feature throws some light on the approach to be adopted when interpreting s 6(3)(b). Giving a generously wide scope to the expression "public function" in s 6(3)(b) will further the statutory aim of promoting the observance of human rights values without depriving the bodies in question of the ability themselves to rely on convention rights when necessary.

'[12] What, then, is the touchstone to be used in deciding whether a function is public for this purpose? Clearly there is no single test of universal application. There cannot be, given the diverse nature of governmental functions and the variety of means by which these functions are discharged today. Factors to be taken into account include the extent to which in carrying out the relevant function the body is publicly funded, or is exercising statutory powers, or is taking the place of central government or local authorities, or is providing a public service.

'[13] Turning to the facts in the present case, I do not think PCCs are "core" public authorities. Historically the Church of England has discharged an important and influential role in the life of this country. As the established Church it still has special links with central government. But the Church of England remains essentially a religious organisation. This is so even though some of the emanations of the Church discharge functions which may qualify as governmental. Church schools and the conduct of marriage services are two instances. The legislative powers of the General Synod of the Church of England are another. This should not be regarded as infecting the Church of England as a whole, or its emanations in general, with the character of a governmental organisation.

'[14] As to PCCs, their constitution and functions lend no support to the view that they should be characterised as governmental organisations or, more precisely, in the language of the statute, public authorities. PCCs are established as corporate bodies under a Church measure, now the Parochial Church Councils (Powers) Measure 1956. For historical reasons this unique form of legislation, having the same force as a statute, is the way the Church of England governs its affairs. But the essential role of a PCC is to provide a formal means, prescribed by the Church of England, whereby ex officio and elected members of the local church promote the mission of the Church and discharge financial responsibilities in respect of their own parish church, including responsibilities regarding maintenance of the fabric of the building. This smacks of a Church body engaged in self-governance and promotion of its affairs. This is far removed from the type of body whose acts engage the responsibility of the state under the convention.

'[15] The contrary conclusion, that the Church authorities in general and PCCs in particular are "core" public authorities, would mean these bodies are not capable of being victims within the meaning of the Human Rights Act. Accordingly they are not able to complain of infringements of convention rights. That would be an extraordinary conclusion. The Human Rights Act goes out of its way, in s 13, to single out for express mention the exercise by religious organisations of the convention right of freedom of thought, conscience and religion. One would expect that these and other convention rights would be enjoyed by the Church of England as much as other religious bodies.

'[16] I turn next to consider whether a PCC is a hybrid public authority. For this purpose it is not necessary to analyse each of the functions of a PCC and see if any of them is a public function. What matters is whether the particular act done by the PCC of which complaint is made is a private act as contrasted with the discharge of a public function. The impugned act is enforcement of Mr and Mrs Wallbank's liability, as lay rectors, for the repair of the chancel of the church of St John the Baptist at Aston Cantlow. As I see it, the only respect in which there is any "public" involvement is that parishioners have certain rights to attend church services and in respect of marriage and burial services. To that extent the state of repair of the church building may be said to affect rights of the public. But I do not think this suffices to characterise actions taken by the PCC for the repair of the church as "public". If a PCC enters into a contract with a builder for the repair of the chancel arch, that could be hardly be described as a public act. Likewise when a PCC enforces, in accordance with the provisions of the Chancel Repairs Act 1932, a burdensome incident attached to the ownership of certain pieces of land: there is nothing particularly "public" about this. This is no more a public act than is the enforcement of a restrictive covenant of which Church land has the benefit.

'[17] For these reasons this appeal succeeds. A PCC is not a core public authority, nor does it become such by virtue of s 6(3)(b) when enforcing a lay rector's liability for chancel repairs. Accordingly the Human Rights Act affords lay rectors no relief from their liabilities … '

...

'[58] There is no doubt that PCCs are an essential part of the administration, on the authority of the General Synod, of the affairs of the Church of England. The parish itself has been described as the basic building block of the Church and the PCC as the central forum for decision-making and discussion in relation to parish affairs: Mark Hill *Ecclesiastical Law* (2nd edn, 2001) pp 48–49 and 74 (paras 3.11 and 3.74). It is constituted by s 3 of the 1956 measure [Parochial Church Councils (Powers) Measure 1956] as a body corporate. It has statutory powers which it may exercise under s 2 of the [Chancel Repairs Act 1932] against any person who appears to it to be liable to repair the chancel, irrespective of whether that person is resident in the parish and is a member of the Church of England. In that context, perhaps, it may be said in a very loose sense to be a public rather than a private body.

'[59] But none of these characteristics indicate that it is a governmental organisation, as that phrase is understood in the context of art 34 of the convention. It plainly has nothing whatever to do with the process of either central or local government. It is not accountable to the general public for what it does. It receives no public funding, apart from occasional grants from English Heritage for the preservation of its historic buildings. In that respect it is in a position which is no different from that of any private individual. The statutory powers which it has been given by the 1932 Act are not exercisable against the public generally or any class or group of persons which forms part of it. The purpose of that Act, as its long title indicates, was to abolish proceedings in ecclesiastical courts for enforcing the liability to repair. The only person against whom the liability may be enforced is the person who, in that obscure phrase, "would, but for the provisions of this Act, have been liable to be admonished to repair the chancel by the appropriate Ecclesiastical Court in a cause of office promoted against him in that Court on the date when the notice was served" (see s 2(3); *Wickhambrook Parochial Church Council v Croxford* [1935] 2 KB 417 at 429 per Lord Hanworth MR).

'[60] Then there is the fact that the PCC is part of the Church of England. The Court of Appeal said that it exemplifies the special status of the Church of which it forms part ([2001] 3 All ER 393 at [32]). The fact that it forms part of the Church by law established showed, it was said (at [35]), that the PCC is a public authority. The implication of these observations is that other bodies such as diocesan and deanery synods and the General Synod itself fall into the same category. In my opinion however the legal framework of the Church of England as a Church by law established does not lead to this conclusion.

'[61] The Church of England as a whole has no legal status or personality. There is no Act of Parliament that purports to establish it as the Church of England: Sir Lewis Dibdin *Establishment in England: Essays on Church and State* (1932) p 111. What establishment in law means is that the state has incorporated its law into the law of the realm as a branch of its general law. In *Marshall v Graham, Bell v Graham* [1907] 2 KB 112 at 126 Phillimore J said:

> "A Church which is established is not thereby made a department of the State. The process of establishment means that the State has accepted the Church as the religious body in its opinion truly teaching the Christian faith, and given to it a certain legal position, and to its decrees, if rendered under certain legal conditions, certain civil sanctions."

The Church of England is identified with the state in other ways, the monarch being head of each: see Norman Doe *The Legal Framework of the Church of England* (1996) p 9. It has regulatory functions within its own sphere, but it cannot be said to be part of government. The state has not surrendered or delegated any of its functions or powers to the Church. None of the functions that the Church of England performs would have to be performed in its place by the state if the Church were to abdicate its responsibility: see *R v Chief Rabbi of the United Hebrew Congregations of Great Britain and the Commonwealth, ex p Wachmann* [1993] 2 All ER 249 at 254, [1992] 1 WLR 1036 at 1042 per Simon Brown J. The relationship which the state has with the Church of England is one of recognition, not of the devolution to it of any of the powers or functions of government.

'[62] The decisions of the Strasbourg court in *Holy Monasteries v Greece* (1995) 20 EHRR 1 and *Hautanemi v Sweden* (1996) 22 EHRR CD 155 support this approach. It is also worth noting that, while the two main churches in Germany (Roman Catholic and Lutheran) have public legal personality and are public authorities bound by the provisions of art 19(4) of the German constitution (Grundgesetz) or Basic Law which guarantees recourse to the court should any person's basic rights be violated by public authority, they are in general considered to be "non-governmental organisations" within the meaning of art 34 of the convention. As such, they are entitled to avail

themselves of, for example, the right to protection of property under art 1 of the First Protocol: Frowein and Peukert *Kommentar zur Europäishen Menschenrechtskonvention* (2nd edn, 1996) art 25, para 16. Maunz and Dürig *Kommentar zum Grundgesetz* (looseleaf) art 33, para 38 explain the position in this way:

> "Keine hoheitsrechtlichen Befugnisse nehmen die Amtsträger der Kirchen wahr, soweit sie nicht kraft staatlicher Ermächtigung (etwa in Kirchensteuerangelegenheiten) tätig werden; die Kirchen sind, auch soweit sie öffentlich-rechtlichen Status haben, nicht Bestandteile der staatlichen Organisation."

[Church officeholders do not exercise sovereign power so long as they are not acting by virtue of state empowerment (for example, in matters concerning church taxes); the churches do not, even though they have public law status, form an integral part of the organisation of the state.] This reflects the view of the German Constitutional Court in its 1965 decision (BVerfGE 18, 385) that measures taken by a church relating to purely internal matters which do not reach out into the sphere of the state do not constitute acts of sovereign power. The churches are not, as we would put it, "core" public authorities although they may be regarded as "hybrid" public authorities for certain purposes.

'[63] For these reasons I would hold that the PCC is not a "core" public authority. As for the question whether it is a "hybrid" public authority, I would prefer not to deal with it in the abstract. The answer must depend on the facts of each case. The issue with which your Lordships are concerned in this case relates to the functions of the PCC in the enforcement of a liability to effect repairs to the chancel. Section 6(5) of the Human Rights Act provides that a person is not a public authority by virtue only of sub-s (3) if the nature of the act which is alleged to be unlawful is private. The Court of Appeal said that the function of chancel repairs is of a public nature ([2001] 3 All ER 393 at [35]). But the liability of the lay rector to repair the chancel is a burden which arises as a matter of private law from the ownership of glebe land.

'[64] It is true, as Wynn-Parry J observed in *Chivers & Sons Ltd v Secretary of State for Air (Queens' College, Cambridge, Third Party)* [1955] 2 All ER 607 at 609, [1955] Ch 585 at 593, that the burden is imposed for the benefit of the parishioners. It may be said that, as the church is a historic building which is open to the public, it is in the public interest that these repairs should be carried out. It is also true that the liability to repair the chancel rests on persons who need not be members of the church and that there is, as the Court of Appeal observed (at [34]), no surviving element of mutuality or mutual governance between the church and the impropriator. But none of these factors leads to the conclusion that the PCC's act in seeking to enforce the lay rector's liability on behalf of the parishioners is a public rather than a private act. The nature of the act is to be found in the nature of the obligation which the PCC is seeking to enforce. It is seeking to enforce a civil debt. The function which it is performing has nothing to do with the responsibilities which are owed to the public by the state. I would hold that s 6(5) applies, and that in relation to this act the PCC is not for the purposes of s 6(1) a public authority.' *Aston Cantlow and Wilmcote with Billesley Parochial Church Council v Wallbank* [2003] UKHL 37 at [6]–[17], [58]–[64], [2003] 3 All ER 1213, HL, per Lord Nicholls of Birkenhead, and Lord Hope of Craighead

Canada '2. Under subparagraph 9(1)(*n*)(iii) of the *Trade-marks Act* does public authority refer to a Canadian public authority?

'[39] In order for a mark to be a proper official mark pursuant to subparagraph 9(1)(*n*)(iii) of the Act, the official mark must have been "adopted and used by any public authority, in Canada as an official mark for wares or services".

'[40] The Act does not define "public authority".

'[41] The applicant argues that pursuant to section 9 of the Act, it is not enough that an entity be a public authority, the entity must be a "Canadian" public authority.

'[42] In my opinion, if the intent was to restrict the application to only "Canadian" public authorities, the legislator would have used the words "Canadian public authority". I am unable to find either in English or in French that the words "in Canada"/"*au Canada*" would grammatically and in an ordinary meaning apply to public authority.

'[43] In statutory interpretation, according to P.-A. Côté, words in a statute should be given their ordinary meanings:

As it is presumed that the legislator wishes to be understood by the citizen, the law is deemed to have been drafted in accordance with the rules of language in common use. In particular, Parliament is presumed to use words in the same sense as would the "man in

the street". The authorities refer frequently to this prototypical subject and to the ordinary meanings of words …

'[44] Therefore, on a plain reading of the section, I agree with the respondent that the term "public authority" is not restricted to Canadian public authority.' *Canada Post Corp v Post Office* [2001] 2 FC 63 at 76–77, TD, per Tremblay-Lamer JA

PUBLIC BENEVOLENT INSTITUTION

Australia 'In my opinion the authorities since [*Perpetual Trust Co Ltd v Federal Commissioner of Taxation* (1931) 45 CLR 224] do not establish, any more than that case did, that to be a public benevolent institution it must serve only those in financial need without charge or for a small charge. In my opinion the authorities deny that relief of poverty or the provision of services only to those in financial need are essential characteristics of benevolence. Nor do they establish that the levying of a charge for the service removes the element of benevolence.' *Commissioner of Pay-roll Tax v Cairnmillar Institute* [1992] 2 VR 706 at 711, per Gobbo

Australia 'Whether or not an institution is accurately described as a public institution because it performs public functions and is publicly controlled and funded or is correctly described as a benevolent institution because of the nature of the benefits it provides, an institution is not a public benevolent institution unless benefits of the requisite character [namely, for the relief of poverty, suffering, distress or misfortune] are provided or available to the general public or a sufficient section of the public. An institution, whether or not a public institution, must provide or promote public benevolence if it is to meet the description "public benevolent institution" …' *Re Royal Society for the Prevention of Cruelty to Animals, Qld Inc* [1993] 1 Qd R 571 at 577, per Fitzgerald P

Australia 'The expression "public benevolent institution" is a compound expression and not one to be fragmented into its component parts ([*Public Trustee (NSW) v Federal Commissioner of Taxation* (1934) 51 CLR 75; 8 ALJR 74]). Whilst "public charity" is not synonymous with "public benevolent institution", the ordinary meanings of the two expressions are somewhat similar: see [*Metropolitan Fire Brigades Board v Federal Commissioner of Taxation* (1990) 27 FCR 279; 97 ALR 335; 21 ATR 1137; 91 ATC 4052] at 283. It is not enough that a particular institution exists for the promotion of the public good. Hence, applying *Perpetual Trustee*, while it is acknowledged that the relief of financial hardship is not an essential characteristic ([*Commissioner of Pay-Roll Tax (Vic) v The Cairnmillar Institute* [1992] 2 VR 706; (1992) 23 ATR 314; 92 ATC 4307]; [*Australian Council of Social Services Inc v Commissioner of Pay-roll Tax (NSW)* [1985] 1 NSWLR 567; (1985) 16 ATR 394; 85 ATC 4235]), the body will not qualify as a "public benevolent institution" unless it promotes the relief of *one or other* of poverty, suffering, distress or misfortune.

'[30] Furthermore, as Thomas J explained in [*Federal Commissioner of Taxation v Royal Society for the Prevention of Cruelty to Animals* (1992) ATC 4,441], the authorities have basically confined the concept of "public benevolent institution" to institutions whose primary activities are eleemosynary. That is the authorities import an underlying conception of "charity" or "gratuity" as the fundamental foundation for their understanding of "benevolence" in this context. In short the authorities propound, and I adopt, a notion of benevolence which involves an act of *kindness*, or perhaps most particularly, the rendering of assistance *voluntarily* to those who, for one reason or another are in need of help and who cannot help themselves.' *Mines Rescue Board of New South Wales v Federal Commissioner of Taxation* (2000) 44 ATR 107; ATC 4191; BC200001378; [2000] FCA 382 at [29], [30], per Hely J

Australia 'I agree with the opinion of the learned trial judge expressed in *Tangentyere Council v Cmr of Taxes* (1990) 99 FLR 363 at 364, that the term "public benevolent institution" is not a term of art, but a compound expression which takes its meaning from ordinary English usage of the day. I would add to that, "and from the legislative context in which it finds itself if that context throws particular light on the intended meaning." In *Perpetual Trustee Co v Federal Cmr of Taxation* (1931) 45 CLR 224, both the context of the expression and the legislative history of the provisions of the Estate Duty Assessment Act 1914–1928 (Cth) were relied upon by Starke J (at 231–2) and by Dixon J (at 233) as showing that the meaning was narrower than "charitable institution" in its technical legal sense. Therefore, a public benevolent institution (PBI) may be a charity in the legal sense, but not every such charity is a PBI. Whilst there is nothing in the history of the Pay-roll Tax Act 1978 (NT) which throws any light on the matter, the expression finds

itself in the same company as religious institutions and public hospitals and there is no reason to depart from this view.

'In the *Perpetual Trustee Co* case, supra, Starke J said at 232 that a PBI was in the context in which it was found and in ordinary English usage "an institution organised for the relief of poverty, sickness, destitution, or helplessness." Dixon J expressed the matter negatively, at 233–4, when he said that "I am unable to place upon the expression 'public benevolent institution' in the exemption a meaning wide enough to include institutions which do not promote the relief of poverty, suffering, distress or misfortune.

'Evatt J said, at 235–6, that:

"... a characteristic of most of these organisations is the absence of any charge for services or the fixing of a purely nominal charge. Such bodies vary greatly in scope and character. But they have one thing in common: they give relief freely to those who are in need of it and who are unable to care for themselves. Those who receive aid or comfort in this way are the poor, the sick, the aged and the young. Their disability or distress arouses pity, and the institutions are designed to give them protection."

'McTiernan J who dissented in the result said, at 241, that:

"... while I do not think that the legislature intended strictly to confine the exemption to gifts to an institution of a strictly eleemosynary character, yet it may be difficult to bring within the scope of the exemption ... a gift to an institution which is of a public character, but does not exist for the relief of distress or misfortune occasioned by poverty."

'Subsequent decisions of the High Court provide further guidance. Although an institution is not subject to public ownership and control, this does not necessarily compel the conclusion that it is not a public benevolent institution. It is a question of fact and degree in each case which depends not so much on how it was established or financed, but upon the character of the institution and the nature of the services rendered: per Starke J in *The Little Company of Mary (SA) Inc v Commonwealth* (1942) 66 CLR 368 at 386: *Maughan v Federal Cmr of Taxation* (1942) 66 CLR 388 at 395–6 per McTiernan J. An institution which aims at benefiting an appreciable, but not necessarily appreciable needy, section of the community is a public institution: per Williams J with whom Rich J agreed in *Maughan v Federal Cmr of Taxation*, supra, at 397–98; *Lemm v Federal Cmr of Taxation* (1942) 66 CLR 399 at 410, 411; per Williams J with whom Rich J agreed. A constitution which provides for those members of the public who are sufficiently interested in the work of the institution to subscribe to its funds and thereby become annual members and as such eligible to vote at the election of the controlling body, creates a control which is public in its nature: *Maughan v Federal Cmr of Taxes*, supra, at 397.

'Decisions of state appellate courts in more recent times offer further illumination. In *Australian Council of Social Services Inc v Cmr of Pay-roll Tax* (1985) 1 NSWLR 567, the New South Wales Court of Appeal held that:

> '"benevolence' in the composite phrase 'public benevolent institution' carries with it the idea of benevolence towards persons in need of benevolence, however manifested. Benevolence in this sense … (is) quite a different concept from benevolence exercised at large and for the benefit of the community as a whole even if such benevolence results in relief of or reduction in poverty and distress." (per Priestley JA, at 575, with whom Mahony JA agreed.)

'In *Cmr of Pay-roll Tax v Cairnmiller Institute* [1992] 2 VR 706 at 709, the Court of Appeal of Victoria held that the relief of poverty is not an essential prerequisite because the relief of suffering, distress or misfortune is also a characteristic of a benevolent institution. In order to qualify as a benevolent institution, it is not necessary to show that the services provided are only to those in financial need or without charge or for a small charge. At 712, the Court observed that it is no less benevolent to assist an AIDS sufferer because that person can afford to pay, for the issue is not the relief of poverty, but the relief of distress.

'In *Royal Society for the Prevention of Cruelty to Animals, Queensland Inc* (1993) 1 Qld R 571, the Court of Appeal of Queensland held that the benevolence must be directed towards the public or a section of it, so that a body which provides those benefits to animals or otherwise indirectly for the benefit of mankind, is not within the meaning of the expression.

'In a number of cases, individual judges have expressed differing views on whether or not the expression is similar to the present popular meaning of 'public charity': see *Royal Society for the Prevention of Cruelty to Animals, Queensland Inc*, supra, at 574 per Fitzgerald P and at 582 per

Thomas J, where it was held that this was "not to the point"; cf *Metropolitan Fire Brigades Board v Cmr of Taxation*, 27 FC R 279 at 283 where the Full Federal Court held, after referring to the speech of Lord Wilberforce in *Ashfield Municipal Council v Joyce* [1978] AC 122 at 137, that the notions, whilst not identical, were similar.

'An institution may have independent or collateral objects and powers which enable its funds to be devoted to purposes which are not benevolent which can have the result of the institution losing the status it would otherwise possess as being a benevolent institution. The distinction to be drawn is between objects and powers which are independent and collateral, even if subsidiary, which have a disqualifying effect and those which are 'merely ancillary, incidental, dependent or concomitant' which do not: see *Maclean Shire Council v Nungera Co-operative Society Ltd* (1995) 86 LGERA 430 at 432–3 (per Handley JA with whom Priestly and Sheller JJA agreed.)

' … As to the question of whether or not the appellant is a charity in the popular sense, I consider that consideration of this question diverts attention from the true question. In particular, I agree with Thomas J in *Royal Society for the Prevention of Cruelty to Animals, Queensland Inc*, supra, at 582 that this is "not to the point". As Lord MacNaughton said in *Cmrs for Special Purposes of the Income Tax v Pemsel* [1891] AC 531 at 583, "… no one as yet has succeeded in defining the popular meaning of the word 'charity'." The uncertainty of the term has often been remarked on: see *Ashfield Municipal Council v Joyce*, supra, at 135 and the cases therein referred to. As to whether benevolence is limited to benevolence in the eleemosynary sense, which I take to mean "by the giving of welfare assistance", it is plain from a number of decisions that this is not essential if by welfare assistance one is speaking of the provision of money, housing, food, medicine, or other basic essentials. The provision of services to relieve distress may be sufficient for example, even if the services are not provided only to those in financial need or without charge or for a small charge: *Cmr of Pay-roll Tax v Cairnmiller Institute*, supra, *Cmr of Taxation v Launceston Legacy* (1987) 15 FCR 527; *Tangentyere Council Incorporated v Cmr of Taxes* (1990) 99 FLR 363 at 372. The fact that not all those who are assisted are needy, or in states of distress, or objects of compassion, is also not necessarily conclusive, so long as the section of the public to whom assistance is directed may be so described as a class and so long as that class may be described as disadvantaged and appreciable: *Lemm v Cmr of Taxation*, supra, at 411 per Williams J (with whom Rich and McTiernan JJ agreed); *Tangentyere Council Incorporated v Cmr of Taxes*, supra, at 366, 374; *Gumbangerrii Aboriginal Corporation v Nambucca Council* (1996) 131 FLR 115 at 121; *Aboriginal Hostels Ltd v Darwin City Council* (1985) 75 FLR 197 at 212.' *Northern Land Council v Cmr of Taxes* (2002) 141 NTR 1; 171 FLR 255; BC200207130; [2002] NTCA 11 at [15]–[23], per Mildren J

PUBLIC FUNCTION

New Zealand [New Zealand Bill of Rights Act 1990, s 3(b).] 'The reference to "public" function [in the New Zealand Bill of Rights Act 1990, s 3(b)] reflects the principle that the Bill of Rights applies only to public and governmental action and not to private actions ...' *M v Board of Trustees of Palmerston North Boys' High School* [1997] 2 NZLR 60 at 71, per Goddard J

PUBLIC HOUSE

[For 24 Halsbury's Laws (4th edn) para 1209 see now 24 Halsbury's Laws (4th edn) (Reissue) para 1109.]

PUBLIC INTEREST

Australia [The Credit Act 1984 (Vic) gives power to the Credit Tribunal to reopen an unjust transaction that gave rise to contract. Under s 147(1), the tribunal is to have regard to, inter alia, the 'public interest' in considering what is unjust.] 'The "public interest" is a difficult concept but may perhaps be adequately understood as directing the tribunal's attention to a consideration whether the credit provider's conduct in connection with the regulated contract offended against community standards of business morality: see Peden, *The Law of Unjust Contracts*, 1982, p 122.' *Custom Credit Corpn Ltd v Lupil* [1992] 1 VR 92 at 105, per Murphy J

Canada [Bail pending appeal was available if detention was not shown to be necessary in the public interest.] 'The "public interest" criterion in s 679(3)(c) of the Code requires a judicial assessment of the need to review the conviction leading to imprisonment, in which case execution of the sentence may have to be temporarily suspended, and the need to respect the general rule of immediate enforceability of judgments ...

'There may have been a time when appellate delays were so short that bail pending appeal could safely be denied, save in exceptional circumstances, without rendering the appeal illusory. Such is no longer the case. In both civil and criminal cases, appellate court judges are often required to balance two competing principles of justice: reviewability and enforceability. Ideally, judgments should be reviewed before they have been enforced. When this is not possible, an interim regime may need to be put in place which must be sensitive to a multitude of factors including the anticipated time required for the appeal to be decided and the possibility of irreparable and unjustifiable harm being done in the interval. This is largely what the public interest requires be considered in the determination of entitlement to bail pending appeal. This is what appellate judges do, sitting alone or on a review panel; this is what appellate judges have always understood their mandate to be. Any difference of opinion as to whether an individual applicant should or should not be granted bail merely reflects a different judgment in the application of the legal standard to the facts. It does not suggest that there is no discernible standard to be applied.' *R v Farinacci* (1993) 109 DLR (4th) 97 at 113–114, Ont CA, per Arbour JA

PUBLIC MEETING

[A newspaper published an article relating to the subject of a press conference, reporting critical remarks made about a firm of solicitors, which sued for libel. The newspaper relied on the defence of qualified privilege under the Defamation Act (Northern Ireland) 1955 s 7 and Schedule para 9, which attaches to the fair and accurate report by a newspaper of 'the proceedings at any public meeting' in the United Kingdom, 'that is to say, a meeting ... for the furtherance or discussion of any matter of public concern, whether the admission to the meeting is general or restricted'. The judge instructed the jury that the meeting was not a public meeting, that accordingly the occasion was not privileged and that the solicitors were therefore entitled to succeed on liability. His decision was affirmed by the Court of Appeal in Northern Ireland.] 'The first and major question for decision is one of statutory construction: whether the press conference on 23 January 1995 was a public meeting within the meaning of s 7 of and para 9 of the Schedule to the 1955 Act.

...

'I am of the clear opinion that the press conference held on 23 January was a public meeting within the meaning of s 7 and para 9. I reach that conclusion for these reasons.

...

'The principal issue is whether the press conference was a "public meeting" within the meaning of s 7 of the 1955 Act and para 9 of the Schedule thereto. The development by the House of Lords in *Reynolds v Times Newspapers Ltd* [1999] 4 All ER 609, [1999] 3 WLR 1010 of a new common law qualified privilege came too late to be of assistance in this case. It is therefore necessary to concentrate on the point of interpretation regarding the width of the expression "public meeting" in its statutory context.

...

'... Normal methods of construction can solve the question of construction before us. The question of interpretation before us must, as it is put in Cross *Statutory Interpretation*, be considered in the light of the legal norms of the contemporary legal system. And freedom of expression is a basic norm of our constitution. Girvan J and the Court of Appeal held that a gathering did not qualify as a public meeting for the purposes of para 9 where the organisers had invited to it a group of persons with a particular nexus, rather than throwing it open to the public in general. This is an interpretation which will needlessly complicate a branch of the law where legal certainty is of prime importance. In any event, given the extensive statutory safeguards attached to the privilege, as well as the importance of the press acting as the "eyes and ears" of the public, I regard this interpretation as unnecessarily narrow. In the context a purposive and indeed generous interpretation as to the meaning of "public meeting" in para 9 is to be preferred.

'In my view the test must be the objective of the organisers of a meeting. It is sufficient to say that when they organise a general press conference to which the media, or an interested sector of the media, are invited in order to publicise to the public at large what the organisers regard as ideas of public concern the requirement of para 9 that the meeting must be public as opposed to a private one is satisfied. On the facts pertaining to the highly organised press conference in the present case this test is amply satisfied.' *McCartan Turkington Breen (a firm) v Times Newspapers Ltd* [2000] 4 All ER 913 at 925, 928–929, HL, per Lord Steyn

PUBLIC MONEY

Canada [A road would be public if 'public money' had been expended in maintenance.] 'It is my view

that the expression "public money", as used in s 4 of the Highway Act, refers to money expended by departments of the provincial, municipal and other governments for highway purposes, and does not include money spent by autonomous, or "*quasi-autonomous*", Crown corporations such as the Hydro Authority in carrying on their businesses as trading entities, or public utilities. Such an interpretation is in harmony with the definition of "public money" found in the Financial Administration Act, SBC 1981, c 15.' *British Columbia v Hilyn Holdings Ltd* (1991) 78 DLR (4th) 27 at 35, BC CA, per Taylor JA

PUBLIC PEACE

Canada '63 The foundational notion of the "public peace" reaches back to the roots of Anglo-Canadian history prior to the Norman Conquest.

> A self-respecting Anglo-Saxon king would always try to bring order and tranquillity to his people, and in Ethelbert's laws there was already one principle by which kings could extend their influence. That was the principle of the *peace*.
>
> ...
>
> The mitigation of the disastrous effects of "self-help" was attained by the extension of the idea of the king's peace and the responsibility of all, not just of the parties to a quarrel, to see that it was observed. [Italics in original; underlining added.]

(A. Harding, *A Social History of English Law* (1966), at pp. 15–21)

The general purpose of "the peace" was to reduce the resort to violence. "The Crown developed the scope of breach of the king's peace in order to preserve public order" (J. H. Baker, *An Introduction to English Legal History* (2nd ed. 1979), vol. 1, at p. 13).

'64 The concept of the "public peace" thus aims at a state of order, the very opposite of a state of violent confrontation, and is not much concerned with who is the aggressor and who claims to be defending themselves. As Professor G. Williams wrote in "Arrest for Breach of the Peace", [1954] *Crim. L. Rev.* 578, at p. 578:

> ... "breach of the peace" as a technical expression has a narrower meaning than the breach of the Queen's peace which is supposed to underlie every crime ... . The most flagrant instance of a breach of the peace is a riot ... . So also a fight between two or more

persons is a breach of the peace; and both parties may be arrested, for the arrester <u>does not have to decide the merits of the affair.</u> [Emphasis added.]

'Authority for this proposition includes the observations of Baron Parke made in the course of a 1835 case:

> If no one could be restrained of his liberty, in cases of mutual conflict, except the party who did the first wrong, and <u>the bystanders acted at their peril in this</u> respect, there would be very little chance of the public peace being preserved by the interference of private individuals, nor indeed of police officers, whose power of interposition on their own view appears not to differ [at common law] from that of any of the King's other subjects. [Emphasis added.]

(*Timothy v. Simpson* (1835), 1 C.M. & R. 757, 149 E.R. 1285, at p. 1288; see now *Criminal Code*, R.S.C. 1985, c. C-46, ss. 30–31; *R. v. Biron*, [1976] 2 S.C.R. 56; and *R. v. Lefebvre* (1984), 15 C.C.C. (3d) 503 (B.C.C.A.).)

'65 In *R. v. Howell* (1981), 73 Crim. App. Rep. 31 (Eng. C.A.), the court noted with approval that violence is "of the essence of a breach of the peace" (p. 37), and affirmed that the "reasonable apprehension of imminent danger of a breach of the peace" justifies arrest not only by a police constable but by "the ordinary citizen" (p. 36). See also *Black's Law Dictionary* (6th ed. 1990), at p. 189:

> Breach of the peace is a generic term, and includes all violations of public peace or order and acts tending to a disturbance thereof.

'66 In *R. v. Magee* (1923), 40 C.C.C. 10 (Sask. C.A.), it was noted by Haultain C.J.S., at pp. 11–12:

> "Public peace" may be taken as equivalent to "the King's Peace," in its broader and later signification. The King's Peace is "the legal name of the normal state of society" (Stephen's <u>History of the Criminal Law</u>, vol. 1, p. 185). "The Peace" is defined in Murray's New English Dictionary, vol. 7, p. 582, as being "the king's peace in its wider sense, the general peace and order of the realm, as <u>provided for by law." [Emphasis added.]</u>

R v Kerr [2004] SCJ No 39, [2004] 2 SCR 371, 240 DLR (4th) 257, per Binnie J

PUBLIC PERFORMANCE

[For 9 Halsbury's Laws (4th edn) para 918 see now 9(2) Halsbury's Laws (4th edn) (Reissue) para 324.]

PUBLIC PLACE

'I think that, when the statute [Road Traffic Act 1930 (repealed); see now the Road Traffic Act 1988, ss 2, 3] speaks of "the public" in this connection, what is meant is the public generally, and not the special classes of members of the public who have occasion for business or social purposes to go to the farmhouse ... . I think also that, when the statute speaks of the public having "access" to the road what is meant is neither (at one extreme) that the public has a positive right of its own to access, nor (at the other extreme) that there exists no physical obstruction, of greater or less impenetrability, against physical access by the public; but that the public actually and legally enjoys access to it ... There must be, as matter of fact, walking or driving by the public on the road, and such walking or driving must be lawfully performed—that is to say, must be permitted or allowed, either expressly or implicitly, by the person or persons to whom the road belongs.' *Harrison v Hill* 1932 JC 13 at 16, 1931 SLT at 600, per the Lord Justice-General (Clyde)

'The distinction, then, is between persons who are there in response to an invitation, permission or request not issued to the public generally, and those members of the public who choose to go to the place because it is open to the public or because the public are permitted to have access to it.' *Rodger v Normand* 1995 SLT 411 at 414, per the Lord Justice-General (Hope)

PUBLIC POLICY

[For 9 Halsbury's Laws (4th edn) para 391 et seq see now 9(1) Halsbury's Laws (4th edn) (Reissue) paras 841–843.]

PUBLIC PURPOSE

New Zealand [Land Act 1948, s 167.] 'Section 167(4) of the Land Act 1948 refers to Crown land set apart as a reserve under s 167 "for any public purpose which is a government work within the meaning of the public Works Act 1981". The Stony Batter historic reserve was plainly not set apart for a public purpose which is a government work within the meaning of the Public Works Act. It is land which in 1983 was set apart as a historic reserve, this being a purpose clearly within the scope of s 167(1) of the Land Act 1948 which authorises the Minister to set apart land for any purpose which in the Minister's opinion is desirable in the public interest. In terms of s 2(2) of the Reserves Act 1977 the particular setting apart was a setting apart for the use, benefit and enjoyment of the people of New Zealand and the inhabitants of the district and locality and was therefore a setting apart for a public purpose.' *Auckland City Council v Man O'War Station Ltd* [1996] 3 NZLR 460 at 464, per Anderson J

PUBLIC SERVANTS

Canada '[13] As I have already indicated, the only question to be decided in this appeal is whether, as judges of the Provincial Court of Alberta, the appellants are "public servants" and the Association to which they have paid the membership dues that they are claiming to deduct is an "association of public servants". This is an issue of statutory interpretation and, as such, the Tax Court Judge's conclusion is reviewable on a standard of correctness.

...

'[16] Before embarking on any exercise of statutory interpretation a court should recall the sentence that the Supreme Court of Canada has often said best captures the approach followed by Canadian courts. It is found in Driedger, *Construction of Statutes*, 2nd ed. (Toronto: Butterworths, 1983), at page 87:

> Today there is only one principle or approach, namely, the words of an Act are to be read in their entire context and in their grammatical and ordinary sense harmoniously with the scheme of the Act, the object of the Act, and the intention of Parliament.

"public servants": ordinary meaning
'[17] If, instead of "public servants", Parliament had used the words "civil servants", judges would not have been included. Conversely, if Parliament had used the words "public servants or holders of public office" judges might well have been included. However, counsel for the appellants submits, the meaning of "public servants" is less clear-cut and could well include judges who are serving the public by administering justice.
'[18] In my opinion, however, the balance of the evidence favours the conclusion that, as ordinarily understood, the term "public servants" does not include judges but approximates to "civil servants" or "government employees", not

independent office holders. It does not include members of the judicial branch of government which performs its work independently of the executive and legislative branches.
'[19] For example, *The Canadian Oxford Dictionary* (Toronto: Oxford University Press, 2001) defines a "public servant" as a "government employee, esp. of a federal government". The definition in *Merriam- Webster's Collegiate Dictionary*, 10th ed. (Springfield, Mass.: Merriam-Webster, 1998) is very similar, namely, "government official or employee". The *ITP Nelson Canadian Dictionary of the English Language: An Encyclopedic Reference* (Toronto: ITP Nelson, 1997) defines "public servant" to mean "civil servant". A somewhat broader range of meanings is reported in *Webster's Third New International Dictionary of the English Language* (Springfield, Mass.: Merriam-Webster, 1986), including "a holder of public office" and "an individual ... rendering public service".
'[20] The French text of subparagraph 8(1)(*i*)(iv) uses the word "*fonctionnaire*", which is defined in *Le Nouveau Petit Robert: dictionnaire alphabétique et analogique de la langue française* (Paris: Dictionnaires Le Robert, 1996) as "*personne qui remplit une fonction publique; personne qui occupe, en qualité de titulaire, un emploi permanent dans les cadres d'une administration publique (spécialit. l'État)*".
'[21] Similarly, *Le Robert & Collins super senior: grand dictionnaire français-anglais, anglais-français*, 2nd ed. (Paris: Dictionnaires Le Robert; Glasgow: HarperCollins, 2000) defines "*fonctionnaire*" as "state employee; (*dans l'administration*) [*ministère*] government official, civil servant; [*municipalité*] local government officer *ou* official". This dictionary also notes that, in France, "*le service public*" has a wider connotation than "civil service" and includes "teachers, social service staff, post office workers and employees of the French rail service." Despite the variety of the positions in this list, it notably does not include judge.' *Crowe v Canada* [2003] 4 FC 321 at 331–333 (FCA), per Evans JA

PUBLIC WORK

New Zealand '... by no stretch of the imagination can a casino or an hotel development be seen as a "public work".' *Auckland City Council v Taubmans (New Zealand) Ltd* [1993] 3 NZLR 361 at 365, per Barker J

PUBLICATION

Australia [By the Interpretation of Legislation Act 1984 (Vic), s 11(2), the publication in the Government Gazette of a proclamation of commencement of an Act is an essential condition precedent to the coming into operation of the Act.] '"Publication" in the present context means, I believe, make generally known and available to the public so that it may be read, and this requires that the proclamation itself be printed, so that its authority and provenance may be seen in the Gazette itself … A proclamation within ss 10A and 11 of the Interpretation of Legislation Act 1984 involves a formal Act of State by the Governor in Council under the Public Seal and published in the Government Gazette. The publication must, in my opinion, show on its face that the necessary solemnity attendant upon a Royal proclamation has preceded the proclamation.' *Flinn v James McEwan & Co Pty Ltd* [1991] 2 VR 434 at 442, per Murphy J

Australia [Section 55(1) of the Australian Securities Commission Act 1989 (Cth) (the ASC Law) provides inter alia, that the Commission may give directions at a hearing preventing or restricting the 'publication' of evidence given before, or of matters contained in documents lodged with, the Commission.] 'In my view, the word "publication" as it occurs in s 55(1) of the ASC Law is not apt to catch, and was not intended to catch, production to a court pursuant to the coercive power of a subpoena or of a notice to produce having the effect of a subpoena.' *Potts v Dennis Jones & Co Ltd* (1995) 58 FCR 61 at 70, per Lindgren J

PUBLICLY AVAILABLE

Canada 'The Crown argues that the trial judge erred in charging the jury to the effect that "publicly available" is to be understood as "open to the public generally, without qualification". To assess the trial judge's definition, I will examine the purpose and context of the *National Transportation Act* to determine Parliament's intention as to the meaning to be accorded to "publicly available" and examine the applicable jurisprudence to determine whether a service offered to a subset of society remains publicly available.'

...

'The Crown argues that a service can still be "publicly available" despite the fact that qualifications exist. The Crown offers two examples.

'The first example is that of an air ambulance service. A member of the general public can utilize this service, but a person must be ill, injured or incapacitated [to] do so. Nevertheless, this type of service has been acknowledged as publicly available. (See *Manitoba v Canada* (*National Transportation Agency*) (1994) 178 NR 14 (FCA).)

'The second example the Crown puts forward pertains to social welfare benefits. Such benefits have been held to be "offered to the public" despite the fact that only a segment of the population qualifies to receive the benefits. (See *Saskatchewan Human Rights Commission v Saskatchewan* (*Department of Social Services*) (1988) 52 DLR (4th) 253 (Sask CA).) The service is not without qualification yet it remains a public one.

'In *Saskatchewan Human Rights Commission*, a board of inquiry held that social assistance was not a service "customarily offered to the public". Since not everyone is entitled to receive financial assistance, the board of inquiry decided that the service was not of a public character. This Court concluded otherwise. Certain eligibility requirements had to be met before a person could receive social assistance but this did not change the service from one offered to the public to one that was not. Any member of the public who qualified to receive benefits could do so.

'Similarly in *Rosin v Canada* (1990) 131 NR 295 at 301, the Federal Court of Appeal held that requirements, qualifications and conditions do not necessarily rob an activity of its public character. In *Rosin* the Court had to determine whether a parachuting course offered by the Canadian Forces was a service or [f]acility "customarily available to the public". The appellant argued that it was a specialist course available only to a limited number of cadets. While this was true, the respondent argued that any young person between the ages of 12 and 18 could join the Royal Canadian Army Cadets. The Court accepted the respondent's arguments and agreed that the parachuting course was one which is "customarily available to the public".

'In *University of British Columbia v Berg* [1993] 2 SCR 353 at 383, 102 DLR (4th) 665, Lamer CJC, speaking for the majority, rejected any definition of "public" which refuses to recognize that "any accommodation, service or facility will only ever be available to a subset of the public". He explained that every service has its own public. In other words, a subset of the population can still constitute "the public". The test enunciated in *Berg*, for whether or not a service should be characterized as "publicly available" (in that case "services customarily available to the public"), must focus on the nature of the service in question and the relationship that it establishes between provider and user.

'In *Berg* a graduate student was denied a rating sheet and an after hours key on the basis that she suffered from a recurrent depressed condition. As a threshold issue, the Court had to decide whether the university services (the granting of a rating sheet and an after hours key) were services "customarily available to the public". The Court looked at the nature of the relationship between the university and its students. The university in question was publicly funded. Educational and recreational resources were available to all those admitted. There was nothing in the nature of the student body which suggested that the university and its students came together as a result of a private selection process. Focussing then on the nature of the service-provider and the nature of the service-user, the Court concluded that there existed a very public relationship between the university and its students. The rating sheet and after hours key were found to be "incidents of the public relationship".

'Where the service provider is a public body, the relationship between the provider and user is much more likely to be public in nature. Nevertheless, a service can be publicly available despite the fact that it is provided by a private organization or individual. In *Struthers v Sudbury* (1900) 27 OAR 217 (CA), a privately owned hospital was found to be a public facility offering a public service. Osler JA wrote, "that an institution is established for private gain or is held in a private hand is not necessarily inconsistent with its being in its nature of a public character" (see p. 221).

'In *Applin v Race Relations Board* [1974] 2 All ER 73, the House of Lords held that a family who takes in foster children without any type of compensation or reward can still be found to be carrying out a public service. While Lord Wilberforce dissented, the majority of the Court held that by their course of conduct, the Watson family had made it a practice to provide a public service. While they could no doubt refuse a child that they considered "obviously unsuitable", they did not select which children could come and stay at their home. The Court estimated that the Watsons had looked after at least fifty children each year and in total had probably housed more than three hundred children. Through the course of the family's conduct, their establishment extended past that of a private household and was declared

to be a public service. The nature of the relationship between the provider and the user was public in nature.

'Returning to the case on appeal, by looking at the purpose of the legislation, the overall legislative and regulatory context of s 67(1) and the relevant jurisprudence, I must conclude that the trial judge erred in charging the jury as he did. The presence of a qualification is not a tenable means by which to determine whether a service is publicly available. While Mr. Biller's passengers must be guests before they can use the flight service, such a qualification does nothing more than define a subset of the public using the service. A service may be publicly available despite the fact that it is not ... "without qualification".' *R v Biller* (1999) 174 DLR (4th) 721 at 745, 746, 747, Sask CA, per Jackson JA

PUBLISH

Australia [The articles of association of the applicant expressly provides that 'notice of every general meeting shall be given by the applicant to members by advertisement published in each of the capital cities of the States of Australia and in Wellington, New Zealand'. It was contended that the requisitionists' notice was not 'published' as required because the *Australian* newspaper was not 'published' in Hobart.] '"Published" in this context is to be used in the same sense as it is in the law of defamation, and that it is sufficient if the daily newspaper in question is sold or made available for sale in the relevant State.' *National Mutual Life Association of Australasia Ltd v Windsor* (1991) 100 ALR 585 at 598, per Heerey J

Australia [Section 31(1) of the Copyright Act 1968 (Cth) provides, inter alia, that copyright is an exclusive right to 'publish' work.] 'The words "to publish" in s 31(1) should be read as meaning to make public that which has not previously been made public in the copyright territory.' *Avel Pty Ltd v Multicoin Amusements Pty Ltd* (1990) 171 CLR 88 at 93, per Mason CJ, Deane and Gaudron JJ

PUNISHMENT

[For 11 Halsbury's Laws (4th edn) para 3 see now 11(1) Halsbury's Laws (4th edn) (Reissue) para 3.]

Canada 'Punishment means "the imposition of a penalty" and a penalty is, in a broad sense, a "disadvantage of some kind" imposed as a consequence of a misbehavior which, it seems to me, may include a loss of reward.' *Knockaert v*

Canada (Commissioner of Corrections) [1987] 2 FCR 202 at 205, FCA, per Marceau J

PURCHASER

Australia 'The avoidance effect of s 120(1) of the Bankruptcy Act 1966 (Cth) does not apply to a "settlement … made in favour of a purchaser … in good faith and for valuable consideration": see para (a). The word "purchaser" is used in a technical sense; the person need not have paid money for the property.' *Re Pearson; Ex p Wensley v Pearson* (1993) 46 FCR 55 at 64, per Wilcox J

PURPORT

Australia [Section 9(4) of the Property Law Act 1969 (WA) provides: 'Every instrument expressed or purporting to be an indenture or a deed or an agreement under seal or otherwise purporting to be a document executed under seal and which is executed as required by this section has the same effect as a deed duly executed in accordance with the law in force immediately prior to the coming into operation of this Act.'] '"Purport" according to the Macquarie Dictionary means "to profess or claim … to convey to the mind as the meaning or thing intended; express, imply, … tenor, import or meaning, … purpose or object …".' In the context of s 9(4) of the Property Law Act "purporting" is used in contra-distinction to "expressed". Thus, in my view, an instrument which is not clearly indicated or distinctly stated to be a deed, but which otherwise conveys to the mind, by implication, through its tenor and the words used therein, that it is intended to be a deed, is an instrument purporting to be a deed.' *Dean and Westham Holdings Pty Ltd v Lloyd* [1991] 3 WAR 235 at 252, per Ipp J

Australia [Section 9 of the Corporations Law defines statutory demand as meaning, inter alia, a document that is, or 'purports' to be a demand served under s 459E.] 'The word "purport" is defined relevantly in the *Macquarie Dictionary*, 2nd ed, rev as:

'1. to profess or claim: "a document purporting to be official". 2. to convey to the mind as the meaning or thing intended; express; imply.

'In some contexts the word may merely mean "has the effect of": cf *Joseph v Joseph* [1966] 3 All ER 486. However, in the present context, in my view, it has its more usual meaning of "profess" or

"claim".' *Kalamunda Meat Wholesalers Pty Ltd v Reg Russell & Sons Ltd* (1994) 128 ALR 149 at 155, per Hill J

PURPORTING TO DISCHARGE

New Zealand [Section 6(5) of the Crown Proceedings Act 1950 provides that "No proceedings shall lie against the Crown by virtue of this section in respect of anything done or omitted to be done by any person while discharging or purporting to discharge any responsibilities …] 'The phrase "discharging or purporting to discharge" conveys the meaning of actually discharging the responsibilities; or of intending or professing to do so.' *Simpson v Attorney-General [Baigent's Case]* [1994] 3 NZLR 667 at 690, CA, per Casey J

'*The Oxford Dictionary* (2nd ed, 1989) gives the relevant meaning of the verb "purport" as "to profess or claim by its tenor". The concept in s 6(5) is therefore one of a claim, explicit or implicit from conduct, to authority under the warrant.' *Simpson v Attorney-General [Baigent's Case]* [1994] 3 NZLR 667 at 696, CA, per Hardie Boys J

PURPOSE

Canada [Criminal liability was imposed on anyone performing an act or omission 'for the purpose' of aiding any person to commit an offence.] 'It is impossible to ascribe a single fixed meaning to the term "purpose". In ordinary usage, the word is employed in two distinct senses. One can speak of an actor doing something "on purpose" (as opposed to by accident) thereby equating purpose with "immediate intention". The term is also used, however, to indicate the ultimate ends an actor seeks to achieve, which imports the idea of "desire" into the definition. This dual sense is apparent in the word's dictionary definition. For instance, the Oxford English Dictionary (2nd ed, 1989) defines "purpose" alternatively as "[t]hat which one sets before oneself as a thing to be done or attained; the object which one has in view" and as "[t]he action or fact of intending or meaning to do something; intention, resolution, determination". The first of these definitions reflects the notion of one's "purpose" as relating to one's ultimate object or desire, while the latter conveys the notion of "purpose" as being synonymous with "intention".

'… in the context of s 21(l)(*b*) of the *Code*, the second of the two meanings of "purpose" discussed above—that is, the interpretation that equates "purpose" with "intention"—best reflects the legislative intent underlying the subsection. In contrast, adopting the first interpretation of "purpose" (the "purpose" equals "desire" interpretation) to describe the *mens rea* for aiding in s 21(1)(*b*) would, in my view, create a number of theoretical and practical difficulties that Parliament is unlikely to have envisioned or intended.' *R v Hibbert* [1995] 2 SCR 973 at 995, 997, SCC, per Lamer J

PURPOSES

Canada [Section 55(2) of the *Income Tax Act*, RSC 1985 (5th Supp), c 1, is an anti-avoidance provision concerning shares disposed of by a corporation.]

'Putting aside these evidential matters, it remains to be decided whether the term "purposes" as employed in subsection 55(2) of the Act is to be understood in an objective sense. Standing alone that term is neutral. It is only when it is placed in a particular context that its meaning can be ascertained. While there may be instances where the term "purposes" is modified by words or phrases suggesting something other than a subjective understanding, that is not the case with respect to subsection 55(2) of the Act. The words of that subsection provide that in certain circumstances the "purpose" of a transaction will determine whether the subsection applies while in another (i.e., where the dividend is deemed to arise under subsection 84(3)) the "result" of a transaction will be determinative. Parenthetically, I note that subsection 55(1), a general anti-avoidance provision (since repealed) [as rep. by SC 1988, c 55, s 33] is limited to circumstances in which the "result" of a transaction is to artificially or unduly reduce the amount of gain. No one can doubt that the term "result" invites an objective appreciation of the factual circumstances. In this context I do not see how one can argue persuasively that both the words "purpose" and "result" are to be interpreted as embracing an objective criterion. In my opinion, it is clear that the use of the term "purpose" in one context and "result" in another requires that a different meaning be attributed to each that is consistent with their use and context within subsection 55(2).

'The foregoing conclusion is reinforced by the decision of the House of Lords in *Commissioners of Inland Revenue v Brebner* (1967), 43 TC 705. That case involved subsection 28(1) of the *Finance Act*, 1960 [(UK), 1960, c 44] which draws a clear distinction between the terms "effect" and "object". It was held that the "object" which had to be considered involved a subjective matter of intention (at page 715). To the extent that the term "object" is synonymous with "purpose", the reasoning in *Brebner* seems equally applicable to the case at hand.' *Canada v Placer Dome Inc* [1997] 1 FC 780 at 794–795, FCA, per Robertson JA

Canada 'Subsection 55(5) [of the *Income Tax Act*] is framed in the legislation as follows:

55. . .

(5) For the purposes of this section,

   . . .

   (*b*) the income earned or realized by a corporation for a period throughout which it was resident in Canada and not a private corporation shall be deemed to be the aggregate of

   . . .

   (*c*) the income earned or realized by a corporation for a period throughout which it was a private corporation shall be deemed to be … .

   (*d*) the income earned or realized by a corporation for a period ending at a time when it was a foreign affiliate of another corporation shall be deemed to be the aggregate of the … . [My emphasis.]

'It is argued by the Minister that paragraphs 55(5)(*b*) to (*d*) create computation rules for those corporations which have safe income under subsection 55(2). The statutory scheme, as evidenced in paragraphs 55(5)(*b*) to (*d*), confirms that safe income consists of income which has been subject to tax in Canada or can be repatriated to Canada free of tax. In this respect, the statutory scheme furthers the goal of preventing double taxation at the corporate level (i.e. the payment of Canadian tax at the corporate level justifies the payment of a tax-free intercorporate dividend to another Canadian corporation). He further submitted that common sense dictates that Parliament, having turned its mind to enacting rules for calculating safe income for these types of corporations, did not intend that corporations not dealt with in paragraphs 55(5)(*b*) to (*d*) should also have safe income.

'I agree with the learned Tax Court Judge's reasoning. I am of the view that by drafting subsection 55(5) as above, Parliament intended that section 55 as a whole be governed by the applicable rules for the purposes of this section. "Purpose" means "object to be attained, thing intended". Literally stated, this means "For the objectives expressly intended by Parliament in section 55 the permitted calculations are as follows".' *Lamont Managament v MNR* [2000] 3 FC 508 at 526–527, FCA, per Malone JA

PURSUANT TO

Canada '[42] The phrase "pursuant to" was applied by this Court in *M.N.R. v. Armstrong*, [1956] S.C.R. 446. The taxpayer had been ordered to pay $100, per month to his former wife for child support. After payments had been made for two years, the taxpayer gave her a cash settlement of $4,000 in full satisfaction of her claim to further payments under the divorce decree. The issue before the Court was whether the lump sum payment was made "pursuant to" an order or judgment in a divorce or separation action, a condition precedent to taxation under the relevant section of the *Income Tax Act*. All three justices who wrote reasons agreed that the payment was not made "pursuant to" a decree, order or judgment. In the words of Locke J.:

> It cannot ... be properly said that this lump sum was paid, in the words of the section, *pursuant* to the divorce decree. It was, it is true, paid *in consequence* of the liability imposed by the decree for the maintenance of the infant, but that does not fall within the terms of the section. [Emphasis in original; p. 449.]

'[43] Kerwin C.J. applied "pursuant to" similarly:

> The test is whether it was paid in pursuance of a decree, order or judgment and not whether it was paid by reason of a legal obligation imposed or undertaken. [Emphasis added; p. 447.]

'[44] Kellock J. reached the same conclusion:

> In my opinion, the payment here in question is not within the statute. It was not an amount payable "pursuant to" or "conformément à" ... the decree but rather an amount paid to obtain a release from the liability thereby imposed. [p. 448]

See also *The Queen v. Sills*, [1985] 2 F.C. 200 (C.A.), at pp. 204–5.

'[45] Even though *Armstrong* dealt with a settlement paid to extinguish a claim for future, not past benefits, that does not diminish its interpretive value. I share the view that "pursuant to" is different from and narrower than "as a result of". *Black's Law Dictionary* (8th ed. 2004) also attributes a narrower definition to the phrase: "[i]n compliance with" or "in accordance with"; "[a]s authorized by"; and "[i]n carrying out". In this case, the lump sum settlement payment was not paid to Ms. Tsiaprailis "in compliance with" or "in accordance with" a disability insurance plan, it was paid "in compliance with" and "in accordance with" a settlement agreement.' *Tsiaprailis v Canada* [2005] 1 SCR 113 at [42]–[45], [2005] SCJ No 9 (SCC), per Abella J

New Zealand [Children and Young Persons and Their Families Act 1989, s 16.] 'In the way in which "pursuant to" is ordinarily used in legal language in New Zealand, I am of the view the words concerned in s 16 of the Act, mean "under" or "in accordance with". That is certainly a use which has been given in Australia, is referred to by Garner and supported by *The Shorter Oxford*. *Collins* uses the word "conformity" which may mean in compliance with ...' *Davidson v Ross and Attorney-General* [1996] 3 NZLR 340 at 347, per Kerr J

Q

QUALIFY

[The Food Act 1984 is largely repealed. See now the Food Safety Act 1990, s 14.]

QUALIFYING SERVICE

[The Pension Schemes Act 1993, s 1 defines an occupational pension scheme with reference to 'earners with qualifying service' in the particular employment.] 'The phrase "qualifying service" is not defined in the 1993 Act but it was pointed out that its use elsewhere in the 1993 Act (in particular in ss 70 and 71 dealing with entitlement to long service and short service benefits) pointed to a concept of service of some identifiable and relevant duration, rather than to the mere fact of employment itself. There is considerable force in that point. One of the critical functions of the definition is to provide a criterion for determining when preservation of benefits is mandatory. It is difficult to see why the preservation requirements should be held to apply to benefits which do not accrue by reference to the duration of service, but to which eligibility exists by virtue of the mere fact of employment itself. On the other hand, the weakness of the point is revealed by the consideration that, if *any* period of service, however small, is stipulated as a condition of eligibility to the benefit, a scheme providing for that benefit would, on this argument, be an occupational pension scheme; whereas if no period is stipulated, the scheme would not be. This seems arbitrary, especially where, as here, the condition of eligibility (the suffering of an injury or the contracting of a disease as a result of something required by the employment) necessarily implies that the employment will have lasted for more than a scintilla temporis.

'I am unable, therefore, to conclude that "qualifying service" means anything more than "such service as qualifies" the earner for the benefit in question. I reach that conclusion with some surprise, since it produces the counter-intuitive result that a scheme, such as that contained in Pt L [of the Local Government Superannuation Regulations 1986], is an occupational pension scheme, whether or not it forms part of a wider scheme which admittedly is.' *Swansea City and County v Johnson* [1999] 1 All ER 863 at 869–870, per Hart J

QUANTUM MERUIT

[For 9 Halsbury's Laws (4th edn) para 692 see now 9(1) Halsbury's Laws (4th edn) (Reissue) para 1155.]

QUARRY

[For 31 Halsbury's Laws (4th edn) para 2 see now 31 Halsbury's Laws (4th edn) (2003 Reissue) para 6.]

QUARTER DAYS

[For 45 Halsbury's Laws (4th edn) para 1106 see now 45(2) Halsbury's Laws (4th edn) (Reissue) para 206.]

QUASHING ORDER *SEE* CERTIORARI

QUASI CONTRACT

[For 9 Halsbury's Laws (4th edn) para 212 see now 9(1) Halsbury's Laws (4th edn) (Reissue) para 618.]

QUASI EASEMENT

[For 12 Halsbury's Laws (4th edn) para 429, 429n see now 12(1) Halsbury's Laws (4th edn) (Reissue) para 629, 629n.]

QUIET ENJOYMENT

[For 27 Halsbury's Laws (4th edn) paras 322–323 see now 27(1) Halsbury's Laws (4th edn) (Reissue) para 406 et seq.]

QUO WARRANTO

[For 1 Halsbury's Laws (4th edn) para 169 see now 1(1) Halsbury's Laws (4th edn) (2001 Reissue) para 251 et seq.]

QUORUM

United States Unless the articles of incorporation or bylaws require a greater number, a quorum of a board of directors consists of: (1) a majority of the fixed number of directors if the corporation has a fixed board size; or (2) a majority of the number of directors prescribed, or if no number is prescribed the number in office immediately before the meeting begins, if the corporation has a variable-range size board. (Revised Model Business Corporation Act 1984, s 8.24(a))

R

RADIOED

Australia [The respondent was injured in a sky-diving accident and sought damages from the appellants. The respondent relied upon a representation said to have been made on behalf of the appellants, namely that the jump was safe because the pilot (Mr Spinks) had not been radioed with regard to wind by the Drop Zone Safety Officer (Mr Lewis).] '… it seems to me that the expression means no more than that Mr Lewis had not established an effective communication by radio. A number of possibilities suggest themselves: a breakdown of equipment at either end; radio traffic congestion; some accident or illness befalling either Mr Lewis or Mr Spinks; or atmospheric or solar conditions inhibiting efficient radio communication.' *Palmer and Jamieson t/as Byron Bay Skydiving Centre v Griffin* BC200201800; [2002] NSWCA 100 at [23], per Brownie AJA

RAINFALL

[The Water Resources Act 1963 has been repealed.]

RANSOM

[For 37 Halsbury's Laws (4th edn) para 1341 see now 36(2) Halsbury's Laws (4th edn) (Reissue) para 841.]

RAPE

Marital exemption

[According to Sir Matthew Hale (*History of the Pleas of the Crown* (1736)) a husband could not be guilty of a rape committed by himself upon his lawful wife, on account of her matrimonial consent to intercourse, which could not be retracted.] 'I am … of the opinion that s 1(1) of the 1976 [Sexual Offences (Amendment)] Act [see Main Volume 4, p 5] presents no obstacle to this House declaring that in modern times the supposed marital exemption in rape forms no part of the law of England. The Court of Appeal, Criminal Division [the court below] took a similar view. Towards the end of the judgment of that court Lord Lane CJ said [[1991] 2 All ER at 266]: "The remaining and no less difficult question is whether … this is an area where the court should step aside to leave the matter to the parliamentary process. This is not the creation of a new offence, it is the removal of a common law fiction which has become anachronistic and offensive and we consider that it is our duty having reached that conclusion to act upon it". I respectfully agree.' *R v R— (rape: marital exemption)* [1991] 4 All ER 481 at 489–490, HL, per Lord Keith of Kinkel

RATCHET CLAUSE

New Zealand 'The expression "ratchet clause" is well understood in New Zealand to mean a particular type of clause, … which prevents the reviewed rent from being lower than the previous rent. This is not the same as a clause giving the landlord an option to initiate review proceedings, even if in practice the economic effect is likely in most (thought not necessarily all) cases to be the same. McGechan J said:

> "[Brierley's] agreement to provide a lease without a ratchet clause did not require provision of a lease with a mandatory review clause. The two were different and were not spoken of as the same."

'The Court of Appeal agreed. In view of these concurrent opinions as to the meaning of what is in effect a term of art in New Zealand commercial property transactions, Their Lordships would be very reluctant to take a different view.' *Board of Trustees of National Provident Fund v Brierley Investments Ltd* [1997] 1 NZLR 1 at 5, PC, per cur

RATIFICATION

[For 1 Halsbury's Laws (4th edn) para 756 see now 1(2) Halsbury's Laws (4th edn) (Reissue) para 72.]

RATIO DECIDENDI

[For 26 Halsbury's Laws (4th edn) para 573 see now 26 Halsbury's Laws (4th edn) (Reissue) para 573.]

REAL

Australia 'The decisions in *Chan v Minister for Immigration and Ethnic Affairs* (1989) 169 CLR 379; 87 ALR 412 and *Boughey v R* (1986) 161 CLR 10; 65 ALR 609 demonstrate that as a matter of usage the word "real", when used as an adjective to describe a "chance" or "risk", means that the chance of the event happening or the risk becoming a reality is not remote even though the chance or risk is less than 50%. "Remote" in this context means something that is extremely unlikely to occur. This is to use the word "real" in the context of a quantitative assessment of the chance or risk. The decisions in *Chan* and *Boughey* mean no more than that in the context of the enactments there being considered, the chance of the event occurring, assessed in a quantitative sense, had to be substantial and not remote even though the chance may be less than 50%. However, neither the meaning of the word "real" when used to describe a chance or risk, nor any requirement of the law, requires that a "real risk" or a "real chance" be assessed solely on a quantitative basis ... there is no inconsistency in finding that a risk is real, in the sense that it is not far-fetched or fanciful, yet the degree of probability of its occurrence is quantitatively low. Such a course is rationally open provided that the word "real" is used in a qualitative and not a quantitative sense to describe the risk.' *Minister for Immigration, Local Government and Ethnic Affairs v Batey* (1993) 112 ALR 198 at 205–206, per cur

Australia '... neither the meaning of the word "real" when used to describe a chance or risk nor any requirement of the law, requires that a "real risk" or a "real chance" be assessed solely on a quantitative basis.'

'The word "real" may be used to describe the quantitative nature of a risk or chance. In this sense it is used to describe something which is not far-fetched or fanciful. Use of the word in its qualitative sense is most clearly seen in the treatment of risk of injury in the law of negligence.' *Minister for Immigration, Local Government and Ethnic Affairs v Batey* (1993) 40 FCR 493 at 501, per cur

REAL AND SUBSTANTIAL PRESENCE

Canada 'In the circumstance of no purposeful commercial activity alleged on the part of Kostiuk and the equally material absence of any person in that jurisdiction having "read" the alleged libel all that has been deemed to have been demonstrated was Kostiuk's passive use of an out of state electronic bulletin. The allegation of publication fails as it rests on the mere transitory, passive presence in cyberspace of the alleged defamatory material. Such a contact does not constitute a real and substantial presence. On the American authorities this is an insufficient basis for the exercise of an *in personam* jurisdiction over a non-resident.' *Braintech Inc v Kostiuk* (1999) 171 DLR (4th) 46 at 62, BC CA, per Goldie JA

REAL PROPERTY

[For 39 Halsbury's Laws (4th edn) para 301 see now 39(2) Halsbury's Laws (4th edn) (Reissue) para 1.]

REASON TO BELIEVE

[A person who has published a statement alleged to be defamatory may offer to make amends under the Defamation Act 1996 s 2. If an offer to make amends under s 2 is not accepted, the fact that the offer was made is a defence to the defamation proceedings under s 4; but s 4(3) provides that 'There is no such defence if the person by whom the offer was made knew or had reason to believe that the statement complained of—(a) referred to the aggrieved party or was likely to be understood as referring to him, and (b) was both false and defamatory of that party; but it shall be presumed until the contrary is shown that he did not know and had no reason to believe that was the case'.]

'[27] As will be seen, this court considers that Eady J's construction of s 4(3) of the 1996 Act in his first judgment was entirely correct for the reasons which he gave. It is necessary to summarise his reasons in this judgment in order to address Mr Parkes's more limited submission. We shall do so briefly without intending to detract from or modify the judge's judgment, which may be referred to in full.

...

'[36] Then (at [[2002] EWHC 2564 (QB)] [44]) the judge said:

"I am quite satisfied that 'reasonable grounds to believe' is not to be equated with either 'reasonable grounds to suspect' or with constructive knowledge. Of course, it is right to say that the use of the phrase imports an objective element. In this context, as in *Swain v Puri* [1996] PIQR P442, what is required first is to demonstrate that the identifiable individual responsible for the article knew of a relevant fact or facts. The objective test then comes into play when the court decides, in applying the s 4 defence provisions, whether such knowledge provided reasonable grounds to believe positively that the words complained of were false. Here there is nothing of the kind."

'There is a minor slip in this paragraph of the judge's judgment. The statutory words in s 4(3) are not that the defendant had "reasonable grounds to believe" but that he had "reason to believe". The first of these expressions is that used in s 1(3)(b) of the 1984 Act. In our view, the expression in s 4(3) of the 1996 Act, which is the expression used by Lord Kilbrandon in the passage from *Cassell & Co Ltd v Broome* [1972] 1 All ER 801, [1972] AC 1927 to which we have referred, more strongly favours the judge's conclusion in the present case. The expression used also more strongly favours Mr Shaw's first submission, that Parliament intended to implement without modification the recommendation of the Neill committee. Where a journalist does not know that what he publishes is false, he might arguably have "reasonable grounds to believe" that it was false if he ought reasonably so to have believed from what he did know. As we explain below, "reason to believe", in our judgment, does not in this statute apply to anything short of recklessness.

...

'[46] It is obviously correct that Parliament intended to and did shift the balance in favour of the making of offers to make amends. This is not perhaps to say that the balance is shifted in favour of defendants, since claimants also benefit. Since the offer tenders appropriate vindication and proper compensation, it is not surprising that s 4(3) of the 1996 Act sets a high hurdle and places the burden of surmounting it squarely on the claimant. We are not persuaded that the judge's construction, if it is correct, places the hurdle insurmountably high. There may be cases where a claimant can establish that a defendant knew that his defamatory publication was false. It may also be possible to establish that he "had reason to believe" that it was false in the sense of the judge's construction. We do not consider that a mechanism which offers appropriate vindication and proper compensation is a recipe for irresponsible journalism. Further, the legislation does not apply only to journalists.

'[47] The question remains whether the judge's construction was correct ... There is no doubt but that the judge decided that s 4(3) of the 1996 Act was to be construed as an unmodified implementation of the recommendations of the Neill committee and that the words "had reason to

believe that the statement complained of ... was ... false" import the concept of recklessness from Lord Diplock's judgment in *Horrocks v Lowe* [[1974] 1 All ER 662, [1975] AC 135, HL]. This may be seen from his references to malice or bad faith in [36], [40] and [41] of his first judgment. It is put beyond doubt by [21] of his second judgment [[2003] EWHC 1843 (QB)], in which he said:

> "I have come to the conclusion that this second attempt to muster a case of bad faith against the defendant, or 'recklessness' (in the sense explained in the previous judgment at [15]–[20]), does not meet the rigorous criteria which must always be applied to such an allegation ..."

...

'[48] There is no indication that Parliament intended to do other than implement the recommendations of the Neill committee. We find no such indication in the change of wording between the draft Bill and the statute. The words in the statute correspond with those of Lord Kilbrandon in *Cassell & Co Ltd v Broome* [1972] 1 All ER 801 at 876, [1972] AC 1027 at 1133 that the publisher does not care whether the material is libellous.

...

'[50] Although Mr Shaw advanced and the judge summarised an alternative lesser submission, sufficient for Mr Shaw's purposes at the first hearing, we do not consider that, in the context of s 4(3) of the 1996 Act, there is a distinct possible meaning of the words "had reason to believe" lying between recklessness on the one hand and constructive or imputed knowledge based on negligence on the other. Mr Shaw drew our attention to other statutes in which the expression had or has "reason to believe" is or was used. These were s 1(3) of the Law Reform (Miscellaneous Provisions) Act 1949 (now repealed); s 22 of the Copyright, Designs and Patents Act 1988; s 143(3) of the Road Traffic Act 1988; s 3 of the Sludge (Use in Agriculture) Regulations 1989, SI 1989/1263; and para 12(2) of the Genetically Modified Organisms (Northern Ireland) Order 1991, SI 1991/1714. We accept Mr Shaw's general submission with particular reference to the 1996 Act that the phrase "knew or had reason to believe" requires an inquiry into what facts were in a person's head, not into what facts ought to have been in his head. Mr Parkes rightly disclaims the second of these, but seeks to find room for a state of mind objectively deduced from facts known to the defendants which is neither actual knowledge nor reckless indifference to the truth. We do not think that there is such an intermediate state of mind in the context of a defamatory publication. In that context, shutting your eyes to an obvious truth is the same as reckless indifference to that truth. Move away from that, and you immediately arrive at constructive knowledge.

'[51] In our judgment, therefore, Eady J's first judgment contains a correct construction of s 4(3) of the 1996 Act for the reasons which he gave ... ' *Milne v Express Newspapers Ltd* [2004] EWCA Civ 664, [2005] 1 All ER 1021 at [27], [36], [46]–[48], [50], per May LJ

New Zealand '... one should not, it seems to me, approach the words "reason to believe" with a preconception that they in fact comprehend the same as and no more than imputed knowledge ... it seems to me that "reason to believe" must involve the concept of knowledge of facts from which a reasonable man would arrive at the relevant belief. Facts from which a reasonable man might suspect the relevant conclusion cannot be enough. Moreover, as it seems to me, the phrase does connote the allowance of a period of time to enable the reasonable man to evaluate those facts so as to convert the facts into a reasonable belief.' *LA Gear Inc v Hi-Tec Sports plc* [1991] FSR 121, ChD and CA, per Morritt J; followed in *Husqvarna Forest and Garden Ltd v Bridon NZ Ltd* [1997] 3 NZLR 215 at 226, per Smellie J

REASONABLE

Australia '*Modern Legal Usage* defines "reasonable" and "rational" together as follows: "*reasonable*; *rational*. Generally, *reasonable* = according to reason; *rational* = having reason. Yet reasonable is often used in reference to persons in the sense 'having the faculty of reason' (reasonable man). When applied to things, the two words are perhaps more clearly differentiated: 'In application to things reasonable and rational both signify according to reason, but the former is used in reference to the business of life, as a reasonable proposal, wish, etc; rational to abstract matters, as rational motives, grounds, questions etc' ... "

'In my opinion, there is nothing in this definition which indicates that something reasonable may be irrational. To the extent that any distinction is made between the two words, it is reference to their application, not to their meaning. I am also of the opinion that the definition of "reasonable" and "rational" in *Modern Legal Usage* supports the statement of Davies J in *Burchill [Department of Industrial Relations v Burchill* (1991) 33 FCR 122;

105 ALR 327] which was relied upon by the tribunal. In addition, the *Shorter Oxford Dictionary* defines "reasonable" to mean, relevantly: "Agreeable to reason; not irrational, absurd or ridiculous." This is the very meaning applied to the word "reasonable" by Davies J and in my opinion accords with the ordinary common sense meaning of the word.' *Australian Doctors' Fund Ltd v Commonwealth of Australia* (1994) 126 ALR 273 at 281, per Beazley J

Australia [Transport Accident Act 1986 (Vic) s 3, 60.] 'The relevant provisions of the Transport Accident Act are to be found in s 3 and s 60. Section 3(1) defines the word "reasonable". In so far as is relevant for present purposes, the definition is as follows. "Reasonable", and I interpolate the word, "means", "having regard to ... (c) the determination by the Commission of reasonable costs or expenses of, or fees for, the service or provision having regard to, (i) the service or provision actually rendered, and, (ii) the necessity of the service or provision, or of the incurring of the expense, in the circumstances".

'Section 60 then imposes liability on the Commission to pay as compensation to a person who is injured as a result of a transport accident, the "reasonable costs of ... medical services ... [and] rehabilitation services ... received because of the transport accident". These provisions, it seems to me, require a body in the position of the Tribunal to ask, when questions whether services would continue to be funded are raised, whether the continued funding of those services is reasonable, having regard to their necessity in the appropriate treatment of the victim of the accident.' *Russell v Transport Accident Commission* [2004] VSC 442 at [8], per Harper J; BC200407291

New Zealand 'The expression "all reasonable steps" does not require the defendant to take any steps other than reasonable ones which are available. A defendant may invoke the protection of the section without having taken any steps if he satisfies the court no reasonable one was open.' *Department of Health v Multichem Laboratories Ltd* [1987] 1 NZLR 334 at 338, per Eichelbaum J

Reasonable assurance

Canada '[14] The words "reasonable assurance", in context and in their natural meaning, imply some measurable form of guarantee. "Assurance" is defined in *Black's Law Dictionary*, 7th ed. (St. Paul: West Group, 1999), as "2. A pledge or guarantee", in *The Concise Oxford Dictionary* ,

10th ed. (Oxford: Oxford University Press, 1999), as "1. a positive declaration intended to give confidence" and in the *Merriam-Webster On line Dictionary* (http://www.merriam-webster.com/cgi-bin /dictionary), as 2b:, "a being certain in the mind". "*Assurance*", in French, is defined in *Le Nouveau Petit Robert* , 2000, page 159, as "4. *Promesse ou garantie qui rend certain de qqch.*" and in *Le Petit Larousse illustré*, 1996, page 97, as "1... *certitude, garantie formelle*". The use of the word "reasonable" has softened the more stringent meaning otherwise associated with the word "assurance": something short of a formal assurance may qualify as "reasonable assurance".' *Canada (Attorney General) v Sacrey* [2004] 1 FCR 733 at 742 (FCA), per Décary JA

Reasonable cause

Australia [Section 592(2)(b)(i) of the Corporations Law refers to a defence of a director not having 'reasonable cause' to expect that the company would not be able to pay all its debts as and when they became due.] 'The test of "reasonable cause" in the context in which the expression appears imports an objective standard, but it must be applied to the facts and circumstances known to the defendant and facts and circumstances which, by reason of the defendant's duties as a director or officer of the company, ought to have been known to him. It would be absurd for a defendant to be able to establish a defence simply on the basis of what he in fact knew. This would reward the incompetent director who ought to have known a great deal more than he in fact knew.' *Rema Industries and Services Pty Ltd v Coad* (1992) 107 ALR 374 at 382, per Lockhart J

Reasonable consequence

Australia [Section 98 of the Planning and Environment Act 1987 (Vic) provides that compensation may be claimed from the planning authority for financial loss suffered as the natural, direct and 'reasonable consequence' of, inter alia, land being reserved for a public purpose.] 'I would propose to follow the same path [as Romer LJ in *Harvey v Crawley Development Corpn* [1957] 1 QB 485 at 494] in deciding what is a reasonable consequence which, so read, means that the loss is one that was a reasonable response to the refusal, in particular that any expense was reasonably incurred. The alternative is that it means a reasonably foreseeable consequence but the latter concept is an awkward one in statutory

compensation law and should not be preferred.' *Mario Piraino Pty Ltd v Roads Corpn (No 2)* [1993] 1 VR 130 at 142, per Gobbo J

Reasonable excuse

[Section 19 of the Firearms Act 1968 makes it an offence for a person, 'without lawful authority or reasonable excuse (the proof whereof lies on him)' to have with him in a public place a loaded shotgun or air weapon, or any other firearm (whether loaded or not) together with ammunition suitable for use in that firearm.] 'The first issue is whether a certificate for a firearm and ammunition is in itself lawful authority for the holder of the certificate to have the firearm and ammunition for it in a public place.

'The second issue is whether, if a firearm certificate is lawful authority for that purpose, mistaken belief by the holder of an invalid certificate that his certificate is valid is capable of being a reasonable excuse and, therefore, a defence under s 19.

'The third issue is whether, if a firearm certificate is not lawful authority for that purpose, mistaken belief by the holder of an invalid certificate that it is valid and that it is lawful authority, is capable of being a reasonable excuse and, therefore, a defence under s 19...

'[I]n our judgment, a holder in a public place of a shotgun or any other firearm in the respective circumstances specified in s 19 may be without lawful authority and in breach of the section for that reason, whether or not he holds a valid firearm or shotgun certificate ...

'Whether matters believed by a defendant are capable, if true, of amounting to a defence of reasonable excuse is for the judge to determine. Whether he did have that belief and, if so, whether it amounts in the circumstances of the case to a reasonable excuse are for the jury to decide, the burden of proof being on the defendant on a balance of probabilities (cf *R v Lennard* [1973] 2 All ER 831, [1973] 1 WLR 483 and *R v Reid (Philip)* [1973] 3 All ER 1020, [1973] 1 WLR 1283). In our view, where there is an honest, but mistaken, belief of facts which, if true, would have constituted lawful authority, it is capable of being a reasonable excuse within the section, and the judge should so direct the jury, leaving them to determine whether the defendant has proved his belief of the requisite facts and whether in the circumstances that belief amounts to a reasonable excuse ...

'The critical issue of law in this case is the third, whether the appellant's mistaken belief both that his certificate was valid and that it constituted lawful authority, was capable of being a reasonable excuse. The judge did not consider that issue because he assumed that a valid certificate would have been lawful authority ... We have no hesitation in ruling that a belief in lawful authority based on facts which, if true, could not amount to lawful authority, is not capable of being a defence of reasonable excuse to a charge under s 19.' *R v Jones* [1995] 3 All ER 139 at 141, 143–144, CA, per Auld J

Australia [Section 4 of the Summary Offences Act 1988 (NSW) provides that it is a defence to a prosecution for an offence of using offensive language in a public place if the defendant had a 'reasonable excuse' for conducting himself or herself in such a manner.] 'Ultimately what must be construed is the meaning of the words in the context of s 4 of the Summary Offences Act 1988. In my opinion, reasonable excuse involves both subjective and objective considerations, but these considerations must be related to the immediately prevailing circumstances in which the offensive words etc are used, just as in self-defence or provocation the response of the accused must be related in some way to the actions of the victim and the particular circumstances. Although in an appropriate case it may also be proper to look at the immediate surrounding circumstances against the background of the defendant's antecedents, prior experiences (both recent and less recent), and other related events, there must, in my view, always be something involved in the immediate particular circumstances before there can be reasonable excuse.' *Conners v Craigie* (1994) 76 A Crim R 502 at 507, per Dunford J

Australia [Section 63 of the Australian Securities Commission Law provides that a person should not, without 'reasonable excuse', fail to comply with a requirement made under s 33 to produce specified books relating to a corporation.] 'That exemption of "reasonable excuse" has been held to apply to physical or practical difficulties in conforming to a statutory notice. It has been held inappropriate to a claimed reliance upon the privilege against self incrimination.' *Australian Securities Commission v Ampolex Ltd* (1995) 18 ACSR 735 at 748, per Kirby P

Australia [Whether the appellant who was carrying a pressurised canister of formaldehyde to defend herself if she happened to be attacked had a reasonable excuse for possessing it within the meaning of the Crimes Act 1900 (NSW) s 545E(2).]

'The term "reasonable excuse" has been used in many statutes and is the subject of many reported decisions. But decisions on other statutes provide no guidance because what is a reasonable excuse depends not only on the circumstances of the individual case but also on the purpose of the provision to which the defence of "reasonable excuse" is an exception ... [W]hen legislatures enact defences such as "reasonable excuse" they effectively give, and intend to give, to the courts the power to determine the content of such defences. Defences in this form are categories of indeterminate reference that have no content until a court makes its decision. They effectively require the courts to prescribe the relevant rule of conduct after the fact of its occurrence ... [P]ossession of a prohibited article or weapon for the purpose of "self-defence" is not of itself a "reasonable excuse". There must be a perceived threat, and its immediacy is also a relevant factor. So is the time, the location, the nature of the prohibited article and the personal history of the defendant.' *Taikato v R* (1996) 139 ALR 386 at 393, 395, 396, per Brennan CJ, Toohey, McHugh and Gummow JJ

New Zealand [Section 49(1) of the Domestic Violence Act 1995 provides that 'Every person commits an offence who, without reasonable excuse, – (a) Does any act in contravention of a protection order; or (b) Fails to comply with any condition of a protection order ...'.] 'It therefore becomes necessary to consider the meaning of "reasonable excuse" which Parliament has stipulated by way of protection for a defendant. I respectfully adopt the formulation of Randerson J in *Hargrave v Police* (1998) 17 FRNZ 124 at p 132 where he stated:

"In my judgment, the scheme of the Act, including in particular s 49, is that the prosecution need only prove the act of contravention of the order and knowledge by the defendant of the order and its terms (refer *MOT v Millar* [1986] 1 NZLR 660 in the context of the offence of driving while disqualified). It is then for the defendant to prove the existence of 'reasonable excuse' on the balance of probabilities (s 67(8) of the Summary Proceedings Act 1957 and *Te Weehi v Regional Fisheries Officer* [1986] 1 NZLR 680, 684–685 per Williamson J)."

'I accordingly reject the argument that the term "reasonable excuse" means "reasonable" only in the subjective perception of the defendant. Such construction would allow the insensitive defendant to engage in violence without sanction. "Reasonable" has been adopted by the law in a

range of contexts as imposing an objective standard as a societal norm. In this context I consider it to mean an excuse which an ordinary New Zealander would consider to be reasonable in all the circumstances. Those circumstances will include:
(a) The need for protection which has given rise to the protection order.
(b) The order and its terms.
(c) The fact that the applicant is ex hypothesi vulnerable to injury including psychological injury.
'Whether there is an "excuse" for the conduct will turn on whether it was objectively "reasonable" for the defendant to engage in it.' *A v Police* [1999] 2 NZLR 501 at 506, per Baragwanath J

Reasonable expectation

Australia [Section 177C(1) of the Income Tax Assessment Act 1936 (Cth) refers to, inter alia, an amount 'reasonably' to be 'expected' to have been included in assessable income.] '... the meaning of words such as "reasonable expectation" depends upon the context in which they appear. Nevertheless, in the present context, as in *Attorney-General's Department v Cockcroft* (1986) 10 FCR 180, the words were intended to receive, and should receive, their ordinary meaning. So too, as in Cockcroft, the word "reasonable" is used in contradistinction to that which is "irrational, absurd or ridiculous". The word "expectation" requires that the hypothesis be one which proceeds beyond the level of a mere possibility to become that which is the expected income. If it were necessary to substitute one ordinary English phrase for another, it might be said that it requires consideration of the question whether the hypothesised outcome is a reasonable probability: c f *Davies v Taylor* [1974] AC 207.' *Peabody v Federal Commissioner of Taxation* (1993) 40 FCR 531 at 541, per Hill J

Reasonable ground

Australia [Section 592(1) of the Corporation Law relevantly provides that 'where (a) a company has incurred a debt; (b) immediately before the time when the debt was incurred: (i) there were "reasonable grounds" to expect that the company will not be able to pay its debts and when they become due; ... any person who was a director of the company ... contravenes this section ...'] 'In my opinion when sub-s (1) of s 592 refers to "reasonable grounds" it requires the establishment of grounds which are reasonable according to the standards of directors or officers of companies of

reasonable ability. Reasonable ability is a relative concept designed to be applied with some flexibility. The test is objective and is not measured by subjective considerations personal to the defendant.' *Rema Industries and Services Pty Ltd v Coad* (1992) 107 ALR 374 at 382, per Lockhart J

Canada [Search warrants were justifiable where there were 'reasonable grounds' to believe that documents were on premises.] 'The standard of "reasonable ground to believe" is not to be equated with proof beyond reasonable doubt as in a criminal offence, but merely the civil standard of reasonable probability.' *Solvent Petroleum Extraction Inc v Canada (MNR)* [1989] 3 FCR 465 at 474, Fed TD, per Dube J

Reasonable grounds

Australia [The Administrative Appeals Tribunal is required by s 58(5) of the Freedom of Information Act 1982 (Cth) to determine whether there exist "reasonable grounds" for a claim that disclosure of documents would be contrary to public interest.] 'In my opinion, "reasonable grounds" for the purposes of s 58(5) are grounds based on reason ... The phrase is not qualified by reference to grounds which moderate and sensible persons might consider to be reasonable ... ' *Australian Doctors' Fund v Commonwealth of Australia* (1994) 49 FCR 479 at 488, per Beazley J

Reasonable hypothesis

Australia [Section 120(3) of the Veterans' Entitlement Act 1986 (Cth) is concerned with whether the material before the Repatriation Commission raises a 'reasonable hypothesis' that the relevant injury, disease or death was connected with the service of the veteran.] 'The material will raise a reasonable hypothesis within the meaning of s 120(3) if the material points to some fact or facts ("the raised facts") which support the hypothesis and if the hypothesis can be regarded as reasonable if the raised facts are true. Clearly enough, a relevant consideration in forming an opinion whether a particular hypothesis is reasonable is whether, as a matter of common or medical experience, the occurrence of an injury etc. of the kind sustained by the veteran is commonly accompanied by or associated with the occurrence of raised facts of the kind which constitute the relevant incidents of the service of the veteran. However, a hypothesis may still be reasonable even though such an accompaniment or association is not demonstrated or even if it is shown to be uncommon. So, in determining whether a hypothesis is reasonable for the purpose of s 120(3), it is not decisive that a connexion has not been proved between the kind of injury which occurred and circumstances of the kind which constitute the relevant incidents of the veteran's service. Nor is it decisive that the medical or scientific opinion which supports the hypothesis has little support in the medical profession or among scientists ... the case must be rare where it can be said that a hypothesis, based on the raised facts, is unreasonable when it is put forward by a medical practitioner who is eminent in the relevant field of knowledge. Conflict with other medical opinions is not sufficient to reject a hypothesis as unreasonable.' *Bushell v Repatriation Commission* (1992) 175 CLR 408 at 414–415, per Mason CJ, Deane and McHugh JJ

Reasonable man

[Under the Homicide Act 1957, s 3 the defence of provocation is to be determined by the jury in terms of whether the provocation was enough to make a reasonable man do as the person charged with murder did, and the jury must take into account everything both done and said according to the effect which, in their opinion, it would have on a reasonable man. The appellant had been taunted about his glue sniffing by the deceased, whom he had stabbed and who subsequently died. The appellant was charged with murder and convicted. On appeal, the question was whether the defendant's addiction to glue sniffing should have been taken into account as affecting the gravity of the provocation.] 'Judging from the speeches in *DPP v Camplin* ([1978] 2 All ER 168, [1978] AC 705, HL), it should indeed have been taken into account. Indeed, it was a characteristic of particular relevance, since the words of the deceased which were said to constitute provocation were directed to the appellant's shameful addiction to glue sniffing and his inability to break himself of it. Furthermore, there is nothing in the speeches in *DPP v Camplin* to suggest that a characteristic of this kind should be excluded from consideration. On the contrary, ... Lord Diplock spoke of the jury taking into consideration "all those factors" which would affect the gravity of the taunts or insults when applied to the defendant ...

'Even so, the Court of Appeal felt that the appellant's addiction to glue sniffing should be excluded because it was a characteristic which was repugnant to the concept of a reasonable man. It seems to me, with all respect, that this conclusion

flows from a misunderstanding of the function of the so-called "reasonable person" test in this context. In truth the expression "reasonable man" or "reasonable person" in this context can lead to misunderstanding. Lord Diplock described it in *DPP v Camplin* [1978] 2 All ER 168 at 173, [1978] AC 705 at 716 as an "apparently inapt expression". This is because the "reasonable person test" is concerned not with ratiocination, nor with the reasonable man whom we know so well in the law of negligence (where we are concerned with reasonable foresight and reasonable care), nor with reasonable conduct generally. The function of the test is only to introduce, as a matter of policy, a standard of self-control which has to be complied with if provocation is to be established at law: see *DPP v Camplin* [1978] 2 All ER 168 at 173, 181–182, [1978] AC 705 at 716, 726 per Lord Diplock and Lord Simon of Glaisdale. Lord Diplock himself spoke of "the reasonable or ordinary person", and indeed to speak of the degree of self-control attributable to the ordinary person is (despite the express words of the statute) perhaps more apt, and certainly less likely to mislead, than to do so with reference to the reasonable person ... In my opinion it would be entirely consistent with the law as stated in s 3 of the 1957 Act, as properly understood, to direct the jury simply with reference to a hypothetical person having the power of self-control to be expected of an *ordinary* person of the age and sex of the defendant, but in other respects sharing such of the defendant's characteristics as they think would affect the gravity of the provocation to him: see *DPP v Camplin* [1978] 2 All ER 168 at 175, [1978] AC 705 at 718 per Lord Diplock ...

'In truth, the mere fact that a characteristic of the defendant is discreditable does not exclude it from consideration ... Indeed, even if the defendant's discreditable conduct causes a reaction in another, which in turn causes the defendant to lose his self-control, the reaction may amount to provocation ...

'At all events it follows that, in a case such as the present, a distinction may have to be drawn between two different situations. The first occurs where the defendant is taunted with his addiction (for example, that he is an alcoholic, or a drug addict, or a glue sniffer), or even with having been intoxicated (from any cause) on some previous occasion. In such a case, however discreditable such a condition may be, it may where relevant be taken into account as going to the gravity of the provocation. The second is the simple fact of the defendant being intoxicated—being drunk, or high on drugs or with glue—at the relevant time, which may not be so taken into account, because that, like displaying a lack of ordinary self-control, is excluded as a matter of policy. Although the distinction is a fine one, it will, I suspect, very rarely be necessary to explain it to a jury.' *R v Morhall* [1995] 3 All ER 659 at 665–667, HL, per Lord Goff of Chieveley

Reasonable period

[By the Administration of Justice Act 1970, s 36 and the Administration of Justice Act 1973, s 8 the court is enabled to exercise discretionary powers in an action for possession of mortgaged land which consists of or includes a dwelling house if it appears that the mortgagor will be able within a 'reasonable period' to pay mortgage arrears or remedy other defaults.] 'It is not surprising that [district judges] have found it convenient to adopt a relatively short period of years as the rough rule of thumb which aids a just determination of the "reasonable period" for the purposes of ss 36 and 8. Nevertheless, although I would not go quite so far with Mr Croally as to say it should be an "assumption", it does seem to me that the logic and spirit of the legislation require ... that the court should take as its starting point the full term of the mortgage and pose at the outset the question: would it be possible for the mortgagor to maintain payment-off of the arrears by instalments over that period?' *Cheltenham and Gloucester Building Society v Norgan* [1996] 1 All ER 449 at 458, CA, per Waite LJ

'... A "reasonable period" implies that the interests of both parties have to be taken into account. When the borrower is likely to be able to make regular payments, of whatever amount, then in general it can be said that the longer the period then the more "reasonable" it will be for him. Although it may not often be reasonable to expect the lender to wait longer than the original term, the question of principle raised by this appeal is whether he can reasonably be required to wait until then ... [M]ortgage lenders such as the respondents have a number of options available to them, when payments are in arrears. They include even extending the term of the loan ... as well as deferring payments of interest ... and, of direct relevance in circumstances such as these, capitalising the interest payments which are in arrears ... I do not see how the respondents can properly say that it is not appropriate to take into account the whole of the remaining part of the original term when assessing a "reasonable period"

for the payment of arrears.' *Cheltenham and Gloucester Building Society v Norgan* [1996] 1 All ER 449 at 461–462, CA, per Evans LJ

Reasonable person

Canada 'The "reasonable person" using the inquiry function of the [personal property security] registration system for the purpose described above must also be regarded as a person who is familiar with the search facilities provided by the system. That is not to say that the standard is that of the most sophisticated and skilled user. The standard must be that of a reasonably competent user of the system ...' *Re Lambert* (1994) 119 DLR (4th) 93 at 107, Ont CA, per Doherty JA

Reasonable suspicion

Australia 'It was argued on behalf of the appellants that to have inconsistent suspicions prevents them being reasonable. I do not accept that argument. It is in the nature of suspicions that it is possible to hold more than one suspicion at the same time and to hold suspicions which are inconsistent. This, as I see it, is inevitable in many cases. A person might have preferred suspicions—for example in this case, drug dealing—but this does not mean that a person could not fairly and reasonably hold other suspicions in relation to the source of the money ... Several elements of the concept of reasonable suspicion are well established by authority. First, the reasonable suspicion had to be entertained at the time the persons were in possession of the property in question: e.g. *Rowe v Galvin* [1984] VR 350 and *McDonald v Webster* [1913] VLR 506. Secondly, the reasonable suspicion must attach to the property and not merely to the person in possession: *O'Sullivan v Tregaskis* [1948] SASR 12 and *Yeo v Capper* [1964] SASR 1. Thirdly, the suspicion must be entertained upon reasonable grounds: *Wallace v Hansberry* [1959] SASR 20; *George v Rockett* (1990) 170 CLR 104; 93 ALR 483; 64 ALJR 384; *Nicholas v Fleming* [1959] Tas SR 165 and *Deudney v Paulston* (1940) 57 WN (NSW) 40. Fourthly, the mere fact that a man makes an untrue statement as to how he came into possession of goods when questioned is not in itself a ground for believing them to be stolen: *McDonald v Webster*. *Nicholls v Young* [1992] 2 VR 209 at 214–215, per Smith J

Reasonable time

[For 45 Halsbury's Laws (4th edn) para 1147 see now 45(2) Halsbury's Laws (4th edn) (Reissue) para 248.]

REASONABLY

Australia '[66] The word "reasonably" and the reference to "all the circumstances" import an objective test of the likelihood unaffected by the intention of the person doing the act — *Hagan v Trustee of Toowoomba Sportsground Trust* [2000] FCA 1615 at [15] (Drummond J); *Creek v Cairns Post Pty Ltd* (2001) 112 FCR 352 at [12] (Kiefel J). That test is not in dispute in the present case.

...

'[78] There is a number of definitions of "reasonable" in the *Shorter Oxford English Dictionary*. The relevant ones are:

3. Agreeable to reason; not irrational, absurd or ridiculous.

4. Not going beyond the limit assigned by reason; not extravagant or excessive; moderate."

The adverb "reasonably" is defined as "in a reasonable manner; sufficiently, fairly".

'[79] There are elements of rationality and proportionality in the relevant definitions of reasonably. A thing is done "reasonably" in one of the protected activities in para (a), (b) and (c) of s 18D if it bears a rational relationship to that activity and is not disproportionate to what is necessary to carry it out. It imports an objective judgment. In this context that means a judgment independent of that which the actor thinks is reasonable. It does allow the possibility that there may be more than one way of doing things "reasonably". The judgment required in applying the section, is whether the thing done was done "reasonably" not whether it could have been done more reasonably or in a different way more acceptable to the court. The judgment will necessarily be informed by the normative elements of ss 18C and 18D and a recognition of the two competing values that are protected by those sections.

'[80] An act will be done reasonably in the performance, exhibition or distribution of an artistic work if it is done for the purpose and in a manner calculated to advance the purpose of the artistic expression in question. An act is done reasonably in relation to statements, publications, discussions or debates for genuine academic, artistic or scientific purposes, if it bears a rational relationship to those purposes. The publication of a genuine scientific paper on the topic of genetic differences between particular human populations might, for one reason or another, be insulting or offensive to a group of people. Its discussion at a scientific conference would no doubt be reasonable. Its presentation to a meeting convened by a racist organisation and its use to support a view that a particular group of persons is morally or otherwise "inferior" to another by reason of their race or ethnicity, may not be a thing reasonably done in relation to para (b) of s 18D.

'[81] The same kind of criterion may be applied to acts done in reports or comments on events or matters of public interest. A presentation of a report or comment which highlights, in a way that is gratuitously insulting or offensive, a matter that is irrelevant to the purported question of public interest under discussion may not be done "reasonably". A feature article on criminal activity said to be associated with a particular ethnic group would in the ordinary course be expected to fall within the protection of (c). If it were written in a way that offered gratuitous insults by, for example, referring to members of the group in derogatory racist slang terms, then it would be unlikely that the comment would be offered "reasonably".' *Bropho v Human Rights and Equal Opportunity Commission* [2004] FCAFC 16 per French J; BC200400209

REASONABLY PRACTICABLE

Australia 'The words "reasonably practicable" have, somewhat surprisingly, been the subject of much judicial consideration. It is surprising because the words "reasonably practicable" are ordinary words bearing their ordinary meaning. And the question whether a measure is or is not reasonably practicable is one which requires no more than the making of a value judgment in the light of all the facts. Nevertheless, three general propositions are to be discerned from the decided cases:

- the phrase "reasonably practicable" means something narrower than "physically possible" or "feasible";
- what is "reasonably practicable" is to be judged on the basis of what was known at the relevant time;
- to determine what is "reasonably practicable" it is necessary to balance the likelihood of the risk occurring against the cost, time and trouble necessary to avert that risk.' (footnotes omitted)

Slivak v Lurgi (Australia) Pty Ltd (2001) 177 ALR 585; (2001) 75 ALJR 481; BC200100264; [2001] HCA 6 at [53], per Gaudron J

REASONABLY REQUIRES

Australia [Section 530A(3) of the Corporations Law provides that an officer of a company that is being wound up must do whatever the liquidator 'reasonably requires' the officer to do to help in the winding up.] 'The phrase "reasonably requires" has been the subject of considerable judicial interpretation in various statutes over the ages; sometimes the phrase means "reasonably necessary" as opposed to "reasonably demanded": see *Crooks National Stores Pty Ltd v Collie* (1957) 97 CLR 581 and *Watney Mann Ltd v Langley* [1966] 1 QB 457. However the phrase can sometimes connote "reasonably demanded": see for instance the cases before *Crooks v Collie* such as *Kiely v Loose* [1948] VLR 181. I think the words "liquidator reasonably requires" carry the connotation that the liquidator considers that the act which he has indicated that the director should do is one which is needed to be done for the proper conduct of the winding up.' *ERS Engines Pty Ltd v Wilson* (1994) 14 ACSR 531 at 537, per Young J

REBATE

Canada 'There is no doubt that the plaintiff met the requirements for entitlement to a rebate. That question is not at issue in this case.

'In subsection 120(5) it can be seen that the method of calculating the tax rebate is not included. Nonetheless, this subsection, by use of the word "prescribed", delegates to a regulatory authority the power to make regulations to set out the necessary parameters for effective implementation of the rebate. Subsection 2(1) of the Act gives the meaning of the word "prescribed" [as am. by SC 1990, c 45, s 1]:

> **2.** (1) ...
> "prescribed" means
> (*a*) in the case of a form, the information to be given on a form or the manner of filing a form, prescribed by the Minister, and
> (*b*) in any other case, prescribed by <u>regulation or determined in accordance with rules prescribed by regulation</u>. [My emphasis.]

'However, this Act contains no definition of the word "*remboursement*": accordingly, again applying the rules of statutory interpretation I have examined the ordinary meaning of this word and the related word "*rembourser*", as well as the word "rebate" used in the English version. According to *Petit Robert 1: Dictionnaire alphabétique et analogique de la langue française*, these words mean:

[TRANSLATION]

Refund: *n. m* ... . Act of refunding.

Refund: v *tr*... Pay (sthg.), to return expenses to someone ... . Return expenses to someone; return to someone.

'The *Petit Larousse Illustré* defines these words as follows:

[TRANSLATION]

Refund: *n. m*. Act of refunding; payment of amount due ...

Refund: v *tr*. (of *fund*) **1.** Return money loaned to someone. **2.** Return money spent to someone.

'The New Shorter Oxford English Dictionary on Historical Principles defines it as follows:

rebate ... A deduction from a sum of money to be paid; a discount. Also, a partial rebate of money paid.

rebate v.t. Deduct (a certain amount) from a sum; subtract; reduce or diminish (a sum or amount) ... Give or allow a reduction to (a person) ... Pay back (a sum of money) as a rebate; give a rebate on.

'As can be seen, the use by Parliament of the word "*remboursement*" (rebate) allows us to conclude with greater certainty that its intent was in fact to require the rebate of a sum of money and that the sum of money owed must as a general rule be rebated in its entirety.' *Société des Alcools du Québec c Canada* [2001] 1 FC 386 at 401–403, FCTD, per Lemieux J

REBUILD

[For 42 Halsbury's Laws (4th edn) para 815 see now 42 Halsbury's Laws (4th edn) (Reissue) para 816.]

RECEIVED BY THE REMOVAL REVIEW AUTHORITY

New Zealand [Regulation 26(2) of the Immigration Regulations 1991 provides: 'The appellant shall ensure that, within 42 days after the date on which the removal order was served on the appellant, the appeal form and the appropriate fee are received by the Removal Review Authority at its Wellington address, being PO Box 1674, Wellington'.] 'I believe that a case could be made for interpreting the words in reg 26(2) so as to include the sending of the appeal form by facsimile. The expression "received by the Removal Authority at its Wellington address, being PO Box 1674, Wellington" is an awkward one. It would be clearer if it said either "received by the Removal Authority at its Wellington address" or "received by the Removal Authority at its Wellington postal address, being PO Box 1674, Wellington". As it is, a literal interpretation would falsely imply that the authority's only Wellington address is a post-office box. The authority is not crouched inside the post-office box waiting for the notice to be thrust into his or her hands. The dominant words in the provision seem to be "received by the Removal Review Authority at its Wellington address". On one possible interpretation, the further words "being PO Box 1674, Wellington" may be there as a matter of mere information rather than prescription. Accordingly they may not preclude reception by the authority at its physical Wellington address ...

'Language is elastic to a certain point but snaps when asked to part company altogether with previously accepted meanings. It could be stretched here to accommodate facsimiles but not, I fear, fees posted but not received within the time limit.' *Wielgus v Removal Review Authority* [1994] 1 NZLR 73 at 78–79, per Fisher J

RECEIVER

[For 39 Halsbury's Laws (4th edn) para 801 see now 39(2) Halsbury's Laws (4th edn) (Reissue) para 301.]

RECEIVES

Australia [Section 10 of the Criminal Code (Qld) provides that a person who 'receives' or assists another who is to his knowledge guilty of an offence, in order to enable him to escape punishment, is said to become an accessory after the fact to the offence.] 'Section 10 defines the offence as "receiving or assisting" another. The section is derived from Stephen's Draft Code of 1880, which has been adopted in various parts of the common law world. In Canada it now appears in s 21(1) of the Criminal Code. The expression in s 21(1) is "receives, comforts, or assists that person". The word "receives" in this context has an ancient lineage. Coke ascribes it to the Statute of Westminster 1275, 3 Edw 1 St 1 c 9, where the French word "receiptment" is used. In its original sense it seems to have meant "harbour": cf J H Baker, *Manual of Law French*, p 182: recever. In discussing accessories after the fact, *Russell on*

Crime, 12th ed, 1964, vol 1, p 163, gives as examples from the old texts, a person harbouring and concealing in his house a felon under pursuit, so that pursuers cannot find him; "and, much more, where one harbours in his house and openly protects such a felon, by reason whereof the pursuers dare not take him".

'In *Sykes v DPP* [1962] AC 528 at 561; (1961) 45 Cr App R 230 at 247, Lord Denning said the words "receives, relieves, comforts or assists" described *active* acts of assistance. What he said reflects the statement in Glanville Williams, *Criminal Law*, 2nd ed, 1961, para 138, p 411, that a positive act of assistance is needed to constitute someone an accessory.' *Re Winston* (1994) 74 A Crim R 312 at 314–315, per McPherson and Pincus JJA

Australia 'It is probably more helpful to consider its meaning principally in the association which the Code [Criminal Code (Qld)] makes of it with the word "assists". It can be said that to "receive" implies an act of acceptance of the offender into an area or location which the accessory controls or over which he exercises some influence and it will involve some measure of positive support for the offender. It can be expected that it will be included within the scope of assisting, which is a more embracing term. Viewed in this way receiving will constitute a particular form of assistance and a whole range of acts of assisting will not involve any aspect of receiving.' *Re Winston* (1994) 76 A Crim R 113 at 118, per cur

RECEPTION, FUNCTION, OR OTHER SOCIAL GATHERING

New Zealand [Sale of Liquor Act 1989, s 51(2).] ' "Reception", "function" and "social gathering" are terms that suggest a gathering for an event of a private nature, although not necessarily attended by "invitation only". Certainly, the terms do not convey the same image as "occasion or events" of a totally public nature such as cricket matches, football matches, race meetings, rock concerts and the like.' *Bar Systems (New Zealand) Ltd v Wellington District Licensing Agency* [1996] 3 NZLR 100 at 108, per Goddard J

RECKLESS

[*R v Lawrence* [1981] 1 All ER 974, HL, was followed in *R v Reid* [1992] 3 All ER 673 HL.

In the former case, the charge was that of reckless driving under the provisions of ss 1, 2 of the Road Traffic Act 1972, which were re-enacted in ss 1, 2 of the Road Traffic Act 1988.

It should be noted that under s 1 of the Road Traffic Act 1991, which came into force in July 1992, there were substituted for ss 1, 2 of the Act of 1988, as from a date to be appointed, new ss 1, 2 and 2A, under which the offence of reckless driving will cease to exist and be replaced by that of dangerous driving.

See DRIVE–DRIVER.]

Australia 'The authorities suggest that there the word "reckless" has been used in the criminal law in the following senses:

1   as conveying the concept of doing an act whilst contemplating the probability of it having the relevant consequence or quality with indifference to that consequence or quality (*R v Crabbe* (1985) 156 CLR 464, explaining *Pemble v R* (1971) 124 CLR 107 at 119; *Jackson v Butterworth* [1946] VLR 330; *Mattingley v Tuckwood* (1989) 43 A Crim R 111 at 121; *R v Nuri* [1990] VR 641; *Filmer v Barclay* [1994] 2 VR 26);

2   as conveying the concept of doing an act whilst contemplating the possibility of it having the relevant consequence or quality with indifference to that consequence or quality (*R v Coleman* (1990) 19 NSWLR 467; *Jackson v Butterworth* (supra));

3   as conveying the concept of doing an act whilst knowing or recognising the existence of a substantial risk of it having the relevant consequence or quality but nevertheless doing that act (*R v Smith* (1982) 7 A Crim R 437);

4   as conveying the concept of doing an act which has the relevant consequence or quality without caring whether it will have that consequence or has that quality (*Williams Brothers Direct Supply Stores Ltd v Cloote* (1944) 60 TLR 270; *R v McKinnon* [1959] 1 QB 150 at 153);

5   as conveying the concept of doing an act which creates an obvious risk that it will have the relevant consequence or quality but nevertheless doing that act without having given any thought to the possibility to the risk of it having that consequence or quality or with a recognition of the risk (*Commissioner of Police of the Metropolis v Caldwell* [1982] AC 341).

'... The Australian authorities take approaches which have an underlying common feature, namely

that recklessness is doing an act whilst contemplating the chance of it having the relevant consequence or quality with indifference to that consequence or quality.' *Dreezer v Duvnjak* (1996) 6 Tas R 294 at 299–300; BC9606360, per Zeeman J

RECOMMENDATION

Canada [At issue was whether deputy minister was required to follow 'recommendation' of committee to grant security clearance.] '... The simple term "recommendations" should be given its ordinary meaning. "Recommendations" ordinarily means the offering of advice and should not be taken to mean a binding decision.' *Thomson v Canada* (*Deputy Minister of Agriculture*) [1992] 1 SCR 385 at 399, per La Forest J (Can SC)

RECONSTRUCTION

[For 7 Halsbury's Laws (4th edn) para 2149 see now 7(2) Halsbury's Laws (4th edn) (1996 Reissue) para 1461.]

RECORD

Australia [Regulation 38 of the Income Tax Regulations (Cth) provides that the address of a person, as described in any 'record' in the custody of the Commissioner, should be his address for service.] '... the word "record" in reg 38 should be given a wide ambit. In my opinion, the word "record" is used to refer to that by which information is recorded, and covers not only documents but computer information and suchlike ... it seems to me at least to require a bona fide recording of information.' *Sunrise Auto Ltd v Deputy Commissioner of Taxation (Cth)* (1994) 124 ALR 425 at 434, per Spender J

Australia [Regulation 38 of the Income Tax Regulations (Cth) provides, inter alia, that where no address for service has been given to the Commissioner of Taxation then the address of the person, as described in any 'record' in the custody of the Commissioner, shall be his address for service.] '... the meaning of "record" in the present context is not the subject of any authoritative decision, although the recent English cases indicate a less rigorous approach than previously; the word does not appear to be used here as a term of art, or to have any special or technical meaning; and it appears to have been intended to have its ordinary dictionary meaning which emphasises that the writing is meant to preserve, for an appreciable time, the memory or knowledge of a fact or an event, even in an informal, or unofficial, fashion with the object of subsequent retrieval of the information; a writing may constitute an official or formal, or an unofficial or informal, record of a fact or event; but the latter type of writing could none the less fairly be described as a "record" for the purposes of reg 38 as, no doubt, could an official record, for instance, a formal document such as the electoral roll'. *Sunrise Auto Ltd v Deputy Commissioner of Taxation* (1995) 133 ALR 274 at 287–288, per Beaumont and Beazley JJ

RECORD (DISC)

[The Dramatic and Musical Performers' Protection Act 1958 has been repealed. See now the definition of 'sound recording' in the Copyright, Designs and Patents Act 1988, s 8.]

RECORD OF BUSINESS

Australia 'In my opinion, a record, brought into existence once only in a business, is not deprived of the quality of a "record of a business" merely because the typical example of a business record is one which is part of systematic record keeping of a business involving more than a single document.' *Feltafield Pty Ltd v Heidelberg Graphic Equipment* (1995) 56 FCR 481 at 483, per Beazley J

RECOVER

Australia ' "Recover" means to get back into one's hands or possession something lost or taken away.' *Cinema Plus Ltd (Administrators Apptd) v Australian and New Zealand Banking Group Ltd* (2000) 49 NSWLR 513; 157 FLR 204; 35 ACSR 1; BC200004226; [2000] NSWCA 195 at [121], per Sheller JA

REDUCED INTO WRITING

Australia [Section 29 of the Evidence Act 1929 (SA) provides, inter alia, that a witness may be cross-examined as to previous statements made by him in writing, or 'reduced to writing', relative to the subject matter of the case without the writing being shown to him.] 'I am of the opinion, therefore, that a previous statement, not actually made in writing by the witness himself, cannot be said to have been "reduced into writing" for the purpose of s 29 unless the writing has been verified or adopted in some way by the witness. He could do

this by signing it (as was the case in *McLellan v Bowyer* (1961) 106 CLR 95) or in some less formal manner — say, by reading it and acknowledging orally to the recorder or someone else that it is accurate — but some form of assent is needed.' *Re Walker* (1993) 70 A Crim R 440 at 443, per Cox J

REDUNDANCY

Australia [In the context of whether an employee's position became redundant following the reorganisation of the company. Workplace Relations Act 1996 (Cth).] '[10] The key concept upon which the operation of cl 55.1.1 in the present case depends is that of a position becoming redundant. The appellants contend that, in this context, "position" means a position in a business, and that, in the circumstances of the demerger, in which a conglomerate enterprise involving a packaging business and a paper operations business was split into two parts, each of which continued to function as before, with the employees performing the same functions, on the same terms and conditions, those employees' positions did not become redundant. The respondents contend, and the Federal Court accepted, that there was a critical change in the employment situation, namely the identity of the employer. That is, even if it is a case of succession, so that the employees had the protection of s 170MB of the Workplace Relations Act 1966 (Cth), at the time of the termination by Amcor of their employment, the employees lost their positions, and they lost them because Amcor no longer needed their services. Accordingly, as between Amcor and the employees, the positions of the employees became redundant, and for that reason the employees were retrenched by Amcor, even though they were immediately re-employed by Paper Australia.

...

'[12] ... In the industrial context, redundancy of position is not a concept of clearly defined and inflexible meaning. Whether cases of succession to a business following corporate restructuring are regarded as justifying an award of redundancy payments is dealt with "on the particular merits of the case rather than by way of broad prescription." Here, however, it is necessary to apply an agreement that contains a "broad prescription", and the task is to decide how that broad prescription operates in the particular circumstances.

...

'[35] The provisions of the Act to which cl 55.7.1 referred (Subdiv C of Div 3 of Pt VIA of the Act)

regulated the termination of employment by an employer. They included provisions (s 170CL) obliging the employer to give written notice to the Commonwealth Employment Service of the intention to terminate the employment of 15 or more employees "for reasons of an economic, technological, structural or similar nature". Evidently then, cl 55.7 used the expression "retrenched employees" to refer to those whose employment had been terminated and terminated "on account of redundancy". Were this not so, the reference to provisions dealing with termination of employment and requiring notice to the Commonwealth Employment Service would not have been apt.

…

'[43] The Commission said, in its supplementary decision, that it had "some difficulty in finding a suitable expression" to make its intention clear about what constituted "redundancy". In its earlier decision, it had referred to a number of definitions of redundancy. Chief among those was the decision by Bray CJ in *R v Industrial Commission (SA); Ex parte Adelaide Milk Supply Co-operative Ltd* which was understood as emphasising that redundancy refers "to a job becoming redundant and not to a worker becoming redundant".

…

'[54] Secondly, reading the provisions as focusing upon a position in a business is consistent with the approach to redundancy taken by the Commission in the *Termination, Change and Redundancy Case*. There, as already noted, the emphasis was upon a "job" becoming redundant rather than a worker becoming redundant. As the Commission pointed out, the definition of "redundancy" which it adopted from the *Adelaide Milk Supply Co-operative Case* recognised that "redundancy situations may not necessarily involve dismissals" and emphasised that the job or work had disappeared through no fault on the part of the employee. To find that a position is redundant whenever an employer leaves an industry (regardless of whether another employer continues to operate the business concerned) would give insufficient emphasis to the need to identify whether a "job" had become redundant.

…

'[99] *"Redundant" in the Agreement*: For cl 55.1.1 to be engaged, the first requirement is that a position become "redundant". Clauses 55.2 and 55.5 refer to employees becoming "redundant" in two situations, "transfer to a lower paid job" and "transfer to another location" within the company. Necessarily, the reason such employees are

considered "redundant" by the Agreement is that the positions in which they were formerly employed have *come to an end*. Otherwise, such a transfer would constitute no more than a demotion or relocation. Reference in cl 55.2 to the effect that an employee "become redundant *and* be transferred to a lower paid job" indicates that something has happened to the original position to cause the transfer to occur. Secondly, although their employment continues, the employees in these situations are *no longer performing the same task*. By definition, were they to continue performing the same task, the position would not have become redundant. Nowhere in the Agreement is there reference to a "redundancy" where the position continues to exist, or where the employee continues to perform the identical function as he or she has previously done.

…

'[105] *Redundancy under the Act*: The fact that the Agreement was prepared for the certification of the Commission in accordance with the Act reinforces the lastmentioned point. It gives emphasis to the consideration that, where the Agreement talks of "redundancy", as it does in the heading to cl 55 and in the use of the adjective "redundant" throughout that clause, it does so in the special context of the meaning that has gathered around that word in Australia generally and in the industrial relations context in particular.

'[106] So viewed, judicial and arbitral decisions and statutory provisions suggest that what is essentially of concern in relation to redundancy in this context is the deprivation of long-term employment without fault on the part of the employee. From the earliest considerations of the notion of redundancy by Australian industrial tribunals, the concern has been over the specific injustice that results for employees who are retrenched after lengthy service and, as a result, face particular problems of re-employment arising from their past specialised skills, the unavailability of alternative work, the diminished career and security expectations and, in some cases, their age consequent upon long service with the employer who retrenches them for redundancy reasons. In such circumstances, the immediate re-engagement of the relevant employees under identical or closely equivalent conditions would usually be regarded as a circumstance taking the case out of classification as one involving industrial "redundancy".

…

'[142] The construction which I prefer has the advantage also, that it gives better effect to the primary meaning of the word "redundant" which the Oxford English Dictionary (2nd ed) 1989 gives as "abundant" and "superfluous, excessive, unnecessary; having some additional or unneeded feature or part". Although the employees here may have become superfluous to the requirements of the appellant, their positions did not.' *Amcor Ltd v Construction, Forestry, Mining and Energy Union* [2005] HCA 10 at [10], [12], per Gleeson CJ and McHugh J, [35], [43], [54], per Gummow, Heyne and Heydon JJ, [99], [105]–[106], per Kirby J, [142], per Callinan J; BC200500901

REDUNDANT

Australia 'I will begin the resolution of this dispute by considering the meaning of the word "redundant". In the context of employment law it is generally accepted that becoming redundant means that the employee is no longer required by his (or her) employer because the employer no longer has a need for the work that the employee was performing. In examining the relevant authorities it is convenient to begin with *Re Clerks (State) Award* [1976] IAS Current Review 166, a decision of the New South Wales Industrial Commission. The NSW Commission was considering an application to vary an award to make provision for redundancy payments. In the course of its decision, the NSW Commission said (at 175):

"It can fairly be said that in industrial circles the term redundancy payment has come to mean compensation for losses of various kinds suffered by employees who have given substantial service to an employer and whose services are terminated because, for one reason or another, the employer no longer needs them."

'An important case to which reference should be made is the decision of the Full Court of the Supreme Court of South Australia in *R v Industrial Commission of South Australia; Ex parte Adelaide Milk Supply Co-op Ltd* (1977) 16 SASR 6. The question at issue was whether the State's Industrial Commission had jurisdiction to make provision by award for redundancy. In the course of dealing with that question each member of the court considered the meaning of the word "redundancy". Bray CJ presided over the court and delivered a separate judgment, but I will first refer to the judgment of Bright J. He said (at 26):

"The word 'redundant' does not occur in the [Industrial Conciliation and Arbitration] Act.

In its industrial sense it is not defined in the *Oxford Dictionary*. The application which I have already set out attempts a definition for the purpose of the proposed award. A consideration of the cases leads me to think that the question of the redundancy of an employee is linked to the question of the continued utility of the job which he is performing. In other words it does not relate to the personal competence of the employee in the job which he is performing. If I am right in this, then in its widest form the concept of redundancy connotes that an employee becomes redundant whenever (and for whatever reason) his employer no longer desires to have performed the job which that employee is doing."

'The Chief Justice said (at 8):

"I should begin by saying that I agree with Bright J that the concept of redundancy in the context we are discussing seems to be simply this, that a job becomes redundant when the employer no longer desires to have it performed by anyone. A dismissal for redundancy seems to be a dismissal, not on account of any personal act or default of the employee dismissed or any consideration peculiar to him, but because the employer no longer wishes the job the employee has been doing to be done by anyone."

'Mitchell J, the remaining member of the court, cited with approval the passage from the decision in *Re Clerks (State) Award* previously mentioned.

'The meaning which Bray CJ gave to the word "redundancy" has been applied in a number of cases including the *Termination, Change and Redundancy Case* (1984) 8 IR 34; *Short v FW Hercus Pty Ltd* (1993) 40 FCR 511; *Hollows v Federal Cmr of Taxation* (1994) 94 ATC 2032; and *Steppes Pty Ltd v Australian Liquor, Hospitality and Miscellaneous Workers Union* (1998) 86 IR 337.

'It has always been assumed that an employee has been made redundant if his employment is terminated because the employer has sold the business in which the employee was working. That the employer has been able to arrange for the new owner to engage the employee is beside the point. In *Re Government Cleaning Services (Privatisation) Award No 2* (1994) 55 IR 199 the NSW Commission was required to consider whether certain employees had become redundant when the Government Cleaning Services was privatised although they had been offered employment by the new operators. The NSW Commission found that the employees had been made redundant. Schmidt J referred to Bray CJ's judgment in *Ex parte Adelaide Milk Supply Co-op Ltd* and then continued (at 218):

> "When a business is sold, or a governmental undertaking privatised, the original employment comes to an end. Employees do not always obtain work with a new employer. The fact that the old employer assists the employees to obtain work with the new employer, does not alter the consequence, that the termination of the original employment arose as a result of the employer's decision, that it no longer wished any of its employees to perform the jobs they were performing and not through any fault on the employee's part. It seems to me that employees in that situation have been made redundant, whether or not they are assisted in obtaining alternate employment."

...

'... [The authorities] establish that the word "redundant" refers to the situation where an employee has been dismissed for a particular reason. They do not suggest that there will be no redundancy if the position established by the employer is continued by another employer. That is to say, "redundancy" is a word which describes the reason why an employee has been dismissed.' *Construction, Forestry, Mining and Energy Union v Amcor Ltd* (2002) 113 IR 112; BC200202317; [2002] FCA 610 at [9]–[12], [16], per Finkelstein J

REFERENTIAL BID

Canada [Referential bid was not acceptable in judicial approval of sale by receiver.] "'Referential bid' refer[s] to a bid which does not stand on its own, which is not understandable without reference to another bid.' *Bank of Nova Scotia v Yoshikuni Lumber Ltd* (1992) 99 DLR (4th) 289 at 309, BC CA, per Gibbs JA

REFUGEE

[Convention and Protocol relating to the Status of Refugees, art 1A(2).] 'Whilst therefore I readily accept that [the issue] is one of very considerable difficulty, and that anomalies may appear to arise on either view, I have concluded that ... an asylum seeker unable to return to his country of origin may indeed be entitled to recognition as a refugee provided only that the fear or actuality of past persecution still plays a causative part in his presence here.' *Adan v Secretary of State for the Home Department* [1997] 2 All ER 723 at 733, CA, per Simon Brown LJ; revsd [1998] 2 All ER 453, HL: see below [Whether to be recognised as a 'refugee' required a current well-founded fear of persecution for a convention reason or if it was sufficient to have had such a fear when leaving country of origin.] 'But having said that, the starting point must be the language itself. The most striking feature is that it is expressed throughout in the present tense: "is outside", "is unable", "is unwilling". Thus in order to bring himself within category (1) Mr Adan must show that he is (not was) unable to avail himself of the protection of his country. If one asks "protection against what?" the answer must surely be, or at least include, protection against persecution. Since "is unable" can only refer to current inability, one would expect that the persecution against which he needs protection is also current (or future) persecution. If he has no current fear of persecution it is not easy to see why he should need current protection against persecution, or why, indeed, protection is relevant at all.

'But the point becomes even clearer when one looks at category (2), which includes a person who is (a) outside the country of his nationality owing to a well-founded fear of persecution, and (b) is unwilling, owing to such fear, to avail himself of the protection of that country. "Owing to such fear" in (b) means owing to well-founded fear of being persecuted for a convention reason. But "fear" in (b) can only refer to current fear, since the fear must be the cause of the asylum-seeker being unwilling now to avail himself of the protection of his country. If fear in (b) is confined to current fear, it would be odd if "owing to well-founded fear" in (a) were not also confined to current fear. The word must surely bear the same meaning in both halves of the sentence.

...

'So with great respect to the majority of the Court of Appeal, I would hold that on the first issue the views of Thorpe LJ are to be preferred. I am glad to have reached that conclusion. For a test which required one to look at historic fear, and then ask whether that historic fear which, ex hypothesi, no longer exists is nevertheless the cause of the asylum-seeker being presently outside his country is a test which would not be easy to apply in practice. This is not to say that historic fear may not be relevant. It may well provide evidence to establish present fear. But it is the existence, or otherwise, of present fear which is determinative.' At 458, 460, per Lord Lloyd of Berwick

REGISTER

[For 7 Halsbury's Laws (4th edn) para 357 see now 7(1) Halsbury's Laws (4th edn) (2004 Reissue) para 777.]

REGISTERED

Australia 'In the circumstances I think the Part A statement must be taken as having been "registered" when, having been physically received, it was finally accepted by the [Australian Securities and Investment] Commission as being in accordance with the requirements of the Corporations Law.' *SSG Industries Pty Ltd v Australian National Industries Ltd* (1999) 17 ACLC 313; BC9900005, per Heerey J

REGULARLY

Canada [Entitlement to unemployment insurance depended on whether claimant was regularly engaged at time of work stoppage.] ' "Regularly" implies "continuity" and is to be contrasted with "casual and intermittent".' *Canada (A-G) v McKenzie* (1993) 104 DLR (4th) 261 at 264, FCA, per Desjardins JA

REGULATE

Canada '13 Applying a broad and purposive interpretation, ss. 7 and 8 [of the Alberta *Municipal Government Act*] grant the City the power to pass bylaws limiting the number of taxi plate licences. As discussed, s. 8 supplements s. 7 by illustrating some of the broad powers exercisable by a municipality. Here the power to limit the number of licences could fall under either s. 8(a), the power to regulate, or s. 8(c), the power to provide for a system of licences. To "regulate", as defined in the *Oxford English Dictionary* (2nd ed. 1989), vol. XIII, is "subject to … restrictions". Thus, as O'Leary J.A. in dissent aptly stated, the "jurisdiction to regulate the taxi business necessarily implies the authority to limit the number of TPLs [taxi plate licences] issued": para. 202. This accords with the legislative history.' *United Taxi Drivers' Fellowship of Southern Alberta v Calgary (City)* [2004] SCJ No 19, [2004] 1 SCR 485, per Bastarache J

REGULATING

New Zealand [Section 17(2)(g) of the Law Practitioners Act 1988.] 'To "regulate" is defined in *The Oxford English Dictionary* as "to control, govern or direct by rule or regulation".' *Strachan v Marriott* [1995] 3 NZLR 272 at 291, CA, per Blanchard J

REHABILITATION

Australia [Section 26 of the Workers Compensation Act 1958 (Vic) defines medical services to include, amongst others, the provision to the worker of medical aids to 'rehabilitation'.] 'A restrictive meaning should not be given to "rehabilitation" having regard to the nature of the legislation. The evidence showed it is medically desirable that the respondent should enjoy mobility by means of an electric chair. The word "rehabilitation" comprehends not only restoration to former health (the narrow meaning) but also to restore partially or completely to a better condition: The Oxford English Dictionary (1989), vol 13. Rehabilitative medicine in our community is not confined to persons who can or will be restored to former health but is available to assist persons whose health would otherwise deteriorate.' *GC Wood & Son (Australia) Pty Ltd v Cullen* [1991] 2 VR 214 at 225, per O'Bryan J

Canada 'The primary question to be resolved by the Minister is whether Mr. Dee has rehabilitated himself following the charges levelled at him under the Marcos régime. The *Immigration Act* does not contain a definition of rehabilitation, and no case law has considered the exact meaning of rehabilitation in the context of this Act. According to *Black's Law Dictionary*, 7th ed, "rehabilitation" means

> The process of seeking to improve a criminal's character and outlook so that he or she can function in society without committing other crimes.

'Mr. Dee has the burden of showing to the Minister that he is of suitable character and that he can function in Canadian society without committing crimes.' *Dee v Canada (Minister of Citizenship and Immigration)* [2000] 3 FC 345 at 358, FCTD, per MacKay J

REHEARING

New Zealand ' "Rehearing" of course is a technical term and does not mean literally a rehearing of the evidence: see *Pratt v Wanganui Education Board* [1977] 1 NZLR 476, 490.' *Society for the Promotion of Community Standards Inc v Waverley International (1988) Ltd* [1993] 2 NZLR 709 at 715, per Tipping and Jaine JJ

REIMBURSED

[Insolvency Rules 1986, r 4.30(3).] 'Rule 4.30(3) provides that the amount of any expenses incurred by the provisional liquidator shall be reimbursed out of the assets. The word "reimbursed" in my view restricts the application of the rule to expenses paid by the provisional liquidator out of his own pocket or for which he is personally liable.' *Re Grey Marlin Ltd* [1999] 4 All ER 429 at 432, per David Donaldson QC

REIMBURSEMENT

Canada 'The word reimbursement in the ordinary sense, as defined in the Shorter Oxford English Dictionary, is as follows: "Reimburse … To repay or make up to a person (a sum expended.) 2. To repay, recompense (a person)… Reimbursement, the act of reimbursing, repayment". Black's Law Dictionary also defines the word reimburse as: "to pay back, to make restoration, to repay that expended; to indemnify or make whole". Examples of the word reimbursement in different legal relationships were cited. First, there is a compulsory payment. This is a situation where a person has been compelled by law to pay and pays money for which another is ultimately liable. The payer can make a claim for reimbursement from the latter individual. Second, there is the example of where a person makes repairs or improvements to property which he believes to be his own. He can claim a reimbursement against the owner of the property. Third, there is the situation where a person, such as a guarantor, discharges more than his proportionate part of a debt. He can take action for reimbursement against the co-guarantors. Finally, in the law of agency, a principal is liable to reimburse his agent for reasonable expenses incurred in an emergency, even if the agent exceeded his actual authority … In all of the examples of the word reimbursement, there exists a flow of benefits between the respective parties. The person who benefits is under a legal obligation to pay back the amount expended … It is my conclusion that reimbursement does not include damage awards.' *Westcoast Energy Inc v Canada* [1991] 3 FCR 302 at 319–320, FCTD, per Denault J; affd 92 DTC 6253, FCA

REINSURANCE *SEE* INSURANCE BUSINESS

REINSTATEMENT (TO POSITION) *SEE* POSITION

RELATED SERIES OF ACTS OR OMISSIONS

[Claimants' representatives selling personal pensions had frequently failed to comply with Life Assurance and Unit Trust Regulatory Organisation (LAUTRO) code of conduct. Some 22,000 claims for mis-selling were made by investors against the claimants. No single claim was for more than £35,000 but the total paid out by the claimants exceeded £125m. The claimants held an insurance policy with the defendant insurers which included an indemnity in respect of their legal liabilities to third parties for third party claims. The mis-selling claims fell within the terms of the policy but the policy covered only the part of each and every third party claim which exceeded the deductible amount of £1m. However, an aggregation clause provided that if a series of third party claims resulted from 'any single act or omission (or related series of acts or omissions)' then all such claims were to be considered to be a single third party claim for the purposes of the application of the deductible.] '[8] The question in this appeal is whether the TSB companies can recover any part of this money under a bankers composite insurance policy under which they and other members of the TSB group were then insured. This policy, as its name suggests, covered the group companies against a variety of risks …

…

'[10] The risk of liability for mis-selling under the FSA fell within the insuring clause of section 3 of the policy …

'[11] There is no dispute that each of the claims for mis-selling satisfied these requirements [of the policy]. But the policy included a "Schedule of Underlying Deductibles" which was said to form part of sections 1, 2 and 3. For section 3, there was to be a deductible of £1m "each and every claim". The same was repeated in item 7 of the schedule to section 3. The effect of the deductible in section 3 was stated in para 2 of the conditions:

> "… the Underwriters shall be liable only for that part of each and every third party claim during the Policy Period … which exceeds the Deductible stated in Item 7 of the Schedule … The Deductible shall apply to each and every third party claim and shall be subject to no aggregate limitation."

'[12] So far, so bad—from the TSB companies' point of view. No single claim came anywhere near exceeding the £1m deductible. But the TSB companies rely, and have so far succeeded, on the "aggregation clause" which follows the clauses I have already quoted:

"If a series of third party claims shall result from any single act or omission (or related series of acts or omissions) then, irrespective of the total number of claims, all such third party claims shall be considered to be a single third party claim for the purposes of the application of the Deductible."

...

'[14] Moore-Bick J said ([2001] 1 All ER (Comm) 13 at 24 (para 24)) that the purpose of an aggregation clause was:

"... to enable two or more separate losses covered by the policy to be treated as a single loss for deductible or other purposes when they are linked by a unifying factor of some kind."

'[15] That seems to me a fair description. The unifying factor is often a common origin in some act or event specified by the clause. But much will turn upon the precise nature of the act or event which, for the purposes of aggregation, the clause treats as a unifying factor. The more general the description of that act or event, the wider the scope of the clause. For example, in *Municipal Mutual Insurance Ltd v Sea Insurance Co Ltd* [1998] Lloyd's Rep IR 421 the unifying cause was expressed in very general terms: "... all occurrences of a series consequent on or attributable to one source or original cause ..."

'[16] This meant that as long as one could find any act, event or state of affairs which could properly be described as a cause of more than one loss, they formed part of a series for the purposes of the aggregation clause. Hobhouse LJ held that a series of losses caused by theft and vandalism from the port of Sunderland over a period of time were attributable to one original cause, namely the inadequacy of the port's system for protecting the goods of which it was bailee. On the other hand, in *AXA Reinsurance (UK) Ltd v Field* [1996] 3 All ER 517 at 526–527, [1996] 1 WLR 1026 at 1035 Lord Mustill contrasted the words "arising from one originating cause" which had been used in *Cox v Bankside Members Agency Ltd* [1995] 2 Lloyd's Rep 437 with the words "arising out of one event" which was the unifying factor designated by the clause then before the House. An "event", he said,

was "something which happens at a particular time, at a particular place, in a particular way". A "cause" on the other hand, was less constricted: it could be a continuing state of affairs or the absence of something happening. The word "originating" was also in his opinion chosen to "open up the widest possible search for a unifying factor". This meant that in the *AXA* case the incompetence of a Lloyds underwriter was not an "event" giving rise to the losses under a number of separate policies which he had written on behalf of various syndicates, whereas in *Cox*'s case it had been held to be the "originating cause" of such losses.

'[17] The choice of language by which the parties designate the unifying factor in an aggregation clause is thus of critical importance and can be expected to be the subject of careful negotiation; as Lord Mustill observed in the *AXA* case [1996] 3 All ER 517 at 526, [1996] 1 WLR 1026 at 1035, among players in the reinsurance market "keen interest [is] shown ... in the techniques of limits, layers and aggregations".

'[18] In the present case the unifying factor is, as in the examples so far given, a common cause, but that cause must be a "single act or omission" or, by an extension in the parenthesis, a "related series of acts and omissions". So the question turns upon the meaning of an "act or omission" or "related series of acts or omissions".

'[19] Moore-Bick J said ([2001] 1 All ER (Comm) 13 at 24 (para 24)) that an "act or omission" included any acts or omissions "of the kinds described in the insuring clause". In his view, this included the TSB companies' breach of their duty under the LAUTRO rules to establish training schemes for their employees and to make arrangements for monitoring their performance. For the purposes of the preliminary issue the TSB companies admitted, indeed, asserted, that they had been in breach of these duties. Moore-Bick J held that these breaches were an act or omission or series of acts and omissions within the meaning of the aggregation clause and that they had been the cause of all the 22,000 claims. So they could all be aggregated and treated as a single claim for the purposes of the deductible.

'[20] The Court of Appeal (Potter, Hale and Longmore LJJ) ([2001] EWCA Civ 1643, [2002] 1 All ER (Comm) 42) did not agree. They drew attention to cl 2(g) of the endorsement to section 3 of the policy, which defines the term "act or omission". For present purposes, the relevant part of the definition is that the words are deemed to mean a breach of the provisions of the LAUTRO rules "as described in the insuring clause". The relevant part of the insuring clause is para (iii)(g), which insures against a breach "in respect of which civil liability arises on the part of the assured". The Court of Appeal said that an "act or omission" must therefore be something which constitutes the investor's cause of action. It cannot mean an act or omission which is causally more remote.

'[21] It is therefore necessary to examine the nature of the cause of action asserted by the 22,000 claimants. It is a contravention of r 3.4(4)(a); to "ensure that" company representatives comply with the code of conduct. A duty to "ensure that" something does or does not happen is the standard form of words used to impose a contingent liability which will arise if the specified act or omission occurs. Even if the act or omission is that of a third party, such as a company representative, the liability is not vicarious. The company is not liable for the representative's act or omission: that is simply the contingency giving rise to the company's own liability. Nor should one be misled by the word "ensure" into thinking that the effect is to impose upon the company a duty to do something. No doubt the company will be well advised to take whatever steps it can to prevent the contingency from happening, but the question of whether it took such steps or not is legally irrelevant to its liability. It is liable simply upon proof that the contingency has occurred.

'[22] It follows that the absence of a training or monitoring system, even though an independent breach of the rules, was legally irrelevant to the civil liability of the TSB companies. Even without any such system, they would not have been liable unless their representatives actually contravened the code. Likewise, any such contravention would have given rise to liability whether they had a training and monitoring system or not. It cannot therefore have been an act or omission from which liability resulted.

'[23] Thus far I respectfully agree with the Court of Appeal. The language of the aggregation clause, read with the definition of "act or omission", shows that the insurers were not willing to accept as a unifying factor a common cause more remote than the act or omission which actually constituted the cause of action. An act or omission could qualify as a unifying factor in respect of more than one loss only if it gave rise to civil liability in respect of both losses. In the present case, the act or omission which gave rise to the civil liability in respect of each claim (failure to give best advice to that investor) was different from the acts or omissions giving rise to the other claims.

'[24] But the Court of Appeal then turned to the words in parenthesis "(or related series of acts or omissions)". And in construing these words, they produced exactly the result which they had rejected in their construction of the primary words "single act or omission". They said that acts or omissions could be "related" and form a "series" if they had a "single underlying cause" or common origin (Potter LJ at [50], Hale LJ at [55]) or if they were "the same omission" which had occurred on more than one occasion (Longmore LJ at [58]). The appeal was therefore dismissed.

'[25] This result seems to me paradoxical. It means that the parties started by choosing a very narrow unifying factor: not "any underlying cause", not "any event" or even "any act or omission", but only and specifically an act or omission which gives rise to the civil liability in question. Having chosen this as the opening and, one must assume, primary concept to act as unifying factor, they have then, by a parenthesis, produced a clause in which the unifying factor is as broad as one could possibly wish. It is sufficient that all the claims have a common underlying cause or (on the view of Longmore LJ) the breaches of duty are the same, which I take to mean sufficiently similar. In my opinion this construction is allowing the tail to wag the dog. I do not think that it is reasonable to understand the parties as having intended the parenthesis to stand the rest of the clause on its head.

'[26] When one speaks of events being "related" or forming a "series", the nature of the unifying factor or factors which makes them related or a series must be expressed or implied by the sentence in which the words are used. It may sometimes be necessary to imply a unifying factor from the general context. But the express language may make such an implication unnecessary or impermissible.

'[27] In the present case, the only unifying factor which the clause itself provides for describing the acts or omissions in the parenthesis as "related" and a "series" is that they "result" in a series of third party claims. In other words, the unifying element is a common causal relationship. But that common causal relationship is, so to speak, downstream of the acts and omissions within the parenthesis. They must have resulted in each of the claims. This obviously does not mean that it is enough that one act should have resulted in one claim and another act in another claim. That provides no common causal relationship. It can only mean that the acts or events form a related series if they together resulted in each of the claims. In this way, the parenthesis plays a proper subordinate role of covering the case in which liability under each of the aggregated claims cannot be attributed to a single act or omission but can be attributed to the same acts or omissions acting in combination.

'[28] The Court of Appeal was unwilling to accept that the clause itself provided the unifying factor to justify the use of the words "related" and "series". They appear to have thought that it was in practice unlikely that acts or omissions having a common causal relationship with a series of claims would occur. So the Court of Appeal sought the unifying factor outside the clause, by implying a reference to a common underlying cause upstream of the acts or omissions in the parenthesis, or some similarity between them. The clause itself says nothing about such unifying factors. Not only that; the narrow formulation of the primary concept, "single act or omission", suggests that it was anxious to avoid them. In my view, such an implication of an unstated unifying factor is impermissible. I would reserve my opinion on the example given by my noble and learned friend Lord Hobhouse of Woodborough of the salesman who presents the identical document to a number of customers in succession. I would not be inclined to accept that these acts are a series just because they are very similar, although I can see it might be said that the relevant single act or series of acts can be described as the distribution of the document and the method of distribution (sending it simultaneously to a number of people, showing it to them in succession or reading it to them at a meeting) is causally irrelevant.

'[29] It is in my opinion quite possible that one could have separate losses caused to a number of people by the combination of more than one act or omission, none of which would have been caused by the one without the other. For example, to adapt an example of my noble and learned friend Lord Hobhouse, they may have been caused by the distribution of a misleading document in identical terms by someone who was not himself negligent but ought to have been corrected by someone else who was. The two acts or omissions would be a series which together caused each of the losses. But in any case, I think that it is wrong to allow doubts about the possibly practical application of the parenthesis (particularly when the clause may have to be applied to the wide variety of circumstances covered by the insuring clause of section 3 of the policy) to produce a construction which undermines the balance of the clause. Each of the claims did not arise from a "single act or

omission". Nor did each of them arise from a "related series of acts or omissions". Each arose from a separate contravention of r 3.4(4)(a). I would therefore allow the appeal, dismiss the cross-appeal, and answer each of the preliminary issues, No.' *Lloyds TSB General Insurance Holdings Ltd v Lloyds Bank Group Insurance Co Ltd* [2003] UKHL 48 at [8], [10]–[12], [14]–[29], [2003] 4 All ER 43 per Lord Hoffmann

RELATIONS

[For 50 Halsbury's Laws (4th edn) para 531 see now 50 Halsbury's Laws (4th edn) (Reissue) para 585.]

RELATIONSHIP IN THE NATURE OF MARRIAGE

New Zealand [Social Security Act 1964, 63 (b).] 'In our view a relationship in the nature of marriage for the purpose of the Social Security Act is one in which the essential element is that there is an acceptance by one partner that (to take the stereotypical role) he will support the other partner and any child or children of the relationship if she has no income of her own or to the extent that it is or becomes inadequate. The commitment must go beyond mere sharing of living expenses, as platonic flatmates or siblings living together may do; it must amount to a willingness to support, if the need exists. There must be at least that degree of financial engagement or understanding between the couple. It will not, however, be negated by a refusal to support, or an arrangement that support will not be given, which is motivated by the knowledge that the dependent partner will then be able to claim a benefit. Such a stratagem cannot create a genuine absence of support.

'Where financial support is available nevertheless there will not be a relationship in the nature of marriage for this purpose unless that support is accompanied by sufficient features evidencing a continuing emotional commitment not arising from a blood relationship. Of these, the sharing of the same roof and of a sexual relationship (especially if it produces offspring) are likely to be the most significant indicators. But, since the amendment to s 63 in 1978, the sharing of a household is not essential. And, particularly in the case of older couples, the absence of sexual activity will not in itself deprive the relationship of the character of a marriage.

'The statutory context is of great importance in determining what is a "relationship in the nature of marriage". Other statutes use the same expression but for different legislative purposes. For example, absence of financial support will be of much less significance when a relationship is considered under the Domestic Violence Act 1995. It is also to be noted that Parliament appears in that Act to have recognised the limitations of the expression and has extended the protection beyond a "partner" (including someone in a relationship in the nature of marriage) to a family member, a person who ordinarily shares a household and someone in a close personal relationship with another.

'The expression "relationship in the nature of marriage" necessarily requires a comparison with a legal marriage but that is not a straightforward exercise. A simple balancing of equivalent features is not possible because for married persons financial obligations are not voluntary: the dependent spouse has some *right* to maintenance. Furthermore, it is not thought that because certain negative features (e g physical abuse, lack of emotional commitment) are found in some de jure marriages, the same factors in a relationship between a man and a woman who are not married are to be disregarded in determining whether that relationship is in the nature of marriage. The comparison must seek to identify whether there exist in the relationship of two unmarried persons those key positive features which are to be found in most legal marriages which have not broken down (cohabitation and a degree of companionship demonstrating an emotional commitment). Where these are found together with financial interdependence there will be such merging of lives as equates for the purposes of the legislation to a legal marriage.' *Ruka v Department of Social Welfare* [1997] 1 NZLR 154 at 161–162, per Richardson P and Blanchard J

'In the context of s 63(b) this [mutual commitment to the maintenance of their relationship] must necessarily include, not only a commitment to the relationship, but some form of financial support or interdependence. The financial interdependence may be direct, being actual support, or indirect, reflecting a mutual understanding about the financial arrangements relating to the relationship …

'The necessary mental and emotional commitment by the man and woman to their relationship was articulated by Tipping J in *Thompson v Department of Social Welfare* in these terms (supra) at p 374:

"It need not necessarily be a commitment intended to last for ever or indefinitely. Nor need it be a commitment to a long-term rela-

tionship. But it must, at least, be a commitment for the foreseeable future. Any lesser commitment would … be neither sufficient for nor consistent with a relationship in the nature of marriage."

'I agree. There is also considerable merit in the way the point was put by Judge Shaw in *Department of Social Welfare v Te Moananui* (District Court, Henderson, CRN 5090016020–21, 5090015857–60, 18 March 1996) at p 7. Addressing the question of a commitment the learned Judge said:

"More problematical is the mental aspect. I believe that to simply view the physical aspects of the relationship and draw an inference from those is to take a naive approach to the complex and subtle dynamic which makes up a commitment between two people. In the late twentieth century it is no longer appropriate that the definition of a marriage or a relationship in the nature of marriage includes violence as an accepted ingredient; certainly not to the point where that violence means that the parties are bound only by fear. At the heart of this case is the term "commitment". This term implies a degree of mutuality towards a relationship i.e. that both parties want the relationship … "

'It is this underlying commitment to the relationship which distinguishes marriage from the relationship of couples who may nevertheless share premises and living expenses. A relationship will not be a relationship in the nature of marriage for the purposes of s 63(b), therefore, unless it exhibits this mutual commitment and assumption of responsibility. In the context of the Social Security Act, this will necessarily include financial support or interdependence or, at least, a mutual understanding about the parties' financial arrangements of the kind I have suggested.

'The circumstances in which this financial responsibility may be discharged will vary greatly. In the stereotypical marriage it is the husband who assumes primary responsibility for providing financial support of his wife and family. In other marriages the responsibility for providing financial support may be shared. In yet other relationships the independent means of one spouse may be such that no financial contribution is required. But in all such cases a mutual understanding as to how the "conjugal" unit is to be supported will be implicit in the relationship. Other features, such as living under the same roof, or having a sexual relationship, especially if it produces children, may be of significance. But for the purpose of the Social

Security Act, concerned as it is in providing income support for those with no other means of support, an assumption of financial interdependence is essential before a relationship can be regarded as being in the nature of a marriage.

...

'Emphasising the necessity for the parties to have so merged their lives that they can be regarded as having assumed responsibility, including financial responsibility, for each other does not mean that the physical aspects put forward as indicia for determining whether a relationship is in the nature of marriage are irrelevant. On the contrary, indicia of the kind listed by Tipping J remain relevant, but they must be taken into account having regard to the effects of the battering relationship or violence on the woman. Thus, less weight, if any, would need to be given to the fact that the parties live together when the woman is staying under the same roof as the batterer out of fear and helplessness. Similarly, the fact that the parties may be said to have a sexual relationship loses its significance as an indicia of marriage if the woman's consent to sexual intercourse is coerced and she is regularly raped. Nor can it properly be concluded that the woman is offering the man emotional support and companionship when any such apparent support is induced by the man's violence and can more accurately be described as "traumatic bonding". The fact that the parties may socialise together and attend activities together and go on holidays as a couple would also be given less weight when the wife's involvement is compelled by fear of the man's irrational violence. Again, the appearance of shared responsibility for bringing up and supporting any children would need to be discounted if the mother's care is tendered without any sense of responsibility or obligation to the father. Nor may it be regarded as particularly material that the parties share household and other domestic tasks or run a common household, or the like, when the wife's participation is governed by the man's will and dictated by the unending rule of terror, violence and abuse.

'... Yet, the phrase "relationship in the nature of marriage" clearly cannot be equated with the worst marriage relationship which may be envisaged or with the common denominator of both good and bad marriages. In a real sense the reference to a relationship in the nature of marriage refers to an abstraction which, in essence, is a commitment to a sharing of the parties' lives in a manner which gives rise to an assumption of responsibility to and for each other. In entering into a legal marriage the parties are in effect deemed to have assumed that

responsibility, including an assumption of financial responsibility and interdependence. In a de facto relationship that assumption of responsibility must exist in fact before it can be said that the relationship is one in the nature of marriage.

'... I consider that having regard to the policy of the Social Security Act, the legislative history of s 63 and the objective of s 63(b) the phrase "relationship in the nature of marriage" can only apply to relationships where the mutual commitment described above, with the appropriate emphasis on the need for financial responsibility and interdependence exists as a matter of fact.' *Ruka v Department of Social Welfare* [1997] 1 NZLR 154 at 179–182, per Thomas J

RELATIVE

[The Child Care Act 1980 has been repealed. A definition is now contained in the Children Act 1989, s 105(1), as follows.] 'Relative', in relation to a child, means a grandparent, brother, sister, uncle or aunt (whether of the full blood or half blood or by affinity) or step-parent.

Canada 'Black's Law Dictionary, 5th edn gives an extended definition of the term relative, as follows: "A kinsman; a person connected with another by blood or affinity. When used generically, includes persons connected by ties of affinity as well as consanguinity and, when used with a restrictive meaning, refers to those only who are connected by blood". I believe that relative is commonly understood to refer to a relation of consanguinity, close or distant, and to a legally recognised affinity created for instance, by marriage or adoption.' *Leroux v Co-operators General Insurance Co* (1990) 65 DLR (4th) 702 at 707, Ont HCJ, per Arbour J

Canada 'As I have indicated, Mr Tessier purchased this optional underinsured coverage as part of his Pilot policy. The endorsement provided additional underinsured coverage to Mr Tessier and those covered by its terms beyond the standard $200,000 required by s 265 of the Act up to the policy limit of $1 million.

'The endorsement extends coverage to any dependent relative of the named insured. It does this by defining "insured person" to include the named insured, his or her spouse and any dependent relative of either. It then defines the term "dependent relative" as follows:

OPCF 44 — FAMILY PROTECTION COVERAGE

1.2 "dependent relative" means

(a) a person who is principally dependent for financial support upon the named insured or his or her spouse, and who is
   (i) under the age of 18 years;
   (ii) 18 years or over and is mentally or physically incapacitated;
   (iii) 18 years or over and in full time attendance at a school, college or university;
(b) a relative of the named insured or of his or her spouse, who is principally dependent on the named insured or his or her spouse for financial support;

'Since John Taggart was over 18 at the date of the accident, and was not mentally or physically handicapped nor going to school, he does not come within s 1.2(a) of this definition. Rather, this claim for indemnity requires that he bring himself within s 1.2(b) of the definition.

'Killeen J allowed Pilot's motion for summary judgment dismissing John Taggart's claim under the OPCF 44–Family Protection Coverage endorsement. He found that the term "relative" must be given its "ordinary work-a-day meaning" and agreed with the position of Pilot that this term provides coverage only to a person connected to the named insured by blood, marriage or adoption. Since John Taggart was not within these categories, Killeen J found that he could not fall within the "dependent relative" coverage of this endorsement and his claim for indemnity on this basis was therefore doomed to failure.

'In my view, on the facts of this case, it is too narrow an approach to exclude John Taggart because he is not connected to Mr Tessier by blood, marriage or adoption. The term "relative" is not defined either in the endorsement or in the Act. The question is whether in the context of its use in this endorsement it can take in someone with the relationship John Taggart has to Mr Tessier.

'Unlike Killeen J, I do not find dictionary definitions helpful in answering this question. The *Concise Oxford Dictionary* defines "relative" as "a person connected by blood or marriage". This would exclude an adopted family member. On the other hand, *Black's Law Dictionary* defines "relation" to include the connection between two persons "… who are associated whether by law, by their own agreement or by kinship in some social status or union for the purposes of domestic life".

'Equally, I do not find helpful the express definition of "relative" in the several Ontario statutes that have specifically defined the term. For example, in the *Credit Union and Caisses Populaires Act, 1994*, SO 1994, c 11, "relative" is defined to mean

"a relative by blood marriage or adoption; ("parent")". While this is the meaning taken by Killeen J, this definition also leaves the implication that this definition describes a subset of "relative" and that there can be relatives who are not connected by blood, marriage or adoption. More importantly, however, this statute was designed for a specific purpose quite unrelated to automobile insurance. The legislature chose not to specify the same definition for "relative" in the Act.

'The respondent also relies on *Leroux v Co-Operators General Insurance Co* (1990), 71 OR (2d) 641 (HC). That case did not involve the endorsement we are dealing with in this case. Moreover, while Arbour J. enunciated a definition of "relative" essentially similar to that used by Killeen J here, I regard her comment as *obiter* because although she did not extend coverage to the plaintiff on the basis that he was a relative of the named insured, she did extend coverage to the plaintiff on another basis.

'In my view, the task of determining whether John Taggart is a "relative" of Mr. Tessier in the circumstances of this case must begin with the endorsement itself. There is nothing in the definition of "dependent relative" that expressly limits this class of insured persons to those linked by marriage, blood or adoption to the named insured. Clearly s 1.2(a) of the definition quoted above does not do so. Indeed, it focuses on dependancy on the named insured rather than on any particular familial relationship with the named insured. It would be inconsistent with this approach to narrowly circumscribe the familial relationship contemplated by s 1.2(b) of the same provision by limiting it to a connection with the named insured by blood, marriage or adoption.

'Moreover, it is to be remembered that we are dealing with an endorsement that extends coverage. Such a provision is to be interpreted liberally or broadly in favour of the insured. See *Lloyd's London Nonmarine Underwriters v Chu,* [1977] 2 SCR 400.

'Finally, as its title makes clear, this endorsement was sold to Mr Tessier as "Family Protection Coverage". Mr Tessier clearly (and I think reasonably) regarded John Taggart as family.

'Given these considerations I think, a liberal approach to the term "relative" requires that the coverage extend to someone with whom the named insured has a *de facto* parent-child relationship. In this case, Mr Tessier regarded John Taggart as his son and vice versa. John's natural father has not been around for many years. Mr Tessier and John Taggart have been living together as family with

Mr Tessier supporting him, looking after him and seeing to his education as any father would.

'In these circumstances, it is my view that the family protection coverage provided by this endorsement extends to John Taggart as a "relative" of Mr Tessier, provided he can demonstrate at trial the dependancy also required by s 1.2(b) of the endorsement.' *Taggart* (*Litigation guardian of*) *v Simmons* (2001) 197 DLR (4th) 522 at 530–532, Ont CA, per Goudge JA

Dependent relative

[The Capital Gains Tax Act 1979 has been repealed. The definition is re-enacted in the Taxation of Chargeable Gains Act 1992, s 226(6).]

RELEVANT

Canada [All 'relevant' evidence was required to be considered on an application for firearms prohibition.] 'The meaning of "all relevant evidence" was the principal basis upon which the majority of the Court of Appeal rested its decision. In my opinion, this expression means all facts which are logically probative of the issue.' *R v Zeolkowski* [1989] 1 SCR 1378 at 1386, SCC, per Sopinka J

Relevant circumstances

Australia 'The argument was that, in the particular circumstances of the present case, which included the fact that some of the delay in bringing the appellant to trial occurred as a result of the conduct of the complainant, and was not the fault of the appellant, fairness and "equal justice" required that the appellant should not be punished more severely than he would have been had he been sentenced before the commencement of the Act [Sentencing Act 1995 (NT)]. Thus, on the individual facts of this particular case, the consideration that the appellant was being punished for an offence committed before the operation of the Act was a "relevant circumstance".' *Siganto v R* (1999) 159 ALR 94 at 98; (1998) 19 LegRepC 1; (1998) 73 ALJR 162; BC9806357, per Gleeson CJ, Gummow, Hayne and Callinan JJ

Relevant disposal

[By s 5 of the Landlord and Tenant Act 1987, where a landlord proposes to make a 'relevant disposal' affecting premises he must serve a notice on qualifying tenants affording them the right of first refusal.] 'It would be absurd if, in a transaction of this kind, there were two relevant disposals, one on the exchange of contracts and another on completion, and neither party contended for this construction. It is therefore necessary to choose between these two events as the "relevant disposal".

...

'With any other Act we would think it extraordinary that doubt should exist on a point as fundamental as this. We have to say that we do not find the answer indicated with an acceptable degree of clarity in the language of the section itself or elsewhere in the 1987 Act. It would, however, appear that in sub-s (2) of the section the draftsman has been primarily (although not consistently) concerned to exclude as relevant disposals certain forms of final transfer, which may perhaps indicate that it was the final transfer and not the preliminary agreement which he intended to be treated as the relevant disposal ... On balance, therefore, we prefer Mr Neuberger's argument on this point and would hold that there has not been a relevant disposal of the building [by exchange of contracts].' *Mainwaring v Trustees of Henry Smith's Charity* [1996] 2 All ER 220 at 232, 233, CA, per Sir Thomas Bingham MR

Relevant person

Australia 'The focal point of the argument was whether the appellants satisfied the description of "a relevant person". S[ection] 3(1) [of the Admiralty Act 1988 (Cth)] contains the following definition: "'relevant person', in relation to a maritime claim, means a person who would be liable on the claim in a proceeding commenced as an action in personam" ... The earliest English authority on the meaning of the critical words ... was *The "St Elefterio"* [1957] P 179, which was decided in 1957... His Lordship [Willmer J] said: "In my judgment the purpose of ... the words 'the person who would be liable on the claim in an action in personam' is to identify the person or persons whose ship or ships may be arrested in relation to this new right (if I may so express it) of arresting a sister ship. The words used, it will be observed, are 'the person who would be liable' not 'the person who is liable', and it seems to me, bearing in mind the purpose of the Act, that the natural construction of those quite simple words is that they mean the person who would be liable on the assumption that the action succeeds"... The Australian legislation having been enacted against the background of English legislation and authority set out above, the definition of "relevant person" should be understood as having the same meaning as the courts had given to the corresponding words in the English statute. When the Parliament has enacted legislation, affecting the subject of international shipping, and followed a statutory precedent from overseas which has by then received a settled construction, there is every reason to construe the statutory language in the same way in this country unless such construction is unreasonable or inapplicable to Australian circumstances. The Full Court of the Supreme Court of Queensland in *Ocean Industries Pty Ltd v The Owners of the Ship MV "Steven C"* (1991) 104 ALR 353, applied the reasoning in *The "St Elefterio"* to the Australian legislation. It was correct to do so.' *Owners of the Motor Vessel 'Iran Amanat' v KMP Coastal Oil Pte Ltd* (1999) 161 ALR 434 at 437–439; 73 ALJR 559; BC9901016, per Gleeson CJ, McHugh, Kirby, Gummow and Hayne JJ

RELIGION

Australia 'The meaning of "religion" in art 1A(2) of the Convention has been considered by the Full Court of this Court in *Wang v Minister for Immigration and Multicultural Affairs* (2001) 179 ALR 1. At [81], Merkel J said on this issue:

"Accordingly, it is appropriate to consider art 18 of the Universal Declaration and the objects of the convention in interpreting art 1A(2). When regard is had to those matters it is clear that there are two elements to the concept of religion for the purposes of art 1A(2): the first is as a manifestation or practice of personal faith or doctrine, and the second is the manifestation or practice of that faith or doctrine in a like-minded community. I would add that that interpretation is consistent wit the commonly understood meaning of religion as including its practice in or with a like-minded community."

'At [5], Wilcox J agreed with Merkel J with one reservation. He did not agree with Merkel J that reference should be made to art 18 of the Universal Declaration [of Human Rights] in determining the meaning of "religion" for the purposes of art 1A(2) of the Convention. He said:

"I regard my reservation as immaterial to the result because, as it seems to me, the concept of 'religion, in art 1A(2) of the Convention on Refugees, anyway includes the element of manifestation or practice of a religious faith in community with others. This element is inherent in the ordinary meaning of the word. For

example, the first two definitions of the word in the *Macquarie Dictionary* are:
1. the quest for the values of the ideal life, involving three phases, the ideal, *the practices for attaining the values of the ideal*, and the theology or world view relating the quest to the environing universe.
   a particular system in which the quest for the ideal life has been embodied [Emphasis added].

"The *Shorter Oxford English Dictionary* gives the following relevant definitions of religion:

Action or conduct indicating a belief in, reverence for, and desire to please, a divine ruling power; the *exercise or practice of rites or observances* implying this; A particular *system of faith and worship* [Emphasis added].

"Some religious rites may be privately practised by individual believers; but the major world religions, at least, also require or encourage their adherents to participate in communal rites or practices. Most Christian denominations, for example, require or encourage adherents to attend mass or holy communion. Muslims are expected to attend prayers, especially on Fridays.
"The form and content of communal rites and practices is often a matter of enormous importance to adherents of a particular faith, as is their system of governance. Many wars have been fought, and many people martyred, because of disagreements on such matters." ' *W244/01A v Minister for Immigration and Multicultural Affairs* BC200200132; [2002] FCA 52 at [35], per Nicholson J

Canada '[39] In order to define religious freedom, we must first ask ourselves what we mean by "religion". While it is perhaps not possible to define religion precisely, some outer definition is useful since only beliefs, convictions and practices rooted in religion, as opposed to those that are secular, socially based or conscientiously held, are protected by the guarantee of freedom of religion. Defined broadly, religion typically involves a particular and comprehensive system of faith and worship. Religion also tends to involve the belief in a divine, superhuman or controlling power. In essence, religion is about freely and deeply held personal convictions or beliefs connected to an individual's spiritual faith and integrally linked to one's self-definition and spiritual fulfilment, the practices of which allow individuals to foster a connection with the divine or with the subject or object of that spiritual faith.' *Syndicat Northcrest v Amselem* [2004] SCJ No 46, [2004] 2 SCR 551, 241 DLR (4th) 1, per Iacobucci J

RELIGIOUS PURPOSES

[For 5 Halsbury's Laws (4th edn) para 528 see now 5(2) Halsbury's Laws (4th edn) (2001 Reissue) para 31.]

RELOCATION

[The Town and Country Planning Act 1971 has been repealed. The definition is not re-enacted in the Town and Country Planning Act 1990.]

REMOVAL OR RETENTION

Australia [In the context of Hague Convention on the Civil Aspects of Child Abduction Arts 1, 3] 'As a general observation, we think it correct to say that in their ordinary primary meaning the words "remove" and "return" are co-relative terms, each being the converse of the other, and each importing a notion of physical movement of a material object, in the former case "from" and in the latter case "to" a place in the material world. This, we think, is borne out by reference to dictionary definitions ... [I]t is clearly the notion of continuing to hold possession of a child which is the meaning borne by "retention" in Art 3 and by "retained" in Art 1(a).' *In the Marriage of Hanbury-Brown* (1996) 20 Fam LR 334 at 358–359; 130 FLR 252 at 278; (1996) FLC 92–671, per cur

REMUNERATION *SEE ALSO* WAGES

REMUNERATIVE

Australia [A mortgage protection policy defined 'disablement' in part to mean total inability to engage in or attend to a 'remunerative' occupation.] '... it appears to us that notwithstanding the practical difficulties to which it may give rise, the parties must have contemplated that the word "remunerative" was being used in its popular sense as suggested by Brightman LJ [in *Perrot v Supplementary Benefits Commission* [1980] 1 WLR 1153], that is, as meaning "profitable". This construction is, in any event, supported by the *contra proferentem* rule—as to which, see generally *MacGillivary and Parkington on Insurance Law,*

8th ed, 1988 pp 454–5; Colinvaux, *The Law of Insurance*, 5th ed, 1984, pp 37–8 and Sutton, *Insurance Law in Australia*, 2nd ed, 1991, pp 534ff.' *National Mutual Life Association Ltd v Richards* (1995) 12 WAR 351 at 355–356, per cur

RENT

[For 27 Halsbury's Laws (4th edn) para 211 see now 27(1) Halsbury's Laws (4th edn) (Reissue) para 212.]

[For 39 Halsbury's Laws (4th edn) para 384 see now 39(2) Halsbury's Laws (4th edn) (Reissue) para 83.]

[The question arose in proceedings for relief against forfeiture of long leasehold interests in residential property granted for a premium and at a low rent, whether the word 'rent' in the County Courts Act 1984, s 138 and the Supreme Court Act 1981, s 38 included service charges which were deemed by the terms of the lease to be sums due by way of additional rent and recoverable as such but not reserved as rent by the reddendum.] 'Because the statutory provisions relating to non-payment of rent differ from those relating to other breaches of covenant, for example for payment of service charge, the first point to be decided ... is into which category the case falls ...

'The question is whether a provision that service charge shall be deemed to be sums due by way of additional rent and shall be recoverable by the landlord as such invests the charge with the character of rent, even though it is not reserved as such by the reddendum. Curiously enough, there appears to be no reported decision directly in point. Several authorities were cited, for example *Property Holding Co Ltd v Clark* [1948] 1 KB 630, but they went rather to the question whether service charge can be "rent" without any deeming provision such as that found here. What we have to do is decide, first, what is meant by "rent" in the statutory provisions and, secondly, whether the relevant provision in each lease had the effect of converting service charge into rent in that sense.

'Seeing that the current statutory provisions derive from others enacted in the 18th and 19th centuries, I regard it as axiomatic that they refer to rent in its correct sense being (i) a periodical sum, (ii) paid in return for the occupation of land, (iii) issuing out of the land, (iv) for non-payment of which a distress is leviable. All those attributes were enjoyed by the rents payable under the leases ... Each of those leases, by providing that service charge should be deemed to be sums payable by way of *additional* rent, had the effect of conferring the like attributes on the service charge, an effect confirmed by the further provision that it should be recoverable as rent. To hold thus is to do no more than give full effect to the agreement between the parties. That agreement is not defeated or modified by the omission to reserve the service charge as rent in the reddendum.' *Escalus Properties Ltd v Robinson* [1996] QB 231 at 243–244, [1995] 4 All ER 852 at 857–858, CA, per Nourse LJ

RENTCHARGE

[For 32 Halsbury's Laws (4th edn) paras 1203, 1204 see now 39(2) Halsbury's Laws (4th edn) (Reissue) paras 753–754.]

REPAIR

[In proceedings for infringement of the plaintiffs' patents for improvements to sifting screens, used to recycle drilling fluid in the offshore oil-drilling industry, the defendants (who acquired frames from the plaintiffs' customers, stripped them down to the bare metal, recoated them with adhesive, attached the mesh and then sold the screens to customers) contended that, in marketing the screens, the plaintiffs had impliedly licensed anyone who acquired a screen to prolong its life by repair, that such marketing constituted an exhaustion of any rights which a repair might infringe and that a person who repaired a screen did not 'make' it within the meaning of s 60(1)(a) of the Patents Act 1977.] 'I do not think that in a case such as the present this question is best approached by considering whether the defendant has "repaired" the patented product. For repair may involve no more than remedial action to make good the effects of wear and tear, involving perhaps no replacement of parts; or it may involve substantial reconstruction of the patented product, with extensive replacement of parts. Both activities might, without abuse of language, be described as repair, but the latter might infringe the patentee's rights when the former did not.' *United Wire Ltd v Screen Repair Services (Scotland) Ltd* [2000] 4 All ER 353 at 355, HL, per Lord Bingham of Cornhill

'… Thirdly, it is said that a person who repairs a screen does not "make" that screen within the meaning of the definition of an infringement in s 60(1)(a) of the Patents Act 1977.

… The concept of an implied licence to do various acts in relation to a patented product is well established in the authorities. Its proper function is to explain why, notwithstanding the apparent breadth of the patentee's rights, a person who has acquired the product with the consent of the patentee may use or dispose of it in any way he pleases. The traditional Royal Command in the grant of a patent forebode others not only to "make" but also to "use, exercise or vend" the invention. Similarly, s 60(1)(a) provides that a person infringes a patent for a product not only if he "makes" it but also if, without the consent of the proprietor, he "disposes of, offers to dispose of, uses or imports the product or keeps it whether for disposal or otherwise"…

'An alternative explanation, adopted in European patent systems, is that of exhaustion of rights. The patentee's rights in respect of the product are exhausted by the first sale (see *Merck & Co Inc v Primecrown Ltd, Beecham Group plc v Europharm of Worthing Ltd* Joined cases C-267/95 and C-268/95 [1996] ECR I-6285 at 6322). The difference in the two theories is that an implied licence may be excluded by express contrary agreement or made subject to conditions while the exhaustion doctrine leaves no patent rights to be enforced.

'Where however it is alleged that the defendant has infringed by making the patented product, the concepts of an implied licence or exhaustion of rights can have no part to play. The sale of a patented article cannot confer an implied licence to make another or exhaust the right of the patentee to prevent others from being made. A repair of the patented product is by definition an act which does not amount to making it: as Lord Halsbury said of the old law in *Sirdar Rubber Co Ltd v Wallington, Weston & Co* (1907) 24 RPC 539 at 543, "you may prolong the life of a licensed article but you must not make a new one under the cover of repair".

'Repair is one of the concepts (like modifying or adapting) which shares a boundary with "making" but does not trespass upon its territory. I therefore agree with the Court of Appeal that in an action for infringement by making, the notion of an implied licence to repair is superfluous and possibly even confusing. It distracts attention from the question raised by s 60(1)(a), which is whether the defendant has made the patented product. As a matter of ordinary language, the notions of making and repair may well overlap. But for the purposes of the statute, they are mutually exclusive. The owner's right to repair is not an independent right conferred upon him by licence, express or implied. It is a residual right, forming part of the right to do whatever does not amount to making the product.'

United Wire Ltd v Screen Repair Services (Scotland) Ltd [2000] 4 All ER 353 at 357–358, HL, per Lord Hoffmann

REPEAL

Australia 'The common law approach seems to have been based upon a technical interpretation of the word "repeal", fairly inflexibly applied. The central pillar of this doctrine may be found in the statement of Lord Tindal CJ in *Kay v Goodwin* (1830) 6 Bing 576 at 582–3, 130 ER 1402 at 1405 that: "I take the effect of repealing a statute to be, to obliterate it as completely passed from the records of the Parliament as if it had never passed; and, it must be considered as a law that never existed, except for the purpose of those actions which were commenced, prosecuted, and concluded whilst it was an existing law." ... However, this is not in my opinion an approach that should be adopted today by analogy in relation to the effect of statutes upon the common law ... [A] technical rule as to the meaning of "repeal" should never prevail over the intention of Parliament in using that word.' *Question of Law Reserved (No 2 of 1996)* (1996) 67 SASR 63 at 68–9, per Doyle CJ

REPLEVIN

[For 13 Halsbury's Laws (4th edn) para 373 see now 13 Halsbury's Laws (4th edn) (Reissue) para 781.]

REPREHENSIBLE

Canada '... the word "reprehensible" is a word of wide meaning. It encompasses scandalous or outrageous conduct but it also encompasses milder forms of misconduct deserving of reproof or rebuke. Accordingly, the standard represented by the word "reprehensible", taken in that sense, must represent a general and all encompassing expression of the applicable standard for the award of special costs.' *Garcia v Crestbrook Forest Industries Ltd* (1994) 119 DLR (4th) 740 at 747, BCCA, per Lambert JA

REPRESENT *SEE* DEPICT

REPRESENTATION

[For 25 Halsbury's Laws (4th edn) para 237 see now 25 Halsbury's Laws (4th edn) (2003 Reissue) para 408.]

[For 31 Halsbury's Laws (4th edn) paras 1005, 1017–1020 see now 31 Halsbury's Laws (4th edn) (2003 Reissue) paras 703, 717–718.]

Canada [Under freedom of information legislation, no person may have access as of right to representations made to the Commissioner in the course of an investigation.] 'In my view, the term representations must, by necessary implication, include the documents leading to the submissions that are ultimately made to the Information Commissioner. Any other interpretation would defeat the purpose of section 35.

'I am of the opinion that the term representations in section 35 is wide enough to include all drafts and supporting documentation generated within the government institution for the purpose of communicating with the Information Commissioner. By the same reasoning, communications prepared by the Information Commissioner for a government institution would also be covered by the restriction to access in section 35 if they deal with the submissions made by the government institution.' *Rubin v Canada (Clerk of the Privy Council)* [1993] 2 FCR 391 at 401–402, per Rothstein J (Fed TD)

REPRESENTATIVES

In a will

[For 50 Halsbury's Laws (4th edn) para 541 see now 50 Halsbury's Laws (4th edn) (Reissue) para 597.]

REPRODUCTION

[For 9 Halsbury's Laws (4th edn) para 912 see now 9(2) Halsbury's Laws (4th edn) (Reissue) para 315.]

Canada '[42] The historical scope of the notion of "reproduction" under the Copyright Act should be kept in mind. As one would expect from the very word "copyright", "reproduction" is usually defined as the act of producing additional or new copies of the work in any material form. Multiplication of the copies would be a necessary consequence of this physical concept of "reproduction". In *Massie & Renwick, Ltd. v. Underwriters' Survey Bureau, Ltd.*, [1940] S.C.R. 218, at p. 227, Duff C.J. viewed copyright law as essentially about protecting the right to multiply copies of a work:

> I think there can be no doubt that material of that character was subject matter for copyright and, not being published, the exclusive

right of multiplying copies of it, or of publishing it, was a right which the common law, prior to the statute of 1921, gave primarily to the authors of it. [Emphasis added.]

See also *Tom Hopkins International, Inc. v. Wall & Redekop Realty Ltd.* (1984), 1 C.P.R. (3d) 348 (B.C.S.C.). In *Underwriters' Survey Bureau Ltd. v. Massie & Renwick Ltd.*, [1937] Ex. C.R. 15, Maclean J., for the Exchequer Court, defined copyright as (at p. 20):

> ... the right to multiply copies of a published work, or the right to make the work public and still retain the beneficial interest therein. [Emphasis added.]

'[43] More pertinent still is the Ontario case of *Fetherling v. Boughner* (1978), 40 C.P.R. (2d) 253 (Ont. H.C.), relied on by the motions judge in this case, which dealt with a similar fact situation. Southey J. concluded in his oral judgment, at p. 256:

> The second question is whether the transfer process constitutes copying. My conclusion, after listening to the argument of counsel, but without hearing any evidence, is that such process does not constitute copying, because it involves the transfer physically of the picture on the copy of The Canadian from which the defendant's product is made. After such transfer there was no picture on the page of The Canadian. I am satisfied that the defendant would have been entitled to purchase a copy of The Canadian; cut out one of the strip photographs; paste it on a piece of paper; put a border around it; frame it; and sell it, without infringing copyright, just as she would have been entitled to sell the issue of The Canadian itself and just as any person, who purchases the work of an artist, is entitled to resell that work, or a piece of it. In my view that is essentially what was done by the defendant in this case.

See also to the same effect: *No Fear, Inc. v. Almo-Dante Mfg. (Canada) Ltd.* (1997), 76 C.P.R. (3d) 414 (F.C.T.D.).

'[44] A similar understanding of "reproduction" is reflected in decisions under the English Act on which s. 3(1) of our Act is based, i.e., the physical making of something which did not exist before (*Laddie et al., supra*, at p. 614). As stated by the Earl of Halsbury in *Walter v. Lane*, [1900] A.C. 539 (H.L.), at p. 545:

The law which I think restrains it is to be found in the Copyright Act, and that Act confers what it calls copyright – which means the right to multiply copies – which it confers on the author of books first published in this country. [Emphasis added.]'

Théberge v Galerie d'Art du Petit Champlain inc [2002] 2 SCR 336 at 359–360, per Binnie J

REPUGNANT TO JUSTICE

New Zealand 'A test of repugnancy to justice uses words which are not usually found in legislation. They are strong, vivid and forceful. It is not just a matter of inequity or a state of being unjust. It has to be repugnant to justice. That, I think, is not merely the standard dictionary meaning of repugnancy, connoting contradiction and incompatibility, but gives a more forcible meaning to provide for a situation which is striking and immediate. It has to have the same effect as in the law of contract, a certain situation impels the right thinking person to the kind of answer which recognises an implied term in a contract because it is so obvious that it goes without saying ... Thus in the particular circumstances a rational and fully-informed bystander, not actuated by vindictiveness or by undue compassion, on being informed of the circumstances and being asked whether rehabilitation and compensation should be granted, would immediately reply "of course not".' *Accident Compensation Corpn v Curtis, Accident Compensation Corpn v McKee* [1993] 3 NZLR 558 at 566, per Greig J

REQUEST UNDER

Australia [Sections 41 and 43(1) of the Extradition Act 1988 (Cth) refer to requests under s 40 of the Act for the surrender of a person.] 'In my opinion the expression "a request under s 40" in these two provisions means "a request made in accordance with s 40" (cf The Oxford English Dictionary, "under", 20d), that is, "a request made by or with the authority of the Attorney-General as required by s 40", not "a request made in exercise of a power given by s 40".' *Oates v A-G (Cth)* BC200100287; [2001] FCA 84 at [29], per Lindgren J

RES GESTAE

Australia [Section 36BC(1) of the Evidence Act 1906 (WA) provides that in 'proceedings for a sexual offence, evidence relating to the sexual experiences of the complainant, being sexual experiences of any kind, at any time and with any person, not being part of the res gestae of the proceedings, shall not be adduced or elicited by or on behalf of a defendant unless leave of the court has first been obtained …'.] 'In his article "Res Gesta Reagitata", Professor Stone described the law as to res gestae as "the lurking place of a motley crowd of conceptions in mutual conflict and reciprocating chaos". Professor Stone pointed out that:

> "evidence admitted under the res gesta decisions falls, *on a proper analysis*, into five distinct categories. First, the facts in issue; second, facts relevant to the facts in issue; third, declarations not in themselves in issue or relevant, but constituting a verbal part of either a fact in issue or a relevant fact; fourth, facts of all kinds, which, though not facts in issue or relevant, are so inextricably bound up with either, that effective proof of the one cannot be made without proof of the other; and fifth, statements admitted as hearsay under what constitute in effect three exceptions to the hearsay rule." (emphasis added)

'[109] Perhaps Professor Stone was right when he complained that the requirement that a fact be part of the res gestae is usually nothing more than a requirement that it be relevant. However, in assigning a meaning to the words "res gestae" in s 36BC, we do not think that the term can cover all of the five categories to which Professor Stone referred. Section 36BC prima facie forbids the chain of "reasoning" that asserts that, because the complainant has a certain sexual reputation or disposition in sexual matters or has had certain sexual experiences, he or she is the "kind of person" who is likely to have consented to the sexual activity which is the subject of the charge. Yet such evidence would be relevant to the charge. If s 36B and s 36BA are to have meaning, res gestae in s36BC must embrace more than relevance and not be so wide a concept that it would admit any evidence of reputation or disposition that fell within Professor Stone's five categories.

'[110] One recognised meaning of res gestae is that it refers to "[t]hings so close in time or space to the matter being proved as to be inseparable from it." [*Butterworths Australian Legal Dictionary* (1997) at 1015] Given the object of s 36B and s 36BA, this seems the most likely meaning of res gestae in s 36BC. The evidence relating to the sexual experiences of the complainant must be part

of the thing that happened if it is to qualify for automatic admission under s 36BC. That is to say, the evidence relating to sexual experiences must be part of the "transaction" which gives rise to the charge. If it is not, it can only be admitted with the leave of the Court.

'[111] In *Dawson v The Queen*, Dixon CJ said:

> "It is the thesis of English law that the ingredients of a crime are to be proved by direct or circumstantial evidence of the events, that is to say, the parts and details of the transaction amounting to the crime, and are not inferred from the character and tendencies of the accused."

'[112] This statement provides an insight as to what constitutes the "res gestae" for the purpose of s 36BC. The existence of consent, for example, is not to be "inferred from the character and tendencies of the [complainant]", but is to "be proved by direct or circumstantial evidence of the events, that is to say, the parts and details of the transaction amounting to the crime". Where an act or statement is intimately connected with the particular sexual conduct which is the subject of the charge, or in other words with "the parts and details of the transaction amounting to the crime", it is part of the res gestae and so is admissible under s 36BC without leave. That applies to acts or matters tending to prove the disposition of the complainant, as well as to other acts or matters relating to the sexual experiences of the complainant.' (footnotes omitted) *Bull v R* (2000) 171 ALR 613; BC200002276; [2000] HCA 24 at [108]–[112], per McHugh, Gummow and Hayne JJ

RES IPSA LOQUITUR

[For 34 Halsbury's Laws (4th edn) para 57 see now 33 Halsbury's Laws (4th edn) (Reissue) para 664.]

Australia 'res ipsa loquitur is merely a mode of inferential reasoning and is *not* a rule of law … The fact that a plaintiff falls outside the "proper scope" of the rule does not mean that he or she may not avail himself or herself of inferential reasoning. There is therefore no need to subsume the maxim into the general body of tort law: it is already fully consonant with it.' *Schellenberg v Tunnel Holdings Pty Ltd* BC200001743; [2000] HCA 18 at [47], per Gleeson CJ and McHugh J

RES JUDICATA *SEE ALSO* ESTOPPEL

'Res judicata, whether cause of action estoppel or issue estoppel, is based on the fundamental principle that it is unjust for a man to be vexed twice with litigation on the same subject matter coupled with the public interest in seeing an end to litigation. So far as cause of action estoppel is concerned, the rule is absolute: you cannot sue twice for the same relief based on the same cause of action even if new facts or law have subsequently come to light. But it is clear that the rule as to issue estoppel is different ... there are circumstances in issue estoppel where the injustice of not allowing the matter to be relitigated outweighs the hardship to the successful party in the first action in having to relitigate the point.' *Arnold v National Westminster Bank plc* [1988] 3 All ER 977 at 982, per Browne-Wilkinson VC

'Res judicata is a special form of estoppel. It gives effect to the policy of the law that the parties to a judicial decision should not afterwards be allowed to relitigate the same question, even though the decision may be wrong. If it is wrong, it must be challenged by way of appeal or not at all. As between themselves, the parties are bound by the decision, and may neither relitigate the same cause of action nor reopen any issue which was an essential part of the decision. These two types of res judicata are nowadays distinguished by calling them "cause of action estoppel" and "issue estoppel" respectively.' *Crown Estate Commissioners v Dorset County Council* [1990] 1 All ER 19 at 23, per Millett J

Canada '[19] Before the adjudicator the applicant raised the defences of *res judicata* and issue estoppel. *Res judicata* is defined in *Black's Law Dictionary* (St. Paul, MN: West Group, 1999) as:

[*res judicata*... Latin "a thing adjudicated"] 1. An issue that has been definitively settled by judicial decision 2. An affirmative defense barring the same parties from litigating a second lawsuit on the same claim, or any other claim arising from the same transaction or series of transactions and that could have been – but was not – raised in the first suit. [...]

'[20] While in substance the applicant has raised two different defences, at common law, issue estoppel is merely one of two forms of *res judicata*. The other form of *res judicata* is properly referred to as cause of action estoppel, see *Danyluk v. Ainsworth Technologies Inc.*, [2001] 2 S.C.R. 460. Although the concepts of *res judicata,* issue estoppel and cause of action estoppel are often intertwined, they have distinct meanings. The principles of these two forms of estoppel can be seen in the two-part definition of *res judicata* cited above and

were recently summarized by the Federal Court of Appeal in *Apotex Inc. v. Merck and Co.*, 2002 FCA 210 at paras. 24–25:

The relevant principles behind the doctrine of *res judicata* were established in two leading Supreme Court of Canada decisions: *Angle v. M.N.R.*, [1975] 2 S.C.R. 248 and *Doering v. Town of Grandview*, [1976] 2 S.C.R. 621. In *Angle, supra*, at 254 Dickson J. noted that *res judicata* essentially encompasses two forms of estoppel, being "cause of action estoppel" and "issue estoppel," both based on similar policies. First, there should be an end to litigation, and second, an individual should not be sued twice for the same cause of action.

These two estoppels, while identical in policy, have separate applications. Cause of action estoppel precludes a person from bringing an action against another where the cause of action was the subject of a final decision of a court of competent jurisdiction. Issue estoppel is wider, and applies to separate causes of action. It is said to arise when the same question has been decided, the judicial decision which is said to create the estoppel is final, and the parties to the judicial decision or their privies are the same persons as the parties to the proceedings in which the estoppel is raised (see *Carl Zeiss Stiftung v. Rayner & Keeler Ltd. (No. 2)*, [1967] 1 A.C. 853., at p. 93, cited by Dickson J. in *Angle supra.*, at 254). [emphasis added]'

Al Yamani v Canada (Minister of Citizenship and Immigration) [2003] 3 FC 345 at 362–363 (FCC), per Kelen J

[For 16 Halsbury's Laws (4th edn) paras 1526–1527 see now 16(2) Halsbury's Laws (4th edn) (Reissue) para 987.]

RESCUE

[For 11 Halsbury's Laws (4th edn) para 968 see now 11(1) Halsbury's Laws (4th edn) (Reissue) para 326.]

[For 13 Halsbury's Laws (4th edn) para 362 see now 13 Halsbury's Laws (4th edn) (Reissue) para 770.]

RESELL

New Zealand [Chattels Transfer Act 1924, Fourth Schedule, cl 7.] 'In this case, the parties differ on the meaning of the relevant provision of cl 7 which states:

"... and take possession thereof, and sell and dispose of the same or any part thereof by private sale or public auction, separately or together in such lots and generally in such manner in every respect as the grantee deems expedient, with power to allow time for payment of purchase money, or to buy in the said chattels or any part thereof at such auction, and to rescind or vary the terms of any contract or sale, *and to resell without being answerable for any loss or expense occasioned thereby* ..." (Emphasis added)

'Both counsel submit that the words "without being answerable for any loss or expense occasioned thereby" relate to the words "to resell" ... When interpreted in context there is clearly a right of sale after a grantee takes possession and then there is a right of resale if the grantee is required to rescind the sale. The relevant point is whether the phrase "without being answerable for any loss or expense occasioned thereby" qualifies the words "to resell" or the earlier provisions including the words "and sell and dispose of the same". Similar wording is used in cl 8 of the Fourth Schedule of the Property Law Act 1952 and there appear to be no cases interpreting that provision. In my view the phrase applies to the words "to resell". If it was to have general application, it would have appeared later in the clause and would also have applied "all such assurances and do all such things for giving effect to any such sale" ...' *Leech v National Bank of New Zealand* [1996] 3 NZLR 707 at 713–714, per Paterson J

RESERVATION

[For 12 Halsbury's Laws (4th edn) para 1531 see now 12(1) Halsbury's Laws (4th edn) (Reissue) para 238.]

[For 27 Halsbury's Laws (4th edn) para 138 see now 27(1) Halsbury's Laws (4th edn) (Reissue) para 219.]

Australia [A form prescribed by regulations contained a "reservation" in favour of the Crown of a right of access to search for minerals and also for any person authorised by the Governor-in-Council to go upon the land for any purpose whatsoever.] 'The term "reservation" in strict usage identifies something newly created out of the land or tenement demised and is inappropriate to identify an exception or keeping back from that which is the subject of the grant [*Norton on Deeds*, 2nd ed (1928), pp 268–72]. However, in accordance with the Australian usage referred to by Windeyer J in

Wade v New South Wales Rutile Mining Co Pty Ltd [(1969) 121 CLR 177 at 194], "reservation" was apt in [the form] to identify that which was withheld or kept back by the grants made by the Governor-in-Council under the 1910 Act.' *Wik Peoples v Queensland* (1996) 141 ALR 129 at 245; 71 ALJR 173, per Gummow J

RESERVE

New Zealand [Reserves Act 1977, s 2(1). In rejecting the submission that the Stony Batter historic reserve is excluded from the definition of 'reserve' in the Reserves Act 1977 by virtue of s 2(1)(j), His Honour said:] 'A comprehensive definition of "reserve" for the purposes of the Reserves Act 1977 is stipulated in s 2(1). The word:

'... means any land set apart for any public purpose, and includes—

...

(i) Any land taken or otherwise acquired or set apart by the Crown under the Public Works Act 1981 or any corresponding former Act, whether before or after the commencement of this Act, for the purposes of a reserve, a recreation ground, a pleasure ground, an agricultural showground, or a tourist and health resort.

But does not include—

(j) Any land taken or otherwise acquired or set apart under the Public Works Act 1928 or any corresponding former Act, whether before or after the commencement of this Act, for any purpose not specified in paragraph (i) of this definition:

(k) Any land to which this section 167(4) of the Land Act applies.

...

'Section 2(2) of the Reserves Act 1977 provides as follows:

(2) Any land, whether Crown land or not, shall be deemed to be set apart for a public purpose within the meaning of this Act if it is granted, reserved, or set apart or purchased or given or dedicated in any lawful manner, whether by or pursuant to any Act, or by the will, or by the deed, or by other like instrument, for the use, benefit, enjoyment, safety, or defence of the people of New Zealand or the inhabitants of any district or locality therein.

...

'Reason and the provisions of s 5(j) of the Acts Interpretation Act 1924 compel me to find that the participial connotation in s 2(1) of the Reserves Act is current status, not superseded historical dealings.' *Auckland City Council v Man O'War Station Ltd* [1996] 3 NZLR 460 at 464, per Anderson J

RESIDE

[For 15 Halsbury's Laws (4th edn) para 415 see now 15 Halsbury's Laws (4th edn) (Reissue) para 318 et seq.

RESIDENT

Australia 'In my opinion, the term "resident" in the Adoption of Children Act 1965 (ACT) is used in the sense that the person referred to is "ordinarily", "habitually" or "usually" so resident. Residence for a short period, merely to satisfy local jurisdictional requirements, based merely on presence for a short period of time, does not qualify.

'If the term "resident" in the Adoption Act was intended to encompass a temporary stay to qualify for adoption, a view that would not be acceptable, I believe, if the position was reversed, one would expect a specific qualifying period to be nominated.' *Re Application for Adoption of M* (1992) 112 ACTR 39 at 46, per Higgins J

Australia [Section 10A of the Local Government Amendment (Meetings) Act 1998 (NSW) indicates that a Council meeting, or part thereof, may be closed to the public for a number of reasons, including the discussion of the personal hardship of any resident or ratepayer.] 'The interpretive task must, I think, begin with the ordinary meaning of the word "resident". That meaning is well known. According to the *Shorter Oxford English Dictionary*, it means inter alia: "One who resides permanently in a place".

'To similar effect, is the meaning given by the *Macquarie Dictionary*: "One who resides in a place", the word "reside" having the following meanings:

"to dwell permanently or for a considerable time; having one's abode for a time."

'The expression "ordinary resident" is often encountered in legislation and has been the subject of many judicial decisions. For example in *R v Barnet London Borough Council: Ex parte Shah* [1983] 2 AC 309 (a case involving the expression "ordinarily resident in the United Kingdom" in the context of the Education Acts) Lord Scarman said at 343:

"Unless, therefore, it can be shown that the statutory framework or the legal context in which the words are used requires a different meaning, I unhesitatingly subscribe to the view that *ordinarily resident* refers to a man's abode in a particular place or country which he has adopted voluntarily and for settled purposes as part of the regular order of his life *for the time being* (my emphasis), whether of short or of long duration."

'In its context in s 10A(2)(b), I think it clear that the word "resident" is to be given its ordinary meaning such as is provided in the standard English dictionaries and that in that context, prima facie it *is residency at the time that the statutory power is exercised* that is meant.

'The Council's argument urging a purposive construction justifying a broad meaning of the word "resident" encounters the obvious difficulty of precisely delimiting the extent to which prior and past residency by a person qualifies that person as a "resident" within the meaning of s 10A(2)(b). Granted that the clear purpose of the statutory provision is to preserve the confidentiality of the personal hardship of a resident would, prior residency within living memory qualify the person as a "resident"? Such an open-ended result, I think, demonstrates the intrinsic difficulty and ultimate illegitimacy of departing from the ordinary meaning of the word "resident" and of ignoring the contextual considerations which indicate that what is required is current residency at the time the statutory power is purported to be exercised. The decision of the Court of Appeal in *Perez v Leslie* (1973) 1 NSWLR 195 can be cited as an example where the Court interpreted the defined term "resident" in the context of the Landlord and Tenant (Amendment) Act 1948 to mean resident at the time that a current value rental determination is made by the Fair Rents Board rather than a resident living at the demised premises in the past (e g during the immediately past financial year).' *Wykanak v Rockdale City Council* BC200102297; [2001] NSWLEC 65 at [35]–[40], per Bignold J

RESIDENTIAL PURPOSE

Canada 'I turn first to the plain and ordinary meaning of the phrase "residential purpose". Those words, in my view, are clearly capable of embracing units for parking and storage in condominiums such as those involved in this case. The Oxford English Dictionary definition of "residential" includes the following: "connected with, pertaining or relating to, a residence or residences (in a general or specific sense)". Spaces to park a car and store items in close proximity to the place of other domestic functions and activities are common elements of a residence. Residences, including apartment-type residences in multiple-dwelling buildings, almost always provide space for parking and storage. The exigencies of modern life require that parking and storage facilities be made available to be used in connection with one's dwelling. Parking and storage units may, accordingly, be regarded as incidental or ancillary aspects or elements of a residence and, accordingly, in my view, may be said to fall within the ordinary meaning of the phrase "used for residential purposes" in the present context.' *Windisman v Toronto College Park Ltd* (1996) 132 DLR (4th) 512 at 519, Ont Gen Div, per Sharpe J

RESOLVE

New Zealand '[45] We accept that the word "resolve" in [the Employment Relations Act 2000] s 144(2)(d) ([mediation] services that assist persons to resolve, promptly and effectively, their employment relationship problems:") means to "settle or find a solution to": *Concise Oxford Dictionary*, 10th edition. It does not simply mean to bring matters to an end, but requires a conclusion in the sense of a mutually agreed settlement or solution.' *Jesudhass v Just Hotel Ltd* (2006) 3 NZELR 106 at [45], per G L Colgan CJ

RESTITUTIO IN INTEGRUM

[For 12 Halsbury's Laws (4th edn) para 1129 see now 12(1) Halsbury's Laws (4th edn) (Reissue) para 885.]

'At common law in a case of bailment, the general principle is restitutio in integrum, which means that the party damnified is entitled to such a sum of money as will put him in as good a position as if the goods had not been lost or damaged. This is subject, however, to the qualification that the damages must not be too remote, ie they must be such damages as flow directly and in the usual course of things from the loss or damage.' *Building and Civil Engineering Holidays Scheme Management Ltd v Post Office* [1966] 1 QB 247 at 261, [1965] 1 All ER 163 at 168, CA, per Lord Denning MR

RESTRAINT OF PRINCES

[For 25 Halsbury's Laws (4th edn) para 161 see now 25 Halsbury's Laws (4th edn) (2003 Reissue) para 339.]

RESTRAINT OF TRADE

[For 47 Halsbury's Laws (4th edn) paras 10, 13, 14 see now 47 Halsbury's Laws (4th edn) (Reissue) paras 13, 15–17.]

RETAIL

Sale of milk

[The Food Act 1984 is largely repealed. The definition is not re-enacted in the Food Safety Act 1990.]

RETAIL SALE

Australia [Schedule 3 to the Customs Tariff Act 1987 (Cth) contains a heading and note specifying that herbicides put up in forms or packings for 'retail sale' or as preparations are subject to customs duty.] 'The weight of authority seems to us to support a conclusion that the words "retail sale" have generally acquired a specialised meaning of a sale to an ultimate customer. We do not think that the usage of the term limits such consumers to ordinary members of the public. The fact that in the present case almost all of the goods imported by the respondent were directly sold to professional horticulturalists and not ordinary gardeners as ultimate customers is, in our opinion, irrelevant. Professionals can still be described as ultimate customers.' *Collector of Customs v Chemark Services Pty Ltd* (1993) 42 FCR 585 at 591; 114 ALR 531 at 537, per cur

RETAINER

[For 44 Halsbury's Laws (4th edn) para 83 see now 44(1) Halsbury's Laws (4th edn) (Reissue) para 99.]

RETIREMENT

Australia [Stamp Duties Act 1923 (SA) s 71(5)(d).] 'It is necessary to determine the meaning of the word "retirement" in s 71(5)(d). In this context, retirement, I think, is not intended to be limited to those occasions where a trustee voluntarily retires from the office of trustee. In ordinary usage, "retirement" has a number of shades of meaning. It denotes, among other things, withdrawal from an office or occupation, or being withdrawn from an office or occupation: see Oxford English Dictionary. It therefore includes removal from an office or occupation: see Macquarie Dictionary. It was held in *Re Stoneham Settlement Trusts* [1953] Ch 59 that a trustee who has been removed against will is not a "retiring trustee" within the meaning of s 36(8) of the Trustee Act 1925 (UK). However, the decision is plainly distinguishable in that the purpose and effect of s 36(8) of the United Kingdom Act is quite different from that of s 71(5)(d). Plainly, the meaning of "retirement" may vary according to the purpose and intent of each statutory provision. In my view, "retirement" in s 71(5)(d) includes both voluntary and involuntary retirement, that is to say, it includes retirement and removal from the office of trustee. That meaning accords with the spirit and intent of s 71(5)(d). The act of retirement and removal has the same consequence, namely, that the trustee no longer acts as trustee. If the exemption did not apply in the case of removal as well as in the case of retirement of a trustee, the intended operation of s 71(5)(d) would be significantly curtailed.' *Dadeeton Pty Ltd v Commissioner of State Taxation* (2004) 88 SASR 109, (2004) 233 LSJS 53, 2004 ATC 4355, (2004) 55 ATR 301, [2004] SASC 88 at [28], per Debelle J; BC200401586

RETROACTIVE

Canada 'A retroactive statute is one that operates backwards, i.e., that is operative as of a time prior to its enactment, either by being deemed to have come into force at a time prior to its enactment (e.g., budgetary measures) or by being expressed to be operative with respect to past transactions as of a past time (e.g., acts of indemnity). A retroactive statute is easier to recognise because the retroactivity is usually express.' *Re Royal Canadian Mounted Police Act (Can)* [1991] 1 FCR 529 at 548, FCA

RETROCESSION

'The only specific legislative reference to retrocession which [Counsel] was able to draw to my attention was that in the definition of the [Insurance Companies (Accounts and Statements) Regulations 1983, SI 1983/1811] which provides that "reinsurance" includes retrocession ... The ordinary meaning of words ... suffices in my view to indicate that retrocession is within "insurance" [for the purposes of the Insurance Companies Act 1982]... Without labouring the point further, I

conclude that retrocession is insurance and, as with reinsurance, is divisible into classes by reference to the classes of initial direct insurance to which it relates.' *Re NRG Victory Reinsurance Ltd* [1995] 1 WLR 239 at 242–243, per Lindsay J

RETROSPECTIVE

[For 44 Halsbury's Laws (4th edn) paras 921, 922 see now 44(1) Halsbury's Laws (4th edn) (Reissue) paras 1284–1285.]

Canada 'A retrospective statute ... changes the law only for the future but looks backward by attaching new consequences to completed transactions. It thus opens up closed transactions and changes their consequences as of the future.' *Re Royal Canadian Mounted Police Act (Can)* [1991] 1 FCR 529 at 548, FCA

RIGHT

Enjoyment as of right

[For 12 Halsbury's Laws (4th edn) para 423 see now 12(1) Halsbury's Laws (4th edn) (Reissue) para 623.]

RIGHT IN PERSONAM

Australia ' ... I am of the view that the expressions "personal equity" and "right in personam" encompass only known legal causes of action or equitable causes of action, albeit that the relevant conduct which may be relied upon to establish "a personal equity" or "right in personam" extends to include conduct not only of the registered proprietor [of an estate or interest in land recorded in the Land Titles Register] but also of those for whose conduct he is responsible, which conduct might antedate or postdate the registration of the dealing which it is sought to have removed from the Register.' *Grgic v Australian and New Zealand Banking Group Ltd* (1994) 33 NSWLR 202 at 222–223, per Powell JA

RIGHT OF ACTION

[By the Limitation Act 1980, s 32, in the case of any action for which a period of limitation is prescribed by the Act, the start of the period of limitation is postponed where, inter alia, any fact 'relevant to the plaintiff's right of action' has been deliberately concealed.] 'I find great difficulty in applying the language of s 32 to the time limit prescribed by s 24(2). The recovery of interest by way of execution on a judgment is not a "right of action" within the meaning of s 32(1)(*b*). Even if it were, I doubt whether the defendant's concealment of himself or his assets would be the concealment of a fact relevant to such a right of action.' *Lowsley v Forbes (t/a L E Design Services)* [1998] 3 All ER 897 at 907, HL, per Lord Lloyd of Berwick

See also ACTION

RIGHT OF FIRST REFUSAL *SEE*
PREFERRED SUPPLIER

RIGHT OF WAY

[For 12 Halsbury's Laws (4th edn) para 436 see now 12(1) Halsbury's Laws (4th edn) (Reissue) para 636.]

RIOT

[For 11 Halsbury's Laws (4th edn) para 861 see now 11(1) Halsbury's Laws (4th edn) (Reissue) para 149.]

RISK

Canada [An applicant for life insurance authorised disclosure of hospital records for 'risk' assessment and 'loss' analysis.] 'The plain meanings of the words "risk" and "loss" ... refer to two distinct events (translation): "These definitions [dictionary definitions] clearly show that the word 'risk' refers to a future event, certain or uncertain, which may occasion loss, while the word 'loss' simply means the occurrence of the event giving rise to the claim". This view is reinforced when looked at in the particular context in which these terms have been used. Indeed, it must be kept in mind that "risk" and "loss" are elements which are central to the foundation of insurance contracts. Hence, "risks" in insurance contracts refer to the very object of the contract of insurance, the happening of which— the "loss"— triggers the obligation of the insurer to indemnify the insured or his beneficiary.' *Frenette v Metropolitan Life Insurance Co* (1992) 89 DLR (4th) 653 at 667, SCC, per L'Heureux-Dubé J

Risk of contamination

[The Food Act 1984 is largely repealed. See now the Food Safety Act 1990, s 16.]

ROAD

Any way (other than a waterway) over which there is a public right of passage (by whatever means) and includes the road's verge, and any bridge (whether permanent or temporary) over which, or tunnel through which, the road passes; and any reference to a road includes a part thereof. (Roads (Scotland) Act 1984, s 151)

[Road Traffic Act 1988, s 145(3)(c).] 'The question for the court in this appeal is whether an injury sustained by the passenger in a car in a multi-storey car park was caused by or arose out of the use of the vehicle on a *road*.

...

'It seems to me that ... too great an emphasis was placed on seeking an answer to the question: is the car park a road? I consider the question would more correctly be posed by asking: is there within the car park a roadway? In the present case, I think that there is within the Great Hall car park a roadway, ie a way marked out for the passage of vehicles controlled by conventional traffic signs and markings and regularly used by members of the public seeking a car parking space.' *Cutter v Eagle Star Insurance Co Ltd* [1997] 2 All ER 311 at 312, 318, CA, per Beldam LJ

ROOF PITCH

Australia 'Although the parties are at issue over the meaning of the words "roof pitch" there is no suggestion that the meaning to be adopted should be other than an ordinary meaning of those words. The ordinary meaning of a word, or its non-legal technical meaning, is a question of fact (see authorities cited in *Collector of Customs v Agfa-Gevaert Ltd* (1996) 186 CLR 389).

'It was, in the Court's opinion, open for the council to determine that the roof pitch is a reference to the line of the angle of the roof so far as the roof physically extends ...' *Wunsch v Rockdale City Council* (2002) 121 LGERA 383; BC200203736; [2002] NSWLEC 103 at [21]–[22], per Talbot J.

ROYAL ASSENT

[For 34 Halsbury's Laws (4th edn) paras 1301–1303 see now 34 Halsbury's Laws (4th edn) (Reissue) paras 833–835.]

ROYALTY

[For 31 Halsbury's Laws (4th edn) para 236 see now 31 Halsbury's Laws (4th edn) (2003 Reissue) para 334.]

ROYALTY VALUE

[The Capital Allowances Act 1968 s 60 has been repealed. The definition is not re-enacted in the Capital Allowances Act 1990.]

RULES

New Zealand [Resource Management Act 1991, s 76(2). Section 4 of the Acts Interpretation Act 1924 defines 'Act' to include all rules and regulations made under an Act. Section 76(2) of the Resource Management Act provides that every rule in a district plan has the force and effect of a regulation unless inconsistent with any regulation. Did district plan rules qualify as 'rules' in terms of s 4?] 'The word "rules" used in s 4 is not defined. But in my opinion "rules" are confined to those made as part of the legislative process by the Governor-General in Council or by any Minister of the Crown under the authority of any Act. Such an interpretation would be consistent with rules and regulations being grouped with statutes under the definition of "Act". Instruments made by local authorities are not, in my opinion, "rules" for the purposes of s 4 just because they have the statutory tag of "rules". In *Stock Exchange Association of New Zealand v Commerce Commission* [1980] 1 NZLR 663, legislative control of the process by which rules were made was an important prerequisite to stock exchange rules qualifying as "rules" in terms of s 4. On that basis district rules would not qualify as "rules" in terms of s 4.' *Christchurch International Airport Ltd v Christchurch City Council* [1997] 1 NZLR 573 at 593, per Tipping J

RUNNING ACCOUNT

Australia 'A running account between traders is merely another name for an active account running from day to day, as opposed to an account where further debits are not contemplated. The essential feature of a running account is that it predicates a continuing relationship of debtor and creditor with an expectation that further debits and credits will be recorded. Ordinarily, a payment, although often matching an earlier debit, is credited against the balance owing in the account. Thus, a running account is contrasted with an account where the expectation is that the next entry will be a credit entry that will close the account by recording the payment of the debt or by transferring the debt to the bad or doubtful debt a/c.' *Airservices Australia v Ferrier* (1996) 185 CLR 483 at 504–505; 137 ALR 609 at 625, per Dawson, Gaudron and McHugh JJ

S

SAFE PORT

[For 43 Halsbury's Laws (4th edn) para 647 see now 43(2) Halsbury's Laws (4th edn) (Reissue) para 1704.]

SAFETY

Place of safety

[The Foster Children Act 1980 has been repealed.]

SAFETY OF THE COMMUNITY

Canada 'The issue here is whether "safety of the community" refers only to the threat posed by the specific offender or whether it also extends to the broader risk of undermining respect for the law. The proponents of the broader interpretation argue that, in certain cases where a conditional sentence could be imposed, it would be perceived that wrongdoers are receiving lenient sentences, thereby insufficiently deterring those who may be inclined to engage in similar acts of wrongdoing, and, in turn, endangering the safety of the community.

'Leaving aside the fact that a properly crafted conditional sentence can also achieve the objectives of general deterrence and denunciation, I think the debate has been rendered largely academic in light of an amendment to s 742.1(b) [of the Criminal Code (SC 1997, c 18, s 107.1) which clarified that courts must take into consideration the fundamental purpose and principles of sentencing set out in ss 718 to 718.2 in deciding whether to impose a conditional sentence. This ensures that objectives such as denunciation and deterrence will be dealt with in the decision to impose a conditional sentence. Since these factors will be taken into account later in the analysis, there is no need to include them in the consideration of the safety of the community.

'In my view, the focus of the analysis at this point should clearly be on the risk posed by the individual offender while serving his sentence in the community. I would note that a majority of appellate courts have adopted an interpretation of the criterion referring only to the threat posed by the specific offender: see *Gagnon, supra,* at pp. 2640–41 (per Fish JA); *R v Parker* (1997), 116 CCC (3d) 236 (NSCA) at pp. 247–48; *Ursel, supra,* at p 260; *R v Horvath,* [1997] 8 WWR 357 at p 374, 117 CCC (3d) 110 (Sask. C.A.); *Brady, supra,* at paras 60–61; *Wismayer, supra,* at p 44.

'(c) *How Should Courts Evaluate Danger to the Community?*

'In my opinion, to assess the danger to the community posed by the offender while serving his or her sentence in the community, two factors must be taken into account: (1) the risk of the offender re-offending; and (2) the gravity of the damage that could ensue in the event of re-offence. If the judge finds that there is a real risk of re-offence, incarceration should be imposed. Of course, there is always some risk that an offender may re-offend. If the judge thinks this risk is minimal, the gravity of the damage that could follow were the offender to re-offend should also be taken into consideration. In certain cases, the minimal risk of re-offending will be offset by the possibility of a great prejudice, thereby precluding a conditional sentence.'

...

'The meaning of the phrase "would not endanger the safety of the community" should not be restricted to a consideration of the danger to physical or psychological safety of persons. In my view, this part of s 742.1(b) [of the Criminal Code] cannot be given this narrow meaning. As Finch JA stated in *Ursel, supra,* at p. 264 (dissenting in part but endorsed by the majority on this issue, at p. 287):

"I would not give to this phrase the restricted meaning for which the defence contends. Members of our community have a reasonable expectation of safety not only in respect of their persons, but in respect as well of their property and financial resources. When homes are broken into, motor vehicles are stolen, employers are defrauded of monies, or financial papers are forged, the safety of the community is. in my view endangered. We go to considerable lengths to protect and secure ourselves against the losses that may result from these sorts of crimes, and I think most ordinary citizens would regard themselves as threatened or endangered where their property or financial resources are exposed to the risk of loss."

'I agree with this reasoning. The phrase "would not endanger the safety of the community" should be construed broadly, and include the risk of any criminal activity. Such a broad interpretation encompasses the risk of economic harm.' *R v Proulx* (2000) 182 DLR (4th) 1 at 33, 34, 35, 36, SCC, per Lamer CJC

SAILING VESSEL

[For 43 Halsbury's Laws (4th edn) para 937 see now 43(1) Halsbury's Laws (4th edn) (Reissue) para 853.]

SALARY

Australia 'The words "salary" and "wage" denote an amount of money payable, the consideration for which is the performance of work or services. That meaning is reflected in the definitions provided for the terms in the *Oxford English Dictionary*, 2nd ed:

> *Salary*: fixed payment made periodically to a person as *compensation* for regular work.
>
> *Wage*: a payment to a person *for* services rendered.'

Deputy Commissioner of Taxation v Applied Design Development Pty Ltd (in liq) (2002) 20 ACLC 463; 2002 ATC 4193; BC200200894; [2002] FCA 205 at [8], per Mansfield J

SALE

[The Deer Act 1980 has been repealed. The definition is re-enacted in the Deer Act 1991, s 10(5).]

'A sale is a contract by which the seller transfers or agrees to transfer the property in goods to the purchaser for a money consideration called the price. It is completed by entering into an agreement.' *Major v Normand* 1996 SLT 297 at 298, per the Lord Justice-General (Hope)

Australia 'There is considerable authority for the proposition that the ordinary meaning of the word "sale" in a variety of statutory and common law

settings is an exchange of commodities for money – *J & P Coats Ltd v Commissioners of Inland Revenue* [1897] 1 QB 778 at 783; *Simpson v Connolly* [1953] 1 WLR 911; *Robshaw Brothers Ltd v Mayer* [1957] 1 Ch 125; *Re Westminster Property Group PLC* [1984] 1 WLR 1117, [1985] 1 WLR 676. That meaning may be extended by statute expressly or by necessary implication – *J & P Coats Ltd v Commissioners of Inland Revenue* (supra) at 783 and see generally the authorities reviewed in *FCT v Salenger* (1988) 81 ALR 25 at 29–32 in relation to the treatment of compulsory acquisitions as "sales" for revenue purposes ... In my opinion the disposition of plant or reproductive material which is an element of an assignment of a right to apply for plant variety rights in respect of the relevant plant variety is not a sale of that plant or reproductive material for the purposes of [the Plant Variety Rights Act 1987 (Cth)] s 14.' *Sun World Inc v Registrar, Plant Variety Rights* (1997) 75 FCR 528 at 540, 542; (1997) 148 ALR 447 at 458, 460; (1997) 39 IPR 161 at 172, 174; (1997) 25 AAR 414; BC9704229, per French J

SALE OF GOODS

[For 41 Halsbury's Laws (4th edn) para 601 see now 41 Halsbury's Laws (4th edn) (Reissue) para 1.]

By description

[For 41 Halsbury's Laws (4th edn) para 688 see now 41 Halsbury's Laws (4th edn) (Reissue) para 72.]

'While "description" itself is an ordinary English word, the Act contains no definition of what it means when it speaks in that section [s 13 of the Sale of Goods Act 1979] of a contract for the sale of goods being a sale "*by* description". One must look at the contract as a whole to identify the kind of goods that the seller was agreeing to sell and the buyer to buy ... where, as in the instant case, the sale (to use the words of s 13) is "*by* sample as well as *by* description", characteristics of the goods which would be apparent on reasonable examination of the sample are unlikely to have been intended by the parties to form part of the "description" *by* which the goods were sold, even though such characteristics are mentioned in references in the contract to the goods that are its subject matter.' *Gill & Duffus SA v Berger & Co Inc* [1984] 1 All ER 438 at 445–446, HL, per Lord Diplock

'We were ... referred to the decision of Sellers J in *Joseph Travers & Sons Ltd v Longel Ltd* (1947) 64 TLR 150, where it was held that, since the buyers had placed no reliance on a descriptive name for rubber boots, the sale was not one by description. The decision is chiefly of value for Sellers J's approval (at 153) of the following passage in *Benjamin on Sale*, 7th edn (1931), p 641: "Sales by description may, it seems, be divided into sales: 1. Of unascertained or future goods, as being of a certain kind or class, or to which otherwise a 'description' in the contract is applied. 2. Of specific goods, bought by the buyer in reliance, at least in part, upon the description given, or to be tacitly inferred from the circumstances, and which identifies the goods. So far as any descriptive statement is a mere warranty or only a representation, it is no part of the description. It is clear that there can be no contract for the sale of unascertained or future goods except by some description. It follows that the only sales not by description are sales of specific goods *as such*. Specific goods may be sold as such when they are sold without any description, express or implied; or where any statement made about them is not essential to their identity; or where, though the goods are described, the description is not relied upon, as where the buyer buys the goods such as they are". It is suggested that the significance which some of these authorities attribute to the buyer's reliance on the description is misconceived. I think that that criticism is theoretically correct. In theory it is no doubt possible for a description of goods which is not relied on by the buyer to become an essential term of a contract for their sale. But in practice it is very difficult, and perhaps impossible, to think of facts where that would be so. The description must have a sufficient influence in the sale to become an essential term of the contract and the correlative of influence is reliance. Indeed, reliance by the buyer is the natural index of a sale by description.' *Harlingdon and Leinster Enterprises Ltd v Christopher Hall Fine Art Ltd* [1990] 1 All ER 737 at 743–744, CA, per Nourse LJ

By sample

[For 41 Halsbury's Laws (4th edn) para 697 see now 41 Halsbury's Laws (4th edn) (Reissue) para 94.]

SALMON

Unseasonable

'The word "unseasonable", although imprecise, can be taken to extend also, for the purposes of the penal sanction, to the period when the fish, although not yet unclean, has reached the condition of being ready to spawn. It is not enough that it is full of spawn, as fish which are in spawn but whose tissues have not yet begun to degenerate to permit spawning are in this respect undoubtedly wholesome ... But when the tissues have degenerated to the point when spawning has become possible, although it has not yet begun, perhaps because the fish has not reached the spawning ground, then there is a physical condition which can be identified by pressing the belly gently towards the vent without killing the fish or subjecting it to serious injury. It is at that period, when it is plainly on the eve of spawning, that it can be taken to be "unseasonable" within the meaning of section 20 [of the Salmon Fisheries (Scotland) Act 1868].' *Brady v Barbour* 1995 SCCR 258 at 264, per the Lord Justice-General (Hope)

SALVAGE

[For 43 Halsbury's Laws (4th edn) para 1027 see now 43(1) Halsbury's Laws (4th edn) (Reissue) para 931.]

[For 25 Halsbury's Laws (4th edn) para 263 see now 25 Halsbury's Laws (4th edn) (2003 Reissue) para 434.]

SAME DAMAGE

[Section 1(1) of the Civil Liability (Contribution) Act 1978 provides that any person liable in respect of any damage suffered by another person may recover contribution from any other person in respect of 'the same damage'.] 'I see no reason to construe s 1(1) of the Act otherwise than directly and simply as it stands. Any person who is liable (see s 6(1)) in respect of any damage suffered by another may recover contribution, partial help, from another person liable in respect of the same damage. The simple direct reading of the subsection must in my opinion lead one to conclude, first, that "the same damage" can only refer to the damage spoken of some dozen or so words earlier in the subsection. Further, the simple approach necessarily involves that the statutory draftsman intended that "the same damage" should be damage suffered by the *same* person.' *Birse Construction Ltd v Haiste Ltd* (*Watson and ors, third parties*) [1996] 2 All ER 1 at 6, CA, per Sir John May

See also TORT-FEASOR LIABLE IN RESPECT OF THAT DAMAGE; WHO IS, OR WOULD IF SUED HAVE BEEN, LIABLE IN RESPECT OF THE SAME DAMAGE

SAME TRANSACTION OR OCCURRENCE

Canada [Joinder of parties to a libel action was available for a claim arising out of the same transaction or occurrence.] 'The same incidents giving rise to a news story may be written in a libellous manner by one publisher and not another. One article names the respondent, the other does not. This may of itself lead to different defences. The newspapers distribute to different audiences in addition to their common market area. Each publisher's defences may differ because it is the publication that is the essence of a libel. These publications are separate and lead to separate causes of action. The story may be the same, but the publication is different.' *Dickhoff v Armadale Communications Ltd* (1993) 108 DLR (4th) 464 at 470, Sask CA, per Lane JA

SANITARY CONVENIENCE

[The Food Act 1984 is largely repealed. The definition is not re-enacted in the Food Safety Act 1990.]

SATISFACTION

[For 16 Halsbury's Laws (4th edn) para 1407 see now 16(2) Halsbury's Laws (4th edn) (Reissue) para 739.]

Australia 'The appellant suggested that the term "satisfaction" was amphibolous in the same way as "discharge". However, in my view, that is not so. The matter was explained by Dixon J in *McDermott v Black* [(1940) 63 CLR 161 at 183–185] in terms which indicate that the essence of accord and satisfaction "is the acceptance by the plaintiff of something in place of his cause of action", that the accord is the agreement or consent to accept the satisfaction and that, upon provision of the satisfaction, there is a discharge which extinguishes the cause of action.' *Federal Commissioner of Taxation v Orica Ltd* (1998) 154 ALR 1 at 34; [1998] HCA 33 at [116]; BC9801652 at 48, per Gummow J

SATISFACTORY TO THE LESSEE

Australia 'Whether particular terms and conditions are "satisfactory to the Lessee" involves, as I see it, a question of fact, namely, whether the lessee is subjectively honestly not content with the terms and conditions: *Meehan v Jones* (1982) 149 CLR 571; *Zieme v Gregory* [1963] VR 214. Unless, on the evidence, the lessee is found to have been subjectively honestly not content with the terms and conditions, those terms and conditions will be taken to have been satisfactory to it. Such a "not

content" approach seems to me to be compelled by the unreality that attends any attempt to prove in any positive way that someone affirmatively finds something "satisfactory", given that what is "satisfactory" to a person often turns in whole or in part on no more than neutrality or lack of objection, as distinct from active approval or endorsement. The general issue must therefore be approached in the light of whatever the evidence shows to be what might best be described as the demonstrated requirements of the defendant with respect to the subject matter of the terms and conditions actually imposed.

'The approach to the meaning of "satisfactory to the Lessee" just outlined is, I think, consistent with that taken by Beaumont J in *Koryar, Koryar & Clarke v Perry & Allen* (unreported, FCA, 4 December 1997) to the following provision of a joint venture agreement:

> "Perry/Allen shall have the right to retain ownership of the fishing vessels and equipment and are at liberty to withdraw their vessels and equipment if not jointly satisfied."

'Dealing with the meaning of "satisfied", Beaumont J said:

> "The primary dictionary meanings (*Macquarie Dictionary*) of the transitive verb 'satisfy' are:
>
> > '1. to fulfil the desires, expectations, needs, or demands of, or content (a person, the mind etc); supply fully the needs of (a person etc). 2. to fulfil (a desire, expectation, want, etc)…'
>
> As an intransitive verb, 'satisfy' means 'to give satisfaction'. The primary meanings of 'satisfaction' are:
>
> > '1. the act of satisfying. 2. the state of being satisfied.'
>
> The present context indicates, in my view, that the words 'not satisfied', here used intransitively, were intended to mean that the joint venture had not fulfilled the defendants' desires or expectations of the venture."

'The present context seems to me to entail an equivalent conclusion, namely, that consent will not have been obtained on terms and conditions satisfactory to the lessee if the consent does not fulfil the lessee's desires or expectations of the consent – what I have termed the demonstrated requirements of the lessee.' *Barak Pty Ltd v WTH*

Pty Ltd BC200300151; [2003] NSWSC 15 at [38]–[41], per Barrett J

SCHEME

Australia [Income Tax Assessment Act 1936 (Cth).] '[9] ... The definition of "scheme" in s 177A is wide, but it must be related to the tax benefit obtained. The deduction here was for the incurring of a liability to pay interest on borrowed money. The tax benefit in connection with the relevant scheme was part of an allowable deduction for interest. This, it seems to us, is what was meant by references in the judgments in the Full Court to the scheme being capable of standing on its own feet. The judges were making the point, which is undoubtedly correct, that, where the tax benefit in question is part of an allowable deduction for interest, a search for the purpose of a scheme, identified in a manner that does not include the borrowing, is not an undertaking that conforms with the requirements of the legislation. In a given case, a wider or narrower approach may be taken to the identification of a scheme, but it cannot be an approach which divorces the scheme from the tax benefit. Here, the borrowing was an indispensable part of that which produced the tax benefit. A description of the scheme that did not include the borrowing would make no sense.

...

'[16] Even so, a transaction may take such a form that there is a particular scheme in respect of which a conclusion of the kind described in s 177D is required, even though the particular scheme also advances a wider commercial objective. In *Federal Commissioner of Taxation v Spotless Services Ltd*, Brennan CJ, Dawson, Toohey, Gaudron, Gummow and Kirby JJ, after noting that revenue law considerations influence the form of most business transactions, and that the presence of a fiscal objective does not mean that a person entered into or carried out a scheme for the dominant purpose of obtaining a tax benefit, said:

Much turns upon the identification, among various purposes, of that which is "dominant". In its ordinary meaning, dominant indicates that purpose which was the ruling, prevailing, or most influential purpose. In the present case, if the taxpayers took steps which maximised their after-tax return and they did so in a manner indicating the presence of the "dominant purpose" to obtain a "tax benefit", then the criteria which were to be met before the Commissioner might make determinations under s 177F were satisfied.

'[17] Their Honours went on to say of the facts of that case:

In those circumstances, a reasonable person would conclude that the taxpayers in entering into and carrying out *the particular scheme* had, as their most influential and prevailing or ruling purpose, and thus their dominant purpose, the obtaining thereby of a tax benefit, in the statutory sense. The scheme was the particular means adopted by the taxpayers to obtain the maximum return on the money invested after payment of all applicable costs, including tax. The dominant purpose in the adoption of the particular scheme was the obtaining of a tax benefit ... It is true that the taxpayers were concerned with obtaining what was regarded as adequate security for an investment made "off-shore". However, the circumstance that the Midland Letter of Credit afforded the necessary assurance to the taxpayers does not detract from the conclusion that, viewed objectively, it was the obtaining of the tax benefit which directed the taxpayers in *taking steps they otherwise would not have taken by entering into the scheme.*'

...

'[34] The schemes to which Pt IVA applies are identified in s 177D. Leaving aside what s 177D says about the time and place at which a scheme is entered into or carried out, there are two elements that must be satisfied. First, it must be shown that the relevant taxpayer has obtained, or would but for s 177F obtain, a tax benefit in connection with the scheme. Secondly, it must be shown that having regard to eight matters "it would be concluded that the person, or one of the persons, who entered into or carried out the scheme or any part of the scheme did so for the purpose of enabling the relevant taxpayer to obtain a tax benefit in connection with the scheme" or enabling the relevant taxpayer and one or more other taxpayers to obtain a tax benefit in connection with the scheme.

'[35] The "person" whose purpose is to be identified under s 177D is the person, or one of the persons, who entered into or carried out the scheme or any part of the scheme. Section 177D makes plain that the person whose purpose is to be identified may be (but need not be) the relevant taxpayer or one of the other taxpayers mentioned in the section.

...

'[37] ... "Scheme" is defined in s 177A(1) as meaning:

(a) any agreement, arrangement, understanding, promise or undertaking, whether express or implied and whether or not enforceable, or intended to be enforceable, by legal proceedings; and

(b) any scheme, plan, proposal, action, course of action or course of conduct

'It includes a reference to a unilateral scheme, plan, proposal, action, course of action or course of conduct. A reference to a scheme or a part of a scheme being entered into or carried out by a person for a particular purpose is to be read as including a reference to the scheme, or part of the scheme, being entered into or carried out by the person for two or more purposes of which the particular purpose is the dominant purpose.

...

'[43] Moreover, it is important to notice that "scheme" is defined, in s 177A(1), in terms that may not always permit the precise identification of what are said to be all of the integers of a particular "scheme". So much follows from the inclusion, within the statutory meaning, not only of arrangements that are not and are not intended to be enforceable by legal proceedings, but also of "any scheme, plan, proposal, action, course of action or course of conduct". This definition is very broad. It encompasses not only a series of steps which together can be said to constitute a "scheme" or a "plan" but also (by its reference to "action" in the singular) the taking of but one step. The very breadth of the definition of "scheme" is consistent with the objective nature of the inquiries that are to be made under Pt IVA.

...

'[55] What the Commissioner identified in these matters as the wider scheme falls within the definition of "scheme". That is, all of the steps leading to, and the entering into, and the implementation of the loan arrangements can be understood as together constituting a "scheme". Those steps were a scheme, plan, or course of action. One of the purposes of that scheme was, of course, to provide money for the financing and refinancing of the two properties. But so, too, the steps said by the Commissioner to have constituted the narrower scheme (the provision of the loan permitting both the division of the loan and the direction of repayments to one portion, coupled with the respondents' direction of their repayments to the home loan portion of the loan) can also be identified as a course of action, scheme, plan or action. Not only is that so, the steps identified as

constituting the narrower scheme can be seen to have formed a part of the wider scheme.' Per Gummow and Hayne JJ.

...

'[87] Read literally, the definition of a scheme is easily wide enough to include something much less than an agreement or arrangement: indeed to include an "action", or "course of action", or a promise made pursuant to, or as part of an agreement or arrangement, or of a scheme. A scheme, however it is to be described, must nonetheless be something which is, or can be the object of a particular, that is to say, a dominant purpose as required by s 177A(5). Further requirements are that what is sought to be identified as a scheme, must be something to which the matters referred to in s 177D(b) can or may be relevant.

'[88] Those matters, especially those of relevance here, do not operate, however, to narrow the meaning of a scheme. The reference in s 177D(b)(ii) to the "substance of the scheme" invites attention to what in fact the taxpayer may achieve by carrying it out, that is to matters whether forming part of, or not to be found within the four corners of an agreement or an arrangement. They also require that substance rather than form be the focus. And s 177D(b)(v) requires reference to the financial position, actual or prospective, of the taxpayer before and after the scheme.

'[89] The first step is to ascertain whether the transactions, or any action taken in relation to, or as part of them, are capable of constituting a scheme within the meaning of s 177A(1). In my opinion there is no doubt that there was a scheme here within that meaning, and that there is more than one way in which what passed between the respondents, Austral and the lender, can be seen to answer the statutory definition of a scheme. The arrangement that the respondents might elect to have interest debited exclusively to one account was each of, an "agreement", "understanding", "promise" or "undertaking", and although the definition does not require as an element of it, legal enforceability, each was legally enforceable as such. The election as to the application of the payments also answers the description of an "action" or "course of action" within the meaning of those words in s 177A(1)(b). This was so despite that the Court said in *Federal Commissioner of Taxation v Peabody*, that "Pt IVA does not provide that a scheme includes part of a scheme". An action or course of action undertaken in the course of, or as part of a transaction or series of transactions, is not the same as part of a scheme. The use of the

Scheme 756

singular, narrow words, proposal, action or course of action in s 177A(1)(b) in juxtaposition with, for example, agreement or arrangement in s 177A(1)(a) indicates that something done which is less than the whole of an arrangement or agreement may be capable of itself being a scheme. This view is I think not only consistent with, and a true reflection of the statutory language, but also with the legislative intention discernible from the Explanatory Memorandum. It is also consistent with the approach of this Court in *Federal Commissioner of Taxation v Consolidated Press Holdings Ltd* in which the Court looked to part only of the activity of the corporate taxpaying group. Furthermore, there is no reason why the promotion of the Wealth Optimiser, its utilization by the respondents, the agreements and mortgages giving effect to it, and the election as to the repayments and debiting of interest, should not be collectively regarded as an arrangement, a course of action or a course of conduct. The arrangement was in fact a tripartite one, involving the broker, the respondents and the lender. Under s 177A(3) a unilateral course of action, for example, the giving of notice of election and payment according to it, by the respondents would have been sufficient to constitute a scheme.' *Commissioner of Taxation v Hart* [2004] HCA 26 at [9], [16]–[17], per Gleeson CJ and McHugh J, [24][35], [37], 43], [55], Gummow and Hayne JJ, [87]–[89], per Callinan J; BC200403006

New Zealand 'The use of the word "scheme" in its context in my judgment takes some colour from its association with the word "competition" and also by dint of the fact that it forms but one ingredient of a composite definition of the expression "prize competition". In my judgment when Parliament used the word "scheme" it was referring to a scheme which was, ex hypothesi, not a competition but which was a scheme in the nature of a competition.' *Department of Internal Affairs v Machirus* [1992] 1 NZLR 503 at 507, per Tipping J

SCHOOL

[For 15 Halsbury's Laws (4th edn) para 296 see now 15 Halsbury's Laws (4th edn) (Reissue) para 96.]

Australia '... [I]t is not open to serious argument that the definition given by Barwick CJ in the *Cromer Golf Club* case [[1972–73] ALR 1295] was intended to be other than its ordinary meaning and has been so regarded subsequently: see

Australian Airlines Ltd v Federal Commissioner of Taxation, [(1996) 65 FCR 341 at 345] ...' *Commissioner of Taxation v Leeuwin Sail Training Foundation Ltd* (1996) 68 FCR 197 at 203; 96 ATC 4721; BC9603368, per Northrop and Finn JJ

New Zealand [Education Act 1989 s 13. The issue was whether 'the school' as referred to in the Education Act 1989 relates only to the educational facility of a boarding school or whether it includes the school's boarding establishment.] '... the reference to "the school" in the Act is a reference to the educational facility [only].' *M v Board of Trustees of Palmerston North Boys' High School* [1997] 2 NZLR 60 at 66, per Goddard J

SCIENCE

Applied science

Australia [Section 73A(6) of the Income Tax Assessment Act 1936 (Cth) defines scientific research for purposes of allowing deduction to mean any activities in the fields of natural or 'applied science' for the extension of knowledge.] 'Applied science is not a term defined in the legislation. It has its ordinary meaning of putting scientific discovery to practical use. As Mr O'Neill observed in Case D81 (72 ATC 480 at 494) in a passage which I would adopt: "Applied science is the practical application of science directed to a solution of practical problems in industry and commerce".' *Goodman Fielder Wattie Ltd v Federal Commissioner of Taxation* (1991) 101 ALR 329 at 347, per Hill J

SCIENTIFIC RESEARCH

[The Capital Allowances Act 1968 has been repealed. The definitions are re-enacted in the Capital Allowances Act 1990, s 139(1).]

SCIENTIST

Australia 'We think that employed "as a scientist" ... ought to be construed as meaning employed in a position which involves the use by the employee of the relevant scientific knowledge ... In *Municipal Officers' Association of Australia v Association of Professional Scientists of Australia* (1980) 280 CAR 779 at 786 Cohen J said ... "The words 'employed as a scientist' ... should be seen as referring to the performance of general functions and, in my view, mean employed on the basis of scientific qualifications which in the judgment of the employer are required for an understanding of the functions to be performed and which would enable research to be carried out if necessary." ' *Orr v Association of Professional Engineers, Scientists and Managers, Australia* (1996) 71 IR 241 at 245, per the Commission

SCIRE FACIAS

[For 11 Halsbury's Laws (4th edn) para 1578 see now 1(1) Halsbury's Laws (4th edn) (2001 Reissue) para 264.]

SEA

[The Dumping at Sea Act 1974 has been repealed. The definition is re-enacted in the Food and Environment Protection Act 1985, s 24(1).]

SEARCH

Australia ' "Search" is an ordinary English word. The *Oxford English Dictionary* (2nd Ed 1989 pp 804–5) defines the verb "to search" when used in relation to a person to mean "to examine by handling, removal of garments, and the like to ascertain whether any article (usually, something stolen or contraband) is concealed in his clothing". In the *New Oxford Dictionary of English* the word search, when used as a verb, conveys trying to find something by looking or otherwise seeking carefully and thoroughly. (1998 Ed, p 1677). The *Macquarie Dictionary* defines the verb "to search" as meaning to go through or look through carefully in seeking to find something; to examine (someone) for concealed objects by going through their pockets. (Third Edition, p 1916) In *Chambers English Dictionary* the same verb is defined as meaning to explore all over with a view to finding something; to examine closely; to examine for hidden articles by feeling all over. (1988 Edition, p 1328) In *Collins Concise English Dictionary* the word "search" when used as a verb is defined as meaning to look through (a place, etc) in order to find someone or something (Australian Edition 1984, p 1040).

'Relevantly the generally accepted connotation of search is that it involves looking carefully in order to find something that is hidden. When it relates to a person, it carries the implication of some physical intrusion onto the person (for example by patting down the clothing of such person) or into the clothing or body of the person the subject of the search.

'The concept of what constitutes a search has been the subject of a large number of decided case in the United States as a result of the protections afforded by the Fourth Amendment to the Constitution of the United States. The Fourth Amendment protects the "right of the people to be secure in their persons, houses, papers and effects against unreasonable searches and seizures." Being a constitutional protection, its ambit has been widely interpreted. It has been held that it "protects people from unreasonable government intrusions into their legitimate expectations of privacy." (*United States v Chadwick* (433 US (1977) 1 at 7) However, even under such a constitutional safeguard, the actions of a sniffer dog in detecting the presence of drugs have been held not to constitute a search.

'In *United States v Bronstein* (521 F 2d 459 (1975)) the Second Circuit of the United States Court of Appeals considered a case in which a quantity of marijuana had been detected in the baggage of the respondents through the use of a police sniffer-dog trained to detect the presence of such drug …

'The court held:

"We find no search or seizure violative of the Fourth Amendment." (supra at 462).

'A like submission had previously been made to the District Court of Columbia Circuit in *United States v Fulero* (498 F 2d 748 (1974)), in which the submission was described as "frivolous".

'In *United States v Place* (462 US 696 (1982)) the Supreme Court of the United States considered the actions of a trained narcotics detection dog that reacted positively to a suitcase in the possession of the defendant (Place)…

'Having considered the characteristics of the activities of the narcotics detection dog, including its non-intrusive character, limited information that results, etc, O'Connor J said:

"In these respects, the canine sniff is sui generis … therefore, we conclude that the … exposure of respondent's luggage, which was located in a public place, to a trained canine – did not constitute a 'search' within the meaning of the Fourth Amendment." (supra at 707)

'Brennan J, who thought it unnecessary to address the issue (supra at 719), concurred in the result but adhered to the view that he had expressed in a dissenting opinion in *Doe v Renfrow* (451 US 1022 at 1025–6 (1981)) (see below). Blackmun J (at 724) concurred in the judgment of the court but also thought it was unnecessary to decide, in the case then before the court, what did or did not constitute a search (at 723).

...

'In some earlier cases, eg *Horton v Goose Creek Independent School District* (690 F 2d 470 (1982), Fifth Circuit), *Doe v Renfrow* (supra (1981)), it had been held or said that the use of a sniffer dog in relation to individuals may be offensive at best, or harrowing at worst to "the innocent sniffee," notwithstanding that the rubric in the Fourth Amendment is the same in relation to persons as it is to objects – whether such objects be houses, papers or other effects.

'In *Horton v Goose Creek Independent School District* (supra) the court was of the view that in the long list of cases cited:

"The majority view is that the sniffing of objects by a dog is not a search" (at 476);

and that:

"... the courts have concluded that the sniffing of a dog is 'no different' or that the dog's olfactory sense merely 'enhances' that of a police officer in the same way that a flashlight enhances the officer's sight." (at 477)

'However, in determining in 1982, ie before the decision in 1984 in *United States v Jacobsen* (supra) that the use of a sniffer dog in relation to school students in the circumstances of that case breached the Fourth Amendment, the United States Court of Appeals, Fifth Circuit, founded its decision on two bases. First, on the student's expectations of privacy (at 478) and secondly, on the nature of the search which was, in the circumstances, unreasonable. (at 481–2)

'In *Doe v Refrow* (supra) the court below had upheld as constitutional the use of a sniffer dog in relation to a teenage school girl. An application was made to the Supreme Court of the United States for a writ of certiorari in relation to such decision. The court denied certiorari, with Brennan J dissenting. Thus the majority decision favoured the application of the same rubric to persons as that which applied to property.

'In this regard it should be noted that the United States commentary on *Doe v Renfrow* (supra) (W R LaFave *Search and Seizure – A Treatise on the Fourth Amendment*, Chapter 2.2(f) p 280 et seq and 1984 supplement at pp 83–4) treats the sniffing of a person as objectionable under the Fourth Amendment because it amounts to "a public accusation of crime". In my opinion, such a basis of distinction, even if applicable in the United States, is not applicable under the law of Australia.

Furthermore, it is clear from Chapter 2.2 of the commentary (pp 281–3) that although "a few courts" in the United States have held that reliance on the olfactory capabilities of a dog to detect that which a law enforcement officer could not discover by his own sense of smell constitutes a search,

"most courts ... have either held or assumed otherwise, sometimes characterising the defendant's argument to the contrary as frivolous" (at 282–3)

'The distinction between the use of trained dogs to sniff objects on the one hand and people on the other which has been drawn by some lower courts and in dissenting judgments in the United States has not been applied in Australia. The logic of the majority judgments in those United States decisions that deal with objects has prevailed in Australia in relation to people.

'In *Questions of Law Reserved* (*No 3 of 1998*) (1998) 71 SASR 223 , the question of the use of a sniffer dog to detect the presence of drugs was considered. The principal judgment was delivered by Olsson J with whom Prior J agreed. Olsson J, said:

"In essence the situation, apropros the accused, was, conceptually, no different than if he happened to be at the bus depot holding the suitcase and the police officer lawfully, but casually, walked past with a sniffer dog who reacted positively when it came near the suitcase.

"In both instances, the reaction of the sniffer dog was plainly adequate to arouse in the mind of the police officer a reasonable apprehension that the accused was in possession of an illegal drug – so as to warrant an actual search of the suitcase itself." (supra at 226)

'He went on to explain why the finding of the trial judge that "... the search of the accused's luggage began when the dog commenced sniffing around it ..." was an error, saying:

"... it is incorrect to say that a mere sniffing of the scent emanating from the suitcase in the air in close proximity of the suitcase constituted a 'search' of it. According to its normal connotation the word 'search' implies some physical intrusion into what is searched, for the purpose of examining what is in it. The word is not apt to describe the mere detection of an odour generated by the content of the item searched, which is released into the atmosphere surrounding it without any positive acts of a third person to effect that release. If it were otherwise, ridiculous questions would arise as to how close one would need to get to an item generating an odour before one could be said to be searching it." (supra at 226)

and he applied those United States authorities which dealt with objects, rather than people. He did so on the basis that insofar as people were concerned, any contrary decisions in the United States depended upon reasonable expectations of privacy of the individual. I agree. Such an approach is a reflection of specific constitutional concepts in the United States that have no counterpart in Australia either by way of constitutional guarantee or in relevant legislation.

'Having concurred with the reasons given by Olsson J, Prior J added:

"I agree in particular with the submission put by the Director of Public Prosecutions that mere sensory perception, whether by eye, ear or nose, cannot of itself constitute a search. It follows that odours which emit from a person's bag are exposed to the plain perception of the public at large. Thus a dog sniffing the area around a bag or parcel does not effect a search of that bag or parcel. It could perhaps be described as an act of identification, but certainly not a search." (supra at 224)

'Williams J in holding that the use of the sniffer dog was not unlawful said:

"Sniffing around the luggage does not, relevantly constitute 'search'." (supra at 227)'

Director of Public Prosecutions (*NSW*) *v Darby* BC200207203; [2002] NSWSC 1157 at [25]–[33], [36]–[45], per O'Keefe J

Canada 'The word "search" is defined by *The Oxford English Dictionary* (2nd ed 1989), vol XIV as: "1. a. The action or an act of searching; examination or scrutiny for the purpose of finding a person or thing ... Also, investigation of a question; effort to ascertain something." In this sense, every investigatory method used by the police will in some measure constitute a "search". However, the scope of s 8 [under the *Canadian Charter of Rights and Freedoms*] is much narrower than that, and protects individuals only against police conduct which violates a reasonable expectation of privacy. To hold that every police inquiry or question constitutes a search under s 8 would disregard entirely the public's interest in law enforcement in favour of an absolute but unrealistic right of privacy of all individuals against

any state incursion however moderate. This is not the intent or the effect of s 8...

...

'The police conduct in this case did not constitute a search within the meaning of s 8 of the *Charter*. In approaching the front door of the residence in broad daylight and knocking at the door, the police officers were exercising an implied licence at common law ... ' *R v Evans* [1996] 1 SCR 8 at 32–33, per Major J

New Zealand [Bill of Rights Act 1990, s 21.] 'In broad terms a search is an examination of a person or property ... Entry and search of private property by officers of the state without permission of the owner or occupier is an actionable trespass unless authorised by the common law or under specific statutory provision. While not ordinarily a crime it is customary to refer to such trepassory intrusion as unlawful and illegal.' *R v Grayson and Taylor* [1997] 1 NZLR 399 at 406, CA, per cur

SEASHORE

[For 49 Halsbury's Laws (4th edn) paras 287–289 see now 49(2) Halsbury's Laws (4th edn) (Reissue) paras 4–6.]

SEAWORTHY

[For 25 Halsbury's Laws (4th edn) paras 66–67 see now 25 Halsbury's Laws (4th edn) (2003 Reissue) paras 248–249.]

[For 43 Halsbury's Laws (4th edn) para 553 et seq see now 43(2) Halsbury's Laws (4th edn) (Reissue) para 1650 et seq.]

SECONDHAND GOODS

New Zealand [The term 'secondhand goods' is defined in s 2 of the Goods and Services Tax Act 1985, as amended by s 2 of the Goods and Services Tax Amendment Act 1988, s 2.] 'The original definition put the focus on use or intended use. The amendment in 1988 adopted in its place the ordinary meaning of the words ... The ordinary meaning of "secondhand" can include both previous use and previous ownership, as is shown in the dictionary meanings [several examples then follow].

...

'Although the term can be used of goods that have been previously owned even if not used, prior ownership does not always have the effect of making goods "secondhand".' *L R McLean*

& *Co Ltd v Commissioner of Inland Revenue*
[1994] 3 NZLR 33 at 40–41, CA, per McKay J

SECONDMENT

Australia 'The words "secondment" and
"seconded" in s 40F and s 40G [of the Australian
Federal Police Act 1979 (Cth)] are not defined in
the ... Act. The verb "to second" is defined in the
Oxford English Dictionary (2nd Ed) as follows:

> To remove (an officer) temporarily from his
> regiment or corps, for employment on the
> staff, or in some other extra-regimental ap-
> pointment. Also transf. Of employees in other
> occupations and employments. Hence sec-
> onded.

'The *Macquarie Dictionary* (Revised Edition, 1985)
defines "to second" as: to transfer (a military
officer or other) temporarily to another post,
organisation, or responsibility.' *Eaton v Overland*
BC200108276; [2001] FCA 1834 at [190]–[191],
per Allsop J

SECRETED ON OR ABOUT HIS PERSON

Canada 'In order to assess whether the search
conducted by the customs officials on the
respondent was authorized by s 98 of the *Customs
Act*, it is necessary first to determine whether the
phrase "on or about his person" in s 98(1) refers
not only to contraband which is concealed by a
traveller in luggage, under clothes or in some other
manner external to the traveller's body, but includes
as well contraband which the traveller has ingested.
The respondent argues that as a matter of common
parlance, standard dictionary definitions of the
words "on" and "about" do not support an
interpretation of the phrase "on or about his person"
which is sufficiently broad to include items which
a traveller has ingested and which are subsequently
located internally within the traveller's digestive
system. Further, s 98 requires a customs official to
conduct the search "within a reasonable time". The
respondent argues that the inclusion of a time
restriction within s 98 necessarily leads to the
conclusion that the phrase "on or about his person"
is not meant to apply to ingested narcotics. A
passive "bedpan vigil" such as was necessary to
confirm the presence of heroin pellets within the
respondent's digestive tract at the time he attempted
to cross the Canadian border involves a lengthy
detention process and therefore cannot be conducted
"within a reasonable time".

'Admittedly, statutory interpretation in the
context of constitutional review is not an exact
science. While reference to common parlance and
standard dictionary definitions are often of
assistance in interpreting legislative provisions,
regard must be had not only to the ordinary and
natural meaning of the words, but also to the
context in which they are used and the purpose of
the provision as a whole: *R v Lewis* [1996] 1 SCR
921, 105 CCC (3d) 523, 133 DLR (4th) 700. The
most significant element of this analysis is the
determination of legislative intent. In light of these
guidelines, the respondent's interpretation of the
phrase "on or about his person" is, with respect,
misguided. As Weiler JA noted in her dissenting
judgment in the Court of Appeal, when read in
context, the words "on or about his person" are
contained within the larger phrase "secreted on or
about his person". In my view, an examination of
this context demonstrates that Parliament intended
to confer authority on customs officers, so far as
the *Charter* permits, to search for prohibited
material not only on or about the surface of the
traveller's body, but also secreted or concealed
within the traveller's body. Fundamentally, the
legislative intent of s 98 was to grant officers the
necessary authority to control the smuggling of
contraband into Canada. As this Court reiterated in
Lewis, a legislative phrase should be given a
meaning consonant with the purpose of the statutory
provision unless the contrary is indicated, provided,
of course, that such an interpretation is consistent
with constitutional limitations and conventional
rules of interpretation.

'The respondent's suggested interpretation of
s 98 is unnecessarily restrictive, in terms of both
the literal text and Parliamentary intent. The
provision does not refer to a traveller who has
"placed' items on or about his or her person, in
which case a more compelling argument could be
made that the legislative intent was to restrict the
authority of customs officers to searches of a
person's exterior physical body and associated
personal effects. Instead, the English version of the
provision refers to material which the traveller has
"secreted" on or about his or her person. The verb
"secrete" refers to the act of placing material into a
concealed location: *Concise Oxford Dictionary* (9th
ed 1995). The French text confirms this
interpretation, as the verb *"dissimuler"* refers to
the act of hiding (*cacher*) or concealing (*celer*): *Le
Nouveau Petit Robert 1* (1996). The concept of
concealment, rather than the distinction between

the interior or exterior of the traveller's physical body, is the fulcrum of the search power in s 98 of the Act.

'Parliament's intent in extending the authority of customs officers to search for any concealed material, whether located internal or external to the traveller's physical body, is further supported by the illogical outcome that would ensue if the Court were to adopt a more restrictive interpretation. A traveller intent on smuggling narcotics across the Canadian border would be able to defeat the purpose of the provision simply by concealing contraband inside his or her mouth rather than under his or her clothing or elsewhere on his or her body. Interpreting s 98 in light of the provision's purpose, which is to restrict the entry of contraband material into Canada, the phrase "secreted on or about his person" cannot have been intended to permit such an absurd result.' *R v Monney* (1999) 171 DLR (4th) 1 at 15–17, SCC, per Iacobucci J

SECURELY FENCED

[For 20 Halsbury's Laws (4th edn) para 563 see now 20(1) Halsbury's Laws (4th edn) (Reissue) para 687.]

SECURITY—SECURITIES

Australia [Section 230 of the Companies (Vic) Code prohibits, inter alia, a company from providing 'security' in connection with a loan made to a director of the company, his spouse or relative of such director or spouse.] 'There is no doubt that the word "security" may have different meanings according to the context in which it is found. The concept that a security may be either a "real security" or a "personal security" goes back at least to the judgment of Chitty J in *Grimwade v Mutual Society* (1884) 52 LT(NS) 409... More recently the issue was discussed by Lee J in *Broad v Commissioner of Stamp Duties* [1980] NSWLR 40 at 44–45: "The word 'security' has a wide meaning. Jowitt's Dictionary of English Law defines 'security' as 'something which makes the enjoyment or enforcement of a right more secure or certain'. It is defined in Stroud's Judicial Dictionary as 'Speaking generally ... anything that makes the money more assured in its payment or more readily recoverable".' I prefer the description given by Professor Sykes at the outset of his work on *The Law of Securities*, 4th edn, p 3: "The general concept of security involves a transaction whereby a person to whom an obligation is owed by another person called the 'debtor' is afforded, in addition to

the personal promise of the debtor to discharge the obligation, rights exercisable against some property of the debtor in order to enforce discharge of the obligation". Cf per Lord Wrenbury in *Singer v Williams* [1921] 1 AC 41 at 59. Moreover, as a matter of principle, Professor Sykes rightly concludes, in my opinion, when considering "securities" by way of guarantee, that "the so called personal security is not a security at all": at p 11. Why the word "securities" has in certain contexts been given such a broad meaning need not further be examined here, although I would not doubt that in the authorities cited above the words "securities" and "security" have both been considered in particular contexts to comprehend the giving of a guarantee.' *Brick and Pipe Industries v Occidental Life Nominees Pty Ltd* (1990) 3 ACSR 649 at 708–709, per Ormiston J

Australia [Section 230 of the Companies (Vic) Code provides that a company should not give a guarantee or 'security' in connection with a loan made to a director or related company.] 'The position is similar with the word "security". It can be used to comprehend a personal security such as a guarantee or indemnity ... the notion of security usually conveys that rights exercisable against some property are given. In our opinion the word has that meaning in s 230... the use of the word in the expression in s 230(1)(b) "give a guarantee or provide security" tends to confirm that the word "security" is used in that sense. There is no context to indicate that the word was intended to include a personal security.' *Brick and Pipe Industries Ltd v Occidental Life Nominees Pty Ltd* [1992] 2 VR 279 at 371; (1991) 6 ACSR 484 at 486, per cur

For repayment of money

'A right in security is a right over property given by a debtor to a creditor whereby the latter in the event of the debtor's failure, acquires priority over the property against the general body of creditors of the debtor. It is of the essence of a right in security that the debtor possesses in relation to the property a right which he can transfer to the creditor, which right must be retransferred to him on payment of the debt.' *Armour v Thyssen Edelstahlwerke A-G* [1990] 3 All ER 481 at 486, HL, per Lord Jauncey of Tullichettle

In will

[For 50 Halsbury's Laws (4th edn) para 479 see now 50 Halsbury's Laws (4th edn) (Reissue) para 533.]

SECURITY INTEREST

Canada 'Basically, security is something which is given to ensure the repayment of a loan. *Black's Law Dictionary* (6th ed 1990), at p 1357, gives a clear definition of a "security interest" in these terms:

> "The term 'security interest' means any interest in property acquired by contract for the purpose of securing payment or performance of an obligation or indemnifying against loss or liability. A security interest exists at any time, (A) if, at such time, the property is in existence and the interest has become protected under local law against a subsequent judgment lien arising out of an unsecured obligation, and (B) to the extent that at such time, the holder has parted with money or money's worth." '

Alberta (Treasury Branches) v MNR [1996] 1 SCR 963 at 979, per Cory J

SEDITION

'In our judgment the common law of sedition and seditious libel was accurately stated in the Supreme Court of Canada in *Boucher v R* (1951) 2 DLR 369 ... So far as material the court held that the seditious intention on which a prosecution for seditious libel must be founded is an intention to incite to violence or to create public disturbance or disorder against His Majesty or the institutions of government. Proof of an intention to promote feelings of ill-will and hostility between different classes of subjects does not alone establish a seditious intention. Not only must there be proof of an incitement to violence in this connection, but it must be violence or resistance or defiance for the purpose of disturbing constituted authority. We agree, with respect, with that too. By constituted authority what is meant is some person or body holding public office or discharging some public function of the State.' *R v Chief Metropolitan Stipendiary Magistrate, ex p Choudhury* [1991] 1 All ER 306 at 322–323, per cur

[For 11 Halsbury's Laws (4th edn) para 827 see now 11(1) Halsbury's Laws (4th edn) (Reissue) para 89.]

SEIZURE

New Zealand [Bill of Rights Act 1990, s 21.] 'In broad terms a search is an examination of a person or property and seizure is a taking of that which is discovered.' *R v Grayson and Taylor* [1997] 1 NZLR 399 at 406, CA, per cur

Of ship

[For 25 Halsbury's Laws (4th edn) para 157 see now 25 Halsbury's Laws (4th edn) (2003 Reissue) para 337.]

Australia ' "Seizure" is not defined in the Act [Customs Act 1901 (Cth)], but the following definition appears in 17 Halsbury's Laws (4th edn) para 489, p 296: "For an act of the sheriff or his bailiff to constitute a seizure of goods it is not necessary that there should be any physical contact with the goods seized, nor does such contact necessarily amount to seizure. An entry upon the premises on which the goods are situate, together with an intimation of an intention to seize the goods, will amount to a valid seizure, even where the premises are extensive and the property seized widely scattered, but some act must be done sufficient to intimate to the judgment debtor or his employees that a seizure has been made, and it is not sufficient to enter upon the premises and demand the debt. Any act which, if not done with the court's authority, would amount to a trespass to goods will constitute a seizure of them when done under the writ. Whether or not there has been a seizure is a question of fact". That passage has been quoted with approval in the United Kingdom in *Lloyds and Scottish Finance Ltd v Modern Cars and Caravans (Kingston) Ltd* [1966] 1 QB 764 at 776 and in this court in *O'Neil v Wratten* [(1986) 65 ALR 451 at 457]. The authorities seem to make it clear that a mere oral announcement of seizure is not enough ... There must be some act of dominion which, of its nature, is such that there would be no doubt in the mind of a reasonable observer that seizure has taken place.' *Whim Creek Consolidated NL v Colgan* (1991) 103 ALR 204 at 216, per O'Loughlin J

SELF-DEFENCE

[For 45 Halsbury's Laws (4th edn) para 1257 see now 45(2) Halsbury's Laws (4th edn) (Reissue) para 369.]

'In a case of self-defence, where self-defence or the prevention of crime is concerned, if the jury come to the conclusion that the defendant believed, or may have believed, that he was being attacked or that a crime was being committed, and that force was necessary to protect himself or to prevent the crime, then the prosecution have not proved their case. If, however, the defendant's alleged belief was mistaken and if the mistake was an unreasonable one, that may be a powerful reason for coming to the conclusion that the belief was not honestly held and should be rejected. Even if the jury come to the conclusion that the mistake was an unreasonable one, if the defendant may genuinely have been labouring under it, he is entitled to rely on it.' *R v Williams* [1987] 3 All ER 411 at 415, CA, per Lord Lane CJ

'The common law recognises that there are many circumstances in which one person may inflict violence on another without committing a crime, as for instance in sporting contests, surgical operations or, in the most extreme example, judicial execution. The common law has always recognised as one of these circumstances the right of a person to protect himself from attack and to act in the defence of others and if necessary to inflict violence on another in so doing. If no more force is used than is reasonable to repel the attack such force is not unlawful and no crime is committed. Furthermore, a man about to be attacked does not have to wait for his assailant to strike the first blow or fire the first shot: circumstances may justify a pre-emptive strike. It is because it is an essential element of all crimes of violence that the violence or the threat of violence should be unlawful that self-defence, if raised as an issue in a criminal trial, must be disproved by the prosecution. If the prosecution fail to do so the accused is entitled to be acquitted because the prosecution will have failed to prove an essential element of the crime, namely that the violence used by the accused was unlawful.' *Beckford v R* [1987] 3 All ER 425 at 431, PC, per Lord Griffiths

SELF-EMPLOYED

[The Social Security Act 1975 has been repealed. The definition is re-enacted in the Social Security Contributions and Benefits Act 1992, s 2(1).]

SELL

Sale of food

[The Food Act 1984 is largely repealed. See now the Food Safety Act 1990, s 7.]

SELLS

[An accused was convicted of selling obscene material contrary to s 51(2) of the Civic Government (Scotland) Act 1982. The accused did not deny that there was obscene material on display in his shop,

but he appealed against conviction on the ground that there was no proof that he had sold any obscene material.] 'We ... agree with the sheriff that the word "sells" includes "offers for sale" and does not require to be construed in the restricted sense of an actual completed sale.' *Rees v Lees* 1997 SLT 872 at 877, per the Lord Justice-Clerk (Ross)

SEND

Australia [In the context of prohibited drug transfer and liability under s 6(1)(c) of the Misuse of Drugs Act 1981 (WA).] 'The Drugs Act does not define "to send". As a result, and in the absence of any indication to the contrary, the verb must be given its ordinary meaning. The New Oxford Dictionary of English relevantly defines to "send" as to "arrange for the delivery of, especially by post". The New Shorter Oxford English Dictionary speaks of ordering or causing a thing to be conveyed, transported or transmitted by an intermediary to a person or place for a particular purpose. The Macquarie Dictionary speaks in similar terms. The definitions focus upon acts initiating, and contributing to, the process of transmission of an object to a particular destination, with a view to the ultimate receipt of the object by a particular person at that destination. None of the definitions suggest that actual receipt of the object by its intended recipient, at the end of the process of transmission, is a necessary element of the expression.

'That circumstance accords with common experience. The mere fact that a parcel, upon reaching its intended destination, may not thereafter reach its intended recipient does not mean that the parcel was not sent to another or that it has no sender. In *The Petrofina*, the House of Lords, in discussing the finding of an arbitrator that the accepted method of payment under a charterparty involved the "sending" of a cheque by post, reached a similar conclusion. The ordinary meaning of "to send" may thus be distinguished from the expression "to deliver to another"; the latter expression connotes a completed transaction, ending in receipt of the object in question. Although "to send" may, in some contexts, be construed as incorporating an element of "deemed delivery", such a construction does not assist in the present case

'It follows that a person is liable under s 6(1)(c) for sending a prohibited drug to another person once he or she has knowingly placed the drug in a mail delivery system with the intention that it be received by that person at a particular place.' *Pinkstone v R* [2004] HCA 23 at [51], per McHugh and Gummow JJ; BC200402837

New Zealand [Regulation 30(1) of the Sports Drugs (Urine Testing) Regulations 1994 (SR 1994/285) at the material time provided that 'As soon as practicable after the receipt at the [Sports Drug Agency] of any carrier bag delivered or sent to it ..., a drug testing official at the Agency shall ... (f) Send the bag by a secure means to a laboratory ...'] 'That can only sensibly point to the process of delivering the sample to the chosen laboratory. Reference to any standard dictionary will confirm that "send" may be used in various senses and the particular meaning depends on the context in which the word appears. Where, as here, the context links the sending to a particular destination and without any qualification as to the means to be employed, "Send ... to" must in our view be given its established meaning of to cause (the sample) to be conveyed to the destination, rather than simply to start it on its way.' *Bray v New Zealand Sports Drug Agency* [2001] 2 NZLR 160 at 162, CA, per cur

SENIORITY

Australia 'I would think it appropriate that this court declare that, until the contrary is provided by competent authority, the word "seniority" in s 33(1) of the Ordinance [Fire Brigade (Administration) Ordinance 1974] is to be taken to mean the tenure of higher rank than, or the tenure for a longer period of the same rank as, is held by the person to whom reference is made in that sub-section by the words "the member provisionally promoted".' *Kerr v Vernon* (1989) 88 ALR 125 at 137, per Jenkinson J

SENTENCE

[Under the United States of America (Extradition) Order 1976, SI 1976/2144, Sch 1 art III(4), 'A person convicted of and sentenced for an offence shall not be extradited therefor unless he was sentenced to imprisonment or other form of detention for a period of four months or more or, subject to the provisions of Article IV, to the death penalty' Art VII(4) requires that 'If the request relates to a convicted person, it must be accompanied by a certificate or the judgment of conviction imposed in the territory of the requesting Party, and by evidence that the person requested is the person to whom the conviction refers and, if the person was sentenced, by evidence of the sentence imposed and a statement showing to what extent the sentence has not been carried out'.] 'The issue which is before your Lordships in this appeal is whether a person whose extradition is sought by the government of the United States of America as a person who has been convicted and sentenced for an extradition crime can be surrendered for extradition when he has served the entirety of his custodial sentence but there remains outstanding a portion of his sentence which requires him to serve a period of supervised release.

...

'The argument for the appellant is directed to the provisions of para (4) of art III and to the concluding words of para (4) of art VII. He points to the fact that he has served the entirety of his custodial sentence and to the fact that the only reason why his return is sought is because he is alleged to be in breach of a condition of his supervised release. Paragraph (4) of art III provides that a person convicted and sentenced for an offence shall not be extradited unless he was sentenced to imprisonment or other form of detention for a period of four months or more. He submits that the reference in the concluding words of para (4) of art VII to "a statement showing to what extent the sentence has not been carried out" must be taken to refer, and to refer only, to the sentence of imprisonment or detention for a period of four months or more laid down by para (4) of art III. It follows that a person is not to be regarded as subject to extradition as a convicted person who has been sentenced unless he has been sentenced to a custodial sentence of or in excess of the stipulated minimum period and the whole or a part of that custodial sentence has not yet been carried out. So the criterion for his extradition is, according to this argument, whether the person is unlawfully at large because he is still subject to a term of imprisonment. As the appellant has served the entirety of his custodial sentence that requirement is not satisfied, so he is not a person who under the terms of the treaty is liable to be extradited. Alternatively he submits that, on a proper analysis of the facts of his case, his extradition is being sought not as a person who has been convicted and sentenced but as a person accused of being in breach of a condition of supervised release. That is an offence which, if proved, would not amount to an extradition crime.

'These arguments were rejected by the Divisional Court. Rose LJ said that in his judgment the sentence for the non-completion of which the appellant's extradition was sought was the whole of the sentence which was imposed on him, including the four and a half years of supervised release which has not been carried out. He said that he was unable to construe the words "the sentence" in para (4) of art VII as being confined merely to the sentence of imprisonment. He observed that there was no requirement in the treaty for a person to be unlawfully at large before he could be extradited.

...

'The scheme of the treaty is that the substantive conditions which must be satisfied as regards the offence and the minimum custodial penalty are set out in art III. The information to be provided when extradition is being sought through the diplomatic channel is set out in art VII. The provision in para (4) of art III about the minimum custodial penalty sets out a threshold which must be crossed before the offence of which the person has been convicted can be regarded as sufficiently serious for him to be extradited. But it says nothing about any other forms of punishment, apart from the death penalty. Nor does it say that a person whose offence qualifies because he has received a sentence of imprisonment or other form of detention for a period of four months or more ceases to be liable to be extradited when he has served his custodial sentence, or that he ceases to be liable to extradition if the period which remains to be served in custody is less than the minimum period of four months. There is nothing in the language of art III which suggests that para (4) was intended to do anything more than set out a threshold condition whose purpose was to show that for the purposes of extradition the particular offence was sufficiently serious. It is enough for the person to be liable to be extradited that the offence of which he has been convicted is one of the serious offences mentioned in art III and that he has received a custodial sentence of sufficient length to satisfy the requirements of para (4).

'The only words of limitation contained in the treaty which are relevant to this issue are to be found in para (4) of art VII. These are to be found in the requirement that a request for extradition through the diplomatic channel which relates to a convicted person must be accompanied by evidence of the sentence imposed and a statement showing to what extent the sentence has not been carried out. It is implicit in the concluding phrase of this paragraph that the process of extradition is not to be resorted to in a case where the sentence has been carried out and there remains no unsatisfied element of punishment. This is consistent with the fact that extradition treaties are designed to ensure that persons who are convicted and sentenced in one country do not escape punishment by fleeing to another country before they have satisfied the sentence imposed by the court. If his sentence has

been carried out, with the result that his punishment for the offence is over and done with, the person is not to be regarded as seeking to escape punishment and there is no longer any purpose to be served by his being extradited.

'But it is significant that the word "sentence" in each of the two phrases where it appears in the concluding words of this paragraph is not otherwise qualified. It is not said that the requirement to provide evidence of "the sentence imposed" is satisfied by producing evidence to show that it met the requirements of para (4) of art III. What requires to be produced is evidence of the sentence imposed by the court. As the present case illustrates, this may include other penalties as well as a custodial sentence. Nor is it said that the requirement to provide a statement showing to what extent "the sentence: has not been carried out is satisfied by producing evidence which relates only to that part of the sentence imposed by the court which relates to the custodial sentence. I consider that the word "sentence" in the concluding phrase refers to the whole of the sentence described in the preceding phrase as "the sentence imposed". The wording of this paragraph lends no encouragement to the idea that it is appropriate to separate out the custodial element in that sentence from the other elements.

'In the present case the judgment of the United States District Court for the Northern District of Illinois states: "The defendant is sentenced as provided in pages 2 through 5 of this judgment." It is made up of a printed form, which provides on page 2 for imprisonment, on page 3 for supervised release, on page 4 for a fine and on page 5 for restitution and forfeiture. Entries have been made on each of these pages, and the sentence of the court comprises the totality of the orders made under each entry. That is the sentence of which evidence required to be provided under para (4) of art VII and in regard to which a statement was to be produced under that paragraph showing to what extent it has not been carried out.

...

'In my opinion the fact that the appellant has served the entirety of his custodial sentence does not have the effect for which he contends of removing his liability as a person who, because he has been sentenced to a period of four months or more in custody, can be returned to the United States as a person convicted of an extradition crime. I would hold that he remains liable to extradition because he received a custodial sentence which satisfies the requirements of para (4) of art III of the treaty, and I would also hold that the order for his supervised release forms part of his sentence for the purposes of para (4) of art VII. I would dismiss the appeal.' *Re Burke* [2000] 3 All ER 481 at 483, 485, 486–488, HL, per Lord Hope of Craighead

Australia [The Fisheries Act 1952 (Cth), s 13c(2), empowers the court to make an order for forfeiture of property on the conviction of a person for "… an offence arising out of his having in his possession or in his charge a boat for taking fish …".] 'By s 2 of the Criminal Appeal Act 1912 (NSW) the word "sentence" is defined to include "any order made by the court of trial on conviction with reference to the person convicted, or his property …". The vessel the subject of the order of forfeiture was not the property of [the person convicted]. Accordingly, the order does not fall within the words of inclusion in the definition of the word "sentence". The significance of the reference in that definition to the property in question as being the property of the person convicted has been emphasised in a number of cases: *Griffiths v The Queen* (1977) 137 CLR 293 at 312, 324, 345; *R v Forsythe* [1972] 2 NSWLR 951 and *R v McDonald* [1979] 1 NSWLR 451. This aspect of the language of the definition of "sentence" in the Criminal Appeal Act of New South Wales has remained unchanged since 1912. It is to be contrasted with the position elsewhere. In Victoria, the Crimes Act 1958 defines "sentence" to include "any order of the court or of the judge thereof made on or in connection with a conviction with reference to the person convicted or any property …". The definition of "sentence" in the corresponding English legislation is also different. In the Criminal Appeal Act 1907 (UK) the word "sentence" was defined to include "any order of the court made on conviction with reference to the person convicted or his wife or children". In the Criminal Appeal Act 1968 (UK) "sentence" was defined to include "any order made by a court when dealing with an offender", and the same language appears in the definition of "sentence" in the Courts Act 1971 (UK)… It does not seem to me that an order of forfeiture of property not belonging to a convicted person is within the ordinary meaning of the word "sentence" and, as has been noted, Lord Parker CJ said exactly that in 1963 [see *R v Surrey Quarter Sessions, ex p Commissioner of Metropolitan Police* [1963] 1 QB 990 at 996].' *R v Kakura* (1990) 20 NSWLR 638 at 643–644, per Gleeson CJ

Australia 'The ordinary meaning of the word "sentence", as well as its use in the Criminal Appeal Act 1912 (NSW) was considered by the High Court in *Griffiths v R* (1977) 137 CLR 293, and it was variously described there. The most appropriate description, in my view, was that of an order which "definitively disposes of the consequences of the conviction" or "a definitive decision by the judge on the punishment or absence of it which is to be the consequence of the conviction": per Barwick CJ (at 304, 307). A sentence imposed following a sentence indication hearing is indisputably such an order.' *R v Warfield* (1994) 34 NSWLR 200 at 205–206, per cur

SEPARATE PROPERTY

New Zealand [Section 8 of the Valuation of Land Act 1951] 'Before turning to the matters which the Judge and counsel considered in giving meaning to the expression "separate property", we begin with the expression itself in its context. Part of that context is land law. The ordinary meaning of "separate property" in that context would be the distinct pieces of land identified as such through the land transfer system and in particular by the relevant certificate of title.' *Rodney District Council v Attorney-General* [2000] 3 NZLR 678 at 685–686, CA, per cur

SERIOUS

Canada [Claims for personal injuries in motor vehicle accidents were restricted to serious disfigurement or serious impairment of bodily function.] ' "Serious" is a word which by its very nature imports a sense of degree and probably imports a range. The courts must avoid qualifying the word "serious". If the legislature had wanted to do so it could have said "very serious" to indicate that it was only those impairments which were at the upper end of the range which would permit an injured person to sue for damages.

'There is no justification in the statute for qualifying "serious" as significant or as approaching the catastrophic. While obviously an impairment which was significantly serious or almost catastrophically serious would be a serious impairment, there is no necessity for the impairment to be that serious in order to qualify as being a serious one.' *Meyer v Bright* (1993) 110 DLR (4th) 354 at 364–365, Ont CA

SERIOUS CIRCUMSTANCE

Australia [Regulation 2(1) of the Migration Regulations 1989 (Cth) refers to a citizen or resident needing assistance from a relative because of death, disability, prolonged illness or other 'serious circumstances'.] '... a "serious circumstance" may be a circumstance not of a medical nature. This being so, it would appear that it is sufficient for a circumstance to be "serious", that it is "weighty and important": *Macquarie Dictionary*. The relationship between a young child and his or her parents, particularly the mother, is of course a weighty or important matter, as the Declaration of the Rights of the Child recognises.' *Chen v Minister for Immigration and Ethnic Affairs* (1994) 51 FCR 322 at 327; 123 ALR 126 at 131, per Davies J

SERIOUS DANGER TO THE COMMUNITY

Australia [Dangerous Prisoners (Sexual Offenders) Act 2003 (Qld) s 13.] 'Such an order may only be made where the Attorney-General proves that the prisoner is a "serious danger to the community": s 13(7). By s 13(2),

A prisoner is a serious danger to the community ... if there is an unacceptable risk that the prisoner will commit a serious sexual offence

—

(a) if ... released from custody; or
(b) if ... released from custody without a supervision order ...

'A conclusion that a prisoner is a "serious danger to the community" depends on the Court's satisfaction of that matter based on "acceptable, cogent evidence" proving the pertinent risk "to a high degree of probability": s 13(3). In considering that issue, "the Court must have regard" to the several matters specified in s 13(4).

'In deciding whether to make an order for continuing detention or a supervision order, "the paramount consideration is to be the need to ensure adequate protection of the community": s 13(6).' *Attorney-General (Qld) v Francis* [2004] QSC 233 at [2], per Byrne J; BC200405103

SERIOUS INJUSTICE

New Zealand [The Property (Relationships) Act 1976, s 14A(2) provides in relation to de facto relationships of short duration that an order cannot be made under the Act for the division of relationship property 'unless ... (b) the Court is satisfied that failure to make the order would result in serious injustice'.] '[22] The first issue for me to determine is whether it would cause "serious injustice" if an order is not made.

'[23] What then is meant by "serious injustice"?

'[24] The wording "serious injustice" surfaces on a number of occasions in the Property Relationships Act. Not only does it emerge in s 14A but also s 21J (setting aside agreements), s 85 (post mortem resolution of de facto relationships of short duration) and s 88(2) (regarding the test to be applied in granting leave to a personal representative of a spouse or de factor partner to apply for relief). It can be fairly assumed that the legislature intended the term to be interpreted in a similar fashion where it is used throughout the Act. The draftsman has made a valiant attempt to frame the wording of the statute in a manner digestible by the layman, as is apparent from a reading of part one of the Act in particular.

'[25] The meaning of "serious injustice" was considered by Heath J in *Re Williams* [2004] 2 NZLR 132 at p 140 where he said :

In my view, the term "serious injustice" suggests injustice of a type that the Court cannot tolerate. While not creating a standard as high as the "repugnant to the interests of justice" test used in s 13 of the 1976 Act (as a threshold test for departure from equal sharing provisions of that Act) the term requires a degree of injustice sufficient *to require* the Court to intervene.

In my judgment, having regard to the context in which s 88(2) appears in the statute, the Court may grant leave only if it is satisfied that refusing leave would create an injustice is intolerable. The need for predictability in the law of succession, so that a testator or testatrix can order his or her affairs on death, militates against a lower threshold test.

'[26] The same words have been considered in the Court of Appeal in the decision of *Harrison v Harrison* [2005] NZFLR 252. There, the Court appears to have adopted an approach confirming the threshold test outlined in defining "serious injustice", in *MacKenzie v MacKenzie* (1983) 2 NZFLR 155 as:

requiring one's conscience to be materially disturbed.

'[27] In the High Court, in *Harrison*, Fogarty J had concluded the serious injustice test had to be applied in the light of the concept of justice provided for in the Property Relationships Act, of which the most important was the strong presumption of equal sharing once qualifying criteria had been satisfied. The Court of Appeal disagreed with the weight Fogarty J had allocated to the presumption of equal sharing, but certainly treated the purpose of the statutory provisions (in that case s 21J, as the foundation on which the interpretation of "serious injustice" should be constructed (see paras [110]–[113])).

'[28] I approach the term as connoting a considerable injustice, which would be intolerable to standards of justice which are themselves shaped within the purposes and intention of the statute.

'[29] Another question arising is, who must be the one who suffers the "serious injustice"?

'[30] The relevant part of s 14A creates a threshold test requiring that "the Court is satisfied that *failure to make the order* would result in serious injustice". (Emphasis added.) That might suggest that the injustice should be seen only from the perspective of the claimant partner, because the statute is silent as to the effects of making an order.

'[31] It would be an unusual outcome if the Court were required to be blind to the co-relative impact on a party arising from the *making* of an order by a myopic concentration only upon the consequences upon the other party of *failing* to make an order. In *Gibbons v Vowles* (2003) 22 FRNZ 946, Judge B D Inglis QC noted at para [5]:

> In relation to s 14A, however, it is left to the Court to determine without any such guidance whether the result of applying the section so as to exclude division of relationship property under s 14A(3) would produce "serious injustice", a concept which must of course take into account the impact on the position of either party.

'[32] I agree that in assessing whether failure to make an order would result in serious injustice to a claimant, the Court must take into account the effect on the other party of actually making an order. Justice in this concept is addressing the interests of both parties.

'[33] In the same case, Judge Inglis QC derived from the Court of Appeal decision in *Martin v Martin* [1979] 1 NZLR 97 (CA) at p 102 the same directive as to a consideration of the concept of justice which I have applied in this case, namely that:

> the reference to justice is clearly to the broad statutory concepts of justice outlined in the Act and not to the varying standards which might appeal to individuals.'

TF v AH [2006] NZFLR 86 at [22]–[33], per Judge R J Murfitt

SERIOUS NON-POLITICAL CRIME

[The Geneva Convention relating to the Status of Refugees 1951, art 1F excludes from the protection of the convention an applicant for political asylum who has committed a 'serious non-political crime' outside the United Kingdom.] 'The question here is, whether or not the offences which the tribunal found T to have committed in Algeria were properly characterised as "terrorist", were they "serious non-political crimes"? ... [The] real question is whether the part which the tribunal found T to have played in those offences made him guilty of crimes which were properly described as non-political ...

'To adopt Lord Diplock's words, a crime committed with the object of overthrowing or changing the government of a state or inducing it to change its policy is to be regarded as a political crime, provided that the commission of the crime is not too remote from the objective.

'... The less proportionate is the criminal offence to the political objective sought to be achieved, the more it savours of ordinary common law criminality, and the less of political crime.

'Indeed, there is in our judgment a common thread running through each of these four sub-paragraphs [of para 152 of the handbook relating to the convention]: before any crime can be said to have a genuinely political purpose it must in some coherent sense be calculated to promote that purpose. That will simply not be so if the crime is wholly disproportionate to the purpose to be served. The more atrocious it is, the more gratuitous violence it involves, the more likely it is to be disproportionate. The more disproportionate it is, the more difficult will it be to establish one close and direct causal link that must exist between the crime and its suggested political object ...

'... We too think it inappropriate "to characterise indiscriminate bombings which lead to the deaths of innocent people as political crimes". Our reason is not that all terrorist acts fall outside the protection of the convention. It is that it cannot properly be said that these particular offences qualify as political. In our judgment the airport bombing in particular was an atrocious act, grossly out of proportion to any genuine political objective. There was simply no sufficiently close or direct causal link between it and T's alleged political purpose.' *T v Secretary of State for the Home Department* [1995] 2 All ER 1042 at 1051, 1054–1055, CA, per Glidewell LJ; affd [1996] 2 All ER 865, HL

Australia [Article 1F(b) of the Convention relating to the Status of Refugees 1951 (Geneva,

28 July1951; Aust TS 1954 No 5; 189 UNTS 150) as amended by the Protocol relating to the Status of Refugees 1967 (New York, 31 January) excludes from the protection of the Convention an applicant for political asylum who has committed a 'serious non-political crime'. The respondent had been a senior member of the Khalistan Liberation Force (KLF) in India and had been involved in the killing of a police officer who, the respondent claimed, had tortured a KLF member.] 'The history of Art 1F(b), and of the expression "serious non-political crime", was considered by the House of Lords in *T v Home Secretary* [1996] AC 742. The task of characterising a crime such as unlawful homicide as either political, or non-political, is difficult to relate to Australian concepts of criminal responsibility. But it has confronted courts in common law jurisdictions for more than a century; originally in the context of the Extradition Act 1870 (UK), and more recently in the context of the Convention. As one of the exceptions to an international obligation to afford protection on certain grounds, it recognises a state's interest in declining to receive and shelter those who have demonstrated a propensity to commit serious crime. The qualification to the exception is that the crime must be non-political. Part of the problem is that the concept of a political crime is not limited to conduct such as treason, sedition, or espionage, which in some cases might readily be recognised as related entirely to the political circumstances of the locality where it occurred, and as unlikely to carry any possible threat to public safety or order in the country of refuge.

'That unlawful killing can, at least in some circumstances, be political, has long been accepted in extradition cases. It may be doubted that the image of the clinical assassin, with a narrow focus upon an oppressive dictator, taking care to avoid what would now be called collateral damage, ever bore much relation to reality. While homicide is foreign to our experience of political conflict, that is because we have been favoured with a relatively peaceful history. At other times, and in other places, the taking of life has been, and is, an incident of political action. Even so, when courts have endeavoured to state the principles according to which a decision is to be made as to whether a crime which, by hypothesis, has been committed in another country, in circumstances utterly different from those that prevail in the country of refuge, is political, they have taken pains to confine the concept so as to avoid the consequence that all offences committed with a political motivation fall within it. An example is to be found in the definition proposed by Lord Lloyd of Berwick, and agreed in by Lord Keith of Kinkel and Lord Browne-Wilkinson, in *T v Home Secretary* [at 786–7]:

"A crime is a political crime for the purposes of article 1F(b) of the Geneva Convention if, and only if (1) it is committed for a political purpose, that is to say, with the object of overthrowing or subverting or changing the government of a state or inducing it to change its policy; and (2) there is a sufficiently close and direct link between the crime and the alleged political purpose. In determining whether such a link exists, the court will bear in mind the means used to achieve the political end, and will have particular regard to whether the crime was aimed at a military or governmental target, on the one hand, or a civilian target on the other, and in either event whether it was likely to involve the indiscriminate killing or injuring of members of the public."

'Terrorist activities are not political crimes, for the reason given in that passage ...

'While the authorities accept the possibility that murder might, in some circumstances, be a political crime, they recognise one further qualification ... Even if a killing occurs in the course of a political struggle, it will not be regarded as an incident of the struggle if the sole or dominant motive is the satisfaction of a personal grudge against the victim. But it is only necessary to state the qualification in order to see the danger of over-simplification. People engaged in any kind of prolonged conflict, including military battle, and ordinary democratic politics, will have scores to settle with their adversaries. It is difficult to imagine serious conflict of any kind without the possibility that parties to the conflict will seek retribution for past wrongs, real or imagined. Revenge is not the antithesis of political struggle; it is one of its most common features.

'The respondent claimed that the Sikhs in India were victims of oppression and brutality that was sometimes condoned, sometimes instigated, and sometimes engaged in, by government agents, including the police. That claim may not be true. As the submissions of counsel for the Minister before the Tribunal plainly suggested, it may be an outrageous slur upon the Indian authorities. But the Tribunal made no finding about that. The respondent claimed that one of the political objectives of the KLF was to prevent oppression of the Sikhs, its ultimate objective, the establishment of an independent Sikh state, being only the final and most complete form of relief in contemplation. Counsel for the Minister, on the other hand, submitted that the KLF was a terrorist organisation involved in revenge killings against people who were violent towards Sikhs. The Tribunal found it unnecessary "to enquire into the political nature ... of the KLF". The Tribunal said that the political objectives of the KLF had no bearing because this particular killing of a government agent was done "out of retribution". I agree with the conclusion of all four judges of the Federal Court. The reasoning of the Tribunal was legally erroneous, and cannot be explained upon the basis suggested by the appellant. It was not merely a finding of fact related to the particular circumstances of the case. There was no evidence to warrant a conclusion that the police officer was killed for reasons of personal animus or private retribution. On the respondent's account, which the Tribunal evidently accepted, the police officer became a "target" because he had tortured a KLF member. That can be described as a form of vengeance or retribution, but, if it were accepted that one of the political objectives of the KLF was to resist oppression of Sikhs, it is not vengeance or retribution of a kind that is necessarily inconsistent with political action in the circumstances which the respondent claimed existed in India. For the Tribunal to say, even by reference to the facts of the case, that such retribution cannot be political, was wrong.

'The very fact that the Tribunal found it unnecessary to form a view as to the political nature of the KLF, or as to whether it was a terrorist organisation, demonstrates that it was proceeding upon a view that there is a necessary antithesis between violent retribution and political action. That was an error of law.

'I do not suggest that, on the respondent's account of events and circumstances in India, and of the aims of the KLF, and of the circumstances of the killing of the police officer, it must follow that the crime was political. Once it was accepted that the concept of a political crime was not limited to offences such as treason, sedition, and espionage, and could extend to what would otherwise be "common" crimes, including unlawful homicide, then it became necessary to find means of avoiding the consequence that any crime could be political if one of the motives for which it was committed was directly or indirectly political. There is no bright line between crimes that are political and those that are non-political. But, as the Tribunal rightly recognised in part of the reasoning quoted above, there must be a sufficiently close connection between the criminal act and some objective

identifiable as political to warrant its characterisation as a political act. And the achievement of that objective must be the substantial purpose of the act. The UNHCR Handbook [Office of the United Nations High Commissioner for Refugees, *Handbook on Procedures and Criteria for determining Refugee Status*, para 152] states:

"There should also be a close and direct causal link between the crime committed and its alleged political purpose and object. The political element of the offence should also outweigh its common-law character. This would not be the case if the acts committed are grossly out of proportion to the alleged objective. The political nature of the offence is also more difficult to accept if it involves acts of an atrocious nature."

'To identify homicide as a political act ordinarily requires a close and direct connection between the act and the achievement of an objective such as a change of government, or change of government policy, which might include relief from government sponsored or condoned oppression of a social group. In the present case, upon an evaluation of the circumstances in India at the time of the killing, the relevant policies of the government, the observance of the rule of law by the agencies of government, including the police, and the objectives and methods of the KLF, the Tribunal might well reach the same conclusion as that which it reached in the first place. Even so, the respondent is entitled to have his case considered according to law. The path by which the Tribunal came to its original decision took an impermissible short-cut.' (footnotes omitted) *Minister for Immigration and Multicultural Affairs v Singh* (2002) 186 ALR 393; (2002) 23(4) Leg Rep 18; BC200200665; [2002] HCA 7 at [15]–[22], per Gleeson CJ

Australia [Article 1F(b) of the Convention relating to the Status of Refugees 1951 (Geneva, 28 July1951; Aust TS 1954 No 5; 189 UNTS 150) as amended by the Protocol relating to the Status of Refugees 1967 (New York, 31 January) excludes from the protection of the Convention an applicant for political asylum who has committed a 'serious non-political crime'. The respondent had been a senior member of the Khalistan Liberation Force (KLF) in India and had been involved in the killing of a police officer who, the respondent claimed, had tortured a KLF member.] 'Defining a "serious non-political crime" has been described as a problem that presents "the gravest difficulties". In an earlier manifestation of the phrase, it was said to present one of the "most acute" dilemmas of extradition law. So far as the Australian law on refugees is concerned, the scope of offences "of a political character" is not fixed ...

'The difficulties of definition derive, in part, from the absence of any settled international consensus about the expression and the changing views of national courts and tribunals about its meaning. The content of the expression depends on an almost infinite variety of factors. It has been influenced by the changing nature of crimes, of weapons, of the transport of criminals and of the global political order, and the increased vulnerability of modern societies to violent forms of political expression.

'Long before the Convention was adopted, Grotius wrote that asylum was accepted by international law as available for those fugitives who suffered undeserved enmity but not for those who had done something injurious to human society. Since that distinction was propounded, first in the field of extradition law and more recently in the Convention, courts have struggled to find a point that will allow decision-makers to differentiate between fugitives accused of a serious political crime and those in respect of whom there are "serious reasons for considering" that they have committed a serious non-political crime.

'Given that this kind of differentiation has troubled courts for more than a hundred years, there is wisdom in Viscount Radcliffe's warning, that it is now unlikely that the point of distinction will receive a definitive answer accepted by everyone as universally applicable. On the other hand, where important rights and duties turn on the meaning of the expression, being rights and duties that must be considered by judges and other decision-makers, it is reasonable to demand that there should be a measure of clarity about the concept. Even if the best that courts can do is describe the idea, and the appropriate ways to approach it, they should attempt to do so. The alternative is a negation of the rule of law and the surrender of such questions to idiosyncratic opinions that may have little or nothing to do with the context of the case at hand.

...

'... A person who is otherwise entitled to protection as a "refugee" has, on the face of things, a high claim to that status. It is one written in Australia's own law. It also reflects obligations of international law, which Australia has accepted and by which it is bound. Even the existence of serious grounds for believing that he or she has committed a "serious" crime will not disqualify a person from protection, if a proper view of the crime in question,

looked at as a whole, is that it is "political" rather than "non-political" in character.

'The motives for the crime are not conclusive as to its character. But because crime in most societies, including our own, ordinarily involves a mental element, the perpetrator's intention may well be relevant to the character of the crime. It may, for example, constitute a reason for classifying a crime, performed by a person who happens to be a member of a political movement, as "non-political", if its purpose was mainly for extraneous, personal or selfish reasons. On the other hand, the mere fact that the crime has been committed by a person involved in a political movement, or during disorder associated with that movement, is not enough to warrant its classification as "political" rather than "non-political". Neither does the existence of some degree of personal motivation necessarily warrant the classification of the offence as non-political. The sometimes complex array of motivations for any offence must be considered before a characterisation of the offence for the purposes of the Convention is determined.

'Nor are the consequences of the crime in question, known or implied, determinative of its character. The history of liberation movements, and rebellion against autocratic, colonial and tyrannical governments, has witnessed too many instances of serious crimes, involving innocent victims, to permit a hard and fast exclusion of otherwise "political" crimes because they had terrible outcomes. It is not possible, conformably with long established case law, to exclude, as such, the crime of murder.

'If the target of the crime is an armed adversary or armed agent of the State (such as a police officer or other public official), it is more likely that the crime should be classified as "political", than if the target comprises innocent civilians, or if there is no particular target and just the indiscriminate use of violence against other human beings. In such cases it is open to the decision-maker, in the context of "non-political crimes" in art 1F(b) of the Convention, to conclude that the crimes are "serious" but outside the scope of the protection for serious "political" crimes.

'In the context of a phrase used in an international treaty it would be inappropriate to apply to its elucidation, doctrines developed peculiarly by the common law, either to exclude classification as "political" by reference to notions of remoteness, or to inculpate persons on the basis of their indirect involvement in a joint criminal enterprise with others. On the other hand, where the achievement of "political" objectives may be viewed as "remote" from the conduct in question, this may just be another way of saying that the true character of the serious crime is "non-political" rather than "political". The mere fact that the person did not actually "pull the trigger" does not necessarily exculpate him or her from involvement in a "serious crime" of the disqualifying kind. Each case must be classified by reference to its own facts.

'Given that what is posited is a "serious crime" and that, ordinarily, the "country of refuge" would be fully entitled to exclude a person suspected of such "criminal conduct" from its community, a duty of protection to refugees that exists under the Convention and municipal law giving it effect, must be one that arises in circumstances where the political element can be seen to outweigh the character of the offence as an ordinary crime. If the humanitarian purpose of the Convention is kept in mind and the decisions are made by people who have some knowledge of the history of the political movements of the world in recent times, the application of the foregoing criteria will be unlikely to involve error of law.' (footnotes omitted) *Minister for Immigration and Multicultural Affairs v Singh* (2002) 186 ALR 393; 23(4) Leg Rep 18; BC200200665; [2002] HCA 7 at [64]–[67], [121]–[126], per Kirby J

SERVANT

Household servant

[For 50 Halsbury's Laws (4th edn) para 543 see now 50 Halsbury's Laws (4th edn) (Reissue) para 599.]

SERVICE

Australia [Infertility Treatment Act 1995 (Vic) s 8 precluded in vitro fertilization techniques to single women inconsistent with (Cth) Sex Discrimination Act 1984 s 22] 'Section 22 deals with discrimination in relation to the provision of goods and services. The word "services" is defined in s 4 so as to include "services of the kind provided by the members of any profession or trade". The primary meaning of "service" given by the *Macquarie Dictionary* as "an act of helpful activity"... In the ordinary use of language, the medical processes answer the description "services of the kind provided by the members of any profession". In legislation such as the Commonwealth Act the word "services" should be given a liberal meaning.'

McBain v Victoria (2000) 99 FCR 116; 177 ALR 320; BC200004187; [2000] FCA 1009 at [10], per Sundberg J

SERVICE (OF DOCUMENTS)

Personally

'It is a method of service which can be effected only in the case of an individual and then only by placing the writ into the hands of the defender or arrestee personally. The writ cannot be said to have been served on him personally if it is put into the hands of someone else, such as an employee, even though this is done at his place of business or at his dwelling place.' *Rae v Calor Gas Ltd* 1995 SCLR 261 at 267, per Lord President Hope

SERVICES

Australia [Section 4(3)(m) of the Admiralty Act 1988 (Cth) provides that: 'A reference in this Act to a general maritime claim is a reference to: ... (m) a claim in respect of goods, materials or services (including stevedoring and lighterage services) supplied or to be supplied to a ship for its operation or maintenance ...'] 'Although it is reasonable to envisage some overlapping between the various subparagraphs of s 4(3), it is also reasonable, in my opinion, to assume that the word "services" in s 4(3)(m) was intended to do extra work and cover more areas than those specifically provided for elsewhere in the other subsections. Clearly enough, it would cover assistance in the mooring of the vessel by line-handling and the like, activities which were held in *Corps v Owners of the Paddle Steamer "Queen of the South"* (*The "Queen of the South"*) [1968] P 449 not to fall within the concept of the supply of goods and materials.

'I can see no warrant for restricting the term "services" to benefits provided by way of work and labour as opposed to the provision of goods and materials. I reject this narrow view of the meaning of the word ...

'Although the word "service" is one in very common use, it has a surprisingly diverse range of meanings. Reference to standard dictionaries demonstrates that from an etymological origin in the latin words for "slavery" and "slave", the word has come to be applied in fields as disparate as domestic employment, the armed forces, state bureaucracy, the provision of gas, water and electricity to buildings, transport in accordance with regular timetables, legal procedures, animal procreative activity, religious ritual, and tennis. There is undoubted difficulty in finding a common thread of meaning. Nevertheless, meaning must be attributed to the word as used in this subsection.

'In my view, it may be regarded as plain that the use of the term "services" is indicative of an intention by the legislature to cover a wider field of activity than that previously covered by the concept of the supply of "necessaries" although, clearly enough, claims previously held as being for necessaries such as dock dues, canal dues, custom house and immigration service fees, telegrams and disbursements for quay rent would fall within the concept: see Hetherington, *Annotated Admiralty Legislation*, p 47.' *Port of Geelong Authority v The Ship 'Bass Reefer'* (1992) 109 ALR 505 at 517–518, per Foster J

Australia 'The term "services" [in the Equal Opportunity Act 1984 (WA) s 4(1)] has a wide meaning. The *Macquarie Dictionary* relevantly defines it to include "an act of helpful activity"; "the providing or a provider of some accommodation required by the public, as messengers, telegraphs, telephones, or conveyance"; "the organised system of apparatus, appliances, employees, etc., for supplying some accommodation required by the public"; "the supplying or the supplier of water, gas, or the like to the public"; and "the duty or work of public servants".' *IW v City of Perth* (1997) 146 ALR 696 at 701; BC9703257 at 6, per Brennan CJ and McHugh J

New Zealand [Section 2 of the Goods and Services Tax Act 1985 provides that ' "Services" means anything which is not goods or money' and by Section 8 of the Goods and Services Tax Act 1985 'Subject to this Act, a tax, to be known as goods and services tax, shall be charged in accordance with the provisions of this Act at the rate of [12.5 percent] on the supply (but not including an exempt supply) in New Zealand of goods and services, …'.] 'While I recognise the width of the definitions of services and supply, I regard it as conceptually unsound in legal terms to say that trustees of a voluntary settlement supply services to the settlor of the trust or to the beneficiaries when all they are doing is to perform the terms of the trust.

'When coupled with the definitions of taxable activity and consideration, to which I shall come, and in spite of the width of those definitions, the concept of supplying services has a reciprocal connotation. It is not apt to catch the fulfilment by trustees of their duties as such, albeit that such fulfilment will necessarily, in a direct or indirect way, be of benefit to the beneficiaries and the

settlor. For these reasons, I do not consider that the trustees engaged in any supply of services in terms of s 8.' *Chatham Islands Enterprise Trust v Commissioner of Inland Revenue* [1999] 2 NZLR 388 at 395, CA, per Tipping J

Canada '[16] If one strips s 2(1) [of the *Builders Lien Act*] to its essentials, and substitutes for the defined words the definitions contained in s 1, s 2(1) would read this way:

> A person engaged by an owner to provide *a service in relation to any physical improvement* attached to or intended to become part of the land has a lien for the price of the unpaid service on …

'[17] In construing the section, the definition of "services" which specifically includes those provided by an architect or engineer and the rental of equipment with operator, must be kept in mind.

'[18] The question in this case is, having regard for the definition of services, whether it can be said that air transportation of personnel to the site of an improvement is a service "in relation to" that improvement.

…

'[52] I come then to the meaning of the word "services" as defined in the Act. Counsel for the plaintiff says that, given the inclusive nature of the definition, there is no reason to limit its meaning to the services specifically identified as coming within its scope.

'[53] There are two matters that I would note in this connection. The first is that in the 1996 Act, services was not a defined term. The word "work" was defined in the old Act, as in the new, to mean "work, labour or *services*, skilled or unskilled, on an improvement". The second matter is that there had been much prior litigation as to whether provision of architectural services gave rise to lien entitlement. For example, in the *John Perkins* case (*supra*) in 1984, the court held that it did not have to decide whether a lien could have been claimed, because there was no improvement to the land to or for which the architectural services could have been said to be provided. The entitlement to a lien for architectural services was left in doubt.

'[54] With those two factors in mind, it seems to me the addition of the present definition of services to the 1997 Act was intended to remedy the uncertainty that previously existed with respect to the three types of services identified in the definition. It may well be, as counsel for the plaintiff contends, that that goal could have been achieved without resorting to the "inclusive" definition of services. However, viewed against the history of builders' lien litigation involving architects, a reasonable interpretation of the definition, in a statute which affects property rights, would be to limit the definition to those services specifically identified as included, rather than read it as a limitless expansion of services that could come within its meaning.

...

'[55] We were referred to many other cases from British Columbia and elsewhere in addition to those already cited, but I do not find it necessary or helpful to refer to most of them. *Redheugh Construction Ltd. v. Coyne Contracting Ltd.* (1996), 26 B.C.L.R. (3d) 3 (C.A.) was particularly relied on by counsel for the plaintiff. In that case, this court held that administrative costs claimed by a subcontractor were recoverable because they contributed directly to improvements on the construction project. The argument on the plaintiff's behalf is that if the costs of air transport for personnel had been included as an administrative cost of subcontractors providing a service to the development of this mine, such costs could have been included in the subcontractor's lien. In my view, whether that result would follow depends on whether the subcontractor's services related directly to the construction of the mine, or formed an integral part of its physical construction.

'[56] I conclude that the phrase "in relation to" in s 2(1) and in the definition of contractor is to be read as meaning "in direct relation to", or "in relation to an integral part of the improvement", and that the definition of "services" is not to be read as limitless, despite its inclusive nature. Rather, it is to be read as remedial, to include those specified services whose inclusion might previously have been in doubt.' *Northern Thunderbird Air Ltd v Royal Oak Mines Inc* (2002) 209 DLR (4th) 681 at 686, 692–694, BCCA, per Finch CJBC

SERVICING

Canada [Insurance coverage applied to use of replacement vehicle substituted on servicing of insured vehicle. Insured was injured when going in second vehicle to get gas for insured vehicle.] '... "service" [includes] "supply the needs of" (Shorter Oxford English Dictionary) and "provision of what is necessary for due maintenance of thing *or operation*" (Concise Oxford Dictionary), and "to make fit for service, as by inspecting, adjusting, repairing, *refuelling* etc." (Webster's New World Dictionary, College Edition).' *Clark v Waterloo Insurance Co* (1992) 98 DLR (4th) 689 at 693, per Zalev J (Ont Ct (Gen Div))

SET-OFF

[For 42 Halsbury's Laws (4th edn) para 406 see now 42 Halsbury's Laws (4th edn) (Reissue) para 406.]

SETTLE

Australia [Section 112 of the Victorian Civil and Administrative Tribunal Act 1998 (Vic) provides that a party who makes an offer to settle a proceeding is entitled to an order that the party who did not accept the offer pay all the costs incurred by the offering party after the offer was made.] 'What is critical, I think, is the use made of the word "settle" in other and neighbouring sections of the [Victorian Civil and Administrative Tribunal Act 1998 (Vic)]. As Mr Justice Batt pointed out in the course of argument, s 83(2)(b) describes one function of a compulsory conference as being "to promote a settlement of the proceeding", and s 84 authorises the Tribunal to require the personal attendance at a compulsory conference of the party personally or "a representative who has authority to settle the proceeding on behalf of the party". In s 90, the mediator must notify the Tribunal if the parties "agree to settle a proceeding as a result of mediation", which means no more than that the mediation has been successful. By s 93, the Tribunal is authorised to make "any orders necessary to give effect to the settlement" if "the parties agree to settle a proceeding at any time". In all of these sections, it cannot be the case that the word "settle", or its derivative "settlement", is used to require some element of compromise; it would surely be enough, in any of these cases, if one party were to concede everything and the other party were to succeed wholly. And according to the dictionaries the word "settle" can wear a meaning that imports no element of compromise [*Butterworths Australian Legal Dictionary* (1997) "settlement", contrast "compromise" and "offer of compromise"; *Oxford English Dictionary* (2nd ed) "settle" (meanings 33 and 34), contrast "compromise" (meanings 3 and 4), *Macquarie Dictionary* (1981) "settle" (meaning 16), *Black's Law Dictionary* (7th ed) "settlement" (meaning 2).]. For example, in *Black's Law Dictionary* (7th ed) the meaning of "settlement" is given as simply "an agreement ending a dispute or law suit".' *Transport Accident Commission v Coyle* BC200108110; [2001] VSCA 236 at [27], per Phillips JA

SETTLEMENT

[For 42 Halsbury's Laws (4th edn) para 601 see now 42 Halsbury's Laws (4th edn) (Reissue) para 601.]

Compound settlement

[For 42 Halsbury's Laws (4th edn) para 601 see now 42 Halsbury's Laws (4th edn) (Reissue) para 601.]

Marriage settlement

[For 42 Halsbury's Laws (4th edn) para 603 see now 42 Halsbury's Laws (4th edn) (Reissue) para 603.]

Post-nuptial settlement

[For 42 Halsbury's Laws (4th edn) para 604 see now 42 Halsbury's Laws (4th edn) (Reissue) para 604.]

Protective settlement

[For 42 Halsbury's Laws (4th edn) para 607 see now 42 Halsbury's Laws (4th edn) (Reissue) para 607.]

Strict settlement

[For 42 Halsbury's Laws (4th edn) para 606 see now 42 Halsbury's Laws (4th edn) (Reissue) para 606.]

SETTLEMENT OF PROPERTY

Australia [Section 120(8) of the Bankruptcy Act 1966 (Cth) provides that 'settlement of property' includes any disposition of property. Section 120(1) voids a settlement of property occurring within two years before bankruptcy or after it where the settlement is not made in favour of a purchaser or encumbrancer in good faith and for valuable consideration.] 'I consider that in the light of the decision of the Full Court of the Supreme Court of Queensland in *Tri-Continental* (1987) 73 ALR 433 and the reasoning of that court in relation to the authorities, the view stated by Gough [W J Gough, *Company Charges*, Butterworths, London, 1978, pp 17, 120] is the present correct position of the law in Australia. It is consistent with the first instance decisions of judges of this court in *McGoldrick* (Olney J, 26 February 1992, unreported) and *Zampatti* (Lee J, 21 April 1993, unreported). In short, an equitable charge which is not a floating charge confers an equitable interest and a proprietary interest so that its creation is capable of being a disposition of property and therefore a settlement within s 120 of the Act. However, in the case of a floating charge, no

equity is created until crystallisation so that there is no conferral of an equitable interest or a proprietary interest by the creation of a floating charge. The consequence is that a floating charge cannot be a disposition of property for the purposes of s 120 of the Act.' *Lyford v Commonwealth Bank of Australia* (1995) 130 ALR 267 at 273, per Nicholson J

SETTLOR

New Zealand '[39] The most common definition of "settlor" appears to be "one who makes a settlement". This seems obvious, and is less than helpful as "settlement" appears to be equally amorphous in meaning. 42 *Halsbury's Laws of England* states at para 601 (p 303) that "settlement" has no generally accepted definition, but that:

> "A possible definition of 'settlement' is any disposition of property, of whatever nature, by any instrument or instruments, by which trusts are constituted for the purpose of regulating the enjoyment of the settled property successively among the persons or classes of persons nominated by the settlor."

'[40] Thus the main factor which may define the act of settlement, at least in the context of a trust, is that it results in the creation of trust obligations in respect of the property settled. The act of creating a trust occurs when trust obligations are created in the trustees with respect to a particular item of property. This means that, technically, a trust is created every time further property is added to a trust fund, because the trustees are acquiring obligations in respect of further property.' *Commissioner of Inland Revenue v Dick* [2002] 2 NZLR 560 at 546 per Glazebrook J

SEVERAL

New Zealand [The plaintiff and defendants agreed that security for a loan would be supported by the 'several' (but not joint) guarantees of the shareholders.] 'In my view the proper interpretation is that those words conveyed not necessarily the legal meaning of the word "several" as contrasted with "joint", but the word in its meaning as "distinct" or "individual" or "respective". In the context of this arrangement it meant the guarantors would be liable proportionate to their shareholding under their guarantees to the extent of the company's indebtedness to the bank at any time. Not to give effect to this carefully expressed formula would in effect involve the individual shareholders in a form of joint liability by reason now of the default of some of them.' *National Bank of New Zealand Ltd v Murland* [1991] 3 NZLR 86 at 92, per Heron J

SEVERANCE

Canada 'There must be a "severance" of the portion from the public service. The term should be given its ordinary meaning. The *Oxford English Dictionary*, 2nd ed., defines "sever" as "To put apart, set asunder …; to part or separate by putting in different places … To disjoin, dissociate, disunite". The requirement is minimal; it involves the splitting-off of certain employees from a portion of the public service. This separation might occur in many different ways, including the letting-go, release or dropping of the employees from the public service. It should be noted that there is nothing in the meaning of the word "severance" ("*séparation*" in the French version) or in the wording of section 47 [of the *Public Service Staff Relations Act*] which requires a "sale", "transfer", "lease" or "other disposition", which apply to situations governed by section 44. This does not mean, however, that a sale of a portion of the public service, if such were entered into, might not amount to a severance.' *Public Service Alliance of Canada v Bombardier Inc* [2001] 2 FC 429 at 442, CA, per Linden JA

SEVERE

Canada '[36] It is evident from a review of the Board's disability decisions, particularly its recent case law, that the Board's position regarding the severity requirement in subparagraph 42(2)(*a*)(i) of the [*Canada Pension*] *Plan* has been applied inconsistently. In the recent cases, there has been no discernible reason for the change in approach to the definition of "severe" in the *Plan*. For this reason, it becomes necessary for this Court to give direction concerning the proper legal test to be applied in determining whether an applicant suffers from a "severe" disability within the meaning of the *Plan*.

(c) *The Appropriate Legal Test for Disability under the Plan*

'[37] Except for one case, none of the recent decisions of the Board has analyzed fully the text of subparagraph 42(2)(*a*)(i) of the *Plan*. That one occasion was the Board's relatively recent decision in *Barlow v. Minister of Human Resources Development* (1999), C.E.B. & P.G.R. 8846 (P.A.B.). It is worth repeating the central passage of the Board's decision in that case:

Is her disability sufficiently severe that it prevents her from regularly pursuing any substantially gainful occupation?

To address this question, we deem it appropriate to analyze the above wording to ascertain the intent of the legislation:

> Regular is defined in the *Greater Oxford Dictionary* as "usual, standard or customary".
>
> Regularly—"at regular intervals or times."
>
> Substantial—"having substance, actually existing, not illusory, of real importance or value, practical."
>
> Gainful—"lucrative, remunerative paid employment."
>
> Occupation—"temporary or regular employment, security of tenure."

Applying these definitions to Mrs. Barlow's physical condition as of December, 1997, it is difficult, if not impossible, to find that she was at age 57 in a position to qualify for any usual or customary employment, which actually exists, is not illusory, and is of real importance.

'[38] This analysis of subparagraph 42(2)(*a*)(i) strongly suggests a legislative intention to apply the severity requirement in a "real world" context. Requiring that an applicant be incapable *regularly* of pursuing any *substantially gainful* occupation is quite different from requiring that an applicant be incapable *at all times* of pursuing *any conceivable* occupation. Each word in the subparagraph must be given meaning and when read in that way the subparagraph indicates, in my opinion, that Parliament viewed as severe any disability which renders an applicant incapable of pursuing with consistent frequency any truly remunerative occupation. In my view, it follows from this that the hypothetical occupations which a decision-maker must consider cannot be divorced from the particular circumstances of the applicant, such as age, education level, language proficiency and past work and life experience.

…

'[42] … The test for severity is not that a disability be "total". In order to express the more lenient test for severity under the *Plan*, therefore, the drafters introduced the notion of severity as the inability regularly to pursue any substantially gainful occupation. The clear wording of the legislation, the companion provisions in the *Regulations*, and the clear intent of the drafters all indicate with equal force that the crucial phrase in subparagraph 42(2)(*a*)(i)'s severity definition cannot be ignored or pared down.

'[43] But this is precisely what the Board has done in the present case. The Board has adopted the strict abstract approach to the severity requirement in subparagraph 42(2)(*a*)(i) without analysing all of the legislative language. For ease of reference, the Board's analysis of the severity definition in subparagraph 42(2)(*a*)(i) is repeated below (see page 10 of the decision):

> It is very important to note that the words "regularly pursuing any substantially gainful occupation ..." means just that: *any* occupation. It is not, as some insurance policies say, "... any occupation for which the applicant is reasonably suited ..." It is *any* occupation, even though the applicant may lack education, special skills, or basic language.
> A second factor is availability of work. This is not a matter that is or can be considered by this Board. So the state of the local job market is irrelevant: It is legally assumed that work is available to do. [Emphasis in original.]

'It is evident, to my mind, that the Board in this case has effectively read out of the severity definition the words "regularly", "substantially" and "gainful". In this way, the Board has reduced the legal test to the following: is the applicant incapable of pursuing any occupation? This approximates the "total" disability test eschewed by the drafters of the *Plan*. Indeed, the Board's repeated emphasis on the word "any" appears to have been a contributing factor in its misinterpretation of the statutory test for severity.' *Villani v Canada (Attorney General)* (2001) 205 DLR (4th) 58 at 74–75, 77, FCA, per Isaac JA

SEWER

[For 38 Halsbury's Laws (4th edn) para 339 see now 38 Halsbury's Laws (4th edn) (Reissue) para 517.]

SEX

See also DISCRIMINATION

[Appeal by applicant appellant against a decision of the employment tribunal in respect of his claim that he had been discriminated against unlawfully on grounds of sex, contrary to Council Directive (EEC) 76/207 (OJ 1976 L39 p 40) (the equal treatment directive) and s 6 of the Sex Discrimination Act 1975 (SDA).] 'It was not disputed that the appellant's employment in the Royal Air Force was terminated by reason of his admitted homosexuality but the substance of the decision against him is that the SDA, in so far as it refers to the word "sex", is concerned with gender and not sexual orientation. The admitted reason therefore for the termination of the appellant's employment does not fall, in the view of the employment tribunal, within the scope of discrimination envisaged by the SDA.

'It has to be noted that the principal argument before the tribunal concerned whether or not, there being uncertainty in the law as to the proper definition or construction to put upon the word "sex" in the SDA, the tribunal should make a reference to the Court of Justice of the European Communities. It also has to be noted that subsequent to the hearing but prior to the issue of the judgment, the European Court of Human Rights in Strasbourg issued a judgment best found as *Smith and Grady v UK* (1999) 29 EHRR 493 in which it held that investigations by the Ministry of Defence into the homosexual orientation of the two appellants violated their human rights in terms of art 8 of the European Convention for the Protection of Human Rights and Fundamental Freedoms (Rome, 4 November 1950; TS 71 (1953); Cmnd 9885 (the convention). The basic facts of this case and its sister case, *Lustig-Prean and Beckett v UK* (1999) Times, 11 October, are indistinguishable from the present case inasmuch that all four applicants in the Strasbourg court were maintaining violation of their human rights in terms of the convention by reason of being dismissed from the services as a consequence of being homosexual, in terms of the policy then adopted by the Ministry of Defence which was to the effect that homosexuality is incompatible with service in the Armed Forces and that persons who were known to be homosexual and to engage in homosexual activity are administratively discharged from the Armed Forces. The European Court of Human Rights upheld their contention with the result that subsequent to the hearing in this case before the tribunal below, for the first time the European Court of Human Rights has interpreted the convention so as to protect the rights of homosexuals, albeit under the right to privacy.

...

'The current state of the law before us is, therefore, within the United Kingdom, that it has been established by the English courts that the word "sex" has been clearly interpreted as being restricted to a gender interpretation and not a sexual orientation interpretation while the opposite interpretation has been put upon the word both indirectly in *Smith and Grady v UK* [(1999) 29 EHRR 493] and directly in *Salgueiro's* case [*Salgueiro da Silva Mouta v Portugal*, unreported case of the European Court of Human Rights dated 29 December 1999] by the European Court of Human Rights ...

...

'We do not consider that the two recent decisions of the European Court of Human Rights and, in particular, the Portuguese case of *Salgueiro*, have created an ambiguity but rather that they have focussed one in the relevant word "sex" found both in the SDA and art 14 of the convention. Intrinsically, the Oxford University Dictionary (1989 edn) inter alia includes a definition under the word "sex" of "a third sex" which undoubtedly refers to homosexuality in both men and women. Since the word also can obviously mean "gender" as interpreted by the English courts an obvious ambiguity arises on the face of the record. Extrinsically, the European Court of Human Rights has now expressly included sexual orientation in the definition of the word "sex", as found in their convention, we consider there is the classic example of a statutory ambiguity before us from two competent authorities and we therefore consider we have a choice of interpretation.

'If this analysis is correct we have thereafter no hesitation in favouring the wider interpretation. The only case presented to us since the obvious change of circumstances created by the two recent European Court of Human Rights cases, is that of *Pearce* [*Pearce v Governing Body of Mayfield Secondary School* [2000] ICR 920] which seems to have concentrated upon the existing state of the English law and certainly there is no indication that the convention cases were laid before the tribunal. In any event the substance of that case was dealing with comparators and applied *Smith v Gardner Merchant Ltd* [[1998] 3 All ER 852, [1999] ICR 134, CA] which in its terms is very clear.

'In reaching our conclusion we have not been greatly influenced by the case of *Grant v South-West Trains Ltd* [Case C–249/96 [1998] All ER (EC) 193, [1998] ECR I–621, ECJ], since the European Court of Justice was then considering the issue of equal pay and not concerned directly with the definition of the word "sex".

'In our opinion, accordingly, on the present state of the law, stated at the date of the dissemination of this judgment, the word "sex" in the SDA should be interpreted to include "on grounds of sexual orientation". In reaching this conclusion, we admit no criticism of the tribunal below who were directed to the essential issue of the reference against what appeared to be settled law. It is simply, that in our opinion, by the time the matter has reached us, matters have moved on.' *MacDonald v Ministry of Defence* [2001] 1 All ER 620 at 623, 626, 630, EAT, per Lord Johnston

New Zealand [Section 3 of the Films, Videos, and Publications Classifications Act 1993 provides:

3. Meaning of "objectionable" — (1) For the purposes of this Act, a publication is objectionable if it describes, depicts, expresses, or otherwise deals with matters such as sex, horror, crime, cruelty, or violence in such a manner that the availability of the publication is likely to be injurious to the public good.]

'In an enactment directed at discrimination, the word "sex" may be tenably defined to include "gender", but that extension would not ordinarily be appropriate in a statute dealing with the censorship of pornographic sex. The word must necessarily take its meaning from its statutory context. A meaning excluding sexual orientation is also intimated by the other words with which the word "sex" is associated, that is, "horror, crime, cruelty, or violence". Pornographic sex is compatible with these concepts; sexual orientation is not. Subsections (2) and (3) further contribute to this meaning referring to socially unacceptable acts for sexual purposes or various forms of deviant sexual conduct. Consequently, in using the word "sex", subs (1) is essentially concerned with the depiction of unacceptable sexual conduct or activity. The concept of sexual orientation does not fit this description. Nor can comment on sexual orientation as a "lifestyle" tenably fall within the rubric of sex or a matter such as sex.' *Living Word Distributors Ltd v Human Rights Action Group Inc (Wellington)* [2000] 3 NZLR 570 at 592, CA, per Thomas J

SEX
DISCRIMINATION *SEE* DISCRIMINATION

SEXUAL ADVANCES

Australia 'I do not accept that the expression "sexual advances" is intended to refer only to repeated acts to the exclusion of a single event. In ordinary usage, "advance" may mean (as the *Oxford English Dictionary* 2nd ed tells us) "a personal approach, a movement towards closer acquaintance and understanding; an overture" and, especially in the plural, it may mean "amorous overtures or approaches". As the examples given in that dictionary make plain, "advances", in the sense of amorous overtures or approaches, can refer to a single event just as much as to a series of events.' *Spencer v Dowling* [1997] 2 VR 127 at 156; BC9603333 at 17, per Hayne JA

SEXUAL ASSAULT

Canada 'To begin with, I agree, as I have indicated, that the test for the recognition of sexual assault does not depend solely on contact with specific areas of the human anatomy. I am also of the view that sexual assault need not involve an attack by a member of one sex upon a member of the other; it could be perpetrated upon one of the same sex. I agree as well with those who say that the new offence is truly new and does not merely duplicate the offences it replaces. Accordingly, the definition of the term "sexual assault" and the reach of the offence it describes is not necessarily limited to the scope of its predecessors. I would consider as well that the test for its recognition should be objective.

'While it is clear that the concept of a sexual assault differs from that of the former indecent assault, it is nevertheless equally clear that the terms overlap in many respects and sexual assault in many cases will involve the same sort of conduct that formerly would have justified a conviction for an indecent assault.' *R v Chase* (1987) 45 DLR (4th) 98 at 103–104, SCC, per McIntyre J

SEXUAL CONNECTION

New Zealand [Section 128 of the Crimes Act 1961 states:

'...
(5) For the purposes of this section, sexual connection means—
(a) Connection occasioned by the penetration of the [genitalia] or the anus of any person by—
(i) Any part of the body of any other person; or
(ii) Any object held or manipulated by any other person,—
otherwise than for bona fide medical purposes:
(b) Connection between the mouth or tongue of any person and any part of the genitalia of any other person:

(c) The continuation of sexual connection as described in either paragraph (a) or paragraph (b) of this subsection.']

'[17] As a matter of statutory interpretation it must follow, as Mr France submitted, that a person, whether male or female, can be charged with unlawful sexual connection with another person, again whether male or female, if, without the consent of that other person or without the actor believing in the other person's consent on reasonable grounds, the actor does acts which come within the definition of "sexual connection" in s 128(5). The prosecution's first task under s 128(5) is to prove sexual connection. That can arise through proof of:
●penetration of the genitalia or anus of any person, male or female, by any part of the body or any object held by any other person, again male or female (other than for bona fide medical purposes); or
●connection between the mouth or tongue of any person, male or female, and any part of the genitalia of any other person, again either male or female; or
●continuation of such sexual connection (s 128(5)(c)).
(The fact that penetration of the male genitalia would only arise in most unusual circumstances does not affect the question of interpretation.)' *R v A* [2003] 1 NZLR 1 at 5, per cur

SHACK

[For 6 Halsbury's Laws (4th edn) para 520 see now 6 Halsbury's Laws (4th edn) (2003 Reissue) para 420.]

SHALL

Australia 'The *Interpretation Act* 1967 (ACT) (the *Interpretation Act*) and its effect on the use in statutes of the expressions "shall" and "may" was considered by me in *Commissioner for Housing for the Australian Capital Territory v Smith* (unreported, Supreme Court, ACT, Higgins J, 14 March 1995). The submission there being considered was whether a power conferred in terms that some act "may" be performed created a mandatory obligation to perform it. The present contention refers to the obverse proposition, that is, that "shall" might, at times, import a discretion rather than a duty to act. It is now to be assumed, it seems to me, that the legislature will always have intended to confer a discretion where "may" has been used in an enactment and to have created a duty to act when the term "shall" has been used. That, at least, is the case with enactments to which the *Interpretation Act* applies.' *R v Medical Board of Australian Capital Territory; Ex parte Davis* (1995) 125 FLR 401 at 406, per Higgins J

SHALL HAVE REGARD TO THE LAW

New Zealand [Section 18(6) of the Disputes Tribunals Act 1988 requires that the Disputes Tribunal 'shall have regard to the law when determining disputes'.] 'In my view, that obligation requires the referee to consider any legal principles of which he or she is or may be aware in a fair and unbiased manner, and to apply the law as he or she understands it in an impartial manner to the facts as the referee finds them, save only when strict observance of those rules would, in the referee's view, prevent determination of the dispute according to the substantial merits and justice of the case.' *NZI Insurance New Zealand Ltd v Auckland District Court* [1993] 3 NZLR 453 at 464, per Thorp J

SHAM

Australia 'A "sham" is therefore, for the purposes of Australian law, something that is intended to be mistaken for something else or that is not really what it purports to be. It is a spurious imitation, a counterfeit, a disguise or a false front. It is not genuine or true, but something made in imitation of something else or made to appear to be something which it is not. It is something which is false or deceptive.' *Sharrment Pty Ltd v Official Trustee in Bankruptcy* (1988) 18 FCR 449 at 454, per Lockhart J

Australia 'A common intention between the parties to the apparent transaction that it be a disguise for some other and real transaction or for no transaction at all.' *Richard Walter Pty Ltd v Commissioner of Taxation* (1996) 67 FCR 243 at 257–258, per Hill J

SHARE OF THE PARTNERSHIP ASSETS

'[1] The issue in this appeal centres on the meaning of the words "his share of the partnership assets" in s 42(1) of the Partnership Act 1890 (the 1890 Act, and references in this judgment to sections are to sections of that Act). In his judgment, which is reported at [2005] EWHC 43 (Ch), [2005] 1 All ER 990, [2005] 1 WLR 1979, Lightman J, upholding Master Bowles, held that the reference to a share in s 42(1) was to the partner's share in the proprietary ownership of the assets belonging to the partnership.

He also held that, in a case such as this, where there were two partners and there was nothing to displace what might be called the presumption of equality, it effectively meant half the gross assets of the partnership.

...

'[14] The resolution of the first issue turns substantially on s 42(1), which provides as follows:

"Where any member of a firm has died or otherwise ceased to be a partner, and the surviving or continuing partners carry on the business of the firm with its capital or assets without any final settlement of accounts as between the firm and the outgoing partner or his estate, then, in the absence of any agreement to the contrary, the outgoing partner or his representatives is entitled at the option of himself or his representatives to such share of the profits made since the dissolution as the Court may find to be attributable to the use of his share of the partnership assets, or to interest at the rate of five per cent. per annum on the amount of his share of the partnership assets."

...

'[18] With that, I now turn to the meaning of s 42(1). The concept of "a partner's share of the partnership assets", at any time before the end of the winding-up process in accordance with s 44, is conceptually somewhat opaque. In a case to which I will have to return, *Popat v Shonchhatra* [1997] 3 All ER 800 at 804, [1997] 1 WLR 1367 at 1372, in an uncontroversial passage, Nourse LJ said this:

"Although it is both customary and convenient to speak of a partner's 'share' of the partnership assets, that is not a truly accurate description of his interest in them, at all events so long as the partnership is a going concern. While each partner has a proprietary interest in each and every asset, he has no entitlement to any specific asset and, in consequence, no right, without the consent of the other partners or partner, to require the whole or even a share of any particular asset to be vested in him. On dissolution the position is in substance not much different, the partnership property falling to be applied, subject to ss 40 to 43 (if and so far as applicable), in accordance with ss 39 and 44 ... As part of that process, each partner in a solvent partnership is presumptively entitled to payment of what is due from the firm to him in respect of capital before division of the ultimate residue in the shares in which profits are divisible; see s 44 ... It is only at that stage that a partner can accurately be said to be entitled to a share of anything, which, in the absence of agreement to the contrary, will be a share of cash."

...

'[49] ... I am disposed to reach a different conclusion from that reached by Lightman J in that it appears to me that the reference in s 42(1) to "the partnership assets" is to the net partnership assets, and not the gross partnership assets. However, that would not necessarily be determinative of the first of the two issues on this appeal, because the basis for assessing the "share" in that section must also be determined. Having said that, many of the reasons for arriving at the conclusion that the reference to "assets" is to net assets appear to me to carry with them the notion that the "share" referred to is the actual share of those assets attributable to the partner concerned in the net assets in the winding-up process in accordance with s 44. Further, logic and commercial common sense (which often, but not invariably, march together) suggest that if the value of "the partnership assets" in s 42(1) is to be assessed by reference to the present value of the prospective surplus, then the partner's "share" under that section must be based on the actual proportion of those assets to which he would be entitled.

'[50] In other words, if the reference to "the partnership assets" in s 42(1) is to what Buckley J called the surplus, i e what remains out of the gross assets, for distribution between the partners, after all debts and other liabilities of the partnership have been met, it seems to follow that the "share" for the purposes of s 42(1) is to be assessed by reference to the share which the partner in question is entitled to receive at the conclusion of the winding-up process. Indeed, it seems to me that the way in which the observations in the cases and textbook to which I have referred are expressed make that conclusion virtually inescapable.' *Sandhu v Gill* [2005] EWCA Civ 1297 at [1], [14], [18], [49]–[50], [2006] 2 All ER 22, per Neuberger LJ

SHARES

Company

[For 7 Halsbury's Laws (4th edn) para 415 see now 7(1) Halsbury's Laws (4th edn) (2004 Reissue) para 820.]

Preference

[For 7 Halsbury's Laws (4th edn) para 176 see now 7(1) Halsbury's Laws (4th edn) (2004 Reissue) para 776.]

New Zealand [Section 21(4)(b) of the Waikato Electricity Authority Act 1988 begins 'The Authority shall have the power, on such terms as it thinks fit, to—... (b) Subscribe for, purchase, acquire, hold, sell, transfer, or dispose of shares ...'.] 'As to that word, "shares", a pre-emptive right is not a present right in the form of a share. A pre-emptive right to a share is an inchoate right. It is a right of first refusal. Moreover, a share has to come into existence—it has to "issue". Certain formalities are required. Under s 90 of the Companies Act 1955 every company must issue a share certificate within two months of allotment (unless the conditions of issue otherwise provide). The certificate is the (presumptive: s 91 of the Companies Act 1955) documentary evidence of title. Once the share has come into existence it amounts to a chose in action.' *Hamilton City Council v Waikato Electricity Authority* [1994] 1 NZLR 741 at 751, per Hammond J

SHIP

[For 43 Halsbury's Laws (4th edn) para 91 see now 43(1) Halsbury's Laws (4th edn) (Reissue) para 102.]

[An offence under the Merchant Shipping Act 1995, s 58 of doing of an act which causes death or serious injury to any person applies, inter alia, to the master of a ship, and under s 313(1) 'ship' includes 'every description of vessel used in navigation'. The question arose whether a jet ski was a 'ship'.] '[11] Part 1 of the 1995 Act deals with the registration of British ships. Section 10 requires the Secretary of State to make regulations providing for the registration of such ships. He has done so. Under these regulations a register of British ships is maintained. A witness statement from the operations manager responsible for this register informs us that 646 "wet bikes" are registered. (For copyright reasons jet skis are described as wet bikes on the register). Provided that a British owner can submit all the appropriate documentation, which includes a survey certificate for tonnage measurement and a completed "carving and marking note", a wet bike will be registered.

'[12] ... We suspect that the reason why so many jet skis have been registered may be because those providing finance for their purchase have required this. We can see the attraction of giving a broad definition to "ship" for the purposes of registration of title. Nonetheless, the fact that such craft are registered does not demonstrate conclusively that they fall within the definition of "ships" under the 1995 Act–see *European and*

Australian Royal Mail Co Ltd v P & O Steam Navigation Co (1866) 14 LT 704.

...

'[14] Mr Teare accepted that one would not describe the Waverunner [jet ski] as a "ship", giving that word its normal English meaning. He submitted, however, that the normal meaning was extended by the definition in s 313 of the 1995 Act as including "every description of vessel used in navigation". Mr Persey argued that there were two reasons why the Waverunner did not fall within the definition of a "ship". The first was that by reason of the nature of its construction, the Waverunner could not be described as a vessel: the second was that the Waverunner was not "used in navigation".

'[15] Mr Persey, understandably, put at the forefront of his case the decision of Sheen J, sitting in the Admiralty Court, in *Steedman v Scofield* [1992] 2 Lloyd's Rep 163. That case involved a collision between a jet ski and a speedboat. The owner of the latter brought a claim in negligence and the defendants sought to have it struck out as time barred under s 8 of the Maritime Conventions Act 1911. The time limit under that section related to any claim against a "vessel". Section 10 of the 1911 Act provided that it was to be construed as one with the Merchant Shipping Acts. Section 742 of the Merchant Shipping Act 1894 provided:

> "'VESSEL' includes any ship or boat, or any other description of vessel used in navigation; 'SHIP' includes every description of vessel used in navigation not propelled by oars ..."

Sheen J held that the jet ski did not fall within this definition.

...

'[17] The recorder, understandably, contrasted Sheen J's jet ski with the Waverunner which is the subject of this appeal. The latter has a concave hull that gives the craft sufficient buoyancy to enable three riders to sit astride the saddle. The craft bears a much closer resemblance to a boat than that which Sheen J had to consider. We do not consider that it is possible to conclude, on the basis of its construction alone, that it is incapable of falling within the first part of the definition of a ship in s 313 of the 1995 Act, namely "every description of vessel". Of much more importance is the qualification that the definition adds to that phrase, namely "used in navigation".

...

'[27] ... [W]e have come to the conclusion that for a vessel to be "used in navigation" under the Merchant Shipping Acts it is not a necessary requirement that it should be used in transporting persons or property by water to an intended destination, although this may well have been what navigation usually involved when the early Merchant Shipping Acts were enacted. What is critical in the present case is, however, whether, for the purposes of the Merchant Shipping Act 1995 definition of ship, navigation is "the planned or ordered movement from one place to another" or whether it can extend to "messing about in boats" involving no journey at all. As to this question there are a number of relevant authorities to which we have not yet referred.

...

'[32] In considering the effect of these authorities one must not lose sight of the context in which the issue of the meaning of a "ship" arises. This is not easy, as the 1995 Act consolidates a number of statutes dealing with shipping, not least of which is the Merchant Shipping Act 1894, itself a consolidating Act. Whilst, as we have observed, there may be reasons for giving "ship" a wide meaning for the purposes of Pt I which deals with registration, one must not adopt a meaning that makes a nonsense of other provisions which govern the use and operation of ships. Those provisions, as the title "Merchant Shipping" suggests, are primarily aimed at shipping as a trade or business. While it may be possible to extend the meaning of ship to vessels which are not employed in trade or business or which are smaller than those which would normally be so employed, if this is taken too far the reduction can become absurd.

'[33] The meaning that Mr Teare would give to "used in navigation" adds nothing to the ordinary meaning of vessel. We have concluded that those authorities which confine "vessel used in navigation" to vessels which are used to make ordered progression over the water from one place to another are correctly decided. The words "used in navigation" exclude from the definition of "ship or vessel" craft that are simply used for having fun on the water without the object of going anywhere, into which category jet skis plainly fall. Mr Teare pointed out, by reference to a chart of Weymouth Harbour, that jet skis were required to follow a channel from the shore before reaching more open waters in which they could be driven. He argued that this demonstrated that jet skis are used in navigation. We do not agree. Following the channel was merely the means of getting to the area where the jet skis could be used for racing around in the manner which led to the accident with which this case is concerned.' *R v Goodwin* [2005] EWCA

Crim 3184 at [11]–[12], [14]–[15], [17], [27], [32]–[33], [2006] 2 All ER 519, per Lord Phillips of Worth Matravers CJ

Home-going ship

[The Food Act 1984 is largely repealed. The definition is not re-enacted in the Food Safety Act 1990.]

Sea-going ship

'[35] We had little argument as to what was meant by a "*sea-going* ship", perhaps because counsel only realised late in the day that s 58 [of the Merchant Shipping Act 1995] only applied to the Waverunner [jet ski] if it was a sea-going ship. Mr Teare submitted that the craft was a sea-going ship because it was being used on the sea as opposed to on inland waters. Mr Persey submitted that the craft was not sea-going because it was being used, as the evidence showed, within the limits of the port of Weymouth.

'[36] Part III of the 1995 Act is headed "Masters and Seamen". Section 24 provides that, with the exception of certain specified sections, Pt III applies only to "ships which are sea-going ships and masters and seamen employed in sea-going ships". Section 58 is one of the excepted sections but, as we have explained at [8] and [9], above, only applies to unregistered ships if they are seagoing ships.

'[37] There is no statutory definition of "sea-going" but a clue to its meaning is given by another excepted section, s 49. This provides:

"(1) Subject to section 48, if a ship to which this section applies goes to sea or attempts to go to sea without carrying such officers and other seamen as it is required to carry under section 47, the owner or master shall be liable–(a) on summary conviction, to a fine not exceeding the statutory maximum; (b) on conviction on indictment, to a fine; and the ship, if in the United Kingdom, may be detained.

(2) This section shall, in its application to ships which are not sea-going ships, have effect as if for the words 'goes to sea or attempts to go to sea' there were substituted the words 'goes on a voyage or excursion or attempts to do so' and the words 'if in the united Kingdom' were omitted."

The inference is that a sea-going ship is a ship which "goes to sea" and that a ship which remains within the United Kingdom is not a sea-going ship.

What is not clear is whether a ship which remains within coastal waters is or is not a sea-going vessel. We need not resolve this question. Section 49 buttresses our conclusion that a vessel used in navigation is a vessel which is used to make ordered progression from one place to another, though we accept that an excursion arguably extends this concept to embrace a round trip.

'[38] A sea-going vessel is a vessel which sets out to sea on a voyage. Thus s 42, which applies only to sea-going ships, implies a term into the contract of employment of seamen that the owner and the master will use all reasonable means to ensure the seaworthiness of the ship "*for the voyage.*"

'[39] The suggestion that the Waverunner was a sea-going ship is worthy of AP Herbert. By no stretch of the imagination could that craft be so described. While jet-skis are used on the sea in proximity to land, they do not go to sea on voyages nor, we suspect would they be seaworthy in heavy weather … ' *R v Goodwin* [2005] EWCA Crim 3184 at [35]–[39], [2006] 2 All ER 519, per Lord Phillips of Worth Matravers CJ

SHIPMENT

[For 41 Halsbury's Laws (4th edn) para 915 see now 42 Halsbury's Laws (4th edn) (Reissue) para 327.]

SHOCK *SEE* NERVOUS

SHOP

[For 20 Halsbury's Laws (4th edn) para 419 see now 20(1) Halsbury's Laws (4th edn) (Reissue) para 530.]

Large shop

[The Sunday Trading Act 1994 provides for restricted opening hours on Sundays for 'large shops'.] 'Large shop' means a shop which has a relevant floor area exceeding 280 square metres; 'relevant floor area', in relation to a shop, means the internal floor area of so much of a shop as consists of or is comprised in a building, but excluding any part of the shop which, throughout the week ending with the Sunday in question (on which the shop is to open), is used neither for the serving of customers in connection with the sale of goods nor for the display of goods. Sunday Trading Act 1994, Sch 1 para 1

See 47 Halsbury's Laws (4th edn) (Reissue) paras 729–735.

Australia [Section 5(1) of the Trading Hours Act 1962 (ACT) defines 'shop' as, inter alia, 'a place, building, stall or tent in which: (a) goods are sold or exposed for sale …'] 'The use of the word "in" gives some guidance to the degree of exclusivity and definition required for a "shop". Ordinarily, a market stall would not be regarded as a "shop": see, for example, *Summers v Roberts* [1944] KB 106; *Greenwood v Whelan* [1967] 1 QB 396. This is said to be because it lacks the necessary degree of permanency, although it seems that the structure, if any, for use in storing or displaying goods need not be more than bare ground, for example, a place or yard for selling vehicles: see *Warley Caravans v Wakelin* (1968) 66 LGR 534.

'Depending on context, however, there is no reason why a market stall could not be a "shop": see, for example, *Barking and Dagenham London Borough Council v Essexplan* (1983) 81 LGR 408.

'In my opinion, the use of the terms "stall or tent" indicate that the Act was intended to apply to any place being occupied for the purpose of the sale of goods, even if the occupation was to be temporary and the associated structures were minimal. That is to be contrasted with the term "shop" in s 6A(1) of the Hawkers Act 1936 (ACT). There a fixed place occupied for the purpose of trading is plainly intended.' *A-G (ACT) v Australian Capital Territory Minister for Land and Planning* (1992) 110 ACTR 1 at 10, per Higgins J

SHORT TERM BASIS

Australia 'The next question is what is meant by "short term basis"? The adjective "short" is used as a measure. Usually these types of adjectives come in pairs, one for each opposite end of a range or scale. Examples abound – old:young; thick:thin; wide:narrow – to mention but a few. The scale that is to be measured by the use of these adjectives will often be imprecise. Thus the opposites in the range may not be identified easily.

'In this case, what is to be measured is a "term" which, in the phrase "short term basis" is a period of time. Presumably the term that is to be measured must be either short or long: though some might say that the term may be short, medium or long. Here we must identify what is a short period. Because there is no definitive measurement available, whether a term is short or not will often be a question of degree. How does one determine on what side of the line a particular term will fall?

'Quite obviously, whether or not a particular term is a short term, cannot be determined as an abstract question. It is necessary to have regard to the thing that is being measured. For example if the thing is a lease, one might say that a three months' lease is a short term lease, but a three year lease is not. If the thing is marriage, a three year marriage might be regarded as of short term, but not if it lasts for fifteen years. If the thing is the life of a human being, fifteen years may be short, while one hundred years would be long.

'How have I been able to make these observations? They are certainly not a priori propositions. The examples chosen are of matters that fall within the ordinary experience of most people. Having regard to that experience, one is able to observe the usual duration of the thing in question, whether it be a lease, a marriage or a life. Then there exists a yardstick against which it is possible to measure whether the duration of the thing under consideration is short or long. This is not to suggest that the answer will always be obvious. Take for example an eighteen month lease, an eight year marriage or a life span of forty-five years? For those cases there may not be a "correct answer". The choice is an exercise of judgment about which reasonable minds may differ.' *Australian Trade Commission v Hellay Laboratories Pty Ltd* BC200106310; [2001] FCA 1436 at [47]–[49], per Wilcox and von Doussa JJ.

SHORTLY AFTER

Australia [Section 65(2)(b) of the Evidence Act 1995 (Cth) provides that the hearsay rule does not apply to evidence of a previous representation that is given by a person 'who saw, heard or otherwise perceived' the representation being made if the representation was 'made when or shortly after the asserted fact occurred and in circumstances that make it unlikely that the representation is a fabrication'.] 'The primary objective which underlies the requirement in s 65(2)(b) of the Act that the representation be made "when" or "shortly after" the asserted fact occurred seems to be to ensure that the matters conveyed are either strictly contemporaneous or, if narrative of a past event, still fresh in the mind of the person recounting that narrative. The expression "shortly after" makes it clear that there need not be anything like the strict contemporaneity required at common law to render the evidence admissible as res gestae.

'[134] In *R v Mankotia* [1998] NSWSC 295, Sperling J had occasion to deal with the meaning of the expression "shortly after" in s 65(2)(b) of the Evidence Act 1995 (NSW). His Honour said:

"The phrase 'shortly after' is not defined. The legislature has chosen not to specify a time. That implies that a normative judgment is to be made dependent on the circumstances of the case. For a judgment to be made, considerations of some kind or other have to taken into account but – as in the case of normative judgments generally – it may be difficult or impossible to articulate in a precise way what they are. I think the predominant factor in the phrase 'shortly after' must be the actual time that has elapsed and whether that fits the ordinary usage of the expression 'shortly after' in the circumstances of the case. The judgment should, however, be influenced by the policy behind the provision. That is to put a brake on evidence being given of a recollection which may have faded in its accuracy with the passage of time. The judgment may therefore be influenced by the subject matter of the event and by how long the memory of such an event is likely to have remained clear in the mind" '

Conway v R BC200001718; [2000] FCA 461 at [133]–[134], per Miles, von Doussa and Weinberg JJ

SHOULD NOT HAVE BEEN RESERVED

New Zealand [Companies Act 1955, s 32B91)(b).] '[T]he requirement under s 32B (1)(b) that the Registrar is to consider whether the name "should not have been reserved under that section" is subject to the important qualification "other than by reason only of the fact that the name was similar to the name of another company and might have been confused with it"… Nor is it irrelevant that in applying residual aspects of deciding whether the name was "undesirable" within the meaning of the original s 31(1)(a), the whole direction under s 32B(1)(b) forms part of a package of reforms effected in 1993. Part of that package is that pursuant to s 32(2) "The Registrar must not reserve a name (a) the use of which would contravene an enactment". Bearing those considerations in mind … a proper approach to an application of the modified s 31 test for "undesirability" properly involves the question whether it is undesirable:

because its use would contravene an enactment; or

because it is identical to, or almost identical to, the name of another company or name reserved for another company; or

because, in the opinion of the Registrar, it is offensive; or

because there is some other exceptional circumstance which would make use of the name undesirable.'

New Zealand Conference of Seventh-Day Adventists v Registrar of Companies [1997] 1 NZLR 751 at 758, per Fisher J

SICK

New Zealand [Section 30A of the Holidays Act 1981.] '[8] "Sick" is a word of variable meaning and the sense in which it is used necessarily depends on the context in which it is employed. The primary meaning given in *The Oxford English Dictionary* (2nd ed, 1989) is "Suffering from illness of any kind; ill, unwell, ailing"; the various meanings given in *Chambers Twentieth Century Dictionary* are "unwell, ill: diseased: vomiting or inclined to vomit: pining: mortified: thoroughly wearied: out of condition"; *The Heritage Illustrated Dictionary of the English Language* (International ed) gives as the primary meaning: "Ailing, ill, unwell" and as synonyms, "sick, ill, indisposed, unwell", continuing, "These adjectives describe persons not in good health. Sick applies to such a condition of any nature or severity. Unwell … has the wide range of sick". And in *Maloney v St Helens Industrial Co-operative Society Ltd* [1933] 1 KB 293 at p 297 Scrutton LJ observed that there were three well-recognised meanings of the word "sickness": affected by nausea as when seasick, incapacitated through disease, and "the well-recognized meaning by which sickness is contrasted with health, that is, sickness is bodily incapacity as distinguished from bodily health." ' *Kelcold Ltd v O'Brien* [1999] 3 NZLR 261 (CA) at 264 per cur

SIGNATURE

[Section 9 of the Wills Act 1837 provides that no will is to be valid unless (a) it is in writing, and signed by the testator, or by some other person in his presence and by his direction; and (b) it appears that the testator intended by his signature to give effect to the will; and (c) the signature is made or acknowledged by the testator in the presence of two or more witnesses present at the same time; and (d) each witness either (i) attests and signs the will; or (ii) acknowledges his signature, in the presence of the testator (but not necessarily in the presence of any other witness), but no form of attestation is necessary. A testarix wrote a will by hand on a printed will form. The final clause read: 'Signed by the said Testator Doris Weatherhill in the presence of us present at the same time who at her request in her presence and in the presence of each other have subscribed our names as witnesses.' but the testatrix's handwriting ended there and was followed by the signatures of the witnesses. The question arose whether the will was validly executed.] 'I turn then to the first issue in this case: does the presence of Doris Weatherhill's name in the attestation clause amount to a "signature" for the purposes of s 9(a) of the 1837 Act. Speaking of that provision in *Wood v Smith* [1992] 3 All ER 556 at 561, [1993] Ch 90 at 111 Scott LJ said:

> "There can be no doubt but that the parliamentary intention in substituting the new s 9 for the original section was to simplify the requirements for the execution and witnessing of a will. The requirements of paras (a) and (b) are in my judgment complementary. Paragraph (a) requires a signature. Paragraph (b) requires that the signature be intended to give effect to the will. These requirements demand a practical approach."

'[Counsel] argued that the presence of Doris Weatherhill's name in the attestation clause could amount to a signature …

'In my judgment it is to be inferred from the facts that Doris Weatherhill wrote out her will in one operation on 10 June 1985. Having referred to her will at the head of page 1 where it is printed she reached the attestation clause and wrote "Signed by the said testator, Doris Weatherhill". In such circumstances and bearing in mind the observations of Scott LJ in *Wood v Smith* which I have already referred to and the authorities to which I was directed in my judgment the appearance of the name "Doris Weatherhill" in the testator's handwriting in the attestation clause is a sufficient signature for the purposes of s 9 of the Act.'
Weatherhill v Pearce [1995] 2 All ER 492 at 494–496, per Judge Kolbert

[Whether an e-mail satisfied the requirements of the Statute of Frauds (1677), s 4, as a signed agreement or personal guarantee to enable an action to be brought on any special promise to answer for the debt of another person.] '[9] Section 4 of the Statute of Frauds provides:

> "no action shall be brought … whereby to charge the defendant upon any special promise to answer for the debt default or miscarriages of another person … unless the agreement upon which such action shall be brought

or some memorandum or note thereof shall be in writing and signed by the party to be charged therewith or some other person thereunto by him lawfully authorised."

It follows that: (1) the agreement in question must be in writing or, if the agreement is made orally, there must be a memorandum or note evidencing the oral agreement; and (2) the agreement or memorandum must be signed by either (2.1) the guarantor, or (2.2) someone authorised by the guarantor to sign the agreement or memorandum on his behalf. The effect of a non-compliance with s 4 is that the contract is unenforceable.

'[10] There were thus two issues that were argued at the hearing of the appeal namely: (1) whether the e-mail constituted a sufficient note or memorandum of the alleged agreement for the purposes of s 4; and (2) assuming the e-mail was a sufficient note or memorandum, whether it was sufficiently signed by or on behalf of Mr Mehta, it being contended on behalf of JPF that the presence of the e-mail address on the copy of the e-mail received by JPF's solicitors was a sufficient signature for these purposes.

…

'[16] Given that nothing has been formally cited to me other than *Lever v Koffler* [[1901] 1 Ch 543], identifying some generally applicable principle is not easy. The purpose of the statute of frauds is to protect people from being held liable on informal communications because they may be made without sufficient consideration or expressed ambiguously or because such a communication might be fraudulently alleged against the party to be charged. That being so, the logic underlying the authorities I have referred to would appear to be that where (as in this case) there is an offer in writing made by the party to be bound which contains the essential terms of what is offered *and* the party to be bound accepts that his offer has been accepted unconditionally, albeit orally, there is a sufficient note or memorandum to satisfy s 4. I say nothing about the position where there is a dispute as to whether or not the written offer has been accepted orally. Such a situation does not arise on this appeal. In the result, subject to the signature issue to which I turn below, I conclude that the e-mail referred to at [3], above, is capable of being a sufficient note or memorandum for the purpose of s 4 because it is in writing, and it is not disputed by Mr Mehta that the offer was accepted orally on behalf of JPF as described by Ms Albaster in para 7 of her witness statement.

…

'[18] The e-mail referred to at [3], above, is not signed by anyone in a conventional sense. Mr Mehta's name or initials do not appear at the end of the e-mail or, indeed, anywhere else in the body of the e-mail. Inevitably, therefore, JPF must contend that the presence of the e-mail address at the top of the e-mail constitutes a signature sufficient to satisfy the requirements of s 4.

'[19] As is well known to anyone who uses e-mail on a regular basis, what is relied upon is not inserted by the sender of the e-mail in any active sense. It is inserted automatically. My knowledge of the technicalities of e-mail is not sufficiently detailed to enable me to know whether it is inserted by the internet service provider (ISP) with whom the sender or the recipient has his e-mail account. However, I accept Mr Aslett's submission that as a matter of obvious inference, if it is inserted by the latter it can only be from information supplied by the former. Mr Mehta suggested that the address was inserted by his employee. I do not see how this could be so and certainly Mr Mehta was not able to give me a coherent explanation of how that might be so. It is possible that Mr Mehta's employee was authorised to use Mr Mehta's e-mail account remotely but, even if that is so, I do not see how that can impact on any of the issues I have to resolve since it is not in dispute that the e-mail was sent on the instructions of Mr Mehta and the method by which the sender address came to be inserted would not be affected even if that was the position.

'[20] It is submitted on behalf of JPF that the appearance of the sender's address at the top of the document constitutes a signature either by the sender or by "some other person thereunto by him lawfully authorised" because it is well known to all users of e-mail that the recipient of the e-mail will always be told the e-mail address of the e-mail account from which the e-mail is sent in the form it appears on the e-mail referred to at [3], above. That being so, it is submitted that by authorising an agent to send an e-mail using the sender's e-mail account, to a third party the sender knows that his her or its e-mail address will appear on the recipient's copy and that is sufficient for it to be held to be a signature for the purposes of s 4.

'[21] It was submitted by Mr Aslett that intention was irrelevant–all that was required was a document that constituted a sufficient memorandum (which, as I have held, the e-mail was) and the signature somewhere on the note or memorandum of either the person to be bound or his duly authorised agent. In support of this contention, Mr Aslett relied on the decision of the House of Lords in

Elpis Maritime Co Ltd v Marti Chartering Co Inc, The Maria D [1991] 3 All ER 758, [1992] 1 AC 21. The facts of that case were very different to the facts of this case. There was no dispute in that case that the party to be charged had signed the document. The dispute in that case concerned whether or not the fact that the party to be bound signed the relevant document as agent made any difference given that there was a clause within the document that purported to create a guarantee by the party purporting to sign only as agent. It had been contended that if such was the case then the fact the agreement contained a clause under which the signing party personally agreed to guarantee certain obligations was not relevant. It was this last argument that was rejected by the House of Lords by reference to *Re Hoyle, Hoyle v Hoyle* [1893] 1 Ch 84, [1891–4] All ER Rep Ext 1800 in which AL Smith LJ said ([1893] 1 Ch 84 at 100): "The question is not what is the intention of the person signing the memorandum, but is one of fact, viz., is there a note or memorandum of the promise signed by the party to be charged?" (See also [1891–4] All ER Rep Ext 1800 at 1804–1805.) It is because this is so that in other cases the courts have accepted letters to third parties, instructions to telegraph companies signed by the sender, and affidavits in unconnected actions as being a sufficient memorandum providing they are signed by the parties to be bound. It was this that led the House of Lords to conclude that it was irrelevant in what capacity or with what intention the document there being considered was signed.

'[22] In my judgment, the issue that arises in this case is not the issue that the House of Lords considered in the *Elpis Maritime* case. Here the issue is not with what intention or with what capacity did Mr Mehta or his employee sign the relevant document–rather the issue is whether it has been signed at all.

'[23] What is relied upon is an e-mail address. It is the e-mail equivalent of a fax or telex number. It is well known that the recipient of a fax will usually receive a copy that has the name and/or number of the sender automatically printed at the top together with a transmission time. Can it sensibly be suggested that the automatically generated name and fax number of the sender of a fax on a faxed document that is otherwise a s 4 note or memorandum would constitute a signature for these purposes? If Mr Aslett is right then the answer depends solely upon whether the sender (or the sender's principal where the sender was an agent) knew that the number or address would appear on the recipient's copy.

...

'[26] In the light of the dicta cited above, it seems to me that a party can sign a document for the purposes of s 4 by using his full name or his last name prefixed by some or all of his initials or using his initials, and possibly by using a pseudonym or a combination of letters and numbers (as can happen for example with a Lloyds slip scratch), providing always that whatever was used was inserted into the document in order to give, and with the intention of giving, authenticity to it. Its inclusion must have been intended as a signature for these purposes ...

...

'[28] I have no doubt that if a party creates and sends an electronically created document then he will be treated as having signed it to the same extent that he would in law be treated as having signed a hard copy of the same document. The fact that the document is created electronically as opposed to as a hard copy can make no difference. However, that is not the issue in this case. Here the issue is whether the automatic insertion of a person's e-mail address after the document has been transmitted by either the sending and/or receiving ISP constitutes a signature for the purposes of s 4.

'[29] In my judgment the inclusion of an e-mail address in such circumstances is a clear example of the inclusion of a name which is incidental in the sense identified by Lord Westbury in the absence of evidence of a contrary intention. Its appearance divorced from the main body of the text of the message emphasises this to be so. Absent evidence to the contrary, in my view it is not possible to hold that the automatic insertion of an e-mail address is, to use Cave J's language, "intended for a signature". To conclude that the automatic insertion of an e-mail address in the circumstances I have described constituted a signature for the purposes of s 4 would I think undermine or potentially undermine what I understand to be the Statute's purpose, would be contrary to the underlying principle to be derived from the cases to which I have referred and would have widespread and wholly unintended legal and commercial effects. In those circumstances, I conclude that the e-mail referred to at [3], above, did not bear a signature sufficient to satisfy the requirements of s 4.

'[30] Before leaving this issue I ought to mention the Electronic Communications Act 2000. This Act empowers the appropriate minister to issue statutory instruments in order to modify any other statute or statutory instrument in order to facilitate electronic communications. My understanding is that this Act was enacted in order to give effect to the European Union Directive on Electronic Commerce (EP and Council Directive (EC) 2000/31 (OJ 2000 L178 p 1)). No relevant statutory instrument made under this Act has been drawn to my attention. It is noteworthy that the Law Commission's view in relation to this directive is that no significant changes are necessary in relation to statutes that require signatures because whether those requirements have been satisfied can be tested in a functional way by asking whether the conduct of the would be signatory indicates an authenticating intention to a reasonable person. This approach is consistent with what I have said so far in this judgment. Thus, as I have already said, if a party or a party's agent sending an e-mail types his or her or his or her principal's name to the extent required or permitted by existing case law in the body of an e-mail, then in my view that would be a sufficient signature for the purposes of s 4. However that is not this case.

'[31] In those circumstances, whilst I conclude that the e-mail referred to at [3], above, is in principle capable of being a s 4 note or memorandum notwithstanding that it contains an offer and thus came into existence before not after the contract which it is said to memorialise, it does not bear the signature within the meaning of s 4 of the Statute of Frauds of either Mr Mehta or his duly authorised agent ... ' *J Pereira Fernandes SA v Mehta* [2006] EWHC 813 (Ch) at [9]–[10], [16], [18]–[23], [26], [28]–[31], [2006] 2 All ER 891, per Judge Pelling QC

Australia [In the context of the Bills of Exchange Act 1909 (Cth) ss 28–29.] '[In *Goodman v J Eban Ltd* [1954] 1 QB 550 Denning LJ, at 561–2, said] ... [W]hen a document is required to be "signed by" someone, what is meant is that "he must write his signature with his own hand" ... The remarks of Lord Denning on this subject were, it may be noticed, made in the course of a dissenting judgment, but they have received a measure of approval in subsequent English decisions, such as *London County Council v Agricultural Food Products Ltd* [1955] 2 QB 218, and, more recently, *Firstpost Homes Ltd v Johnson* [1995] 1 WLR 1567. His Lordship's persistence has, however, not been similarly rewarded in Australia, where there are now decisions to the contrary in three different courts at appellate level: see *McRae v Coulton* (1986) 7 NSWLR 644 (CA(NSW)); *DCT (Vic) v Boxshall* (1988) 83 ALR 175 and *Vincent v Johnstone Shire Council* (CA(Qld), App 87 of 1995). See also *R v Burchill and Salway; Ex parte Kretschmar* [1947] St R Qd 249. Unless and until constrained by higher authority, it is conceived that the rule to be followed in this country is that, in the absence of express provision or other indication to the contrary, legislation requiring "signature" of a document is not to be taken to preclude signature by agent, whether that signature is written in the name of the principal or of the agent: see *McRae v Coulton*, at 663–4 (Hope J, with whom Kirby P and McHugh JA agreed)… "Signature" may perhaps be defined as the writing of a person's name on a bill or notice in order to authenticate and give effect to some contract thereon.' *Muirhead v Commonwealth Bank of Australia* (1996) 139 ALR 561 at 565, 567; 127 FLR 434, per McPherson JA

SIGNED BY THE PRINCIPAL

[A form of proxy for the purposes of the Insolvency Rules 1986, SI 1986/1925, r 8.2(3) must be 'signed by the principal' or by some person authorised by him. A question arose whether a proxy form sent by fax was duly signed.] 'Although the rules stipulate that the form of proxy must be signed, it was, I believe, common ground that "signing" in the context could not be restricted to the narrow concept of marking a substrate manually by direct use of a pen or similar writing instrument. It was conceded that a proxy form could be "signed" by use (by the creditor or his agent) of a stamp. Similarly, if a form had a signature impressed on it by a printing machine in the way that share dividend cheques frequently are signed by company secretaries, the form can be said to be "signed".
…
'With these considerations in mind, I have come to the conclusion that a proxy form is signed for the purpose of r 8.2(3) if it bears upon it some distinctive or personal marking which has been placed there by, or with the authority of, the creditor. When a creditor faxes a proxy form to the chairman of a creditors' meeting he transmits two things at the same time, the contents of the form and the signature applied to it. The receiving fax is in effect instructed by the transmitting creditor to reproduce his signature on the proxy form which is itself being created at the receiving station. It follows that, in my view, the received fax is a proxy form signed by the principal or by someone authorised by him. The view which I have reached appears to me to be consistent with the realities of modern technology. If it is legitimate to send by post a proxy form signed with a rubber stamp, why should it not be at least as authentic to send the form by fax?
'… [T]he views I express as to whether a fax document bearing a fax signature is "signed" ha[ve]

only been considered in this case in relation to Pt 8 of the Insolvency Rules 1986. Different considerations may apply to faxed documents in relation to other legislation.' *Re a debtor (No 2021 of 1995), ex p IRC v The debtor* [1996] 2 All ER 345 at 349, 351, 352, per Laddie J

SIGNIFICANT

[In claims for damages for negligence, nuisance, or breach of duty, where the damages claimed were for personal injury, s 11 of the Limitation Act 1980 provides a special time limit of three years from the accrual of the cause of action or 'the date of knowledge (if later) of the person injured'. Under s 14(1)(a), 'date of knowledge' is defined as the date on which the person first had knowledge 'that the injury in question was significant' and under s 14(2) an injury is 'significant' if the person would 'reasonably have considered it sufficiently serious to justify' the institution of proceedings against a compliant defendant who could satisfy judgment. These factors had to be considered in relation to sexual abuse cases.] '[28] The main issue for the judge under s 14 was as to knowledge of "significant" injury, not, in the circumstances, of attributability. It did not seem to us that the judge, in applying Lord Griffiths' observation to every claim in the way that he did, can have had sufficient regard to the special and partly subjective meaning of the word "significant" in s 14(2) or to the confining effect of the words "the injury in question" in s 14(1)(a), identifying as one of the facts required for the date of knowledge that a claimant knew "that the injury in question" was "significant". In short, of what knowledge and of what injury was the judge speaking when he held that all these claimants "had the relevant knowledge before they left the community"?
…
'[39] In any s 14 case, it is important to distinguish between the occurrence of initial damage that may itself amount to a significant injury in a s 14(2) sense and that which, although the claimant could have successfully sued for it, does not. It is not apparent from the judge's reasoning in this case that he has done that, either in his general treatment of the provision or in his individual consideration of each claim. We say that for a number of reasons, all of which we should preface by a consideration of how s 14(2) can be made to fit the circumstances of claims like these of child abuse causing immediate physical and mental injury and later long-term psychiatric injury first diagnosed when well into adulthood.

'[40] Section 14(2) was designed principally to provide for cases of late diagnosis of physical diseases, such as asbestosis or byssinosis, the deadly development of which may be unknown until their symptoms eventually appear. At first sight, it does not fit so readily the circumstances of abused children who, because of their immaturity and vulnerable position, might never consider or seek advice about suing their abusers, or those responsible for them, for damages. The test, properly interpreted, is likely to be somewhat unrealistic in many child abuse cases when applied to claims for immediate injury. Such injury is likely to include, in addition to any physical injury, a mix of emotions and other mental effects, for example, humiliation, distress, shame, guilt and fear of being disbelieved or of disclosure. In such circumstances, depending on the severity of the victim's condition and the dates of the abuse, it could have been unreasonable and unreal to have expected him, as he moved from childhood to three years beyond majority, to consider recourse to the civil courts for damages for something he just wanted to put behind him. Given the circumstances of the abuse and his subsequent way of life, making such a claim, or seeking advice about it, might reasonably never occur to him. He might have known at the time of the abuse that it was wrong; he might have harboured resentment, great grievance, or even a desire for revenge, perhaps even a wish to report it to the police, but not necessarily to litigate for damages.

'[41] Application of the s 14(2) meaning of "significance" to child victims of abuse is often the more difficult because many of them, as in the case of these claimants, come to it already damaged and vulnerable because of similar ill-treatment in other settings. For some such behaviour is unpleasant, but familiar. As Mr Owen put it in his supplemental submissions, such misconduct was for many of these claimants "the norm"; it was committed by persons in authority; and they, the claimants, were powerless to do anything about it. Some victims of physical abuse may have believed that, to some extent, they deserved it. And, in cases of serious sexual abuse unaccompanied by serious physical injury of any permanent or disabling kind, it is not surprising, submitted Mr Owen that they did not see the significance of the conduct in s 14(2) terms, and simply tried to make the best of things.

'[42] However artificial it may seem to pose the question in this context, s 14 requires the court, on a case-by-case basis, to ask whether such an already damaged child would reasonably turn his mind to litigation as a solution to his problems? The same applies to those, as in the case of many of these claimants who, subsequent to the abuse, progress into adulthood and a twilight world of drugs, further abuse and violence and, in some cases, crime. Some would put the abuse to the back of their minds; some might, as a result or a symptom of an as yet undiagnosed development of psychiatric illness, block or suppress it. Whether such a reaction is deliberate or unconscious, whether or not it is a result of some mental impairment, the question remains whether and when such a person would have reasonably seen the significance of his injury so as turn his mind to litigation in the sense required by s 14(1)(a) and (2) to start the period of limitation running. At this stage the s 14(1)(b) issue of actual or constructive knowledge of attributability becomes more of a live issue than it would have been at or shortly after the abuse, because in some cases it might only be after the intervention of a psychiatrist that a claimant realises that there could have been a causal link between the childhood abuse and the psychiatric problems suffered as an adult, an argument accepted by the Court of Appeal, but which Lord Griffiths found difficult to accept, in *Stubbings'* case [*Stubbings v Webb* [1993] AC 498, [1993] 1 All ER 322, HL].

'[43] The posing of such questions may have become less artificial in recent years as a result of the publicity given to inquiries of the sort conducted by Sir Ronald Waterhouse in 1997 and 1998 and the disturbing increase in the number of criminal prosecutions and civil suits for child abuse, some of it a very long time ago. The momentum of increase in public awareness of such conduct, of which Bingham LJ spoke in 1992 in *Stubbings'* case is likely to have begun to usher in a generation more sensitive to its seriousness and "significance" in a s 14(2) sense ...

...

'[45] . . To paraphrase Bingham LJ, whether a particular claimant would reasonably have not regarded a particular injury from such abuse when it occurred, as significant for this purpose is still likely to be a "highly judgmental question". It is a fact-sensitive question that needs to be considered on a case-by-case basis. It is plain that the judge ([2001] All ER (D) 322 (Jun)) did not do that. First, it looks as if he construed the word "significant" in s 14(1) without reference to the special meaning given to it in this context by s 14(2). And, second, even if he had its partly subjective meaning in mind, he does not appear to have considered its application on a claim-by-claim basis, in particular as to the nature, condition and circumstances of the individual claimant or to "the injury in question". A sure sign of his erroneous approach is that he felt able to credit all of the claimants with "the relevant knowledge before they left the community", namely at a time when all or most of them were still as or more vulnerable than when they had first arrived there and when each of them had still to go out into the world.

…

'[47] … It was for the judge to determine in the case of each claimant whether, within three years after majority, he or she had significant knowledge within the meaning of s 14(2) and in respect of what injury, whether physical and/or mental. In the case of each claimant, the judge had to consider, among other things, his or her individual history and circumstances, the nature, severity and duration of the abuse, the period of time when it occurred and its physical and/or mental effects evident to the claimant within three years after reaching majority. He then had to relate them all to the question whether that claimant, given those and any other relevant circumstances, would have considered the injury of which he knew (the injury in question) sufficiently serious to institute proceedings against a solvent and compliant defendant.

'[48] There are no short cuts in such an exercise, such as, for example, that adopted by Mr Faulks of asking each claimant whether they knew at the time that what had happened to them was "wrong", although, as he submitted to the court, it may be a step on the way to identifying whether any particular claimant had relevant knowledge. Nor did the judge's reliance on Lord Griffiths' qualified and obiter remark in *Stubbings v Webb* [1993] 1 All ER 322 at 328, [1993] AC 498 at 506 for his general conclusion on the matter ([2001] All ER (D) 322 (Jun) at [29] and [30]) come close to focusing on the true test of significance in s 14(2) or on the case-sensitive nature of the examination that it called for, namely that each claimant—

> "must have known at the time that he or she was the victim of [a physical and/or sexual] assault which caused at the least some distress and more often profound disquiet, pain and resentment. They knew, in ordinary language, that they had been injured in a manner which could not properly be described as trivial, but which was significant. They also knew, as I conclude that the distress suffered was attributable to the actions upon which they now rely to found their claims. Their situations were similar to the actions of the victim … in *Stubbings'* case …"

As we have already indicated, in so expressing himself, the judge did not have the benefit of the basis upon which the Court of Appeal proceeded in that case, namely that, on the facts and for the reasons all three members of the court gave, there was no early knowledge of significant injury. In the climate of public knowledge and awareness at the time of the abuse in question, as Bingham LJ put it ([1991] 3 All ER 949 at 956, [1992] QB 197 at 207):

> "… in purely physical terms the impairment of the plaintiff's condition was minor … there would have been very little to support an indictment of causing actual bodily harm or to plead as particulars of personal injury."

'[49] In addition, it should be remembered that it is not normally for a defendant to establish when, if at all, a claimant had the relevant knowledge. It is for the claimant to prove how long he was without it. The issue of limitation having been raised, it was for each claimant to satisfy the court of the date upon which the cause of action accrued and, where relevant, the later date when he first had knowledge of the facts, including as to the significance of the injury within s 14(1) and (2), but possibly not as to constructive knowledge under s 14(3); see *Crocker v British Coal Corp* (1995) 29 BMLR 159 per Mance J; and *Parry v Clwyd Health Authority* [1997] PIQR P1 per Colman J.' *KR v Bryn Alyn Community (Holdings) Ltd (in liquidation)* [2003] EWCA Civ 85 at [28], [39]–[43], [45], [47]–[49], [2004] 2 All ER 716, CA, per Auld LJ

SITUATED ON RESERVE

Canada [Property situated on a reserve was exempt from garnishment.] 'It is plain that what we are talking about here is personal property, and where it is situated. That is commonly called its situs. It is also very clear that a bank account with a positive balance is a debt owed by the bank to the account holder. Similar accounts in trust companies work the same way and are always treated the same at common law …

'But neither the board nor the collection agency is a party to the present contract or bound by it. I cannot see that an Indian or a band can render all of his or its property exempt simply by signing a contract with someone else who is not a creditor or connected with a creditor, deeming his or its property to be where it is not. That is not what the Indian Act says, and it would violate every principle of contracts.

'Of course the Indian or the band may do that indirectly with respect to debts owing to him or it. For example, he or it may contract with his debtor (the trust company) that the debt will be payable at a named place, which is in fact on a reserve ...

'Therefore, it is clear that the only place at which the customer band could require payment out from its account was at the branch in downtown Edmonton, and that was the only place that the parties could deal with each other. There is no evidence that they ever dealt with each other anywhere else. Therefore, if place of payment or dealing has any relevance, the situs of the account was in downtown Edmonton, and not on any Indian reserve.' *Alberta* (*Workers' Compensation Board*) *v Enoch Indian Band* (1993) 106 DLR (4th) 279 at 289, 291–292, Alta CA, per Côté J

SITUATION THAT GAVE RISE TO THE PERSONAL GRIEVANCE

New Zealand [The Employment Contracts Act 1991, ss 40(2), 41(3) provide that where an employee has a personal grievance by reason of being unjustifiably dismissed, the tribunal or court must consider whether the employee contributed towards 'the situation that gave rise to the personal grievance' in deciding on any remedy to be awarded.] '[30] These sections refer to "the situation that gave rise to the personal grievance". This language must be considered broadly and, in the present context, extend to the entire history of the dispute between Mr Ioane and his superiors. In other words, the assessment required by ss 40(2) and 41(3) is not confined to considering whether the actions of Mr Ioane were causally linked to the procedural infelicities that resulted in the decision that his dismissal was procedurally unjustified, see *Ark Aviation Ltd v Newton* [2002] 2 NZLR 145 at para [42].' *Waitakere City Council v Ioane* (*No 2*) (2005) 2 NZELR 537, CA, per Anderson P, Hammond and William Young JJ

SLANDER

[For 28 Halsbury's Laws (4th edn) para 12 see now 28 Halsbury's Laws (4th edn) (Reissue) para 12.]

Slander of goods

[For 28 Halsbury's Laws (4th edn) para 263 see now 28 Halsbury's Laws (4th edn) (Reissue) para 277.]

Slander of title

[For 28 Halsbury's Laws (4th edn) para 262 see now 28 Halsbury's Laws (4th edn) (Reissue) para 276.]

SLAUGHTERHOUSE

[The Food Act 1984 is largely repealed. The definition is re-enacted in the Food Safety Act 1990, s 53(1).]

SLAVE

New Zealand [Section 98 of the Crimes Act 1961 provides that 'Every one is liable to imprisonment ... who, within or outside New Zealand ... in any way whatsoever deals with any person as a slave'.]

[The High Court judge in this case on a pretrial application on behalf of the accused under s 347 of the Crimes Act 1961 treated as applicable a definition of 'slave' contained in both the Oxford English Dictionary and the Shorter Oxford English Dictionary — 'a servant completely divested of freedom and personal rights'. However, in summing up, apparently because on further thought the judge regarded the concept of 'servant' as inappropriate in current New Zealand usage, he offered to the jury as well an alternative and preferred definition found by him in Chambers English Dictionary — 'one who is submissive under domination'. He went on to say:

'One who is submissive under domination. So let us consider what that means. "Domination", I guide you as a matter of law in the circumstances of this case, means "control and authority that brooks no opposition or disobedience". That is domination. Control or authority that brooks no opposition or disobedience. And submissive means "acceptance of that domination". Acceptance of that domination, whether willingly or unwillingly. You might add an inability to cast off the domination. So "submissive" means acceptance of that domination, whether willingly or unwillingly. So one who is submissive under domination, who accepts it, unable to cast it off, can properly be described as a slave'.]

[The Chambers English Dictionary gives as its first definition of 'slave', 'a person held as property'.]

'... "a person held as property" is more apt and quite sufficient in the context of s 98 of the Crimes Act. It is much the same as but more succinct than the *Oxford* definition, which can usefully be given to a jury in amplification of the terser definition if the trial Judge thinks amplification necessary …

'While preferring the first definition in *Chambers* for the purpose of s 98, we think that [the High Court judge's explanation] was enough in the circumstances of the present case to bring home the same concept to the jury.' *R v Decha-Iamsakun* [1993] 1 NZLR 141 at 144, CA, per cur

SMOKE

[The Clean Air Act 1956 has been repealed. The definition is re-enacted in the Clean Air Act 1993, s 64(1).]

Dark smoke

[The Clean Air Act 1956 has been repealed. The definition is now contained in the Clean Air Act 1993, s 3, as follows.]

(1) In this Act 'dark smoke' means smoke which, if compared in the appropriate manner with a chart of the type known on 5th July 1956 (the date of the passing of the Clean Air Act 1956) as the Ringelmann Chart, would appear to be as dark as or darker than shade 2 on the chart.

(2) For the avoidance of doubt it is hereby declared that in proceedings—

    (a) for an offence under section 1 or 2 (prohibition of emissions of dark smoke); or

    (b) brought by virtue of section 17 (smoke nuisances in Scotland),

the court may be satisfied that smoke is or is not dark smoke as defined in subsection (1) notwithstanding that there has been no actual comparison of the smoke with a chart of the type mentioned in that subsection.

(3) Without prejudice to the generality of subsections (1) and (2), if the Secretary of State by regulations prescribes any method of ascertaining whether smoke is dark smoke as defined in subsection (1), proof in any such proceedings as are mentioned in subsection (2)—

    (a) that that method was properly applied, and

    (b) that the smoke was thereby ascertained to be or not to be dark smoke as so defined,

shall be accepted as sufficient.

SOCIAL SERVICES

Canada ' "Social services" is not a defined term in the *Immigration Act*. Paragraph 114(1)(m.1) [as

amended by SC 1992, c 49, s 102] authorizes the Governor in Council to prescribe social services for the purposes of subparagraph 19(1)(a)(ii) but nothing has been prescribed to date.

'The *Concise Oxford Dictionary of Current English*, 9th edition defines "social service" as:

"… services provided by the state for the community, esp. education, health and housing."

According to the dictionary definition of the term, "social services" would include special education.

'More significantly, the context in which the term is used in subparagraph 19(1)(a)(ii) also points in the same direction. Health and social services are not unlimited and not costless. Subparagraph 19(1)(a)(ii) is clearly intended to ensure, as far as possible, that access to health and social services by Canadian citizens and permanent residents should not be denied or impaired by reason of excessive demands for those services by prospective immigrants. Paragraph 19(1)(a) is only triggered when a prospective immigrant is found to be suffering from a disease, disorder, disability or other health impairment. Social services in subparagraph 19(1)(a)(ii) contemplates services provided to those in need after assessment of the nature, severity or probable duration of their disease, disorder, disability or other health impairment. Considering that the requirement for publicly funded special education arises from the assessment of the nature, severity and probable duration of a mental disability, there is no obvious reason why Parliament would have intended to exclude special education for the mentally retarded from the ambit of social services in subparagraph 19(l)(a)(ii).'

…

'It appears that a policy of institutionalization of the mentally disabled has been replaced by a policy aimed at integrating such persons into the mainstream of society. There is no doubt that for purposes of subparagraph 19(l)(a)(ii), institutionalization would constitute a social service. A substitute publicly provided program such as special education to assist the mentally disabled must also be a social service for purposes of that provision.

'The learned Motions Judge was of the view that social services in subparagraph 19(l)(a)(ii) is to be read [at paragraph 6] "in a narrow sense, as meaning social services akin to welfare". In her view, the phrase "health or social services" indicates that health services are distinct from social services and that education, including special education, provided within the school system, is also distinct. With respect, we are unable to agree.

'While social services would include welfare, the term means something more than welfare. In paragraph 19(1)(b) [as am by SC 1992, c. 49, s 11 Parliament uses the term "social assistance" in the context of care and support of persons unable or unwilling to support themselves:

19....

> (b) persons who there are reasonable grounds to believe are or will be unable or unwilling to support themselves and those persons who are dependent on them for care and support, except persons who have satisfied an immigration officer that adequate arrangements, other than those that involve social assistance, have been made for their care and support; [Emphasis added.]

Social assistance as used in paragraph 19(1)(b), connotes welfare. Social services in subparagraph 19(1)(a)(ii) includes welfare, but also broader considerations.

'Further, in paragraph 19(1)(a) there is a link between a disease, disorder, disability or health impairment and social services. Here, the disability is mental retardation and that is what lead to the requirement, in the opinion of the medical officers, for special education. To exclude special education from the term "social services" would be to arbitrarily preclude the term from applying to the very type of services found to be required because of a determined disability. As we said above, if institutionalization of the mentally retarded is a social service, and we think it indisputable that it is, a substitute more modern program, special education, is also a social service.' *Thangarajan v Canada* (1999) 4 FC 167 at 171, 172, 173, 174, CA, per Rothstein JA

SOCIETY *SEE* ASSOCIATION

SOLE OR MAIN RESIDENCE

[The claimant council taxpayer owned a cottage. Between January 1993 and August 1996 he was employed as a housemaster by a nearby school. The school provided him with a house, in which he and his wife lived during his employment and following his retirement, until July 1997. The cottage and the house were in different billing authority areas for the purposes of council tax. The school declared that the house was the taxpayer's main home for council tax purposes and paid council tax in full on his behalf. The taxpayer had continued to pay council tax in full in relation to the cottage, and applied for a 50% rebate from the defendant council for the period from January 1993 to July 1997. The council considered that during that period the cottage fell to be considered as the taxpayer's sole or main residence for the purposes of s 6 of the Local Government Finance Act 1992.] '[23] There was and could be no suggestion that Pump Cottage constituted the Williams' sole residence during the relevant period. The issue before the tribunal was whether during that period Pump Cottage or The Oaks was their main residence. The tribunal's starting point should have been to consider the meaning of this phrase. *Frost v Feltham* might have assisted them in that task. Nourse J appears to have accepted that "main" in this context means "principal" or "most important" (see [1981] STC 115 at 117, [1981] 1 WLR 452 at 455). Perhaps more significantly, he made the observation that a residence is a place where someone lives. The precise meaning of the word "residence" can vary according to its context. The *Shorter Oxford English Dictionary* (3rd edn, 1944) includes the following material definitions of residence: "a) the place where a person resides; his dwelling place; the abode of a person; b) a dwelling, esp. one of a superior kind."

'[24] Mr Easton submitted that we should give "residence" the latter meaning in the present context. We do not agree.

'[25] Where an estate agent's brochure speaks of a "desirable residence" it gives the word the latter meaning. In the present case, residence is used as part of the definition of the word "resident". The primary meaning of "resident" given by the dictionary is: "One who resides permanently in a place." The relevant definition of "reside" is: "To dwell permanently or for a considerable time; to have one's settled abode; to live in or at a particular place."

'[26] All this reinforces the conclusion (which is one that we would have reached without reference to the dictionary) that in s 6(5) of the 1992 Act "sole or main residence" refers to premises in which the taxpayer actually resides. The qualification "sole or main" addresses the fact that a person may reside in more than one place. We think that it is probably impossible to produce a definition of "main residence" that will provide the appropriate test in all circumstances. Usually, however, a person's main residence will be the dwelling that a reasonable onlooker, with knowledge of the material facts, would regard as that person's home at the material time. That test may not always be an easy one to apply, but we have no doubt as to the conclusion to which it leads in the present case.

'[27] Mr Williams, upon whom we did not need to call, in a lengthy and lucid written argument, contended that the facts of his case are very different from the three considered by the tribunal. We agree. In each of those cases there was: a matrimonial home in which the wife resided; the taxpayer had to live elsewhere as a condition of his employment, but when on leave or holiday returned to the matrimonial home; and in each of those cases the reasonable onlooker would have concluded that the residence subject to community charge or council tax remained at all material times the taxpayer's home. Where a person ceases to reside in the house which has been his sole or main residence for a period of time, an issue may arise as to whether during that period the house in question ceases to be his sole or main residence. The answer will depend on the particular circumstances; it will be a matter of fact and degree.

'[28] In the present case the tribunal had regard to the fact that, during the material period, Mr and Mrs Williams never stayed at Pump Cottage, but failed to have regard to a number of circumstances that made that fact of particular significance. The first is the length of time that they lived elsewhere. Then there is the fact that Pump Cottage in West Sussex is very close to The Oaks in Mid-Sussex. That explains why Mr and Mrs Williams kept their doctor and dentist. According to Mr Williams, a visit to either only entailed driving for an extra 15 minutes or so. Another factor is that schoolmasters have much longer holidays than most people. Had Mr and Mrs Williams wished to live in Pump Cottage, there must have been lengthy periods when they would have been free to do so. Certainly the proximity of the two houses would have facilitated this. The next circumstance is that they opted to stay on in The Oaks at their own expense for nearly a year after Mr Williams' employment as housemaster ceased.

'[29] These circumstances would, in our view, lead any reasonable onlooker to conclude that Mr and Mr Williams moved their home from Pump Cottage to The Oaks, and that between January 1993 and July 1997, a period of four-and-a-half years, The Oaks was their home. Furthermore, we do not consider that any reasonable tribunal that applied a proper test to the material facts could have come to any conclusion other than that The Oaks, rather than Pump Cottage, was Mr and

Mrs Williams' main residence during the relevant period. Indeed it could be argued that it was their sole residence.' *Williams v Horsham District Council* [2004] EWCA Civ 39 at [23]–[29], [2004] 3 All ER 30, CA, per Lord Phillips of Worth Matravers MR

SOLICIT

Australia [Section 19 of the Summary Offences Act 1988 (NSW) prohibits soliciting for the purposes of prostitution contrary to section s 19(1) of the Summary Offences Act 1988 (NSW).] 'The word solicit has a number of possible meanings, depending on the context. The plaintiff ... put before the Court a number of dictionary meanings of solicit. The first was the American Dictionary of the English Language. This dictionary is in a form somewhat different from that of Australian and English dictionaries. It does not include any specific reference to the meaning of solicit in the context of prostitution, but does indicate that the meaning of solicit is:

> "to ask with some degree of earnestness; to make petition to; to apply to for obtaining something. This word implies earnestness in seeking, but I think less earnestness than beg, implore and importune, and more than ask or request."

'The plaintiff then referred to the New Shorter Oxford Dictionary which listed a number of meanings. One is "entreat, petition, urge (a person); ask earnestly or persistently"; another, related to prostitution, is "accost a person and offer oneself or another as a prostitute". Her next reference was to Webster's 9th New Collegiate Dictionary from which she referred to the word accost as meaning "to approach and speak to, *often* in a challenging or aggressive way" (Italics added). This was done because in the Oxford Pocket Dictionary (her next reference), the word solicit is defined to include "accost as a prostitute". It is to be noted that in this Webster's Dictionary definition, the manner of the approach and speaking are only a frequent, nor a necessary, accompaniment. The necessary elements are approaching and speaking to.

'No reference was made by the plaintiff to any of the following dictionary meanings:

(1) The Macquarie Dictionary (2nd Edition, 1991) gives solicit a particular meaning in relation to prostitution namely, "to accost (another) with immoral intention as a prostitute".

(2) The Oxford English Dictionary (2nd Edition, 1989) gives two meanings appropriate in the context of prostitution: "Of women: to accost and importune (men) for immoral purposes"; "to tempt, entice, allure, to attract or draw by enticement". One of the examples given in respect of the first mentioned meaning is a reference to a person who "persistently solicited in a public place." This would suggest that, unless the authors of the Oxford English Dictionary used an oxymoron (which is unlikely for authors of such dictionary), the word solicit per se, ie when used alone, does not necessarily involve any sense of persistence. The same dictionary relevantly defines "importune" as "to solicit for purposes of prostitution". Accosting in the sense of approaching and offering the services usual for a prostitute, is the primary or essential meaning in this dictionary, with a linked appropriate meaning which involves allurement, enticement and the like.

(3) In the Australian Concise Oxford Dictionary (1986) solicit, when used as a verb, has as the relevant meaning "to invite or make appeals to or to importune".

(4) In Collins Concise English Dictionary (Australian Edition, 1984), solicit is given the meaning "make a request, accost with an offer of sexual relations in return for money".

(5) Chambers English Dictionary (1988) relevantly defines solicit as "to invite to immorality" and ("of prostitutes") "the making of advances".

(6) In Webster's Third International Dictionary (1976) the meaning appropriate to the context of prostitution is "to accost (a man) for immoral purposes" Accost is defined as "to approach and speak to."

'Soliciting is not restricted to prostitutes. A person may solicit a bribe. The word solicit is derived from the Latin verb "sollicitare". When used in relation to bribes it bears the meaning "seek to obtain": thus sollicitare iudicium donis (Ovid). There is no need for persistence or like behaviour. Furthermore, authority indicates that a mere request for a bribe is sufficient to constitute a solicitation.

Putting one's hand out in a particular way in appropriate circumstances can amount to soliciting ie seeking to obtain, a bribe. A person may solicit alms. This may be done by actually asking for money, or by sitting or standing on the pavement with a bowl, saucepan or equivalent receptacle and either holding it out to passers by or so placing it that there is an invitation to put money in it. This may or may not be accompanied by words. If words are used they may be no more than "Spare some change?" "Can you help me?", or equivalents. Neither the acts nor the words need be persistent, repetitive or aggressive. Indeed, this is highlighted by the fact that in some American States where, to introduce an element of persistence or aggression into such begging offences, *aggressive* pan-handling is required – a reference to a saucepan being held by the handle and extended to the potential donor.

'Having examined these various dictionary meanings, I am of opinion, that the ordinary dictionary meaning of solicit in the context of prostitution in this day and age involves a personal approach for the purpose of, or which is accompanied by, or which constitutes or conveys, an offer that some form of sexual activity will be engaged in by the person making the approach in return for monetary gain. The approach need not be aggressive persistent, pestering, or repeated nor is it necessary that it should constitute an annoyance to the person approached.

...

'An examination of the ordinary dictionary meaning and derivation of the word solicit when used in the context of prostitution, the legislative history and form of s 19 of the Summary Offences Act 1988, and relevant decided cases leads to the conclusion that when used in s 19 of the Summary Offences Act 1988, solicit involves a personal approach, for the purpose of, or which is accompanied by, or which constitutes or conveys, an offer that some form of sexual activity will be engaged in by the person making the approach in return for monetary gain.

'It is unnecessary, according to the ordinary meaning of the word solicit, when used in the context of prostitution, for there to be any element of aggressive persistence, pestering, pressure, or harassment or annoyance to the person approached. Nor is there a need for distress or embarrassment to be caused by or result from the approach or offer. If there are any of those elements present they may evidence a breach of s 19(3) [which provides that a "person shall not ... solicit another person, for the purpose of prostitution, in a manner that harasses or distresses the other person"]. The mere approach by a prostitute to a person who is a potential customer, when she is dressed in a suggestive manner, perhaps with appropriate gestures or words, or is presented in a particular way is sufficient to constitute an offer of services as a prostitute.' *Coleman v DPP* (2000) 49 NSWLR 371; BC200004089; [2000] NSWSC 275 at [9]–[13], [41]–[42], per O'Keefe J

SOLICITING

[The Summary Offences Act 1988 (NSW) s16 provides 'A person shall not use, for the purpose of prostitution or of soliciting for prostitution, any premises held out as being available [inter alia] for the provision of massage, sauna baths, steam baths or facilities for physical exercise'.] 'There is no doubt that "soliciting" in relation to prostitution commonly conveys an element of pestering by way of accosting, importuning or flaunting. Standard dictionary definitions reflect that common element. But the expression "soliciting" does not necessarily convey that element. A commercial traveller, for example, is still soliciting for orders if he offers his company products politely and succinctly without any element of pestering … From the nature of the services held out as provided in the premises, be it massage, saunas, steam baths or any of the other services referred to in s 16, it is likely that people will attend for those respectable services and approach, accordingly, the person who is in the premises whom they may assume is there to provide them … In that setting it is in my judgment a natural use of the expression "soliciting for prostitution" that it suffices that the prostitute personally offers to the person attending the premises her services as a prostitute … Cases such as *Weisz v Monahan* [1962] 1 All ER 664; *Behrendt v Burridge* [1976] 3 All ER 285; *Hutt v The Queen* (1978) 82 DLR (3d) 95 and *Fingleton v Bryson* (1980) 26 SASR 208 are to be distinguished on that ground.' *Jitjarden v Thompson* (1995) 85 A Crim R 24 at 26, per Allen J

SOLICITOR

[For 44 Halsbury's Laws (4th edn) para 1 et seq see now 44(1) Halsbury's Laws (4th edn) (Reissue) para 1 et seq.]

Acting as a solicitor

[The Solicitors Act 1974, s 25(1) disallows costs in respect of anything done by an unqualified person 'acting as a solicitor'.] '… it seems clear to me that the words 'acting as a solicitor' are limited to the doing of acts which only a solicitor may perform and/or the doing of acts by a person pretending or holding himself out to be a solicitor. Such acts are not to be confused with the doing of acts of a kind commonly done by solicitors, but which involve no representation that the actor is acting as such.' *Piper Double Glazing Ltd v D C Contracts (1992) Ltd* [1994] 1 All ER 177 at 186, per Potter J

SOME OTHER PERSON

New Zealand [Section 3(2) of the Trespass Act 1980 provides 'It shall be a defence to a charge under subsection (1) of this section if the defendant proves that it was necessary for him to remain in or on the place concerned for his own protection or for the protection of some other person, or because of some emergency involving his property or the property of some other person'.] 'Obviously relevant mothers of the unborn children come within the phrase …

'When subs (2) speaks of "the property of some other person" it is clearly denoting that some other person owns the property in question, ie the property that is the subject of the emergency. An unborn child cannot own property in this sense. At most the property may be owned by someone else on behalf of or in trust for the unborn child. Thus in the last line of subs (2) the reference to "some other person" cannot be construed as referring to an unborn child.

'The question is whether two lines earlier the same expression should be read as being intended to include an unborn child. It is unusual, although not impossible, for the same word or phrase to carry materially different meanings within the same subsection. It is, however, unlikely that this should be so. If a distinction is intended the draftsman will ordinarily use another expression clearly denoting the distinction, or will signal the distinction in some other appropriate way. Thus, within the confines of subs (2) itself there is already an indication that the expression "some other person", where it first appears, is not intended to encompass an unborn child. I reach the same conclusion when considering s 3(2) in the wider context of the Trespass Act as a whole. When Parliament gave trespassers a defence if they could prove that their continued presence was necessary for the protection of "some other person" I regard it as most unlikely that unborn children were intended to be within the ambit of that phrase. This conclusion is reinforced by reference to relevant case law.' *Wilcox v Police* [1994] 1 NZLR 243 at 248–249, per Tipping J

SOVEREIGNTY

Australia ' "Sovereignty" is a concept that legal scholars have spent much time examining. It is a word that is sometimes used to refer to very different legal concepts and for that reason alone, care must be taken to identify how it is being used. H L A Hart said of the idea of sovereignty that [H L A Hart, *The Concept of Law* (1961), at 218]: "It is worth observing that an uncritical use of the idea of sovereignty has spread similar confusion in the theory both of municipal and international law, and demands in both a similar corrective. Under its influence, we are led to believe that there must in every municipal legal system be a sovereign legislator subject to no legal limitations; just as we are led to believe that international law must be of a certain character because states are sovereign and incapable of legal limitation save by themselves. In both cases, belief in the necessary existence of the legally unlimited sovereign prejudges a question which we can only answer when we examine the actual rules. The question for municipal law is: what is the extent of the supreme legislative authority recognised in this system? For international law it is: what is the maximum area of autonomy which the rules allow to states?" ' *Joosse v Australian Securities and Investment Commission* (1998) 159 ALR 260 at 263–264; 73 ALJR 232; BC9806758, per Hayne J

SPECIAL

Australia [Section 51(xxvi) of the Commonwealth Constitution confers on the Commonwealth Parliament power to make laws with respect to the people of any race for whom it is deemed necessary to make 'special' laws.] 'The races power, unlike the aliens power or the corporations power, is not expressed to be a power to make laws simply with respect to persons of a designated character. It must be "deemed necessary" that "special laws" be made for "the people of any race ... "

' "Special" qualifies "law"; it does not relate to necessity. Therefore the special quality of a law must be ascertained by reference to its differential operation upon the people of a particular race (*Koowarta v Bjelke-Peterson* (1982) 153 CLR 168 at 186, 245, 261) not by reference to the circumstances which led the parliament to deem it necessary to enact the law. A special quality appears when the law confers a right or benefit or imposes an obligation or disadvantage especially on the people of a particular race. The law may be special even when it confers a benefit generally, provided the benefit is of special significance or importance to the people of a particular race.' *State of Western Australia v Commonwealth* (1995) 128 ALR 1 at 43–44, per Mason CJ, Brennan, Deane, Toohey, Gaudron and McHugh JJ

SPECIAL CIRCUMSTANCES

Australia [Pursuant to court directions, a written statement had been made in proceedings, however the statement was never read in open court as the proceedings settled. A party to other proceedings filed a notice seeking the Federal Court's leave to use the statement in Supreme Court proceedings. The author of the statement had refused to consent to use of the statement in the Supreme Court proceedings. The motion was opposed on the basis that the court could only grant leave to use the statement if the applicant demonstrated there were 'special circumstances' allowing the court to override the implied undertaking attaching to a statement of evidence that it will not be used for any collateral purpose.] 'For "special circumstances" to exist it is enough that there is a special feature of the case which affords a reason for modifying or releasing the undertaking and is not usually present. The matter then becomes one of the proper exercise of the court's discretion, many factors being relevant. It is neither possible nor desirable to propound an exhaustive list of those factors. But plainly they include the nature of the document, the circumstances under which it came into existence, the attitude of the author of the document and any prejudice the author may sustain, whether the document pre-existed litigation or was created for that purpose and therefore expected to enter the public domain, the nature of the information in the document (in particular whether it contains personal data or commercially sensitive information), the circumstances in which the document came into the hands of the applicant for leave and, perhaps most important of all, the likely contribution of the document to achieving justice in the second proceeding.' *Springfield Nominees Pty Ltd v Bridgelands Securities Ltd* (1992) 110 ALR 685 at 693, per Wilcox J

Australia [Section 21(6)(f)(iv) of the Extradition Act 1988 (Cth) provides that the Federal Court of Australia has jurisdiction, if there are 'special circumstances' justifying such a course, to order the release on bail of a person.] 'The special circumstances which the applicant for bail must establish are those which satisfy the court that it is justified in departing from the presumption implicit in s 21(6)(f)(iv) of the Act that ordinarily bail is not to be granted. This is the same approach taken at common law where "special" or "exceptional" circumstances must be demonstrated (see for example *R v Ladd* (1958) 75 WN(NSW) 431 at 432–3). Of course, unless the court was satisfied that it was not probable that the applicant would abscond, it is hard to imagine any situation where special circumstances would be made out. But in assessing that probability regard may be had to the personal circumstances of the applicant and the ability of the court to impose conditions which maximise the likelihood that an applicant will answer bail. It is not in my view that the circumstances are so exceptional or special that it is not probable that the applicant will abscond which is the sole or appropriate, test required by s 21(6)(f)(iv), but rather whether the circumstances are such as to displace the ordinary rule against bail because the personal and other public interests underlying the proven circumstances outweigh the statutory interests and concerns evident in ss 3 and 21(6)(f)(iv) of the Act. Certain matters which touch a particular applicant, for example the time already spent in custody and the time the applicant faces in custody until the court can determine the merits of the appeal, are matters which may be given considerable weight although in themselves they may not be decisive of the outcome in any particular case.' *Holt v Hogan* (1993) 44 FCR 572 at 579; 117 ALR 378 at 385, per Cooper J

Australia 'The words "special circumstances" are not so imprecise as to require judicial gloss: *Beadle v Director-General of Social Security* (1985) 60 ALR 225, 228. In *Groth v Secretary, Department of Social Security* (1995) 40 ALD 541, 545 I expressed the view that the words require something which distinguishes a person's case from others, something that sets it apart from the usual or ordinary case.' *Secretary, Department of Family and Community Services v Chamberlain* (2002) 5(1) SSR 9; BC200200276; [2002] FCA 67 at [19], per Keifel J

Australia 'The word "special" is an ordinary English word. The relevant definition of it as used in the present context appears to me to be that given in the *Macquarie Dictionary* (3rd ed, 1997) as follows:

"6 Distinguished or different from what is ordinary or usual: a special occasion"

The thrust of that definition is that "special" is used in contradistinction to "ordinary" or "common". "Special circumstances" is an expression that has been used in other statutes. One must always bear in mind in an exercise of statutory interpretation that one is interpreting the particular words in the context of the particular statute. However, cases decided on other statutes, whilst they cannot govern the situation, indicate that, where "special circumstances" is used in contexts like the present, it is used in the sense of the definition which I have quoted from the *Macquarie Dictionary*. Its essential meaning is that it denotes a particular situation which can be regarded as distinguished from the ordinary or common runs of situations. It has been found to bear this meaning in a number of other statutory contexts of a widely varying nature: e g *Re Norman* (1886) 16 QBD 673 per Lopes LJ at 677; *Re Hunter (a Bankrupt), Ex Parte Exclusive English Imports Ltd (in liq)* [1954] NZLR 747 per F B Adams J at 754; *Clarks of Hove Ltd v Bankers' Union* [1978] 1 WLR 1207 per Geoffrey Lane LJ at 1215; *Springfield Nominees Pty Ltd v Bridgelands Securities Ltd* (1992) 38 FCR 217 per Wilcox J at 225; *Lyon v Wilcox* [1994] 3 NZLR 422 CA per Casey J at 431; *Peninsula Watchdog Group (Inc) v Minister of Energy* [1996] 2 NZLR 529 CA per Richardson P at 536.

'The other thing that may be said about the meaning of the words "special circumstances" in this context is that there should be no exhaustive attempt to define or list the matters which may come within the rubric "special circumstances" as used here: *Re Norman* ibid; *Springfield Nominees* ibid ...' *Expile Pty Ltd v Jabb's Excavations Pty Ltd* (2002) 194 ALR 138; BC200205437; [2002] NSWSC 851 at [5]–[6], per Hamilton J

New Zealand [The Court of Appeal, per cur, adopted the meaning adopted by Tipping J in the High Court proceeding of this case at [1993] NZFLR 716 who applied the Full Court's general description of 'special circumstances' in *Re M* [1993] NZFLR 74 as] '... facts peculiar to the particular case which set it apart from other cases.' *Lyon v Wilcox* [1994] 3 NZLR 422 at 431, CA, per cur

New Zealand [Section 109(2) of the Mining Act 1971.] 'A special consideration is one outside the common run of things, one which ... is exceptional, abnormal, or unusual, but something less than extraordinary or unique.' *Peninsula Watchdog Group (Inc) v Minister of Energy* [1996] 2 NZLR 529 at 536, CA, per cur

SPECIAL DELIVERY

Australia ' "Special" is relevantly defined in the Shorter Oxford English Dictionary on Historical Principles (Vol 11, Clarendon Press Oxford) as:

"A. adj 1. Of such a kind as to exceed or excel in some way that which is usual or common; exceptional in character, quality, or degree. 2. Of friends: Admitted to particular intimacy; held in particular esteem ME. 3. Marked off from others of the kind by some distinguishing qualities or features; having a distinct or individual character; also, in weakened sense, particular, certain ME. B. Additional to the usual or ordinary 1840... "

'In *Boscolo v Secretary, Department of Social Security* [1999] FCA 106 at 531, French J referred to other court decisions which have defined the word "special". French J stated:

"The word 'special' conditioning 'reasons' or 'circumstances' guards the entrance to the exercise of many different statutory discretions. It is generally futile to search for its meaning in terms of other words. It is in essence instrumental, a direction to the decision-maker that the discretion it constrains is not lightly to be enlivened. A Full Court has spoken of it as having content which is '... sufficiently understood not to require judicial gloss": *Beadle v Director-General of Social Security* (1985) 60 ALR 225 at 228. If helpful to speak in terms of its meaning almost all of it comes from context. Thus man may be 'special' in relation to animals generally but '... when you are speaking of poets, he may need to be a Milton': *Holpitt Pty Ltd v Varimu Pty Ltd* (1991) 29 FCR 576 at 578; 103 ALR 684 at 686 per Burchett J. It is an elastic instruction suitable for application across a range of situations: *Jess v Scott* (1986) 12 FCR 187; 70 ALR 185. This is just another way of pointing to its instrumental character. That application is not to be confined by precise limits or rules: *Beadle* at 228. Circumstances or reasons will not necessarily fall outside the designation of 'special' because they fall within a class which is widely defined or because they are circumstances or reasons which can be foreseen before they arise: *Hutchins*; *Jarlas Pty Ltd v Commissioner of Taxation (Cth)* (1987) 14 FCR 510 at 527; 74 ALR 455 at 473. The core of the requirement for 'special circumstances' or 'special reasons' is that there be something unusual or different to take the matter the subject of the discretion out of the ordinary course: *Minister for Community Services and Health v Chee Keong Thoo* (1988) 8 AAR 245 at 261–262; 78 ALR 307 at 324 (Burchett J). But that does not require that the case be extremely unusual, uncommon or exceptional: *Secretary, Department of Social Security v Hodgson* (1992) 37 FCR 32; 108 ALR 322."

' "Special" can be said to be exceptional, has a distinct, individual or instrumental character. "Special" indicates to the decision maker that the discretion is one which is not lightly enlivened. However "special reasons" is an elastic instruction suitable for application across a range of situations.' *Binks v North Sydney Council* BC200100103; [2001] NSWSC 27 at [8]–[10], per Harrison M

SPECIAL EDUCATION

New Zealand [Section 2(1) of the Special Education Act 1989 provides that: 'Special education means education or help from a special school, special class, special clinic, or special service:'] '[49] This definition is to be contrasted with that in the 1964 Act. While the 1964 definition emphasises the handicap or difficulty of the child and the consequent need for educational treatment beyond that normally obtained in ordinary classes, the new definition is written solely in terms of institutions. It does that simply by listing the special facilities provided for in s 98 of the 1964 Act and established or authorised by the Minister. Section 2(2) of the 1989 Act underlines the limiting of "special education" in the 1989 Act to those special facilities:

(2) In this Part, and Parts 2 and 3, of this Act, unless the context otherwise requires, the terms special class, special clinic, special school, and special service have the meanings assigned to them by section 2 of the Education Act 1964.

'[50] Although that attempted definition misfires, since there is no definition of those four terms in s 2 of the 1964 Act, or anywhere else in it, the definition is significant because it ties the various types of special facilities and the expression "special education" in ss 2 and 9 of the 1989 Act back to the specific institutions and facilities established or authorised by the Minister under s 98 of the 1964 Act, and to nothing else. It does not have the broader emphasis of the 1964 definition.

'[51] Notwithstanding the availability of the shorthand allowed by the new definition, Parliamentary Counsel did not in fact rely solely on it and in the substantive provisions of s 9(1) and (2) of the 1989 Act effectively equated "special education" with the four special facilities. For instance, the former provides:

> 9. Special education — (1) If satisfied that a person under 21 should have special education, the Secretary shall –
>
> > (a) Agree with the person's parents that the person should be enrolled, or direct them to enrol the person, at a particular state school, special school, special class, or special clinic; or
> >
> > (b) Agree with the person's parents that the person should have, or direct them to ensure that the person has, education or help from a special service.

(The reference to "a particular state school" was added to the Bill in the course of its passage through Parliament to enable the secretary to use his power of direction where a parent is refusing to enrol a child in the school in question. The power, which has been used in practice for instance to override an enrolment scheme, appears to be of no consequence in this case.)

'[52] The equation in the 1989 Act of special education with the institutions established or authorised by the Minister under s 98 also appears in the critical s 9(4) which requires a s 9 agreement or direction if "special education" within its terms is to be provided:

> (4) No person shall be or continue to be enrolled at a special school, special class, or special clinic, or have or continue to have education or help from a special service, except pursuant to an agreement or direction under subsection (1) of this section.

...

'[56] We do not see the legislation in that way. To repeat, the 1989 definition of "special education" ties back to the 1964 Act by reference to "special school, special class, special clinic, or special service" and the misfiring but nevertheless significant definition of those expressions. Under the 1964 Act those special facilities are established or authorised only by the Minister (or authorised delegate). While the predecessors to the ORRS were so established under s 98 the record before us indicates that the other SE2000 programmes were not. Rather, they were and are provided through

the decisions of school boards of trustees, sometimes operating on a cluster basis (as with RTLB), on the basis of the additional funding provided under the relevant aspects of SE2000. It follows that it is only the provision of education in special schools and through the ORRS that at present requires the ministry to make decisions under s 9 about individual students. (See also the power in s 9(1) in respect of regular state schools: see para [51] above.) The remaining resources are directed for the benefit of those with special educational needs who under s 8 attend local schools which are to provide the relevant services through the other SE2000 programmes and the related funding.' *Attorney-General v Daniels* [2003] 2 NZLR 743

SPECIAL NEED RELATIVE

Australia [Regulation 2(1) of the Migration Regulations 1989 (Cth) defines 'special need relative'.] '... the definition of "special need relative" may encompass the relationship of parent and child, and so authorise the grant of a permit to a parent who is an illegal entrant in Australia, if the child in Australia has a need for the presence in Australia of that parent.' *Chen v Minister for Immigration and Ethnic Affairs* (1994) 51 FCR 322 at 326–327; 123 ALR 126 at 130, per Davies J

SPECIAL REASONS

[Under the Road Traffic Act 1972 (repealed; see now the Road Traffic Offenders Act 1988, s 34(1)) a court is empowered not to order disqualification for certain offences where 'special reasons' are considered to exist.] 'In the course of this case Watkins LJ indicated seven matters which ought to be taken into account by justices if a submission is made that special reasons exist for the defendant not being disqualified. First of all they should consider how far the vehicle was in fact driven; second, in what manner it was driven; third, what was the state of the vehicle; fourth, whether it was the intention of the driver to drive any further; fifth, the prevailing conditions with regard to the road and the traffic on it; sixth, whether there was any possibility of danger by contact with other road users; and, finally, what was the reason for the vehicle being driven at all.' *Chatters v Burke* [1986] 3 All ER 168 at 171–172, per Taylor J

Australia [Section 48(7)(c) of the Police (Complaints and Disciplinary Proceedings) Act 1985 (SA) stipulates that a person appointed to be the Police Complaints Authority or the Commissioner of Police cannot be required to divulge information disclosed or obtained under the Act in the course of an investigation except where such a requirement is made by a court in the interests of justice.] 'So far as relevant, the section provides that neither the Commissioner nor the Authority can be required to disclose records of the type here in question, unless the Court is satisfied that there are special reasons requiring the making of an order for disclosure and that the interests of justice cannot adequately be served, except by the making of such an order.

'A consideration of the history of legislation, as particularly revealed by relevant second reading speeches, indicates that the confidentiality provisions of the statute were directed towards what was, on the occasion of the 2000 amendment, described as the "sometime practice of defence counsel in a criminal trial subpoenaing the records of the Police Complaints Authority in relation to officers involved in the case in order to see if there was anything discreditable in their records which could be used to attack police testimony". The section was therefore sought to be amended to "tighten this up", by requiring the existence of special reasons and satisfaction that the interests of justice could not adequately be served, except by the making of an order for disclosure.

'It is to be noted that this explanation was given subsequently to what was said in a second reading speech related to earlier amendments to s 48, in 1998. At that time the Minister commented:

> "This provision was amended in 1996 to provide that it must be in the interests of justice before the Court can require information to be divulged. This change was a result of defence counsel conducting 'fishing expeditions' in the hope of finding something in Police Complaints Authority files that would discredit police witnesses in criminal trials. These 'fishing expeditions' are disruptive not only to the Authority and the Police but also to the trials of criminal matters, when subpoenas are sought as a matter goes to trial.
> "'Fishing expeditions' have not ceased and the provision is now further amended to require applicants to satisfy the court that there are special reasons requiring the making of an order and the interests of justice cannot be adequately served except by making the order. Where the information in the files is necessary

to ensure that justice is done the information will be made available to the defence, but only then."

'It is thus abundantly clear as to what was the evil sought to be addressed by the legislation. The phrase "special reasons" has not been judicially defined in the context of s 48 in its present form, but, clearly, it establishes a requirement that an applicant for disclosure must establish the existence of a situation which, to paraphrase the language of Chernov J in *Telstra Corp Ltd v CXA Communications Ltd* (1998) 146 FLR 481, takes the case out of the mainstream of the obvious legislative intent that proceedings under the statute are to be confidential. The reasons must be special to the particular case, the features of which are out of the ordinary; and by reason of which it can also fairly be said that the interests of justice cannot adequately be served, absent the disclosure sought.

'This is consistent with the reasoning of King CJ in *Goldsmith v Newman* (1992) 59 SASR 404 at 409–11. As the learned Chief Justice there pointed out at 409, the expression "special reasons" takes its colour, necessarily, from the context in which it is found and, in particular, the purpose which the relevant statutory provision is intended to serve. But, the expression "special reasons" necessarily connotes the existence of some situation which is, patently, a substantial departure from the normal disadvantage of not having access to the restricted information in issue.' *R v Ferri* (2002) 220 LSJS 155; BC200203839; [2002] SASC 217 at [12]–[16], per Olsson AJ

Special reasons relating to the offence

New Zealand [Section 107B(2) of the Fisheries Act 1983 uses the term 'special reasons relating to the offence'.] 'It is commonplace that the term "special" in s 107B(2) means something exceptional and not something general nor found in the common run of cases.' *Atwill v Basile* [1995] 1 NZLR 712 at 713, per Doogue J

New Zealand [Section 107B(2) of the Fisheries Act 1983.] 'In the statutory context "special" is a limiting adjective. A special reason is one that is not found in the common run of cases. While not necessarily being categorised as "exceptional" or "extraordinary" it is one that may properly be characterised as not ordinary or common or usual.' *Basile v Atwill* [1995] 2 NZLR 537 at 539, CA, per cur

SPECIAL RELATIONSHIP

New Zealand [Evidence Amendment Act (No 2) 1980, s 35.] 'The New Zealand Court of Appeal approach invokes a definition which is peculiar to s 35 of the Evidence Amendment Act. The test is in two parts. First, there must be "a relationship of a kind that would encourage the imparting of confidences" *and* "that has a public interest element in it". The first is necessarily fact dependent. The second phrase is more difficult.' *R v Lory (Ruling 8)* [1997] 1 NZLR 44 at 48, per Hammond J

SPECIALTY

Canada '[27] The words "specialty" and "deed", as well as the expression "sealed instrument" are often treated as equivalents for general legal purposes in English and Canadian dictionaries. As well, most dictionaries draw a sharp distinction between a "specialty" and a "specialty debt". The following inventory does not purport to be exhaustive:

A Concise Dictionary of Law, 2nd ed., (Oxford: Oxford University Press, 1990) s *v.* "specialty", "deed":

specialty n. See deed.

deed n. A written document that is signed, sealed, and delivered. *If it is a contractual document, it is referred to as a contract under seal (or a specialty).*

[Emphasis added]

(*b*) Osborn's *Concise Law Dictionary*, 8th ed., (London: Sweet & Maxwell, 1993) s *v.* "specialty":

specialty. A somewhat archaic term used to refer to a contract under seal (*q.v.*). A specialty debt is one due under a deed (*q.v.*).

(*c*) Jowitt's *Dictionary of English Law*, vol. 2, 2nd ed., (London: Sweet & Maxwell Limited, 1977) s *v.* "specialty":

Specialty, a contract under seal.

(*d*) D.A. Dukelow & B. Nuse, *The Dictionary of Canadian Law*, (Ontario: Carswell, 1991) s *v.* "specialty":

Specialty. *n.* A contract under seal.

(*e*) *The Canadian Oxford Dictionary*, (Toronto, Ont.: Oxford University Press, 1998) s *v.* "specialty":

specialty ... 4 *Law* an instrument under seal; a sealed contract. [Middle English from Old French (e)specialité (as SPECIAL)]

(*f*) *The Oxford English Dictionary*, vol. X, (Oxford: Clarendon Press, 1970) s *v.* "specialty":

Specialty

7. *Law.* A special contract, obligation, or bond, expressed in an instrument under seal.

c 1482 in *Cal. Proc. Chanc. Q. Eliz.* (1830) II. Pref. 63 Your besecher can have noo remedy by cours of the comen lawe, for asmoche as he hath noo specialte in writyng. 1483 *Cely Papers* (Camden) 134 To receyve yn thys martt all syche specyalltes of yowrs payabull yn thys martt. 1528 in *Lett. Suppress. Monast.* (Camden) 3 Certen munimentes, evidencez, and specialties, tochinge and apperteynynge unto our monastery. 1594 WEST *2nd Pt. Symbol., Chancerie* § 120 He neither tooke any specialtie or securitie of him, ... nor provided any witnesses to be present. 1621 *Galway Arch.* In *10th Rep. Hist. MSS. Comm.* App. V. 470 Those persons whoe have neglected to produce theire said evidences, grauntes, and specialties, to bee looked into by the Maior. 1644 HOWELL *Twelve Treat.* (1661) 238 There's no legall Instrument, no Bond, Bill, or Specialty can be writ but upon his seal'd paper. 1768 BLACKSTONE *Comm.* III. 154 Where the debt arises upon a specialty, that is, upon a deed or instrument under seal. 1781 M. MADAN *Thelyphthora* III. 309 Marriage-settlements, mortgage-deeds, and specialties of various kinds. 1856 H. BROOM *Comm. Common Law* II.i. 274 *A specialty ... is distinguished from a simple contract in writing by certain solemnities attendant on its execution – viz. by sealing and delivery. 1883 H.G. Wood Limitation of Actions 64 All instruments under seal of record, and liabilities imposed by statute, are specialties within the meaning of the Stat. 21 James I.* [Emphasis added]

'[28] I note parenthetically that the English statute of 1623 (*An Act for Limitation of Actions, and for avoiding of Suits in Law* 21 James I Cap. 16) to which reference is made in *The Oxford English Dictionary* definition reproduced above was the first *Statute of Limitations* to employ the term "specialty". It provided, *inter alia*, a six-year limitation period for "all Actions of Debt grounded upon any Lending or Contract without Specialty ...". That provision did not apply to an action of debt or covenant upon a contract under seal. See J.K. Angell, *A Treatise on the Limitations of Actions at Law*, 6th ed. (Boston: Little, Brown, and Company, 1876) at 88–89.

'[29] I have not come across any legal dictionary that limits the meaning of the word "specialty" to a contract involving a debt obligation for a fixed sum or an instrument under seal given as security for the payment of a sum certain. The few legal dictionaries that include definitions of that nature select more general phrases, such as "a contract under seal" or "[a] writing sealed and delivered, containing some agreement or promise ..." as the primary meaning of the word "specialty". See *Black's Law Dictionary*, 5th ed., (St. Paul, Minn.: West Publishing Co., 1979) s *v.* "specialty" at p. 1571 and *Bouvier's Law Dictionary and Concise Encyclopedia*, vol. 3, 8th ed., (Buffalo, New York: William s Hein Company, 1984) s *v.* "specialty" at page 3100.

'[30] The leading English legal history textbooks explain that, by the 17th century, the term "specialty", at least when used to designate a document giving rise to legal obligations, was commonly equated to "deed". See W. Holdsworth, *A History of English Law*, vol. III (London: Sweet & Maxwell, 1966) at 417–429; and Salmond, *Essays in Jurisprudence* 93, 94, cited in Holdsworth's *A History of English Law*, at p. 103, footnote 5. A wider meaning was ascribed to the term in the context of limitation statutes. That point is illustrated quite nicely in the jurisprudence-rich explanation of the term "specialty" found in J.S. James, *Stroud's Judicial Dictionary of Words and Phrases*, vol. 5, 5th ed., (London: Sweet & Maxwell Limited, 1986) s *v.* "specialty":

SPECIALTY.

(1) A *"specialty" is a contract under seal; and a "specialty debt" is an obligation secured by such a contract, e.g. a bond, or mortgage. So, also, an obligation arising under a statute is a "specialty" within the meaning of the Statutes of Limitation; e.g. an action under 2 Edw. 6, c. 13, for carrying away corn without setting out tithes (Talory v.*

Jackson Cro. Car. 513); an action for an escape (*Jones v. Pope* 1 Wms. Saund. 36); or for calls on a shareholder in a company formed by Act of Parliament (*Cork & Bandon Railway v. Goode* 13 C.B. 826), or under the Companies Act 1862 (c. 89), ss 16, 75, 90, 134 (see Companies Act 1948 (c. 38), s 260): (*Buck v. Robson* L.R. 10 Eq. 629); or under a deed of settlement (*Re Portsmouth Banking Co.* L.R. 2 Eq. 167); or a shareholder's right to a dividend or to an authorised return of capital duly certified by the seal of the company (*Re Drogheda Steam Packet Co.* [1903] 1 Ir. R. 512; *Re Artizans' Land & Mortgage Corporation* [1904] 1 Ch. 796); or debentures issued by a company under statutory powers (*Re Cornwall Railway* [1897] 2 Ch. 74); or for dues authorised by Parliament (*Shepherd v. Hills* 11 Ex. 55). But a penalty under a bye-law of a company founded by charter under the Great Seal, is not a "specialty," for such a liability springs out of the member's implied consent to obey the bye-laws, which is in effect a contract without specialty (*Tobacco Pipe Co. v. Loder* 16 Q.B. 765); so also the mere recital in a deed of a simple contract debt does not make the debt a specialty (*Ivens v. Elwes* 24 L.J. Ch. 249), so, of an acknowledgment by deed of such a debt (*Brook v. Harwood* 3 Ch. 225); but if the deed secures such debt, the debt merges and becomes a specialty (*Commissioners of Stamps v. Hope* [1891] A.C. 476), so if the deed agrees to give a specialty security (*Saunders v. Milsome* L.R. 2 Eq. 573).

(2) For a statement of the nature of a specialty debt, see *per* Lord Maugham, *R. v. Williams* [1942] A.C. 541, at pp. 554 *et seq*. Share certificates, though under seal, are not specialties, *ibid*.

(3) An action by an agricultural labourer for the difference between the wages paid to him as agreed, and those to which he had been entitled under the Agricultural Wages (Regulation) Act 1924 (c. 37), held not be an action for a specialty debt upon that statute, but an action on the simple contract with his employer, as varied by the statute (*Gutsell v. Reeve* [1936] 1 K.B. 272).

(4) (*Limitation Act 1939* (c. 21), s 2(3)) meant deeds and contracts under seal (*Leivers v. Barber, Walker & Co.* [1943] K.B. 385).

(5) "Specialty" (*Limitation Act 1980* (c.58), s 8). An action to enforce a tenant's right of franchisement under the Leasehold Reform Act 1967 (c.88) was an action on a "specialty" within the meaning of this section (*Collin v. Duke of Westminster* [1985] 2 W.L.R. 553).

(6) As to rent: see *Kidd v. Boone* L.R. 12 Eq. 89; *Re Hastings* 6 Ch. D. 610.

(7) The action of debt upon "bonds and specialties" given by Fraudulent *Devises Act* 1691 (c. 14), s 6, against heirs and devisees of obligors, did not extend to damages on a covenant, for the context limited the "specialties" to those on which the action of debt lay (*Wilson v. Knubley* 7 East, 128).

Cp. PAROL; SIMPLE CONTRACT.
[Emphasis added]

'[31] The *Report of the Ontario Law Reform Commission on Limitation of Actions*, (Ontario: Department of the Attorney General, 1969) at 42–43 joins the English authorities mentioned above in recognizing that the term "specialty" in *Statutes of Limitations* has historically included any contract under seal:

3. *Specialties and Recognizances*

The term "specialty" is described by Franks (at p. 188) as "an archaic word of somewhat imprecise meaning".

Usually, a specialty is thought to refer to a contract under seal, which, unlike the simple contract, does not require for its validity consideration for a promise. However, an obligation to pay money arising under a statute is also said to be a specialty. Thus, actions for taxes, or for compensation for land expropriated by statute, or for interest charged contrary to statute have been said to be actions on specialties for the purposes of limitations. (Actions to recover penalties, damages or sums of money given by a statute are the subject of special limitation periods. See s 45(1)(h) and (m) and the 1936 English Report at para. 4.)

Sometimes it has been said that a judgment is a specialty, and, to a lesser extent the term has been applied to a recognizance. (See Weaver, at p. 301, Preston and Newsom, at p. 57, and s 3(1)(f) of the Uniform Act.) These latter applications of "specialty" must be regarded as doubtful.

Historically, contracts are classified in three categories:
1. Contracts of record,
2. *Contracts under seal, usually referred to as a specialty*,
3. Simple contracts.

"Contract of record" applies to judgments and recognizances, which are entered in the record of court proceedings. Where money was owing under a judgment or recognizance, the law implied a debt, which arose from the entry on the record and not from agreement between the parties. The liability to pay is independent of consent and thus the application of the term contract to judgments and recognizances is not a satisfactory one.

The recognizance is an obligation acknowledged before some court or judge to secure the performance of some act, the obligation being entered on the court record. If the act is not performed, the recognizance is forfeited and the person giving it becomes a debtor to the Crown for the sum he bound himself to pay. The procedure by which forfeited recognizances are dealt with is set out in *The Estreats Act* (R.S.O. 1960, c. 124).

So far as limitations are concerned, considerable clarification would result if the term specialty were not used and the various matters treated separately, as follows:
1. *Judgments*,
2. *Recognizances*,
3. *Contracts under seal*.
4. *Obligations arising under statute.*
[Emphasis added]

'[32] New Brunswick *Statutes of Limitations* have used the word "specialty" in its wider sense to refer to both sealed contracts and contracts of record such as judgments and recognizances. Indeed, s 2 of the various *Statutes of Limitations* in effect in this Province from 1877 to 1993 included judgments in the list of specialties within their purview. Judgments were removed from that list with the adoption in 1993 of s 2.1 of the *Act*, which changed the starting point for the tolling of the 20-year limitation period on a judgment from the date when "the cause of action arose" to "the date of the judgment".

'[33] In T. Parsons, *Law of Contracts: Historical Writings in Law and Jurisprudence,* vol. 1 (Buffalo: William F. Hein & Company, 1980) at 7, the author explains that contracts are generally divided into contracts by specialty and simple contracts. He goes on to define contracts by specialty as follows:

> Contracts by specialty are those which are reduced to writing and attested by seal – or, to use the common phrase, contracts under seal; and contracts of record. These last are judgments, recognizances, and statutes staple. But the term "contracts by specialty" is sometimes confined to contracts under seal ...

'[34] Oliver L.J. was surely right when he stated in *Collin v. Duke of Westminster*, [1985] 1 All E.R. 463 (C.A.), at p. 472, that "[t]he obvious and most common case of an action on a specialty is an action based on a contract under seal ...". See, as well, *Aiken v. Stewart Wrightson*, [1995] 3 All E.R. 449 (Q.B., Potter J., as he then was), at p. 460 and *Raja v. Lloyd's TSB Bank plc*, [2001] E.W.J. No. 606 at para. 12 (C.A.), online: QL (EWJ).

'[35] Thus, when the New Brunswick legislature resorted to the word "specialty" to express its will in the successive *Statutes of Limitations* enacted since 1836, it used a word that has been understood since the very first *Statutes of Limitations* to include any sealed contract or deed.' *Kenmont Management Inc v Saint John Port Authority* (2001) 210 DLR (4th) 676 at 726–731, NBCA, per Robertson JA

SPECIALTY ARRANGEMENTS/ SPECIALTY RULE

[The Criminal Justice Act 1987, s 95(1) provides that the Secretary of State must not order a person's extradition to a category 2 territory if there are no 'speciality arrangements' with the category 2 territory.] '[10] Section 95 is cross-headed "Speciality". For some reason which we have not fathomed the legislature chose this word to mean the same as "specialty", which is the term long used in the law of extradition to refer to the rule (I summarise) that an extradited person may only be tried in the requesting state for the crime or crimes

for which he has been extradited. In this judgment I shall use the expression "specialty rule"... ' *R (on the application of Bermingham) v Director of the Serious Fraud Office; Bermingham v Government of the United States of America* [2006] EWHC 200 (Admin) at [10], [2006] 3 All ER 239, per Laws LJ

SPECIFIC PERFORMANCE

[For 44 Halsbury's Laws (4th edn) para 401 see now 44(1) Halsbury's Laws (4th edn) (Reissue) para 801.]

SPECIFIED FUND

[CPR 25.1(1)(l) empowers the court to order, as an interim remedy, a 'specified fund' to be paid into court where there is a dispute over a party's right to that fund.] '[1] ... The short issue of law raised on this application is whether the court had jurisdiction to make such an order under CPR 25.1(1)(l) (the rule) which provides that amongst the interim remedies which the court may grant the court may make "an order for a specified fund to be paid into court or otherwise secured, where there is a dispute over a party's right to the fund ...".

'[2] This turns on the question whether the alleged debt owed by the defendant to the claimant constitutes a "specified fund" which the court can under the rule order to be paid into court or otherwise secured. The rule replaces and (in the language of the *White Book Service* (Autumn 2002), vol 1, p 502 (para 25.1.31)) "is based on" RSC Ord 29, r 2(3). There is apparently no authority providing guidance on the current rule or its predecessor.

...

'[6] Whether the claimant is entitled to invoke the rule turns on the question whether on a claim by the creditor against the debtor the debt itself constitutes a "specified fund" within the meaning of the rule. In my judgment it clearly does not do so.

'[7] The word "fund" is not a term of art and (like so many other words) is capable of a variety of meanings depending on the context in which it is used. Two authorities have been cited to me which exemplify this fact. In *Allchin v Coulthard (Treasurer of the County Borough of South Shields)* [1942] 2 All ER 39 at 44, [1942] 2 KB 228 at 234 Lord Greene MR referred to two distinct meanings of the word. He said:

> "The word 'fund' may mean actual cash resources of a particular kind (e.g., money in a

drawer or a bank) or it may be a mere accountancy expression used to describe a particular category which a person uses in making up his accounts. The words 'payment out of' when used in connection with the word 'fund' in its first meaning connote actual payment, e.g., by taking the money out of the drawer or drawing a cheque on the bank. When used in connection with the word "fund" in its second meaning they connote that for the purposes of the account in which the fund finds a place, the payment is debited to that fund, an operation which, of course, has no relation to the actual method of payment or the particular cash resources out of which the payment is made ... A fund in the second sense is merely an accountancy category. It has a real existence in that sense, but not in the sense that a real payment can be made out of it as distinct from being debited to it."

'[8] In the case of *Shamia v Joory* [1958] 1 All ER 111, [1958] 1 QB 448 another meaning was given to the word in a different context. In that case Barry J held that in accordance with the principle stated by Blackburn J in *Griffin v Weatherby* (1868) LR 3 QB 753 at 758 (the principle) if a creditor wishes to make a gift of that debt to a third party and with that intention in mind instructs the debtor to pay the third party, and if the debtor subsequently promises to pay the debt to the third party, the third party may sue the debtor for the debt. For the purpose of the principle the authorities speak of the essential need for the existence of what is referred to as "a fund" over which the transferor has a right of disposal and for this purpose a debt owed to the transferor is such a fund. In this context Barry J said ([1958] 1 All ER 111 at 114, [1958] 1 QB 448 at 458):

"... there is, of course, no magic in [the word 'fund']; nor is it to be regarded as though it were a word used in a statute. It was clearly chosen by Blackburn J not as a term of art, but as a word which aptly fitted the facts which were then under consideration."

'[9] Whilst therefore in the context of the principle the word "fund" is apt to mean or include a debt, contrary to the submissions of Mr Nicholls (counsel for the claimant) the authorities referred to lend no support to the proposition that the word "fund" has that meaning in any other, let alone the present, context.' *Myers v Design Inc (International) Ltd* [2003] EWHC 103 (Ch) at [1]–[2], [6]–[9], [2003] 1 All ER 1168, per Lightman J

SPORTS AND PASTIMES

[In an application for registration of a village green as a common, one ground under the Commons Registration Act 1965, s 22 is that there is a 'customary right to indulge in lawful sports and pastimes'; it was sought to justify refusal of registration on the ground, inter alia, of lack of evidence of the use of the land for sports as opposed to pastimes, and that such sports and pastimes had to be the same as those which would give rise to customary rights under s 22(1), namely an activity with a communal element such as playing cricket, shooting at butts or dancing around the maypole.] 'The first point concerned the nature of the activities on the glebe. They showed that it had been used for solitary or family pastimes (walking, tobogganing, family games) but not for anything which could properly be called a sport. Miss Cameron said that this was insufficient for two reasons. First, because the definition spoke of "sports and pastimes" and therefore, as a matter of language, pastimes were not enough. There had to be at least one sport. Secondly, because the "sports and pastimes" in class "c" had to be the same sports and pastimes as those in respect of which there could have been customary rights under class "b" and this meant that there had to be some communal element about them, such as playing cricket, shooting at butts or dancing round the maypole. I do not accept either of these arguments. As a matter of language, I think that "sports and pastimes" is not two classes of activities but a single composite class which uses two words in order to avoid arguments over whether an activity is a sport or a pastime. The law constantly uses pairs of words in this way. As long as the activity can properly be called a sport or a pastime, it falls within the composite class. As for the historical argument, I think that one must distinguish between the concept of a sport or pastime and the particular kind of sports or pastimes which people have played or enjoyed at different times in history. Thus in *Fitch v Rawling* (1795) 2 Hy Bl 393, [1775–1802] All ER Rep 571, 126 ER 614 Buller J recognised a custom to play cricket on a village green as having existed since the time of Richard I, although the game itself was unknown at the time and would have been unlawful for some centuries thereafter: see *Mercer v Denne* [1904] 2 Ch 534 at 538–539, 553, [1904–7] All ER Rep 71 at 76. In *Abercromby v Fermoy Town Comrs* [1900] 1 IR 302 the Irish Court of Appeal upheld a custom for the inhabitants of Fermoy to use a strip of land along the river for their evening passeggiata. Holmes LJ (at 314) said that popular amusement took many shapes: ". . legal principle does not require that rights of this nature should be limited to certain ancient pastimes". In any case, he said, the Irish had too much of a sense of humour to dance around a maypole. Class "c" is concerned with the creation of town and village greens after 1965 and in my opinion sports and pastimes includes those activities which would be so regarded in our own day. I agree with Carnwath J in *R v Suffolk CC, ex p Steed* (1995) 70 P & CR 487 at 503, when he said that dog walking and playing with children were, in modern life, the kind of informal recreation which may be the main function of a village green. It may be, of course, that the user is so trivial and sporadic as not to carry the outward appearance of user as of right. In the present case, however, Mr Chapman found "abundant evidence of use of the glebe for informal recreation" which he held to be a pastime for the purposes of the Act.' *R v Oxfordshire County Council, ex p Sunningwell Parish Council* [1999] 3 All ER 385 at 396–397, HL, per Lord Hoffmann

SPOUSE

[The Rent Act 1977, Sch 1 para 2(1), allows the 'surviving spouse' of a statutory tenant to succeed to the tenancy on the death of the original tenant. Where a homosexual couple had lived together for a long period, the surviving partner claimed to be entitled to succeed to the statutory tenancy as 'a person who was living with the original tenant as his or her wife or husband' as permitted by Sch 1 para 1(2), or alternatively to succeed to an assured tenancy as a 'member of the original tenant's family' within Sch 1 para 3(1).] 'The question is, therefore, was the appellant the spouse of, or a member of the family of, Mr Thompson within the meaning of this Act? I stress "within the meaning of this Act" since it is all that your Lordships are concerned with. In other statutes, in other contexts, the words may have a wider or a narrower meaning than here. I refer to the judgment of McHugh J in *Re Wakim, ex p McNally, Re Wakim, ex p Darvall, Re Brown, ex p Amann, Spinks v Prentice* (1999) 73 ALJR 839 at 850 in the High Court of Australia which recognises that changes in attitudes and perceptions may require a wider meaning to be given to a word such as "marriage", at any rate in some contexts.

'The first question then is whether the appellant was the "spouse" of Mr Thompson within the meaning of para 2 of Sch 1 to the 1977 Act as amended. I recognise that if the non-gender specific noun "spouse" stood alone the matter might be

more debatable as Mr Blake QC contends, though the ordinary meaning is plainly "husband" or "wife". In the context of this Act, however, "spouse" means in my view legally a husband or wife. The 1988 amendment extended the meaning to include as a "spouse" a person living with the original tenant "as his or her wife or husband". This was obviously intended to include persons not legally husband and wife who lived as such without being married. That prima facie means a man and a woman, and the man must show that the woman was living with him as "his" wife; the woman that he was living with her as "her" husband. I do not think that Parliament as recently as 1988 intended that these words should be read as meaning "my same-sex partner" rather than specifically "my husband" or "my wife". If that had been the intention, it would have been spelled out. The words cannot in my view be read as the appellant contends. I thus agree as to the result with the decision in *Harrogate BC v Simpson* (1984) 17 HLR 205. The appellant accordingly fails in the first way he puts his appeal. Whether that result is discriminatory against same-sex couples in the light of the fact that non-married different sex couples living together are to be treated as spouses, so as to allow one to succeed to the tenancy of the other, may have to be considered when the Human Rights Act 1998 is in force. Whether the result is socially desirable in 1999 is a matter for Parliament.' *Fitzpatrick v Sterling Housing Association Ltd* [1999] 4 All ER 705 at 710, HL, per Lord Slynn of Hadleigh

'[1] My Lords, on the death of a protected tenant of a dwelling house his or her surviving spouse, if then living in the house, becomes a statutory tenant by succession. But marriage is not essential for this purpose. A person who was living with the original tenant "as his or her wife or husband" is treated as the spouse of the original tenant: see para 2(2) of Sch 1 to the Rent Act 1977. In *Fitzpatrick v Sterling Housing Association Ltd* [1999] 4 All ER 705, [2001] 1 AC 27 your Lordships' House decided this provision did not include persons in a same-sex relationship. The question raised by this appeal is whether this reading of para 2 can survive the coming into force of the Human Rights Act 1998. In *Fitzpatrick*'s case the original tenant had died in 1994.

'[2] In the present case the original tenant died after the 1998 Act came into force on 2 October 2000. In April 1983 Mr Hugh Wallwyn-James was granted an oral residential tenancy of the basement flat at 17 Cresswell Gardens, London SW5. Until his death on 5 January 2001 he lived there in a stable and monogamous homosexual relationship with the defendant Mr Juan Godin-Mendoza. Mr Godin-Mendoza is still living there. After the death of Mr Wallwyn-James the landlord, Mr Ahmad Ghaidan, brought proceedings in the West London County Court claiming possession of the flat. Judge Cowell held that on the death of Hugh Wallwyn-James, Mr Godin-Mendoza did not succeed to the tenancy of the flat as the surviving spouse of Hugh Wallwyn-James within the meaning of para 2 of Sch 1 to the 1977 Act, but that he did become entitled to an assured tenancy of the flat by succession as a member of the original tenant's "family" under para 3(1) of that schedule.

'[3] Mr Godin-Mendoza appealed, and the Court of Appeal, comprising Kennedy, Buxton and Keene LJJ, allowed the appeal ([2002] EWCA Civ 1533, [2002] 4 All ER 1162, [2003] Ch 380). The court held he was entitled to succeed to a tenancy of the flat as a statutory tenant under para 2. From that decision Mr Ghaidan, the landlord, appealed to your Lordships' House.

...

'[5] On an ordinary reading of this language para 2(2) draws a distinction between the position of a heterosexual couple living together in a house as husband and wife and a homosexual couple living together in a house. The survivor of a heterosexual couple may become a statutory tenant by succession, the survivor of a homosexual couple cannot. That was decided in *Fitzpatrick*'s case. The survivor of a homosexual couple may, in competition with other members of the original tenant's "family", become entitled to an assured tenancy under para 3. But even if he does, as in the present case, this is less advantageous. Notably, so far as the present case is concerned, the rent payable under an assured tenancy is the contractual or market rent, which may be more than the fair rent payable under a statutory tenancy, and an assured tenant may be evicted for non-payment of rent without the court needing to be satisfied, as is essential in the case of a statutory tenancy, that it is reasonable to make a possession order. In these and some other respects the succession rights granted by the statute to the survivor of a homosexual couple in respect of the house where he or she is living are less favourable than the succession rights granted to the survivor of a heterosexual couple.

'[6] Mr Godin-Mendoza's claim is that this difference in treatment infringes art 14 of the European Convention for the Protection of Human Rights and Fundamental Freedoms 1950 (as set out in Sch 1 to the 1998 Act) read in conjunction

with art 8. Article 8 does not require the state to provide security of tenure for members of a deceased tenant's family. Article 8 does not in terms give a right to be provided with a home: see *Chapman v UK* (2001) 10 BHRC 48 at 72 (para 99). It does not "guarantee the right to have one's housing problem solved by the authorities": see *Marzari v Italy* (1999) 28 EHRR CD 175 at 179. But if the state makes legislative provision it must not be discriminatory. The provision must not draw a distinction on grounds such as sex or sexual orientation without good reason. Unless justified, a distinction founded on such grounds infringes the convention right embodied in art 14, as read with art 8. Mr Godin-Mendoza submits that the distinction drawn by para 2 of Sch 1 to the 1977 Act is drawn on the grounds of sexual orientation and that this difference in treatment lacks justification.

'[7] That is the first step in Mr Godin-Mendoza's claim. That step would not, of itself, improve Mr Godin-Mendoza's status in his flat. The second step in his claim is to pray in aid the court's duty under s 3 of the 1998 Act to read and give effect to legislation in a way which is compliant with the convention rights. Here, it is said, s 3 requires the court to read para 2 so that it embraces couples living together in a close and stable homosexual relationship as much as couples living together in a close and stable heterosexual relationship. So read, para 2 covers Mr Godin-Mendoza's position. Hence he is entitled to a declaration that on the death of Mr Wallwyn-James he succeeded to a statutory tenancy.

...

'[13] In the present case para 2 of Sch 1 to the 1977 Act draws a dividing line between married couples and cohabiting heterosexual couples on the one hand and other members of the original tenant's family on the other hand. What is the rationale for this distinction? The rationale seems to be that, for the purposes of security of tenure, the survivor of such couples should be regarded as having a special claim to be treated in much the same way as the original tenant. The two of them made their home together in the house in question, and their security of tenure in the house should not depend upon which of them dies first.

'[14] The history of the 1977 Act legislation is consistent with this appraisal. A widow, living with her husband, was accorded a privileged succession position in 1920. In 1980 a widower was accorded the like protection. In 1988 para 2(2) was added, by which the survivor of a cohabiting heterosexual couple was treated in the same way as a spouse of the original tenant.

'[15] Miss Carss-Frisk QC submitted there is a relevant distinction between heterosexual partnerships and same-sex partnerships. The aim of the legislation is to provide protection for the traditional family. Same-sex partnerships cannot be equated with family in the traditional sense. Same-sex partners are unable to have children with each other, and there is a reduced likelihood of children being a part of such a household.

'[16] My difficulty with this submission is that there is no reason for believing these factual differences between heterosexual and homosexual couples have any bearing on why succession rights have been conferred on heterosexual couples but not homosexual couples. Protection of the traditional family unit may well be an important and legitimate aim in certain contexts. In certain contexts this may be a cogent reason justifying differential treatment: see *Karner v Austria* (2003) 14 BHRC 674 at 682 (para 40). But it is important to identify the element of the "traditional family" which para 2, as it now stands, is seeking to protect. Marriage is not now a prerequisite to protection under para 2. The line drawn by Parliament is no longer drawn by reference to the status of marriage. Nor is parenthood, or the presence of children in the home, a precondition of security of tenure for the survivor of the original tenant. Nor is procreative potential a prerequisite. The survivor is protected even if, by reasons of age or otherwise, there was never any prospect of either member of the couple having a natural child.

'[17] What remains, and it is all that remains, as the essential feature under para 2 is the cohabitation of a heterosexual couple. Security of tenure for the survivor of such a couple in the house where they live is, doubtless, an important and legitimate social aim. Such a couple share their lives and make their home together. Parliament may readily take the view that the survivor of them has a special claim to security of tenure even though they are unmarried. But the reason underlying this social policy, whereby the survivor of a cohabiting heterosexual couple has particular protection, is equally applicable to the survivor of a homosexual couple. A homosexual couple, as much as a heterosexual couple, share each other's life and make their home together. They have an equivalent relationship. There is no rational or fair ground for distinguishing the one couple from the other in this context: see the discussion in *Fitzpatrick*'s case [1999] 4 All ER 705 at 720, [2001] 1 AC 27 at 44.

'[18] This being so, one looks in vain to find justification for the difference in treatment of homosexual and heterosexual couples. Such a difference in treatment can be justified only if it pursues a legitimate aim and there is a reasonable relationship of proportionality between the means employed and the aim sought to be realised. Here, the difference in treatment falls at the first hurdle: the absence of a legitimate aim. None has been suggested by the First Secretary of State, and none is apparent. In so far as admissibility decisions such as *S v UK* (1986) 47 DR 274 and *Roosli v Germany* (1996) 85 DR 149 adopted a different approach from that set out above, they must now be regarded as superseded by the recent decision of the European Court of Human Rights in *Karner's* case.

...

'[24] In my view, therefore, Mr Godin-Mendoza makes good the first step in his argument: para 2 of Sch 1 to the 1977 Act, construed without reference to s 3 of the 1998 Act, violates his convention right under art 14 taken together with art 8.

'[25] I turn next to the question whether s 3 of the 1998 Act requires the court to depart from the interpretation of para 2 enunciated in *Fitzpatrick*'s case.

'[26] Section 3 is a key section in the 1998 Act. It is one of the primary means by which convention rights are brought into the law of this country. Parliament has decreed that all legislation, existing and future, shall be interpreted in a particular way. All legislation must be read and given effect to in a way which is compatible with the convention rights "so far as it is possible to do so". This is the intention of Parliament, expressed in s 3, and the courts must give effect to this intention.

...

'[35] In some cases difficult problems may arise. No difficulty arises in the present case. Paragraph 2 of Sch 1 to the 1977 Act is unambiguous. But the social policy underlying the 1988 extension of security of tenure under para 2 to the survivor of couples living together as husband and wife is equally applicable to the survivor of homosexual couples living together in a close and stable relationship. In this circumstance I see no reason to doubt that application of s 3 to para 2 has the effect that para 2 should be read and given effect to as though the survivor of such a homosexual couple were the surviving spouse of the original tenant. Reading para 2 in this way would have the result that cohabiting heterosexual couples and cohabiting heterosexual couples would be treated alike for the purposes of succession as a statutory tenant. This would eliminate the discriminatory effect of para 2 and would do so consistently with the social policy underlying para 2. The precise form of words read in for this purpose is of no significance. It is their substantive effect which matters.' *Ghaidan v Mendoza* [2004] UKHL 30 at [1]–[3], [5]–[7], [13]–[18], [24]–[26], [35], [2004] 3 All ER 411, HL, per Lord Nicholls of Birkenhead

Canada [An automobile insurance policy provided coverage for a 'spouse'.] 'In my opinion the plain, ordinary, grammatical meaning of the word "spouse" in the relevant context herein refers to a man or a woman who is legally married to a person of the opposite sex. In Jowitt's Dictionary of English Law, 2nd edn, p 1687, "spouse" is defined as "a husband or wife". See also the Shorter Oxford English Dictionary, p 2087, where the meaning of "spouse" is said to be: "1. To join in marriage or wedlock. 2. To give in marriage; to promote or procure the marriage of; to marry. (3) To take (a woman) as a wife; to marry, wed".' *Fraser v Haight* (1987) 36 DLR (4th) 459 at 462–463, Ont HCJ, per Craig J

Canada 'As stated above, the *DRA* [Drug Relief Act] does not define the word "spouse". Thus, Taylor's first argument was that the word "spouse" could be interpreted as including unmarried cohabitants. The trial judge rejected this argument. He held that the legislature did not intend to include unmarried cohabitants in the definition of "spouse". We note that those Canadian jurisdictions which have extended support rights to unmarried cohabitants have done so expressly through the revision of their legislation. In addition, there is little consistency in the definitions of "common law spouse" in the jurisdictions which have amended their legislation. Specifically, they have each defined "common law spouse" as requiring a certain qualifying period of cohabitation, but the periods range from a cohabitation of "some permanence" to a cohabitation of five years. Periods of one, two and three years are also used. Some provide that application for support must be made within three months, or within one year, after the cessation of cohabitation. Most jurisdictions recognize relationships of some permanence in which there is a child of the relationship. 'Justice Richard of the Northwest Territories Supreme Court considered whether the word "spouse" could be interpreted as including "common law spouse" in the case *Andre v Blake* [1991] NWTR 351, 37 RFL (3d) 322 (SC). He held that it could not since the ordinary meaning of

the word "spouse" is a person joined in lawful marriage to another person. Veit J distinguished this case in the context of the *Alberta Family Relief Act* in *Armstrong v McLaughlin Estate* (1994) 112 DLR (4th) 745, 150 AR 343 (QB), but her decision was overturned on appeal on other grounds: (1995) 130 DLR (4th) 766, 178 AR 125 (CA). In our view, the following reasoning of Richard J is applicable in Alberta:

> In interpreting the word "spouse," the court must give effect to the ordinary meaning of the word, in the general context of the statute, unless to do so produces a result which is contrary to the purpose of the statute: see Sir Rupert Cross, S*tatutory Interpretation*, 2d ed, (London: Butterworths, 1987) p 47. And the court must not read in words that are not in the statute unless they are necessarily there by implication: Cross, p 47. [*Andre v Blake*, *supra* at 326–327 (RFL).]

'The ordinary meaning of the word "spouse" is a person who is joined in lawful marriage to another person. Richard J. stated that the "French word conjoint used in the statute has the same ordinary meaning". To give effect to this ordinary meaning of the word "spouse", it cannot be said to produce a result which is contrary to the purpose of the statute. Further, it cannot be said that the legislature, by using the word "spouse", was by inference, including "cohabitee". As Richard J stated:

> 'If the legislature had intended that a cohabitee be considered a spouse for the purposes of this statute, then such an intention would have been clearly expressed in the statute, or by a subsequent amendment to the statute.

'When one looks to other statutes in pari materia, one indeed finds that the legislature can, and does, distinguish between a spouse and a cohabitee. Both the [Northwest Territories] *Dependants Relief Act*, enacted in 1971 ... and the [Northwest Territories] *Criminal Injuries Compensation Act*, enacted in 1973 ... define a "dependant" to include a cohabitee in addition to a spouse, for purposes of those statutes. In the [Northwest Territories] *Workers' Compensation Act*, in 1974 ... the legislature provided for compensation to be paid to a cohabitee, separate and distinct from compensation to be paid to a spouse.

'It is for the legislature, if and when it sees fit, to amend the *Maintenance Act* to include cohabitees (as the legislature might specifically define that term) within the ambit of the legislation; however, the legislature has not done so. The Court must interpret and apply the legislation as it is written at present, not as it might be written. [*Andre v Blake*, *supra* at 327 (RFL).]

'In our view, it is not for this Court to interpret the word "spouse" as encompassing "common law spouses who have cohabited for at least [a certain period of time]" when there is clearly no consensus on the appropriate duration of cohabitation. We agree with the trial judge that the word "spouse" in the support provisions of the *DRA* cannot be interpreted as including "common law spouse".' *Taylor v Rossu* (1998) 161 DLR (4th) 266 at 297–298, Alta CA, per cur.

Canada '[3] … The parties and Canada agree it therefore follows that the definition of "spouse" in the *Divorce Act* must also infringe s. 15(1) of the *Charter*, and also cannot be justified under s. 1, since the definition of "spouse" is essentially a definition of marriage that requires the parties to be of opposite sexes.

'[4] Regardless of their agreement concerning the *Charter* breach, agreement alone is insufficient to support the finding. [See *Schachter v. Canada*, [1992] 2 S.C.R. 679 at p. 695.] The court must embark on its own analysis, and reach its own conclusion. Unlike the situation in *Schachter*, I have been provided with comprehensive evidence concerning both the s. 15 issue on its merits, the question of a s. 1 justification, and the question of legislative objectives to assist with the consideration of a remedy.

'[5] At the end of the hearing, I indicated that I was in agreement with the constitutional analysis presented, and would make a finding that the definition of spouse was unconstitutional, inoperative, and of no force and effect, with my reasons for doing so to follow. I also indicated that I would address the issue of the appropriate remedy for the *Charter* breach.' *MM v JH* [2004] OJ No 5314, 247 DLR (4th) 361 (SCJ), per Mesbur J

STAFF

Australia [Section 120(1) of the ASC Law provides that the Commission's 'staff' shall be persons appointed or employed under the Public Service Act 1922 (Cth).] 'The word "staff" as used in the ASC Law is not a term of art and has no particular technical meaning. While in some contexts the term "staff" might comprehend only persons who were actually engaged in the work of a particular establishment at a given time, see for example *Parker v Westby* [1941] St R Qd 47 at 53, the word is very frequently used to include persons who might be absent from their place of employment, perhaps for some considerable time and perhaps without pay. Persons on leave whether annual, long service, compassionate or for study purposes, would ordinarily be regarded as still being on the staff of their employer. There is in my opinion nothing in the ASC Law to indicate that the word "staff" is used in a restricted sense.' *Johns v Australian Securities Commission* (1992) 108 ALR 277 at 290, per Heerey J

Australia 'There is nothing in the ASC Law to indicate that the word "staff" is used in a restricted sense to exclude persons who may be absent from their place of employment on leave … persons on leave whether annual leave, long service leave or leave for study purposes would ordinarily be regarded as being on the "staff" of their employer. Moreover, the inclusion within the definition of staff member of persons engaged by the ASC as consultants under s 121 of the ASC Law shows that it was not intended that the class of persons, staff members, to whom powers may be delegated, should be confined to those actually performing full-time duties with the ASC.' *Johns v Australian Securities Commission* (1992) 108 ALR 405 at 434, per Black CJ and von Doussa J (on appeal)

STANDARD

Australia 'A standard in the context of something "to be observed by commercial television broadcasting licensees" is a measure of performance to which licensees must attain. As the standard must relate to "the Australian content of programs", a standard to be observed by broadcasting licensees is a standard which is calculated to ensure that they broadcast programs of Australian content. A transmission quota for programs is a standard of that kind.' *Project Blue Sky Inc v Australian Broadcasting Authority* (1998) 153 ALR 490 at 497; 72 ALJR 841; BC9801389, per Brennan J

Australia 'In *Herald-Sun* [*Herald-Sun TV Pty Ltd v Australian Broadcasting Tribunal* (1985) 156 CLR 1] the Court was concerned with s 16(1) of the Broadcasting and Television Act 1942 (Cth) ("BT Act") which gave power to the Australian Broadcasting Tribunal ("ABT") to determine standards to be observed by licensees in respect of the broadcasting or televising of programmes. In that case the Court was concerned with a requirement that went to the quality of a television programme. The relevant dictionary meaning adopted by the Court was that in the *Shorter Oxford English Dictionary*, namely:

> A definite level of excellence, attainment, wealth or the like, or a definite degree of any quality, viewed as a prescribed objective of endeavour or as the measure of what is adequate for some purpose.

The Court said at 4:

> A standard determined for a television programme must fix the quality or nature of the programme in such a way that both the licensee required to observe the standard and the court or other body called upon to decide whether it has done so can determine whether the programme answers the criteria set by the standard. That is not to say that the test should be entirely objective, for it may involve questions of taste, but it does mean that the standard is to be found in the determination itself. The power to fix a standard which is to be generally applied is quite different from a power to decide ad hoc, from case to case, whether a particular programme may be televised. A power of the latter kind is not a power to fix standards.

'In *Saatchi & Saatchi* [*Australian Broadcasting Tribunal v Saatchi & Saatchi Compton (Vic) Pty Ltd* (1985) 10 FCR 1], the issue before the Court related to s 100 of the BT Act which provided that "a licensee shall comply with such standards as the Tribunal determines in relation to ... advertisements." Beaumont J, at first instance, (1984) 5 FCR 431, said, at 436:

> In my opinion, the ordinary meaning of "standards" and its context suggest that it is the quality of the product, rather than its quantity, that is the subject matter of the Tribunal's power of determination ... the Tribunal may regulate the content of the advertised material in terms of its quality in the sense of what is regarded as socially desirable or acceptable.

'His Honour referred to the *Macquarie Dictionary*, the third edition of which defines the word "standard" as:

> 1. anything taken by general consent as a basis of comparison; an approved model ... 6. a grade or level of excellence, achievement, or advancement: a high standard of living ... 7. a level of quality which is regarded as normal, adequate or acceptable ... 9. (usu pl), behav-

iour, beliefs etc, regarded as socially desirable or acceptable ... 22. serving as a basis of weight, measure, value, comparison or judgment.

'In the present case the last mentioned definition (22) appears pertinent. In the particular context of the quality of television programmes, Beaumont J was of the view that the ninth definition which relates to behaviour and beliefs regarded as socially desirable or acceptable, was the appropriate standard. This illustrates that in *Saatchi & Saatchi*, the context in which the term standard was used carried a strong qualitative connotation.

'The range of diverse descriptions of the term "standard" in relation to different subject matters illustrates the overriding importance of context when determining whether a provision is a standard or not.' *Visa International Service Assn v Reserve Bank of Australia* [2003] FCA 977 at [383]–[388] per Tamberlin J; BC200305436

STANDING

Australia 'Standing simply means the capacity or right of a person to be heard in courts or tribunals: *Butterworths Australian Legal Dictionary*, 1997, p 1106. In *Locus Standi*, Stein, 1979, the author says, at p 3:

> "The [term] ... 'standing to sue' ... denote[s] the right of an individual or a group of individuals (not necessarily constituting a legal entity) to have a court enter upon an adjudication of an issue brought before the court by proceedings instigated by the individual or the group. That right, once found, exists apart from the factual or legal merits of the issue before the court or the jurisdiction of the court to adjudicate on the issue." '

Conlan (as liquidator of Oakleigh Acquisitions Pty Ltd) v Registrar of Titles (2001) 24 WAR 299; BC200104400; [2001] WASC 201 at [339], per Owen J

STATE INSTRUMENTALITY

Australia 'However, the expression "State instrumentality" is one that carries much the same meaning in popular usage as in a legal context. That meaning directs attention to the purpose or end served, so that a body is a State instrumentality if it is empowered to and does, in fact, serve some State government purpose. And that is so even if it is neither a servant nor an agent of the State.' *Re*

Anti-Cancer Council v Victoria: ex p State Public Services Federation (1992) 109 ALR 240 at 242–243, per cur

STATION

Canada '[17] The scheme of the *Libel and Slander Act*, R.S.O. 1990, c. L.12 also suggests that the use of a microphone and a loudspeaker does not constitute a broadcast. Section 7 of the act limits the application of s. 5(1) (Notice of Action) and s. 6 (Limitation Period) to "broadcasts from a station in Ontario". (emphasis added) While "station" is not defined in the act, it is defined in the *Oxford English Dictionary*, among other things, as:

> A place where men are stationed and apparatus set up for some particular kind of industrial work, scientific research, or the like. Often with a defining word, as ...

> A broadcasting station; an establishment or organization transmitting radio or television signals.

'Thus, it is difficult to see how a person speaking into a microphone could constitute a "station". Therefore, even if the speaker was situated in Ontario, they would be deprived of the protections afforded defendant "stations" by ss. 5(1) and 6. This would make no sense especially as these protections have been found to apply to both media and non-media defendants: *Watson v. Southam Inc.* (2000), 189 D.L.R. (4th) 695 (Ont. C.A.).' *Romano v D'Onofrio* [2004] OJ No 4989, 246 DLR (4th) 720 (SCJ), per Ducharme J

STEP IN THE PROCEEDINGS

[Proceedings under an agreement for the allotment of preference shares were stayed by the master under s 9(4) of the Arbitration Act 1996 on the ground that the parties had agreed that the claim should be submitted to arbitration. The claimant's appeal against the master's order was dismissed. The claimant further appealed and the question arose whether the defendant had taken a 'step in the proceedings' within the terms of s 9(3) of the 1996 Act by making an application, subsequent to its application for a stay, for summary judgment in the event that the application for a stay was unsuccessful.] '[54] As indicated above, CTIL [Capital Trust Investments Ltd] asserted before the judge, but not before the master, that Radio Design was not entitled to apply for a stay of this action because it took a "step in the proceedings" within

the meaning of s 9(3) of the [Arbitration Act 1996]. Section 9(3) and (4) provides as follows:

> "(3) An application may not be made by a person before taking the appropriate procedural step (if any) to acknowledge the legal proceedings against him or after he has taken any step in those proceedings to answer the substantive claim.

> (4) On an application under this section the court shall grant a stay unless satisfied that the arbitration agreement is null and void, inoperative, or incapable of being performed."

'[55] It is common ground that, on the assumption that these claims are within the arbitration agreement to which both Radio Design and CTIL are parties, Radio Design is entitled to a stay unless it took a step in the proceedings within the meaning of s 9(3). Section 9(3) is for present purposes in similar terms to s 1(1) of the Arbitration Act 1975 and s 4 of the Arbitration Act 1950. The question what amounts to a step in the proceedings has been considered a number of times under those sections and their predecessors: see e g *Pitchers Ltd v Plaza (Queensbury) Ltd* [1940] 1 All ER 151, *Eagle Star Insurance Co Ltd v Yuval Insurance Co Ltd* [1978] 1 Lloyd's Rep 357, *Kuwait Airways Corp v Iraq Airways Corp* [1994] 1 Lloyd's Rep 276 and *Patel v Patel* [1999] 1 All ER (Comm) 923, [2000] QB 551.

...

'[60] It appears to us that that application was not a "step in the proceedings" on the basis of the principles set out above. Thus, it did not (in the words of Lord Denning) express the willingness of Radio Design to go along with a determination of the courts instead of arbitration. On the contrary, it made it clear that the application for summary judgment was only advanced "in the event that its application for a stay is unsuccessful". In Merkin's words, approved by Otton LJ, the application made it clear that it was specifically seeking a stay, with the result that a step which would otherwise be a step in the proceedings, namely an application for summary judgment, is not so treated.

'[64] We have already expressed our view, in agreement with the judge, that Radio Design did not take a step in the proceedings when it made its application for summary judgment on 2 May. Nor, in our judgment, did it do so thereafter. The hearing before the master was conducted on the same basis as set out in the summons, namely that Radio Design's application for summary judgment was being made only if a stay was refused. We do not think it can fairly be held that that position changed when the parties asked the master to deliver a judgment on the summary judgment application because they only did so in case an appeal against the stay failed. There was equally no change before the judge.' *Capital Trust Investments Ltd v Radio Design TJ AB* [2002] EWCA Civ 135 at [54], [55], [60], [64], [2002] 2 All ER 159 at 174–176, CA, per Clarke LJ

STEP-FATHER

Australia [Section 73 of the Crimes Act 1900 (NSW) states that a 'step-father' who, unlawfully and carnally knows his 'step-daughter' above the age of 16 years, and under the age of 17 years, is liable to imprisonment for 8 years.] 'Dictionary definitions of these words involve marriage between the putative step-father and the mother of the putative step-daughter. As examples, in the *Oxford English Dictionary* (2nd ed, 1989) step-father is defined as "a man who has married one's mother after one's father's death or divorce", and step-daughter is defined as "a daughter, by a former marriage, of one's husband or wife"; in the *Macquarie Dictionary* (3rd ed, 1997) step-father is defined as "a man who occupies one's father's place by marriage to one's mother", step-daughter is defined as "a daughter of one's husband or wife by a former marriage", and "step–" is defined as "a prefix indicating connection between members of a family by the remarriage of a parent and not by blood".

'These meanings have been taken up in, for example, the Family Law Act 1975 (Cth) in its provisions concerning proper parenting of children: the definition of "step-parent" in s 60D is a person who is not a parent of the child, is or has been married to the parent of the child, and treats or at any time during the marriage treated the child as a member of the family formed with the parent.

'The meanings have also been recognised in the cases as the meaning according to ordinary usage, with marriage between the step-parent and the parent of the child a necessary ingredient.' *R v Miller* BC200102556; [2001] NSWCCA 209 at [27]–[29], per Giles JA

STEP-PARENT

Canada 'This issue centres on what the legislature intended by its use of the term "step-parent" in sections 59(3) and 64(3) [of the Child Welfare Act]. The statute itself is silent on this point.

Therefore, the court must formulate a definition that gives effect to the wishes of the legislature. That task requires an application of the standard rules of statutory interpretation.

'The petitioners suggest that the rules of interpretation lead to the conclusion that the term "step-parent" as used in the private adoption provisions is intended to include, *inter alia*, same-sex couples, and further they argue that this interpretation is supported by the extrinsic information surrounding the amendments. They say that all the evidence indicates that the purpose of the amendments was to remove the spousal requirement traditionally associated with the term "step-parent", focusing instead on the type of parental relationship which the petitioner has with the child.

...

'... there can be no doubt that by enacting the amendments to sections 59(3) and 65(3) of the *Child Welfare Act*, and section 9(2.1) of the *Vital Statistics Act*, the government intended to permit a partner in a same-sex relationship to be able to apply for a private adoption in the same manner as a heterosexual partner of a parent.

...

'Furthermore, it is reasonable and just to interpret the term "step-parent" to include same-sex couples. The legislature has acknowledged that there are diverse family structures in which private adoptions may be warranted, but would not have been permitted under the former spousal adoption provisions. Same-sex couples may constitute "families" as defined by the criteria set out in the Family Policy Grid since they are able to perform the enumerated functions to the same extent as are traditional families. Thus, this interpretation is consistent with the government's policy relating to family law legislation because it reflects the current and evolving family structures.

'The amendments to the *Vital Statistics Act* also suggest that same-sex couples may be included in the term "step-parent". These amendments would have no meaning if "step-parent" is limited to the traditional mother and father model, as that was contemplated in the pre-existing legislation. A broader meaning must have been intended. As the rules of legislative interpretation require the court to presume the legislation has a purpose, in these circumstances it is reasonable to infer that the legislature intended to enable persons other than a mother and father to register as adopted parents by virtue of the amendments.

'Finally, it must be recognized that this interpretation is consistent with the overall purpose and goal of the adoption legislation, which is to permit adoptions when it is in the best interests of the child. Clearly the best interests of the child are served by giving legal recognition to that child's relationship with a step-parent, regardless of that step-parent's legal status *vis-a-vis* the natural parent.

...

'The evidence demonstrates unequivocally that the legislature intended to permit same sex adoptions by replacing "spouse" with "step-parent" in the *Child Welfare Act* and the *Vital Statistics Act*.' *A (Re)* (1999) 181 DLR (4th) 300 at 306, 307, 309, 311, 312, Alta QB, per Martin J

STATEMENT

'Statement' means words, pictures, visual images, gestures or any other method signifying meaning (Defamation Act 1996, s 17(1))

STATUTE

[For 44 Halsbury's Laws (4th edn) paras 801, 804–807 see now 44(1) Halsbury's Laws (4th edn) (Reissue) paras 1205–1211.]

STATUTORY INSTRUMENT

[For 44 Halsbury's Laws (4th edn) para 984 see now 44(1) Halsbury's Laws (4th edn) (Reissue) para 1503.]

STEP

[For 2 Halsbury's Laws (4th edn) para 563 see now 2(3) Halsbury's Laws (4th edn) (Reissue) para 20.]

New Zealand [Defamation Act 1992, s 50.] 'There is no particular mystery in the concept of "step" "in a proceeding" given contexts. The section and rule envisage some genuine and authorised procedural act within the limits of the rules and recognised practice of the Court. Usually that will involve the filing of a document in the registry: but even that is not essential. As R 432(2) implicitly recognises, a "step" may be wider than the filing of pleadings or the making of interlocutory applications. I have no doubt an oral interlocutory application ... would constitute a "step". While the act concerned more usually will be within the registry or courtroom, actions outside Court premises governed by the rules of Court ... would qualify. The act must, however, be one within and governed by the rules or recognised practice of the Court. Actions outside that area, albeit connected

with the litigation, are not "steps" for this purpose. Mere correspondence, or negotiations, or briefing of witnesses are not included.' *Mountain Rock Productions Ltd v Wellington Newspapers Ltd* [1997] 3 NZLR 31 at 36–37, per McGechan J

STEPCHILD

Australia [The issue in this case was whether the applicants were still the stepchildren of the testatrix after the termination of the marriage by death of their father. Section 89 of the Succession Act 1867 (Cth) defines 'stepchild—in relation to any person, [means] a child by a former marriage of that person's husband or wife'.] 'There are three possible meanings which, arguably, may have been intended by the reference to "that person's husband or wife". To avoid disjunctive references I take the case of a husband in relation to a testatrix. The possible meanings of "husband" seem to be: (a) her husband while that marriage still subsists, (viz to whom she is still married at the time of her death); (b) her last husband, (whether alive, dead or divorced); (c) all her husbands, (whether alive, dead or divorced)... In my view, the reference in the definition of "stepchild" to the "husband or wife" of the person against whose estate the claim is made is to one husband (or wife) only. This means that the correct construction must be (a) or (b) of the three possible meanings set out above. The status of stepchild, as ordinarily understood, does not apply to a case in which the natural parent has been divorced from the step-parent, and probably does not survive the death of the natural parent. If the latter part of this proposition is correct, the better interpretation seems to be that in para (a), that is to say, that stepchildren are children by a former marriage of the testatrix's husband (or testator's wife) provided that the later marriage is still subsisting at the date of death of the testator/testatrix.' *Re Burt* [1988] 1 Qd R 23 at 30–32, per Thomas J

STRANDED

New Zealand [Maritime Transport Act 1994, s 110.] 'The term has come to have a special meaning in insurance law. That was recognised as far back as 1827 by Littledale J in *Bishop v Pentland* [(1827) 7 B & C 219]...

'It must be kept in mind, as Mrs Barratt submitted, that the term is used in the context of maritime safety ...

'First, a ship or vessel is "stranded" when all or part of it has grounded, whether this occurs accidentally or deliberately. The subsection is not concerned with the ordinary course of navigation; or how the ship or vessel became grounded.

'Secondly, it is immaterial whether the ship or vessel is in contact with the ground at its bow or its stern or its mid-length or over its entire length, or only on one side or part thereof.

'Thirdly, the ship or vessel which has "stranded" is one which is all or partly above the water-line, for if it is totally below the water-line it would have sunk.

'Fourthly, the grounding of a ship or vessel can be either temporary in the sense that the ship or vessel can be towed off or manoeuvred off under its own power or with assistance, or permanent in the sense that it is immovable and therefore a wreck. In both situations the ship or vessel is "stranded".

'Fifthly, a vessel can be considered to be "stranded" even although it may move or drag as the result of the wind or the tide or the currents, or a combination of these matters, provided that there is some contact with the ground at least on the ebbing of the tide; or to use the old phraseology, it is then "on the strand".

'Sixthly, I reject the notion that for a vessel to be "stranded", its adventure or life is necessarily at an end. It may be; it may not be. It depends on the particular circumstances.

'And seventhly, I see no distinction between a "stranding" and "stranded". I notice that even Mr Cooke found it difficult to maintain this distinction as he developed his argument. The only distinction lies in English grammar and not in the law. A "stranding" is the noun; "stranded" is the verb.' *Dorn v Maritime Safety Authority of New Zealand* [1999] 2 NZLR 482 at 499–500, per Penlington J

STRANDING

[For 25 Halsbury's Laws (4th edn) para 277 see now 25 Halsbury's Laws (4th edn) (2003 Reissue) para 349.]

STREET

[For 21 Halsbury's Laws (4th edn) paras 795–797 see now 21 Halsbury's Laws (4th edn) (2004 Reissue) para 9.]

STRIKE

[For 47 Halsbury's Laws (4th edn) para 567 see now 47 Halsbury's Laws (4th edn) (Reissue) para 1401.]

Canada [One-day work stoppage occurred for political reasons. Force majeure clause relieved plaintiff in event of 'strike'.] 'The ordinary and natural meaning of the word "strike" in that clause of the "agreement" must include any circumstances in which the employees of MacMillan Bloedel, acting in concert, refuse to work. If such a strike results in a reduction of the electricity required by MacMillan Bloedel in its operations, the force majeure clause is triggered.' *MacMillan Bloedel Ltd v British Columbia Hydro and Power Authority* (1992) 98 DLR (4th) 492 at 502, BC CA, per Cumming JA

New Zealand 'Strike in the statutory sense is a collective withdrawal of labour. Underlying the descriptive expressions "combination", "agreement", "common understanding" and "concerted action" [in s 61 of the Employment Contracts Act 1991] is the theme of workers acting in concert to achieve an agreed end. It necessarily involves communication between them and not simply simultaneous actions occurring spontaneously.

'Further, the collective decision is one that is "made or entered into" by employees. It is implicit in the collective decision which may be "express or implied" that a decision imposed on employees under duress or other pressure does not qualify.' *Collins v Independent Fisheries Ltd* [1993] 2 NZLR 290 at 294, CA, per Richardson J

STRIKING

Australia '… whatever may be the precise limits of the concept of striking, it appears to me to be the essence of the ordinary understanding of the word that there should be an impact upon the person or thing struck. In its ordinary meaning relevant to this context, to strike is to hit. There is a distinction between the delivery of a blow by the hand which passes through space and impacts upon the body of the victim and a push constituted by the placing of the hand on the body of the victim in a manner not aptly described as hitting or striking or delivering a blow and only then applying force in the form of a push.' *Re Clarke* (1993) 71 A Crim R 58 at 62–63, per Badgery-Parker J

STRUCTURE

New Zealand [Clause 102(3) of the Local Government (Auckland Region) Reorganisation Order 1989] ' "Structure", as the High Court recognised, is a word with a range of meanings. It takes its precise meaning from the context. We were referred to a number of statutory definitions of the term, dictionary meanings and cases where the term is discussed. Apart from indicating it can have a wide or narrow meaning we have not found the statutory definitions helpful. Of the dictionary meanings of "structure" that which is most apt in the context of the commission's discussion is "a thing which is built or constructed, a building, an edifice". In *R v Rose* [1965] QWN 42 at p 43 Gibbs J said the "most natural and ordinary meaning" of structure is a building "but the word is capable of having the wider meaning of anything constructed out of material parts". The commission was principally concerned with buildings that straddled the mean high-water mark boundary. It is our view that in the context the term "structure" means a thing built or constructed to remain permanently in one place on land within the city's seaward boundary even if it was also partly situated outside that boundary. Applying that interpretation, we hold that under cl 102(3) fixed piers, jetties, grids and slipways are "structures" but that the floating jetties and pontoons of the Westhaven waterspace areas are not. Nor in our view are the piles which retain them in place, as they should not in this context be regarded as separate from the pontoons of which they are an integral part. The fixed piers and grids at those locations are structures.' *Auckland City Council v Ports of Auckland Ltd* [2000] 3 NZLR 614 at 629–630, CA, per cur

STRUCTURE PLAN

[The Town and Country Planning Act 1971 has been repealed. The definition is re-enacted in the Town and Country Planning Act 1990, s 31(2).]

SUBJECT

Canada '[17] The application to strike will be allowed if it is established that the ship and cargo are not the subject of the action within the meaning of subsection 43(2), in the context of an action "arising out of any agreement relating to the carriage of goods in or on a ship ... whether by charter party or otherwise" (paragraph 22(2)(*i*) of the Act). It is not possible to separate procedure from jurisdiction and increase by the procedure used the jurisdiction that would otherwise devolve on the Court. The *in rem* proceeding in the case at bar can only apply to a ship or a cargo which is the subject of an action over which the Court has jurisdiction. Thus, although the words "*action portant sur*" in

subsection 43(2) of the Act, and still more in the English wording, "the subject of the action", are the key words which the Court must interpret, we have to examine them in terms of the field of jurisdiction applicable in a specific case.

'[18] I said that I prefer the English wording, "the subject of the action", to the French one, "*action portant sur*", because in subsection 43(3) the same English phrase is rendered in French by "*navire [...] en cause*". The common feature of the variants in the French versions is, it seems to me, that this provision applies to the ship or cargo which is the subject or cause of the action. I note that according to the *Oxford Hachette Dictionary, English-French*, Oxford Superlex Three in One, CD-ROM (version 1.1), Oxford University Press, 1994–1996, the word "subject" in this context is translated by "objet". While I am dealing with dictionaries, I should say at once that the word "subject" is defined *inter alia* in *The Oxford English Dictionary*, Vol. X, Oxford, Clarendon Press, 1970, as "9. A thing or person giving rise to specified feeling, action, etc.; a ground, a motive, a cause".' *Paramount Enterprises Inc v An Xin Jiang (The)* [2001] 2 FC 551 at 561, CA, per Décary JA

SUBJECT OF PUBLIC INTEREST

Australia 'Thus, when the law of defamation in Queensland was codified in the Defamation Act 1889, a "subject of public interest" was understood in the law of defamation to refer to the *conduct* of a person engaged in activities that either inherently, expressly or inferentially invited public criticism or discussion ... It may be debatable whether the term "subject of public interest" had acquired a technical meaning in the law of defamation by 1889. But it was a term used in a special sense to describe the conduct of a person whose conduct invited public criticism or discussion. That being so, it is perfectly legitimate to give the words "subject of public interest" the same meaning in [the Criminal Code (Qld)] s 377(8) that they had, and still have, in that branch of the common law of defamation known as the doctrine of fair comment.' *Bellino v Australian Broadcasting Corp* (1996) 185 CLR 183 at 219–221; (1996) 135 ALR 368 at 396–397; (1996) 70 ALJR 387; (1996) Aust Torts Reports 81–377; BC9600872 at 45–47, per Dawson, McHugh and Gummow JJ

SUBJECT TO

Australia [Section 38(1) of the Occupational Health and Safety Act 1985 (Vic) provides that 'subject to' the Public Service Act 1974 (Vic), inspectors shall be appointed as are necessary for the purposes of the first mentioned Act.]

'In my view, the expression "subject to the Public Service Act" was not used simply as a draftsman's precaution against possibly conflicting statutory provisions. Rather it was used in conjunction with the passive voice expression "there shall be appointed" with the intention that the provisions of the Public Service Act should be applied, and should be applied to regulate not only the terms and conditions upon which an inspector would hold office but also to regulate the way in which an inspector would be appointed to office. That is, the expression was intended to apply to the office of inspector the whole of the provisions of the Public Service Act 1974, an Act which is, according to its terms to "take effect notwithstanding anything in section 88 of the Constitution Act 1975' [(Vic) by which appointment to public offices was vested in the Governor in Council]. It was not used to indicate simply a qualification for office for in my view its words are simply not apt to that purpose. Rather it was intended as indicating that the appointment should be made "subject to", i.e. in the manner prescribed by, the Public Service Act and indicating that the appointee was thereafter to be "subject to" that Act.' *Davis v Grocon Ltd* [1992] 2 VR 661 at 668, per Hayne J

SUBORDINATE LEGISLATION

[For 44 Halsbury's Laws (4th edn) paras 981, 982 see now 44(1) Halsbury's Laws (4th edn) (Reissue) paras 1499, 1500.]

SUBROGATION

[For 16 Halsbury's Laws (4th edn) para 1438 see now 16(2) Halsbury's Laws (4th edn) (Reissue) para 770.]

[For 25 Halsbury's Laws (4th edn) para 330 see now 25 Halsbury's Laws (4th edn) (2003 Reissue) paras 314, 505 et seq.]

Australia 'Subrogation is the substitution of one person for another in respect of a lawful claim or right, so that the person substituted succeeds to or acquires the rights, remedies or securities of the other in relation to the claim. The person who is subrogated to another stands in that other person's shoes: *Butterworths Australian Legal Dictionary* at p 1127.

'In *Orakpo v Manson Investments Ltd* [1978] AC 95 Lord Diplock held at 104 that there was no

general doctrine of unjust enrichment recognised by English law but that specific remedies were allowed in particular cases. He continued:

"There are some circumstances in which the remedy takes the form of 'subrogation', but this expression embraces more than a single concept in English law. It is a convenient way of describing a transfer of rights from one person to another, without assignment or assent of the person from whom the rights are transferred and which takes place by operation of law in a whole variety of widely different circumstances. Some rights by subrogation are contractual in their origin, as in the case of contracts of insurance. Others, such as the right of an innocent lender to recover from a company moneys borrowed ultra vires to the extent that these have been expended on discharging the company's lawful debts, are in no way based on contract and appear to defeat classification except as an empirical remedy to prevent a particular kind of unjust enrichment."

'In *Banque Financiere de la Cite v Parc (Battersea) Ltd* [1999] 1 AC 221 at 231–2 Lord Hoffmann said:

"My Lords, the subject of subrogation is bedevilled by problems of terminology and classification which are calculated to cause confusion. For example, it is often said that subrogation may arise either from the express or implied agreement of the parties or by operation of law in a number of different situations: see, for example, Lord Keith of Kinkel in *Orakpo v Manson Investments Ltd* [1978] AC 95, 119. As a matter of current terminology, this is true. Lord Diplock, for example, was of the view that the doctrine of subrogation in contracts of insurance operated entirely by virtue of an implied term of the contract of insurance (*Hobbs v Marlowe* [1978] AC 16, 39) and although in Lord Napier and *Ettrick v Hunter* [1993] AC 713 your Lordships rejected the exclusivity of this claim for the common law and assigned a larger role to equitable principles, there was no dispute that the doctrine of subrogation in insurance rests upon the common intention of the parties and gives effect to the principle of indemnity embodied in the contract. Furthermore, your Lordships drew attention to the fact that it is customary for the assured, on payment of the loss to provide the insurer with a letter of subrogation, being no more nor less than an express assignment of his rights of recovery against any third party. Subrogation in this sense is a contractual arrangement for the transfer of rights against third parties and is founded upon the common intention of the parties. But the term is also used to describe an equitable remedy to reverse or prevent unjust enrichment which is not based upon any agreement or common intention of the party enriched and the party deprived. The fact that contractual subrogation and subrogation to prevent unjust enrichment both involve transfers of rights or something resembling transfers of rights should not be allowed to obscure the fact that one is dealing with radically different institutions. One is part of the law of contract and the other part of the law of restitution. Unless this distinction is borne clearly in mind, there is a danger that the contractual requirement of mutual consent will be imported into the conditions for the grant of the restitutionary remedy or that the absence of such a requirement will be disguised by references to a presumed intention which is wholly fictitious. There is an obvious parallel with the confusion caused by classifying certain restitutionary remedies as quasi-contractual and importing into them features of the law of contract."

...

'One recognised contract in which the doctrine of subrogation applies is a contract of indemnity where one party has with the consent of another indemnified that other against certain liability or expense. The former is entitled to be subrogated to the personal and proprietary rights of the latter as against any third party or property. It is thought that the basis of subrogation of this type arises as a matter of contract of indemnity under which the person giving the indemnity is given rights of recourse in the name of the person indemnified against third parties. However, there can be no doubt that the doctrine of subrogation is at least in part an equitable doctrine.

'Two common examples of the use of the doctrine of subrogation in relation to indemnities are as follows:

An indemnity, express or implied given by the principal debtor to the guarantor in a contract of guarantee. In that case, the party giving the indemnity will be subrogated to the rights of the party indemnified. On payment in full to

the creditor, the guarantor will be entitled to recover, if necessary using the name of the creditor.

A contract of insurance. On the insurer paying a claim, he is entitled to recover the amount of the loss from a third party in a case where the third party is liable to the insured in respect of the loss. In that case, the insurer is entitled, with the consent of the insured, which is usually given in the policy, to recover the amount of any loss incurred, using the name of the insured in any legal proceedings which it may be necessary to commence.'

Emanuel Management Pty Ltd (in liq) v Emanuele (2002) 83 SASR 501; (2002) 220 LSJS 435; BC200204687; [2002] SASC 170 at [42]–[46], per Wicks J

SUBSCRIPTION PROGRAMMING SIGNAL

Canada '[32] In its basic form, s. 9(1)(c)[of the *Radiocommunication Act*] is structured as a prohibition with a limited exception. Again, with the relevant portions emphasized, it states that:

9   (1) *No person shall*

...

(c) decode an encrypted subscription programming signal or encrypted network feed otherwise than under and in accordance with authorization from the lawful distributor of the signal or feed ... [Emphasis added.]

...

The provision opens with the announcement of a broad prohibition ("No person shall"), follows by announcing the nature ("decode") and object ("an encrypted programming signal") of the prohibition, and then announces an exception to it ("otherwise than under and in accordance with authorization from the lawful distributor"). The French version shares the same four features, albeit in a modified order (see Provost C.Q.J. in *Pearlman, supra,* at p. 2031).

'[33] The forbidden activity is decoding. Therefore, as noted by the Court of Appeal, the prohibition in s. 9(1)(c) is directed towards the *reception* side of the broadcasting equation. Quite apart from the provenance of the signals at issue, where the impugned decoding occurs within Canada, there can be no issue of the statute's having an extraterritorial reach. In the present case, the reception that the appellant seeks to enjoin occurs entirely within Canada.

'[34] The object of the prohibition is of central importance to this appeal. What is interdicted by s. 9(1)(c) is the decoding of "*an* encrypted subscription programming signal" (in French, "un signal d'abonnement") (emphasis added). The usage of the indefinite article here is telling: it signifies "one, some [or] any" (*Canadian Oxford Dictionary* (1998)). Thus, what is prohibited is the decoding of any encrypted subscription programming signal, subject to the ensuing exception.

'[35] The definition of "subscription programming signal" suggests that the prohibition extends to signals emanating from other countries. Section 2 of the Act defines that term as, "radiocommunication that is intended for reception either directly or indirectly by the public in Canada *or elsewhere* on payment of a subscription fee or other charge" (emphasis added). I respectfully disagree with the respondents and Weiler J.A. in *Branton, supra*, at para. 26, "that the wording 'or elsewhere' is limited to the type of situation contemplated in s. 3(3)" of the Act. Subsection 3(3) reads:

> 3(3) This Act applies within Canada and on board
>   (a)   any ship, vessel or aircraft that is
>   (i) registered or licensed under an Act of Parliament, or
>   (ii) owned by, or under the direction or control of, Her Majesty in right of Canada or a province;
>   (b)   any spacecraft that is under the direction or control of
>   (i) Her Majesty in right of Canada or a province,
>   (ii) a citizen or resident of Canada, or
>   (iii) a corporation incorporated or resident in Canada; and
>   (c)   any platform, rig, structure or formation that is affixed or attached to land situated in the continental shelf of Canada.

'[36] This provision is directed at an entirely different issue from that which is at play in the definition of "subscription programming signal". Section 3(3) specifies the geographic scope of the *Radiocommunication Act* and all its constituent provisions, as is confirmed by the marginal note accompanying the subsection, which states "*Geographical application*". To phrase this in the context of the present appeal, any person within Canada or on board any of the things enumerated in s. 3(3)(a) through (c) could potentially be subject to liability for unlawful decoding under s. 9(1)(c);

in this way, s. 3(3) addresses the "where" question. On the other hand, the definition of "subscription programming signal" provides meaning to the s. 9(1)(c) liability by setting out the class of signals whose unauthorized decoding will trigger the provision; this addresses the object of the prohibition, or the "what" question. These are two altogether separate issues.

'[37] Furthermore, it was not necessary for Parliament to include the phrase "or elsewhere" in the s. 2 definition if it merely intended "subscription programming signal" to be interpreted as radiocommunication intended for direct or indirect reception by the public on board any of the s. 3(3) vessels, spacecrafts or rigs. In my view, the words "or elsewhere" were not meant to be tautological. It is sometimes stated, when a court considers the grammatical and ordinary sense of a provision, that "[t]he legislator does not speak in vain" (*Quebec (Attorney General) v. Carrières Ste-Thérèse Ltée*, [1985] 1 S.C.R. 831 at p. 838, 20 D.L.R. (4th) 602). Parliament has provided express direction to this effect through its enactment of s. 10 of the *Interpretation Act*, which states in part that "[t]he law shall be considered as always speaking". In any event, "or elsewhere" ("ou ailleurs", in French) suggests a much broader ambit than the particular and limited examples in s. 3(3), and I would be reticent to equate the two.

'[38] In my opinion, therefore, the definition of "subscription programming signal" encompasses signals originating from foreign distributors and intended for reception by a foreign public ... ' *Bell ExpressVu Limited Partnership v Rex* (2002) 212 DLR (4th) 1 at 22–24 (SCC), per Iacobucci J

SUBSTANCE

[The Food Act 1984 is largely repealed. The definition is now contained in the Food Safety Act 1990, s 53(1), as follows.] 'Substance' includes any natural or artificial substance or other matter, whether it is in solid or liquid form or in the form of a gas or vapour.

SUBSTANTIAL

'In *R v Lloyd* [[1966] 1 All ER 107] directions as to the word "substantial" [of mental responsibility] to the effect that (1) the jury should approach the word in a broad commonsense way, or (2) the word meant "more than some trivial degree of impairment which does not make any appreciable difference to a person's ability to control himself, but it means less than total impairment" were both approved ... For the avoidance of doubt, we advise judges of guidance as to the meaning of "substantial" should be explicitly provided for the jury by one or other of the two meanings in *R v Lloyd*.' *R v Egan* [1992] 4 All ER 470 at 476, 480, CA, per Watkins LJ

Australia [Section 9(a) of the Succession Act 1981 (Qld) states that the court may admit to probate a testamentary instrument executed in 'substantial' compliance with legislative formalities.]

'It seems to me that proviso (a) clearly indicates that Parliament wanted to allow clear testamentary intention to override a lack of formality. It chose the words "substantial compliance" to define a judicial discretion. As Deane J observed in *Tillmanns Butcheries Pty Ltd v Australasian Meat Industry Employees' Union* (1979) 42 FLR 331, at 348, "['substantial'] is a word calculated to conceal a lack of precision". When used in a quantitative sense it does not necessarily mean "most", but may mean only "much" or "some" e.g. see *Terry's Motors Ltd v Rinder* [1948] SASR 167 at 180.' *Re Cashin* [1992] 2 Qld R 63 at 65, per Demack J

Australia [After citing *Tillmanns Butcheries Pty Ltd v Australasian Meat Industry Employees' Union* (1979) 42 FLR 331 at 348, per Deane J] 'When used in [the Corporations Law] s 445G(3)(a), the word "substantially" involves a matter of the degree of compliance. It is used in a relative sense rather than any absolute sense.' *Commissioner of Taxation v Comcorp Australia Ltd* (1996) 70 FCR 356 at 395; (1996) 21 ACSR 590 at 628; (1996) 14 ACLC 1616; BC9604542, per Carr J

Australia 'Indeed, his Worship's use of the phrase "special or substantial" in that very passage suggests that he has blurred the distinction between the two adjectives ... The first meaning assigned to the word in *Butterworth's Australian Legal Dictionary* is "Real or of substance, as distinct from ephemeral or nominal". On the question of substantial impairment of mental responsibility for the purpose of the law of diminished responsibility in murder cases, juries are commonly directed that "substantial" means "less than total, but more than trivial or minimal": *R v Lloyd* [1967] 1 QB 175. Accordingly, "substantial" does not mean "special", and to establish substantial reasons for the attendance of witnesses at committal proceedings it is not necessary to show that the case is exceptional or unusual.' *Losurdo v DPP* (1998) 101 A Crim R 162 at 166; BC9800566 at 7, per Hidden J

Substantial loss or damage

Australia [Section 45D(1) of the Trade Practices Act 1974 (Cth) refers to 'substantial loss or damage' to the business.] 'The word "substantial" requires loss or damage that is more than trivial or minimal. It cannot be said that it requires any specific level of loss or damage. In the context in which it appears it imports a notion of relativity. That is to say one needs to know something of the circumstances of the business affected before one can arrive at a conclusion whether the loss or damage in question should be regarded as substantial in relation to that business: *Tillmanns Butcheries Ltd v Australasian Meat Industry Employees' Union* at FLR 338 per Bowen CJ (Evatt J agreeing). In the same case Deane J said at ALR 382; FLR 348: "In the context of s 45D(1) of the Act, the word 'substantial' is used in a relative sense in that, regardless of whether it means large or weighty on the one hand or real or of substance as distinct from ephemeral or nominal on the other, it would be necessary to know something of the nature and scope of the relevant business before one could say that particular, actual or potential loss or damage was substantial. As at present advised, I incline to the view, that the phrase 'substantial loss or damage', in s 45D(1) includes loss or damage that is in the circumstances, real or of substance and not insubstantial or nominal".' *J-Corp Pty Ltd v Australian Builders Labourers Federated Union of Workers—Western Australian Branch* (1992) 111 ALR 502 at 537–538, per French J

Substantial part

Australia [In considering whether there had been an infringement of published edition copyright, the issue of substantiality, in the sense used in s 14(1) of the Copyright Act 1968 (Cth), is relevant]. 'The cases concerned with substantiality in relation to works cannot necessarily be applied uncritically to allegations of infringement of published edition copyright ...

'It has been said that the phrase "substantial part" as used in s 14(1) of the Act refers to the quality of what is taken, rather than the quantity: *Autodesk Inc v Dyason (No 2)* (1993) 176 CLR 300 at 305; 111 ALR 385, per Mason CJ. It has also been said that the reproduction of a part of a work which has no originality will not normally be a substantial part of the copyright and therefore will not be protected: *Ladbroke (Football) Ltd v William Hill (Football) Ltd* [1964]1 All ER 465 at 481, per Lord Pearce. As Mason CJ observed, in determining whether the quality of what is taken makes it a substantial part of the work, the importance of what is taken should be considered in relation to the work as a whole and, for that purpose, it is appropriate to consider whether it is, an "essential" or "material" part of the work: *Autodesk (No 2)*, at CLR 305.' *Nationwide News Pty Ltd v Copyright Agency Ltd* (1996) 136 ALR 273 at 290, per Sackville J

Substantial risk

Canada [Protection order for child could be made on proof of substantial risk to health or safety.] 'The case law suggests that there are two distinct approaches in defining "substantial risk". One approach is to ascribe ordinary and plain meaning to the words "substantial risk". The words are interpreted in the context of the statement of purposes of the Act. The other is to add words to qualify the words "substantial risk" giving to it added meaning and placing a massive burden upon the CAS. I find the second approach narrow, restrictive and contrary to the purposes of the Act. I prefer and adopt the first approach.

'I conclude based upon the case law referred to that the correct interpretation of "substantial" in s 51(3) means actual, real, not illusory or speculative. "Risk" means a real chance of danger to the health or safety of a child.' *Catholic Children's Aid Society of Metropolitan Toronto v D (A)* (1994) 111 DLR (4th) 151 at 156, 158–159, Ont Gen Div, per Wilson J

SUBSTANTIALITY

New Zealand [Contractual Remedies Act 1979, s 7.] 'To amount to derogation from the grant the interference with a use for which the premises were let must be substantial: *Mount Cook National Park Board v Mount Cook Motels Ltd; O'Cedar Ltd v Slough Trading Co Ltd*... Mere interference with convenience or amenities such as privacy or tranquillity in the absence of a use known to be particularly susceptible to such interference will not be sufficient to constitute a derogation from the grant: *Kelly v Battershell*; *O'Cedar Ltd v Slough Trading Co Ltd*.' *Nordern v Blueport Enterprises Ltd and Others* [1996] 3 NZLR 450 at 455, per Elias J

SUBSTANTIALLY

Australia [The Social Security Act 1947 (Cth) defines, for the purposes of the sole parent's pension, the expression 'dependent child' as including a child who is being wholly or 'substantially' maintained by a person.] 'In the present context the word "substantially" appears in contrast to the word "wholly" but forms a phrase with it. If "substantially" bore the meaning suggested by the tribunal, namely, something more than merely incidental, there would have been no need at all for the word "wholly" to have appeared. It is the word "wholly" that gives context here to the word "substantially". In the context, in my view, the word means something less than "wholly" but more than merely "insubstantial" or "insignificant" and is appropriately paraphrased by the word "in the main" or "as to the greater part". I am reinforced in my view by the adoption of the same view by the Full Court of this court in *Commissioner for Superannuation v Scott* (1987) 71 ALR 408 at 411–13 in a similar context.' *Secretary, Dept of Social Security v Wetter* (1993) 40 FCR 22 at 29–30; 112 ALR 151 at 159, per Hill J

SUBSTITUTION

New Zealand 'In normal usage I think the words clearly denote an element of replacement or exchange. One document or transaction takes the place of another.' *Re Kerr* [1993] 2 NZLR 378 at 382, per Gallen J

SUBVERSION

Canada ' "Subversion", I am satisfied, is an extraordinarily elusive concept.

...

'The *Immigration Act* neither expressly defines nor sets out any criteria by which to gauge the meaning of the term "subversion". The language of paragraph 19(1)(*e*) is very broad; not only does it contemplate activities taking place within Canada but aimed towards the undermining of foreign countries, but it also captures both violent and non-violent acts of espionage and subversion. One thing is clear from the terminology of paragraph 19(1)(*e*): it employs the words "espionage" and "subversion" disjunctively. Thus, whatever "subversion" is intended to mean, it is not intended to encompass "espionage".

...

'It is therefore evident that the policy and purpose behind the exclusion from Canada pursuant to paragraph 19(1)(*e*) of the Act of persons who either have engaged in or who may engage in espionage or subversion is to promote international order and justice by denying the use of Canada as a base for espionage or subversion or, in the words of paragraph 3(*j*), for "criminal activity", an expression that is clearly not coextensive with espionage and subversion.

...

'Given the absence of a definition of "subversion" within the *Immigration Act* and its failure to set out any factors or determinative elements for identifying the parameters of activities falling within the scope of "subversion", I turn to the related provisions of the *Canadian Security Intelligence Service Act* for guidance.

'It is interesting to note that the *Canadian Security Intelligence Service Act* simply does not use the term "subversion". Paragraph (*d*) of the definition "threats to the security of Canada" in section 2 of that Act is apparently as close as the Act gets to a concept of subversion. Further, that paragraph, as with all elements of the definition, is specifically limited to exclude lawful advocacy, protest or dissent unless the advocacy, protest or dissent is carried on in conjunction with the activities referred to in the elements of the definition.

...

'In contrast to paragraph 19(1)(*e*) of the *Immigration Act*, the *Canadian Security Intelligence Service Act* confines the concept of "subversion" to acts directed toward either the undermining by covert unlawful acts or the overthrow by violence of the constitutionally established system of government in Canada. It therefore is much more specific or focussed than the concept "subversion" in the *Immigration Act* in that it requires acts to be directed at the Canadian system of government, and to be either covert and unlawful or violent.

'The uncertainty surrounding any attempt to distinguish between permissible and impermissible conduct in relation to "subversion" is compounded when one considers the broad definition of "subversive or hostile activities" found in subsection 15(2) of the *Access to Information Act*. The relevant portion of that provision reads:

15. (1) ...
(2) In this section,

...

"subversive or hostile activities" means
(*a*) espionage against Canada or any state allied or associated with Canada,
(*b*) sabotage,
(*c*) activities directed toward the commission of terrorist acts, including hijacking, in or against Canada or foreign states,
(*d*) activities directed toward accomplishing government change within Canada or foreign states by the use of or the encouragement of the use of force, violence or any criminal means,
(*e*) activities directed toward gathering information used for intelligence purposes that relates to Canada or any state allied or associated with Canada, and
(*f*) activities directed toward threatening the safety of Canadians, employees of the Government of Canada or property of the Government of Canada outside Canada.

'The foregoing definition would appear to contemplate "subversive activities" which may or may not involve violence and that target Canada or any state allied or associated with Canada. It does not distinguish between activities which would be considered subversive as opposed to hostile; rather, it lumps together a broad mix of activities ranging from intelligence-gathering to terrorism.

'Given the ambiguity and lack of determinative elements regarding the term subversion in the *Immigration Act*, it is perhaps surprising that the term has been rarely judicially considered. In fact, Mr Justice Cullen appears to be alone in his attempt to give meaning to the term. In *Shandi, Re*, in the context of a judicial review of the validity of a certificate issued pursuant to subsection 40.1(4) [as enacted by RSC, 1985 (4th Supp), c 29, s 4] of the *Immigration Act*, Mr Justice Cullen, as noted earlier in these reasons, wrote:

Espionage and subversion are not limited to the actual act but to be engaged in these activities the words envisage participation by one who assists or facilitates the objective as one who commits the *actus reus*. Any act that is intended to contribute to the process of overthrowing a government is a subversive act. It perplexes me that so much has been written about subversion, or that the word should not be used because it runs contrary to a person's rights under the **Charter** to be a dissident. Certainly CSIS investigators must be aware of the difference (which may not always have been the case), but subversive acts are not difficult to distinguish from acts of protest that should not be subject to investigations. For example, if funds are raised or guns sent to the IRA from Canada, is that not clearly subversion? However, vocal comment or written treaties on the "Struggle" are clearly protected under the **Charter**. Examples of subversive acts are not difficult to find. [Emphasis added.]

'Mr Justice Cullen's terminology would appear to be remarkably broad. The highlighted sentence involves no concept of covertness, violence or unlawfulness; rather, it would appear to encompass open, non-violent, lawful activities of legitimate political opposition parties, albeit that this breadth would appear to be qualified somewhat later in the quoted paragraph. In the end, Justice Cullen appears to be saying, we will know subversion when we see it. In this, he appears to draw support from reputable dictionaries.

'The *Oxford English Dictionary*, 2nd edition, defines "subversion" as including "the action of subverting or state of being subverted":

> **1.** Overthrow, demolition (of a city, stronghold, etc.).
> …
> **4.** In immaterial senses: Overthrow, ruin.
>
> > **a.** of a law, rule, system, condition, faculty, character, etc.
> >
> > …
> >
> > **b.** of persons, countries, peoples or their lives or fortunes.

'The ITP Nelson Canadian Dictionary of the English Language provides the following relevant definitions:

> subversion **1.a.** The act or an instance of subverting. **b.** The condition of being subverted. **2.…** . A cause of overthrow or ruin.
>
> subversive Intended or serving to subvert, esp. intended to overthrow or undermine an established government.
>
> subvert **1.** To destroy completely; ruin. **2.** To undermine the character, morals, or allegiance of; corrupt. **3.** To overthrow completely.

'*Black's Law Dictionary*, 7th edition, provides:

> **subversion**. The process of overthrowing, destroying, or corrupting.
>
> **subversive activity**. A pattern of acts designed to overthrow a government by force or other illegal means.

'While Mr Justice Cullen's definition and the dictionary definitions of "subversion" and related terms are helpful in providing a general understanding of the concept, they do not clarify its legal parameters. In particular, they do not aid in distinguishing between subversion and lawful dissent, nor do they provide guidance to define the boundary between the two. They provide no basis or guidance for legal debate.' *Al Yamani v Canada (Minister of Citizenship and Immigration)* [2000] 3 FC 433 at 454–460, FCTD, per Gibson J

SUCH OF THE PROPERTY

New Zealand [Under section 15(1) of the Proceeds of Crimes Act 1991 '… the Court may … order that such of the property as is specified by the Court is forfeited to the Crown'.] 'The words "such of the property" clearly enable some items only to be selected for forfeiture. They do not, in their ordinary meaning, authorise the forfeiture in part of a particular item.

…

'There is no reason to go beyond the ordinary meaning of the words "such of the property", and to read them as if they continued "or such part thereof as is specified by the Court".'*R v Dunsmuir* [1996] 2 NZLR 1 at 3, CA, per cur

SUCCESSOR

Canada [Employers' organization claimed successor rights relating to pension trust fund.] 'I am also satisfied that, in this context, the word "successor" should be interpreted as meaning a person or entity that takes over and assumes all of the existing responsibilities of such associations, and that the applicant, having only the exclusive right to collective bargain, has not assumed or taken over the overall mandate of the employers associations.' *Construction Labour Relations v SMW, Local No 8* (1994) 111 DLR (4th) 569 at 575, Alta QB, per Lefsrud J

SUE

[Brussels Convention on Jurisdiction and the Enforcement of Judgments in Civil and Commercial Matters 1968 (as set out in the Civil Jurisdiction and Judgments Act 1982 Sch 1) art 2. '… persons domiciled in a Contracting State shall, whatever their nationality, be sued in the courts of that State'. The question was whether a claim for unpaid costs under the Supreme Court Act 1981, s 51 was encompassed by the Convention.] 'My inclination is to the view that a summons issued in an action relating to costs does not "sue" the non-party. I would agree with the judge that "suing" contemplates pursuing a substantive cause of action. It does not relate to the making of orders ancillary to substantive proceedings pending before a particular court. To proceed to commit for contempt, for example, would in my view not be to "sue" the alleged contemnor. A proceeding to obtain an order for costs because someone has interfered with or been responsible for the bringing of substantive proceedings is not in my view to "sue" as contemplated in Titles I to III of the Brussels Convention.' *National Justice Compania Naviera SA v Prudential Assurance Co Ltd, The Ikarian Reefer* [2000] 1 All ER 37 at 48, CA, per Waller LJ

SUED

[Lugano Convention on Jurisdiction and the Enforcement of Judgments in Civil and Commercial Matters 1988 arts 2 and 6.] 'Article 2 states the general principle in the following terms:

"Subject to the provisions of this Convention, persons domiciled in a Contracting State shall, whatever their nationality, be sued in the courts of that State. Persons who are not nationals of the State in which they are domiciled shall be governed by the rules of jurisdiction applicable to nationals of that State."

'Article 6 contains a special rule of jurisdiction. It provides, so far as material, as follows:

"A person domiciled in a Contracting State may also be sued: 1. where he is one of a number of defendants, in the courts for the place where any one of them is domiciled."

'The principal question of law before the House is whether the concept "sued" in arts 2 and 6, when applied to legal proceedings taken in England, means the date of issue of the writ (as the plaintiff respondents contend) or the date of service of the writ (as the appellants contend)...

...

'The problem inherent in the application of the concepts of the convention in national legal systems requires a twofold classificatory enquiry. In the first place it is necessary to interpret a particular concept used in the convention independently by reference to the language, structure, system and objectives of the convention. Secondly, recognising that a concept of the convention may have a different content in various national legal systems, it is necessary to apply it to the procedural regime of the particular legal system: see *Shearson Lehman Hutton Inc v Treuhand für Vermögensverwaltung und Beteiligungen (TVB) mbH* Case C-89/91 [1993]

ECR I-139 at 186 (para 13). The starting point is therefore the ascertainment of the meaning of the concept of being "sued" in arts 2 and 6.

'In examining the problem before the House one can safely proceed from two premises. First, the word "sued" must bear the same meaning in arts 2 and 6. Secondly, in a convention of which the major purpose is the attainment, so far as possible, of certainty and uniformity, it is obvious that the search must be for a single meaning of the concept "sued" which can apply across the spectrum of national legal systems and the diversity of procedures potentially involved.

'The answer to the central question must be found in the principal sources of treaty or convention interpretation, viz the text, its context and the object and purpose of the treaty or convention: see arts 31 and 32 of the Vienna Convention on the Law of Treaties (Vienna, 23 May 1969; Misc 19 (1971); Cmnd 4818); Aust *Modern Treaty Law and Practice* (2000) pp 184–191. I turn first to the language and structure of the convention. One can perhaps accept as a general proposition that the word "sued" as used in arts 2 and 6 and elsewhere in the convention is equally capable as a matter of language of indicating the moment of initiation of the proceedings or the date of service of the initiating process. But the convention also uses the concept that a party may "bring proceedings" in a number of articles: see arts 10, 11, 12, 14, 21 and 22. The words "to bring proceedings" in the context of the convention appear to point to the initiation of the proceedings. Moreover, as my noble and learned friend Lord Cooke of Thorndon pointed out during the argument the point is reinforced by the contextual meaning of art 14.

...

'... Moreover, the convention uses yet other language as pinpointing the time for the coming into operation of the various rules, viz the concept of 'instituting' legal proceedings: see arts 6 and 20. Where this language is used it points tolerably clearly to the initiation of proceedings. Standing back from this review of the particular provisions of the convention one is entitled to make the provisional judgment that the concepts 'sued', 'bring proceedings' and 'instituted proceedings' have been used interchangeably. Significantly, that is how the matter was viewed in the Jenard Report (OJ 1979 C59, p 1) Ch IV, section B (Jurisdiction in matters relating to insurance). If this view is correct, as it appears to be, it may afford a substantial basis for concluding that "sued" in arts 2 and 6 refer to the initiation of the proceedings.

'It is also necessary to consider the rival arguments from the point of view of the attainment of the principal objectives of the convention. The preamble of the Lugano Convention records the desire "to ensure as uniform an interpretation as possible of this instrument": see also Protocol No 2 "On the Uniform Interpretation of the Convention", arts 1 and 2. It may be that either interpretation would meet this criterion. Certainly, the date of initiation of proceedings can meet this criterion in all national systems albeit that the point may be differently determined in different countries. The second major aim of the convention is the achievement of predictability and certainty at all stages for all concerned, viz at the time of the conclusion of the transaction, when the dispute has arisen and when it has to be ruled on. In *Mulox IBC Ltd v Geels* Case 125/92 [1993] ECR I-4075 at 4103 (para 11) the European Court of Justice said of its judgment that the aim is to allow "the plaintiff easily to identify the court before which he may bring an action and the defendant reasonably to foresee the court before which he may be sued". From this perspective there is an advantage in selecting the time of lodging of the process with the court as the operative time. It will presumably be a matter of record in all national legal systems. It will have the advantage of certainty. On the other hand, proof of valid service depends on evidence. Moreover, even if there are differences between systems as to how proceedings are initiated, the date of initiation appears to be a readily available point of reference. On balance selecting the time of initiation of the proceedings as the critical point promotes certainty.

...

'Looking at the matter in the round I am satisfied that "sued" in arts 2 and 6 should be interpreted as referring to the initiation of the proceedings.' *Canada Trust Co v Stolzenburg (No 2)* [2000] 4 All ER 481 at 484, 486–487, 489–490, HL, per Lord Steyn

SUGGEST

Canada [An applicant for a declaration of significant discovery of petroleum was required to show reasonable grounds to suggest the potential of sustained production.] 'Webster's New Dictionary and Thesaurus (1989), defines "suggest" as "to bring to one's mind by association of ideas". It defines "potential" as "possibility; powers or resources not yet developed". It defines "possibility" as "that which may be possible; a contingency" and "possible" as "not contrary to the nature of things; that may be or happen; that may be done, practicable".' *Petro-Canada v Canada-Newfoundland Offshore Petroleum Board* (1995) 127 DLR (4th) 483 at 500, Nfld SC, per Barry J

SUITABILITY OF THE APPLICANT

New Zealand [Section 13(1)(a) of the Sale of Liquor Act 1989.] 'Suitability is a word commonly used in the English language and is well understood. In an earlier decision the [Liquor Licensing Authority] has adopted the definition in *The Concise Oxford* dictionary as "well fitted for the purpose; appropriate".

'I do not find it helpful to refer to other decisions on different facts as to the meaning of that word. Where a statute uses an unambiguous and well understood word or expression and chooses not to enlarge on the ordinary definition of the word or expression by a special interpretation in the statute it is usually unwise for a Court to add to the ordinary meaning of the word as a general guide for all cases, as distinct from applying the word to the particular facts before it. *Re Sheard* [1996] 1 NZLR 751 at 755 per Holland J

SUITABLE EDUCATION

[Education Act 1993, s 298 (re-enacted in Education Act 1996, s 19): local education authority required to make arrangements for the provision of suitable full-time or part-time education for children who might not otherwise receive 'suitable education'.] 'There is nothing in the 1993 Act to suggest that resource considerations are relevant to the question of what is "suitable education". On their face those words connote a standard to be determined purely by educational considerations. This view is much strengthened by the definition of "suitable education" in s 298(7), which spells out expressly the factors which are relevant to the determination of suitability, viz the education must be "efficient" and "suitable to his age, ability and aptitude" and also suitable to "any special educational needs he may have". All these express factors relate to educational considerations and nothing else. There is nothing to indicate that the resources available are relevant. Moreover, there are other provisions in the Act which do refer expressly to the efficient use of resources: see ss 160, 161(4) and Sch 10, para 3.

...

'For these reasons as a matter of pure construction I can see no reason to treat the resources of the LEA as a relevant factor in

determining what constitutes "suitable education".'
R v East Sussex County Council, ex p Tandy [1998]
2 All ER 769 at 774, 775, HL, per Lord Browne-
Wilkinson

SUM

Sum actually paid

[Three excess of loss reinsurance contracts in
respect of catastrophe loss and aviation loss
contained a liability clause which provided that the
reinsurers would only be liable if and when the
ultimate loss sustained by the insurers exceeded a
specified amount, and an ultimate net loss
clause defining net loss as 'the sum actually paid
by the [insurers] in settlement of losses or liability'.]
'The appeal was argued on the basis that it raises a
short point of construction: does the phrase in
these reinsurance policies "the sum actually paid"
mean what it appears to mean or does it mean "the
sum actually payable"? In other words, for the
reinsurers to be liable, must the reinsured actually
have disbursed (or otherwise satisfied) the claim
against which the reinsurance is to indemnify them,
or is it sufficient that such claim has been
established to be immediately payable?
...
'Is the apparent meaning of the words used
here—"the sum actually paid"—so abundantly clear
in context, does it so obviously involve actual
disbursement, that, however unreasonable this result,
one must so construe them?
'Powerful though the arguments are to that
effect, and hesitant though I am to disagree with
Staughton LJ's conclusions, I have finally reached
the view that the words here are not so clear ...
'To say that words of yet clearer meaning could
have been used is not, however, I accept, a sufficient
answer to the submission that the words used here
are themselves unambiguously clear ... Additional
responses need to be given. First is that, as always,
the words have to be construed in their context.
That context here has two aspects. One, the wider
aspect, is that these words appear in an excess of
loss reinsurance contract, a context in which it is
unlikely that the reinsurers' duty to pay will be
made conditional upon the reinsureds' prior
disbursement of incoming insurance claims ...
'The second and narrower aspect is that the
words are used in an "ultimate net loss clause", a
clause which on any view is concerned essentially
with the measurement of reinsurance recoveries
and where it would be surprising to find imposed a
condition requiring prior disbursement.

...

'Mance J furthermore pointed out that, read
literally, the liability clause in the first two contracts
is inconsistent with the ultimate net loss clause,
there being no liability under the former to pay on
an interim basis despite the clear implication to
this effect in the proviso to the later clause. This to
my mind is another factor justifying a less literal
approach to the words in question.
'... I conclude that it is possible to construe the
words as not requiring disbursement but rather as
emphasising that the recoverable loss must be
immediately due and net of all deductions.' *Charter
Reinsurance Co Ltd (in liq) v Fagan* [1996] 1 All ER
406 at 425–426, CA, per Simon Brown LJ

Sum due

[The Insolvency Act 1986, s 74(2)(f) provides that
a 'sum due' to any member of the company (in his
character of a member) by way of dividends,
profits or otherwise is not deemed to be a debt of
the company.] 'Is the sum referred to in the
paragraph a liquidated sum? To my mind, the
language of para (f) strongly suggests that it is.
The sum "due" is not deemed to be "a debt" which
is "payable" to a member. There is no reference to
the looser term "liability" in the paragraph and that
contrasts with sub-s (1) and para (b) of the same
subsection as that in which para (f) is found; the
absence of any reference to "liability" in the
paragraph must be taken to be deliberate.
Accordingly, a claim for unliquidated damages
would not appear to be a sum due within s 74(2)(f),
unless statute has intervened to deem it so.

...

'... We are not persuaded that extraordinary
anomalies arise if only liquidated claims are
postponed by s 74(2)(f) on the interpretation which
we favour of the other parts of para (f).
'However, Mr Potts advanced a further
substantial argument based on the 1986 Act and
r 13.12 of the Insolvency Rules 1986... There is no
doubt that by reason of s 411 of, and paras 12 and
13 of Sch 8 to, the 1986 Act, the 1986 rules can
and do affect the meaning of terms used in that
Act. Accordingly, we would accept that the
reference to a "sum due" in s 74(2)(f) includes a
liability for unliquidated damages for tort.' *Soden v
British and Commonwealth Holdings plc (in
administration)* [1996] 3 All ER 951 at 958,
964–965, CA, per Peter Gibson LJ

SUPERANNUATION SCHEME

[The Wages Councils Act 1979 has been repealed.]

New Zealand [Matrimonial Property Act 1976, s 8(i).] 'The subsection is concerned with a benefit only if there is an entitlement to it under a superannuation scheme. The deed in question does not establish anything which has the character of a superannuation scheme – there is no separate fund or fund manager. Furthermore, there is no provision for contributions either by a partner or by the firm itself. Entitlement therefore is not derived from contributions. Nor does entitlement derive from employment or an office which is held. The husband is not employed by the firm – he is one of the partners who constitute the firm. Neither does his status as a partner fit easily with the term "office" as it is used in the subsection. It is also of some significance that a retiring partner is subject to a number of undertakings, including a restraint of trade and other ongoing obligations to the firm. This lends support to the conclusion that the retirement benefit provisions are not part of a superannuation scheme, as that phrase is commonly understood.' *Z v Z (No 2)* [1997] 2 NZLR 258 at 286, CA

SUPERSEDE

Canada 'Counsel for the respondent submits that the Tribunal acted within its jurisdiction given that the first notice of suspension was never actually withdrawn and was thus revived as a consequence of the invalidity of the second notice.

'I disagree with counsel for the respondent.

'A reading of the Minister's letter accompanying the second notice clearly indicates that the intention of the Minister in issuing the second notice was to replace and supersede the first notice.

'As submitted by the applicant, in all the dictionary definitions, the word supersede does not mean "to amend":

> **Supersede**: Obliterate, set aside, annul, replace, make void, inefficacious or useless, repeal ... To set aside, render unnecessary, suspend or stay. [*Black's Law Dictionary*, 5th ed.]

> **Supersede**: ... 1) To desist from, discontinue (a procedure, an attempt, etc.); not to proceed with. To desist, forbear, refrain. 2) To refrain from (disclosure, disquisition); to omit to mention, refrain from mentioning. 3) To put a stop to (legal proceedings, etc.); to stop, stay. *Law.* To discharge by a writ of supersedeas. 4) To render superfluous or unnecessary. 5) To make of no effect; to render void, nugatory, or useless; to annul; to override. 6) To be set

aside as useless or obsolete; to be replaced by something regarded as superior. 7) To take the place of (something set aside or abandoned); to succeed to the place occupied by; to serve, be adopted or accepted instead of. 8) To supply the place of (a person deprived of or removed from an office or position) by another; also to promote another over the head of; to be removed from office to make way for another; to supply the place of (a thing). [Underlining added.] [*Shorter Oxford English Dictionary*, 3rd ed.]

> **Replace**: To place again, to restore to a former condition ... Term, given its plain, ordinary meaning, means to supplant with substitute or equivalent ... To take the place of. [Underlining added.] [*Black's Law Dictionary*, 5th ed.]

> **Replace**: ... 1) To restore to a previous place or position; to put back again *in* a place, 2) to take the place of, become a substitute for (a person or thing), 3) to fill the place of (a person or thing) *with* or *by* a substitute, to provide or procure a substitute or equivalent in place of (a person or thing). [*Shorter Oxford English Dictionary*, 3rd ed.]

'Therefore, I am of the opinion that the first notice was revoked as of November 13, 1998, and was thus not in effect.

'It was not open to the Tribunal to second-guess the Minister's intention and declare that the second notice was in fact intended to amend the first notice. This goes well beyond the jurisdiction of the Tribunal.' *Air Nunavut v Canada (Minister of Transport)* [2001] 1 FC 138 at 151–152, FCTD, per Tremblay-Lamer J

New Zealand 'In my opinion a determination is "superseded" in the sense in which that word is used in s 7 [of the Health Service Personnel Amendment Act (No 2) 1985] by a later determination when the latter takes the place of, or replaces, or is the successor of, the former. A later determination would only supersede an earlier one where it deals with the same subject-matters or topics. If the later determination deals with matters not dealt with by the earlier the latter would not supersede the former.' *Mawson v Auckland Area Health Board* [1991] 3 NZLR 599 at 607, per Tompkins J

SUPPLY

'The word "supply", in its ordinary natural meaning, conveys the idea of furnishing or providing to another something which is wanted or required in order to meet the wants or requirements of that other. It connotes more than the mere transfer of physical control of some chattel or object from one person to another. No one would ordinarily say that to hand over something to a mere custodier was to supply him with it. The additional concept is that of enabling the recipient to apply the thing handed over to purposes for which he desires or has a duty to apply it. In my opinion it is not a necessary element in the conception of supply that the provision should be made out of the personal resources of the person who does the supplying.' *R v Maginnis* [1987] 1 All ER 907 at 909, HL, per Lord Keith of Kinkel

'The primary rule of construction is that we should attribute to words their natural and ordinary meaning, unless the context otherwise requires. So what is the natural and ordinary meaning of the word "supply"? I hesitate to attempt a definition, especially as the word under consideration is not always very precisely used; but to me the word, as used in relation to goods, connotes the idea of making goods available to another from resources other than those of the recipient.' Ibid at 913, per Lord Goff of Chieveley

Australia [In determining '... the extent to which the conduct of the appellant amounted to the "supply" of a prohibited drug within the meaning of s 6(1)(c) of the [Misuse of] Drugs Act [1981 (WA)]'.] '[43] ... In the present case, there is not suggestion that the appellant sold or offered to sell methylamphetamine to another person within the meaning of para (c). Accordingly, consideration may be given wholly to the proper meaning in para (c) of "supply ... to another".

...

'[49] ... However, reference must also be made to s 3. That section is headed "Interpretation". Section 3(1) defines "to supply" as including:

> to *deliver*, dispense, distribute, *forward*, furnish, make available, provide, return or *send*, and it does not matter that something is supplied on behalf of another or on whose behalf it is supplied.

(emphasis added)

'The definition of "to supply" contained in s 3(1) significantly expands the meaning otherwise to be attributed to that phrase in the context of s 6(1)(c). It follows that, among other things, the forwarding or sending of a prohibited drug to another will, by operation of s 3(1), amount to the supply of that drug to another in contravention of s 6(1)(c). That such a result may, in the eyes of some, appear

unduly burdensome is not a reason for denying the plain words of the statute their proper meaning and effect.

...

'[53] It follows that a person is liable under s 6(1)(c) for sending a prohibited drug to another person once he or she has knowingly placed the drug in a mail delivery system with the intention that it be received by that person at a particular place. Whether or not the drug in question ultimately reaches the intended recipient once it has arrived at its intended destination is, for this purpose, irrelevant. For these reasons, the actions of the appellant in arranging for the delivery of a prohibited drug with the intention that the drug would be received by Mr Yanko at Perth Airport, when combined with the actions of Ansett in causing the drug to reach, and be unloaded at, Perth Airport, amounted to the "supply" of that drug to another within the meaning of s6(1)(c) of the Drugs Act ...'

...

'[100] It is from the context of the Act, that "supply" of prohibited drugs, in its ordinary sense, has generally attracted a meaning proper for the supply of a thing for use or sale as drugs. This is why the mere transfer of physical control over drugs does not, as such, constitute "supply", within the Drugs Act ...

'[101] In some of the cases concerned with the meaning of "supply", attention has been paid to the question whether the alleged supplier owned, or had physical possession and control of, the goods in question. Whilst this is an understandable inquiry in circumstances where the act said to constitute "supply" is claimed to be nothing more than a transfer pursuant to an arrangement of bailment, the word "supply" does not necessarily say anything about the interest of the alleged supplier in the goods "supplied". It is sufficient for the offence if the supplier has control over the goods for the purpose of the "supply" in question. In some cases, control will derive from ownership or the right to possession. In other cases it will involve nothing more than temporary custody. In the present case, there is no doubt that the police officers at Perth Airport who took control of the drugs in question had, and exercised, control over them sufficient to "supply" them to a recipient. The appellant may have owned the drugs. However, after he consigned them by Ansett cargo, he lost physical control over them. That control was entrusted to Ansett cargo. They constituted the appellant's agent for the purpose of supplying the drugs to the named recipient. They were not his agent for the purpose of supplying the drugs to police officers. Still less were the police officers the appellant's agents to take control of the drug and to "supply" it to Mr Yanko.

...

'[109] In the present case, however, two considerations make it impossible to attribute to the appellant the eventual "supply" of the drug to Mr Yanko. The first is that the physical acts constituting the "supply" were ultimately those of Officer Kanawati, who interposed himself between the appellant and Mr Yanko and was not an innocent agent of the appellant. Secondly, that interposition broke the chain of causation between the appellant's consignment of the cargo to Mr Yanko and the latter's receipt of it. It introduced a "new cause" in the effectuation of the "supply". It was one performed without the request or authority of the appellant. It was wholly performed as a voluntary act on the part of police for their own purposes.

'[110] *Police supply is not appellant's supply*: To say the least, the police action of "supply" to Mr Yanko for their purposes was not intended, or authorised, by the appellant. It involved a new operative cause of the "supply". This meant that the act of "supply", as it occurred, did not coincide with the "supply" as arranged and intended by or on behalf of the appellant. In these circumstances the contemporaneity between the relevant criminal act and the criminal intention required in this case to establish the offence of "supply" was missing. Although doubtless well intended in the circumstances, the intervention of Officer Kanawati meant that, as a matter of law, the "supply" was solely that of the police. Neither by innocent agency nor otherwise could it be attributed in law to the appellant.' *Pinkstone v R* [2004] HCA 23 at 51 at [43], [49], [53], per per McHugh and Gummow JJ, [100]–[101], [109]–[110], per Kirby J (dissenting); BC200402837

New Zealand 'It is plain ... within the context of this legislative scheme [Fair Trading Act 1986] the word supply has a very wide meaning. In its natural and ordinary primary meaning it is used to mean to provide or furnish but that definition is expanded in two important ways. First, supply is not confined to one method of acquisition such as sale, but is expanded quite widely to include both commercial and non-commercial ways of passing or acquiring goods. Secondly, the definition in s 2(3) by including "agreeing to supply" widens the relevant time span so that supply is not confined to the point at which the contract is consummated by the passing of the goods and the paying of the price. The totality of the transaction embraced by the provision and furnishing of goods can be affected by conduct prior to that final event.' *Foodtown Supermarkets Ltd v Commerce Commission* [1991] 1 NZLR 466 at 469, per Jeffries J

New Zealand 'Granted that the meaning of "supply" generally includes some element of benefit to the person supplied, we do not consider that element of such plain and central significance to its use that a delivery of firearms into the possession and control of a volunteer who does not thereby receive any personal benefit cannot sensibly be described as a "supply" of the firearms.' *Police v Coory* [1991] 3 NZLR 686 at 688, CA, per cur

New Zealand [Section 2 of the Goods and Services Tax Act 1985 provides that ' "Services" means anything which is not goods or money" and by Section 8 of the Goods and Services Tax Act 1985 'Subject to this Act, a tax, to be known as goods and services tax, shall be charged in accordance with the provisions of this Act at the rate of [12.5 percent] on the supply (but not including an exempt supply) in New Zealand of goods and services, ...'.] 'While I recognise the width of the definitions of services and supply, I regard it as conceptually unsound in legal terms to say that trustees of a voluntary settlement supply services to the settlor of the trust or to the beneficiaries when all they are doing is to perform the terms of the trust.

'When coupled with the definitions of taxable activity and consideration, to which I shall come, and in spite of the width of those definitions, the concept of supplying services has a reciprocal connotation. It is not apt to catch the fulfilment by trustees of their duties as such, albeit that such fulfilment will necessarily, in a direct or indirect way, be of benefit to the beneficiaries and the settlor. For these reasons, I do not consider that the trustees engaged in any supply of services in terms of s 8.' *Chatham Islands Enterprise Trust v Commissioner of Inland Revenue* [1999] 2 NZLR 388 at 395, CA, per Tipping J

Of drugs

Australia 'By definition under the Poisons and Narcotic Drugs Ordinance [1978 Act], "supply" includes sale and sell (but is not limited to these), and does not include "administer" (by virtue of s 4(10)). Apart from the foregoing, "supply" therefore, as I understand it, has its ordinary meaning, in the English language. It generally means to furnish or provide, or give.' *Excell v Dellaca* (1987) 82 ACTR 8 at 9, per Kelly J

Australia 'The word "supply" where secondly appearing in s 29 of the [Drug Misuse and Trafficking Act 1985 (NSW)] … does not include the mere transfer of physical control of the drugs from a person who has had the drugs deposited with him to their owner or to the person reasonably believed to be such. The same construction must also be applied to the word "supply" in the phrase "having in possession for supply" in the definition of "supply" in s 3.' *R v Carey* (1990) 50 A Crim R 163 at 167, per Hunt J

Of intoxicating liquor

New Zealand 'It is my conclusion that in the context of s 249(1) [of the Sale of Liquor Act 1962] where there has been a completed sale and property in the goods has passed to the purchaser, the subsequent obtaining of possession of the goods by the purchaser on the licensed premises does not involve a supply by the licensee or manager.' *Police v Matheson* [1989] 3 NZLR 682 at 687, per Tompkins J

SUPPORT

Easement of

[For 31 Halsbury's Laws (4th edn) para 47 see now 31 Halsbury's Laws (4th edn) (2003 Reissue) paras 116, 118.]

SURETY

[For 20 Halsbury's Laws (4th edn) para 105 see now 20(1) Halsbury's Laws (4th edn) (Reissue) para 106.]

SURFACE

[For 31 Halsbury's Laws (4th edn) para 16 see now 31 Halsbury's Laws (4th edn) (2003 Reissue) para 19.]

SURPRISE

[For 16 Halsbury's Laws (4th edn) para 1226 see now 16(2) Halsbury's Laws (4th edn) (Reissue) para 434.]

SURRENDER

[For 27 Halsbury's Laws (4th edn) para 444 see now 27(1) Halsbury's Laws (4th edn) (Reissue) para 524.]

SURVIVE–SURVIVOR

[For 50 Halsbury's Laws (4th edn) paras 500, 501 see now 50 Halsbury's Laws (4th edn) (Reissue) paras 554–555.]

SUSPECTED

Australia [Section 464H of the Crimes Act 1958 (Vic) refers to evidence of a confession made by a person who is 'suspected' of having committed an offence.] 'The distinction between suspicion and belief as a state of mind was analysed by Vincent J in *Walsh v Loughnan* [1991] 2 VR 351 at 356–7. Vincent J observed in his ruling: "Although the creation of a suspicion requires a lesser factual basis than the creation of a belief, it must, nonetheless, be built upon some factual foundation".

'In our opinion, this observation is plainly correct. The section is not concerned with a state of mind founded upon speculation or "mere idle wondering" (Kitto J in *Queensland Bacon Pty Ltd v Rees* (1966) 115 CLR 266 at 303) but is concerned with a state of mind arrived upon consideration of known facts out of which an apprehension that a person might possibly have committed an offence is created.' *R v Heaney* [1992] 2 VR 522 at 547–548, per cur

SUSPECTS *SEE ALSO* KNOWS OR REASONABLY SUSPECTS

SUSPENSION

Australia [Under the University of New South Wales (Academic Staff) Enterprise Agreement 2000 (the Agreement), the University could take action to discipline an academic for unsatisfactory performance, misconduct or serious misconduct, including suspending the academic with or without pay. The applicant was suspended from his position as Head of School until the day his appointment ended.] 'It is appropriate to consider first the ordinary meaning of "suspension". The *Macquarie Dictionary* (3rd ed, 1997) defines "suspension" relevantly as "3. temporary abrogation, as of a law or privilege". The verb "suspend" is defined as "8. to debar, usually for a time, from the exercise of an office or function or the enjoyment of a privilege". Suspension, in the ordinary sense, thus has a temporary character.

'In cl 3 of the Agreement, the word appears in a list of disciplinary actions, which appears to be ordered from least to most severe: "counselling", "formal censure", "demotion by one or more classification levels or increments", "withholding of an increment", "suspension with or without pay" and "termination of employment". There is nothing to suggest that the word "suspension" is used in anything but its ordinary sense. That is, a suspension must be for a period, however that period is specified.

'The distinction between a suspension and a dismissal was adverted to by Allen J in *Ford v Lismore City Council* (1989) 28 IR 68, though in a different legal and factual context. There, a council purported to terminate the employment of a librarian. However, s 99 of the Local Government Act 1919 (NSW) required the council to first suspend an employee whose employment it proposed to terminate and allow the employee to request an inquiry. The council submitted that it had suspended the employee. Allen J rejected that submission, stating (at IR 77):

> "A suspension, within the meaning of that section, is essentially different from a purported dismissal. It is not a repudiation of contract of service. It is, indeed, an affirmation that the contract of service continues – albeit that the statutory scheme contains provisions pursuant to which the servant may be dismissed at some time in the future. What [the council] did, in quite clear terms, was not to suspend the plaintiff but to declare that it regarded her contract of service with it as terminated [...]. She remained an employee, not suspended, up to that time. [The council] did not affirm the contract by suspending the plaintiff."

'The suspension in the present case was expressed in the letter from the Acting Vice-Chancellor ... to be for a period. Nevertheless, it should be inferred from the fact that this period ended on the day the applicant's appointment ended, from the conclusive measures taken by the University to remove the applicant from his position, described in the letter from the Dean to the applicant ..., and from the fact that an Acting Head of School was appointed for a period extending beyond [the day the applicant's appointment ended], that the University sought to effectively terminate the applicant's appointment as Head of School. A suspension need not, in fact, result in a restoration to former duties, such as might be the case where an employee is suspended pending the outcome of a short investigation and is then dismissed. However, it is inappropriate to characterise the action taken by the University as a "suspension". It is apt to be described as a termination of the applicant's

appointment as Head of School.' *Moshirian v University of New South Wales* BC200200557; [2002] FCA 179 at [63]–[66], per Moore J

SUSPICION *SEE ALSO* KNOWS OR REASONABLY SUSPECTS

SUSTAINED

Canada [A limitation period was calculated from the time when damages were sustained.] '... the word "sustained" is not the equivalent of "discovered" or "identified". The word has several meanings cited in the Shorter Oxford English Dictionary, 3rd ed, but the one most apt to its usage in this section is:

> "To undergo, experience, have to submit to (evil, hardship or damage; now chiefly with injury, *loss as obj.*); to have inflicted upon one, suffer the infliction of." '

Peixeiro v Haberman (1995) 127 DLR (4th) 475 at 482, Ont CA, per Carthy JA

SUSTAINED LOSS OF TRACTION

New Zealand [Offence under the Land Transport Act 1998, s 22A, of operating a motor vehicle in a manner that caused the vehicle to undergo sustained loss of traction.] '[33] After considering the words *sustained loss of traction* in s 22A(3) of the Act by reference to the commentary to the relevant amending legislation, dictionaries and case law, Judge Walsh determined that the word "sustained" means to carry on, to keep up or keep going without intermission, which was synonymous with the word "continuously", meaning uninterrupted, in unbroken sequence, without intermission or cessation, without intervening time. He found that applying that interpretation to s 22A(3), "sustained" meant to keep up or keep going the action or process of loss of traction. I respectfully agree with Judge Walsh's definition of the word "sustained" which, of course, must always be applied in the context of the facts of the case.' *Police v Bisley* [2006] DCR 176 at [33], per Judge P F Barber

SWORN

New Zealand [Section 198(1) of the Summary Proceedings Act 1957 provides that a search warrant may be issued 'on application in writing made on oath'.] 'Section 198(1) makes it plain that the facts are to be drawn from sworn evidence. "Sworn" in this context means that there must be an assertion of personal belief accompanied by an oath given in accordance with the requirements of ss 3, 4 and 15 of the Oaths and Declarations Act 1957.

'... the very fact that the statute requires sworn evidence indicates that the deponent must expressly or impliedly assert his or her personal belief in the truth of the primary facts to which he or she is deposing.' *R v Sanders* [1994] 3 NZLR 450 at 460, CA, per Fisher J

T

TAKE

Canada [A father was charged with child abduction under s 283(1) of the *Criminal Code*, which makes it an offence for a parent to take a child, not subject to custody order, with intent to deprive the other parent of possession of that child.] '... The word "take", for example, used in the English text of the section, is commonly understood to mean, *inter alia*, "to cause (a person or animal) to go with one": *Oxford English Dictionary*, 2nd ed (Oxford: Claredon Press, 1989), vol XVII, at p 564; see also D Watt, *The New Offences Against the Person: The Provisions of Bill C-127* (Toronto: Butterworths, 1984), at p 141. The verb "*enlever*", which appears in the French text, is somewhat more precise, as it connotes the action of "*soustraire (une personne) à l'autorité de ceux qui en ont la garde*": *Le Grand Robert de la langue française*, 2nd ed (Paris, 1986), t. III, at p 1002. Reading the two texts together, I conclude that a "taking" or "*enlèvement*" occurs where the accused causes the child to come or go with him or her, and, in the process, excludes the authority of another person who has lawful care or charge of the child. There is nothing in s 283 to suggest that the deprived parent, guardian or other person having lawful care or charge of the child must actually have had possession of the child at the moment of the offence.' *R v Dawson* (1996) 141 DLR (4th) 257 at 260, [1996] 3 SCR 783, per L'Heureux-Dubé J

TAKE-OVER OFFER

New Zealand [Companies Amendment Act 1963, First Schedule, Part A, para 1.] '[T]he terms ["offer" and "take-over offer"] are used in an extended sense encompassing not only offers in the strict sense but conditional contracts resulting from their acceptance.' *Southfert Co-operative Ltd v Ravensdown Corporation Ltd* [1996] 3 NZLR 196 at 200, 203–204, per Tipping J

TAKEN

[The Consumer Credit Act 1974, s 116(1) provides that a pawn is redeemable at any time within six months after it was taken.] '[26] Mr Cook also places particular reliance on the fact that s 116(1) refers to the six-month period running from the date on which the pawn "was taken". He argues that there is significance in the fact that the legislation does not state that the period should run from the date of execution of the agreement. He says that the watch was put in the hands of the respondent on the date of contract no 61360, namely 22 May 1995 and remained there thereafter. It was therefore legitimate to treat it as taken at the date on which contract no 66330 was deemed to commence, namely 21 December 1995.

'[27] It is not clear that this was an argument which was put before Judge Rose and it does not figure in his judgment nor is it raised in any respondent's notice. But in any event, I think there is nothing in it. If one considers "taken" to refer to the time when the pawn first passes into the lender's possession, that would have been in May 1995. The six-month minimum period would have expired before contract no 66330 was entered into, so it would not help the respondent. Alternatively, if one is allowed to select whatever date one likes for the date on which the pawn is taken, this is simply a way of contracting out of the statutory six-month period, something which is not open to the parties.

'[28] As I understand it, there is no definition of "taken" in the 1974 Act. It seems to me that the natural meaning of it in the context is that it refers to the date on which the pawn is taken by the lender under the agreement. It cannot be earlier than the date on which the agreement is entered into by the parties.' *Wilson v Robertsons (London) Ltd* [2005] EWHC 1425 (Ch) at [26]–[28], [2005] 3 All ER 873, per Laddie J

TAKING ACTION

Canada [Notice was required to be given of the taking of any action under security against farmland.] 'I think the more appropriate way of implementing the intent of the statute is to give words their plain meaning, which would include the institution of a proceeding in court in "taking of any action". Thus, the notice should be given before taking action.' *Calvert v Salmon* (1994) 113 DLR (4th) 156 at 160, Ont CA, per Carthy JA

TANGIBLE PERSONAL PROPERTY

Australia 'In my view, both dictionary definitions [The Oxford English Dictionary (2nd ed and the Macquarie Dictionary (Revised ed)] suggest that "property" denotes concepts of ownership or belonging. Whilst I accept ... that electricity is something capable of quantification, I do not regard that capability as enabling it to be regarded as "tangible personal property".' *State Electricity Commission (Vic) v FCT* (1999) 99 ATC 4274 at 4283; BC9900759, per Ryan J

TAX AFFAIRS

Australia 'It is clear that Parliament did not intend that the expression "tax affairs" as used in s 69 of the 1936 Act should be limited to the income tax affairs of a taxpayer in the strict sense of the tax which is the subject of assessment under s 166 of the 1936 Act. If Parliament had so intended, it could have said so very simply. Take for example expenditure incurred by a taxpayer for advice on or in connection with the calculation of provisional tax. Strictly provisional tax is not itself income tax. While it is a tax and is payable under s 221YB of the 1936 Act it is not assessed under any act. The liability to provisional tax is ancillary to the liability to income tax and is not a separate tax: *Commissioner of Taxation v Clyne* (1958) 100 CLR 246 at 260 per Dixon CJ. The liability arises for the purpose of enabling the income tax of certain taxpayers to be collected during the financial year for which it is levied and in advance of assessment. Advice in relation to compliance with requirements for provisional tax clearly would involve a tax-related matter within the meaning of s 69 of the 1936 Act and thus potentially deductible under that section if all other requirements of the section were fulfilled.

'Likewise, group tax, and prescribed payments tax are both taxes which are not the subject of assessment. They are both amounts which a taxpayer is required to deduct from amounts payable to others, the one from salary and wages paid to an employee and the other from amounts paid to contractors in certain industries. Like provisional tax group tax and prescribed payments tax are ancillary to the liability imposed for income tax on a person not being the payer of the amount from which deduction is to be made. They arise to

ensure that income tax of a taxpayer will be paid to the Commissioner concurrently with the derivation of income and the liability to pay to the Commissioner is there to protect against payment of income tax being evaded. In my view advice concerning both would thus fall within the expression "tax affairs" as used in the 1936 Act.' *Bartlett v FC* [2003] FCA 1125 at [63], [64] per Hill J; BC200306214

TAX ON PROPERTY

Australia [Section 114 of the Commonwealth Constitution provides that the Commonwealth shall not impose any tax on property of any kind belonging to a State.] 'A tax on the use of property, without more, would not be properly characterized as a "tax on property" for the purposes of s 114. On the other hand, a tax imposed upon the use or occupation of land by the owner would be a "tax on property" for the purposes of the section for the reason that it is tantamount to a tax upon the ownership or holding of the relevant property. The Court has accepted and applied that distinction in *South Australia v Commonwealth* [(1992) 174 CLR 235.] *Deputy Commissioner of Taxation v State Bank of New South Wales* (1992) 174 CLR 219 at 227; 105 ALR 161, per cur

TAXABLE ACTIVITY

New Zealand [Goods and Services Tax Act 1985, s 6.] 'The term "taxable activity" which is given a very wide meaning in s 6, is directed to "the supply of goods and services to any other person for a consideration". Where the consideration for the supply is money, then by s 10 the value of the supply is the amount of the money. The Act does not require that the supply be to the person who pays the consideration. The term "consideration" is defined in s 2 as follows:

> "Consideration" in relation to the supply of goods and services to any person includes any payment made or any act or forbearance, whether or not voluntary, in respect of, in response to, or for the inducement of, the supply of any goods and services, whether by that person or any other person; but does not include any payment made by any person ... as an unconditional gift to any non-profit body.

'As noted in *Turakina Maori Girls College Board of Trustees v Commission of Inland Revenue* (1993) 15 NZTC 10,032 at 10,036–10,037, it is clear from this definition that the supply of any service for consideration is part of a "taxable activity" under s 6, even though it is to a person other than the person who provides the consideration.' *Director-General of Social Welfare v De Morgan* [1996] 3 NZLR 677 at 682, CA, per cur

New Zealand [Goods and Services Tax Act 1985, s 6.] 'Although the linkage or nexus between a payment and the activity to which it gives rise may be very broad, it is still necessary to have regard to the legal form which is being employed:

> "... in taxation disputes the Court is concerned with the legal arrangements actually entered into ... not with the economic or other consequences of the arrangements."

(*Commissioner of Inland Revenue v New Zealand Refining Co Ltd* (1997) 18 NZTC 13,187 at 13,192 citing *Marac Life Assurance Ltd v Commissioner of Inland Revenue* [1986] 1 NZLR 694 at p 706.) The tax being one on transactions, it is necessary to pay close attention to the legal nature of what has been done.' *Chatham Islands Enterprise Trust v Commissioner of Inland Revenue* [1999] 2 NZLR 388 at 393, CA, per Keith and Blanchard JJ

TENANCY

'If all that is disclosed is the granting of exclusive possession for a fixed term for payment of a rental fee, then, in the absence of any feature indicating to the contrary, the intention of the parties as expressed by their agreement must be to create a tenancy. If, however, the context in which the right to exclusive occupation is granted specifically and definitively negatives an intention to create a tenancy, then some other interest [eg a licence] appropriate to the intention established by that context will be created.' *Ogwr Borough Council v Dykes* [1989] 2 All ER 880 at 886, CA, per Purchas LJ

[But see *Family Housing Association v Jones* [1990] 1 All ER 385, CA (esp at 393, per Balcombe LJ) in which the above case was not followed.]

[For 27 Halsbury's Laws (4th edn) paras 1–2 see now 27(1) Halsbury's Laws (4th edn) (Reissue) paras 1–2.]

Periodic

[For 27 Halsbury's Laws (4th edn) para 202 see now 27(1) Halsbury's Laws (4th edn) (Reissue) para 203.]

At sufferance

[For 27 Halsbury's Laws (4th edn) para 175 see now 27(1) Halsbury's Laws (4th edn) (Reissue) para 176.]

At will

[For 27 Halsbury's Laws (4th edn) para 167 see now 27(1) Halsbury's Laws (4th edn) (Reissue) para 168.]

From year to year

[For 27 Halsbury's Laws (4th edn) para 177 see now 27(1) Halsbury's Laws (4th edn) (Reissue) para 178.]

TENANT OF THE FLAT

[Leasehold Reform Act 1967 s 1(1ZB).] '[4] Under s 101(3) of the Leasehold Reform, Housing and Urban Development Act 1993 (the 1993 Act), a head lessee can be a "qualifying tenant" for the purposes of Chs 1 and 2 of Pt 1 of the 1993 Act. This was held to be the case in *Crean Davidson Investments Ltd v Earl Cadogan* [1998] 2 EGLR 96 and is agreed to be so by the parties. Under s 39(4) of the 1993 Act, a person can be the qualifying tenant of each of two or more flats at the same time, whether he is tenant of those flats under one lease or under two or more separate leases. In this case the parties agree that, because the flats in the premises are sublet on short-term tenancies, the tenant under the headlease, the appellant, is the "qualifying tenant" of each flat. On the facts of this case, by virtue of the headlease, the appellant is also the tenant of the whole house. It is because the appellant is both the tenant of the house and a qualifying tenant of the flats under the 1993 Act that the current dispute has arisen.

'[5] Section 1(1ZB) of the 1967 Act provides:

> "Where a flat forming part of a house is let to a person who is a qualifying tenant of the flat for the purposes of Chapter 1 or 2 of Part 1 of the [1993 Act], a tenant of the house does not have any right under this Part of the Act unless, at the relevant time, he has been occupying the house, or any part of it, as his only or main residence (whether or not he has been using it for other purposes)—(a) for the last two years; or (b) for periods amounting to two years in the last ten years."

'[6] The respondents' argument, accepted by the judge, is as follows. All of the flats, each of which is for part of the house, is let to a qualifying tenant, namely the appellant. Because that is so, the tenant of the house, who is also the appellant, does not have any right to enfranchise unless it meets the occupancy requirements set by s 1(1ZB). However, it is not in dispute that the appellant cannot meet this requirement because it is a company; s 37(5) of the 1967 Act provides that a company cannot occupy property as its residence for the purposes of this legislation. It follows that the appellant has no right to enfranchise.

'[7] The appellant argues that this is not the correct construction of s 1(1ZB). It says that, read purposively, the tenant of the house cannot be the same person as the qualifying tenant. It is inherent in the provision that they are different.

'[8] To determine the scope of s 1(1ZB) it is useful to have in mind the legislative history. Until amendment of the 1967 Act, including the introduction of s 1(1ZA) and (1ZB), by s 138(2) of the Commonhold and Leasehold Reform Act 2002 (the 2002 Act), a tenant of a house who wished to enfranchise under that Act or a tenant of a flat who wanted to obtain an extended lease under Ch 2 of the 1993 Act had to demonstrate that he had been occupying the premises as his only or main residence or principal home for three years. This requirement had two effects. First, in most cases it resolved conflicts between different people who might be interested in enfranchisement of the same premises. Second, it severely restricted the ability of companies to seek enfranchisement because they were incapable of meeting the residency requirements as explained above. They could only seek enfranchisement under the group provisions of Ch 1 of Pt 1 of the 1993 Act. The consequence of this was that landlords used the residency requirement to curtail severely their exposure to successful applications for enfranchisement. So long as they only granted long leaseholds to companies and would only permit assignment to companies, they ensured that the tenant could never be treated as resident in the premises.

'[9] The amendments introduced under the 2002 Act largely removed the residency requirement for enfranchisement and thereby allowed company tenants to qualify for enfranchisement.

'[10] The 2002 Act introduced s 1(1ZA) and (1ZB). The former is in the following terms:

> "Where a house is for the time being let under two or more tenancies, a tenant under any of those tenancies which is superior to that held

by any tenant on whom this Part of this Act confers a right does not have any right under this Part of this Act."

'[11] The clear intention of this was to resolve conflicts between different tenants which would have surfaced because of the removal of the residency requirement. The subtenant can enfranchise, those higher up the ladder cannot.

...

'[15] … As explained above, one of the purposes of the changes to the 1967 Act effected by the 2002 Act was to change the law so as to allow companies to obtain enfranchisement. To do that the residence requirement was removed from most of the enfranchisement provisions. Since that is so, one has to inquire why, in the special circumstances of s 1(1ZB), the residence requirement is retained. [Counsel for the appellants'] construction is consistent with a logical purpose to the section, namely to resolve which of two or more people should have the right to seek enfranchisement. In this respect it seeks to achieve a similar result to s 1(1ZA). By contrast, it is difficult to see what purpose would be served were [counsel for the respondents'] construction correct. Indeed, as [counsel for the appellants] points out, were one to accept [counsel for the respondents'] construction, it would have the effect that, in a situation like the present one, although the appellant could not obtain enfranchisement of its interest in the house, it could still obtain extension of each of the leases for all the individual flats of which it is the qualifying tenant. This would mean that it would have longer leases for the flats than it would have for the common parts. [Counsel for the appellants] described such an outcome as bizarre. I agree.

'[16] In the result I accept [counsel for the appellants'] argument that the reference in s 1(1ZB) to a situation "[w]here a flat forming part of a house is let to a person who is a qualifying tenant of the flat for the purposes of Chapter 1 or 2 of Part 1 of the [1993 Act]", the tenant of the flat is someone other than the tenant of the house. So construed, the section does not apply to the appellant and, therefore, does not prevent it from obtaining enfranchisement.' *Cadogan v Search Guarantees plc* [2004] EWCA Civ 969, [2005] 1 All ER 280 at [4]–[11], [15]–[16], per Laddie J

TENANT RIGHT

[For 1 Halsbury's Laws (4th edn) para 1071 see now 1(2) Halsbury's Laws (4th edn) (Reissue) para 376.]

TENEMENT

[For 27 Halsbury's Laws (4th edn) para 131 see now 27(1) Halsbury's Laws (4th edn) (Reissue) para 132.]

[For 39 Halsbury's Laws (4th edn) paras 375, 379 see now 39(2) Halsbury's Laws (4th edn) (Reissue) paras 74, 78.]

Australia 'The popular meaning of "tenement" appears to be generally linked to its use as a dwelling house for I have been unable to find an example in the cases of its use, standing alone, as representing building rather than merely a house. There are, however, examples of its use in association with other words as meaning "property capable of visible and physical occupation"; see *Redington v Millar* (1888) 24 LR Ir 65, at p 67.' *Australian Shipping Commission v City of Port Melbourne* [1990] VR 439 at 441, per Clarke J

TENURE

[For 39 Halsbury's Laws (4th edn) para 376 see now 39(2) Halsbury's Laws (4th edn) (Reissue) para 75.]

TERM OF IMPRISONMENT

Australia [Whether a sentence of imprisonment to the rising of the court is a "term of imprisonment".] 'The ordinary meaning of the word "term" is a limit in space, duration, etc; that which limits the extent of anything; a limit, extremity, boundary or bound (*Shorter Oxford English Dictionary*). The fact that the limit of the period fixed by the judgment is fluid and dependent upon the happening of some inevitable event other than the passage of a given period of time does not deprive it of the character of being a "term"... Resort to the dictionary shows that the ordinary meaning of the verb "to imprison" is to put in prison; to detain in custody and to confine (ibid)... If a magistrate orders a convicted person by way of sentence to be detained until the rising of the court ... it cannot be said not to be a term of imprisonment.' *Harriss v Walker* (1996) 89 A Crim R 257 at 261, per Cox J

Australia 'I agree, for the reasons given by Davies JA, that the expression "term of imprisonment" in section 175(1)(a)(i)(A) of the Corrective Services Act 1988 (Qld) means the term of imprisonment imposed by the sentencing judge, and not the duration of the period for which the prisoner is in fact detained. That is, as has been accepted, the "natural prima facie meaning" of

those words: *Winsor v Boaden* (1953) 90 CLR 345, 347; as well as being their "ordinary" meaning: *Husson v Slattery* [1982] 3 NSWLR 389, 393.' *Smith v Queensland Community Corrections Board* BC200100235; [2001] QCA 30 at [1], per McPherson JA

TERM OF TENANCY FOR FIXED TERM

Canada 'The initial term plus the term of all option periods constitute in my opinion "the term of a tenancy for a fixed term" so that if the tenant exercises her options, and is otherwise in good standing under her tenancy agreement, she cannot be evicted under the provisions of s 103 of the *Landlord and Tenant Act* until the end of the resulting term.' *Wise v Frankel* (1996) 132 DLR (4th) 463 at 469, Ont Gen Div, per Sutherland J

TERM OF YEARS

[For 27 Halsbury's Laws (4th edn) para 204 see now 27(1) Halsbury's Laws (4th edn) (Reissue) para 205.]

TERMINATE

Canada [Insurer alleged that coverage had terminated.] ' "Terminate" is a broad term, as the Insurance Bureau of Canada must have been aware. It is broad enough to include discontinuance of insurance coverage for any reason, including cancellation, non-renewal, lapse or expiry. It is used in this broad sense as the heading or para 5, following which were references to both the term of the policy and to cancellation. If it was intended that different types of termination carried different duties to notify, the standard mortgage clause had only to say so ...

'The source of the definition of "termination" in Black's Law Dictionary is *Waynesville Security Bank v Stuyvesant Insurance Company*, 499 SW 2d 218 (1973) at p 220, in which the Missouri Court of Appeal stated:

> "Cancellation" as used in insurance law means termination of a policy prior to the expiration of the policy period by the act of one or all of the parties; "termination" refers to the expiration of a policy by lapse of the policy period.'

Bank of Nova Scotia v Commercial Union Assurance Co of Canada (1993) 104 DLR (4th) 318 at 328, NS CA, per Freeman JA

Canada '[39] In *Black's Law Dictionary*, 7th ed., the word "terminate" means "to put an end to; to conclude." In the *Concise Oxford Dictionary*, 10th ed., "terminate" is defined as "bring to an end; end the employment of." In the present case, the applicants' terms of employment are all governed by the following unambiguous termination provisions in the *School Act*:

79...
(3) A probationary contract of employment shall terminate on the June 30 next following the commencement date specified in the contract.

...

82...
(2) A temporary contract of employment entered into under subsection (1) shall
   (a) specify the date on which the teacher commences employment with the board, and
   (b) terminate
      (i) on the June 30 next following the commencement date specified in the contract, or
      (ii) on a date provided for in the contract,
   whichever is earlier.

...

83...
(3) An interim contract of employment terminates on the June 30 next following the commencement date specified in the contract unless otherwise specified in the contract. [Emphasis added.]

On a plain reading of these provisions, the applicants' contracts all came to an end on June 30, 1999. The question then becomes, how these sections of the *School Act* affect the applicants' entitlement to employment insurance benefits under paragraph 33(2)(*a*) of the Regulations.

'[40] In his search for the true intention of Parliament in using the word "terminated" in paragraph 33(2)(*a*), the Umpire applied the well-established principle of interpretation that the words of a statute are to be read in their entire context and in their grammatical and ordinary sense harmoniously with the scheme of the Act, the object of the Act, and the intention of Parliament (*Rizzo & Rizzo Shoes Ltd. (Re)*, [1998] 1 S.C.R. 27). While this principle is important, such analysis cannot alter the result where the words of a statute are clear and plain. (See *Canada v. Antosko*, [1994]

2 S.C.R. 312; *65302 British Columbia Ltd. v. Canada*, [1999] 3 S.C.R. 804 (*65302 British Columbia Ltd.*).) Like the *Income Tax Act* [R.S.C., 1985 (5th Supp.), c. 1], employment insurance legislation is detailed, complex and comprehensive, and accordingly, umpires and this Court must be cautious in adopting unexpressed notions of policy or principle under the modern rules of statutory interpretation (*65302 British Columbia Ltd.*, at paragraph 51).

'[41] In my opinion, the learned Umpire committed an error of law in ignoring the clear legal effect of the above-quoted sections of the *School Act* and in adopting the unexpressed notion that Parliament intended the word "terminate" to only apply to situations where teachers are "in the true sense of the word 'unemployed', ... which is not synonymous with 'not working'" (Umpire's reasons for judgment).' *Oliver v Canada (Attorney General)* [2003] 4 FC 47 at 62–64 (FCA), per Létourneau JA

TERMINATED BY THE EMPLOYER

Canada 'As I see the matter, when the express words of ss 40 and 40*a* of the *ESA* [Employment Standards Act] are examined in their entire context, there is ample support for the conclusion that the words "terminated by the employer" must be interpreted to include termination resulting from the bankruptcy of the employer. Using the broad and generous approach to interpretation appropriate for benefits-conferring legislation, I believe that these words can reasonably bear that construction (see *R v Z (DA)*, [1992] 2 SCR 1025). I also note that the intention of the Legislature as evidenced in s 2(3) of the *ESAA*, clearly favours this interpretation. Further, in my opinion, to deny employees the right to claim *ESA* termination and severance pay where their termination has resulted from their employer's bankruptcy, would be inconsistent with the purpose of the termination and severance pay provisions and would undermine the object of the *ESA*, namely, to protect the interests of as many employees as possible.' *Re Rizzo & Rizzo Shoes Ltd* [1998] 1 SCR 27 at 48–49, per Iacobucci J

TERMS AND CONDITIONS OF EMPLOYMENT

[The Trade Union and Labour Relations (Consolidation) Act 1992 s 244(1)(a) provides that a trade dispute is a dispute between workers and their employer which relates wholly or mainly to "terms and conditions of employment". On appeal to the House of Lords, it was contended that "terms and conditions of employment" meant the rules which governed the employment relationship, that there was a rule that teachers should comply with the directions of the headmaster and the dispute was not about that rule but about its application.] '[24] In my opinion this was plainly a dispute over terms and conditions of employment, which I regard as a composite phrase chosen to avoid arguments over whether something should properly be described as a "term" or "condition" of employment. It is sufficient that it should be one or the other. Furthermore, the use of such a composite expression shows that it was intended to be given a broad meaning (see Roskill LJ in *British Broadcasting Corp v Hearn* [1978] 1 All ER 111 at 120, [1977] ICR 685 at 696).

'[25] In the present case, it seems to me that the dispute was about the contractual obligation of the teachers to teach P. It could be characterised as a dispute over whether there was such a contractual obligation: the union, as we have seen, contended that the head teacher's direction was unreasonable. Alternatively it could be characterised as a dispute over whether there should be such a contractual obligation. It does not seem to me profitable to try to analyse it one way or the other. The dispute arose because the head teacher said that the teachers were obliged to teach P and they said that they were not willing to do so. That seems to me a dispute which does not merely "relate to" but is about their terms and conditions of employment.' *P v National Association of Schoolmasters/Union of Women Teachers* [2003] UKHL 8 at [24]–[25], [2003] 1 All ER 993, per Lord Hoffmann

TERRITORY

Australia 'The term "territory" may, according to its context, identify no more than a tract of land or an area of the earth's surface. In the law construed in *R v Governor of Brixton Prison; Ex parte Schtraks* [[1964] AC 556 at 579, 587, 593, 604] "territory" included any area under the effective jurisdiction of a particular state. The term may also identify a geo-political entity with some attributes of a distinct governmental organisation, such as a local administration operating in a particular area.' *Attorney-General (Cth) v Chu-Fai* (1998) 153 ALR 128 at 140–141; [1998] HCA 25 at [44]; BC9800991 at 20, per Gaudron, McHugh, Gummow, Kirby, Hayne and Callinan JJ

TERRORISM

Canada '[93] The term "terrorism" is found in s. 19 of the *Immigration Act*, dealing with denial of refugee status upon arrival in Canada. The Minister interpreted s. 19 as applying to terrorist acts post-admission and relied on alleged terrorist associations in Canada in seeking Suresh's deportation under s. 53(1)(*b*), which refers to a class of persons falling under s. 19. We do not in these reasons seek to define terrorism exhaustively – a notoriously difficult endeavour – but content ourselves with finding that the term provides a sufficient basis for adjudication and hence is not unconstitutionally vague. We share the view of Robertson J.A. that the term is not inherently ambiguous "even if the full meaning ... must be determined on an incremental basis" (para. 69).

'[94] One searches in vain for an authoritative definition of "terrorism". The *Immigration Act* does not define the term. Further, there is no single definition that is accepted internationally. The absence of an authoritative definition means that, at least at the margins, "the term is open to politicized manipulation, conjecture, and polemical interpretation"...

...

'[96] We are not persuaded, however, that the term "terrorism" is so unsettled that it cannot set the proper boundaries of legal adjudication. The recently negotiated *International Convention for the Suppression of the Financing of Terrorism*, GA Res. 54/109, December 9, 1999, approaches the definitional problem in two ways. First, it employs a functional definition in Article 2(1)(*a*), defining "terrorism" as "[a]n act which constitutes an offence within the scope of and as defined in one of the treaties listed in the annex". The annex lists nine treaties that are commonly viewed as relating to terrorist acts, such as the *Convention for the Suppression of the Unlawful Seizure of Aircraft*, Can. T.S. 1972 No. 23, the *Convention on the Physical Protection of Nuclear Material*, 18 I.L.M. 1419, and the *International Convention for the Suppression of Terrorist Bombings*, 37 I.L.M. 249. Second, the Convention supplements this offence-based list with a stipulative definition of terrorism. Article 2(1)(*b*) defines "terrorism" as:

> Any ... act intended to cause death or serious bodily injury to a civilian, or to any other person not taking an active part in the hostilities in a situation of armed conflict, when the purpose of such act, by its nature or context, is to intimidate a population, or to compel a

government or an international organization to do or to abstain from doing any act.

'[97] In its submission to this Court, the CAF argued that this Court should adopt a functional definition of terrorism, rather than a stipulative one. The argument is that defining terrorism by reference to specific acts of violence (e.g. "hijacking, hostage taking and terrorist bombing") would minimize politicization of the term (CAF factum, at paras. 11–14). It is true that the functional approach has received strong support from international law scholars and state representatives – support that is evidenced by the numerous international legal instruments that eschew stipulative definitions in favour of prohibitions on specific acts of violence. While we are not unaware of the danger that the term "terrorism" may be manipulated, we are not persuaded that it is necessary or advisable to altogether eschew a stipulative definition of the term in favour of a list that may change over time and that may in the end necessitate distinguishing some (proscribed) acts from other (non-proscribed) acts by reliance on a term like "terrorism". (We note that the CAF, in listing acts, at para. 11, that might be prohibited under a functional definition, lists "terrorist bombing" – a category that clearly would not avoid the necessity of defining "terrorism".)

'[98] In our view, it may safely be concluded, following the *International Convention for the Suppression of the Financing of Terrorism*, that "terrorism" in s. 19 of the Act includes any "act intended to cause death or serious bodily injury to a civilian, or to any other person not taking an active part in the hostilities in a situation of armed conflict, when the purpose of such act, by its nature or context, is to intimidate a population, or to compel a government or an international organization to do or to abstain from doing any act". This definition catches the essence of what the world understands by "terrorism" …' *Suresh v Canada (Minister of Citizenship and Immigration)* [2002] 1 SCR 3 at 54–55, per the Court

TESTAMENT

[For 50 Halsbury's Laws (4th edn) para 201 see now 50 Halsbury's Laws (4th edn) (Reissue) para 251.]

TESTAMENTARY

Testamentary expenses

[For 17 Halsbury's Laws (4th edn) paras 1185, 1186 see now 17(2) Halsbury's Laws (4th edn) (Reissue) paras 432–433.]

THE

Canada '[31] … Counsel for the applicant referred to the dictionary definition of the word "the" to support a submission that the words "the relationship of mother and child" in subsection 4(3) should be "understood generically" or "to indicate reference to a group as a whole". These are two of sixteen different usages of the word "the" identified by the dictionary. The examples of these particular usages in the dictionary quoted are "the dog is a domestic animal" and "the elite". These usages of the word "the" connote a much different meaning than can reasonably be afforded to section 4(3) of the *Children's Law Reform Act*, particularly in the context of section 4(1). The dictionary reference fails to create any contextual ambiguity.

'[32] Legislation is presumed to be accurate and well crafted. As long ago as 1891, in *Commissioner for Special Purposes of the Income Tax v. Pemsel*, [1891] A.C. 531 at 549 (H.L.). Lord Halsbury wrote:

> … I do not think it is competent to any court to proceed upon the assumption that the legislature has made a mistake. Whatever the real fact may be, I think a Court of Law is bound to proceed upon the assumption that the legislature is an ideal person that does not make mistakes.

'[33] More than a hundred years later the Ontario Court of Appeal said much the same in *Joe Moretta Investments Ltd. v. Ontario (Minister of Housing)* (1992), 8 O.R. (3d) 129:

> There is another fundamental principle of statutory interpretation which is particularly important in this case. That principle is set out in several decisions of the Supreme Court of Canada. In *Grand Trunk Pacific Railway v. Dearborn* (1919), 58 S.C.R. 315, 47 D.L.R. 27, Sir Louis Davies C.J. said at pp. 320–21 S.C.R., p. 31 D.L.R.:
>
>> I cannot admit the right of the courts where the language of a statute is plain and unambiguous to practically amend such statute either by eliminating words or inserting limiting words unless the grammatical and ordinary sense of the words as enacted leads to some absurdity or some repugnance or inconsistency with the rest of the enactment, and in those cases only to the extent of avoiding that absurdity, repugnance and inconsistency.

In *Williams v. Box* (1910), 44 S.C.R. 1, Anglin J., speaking for a majority of the court, said at p. 24 S.C.R.:

> To treat any part of a statute as ineffectual, or as mere surplusage, is never justifiable if any other construction be possible. The rejection or excision of a word or phrase is permissible only where it is impossible otherwise to reconcile or give effect to the provisions of the Act.

'[34] When the legislation uses a word such as "the", it is presumed to do so precisely and for a purpose. It represents a choice of the definite article over the indefinite article. Considerable weight must be given to its clear and ordinary meaning.

'[35] A conclusion that Part II of the *Children's Law Reform Act* contemplates a single mother and a single father (outside the adoption exception already noted) is reinforced by its consistency with another provision in the Act. Section 8(1) provides a list of certain rebuttable presumptions whereby a male person "shall be recognized in law to be the father of a child". For example, a person who is married to the mother of the child at the time of the child's birth, or within 300 days before the child's birth, or who cohabited with the mother within that time is presumed to be the father. The presumption also arises if the person has "certified" the child's birth as provided in the *Vital Statistics Act* or if the person marries the child's mother after the child's birth and "acknowledges" that he is the natural father. Significantly, subsection (3) provides

> 8(3) Where circumstances exist that give rise to a presumption or presumptions of paternity by more than one father under subsection (1), no presumption shall be made as to paternity and no person is recognized in law to be the father.

The legislator could have left open the possibility of more than one father but, instead, made an express opposite choice. There is no logical reason to suppose the legislator would choose to limit the number of fathers to one while allowing for more than one mother.

'[36] This conclusion is also consistent with other legislation, namely the adoption provision in the *Child and Family Services Act*, whereby no more than two persons can apply for an adoption order and the order extinguishes other parental status. Adoption thus limits the number of parents to a maximum of two.

'[37] Therefore, the plain and ordinary meaning of the word "the" is unambiguous, consistent with other expression of legislative intent and not inconsistent with any *Charter* or common law principle.' *A (A) v B (B)* (2003) 225 DLR (4th) 371 at 380–382 (Ont SCJ), per Aston J

THEREUNDER

New Zealand [Companies Amendment Act 1963, First Schedule, Part A, para 1.] 'The expression of immediate relevance is "every obligation incurred thereunder". Whether one reads the word "thereunder" as referring to the take-over scheme or to the offer originally made (that latter I think being preferably) it is clear that the draftsman is proceeding on the basis that obligations can arise under the offer or series of offers which constitute the scheme.' *Southfert Co-operative Ltd v Ravensdown Corporation Ltd* [1996] 3 NZLR 196 at 201, per Tipping J

THOSE OF MY CHILDREN THAT SURVIVE ME

Australia [Part of a clause in the testatrix's will divided] 'the whole of her estate equally "among those of my children that survive me". I consider the natural and ordinary meaning of those words refer to those children that survived the testatrix. "Survive" means alive at the date of her death: see in *The Will of Arndt* [1990] WAR 5 and *Re Hodgson* [1952] 1 All ER 769. The phrase refers to every child alive at her death ...' *Shelton v Kilsby* BC200003993; [2000] WASC 180 at [5], per Bredmeyer M

THREAT

[For 35 Halsbury's Laws (4th edn) para 644 see now 35 Halsbury's Laws (4th edn) (Reissue) para 642.]

Australia [Section 30 of the Crimes Act 1900 (ACT) provides that it is an offence to, inter alia, make a 'threat' to another person to kill that other person or any third person.] 'There is no real question as to what is meant by the word "threat". It is a declaration of intention: see *Concise Oxford Dictionary*, 1984, Oxford, Clarendon. The intention so declared has to be that of ending the life of the person or persons allegedly so threatened.' *R v Leece* (1995) 125 ACTR 1 at 4–5, per Higgins J

Canada 'The issue to be decided in the case before me therefore, is whether it can be said that, at the time they arrested the plaintiff, the defendant police officers had reasonable grounds to believe that he had committed the indictable offence of threatening death. In dealing with this issue, I accept the evidence of the officers that from the statement of Mrs Thornton, they believed that the accused had committed the offence of threatening death. From the testimony of the officers at trial, it is clear that the crux of the threat upon which the charge was based, are the words:

"Scott came in at 1:45 a.m. and started yelling at me and telling me he wished I was dead."

...

'Based on the foregoing, the narrower issue to be decided is, applying the test propounded by Cory J, would a reasonable person placed in the position of the officers be able to conclude that a threat of death was uttered or conveyed by the accused. In my view the question must be answered in the negative. "Threat" is defined in the *Oxford Illustrated Dictionary*, Oxford University Press (1962) as follows:

"Declaration of intention to punish or hurt;"

and by *Black's Law Dictionary* (5th edition) as follows:

"A communicated intent to inflict physical or other harm on any person or property. A declaration of an intention to injure another or his property by some unlawful act ... A declaration of intention or determination to inflict punishment, loss, or pain on another, or to injure another by the commission of some unlawful act ... A menace; especially any menace of such a nature and extent as to unsettle the mind of the person on whom it operates and to take away from his acts that free and voluntary action which alone constitutes consent. A declaration of one's purpose of intention towards injury to the person, property or right of another, with a view of restraining such person's freedom of action."

'Defence counsel argues that in considering whether reasonable grounds for arrest existed, one must look at the dynamics of the situation as well as considering societal interests particularly in light of unfortunate events which have led to two recent inquests in this area as a result of domestic violence. He urges that the policemen were, by circumstances, placed in a position where, if there seemed to be the existence of reasonable grounds for arrest, they must react.

'In my view, the words of Mr. Thornton, looked at objectively, do not constitute a "*threat*" within the ordinary meaning of that word. Further, there was nothing arising from the circumstances which could be said to elevate words which do not constitute a threat to the level of a threat.' *Thornton v Byers* (1999) 173 DLR (4th) 568 at 572, 573, Ont Gen Div, per Lofchik J

THREAT TO KILL

Australia '... to be a threat to kill, the relevant utterance or communication must convey, objectively, to the hypothetical reasonable person in the position of the listener or recipient that the publisher proposes to kill the listener or recipient or another person. If it conveys a merely hypothetical proposal that will not suffice, but a conditional threat, particularly when the person threatened is entitled not to meet such conditions, will suffice as "a threat".' *R v Leece* (1995) 125 ACTR 1 at 6, per Higgins J

THREATEN

Australia 'To "threaten" means "1. to utter a threat against; menace. 2. to be a menace or source of danger to. 3. to offer (a punishment, injury, etc) by way of a threat. 4. to give an ominous indication of: the clouds threaten rain. v i 5. to utter or use threats. 6. to indicate impending evil or mischief." ' *Coleman v P* BC200107434; [2001] QCA 539 at [11], per McMurdo P

THRIFT SCHEME

[The Wages Councils Act 1979 has been repealed.]

TILLAGE

[For 1 Halsbury's Laws (4th edn) para 1073 see now 1(2) Halsbury's Laws (4th edn) (Reissue) para 377.]

TIMBER

[For 19 Halsbury's Laws (4th edn) para 33 see now 19(1) Halsbury's Laws (4th edn) (Reissue) para 32.]

TIME

[For 45 Halsbury's Laws (4th edn) paras 1115, 1116 see now 45(2) Halsbury's Laws (4th edn) (Reissue) paras 215–216.]

TIME IMMEMORIAL

[For 6 Halsbury's Laws (4th edn) para 590 see now 6 Halsbury's Laws (4th edn) (2003 Reissue) para 485.]

[For 12 Halsbury's Laws (4th edn) para 407 see now 12(1) Halsbury's Laws (4th edn) (Reissue) para 607.]

TO STAND TRIAL

Australia [Transfer of Prisoners Act 1983 (Cth), s 10.] 'In my view the words "to stand trial" are not limited to the next step after the transfer. What the Act requires as a condition precedent to an application for a trial transfer order is the certification from the Attorney-General that it is desirable that the prisoner be transferred "to stand trial". I am satisfied that in this context the words "to stand trial" is a generic term and includes all necessary preliminary steps to the prisoner standing trial, including, as necessary, charging, service of the Crown witness statements, committal and arraignment.' *Muir v DPP (Cth)* [2004] NSWSC 983 at [14], per Dunford J; BC200406991

TO SUCH PROPERTY

[Agreement by bank to make secured advance to customer to purchase land. Undertaking by customer's solicitor to bank in standard form to apply sums received from bank or client solely for acquiring a good marketable title 'to such property'.] 'It follows from what I have said so far that the expression "a good marketable title" leaves open the question "a good marketable title to what?" Where the expression is contained in a contract for the sale of land, it must mean "to the property contracted to be sold". It can have no other meaning. Where the contract is an open contract, that is to say one which describes the property in general terms without mentioning whether it is freehold or leasehold and without stating that it is subject to incumbrances, it means "to the fee simple free from incumbrances": see *Cato v Thompson* (1882) 9 QBD 616.' *Barclays Bank plc v Weeks Legg & Dean (a firm)* [1998] 3 All ER 213 at 222–223, CA, per Millett LJ

TO THE PUBLIC

Australia [The Copyright Act 1968 (Cth) s 10(1) defines 'broadcast' as, 'transmit by wireless telegraphy to the public'.] 'Section 31(1)(a)(iii) [of the Copyright Act 1968 (Cth)] speaks of the right to perform a work "in public", but the definition of "broadcast", with which we are concerned, speaks of transmission "to the public". If anything, the use of the words "to the public" conveys a broader concept than the use of the words "in public" since it makes clear that the place where the relevant communication occurs is irrelevant. That is to say, there can be a communication to individual members of the public in a private or domestic setting which is nevertheless a communication to the public. A broadcast by a radio station is just such a communication.' *Telstra Corp Ltd v Australian Performing Rights Association Ltd* (1997) 146 ALR 649 at 657; BC9703567 at 9, per Dawson and Gaudron JJ

Canada '[100] ... In my view, the ordinary meaning of the phrase "to the public" indicates that a communication must be aimed or targeted toward "people in general" or "the community" (see the *New Oxford Dictionary of English, s.v.* "public" (Oxford: Clarendon Press, 1998). Article 1721(2) of NAFTA, *supra*, which is not binding on this Court but is nevertheless helpful since "public" is not otherwise defined, states that the public includes "any aggregation of individuals intended to be the object of, and capable of perceiving, communications". A communication that is targeted only at a segment of the public, may however, also be a communication to the public. Paragraph 2.4(1)(*a*), which was added to the [*Copyright*] *Act* to overrule the conclusion in *Canadian Admiral, supra* (see *Fox, supra*, at 498; S.C. 1997, c. 24, s. 2), clarifies that a communication may be to the public if it is "intended to be received" by a "part of the public", specifically persons who occupy apartments, hotel rooms, or dwelling units in the same building. Thus, to be "to the public" a communication must be targeted at an aggregation of individuals, which is more than a single person but not necessarily the whole public at large.' *CCH Canadian Ltd v Law Society of Upper Canada* (2002) DLR (4th) 385 at 433 (FCA), per Linden JA

TO THE PUBLIC OR TO ANY SECTION OF THE PUBLIC

New Zealand 'The cited cases show that the terms "public" and "section of the public" can encompass a variety of meanings, and must be construed having regard to the purpose of the statute in which they are used.' *Coburn v Human Rights Commission* [1994] 3 NZLR 323 at 336, per Thorp J

TOLL

Toll thorough

[For 21 Halsbury's Laws (4th edn) para 138 see now 21 Halsbury's Laws (4th edn) (2004 Reissue) para 210.]

Toll traverse

[For 21 Halsbury's Laws (4th edn) para 138 see now 21 Halsbury's Laws (4th edn) (2004 Reissue) para 210.]

TONTINE

[For 25 Halsbury's Laws (4th edn) para 298 see now 25 Halsbury's Laws (4th edn) (Reissue) para 282.]

TORT-FEASOR LIABLE IN RESPECT OF THAT DAMAGE

Australia 'Para(c) [of s 5(1) Law Reform (Miscellaneous Provisions) Act 1946 (NSW)] applies where damage is suffered by any person as a result of a tort (whether a crime or not) and states: "any tort-feasor liable in respect of that damage may recover contribution from any other tort-feasor who is, or would if sued have been, liable in respect of the same damage, whether as a joint tort-feasor or otherwise, so, however, that no person shall be entitled to recover contribution under this section from any person entitled to be indemnified by that person in respect of the liability in respect of which the contribution is sought" ... It is necessary that the claimant for contribution should be a "tort-feasor liable in respect of that damage". By the authority of this Court, that phrase refers to a tortfeasor whose liability has been ascertained, including ascertained by judgment.' *James Hardie & Co Pty Ltd v Seltsam Pty Ltd* (1998) 159 ALR 286 at 270 and 289; 73 ALJR 238; BC9806759, per Gaudron and Gummow JJ

TOTAL LOSS

[For 19 Halsbury's Laws (4th edn) para 104n see now 19(1) Halsbury's Laws (4th edn) (Reissue) para 107n.]

TOUCHING

[Under the Sexual Offences Act 2003, s 3(1) a person commits an offence if (a) he intentionally touches another person (B), (b) the touching is sexual, (c) B does not consent to the touching, and (d) A does not reasonably believe that B consents. 'Touching' in s 3 has to be considered together with s 79(8), which provides that 'touching includes touching— (a) with any part of the body, (b) with anything else, (c) through anything, and in particular includes touching amounting to penetration'. The term 'sexual' is defined in s 78.] '[23] At the end of the prosecution case there was a submission of no case to answer. Two arguments were advanced by Mr West on behalf of the appellant. The first was based upon the interpretation of the statutory provisions of the 2003 Act. He submitted that the touching of the tracksuit bottoms alone did not amount to the touching of another person.

'[24] The judge rejected that submission. We consider that he was right to do so. Where a person is wearing clothing we consider that touching of the clothing constitutes touching for the purpose of the s 3 offence.

'[25] As against that approach Mr West relied on s 79(8) (set out above). He submits that under s 79(8)(c) touching through anything (through clothing), if pressure in some form is not brought against the body of the person concerned, there cannot be touching; there has to be some form of touching of the body of the individual who is alleged to have been assaulted, even if it be through clothing. Mr West submits that, having regard to the complainant's evidence in this case, there was no such touching.

'[26] It is important to note that the opening words of s 79(8) are "[t]ouching includes touching" and in particular "through anything". Subsection (8) is not a definition section. We have no doubt that it was not Parliament's intention by the use of that language to make it impossible to regard as a sexual assault touching which took place by touching what the victim was wearing at the time.' *R v H* [2005] EWCA Crim 732, [2005] 2 All ER 859 at [23]–[26], per Lord Woolf CJ

TOWAGE

[For 43 Halsbury's Laws (4th edn) para 872 et seq see now 43(1) Halsbury's Laws (4th edn) (Reissue) para 789 et seq.]

TOWER

Australia [In the context of whether a stobie pole was a tower within the meaning of the Telecommunications Act 1993 (Cth) Sch 3.] '[111] The ordinary, natural meaning of the word "tower" is commonly confined to something more in the nature of a building, as in the case of a church tower, or a more substantial structure than a mere pole.

'[112] The Shorter Oxford Dictionary defines a tower as:

1. A building or structure high in proportion to its lateral dimensions, either isolated or forming part of any building.
2. Such a structure used as or intended for a stronghold, fortress, prison, etc.
3. Any of various tower-like structures, contrivances or objects.
4. A tall, moveable structure used in ancient and mediaeval warfare and storming a fortified place.

...

'[114] If the word "tower" was to be given its ordinary meaning, I have some doubt as to whether or not the stobie poles would answer to that description.

...

'[116] ... I take the view that the definition of a tower ... means "a tower, pole or mast".

'[117] In any event, the word "tower" is separately defined ... as meaning "a pole or mast".

'[118] The inclusion in the definition of the word "pole", means that the stobie poles referred to in this question are properly to be regarded as towers ...

'[119] In my view, they do not lose their character as such, by reason of the fact that they are also used to carry ... transmission lines.' *City of Mitcham v Hutchison 3G Australia Ltd* [2005] SASC 78 at [111]–[112], [114], [116]–[119], per Perry J; BC200500962

TRACING (OF FUNDS)

At common law

'Tracing at law does not depend upon the establishment of an initial fiduciary relationship. Liability depends upon receipt by the defendant of the plaintiff's money and the extent of the liability depends on the amount received. Since liability depends upon receipt the fact that a recipient has not retained the asset is irrelevant. For the same reason dishonesty or lack of inquiry on the part of the recipient are irrelevant. Identification in the defendant's hands of the plaintiff's asset is, however, necessary. It must be shown that the money received by the defendant was the money of the plaintiff.'

Agip (Africa) Ltd v Jackson [1992] 4 All ER 451 at 463–464, CA, per Fox LV.

In equity

'Both common law and equity accepted the right of the true owner to trace his property into the hands of others while it was in an identifiable form. The common law treated property as identified if it had not been mixed with other property. Equity, on the other hand, will follow money into a mixed fund and charge the fund ... It is, however, a prerequisite to the operation of the remedy in equity that there must be a fiduciary relationship which calls the equitable jurisdiction into being.' Ibid at 466, per Fox LJ

TRACK

Australia ' ... it is necessary to define a track vis-à-vis a road. A track is not a road. A track traces the contours of the land avoiding natural obstacles; a road is a specific construction for vehicular use, often involving earthworks.' *Shire of Gisborne v King* [1994] 1 VR 364 at 370, per Nathan J

TRADE

[For 47 Halsbury's Laws (4th edn) para 1 see now 47 Halsbury's Laws (4th edn) (Reissue) para 5.]

TRADE MARK

[The Trade Marks Act 1938 is repealed by the Trade Marks Act 1994, as from a day to be appointed. In the 1994 Act, 'trade mark' means any sign capable of being represented graphically which is capable of distinguishing goods or services of one undertaking from those of other undertakings. A trade mark may, in particular, consist of words (including personal names), designs, letters, numerals or the shape of the goods or their packaging. (Trade Marks Act 1994, s 1(1))

A collective mark is a mark distinguishing the goods or services of a member of the association which is the proprietor of the mark from those of other undertakings. (ibid s 49(1))

A certification mark is a mark indicating that the goods or services in connection with which it is used are certified by the proprietor of the mark in respect of the origin, material, mode of manufacture of goods or performance of services, quality, accuracy or other characteristics. (ibid s 50(1))]

Australia [Section 6(1) of the Trade Marks Act 1955 (Cth) defines 'trade mark' as meaning: 'a mark used or proposed to be used in relation to goods or services for the purpose of indicating, or so as to indicate, a connexion in the course of trade between the goods or services and a person who has the right ... to use the mark, whether with or without an indication of the identity of that person.'] 'Essentially, so far as relevant, it is a mark used in trade to distinguish the goods of the person who uses it. It is a badge of origin of the goods indicating a connection in the course of trade between the goods and the person who applies it to the goods: see *Attorney-General (NSW) v Brewery Employees Union of New South Wales* (1908) 6 CLR 469; *Mark Foy's Ltd v Davies Coop and Co Ltd* (the *Tub Happy* case) (1956) 95 CLR 190; *Shell Co of Australia Ltd v Esso Standard Oil (Australia) Ltd* (the *Esso* case) (1963) 109 CLR 407.' *Johnson & Johnson Australia Pty Ltd v Sterling Pharmaceuticals Pty Ltd* (1991) 101 ALR 700 at 709, per Lockhart J

New Zealand '... the definitions of "mark" and "trade mark" in the Trade Marks Act are very broad and encompass virtually anything which indicates a connection between goods or services and some person having the right to use the mark ...

'Although I accept the substance of Mr Brown's broad contention ... that a mark is a visual device in the sense that it is a symbol to give "an indication to the eye" of the trade source, the fact that the modern definitions in the Act allow such contrivances as names, words, letters or numerals to qualify as marks, undermines any suggestion that trade marks can only be accurately portrayed in the register by pictorial representation. Obviously it is simple to compose a written description for registration of a trade mark which consists of a written word only. Additionally, there is no reason in principle, or practice, why an effective statutory system of trade mark registration must depend solely and exclusively upon a visual representation.' *Levis Strauss & Co v Kimbyr Investments Ltd* [1994] 1 NZLR 332 at 347–348, per Williams J

TRADE QUALIFICATION

Australia 'The reference to apprenticeships and non-apprenticed entry tend to suggest that the word "trade" [in (CTH) Migration Regulations 1989 reg 816.721(2)(b)(ii)] in both the expression "trade certificate" and "trade training" is a reference to trades in the more traditional conception of skilled manual labour. That is, it is a reference to trades the skills for which might be gained by on the job training as an apprentice.' *Subraju v Minister for Immigration and Ethnic Affairs* (1996) 68 FCR 313 at 317, per Moore J

TRADE SECRETS

Australia 'The term may have been used more frequently in judicial decisions than in common parlance to described secrets the confidentiality of which courts of law will protect. In the legal area the term is particularly used in cases where an employee/employer relationship is involved and the issue is the extent of the employee's implied obligations to the employer as to confidentiality or as to whether an express obligation is invalid as being too wide and in restraint of trade. Gummow J in *Corrs Pavey Whiting & Byrne v Collector of Customs (Vic)* (1987) 14 FCR 434 at 449; 74 ALR 428, went so far as to say that the term "trade secrets" in s 43(1)(a) was prima facie a "technical legal expression". At least in the context of the Freedom of Information Act 1982 (Cth), we think that the term does not have a technical legal meaning but is an ordinary term of the English language, though used perhaps more commonly in legal judgments and legal writings than elsewhere.' *Searle Australia Pty Ltd v Public Interest Advocacy Centre* (1992) 108 ALR 163 at 172, per cur

TRADE UNION

[The Trade Union and Labour Relations Act 1974 has been repealed. The definition is now contained in the Trade Union and Labour Relations (Consolidation) Act 1992, as follows.] '... trade union' means an organisation (whether temporary or permanent) —
(a) which consists wholly or mainly of workers of one or more descriptions and whose principal purposes include the regulation of relations between workers of that description or those descriptions and employers or employers' associations; or
(b) which consists wholly or mainly of —
  (i) constituent or affiliated organisations which fulfil the conditions in paragraph (a) (or themselves consist wholly or mainly of constituent or affiliated organisations which fulfil those conditions), or
  (ii) representatives of such constituent or affiliated organisations,

and whose principal purposes include the regulation of relations between workers and employers or between workers and employers' associations, or the regulation of relations between its constituent or affiliated organisations. (Trade Union and Labour Relations (Consolidation) Act 1992, s 1)

'Federated trade union' means a trade union which consists wholly or mainly of constituent or affiliated organisations, or representatives of such organisations, as described in paragraph (b) above. (ibid s 118(1))

[For 47 Halsbury's Laws (4th edn) para 491 see now 47 Halsbury's Laws (4th edn) (Reissue) para 1001.]

TRADER OR DEALER

Canada [Optional tax treatment for certain capital gains was denied to traders or dealers.] 'In my view, the words "a trader or dealer" should be given their ordinary meaning. They normally refer to a person who deals in merchandise, is engaged in buying and selling or whose business is trade or commerce. In Black's Law Dictionary, a "dealer" is defined as "any person engaged in the business of buying and selling securities for his own account, through a broker or otherwise, but does not include a bank, or any person in so far as he buys or sells securities for his own account, either individually or in some fiduciary capacity, *but not as part of a regular business*". (My emphasis.)

'I note in passing that the word "dealer" has been loosely translated in French by "*courtier*". A "*courtier*" is a "broker", that is to say a person employed as a middleman to transact business or negotiate bargains. The notion of "broker" necessarily involves the buying and selling on behalf of others. It is, therefore, narrower than either the term "trader" or "dealer". I hasten to add that it has no impact on the question submitted to us as the English version of paragraph 39(5)(a) contains no such ambiguity and the French word "*commerçant*" is, in any event, broad enough to include a broker.' *Vancouver Art Metal Works Ltd v Canada* [1993] 2 FCR 179 at 186, 187, FCA, per Letourneau JA

TRADING STOCK

Australia 'The Act [Income Tax Assessment Act 1936] defines "trading stock" in s 6(1) as including "anything produced, manufactured, acquired or purchased for purposes of manufacture, sale or exchange, and also includes live stock".

The definition looks to the nature of goods that may constitute trading stock and posits that they will constitute trading stock if acquired for any of the specified purposes, including sale. It presupposes that the person by whom they are produced, manufactured, acquired or purchased is or will be engaged in trade in those goods. But it does not render an inquiry into whether or not the person is or will be engaged in that trade irrelevant. A single transaction does not render a person a trader, although, of course, a single transaction may constitute an adventure in the nature of trade. Nor, we think, is a single item acquired for the purpose of manufacture, sale or exchange an item of trading stock, unless the purchaser is or will be engaged in trading goods of that nature. Thus it is relevant to inquire whether the person who acquires an item claimed to be trading stock is a trader in the sense that he is engaged or will be engaged in trading goods of the nature of the item acquired.' *John v Taxation Commissioner of the Commonwealth of Australia* (1989) 166 CLR 417 at 429, per cur

Australia [Section 6(1) of the [Income Tax Assessment Act 1936 (Cth)] provides: '"trading stock" includes anything produced, manufactured, acquired or purchased for purposes of manufacture, sale or exchange, and also includes live stock.'] 'Although the word "stock" may sometimes be used in ordinary parlance to describe the goods which a trader, particularly a retailer, has ready for sale, the term "trading stock" is not limited to that sense in the Act nor is it limited to that sense when what is in issue is the calculation of the annual profits or income of the trader. Section 6(1) of the Act does not require that goods be ready for sale or even that they be purchased or acquired in the ordinary course of business. It simply requires that goods be produced, manufactured, acquired or purchased for purposes of manufacture, sale or exchange. Work in progress is thus trading stock for the purposes of the Act, as it is in ordinary commercial and accounting concepts of stock on hand … The words "trading stock on hand" in s 28 thus refer to the trading stock held by the taxpayer at the specified time. Because the trading stock provisions are based upon well known concepts of trade and accountancy, those concepts of what stock a trader holds and thus what should be brought to account in a calculation of the profits or income of the year provide a guide as to the stock "on hand" at the relevant date. In the present case, that stock included the goods in respect of which bills of lading were held.' *Federal Commissioner of Taxation v All States Frozen Food Pty Ltd* (1989) 88 ALR 575 at 580–581, per Davies J

TRADITION

Australia 'The meaning of "traditional" is that which is "handed down by tradition" and "tradition" is "the handing down of statements, beliefs, legends, customs, etc from generation to generation, especially by word of mouth or by practice": The Macquarie Dictionary, 3rd ed.' *Commonwealth v Yarmirr* (1999) 101 FCR 171; 168 ALR 426; BC9907888; [1999] FCA 1668 at [65], per Beaumont and von Doussa JJ

TRADITIONAL

Australia 'Section 223(1) of the Native Title Act 1993 (Cth) speaks not of traditionally based laws and customs but rather of "the traditional laws acknowledged, and traditional customs observed". However, reference to the extrinsic materials ... demonstrates that the legislature did not intend the words "the traditional laws acknowledged, and traditional customs observed" in para 223(1)(a) to narrow the common law concept of native title.

'The language of section 223(1) of the Native Title Act 1993 (Cth) is consistent, in our view, with the common law in this regard. The Macquarie Dictionary 3rd Edition gives as its first three meanings of "traditional":

"1. relating to tradition. 2. handed down by tradition. 3. in accordance with tradition."

'The Oxford English Dictionary 2nd Edition gives as the first meaning of "traditional":

"Belonging to, consisting in, or of the nature of tradition; handed down by or derived from tradition."

'The Macquarie Dictionary and the Oxford English Dictionary define "tradition" in the relevant sense similarly. The definition in the Macquarie Dictionary is:

"1. the handing down of statements, beliefs, legends, customs, etc, from generation to generation, especially by word of mouth or by practice: a story that has come down to us by popular tradition. 2. that which is so handed down: the traditions of the Inuits."

'Nothing in the above dictionary definitions suggests that the terms "traditional" and "tradition" as ordinarily used are inconsistent with the notion of evolutionary or adaptive changes to the subject matter of a tradition. Indeed, it is common for something to be described as traditional which has long established roots notwithstanding that it incorporates some modern elements. The courtroom ceremonies by which newly appointed judges publicly present their commissions as judges do not fail to be traditional within the ordinary usage of that term where women present their commissions simply because the appointment of women as judges is a relatively recent phenomenon. By analogy, a tradition of hunting in a certain area may be maintained notwithstanding that the wildlife available to be hunted may have changed over time (e g from possum to rabbit) or the tools used may have changed over time (e g from spear or throwing stick to rifle).' *Members of the Yorta Yorta Aboriginal Community v Vic* (2001) 180 ALR 655; BC200100153; [2001] FCA 45 at [123]–[125], per Branson and Katz JJ

'It is wrong, however, to see "traditional" as, of its nature, a concept concerned with what is dead, frozen or otherwise incapable of change. As Beaumont and von Doussa JJ observed in *Commonwealth v Yarmirr* (1999) 168 ALR 426 at [65], citing The Macquarie Dictionary, 3rd ed, the meaning of "traditional" is that which is "'handed down by tradition' and 'tradition' is 'the handing down of statements, beliefs, legends, customs etc, from generation to generation, especially by word of mouth or by practice'". The Oxford English Dictionary gives a very similar definition, again emphasising that tradition is the handing down of statements etc, especially by word of mouth or by practice, and not by writing. Far from being concerned with what is static, the very notion of "tradition" as involving the transmission from generation to generation of statements, beliefs, legends and customs orally or by practice implies recognition of the possibility of change.' *Members of the Yorta Yorta Aboriginal Community v Vic* (2001) 180 ALR 655; BC200100153; [2001] FCA 45 at [35], per Black CJ

TRANSACTION

Australia [In the context of voidable transactions under (Cth) Corporations Act 2001.] '[20] The various references to "transaction" are to be understood in the light of the definition of that term in s 9:

transaction, in Part 5.7B, in relation to a body corporate or Part 5.7 body, means a transaction to which the body is a party, for example (but without limitation):
(a) a conveyance, transfer or other disposition by the body of property of the body; and

(b) a charge created by the body on property of the body; and

(c) a guarantee given by the body; and

(d) a payment made by the body; and

(e) an obligation incurred by the body; and

(f) a release or waiver by the body; and

(g) a loan to the body;

and includes such a transaction that has been completed or given effect to, or that has terminated.

...

'[24] The relevant concept of "transaction" is, as the definition implies, very broad. Its breadth is illustrated by a number of cases in which a series of steps over a period, involving several parties and not always contractual consequences, have been held to be a "transaction". "Transaction" includes an arrangement giving rise to an estoppel under which one party may not resile from a position. And, as the definition itself makes clear (for example, by referring to a disposition of property), a "transaction" may be unilateral in character. These matters are made clear by the decision of the Full Federal Court in *Re Emanuel (No 14) Pty Ltd*; *Macks v Blacklaw & Shadforth Pty Ltd* (1997) 24 ACSR 292 and those of the Court of Appeal in *Bartercard Ltd v Wily* (2001) 39 ACSR 94 and *Somerset Marine Inc v New Cap Reinsurance Corporation* [2003] NSWCA 338'. *Australian Kitchen Industries Pty Ltd v Albarran (as liq of W & J Kitchens Pty Ltd)* 2004 NSWSC 1047 at [20], [24], 51 ACSR 604, per Barrett J

TRANSFER

Australia 'The learned judge also referred to an almost identical definition in the *Macquarie Dictionary*, but it may be thought more useful now to cite that appearing in the *Encyclopaedic Australian Legal Dictionary*: "The passing of a legal right from one person to another so as to vest that right in the other." Although the word "transfer" is not a term of art and is a word of wide connotation, to my way of thinking it is the passing of rights to another, so as to vest them in that other person, which is essential to a transfer, properly understood. It is not a mere disposition, a ridding oneself of the right or interest, it is the vesting in the transferee of that right or interest, precisely or substantially, which is necessary to effect a transfer, as ordinarily understood in the law.' *Coles Myer Ltd v Commissioner of State Revenue* (1998) 98 ATC 4537 at 4546; BC9801479 at 18, per Ormiston JA (Winneke P concurring)

TRANSGENIC

Canada 'In my opinion, the oncomouse must be considered to be the result of both ingenuity and the laws of nature — ingenuity in the initial genetic engineering involving the assembly of the oncogene, incorporating it into the plasmid and injecting the plasmid into the zygote; and the laws of nature, with the oncogene then affecting all the cells of the oncomouse in the course of gestation, the subsequent mating of an oncomouse and an uninjected mouse, and the reliance on Mendelian laws of inheritance to obtain offspring oncomice. However, the use of the laws of nature by inventors does not disqualify a product from being an invention, provided inventiveness or ingenuity is also involved. As Professor Vaver has explained:

Patents can, of course, be granted for a new practical application of the theory of gravity- –for example, on an improved gravity pump.

'Indeed, substantially more is involved here than merely the operation of the laws of nature. By definition, transgenic organisms come into being through human manipulation at the genetic or molecular level. The *New Oxford Dictionary of English* defines "transgenic" as:

... of, relating to, or denoting an organism that contains genetic material into which DNA from an unrelated organism has been artificially introduced.'

Harvard College v Canada (Commissioner of Patents) (2000) 189 DLR (4th) 385 at 404, FCA, per Rothstein JA

TRANSIT

[For 41 Halsbury's Laws (4th edn) para 830 see now 41 Halsbury's Laws (4th edn) (Reissue) para 251.]

TRANSLATION

Canada [It was alleged that conversion of programs from assembly language to machine language was 'translation' within the contemplation of the Copyright Act, RSC 1970, c C-30.] 'I agree with the learned trial judge that the conversion of a text into Morse code or shorthand does not result in a different literary work and that the text, so converted, does retain the character of the original. That, however, does not lead to the conclusion that such conversion is translation for purposes of the Act. A person knowledgeable of Morse code or the particular shorthand system could read the converted version and what would be heard would be the original text verbatim. Such a conversion is not, in my opinion a translation within the contemplation of the Copyright Act. It is rather a reproduction of the original, the making of which was equally the exclusive right of the owner of the copyright in that original.' *Apple Computer Inc v Macintosh Computers Ltd* (1987) 44 DLR (4th) 74 at 83, FCA, per Mahoney J

New Zealand 'Giving the term "translation" a "fair, large, and liberal" interpretation, therefore, as required by s 5(j) of the Acts Interpretation Act 1924, I apply the secondary meaning of "the expression or rendering of something in another medium or form". Furthermore, object code fits squarely within this definition. It is essentially the expression of source code in a different form. English words and mathematical symbols are expressed by the compiler in the form of electrical impulses, which can be represented in binary code. Any source code run through the compiler program will be translated into the corresponding object code form. The compiler does not act upon the source code instructions—it merely translates them. Once in object code form, the instructions may be implemented by the CPU.' *International Business Machines Corpn v Computer Imports Ltd* [1989] 2 NZLR 395 at 413, per Smellie J

TRANSMISSION

Australia [Whether a vesting order made by the Supreme Court pursuant to s 71 of the *Trustee Act* 1925 (NSW) is a 'transmission'.] 'In *Wolfson v Registrar General (NSW)* (1934) 51 CLR 300 at 311–312, Starke J defined "transmission" as follows: "Transmission" in its strictest sense is the devolution of property upon some person by operation of law, unconnected with any direct act of the party to whom the property is transmitted—as, by death, bankruptcy, insolvency or marriage ..." ... Section 78(1) of the [*Trustee Act* 1925 (NSW)] ... support[s] the conclusion that a vesting order, of itself, vests ownership by operation of law, just as the case of a will or bankruptcy, so characterising a vesting order as a transmission.' *Andco Nominees Pty Ltd v Lestato Pty Ltd* (1995) 126 FLR 404 at 421, 422, per Santow J

New Zealand 'In terms of s 36 [of the Ship Registration Act 1992] "where a ship ... passes by transmission to a person by any lawful means other than by a transfer under s 35 ..." a declaration of transmission made by that person is lodged with the Registrar who then enters in the register the name of that person as owner of the ship. Transmission is used to express the legal result which follows through change in ownership by operation of law.' *Equal Enterprise Ltd v Attorney-General* [1995] 3 NZLR 293 at 298, per cur

TRANSPORTATION COMPANY

Canada [Obligations and fees were imposed by the immigration regulatory scheme on transportation companies.] 'In my opinion, the applicants fall within the definition of "transportation company" under the *Immigration Act*. While a number of their vessels are primarily engaged in fishing operations, or work incidental to those operations, they do transport the crew on board their vessels. They are required, as are the operators of any other vessel or vehicle transporting persons to Canada, to undertake certain acts in rela–tion to their crews and immigration requirements. The Act and Regulations have specific provisions for dealing with arrangements for crew members on arrival to and departure from Canada, and for the obligations of companies operating the vessels to meet costs that may be incurred to remove persons transported to Canada, whether as crew members or otherwise; if they have no right to remain here under the Act. Thus the Act is broad enough to include operators of vehicles or vessels who arrive in Canada with stow-aways aboard who seek to leave the carrying ship in a Canadian port. The primary purpose of operating the vessel surely has little bearing on the obligations of operators and masters to avoid creating immigration problems for this country when they visit.' *Flota Cubana de Pesca (Cuban Fishing Fleet) v Canada (Minister of Citizenship and Immigration)* [1995] 3 FC 383 at 392, Fed TD, per MacKay J

TRANSSEXUAL

'[7] Transsexual people are to be distinguished from inter-sexual people. Transsexual is the label given, not altogether happily, to a person who has the misfortune to be born with physical characteristics which are congruent but whose self-belief is incongruent. Transsexual people are born with the anatomy of a person of one sex but with an unshakeable belief or feeling that they are persons of the opposite sex. They experience themselves as being of the opposite sex. Mrs Bellinger is such a person. The aetiology of this condition remains uncertain. It is now generally recognised as a psychiatric disorder, often known as gender dysphoria or gender identity disorder. It can result in acute psychological distress.' *Bellinger v Bellinger* [2003] UKHL 21, [2003] 2 All ER 593, per Lord Nicholls of Birkenhead (affirming *Bellinger v Bellinger* [2001] EWCA Civ 1140, [2002] 1 All ER 311)

TRANSSEXUALISM

'[47] Transsexualism is, therefore, according to the present accepted medical knowledge, recognised as a psychiatric condition, coming within gender dysphoria or gender identity disorder. There is the possibility that it is a medical condition with a biological basis by reason of sexual differentiation of the brain after birth. Another disorder within the same group is the condition called inter-sex, which has certain similarities to transsexualism but is recognised as a distinct disorder. An inter-sexed person is someone whose biological criteria at birth are not congruent, and is, therefore, of uncertain sex and, as Professor Gooren and Professor Green described, would be assigned to the sex the medical profession considered most appropriate for psychological reasons rather than biological reasons. By contrast the transsexual would be born with congruent biological criteria and would be appropriately assigned to one sex, but would become seriously discontented with that "label" as he/she grew up. At some stage a transsexual would be likely to seek medical advice. As Professor Gooren said, it would be a stepwise procedure.' *Bellinger v Bellinger* [2001] EWCA Civ 1140 at [47], [2002] 1 All ER 311 at 323–324, CA, per Dame Elizabeth Butler-Sloss P and Robert Walker LJ

TRAVELLER

See also GIPSY

'Like most English words, the meaning of the word "traveller" depends on the context in which it is being used. It has one meaning when seen on a railway station. For some time now the refreshment service provided at railway stations and on trains has been styled "Travellers Fare". The word has a different meaning when in its context it is directed at travelling salesmen. In my view, in the windows of the Cat and Mutton [a local public house] "No travellers" will be understood by those to whom it is directed, namely potential customers, as meaning persons who are currently leading a nomadic way of life, living in tents or caravans or other vehicles. Thus the notices embrace gipsies who are living in

that way. But the class of persons excluded from the Cat and Mutton is not confined to gipsies. The prohibited class includes all those of a nomadic way of life mentioned above. As the judge said, they all come under the umbrella expression 'travellers', as this accurately describes their way of life.' *Commission for Racial Equality v Dutton* [1989] 1 All ER 306 at 311, CA, per Nicholls LJ

TREASON

[For 11 Halsbury's Laws (4th edn) para 823 see now 11(1) Halsbury's Laws (4th edn) (Reissue) para 76.]

TREASURE TROVE

[As to the coroner's jurisdiction, formerly to be found in the repealed Coroners Act 1887, see now the Coroners Act 1988, s 30.]

[The common law position has been replaced by the Treasure Act 1996. For the definition of treasure see now s 1(1) and 9(2) Halsbury's Laws (4th edn) (Reissue) para 976.]

'Property is only capable of being treasure trove if its last owner left it, intending to recover it. If he deliberately abandoned it or accidentally lost it, it is not treasure trove. If, as was the defence case here, silver coins were buried at a religious site or burial ground as sacrifices or votive offerings, they are unlikely to be treasure trove.' *R v Hancock* [1990] 3 All ER 183 at 186, CA, per cur

TREASURY BILL

[For 4 Halsbury's Laws (4th edn) para 524 see now 4(1) Halsbury's Laws (4th edn) (2002 Reissue) para 513.]

TREATING

[For 15 Halsbury's Laws (4th edn) para 781 see now 15 Halsbury's Laws (4th edn) (Reissue) para 696.]

TRESPASS

Trespass ab initio

[For 45 Halsbury's Laws (4th edn) para 1389 see now 45(2) Halsbury's Laws (4th edn) (Reissue) para 510.]

Trespass to goods

[For 45 Halsbury's Laws (4th edn) para 1491 see now 45(2) Halsbury's Laws (4th edn) (Reissue) para 659.]

Trespass to land

[For 45 Halsbury's Laws (4th edn) paras 1384, 1385 see now 45(2) Halsbury's Laws (4th edn) (Reissue) paras 505–506.]

Trespass to the person

[For 45 Halsbury's Laws (4th edn) para 1308 see now 45(2) Halsbury's Laws (4th edn) (Reissue) para 425.]

TRESPASSES

New Zealand [Section 3 of the Trespass Act 1980 provides that 'Every person commits an offence against this Act who trespasses on any place …'.] 'The civil wrong of trespass consists of setting foot on the land of another, or remaining there, without that other's permission, express or implied, unless there is some other legal justification for doing so …

'… the concept of trespass for the purposes of s 3(1) involves simply entering or remaining on the land of another without that other's authority, express or implied. If there is entry onto the land of another with authority, it is necessary for that authority to be revoked before the person concerned can become a trespasser.' *Wilcox v Police* [1994] 1 NZLR 243 at 246–247, per Tipping J

New Zealand [Section 3(1) of the Trespass Act 1980.] '… the reference in subs (1) to a person who "trespasses" on any place should be read as meaning a person who was [there] without the leave or licence of the occupier.' *Wilcox & Others v Police* [1995] 2 NZLR 160 at 164, CA, per cur

TRIAL

Australia 'The term "trial" is not defined in the Rules [of the Supreme Court (Qld)]. Counsel for the appellant referred the court to the discussion of the term "trial" in *Jowitt's Dictionary of English Law*. To that may be added the primary definition appearing in *Butterworths Australian Legal Dictionary*: "A fact finding process, by which the court resolves disputed issues of fact presented by the parties and applies appropriate legal rules, culminating in a judgment". That, in my view, is

an accurate description of what is meant by the term "trial" when used in the Rules.' *W R Carpenter Australia Ltd v Ogle* (CA(QLD), Pincus JA, Williams and Cullinane JJ, No 5023/96, 28 October 1997, unreported, BC9705919) at 8–9, per Williams J

The trial

New Zealand [Section 344A of the Crimes Act 1961 repeatedly uses the words 'the trial'.] '… we are satisfied that the words "the trial" where they appear in subss (1) and (4) mean the trial contemplated at the time the application is made.' *R v Gallagher* [1993] 1 NZLR 659 at 661, CA, per cur

TRIBUNAL

Australia 'The word in its ordinary meaning signifies something more than an official performing this function. The dictionaries tell us that, in its primary sense, "tribunal" means a place or seat of judgment (*Shorter Oxford Dictionary*), a body appointed to adjudicate disputes (*Butterworths Australian Legal Dictionary*) and (according to the *Dictionary of English Law*) a person or body exercising judicial or quasi-judicial functions outside the regular judicial system, and, in these senses, the word is quite inapt to describe the office of Director [of Conciliation and Review] in the performance of the essentially administrative task of examining doctors' reports for compliance with the medical evidence requirements of s 93D(6) of the Workers' Compensation and Rehabilitation Act 1981 (WA) and deciding whether they do or do not comply.' *Re Monger; Ex parte WMC Resources Ltd* BC200202528; [2002] WASCA 129 at [76], per Anderson J

TRIBUNAL ESTABLISHED BY LAW

'[5] The Lord Chancellor has power under s 9(1) of the [Supreme Court Act 1981] to authorise circuit judges to sit as justices of the High Court. This power is routinely exercised on the appointment of a circuit judge to the [Technology and Construction Court], but by a most regrettable oversight it had not been exercised in respect of Judge Seymour or (as has now been ascertained) Judge Toulmin QC. Accordingly it is accepted both by the commissioners and by counsel for the Lord Chancellor that the judge sat and adjudicated in Mr Coppard's case without legal authority.

…

DOES A JUDGE IN FACT COME WITHIN ART 6?

'[33] The answer to the question of convention-compliance, in our judgment, depends on at least two things: first, what the substantive content of the phrase "established by law" is; and secondly, whether the de facto doctrine, even in the shape in which we have now construed it, matches that content.

ESTABLISHED BY LAW

'[34] There is no decision of either the European Court of Human Rights or the European Commission of Human Rights which deals comprehensively with the content of the expression "established by law". But in *Zand v Austria* (1978) 15 DR 70 at 80 (para 69) the Commission of Human Rights, in debating the status of the Austrian labour courts, which had been set up only under elective ministerial powers, said that the object and purpose of the provision was—

> "that the judicial organization in a democratic society must not depend on the discretion of the Executive, but that it should be regulated by law emanating from Parliament."

The Court of Human Rights has made it clear (see *Sunday Times v UK* (1979) 2 EHRR 245) that law declared by the courts ranks for these purposes with that made by Parliament. We do not consider, however, that this passage in *Zand*'s case (which s 2 of the 1998 Act requires us to take into account) answers the question. First of all, it is addressed to the issue then before the Commission of Human Rights, which concerned the use of ministerial powers to create courts—hence the focus on the executive. Secondly, it seems to us that independence from the executive is what the word 'independent' in art 6(1) is principally concerned with. Thirdly, and perhaps most importantly, it is plain that much more than this is involved in the concept of a tribunal established by law. Among other things, the purpose (especially when one remembers the period of European history of which the convention was intended to mark a definitive end) is to ensure that justice is administered by, and only by, the prescribed exercise of the judicial power of the state, not by ad hoc 'people's courts' and the like. Such a principle must be fundamental to any concept of the rule of law. Implicit in it is that the composition and authority of a court must not be arbitrary.

…

COMPATIBILITY WITH THE CONVENTION

'[35] This brings us to the second question: does the de facto doctrine meet this standard? To the extent that, as we hold, it validates the authority of the tribunal and not merely its acts, it does. But Mr Macpherson submits that it does not exclude, as it needs to, a validation of the authority of a person who is so incompetent to sit that to ratify him in office would amount to arbitrariness or irrationality offensive to the rule of law.

'[36] This argument is in very large part already addressed by our holding that the doctrine cannot validate the authority of a usurper, for it will be a rare case in which an incompetent person who lacks legal authority does not know that he or she ought not to be sitting as a judge. The freak case of a person without either professional competence or legal authority who believes despite his incompetence that he is authorised to sit as a judge can be addressed if and when it arises. What matters to the present issues is that the de facto doctrine ratifies the authority only of persons believed by themselves and the world to possess the judicial power they are exercising. It does not protect people who have deluded themselves or others into thinking they have authority.

'[37] But there is a second and more troubling ground on which Mr Macpherson contends that a judge in fact is not a tribunal established by law. "Established" in his contention requires a tribunal to have been established by the time the individual's civil rights and obligations come before it. We are not disposed to accept Mr Sales' argument that the common law gives de facto tribunals this legal status proleptically. To accept this would be to establish, in effect, a prior dispensation for avoidable error, with undesirable consequences for legal certainty and good administration. If the de facto doctrine establishes a tribunal by law, it seems to us that it does so by recognising the authority, in an appropriate and legally controlled situation, of what would otherwise not be a lawful tribunal.

'[38] The convention itself is silent on this question. So is the International Covenant on Civil and Political Rights (New York, 16 December 1966; TS 6 (1977); Cmnd 6702), though by art 14(1) it adds the adjective "competent" to the requisite qualities of a tribunal established by law. But art 47 of the Charter of Fundamental Rights of the European Union (OJ 2000 C364 p 1), a non-binding instrument adopted by the United Kingdom and the other member states in December 2000, says: "Everyone is entitled to a fair and public hearing within a reasonable time by an independent and impartial tribunal previously established by law." This reproduces the language of art 6(1) of the convention with the striking addition of the word "previously". If it were part of the language of the convention we might well have been driven to hold that the de facto doctrine did not comply with it. But is it, as Mr Macpherson urges, implicit in the convention? No jurisprudence of the Commission or Court of Human Rights indicates that it is, but that could be because the question has not yet come before either body.

'[39] We remind ourselves that the convention is not a United Kingdom statute, and that we should be concerned less with close analysis of its language than with the principles which animate it. We remind ourselves that the legal system of every member state will contain ways of dealing with errors and omissions in the appointment of persons to judicial office, whether by ratifying or by nullifying what has happened. Provided that the United Kingdom's legal response, at least as it has developed in England and Wales, is not such as to ratify the acts of usurpers or to operate arbitrarily and is limited, in effect, to the correction of mistakes of form rather than of substance—and in our judgment it meets all these tests—we do not consider that the convention requires the disqualification of a judge purely because his authority was not formally established before he sat.

CONCLUSION

'[40] A person who sits as a judge of the High Court of England or Wales in the circumstances in which Judge Seymour sat is in our judgment a judge in fact and a tribunal established by law. In spite, therefore, of the novel and difficult issues which this appeal has raised, it must be dismissed.'
Coppard v Customs and Excise Comrs [2003] EWCA Civ 511 at [35]–[40], [2003] 3 All ER 351, per Sedley LJ

TRIFLING

Australia [Section 47B(3)(b) of the Road Traffic Act 1961 (SA) states that 'disqualification [from holding or obtaining a driver's licence] ... cannot be reduced or mitigated in any way or be substituted by any other penalty or sentence unless, in the case of a first offence, the court is satisfied, by evidence given on oath, that the offence is trifling, in which case it may order a period of disqualification that is less than the prescribed minimum period but not less than one month'.] 'A number of statutes have given and still give the courts power to impose a lesser penalty than would otherwise be required, if the court finds an offence to be trifling. Sometimes such provisions relate to offences generally: see s 15, s 16 and s 17 of the Criminal Law (Sentencing) Act 1988 (SA) ... Sometimes the provision relates

only to a particular offence, as in the case of s 47B(3)(b). Other examples of this kind are found in the Act. Sometimes the trifling nature of the offence is one of a number of bases for imposing a lesser penalty: see s 16 and s 17 of the Sentencing Act. Sometimes the trifling nature of the offence is the only basis for reducing the minimum penalty, as in s 47B(3)(b) and in s 15(1) of the Sentencing Act.

'My view is that the same meaning is to be given to "trifling" in each circumstance.

'It is the offending conduct that must be trifling ...

...

'As Parliament has conferred the relevant power in relation to all three categories of offence under s 47B, one cannot say that simply because the offence is a category 2 offence it cannot be trifling. In *Walden v Hensler* (1987) 163 CLR 561 Brennan J said at 577:

> "Triviality must be ascertained by reference to the conduct which constitutes the offence for which the offender is liable to be convicted and to the actual circumstances in which the offence is committed. It was erroneous to ascertain the triviality of the offence by reference simply to the statutory provision which prescribes the maximum penalty."

Dawson J expressed a similar view at 595.

'... one should begin by bearing in mind the ordinary meaning of "trifling". That meaning in this context is trifling in the sense of being of slight importance, insignificant or of little moment.

'A point made in many of the cases is that an offence which is a normal or typical example of its type will not be trifling. The reason is that Parliament could not have intended that the normal or typical offence would be treated in an exceptional manner. Nor could Parliament have intended that something which it has treated as an offence should routinely be regarded as of trifling significance. The intention behind a provision like s 47B(3)(b) must be to deal with unusual or exceptional cases, the circumstances of which call for the usual minimum to be put to one side: see *Verran v Roberts* [1938] SASR 256 at 259–60: *Mancini v Vallelonga* (1981) 28 SASR 236 at 239. The offence might be unusual or exceptional in this sense, if it is "a trivial example of the forbidden act": *Brebner v Hersey* [1963] SASR 1 at 11.' *Siviour-Ashman v Police* (2003) 225 LSJS 335; BC200300335; [2003] SASC 29 at [19]–[21], [23]–[25], per Doyle CJ

TRINITY HOUSE

[For 43 Halsbury's Laws (4th edn) para 33 see now 43(2) Halsbury's Laws (4th edn) (Reissue) para 1102.]

TRIVIAL *SEE* NOMINAL, TRIVIAL OR COLOURABLE

TRUST

[For 48 Halsbury's Laws (4th edn) paras 501, 504, 523 see now 48 Halsbury's Laws (4th edn) (2000 Reissue) paras 501, 504, 524.]

Bare trust

Australia '... The term "bare trustee" is often used in statutes where its meaning depends on its context: *Corumo Holdings Pty Ltd v C Itoh Ltd* (1991) 24 NSWLR 370 at 398; *Thorpe v Bristile Ltd* (1996) 16 WAR 500 at 505–6.

'In the context of the companies legislation considered in *Coruma Holdings* (supra), the term was held to mean a trustee who was no more than a nominee or cypher in a common sense commercial view.

'In *Thorpe v Bristile Ltd* (supra) Malcolm CJ (at 505), with whom Pidgeon and Owen JJ agreed (at 507), referred with approval to the statement in *Jacob's Law of Trusts in Australia* to the effect that:

> "A 'bare trust' is simply a trust in which the trustee has no active duties to perform. In its classic form it occurs when a principal vests property in his agent as his nominee, but obviously can occur in other circumstances. There are only two circumstances in which it is relevant to consider whether or not a trust is a 'bare trust'. The first concerns the question of possession: a cestui que trust is entitled to the possession of the trust assets if a trust be a 'bare trust', but not otherwise. The second concerns the effect of the creation of a sub-trust. If A holds property on trust for B, and B declares himself a trustee of his interest for C, if the intermediate trust is a 'bare trust', but not otherwise, it is arguable (but not certain) that the effect of B's declaration of trust is to bring A and C into a direct relationship, so that A becomes a trustee for C."

'Although the beneficiary of a bare trust is "entitled to possession" of the trust property, it does not necessarily follow that it is in actual possession.

Further, as Meagher JA observed in *Corumo Holdings* (at 398), in reality almost no situation can be postulated when a trustee cannot in some circumstances have active duties to perform. However, by no stretch of the imagination can it be said that a trustee carrying on a business would or could be a bare trustee.

'... However, such power [to carry on a business] may be implied from the trust instrument and it has been suggested that there is statutory authority to do so: Ford H A J and Lee W A, *Principles of the Law of Trusts*, 3rd ed, Law Book Co, Australia, 1996, para 12,500.' *Old Papa's Franchise Systems Pty Ltd v Camisa Nominees Pty Ltd* BC200300206; [2003] WASCA 11 at [54]–[58], per Murray, Parker and McLure JJ

Constructive trust

[For 16 Halsbury's Laws (4th edn) para 1453 see now 16(2) Halsbury's Laws (4th edn) (Reissue) para 852. For 48 Halsbury's Laws (4th edn) para 584 see now 48 Halsbury's Laws (4th edn) (2000 Reissue) para 587.]

Discretionary trust

[For 48 Halsbury's Laws (4th edn) para 577 see now 48 Halsbury's Laws (4th edn) (2000 Reissue) para 579.]

Executed or executory trust

[For 48 Halsbury's Laws (4th edn) para 525 see now 48 Halsbury's Laws (4th edn) (2000 Reissue) para 526.]

Express trust

[For 16 Halsbury's Laws (4th edn) para 1452 see now 16(2) Halsbury's Laws (4th edn) (Reissue) para 851.]

Precatory trust

[For 48 Halsbury's Laws (4th edn) para 526 see now 48 Halsbury's Laws (4th edn) (2000 Reissue) para 527.]

Private trust

[For 48 Halsbury's Laws (4th edn) para 530 see now 48 Halsbury's Laws (4th edn) (2000 Reissue) para 531.]

Public trust

[For 48 Halsbury's Laws (4th edn) para 529 see now 48 Halsbury's Laws (4th edn) (2000 Reissue) para 530.]

Resulting trust

[For 16 Halsbury's Laws (4th edn) para 1453 see now 16(2) Halsbury's Laws (4th edn) (Reissue) para 853. For 48 Halsbury's Laws (4th edn) para 597 see now 48 Halsbury's Laws (4th edn) (2000 Reissue) para 604.]

Secret trust

[For 48 Halsbury's Laws (4th edn) paras 527, 570 see now 48 Halsbury's Laws (4th edn) (2000 Reissue) paras 528, 572.]

Voluntary trust

[For 48 Halsbury's Laws (4th edn) para 528 see now 48 Halsbury's Laws (4th edn) (2000 Reissue) para 529.]

TRUSTEE

Bare trustee

[For 48 Halsbury's Laws (4th edn) para 641 see now 48 Halsbury's Laws (4th edn) (2000 Reissue) para 650.]

Australia 'The expression "bare trustee" was used by Lord Hardwicke LC in *Fell v Lutwidge* (1740) Barn (Ch) 319; 27 ER 662, to describe the interest of the defendant in proceeds of an insurance policy on a merchant ship, the policy having been taken out in his name but on behalf of and at the direction of one of the owners of the ship. Today the usually accepted meaning of "bare" trust is a trust under which the trustee or trustees hold property without any interest therein, other than that existing by reason of the office and the legal title as trustee, and without any duty or further duty to perform, except to convey it upon demand to the beneficiary or beneficiaries or as directed by them, for example, on sale to a third party.' *Herdegen v Federal Commissioner of Taxation* (1988) 84 ALR 271 at 281, per Gummow J

Charity trustee

[The Charities Act 1960 is largely repealed. The definition is re-enacted in the Charities Act 1993, s 97(1).]

TRUSTWORTHINESS

Australia [Section 40A(1) of the Evidence Act 1910 (Tas) provides that writings purporting to be a memorandum or record of any event is admissible in evidence as proof of the facts if it appears to the court that the source of information, and the method and time of the preparation, were such as to indicate its 'trustworthiness']. 'So far as we are aware, the concept of "trustworthiness" embodied in s 40A(1)(b) has not been the subject of prior judicial pronouncement. In our opinion, having regard to the context in which it appears in the section, the word has a dual connotation. In the first place the writing in question must come from a source which obviates any reasonable suspicion that the document may have been prepared for the ulterior purpose of assisting the case for the party on whose behalf the document is tendered. Secondly, the nature and source of the information recorded must provide a basis for positively inferring that the recorded material is reasonably reliable and accurate.' *Durovic v R* (1994) 4 Tas R 113 at 126–127, per cur

TURBARY

[For 6 Halsbury's Laws (4th edn) para 576 see now 6 Halsbury's Laws (4th edn) (2003 Reissue) para 471.]

TYPE

'Interpreting the phrase "of the type known as the pit bull terrier" in s 1(1) of the [Dangerous Dogs Act 1991] simply by the normal canon of construction, ie by giving the words their ordinary meaning, I entirely agree with the decision of the Crown Court ... that the word "type" is not synonymous with the word "breed". The definition of a breed is normally that of some recognised body such as the Kennel Club in the United Kingdom ... the word "type" in this context has a meaning different from and wider than the word "breed".' *R v Crown Court at Knightsbridge, ex p Dunne* [1993] 4 All ER 491 at 496–497, DC, per Glidewell LJ

U

ULTRA VIRES

[For 7 Halsbury's Laws (4th edn) para 945 see now 7(2) Halsbury's Laws (4th edn) (1996 Reissue) para 1097.]

UNABLE/UNWILLING

Canada [Refugee status was available to certain persons who inter alia were unable or unwilling to seek the protection of their home state.] 'I would agree with the court below that "unable" and "unwilling" have different meanings, which are fairly apparent on their face. One can say that "unable" means physically or literally unable, and that "unwilling" simply means that protection from the state is not wanted for some reason, though not impossible. This would, at first sight, seem to be a clear distinction, but as we shall see it has become somewhat blurred …

'With respect to "unable", it would appear that physical or literal impossibility is *one* means of triggering the definition, but it is not the *only* way. Thus ineffective state protection is encompassed within the concept of "unable" and "unwilling", and I am left with the conclusion that the appellant here could have pursued his claim under either category.' *Canada (A-G) v Ward* [1993] 2 SCR 689 at 717, 718, 719, per La Forest J

UNABLE TO PAY

Australia [Section 1335 of the Corporations Law provides that the court may require security for costs where there is reason to believe that the plaintiff corporation will be 'unable to pay' the costs of the defendant if successful.] 'A corporation "will be unable to pay" the costs within the meaning of the section if it can only do so if given extended time to realise assets which might be difficult to realise, at least at a price sufficient to provide a surplus over other liabilities, sufficient to pay the costs: see *Southern Cross Exploration NL v Fire & All Risks Insurance Co Ltd* (1985) 1 NSWLR 114 at 121. The company will also be unable to pay the costs within the meaning of the section if the

payment would be one that will amount to a preference of the defendant over other creditors such that the payment would be liable to be set aside either as a preference or as a fraudulent disposition (that is a payment made by the plaintiff corporation with the intention to defeat or delay one or more other creditors) in the event of the plaintiff corporation later going into liquidation.' *Beach Petroleum NL v Johnson* (1992) 7 ACSR 203 at 205, per von Doussan J

UNABLE TO SERVE

[Under CPR 7.6(1) a claimant may apply for an order extending the period within which the claim form may be served. CPR 7.6(2) provides that the general rule is that an application to extend the time for service must be made (a) within the period for serving the claim form specified by r 7.5; or (b) where an order has been made under r 7.6, within the period for service specified by that order. Under CPR 7.6(3), if the claimant applies for an order to extend the time for service of the claim form after the end of the period specified by r 7.5 or by an order made under r 7.6, the court may make such an order only if (a) the court has been 'unable to serve' the claim form; or (b) the claimant has taken all reasonable steps to serve the claim form but has been unable to do so; and, (c) in either case, the claimant has acted promptly in making the application.] '[29] We conclude, therefore, even without regard to the [Human Rights Act 1998], the words "has been unable to serve" in r 7.6(3)(a) include all cases where the court has failed to serve, including mere oversight on its part. It is therefore unnecessary to consider the position under the 1998 Act. If it had been necessary to do so, we would not have hesitated to adopt what might be considered to be a linguistically strained interpretation in order to read r 7.6(3)(a) in a way which is compatible with art 6 of the European Convention for the Protection of Human Rights and Fundamental Freedoms 1950 (as set out in Pt I of Sch 1 to the 1998 Act), so as to ensure that litigants are not denied access to the courts, where it is the fault of the courts that the claim form has not been served in time.' *Cranfield v Bridgegrove Ltd* [2003] EWCA Civ 656 at [29], [2003] 3 All ER 129, per Dyson LJ

UNCONFINED SURFACE WATER

Australia [The definition of 'waters' in the Clean Waters Act 1970 (NSW) was amended by including swamp, wetlands and 'unconfined surface water'.] 'I understand unconfined surface water to mean surface water whose area is not limited by any significant natural or artificial barrier.' *Genkem Pty Ltd v Environment Protection Authority* (1994) 35 NSWLR 33 at 38, per Gleeson CJ

UNCONSCIONABLE BARGAIN

[For 18 Halsbury's Laws (4th edn) para 344 see now 31 Halsbury's Laws (4th edn) (2003 Reissue) para 854.]

UNCONSCIONABLE. *SEE*
UNCONSCIONABLE CONDUCT

UNCONSCIONABLE CONDUCT

Australia [Section 51AA(1) of the Trade Practices Act 1974 (Cth) provides that a 'corporation must not, in trade or commerce, engage in conduct that is unconscionable within the meaning of the unwritten law, from time to time, of the States and Territories.'] 'It may be seen from the preceding that the concept of unconscionable conduct "within the meaning of the unwritten law" is presently confined in its operation by reference to specific doctrines. Nevertheless the cases indicate that its use is a matter of taxonomy which may be subject to substantial change. As Hardingham has suggested:

> "... the boundaries between traditional heads of intervention against unconscionable behaviour – specifically between common law duress and actual undue influence or pressure, between presumed undue influence and unconscionable dealing as such – are shifting. Lines of demarcation are not now as clearly defined as they may have been in the past. As a consequence, the traditional heads themselves may be ready for some redefinition or rationalise." – [Hardingham, "Unconscionable Dealing" in Finn (ed), *Essays on Equity* (1985) LBC] at p 2

'[21] In considering the contention that "unconscionable conduct within the meaning of the unwritten law" in s 51AA refers to some kind of legal dictionary, it is important to observe that it has no settled technical meaning. It is, as Mahoney JA said [in *Antonovic v Volker* (1986) 7 NSWLR 151 at 165], "better described than defined". It offers a standard determined by judicial decision-making rather than a rule, albeit it may for the present be subject to limitation in its factual field of operation by the existence of specific doctrines.' *Australian Competition and Consumer Commission v C G Berbatis Holdings Pty Ltd* (2000) 169 ALR 324; (2000) ATPR 41–755; BC200000015; [2000] FCA 2 at [20], [21], per French J

Australia 'The unconscionable conduct prohibited by s 51AC has not been considered to be limited by reference to "specific equitable doctrines": *Australian Competition & Consumer Commission v Berbatis Holdings Pty Ltd* (2000) 169 ALR 324 at 335 per French J; *Australian Competition & Consumer Commission v Simply No-Knead (Franchising) Pty Ltd* [2000] FCA 1365 at [31]. And in *Hurley v McDonald's Australia Ltd* (2000) ATPR 41–741 at 40,585 a Full Court of this Court (Heerey, Drummond and Emmett JJ) said that whatever "unconscionable" means in ss 51AB and 51AC, the term carries the dictionary meaning namely actions "'showing no regard for conscience' or that are 'irreconcilable with what is right or reasonable' — *Qantas Airways Ltd v Cameron* (1996) 66 FCR 246 at 262. The various synonyms used in relation to the term 'unconscionable' import a pejorative moral judgment — *Qantas Airways Ltd v Cameron* ... at 283–4 and 298'." Whilst the circumstances of the consumer no doubt remain relevant under s 51AC, the focus would appear to be upon the conduct of the supplier.' *Australian Competition and Consumer Commission v Oceana Commercial Pty Ltd* [2003] FCA 1516 at [336] per Kiefel J; BC200307835

UNCROPPED

Canada [Non-conforming use for non-agricultural purposes was not available in respect of 'uncropped' land.] "'To leave land uncropped" means "not to cultivate land for the purpose of obtaining a crop from it". This is what happens, for example, when land is left fallow so that it can rest and regenerate, although it may cease to be cultivated for other reasons. Eventually, land that is no longer cultivated will be covered with vegetation ...

'The English expression "to leave land uncropped" suggests essentially that the land not being cultivated is nevertheless suitable for agriculture ... Accordingly, I believe that "uncropped" and *"sous couverture vegetale"* are expressions which both mean "covered by vegetation".' *Veilleux v Quebec (CPTA)* [1989] 1 SCR 839 at 857–858, SCC, per Beetz J

UNDER

Australia [The court considered whether the Curtin University of Technology was established 'by' the Curtin University of Technology Act 1966 (WA) rather than 'under' it]. 'While in particular contexts [a distinction between "by" and "under"] may be made, there are also contexts where "by" and "under" have the same meaning. For example, both "by" and "under" are commonly used in contexts where the meaning is "pursuant to" or "in accordance with".

'While the word "under" has a primary meaning in the sense of denoting a position beneath or below something which is overhead or above or covered by it, it also has a meaning as an adverb implying covered by or in accordance with some regulative power or principle: *Shorter Oxford English Dictionary* (3rd Ed) Vol II, 2290.

'The word "under" as an adverb also has a meaning in denoting a state or condition including in the sense of denoting inclusion in a group, category or class. Thus the reference to "a member, officer or employee of any ... corporation ... established under a written law" identifies a corporation as one member of a class of various bodies established under a written law ... In this context it matters not that the University was in terms established as a body corporate "by" the Act, as distinct from "under" the Act in the general sense, as it is clear from the definition in the Act that "under" was being used as an equivalent to "by" in the relevant sense. That sense is roughly the equivalent to "in accordance with" or "pursuant to". For example, "by and with" is described in *A Dictionary of Modern Legal Usage* (Oxford 2nd Edn) at 124 as follows:

> "by and with is a classic legal REDUN-DANCY with but one legitimate use: 'For appointments to constitutional offices the phrase by and with the advice of the Senate is a TERM OF ART and should not be changed.' Reed Dickenson Legislative Drafting 75 n 4 (1954)."

'The terms "by law" and "under law" are regarded as synonymous: ibid at 897. The word "under",

like "by", is used in the sense of inclusion in a class or category or "in accordance with some regulatory power or principle": *Shorter Oxford English Dictionary* (3rd Ed) Vol II at 2290. Another example is a warrant "under" the King's "own hand": ibid; and see *The Macquarie Dictionary* (3rd Ed) at 229 where the meanings of "under" include "in accordance with" law.' *R v Tkacz* BC200107679; (2001) 25 WAR 77; [2001] WASCA 391 at [23]–[26], per Malcolm CJ

Australia 'Dictionaries give the relevant definition as "in accordance with" (*The New Shorter Oxford English Dictionary* (1993), 16b; *The Macquarie Dictionary* (1988), 16). Meanings recognised as possibilities in the cases include "in accordance with" (*Gilbert v Western Australia* (1962) 107 CLR 494 at 516), "pursuant to" and "by virtue of" (*R v Clyne; Ex parte Harrap* [1941] VLR 200 at 201 per O'Bryan J) and "by" (*R v Tkacz* (2001) 25 WAR 77 at [23]–[26] per Malcolm CJ). The word "under" admits of degrees of precision and exactness on the one hand, and of looseness and inexactness on the other.' *Energy Resources of Australia Ltd v Cmr of Taxation* (2003) ATC 4024; 52 ATR 120; BC200300062; [2003] FCA 26 at [37], per Lindgren J

UNDER A DISABILITY

New Zealand [Sections 2(2), 2(3) and 24(a) of the Limitation Act 1950.] 'The expression "under a disability" has a particular although not precise meaning in law, well conveyed by the second of the meanings of "disability" in *The Oxford English Dictionary* (2nd ed, 1989) "2. Incapacity in the eye of the law, or created by the law; a restriction framed to prevent any person or class of persons from sharing in duties or privileges which would otherwise be open to them; legal disqualification". See *Re Carew* [1896] 2 Ch 311, where Lindley LJ gave as examples under the law of that time bankruptcy, conviction for felony, attainder for treason and lunacy. At times, statutes have contained their own definition, such as that in the Naturalization Act 1870 (UK): "the status of being an infant, lunatic, idiot or married woman". But times change, and today the only complete disabilities imposed by law are infancy and unsoundness of mind. To a limited extent, an undischarged bankrupt and certain inmates of penal institutions may be said to be under a disability, but not one that could affect their ability to sue for damages for personal injury.

'Thus while subss (2) and (3) of s 2 of the Limitation Act do not purport to give an exhaustive definition of "under a disability", it is unlikely that in the context of that Act the expression now goes beyond the two deemed circumstances, infancy and unsoundness of mind. In *Matai Industries Ltd v Jensen* [1989] 1 NZLR 525 Tipping J held that it does not include a company in receivership "legally capable of suing but unlikely to be able to do so" (p 541). It certainly does not extend to physical disability, or a mental inability or incapacity short of unsoundness of mind.' *T v H* [1995] 3 NZLR 37 at 48, CA, per Hardie Boys J

UNDER WAY

[For 43 Halsbury's Laws (4th edn) para 884 see now 43(1) Halsbury's Laws (4th edn) (Reissue) para 805.]

UNDERGROUND STRATA

[The Water Resources Act 1963 has been repealed. The definition is now contained in the Water Resources Act 1991, s 221(1), as follows.] 'Underground Strata' means strata subjacent to the surface of any land.

UNDERTAKING

[The Radioactive Substances Act 1960 has been repealed. The definition is re-enacted in the Radioactive Substances Act 1993, s 47(1).]

UNDERWRITING

[For 7 Halsbury's Laws (4th edn) para 190 see now 7(1) Halsbury's Laws (4th edn) (2004 Reissue) para 577.]

UNDESIRABLE

New Zealand [Companies Act 1955, s 32B(1)(b).] '[A] proper approach to an application of the modified s 31 test for "undesirability" properly involves the question whether it is undesirable:

because its use would contravene an enactment; or

because it is identical to, or almost identical to, the name of another company or name reserved for another company; or

because, in the opinion of the Registrar, it is offensive; or

because there is some other exceptional circumstance which would make use of the name undesirable.'

New Zealand Conference of Seventh-Day Adventists v Registrar of Companies [1997] 1 NZLR 751 at 758, per Fisher J

UNDUE

Canada 'While "undue" is a word of common usage which does not have a precise technical meaning the Supreme Court has variously defined "undue" to mean "improper, inordinate, excessive or oppressive" or to express "a notion of seriousness or significance." To this list of synonyms, the *Concise Oxford Dictionary of Current English* adds "disproportionate."

'What is clear from all of these terms is that "undueness" is a relative concept. I agree with the position expressed by Cartwright J, as he then was:

"Undue" and "unduly" are not absolute terms whose meaning is self-evident. Their use pre-supposes the existence of a rule or standard defining what is "due". Their interpretation does not appear to me to be assisted by substituting the adjectives "improper", "inordinate", "excessive", "oppressive" or "wrong", or the corresponding adverbs, in the absence of a statement as to what, in this connection, is proper, ordinate, permissible or right.

'The proper approach to determining if something is "undue", then, is a contextual one. Undue-ness must be defined in light of the aim of the relevant enactment. It can be useful to assess the consequences or effect if the undue thing is allowed to remain in place.

'The Supreme Court has also recognized that the term implies a requirement to balance the interests of the various parties. In a case dealing with whether an employer had accommodated an employee's right to exercise his religious beliefs up to the point of undue hardship, Wilson J, writing for the majority, found it helpful to list some of the factors relevant to such an appraisal. She concluded by stating: "This list is not intended to be exhaustive and the results which will be obtained from a balancing of these factors against the right of the employee to be free of discrimination will necessarily vary from case to case." ' *VIA Rail Canada Inc. v Canada (National Transportation Agency)* (2000) 193 DLR (4th) 357 at 367, FCA, per Sexton JA

Canada '[15] Tribunal Chairperson Barton, who delivered both of the Tribunal's decisions, found that the word "undue" in paragraph 138(2)(*a*) of the Regulations had the same meaning as the word "excessive". In support of this interpretation, Tribunal Chairperson Barton relied on a dictionary definition, without giving the reader any specific reference. The following is the relevant passage from the decisions [at paragraph 8]:

> [TRANSLATION] According to the dictionary definition, the word "undue" means "excessive".

...

'[17] In my opinion, the interpretation of the word "undue"and consequently of the words "undue suffering" adopted by the Tribunal is wrong. Although it appears from the dictionary definitions (to which I will refer later) that the words "undue" and "*indu[e]*" may, in certain circumstances, have the same meaning as the word "excessive", I am of the opinion that this is not the case in this instance.

...

'[21] According to Tribunal Chairperson Barton, therefore, demonstrating that the animal was suffering before being loaded and that it would continue to suffer during its transportation does not constitute sufficient evidence to conclude that the respondents' conduct was in breach of paragraph 138(2)(*a*). The interpretation proposed by Tribunal Chairperson Barton would, in my opinion, allow the loading and transportation of suffering animals.

'[22] Here are a few definitions from English and French dictionaries of the words "undue" and "*indu[e]*" used in the English and French versions of paragraph 138(2)(*a*) of the Regulations. *Le Nouveau Petit Robert: dictionnaire alphabétique et analogique de la langue française*, Paris: Dictionnaires Le Robert, 1993, defines "*indu[e]*" in these words:

> *Qui va à l'encontre des exigences de la raison, de la règle, de l'usage ... où il ne convient pas de faire telle ou telle chose ... Qui n'est pas fondé ... Ce qui n'est pas dû ... CONTR. Convenable, normal, régulier. Dû.*

According to the *Dictionnaire des synonymes et antonymes*, Hector Dupuis and Romain Légaré, Québec: Éditions Fides, 2003, the word "*indu*" means:

> *Indu: Syn. 1. Inapproprié, inconvénient, inopportun. 2. Infondé, injustifié. Ant. Approprié, convenable, opportun, fondé, justifié.*

As for *Thésaurus Larousse*, Paris: Larousse, 1999, it defines "*indu*" as follows:

> *Inopportun; déplacé, déraisonnable, fâcheux, importun, incongru, indu, intempestif, maladroit, malencontreux; malvenu, prématuré, saugrenu: – Hors de saison; hors de propos; mal choisi; à côté de la plaque.*

According to *Roget's International Thesaurus*, 5th ed., HarperCollins Publishers, 1992, the word "undue" means:

> UNDUE: overpriced, wrong, unowed, unjust, excessive.
>
> **Undue, unowed, unowing**, not coming, not outstanding; **undeserved, unmerited**, unearned; **unwarranted, unjustified**, unprovoked; unentitled, undeserving, unmeriting, nonmeritorious, unworthy; preposterous, outrageous.

The *Oxford English Dictionary*, 2nd ed., 1989, defines the word "undue" as follows:

> **Undue**: 1. Not properly owing or payable 2. Not appropriate or suitable, improper. Also of times, etc. Unseasonable 3. Not in accordance with what is just and right; unjustifiable; illegal.

The *Oxford Compact Thesaurus*, 2nd ed., Oxford University Press, 2001, page 913, defines the word "undue" as follows:

> UNDUE adj. = excessive, immoderate, intemperate, inordinate, disproportionate, uncalled for, unneeded, unnecessary, non-essential, needless, unwarranted, unjustified, unreasonable, inappropriate, unmerited, unsuitable, improper.

According to the *Dictionary of Synonyms and Antonyms*, Oxford University Press, 1999, the word "undue" is defined as follows:

> UNDUE adj. = excessive.

'[23] From these definitions, it appears that only the *Dictionary of Synonyms and Antonyms* confines itself to defining the word "undue" as meaning "excessive".

'[24] The applicant is asking that we reject the Tribunal's interpretation and adopt the meaning of the word "undue" which, in his opinion, is the most reasonable, namely: [TRANSLATION] "which is contrary to reason, rules or usage". The applicant characterizes the words "undue suffering" as meaning [TRANSLATION] "unnecessary suffering". This interpretation, he argues, is consistent with the objectives and scheme of the *Health of Animals Act*, S.C. 1990, c. 21. The applicant notes that the Regulations, and more particularly paragraph 138(2)(*a*), were adopted by the Governor in Council under paragraph 64(1)(*i*) of the *Health of Animals Act*, which provides:

> **64.**(1) The Governor in Council may make regulations for the purpose of protecting human and animal health through the control or elimination of diseases and toxic substances and generally for carrying out the purposes and provisions of this Act, including regulations
>
> ...
>
> (*i*) for the humane treatment of animals and generally
>
>> (i) governing the care, handling and disposition of animals,
>>
>> (ii) governing the manner in which animals are transported within, into or out of Canada, and
>>
>> (iii) providing for the treatment or disposal of animals that are not cared for, handled or transported in a humane manner; [Emphasis added.]

'[25] Based on these provisions, the applicant submits that the clear purpose of the Regulations is, *inter alia*, to protect the health of animals. Accordingly, he says, paragraph 138(2)(*a*) cannot be interpreted in such a way as to allow the transportation of suffering animals.

'[26] In my opinion, the applicant's arguments are well founded. It does not seem reasonable to me to interpret the words "undue" and "*indu[e]*" as meaning "excessive" and "*excessif*". In my opinion, a reasonable interpretation of undue" and "*indu[e]*", in the context of the relevant legislation, can only lead to the conclusion that these words mean instead "undeserved", "unwarranted", "unjustified", "unmerited" or "*inappro-prié*", "*inopportun*", "*injustifié*", "*déraisonnable*". This interpretation ensures that a suffering animal cannot be loaded and transported, since any such loading or transportation will cause "unjustified" and "unreasonable" suffering to the animal. It is appropriate to recall that Dr. Villeneuve, in his written observations, stated that the hog had [TRANSLATION] "an open fracture with a lot of necrosis of the skin, muscle and bone tissue." In Dr. Villeneuve's opinion, the owner of the animal "displayed negligence and cruelty toward this animal".

'[27] I conclude, therefore, that the transportation of an injured (and therefore suffering) animal could only cause unjustifiable or inappropriate suffering to that animal. Using the English text of paragraph 138(2)(*a*) of the Regulations, the suffering that will be caused to the animal while being transported will be "unjustified" or "unwarranted".'

Canada (AG) v Porcherie des CEDRES Inc (2005) 254 DLR (4th) 676 at [15], [17], [21]–[27], [2005] 3 FCR 539, [2005] FCJ No 273 (Fed CA), per Nadon JA

UNDUE COERCION

Australia [Section 60 of the Trade Practices Act 1974 (Cth) states that a 'corporation shall not use physical force or undue harassment or coercion in connection with the supply or possible supply of goods or services to a consumer or the payment for goods or services by a consumer'.] 'The word "coercion" is defined in the Shorter Oxford English Dictionary thus:

> "1. The action of coercing; constraint, re-straint, compulsion.
> 2. Government by force; the employment of force to suppress political disaffection and disorder.
> 3. Physical pressure; compression.
> 4. Coercitive power or jurisdiction."

'The verb "coerce" is defined as:

> "1. To constrain or restrain by force, or by authority resting on force.
> 2. To subject to restraint in the matter of (rare) 1780.
> 3. To effect by compulsion."

'The collection of debts may involve coercion in the sense that the debtor is subjected to the pressure of the demand and the legitimate threat of civil process for recovery with the additional cost and damage to credit which that can involve. Such pressure may be thought of as coercion but is entirely legitimate and not "undue". Where the demand includes content which does not serve legitimate purposes of reminding the debtor of the obligation and threatening legal proceedings for recovery but is calculated otherwise to intimidate or threaten the debtor, then the coercion may be undue. So if a threat is made of criminal proceedings, or of the immediate seizure and sale of house and property, a remedy not available in the absence of retention of title or some form of security, the coercion is likely to be seen as undue. The threat of criminal proceedings itself may be an offence against State laws. Quite apart from content the manner or circumstances of a demand or communication, including the language used, the time and place at which it is made and the person to whom it is communicated, may go beyond the legitimate purposes of drawing attention to the existence of the obligation and the consequences for non-compliance. Again such a communication may amount to undue coercion. Obvious examples include the use of personally abusive or obscene language, conveying the demand to uninvolved family members, particularly children, or conveying the demand through a third party in order to embarrass the debtor when the debtor could reasonably have been the subject of a direct communication. Each case will turn on its own facts. Some useful examples of situations that may give rise to contraventions of s 60 are set out in the ACCC guidelines entitled "Debt Collection and the Trade Practices Act" published in July 1999. As pointed out of course that publication is not a statement of the law. It can only be a guide. The recovery of unpaid debts can be pursued with firmness, determination and civility. It can do all those things without resorting to bullying, bluff, misrepresentation or stand-over tactics. If it does the first and avoids the second it is unlikely to contravene the law.' *Australian Competition and Consumer Commission v McCaskey* (2000) 104 FCR 8; BC200004335; [2000] FCA 1037 at [50]–[51], per French J

UNDUE DELAY

Australia [Section 212 of the Customs Act 1901 (Cth) provides that every person arrested may be detained until such time as he can without 'undue delay' be taken before a justice.] 'So far as s 212 of the Customs Act is concerned, the section recognises that there may be a delay so long as it is not undue. Inevitably there will be an interval of time between the arrest of a person and the bringing of that person before a justice. It may be short or it may be long, depending on the circumstances. In ordinary language that does not necessarily constitute a delay because the term has a pejorative overtone of putting something off. But, as the section and its counterparts have been interpreted over the years, undue delay should be seen as a composite expression which accepts that there may be an interval of time before a person is brought before a justice, so long as the lapse of time which ensues is not excessive in the circumstances. Undue delay has been treated as synonymous with the statutory expressions "as soon as is practicable" in s 34A (1) of the Justices Act 1959 (Tas) and "without delay" in s 303(1) of the Criminal Code (Tas) respectively and with the common law expression "as soon as is reasonably possible": [*Re Williams* (1986) 161 CLR 278 at 300, 313].' *Re Michaels* (1995) 80 A Crim R 542 at 545, per Brennan, Deane, Toohey and McHugh JJ

New Zealand [Section 25(b) of the New Zealand Bill of Rights Act 1990 provides "Everyone who is charged with an offence has, in relation to the determination of the charge, the following minimum rights: ...(b) The right to be tried without undue delay."] ' "Undue delay" cannot be defined, and although broad principles governing the application of the subsection are being and will continue to be established, it must always be the evaluation of the particular case which is determinative. What is an undue lapse of time in one set of circumstances may not be undue in another. There are necessarily a varying number of factors contributing to the lapse of time from arrest to trial which we think render it impossible to lay down a general time framework.' *R v B* [1996] 1 NZLR 385 at 387, CA, per cur

UNDUE HARASSMENT

Australia [Section 60 of the Trade Practices Act 1974 (Cth) states that a 'corporation shall not use physical force or undue harassment or coercion in connection with the supply or possible supply of goods or services to a consumer or the payment for goods or services by a consumer.'] 'The words of [s 60] are to be given their ordinary meanings relevant to the context in which they appear. The term "harass" as defined in the new Shorter Oxford English Dictionary derives from the French "harasser", a pejorative derivation of the word "harer" meaning "to set a dog upon". The definitions of the word are thus:

> "1. Trouble by repeated attacks. Now Freq; subject to constant molesting or persecution.
> 2. Lay waste, devastate.
> 3. Tire out, exhaust.
> 4. Overwhelm with cares and misfortunes etc – Chiefly as harassed."

'The meaning of primary relevance here is the first, but it is important to have regard to context in considering its application in s 60... Certainly it is consistent with the ordinary meaning of "harass" as involving an element of repetition to speak of a harassed state of mind arising out of one or more events – *Johnston v Collier* (1997) 142 FLR 409 at 412 (Anderson J). But there, "harassed" is used in the fourth of the defined meanings and relates to the state of mind of a person induced by an event or events none of them necessarily amounting to harassment. A person can feel harassed because something has gone wrong for which nobody is to blame.

'The word "harassment" as used in s 60 must serve two broad purposes. It describes a range of conduct, in connection with the supply of goods or services which involve, inter alia, applying repeated pressure to a consumer who is under no pre-existing obligation to acquire. It also describes conduct in relation to a consumer who is under an unfulfilled obligation to pay for goods or services. Given the range of cases that it can cover, the question whether or not there is harassment involves evaluative judgment. The word "undue" adds an extra layer of evaluation which is more relevant to the case of debt recovery than to the sale of goods or services. Repeated unwelcome approaches to a potential acquirer of goods or services could qualify as harassment and, so qualified, require very little additional evidence, if any, to attract the characterisation of "undue harassment". On the other hand a consumer who owes money to a supplier can expect repeated unwelcome approaches requesting payment of the debt if he or she does not pay. No doubt such approaches might also qualify as harassment. If legitimate demands are reasonably made, on more than one occasion, for the purpose of reminding the debtor of his or her obligation and drawing the debtor's attention to the likelihood of legal proceedings if payment is not made, then that conduct, if it be harassment, is not undue harassment. If, however, the frequency, nature or content of the approaches and communications associated with them is such that they are calculated to intimidate or demoralise, tire out or exhaust a debtor rather than convey the demand and an associated legitimate threat of proceedings, the harassment will be undue.' *Australian Competition and Consumer Commission v McCaskey* (2000) 104 FCR 8; BC200004335; [2000] FCA 1037 at [47]–[48], per French J

Australia [Section 60 of the Trade Practices Act 1974 (Cth) provides that a 'corporation shall not use physical force or undue harassment or coercion in connection with the supply or possible supply of goods or services to a consumer or the payment for goods or services by a consumer'.] 'The word "harassment" in my view connotes conduct which can be less serious than conduct which amounts to coercion. The word "harassment" means in the present context persistent disturbance or torment. In the case of a person employed to recover money owing to others, as was the first respondent in *Australian Competition and Consumer Commission v McCaskey* (2000) 104 FCR 8, it can extend to cases where there are frequent unwelcome approaches requesting payment of a debt. However, such unwelcome approaches

would not constitute undue harassment, at least where the demands made are legitimate and reasonably made. On the other hand where the frequency, nature or content of such communications is such that they are calculated to intimidate or demoralise, tire out or exhaust a debtor, rather than merely to convey the demand for recovery, the conduct will constitute undue harassment (see per French J in *McCaskey* at [48]). Generally it can be said that a person will be harassed by another when the former is troubled repeatedly by the latter. The reasonableness of the conduct will be relevant to whether what is harassment constitutes undue harassment. Like French J in *McCaskey* at [47] I get little assistance from cases in the context of sexual harassment where the word has almost taken on a technical meaning.

...

'It is clear that the word "undue" suggests that what is done must, having regard to the circumstances in which the conduct occurs, extend beyond that which is acceptable or reasonable. It thus adds, as French J observes at [48] in *Australian Competition and Consumer Commission v McCaskey* (2000) 104 FCR 8, "an extra layer of evaluation". The word "undue", when used in relation to harassment, ensures that conduct which amounts to harassment will only amount to a contravention of the section where what is done goes beyond the normal limits which, in the circumstances, society would regard as acceptable or reasonable and not excessive or disproportionate ... I am of the view that qualitatively the word "undue" adds the quality of unreasonableness, unacceptability or lack of proportionality to the general concept of harassment.' *Australian Competition and Consumer Commission v Maritime Union of Australia* (2001) 187 ALR 487; (2002) ATPR ¶41–849; BC200106710; [2001] FCA 1549 at [60], [62], per Hill J

UNDUE INFLUENCE

'Undue influence is of two kinds: (1) express or, as it is nowadays more usually known, actual undue influence; and (2) that which in certain circumstances is presumed from a confidential relationship, by which in this context is meant a relationship wherein one party has ceded such a degree of trust and confidence as to require the other, on grounds of public policy, to show that it has not been betrayed or abused. In cases where there is no confidential relationship actual undue influence must be proved. In cases where there is such a relationship it is sometimes alleged, but need not be proved and may never have occurred ... At least since the time of Lord Eldon LC, equity has steadfastly and wisely refused to put limits on the relationships to which the presumption can apply. Nor do I believe that it has ever been distinctly held that there is any relationship from which it cannot in any circumstances be dissociated. But there are several well-defined relationships, such as parent and child, superior and member of a sisterhood, doctor and patient and solicitor and client, to which the presumption is, as it were, presumed to apply unless the contrary is proved. In such relationships it would seem that you only have to look at the relative status of the parties in order to presume that the requisite degree of trust and confidence is there. But there are many and various other relationships lacking a recognisable status to which the presumption has been held to apply. In all of these relationships, whether of the first kind or the second, the principle is the same. It is that the degree of trust and confidence is such that the party in whom it is reposed, either because he is or has become an adviser of the other or because he has been entrusted with the management of his affairs or everyday needs or for some other reason, is in a position to influence him into effecting the transaction of which complaint is later made.' *Goldsworthy v Brickell* [1987] 1 All ER 853 at 865, CA, per Nourse LJ

'To make a good will a man must be a free agent. But all influences are not unlawful. Persuasion, appeals to the affections or ties of kindred, to a sentiment of gratitude for past services, or pity for future destitution, or the like, these are all legitimate, and may be fairly pressed on a testator. On the other hand, pressure of whatever character, whether acting on the fears or the hopes, if so exerted as to overpower the volition without convincing the judgment, is a species of restraint under which no valid will can be made. Importunity or threats, such as the testator has not the courage to resist, moral command asserted and yielded to for the sake of peace and quiet, or of escaping from distress of mind or social discomfort, these, if carried to a degree in which the free play of the testator's judgment, discretion or wishes, is overborne, will constitute undue influence, though no force is either used or threatened. In a word, a testator may be led but not driven; and his will must be the offspring of his own volition, and not the record of someone else's.' *Hall v Hall* (1868) LR 1 P & D 481 at 482, per cur

[See also *Re T*, [1992] 4 All ER 649, CA.]

'Leaving aside proof of manifest disadvantage, we think that a person relying on a plea of actual undue influence must show: (a) that the other party to the transaction (or someone who induced the transaction for his own benefit) had the capacity to influence the complainant; (b) that the influence was exercised; (c) that its exercise was undue; (d) that its exercise brought about the transaction.' *Bank of Credit and Commerce International SA v Aboody* [1992] 4 All ER 955 at 976 CA, per cur

'A person who has been induced to enter into a transaction by the undue influence of another (the wrongdoer) is entitled to set that transaction aside as against the wrongdoer. Such undue influence is either actual or presumed. In *Bank of Credit and Commerce International SA v Aboody* [1988] 4 All ER 955 at 964, [1990] 1 QB 923 at 953 the Court of Appeal helpfully adopted the following classification.

Class 1: actual undue influence. In these cases it is necessary for the claimant to prove affirmatively that the wrongdoer exerted undue influence on the complainant to enter into the particular transaction which is impugned.

Class 2: presumed undue influence. In these cases the complainant only has to show, in the first instance, that there was a relationship of trust and confidence between the complainant and the wrongdoer of such a nature that it is fair to presume that the wrongdoer abused that relationship in procuring the complainant to enter into the impugned transaction. In class 2 cases therefore there is no need to produce evidence that actual undue influence was exerted in relation to the particular transaction impugned: once a confidential relationship has been proved, the burden then shifts to the wrongdoer to prove that the complainant entered into the impugned transaction freely, for example by showing that the complainant had independent advice. Such a confidential relationship can be established in two ways, viz:

Class 2A. Certain relationships (for example solicitor and client, medical advisor and patient) as a matter of law raise the presumption that undue influence has been exercised.

Class 2B. Even if there is no relationship falling within class 2A, if the complainant proves the de facto existence of a relationship under which the complainant generally reposed trust and confidence in the wrongdoer, the existence of such relationship raises the presumption of undue influence. In a class 2B case therefore, in the absence of evidence disproving undue influence, the complainant will succeed in setting aside the impugned transaction merely by proof that the complainant reposed trust and confidence in the wrongdoer without having to prove that the wrongdoer exerted actual undue influence or otherwise abused such trust and confidence in relation to the particular transaction impugned.' *Barclays Bank plc v O'Brien* [1993] 4 All ER 417 at 423, HL, per Lord Browne-Wilkinson

[For 9 Halsbury's Laws (4th edn) para 298 see now 9(1) Halsbury's Laws (4th edn) (Reissue) para 712.]

[For 16 Halsbury's Laws (4th edn) para 1227 see now 16(2) Halsbury's Laws (4th edn) (Reissue) para 417.]

[For 17 Halsbury's Laws (4th edn) para 911 see now 17(2) Halsbury's Laws (4th edn) (Reissue) para 323.]

[For 18 Halsbury's Laws (4th edn) para 330 see now 31 Halsbury's Laws (4th edn) (2003 Reissue) para 839.]

UNENCLOSED

Australia [Pastoral leases granted under the Land Regulations (WA) and the Land Act 1933 (WA) reserved to Aboriginal people rights to enter upon 'unenclosed or enclosed but otherwise unimproved', and 'unenclosed and unimproved' parts of the lease.] 'To "enclose" means "(1) to shut in: close in on all sides; (2) to surround as with a fence or wall: *to enclose land* ..." (*The Macquarie Concise Dictionary*, 3rd ed). The meaning of "enclosed" is to be ascertained having regard both to the reservation in favour of Aborigines, and the reservation in respect of the right of any person to pass over unenclosed, or enclosed but otherwise unimproved land with or without horses, stock or vehicles (the reservation now contained in s 106(1)(f) [of the Land Act 1933 (WA)]). In that reservation we think it is clear that "unenclosed" means unfenced so that entry with or without horses, stock or vehicles is unrestricted, and "enclosed" means "fenced".' *Western Australia v Ward* (2000) 170 ALR 159; BC200000641; [2000] FCA 191 at [321], per Beaumont and von Doussa JJ

UNFAIRNESS

Australia 'The term "unfairness" necessarily lacks precision; it involves an evaluation of circumstances. But one thing is clear: "[T]he question is not whether the police have acted unfairly; the question is whether it would be unfair to the accused to use his statement against him ... Unfairness, in this sense, is concerned with the accused's right to a

fair trial, a right which may be jeopardised if a statement is obtained in circumstances which affect the reliability of the statement." [*Van der Meer v The Queen* (1988) 82 ALR 10 at 26; 62 ALJR 656 per Wilson, Dawson and Toohey JJ]. Unfairness then relates to the right of an accused to a fair trial; in that situation the unfairness discretion overlaps with the power or discretion to reject evidence which is more prejudicial than probative, each looking to the risk that an accused may be improperly convicted. While unreliability may be a touchstone of unfairness, it has been said not to be the sole touchstone. It may be, for instance, that no confession might have been made at all, had the police investigation been properly conducted. And once considerations other than unreliability are introduced, the line between unfairness and policy may become blurred.' *R v Swaffield* (1998) 192 CLR 159 at 189–190; 151 ALR 98 at 117, 118; 72 ALJR 339; 96 A Crim R 96; BC9800011, per Toohey, Gaudron and Gummow JJ

UNIMPROVED LAND

Canada 'The leases list four factors in the rent review section which are to be taken into account in determining the "current land value." Clause 2(2)(a) requires that one assume that the lands are "unimproved lands in the same state as they were on the date of this agreement". The Band cross-appeals on the meaning of "this agreement" and on whether "unimproved" means simply without buildings or whether it means without services as well. If the latter, some amount must be deducted from the "current land value" notionally to return the land to its unserviced condition.

'The debate in the courts below about whether "this agreement" refers to the Master Agreement or to the leases turns out to be irrelevant, given my decision on the meaning of "unimproved" land. On the basis of the plain meaning of the word "unimproved" and of its use in the leases, I conclude that "unimproved lands" means "unserviced" lands, not just lands without buildings. As the Federal Court of Appeal noted, *"Black's Law Dictionary*, 6th ed, (at page 757) defines 'improved land' as '(r)eal estate whose value has been increased by landscaping and the addition of sewers, roads, utilities, and the like'. Similarly, the term 'improvement' generally refers 'to buildings, but may also include any permanent structure or other development, such as a street, sidewalks, sewers, utilities, etc.'" (para 87). In *Re Planet Parking Ltd and Assessment Commissioner of Metropolitan*

Toronto, [1970] 3 OR 657 (HC), the court found that the word "unimproved" in the context of the *Assessment Act* related to the "ordinary and natural" meaning of "improvement" as in "making … better" (p 661). The court rejected "the contention that unimproved land as distinguished from improved land means land without buildings erected thereupon" (p 662).

'In the Musqueam leases, the word "improvement" is used to refer to things other than buildings. Clause 8(a), for example, refers to "any buildings … and … such other improvements, including construction of roads, water, sewer, electricity and/or gas systems". Similar phrases are found throughout the leases. Improvements include services, and conversely "unimproved" means without services. The internal coherence of the rent review clause also supports the view that "unimproved" means unserviced. The leases were signed before any buildings were built, so the word "unimproved" would have added nothing to the phrase "unimproved lands in the same state as they were on the date of this agreement" unless it referred to the pre-existing servicing.' *Musqueam Indian Band v Glass* (2000) 192 DLR (4th) 385 at 406–407, SCC, per Bastarache J

UNIT TRUST

[For 45 Halsbury's Laws (4th edn) para 65 see now 45(1) Halsbury's Laws (4th edn) (Reissue) para 65.]

UNJUST OR OPRRESSIVE OR TOO SEVERE A PUNISHMENT

Australia [Under reg 7 of the Extradition (Commonwealth Countries) Regulations (Cth), the Attorney-General, when considering the surrender of a person in relation to an extradition offence, must be satisfied that the surrender is not 'unjust or oppressive or too severe a punishment'.] 'At least for most purposes, the words "unjust or oppressive or too severe a punishment" will be better understood as providing a single description of the relevant criterion which is to be applied rather than as three distinctly different criteria. The use of the disjunctive "or" might suggest the need to consider each element of the expression separately but for several reasons we think it preferable not to approach the provision in that way. First, there is the fact that the terms used are, as we have already said, qualitative descriptions requiring assessment and judgment. Secondly, the use of the words "too severe" suggests a need for comparison with some standard of punishment that is regarded as correct

or just or, at least, not too severe. Thirdly, the considerations which may contribute to the conclusion that something is "unjust" will overlap with those that are taken into account in considering the other two descriptions. It would, then, be artificial to treat the three ideas as rigidly distinct. Each takes its content, in part, from the use of the others.' *Foster v Minister for Customs and Justice* (2000) 200 CLR 442; 173 ALR 585; BC200004310; [2000] HCA 38 at [41], per Gaudron and Hayne JJ

UNJUSTLY BURDENSOME

New Zealand [Credit Contracts Act 1981, s 9.] 'The term "unjustly burdensome" is closer to the Chancery conception of hardship; hardship amounting to injustice.' *Prudential Building and Investment Society of Canterbury v Hankins* [1997] 1 NZLR 114 at 124, per Hammond J

UNLAWFUL

[For further consideration of *R v Chapman* [1958] 3 All ER 143 see *R v R— (rape: marital exemption)* [1991] 4 All ER 481 at 488–489, HL, per Lord Keith of Kinkel.]

Australia 'The word "unlawful" may be used in various senses. Two of these were discussed by Griffith CJ in *Lyons v Smart* [(1908) 6 CLR 143 at 147–8]. His Honour spoke as follows … "Now, the word "unlawfully" is a word commonly used in statutes creating crimes, misdemeanours and minor offences, and in such Acts it is used in two shades of meaning, one when referring to an act which is wrong or wicked in itself—recognised by everybody as wicked—as, for instance, when it is used with reference to certain sexual offences, or with reference to acts which are absolutely prohibited under all circumstances; the other when referring to some prohibition of positive law …"… In *Lyons v Smart*, [(1908) 6 CLR 143 at 155, 160] Barton J and O'Connor J treated the ordinary meaning of an unlawful act as one "forbidden by some definite law", whether statute law or common law … Finally, in his dissenting judgment in *Lyons v Smart* [(1908) 6 CLR 143 at 164], Isaacs J referred to that construction of "unlawfully" as meaning without any bona fide claim of right or colour of justification.' *Wik Peoples v Queensland* (1996) 141 ALR 129 at 239–240; 71 ALJR 173, per Gummow J

UNLAWFUL ACT

New Zealand 'The expression "unlawful act" in the context of the law of manslaughter is not one upon which the present case calls for any attempt at exhaustive definition; but an unlawful assault intended to cause some, even though minor, physical harm or hurt to the victim is undoubtedly within it.' *R v Renata* [1992] 2 NZLR 346 at 349, CA, per cur

UNLAWFULLY

Australia [Environmental Management and Pollution Control Act 1994 s 53(2) provides: (2) A person who unlawfully causes an environmental nuisance is guilty of an offence.] 'It is common ground that the word "unlawfully" in s 53(2) means "unauthorised or unjustified by law" or "without lawful justification", as distinct from "contrary to law". Wright J took the view that the word "unlawfully" had such a meaning in *Re The Environmental Management and Pollution Control Act 1994* (1999) 8 Tas R 419, and I think he was right in taking that view. Thus, a person who causes an "environmental nuisance" commits an offence if he or she has no lawful authority to do so, even if his or her conduct is not otherwise prohibited or unlawful.' *Gard v Gibsons Ltd* [2004] TASSC 108 at [35], per Blow J; BC200406175

Canada [Accused alleged unconstitutionally of offence of unlawfully causing bodily harm.] '... the most principled approach to the meaning of "unlawful" in the context of s 269 is to require that the unlawful act be at least objectively dangerous. This conclusion is both supported by the meaning given to the word "unlawful act" by virtually all of the lower courts and also is in accord with the emerging jurisprudence of this court in regard to personal fault ...

'Objective foresight of bodily harm should be required for both criminal and non-criminal unlawful acts which underlie a s 269 prosecution. I can see no reason why there should be a difference between the two categories of acts. There is no need to differentiate between criminal and non-criminal unlawful acts when one unifying concept is available. Thus the test is one of objective foresight of bodily harm for all underlying offences. The act must be both unlawful, as described above, *and* one that is likely to subject another person to danger of harm or injury. This bodily harm must be more than merely trivial or transitory in nature and will in most cases involve an act of violence done deliberately to another person. In interpreting what constitutes an objectively dangerous act, the courts should strive to avoid attaching penal sanctions to mere inadvertence.' *R v DeSousa* (1992) 95 DLR (4th) 595 at 608–609, per Sopinka J (Can SC)

Canada ' ... "unlawfully" has been equated with, amongst other things, "without lawful authority" in the sense of absence of parental authority over the child or "without lawful justification, authority or excuse" ...

'It is appropriate to interpret the expression "unlawfully" as meaning "without lawful justification, authority or excuse", as that term is used in s 281 of the Criminal Code [RSC 1985, c C-46]; this interpretation is in accord with the purpose of the section which is to prevent and punish strangers intending to deprive a parent (guardian, etc) of his or her child (the child for whom they act as guardian, etc). To require that an additional unlawful act occur beyond the physical act of taking the child is at cross-purposes with the mischief Parliament wanted to cure; such an interpretation would not adequately achieve the goal of prevention, and the rights of the parents could not be vindicated.' *R v Chartrand* (1994) 116 DLR (4th) 207 at 220–221, SCC, per L'Heureux-Dubé J

UNLICENSED DRIVER

New Zealand [Section 113(2)(e) of the Land Transport Act 1998 provides that 'Without limiting any other powers conferred on an enforcement officer, an enforcement officer, in enforcing any provisions referred to in subsection (1), may at any time—

...

(e) Forbid an unlicensed driver to drive a motor vehicle.]

'[27] The view I take in this case is that the legislation has deliberately or unintentionally, probably the latter, omitted words which would have put their intention beyond doubt. Having regard however to the general words used, I am prepared to find that the broad definition of "unlicensed" covers the situation of someone who has allowed his or her driver licence to expire.

'[28] In doing so, I am doing no more than I am required by law to do, under s 5 of the Interpretation Act 1999, which is to ascertain the meaning of an enactment from its text and in the light of its purpose.

'[29] One of the purposes of this legislation was to reform the rules relating to motor vehicle licensing and to enforce those rules by sanctions which included forbidding people to drive and confiscating their vehicles if they did so. By reference to context and those other matters referred to, all of which I consider fall under s 5(3) of the

Interpretation Act 1999, I have no doubt that expired licence holders were intended to fall into the net. Had the legislation used language inconsistent with or irrelevant to the status of expired licence holders, I would be bound by the text of the statute, but I have no difficulty in bridging the gap caused by omitting precise reference to a category when the general meaning of unlicensed is considered. But for the text of ss 113 and 96 of the Land Transport Act, it is easy enough to equate the status of unlicensed driver with someone whose licence has expired and a new application to obtain a licence is required. No authority was cited to me that could justify or explain any perceivable difference.' *Police v Sinclair* [2001] 1 NZLR 355 at 361, per Heron ACJ

UNOCCUPIED

Australia [A fire insurance policy issued in relation to a dwelling-house owned by the insured provided, inter alia, that the policy would be avoided with respect to any item to which there was any alteration after commencement of the insurance where the building insured became 'unoccupied' and remained so for more than 30 days.] ' "Occupation" does not seem to require either residence or permanent physical presence broken only by temporary absences. On the other hand, it is unlikely that even the most fleeting single visit involving entry into a dwelling would be sufficient for it to be considered to be occupied. A right to possession and physical presence coupled with a sufficient degree of control are needed. These are patently questions of fact and degree, to be determined by the tribunal of fact, in this case the jury, having regard to all the circumstances, including the nature of the property and the activities engaged in on the property by the person by whom it is said to be occupied.' *Livock v Suncorp Insurance and Finance* [1993] 1 Qd R 206 at 211–212, per cur

UNREASONABLE

Australia [Section 59 of the Legal Practitioners Act 1893 (WA) provides that a practitioner may make a remuneration agreement with a client. The agreement may be reviewed by the Supreme Court and if it is 'unreasonable' the amount payable may be reduced or the agreement cancelled and costs taxed.] 'In our opinion, his Honour was correct to hold that a remuneration agreement may be unreasonable because of the circumstances under which it came into being as well as because its terms are unreasonable or because its effects upon

the client is unreasonable.' *Stoddart & Co v Jovetic* (1993) 8 WAR 420 at 430, per cur

UNREASONABLE SEARCH AND SEIZURE

New Zealand 'A search is unreasonable if the circumstances giving rise to it make the search itself unreasonable or if a search which would otherwise be reasonable is carried out in an unreasonable manner. So to seizure. Whether a police search or seizure is unreasonable depends on both the subject-matter and the particular time, place and circumstance.' *R v Grayson and Taylor* [1997] 1 NZLR 399 at 407, CA, per cur

UNREASONABLE ... SEIZURE

New Zealand [Section 21 of the New Zealand Bill of Rights Act 1990.] 'Leaving aside the question whether or not the "seizure" is "unreasonable" within the ambit of s 21, it may also be questioned whether the erosion of property by the constitutes a "seizure" on the natural and ordinary meaning of that word. The word is suggestive of the forcible taking of possession, capture or confiscation [authorities then cited]. The word "seizure" is also suggestive of some sort of human agency rather than of a gradual process of nature, albeit one which could be prevented by human intervention.' *Falkner v Gisborne District Council* [1995] 3 NZLR 622 at 633, per Barker J

UNREASONABLY DISPROPORTIONATE

Australia [Section 442B of the Crimes Act 1900 (NSW) provides that, in determining the sentence to be passed on a person convicted of an offence, a court may reduce the sentence it would otherwise impose, having regard to the degree to which the person has, inter alia, assisted law enforcement authorities in the investigation of the offence. Subsection (2) provides that a court must not reduce a sentence so that the sentence becomes 'unreasonably disproportionate' to the nature and circumstances of the offence.] ' ... the proscription imposed by s 442B(2) was not absolute proscription. The provision did not proscribe sentences which were disproportionate; it proscribed only those which were "unreasonably disproportionate". It was clearly intended that, in determining what was "unreasonable" for this purpose, the court should be able to take into account the assistance given to law enforcement authorities and, taking that into account, to reduce a sentence below what otherwise would be required by the nature and circumstances of the offence. The use of the term "unreasonably" for such a purpose involves at least two things: that the sentence, following reduction for the assistance will be "disproportionate" to the offence but not unreasonably so; and that, in deciding what is "unreasonable" for this purpose, the court may take into account the nature and extent of the assistance given.' *Re C* (1994) 75 A Crim R 309 at 315, per Mahoney JA

UNSAFE AND UNSATISFACTORY

Australia 'The expression "unsafe and unsatisfactory" has no very precise meaning. It is commonly used to indicate that, although there was evidence to sustain a verdict of guilty, the jury ought, nonetheless, to have entertained a reasonable doubt as to guilt. That is the sense in which it was understood by the Court of Appeal in this case. However, it, or an equivalent expression such as "unjust or unsafe", may be used to indicate that there is some defect in the summing up or "some feature of the case raising a substantial possibility that, either in the conclusion itself, or in the manner in which it has been reached, the jury may have been mistaken or misled" [*Davies and Cody v The King* (1937) 57 CLR 170 at 180]. It is well settled that, where it is contended that a verdict is unsafe or unsatisfactory, in the sense that the jury should have entertained a reasonable doubt as to guilt, "[a]n appellate court must itself consider the evidence in order to determine whether it was open to the jury to convict" [*Carr v The Queen* (1988) 165 CLR 314 at 331 per Brennan J]. And "[i]f the evidence, upon the record itself, contains discrepancies, displays inadequacies, is tainted or otherwise lacks probative force in such a way as to lead the court of criminal appeal to conclude that, even making full allowance for the advantages enjoyed by the jury, there is a significant possibility that an innocent person has been convicted, then the court is bound to act and to set aside a verdict based upon that evidence" [*M v The Queen* (1994) 181 CLR 487 at 494 per Mason CJ, Deane, Dawson and Toohey JJ, referring to *Chamberlain v The Queen [No 2]* (1984) 153 CLR 521 at 618–619 and *Chidiac v The Queen* (1991) 171 CLR 432 at 443–444]. In that exercise, it is necessary for an appellate court to have regard to the whole of the evidence. And ordinarily, it will also be necessary to have regard to the trial judge's summing up.' *Gipp v R* (1998) 155 ALR 15 at 21; 72 ALJR 1012; BC9802404, per Gaudron J

UNSEAWORTHY

[For 43 Halsbury's Laws (4th edn) paras 554–555 see now 43(2) Halsbury's Laws (4th edn) (Reissue) paras 1605–1606.]

UNSOUND MIND

[Section 17(3) of the Prescriptions and Limitation (Scotland) Act 1973 provides that in the computation of a period of three years there shall be disregarded any time during which a person is under a legal disability by reason of 'unsoundness of mind'.] 'There must be many conditions short of insanity which disable a person from fully appreciating all the implications of a court action and from forming a reasoned judgment as to his rights and interests in regard not only to the raising of an action but also to its conduct. I do not consider that unsoundness of mind in this section means only insanity. Every insane person is, I suppose, of unsound mind but every person suffering from some unsoundness of mind is not necessarily insane. If the intention in the 1973 Act was to make the relevant legal disability insanity, that word could have been used as it is used in modern legislation in other contexts, unlike the word lunacy, which is seldom used, no doubt because of its disagreeable connotations.' *Macdonald (Curator Bonis) v Graham* 1992 SCLR 920 at 924, per cur

UNTIL THE DATE THAT THE SURVIVING SPOUSE DIES

Canada 'Counsel could not produce any authorities bearing on this issue and I was unable in the short time available to me to discover any. I did examine some of the texts dealing with words and phrases in a legal context. One which I found to some degree helpful was that contained in *Black's Law Dictionary*, 5th edition (St Paul's, Minnesota: West Publishing Co, 1979) at p 1380 which discussed the meaning of the word "until". I quote:

> "*Until*. Up to time of. A word of limitation, used ordinarily to restrict that which precedes to what immediately follows it, and its office is to fix some point of time or some event upon the arrival or occurrence of which what precedes will cease to exist."

'The parties are agreed that the key words in s 146 [of The Automobile Accident Insurance Act] are "until the date that the surviving spouse dies". Saskatchewan Government Insurance maintains that

that contemplates a day beyond the date on which the first spouse died and of necessity would mean a date subsequent to the fatal accident. The applicant takes the position that the section contemplates a payment to the surviving spouse however brief his or her lifespan may be after the death of the other spouse.

'In my respectful view, the words "until the date" connote a passage of time, a date subsequent to the date of death of the first spouse. As *Black's* definition indicates, there is a discernable progression from one day to another. Using the words "until the date that the surviving spouse dies" has to mean that the survivor lives past the date of the accident.' *Fehr Estate v Saskatchewan Government Insurance* (1999) 182 DLR (4th) 747 at 749, 750, Sask QB, per Wright J

UNTRUE REPRESENTATION

Australia [By the Crimes Act 1900 (NSW), s 410, evidence obtained relying on an 'untrue representation' was inadmissible.] 'Almost 100 years ago the Full Court of the Supreme Court of this State held that, in the context of the direct legislative precursor of s 410, the word "untrue" meant "deliberately untrue": *Davidson* (1895) 16 LR (NSW) 149. The section was re-enacted, in the language that had been authoritatively construed in *Davidson*, not long after that decision.' *R v Connors* (1990) 48 A Crim R 260 at 267, per Gleeson CJ

UPBRINGING

[By s 1(1)(a) of the Children Act 1989, it is provided that where a court determines any question with respect to the upbringing of a child, the child's welfare must be the paramount consideration. In a case where the BBC broadcast an interview with a ward of court and an injunction was granted to restrain publication of the interview, and the BBC appealed, the question of the court's jurisdiction arose. The 'custodial jurisdiction' would only be engaged where the court was concerned with media activities which either related directly to the child's 'upbringing', as that word was used in s 1(1)(a) of the Children Act 1989.] 'So far as concerns relief in rem or contra mundum, I read Ward LJ's analysis [in *Re Z (a minor)*] as indicating that the child's welfare will be paramount only if the court is determining a question with respect to the child's upbringing: see the discussion at [1995] 4 All ER 961 at 982–983, [1997] Fam 1 at 28–29. That being so, the critical question then becomes, what is meant by "upbringing"? As Ward LJ

commented wryly: "It is not always easy to decide when a question of upbringing is being determined." (See [1995] 4 All ER 961 at 982, [1997] Fam 1 at 28.) I agree with Mr Tugendhat when he submits that not everything a child does is a matter of upbringing. Ward LJ's conclusion was that "a question of upbringing is determined whenever the central issue before the court is one which relates to how the child is being reared" (see [1995] 4 All ER 961 at 983, [1997] Fam 1 at 29). The reference to how the child is being "reared" (which I observe reflects the dictionary meaning of the word "upbringing") is revealing. Both words carry the connotation of the bringing up, care for, treatment, education and instruction of the child throughout childhood by its parents or by those in loco parentis. Upbringing thus involves a process in which the parent, or other person in loco parentis, is the subject and of which the child is the object. In formal grammatical terms the statutory phrase "upbringing of a child" is an objective genitive, not a subjective genitive. Section 1(1)(a) of the 1989 Act therefore applies only to those processes or actions of which the child is the object, and not to those in which the child is the subject.

...

'It follows, in my judgment, that Bobby's participation in the interview with the BBC— something done, I might add, without reference to either his mother or his grandmother—does not raise any question with respect to his upbringing. I agree therefore with Mr Tugendhat that the present case falls into the second and not the third category. As a consequence Bobby's welfare is not the paramount consideration.' *Kelly v BBC* [2001] 1 All ER 323 at 348, 350, per Munby J

UPON DELIVERY (AEROPLANE LEASE)

New Zealand 'The critical words are "upon re-delivery of the Aircraft". Although construction of particular words and phrases in other contexts can provide only limited guidance, it is a convenient starting point to refer to what was said of possible meanings of the word "upon" in statutory contexts in *R v Humphrey* (1839) 10 Ad & E 335, 370:

> "... the word 'upon' ... in different cases, may undoubtedly either mean before the act to be done to which it relates, or simultaneously with the act done, or after the act done, according as reason and good sense require the interpretation, with reference to the context, and the subject matter of the enactment."

'This was cited in *Kuratau Land Co Ltd v Kahu Te Kuru* [1966] NZLR 544, 547 as were other English decisions to similar effect.

'It seems to us that, in the context, to require a payment in respect of modifications to the aeroplane "upon" its re-delivery at the expiry of the lease is unlikely to reflect an intention by the parties that the payment is to be made before re-delivery. The real alternatives are that payment is to be made immediately (or within a reasonable time) after re-delivery or is to be made at the time of re-delivery—so long as the lessee has provided accurate documentation and is not then in breach of the lease.

...

'It is necessary to look beyond the express words of the clause to the purpose of the provision and to any other indications in the document.' *Air New Zealand Ltd v Nippon Credit Bank Ltd* [1997] 1 NZLR 218 at 221–222, CA, per cur

URGENT

[A bankrupt may obtain an automatic discharge from his bankruptcy, pursuant to the provisions of s 279 of the Insolvency Act 1986, three years from the date of his bankruptcy order. However, an application may be made under s 279(3) for suspension of the automatic discharge. Such an application is governed by the Insolvency Rules 1986, Ch 1 of Pt 7, of which r 6.215(4) requires 21 days' notice of the application to be given. Rule 7.4(6) provides that where the case is one of 'urgency', the court may hear the application immediately, either with or without notice, to the other parties.] '[16] It is clear that an application under s 279(3) of the 1986 Act is governed by Ch 1 of Pt 7 of the 1986 rules. Rules 7.4(6) and 7.5 provide:

"7.4 ... (6) Where the case is one of urgency, the court may (without prejudice to its general power to extend or abridge time limits)—(a) hear the application immediately, either with or without notice to, or the attendance of, other parties ...

"7.5 Other hearings ex parte.—(1) Where the relevant provisions of the Act or Rules do not require service of the application on, or notice of it to be given to, any person, the court may hear the application ex parte.

"(2) Where the application is properly made ex parte, the court may hear it forthwith, without fixing a venue as required by Rule 7.4(2) ..."

'[17] Rule 7.5(1) appears to have a limited operative effect, if any. It would seem to follow that where relevant provisions do not require service of an application or notice of that application to be given to a party the court is able to deal with it without that party being present. Its effect however may be, when read with r 7.51, to exclude any inherent power or power under the CPR for the court to hear applications ex parte other than as provided for in the 1986 rules. In any event it seems to me that r 7.5(1) is a "sweeping up" provision supplemental to the powers conferred on the court by r 7.4(6).

'[18] There does not appear to be any authority on the operation of r 7.4(6) and in particular on what constitutes a case of "urgency" within that rule. The obtaining of a particular order may appear urgent to the applicant but not urgent at all to persons affected by the order when made.

'[19] It seems to me that whether a particular order is to be treated as urgent within r 7.4(6) is a matter for the court in deciding whether or not to make the order. An application for an order is urgent within the rule in circumstances where, if the order is not made, the situation of the relevant parties or one of them will irretrievably alter. The court will then go on to consider whether in fact to make the order on familiar principles of balance of convenience.

'[20] The decision of Mr Michael Burton QC in *Jacobs v Official Receiver* [1998] 3 All ER 250, [1999] 1 WLR 619 is authority for the proposition that a court considering an application under s 279(3) of the 1986 Act may make an interim order suspending a bankrupt's automatic discharge pending a full hearing of the Official Receiver's application for such suspension. In that case, however, the order appealed from, which was upheld, was made after there had been full compliance with r 6.215 of the 1986 rules and inter partes in the sense that it was made at a preliminary hearing where the bankrupt was present and able to argue against the making of the interim order in circumstances where he had not been able to put his own evidence before the court or to challenge that of the Official Receiver. It does not appear from the report that the court considered the provisions of rr 7.4(6) or 7.5(1).

...

'[24] In my judgment the provisions of r 7.4(6) of the 1986 rules confer power on the court to make an interim order suspending a bankrupt's automatic discharge, ex parte and before the provisions of r 6.215 have been complied with in a case where the court can properly regard the making of such an order as urgent and has concluded that, on the balance of convenience between the Official Receiver, as representing the interests of the creditors, and the bankrupt, it is appropriate that such an order should be made. I am satisfied that when Deputy District Judge Radcliffe made the order of suspension of 2 August 2002 he had the power to make such an order and, subject to questions arising under art 6 of the convention, there was material before him upon which he could conclude that it was appropriate for him to do so. Suspension of discharge is one of the weapons available to those administering insolvent estates to coerce a bankrupt into duly performing his duty to co-operate with the trustee in bankruptcy in realising his assets for the benefit of his creditors. Had the order of 2 August not been made this weapon would have been removed before proper consideration could take place at a full hearing of whether the Official Receiver was justified in seeking an order of suspension. The prejudice to the bankrupt in the prolongation of his status as a bankrupt in the interim was outweighed by the prejudice to the creditors in irretrievably losing the coercive effect of the continuation of the bankruptcy, without being able, through the Official Receiver's application, to justify and so obtain an order of suspension.' *Bagnall v Official Receiver* [2003] EWHC 1398 (Ch) at [16]–[20], [24], [2003] 3 All ER 613, per Evans-Lombe J

USAGE

[For 12 Halsbury's Laws (4th edn) para 445 see now 12(1) Halsbury's Laws (4th edn) (Reissue) para 650.]

USE

[Under section 5(2)(b) of the Data Protection Act 1984 it is an offence for a registered data user to 'use' personal data for any purpose other than the purpose described in the relevant entry in the register of data users.] 'Now the only action taken by the defendant in relation to the relevant data was that he caused another police officer to operate the computer and so caused the information which constituted the data to be displayed on a screen. The defendant then read the information so displayed, and observed what it consisted of, but took no other action in relation to it. The question is whether by so acting he *used* the data, contrary to s 5(2)(b).

...

'I approach the matter as follows. I accept that, since the word "use" is not defined in the Act, it must be given its natural and ordinary meaning. Synonyms of the verb "use" are to "make use of" or to "employ for a purpose". Here the word is used in relation to "data", and data means information recorded in a computer-readable form. I must confess that at first sight I would not have thought that simply retrieving such information from the database in which it is stored, so that it appeared on a screen or a print-out and could therefore be read by a human being could properly be described as "using" the information so recorded. Of course, the computer would be used to retrieve it; but the retrieval of the information would not of itself be "using" the information so retrieved. It would simply be transferring the information into a different form. This to my mind underlines the fact that the definition of data as information in a computer-readable form does not mean that such information is only data while it is so recorded. It means rather that, if information is so recorded, it becomes data for the purposes of the Act; and if such information from that source is thereafter made use of it is used within the meaning of the Act. So if for example a police constable with the Kent Constabulary operates the police computer to retrieve personal data from the database so that he becomes aware of its contents, and then proceeds to make use of that information, he uses the personal data within the meaning of the statute. In such a case, the retrieval is not the use; it is simply a prerequisite of the use. Moreover, if the police officer, who is the servant or agent of the data user (the chief constable) knowingly or recklessly puts the information to an improper use, he will be guilty of an offence under the Act. This may occur not only where the police officer retrieves the personal data from the database and then puts the information to an improper use, but also where, for example, he improperly makes use of personal data which has come to his knowledge when he operated the police computer innocently on a previous occasion, or where the data has been communicated to him by a colleague who had innocently operated the computer.' *R v Brown* [1996] 1 All ER 545 at 548–549, HL, per Lord Goff of Chieveley

Australia [Section 10 of the Crimes (Confiscation of Profits) Act 1988 (WA) allows the forfeiture of property 'used' in connection with the commission of an offence.] 'The phrase "used in, or in connection with, the commission of an offence" connotes a use of a thing which has a relationship with the commission of the offence. The relationship may be direct or indirect depending on whether the thing is used in the commission of the offence or used only in connection with the commission of the offence. Thus, where land is used for the cultivation of a cannabis crop, for example, in my opinion the land is used directly in the commission of the offence of cultivation under s 7(1)(a) of the Misuse of Drugs Act ... In the present case, the use of the house as the place to store, prepare and sell or supply the drugs represented a state of affairs which, in my opinion, constituted a use of the house for those purposes. The house was "used" by the respondent for those purposes in the ordinary meaning of the word "used". The ordinary meaning of the verb "to use" is "to employ for a purpose" and the ordinary meaning of "use" is utilization or employment for or with some aim or purpose": see the Shorter Oxford English Dictionary, p 2325.' *R v Rintel* (1991) 52 A Crim R 209 at 210–211, per Malcolm CJ

'I agree with the conclusion that the words in s 10(1)(a) should have their ordinary grammatical meaning. There is no warrant to import the adjective "substantial" to modify them. I would, however, see some limitation in the meaning of the verb "to use" when it is used in the context of land. The most concise definitions are, I feel, contained in the Macquarie Dictionary inasmuch as they do not contain the word to be defined. The definitions are "to employ for some purpose"; "to put into service"; "to avail oneself of" and "to apply to one's own purposes"... In the present case a statute is being interpreted where the result is forfeiture, in some instances, by way of further punishment. In my view it would be going beyond the intent of the legislation to adopt an interpretation that would result in a liability to forfeiture every time an activity is carried out on that land when in ordinary speech it would not be regarded as being so carried out. The position can be contrasted if it was shown that the land or house was used in a way equivalent to a warehouse or possibly if the house was used as a "safe house". Cultivation would be a clear use of the land. The mere presence of the drug on the land would not, in my view, be sufficient to regard the land as being "used".' Ibid at 224, per Pidgeon J

Australia [Residential Tenancies Act 1987 s 23(1) provides: (1) It is a term of every residential tenancy agreement that: (a) the tenant shall not use the residential premises, or cause or permit the premises to be used, for any illegal purpose, (b) the tenant shall not cause or permit a nuisance, and (c) the tenant shall not interfere, or cause or permit any interference, with the reasonable peace, comfort or privacy of any neighbour of the tenant.] '[12] ...

according to the plaintiff, the activity of growing cannabis plants does not fall into the definition of "use" in s 23(1).

...

'[15] The plaintiff referred to *R v Rintel* (1991) 52 A Crim R 209 a decision of the Western Australian Court of Criminal Appeal where Pidgeon J in discussing s 10 of the Crimes (Confiscation of Profits) Act 1988 (WA) stated:

> ... I would, however, see some limitation in the meaning of the verb "to use" when it is used in the context of land. The most concise definitions are, I feel, contained in the Macquarie Dictionary inasmuch as they do not contain the word to be defined. The definitions are "to employ for some purpose"; "to put into service"; "to avail oneself of" and "to apply to one's own purpose". I would consider that in some contexts in ordinary speech the lesser is capable of excluding the greater. If one is having a bath, then the bath itself is being used for that purpose. Ordinary speech would indicate that the bathroom is also being used for the same purpose. That is the use for which it is set aside and it is also used for the purpose of drying. However I do not consider that it would normally be said, in ordinary speech, that the land on which the bathroom is situate is being used for the purpose of having a bath. If, therefore, the scales are used in a room for weighing, the scales are being used but I do not consider it could be said, if that was the only operation, that the land was being used. One of the factors to consider is that the act of weighing can be performed anywhere and does not need any particular place. If it could be said that the land is also being used, then it would follow that land must be used in respect of every act performed by mankind, unless the act was performed at sea or in the air.

'[16] The plaintiff further submitted that "use" should be interpreted as being protective of the landlord's interest. The plaintiff seeks a technical, restricted interpretation of s 23(1)(a) of the RT Act. The word "use" is not defined in the RT Act. The word "use" should be given its natural and ordinary meaning. The ordinary meaning of the verb "use" is utilization or employment for or with some aim or purpose — Shorter Oxford English Dictionary. The Macquarie Dictionary definitions of "use" include "to put into service", to "avail oneself of", "to exploit to one's own end" and "to apply to one's own purposes".

'[17] The use does not have to involve the "use" of the whole residential premises. It is my view that the plaintiff's hydroponic cultivation of cannabis within two areas of the residential premises falls within the definition of "use" in s 23(1) of the RT Act.' *McAuliffe v Consumer, Trader and Tenancy Tribunal* [2004] NSWSC 824 at [12], [15]–[17], per Harrison M; BC200406014

Canada [Insurance coverage applied to damage from ownership, use or operation of vehicle. Claim was made in respect of fire damage to third party premises resulting from repairs being performed on vehicle by husband of owner.] 'The work being done went to the "use" of the vehicle. It was not repair work without which the vehicle was immobile, unsafe or underperforming but it was consonant with, and not severable from, its use during a hoped-for period of long service. Prevention of deterioration by a family member is an integral part of use. Repair work need not be necessary to immediate driveability to come within the meaning of "use" in the regulation.' *Elias v Insurance Corpn of British Columbia* (1992) 95 DLR (4th) 303 at 307–308, per Boyle J (BC SC)

Canada 'I am satisfied that the repair of an automobile (by a person who not one of a "garage personnel") falls within the auto insurer's agreement to indemnify both the named and unnamed insured against liability "for loss or damage arising from the use or automobile".

...

'... I find that when the defendant Priore was repairing the body damage on the defendant Pennacchio's vehicle (which Priore had with consent and authority to use or operate by the owner) the act of repair was a "use" of the vehicle within the meaning of the automobile policy albeit not done by the owner or his agent ... ' *Pilliteri v Priore* (1997) 145 DLR (4th) 531 at 540, 542 per Kovacs J (Ont Gen Div)

Canada '28 The central question on this appeal is whether Schmeiser, by collecting, saving and planting seeds containing Monsanto's patented gene and cell, "used" that gene and cell.

'29 The onus of proving infringement lies on the plaintiff, Monsanto.

'30 Infringement is generally a question of fact (see *Whirlpool, supra*). In most patent infringement cases, once the claim has been construed it is clear on the facts whether infringement has taken place: one need only compare the thing made or sold by the defendant with the claims as construed. Patent infringement cases that turn on "use" are more

unusual. In those rare cases where a dispute arises on this issue, as in this case, judicial interpretation of the meaning of "use" in s. 42 of the [*Patent*] *Act* may be required.

'31 Determining the meaning of "use" under s. 42 is essentially a matter of statutory construction. The starting point is the plain meaning of the word, in this case "use" or "*exploiter*". *The Concise Oxford Dictionary* defines "use" as "cause to act or serve for a purpose; bring into service; avail oneself of": *The Concise Oxford Dictionary of Current English* (9th ed. 1995), at p. 1545. This denotes utilization for a purpose. The French word "*exploiter*" is even clearer. It denotes utilization with a view to production or advantage: "*tirer parti de (une chose), en vue d'une production ou dans un but lucratif. [...] Utiliser d'une manière avantageuse*": *Le Nouveau Petit Robert* (2003), at p. 1004.' *Monsanto Canada Inc v Schmeiser* [2004] SCJ No 29, [2004] 1 SCR 902, 239 DLR (4th) 271, per McLachlin CJC and Fish J

Use ... a dominant position in a market

New Zealand [Section 36 of the Commerce Act 1986 provides 'No person who has a dominant position in a market shall use that position'] 'In their Lordships' view it cannot be said that a person in a dominant market position "uses" that position for the purposes of s 36 unless he acts in a way which a person not in a dominant position but otherwise in the same circumstances would have acted.' *Telecom Corporation of New Zealand Ltd v Clear Communications Ltd* [1995] 1 NZLR 385 at 403, PC, per cur

Use any land

New Zealand [Section 9(1) of the Resource Management Act 1991 provides that "No person may use any land in a manner that contravenes a rule in a district plan or proposed district plan ... .] '... I think that for a person to walk or stand upon land involves using that land for the purpose of s 9(4)(e). Similarly, carrying out some activity on land such as wielding a chainsaw is using the land for that purpose. Once that use contravenes a rule in the district plan then, in my view, that element of s 9 is satisfied. That would accord with the commonly understood meaning of the word "use".' *Smith v Auckland City Council* [1996] 1 NZLR 634 at 639, per Fisher J

USE OR OPERATION OF A MOTOR VEHICLE

Canada 'Here we are asked to interpret Section A of the standard automobile policy which reads as follows:

"The insurer agrees to indemnify the insured and, in the same manner and to the same extent as if named herein as the insured, the other person who with his consent personally drives the automobile or personally operates any part thereof, *against the liability imposed by law* upon the insured or upon any such other person for loss or damage *arising from the ownership, use or operation* of the auto-mobile and resulting from ... [Emphasis added.]"

'It is not necessary to decide in this case whether the phrase "result from" is equivalent to the phrase "caused by", as all counsel have agreed that the test set out by Major J, in *Amos* should be adopted. In view of my conclusion respecting this appeal, the difference in wording between Section 79(1) and Section A is not determinative.

'The interpretation of the phrase "ownership, use or operation" is the central issue.'

...

'The words "use or operation" connote different activities (*Stevenson v Reliance Petroleum Ltd* [1956] SCR 936, 5 DLR (2d) 673).

'In order to meet the purpose test, Best Print need only establish that the "accident" resulted from either the use, or operation, of the Truck. (See comments of Laskin JA on behalf of the Ontario Court of Appeal in *Vijeyekumar v State Farm Mutual Automobile Insurance Co* (1999), 175 DLR (4th) 154 at 162. An application for leave to appeal to the Supreme Court of Canada, filed on behalf of State Farm on September 15, 1999 (SCCA 438), is presently outstanding [since refused SCC Bull 5/5/00, p 796].)

'Counsel for Best Print submits the words "use or operation" should be interpreted broadly, as mandated by *Amos*, and refers us to the definition of the word "use" as found in the *Random House College Dictionary* (New York: Random House Inc, 1984) as:

"To employ for some purpose, put into serv-ice, make use of."

'Counsel for Best Print submits we should frame Mr Emeneau's activities by characterizing his individual actions with respect to the employment of the gasoline, and its ignition, more generally, as a use of the Truck to commit suicide.

'Counsel's position is expressed in his factum in this way:

"Using a motor vehicle to commit suicide is a recognized activity to which motor vehicles are sometimes put. Indeed, it is common knowledge that motor vehicles are used to commit suicides in various ways.
Sometimes the suicide is accomplished by carbon monoxide poisoning, as in *Vijeyekumar*. Perhaps even more frequent is a suicide accomplished by driving the vehicle into a stationary object or into oncoming traffic. Sometimes the vehicle is set afire. Whatever method is used, the motor vehicle is not merely the situs of act. On the contrary, the motor vehicle is used because it is a motor vehicle and as such is suited in a certain way to accomplishing the suicide."

'I do not agree with this submission.

'Even if we framed the activities as simply an innovative mode of committing suicide, they most certainly do not constitute "ordinary" activity.

'The word "ordinary" is defined in the *Random House Dictionary* (1971) as:

... of the usual kind, not exceptional: com-monplace ... something regular customary, or usual ...

'I agree with Justice Wright's characterization of Mr Emeneau's activities as "highly extraordinary".

'I further agree with Justice Wright's conclusion [*supra*] that:

"The truck was merely the situs of that act of destruction which sets this case apart from many of the others."

'Any confined space would have served Mr. Emeneau's objective. (I note that counsel were in agreement that the "explosion" described in the 1994 statement, which led to the fire, resulted from the ignition of the match in the volatile atmosphere of the Truck's cab, not from an explosion of the gas tank.)

'Here the Truck was not "used" as an automobile but as a receptacle to accumulate and store gas fumes.' *Holdbrook v Emeneau* (2000) 184 DLR (4th) 606 at 613, 614, 615, NSCA, per Pugsley JA

USED IN NAVIGATION *SEE* SHIP

USUAL PROFESSIONAL CHARGES

Australia [A will provided, inter alia, that the trustee, being a solicitor, could make all 'usual professional charges' for work done by him in relation to the estate's administration or trusts.] 'The first point to be made is that the expression "usual professional charges" in cl 23 must be construed as a reference not to what [the solicitor] usually charges but to what is "usual" in the profession generally. In practical terms such charges would be calculated in accordance with the provisions in force from time to time prescribing costs to be charged by solicitors ...' *Sacks v Gridiger* (1990) 22 NSWLR 502 at 514, per McLelland J

V

VACANT

Canada 'It is also helpful to consider how "vacant" and "unoccupied" are defined in *Black's Law Dictionary*, 6th ed, abridged (1990) at 1548 and 1538 respectively:

> "*Vacant.* Empty; unoccupied; as, a 'vacant' office or parcel of land. Deprived of contents, without inanimate objects. *It implies entire abandonment, nonoccupancy for any purpose.* Foley v Sonoma County Farmers' Mut Fire Ins Co of Sonoma, Cal App, 108 P 2d 939, 942. Absolutely free, unclaimed, and unoccupied.
>
> "In fire policy insuring dwelling, term 'vacant' means empty, without inanimate objects, deprived of contents; a thing is vacant when there is nothing in it; *'vacant' means abandoned and not used for any purpose.* Alcock v Farmers' Mut Fire Ins Co of DeKalb County, Mo App 591 SW 2d 126, 128.
>
> "*Unoccupied.* Within fire policy exempting insurer from liability in case dwelling is 'unoccupied', means when it is not used as a residence, when it is no longer used for the accustomed and ordinary purposes of a dwelling or place of abode, or when it is not the place of usual return and habitual stoppage. Hence a mere temporary absence of occupants of dwelling house from such premises, with intention to return thereto does not render dwelling 'unoccupied'. Foley v Sonoma County Farmers' Mut Fire Ins Co, 18 Cal 2d 232, 115 P 2d 1, 2, 3. [Emphasis added.]"

...

... On the basis of the agreed facts, I am satisfied that it was never the intention of the insured to abandon the cabin, and that to the extent it had not been used as a seasonal home for several months, this was to permit renovations to be made, following which it was to be used as a seasonal home. In this regard, the following statement was made in an early treatise:

> "'*Vacant*' *premises.* — The mere temporary absence of the occupant of a building will not avoid a policy conditioned to be void in case the building becomes 'vacant'. To render the building vacant there must be a permanent removal from the house, and an abandonment of the same as a place of residence. And a mere temporary absence from one's dwelling house with intent to return and occupy the premises is not a vacancy."

'Joyce, *A Treatise on the Law of Insurance of Every Kind,* 2nd ed (Rochester, New York: The Lawyers Co-operative Publishing Co, 1918) vol IV, 3795. In my view, an exclusionary clause based on the vacancy of a property should be construed in respect to the character or class of property to which it applies in the context of the circumstances of each case. For example, it would not likely have the same interpretation when applied to churches as when applied to dwellings, or when applied to a seasonal dwelling in the country as when applied to a permanent dwelling in a city or town. Similarly, a house that is not occupied because it is being renovated is different from one that is unoccupied because a tenant or a purchaser cannot be obtained.' *Nicoli v Liberty Mutual Insurance Co* (1996) 141 DLR (4th) 372 at 382, 383, 384, per Borins J (Ont Gen Div)

VACANT POSSESSION

[For 42 Halsbury's Laws (4th edn) para 129 see now 42 Halsbury's Laws (4th edn) (Reissue) para 123.]

VALUABLE BENEFIT

Australia [Section 6(1) of the Family Provision Act 1982 (NSW) provides that 'property' includes real and personal property and, inter alia, any 'valuable benefit'.] '... the increase in the value of ... shares in [a] company on the death of the deceased [is] a "valuable benefit" [as defined in s 6(1) of the Family Provision Act].' *Schaeffer v Schaeffer* (1994) 36 NSWLR 315 at 319, per Handley JA

VALUATION

Just valuation

'Clause 15 of the 1949 deed required that in taking a general account of "all the capital stock-in-trade property engagements and liabilities for the time being of the partnership ... a just valuation shall be made of all particulars requiring and capable of valuation". It is, to my mind, pertinent to note that the requirement is not for "a true valuation" or for "a market valuation" or even for "a fair valuation". Those are all expressions which, in an appropriate context, may have the same meaning as "a just valuation"; but it does not follow that that will be the meaning to be placed on the expression "a just valuation" when construing the 1949 deed in the circumstances known to Mr Dennis White and Mr Lawrence White in July 1961. The question of construction in the present case is not answered by recognising that "a just valuation" may have been held, in other cases, to have the same meaning as "a market valuation". The task, in the present case, is to determine what that expression meant to the two brothers when they adopted it in the context of their partnership agreement.

'There are, as it seems to me, six factors which lead to the conclusion that, in relation to the Brantwood Road property, a just valuation for the purposes of the general account to be taken each year was to be the historic cost.

...

'Taking these factors together, I am satisfied that the answer to the question "what did the expression 'a just valuation' mean to the two brothers, in relation to the treatment of the Brantwood Road property in a general account of the partnership, when they adopted the terms of the 1949 deed (including cl 15) on entering into a new partnership on 28 July 1961" is not open to any serious doubt. The expression required the Brantwood Road property to be included in a general account at historic cost. That was how they had always dealt with the matter. In particular, that was the basis upon which they had come into the partnership in 1949; that was the basis on which they had paid out their father's estate; and that was the basis upon which they had dealt with their sister on her retirement. I have no doubt that each brother would have thought it "unjust" for the other to seek to insist (in the absence of agreement) on the inclusion of the property in a general account at market value. And I have no doubt that each brother would have been right to take that

view.' *Re White (decd), White v Minnis* [2000] 3 All ER 618 at 629, 631–632, CA, per Chadwick LJ

VALUE

Canada [Business tax assessment was based on the 'annual rental value' of property.] 'The principal noun in the phrase is "value", and it is value that has to be determined. Among the dictionary definitions of "value" that appear more or less appropriate in the context are worth, estimate of worth, price equal to the worth, and money for which a thing is sold or will sell, a fair or adequate equivalent or return of the material or monetary worth of a thing. The adjective annual gives no difficulty. The noun rental, here used attributively, is variously defined as follows: income from rents, amount paid or received as rent, an income arising from rents received, the amount paid or received as rent. In the Random House Dictionary (USA) rental is shown as an adjective as well as a noun, and its meaning as an adjective is given as "pertaining to rent".

'I am confident that the most appropriate synonym of "value" is "worth". Money paid by a tenant for the right to occupy property becomes rent only when it is received by the landlord and it can only be the worth to the landlord of what he receives that represents the value. If he cannot keep the whole of the rents that he receives, but is in effect required by law to pay part of them away to a municipality, the value is what remains after that payment away. To my mind and so far as it is relevant here, rental value connotes the net worth to the landlord of the income arising from rents received. This reasoning has strong support.' *Re MacMillan Bloedel Ltd and City of Port Alberni* (1972) 28 DLR (3d) 688 at 693, per Robertson JA,BC CA; affd on this point (1973) 36 DLR (3d) 229, SCC

VALUER

[For 49 Halsbury's Laws (4th edn) paras 1, 6 see now 49(1) Halsbury's Laws (4th edn) (Reissue) paras 401, 410.]

VANDALISM

Canada 'Vandalism is not defined in the *Regulation* or in the *Insurance (Motor Vehicle) Act*, RSBC 1996, c 231.

'The *Concise Oxford Dictionary of Current English*, 8th edition (1990), defines "vandalism" as "wilful or malicious destruction or damage to works of art or other property". The *Canadian Oxford Dictionary* (1998) defines "vandalism" as "wilful or malicious destruction of or damage to private or public property".

'*Black's Law Dictionary* (4th edition) defines "vandalism" as "willful or ignorant destruction of artistic or literary treasures; hostility to or contempt for what is beautiful or venerable".

'There does not appear to be any assistance on the meaning of "vandalism" in the Canadian or Commonwealth case law.

'One definition often cited in the United States case authorities is *Livaditis v American Casualty Company of Reading, Pa*, 160 SE 2d 449 (Ga App 1968), at 450:

Vandalism means the destruction of property generally ... It must also, of course, be willful and malicious, meaning that the act must have been intentional or in such reckless and wanton disregard of the rights of others as to be the equivalent of intent. As to malice, this may be inferred from the act of destruction.

'None of these definitions suggests that property may not be vandalized by its owner.' *Bevacqua v Insurance Corp of British Columbia* (1999) 179 DLR (4th) 219 at 224, BCCA, per Finch JA

VARY

New Zealand [Sections 32(1)(a) and 33(11)(a) of the Income Tax Act 1976.] 'Our ss 32(1)(a) and 33(11)(a) use the words "confirm or cancel or vary the assessment". The word "vary" permits an increase or decrease ...' *Golden Bay Cement Co Ltd v Commissioner of Inland Revenue* [1996] 2 NZLR 665 at 672, CA, per cur

VEHICLE

'[T]he expression "vehicle" ... as used in right of way cases ... is in my opinion apt to express a sharp distinction between machines for carrying passengers over the country by some sort of motive power which precludes them from using their own legs for the purpose, and, on the other hand, any form of contrivance, such as a skate or roller skate or ski or snowshoe, which merely facilitates the use of the individual's own muscle to cover ground more quickly. Accordingly I take the view that the pedal cycle is only an aid to pedestrianism. I think it would be unfortunate in Scotland to take any other view, for otherwise tracks which had only been used by the comparatively innocuous two

wheeled pedal cycle might be appropriated by the public thereby to all purposes of traffic.' *Aberdeenshire County Council v Lord Glentanar* 1999 SLT (Notes) 1456, per Lord Mackay

Australia 'The real issue is whether a ride-on motor mower is "a vehicle". Mr Cawthorn contended it was not and started with the definition of vehicle in the *Oxford English Dictionary* (2nd ed, 480) referring to the sixth and seventh definitions as follows:

"6. A means of conveyance provided with wheels or runners and used for the carriage of persons or goods; a carriage cart wagon sled or similar contrivance.
7. A. Any means of carriage conveyance or transport; a receptacle which in anything is placed in order to be moved."

'[24] He referred also to the *Macquarie English Dictionary* (2nd ed) in which a vehicle is defined as:

"1. Any receptacle, or means of transport, in which something is carried or conveyed or travels.
2. A carriage or conveyance moving on wheels or runners."

'[25] However, *Butterworths Australian Legal Dictionary* (p 1240) sets out the following definitions:

"Vehicle (1) a conveyance designed to be propelled or drawn by any means, whether or not capable of being propelled or drawn, and includes a bicycle or other pedal-powered vehicle, trailer tramcar or air-cushioned vehicle but does not include railway locomotives or railway rolling stock"

referring there to the definition in the Road Safety Act 1986 s 31. Butterworths goes on to say:

"2. Apart from any statutory definition the term is given its ordinary and popular meaning ... in this sense, the term means a contrivance or instrument used for the carriage of something, or a conveyance *capable of being used as a means of transportation*." (My emphasis.)

Counsel for the plaintiffs' submission was that the proper definition involves that a vehicle (a) must be capable of carrying goods or animals or transporting persons; and (b) must have as its principal primary or customary use the carriage of goods or animals or the transporting of persons.

Thus, he submitted, a ride-on mower does not have these characteristics because its primary purpose is cutting grass and it is not customarily used for transporting persons or goods.

...

'[27] I have concluded that a ride-on motor mower is a vehicle within the meaning of the exclusion clause in this policy. It seems almost absurd not to characterize it as such. It is not necessary that I add to the already overburdened attempts at definition, although I am of the view that the definition as propounded in *Butterworths Australian Legal Dictionary* is probably correct. None of the definitions support, and as matter of my own judgment I reject, that there is some "primary purpose" criteria which must be satisfied before conforming with the definition of "vehicle".' *QBE Insurance Ltd v Fortis Insurance Ltd* BC9903972; [1999] VSC 212 at [25], [27], per Hedigan J

Canada 'I also note that though the word "vehicle" has often been associated with conveyances running on land, it is often shorthand for a motor vehicle. "Vehicle" standing alone, may in a legislative context be justifiably restricted to conveyances running on land.

'In the statute before me, a proper construction of its charging provision is to impose a tax on diesel fuel, including of course, a tax on diesel fuel used primarily in the operation of a vehicle. The exemption *only* applies when such fuel is for use in the generation of electricity. The general rule is therefore that fuel for vehicles is taxable and any exception invites a narrow interpretative approach. *A contrario*, therefore, the word "vehicle" invites a more generic or wider approach. It could be said that the narrower the approach to "use in the generation of electricity", the wider the interpretation of the wording used in taxing an item generally including of course diesel fuel, no matter for what general purpose it might be used.

'In this regard, one must avoid becoming preoccupied with the double exception in the structure of the statute. I would repeat, diesel fuel is taxable when used in vehicles. The exemption *only* applies in the generation of electricity.

'One can then look into the intent of Parliament with special regard to a vehicle which uses fuel oil generated electricity for its operation. Such a propulsive or motive force is not the exclusive habitat of motor vehicles or other conveyances running on land. It is found in probably more marine installations than otherwise.' *Seaspan International Ltd v* Canada [1994] 1 FCR 524 at 543, per Joyal J (Fed TD)

VEIN

[For 31 Halsbury's Laws (4th edn) para 12 see now 31 Halsbury's Laws (4th edn) (2003 Reissue) para 16.]

VENISON

[The Deer Act 1980 has been repealed. The definition is now contained in the Deer Act 1991, s 16, as follows.] 'Venison' includes imported venison and means—

    (a) the carcase of a deer, or

    (b) any edible part of the carcase of a deer,

which has not been cooked or canned.

VENTURE

Canada '[62] Thus, the question is whether property which a man, unbeknownst to his wife, purchases in his own name as a residence for his mistress, in which she thereafter resides and to which he from time to time resorts, is a "venture".

'[63] I put the question in those terms because, if the answer to that question is "no", the answer is also "no" on the facts here which are, in their essentials, the same. To put it another way, that the second respondent was unaware that she was not the lawful wife of the first respondent is irrelevant to the issue as between the petitioner and the first respondent.

'[64] The word "venture" is not easy to construe. This Court considered it in *Hopkinson v. Hopkinson* (1997), 34 R.F.L. (4th) 137, 43 B.C.L.R. (3d) 232 (C.A.), in which a husband had obtained an interest in some property for the purpose of providing a home for himself and his first family. Here, of course, the situation is reversed, for Sherlock Avenue was acquired for the purpose of providing a home for the first respondent's second family.

'[65] Proudfoot J.A. said, at 143 (R.F.L.):

Does the Husband's Interest Qualify as a "Venture"?

23 Mr. Justice Wood in Joki-Hollanti v. Joki-Hollanti, [[1990] B.C.J. No. 585 (Q.L.)] (B.C.S.C.), said of the word "venture" as used in s. 45(3)(e), the following:

I see no reason to give the word "venture" a restrictive interpretation such as that suggested by the defendant. By that I mean that I see no need to restrict its meaning exclusively to that of "... an undertaking attended with risk, especially one aiming at making money; business speculation ...". In my view any investment, in which there is an element of risk, and which has the potential for profit, even though its primary function may be to serve some other purpose, may qualify as a venture under s. 45(3)(e) of the Act. Whether it does qualify or not, in any given case, will depend upon all of the circumstances in which it was acquired and used.

24 Relying on the meaning given to the word "venture" by Mr. Justice Wood, the trial judge held that the husband's interest in the property lacked the "aura" of an "investment" or a "venture" as envisaged by s. 45(3)(e) of the Act. I agree. The Garrow Bay property was essentially held for purposes of the husband's first marriage, and there was no evidence it was regarded as an investment that could be disposed of at a later date for profit. Indeed, being held by husband and first wife, it likely could not be sold without her co-operation or consent; nor could it be mortgaged in practical terms. Thus the circumstances of its acquisition and use do not accord with its characterization as an "investment". Further, if I am incorrect in my interpretation as to what qualifies as a venture, I would still find that the Garrow Bay property does not meet the family asset definition set out in s. 45(3)(e) of the Act due to the fact the wife did not contribute directly or indirectly to the property, nor did the husband contribute on her behalf.

'[66] I am of the opinion that Sherlock Avenue lacks the "aura" of an investment and, thus, the first respondent's interest in it is not within the statute [the *Family Relations Act* (B.C.)] as between himself and the petitioner.' *Yang v Yang* (2003) 230 DLR (4th) 605 at 627–628 (BCCA), per Southin JA

VERDICT

[For 26 Halsbury's Laws (4th edn) para 642 see now 26 Halsbury's Laws (4th edn) (Reissue) para 444.]

VERIFY

Australia [Section 459E(3) of the Corporations Law provides that a statutory demand must be accompanied by an affidavit 'verifying', inter alia, that the debt is due and payable by the company.] 'The kind of distinction which lies beneath the competing contentions of the parties is the kind of distinction drawn in an entirely different statutory context by Lee J in *Re Powell* (1992) 35 FCR 133, where in relation to certain industrial legislation of the Commonwealth his Honour drew the distinction between "verify" in the sense of "prove or demonstrate by good evidence or otherwise substantiate" certain matters; and "verify" used in the sense of "a formal affirmation".

'In my opinion, s 459E(3) uses the expression "verify" in that latter sense rather than in the former sense contended for by the applicant.' *Azed Developments Pty Ltd v Frederick & Co Ltd (in liq)* (1994) 14 ACSR 54 at 56, per Hayne J

VESSEL

[For 43 Halsbury's Laws (4th edn) para 91 see now 43(1) Halsbury's Laws (4th edn) (Reissue) para 102.]

Canada '[35] I begin this part of my analysis by considering the relevant statutory definitions:

'[36] The *Canada Shipping Act*, R.S.C. 1985, c. S-9 defines a "ship" as:

(a) any description of vessel used in navigation and not propelled by oars, and

(b) for the purpose of Part I and sections 574 to 581, any description of lighter, barge or like vessel used in navigation in Canada however propelled ...

'[37] Under this Act, a "vessel", meanwhile includes,

any ship or boat or any other description of vessel used or designed to be used in navigation;

'[38] The interpretation provisions of the *Canada Shipping Act, 2001*, S.C. 2001, c. 26, s. 2 (not yet in force) will replace these two definitions with a single definition of "vessel":

"vessel" means a boat, ship or craft designed, used or capable of being used solely or partly for navigation in, on through or immediately above water, without regard to method or lack of propulsion, and includes such a vessel that is under construction. It does not include a floating object of a prescribed class.

'[39] The authors of the recent test *Maritime Law* (2003) (E. Gold, A. Chircop and H. Kindred, [Irwin Law, 2003]) at page 144 suggest that this "streamlined and more expansive definition of "vessel" will represent a "significant change" when it comes into force:

The new definition – by including boat and craft, partial navigational use, capability of navigation, navigation through and above water, and vessel under construction, while disregarding mode of propulsion – has fused together elements that appeared in separate definitions as well as adding new elements. The effect is a more expansive definition of "vessel", clearly a definition that intends to include, more than exclude. Exclusions apply only in relation to floating objects of a prescribed class.

'[40] Meanwhile, the *Federal Courts Act*, R.S.C., 1985, c. F-7, defines "ship" in this manner:

> "ship" means any vessel or craft designed, used or capable of being used solely or partly for navigation, without regard to method or lack of propulsion, and includes
> (a) a ship in the process of construction from the time that it is capable of floating, and
> (b) a ship that has been stranded, wrecked or sunk and any part of a ship that has broken up.

'[41] From all these definitions, two things become clear. First of all, a ship includes a vessel so the Plaintiff, to be successful, need only meet the latter definition. Secondly, whether completed or under construction, whether self-propelled or not; whether able to navigate or not, a structure should be at least capable of floating in order to be considered a "vessel". In the case at Bar, the *Topside* will be carried to the ocean site by barge to rest on the ocean floor. It is not designed to ever float. These material facts are set out in the Neale Affidavit and are undisputed. Furthermore, should the *Topside* be considered as an appurtenance of the platform, there is nothing to suggest that the platform once completed will ever float.

'[42] On this basis, I find that the *Topside* could never be considered a "vessel" nor an appurtenance to a "vessel". As noted above, if it is not a vessel, it is not a ship. Therefore, on this point as well, I find there is no arguable issue of material fact to be tried.' *TJ Inspection Services v Halifax Shipyards, a division of Irving Shipbuilding Inc* [2004] NSJ No 347, 245 DLR (4th) 171 (SC), per MacDonald ACJSC

VEST

[For 50 Halsbury's Laws (4th edn) para 588 see now 50 Halsbury's Laws (4th edn) (Reissue) para 644.]

VESTED AND INDEFEASIBLE INTEREST

Australia 'The words "vested" and "indefeasible" in the context of trust law are technical legal words of limitation, which have a well understood meaning to property conveyancers. Estates may be vested in interest or vested in possession, the difference being between a present fixed right of future enjoyment where the estate is said to be vested in interest and a present right of present enjoyment of the right, where the estate is said to be vested in possession: *Glenn v Federal Commissioner of Land Tax* (1915) 20 CLR 490 at 496, per Griffith CJ, at 501 per Isaacs J. A person with an interest in remainder, subject to a pre-existing life interest, has an interest which is vested in interest, but being a future interest is not yet vested in possession. That person's interest will vest in possession on the death of the life tenant. In the present context the word "vested" is used in contradistinction to contingent.

'An interest is said to be defeasible where it can be brought to an end and indefeasible where it can not. Thus, a beneficiary with an interest which is not contingent but which interest may be brought to an end by the exercise of a power of appointment, would be said to have a vested but defeasible interest: see *Queensland Trustees Ltd v Commissioner of Stamp Duties* (1952) 88 CLR 54 at 63 and *Re Kilpatrick's Policies Trusts* [1966] Ch 730.

'An interest may be vested and indefeasible, notwithstanding that it is subject to a security interest in another. The mere existence of a lien or charge over the property does not convert an interest otherwise vested and indefeasible into one that is vested but defeasible, or not vested at all.' *Dwight v Federal Commissioner of Taxation* (1992) 37 FCR 178 at 192, 107 ALR 407 at 422, per Hill J

VEXATIOUS PROCEEDINGS

Australia 'It is unhelpful to embark upon an analysis of what other courts have decided constitutes vexatious proceedings. Section 39(5) of the Supreme Court Act provides an exhaustive definition of what constitutes vexatious proceedings for the purpose of the section. Each paragraph of the definition requires the court to examine the circumstances surrounding the institution of the proceedings. It is not concerned with the manner in which the defendant conducted himself during the proceedings save to the extent that that may be an indicator of whether the proceedings were instituted for a purpose described in para(a) of subs (5), or in order to ascertain whether there was any reasonable ground for instituting the proceedings. If the proceedings are utterly hopeless they will satisfy that description: *Attorney-General for the State of Victoria v Weston* [2004] VSC 314 at [22]. If the proceedings have no prospect of success, or could have been or were in fact struck out as disclosing no reasonable cause of action, it is likely that they will be held to have been commenced vexatiously. Most of the proceedings alleged by the plaintiff to be vexatious are said to have been instituted without reasonable ground. However, some of the plaintiff's allegations venture into the territory covered by para(a) of subs (5).' *Mitsubishi Motors Australia Ltd v Kowalski* [2005] SASC 154 AT [58], per Bleby J; BC200502250

VICINITY

Canada ' "Vicinity" is a relative term, not defined in the Act, and is usually found to be a smaller area than an entire municipality. If the proportion of market value used to arrive at an assessed value for a particular class of property within the municipality were to vary between vicinities, s 63(3) [of Assessment Act, RSO 1980, c 31] would not only be violated, but its entire purpose would be defeated. The sections can only be reconciled if the term "vicinity" is interpreted to mean "municipality" in a s 63(3) municipality ... It logically follows that in any municipality where s 63(3) has been implemented "vicinity" in s 65(2) can only mean the entire municipality. It is important to note that s 63(3) was passed four years after s 65 and was designed to correct inequities. This is a reasonable reconciliation of the two sections and in my view is in compliance with the objectives of the Act.' *Re Regional Assessment Commissioner, Region No 3 and Graham* (1987) 39 DLR (4th) 154 at 157, Ont HCJ, per McRae J

Canada [Assessment for condominium units was based on values applicable to single family residences in vicinity.] ' "Vicinity" is not defined in the Act. The cases which have previously dealt with the definition of the term "vicinity" in the context of s 65(1) of the Act have stressed that whether something is or is not "in the vicinity" must depend on the particular facts in issue: see *Re Fogh-Dohmstadt and Regional Assessment Commissioner, Region No 32* (1981) 16 MPLR 199 (Ont Dist Ct); *Joshi v Regional Assessment Commissioner, Region 11* (1985) 18 OMBR 88; *Mount Citadel Ltd v Regional Assessment Commissioner, Region 11* (1980) 13 OMBR 242.

As was pointed out by the board in this case, "vicinity", in appropriate circumstances can mean an entire municipality, but may also mean a smaller portion thereof, depending on the appropriate geographical base that will yield meaningful comparables. The flexibility in the term does not mean that it is unclear or ambiguous and that violence should be done to its accepted ordinary and grammatical meaning, and to the meaning that it clearly has in other parts of the Act. Departure from the ordinary, plain meaning of the word should only be resorted to in the face of absurdity or inconsistency that is apparent from the very language of the statute (Driedger, *Construction of Statutes*, 2nd edn (Toronto: Butterworths, 1983), at pp 47–57).

'The respondents' main argument is that there is some repugnancy or inconsistency between ss 63(3) and 65(2) and thus, "vicinity" must be interpreted as "municipality" in order to avoid that repugnancy or inconsistency. I note at the outset that had the legislature intended that the municipality be the area of comparison in all cases, it would not have used the word "vicinity".' *Ontario (Regional Assessment Commissioner, Region No 3) v Graham* (1993) 106 DLR (4th) 577 at 583, Ont CA, per Arbour JA

VICTIM

Australia [Section 69a of the Evidence Act 1929 (SA) refers to a suppression order being made to prevent undue hardship, inter alia, to a 'victim' of crime.] 'The word "victim" in s 69a is not to be given a figurative or fanciful or strained interpretation. Simply to show that someone has been adversely affected in some way by the commission of a crime does not, in my judgment, make him a victim within the meaning of s 69a.' *Martin v M* (1991) 54 A Crim R 173 at 179–180, per Cox J

VIOLENCE

[For 25 Halsbury's Laws (4th edn) para 602 see now 25 Halsbury's Laws (4th edn) (2003 Reissue) para 577.]

VIOLENT

'The word "violent" is an ordinary English word, which here appears in a common commercial document [an insurance policy]. It seems to me that there is no reason why its meaning should be in any way different from what any ordinary person would understand. At first sight I therefore conclude that there should be no need to resort either to a dictionary, or to authorities, to interpret this work; nor to the rule that, this being an insurers' document, it must be construed against them. On that basis I would take the ordinary meaning of the word "violent" in this context to be that it is intended to convey that the use of *some* force to effect entry, which may be minimal, such as the turning of a key in a lock or the turning of a door handle, if accentuated or accompanied by some physical act which can properly be described as violent in its nature or character. An obvious picture that springs to mind is the breaking down of a door or the forcing open of a window, which would be acts of violence directed to the fabric of the premises to effect entry. Or there might be violence to a person, such as knocking down someone who seeks to prevent entry, irrespective of whatever may be contained within para (b) of that part of the cover.

'Accordingly, on that basis I would not consider for one moment that the ordinary meaning of the phrase "entry to premises by forcible and violent means" can be applied to the action of moving the lever of a lock into its open position by means of its proper key and then turning a knob or pushing the door open to go inside. That would be "forcible" in the sense which I have explained, as is conceded on the authorities. But there would be nothing violent about it at all.' *Dino Services Ltd v Prudential Assurance Co Ltd* [1989] 1 All ER 422 at 426, CA, per Kerr LJ

Violent conduct

Australia [The defendant had pleaded guilty to dangerous driving occasioning death and grievous bodily harm under Crimes Act (NSW) s 52A. It was determined that the defendant had been charged with offences involving 'violent conduct' within s 5(2)(b) of the Drug Court Act 1998 (NSW), and that accordingly he was ineligible for sentencing under s 7(2) of that Act. The defendant appealed the finding.] 'There is some force in the submission that driving would not normally be regarded as violent conduct. There seem to me to be two possible reasons why this might be so. First, there is the circumstance that any violence is indirect, in that it is mediated by the vehicle: in this respect, it might be similar to violence to a person caused by pulling a trigger or pushing a button. The second reason relates to the circumstance that the dangerousness of the driving and the violent outcome need not be intended and may possibly not even be adverted to.

'[49] As to the first reason, in my opinion the circumstance that violence is done to a person, not by vigorous physical activity, but through some instrument that may be activated without any vigorous physical activity, does not prevent the doing of violence to a person by those means being properly described as violent conduct. There is perhaps a latent conflict in ordinary usage here: the use of a weapon which does violence to a person would ordinarily be regarded as aggravating violent conduct, whereas on the other hand, it may be seen as negativing violent conduct because it reduces to near-inactivity the physical action required from the person causing the violence. Even though one must ultimately apply the ordinary meaning of words, I think this should be done with due consideration; and on the basis of due consideration, my view is that the circumstance that violence is caused to a person by an instrument activated by minimal physical activity does not make that activity other than violent conduct.

'[50] Turning to the second reason, that which concerns intention or advertence, my opinion is that, so long as the conduct itself is voluntary, the circumstance that there may be no advertence to its dangerousness, and no intention of the violent outcome, does not prevent the conduct being called violent conduct. The elements of the offence in question here include voluntary conduct, which is objectively dangerous, and which does in fact do violence to a person. The conduct involves what can be regarded as a dangerous weapon; so it is not as if the objective dangerousness of the conduct, or the violent outcome, are matters that could be considered foreign to the voluntary conduct.' *Chandler v DPP* (NSW) BC200002480; [2000] NSWCA 125 at [48]–[50] per Hodgson CJ in Eq

Violent offence

[Under s 2(2)(b) of the Criminal Justice Act 1991 an extended custodial sentence may be imposed on a person convicted of a 'violent offence' as defined in s 31(1).] 'The point taken by counsel for the appellant on this appeal is that neither of the offences of threatening to kill which the appellant committed was a "violent offence" within the definition of that term, which is to be found in s 31(1) of the 1991 Act. That is an interpretation section and provides, so far as relevant: ''"violent offence' means an offence which leads, or is intended or likely to lead, to a person's death or to physical injury to a person".

'The argument is, first, that the offence of threatening to kill is not per se within this definition.

With that submission we agree ... In the ordinary way the threat of itself will not lead, or be likely to lead, to death or physical injury. Such a dismal consequence would not arise unless there followed an intervening offence of actual violence, or an attempt at it.

'There may, however, be cases in which a threat to kill will constitute an offence of violence within s 31(1). They are likely to be relatively rare. They fall into two classes: first, where the threat was *intended* to lead to death or injury: that might happen in a case where to the defendant's knowledge the victim's health was delicate and he intended by making the threat that the victim should be so frightened as to suffer physical harm. It might arise, for instance, if the victim suffered from a serious heart condition. This class of case shades into the second, which arises when the circumstances of the offence are such that the threat makes it likely that death or injury will happen. This class of case would include, as Pill LJ pointed out in the course of argument, a state of affairs in which the threat was made when the victim was standing on a balcony or precipice and was likely as a result to recoil and fall.

'But these are special cases. We think it right to acknowledge their possible existence; however, unless there exist particular circumstances such that the prosecution can prove either that the defendant intended death or injury to result from the threat itself, or that on the facts such a consequence flowed or was likely to flow from the threat itself, the offence of threatening to kill is not within the statutory definition.' *R v Ragg* [1995] 4 All ER 155 at 157–158, CA, per Laws J

Canada '[1] In these appeals, this Court is being asked to define the term "violent offence" for purposes of the *Youth Criminal Justice Act*, S.C. 2002, c. 1 ("*YCJA*" or the "Act"). This term is found in s. 39(1) of the Act, and it represents one of only four gateways to a custodial youth sentence. Specifically, s. 39(1) provides that a youth justice court shall not commit a young person to custody under s. 42 (youth sentences) unless:

(a) the young person has committed a violent offence;

(b) the young person has failed to comply with non-custodial sentences;

(c) the young person has committed an indictable offence for which an adult would be liable to imprisonment for a term of more than two years and has a history that indicates a pattern of findings of guilt under this Act or the *Young*

Offenders Act, chapter Y-1 of the Revised Statutes of Canada, 1985; or

(d) in exceptional cases where the young person has committed an indictable offence, the aggravating circumstances of the offence are such that the imposition of a non-custodial sentence would be inconsistent with the purpose and principles set out in section 38.

'[2] The definition of "violent offence" is at issue in these appeals because the appellants, who are young persons within the meaning of the *YCJA*, were both found to be eligible for the custodial sentence they ultimately received on the basis that they had committed a "violent offence" under s. 39(1)(a) of the *YCJA*.

...

3.2.2.3 Preferred Definition: Causes, Attempts to Cause or Threatens to Cause Bodily Harm

'[81] Although I do not favour extending the definition of "violent offence" to those offences where bodily harm is merely reasonably foreseeable, in general, I still support extending this definition beyond those offences in which bodily harm is caused or attempted, in order to make the definition of "violent offence" something more than simply a replica of the definition of "serious violent offence" with the word "serious" omitted. Specifically, as indicated above, I support extending the definition to capture those offences in which bodily harm is threatened. This would make the definition of "violent offence" an offence in the commission of which a young person causes, attempts to cause or threatens to cause bodily harm.

...

'[83] With that preliminary issue resolved, I will now explain why I am in favour of incorporating threats of bodily harm into the definition of "violent offence".

'[84] First, including threats of bodily harm in the definition of "violent offence" accords with ss. 98(4)(a)(iv) and 104(3)(a)(iv) of the *YCJA*. These sections both provide that for the purpose of determining whether the test for continuation of custody is met

the youth justice court shall take into consideration any factor that is relevant to the case of the young person, including

(a) evidence of a pattern of persistent violent behaviour and, in particular,

...

(iv) explicit threats of violence,

Although the term "violent behaviour" is used in a context that is somewhat different than that associated with s. 39(1)(*a*), the fact that in ss. 98 and 104 this term is linked with threats and not simply actions strongly supports the inclusion of threats of bodily harm in the definition of "violent offence".

'[85] Second, a definition of "violent offence" that includes offences in which the young person threatens bodily harm is to be preferred because it accords with the commonly held view that a threat to cause bodily harm is, at base, an act of violence. For example, Scassa argues that:

> Threats of violence are violence itself. Those who are threatened know that the violence they fear has already begun with the threat. The threat is a taste of violence and a promise of more. It is the slap that foreshadows the beating. [p. 818]

Similarly, in his treatise *Youth Criminal Justice Law*, Bala argues that "a spoken threat to do physical harm is the offence of 'uttering threats' contrary to section 264.1 of the *Criminal Code* and is also likely to be regarded as a violent offence [within the meaning of s. 39(1)(*a*) of the *YCJA*], even if there is no proof of intent to cause actual physical injury" (p. 448, citing *McCraw* in support). This is also the view expressed by Professor Cornu quoted in these reasons at para. 68. Additionally, in his reasons for judgment in *R. v. D.L.C.*, [2003] N.J. No. 94 (QL) , Gorman Prov. Ct. J. opined that a threat to commit rape could be considered a "violent offence":

> It is not necessary for the Court in this case to provide a definitive definition of what will and will not constitute a violent offence within the meaning of subsection 39(1)(*a*) of the Act. It is suffice to say that it does not require that the offence involve the application or attempted application of physical force. Such a definition would be overly narrow. For instance, uttering a threat to rape someone could constitute a violent offence (see *R. v. McCraw* (1991), 66 C.C.C. (3d) 517 (S.C.C.) and *R. v. Young* (1998), 159 Nfld. & P.E.I.R. 136 (N.L.C.A.)). [para. 61]

The view that threats of bodily harm are essentially acts of violence is likely based on the fact that threatening to cause bodily harm can often perform the same function as actually causing it, in that both can instill the level of fear in the victim that is needed to achieve the offender's goal: see *McCraw*, at pp. 81–82. In this sense, it can be said that irrespective of whether an offender threatens to cause bodily harm or actually causes bodily harm, in both cases he or she is "wielding violence" to satisfy his or her object(s).

'[86] The final reason why I am in favour of incorporating threats of bodily harm into the definition of "violent offence" is that, as noted above, it will make the definition sufficiently distinct from the statutory definition of "serious violent offence", since it will no longer be a simple copy of the statutory definition with the word "serious" omitted. However, the inclusion of threats of bodily harm will not make the definition of "violent offence" so distinct that it creates a situation where a "serious violent offence" might not also be considered a "violent offence". Accordingly, it can be said that a definition of "violent offence" that includes offences in which bodily harm is threatened, as well as caused or attempted, pays adequate attention to Parliament's decision to leave the term "violent offence" undefined, while also ensuring that the *YCJA* operates properly and does not produce absurd results.

'[87] For all these reasons, I support extending the definition of "violent offence" to capture those offences in which bodily harm is threatened. Accordingly, I am of the view that, for purposes of s. 39(1)(*a*) of the *YCJA*, the term "violent offence" must be defined as an offence in the commission of which a young person causes, attempts to cause or threatens to cause bodily harm. Since the Alberta Court of Appeal defined this term differently, I must respectfully conclude that it erred in law in doing so.' *R v D (C); R v K (CD)* (2005) 261 DLR (4th) 257 at [1]–[2], [81], [83]–[87], [2005] SCJ No 79 (SCC), per Bastarache J

VISITOR

To university

'The action for wrongful dismissal has largely been superseded by the far wider protection afforded to employees by the Employment Protection (Consolidation) Act 1978. All these rights are available to all university academic staff because Parliament can of course invade the jurisdiction of the visitor if it chooses to do so. If in the course of such proceedings any question arises concerning the interpretation or application of the internal laws of the university, it will have to be resolved for the purpose of the case by the tribunal hearing the application. Such power must be implicit in the remedies provided by the Act, and to this extent, Parliament has given rights that enter and supersede the jurisdiction of the visitor ... [But] the visitatorial jurisdiction subject to which all our modern universities have been founded is not an ancient anachronism which should now be severely curtailed, if not discarded. If confined to its proper limits, namely the laws of the foundation and matters deriving therefrom, it provides a practical and expeditious means of resolving disputes which it is in the interests of the universities and their members to preserve.' *Thomas v University of Bradford* [1987] 1 All ER 834 at 849–850, HL, per Lord Griffiths

[See also *Page v Hull University Visitors* [1993] 1 All ER 97, HL, in which the above case is further explained. See *R v Visitors to the Inns of Court, ex p Calder, ex p Persaud* [1993] 2 All ER 876, CA, as to visitors to the Inns of Court.]

VOID

Australia 'Windeyer J said of the term "void" that it "has never been an easy word" and pointed out that it did not necessarily mean that the void act had no legal effect at all. In particular, where (as here) a disposition between two parties is described as "void" at the will of a third, the preferred construction is to read "void" as "voidable".' *Victoria v Sutton* (1998) 156 ALR 579 at 589; 72 ALJR 1386; BC9804343, per Gaudron, Gummow and Hayne JJ

New Zealand [Matrimonial Property Act 1976, s 21.] '[25] It can be seen that non-compliance renders the agreement "void". However, the Court is given a limited discretion to give effect if it is satisfied that the "non-compliance" has not materially prejudiced the affected party (s 21(9)).

'[26] Secondly, the Court is given a general discretion to not give effect to an agreement if satisfied that to do so would be unjust (s 21(8)(b)). Section 21(10) then sets out mandatory considerations in exercising the discretion ... If the Court decides not to give effect to the agreement under this provision, the agreement similarly is "void".

'[27] Mr Walker advanced his submission on the basis that the effect of non-compliance was that the agreement was void from the outset. Given that, it was indisputable that Mr Thom had suffered loss because he did not have the benefit of the protection of the agreement. Issues of how much it would cost him were matters of quantum and not contingency.

'[28] Pivotal to Mr Walker's argument is the proposition, contested by Mr Cox, that non-compliance with the execution requirements means

the agreement is immediately ineffective. In Mr Cox's submission it is not ineffective until a Court refuses to give effect to it. Further, the ultimate disposition of property under a matrimonial property order goes beyond quantum; it determines whether the wrong (the negligent execution of the agreement) has actually produced an adverse burden (the loss).

'[29] I queried with Mr Walker the "void from the outset" interpretation because it is plain that the word "void" as it is used at the start of s 21(8) applies equally to the general discretion in s 21(8)(b). Since an agreement might become unjust and be held to be void because of events occurring long after execution, it seemed to me impossible to give void the meaning of "ineffective from the outset" in relation to a s 21(8)(b) situation. Mr Walker replied that ineffective from the outset was nevertheless the only meaning that could be given to a s 21(8)(a) infirmity. In support of dual meanings he pointed to s 21(12) which provides that:

> (12) Where any agreement purporting to be made pursuant to this section is *void* or is *avoided* or is unenforceable, the provisions of this Act (other than this section) shall have effect as if the agreement has never been made. (Emphasis added.)

'[30] In his submission "void" refers to s 21(8)(a), and "avoided" refers to s 21(8)(b). Mr Walker also referred to the way the provisions are now drafted. Sections 21F and 21H of the Property (Relationships) Act 1976 reflect almost identically s 21(8)(a) and s 21(9). However, the general discretion formerly contained in s 21(8)(b) is now in a separate section, s 21J. More importantly, an exercise of the discretion against enforceability no longer renders the agreement void, but amounts only to not giving effect to the agreement.

'[31] I accept that the use of void is capable of bearing the analysis Mr Walker gives it, although the same word having different meaning on the same occasion of its use is not an interpretation that is likely to be correct. More importantly, however, in my view void from the outset is not a meaning that reflects the scheme and reality of s 21 agreements.

'[32] Section 21 agreements are creatures of statute that are contingent on Court decisions both in relation to the enforceability of the agreement, and the overall disposition of property. Until these decisions are taken, it is incorrect to say loss has accrued. *Fisher on Matrimonial and Relationship Property* (LexisNexis) describes a non-complying agreement as "prima facie void" and a complying agreement as "prima facie valid". These terms reflect, I consider, the reality of the statutory context.' *Thom v Burton* [2006] NZFLR 116 at [25]–[32], per Simon France J

VOID MARRIAGE

[Section 1(1) of the Legitimacy Act 1976 provides that the child of a 'void marriage' shall be treated as the legitimate child of his parents if, at the time of the act of intercourse, the parents reasonably believed that their marriage was valid.] 'A void marriage, both as a matter of language and by definition (see s 10(1) of the 1976 Act) is a nullity. It is only an idle ceremony. It achieves no change in the status of the participants. It achieves nothing of substance. How then can you sensibly refer to the child of a void marriage? You cannot be referring to the child of a ceremony. There is no such thing.' *Re Spence (decd), Spence v Dennis* [1990] 2 All ER 827 at 832, CA, per Nourse LJ

[Held: Section 1(1) does not apply to children born before the entry of the parents into the void marriage.]

VOLENTI NON FIT INJURIA

[For 34 Halsbury's Laws (4th edn) para 62 see now 33 Halsbury's Laws (4th edn) (Reissue) para 669.]

[For 45 Halsbury's Laws (4th edn) para 1262 see now 45(2) Halsbury's Laws (4th edn) (Reissue) para 375.]

VOLUNTARY *SEE ALSO* CONSCIOUS, VOLUNTARY AND DELIBERATE ACT; FREE

VOLUNTARY HOME

[The Child Care Act 1980 has been repealed. The definition is now contained in the Children Act 1989, s 60(3), as follows.]

In this Act 'voluntary home' means any home or other institution providing care and accommodation for children which is carried on by a voluntary organisation but does not include—

(a) a nursing home, mental nursing home or residential care home;
(b) a school;
(c) any health service hospital;
(d) any community home;
(e) any home or other institution provided, equipped and maintained by the Secretary of State; or

(f) any home which is exempted by regulations made for the purposes of this section by the Secretary of State.

VULNERABILITY

Australia [In the context of the duty of care owed by a private building surveyor to a subsequent purchaser of a dwelling.] '[84] In my view the authorities do not support the narrow concept of "vulnerability" advanced by the appellants. Insofar as the appellants relied upon *Perre v Apand*, it must be borne in mind that in that case the defendant had not assumed responsibility to others in the way that the defendant did in *Bryan v Maloney, Hawkins v Clayton* and *Hill v Van Erp*. "Vulnerability" is a broad concept. Reference should be made to the majority judgment in *Woolcock* in which the concept of "vulnerability" is discussed. Their Honours treat as coming within that concept not only situations where plaintiffs are unable to protect themselves from the consequences of a defendant's want of reasonable care (either entirely or at least in a way which would cast the consequences of loss on another) but also

• situations where the defendant has assumed responsibility and there is "known reliance" and
• the negligent misstatement cases, where central to the plaintiff's allegation is the contention that the defendant knew that the plaintiff would rely on the accuracy of the information provided by the defendant.

'Their Honours comment that the two latter examples can be explained as suggested by Professor Stapleton by reference to notions of vulnerability. Their Honours declined however to attempt to "identify or articulate the breadth of any general proposition about the importance of vulnerability". I suggest that it is clear from the majority judgment that the concept of "vulnerability" is much wider than the concept put forward by counsel for the appellants.

'[85] As to the use of the concept of "vulnerability", the recent authorities refer to "vulnerability" for the purpose of identifying a limited class of plaintiff whom, to quote Lord Atkin, the defendant "ought reasonably to have … in contemplation as being … affected" by his "act or omission". It is, however, a name for a category and does not exclude other relationships with other features and its own definition is yet to be finalised. The concept may be used to define a neighbour relationship sufficient to warrant the imposition of a duty of care to the plaintiff by requiring, for example, that it be shown that the plaintiff belonged to an identifiable class of people at risk of economic loss as a result of the negligence of the defendant and that it was reasonably foreseeable to the defendant that they either could not protect themselves or there was a likelihood that they would not do so. So articulated, the issue whether *particular plaintiffs* could have protected themselves remains relevant to the defence of contributory negligence but not to the question of the existence of a duty.

...

'[126] If more is required before a duty of care can be imposed, however, the following additional features of "vulnerability" in subsequent purchasers are relevant.

(a) Known reliance. A building surveyor in the position of Mellis would be or ought to have been aware that subsequent purchasers would be likely to assume that the house had been competently built and that the footings were in fact adequate.

(b) Dependency. Subsequent purchasers are a class of people linked to and dependent upon the building surveyor in the sense that there is nothing that they can do to undo the defective design or defective work. The building surveyor is in fact intended under the statutory scheme to ensure that standards are met and so give protection to building owners — initial and subsequent. The most they can do is to take additional steps to try to protect themselves after the event, from possible want of care on the part of the person intended to give protection, by informing themselves about the building, attempting to renegotiate the contract or refusing to proceed with the purchase.

(c) Limited ability of the class of plaintiffs to secure protection.

   (i) *Practical protection*. For most purchasers of dwellings, the only way they can inform themselves of structural deficiencies is by engaging another expert to inspect thoroughly the premises and all plans and specifications and, to a large extent, repeat the work the building surveyor undertook to perform. A detailed inspection of the kind needed is likely to be costly. Much depends on what a purchaser can afford to pay and a significant proportion of purchasers of dwellings will have difficulty funding a complete inspection by experts. Many, if not most purchasers will rely upon a visual inspection and an assumption that the original work has been done properly. Such an assumption is reasonable (and to be expected) when there is, as here, a comprehensive system of building regulation under which building surveyors undertake to monitor the design and critical aspects of the construction.

   I note also, the Tribunal's finding about the problems of gaining access to the private building surveyor's file compared with the situation where the relevant Council officer did the work. It may be said that engagement of the private building surveyor increases the vulnerability of a subsequent purchaser.

   (ii) *Legal protection*. It is unrealistic to expect purchasers of dwellings as a class generally to be able to obtain, let alone know about, contractual protections. Further, there can be no guarantees that such action will provide adequate protection.

For these additional reasons subsequent purchasers form a class of people that is "vulnerable" to the negligence of the private building surveyor.'
Moorabool Shire Council v Taitapanui [2004] VSC 239 at [84]–[85], [126], per Smith J; BC200403987

W

WAGE

Australia 'The words "salary" and "wage" denote an amount of money payable, the consideration for which is the performance of work or services. That meaning is reflected in the definitions provided for the terms in the *Oxford English Dictionary*, 2nd ed:

> *Salary*: fixed payment made periodically to a person as *compensation* for regular work.

> *Wage*: a payment to a person *for* services rendered.'

Deputy Commissioner of Taxation v Applied Design Development Pty Ltd (in liq) (2002) 20 ACLC 463; 2002 ATC 4193; BC200200894; [2002] FCA 205 at [8], per Mansfield J

WAGES

Australia [The Payroll Tax Commissioner contended that the provision of a car to an employee to drive to and from work was 'wages' paid in kind.] '"Wages" meaning an amount agreed to be paid to an employee is the meaning adopted in the Industrial Arbitration Act 1940 (NSW), s 5 (as amended) under which elaborate provision is made for the making of awards which fix "rates of wages" and "allowances as compensation for overtime, holidays or other special work": ss 22, 30... The definition of "wages" in the Payroll Tax Act 1971 (NSW) is not intended to attribute to the words "wages, salary" used in the definition a meaning other than their ordinary meaning and that the meaning is one which contemplates an agreement between employer and employee that an agreed amount of money shall be paid as wages. The definition of "wages", as I have said, in using the words "paid or payable (... in cash or in kind)" in no way alters the meaning of the word "wages" as being the monetary amount agreed upon as the price or remuneration for the work done by the employee. It is of significance that in the one instance where the section deals with a provision of other than agreed monetary reward there is a specific provision in sub-s (2) to give that provision a precise monetary import. If the Commissioner is right here as to the meaning of "wages" or "allowance" the need for para (e) disappears ... The provision of a car for private use is certainly not within the concept of wages as understood in this country. It does not therefore come within the words "wages" or "salary" used in s 3(1).' *Terry Shields Pty Ltd v Chief Commissioner of Payroll Tax* (1989) 98 ALR 559 at 563–567, per Lee CJ

Australia [Section 21(4) of the Builders Licensing Act 1967 (SA) refers to an amount charged by a person for building work being wholly 'in the nature of wages'.] 'Reference to the considerable body of case law in which the meaning of "wages" is discussed is of little assistance as many cases were concerned with the interpretation of statutory definitions. It seems to me that what Parliament had in mind in the employment of the expression "in the nature of wages" is that there may be a fee charged which could not be accurately categorised as wages, perhaps because the relationship of master and servant was absent. However, the fee would be for labour and skill only and would be payable only to the person who undertook the work. If these features are present and there is no component in the fee for other than the provision of labour and skill, such as for administration or some other overhead, the fee will be in the nature of wages. I do not think that it is necessary for there to have been regular periodic payments of the fees charged for them to be in the nature of wages.' *Saunders v Cadman* (1990) 54 SASR 534 at 538–539, per Mullighan J

Australia 'A number of the authorities deal with the meaning to be attributed to the word "wages" in various statutory contexts. A good deal of caution must be exercised in placing any reliance upon observations made in cases of that kind, as frequently they relate to specific definitions set out in the statutes in question. Even if that is not so, different statutory contexts may nonetheless operate to colour the meaning to be attributed to the word.

'While accepting, for the reasons which I have given, the need for caution, I have nonetheless been considerably assisted by two decisions of Wilcox CJ, sitting in the Industrial Relations Court of Australia.

'In *May v Lilyvale Hotel Pty Ltd* (1995) 68 IR 112, Wilcox CJ had occasion to address the question of the amount of compensation to be paid to an employee whose employment had been terminated unlawfully within the meaning of the Industrial Relations Act 1988 (Cth). Section 170EE(3) of the Act provided that in determining the amount of compensation to be paid to an employee whose employment had been unlawfully terminated [at 115]:

> "… the Court is to have regard to the remuneration that the employee would have received, or would have been likely to have received, if the employer had not terminated the employment …" (emphasis added)

'In the course of his decision in that case, Wilcox CJ observed [at 116–17]:

> "Plainly, the word 'remuneration' was chosen, for s 170EE(3), in order to denote a concept other than wages. Non-monetary benefits are not wages: see *Ardino v Count Financial Group Pty Ltd* (1994) 1 IRCR 221 at 228–9; 57 IR 89 at 94–5; 126 ALR 49. But they fall within the concept of remuneration."

'In *Ardino v Count Financial Group Pty Ltd*, Wilcox CJ had regard to other provisions in the Industrial Relations Act 1988 which concerned the meaning to be attributed to the words "relevant wages". The expression was defined in s 170CD(4) of the Act to mean "… the total amount of the wages that the employee received, or was entitled to receive, from the employer in respect of" certain stated periods of employment. In the course of his judgment in that case, Wilcox CJ said [at 54–5]:

> "I agree with counsel that the definition of 'relevant wages' is concerned only with payments that are wages, strictly so-called. I do not think it includes payments made by an employer on behalf of an employee pursuant to a binding antecedent obligation, whether statutory or contractual …

> "In relation to non-pecuniary benefits, I cannot see how they can ever be regarded as 'wages' for the purpose of the definition. The word 'wages' is not defined by the Industrial Relations Act, so in s170CD it bears it ordinary meaning. The Shorter Oxford English Dictionary defines 'wage' as:

> 'A payment to a person for service rendered; now esp the amount paid periodically for the labour or service of a workman or servant. Freq pl.'

"The *Macquarie Dictionary* gives the primary meaning of 'wage', noting that it is often plural, as 'that which is paid for work or services, as by the day or week; hire; pay'. I think these definitions' emphasis on payment makes it difficult to argue that benefits that do not take the form of money payments are 'wages'."

'Other authorities which confirm a similar approach to the definition of the word "wages" are *Terry Shields Pty Ltd v Chief Cmr of Payroll Tax* (1989) 98 ALR 559 and *Hargraves v National Safety Council of Australia Ltd* (1997) 77 FCR 272.

'In *Rofin Aust Pty Ltd v Newton* (1997) 78 IR 78, the full bench of the Australian Industrial Relations Commission (Williams SDP, Acton DP and Eames C) observed [at 80–1]:

> "Prior to the amendments made to the Act by the Workplace Relations and Other Legislation Amendment Act 1996 (Cth) (the WROLA Act), the 'salary cap' for the purposes of excluding non-award employees from the operation of the termination of employment provisions was expressed in terms of 'relevant wages'. The term now used is 'remuneration', a term which denotes a broader concept than salary or wages. 'Remuneration', in our view, is properly defined as the reward payable by an employer to an employee for the work done by that employee in the course of his or her employment with that employer. It is a term that is confined neither to cash payments nor, necessarily, to payments actually made to the employee. It would include non-pecuniary benefits and payments made on behalf of and at the direction of the employee to another person out of moneys otherwise due to that employee as salary or wages."

'In his submission, Mr Armour of counsel for Bibby and Kelm referred to two cases under the Workers Rehabilitation and Compensation Act 1986 (SA). He submitted that the cases were examples of the fact that "the term 'wages' has been defined to mean something much wider than just salary".

'In the first of them, *Cleggett v Coca Cola Amatil* (1995) A 156/1995, Gilchrist DP observed [at 4–5]:

"The Act, like its predecessors, provides for the payment of weekly payments to compensate disabled workers for the duration of their incapacity. The amount of that payment is reckoned by reference to the worker's average weekly earnings. But, the problem is, not all earnings take the form of a monetary payment. Remuneration can take a variety of forms. These may include, access to cheap loans, payment of school fees, hospital insurance, medical benefits, entertainment allowances, accommodation and the provision of a company vehicle for private use. If the provision of such a benefit is in substitution for wages that would otherwise be payable, it forms part of the earnings of the worker and therefore ought to feature in the assessment of weekly payments. That, is a well established principle of worker's compensation."

'However, under the Workers Rehabilitation and Compensation Act 1986, consideration of which provides the context for those observations, the relevant payments to disabled workers are described as "income maintenance", which falls to be calculated by reference to "weekly earnings" or "notional weekly earnings".

'In the passage which I have just cited, Gilchrist DP refers to "average weekly earnings" as well as to "remuneration". While he also refers to "wages that would otherwise be payable", it is clear that his observations do not relate to "wages" strictly so-called. The relevant word in the Act there in question is "earnings".

'The same comment may be made about the other case under the Workers Rehabilitation and Compensation Act 1986 to which Mr Armour made reference. This was *Phillis v WorkCover Corp/MMI Workers Compensation (SA) Ltd (O'Brien Glass Industries Ltd)* [1999] SAWCT 64. In that case, the Full Bench of the Workers Compensation Tribunal dealt with a dispute concerning the calculation of the worker's "average weekly earnings". In the course of their judgment they said [at 16]:

"... the focus of the enquiry has to be to identify whether the allowance [a 'pager' allowance paid in consideration of the employee being on call] is paid in exchange for the sale of the worker's skill and labour. If it is, then subject to s 4(8)(b) such amount is to be included in the assessment of the worker's average weekly earnings.

'In *Cleggett v Coca Cola Amatil* (supra), Gilchrist DP referred to the judgment of Cozens-Hardy LJ

in *Great Northern Railway Co v Dawson* [1905] 1 KB 331 at 334–5, where the latter said:

"It must, I think, upon the authorities, be taken to be a fallacy that the wages in money are necessarily to be the measure of the worker's earnings for the purposes of the Act. It cannot be doubted, for instance, that, if a workman is, in addition to his wages in money, allowed to occupy a house belonging to his employer, the value of that occupation must generally be considered as part of his earnings, because the necessary inference would be that, but for this privilege, the amount of his wages in money would be higher."

'As to that dictum, I make the same comment; Cozens-Hardy LJ was referring to quantification of the worker's "earnings" and not to "wages" as such.

'After considering the authorities referred to by counsel and to their submissions, I have reached the conclusion that the clear weight of authority is in favour of the view that ordinarily the meaning of the word "wages" does not extend to include non-pecuniary benefits.

'The only remaining questions are whether or not there is anything in the Act which should lead to the conclusion that another meaning is intended, and if not, whether there are any other provisions of the Act pursuant to which an order could be made for the payment of monetary compensation for loss of the benefit of the provision of accommodation or meals.

'As to the first point, the Act does not define "wages". Furthermore, the word "wages" in s 40(3)(f) is not used in conjunction with any other words or phrases which might suggest a more expanded meaning.

'In all the circumstances, there is no reason why it should not be given its ordinary and natural meaning.' (some footnotes omitted) *Quality Lodges International Pty Ltd v Bibby (No 2)* BC200202206; [2002] SASC 147 at [16]–[33], per Perry J

WAITING FOR

Australia [Section 54Q(3) of the Migration Act 1958 (Cth) provides that a person is in application custody unless, inter alia, the Department of Immigration is 'waiting for' information relating to the application to be given.] 'In our view, Neaves J [at first instance] was correct in holding that some notion of delay is inherent in the concept of "waiting for" something;

and in rejecting the appellants' argument that any lapse of time, whether ordinate or inordinate, qualifies as part of a "waiting" period.' *Minister for Immigration and Ethnic Affairs v Tang* (1993) 47 FCR 176 at 187, per cur

WAIVER

[For 16 Halsbury's Laws (4th edn) para 1471 see now 16(2) Halsbury's Laws (4th edn) (Reissue) para 907.]

[For 45 Halsbury's Laws (4th edn) para 1269 see now 45(2) Halsbury's Laws (4th edn) (Reissue) para 385.]

[Each of the defendants had either pleaded guilty to, or been convicted of, criminal charges in proceedings before temporary sheriffs in Scotland, and had been sentenced by such sheriffs. After the conclusion of the proceedings against the defendants, the High Court of Justiciary held in another case that a temporary sheriff was not an independent and impartial tribunal for the purposes of the right to a fair hearing under art 6(1) of the European Convention for the Protection of Human Rights and Fundamental Freedoms 1950 (as set out in Sch 1 to the Human Rights Act 1998). Relying on that decision, the defendants contended in conjoined appeals to the High Court that their prosecutions had been unlawful since, under s 57(2) of the Scotland Act 1998, the Lord Advocate had no power to do any act that was incompatible with a convention right. The High Court dismissed the appeals, holding that the defendants' agents had, through failing to take the point at trial, waived their clients' right to object to the hearing of their cases by temporary sheriffs. The defendants appealed to the Privy Council.] '[27] I accept the argument for the accused on this point. The Lord Advocate had no power to act in a way which infringed any convention right of the accused. By continuing to prosecute the accused before a tribunal which was not independent and impartial, he infringed the right of the accused to have the criminal charges against them determined by a tribunal which was independent and impartial. Unless the accused validly waived their entitlement to trial before an independent and impartial tribunal, he acted in a way which [the Scotland Act 1998] s 57(2) denied him power to do. I think this is the view taken by the High Court.

...

Waiver

'[31] In most litigious situations the expression "waiver" is used to describe a voluntary, informed and unequivocal election by a party not to claim a right or raise an objection which it is open to that party to claim or raise. In the context of entitlement to a fair hearing by an independent and impartial tribunal, such is in my opinion the meaning to be given to the expression. That the waiver must be voluntary is shown by *Deweer v Belgium* (1980) 2 EHRR 439 at 465 (para 54), where the applicant's failure to insist on his right to a fair trial was held not to amount to a valid waiver because it was tainted by constraint. In *Pfeifer v Austria* (1992) 14 EHRR 692 at 713 (para 38) there was held to be no waiver where a layman had not been in a position to appreciate completely the implication of a question he had been asked. In any event, it cannot meaningfully be said that a party has voluntarily elected not to claim a right or raise an objection if he is unaware that it is open to him to make the claim or raise the objection. It is apparent from passages already cited from cases decided by the European Court of Human Rights that a waiver, to be effective, must be unequivocal, which I take to mean clear and unqualified. I infer that the High Court was of this opinion (see 2000 JC 648 at 654–655 (paras 12, 13)).' *Millar v Dickson (Procurator Fiscal, Elgin)* [2001] UKPC D4 at [27], [31], [2002] 3 All ER 1041, per Lord Bingham of Cornhill

Australia 'The doctrine of waiver was considered in the context of promissory estoppel by the High Court in *Commonwealth v Verwayen* (1990) 170 CLR 394. At 406, Mason CJ pointed out that often the term "waiver" is used to describe the result of the application of various principles rather than to designate a particular legal concept or doctrine. He went on to say: "According to its strict connotation, waiver is an intentional act done with knowledge whereby a person abandons a right by acting in a manner inconsistent with that right: *Craine v Colonial Mutual Fire Insurance Co Ltd* ((1920) 28 CLR 305 at 326). ... However, the better view is that, apart from estoppel and new agreement, abandonment of a right occurs only where the person waiving the right is entitled to alternative rights inconsistent with one another such as the right to insist on performance of a contract and the right to rescind for essential breach. See *Kammins* ([1971] AC at 883). This category of waiver is an example of the doctrine of election." ... In my view, the reasons of the majority of the High Court in *Verwayen's* case (supra) support the view that there is no independent doctrine of waiver as distinct from election, variation of contract or estoppel.' *Mowie Fisheries Pty Ltd v Switzerland Insurance Australia Ltd* (1996) 140 ALR 57 at 79–80; BC9604822 at 56–58, per Tamberlin J

WAIVER OF TORT

Canada 'Fridman, *Restitution*, Second edition 1992, pp 355–56 what is meant by "waiver of tort":

The law of restitution provides for the granting of restitutionary relief where a defendant has acquired a benefit as a result of his wrongful act. If there was a pre-existing relationship between the parties, the receipt of the benefit, if referable to this relationship, may be dealt with in terms of the breach of a fiduciary relationship. Where there was no pre-existing relationship between the parties, the ability of the plaintiff to obtain restitutionary relief as a consequence of the wrongful act depends on whether he is entitled to bring his situation within the scope of the doctrine of waiver of tort. This curious and anomalous doctrine, the nature, utility, and even existence of which have been questioned in recent years, originated after the development of the writs of *assumpsit* and *indebitatus assumpsit*. Although the expression "waiver of tort" has been said to have three distinct senses or meanings, its most pertinent use is procedural, in relation to a claim for restitution, based on unjust enrichment, in respect of a tort committed by the defendant against the plaintiff, in place of an action in tort that could have been maintained by the plaintiff, arising out of the conduct of the defendant. The basis of the doctrine is described in these terms by the American *Restatement of Restitution*. "A person upon whom a tort has been committed and who brings an action for the benefits received by the tortfeasor is sometimes said to 'waive the tort'." In the case of certain torts, where, by a wrongful act, the defendant acquired a liquidated sum of money or other tangible benefit, it was a frequent practice under the old forms of procedure for the plaintiff to "waive" the tort and sue for the liquidated sum as money had and received by suing in the action for *indebtedness assumpsit* rather than claiming damages by bringing the appropriate writ for the particular tort in issue. The term "waiver of tort" is somewhat of a misnomer in the context. The plaintiff does not "waive" the tort in the sense that he forgives the defendant for his wrongful acts. Rather, the plaintiff waives the tort in the sense that he forgoes his right to sue for common law damages as a result of the wrongful act and elects rather to sue in what was quasi-contract to recover the benefit received by the defendant as a result of his wrongful act. To waive a tort, then, is to make an election of remedies. On the same set of facts, the plaintiff can sue in either tort or what was quasi-contract. It is not the tort itself which is waived, but rather the right to recover damages as a result of its commission. Much of the current confusion surrounding waiver of tort has arisen because of the fact that the old forms of action required the court to "imply" a contract between the plaintiff and the tortfeasor as to the benefit in question. This contract was not based on the intention of the parties, but was implied by operation of law. In cases falling within the general area of waiver in tort, the facts present two distinct remedies: the remedy in quasi-contract by way of restitutionary relief for the benefit conferred and a remedy in tort by way of compensation. The real nature of a claim in waiver of tort lies, then, in the defendant's wrongdoing. The tort is an essential aspect of the plaintiff's cause of action. [Footnotes omitted.]

'Thus, a waiver of tort is a means by which a party can claim a specified amount as compensation for certain wrongful acts instead of pursuing a claim for damages. The claim remains grounded in tort.' *Ross v HVLD Systems (1997) Ltd* (1999) 170 DLR (4th) 600 at 605–606, Sask CA, per Jackson JA

WANT OF JURISDICTION. *SEE* EXCESS OF JURISDICTION

WAR

[For 48 Halsbury's Laws (4th edn) para 101 see now 49(1) Halsbury's Laws (4th edn) (Reissue) para 506.]

WARD OF COURT

[For 24 Halsbury's Laws (4th edn) para 576 see now 5(3) Halsbury's Laws (4th edn) (Reissue) para 317.]

WARRANT

Extradition proceedings

[The Extradition Act 1870 has been repealed. The definition is re-enacted in the Extradition Act 1989, Sch 1, para 20.]

[For 18 Halsbury's Laws (4th edn) para 225 see now 17(2) Halsbury's Laws (4th edn) (Reissue) paras 1193, 1216.]

WARRANT IN FORCE FOR THE ARREST OF A PERSON

Australia '... there is little significant difference between the notion of a "warrant in force for the arrest of a person" in s 6(a)(i) and "a duly authenticated warrant ... for the arrest of the person" in s 19(3) of the [Extradition Act 1988 (Cth)]. The words "for the arrest, etc" are in both instances merely descriptive of the warrant. That is, the warrant must authorise arrest. The "due authentication" requirement in s 19(3), which is not found in s 6(a)(i), simply reflects the fact that the requirement for formal proof is postponed until a more advanced stage in the extradition process. On this approach, the expression "a warrant in force for the arrest of a person" refers to a warrant that is valid (or, which is the same thing, operational or effective). The fact that a valid warrant is stayed (for a limited time and purpose and upon conditions designed to secure the suspect's presence in the criminal proceeding initiated against him) does not deprive the warrant of relevant "force".' *Bertran v Vanstone* BC200001210; [2000] FCA 359 at [57], per Kenny J

WARRANTY

[For 9 Halsbury's Laws (4th edn) para 57 see now 9(1) Halsbury's Laws (4th edn) (Reissue) para 664.]

Insurance generally

[For 25 Halsbury's Laws (4th edn) para 420 see now 25 Halsbury's Laws (4th edn) (2003 Reissue) para 94.]

Marine insurance

[For 25 Halsbury's Laws (4th edn) para 52 see now 25 Halsbury's Laws (4th edn) (Reissue) para 235.]

Sale of goods

[For 41 Halsbury's Laws (4th edn) paras 681, 682 see now 41 Halsbury's Laws (4th edn) (Reissue) para 63.]

WASTE

[For 27 Halsbury's Laws (4th edn) paras 279–280 see now 27(1) Halsbury's Laws (4th edn) (Reissue) para 345.]

[For 42 Halsbury's Laws (4th edn) para 992 see now 42 Halsbury's Laws (4th edn) (Reissue) para 986.]

Equitable waste

[For 42 Halsbury's Laws (4th edn) para 1003 see now 42 Halsbury's Laws (4th edn) (Reissue) para 997.]

Meliorating waste

[For 42 Halsbury's Laws (4th edn) para 999 see now 42 Halsbury's Laws (4th edn) (Reissue) para 993.]

Permissive waste

[For 42 Halsbury's Laws (4th edn) para 1001 see now 42 Halsbury's Laws (4th edn) (Reissue) para 995.]

Voluntary waste

[For 42 Halsbury's Laws (4th edn) para 993 see now 42 Halsbury's Laws (4th edn) (Reissue) para 987.]

WASTE LAND

[*Box Parish Council v Lacey* was overruled by the House of Lords in *Hampshire County Council v Milburn*, from which the following is an extract.] 'The manorial system which the Normans partly inherited and partly established displayed a variety of local laws and customs but in general there were three categories of land comprised in a manor. The demesne land belonged to the lord of the manor. The copyhold land was divided between the tenants of the lord of the manor. The remainder of the land consisted of uncultivated land, referred to as the waste of the manor. The waste land was the natural source of grazing, fodder and fuel for all the inhabitants of the manor. The waste land belonged to the lord of the manor subject to the rights of the tenants to enjoy in common the fruits or some of the fruits of the soil in the manner of a "profit a prendre".' *Hampshire County Council v Milburn* [1990] 2 All ER 257 at 258, HL, per Lord Templeman

WATER RESOURCES

[The Water Resources Act 1963 has been repealed. The Water Resources Act 1991 gives a definition of 'source of supply' in place of 'water resources'.]

'Source of supply' means—
(a) any inland waters except, without prejudice to subsection (3) below in its application to paragraph (b) of this definition, any which are discrete waters; or
(b) any underground strata in which water is or at any time may be contained;
(Water Resources Act 1991, s 221(1))

Any reference in this Act to water contained in underground strata is a reference to water so contained otherwise than in a sewer, pipe, reservoir, tank or other underground works constructed in any such strata; but for the purposes of this Act water for the time being contained in—
(a) a well, borehole or similar work, including any adit or passage constructed in connection with the well, borehole or work for facilitating the collection of water in the well, borehole or work; or
(b) any excavation into underground strata, where the level of water in the excavation depends wholly or mainly on water entering it from those strata,
shall be treated as water contained in the underground strata into which the well, borehole or work was sunk or, as the case may be, the excavation was made. (Water Resources Act 1991, s 221(3))

WATERCOURSE

[The Water Resources Act 1963 and the definition in the Water Act 1989, s 189(1) have been repealed. The definition is now contained in the Water Resources Act 1991, s 221(1), as follows.]
'Watercourse' includes all rivers, streams, ditches, drains, cuts, culverts, dykes, sluices, sewers and passages through which water flows, except mains and other pipes which—
(a) belong to the Authority or a water undertaker; or
(b) are used by a water undertaker or any other person for the purpose only of providing a supply of water to any premises.

WATERCOURSE

[Public Health Act 1936, s 259(1)(a).] 'This appeal raises the discrete but vital question of whether Carrick Roads is a "watercourse" within the meaning of s 259(1)(a)of the Public Health Act 1936. If it is not, the Port Health Authority had no power to issue the abatement notice.

'2. Section 79(1) of the Environmental Protection Act 1990 defines a number of "statutory nuisances" for the purpose of Pt III of that Act, including "(h) any other matter declared by any enactment to be a statutory nuisance". One such enactment is s 259(1) of the 1936 Act. As amended by the 1990 Act, and as material for present purposes, this provides:

"The following matters shall be statutory nuisances for the purposes of Pt III of the Environmental Protection Act 1990, that is to say—(a) any pond, pool, ditch, gutter or watercourse which is so foul and in such a state as to be prejudicial to health or a nuisance; (b) any part of a watercourse, not being a part normally navigated by vessels employed in the carriage of goods by water, which is so choked or silted up as to obstruct or impede the proper flow of water and thereby cause a nuisance, or give rise to conditions prejudicial to health ..."

'3. Mr Havers QC, for South West Water, argues that a "watercourse" in s 259(1)(a) cannot possibly extend to an estuary or other large body of water such as Carrick Roads. He relies upon the ejusdem generis principle coupled with the statutory history of para (a) which dates back to 1855. Mr Gordon QC, for the Port Health Authority, argues that the word "watercourse" is capable of extending to a river or estuary, as is clear from para (b) of s 259(1), and that Parliament cannot have intended that the same word should have a different meaning in two paragraphs of the same subsection. He also argues that in setting up the Port Health Authority it must have been intended that it would have these powers in relation to the waters within its jurisdiction.

'4. We have therefore looked in detail at the statutory history of both these provisions and at other uses of the term "watercourse" in the same legislation. We have also been referred to the common law and opinio juris. It may be helpful, therefore, to begin at the beginning.

'5. The definition of a "watercourse" in the *Shorter Oxford English Dictionary on Historical Principles* (3rd edn, 1944) is: "1510 1. A stream of water, a river or brook; also, an artificial channel for the conveyance of water. 2. The bed or channel of a river or stream 1566."

'6. At common law there were important distinctions between the rights of landowners to surface water, percolating water and water flowing in a known and defined channel or "watercourse". But there was also an important distinction between tidal and non-tidal waters ... [T]he concept of a watercourse was capable of encompassing anything from a beck or small stream to a sizeable river but did not, it appears, extend to tidal waters (see also 49(2) *Halsbury's Laws* (4th edn reissue) paras 98–107).

...

'18. Section 259(1), as seen in para 2 above, provides for two different statutory nuisances. Paragraph (a) repeats the old s 91.2 of the 1875 Act (see para 15), itself derived from s 8 of the 1855 Act (see para 9), but not in identical terms (see para 20 below). Paragraph (b) has its origins in s 54(1) of the Public Health Act 1925, although it is not in exactly the same terms. Section 54(1) provided that choked or silted up parts of watercourses which were likely to cause overflows or "hinder the usual effectual drainage of water through the same" should be deemed to be a nuisance for the purpose of s 91 of the 1875 Act "notwithstanding that the same may not be injurious to health". It is difficult to see what those last words were doing there unless the intention was to make this a specific example of a watercourse in such a state as to be a nuisance under s 91.2. However, the draftsman added what was then a proviso, excluding those parts of such watercourses as were used for the carriage of goods by water. Obviously, he must have contemplated that a watercourse could include a sizeable river or canal.

'19. The construction of "watercourse" as it now appears in s 259(1)(a) of the 1936 Act is thus no easy matter. Although its history can be traced back to s 8 of the 1855 Act, that does not necessarily mean that it has retained exactly the same meaning throughout. It is clearly a word which is capable of bearing different meanings according to the context and purpose of the provision in which it appears. The 1855 provision referred to any pool etc "so *foul* as to be a Nuisance or injurious to health" (my emphasis). Whatever else might make a place foul it clearly contemplated that human waste might do so. This is reinforced by the list which covered exactly the sort of places where human waste might accumulate in such a way. It is therefore extremely unlikely that at that stage it was intended to include watercourses into which it was generally thought proper to discharge such matter. By no stretch of the imagination could it have included an estuary such as Carrick Roads or indeed any tidal waters ...

'20. But by 1936 both the provision and the surrounding circumstances had changed. First, the 1875 Act had referred to a pool etc which was "so foul *or in such a state*" (my emphasis) thus preserving the connection with foul waste but

widening it to encompass other causes of nuisance or injury to health. Secondly, in the 1936 Act the word "pool" was added at the beginning of the list and the words "privy urinal cesspool drain or ashpit" were dropped. Cesspools and drains turned up in s 39(1), and "closets" (which include privies) in s 44(1), not as statutory nuisances but remedied in a very similar way. The effect is to make the 1936 list look very different from the 1855 and 1875 lists, giving the impression that the scope of the provision is now broader than it had been before. That impression is reinforced by the addition of para (b), which clearly assumes that "watercourse" can refer to a much larger body of water. It is of course possible for the same word to mean different things in the same statute, but it is improbable that it means different things in the same subsection, especially when a deliberate (and quite unnecessary) decision has been taken to put them together.

'21. Furthermore, applying the ejusdem generis principle to the provision as it now stands, in the light of the statutory history, one can see that, whatever else it is concerned with, it has always been concerned with protecting the public from threats to health posed by accumulations of human waste. What was an acceptable place of discharge in 1855 was no longer so in 1936. It may very well be, therefore, that the meaning of "watercourse" in s 259(1)(a) of the 1936 Act is wider than it was in 1855 or 1875. But it cannot be insignificant that pollution control was not fully established over tidal waters such as Carrick Roads until much later. It cannot have been contemplated in 1936 that the Port Health Authority could take action under this legislation against the local health authorities who were responsible for the old outfalls. In many places the responsible authorities would be one and the same.

'22. Since then, of course, things have moved on again. Control is now exercised over tidal waters. Recognition that sewage discharged into such waters may indeed cause health hazards has grown. Their use not only for sailing but also for contact water sports has also grown. Local health authorities are no longer responsible for receiving and disposing of sewage. They not only can but must use their statutory nuisance powers to protect their beaches from accumulations or deposits which are prejudicial to health or a nuisance within the meaning of s 79(1)(e) of the Environmental Protection Act 1990: see *R v Carrick DC, ex p Shelley* [1996] JPL 857. Is it therefore possible to hold that the meaning of the term is now broader than it was in 1936? To do so would of course involve applying the principles stated by Lord Wilberforce in *Royal College of Nursing of the UK v Dept of Health and Social Security* [1981] 1 All ER 545 at 564–565,[1981] AC 800 at 822, and recently applied by a majority of their lordships to the term "family" in the Rent Act 1977 in *Fitzpatrick v Sterling Housing Association Ltd* [1999] 4 All ER 705, [1999] 3 WLR 1113.

'23. In my view it is not possible to do so. One reason is that the social purpose of protecting such waters from the health hazards arising from sewage pollution can be achieved in other ways. Although the Environment Agency has a wider brief it could have refused consent to this new discharge. Another is that by no linguistic contortions can a "watercourse" be made to include the open sea. Yet the social purpose now sought to be achieved would require jurisdiction over discharges into the open sea as well as estuaries such as Carrick Roads. If Carricks Roads is a watercourse, the Port Health Authority would have power to control nuisances arising from the new Black Rock and the old Middle Point discharges which are within the estuary but not from the old Pennance Point discharge which is into Falmouth Bay.

'24. This brings me to Mr Gordon's final argument. This is a port health authority, successor to the port sanitary authority first set up permanently in 1888 by order made under s 287 of the Public Health Act 1875. This gave the authority jurisdiction over the port of Truro and as much of the port of Falmouth as lay within a line drawn from Pennance Point (in the west) to Zoze Point (in the east). Most of the waters within this line were in the Carrick Roads estuary but some were in Falmouth Bay. The jurisdiction was extended in 1893 to a line drawn from Zoze Point (in the east) to Dennis Head (in the west), thus covering more of Falmouth Bay and some of the Helford River. (In 1988 it was extended further west and out to sea.) The 1888 authority was given various functions of an urban sanitary authority, including those under ss 91 to 111 of the 1875 Act relating to nuisances. Mr Gordon therefore argues that "watercourse" in s 91.2 must even then have included Carrick Roads for why else was the authority given these powers? One answer to that is that s 110 of the 1875 Act (repeated from s 32 of the Public Health Act 1866) provided that ships and vessels lying within an authority's jurisdiction were to be treated as houses for the purpose of the Act's provisions as to nuisances. Another answer is that their jurisdiction extended over "docks, basins, harbours, creeks, rivers, channels, reads, bays and streams" belonging to the ports in question. Some of these might well

be watercourses and some might give rise to other forms of statutory nuisance. Above all, however, from the very beginning it appears that this authority has had jurisdiction over waters which were beyond the mouth of the estuary and cannot ever have been a "watercourse". Yet it was thought worthwhile creating a port sanitary authority with jurisdiction over them. This argument cannot therefore persuade me that Carrick Roads is a watercourse for the purpose of s 259(1)(a) of the 1936 Act.

'25. For those reasons, I agree with Harrison J that Carrick Roads is not a watercourse and that the abatement notice was invalid. I would therefore dismiss this appeal.' *R v Falmouth and Truro Port Health Authority, ex p South West Water Ltd* [2000] 3 All ER 306 at 337–338, 342–344, CA, per Hale LJ

WATERS

Australia [The Clean Waters Act 1970 (NSW) s 16(1) creates an offence of polluting 'waters'. 'Waters' is defined in s 5 of the Act.] 'There is no doubt that the legislature intended that the term "waters" should include waters on privately-owned or occupied land. One reason is obvious. Water flows. Many of the forms of waters referred to in the statutory definition are located upon, or would flow through or over, private land.' *Electricity Commission of New South Wales v Environment Protection Authority* (1992) 28 NSWLR 474 at 498, per Gleeson CJ

WATERWAY

[See also the Water Resources Act 1963, s 135(1), as amended by the Water Act 1989, s 128, Sch 13, para 31(1)(b).]

WAYLEAVE

[For 31 Halsbury's Laws (4th edn) para 237 see now 31 Halsbury's Laws (4th edn) (2003 Reissue) para 335.]

WEAPON

Canada 'In my view, a firearm must come within the definition of a weapon. A firearm is expressly designed to kill or wound. It operates with deadly efficiency in carrying out the object of its design. It follows that such a deadly weapon can, of course, be used for purposes of threatening or intimidating. Indeed, it is hard to imagine anything more intimidating or dangerous than a brandished firearm.

A person waving a gun and calling "hands up" can be reasonably certain that the suggestion will be obeyed. A firearm is quite different from an object such as a carving knife or an ice pick which will normally be used for legitimate purposes. A firearm, however, is always a weapon. No matter what the intention may be of the person carrying a gun, the firearm itself presents the ultimate threat of death to those in its presence.

'The definition of "weapon" in s 2 must include a firearm as defined in s 84. For example s 88 of the Criminal Code provides that anyone who, without lawful excuse, has a weapon in his possession while he is attending or on his way to attending a public meeting is guilty of an offence. The presence of a firearm at a public meeting would, in itself, present a threat and result in the intimidation of all who were present. It really cannot have been the intention of the framers of the legislation that people would be permitted to brazenly take their guns with them to public meetings provided that they did not use them or intend to use them to cause injury or to threaten or intimidate. Indeed, to state the proposition reveals that a definition with such a result is unthinkable.' *R v Felawka* [1993] 4 SCR 199 at 211–212, per Cory J

WEEK

[For 45 Halsbury's Laws (4th edn) para 1112 see now 45(2) Halsbury's Laws (4th edn) (Reissue) para 212.]

WHENEVER POSSIBLE

New Zealand [Rule 9 of the Judges' Rules begins 'Any statement made in accordance with the above rules, should, whenever possible, be taken down in writing …'.] 'In my opinion the words … can refer to any circumstances at all which would affect the possibility of a statement being made in accordance with the procedure prescribed in the rule. The refusal of an accused to speak when notes, notepaper or pen are available is a circumstance which, in my view, would be relevant to an application of the rule.' *R v Gordon* [1993] 2 NZLR 209 at 223, per Williamson J

WHO IS, OR WOULD IF SUED HAVE BEEN, LIABLE IN RESPECT OF THE SAME DAMAGE

Australia 'Para (c) [of s 5(1) Law Reform (Miscellaneous Provisions) Act 1946 (NSW)] applies where damage is suffered by any person as a result of a tort (whether a crime or not) and states: "any tort-feasor liable in respect of that damage may recover contribution from any other tort-feasor who is, or would if sued have been, liable in respect of the same damage, whether as a joint tort-feasor or otherwise, so, however, that no person shall be entitled to recover contribution under this section from any person entitled to be indemnified by that person in respect of the liability in respect of which the contribution is sought"… The words "would if sued have been" in para(c) … envisage a completed action where the target tortfeasor has been sued to judgment and the action has been fully dealt with on its merits. Lord Denning suggested this construction of the paragraph in *Hart* [[1969] 1 QB 405 at 411]. Windeyer J implied as much in *Brambles* when he said [(1966) 114 CLR 213 at 221]: "The description, a tort-feasor who if sued would have been liable, denotes any person who would have been held liable in tort had he been sued in a competent court, by proper process, at a proper time and on evidence properly presented – that is anyone whose liability as a tort-feasor could have been ascertained in an action". Clearly, in the context, the ascertainment of liability means ascertainment on its merits, not ascertainment by private arrangement between only some of the parties by which, unilaterally, they deprive others of rights which, for good purpose, Parliament has conferred on them by reforming legislation.' *James Hardie & Co Pty Ltd v Seltsam Pty Ltd* (1998) 159 ALR 268 at 270 and 291; 73 ALJR 238; BC9806759, per Kirby J

WHOLESALE

Australia 'I respectfully agree with Samuels JA [in *Attorney-General (NSW) (Ex rel Franklins Stores Pty Ltd) v Lizelle Pty Ltd* [1977] 2 NSWLR 955; (1977) 36 LGRA 1] that the "essence of a wholesale business is the nature and purpose of the activity". Wholesaling normally does, but does not necessarily, involve the sale of significant quantities of goods. It normally does, but does not necessarily, involve sales to retailers. A wholesale warehouse is not a place to which members of the public are invited and it is not a place where retail sales occur in the sense that a sale is made to the ultimate consumer.' *Woolworths Ltd v Campbells Cash and Carry Pty Ltd* (1996) 92 LGERA 244 at 258; BC9605638 at 15, per Cole JA

WHOLLY OR MAINLY

[The Broadcasting Act 1990, s 92(2)(a) prohibits the broadcasting of any advertisement inserted by or on behalf of a body whose objects are 'wholly or mainly' of a political nature.] ' "Wholly or mainly" is a phrase the meaning of which is not free from ambiguity. Clearly it requires a proportion which is more than half. But how much more? 51% or 99% and anything between are candidates.
...

'The issue is not whether the restriction contained in the first rule is justifiable but how the restriction should be construed having regard to its blanket or discriminative effect in relation to a political body. In view of this restriction the ambiguous words "wholly or mainly" should be construed restrictively. By that I mean they should be construed in a way in which [sic] limits the application of the restriction to bodies whose objects are substantially or primarily political ... Certainly a body to fall within the provision must be at least midway between the two percentages I have identified i e more than 75%.' *R v Radio Authority, ex p Bull* [1997] 2 All ER 561 at 570, CA, per Lord Woolf MR

'The words "wholly or mainly" are words of degree. They are not coterminous in meaning. A person who is wholly to blame will bear a greater burden of fault than a person who is mainly to blame. They are, however, ordinary English words and the question whether something is "wholly or mainly" is of its nature one which is a jury type question.' *R v Radio Authority, ex p Bull* [1997] 2 All ER 561 at 575, CA, per Aldous LJ

WILFULLY

Australia [The Criminal Code (Tas) provides, by s 268, that 'a person who unlawfully sets fire to any building ... is guilty of a crime which is called arson' and, by s 267(3), that 'an act causing injury to property shall not constitute a crime ... unless it is done wilfully ...'. A house was substantially damaged by fires deliberately lit in several places.] ' "Wilful" and "wilfully" have been used in a variety of legal contexts, criminal, quasi-criminal and civil — see, e.g., *Words and Phrases Legally Defined*, 2nd edn, vol 5, pp 333–340 [see 3rd edn, vol 4, pp 434–439]. In the great majority of cases involving conduct which is criminal or constitutes a statutory offence it will be found that the word (I treat them here as one) implies something blameworthy in the state of mind accompanying the conduct which is to be "wilful"... Even in a

civil context, "wilful" will be found often used in respect of conduct which is unreasonable or captious — for example, in the field of contract law, *Bennett v Stone* [1903] 1 Ch 509 at 514–515 — "wilful default"; or acquisition of land, *Re East End Docks & Birmingham Junction Railway Act, ex p Bradshaw* (1848) 16 Sim 174 at 175–176 — "wilful refusal". This usage accords with the most appropriate of the dictionary definitions. The word is capable in ordinary speech of a wide range of meaning. Thus, the Shorter Oxford English Dictionary (vol 2, p 2549) gives the following for "wilfully": "1. willingly, readily; patiently, submissively. 2. Of one's own free will, of one's own accord, voluntarily. According to one's own will; at will, freely. 3. Purposely, on purpose, intentionally, deliberately. Chiefly, now always, in bad sense; occasionally implying maliciously. 4. In a self-willed manner; perversely, obstinately, stubbornly". Of these meanings, the third is the nearest to being appropriate for the present purpose. The applicable law for us is that recklessness of the kind described in *R v Cunningham* (1957) 2 QB 396 is conduct which satisfies in respect of arson the meaning of "wilfully" in s 267(3).' *Gardenal-Williams v R* (1989) Tas R 62 at 74, 78, per Neasey J

Australia [Section 5(1) of the Environmental Offences and Penalties Act 1989 (NSW) provides that a person who 'wilfully' disposed of waste in a manner which did or was likely to harm the environment, was guilty of an offence.]
'Perhaps the only assistance which can be obtained from [*Iannella v French* (1968) 119 CLR 84] is to be found in the statements by Barwick CJ (at 93, 95) that the denotation of the word "wilfully" depends upon its context and the subject matter of the provision in which it is found, and by Windeyer J (at 108) that an exercise in the science of language and meaning of words (semasiology) will not yield the true interpretation of the word "wilfully"; its importance is in the meaning which it gives to (rather than takes from) its context.

'The immediate context of the word "wilfully" in s 5(1) of the Act with which this appeal is concerned is that, as an adverb, it qualifies the verb "disposes". That word, however, already imports the notion of intention. To dispose of waste means to get rid of it; such an action is necessarily deliberate or intentional. As a general rule, a court will adopt that construction of a statutory provision which will give some effect to all of the words which it contains; *Beckwith v R* (1976) 135 CLR 569 at 574. The interpretation given to "wilfully" by the majority in *Iannella v French* would give it no operation at all in s 5 if the qualification which it creates were limited to the verb "disposes". The only additional ingredient of the offence is that the manner of disposal was one which harms or is likely to harm the environment. Thus, in order to give the word "wilfully" any operation at all to perform, in my view, it must qualify the stated consequence of the manner in which the disposal is effected.' *Environment Protection Authority v N* (1992) 26 NSWLR 352 at 355, per Hunt CJ at CL

Australia [Section 5(1) of the Environmental Offences and Penalties Act 1989 (NSW) provides that a person who, without lawful authority, 'wilfully' or negligently disposes of waste in a manner harmful or likely to harm the environment, is guilty of an offence.] 'The immediate context of the word "wilfully" in s 5(1) of the Act with which this appeal is concerned is that, as an adverb, it qualifies the verb "disposes". That word, however, already imports the notion of intention. To dispose of waste means to get rid of it; such an action is necessarily deliberate or intentional ... in order to give the word "wilfully" any operation at all to perform, in my view, it must qualify the stated consequence of the manner in which the disposal is effected.' *Environment Protection Authority v N* (1992) 59 A Crim R 408 at 411, per Hunt CJ at CL

WILL (TESTAMENT)

[The definition in s 1 of the Wills Act 1837 has been amended. For the words 'and also to a disposition by will and testament or devise of the custody and tuition of any child' there have been substituted the words 'and also to an appointment by will of a guardian of a child.' See the Children Act 1989, Sch 13, para 1.]

[For 50 Halsbury's Laws (4th edn) para 201 see now 50 Halsbury's Laws (4th edn) (Reissue) para 251.]

Informal or nuncupative will

[For 50 Halsbury's Laws (4th edn) para 272 see now 50 Halsbury's Laws (4th edn) (Reissue) para 323.]

WILL

Australia [Section 24 of the Criminal Assets Recovery Act 1990 (NSW) provides that 'if the Supreme Court is satisfied that an assets forfeiture order will operate to cause hardship to any

dependant' the Court may alleviate such hardship.] 'It is submitted ... that [s 24] speaks in the future tense.

'I accept that the use of the future tense of the verb in the relevant section is of some significance. However, as revealed by the *Macquarie Dictionary* the word "will" does not only indicate "future likelihood" but can also indicate "capability".' *New South Wales Crime Commission v Kelly* BC200300431; [2003] NSWSC 56 at [8], [9], per Shaw J

WINDING UP

Australia [Section 601 of the Corporations Law provides that: 'The provisions of this law with respect to winding up do not apply to any body corporate the winding up of which was started before the commencement of this Chapter ...'] 'What is meant by "winding up" in this context? In my opinion it does not comprehend steps or proceedings taken for the purpose of obtaining an order that the company be wound up. Winding up is a process that consists of collecting the assets, realising and reducing them to money, dealing with proofs of creditors by admitting or rejecting them, and distributing the net proceeds, after providing for costs and expenses, to the persons entitled. It is a process, comparable to an administration in equity, that begins or "starts" with an order of the Court. However, it is not the court order itself that "winds up" the company; the order does no more than direct that the company be wound up, which is then carried into effect by an officer of court, the liquidator, who does the things I have identified in order to liquidate the company's assets and wind up its affairs. In referring to "winding up" or to the company being "wound up", and to the manner and the incidents of doing so, s 601 therefore speaks not of proceedings aimed at obtaining an order of court to wind up the company but of the process that ensues from and follows such an order. Leaving aside the case of a successful appeal, winding up thus "starts" when, and not before, an order to wind up is made appointing a liquidator.' *Re Crust 'N' Crumb Bakers (Wholesale) Pty Ltd* [1992] 2 Qld R 76 at 78, per McPherson SPJ

WITH A VIEW TO GIVING THAT CREDITOR A PREFERENCE

New Zealand [Section 309 of the Companies Act 1955 provides that, subject to a number of conditions, if an agreement is made in favour of a creditor less than two years before the liquidation of the indebted company, 'with a view to giving that creditor ... a preference over other creditors', the agreement will be voidable as against the liquidator.] '... a line of decisions holding that the words "with a view to ... giving a preference" imply both an act of free will on the part of the insolvent, ie free from pressure by others; and a dominant intention to prefer the creditor over others. It is not enough that the creditor was in fact preferred.' *Tyree Power Construction Ltd v D S Edmonds Electrical Ltd (In Liquidation)* [1994] 2 NZLR 268 at 272, CA, per cur

WITHDRAW

Australia [Under the Supreme Court Rules 1970 (NSW) Pt 55 r 10(b) the Supreme Court may issue a warrant for the arrest of a contemnor and his or her detention in custody until he or she is brought before the Court to answer the contempt charge where 'it appears that the contemnor is likely to abscond or otherwise withdraw himself from the jurisdiction'.] 'The word "withdraw" as used in the rule is relevantly defined in the [*Macquarie Dictionary* (3rd ed, 1997)] as "to retire; retreat; go apart or away." I do not think there is a notion in the word "withdraw" of a purpose of avoidance. However, I do not think that the word is used in the rule to refer to a fleeting or a short absence. It seems to me that the word suggests an absence that is of some considerable length or indefinite. This is because it is in a context where what is contemplated is that the alleged contemnor will not appear in answer to the proceedings. The absence, in any event, of a sense of purpose from the meaning of "withdraw" in the context is confirmed by what Kirby P said in [*Registrar, Court of Appeal v Ritter* (1985) 34 NSWLR 641].' *Schnabel v Lui* BC200208087; [2002] NSWSC 1184 at [17], per Hamilton J

WITHIN

[A person aggrieved by a compulsory purchase order under the Acquisition of Land Act 1981 may apply to the court to determine the validity of the order on specified grounds; by s 23(4), an application must be made 'within six weeks' from the date on which notice of the confirmation or making of the order is first published.] 'In my judgment, a time limit which for sound policy reasons is incapable of extension and yet which may be critical to the vindication of the property rights of individuals, is not to be narrowly construed ... I prefer the view, corresponding with both colloquial usage and legal principle, that six weeks beginning on a Tuesday end six Tuesdays later, and that an act done on the final Tuesday is therefore an act done "within" the six weeks.' *Okolo v Secretary of State for the Environment* [1997] 2 All ER 911 at 915, 916, per Sedley J

Australia [Section 44(3)(b)(1) of the Limitation Act 1981 (NT) prohibits the exercise of discretion to extend the time to lodge an action for damages arising from a motor vehicle accident unless the court is satisfied that the action has been instituted 'within' twelve months after the ascertainment of the material facts by the plaintiff.] 'So far as the Oxford English Dictionary defines "within" in temporal terms, those definitions are as follows: "In the limits of (a period of time); most usually, before the end of, after not more than; also, since the beginning of, not more than ... ago; or *generally* between the beginning and end of, in the course of, during". Clearly some of those definitions favour the appellant, ("before the end of"), some, the respondent ("during"). In the context, however, and to avoid an otherwise absurd result I consider that the former meaning is appropriate. A reading of "within" as meaning "before the end of" appears in *Earl of Morton's Trustees v McDougal* [1944 SC 410]... Lord Justice-Clerk Cooper said [at 443]; "It is to be noted that the words are 'within one month' and not 'within the month'. According to its normal significance, as evidenced by the dictionaries, 'within' when applied to a period of time most usually means 'before the end of'... It seems to me that that is a sufficient meaning to give to the words of the statute—in other words to read them as prescribing a time limit on the expiry of which, if the claim and particulars have not been given, the claim will prescribe".' *Ward v Walton* (1989) 10 MVR 537 at 541, per Asche CJ

WITHOUT

Australia [Section 556(2) of the Companies (NSW) Code provides that in any proceedings against a director of a company which incurred debts while unable to pay its debts when they became due, it is a defence if the defendant proves that the debt was incurred without his express or implied authority or consent. It was argued that the words 'without' in the context meant 'beyond the compass, limits, range or scope of' or 'outside of, not in the limits of, external ... beyond the extent of, beyond the scope or sphere of action of ...' the relevant authority or consent.] 'I do not consider this to be the natural meaning of "without" in the context. The Oxford Dictionary suggests that such meaning is now somewhat obsolescent and is generally confined to literary use. The primary meaning, and that suggested by s 556(2)(a) itself, is that of the absence or negation of something; not accompanied by; or which lacks that without which it is said to be. The Macquarie Dictionary confirms this meaning: see ibid (at 1959).' *Metal Manufacturers Pty Ltd v Lewis* (1988) 13 NSWLR 315 at 320, per Kirby J

WITHOUT AUTHORITY

New Zealand '[1] The issue which I must decide in this case is whether a person who enters retail premises commits a burglary if he or she either enters with the intention of committing a crime in the premises or forms that intention while inside the premises.

'[2] The decision on this issue depends on the meaning of the words "without authority" in s 231(1) of the Crimes Act 1961, which provides:

> **231. Burglary** – Every one commits burglary and is liable to imprisonment for a term not exceeding 10 years who–
> (a) enters any building or ship, or part of a building or ship, without authority and with intent to commit a crime in the building or ship; or
> (b) having entered any building or ship, remains in it without authority and with intent to commit a crime in the building or ship.

'[3] The term "without authority" is not defined in the Crimes Act. However, s 231(3)(b) provides that a person "who gains entrance to a building or ship by any threat or artifice used for that purpose is to be treated as having entered without authority".

'[4] Mr Barwell faces 24 charges of burglary, all of which relate to service stations and other retail premises which were open to the public at the time.

...

'[63] ... I acknowledge that there is some force in Mr Ruane's argument. After all, if he or she was asked the specific question, an owner or a manager of retail premises would be unlikely to allow someone who intends to steal from his or her shop to enter or remain in the shop.

'[64] However, Mr Glover's submission that a shopkeeper has to assume that everyone who enters his or her shop is bona fide has force.

'[65] Furthermore, there are two significant difficulties with the interpretation of s 231(1) for which Mr Ruane contended.

'[66] Firstly, it involves a person's status, ie the lawfulness or otherwise of his or her presence in a building, being determined solely by reference to his or her own state of mind, rather than by reference to any objective or independent fact or to any action by or on behalf of the owner or lessee of the building.

'[67] That problem is compounded in the case of a person who, having entered a shop without a dishonest intent, then decides to steal something from the shop. That is because, on Mr Ruane's argument, that change in state of mind alone would render his or her presence in the building unlawful and would mean that he or she would have committed the crime of burglary, without the manager or owner of the shop having to say or do anything.

'[68] By comparison, a person who enters a building contrary to a trespass notice or in breach of a protection order under the Domestic Violence Act 1995 does so "without authority" (and did so "unlawfully" until 2003), and that element of the offence would thereby be proved. Although it might be regarded as somewhat anomalous, the same would apply in respect of an under-age person who enters a bottle store.

'[69] Secondly, the concept of "without authority" is generally inconsistent with a scenario where a person remains in a building with the consent of either the occupier of those premises or someone who is acting on his or her behalf.

...

'[82] The conclusion that merely walking into a shop which is open to the public, although with a dishonest intent, cannot constitute entering that shop "without authority" is also supported by the comment of the Court of Appeal in *R v Panine* (2003) 20 CRNZ 37 that "a construction [of s 240A(1)(b), which provided for one of the three forms of aggravated burglary] that abandons the element of unlawful passage to or from the building, seen as essential throughout both simple burglary and other forms of aggravated burglary, gives cause for reflection" (p 45, para [26]).

'[83] Returning to the proposition to which I referred in para [63], in my view a shopkeeper who opens his or her shop to the public at large in effect takes the risk that some of the persons who enter the shop may be dishonest and may steal items from inside the shop or may otherwise act dishonestly in their dealings with shop staff.

'[84] In my view it therefore cannot be said, as a general proposition, that any shopkeeper prohibits an individual, but unknown, member of the public from entering his or her shop because that person has the intention to shoplift or otherwise act dishonestly inside the shop.

'[85] Indeed, it is a common practice in the retailing industry to attempt to deter people who might be tempted to shoplift, while still allowing them access.

'[86] For example, the function of "shoplifters will be prosecuted" signs is to warn potential shoplifters not against entering a store but against stealing inside it, while in-store video security cameras and security personnel, either at the door or inside the shop, have the dual purpose of detecting both offending and offenders and deterring people from stealing.

'[87] As I have already mentioned, the position regarding the "without authority" issue is otherwise if an offender is apprehended and is then served with a trespass notice in respect of the premises in question.' *Police v Barwell* [2006] DCR 198 at [1]–[4], [63]–[69], [82]–[87], per Judge T M Abbott

WITHOUT DELAY

New Zealand 'The temporal expression "without delay" is not synonymous with instantly or immediately. It is a negative injunction — not to delay — which in the absence of any further qualification necessarily imports as the test whether the delay is reasonable in all the circumstances having regard to the purpose of the right.' *R v Mallinson* [1993] 1 NZLR 528 at 530, CA, per cur

New Zealand 'The phrase "without delay" in s 23 [of the New Zealand Bill of Rights Act 1990] refers to consultation and instruction. It does not specifically refer to the right to be informed but it follows that if a person has a right to consult a lawyer without delay then he or she should be advised of that right at a point in time where it can be effectively exercised.' *Barr v Ministry of Transport* [1993] 1 NZLR 703 at 705–706, per Williams J

WITHOUT GOOD CAUSE

New Zealand [New Zealand Law Society Rules of Professional Conduct for Barristers and Solicitors, R 1.02.] 'It is to be noted that the obligation contains the exception "without good cause"—it is and could not be absolute. Examples of good cause in this context include instructions for services which are outside the field of competence of the practitioner, the unavailability of a proper fee, and the instructions regarding deception of the Court.

The circumstances which may constitute good cause are many and varied. They cannot be defined either exhaustively or with particularity.' *Wells v Wellington District Law Society* [1997] 1 NZLR 660 at 663, CA, per cur

WITHOUT ISSUE

[For 50 Halsbury's Laws (4th edn) para 619 see now 50 Halsbury's Laws (4th edn) (Reissue) para 572.]

WITHOUT LIMIT OF TIME

New Zealand 'The words mean no more than the term of the agreement is not specified. They are not synonymous with "indefinitely" or "forever". They do not relate to the right of termination of the agreement. In other words, merely because the agreement is without period of time, that is to say the agreement is unspecified as to duration, it does not mean that the parties intended that the agreement should go on indefinitely or forever and that a right of termination by reasonable notice was precluded by those words.' *Anchor Butter Co Ltd v Tui Foods Ltd* [1997] 3 NZLR 107 at 116, per Penlington J

WITHOUT PREJUDICE

New Zealand [Document and discussion.] 'The "without prejudice" privilege is based primarily on the public policy that parties should be encouraged so far as possible to settle their disputes without resort to litigation. The law gives effect to this public policy by excluding evidence of anything said or done or omitted to be said or done in the course of the settlement negotiations which can be construed as an admission of liability of the party against whom the evidence is sought to be admitted. The privilege provided by public policy may be reinforced or qualified by agreement between the parties, for example, the parties may agree that the settlement negotiations will be "without prejudice" save as to costs. The privilege applies only where an attempt is being made to settle a dispute between the parties. The admission in evidence of "without prejudice" discussions or documents to prove that a settlement was reached or to establish a claim to rectification of a written agreement entered into after settlement negotiations to reflect the actual agreement is not inconsistent with the policy and is therefore not an exception to it. The privilege does not extend to facts and statements which are independent of the settlement negotiations, notwithstanding that they occur or are made in the course of the negotiations. The law will not permit the privilege to be used to prevent proof of an act which gives statutory rights of action to other parties. The law will not permit the privilege to be used to exclude evidence of the making of a threat. The Court will override the privilege if the interests of justice require it.' *Cedenco Foods Ltd v State Insurance Ltd* [1996] 3 NZLR 205 at 210–212, per Master Kennedy-Grant

WITHOUT PREJUDICE TO LIABILITY

[The owners of a flat in a tenement carried out building works which damaged a neighbouring flat. It was clear from subsequent correspondence that the owners never disputed liability for the damage: what was disputed was the extent and effect of the damage. One of the owners' letters was headed 'Without prejudice to liability' and counsel for the owners argued that it should not therefore be referred to in court. The owners also argued that the case was time-barred. The Prescription and Limitation (Scotland) Act 1973, s 6, states that obligations shall be extinguished after five years unless a relevant claim has been made or the subsistence of the obligation has been relevantly acknowledged. Section 10(1) of the 1973 Act states, in brief, that 'relevantly acknowledged' means either performance by the debtor or an unequivocal written admission by the debtor to the creditor that the obligation still subsists.] '[E]ach situation must be judged upon its own facts ... I am satisfied that in considering the issues ... it is not appropriate to look at individual letters or individual events in isolation only. If, looking at them in conjunction and taking this letter into account, it appears that there is no clear indication, or no clear acknowledgment by written admission, that the obligation still subsists, then it may well be that, along with a conclusion to that effect, one might conclude that the terms of this letter lacked sufficient substance to overcome the words "without prejudice to liability". But if overall the substance of this letter, taken with the substance of prior events or writings, could be seen as satisfying the conditions set out in section 10(1), it would, in my opinion, be quite wrong to have decided a priori that the terms of this letter were of insufficient substance to overcome the docquet. If the terms of this letter, whether alone or with other material, are sufficient to satisfy either of those conditions in section 10(1), then in my opinion they are sufficient to render the docquet ineffectual.' *Richardson v Quercus Ltd* 1999 SCLR 133 at 138, per Lord Prosser

WITHOUT SUFFICIENT CAUSE

New Zealand [Commissions of Inquiry Act 1908, s9(2)(b).] '[I]n the present case the statutory "sufficient cause" and "just cause" exceptions provide ample scope for all the circumstances to be taken into account. Inherent in these two expressions, which are synonymous in this context, is the concept of weighing all the consequences of the refusal to give evidence: the adverse consequences to the inquiry if the questions are not answered, and the adverse consequences to the witness if he is compelled to answer.' *Brannigan v Sir Ronald Davison* [1997] 1 NZLR 140, at 147–148, PC, per cur

WOMAN

Australia 'In my opinion the ordinary meaning of ["woman"] where appearing in s 37(1) [of the Social Security Act 1947 (Cth)] includes a post-operative male-to-female transsexual who is both anatomically and psychologically female.' *Secretary, Department of Social Security v SRA* (1993) 118 ALR 467 at 496, per Lockhart J

WORD

[For 50 Halsbury's Laws (4th edn) para 430 see now 50 Halsbury's Laws (4th edn) (Reissue) para 484.]

WORK

Australia [In the context of the Veterans' Entitlements Act 1986 (Cth) s 37(1) and the Veterans' Entitlements (Income Support Supplement – Permanent Capacity for Work) Determination 1999 (Cth).] '[50] The facts of the present case illustrate the difficulty that can arise in determining the limits that are to be imposed upon the term "work" in the context of the VE Act. Plainly, "work" connotes voluntary action of some kind. It may also be accepted that "work" is purposive, rather than random. However, it is by no means easy to distinguish between work and other purposive activity, much of which may be valuable. What differentiates work from play, sport, exercise, study, or leisure?

...

'[57] In our view, the expression to "do work" in cl 5(2)(b), when read in context, requires the decision-maker to focus upon the applicant, and not some hypothetical person. Consideration must be given to whether a person of the applicant's background, suffering from his or her condition, is, solely by reason of the impairment, permanently unable to do remunerative work of the type that he or she would otherwise be fitted to undertake. In answering that question, it must be determined whether the applicant can undertake such work for more than eight hours per week. In other words, the test looks at the individual applicant, treats "work" as remunerative activity, and assesses the applicant's ability to carry out that activity by reference to that person's qualifications, background and skills." *Repatriation Commission v Hill* [2005] FCAFC 7 at [50], [57], per Wilcox, French and Weinberg JJ

WORK OF ARTISTIC CRAFTMANSHIP

Australia '[63] There is apparently some debate, see Lahore *"Copyright and Designs"* Vol 1 p 64,115 about whether the term "work of artistic craftsmanship" in s 77(1)(a) has the same meaning as "work of artistic craftsmanship" within the definition of "artistic work" in s 10(1)(c) of the Copyright Act. The author says that "presumably, this is the intended meaning". For present purposes I shall work on that assumption.

'[64] Section 10(1) relevantly provides as follows:

artistic work means:
(a) a painting, sculpture, drawing, engraving or photograph, whether the work is of artistic quality or not;
(b) a building or a model of a building, whether the building or model is of artistic quality or not; or
(c) a work of artistic craftsmanship to which neither of the last two preceding paragraphs applies;

but does not include a circuit layout within the meaning of the Circuit Layouts Act 1989.

...
'[78] I am comforted to find that the same view is expressed in Lahore at Vol 1 para [6125], where the author says this:

Works of artistic craftsmanship comprise only those works not falling within the other categories of artistic work, although it is not clear whether a work such as a sculpture, included in category (a) of the definition, may not also be a work of artistic craftsmanship. Category (c) does not exclude this possibility. On the contrary, the definition suggests that categories (a) and (b) may apply to a work of

artistic craftsmanship. Such works will, however, include all kinds of applied art such as jewellery, metal work, pottery, furniture, glassware, and works of "artistic" design or representation. In many cases preliminary sketches or drawings will be made and copyright may subsist in these as artistic works. But the finished work of artistic craftsmanship may itself be a separate subject-matter of copyright".'

Swarbrick v Burge [2003] FCA 1176 per Carr J; BC200306237

WORKER

[The Wages Councils Act 1979 has been repealed. The definition is now contained in the Wages Act 1986, s 8(1), (2), as follows.]
'Worker' means (subject to subsection (2)) an individual who—
(a) has entered into or works under (or, where the employment has ceased, worked under) one of the contracts referred to in section 8(2) [of the Wages Act 1986], or
(b) whether or not he falls within paragraph (a) above, is a homeworker,
and any reference to a worker's contract shall be construed as a reference to any such contract as is referred to in paragraph (a) above or, in the case of a homeworker, to the contract by virtue of which he is a homeworker.
(2) In this Part 'worker' does not include an individual who is wholly employed otherwise than for the purposes of the business of the person employing him.

[Under reg 2 of the Working Time Regulations 1998, SI 1998/1833, the meaning of 'worker' includes an individual who works under a contract whereby the individual 'undertakes to do or perform personally any work or services for another party to the contract'. In two separate applications to employment tribunals, the issue arose whether the applicant bricklayers were 'workers' within the meaning of the 1998 regulations and so entitled to the compensation relating to entitlement to leave in reg 14.] '[23] The tribunals were entitled to construe the contracts in the light of the circumstances in which they were made. An important issue is whether, in those circumstances, condition 6 was a term of these particular contracts. Light may be thrown on that issue by considering, for example, the agreement as to how the contract was to be performed, the method of payment. It is not a question of looking at prior negotiations but "absolutely anything which would have affected the way in which the language of the document would have been understood by a reasonable man" (see *Investors' Compensation Scheme Ltd v West Bromwich Building Society, Investors' Compensation Scheme Ltd v Hopkins & Sons (a firm), Alford v West Bromwich Building Society, Armitage v West Bromwich Building Society* [1998] 1 All ER 98 at 114, [1998] 1 WLR 896 at 913 per Lord Hoffmann). While respecting the tribunals' findings of fact, and admitted facts, this court is in as good as a position as the tribunals to consider that question.

'[24] Relevant considerations are: (a) Redrow's printed form of contract was plainly intended to cover a wide range of situations, from contracts with substantial contractors to contracts with applicants such as the present applicants. (b) Arrangements between house-builders such as Redrow and small gangs of workers, such as the bricklayers in these cases, are common in the house-building industry. Both Redrow and the present applicants were accustomed to them. (c) Condition 1 binds the applicants to the conditions "insofar as they are applicable to his subcontract". Having regard to the wide range of contracting parties by whom the conditions were intended to be used, that provision is totally unsurprising. (d) There is no evidence that Redrow sought to enforce, or intended to enforce against these parties the conditions relating to depositing a current health and safety policy and relevant VAT registration. It can be inferred, as an illustration of the flexibility permitted by condition 1, that these provisions were not considered appropriate to the contracts with these applicants, as distinct from bigger contractors. (e) The items of work specified were not beyond the capacity of the men to do it themselves. (f) The agreed method of payment was not payment to the named contractor, Mr Wright, but to each individual doing the work. The suggestion that, by agreeing to pay Mr Milner, Redrow was acting as agent for Mr Wright, produces an unnecessary and unlikely complexity. While Mr Milner is not an applicant, it is difficult to discern an intention that his position be different from that of Mr Wright. (g) In Roberts's case, it was not suggested by Redrow that the other members of the gang were in a position different from that of Mr Roberts. (h) The requirement in condition 6 for a "competent foreman or chargehand" is foreign to arrangements made, and customarily made, with members of a small gang of bricklayers and it is difficult to conclude that the parties intended it to be included in these contracts.

'[25] Against that background, each of the tribunals was in my judgment entitled to find that there was "a mutuality of obligation" (Roberts's case), or "a personal provision of services' (Wright's case). Criticism can be made of the reasoning in each case but, in context, the conclusion was correct and should be upheld in this court upon a consideration of the evidence. In these contracts, condition 6 was not intended to be included so as to permit others to do the work. (When the tribunal in Wright's case used the word "expectation" (see [14], above), I believe they meant to convey the state of mind of intention but that finding is not essential to my general conclusion upon condition 6.)

'[26] In my judgment, the intention of the parties when the contracts were made involved, in each case, an obligation on the applicants to do the work personally. That makes sense of Redrow's decision to contract with bricklayers individually. The scheme for payment points strongly in the direction of contracts with individual bricklayers to do the work personally. Had the intention been otherwise, Redrow would have been likely to make arrangements with Mr Wright and with Mr Roberts alone and arrange for the payments to be made to them. On the evidence, the finding that the obligation to Redrow of each of the men was personal was justified. An analysis has not been attempted by the parties as to what the position would, on my conclusion, be as between members of the gang, or as between one of them and Redrow, if a member failed to do his share of specified work, and that does not need to be determined in this case.

'[27] I agree with the EAT that it was the intention of the parties that personal services be provided and I would dismiss these appeals.' *Roberts v Redrow Homes (North West) Ltd* [2004] EWCA Civ 469 at [23]–[27], [2004] 3 All ER 98, CA, per Pill LJ

WORKERS COMPENSATION

Australia 'The phrase "workers compensation" has long been understood as referring to an entitlement to periodic payments to compensate an injured worker for medical expenses and/or loss of wages due to injury sustained during the course of the worker's employment, irrespective of whether there has been any breach of duty by the employer. The concept is quite different from that of liability for common law damages obtained by a worker as a consequence of establishing that his injuries were attributable to negligence or breach of statutory duty on the part of the employer.' *Allianz Australia Workers Compensation (NSW) Ltd v PPG Industries Australia P/L* [2004] ACTCA 28, at [27], per Higgins CJ, Crispin P, Weinberg J; BC200408769

WORKING CLASSES

'I was referred to a series of cases in which distinguished judges have found the words [working class] difficult to define. In *Rodwell v Minister of Health* [1947] 1 All ER 80 at 82, [1947] KB 404 at 411 Morris J said that the words were "neither happy nor precise". Nonetheless he decided that a particular occupation was not that of one of the working classes. In *H E Green & Sons v Minister of Health* [1947] 2 All ER 469 at 471, [1948] 1 KB 34 at 38 Denning J (as he then was) said that "the words 'working classes' used in the Acts are quite inappropriate to modern social conditions". Despite that the learned judge reached a conclusion. In *Belcher v Reading Corp* [1949] 2 All ER 969 at 984, [1950] Ch 380 at 392 Romer J said: "The phrase has a far wider and less certain signification than it used to possess … ". Nonetheless he decided that a certain section of the public were, on the evidence before him, within the phrase. In *Guinness Trust (London Fund) v Green* [1955] 2 All ER 871 at 873, [1955] 1 WLR 872 at 875 Denning LJ (as he had then become) repeated his criticism of the words from *Green*'s case, but held that the way to apply the test was "to ask whether the house is provided for people in the lower income range … ". That seems to me a useful illustration of how common sense can be applied to difficult circumstances where matters have become obscure by passage of time or changing circumstances. Finally, in *Re Niyazi's Will Trusts* [1978] 3 All ER 785 at 788, [1978] 1 WLR 910 at 915 Megarry V-C, a judge noted for his extreme precision in the use of words, found himself able to express the phrase as having "not lost [its] general connotation of 'lower income' ". None of these cases shows any suggestion that the courts cannot comprehend or deal with questions arising on the meaning of the words "working classes", although all of them agree that the words are much less clear now than formerly. In my judgment those authorities contradict rather than support a suggestion that the words "working classes" are incapable of any meaning today.' *Westminster City Council v Duke of Westminster* [1991] 4 All ER 136 at 144–145, per Harman J

WOULD

Australia [Under s 151A(5) of the Workers Compensation Act 1987 (NSW), a person who has elected to claim permanent loss compensation in respect of an injury may revoke the election and commence proceedings in the court for the recovery of damages in respect of the injury if there has been a further deterioration in the person's medical condition that, had it existed at the time of the election, would have entitled the person to additional permanent loss compensation. The election may only be revoked, though, if at the time of the election, there was "no reasonable cause to believe that the further deterioration would occur": s 151A(5)(c).] '… [I]t is important to note the word "would", appearing in para (c). Obviously, it was appropriate to use a word in the conditional tense because the postulate of the paragraph is that "a further material deterioration in the person's medical condition" has been established. Para (c), in a sense, turns the clock back to consider what was the position at the time of the election. If the purpose of Parliament had been to exclude revocation of an election where mere possibilities, as distinct from likelihood, were taken into account, the word "would" in para (c) would probably have appeared as "might". The word "would" addresses attention, instead, to a real likelihood of further deterioration that, for reasonable cause, *would* have produced a "belief" that (by inference) was, or should have been, taken into account in *making* an election "at the *time* of the election".' (footnote omitted) *New South Wales v Taylor* (2001) 178 ALR 32; BC200100871; [2001] HCA 15 at [63], per Kirby J

New Zealand [Companies Act 1955, s 32(2)(a).] 'The word "would" is not concerned with mere probabilities or likelihoods. Although subjunctive, the condition relates to the use of the name, not the contravention which would follow. In this context, "would" is therefore absolute.' *New Zealand Conference of Seventh-Day Adventists v Registrar of Companies* [1997] 1 NZLR 751 at 759, per Fisher J

WOUND

[For 11 Halsbury's Laws (4th edn) para 1199 see now 11(1) Halsbury's Laws (4th edn) (Reissue) para 470.]

WRECK

[For 43 Halsbury's Laws (4th edn) para 1008 see now 43(1) Halsbury's Laws (4th edn) (Reissue) para 1031.]

WRONGFUL

Australia 'The word "wrongfully" is a word of wide and uncertain import: *Felix v General Dental Council* [1960] AC 704 at 717. The Privy Council pointed out in that case that, where the conduct to which the word was applied was itself wrongful, the word "wrongfully" added nothing. On the other hand, if the conduct was otherwise innocent, the addition of the word "wrongfully" may be regarded as imputing to that conduct an unspecified degree of culpability of an undefined character, ranging (in that case) from mere carelessness to fraud or dishonesty. As with the word "improperly", therefore, the words "wrongfully" and "wrongly" should not be used in imputations unless the context in which they are so used makes clear their intended meaning (and the degree of wrongfulness involved). The context, however, should in some cases be of more assistance than it usually is for the word "improperly".' *McCormick v John Fairfax & Sons Ltd* (1989) 16 NSWLR 485 at 494, per Hunt J

Australia [Section 191 of the Real Property Act (NT) provides for damages where a caveat is lodged wrongfully and without reasonable cause.] 'Its juxtaposition with the expression "without reasonable cause" indicates that something beyond mere mistake or misapprehension of one's rights is contemplated, that is, something done which is not only without reasonable cause but morally blameworthy: see Oxford English Dictionary: "in a manner contrary to the principles of justice or equity; unjustly, unfairly". On this interpretation a person who had a genuine, though mistaken or even irrational, belief in his right to lodge a caveat would not be liable in compensation; but a person lodging a caveat knowing full well he had no reasonable cause to do so would be liable.' *Terri Co Pty Ltd v Aldoth Pty Ltd* (1989) 94 FLR 245 at 270, per Asche CJ

WRONGFUL ACT OR INSULT

Australia [Section 160(2) of the Criminal Code (Tas) provides: 'Any wrongful act or insult of such a nature as to be sufficient to deprive an ordinary person of the power of self-control ... is provocation ...'] 'The composite phrase "wrongful act or insult" appears in a number of other statutory provisions dealing with provocation, including the Queensland and Western Australian Criminal Codes. The phrase did not, however, have any settled legal meaning when the Code was enacted in 1924 and it should not be seen as a technical one. Its critical words — "wrongful", "act" and "insult" — are words of wide general import which should be given their ordinary meaning. In the Report of the Criminal Code Bill Commission of 1879, the Commissioners — Lord Blackburn, Barry J (of the High Court of Justice in Ireland), Lush J and Sir James Stephen — commented (pp 24–5) that they had used the words "wrongful act or insult" in the draft s 176 to introduce "an alteration of considerable importance into the common law": see, also, Sir James Stephen, *A History of The Criminal Law of England*, 1883, vol 3, pp 81–2, 85. In that context, the adoption of the phrase in s 160(2) of the Code should be seen as involving a deliberate departure from the long prevalent common law approach that the kinds of conduct which could, as a matter of law, constitute provocation reducing murder to manslaughter were somewhat artificially confined and, putting to one side a confession of adultery, did not include a case of "mere words": see e.g., Stephen, *A Digest of the Criminal Law*, 3rd edn (1883), pp 161–4; *R v Palmer* [[1913] 2 KB 29 at 30–31]; *R v Withers* [(1925)] SR (NSW) 382 at 389–391]; *R v Camplin* [[1978] AC 705 at 714–715]; *Moffa v R* [(1977) 138 CLR 601 at 605, 616–617, 619–621]. Accordingly, the scope of the word "insult" in s 160(2) should not be restricted by reference to earlier common law doctrine. In particular, it can denote an insulting word or gesture which is neither accompanied by nor in the context of physical violence or the conveyance of information.' *Stingel v R* (1990) 171 CLR 312 at 321–322, per cur

WRONGFUL CONVICTIONS

'[4] The expression "wrongful convictions" is not a legal term of art and it has no settled meaning. Plainly the expression includes the conviction of those who are innocent of the crime of which they have been convicted. But in ordinary parlance the expression would, I think, be extended to those who, whether guilty or not, should clearly not have been convicted at their trials. It is impossible and unnecessary to identify the manifold reasons why a defendant may be convicted when he should not have been ... It may be because evidence helpful to the defence was concealed or withheld ... In cases of this kind, it may, or more often may not, be possible to say that a defendant is innocent, but it is possible to say that he has been wrongly convicted. The common factor in such cases is that something has gone seriously wrong in the investigation of the offence or the conduct of the trial, resulting in the conviction of someone who should not have been convicted.' *R (on the application of Mullen) v Secretary of State for the*

Home Dept [2004] 3 All ER 65, [2005] 1 AC 1 at [4], per Lord Bingham of Cornhill

WRONGFULLY

Australia [Section 74P(1) of the Real Property Act 1900 (NSW) provides that a person who 'wrongfully' lodges a caveat is liable to pay compensation.] 'It is my opinion that the purpose intended to be served by the word "wrongfully" was to limit liability to compensation to the deliberate acts of a person and to exclude from its operation those acts, such as negligent or careless ones, which were not deliberate invasions of the registered proprietor's interest in his land. I would thus construe "wrongfully" as meaning "in deliberate infringement of the rights of the registered proprietor or interested person".' *Beca Developments Pty Ltd v Idameneo (No 92) Pty Ltd* (1990) 21 NSWLR 459 at 474, per Clarke JA

Y

YEAR

[For 45 Halsbury's Laws (4th edn) paras 1103–1105 see now 45(2) Halsbury's Laws (4th edn) (Reissue) paras 203–205.]

Australia [It was contended that the word 'yearly', for the purpose of calculating a bank's claim for interest, referred to a year which consisted of 365 days.] 'In *R v Inhabitants of Roxley* (1829) 5 Man & Ry KB 40 ... Lord Tenterden CJ is reported as contenting himself with saying: "When a leap year occurs, a year must be understood to mean 366 days". But Bayley J relied on the statute law to justify the same conclusion. He said: "The statute 24 Geo 2, c 23, s 2, speaks of bissextile, or leap year, consisting of 366 days"... To like effect is the decision of the majority in the somewhat earlier case *R v Inhabitants of Worminghall* (1817) 6 M & S 350; 105 ER 1274, where virtually the same question had arisen. Lord Ellenborough CJ said: "In those years which consist of 366 days, a hiring and service for a year must be for that same number of days; in like manner as when the year has 365 days, it must have continuance during that number". Bayley J said: "One day was wanting to complete the year; for in leap year, the statute (24 Geo 2, c 23) enacts that the year shall consist of 366 days"... The courts declined to treat 365 days as a standard or conventional year when a leap year was involved. The position is *a fortiori* in respect of a shorter period of days falling within a leap year. There is nothing nominal about 29 February; it takes its place in the succession of days of the week as a Sunday or other designated day — there are not two Sundays (allowing the added day to be nominal) because one is an intercalary day. It is the year which is conventional, its length being adjusted artificially to correct an error of approximation in the calendar.' *Re Clubb; ex p Clubb v Westpac Banking Corpn* (1990) 93 ALR 123 at 128–129, per Burchett J

YEAR AND A DAY RULE

The rule known as the 'year and a day rule' (that is, the rule that, for the purposes of offences involving death and of suicide, an act or omission is conclusively presumed not to have caused a person's death if more than a year and a day elapsed before he died) is abolished for all purposes (Law Reform (Year and a Day Rule) Act 1996, s 1)